Timeline

The Story of Psychology: A Timeline

by Charles L. Brewer, Furman University

B.C.

387 — Plato, who believed in innate ideas, suggests that the brain is the seat of mental processes.

335 — Aristotle, who denied the existence of innate ideas, suggests that the heart is the seat of mental processes.

A.D.

1604 — Johannes Kepler describes inverted image on the retina.

1605 — Francis Bacon publishes *The Proficiency and Advancement of Learning.*

1636 — Harvard College is founded.

1637 — René Descartes, the French philosopher and mathematician who proposed mind-body interaction and the doctrine of innate ideas, publishes *A Discourse on Method.*

1690 — John Locke, the British philosopher who rejected Descartes' notion of innate ideas and insisted that the mind at birth is a "blank slate" (*tabula rasa*), publishes *An Essay Concerning Human Understanding,* which stresses empiricism over speculation.

1774 — Franz Mesmer, an Austrian physician, performs his first supposed cure using "animal magnetism" (later called Mesmerism and hypnosis). In **1777** he was expelled from the practice of medicine in Vienna.

1793 — Philippe Pinel releases the first mental patients from their chains at the Bicêtre asylum in France and advocates more humane treatment of mental patients.

1802 — Thomas Young publishes *A Theory of Color Vision* in England (his theory was later called the trichromatic theory).

1808 — Franz Joseph Gall, a German physician, describes phrenology, the belief that the shape of a person's skull reveals mental faculties and character traits.

1834 — Ernst Heinrich Weber publishes *The Sense of Touch,* in which he discusses the just noticeable difference (*jnd*) and what we now call Weber's Law.

1848 — Phineas Gage suffers massive brain damage when a large iron rod accidentally pierces his brain, leaving his intellect and memory intact but altering his personality.

1859 — Charles Darwin publishes *On the Origin of Species by Means of Natural Selection,* synthesizing much previous work on the theory of evolution, including that of Herbert Spencer, who coined the phrase "survival of the fittest."

1861 — Paul Broca, a French physician, discovers an area in the left frontal lobe of the brain (now called Broca's area) that is critical for the production of spoken language.

1905 — Ivan Petrovich Pavlov begins publishing studies of conditioning in animals.

Alfred Binet and Théodore Simon produce the first intelligence test for assessing the abilities and academic progress of Parisian schoolchildren.

1913 — John B. Watson outlines the tenets of behaviorism in a *Psychological Review* article, "Psychology as the Behaviorist Views It."

1914 — During World War I, Robert Yerkes and his staff develop a group intelligence test for evaluating U.S. military personnel, which increases the U.S. public's acceptance of psychological testing.

1920 — Leta Stetter Hollingworth publishes *The Psychology of Subnormal Children,* an early classic. In **1921** she was cited in *American Men of Science* for her research on the psychology of women.

Francis Cecil Sumner receives a Ph.D. degree in psychology from Clark University, becoming the first African-American to earn a psychology doctorate.

John B. Watson and Rosalie Rayner report conditioning a fear reaction in a child called "Little Albert."

1921 — Hermann Rorschach, a Swiss psychiatrist, introduces the Rorschach inkblot test.

1923 — Developmental psychologist Jean Piaget publishes *The Language and Thought of the Child.*

1924 — Mary Cover Jones reports reconditioning a fear reaction in a child (Peter), a forerunner of systematic desensitization developed by Joseph Wolpe.

1927 — In *Introduction to the Technique of Child Analysis,* Anna Freud discusses psychoanalysis in the treatment of children.

1929 — Wolfgang Köhler publishes *Gestalt Psychology,* which criticizes behaviorism and outlines essential elements of the Gestalt position and approach.

1931 — Margaret Floy Washburn becomes the first female psychologist (and the second female scientist in any discipline) elected to the U.S. National Academy of Sciences.

1932 — In *The Wisdom of the Body,* Walter B. Cannon coins the term *homeostasis,* discusses the fight-or-flight response, and identifies hormonal changes associated with stress.

1933 — Inez Beverly Prosser becomes the first African-American woman to receive a doctoral degree in psychology from a U.S. institution (Pd.D., University of Cincinnati).

Turn the page to continue

1935 — Christiana Morgan and Henry Murray introduce the Thematic Apperception Test to elicit fantasies from people undergoing psychoanalysis.

1936 — Egas Moniz, Portuguese physician, publishes work on the first frontal lobotomies performed on humans.

1938 — B. F. Skinner publishes *The Behavior of Organisms*, which describes operant conditioning of animals.

In *Primary Mental Abilities*, Louis L. Thurstone proposes seven such abilities.

Ugo Cerletti and Lucino Bini use electroshock treatment with a human patient.

1939 — David Wechsler publishes the Wechsler-Bellevue intelligence test, forerunner of the Wechsler Intelligence Scale for Children (WISC) and the Wechsler Adult Intelligence Scale (WAIS).

Mamie Phipps Clark receives a master's degree from Howard University. In collaboration with Kenneth B. Clark, she later extended her thesis, "The Development of Consciousness of Self in Negro Preschool Children," providing joint research cited in the U.S. Supreme Court's **1954** decision to end racial segregation in public schools.

Edward Alexander Bott helps found the Canadian Psychological Association. He becomes its first president in **1940**.

World War II provides many opportunities for psychologists to enhance the popularity and influence of psychology, especially in applied areas.

1943 — Psychologist Starke Hathaway and physician J. Charnley McKinley publish the Minnesota Multiphasic Personality Inventory (MMPI).

1945 — Karen Horney, who criticized Freud's theory of female sexual development, publishes *Our Inner Conflicts*.

1946 — Benjamin Spock's first edition of *The Commonsense Book of Baby and Child Care* appears; the book will influence child rearing in North America for several decades.

1948 — Alfred Kinsey and his colleagues publish *Sexual Behavior in the Human Male*.

B. F. Skinner's novel, *Walden Two*, describes a Utopian community based on positive reinforcement, which becomes a clarion call for applying psychological principles in everyday living, especially communal living.

Ernest R. Hilgard publishes *Theories of Learning*, which was required reading for several generations of psychology students in North America.

1949 — Raymond B. Cattell publishes the Sixteen Personality Factor Questionnaire (16PF).

Continued on inside back cover

1869 — Francis Galton, Charles Darwin's cousin, publishes *Hereditary Genius*, in which he claims that intelligence is inherited. In **1876** he coined the expression "nature and nurture" to correspond with "heredity and environment."

1874 — Carl Wernicke, a German neurologist and psychiatrist, shows that damage to a specific area in the left temporal lobe (now called Wernicke's area) disrupts ability to comprehend or produce spoken or written language.

1878 — G. Stanley Hall receives from Harvard University the first Ph.D. degree in psychology awarded in the United States.

1879 — Wilhelm Wundt establishes at the University of Leipzig, Germany, the first psychology laboratory, which becomes a Mecca for psychology students from all over the world.

1883 — G. Stanley Hall, student of Wilhelm Wundt, establishes the first formal U.S. psychology laboratory at Johns Hopkins University.

1885 — Hermann Ebbinghaus publishes *On Memory*, summarizing his extensive research on learning and memory, including the "forgetting curve."

1889 — Alfred Binet and Henri Beaunis establish the first psychology laboratory in France at the Sorbonne, and the first International Congress of Psychology meets in Paris.

1890 — William James, Harvard University philosopher and psychologist, publishes *The Principles of Psychology*, describing psychology as "the science of mental life."

1891 — James Mark Baldwin establishes the first psychology laboratory in the British Commonwealth at the University of Toronto.

1892 — G. Stanley Hall spearheads the founding of the American Psychological Association (APA) and becomes its first president.

1893 — Mary Whiton Calkins (pictured) and Christine Ladd-Franklin are the first women elected to membership in the APA.

1894 — Margaret Floy Washburn is the first woman to receive a Ph.D. degree in psychology (Cornell University).

Harvard University denies Mary Whiton Calkins admission to doctoral candidacy because of her gender, despite Hugo Münsterberg's claim that she was the best student he had ever had there.

1896 — John Dewey publishes "The Reflex Arc Concept in Psychology," helping to formalize the school of psychology called functionalism.

1898 — In "Animal Intelligence," Edward L. Thorndike, Columbia University, describes his learning experiments with cats in "puzzle boxes." In **1905**, he proposed the "law of effect."

1900 — Sigmund Freud publishes *The Interpretation of Dreams*, his major theoretical work on psychoanalysis.

1901 — Ten founders establish the British Psychological Society.

1905 — Mary Whiton Calkins becomes the first woman president of the APA.

Psychology
EIGHTH EDITION

David G. Myers

Hope College
Holland, Michigan

WORTH PUBLISHERS

Publisher: Catherine Woods

Senior Acquisitions Editors: Kevin Feyen, Renée Altier

Associate Marketing Director: Carlise Stembridge

Senior Marketing Manager: Katherine Nurre

Development Editors: Christine Brune, Nancy Fleming

Media Editor: Andrea Musick

Photo Editor: Bianca Moscatelli

Photo Researchers: Christina Micek, Julie Tesser

Art Director, Cover Designer: Babs Reingold

Interior Designer: Lissi Sigillo

Layout Designer: Lee Ann Mahler

Associate Managing Editor: Tracey Kuehn

Illustration Coordinator: Bill Page

Illustrations: TSI Graphics, Alan Reingold, Matthew Holt, Christy Krames, Shawn Kenney, Bonnie Hofkin, and Demetrios Zangos

Production Manager: Sarah Segal

Composition: TSI Graphics

Printing and Binding: R. R. Donnelley and Sons

Cover Painting: Pierre Bonnard (1867–1947), *The Open Window,* 1921 (oil on canvas), Phillips Collection, Washington DC, USA

ISBN-10: 0-7167-2830-3
ISBN-13: 978-0-7167-2830-6

Printed in the United States of America

Third printing

All royalties from the sale of this book are assigned to the David and Carol Myers Foundation, which exists to receive and distribute funds to other charitable organizations.

Worth Publishers
41 Madison Avenue
New York, NY 10010
www.worthpublishers.com

In memory of
Phyllis J. Vandervelde (1939-2005)
Beloved friend of four decades and manuscript developer for
all eight editions of this book, with deep gratitude for her
extraordinary commitment to excellence.

Grateful acknowledgment is given for permission to reprint the following:

Prologue   *Illustration:* Gina Triplett c/o FrankSturgesReps; *Excerpt:* "Human Family," copyright © 1990 by Maya Angelou, from *I Shall Not Be Moved* by Maya Angelou. Used by permission of Random House, Inc.

Chapter 1   *Illustration:* Stephan Daigle; *Excerpt:* From *The Collected Poems of Langston Hughes* by Langston Hughes, copyright © 1994 by The Estate of Langston Hughes. Used by permission of Alfred A. Knopf, a division of Random House, Inc.

Chapter 2   *Illustration:* Brad Holland; *Excerpt:* Reprinted by permission of the publishers and the Trustees of Amherst College from *The Poems of Emily Dickinson*, Thomas H. Johnson, ed., Cambridge, Mass: The Belknap Press of Harvard University Press, Copyright © 1951, 1955, 1979, 1983 by the President and Fellows of Harvard College.

Chapter 3   *Illustration:* Cathy Gendron c/o theispot.com; *Excerpt:* Reprinted from *Prairie Schooner*, volume 66, number 3 (fall 1992) by permission of the University of Nebraska Press. Copyright © 1992 by the University of Nebraska Press.

Chapter 4   *Illustration* by Stefano Vitale; *Excerpt:* From *Namesake* by Jhumpa Lahiri. Copyright © 2003 by Jhumpa Lahiri. Reprinted by permission of Houghton Mifflin Company. All rights reserved.

Chapter 5   *Illustration:* Brian Stauffer c/o theispot.com; *Excerpt:* From Helen Keller, "Before the Soul Dawn"

Chapter 6   *Illustration:* Michael Morgenstern, © 2006; *Excerpt:* From *Slackjaw* by James Knipfel, copyright © 1997 by James Knipfel. Used by permission of Jeremy P. Tarcher, a imprint of Penguin Group (USA) Inc.

Chapter 7   *Illustration:* Stefano Vitale; *Excerpt:* Excerpted from "A Prison Daybreak" by Faiz Ahmed Faiz, with grateful acknowledgment

Chapter 8   *Illustration:* Robert Frankle c/o theispot.com; *Excerpt:* From *Superman and Me* by Sherman Alexie. *Los Angeles Times*, April 19, 1998. © 1998. Reprinted by permission of the author.

Chapter 9   *Illustration:* Family Tree by Antonis Ampatzis, Courtesy of Trinity Gallery, Atlanta, GA; *Excerpt:* "The Bean Eaters" by Gwendolyn Brooks is reprinted by consent of Brooks Permissions.

Chapter 10   *Illustration:* Rafael Lopez c/o theispot.com; *Excerpt:* Reprinted from *Imitation of Life:* "On Being Told I Don't Speak Like a Black Person," by permission of Carnegie Mellon University Press © 1999 by Allison Joseph.

Chapter 11   *Illustration:* Norma Bliss; *Excerpt:* "Two Loves" by Will Coffey in *I Thought My Father Was God*, edited by Paul Auster. Copyright © 2002. Reprinted by permission of the Carol Mann Agency.

Chapter 12   *Illustration:* Philippe Lardy; *Excerpt:* From *The Life of Pi* by Yann Martel.b (Orlando, FL: Harcourt Books) Originally published in Canada by Random House of Canada. © 2001.

Chapter 13   *Illustration:* Dave Cutler; *Excerpt:* Remarks by Admiral Dennis Blair, Commander of U.S. Pacific Forces, are gratefully acknowledged.

Chapter 14   *Illustration:* Philippe Lardy; *Excerpt:* "Later" by Audre Lorde From *The Cancer Journal,* © 1980. Reprinted by permission of Regula Noetzli, Literary Agent, affiliate of the Charlotte Sheedy Literary Agency, Inc.

Chapter 15   *Illustration:* Philippe Lardy; *Excerpt:* From "Sonny's Blues" © 1957 by James Baldwin. Originally published in Partisan Review. Copyright Renewed. Collected in *Going to Meet the Man*, published by Vintage Books. Reprinted by arrangement with the James Baldwin Estate.

Chapter 16   *Illustration:* Jon Krause c/o theispot.com; *Excerpt:* From *Sap Rising* by Christine Lincoln. (New York: Pantheon Books, 2001)

Chapter 17   *Illustration:* Jon Krause c/o theispot.com; *Excerpt:* The Healers" from *Poems From the Same Ghost* and *Between* by Jack Ridl. © 1984 and 1988. Reprinted by permission of the author.

Chapter 18   *Illustration:* Rafael Lopez c/o theispot.com; *Excerpt:* From "Blink Your Eyes" by Sekou Sundiata, with grateful acknowledgment

Credits for timeline photos, inside front and back covers (by date): 1637, Corbis-Bettmann; 1859, Granger Collection; 1878, 1879, 1890, Brown Brothers; 1893, 1894, Wellesley College Archives; 1898, Yale University Library; 1905, Sovfoto; 1913, 1920, 1933, 1939, Archives of the History of American Psychology, University of Akron; 1924, Larsen/Watson Papers, Archives of the History of American Psychology, University of Akron; 1938, Bettmann/Corbis; 1945, Corbis; 1951, Courtesy of Carl Rogers Memorial Library; 1954, Ted Polumbaum/*Life* magazine, © 1968 TimeWarner, Inc.; 1959, Chris Felver/Archive Images; 1963, Courtesy of CUNY Graduate School and University Center; 1966 (Johnson), © Art Shay; 1966 (Garcia), Courtesy of John Garcia; 1971, Courtesy of Albert Bandura, Stanford University; 1974, Russell Fernald, Courtesy of the Stanford University News Service; 1979, Courtesy of Elizabeth Loftus, University of California, Irvine; 1981, Courtesy of the Archives, California Institute of Technology; 1987, Wellesley College Archives; 1993, Chet Snedden/American Airlines Corporate Communications.

About the Author

David Myers received his psychology Ph.D. from the University of Iowa. He has spent his career at Hope College, Michigan, where he is the John Dirk Werkman Professor of Psychology and has taught dozens of introductory psychology sections. Hope College students have invited him to be their commencement speaker and voted him "outstanding professor."

Myers' scientific articles have, with support from National Science Foundation grants, appeared in more than two dozen scientific periodicals, including *Science, American Scientist, Psychological Science,* and the *American Psychologist*. In addition to his scholarly writing and his textbooks for introductory and social psychology, he also digests psychological science for the general public. His writings have appeared in three dozen magazines, from *Today's Education* to *Scientific American*. He also has authored five general audience books, including *The Pursuit of Happiness* and *Intuition: Its Powers and Perils*.

David Myers has chaired his city's Human Relations Commission, helped found a thriving assistance center for families in poverty, and spoken to hundreds of college and community groups. He bikes to work year-round and plays daily pick-up basketball. David and Carol Myers have raised two sons and a daughter.

Brief Contents

Contents

CHAPTER 6:

Perception   237

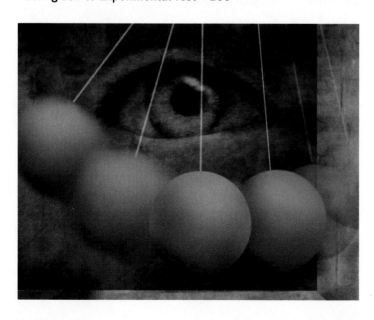

CHAPTER 7:

States of Consciousness   271

CHAPTER 8:

Learning   313

CHAPTER 9:

Memory   349

CHAPTER 10:

Thinking and Language 395

CHAPTER 11:

Intelligence 431

CHAPTER 12:

Motivation and Work 469

CHAPTER 16:

Psychological Disorders   639

CHAPTER 17:

Therapy   685

| Preface |

Two decades of time's ever rolling stream have flowed swiftly by since publication of this book's first edition. And what an amazing two decades it has been. Hardly a day goes by without my feeling gratitude for the privilege of assisting with the teaching of psychology to so many students, in so many countries, through so many different languages. To be entrusted with discerning and communicating the wisdom of this humanly significant discipline is both an exciting honor and a great responsibility.

What sustains my motivation is, first, my continuing appreciation for psychological science and its ever-expanding understandings, and, second, my commitment to the students and teaching colleagues with whom this book enables me to have conversation. I love the mind-expanding learning that comes from my day-to-day reading of psychological science, and I love connecting with so many people (many hundreds of whom have written to share their experiences and gentle words of advice).

Although each new edition of this text appears every three years, it is a rare day in between those editions when I do not harvest new information about the field I love and its application to everyday life. Week by week, new information surprises us with discoveries about, for example, the neuroscience of our moods and memories, the reach of our adaptive unconscious, and the shaping power of our social and cultural context. No wonder this book has changed dramatically since I set to work on the first edition 23 years ago. Today's psychological science is more attuned to the relative effects of nature and nurture, to gender and cultural diversity, to our conscious and unconscious information processing, and to the biology that underlies our behavior (see **TABLES 1** and **2,** page xvi). We today can also harness new ways to present information, both in books and via electronic media. These changes are exhilarating! Keeping up with new discoveries fills each day and connects me with many colleagues and friends.

The thousands of instructors and millions of students across the globe who have studied this book have contributed immensely to its development. Much of this has occurred spontaneously, through correspondence and conversations. For this edition, we also formally involved over 800 researchers and teaching psychologists, along with many students, in our efforts to gather accurate and up-to-date information about the field of psychology and the content, pedagogy, and supplements needs of instructors and students in the introductory course. Moreover, we look forward to continuing feedback as we strive, over future editions, to create an ever better book.

What Continues?

Throughout its eight editions, however, my vision for *Psychology* has not wavered: *to merge rigorous science with a broad human perspective in a book that engages both mind and heart.* My aim has been to create a state of the art introduction to psychology, written with sensitivity to students' needs and interests. I aspire to help students understand and appreciate the wonder of important phenomena of their lives. I also want to convey the inquisitive spirit in which psychologists *do* psychology. The study of psychology, I believe, enhances our abilities to restrain intuition with critical thinking, judgmentalism with compassion, and illusion with understanding.

Believing with Thoreau that "Anything living is easily and naturally expressed in popular language," I seek to communicate psychology's scholarship with crisp narrative and vivid storytelling. Writing as a solo author, I hope to tell psychology's story in

Table 1: Evolutionary Psychology and Behavior Genetics

In addition to the coverage found in Chapter 3, *the **evolutionary perspective** is covered on the following pages:*

Aging, p. 178

Anxiety disorders, pp. 654–655

Attraction, pp. 111–112, 758–759

Biological predispositions in learning, pp. 321–323, 335–336

Brainstem, p. 71

Charles Darwin, p. 9

Electromagnetic spectrum, sensitivity to, p. 204

Emotion, pp. 404–405, 529, 530, 534

Emotion-detecting ability, p. 464

Evolutionary perspective, defined, p. 11

Exercise, p. 569

Fear, pp. 404–405, 533–534

Hearing, p. 215

Hunger and taste preference, pp. 477–478

Instincts, pp. 470–471

Intelligence, pp. 459–461

Language, pp. 410, 414–415

Love, p. 187

Need to belong, p. 495

Obesity, pp. 581–582

Overconfidence, p. 403

Puberty, onset of, pp. 173–174

Risk taking, p. 111

Sensation, pp. 198, 224

Sensory adaptation, pp. 202–203, 256

Sexual attraction, pp. 111–112

Sexual orientation, pp. 490–491

Sexuality, p. 481

Signal detection theory, p. 199

Sleep, pp. 276, 282

Smell, pp. 231–233

Stress and the immune system, pp. 557–558

In addition to the coverage found in Chapter 3, **behavior genetics** *is covered on the following pages:*

Abuse, intergenerational transmission of, p. 343

Aggression, p. 749

Biomedical therapies, pp. 711–718

Depth perception, p. 245

Drives and incentives, p. 471

Drug use, pp. 305–307

Emotion and cognition, pp. 521–523

Fear, pp. 534–535

Happiness, pp. 542–544

Hunger, taste preference, pp. 477–478

Intelligence, pp. 423, 440, 452–464

Learning, pp. 321–323, 335–336

Motor development, p. 145

Obesity and weight control, pp. 585–587

Perception, pp. 254–261

Personality traits, pp. 619–621

Psychological disorders:

anxiety disorders, pp. 649–650

biopsychosocial approach, p. 643

mood disorders, pp. 658–668

personality disorders, pp. 656–657, 677–679

schizophrenia, pp. 669–676

Romantic love, p. 187

Sexuality, p. 481

Sexual orientation, p. 490–491

Smell, pp. 231–233

Stress, personality, and illness, pp. 555–556, 559–561, 570–571

Traits, p. 460

Table 2: Neuroscience

In addition to coverage found in Chapter 2, **neuroscience** *can be found on the following pages:*

Antisocial personality disorder, pp. 677–678

Autism, p. 152

Biofeedback, pp. 561–572

Brain activity and

aging, pp. 179–180, 183–185, 376

aggression, p. 522

dementia and Alzheimer's, pp. 180–181, 365

disease, p. 220

dreams, pp. 287–288

emotion, pp. 166, 233, 366, 517–520, 522

sleep, pp. 275–278

Brain development:

adolescence, p. 166–167

experience and, pp. 114–116

infancy and childhood, pp. 144–145

sexual differentiation in utero, p. 130

Consciousness, p. 273

Drug dependence, p. 306

Emotion and cognition, pp. 521–522

Fear-learning, p. 654

Fetal alcohol syndrome and brain abnormalities, p. 142

Hallucinations and:

sleep, p. 288

hallucinogens, pp. 302–303

near-death experiences, p. 309

Hormones and:

abuse, p. 159

development, pp. 129–130, 165–167

emotion, pp. 516–517

memory, pp. 365–367

sex, pp. 129–130, 165–166, 176, 463, 482–483, 516

stress, pp. 516–517, 533, 551–553, 555, 557, 566

weight control, pp. 475–476

Hunger, pp. 475–476

Insight, p. 398

Intelligence, pp. 440–441, 455

Language, statistical learning, pp. 415–417

Memory,

physical storage of, pp. 364–366, 368, 369

sleep, pp. 283, 287–288

Mirror neurons, pp. 341–342

Neuroscience perspective, defined, p. 11

Neurotransmitters and:

biomedical therapy:

depression, pp. 664–665, 713–715

ECT, pp. 715–717

obsessive-compulsive disorder, p. 697

psychosurgery, pp. 717–718

schizophrenia, pp. 672–673, 711–712

child abuse, p. 159

depression, pp. 643, 664–665

drugs, pp. 298–299, 300–303

exercise, p. 568

narcolepsy, p. 284

obsessive-compulsive disorder, p. 697

schizophrenia, pp. 672–673

smoking, p. 578

Pain, pp. 226–229

phantom limb pain, pp. 226–227

Parallel vs. serial processing, p. 210

Perception:

brain damage and, pp. 198, 210–211

color vision, pp. 212–214

feature detection, pp. 209–210

transduction, p. 115

visual information processing, pp. 208–211

Schizophrenia and brain abnormalities, pp. 672–673

Sensation:

body position and movement, pp. 233–234

deafness, pp. 220–221

hearing, pp. 219–221

sensory adaptation, p. 203

smell, pp. 231–233

taste, pp. 229–231

Sexual orientation, pp. 489–492

Sleep,

memory and, p. 283

recuperation during, pp. 282–283

a way that is warmly personal as well as rigorously scientific. I love to reflect on connections between psychology and other realms, such as literature, philosophy, history, sports, religion, politics, and popular culture. And I love to provoke thought, to play with words, and to laugh.

Although supplemented by added story telling, this new edition retains its predecessors' voice and much of its content and organization. It also retains the goals—the guiding principles—that have animated the previous seven editions:

1. **To exemplify the process of inquiry** I strive to show students not just the outcome of research, but how the research process works. Throughout, the book tries to excite the reader's curiosity. It invites readers to imagine themselves as participants in classic experiments. Several chapters introduce research stories as mysteries that progressively unravel as one clue after another falls into place. (See, for example, the historical story of research on the brain's processing of language on pages 80–82.)

2. **To teach critical thinking** By presenting research as intellectual detective work, I exemplify an inquiring, analytical mind-set. Whether students are studying development, cognition, or statistics, they will become involved in, and see the rewards of, critical reasoning. Moreover, they will discover how an empirical approach can help them evaluate competing ideas and claims for highly publicized phenomena—ranging from subliminal persuasion, ESP, and alternative therapies to astrology, hypnotic regression, and repressed and recovered memories.

3. **To put facts in the service of concepts** My intention is not to fill students' intellectual file drawers with facts, but to reveal psychology's major concepts—to teach students how to think, and to offer psychological ideas worth thinking about. In each chapter I place emphasis on those concepts I hope students will carry with them long after they complete the course. Always, I try to follow Albert Einstein's dictum that "Everything should be made as simple as possible, but not simpler."

4. **To be as up-to-date as possible** Few things dampen students' interest as quickly as the sense that they are reading stale news. While retaining psychology's classic studies and concepts, I also present the discipline's most important recent developments. Nearly 500 references in this edition are dated 2004 or 2005.

5. **To integrate principles and applications** Throughout—by means of anecdotes, case histories, and the posing of hypothetical situations—I relate the findings of basic research to their applications and implications. Where psychology can illuminate pressing human issues—be they racism and sexism, health and happiness, or violence and war—I have not hesitated to shine its light.

6. **To enhance comprehension by providing continuity** Many chapters have a significant issue or theme that links subtopics, forming a thread that ties the chapter together. The Learning chapter conveys the idea that bold thinkers can serve as intellectual pioneers. The Thinking and Language chapter raises the issue of human rationality and irrationality. The Psychological Disorders chapter conveys empathy for, and understanding of, troubled lives. "The uniformity of a work," observed Edward Gibbon, "denotes the hand of a single artist." Because the book has a single author, other threads, such as behavior genetics and cultural diversity, weave throughout the whole book, and students hear a consistent voice.

7. **To reinforce learning at every step** Everyday examples and rhetorical questions encourage students to process the material actively. Concepts presented earlier are frequently applied, and thereby reinforced, in later chapters. For instance, in Chapter 5 students learn that much of our information processing occurs *outside* of our conscious awareness. Ensuing chapters reinforce this concept. Learning Objectives, Learning Outcomes, self-tests, a marginal glossary, and end-of-chapter key terms lists help students master important concepts and terminology.

8. **To convey respect for human unity and diversity** Especially in newly revised Chapter 3, Nature, Nurture, and Human Diversity, but also throughout the book, readers will see evidence of our human kinship—our shared biological heritage, our common mechanisms of seeing and learning, hungering and feeling, loving and hating. They will also better understand the dimensions of our diversity—our *individual* diversity in development and aptitudes, temperament and personality, and disorder and health; and our *cultural* diversity in attitudes and expressive styles, childrearing and care for the elderly, and life priorities.

What's New?

Despite the overarching continuity, there is change on every page. In addition to updates everywhere and 900 new references—comprising 24 percent of the bibliography—I have introduced the following major changes to *Psychology,* eighth edition:

Increased Coverage of Cultural and Gender Diversity

This edition presents an even more thoroughly cross-cultural perspective on psychology (**TABLE 3**)—reflected in research findings, and text and photo examples. Coverage of the psychology of women and men is thoroughly integrated (see **TABLE 4**). In addition, I am working to offer a world-based psychology for our worldwide student readership.

Table 3: Culture and Multicultural Experience

From the Prologue to Chapter 18, coverage of **culture and multicultural experience** *can be found on the following pages:*

Aging population, pp. 177–178

Aggression, pp. 749, 752, 753

AIDS, pp. 190, 406, 558–559

Alcoholism, pp. 299–300

Anger, pp. 535–537

Animal research ethics, p. 47

Attractiveness, pp. 110–111, 759–762

Behavioral effects of culture, pp. 47–48, 103–104

Categorization, p. 397

Conformity, pp. 731, 733, 734

Corporal punishment practices, pp. 332–333

Cultural norms, pp. 120, 131–132

Culture and the self, pp. 121–123

Culture context effects, p. 260

Culture shock, pp. 120–121, 553

Deaf culture, pp. 83, 86, 88, 220–223, 411, 412, 413–414, 417, 420

Depression, p. 662

Development:

adolescence, p. 165

attachment, pp. 157–161

child-rearing, p. 124

cognitive development, p. 154

developmental similarities, p. 125

moral development, p. 168

motor development, p. 142

social development, p. 157

Dieting, p. 582

Drugs, psychological effects of, p. 300

Emotion:

emotion-detecting ability, pp. 524–525

expressing, pp. 526, 528–531, 536, 537

experiencing, pp. 535–536, 537, 540–541

Enemy perceptions, p. 758

Flynn effect, pp. 447–448

Gender:

roles, pp. 131–132

social connectedness, p. 170

Grief, expressing, p. 191

Happiness, pp. 539–541, 543–544

Hindsight bias, p. 21

History of psychology, pp. 3–7

Homosexuality, views on, p. 27

Human diversity/kinship, pp. 47–48, 120–124

Hunger, p. 477

Individualism/collectivism, pp. 121–124

Intelligence, pp. 446–448, 459–461

bias, pp. 464–466

Language, pp. 119, 411, 414–415, 418–420

Leaving the nest, pp. 173–174

Life-expectancy, pp. 177–178

Life satisfaction, pp. 538–541

Management styles, p. 509

Marijuana use, p. 307

Marriage, p. 187

Medical risk, p. 460

Meditation, pp. 571–572

Memory, encoding, pp. 360, 559

Mental illness rate, p. 680

Need to belong, pp. 495–496

Obesity, pp. 586–587

Observational learning:

television viewing, p. 160

television and aggression, pp. 344–345

Pace of life, pp. 30, 120–121

Parapsychology, pp. 264, 268

Participative management, p. 509

People with disabilities, p. 539

Perception, pp. 237, 252

Personal space, p. 120

Poverty and inequality, p. 31

Prejudice, pp. 743–748

Prejudice prototypes, p. 397

Psychological disorders:

antisocial personality disorder, p. 679

dissociative personality disorder, p. 657

eating disorders, pp. 478–480, 643

rates of, pp. 680–681

schizophrenia, p. 643

susto, p. 643

taijin-kyofusho, p. 643

Psychotherapy:

EMDR training, p. 706

Psychoanalysis, p. 687

Psychotherapists and values, pp. 708–710

Puberty and adult independence, pp. 173–174

Self-esteem, pp. 543–544, 633

Self-serving bias, p. 634

Sexual attraction, p. 111

Sexual orientation, pp. 487–488

Size-distance relationship, pp. 251–252

Smoking, pp. 575–581

Social-cultural perspective, pp. 10–13

Social clock, p. 186

Stress:

adjusting to a new culture, pp. 553–554

poverty and inequality/life-expectancy, pp. 563, 564, 565

Suicide, p. 662

Teen sexuality, pp. 485–487

Testing bias, pp. 464–466

See also Chapter 18, Social Psychology, pp. 722–772

Table 4: The Psychology of Men and Women

*Coverage of the **psychology of men and women** can be found on the following pages:*

ADHD, p. 641
Aggression, pp. 749, 750
Alcohol use, pp. 298–300
Autism, p. 152
Behavioral effects of gender, p. 46
Biological sex/gender, pp. 129–130
Body image, p. 479
Changes in physical development, pp. 176–177
Depression, pp. 659, 667
Dieting, pp. 582–583, 587
Dream content, pp. 286–288
Drugs and addiction, pp. 299, 300
Eating disorders, pp. 478–480
Emotion-detecting ability, pp. 464, 526–527
Emotional expression, pp. 190, 524–526
Empty nest, p. 188
Father care, pp. 157, 486

Fear, p. 534
Freud's views, pp. 598–599, 604
Gender and child-rearing, pp. 132–133, 479, 486
Gender roles, pp. 131–132
Gender prejudice, p. 745
Gendered brain, pp. 130–131, 479, 482, 484, 492
Generic pronoun "he," p. 419
Happiness, p. 544
Heart disease, pp. 555–556
Help-receiving, p. 766
Hormones and:
  aggression, pp. 750
  sexual behavior, pp. 482–483
  sexual development, pp. 129–130, 165–167
Immune system, p. 557
Intelligence, pp. 461–464
  bias, p. 465

Life expectancy, p. 178
Marriage, p. 566
Maturation, pp. 165–167
Menarche, p. 166
Menopause, pp. 176–177
Midlife crisis, pp. 185–186
Obesity, pp. 582–584
Pornography, pp. 484, 752–754
Prejudice, pp. 397, 745–746
Psychological disorders, rates of, pp. 680–681
Rape, pp. 325, 753–754
REM sleep, arousal in, p. 278
Risk taking, p. 111
Savant syndrome, pp. 433–434
Schizophrenia, pp. 669, 671
Sense of smell, p. 232
Sexual abuse, pp. 109, 158–159, 299, 567

Sexual attraction, pp. 111–112
Sexual disorders, p. 482
Sexual fantasies, pp. 484, 485
Sexual orientation, pp. 487–493
Sexuality, pp. 110–111, 481–485
Sleep, pp. 280, 281
Smoking, pp. 111, 141, 579–580
Social connectedness, pp. 565–566
Stereotyping, p. 261
Stress, pp. 555–556
  response, p. 553
  in marriage, pp. 565–566
  sexual abuse, p. 566
Suicide, pp. 662–663
Weight discrimination, pp. 583–584
Women and work, p. 189
Women in psychology, p. 6
See also Chapter 18, Social Psychology, pp. 722–771

Thus, I continually search the world for research findings and text and photo examples, conscious that readers may be in Melbourne, Sheffield, Vancouver, or Nairobi. North American and European examples come easily, given that I reside in the United States, maintain contact with friends and colleagues in Canada, subscribe to several European periodicals, and live periodically in the U.K. This edition, for example, offers 82 explicit Canadian and 142 British examples, and 82 mentions of Australia and New Zealand. We are all citizens of a shrinking world, thanks to increased migration and the growing global economy. Thus, American students, too, benefit from information and examples that internationalize their world-consciousness. And if psychology seeks to explain *human* behavior (not just American or Canadian or Australian behavior), the broader the scope of studies presented, the more accurate is our picture of this world's people. My aim is to expose all students to the world beyond their own culture. Thus, I continue to welcome input and suggestions from all readers. Our **revised Chapter 3, retitled Nature, Nurture, and Human Diversity,** encourages students to appreciate cultural and gender differences and commonalities, and to consider the interplay of nature and nurture.

Each chapter opening art page now includes a **brief literary excerpt from varied cultural perspectives.** These excerpts, from Maya Angelou, Judith Ortiz Cofer, Jhumpa Lahiri, Faiz Ahmed Faiz, Gwendolyn Brooks, and others offer "Another Voice" on the chapter's topic. In addition, **many new photos** showcase the diversity of cultures within North America, as well as across the globe. In addition to significant cross-cultural examples and research presented within the narrative, these new photos with informative captions freshen each chapter and broaden students' perspectives in applying psychological science to their own world and to the worlds across the globe.

A Revised and Thoroughly Considered Pedagogical Program

In addition to the new chapter-opening literary excerpts, this edition includes the following new study aids.

- **New numbered Learning Objectives** introduce significant sections of text (around 15-30 per chapter) and direct student reading. These Learning Objectives organize the Study Guide and the Test Banks and are listed in the Instructor's Resources.

- *New Learning Outcomes,* found at the end of each major section of text, repeat the Learning Objectives and address them with a narrative summary.
- The Learning Outcomes sections also include at least one *Ask Yourself question,* which encourages students to apply new concepts to their own experiences.
- *Chapter-ending Review sections* contain 3-5 short-answer *Test Yourself questions* (with answers in an appendix) that assess student mastery and encourage big picture thinking, followed by page-referenced *Terms and Concepts to Remember.*

Greater Emphasis on the Biological-Psychological-Social/Cultural Levels of Analysis Approach in Psychology

This edition now systematically includes coverage of the biological, psychological, and social-cultural influences on our behavior. A significant new section in the Prologue introduces the levels-of-analysis approach, setting the stage for future chapters, and new levels-of-analysis figures in most chapters help students understand concepts in the biopsychosocial context. Richard Straub's new, accompanying interactive Visual Concept Review booklet also includes levels-of-analysis visual summary reviews.

Greater Sensitivity to the Clinical Perspective

With helpful guidance from clinical psychologist colleagues, I have been more mindful in this edition of the clinical angle on various concepts within psychology, which has sensitized and improved the Personality, Psychological Disorders, and Therapy chapters, among others. For example, I now cover problem-focused and emotion-focused coping strategies in the Stress and Health chapter, and the Intelligence chapter includes several mentions of how intelligence tests are used in clinical settings.

New Teaching and Learning Resources

Our supplements and media have been celebrated for their quality, abundance, and accuracy. The package available for *Psychology,* Eighth Edition, raises the bar even higher. New media items include the *ActivePsych* classroom activity CD-ROMs, the new Online Study Center 2.0 for students, and enhanced course management solutions. New print supplements include Martin Bolt's Instructor's Media Guide, Richard Straub's Visual Concept Reviews, and a thoroughly revised Test Bank. See page xxvi for details.

New Careers in Psychology Appendix, by Jennifer Zwolinski, University Of San Diego

This highly applied and research-based appendix provides guidance to students considering a psychology major and/or career. Topics covered include the benefits of studying psychology and obtaining a psychology degree, psychology careers available and the job market landscape for students at all levels (bachelors, masters, doctorate), career options within the sub-fields in psychology (such as clinical, counseling, community, school, forensic, and sports psychology), and early preparation tips for those considering graduate school.

Enhanced Critical Thinking Coverage

I aim to introduce students to critical thinking in a natural way throughout the book, with even more in the narrative that encourages active learning of psychology's key concepts. In addition to the new Learning Objectives and Learning Outcomes, which encourage critical reading to glean an understanding of important concepts, the eighth edition includes the following opportunities for students to learn or practice their critical thinking skills.

- ***Chapter 1 takes a unique, critical thinking approach to introducing students to psychology's research methods,*** emphasizing the fallacies of our everyday intuition and common sense and, thus, the need for psychological science. Critical thinking is introduced as a key term in this chapter (p. 24). The discussions of Statistical Reasoning encourages students to "focus on thinking smarter by applying simple statistical principles to everyday reasoning" (pp. 39–40).
- ***"Thinking Critically About . . ." boxes*** are found throughout the book, modeling for students a critical approach to some key issues in psychology. For example, see the new box "Thinking Critically About: ADHD—Pathologizing Rambunctiousness or Genuine Disorder?" on p. 641.
- ***Detective-style stories*** throughout the narrative get students thinking critically about psychology's key research questions.
- ***"Apply this"*** and ***"Think about it"*** style discussions keep students active in their study of each chapter.
- ***Critical examinations of pop psychology*** spark interest and provide important lessons in thinking critically about everyday topics.

See **TABLE 5** for a complete list of this text's coverage of critical thinking topics and Thinking Critically About boxes.

Table 5: Critical Thinking and Research Emphasis

*Critical thinking coverage, and in-depth stories of psychology's **scientific research** process, can be found on the following pages:*

Thinking Critically About . . . boxes:

Desegregation and the Death Penalty—When Beliefs Collide With Psychological Science, p. 50

Left Brain/Right Brain, p. 87

The Fear Factor—Do We Fear the Right Things?, pp. 404–405

Lie Detection, pp. 520–521

Alternative Medicine: New Ways to Health or Old Snake Oil?, pp. 570–571

How to Be a "Successful" Astrologer or Palm Reader, pp. 616–617

ADHD—Pathologizing Rambunctiousness or Genuine Disorder?, p. 641

Insanity and Responsibility, p. 648

Dissociation and Multiple Personalities, pp. 656–657

"Regressing" from Unusual to Usual, p. 701

Critical Examinations of Pop Psychology:

Do Video Games Teach or Release Violence?, pp. 754–756

Perceiving order in random events, pp. 34–35

Do we use only 10 percent of our brains?, pp. 79–80

Critiquing the evolutionary perspective, pp. 112–113

How great is the power of parenting?, pp. 116–117

Sensory restriction, pp. 255–256

Is there extrasensory perception?, pp. 264–268

Can hypnosis enhance recall? Coerce action? Be therapeutic? Alleviate pain?, pp. 292–293

Has the concept of "addiction" been stretched too far?, pp. 297–298

Near-death experiences, pp. 309–310

Do animals exhibit language?, pp. 425–428

Is aerobic exercise therapeutic?, pp. 567–569

Spirituality and faith communities, pp. 572–575

How valid is the Rorschach test?, pp. 602–603

Is repression a myth?, pp. 604–605

Is Freud credible?, pp. 604–607

Post-traumatic stress disorder, pp. 652–653

Is psychotherapy effective?, pp. 700–705

Evaluating alternative therapies, pp. 705–707

Thinking Critically with Psychological Science:

The limits of intuition and common sense, pp. 19–22

"Critical thinking" introduced as a key term, p. 24

The scientific attitude, pp. 23–24

The scientific method, pp. 24–26

Correlation and causation, pp. 32–33

Illusory correlation, pp. 33–34

Exploring cause and effect, pp. 36–37

Evaluating therapies, pp. 37–38

Statistical reasoning, pp. 39–40

Making inferences, pp. 42–44

Scientific Detective Stories:

Is breast milk better than formula?, pp. 36–37

Language in the brain, pp. 80–82

Our divided brains, pp. 83–88

The twin and adoption studies, pp. 97–101

How a child's mind develops, pp. 147–154

Aging and intelligence, pp. 183–185

Parallel processing, pp. 210–211

How do we see in color?, pp. 212–214

Why do we sleep?, pp. 279–283

Why do we dream?, pp. 287–289

Is hypnosis an altered state of consciousness?, pp. 294–295

How do we store memories in our brains?, pp. 364–369

Memory construction, pp. 382–390

Do animals exhibit language?, pp. 425–428

Why do we feel hunger?, pp. 474–477

What determines sexual orientation?, pp. 488–493

The pursuit of happiness: Who is happy, and why?, pp. 537–545

Why—and in whom—does stress contribute to heart disease?, pp. 555–556

How and why is social support linked with health?, pp. 564–567

Self-esteem versus self-serving bias, pp. 633–636

What causes mood disorders?, pp. 658–668

Do prenatal viral infections increase risk of schizophrenia?, pp. 673–674

Is psychotherapy effective?, pp. 700–705

Why do people fail to help in emergencies?, pp. 765–766

Innovative Multimedia Supplements Package

Psychology, Eighth Edition, boasts a host of new electronic and print supplements titles.

Media Supplements

New! ActivePsych Instructor's Classroom Exercise CD-ROMs include interactive activities designed for in-class presentation and group participation, as well as a robust library of new clips and animations. These activities require very little instructor preparation (just load the CD and launch the activity) and are designed to foster class discussion and critical thinking. The ActivePsych suite of instructor presentation CD-ROMs includes the following:

- *More than 30 interactive activities,* including animations, video clips, illustrations, photographs, and critical thinking questions. A number of activities have been adapted from Martin Bolt's Instructor's Resources and Thomas Ludwig's Psych-Sim 5.0 (and are now classroom presentation-friendly). ActivePsych also includes a significant number of completely original, creative activities, all authored (and class-tested) by veteran introductory psychology teachers.
- *Approximately 30 completely new short video clips,* drawn from a variety of sources, and numerous new animations.
- *New! Scientific American Frontiers Teaching Modules, Third Edition,* which have been housed in ActivePsych and edited by Martin Bolt. The Third Edition offers you 15 edited clips from Scientific American Frontiers segments produced between 2003-2005.

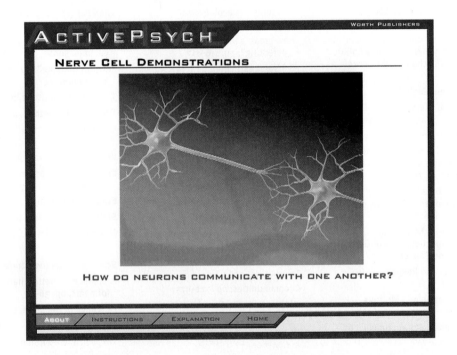

New! Instructor's Media Guide (based on trusted *Instructor's Resources* author Martin Bolt's work) expands the Lecture Guides and offers instructors a simple way to incorporate instructor media, presentation, and video resources into their course.

New! Online Study Center 2.0 for *Psychology,* Eighth Edition The customized Online Study Center (OSC) offers students a variety of tools to help them master the course:

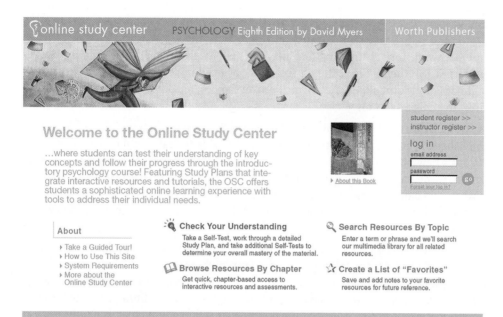

- *A Chapter-by-Chapter Self-Guided Study Plan with Diagnostic Tests.* Students may take a 20–25 question Self-Test to assess their current knowledge of a particular chapter, then view a Study Plan that identifies areas of weakness and offers a variety of resources for learning those concepts.
- *Self-Paced Tutorials* that allow students to revisit and master course concepts on their own.
- *Multiple Assessment and Review Tools,* organized by chapter. In addition to the Study Plan, students can Search by Topic or Browse by Chapter to access interactive demonstrations and review materials.
- *Dozens of Hands-On Activities.* Your students will be able to tackle classic experiments (condition a rat, probe the hypothalamus electronically), encounter perceptual illusions, test their memory, interpret facial expressions, and more.
- *Digitized Video Demonstrations* (for example, the effects of teratogens on development) and Animations (such as neural communication) bring text concepts to life.
- *A Sophisticated Search Engine* (similar to Google®) that allows students to search quickly by topic (not just by chapter).
- *Interactive Study Tools.* Students are able to add resources to their Favorites and even add Notes to specific resources.

New! Enhanced Course Management Solutions (WebCT, Blackboard, Desire2Learn, Angel) allow adopters to access all of this edition's teaching and learning resources in one, central location (through their course management system) through one, seamless, guided experience.

New! eLibrary for Psychology, Eighth Edition brings together the supplementary resources, such as the *Instructor's Resources, PsychSim 5.0,* and *PsychOnline,* in a single, easy-to-use Web site. Through sophisticated and seamless search and browse functions, the eLibrary allows instructors to quickly build free, premium student Web pages, construct lectures, and organize resources.

New! Expanded and Improved Book Companion Site The *Psychology,* Eighth Edition, Book Companion site offers students a virtual study guide, twenty-four hours a day, seven days a week. Best of all, these resources are free and do not require any special access codes or passwords. In addition to self-tests, review materials, annotated web links, simulations, and demonstrations, the site now includes an interactive, historical timeline and new Spanish-English Flashcards. The **password-protected Instructor Site** offers a full array of teaching resources, including a new suite of PowerPoint slides, electronic Lecture Guides, an online quiz grade book, and links to additional tools.

New! iClicker Radio Frequency Classroom Response System Offered by Worth Publishers, in partnership with iClicker and available for fall 2006 classes, iClicker is Worth's new polling system, created by educators for educators. This radio frequency system is the hassle-free way to make your class time more interactive. The system allows you to pause to ask questions and instantly record responses, as well as take attendance, direct students through lectures, gauge your students' understanding of the material, and much more.

Revised! Instructor's Resource CD-ROM Customized for *Psychology,* Eighth Edition, this CD-ROM contains pre-built PowerPoint presentation slide sets for each chapter, a digital photograph library, an electronic version of Martin Bolt's *Instructor's Resources and Lecture Guides,* and a complete illustration library. A new intuitive browser interface makes it easy to preview and use all elements in this CD-ROM.

- *Chapter Art PowerPoint® Slides* feature all of the text art and illustrations (including tables, charts, and graphs) within the PowerPoint format. This program also offers a number of layered PowerPoint slides for key biological and process diagrams.
- *Revised! Lecture PowerPoint® Presentation Slides* Developed by a longtime adopter of Psychology and informed by 20 reviewers, these slides focus on key concepts and themes from the text. The slides feature tables, graphs and figures from the text and from outside sources.
- *New! Step Up to Psychology: A PowerPoint Review Game by John Schulte, University of North Carolina–Wilmington.* This PowerPoint-based review adopts a game-show approach where students divide into teams to compete for points by answering questions related to chapter material. The questions are ranked for difficulty (four levels), and include both factual/definitional and conceptual/application questions.
- *New! Digital Photo Library* gives you access to all of the photographs from the eighth edition, organized by chapter.

PsychSim 5.0, Thomas Ludwig, Hope College, CD-ROM and Booklet These 42 interactive simulations involve students in the practice of psychological research by having them play the role of experimenter (conditioning a rat, probing the hypothalamus electrically, working in a sleep lab) or participant (responding to tests of memory or visual illusions, interpreting facial expressions). Other simulations provide dynamic tutorials or demonstrations. In addition, 5-question multiple choice quizzes are available for each activity on the Companion Web site.

PsychInquiry for *Psychology,* Eighth Edition: Student Activities in Research and Critical Thinking CD-ROM, Thomas Ludwig, Hope College Customized to work specifically with this new edition, this CD-ROM contains dozens of interactive activities designed to help students learn about psychological research and to improve their critical thinking skills.

PsychOnline (Course Management Version), Thomas Ludwig, Hope College Housed in both WebCT and Blackboard, *PsychOnline* is a comprehensive instructor and student online solution for introductory psychology. Designed for use as a supplement for either web-enhanced lecture courses or complete online courses, *PsychOnline* offers a rich, web-based collection of interactive tutorials and activities for introductory psychology.

PsychOnline 2.0 (Web-Based Version), Thomas Ludwig, Hope College
PsychOnline 2.0 is a comprehensive online resource for introductory psychology. *PsychOnline 2.0* looks like a Worth Web site, includes more than 100 interactive tutorials and over 250 activities, and also contains the following new features:

- A Web-based interface that is easy to use and incorporate within your course
- A self-guided study plan that includes a multiple-choice Diagnostic Test for each topic. After the student completes the Diagnostic Test, the student is given a Diagnostic Test Report that offers test results and suggestions for re-examining and studying material.
- 20 modules from Thomas Ludwig's *PsychSim 5.0*

Diploma Computerized Test Bank (Available in Windows and Macintosh on One CD-ROM) The CD-ROM allows you to add an unlimited number of questions, edit questions, format a test, scramble questions, and include pictures, equations, or multimedia links. With the accompanying grade book, you can record students' grades throughout a course, sort student records and view detailed analyses of test items, curve tests, generate reports, add weights to grades, and more. This CD-ROM is the access point for Diploma Online Testing. Blackboard and WebCT formatted versions of the Test Bank are also available within the Course Cartridge and ePack.

Diploma Online Testing at www.brownstone.net With Diploma, you can easily create and administer exams over the Internet, with questions that incorporate multimedia and interactivity. Students receive instant feedback and can take the quizzes multiple times. Instructors can sort and view results, and can take advantage of various grade book and result-analysis features, as well as restrict tests to specific computers or time blocks.

Online Quizzing at worthpublishers.com/myers Now you can easily and securely quiz students online using prewritten multiple-choice questions for each chapter. Students receive instant feedback and can take the quizzes multiple times. As the instructor, you can view results by quiz, student, or question, or you can get weekly results via email.

Worth Image and Lecture Gallery at www.worthpublishers.com/ilg Using the *Image and Lecture Gallery*, you can browse or search and download text art, illustrations, outlines, and pre-built PowerPoint slides for ALL Worth titles. Users can also create personal folders for easy organization of the materials.

Video/DVD Resources

New! Moving Images: Exploring Psychology Through Film Available in VHS and DVD and edited by Martin Bolt (Calvin College), this completely new series (drawn from the Films for the Humanities and Sciences) contains 25 one-to-eight minute clips of real people, real experiments, and real patients. The series combines historical footage with cutting-edge research and news programming. Highlights include: "Brain and Behavior: A Contemporary Phineas Gage," "Firewalking: Mind Over Matter," and "Social Rejection: The Need to Belong."

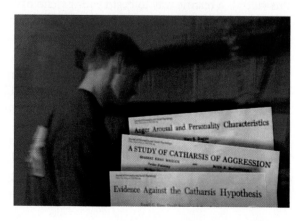

**Moving Images:
Exploring Psychology Through Film**
(edited by Martin Bolt)

New! Scientific American Frontiers Teaching Modules, Third Edition. Housed on ActivePsych Instructor's Classroom Exercise CD-ROMs and also available separately on CD-ROM, DVD, and VHS, this series was edited by Martin Bolt (Calvin College). The Third Edition of this acclaimed series offers you 15 new clips from contemporary segments produced between 2003–2005. Featuring Alan Alda, the series presents both current research and real-world applications, and offers yet another terrific way to encourage discussion and debate in your introductory psychology course.

Worth Digital Media Archive (available in dual platform CD-ROMs, VHS, and DVD) This rich presentation tool contains 42 digitized video clips of classic experiments and research. Footage includes Bandura's Bobo doll experiment, Takooshian's bystander studies, Piaget's conservation experiment, Harlow's monkey experiments, and Milgram's obedience studies. The Digital Media Archive CD-ROM clips are available in MPEG for optimal visual presentation, and are compatible with PowerPoint.

Psychology: The Human Experience Teaching Modules This series includes more than 3 hours of footage from the Introductory Psychology telecourse, *Psychology: The Human Experience,* produced by Coast Learning Systems in collaboration with Worth Publishers. Footage contains noted scholars, the latest research, and striking animations.

The Many Faces of Psychology Video (available in VHS and DVD) Created and written by Frank J. Vattano, Colorado State University, and Martin Bolt, Calvin College (produced by the Office of Instructional Services, Colorado State University), this video is a terrific way to begin your psychology course. *The Many Faces of Psychology* introduces psychology as a science and a profession, illustrating basic and applied methods. The 22-minute video presents some of the major areas in which psychologists work and teach.

Scientific American Frontiers Video Collection, Second Edition (available in VHS and DVD) Hosted by Alan Alda, these 8- to 12-minute teaching modules from the highly praised Scientific American series feature the work of such notable researchers as Steve Sumi, Renée Baillargeon, Carl Rosengren, Laura Pettito, Steven Pinker, Barbara Rothbaum, Bob Stickgold, Irene Pepperberg, Marc Hauser, Linda Bartoshuk, and Michael Gazzaniga.

The Mind Video Teaching Modules, Second Edition (available in VHS and DVD) Edited by Frank J. Vattano, Colorado State University, with the consultation of

Charles Brewer, Furman University, and myself in association with WNET, these 35 brief, engaging video clips dramatically enhance and illustrate your lectures. Examples include segments on language processing, infant cognitive development, genetic factors in alcoholism, and living without memory (featuring a dramatic interview with Clive Wearing).

The Brain Video Teaching Modules, Second Edition (available in VHS and DVD) Edited by Frank J. Vattano and Thomas L. Bennet from Colorado State University, and Michelle Butler, from the United States Air Force Academy, this collection of 32 short clips provides vivid examples for myriad topics in introductory psychology.

Print Supplements for Instructors

New! Significantly Revised and Enhanced Printed Test Bank, Volumes 1 and 2, John Brink, Calvin College Broken down into two volumes of tests, the Test Bank provides over 5,000 multiple-choice factual/definitional, conceptual/application, and conceptual questions, plus essay questions. In response to review input from over a dozen reviewers, Brink has changed the number of distracters from 5 to 4 to avoid confusion, and he has carefully edited each question for effectiveness and comprehension. As a result, this eighth edition set includes over 20 percent new and significantly revised questions. Each question is keyed to a learning objective from the text, page-referenced to the text, and rated for level of difficulty. Also included are copies of the Student Book Companion site quizzes. The first Test Bank includes optional questions from the Study Guide (for instructors who incorporate or require the Study Guide in their courses). The second Test Bank includes optional questions on key Worth media tools, such as PsychSim 5.0, The Brain and The Mind video series, the Scientific American videos, the Digital Media Archive, and Moving Images: Exploring Psychology Through Film.

New! Instructor's Media Guide: This handy guide quickly and visually organizes the extensive instructor and student media resources available for *Psychology,* Eighth Edition, including every video, animation, student web activity (including PsychSim), PowerPoint®, and more—all organized by chapter.

Instructor's Resources, Martin Bolt, Calvin College (also available electronically within the eLibrary) Well-known in the psychology community for its comprehensiveness and innovative teaching ideas, Martin Bolt's revised Instructor's Resources feature more than 30 percent new, revised, and updated material and include the following:

- Outline of Resources, organized by text topic, includes the relevant Instructor's Resource items by type (classroom exercise, lecture/discussion topic, etc.) with appropriate Instructor's Resources page numbers.
- Chapter Objectives from the text highlight main concepts and terms and detail the key points of each text chapter. They can be used as essay questions in classroom examinations. Test Bank and Study Guide fill-in questions are keyed to the Objectives.
- Chapter Outlines follow the major text section headings (with page references), providing relevant instructional materials for each topic—including dozens of ready-to-use detailed lecture/discussion ideas, student projects, classroom exercises (many with ready-to-use handouts for in- or out-of-class use), and suggestions about how to use the videos provided by Worth Publishers (see above), PsychSim modules, and feature films (as they apply to psychological concepts discussed in the text). Note that the films and videos from other sources are outlined in the Book Companion site. Other Web sites are also listed and described here and the feature film descriptions are repeated on the Book Companion site.

Martin Bolt's Lecture Guides, available in both print and easily modifiable Microsoft Word formats (as well as at the end of the Instructor's Resources), offer you a terrific integrating resource for lecture preparation. For each text chapter, the Lecture Guides summarize the main ideas by major section and by Learning Objective. The Lecture Guides also list the lecture/discussion topics, exercises, projects, feature films, transparencies, PsychSim modules, and video segments (from the Worth library) that complement the topics within each major section.

Overhead Transparencies Our transparency set includes over 150 text images, charts, and tables from *Psychology,* Eighth Edition, and other sources.

Print Supplements for Students

New! Visual Concept Reviews, Richard Straub, University of Michigan-Dearborn This full-color booklet—available for free when shrink-wrapped with the book or Study Guide—offers fill-in-the-blank style concept charts that allow students to apply their understanding of the concepts to real-life situations (with answers in an appendix). Some of the Concept Reviews focus on the biopsychosocial approach, thus extending the levels of analysis theme that I have further applied in the text for this edition.

Study Guide, Richard Straub, University of Michigan-Dearborn Following the text's content, Richard Straub offers a Chapter Overview and Chapter Review, divided by major section (each group of fill-in-the-blank and short-essay questions is preceded by the relevant Learning Objective from the text). The Study Guide also includes three self-tests (one of which encourages students to think critically about the chapter's concepts), answers (with page references for the self-tests and explanations of why a choice is correct or incorrect), and a Focus on Language and Vocabulary section, which explains idioms and other phrases from the text that may not be clear to some readers.

***Pursuing Human Strengths: A Positive Psychology Guide,* Martin Bolt, Calvin College** By using the scientific method in its efforts to assess, understand, and then build human strengths, positive psychology balances the investigation of weakness and damage with a study of strength and virtue. This brief *Positive Psychology Guide* gives instructors and students alike the means to learn more about this relevant approach to psychology.

***Critical Thinking Companion,* Second Edition, Jane Halonen, University of West Florida, and Cynthia Gray, Alverno College** Tied to the main topics in *Psychology,* this engaging handbook includes six categories of critical thinking exercises: pattern recognition, practical problem solving, creative problem solving, scientific critical thinking, psychological reasoning, and perspective taking, which connect to the six categories used in the Critical Thinking Exercises available in the Student Study Guide.

Scientific American Reader I hand picked these 14 classic and current articles to provide another tool for enhancing lectures, encouraging discussions, and emphasizing the relevance of psychology to everyday life.

Scientific American Mind This special issue explores riveting breakthroughs in neuroscience and related fields, and investigates, analyzes, and reveals new thinking on: Dreaming and Consciousness, Intelligence and Cognition, Imagination and Emotions, Depression and Mental Illness, and Perception and Understanding.

***Improving the Mind and Brain:* A Scientific American Special Issue** This single-topic issue from Scientific American magazine features findings from the most distinguished researchers in the field.

***Scientific American Explores The Hidden Mind:* A Collector's Edition** This collector's edition includes feature articles that explore and reveal the mysterious inner workings of our minds and brains.

In Appreciation

If it is true that "whoever walks with the wise becomes wise" then I am wiser for all the wisdom and advice received from expert colleagues. Aided by nearly a thousand consultants and reviewers over the last two decades, this has become a better, more accurate book than one author alone (this author, at least) could write. As my editors and I keep reminding ourselves, all of us together are smarter than any one of us.

My indebtedness continues to each of the teacher-scholars whose influence I acknowledged in the seven previous editions, and also to the innumerable researchers who have been so willing to share their time and talent to help me accurately report their research. This new edition also benefited from the creative input and assistance of Jennifer Peluso, Florida Atlantic University, in revising Chapters 9 (Memory) and 10 (Thinking and Language).

My gratitude extends to the colleagues who contributed criticism, corrections, and creative ideas related to the content, pedagogy, and format of this new edition and its supplements package. For their expertise and encouragement, and the gifts of their time to the teaching of psychology, I thank the reviewers, consultants, and focus group participants listed below.

Julie Allison,
Pittsburg State University

Aneeq Ahmad,
Henderson State University

Emir Andrews,
Memorial University

Willow Aureala,
University of Hawaii Center, West Hawaii

Debra K. Bagley,
Mount Aloysius College

David Barkmeier,
Northeastern University

Marcelle Bartolo-Abela,
Holyoke Community College

Scott Bates,
Utah State University

Rochelle Battersby,
Sanford H. Calhoun High School

Susan Becker,
Mesa State University

Stefanie Bell,
Pikes Peak Community College

Suzanne T. Bell,
DePaul University

Sheryl Bereziuk,
Grande Prairie Regional College

Denise Berg,
Santa Monica College

Kathleen Bey,
Palm Beach Community College

Patricia Bishop,
Cleveland State Community College

Marilyn Blumenthal
Farmingdale State University

Linda Bradford,
Community College of Aurora

Suzanne Brayer,
North Canyon High School

June Breninger,
Cascade College

Gayle Brosnan-Watters,
Slippery Rock University

Jay Brown,
Southwest Missouri State University

Michelle A. Butler,
United States Air Force Academy

Hazel Caldwell,
Central Georgia Technical College

Cari Cannon,
Santiago Canyon College

William Canu,
University of Missouri-Rolla

Maureen Carrigan,
University of South Carolina Aiken

Pamela Carroll,
Three Rivers Community College

Richard G. Cavasina,
California University of Pennsylvania

Gabriela Chavira and her graduate student teachers,
California State University-Northridge

Dorothy Chin,
Santa Monica College

Stephen M. Colarelli,
Central Michigan University

Kaye Cook,
Gordon College

Mary Coplen,
Hutchinson Community College

Pamela Costa,
Tacoma Community College

Kathleen Cramm,
Community College of Aurora

Katherine Demtrakis,
Albuquerque Technical Vocational Institute

Vicki DiLillo,
Ohio Wesleyan University

Roberta Eveslage,
Johnson County Community College

Ellie Ezatti,
Santa Monica College

Gaithri Fernando,
California State University, Los Angeles

Gloria Fisher,
Mississippi College

Jim Frailing,
Neenah High School

Sue Frantz,
Highline Community College

Rick Froman,
John Brown University

Gary Gargano,
Merced College

Carol B. George,
St. Johns School

Andrew R. Getzfeld,
New Jersey City University

Kristy Gould,
Luther College

David Gramling,
Austin Preparatory School

Nicholas Greco,
College of Lake County

Toby Green,
Santa Monica College

Laura Gruntmeir,
Redlands Community College

Mary Hannah,
University of Detroit Mercy

Peg Hanson,
College of Lake County

Chris Heavey,
University of Nevada-Las Vegas

Paul Hillock,
Algonquin College

Len Hudzinski,
Lake Tahoe Community College

Steven Isonio,
Golden West College

Charles Ivey,
Winter Park High School

Maria Janicki,
Douglas College

Robert Jensen,
California State University-Sacramento

Andrew T. Johnson
Park University

Suzanne R. Jones,
Webster University

Oscar Joseph Harm,
University of South Carolina Aiken

Misty Hull,
Pikes Peak Community College

Wendy Kallina,
Macon State College

Cindy Kamilar,
Pikes Peak Community College

Jeffry Kellogg,
Marian College

Arthur D. Kemp,
Central Missouri State University

Raymond Kilduff,
Community College of Rhode Island

Rosalyn King,
Northern Virginia Community College-Loudon

Kristina T. Klassen,
North Idaho College

Gary Klatsky,
SUNY Oswego

Timothy Klitz,
Washington and Jefferson College

Jean E. Kubeck,
Adams State College

Samuel H. Lamb III,
Tidewater Community College

Claudia Lampman,
University of Alaska

Jackie Lanum,
Santa Monica College

Elizabeth Levin,
Laurentian University

Deborah Licht,
Pikes Peak Community College

Rachelle Lipschultz,
Anne Arundel Community College

Nancey Lobb,
Alvin Community College

Jann Longman,
Liberty High School

Wade C. Lueck,
College of Eastern Utah

Angie Mackewn,
University of Tennessee at Martin

Laura Madson,
New Mexico State University

Brian Malley,
University of Michigan

Nancy B. Mann,
Southern Wesleyan University

Cindy Marriot,
Schoolcraft College

Jerry Marshall,
Green River Community College

Diane Martichuski,
University of Colorado Boulder

Cathy Matresse,
North Idaho College and Bay Mills Community College

Donna Wood McCarty,
Clayton State University

David McCone,
United States Air Force Academy

Lisa McCone,
Pine Creek High School

Donna McEwen,
Friends University

Lesley McIntyre,
SUNY Cobleskill

Polly McMahon,
Spokane Falls Community College

Jennifer Meehan Brennom,
Kirkwood Community College

Joni Mihura,
University of Toledo

Antoinette Miller,
Clayton College and State University

Jeannie Mitchell,
Rend Lake College

Mark Mitchell,
Clarion University of Pennsylvania

Marta Mohr,
Kilian Community College

Joann Morgan,
Albuquerque Technical Vocational Institute

Karlyn Musante,
Santa Monica College

Barbara Nash,
Bentley College

Nathaniel Naughton,
Arlington Catholic High School

Michael Nelson,
University of Missouri-Rolla

Benjamin Newberry,
Kent State University

Cynthia O'Dell,
Indiana University Northwest

Peggy O'Neil-Chromey,
Northfield Mount Hermon School

William H. Overman,
University of North Carolina, Wilmington

Dan Patanella,
John Jay College of Criminal Justice

Marcus D. Patterson,
University of Massachusetts-Boston

Marilyn Patterson,
Lindenwood University

Andrew Peck,
Pennsylvania State University

Jennifer Peluso,
Florida Atlantic University

Pete Petersen,
Johnson County Community College

John Petraitis,
University of Alaska

Stephen Phillips,
Broward Community College

Michelle Pilati,
Rio Hondo College

Colleen Pilgrim,
Schoolcraft College

Debbie Podwika,
Kankakee Community College

Scott Plous,
Wesleyan University

Kathryn Potoczak,
Saint Lawrence University

Michael Poulin,
University of California-Irvine

Psi Chi Honors Society and other students,
Montana State University

Jennifer Puente,
William Rainey Harper College

Diane Quartarolo,
Union Institute and University

Christopher Randall,
Troy University, Montgomery Campus

Louise Rasmussen,
Wright State University

Judith S. Rauenzahn,
Kutztown University

Celia Reaves,
Monroe Community College

Brad Redburn,
Johnson County Community College

Darrel Regier,
American Psychiatric Association

Leonard Riley,
Pikes Peak Community College

Alan Roberts,
Indiana University

June Rosenberg,
Lyndon State College

Steve Rouse,
Pepperdine University

Lisa Routh,
Pikes Peak Community College

Patricia Sampson,
University of Maryland Eastern Shore

Don Saucier,
Kansas State University

Sherry Schnake,
Saint Mary of the Woods College

John Schwoebel,
Cazenovia College

Eric Seelau,
Indiana University of Pennsylvania

Jane Sheldon,
University of Michigan—Dearborn

Mark Sibicky,
Marietta College

Cynthia Silovich,
Fargo South High School

David Simpson,
Valparaiso University

Stephanie Smith,
Indiana University Northwest

Ross B. Steinman,
Rowan University

Betsy Stern,
Milwaukee Area Technical College

Robby Stewart,
Oakland University

Christine Sutow,
Rio Hondo College

Amy Sweetman,
Los Angeles City College

Patricia Toney,
Sandhills Community College

Meral Topcu-LeCroix,
Ferris State University

Michael Trumbull,
Pikes Peak Community College

Gopakumar Venugopalan,
University of Alaska

Jeanne M. Viviani,
LaGuardia Community College

Steven L. Voss,
Moberly Area Community College

Dennis Wanamaker,
Bellevue Community College

Kathryn M. Wescott,
Juniata College

Fred Whitford,
Montana State University

Gordon Whitman,
Tidewater Community College

Eric Wiertelak,
Macalester College

Jacquie Witsberger,
Wheeling Jesuit University

Leland Woodson,
Kwantlen University College

At Worth Publishers a host of people played key roles in creating this eighth edition.

Although the information gathering is never ending, the formal planning began as the author-publisher team gathered for a two day retreat in October, 2004. This happy and creative gathering included John Brink, Martin Bolt, Thomas Ludwig, Richard Straub, and me from the author team, along with my assistant Kathryn Brownson and manuscript developer Phyllis Vandervelde. We were joined by Worth Publishers' publisher Catherine Woods; editors Christine Brune, Renee Altier, Nancy Fleming, Tracey Kuehn, and Betty Probert; and sales and marketing executives Kate Nurre, Tom Kling, Guy Geraghty, Greg David, and Chuck Linsmeier. The input and brainstorming during this meeting of minds gave birth, among other things, to the new pedagogy in this edition, and to the thoroughly revised Chapter 3, Nature, Nurture, and Human Diversity.

Christine Brune, chief editor for the last six editions, is a wonder worker. She offers just the right mix of encouragement, gentle admonition, attention to detail, and passion for excellence. An author could not ask for more.

Renee Altier, who is now the Director of Product and New Business Development for Bedford, Freeman, and Worth Publishers, helped connect me with many colleagues throughout the revision process, and spearheaded a creative new photo program. Renee also played an essential role in expanding and improving the impressive multimedia supplements that accompany this edition. As Renee's supportive role shifted, she passed the baton for editorial management of our teaching package to acquisitions editor, Kevin Feyen, with whom we are pleased to now be working.

Development editor Nancy Fleming is one of those rare editors who is gifted both at "thinking big" about a chapter—and with a kindred spirit to my own—while also applying her sensitive, graceful, line-by-line touches. Nancy also displayed her gifts in leading the creation of the new Learning Objectives and Learning Outcomes.

Publisher Catherine Woods helped construct and execute the plan for this new edition and its supplements. Catherine was also a trusted sounding board as we faced the myriad discrete decisions along the way. Media and Supplements Editor Andrea Musick coordinated production of the huge supplements package for this edition. Betty Probert efficiently edited and produced the print supplements, and, in the process, also helped fine-tune the whole book. Editorial Assistants Sarah

Berger and Matthew Driskill provided invaluable support in commissioning and organizing the multitude of reviews, mailing information to professors, and numerous other daily tasks related to the book's development and production. Lee Mahler did a splendid job of laying out each page. Patricia Marx, Bianca Moscatelli, Christina Micek, and Julie Tesser worked together to locate the myriad new photographic illustrations.

Associate Managing Editor Tracey Kuehn displayed tireless tenacity, commitment, and impressive organization in leading Worth's gifted artistic production team and coordinating editorial input throughout the production process. Production Manager Sarah Segal masterfully kept the book to its tight schedule, and Babs Reingold skillfully directed creation of the distinctive design and art program. Production Manager Stacey Alexander, along with supplements production editor Eve Conte, did their usual excellent work of producing the many supplements.

To achieve our goal of supporting the teaching of psychology, this teaching package not only must be authored, reviewed, edited, and produced, but also made available to teachers of psychology. For their exceptional success in doing that, our author team is grateful to Worth Publishers' professional sales and marketing team. We are especially grateful to Associate Marketing Director Carlise Stembridge and Senior Marketing Manager Kate Nurre both for their tireless efforts to inform our teaching colleagues of our efforts to assist their teaching, and for the joy of working with them.

At Hope College, the supporting team members for this edition included Kathryn Brownson, who researched countless bits of information, proofed hundreds of pages, and, with the assistance of Sara Neevel and Megan Rapelje, prepared the bibliography and name index. Kathryn has become a knowledgeable and sensitive adviser on many matters. With diligence and delight, Travis Goldwire and Erin Darlington supported all of Kathryn's efforts by sleuthing information, photocopying, and proofreading. Laura Luchies helped compile the cross-reference table on new coverage of gender in this edition, and Laura Myers updated, with page citations, all the cross-reference tables.

Manuscript developers Phyllis and Richard Vandervelde worked faithfully to enter or revise every one of the more than 400,000 words. Over more than two decades they have processed some 10 million words of two dozen text editions and trade books, with timely diligence, a passion for excellence, a guiding voice, and an infectious joy. Amid the pleasures of creating this new edition was the enormous sadness, after four decades of close family and professional friendship, of losing Phyllis to cancer. Even its associated pain could not, however, deter her from completing her last chapter less than two weeks before her death.

Because of this unexpected loss, we are especially grateful to Marilyn Essink and Sara Neevel for so ably stepping in to do the meticulous completion of *Psychology*, Eighth Edition.

Again, I gratefully acknowledge the influence and editing assistance of my writing coach, poet Jack Ridl, whose influence resides in the voice you will be hearing in the pages that follow. He, more than anyone, cultivated my delight in dancing with the language, and taught me to approach writing as a craft that shades into art.

After hearing countless dozens of people say that this book's supplements have taken their teaching to a new level, I reflect on how fortunate I am to be a part of a team on which everyone has produced on-time work marked by the highest professional standards. For their remarkable talents, their long-term dedication, and their friendship, I thank Martin Bolt, John Brink, Thomas Ludwig, and Richard Straub.

Finally, my gratitude extends to the many students and instructors who have written to offer suggestions, or just an encouraging word. It is for them, and those about to begin their study of psychology, that I have done my best to introduce the field I love.

The day this book went to press was the day I started gathering information and ideas for the ninth edition. Your input will again influence how this book continues to evolve. So, please, do share your thoughts.

David Myers

Hope College
Holland, Michigan 49422-9000 USA
davidmyers.org

| For Advanced Placement Teachers |

Why Should I Use Myers: *Psychology*, Eighth Edition, for AP Psychology?

If you're a high school teacher trying to decide on a text for your Advanced Placement (AP) Psychology course, you cannot do better than the book you're holding right now. Student evaluations from our own classes are filled with enthusiatic observations:

- "I actually liked this book!"
- "David Myers rocks."
- "I have never wanted to read a textbook before this one."

The language is accessible and the narrative flows. Students enjoy the clear explanations of difficult concepts, the evenhanded treatment of unresolved issues, the use of humor, and the engaging examples and quotations used to illustrate content.

From our perspective as teachers, we could not hope for a better partner as we prepare students for the challenge of the AP exam. The comprehensive coverage in this text, with its emphasis on up-to-date research findings, will prepare your students to excel on exam day. Whether you are a veteran with vast files of supplementary materials or a rookie just beginning the adventure of teaching AP Psychology, you will appreciate the support of this text and its package. (See Preface, p. xxii, for more details.)

What Is in the Myers AP Psychology Package?

The eighth edition of *Psychology* is specially designed for the AP course. The Myers text solidly presents the content your students will need to succeed. The package includes a host of top-quality supplements available to adopters of the text. The amazing Instructor's Resources binder, several sets of video clips, PowerPoint® presentations, and transparencies are all available to help you.

In addition, special resources are available just for AP teachers and students.

- **The AP Psychology Test Bank** This resource, available in both print and electronic versions, allows you to assess student progress with multiple-choice and free-response (essay) questions. For each chapter, the Test Bank offers 100 or more multiple-choice questions formatted like those found on the AP Exam. You may use these items to create quizzes and tests for your teaching units. You will also find two complete AP Psychology practice exams, each with 100 multiple-choice and two free-response questions, designed to parallel the real test. You may use these tests as your course final exam, or as AP exam preparation for your students. Finally, this specially designed Test Bank includes a wealth of information based on our extensive experiences on the AP Psychology Test Development Committee and at the annual exam scoring sessions. (Call us crazy. We have worked them all—from 1992 to the present!). You will learn about the philosophy of the test and how your students can maximize the credit they receive for their knowledge.
- **The AP Psychology Study Guide** The exercises in this book will help your students master the core concepts of psychology. They will gain both competence and confidence as they work their way through the curriculum. They will also get practical advice for succeeding in the course based on our own experiences in the AP classroom.

- ***The AP Psychology Web Site*** This robust Web site includes AP-specific content for both students and teachers, including tips for preparing for and taking the AP exam; special handouts, activities, and information for new AP teachers; interactive flashcards; Web quizzes; simulations and demonstrations; Web links; and extra content coverage such as a discussion of somatoform disorders.

Why Is Psychology the Perfect AP Class?

AP teachers are a special breed. If you've taught AP courses, you know what we're talking about. It takes extra effort to prepare for an AP class and extra enthusiasm to teach it. There is more stress involved as we work to make sure our students are ready for the AP exams in May.

For most of us, though, the extra effort is worth it. There is something particularly satisfying about leading students to new levels of commitment and academic achievement. The rewards of watching them grow in confidence and ability more than compensate for the additional demands of teaching AP.

Although all AP courses are special in these ways, the topic of psychology lends a unique freshness to the AP teaching experience. Last fall, one of our students introduced herself by saying, "I've been waiting since eighth grade to take this class!"

How can a student *not* be interested in behavior and mental processes? Our subject has a relevance that no other course can match. Our discipline has a breadth that leads students on a fantastic journey from the impact of neurotransmitters at the synapse to the dynamics of decision making on a jury; from the psychophysics of depth perception to the stability of babies' temperaments in their developing personalities. Even if students happen not to be interested in the topic of this week's lessons, by next week we will have moved on to something new and different.

The content, of course, is only part of the story. The *process* of psychology also serves students well as they chart their courses toward the future. The scientific nature of psychology allows us to teach the critical thinking skills that are so important for personal and society-level decision making. While most of our students will not end up as researchers, all of them need to have enough scientific literacy to understand what they hear in the media. Psychology shares methods with chemistry, astronomy, and other sciences, but students tend to be more interested in psychological research because it's more directly relevant to their lives. Through our classes, they learn the tools that allow them to evaluate claims effectively and make rational decisions. In a world where noncritical thinking and pseudoscience have powerful footholds, students need all the help they can get to sort the wheat from the chaff.

How Is the AP Psychology Examination Formatted and Administered?

The AP Psychology Exam has been administered annually in May since 1992. Except for the difficulty level (it's harder now than it used to be), little has changed since that first year. Every exam consists of two sections:

1. 100 multiple-choice items

2. 2 free-response prompts (often called "essay questions").

Let's take a closer look at each section in the order students will encounter them on exam day.

Multiple Choice Students have 70 minutes to complete this part of the test. Rigorously pretested, the questions (each with five options) are arranged by difficulty level, with the easier questions at the beginning of the exam. Correct answers are worth 1 point, but incorrect answers cost students only $^{1}/_{4}$ point. The point total earned on this section is 66.7 percent of the final score. Most students finish this section ahead of the time limit, but they must wait the full 70 minutes before starting the second section of the test.

Free Response Students have 50 minutes to address both free-response prompts. The integrated nature of the prompts challenges students to apply their knowledge of several content areas (for example, scientific methods, biological foundations, and motivation) in the same answer. While potential point totals for each prompt may vary, the two answers are weighted equally and together contribute 33.3 percent of the final score.

What Are Some Helpful Strategies for Teaching AP Psychology?

It is hard to beat a well-planned, well-taught course when preparing students for the AP Psychology exam. We've generated the following tips for establishing a successful course from personal experience and discussions with dozens of successful (and unsuccessful) AP teachers.

1. **Establish a schedule and stick to it.** Assemblies, weather, and illness can derail progress, but do all you can to stay on track.

2. **Incorporate active learning in your classroom.** Your students will retain more of the knowledge you are imparting if your teaching includes demonstrations, experiments, writing exercises, and other active learning resources, such as those found in the supplements package for this AP text.

3. **Require textbook reading.** You can't cover everything in class. Use quizzes, assignments, and exams to hold students accountable for text material you don't cover. Teach students how to take effective reading notes.

4. **Give tests resembling the AP test format.** If you're on a block schedule, 50 multiple-choice questions and one free-response prompt will easily fit into a class period. Cut down on the number of multiple-choice questions for more traditional-length class periods.

5. **Teach writing.** If writing is not your strength, ask a trusted English teacher to give you a hand. Students need to be able to convey information clearly in high-pressure testing situations. Remember that parroting the prompt in a long introduction is unnecessary and never earns points.

6. **Use grading rubrics to score exams.** Every summer at the AP Exam Reading, a rubric is developed to score the free-response answers. Rubrics add grading speed and reliability to test scoring and allow you to explain why a particular answer did or did not earn points.

7. **Give cumulative or review tests regularly.** Chapter tests are fine, but cumulative tests more closely resemble the AP exam, help students keep previously learned material in mind, and allow students to make connections among all that they are learning.

8. **Obtain and administer actual AP exams.** Every free-response question is released 48 hours after the test is given in May. Rubrics for each exam are also available either from the College Board or from seasoned AP teachers who keep good files. Three of the multiple-choice tests have also been released. The most recent test may be purchased online from the College Board (http://apcentral.collegeboard.com/).

Especially if you are new to teaching the AP course, you should consider attending an all-day, AP Psychology teaching workshop. Dozens of these workshops take place across North America each year. AP Psychology teachers also benefit tremendously when they participate in a five-day AP summer institute The AP coordinator in your school will receive information on the workshops and institutes nearest you.

Networking with other AP teachers is also invaluable. You may achieve this by attending a workshop or institute or by joining a listserv dedicated to teaching AP Psychology. The College Board AP psychology list is a good place to start (http://ap-central.collegeboard.com/). Joining organizations such as APA's Teachers of Psychology in Secondary Schools (TOPSS: http://www.apa.org/ed/topss/) and the Society for the Teaching of Psychology (http://teachpsych.lemoyne.edu/teachpsych/div/divindex.html) will also help you network while providing access to excellent content and pedagogical resources.

We hope these tips, and this comprehensive and unparalleled Myers: *Psychology*, Eighth Edition, AP package will help you and your students build a successful AP Psychology program.

We look forward to hearing your success stories as well as continuing input as we strive to help David Myers maintain the best possible package for AP Psychology course.

Charles T. Blair-Broeker
Cedar Falls High School, Iowa

Randal M. Ernst
Lincoln High School, Nebraska

ANOTHER VOICE ON: THE STORY OF PSYCHOLOGY

LANGSTON HUGHES (1902–1967), FROM "I DREAM A WORLD," 1945, *THE COLLECTED POEMS OF LANGSTON HUGHES*

I dream a world where man
No other man will scorn,
Where love will bless the earth
And peace its paths adorn.
I dream a world where all
Will know sweet freedom's way,

Where greed no longer saps the soul
Nor avarice blights our day.
A world I dream where black or white,
Whatever race you be,
Will share the bounties of the earth
And every man is free,

Where wretchedness will hang its head
And joy, like a pearl,
Attends the needs of all mankind–
Of such I dream, my world!

Prologue: The Story of Psychology

"I have made a ceaseless effort not to ridicule, not to bewail, not to scorn human actions, but to understand them."

Benedict Spinoza, *A Political Treatise, 1677*

"What's it like being married to a psychologist?" people occasionally ask my wife. "Does he use his psychology on you?"

"So, does your Dad, like, analyze you?" my children have been asked many times by friends.

"What do you think of me?" asked one barber, hoping for an instant personality analysis after learning that I was a psychologist.

For these questioners, as for most people whose exposure to psychology comes from popular books, magazines, and TV, psychologists analyze personality, offer counseling, and dispense child-rearing advice.

Do they? Yes, and much more. Consider some of psychology's questions that from time to time you may wonder about:

Have you ever found yourself reacting to something just as one of your biological parents would—perhaps in a way you vowed you never would—and then wondered how much of your personality you inherited? *To what extent are person-to-person differences in personality predisposed by one's genes? To what extent by the home and neighborhood environments?*

Have you ever played peekaboo with a 6-month-old and wondered why the baby finds the game so delightful? The infant reacts as though, when you momentarily move behind a door, you actually disappear—only to reappear later out of thin air. *What do babies actually perceive and think?*

Have you ever awakened from a nightmare and, with a wave of relief, wondered why you had such a crazy dream? *How often, and why, do we dream?*

Have you ever wondered what leads to school and work success? Are some people just born smarter? *Does sheer intelligence explain why some people get richer, think more creatively, or relate more sensitively?*

Have you ever become depressed or anxious and wondered whether you'll ever feel "normal"? *What triggers our bad moods—and our good ones?*

Have you ever worried about how to act among people of a different culture, race, or gender? *In what ways are we alike as members of the human family? How do we differ?*

Such questions provide grist for psychology's mill because psychology is a science that seeks to answer all sorts of questions about us all: how we think, feel, and act.

A smile is a smile the world around
Throughout this book, you will see examples not only of our cultural and gender diversity but also of the similarities that define our shared human nature. People in different cultures vary in when and how often they smile, but a smile *means* the same thing anywhere in the world.

Psychology's Roots

OBJECTIVE **1** | Define *psychology.*

Once upon a time, on a planet in your neighborhood of the universe, there came to be people. Soon thereafter, these creatures became intensely interested in themselves and in one another. They wondered, *"Who are we? From where come our thoughts? Our feelings? Our actions? And how are we to understand—and to master or manage—those around us?"* Psychology's answers to these wonderings have developed from international roots in philosophy and biology into a science that aims to describe and explain how we think, feel, and act. Today we define **psychology** as *the scientific study of behavior and mental processes.* Let's unpack this definition. *Behavior* is anything an organism *does*—any action we can observe and record. Yelling, smiling, blinking, sweating, talking, and questionnaire marking are all observable behaviors. *Mental processes* are the internal, subjective experiences we infer from behavior—sensations, perceptions, dreams, thoughts, beliefs, and feelings.

The key word in psychology's definition is *science.* Psychology, as I will emphasize in Chapter 1 and throughout this book, is less a set of findings than a way of asking and answering questions. As a science, psychology evaluates competing ideas with careful observation and rigorous analysis. In its attempt to describe and explain human nature, psychological science welcomes hunches and plausible-sounding theories. And it puts them to the test. If a theory works—if the data support its predictions—so much the better for that theory. If the predictions fail, the theory will be revised or rejected.

My aim in this text, then, is not merely to report results but also to show you how psychologists play their game. You will see how researchers evaluate conflicting opinions and ideas. And you will learn how all of us, whether scientists or simply curious people, can think smarter when describing and explaining the events of our lives.

But first, let's consider the roots of today's psychology to help us appreciate psychologists' varied perspectives.

Prescientific Psychology

OBJECTIVE **2** | Trace psychology's prescientific roots, from early understandings of mind and body to the beginnings of modern science.

We can trace many of psychology's current questions back through human history. These early thinkers wondered: How do our minds work? How do our bodies relate to our minds? How much of what we know comes built in? How much is acquired through experience? In India, for example, Buddha pondered how sensations and perceptions combine to form ideas. In China, Confucius stressed the power of ideas and of an educated mind. In ancient Israel, Hebrew scholars anticipated today's psychology by linking mind and emotion to the body; people were said to think with their hearts and feel with their bowels.

In ancient Greece, the philosopher-teacher Socrates (469–399 B.C.) and his student Plato (428–348 B.C.) concluded that mind is separable from body and continues after the body dies, and that knowledge is innate—born within us. As Socrates lay dying, Plato's future student, a teenager named Aristotle (384–322 B.C.), was developing a sharp mind in another part of Greece. Aristotle's love of data distinguished him from Socrates and Plato, who derived principles by logic. An intellectual ancestor of today's scientists, Aristotle derived principles from careful observations. His observations told him that "the soul is not separable from the body, and the same holds good of particular parts of the soul" (*De Anima*). Moreover, he said knowledge is *not* preexisting (sorry, Socrates and Plato); instead, it grows from the experiences stored in our memories.

■ **psychology** the scientific study of behavior and mental processes.

■ **empiricism** the view that (a) knowledge comes from experience via the senses, and (b) science flourishes through observation and experiment.

The next 2000 years brought few enduring new insights into human nature, but that changed in the 1600s, when modern science began to flourish. With it came new theories of human behavior, and new versions of the ancient debates. A frail but brilliant Frenchman named René Descartes (1595–1650) agreed with Socrates and Plato about the existence of innate ideas and the mind's being "entirely distinct from the body" and able to survive its death. Descartes' concept of mind forced him to conjecture, as people have ever since, how the immaterial mind and physical body communicate. A scientist as well as a philosopher, Descartes dissected animals and concluded that the fluid in the brain's cavities contained "animal spirits." These spirits, he surmised, flowed from the brain through what we call the nerves (which he thought were hollow) to the muscles, provoking movement. Memories formed as experiences opened pores in the brain, into which the animal spirits also flowed.

Descartes was right that nerve paths are important and that they enable reflexes. Yet, genius though he was, and standing upon the knowledge accumulated from 99+ percent of our human history, he hardly had a clue of what today's average 12-year-old knows. Indeed, most of the scientific story of our self-exploration—the story told in this book's chapters—has been written in but the last historical eye blink of human time.

Meanwhile, across the English channel in Britain, science was taking a more down-to-earth form, centered on experiment, experience, and common-sense judgment. Francis Bacon (1561–1626) became one of the founders of modern science, and his influence lingers in the experiments of today's psychological science. Bacon also was fascinated by the human mind and its failings. Anticipating what we have come to appreciate about our mind's hunger to perceive patterns even in random events, he wrote that "the human understanding, from its peculiar nature, easily supposes a greater degree of order and equality in things than it really finds" (*Novum Organuum*). He also foresaw research findings on our noticing and remembering events that confirm our beliefs: "All superstition is much the same whether it be that of astrology, dreams, omens . . . in all of which the deluded believers observe events which are fulfilled, but neglect and pass over their failure, though it be much more common."

Some 50 years after Bacon's death, John Locke (1632–1704), a British political philosopher, sat down to write a one-page essay on "our own abilities" for an upcoming discussion with friends. After 20 years and hundreds of pages, Locke had completed one of history's latest and greatest late papers (*An Essay Concerning Human Understanding*), in which he famously argued that the mind at birth is a blank slate—a "white paper"—on which experience writes. This idea, adding to Bacon's ideas, helped form modern **empiricism,** the view that knowledge originates in experience and that science should, therefore, rely on observation and experimentation.

Bettmann/Corbis

A seventeenth-century view of nerves
In his *Treatise of Man*, Descartes proposed the hydraulics of a simple reflex.

Psychological Science Is Born

OBJECTIVE 3 | Explain how the early psychologists sought to understand the mind's structure and functions, and identify some of the leading psychologists who worked in these areas.

Philosophers' thinking about thinking continued until the birth of psychology as we know it, on a December day in 1879, in a small room on the third floor of a shabby building at Germany's University of Leipzig. There, two young men were helping an austere, middle-aged professor, Wilhelm Wundt, create an experimental apparatus. Their machine measured the time lag between people's hearing a ball hit a platform and their pressing a telegraph key (Hunt, 1993). Later, the researchers compared this lag with the time required for slightly more complex tasks. Curiously, people responded in about one-tenth of a second when asked to press the key as soon as the sound occurred—and in about two-tenths of a second when asked to press the key as soon as they were consciously aware of perceiving the sound. (To be aware of one's awareness

Information sources are cited in parentheses, with name and date, then provided fully in the References section at the book's end.

Wilhelm Wundt
Wundt (far left) established the first psychology laboratory at the University of Leipzig, Germany.

takes a little longer.) Wundt was seeking to measure "atoms of the mind"—the fastest and simplest mental processes. Thus began what many consider psychology's first experiment, launching the first psychological laboratory, staffed by Wundt and psychology's first graduate students.

Before long this new science of psychology became organized into different branches, or schools of thought, each promoted by pioneering thinkers. These early schools included *structuralism* and *functionalism,* described here, and Gestalt psychology, behaviorism, and psychoanalysis, described in later chapters.

Thinking About the Mind's Structure

Soon after receiving his Ph.D. in 1892, Wundt's student Edward Bradford Titchener joined the Cornell University faculty and introduced **structuralism.** As physicists and chemists discerned the structure of matter, so Titchener aimed to discover the elements of mind. His method was to engage people in self-reflective *introspection* (looking inward), training them to report elements of their experience as they looked at a rose, listened to a metronome, smelled a scent, or tasted a substance. What were

■ **structuralism** an early school of psychology that used introspection to explore the elemental structure of the human mind.

Edward Bradford Titchener
Used introspection to search for the mind's structural elements.

their immediate sensations, their images, their feelings? And how did these relate to one another? Titchener shared with the English essayist C. S. Lewis (1960, pp. 18–19) the view that "there is one thing, and only one in the whole universe which we know more about than we could learn from external observation." That one thing, Lewis said, is ourselves. "We have, so to speak, inside information."

Alas, structuralism waned as introspection waned. Introspection required smart, verbal people. It also proved somewhat unreliable, its results varying from person to person and experience to experience. Moreover, recent studies indicate that people's recollections frequently err. So do their self-reports about what, for example, has caused them to help or hurt another (Myers, 2002). Often we just don't know why we feel what we feel and do what we do.

Thinking About the Mind's Functions

Unlike those hoping to assemble the structure of mind from simple elements—which was rather like trying to understand a car by examining its disconnected parts—philosopher-psychologist William James thought it more fruitful to consider the evolved *functions* of our thoughts and feelings. Smelling is what the nose does; thinking is what the brain does. But why do the nose and brain do these things? Under the influence of evolutionary theorist Charles Darwin, James assumed that thinking, like smelling, developed because it was adaptive—it contributed to our ancestors' survival. Consciousness serves a function. It enables us to consider our past, adjust to our present circumstances, and plan our future. As a **functionalist,** James encouraged explorations of down-to-earth emotions, memories, will power, habits, and moment-to-moment streams of consciousness.

James' greatest legacy, however, came less from his laboratory than from his Harvard teaching and his writing. When not plagued by ill health and depression, James was an impish, outgoing, and joyous man, who once recalled that "the first lecture on psychology I ever heard was the first I ever gave." During one of his wise-cracking lectures, a student interrupted and asked him to get serious (Hunt, 1993). He was reportedly one of the first American professors to solicit end-of-course student evaluations of his teaching. He loved his students, his family, and the world of ideas, but tired of painstaking chores such as proofreading. "Send me no proofs!" he once told an editor. "I will return them unopened and never speak to you again" (Hunt, 1993, p. 145).

James displayed the same spunk in 1890, when—over the objections of Harvard's president—he admitted Mary Calkins into his graduate seminar (Scarborough &

■ **functionalism** a school of psychology that focused on how mental and behavioral processes function—how they enable the organism to adapt, survive, and flourish.

"You don't know your own mind."
Jonathan Swift, *Polite Conversation*, 1738

Monika Suteski

William James and Mary Whiton Calkins
James, legendary teacher-writer, mentored Calkins, who became a pioneering memory researcher and American Psychological Association president.

Margaret Floy Washburn
The first woman to receive a psychology Ph.D.; synthesized animal behavior research in *The Animal Mind*.

■ **humanistic psychology** historically significant perspective that emphasized the growth potential of healthy people; used personalized methods to study personality in hopes of fostering personal growth.

Sigmund Freud
Famed personality theorist and therapist, whose controversial ideas influenced humanity's self-understanding.

Furumoto, 1987). When Calkins joined, all the other students dropped. (In those years women lacked even the right to vote.) So James tutored her alone. Later she finished all the requirements for a Harvard Ph.D., outscoring all the male students on the qualifying exams. Alas, Harvard denied her the degree she had earned, offering her instead a degree from Radcliffe College, its undergraduate sister school for women. Calkins resisted the unequal treatment and refused the degree. More than a century later, psychologists and psychology students were lobbying Harvard to posthumously award the Ph.D. she earned (*Feminist Psychologist,* 2002).

Calkins nevertheless became a distinguished memory researcher and the American Psychological Association's (APA's) first female president in 1905. What a different world from the recent past—1996 to 2005—when women claimed two-thirds or more of new psychology Ph.D.s and were 5 of the 10 elected presidents of the science-oriented American Psychological Society. In Canada and Europe, too, most recent psychology doctorates have been earned by women.

When Harvard denied Calkins the claim to being psychology's first female psychology Ph.D., that honor fell to Margaret Floy Washburn, who later wrote an influential book, *The Animal Mind,* and became the second female APA president in 1921. Although Washburn's thesis was the first foreign study Wundt published in his journal, her gender meant she was barred from joining the organization of experimental psychologists founded by Titchener, her own graduate adviser (Johnson, 1997).

James' influence reached even further through his dozens of well-received articles, which moved the publisher Henry Holt to offer a contract for a textbook of the new science of psychology. James agreed and began work in 1878, with an apology for requesting two years to finish his writing. The work proved an unexpected chore and actually took him 12 years. (Why am I not surprised?) More than a century later, people still read the resulting *Principles of Psychology* and marvel at the brilliance and elegance with which James introduced psychology to the educated public.

Psychological Science Develops

OBJECTIVE 4 | Describe the evolution of psychology as defined from the 1920s through today.

This young science of psychology developed from the more established fields of philosophy and biology. Wundt was both a philosopher and a physiologist. James was an American philosopher. Ivan Pavlov, who pioneered the study of learning, was a Russian physiologist. Sigmund Freud, who developed an influential theory of personality, was an Austrian physician. Jean Piaget, the last century's most influential observer of children, was a Swiss biologist. This list of pioneering psychologists—"Magellans of the mind," as Morton Hunt (1993) has called them—illustrates psychology's origins in many disciplines and countries.

The rest of the story of psychology—the subject of this book—develops at many levels. With activities ranging from psychotherapy to the study of nerve cell activity, *psychology* is not easily defined. Wundt and Titchener focused on *inner* sensations, images, and feelings. James, too, engaged in introspective examination of the stream of consciousness and of emotion. Freud emphasized the ways emotional

Monika Suteski

John B. Watson and Rosalie Rayner
Working with Rayner, Watson championed psychology as the science of behavior and demonstrated conditioned responses on a baby who became famous as "Little Albert."

Monika Suteski

B. F. Skinner
A leading behaviorist, who rejected introspection and studied how consequences shape behavior.

responses to childhood experiences and our unconscious thought processes affect our behavior. Thus, until the 1920s, *psychology* was defined as "the science of mental life."

From the 1920s into the 1960s, American psychologists, initially led by flamboyant and provocative John B. Watson and later by the equally provocative B. F. Skinner, dismissed introspection and redefined *psychology* as "the scientific study of observable behavior." After all, said these *behaviorists,* science is rooted in observation. You cannot observe a sensation, a feeling, or a thought, but you *can* observe and record people's *behavior* as they respond to different situations.

Humanistic psychology was a softer, 1960s response to Freudian psychology and to behaviorism, which pioneers Carl Rogers and Abraham Maslow found too mechanistic. Rather than calling up childhood memories or focusing on learned behaviors, Rogers and Maslow both emphasized the importance of current environmental influences on our growth potential, and the importance of meeting our needs for love and acceptance.

In the 1960s, psychology began to recapture its initial interest in mental processes through studies of how our mind processes and retains information. This *cognitive revolution* supported ideas developed by earlier psychologists, such as the importance of considering internal thought processes, but it expanded upon those ideas to explore scientifically the ways we perceive, process, and remember information. Cognitive psychology and more recently *cognitive neuroscience* (the study of the interaction of thought processes and brain function) have been especially beneficial in helping to develop new ways to understand and treat disorders such as depression, as we shall see in Chapter 16.

To encompass psychology's concern with observable behavior *and* with inner thoughts and feelings, we define *psychology* today as the scientific study of behavior *and* mental processes.

Psychology's scope and history
In her quilt, "Crazy About Psychology," Nancy S. Breland, a psychology professor at the College of New Jersey, captures images and people from psychology's first century.

Courtesy Nancy S. Breland

≫ LEARNING OUTCOMES

Psychology's Roots

OBJECTIVE 1 | **Define** *psychology.*

Psychology is the scientific study of behavior (anything an organism does) and mental processes (subjective experiences inferred from behavior). The key word in this definition is *science*.

OBJECTIVE 2 | **Trace psychology's prescientific roots, from early understandings of mind and body to the beginnings of modern science.**

Psychology traces its roots back through recorded history to India, China, the Middle East, and Europe, where many scholars spent their lives wondering about people. In their attempt to understand human nature, they looked carefully at how our minds work and how our bodies relate to our minds.

More than 2000 years ago, Buddha and Confucius focused on the power and origin of ideas. In other parts of the world, the ancient Hebrews, Socrates, his student Plato, and Plato's student Aristotle pondered whether mind and body are connected or distinct, and whether human ideas are innate or result from experience. In the 1600s, René Descartes and John Locke reengaged aspects of those ancient debates, and Locke coined his famous description of the mind as a "white paper." The ideas of Francis Bacon and John Locke were important ingredients in the development of modern empiricism, the view that knowledge comes from experience through the senses and that science should rely on observation and experimentation.

OBJECTIVE 3 | **Explain how the early psychologists sought to understand the mind's structure and functions, and identify some of the leading psychologists who worked in these areas.**

Psychology as we know it today was born in a laboratory in Germany in the late 1800s, when Wilhelm Wundt ran the first true experiments in psychology's first lab. Soon, the new discipline formed branches. Edward Bradford Titchener and other structuralists searched for the basic elements of the mind by training people to look inward and describe the smallest units of their experiences. In an attempt to understand how mental and behavioral processes help us to adapt, survive, and flourish, William James and other functionalists tried to explain why we do what we do. James also wrote a popular text for the new discipline.

OBJECTIVE 4 | **Describe the evolution of psychology as defined from the 1920s through today.**

Until the 1920s, psychology was a "science of mental life" studied through introspection. Then American behaviorists, led by John B. Watson and later by B. F. Skinner, changed psychology's focus to the study of observable behavior. In the 1960s, humanistic psychologists drew attention to the importance of environmental influences, personal growth, and the needs for love and acceptance. Also in the 1960s, the cognitive revolution began to refocus psychology's interest in mental processes, with special attention to perception, information processing, and memory. Cognitive neuroscientists are broadening our understanding of these and other processes in today's psychology, which views itself as a "science of behavior and mental processes."

ASK YOURSELF: **How do you think psychology might change as more people from non-Western countries contribute their ideas to the field?***

*The Ask Yourself questions will help you reflect on the key issues and connect them to your own life. Making these issues personally meaningful will make them memorable.

Contemporary Psychology

Like its pioneers, today's psychologists are citizens of many lands. The International Union of Psychological Science has 69 member nations, from Albania to Zimbabwe. Nearly everywhere, membership in psychological societies is mushrooming—from 4183 American Psychological Association members and affiliates in 1945 to more than 160,000 today, with similarly rapid growth in Britain (from 1100 to 34,000). In China, five universities had psychology departments in 1985; by the century's end, there were 50 (Jing, 1999). Worldwide, some 500,000 people have been trained as psychologists, and 130,000 of them belong to European psychological organizations (Tikkanen, 2001). Moreover, thanks to international publications, joint meetings, and the Internet, collaboration and communication cross borders more now than ever: "We are moving rapidly towards a single world of psychological science," reports Robert Bjork (2000). Psychology is *growing* and it is *globalizing*.

Today's psychologists debate some enduring issues and view behavior from differing perspectives. They also teach, work, and do research in many different subfields.

■ **nature-nurture issue** the longstanding controversy over the relative contributions that genes and experience make to the development of psychological traits and behaviors.

■ **natural selection** the principle that, among the range of inherited trait variations, those contributing to reproduction and survival will most likely be passed on to succeeding generations.

Psychology's Big Debate

OBJECTIVE 5 | Summarize the nature-nurture debate in psychology, and describe the principle of natural selection.

During its short history, psychology has wrestled with some issues that will reappear throughout this book. The biggest and most persistent issue (and the focus of Chapter 3) concerns *the relative contributions of biology and experience.* As we have seen, the origins of this **nature-nurture** debate are ancient. Do our human traits develop through experience, or do we come equipped with them? The ancient Greeks debated this, with Plato assuming that character and intelligence are largely inherited and that certain ideas are also inborn, and Aristotle countering that there is nothing in the mind that does not first come in from the external world through the senses. In the 1600s, philosophers rekindled the debate. Locke rejected the notion of inborn ideas, offering his notion that the mind is a blank sheet on which experience writes. Descartes disagreed, believing that some ideas are innate.

Charles Darwin
Argued that natural selection shapes behaviors as well as bodies.

Two centuries later, Descartes' views gained support from a curious naturalist. In 1831, an indifferent student but ardent collector of beetles, mollusks, and shells set sail on what was to prove a historic round-the-world journey. The 22-year-old voyager was Charles Darwin, and for some time afterward, he pondered the incredible species variation he had encountered, including tortoises on one island that differed from those on other islands of the region. Darwin's 1859 *Origin of Species* explained this diversity of life by proposing an evolutionary process. From among chance variations in organisms, he believed, nature selects those that best enable an organism to survive and reproduce in a particular environment. Darwin's principle of **natural selection**—"the single best idea anyone has ever had," says philosopher Daniel Dennett (1996)—is still with us nearly 150 years later as an organizing principle of biology. Evolution also has become an important principle for twenty-first century psychology. This would surely have pleased Darwin, for he believed his theory explained not only animal structures (such as why polar bear coats are white) but also animal behaviors (such as the emotional expressions associated with lust and rage).

The nature-nurture debate weaves a thread from the distant past to our time. Today's psychologists have continued the debate by asking:

- How are differences in intelligence, personality, and psychological disorders influenced by heredity and by environment?
- Is children's grammar mostly innate or formed by experience?

A nature-made nature-nurture experiment
Because identical twins have the same genes, they are ideal participants in studies designed to shed light on hereditary and environmental influences on temperament, intelligence, and other traits. Studies of identical and fraternal twins provide a rich array of findings—described in later chapters—that underscore the importance of both nature and nurture.

■ **levels of analysis** the differing complementary views, from biological to psychological to social-cultural, for analyzing any given phenomenon.

■ **biopsychosocial approach** an integrated perspective that incorporates biological, psychological, and social-cultural levels of analysis.

- Are sexual behaviors more "pushed" by inner biology or "pulled" by external incentives?
- Should we treat depression as a disorder of the brain or a disorder of thought—or both?
- How are we humans alike (because of our common biology and evolutionary history) and different (because of our differing environments)?
- Are gender differences biologically predisposed or socially constructed?

The debate continues. Yet over and over again we will see that in contemporary science the nature-nurture tension dissolves: *Nurture works on what nature endows.* Our species is biologically endowed with an enormous capacity to learn and adapt. Moreover, every psychological event (every thought, every emotion) is simultaneously a biological event. Thus depression can be *both* a thought disorder and a brain disorder.

Psychology's Three Main Levels of Analysis

OBJECTIVE **6** | Identify the three main levels of analysis in the biopsychosocial approach, and explain why psychology's varied perspectives are complementary.

Each of us is a complex system that is part of a larger social system, but each of us is also composed of smaller systems, such as our nervous system and body organs, which are composed of still smaller systems—cells, molecules, and atoms.

These different systems suggest different **levels of analysis,** which offer complementary outlooks. It's like explaining why grizzly bears hibernate. Is it because hibernation enhanced their ancestors' survival and reproduction? Because their inner physiology drives them to do so? Because cold environments hinder food gathering during winter? Such perspectives are complementary, because "everything is related to everything else" (Brewer, 1996). Together, different levels of analysis form an integrated **biopsychosocial approach,** which considers the influences of biological, psychological, and social-cultural factors (**FIGURE 1**). Each level provides a valuable vantage point for looking at behavior, yet each by itself is incomplete.

FIGURE 1
Biopsychosocial approach
This integrated viewpoint incorporates various levels of analysis and offers a more complete picture of any given behavior or mental process.

Biological influences:
- genetic predispositions
- genetic mutations
- natural selection of adaptive physiology and behaviors
- genes responding to the environment

Psychological influences:
- learned fears and other learned expectations
- emotional responses
- cognitive processing and perceptual interpretations

Behavior or mental process

Social-cultural influences:
- presence of others
- cultural, societal, and family expectations
- peer and other group influences
- compelling models (such as the media)

TABLE

PSYCHOLOGY'S CURRENT PERSPECTIVES

Perspective	Focus	Sample Questions
Neuroscience	How the body and brain enable emotions, memories, and sensory experiences	How are messages transmitted within the body? How is blood chemistry linked with moods and motives?
Evolutionary	How the natural selection of traits promotes the perpetuation of one's genes	How does evolution influence behavior tendencies?
Behavior genetics	How much our genes and our environment influence our individual differences	To what extent are psychological traits such as intelligence, personality, sexual orientation, and vulnerability to depression attributable to our genes? To our environment?
Psychodynamic	How behavior springs from unconscious drives and conflicts	How can someone's personality traits and disorders be explained in terms of sexual and aggressive drives or as the disguised effects of unfulfilled wishes and childhood traumas?
Behavioral	How we learn observable responses	How do we learn to fear particular objects or situations? What is the most effective way to alter our behavior, say, to lose weight or stop smoking?
Cognitive	How we encode, process, store, and retrieve information	How do we use information in remembering? Reasoning? Solving problems?
Social-cultural	How behavior and thinking vary across situations and cultures	How are we—as Africans, Asians, Australians, or North Americans—alike as members of one human family? As products of different environmental contexts, how do we differ?

Consider, for example, how psychology's varied perspectives described in TABLE 1, can supplement one another and shed light on anger.

- Someone working from the *neuroscience perspective* might study the brain circuits that produce the physical state of being "red in the face" and "hot under the collar."
- Someone working from the *evolutionary perspective* might analyze how anger facilitated the survival of our ancestors' genes.
- Someone working from the *behavior genetics perspective* might study how heredity and experience influence our individual differences in temperament.
- Someone working from the *psychodynamic perspective* might view an outburst as an outlet for unconscious hostility.
- Someone working from the *behavioral perspective* might study the facial expressions and body gestures that accompany anger, or might attempt to determine which external stimuli result in angry responses or aggressive acts.

Gabe Palmer/Corbis

Views of anger
How would each of psychology's levels of analysis explain what's going on here?

Want to learn more? See Appendix A, Careers in Psychology, at the end of this book for more information about psychology's subfields and to learn about the many interesting options available to those with bachelor's, master's, and doctoral degrees in psychology.

- Someone working on the *cognitive perspective* might study how our interpretation of a situation affects our anger and how our anger affects our thinking.
- Someone working on the *social-cultural perspective* might explore which situations produce the most anger, and how expressions of anger vary across cultural contexts.

This important point—that different perspectives can complement one another—is also true of the different academic disciplines. Each academic perspective has its questions and its limits. A perfume manufacturer needs chemistry to create its products, psychology to know what will sell, and marketing and business to turn a profit. Differing academic perspectives are like different two-dimensional views of a three-dimensional object. Each two-dimensional perspective is helpful, but by itself fails to reveal the whole picture.

So bear in mind psychology's limits. Don't expect it to answer the ultimate questions, such as those posed by Russian novelist Leo Tolstoy (1904): "Why should I live? Why should I do anything? Is there in life any purpose which the inevitable death that awaits me does not undo and destroy?" Instead, expect that psychology will help you understand why people think, feel, and act as they do. Then you should find the study of psychology fascinating and useful.

Psychology's Subfields

OBJECTIVE 7 | Identify some of psychology's subfields, and explain the difference between clinical psychology and psychiatry.

Psychology is a collection of diverse subfields. Some psychologists do basic research, some do applied research, and some provide professional services. Picturing a chemist at work, you probably envision a white-coated scientist surrounded by glassware and high-tech equipment. Picture a psychologist at work and you would be right to envision

- a white-coated scientist probing a rat's brain.
- an intelligence researcher measuring how quickly an infant becomes bored with (looks away from) a familiar picture.
- an executive evaluating a new "healthy life-styles" training program for employees.
- someone at a computer keyboard analyzing data on whether adopted teens' temperaments more closely resemble those of their adoptive parents or those of their biological parents.
- a therapist listening carefully to a client's depressed thoughts.
- a traveler en route to another culture to collect data on variations in human values and behaviors.
- a teacher or writer sharing the joy of psychology with others.

The cluster of subfields we call psychology has less unity than most other sciences. But there is a payoff: Psychology is a meeting ground for different disciplines and is thus a perfect home for those with wide-ranging interests. In their diverse activities, from biological experimentation to cultural comparisons, a common quest unites the tribe of psychology: to describe and explain behavior and the mind underlying it.

Some psychologists conduct **basic research** that builds psychology's knowledge base. In the pages that follow we will meet a wide variety of such researchers:

- *Biological psychologists* exploring the links between brain and mind
- *Developmental psychologists* studying our changing abilities from womb to tomb
- *Cognitive psychologists* experimenting with how we perceive, think, and solve problems
- *Personality psychologists* investigating our persistent traits
- *Social psychologists* exploring how we view and affect one another

"I'm a social scientist, Michael. That means I can't explain electricity or anything like that, but if you ever want to know about people I'm your man."

Michael Newman/Photo Edit

Jeff Greenberg/PhotoEdit

These psychologists also may conduct **applied research** that tackles practical problems. So do other psychologists, such as *industrial/organizational psychologists* as they study and advise on behavior in the workplace. They use psychology's concepts and methods to help organizations and companies select and train employees more effectively, to boost morale and productivity, to design products, and to implement systems.

Although most psychology textbooks focus on psychological science, psychology is also a helping profession devoted to such practical issues as how to have a happy marriage, how to overcome anxiety or depression, and how to raise thriving children. **Counseling psychologists** help people cope with challenges (including academic, vocational, and marital issues) by recognizing their strengths and resources. **Clinical psychologists** assess and treat mental, emotional, and behavior disorders (APA, 2003). Both counseling and clinical psychologists administer and interpret tests, provide counseling and therapy, and sometimes conduct basic and applied research. By contrast, **psychiatrists,** who also often provide psychotherapy, are medical doctors licensed to prescribe drugs and otherwise treat physical causes of psychological disorders. (Some clinical psychologists are lobbying for a similar right to prescribe mental health–related drugs, and in 2002 the state of New Mexico granted that right to specially trained and licensed psychologists.)

With perspectives ranging from the biological to the social, and with settings from the laboratory to the clinic, psychology relates to many disciplines. More and more, psychology connects with fields ranging from mathematics to biology to sociology to philosophy. And more and more, psychology's methods and findings aid other disciplines. Psychologists teach in medical schools, law schools, and theological seminaries, and they work in hospitals, factories, and corporate offices. They engage in interdisciplinary studies, such as psychohistory (the psychological analysis of historical characters), psycholinguistics (the study of language and thinking), and psychoceramics (the study of crackpots).[1]

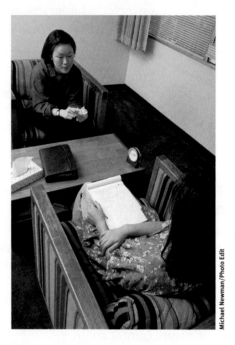

Michael Newman/Photo Edit

Psychology: A science and a profession
Psychologists experiment with, observe, test, and treat behavior. Here we see psychologists testing a child, recording children's behavior, and doing face-to-face therapy.

■ **basic research** pure science that aims to increase the scientific knowledge base.

■ **applied research** scientific study that aims to solve practical problems.

■ **counseling psychology** a branch of psychology that assists people with problems in living (often related to school, work, or marriage) and in achieving greater well-being.

■ **clinical psychology** a branch of psychology that studies, assesses, and treats people with psychological disorders.

■ **psychiatry** a branch of medicine dealing with psychological disorders; practiced by physicians who sometimes provide medical (for example, drug) treatments as well as psychological therapy.

[1]Confession time: I wrote the last part of this sentence on April Fools' Day.

I see you!
A biological psychologist might view this child's delighted response as evidence for brain maturation. A cognitive psychologist might see it as a demonstration of the baby's growing knowledge of his surroundings. For a cross-cultural psychologist, the role of grandparents in different societies might be the issue of interest. As you will see throughout this book, these and other perspectives offer complementary views of behavior.

Laura Dwight

> "Once expanded to the dimensions of a larger idea, [the mind] never returns to its original size."
>
> Oliver Wendell Holmes, 1809–1894

Psychology also influences modern culture. Knowledge transforms us. Learning about the solar system and the germ theory of disease alters the way people think and act. Learning psychology's findings also changes people: They less often judge psychological disorders as a moral failing, treatable by punishment and ostracism. They less often regard and treat women as men's mental inferiors. They less often view and rear children as ignorant, willful beasts in need of taming. "In each case," notes Morton Hunt (1990, p. 206), "knowledge has modified attitudes, and, through them, behavior." Once aware of psychology's well-researched ideas—about how body and mind connect, how a child's mind grows, how we construct our perceptions, how we remember (and misremember) our experiences, how people across the world differ (and are alike)—your mind may never again be quite the same.

>> LEARNING OUTCOMES

Contemporary Psychology

Psychology is growing and globalizing, as psychologists in 69 countries around the world work, teach, and do research in many subfields.

OBJECTIVE 5 | **Summarize the nature-nurture debate in psychology, and describe the principle of natural selection.**
Psychology's biggest and most enduring issue concerns the balance between the influences of nature (genes) and nurture (all other influences, from conception to death). Philosophers had long debated whether nature (the view of Plato and Descartes) or nurture (the view of Aristotle and Locke) was more important. Charles Darwin proposed a mechanism—the principle of natural selection—by which nature selects chance variations that enable organisms to survive and reproduce in particular environments. Psychologists now believe that in most cases, every psychological event is simultaneously a biological event. A great deal of research, including studies of identical and fraternal twins, sheds light on the relative importance of these two sets of influences on such traits as personality and intelligence.

OBJECTIVE 6 | **Identify the three main levels of analysis in the biopsychosocial approach, and explain why psychology's varied perspectives are complementary.**
The biopsychosocial approach integrates information from the biological, psychological, and social-cultural levels of analysis. Psychologists study human behaviors and mental processes from many different perspectives (including the neuroscientific, evolutionary, behavior genetics, psychodynamic, behavioral, cognitive, and social-cultural perspectives). Melding the information gathered from these many lines of research creates a more complete understanding of behaviors and mental processes than would be available from any one viewpoint alone.

OBJECTIVE 7 | **Identify some of psychology's subfields, and explain the difference between clinical psychology and psychiatry.**
Psychology's subfields encompass basic research (often done by biological, developmental, cognitive, personality, and social psychologists), applied research (sometimes conducted by industrial/organizational psychologists), and clinical applications (the work of counseling and clinical psychologists). Clinical psychologists study, assess, and treat (with psychotherapy) people with psychological disorders; psychiatrists also study, assess, and treat people with disorders, but they are medical doctors who can prescribe medication as well as offer psychotherapy.

ASK YOURSELF: **When you signed up for this course, what did you think psychology would be all about?**

CLOSE-UP:

YOUR STUDY OF PSYCHOLOGY

OBJECTIVE 8 | Describe some effective study techniques.

The investment you are making in studying psychology should enrich your life and enlarge your vision. Although many of life's significant questions are beyond psychology, some very important ones are illuminated by even a first psychology course. Through painstaking research, psychologists have gained insights into brain and mind, depression and joy, dreams and memories. Even the unanswered questions can enrich us, by renewing our sense of mystery about "things too wonderful" for us yet to understand. What is more, your study of psychology can help teach you *how to ask and answer important questions*—how to think critically as you evaluate competing ideas and claims.

Having your life enriched and your vision enlarged (and getting a decent grade) requires effective study. As you will see in Chapter 9, to master information you must *actively process* it. Your mind is not like your stomach, something to be filled passively; it is more like a muscle that grows stronger with exercise. Countless experiments reveal that people learn and remember material best when they put it in their own words, rehearse it, and then review and rehearse it again.

A simple study method incorporates these principles. You can remember it as SQ3R: *Survey, Question, Read, Review,* and *Reflect*.

First, *survey* what you're about to read, including chapter outlines and section heads. Note a section's main topic, as indicated by the learning objective at the beginning. This will focus your reading and study.

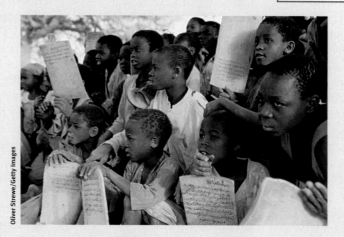

Oliver Strewe/Getty Images

Learning how to ask and answer important questions
The basic study tips in this box are beneficial to students at all levels and in all places, including these children at a village school in Niger.

Keep the learning objective in mind as a *question* you will attempt to answer as you *read* the section. Usually a single main chapter section will be as much as you can absorb without tiring. Treat each main chapter section as if it were a whole chapter. Read actively and critically. Ask questions. Make notes. Consider implications: How does what you've read support or challenge your assumptions? How convincing is the evidence? How does it relate to your own life?

Finally, *review* and *reflect*. To root a section's organization more deeply in your memory, rescan the section and the marginal definitions of key terms. Study the Learning Outcomes at the end of each section. Quiz yourself with the Test Yourself questions at the end of each chapter and, perhaps, by taking quizzes in the book's accompanying study guide and online learning resources (see page 17). Glance over your notes or highlighting. Then stop and let it all sink in. Better yet,

summarize the material for a friend or lecture about it to an imaginary audience.

Survey, question, read, review, reflect. I have organized the chapters to facilitate your using the SQ3R study method. Each chapter begins with an outline that helps you survey what is upcoming, and each main section begins with a learning objective. I have divided chapters into three to five main sections of readable length. To assist your reviewing, each main section ends with a Learning Outcomes narrative summary. End-of-section Ask Yourself questions are designed to help you reflect—applying what you've learned to your own life to make the material more meaningful and memorable. The chapter ends with big-picture Test Yourself review questions and an organized reminder of key terms. Survey, question, read, review, reflect.

Five additional study hints may further boost your learning:

Distribute your study time. One of psychology's oldest findings is that spaced practice promotes better retention than massed practice. You'll remember material better if you space your time over several study periods—perhaps one hour a day, six days a week—rather than cram it into one long study blitz. Spacing your study sessions requires a disciplined approach to managing your time. (Richard O. Straub explains time management in the helpful *Study Guide* that accompanies this text.) For example, rather than trying to read a whole chapter in a single sitting, read just one of the chapter's main sections and then turn to something else.

In class, listen actively. As psychologist William James urged some 100 years ago, *"No reception without reaction, no impression without . . . expression."* Listen for the main idea and subideas in lectures. *Write them down.* Ask questions during and after class. In class, as in your private study, process the information actively and you will understand and retain it better.

Overlearn. Psychology tells us that "overlearning improves retention." The more often students read a chapter and the fewer classes they miss, the better their exam scores are (Woehr & Cavell, 1993). Students frequently stop short of overlearning and overestimate how much they know. Really *learning* something requires more than momentarily understanding it. You may understand a chapter as you read it, but if you devote extra study time to rereading, to testing yourself, and to reviewing what you think you know, you will actually *learn* the material and retain your new knowledge longer.

Focus on the big ideas. It helps to step back periodically and see the big picture so that you know how all the facts and research fit together. To understand and appreciate psychology's lessons, for example, it's important to read about the research that informs them, but it is also important to watch for the bigger concepts and themes that psychologists construct from these smaller findings. Among this book's big ideas are these:

- Critical thinking and scientific scrutiny help us think smarter about many things.

- We gain understanding by viewing a phenomenon from the biological, psychological, and social-cultural levels. Everything psychological is simultaneously biological. Yet our behavior is often influenced by our environment and our culture.
- Nature (our genes and our biological makeup) and nurture (our environment, our culture, and the world around us) work together in forming our traits and behaviors.
- We are creatures of our culture and gender, yet we are far more alike than different.
- Much of our human information processing is unconscious, below the radar screen of our awareness.

Be a smart test-taker. If a test contains both multiple-choice questions and an essay question, turn first to the essay. Read the question carefully, noting exactly what the instructor is asking. On the back of a page, pencil in a list of points you'd like to make, and then organize them. Before writing, put the essay aside and work through the multiple-choice questions. (As you do so, you may continue to mull over the essay question. Sometimes the objective questions will bring pertinent thoughts to mind.) Then reread the essay question, rethink your answer, and start writing. When you finish, proofread your work to eliminate spelling and grammatical errors that make you look less competent than you are.

When reading multiple-choice questions, don't confuse yourself by trying to imagine how each choice might be the right one. Try instead to answer the question as if it were a fill-in-the-blank. First, cover the answers, recall what you know, and complete the sentence in your mind. Then read the answers on the test and find the alternative that best matches your own answer.

As you read psychology, you will learn much more than effective study techniques. Psychology teaches us how to ask important questions—how to think critically as we evaluate competing ideas and popular claims. It deepens our appreciation for how we humans perceive, think, feel, and act. By so doing, it informs our living and enlarges our compassion. Through this book I hope to help guide you toward that end. As educator Charles Eliot said a century ago, "Books are the quietest and most constant of friends, and the most patient of teachers."

>> LEARNING OUTCOMES

OBJECTIVE **8** | **Describe some effective study techniques.**
SQ3R is an effective study method in which you *survey* material before reading it, keep in mind a *question* you will try to answer as you *read*, and then *review* the material you have read and *reflect* on it to make it meaningful and memorable. Five additional types are to distribute study time, listen actively in class, overlearn, focus on big ideas, and be a smart test-taker.

REVIEW: **The Story of Psychology**

Test Yourself

1. What events defined the founding of scientific psychology?

2. What are psychology's major levels of analysis?

The Test Yourself questions offer you a handy self-test on the material you have just read. Answers to these questions can be found in Appendix B at the back of the book.

Terms and Concepts to Remember

psychology, p. 2

empiricism, p. 3

structuralism, p. 4

functionalism, p. 5

humanistic psychology, p. 7

nature-nurture issue, p. 9

natural selection, p. 9

levels of analysis, p. 10

biopsychosocial approach, p. 10

basic research, p. 12

applied research, p. 13

counseling psychology, p. 13

clinical psychology, p. 13

psychiatry, p. 13

WEB

 To continue your study and review of The Story of Psychology, visit this book's Web site at www.worthpublishers.com/myers. You will find practice tests, review activities, and many interesting articles and Web links for more information on topics related to The Story of Psychology.

1: Thinking Critically With Psychological Science

What good fortune for those in power that people do not think.

Adolf Hitler, 1889-1945

Hoping to satisfy their curiosity about people and to remedy their own woes, millions turn to "psychology." They listen to talk-radio counseling, read articles on psychic powers, attend stop-smoking hypnosis seminars, and absorb self-help books on the meaning of dreams, the path to ecstatic love, and the roots of personal happiness.

Others, intrigued by claims of psychological truth, wonder: Do mothers and infants bond in the first hours after birth? Should we trust childhood sexual abuse memories that get "recovered" in adulthood—and prosecute the alleged predators? Are first-born children more driven to achieve? Does handwriting offer clues to personality? Does psychotherapy heal?

In working with such questions, how can we separate uninformed opinions from examined conclusions? *How can we best use psychology to understand why people think, feel, and act as they do?*

The Need for Psychological Science

As we familiarize ourselves with psychological science's strategies and incorporate its underlying principles into our daily thinking, our thinking becomes smarter. Two phenomena—hindsight bias and judgmental overconfidence—illustrate why we cannot rely solely on intuition and common sense. The critical inquiry that flows from a scientific approach—undergirded by curiosity, skepticism, and humility—helps winnow sense from nonsense.

The Limits of Intuition and Common Sense

Some people think psychology merely documents what people already know and dresses it in jargon: "So what else is new—you get paid for using fancy methods to prove what my grandmother knew?" Others scorn a scientific approach because of their faith in human intuition. Advocates of "intuitive management" urge us to distrust statistical predictors and tune into our hunches when hiring, firing, and investing. Like *Star Wars'* Luke Skywalker, should we trust the force within?

The limits of intuition
Personnel interviewers tend to be overconfident of their gut feelings about job applicants. Their confidence stems partly from their recalling cases where their favorable impression proved right, and partly from their ignorance about rejected applicants who succeeded elsewhere.

Taxi/Getty Images

■ **hindsight bias** the tendency to believe, after learning an outcome, that one would have foreseen it. (Also known as the *I-knew-it-all-along phenomenon*.)

Actually, notes writer Madeleine L'Engle, "The naked intellect is an extraordinarily inaccurate instrument" (1972). Our intuition can lead us astray.

1. Imagine (or ask someone to imagine) folding a sheet of paper on itself 100 times. Roughly how thick would it then be?
2. A rope is placed around the Earth at the equator. How much more rope would have to be added for the rope to be 1 foot above the Earth all the way around? (See page 22 for the answers.)

Our notions of common sense similarly err. We're all wise after the fact, presuming that we could have foreseen what happened.

Did We Know It All Along? Hindsight Bias

OBJECTIVE 1 | Describe *hindsight bias,* and explain how it can make research findings seem like mere common sense.

How easy it is to seem astute when drawing the bull's eye after the arrow has struck. *After* each stock market downswing—after the bursting of the dot-com bubble, for example—investment gurus say "the market was obviously overdue for a correction." After the first World Trade Center tower in New York was hit on September 11, 2001 (9/11), commentators said people in the second tower *should* have immediately evacuated (it became obvious only later that it was not an accident). And after physicians receive case information *plus* an autopsy report, they find the cause of death to be self-evident—something they presume they easily could have foreseen, knowing the symptoms. But *before* the arrow strikes, the stock market drops, the terrorists attack, and death occurs, these results are anything but obvious. Causes of death, for example, are not so clear to doctors told the same symptoms without the autopsy report (Dawson & others, 1988). Finding that something has happened makes it seem inevitable. Psychologists Paul Slovic and Baruch Fischhoff (1977) have called this 20/20 hindsight vision **hindsight bias,** also known as the *I-knew-it-all-along phenomenon.*

This phenomenon is easy to demonstrate: Give half the members of a group some purported psychological finding, and the other half an opposite result. Tell the first group, "Psychologists have found that separation weakens romantic attraction. As the saying goes, 'Out of sight, out of mind.'" Ask them to imagine why this might be true. Most people can, and nearly all will then regard this true finding as unsurprising.

Tell the second group just the opposite—that "psychologists have found that separation strengthens romantic attraction. As the saying goes, 'Absence makes the heart grow fonder.'" People given this untrue result can also easily explain it, and they overwhelmingly see it as unsurprising common sense. Obviously, when both a supposed finding and its opposite seem like common sense, there is a problem.

Such errors in our recollections and explanations show why we need psychological research. Just asking people how and why they felt or acted as they did can sometimes be misleading—*not* because common sense is usually wrong, but because it is after the fact.

> "Life is lived forwards, but understood backwards."
>
> Philosopher Søren Kierkegaard, 1813–1855

> "History is written through a rearview mirror, but it unfolds through a foggy windshield."
>
> Samuel Berger, President Clinton's national security adviser, in testimony before the 9/11 Commission, 2004

> "Anything seems commonplace, once explained."
>
> Dr. Watson to Sherlock Holmes

Non Sequitur

THE IRRESISTIBLE FORCE MEETS THE IMMOVABLE OBJECT

THE FACTS AS THEY ARE

THE TRUTH AS I SEE IT

WILEY 5-16

Common sense describes what has happened more easily than it predicts what will happen. As physicist Neils Bohr reportedly said, "Prediction is very difficult, especially about the future."

The phenomenon is widespread. Some 100 studies have observed hindsight bias in various countries and among both children and adults (Bernstein & others, 2004; Guilbault & others, 2004). Nevertheless, Grandmother is often right. As Yogi Berra once said, "You can observe a lot by watching." (We have Berra to thank for other gems, such as "Nobody ever comes here—it's too crowded," and "If the people don't want to come out to the ballpark, nobody's gonna stop 'em.") Because we're all behavior watchers, it would be surprising if many of psychology's findings had *not* been foreseen. Many people believe that love breeds happiness, and they are right (we have what Chapter 12 calls a deep "need to belong"). Indeed, note Daniel Gilbert, Brett Pelham, and Douglas Krull (2003), "Good ideas in psychology usually have an oddly familiar quality, and the moment we encounter them we feel certain that we once came close to thinking the same thing ourselves and simply failed to write it down."

But sometimes Grandmother's intuition has it wrong. Informed by countless casual observations, our intuition may tell us that familiarity breeds contempt, that dreams predict the future, and that emotional reactions coincide with menstrual phase. As we will see in later chapters, the available evidence suggests that these common-sense ideas are wrong, wrong, and wrong. Do you know which of the popular ideas in **TABLE 1.1** have been confirmed by psychology's research, and which have been refuted? Throughout this book we will see how research has both inspired and overturned popular ideas—about aging, about sleep and dreams, about personality. And we will also see how it has surprised us with discoveries about how the brain's chemical messengers control our moods and memories, about animal abilities, and about the effects of stress on our capacity to fight disease.

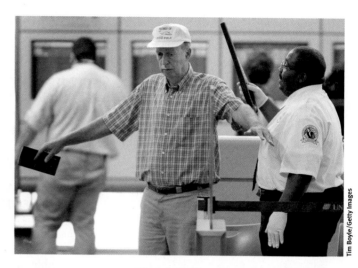

Hindsight bias *After* the horror of 9/11, it seemed obvious that the U.S. intelligence analysts should have taken advance warnings more seriously, that airport security should have anticipated box-cutter–wielding terrorists, that occupants of the second World Trade Center tower should have known to play it safe and leave. With 20/20 hindsight, everything seems obvious. Thus we now spend billions to protect ourselves against what the terrorists did last time.

Tim Boyle/Getty Images

TABLE 1.1

TRUE OR FALSE?

Psychological research discussed in chapters to come will either confirm or refute each of these statements (adapted, in part, from Furnham & others, 2003).

1. If you want to teach a habit that persists, reward the desired behavior every time, not just intermittently (see pages 330–332).

2. Patients whose brains are surgically split down the middle survive and function much as they did before the surgery (see pages 83–85).

3. Traumatic experiences, such as sexual abuse or surviving the Holocaust, are typically "repressed" from memory (see pages 381, 387–390, 604–605).

4. Most abused children do *not* become abusive adults (see pages 158–159).

5. Most infants recognize their own reflection in a mirror by the end of their first year (see page 161).

6. Adopted siblings tend not to develop similar personalities, even though reared by the same parents (see pages 100–101).

7. Fears of harmless objects, such as flowers, are just as easy to acquire as fears of potentially dangerous objects, such as snakes (see pages 534–535).

8. Lie detection tests often lie (see pages 520–521).

(For answers, see page 23.)

Overconfidence

OBJECTIVE **2** | Describe how overconfidence contaminates our everyday judgments.

Our everyday thinking is limited not only by our after-the-fact common sense but also by our human tendency to be overly confident. As Chapter 10 explains, we tend to think we know more than we do. Asked how sure we are of our answers to factual questions (Is Boston north or south of Paris?), we tend to be more confident than correct.[1] Or consider these three anagrams, which Richard Goranson (1978) asked people to unscramble:

WREAT → WATER
ETRYN → ENTRY
GRABE → BARGE

Reflect for a moment: About how many seconds do you think it would have taken you to unscramble each of these?

Once people know the target word, hindsight makes it seem obvious—so much so that they become overconfident. They think they would have seen the solution in only 10 seconds or so, when in reality the average problem solver spends 3 minutes, as you also might, given a similar anagram without the solution: OCHSA (see page 24 to check your answer).

Are we any better at predicting our social behavior? To find out, Robert Vallone and his associates (1990) had students predict at the beginning of the school year whether they would drop a course, vote in an upcoming election, call their parents more than twice a month, and so forth. On average, the students felt 84 percent confident in making these self-predictions. Later quizzes about their actual behavior showed their predictions were correct only 71 percent of the time. Even when they were 100 percent sure of themselves, their self-predictions erred 15 percent of the time.

It's not just collegians. For a dozen years, Ohio State University psychologist Philip Tetlock (1998) collected experts' predictions of political, economic, and military situations. In the late 1980s, for example, he invited expert professors, think-tank analysts, government experts, and journalists to project the governance of the Soviet Union or of South Africa five years later, and to rate how confident they felt. Others did the same for the future of Canada in 1992. After the five years had elapsed (and Communism had collapsed in the Soviet Union, South Africa had become a multiracial democracy, and the Canadian constitution continued), Tetlock invited the experts to recall and reflect on their predictions—which, as in laboratory studies, were far more confident than correct. Experts who had felt more than 80 percent confident were right less than 40 percent of the time.

Despite their lackluster predictions, those who erred were nearly as likely as those who got it right to convince themselves that their initial analysis was *still basically right*. I was "almost right," many of them felt. "The hardliners almost succeeded in their coup attempt against Gorbachev." "The Quebecois separatists almost won the secessionist referendum." "But for the coincidence of de Klerk and Mandela, the transition to black majority rule in South Africa would have been a lot bloodier." The overconfidence of political experts (and stock market forecasters and sports prognosticators) is therefore hard to dislodge, no matter what the outcome.

The point to remember: Hindsight bias and overconfidence often lead us to overestimate our intuition. But scientific inquiry, fed by curious skepticism and by humility, can help us sift reality from illusions.

Fun anagram solutions from Wordsmith.org:
Elvis = lives
Dormitory = dirty room
Slot machines = cash lost in 'em

"We don't like their sound. Groups of guitars are on their way out."

Decca Records, in turning down a recording contract with the Beatles in 1962

"Computers in the future may weigh no more than 1.5 tons."

Popular Mechanics, 1949

"The telephone may be appropriate for our American cousins, but not here, because we have an adequate supply of messenger boys."

British expert group evaluating the invention of the telephone

"They couldn't hit an elephant at this dist—."

General John Sedgwick's last words, uttered during a U.S. Civil War battle, 1864

Answers to questions on page 20:
1. Given a 0.1-millimeter-thick sheet, the thickness after 100 folds would be 800 trillion times the distance between the Earth and the Sun (Gilovich, 1991).
2. About 6 more feet of rope. The circumference of a circle, or of the Earth, is $2\pi r$. The circumference of a rope elevated one foot is $2\pi(r + 1)$. Thus the added length is $2\pi(r + 1) - 2\pi r = 2\pi$, or about 6 feet.

---

[1]Boston is south of Paris.

The Scientific Attitude

OBJECTIVE **3** | Explain how the scientific attitude encourages critical thinking.

Underlying all science is, first, a hard-headed *curiosity,* a passion to explore and understand without misleading or being misled. Some questions (Is there life after death?) are beyond science. To answer them in any way requires a leap of faith. With many other ideas (Can some people demonstrate ESP?), the proof is in the pudding. No matter how sensible or crazy-sounding an idea, the hard-headed question is, Does it work? When put to the test, can its predictions be confirmed?

This scientific approach has a long history. As ancient a figure as Moses used such an approach. How do you evaluate a self-proclaimed prophet? His answer: Put the prophet to the test. If the predicted event "does not take place or prove true," then so much the worse for the prophet (*Deuteronomy* 18:22). Magician James Randi uses Moses' approach when testing those claiming to see auras around people's bodies:

> **Randi:** Do you see an aura around my head?
> **Aura-seer:** Yes, indeed.
> **Randi:** Can you still see the aura if I put this magazine in front of my face?
> **Aura-seer:** Of course.
> **Randi:** Then if I were to step behind a wall barely taller than I am, you could determine my location from the aura visible above my head, right?

Randi has told me that no aura-seer has agreed to take this simple test.

When subjected to such scrutiny, crazy-sounding ideas sometimes find support. During the 1700s, scientists scoffed at the notion that meteorites had extraterrestrial origins. When two Yale scientists dared to deviate from the conventional opinion, Thomas Jefferson jeered, "Gentlemen, I would rather believe that those two Yankee Professors would lie than to believe that stones fell from heaven." Sometimes scientific inquiry refutes skeptics.

More often, science relegates crazy-sounding ideas to the mountain of forgotten claims of perpetual motion machines, miracle cancer cures, and out-of-body travels into centuries past. To sift reality from fantasy, sense from nonsense, therefore requires a scientific attitude: being skeptical but not cynical, open but not gullible.

As scientists, psychologists approach the world of behavior with a *curious skepticism.* They persistently ask two questions: What do you mean? How do you know? In business, the motto is "Show me the money." In science, it is "Show me the evidence."

Do parental behaviors determine their children's sexual orientation? Can astrologers analyze your character and predict your future based on the position of the planets at your birth? As you will see in the chapters that follow, putting such claims to the test has led most psychologists to doubt them. In the arena of competing ideas, skeptical testing can reveal which ones best match the facts. "To believe with certainty," says a Polish proverb, "we must begin by doubting."

Putting a scientific attitude into practice requires not only skepticism but also *humility,* because we may have to reject our own ideas. In the last analysis, what matters is not my opinion or yours, but the truths nature reveals in response to our questioning. If people don't behave as our ideas predict, then so much the worse for our ideas. This is the humble attitude expressed in one of psychology's early mottos: "The rat is always right."

Historians of science tell us that these attitudes of curiosity, skepticism, and humility helped make modern science possible. Many of its founders, including Copernicus and Newton, were people whose religious convictions made them humble before nature and skeptical of mere human authority (Hooykaas, 1972; Merton, 1938). Today's deeply religious people sometimes view science, especially psychological science, as a threat. Yet, notes sociologist Rodney Stark (2003a,b), the scientific revolution was led

> "The scientist . . . must be free to ask any question, to doubt any assertion, to seek for any evidence, to correct any errors."
> Physicist J. Robert Oppenheimer, *Life,* October 10, 1949

The amazing Randi The magician James Randi exemplifies skepticism. He has tested and debunked a variety of psychic phenomena.

> "A skeptic is one who is willing to question any truth claim, asking for clarity in definition, consistency in logic, and adequacy of evidence."
> Philosopher Paul Kurtz, *The Skeptical Inquirer,* 1994

> "My deeply held belief is that if a god anything like the traditional sort exists, our curiosity and intelligence are provided by such a god. We would be unappreciative of those gifts . . . if we suppressed our passion to explore the universe and ourselves."
> Carl Sagan, *Broca's Brain,* 1979

Courtesy of the James Randi Education Foundation

■ **critical thinking** thinking that does not blindly accept arguments and conclusions. Rather, it examines assumptions, discerns hidden values, evaluates evidence, and assesses conclusions.

" The real purpose of the scientific method is to make sure Nature hasn't misled you into thinking you know something you don't actually know."

Robert M. Pirsig, *Zen and the Art of Motorcycle Maintenance*, 1974

mostly by deeply religious people acting on the religious idea that "in order to love and honor God, it is necessary to fully appreciate the wonders of his handiwork."

Of course, scientists, like anyone else, can have big egos and may cling to their preconceptions. We all view nature through the spectacles of our preconceived ideas. Nevertheless, the ideal that unifies psychologists with all scientists is the curious, skeptical, humble scrutiny of competing ideas. As a community, scientists check and recheck one another's findings and conclusions.

This scientific attitude prepares us to think smarter. Smart thinking, called **critical thinking,** examines assumptions, discerns hidden values, evaluates evidence, and assesses conclusions. Whether reading a news report or listening to a conversation, critical thinkers ask questions. Like scientists, they wonder, How do they know that? What is this person's agenda? Is the conclusion based on anecdote and gut feelings, or on evidence? Does the evidence justify a cause-effect conclusion? What alternative explanations are possible? Carried to an extreme, healthy skepticism can degenerate into a negative cynicism that scorns any unproven idea. Better to have a critical attitude that produces humility—an awareness of our own vulnerability to error and an openness to surprises and new perspectives.

Has psychology's critical inquiry been open to surprising findings? The answer, as ensuing chapters illustrate, is plainly yes. Believe it or not . . .

- massive losses of brain tissue early in life may have minimal long-term effects (see page 83).
- within days, newborns can recognize their mother's odor and voice (see page 143).
- brain damage can leave a person able to learn new skills, yet be unaware of such learning (see pages 367–368).
- diverse groups—men and women, old and young, rich and working class, those with disabilities and without—report roughly comparable levels of personal happiness (see pages 537–544).
- electroconvulsive therapy (delivering an electric shock to the brain) is often a very effective treatment for severe depression (see pages 715–716).

And has critical inquiry convincingly debunked popular presumptions? The answer, as ensuing chapters also illustrate, is again yes. The evidence indicates that . . .

- sleepwalkers are *not* acting out their dreams and sleeptalkers are *not* verbalizing their dreams (see Chapter 7).
- our past experiences are *not* all recorded verbatim in our brains; with brain stimulation or hypnosis, one *cannot* simply "play the tape" and relive long-buried or repressed memories (see pages 364–369).
- most people do *not* suffer from unrealistically low self-esteem, and high self-esteem is not all good (see pages 633–636).
- opposites do *not* generally attract (see pages 758–759).

In each of these instances and more, what has been learned is not yet what is widely believed.

The Scientific Method

OBJECTIVE 4 | Describe how psychological theories guide scientific research.

Psychologists arm their scientific attitude with the *scientific method:* They make observations, form theories, and then refine their theories in the light of new observations. In everyday conversation, we tend to use *theory* to mean "mere hunch." In science, however, *theory* is linked with observation. A scientific **theory** *explains* through an integrated set of principles that *organizes* and *predicts* behaviors or events. By organizing isolated facts, a theory simplifies things. There are too many facts about behavior to remember

Solution to anagram on page 22: CHAOS.

them all. By linking facts and bridging them to deeper principles, a theory offers a useful summary. When we connect the observed dots, we may discover a coherent picture.

A good theory of depression, for example, helps us organize countless observations concerning depression into a short list of principles. Imagine we observe over and over that people with depression describe their past, present, and future in gloomy terms. We might therefore theorize that low self-esteem contributes to depression. So far so good: Our self-esteem principle neatly summarizes a long list of facts about people with depression.

Yet no matter how reasonable a theory may sound—and low self-esteem seems a reasonable explanation of depression—we must put it to the test. A good theory doesn't just sound appealing. It must produce testable predictions, called **hypotheses.** By enabling us to test and reject or revise the theory, such predictions give direction to research. They specify what results would support the theory and what results would disconfirm it. To test our self-esteem theory of depression, we might assess people's self-esteem by having them indicate their agreement to statements such as "I have good ideas" and "I am fun to be with." Then we could see whether, as we hypothesized, people who report poorer self-images also score higher on a depression scale (**FIGURE 1.1**).

In testing our theory, we should be aware that it can bias subjective observations. Having theorized that depression springs from low self-esteem, we may see what we expect. We may perceive depressed people's neutral comments as self-disparaging. The urge to see what we expect is an ever-present temptation for all of us. For example, according to the bipartisan U.S. Senate Select Committee on Intelligence (2004), preconceived expectations that Iraq had weapons of mass destruction led intelligence analysts to wrongly interpret ambiguous observations as confirming that theory, and this theory-driven conclusion then led to the preemptive U.S. invasion of Iraq.

As a check on their biases, psychologists report their research—with precise **operational definitions** of concepts that allow anyone to **replicate** (repeat) their observations. If other researchers re-create a study with different participants and materials and get similar results, then our confidence in the finding's reliability grows. The first study of hindsight bias aroused psychologists' curiosity. Now, after many successful replications with differing people and questions, we feel sure of the phenomenon's power.

■ **theory** an explanation using an integrated set of principles that organizes observations and predicts behaviors or events.

■ **hypothesis** a testable prediction, often implied by a theory.

■ **operational definition** a statement of the procedures (operations) used to define research variables. For example, *human intelligence* may be operationally defined as what an intelligence test measures.

■ **replication** repeating the essence of a research study, usually with different participants in different situations, to see whether the basic finding extends to other participants and circumstances.

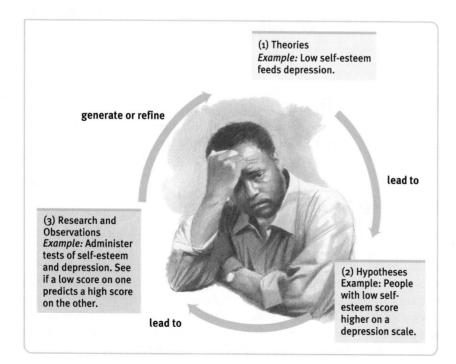

(1) Theories
Example: Low self-esteem feeds depression.

generate or refine

lead to

(3) Research and Observations
Example: Administer tests of self-esteem and depression. See if a low score on one predicts a high score on the other.

(2) Hypotheses
Example: People with low self-esteem score higher on a depression scale.

lead to

FIGURE 1.1

The scientific method A self-correcting process for asking questions and observing nature's answer.

Good theories explain by
1. organizing and linking observed facts.
2. implying hypotheses that offer testable predictions and, sometimes, practical applications.

In the end, our theory will be useful if it (1) effectively *organizes* a range of self-reports and observations and (2) implies clear *predictions* that anyone can use to check the theory or to derive practical applications. (If we boost people's self-esteem, will their depression lift?) Eventually, our research will probably lead to a revised theory (such as the one on pages 665–668) that better organizes and predicts what we know about depression.

As we will see next, we can test our hypotheses and refine our theories using descriptive, correlational, and experimental methods. To think critically about popular psychology claims, we need to recognize these methods and know what conclusions they allow.

>> LEARNING OUTCOMES

The Need for Psychological Science

OBJECTIVE 1 | **Describe *hindsight bias*, and explain how it can make research findings seem like mere common sense.**

Hindsight bias (also called the *I-knew-it-all-along phenomenon*) is the tendency to believe, after learning an outcome, that we would have foreseen it. Thus, learning the outcome of a study can make it seem like obvious common sense. Scientific inquiry and critical thinking can help us overcome this tendency to overestimate our unaided intuition.

OBJECTIVE 2 | **Describe how overconfidence contaminates our everyday judgments.**

We are routinely *overconfident* of our judgments, thanks partly to our bias to seek information that confirms them. Science, with its procedures for gathering and sifting evidence, restrains error by taking us beyond the limits of our intuition and common sense.

OBJECTIVE 3 | **Explain how the scientific attitude encourages critical thinking.**

Although limited by the testable questions it can address, a scientific approach helps us sift reality from illusion. Scientific inquiry begins with an attitude—a curious eagerness to *skeptically* scrutinize competing ideas and an open-minded *humility* before nature. This attitude carries into everyday life as *critical thinking*, which examines assumptions, discerns hidden values, evaluates evidence, and assesses outcomes. Putting ideas, even crazy-sounding ideas, to the test helps us winnow sense from nonsense.

OBJECTIVE 4 | **Describe how psychological theories guide scientific research.**

Psychological *theories* organize *observations* and imply predictive *hypotheses*. After constructing precise operational definitions of their procedures, researchers test their hypotheses (predictions), validate and refine the theory, and, sometimes, suggest practical applications. If other researchers can replicate the study with similar results, we can then place greater confidence in the conclusion.

ASK YOURSELF: **How might the scientific method help us understand the roots of terrorism?**

Description

The starting point of any science is description. In everyday life, all of us observe and describe people, often drawing conclusions about why they behave as they do. Professional psychologists do much the same, though more objectively and systematically.

The Case Study

OBJECTIVE 5 | Identify an advantage and a disadvantage of using case studies to study behavior.

Among the oldest research methods is the **case study,** in which psychologists study one individual in great depth in the hope of revealing things true of us all. Some examples: Much of our early knowledge about the brain came from case studies of individuals who suffered a particular impairment after damage to a certain brain region. Jean Piaget taught us about children's thinking after carefully observing and questioning but a few

■ **case study** an observation technique in which one person is studied in depth in the hope of revealing universal principles.

The case of the conversational chimpanzee In intensive case studies of chimpanzees, psychologists have explored the intriguing question of whether language is uniquely human. Here Nim Chimpsky signs *hug* as his trainer, psychologist Herbert Terrace, shows him the puppet Ernie. But is Nim really capable of using language? We'll explore that issue in Chapter 10.

children. Studies of only a few chimpanzees have revealed their capacity for understanding and language. Intensive case studies are sometimes very revealing.

Case studies can suggest hypotheses for further study. They also show us what *can* happen. In everyday life, however, individual cases sometimes mislead us: An individual may be atypical. Unrepresentative information can lead to mistaken judgments and false conclusions. Indeed, anytime a researcher mentions a finding ("Smokers die younger: 95 percent of men over 85 are nonsmokers") someone is sure to offer a contradictory case ("Well, I have an uncle who smoked two packs a day and lived to be 89"). Anecdotal cases—dramatic stories, personal experiences, even psychological case examples—have a way of overwhelming general truths. Highly publicized school shootings can raise alarm about school violence even while school violence rates are subsiding. Numbers can be numbing (in one study of 1300 dream reports concerning a kidnapped child, only 5 percent correctly envisioned the child as dead—see page 266). Anecdotes are often more startling. ("But I know a man who dreamed his sister was in a car accident, and two days later she was.") As psychologist Gordon Allport (1954, p. 9) said, "Given a thimbleful of [dramatic] facts we rush to make generalizations as large as a tub."

The point to remember: Individual cases can suggest fruitful ideas. What's true of all of us can be glimpsed in any one of us. But to discern the general truths that cover individual cases, we must answer questions with other methods.

> 'Well my dear,' said Miss Marple, 'human nature is very much the same everywhere, and of course, one has opportunities of observing it at closer quarters in a village.'"
> Agatha Christie, *The Tuesday Club Murders*, 1933

The Survey

OBJECTIVE 6 | Identify the advantages and disadvantages of using surveys to study behavior and mental processes, and explain the importance of wording effects and random sampling.

The **survey** method looks at many cases in less depth. A survey asks people to report their behavior or opinions. Questions about everything from sexual practices to political opinions get put to the public. It's hard to think of a significant question that survey researchers have not asked. For example, Harris and Gallup polls have revealed that 72 percent of Americans think there is too much TV violence, 84 percent favor equal job opportunities for homosexual people, 89 percent say they face high stress, 95 percent believe in God, and 96 percent would like to change something about their appearance. In Britain, seven in ten 18- to 29-year-olds support gay marriage; among those over 50, about the same percentage oppose it (a generation gap found in many Western countries). But asking questions is tricky, and the answers may well depend on your wording and your choice of respondents.

■ **survey** a technique for ascertaining the self-reported attitudes or behaviors of people, usually by questioning a representative, random sample of them.

■ **false consensus effect** the tendency to overestimate the extent to which others share our beliefs and behaviors.

■ **population** all the cases in a group, from which samples may be drawn for a study. (*Note:* Except for national studies, this does *not* refer to a country's whole population.)

■ **random sample** a sample that fairly represents a population because each member has an equal chance of inclusion.

■ **naturalistic observation** observing and recording behavior in naturally occurring situations without trying to manipulate and control the situation.

This Modern World by Tom Tomorrow © 1991.

With very large samples, estimates become quite reliable. *E* is estimated to represent 12.7 percent of the letters in written English. *E*, in fact, is 12.3 percent of the 925,141 letters in Melville's *Moby Dick*, 12.4 percent of the 586,747 letters in Dickens' *A Tale of Two Cities*, and 12.1 percent of the 3,901,021 letters in 12 of Mark Twain's works (*Chance News*, 1997).

Wording Effects

Even subtle changes in the order or wording of questions can have major effects. Should cigarette ads or pornography be allowed on television? People are much more likely to approve "not allowing" such things than "forbidding" or "censoring" them. In one national survey, only 27 percent of Americans approved of "government censorship" of media sex and violence, though 66 percent approved of "more restrictions on what is shown on television" (Lacayo, 1995). People are similarly much more approving of "aid to the needy" than of "welfare," of "affirmative action" than of "preferential treatment," and of "revenue enhancers" than of "taxes." Because wording is such a delicate matter, critical thinkers will reflect on how the phrasing of a question might have affected the opinions respondents expressed.

Random Sampling

In our everyday experience we spend most of our time with a biased sample of people—mostly those who share our attitudes and habits. Thus, when we wonder how many people hold a particular belief, those who think as we do come to mind most readily. This tendency to overestimate others' agreement with us is the **false consensus effect** (Ross & others, 1977). Vegetarians will think more people are vegetarians than will meat-eaters, and conservatives will perceive more support for conservative views than will liberals.

You can describe human experience using your estimates of others, perhaps supplemented by dramatic anecdotes and personal experience. But for an accurate picture of the experiences and attitudes of a whole population, there's only one game in town—the representative sample.

We can extend this point to everyday thinking, as we generalize from samples we observe, especially vivid cases. Given (a) a statistical summary of a professor's student evaluations and (b) the vivid comments of two irate students, an administrator's impression of the professor may be influenced as much by the two unhappy students as by the many favorable evaluations in the statistical summary. Standing in the checkout line at the supermarket, George sees the woman in front of him pay with government-provided food stamps and then watches with dismay as she drives away in a fancy car. In both situations, the temptation to generalize from a few vivid but unrepresentative cases is nearly irresistible.

The point to remember: The best basis for generalizing is from a representative sample of cases.

If you wish to survey the students at your college or university, how could you survey a representative sample of the total student **population**—the whole group you want to study and describe? Typically, you would choose a **random sample,** one in which every person in the entire group has an equal chance of participating.

To sample the students randomly, you would *not* send each of them a questionnaire. (The conscientious people who return it would not be a random sample.) Rather, you would aim for a representative sample by, say, using a table of random numbers to pick participants from a student listing and then making sure you involve as many as possible. Large representative samples are better than small ones, but a small representative sample of 100 is better than an unrepresentative sample of 500.

The point to remember: Before believing survey findings, think critically: Consider the sample. You cannot compensate for an unrepresentative sample by simply adding more people.

The random-sampling principle also works in national surveys. Imagine that you had a giant barrel containing 60 million white beans mixed with 40 million red beans. A scoop that randomly sampled 1500 of them would contain about 60 percent white and 40 percent red beans, give or take 2 or 3 percent. Sampling voters in a national election survey is like sampling the beans; 1500 randomly sampled people, drawn from all areas of a country, provide a remarkably accurate snapshot of the opinions of a nation. Without random sampling, large samples—including call-in phone samples and TV website polls—often merely give misleading results.

Naturalistic Observation

OBJECTIVE 7 | Identify an advantage and a disadvantage of using naturalistic observation to study behavior.

A third descriptive research method involves watching and recording the behavior of organisms in their natural environment. These **naturalistic observations** range from watching chimpanzee societies in the jungle, to unobtrusively videotaping (and later systematically analyzing) parent-child interactions in different cultures, to recording students' self-seating patterns in the lunchrooms of multiracial schools.

Like the case study and survey methods, naturalistic observation does not *explain* behavior. It *describes* it. Nevertheless, descriptions can be revealing. We once thought, for example, that only humans use tools. Then naturalistic observation revealed that chimpanzees sometimes insert a stick in a termite mound and withdraw it, eating the stick's load of termites. Such unobtrusive naturalistic observations, recalls chimpanzee observer Jane Goodall (1998), paved the way for later studies of animal thinking, language, and emotion: "Observations, made in the natural habitat, helped to show that the societies and behavior of animals are far more complex than previously supposed," thus expanding our understanding of our fellow animals. We later learned that chimps and baboons also use deception to achieve their aims. Psychologists Andrew Whiten and Richard Byrne (1988) repeatedly saw one young baboon pretending to have been attacked by another as a tactic to get its mother to drive the other baboon away from its food.

Naturalistic observations are also done with humans. Here are three examples I think you will enjoy.

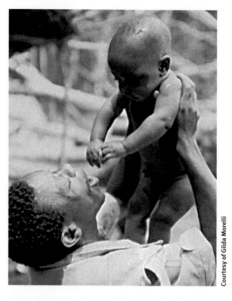

Naturalistic observation Psychologist Gilda Morelli has lived among and observed the Efe people of Central Africa for more than 20 years, studying paternal and maternal care and observing children's development.

- *A funny finding.* We humans laugh 30 times more often in social situations than in solitary situations. (Have you noticed how seldom you laugh when alone?) When we do laugh, 17 muscles contort our mouth and squeeze our eyes, and we emit a series of 75-millisecond vowel-like sounds that are spaced about one-fifth of a second apart (Provine, 2001).

- *Sounding out students.* What, really, are introductory psychology students saying and doing during their everyday lives? To find out, Matthias Mehl and James Pennebaker (2003) equipped 52 such University of Texas students with a belt-worn tape recorder that, for up to four days, captured 30 seconds of their waking hours every 12.5 minutes—thus enabling the researchers to eavesdrop on more than 10,000 half-minute life slices. On what percentage of the slices do you suppose they found the students talking with someone? What percentage captured the students at a computer keyboard? The answers: 28 and 9 percent, respectively. (What percentage of *your* waking hours are spent in these activities?)

"How would you like me to answer that question? As a member of my ethnic group, educational class, income group, or religious category?"

■ **correlation** a measure of the extent to which two factors vary together, and thus of how well either factor predicts the other. The *correlation coefficient* is the mathematical expression of the relationship, ranging from –1 to +1.

■ **scatterplot** a graphed cluster of dots, each of which represents the values of two variables. The slope of the points suggests the direction of the relationship between the two variables. The amount of scatter suggests the strength of the correlation (little scatter indicates high correlation). (Also called a *scattergram* or *scatter diagram*.)

• *Culture, climate, and the pace of life.* Naturalistic observation also enabled Robert Levine and Ara Norenzayan (1999) to compare the pace of life in 31 countries. By operationally defining *pace of life* as walking speed, the speed with which postal clerks completed a simple request, and the accuracy of public clocks, they concluded that life is fastest paced in Japan and Western Europe, and slower paced in economically less-developed countries. People in colder climates also tend to live at a faster pace (and are more prone to die from heart disease). Naturalistic observation describes behavior more than it explains it. But this study illustrates how naturalistic observation can also be used with correlational research, our next topic.

>> LEARNING OUTCOMES

Description

OBJECTIVE **5** | **Identify an advantage and a disadvantage of using case studies to study behavior.**
Researchers using case studies focus in depth on one individual, in the hope of revealing universal principles. Case studies describe behavior. They can suggest hypotheses, but studying an unrepresentative individual may lead to false conclusions.

OBJECTIVE **6** | **Identify the advantages and disadvantages of using surveys to study behavior and mental processes, and explain the importance of wording effects and random sampling.**
Surveys describe behavior by gathering information from a large number of people. This technique relies on people giving accurate self-reports of their attitudes or behaviors. Wording effects—subtle influences in the sequence or phrasing of questions—can affect responses. Random sampling helps researchers achieve a sample that fairly represents the population under study. Because random sampling chooses people by chance, each person in the entire group has an equal chance of participating.

OBJECTIVE **7** | **Identify an advantage and a disadvantage of using naturalistic observation to study behavior.**
Naturalistic observation gives researchers an opportunity to watch and record behavior in naturally occurring situations. Like other forms of description, naturalistic observation cannot explain behaviors, but it can expand our understanding and lead to hypotheses that can be studied by other methods.

ASK YOURSELF: **Can you recall examples of misleading surveys you have experienced or read about? What principles for a good survey did they violate?**

FIGURE 1.2
How to read a correlation coefficient

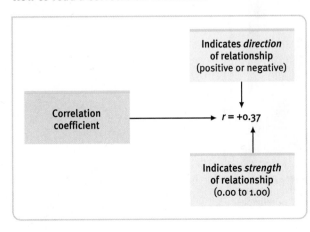

Indicates *direction* of relationship (positive or negative)

Correlation coefficient → *r* = +0.37

Indicates *strength* of relationship (0.00 to 1.00)

Correlation

OBJECTIVE **8** | Describe positive and negative correlations, and explain how correlational measures can aid the process of prediction.

Describing behavior is a first step toward predicting it. When surveys and naturalistic observations reveal that one trait or behavior accompanies another, we say the two **correlate**. The *correlation coefficient* is a statistical measure of a relationship (**FIGURE 1.2**): It reveals how closely two things vary together and thus how well either one *predicts* the other. Knowing how much aptitude test scores *correlate* with school success tells us how well the scores *predict* school success.

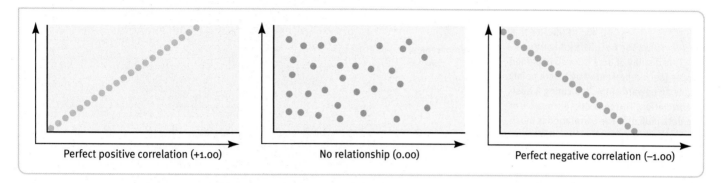

FIGURE **1.3**

Scatterplots, showing patterns of correlation Correlations can range from +1.00 (scores on one measure increase in direct proportion to scores on another) to –1.00 (scores on one measure decrease precisely as scores rise on the other).

Throughout this book we will often ask how strongly two things are related: For example, how closely related are the personality scores of identical twins? How well do intelligence test scores predict achievement? How closely is stress related to disease?

FIGURE 1.3 illustrates perfect positive and negative correlations, which rarely occur in the "real world." These graphs are called **scatterplots,** because each point *plots* the value of two variables. A positive correlation means that two sets of scores, such as height and weight, tend to rise or fall together. A correlation's being negative has nothing to do with its strength or weakness; a negative correlation means two things relate inversely (one set of scores goes up as the other goes down). As toothbrushing goes up from zero, tooth decay goes down; brushing and decay correlate (negatively). A weak correlation, indicating little or no relationship, has a coefficient near zero.

Here are some recent news reports of correlational research. Can you spot which are reporting positive correlations, which negative?

- The more TV is on in the homes of young children, the less time they spend reading (Kaiser, 2003).
- The more sexual content teens see on TV, the more likely they are to have sex (Collins & others, 2004).
- The longer children are breast-fed, the greater their later academic achievement (Horwood & Fergusson, 1998).
- The more income rose among a sample of poor families, the fewer psychiatric symptoms their children experienced (Costello & others, 2003).

(These are negative, positive, positive, and negative correlations, respectively.)

Statistics can help us see what the naked eye sometimes misses. To demonstrate this for yourself, try an imaginary project. Wondering if tall men are more or less easygoing, you collect two sets of scores: men's heights and men's temperaments. You measure the heights of 20 men, and have someone else independently assess their temperaments (from zero for extremely calm to 100 for highly reactive).

With all the relevant data (**TABLE 1.2**) right in front of you, can you tell whether there is (1) a positive correlation between height and reactive temperament, (2) very little or no correlation, or (3) a negative correlation?

Comparing the columns in Table 1.2, most people detect very little relationship between height and temperament. In fact, the correlation in this imaginary example is moderately positive, +0.63, as we can see if we display the data as a scatterplot. In **FIGURE 1.4** (page 32), moving from left to right, the upward, oval-shaped slope of the cluster of points shows that our two imaginary sets of scores (height and reactivity) tend to rise together.

If we fail to see a relationship when data are presented as systematically as in Table 1.2, how much less likely are we to notice them in everyday life? To see what is right in front of us, we sometimes need statistical illumination. We can easily see evidence of gender discrimination when given statistically summarized information about job level, seniority, performance, gender, and salary. But we often see no discrimination when the same information dribbles in, case by case (Twiss & others, 1989).

TABLE 1.2

HEIGHT AND TEMPERAMENT OF 20 MEN

	Height in Inches	Temperament
1	80	75
2	63	66
3	61	60
4	79	90
5	74	60
6	69	42
7	62	42
8	75	60
9	77	81
10	60	39
11	64	48
12	76	69
13	71	72
14	66	57
15	73	63
16	70	75
17	63	30
18	71	57
19	68	84
20	70	39

FIGURE 1.4

Scatterplot for height and temperament This display of data from 20 imagined people (each represented by a data point) reveals an upward slope, indicating a positive correlation. The considerable scatter of the data indicates the correlation is much lower than +1.0.

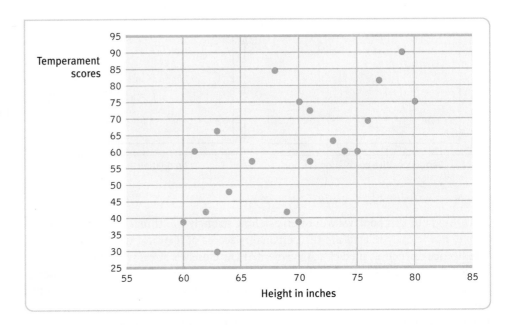

Though informative, psychology's correlations usually leave most of the variation among individuals unpredicted. As we will see, there is a correlation between parents' abusiveness and their children's later abusiveness when they become parents. But this does not mean that most abused children become abusive. The correlation simply indicates a statistical relationship: Although most abused children do not grow into abusers, nonabused children are even less likely to become abusive.

The point to remember: A correlation coefficient helps us see the world more clearly by revealing the extent to which two things relate.

Correlation and Causation

FIGURE 1.5

Three possible cause-effect relationships People low in self-esteem are more likely to report depression than are those high in self-esteem. One possible explanation of this negative correlation is that a bad self-image causes depressed feelings. But, as the diagram indicates, other cause-effect relationships are possible.

OBJECTIVE 9 | Explain why correlational research fails to provide evidence of cause-effect relationships.

Correlations help us predict, and they restrain the illusions of our flawed intuition. Watching violence correlates with (and therefore predicts) aggression. But does that mean it *causes* aggression? Does low self-esteem *cause* depression? If, based on the correlational evidence, you assume that they do, you have much company. A nearly irresistible thinking error is assuming that correlation proves causation. But no matter how strong the relationship, it does not!

For example, what about the negative correlation between self-esteem and depression? Perhaps low self-esteem does cause depression. But as **FIGURE 1.5** suggests, we'd get the same correlation between low self-esteem and depression if depression caused people to be down on themselves, or if something else—a third factor such as heredity or brain chemistry—caused both low self-esteem and depression. Among men, length of marriage correlates positively with hair loss—because both are associated with a third factor, age. And people who wear hats are *more* likely to suffer skin cancer—because both are associated with fair-skinned people (who are vulnerable to skin cancer and more likely to wear protective hats).

| (1)
Low self-esteem | could cause → | Depression |

or

| (2)
Depression | could cause → | Low self-esteem |

or

| (3)
Distressing events
or biological
predisposition | could cause | Low self-esteem
and
Depression |

R. Sidney/The Image Works

Correlation need not mean causation
Length of marriage correlates with hair loss in men. Does this mean that marriage causes men to lose their hair (or that balding men make better husbands)? In this case, as in many others, a third factor obviously explains the correlation: Golden anniversaries and baldness both accompany aging.

This point is so important—so basic to thinking smarter with psychology—that it merits one more example, from a survey of over 12,000 adolescents: The more teens feel loved by their parents, the less likely they are to behave in unhealthy ways—having early sex, smoking, abusing alcohol and drugs, exhibiting violence (Resnick & others, 1997). "Adults have a powerful effect on their children's behavior right through the high school years," gushed an Associated Press (AP) story on the study. But the correlation comes with no built-in cause-effect arrow. Said differently (turn the volume up here), *correlation does not prove causation.* Thus, the AP could as well have said, "Well-behaved teens feel their parents' love and approval; out-of-bounds teens more often think their parents are disapproving jerks."

The point to remember: Correlation indicates the *possibility* of a cause-effect relationship, *but it does not prove causation.* Knowing that two events are correlated need not tell us anything about causation. Remember this principle and you will be wiser as you read and hear news of scientific studies.

Illusory Correlations

OBJECTIVE 10 | Describe how people form illusory correlations.

Correlations make visible the relationships we might otherwise miss. They also restrain our "seeing" relationships that actually do not exist. A perceived nonexistent correlation is an **illusory correlation.** When we *believe* there is a relationship between two things, we are likely to *notice* and *recall* instances that confirm our belief (Trolier & Hamilton, 1986).

Illusory correlations help explain many a superstitious belief, such as the presumption that more babies are born when the moon is full or that infertile couples who adopt become more likely to conceive (Gilovich, 1991). Those who conceive after adopting capture our attention. We're less likely to notice those who adopt and never conceive, or those who conceive without adopting. In other words, illusory correlations occur when we over-rely on the top left cell of **FIGURE 1.6** (on page 34), ignoring equally essential information in the other cells.

Such illusory thinking helps explain why for so many years people believed (and many still do) that sugar made children hyperactive, that getting cold and wet caused one to catch a cold, and that weather changes trigger arthritis pain. Physician Donald Redelmeier, working with psychologist Amos Tversky (1996), followed 18 arthritis patients for 15 months. The researchers recorded both the patients' pain reports and the daily weather—temperature, humidity, and barometric pressure. Despite patients' beliefs, the weather was uncorrelated with their discomfort, either on the same day or

A *New York Times* writer reported a massive survey showing that "adolescents whose parents smoked were 50 percent more likely than children of nonsmokers to report having had sex." He concluded (would you agree?) that the survey indicated a causal effect—that "to reduce the chances that their children will become sexually active at an early age" parents might "quit smoking" (O'Neil, 2002).

■ **illusory correlation** the perception of a relationship where none exists.

FIGURE 1.6

Illusory correlation in everyday life
Many people believe infertile couples become more likely to conceive a child after adopting a baby. This belief arises from their attention being drawn to such cases. The many couples who adopt without conceiving or conceive without adopting grab less attention. To determine whether there actually is a correlation between adoption and conception, we need data from all four cells in this figure. (From Gilovich, 1991)

	Conceive	**Do not conceive**
Adopt	confirming evidence	disconfirming evidence
Do not adopt	disconfirming evidence	confirming evidence

Michael Newman Jr./PhotoEdit

up to two days earlier or later. Shown columns of random numbers labeled "arthritis pain" and "barometric pressure," even college students saw a correlation where there was none. We are, it seems, prone to perceiving patterns, whether they're there or not.

Because we are sensitive to dramatic or unusual events, we are especially likely to notice and remember the occurrence of two such events in sequence—say, a premonition of an unlikely phone call followed by the call. When the call does not follow the premonition, we are less likely to note and remember the nonevent.

Likewise, instances of positive-thinking people being cured of cancer impress those who believe that positive attitudes counter disease. But to assess whether positive thinking actually affects cancer, we need three more types of information. We need an estimate of how many positive thinkers were *not* cured. Then we need to know how many cancer patients were and were not cured among those not using positive thinking. Without these comparison figures, the positive examples of a few tell us nothing about the actual correlation between attitudes and disease. (Chapter 14 explores the effects of emotions on health and illness.)

The point to remember: When we notice random coincidences, we may forget that they are random and instead see them as correlated. Thus, we can easily deceive ourselves by seeing what is not there.

Perceiving Order in Random Events

OBJECTIVE **11** | Explain the human tendency to perceive order in random sequences.

Illusory correlations arise from our natural eagerness to make sense of our world—what poet Wallace Stevens called our "rage for order." Given even random data, we look for order, for meaningful patterns. And we usually find such, because *random sequences often don't look random.* Consider a random coin flip: If someone flipped a coin six times, which of the following sequences of heads (H) and tails (T) would be most likely: HHHTTT or HTTHTH or HHHHHH?

FIGURE 1.7

Two random sequences
Your chances of being dealt either of these hands are precisely the same: 1 in 2,598,960.

Daniel Kahneman and Amos Tversky (1972) found that most people believe HTTHTH would be the most likely random sequence. Actually, all three are equally likely (or, you might say, equally unlikely) to occur. A bridge or poker hand of 10 through Ace, all of hearts, would seem extraordinary; actually, it would be no more or less likely than any other specific hand of cards (**FIGURE 1.7**).

In actual random sequences, patterns and streaks (such as repeating digits) occur more often than people expect. To demonstrate this phenomenon for myself (as you can do), I flipped a coin 51 times, with these results:

1. H	11. T	21. T	31. T	41. H	51. T
2. T	12. H	22. T	32. T	42. H	
3. T	13. H	23. H	33. T	43. H	
4. T	14. T	24. T	34. T	44. H	
5. H	15. T	25. T	35. T	45. T	
6. H	16. H	26. T	36. H	46. H	
7. H	17. T	27. H	37. T	47. H	
8. T	18. T	28. T	38. T	48. T	
9. T	19. H	29. H	39. H	49. T	
10. T	20. H	30. T	40. T	50. T	

Looking over the sequence, patterns jump out: Tosses 10 to 22 provided an almost perfect pattern of pairs of tails followed by pairs of heads. On tosses 30 to 38 I had a "cold hand," with only one head in eight tosses. But my fortunes immediately reversed with a "hot hand"—seven heads out of the next nine tosses. Similar streaks happen, about as often as one would expect in random sequences, in basketball shooting, baseball hitting, and mutual fund stock pickers' selections (Gilovich & others, 1985; Malkiel, 1989, 1995; Myers, 2002). Whether flipping coins, watching basketball, or monitoring investment adviser performance, random sequences often don't look random, and so get overinterpreted ("When you're hot, you're hot—give her the ball!").

What explains these streaky patterns? Was I exercising some sort of paranormal control over my coin? Did I snap out of my tails funk and get in a heads groove? No such explanations are needed, for these are the sorts of streaks found in any random data. Comparing each toss to the next, 24 of the 50 comparisons yielded a changed result—just the sort of near 50-50 result we expect from coin tossing. Despite the seeming patterns in these data, the outcome of one toss gives no clue to the outcome of the next toss.

However, some happenings seem so extraordinary that we struggle to conceive an ordinary, chance-related explanation (as applies to our coin-tosses). In such cases, statisticians often are less mystified. When Evelyn Marie Adams won the New Jersey lottery *twice*, newspapers reported the odds of her feat as 1 in 17 trillion. Bizarre? Actually,

1 in 17 trillion are the odds that a given person who buys a single ticket for two New Jersey lotteries will win both times. But statisticians Stephen Samuels and George McCabe (1989) report that, given the millions of people who buy U.S. state lottery tickets, it was "practically a sure thing" that someday, somewhere, someone would hit a state jackpot twice. Indeed, say fellow statisticians Persi Diaconis and Frederick Mosteller (1989), "with a large enough sample, any outrageous thing is likely to happen." "The really unusual day would be one where nothing unusual happens," adds Diaconis (2002). An event that happens to but one in 1 billion people every day occurs about six times a day, 2000 times a year.

BIZARRE SEQUENCE OF COMPUTER-GENERATED RANDOM NUMBERS

© 1990 by Sidney Harris/American Scientist Magazine.

Bizarre-looking, perhaps. But actually no more unlikely than any other number sequence.

On March 11, 1998, Utah's Ernie and Lynn Carey gained three new grandchildren when three of their daughters gave birth—on the same day (*Los Angeles Times*, 1998).

Jerry Telfer/San Francisco Chronicle

Given enough random events, something weird will happen Angelo and Maria Gallina were the beneficiaries of one of those extraordinary chance events when they won two California lottery games on the same day.

>> Learning Outcomes

Correlation

OBJECTIVE 8 | Describe positive and negative correlations, and explain how correlational measures can aid the process of prediction.

A *correlation coefficient* is a statistical measure of the strength and duration of the relationship between two factors. In a positive correlation (ranging from 0 to +1.00), the two factors rise or fall together. In a negative correlation (ranging from 0 to −1.00), one item rises as the other falls. Scatterplots and the correlations they reveal help us to see relationships that the naked eye might miss.

OBJECTIVE 9 | Explain why correlational research fails to provide evidence of cause-effect relationships.

A correlation indicates the *possibility* of a cause-effect relationship, but it does not prove causation or, if causation exists, the direction of the influence. A third factor may be the cause of the correlation.

OBJECTIVE 10 | Describe how people form illusory correlations.

Illusory correlations are random events that we notice and falsely assume are related. They arise from our sensitivity to dramatic or unusual events. Once we believe two things are related, we tend to notice and recall instances that confirm this belief.

OBJECTIVE 11 | Explain the human tendency to perceive order in random sequences.

We search for patterns in an attempt to make sense of the world around us. Patterns or sequences occur naturally in sets of random data, but we tend to interpret these patterns as meaningful connections.

ASK YOURSELF: Can you think of an example of correlational research that you recently heard about from a friend or on the news? Was an unwarranted conclusion drawn?

Experimentation

Happy are they, remarked the Roman poet Virgil, "who have been able to perceive the causes of things." We endlessly wonder and debate *why* we act as we do. Why do people smoke? Have babies while they are still children? Do stupid things when drunk? Become troubled teens and open fire on their classmates? Though psychology cannot answer these questions directly, it has helped us to understand what influences drug use, sexual behaviors, thinking when drinking, and aggression.

Exploring Cause and Effect

OBJECTIVE 12 | Explain how experiments help researchers isolate cause and effect.

Many factors influence our everyday behavior. To isolate cause and effect—say, in looking for causes of depression—psychologists statistically control for other factors. For example, many studies have found that breast-fed infants grow up with somewhat higher intelligence scores than those of infants bottle-fed with cow's milk (Angelsen & others, 2001; Mortensen & others, 2002; Quinn & others, 2001). Mother's milk correlates modestly but positively with later intelligence. But does this mean that smarter mothers (who more often breast-feed) have smarter children? Or, as some researchers believe, do the nutrients of mother's milk contribute to brain development? To help answer this question, researchers have "controlled for" (statistically removed differences in) maternal age, education, and intelligence. Still, breast-fed infants exhibit slightly higher intelligence as young children.

The clearest and cleanest way to isolate cause and effect is, however, to **experiment**. Experiments enable a researcher to focus on the possible effects of one or more factors by (1) *manipulating the factors of interest* and (2) *holding constant ("controlling") other factors*. Knowing that correlations of infant nutrition and later intelligence can't possibly control for all other possible factors, a British research team led by Alan Lucas (1992) decided to experiment, using 424 hospital preterm infants. With parental

■ **experiment** a research method in which an investigator manipulates one or more factors (independent variables) to observe the effect on some behavior or mental process (the dependent variable). By random assignment of participants, the experimenter aims to control other relevant factors.

permission, the researchers randomly assigned some infants to the usual infant formula feedings and others to donated breast milk feedings. When given intelligence tests at age 8, the children nourished with breast milk had significantly higher intelligence scores than their formula-fed counterparts. No single experiment is conclusive, of course, but by randomly assigning infants to a feeding condition, these researchers were able to hold constant all factors except nutrition. This eliminated alternative explanations and supported the conclusion that, so far as the developing intelligence of preterm infants is concerned, breast is best. (*Note:* The other infants were not harmed by the experiment, because they received the standard feeding.)

If a behavior (such as test performance) changes when we vary an experimental factor (such as infant nutrition), then we know the factor is having an effect. *The point to remember:* Unlike correlational studies, which uncover naturally occurring relationships, an experiment manipulates a factor to determine its effect.

Understanding experimentation is central to thinking critically with psychological science. So, let's consider further how we experiment.

Evaluating Therapies

OBJECTIVE **13** | Explain why the double-blind procedure and random assignment build confidence in research findings.

Our tendency to seek new remedies when we are ill or emotionally down can produce misleading testimonies. If three days into a cold we start taking vitamin C tablets and find our cold symptoms lessening, we may credit the pills rather than the cold naturally subsiding. If, after nearly failing the first exam, we listen to a "peak learning" subliminal tape and then improve on the next exam, we may credit the tape rather than conclude that our performance has returned to our average. In the 1700s, blood-letting *seemed* effective. Sometimes people improved after the treatment; when they didn't, the practitioner inferred the disease was just too advanced to be reversed. (We, of course, now know that blood-letting is a *bad* treatment.) So, whether or not a remedy is truly effective, enthusiastic users will probably endorse it. To find out whether it actually is effective, we must experiment.

And that is precisely how new drug treatments and new methods of psychological therapy are evaluated (Chapter 17). In many of these studies, the participants are *blind* (uninformed) about what treatment, if any, they are receiving. One group receives the treatment. Others receive a pseudotreatment—an inert *placebo* (perhaps a pill with no drug in it). Often, neither the participant nor the research assistant collecting the data knows whether the participant's group is receiving the treatment. This **double-blind procedure** enables researchers to check a treatment's actual effects apart from the research participants' (and their own) enthusiasm for it and from the healing power of belief. The **placebo effect** is well documented in reducing pain, depression, and anxiety (Kirsch & Sapirstein, 1998). Just *believing* you are getting a treatment can boost your spirits, relax your body, and relieve your symptoms.

The double-blind procedure is one way to create an **experimental condition** in which people receive the treatment and a contrasting **control condition** without the treatment. By **randomly assigning** people to these conditions, researchers can be fairly certain the two groups are otherwise identical. Random assignment roughly equalizes the two groups in age, attitudes, and every other characteristic. With random assignment, as occurred with the infants in the breast milk experiment, we also can know that any later differences between people in the experimental and control conditions will usually be the result of the treatment.

Another example: On the advice of their physicians, millions of postmenopausal women turned to hormone replacement therapy after correlational studies found

■ **double-blind procedure** an experimental procedure in which both the research participants and the research staff are ignorant (blind) about whether the research participants have received the treatment or a placebo. Commonly used in drug-evaluation studies.

■ **placebo** [pluh-SEE-bo; Latin for "I shall please"] **effect** experimental results caused by expectations alone; any effect on behavior caused by the administration of an inert substance or condition, which is assumed to be an active agent.

■ **experimental condition** the condition of an experiment that exposes participants to the treatment, that is, to one version of the independent variable.

■ **control condition** the condition of an experiment that contrasts with the experimental condition and serves as a comparison for evaluating the effect of the treatment.

■ **random assignment** assigning participants to experimental and control conditions by chance, thus minimizing preexisting differences between those assigned to the different groups.

■ **independent variable** the experimental factor that is manipulated; the variable whose effect is being studied.

■ **dependent variable** the outcome factor; the variable that may change in response to manipulations of the independent variable.

that women on replacement hormones had lower rates of heart disease, stroke, and colon cancer. But these women may also have been more likely to receive medical care, to exercise, and to eat well. So, did the hormones make women healthy or did healthy women take the hormones? In 2002, the National Institutes of Health announced the surprising results of a massive experiment that randomly assigned 16,608 healthy women to either replacement hormones or a placebo. The shocking result: Compared with women in the control condition, women receiving the hormones had *more* health problems (Love, 2002).

Independent and Dependent Variables

OBJECTIVE 14 | Explain the difference between an independent and a dependent variable.

Here is an even more potent example: The drug Viagra was approved for use after 21 clinical trials, including an experiment in which researchers randomly assigned 329 men with impotence to either an experimental condition (Viagra) or a control condition (a placebo). It was a double-blind procedure—neither the men nor the person who gave them the pills knew which drug they were receiving. The result: At peak doses, 69 percent of Viagra-assisted attempts at intercourse were successful, compared with 22 percent for men receiving the placebo (Goldstein & others, 1998). Viagra had an effect.

This simple experiment manipulated just one drug factor. We call this experimental factor the **independent variable** because we can vary it independently of other factors, such as the men's age, weight, and personality (which random assignment should control). Experiments examine the effect of one or more independent variables on some measurable behavior, called the **dependent variable** because it can vary *depending* on what takes place during the experiment. Both variables are given precise operational definitions, which specify the procedures that manipulate the independent variable (the precise drug dosage and timing in this study) or measure the dependent variable (the questions that assessed the men's responses). These definitions answer the "What do you mean?" question with a level of precision that enables others to repeat the study. (See **FIGURE 1.8** for another experiment's design.)

Experiments can also help us evaluate social programs. Do early childhood education programs boost impoverished children's chances for success? What are the effects of different anti-smoking campaigns? Do school sex-education programs reduce teen pregnancies? To answer these questions, we can experiment: If an intervention is welcomed but resources are scarce, we could use a lottery to randomly assign some people (or regions) to experience the new program and others to a control condition. If later the two groups differ, the intervention's effect will be confirmed (Passell, 1993).

FIGURE 1.8

Experimentation To discern causation, psychologists may randomly assign some participants to an experimental treatment, others to a control condition. Measuring the dependent variable (intelligence score) will determine the effect of the independent variable (type of milk).

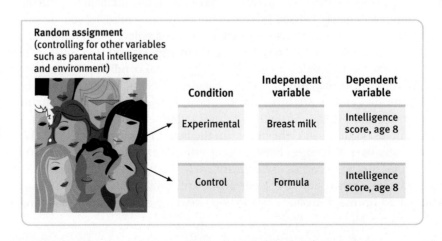

TABLE 1.3

COMPARING RESEARCH METHODS

Research Method	Basic Purpose	How Conducted	What Is Manipulated	Weaknesses
Descriptive	To observe and record behavior	Do case studies, surveys, or naturalistic observations	Nothing	No control of variables; single cases may be misleading
Correlational	To detect naturally occurring relationships; to assess how well one variable predicts another	Compute statistical association, sometimes among survey responses	Nothing	Does not specify cause and effect
Experimental	To explore cause and effect	Manipulate one or more factors; use random assignment	The independent variable(s)	Sometimes not feasible; results may not generalize to other contexts; not ethical to manipulate certain variables

Let's recap. A variable is anything that can vary (infant nutrition, intelligence, TV exposure—anything within the bounds of what is feasible and ethical). Experiments aim to *manipulate* an *independent* variable, *measure* the *dependent* variable, and *control* all other variables. An experiment has at least two different conditions: an experimental condition and a comparison or control condition. Random assignment works to equate the conditions before any treatment effects. In this way, an experiment tests the effect of at least one independent variable (what we manipulate) on at least one dependent variable (the outcome we measure). **TABLE 1.3** compares the features of psychology's research methods.

Note the distinction between random *sampling* (typically associated with surveys) and random *assignment* in experiments. Random sampling helps us generalize to a larger population. Random assignment controls extraneous influences, which helps us infer cause and effect.

>> LEARNING OUTCOMES

Experimentation

OBJECTIVE 12 | **Explain how experiments help researchers isolate cause and effect.**
To discover cause-effect relationships, psychologists conduct *experiments*. By manipulating one or more factors of interest, and controlling other factors, experimenters can determine the effect on some behavior or mental process.

OBJECTIVE 13 | **Explain why the double-blind procedure and random assignment build confidence in research findings.**
In a double-blind procedure, neither the researchers nor the participants know whether participants are receiving the treatment or a placebo. This counteracts the possibility that a placebo effect or researchers' expectations will unintentionally influence the study's results. Random assignment minimizes preexisting differences between the groups by selecting people by chance for the experimental condition (the group exposed to the treatment) or the control condition (a group that experiences no treatment or a different version of the treatment).

OBJECTIVE 14 | **Explain the difference between an independent and a dependent variable.**
The independent variable is the factor you manipulate to study its effect. The dependent variable is the factor you measure to discover any changes that occur in response to these manipulations.

ASK YOURSELF: **If you were to become a research psychologist, what questions would you like to explore with experiments?**

Statistical Reasoning

OBJECTIVE 15 | Explain the importance of statistical principles, and give an example of their use in everyday life.

Having gathered data, we must next organize, summarize, and make inferences from it, using statistics. Today's statistics are tools that help us see and interpret what the unaided eye might miss.

"Figures can be misleading—so I've written a song which I think expresses the real story of the firm's performance this quarter."

Off-the-top-of-the-head estimates often misread reality and then mislead the public. Someone throws out a big round number. Others echo it and before long the big round number becomes public misinformation. A few examples:

- *One percent of Americans (2.7 million) are homeless.* Or is it 300,000, an earlier estimate by the federal government? Or 600,000, an estimate by the Urban Institute (Crossen, 1994)?
- *Ten percent of people are lesbians or gay men.* Or is it 2 to 3 percent, as suggested by various national surveys (Chapter 12)?
- *We ordinarily use but 10 percent of our brain.* Or is it closer to 100 percent? (Chapter 2; which 90 percent, or even 10 percent, would you be willing to sacrifice?)
- *We remember 10 percent of what we read, 20 percent of what we hear, 30 percent of what we see, and 80 percent of what we say.* So reported the British Audio Visual Society (Genovese, 2004). Or is it, as a book on accelerated learning declares, 20 percent of what we read, 30 percent of what we hear, 40 percent of what we see, and 50 percent of what we say?

The point to remember: Doubt big, round, undocumented numbers. Rather than swallow top-of-the-head estimates, focus on thinking smarter by applying simple statistical principles to everyday reasoning.

Describing Data

OBJECTIVE 16 | Explain how bar graphs can misrepresent data.

Once researchers have gathered their data, their first task is to *organize* them. One way is to use a simple *bar graph,* as in **FIGURE 1.9**, which displays a distribution of trucks of different brands still on the road after a decade. When reading statistical graphs such as this, take care. As you can see, people can design a graph to make a difference look small or big, depending on what they want to emphasize.

The point to remember: Think smart. When viewing figures in magazines and on television, read the scale labels and note their range.

FIGURE 1.9
Read the scale labels An American truck manufacturer offered a graph (a)—with actual brand names included—to suggest the much greater durability of its trucks. Note, however, how the apparent difference shrinks as the vertical scale changes (graph b).

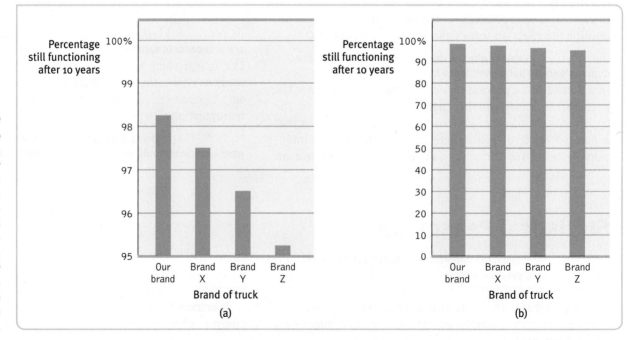

Measures of Central Tendency

OBJECTIVE **17** | Describe the three measures of central tendency, and tell which is most affected by extreme scores.

The next step is to summarize the data using some *measure of central tendency,* a single score that represents a whole set of scores. The simplest measure is the **mode,** the most frequently occurring score or scores. The most commonly reported is the **mean,** or arithmetic average—the total sum of all the scores divided by the number of scores. On a divided highway, the median is the middle. So, too, with data: The **median** is the midpoint—the 50th percentile. If you arrange all the scores in order from the highest to the lowest, half will be above the median and half will be below it.

Measures of central tendency neatly summarize data. But consider what happens to the mean when a distribution is lopsided or *skewed.* With income data, for example, the mode, median, and mean often tell very different stories (**FIGURE 1.10**). This happens because the mean is biased by a few extreme scores. When Microsoft founder Bill Gates sits down in an intimate cafe, its average (mean) patron instantly becomes a billionaire. Understanding this, you can see how a British newspaper could accurately run the headline "Income for 62% Is Below Average" (Waterhouse, 1993). Because the bottom *half* of British income earners receive only a *quarter* of the national income cake, most British people, like most people everywhere, make less than the mean.

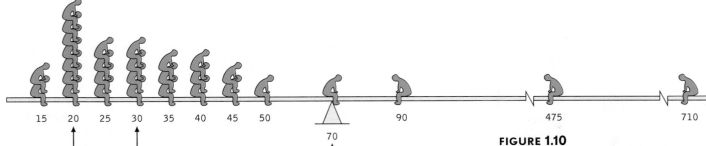

Mode   **Median**   **Mean**

One family   Income per family in thousands of dollars

mode the most frequently occurring score(s) in a distribution.

mean the arithmetic average of a distribution, obtained by adding the scores and then dividing by the number of scores.

median the middle score in a distribution; half the scores are above it and half are below it.

FIGURE 1.10
A skewed distribution This graphic representation of the distribution of incomes illustrates the three measures of central tendency—mode, median, and mean. Note how just a few high incomes make the mean—the fulcrum point that balances the incomes above and below—deceptively high.

The average person has one ovary and one testicle.

In the United States, advocates and critics described the 2003 tax cut with different statistics, both true. The White House explained that "92 million Americans will receive an average tax cut of $1083." Critics agreed, but also noted that 50 million taxpayers got no cut, and half of the 92 million who did benefit received less than $100 (Krugman, 2003). Mean and median tell different true stories.

The point to remember: Always note which measure of central tendency is reported. Then, if it is a mean, consider whether a few atypical scores could be distorting it.

Measures of Variation

OBJECTIVE **18** | Describe two measures of variation.

Knowing the value of an appropriate measure of central tendency can tell us a great deal. But it also helps to know something about the amount of *variation* in the data—how similar or diverse the scores are. Averages derived from scores with low variability are more reliable than averages based on scores with high variability. Consider a basketball player who scored between 13 and 17 points in each of her first 10 games in a season. Knowing this, we would be more confident that she would score near 15 points in her next game than if her scores had varied from 5 to 25 points.

TABLE 1.4

STANDARD DEVIATION IS MUCH MORE INFORMATIVE THAN MEAN ALONE

Note that the test scores in Class A and Class B have the same mean (80), but very different standard deviations, which tell us more about how the students in each class are really faring.

Test Scores in Class A			Test Scores in Class B		
Score	Deviation From the Mean	Squared Deviation	Score	Deviation From the Mean	Squared Deviation
72	−8	64	60	−20	400
74	−6	36	60	−20	400
77	−3	9	70	−10	100
79	−1	1	70	−10	100
82	+2	4	90	+10	100
84	+4	16	90	+10	100
85	+5	25	100	+20	400
87	+7	49	100	+20	400
Total = 640		Sum of (deviations)² = 204	Total = 640		Sum of (deviations)² = 2000
Mean = 640 ÷ 8 = 80			Mean = 640 ÷ 8 = 80		

Standard deviation =

$$\sqrt{\frac{\text{Sum of (deviations)}^2}{\text{Number of scores}}} = \sqrt{\frac{204}{8}} = 5.0$$

Standard deviation =

$$\sqrt{\frac{\text{Sum of (deviations)}^2}{\text{Number of scores}}} = \sqrt{\frac{2000}{8}} = 15.8$$

"The poor are getting poorer, but with the rich getting richer it all averages out in the long run."

The **range** of scores—the gap between the lowest and highest scores—provides only a crude estimate of variation because a couple of extreme scores in an otherwise uniform group, such as the $475,000 and $710,000 incomes in Figure 1.10, will create a deceptively large range.

The more useful standard for measuring how much scores deviate from one another is the **standard deviation.** It better gauges whether scores are packed together or dispersed, because it uses information from each score (**TABLE 1.4**). (The computation assembles information about how much individual scores differ from the mean.) If your college or university attracts students of a certain ability level, their intelligence scores will have a smaller standard deviation than the one found in the more diverse community population outside your school.

Making Inferences

Data are "noisy." One group's average score (breast-fed babies' intelligence scores) could conceivably differ from another's (the formula-fed babies) not because of any real difference but merely because of chance fluctuations in the people sampled. How confidently, then, can we infer that an observed difference accurately estimates the true difference?

When Is an Observed Difference Reliable?

OBJECTIVE 19 | Identify three principles for making generalizations from samples.

In deciding when it is safe to generalize from a sample, we should keep three principles in mind. Let's look at each in turn.

1. *Representative samples are better than biased samples.* The best basis for generalizing is not from the exceptional and memorable cases one finds at the extremes (remember Bill Gates' income?) but from a representative sample of cases. No research involves a representative sample of the whole human population. Thus, it pays to keep in mind what population a study has sampled.

2. ***Less-variable observations are more reliable than those that are more variable.*** As we noted in the example of the basketball player whose points scored were consistent, an average is more reliable when it comes from scores with low variability.

3. ***More cases are better than fewer.*** An eager prospective university student visits two college campuses, each for a day. At the first, the student randomly attends two classes and discovers both instructors to be witty and engaging. At the next campus, the two sampled instructors seem dull and uninspiring. Returning home, the student (discounting the small sample size of only two teachers at each institution) tells friends about the "great teachers" at the first school, and the "bores" at the second. Again, we know it but we ignore it: *Averages based on many cases are more reliable* (less variable) than averages based on only a few cases.

The point to remember: Don't be overly impressed by a few anecdotes. Generalizations based on a few unrepresentative cases are unreliable.

When Is a Difference Significant?

OBJECTIVE 20 | Explain how psychologists decide whether differences are meaningful.

Statistical tests also help us determine whether differences are meaningful. Here is the underlying logic: When *averages* from two samples are each *reliable* measures of their respective populations (as when each is based on many observations that have small variability), then their difference (sometimes even a very small difference) is likely to be reliable as well. (The less the variability in women's and in men's aggression scores, the more confidence we would have that any observed gender difference is reliable.) But when the *difference* between the sample averages is *large,* we have even more confidence that the difference between them reflects a real difference in their populations.

In short, *when the sample averages are reliable and the difference between them is relatively large,* we say the difference has **statistical significance.** This simply means that the difference we observed is probably not due to chance variation between the samples.

In judging statistical significance, psychologists are conservative. They are like juries who must presume innocence until guilt is proven. For most psychologists, proof beyond a reasonable doubt means not making much of a finding unless the odds of its occurring by chance are less than 5 percent (an arbitrary criterion).

When reading about research, you should remember that, given large enough or homogeneous enough samples, a difference between them may be "statistically significant" yet have little practical significance. For example, comparisons of intelligence test scores among hundreds of thousands of first-born and later-born individuals indicate a highly significant tendency for first-born individuals to have higher average scores than their later-born siblings (Zajonc & Markus, 1975). But because the scores differ by only one or two points, the difference has little practical importance. Such findings have caused some psychologists to advocate alternatives to significance testing (Hunter, 1997). Better, they say, to use other ways to express a finding's "effect size"—its magnitude and reliability.

■ **range** the difference between the highest and lowest scores in a distribution.

■ **standard deviation** a computed measure of how much scores vary around the mean score.

■ **statistical significance** a statistical statement of how likely it is that an obtained result occurred by chance.

PEANUTS

The point to remember: Statistical significance indicates the *likelihood* that a result will happen by chance. It does not indicate the *importance* of the result.

Using the principles discussed in this chapter will help us to think critically—to see more clearly what we might otherwise miss or misinterpret, and to generalize more accurately from our observations. We do think smarter when we understand and use the principles of research methods and statistics (Fong & others, 1986; Lehman & others, 1988; VanderStoep & Shaughnessy, 1997). It requires training and practice, but developing clear and critical thinking abilities is part of becoming an educated person. The report of the Project on Redefining the Meaning and Purpose of Baccalaureate Degrees (1985) eloquently asserts why there are few higher priorities in a college education:

> If anything is paid attention to in our colleges and universities, thinking must be it. Unfortunately, thinking can be lazy. It can be sloppy. . . . It can be fooled, misled, bullied. . . . Students possess great untrained and untapped capacities for logical thinking, critical analysis, and inquiry, but these are capacities that are not spontaneous: They grow out of wide instruction, experience, encouragement, correction, and constant use.

>> LEARNING OUTCOMES

Statistical Reasoning

OBJECTIVE **15** | **Explain the importance of statistical principles, and give an example of their use in everyday life.**

Statistics help us to organize, summarize, and make inferences from data. We need not remember complicated formulas to think more clearly and critically about the data we encounter in everyday life. For example, understanding statistical concepts teaches us the importance of doubting big, round, undocumented numbers.

OBJECTIVE **16** | **Explain how bar graphs can misrepresent data.**

Scale labels and ranges used in bar graphs can be designed to minimize or maximize differences. When looking at statistical graphs in books and magazines and on TV and the Internet, think critically.

OBJECTIVE **17** | **Describe the three measures of central tendency, and tell which is most affected by extreme scores.**

The *median* is the middle score in a group of data. The *mode* is the most frequently occurring score. The *mean*, the arithmetic average, is most easily distorted by a few very high or very low scores.

OBJECTIVE **18** | **Describe two measures of variation.**

Measures of variation tell us how similar or diverse data are. A *range* describes the gap between the highest and lowest scores. The more useful measure, the *standard deviation*, states how much scores vary around the mean, or average, score.

OBJECTIVE **19** | **Identify three principles for making generalizations from samples.**

1. Representative samples are better than biased samples.

2. Less-variable observations are more reliable than those that are more variable.

3. More cases are better than fewer.

OBJECTIVE **20** | **Explain how psychologists decide whether differences are meaningful.**

When averages from two samples are each reliable measures of their own populations, and the difference between them is relatively large, we can assume the difference is significant—that the result did not occur by chance alone. Statistical significance indicates the likelihood of a result's occurring, not the importance of the result.

ASK YOURSELF: **Find a graph in a popular magazine ad. How does the advertiser use (or abuse) statistics to make a point?**

Frequently Asked Questions About Psychology

We have seen how case studies, surveys, and naturalistic observations help us describe behavior. We have also noted that correlational studies assess the relationship between two factors, which indicates how well one thing predicts another. We have examined the logic that underlies experiments, which use control conditions and random assignment of participants to isolate the effects of an independent variable on a dependent variable. We have reflected on how a scientific approach, aided by statistics, can restrain biases.

You are now prepared to understand what lies ahead and to think critically about psychological matters. Yet, even knowing this much, you may still be approaching psychology with a mixture of curiosity and apprehension. So before we plunge in, let's address some frequently asked questions.

■ **culture** the enduring behaviors, ideas, attitudes, and traditions shared by a large group of people and transmitted from one generation to the next.

Can Laboratory Experiments Illuminate Everyday Life?

OBJECTIVE **21** | Explain the value of simplified laboratory conditions in discovering general principles of behavior.

When you see or hear about psychological research, do you ever wonder whether people's behavior in the lab will predict their behavior in real life? For example, does detecting the blink of a faint red light in a dark room have anything useful to say about flying a plane at night? Does our tendency to remember best the first and last items in a list of unrelated words tell us anything about why we remember the names of certain people we meet at a party? After viewing a violent, sexually explicit film, does an aroused man's increased willingness to push buttons that he thinks will electrically shock a woman really say anything about whether violent pornography makes a man more likely to abuse a woman?

Before you answer, consider: The experimenter *intends* the laboratory environment to be a simplified reality—one that simulates and controls important features of everyday life. Just as an aeronautical wind tunnel enables an engineer to re-create atmospheric forces under controlled conditions, a laboratory experiment enables a psychologist to re-create psychological forces under controlled conditions.

People in the lab are not different creatures from their out-of-lab selves. For example, Cecilia Cheng (2001) observed that Hong Kong adults who coped flexibly with laboratory stresses also coped flexibly with stress in their marriages. In aggression studies, deciding whether to push a button that delivers a shock may not be the same as slapping someone in the face, but the *principle* is the same. And the experiment's purpose, notes Douglas Mook (1983), is not to re-create the exact behaviors of everyday life but to test theoretical principles. *It is the resulting principles—not the specific findings—that help explain everyday behaviors.*

When psychologists apply laboratory research on aggression to actual violence, they are applying theoretical *principles* of aggressive behavior, principles they have refined through many experiments. Similarly, it is the principles of the visual system, developed from experiments in artificial settings (such as looking at red lights in the dark), that we apply to more complex behaviors such as night flying. And many investigations show that principles derived in the laboratory *do* typically generalize to the everyday world (Anderson & others, 1999).

The point to remember: As psychologists, our concerns lie less with particular behaviors than with the general principles that help explain many behaviors.

A cultured greeting Because culture shapes people's understanding of social behavior, actions that seem ordinary to us may seem quite odd to visitors from far away. Yet underlying these differences are powerful similarities. Supporters of newly elected leaders everywhere typically greet them with pleased deference, though not necessarily with bows and folded hands, as in India. Here influential and popular politician Sonia Gandhi greets some of her constituents shortly after her election.

Does Behavior Depend on One's Culture?

OBJECTIVE **22** | Discuss whether psychological research can be generalized across cultures and genders.

If culture shapes behavior, what can psychological studies done in one culture, often with white Europeans or North Americans, really tell us about people in general? As we will see time and again, **culture**—shared ideas and behaviors that one generation passes on to the next—matters. Our culture influences our standards of promptness and frankness, our attitudes toward premarital sex and varying body shapes, our tendency to be casual or formal, our eye contact, our conversational distance, and much, much more. Being aware of such differences, we can restrain our assumptions that others will think and act as we do. Given the growing mixing and clashing of cultures, our need for such awareness is urgent.

Ami Vitale/Getty Images

Our shared biological heritage does, however, unite us as a universal human family. The same underlying processes guide people everywhere:

- People diagnosed with dyslexia, a reading disorder, exhibit the same brain malfunction whether they are Italian, French, or British (Paulesu & others, 2001).
- Variation in languages—spoken and gestured—may impede communication across cultures. Yet all languages share deep principles of grammar, and people from opposite hemispheres can communicate with a smile or a frown.
- People in different cultures do vary in feelings of loneliness. But across cultures, loneliness is magnified by shyness, low self-esteem, and being unmarried (Jones & others, 1985; Rokach & others, 2002).
- Most Japanese prefer their fish raw and most North Americans prefer theirs cooked. But the same principles of hunger and taste influence all of us when we sit down to a meal. We are each in certain respects like all others, like some others, and like no other. Studying people of all races and cultures helps us discern our similarities and our differences, our human kinship and our diversity.

The point to remember: Even when specific attitudes and behaviors vary across cultures, as they often do, the underlying processes are much the same.

Does Behavior Vary With Gender?

At your birth, friends and family immediately wondered which of the two human types you were: male or female. Given how important gender is to our identity and to others' perceptions of us, do we need a different psychology for women and for men?

You will see throughout this book that gender issues permeate psychology. Researchers report gender differences in what we dream, in how we express and detect emotions, and in our risk for alcoholism, depression, and eating disorders. Not only is studying such differences interesting, it also is potentially beneficial. For example, many researchers believe that women carry on conversations more readily to build relationships, while men talk more to give information and advice (Tannen, 1990). Knowing this difference can help us prevent conflicts and misunderstandings in everyday relationships.

Nevertheless, it's important to remember that psychologically as well as biologically, women and men are overwhelmingly similar. Whether female or male, we learn to walk at about the same age. We experience the same sensations of light and sound. We feel the same pangs of hunger, desire, and fear. We exhibit similar overall intelligence and well-being. We also tend to exhibit and perceive the very behaviors our culture expects of males and females.

So, gender matters. Biology determines our sex, and then culture further bends the genders. Yet in many ways female and male are similarly human.

Why Do Psychologists Study Animals?

OBJECTIVE 23 | Explain why psychologists study animals, and discuss the ethics of experimentation with both animals and humans.

Many psychologists study animals because they find them fascinating. They want to understand how different species learn, think, and behave. Psychologists also study animals to learn about people, by doing experiments that are permissible only with animals. Human physiology resembles that of many other animals. We humans are not *like* animals; we *are* animals. Animal experiments have therefore led to treatments for human diseases—insulin for diabetes, vaccines to prevent polio and rabies, transplants to replace defective organs.

Likewise, the same processes by which humans see, exhibit emotion, and become obese are present in rats and monkeys. To discover more about the basics of human learning, researchers even study sea slugs. To understand how a combustion engine works, you would do better to study a lawn mower's engine than a Mercedes'. Like

"All people are the same; only their habits differ."

Confucius, 551–479 B.C.

"Rats are very similar to humans except that they are not stupid enough to purchase lottery tickets."

Dave Barry, July 2, 2002

Mercedes engines, humans are complex. But the simplicity of the sea slug's nervous system is precisely what makes it so revealing of the neural mechanisms of learning.

Is It Ethical to Experiment on Animals?

If we share important similarities with other animals, then should we not respect them? "We cannot defend our scientific work with animals on the basis of the similarities between them and ourselves and then defend it morally on the basis of differences," noted Roger Ulrich (1991). The animal protection movement protests the use of animals in psychological, biological, and medical research. Researchers remind us that the world's 30 million mammals used each year in research are but a fraction of 1 percent of the billions of animals killed annually for food (which means the average person eats 20 animals a year). While researchers each year conduct experiments on some 200,000 dogs and cats cared for under humane regulations, humane animal shelters are forced to kill 50 times that many (Goodwin & Morrison, 1999).

Animal protection organizations, such as Psychologists for the Ethical Treatment of Animals, advocate naturalistic observation of animals rather than laboratory manipulation. Animal researchers have responded that the issue is not the morality of good versus evil but of compassion for animals versus compassion for people. How many of us would have attacked Pasteur's experiments with rabies, which caused some dogs to suffer but led to a vaccine that spared millions of people (and dogs) from agonizing death? And would we really wish to have deprived ourselves of the animal research that led to effective methods of training children with mental disorders; of understanding aging; of relieving fears and depression; and of controlling obesity, alcoholism, and stress-related pain and disease? The answers to such questions vary by culture. In Gallup surveys in Canada and the United States, about 6 in 10 adults deem medical testing on animals "morally acceptable." In Britain, only 37 percent do (Mason, 2003).

Out of this heated debate, two issues emerge. The basic one is whether it is right to place the well-being of humans above that of animals. In experiments on stress and cancer, is it right that mice get tumors in hopes that people might not? Should some monkeys be exposed to an HIV-like virus in the search for an AIDS vaccine? Is our use of other animals as natural as the behavior of carnivorous hawks, cats, and whales? Defenders of research on animals argue that anyone who has eaten a hamburger, worn leather shoes, tolerated hunting and fishing, or supported the extermination of crop-destroying or plague-carrying pests has already agreed that, yes, it is sometimes permissible to sacrifice animals for the sake of human well-being.

Scott Plous (1993) notes, however, that our compassion for animals varies, as does our compassion for people—based on their perceived similarity to us. As Chapter 18 explains, we feel more attraction, give more help, and act less aggressively toward similar others. Likewise, we value animals according to their perceived kinship with us. Thus, primates and companion pets get top priority. (Western people raise or trap mink and foxes for their fur, but not dogs or cats.) Other mammals occupy the second rung on the privilege ladder, followed by birds, fish, and reptiles on the third rung, with insects at the bottom. In deciding which animals have rights, we each draw our own cut-off line somewhere across the animal kingdom.

If we give human life first priority, the second issue is the priority we give to the well-being of animals in research. What safeguards should protect them? Most researchers today feel ethically obligated to enhance the well-being of captive animals and protect them from needless suffering. In one survey of animal researchers, 98 percent or more supported government regulations protecting primates, dogs, and cats, and 74 percent supported regulations providing for the humane care of rats and mice (Plous & Herzog, 2000). Many professional associations and funding agencies

Animal research benefiting animals
Thanks partly to research on the benefits of novelty, control, and stimulation, these Bronx Zoo gorillas are enjoying improved quality of life.

"I believe that to prevent, cripple, or needlessly complicate the research that can relieve animal and human suffering is profoundly inhuman, cruel, and immoral."
Psychologist Neal Miller, 1983

"Please do not forget those of us who suffer from incurable diseases or disabilities who hope for a cure through research that requires the use of animals."
Psychologist Dennis Feeney (1987)

"The righteous know the needs of their animals."
Proverbs 12:10

now have guidelines for the humane use of animals. For example, British Psychological Society guidelines call for housing animals under reasonably natural living conditions, with companions for social animals (Lea, 2000). American Psychological Association (2002) guidelines mandate ensuring the "comfort, health, and humane treatment" of animals, and of minimizing "infection, illness, and pain of animal subjects." Humane care also leads to more effective science, because pain and stress would distort the animals' behavior during experiments.

Animals have themselves benefited from animal research. One Ohio team of research psychologists measured stress hormone levels in samples of millions of dogs brought each year to animal shelters, and they devised methods of handling and stroking them that reduced stress and eased their transition to adoptive homes (Tuber & others, 1999). Thanks to animal behavior studies, formerly idle Bronx Zoo animals are now staving off listless boredom by working for their supper, as would their counterparts in the wild (Stewart, 2002). Other studies have helped improve care and management in animals' natural habitats. By revealing our behavioral kinship with animals and the remarkable intelligence of chimpanzees, gorillas, and other animals, experiments have also led to increased empathy and protection for them. At its best, a psychology concerned for humans and sensitive to animals serves the welfare of both.

Is It Ethical to Experiment on People?

If the image of animals or people receiving supposed electric shocks troubles you, you may be relieved to know that most psychological research involves no such stress. With people, blinking lights, flashing words, and pleasant social interactions are more common.

Occasionally, though, researchers do temporarily stress or deceive people, but only when they believe it is essential to a justifiable end, such as understanding and controlling violent behavior or studying mood swings. Such experiments wouldn't work if the participants knew all there was to know about the experiment beforehand. Either the procedures would be ineffective or the participants, wanting to be helpful, might try to confirm the researchers' predictions.

Ethical principles developed by the American Psychological Association (1992) and the British Psychological Society (1993) urge investigators to (1) obtain the informed consent of potential participants, (2) protect them from harm and discomfort, (3) treat information about individual participants confidentially, and (4) fully explain the research afterward. Moreover, most universities today screen research proposals through an ethics committee that safeguards the well-being of every participant.

Much research, however, occurs outside of university laboratories, in places where there may be no ethics committees. For example, retail stores routinely survey people, photograph their purchasing behavior, track their buying patterns, and test the effectiveness of advertising. Curiously, such research attracts less attention than the scientific research done to advance human understanding.

Is Psychology Free of Value Judgments?

OBJECTIVE 24 | Describe how personal values can influence psychologists' research and its application, and discuss psychology's potential to manipulate people.

Psychology is definitely not value-free. Values affect what we study, how we study it, and how we interpret results. Consider: Researchers' values influence their choice of research topics—whether to study worker productivity or worker morale, sex discrimination or gender differences, conformity or independence. Values can also color "the facts." As we noted earlier, our preconceptions can bias our observations and interpretations; sometimes we see what we want or expect to see (**FIGURE 1.11**).

Even the words we use to describe a phenomenon can reflect our values. Labeling the sex acts we do not practice as "perversions" or as "sexual variations" conveys a value judgment. The same holds true in everyday speech, when one person's "rigidity" is another's "consistency," or one person's "faith" is another's "fanaticism." Our labeling

"The greatness of a nation can be judged by the way its animals are treated."
Mahatma Gandhi, 1869–1948

FIGURE 1.11

What do you see? People interpret ambiguous information to fit their preconceptions. Did you see a duck or a rabbit? Before showing some friends this image, ask them if they can see the duck lying on its back (or the bunny in the grass). (From Shepard, 1990.)

© Roger Shepard

someone as "firm" or "stubborn," "careful" or "picky," "discreet" or "secretive" reveals our feelings. Both in and out of psychology, labels describe and labels evaluate.

Popular applications of psychology also contain hidden values. If you defer to "professional" guidance about how to live—how to raise children, how to achieve self-fulfillment, what to do with sexual feelings, how to get ahead at work—you are accepting value-laden advice. A science of behavior and mental processes can certainly help us reach our goals, but it cannot decide what those goals should be. (See Thinking Critically About Desegregation and the Death Penalty on page 50.)

Is Psychology Potentially Dangerous?

If some people see psychology as merely common sense, others have a different concern—that it is becoming dangerously powerful. Is it an accident that astronomy is the oldest science and psychology the youngest? Exploring the external universe is one thing, but exploring our own inner universe seems more dangerous and threatening. Might psychology be used to manipulate people?

Knowledge, like all power, can be used for good or evil. Nuclear power has been used to light up cities—and to demolish them. Persuasive power has been used to educate people—and to deceive them. The power of mind-altering drugs has been used to restore sanity—and to destroy it.

Although psychology does indeed have the power to deceive, its purpose is to enlighten. Every day, psychologists are exploring ways to enhance learning, creativity, and compassion. Psychology also speaks to many of our world's great problems—war, overpopulation, prejudice, family dysfunction, crime—all of which involve attitudes and behaviors. And psychology speaks to our deepest longings—for nourishment, for love, for happiness. True, psychology cannot address all of life's great questions, but it speaks to some mighty important ones.

> "It is doubtless impossible to approach any human problem with a mind free from bias."
>
> Simone de Beauvoir, *The Second Sex*, 1953

>> LEARNING OUTCOMES

Frequently Asked Questions About Psychology

OBJECTIVE 21 | **Explain the value of simplified laboratory conditions in discovering general principles of behavior.**
Researchers test theoretical principles by intentionally creating a controlled, simplified environment in the lab. Their concern is not the particular behavior being studied, but rather the underlying general principles that help explain many behaviors.

OBJECTIVE 22 | **Discuss whether psychological research can be generalized across cultures and genders.**
Behaviors, ideas, attitudes, and traditions vary across cultures, but the principles that underlie them are shared, in part because of our common biological heritage. Biology also determines our sex, but our culture sets up expectations about what it means to be male or female. Males and females do differ in some ways, but they are biologically and psychologically much more alike than different.

OBJECTIVE 23 | **Explain why psychologists study animals, and discuss the ethics of experimentation with both animals and humans.**
Some psychologists study animals out of an interest in animal behavior. Others do so because knowledge of the physiological and psychological processes of animals gives them a better understanding of the similar processes operating in humans.

Under ethical and legal guidelines, animals used in psychological experiments rarely experience pain. Nevertheless, animal rights groups raise an important issue: Even if it leads to the relief of human suffering, is an animal's temporary suffering justified?

Occasionally researchers temporarily stress or deceive people to learn something important. Professional ethical standards provide guidelines concerning the treatment of research participants, and university ethics committees safeguard participants' well-being.

OBJECTIVE 24 | **Describe how personal values can influence psychologists' research and its application, and discuss psychology's potential to manipulate people.**
Psychology is not value-free. Psychologists' own values influence their choice of research topics, their theories and observations, their labels for behavior, and their professional advice. In psychology as elsewhere, knowledge is power that can be used for good or evil. Psychology has the power to deceive, but so far, applications of psychology's principles have been overwhelmingly for the good. Psychology can help us reach our goals, but it cannot decide what those goals should be.

ASK YOURSELF: **Were any of the Frequently Asked Questions your questions? Do you have other questions or concerns about psychology?**

THINKING CRITICALLY ABOUT :

DESEGREGATION AND THE DEATH PENALTY—WHEN BELIEFS COLLIDE WITH PSYCHOLOGICAL SCIENCE

An influential modern viewpoint, ironically called *postmodernism*, questions scientific objectivity. Rather than mirroring the real world, say postmodernists, scientific concepts are socially constructed fictions. Like all knowledge, they reflect the culture that formed them. "Intelligence," for instance, is a concept psychologists created and defined. Because personal values guide theory and research, "truth" is said to be personal and subjective. (What behaviors shall we call "intelligent"?) In our quest for truth, we cannot help following our hunches, our biases, our cultural bent.

Psychological scientists agree that many important questions lie beyond the reach of science. And they agree that personal beliefs often shape perceptions. But they also believe that there is a real world out there, and that we advance truth by checking our hunches against it. Marie Curie did not just construct the concept of radium, she *discovered* radium. It really exists. In the behavioral sciences, pure objectivity, like pure love, may be unattainable. Yet most would argue that it is better to humble ourselves before reliable evidence than to cling to untested presumptions.

Humbling itself before the evidence is what the U.S. Supreme Court did in making its historic 1954 decision declaring segregated schools unconstitutional. This was the Court's first case in which social psychologists participated actively. They did so as expert witnesses and as authors, led by Kenneth Clark (1952), of an influential social science brief that formed part of the case presented. The Court found it noteworthy that when Kenneth Clark and Mamie Phipps Clark

Psychologists Mamie Phipps Clark and Kenneth B. Clark
Their work was cited in the historic U.S. Supreme Court school desegregation decision in 1954.

Office of Public Affairs at Columbia University

(1947) gave African-American children a choice between Black dolls and White dolls, most chose the White, which suggested that under segregation Black children were internalizing anti-Black prejudice.

This social science success inspired hundreds more studies that researchers hoped would inform future judicial decisions. More recently, however, the Court has joined postmodernists in discounting behavioral science research. In deciding whether the death penalty falls under the Constitution's ban on "cruel and unusual punishment," the Court wrestled with whether society defines execution as cruel and unusual, whether courts inflict the penalty arbitrarily, whether they apply it with racial bias, and whether execution deters crime more than all other available punishments. The behavioral science answers to each of these questions, note psychologists Mark Costanzo (1997) and Craig Haney and Deana Logan (1994), could

hardly be clearer. And yet, on two of these issues—the fairness of the death penalty and its effectiveness—the Court has disregarded social science research.

Is the death penalty applied fairly? Studies show that those eligible to serve as jurors in capital punishment cases—namely, those who accept the death penalty—do not represent the greater population. Compared with people excluded by virtue of their qualms about capital punishment, those chosen as jurors are less likely to be minorities and women. They are also more likely to believe the prosecution's arguments, and they are more conviction-prone.

Does the death penalty work—does it deter crime? The evidence is consistent: States with a death penalty do not have lower homicide rates. After instituting the death penalty, these states did not see their rates drop. And homicide has not risen in states that have abandoned the death penalty. A person committing a crime of passion doesn't pause to calculate the consequences (and, if she or he did, would likely consider life in a prison cell an ample deterrent). Yet the Court persists in its belief that "the death penalty undoubtedly is a significant deterrent."

Beliefs guide perceptions. And that, say psychological scientists responding to postmodernists, is why we *need* to think smarter—to restrain our hunches, our biases, and our cultural leanings by checking them against available evidence. Why not put our testable beliefs to the test? If they find support, so much the better for them. If they collide against a wall of observation, so much the worse for them. These ideals of skeptical scrutiny and humility fuel all scientific endeavor.

REVIEW CHAPTER 1: Thinking Critically With Psychological Science

Test Yourself

1. What is the scientific attitude, and why is it important for critical thinking?

2. What are the strengths and weaknesses of the three different methods psychologists use to describe behavior—case studies, surveys, and naturalistic observation?

3. Here are some recently reported correlations, with interpretations drawn by journalists. Further research, often including experiments, has clarified cause and effect in each case. Knowing just these correlations, can you come up with other possible explanations for each of these?

   a. Alcohol use is associated with violence. (One interpretation: Drinking triggers or unleashes aggressive behavior.)

   b. Educated people live longer, on average, than less-educated people. (One interpretation: Education lengthens life and enhances health.)

   c. Teens engaged in team sports are less likely to use drugs, smoke, have sex, carry weapons, and eat junk food than are teens who do not engage in team sports. (One interpretation: Team sports encourage healthy living.)

   d. Adolescents who frequently see smoking in movies are more likely to smoke. (One interpretation: Movie stars' behavior influences impressionable teens.)

4. Why, when testing a new drug for blood pressure, would we learn more about its effectiveness from giving it to half of the participants in a group of 1000 than to all 1000 participants?

5. Consider a question posed by Christopher Jepson, David Krantz, and Richard Nisbett (1983) to University of Michigan introductory psychology students:

   The registrar's office at the University of Michigan has found that usually about 100 students in Arts and Sciences have perfect marks at the end of their first term at the University. However, only about 10 to 15 students graduate with perfect marks. What do you think is the most likely explanation for the fact that there are more perfect marks after one term than at graduation?

6. How are human and animal research subjects protected?

Answers to the Test Yourself questions can be found in Appendix B at the end of the book.

Terms and Concepts to Remember

hindsight bias, p. 20

critical thinking, p. 24

theory, p. 24

hypothesis, p. 25

operational definition, p. 25

replication, p. 25

case study, p. 26

survey, p. 27

false consensus effect, p. 28

population, p. 28

random sample, p. 28

naturalistic observation, p. 29

correlation, p. 30

scatterplot, p. 31

illusory correlation, p. 33

experiment, p. 36

double-blind procedure, p. 37

placebo effect, p. 37

experimental condition, p. 37

control condition, p. 37

random assignment, p. 37

independent variable, p. 38

dependent variable, p. 38

mode, p. 41

mean, p. 41

median, p. 41

range, p. 42

standard deviation, p. 42

statistical significance, p. 43

culture, p. 45

WEB

> To continue your study and review of Thinking Critically With Psychological Science, visit this book's Web site at www.worthpublishers.com/myers. You will find practice tests, review activities, and many interesting articles and Web links for more information on topics related to Thinking Critically With Psychological Science.

2: Neuroscience and Behavior

OBJECTIVE 1 | Explain why psychologists are concerned with human biology, and describe the ill-fated phrenology theory.

No principle is more central to today's psychology, or to this book, than this: *Everything psychological is simultaneously biological.* Your every idea, every mood, every urge is a biological happening. You love, laugh, and cry with your body. Without your body—your genes, your brain, your appearance—you are, indeed, nobody. Although we find it convenient to talk separately of biological and psychological influences on behavior, we need to remember: To think, feel, or act without a body would be like running without legs.

Today's science is riveted on our body's most amazing parts—the brain, its component neural systems, and their genetic instructions. The brain's ultimate challenge? To understand itself. How does our brain organize and communicate with itself? How do our heredity and our experience together wire our brain? How does the brain process the information we need to shoot a basketball? To delight in a guitarist's notes? To remember our first kiss?

Our understanding of how the brain gives birth to the mind has come a long way. The ancient philosopher Plato correctly located the mind in the spherical head—his idea of the perfect form. His student, Aristotle, believed the mind was in the heart, which pumps warmth and vitality to the body. The heart remains our symbol for love, but science has long overtaken philosophy on this issue. It's your brain, not your heart, that falls in love.

We have come far since the early 1800s, when the German physician Franz Gall invented *phrenology,* a popular but ill-fated theory that claimed bumps on the skull could reveal our mental abilities and our character traits (**FIGURE 2.1**). At one point, Britain had 29 phrenological societies, and phrenologists traveled North America giving skull readings (Hunt, 1993). Humorist Mark Twain put one famous phrenologist to the test when he came, using a pseudonym, for a skull-reading. "He found a cavity

Bettman/Corbis

FIGURE 2.1
A wrongheaded theory
Despite initial acceptance of Franz Gall's speculations, bumps on the skull tell us nothing about the brain's underlying functions. Nevertheless, some of Gall's assumptions have held true. Different parts of the brain do control different aspects of behavior, as you will see throughout this chapter.

■ **biological psychology** a branch of psychology concerned with the links between biology and behavior. (Some biological psychologists call themselves *behavioral neuroscientists, neuropsychologists, behavior geneticists, physiological psychologists,* or *biopsychologists.*)

" If I were a college student today, I don't think I could resist going into neuroscience."

Novelist Tom Wolfe, 2004

[and] startled me by saying that that cavity represented the total absence of the sense of humor!" Three months later, Twain sat for a second reading, this time identifying himself. Now "the cavity was gone, and in its place was . . . the loftiest bump of humor he had ever encountered in his life-long experience!" (Lopez, 2002). Phrenology did, however, correctly focus attention on the idea that various brain regions have particular functions.

Within little more than the last century, we have also realized that the body is composed of cells; that among these are nerve cells that conduct electricity and "talk" to one another by sending chemical messages across a tiny gap that separates them; that specific brain systems serve specific functions (though not the functions Gall supposed); and that from the information processed in these different brain systems, we construct our experience of sights and sounds, meanings and memories, pain and passion. You and I are privileged to live in a time when discoveries about the interplay of our biology and our behavior and mental processes are occurring at an exhilarating pace.

Throughout this book you will find examples of this interplay. By studying the links between biological activity and psychological events, **biological psychologists** are gaining a better understanding of sleep and dreams, depression and schizophrenia, hunger and sex, stress and disease. We therefore begin our study of psychology with a look at its biological roots.

Neural Communication

OBJECTIVE 2 | Explain how viewing each person as a biopsychosocial system helps us understand human behavior, and discuss why researchers study other animals in search of clues to human neural processes.

The body's information system is built from billions of interconnected cells called *neurons*. To fathom our thoughts and actions, memories and moods, we must first understand how neurons work and communicate.

We are each a system composed of subsystems that are in turn composed of even smaller subsystems. Tiny cells organize to form such body organs as the stomach, heart, and brain. These organs in turn form larger systems for digestion, circulation, and information processing. And those systems are part of an even larger system—the individual, who in turn is a part of a family, culture, and community. We are *biopsychosocial* systems. To understand our behavior, we need to study how these biological, psychological, and social-cultural systems work and interact.

In this book we start small and build from the bottom up—from nerve cells up to the brain in this chapter, and to the environmental and cultural influences that interact with our biology in later chapters. We will also work from the top down, as we consider how our thinking and emotions influence our brain and our health. At all levels, psychologists examine how we process information—how we take in information; how we organize, interpret, and store it; and how we use it.

For scientists, it is a happy fact of nature that the information systems of humans and other animals operate similarly—so similarly, in fact, that you could not distinguish between small samples of brain tissue from a human and a monkey. This similarity allows researchers to study relatively simple animals, such as squids and sea slugs, to discover how our neural systems operate. It allows them to study other mammals' brains to understand the organization of our own. Cars differ, but all have engines, accelerators, steering wheels, and brakes. A Martian could study any one of them and grasp the operating principles. Likewise, animals differ, yet their nervous systems operate similarly. Though the human brain is more complex than a rat's, both follow the same principles.

Neurons

OBJECTIVE 3 | Describe the parts of a neuron, and explain how its impulses are generated.

Our body's neural information system is complexity built from simplicity. Its building blocks are neurons, or nerve cells. There are many different types of **neurons,** but all are variations on the same theme (**FIGURE 2.2**). Each consists of a cell body and its branching fibers. The bushy **dendrite** fibers receive information and conduct it toward the cell body. From there, **axon** fibers pass the message along to other neurons or to muscles or glands. Axons speak. Dendrites listen.

Unlike the short dendrites, axons are sometimes very long, projecting several feet through the body. Motor neurons, which control muscles, are the neural system's giant redwoods. A neuron carrying orders to a leg muscle has a cell body and axon roughly on the scale of a basketball attached to a rope 4 miles long. A layer of fatty tissue, called the **myelin sheath,** insulates the axons of some neurons and helps speed their impulses. The myelin sheath's importance is evident in multiple sclerosis, a disease in which the myelin sheath degenerates. The result is a slowing of all communication to muscles and the eventual loss of muscle control.

Depending on the type of fiber, the neural impulse travels at speeds ranging from a sluggish 2 miles per hour to a breakneck 200 or more miles per hour. But even this top speed is 3 million times slower than that of electricity through a wire. We measure brain activity in milliseconds (thousandths of a second) and computer activity in nanoseconds (billionths of a second). That helps to explain why, unlike the nearly instantaneous reactions of a high-speed computer, your reaction to a sudden event, such as a child darting in front of your car, may take a quarter-second or more. Your brain is vastly more complex than a computer, but not faster at executing simple responses.

A neuron fires an impulse when it receives signals from sense receptors stimulated by pressure, heat, or light, or when it is stimulated by chemical messages from neighboring neurons. The impulse, called the **action potential,** is a brief electrical charge that travels down the axon.

Neurons, like batteries, generate electricity from chemical events. The chemistry-to-electricity process involves the exchange of electrically charged atoms, called *ions.* The fluid interior of a resting axon has an excess of negatively charged ions, while the fluid outside the axon membrane has more positively charged ions. This

▪ **neuron** a nerve cell; the basic building block of the nervous system.

▪ **dendrite** the bushy, branching extensions of a neuron that receive messages and conduct impulses toward the cell body.

▪ **axon** the extension of a neuron, ending in branching terminal fibers, through which messages pass to other neurons or to muscles or glands.

▪ **myelin** [MY-uh-lin] **sheath** a layer of fatty tissue segmentally encasing the fibers of many neurons; enables vastly greater transmission speed of neural impulses as the impulse hops from one node to the next.

▪ **action potential** a neural impulse; a brief electrical charge that travels down an axon. The action potential is generated by the movement of positively charged atoms in and out of channels in the axon's membrane.

" I sing the body electric."
Walt Whitman, "Children of Adam," 1855

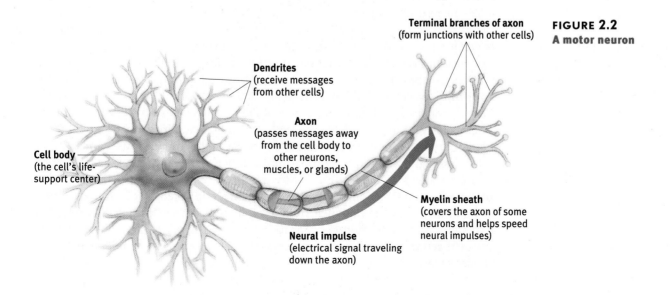

FIGURE 2.2
A motor neuron

Dendrites
(receive messages from other cells)

Terminal branches of axon
(form junctions with other cells)

Axon
(passes messages away from the cell body to other neurons, muscles, or glands)

Cell body
(the cell's life-support center)

Myelin sheath
(covers the axon of some neurons and helps speed neural impulses)

Neural impulse
(electrical signal traveling down the axon)

2. This depolarization produces another action potential a little farther along the axon. Gates in this neighboring area now open, and charged sodium atoms rush in. Meanwhile, a pump in the cell membrane (the sodium/potassium pump) transports the sodium ions back out of the cell.

3. As the action potential continues speedily down the axon, the first section has now completely recharged.

Cell body end of axon

1. Neuron stimulation causes a brief change in electrical charge. If strong enough, this produces depolarization and an action potential.

Direction of neural impulse: toward axon terminals

FIGURE 2.3
Action potential

positive-outside/negative-inside state is called the *resting potential*. Like a tightly guarded facility, the axon's surface is very selective about what it allows in. We say the axon's surface is *selectively permeable*. For example, a resting axon has gates that block positive sodium ions.

When a neuron fires, however, the security parameters change: The first bit of the axon opens its gates, rather like manhole covers flipping open, and the positively charged sodium ions flood through the membrane (**FIGURE 2.3**). This *depolarizes* that part of the axon, causing the axon's next channel to open, and then the next, like dominoes falling, each one tripping the next. During a resting pause (the *refractory period,* rather like a camera flash pausing to recharge), the neuron pumps the positively charged sodium ions back outside. Then it can fire again. (In myelinated neurons, as in Figure 2.2, page 55, the action potential speeds up by hopping from one myelin "sausage" to the next.) The mind boggles when imagining this electrochemical process repeating up to 100 or even 1000 times a second. But this is just the first of many astonishments.

The neuron is a miniature decision-making device that performs some complex calculations. From hundreds, even thousands of other neurons, it receives signals on its dendrites and cell body. Most of these signals are *excitatory,* somewhat like pushing a neuron's accelerator. Other signals are *inhibitory,* more like pushing its brake. If excitatory signals minus inhibitory signals exceed a minimum intensity, called the **threshold,** the combined signals trigger an action potential. (Think of it this way: If the excitatory party animals outvote the inhibitory party poopers, the party's on.) The action potential transmits down the axon, which branches into junctions with hundreds or thousands of other neurons and with the body's muscles and glands.

Increasing the stimulus above the threshold, however, will not increase the action potential's intensity. The neuron's reaction is an *all-or-none response:* Like guns, neurons either fire or they don't. How then do we detect the intensity of a stimulus? How do we distinguish a gentle touch from a big hug? A strong stimulus—a slap rather than a tap—can trigger more neurons to fire, and to fire more often. But it does not affect the action potential's strength or speed. Squeezing a trigger harder won't make a bullet go faster.

"What one neuron tells another neuron is simply how much it is excited."
Francis Crick, *The Astonishing Hypothesis*, 1994

■ **threshold** the level of stimulation required to trigger a neural impulse.

How Neurons Communicate

OBJECTIVE 4 | Describe how nerve cells communicate.

Neurons interweave so intricately that even with a microscope it is hard to see where one neuron ends and another begins. Scientists once believed that the branching axon of one cell fused with the dendrites of another in an uninterrupted fabric. Then a Spanish anatomist, Santiago Ramon y Cajal (1852–1934), described gaps between individual nerve cells and concluded that the individual neurons must function as independent agents within the nervous system. At the same time, the British physiologist Sir Charles Sherrington (1857–1952) noticed that neural impulses were taking an unexpectedly long time to travel a neural pathway. Sherrington inferred there must be a brief interruption in the transmission.

We now know that the axon terminal of one neuron is in fact separated from the receiving neuron by a gap less than a millionth of an inch wide. Sherrington called this junction the **synapse,** and the gap is called the *synaptic gap* or *cleft*. To Cajal, these near-unions of neurons—"protoplasmic kisses," he called them—were another of nature's marvels. "Like elegant ladies air-kissing so as not to muss their makeup, dendrites and axons don't quite touch," notes Diane Ackerman (2004). How do the neurons execute this protoplasmic kiss? How does information cross the tiny synaptic gap? The answer is one of the important scientific discoveries of our age.

When the action potential reaches the knoblike terminals at an axon's end, it triggers the release of chemical messengers, called **neurotransmitters** (**FIGURE 2.4**).

■ **synapse** [SIN-aps] the junction between the axon tip of the sending neuron and the dendrite or cell body of the receiving neuron. The tiny gap at this junction is called the *synaptic gap* or *cleft*.

■ **neurotransmitters** chemical messengers that traverse the synaptic gaps between neurons. When released by the sending neuron, neurotransmitters travel across the synapse and bind to receptor sites on the receiving neuron, thereby influencing whether that neuron will generate a neural impulse.

"All information processing in the brain involves neurons 'talking to' each other at synapses."

Neuroscientist Solomon H. Snyder (1984)

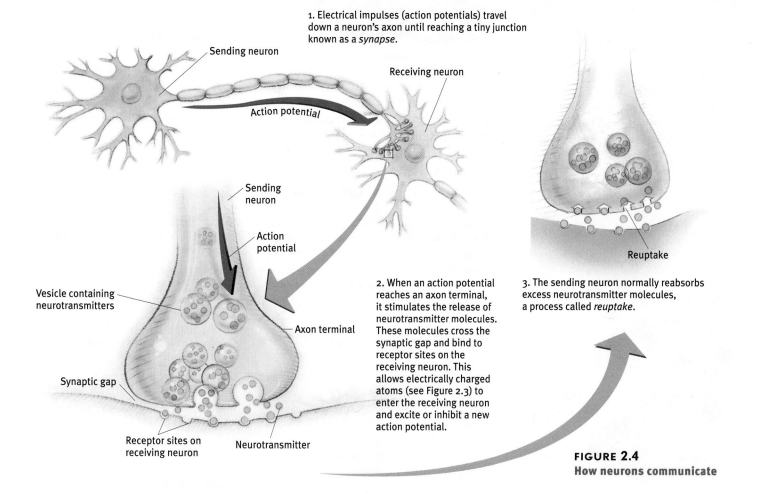

1. Electrical impulses (action potentials) travel down a neuron's axon until reaching a tiny junction known as a *synapse*.

Sending neuron

Receiving neuron

Action potential

Sending neuron

Action potential

Vesicle containing neurotransmitters

Axon terminal

Synaptic gap

Receptor sites on receiving neuron

Neurotransmitter

2. When an action potential reaches an axon terminal, it stimulates the release of neurotransmitter molecules. These molecules cross the synaptic gap and bind to receptor sites on the receiving neuron. This allows electrically charged atoms (see Figure 2.3) to enter the receiving neuron and excite or inhibit a new action potential.

3. The sending neuron normally reabsorbs excess neurotransmitter molecules, a process called *reuptake*.

Reuptake

FIGURE 2.4
How neurons communicate

■ **acetylcholine** [ah-seat-el-KO-leen] **(ACh)** a neurotransmitter that enables learning and memory and also triggers muscle contraction.

Within 1/10,000th of a second, the neurotransmitter molecules cross the synaptic gap and bind to receptor sites on the receiving neuron—as precisely as a key fits a lock. For an instant, the neurotransmitter unlocks tiny channels at the receiving site. This allows ions to enter the receiving neuron, thereby either exciting or inhibiting its readiness to fire. Excess neurotransmitters are reabsorbed by the sending neuron in a process called *reuptake*.

How Neurotransmitters Influence Us

OBJECTIVE 5 | Explain how neurotransmitters affect behavior, and outline the effects of acetylcholine and the endorphins.

"When it comes to the brain, if you want to see the action, follow the neurotransmitters."

Neuroscientist Floyd Bloom (1993)

As researchers discovered dozens of different neurotransmitters, they also encountered new questions: Are certain neurotransmitters found only in specific places? How do they affect our moods, memories, and mental abilities? Can we boost or diminish these effects through drugs or diet?

In later chapters we will examine neurotransmitter influences on depression and euphoria, hunger and thinking, addictions and therapy. For now, let's glimpse how neurotransmitters influence our motions and our emotions. We now know that a particular neural pathway in the brain may use only one or two neurotransmitters (**FIGURE 2.5**), and that particular neurotransmitters may have particular effects on behavior and emotions. (**TABLE 2.1** offers examples.)

Serotonin pathways

Dopamine pathways

FIGURE 2.5
Neurotransmitter pathways
Each of the brain's differing chemical messengers has designated pathways where it operates, as shown here for serotonin and dopamine (Carter, 1998).

Acetylcholine (ACh) is one of the best-understood neurotransmitters. In addition to its role in learning and memory, ACh is the messenger at every junction between a motor neuron and skeletal muscle. When ACh is released to our muscle cells, the muscle contracts. If ACh transmission is blocked, the muscles cannot contract.

Both photos from Mapping the Mind, Rita Carter, © 1989 University of California Press

Stanley Chou/Getty Images

TABLE 2.1

SOME NEUROTRANSMITTERS AND THEIR FUNCTIONS

Neurotransmitter	Function	Examples of Malfunctions
Acetylcholine (ACh)	Enables muscle action, learning, and memory.	With Alzheimer's disease, ACh-producing neurons deteriorate.
Dopamine	Influences movement, learning, attention, and emotion.	Excess dopamine receptor activity linked to schizophrenia. Starved of dopamine, the brain produces the tremors and decreased mobility of Parkinson's disease.
Serotonin	Affects mood, hunger, sleep, and arousal.	Undersupply linked to depression; Prozac and some other antidepressant drugs raise serotonin levels.
Norepinephrine	Helps control alertness and arousal.	Undersupply can depress mood.
GABA (gamma-aminobutyric acid)	A major inhibitory neurotransmitter.	Undersupply linked to seizures, tremors, and insomnia.
Glutamate	A major excitatory neurotransmitter; involved in memory.	Oversupply can overstimulate brain, producing migraines or seizures (which is why some people avoid MSG, monosodium glutamate, in food).

An exciting discovery about neurotransmitters occurred when Candace Pert and Solomon Snyder (1973) attached a radioactive tracer to morphine, showing them where it was taken up in an animal's brain. Their discovery: The morphine, an opiate drug that elevates mood and eases pain, bound to receptors in areas linked with mood and pain sensations.

It was hard to imagine why the brain would contain these "opiate receptors" unless it had its own naturally occurring opiates. Why would the brain have a chemical lock, unless it also had a corresponding key? Researchers soon confirmed that the brain does indeed contain several types of neurotransmitter molecules similar to morphine. Named **endorphins** (short for *endo*genous [produced within] *morphin*e), these natural opiates are released in response to pain and vigorous exercise. They may therefore help explain good feelings such as the "runner's high," the painkilling effects of acupuncture, and the indifference to pain in some severely injured people, such as David Livingstone reported in his 1857 *Missionary Travels:*

> I heard a shout. Starting, and looking half round, I saw the lion just in the act of springing upon me. I was upon a little height, he caught my shoulder as he sprang, and we both came to the ground below together. Growling horribly close to my ear, he shook me as a terrier does a rat. The shock produced a stupor similar to that which seems to be felt by a mouse after the first shake of the cat. It caused a sort of dreaminess in which there was no sense of pain nor feeling of terror, though [I was] quite conscious of all that was happening. . . . This peculiar state is probably produced in all animals killed by the carnivora; and if so, is a merciful provision by our benevolent Creator for lessening the pain of death.

How Drugs and Other Chemicals Alter Neurotransmission

OBJECTIVE 6 | Explain how drugs and other chemicals affect neurotransmission, and describe the contrasting effects of agonists and antagonists.

If indeed the endorphins lessen pain and boost mood, why not flood the brain with artificial opiates, thereby intensifying the brain's own "feel-good" chemistry? One problem is that when flooded with opiate drugs such as heroin and morphine, the brain may stop producing its own natural opiates. When the drug is withdrawn, the brain may then be deprived of any form of opiate. For a drug addict, the result is discomfort that persists until the brain resumes production of its natural opiates or receives more artificial opiates. As we will see in later chapters, mood-altering drugs, from alcohol to nicotine to heroin, share a common effect: They trigger unpleasant, lingering aftereffects. For suppressing the body's own neurotransmitter production, nature charges a price.

Various drugs affect communication at the synapse, often by either exciting or inhibiting neurons' firing. *Agonists* excite. An agonist molecule may be similar enough to the neurotransmitter to mimic its effects (**FIGURE 2.6b** on page 60) or it may block the neurotransmitter's reuptake. Some opiate drugs, for example, produce a temporary "high" by amplifying normal sensations of arousal or pleasure. Not so pleasant are the effects of black widow spider venom, which floods synapses with ACh. The result? Violent muscle contractions, convulsions, and possible death.

Antagonists inhibit. An antagonist can be a drug molecule that inhibits a neurotransmitter's release. Botulin, a poison that can form in improperly canned food, causes paralysis by blocking ACh release from the sending neuron. (Injections of botulin—Botox—smooth wrinkles by paralyzing the underlying facial muscles.) Or it may be enough like the natural neurotransmitter to occupy its receptor site and block its effect, as in **FIGURE 2.6c,** but not similar enough to stimulate the receptor (rather like foreign coins that fit into, but won't operate, a soda or candy machine). Curare, a poison that certain South American Indians apply to the tips of their hunting darts,

■ **endorphins** [en-DOR-fins] "morphine within"—natural, opiatelike neurotransmitters linked to pain control and to pleasure.

" Physician Lewis Thomas, on the endorphins: "There it is, a biologically universal act of mercy. I cannot explain it, except to say that I would have put it in had I been around at the very beginning, sitting as a member of a planning committee."

The Youngest Science, 1983

This neurotransmitter molecule fits the receptor site on the receiving neuron, much as a key fits a lock.

Receptor site on receiving neuron

(a)

This agonist molecule excites. It is similar enough in structure to the neurotransmitter molecule to mimic its effects on the receiving neuron. Morphine, for instance, mimics the action of endorphins.

Agonist mimics neurotransmitter

(b)

This antagonist molecule inhibits. It has a structure similar enough to the neurotransmitter to occupy its receptor site and block its action, but not similar enough to stimulate the receptor. Curare poisoning paralyzes its victims by blocking ACh receptors involved in muscle movement.

Antagonist blocks neurotransmitter

(c)

Neurotransmitters carry a message from a sending neuron across a synapse to receptor sites on a receiving neuron.

FIGURE 2.6
Agonists and antagonists

occupies and blocks ACh receptor sites, leaving the neurotransmitter unable to affect the muscles. Struck by one of these darts, an animal becomes paralyzed.

Neurotransmitter research is leading to new therapeutic drugs to alleviate depression, schizophrenia, and other disorders. But designing a drug can be harder than it sounds. A *blood-brain barrier* enables the brain to fence out unwanted chemicals circulating in the blood. Scientists know, for example, that the tremors of Parkinson's disease result from the death of nerve cells that produce dopamine. Giving the patient dopamine doesn't help, because dopamine cannot cross the blood-brain barrier. But some chemicals can slither through this barrier. One, L-dopa, a raw material the brain can convert to dopamine, enables many patients to regain better muscular control.

>> LEARNING OUTCOMES

Neural Communication

OBJECTIVE 1 | Explain why psychologists are concerned with human biology, and describe the ill-fated phrenology theory.

For convenience, we may talk separately about biological or psychological influences on behavior, but in reality, everything psychological is simultaneously biological. Franz Gall did not subject his beliefs about phrenology to scientific tests, but this early theory did help scientists to begin thinking about links among our biology, behavior, and mental processes.

OBJECTIVE 2 | Explain how viewing each person as a biopsychosocial system helps us understand human behavior, and discuss why researchers study other animals in search of clues to human neural processes.

Viewing each person as a biopsychosocial system lets us study behavior from multiple levels of analysis. At the biological level, neurons and other cells compose organs, which form larger systems (digestion, circulation, information processing). At the social-cultural level, people live in specific times and places and are subject to specific environmental and social-cultural influences. At the psychological level, people's thoughts and emotions interact with their biology and personal history to produce that unique individual. Scientists gain much from their study of neural processes in other mammals and in relatively simple animals because humans and other animals have similar neural systems.

OBJECTIVE 3 | **Describe the parts of a neuron, and explain how its impulses are generated.**

The body's circuitry, the nervous system, consists of billions of individual cells called neurons. Neurons send signals through their *axon,* which is sometimes encased in a myelin sheath. Neurons receive signals from other cells through their branching *dendrites* and their *cell body.* If the combined signals are strong enough, the neuron fires, transmitting an electrical impulse (the action potential) down its axon, by means of a chemistry-to-electricity process in which ions are exchanged. The neuron's reaction is an all-or-none response.

OBJECTIVE 4 | **Describe how nerve cells communicate.**

When action potentials reach the end of an axon (the axon terminals), they stimulate the release of neurotransmitters. These chemical messengers carry a message from the sending neuron across a synapse to receptor sites on a receiving neuron. The sending neuron, in a process called *reuptake,* then normally absorbs the excess neurotransmitter molecules in the synaptic gap. The receiving neuron, if the signals from that neuron and others are strong enough, generates its own action potential and relays the message to other cells.

OBJECTIVE 5 | **Explain how neurotransmitters affect behavior, and outline the effects of acetylcholine and the endorphins.**

Each neurotransmitter travels a designated path in the brain and has a particular effect on behavior and emotions. Acetylcholine, one of the best-understood neurotransmitters, affects muscle action, learning, and memory. The endorphins are natural opiates released in response to pain and exercise.

OBJECTIVE 6 | **Explain how drugs and other chemicals affect neurotransmission, and describe the contrasting effects of agonists and antagonists.**

Drugs and other chemicals affect communication at the synapse. Agonists, such as some of the opiates, excite by mimicking particular neurotransmitters or by blocking their reuptake. Antagonists, such as curare, inhibit a particular neurotransmitter's release or block its effect.

ASK YOURSELF: **Can you recall a time when the endorphin response may have protected you from feeling extreme pain?**

The Nervous System

OBJECTIVE 7 | Describe the nervous system's two major divisions, and identify the three types of neurons that transmit information through the system.

To live is to take in information from the world and the body's tissues, to make decisions, and to send back information and orders to the body's tissues. Neurons are the elementary components of our **nervous system,** our body's speedy electrochemical information network (**FIGURE 2.7**). The brain and spinal cord form the **central nervous system (CNS).** The **peripheral nervous system (PNS)** links the central nervous system with the body's sense receptors, muscles, and glands.

■ **nervous system** the body's speedy, electrochemical communication network, consisting of all the nerve cells of the peripheral and central nervous systems.

■ **central nervous system (CNS)** the brain and spinal cord.

■ **peripheral nervous system (PNS)** the sensory and motor neurons that connect the central nervous system (CNS) to the rest of the body.

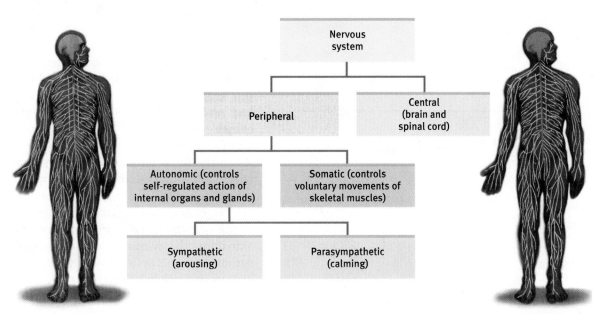

**FIGURE 2.7
The functional divisions of the human nervous system**

■ **nerves** neural "cables" containing many axons. These bundled axons, which are part of the peripheral nervous system, connect the central nervous system with muscles, glands, and sense organs.

■ **sensory neurons** neurons that carry incoming information from the sense receptors to the central nervous system.

■ **motor neurons** neurons that carry outgoing information from the central nervous system to the muscles and glands.

■ **interneurons** central nervous system neurons that internally communicate and intervene between the sensory inputs and motor outputs.

The axons carrying this PNS information are bundled into the electrical cables that we know as **nerves.** The optic nerve, for example, bundles a million axon fibers into a single cable carrying the information that each eye sends to the brain (Mason & Kandel, 1991).

Information travels in the nervous system through three types of neurons. The **sensory neurons** send information from the body's tissues and sensory organs inward to the central nervous system's brain and spinal cord, which process the information. The central nervous system then sends instructions out to the body's tissues via the **motor neurons.** In between the sensory input and motor output, information is processed by the central nervous system's internal communication via its **interneurons.** Our complexity resides mostly in our interneuron systems. Our nervous system has a few million sensory neurons, a few million motor neurons, and billions and billions of interneurons.

The Peripheral Nervous System

OBJECTIVE 8 | Identify the subdivisions of the peripheral nervous system, and describe their functions.

Our peripheral nervous system has two components—somatic and autonomic. The **somatic nervous system** enables voluntary control of our skeletal muscles. As you reach the bottom of this page, the somatic nervous system will report to your brain the current state of your skeletal muscles and carry instructions back, triggering your hand to turn the page.

Our **autonomic nervous system** controls the glands and the muscles of our internal organs. Like an automatic pilot, this system may be consciously overridden. But usually it operates on its own (autonomously) to influence our internal functioning, including our heartbeat, digestion, and glandular activity.

The autonomic nervous system is a dual system (**FIGURE 2.8**). The **sympathetic nervous system** arouses. If something alarms, enrages, or challenges you (such as a longed-for job interview), the sympathetic system will accelerate your heartbeat, raise your blood pressure, slow your digestion, raise your blood sugar, and cool you with perspiration, making you alert and ready for action. (Lie-detection machines measure such stress responses, which sometimes also accompany lies.) When the stress subsides, the **parasympathetic nervous system** produces opposite effects. It conserves energy as it calms you by decreasing your heartbeat, lowering your blood sugar, and so forth. In everyday situations, the sympathetic and parasympathetic nervous systems work together to keep us in a steady internal state.

FIGURE 2.8
The dual functions of the autonomic nervous system
The autonomic nervous system controls the more autonomous (or self-regulating) internal functions. Its sympathetic division arouses and expends energy. Its parasympathetic division calms and conserves energy, allowing routine maintenance activity. For example, sympathetic stimulation accelerates heartbeat, whereas parasympathetic stimulation slows it.

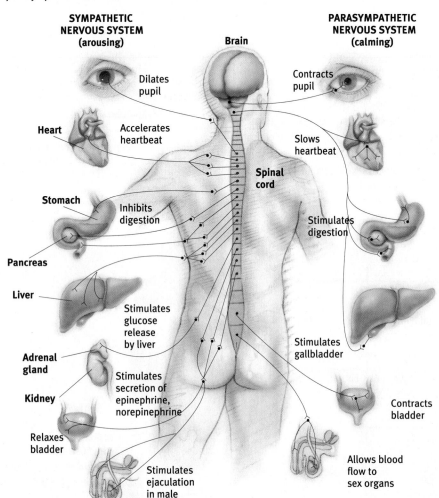

SYMPATHETIC NERVOUS SYSTEM (arousing)

PARASYMPATHETIC NERVOUS SYSTEM (calming)

Brain

Dilates pupil

Contracts pupil

Heart
Accelerates heartbeat

Slows heartbeat

Spinal cord

Stomach
Inhibits digestion

Stimulates digestion

Pancreas

Liver
Stimulates glucose release by liver

Stimulates gallbladder

Adrenal gland
Stimulates secretion of epinephrine, norepinephrine

Kidney

Contracts bladder

Relaxes bladder

Stimulates ejaculation in male

Allows blood flow to sex organs

The Central Nervous System

OBJECTIVE 9 | Contrast the simplicity of the reflex pathways with the complexity of neural networks.

From the simplicity of neurons "talking" to other neurons arises the complexity of the central nervous system that enables our humanity—our thinking, feeling, and acting. Tens of billions of neurons, each communicating with thousands of other neurons, yield an ever-changing wiring diagram that dwarfs a powerful computer. One of the great remaining scientific mysteries is how this neural machinery organizes itself into complex circuits capable of learning, feeling, and thinking.

The Spinal Cord and Reflexes

The central nervous system's spinal cord is an information highway connecting the peripheral nervous system to the brain. Ascending neural fibers send up sensory information, and descending fibers send back motor-control information.

The neural pathways governing our **reflexes,** our automatic responses to stimuli, illustrate the spinal cord's work. A simple spinal reflex pathway is composed of a single sensory neuron and a single motor neuron. These often communicate through an interneuron. The knee-jerk response, for example, involves one such simple pathway; a headless warm body could do it.

Another such pathway enables the pain reflex (**FIGURE 2.9**). When your finger touches a flame, neural activity excited by the heat travels via sensory neurons to interneurons in your spinal cord. These interneurons respond by activating motor neurons to the muscles in your arm. That's why it feels as if your hand jerks away not by your choice, but on its own.

Because the simple pain reflex pathway runs through the spinal cord and out, your hand jerks from the candle's flame *before* your brain receives and responds to the information that causes you to feel pain. Information travels to and from the brain by way of the spinal cord. Were the top of your spinal cord severed, you would not feel such pain. Nor would you feel pleasure. Your brain would literally be out of touch with your body. You would lose all sensation and voluntary movement in body regions whose sensory and motor neurons connect with the spinal cord below its point

> You are your synapses."
> Joseph Le Doux, *The Synaptic Self*, 2002

■ **somatic nervous system** the division of the peripheral nervous system that controls the body's skeletal muscles. Also called the *skeletal nervous system.*

■ **autonomic** [aw-tuh-NAHM-ik] **nervous system** the part of the peripheral nervous system that controls the glands and the muscles of the internal organs (such as the heart). Its sympathetic division arouses; its parasympathetic division calms.

■ **sympathetic nervous system** the division of the autonomic nervous system that arouses the body, mobilizing its energy in stressful situations.

■ **parasympathetic nervous system** the division of the autonomic nervous system that calms the body, conserving its energy.

■ **reflex** a simple, automatic, inborn response to a sensory stimulus, such as the knee-jerk response.

> If the nervous system be cut off between the brain and other parts, the experiences of those other parts are nonexistent for the mind. The eye is blind, the ear deaf, the hand insensible and motionless."
> William James, *Principles of Psychology*, 1890

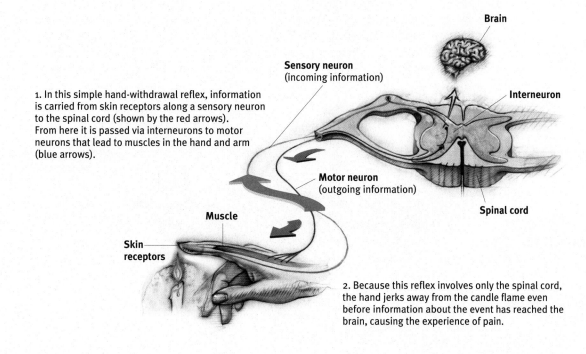

1. In this simple hand-withdrawal reflex, information is carried from skin receptors along a sensory neuron to the spinal cord (shown by the red arrows). From here it is passed via interneurons to motor neurons that lead to muscles in the hand and arm (blue arrows).

2. Because this reflex involves only the spinal cord, the hand jerks away from the candle flame even before information about the event has reached the brain, causing the experience of pain.

FIGURE 2.9
A simple reflex

■ **neural networks** interconnected neural cells. With experience, networks can learn, as feedback strengthens or inhibits connections that produce certain results. Computer simulations of neural networks show analogous learning.

© Tom Swick

"The body is made up of millions and millions of crumbs."

of injury. You would exhibit the knee-jerk without feeling the tap. With the severing of the brain center that keeps the brakes on erections, men paralyzed below the waist are often capable of an erection (a simple reflex) if their genitals are stimulated (Goldstein, 2000). Females similarly paralyzed may respond with vaginal lubrication. But, depending on where and how completely the spinal cord is severed, they may be genitally unresponsive to erotic images and have no genital feeling (Kennedy & Over, 1990; Sipski & Alexander, 1999). To produce bodily pain or pleasure, the sensory information must reach the brain.

The Brain and Neural Networks

The other part of your central nervous system, your brain, receives information, interprets it, and decides responses. In doing so, the brain functions rather like a computing machine. It receives slightly differing images of an object from the two eyes, computes their difference, and instantly infers how far away the object must be to project such a difference. As basketball star LeBron James releases his falling-away jump shot, his agile brain performs an incredible number of instant computations, adjusting for body position and movement, distance, and angle.

How does James' brain perform such computations? First, each neuron connects with thousands of others. To get a feel for the complexity of these interconnections, consider: You could join two 8-studded Lego bricks 24 ways, and six bricks nearly 103 million ways. With some 40 billion neurons, each having roughly 10,000 contacts with other neurons, we end up with perhaps 400 trillion synapses—places where neurons meet and greet their neighbors (de Courten-Myers, 2005). A grain-of-sand–sized speck of your brain contains 100,000 neurons and one billion "talking" synapses (Ramachandran & Blakeslee, 1998). Being human takes a lot of nerve.

Neurons cluster into work groups called **neural networks.** To understand why neurons tend to connect with nearby neurons, Stephen Kosslyn and Olivier Koenig (1992, p. 12) invite us to "think about why cities exist; why don't people distribute themselves more evenly across the countryside?" Like people networking with people, neurons network with nearby neurons with which they can have short, fast connections. As in **FIGURE 2.10,** the cells in each layer of a neural network connect with various cells in the next layer. Learning occurs as feedback strengthens connections that produce certain results. Piano practice, for example, builds neural connections. Neurons that fire together wire together.

New computer models simulate neural networks, complete with excitatory and inhibitory connections that gain strength with experience—and mimic the brain's capacity for learning. Of course, our own neural networks are more complicated than the networks depicted in Figure 2.10. In our brains, one neural network is intercon-

FIGURE 2.10
A simplified neural network
Neurons network with nearby neurons. Encoded in these networks of interrelating neurons is your own enduring identity, your sense of self that extends across the years.

Neurons in the brain connect
with one another to form networks

Inputs   Outputs

The brain learns by modifying
certain connections in response to feedback

nected with other networks that do different things. Open the brain and you will see no arrows that tell you where one network ends and the next begins; what distinguishes them is their specific functions. Each is a subnetwork, contributing its little bit of information to the whole information-processing system that we call the brain.

>> LEARNING OUTCOMES

The Nervous System

OBJECTIVE 7 | Describe the nervous system's two major divisions, and identify the three types of neurons that transmit information through the system.

One major division of the nervous system is the *central nervous system (CNS)*, which consists of the brain and spinal cord. The other is the *peripheral nervous system (PNS)*, which consists of the neurons that connect the CNS to the rest of the body by means of nerves (bundled axons of the sensory and motor neurons). *Sensory neurons* carry incoming information from sense receptors to the CNS, and *motor neurons* carry information from the CNS out to the muscles and glands. *Interneurons* communicate within the CNS and between sensory and motor neurons.

OBJECTIVE 8 | Identify the subdivisions of the peripheral nervous system, and describe their functions.

The peripheral nervous system has two main divisions. The *somatic nervous system* enables voluntary control of the skeletal muscles. The *autonomic nervous system,* through its sympathetic and parasympathetic divisions, controls our involuntary muscles and glands.

OBJECTIVE 9 | Contrast the simplicity of the reflex pathways with the complexity of neural networks.

Reflex pathways are automatic inborn responses to stimuli, and they do not rely on conscious decisions made in the brain. A single sensory neuron, excited by some stimulus (such as a flame), passes a message to an interneuron in the spinal cord. The interneuron activates a motor neuron, causing some muscle reaction (such as jerking away from the heat source). In contrast, neural networks, found in the brain, are clusters of many neurons that together share some special task. These complex networks strengthen with use, learning from experience. Each neural network connects with other networks performing different tasks.

ASK YOURSELF: Does our nervous system's design—with its synaptic gaps that chemical messenger molecules cross in an imperceptibly brief instant—surprise you? Would you have designed yourself differently?

The Endocrine System

OBJECTIVE 10 | Describe the nature and functions of the endocrine system and its interaction with the nervous system.

So far we have focused on the body's speedy electrochemical information system. There is, however, another communication system. Interconnected with the nervous system is the second of the body's communication systems, the **endocrine system** (**FIGURE 2.11** on page 66). The endocrine system's glands secrete another form of chemical messengers, **hormones.** Hormones originate in one tissue, travel through the bloodstream, and affect other tissues, including the brain. When they act on the brain, they influence our interest in sex, food, and aggression.

Some hormones are chemically identical to neurotransmitters (those chemical messengers that diffuse across a synapse and excite or inhibit an adjacent neuron). The endocrine system and nervous system are therefore kindred systems: They both secrete molecules that activate receptors elsewhere. But unlike the speedy nervous system, zipping messages from eyes to brain to hand in a fraction of a second, endocrine messages trudge along. If the nervous system's communication delivers messages rather like e-mail, the endocrine system is the body's snail mail. Several seconds or more may elapse before the bloodstream carries a hormone from an endocrine

■ **endocrine** [EN-duh-krin] **system** the body's "slow" chemical communication system; a set of glands that secrete hormones into the bloodstream.

■ **hormones** chemical messengers, mostly those manufactured by the endocrine glands, that are produced in one tissue and affect another.

FIGURE 2.11
The endocrine system

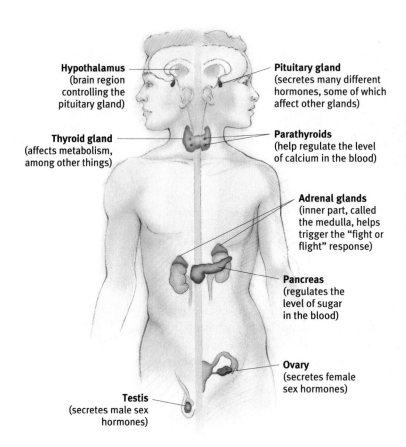

Hypothalamus
(brain region
controlling the
pituitary gland)

Pituitary gland
(secretes many different
hormones, some of which
affect other glands)

Thyroid gland
(affects metabolism,
among other things)

Parathyroids
(help regulate the level
of calcium in the blood)

Adrenal glands
(inner part, called
the medulla, helps
trigger the "fight or
flight" response)

Pancreas
(regulates the
level of sugar
in the blood)

Ovary
(secretes female
sex hormones)

Testis
(secretes male sex
hormones)

gland to its target tissue. But these endocrine messages are often worth the wait because their effects usually outlast the effects of a neural message. And that helps explain why sometimes, after our conscious mind is distracted from some mildly stressful news, we may have a lingering feeling that something isn't quite right. Under the influence of hormones and nonverbal brain areas, the feeling outlasts the thought—until we recapture the awareness and perhaps feel relief at recalling the reason for our discomfort.

The endocrine system's hormones influence many aspects of our lives—growth, reproduction, metabolism, mood—working to keep everything in balance while we respond to stress, exertion, and our own thoughts. In a moment of danger, for example, the autonomic nervous system orders the **adrenal glands** on top of the kidneys to release *epinephrine* and *norepinephrine* (also called *adrenaline* and *noradrenaline*). These hormones increase heart rate, blood pressure, and blood sugar, providing us with a surge of energy. When the emergency passes, the hormones—and the feelings of excitement—linger a while.

The most influential endocrine gland is the **pituitary gland,** a pea-sized structure located in the core of the brain, where it is controlled by an adjacent brain area called the *hypothalamus.* The pituitary releases hormones that influence growth, and its secretions also influence the release of hormones by other endocrine glands. The pituitary, then, is really a sort of master gland (whose own master is the hypothalamus). For example, under the brain's influence, the pituitary triggers your sex glands to release sex hormones. These in turn influence your brain and behavior.

This feedback system (brain → pituitary → other glands → hormones → brain) reveals the intimate connection of the nervous and endocrine systems: the nervous system directing endocrine secretions, which then affect the nervous system. In fact, the two systems so closely interconnect that the distinction between them sometimes

■ **adrenal** [ah-DREEN-el] **glands** a pair of endocrine glands just above the kidneys. The adrenals secrete the hormones epinephrine (adrenaline) and norepinephrine (noradrenaline), which help to arouse the body in times of stress.

■ **pituitary gland** the endocrine system's most influential gland. Under the influence of the hypothalamus, the pituitary regulates growth and controls other endocrine glands blurs. Researchers have discovered that neurotransmitters can drift in the brain's fluid to nerve receptors at distant sites, thereby affecting overall alertness or mood (Agnati & others, 1992; Pert, 1986). In such cases, the distinction between certain neurotransmitters and their chemical twins—which are called hormones when released by glands—is no longer so clear. Conducting and coordinating this whole electrochemical orchestra is that maestro we call the brain.

>> LEARNING OUTCOMES

The Endocrine System

OBJECTIVE 10 | **Describe the nature and functions of the endocrine system and its interaction with the nervous system.**

The endocrine system is a set of glands that secrete hormones into the bloodstream. These chemical messengers travel through the body and affect other tissues, including the brain. Some hormones are chemically identical to neurotransmitters. The endocrine system's master gland, the pituitary, influences hormone release by other glands. In an intricate feedback system, the brain's hypothalamus influences the pituitary gland, which influences other glands, which release hormones, which in turn influence the brain.

ASK YOURSELF: **Can you remember feeling an extended period of discomfort after some particularly stressful event? How long did those feelings last?**

The Brain

In a jar on a display shelf in Cornell University's psychology department resides the well-preserved brain of Edward Bradford Titchener, a great turn-of-the-century experimental psychologist and proponent of the study of consciousness. Imagine yourself gazing at that wrinkled mass of grayish tissue, wondering if in any sense Titchener is still in there.[1]

You might answer that, without the living whir of electrochemical activity, there could be nothing of Titchener in his preserved brain. Consider then an experiment about which the inquisitive Titchener himself might have daydreamed. Imagine that just moments before his death, someone removed Titchener's brain from his body and kept it alive by floating it in a tank of cerebral fluid while feeding it enriched blood. Would Titchener now still be in there? Further imagine that someone then transplanted the still-living brain into the body of a person with severe brain damage. To whose home should the recovered patient return?

That we can imagine such questions illustrates how convinced we are that we live in our heads. And for good reason: The brain enables the mind—seeing, hearing, smelling, feeling, remembering, thinking, speaking, dreaming. The brain is what poet Diane Ackerman (2004, p. 3) calls "that shiny mound of being . . . that dream factory . . . that huddle of neurons calling all the plays . . . that fickle pleasuredrome."

Moreover, it is the brain that self-reflectively analyzes the brain. When we're thinking about our brain, we're thinking *with* our brain—by firing countless millions of synapses and releasing billions of neurotransmitter molecules. Indeed, say neuroscientists, the *mind is what the brain does*. But precisely where and how are the mind's functions tied to the brain? Let's first see how scientists explore such questions.

"You're certainly a lot less fun since the operation."

"I am a brain, Watson. The rest of me is a mere appendix."

Sherlock Holmes, in Arthur Conan Doyle's "The Adventure of the Mazarin Stone"

---

[1]Carl Sagan's *Broca's Brain* (1979) inspired this question.

■ **lesion** [LEE-zhuhn] tissue destruction. A brain lesion is a naturally or experimentally caused destruction of brain tissue.

■ **electroencephalogram (EEG)** an amplified recording of the waves of electrical activity that sweep across the brain's surface. These waves are measured by electrodes placed on the scalp.

The Tools of Discovery

OBJECTIVE **11** | Describe several techniques for studying the brain.

For centuries, we had no tools high-powered yet gentle enough to explore the living human brain. Now, within a lifetime, all that has changed. The known universe's most amazing organ is being probed and mapped by a new generation of neural cartographers. Whether in the interests of science or medicine, we can selectively **lesion** (destroy) tiny clusters of normal or defective brain cells, leaving their surroundings unharmed. We can probe the brain with tiny electrical pulses. We can snoop on the messages of individual neurons and eavesdrop on the chatter of billions of neurons. We can see color representations of the brain's energy-consuming activity. These techniques for peering into the thinking, feeling brain are doing for psychology what the microscope did for biology and the telescope did for astronomy.

Clinical Observation

Banking brains
Francine Benes, director of McLean Hospital's Brain Bank, sees the collection as a valuable database.

The oldest method of studying brain-mind connections is to observe the effects of specific brain diseases and injuries. Such observations were first recorded some 5000 years ago. But it was not until the last two centuries that physicians began systematically recording the results of damage to specific brain areas. Some noted that damage to one side of the brain often caused numbness or paralysis on the body's opposite side, suggesting that the right side of the body is wired to the brain's left side, and vice versa. Others noticed that damage to the back of the brain disrupted vision, and that damage to the left-front part of the brain produced speech difficulties. Gradually, these early explorers were mapping the brain. Today, records of more than 1500 brain-injured patients have been assembled by University of Iowa researchers into the largest-ever brain-damage registry. The Harvard Brain Bank at Boston's McLean Hospital stores 3000 brains from both "normal" people and those who suffered various psychiatric or neurological disorders. Their stories provide clues to our own brains' inner workings.

Manipulating the Brain

Today's scientists do not need to await brain injuries. They can electrically, chemically, or magnetically *stimulate* various parts of the brain and note the effects. They can also surgically lesion tissue in specific brain areas in animals. For example, a lesion in one area of the hypothalamus in a rat's brain reduces eating, causing the rat to starve unless force-fed. A lesion in another area produces *over*eating.

FIGURE 2.12

An electroencephalograph providing amplified tracings of waves of electrical activity in the brain
Here it is displaying the brain activity of this 4-year-old who has epilepsy.

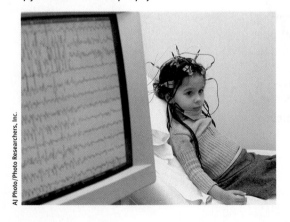

Recording the Brain's Electrical Activity

Right now, your mental activity is giving off telltale electrical, metabolic, and magnetic signals that would enable neuroscientists to observe your brain at work. The tips of modern microelectrodes are so small they can detect the electrical pulse in a single neuron, providing some astonishingly precise findings. For example, we can now detect exactly where the information goes in a cat's brain when someone strokes its whisker.

Electrical activity in the brain's billions of neurons sweeps in regular waves across its surface. The **electroencephalogram (EEG)** is an amplified readout of such waves. Studying an EEG of the brain's activity is like studying a car engine by listening to its hum. However, by presenting a stimulus repeatedly and having a computer filter out brain activity unrelated to the stimulus, one can identify the electrical wave evoked by the stimulus (**FIGURE 2.12**).

Neuroimaging Techniques

Newer windows into the brain give us a Supermanlike ability to see inside the living brain. One such tool, the **PET (positron emission tomography) scan** (**FIGURE 2.13**), depicts brain activity by showing each brain area's consumption of its chemical fuel, the sugar glucose (see Figure 2.33, page 82). Active neurons are glucose hogs. A person is given a temporarily radioactive form of glucose, and the PET scan locates and measures the radioactivity, thereby detecting where this "food for thought" goes. PET scans show that the brain areas that light up when people silently say the name of an animal differ from those that light up when they say the name of a tool (Martin & others, 1996). Rather like weather radar showing rain activity, PET scan "hot spots" show which brain areas are most active as the person performs mathematical calculations, listens to music, or daydreams.

Another new way of having one's head examined exploits the fact that the centers of atoms, including those in our brains, spin like tops. In **MRI (magnetic resonance imaging)** scans, the head is put in a strong magnetic field, which aligns the spinning atoms. Then a brief pulse of radio waves disorients the atoms momentarily. When the atoms return to their normal spin, they release signals that provide images of their concentrations, resulting in a detailed picture of the brain's (and the body's) soft tissues. MRI scans reveal a larger-than-average neural area in the left brain of musicians who display perfect pitch (Schlaug & others, 1995). MRI scans can also reveal enlarged fluid-filled brain areas in some patients who have schizophrenia, a disabling psychological disorder (**FIGURE 2.14**).

A special application of MRI, **fMRI (functional MRI),** can reveal the brain's functioning as well as its structure. Where the brain is especially active, blood goes. By comparing MRI scans taken less than a second apart, researchers can watch the brain light up (with increased oxygen-laden bloodflow) as a person performs different mental functions. As the person looks at a face, for example, the fMRI machine detects blood rushing to the back of the brain, which processes visual information (see Figure 2.28, page 79). Such snapshots of the brain's changing activity provide new insights into how the brain divides its labor.

■ **PET (positron emission tomography) scan** a visual display of brain activity that detects where a radioactive form of glucose goes while the brain performs a given task.

■ **MRI (magnetic resonance imaging)** a technique that uses magnetic fields and radio waves to produce computer-generated images that distinguish among different types of soft tissue; allows us to see structures within the brain.

■ **fMRI (functional magnetic resonance imaging)** a technique for revealing blood flow and, therefore, brain activity by comparing successive MRI scans. MRI scans show brain anatomy; fMRI scans show brain function.

Courtesy of Brookhaven National Laboratories

FIGURE 2.13
The PET scan

To obtain a PET scan, researchers inject volunteers with a low and harmless dose of a short-lived radioactive sugar. Detectors around the subject's head pick up the release of gamma rays from the sugar, which has concentrated in active brain areas. A computer then processes and translates these signals into a map of the brain at work. (See page 82 for an example of PET scans.)

Both photos from Daniel Weinberger, M.D., CBDB,NIMH

FIGURE 2.14
MRI scan of a healthy individual (left) and a person with schizophrenia (right)

Note the enlarged fluid-filled brain region in the image on the right.

FIGURE 2.15
Brain reading
An fMRI scan identified two brain areas that became especially active when a participant lied about holding a five of clubs.

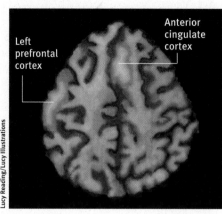

Left prefrontal cortex

Anterior cingulate cortex

In one intriguing study, neuroscientist Daniel Langleben and his colleagues (2002) discovered that fMRI scans located increased brain activity associated with lying. When participants lied about a playing card they held in their hand, the telltale fMRI revealed increased activity in two brain regions (**FIGURE 2.15**). One was the anterior cingulate cortex, an area typically active when we experience conflicting urges. Some researchers speculate that more portable methods of measuring brain activity might someday detect lies in real-life situations.

To be learning about the neurosciences now is like studying world geography while Magellan was exploring the seas. The number of explorers grows: The growing membership of the interdisciplinary Society for Neuroscience, founded in 1969, surpassed 36,000 in 2004. Every year the explorers announce new discoveries, which also generate new interpretations of old discoveries.

Researchers are assembling this wealth of new information in computer databases. This brain cartography will give all researchers instant access through electronic networks to PET or MRI studies that reveal activity in a particular brain area while a person, for example, solves math problems. Clearly, this is the golden age of brain science.

Older Brain Structures

OBJECTIVE **12** | Describe the components of the brainstem, and summarize the functions of the brainstem, thalamus, and cerebellum.

If you could open the skull and look inside, the first thing you might note is the brain's size. In dinosaurs, the brain represents 1/100,000th of the body's weight, in whales 1/10,000th, in elephants 1/600th, in humans 1/45th. It looks as though a principle is emerging. But keep on. In mice the brain is 1/40th the body's weight, and in marmosets 1/25th. So there are exceptions to the rule that the ratio of brain to body weight provides a clue to a species' intelligence.

More useful indicators about an animal's capacities come from its brain structures. In primitive vertebrate (backboned) animals, such as sharks, the brain primarily regulates basic survival functions: breathing, resting, and feeding. In lower mammals, such as rodents, a more complex brain enables emotion and greater memory. In advanced mammals, such as humans, the brain processes more information, so we are able to act with foresight.

To enable this increasing complexity, species have elaborated new brain systems on top of the old, much as the Earth's landscape covers the old with the new. Digging down, one discovers the fossil remnants of the past—brainstem components still performing much as they did for our distant ancestors. Starting with the brainstem and working up to the newer systems, let's now explore the brain.

The Brainstem

The brain's basement—its oldest and innermost region—is the **brainstem.** It begins where the spinal cord enters the skull and swells slightly, forming the **medulla.** Here lie the controls for your heartbeat and breathing. If the top of a cat's brainstem is severed from the rest of the brain above it, the animal will still breathe and live—and even run, climb, and groom (Klemm, 1990). But cut off from the brain's higher region, it won't purposefully run or climb to get food. Just above the medulla sits the *pons,* which helps coordinate movements.

The brainstem is also the crossover point, where most nerves to and from each side of the brain connect with the body's opposite side. This peculiar cross-wiring is but one of many surprises the brain has to offer.

Inside the brainstem, between your ears, lies the **reticular** ("netlike") **formation,** a finger-shaped network of neurons that extends from the spinal cord right up to the thalamus (**FIGURE 2.16**). As the spinal cord's sensory input travels up to the thalamus, some of it travels through the reticular formation, which filters incoming stimuli and relays important information to other areas of the brain.

In 1949, Giuseppe Moruzzi and Horace Magoun discovered that electrically stimulating the reticular formation of a sleeping cat almost instantly produced an awake, alert animal. When Magoun *severed* a cat's reticular formation from higher brain regions, without damaging the nearby sensory pathways, the effect was equally dramatic: The cat lapsed into a coma from which it never awakened. Magoun could clap his hands by the cat's ear, even pinch it; still, no response. The conclusion? The reticular formation is involved in arousal. Later researchers discovered that elsewhere in the brainstem are neurons whose activity is needed for sleep. (As you will see in Chapter 7, our brains are not idle while we sleep.)

■ **brainstem** the oldest part and central core of the brain, beginning where the spinal cord swells as it enters the skull; the brainstem is responsible for automatic survival functions.

■ **medulla** [muh-DUL-uh] the base of the brainstem; controls heartbeat and breathing.

■ **reticular formation** a nerve network in the brainstem that plays an important role in controlling arousal.

FIGURE 2.16
The brainstem and thalamus
The brainstem, including the pons and medulla, is an extension of the spinal cord. The thalamus is attached to its top. The reticular formation passes through both structures.

■ **thalamus** [THAL-uh-muss] the brain's sensory switchboard, located on top of the brainstem; it directs messages to the sensory receiving areas in the cortex and transmits replies to the cerebellum and medulla.

■ **cerebellum** [sehr-uh-BELL-um] the "little brain" attached to the rear of the brainstem; its functions include processing sensory input and coordinating movement output and balance.

The Thalamus

Atop the brainstem sits the brain's sensory switchboard, a joined pair of egg-shaped structures called the **thalamus** (Figure 2.16). It receives information from all the senses except smell and routes it to the brain regions that deal with seeing, hearing, tasting, and touching. Think of the thalamus as being to sensory input what London is to England's trains: a hub through which traffic passes en route to various destinations. The thalamus also receives some of the higher brain's replies, which it then directs to the medulla and to the cerebellum.

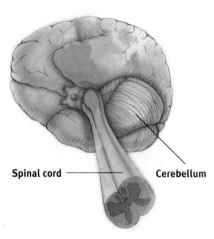

FIGURE 2.17
The brain's organ of agility
Hanging at the back of the brain, the cerebellum coordinates our movements, as when David Beckham directs the ball precisely.

Lluis Gene/AFP/Getty Images

The Cerebellum

Extending from the rear of the brainstem is the baseball-sized **cerebellum,** meaning "little brain," which is what its two wrinkled halves resemble (**FIGURE 2.17**). As you will see in Chapter 9, the cerebellum enables one type of nonverbal learning and memory. New studies reveal that it also helps us judge time, modulate our emotions, and discriminate sounds and textures (Bower & Parsons, 2003). In addition to processing sensory information, the cerebellum coordinates voluntary movement. When soccer great David Beckham fires the ball into the net with a perfectly timed kick, give his cerebellum some credit. If you injured your cerebellum, you would have difficulty walking, keeping your balance, or shaking hands. Your movements would be jerky and exaggerated.

Note: These older brain functions all occur without any conscious effort. This illustrates another of our recurring themes: *Our brain processes most information outside of our awareness.* We are aware of the *results* of our brain's labor (say, our current visual experience) but not of *how* we construct the visual image. Likewise, whether we are asleep or awake, our brainstem manages its life-sustaining functions, freeing our newer brain regions to dream, think, talk, or savor a memory.

The Limbic System

FIGURE 2.18
The limbic system
Limbic structures form a doughnut-shaped neural system between the brain's older parts and its cerebral hemispheres. Although part of the hormonal (endocrine) system, not the brain, the pituitary gland is controlled by the limbic system's hypothalamus, just above it.

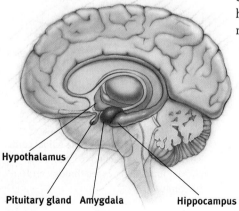

OBJECTIVE 13 | Describe the structures and functions of the limbic system, and explain how one of these structures controls the pituitary gland.

At the border ("limbus") of the brain's older parts and the cerebral hemispheres is the doughnut-shaped **limbic system** (**FIGURE 2.18**). We will see in Chapter 9 how one limbic system component, the *hippocampus,* processes memory. (If animals or humans lose their hippocampus to surgery or injury, they become unable to process new memories of facts and episodes.) For now, let's look at the limbic system's links to emotions such as fear and anger, and to basic motives such as those for food and sex.

The Amygdala In the limbic system, two lima bean-sized neural clusters, called the **amygdala,** influence aggression and fear (**FIGURE 2.19**). In 1939, psychologist Heinrich Klüver and neurosurgeon Paul Bucy surgically lesioned the part of a rhesus monkey's brain that included the amygdala. The result? The normally ill-tempered monkey turned into the most mellow of creatures. Poke it, pinch it, do virtually anything that normally would trigger a ferocious response, and still the animal remained placid. In later studies with other wild animals, including the lynx, wolverine, and wild rat, researchers noted the same effect. What then might happen

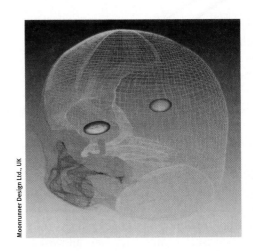

FIGURE 2.19
The amygdala

Moonrunner Design Ltd., UK

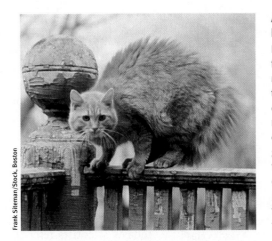

Frank Siteman/Stock, Boston

Aggression as a brain state
Back arched and fur fluffed, this fierce cat is ready to attack. Electrical stimulation of a cat's amygdala provokes reactions such as the one shown here, suggesting its role in emotions like rage. Which division of the autonomic nervous system is activated by such stimulation? (See page 74.)

if we electrically stimulated the amygdala in a normally placid domestic animal, such as a cat? Do so in one spot and the cat prepares to attack, hissing with its back arched, its pupils dilated, its hair on end. Move the electrode only slightly within the amygdala, cage the cat with a small mouse, and now it cowers in terror.

These experiments confirm the amygdala's role in rage and fear, not to mention the perception of such emotions and the processing of emotional memories (Anderson & Phelps, 2000; Poremba & Gabriel, 2001). Still, we must be careful. The brain is *not* neatly organized into structures that correspond to our categories of behavior. Actually, both aggressive and fearful behavior involve neural activity in all levels of the brain, not solely in the amygdala. Even within the limbic system, stimulating neural structures other than the amygdala can evoke such behavior. If you put a charge to your car's dead battery, you can activate the engine. Yet the battery is merely one link in an integrated system.

Given that amygdala lesions can transform violent monkeys into mellow ones, might such lesions do the same in violent humans? You might think so. But such "psychosurgery" has produced varied results (Mark & Ervin, 1970; Valenstein, 1986). In a few cases involving patients who suffered brain abnormalities, it reduced fits of rage, though sometimes with devastating side effects on the patient's everyday functioning. For ethical reasons, and because of the uncertainties involved, drastic psychosurgery is rarely used. Perhaps, though, as we learn more about how the brain controls behavior, we will learn to alleviate brain disorders without creating new ones.

The Hypothalamus Another of the limbic system's fascinating structures lies just below (*hypo*) the thalamus, and so is called the **hypothalamus** (**FIGURE 2.20**). By either lesioning or stimulating different areas, neuroscientists have identified hypothalamic neural networks that perform specific bodily maintenance duties. Some neural clusters influence hunger; others regulate thirst, body temperature, and sexual behavior.

The hypothalamus both monitors blood chemistry and takes orders from other parts of the brain. For example, thinking about sex (in your brain's cerebral cortex) can stimulate your hypothalamus to secrete hormones. Through these hormones, the hypothalamus controls the adjacent "master gland," the pituitary (see Figure 2.18), which in turn influences hormone release by other glands. (Note the interplay between the nervous and hormone systems: The brain influences the hormone system, which in turn influences the brain.)

The story of a remarkable discovery about the hypothalamus illustrates how progress in scientific research often occurs--when curious,

■ **limbic system** a doughnut-shaped system of neural structures at the border of the brainstem and cerebral hemispheres; associated with emotions such as fear and aggression and drives such as those for food and sex. Includes the hippocampus, amygdala, and hypothalamus.

■ **amygdala** [uh-MIG-duh-la] two lima bean-sized neural clusters that are components of the limbic system and are linked to emotion.

■ **hypothalamus** [hi-po-THAL-uh-muss] a neural structure lying below (*hypo*) the thalamus; it directs several maintenance activities (eating, drinking, body temperature), helps govern the endocrine system via the pituitary gland, and is linked to emotion.

FIGURE 2.20
The hypothalamus
This small but important structure, colored yellow/orange in this MRI scan photograph, helps keep the body's internal environment in a steady state by regulating thirst, hunger, and body temperature. Its activity also influences experiences of pleasurable reward.

ISM/Phototake

FIGURE 2.21
Rat with an implanted electrode
With an electrode implanted in a reward center of its hypothalamus, the rat readily crosses an electrified grid, accepting the painful shocks, to press a lever that sends electrical impulses to its "pleasure centers."

> "If you were designing a robot vehicle to walk into the future and survive, . . . you'd wire it up so that behavior that ensured the survival of the self or the species—like sex and eating—would be naturally reinforcing."
>
> Candace Pert (1986)

The cat on page 73 is aroused via its sympathetic nervous system.

FIGURE 2.22
Ratbot on a pleasure cruise
When stimulated by remote control, this rat could be guided to navigate across a field and even up a tree.

Sanjiv Talwar, SUNY Downstate

open-minded investigators make an unexpected observation. Two young McGill University neuropsychologists, James Olds and Peter Milner (1954), were trying to implant electrodes in the reticular formations of white rats when they made a magnificent mistake. In one rat, they incorrectly placed an electrode in what was later discovered to be a region of the hypothalamus (Olds, 1975). Curiously, the rat kept returning to the place on its tabletop enclosure where it had been stimulated by this misplaced electrode, as if seeking more stimulation. Upon discovering their mistake, Olds and Milner alertly recognized that they had stumbled upon a brain center that provides a pleasurable reward.

In a meticulous series of experiments, Olds (1958) went on to locate other "pleasure centers," as he called them. (What the rats actually experience only they know, and they aren't telling. Rather than attribute human feelings to rats, today's scientists refer to *reward centers,* not "pleasure centers.") When allowed to trigger their own stimulation in these areas by pressing a pedal, rats would sometimes do so at a feverish pace—up to 7000 times per hour—until they dropped from exhaustion. Moreover, they would do anything to get this stimulation, even cross an electrified floor that a starving rat would not cross even to reach food (**FIGURE 2.21**).

Similar reward centers in or near the hypothalamus were later discovered in many other species, including goldfish, dolphins, and monkeys. In fact, animal research has revealed both a general reward system that triggers the release of the neurotransmitter dopamine and specific centers associated with the pleasures of eating, drinking, and sex. Animals, it seems, come equipped with built-in systems that reward activities essential to survival.

More recent experiments have found new ways of using limbic stimulation to control animals' actions. By using brain stimulation to reward rats for turning left or right, Sanjiv Talwar and his colleagues (2002) trained rats that had never been outdoors to navigate natural environments (**FIGURE 2.22**). By pressing buttons on a laptop, the researchers can direct a rat—which carries a receiver, power source, and video camera on a backpack—to turn on cue, climb trees, scurry along branches, and turn around and come back down. Their work suggests future applications in search-and-rescue operations.

Dramatic findings like these have led people to wonder whether humans, too, might have limbic centers for pleasure. Indeed we do. One neurosurgeon used electrodes to calm violent patients. Stimulated patients reported mild pleasure; however, unlike Olds' rats, they were not driven to a frenzy (Deutsch, 1972; Hooper & Teresi, 1986). Some researchers believe that addictive disorders, such as alcoholism, drug abuse, and binge eating, may stem from a *reward deficiency syndrome*—a genetically disposed deficiency in the natural brain systems for pleasure and well-being that leads people to crave whatever provides that missing pleasure or relieves negative feelings (Blum & others, 1996).

The Cerebral Cortex

OBJECTIVE **14** | Define *cerebral cortex,* and explain its importance for the human brain.

Older brain networks sustain basic life functions and enable memory, emotions, and basic drives. Newer neural networks within the cerebral hemispheres form specialized work teams that enable our perceiving, thinking, and speaking. Your **cerebral cortex** is an intricate covering of interconnected neural cells that, like bark on a tree, forms a thin surface layer on your cerebral hemispheres. It is

Corpus callosum: axon fibers connecting two cerebral hemispheres

Cerebral cortex: ultimate control and information-processing center

Right hemisphere

Left hemisphere

Thalamus: relays messages between lower brain centers and cerebral cortex

Hypothalamus: controls maintenance functions such as eating; helps govern endocrine system; linked to emotion and reward

Amygdala: neural centers in the limbic system linked to emotion

Pituitary: master endocrine gland

Reticular formation: helps control arousal

Medulla: controls heartbeat and breathing

Hippocampus: a structure in the limbic system linked to memory

Spinal cord: pathway for neural fibers traveling to and from brain; controls simple reflexes

Cerebellum: coordinates voluntary movement and balance

FIGURE 2.23 Brain structures and their functions

■ Cerebral cortex   ■ Limbic system   ■ Brainstem

your body's ultimate control and information-processing center. (**FIGURE 2.23** locates the cerebral cortex as well as other brain areas discussed in this chapter.)

With the expansion of the cerebral cortex, tight genetic controls relax and the organism's adaptability increases. Frogs and other amphibians have a small cortex and operate extensively on preprogrammed genetic instructions. The larger cortex of mammals offers increased capacities for learning and thinking, enabling them to be more adaptable. What makes us distinctively human mostly arises from the complex functions of our brain's thinking crown, its cerebral cortex.

Structure of the Cortex

OBJECTIVE 15 | Identify the four lobes of the cerebral cortex.

If you opened a human skull, exposing the brain, you would see a wrinkled organ, shaped somewhat like the meat of an oversized walnut. Eighty percent of the brain's weight lies in the ballooning left and right cerebral hemispheres, which are mostly filled with axon connections between the brain's surface and its other regions. The cerebral cortex—the brain hemispheres' thin surface layer—contains some 20 to 23 billion nerve cells (an estimate projected by sampling square-millimeter columns of cortical tissue [de Courten-Myers, 2002]).

Supporting these billions of nerve cells are nine times as many spidery **glial cells**— "glue cells" that guide neural connections, provide nutrients and insulating myelin, and mop up ions and neurotransmitters. Neurons are like queen bees; on their own they cannot feed or sheathe themselves. Glial cells are neural nannies. New evidence suggests they may also play a role in learning and thinking. By "chatting" with neurons they may participate in information transmission and memory (Travis, 1994). Moving up the ladder of animal life, the proportion of glia to neurons increases. A recent post-mortem analysis of Einstein's brain did not find more or larger-than-usual neurons,

The people who first dissected and labeled the brain used the language of scholars—Latin and Greek. Their words are actually attempts at graphic description: For example, *cortex* means "bark," *cerebellum* is "little brain," and *thalamus* is "inner chamber."

■ **cerebral** [seh-REE-bruhl] **cortex** the intricate fabric of interconnected neural cells that covers the cerebral hemispheres; the body's ultimate control and information-processing center.

■ **glial cells (glia)** cells in the nervous system that support, nourish, and protect neurons.

FIGURE 2.24
The cerebral cortex
If flattened, a human cortex would cover about four pages of this book. A chimpanzee's would cover one page, a monkey's a postcard, and a rat's a postage stamp (Calvin, 1996).

but it did reveal a much greater concentration of glia than found in an average Albert's head (Fields, 2004).

Looking at a human brain, the first thing you would notice about the cerebral cortex is its wrinkled surface, only about one-third of which would be visible. These folds greatly increase the brain's surface area. If flattened, the brain's surface would be roughly the size of a large pizza. (To fit a thin pizza crust inside a skull, we would need to crumple it up.) In rats and other lower mammals, the cortex surface is smoother, with less neural fabric (**FIGURE 2.24**).

Each brain hemisphere is divided into four *lobes,* geographic subdivisions separated by prominent *fissures,* or folds (**FIGURE 2.25**). Starting at the front of your brain and going around over the top, there are the **frontal lobes** (behind your forehead), the **parietal lobes** (at the top and to the rear), the **occipital lobes** (at the back of your head), and the **temporal lobes** (on the sides of your head, just above your ears). Each lobe carries out many functions, and many functions require the interplay of several lobes.

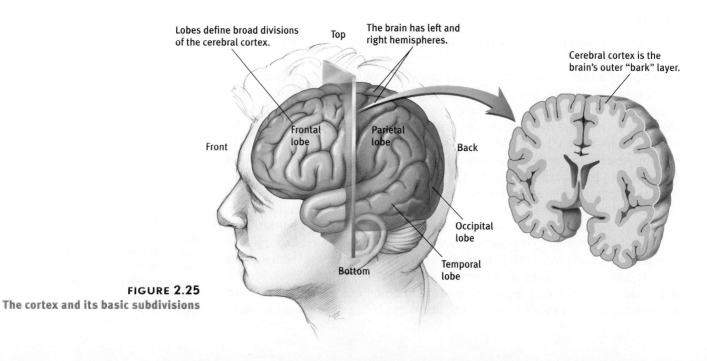

FIGURE 2.25
The cortex and its basic subdivisions

Functions of the Cortex

OBJECTIVE **16** | Summarize some of the findings on the functions of the motor cortex and the sensory cortex, and discuss the importance of the association areas.

More than a century ago, autopsies of people partially paralyzed or speechless revealed damaged cortical areas. But this rather crude evidence did not convince researchers that specific parts of the cortex perform specific functions. After all, if control of speech and movement were diffused across the cortex, damage to almost any area might produce the same effect. A television would go dead with its power cord cut, but we would be deluding ourselves if we thought we had "localized" the picture in the cord.

This analogy reminds us how easy it is to err when trying to localize brain functions. Complex activities such as speaking, drawing, and shooting pool involve many brain areas. For example, our experience of vocal music integrates brain activity in areas involved in speech and music processing. Mereille Besson and colleagues (1998) discovered this when recording electrical activity in the brains of French musicians listening to unaccompanied operatic solos. The musicians' brains processed the lyrics and tunes in separate brain areas en route to their experiencing "the exquisite unity of vocal music." Moreover, the spine-tingling thrills that music lovers enjoy appear to activate the same brain reward systems that are stimulated by sex and pleasing foods (Weinberger, 2004). As with other complex activities and experiences, music engages multiple brain areas.

Motor Functions Scientists have, however, localized simpler brain functions. For example, in 1870, when German physicians Gustav Fritsch and Eduard Hitzig applied mild electrical stimulation to the cortexes of dogs, they made an important discovery: They could make different body parts move. The effects were selective: Stimulation caused movement only when applied to an arch-shaped region at the back of the frontal lobe, running roughly from ear to ear across the top of the brain. This arch we now call the **motor cortex** (**FIGURE 2.26**). Moreover, when the researchers stimulated specific parts of this region in the left or right hemisphere, specific body parts moved on the *opposite* side of the body.

■ **frontal lobes** the portion of the cerebral cortex lying just behind the forehead; involved in speaking and muscle movements and in making plans and judgments.

■ **parietal** [puh-RYE-uh-tuhl] **lobes** the portion of the cerebral cortex lying at the top of the head and toward the rear; receives sensory input for touch and body position.

■ **occipital** [ahk-SIP-uh-tuhl] **lobes** the portion of the cerebral cortex lying at the back of the head; includes the visual areas, which receive visual information from the opposite visual field.

■ **temporal lobes** the portion of the cerebral cortex lying roughly above the ears; includes the auditory areas, each of which receives auditory information primarily from the opposite ear.

■ **motor cortex** an area at the rear of the frontal lobes that controls voluntary movements.

FIGURE 2.26

Left hemisphere tissue devoted to each body part in the motor cortex and the sensory cortex

As you can see from this classic though inexact representation, the amount of cortex devoted to a body part is not proportional to that part's size. Rather, the brain devotes more tissue to sensitive areas and to areas requiring precise control. Thus, the fingers have a greater representation in the cortex than does the upper arm.

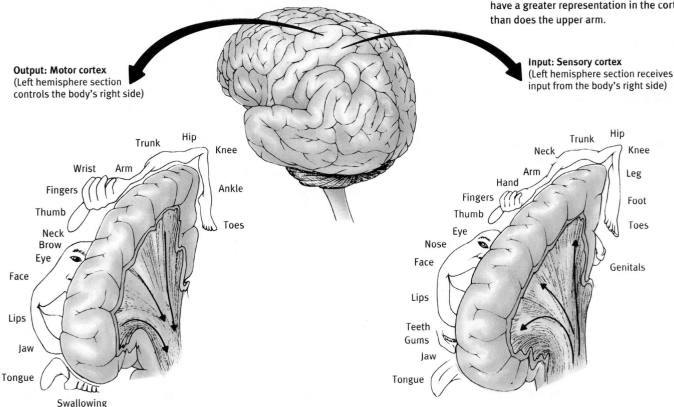

Output: Motor cortex
(Left hemisphere section controls the body's right side)

Input: Sensory cortex
(Left hemisphere section receives input from the body's right side)

Demonstration: Try moving your right hand in a circular motion, as if polishing a table. Now start your right foot doing the same motion synchronized with the hand. Now reverse the foot motion (but not the hand). Tough, huh? But easier if you try moving the *left* foot opposite to the right hand. The left and right limbs are controlled by opposite sides of the brain. So their opposed activities interfere less with one another.

FIGURE 2.27
Mind over matter
Can just thinking make something happen? A California Institute of Technology research team led by Sam Musallam implanted electrodes in a parietal lobe region and recorded neural activity as a monkey planned to reach. When programmed into a computer's memory, this activity then enabled the monkey to move a cursor merely by thinking about it.

■ **sensory cortex** the area at the front of the parietal lobes that registers and processes body touch and movement sensations.

■ **association areas** areas of the cerebral cortex that are not involved in primary motor or sensory functions; rather, they are involved in higher mental functions such as learning, remembering, thinking, and speaking.

Mapping the Motor Cortex A half-century ago, neurosurgeons Otfrid Foerster in Germany and Wilder Penfield in Montreal mapped the motor cortex in hundreds of wide-awake patients. Before putting the knife to the brain, the surgeons needed to know the possible side effects of removing different parts of the cortex. They painlessly (the brain has no sensory receptors) stimulated different cortical areas and noted the body responses. Like Fritsch and Hitzig, they found that when they stimulated different areas of the motor cortex at the back of the frontal lobe, different body parts moved. (Kids, don't try this without parental supervision.) They were now able to map the motor cortex according to the body parts it controlled (Figure 2.26). Interestingly, those areas of the body requiring precise control, such as the fingers and mouth, occupied the greatest amount of cortical space.

Neuroscientist José Delgado repeatedly demonstrated the mechanics of motor behavior. In one human patient, he stimulated a spot on the left motor cortex that triggered the right hand to make a fist. Asked to keep the fingers open during the next stimulation, the patient, whose fingers closed despite his best efforts, remarked, "I guess, Doctor, that your electricity is stronger than my will" (Delgado, 1969, p. 114). Scientists have also been able to predict a monkey's arm motion a tenth of a second before it moves—by repeatedly measuring motor cortex activity preceding specific arm movements (Gibbs, 1996).

Neural Prosthetics By similarly eavesdropping on the brain, could we enable someone—perhaps a paralyzed person—to move a robotic limb or command a cursor to write e-mail or surf the Web? To find out, Brown University brain researchers implanted 100 tiny recording electrodes in the motor cortexes of three monkeys (Nicolelis & Chapin, 2002; Serruya & others, 2002). As the monkeys used a joystick to move a cursor to follow a moving red target (to gain rewards), the researchers matched the brain signals with the arm movements. Then they let their computer operate the joystick. When a monkey merely thought about a move, the mind-reading computer moved the cursor with nearly the same proficiency as the monkey.

Newer research has recorded messages not from the motor neurons that directly control a monkey's arm, but from a brain area involved in planning and intention (Musallam & others, 2004). While the monkeys awaited a cue that told them to reach toward a spot (to get a juice reward) that had flashed on a screen in one of up to eight locations, a computer program recorded their neural activity. By matching the brain activity to a monkey's subsequent pointing, the mind-reading researchers could now program a cursor to move in response to the monkey's thinking (**FIGURE 2.27**). Monkey think, computer do.

In 2004, the U.S. Food and Drug Administration approved the first clinical trial of neural prosthetics with paralyzed humans (Pollack, 2004). The first patient, a paralyzed 25-year-old man, is now able to mentally control a television, draw shapes on a computer screen, and play video games—all thanks to an aspirin-sized chip with 100 microelectrodes recording activity in his motor cortex (Patoine, 2005).

Sensory Functions If the motor cortex sends messages out to the body, where does the cortex receive the *incoming* messages? Penfield identified a cortical area that specializes in receiving information from the skin senses and from the movement of body parts. This area, parallel to the motor cortex and just behind it at the front of the parietal lobes, we now call the **sensory cortex** (Figure 2.26). Stimulate a point on the top of this band of tissue, and a person may report being touched on the shoulder; stimulate some point on the side, and the person may feel something on the face.

The more sensitive a body region, the larger the area of the sensory cortex devoted to it; your supersensitive lips project to a larger brain area than do your toes (Figure 2.26). (That's one reason we kiss with our lips rather than touch toes.) Similarly, rats have a large area of the brain devoted to their whisker sensations, owls to their hearing sensations, and so forth.

Scientists have identified other areas where the cortex receives input from senses other than touch. At this moment, you are receiving visual information in the occipital lobes at the very back of your brain (**FIGURE 2.28**). A bad enough bash there would make you blind. Stimulated there, you might see flashes of light or dashes of color. (In a sense, we *do* have eyes in the back of our head!) From your occipital lobes, visual information goes to other areas that specialize in tasks such as identifying words, detecting emotions, and recognizing faces.

Any sound you now hear is processed by the auditory areas in your temporal lobe (**FIGURE 2.29**). (If you think of your clenched fist as a brain, and hold it in front of you, your thumb would roughly correspond to the temporal lobe.) Most of this auditory information travels a circuitous route from one ear to the auditory receiving area above your opposite ear. If you were stimulated there, you might hear a sound. The sound needn't be real. MRI scans of people with schizophrenia reveal that auditory areas of the temporal lobe are active during auditory hallucinations (Lennox & others, 1999). Even the phantom ringing sound experienced by people with hearing loss is—if heard in one ear—associated with activity in the temporal lobe on the brain's opposite side (Muhlnickel, 1998).

Courtesy of V. P. Clark, K. Keill, J. Ma. Maisog, S. Courtney, L. G. Ungerleider, and J. V. Haxby, National Institute of Mental Health

FIGURE 2.28
New technology shows the brain in action
This functional MRI scan shows the visual cortex—the occipital lobes—activated (color representation of increased bloodflow) as the subject looks at faces. When the person stops looking at faces, the region instantly calms down.

FIGURE 2.29
The visual cortex and auditory cortex
The occipital lobes at the rear of the brain receive input from the eyes. An auditory area of the temporal lobes receives information from the ears.

Visual cortex

Auditory cortex

Association Areas So far, we have pointed out small areas of the cortex that either receive sensory input or direct muscular output. In humans, that leaves a full three-fourths of the thin wrinkled layer, the cerebral cortex, uncommitted to sensory or muscular activity. What then goes on in this vast region of the brain? Neurons in these **association areas** (the peach-colored areas in **FIGURE 2.30**) integrate information. They associate various sensory inputs with stored memories—a very important part of thinking.

Electrically probing the association areas doesn't trigger any observable response. So, unlike the sensory and motor areas, we can't so neatly specify the functions of the

Rat

Cat

Chimpanzee

Human

■ Motor areas
■ Sensory areas
■ Association areas

FIGURE 2.30
Areas of the cortex in four mammals
More intelligent animals have increased "uncommitted" or association areas of the cortex. These vast areas of the brain are responsible for integrating and acting on information received and processed by sensory areas.

FIGURE 2.31
Phineas Gage reconsidered
Using measurements of his skull (which was kept as a medical record) and modern neuroimaging techniques, researcher Hanna Damasio and her colleagues (1994) have reconstructed the probable path of the rod through Gage's brain.

association areas. Their silence seems to have led to one of pop psychology's most widespread falsehoods: that we ordinarily use only 10 percent of our brains (as if the odds are 90 percent that a bullet to your brain would land in an area you don't use). This fabrication—"one of the hardiest weeds in the garden of psychology," writes Donald McBurney (1996, p. 44)—implies that if we could activate our whole brain, we would be far smarter than those who drudge along on 10 percent brain power. But surgically lesioned animals and brain-damaged humans bear witness that the association areas are not dormant. (The brain has no appendix—no apparently purposeless tissue. Moreover, given that brain tissue demands a lot of energy, nature would not squander resources on unused brain.) Rather, these areas interpret, integrate, and act on information processed by the sensory areas.

Association areas are found in all four lobes. In the frontal lobes, these areas enable us to judge, plan, and process new memories. People with damaged frontal lobes may have intact memories, score high on intelligence tests, and be able to bake a cake—yet be unable to plan ahead to *begin* baking the cake for the birthday party.

Frontal lobe damage also can alter personality, removing a person's inhibitions. Consider the classic case of railroad worker Phineas Gage. One afternoon in 1848, Gage, then 25 years old, was packing gunpowder into a rock with a tamping iron. A spark ignited the gunpowder, shooting the rod up through his left cheek and out the top of his skull, leaving his frontal lobes massively damaged (**FIGURE 2.31**). To everyone's amazement, Gage was immediately able to sit up and speak, and after the wound healed he returned to work.

Although his mental abilities and memories were intact, his personality was not. The affable, soft-spoken Phineas Gage was now irritable, profane, and dishonest. He eventually lost his job and ended up earning his living as a fairground exhibit. This person, said his friends, was "no longer Gage." With his frontal lobes ruptured, Gage's moral compass became disconnected from his behavior.

The same loss of moral compass was recently discovered to be true of two people who as young children had experienced frontal lobe damage similar to Gage's. Both of these individuals recovered, but they also matured as morally deficient—stealing, lying, and abusing and neglecting their out-of-wedlock children without remorse (Dolan, 1999). Although raised in good homes, they seemingly didn't know right from wrong.

Other association areas also perform mental functions. For example, the parietal lobes, parts of which were large and unusually shaped in Einstein's normal-weight brain, enable mathematical and spatial reasoning (Witelson & others, 1999). An area on the underside of the right temporal lobe enables us to recognize faces. If a stroke or head injury destroyed this area of your brain, you would still be able to describe facial features and to recognize someone's gender and approximate age, yet be strangely unable to identify the person as, say, Britney Spears or even your grandmother. But by and large, complex mental functions such as learning and memory don't reside in any one place. There is no one spot in a rat's small association cortex that, when damaged, will obliterate its ability to learn or remember a maze. Complex human abilities, such as memory and language, result from the intricate coordination of many brain areas.

Language

OBJECTIVE **17** | Describe the five brain areas that would be involved if you read this sentence aloud.

Consider this curious finding: Damage to any one of several cortical areas can cause **aphasia,** an impaired use of language. It is even more curious that some people with aphasia can speak fluently but cannot read (despite good vision), while others can comprehend what they read but cannot speak. Still others can write but not read, read but not write, read numbers but not letters, or sing but not speak. This is puzzling, because we think of speaking and reading, or writing and reading, or singing and speaking as merely different examples of the same general ability. So, how did researchers solve the mystery of how we use language? Consider these clues, which fit together as neatly as Lego blocks in a toy house.

Clue 1 In 1865, French physician Paul Broca reported that after damage to a specific area of the left frontal lobe (later called **Broca's area**) a person would struggle to speak words while still being able to sing familiar songs and comprehend speech.

Clue 2 In 1874, German investigator Carl Wernicke discovered that after damage to a specific area of the left temporal lobe (**Wernicke's area**) people could speak only meaningless words. Asked to describe a picture that showed two boys stealing cookies behind a woman's back, one patient responded: "Mother is away her working her work to get her better, but when she's looking the two boys looking the other part. She's working another time" (Geschwind, 1979).

Clue 3 It was later discovered that reading aloud involves a third brain area. The *angular gyrus* receives the visual information from the visual area and recodes it into the auditory form, which Wernicke's area uses to derive its meaning.

Clue 4 Nerve fibers interconnect these brain areas.

Norman Geschwind assembled these clues into an explanation of how we use language (**FIGURES 2.32 AND 2.33**, page 82). When you read aloud, the words (1) register in the visual area, (2) are relayed to a second brain area, the *angular gyrus*, which transforms the words into an auditory code that is (3) received and understood in the nearby Wernicke's area and (4) sent to Broca's area, which (5) controls the motor cortex as it creates the pronounced word. Depending on which link in this chain is damaged, a different form of aphasia occurs. Damage to the angular gyrus leaves the person able to speak and understand but unable to read. Damage to Wernicke's area disrupts understanding. Damage to Broca's area disrupts speaking. The now-familiar principle bears repeating: *Complex abilities result from the intricate coordination of many brain areas.*

Said another way, the brain operates by dividing its mental functions—speaking, perceiving, thinking, remembering—into subfunctions. Our conscious experience

■ **aphasia** impairment of language, usually caused by left hemisphere damage either to Broca's area (impairing speaking) or to Wernicke's area (impairing understanding).

■ **Broca's area** controls language expression—an area of the frontal lobe, usually in the left hemisphere, that directs the muscle movements involved in speech.

■ **Wernicke's area** controls language reception—a brain area involved in language comprehension and expression; usually in the left temporal lobe.

5. Motor cortex (word is pronounced)

4. Broca's area (controls speech muscles via the motor cortex)

2. Angular gyrus (transforms visual representations into an auditory code)

1. Visual cortex (receives written words as visual stimulation)

3. Wernicke's area (interprets auditory code)

FIGURE 2.32
Specialization and integration in language

(a)
Hearing words
(auditory cortex and
Wernicke's area)

(b)
Seeing words
(visual cortex and
angular gyrus)

(c)
Speaking words
(Broca's area and
the motor cortex)

seems indivisible. Right now, assuming you have sight, you are experiencing a whole visual scene as if your eyes were video cameras projecting the scene into your brain. Actually, as you will see in Chapter 5, your brain breaks vision into specialized subtasks, such as discerning color, depth, movement, and form. (After a localized stroke that destroys one of these neural work teams, people may lose just one aspect of vision, such as the ability to perceive movement.) Each of these specialized neural networks, having simultaneously done its own thing, then feeds its information to "higher-level" networks that combine the atoms of experience and relay them to progressively higher-level association areas, enabling us to recognize a face as "Grandmother."

The same is true of reading a word: The brain computes the word's form, sound, and meaning using different neural networks (Posner & Carr, 1992). Thus fMRI scans show that jokes playing on meaning ("Why don't sharks bite lawyers? . . . Professional courtesy") are processed in a different brain area than jokes playing on words ("What kind of lights did Noah use on the ark? . . . Flood lights") (Goel & Dolan, 2001). Think about it: *What you experience as a continuous, indivisible stream of perception is actually but the visible tip of the information-processing iceberg, most of which lies beneath the surface of your conscious awareness.*

To sum up, the mind's subsystems are localized in particular brain regions, yet the brain acts as a unified whole. Moving your hand; recognizing faces; even perceiving color, motion, and depth—all depend on specific neural networks. Yet complex functions such as listening, learning, and loving involve the coordination of many brain areas. Together, these two principles—specialization and integration—describe the brain's functioning.

The Brain's Plasticity

OBJECTIVE 18 | Discuss the brain's plasticity following injury or illness.

The brain is sculpted not only by our genes but also by our experiences. In Chapter 3, we'll focus more on how experience molds the brain, but for now, let's turn to evidence from studies of the brain's **plasticity,** its ability to modify itself after some types of damage.

Most severed neurons will not regenerate (if your spinal cord were severed, you likely would be permanently paralyzed). And some brain functions seem preassigned to particular areas. A newborn who suffered damage to the facial recognition areas on both temporal lobes never regained a normal ability to recognize faces (Farah & others, 2000). But some neural tissue can *reorganize* in response to damage. It happens within all of us, as the brain repairs itself after little mishaps. Plasticity is especially evident after serious damage. Lose a finger and the sensory cortex that received

■ **plasticity** the brain's capacity for modification, as evident in brain reorganization following damage (especially in children) and in experiments on the effects of experience on brain development.

its input will begin to receive input from the adjacent fingers, which then become more sensitive (Fox, 1984). MRI scans show that well-practiced pianists likewise have a larger-than-usual auditory cortex area that encodes piano sounds (Bavelier & others, 2000; Pantev & others, 1998). Our brains are most plastic when we are young children (Kolb, 1989; see **FIGURE 2.34**).

The brain's plasticity is good news for those blind or deaf. If a blind person uses one finger to read Braille, the brain area dedicated to that finger expands as the sense of touch invades the visual cortex that normally helps people see (Barinaga, 1992a; Sadato & others, 1996). Temporarily "knock out" the visual cortex with magnetic stimulation, and a lifelong-blind person will make more errors on a *language* task (Amedi & others, 2004). In deaf people whose native language is sign, the temporal lobe area normally dedicated to auditory information waits in vain for stimulation. Finally, it looks for other signals to process, such as those from the visual system. That helps explain why some studies find that deaf people have enhanced peripheral vision (Bosworth & Dolkins, 1999).

If a body part is amputated, sensory fibers that terminate on adjacent areas of the sensory cortex may invade the brain tissue that's no longer receiving sensory input. As Figure 2.26 on page 77 shows, the hand is between the face and the arm regions on the sensory cortex. This explains a mysterious phenomenon: When stroking the face of someone whose hand had been amputated, V. S. Ramachandran found the person felt the sensations not only on his face but also on his nonexistent ("phantom") fingers. Ditto when stroking the arm, whose sensory fibers had also invaded the brain area vacated by the hand. Note, too, that the toes region is adjacent to the genitals. So what do you suppose was the sexual intercourse experience of another Ramachandran patient whose lower leg had been amputated? "I actually experience my orgasm in my foot. And there it's much bigger than it used to be because it's no longer just confined to my genitals" (Ramachandran & Blakeslee, 1998, p. 36).

Although brain modification often takes the form of reorganization, new evidence suggests that, contrary to long-held belief, adult mice and humans can also, in two older brain regions, generate new brain cells (Kempermann & Gage, 1999; Van Praag & others, 2002). Moreover, monkey brains form thousands of new neurons each day. These baby neurons originate deep in the brain and may then migrate to the thinking frontal lobe and form connections with neighboring neurons (Gould & others, 1999). Master stem cells that can develop into any type of brain cell have also been discovered in the human embryo. If mass-produced in a lab and injected into a damaged brain, might neural stem cells turn themselves into replacements for lost brain cells? Might we someday be able to rebuild damaged brains, much as we reseed damaged lawns? Might new drugs spur the production of new nerve cells? Stay tuned. Today's biotech companies are hard at work on such possibilities (Gage, 2003).

FIGURE 2.34
Brain plasticity
If an injury or a surgical procedure destroys one part of a child's brain or, as in the case of this 6-year-old, even an entire *hemisphere* (to eliminate seizures), the brain will compensate by putting other surplus areas to work. One Johns Hopkins medical team, reflecting on the 58 child hemispherectomies they had performed, reports being "awed" by how well children retain their memory, personality, and humor after removal of either brain hemisphere (Vining & others, 1997).

Our Divided Brain

OBJECTIVE 19 | Describe split-brain research, and explain how it helps us understand the functions of our left and right hemispheres.

For more than a century, clinical evidence has shown that the brain's two sides serve differing functions. Accidents, strokes, and tumors in the left hemisphere generally impair reading, writing, speaking, arithmetic reasoning, and understanding. Similar lesions in the right hemisphere seldom have such dramatic effects.

By 1960 the left hemisphere was therefore described as the "dominant" or "major" hemisphere, and its silent companion to the right as the "subordinate" or "minor"

"You wouldn't want to have a date with the right hemisphere."

Michael Gazzaniga (2000)

FIGURE 2.35
The corpus callosum
This large band of neural fibers connects the two brain hemispheres. To photograph the half brain shown at left, the hemispheres were separated by cutting through the corpus callosum and lower brain regions. In the view on the right, a surgeon has cut back brain tissue to expose the corpus callosum and bundles of fibers coming out from it.

■ **corpus callosum** [KOR-pus kah-LOW-sum] the large band of neural fibers connecting the two brain hemispheres and carrying messages between them.

■ **split brain** a condition in which the two hemispheres of the brain are isolated by cutting the connecting fibers (mainly those of the corpus callosum) between them.

FIGURE 2.36
The information highway from eye to brain
Information from the left half of your field of vision goes to your right hemisphere, and information from the right half of your visual field goes to your left hemisphere, which usually controls speech. (Note, however, that each eye receives sensory information from both the right and left visual fields.) The data received by either hemisphere are quickly transmitted to the other across the corpus callosum. In a person with a severed corpus callosum, this information sharing does not take place.

hemisphere. Then researchers found that the "minor" right hemisphere was not so limited after all. The story of this discovery is a fascinating chapter in psychology's history.

Splitting the Brain

In 1961, two Los Angeles neurosurgeons, Philip Vogel and Joseph Bogen, speculated that major epileptic seizures were caused by an amplification of abnormal brain activity that reverberated between the two cerebral hemispheres. They wondered whether they could reduce seizures in their patients with uncontrollable epilepsy by cutting communication between the hemispheres. To do this, Vogel and Bogen knew they would have to sever the **corpus callosum,** the wide band of axon fibers connecting the two hemispheres (**FIGURE 2.35**).

The surgeons had reason to believe such an operation would not be incapacitating. Psychologists Roger Sperry, Ronald Myers, and Michael Gazzaniga had divided the brains of cats and monkeys in this manner with no serious ill effects. So Vogel and Bogen operated. The result? The seizures were all but eliminated and the patients with these **split brains** were surprisingly normal, their personality and intellect hardly affected. Waking from the surgery, one patient even managed to quip that he had a "splitting headache" (Gazzaniga, 1967).

Only a decade earlier, neuropsychologist Karl Lashley had jested that maybe the corpus callosum served only "to keep the hemispheres from sagging." The ingenious experiments of Sperry and Gazzaniga revealed that this broad band of more than 200 million nerve fibers, capable of transferring more than a billion bits of information per second between the hemispheres, has a more significant purpose. Their studies of split-brain people—"the most fascinating people on Earth"—provided a key to understanding the two hemispheres' complementary functions.

As **FIGURE 2.36** explains, the peculiar nature of our visual wiring enabled the researchers to send information to the patient's left or right brain—by having the patient stare at a spot and then flashing a stimulus to its right or left. They could do this with you, too, but in your intact brain the hemisphere that received the information would instantly pass the news to its partner across the valley. The split-brain surgery severed the phone cables—the corpus callosum—across the valley, enabling the researchers to quiz each hemisphere separately.

In an early experiment, Gazzaniga (1967) asked split-brain patients to stare at a dot as he flashed HE•ART on a screen (**FIGURE 2.37**). Thus, HE appeared in their left visual field (which transmits to the right brain) and ART in

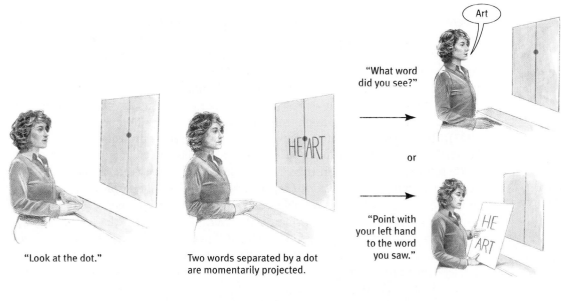

"What word did you see?"

or

"Point with your left hand to the word you saw."

"Look at the dot."

Two words separated by a dot are momentarily projected.

Art

FIGURE 2.37
Testing the divided brain
When an experimenter flashes the word HEART across the visual field, the split-brain person reports seeing the portion of the word transmitted to her left hemisphere. However, if asked to indicate with her left hand what she saw, she points to the portion of the word transmitted to her right hemisphere. (From Gazzaniga, 1983.)

the right field (which transmits to the left brain). When he then asked what they had seen, the patients *said* they had seen ART. But when asked to *point* to the word, they were startled when their left hand (controlled by the right brain) pointed to HE. Given an opportunity to express itself, each hemisphere reported only what it had seen. The right brain (controlling the left hand) intuitively knew what it could not verbally report.

When a picture of a spoon was flashed to their right hemisphere, the patients could not say what they had viewed. But when asked to identify what they had viewed by feeling an assortment of hidden objects with their left hand, they readily selected the spoon. If the experimenter said, "Right!" the patient might reply, "What? Right? How could I possibly pick out the right object when I don't know what I saw?" It is, of course, the left hemisphere doing the talking here, bewildered by what the nonverbal right hemisphere knows.

A few people who have had split-brain surgery have been for a time bothered by the unruly independence of their left hand, which might unbutton a shirt while the right hand buttoned it, or put grocery store items back on the shelf after the right hand put them in the cart. It was as if each hemisphere was thinking "I've half a mind to wear my green (blue) shirt today." Indeed, said Sperry (1964), split-brain surgery leaves people "with two separate minds." With a split brain, both hemispheres can comprehend and follow an instruction to copy—*simultaneously*—different figures with the left and right hand (Franz & others, 2000; see **FIGURE 2.38**). (Reading these reports, I fantasize a split-brain person enjoying a solitary game of "rock, paper, scissors"—left versus right hand.)

When the "two minds" are at odds, the left hemisphere does mental gymnastics to rationalize reactions it does not understand. If a patient follows an order sent to the right hemi-

"Do not let your left hand know what your right hand is doing."

Matthew 6:3

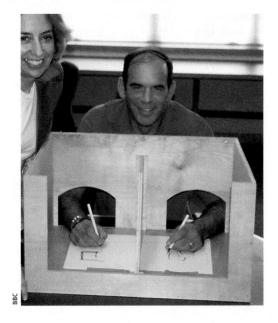

FIGURE 2.38
Try this!
Joe, a split-brain patient, can simultaneously draw two different shapes.

Question: If we flashed a red light to the right hemisphere of a split-brain patient and flashed a green light to the left hemisphere, would each observe its own color? Would the person be aware that the colors differ? What would the person verbally report seeing? (Answers on page 86.)

BBC

Which one is happier?
Look at the center of one face, then the other. Does one appear happier? Most people say the right face does. Some researchers think this is because the right hemisphere, which is skilled in emotion processing, receives information from the left half of each face (when looking at its center).

sphere ("Walk"), the interpretive left hemisphere will offer a ready explanation ("I'm going into the house to get a Coke"). Thus, Michael Gazzaniga (1988) concludes that the conscious left hemisphere is an "interpreter" that instantly constructs theories to explain our behavior. Unlike the unconscious mind that runs our lives rather like the autopilot that operates a jumbo jet, the conscious mind acts like the pilot who occasionally takes control of the jet. It also acts as the mind's press secretary (and sometimes its storyteller), by explaining decisions made behind closed doors (Wegner, 2002; Wilson, 2002). These reports illustrate a core concept we will re-visit throughout this book: *The unconscious brain can control our behavior without our conscious effort or will.*

These experiments demonstrate that the left hemisphere is more active when a person deliberates over decisions (Rogers, 2003). The right hemisphere understands simple requests, easily perceives objects, and is more engaged when quick, intuitive responses are needed. The right side of the brain also surpasses the left at copying drawings and at recognizing faces, perceiving differences, perceiving emotion, and expressing emotion through the more expressive left side of the face. Right-hemisphere damage therefore more greatly disrupts emotion processing and social conduct (Tranel & others, 2002).

Most of the body's paired organs—kidneys, lungs, breasts—perform identical functions, providing a backup system should one side fail. Not so the brain's two halves, which can simultaneously carry out different functions with minimal duplication of effort. The result is a biologically odd but smart couple, each seemingly with a mind of its own.

Studying Hemispheric Differences in the Intact Brain

So, what about the 99.99+ percent of us with undivided brains? Have scientists found *our* hemispheres to be similarly specialized? With a warning that these findings are not meant to be overestimated (see Thinking Critically About Left Brain/Right Brain), the answer is yes.

When a person performs a *perceptual* task, for example, brain waves, bloodflow, and glucose consumption reveal increased activity in the *right* hemisphere; when a person speaks or calculates, activity increases in the *left* hemisphere. On occasion, hemispheric specialization (called *lateralization*) has been dramatically shown by using magnetic stimulation to temporarily disrupt left- or right-brain activity (Knecht & others, 2002), or by briefly sedating an entire hemisphere. To check for the locus of language before surgery, a physician may inject a sedative into the neck artery that feeds blood to the hemisphere on its side of the body. Before the drug is injected, the patient is lying down, arms in the air, conversing easily. You can likely predict what happens when the drug flows into the artery going to the left hemisphere: Within seconds, the person's right arm falls limp. If the left hemisphere controls language, the patient also becomes speechless until the drug wears off. When the drug enters the artery to the right hemisphere, the *left* arm falls limp, but the person can still speak. With the right rather than left hemisphere asleep, people also have difficulty recognizing themselves in an altered photo (Keenan, 2001).

Other tests confirm hemispheric specialization. For example, most people recognize a picture faster and more accurately when it is flashed (via the left visual field) to the right hemisphere. But they recognize a word faster and more accurately when it is flashed to the left hemisphere. If a word is flashed to your right hemisphere, perception takes a fraction of a second longer—the length of time it takes to send the information through the corpus callosum to the more verbal left hemisphere.

Which hemisphere would you suppose enables sign language among deaf people? The right, because of its visual-spatial superiority? Or the left, because of its processing language? Studies reveal that, just as hearing people usually use the left hemisphere

Answers to questions on page 85: Yes. No. Green.

THINKING CRITICALLY ABOUT :

LEFT BRAIN/RIGHT BRAIN

You've heard or read it many times: Some people are "left-brained," others "right-brained." But neuroscientists raise a caution flag: Beware the fad of locating complex human abilities such as science or art in either hemisphere. "The left-right dichotomy in cognitive mode is an idea with which it is very easy to run wild," warned Roger Sperry (1982).

Why do the popularizations of brain research so greatly exaggerate the findings? In *The Left-Hander Syndrome,* University of British Columbia psychologist Stanley Coren (1993) illustrates how journalism often oversimplifies and embellishes science. He recalls hearing a convention talk by Doreen Kimura, a psychologist then at the University of Western Ontario in London, Ontario. Kimura reported that melodies fed to the left ear were more easily recognized than melodies fed to the right ear. Knowing that the left ear sends most of its information to the right hemisphere, she concluded that, among her right-handed student volunteers, the right brain was better at recognizing melodies.

A few days later, the *New York Times* reported that "Doreen Kimura, a psychologist from London, Ontario, has found that *musical ability* is controlled by the right side of the brain" (italics highlight the embellishment). Apparently drawing from the *Times* story, a syndicated newspaper story then reported that "London psychologist, Dr. Doreen Kimura, claims that musicians

are right-brained!" (But Kimura studied university students, not musicians.) Later, a follow-up newspaper article further distorted the study: "An English psychologist has finally explained why there are so many great left-handed musicians."

Knowing that Kimura is not English, did not study musicians, and did not study left-handers, Coren recalled the words of an American editor: "Everything you read in the newspaper is absolutely true, except for the rare story of which you happen to have first-hand knowledge."

What can happen is this: As information flows from scientist to reader, it gets simplified as well as

> "Error flies from mouth to mouth, from pen to pen, and to destroy it takes ages." —Voltaire 1694–1778

embellished, much as gossip does in passing from one person to the next. A TV network picks up an interesting finding, then reduces it to a 30-second report with an 11-second sound bite from the researcher. This alerts a major newspaper to a story angle, which in turn gets picked up by popular science magazines and, eventually, by supermarket magazines and tabloids.

At each step, notes Coren, "Ideas become more speculative and more distant from the actual research. . . . After a while, the neuropsychologist is no longer even visible in the communication chain." The rumors grow, accumulate, and evolve into scientific misinformation that becomes "'accepted truths,' which show up in conversation and writing in sentences that begin with, 'As everybody knows . . . ,' or 'Scientists have shown that. . . .'" In the end, sighs Coren, the public myth drowns out the voices of dissenting scientists.

The moral is not to discount everything you read, but to beware. Reporters want their stories to be newsworthy. When at their best, their ideal (and mine, in writing this book) is to extract the essence—to simplify without becoming simplistic. When at their worst, they distort a pretzel-shaped finding into a breadstick-shaped story: Some people are left-brained, others right-brained. . . .

Robert Brenner/PhotoEdit

Left brain/right brain
Is the artist a "right-brained" person? Such notions distort scientific findings regarding the cerebral hemispheres. While some areas of each hemisphere specialize in different tasks, the brain's two sides cooperate to enable whatever we do.

to process speech, deaf people use the left hemisphere to read signs (Corina & others, 1992; Hickok & others, 2001). A stroke in the left hemisphere will disrupt a deaf person's signing, much as it would disrupt a hearing person's speaking. Broca's area is similarly involved in both spoken and signed speech production (Corina, 1998). To the brain, language is language, whether spoken or signed.

Although the left hemisphere is adept at making quick, literal interpretations of language, the right hemisphere excels in making subtle inferences (Beeman & Chiarello, 1998; Bowden & Beeman, 1998; Mason & Just, 2004). If primed with the flashed word *foot,* the left hemisphere will be especially quick to then recognize the closely associated word *heel.* But if primed with *foot, cry,* and *glass,* the right hemisphere will more quickly recognize another word that is distantly related to all three (*cut*). And if given an insightlike problem—what word goes with *pie, luck,* and *belly?*— the right hemisphere more quickly than the left recognizes that the solution is *pot.* As one patient explained after suffering right-hemisphere stroke damage, "I understand words, but I'm missing the subtleties." The right hemisphere also helps us modulate our speech to make meaning clear—as when we ask "What's that in the road ahead?" instead of "What's that in the road, a head?" (Heller, 1990).

From simply looking at the two hemispheres, which appear alike to the naked eye, who would suppose that they contribute so uniquely to the harmony of the whole? Yet a variety of observations—of people with split brains and people with normal brains—converge beautifully, leaving little doubt that we have unified brains with specialized parts.

Brain Organization and Handedness

OBJECTIVE 20 | Discuss the relationships among brain organization, handedness, and mortality.

Nearly 90 percent of us are primarily right-handed (Medland & others, 2004). Some 10 percent of us (somewhat more among males, somewhat less among females) are left-handed. (A few people write with their right hand and throw a ball with their left, or vice versa.) Almost all (95 percent) right-handers process speech primarily in the left hemisphere, which tends to be the slightly larger hemisphere (Springer & Deutsch, 1985). Left-handers are more diverse. More than half process speech in the left hemisphere, as right-handers do. About a quarter process language in the right hemisphere; the other quarter use both hemispheres.

Is Handedness Inherited? Judging from prehistoric human cave drawings, tools, and hand and arm bones, this veer to the right occurred long ago (Corballis, 1989; Steele, 2000). Right-handedness prevails in all human cultures. Moreover, it appears prior to culture's impact. Ultrasound observations of fetal thumb-sucking reveal that more than 9 in 10 fetuses suck the right hand's thumb (Hepper & others, 1990, 2004). This bias for the right hand is unique to humans and to the primates most like us: chimpanzees (Hopkins & others, 2005) and gorillas—only about 35 percent of whom are left-handed. Other primates are more evenly divided between lefties and righties.

Observing 150 human babies during the first two days after their birth, George Michel (1981) found that two-thirds consistently preferred to lie with their heads turned to the right. When he again studied a sample of these babies at age 5 months, almost all of the "head-right" babies reached for things with their right hands, and almost all of the "head-left" babies reached with their left hands. Such findings, along with the universal prevalence of right-handers, indicate that either genes or some prenatal factors influence handedness.

So, Is It All Right to Be Left-Handed? Judging by our everyday conversation, left-handedness is not all right. To be "coming out of left field" or to offer a "left-handed compliment" is hardly better than to be "gauche" or "sinister" (words de-

Most people also kick with their right foot, look through a microscope with their right eye, and (had you noticed?) kiss with their head and nose tilted to the right (Güntürkün, 2003).

Evidence that challenges a genetic explanation of handedness: Handedness is one of but a few traits that genetically identical twins aren't especially likely to share (Halpern & Coren, 1990).

rived from the French and Latin for "left"). On the other hand, right-handedness is "right on," which any "righteous" "right-hand man" "in his right mind" usually is.

Left-handers are more numerous than usual among those with reading disabilities, allergies, and migraine headaches (Geschwind & Behan, 1984). But in Iran, where students report which hand they write with when taking the university entrance exam, lefties outperform righties in all subjects (Noroozian & others, 2003). Left-handedness is also more common among musicians, mathematicians, professional baseball and cricket players, architects, and artists, including such luminaries as Michelangelo, Leonardo da Vinci, and Picasso.[2] Although left-handers must tolerate elbow jostling at dinner parties, right-handed desks, and awkward scissors, the pros and cons of being a lefty seem roughly equal. But researchers have turned up one con that deserves more attention: Left-handers seem to disappear with age!

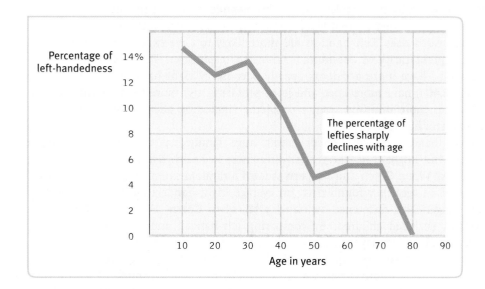

FIGURE 2.39
The disappearing southpaws
The percentage of left-handers decreases sharply in samples of older people. (Adapted from Coren, 1993b.)

A Scientific Mystery: The Case of the Disappearing Southpaws While studying handedness, psychologist Stanley Coren (1993) stumbled upon a rather stunning fact: With age, the percentage of left-handers declines dramatically. In his initial sample of 5147 people, he found that 15 percent of 10-year-olds, 5 percent of 50-year-olds, and less than 1 percent of those over age 80 were left-handers (**FIGURE 2.39**). Other researchers around the world have confirmed Coren's finding. Intrigued, Coren and fellow sleuth Diane Halpern (1991; Halpern & Coren, 1988, 1991, 1993) set out in search of an answer. (If you were one of them, what explanations might have come to mind?)

Perhaps, Coren and Halpern first thought, childhood coercion causes natural lefties to become right-handed as they age. (Many older people can recall having their left hand slapped, tied down, or even balled into a fist with surgical tape when they tried to use it.) If today's parents and teachers are more accepting of left-handedness than were those of earlier times, the result might be more young left-handers. But North American and European studies suggest that during the twentieth century, left-handers increased only from about 6 percent of the population to 10 percent (Porac & others, 1980), too little to explain the much greater percentage of left-handers among the very young. Coren and his colleagues found further support for the stability of left-

[2]Strategic factors explain the higher-than-normal percentage of lefties in sports. For example, it helps a soccer team to have left-footed players play the left side of the field (Wood & Aggleton, 1989). In golf, however, no left-hander won the American Masters tournament until Canadian Mike Weir did so in 2003.

handedness in art works dated from 15,400 to 3000 B.C., where 10 percent of the people were depicted as left-handed. In modern art works, 11 percent are left-handers.

Might simple learning explain the slow and gradual disappearance of left-handers? Might the world's being designed for right-handers make it easier for lefties to learn *gradually* to use their right hands? But again, no. Preschoolers who switch handedness complete the process before adolescence. Handedness rarely switches after age 8 or 9, and even before then it occurs only for specific coerced actions (such as eating or writing).

What else remains? Coren and Halpern dared to think the unthinkable: that left-handers die younger. "That can't be true," skeptical colleagues replied when Coren first voiced the idea. "If true, surely someone would have noticed by now. Besides, my paternal grandmother was left-handed and lived to 91." But vivid anecdotes ("I know a person who . . .") are no substitute for conclusions based on large and representative samples. Neither examples nor counterexamples prove a generality.

So to explore their morbid idea, Coren and Halpern first reflected on the lefties' known health risks. Left-handers are more likely to have experienced birth stress, such as prematurity or the need for assisted respiration. They also endure more headaches, have more accidents (partly because of right-handed equipment; see **FIGURE 2.40**), have more knee and joint problems, use more tobacco and alcohol, and suffer more immune system problems (including allergies such as asthma, eczema, and hay fever).

These handedness differences aren't huge (individual differences are much greater). But might they, like gender differences in health risks, add up to differing life spans? When Coren and Halpern studied a random sample of recently deceased people of all ages they found that, on average, right-handers did live eight or nine years longer. This difference dwindled a bit when Coren, Halpern, and other researchers excluded children. By comparing left-handed and right-handed former baseball and cricket players, they found the life-span difference reduced—three years, Coren estimated—but still apparent (Aggleton & others, 1993; Rogerson, 1994).

This stunning finding triggered an avalanche of publicity, much of it distorted, which in turn triggered nasty responses: "Dear professor . . . we strongly suggest that you beware of sinister lefties bearing grudges—and chain saws," and "You right-handers think that you'll live longer than left-handers but you won't if we kill you first" (Halpern & others, 1996). The finding also stimulated some follow-up research that produced no life-expectancy advantage for right-handers (Harris, 1993). One National Institute on Aging research team followed 3800 East Boston adults for six years and found that, at any age, left-handers were *not* more likely to die (Salive &

> "Truth is arrived at by the painstaking process of eliminating the untrue. When you have eliminated the impossible, whatever remains, *however improbable*, must be the truth."
>
> Sherlock Holmes in Arthur Conan Doyle's "The Sign of the Four," 1890

Long-lived left-handers:
• Benjamin Franklin (84)
• Charlie Chaplin (88)
• Pablo Picasso (92)
• The Queen Mother (101)

Short-lived left-handers:
• Babe Ruth (53)
• Marilyn Monroe (36)
• Alexander the Great (33)
• Kurt Cobain (27)

FIGURE 2.40
The southpaw's hazardous life
In the book *The Left-Hander Syndrome*, Stanley Coren illustrates risks posed by a world made for right-handers. When left-handers use a drill press, their left arm may obscure their view.

others, 1993). Coren (1993) responded that six years is not long enough to catch a statistically significant handedness effect in a sample this small.

The unfinished case of the disappearing southpaws illustrates the very heart of science—how it dares to ask researchable questions, even those with unsettling implications. In the court of scientific judgment, researchers are welcome to state new ideas but they must expose themselves to counterexamination from opposing views and to heated debate. Over time, science has a way of unmasking error, taking us closer to truth, and often to an improved world. As it explains the absence of elder left-handers, it may also point the way to safer, more comfortable environments for left-handed people.

We have glimpsed the truth of this chapter's overriding principle: Everything psychological is simultaneously biological. This chapter has focused on how our thoughts, feelings, and actions arise from our specialized yet integrated brain. In chapters to come, we will further explore the significance of the biological revolution in psychology. We will see, for example, how

- genes and experience jointly influence our personality, emotions, and intelligence.
- brain development underlies a child's mental development.
- our sense organs and our brain enable us to see and hear.
- the brain stores memories.
- our brain and body work to create our experiences of hunger and sexuality, anger and fear, sleep and dreams.
- mind and body together influence our vulnerability to disease and our capacity for healing.
- aberrant brain anatomy and chemistry influence depression and schizophrenia; and we'll see how biological treatments can alleviate these conditions.
- our species' evolutionary history may predispose us to hurt, help, or love certain others.

From nineteenth-century phrenology to today's neuroscience, we have come a long way. Yet what is unknown still dwarfs what is known. We can describe the brain. We can learn the functions of its parts. We can study how the parts communicate. But how do we get mind out of meat? How does the electrochemical whir in a hunk of tissue the size of a head of lettuce give rise to elation, a creative idea, or that memory of Grandmother?

Much as gas and air can give rise to something different—fire—so also, believed Sperry, does the complex human brain give rise to something different: consciousness. The mind, he argued, emerges from the brain's dance of ions, yet is not reducible to it. Cells cannot be fully explained by the actions of atoms, nor minds by the activity of cells. Psychology is rooted in biology which is rooted in chemistry which is rooted in physics. Yet psychology is more than applied physics. As Jerome Kagan (1998) reminds us, the meaning of the Gettysburg Address is not reducible to neural activity. Sexual love is more than blood flooding to the genitals. Morality and responsibility become possible when we understand the mind as a "holistic system," said Sperry (1992). We are not mere jabbering robots.

The mind seeking to understand the brain—that is indeed among the ultimate scientific challenges. And so it will always be. To paraphrase cosmologist John Barrow, a brain simple enough to be understood is too simple to produce a mind able to understand it.

Mind and brain as holistic system
In Roger Sperry's view, the brain creates and controls the emergent mind, which in turn influences the brain. (Think vividly about biting into a lemon and you may salivate.)

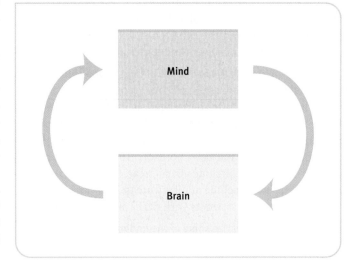

>> LEARNING OUTCOMES

The Brain

OBJECTIVE 11 | **Describe several techniques for studying the brain.**
Clinical observations have long revealed the general effects of damage to various areas of the brain. But MRI scans now reveal brain structures, and EEG, PET, and fMRI (functional MRI) recordings reveal brain activity. By surgically lesioning or electrically stimulating specific brain areas, by recording the brain's surface electrical activity, and by displaying neural activity with computer-aided brain scans, neuroscientists explore the connections among brain, mind, and behavior.

OBJECTIVE 12 | **Describe the components of the brainstem, and summarize the functions of the brainstem, thalamus, and cerebellum.**
The brainstem is the oldest part of the brain and is responsible for automatic survival functions. Its components are the medulla (which controls heartbeat and breathing), the pons (which helps coordinate movements), and the reticular formation (which affects arousal). The thalamus, the brain's sensory switchboard, sits above the brainstem. The cerebellum, attached to the rear of the brainstem, coordinates muscle movement and helps process sensory information.

OBJECTIVE 13 | **Describe the structures and functions of the limbic system, and explain how one of these structures controls the pituitary gland.**
Between the brainstem and cerebral cortex is the limbic system, which is linked to emotions, memory, and drives. One of its neural centers, the amygdala, is involved in responses of aggression and fear. Another, the hypothalamus, is involved in various bodily maintenance functions, pleasurable rewards, and the control of the hormonal system. The hypothalamus sits just above the pituitary (the "master gland") and controls it by stimulating it to trigger the release of hormones. The hippocampus, also part of the limbic system, processes memory.

OBJECTIVE 14 | **Define *cerebral cortex*, and explain its importance for the human brain.**
The cerebral cortex is the thin surface layer of interconnected neurons covering the brain's hemispheres. The human brain's cortex is larger than that of other animals, and it enables learning, thinking, and the other complex forms of information processing that make us uniquely human.

OBJECTIVE 15 | **Identify the four lobes of the cerebral cortex.**
Each cerebral hemisphere has four geographic areas. The frontal lobe, just behind the forehead, is involved in speaking, muscle movements, and planning and judgments. The parietal lobes, at the top of the head and toward the rear, receive sensory input for touch and body position. The occipital lobes, at the back of the head, include visual areas. The temporal lobes, just above the ears, include auditory areas. Each lobe performs many functions and interacts with other areas of the cortex.

OBJECTIVE 16 | **Summarize some of the findings on the functions of the motor cortex and the sensory cortex, and discuss the importance of the association areas.**
Some areas of the brain serve specific functions (see Figure 2.23 on page 75). One such area is the motor cortex, an arch-shaped region at the rear of the frontal lobes that controls voluntary movements. Another is the sensory cortex, a region at the front of the parietal lobes that registers and processes body sensations. In these regions, body parts requiring precise control (in the motor cortex) or those that are especially sensitive (in the sensory cortex) occupy the greatest amount of space. Most of the brain's cortex—the major portion of each of the four lobes—is devoted to uncommitted association areas, which integrate information involved in learning, remembering, thinking, and other higher-level functions.

OBJECTIVE 17 | **Describe the five brain areas that would be involved if you read this sentence aloud.**
Language results from the integration of many specific neural networks performing specialized subtasks. When you read aloud, your brain's *visual cortex* registers words as visual stimuli, the *angular gyrus* transforms those visual representations into auditory codes, *Wernicke's area* interprets those codes and sends the message to *Broca's area*, which controls the *motor cortex* as it creates the pronounced words.

OBJECTIVE 18 | **Discuss the brain's plasticity following injury or illness.**
If one hemisphere is damaged early in life, the other will pick up many of its functions. This plasticity diminishes later in life, although nearby neurons may partially compensate for damaged ones after a stroke or other brain injury.

OBJECTIVE 19 | **Describe split-brain research, and explain how it helps us understand the functions of our left and right hemispheres.**
Clinical observations long ago revealed that the left cerebral hemisphere is crucial for language. Split-brain research (experiments on people with a severed corpus callosum) has confirmed that in most people the left hemisphere is the more verbal, and that the right hemisphere excels in visual perception and the recognition of emotion. Studies of healthy people with intact brains confirm that each hemisphere makes unique contributions to the integrated functioning of the brain.

OBJECTIVE 20 | **Discuss the relationships among brain organization, handedness, and mortality.**
About 10 percent of us are left-handed. Almost all right-handers process speech in the left hemisphere, as do more than half of all left-handers. The remainder of left-handers split about evenly in processing language in the right hemisphere or in both hemispheres. The percentage of lefties decreases sharply with age, from about 15 percent at age 10 to less than 1 percent at age 80. This decline may reflect a higher risk of accidents.

ASK YOURSELF: How might you feel with two separate brain hemispheres, both of which controlled your thought and action but one of which dominated your consciousness and speech? How might that affect your sense of self, as one indivisible person?

REVIEW CHAPTER 2: **Neuroscience and Behavior**

Test Yourself

1. How do neurons communicate with one another?

2. How does information flow through your nervous system as you pick up a fork? Can you summarize this process?

3. Why is the pituitary gland called the "master gland"?

4. Within what brain region would damage be most likely to disrupt your ability to skip rope? Your ability to sense tastes or sounds? In what brain region would damage perhaps leave you in a coma? Without the very breath and heartbeat of life?

5. As you look straight ahead, how is the visual information sent to your two brain hemispheres?

Answers to the Test Yourself questions can be found in Appendix B at the end of the book.

Terms and Concepts to Remember

biological psychology, p. 54

neuron, p. 55

dendrite, p. 55

axon, p. 55

myelin [MY-uh-lin] sheath, p. 55

action potential, p. 55

threshold, p. 56

synapse [SIN-aps], p. 57

neurotransmitters, p. 57

acetylcholine [ah-seat-el-KO-leen] (ACh), p. 58

endorphins [en-DOR-fins], p. 59

nervous system, p. 61

central nervous system (CNS), p. 61

peripheral nervous system (PNS), p. 61

nerves, p. 62

sensory neurons, p. 62

motor neurons, p. 62

interneurons, p. 62

somatic nervous system, p. 62

autonomic [aw-tuh-NAHM-ik] nervous system, p. 62

sympathetic nervous system, p. 62

parasympathetic nervous system, p. 62

reflex, p. 63

neural networks, p. 64

endocrine [EN-duh-krin] system, p. 65

hormones, p. 65

adrenal [ah-DREEN-el] glands, p. 66

pituitary gland, p. 66

lesion [LEE-zhuhn], p. 68

electroencephalogram (EEG), p. 68

PET (positron emission tomography) scan, p. 69

MRI (magnetic resonance imaging), p. 69

fMRI (functional MRI), p. 69

brainstem, p. 71

medulla [muh-DUL-uh], p. 71

reticular formation, p. 71

thalamus [THAL-uh-muss], p. 72

cerebellum [sehr-uh-BELL-um], p. 72

limbic system, p. 72

amygdala [uh-MIG-duh-la], p. 72

hypothalamus [hi-po-THAL-uh-muss], p. 73

cerebral [seh-REE-bruhl] cortex, p. 74

glial cells (glia), p. 75

frontal lobes, p. 76

parietal [puh-RYE-uh-tuhl] lobes, p. 76

occipital [ahk-SIP-uh-tuhl] lobes, p. 76

temporal lobes, p. 76

motor cortex, p. 77

sensory cortex, p. 78

association areas, p. 79

aphasia, p. 80

Broca's area, p. 81

Wernicke's area, p. 81

plasticity, p. 82

corpus callosum [KOR-pus kah-LOW-sum], p. 84

split brain, p. 84

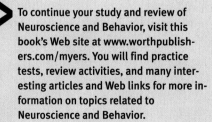

WEB

> To continue your study and review of Neuroscience and Behavior, visit this book's Web site at www.worthpublishers.com/myers. You will find practice tests, review activities, and many interesting articles and Web links for more information on topics related to Neuroscience and Behavior.

Another Voice On: Nature, Nurture, and Human Diversity

Reprinted from *Prairie Schooner*, vol. 66, no 3 (fall 1992) by permission of the University of Nebraska Press. Copyright © 1992 by the University of Nebraska Press

As a young girl
vying for my father's attention,
I invented a game that made him look up
from his reading and shake his head
as if both baffled and amused.

In my brother's closet, I'd change
into his dungarees—the rough material
molding me into boy shape; hide
my long hair under an army helmet
he'd been given by Father, and emerge

transformed into the legendary Che
of grown-up talk.

Strutting around the room,
I'd tell of life in the mountains,
of carnage and rivers of blood,
and of manly feasts with rum and music
to celebrate victories para la libertad.
He would listen with a smile
to my tales of battles and brotherhood
until Mother called us to dinner.

She was not amused
by my transformations, sternly
    forbidding me
from sitting down with them as a man.
She'd order me back to the dark cubicle
that smelled of adventure, to shed
my costume, to braid my hair furiously
with blind hands, and to return invisible,
as myself,
to the real world of her kitchen.

3: Nature, Nurture, and Human Diversity

OBJECTIVE **1** | Give examples of differences and similarities within the human family.

What makes you you? In important ways, we are each unique. We look different. We sound different. We have varying personalities, interests, and cultural and family backgrounds. But how different are we really?

We are also the leaves of one tree. Our human family shares not only a common biological heritage—cut us and we bleed—but also common behavioral tendencies. Our shared brain architecture predisposes us to sense the world, develop language, and feel hunger through identical mechanisms. Whether we live in the Arctic or the tropics, we prefer sweet tastes to sour. We divide the color spectrum into similar colors. And we feel drawn to behaviors that produce and protect offspring.

Our kinship appears in our social behaviors as well. Whether our last name is Wong, Nkomo, Smith, or Gonzales, at about eight months we start fearing strangers, and as adults we prefer the company of those whose attitudes and attributes are similar to our own. Coming from different parts of the globe, we know how to read one another's smiles and frowns. As members of one species, we affiliate, conform, reciprocate favors, punish offenses, organize hierarchies of status, and grieve a child's death. A visitor from outer space could drop in anywhere and find humans dancing and feasting, singing and worshiping, playing sports and games, laughing and crying, living in families, and forming groups. Taken together, such universal behaviors reveal our human nature.

What causes our striking diversity and our shared human nature? This chapter begins to tell this complex story. We start with *behavior genetics,* which studies the relative effects of our genes *(nature)* and our environments *(nurture)* on our individual differences in behavior and mental processes. Together, our genes and environments design our unique body-mind system and define the things that make us different. Genes matter. Culture, and everything we experience from womb to tomb, matter, too.

We will consider how nature and nurture together shape us by focusing on:

● *Evolutionary psychology,* which studies behaviors, emotions, and thinking capacities that seemingly allowed our distant ancestors to survive, reproduce, and send their genes into the future. We humans tend to fear snakes and spiders, and to avoid heights and bitter-tasting foods, because such fears and behaviors helped our ancestors to survive.

● *Parents, peers, and culture,* which influence our beliefs and values, our interests and food tastes, and our language and appearance. Even before hearing

The nurture of nature
Parents everywhere wonder: Will my baby grow up to be peaceful or aggressive? Homely or attractive? Successful or struggling at every step? What comes built in, and what is nurtured—and how? Research reveals that nature and nurture together shape our development—every step of the way.

Jeffrey W. Myers/Stock, Boston

their accent, my Scottish friends can spot American tourists by the way they look and walk.

- *Gender* and all its associated expectations, which influence how others perceive us and how we think about ourselves. Yet for all their publicized differences, women and men are, as we will see, more alike than different.

Behavior Genetics: Predicting Individual Differences

OBJECTIVE 2 | Describe the types of questions that interest behavior geneticists.

How much are our behavior differences shaped by our genetic differences? And how much by our **environment**—every external influence, from maternal nutrition while in the womb to social support while nearing the tomb—reacting to our genetic traits? More specifically, to what extent are we formed by our upbringing? By our culture? By our current circumstances? If Jaden Agassi, son of tennis stars Andre Agassi and Stephanie Graf, grows up to be a tennis star, should we attribute his talent to his Grand Slam genes? To his growing up in a tennis-rich environment? To high expectations? Equally to all three? **Behavior geneticists** study our differences and weigh the relative effects of heredity and environment.

Genes: Our Codes for Life

OBJECTIVE 3 | Define *chromosome, DNA, gene,* and *genome,* and describe their relationships.

Behind the story of our body and of our brain—surely the most awesome thing on our little planet—is the heredity that interacts with our experience to create both our universal human nature and our individual and social diversity. Barely more than a century ago, few would have guessed that every cell nucleus in your body contains the genetic master code for your entire body. It's as if every room in the Empire State Building had a book containing the architect's plans for the entire structure. The plans for your own book of life run to 46 chapters—23 donated by your mother (from her egg) and 23 by your father (from his sperm). These chapters, called **chromosomes,** are each composed of a coiled chain of the molecule **DNA** (*deoxyribonucleic acid*). **Genes,** small segments of the giant DNA molecules, form the words of these chromosome books (**FIGURE 3.1**). All told, each of us has 30,000 or so of these gene words, each a self-replicating unit capable of synthesizing proteins. Genes do not directly guide our behavior. They simply, when "turned on," provide the code for creating protein molecules, the building blocks of our physical development.

Genetically speaking, every other human is close to being your identical twin. Even the person you like least is your near-clone, sharing about 99.9 percent of your DNA (Plomin & Crabbe, 2000). But that 0.1 percent difference, in interaction with differing environments, can give us a Nelson Mandela or an Adolf Hitler.

Human **genome** researchers have discovered the common sequence within human DNA. It is this shared genetic profile that makes us humans, rather than chimpanzees or tulips. Actually, we aren't all that different from our chimpanzee cousins; with them we share, depending on how the count is done, 96 percent of our DNA sequence (Mikkelsen & others, 2005). At "functionally important" DNA sites, reports one molecular genetics team, the human–chimpanzee DNA similarity is 99.4

"Thanks for almost everything, Dad."

■ **environment** every nongenetic influence, from prenatal nutrition to the people and things around us.

■ **behavior genetics** the study of the relative power and limits of genetic and environmental influences on behavior.

■ **chromosomes** threadlike structures made of DNA molecules that contain the genes.

■ **DNA (deoxyribonucleic acid)** a complex molecule containing the genetic information that makes up the chromosomes.

■ **genes** the biochemical units of heredity that make up the chromosomes; a segment of DNA capable of synthesizing a protein.

■ **genome** the complete instructions for making an organism, consisting of all the genetic material in that organism's chromosomes.

■ **identical twins** twins who develop from a single fertilized egg that splits in two, creating two genetically identical organisms.

Nucleus
(the inner area of a cell that houses chromosomes and genes)

Chromosome
(threadlike structure made largely of DNA molecules)

Gene
(segment of DNA containing the code for a particular protein; determines our individual biological development)

Cell
(the basic structural unit of a living thing)

DNA
(a spiraling, complex molecule containing genes)

FIGURE 3.1

The genes: Their location and composition

Contained in the nucleus of each of the trillions of cells in your body are chromosomes. Each chromosome contains a coiled chain of the molecule DNA. Genes are DNA segments that, when expressed (turned on), form templates for the production of proteins. By directing the manufacture of proteins, the genes determine our individual biological development.

percent (Wildman & others, 2003). Yet that wee difference matters. Despite some remarkable abilities, chimpanzees grunt. Shakespeare intricately wove some 24,000 words to form his literary masterpieces. And small differences matter among chimpanzees, too. Two species that differ by much less than 1 percent of their genomes also display obvious behavior differences. Common chimpanzees are aggressive and male-dominated. Bonobos are peaceable and female led.

Geneticists and psychologists are interested in the occasional variations found at particular gene sites in the DNA—variations that in their many combinations define each person's uniqueness. Slight person-to-person variations from the common pattern give clues to why one person has a disease that another does not, why one person is short and another tall, why one is happy and another depressed.

Human traits are influenced by *gene complexes*—many genes acting in concert. How tall you are, for example, reflects the height of your face, the size of your vertebrae, the length of your leg bones, and so forth—each of which may be influenced by different genes interacting with your environment. Complex human traits such as intelligence, happiness, and aggressiveness are similarly influenced by groups of genes. Thus our genetic predispositions help explain both our shared human nature and our human diversity.

> "We share half our genes with the banana."
>
> Evolutionary biologist Robert May, president of Britain's Royal Society, 2001

Twin Studies

OBJECTIVE 4 | Explain how identical and fraternal twins differ, and cite ways that behavior geneticists use twin studies to understand the effects of environment and heredity.

To disentangle the threads of heredity and environment, behavior geneticists often use two sets of tweezers: twin studies and adoption studies.

Identical Versus Fraternal Twins

To scientifically tease apart the influences of environment and heredity, we would need to control the home environment while varying heredity. Happily for our purposes, nature has given us ready-made subjects for this experiment: identical versus fraternal twins. **Identical twins,** who develop from a single fertilized egg that splits in two, are *genetically* identical (**FIGURE 3.2** on page 98). They are nature's own human clones—indeed, clones who share not only the same genes but the same conception, uterus, birth date, and usually the same cultural history.

Identical?

Twins Morgan Hamm and Paul Hamm, world-class gymnasts, are identical, yet their achievements are not. In the 2004 Olympics, Paul won more medals than the brother with whom he grew up. This small difference suggests the influence of slightly different environments (perhaps even prenatal environments) as well as the influence of their individual interactions with their environments after birth.

Adrian Dennis/AFP/Getty Images

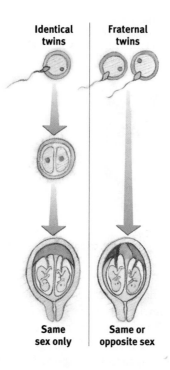

FIGURE 3.2
Same fertilized egg, same genes; different eggs, different genes
Identical twins develop from a single fertilized egg, fraternal twins from two.

Curiously, twinning rates vary by race. The rate among Caucasians is roughly twice that of Asians and half that of Africans. In Africa and Asia, most twins are identical. In Western countries, most twins are fraternal, and fraternal twins are increasing with the use of fertility drugs (Hall, 2003; Steinhauer, 1999)

Fraternal twins, who develop from separate fertilized eggs, are genetically no more similar than ordinary brothers and sisters. A person whose identical twin has Alzheimer's disease has a 60 percent risk of sharing the disease; if the affected twin is fraternal, the risk is only 30 percent (Plomin & others, 1997). Such a difference suggests a genetic influence. But behavior geneticists also work to tease out the influences of siblings' unique experiences and shared environments (such as being in the same family, neighborhood, and schools); see **FIGURE 3.3.**

Are identical twins, being genetic clones of one another, behaviorally more similar than fraternal twins (Bouchard, 2004)? Studies of nearly 13,000 pairs of Swedish twins, of 7000 Finnish twin pairs, and of 3810 Australian twin pairs provide a consistent answer: On both extraversion (outgoingness) and neuroticism (emotional instability), identical twins are much more similar than fraternal twins. In explaining individual differences, genes matter.

If genes influence traits such as emotional instability, might they also influence the social effects of such traits? To find out, Matt McGue and David Lykken (1992) studied divorce rates among 1500 same-sex, middle-age twin pairs. Their result: If you have a fraternal twin who has divorced, the odds of your divorcing go up 1.6 times (compared with having a not-divorced twin). If you have an identical twin who has divorced, the odds of your divorcing go up 5.5 times. From such data, McGue and Lykken estimate that people's differing divorce risks are about 50 percent attributable to genetic factors.

Other dimensions also reflect genetic influences. When John Loehlin and Robert Nichols (1976) gave a battery of questionnaires to 850 U.S. twin pairs, identical twins were much more similar than fraternals in many ways—in abilities, personal traits, and interests. However, the identical twins, more than fraternal twins, also reported

FIGURE 3.3
Twin studies
Behavior geneticists have used twin studies to disentangle the influence of *genes*, the *shared environment*, and the unique or *nonshared environment*. (Adapted from Lisa Legrand, William Iacono, and Matt McGue, 2005.)

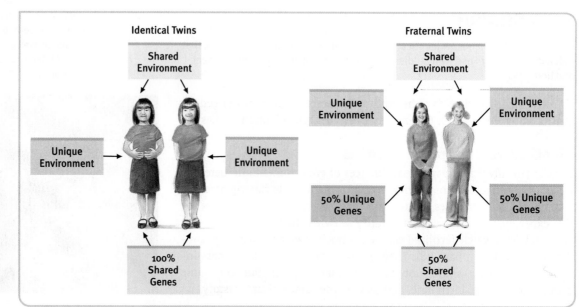

being treated alike. So, did their experience rather than their genes account for their similarity? No, said Loehlin and Nichols; identical twins whose parents treated them alike were *not* psychologically more alike than identical twins who were treated less similarly.

Separated Twins

Imagine the following science fiction experiment: A mad scientist decides to separate identical twins at birth, then rear them in differing environments. Better yet, consider a true story:

On a chilly Ohio Saturday morning in February 1979, some time after divorcing his first wife, Linda, Jim Lewis awoke in his modest, middle-class home next to his second wife, Betty. Jim—a romantic, affectionate type—was determined that this marriage would work and made a habit of leaving love notes to Betty around the house. As Jim lay in bed he thought about others he had loved, including his son, James Alan, and his faithful dog, Toy.

Having outfitted a workshop in a corner of his basement, Jim looked forward to spending some of the day's free time on his woodworking hobby. He had derived many hours of satisfaction from building furniture, picture frames, and an assortment of other items, including a circular white bench around a tree in his front yard. Jim also liked to spend free time driving his Chevy, watching stock-car racing, and drinking Miller Lite beer.

Jim was basically healthy. Having undergone a vasectomy, he was done having children. His blood pressure was a little high, perhaps related to his chain-smoking habit. He chewed his fingernails to the nub. And he suffered occasional half-day migraine headaches—"like somebody's hitting you with a two-by-four in the back of the neck." He had become overweight a while back but had shed some of the pounds.

What was extraordinary about Jim Lewis, however, was that at that same moment (I am not making this up) there existed another man—also named Jim—for whom all these things (right down to the dog's name) were also true.[1] This other Jim—Jim Springer—just happened, 38 years earlier, to have been his womb-mate. Thirty-seven days after their birth, these two genetically identical twins were separated, adopted by blue-collar families, and reared with no contact or knowledge of each other's whereabouts until one February day when Jim Lewis' phone rang. The caller was his genetic clone (who, having been told he had a twin, set out to find him).

One month after that fateful encounter, the brothers became the first twin pair tested by University of Minnesota psychologist Thomas Bouchard and his colleagues, thus beginning a study of separated twins that extends to the present (Holden, 1980a,b; Wright, 1998). When given tests measuring their personality, intelligence, heart rate, and brain waves, the Jim twins—despite 38 years of separation—were virtually as alike as the same person tested twice. Their voice intonations and inflections were so similar that, hearing a playback of an earlier interview, Jim Springer guessed "That's me." Wrong—it was his brother.

■ **fraternal twins** twins who develop from separate fertilized eggs. They are genetically no closer than brothers and sisters, but they share a fetal environment.

Sweden has the world's largest national twin registry—140,000 living and dead twin pairs—which form part of a massive European registry of 600,000 twins currently being sampled in the world's largest twin study (Wheelwright, 2004). www.genomeutwin.org

Twins Lorraine and Levinia Christmas, driving to deliver Christmas presents to each other near Flitcham, England, collided (Shepherd, 1997).

Bob Sacha

Identical twins are people two
Identical twins Gerald Levey and Mark Newman were separated at birth and raised in different homes. When reunited at age 31, they discovered that they both volunteered as firefighters. Research has shown remarkable similarities in the life choices of separated identical twins, lending support to the idea that genes influence personality.

[1]Actually, this description of the two Jims errs in one respect: Jim Lewis named his son James Alan. Jim Springer named his James Allan.

"In some domains it looks as though our identical twins reared apart are . . . just as similar as identical twins reared together. Now that's an amazing finding and I can assure you none of us would have expected that degree of similarity."

Thomas Bouchard (1981)

Coincidences are not unique to twins. Patricia Kern of Colorado was born March 13, 1941, and named Patricia Ann Campbell. Patricia DiBiasi of Oregon also was born March 13, 1941, and named Patricia Ann Campbell. Both had fathers named Robert, worked as bookkeepers, and at the time of this comparison had children ages 21 and 19. Both studied cosmetology, enjoyed oil painting as a hobby, and married military men, within 11 days of each other. They are not genetically related (from an AP report, May 2, 1983).

Identical twins Oskar Stohr and Jack Yufe presented equally striking similarities. One was raised by his grandmother in Germany as a Catholic and a Nazi, while the other was raised by his father in the Caribbean as a Jew. Nevertheless, they share traits and habits galore. They like spicy foods and sweet liqueurs, have a habit of falling asleep in front of the television, flush the toilet before using it, store rubber bands on their wrists, and dip buttered toast in their coffee. Stohr is domineering toward women and yells at his wife, as did Yufe before he and his wife separated. Both married women named Dorothy Jane Scheckelburger. Okay, the last item is a joke. But as Judith Rich Harris (2006) notes, it is hardly weirder than some other reported coincidences.

Aided by publicity in magazine and newspaper stories, Bouchard and his colleagues (1990; DiLalla & others, 1996; Segal, 1999) have located and studied 80 pairs of identical twins reared apart. They continue to find similarities not only of tastes and physical attributes but also of personality, abilities, attitudes, interests, and even fears.

In Sweden, Nancy Pedersen and her co-workers (1988) identified 99 separated identical twin pairs and more than 200 separated fraternal twin pairs. Compared with equivalent samples of identical twins reared together, the separated identical twins had more dissimilar *personalities*—characteristic patterns of thinking, feeling, and acting. Still, separated twins were more alike if genetically identical than if fraternal. Separation shortly after birth (rather than, say, at age 8) didn't amplify their personality differences.

The stories of startling twin similarity do not impress Bouchard's critics, who remind us that "the plural of anecdote is not data." They contend that if any two strangers were to spend hours comparing their behaviors and life histories, they would probably discover many coincidental similarities. If researchers created a control group of biologically unrelated pairs of the same age, sex, and ethnicity, who had not grown up together but who were as similar to one another in economic and cultural background as are many of the separated twin pairs, wouldn't these pairs also exhibit striking similarities (Joseph, 2001)? (Bouchard replies that separated fraternal twins do not exhibit similarities comparable to those of separated identical twins, and twin researcher Nancy Segal [2000] notes that "virtual twins"—same-age, biologically unrelated siblings—are also much more dissimilar.)

Even the more impressive data from the personality assessments are clouded by the reunion of many of the separated twins some years before they were tested. Moreover, separated twins share an appearance, and the responses it evokes. And adoption agencies tend to place separated twins in similar homes. Despite these criticisms, the striking twin study results have helped shift scientific thinking toward a greater appreciation of genetic influences.

Adoption Studies

OBJECTIVE 5 | Cite ways that behavior geneticists use adoption studies to understand the effects of environment and heredity.

For behavior geneticists, another handy real-life experiment—adoption—creates two groups of relatives: the adoptees' genetic relatives (biological parents and siblings) and their environmental relatives (adoptive parents and siblings). For any given trait we can therefore ask whether adopted children are more like their adoptive parents, who contribute a home environment, or their biological parents, who contributed their genes. While sharing the same home environment, do adopted siblings come to share traits?

The stunning finding from studies of hundreds of adoptive families is that people who grow up together, whether biologically related or not, do not much resemble one another in personality (McGue & Bouchard, 1998; Plomin & others, 1998; Rowe,

1990). Adoptees' traits (their outgoing-ness, agreeableness, and so forth) bear more similarities to their biological parents than to their caregiving adoptive parents.

The finding is important enough to bear repeating: Environmental factors shared by a family's children have virtually no impact on their personalities. Two adopted children reared in the same home are no more likely to share personality traits with each other than with the child down the block. Heredity shapes other primates' personalities, too. For chimpanzees, being raised in the same zoo hardly matters (Weiss & others, 2000). Similarly, macaque monkeys raised by foster mothers exhibit social behaviors that resemble their biological, rather than foster, mothers (Maestripieri, 2003). Add all this to the finding that identical twins are about as similar as we would expect from their shared genes, whether they grow up together or apart, and the effect of a shared rearing environment seems shockingly modest.

What we have here is perhaps "the most important puzzle in the history of psychology," contends Steven Pinker (2002): Why are children in the same family so different? (Even biological siblings tend to be strikingly different.) Why do the shared genes and the shared family environment (the family's social class, the parents' personalities and marital status, day care versus home care, the neighborhood) have so little discernible effect on children's personalities? Is it because each sibling nevertheless has differing experiences—differing peer influences and life events? Is it because sibling relationships ricochet off each other, amplifying their differences? Is it because siblings—despite sharing half their genes—have very different combinations of genes? Does parental influence therefore affect an easygoing child one way, an emotionally reactive child another? "Child-rearing is not something a parent does to a child," notes Judith Rich Harris (1998). "It is something the parent and the child do together. . . . I would have been pegged as a permissive parent with my first child, a bossy one with my second."

So is adoptive parenting a fruitless venture? No. The genetic leash may limit the family environment's influence on personality, but parents do influence their children's attitudes, values, manners, faith, and politics (Brodzinsky & Schechter, 1990). A pair of adopted children or identical twins *will* have more similar religious beliefs, especially while still at home during adolescence, if reared together (Kelley & De Graaf, 1997; Koenig & others, 2005; Rohan & Zanna, 1996). Parenting matters!

Moreover, in adoptive homes, child neglect and abuse and even parental divorce are rare. (Adoptive parents are carefully screened; natural parents are not.) So it is not surprising that, despite a somewhat greater risk of psychological disorder, most adopted children thrive, especially when adopted as infants (Benson & others, 1994; Wierzbicki, 1993). They score higher than their biological parents on intelligence tests. Seven in eight report feeling strongly attached to one or both adoptive parents. As children of self-giving parents, they grow up to be more self-giving and altruistic than average (Sharma & others, 1998). And they generally become happier and more stable people than they would have been in a stressed or neglectful environment. In one Swedish study, infant adoptees grew up with fewer problems than were experienced by children whose biological mothers had initially registered them for adoption but then decided to raise the children themselves (Bohman & Sigvardsson, 1990). Regardless of personality differences between parents and their adoptees, children benefit from adoption.

Family ties
Studies of adoptive families have provided clues to hereditary and environmental influences. Adopted children share many values and attitudes with their adoptive parents, but adopted children's *personalities* tend to display the genetic legacy of their biological parents.

"Mom may be holding a full house while Dad has a straight flush, yet when Junior gets a random half of each of their cards his poker hand may be a loser."

David Lykken (2001)

The greater uniformity of adoptive homes—mostly healthy, nurturing homes—helps explain the lack of striking differences when comparing child outcomes of different adoptive homes (Stoolmiller, 1999).

■ **temperament** a person's characteristic emotional reactivity and intensity.

■ **heritability** the proportion of variation among individuals that we can attribute to genes. The heritability of a trait may vary, depending on the range of populations and environments studied.

Temperament Studies

OBJECTIVE 6 | Discuss how the relative stability of our temperament illustrates the influence of heredity on development.

As most parents will tell you after having their second child, babies differ even before gulping their first breath. Consider one quickly apparent aspect of personality. An infant's **temperament** is its emotional excitability—whether reactive, intense, and fidgety, or easygoing, quiet, and placid. From the first weeks of life, *difficult* babies are more irritable, intense, and unpredictable. *Easy* babies are cheerful, relaxed, and predictable in feeding and sleeping (Chess & Thomas, 1987).

Parents, being keenly sensitive to their children's differences, perceive their temperaments as even more different than they are (Saudino & others, 2004). Yet actual temperament differences do exist and do persist. Consider these findings:

- The most emotionally reactive newborns tend also to be the most reactive 9-month-olds (Wilson & Matheny, 1986; Worobey & Blajda, 1989).
- Four-month-olds who react to changing scenes with arched back, pumping legs, and crying are usually fearful and inhibited in their second year. Those who react with relaxed smiles are usually fearless and sociable in their second year (Kagan, 1990).
- Exceptionally inhibited and fearful 2-year-olds often are still relatively shy as 8-year-olds; about half will become introverted adolescents (Kagan & others, 1992, 1994).
- The most emotionally intense preschoolers tend to be relatively intense as young adults (Larsen & Diener, 1987). In one ongoing study of more than 900 New Zealanders, emotionally reactive and impulsive 3-year-olds have developed into somewhat more impulsive, aggressive, and conflict-prone 21-year-olds (Caspi, 2000).

Compared with fraternal twins, identical twins have more similar temperaments, indicating that heredity may predispose temperament differences (Emde & others, 1992; Gabbay, 1992; Robinson & others, 1992). Another line of evidence comes from physiological tests which reveal that anxious, inhibited infants have high and variable heart rates and a reactive nervous system, and that they become more physiologically aroused when facing new or strange situations (Kagan & Snidman, 2004). Such evidence adds to the emerging conclusion that our biologically rooted temperament helps form our enduring personality (McCrae & others, 2000; Rothbart & others, 2000).

"Oh, he's cute, all right, but he's got the temperament of a car alarm."

Heritability

OBJECTIVE 7 | Discuss heritability's application to individuals and groups, and explain what we mean when we say genes are *self-regulating*.

Using the twin and adoption methods, behavior geneticists can mathematically estimate the **heritability** of a trait—the extent to which variation among individuals can be attributed to their differing genes. As Chapter 11 will emphasize, if the heritability of intelligence is, say, 50 percent, this does *not* mean that your intelligence is 50 percent genetic. (If the heritability of height is 90 percent, this does not mean that a 60-inch-tall woman can credit her genes for 54 inches and her environment for the other 6 inches.) Rather, it means that we can attribute to genetic influence 50 percent of the observed variation among people. This point is so often misunderstood that I repeat: We can never say what percentage of an *individual's* personality or intelligence is inherited. It makes no sense to say that your personality is due *x* percent to your heredity and *y* percent to your environment. Heritability refers instead to the extent to which *differences among people* are attributable to genes.

Even this conclusion must be qualified, because heritability can vary from study to study. If we were to follow humorist Mark Twain's (1835–1910) proposal to raise boys in barrels to age 12, feeding them through a hole, they would emerge with lower-than-normal intelligence scores. Yet, given their equal environments, their individual IQ score differences at age 12 could be explained only by their heredity. In other words, heritability for their differences would be near 100 percent. *As environments become more similar, heredity as a source of differences necessarily becomes more important.* If all schools were of uniform quality, all families equally loving, and all neighborhoods equally healthy, heritability—differences due to genes— would *increase* (because differences due to environment would decrease). At the other extreme, if all people had similar heredities but were raised in drastically different environments (some in barrels, some in luxury homes), heritability would be much lower.

"The title of my science project is 'My Little Brother: Nature or Nurture.'"

Group Differences

If genetic influences help explain individual diversity in traits such as aggressiveness, can the same be said of group differences between men and women, or between people of different races? Not necessarily. Individual differences in height and weight, for example, are highly heritable; yet nutritional rather than genetic influences explain why, as a group, today's adults are taller and heavier than those of a century ago. The two groups differ, but not because human genes have changed in a mere century's eyeblink of time.

As with height and weight, so with personality and intelligence scores: Heritable individual differences need not imply heritable group differences. If some *individuals* are genetically disposed to be more aggressive than others, that doesn't explain why some *groups* are more aggressive than others. Putting people in a new social context can change their aggressiveness. Today's peaceful Scandinavians carry many genes inherited from their Viking ancestors.

Nature *and* Nurture

Among our similarities, the most important—the behavioral hallmark of our species— is an enormous adaptive capacity. Some human traits, such as having two eyes, develop the same in virtually every environment. But most psychologically interesting traits are expressed in particular environments. We all are driven to eat, but depending on our culturally learned tastes, we may have a yen for fish eyes, black bean salad, or chicken legs. Go barefoot for a summer and you will develop toughened, callused feet—a biological adaptation to friction. Meanwhile, your shod neighbor will remain a tenderfoot. The difference between the two of you is, of course, an effect of environment. But it is also the product of a biological mechanism. Our shared biology enables our developed diversity (Buss, 1991).

An analogy may help: Genes and environment—nature and nurture—work together like two hands clapping. Genes not only code for particular proteins, they also respond to environments. An African butterfly that is green in summer turns brown in fall, thanks to a temperature-controlled genetic switch. "The genome is giving the butterfly two different choices, two different opportunities. It's not dictating, 'You must take this form,'" Gary Marcus (2004) explains. "It's saying, 'If you're in this situation you can take this form, if you're in this other situation you can take this other form.'" Thus, genes are *self-regulating*. Rather than acting as blueprints that

> " Men's natures are alike; it is their habits that carry them far apart."
>
> Confucius, *Analects*, 500 BC

lead to the same result no matter the context, genes react. People with identical genes but differing experiences therefore have similar though not identical minds. One twin may fall in love with someone quite different from the co-twin's love. And, as we will see in Chapter 16, at least one known gene will, in response to major life stresses, code for a protein that controls neurotransmitter functions underlying depression. By itself, the gene doesn't cause depression, but it is part of the recipe.

Thus, asking whether your personality is more a product of your genes or your environment is like asking whether water's wetness is due more to its hydrogen or its oxygen, or whether the area of a field is more the result of its length or its width. We could, however, ask whether the *differing* areas of various fields are more the result of differences in their length or width and whether person-to-person personality *differences* are influenced more by nature or nurture. For psychological phenomena, human differences are nearly always the result of both genetic and environmental influences. Thus (to give a preview of coming attractions), eating disorders are genetically influenced: Some individuals are more at risk than others. But culture also bends the twig, for eating disorders are primarily a contemporary Western cultural phenomenon.

> "Genes are as important to the brain as sparking plugs are to car engines, but there is a big difference between something being necessary and sufficient. The potential of a sparking plug is only realized when it is placed in an engine, the engine is in a car, and the car has a driver."
>
> Neuroscientist Susan Greenfield, "Alcohol on the Brain," 2002

Gene-Environment Interaction

OBJECTIVE **8** | Give an example of a genetically influenced trait that can evoke responses in others, and give another example of an environment that can trigger gene activity.

To say that genes and experience are *both* important is true. But more precisely, they interact. Imagine two babies, one genetically predisposed to be attractive, sociable, and easygoing, the other less so. Assume further that the first baby attracts more affectionate and stimulating care than the second and so develops into a warmer and more outgoing person. As the two children grow older, the more naturally outgoing child more often seeks activities and friends that encourage further social confidence.

> "Heredity deals the cards; environment plays the hand."
>
> Psychologist Charles L. Brewer (1990)

What has caused their resulting personality differences? Neither heredity nor experience dances alone. Environments trigger gene activity. And our genetically influenced traits *evoke* significant responses in others. Thus, a child's impulsivity and aggression may evoke an angry response from a teacher who reacts warmly to the child's model classmates. Parents, too, may treat their children differently; one

Gene-environment interaction
People respond differently to a Rowan Atkinson (here playing Mr. Bean) than to fellow actor Orlando Bloom.

child elicits punishment, another does not. In such cases, the child's nature and the parents' nurture interact. Neither operates apart from the other. Gene and scene dance together.

Evocative interactions may help explain why identical twins reared in different families recall their parents' warmth as remarkably similar—almost as similar as if they had had the same parents (Plomin & others, 1988, 1991, 1994). Fraternal twins recall greater variations in their early family life—even if reared in the same family! "Children experience us as different parents, depending on their own qualities," notes Sandra Scarr (1990). Moreover, as we grow older we also *select* environments well suited to our natures.

So, from conception onward, we are the product of a cascade of **interactions** between our genetic predispositions and our surrounding environments. Our genes affect how people react to and influence us. Biological appearances have social consequences. Asking whether genes or experiences are more important is therefore like asking whether an engine or a steering wheel is more important for driving a car. So, forget nature *versus* nurture; think nurture *via* nature.

The New Frontier: Molecular Genetics

OBJECTIVE 9 | Identify the potential promise and perils of molecular genetics research.

Behavior geneticists have progressed beyond asking, "Do genes influence behavior?" The new frontier of behavior-genetics research is the "bottom-up" **molecular genetics** quest to identify *specific genes* influencing behavior. As psychologist Robert Plomin (1997) observes, "The DNA train [is] pulling out of the station," and psychologists are climbing aboard.

As we have already seen, most human traits are influenced by teams of genes. For example, twin and adoption studies tell us that heredity influences body weight, but there is no single "obesity gene." More likely, some genes influence how quickly the stomach tells the brain, "I'm full." Others might dictate how much fuel the muscles need, how many calories are burned off by fidgeting, and how efficiently the body converts the extra calories into fat (Vogel, 1999). The goal of molecular behavior genetics is to find some of the many genes that influence normal human traits, such as body weight, sexual orientation, and extraversion.

Genetic tests can now reveal at-risk populations for at least a dozen diseases. The search continues in labs worldwide, where molecular geneticists are teaming with psychologists to pinpoint genes that put people at risk for such genetically influenced disorders as learning disabilities, depression, schizophrenia, aggressiveness, and alcoholism. In Chapter 16, for example, we will take note of a worldwide research effort to sleuth the genes that make one vulnerable to the emotional swings of bipolar disorder (formerly known as manic-depressive disorder). To tease out the implicated genes, molecular geneticists seek links between certain genes or chromosome segments and specific disorders. First, they find families that have had the disorder across several generations. Then they draw blood or take cheek swabs from both affected and unaffected family members and examine their DNA, looking for differences. "The most powerful potential for DNA," note Robert Plomin and John Crabbe (2000), "is to predict risk so that steps can be taken to prevent problems before they happen."

Aided by inexpensive DNA-scanning techniques, medical personnel may soon be able to give would-be parents a readout on how their fetus' genes differ from the normal pattern and what this might mean. With this benefit come risks. Might labeling a fetus, for example, "at risk for a learning disorder" lead to discrimination?

> "We predict that DNA will revolutionize psychological research and treatment early in the twenty-first century."
>
> Robert Plomin and John Crabbe (2000)

■ **interaction** the effect of one factor (such as environment) depends on another factor (such as heredity).

■ **molecular genetics** the subfield of biology that studies the molecular structure and function of genes.

"I thought that sperm-bank donors remained anonymous."

Prenatal screening poses ethical dilemmas. In China and India, where boys are highly valued, testing for an offspring's sex has enabled selective abortions resulting in millions—yes, millions—of "missing women." A new technique for sorting sperm carrying male or female chromosomes can provide expectant parents a reasonable chance of success at choosing a child's sex before conception.

Blueprints for "designer babies" are, of course, constrained by the reality that it takes many genes to influence behavior in combination with complex environments. But assuming it were possible, should prospective parents take their eggs and sperm to a genetics lab for screening before combining them to produce an embryo? Before scoffing at this possibility, recall that a quarter century ago people were horrified at the prospect of in vitro fertilization ("test-tube" conception). Today, infertile couples demand it. A half-century ago, people worried about the kind of control that novelist Aldous Huxley imagined in his *Brave New World,* in which government social engineers bred hothouse babies genetically assigned to roles, such as clever "Alphas" and dim-witted "Epsilons." In today's more plausible new world, notes Robert Wright (1999), millions of parents will freely select for health, and perhaps for brains, beauty, and athleticism. But as always, progress is a two-edged sword, raising both hopeful possibilities and difficult problems. By selecting out certain traits, we may deprive ourselves of future Handels and van Goghs, Churchills and Lincolns, Tolstoys and Dickinsons—troubled people all.

>> LEARNING OUTCOMES

Behavior Genetics: Predicting Individual Differences

OBJECTIVE **1** | **Give examples of differences and similarities within the human family.**

We humans differ from and resemble one another in many ways. We differ in personality, interests, physical appearance, family background, culture, and native language. Our similarities include our biological heritage and needs, our shared brain architecture, our ability to use language, the senses with which we explore the world around us, and our social behaviors.

OBJECTIVE **2** | **Describe the types of questions that interest behavior geneticists.**

Behavior geneticists are especially interested in the extent to which genetics and environment influence our behavior, creating individual differences. In this context, *environment* means every external, nongenetic aspect of our lives, from prenatal nutrition to the people and things around us now.

OBJECTIVE **3** | **Define *chromosome, DNA, gene,* and *genome,* and describe their relationships.**

We have 46 chromosomes in each cell—23 from our mother and 23 from our father. *Chromosomes* are threadlike structures made of *DNA,* a spiraling complex molecule containing genes. Our approximately 30,000 *genes* are DNA segments that, when "turned on" (expressed) form templates for the creation of various protein molecules, the building blocks of our physical and behavioral development. A *genome* is an organism's genetic profile—the complete set of instructions for making that organism, consisting of all the genetic material in its chromosomes. Combinations of variations at particular gene sites help define our differences. Most human traits are influenced by many genes acting together, not by the influence of a single gene acting alone.

OBJECTIVE **4** | **Explain how identical and fraternal twins differ, and cite ways that behavior geneticists use twin studies to understand the effects of environment and heredity.**

Identical twins develop from one egg that splits after being fertilized. They share the same set of genes, a similar prenatal environment, and—usually—the same family and culture after birth. *Fraternal twins* develop from separate fertilized eggs and share a prenatal environment, family, and social-cultural environment after birth, so they are genetically no more similar than any other two siblings. When some trait (such as extraversion) is present in both members of identical twin pairs but in only one member of fraternal twin pairs, researchers have a clue that heredity may be important in the development of that trait. Such comparisons are especially rich sources of information when twins have been separated at (or shortly after) birth, letting researchers see more clearly the effects of heredity in different environments.

OBJECTIVE **5** | **Cite ways that behavior geneticists use adoption studies to understand the effects of environment and heredity.**

Adopted children carry the genetic inheritance from their biological parents into an environment created by their adoptive families. Similarities between the child and the biological relatives give clues to the influence of heredity. Similarities between the child and the adoptive relatives give clues to the influence of environment. Adopted children tend to resemble their biological parents in their personality (their characteristic pattern of thinking, feeling, and acting), and their adoptive parents in their values, attitudes, manners, faith, and politics.

OBJECTIVE 6 | Discuss how the relative stability of our temperament illustrates the influence of heredity on development.

Temperament, a person's characteristic level of emotional reactivity and intensity, is apparent soon after birth and tends to continue relatively unchanged into adulthood. This suggests that heredity plays a much larger role than environment in the development of temperament.

OBJECTIVE 7 | Discuss heritability's application to individuals and groups, and explain what we mean when we say genes are *self-regulating*.

Heritability describes the extent to which variation among individuals can be attributed to genes. It applies only to differences *among individuals*—never to any one person. In an imaginary experiment that could create identical environments, any observed differences (in, for example, weight) among people would be the result of their heredity, and heritability would be 100 percent for that trait. Heritable individual differences in traits such as height or intelligence need not explain *group* differences. Genes mostly explain why some are taller than others, but not why people today are taller than a century ago. Saying that genes are *self-regulating* means that genes are not blueprints; they can react differently in different environments.

OBJECTIVE 8 | Give an example of a genetically influenced trait that can evoke responses in others, and give another example of an environment that can trigger gene activity.

Some human traits (such as having two eyes) develop in any environment, but many important psychological traits are a product of the interaction of our genetic predispositions and our surrounding environment. For example, a genetic predisposition that causes a child to be restless and hyperactive can evoke angry responses from parents or teachers. And a stressful environment can trigger genes that affect the production of neurotransmitters contributing to depression.

OBJECTIVE 9 | Identify the potential promise and perils of molecular genetics research.

Molecular geneticists study the molecular structure and function of genes in search of those that influence behaviors. Psychologists and molecular geneticists are cooperating in a search to identify specific genes—or more often, teams of genes—that put people at risk for disorders. Knowledge of such links will enable medical personnel to inform expectant parents of some situations in which a fetus deviates from normal patterns. The ethical implications of such choices will be debated if parents choose to abort children who do not conform to their image of an ideal child.

ASK YOURSELF: Would you want genetic tests on your unborn offspring, in the uterus? What would you do if you knew your child would be destined for hemophilia? A learning disability? Would society benefit or lose if such embryos were aborted?

Evolutionary Psychology: Understanding Human Nature

OBJECTIVE 10 | Describe the area of psychology that interests evolutionary psychologists.

Molecular genetics involves a here-and-now way to select for certain behaviors and traits that make individuals distinct. **Evolutionary psychologists** instead focus mostly on what makes us so much alike as humans. To understand how these principles work, let's first consider a straightforward example in foxes.

Natural Selection

OBJECTIVE 11 | State the principle of natural selection, and point out some possible effects of natural selection in the development of human characteristics.

A fox is a wild and wary animal. If you capture a fox and try to befriend it, be careful. Stick your hand in the cage and, if the timid fox cannot flee, it probably will make a snack of your fingers. Familiar with foxes, Dmitry Belyaev, of the Russian Academy of Science's Institute of Cytology and Genetics, wondered how our human ancestors had domesticated dogs from their equally wild wolf forebears. Might he, within a

■ **evolutionary psychology** the study of the evolution of behavior and the mind, using principles of natural selection.

L.N. Trut, *American Scientist* (1999) 87: 160–169

From beast to beauty
More than 40 years into the fox-breeding experiment, most of the offspring are devoted, affectionate, and capable of forming strong bonds with people.

comparatively short stretch of time, accomplish a similar feat by transforming the fearful fox into a friendly fox?

To find out, Belyaev set to work with 30 male and 100 female foxes. From their offspring he selected and mated the tamest 5 percent of males and 20 percent of females. (He measured tameness by the foxes' responses to attempts to feed, handle, and stroke them.) Over more than 30 generations of foxes, Belyaev and his successor, Lyudmila Trut, repeated that simple procedure. Today, more than 40 years and 45,000 foxes later, they have a new breed of foxes that, in Trut's (1999) words, are "docile, eager to please, and unmistakably domesticated. . . . Before our eyes, 'the Beast' has turned into 'beauty,' as the aggressive behavior of our herd's wild [ancestors] entirely disappeared." So friendly and eager for human contact are they, so inclined to whimper to attract attention and to lick people like affectionate cats, that the cash-strapped institute seized on a way to raise funds—marketing its foxes to people as house pets.

As Belyaev and Trut demonstrated, when certain traits are *selected*—by conferring a reproductive advantage to an individual or a species—those traits, over time, will prevail. Over many generations, wild wolves can become tame dogs, and wary foxes can have cuddly descendants. Dog breeders, as Robert Plomin and his colleagues (1997) remind us, have given us sheepdogs that herd, retrievers that retrieve, trackers that track, and pointers that point. Psychologists, too, have bred dogs, mice, and rats whose genes predispose them to be serene or reactive, quick learners or slow learners.

In life outside the laboratory, the same selection process confers an advantage on other organisms. Deep in the sea, many years ago, a mutant shark with keener-than-normal smell was able to find more prey, enabling it to live longer and leave more offspring. As nature continued over countless generations to give an edge to sharks best suited to their ecological niche, an exquisitely effective predator came into being. A much smaller predator has developed in your lifetime. Bacteria that resist a hospital's antibiotics will multiply rapidly, as less-resistant bacteria die off. Over time, the natural result has been many hospitals plagued by antibiotic-resistant bacteria.

Does **natural selection** also explain our human tendencies? Nature has indeed selected advantageous variations from among the **mutations** (random errors in gene replication) and the new gene combinations produced at each human conception. Do we, as suggested earlier, fear snakes and heights because our ancestors who feared them were more likely to survive and spread their genes?

Perhaps. But the tight genetic leash that predisposes a dog's retrieving, a cat's pouncing, or an ant's nest building is looser on humans. The genes selected during our ancestral history provide more than a long leash; they endow us with a great capacity to learn and therefore to adapt to life in varied environments, from the tundra to the jungle. Genes and experience together wire the brain. Our adaptive flexibility in responding to different environments contributes to our fitness—our ability to survive and reproduce.

Yet in the big picture, our lives are remarkably alike. Visit the international arrivals area at London's Heathrow Airport, a world hub where arriving passengers meet their excited loved ones. There you will see the same delighted joy in the faces of Jamaican grandmothers, Chinese children, and homecoming Britons. Although human differences grab our attention, our deep similarities also demand explanation. Evolutionary psychologist Steven Pinker (2002, p. 73) believes our shared human traits "were shaped by natural selection acting over the course of human evolution." No wonder, then, that our emotions, drives, and reasoning "have a common logic across cultures."

Our behavioral and biological similarities arise from our shared human genome. No more than 5 percent of the genetic differences among humans arise from population group differences. Some 95 percent of genetic variation exists

■ **natural selection** the principle that, among the range of inherited trait variations, those that lead to increased reproduction and survival will most likely be passed on to succeeding generations.

■ **mutation** a random error in gene replication that leads to a change.

within populations (Rosenberg & others, 2002). The typical genetic difference between two Icelandic villagers or between two Kenyans is much greater than the *average* difference between the two groups. Thus, noted geneticist Richard Lewontin (1982), if after a worldwide catastrophe only Icelanders or Kenyans survived, the human species would suffer only "a trivial reduction" in its genetic diversity.

Why are we all so much alike? At the dawn of human history, our ancestors faced certain questions: Who is my ally, who my foe? What food should I eat? With whom should I mate? Some individuals answered those questions more successfully than others. For example, some women's experience of nausea in the critical first three months of pregnancy predisposes their avoiding certain bitter, strongly flavored, and novel foods. Avoiding such foods has survival value, since they are the very foods most often toxic to embryonic development (Schmitt & Pilcher, 2004). Those disposed to eat nourishing rather than poisonous food survived to contribute their genes to later generations. Those who deemed leopards "nice to pet" often did not.

Similarly successful were those who mated with someone with whom they could produce and nurture offspring. Over generations, the genes of individuals not so disposed tended to be lost from the human gene pool. As further mutations occurred, genes providing an adaptive edge continued to be selected. The result, say evolutionary psychologists, is behavioral tendencies and thinking and learning capacities that prepared our Stone Age ancestors to survive, reproduce, and send their genes into the future. Nature selected the fittest adaptations, which also include the human diversity that allows Arctic and equatorial dwellers to thrive in their distinct environments.

As inheritors of this prehistoric genetic legacy, we are predisposed to behave in ways that promoted our ancestors' surviving and reproducing. We love the taste of sweets and fats, which once were hard to come by but which prepared our ancestors to survive famines. Ironically, with famine rare in Western cultures, and sweets and fats beckoning us from store shelves, fast-food outlets, and vending machines, obesity has become a growing problem. Our natural dispositions, rooted deep in history, are mismatched with today's junk-food environment (Colarelli & Dettman, 2003). We are, in some ways, biologically prepared for a world that no longer exists.

Evolution has been an organizing principle for biology for a long time. Jared Diamond (2001) notes that "virtually no contemporary scientists believe that Darwin was basically wrong." Darwin's theory lives on as an organizing principle for biology and, more recently, in "the second Darwinian revolution," in psychology. Charles Darwin (1859) anticipated this application of evolutionary principles to psychology. In concluding *On the Origin of Species,* he foresaw "open fields for far more important researches. Psychology will be based on a new foundation" (p. 346).

Evolutionary psychologists are now exploring such questions as these:

- Why do infants start to fear strangers about the time they become mobile?
- Why are biological fathers so much less likely than unrelated boyfriends to abuse and murder the children with whom they share a home?
- Why are most parents so passionately devoted to their children?
- Why do so many more people have phobias about spiders and snakes than about more dangerous threats, such as guns and electricity?
- How are men and women alike? How and why do men and women differ? For example, why are men quicker than women to perceive friendliness as sexual interest, to initiate sexual relations, and to feel jealous rage over a mate's having sex with someone else?

To see how evolutionary psychologists think and reason, let's pause to explore this last question: How—and why, according to evolutionary psychology—do women's and men's sexuality differ?

Those who are troubled by an apparent conflict between scientific and religious accounts of human origins may find it helpful to recall (Chapter 1) that different perspectives of life can be complementary. For example, the scientific account attempts to tell us *when* and *how*; religious creation stories usually aim to tell about an ultimate *who* and *why*. As Galileo explained to the Grand Duchess Christina, "The Bible teaches how to go to heaven, not how the heavens go."

■ **gender** in psychology, the biologically and socially influenced characteristics by which people define *male* and *female*.

An Evolutionary Explanation of Human Sexuality

Gender Differences in Sexuality

OBJECTIVE **12** | Identify some gender differences in sexuality.

Having faced many similar challenges throughout history, men and women have adapted in similar ways. Whether male or female, we eat the same foods, fear the same heights, avoid the same predators, and perceive, learn, and remember similarly. It is only in those domains where we have faced differing adaptive challenges—most obviously in behaviors related to reproduction—that we differ, say evolutionary psychologists. And differ we do, report psychologists Roy Baumeister, Kathleen Catanese, and Kathleen Vohs (2001). They invite us to consider whether women or men have the stronger sex drive. Who desires more frequent sex, thinks more about sex, masturbates more often, initiates more sex, and makes more sacrifices to gain sex? The answers, they report, are men, men, men, men, and men. Indeed, "with few exceptions anywhere in the world," agree cross-cultural psychologist Marshall Segall and his colleagues (1990, p. 244), "males are more likely than females to initiate sexual activity." This difference is among the largest of **gender** differences in sexuality, but there are others:

- In a 2004 survey of 289,452 entering U.S. college students, 60 percent of men but only 35 percent of women agreed that "if two people really like each other, it's all right for them to have sex even if they've known each other for a very short time" (Sax & others, 2004). "I can imagine myself being comfortable and enjoying 'casual' sex with different partners," agreed 48 percent of men and 12 percent of women in another survey of 4901 Australians (Bailey & others, 2000).
- In one careful survey of 3432 U.S. 18- to 59-year-olds, 48 percent of the women but only 25 percent of the men cited affection as a reason for first intercourse. And how often do they think about sex? "Every day" or "several times a day," acknowledged 19 percent of the women and 54 percent of the men (Laumann & others, 1994).
- Such gender differences characterize both heterosexual and homosexual people. Gay men report more interest in uncommitted sex, more responsiveness to visual sexual stimuli, and more concern with their partner's physical attractiveness than do lesbians (Bailey & others, 1994). Compared with their gay male counterparts, American lesbians are nearly twice as likely to have partners (24 percent versus 47 percent, respectively [Doyle, 2005]).

"It's not that gay men are oversexed; they are simply men whose male desires bounce off other male desires rather than off female desires."

Steven Pinker, *How the Mind Works*, 1997

Gender differences in attitudes extend to differences in behavior. Casual, impulsive sex is most frequent among males with traditional masculine attitudes (Pleck & others, 1993). Russell Clark and Elaine Hatfield (1989) observed this striking gender difference in 1978 when they sent some average-looking student research assistants strolling across the Florida State University quadrangle. Spotting an attractive person of the other sex, a researcher would approach and say, "I have been noticing you around campus and I find you to be very attractive. Would you go to bed with me tonight?" The women all declined, some obviously irritated ("What's wrong with you, creep! Leave me alone"). But 75 percent of the men readily agreed, often replying with comments such as "Why do we have to wait until tonight?" Somewhat astonished by their result, Clark and Hatfield repeated their study in 1982 and twice more during the late-1980s U.S. AIDS era (Clark, 1990). Each time, virtually no women, but half or more of the men, agreed to go to bed with a stranger.

Men also have a lower threshold for perceiving warm responses as a sexual come-on. In study after study, men more often than women attribute a woman's friendliness to sexual interest (Abbey, 1987; Johnson & others, 1991). Misattributing women's cordiality as a come-on helps explain, but does not excuse, men's greater sexual assertiveness (Kenrick & Trost, 1987). The unfortunate results can range from sexual harassment to date rape.

Natural Selection and Mating Preferences

OBJECTIVE **13** | Describe evolutionary explanations for gender differences in sexuality.

As biologists use natural selection to explain the mating behaviors of many species, so evolutionary psychologists use natural selection to explain women's more relational and men's more recreational approaches to sex. Their explanation goes like this: While a woman normally incubates and nurses one infant, a male can spread his genes through other females. Our natural yearnings are our genes' way of reproducing themselves. In our ancestral history, women most often sent their genes into the future by pairing wisely, men by pairing widely. "Humans are living fossils—collections of mechanisms produced by prior selection pressures," says evolutionary psychologist David Buss (1995).

And what do heterosexual men and women find attractive in the other sex? Some aspects of attractiveness cross place and time. Men in 37 cultures, from Australia to Zambia, judge women as more attractive if they have a youthful appearance. Evolutionary psychologists say that men who were drawn to healthy, fertile-appearing women—women with smooth skin and a youthful shape suggesting many childbearing years to come—stood a better chance of sending their genes into the future. Regardless of cultural variations in ideal weight, men everywhere feel most attracted to women whose waists are roughly a third narrower than their hips—a sign of future fertility (Singh, 1993).

Women also feel attracted to healthy-looking men, but especially to those who seem mature, dominant, bold, and affluent (Singh, 1995). Such attributes, say the evolutionary psychologists, connote a capacity to support and protect (Buss, 1996, 2000; Geary, 1998). Some 150 studies of gender and risk taking reveal that in 14 of 16 realms (including intellectual risk taking, physical skills, smoking, and sex) men are the greater risk takers (Byrnes & others, 1999). They also tend to be more optimistic about the stock market and more aggressive in trading stocks (Jacobe, 2003; Myers, 2002). In explaining why 16- to 24-year-old men show more bravado—and are therefore nearly three times more likely than young women to die in auto crashes—Victor Nell (2002) speculates that "young men who do crazy things are saying in one voice with the peacock and the buck that prances when the lion approaches, 'Look at me! I have so much strength and skill that I am fearless, I will survive no matter how much I drink or how fast I drive.'"

Evolutionary psychologists note that women also prefer mates with the potential for long-term mating and investment in their joint offspring (Gangestad & Simpson, 2000). They prefer stick-around dads over likely cads. Long-term mates contribute protection and support, which give their offspring greater survival prospects. Thus, for men there are genetic tradeoffs between seeking to distribute one's genes widely and being willing to co-parent.

There is a principle at work here, say evolutionary psychologists: Nature selects behaviors that increase the likelihood of sending one's genes into the future (**FIGURE 3.4,** page 112). As mobile gene machines, we are designed to prefer whatever worked for our ancestors in their environments. They were predisposed to act in ways that would leave grandchildren—had they not been, we wouldn't be here. And as carriers of their genetic legacy, we are similarly predisposed.

Canada's famed Starbuck Holstein bull sired more than 200,000 offspring.

"I had a nice time, Steve. Would you like to come in, settle down, and raise a family?"

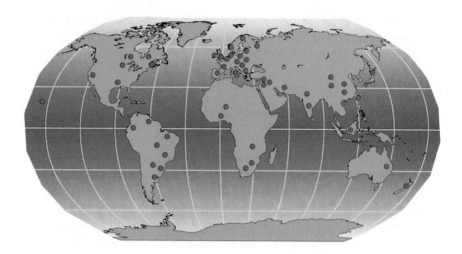

FIGURE 3.4
Worldwide mating preferences
If men more than women prefer attractive physical features suggesting youth and health—and reproductive potential—and if women more than men prefer mates with resources and social status, we can credit (or blame) natural selection. (The red dots indicate the 37 cultures studied [Buss, 1994].)

Critiquing the Evolutionary Perspective

OBJECTIVE 14 | Summarize the criticisms of evolutionary explanations of human behaviors, and describe the evolutionary psychologists' responses to those criticisms.

Without disputing nature's selection of traits that enhance gene survival, critics see problems with evolutionary psychology. It often, they say, starts with an effect (such as the gender sexuality difference) and works backward to propose an explanation. So let's imagine a different observation and reason backward. If men were uniformly loyal to their mates, might we not reason that the children of committed, supportive fathers more often survived to perpetuate their genes? Might not men also be better off bonded to one woman—both to increase the otherwise slim odds of impregnation and to keep her from the advances of competing men? Might not a ritualized bond—a marriage—also spare women from chronic male harassment? Such suggestions are, in fact, evolutionary explanations for why humans tend to pair off monogamously.

Lynn Carol Miller and her colleagues (2002) note, for example, that more men than women desire multiple sexual partners, but the things men and women seek in a mate "are remarkably similar." And what about those species, such as common bonobo chimpanzees, in which ardent females mate with numerous males? Does this ensure that the males, not knowing the true paternity of a female's offspring, will join in tolerating or protecting them? One can hardly lose at hindsight explanation, which is, said paleontologist Stephen Jay Gould (1997), mere "speculation [and] guesswork in the cocktail party mode."

Some worry about the social consequences of evolutionary psychology. Does it suggest a genetic determinism that strikes at the heart of progressive efforts to re-make society (Rose, 1999)? Does it undercut ethical theory and moral responsibility? Could it be used to rationalize "high-status men marrying a series of young, fertile women" (Looy, 2001)? Much of who we are is *not* hard-wired (which evolutionary psychologists do not dispute). Cultural expectations bend the genders, and what's considered attractive does vary somewhat with time and place. The voluptuous Marilyn Monroe ideal of the 1950s has been replaced by the turn-of-the-century leaner, athletic female image. Moreover, if socialized to value lifelong commitment, men may sexually bond with one partner; if socialized to accept casual sex, women may willingly have sex with many partners.

To some extent, gender differences in mate preferences are universal across cultures. But gender differences do vary within a culture's social and family structures. Show Alice Eagly and Wendy Wood (1999; Wood & Eagly, 2002) a culture with gender inequality—where men are providers and women are homemakers—and they will show you a culture where men strongly desire youth and domestic skill in their potential mates, and where women seek status and earning potential in their mates. Show Eagly and Wood a culture with gender equality, and they will show you a culture with smaller gender differences in mate preferences. They draw their conclusions from an analysis of the same 37 cultures studied earlier by David Buss (1994).

Evolutionary psychologists reassure us that the sexes, having faced similar adaptive problems, are far more alike than different. They stress that humans have a great capacity for learning and social progress. (We come equipped to adapt and survive, whether living in igloos or tree houses.) They point to the coherence and explanatory power of evolutionary principles, especially those offering testable predictions (for example, that we will favor others to the extent they share our genes or can later reciprocate our favors). And they remind us that the study of how we came to be who we are need not dictate how we ought to act. Sometimes understanding our propensities helps us overcome them.

>> Learning Outcomes

Evolutionary Psychology: Understanding Human Nature

OBJECTIVE 10 | Describe the area of psychology that interests evolutionary psychologists.
Evolutionary psychologists attempt to understand how natural selection has shaped behaviors found throughout the human species.

OBJECTIVE 11 | State the principle of natural selection, and point out some possible effects of natural selection in the development of human characteristics.
The principle of natural selection states that, among the range of possible variations in an inherited trait, the variations most likely to be passed on to future generations are those that increase the odds of reproducing and surviving. Genes that enabled a capacity to learn and to adapt had survival value for our ancestors, as did those that prepared people to survive in feast-or-famine conditions. We suffer the effects of famine less often, thanks to modern technology, but with a genetic legacy that causes us to store fat and a decrease in rigorous exercise, we become obese. Charles Darwin, whose theory of evolution has for a long time been an organizing principle in biology, anticipated the contemporary application of evolutionary principles in psychology.

OBJECTIVE 12 | Identify some gender differences in sexuality.
Gender refers to the biologically and socially influenced characteristics by which we define *male* and *female*. Men and women differ in their attitudes toward sex: Men are more approving of casual sex, think about sex more often, and are more likely to misinterpret friendliness as sexual interest. Women are more likely to cite affection as a reason for first intercourse and to have a relational view of sexual activity. Similar differences appear in sexual behavior. Men masturbate more often, initiate sexual activity more frequently, and make more sacrifices to gain sex.

OBJECTIVE 13 | Describe evolutionary explanations for gender differences in sexuality.
Applying principles of natural selection, evolutionary psychologists interpret human sexual behavior in terms of its survival value—the tendency for behaviors to be selected if they increase the likelihood of sending one's genes into the future. Thus, being attracted to multiple healthy, fertile-appearing partners increases men's chances of spreading their genes widely and reproducing. Because women incubate and nurse babies, they increase their own and their children's chances of survival by searching for mates with economic resources and social status, who have the potential for long-term mating and investment in their joint offspring.

OBJECTIVE 14 | Summarize the criticisms of evolutionary explanations of human behaviors, and describe the evolutionary psychologists' responses to those criticisms.
One criticism is that evolutionary psychologists start with an effect and work backward to an explanation. Another is that the evolutionary perspective underestimates cultural expectations and socialization. A third is that the evolutionary viewpoint absolves people from taking ethical and moral responsibility for their sexual behavior. Evolutionary psychologists respond that understanding our predispositions can help us overcome them. They also cite the value of testable predictions based on evolutionary principles, as well as the coherence and explanatory power of those principles.

ASK YOURSELF: Whose reasoning do you find most persuasive—that of evolutionary psychologists or their critics? Why?

Parents and Peers

We have seen how our genes, as expressed in specific environments, influence our developmental differences. But what about the part of us that is *not* hard wired? If we are formed by nature *via* nurture, what are the most influential components of our nurture? How do our prenatal environment, our early experiences, our family, our friends, and our culture guide our development and contribute to our diversity?

Parents and Early Experiences

The formative nurture that conspires with nature begins at conception, with the prenatal environment. After birth, it extends into our family and peer relationships, and to all our other experiences.

Prenatal Environment

OBJECTIVE 15 | Describe some of the conditions that can affect development before birth.

Nurture begins in the womb, as embryos receive differing nutrition and varying levels of exposure to toxic agents (more on this in Chapter 4). Even identical twins may receive not-so-identical prenatal nurture. Two-thirds of identical twins share the same placenta, and thus a more similar prenatal environment (although one might get a richer blood supply and weigh more at birth). Other identical twins have separate placentas (**FIGURE 3.5**). In this arrangement, one placenta sometimes has a more advantageous placement that provides better nourishment and a better placental barrier against viruses. Early indications are that, compared with same-placenta identical twins, those who develop with separate placentas are somewhat less similar in their psychological traits, such as self-control and social competence (Phelps & others, 1997; Sokol & others, 1995).

FIGURE 3.5

Two placental arrangements in identical twins Identical twins may (a) have separate placentas and blood sources, as do all fraternal twins. Or they may (b) share the same placental blood. Researchers are now studying how this variation predicts later differences between identical twins. (From Davis & others, 1995.)

(a)   (b)

Experience and Brain Development

OBJECTIVE 16 | Describe how experience can modify the brain.

Nurture continues outside the womb, where our early experiences foster brain development. Experience helps develop our brain's neural connections. This early learning prepares our brains for thought and language, and also for later experiences. But how do early experiences leave their "marks" in the brain? Mark Rosenzweig and David Krech reared some young rats in solitary confinement and others in a communal playground (**FIGURE 3.6**). When their brains were then analyzed, the rats who died with the most toys had won. Those living in the enriched environment, which simulated a natural environment, usually developed a heavier and thicker brain cortex.

Rosenzweig (1984; Renner & Rosenzweig, 1987) was so surprised by this discovery that he repeated the experiment several times before publishing his findings. The effects are great enough that, shown brief video clips of rats, you could tell from their activity and curiosity whether their rearing was impoverished or enriched (Renner & Renner, 1993). After rats have been housed for 60 days in enriched environments,

Impoverished environment

Impoverished rat brain cell

Enriched environment

Enriched rat brain cell

FIGURE 3.6

Experience affects brain development

Mark Rosenzweig and David Krech reared rats either alone in an environment without playthings, or with others in an environment enriched with playthings that were changed daily. In 14 of 16 repetitions of this basic experiment, the rats placed in the enriched environment developed significantly more cerebral cortex (relative to the rest of the brain's tissue) than did those in the impoverished environment.

report Bryan Kolb and Ian Whishaw (1998), rats' brain weight increases 7 to 10 percent and the number of synapses mushrooms by about 20 percent—"an extraordinary change!" Such results have motivated improvements in the environments we provide for laboratory, farm, and zoo animals—and for children in institutions.

Several research teams have found that the stimulation of touch or massage benefits infant rats and premature babies (Field, 2001; Field & others, 2004). "Handled" infants of both species gain weight more rapidly and develop faster neurologically. Neonatal intensive care units now apply this finding by giving preemies massage therapy, enabling them to develop faster and go home sooner. William Greenough and his University of Illinois colleagues (1987) further discovered that repeated experiences modify a rat's neural tissue—at the very spot in the brain that processes the experience. After brain maturation provides us with an abundance of neural connections, experience preserves our activated connections while allowing our unused connections to degenerate. The result by puberty is a massive loss of unemployed connections (a process known as *pruning*).

Here, then, at the juncture of nurture and nature, is where a child's enriched environment activates and preserves connections that, given impoverished experiences, might have died off from disuse. There is a biological reality to early childhood education. During early childhood—while the excess connections are still on call—youngsters can most easily master the grammar and accent of another language. Lacking any exposure to written or signed language before adolescence, a person will never master any language (see page 417).

Courtesy of C. Brune

Stringing the circuits young

String musicians who started playing before age 12 have larger and more complex neural circuits controlling the note-making left-hand fingers than do string musicians whose training started later (Elbert & others, 1995).

Likewise, lacking visual experience during the early years, people whose vision is restored by cataract removal never achieve normal perceptions (see page 255). The brain cells normally assigned to vision have died or been diverted to other uses. For us to have optimum brain development, normal stimulation during the early years is critical. The maturing brain seems governed by a rule: Use it or lose it.

The brain's development does not, however, end with childhood. Throughout life our neural tissue is changing. Both nature and nurture sculpt our synapses. Sights and smells, touches and tugs activate and strengthen some neural pathways while others weaken from disuse. Similar to pathways through a forest, less-traveled paths gradually disappear and popular paths are broadened. Our genes dictate our overall brain architecture, but experience directs the details. If a monkey is trained to push a lever with a finger several thousand times a day, the brain tissue that controls the

"Genes and experiences are just two ways of doing the same thing—wiring synapses."

Joseph LeDoux, *The Synaptic Self*, 2002

FIGURE 3.7
A trained brain
A well-learned finger-tapping task activates more motor cortex neurons (orange area, right) than were active in the same brain before training (left). (From Karni & others, 1998.)

finger changes to reflect the experience. Human brains work similarly. Whether learning to keyboard or skateboard, we perform with increasing skill as our brain incorporates the learning (**FIGURE 3.7**).

How Much Credit (or Blame) Do Parents Deserve?

OBJECTIVE **17** | Explain why we should be careful about attributing children's successes and failures to their parents' influence.

It may be scary to realize how risky it is to have and raise children. In procreation, a woman and a man shuffle their gene decks and deal a life-forming hand to their child-to-be, who is then subjected to countless influences beyond their control. Parents, nonetheless, feel enormous satisfaction in their children's successes, and guilt or shame over their failures. They beam over the child who wins an award. They wonder where they went wrong with the child repeatedly called into the principal's office. Freudian psychiatry and psychology have been among the sources of such ideas, by blaming problems from asthma to schizophrenia on "bad mothering." And society reinforces such parent-blaming: Believing that parents shape their offspring as a potter molds clay, people readily praise parents for their children's virtues and blame them for their children's vices. Popular culture has endlessly proclaimed the psychological harm toxic parents inflict on their fragile children. "The major source of human misery" is the "neglected, wounded child" within each of us, claimed author-lecturer John Bradshaw (1990, p. 7).

Even among chimpanzees, when one infant is hurt by another, the victim's mother will often attack the offender's mother (Goodall, 1968).

But do parents really produce future adults with an inner wounded child by being (take your pick from the toxic-parent lists) overbearing—or uninvolved? Pushy—or ineffectual? Overprotective—or distant? Are children really so easily wounded? If so, should we then blame our parents for our failings, and ourselves for our children's failings? Should we pass city ordinances that punish parents for their children's misdeeds? Or does all the talk of wounding fragile children through normal parental mistakes trivialize the brutality of real abuse?

Peter Neubauer and Alexander Neubauer (1990, pp. 20–21) illustrate how, with hindsight, we may inappropriately credit or blame our parents:

> Identical twin men, now age 30, were separated at birth and raised in different countries by their respective adoptive parents. Both kept their lives neat— neat to the point of pathology. Their clothes were preened, appointments met precisely on time, hands scrubbed regularly to a raw, red color. When the first was asked why he felt the need to be so clean, his answer was plain.

"So I blame you for everything—whose fault is that?"

"My mother. When I was growing up she always kept the house perfectly ordered. She insisted on every little thing returned to its proper place, the clocks—we had dozens of clocks—each set to the same noonday chime. She insisted on this, you see. I learned from her. What else could I do?"

The man's identical twin, just as much a perfectionist with soap and water, explained his own behavior this way: "The reason is quite simple. I'm reacting to my mother, who was an absolute slob."

Miguel L. Fairbanks

Parents do matter (Collins & others, 2000; Eisenberg & others, 1998a,b; Vandell, 2000). The power of parenting to shape our differences is clearest at the extremes. Chapter 4 will provide the sharpest examples—the abused who become abusive, the neglected who become neglectful, the loved but firmly handled children who become self-confident and socially competent. The power of the family environment also frequently shows up in children's political attitudes, religious beliefs, and personal manners. And it appears in the remarkable academic and vocational successes of children of the refugee "boat people" fleeing Vietnam and Cambodia—successes attributed to close-knit, supportive, even demanding families (Caplan & others, 1992).

Yet in personality measures, at least, shared environmental influences—including the home influences that siblings share—typically account for less than 10 percent of children's differences. In the words of behavior geneticists Robert Plomin and Denise Daniels (1987), "Two children in the same family [are on average] as different from one another as are pairs of children selected randomly from the population." To developmental psychologist Sandra Scarr (1993), this implies that "parents should be given less credit for kids who turn out great and blamed less for kids who don't." Although environments matter, "extreme environmentalism is cruel," contends Michael Gazzaniga (1992, p. 202). Why? "Because it suggests to the parents that their child has been warped by something they did."

Parental nurture is like nutrition. It may not matter much whether we get our protein from eating chicken or beans, but we must have food. Likewise, it may not matter whether we grew up with parents who toilet trained us early or late, but it sure helps to have someone we belong to, someone who cares about us.

> "If you want to blame your parents for your own adult problems, you are entitled to blame the genes they gave you, but you are not entitled—by any facts I know—to blame the way they treated you. . . . We are not prisoners of our past."
>
> Martin Seligman, *What You Can Change and What You Can't*, 1994

Peer Influence

OBJECTIVE 18 | Evaluate the importance of peer influence on development.

As children mature, what other experiences do the work of nurturing? We are subject to group influences (as we will see in Chapter 18) at all ages, as we seek to establish ourselves and to be accepted in various school and other groups. The conformity behavior of children seeking to fit in with various groups is a significant influence on day-to-day behaviors. For example:

- Preschoolers who disdain a certain food despite parents' urgings often will eat the food if put at a table with a group of children who like it.
- A child who hears English spoken with one accent at home and another in the neighborhood and at school will invariably adopt the accent of the peers, not the parents.

Peer power
As we develop, we play, mate, and partner with peers. No wonder children and youths are so sensitive and responsive to peer influences.

Ole Graf/zefa/Corbis

"Men resemble the times more than they resemble their fathers."

Ancient Arab proverb

"It takes a village to raise a child."

African proverb

- Direct parental influences on smoking are less important than many people suppose. Rather, teens who start smoking typically have *friends* who model smoking, who suggest its pleasures, and who offer cigarettes (Rose & others, 1999, 2003). Part of the similarity to peers may result from a *selection effect,* as kids seek out peers with similar attitudes and interests. Those who smoke (or don't) may select as friends those who also smoke (or don't).

Knowing that lives are formed by influences partly beyond parents' control suggests caution in crediting parents for their children's achievements and blaming them for their children's troubling traits. And if our children are not easily sculpted by parental nurture, then perhaps we parents can relax a bit more and love our children for who they are.

Powerful parental influence may, however, occur indirectly. A group of parents can influence the culture that shapes the peer group. Culture is transmitted across generations partly by what Judith Rich Harris (2000b) calls "parents'-group-to-children's-group effects." That being so, parental influence occurs when parents help select their children's neighborhood and peers. Neighborhood influences matter (Kalff & others, 2001; Leventhal & Brooks-Gunn, 2000). Intervention programs for youth had therefore best be aimed at a whole school or neighborhood and not just at isolated individuals. If the vapors of a toxic climate are seeping into a child's life, that climate—not just the child—needs reforming.

Howard Gardner (1998) concludes that parents and peers are complementary:

> Parents are more important when it comes to education, discipline, responsibility, orderliness, charitableness, and ways of interacting with authority figures. Peers are more important for learning cooperation, for finding the road to popularity, for inventing styles of interaction among people of the same age. Youngsters may find their peers more interesting, but they will look to their parents when contemplating their own futures. Moreover, parents [often] choose the neighborhoods and schools that supply the peers.

>> LEARNING OUTCOMES

Parents and Peers

OBJECTIVE 15 | **Describe some of the conditions that can affect development before birth.**
Prenatal environments differ in terms of nutrition and exposure to toxic agents. Even identical twins sharing a placenta can, because of their differing locations, have unequal access to nourishment and protection from viruses.

OBJECTIVE 16 | **Describe how experience can modify the brain.**
During maturation, a child's neural connections increase in areas associated with repetitive activities (vision, for example). Unused synapses degenerate, as happens in the brain cells normally assigned to vision in the cortex of children with congenital and untreated cataracts. Though the process is most evident in the brains of young children, growth and pruning of synapses continue throughout life.

OBJECTIVE 17 | **Explain why we should be careful in attributing children's successes and failures to their parents' influence.**
Freudian psychiatry and extreme environmentalism in early psychology contributed to the idea that parents shape their children's futures. Parents do influence some areas of their children's lives, such as their manners and political and religious beliefs. But in other areas, such as personality, the environment siblings share at home accounts for less than 10 percent of their differences.

OBJECTIVE 18 | **Evaluate the importance of peer influence on development.**
Children, like adults, attempt to fit into groups by conforming. But children also seek out others who share their attitudes and interests; this selection effect contributes to peer group uniformity. Parents and peers are complementary influences in children's lives. Parents are important models for education, discipline, responsibility, orderliness, charitableness, and ways of interacting with authorities. Peers are influential in such areas as learning to cooperate with others, achieving popularity, and finding appropriate styles of interaction with people of a similar age. By choosing the neighborhoods in which their children live, parents can exert some influence over the peer group culture that helps shape children.

ASK YOURSELF: **To what extent, and in what ways, have your peers and your parents helped shape who you are?**

Cultural Influences

OBJECTIVE 19 | Discuss the survival benefits of culture.

Compared with the narrow path taken by flies, fish, and foxes, nature has built for us a longer, wider road along which environment drives us. The mark of our species—nature's great gift to us—is our ability to learn and adapt. We come equipped with a huge cerebral hard drive ready to receive many gigabytes of cultural software.

Culture is the behaviors, ideas, attitudes, values, and traditions shared by a group of people and transmitted from one generation to the next (Brislin, 1988). Human nature, notes Roy Baumeister (2005), seems designed for culture. We are social animals, but more. Wolves are social animals; they live and hunt in packs. Ants are incessantly social, never alone. But "culture is a better way of being social," notes Baumeister. Culture supports survival and reproduction with social and economic systems that enable us to eat fruit in the winter, surf the Internet, and accumulate information. Wolves function pretty much as they did 10,000 years ago. You and I enjoy things unknown to most of our century-ago ancestors, including electricity, indoor plumbing, and antibiotics. Culture works.

As we will see in Chapter 10, primates exhibit the rudiments of culture, with local customs of tool use, grooming, and courtship. Younger chimpanzees and macaque monkeys sometimes invent customs—potato washing, in one famous example—and pass them on to their peers and offspring. But human culture does more. Thanks to our mastery of *language,* we humans not only know how to clean our food, we also enjoy one of culture's hallmarks: the *preservation of innovation*. Within the span of this day, I have, thanks to my culture, made good use of Post-It notes, Google, and a single-shot skinny latté. We also have culture's accumulated knowledge to thank for the last century's extension of our life expectancy from 47 to 76 years. Moreover, culture enables an efficient *division of labor*. Although one lucky person gets his name on this book's cover, the product actually results from the coordination and commitment of a team of women and men, no one of whom is capable of producing it alone.

Across cultures, we differ in our language, our monetary system, our sports, which fork—if any—we eat with, even which side of the road we drive on. But beneath these differences is our great similarity—our capacity for culture, for the shared and transmitted customs and beliefs that enable us to communicate, to exchange money for things, to play, to eat, and to drive with agreed-upon rules and without crashing into one another. This shared capacity for culture enables our striking differences. Human nature manifests human diversity.

If we all lived in homogeneous ethnic groups in separate regions of the world, as some people still do, cultural diversity would be less relevant. In Japan, 99 percent of the country's 126 million people are of Japanese descent. Internal cultural differences are therefore minimal compared with those found in Los Angeles, where the public schools recently taught 82 different languages, or in Toronto or Vancouver, where minorities are one-third of the population and many are immigrants (as are 17 percent of all Canadians and 24 percent of Australians) (Iyer, 1993; Statistics Canada, 2002; Trewin, 2001). I am ever mindful that the readers of this book are culturally diverse. You and your ancestors reach from Australia to Africa and from Singapore to Sweden.

■ **culture** the enduring behaviors, ideas, attitudes, values, and traditions shared by a group of people and transmitted from one generation to the next.

Uniform requirements
People in individualist Western cultures sometimes see traditional Japanese culture as confining. But from the Japanese perspective the same tradition expresses a "serenity that comes to people who know exactly what to expect from each other" (Weisz & others, 1984).

Kevin R. Morris/Corbis

Variation Across Cultures

OBJECTIVE **20** | Describe some ways that cultures differ.

We see our adaptability in cultural variations among our beliefs and our values, in how we raise our children and bury our dead, and in what we wear (or whether we wear anything at all). Riding along with a unified culture is like biking with the wind: As it carries us along, we hardly notice it is there. When we try riding *against* the wind we feel its force. Face to face with a different culture, we become aware of the cultural winds. Visiting Europe, most North Americans notice the smaller cars, the left-handed use of the fork, the uninhibited attire on the beaches. Stationed in Iraq, Afghanistan, and Kuwait, European and American soldiers alike realized how liberal their home cultures were. A decade of working with refugee immigrants sensitized psychologist Mary Pipher (2002) to her own culture:

> Like most Americans I only speak English fluently. I value freedom and personal space. I am time-conscious. I am comfortable with only certain forms of touch. A certain amount of eye contact and distance between bodies seems right to me. Some things seem much more edible than others. Certain clothes—jeans and T-shirts—feel best to me. I do not cover my head when I go out and I wear shoes inside my house. I like to talk.

Arriving in North America, visitors from Japan and India struggle to understand why many people wear their dirty *street* shoes in the house, and others wonder why people find it fun to eat a picnic lunch out in the woods amid flies and ants.

Each cultural group evolves its own **norms**—the rules for accepted and expected behavior. Many South Asians, for example, use only the right hand's fingers for eating. The British have a norm for orderly waiting in line. Sometimes social expectations seem oppressive: "Why should it matter how I dress?" Yet, norms grease the social machinery. Prescribed, well-learned behaviors free us from self-preoccupation. Knowing when to clap or bow, which fork to pick up first at a dinner party, and what sorts of gestures and compliments are appropriate, we can relax and enjoy one another without fear of embarrassment or insult. Likewise, having a well-understood norm for greeting people in one's culture—by shaking hands or kissing each cheek—precludes awkward moments of indecision about whether to lead with one's hand or cheek.

When cultures collide, their differing norms often befuddle. For example, if someone invades our **personal space**—the portable buffer zone we like to maintain around our bodies—we feel uncomfortable. Scandinavians, North Americans, and the British prefer more personal space than do Latin Americans, Arabs, and the French (Sommer, 1969). At a social gathering, a Mexican seeking a comfortable conversation distance may end up walking around a room with a backpedaling American. (You can experience this at a party by playing Space Invader as you talk with someone.) To the American, the Mexican may seem intrusive; to the Mexican, the American may seem standoffish.

Cultures also vary in their expressiveness. Those with roots in northern European culture often perceive people from Mediterranean cultures as warm and charming but inefficient. The Mediterraneans, in turn, see northern Europeans as efficient but cold and preoccupied with punctuality (Triandis, 1981).

Cultures vary in their pace of life, too. A British businessperson may feel frustrated by a Latin American client who arrives 30 minutes after the time set for lunch. People from time-conscious

Cultures differ
Behavior seen as appropriate in one culture may violate the norms of another group. In Arab societies, but not in Western cultures, men often greet one another with a kiss, or hold hands as a sign of friendship, as U.S. President George W. Bush did in 2005 while strolling with Saudi Crown Prince Abdullah.

Japan—where bank clocks keep exact time, pedestrians walk briskly, and postal clerks fill requests speedily—may find themselves growing impatient when visiting Indonesia, where clocks keep less accurate time and the pace of life is more leisurely (Levine & Norenzayan, 1999). In adjusting to their host countries, the first wave of U.S. Peace Corps volunteers reported that two of their greatest culture shocks, after the language differences, were the differing pace of life and the people's differing sense of punctuality (Spradley & Phillips, 1972).

Variation Over Time

OBJECTIVE **21** | Explain why changes in the human gene pool cannot account for culture change over time.

Consider, too, how rapidly cultures may change over time. English poet Geoffrey Chaucer (1342–1400) is separated from a modern Briton by only 20 generations, but the two would converse with great difficulty. In the thinner slice of history since 1960, most Western cultures have changed with remarkable speed. Middle-class people fly to places they once only read about, e-mail those they once snail-mailed, and work in air-conditioned comfort where they once sweltered. They enjoy the convenience of on-line holiday shopping, cell-phone calling, and—enriched by doubled per-person real income—eating out more than twice as often as did their parents back in the culture of 1960. With greater economic independence, today's women are more likely to marry for love and less likely to endure abusive relationships out of economic need. Many minority groups enjoy expanded human rights.

But some changes seem not so wonderfully positive. Had you fallen asleep in the United States in 1960 and awakened a third of a century later, you would have opened your eyes to a culture with a doubled rate of divorce, a nearly tripled rate of teen suicide, a quadrupled rate of reported juvenile violent crime, a quintupled prison population, and an escalating incidence of depression (Myers, 2000). (Thankfully, the teen suicide and crime rates began subsiding after 1993.) You would also find Americans spending more hours at work, fewer hours sleeping, and fewer hours with friends and family (Frank, 1999; Putnam, 2000). Similar cultural transformations have occurred in Canada, Britain, Australia, and New Zealand.

Whether we love or loathe these changes, we cannot fail to be impressed by their breathtaking speed. And we cannot explain them by changes in the human gene pool, which evolves far too slowly to account for high-speed cultural transformations. Cultures vary. Cultures change. And cultures shape our lives.

Culture and the Self

OBJECTIVE **22** | Identify some ways a primarily individualist culture differs from a primarily collectivist culture, and compare their effects on personal identity.

Cultures vary in the event to which they give priority to the nurturing and expression of one's personal identity or of one's group identity. To grasp the difference, imagine that someone were to rip away your social connections, making you a solitary refugee in a foreign land. How much of your identity would remain intact? The answer would depend in large part on whether you give greater priority to the independent self that marks **individualism** or to the interdependent self that marks **collectivism.**

If as our solitary traveler you were an individualist, a great deal of your identity would remain intact—the very core of your being, the sense of "me," the awareness of

> ■ **norm** an understood rule for accepted and expected behavior. Norms prescribe "proper" behavior.
>
> ■ **personal space** the buffer zone we like to maintain around our bodies.
>
> ■ **individualism** giving priority to one's own goals over group goals and defining one's identity in terms of personal attributes rather than group identifications.
>
> ■ **collectivism** giving priority to the goals of one's group (often one's extended family or work group) and defining one's identity accordingly.

Like athletes who take more pleasure in their team's victory than in their own performance, collectivists find satisfaction in advancing their groups' interests, even at the expense of personal needs.

Collectivism

By identifying with family and other groups, these women and children in Pakistan have gained a sense of "we," a set of values, a network of care. This collectivist support system may have helped these people struggle through the devastation of the October 2005 Kashmir earthquake, which leveled the house behind them.

"One needs to cultivate the spirit of sacrificing the *little me* to achieve the benefits of the *big me*."

Chinese saying

your personal convictions and values. Individualists give relatively greater priority to personal goals and define their identity mostly in terms of personal attributes. They strive for personal control and individual achievement. In American culture, with its relatively big "I" and small "we," 85 percent of people say it is possible "to pretty much be who you want to be" (Sampson, 2000). Being more self-contained, individualists more easily move in and out of social groups. They feel relatively free to switch places of worship, leave one job for another, or even leave their extended families and migrate to a new place. Marriage is often for as long as they both shall love.

Individualism varies from person to person within any culture. In the movie, *Antz*, Woody Allen gave voice to an individualist ant who resisted the extreme collectivism of his colony's culture: "It's this whole gung-ho, superorganism thing that—that, you know, I can't get. I try, but I don't get it. I mean, what is it? I'm supposed to do everything for the colony? And—and what about my needs? What about me?"

If set adrift in a foreign land as a collectivist, you might experience a much greater loss of identity than as an individualist. Cut off from family, groups, and loyal friends, you would lose the connections that have defined who you are. In a collectivist culture, group identifications provide a sense of belonging, a set of values, a network of caring individuals, an assurance of security. In return, collectivists give priority to the goals of their groups, often their family, clan, or company, and define their identity accordingly—not as "me" but as "we." In Korea, for example, people place less value on expressing a consistent, unique self-concept, and more on tradition and shared practices (Choi & Choi, 2002).

Collectivists may act shy in new groups and are more easily embarrassed than their individualist counterparts (Singelis & others, 1995, 1999). Compared with Westerners, people in Japanese and Chinese cultures, for example, exhibit greater shyness toward strangers and greater concern for social harmony and loyalty (Bond, 1988; Cheek & Melchior, 1990; Triandis, 1994). They have deeper, more stable attachments to their familiar groups and families. Duty to one's family may trump personal career preference. Compared with students in the United States, for example, students in Japan, China, and India are much less likely to complete the sentence "I am . . ." with personal traits ("I am sincere," "I am confident") and are more likely to declare their social identities ("I am a Keio University student," "I am the third son in my family") (Cousins, 1989; Dhawan & others, 1995; Triandis, 1989a,b). "My parents will be disappointed in me" has been a concern expressed by 7 percent of American and Italian teenagers and 14 percent of Australian teens, but by nearly 25 percent of teens in Taiwan and Japan (Atkinson, 1988).

Relationships are long-term. Loyalties run strong between employer and employees. No wonder, says Harry Triandis (1989b), that modern world colonization was led not by Asians, who were reluctant to cut social and family ties, but by the more individualist Europeans. And no wonder that some countries colonized by Europeans willing to leave friends and family are today highly individualistic. People wanting to resettle in a new country express more concern for work and achievement, and less concern for relationships and family, than do those wanting to remain (Boneva & Frieze, 2001).

Individuals within a culture vary and cultures include varying subgroups (Oyserman & others, 2002a,b). Yet cross-cultural psychologists have discovered some variations across cultures, ranging from the individualism of the United States outside the Deep South to the collectivism of rural Asia (Hofstede, 1980; Triandis, 1994; Vandello & Cohen, 1999). Valuing communal solidarity, people in collectivist cultures place a premium on maintaining harmony and making sure others never lose face. What people say reflects both what they feel (their inner attitudes) and what they presume others feel (Kashima & others, 1992). Elders and superiors are given respect. To preserve group spirit, people avoid direct confrontation, blunt honesty, and uncomfortable topics; they defer to others' wishes and display a polite, self-effacing humility (Markus & Kitayama, 1991). Thus, that individualized latté—

TABLE 3.1

VALUE CONTRASTS BETWEEN INDIVIDUALISM AND COLLECTIVISM

Concept	Individualism	Collectivism
Self	Independent (identity from individual traits)	Interdependent (identity from belonging)
Life task	Discover and express one's uniqueness	Maintain connections, fit in, perform role
What matters	Me—personal achievement and fulfillment; rights and liberties; self-esteem	Us—group goals and solidarity; social responsibilities and relationships; family duty
Coping method	Change reality	Accommodate to reality
Morality	Defined by individuals (self-based)	Defined by social networks (duty-based)
Relationships	Many, often temporary or casual; confrontation acceptable	Few, close and enduring; harmony valued
Attributing behavior	Behavior reflects one's personality and attitudes	Behavior reflects social norms and roles

Sources: Adapted from Thomas Schoeneman (1994) and Harry Triandis (1994).

"decaf, single shot, skinny, extra hot"— that feels so good to a North American in an espresso shop might sound more like a selfish demand in Seoul, note Heejung Kim and Hazel Markus (1999). And Korean ads are also less likely to emphasize personal choice, freedom, and uniqueness, and they more often feature people together (Markus, 2001). In collectivist cultures, people remember those who have done them favors, and reciprocity becomes a social art. The collectivist self is not independent but *inter*dependent (**TABLE 3.1**). Among collectivists—especially those influenced by the Confucian idea of self as embedded in "a web of interrelatedness"—no one is an island (Kim & Lee, 1994). Happiness is being attuned to others (Kitayama & Markus, 2000).

Both individualism and collectivism offer benefits and come at a cost. People in competitive, individualist cultures have more personal freedom, take more pride in personal achievements, are less geographically bound to their families, and enjoy more privacy. Their less-unified cultures offer a smorgasbord of life-styles and invite individuals to construct their own identities. These cultures also celebrate innovation and creativity, and they tend to respect individual human rights. Such may help explain Ed Diener, Marissa Diener, and Carol Diener's (1995) finding that people in individualist cultures report experiencing greater happiness than do those in collectivist cultures. When individualists pursue their own ends and all goes well, life can seem rewarding.

Curiously, though, within individualist cultures, people with the strongest social ties express greatest satisfaction with their lives (Bettencourt & Door, 1997). Moreover, the seeming benefits of individualism can come at the cost of more loneliness, more divorce, more homicide, and more stress-related disease (Popenoe, 1993; Triandis & others, 1988). People in individualist cultures express more self-focused "narcissism," by agreeing, for example, that "I find it easy to manipulate people" (Foster & others, 2003). Individualists also demand more romance and personal fulfillment in marriage, which subjects the marriage relationship to more pressure (Dion & Dion, 1993). In one survey, "keeping romance alive" was rated as important to a good marriage by 78 percent of U.S. women but only 29 percent of Japanese women (*American Enterprise*, 1992). In China, love songs often express enduring commitment and friendship (Rothbaum & Tsang, 1998). As one song put it, "We will be together from now on . . . I will never change from now to forever."

Individualist proverb: "The squeaky wheel gets the grease."
Collectivist proverb: "The quacking duck gets shot."

Culture and Child-Rearing

OBJECTIVE **23** | Describe some ways that child-rearing differs in individualist and collectivist cultures.

Child-rearing practices are not immune to the variations in cultural values from one time and place to another. Do you prefer children who are independent or children who comply with what others think?

If you live in a Westernized culture, the odds are you prefer the former. Most parents in Western societies want their children to think for themselves. "You are responsible for yourself," Western families and schools tell their children. "Follow your conscience. Be true to yourself. Discover your gifts. Think through your personal needs." But these cultural values represent change over time. A half-century ago, Western parents placed greater priority on obedience, respect, and sensitivity to others (Alwin, 1990; Remley, 1988). "Be true to your traditions," they taught their children. "Be loyal to your heritage and country. Show respect toward your parents and other superiors."

Unlike most Westerners, who now raise their children to be independent, many Asians and Africans live in cultures that focus on cultivating emotional closeness. Rather than being given their own bedrooms and entrusted to day care, infants and toddlers have typically slept with their mothers and spent their days close to a family member (Morelli & others, 1992; Whiting & Edwards, 1988). Children in these cultures grow up with a stronger sense of *family self*—a feeling that what shames the child shames the family, and what brings honor to the family, brings honor to the self.

Children across place and time have thrived under various child-rearing systems. Upper-class British parents traditionally handed off routine caregiving to nannies, then sent their children off to boarding school at about age 10. These children generally grew up to be pillars of British society, just like their parents and their boarding-school peers. In the African Gusii society, babies nurse freely but spend most of the day on their mother's back—with lots of body contact but little face-to-face and language interaction. When the mother becomes pregnant, the toddler is weaned and handed over to someone else, often an older sibling. Westerners may wonder about the negative effects of this lack of verbal interaction, but then the African Gusii would in turn wonder about Western mothers pushing

Cultures vary
In Scotland's Orkney Islands' town of Stromness, social trust enables parents to park their toddlers outside of shops.

Parental involvement promotes development
Parents in every culture facilitate their children's discovery of their world, but cultures differ in what they deem important. Asian cultures place more emphasis on school and hard work than does North American culture. This may help explain why Japanese and Taiwanese children get higher scores on mathematics achievement tests.

their babies around in strollers and leaving them in playpens and car seats (Small, 1997). Such diversity in child-rearing cautions us against presuming that our culture's way is the only way to rear children successfully.

Developmental Similarities Across Groups

OBJECTIVE 24 | Describe some ways that humans are similar, despite their cultural differences.

Because we are so mindful of how others differ from us, we often fail to notice the similarities predisposed by our shared biology. Cross-cultural research can help us by leading us to appreciate both our cultural diversity *and* our human kinship. Compared with the person-to-person differences within groups, the differences between groups are small. Regardless of our culture—and culture is itself something that shapes and guides us all—we humans share the same life cycle. We all speak to our infants in similar ways and respond similarly to their coos and cries (Bornstein & others, 1992a,b). All over the world, the children of parents who are warm and supportive feel better about themselves and are less hostile than are the children of parents who are punitive and rejecting (Rohner, 1986; Scott & others, 1991).

Within a culture, ethnic subgroups may behave differently and yet be influenced similarly. Differences sometimes attributed to race may therefore actually result from other factors. David Rowe and his colleagues (1994, 1995) illustrate this with an analogy: Black men tend to have higher blood pressure than white men. Suppose that (1) in both groups salt consumption correlates with blood pressure, and (2) salt consumption is higher among black men than among white men. What then might we expect? A blood pressure "race difference" that may actually be, at least partly, a *diet* difference.

And that, say Rowe and his colleagues, parallels psychological findings: Behavior differences, like blood pressure differences, can result from differing inputs to the same process. Although American Hispanic, Asian, Black, and White ethnic groups differ in school achievement and delinquency, the differences are "no more than skin deep." To the extent that family structure, peer influences, and parental education predict behavior in one ethnic group, they do so for other groups as well.

So in surface ways we may differ, but as members of one species we seem subject to the same psychological forces. As members of different ethnic and cultural groups, our languages vary, yet they reflect universal principles of grammar (Chapter 10). Our tastes vary, yet they reflect common principles of hunger (Chapter 12). Our social behaviors vary, but they reflect pervasive principles of human influence (Chapter 18).

> "We recognize that we are the products of many cultures, traditions, and memories; that mutual respect allows us to study and learn from other cultures; and that we gain strength by combining the foreign with the familiar."
>
> U.N. Secretary-General Kofi Annan, Nobel Peace Prize lecture, 2001

> "When someone has discovered why men in Bond Street wear black hats he will at the same moment have discovered why men in Timbuctoo wear red feathers."
>
> G. K. Chesterton, *Heretics*, 1908

>> LEARNING OUTCOMES

Cultural Influences

OBJECTIVE 19 | Discuss the survival benefits of culture.
Culture is a set of enduring behaviors, ideas, attitudes, values, and traditions shared by a group of people and transmitted from one generation to the next. Culture and our capacity for language let us preserve innovations and pass them on to the next generation, a process that encourages diversity between groups. Despite cultural differences, our shared capacity for culture is a common thread running throughout the human species.

OBJECTIVE 20 | Describe some ways that cultures differ.
Cultures vary in their ideas, attitudes, values, and traditions. Those variations are embedded in each culture's norms, its rules for accepted and expected behavior. Newcomers or visitors to a culture different from their own may experience culture shock—confusion or frustration caused by their lack of understanding of the norms for observing personal space, expressing personal feelings, maintaining a faster or slower pace of life, or educating and caring for children.

OBJECTIVE 21 | **Explain why changes in the human gene pool cannot account for culture change over time.**

Cultures change rapidly. Western cultures, for example, have changed as they have discovered and adapted to new forms of technology. Cultures also change in their values, attitudes, and behaviors. The speed at which such changes occur is much faster than the slow pace of evolutionary changes in the human gene pool.

OBJECTIVE 22 | **Identify some ways a primarily individualist culture differs from a primarily collectivist culture, and compare their effects on personal identity.**

Cultures based on self-reliant *individualism,* like those of most of the United States, Canada, and Western Europe, value personal independence and individual achievement. Relationships tend to be more temporary and casual, confrontation is acceptable, and morality is self-defined. Individualist cultures tend to define identity in terms of self-esteem, personal goals and attributes, and personal rights and liberties. Cultures based on socially connected *collectivism,* like those of many parts of Asia and Africa, value interdependence, tradition, and harmony. Relationships tend to be few, close, and enduring,

and morality is based on duty to one's social network. Collectivist cultures tend to define identity in terms of group goals and commitments and belonging to one's group.

OBJECTIVE 23 | **Describe some ways that child-rearing differs in individualist and collectivist cultures.**

Individualist cultures expect their members to be independent and to think for themselves, and child-rearing practices in those cultures reflect these values. Collectivist cultures, which emphasize a stronger sense of family self, tend to focus more on developing a sense of emotional closeness.

OBJECTIVE 24 | **Describe some ways that humans are similar, despite their cultural differences.**

Although we humans differ in our cultures, we share the same genetic profile, life cycle, capacity for language, biological needs, and need to belong. To the extent that biology and social forces predict behavior in individuals in one group, they often predict similar behaviors in those in other groups.

ASK YOURSELF: **Which concept best describes you—collectivist or individualist? Do you fit completely in either category, or are you sometimes a collectivist and sometimes an individualist?**

Gender Development

As we will see in Chapter 10, Thinking and Language, we humans have an irresistible urge to organize our worlds into simple categories. Among the ways we classify people (and ourselves)—as tall or short, slim or fat, smart or dull—two stand out: race and, especially, sex. At your birth, the one thing everyone wanted to know was, "Boy or girl?" Our biological sex then helps define our *gender* (see page 110), our assumed characteristics as male or female. In considering how nature and nurture together create social diversity, gender is the prime case example. Earlier we considered one significant gender difference—in sexual interests and behaviors. Let's recap this chapter's theme—that nature and nurture together create our differences and commonalities—by considering other gender variations.

Gender Similarities and Differences

OBJECTIVE 25 | Identify some biological and psychological differences between males and females.

In most ways, males and females, having faced similar adaptive challenges, are alike. Men and women are not from different planets—Mars and Venus—but from the same planet Earth. Tell me whether you are male or female and you give me virtually no clues to your vocabulary, your intelligence, your self-esteem, your happiness, or the mechanisms by which you see, hear, learn, and remember. Your "opposite" sex is, in reality, your very similar sex. And should we be surprised? Among your 46 chromosomes, 45 are unisex.

But there also are some differences, and differences we notice. Diversity commands attention. Ask people to describe themselves, and their unique features often come to mind. Redheads will mention their hair color. Tall people will mention their height. In situations where you are the only person of your race or gender, you will be mindful of those unique features (McGuire & others, 1978).

Some male-female differences are obvious. Compared with the average man, the average woman has 70 percent more fat, possesses 40 percent less muscle, and is 5 inches shorter. She also enters puberty two years sooner and will outlive her male counterparts by five years. However, it's worth noting that the women's world records in the 400-meter dash and the marathon are now within 10 percent of men's record times (Leonhardt, 2004). Throughout this book, we will also see some less obvious gender differences. Women are more likely to dream equally of men and women, to become sexually re-aroused immediately after orgasm, to smell faint odors, to express emotions freely, and in some situations to be offered help. They also are doubly vulnerable to depression and anxiety and are at 10 times greater risk for eating disorders. But then men are some four times more likely to commit suicide or suffer alcoholism, and are far more likely to be diagnosed with autism, color-blindness, hyperactivity (as children), and antisocial personality disorder (as adults). Choose your gender and pick your vulnerability.

Let's look more closely at gender and social behavior. Researchers have found differences in aggression, social power, and social connectedness. How much does biology bend the genders, and what portion of such differences are socially constructed—by the gender roles that culture assigns us, and by how we are socialized as children?

Gender and Aggression

OBJECTIVE 26 | Summarize the gender gap in aggression.

In surveys, men admit to more **aggression** than do women, and experiments confirm that men tend to behave more aggressively, such as by administering what they believe are more painful electric shocks (Bettencourt & Kernahan, 1997). The aggression gender gap, which pertains to *physical* rather than verbal aggression, also appears in everyday life in various cultures and at various ages (Archer, 2004). Violent crime rates illustrate the difference. The male-to-female arrest ratio for murder, for example, is 9 to 1 in the United States and 7 to 1 in Canada (FBI, 2004; Statistics Canada, 2003).

Throughout the world, hunting, fighting, and warring are primarily men's activities (Wood & Eagly, 2002). Men also express more support for war. In one 2005 survey, 51 percent of American men but only 34 percent of American women expressed approval of George Bush's Iraq initiative (Gallup, 2005).

Gender and Social Power

OBJECTIVE 27 | Describe some gender differences in social power.

Around the world, from Nigeria to New Zealand, people perceive men as more dominant, forceful, and independent, women as more deferential, nurturant, and affiliative (Williams & Best, 1990). Indeed, in most societies men *are* socially dominant. When groups form, whether as juries or companies, leadership tends to go to males (Colarelli & others, 2005). As leaders, men tend to be more directive, even autocratic; women tend to be more democratic, more welcoming of subordinates' participation in decision making (Eagly & Johnson, 1990; van Engen & Willemsen, 2004). When people interact, men are more likely to utter opinions, women to express support (Aries, 1987; Wood, 1987). In everyday behavior, men are more likely to act as powerful people often do—to talk assertively, to interrupt, to initiate touching, to smile less, to stare (Hall, 1987; Major & others, 1990).

▪ **aggression** physical or verbal behavior intended to hurt someone.

"In the long years liker must they grow;
The man be more of woman, she of man."

Alfred Lord Tennyson, *The Princess*, 1847

Question: Why does it take 200 million
sperm to fertilize one egg?
Answer: Because they won't stop for
directions.

**Sex brought us together, but gender drove
us apart.**

Such behaviors help sustain the inequities of social power. When political leaders
are elected, they usually are men, who held 84 percent of the seats in the world's governing parliaments in 2005 (IPU, 2005). When salaries are paid, those in traditionally male occupations receive more. Gender differences in power do appear to lessen
with maturity, however, as middle-aged women become more assertive and men
more empathic (Maccoby, 1998).

Gender and Social Connectedness

OBJECTIVE 28 | Discuss gender differences in connectedness, or the ability to
"tend and befriend."

To Carol Gilligan and her colleagues (1982, 1990), the "normal" struggle to create
one's separate identity describes individualist males more than relationship-oriented
females. Gilligan believes females differ from males both in being less concerned with
viewing themselves as separate individuals and in being more concerned with "making connections."

These gender differences surface early, in children's play. Boys typically play in
large groups with an activity focus and little intimate discussion. Girls usually play in
smaller groups, often with one friend. Their play is less competitive than boys' and
more imitative of social relationships. Both in play and other settings, females are
more open and responsive to feedback than are males (Maccoby, 1990; Roberts,
1991). Asked difficult questions—"Do you have any idea why the sky is blue?" "Do
you have any idea why shorter people live longer?"—men are more likely than women
to hazard answers rather than admit they don't know, a phenomenon Traci Giuliano
and her colleagues (1998a,b) call the *male answer syndrome*.

As teens, girls spend more time with friends and less time alone (Wong & Csikszentmihalyi, 1991). The gender difference in connectedness continues through
adulthood. Women, being more *interdependent,* use conversation more to explore relationships; men use it to communicate solutions (Tannen, 1990). New studies from
several countries confirm gender differences in communication:

- *New Zealand:* Given a sample of students' e-mail notes, people correctly guessed
  the writer's gender 66 percent of the time (Thomson & Murachver, 2001).
  (Males less often disclosed emotion and personal information, offered apologies,
  and used such hedges as "it was *sort of* interesting.")
- *United States:* When using computers, girls spend less time playing games and
  more time e-mailing friends (Crabtree, 2002).
- *France:* Women make 63 percent of telephone calls, and when talking to a
  woman stay connected longer (7.2 minutes) than men do when talking to other
  men (4.6 minutes) (Smoreda & Licoppe, 2000).

Women emphasize caring and provide most of the care to the very young and the
very old. Women also purchase 85 percent of greeting cards (*Time,* 1997). Although
69 percent of people say they have a close relationship with their father, 90 percent
feel close to their mother (Hugick, 1989).

Like empowered people generally, men emphasize freedom and self-reliance. That
helps explain why at all ages men worldwide assign less importance to religion and
pray less often than their female counterparts (Benson, 1992; Stark, 2002). In a 2003
U.S. Gallup Poll, 53 percent of men and 69 percent of women said religion was "very
important" in their life (Saad, 2003). Men also dominate the ranks of professional
skeptics. Nearly 4 in 5 respondents to one Skeptics Society survey were men (Shermer,
1999). Likewise, the two dozen winners and runners-up on the *Skeptical Inquirer's* list
of outstanding twentieth-century rationalist skeptics were all men. In the Science and
the Paranormal section of the 2004–2005 catalog of Prometheus Books (the leading
publisher of skepticism), I counted 104 male authors and only 4 female authors.

Every man for himself, or tend and befriend? Gender differences in the way we interact with others begin to appear at a very young age.

Women, it appears, are more open to spirituality (and are far more likely to author books on spirituality than on skepticism).

Bonds and feelings of support are also stronger among women than among men (Rossi & Rossi, 1993). Women's ties—as mothers, daughters, sisters, aunts, and grand-mothers—bind families together. As friends, women are more intimate than men; they talk more often and more openly (Berndt, 1992; Dindia & Allen, 1992). While men enjoy doing activities *side-by-side,* women take more pleasure in talking *face-to-face* (Wright, 1989). And when coping with stress, women more often turn to others for support—they *tend and befriend* (Tamres & others, 2002; Taylor, 2002).

Both men and women report their friendships with women to be more intimate, enjoyable, and nurturing (Rubin, 1985; Sapadin,). When wanting understand-ing and someone with whom to share worries and hurts, both men and women usu-ally turn to women.

The Nature of Gender

OBJECTIVE 29 | Explain how biological sex is determined, and describe the role of sex hormones in biological development and gender differences.

What explains our gender diversity? Is biology destiny? Are we shaped by our cul-tures? A biopsychosocial view suggests it is both, thanks to the interplay among what Wendy Wood and Alice Eagly (2002) call "the evolved character of the sexes," our de-velopmental experiences, and our current situations.

In domains where men and women have faced similar challenges—regulating heat with sweat, developing tastes that nourish, growing calluses where the skin meets friction—the sexes are similar. Even when describing the ideal mate, both men and women put traits such as "kind," "honest," and "intelligent" at the top of their lists. But in domains pertinent to mating, evolutionary psychologists con-tend, guys act like guys whether they are elephants or elephant seals, rural peas-ants or corporate presidents. Such gender differences may be influenced genetically, by our differing *sex chromosomes* and, physiologically, from our differ-ing concentrations of *sex hormones.*

Males and females are variations on a single form. Seven weeks after conception, you were anatomically indistinguishable from someone of the other sex. Then your genes activated your biological sex. Your sex was determined by your twenty-third pair of chromosomes, the two sex chromosomes. From your mother you received an **X chromosome.** From your father, you received the one chromosome out of 46 that is not unisex. This was either an X chromosome, making you a girl, or a **Y chromosome,**

■ **X chromosome** the sex chromosome found in both men and women. Females have two X chromosomes; males have one. An X chromosome from each parent pro-duces a female child.

■ **Y chromosome** the sex chromosome found only in males. When paired with an X chromosome from the mother, it produces a male child.

Courtesy of Nick Downes.

"Genes, by themselves, are like seeds dropped onto pavement: powerless to produce anything."

Primatologist Frans B. M. de Waal (1999)

■ **testosterone** the most important of the male sex hormones. Both males and females have it, but the additional testosterone in males stimulates the growth of the male sex organs in the fetus and the development of the male sex characteristics during puberty.

■ **role** a set of expectations (norms) about a social position, defining how those in the position ought to behave.

■ **gender role** a set of expected behaviors for males and for females.

making you a boy. The Y chromosome includes a single gene that throws a master switch triggering the testes to develop and produce the principal male hormone, **testosterone,** which about the seventh week starts the development of external male sex organs. Females also have testosterone, but less of it. Another key period for sexual differentiation falls during the fourth and fifth prenatal months, when different brain-wiring patterns for males and females develop under the influence of the male's greater testosterone and the female's ovarian hormones (Hines, 2004; Udry, 2000).

What do you suppose happens when glandular malfunction or hormone injections expose a female embryo to excess testosterone? These genetically female infants are born with masculine-appearing genitals, which can be corrected surgically. Until puberty, such females tend to act in more aggressive "tomboyish" ways than do most girls, and they dress and play in ways more typical of boys than of girls (Berenbaum & Hines, 1992; Ehrhardt, 1987). Given a choice of toys, they (like boys) are more likely to play with cars and guns than with dolls and crayons. Some develop into lesbians, but most—like nearly all girls with traditionally feminine interests—become heterosexual. Moreover, the hormones do not reverse their gender identity; they view themselves as girls, not boys (Berenbaum & Bailey, 2004).

Is the tomboyish behavior of these girls due to the prenatal hormones? If so, may we conclude that biological sex differences produce behavioral gender differences? Like humans, male vervet monkeys spend more time with "masculine" toys such as trucks, and females with "feminine" toys such as dolls (Hines, 2004). And experiments with many species, from rats to monkeys, confirm that female embryos given male hormones will later exhibit atypically masculine appearance and more aggressive behavior (Hines & Green, 1991). But among humans, such girls frequently *look* masculine and are known to be "different," so perhaps people also treat them more like boys. Early exposure to sex hormones thus affects us both directly, in our biological appearance, and indirectly, by influencing social experiences that shape us. Like a sculptor's two hands shaping a lump of clay, nature and nurture work together.

Further evidence that biology influences gender development comes from studies of genetic males who, despite normal male hormones and testes, are born without penises or with very small ones. In one study of 14 who underwent early sex-reassignment surgery and were raised as girls, six later declared themselves as male, five were living as female, and three had unclear sexual identity (Reiner & Gearhart, 2004). In one famous case, the parents of a Canadian boy who lost his penis to a botched circumcision followed advice to raise him as a girl rather than as a damaged boy. Alas, "Brenda" was not like other girls. "She" didn't like dolls. She tore her dresses with rough-and-tumble play. At puberty she wanted no part of kissing boys. Finally, Brenda's parents explained what had happened, whereupon Brenda immediately rejected her female identity, cut her hair, took a male name and ended up marrying a woman, becoming a stepfather, and, sadly, later committing suicide (Colapinto, 2000). Although socially influenced, gender is not written on a biologically blank slate.

Sex chromosomes control sex hormones that bathe the fetal brain and influence its wiring. Recent research confirms male–female differences during development in brain areas with abundant sex hormone receptors (Cahill, 2005). In adulthood, part of the frontal lobes, an area involved in verbal fluency, is reportedly thicker in women. Part of the parietal cortex, a key area for space perception, is thicker in men. Other studies report gender differences in the hippocampus, the amygdala, and the volume of brain gray matter (the neural bodies) versus white matter (the axons and dendrites). Although further research is needed to confirm these findings and sort out their implications, this much seems clear, reports the National Academy of Sciences (2001): "Sex matters." In combination with the environment, sex-related genes and physiology "result in behavioral and cognitive differences between males and females."

The Nurture of Gender

OBJECTIVE 30 | Discuss the importance of environment in the development of gender roles, and describe two theories of gender-typing.

Although biologically influenced, gender is also socially constructed. What biology initiates, culture accentuates.

Gender Roles

Sex matters. But from a biopsychosocial perspective, culture and the immediate situation matter, too. Culture, as we noted earlier, is everything that is shared by a group and transmitted across generations. We can see culture's shaping power in the social expectations that guide men's and women's behavior. In psychology, as in the theater, a **role** refers to a cluster of prescribed actions—the behaviors we expect of those who occupy a particular social position. One set of norms defines our culture's **gender roles**—our expectations about the way men and women behave. Thirty years ago, it was standard for men to initiate dates, drive the car, and pick up the check, and for women to decorate the home, buy and care for the children's clothes, and select the wedding gifts. Gender roles exist outside the home, too. In the United States, employed men spend about an hour more per day working than do employed women, and about an hour a day less on household activities and in caregiving (Bureau of Labor Statistics, 2004). And, I do not have to tell you which parent, about 90 percent of the time in two-parent families, still stays home with a sick child, arranges for the baby-sitter, or calls the doctor (Maccoby, 1995). In Australia, women devote 54 percent more time to unpaid household work and 71 percent more time to child care than do men (Trewin, 2001).

Gender roles can smooth social relations, saving awkward decisions about who does the laundry this week and who mows the lawn. But they often do so at a cost: If we deviate from such conventions, we may feel anxious.

Do gender roles reflect what is biologically natural for men and women? Or do cultures construct them? The diversity of gender roles across cultures and over time indicates that culture has a big influence. Nomadic societies of food-gathering people have only a minimal division of labor by sex. Boys and girls receive much the same upbringing. However, in agricultural societies, women remain close to home, working in the fields and staying with the children; men often roam more freely, herding cattle or sheep. Such societies typically socialize their children into more distinct gender roles (Segall & others, 1990; Van Leeuwen, 1978).

Among the industrialized countries, gender roles and attitudes nevertheless vary widely. Would you say that life is more satisfying when both spouses work and share child care? A Pew Global Attitudes survey (2003) revealed that in 41 of 44 countries, most people agreed that shared work and child care is most satisfying (rather than women staying home while the husband provides). But the culture-to-culture differences were huge, ranging from Egypt, where people disagreed 2 to 1, to Vietnam, where people concurred by 11 to 1.

Gender roles also vary over time:

- As we began the last century, only one country—New Zealand—granted women the right to vote. As we ended it, only one democracy—Kuwait—did not (Briscoe, 1997).
- With the flick of an apron, the number of U.S. college women hoping to be full-time homemakers plunged during the late 1960s and early 1970s (**FIGURE 3.8**, page 132). In 1960, one in 30 entering U.S. law students were women; by the early twenty-first century, half were (Glater, 2001).

(c) DPA/The Image Works

The gendered tsunami
In Sri Lanka, Indonesia, and India, the gendered division of labor helps explain the excess of female deaths from the 2004 tsunami. In some villages, 80 percent of those killed were women, who were mostly at home while the men were more likely to be out at sea fishing or doing out-of-the-home chores (Oxfam, 2005).

FIGURE 3.8

Changing attitudes about gender roles
U.S. college students' endorsement of the traditional view of women's role has declined dramatically. Men's and women's attitudes have also converged. (From Dey & others, 1991; Sax & others, 2004.)

■ **gender identity** one's sense of being male or female.

■ **gender-typing** the acquisition of a traditional masculine or feminine role.

■ **social learning theory** the theory that we learn social behavior by observing and imitating and by being rewarded or punished.

■ **gender schema theory** the theory that children learn from their cultures a concept of what it means to be male and female and that they adjust their behavior accordingly.

- Over the decades since 1930, women's assertiveness has increased and decreased with their social status—up until the end of World War II, then down until the mid-1960s, then up again (Twenge, 2001). It is "all right for a girl to telephone a boy to ask for a date," agreed 29 percent of Americans in a 1950 Gallup poll and 70 percent a half-century later.

Gender ideas also vary across generations. When families emigrate from Asia to Canada and the United States, the immigrant children often grow up with peers who assume gender roles different from those of the immigrant parents. Daughters, especially, may feel torn between competing sets of norms (Dion & Dion, 2001).

Gender and Child-Rearing

Society assigns each of us to a gender, the social category of male or female. The inevitable result is our strong **gender identity,** our sense of being male or female. To varying extents, we also become **gender-typed.** That is, some boys more than others exhibit traditionally masculine traits and interests, and some girls more than others become distinctly feminine.

Social learning theory assumes that children learn gender-linked behaviors by observing and imitating and by being rewarded or punished. "Nicole, you're such a good mommy to your dolls"; "Big boys don't cry, Alex." But modeling and rewarding is not done by parents alone, because the differences in the way parents rear boys and girls aren't enough to explain gender-typing (Lytton & Romney, 1991). In fact, even when their families discourage traditional gender-typing, children organize themselves into "boy worlds" and "girl worlds," each guided by rules for what boys and girls do.

Gender schema theory combines social learning theory with cognition: In your own childhood, as you struggled to comprehend the world, you—like other children—formed concepts, or *schemas,* including a schema for your own gender (Bem, 1987, 1993). Gender then became a lens through which you viewed your experiences (**FIGURE 3.9**). Before age 1, children begin to discriminate male and female voices and faces (Martin & others, 2002). After age 2, language forces children to begin organizing their worlds on the basis of gender. English,

Gender roles have changed, but not every male has changed with them.

FIGURE 3.9
Two theories of gender-typing
Social learning theory proposes that gender-typing evolves through imitation and reinforcement. Gender schema theory proposes that one's concept of maleness and femaleness influences one's perceptions and behavior.

for example, uses the pronouns *he* and *she;* other languages classify objects as masculine ("*le train*") or feminine ("*la table*"). Through language, dress, toys, and songs, social learning shapes gender schemas. Children then compare themselves with their concept of gender ("I am male—thus, masculine, strong, aggressive," or "I am female—therefore, feminine, sweet, and helpful") and adjust their behavior accordingly.

Young children are "gender detectives," explain Carol Lynn Martin and Diane Ruble (2004). Once they grasp that two sorts of people exist—and they are of one sort—they search for cues about gender. Girls, they may decide, are the ones with long hair. Having divided the human world in half, 3-year-olds will then like their own sex better and seek out their own kind for play. The rigidity of their stereotypes about boys and girls increases to a peak at about age 5 or 6. If the new neighbor is a boy, a 6-year-old girl may just assume that he cannot share her interests. For young children, gender schemas loom large.

"How is it gendered?"

>> Learning Outcomes

Gender Development

Objective 25 | Identify some biological and psychological differences between males and females.
The major way human males and females are similar is in their genetic makeup, where 45 of 46 chromosomes are unisex. Males and females differ biologically in body fat, muscle, height, age of onset of puberty, and life expectancy. They also differ psychologically, for example, in their vulnerability to certain disorders: More women are diagnosed with depression, more men with antisocial personality disorder.

Objective 26 | Summarize the gender gap in aggression.
Men more than women behave aggressively and describe themselves as aggressive. The aggression gender gap appears in many cultures and at various ages, especially for physical aggression.

Objective 27 | Describe some gender differences in social power.
In most societies, men are socially dominant and are perceived as such. Men tend to occupy more leadership positions, and their leadership style is more directive than women's.

OBJECTIVE 28 | Discuss gender differences in connectedness, or the ability to "tend and befriend."

Women, more than men, are concerned with making connections with others. This difference is noticeable in young children's play, and it continues throughout the teen years and into adulthood. Women tend and befriend—they emphasize caring, often being responsible for the very young and very old. Bonds between women seem stronger and more supportive than those between men. Men tend to emphasize freedom and self-reliance.

OBJECTIVE 29 | Explain how biological sex is determined, and describe the role of sex hormones in biological development and gender differences.

Biological sex is determined by the twenty-third pair of chromosomes. In this pair, the mother's contribution is always an X chromosome. The father's contribution—which determines whether a child will be male or female—can be either an X or a Y. An XX combination produces a female; an XY combination produces a male. The Y chromosome contains a master switch for the production of the hormone testosterone, which triggers the growth of external male sex organs in the seventh week of prenatal development. (Females also produce testosterone, but less of it.) The fourth and fifth prenatal months are a second key period for sexual differentiation, influenced by a male fetus' greater testosterone or a female fetus' ovarian hormones. *Gender* is defined as the set of biologically and socially influenced characteristics by which people define *male* and *female*. Sex-related genes and hormones do influence gender differences in behavior, possibly by influencing brain development, but many gender differences are learned.

OBJECTIVE 30 | Discuss the importance of environment in the development of gender roles, and describe two theories of gender-typing.

Our biology influences our gender, but cultures shape gender roles—expectations about how men and women should behave. Gender roles can vary from one place to another, and from one time to another within the same culture. A person's sense of being male or female is called *gender identity*, and some people more than others exhibit gender-typed (traditionally masculine or feminine) behavior. Social learning theory proposes that we learn gender behavior as we learn other things—through reinforcement, punishment, and observation. Gender schema theory proposes that we learn a cultural "recipe" of how to be male or female, which influences our behaviors and perceptions of what is appropriate for "people like us."

ASK YOURSELF: Do you consider yourself strongly gender-typed or *not* strongly gender-typed? What factors do you think have contributed to your feelings of masculinity or femininity?

Reflections on Nature and Nurture

OBJECTIVE 31 | Describe the biopsychosocial approach to development.

"There are trivial truths and great truths," reflected the physicist Niels Bohr on some of the paradoxes of modern science. "The opposite of a trivial truth is plainly false. The opposite of a great truth is also true." It appears true that our ancestral history helped form us as a species. Where there is variation, natural selection, and heredity, there will be, on some scale, evolution. The unique gene combination created when our mother's egg engulfed our father's sperm also helped form us, as individuals. Genes predispose both our shared humanity and our individual differences. This is a great truth about human nature. Genes form us.

But it also is true that our experiences form us. In the womb, in our families, and in our peer social relationships, we learn ways of thinking and acting. Even differences initiated by our nature may be amplified by our nurture. If their genes and hormones predispose males to be more physically aggressive than females, culture may magnify this gender difference through norms that encourage males to be macho and females to be the kinder, gentler sex. If men are encouraged toward roles that demand physical power, and women toward more nurturing roles, each may then exhibit the actions expected of those who fill such roles and find themselves shaped accordingly. Roles remake their players. Presidents in time become more presidential, servants more servile. Gender roles similarly shape us.

But gender roles are converging. As brute strength has become increasingly irrelevant to power and status (think Bill Gates), both women and men have become "fully capable of effectively carrying out organizational roles at all levels," note

FIGURE 3.10
The biopsychosocial approach to development

Wendy Wood and Alice Eagly (2002). And as women's employment in formerly male occupations has increased, gender differences in traditional masculinity/femininity and in what one seeks in a mate have diminished (Twenge, 1997). As the roles we play change over time, we change with them.

* * * * *

If nature and nurture jointly form us, are we "nothing but" the product of nature and nurture? Are we rigidly determined?

We *are* the product of nature and nurture (**FIGURE 3.10**), but we are also an open system. Genes are all-pervasive but not all-powerful. Sometimes people defy their genetic bent to reproduce, by electing celibacy. Culture, too, is all-pervasive but not all-powerful. Sometimes people defy peer pressures, by asserting their freedom and doing the opposite of the expected. When the crowd goes one way, they remember who they are and go another. To excuse our failings by blaming our nature and nurture is what philosopher-novelist Jean-Paul Sartre called "bad faith"—attributing responsibility for one's fate to bad genes or bad influences.

In reality, we are both the creatures and the creators of our worlds. We are—it is a great truth—the products of our genes and environments. Nevertheless—another great truth—the stream of causation that shapes the future runs through our present choices. Our decisions today design our environments tomorrow. Mind matters. The human environment is not like the weather—something that just happens. We are its architects. Our hopes, goals, and expectations influence our future. And that is what enables cultures to vary and to change so quickly.

* * * * *

I know from my mail and from public opinion surveys that some readers feel troubled by the naturalism and evolutionism of contemporary science. They worry that a science of behavior (and evolutionary science in particular) will destroy our sense of the beauty, mystery, and spiritual significance of the human creature. For those concerned, I offer some reassuring thoughts.

When Isaac Newton explained the rainbow in terms of light of differing wavelengths, the poet Keats feared that Newton had destroyed the rainbow's mysterious beauty. Yet, notes Richard Dawkins (1998) in *Unweaving the Rainbow,* Newton's analysis led to Maxwell's theory of electromagnetism and onward to an even deeper mystery—Einstein's theory of special relativity. Moreover, nothing about Newton's optics need diminish our appreciation for the dramatic elegance of a rainbow arching across a rain-darkened sky.

"Let's hope that it's not true; but if it is true, let's hope that it doesn't become widely known."

Lady Ashley, commenting on Darwin's theory

"Is it not stirring to understand how the world actually works—that white light is made of colors, that color measures light waves, that transparent air reflects light . . . ? It does no harm to the romance of the sunset to know a little about it."

Carl Sagan, *Skies of Other Worlds,* 1988

When Galileo assembled evidence that the Earth revolved around the Sun, not vice versa, he did not offer irrefutable proof for his theory. Rather he offered a coherent explanation for a variety of observations, such as the changing shadows cast by the Moon's mountains. His explanation eventually won the day because it described and explained things in a way that made sense, that hung together. Darwin's theory of evolution likewise is a coherent view of natural history. It offers an organizing principle that unifies various observations.

Although some people of faith may find the scientific idea of human origins troubling, many others find it congenial with their spirituality. In the fifth century, St. Augustine (quoted by Wilford, 1999) wrote, "The universe was brought into being in a less than fully formed state, but was gifted with the capacity to transform itself from unformed matter into a truly marvelous array of structures and life forms." Some 1600 years later, Pope John Paul II in 1996 welcomed a science-religion dialogue, finding it noteworthy that evolutionary theory "has been progressively accepted by researchers, following a series of discoveries in various fields of knowledge."

Meanwhile, many people of science are awestruck at the emerging understanding of the universe and the human creature. It boggles the mind—the entire universe popping out of a point some 14 billion years ago, and instantly inflating to cosmological size. Had the energy of this Big Bang been the tiniest bit less, the universe would have collapsed back on itself. Had it been the tiniest bit more, the result would have been a soup too thin to support life. Had gravity been a teeny bit stronger or weaker, or had the weight of a carbon proton been a wee bit different, our universe just wouldn't have worked.

What caused this almost-too-good-to-be-true, finely tuned universe? Why is there something rather than nothing? How did it come to be, in the words of Harvard-Smithsonian astrophysicist Owen Gingerich (1999), "so extraordinarily right, that it seemed the universe had been expressly designed to produce intelligent, sentient beings"? Is there a benevolent superintelligence behind it all? Have there instead been an infinite number of universes born and we just happen to be the lucky inhabitants of one that, by chance, was exquisitely fine-tuned to give birth to us? Or does that idea violate *Occam's razor,* the principle that we should prefer the simplest of competing explanations? On most of these matters, science is silent. Faced with such mind-boggling questions, a humble, awed, scientific silence is appropriate, suggested philosopher Ludwig Wittgenstein: "Whereof one cannot speak, thereof one must be silent."

> "The causes of life's history [cannot] resolve the riddle of life's meaning."
>
> Stephen Jay Gould, *Rocks of Ages: Science and Religion in the Fullness of Life,* 1999

Rather than fearing or restraining science, we can welcome its enlarging our understanding and awakening our sense of awe. In *The Fragile Species,* Lewis Thomas (1992) described his utter amazement that the Earth in time gave rise to bacteria and eventually to Bach's *Mass in B-Minor.* In a short 4 billion years, life on Earth has come from nothing to structures as complex as a 6-billion-unit strand of DNA and the incomprehensible intricacy of the human brain. Nature, says cosmologist Paul Davies (1992, 1999, 2004), seems cunningly and ingeniously devised to produce extraordinary, self-replicating, information-processing systems—us. Although we appear to have been created from dust, over eons of time, the end result is a priceless creature, one rich with potentials beyond our imagining.

>> LEARNING OUTCOMES

Reflections on Nature and Nurture

OBJECTIVE 31 | Describe the biopsychosocial approach to development.

Our biology—established through natural selection as members of the human species or through our unique genetic combination at the time of our conception—provides us with certain abilities and places limits on others. The people and customs in our social environment direct us toward specific roles and reward us for conforming (or punish us for not conforming) to cultural expectations. Our individual biological and psychological characteristics also evoke reactions from those around us, which then influence our behavior. But our choices matter, too. We can study development from any point on this biopsychosocial continuum. Rather than diminishing us, science can enlarge our understanding of ourselves and our appreciation of the world around us.

ASK YOURSELF: Do you believe your heredity and your environment *determined* who you are today or *influenced* who you are today? Can you recall an important time when you determined your own fate in a way that was at odds with your heredity and your environment?

REVIEW CHAPTER 3: Nature, Nurture, and Human Diversity

Test Yourself

1. What is *heritability?*

2. What are the three main criticisms of the evolutionary explanation of human sexuality?

3. To predict whether a teenager smokes, ask how many of the teen's friends smoke. One explanation for this correlation is peer influence. What's another?

4. How do individualist and collectivist cultures differ?

5. What are gender roles, and what do their variations tell us about our human capacity for learning and adaptation?

Answers to the Test Yourself questions can be found in Appendix B at the end of the book.

Terms and Concepts to Remember

environment, p. 96
behavior genetics, p. 96
chromosomes, p. 96
DNA, p. 96
genes, p. 96
genome, p. 96
identical twins, p. 97
fraternal twins, p. 98
temperament, p. 102
heritability, p. 102
interaction, p. 105

molecular genetics, p. 105
evolutionary psychology, p. 107
natural selection, p. 108
mutation, p. 108
gender, p. 110
culture, p. 119
norm, p. 120
personal space, p. 120
individualism, p. 121
collectivism, p. 121
aggression, p. 127

X chromosome, p. 129
Y chromosome, p. 129
testosterone, p. 130
role, p. 131
gender role, p. 131
gender identity, p. 132
gender-typing, p. 132
social learning theory, p. 132
gender schema theory, p. 132

WEB

 To continue your study and review of Nature, Nurture, and Human Diversity, visit this book's Web site at www. worthpublishers.com/myers. You will find practice tests, review activities, and many interesting articles and Web links for more information on topics related to Nature, Nurture, and Human Diversity.

ANOTHER VOICE ON: DEVELOPING THROUGH THE LIFE SPAN

JHUMPA LAHIRI (b. 1967), FROM *THE NAMESAKE*, 2003

Ashima Ganguli . . . is in labor. . . . She is alone, cut off by curtains from the three other women in the room. . . . It is the first time in her life she has slept alone, surrounded by strangers; all her life she has slept either in a room with her parents, or with Ashoke at her side. She wishes the curtains were open, so that she could talk to the American women. Perhaps one of them has given birth before, can tell her what to expect. But she has gathered that Americans, in spite of their public declarations of affections, in spite of their miniskirts and bikinis, in spite of their hand-holding on the street and lying on top of each other on the Cambridge Common, prefer their privacy. She spreads her fingers over the taut, enormous drum her middle has become, wondering where the baby's feet and hands are at this moment. The child is no longer restless; for the past few days, apart from the occasional flutter, she has not felt it punch or kick or press against her ribs. She wonders if she is the only Indian person in the hospital, but a gentle twitch from the baby reminds her that she is, technically speaking, not alone. Ashima thinks it is strange that her child will be born in a place most people enter to either suffer or to die . . . . In India, she thinks to herself, women go home to their parents to give birth, away from husbands and in-laws and household cares, retreating briefly to childhood when the baby arrives.

4: Developing Through the Life Span

OBJECTIVE 1 | State the three areas of change that developmental psychologists study, and identify the three major issues in developmental psychology.

As we journey through life—from womb to tomb—when, how, and why do we develop? We can't help but notice how people differ. However, to **developmental psychologists,** who study physical, cognitive, and social changes throughout the human life cycle, discerning our commonalities is just as important. Virtually all of us began walking around age 1 and talking by age 2. As children, we engaged in social play in preparation for life's work. As adults, we all smile and cry, love and loathe, and occasionally ponder the fact that someday we will die. Psychology's developmental perspective examines how people are continually developing, from infancy through old age. Much of its research centers on three major issues:

1. *Nature/nurture:* How do genetic inheritance (*our nature*) and experience (*the nurture we receive*) influence our development?
2. *Continuity/stages:* Is development a gradual, continuous process like riding an escalator, or does it proceed through a sequence of separate stages, like climbing rungs on a ladder?
3. *Stability/change:* Do our early personality traits persist through life, or do we become different persons as we age?

In Chapter 3, we engaged the nature/nurture issue. At this chapter's end, we will reflect on the continuity and stability issues.

> "Nature is all that a man brings with him into the world; nurture is every influence that affects him after his birth."
>
> Francis Galton, *English Men of Science,* 1874

Study Tip Reminder: Treat each main section of a chapter as if it were a short chapter—an amount suitable for reading in one sitting. To assist your doing so, each unit has several Objectives to draw your attention to important points, and ends with a Learning Outcomes section to help you review and reflect on those points.

Prenatal Development and the Newborn

How, over time, did we come to be who we are? From the union of sperm and egg to the birth of the newborn, development progresses in an orderly, though fragile, sequence.

Conception

OBJECTIVE 2 | Describe the union of sperm and egg at conception.

Nothing is more natural than a species reproducing itself. Yet nothing is more wondrous. Consider human reproduction. The process starts when a woman's ovary releases a mature egg, a cell roughly the size of the period at the end of this sentence, and when the 200 million or more sperm deposited during intercourse begin their race upstream toward it. The woman was born with all the immature eggs she would ever have, although only 1 in 5000 will ever mature and be released. A man, in contrast, begins producing sperm cells at puberty. The manufacturing process

■ **developmental psychology** a branch of psychology that studies physical, cognitive, and social change throughout the life span.

139

FIGURE 4.1
Life is sexually transmitted
(a) Sperm cells surround an ovum. (b) As one sperm penetrates the egg's jellylike outer coating, a series of chemical events begins that will cause sperm and egg to fuse into a single cell. If all goes well, that cell will subdivide again and again to emerge 9 months later as a 100-trillion-cell human being.

(a)

(b)

continues 24 hours a day for the rest of his life, although the rate of production—in the beginning more than 1000 sperm during the second it takes to read this phrase—slows with age.

Like space voyagers approaching a huge planet, the sperm approach a cell 85,000 times their own size. The relatively few that make it to the egg release digestive enzymes that eat away the egg's protective coating, allowing a sperm to penetrate (**FIGURE 4.1**). But the egg is hardly passive. As soon as one sperm begins to penetrate, the egg's surface blocks out the others. Meanwhile, fingerlike projections sprout around the successful sperm and pull it in. Before half a day elapses, the egg nucleus and the sperm nucleus fuse. The two have become one. Consider it your most fortunate of moments. Among 200 million sperm, the one needed to make you, in combination with that one particular egg, won the race. Physician and author Lewis Thomas (1979) appreciated the wonder when the first "test tube baby" was born:

> In mid-1978, the newest astonishment in medicine . . . was the birth of an English baby nine months after conception in a dish. The older surprise, which should still be fazing us all, is that a solitary sperm and a single egg can fuse and become a human being. . . . This has been going on under our eyes for so long a time that we've gotten used to it; hence the outcries of amazement at this really minor technical modification of the general procedure—nothing much, really, beyond relocating the beginning of the process from the fallopian tube to a plastic container.

Prenatal Development

OBJECTIVE 3 | Define *zygote*, *embryo*, and *fetus*, and explain how teratogens can affect development.

"From the very moment that the sperm hits the egg, a precarious trip on the thin edge of biological extinction has begun."
Ralph Blair, *Nevertheless Joy!* 1989

Fewer than half of all fertilized eggs, called **zygotes**, survive beyond the first 2 weeks (Grobstein, 1979; Hall, 2004). But for you and me, good fortune prevailed. Beginning as one cell, each of us became 2 cells, then 4—each cell just like the first. Then, within the first week, when this cell division had produced a zygote of some 100 cells, the cells began to *differentiate*—to specialize in structure and function. How identical cells do this—as if one decides "I'll become a brain, you become intestines!"—is a scientific puzzle that developmental biologists are just beginning to solve.

About 10 days after conception, the increasingly diverse cells attach to the mother's uterine wall, beginning approximately 37 weeks of the closest human relationship. The zygote's outer part attaches to the uterine wall, forming the placenta, through which nourishment passes. The inner cells become the **embryo** (**FIGURE 4.2**). Over the next 6 weeks, organs begin to form and function. The heart begins to beat.

By 9 weeks after conception, the embryo looks unmistakably human. It is now a **fetus** (Latin for "offspring" or "young one"). During the sixth month, organs such as the stomach are sufficiently formed and functional to allow a prematurely born fetus a chance of survival. At this point, the fetus is also responsive to sound. Microphone readings taken inside the uterus have revealed that the fetus is exposed to the sound of its mother's muffled voice (Ecklund-Flores, 1992). Immediately after birth, infants prefer this voice to another woman's voice or their father's (Busnel & others, 1992; DeCasper & others, 1984, 1986, 1994).

At each prenatal stage, genetic *and* environmental factors affect our development. The placenta transfers nutrients and oxygen from mother to fetus, while screening out many potentially harmful substances. But some substances slip by. The placental screen can admit **teratogens**—harmful agents such as certain viruses and drugs. If the mother is a heroin addict, her baby will be born a heroin addict. If she carries the AIDS virus, her baby may also. A pregnant woman never smokes alone; she and her fetus both experience reduced blood oxygen and a shot of nicotine. If she is a heavy smoker, her fetus may receive fewer nutrients and be born underweight and at risk for various problems (Pringle & others, 2005).

■ **zygote** the fertilized egg; it enters a 2-week period of rapid cell division and develops into an embryo.

■ **embryo** the developing human organism from about 2 weeks after fertilization through the second month.

■ **fetus** the developing human organism from 9 weeks after conception to birth.

■ **teratogens** agents, such as chemicals and viruses, that can reach the embryo or fetus during prenatal development and cause harm.

Prenatal development
zygote: conception to 2 weeks
embryo: 2 weeks through 8 weeks
fetus: 9 weeks to birth.

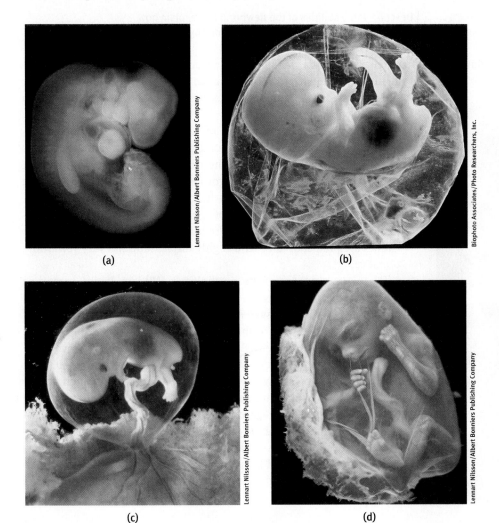

(a)   (b)   (c)   (d)

FIGURE 4.2
Prenatal development
(a) The embryo grows and develops rapidly. At 40 days, the spine is visible and the arms and legs are beginning to grow. (b) Five days later, the inch-long embryo's proportions have begun to change. The rest of the body is now bigger than the head, and the arms and legs have grown noticeably. (c) By the end of the second month, when the fetal period begins, facial features, hands, and feet have formed. (d) As the fetus enters the fourth month, its 3 ounces could fit in the palm of your hand.

■ **fetal alcohol syndrome (FAS)** physical and cognitive abnormalities in children caused by a pregnant woman's heavy drinking. In severe cases, symptoms include noticeable facial misproportions.

■ **rooting reflex** a baby's tendency, when touched on the cheek, to turn toward the touch, open the mouth, and search for the nipple.

"You shall conceive and bear a son. So then drink no wine or strong drink."

Judges 13:7

There is no known safe amount of alcohol for a pregnant woman. Even light drinking can affect the fetal brain, and even a single drinking binge can kill millions of fetal brain cells (Braun, 1996; Ikonomidou & others, 2000). Alcohol enters the woman's bloodstream—and her fetus'—and depresses activity in both their central nervous systems. If she drinks heavily, her baby will be at risk for birth defects and mental retardation. For 1 in 750 infants, the effects are visible as **fetal alcohol syndrome (FAS),** marked by a small, misproportioned head and lifelong brain abnormalities. FAS is now the leading cause of mental retardation (Niccols, 1994; Streissguth & others, 1991). More children suffer from it where maternal drinking has been commonplace (Dorozyaski, 1993; Dorris, 1989). Children of alcoholic mothers are especially at risk. About 4 in 10 alcoholic mothers who drink during pregnancy have babies with FAS.

In many parts of the world, people believe that a woman's psychological state during pregnancy affects her fetus. Exploring this possibility in experiments that stressed pregnant rodents and nonhuman primates, researchers have found that stress does lead to offspring with delayed motor development, increased emotionality, learning deficits, and alterations in neurotransmitter systems associated with human psychological disorders, such as depression (DiPietro, 2004; Huizink & others, 2004). It remains for future studies to determine whether prenatal maternal stress similarly influences human development and, if so, at what level of stress.

The Competent Newborn

OBJECTIVE 4 | Describe some abilities of the newborn, and explain how researchers use habituation to assess infant sensory and cognitive abilities.

Having survived prenatal hazards, we as newborns came equipped with reflexes ideally suited for our survival. We withdrew our limbs to escape pain. If a cloth over our face interfered with our breathing, we turned our head from side to side and swiped at it.

New parents are often in awe of the coordinated sequence of reflexes by which their baby gets food. The **rooting reflex** illustrates this: When something touches their cheek, babies turn toward that touch, open their mouth, and vigorously "root" for a nipple. Finding one, they automatically close on it and begin sucking—which itself requires a coordinated sequence of tonguing, swallowing, and breathing. Failing to find satisfaction, the hungry baby may cry—a behavior parents are predisposed to find highly unpleasant and very rewarding to relieve.

Prepared to feed and eat Animals are predisposed to respond to their offsprings' cries for nourishment.

The pioneering American psychologist William James presumed that the newborn experiences a "blooming, buzzing confusion." Until the 1960s, few people disagreed. It was said that, apart from a blur of meaningless light and dark shades, newborns could not see. But these scientists themselves saw the light, thanks to new investigative techniques that enhance infant studies. They discovered that babies can tell you a lot—if you know how to ask. (See Close-Up: Research Strategies for Understanding Infants' Thinking.) To ask, you must capitalize on what the baby can do—gaze, suck, turn her head. So, equipped with eye-tracking machines and pacifiers wired to electronic gear, researchers set out to answer parents' age-old questions: What can my baby see, hear, smell, and think?

What they discovered was fascinating. We are born preferring sights and sounds that facilitate social responsiveness. As newborns, we turn our heads in the direction of human voices. We gaze longer at a drawing of a facelike image (**FIGURE 4.3**) than at a bull's-eye pattern; yet we gaze more at a bull's-eye pattern—which has contrasts much like those of the human eye—than at a solid disk (Fantz, 1961). We prefer to look at objects 8 to 12 inches away, which, wonder of wonders, just happens to be the approximate distance between a nursing infant's eyes and its mother's (Maurer & Maurer, 1988).

FIGURE 4.3
Newborns' preference for faces
When shown these two stimuli with the same elements, Italian newborns spent nearly twice as many seconds looking at the facelike image (Johnson & Morton, 1991). Canadian newborns—average age 53 minutes in one study—display the same apparently inborn preference to look toward faces (Mondloch & others, 1999).

Our perceptual abilities develop continuously during the first months of life. Within days after birth, our brain's neural networks were stamped with the smell of our mother's body. Thus, a week-old nursing baby, placed between a gauze pad from its mother's bra and one from another nursing mother, will usually turn toward the smell of its own mother's pad (MacFarlane, 1978). At 3 weeks, if given a pacifier that sometimes turns on recordings of its mother's voice and sometimes that of a female stranger's, an infant will suck more vigorously when it hears its now-familiar mother's voice (Mills & Melhuish, 1974). So not only can we as young infants see what we need to see, and smell and hear well, but we are already using our sensory equipment to learn.

■ **habituation** decreasing responsiveness with repeated stimulation. As infants gain familiarity with repeated exposure to a visual stimulus, their interest wanes and they look away sooner.

CLOSE-UP:

RESEARCH STRATEGIES FOR UNDERSTANDING INFANTS' THINKING

Can a newborn see well enough to distinguish shapes? Can a 3-month-old recognize faces? Does a 5-month-old have a concept of number? If babies could talk, we would ask them. But they can't, so psychologists let behavior do the talking. Developmental researchers, for example, exploit a simple form of learning called **habituation**—a decrease in responding with repeated stimulation. A novel stimulus gets attention when first presented. But the more often the stimulus is presented, the weaker the response becomes. This seeming boredom with familiar stimuli gives us a way to ask infants what they see and remember.

Janine Spencer, Paul Quinn, and their colleagues (1997; Quinn, 2002) used a novelty preference procedure to ask 4-month-olds how they recognize cats and dogs. The researchers first

Courtesy Paul Quinn, © John Wiley & Sons

FIGURE 4.4
Quick—which is the cat?
Researchers used cat-dog hybrid images such as these to test how infants categorize animals.

showed the infants a series of images of cats or dogs. Which of the two animals in **FIGURE 4.4** do you think the infants would find more novel (measured in looking time) after seeing a series of cats? It was the hybrid animal with the dog's head (or with a cat's head, if they had previously viewed a series of dogs). This suggests

that infants, like adults, focus first on the face, not the body.

Other researchers using the habituation phenomenon report that infants can also discriminate colors, shapes, and sounds and can understand some basic concepts of numbers and physics (for example, that two solid objects cannot occupy the same space).

Why have such elegantly simple studies been done only recently? Researcher Alan Slater (1994) explains: To recognize a new stimulus as different, an infant must remember the initial stimulus. Until the early 1980s, researchers assumed a newborn's brain was too immature to enable such memory. Then, as their appreciation for a newborn's abilities grew, they devised new ways to test the scope of infant cognition.

>> LEARNING OUTCOMES

Prenatal Development and the Newborn

OBJECTIVE 1 | **State the three areas of change that developmental psychologists study, and identify the three major issues in developmental psychology.**

Developmental psychologists study physical, mental, and social changes throughout the life span. The three major issues are the relative influence of nature (heredity) and nurture (experience); whether development is a continuous process or a series of discrete stages; and whether personality is stable or changes as we age.

OBJECTIVE 2 | **Describe the union of sperm and egg at conception.**

At conception, only one of the man's sperm can penetrate the outer coating of the woman's egg before the egg's surface blocks out all others. Within about 12 hours, the nuclei of the sperm and egg fuse into a single cell.

OBJECTIVE 3 | **Define *zygote*, *embryo*, and *fetus*, and explain how teratogens can affect development.**

A *zygote* is a fertilized egg, whose cells become increasingly diverse. After about 10 days, the outer part of the cell mass attaches to the mother's uterine wall and the inner cells soon become the *embryo*, beginning a stage of development when major organs form and begin to function. From 9 weeks after fertilization until birth, the organism, now known as a *fetus*, continues to develop and grow. *Teratogens* are potentially harmful agents that can pass through the placental screen and harm the developing embryo or fetus.

OBJECTIVE 4 | **Describe some abilities of the newborn, and explain how researchers use habituation to assess infant sensory and cognitive abilities.**

Infants are born with a number of automatic responses (reflexes) that aid survival, including the rooting reflex that helps them locate food. Newborns' rapidly developing senses of sight and hearing seem tuned to social events, such as a caretaker's face or voice. Researchers can discover some of what preverbal infants sense and think by observing how they react to novel stimuli (such as colors, shapes, and forms) and grow bored with (habituate to) familiar stimuli. To recognize a new stimulus as different, an infant must remember the old stimulus, which indicates a simple form of learning.

ASK YOURSELF: Are you surprised by the news of infants' competencies? Or did you "know it all along"?

Infancy and Childhood

During infancy, a baby grows from newborn to toddler, and during childhood from toddler to teenager. We all traveled this path, developing physically, cognitively, and socially. From infancy on, brain and mind, neural hardware and cognitive software, develop together.

> "It is a rare privilege to watch the birth, growth, and first feeble struggles of a living human mind."
>
> Annie Sullivan, in Helen Keller's *The Story of My Life*, 1903

Physical Development

Infants' biological development underlies their psychological development. To understand the emergence of motor skills and memory, we must understand the developing brain.

Brain Development

OBJECTIVE 5 | Describe some developmental changes in a child's brain, and explain why maturation accounts for many of our similarities.

While you resided in your mother's womb, your body was forming nerve cells at the explosive rate of nearly one-quarter million per *minute*. The developing brain cortex actually overproduces neurons, with the number peaking at 28 weeks and then subsiding to a stable 23 billion or so at birth (Rabinowicz & others, 1996, 1999; de Courten-Myers, 2002). On the day you were born, you had most of the brain cells you would ever have. However, at birth your nervous system was immature: After birth, the neural networks that eventually enabled you to walk, talk, and remember had a wild growth spurt (**FIGURE 4.5**). From ages 3 to 6, the brain's neural network is

FIGURE 4.5

Drawings of human cerebral cortex sections

In humans, the brain is immature at birth. As the child matures, the neural networks grow increasingly more complex.

At birth   3 months   15 months

sprouting most rapidly in the frontal lobes, which enable rational planning (and which continue developing into adolescence and beyond). The association areas of the cortex—those linked with thinking, memory, and language—are the last brain areas to develop. As they do, mental abilities surge ahead (Chugani & Phelps, 1986; Thatcher & others, 1987). Fiber pathways supporting language and agility proliferate into puberty, after which a pruning process shuts down excess connections, while strengthening others (Paus & others, 1999; Thompson & others, 2000).

A flower unfolds in accord with its genetic instructions. So do we, experiencing an orderly sequence of genetically designed biological growth processes called **maturation.** Maturation decrees many of our commonalities—from standing before walking, to using nouns before adjectives. Severe deprivation or abuse will retard development, and ample experiences with parents who talk and read to the child will help sculpt neural connections. Yet the genetic growth tendencies are inborn. Maturation sets the basic course of development; experience adjusts it.

Motor Development

OBJECTIVE 6 | Outline four events in the motor development sequence from birth to toddlerhood, and evaluate the effects of maturation and experience on that sequence.

The developing brain enables physical coordination. As an infant's muscles and nervous system mature, more complicated skills emerge. With minor exceptions, the sequence of physical (motor) development is universal. Babies roll over before they sit unsupported, and they usually creep on all fours before they walk (**FIGURE 4.6**). These behaviors reflect not imitation but a maturing nervous system; blind children, too, crawl before they walk.

There are, however, individual differences in the timing of this sequence. In the United States, for example, 25 percent of all babies walk by age 11 months, 50 percent within a week after their first birthday, and 90 percent by age 15 months (Frankenburg & others, 1992). The recommended infant "back-to-sleep" position (putting babies to sleep on their backs to reduce the risk of a smothering crib death) has been associated with somewhat later crawling but not with later walking (Davis & others, 1998; Lipsitt, 2003).

Genes play a major role. Identical twins typically begin sitting up and walking on nearly the same day (Wilson, 1979). Biological maturation—including the rapid development of the cerebellum at the back of the brain—creates our readiness to learn

■ **maturation** biological growth processes that enable orderly changes in behavior, relatively uninfluenced by experience.

"This is the path to adulthood. You're here."

FIGURE 4.6
Triumphant toddlers
Sit, crawl, walk, run—the sequence of these motor development milestones is the same the world around, though babies reach them at varying ages.

walking at about age 1. Experience before that time has a limited effect. This is true for other physical skills, including bowel and bladder control. Before necessary muscular and neural maturation, no pleading, harassment, or punishment will produce successful toilet training.

Maturation and Infant Memory

OBJECTIVE 7 | Explain why we have few memories of experiences during our first three years of life.

Our earliest memories seldom predate our third birthdays. We see this "infantile amnesia" in the memories of some preschoolers who experienced an emergency fire evacuation caused by a burning popcorn maker. Seven years later they were able to recall the alarm and what caused it—*if* they were 4 to 5 years old at the time. Those who experienced the event as 3-year-olds could not remember the cause and usually misrecalled being already outside when the alarm sounded (Pillemer, 1995).

Other studies confirm that the average age of earliest conscious memory is 3.5 years (Bauer, 2002). By 4 to 5 years, childhood amnesia is giving way to remembered experiences (Bruce & others, 2000).

Memories of our preschool years are very few because we organize our memories differently after age 3 or 4. As the brain cortex matures, toddlers gain a sense of self and their long-term storage increases (Howe, 2003). Trying to access memories of those first 4 years is like trying to read a document formatted by an earlier version of a computer operating system (Hayne, 2004; Loftus & Kaufman, 1992). Infants' preverbal memories do not easily translate into their later language.

For parents, children's blank memory for infancy can be disconcerting. After all, we parents spend countless hours with our babies—frolicking on the rug, diapering, feeding, and rocking them to sleep. But what will they consciously remember of us if we die before they reach age 4? Virtually nothing!

Although we consciously recall little from before age 4, some memories exist during and beyond those early years. Given occasional reminders, 3-month-old infants who learn that moving their leg propels a mobile will remember the association for at least a month (**FIGURE 4.7**). Ten-year-olds shown photos of former classmates they had not seen since preschool recognize (amid other photos of preschoolers) only 1 in 5 of their one-time compatriots. Yet their physiological responses (measured as skin perspiration) are greater to their former classmates, whether or not they consciously recognize them (Newcombe & others, 2000). What the conscious mind does not know and cannot express in words, the nervous system somehow remembers.

Can you recall your first day of preschool (or your third birthday party)?

Still building a sense of self
What will Evan remember from his infant experience? Nothing *consciously*, but conscious memories are not everything. His neural networks are wildly expanding with the stimulating experiences his caregivers are providing, and he is busy learning all about his new world.

See Chapter 9 for a discussion of children's eyewitness recall.

FIGURE 4.7
Infant at work
Babies only 3 months old can learn that kicking moves a mobile—and can retain that learning for a month. (From Rovee-Collier, 1989, 1997.)

Cognitive Development

OBJECTIVE **8** | State Piaget's understanding of how the mind develops, and discuss the importance of assimilation and accommodation in this process.

"Who knows the thoughts of a child?" wondered poet Nora Perry. As much as anyone of his generation, developmental psychologist Jean Piaget (pronounced Pee-ah-ZHAY) knew. His interest began in 1920, when he was working in Paris to develop questions for children's intelligence tests. While administering tests to find out at what age children could answer certain questions correctly, Piaget became intrigued by children's *wrong* answers. Where others saw childish mistakes, Piaget saw intelligence at work. The errors made by children of a given age, he noted, were often strikingly similar.

A half-century spent with children convinced Piaget that a child's mind is not a miniature model of an adult's. Piaget revolutionized our understanding of children's minds, much as Copernicus revolutionized our understanding of the solar system, suggests William Damon (1995). Until Piaget, most people—forgetting their own preschool days—assumed children "simply knew less, not *differently*, than adults" (p. 100). Thanks partly to his work, we now understand that "children reason in wildly illogical ways about problems whose solutions are self-evident to adults" (Brainerd, 1996).

Piaget further believed that a child's mind develops through a series of stages, in an upward march from the newborn's simple reflexes to the adult's abstract reasoning power. An 8-year-old child comprehends things a 3-year-old cannot. An 8-year-old might grasp the analogy "getting an idea is like having a light turn on in your head." Trying to teach the same analogy to a 3-year-old would be fruitless. An 8-year-old also understands what the 2-year-olds in **FIGURE 4.8** do not—that the miniature slide is too small for sliding, and the miniature car is much too small to get into. But our adult minds likewise engage in reasoning uncomprehended by 8-year-olds.

■ **schema** a concept or framework that organizes and interprets information.

> "Childhood has its own way of seeing, thinking, and feeling, and there is nothing more foolish than the attempt to put ours in its place."
>
> Philosopher Jean-Jacques Rousseau, 1798

FIGURE 4.8
Scale errors
Psychologists Judy DeLoache, David Uttal, and Karl Rosengren (2004) report that 18- to 30-month-old children may fail to take the size of an object into account when trying to perform impossible actions with it. At left, a 21-month-old attempts to slide down a miniature slide. At right, a 24-month-old opens the door to a miniature car and tries to step inside.

Piaget believed the driving force behind this intellectual progression is our unceasing struggle to make sense of our experiences. His core idea is that "children are active thinkers, constantly trying to construct more advanced understandings of the world" (Siegler & Ellis, 1996). To this end, the maturing brain builds concepts, which Piaget called **schemas.** Schemas (or schemes) are mental molds into which we pour our experiences. By adulthood we have built countless schemas, ranging from cats and dogs to our concept of love (**FIGURE 4.9**).

FIGURE 4.9
An impossible object
Look carefully at the "devil's tuning fork" at left. Now look away—no, better first study it some more—and then look away and draw it. . . . Not so easy, is it? Because this tuning fork is an impossible object, you have no schema for such an image.

Two-year-old Gabriella has learned the schema for "cow" from her picture books.

Gabriella sees a moose and calls it a "cow." She is trying to assimilate this new animal into an existing schema. Her mother tells her, "No, it's a moose."

Gabriella accommodates her schema for large, shaggy animals and continues to modify that schema to include "mommy moose," "baby moose," and so forth.

FIGURE 4.10
Pouring experience into mental molds
We use our existing schemas to assimilate new experiences. But sometimes we need to accommodate (adjust) our schemas to include new experiences.

Jean Piaget
"If we examine the intellectual development of the individual or of the whole of humanity, we shall find that the human spirit goes through a certain number of stages, each different from the other" (1930).

To explain how we use and adjust our schemas, Piaget proposed two processes. First, we **assimilate** new experiences—we interpret them in terms of our current understandings (schemas). Having a simple schema for *dog*, for example, a toddler may call all four-legged animals *doggies*. But we also adjust, or **accommodate,** our schemas to fit the particulars of new experiences. The child soon learns that the original *doggie* schema is too broad and accommodates by refining the category (focusing especially on the head, as we noted earlier). As children interact with the world, they construct and modify their schemas (**FIGURE 4.10**)

Piaget's Theory and Current Thinking

OBJECTIVE 9 | Outline Piaget's four main stages of cognitive development, and comment on how children's thinking changes during these four stages.

Cognition refers to all the mental activities associated with thinking, knowing, remembering, and communicating. Piaget believed that children experience spurts of change followed by greater stability as they move from one cognitive developmental plateau to the next. These plateaus form four stages (**TABLE 4.1**), each with distinctive characteristics that permit specific kinds of thinking. To appreciate how a child's mind grows, let's look at Piaget's stages in the light of our current thinking about cognitive development.

TABLE 4.1

PIAGET'S STAGES OF COGNITIVE DEVELOPMENT

Typical Age Range	Description of Stage	Developmental Phenomena
Birth to nearly 2 years	*Sensorimotor* Experiencing the world through senses and actions (looking, touching, mouthing, and grasping)	• Object permanence • Stranger anxiety
2 to about 6 or 7 years	*Preoperational* Representing things with words and images; use intuitive rather than logical reasoning	• Pretend play • Egocentrism • Language development
About 7 to 11 years	*Concrete operational* Thinking logically about concrete events; grasping concrete analogies and performing arithmetical operations	• Conservation • Mathematical transformations
About 12 through adulthood	*Formal operational* Abstract reasoning	• Abstract logic • Potential for mature moral reasoning

Sensorimotor Stage During Piaget's **sensorimotor stage,** from birth to nearly age 2, babies take in the world through their sensory and motor interactions with objects--through looking, hearing, touching, mouthing, and grasping.

Very young babies seem to live in the present: What is out of sight is out of mind. In one of his tests, Piaget would show an infant an appealing toy and then flop his beret over it to see whether the infant searched for the toy. Before the age of 6 months, the infant did not. Young infants lack **object permanence**—the awareness that objects continue to exist when not perceived (**FIGURE 4.11**). By 8 months, infants begin exhibiting memory for things no longer seen. If you hide a toy, the infant will momentarily look for it. Within another month or two, the infant will look for it even after being restrained for several seconds.

FIGURE 4.11
Object permanence
Infants younger than 6 months seldom understand that things continue to exist when they are out of sight. But for this infant, out of sight is definitely not out of mind.

Doug Goodman

But does object permanence in fact blossom at 8 months, much as tulips blossom in spring? Today's researchers see development as more continuous than Piaget did, and they now view object permanence as unfolding gradually. Even young infants will at least momentarily look for a toy where they saw it hidden a second before.

Researchers believe that Piaget and his followers underestimated young children's competence. Piaget assumed that before age 2, infants cannot think. They can recognize things, smile at them, crawl to them, manipulate them. But they have no abstract concepts or ideas. Theirs is a life lived, but not thought about.

Consider, however, some simple experiments that demonstrate baby logic:

- Like adults staring in disbelief at a magic trick (the "Whoa!" look), infants look longer at an unexpected scene of a car seeming to pass through a solid object, a ball stopping in midair, or an object violating object permanence by magically disappearing (Baillargeon, 1995, 1998, 2004; Wellman & Gelman, 1992). Babies seem to have a more intuitive grasp of simple laws of physics than Piaget realized.

- Babies also have a head for numbers. Karen Wynn (1992, 2000) showed 5-month-olds one or two objects. Then she hid the objects behind a screen, and then visibly removed or added one (**FIGURE 4.12** on page 150). When she lifted the screen, the infants sometimes did a double take, staring longer when shown a wrong number of objects. But were they just responding to a greater or smaller mass of objects, rather than a change in number (Feigenson & others, 2002)? Later experiments showed that babies' number sense extends to larger numbers and such things as drumbeats and motions (Lipton & Spelke, 2003; McCrink & Wynn, 2004; Spelke, 2000; Wynn & others, 2002). If accustomed to a Daffy Duck puppet jumping three times on stage, they show surprise if it jumps only twice. Clearly, infants are smarter than Piaget appreciated. Even as babies, we had a lot on our minds.

The educated public's new appreciation for infant competence enabled a spoof headline in a 2002 *Onion:* "STUDY REVEALS: BABIES ARE STUPID" (based on "research" showing that infants cannot learn to read a map or scuba dive).

■ **assimilation** interpreting one's new experience in terms of one's existing schemas.

■ **accommodation** adapting one's current understandings (schemas) to incorporate new information.

■ **cognition** all the mental activities associated with thinking, knowing, remembering, and communicating.

■ **sensorimotor stage** in Piaget's theory, the stage (from birth to about 2 years of age) during which infants know the world mostly in terms of their sensory impressions and motor activities.

■ **object permanence** the awareness that things continue to exist even when not perceived.

FIGURE 4.12
Baby math
Shown a numerically impossible outcome, infants stare longer. (From Wynn, 1992.)

Then either: possible outcome

5. Screen drops...   revealing 1 object

or: impossible outcome

5. Screen drops...   revealing 2 objects

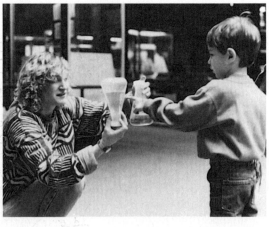

1. Objects placed in case 2. Screen comes up 3. Empty hand enters 4. One object removed

■ **preoperational stage** in Piaget's theory, the stage (from about 2 to 6 or 7 years of age) during which a child learns to use language but does not yet comprehend the mental operations of concrete logic.

■ **conservation** the principle (which Piaget believed to be a part of concrete operational reasoning) that properties such as mass, volume, and number remain the same despite changes in the forms of objects.

■ **egocentrism** in Piaget's theory, the preoperational child's difficulty taking another's point of view.

■ **theory of mind** people's ideas about their own and others' mental states—about their feelings, perceptions, and thoughts and the behavior these might predict.

Preoperational Stage Piaget believed that during the preschool period and up to about age 6 or 7, children are in a **preoperational stage**—too young to perform mental operations. For a 5-year-old, the milk that seems "too much" in a tall, narrow glass may become an acceptable amount if poured into a short, wide glass. Focusing only on the height dimension the child is incapable of performing the *operation* of mentally pouring the milk back. This preoperational child lacks the concept of **conservation**—the principle that quantity remains the same despite changes in shape (**FIGURE 4.13**). Closed beakers with identical volumes seem suddenly to hold different amounts after one is merely inverted.

FIGURE 4.13
Piaget's test of conservation
This preoperational child does not yet understand the principle of conservation of substance. Closed beakers with identical volumes seem suddenly to hold different amounts after one is merely inverted.

Ontario Science Center

Question: If most 2½-year-olds do not understand how miniature dolls and toys can symbolize real objects, should anatomically correct dolls be used when questioning such children about alleged physical or sexual abuse? Judy DeLoache (1995) reports that "very young children do not find it natural or easy to use a doll as a representation of themselves."

Piaget did not view the stage transitions as abrupt. Even so, symbolic thinking appears at an earlier age than he supposed. Judy DeLoache (1987) discovered this when she showed children a model of a room and hid a model toy in it (a miniature stuffed dog behind a miniature couch). The 2½-year-olds easily remembered where to find the miniature toy, but they could not use the model to locate an actual stuffed dog behind a couch in a real room. Three-year-olds—only 6 months older—usually went right to the actual stuffed animal in the real room, showing that they *could* think of the model as a symbol for the room. Piaget probably would have been surprised.

Egocentrism Piaget contended that preschool children are **egocentric:** They have difficulty perceiving things from another's point of view. Asked to "show Mommy your picture," 2-year-old Gabriella holds the picture up facing her own eyes. Three-year-old Gray makes himself "invisible" by putting his hands over his eyes, assuming that if he can't see someone, they can't see him. Children's conversations also reveal their egocentrism, as one young boy demonstrated (Phillips, 1969, p. 61):

"Do you have a brother?"
"Yes."
"What's his name?"
"Jim."
"Does Jim have a brother?"
"No."

TV-watching preschoolers who block your view of the television assume that you see what they see. When relating to a young child, remember that such behaviors reflect a cognitive limitation: The egocentric preschoolers are not intentionally "selfish" or "inconsiderate." They simply have not developed the ability to take another's viewpoint. We never, however, fully outgrow our early childhood egocentrism. Even as adults, we often overestimate the extent to which others share our opinions and perspective, as when we assume that something will be clear to others if it is clear to us (Epley & others, 2004). Children, however, are even more susceptible to this "curse of knowledge" (Birch, 2005).

Parents who abuse their children generally have no understanding of children's greater egocentrism. They see their children as junior adults able to control their behavior (Larrance & Twentyman, 1983). Thus, they misperceive an egocentric child who stands in the way, spills food, disobeys negative instructions, or cries as willfully malicious.

Theory of Mind When Little Red Riding Hood realizes her "grandmother" is really a wolf, she swiftly revises her ideas about the creature's intentions and races away. Preschoolers, although still egocentric, develop this ability to infer others' mental states when they begin forming a **theory of mind** (a term coined by psychologists David Premack and Guy Woodruff, to describe chimpanzees' seeming ability to read intentions).

As their ability to infer others' mental states develops, children will seek to understand what made a playmate angry, when a sibling will share, and what might make a parent buy a toy. The preschooler's growing ability to tease, empathize, and persuade stems from this growing ability to take another's perspective. Between about 3½ and 4½, for example, children worldwide come to realize that others may hold false beliefs (Callaghan & others, 2005; Wellman & others, 2001; Zimmer, 2003). Jennifer Jenkins and Janet Astington (1996) showed Toronto children a Band Aids box and asked them what was inside. Expecting Band Aids, the children were surprised to discover that the box actually contained pencils. Asked what a child who had never seen the box would think was inside, 3-year-olds typically answered "pencils." By age 4 to 5, the children's "theory of mind" had leapt forward, and they delighted in anticipating their friends' false belief that the box would hold Band Aids.

Our theory of mind also enables us to infer others' feelings. Even young preschoolers understand that sad events cause sad feelings, report John Flavell and his Stanford colleagues (2001). Next, children come to understand that thoughts can cause feelings—for example, that reminders of an earlier sad event can trigger a sad feeling. Finally, between ages 5 and 8, children learn that spontaneous self-produced thoughts can also create feelings. If someone's mood suddenly changes for no apparent reason, an 8-year-old will assume the occurrence of a thought.

Researchers explore children's ability to take another person's perspective with seemingly simple experiments. In one experiment (**FIGURE 4.14**), children see a doll named Sally leaving her ball in a red cupboard. Another doll, Anne, then moves the ball to a blue cupboard.

FAMILY CIRCUS ® BIL KEANE

"Don't you remember, Grandma? You were in it with me."

FIGURE 4.14
Testing children's theory of mind
This simple problem illustrates how researchers explore children's presumptions about others' mental states. (Inspired by Baron-Cohen & others, 1985.)

This is Sally. This is Anne.

Sally puts her ball in the red cupboard.

Sally goes away.

Anne moves the ball to the blue cupboard.

Where will Sally look for her ball?

CLOSE-UP:

AUTISM

Autism, a disorder characterized by deficient communication and social interaction, is marked by an impaired theory of mind (Klein & Kihlstrom, 1998; Yirmiya & others, 1998). People with autism are said to be "mind blind." They have difficulty inferring others' thoughts and feelings. They do not appreciate that playmates and parents might view things differently. Mindreading that you do intuitively—is that face conveying a happy smile, a self-satisfied smirk, or a contemptuous sneer?—is difficult for those with autism. Most children learn that another child's pouting mouth signals sadness, and that twinkling eyes mean happiness or mischief. A child with autism (which is related to malfunctions of brain areas that enable attending to others) fails to understand these signals (Frith & Frith, 2001). *Asperger syndrome,* which is sometimes classified as a "high functioning" form of autism, is marked by normal intelligence, often accompanied by exceptional skill or talent in a specific area, but deficient social and communication skills (and thus an inability to form normal peer relationships).

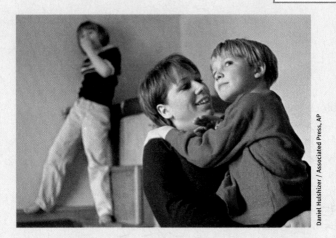

Daniel Hulshizer / Associated Press, AP

Autism

Both of Bobbie Gallagher's children were diagnosed with autism, which is marked by deficient social communication and difficulty in grasping others' states of mind.

Symptoms of autism, which can also include speech difficulty and clumsiness, range from mild to severe, and for reasons still debated, diagnoses of autism have increased in recent years. The underlying cause—altered brain circuitry involving the fibers that connect distant neurons and enable communication among brain regions—appears to result from an unknown number of genes interacting with the environment (Blakeslee, 2005; Wickelgren, 2005).

In a provocative new theory, psychologist Simon Baron-Cohen (2004, 2005) proposes that autism represents an "extreme male brain." Girls are naturally predisposed to be "empathizers," he contends. They are better at reading facial expressions and gestures—a task that challenges those with autism. Although the sexes overlap, boys, he believes, tend to be "systemizers"—of understanding things according to rules or laws, as in mathematical and mechanical systems. "If two 'systemizers' have a child, this will increase the risk of the child having autism," he theorizes. And because of "assortative mating"—people's tendency to seek spouses who share their interests—two systemizers will indeed often mate, he notes. "I do not discount environmental factors; I'm just saying, don't forget about biology." Elizabeth Spelke (2005), however, is skeptical of the supposed inborn, male-systemizing tendency. From other research, she sees "no male advantage for perceiving objects or learning about mechanical systems. In most studies, male and female infants are found to discover the same things at the same times." So, is there any merit to the idea that children with autism (most of whom are male) have extreme male brains? Stay tuned for more research to come.

Researchers then pose a question: When Sally returns, where will she look for the ball? Children with *autism* (see Close-Up: Autism) have difficulty understanding that Sally's state of mind differs from their own—that Sally, not knowing the ball has been moved, will return to the red cupboard. They also have difficulty reflecting on their own mental states. They are, for example, less likely to use the personal pronouns *I* and *me*. Deaf children who have hearing parents and minimal opportunities for communication have similar difficulty inferring others' states of mind (Peterson & Siegal, 1999).

Our abilities to perform mental operations, to think symbolically, and to take another's perspective are not absent in the preoperational stage, and then miraculously present later. Rather, these abilities begin early and develop gradually (Wellman & others, 2001) (**FIGURE 4.15**).

■ **autism** a disorder that appears in childhood and is marked by deficient communication, social interaction, and understanding of others' states of mind.

(a)

(b)

(c)

FIGURE 4.15
Piaget's stages
(a) **Sensorimotor stage**
Infants try to get to know their dog by tasting and touching it.
(b) **Preoperational stage**
Preschoolers see the family pet as yet another playmate, existing purely for them to play with.
(c) **Concrete and formal operational stages**
Older children begin to understand the level of responsibility and work that is associated with keeping a pet.

By age 7, children become increasingly capable of thinking in words and of using words to work out solutions to problems. They do this, noted the Russian psychologist Lev Vygotsky (1896–1934), by no longer thinking aloud. Instead they internalize their culture's language and rely on inner speech. Parents who say "no" when pulling a child's hand away from a cake are giving the child a self-control tool. When later needing to resist temptation the child may likewise say "no." Second-graders who mutter to themselves while doing math problems grasp third-grade math better the following year (Berk, 1994). Whether out loud or inaudible, talking to themselves helps children control their behavior and emotions and master new skills. And when parents give children words, they provide, in Vygotsky's words, a *scaffold* upon which children can step to higher levels of thinking.

Concrete Operational Stage By the time children are about 6 or 7 years of age, said Piaget, they enter the **concrete operational stage.** Given concrete materials, they begin to grasp conservation—that change in shape does not mean change in quantity. They can mentally pour milk back and forth between glasses of different shapes. They also enjoy jokes that allow them to use their new understanding of conservation:

> Mr. Jones went into a restaurant and ordered a whole pizza for his dinner. When the waiter asked if he wanted it cut into 6 or 8 pieces, Mr. Jones said, "Oh, you'd better make it 6, I could never eat 8 pieces!" (McGhee, 1976)

During the concrete operational stage, said Piaget, children fully gain the mental ability to comprehend mathematical transformations and conservation. When my daughter Laura was 6, I was astonished at her inability to reverse arithmetic operations. Asked, "What is 8 plus 4?" she required 5 seconds to compute "12," and another 5 seconds to then compute 12 minus 4. By age 8, she could answer the second question instantly.

■ **concrete operational stage** in Piaget's theory, the stage of cognitive development (from about 6 or 7 to 11 years of age) during which children gain the mental operations that enable them to think logically about concrete events.

Formal Operational Stage By age 12, our reasoning expands from the purely concrete (involving actual experience) to encompass abstract thinking (involving imagined realities and symbols). As children approach adolescence, said Piaget, many become capable of solving hypothetical propositions and deducing consequences: *If this, then that.* Systematic reasoning, what Piaget called **formal operational** thinking, is now within their grasp.

Although full-blown logic and reasoning await adolescence, the rudiments of formal operational thinking begin earlier than Piaget realized. Consider this simple problem:

> If John is in school, then Mary is in school. John is in school. What can you say about Mary?

Formal operational thinkers have no trouble answering correctly. But neither do most 7-year-olds (Suppes, 1982).

Reflecting on Piaget's Theory

OBJECTIVE 10 | Discuss psychologists' current views on Piaget's theory of cognitive development.

Piaget's stage theory has been influential. In some respects, it gets high marks. Studies around the globe, from aboriginal Australia to Algeria to North America, have supported his idea that human cognition unfolds basically in the sequence Piaget proposed (Segall & others, 1990). However, today's researchers see development as more continuous than did Piaget. By detecting the beginnings of each type of thinking at earlier ages, they have revealed conceptual abilities Piaget missed. Moreover, they see formal logic as a smaller part of cognition than he did.

What remains of Piaget's ideas about the child's mind? Plenty—enough to merit his being singled out in 1999 by *Time* magazine as one of the century's 20 most influential scientists and thinkers and rated in a survey of British psychologists as the greatest twentieth-century psychologist (*Psychologist*, 2003). Piaget identified significant cognitive milestones and stimulated worldwide interest in how the mind develops. His emphasis was less on the ages at which children typically reach specific milestones than on their sequence—a sequence that later research has shown is pretty much as he described (Lourenco & Machado, 1996). Piaget would not be surprised that today, as part of our own cognitive development, we are adapting his ideas to accommodate new findings.

What are the implications of all this for parents and teachers? Piaget contended that children construct their understandings from their *interactions* with the world. This implies that children are not passive receptacles waiting to be filled with a teacher's knowledge. Teachers would do better to build on what children already know, engaging them in concrete demonstrations and stimulating them to think for themselves. Future parents and teachers, remember: Young children are incapable of adult logic. Realize that what is simple and obvious to you—that getting off a teeter-totter will cause a friend on the other end to crash—may be incomprehensible to a 3-year-old. And accept children's cognitive immaturity as adaptive. It is nature's strategy for keeping children close to protective adults and providing time for learning and socialization (Bjorklund & Green, 1992).

Social Development

OBJECTIVE 11 | Define *stranger anxiety*.

A human is, as Aristotle said, "a social animal," destined to live in close relationship with important others. How then do the bonds of attachment form? What happens when they form securely, or when they are missing or broken?

> " Assessing the impact of Piaget on developmental psychology is like assessing the impact of Shakespeare in English literature."
>
> Developmental psychologist Harry Beilin (1992)

■ **formal operational stage** in Piaget's theory, the stage of cognitive development (normally beginning about age 12) during which people begin to think logically about abstract concepts.

■ **stranger anxiety** the fear of strangers that infants commonly display, beginning by about 8 months of age.

■ **attachment** an emotional tie with another person; shown in young children by their seeking closeness to the caregiver and showing distress on separation.

From birth, babies are social creatures. In all cultures, infants develop an intense bond with their caregivers. Beginning with a newborn's attraction to humans in general, infants soon come to prefer familiar faces and voices, then to coo and gurgle when given their mother's or father's attention. Soon after object permanence emerges and children become mobile, a curious thing happens: In most cultures, they develop a fear of strangers, called **stranger anxiety.** Beginning at about 8 months, they may greet strangers by crying and reaching for their familiar caregivers. "No! Don't leave me!" their distress seems to say. At about this age, children have schemas for familiar faces; when they cannot assimilate the new face into these remembered schemas, they become distressed (Kagan, 1984). This illustrates an important principle: The brain, mind, and social-emotional behavior develop together.

At 12 months, many infants cling tightly to a parent when they are frightened or expect separation. Reunited after being separated, they shower the parent with smiles and hugs. No social behavior is more striking than this intense and mutual infant-parent bond.

Origins of Attachment

OBJECTIVE 12 | Discuss the effects of nourishment, body contact, and familiarity on infant social attachment.

The **attachment** bond is a powerful survival impulse that keeps infants close to their caregivers. Infants become attached to those—typically their parents—who are comfortable and familiar. For many years, developmental psychologists had reasoned that infants became attached to those who satisfied their need for nourishment. It made sense. But an accidental finding overturned this explanation.

Body Contact During the 1950s, University of Wisconsin psychologists Harry Harlow and Margaret Harlow bred monkeys for their learning studies. To equalize the infant monkeys' experiences and to isolate any disease, they separated them from their mothers shortly after birth and raised them in sanitary individual cages, which included a cheesecloth baby blanket (Harlow & others, 1971). Surprisingly, the infants became intensely attached to their blankets: When the blankets were taken to be laundered, the monkeys became distressed.

The Harlows recognized that this attachment to the blanket contradicted the idea that attachment derives from an association with nourishment. But how could they show this more convincingly? To pit the drawing power of a food source against the contact comfort of the blanket, they created two artificial mothers. One was a bare wire cylinder with a wooden head, the other a cylinder wrapped with terry cloth. By attaching a bottle they could associate either with nourishment.

When reared with both a nourishing wire mother and a non-nourishing cloth mother, the monkeys overwhelmingly preferred the comfy cloth mother (**FIGURE 4.16**). Like human infants clinging to their mothers, the monkeys would cling to their cloth mothers when anxious. They also used her as a secure base from which to venture into the environment, as if attached to the mother by an invisible elastic band that stretched so far and then pulled the infant back. Further studies revealed other qualities—rocking, warmth, and feeding—that made the cloth mother even more appealing.

Human infants, too, become attached to parents who are soft and warm and who rock, feed, and pat. Much of the parent-infant emotional communication occurs via touch (Hertenstein, 2002), which can be either soothing (snuggles) or arousing (tickles). Human attachment also consists of one person providing another with a *safe haven* when distressed and a *secure base* from which to explore. As we mature, our

Stranger anxiety
A newly emerging ability to evaluate people as unfamiliar and possibly threatening helps protect babies 8 months and older.

FIGURE 4.16
The Harlows' mothers
Psychologists Harry Harlow and Margaret Harlow reared monkeys with two artificial mothers—one a bare wire cylinder with a wooden head and an attached feeding bottle, the other a cylinder with no bottle but covered with foam rubber and wrapped with terry cloth. The Harlows' discovery surprised many psychologists: The monkeys much preferred contact with the comfortable cloth mother, even while feeding from the nourishing mother.

Lee Kirkpatrick (1999) reports that for some people a perceived relationship with God functions as do other attachments—by providing a secure base for exploration and a safe haven when threatened.

Alastair Miller

Attachment
When French pilot Christian Moullec takes off in his microlight plane, his imprinted geese, which he reared since their hatching, follow closely.

■ **critical period** an optimal period shortly after birth when an organism's exposure to certain stimuli or experiences produces proper development.

■ **imprinting** the process by which certain animals form attachments during a critical period very early in life.

secure base and safe haven shift—from parents to peers and partners (Cassidy & Shaver, 1999). But at all ages we are social creatures. We gain strength when someone offers, by words and actions, a safe haven: "I will be here. I am interested in you. Come what may, I will actively support you" (Crowell & Waters, 1994).

Familiarity Contact is one key to attachment. Another is familiarity. In many animals, attachments based on familiarity likewise form during a **critical period**—an optimal period shortly after birth when certain events must take place to facilitate proper development (Bornstein, 1989). The first moving object a gosling, duckling, or chick sees during the hours shortly after hatching is normally its mother. From then on, the young fowl follows her, and her alone.

This rigid attachment process, called **imprinting,** was explored by Konrad Lorenz (1937). He wondered: What would ducklings do if *he* was the first moving creature they observed? What they did was follow him around: Everywhere that Konrad went, the ducks were sure to go. Further tests revealed that although baby birds imprint best to their own species, they also will imprint to a variety of moving objects—an animal of another species, a box on wheels, a bouncing ball (Colombo, 1982; Johnson, 1992). And, once formed, this attachment is difficult to reverse.

Children—unlike ducklings—do not imprint. However, they do become attached to what they've known. "Mere exposure" to people and things fosters fondness (see pages 758–759). Children like to reread the same books, rewatch the same movies, reenact family traditions. They prefer to eat familiar foods, live in the same familiar neighborhood, attend school with the same old friends. Familiarity is a safety signal. Familiarity breeds content.

Attachment Differences

OBJECTIVE 13 | Contrast secure and insecure attachment, and discuss the roles of parents and infants in the development of attachment and an infant's feelings of basic trust.

What accounts for attachment differences? Placed in a *strange situation* (usually a laboratory playroom), about 60 percent of infants display *secure attachment*. In their mother's presence they play comfortably, happily exploring their new environment. When she leaves, they are distressed; when she returns, they seek contact with her. Other infants show *insecure attachment*. They are less likely to explore their surroundings; they may even cling to their mother. When she leaves, they either cry loudly and remain upset or seem indifferent to their mother's going and returning (Ainsworth, 1973, 1989; Kagan, 1995; van IJzendoorn & Kroonenberg, 1988).

One possible source of these differences is the mother's behavior. Female rats reared by relaxed, attentive adoptive mothers become more relaxed and attentive to their offspring than do those reared by stress-prone, inattentive adoptive mothers (Francis & others, 1999). Do human infants likewise pick up their mothers' tendencies?

Mary Ainsworth (1979) studied attachment differences by observing mother-infant pairs at home during their first six months. Later she observed the 1-year-old infants in a strange situation without their mothers. Sensitive, responsive mothers—those who noticed what their babies were doing and responded appropriately—had infants who exhibited secure attachment. Insensitive, unresponsive mothers—mothers who attended to their babies when they felt like doing so but ignored them at other times—had infants who often became insecurely attached. The Harlows' monkey studies, in which the artificial structures were certainly the ultimate unresponsive mothers, produced even more striking effects. When put in strange situations without their artificial mothers, the deprived infants were terrified (**FIGURE 4.17**).

Follow-up studies have confirmed that sensitive mothers—and fathers—tend to have securely attached infants (De Wolff & van IJzendoorn, 1997; van IJzendoorn, 1997). But is attachment style the result of parenting, as children's early experiences form their thinking about relationships? Or is attachment style the result of genetically influenced *temperament*—one's characteristic emotional reactivity and intensity? Shortly after birth, some babies are noticeably "difficult"—irritable, intense, and unpredictable. Others are "easy"—cheerful, relaxed, and feeding and sleeping on predictable schedules (Chess & Thomas, 1987). By neglecting such inborn differences, chides Judith Harris (1998), the parenting studies are like "comparing foxhounds reared in kennels with poodles reared in apartments." So, to separate nature and nurture, Dutch researcher Dymphna van den Boom (1990) varied parenting while controlling temperament. (Pause and think: If you were the researcher, how might you have done this?)

Van den Boom's solution was to randomly assign one hundred 6- to 9-month-old temperamentally difficult infants to either an experimental condition, in which mothers received personal training in sensitive responding, or to an untreated control condition in which they did not. At 12 months of age, 68 percent of the experimental-condition infants were rated securely attached; only 28 percent of the control-condition infants received this rating. Other studies have also found that intervention programs can increase parental sensitivity and, to a lesser extent, infant attachment security (Bakermans-Kranenburg & others, 2003).

As these examples indicate, researchers have more often studied mother care than father care. Infants who lack a caring mother are said to suffer "maternal deprivation"; those lacking the care of a father are said merely to experience "father absence." "Fathering a child" has meant impregnating; "mothering" has meant nurturing. But evidence increasingly indicates that fathers are more than just mobile sperm banks. Across nearly 100 studies worldwide, a father's love and acceptance have been comparable to a mother's love in predicting offsprings' health and well-being (Rohner & Veneziano, 2001). In one mammoth British study following 7259 children from birth to adulthood, those whose fathers were most involved in parenting (including outings, reading to them, and taking an interest in their education) tended to achieve more in school, even after controlling for many other factors such as parental education and family wealth (Flouri & Buchanan, 2004).

Whether children stay home or attend a day-care center, whether they live in North America, Guatemala, or the Kalahari Desert, anxiety over separation from parents peaks at around 13 months, then gradually declines (**FIGURE 4.18** on page 158). Does this mean our need for and love of others also fades away? Hardly. Our capacity for love grows, and our pleasure in touching and holding those we love never ceases. The power of early attachment does nonetheless gradually relax, allowing us to move out into a wider range of situations, communicate with strangers more freely, and stay attached emotionally to loved ones despite distance.

Harlow Primate Laboratory, University of Wisconsin

FIGURE 4.17
Social deprivation and fear
Monkeys raised by artificial mothers were terror-stricken when placed in strange situations without their surrogate mothers. (Today's climate of greater respect for animal welfare prevents such primate studies.)

Further discussions of Father Care and Children and Divorce can be found at the Web site accompanying this chapter (www.worthpublishers.com/myers).

© Barry Hewlett

Fantastic father
Among the Aka people of Central Africa, fathers form an especially close bond with their infants, even suckling the babies with their own nipples when hunger makes the child impatient for Mother's return. According to anthropologist Barry Hewlett (1991), fathers in this culture are holding or within reach of their babies 47 percent of the time.

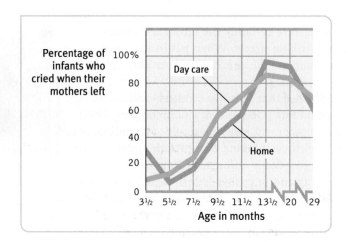

FIGURE 4.18
Infants' distress over separation from parents
In an experiment, groups of infants were left by their mothers in an unfamiliar room. In both groups, the percentage who cried when the mother left peaked at about 13 months. (From Kagan, 1976.) Whether the infant had experienced day care made little difference.

> "Out of the conflict between trust and mistrust, the infant develops hope, which is the earliest form of what gradually becomes faith in adults."
>
> Erik Erikson, 1983

> "What is learned in the cradle, lasts to the grave."
>
> French proverb

■ **basic trust** according to Erik Erikson, a sense that the world is predictable and trustworthy; said to be formed during infancy by appropriate experiences with responsive caregivers.

Developmental theorist Erik Erikson (1902–1994) would not have been surprised. Erikson, in collaboration with his wife, Joan Erikson, said that securely attached children approach life with a sense of **basic trust**—a sense that the world is predictable and reliable. He attributed basic trust not to one's continuing positive environment or inborn temperament, but to early parenting. He theorized that infants blessed with sensitive, loving caregivers form a lifelong attitude of trust rather than fear. Nor would Erikson have been surprised that our adult styles of romantic love exhibit either secure, trusting attachment; insecure, anxious attachment; or the avoidance of attachment (Feeney & Noller, 1990; Mikulincer & Shaver, 2005; Rholes & Simpson, 2004). Although debate continues, many researchers now believe that our early attachments form the foundation for our adult relationships (Fraley, 2002).

Deprivation of Attachment

OBJECTIVE 14 | Assess the impact of parental neglect, family disruption, and day care on attachment patterns and development.

If secure attachment nurtures social competence, what happens when circumstances prevent a child from forming attachments? In all of psychology, there is no sadder research literature. Babies reared in institutions without the stimulation and attention of a regular caregiver, or locked away at home under conditions of abuse or extreme neglect, are often withdrawn, frightened, even speechless. Those abandoned in Romanian orphanages during the 1980s looked "frighteningly like Harlow's monkeys" (Carlson, 1995). If institutionalized more than 8 months, they often bore lasting emotional scars (Chisholm, 1998; Malinosky-Rummell & Hansen, 1993; Rutter & others, 1998).

Harlow's monkeys similarly bore scars if reared in total isolation, without even an artificial mother. As adults, when placed with other monkeys their age, they either cowered in fright or lashed out in aggression. When they reached sexual maturity, most were incapable of mating. If artificially impregnated, females often were neglectful, abusive, even murderous toward their first-born.

In humans, too, the unloved sometimes become the unloving. Most abusive parents report having been neglected or battered as children (Kempe & Kempe, 1978). Many condemned murderers report the same. One study of 14 young men awaiting execution for juvenile crimes found that all but two had histories of brutal physical abuse (Lewis & others, 1988).

But does this mean that today's victim is predictably tomorrow's victimizer? The answer is no. Though most abusers were indeed abused, most abused children do *not* later become violent criminals or abusive parents. Most children growing up under adversity, as did the surviving children of the Holocaust, are resilient; they become normal adults (Helmreich, 1992; Masten, 2001). One study followed 1000 youths who had been maltreated. If the abuse had been restricted to early childhood, its manifestation as delinquency waned by late adolescence (Ireland & others, 2002).

But other children, especially those who experience no sharp break from their abusive past, are not so dramatically resilient. Some 30 percent of those abused do abuse their children—a rate four times higher than the national rate of child abuse (Kaufman & Zigler, 1987; Widom, 1989a, b). Moreover, young children terrorized through physical abuse or wartime atrocities (being beaten, witnessing torture, and living in constant fear) may suffer other lasting wounds—often nightmares, depression, and an adolescence troubled by substance abuse, binge eating, or aggression (Kendall-Tackett & others, 1993; Polusny & Follette, 1995; Trickett & McBride-Chang, 1995). Child sexual abuse, especially if severe and prolonged, places children at increased risk for health problems, psychological disorders, substance abuse, and criminality (Freyd & others, 2005; Tyler, 2002).

Although children are resilient, extreme childhood trauma can leave footprints on the brain. Baby rats deprived of their care-giving adult for several hours a day form fewer new brain neurons later in life (Mirescu & others, 2004). Normally placid golden hamsters that are repeatedly threatened and attacked while young grow up to be cowards when caged with same-sized hamsters, or bullies when caged with weaker ones (Ferris, 1996). Such animals show changes in the brain chemical serotonin, which calms aggressive impulses. A similarly sluggish serotonin response has been found in abused children who become aggressive teens and adults. "Stress can set off a ripple of hormonal changes that permanently wire a child's brain to cope with a malevolent world," concludes abuse researcher Martin Teicher (2002).

Might abuse victims' problems result from something else—perhaps other family troubles, a dysfunctional neighborhood, or a vulnerable temperament? Studies of American and Australian twins reveal that women who suffered child sexual abuse that included intercourse have greater risk of depression, anxiety, and alcohol abuse than do their nonabused identical twins (Kendler & others, 2000; Nelson & others, 2002). Given the same genes, same parents, and same neighborhood, the badly abused twin lives with the aftereffects. Nevertheless, researchers caution against inferring past sexual abuse from current symptoms (Sbraga & O'Donohue, 2003). Although child sex abuse increases the risk of depression, for example, many abused people do not suffer depression and most depressed people have not been sexually abused.

Disruption of Attachment What happens to an infant when attachment is disrupted? Separated from their families, both monkey and human infants become upset and, before long, withdrawn and even despairing (Bowlby, 1973; Mineka & Suomi, 1978). Fearing that the stress of separation might cause lasting damage (and when in doubt, acting to protect parents' rights), courts are usually reluctant to remove children from their homes.

If placed in a more positive and stable environment, most infants recover from the separation distress. In studies of adopted children, Leon Yarrow and his co-workers (1973) found that when children between 6 and 16 months of age were removed from their foster mothers, they initially had difficulties eating, sleeping, and relating to their new mothers. But when these children were studied at age 10, little visible effect remained. Thus, they fared no worse than children placed before the age of 6 months (with little accompanying distress). Likewise, socially deprived but adequately nourished Romanian orphans who were adopted into a loving home during infancy or early childhood usually progressed rapidly, especially in their cognitive development. If removed and adopted after age 2, however, they were at risk for attachment problems. Foster care that prevents attachment by moving a child through a series of foster families can be very disruptive. So can repeated and prolonged removals from a mother.

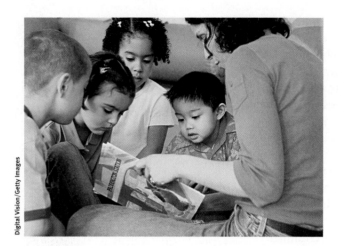

An example of high-quality day care
Research has shown that young children thrive socially and intellectually in safe, stimulating environments with a ratio of one caregiver for every three or four children.

Adults also suffer when attachment bonds are severed. Whether it occurs through death or separation, the break produces a predictable sequence of agitated preoccupation with the lost partner, followed by deep sadness and, eventually, the beginnings of emotional detachment and a return to normal living (Hazan & Shaver, 1994). Newly separated couples who have long ago ceased feeling affection are sometimes surprised at their desire to be near the former partner. Deep and longstanding attachments seldom break quickly. Detaching is a process, not an event.

Does Day Care Affect Attachment? In the mid-twentieth century, when Mom-at-home was the social norm, researchers asked, "Is day-care bad for children? Does it disrupt children's attachments to their parents?" For the high-quality day-care programs usually studied, the answer was no (Belsky, 1990). In *Mother Care/Other Care,* developmental psychologist Sandra Scarr (1986) explained that children are "biologically sturdy individuals . . . who can thrive in a wide variety of life situations." Scarr spoke for many developmental psychologists, whose research has uncovered no major impact of maternal employment on children's development (Erel & others, 2000).

Research then shifted to the effects of differing quality of day care on different types and ages of children. Scarr (1997) explained: Around the world, "high-quality child care consists of warm, supportive interactions with adults in a safe, healthy, and stimulating environment. . . . Poor care is boring and unresponsive to children's needs." Newer research not only confirms that day-care quality matters, but also finds that family poverty often consigns children to lower-quality day care, as well as more family instability and turmoil, more authoritarian parenting, more time in front of the television, and less access to books (Love & others, 2003; Evans, 2004).

One ongoing study in 10 American cities has followed 1100 children since the age of 1 month. The researchers found that at ages 4½ to 6, those children who had spent the most time in day care had slightly advanced thinking and language skills. They also had an increased rate of aggressiveness and defiance (NICHD, 2002; NICHD, 2003). To developmental psychologist Eleanor Maccoby (2003), the positive correlation between increased rate of problem behaviors and time spent in child care suggests "some risk for some children spending extended time in some day-care settings as they're now organized." But the child's temperament, the mother's sensitivity, and the family's economic and educational level mattered more than time spent in day care. Other recent research offers a mixed bag of findings:

- Toddler's stress hormone levels tend to rise during days spent in day care and to diminish during days spent at home (Watamura & others, 2003).
- When mothers transition from welfare to work, their preschool children do not suffer negative outcomes (Chase-Lansdale & others, 2003).
- Although working mothers spend less total time with their infants, they tend to partially compensate by sacrificing other activities (such as socializing) during their off hours, including weekends. As a result, they spend more time during those hours playing with, talking to, and holding their infants than do their nonworking counterparts (Huston & Aronson, 2005).

To be a day-care researcher and "to follow the data" can be controversial, notes researcher Jay Belsky (2003). Both opponents and advocates of day care have strong feelings. "As a result," says Belsky, "the scientist who is willing to report unpopular results is all too frequently blamed for generating them." Just as weather forecasters can report rain but love sunshine, so scientists aim to reveal and report the way things are, even when they wish it were otherwise.

Children's ability to thrive under varied types of responsive caregiving should not surprise us, given cultural variations in attachment patterns. Westernized attachment features one or two caregivers and their offspring. In other cultures, such as the Efe of Zaire, multiple caregivers are the norm (Field, 1996; Whaley & others, 2002). Even before the mother holds her newborn, the baby is passed among several women. In the weeks to come, the infant will be constantly held (and fed), by other women. The result is strong multiple attachments. As the now-famous African proverb says, "It takes a village to raise a child."

There is little disagreement that the many preschool children left *alone* for part of their parents' working hours deserve better. So do the children who merely exist for 9 hours a day in minimally equipped, understaffed centers. What all children need is a consistent, warm relationship with people whom they can learn to trust.

Self-Concept

OBJECTIVE 15 | Trace the onset and development of children's self-concept.

Infancy's major social achievement is attachment. *Childhood's* major social achievement is a positive sense of self. By the end of childhood, at about age 12, most children have developed a **self-concept**—a sense of their own identity and personal worth. Parents often wonder when and how this sense of self develops. "Is my baby girl aware of herself—does she know she is a person distinct from everyone else?"

Of course we cannot ask the baby directly, but we can again capitalize on what she can do—letting her *behavior* provide clues to the beginnings of her self-awareness. In 1877, biologist Charles Darwin offered one idea: Self-awareness begins when we recognize ourselves in a mirror. By this indicator, self-recognition emerges gradually over about a year, starting in roughly the sixth month as the child reaches toward the mirror to touch her image as if it were another child (Courage & Howe, 2002; Damon & Hart, 1982, 1988).

But how can we know when the child recognizes that the girl in the mirror is indeed herself, not just an agreeable playmate? In a simple variation of the mirror procedure, researchers sneakily dabbed rouge on children's noses before placing them in front of the mirror. At about 15 to 18 months, children will begin to touch their own noses when they see the red spot in the mirror (Butterworth, 1992; Gallup & Suarez, 1986). Apparently, 18-month-olds have a schema of how their faces should look, and they wonder, "What is that spot doing on *my* face?"

Beginning with this simple self-recognition, the child's self-concept gradually strengthens. By school age, children start to describe themselves in terms of their gender, group memberships, and psychological traits, and they compare themselves with other children (Newman & Ruble, 1988; Stipek, 1992). They come to see themselves as good and skillful in some ways but not others. They form a concept of which traits, ideally, they would like to have. By age 8 or 10, their self-images are quite stable.

Children's views of themselves affect their actions. Children who form a positive self-concept are more confident, independent, optimistic, assertive, and sociable (Maccoby, 1980). This then raises important questions: Can parents encourage a positive yet realistic self-concept? Does parenting style affect children?

Child-Rearing Practices

OBJECTIVE 16 | Describe three parenting styles, and offer three potential explanations for the link beween authoritative parenting and social competence.

Parenting styles vary. Some parents spank, some reason. Some are strict, some are lax. Some show little affection, some liberally hug and kiss. Do such differences affect children?

■ **self-concept** a sense of one's identity and personal worth.

Laura Dwight

Self-awareness

Mirror images fascinate infants from the age of about 6 months. Only at about 18 months, however, does the child recognize that the image in the mirror is "me."

After prolonged exposure to mirrors, four other species—chimpanzees, orangutans, gorillas, and dolphins—have similarly demonstrated self-recognition of their mirror image (Marino & others, 1994; Wright, 1996). Capuchin monkeys display partial self-recognition (de Waal & others, 2005).

The most heavily researched aspect of parenting has been how, and to what extent, parents seek to control their children. Investigators have identified three parenting styles:

1. *Authoritarian* parents impose rules and expect obedience: "Don't interrupt." "Do keep your room clean." "Don't stay out late or you'll be grounded." "Why? Because I said so."

2. *Permissive* parents submit to their children's desires, make few demands, and use little punishment.

3. *Authoritative* parents are both demanding and responsive. They exert control not only by setting rules and enforcing them but also by explaining the reasons and, especially with older children, encouraging open discussion and allowing exceptions when making the rules.

Too hard, too soft, and just right, these styles have been called. Studies by Stanley Coopersmith (1967), Diana Baumrind (1996), and John Buri and others (1988) reveal that children with the highest self-esteem, self-reliance, and social competence usually have warm, concerned, *authoritative* parents. (Those with authoritarian parents tend to have less social skill and self-esteem, and those with permissive parents tend to be more aggressive and immature.) Although the participants in most studies have been middle-class white families, studies with families of other races and in more than 200 cultures worldwide confirm the social and academic correlates of loving and authoritative parenting (Rohner & Veneziano, 2001; Steinberg & Morris, 2001).

But wait. Before jumping to conclusions about the results of different parenting styles, heed this caution: *Correlation is not causation.* The association between certain parenting styles (being firm but open) and certain childhood outcomes (social competence) is correlational. There are other possible explanations for this parenting-competence link (**FIGURE 4.19**).

• Perhaps children's traits influence parenting more than vice versa. Parental warmth and control vary somewhat from child to child even in the same family (Holden & Miller, 1999). So perhaps socially mature, agreeable, easygoing children *evoke* greater trust and warmth from their parents, and less competent and less cooperative children elicit less. Twin studies support this possibility (Kendler, 1996).

• Perhaps there may be some underlying third factor. Maybe, for example, competent parents and their competent children share genes that predispose social competence.

Parents struggling with conflicting advice and with the stresses of child-rearing should remember that *all advice reflects the advice-giver's values.* For those who prize unquestioning obedience from a child, an authoritarian style may have the desired effect. For those who value children's sociability and self-reliance, authoritative firm-but-open parenting is advisable.

FIGURE 4.19
The correlation between authoritative parenting and social competence in children
Three possible explanations are: (1) parenting may influence children's competence; (2) children's social competence may influence parenting; or (3) both may be influenced by an underlying third factor.

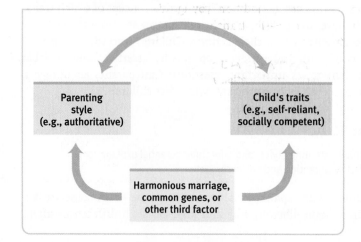

Parenting style (e.g., authoritative)

Child's traits (e.g., self-reliant, socially competent)

Harmonious marriage, common genes, or other third factor

The investment in raising a child buys many years not only of joy and love but of worry and irritation. Yet for most parents, a child is one's biological and social legacy—one's personal investment in the human future. Remind young adults of their mortality and they will express increased desire for children (Wisman & Goldenberg, 2005). To paraphrase psychiatrist Carl Jung, we reach backward into our parents and forward into our children, and through their children into a future we will never see, but about which we must therefore care.

> "You are the bows from which your children as living arrows are sent forth."
>
> Kahlil Gibran, *The Prophet*, 1923

>> Learning Outcomes

Infancy and Childhood

Objective 5 | Describe some developmental changes in a child's brain, and explain why maturation accounts for many of our similarities.

A newborn's immature nervous system undergoes a rapid growth spurt after birth, as neural networks proliferate. Between ages 3 and 6, growth is most pronounced in the frontal lobes. Development in the association areas of the cortex enables thinking, memory, and language. Brain pathways continue to develop and strengthen with use until puberty, when pruning begins to eliminate excess connections. In the absence of severe abuse or neglect, maturation—the orderly sequence of genetically determined biological processes—guides all infants along the same general course of development.

Objective 6 | Outline four events in the motor development sequence from birth to toddlerhood, and evaluate the effects of maturation and experience on that sequence.

Though the timing may vary, almost all babies follow the same sequence of first rolling over, then sitting unsupported, then crawling, then walking. Experience has little influence; maturation, including that of the cerebellum, enables these events.

Objective 7 | Explain why we have few memories of experiences during our first three years of life.

"Infantile amnesia"—an inability to consciously recall events that happened before age 3—results from a change in the way the brain organizes memories at about that age. As the cortex matures, long-term storage increases; in addition, young children's preverbal memories are not easily transformed into language.

Objective 8 | State Piaget's understanding of how the mind develops, and discuss the importance of assimilation and accommodation in this process.

Piaget proposed that children's reasoning develops in a series of stages, and that children actively construct and modify their understanding of the world as they interact with it. They form *schemas* (concepts or frameworks for organizing experience). They then *assimilate* (interpret) information by means of these schemas, or—if the information does not conform to the schema—they *accommodate* (adjust) the schema to incorporate the new information.

Objective 9 | Outline Piaget's four main stages of cognitive development, and comment on how children's thinking changes during these four stages.

In the *sensorimotor stage* (birth to age 2), children experience the world through their senses and actions. In the first six months, infants lack object permanence, or the awareness that things exist when out of sight. In the *preoperational stage* (age 2 to about 6 or 7), children learn to use language and can represent things with words and images, but they are unable to reason logically. They lack a theory of mind and are egocentric, or have difficulty taking another person's point of view (people with the disorder of autism also lack a theory of mind). Preoperational children have no concept of conservation—the understanding that things can change form but retain their mass, volume, or number. In the *concrete operational stage* (about age 7 to 11), children can think logically about concrete events, grasp analogies, and perform arithmetical operations. In the *formal operational stage* (12 through adulthood), they gain the ability to reason abstractly. Piaget viewed the ages connected with these stages as approximate, but the sequence as universal.

Objective 10 | Discuss psychologists' current views on Piaget's theory of cognitive development.

Contemporary research shows that formal logic plays a smaller part in cognitive development than Piaget believed, and that the development of cognitive abilities is more continuous, with stages starting earlier and less abruptly. Nevertheless, Piaget's views about the *sequence* of development of children's cognitive abilities have been supported repeatedly.

Objective 11 | Define *stranger anxiety*.

Stranger anxiety is the fear of strangers that infants begin to display at about 8 months of age. Children of this age have formed schemas for familiar faces, and they become distressed when faces do not match their schemas.

Objective 12 | Discuss the effects of nourishment, body contact, and familiarity on infant social attachment.

Until the Harlows' research in the mid-1950s, many psychologists believed that, through a conditioning process, children become attached (form an emotional tie) to those who provide nourishment. The Harlows' experiments showed that infant monkeys would search out a non-nourishing "mother" that provided comfort in preference to one that provided nourishment without comfort. Ducks and other animals imprint, forming an attachment to a significant organism or object during a *critical period* (a time shortly after birth when proper development depends on exposure to certain stimuli or experiences). Humans do not imprint, but they do become attached to familiar people and things, which provide feelings of safety.

OBJECTIVE 13 | Contrast secure and insecure attachment, and discuss the roles of parents and infants in the development of attachment and an infant's feelings of basic trust.

In the experimental condition called the strange situation, researchers observe a mother and her child in a laboratory playroom, taking note of the child's reactions as the mother leaves and reenters. Securely attached children play and explore comfortably in the mother's presence, are distressed when she leaves, and seek contact when she returns. Insecurely attached children explore less in the mother's presence and may cling to her, cry loudly when she leaves, and remain upset or act indifferent when she returns. Other studies show that sensitive responsive parents tend to have securely attached children. Genetically influenced temperament may evoke responsive parenting, but parental sensitivity has been taught and does increase infant attachment security to some extent. Father love as well as mother love is a predictor of children's health and well-being. Adult relationships tend to reflect the secure or insecure attachment styles of early childhood, lending support to Erik Erikson's idea that basic trust is formed in infancy by our experiences with responsive caregivers.

OBJECTIVE 14 | Assess the impact of parental neglect, family disruption, and day care on attachment patterns and development.

When parental neglect or other trauma deprive children of the opportunity to form attachments, children become withdrawn and frightened and may not develop speech. If prolonged, childhood abuse places children at risk for a variety of physical, psychological, and social problems and may alter the brain's production of serotonin. Damage from disruption of attachment bonds, as happens when children are placed in foster care, appears to be minimal before 16 months of age. Children who are moved repeatedly or otherwise prevented from forming attachments by age 2, however, may be at risk for attachment problems. Quality day care, with responsive adults interacting with children in a safe and stimulating environment, does not appear to harm children's thinking and language skills, but some studies have linked extensive time in day care with increased aggressiveness and defiance.

OBJECTIVE 15 | Trace the onset and development of children's self-concept.

Self-concept, a sense of one's identity and personal worth, emerges gradually, beginning at about 6 months. At 15 to 18 months, children recognize themselves in a mirror. By school age, they can describe many of their own traits, and by age 8 to 10, their self-image is stable.

OBJECTIVE 16 | Describe three parenting styles, and offer three potential explanations for the link between authoritative parenting and social competence.

Authoritarian parents impose rules and expect obedience. *Permissive* parents submit to children's demands, ask little, and punish rarely. *Authoritative* parents are demanding but responsive to their children. Authoritative parenting correlates with social competence, but the cause-effect relationship is not clear. This style of parenting may produce socially competent children, or agreeable easygoing children may evoke authoritative parenting. Or a third factor, such as shared genes, may lead to a temperament that is comfortable with an authoritative parenting style and that manifests itself in agreeable easygoing social interactions.

ASK YOURSELF: Can you recall a time when you have misheard some song lyrics, by *assimilating* them into your own *schema*? (For hundreds of examples of such, visit www.kissthisguy.com.)

Adolescence

■ **adolescence** the transition period from childhood to adulthood, extending from puberty to independence.

■ **puberty** the period of sexual maturation, during which a person becomes capable of reproducing.

■ **primary sex characteristics** the body structures (ovaries, testes, and external genitalia) that make sexual reproduction possible.

■ **secondary sex characteristics** nonreproductive sexual characteristics, such as female breasts and hips, male voice quality, and body hair.

OBJECTIVE 17 | Define *adolescence.*

Many psychologists once believed that childhood sets our traits. Today's developmental psychologists see development as lifelong. At a five-year high school reunion, former soul mates may be surprised at their divergence; a decade later, they may have trouble sustaining a conversation.

As this life-span perspective emerged, psychologists began to look at how maturation and experience shape us not only in infancy and childhood, but also in adolescence and beyond. **Adolescence** is life between childhood and adulthood. It starts with the physical beginnings of sexual maturity and ends with the social achievement of independent adult status.

What are the teen years like? In Leo Tolstoy's *Anna Karenina*, the teen years were "that blissful time when childhood is just coming to an end, and out of that vast circle, happy and gay, a path takes shape." But in her diary, written while hiding from the Nazis, teenager Anne Frank described tumultuous teen emotions:

> My treatment varies so much. One day Anne is so sensible and is allowed to know everything; and the next day I hear that Anne is just a silly little goat who doesn't know anything at all and imagines that she's learned a wonderful lot from books. . . . Oh, so many things bubble up inside me as I lie in bed, having to put up with people I'm fed up with, who always misinterpret my intentions.

To G. Stanley Hall (1904), one of the first psychologists to describe adolescence, the tension between biological maturity and social dependence created a period of "storm and stress." Indeed, after age 30, many who grow up in independence-fostering Western cultures look back on their teenage years as a time they would not want to relive, a time when their peers' social approval was imperative, their sense of direction in life was in flux, and their feeling of alienation from their parents was deepest (Arnett, 1999; Macfarlane, 1964). Humorist Dave Barry (1996) is one such person:

> When my dad pulled up, wearing his poodle hat and driving his Nash Metropolitan—a comically tiny vehicle resembling those cars outside supermarkets that go up and down when you put in a quarter, except the Metropolitan looked sillier and had a smaller motor—I was mortified. I might as well have been getting picked up by a flying saucer piloted by some bizarre multitentacled stalk-eyed slobber-mouthed alien being that had somehow got hold of a Russian hat. I was horrified at what my peers might think of my dad; it never occurred to me that my peers didn't even notice my dad, because they were too busy being mortified by THEIR parents.
>
> Of course eventually my father stopped being a hideous embarrassment to me, and I, grasping the Torch of Dorkhood, became a hideous embarrassment to my son.

Embarrassment is just one of the many adolescent moods. Despite the mood swings, adolescence can also be a time of vitality without the cares of adulthood, a time of rewarding friendships, of heightened idealism and a growing sense of life's exciting possibilities (Coleman, 1980).

Physical Development

OBJECTIVE 18 | Identify the major physical changes during adolescence.

Adolescence begins with **puberty,** the time when one is maturing sexually. Puberty follows a surge of hormones, which may intensify moods and which trigger a two-year period of rapid physical development, usually beginning at about age 11 in girls and at about age 13 in boys. About the time of puberty, boys' growth propels them to greater height than their female counterparts (**FIGURE 4.20**). During this growth spurt, the **primary sex characteristics**—the reproductive organs and external genitalia—develop dramatically. So do **secondary sex characteristics,** the nonreproductive traits such as breasts and hips in girls, facial hair and deepened voice in boys, pubic and underarm hair in both sexes (**FIGURE 4.21** on page 166). A year or two before puberty, however, boys and girls often feel the first stirrings of attraction toward those of the other (or their own) sex (McClintock & Herdt, 1996).

In girls, puberty starts with breast development, which now often begins by age 10 (Brody, 1999). But puberty's landmarks are the first ejaculation in boys, usually by about age 14, and the first menstrual

How will you look back on your life 10 years from now? Are you making choices that someday you will recollect with satisfaction?

FIGURE 4.20
Height differences
Throughout childhood, boys and girls are similar in height. At puberty, girls surge ahead briefly, but then boys overtake them at about age 14. (Data from Tanner, 1978.) Recent studies suggest that sexual development and growth spurts are beginning somewhat earlier than was the case a half-century ago (Herman-Giddens & others, 2001).

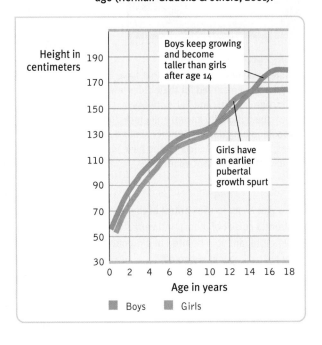

FIGURE 4.21
Body changes at puberty
At about age 11 in girls and age 13 in boys, a surge of hormones triggers a variety of physical changes.

Young rockers
Children are now doing things that have in the past been reserved for their older peers. Chloe, age 11 (left), and her sister Asya, age 13, are the nationally known indie rock duo Smoosh, joining dozens of other similarly young but famous musicians who have hit the rock scene in recent years.

"If a gun is put in the control of the prefrontal cortex of a hurt and vengeful 15-year-old, and it is pointed at a human target, it will very likely go off."
National Institutes of Health brain scientist Daniel R. Weinberger, "A Brain Too Young for Good Judgment," 2001

period in girls, usually within a year of age 12. The first menstrual period, called **menarche** (meh-NAR-key), is a memorable event. Nearly all adult women recall it and remember experiencing a mixture of feelings—pride, excitement, embarrassment, and apprehension (Greif & Ulman, 1982; Woods & others, 1983). Girls who have been prepared for menarche usually experience it as a positive life transition. Most men similarly recall their first ejaculation (*spermarche*), which usually occurs as a nocturnal emission (Fuller & Downs, 1990).

Just as in the earlier life stages, the *sequence* of physical changes in puberty (for example, breast buds and visible pubic hair before menarche) is far more predictable than their *timing*. Some girls start their growth spurt at 9, some boys as late as age 16. Though such variations have little effect on height at maturity, they may have psychological consequences. Early maturation pays dividends for boys. Early developing boys, being stronger and more athletic during their early teen years, tend to be more popular, self-assured, and independent, though also more at risk for alcohol use and premature sexual activity (Steinberg & Morris, 2001). But for girls, early maturation can be stressful. If a young girl's body is out of sync with her own emotional maturity and her friends' physical development and experiences, she may begin associating with older adolescents or may suffer teasing or sexual harassment. It is not only when we mature that counts, but how people react to our genetically influenced physical development. Remember: *Heredity and environment interact.*

Adolescents' brains are also a work in progress. Until puberty, brain cells increase their connections, like trees growing more roots and branches. Then, during adolescence, comes a selective pruning of unused neurons and connections (Durston & others, 2001). What we don't use, we lose. It's rather like traffic engineers reducing congestion by eliminating certain streets and constructing new beltways that move traffic more efficiently.

Frontal lobe development during adolescence also includes the growth of *myelin*, the fatty tissue around axons that speeds neurotransmission. This frontal lobe maturation lags the emotional limbic system. The pubertal hormonal surge and limbic system development helps explain teens' occasional impulsiveness, risky behaviors, emotional storms—slamming doors and turning up the music. With frontal lobe maturation during the teens and early twenties comes improved judgment, impulse control, and the ability to plan for the long term. When university students choose immediate rewards, fMRI scans show their limbic reward system activating; when electing a bigger delayed reward, a part of their calculating frontal lobe area more strongly activates (McClure & others, 2004). No wonder younger teens (whose unfinished frontal lobes aren't yet fully equipped for making long-term plans and curbing impulses) so often succumb to the lure of smoking, which most adult smokers could tell them they will later regret.

So, when Junior drives recklessly and academically self-destructs, should his parents reassure themselves that "he can't help it; his frontal cortex isn't yet fully grown"? They can at least take hope: The brain with which Junior begins his teens differs from the brain with which he will end his teens, and which will continue maturing until about age 25 (Beckman, 2004). In 2004, the American Psychological Association joined seven other medical and mental health associations in filing U.S. Supreme Court briefs, arguing against the death penalty for 16- and 17-years olds. The briefs documented the teen brain's immaturity "in areas that bear upon adolescent decision-making." Teens are "less guilty by reason of adolescence," suggested psychologist Laurence Steinberg and law professor Elizabeth Scott (2003). In 2005, by a 5-to-4 margin, the Court concurred, declaring juvenile death penalties unconstitutional.

Cognitive Development

Adolescents' developing ability to reason gives them a new level of social awareness and moral judgment. As young teenagers become capable of thinking about their thinking, and of thinking about other people's thinking, they begin imagining what other people are thinking about *them*. (Adolescents might worry less about what others think of them if they knew how similarly self-preoccupied their peers are.) As their cognitive abilities mature, many adolescents think about what is ideally possible and criticize their society, their parents, and even their own shortcomings.

Developing Reasoning Power

OBJECTIVE 19 | Describe the changes in reasoning abilities that Piaget called formal operations.

During the early teen years, reasoning is often self-focused. Adolescents may think their private experiences are unique. They may assume their parents just can't understand what it feels like to be dating or to hate school: "But, Mom, *you* don't really know how it feels to be in love" (Elkind, 1978).

Gradually, though, most achieve the intellectual summit that Piaget called *formal operations*. Preadolescents reason concretely, but adolescents become more capable of abstract logic: *If* this, *then* that. We can see this new abstract reasoning power as adolescents ponder and debate human nature, good and evil, truth and justice. Having perhaps envisioned God as an old man in the clouds when they were first capable of symbolic thinking in early childhood, they may now seek a deeper conception of God

■ **menarche** [meh-NAR-key] the first menstrual period.

> ❝When the pilot told us to brace and grab our ankles, the first thing that went through my mind was that we must all look pretty stupid.❞
> Jeremiah Rawlings, age 12, after a 1989 DC-10 crash in Sioux City, Iowa

"Ben is in his first year of high school, and he's questioning all the right things."

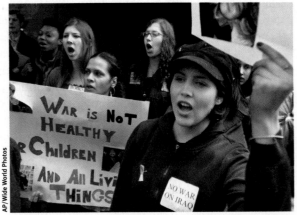

Demonstrating their reasoning ability
Although on opposite sides of the Iraq War debate, these teens demonstrate their newfound ability to think logically about abstract topics. According to Piaget, they are in the final cognitive stage, formal operations.

and existence (Elkind, 1970; Worthington, 1989). Adolescents' ability to reason hypothetically and deduce consequences also enables them to detect inconsistencies in others' reasoning and to spot hypocrisy. This can lead to heated debates with parents and silent vows never to lose sight of their own ideals (Peterson & others, 1986).

Developing Morality

OBJECTIVE **20** | Discuss moral development from the perspectives of moral thinking, moral feeling, and moral action.

> "It is a delightful harmony when doing and saying go together."
>
> Michel Eyquem de Montaigne (1533–1592)

A crucial task of childhood and adolescence is discerning right from wrong and developing character—the psychological muscles for controlling impulses. To be a moral person is to *think* morally and *act* accordingly.

Moral Thinking Piaget (1932) believed that children's moral judgments build on their cognitive development. Agreeing with Piaget, Lawrence Kohlberg (1981, 1984) sought to describe the development of *moral reasoning,* the thinking that occurs as we consider right and wrong. Kohlberg posed moral dilemmas (for example, whether a person should steal medicine to save a loved one's life), and asked children, adolescents, and adults if the action was right or wrong. He then analyzed their answers for evidence of stages of moral thinking.

His findings led him to believe that as we develop intellectually, we pass through three basic levels of moral thinking:

Moral reasoning

New Orleans hurricane and flood victims were faced with a moral dilemma: Should they steal household necessities? Their reasoning likely reflected different levels of moral thinking, even if they behaved similarly.

- *Preconventional morality* Before age 9, most children have a preconventional morality of self-interest: They obey either to avoid punishment or to gain concrete rewards.
- *Conventional morality* By early adolescence, morality usually evolves to a more conventional level that cares for others and upholds laws and social rules simply because they are the laws and rules.
- *Postconventional morality* Some of those who develop the abstract reasoning of formal operational thought may come to a third level. Postconventional morality affirms people's agreed-upon rights or follows what one personally perceives as basic ethical principles.

Kohlberg's claim was that these levels form a moral ladder (**FIGURE 4.22**), from the bottom rung of a young child's immature, preconventional morality, to the top rung of an adult's self-defined ethical principles, which only some attain. As with all stage theories, the sequence is unvarying. We begin on the bottom rung and ascend to varying heights.

Research confirms that children in various cultures progress from the level Kohlberg called preconventional, then into his conventional level (Edwards, 1981, 1982; Snarey, 1985, 1987). And as our *thinking* matures, our *behavior* also becomes less selfish and more caring (Krebs & Van Hesteren, 1994; Miller & others, 1996). However, the postconventional level is more controversial. It appears mostly in the European and North American educated middle class, which prizes individualism—giving priority to one's own goals rather than to group goals (Eckensberger, 1994; Miller & Bersoff, 1995). Critics therefore contend that the theory is biased against the moral reasoning of those in communal societies such as China and India—and also against Western women, whose morality may be based slightly less on abstract, impersonal principles and more on caring relationships.

Moral Feeling The mind makes moral judgments as it makes aesthetic judgments—quickly and automatically. We feel disgust when seeing people engaged in degrading or subhuman acts, and we feel *elevation*—a tingly, warm, glowing feeling in the chest—when seeing people display exceptional generosity, compassion, or courage.

> "I am a bit suspicious of any theory that says that the highest moral stage is one in which people talk like college professors."
>
> James Q. Wilson, *The Moral Sense,* 1993

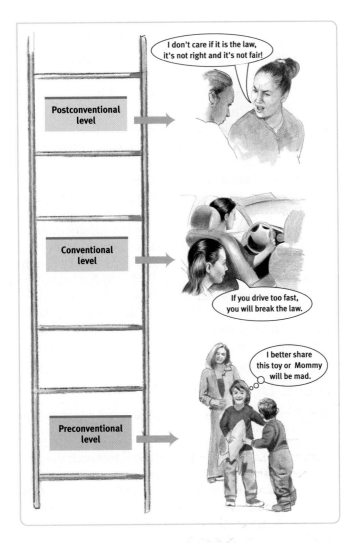

FIGURE 4.22
Kohlberg's moral ladder
As moral development progresses, the focus of concern moves from the self to the wider social world. Kohlberg contended that post-conventional moral thinking, embodied by Martin Luther King, Jr., may be rejected by those who do not comprehend it.

One woman recalled driving through her snowy neighborhood with three young men as they passed "an elderly woman with a shovel in her driveway. I did not think much of it, when one of the guys in the back asked the driver to let him off there. . . . When I saw him jump out of the back seat and approach the lady, my mouth dropped in shock as I realized that he was offering to shovel her walk for her." Witnessing this unexpected goodness triggered elevation: "I felt like jumping out of the car and hugging this guy. I felt like singing and running, or skipping and laughing. I felt like saying nice things about people" (Haidt, 2000).

In Jonathan Haidt's (2001, 2002) *social intuitionist* account of morality, moral feelings precede moral reasoning. "Could human morality really be run by the moral emotions," he wonders, "while moral reasoning struts about pretending to be in control?" Indeed, he surmises, "moral judgment involves quick gut feelings, or affectively laden intuitions, which then trigger moral reasoning." Moral reasoning—our mind's press secretary—aims to convince others of what we intuitively feel.

The social intuitionist explanation of morality finds support from a study of moral paradoxes. Imagine a runaway trolley headed for five people. All will certainly be killed unless you throw a switch that diverts the trolley onto another track, where it will kill one person. Should you throw the switch?

Most say yes. Kill one, save five. Now imagine the same dilemma, except that your opportunity to save the five requires you to push a large stranger onto the tracks, where he will die as his body stops the trolley. Kill one, save five?

The logic is the same, but most say no. Seeking to understand why, a Princeton research team led by Joshua Greene (2001) used brain imaging to spy on people's

"This might not be ethical. Is that a problem for anybody?"

neural responses as they contemplated such dilemmas. Only when given the body-pushing type of moral dilemma did their brain's emotion areas light up. Despite the identical logic, the personal dilemma engaged emotions that altered moral judgment. Moral judgment is more than thinking; it is also gut-level feeling.

Moral Action Our moral thinking and feeling surely affect our moral talk. But sometimes talk is cheap and emotions are fleeting. Morality involves *doing* the right thing, and what we do also depends on social influences. As political theorist Hannah Arendt (1963) observed, many Nazi concentration camp guards during World War II were ordinary "moral" people who were corrupted by a powerfully evil situation.

Today's character education programs tend to focus both on discussions of moral issues and their implications and on *doing* the right thing. Thus, they teach children *empathy* for others' feelings, and also the self-discipline needed to restrain one's own impulses—to delay small gratifications now to enable bigger rewards later. Those who do learn to *delay gratification* become more socially responsible, academically success-ful, and productive (Funder & Block, 1989; Mischel & others, 1988, 1989). They often engage students in responsible action through *service learning*. When teens tutor, clean up their neighborhoods, and assist the elderly, their sense of competence and desire to serve increases and their school absenteeism and drop-out rates dimin-ish (Andersen, 1998; Piliavin, 2003). Moral action feeds moral attitudes.

Social Development

OBJECTIVE 21 | Identify Erikson's eight stages of psychosocial development and their accompanying issues.

Theorist Erik Erikson (1963) contended that each stage of life has its own *psychosocial* task, a crisis that needs resolution. Young children wrestle with issues of *trust* (page 158), then *autonomy* (independence), then *initiative* (**TABLE 4.2**). School-age children

TABLE 4.2

ERIKSON'S STAGES OF PSYCHOSOCIAL DEVELOPMENT

Stage (approximate age)	Issues	Description of Task
Infancy (to 1 year)	*Trust vs. mistrust*	If needs are dependably met, infants develop a sense of basic trust.
Toddlerhood (1 to 2 years)	*Autonomy vs. shame and doubt*	Toddlers learn to exercise will and do things for themselves, or they doubt their abilities.
Preschooler (3 to 5 years)	*Initiative vs. guilt*	Preschoolers learn to initiate tasks and carry out plans, or they feel guilty about efforts to be independent.
Elementary school (6 years to puberty)	*Competence vs. inferiority*	Children learn the pleasure of applying them-selves to tasks, or they feel inferior.
Adolescence (teen years into 20s)	*Identity vs. role confusion*	Teenagers work at refining a sense of self by testing roles and then integrating them to form a single identity, or they become confused about who they are.
Young adulthood (20s to early 40s)	*Intimacy vs. isolation*	Young adults struggle to form close relation-ships and to gain the capacity for intimate love, or they feel socially isolated.
Middle adulthood (40s to 60s)	*Generativity vs. stagnation*	In middle age, people discover a sense of con-tributing to the world, usually through family and work, or they may feel a lack of purpose.
Late adulthood (late 60s and up)	*Integrity vs. despair*	When reflecting on his or her life, the older adult may feel a sense of satisfaction or failure.

strive for *competence,* feeling able and productive. The adolescent's task, said Erikson, is to synthesize past, present, and future possibilities into a clearer sense of self. Adolescents wonder "Who am I as an individual? What do I want to do with my life? What values should I live by? What do I believe in?" Erikson called this quest the adolescent's *search for identity.*

As sometimes happens in psychology, Erikson's interests were bred by his own life experience. As the son of a Jewish mother and a Danish father, Erikson was "doubly an outsider," reports Morton Hunt (1993, p. 391). He was "scorned as a Jew in school but mocked as a Gentile in the synagogue because of his blond hair and blue eyes." Such episodes fueled his interest in the adolescent struggle for identity.

Forming an Identity

OBJECTIVE 22 | Explain how the search for identity affects us during adolescence, and discuss how forming an identity prepares us for intimacy.

To refine their sense of identity, adolescents in Western cultures usually try out different "selves" in different situations—perhaps acting out one self at home, another with friends, and still another at school and work. If two of these situations overlap—as when a teenager brings home friends—the discomfort can be considerable. The teen asks, "Which self should I be? Which is the real me?" This role confusion usually gets resolved by forming a self-definition that unifies the various selves into a consistent and comfortable sense of who one is—an **identity.**

But not always. Erikson noticed that some adolescents forge their identity early, simply by taking on their parents' values and expectations. (Traditional, less individualistic cultures inform adolescents about who they are, rather than letting them decide on their own.) Other adolescents may adopt a negative identity defined in opposition to parents and society but in conformity with a particular peer group—the jocks, the preppies, the geeks, the goths.

Most young people do develop a sense of contentment with their lives. When American teens were asked whether a series of statements described them, 80 percent said yes to "I would choose my life the way it is right now." But others never quite seem to find themselves: About 20 percent agreed with "I wish I were somebody else," and 28 percent with "I often wonder why I exist" (Lyons, 2004). Reflecting on their existence, 75 percent of American collegians say they "discuss religion/spirituality" with friends, "pray," and agree that "we are all spiritual beings" and "search for meaning/purpose in life" (HERI, 2005). This would not surprise Stanford psychologist William Damon and his colleagues (2003), who contend that a key task of adolescent development is to achieve a purpose—a desire to accomplish something personally meaningful that makes a difference to the world beyond oneself.

The late teen years, when many people begin attending college or working full time, provide new opportunities for trying out possible roles. As seniors, many college students have achieved a clearer identity than they had as first-year students (Waterman, 1988). Their identity typically incorporates an increasingly positive self-concept. In several nationwide studies, researchers have given young Americans tests of self-esteem. (Sample item: "I am able to do things as well as most other people.") During the early to mid-teen years, self-esteem falls and for girls, depression scores often increase, but then self-image rebounds during the late teens and twenties (Robins & others, 2002; Twenge & Campbell, 2001; Twenge & Nolen-Hoeksema, 2002).

Identity also becomes more personalized. Daniel Hart (1988) asked youths of various ages to imagine a machine that would clone (a) what you think and feel, (b) your appearance, or (c) your relationships with friends and family. When he then asked which clone would be "closest to being you?" three-fourths of the seventh-graders

identity one's sense of self; according to Erikson, the adolescent's task is to solidify a sense of self by testing and integrating various roles.

Leland Bobbe/Getty Images

Matthias Clamer/Getty Images

Who shall I be today?
By varying the way they look, adolescents try out different "selves." Although we eventually form a consistent and stable sense of identity, the self we present may change with the situation.

"I am becoming still more independent of my parents; young as I am, I face life with more courage than Mummy; my feeling for justice is immovable, and truer than hers. I know what I want, I have a goal, an opinion, I have a religion, and love. Let me be myself and then I am satisfied. I know that I'm a woman, a woman with inward strength and plenty of courage."
Anne Frank, *Diary of a Young Girl,* 1947

■ **intimacy** in Erikson's theory, the ability to form close, loving relationships; a primary developmental task in late adolescence and early adulthood.

chose (*c*), the clone with the same social network. In contrast, three-fourths of the ninth-graders chose (*a*), the one with their individual thoughts and feelings.

Erikson contended that the adolescent identity stage is followed in young adulthood by a developing capacity for **intimacy,** the ability to form emotionally close relationships. Once you have a clear and comfortable sense of who you are, said Erikson, you are ready for close relationships. Such relationships are, for most of us, a source of great pleasure. When Mihaly Csikszentmihalyi (pronounced chick-SENT-me-hi) and Jeremy Hunter (2003) used a beeper to sample the daily experiences of American teens, they found them unhappiest when alone and happiest when with friends. As Aristotle long ago recognized, we humans are "the social animal."

Parent and Peer Influence

OBJECTIVE **23** | Contrast parental and peer influences during adolescence.

As adolescents in Western cultures seek to form their own identities, they begin to separate themselves from their parents (Paikoff & Brooks-Gunn, 1991). The preschooler who can't be close enough to her mother, who loves to touch and cling to her, becomes the 14-year-old who wouldn't be caught dead holding hands with Mom. The transition occurs gradually (**FIGURE 4.23**). By adolescence, arguments occur more often, usually over mundane things—household chores, bedtime, homework (Tesser & others, 1989). From early to late adolescence, parent-adolescent conflicts become temporarily (during early adolescence) more intense but progressively less frequent.

For a minority of parents and their adolescents, differences lead to estrangement and to great stress (Steinberg & Morris, 2001). But for most, disagreement at the level of bickering is not destructive. One study of 6000 adolescents in 10 countries, from Australia to Bangladesh to Turkey, found that most liked their parents (Offer & others, 1988). "We usually get along but . . . ," adolescents often report (Galambos, 1992; Steinberg, 1987). Positive relations with parents support positive peer relations. High school girls who have the most affectionate relationships with their mothers tend also to enjoy the most intimate friendships with girlfriends (Gold & Yanof, 1985). And teens who feel close to their parents tend to be healthy and happy and to do well in school (Resnick & others, 1997). Of course, we can state this correlation the other way: Misbehaving teens are more likely to have tense parental relationships.

Adolescence is typically a time of diminishing parental influence and growing peer influence. Asked in a survey if they had "ever had a serious talk" with their child about illegal drugs, 85 percent of American *parents* answered yes. But the teens sometimes tuned out this earnest advice, for only 45 percent could recall such a serious talk (Morin & Brossard, 1997). Instead, what their friends are—what "everybody's doing"—they often become.

As we noted in Chapter 3, heredity does much of the heavy lifting in forming individual differences in character and personality, and parent and peer influences do much of the rest. Teens are herd animals. They talk, dress, and act more like their peers than their parents. In teen calls to hotline counseling services, peer relationships are the most discussed topic (Boehm & others, 1999). For

"How was my day? How was my day? Must you micromanage my life?"

Compared with teens elsewhere, teens in the United States spend more time watching TV and hanging out with friends (both predictors of negative outcomes) and less time on schoolwork (Larson, 2001).

FIGURE 4.23
The changing parent-child relationship
Interviews from a large, national study of Canadian families reveal that the typically close, warm relationships between parents and preschoolers loosen among children of older ages. (Data from Statistics Canada, 1999.)

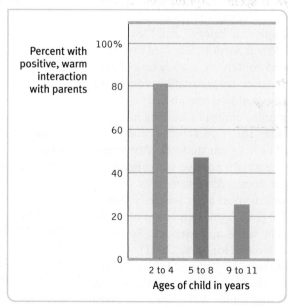

Percent with positive, warm interaction with parents

100%

80

60

40

20

0

2 to 4   5 to 8   9 to 11

Ages of child in years

those who feel excluded, the pain is acute. "The social atmosphere in most high schools is poisonously clique-driven and exclusionary," observes social psychologist Elliot Aronson (2001). Most excluded "students suffer in silence. . . . A small number act out in violent ways against their classmates." When rejected adolescents withdraw, they are vulnerable to loneliness, low self-esteem, and depression (Steinberg & Morris, 2001). Peer approval matters.

Teens see their parents as having more influence in other areas—for example, in shaping their religious faith and practices and in thinking about college and career choices (*Emerging Trends*, 1997). A Gallup Youth Survey reveals that most share their parent's political views, too (Lyons, 2005).

Emerging Adulthood

OBJECTIVE 24 | Discuss the characteristics of emerging adulthood.

As people mature in young adulthood, their emotional ties with parents loosen. During their early twenties, many still lean heavily on their parents. By their late twenties, most feel more comfortably independent of their parents and better able to empathize with them as fellow adults (Frank, 1988; White, 1983). This graduation from adolescence to adulthood is now taking longer.

In the Western world, adolescence now roughly corresponds to the teen years, but at earlier times—and in some developing countries today—adolescence was a brief interlude between the dependence of childhood and the responsibilities of adulthood (Baumeister & Tice, 1986). Shortly after sexual maturity, society bestowed adult responsibilities and status on the young person, often marking the event with an elaborate initiation. The new adult then worked, married, and had children. With compulsory schooling, adult independence began occurring later. In industrialized cultures from Europe to Australia, adolescents are taking more time to finish college, to leave the nest, and to establish careers. In the United States, for example, the average age at first marriage has increased more than 4 years since 1960 (to 27 for men, 25 for women). Today's earlier sexual maturity is related both to increased body fat (which can support pregnancy and nursing) and to weakened parent-child bonds, including absent fathers (Ellis, 2004). Together, later independence and earlier sexual maturity have widened the once-brief interlude between biological maturity and social independence (**FIGURE 4.24**). That gap—the years spent morphing from child to adult—is adolescence.

Nine times out of ten, it's all about peer pressure.

FIGURE 4.24
Adolescence is being stretched from both ends

In the 1890s the average interval between a woman's first menstrual period and marriage, which typically marked a transition to adulthood, was about 7 years; today in industrialized countries it is about 12 years (Guttmacher, 2000). Although many adults are unmarried, later marriage combines with prolonged education and earlier menarche to help stretch out adolescence.

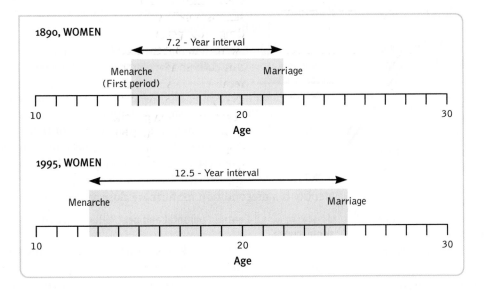

1890, WOMEN
7.2 - Year interval
Menarche (First period)   Marriage
10   20   30
Age

1995, WOMEN
12.5 - Year interval
Menarche   Marriage
10   20   30
Age

The time from 18 to the mid-twenties is an increasingly not-yet-settled phase of life, which some now call *emerging adulthood* (Arnett, 2000). These emerging adults are no longer adolescents, but they have not yet taken on adult-level responsibilities and independence, either. Unlike some non-Western cultures that have public rites of passage marking an abrupt transition to adulthood, Westerners typically have a more gradual transition. Those who leave home for college, for example, are separated from parents and, more than ever before, managing their time and priorities. Yet they may remain dependent on their parents' financial and emotional support and may return home for holidays. For many others out of school, their parents' home may be the only affordable place to live. Adulthood emerges, gradually.

>> LEARNING OUTCOMES

Adolescence

OBJECTIVE 17 | **Define *adolescence*.**

Adolescence is the transition period from childhood to adulthood, extending from puberty to independence.

OBJECTIVE 18 | **Identify the major physical changes during adolescence.**

Adolescence begins with puberty, the period of sexual maturation that enables reproduction. A surge of hormones triggers a two-year growth spurt, beginning at about age 11 in girls and age 13 in boys. Primary sex characteristics (the reproductive organs and external genitalia) and secondary sex characteristics (nonreproductive sexual characteristics such as a girl's breasts and a boy's deepened voice) develop during puberty, though the exact timing varies from one person to another. For most girls, menarche happens within a year of age 12. For most boys, spermarche occurs by about age 14. Heredity and environment interact, and other people's reactions to early or late maturation can influence adolescents' adjustment. There is also significant brain development during adolescence, with frontal lobe maturation and selective pruning of unused neurons and their connections.

OBJECTIVE 19 | **Describe the changes in reasoning abilities that Piaget called formal operations.**

With the development of formal operations, adolescents gain the ability to reason abstractly. This ability lets them form hypotheses and deduce consequences.

OBJECTIVE 20 | **Discuss moral development from the perspectives of moral thinking, moral feeling, and moral action.**

In Piaget's view, moral judgments reflect the developing child's reasoning powers. Lawrence Kohlberg proposed three levels of *moral thinking*. Preconventional morality is self-interested morality based on reasoning that attempts to avoid punishment or gain concrete rewards. Conventional morality is law-abiding morality based on reasoning that existing laws must be upheld. Postconventional morality (not everyone attains this final stage) is self-defined morality based on abstract reasoning about what is ethical, right, and fair. The social intuitionist view of morality proposes that *moral feelings* precede moral thinking and judgments. Some brain-imaging experiments confirm that the brain's emotion areas are active when people consider moral dilemmas. The *moral action* perspective focuses on social influences on decisions to do the right thing. Programs based on the moral action perspective teach children to empathize with others' feelings and to delay gratification to enable bigger rewards later.

OBJECTIVE 21 | **Identify Erikson's eight stages of psychosocial development and their accompanying issues.**

Erik Erikson proposed that we pass through eight stages in life (loosely associated with age), each with its own psychosocial task. In infancy (to 1 year), the issue is trust versus mistrust; in toddlerhood (1 to 2 years), the issue is autonomy versus shame and doubt. Preschoolers (3 to 5) learn initiative or guilt, and elementary school children (6 to puberty), competence or inferiority. A chief task of adolescence (teens to twenties) is solidifying one's sense of self—one's identity. For young adults (twenties to early forties), the issue is intimacy versus isolation, and for middle adulthood (forties to sixties), generativity versus stagnation. Late adulthood's (late sixties and up) task is integrity versus despair.

OBJECTIVE 22 | **Explain how the search for identity affects us during adolescence, and discuss how forming an identity prepares us for intimacy.**

In Western cultures, most adolescents try out different selves before settling into a consistent and comfortable identity. A smaller number unthinkingly adopt the identity of their parents or, rejecting the values of parents and society, take on the identity of peers. Self-esteem increases with identity achievement. Erikson believed that having a clear and comfortable identity is a precondition for forming close relationships.

OBJECTIVE 23 | **Contrast parental and peer influences during adolescence.**

Adolescents in Western cultures do tend to become increasingly independent of their parents, but researchers have found that most teenagers nevertheless relate to their parents reasonably well. Peer approval and relationships are very important, and teens talk, dress, and act like their peers. Parents continue to influence teens in such areas as religiosity and college and career choices.

OBJECTIVE 24 | **Discuss the characteristics of emerging adulthood.**
Emerging adulthood refers to the period from about age 18 to the mid-twenties, when many young people in Western cultures are no longer adolescents but have not yet achieved full independence as adults. During this time, many young people attend college or work but continue to live in their parents' home. In the United States, the age of first marriage now extends into the mid-twenties for men and women.

ASK YOURSELF: **What are the most positive and most negative things you remember about your own adolescence? And who do you credit or blame more—your parents or your peers?**

Adulthood

At one time, psychologists viewed the center-of-life years between adolescence and old age as one long plateau. No longer. Those who follow the unfolding of people's adult lives now believe our development continues.

It is more difficult to generalize about adulthood stages than about life's early years. If you know that James is a 1-year-old and Jamal is a 10-year-old, you could say a great deal about each child. Not so with adults who differ by a similar number of years. The boss may be 30 or 60; the marathon runner may be 20 or 50; a 19-year-old can be a parent who supports a child or a child who gets an allowance. Yet our life courses are in some ways similar. Physically, cognitively, and especially socially, we are at age 50 different from our 25-year-old selves. Although our bodies, minds, and relationships undergo some changes in common with those of our childhood friends, in other ways, we may now seem very different.

> " I am still learning."
> Michelangelo, 1560, at age 85

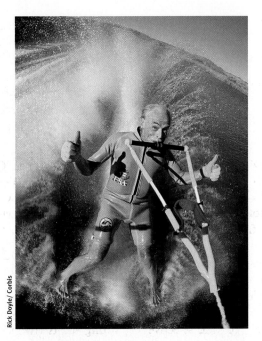

Rick Doyle / Corbis

Adult abilities vary widely
Eighty-seven-year-olds: Don't try this. In 2002, George Blair became the world's oldest barefoot water skier, 18 days after his eighty-seventh birthday.

Physical Development

Our physical abilities—muscular strength, reaction time, sensory keenness, and cardiac output—all crest by the mid-twenties. Like the declining daylight after the summer solstice, the decline of physical prowess begins imperceptibly. Athletes are often the first to notice. World-class sprinters and swimmers peak by their early twenties. Women, because they mature earlier than men, also peak earlier. But most of us—especially those of us whose daily lives do not require top physical performance—hardly perceive the early signs of decline.

Physical Changes in Middle Adulthood

OBJECTIVE 25 | Identify the major physical changes that occur in middle adulthood.

Middle-age (post-40) athletes know all too well that physical decline gradually accelerates (**FIGURE 4.25** on page 176). As a 63-year-old who regularly plays basketball, I now find myself occasionally wondering whether my team really needs me down court. But even diminished vigor is sufficient for normal activities. Moreover, during

How old does a person have to be before you think of him or her as old? The average 18- to 29-year-old says 67. The average person 60 and over says 76 (Yankelovich, 1995).

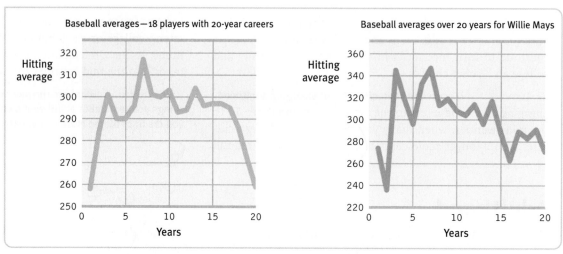

FIGURE 4.25
Gradually accelerating decline
An analysis of aging and batting averages of all twentieth-century major league baseball players revealed a gradual but accelerating decline in players' later years (Schall & Smith, 2000). The career performance record of the great Willie Mays is illustrative.

"There are no life-style changes, surgical procedures, vitamins, antioxidants, hormones or techniques of genetic engineering available today that have been demonstrated to influence the processes of aging."

Position Statement on Human Aging signed by 51 scientists who study aging, 2002

"If the truth were known, we'd have to diagnose [older women] as having P.M.F.— Post-Menstrual Freedom."

Social psychologist Jacqueline Goodchilds (1987)

"Happy fortieth. I'll take the muscle tone in your upper arms, the girlish timbre of your voice, your amazing tolerance for caffeine, and your ability to digest french fries. The rest of you can stay."

early and middle adulthood, physical vigor has less to do with age than with a person's health and exercise habits. Many of today's physically fit 50-year-olds run 4 miles with ease, while sedentary 25-year-olds find themselves huffing and puffing up two flights of stairs.

As in adolescence, the physical changes of adult life may trigger psychological responses, which vary depending on how one views growing older. In some Eastern cultures, where respect and power come with age, outward signs of advancing years are accepted and even welcomed. In Western cultures, where the perceived ideal is smooth skin and a slim torso, middle-age wrinkles and bulges can threaten self-esteem. Millions therefore spend billions in hopes of slowing or reversing the process. But nature will not be denied; inevitably the lines appear (or reappear) and the youthful form changes shape.

For women, aging means a gradual decline in fertility. Among women 35 to 39, a single act of intercourse is half as likely to produce a pregnancy as it would be for a woman 19 to 26 (Dunson & others, 2002). But women's foremost biological sign of aging is **menopause,** the ending of the menstrual cycle, usually beginning within a few years of age 50. Menopause and its physical symptoms accompany a reduction in the hormone estrogen. For 4 or 5 in 10 Canadian and U.S. women, but only 1 in 7 Japanese women, these symptoms include occasional hot flashes (Goode, 1999; Lock, 1998). Like the stereotype of adolescent storm and stress, the image of menopausal emotionality and depression clashes with reality: Menopause usually does *not* create psychological problems for women. Studies following thousands of American and Australian middle-aged women for up to 10 years have all found them no more or less depressed if experiencing menopause (Avis, 2003; Dennerstein & others, 2000).

A woman's expectations and attitudes influence the emotional impact of menopause. Does she see it as a sign that she is losing her femininity and sexual attractiveness and growing old? Or does she view it as liberation from menstrual periods, fears of pregnancy, and children's demands? To learn women's attitudes toward menopause, Bernice Neugarten and her colleagues (1963) did what, a half-century before, no one had ever done: They questioned women whose experience of menopause had *not* led them to seek treatment. When asked whether it is true that after menopause "women generally feel better than they have for years," only one-fourth of the premenopausal women under age 45 guessed yes. Of the older women who had experienced menopause, two-thirds said yes. As one woman said, "I can remember my mother saying that after her menopause she really got her vigor, and I can say the same thing myself." In one MacArthur Foundation study of 3000 midlife adults, most postmenopausal women recalled "only relief" when their periods stopped; just 2 percent felt "only regret" (Goode, 1999).

Perception Laboratory, University of St. Andrews

The aging face
Psychologists Michael Burt and David Perrett (1995) created computer composite images averaged from 20- to 24-year-old and 50- to 54-year-old Caucasian males. Then they applied the age changes to other faces, projecting, for example, what an older Marilyn Monroe would have looked like.

Men experience no equivalent to menopause—no cessation of fertility, no sharp drop in sex hormones. They do experience a more gradual decline in sperm count, testosterone level, and speed of erection and ejaculation. If testosterone levels plummet too fast and far, the result may be depression, irritability, insomnia, impotence, or weakness, which can be treated by testosterone replacement therapy (Sternbach, 1998). Some may also experience psychological distress related to their perception of decreased virility and declining physical capacities. But most men age without such problems. After middle age, most men and women remain capable of satisfying sexual activity. When people over 60 were surveyed by the National Council on Aging, 39 percent expressed satisfaction with the amount of sex they were having and 39 percent said they wished for sex more frequently (Leary, 1998).

> " The things that stop you having sex with age are exactly the same as those that stop you riding a bicycle (bad health, thinking it looks silly, no bicycle)."
> Alex Comfort, *The Joy of Sex,* 2002

Physical Changes in Later Life

OBJECTIVE **26** | Compare life expectancy in the mid-twentieth and early twenty-first centuries, and discuss changes in sensory abilities and health (including frequency of dementia) in older adults.

Is old age "more to be feared than death" (Juvenal, *Satires*)? Or is life "most delightful when it is on the downward slope" (Seneca, *Epistulae ad Lucilium*)? What is it like to grow old? To gauge your own understanding, take the following true/false quiz:

1. Older people become more susceptible to short-term illnesses (see pages 177–178).
2. During old age many of the brain's neurons die (see page 180).
3. If they live to be 90 or older, most elderly people eventually become senile (see pages 179–180).
4. Recognition memory—the ability to identify things previously experienced—declines with age (see pages 181–182).
5. Life satisfaction peaks in the fifties and then gradually declines after age 65 (see pages 189–190).

Life Expectancy The above statements—all false—are among the misconceptions about aging exploded by recent research on the world's most rapidly growing population group. Worldwide, life expectancy at birth increased from 49 years in 1950 to 67

■ **menopause** the time of natural cessation of menstruation; also refers to the biological changes a woman experiences as her ability to reproduce declines.

World record for longevity?
French woman Jeanne Calment, the oldest human in history with authenticated age, died in 1998 at age 122. At age 100, she was still riding a bike. At age 114, she became the oldest film actor ever, by portraying herself in *Vincent and Me*.

Georges Gobet/AP Photo

Swaziland has the world's shortest life expectancy (33 years). Andorrans enjoy the longest expectation of life—almost 84 years (CIA Factbook, 2005).

After age 30, the risk of death doubles every 8 years. A 48-year-old's risk of dying is twice that of a 40-year-old's (National Center for Health Statistics, 1992; Olshansky & others, 1993).

Most stairway falls taken by older people occur on the top step, precisely where the person typically descends from a window-lit hallway into the darker stairwell (Fozard & Popkin, 1978). Our knowledge of aging could be used to design environments that would reduce such accidents (National Research Council, 1990).

in 2004—and to 80 and beyond in some developed countries (PRB, 2004; Sivard, 1996). This increasing life expectancy (humanity's greatest achievement, say some) combines with decreasing birthrates to make the elderly a bigger and bigger population segment. By 2050, about 35 percent of Europe's population likely will be over age 60 (Fernández-Ballesteros, 2003). Clearly, countries that have depended on children to care for the aged are destined for major social changes. Russia and Western Europe are also headed for depopulation—from 146 million to 104 million people in Russia by 2050, projects the United Nations (Brooks, 2005). "When an entire continent, healthier, wealthier, and more secure than ever before, fails to create the human future in the most elemental sense—by creating the next generation—something very serious is afoot," surmises George Weigel (2005).

Life expectancy differs for males and females; males are more prone to dying. Although 126 male embryos begin life for every 100 females who do so, the sex ratio is down to 105 males for every 100 females at birth (Strickland, 1992). During the first year, male infants' death rates exceed females' by one-fourth. Women outlive men by 4 years worldwide and by 5 to 6 years in Canada, the United States, and Australia. (Rather than marrying a man older than themselves, 20-year-old women who want a husband who shares their life expectancy should wait for the 15-year-old boys to mature.) By age 100, females outnumber males 5 to 1.

But few of us live to 100. Even if no one died before age 50, and cancer, heart disease, and infectious illness were eliminated, average life expectancy would still increase only to about 85 or a few years beyond (Barinaga, 1991). The body ages. Its cells stop reproducing. It becomes frail. It becomes vulnerable to tiny insults—hot weather, a fall, a mild flu bug—that at age 20 would have been trivial.

Why do we eventually wear out? Why don't we, like the bristlecone pine trees, rockfish, and some social insect queens, grow older without withering? One theory, proposed by evolutionary biologists, speculates that the answer relates to our survival as a species: We pass on our genes most successfully when we raise our young and then stop consuming resources. Once we've fulfilled our gene-reproducing task, there are no natural selection pressures against genes that cause degeneration in later life (Olshansky & others, 1993; Sapolsky & Finch, 1991).

Sensory Abilities As we have seen, physical decline begins in early adulthood, but we are not usually acutely aware of it until later life. Visual sharpness diminishes, and adaptation to changes in light level slows. Muscle strength, reaction time, and stamina also diminish noticeably, as do hearing, distance perception, and the sense of smell (**FIGURE 4.26**). In later life, the stairs get steeper, the print gets smaller, and people seem to mumble more.

With age, the eye's pupil shrinks and its lens becomes less transparent, reducing the amount of light reaching the retina. In fact, a 65-year-old retina receives only

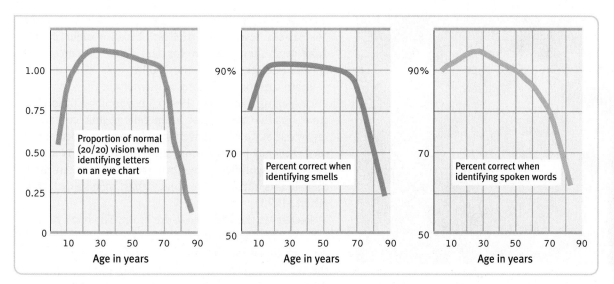

Michael Newman/PhotoEdit

FIGURE 4.26
The aging senses
Sight, smell, and hearing all are less acute among those over age 70. (From Doty & others, 1984.)

about one-third as much light as its 20-year-old counterpart (Kline & Schieber, 1985). Thus, to see as well as a 20-year-old when reading or driving, a 65-year-old needs three times as much light—a reason for buying cars with untinted windshields. This also explains why older people sometimes ask younger people, "Don't you need better light for reading?"

Health For those growing older, there is both bad and good news about health. The bad news: The body's disease-fighting immune system weakens, making the elderly more susceptible to life-threatening ailments such as cancer and pneumonia. The good news: Thanks partly to a lifetime's accumulation of antibodies, older people *less* often suffer short-term ailments, such as common flu and cold viruses. For example, those over 65 are half as likely as 20-year-olds and one-fifth as likely as preschoolers to suffer upper respiratory flu each year (National Center for Health Statistics, 1990). This helps explain why older workers have lower absenteeism rates (Rhodes, 1983).

Aging levies a tax on the brain by slowing our neural processing. Up to the teen years, we process information with greater and greater speed (Fry & Hale, 1996; Kail, 1991). But compared with teens and young adults, older people take a bit more time to react, to solve perceptual puzzles, even to remember names (Bashore & others, 1997; Verhaeghen & Salthouse, 1997). The lag is greatest when tasks become complex (Cerella, 1985; Poon, 1987). At video games, most 70-year-olds are no match for a 20-year-old. And, as **FIGURE 4.27** indicates, fatal accident rates per mile driven

> "For some reason, possibly to save ink, the restaurants had started printing their menus in letters the height of bacteria."
> Dave Barry, *Dave Barry Turns Fifty*, 1998

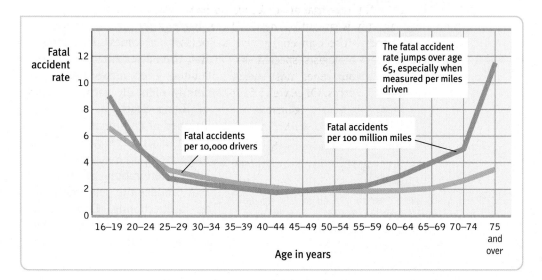

FIGURE 4.27
Age and driver fatalities
Slowing reactions contribute to increased accident risks among those 75 and older, and their greater fragility increases their risk of death when accidents happen (NHTSA, 2000). Would you favor driver exams based on performance, not age, to screen out those whose slow reactions or sensory impairments indicate accident risk?

Keeping the biological clock running smoothly
How quickly people age depends in part on their health habits. As these members of the Young@Heart Chorus make clear, the more active people remain, the more vigor they retain. Here Jeanne Hatch sings solo as the chorus dances and provides backup vocals.

■ **Alzheimer's disease** a progressive and irreversible brain disorder characterized by gradual deterioration of memory, reasoning, language, and, finally, physical functioning.

increase sharply after age 75. By age 85, they exceed the 16-year-old level. Nevertheless, because older people drive less, they account for less than 10 percent of crashes (Coughlin & others, 2004).

Brain regions important to memory begin to atrophy during aging (Schacter, 1996). In young adulthood, a small, gradual net loss of brain cells begins, contributing by age 80 to a brain-weight reduction of 5 percent or so. Aging may proceed more slowly in women. Not only do women worldwide live four years longer than men, their brains shrink more slowly than men's (Coffey & others, 1998).

Exercising the body feeds the brain. The birth of new cells and the proliferation of neural connections, especially in those who remain active, helps compensate for the cell loss (Coleman & Flood, 1986). Physical exercise enhances muscles, bones, and energy and helps prevent obesity and heart disease. It also stimulates brain cell development and connections, thanks perhaps to increased oxygen and nutrient flow (Kempermann & others, 1998). And that may explain why active older adults tend to be mentally quick older adults, and why, across 20 studies, sedentary older adults randomly assigned to aerobic exercise programs have exhibited enhanced memory and sharpened judgment (Colcombe & Kramer, 2003; Colcombe & others, 2004; Weuve & others, 2004). We are more likely to rust from disuse than to wear out from overuse. "Use it or lose it" is sound advice.

Dementia and Alzheimer's Disease Some adults do, unfortunately, suffer a substantial loss of brain cells. Up to age 95, the incidence of mental disintegration doubles roughly every 5 years (**FIGURE 4.28**). A series of small strokes, a brain tumor, or alcoholism can progressively damage the brain, causing that mental erosion we call *dementia*. So, too, can the most feared of all brain ailments, **Alzheimer's disease,** which strikes 3 percent of the world's population by age 75. Alzheimer's symptoms are *not* the same as normal aging. (Occasionally forgetting where you laid the car keys is no cause for alarm; forgetting how to get home does suggest Alzheimer's.)

Alzheimer's destroys even the brightest of minds. First memory, then reasoning, deteriorates. Robert Sayre (1979) recalls his father shouting at his afflicted mother to "think harder," while his mother, confused, embarrassed, on the verge of tears, randomly searched the house for lost objects. As Alzheimer's runs its course, after 5 to 20 years, the person becomes emotionally flat, then disoriented and disinhibited, then incontinent, and finally mentally vacant—a sort of living death, a mere body stripped of its humanity.

Underlying the symptoms of Alzheimer's is a loss of brain cells and deterioration of neurons that produce the neurotransmitter acetylcholine. Deprived of this vital chemical messenger, memory and thinking suffer. An

FIGURE 4.28
Incidence of dementia (mental disintegration) by age
Risk of dementia due to Alzheimer's disease or a series of strokes doubles about every 5 years in later life. (From Jorm & others, 1987, based on 22 studies in industrial nations.)

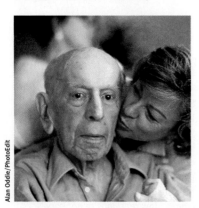

Percentage with dementia

Risk of dementia increases in later years

40%

30

20

10

0

60–64 70–74 80–84 90–95
65–69 75–79 85–89

Age group

autopsy reveals two telltale abnormalities in these acetylcholine-producing neurons: shriveled protein filaments in the cell body and plaques (globs of degenerating tissue) at the tips of neuron branches. In one line of research, scientists are working to develop drugs that will block proteins from aggregating into plaques (Ingram, 2003).

Researchers are gaining insights into the chemical, neural, and genetic roots of Alzheimer's. In people at risk for this disease, brain scans (**FIGURE 4.29**) reveal—before symptoms appear—both the telltale degeneration of critical brain cells and more diffuse brain activity while memorizing words, as if more exertion was required to achieve the same performance (Bookheimer & others, 2000; Fox & others, 2001). Physically active, nonobese people are less at risk for Alzheimer's (Abbott & others, 2004; Gustafson & others, 2003; Marx, 2005). So, too, are those with an active, challenged mind—often the mind of an educated, active reader (Wilson & Bennett, 2003). As with muscles, so with the brain: Those who use it, less often lose it.

FIGURE 4.29
Predicting Alzheimer's disease
During a memory test, MRI scans of the brains of people at risk for Alzheimer's (left) revealed more intense activity (yellow, followed by orange and red) when compared with normal brains (right). As brain scans and genetic tests make it possible to identify those likely to suffer Alzheimer's, would you want to be tested? At what age?

Cognitive Development

Among the most controversial questions in the study of the human life span is whether adult cognitive abilities, such as memory, creativity, and intelligence, parallel the gradually accelerating decline of physical abilities.

Aging and Memory

OBJECTIVE **27** | Assess the impact of aging on recall and recognition in adulthood.

As we age, we remember some things well. Looking back in later life, people most vividly recall not only recent happenings but also their experiences in life's second two decades (Conway & others, 2005; Rubin & others, 1998). Asked to recall the one or two most important events over the last half-century, they tend to name events from their teens or twenties. Whatever one experienced around this stage of life—World War II, the civil rights movement, the Vietnam war, or the events of 9/11—becomes pivotal (Pillemer, 1998; Schuman & Scott, 1989). Our teens and twenties are also the time when we experience so many of life's memorable "firsts"—first date, first job, first going to college, first meeting your parents-in-law.

If you are within five years of 20, what experiences from your last year will you likely never forget? (This is the time of your life you may best remember when you are 50.)

For some types of learning and remembering, early adulthood is indeed a peak time. In one experiment, Thomas Crook and Robin West (1990) invited 1205 people to learn some names. Fourteen videotaped people said their names, using a common format: "Hi, I'm Larry." Then the same individuals reappeared and said, for example, "I'm from Philadelphia"—thus providing a visual and voice cue for remembering the person's name. As **FIGURE 4.30** shows, everyone remembered more names after a second and third replay of the introductions, but younger adults consistently surpassed older adults in their

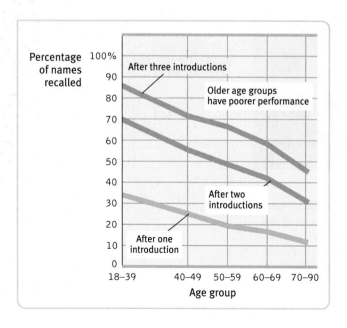

FIGURE 4.30
Tests of recall
Recalling new names introduced once, twice, or three times is easier for younger adults than for older ones. (Data from Crook & West, 1990.)

name recall. Similar results appear in other studies. Within hours after Prime Minister Margaret Thatcher announced her resignation, young and old British people recalled how they heard the news. When asked again 11 months later, 90 percent of the younger group, but only 42 percent of the older group, told the same story (Cohen & others, 1994). Perhaps it is not surprising, then, that nearly two-thirds of people over age 40 say their memory is worse than it was 10 years ago (KRC, 2001).

But consider another experiment. David Schonfield and Betty-Anne Robertson (1966) asked adults of various ages to learn a list of 24 words. Without giving any clues, the researchers asked some to *recall* as many words as they could from the list, and others simply to *recognize* words, using multiple-choice questions. Again, younger adults had better recall (**FIGURE 4.31**). But the researchers found no similar memory decline with age on the recognition tests. Tests also reveal that, unless given a jolt of caffeine, recognition memory is better for older adults early in the day rather than late (May & others, 1993; Ryan & others, 2002). So, how well older people remember depends: Are they being asked simply to *recognize* what they have tried to memorize (minimal decline) or to *recall* it without clues (greater decline)?

Forgetting seems also to depend on the type of information you are trying to remember. If asked to recall meaningless information—nonsense syllables or unimportant events—then the older you are, the more errors you are likely to make. If the information is meaningful, older people's rich web of existing knowledge will help them to catch it, though they may take longer than younger adults to *produce* the words and things they know (Burke & Shafto, 2004). (Quick-thinking game show winners are usually younger to middle-age adults.) Older people's capacity to learn and remember skills also decline less than their verbal recall (Graf, 1990; Labouvie-Vief & Schell, 1982; Perlmutter, 1983).

Prospective memory ("Remember to. . .") remains strong when events help trigger memories, as when walking by a convenience store triggers a ". . . pick up milk" memory. Time-based tasks ("Remember the 3 P.M. meeting") prove somewhat more challenging for older people. Habitual tasks, such as remembering to take medications three times daily, can be especially challenging, report Gilles Einstein, Mark McDaniel, and their colleagues (1990, 1995, 1998). To minimize problems associated with declining prospective memory, older adults rely more on time management and on using reminder cues, such as notes to themselves (Henry & others, 2004).

Taking several pills several times each day can be a challenge for an older adult's declining prospective memory. The simple solution is an external aid: Putting each week's pills into a box that has slots for all the days and times removes confusion about whether one has taken the pills or only thought about doing so. (Pharmacies offer these.)

David Myers

FIGURE 4.31
Recall and recognition in adulthood
In this experiment, the ability to *recall* new information declined during early and middle adulthood, but the ability to *recognize* new information did not. (From Schonfield & Robertson, 1966.)

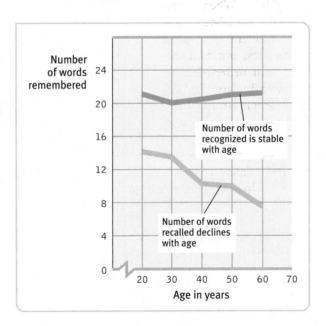

Number of words remembered

Number of words recognized is stable with age

Number of words recalled declines with age

Age in years

Those who study our capacity to learn and remember are aware of one other important complication: Right through our later years, we continue to diverge. Twenty-year-olds differ widely in their abilities to learn and remember, but 70-year-olds differ much more. Some 70-year-olds perform below nearly all 20-year-olds; other 70-year-olds match or outdo the average 20-year-old.

Aging and Intelligence

OBJECTIVE 28 | Summarize the contributions of cross-sectional and longitudinal studies to our understanding of the normal effects of aging on adult intelligence.

What happens to our broader intellectual powers as we age? Do they gradually decline, as does our ability to recall new material? Or do they remain constant, as does our ability to recognize meaningful material? The evolving answer to this question makes an interesting research story, one that illustrates psychology's self-correcting process (Woodruff-Pak, 1989).

Phase I: Cross-Sectional Evidence for Intellectual Decline In **cross-sectional studies,** researchers test and compare people of various ages. When giving intelligence tests to representative samples of people, researchers consistently find that older adults give fewer correct answers than do younger adults. David Wechsler (1972), creator of the most widely used adult intelligence test, therefore concluded that "the decline of mental ability with age is part of the general [aging] process of the organism as a whole."

For a long time, this rather dismal view of mental decline went unchallenged. Many corporations established mandatory retirement policies, assuming the companies would benefit by replacing aging workers with younger, presumably more capable, employees. As everyone "knew," you couldn't teach an old dog new tricks.

Phase II: Longitudinal Evidence for Intellectual Stability After colleges began giving intelligence tests to entering students about 1920, several psychologists saw their chance to study intelligence **longitudinally**—retesting the same people over a period of years. What they expected to find was a decrease in intelligence after about age 30 (Schaie & Geiwitz, 1982). What they actually found was a surprise: Until late in life, intelligence remained stable (**FIGURE 4.32**). On some tests, it even increased.

How then are we to account for the findings from the cross-sectional studies? In retrospect, researchers saw the problem. When cross-sectional studies compared 70-year-olds and 30-year-olds, it compared people not only of two different ages but of two different eras. It compared generally less-educated people (born, say, in the early 1900s) with better-educated people (born after 1950), people raised in large families with people raised in smaller families, people growing up in less affluent families with people raised in more affluent families.

According to this more optimistic view, the myth that intelligence sharply declines with age is laid to rest. As everyone "knows," given good health you're never too old to learn. At age 70, John Rock developed the birth control pill. At age 78, Grandma Moses took up painting, and she was still painting after age 100. At age 81—and 17 years from the end of his college football coaching career—Amos Alonzo Stagg was named coach of the year. At age 89, architect Frank Lloyd Wright designed New York City's Guggenheim Museum.

■ **cross-sectional study** a study in which people of different ages are compared with one another.

■ **longitudinal study** research in which the same people are restudied and retested over a long period.

FIGURE 4.32
Cross-sectional versus longitudinal testing of intelligence at various ages In this test of one type of verbal intelligence (inductive reasoning), the cross-sectional method produced declining scores with age. The longitudinal method (in which the same people were retested over a period of years) produced a slight *rise* in scores well into adulthood. (Adapted from Schaie, 1994.)

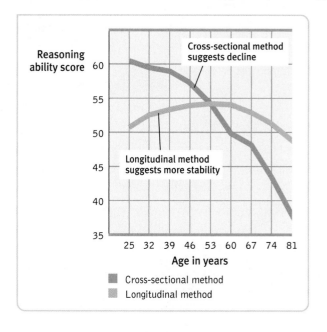

Reasoning ability score

Cross-sectional method suggests decline

Longitudinal method suggests more stability

Age in years

■ Cross-sectional method
■ Longitudinal method

■ **crystallized intelligence** one's accumulated knowledge and verbal skills; tends to increase with age.

■ **fluid intelligence** one's ability to reason speedily and abstractly; tends to decrease during late adulthood.

"In youth we learn, in age we understand."

Marie Von Ebner-Eschenbach, *Aphorisms*, 1883

Phase III: It All Depends But the controversy continues. For one thing, longitudinal studies have their own pitfalls. Those who survive to the end of longitudinal studies may be bright, healthy people whose intelligence is least likely to decline. (Perhaps people who died younger and were removed from the study had declining intelligence.) Adjusting for the loss of subjects, as did a study following more than 2000 people over 75 in Cambridge, England, reveals a steeper intelligence decline. This is especially so as people age after 85 (Brayne & others, 1999).

Research is further complicated by the finding that intelligence is not a single trait (Chapter 11). Intelligence tests that assess speed of thinking may place older adults at a disadvantage because of their slower neural mechanisms for processing information. Meeting old friends on the street, names rise to the mind's surface more slowly—"like air bubbles in molasses," says David Lykken (1999). But slower need not mean less intelligent. When given tests that assess general vocabulary, knowledge, and ability to integrate information, older adults generally fare well (Craik, 1986). Older Canadians surpass younger Canadians at answering questions such as, "Which province was once called New Caledonia?" In four studies, the highest average performance on *New York Times* crossword puzzles (given 15 minutes to fill in words) was achieved by adults in their fifties, sixties, and seventies (**FIGURE 4.33**).

German researcher Paul Baltes and his colleagues (1993, 1994, 1999) have developed "wisdom" tests that assess "expert knowledge about life in general and good judgment and advice about how to conduct oneself in the face of complex, uncertain circumstances." Their results suggest that older adults more than hold their own on such tests. Thus, despite 30-year-olds' quick-thinking smarts, we usually select older people to be president of the company, the college, or the country. Age is sage. To paraphrase one 60-year-old, "Forty years ago I had a great memory, but I was a fool."

So, whether intelligence increases or decreases with age depends on the type of intellectual performance we measure. **Crystallized intelligence**—one's accumulated knowledge as reflected in vocabulary and analogies tests—*increases* up to old age. **Fluid intelligence**—one's ability to reason speedily and abstractly, as when solving novel logic problems—*decreases* slowly up to age 75 or so, then more rapidly, especially after age 85 (Cattell, 1963; Horn, 1982). We can see this pattern in the intelligence scores of a national sample of adults. After adjustments for education, verbal scores (reflecting crystallized intelligence) held relatively steady from ages 20 to 74. Nonverbal, puzzle-solving intelligence declined. Thus, Denise Park and her colleagues (2002) confirm, with age we lose and we win (**FIGURE 4.34**). We lose recall memory and processing speed, but we gain vocabulary and knowledge.

FIGURE 4.33
Word power grows with age
In four studies summarized by Timothy Salthouse (2004), older crossword puzzle players excelled when given 15 minutes with a *New York Times* puzzle.

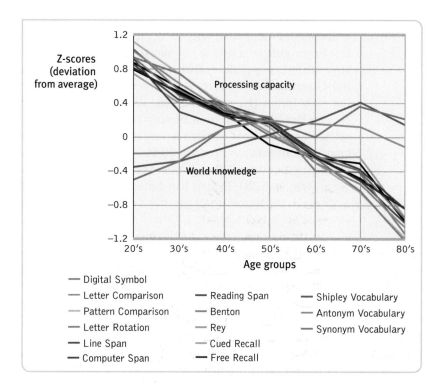

FIGURE 4.34
The downs and ups of aging
Using a variety of reliable measures of processing capacity (such as speed of processing, working memory, and long-term memory) and world knowledge (such as vocabulary), Denise Park and her colleagues (2002) consistently illustrated that with age, our processing capacity declines but our vocabulary and general knowledge increase.

These cognitive differences help explain why mathematicians and scientists produce much of their most creative work during their late twenties or early thirties, whereas those in literature, history, and philosophy tend to produce their best work in their forties, fifties, and beyond, after accumulating more knowledge (Simonton, 1988, 1990). For example, poets (who depend on fluid intelligence) reach their peak output earlier than prose authors (who need a deeper knowledge reservoir), a finding observed in every major literary tradition, for both living and dead languages. So, intellectual performance can either increase or decrease with age, depending on what we assess and how we assess it.

Social Development

Many differences between younger and older adults are created not by the physical and cognitive changes that accompany aging but by life events associated with family relationships and work. A new job means new relationships, new expectations, and new demands. Marriage brings the joy of intimacy and the stress of merging your life with another's. The birth of a child introduces responsibilities and significantly alters your life focus. The death of a loved one creates an irreplaceable loss and a need to reaffirm your own life. Do these normal events of adult life shape a predictable sequence of life changes?

Adulthood's Ages and Stages

OBJECTIVE 29 | Explain why the path of adult development need not be tightly linked to one's chronological age.

As people enter their forties, they undergo a transition to middle adulthood, a time when they realize that life will soon be mostly behind them instead of ahead of them. Some psychologists have argued that for many the *midlife transition* is a crisis, a time of great struggle, of regret, or even of feeling struck down by life. The popular image

"Midway in the journey of our life I found myself in a dark wood, for the straight way was lost."

Dante, *The Divine Comedy,* 1314

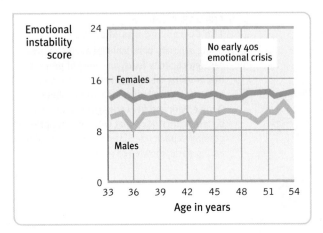

FIGURE 4.35
Early forties midlife crises?
Among 10,000 people responding to a national health survey, there was no early forties increase in emotional instability ("neuroticism") scores. (From McCrae & Costa, 1990.)

" The important events of a person's life are the products of chains of highly improbable occurrences."
Joseph Traub, "Traub's Law," 2003

Resetting the social clock
The social clock once prescribed that university graduation should occur around age 22. Today, more students are earning degrees at other ages.

of the midlife crisis is an early-forties man who forsakes his family for a younger girlfriend and a hot sports car. But the fact—reported by large samples of people—is that unhappiness, job dissatisfaction, marital dissatisfaction, divorce, anxiety, and suicide do *not* surge during the early forties (Hunter & Sundel, 1989; Mroczek & Kolarz, 1998). Divorce, for example, is most common among those in their twenties, suicide among those in their seventies and eighties. One study of emotional instability in nearly 10,000 men and women found "not the slightest evidence" that distress peaks anywhere in the midlife age range (**FIGURE 4.35**). For the 1 in 4 adults who do report experiencing a life crisis, the trigger is not age, but a major event such as illness, divorce, or job loss (Lachman, 2004).

There is another reason skeptics question age-linked stages such as the "midlife crisis." The **social clock**—the cultural prescription of "the right time" to leave home, get a job, marry, have children, and retire—varies from culture to culture and era to era. In Jordan, 40 percent of brides are in their teens; in Hong Kong, only 3 percent are (United Nations, 1992). In Western Europe, fewer than 10 percent of men over 65 remain in the work force, as do 16 percent in the United States, 36 percent in Japan, and 69 percent in Mexico (Davies & others, 1991). And the once rigid sequence for Western women—of student to worker to wife to at-home mom to worker again—has loosened. Contemporary women occupy these roles in any order or all at once.

Life Events and Chance Encounters For women and men, life events—marriage, parenthood, vocational changes, divorce, nest emptying, relocation, and retirement—mark transitions to new life stages whenever they occur, and they are occurring at increasingly unpredictable ages. The social clock still ticks, but people feel freer about being out of sync with it.

Even chance events can have lasting significance because they often deflect us down one road rather than another (Bandura, 1982). Romantic attraction, for example, is often influenced by chance encounters. Albert Bandura (2004) recalls the ironic true story of a book editor who came to one of his lectures on the "Psychology of Chance Encounters and Life Paths"—and ended up marrying the woman who happened to sit next to him.

Consider one study of identical twins and their spouses. Twins, especially identical twins, make similar choices of friends, clothes, vacations, jobs, and so on. So, if your identical twin became engaged to someone, wouldn't you (being in so many ways the same as your twin) expect to also feel attracted to this person? Surprisingly, only half the identical twins recalled really liking their co-twin's selection, and only 5 percent said, "I could have fallen for my twin's partner." Researchers David Lykken and Auke Tellegen (1993) surmise that romantic love is rather like ducklings' imprinting: Given repeated exposure to someone after childhood, you may form a bond (infatuation) with almost any available person who has a roughly similar background and level of attractiveness and who reciprocates your affections.

Adulthood's Commitments

OBJECTIVE **30** | Discuss the importance of love, marriage, and children in adulthood, and comment on the contribution of one's work to feelings of self-satisfaction.

Two basic aspects of our lives do, however, dominate adulthood. Erik Erikson called them *intimacy* (forming close relationships) and *generativity* (being productive and supporting future generations). Researchers have chosen various terms—

affiliation and *achievement*, *attachment* and *productivity*, *commitment* and *competence*. Sigmund Freud (1935) put it most simply: The healthy adult, he said, is one who can *love* and *work*.

Love Across time and place, human societies have nearly always included relatively monogamous pairing. We flirt, fall in love, and commit—one person at a time. "Pair-bonding is a trademark of the human animal," observed anthropologist Helen Fisher (1993). From an evolutionary perspective, the arrangement makes sense: Parents who cooperated to nurture their children to maturity were more likely to have their genes passed along to posterity than parents who didn't. Rivaling or exceeding adult pair-bonding is the love of parent for child. "I feel an overwhelming love for my children unlike anything I feel for anyone else," agreed 93 percent of American mothers in a national survey (Erickson & Aird, 2005). Many fathers feel the same. A few weeks after the birth of my first child I was suddenly struck by a realization: "So *this* is how my parents felt about me!"

Adult bonds of love are most satisfying and enduring when marked by a similarity of interests and values, a sharing of emotional and material support, and intimate self-disclosure (see Chapter 18). Marriage bonds are also likely to last when couples marry after age 20 and are well educated. Compared with their counterparts of 40 years ago, people in Western countries *are* better educated and marrying later. Yet, ironically, they are twice as likely to divorce. This partly reflects women's lessened economic dependence and men and women's rising expectations. We now hope not only for an enduring bond, but also for a mate who is a wage earner, caregiver, intimate friend, and warm and responsive lover. To judge from the divorce rate—both Canada and the United States now have about one divorce for every two marriages—marriage has become a union that often defies management (Bureau of the Census, 2004). In Europe, divorce is only slightly less common.

Might test-driving life together in a "trial marriage" minimize divorce risk? In a 2001 Gallup survey of American twenty-somethings, 62 percent thought it would (Whitehead & Popenoe, 2001). In reality, studies in Europe, Canada, and the United States have repeatedly found that those who cohabited before marriage actually had *higher* rates of divorce and marital dysfunction than those who did not (Dush & others, 2003; Popenoe & Whitehead, 2002). The risk of poor marital outcomes appears greatest for those who cohabit prior to engagement (Kline & others, 2004). Cohabiters tend to be initially less committed to the ideal of enduring marriage, and they become even less marriage-supporting while cohabiting.

Nonetheless, the institution of marriage endures. Worldwide, reports the United Nations, 9 in 10 heterosexual adults marry (Lowy, 2000). In Western countries, 3 in 4 who divorce will remarry—and their second marriages will be virtually as happy as the average first marriage (Vemer & others, 1989). They are not alone. Surveys of more than 40,000 Americans since 1972 reveal that 40 percent of married adults, though only 23 percent of unmarried adults, report being "very happy." Lesbian couples, too, report greater well-being than those who are alone (Wayment & Peplau, 1995). Marriage is a predictor not only of happiness but also of health, sexual satisfaction, and income. Moreover, neighborhoods with high marriage rates typically have low rates of social pathologies such as crime, delinquency, and emotional disorders among children (Myers & Scanzoni, 2005).

> "One can live magnificently in this world if one knows how to work and how to love."
>
> Leo Tolstoy, 1856

Love
Intimacy, attachment, commitment—love by whatever name—is central to healthy and happy adulthood.

■ **social clock** the culturally preferred timing of social events such as marriage, parenthood, and retirement.

What do you think? Does marriage correlate with happiness because marital support and intimacy breed happiness, because happy people more often marry and stay married, or both?

Marriages that last are not always devoid of conflict. Some couples fight but also shower one another with affection. Other couples never raise their voices yet also seldom praise one another or nuzzle. Both styles can last. After observing the interactions of 2000 couples, John Gottman (1994) reported one indicator of marital success: at least a five-to-one ratio of positive to negative interactions. Stable marriages provide five times more instances of smiling, touching, complimenting, and laughing than of sarcasm, criticism, and insults. So, if you want to predict which newlyweds will stay together, do not pay attention to how passionately they are in love. The couples who make it are more often those who restrain putting down their partners. To prevent a cancerous negativity, successful couples learn to fight fair (to state feelings without insulting) and to steer conflict away from chaos with comments like "I know it's not your fault" or "I'll just be quiet for a moment and listen."

Often, love bears children. For most people, the most enduring of life changes, having a child, is a happy event. However, when children begin to absorb time, money, and emotional energy, satisfaction with the marriage itself may decline. This is especially likely among employed women who, more than they expected, carry the traditional burden of doing the chores at home. Putting effort into creating an equitable relationship can thus pay double dividends: a more satisfying marriage, which breeds better parent-child relations (Erel & Burman, 1995).

Although love bears children, children eventually leave home. This departure is a significant event, and a sometimes difficult separation. But national surveys reveal that the empty nest is for most people a happy place (Adelmann & others, 1989; Glenn, 1975). Compared with middle-aged women with children at home, those living in an empty nest report greater happiness and greater enjoyment of their marriage. Many parents experience what sociologists Lynn White and John Edwards (1990) call a "postlaunch honeymoon," especially if they maintain close relationships with their children.

If you have left home, did your parents suffer the "empty nest syndrome"—a feeling of distress focusing on a loss of purpose and relationship? Did they mourn the lost joy of listening for you in the wee hours of Saturday morning? Or did they seem to discover a new freedom, relaxation, and (if still married) renewed satisfaction with their own relationship?

Work For many adults, the answer to "Who are you?" depends a great deal on the answer to "What do you do?" Was Freud right that work, including a career, contributes to self-fulfillment and life satisfaction? It does for those who enter the working world with a positive disposition that helps engender success which, over time, reinforces a positive approach to life. "Alienated and hostile adolescents," on the other hand, tend to have less satisfying work experiences that undermine their achieving a positive transition into the working world (Roberts & others, 2003).

Job satisfaction and life satisfaction
Work can provide us with a sense of identity and competence and opportunities for accomplishment. Perhaps this is why challenging and interesting occupations enhance people's happiness.

Researchers have also studied the work–satisfaction relationship by comparing the roughly equal numbers of North American women who are or are not employed. From their studies at the Wellesley College Center for Research on Women, Grace Baruch and Rosaline Barnett (1986) concluded that what matters is not which roles a woman occupies—paid worker, wife, and/or mother—but the quality of her experience in those roles.

For women and men, choosing a career path is difficult, especially in today's changing work environment. During the first two years of college or university, few students can predict their later careers. Most shift from their initially intended majors, many find their postcollege employment in fields not directly related to their majors, and most will change careers (Rothstein, 1980). In the end, happiness is about having work that fits your interests and provides you with a sense of competence and accomplishment. And for those who choose to marry, it is having a partner who is a close, supportive companion and who sees you as special, and—for some—it includes having loving children whom you like and feel proud of.

Well-Being Across the Life Span

OBJECTIVE 31 | Describe trends in people's life satisfaction across the life span.

We're all aging. This moment marks the oldest you have ever been and the youngest you will henceforth be. To live is to grow older. That means we all can look back with satisfaction or regret, and forward with hope or dread. When people are asked what they would have done differently if they could relive their lives, their most common answer is "taken my education more seriously and worked harder at it" (Kinnier & Metha, 1989). How will you look back on your life 10 years from now? Are you making choices that someday you will recollect with satisfaction? Other regrets—"I should have told my father I loved him," "I regret that I never went to Europe"—also focus less on mistakes made than on the things one *failed* to do (Gilovich & Medvec, 1995).

From early adulthood to midlife, people typically experience a strengthening sense of identity, confidence, and self-esteem (Miner-Rubino & others, 2004; Robins & Trzesniewski, 2005). In later life, challenges arise: Income shrinks, work is often taken away, the body deteriorates, recall fades, energy wanes, family members and friends die or move away, and the great enemy, death, looms ever closer. Small wonder that many presume the over-65 years to be the worst of times (Freedman, 1978). But they are not, as Ronald Inglehart (1990) discovered when he amassed interviews conducted during the 1980s with representative samples of nearly 170,000 people in 16 nations. Older people report as much happiness and satisfaction with life as younger people do (**FIGURE 4.36**).

If anything, positive feelings grow after midlife and negative feelings subside (Charles & others, 2001; Mroczek, 2001). Older adults increasingly use words that convey positive emotions (Pennebaker & Stone, 2003). They attend less and less to negative information. For example, they are slower than younger adults to perceive negative faces (Mather & Carstensen, 2003). Their amygdala, a neural processing center for emotions, shows diminishing activity in response to negative events while maintaining its responsiveness to positive events (Mather & others, 2004). Moreover, the bad feelings we associate with negative events fade faster than do the good feelings we associate with positive events (Walker & others, 2003).

FIGURE 4.36
Age and life satisfaction
With the tasks of early adulthood behind them, many older adults have more time to pursue personal interests. No wonder their satisfaction with life remains high, and may even rise if they are healthy and active. As this graph based on multinational surveys shows, age differences in life satisfaction are trivial. (Data from Inglehart, 1990.)

Biological influences:	Psychological influences:
• no genetic propensity for Alzheimer's, dementia, or other diseases • neural changes that hinder negative thinking • appropriately meeting nutritional needs	• optimistic outlook • physically and mentally active life-style

Successful aging

Social-cultural influences:
• support from family and friends
• access to meaningful work or activities
• positive expectations of the surrounding culture
• stable and safe living conditions

FIGURE 4.37
Biopsychosocial influences on successful aging
Numerous biological, psychological, and social-cultural factors affect the way we age. With the right genes, we have a good chance of aging successfully if we maintain a positive outlook and stay mentally and physically active as well as connected to family and friends in the community.

"The best thing about being 100 is *no peer pressure*."

Lewis W. Kuester, 2005, on turning 100

Death comes too young for too many in AIDS-ravaged Africa

Chris Steele-Perkins/Magnum Photos

This contributes to most older people's sense that life, on balance, has been mostly good. Given that growing older is an outcome of living (an outcome nearly all of us prefer to early dying), the positivity of later life is comforting (**FIGURE 4.37**).

The astonishing stability of well-being across the life span obscures some interesting age-related emotional differences. As the years go by, feelings mellow (Costa & others, 1987; Diener & others, 1986). Highs become less high, lows less low. Thus, although the *average* feeling level may remain stable, with age we find ourselves less often feeling excited, intensely proud, and on top of the world, but also less often depressed. Compliments provoke less elation and criticisms less despair, as both become merely additional feedback atop a mountain of accumulated praise and blame. Psychologists Mihaly Csikszentmihalyi and Reed Larson (1984) mapped people's emotional terrain by periodically signaling them with electronic beepers to report their current activities and feelings. They found that teenagers typically come down from elation or up from gloom in less than an hour. Adult moods are less extreme but more enduring. For most people, old age offers less intense joy but greater contentment and increased spirituality, especially for those who remain socially engaged (Harlow & Cantor, 1996; Wink & Dillon, 2002). As we age, life becomes less an emotional roller coaster, more like paddling a canoe.

Death and Dying

OBJECTIVE 32 | Describe the range of reactions to the death of a loved one.

Most of us will suffer and cope with the deaths of relatives and friends. Usually, the most difficult separation is from one's spouse—a loss suffered by five times more women than men. When, as usually happens, death comes at an expected late-life time, the grieving may be relatively short-lived (**FIGURE 4.38** shows the typical emotions before and after a spouse's death). Grief is especially severe when the death of a loved one comes suddenly and before its expected time on the social clock. The accidental death of a child or the sudden illness that claims a 45-year-old life partner may trigger a year or more of mourning flooded with memories, eventually subsiding to a mild depression that sometimes continues for several years (Lehman & others, 1987). For some, the loss is unbearable. One study, following more than 1 million Danes over the last half of the twentieth century, found that more than 17,000 people had suffered the death of a child under 18. In the five years following that death, their 3 percent rate of first psychiatric hospitalization was 67 percent higher than the rate recorded for parents who had not lost a child (Li & others, 2005).

AIDS, which so often strikes down people in midlife and younger, has left countless grief-stricken partners experiencing bereavement, as well as millions of orphaned children. In 2004, the disease killed more than 3 million people worldwide (UNAIDS, 2005). In sub-Saharan Africa, which is home to 1 in 10 of the world's people and 6 in 10 of those carrying the HIV virus, the resulting death and treatment needs are sapping social resources. In nine African countries, life expectancy at birth has dropped below 40 years (UNAIDS, 2004).

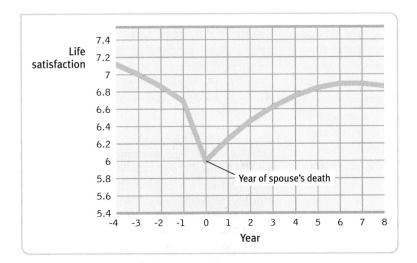

FIGURE 4.38

Life satisfaction before, during the year of, and after a spouse's death Richard Lucas and his collaborators (2003) examined longitudinal annual surveys of more than 30,000 Germans. The researchers identified 513 married people who experienced the death of a spouse and did not remarry. They found that life satisfaction began to dip during the prewidowhood year, dropped significantly during the year of the spouse's death, and then eventually rebounded to nearly the earlier level. (*Source:* Richard Lucas.)

The normal range of reactions to a loved one's death is wider than most suppose. Some cultures encourage public weeping and wailing; others hide grief. Within any culture, some individuals grieve more intensely and openly. Contrary to popular misconceptions, however,

- those who express the strongest grief immediately do not purge their grief more quickly (Bonanno & Kaltman, 1999; Wortman & Silver, 1989).
- for most people, bereavement therapy and self-help groups do little to enhance the healing power of time and supportive friends. Grieving spouses who talk often with others or who receive grief counseling adjust no better than those who grieve more privately (Bonanno, 2001, 2004; Genevro, 2003; Stroebe & others, 2001, 2002, 2005). No amount of talking can eliminate the feeling of being alone and separated from the loved one.
- terminally ill and bereaved people do not go through predictable stages, such as denial, anger, and so forth (Nolen-Hoeksema & Larson, 1999). Given similar losses, some people grieve hard and long, others more lightly and briefly.

We can be grateful for the waning of death-denying attitudes. Facing death with dignity and openness helps people complete the life cycle with a sense of life's meaningfulness and unity—the sense that their existence has been good and that life and death are parts of an ongoing cycle. Although death may be unwelcome, life itself can be affirmed even at death. This is especially so for people who review their lives not with despair but with what Erik Erikson called a sense of *integrity*—a feeling that one's life has been meaningful and worthwhile.

> " Do not go gentle into that good night,
>   Old age should burn and rave at close of day;
>   Rage, rage against the dying of the light."
> Dylan Thomas, "Do not go gentle into that good night," 1952, poem written to his father, who lay dying peacefully

> " Consider, friend, as you pass by, as you are now, so once was I. As I am now, you too shall be. Prepare, therefore, to follow me."
> Scottish tombstone epitaph

>> LEARNING OUTCOMES

Adulthood

OBJECTIVE **25** | **Identify the major physical changes that occur in middle adulthood.**

Muscular strength, reaction time, sensory abilities, and cardiac output begin to decline in the late twenties. Around age 50, menopause ends women's period of fertility, but they may continue to enjoy a satisfying sex life. Most women do not experience depression or other psychological problems with menopause. Men do not undergo a similar sharp drop in hormone levels or fertility.

OBJECTIVE **26** | **Compare life expectancy in the mid-twentieth and early twenty-first centuries, and discuss changes in sensory abilities and health (including frequency of dementia) in older adults.**

Worldwide, life expectancy has increased from 49 years in the mid-twentieth century to 67 in the early twenty-first century, and it exceeds 80 in some developed countries. Women outlive men and outnumber men at most ages past early infancy. In late adulthood, especially after age 70, hearing, distance perception, and the sense of smell diminish, as do muscle strength, reaction time, and stamina. As the body's immune system weakens, the elderly become vulnerable to life-threatening diseases such as cancer and pneumonia, but short-term ailments are fewer. Neural processes slow, especially for complex tasks, and by about age 80, the brain shrinks by about 5 percent. Physical exercise can stimulate the development of some new brain cells and connections. With age, the incidence of dementia—including the progressive deterioration of Alzheimer's disease—increases, doubling every five years from the early sixties on. Dementia is not a normal part of the aging process.

OBJECTIVE 27 | **Assess the impact of aging on recall and recognition in adulthood.**

The ability to recall new information declines during early and middle adulthood, but the ability to recognize such information does not. Older adults recall meaningful information more easily than meaningless information, but they may take longer to produce the words describing what they know. Prospective memory ("remember to . . .") remains strong when cues are available, but without reminder cues, time-based and habitual tasks are vulnerable to memory loss.

OBJECTIVE 28 | **Summarize the contributions of cross-sectional and longitudinal studies to our understanding of the normal effects of aging on adult intelligence.**

Cross-sectional studies (comparing people of different ages with one another) suggested that intelligence declines steadily after early adulthood, but this research failed to consider generational differences in education and other life experiences. *Longitudinal studies* (retesting the same people over a long period of time) suggested intelligence was stable until very late in life. But longitudinal research failed to account for those who dropped out of the studies, who may have been less intelligent than the survivors or in poor health, leaving an above-average group of participants in late life. Today's view is that *fluid intelligence* (the ability to reason speedily and abstractly) declines in later life, but *crystallized intelligence* (accumulated knowledge and skills) does not.

OBJECTIVE 29 | **Explain why the path of adult development need not be tightly linked to one's chronological age.**

Psychologists doubt that adults pass through an orderly sequence of age-bound stages, some accompanied by times of crisis, such as a midlife crisis in the early forties. Life crises tend to be triggered by major events (such as divorce) or chance occurrences (such as meeting a future partner) rather than predictable stages. Stage-defined crises also imply rigid timing of social events, and research shows that the *social clock* (the cultural prescription of the "right time" for such events) varies from place to place and from time to time.

OBJECTIVE 30 | **Discuss the importance of love, marriage, and children in adulthood, and comment on the contribution of one's work to feelings of self-satisfaction.**

Love and work are the defining themes in adult life. Evolutionary psychologists believe commitment had survival value for our ancestors, in that parents who stayed together, cooperated, and raised children to a child-bearing age had a better chance of passing along their genes to posterity. The likelihood of divorce has doubled over the past 40 years, partly because of women's increased economic independence and partly because of men's and women's increased expectations of acceptable qualities in a life partner. Cohabitation before marriage has correlated with higher rates of divorce and marital dysfunction. Most people still expect to marry, and those who do tend to be happier than their single counterparts. The birth of a child is usually a welcome event but may strain a couple's financial and emotional resources. Settling into a career path is difficult and time-consuming, but satisfying work (that fits your interests and gives a sense of competence and accomplishment) also correlates with life satisfaction.

OBJECTIVE 31 | **Describe trends in people's life satisfaction across the life span.**

Well-being and people's feelings of satisfaction are stable across the life span. Studies show that as we age, highs may be less high and lows less low, but the average level of satisfaction remains stable.

OBJECTIVE 32 | **Describe the range of reactions to the death of a loved one.**

There is no "normal" reaction or series of grief stages after the death of a loved one. Grief is most severe when the death is sudden or before its expected time, as in the death of a child. People who in old age achieve a sense of integrity, in Erikson's terms, may meet death by affirming that their own life was meaningful and worthwhile.

ASK YOURSELF: As you reflect on your last four years—four formative years if you are a young adult—what do you most regret? What do you feel best about?

Reflections on Two Major Developmental Issues

OBJECTIVE 33 | Summarize current views on continuity versus stages and stability versus change in lifelong development.

We began our survey of developmental psychology by identifying three pervasive issues: (1) how development is steered by genes and by experience, (2) whether development is a gradual, continuous process or a series of discrete stages, and (3) whether development is characterized more by stability over time or by change. We considered the first issue in Chapter 3. It is time to reflect on the second and third.

Continuity and Stages

Adults are vastly different from infants. But do they differ as a giant redwood differs from its seedling—a difference created by gradual, cumulative growth? Or do they differ as a butterfly differs from a caterpillar—a difference of distinct stages?

Generally speaking, researchers who emphasize experience and learning see development as a slow, continuous shaping process. Those who emphasize biological maturation tend to see development as a sequence of genetically predisposed stages or steps: Although progress through the various stages may be quick or slow, everyone passes through the stages in the same order.

Are there clear-cut stages of psychological development, as there are physical stages such as walking before running? We have considered the stage theories of Jean Piaget on cognitive development, Lawrence Kohlberg on moral development, and Erik Erikson on psychosocial development. And we have seen their stage theories criticized: Young children have some abilities Piaget attributed to later stages. Kohlberg's work reflected a worldview characteristic of educated males in individualistic cultures and emphasized thinking over acting. Adult life does not progress through the fixed, predictable series of steps Erikson envisioned.

Although research casts doubt on the idea that life proceeds through neatly defined, age-linked stages, the concept of stage remains useful. The human brain does experience growth spurts during childhood and puberty that correspond roughly to Piaget's stages (Thatcher & others, 1987). And stage theories contribute a developmental perspective on the whole life span, by suggesting how people of one age think and act differently when they arrive at a later age.

TOO MUCH COFFEE MAN BY SHANNON WHEELER

Stages of the life cycle

Stability and Change

This leads us to the final question: Over time, are people's personalities consistent, or do they change? If reunited with a long-lost grade school friend, would you instantly recognize that "it's the same old Andy"? Or does a person during one period of life seem like a different person at a later period?

Researchers who have followed lives through time have found evidence for both stability and change. There is continuity to personality and yet, happily for troubled children and adolescents, life is a process of becoming: The struggles of the present

As adults grow older, there is continuity of self.

"At 70, I would say the advantage is that you take life more calmly. You know that 'this, too, shall pass'!"

Eleanor Roosevelt, 1954

may be laying a foundation for a happier tomorrow. More specifically, researchers generally agree on the following points:

1. The first two years of life provide a poor basis for predicting a person's eventual traits (Kagan & others, 1978, 1998). Older children and adolescents also change. Although delinquent children have elevated rates of work problems, substance abuse, and crime, many confused and troubled children have blossomed into mature, successful adults (Moffitt & others, 2002; Roberts & others, 2001; Thomas & Chess, 1986). As people grow older, however, personality does gradually stabilize (Johnson & others, 2005; Vaidya & others, 2002).

2. Some characteristics, such as temperament, are more stable than others, such as social attitudes (Moss & Susman, 1980). When a research team led by Avshalom Caspi (2003) studied 1000 New Zealanders from age 3 to 26, they were struck by the consistency of temperament and emotionality across time. But attitudes, too, become more stable with age (Krosnick & Alwin, 1989). For most people, life goals, such as whether one seeks status, pleasure, or close relationships, also are quite stable (Roberts & others, 2004).

3. In some ways, we all change with age. Most shy, fearful toddlers begin opening up by age 4, and most people become calmer and more self-disciplined, agreeable, and self-confident in the years after adolescence (McCrae & Costa, 1994; Roberts & others, 2003). Conscientiousness increases especially during the twenties, and agreeableness during the thirties (Srivastava & others, 2003). Many a 20-year-old goof-off has matured into a 40-year-old business or cultural leader. Such changes can occur without changing a person's position *relative* to others of the same age. The hard-driving young adult may mellow by later life yet still be a relatively hard-driving senior citizen.

Finally, we should remember that life requires *both* stability and change. Stability enables us to depend on others, provides our identity, and motivates our concern for the healthy development of children. Change motivates our concerns about present influences, sustains our hope for a brighter future, and lets us adapt and grow with experience.

>> LEARNING OUTCOMES

Reflections on Two Major Developmental Issues

OBJECTIVE 33 | Summarize current views on continuity versus stages and stability versus change in lifelong development.

Researchers viewing development as a slow continuous process are generally those who emphasize experience and learning. Researchers who emphasize biological maturation see development as a series of genetically predisposed steps. Later research has modified the stage theories of Piaget (cognitive development), Kohlberg (moral development), and Erikson (psychosocial development), but these theories have enriched psychology by alerting us to ways people differ at various points in the life span. Research also shows that lifelong development features both stability and change. Personality gradually stabilizes as people age, but a toddler's traits do not necessarily predict the adult's, and older children and adolescents also change. Some traits, such as temperament, are more stable than others. As we age, we may change relative to our earlier selves while sustaining our characteristic traits in comparison to our age mates.

ASK YOURSELF: Are you the same person you were as a preschooler? A 10-year-old? A mid-teen? How are you different? How are you the same?

REVIEW CHAPTER 4: Developing Through the Life Span

Test Yourself

1. Your friend—a heavy smoker—hopes to become pregnant soon and has stopped smoking. Why is this a good idea? What negative effects does smoking during pregnancy have on the fetus?

2. Use Piaget's first three stages of cognitive development to explain why young children are *not* just miniature adults in the way they think.

3. How has the transition from childhood to adulthood changed in Western cultures in the last 100 years?

4. Research has shown that living together before marriage predicts an increased likelihood of future divorce. Can you imagine two possible explanations for this correlation?

5. What findings in psychology support the stage theory of development and the idea of stability in personality across the life span? What findings challenge these ideas?

Answers to the Test Yourself questions can be found in Appendix B at the end of the book.

Terms and Concepts to Remember

developmental psychology, p. 139

zygote, p. 140

embryo, p. 141

fetus, p. 141

teratogens, p. 141

fetal alcohol syndrome (FAS), p. 142

rooting reflex, p. 142

habituation, p. 143

maturation, p. 145

schema, p. 147

assimilation, p. 148

accommodation, p. 148

cognition, p. 148

sensorimotor stage, p. 149

object permanence, p. 149

preoperational stage, p. 150

conservation, p. 150

egocentrism, p. 150

theory of mind, p. 151

autism, p. 152

concrete operational stage, p. 153

formal operational stage, p. 154

stranger anxiety, p. 155

attachment, p. 155

critical period, p. 156

imprinting, p. 156

basic trust, p. 158

self-concept, p. 161

adolescence, p. 164

puberty, p. 165

primary sex characteristics, p. 165

secondary sex characteristics, p. 165

menarche [meh-NAR-key], p. 166

identity, p. 171

intimacy, p. 172

menopause, p. 176

Alzheimer's disease, p. 180

cross-sectional study, p. 183

longitudinal study, p. 183

crystallized intelligence, p. 184

fluid intelligence, p. 184

social clock, p. 186

WEB

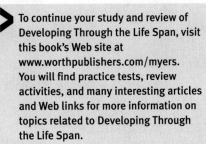

> To continue your study and review of Developing Through the Life Span, visit this book's Web site at www.worthpublishers.com/myers. You will find practice tests, review activities, and many interesting articles and Web links for more information on topics related to Developing Through the Life Span.

ANOTHER VOICE ON: SENSATION

HELEN KELLER (1880–1968), FROM "BEFORE THE SOUL DAWN"

Perhaps my sun shines not as yours. The colors that glorify my world, the blue of the sky, the green of the fields, may not correspond exactly with those you delight in; but they are none the less color to me. The sun does not shine for my physical eyes, nor does the lightning flash, nor do the trees turn green in the spring; but they have not therefore ceased to exist; any more than the landscape is annihilated when you turn your back on it.

I understand how scarlet can differ from crimson because I know the smell of an orange is not the smell of a grapefruit. I can also conceive that colors have shades, and guess what shades are. . . . Odors in certain grasses fade as real to my sense as certain colors do to yours in the sun. I make use of analogies like these to enlarge my conceptions of colors. Some analogies which I draw between qualities in surface and vibration, taste and smell, are drawn by others between sight, hearing, and touch. This fact encourages me to persevere, to try to bridge the gap between the eye and the hand.

5: Sensation

What's going on here?
Our sensory and perceptual processes work together to help us sort out the complex images in this Bev Doolittle painting, "The Forest Has Eyes." Bottom-up processing enables our sensory systems to detect the lines, angles, and colors that form the horses, rider, and surroundings. Using top-down processing we consider the painting's title, notice the apprehensive expressions, and then direct our attention to aspects of the painting that will give those observations meaning.

OBJECTIVE **1** | Contrast sensation and perception, and explain the difference between bottom-up and top-down processing.

Twenty-four hours a day, stimuli from the outside world bombard your body. Meanwhile, in a silent, cushioned, inner world, your brain floats in utter darkness. By itself, it sees nothing. It hears nothing. It feels nothing. This raises a question that predates psychology by thousands of years and helped inspire its beginnings more than a century ago: *How does the world out there get in?*

To modernize the question: How do we construct our representations of the external world? How do a campfire's flicker, crackle, and smoky scent activate neural connections? And how, from this living neurochemistry, do we create our conscious experience of the fire's motion and temperature, its aroma and beauty?

To represent the world in our head, we must detect physical energy from the environment and encode it as neural signals, a process traditionally called **sensation.** And we must select, organize, and interpret our sensations, a process traditionally called **perception.** In our everyday experiences, sensation and perception blend into one continuous process. In this chapter and Chapter 6, we slow down that process to study its parts.

We start with the sensory receptors and work up to higher levels of processing. Psychologists refer to sensory analysis that starts at the entry level as **bottom-up processing.** Chapter 6 focuses on how our mind interprets what our senses detect. As **FIGURE 5.1** (page 198) illustrates, we construct perceptions drawing both on sensations coming bottom-up to the brain and on our experience and expectations, which psychologists call **top-down processing**.

Detail, *The Forest Has Eyes* by Bev Doolittle © The Greenwich Workshop, Inc., Trumbull, CT.

FIGURE 5.1
**Sensation and perception:
One continuous process**

Failures of perception may occur anywhere between sensory detection and perceptual interpretation. After losing a temporal lobe area essential to recognizing faces, patient "E.H." suffers from a condition called *prosopagnosia*. She has complete sensation but incomplete perception. She can sense visual information—indeed may accurately report the features of a face—yet she is unable to recognize it. Shown an unfamiliar face, she does not react. Shown a familiar face, her autonomic nervous system responds with measurable perspiration. Still, she hasn't a clue who the person is. Shown her own face in a mirror, she is again stumped. Because of her brain damage, she cannot process top-down—she cannot relate her stored knowledge to the sensory input.

Sensing the World: Some Basic Principles

Nature's sensory gifts suit each recipient's needs. They enable each organism to obtain the information it needs. Consider:

- A frog, which feeds on flying insects, has eyes with receptor cells that fire only in response to small, dark, moving objects. A frog could starve to death knee-deep in motionless flies. But let one zoom by and the frog's "bug detector" cells snap awake.
- A male silkworm moth has receptors so sensitive to the female sex-attractant odor that a single female need release only a billionth of an ounce per second to attract every male silkworm moth within a mile. That is why there continue to be silkworms.
- We are similarly designed to detect what are, for us, the important features of our environment. Our ears are most sensitive to sound frequencies that include human voice consonants and a baby's cry.

We begin our exploration of those sensory gifts with questions that cut across all our sensory systems: What stimuli cross our threshold for conscious awareness? Could we unknowingly be influenced by subliminal stimuli too weak to be perceived? Why are we unaware of unchanging stimuli, such as the watch pressing against our wrist?

■ **sensation** the process by which our sensory receptors and nervous system receive and represent stimulus energies from our environment.

■ **perception** the process of organizing and interpreting sensory information, enabling us to recognize meaningful objects and events.

■ **bottom-up processing** analysis that begins with the sensory receptors and works up to the brain's integration of sensory information.

■ **top-down processing** information processing guided by higher-level mental processes, as when we construct perceptions drawing on our experience and expectations.

Thresholds

OBJECTIVE **2** | Distinguish between absolute and difference thresholds, and discuss whether we can sense stimuli below our absolute thresholds and be influenced by them.

We exist in a sea of energy. At this moment, you and I are being struck by x-rays and radio waves, ultraviolet and infrared light, and sound waves of very high and very low frequencies. To all of these we are blind and deaf. Other animals detect the world that lies beyond human experience (Hughes, 1999). Birds use their magnetic compass. Bats and dolphins locate prey with sonar (bouncing echoing sound off objects). On a cloudy day, bees navigate by detecting polarized light from an invisible (to us) sun.

The shades on our own senses are open just a crack, allowing us only a restricted awareness of this vast sea of energy. **Psychophysics** is the study of how this physical energy relates to our psychological experience. What stimuli can we detect? At what intensity? How sensitive are we to changing stimulation?

Absolute Thresholds

To some kinds of stimuli we are exquisitely sensitive. Standing atop a mountain on an utterly dark, clear night, most of us could see a candle flame atop another mountain 30 miles away. We could feel the wing of a bee falling on our cheek. We could even smell a single drop of perfume in a three-room apartment (Galanter, 1962).

Our awareness of these faint stimuli illustrates our **absolute thresholds**—the minimum stimulation necessary to detect a particular light, sound, pressure, taste, or odor 50 percent of the time. To test your absolute threshold for sounds, a hearing specialist would expose each of your ears to varying sound levels. For each tone, the test would define where half the time you correctly detect the sound and half the time you do not. For each of your senses, that 50-50 recognition point defines your absolute threshold.

Signal Detection

Detecting a weak stimulus, or signal, depends not only on the signal's strength (such as the hearing-test tone), but also on our psychological state—our experience, expectations, motivation, and alertness. **Signal detection theory** predicts when we will detect weak signals, measured as our ratio of "hits" to "false alarms." Signal detection theorists seek to understand why people respond differently to the same stimuli, and why the same person's reactions vary as circumstances change. Exhausted parents of a newborn will notice the faintest whimper from the cradle while failing to notice louder, unimportant sounds. Responsiveness also increases in a horror-filled wartime situation, where failure to detect an intruder may mean death. Mindful of many comrades' deaths, soldiers and police in Iraq probably became more likely to notice—and fire at—an almost imperceptible noise. With such heightened responsiveness come more false alarms, as when the American military fired on an approaching car that was rushing an Italian journalist to freedom, killing the Italian intelligence officer who had rescued her. In peacetime, when survival is not threatened, the same soldiers require a stronger signal before sensing danger.

Signal detection can also have life-or-death consequences when people are responsible for watching an airport scanner for weapons, monitoring patients from an intensive-care nursing station, or detecting radar blips. Studies have shown, for example, that people's ability to catch a faint signal diminishes after about 30

■ **psychophysics** the study of relationships between the physical characteristics of stimuli, such as their intensity, and our psychological experience of them.

■ **absolute threshold** the minimum stimulation needed to detect a particular stimulus 50 percent of the time.

■ **signal detection theory** a theory predicting how and when we detect the presence of a faint stimulus ("signal") amid background stimulation ("noise"). Assumes there is no single absolute threshold and that detection depends partly on a person's experience, expectations, motivation, and level of fatigue.

Signal detection
How soon would you notice the radar blips of an approaching object? Fairly quickly if (1) you *expect* an attack, (2) it is *important* that you detect it, and (3) you are *alert*.

Carol Lee / Tony Stone Images

minutes. But this diminishing response depends on the task, on the time of day, and even on whether the participants periodically exercise (Warm & Dember, 1986). Experience matters, too. In one experiment, 10 hours of action video game playing—scanning for and instantly responding to any intrusion—increased novice players' signal detection skills (Green & Bavelier, 2003). (See pages 754–756 for research on less positive social effects of violent video games.)

Subliminal Stimulation

In 1956, a national controversy erupted over a report (later shown to be false) that New Jersey movie audiences were unwittingly being influenced by imperceptible flashed messages to DRINK COCA-COLA and EAT POPCORN (Pratkanis, 1992).

Many years later, the controversy erupted anew. Rock recordings were said to contain "satanic messages" that could be heard if the recordings were played backward and that, even when played forward, could unconsciously persuade the unwitting listener (Vokey, 2002). Hoping to penetrate our unconscious, entrepreneurs offer audiotapes to help us lose weight, stop smoking, or improve our memories. These tapes contain soothing ocean sounds that mask unheard messages such as, "I am thin," "Smoke tastes bad," or "I do well on tests. I have total recall of information." Such claims make two assumptions: We can unconsciously sense **subliminal** (literally, "below threshold") stimuli, and without our awareness, these stimuli have extraordinary suggestive powers. Can we? Do they?

Can we sense stimuli below our absolute thresholds? In one sense, the answer is clearly yes. Remember that the "absolute" threshold is merely the point at which we detect a stimulus half the time (**FIGURE 5.2**). At or slightly below this threshold we will still detect the stimulus some of the time. The answer is yes in another sense, too. People who plead total ignorance when asked to make some perceptual judgment—for example, when deciding which of two very similar weights is heavier—usually beat chance. Sometimes we know more than we think we do.

Can we be affected by stimuli so weak as to be unnoticed? Under certain conditions, the answer is again yes. An invisible image or word can briefly **prime** your response to a later question. In a typical experiment, the image or word is quickly flashed, then replaced by a "masking" stimulus that interrupts the brain's processing before conscious perception. For example, one experiment subliminally flashed either emotionally positive scenes (kittens, a romantic couple) or negative scenes (a werewolf, a dead body) an instant before participants viewed slides of people (Krosnick & others, 1992). Although the participants consciously perceived only a flash of light, they gave more positive ratings to people whose photos had been associated with positive scenes. People somehow looked nicer if their photo immediately followed unperceived kittens rather than an unperceived werewolf.

This experiment illustrates an intriguing aspect of the priming effect: Sometimes we *feel* what we do not know and cannot describe. An imperceptibly brief stimulus evidently triggers a weak response

Try out this old riddle on a couple of friends. "You're driving a bus with 12 passengers. At your first stop, 6 passengers get off. At the second stop, 3 get off. At the third stop, 2 more get off but 3 new people get on. What color are the bus driver's eyes?" Do your friends detect the signal—who is the bus driver?—amid the accompanying noise?

How to think uncritically without psychology: James Vicary, an unemployed marketing researcher, masterminded the EAT POPCORN subliminal advertising hoax with the help of uncritical reporters and broadcasters. Vicary reportedly collected big fees from advertising firms for his promised services—and then disappeared (Rogers, 1993, 1994).

FIGURE 5.2
Absolute threshold
Do I taste it or not? When stimuli are detectable less than 50 percent of the time, they are "subliminal." Absolute threshold is the intensity at which we can detect a stimulus half the time.

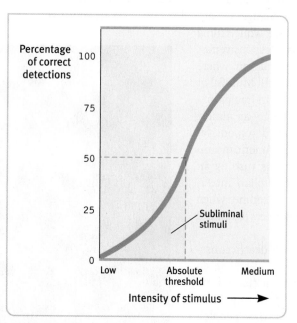

Percentage of correct detections

100

75

50

25

0

Low   Absolute   Medium
        threshold

Subliminal stimuli

Intensity of stimulus ⟶

Kurt Scholz/Superstock

that *can* be detected by brain scanning (Blankenburg & others, 2003). That small brain response may evoke a feeling, though not a conscious awareness of the stimulus. This subliminal priming phenomenon joins much other evidence in pointing to the powers of intuition (Myers, 2002). The conclusion (turn up the volume here): *Much of our information processing occurs automatically, out of sight, off the radar screen of our conscious mind.*

But does the fact of subliminal *sensation* verify entrepreneurial claims of subliminal *persuasion*? Can advertisers really manipulate us with "hidden persuasion"? The near-consensus among research psychologists is no. Their verdict is similar to that of astronomers who say of astrologers, yes, they are right that stars and planets are out there, but no, the celestial bodies don't directly affect us. The laboratory research reveals a *subtle, fleeting* effect. Priming thirsty people with the subliminal word *thirst* might therefore, for a brief interval, make a thirst-quenching beverage ad more persuasive (Strahan & others, 2002). But the subliminal tape hucksters claim something different: a *powerful, enduring* effect on *behavior*.

To test whether commercial subliminal tapes have an effect beyond that of a placebo—the effect of one's belief in them—Anthony Greenwald and his colleagues (1991) randomly assigned university students to listen daily for five weeks to commercial subliminal tapes claiming to improve either self-esteem or memory. On half the tapes they played a very practical joke and switched the labels. Some students *thought* they were receiving affirmations of self-esteem when they actually were hearing the memory enhancement tape. Others got the self-esteem tape but *thought* their memory was being recharged.

Were the tapes effective? Students' scores on tests for both self-esteem and memory, taken before and after the five weeks, revealed no effects. And yet, those who *thought* they had heard a memory tape *believed* their memories had improved. A similar result occurred for those who thought they had heard a self-esteem tape. The tapes had no effects, yet the students *perceived* themselves receiving the benefits they *expected*. When reading this research, one hears echoes of the testimonies that ooze from the mail-order tape catalogs. Some customers, having bought what is not supposed to be heard (and having indeed not heard it!) offer testimonials like, "I really know that your tapes were invaluable in reprogramming my mind." Over a decade, Greenwald conducted 16 double-blind experiments evaluating subliminal self-help tapes. His results were uniform: Not one had any therapeutic effect (Greenwald, 1992). His conclusion: "Subliminal procedures offer little or nothing of value to the marketing practitioner" (Pratkanis & Greenwald, 1988).

Difference Thresholds

To function effectively, we need absolute thresholds low enough to allow us to detect important sights, sounds, textures, tastes, and smells. We also need to detect small differences among stimuli. A musician must detect minute discrepancies in an instrument's tuning. A wine taster must detect the slight flavor difference between two vintage wines. Parents must detect the sound of their own child's voice amid other children's voices.

The **difference threshold** (also called the *just noticeable difference,* or *jnd*) is the minimum difference a person can detect between any two stimuli half the time. The difference threshold increases with the magnitude of the stimulus. Thus, if you add 10 grams to a 100-gram weight, you will detect the difference; add 10 grams to a 1-*kilogram* weight and you will not, because the difference threshold has increased. More than a century ago, Ernst Weber noted that regardless of their magnitude, two stimuli must differ by a constant proportion for their difference to be perceptible. This principle—that the difference threshold is not a constant amount but some constant *proportion* of the stimulus—is so simple and so widely

> "The heart has its reasons which reason does not know."
>
> Pascal, *Pensées,* 1670

Babs Reingold

Subliminal persuasion?
Although subliminally presented stimuli *can* subtly influence people, experiments discount attempts at subliminal advertising and self-improvement. (The playful message here is not actually subliminal—because you can easily perceive it.)

■ **subliminal** below one's absolute threshold for conscious awareness.

■ **priming** the activation, often unconsciously, of certain associations, thus predisposing one's perception, memory, or response.

■ **difference threshold** the minimum difference between two stimuli required for detection 50 percent of the time. We experience the difference threshold as a just noticeable difference. (Also called *just noticeable difference* or *jnd.*)

The difference threshold

In this computer-generated copy of the Twenty-third Psalm, each line of the typeface changes imperceptibly. How many lines are required for you to experience a just noticeable difference?

> "We need above all to know about changes; no one wants or needs to be reminded 16 hours a day that his shoes are on."
>
> Neuroscientist David Hubel (1979)

For 9 in 10 people—but, curiously, for only 1 in 3 of those with schizophrenia—this eye flutter turns off when the eye is following a moving target (Holzman & Matthyss, 1990).

applicable that we still refer to it as **Weber's law.** The exact proportion varies, depending on the stimulus. For the average person to perceive their differences, two lights must differ in intensity by 8 percent. Two objects must differ in weight by 2 percent. And two tones must differ in frequency by only 0.3 percent (Teghtsoonian, 1971).

Weber's law is a rough approximation. It works well for nonextreme sensory stimuli, and it parallels some of our life experiences. If the price of a $1 chocolate bar goes up by 10 cents, shoppers might notice the change; similarly, it might take a £4000 price hike in a £40,000 Mercedes to raise the eyebrows of its potential buyers. In both cases, the price went up by 10 percent. Weber's principle: Our thresholds for detecting differences are a roughly constant proportion of the size of the original stimulus.

Sensory Adaptation

OBJECTIVE 3 | Describe sensory adaptation, and explain how we benefit from being unaware of unchanging stimuli.

Entering your neighbors' living room, you smell a musty odor. You wonder how they can stand it, but within minutes you no longer notice it. Jumping into a swimming pool, you shiver and complain about how cold it is. A short while later a friend arrives and you exclaim, "C'mon in. Water's fine!" These examples illustrate **sensory adaptation**—our diminishing sensitivity to an unchanging stimulus. (To experience this phenomenon, move your watch up your wrist an inch: You will feel it—but only for a few moments.) After constant exposure to a stimulus, our nerve cells fire less frequently.

Why, then, if we stare at an object without flinching, does it not vanish from sight? Because, unnoticed by us, our eyes are always moving, quivering just enough to guarantee that stimulation on the eyes' receptors continually changes.

But what if we actually could stop our eyes from moving? Would sights seem to vanish, as odors do? To find out, psychologists have devised ingenious instruments for maintaining a constant image on the eye's inner surface. Imagine that we have fitted a volunteer, Mary, with one of these instruments—a miniature projector mounted on a contact lens (**FIGURE 5.3a**). When Mary's eye moves, the image from the projector moves as well. So everywhere that Mary looks, the scene is sure to go.

If we project the profile of a face through such an instrument, what will Mary see? At first, she will see the complete profile. But within a few seconds, as her sensory receptors begin to fatigue, things get weird. Bit by bit, the image vanishes, only later to reappear and then disappear—in recognizable fragments or as a whole (**FIGURE 5.3b**).

FIGURE 5.3

Sensory adaptation: Now you see it, now you don't!

(a) A projector mounted on a contact lens makes the projected image move with the eye. (b) Initially the person sees the stabilized image, but soon she sees fragments fading and reappearing. (From "Stabilized images on the retina" by R. M. Pritchard. Copyright © 1961 Scientific American, Inc. All Rights Reserved.)

(a)

(b)

Interestingly, the disappearance and reappearance of an image occurs in meaningful units. If a person is shown a word, it will disappear, and new words made up of parts of that word will appear and then vanish. This phenomenon anticipates the next chapter's major conclusion: Our perceptions are organized by the meanings that our minds impose.

Although sensory adaptation reduces our sensitivity, it offers an important benefit: It enables us to focus on *informative* changes in our environment without being distracted by the uninformative constant stimulation of garments, odors, and street noise. Our sensory receptors are alert to novelty; bore them with repetition and they free our attention for more important things. This reinforces a fundamental lesson: We perceive the world not exactly as it is, but as it is useful for us to perceive it.

Our sensitivity to changing stimulation helps explain television's attention-getting power. Cuts, edits, zooms, pans, and sudden noises demand attention. Even television researchers marvel at the attention-grabbing power of TV. During interesting conversations, notes media researcher Percy Tannenbaum (2002), "I cannot for the life of me stop from periodically glancing over to the screen."

Sensory thresholds and adaptation are not the only commonalities among the senses. All the senses receive sensory stimulation, transform it into neural information, and deliver that information to the brain. How do the senses work? How do we see? Hear? Smell? Taste? Feel pain? Keep our balance? Let's start with vision, the sense people prize the most.

" My suspicion is that the universe is not only queerer than we suppose, but queerer than we can suppose."

J. B. S. Haldane, *Possible Worlds*, 1927

■ **Weber's law** the principle that, to be perceived as different, two stimuli must differ by a constant minimum percentage (rather than a constant amount).

■ **sensory adaptation** diminished sensitivity as a consequence of constant stimulation.

>> LEARNING OUTCOMES

Sensing the World: Some Basic Principles

OBJECTIVE 1 | Contrast sensation and perception, and explain the difference between bottom-up and top-down processing.

Sensation is the process by which our sensory receptors and nervous system receive and represent stimulus energies from our environment. *Perception* is the process by which we organize and interpret this information. Although we view sensation and perception separately to analyze and discuss them, they are actually parts of one continuous process. *Bottom-up processing* is sensory analysis that begins at the entry level, with information flowing from the sensory receptors to the brain. *Top-down processing* is analysis that begins with the brain and flows down, filtering information through our experience and expectations to produce perceptions.

OBJECTIVE 2 | Distinguish between absolute and difference thresholds, and discuss whether we can sense stimuli below our absolute thresholds and be influenced by them.

Each species comes equipped with sensitivities that enable it to survive and thrive. *Psychophysics* is the study of the relationships between the physical characteristics of stimuli and our psychological experience of them.

Our *absolute threshold* for any stimulus is the minimum stimulation necessary for us to be consciously aware of it 50 percent of the time. Signal detection theory demonstrates that individual absolute thresholds vary, depending on the strength of the signal and also on our experience, expectations, motivation, and alertness. Our *difference threshold* (also called *just noticeable difference*, or *jnd*) is the barely noticeable difference we discern between two stimuli 50 percent of the time. As Weber's law states, to be perceptibly different, two stimuli must differ by a constant proportion (such as a 2 percent difference in weight), not a constant amount, of the original stimulus.

The priming effect and other experiments reveal that we *can* process some information from stimuli below our absolute threshold for conscious awareness. But the restricted conditions under which it occurs would not enable unscrupulous opportunists to exploit us with subliminal messages.

OBJECTIVE 3 | Describe sensory adaptation, and explain how we benefit from being unaware of unchanging stimuli.

Sensory adaptation is our diminished sensitivity to constant or routine odors, sounds, and touches. We benefit from this phenomenon because it focuses our attention on informative changes in stimulation, rather than on unchanging elements in our environment.

ASK YOURSELF: What types of sensory adaptation have you experienced in the last 24 hours?

■ **transduction** conversion of one form of energy into another. In sensation, the transforming of stimulus energies, such as sights, sounds, and smells, into neural impulses our brains can interpret.

■ **wavelength** the distance from the peak of one light or sound wave to the peak of the next. Electromagnetic wavelengths vary from the short blips of cosmic rays to the long pulses of radio transmission.

Vision

OBJECTIVE **4** | Define *transduction,* and specify the form of energy our visual system converts into the neural messages our brain can interpret.

One of nature's great wonders is neither bizarre nor remote, but commonplace: How does our material body construct our conscious visual experience? How do we transform particles of light energy into colorful sights?

Part of our genius is our body's ability to convert one sort of energy to another. Sensory **transduction** is the process by which our sensory systems encode stimulus energy as neural messages. Your eyes, for example, receive light energy and manage an amazing feat: They transduce (transform) the energy into neural messages that the brain then processes into what you consciously see. How does such a taken-for-granted yet remarkable thing happen?

FIGURE 5.4
The spectrum of electromagnetic energy
This spectrum ranges from gamma rays as short as the diameter of an atom to radio waves over a mile long. The narrow band of wavelengths visible to the human eye (shown enlarged) extends from the shorter waves of blue-violet light to the longer waves of red light.

The Stimulus Input: Light Energy

Scientifically speaking, what strikes our eyes is not color but pulses of electromagnetic energy that our visual system perceives as color. What we see as visible light is but a thin slice of the whole spectrum of electromagnetic radiation. As **FIGURE 5.4** illustrates, this *electromagnetic spectrum* ranges from imperceptibly short waves of gamma rays, to the narrow band that we see as visible light, to the long waves of radio transmission. Other organisms are sensitive to differing portions of the spectrum. Bees, for instance, cannot see red but can see ultraviolet light (**FIGURE 5.5**).

Two physical characteristics of light help determine our sensory experience of them. Light's **wavelength**—the distance from one

Gamma rays	X-rays	Ultra-violet rays	Infrared rays	Radar	Broadcast bands	AC circuits

10^{-5} 10^{-3} 10^{-1} 10^{1} 10^{3} 10^{5} 10^{7} 10^{9} 10^{11} 10^{13} 10^{15} 10^{17}
Wavelength in nanometers (billionths of a meter)

FIGURE 5.5
Differing eyes
When it comes to vision, humans and bees are on different wavelengths. Compare the way a human eye and a bee's eye register a flower. The bee detects reflected ultraviolet wavelengths, enabling it to see the pollen landing field where it will find nutrients. The differing ecological niches occupied by different species demand sensitivity to different stimuli.

Human eye

Bee's eye

Both photos: Thomas Eisner

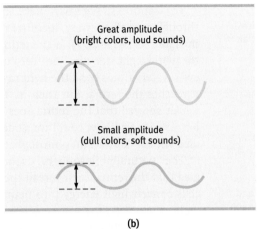

(a)

(b)

FIGURE 5.6
The physical properties of waves

(a) Waves vary in wavelength, the distance between successive peaks. Frequency, the number of complete wavelengths that can pass a point in a given time, depends on the wavelength. The shorter the wavelength, the higher the frequency. (b) Waves also vary in amplitude, the height from peak to trough. Wave amplitude determines the intensity of colors and sounds.

wave peak to the next (**FIGURE 5.6a**)—determines its **hue** (the color we experience, such as blue or green). **Intensity,** the amount of energy in light waves (determined by a wave's *amplitude,* or height), influences brightness (**FIGURE 5.6b**). To understand *how* we transform physical energy into color and meaning, we first need to understand vision's window, the eye.

The Eye

OBJECTIVE **5** | Describe the major structures of the eye, and explain how they guide an incoming ray of light toward the eye's receptor cells.

Light enters the eye through the *cornea,* which protects the eye and bends light to provide focus. The light then passes through the **pupil,** a small adjustable opening (**FIGURE 5.7**). The pupil's size, and therefore the amount of light entering the eye, is regulated by the **iris,** a colored muscle surrounding the pupil. The iris adjusts light intake by dilating and constricting in response to light intensity and even to inner emotions. (When we're feeling amorous, our telltale dilated pupils and dark eyes subtly signal our interest.) The uniqueness of each iris enables iris scanning machines to confirm someone's identity.

Behind the pupil is a **lens** that focuses the incoming rays into an image on the eye's light-sensitive back surface. The lens does this by changing its curvature in a process called **accommodation.** The eyeball's light-sensitive inner surface on which the rays focus is a multilayered tissue, the **retina.**

■ **hue** the dimension of color that is determined by the wavelength of light; what we know as the color names *blue, green,* and so forth.

■ **intensity** the amount of energy in a light or sound wave, which we perceive as brightness or loudness, as determined by the wave's amplitude.

■ **pupil** the adjustable opening in the center of the eye through which light enters.

■ **iris** a ring of muscle tissue that forms the colored portion of the eye around the pupil and controls the size of the pupil opening.

■ **lens** the transparent structure behind the pupil that changes shape to help focus images on the retina.

■ **accommodation** the process by which the eye's lens changes shape to focus near or far objects on the retina.

■ **retina** the light-sensitive inner surface of the eye, containing the receptor rods and cones plus layers of neurons that begin the processing of visual information.

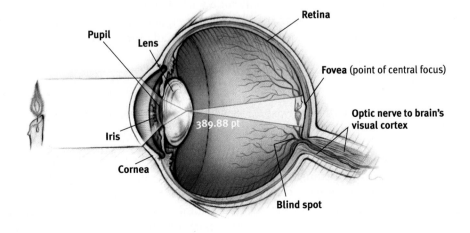

FIGURE 5.7
The eye

Light rays reflected from the candle pass through the cornea, pupil, and lens. The curvature and thickness of the lens change to bring either nearby or distant objects into focus on the retina. Light rays travel in straight lines. So rays from the top of the candle strike the bottom of the retina and those from the left side of the candle strike the right side of the retina. The candle's retinal image is thus upside-down and reversed.

■ **acuity** the sharpness of vision.

■ **nearsightedness** a condition in which nearby objects are seen more clearly than distant objects because distant objects focus in front of the retina.

■ **farsightedness** a condition in which far-away objects are seen more clearly than near objects because the image of near objects is focused behind the retina.

■ **rods** retinal receptors that detect black, white, and gray; necessary for peripheral and twilight vision, when cones don't respond.

■ **cones** retinal receptor cells that are concentrated near the center of the retina and that function in daylight or in well-lit conditions. The cones detect fine detail and give rise to color sensations.

■ **optic nerve** the nerve that carries neural impulses from the eye to the brain.

■ **blind spot** the point at which the optic nerve leaves the eye, creating a "blind" spot because no receptor cells are located there.

■ **fovea** the central focal point in the retina, around which the eye's cones cluster.

For centuries, scientists have known that when the image of a candle passes through a small opening, its mirror image appears inverted on a dark wall behind (as in Figure 5.7, page 205). If the retina receives an upside-down image, how can we see the world right side up? The ever-curious Leonardo da Vinci had an idea: Perhaps the eye's watery fluids bend the light rays, reinverting the image to the upright position as it reaches the retina. But then in 1604, the astronomer and optics expert Johannes Kepler showed that the retina does receive upside-down images of the world (Crombie, 1964). And how could we understand such a world? "I leave it," said the befuddled Kepler, "to natural philosophers."

The "natural philosophers" eventually included research psychologists who discovered that the retina doesn't read the image as a whole. Rather, its millions of receptor cells convert light energy into neural impulses. These impulses are sent to the brain and constructed *there* into a perceived, upright-seeming image.

Acuity, or sharpness of vision, can be affected by small distortions in the eye's shape. Normally the cornea and lens focus the image of any object on the retina (**FIGURE 5.8a**). In **nearsightedness,** the misshapen eyeball focuses the light rays from distant objects in front of the retina (**FIGURE 5.8b**) If you are nearsighted, your perception of near objects is clearer than that of distant objects, but if you are extremely nearsighted you see nothing clearly. Glasses, contact lenses, or, in some cases, laser-assisted (LASIK) surgery to reshape the cornea can correct the problem.

FIGURE 5.8 **(a) Normal vision**
Rays of light converge on the retina of a normal eye. This occurs for both nearby objects and, with appropriate readjustments in the curvature of the lens, for objects far away.

(b) Nearsighted vision
In the eye of a person with nearsighted vision, the light rays from distant objects focus in front of the retina. When their image reaches the retina, the rays are spreading out, blurring the image.

(c) Farsighted vision
In the eye of a person with farsighted vision, the light rays from nearby objects come into focus behind the retina, resulting in blurred images.

When viewing an eye chart, people with normal 20/20 vision can read material of a certain size from a distance of 20 feet. If you're standing 20 feet away and can discriminate only what people with normal vision can see at 50 feet, then you have 20/50 vision.

Farsightedness is the opposite of nearsightedness. Here, the light rays from nearby objects reach the retina before they have produced a focused image, making near objects appear blurry (**FIGURE 5.8c**). In children, the eye's ability to accommodate (thanks to its flexible lens) usually makes up for this problem. So children rarely need glasses—but they may suffer eyestrain from overusing their eye muscles, and some get headaches. People only mildly farsighted often do not discover their condition until middle age, as the lens becomes less flexible and loses its ability to change shape rapidly and they need glasses, especially for reading and seeing other nearby objects.

The Retina

OBJECTIVE 6 | Contrast the two types of receptor cells in the retina, and describe the retina's reaction to light.

If you followed a single particle of light energy into your eye, you would see that it first makes its way through the retina's outer layer of cells to its buried receptor cells, the **rods** and **cones** (**FIGURE 5.9**). Light energy striking the rods and cones produces chemical changes that generate neural signals. These signals activate the neighboring *bipolar cells,* which in turn activate the neighboring *ganglion cells.* The

2. Chemical reaction in turn activates bipolar cells.

3

2

1

Cone

1. Light entering eye triggers photochemical reaction in rods and cones at back of retina.

Light

Ganglion cell

Bipolar cell

Neural impulse

Cross section of retina

Light

3

Rod

2

1

To visual cortex via the thalamus

Optic nerve

3. Bipolar cells then activate the ganglion cells, the axons of which converge to form the optic nerve. This nerve transmits information to the visual cortex (via the thalamus) in the brain's occipital lobe.

FIGURE 5.9
The retina's reaction to light

axons from the network of ganglion cells converge like the strands of a rope to form an **optic nerve** that carries information to your brain (where the thalamus receives and distributes the information). Nearly a million messages can be sent by the optic nerve at once, through nearly a million ganglion fibers. (The auditory nerve, which enables hearing, carries much less information through its mere 30,000 fibers.) Where the optic nerve leaves the eye there are no receptor cells—creating a **blind spot** (**FIGURE 5.10**).

Rods and cones differ in their geography and in the tasks they handle. Cones cluster around the **fovea,** the retina's area of central focus (see Figure 5.7, page 205). In fact, the fovea contains only cones, no rods. Many cones have their own hotline to the brain—bipolar cells that help relay the cone's individual message to the visual cortex, which devotes a large area to input from the fovea. These direct connections preserve the cones' precise information, making them better able to detect fine detail. Rods have no such hotline; they share bipolar cells with other rods, so their individual messages get combined. To illustrate this difference in sensitivity to details, pick a word in this sentence and stare directly at it, focusing

Rod-shaped rods and cone-shaped cones
As the scanning electron microscope shows, rods and cones are well named. The rods are more sensitive to light than are the color-sensitive cones, which is why the world looks colorless at night. Some nocturnal animals, such as toads, mice, rats, and bats, have retinas made up almost entirely of rods, allowing them to function well in dim light. These creatures probably have very poor color vision.

E. R. Lewis, Y. Y. Zeevi, F. S. Werblin, 1969

FIGURE 5.10
The blind spot
There are no receptor cells where the optic nerve leaves the eye (Figure 5.9). This creates a blind spot in our vision. To demonstrate, close your left eye, look at the spot, and move the page to a distance from your face (about a foot) at which the car disappears. The blind spot does not normally impair your vision, because your eyes are moving and because one eye catches what the other misses.

TABLE 5.1

RECEPTORS IN THE HUMAN EYE

	Cones	Rods
Number	6 million	120 million
Location in retina	Center	Periphery
Sensitivity in dim light	Low	High
Color sensitive?	Yes	No
Detail sensitive?	Yes	No

its image on the cones in your fovea. Notice that words a few inches off to the side appear blurred? This happens because their image strikes the more peripheral region of your retina, where the rods predominate (**TABLE 5.1**).

Cones also enable you to see color. But in dim light, the cones become ineffectual, which is why you then see no colors. This is when rods, which enable black-and-white vision, take the lead. Rods remain sensitive in dim light, and several rods will funnel their faint energy output onto a single bipolar cell. Thus, cones and rods each provide a special sensitivity—cones to detail and color, and rods to faint light.

When you enter a darkened theater or turn off the light at night, your pupils dilate to allow more light to reach the rods in the retina's periphery. It typically takes 20 minutes or more before your eyes fully adapt. You can demonstrate dark adaptation by closing or covering one eye for up to 20 minutes. Then make the light in the room not quite bright enough to read this book with your open eye. Now open the dark-adapted eye and read (easily). This period of dark adaptation is yet another instance of the remarkable flexibility of our sensory systems, for it parallels the average natural twilight transition between the sun's setting and darkness.

Knowing just this much about the eye, can you imagine why a cat sees so much better at night than you do?[1]

Visual Information Processing

OBJECTIVE 7 | Discuss the different levels of processing that occur as information travels from the retina to the brain's cortex.

Visual information percolates through progressively more abstract levels. At the entry level, the retina—which is actually brain tissue that migrates to the eye during early fetal development—processes information before routing it via the thalamus to the brain's cortex. The retina's neural layers are not just passing along electrical impulses; they also help to encode and analyze the sensory information. The third neural layer in a frog's eye, for example, contains the "bug detector" cells that fire only in response to moving flylike stimuli.

Information from the retina's nearly 130 million receptor rods and cones is received and transmitted by the million or so ganglion cells, whose axons make up the optic nerve, which shoots information to the brain. Any given retinal area relays its information to a corresponding location in the occipital lobe—the visual cortex in the back of your brain (**FIGURE 5.11**).

The same sensitivity that enables retinal cells to fire messages can lead them to misfire as well. Turn your eyes to the left, close them, and then gently rub the right side of your right eyelid with your fingertip. Note the patch of light to the left, moving as your finger moves. Why do you see light? Why at the left?

Your retinal cells are so responsive that even pressure triggers them. But your brain interprets their firing as light. Moreover, it interprets the light as coming from the left—the direction light normally comes from when it activates the right side of the retina.

FIGURE 5.11

Pathway from the eyes to the visual cortex

Ganglion axons forming the optic nerve run to the thalamus, where they synapse with neurons that run to the visual cortex.

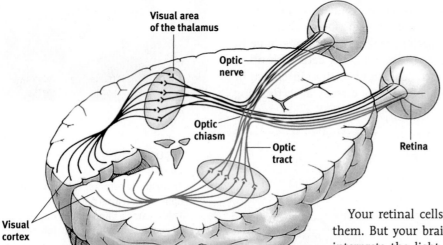

[1]There are at least two reasons: A cat's pupils can open much wider than yours, letting in more light; and a cat has a higher proportion of light-sensitive rods (Moser, 1987). But there is a trade-off: With fewer cones, a cat sees neither details nor color as well as you do.

Ross Kinnaird/Allsport/Getty Images

FIGURE 5.12

Electrodes record how individual cells in this monkey's visual cortex respond to different visual stimuli Hubel and Wiesel won a Nobel Prize for their discovery that most cells in the visual cortex respond only to particular features—for example, to the edge of a surface or to a bar at a 30-degree angle in the upper right part of the field of vision. Other cells integrate information from these simpler ones.

Feature Detection

When individual ganglion cells register information in their region of the visual field, they send signals to the occipital lobe's visual cortex. Nobel prize winners David Hubel and Torsten Wiesel (1979) demonstrated that the visual cortex has **feature detector** neurons that receive this information and respond to a scene's specific features—to particular edges, lines, angles, and movements. For example, one visual cortex cell might respond maximally to a bar flashed at a 2 o'clock tilt (**FIGURE 5.12**). If the bar is tilted further—say, to a 3 o'clock or 1 o'clock position—the cell quiets down.

Feature detection cells in the visual cortex pass such information to other areas of the cortex where cells respond only to more complex patterns. One temporal lobe area just behind your right ear, for example, enables you to perceive faces. If this region were damaged, you would have difficulty recognizing familiar faces but could recognize other objects. Other brain areas light up fMRI scans when a person views images of the human body or of inanimate objects (Downing & others, 2001). Damage in these areas blocks other perceptions while sparing face recognition. Amazingly specific combinations of temporal lobe activity occur as people look at faces, shoes, cats, houses, and other object categories (**FIGURE 5.13**). "We can tell if a person is looking at a shoe, a chair, or a face, based on the pattern of their brain activity," notes researcher James Haxby (2001).

Other high-level brain cells respond to specific visual scenes, such as a face or an arm movement in a particular direction. Psychologist David Perrett and his colleagues (1988, 1992, 1994) reported that for biologically important objects and events, monkey brains (and surely ours as well) have a "vast visual encyclopedia" distributed as cells that respond to one stimulus but not to others. Perrett identified nerve cells that specialize in responding to a specific gaze, head angle, posture, or body movement. Other supercell clusters integrate this information and fire only when the cues collectively indicate the direction of someone's attention and approach. This instant analysis, which aided our ancestors' survival, also helps a soccer goalie anticipate the direction of an impending kick and a pedestrian anticipate another pedestrian's next movement.

▪ **feature detectors** nerve cells in the brain that respond to specific features of the stimulus, such as shape, angle, or movement.

Ishai, Ungerleider, Martin and Haxby/NIMH

■ Faces

■ Houses

■ Chairs

■ Houses and chairs

FIGURE 5.13

The telltale brain Looking at faces, houses, and chairs activates different brain areas in this right-facing brain.

AP Photo/Armando Franca

Well-developed supercells In this 2005 World Cup qualifying match, Brazil's Adriano (in yellow) instantly processed visual information about the positions and movements of Argentina's defenders and goalie and somehow managed to get the ball around them all—heading it into the net.

FIGURE 5.14
How the brain perceives
As you stare at this Necker cube, providing fairly constant stimulation to your retina, your perception—and accompanying neural activity in your brain—will change every couple of seconds.

FIGURE 5.15
An example of the brain's virtual reality: Illusory contours
Simulated neural networks respond to the illusory triangle as humans do—as if it were a real triangle, and not what it really is: merely three Pac-Man faces.

■ **parallel processing** the processing of several aspects of a problem simultaneously; the brain's natural mode of information processing for many functions, including vision. Contrasts with the step-by-step (serial) processing of most computers and of conscious problem solving.

FIGURE 5.16
Parallel processing
Studies of patients with brain damage suggest that the brain delegates the work of processing color, motion, form, and depth to different areas. After taking a scene apart, how does the brain integrate these subdimensions into the perceived image? The answer to this question is the Holy Grail of vision research.

The brain activity that underlies perception combines sensory input with our assumptions and expectations. As your perception of the Necker cube in **FIGURE 5.14** shifts every few seconds, so does neural activity in your visual cortex. Although the same image continues to strike your retina, your brain constructs varying perceptions. Researchers have identified nerve cells that activate or not, depending on how a monkey *perceives* a given image, as reported by the monkey's up or down eye movements (Barinaga, 1997; Logothetis & Schall, 1989). Such studies remind us that our visual system works both bottom-up and top-down.

Researchers continue to explore the features and patterns brain cells detect. Research suggests that any image, such as a face, can be broken down into patterns of changing light intensity that can be described mathematically. Thus, in seeing, your brain may actually be processing mathematical-like codes that represent a perceived image (Kosslyn & Koenig, 1992; Marr, 1982). Neuroscientists working with computer experts are simulating the activity of the brain's interconnected, multilevel neural networks. Their goal is to build artificial vision systems that respond in the ways our own visual system responds. For example, their simulated neural networks respond as humans do to the illusory image of a triangle like that in **FIGURE 5.15**—as if they were reacting to a real triangle (Finkel & Sajda, 1994).

Parallel Processing

OBJECTIVE **8** | Define *parallel processing*, and discuss its role in visual information processing.

Unlike most computers, which do step-by-step *serial processing,* our brain engages in **parallel processing:** doing several things at once. The brain divides a visual scene into subdimensions such as color, depth, movement, and form (**FIGURE 5.16**) and works on each aspect simultaneously (Livingstone & Hubel, 1988). We then construct our perceptions by integrating the work of these different visual teams, working in parallel.

To recognize a face, for example, the brain integrates information that the retina projects to several visual cortex areas, compares it to stored information, and enables you to recognize the image as, say, your grandmother. The whole process of facial recognition requires tremendous brain power—30 percent of the cortex. That is 10 times the area the brain devotes to hearing.

At the instant your brain pulls all this information together, distant clusters of brain neurons momentarily synchronize their activity. With distributed parts of the brain having done their processing, EEG recordings reveal their integration: For about a fourth of a second, thousands of neurons emit equivalent signals at the rate of 40 times a second, creating gamma waves (Rodriguez & others, 1999). For this fleeting moment, distant brain areas collaborate and the result is something no single neural cluster could achieve: a conscious recognition (**FIGURE 5.17**).

Destroy or disable the neural workstation for a visual subtask, however, and something peculiar results, as happened to "Mrs. M." (from Hoffman, 1998). Having suffered stroke damage near the rear of both sides of her brain, she can no longer perceive movement. People moving about a room seem "suddenly here or there but I have not seen them moving." Pouring tea into a cup is a challenge because the fluid appears frozen and she cannot perceive it rising in the cup. (You could experience this same loss of motion detection if given disruptive magnetic stimulation to the corresponding neural area in your brain.)

Others who have lost a portion of their brain's visual cortex to stroke or surgery have experienced blindness in part of their field of vision, a phenomenon called *blindsight* (Weiskrantz, 1986). Shown a series of sticks in the blind field, they report seeing nothing. Yet when asked to guess whether the sticks are vertical or horizontal, they unerringly offer the correct response. When told, "You got them all right," they are astounded. There is, it seems, a second "mind"—a parallel processing system—operating unseen.

Indeed, "sight unseen" is how University of Durham psychologist David Milner (2003) describes the brain's two visual systems—"one that gives us our conscious perceptions, and one that guides our actions." The second he calls "the zombie within." Milner describes a woman with brain damage who can see fine details—the hairs on the back of a hand—without being able to recognize the hand. Asked to use her thumb and forefinger to estimate an object's size, she can't do it. Yet when reaching for the object, her thumb and forefinger are appropriately placed. She knows more than she is aware of.

Other senses process information with similar speed and intricacy. A scientific understanding of sensory information processing left neuropsychologist Roger Sperry awestruck (1985): The "insights of science give added, not lessened, reasons for awe, respect, and reverence." Think about it: As you look at someone, visual information is transduced and sent to your brain as millions of neural impulses, then constructed into its component features, and finally, in some as yet mysterious way, composed into a meaningful perceived image, which you compare with previously stored images and recognize as, for example, your grandmother. The whole process (**FIGURE 5.18**) is more complex than taking a car apart, piece by piece, transporting it to a different location, then having specialized workers reconstruct it. That all of this happens instantly, effortlessly, and continuously is indeed awesome.

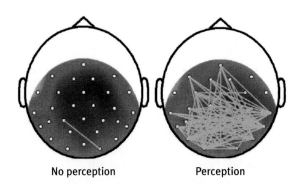

No perception   Perception

FIGURE 5.17
The shadow of a perception
EEG recordings show that shortly after a person sees a face, brain waves (detected by various scalp electrodes) become momentarily synchronized. Green lines between electrode points indicate increased synchrony. (From Rodriguez & others, 1999.)

" I am fearfully and wonderfully made."
King David, Psalms 139:14

Abstraction:
Brain's higher-level cells respond to combined information from feature-detector cells

Feature detection:
Brain's detector cells respond to elementary features—bars, edges, or gradients of light

Recognition:
Brain matches the constructed image with stored images

Retinal processing:
Receptor rods and cones → bipolar cells → ganglion cells

Scene

Tim Bieber/ The Image Bank

FIGURE 5.18
A simplified summary of visual information processing

Color Vision

OBJECTIVE 9 | Explain how the Young-Helmholtz and opponent-process theories help us understand color vision.

We talk as though objects possess color. We say, "A tomato is red." Perhaps you have pondered the old question, "If a tree falls in the forest and no one hears it, does it make a sound?" We can ask the same of color: If no one sees the tomato, is it red?

The answer is no. First, the tomato is everything *but* red, because it *rejects* (reflects) the long wavelengths of red. Second, the tomato's color is our mental construction. As Isaac Newton (1704) noted, "The [light] rays are not coloured." Color, like all aspects of vision, resides not in the object but in the theater of our brains. Even while dreaming, we may perceive things in color.

In the study of vision, one of the most basic and intriguing mysteries is how we see the world in color. How, from the light energy striking the retina, does the brain manufacture our experience of color—and of such a multitude of colors? Our difference threshold for colors is so low that we can discriminate some 7 million different color variations (Geldard, 1972).

At least most of us can. For about 1 person in 50, vision is color-deficient—and that person is usually male, because the defect is genetically sex-linked. To understand why some people's vision is color-deficient, it will help to first understand how normal color vision works.

Modern detective work on the mystery of color vision began in the nineteenth century when Hermann von Helmholtz built on the insights of an English physicist, Thomas Young. Young and von Helmholtz knew that any color can be created by combining the light waves of three primary colors—red, green, and blue. So they inferred that the eye must have three types of color receptors, one for each primary color of light.

Years later, researchers measured the response of various cones to different color stimuli and confirmed the **Young-Helmholtz trichromatic (three-color) theory,** which simply states that the retina has three types of color receptors, each especially sensitive to one of three colors. And surprise! Those colors are, indeed, red, green, or blue. When we stimulate combinations of these cones, we see other colors. For example, there are no receptors especially sensitive to yellow. Yet when both red- and green-sensitive cones are stimulated, we see yellow.

If you are trying to make sense of all this by thinking back to mixing paints, you had better think again. Mixing paints is *subtractive color mixing* because it *subtracts* wavelengths from the reflected light. The more colored paints you add to the mix, the fewer wavelengths can be reflected back. So, mixing blue and yellow paint leaves only green to be reflected back. Combining red, blue, and yellow means no light waves will be reflected and you will see brown or black. But mixing *lights,* as Young and von Helmholtz did, is *additive color mixing,* because the process *adds* wavelengths and thus *increases* light—combining red, blue, and green lights makes white light (**FIGURE 5.19**).

Most color-deficient people are not actually "colorblind." They simply lack functioning red- or green-sensitive cones, or sometimes both. Their vision—perhaps unknown to

FIGURE 5.19
Subtractive and additive color mixing
Mixing paint colors subtracts wavelengths. Mixing all three primary colors leaves you with black. Mixing lights is additive, because wavelengths from each light in the mix reach the eye, and mixing all three primary light colors creates white.

Subtractive color mixing

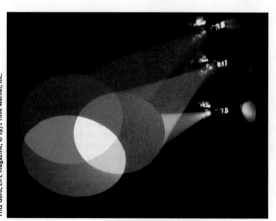

Fritz Goro, LIFE magazine, © 1971 Time Warner, Inc.

Additive color mixing

them, because their lifelong vision *seems* normal—is monochromatic (one-color) or dichromatic (two-color) instead of trichromatic, making it impossible to distinguish the red and green in **FIGURE 5.20** (Boynton, 1979). Dogs, too, lack receptors for the wavelengths of red, giving them only limited, dichromatic color vision (Neitz & others, 1989).

Soon after Young and von Helmholtz proposed the trichromatic theory, physiologist Ewald Hering pointed out that other parts of the color vision mystery remained unsolved. For example, we see yellow when mixing red and green light. But how is it that those blind to red and green can often still see yellow? And why does yellow appear to be a pure color and not a mixture of red and green, the way purple is of red and blue?

Hering found a clue in the well-known occurrence of *afterimages*. When you stare at a green square for a while and then look at a white sheet of paper, you see red, green's *opponent color*. Stare at a yellow square and you will later see its opponent color, blue, on the white paper (as in the flag demonstration in **FIGURE 5.21**). Hering surmised that there were two additional color processes, one responsible for red-versus-green perception, and one for blue-versus-yellow.

A century later, researchers confirmed Hering's **opponent-process theory.** *After* leaving the receptor cells, visual information is analyzed in terms of the opponent colors red and green, blue and yellow, and also black and white. In the retina and in the thalamus (where impulses from the retina are relayed en route to the visual cortex), some neurons are turned "on" by red but turned "off" by green. Others are turned on by green but off by red (DeValois & DeValois, 1975).

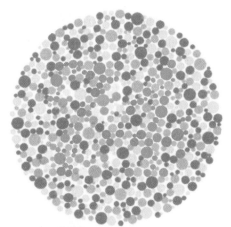

FIGURE 5.20
Color-deficient vision
People who suffer red-green deficiency have trouble perceiving the number within the design.

Opponent processes explain afterimages, such as in the flag demonstration, in which we tire our green response by staring at green. When we then stare at white (which contains all colors, including red), only the red part of the green-red pairing will fire normally.

The present solution to the mystery of color vision is therefore roughly this: Color processing occurs in two stages. The retina's red, green, and blue cones respond in varying degrees to different color stimuli, as the Young-Helmholtz trichromatic theory suggested. Their signals are then processed by the nervous system's opponent-process cells, en route to the visual cortex.

Color Constancy

OBJECTIVE **10** | Explain the importance of color constancy.

Our experience of color depends on something more than the wavelength information received by our trichromatic cones and transmitted through the opponent-process cells.

That something more is the surrounding *context*. If you view only part of a tomato, its color will seem to change as the light changes. But if you see the whole tomato as

FIGURE 5.21
Afterimage effect
Stare at the center of the flag for a minute and then shift your eyes to the dot in the white space beside it. What do you see? (After tiring your neural response to black, green, and yellow, you should see their opponent colors.) Stare at a white wall and note how the size of the flag grows with the projection distance!

■ **Young-Helmholtz trichromatic (three-color) theory** the theory that the retina contains three different color receptors—one most sensitive to red, one to green, one to blue—which when stimulated in combination can produce the perception of any color.

■ **opponent-process theory** the theory that opposing retinal processes (red-green, yellow-blue, white-black) enable color vision. For example, some cells are stimulated by green and inhibited by red; others are stimulated by red and inhibited by green.

■ **color constancy** perceiving familiar objects as having consistent color, even if changing illumination alters the wavelengths reflected by the object.

> From there to here, from here to there, funny things are everywhere."
>
> Dr. Seuss, *One Fish, Two Fish, Red Fish, Blue Fish*, 1960

one item in a bowl of fresh vegetables, its color will remain roughly constant as the lighting and wavelengths shift—a phenomenon known as **color constancy.** Dorothea Jameson (1985) noted that a chip colored blue under indoor lighting matches the wavelengths reflected by a gold chip in sunlight. Yet bring a bluebird indoors and it won't look like a goldfinch. Likewise, a green leaf hanging from a brown branch may, when the illumination changes, reflect the same light energy that formerly came from the brown branch. Yet to us the leaf stays greenish and the branch stays brownish. Put on yellow-tinted ski goggles and the snow, after a second, looks as white as before.

Though we take this color constancy for granted, the phenomenon is truly remarkable. It demonstrates that our experience of color comes not just from the object—the color is not in the isolated leaf—but from everything around it as well. You and I see color thanks to our brains' computations of the light reflected by any object *relative to its surrounding objects*. But only if we grew up with normal light, it seems. Monkeys raised under a restricted range of wavelengths later have great difficulty recognizing the same color when illumination varies (Sugita, 2004).

FIGURE 5.22
Color depends on context
Believe it or not, these three blue disks are identical in color.

R. Beau Lotto at University College, London

In a context that does not vary, we maintain color constancy. But what if we change the context? Because the brain computes the color of an object relative to its context, the perceived color changes (as is dramatically apparent in **FIGURE 5.22**). This principle—that we perceive objects not in isolation but in their environmental context—is especially significant for artists, interior decorators, and clothing designers. Our perception of the color of a wall or of a swatch of paint on a canvas is determined not just by the paint in the can but by the surrounding colors. The take-home lesson: Comparisons govern our perceptions.

>> LEARNING OUTCOMES

Vision

OBJECTIVE 4 | **Define** *transduction,* **and specify the form of energy our visual system converts into the neural messages our brain can interpret.**

Transduction is the process by which our sensory systems encode stimulus energy as neural messages the brain can interpret. In vision, we convert light energy into these neural impulses. The energies we experience as visible light are a thin slice from the broad spectrum of electromagnetic radiation. The hue and brightness we perceive in a light depend on the wavelength and intensity.

OBJECTIVE 5 | **Describe the major structures of the eye, and explain how they guide an incoming ray of light toward the eye's receptor cells.**

Light enters the eye through the cornea, a protective covering that bends the light ray. The iris, a ring of muscle, controls the size of the pupil, through which light enters. The lens changes shape to focus light rays on the retina, the inner

surface of the eye, where receptor cells convert the light energy into neural impulses. After coding in the retina, the impulses travel along the optic nerve to the brain. Although the retina receives an upside-down image, the brain constructs the impulses it receives into an upright-seeming image. Distortions in the eye's shape can affect the sharpness of vision.

OBJECTIVE 6 | **Contrast the two types of receptor cells in the retina, and describe the retina's reaction to light.**

The two types of receptors in the retina are the rods and the cones, and they differ in their shape, number, function, location, and links to the brain. When light enters the eye, it triggers a photochemical reaction in the rods and cones, which in turn activates bipolar cells. The bipolar cells activate ganglion cells, and their axons (combined to form the optic nerve) transmit information (via the thalamus) to the visual cortex in the brain's occipital region. The more numerous rods, located mainly around the periphery of the retina, are more sensitive to light. Multiple rods send combined messages to a bipolar cell, and this pool of information lets us see rough images in dim light. Cones, concentrated in the fovea (at the center of the retina), are sensitive to color and detail. A cone may link directly to a single bipolar cell, and this direct line to the brain preserves fine details in the cone's message.

OBJECTIVE **7** | **Discuss the different levels of processing of visual information traveling from the eye's retina to the brain's cortex.**

Perceptions arise from the interaction of many neuron systems, each performing a simple task. Processing begins in the retina's multiple neural layers, and then the retina's 6 million cones and 120 million rods relay their information via bipolar cells to ganglion cells. Impulses travel along the ganglion cells' axons, which form the optic nerve, to the thalamus, and on to the visual cortex. In the visual cortex, feature detectors respond to specific features of the visual stimulus. Higher-level supercells integrate this pool of data for processing in other cortical areas. As sensory input passes through multiple levels of processing, it is influenced by our assumptions, interests, and expectations.

OBJECTIVE **8** | **Define *parallel processing*, and discuss its role in visual information processing.**

Parallel processing is the brain's natural mode of information processing, in which it handles many aspects of a problem simultaneously. This multitasking ability lets the brain distribute subdimensions of vision (color, movement, depth, and form) to separate neural teams that work separately and simultaneously. Other neural teams collaborate in integrating the results, comparing them with stored information, and enabling perceptions.

OBJECTIVE **9** | **Explain how the Young-Helmholtz and opponent process theories help us understand color vision.**

The *Young-Helmholtz trichromatic (three-color) theory* proposed that the retina contains three types of color receptors. Contemporary research has found three types of cones, each most sensitive to the wavelengths of one of the three primary colors of light (red, green, or blue). Hering's *opponent-process theory* proposed two additional color processes (red-versus-green and blue-versus-yellow) plus a third black-versus-white process. Contemporary research has confirmed that, en route to the brain, neurons in the retina and the thalamus code the color-related information from the cones into pairs of opponent colors, as demonstrated by afterimages. These two theories, and the research supporting them, show that color processing occurs in two stages.

OBJECTIVE **10** | **Explain the importance of color constancy.**

Color constancy is our ability to perceive consistent color in objects, even though the lighting and wavelengths shift. This phenomenon demonstrates that our brains construct our experience of the color of an object through comparisons with other surrounding objects.

ASK YOURSELF: **If you were forced to give up one sense, which would it be? Why?**

Hearing

Somewhat less mysterious, but still amazing, is another aspect of our ordinary experience: the process by which we transduce air pressure waves into neural messages the brain interprets as a meaningful symphony of sound. Like our other senses, our hearing, or **audition,** is highly adaptive. We hear a wide range of sounds, but we hear best those sounds with frequencies in a range corresponding to that of the human voice. We also are remarkably sensitive to faint sounds, an obvious boon for our ancestors' survival when hunting or being hunted, or for detecting a child's whimper. (If our ears were much more sensitive, we would hear a constant hiss from the movement of air molecules.) We are also acutely sensitive to differences in sounds. We easily detect differences among thousands of human voices: Answering the phone, we recognize a friend calling from the moment she says "Hi." A fraction of a second after such events stimulate receptors in the ear, millions of neurons have simultaneously coordinated in extracting the essential features, comparing them with past experience, and identifying the stimulus (Freeman, 1991). For hearing as for seeing, we will consider the fundamental question: How do we do it?

The Stimulus Input: Sound Waves

OBJECTIVE **11** | Describe the pressure waves we experience as sound.

Hit a piano key and the resulting stimulus energy is sound waves—jostling molecules of air, each bumping into the next, like a shove being transmitted through a concert hall's crowded exit tunnel. The resulting waves of compressed and expanded air are like the ripples on a pond circling out from where a stone has been tossed. As we swim in our ocean

■ **audition** the sense or act of hearing.

The sounds of music
A violin's short, fast waves create a high pitch, a cello's longer, slower waves a lower pitch. Differences in the waves' height, or amplitude, also create differing degrees of loudness.

of moving air molecules, our ears detect these brief air pressure changes. Exposed to a loud, low bass sound—perhaps from a nearby tuba—we can also *feel* the vibration, and we hear by both air and bone conduction. (Hearing is a special form of touch sensation.)

The ears then transform the vibrating air into nerve impulses, which our brain decodes as sounds. The strength, or amplitude, of sound waves (recall Figure 5.6, page 205) determines their *loudness*. Waves also vary in length, and therefore in **frequency.** Their frequency determines the **pitch** we experience: Long waves have low frequency—and low pitch. Short waves have high frequency—and high pitch. A piccolo produces much shorter, faster sound waves than does a tuba.

Decibels are the measuring unit for sound energy. The absolute threshold for hearing is arbitrarily defined as zero decibels. Every 10 decibels correspond to a tenfold increase in sound. Thus, normal conversation (60 decibels) is 10,000 times louder than a 20-decibel whisper. And a tolerable 100-decibel passing subway train is 10 billion times louder than the faintest detectable sound. Although our vision system can tolerate a stimulus a trillion times more intense than a barely noticeable glimmer, our hearing is not so forgiving. Prolonged exposure to sounds above 85 decibels can produce hearing loss (**FIGURE 5.23**).

FIGURE 5.23
The intensity of some common sounds
At close range, the thunder that follows lightning has 120-decibel intensity.

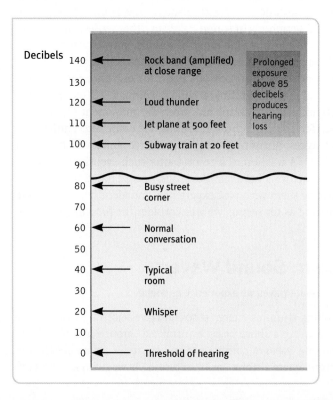

The Ear

OBJECTIVE 12 | Describe the three regions of the ear, and outline the series of events that triggers the electrical impulses sent to the brain.

To hear, we must somehow convert sound waves into neural activity. But how? The human ear accomplishes this feat through an intricate mechanical chain reaction (**FIGURE 5.24**). First, the visible *outer ear* channels the sound waves through the auditory canal to the *eardrum,* a tight membrane that vibrates with the waves. The **middle ear** then transmits the eardrum's vibrations through a piston made of three tiny bones (the *hammer, anvil,* and *stirrup*) to the **cochlea,** a snail-shaped tube in the **inner ear.** The incoming vibrations cause the cochlea's membrane (the *oval window*) to vibrate, jostling the fluid that fills the tube. This motion causes ripples in the *basilar membrane,* which is lined with *hair cells,* so named because of their tiny hairlike projections. At the end of this sequence, the rippling of the basilar membrane bends these hair cells, not unlike the wind bending a wheat field. The movement of the hair cells triggers impulses in the adjacent nerve fibers, which in turn converge to form the auditory nerve. By means of this mechanical chain of events, sound waves cause the hair cells of the inner ear to send neural messages (via the thalamus) to the temporal lobe's auditory cortex. From vibrating air to moving piston to fluid waves to electrical impulses to the brain: Voila! We hear.

My vote for the most magical part of the hearing process is the hair cells, damage to which accounts for most hearing loss. A 1997 Howard Hughes Medical Institute report on these "quivering bundles that let us hear" marvels at their "extreme sensitivity and extreme speed." A cochlea has 16,000 of them, which sounds like a lot until we compare that with an eye's 130 million or so photoreceptors. But consider their responsiveness. Deflect the tiny bundles of cilia on the tip of a hair cell by the width

■ **frequency** the number of complete wavelengths that pass a point in a given time (for example, per second).

■ **pitch** a tone's experienced highness or lowness; depends on frequency.

■ **middle ear** the chamber between the eardrum and cochlea containing three tiny bones (hammer, anvil, and stirrup) that concentrate the vibrations of the eardrum on the cochlea's oval window.

■ **cochlea** [KOHK-lee-uh] a coiled, bony, fluid-filled tube in the inner ear through which sound waves trigger nerve impulses.

■ **inner ear** the innermost part of the ear, containing the cochlea, semicircular canals, and vestibular sacs

FIGURE 5.24

Hear here: How we transform sound waves into nerve impulses that our brain interprets
(a) The outer ear funnels sound waves to the eardrum. The bones of the middle ear amplify and relay the eardrum's vibrations through the oval window into the fluid-filled cochlea. (b) As shown in this detail of the middle and inner ear, the resulting pressure changes in the cochlear fluid cause the basilar membrane to ripple, bending the hair cells on the surface. Hair cell movements trigger impulses at the base of the nerve cells, whose fibers converge to form the auditory nerve, which sends neural messages to the thalamus and on to the auditory cortex.

Enlargement of middle ear and inner ear, showing cochlea partially uncoiled for clarity

CLOSE-UP:

A NOISY NOISE ANNOYS

Modern life is noisy. Traffic roars. Factory machines clatter. Jackhammers tear up pavement. To escape into more pleasant sounds, runners stride to the beat of intense music on their headsets.

All this noise causes a problem. Brief exposure to extremely intense sounds, such as gunfire near one's ear, and prolonged exposure to intense sounds, such as amplified music, can damage receptor cells and auditory nerves (Backus, 1977; West & Evans, 1990). Ironically, even health clubs and fitness spas—which commonly blast 100+ decibel music—may be damaging their patrons' hearing health. Hair cells have been likened to shag carpet fibers. Walk around on them and they will spring back with a quick vacuuming. But leave a heavy piece of furniture on them for a long time and they may never rebound.

As a general rule, if you cannot talk over a noise, it is potentially harmful, especially if prolonged and repeated (Roesser, 1998). Such experiences are common when sound exceeds 100 decibels, as happens in venues from frenzied sports arenas to bagpipe bands. And if we experience ringing of the ears after exposure to loud machinery or music we have been bad to our unhappy hair cells. As pain alerts us to possible bodily harm, ringing of the ears alerts us to possible hearing damage. It is hearing's equivalent of bleeding. People who spend whole days behind a power mower, above a jackhammer, or working in a loud nightclub should definitely be wearing earplugs. "Condoms or, safer yet, abstinence," say sex educators. "Earplugs or walk away," say hearing educators.

Noise affects not only our hearing but also our behavior. On tasks requiring alert performance, people in noisy surroundings work less efficiently and make more errors (Broadbent, 1978). When the new Munich International Airport opened, reading and long-term memory scores improved among students near the now-closed old airport and became slightly impaired among children near the new airport (Hygge & others, 2002). People who live with continual noise in factories, in homes near airports, and in apartments next to trains and highways also suffer elevated rates of stress-related disorders: high blood pressure, anxiety, and feelings of helplessness are common (Evans & others, 1995).

Several laboratory experiments have explored the psychological effects of noise. In one such experiment, David Glass and Jerome Singer (1972) tape-recorded the chatter of office machines and of people speaking a mix of languages. Workers completing various tasks heard this noise, played either loudly or softly, at either predictable or unpredictable intervals. Regardless of the conditions, people soon adapted to the predictable noise and performed well on almost every task. However, those exposed to *unpredictable* loud noise later made more errors on a proofreading task and reacted more quickly to frustration.

The conclusion: Noise is especially stressful when unanticipated or uncontrollable. That explains why the unpredictable and uncontrollable blaring of someone else's stereo can be so much more upsetting than the same decibels from your own. If only our ears had earlids.

Be kind to your inner ear's hair cells
When vibrating in response to sound, the hair cells shown here lining the cochlea produce an electrical signal.

Dr. Fred Hossler/Visuals Unlimited

of an atom—the equivalent of displacing the top of the Eiffel Tower by half an inch—and the alert hair cell, thanks to a special protein at its tip, triggers a neural response (Corey & others, 2004).

At the highest perceived frequency, hair cells can turn neural current on and off a thousand times per second! As you might expect of something so sensitive, they are, however, delicate and fragile. Blast them with hunting rifle shots or headset sounds and the hair cells' cilia will begin to wither or fuse (see Close-Up on noise).

And how do we detect loudness? It is not, as I would have guessed, from the intensity of a hair cell's response. Rather, a soft, pure tone activates only the few hair cells attuned to its frequency. Given louder sounds, its neighbor hair cells also respond. Thus, the brain can interpret loudness from the *number* of activated hair cells.

If a hair cell loses sensitivity to soft sounds, it may still respond to loud sounds. This helps explain another surprise: Really loud sounds may seem loud both to people with hearing loss and to those with normal hearing. As a person with hearing loss, I used to wonder when exposed to really loud music what it must sound like to people with normal hearing. Now I realize it can sound much the same; where we differ is in our sensation of soft sounds. This is why we hard-of-hearing people do not want *all* sounds (loud and soft) amplified. We like sound *compressed*—which means harder-to-hear sounds are amplified more than loud sounds (a feature of today's digital hearing aids).

How Do We Perceive Pitch?

OBJECTIVE 13 | Contrast place and frequency theories, and explain how they help us to understand pitch perception.

How do we know whether a sound is the high-frequency, high-pitched chirp of a bird or the low-frequency, low-pitched roar of a truck? Current thinking on how we discriminate pitch, like current thinking on how we discriminate color, combines two theories.

Hermann von Helmholtz's **place theory** presumes that we hear different pitches because different sound waves trigger activity at different places along the cochlea's basilar membrane. Thus, the brain can determine a sound's pitch by recognizing the place on the membrane from which it receives neural signals. When Nobel laureate-to-be Georg von Békésy (1957) cut holes in the cochleas of guinea pigs and human cadavers and looked inside with a microscope, he discovered that the cochlea vibrated in response to sound, rather like a shaken bedsheet. High frequencies produced large vibrations near the beginning of the cochlea's membrane, low frequencies near the end.

Although place theory explains how we hear high-pitched sounds, it doesn't explain how we hear low-pitched sounds, because the neural signals they generate are not so neatly localized on the basilar membrane. **Frequency theory** suggests an alternative explanation for how we detect pitch. The whole basilar membrane vibrates with the incoming sound wave, triggering neural impulses to the brain at the same rate as the sound wave. If the sound wave has a frequency of 100 waves per second, then 100 pulses per second travel up the auditory nerve. Thus, the brain can read pitch from the frequency of neural impulses.

Frequency theory can explain how we perceive low-pitched sounds. But it, too, is problematic: Individual neurons cannot fire faster than 1000 times per second. How then can frequency theory explain our sensing sounds with frequencies above 1000 waves per second (roughly the upper third of a piano keyboard and above)? Enter the *volley principle:* Like soldiers who alternate firing so that some can shoot while others reload, neural cells can alternate firing. By firing in rapid succession, they can achieve a combined frequency above 1000 times per second.

Thus, place theory best explains how we sense high pitches, frequency theory best explains how we sense low pitches, and some combination of place and frequency seems to handle the pitches in the intermediate range.

How Do We Locate Sounds?

OBJECTIVE 14 | Describe how we pinpoint sounds.

Why don't we have one big ear—perhaps above our one nose? The better to hear you, as the wolf said to Red Riding Hood. As the placement of our eyes allows us to sense visual depth (pages 245–246), so the placement of our two ears allows us to enjoy stereophonic ("three-dimensional") hearing. The slightly different messages sensed by the two microphones used in creating a stereophonic recording mimic the slightly different sound messages received by our two ears.

Two ears are better than one for at least two reasons: If a car to the right honks, your right ear receives a more *intense* sound, and it receives sound slightly *sooner* than your left ear (**FIGURE 5.25**). Because sound travels 750 miles per hour and our ears are but 6 inches apart, the intensity difference and the time lag are extremely small. However, our supersensitive auditory system can detect such minute differences (Brown & Deffenbacher, 1979; Middlebrooks & Green, 1991). A just noticeable difference in the direction of two sound sources corresponds to a time difference of just 0.000027 second!

■ **place theory** in hearing, the theory that links the pitch we hear with the place where the cochlea's membrane is stimulated.

■ **frequency theory** in hearing, the theory that the rate of nerve impulses traveling up the auditory nerve matches the frequency of a tone, thus enabling us to sense its pitch.

FIGURE 5.25

How we locate sounds

Sound waves strike one ear sooner and more intensely than the other. From this information, our nimble brain computes the sound's location. As you might therefore expect, people who lose all hearing in one ear often have difficulty locating sounds.

■ **conduction hearing loss** hearing loss caused by damage to the mechanical system that conducts sound waves to the cochlea.

■ **sensorineural hearing loss** hearing loss caused by damage to the cochlea's receptor cells or to the auditory nerves; also called *nerve deafness*.

■ **cochlear implant** a device for converting sounds into electrical signals and stimulating the auditory nerve through electrodes threaded into the cochlea

To simulate what the ears experience with sound from varying locations, audio software can emit sound from two stereo speakers with varying time delays and intensity. The result: We may perceive a bee buzzing loudly in one ear, then flying around the room and returning to buzz near the other ear (Harvey, 2002).

So how well do you suppose we do at locating a sound that is equidistant from our two ears, such as those that come from directly ahead, behind, overhead, or beneath us? Not very well. Why? Because such sounds strike the two ears simultaneously. Sit with closed eyes while a friend snaps fingers around your head. You will easily point to the sound when it comes from either side, but you will likely make some mistakes when it comes from directly ahead, behind, above, or below. That is why, when trying to pinpoint a sound, you cock your head, so that your two ears will receive slightly different messages.

With auditory as with visual information, the brain uses parallel processing—by putting specialized neural teams to work simultaneously on different subtasks. Owls (and probably humans, too) process timing differences in one neural pathway and intensity differences in another before merging their information to pinpoint a sound's location (Konishi, 1993). Other auditory processing circuits specialize in extracting the features of certain sounds, much like symphonic musicians reading their own parts. For example, some brain neurons respond more to a high-contrast sound stimulus, as might be made by a musical instrument playing solo; others respond more to low-contrast sound, as would be made by the same instrument playing in an orchestra (Barbour & Wang, 2004).

Hearing Loss and Deaf Culture

Objective 15 | Contrast the two types of hearing loss, and describe some of their causes.

The ear's intricate and delicate structure makes it vulnerable to damage. Problems with the mechanical system that conducts sound waves to the cochlea cause **conduction hearing loss**. If the eardrum is punctured or if the tiny bones of the middle ear lose their ability to vibrate, the ear's ability to conduct vibrations diminishes.

Damage to the cochlea's hair cell receptors or their associated nerves can cause the more common **sensorineural hearing loss** (or *nerve deafness*). Occasionally, disease causes sensorineural hearing loss, but more often the culprits are biological changes linked with heredity, aging, and prolonged exposure to ear-splitting noise or music (**FIGURE 5.26**). Once destroyed, these tissues remain dead, though a hearing aid may

FIGURE 5.26
Older people tend to hear low frequencies well but suffer hearing loss for high frequencies
This high-frequency loss results from nerve degeneration near the beginning of the basilar membrane. The finding supports place theory's assumption that different pitches activate different places on the basilar membrane. (From Wever, 1949.)

amplify enough sound to stimulate neighboring hair cells. Digital hearing aids improve hearing by amplifying vibrations for frequencies (usually high frequencies) in which one's hearing is weakest and also by compressing sound (amplifying soft sounds but not loud sounds).

In some animals, such as sharks and birds, hair cells can regenerate, and scientists have discovered ways to stimulate hair cell regeneration in guinea pigs and rat pups (Forge & others, 1993; Warchol & others, 1993; Sage & others, 2005). These findings raise hopes that a way might someday be found to trick the human cochlea into regenerating hair cells—and thereby restore hearing. Someday, we can hope, the human ear will experience life after deaf.

Cochlear Implants

OBJECTIVE 16 | Describe how cochlear implants function, and explain why Deaf culture advocates object to these devices.

For now, the only way to restore hearing for people with nerve deafness is a sort of bionic ear—a **cochlear implant.** This electronic device translates sounds into electrical signals that, wired into the cochlea's nerves, convey some information about sound to the brain. The implant helps children become proficient in oral communication (especially if they receive it as preschoolers) and may also help children become less distractible and impulsive (Dorman & Wilson, 2004; Svirsky & others, 2000). The latest cochlear implants also can help restore hearing for most adults (though not for those whose adult brain never learned to process sound during childhood). By 2003, some 60,000 people worldwide had cochlear implants, and millions more were potential candidates (Gates & Miyamoto, 2003).

The use of cochlear implants is hotly debated. On the one side are the hearing parents of more than 90 percent of all deaf children. Most of these parents want their children to experience their world of sound and talk, and, if an implant is to be effective, they cannot delay the decision until their child reaches the age of consent. On the other side are Deaf culture advocates, who object to using the implants on children deafened before learning to speak. The National Association of the Deaf, for example, argues that deafness is *not* a disability, because native signers are not linguistically disabled. In his 1960 book *Sign Language Structure,* Gallaudet University linguist William Stokoe showed what even native signers had not fully understood: Sign is a complete language with its own grammar, syntax, and semantics. Because American Sign Language (ASL) bears no relationship to other languages such as English, those who learn only ASL (or some other version of sign) during childhood have difficulty later learning to read and write. Some schools and families therefore help deaf children become bilingual both in sign and in their culture's spoken and written language, for example by using cued speech that links signs to English (Holloway, 2000).

Those of us whose hearing has diminished with age or illness—who live outside Deaf culture and have known, then lost, hearing—are more likely to describe ourselves as having an impairment. Among people who experience hearing loss, the National Center for Health Statistics estimates that only about 1 percent were born deaf. Those who lose their hearing need not think of themselves as disabled *people* (which labels the person) to acknowledge that

Good vibrations
Scotland's Evelyn Glennie, who has been profoundly deaf since she was 12 years old, is a full-time percussion soloist. In performance she relates to her instruments through her sense of touch (performing without shoes) and to the conductor through her keen visual sense.

Experiments are also under way to restore vision—with a bionic retina (a 2-millimeter-diameter microchip with photoreceptors that stimulate damaged retinal cells), and with a video camera and computer that stimulates the visual cortex. In test trials, both devices have enabled blind people to gain partial sight (Boahen, 2005; Steenhuysen, 2002).

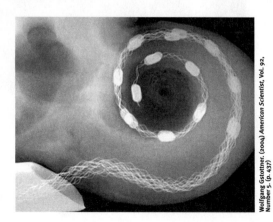

Hardware for hearing
An x-ray image shows a cochlear implant's array of wires leading to 12 stimulation sites on the auditory nerve.

CLOSE-UP:

LIVING IN A SILENT WORLD

Those who live with hearing loss are a diverse group. Some are profoundly deaf; others have limited hearing. Some were deaf prelingually (before developing language); others have known the hearing world. Some sign and identify with the language-based Deaf culture; more, especially those who lost their hearing postlingually, are "oral" and converse with the hearing world by reading lips or reading written notes. Still others move between the two cultures. Children who grow up around other deaf people more often identify with Deaf culture and feel positive self-esteem. If raised in a signing household, whether by Deaf or hearing parents, they also express higher self-esteem and feel more accepted (Bat-Chava, 1993, 1994).

Deaf people face challenges (Braden, 1994). Because academic subjects are rooted in spoken languages, their school achievement may suffer. Social challenges are even greater. Unable to communicate in customary ways, deaf children and their hearing playmates struggle to coordinate their play. Adolescents may experience social exclusion and a resulting low self-confidence. Even adults whose hearing becomes impaired later in life may find that the challenges lead to a sort of shyness. "It's almost universal among the deaf to want to cause hearing people as little fuss as possible," reports Henry Kisor (1990, p. 244), a Chicago newspaper editor and columnist who lost his hearing at age 3. "We can be self-effacing and diffident to the point of invisibility. Sometimes this tendency can be crippling. I must fight it all the time."

I know. My mother, with whom we communicated by writing notes on an erasable "magic pad," spent her last dozen years in a silent world, largely withdrawn from the stress and strain of trying to interact with people outside a small circle of family and old friends. With my own hearing declining on a trajectory toward hers, I find myself sitting front and center at plays and meetings, seeking quiet corners in restaurants, asking my wife to make necessary calls to friends whose accents differ from ours, and using some cool technology that, at the press of a button, can transform my hearing aids into in-the-ear loudspeakers for the broadcast of telephone, TV, and public address system sound (see hearingloop.org). But the greatest frustration comes when, with or without hearing aids, I can't hear the joke everyone else is guffawing over; when, after repeated tries, I just can't catch that exasperated person's question and can't fake my way around it; when family members give up and say, "Oh, never mind" after trying three times to tell me something unimportant.

As she aged, my mother came to feel that seeking social interaction was simply not worth the effort. However, I share newspaper columnist Kisor's belief that communication is worth the effort. "So, . . . I will grit my teeth and plunge ahead" (p. 246). To reach out, to connect, to communicate with others, even across a chasm of silence, is to affirm our humanity as social creatures.

Signs of success
Deaf participants in a spelling bee offer signed applause to a contestant.

AP Photo/Seth Perlman

they are persons with a disability (describing the impairment). For individuals who have never learned to sign, the loss of hearing can indeed be socially disabling. Helen Keller said she "found deafness to be a much greater handicap than blindness. . . . Blindness cuts people off from things. Deafness cuts people off from people."

Sensory Compensation

Deaf culture advocates sometimes further contend that deafness could as well be considered "vision enhancement" as "hearing impairment." People who lose one channel of sensation do seem to compensate with a slight enhancement of their other sensory abilities (Backman & Dixon, 1992; Levy & Langer, 1992). Some examples:

- Blind musicians (think Stevie Wonder) are more likely than sighted ones to develop perfect pitch (Hamilton, 2000).
- With one ear plugged, blind people are also more accurate than sighted people at locating a sound source (Gougoux & others, 2005; Lessard & others, 1998).
- Close your eyes and with your hands indicate the width of a carton with a dozen eggs. Blind individuals, report University of Otago researchers, can do this more accurately than sighted people (Smith & others, 2005).
- Starved for sensory input, deaf people's auditory cortex remains largely intact but becomes responsive to touch and to visual input (Emmorey & others, 2003; Finney & others, 2001; Penhune & others, 2003).

As a result of her lifelong blindness and deafness, Helen Keller's brain had regions normally dedicated to visual and auditory inputs available for other uses, such as discriminating touch sensations. Although deaf people generally do not have superior reading ability, visual compensation may help explain why many are visually skilled engineers, architects, and mathematicians. Cosmologist Stephen Hawking has said that lacking a functional body forced him to use his brain for other activity, making his thinking more original (Uehling, 1998). Close your eyes and immediately you, too, will notice your attention being drawn to your other senses. When kissing, lovers minimize distraction and increase their touch sensitivity by closing their eyes. People with aphasia—having lost the ability to express language—typically become *more* accurate at attending to face, body, and voice clues, and thus at spotting deception. Nancy Etcoff and her colleagues (2000) found that people who developed aphasia after a stroke were able to spot liars 73 percent of the time when focusing on facial expressions (while those without aphasia did no better than chance). You and I might miss the meaning conveyed by someone's intonation and gestures, but a person with aphasia reads these messages readily.

> " By placing my hand on a person's lips and throat, I gain an idea of many specific vibrations, and interpret them: a boy's chuckle, a man's 'Whew!' of surprise, the 'Hem!' of annoyance or perplexity, the moan of pain, a scream, a whisper, a rasp, a sob, a choke, and a gasp."
>
> Helen Keller, 1908

>> LEARNING OUTCOMES

Hearing

OBJECTIVE 11 | Describe the pressure waves we experience as sound.

Sound waves are bands of compressed and expanded air. Our ears detect these changes in air pressure and transform them into neural impulses, which the brain decodes as sound. Sound waves vary in frequency and amplitude, which we perceive as differences in pitch and loudness.

OBJECTIVE 12 | Describe the three regions of the ear, and outline the series of events that triggers the electrical impulses sent to the brain.

The outer ear is the visible portion of the ear. The middle ear is the chamber between the eardrum and cochlea. The inner ear consists of the cochlea, semicircular canals, and vestibular sacs. Through a mechanical chain of events, sound waves traveling through the auditory canal cause minuscule vibrations in the eardrum. The bones of the middle ear amplify the vibrations and relay them to the fluid-filled cochlea. Rippling of the basilar membrane, caused by pressure changes in the cochlear fluid, causes movement of the tiny hair cells, triggering neural messages to be sent (via the thalamus) to the auditory cortex in the brain.

OBJECTIVE 13 | Contrast place and frequency theories, and explain how they help us to understand pitch perception.

Place theory proposes that our brain interprets a particular pitch by decoding the location (thus, "place") where a sound wave has stimulated the cochlea's basilar membrane. *Frequency theory* proposes that the brain deciphers the number and rate (thus "frequency") of the pulses traveling up the auditory nerve to the brain. Research supports both theories, but for different ranges. Place theory cannot explain how we hear low-pitched sounds (which cannot be localized on the basilar membrane), but it can explain our sensation of high-pitched sounds. Frequency theory cannot explain how we hear high-pitched sounds (individual neurons cannot fire fast enough to produce the necessary number of surges), but it can explain our sensation of low-pitched sounds. Some combination of the two explains how we hear sounds in the middle range.

Objective 14 | Describe how we pinpoint sounds.

Sound waves strike one ear sooner and more intensely than the other. Using parallel processing, the brain analyzes the minute differences in the sounds received by the two ears and computes the source of the sound.

Objective 15 | Contrast the two types of hearing loss, and describe some of their causes.

Conduction hearing loss results from damage to the mechanical system that transmits sound waves to the cochlea. *Sensorineural hearing loss* (or nerve deafness) results from damage to the cochlea's hair cells or their associated nerves. Diseases and accidents can cause these problems, but age-related disorders and prolonged exposure to loud noise are more common causes of hearing loss, especially of nerve deafness.

Objective 16 | Describe how cochlear implants function, and explain why Deaf culture advocates object to these devices.

Cochlear implants are wired into various sites on the auditory nerve, allowing them to transmit electrical impulses to the brain. These devices can help deaf children to hear some sounds and to learn to use spoken language. But cochlear implants are most effective when children are very young, which means that parents must make this decision for their deaf children. Deaf culture advocates believe the operation is unnecessary since they do not see deafness as a disability—Deaf people already have a complete language, sign. Some further argue that sensory compensation, which enhances other senses, gives deaf people advantages that the hearing do not have.

ASK YOURSELF: If you had been born deaf, do you think you would want to receive a cochlear implant? Does it surprise you that most lifelong Deaf adults do not desire implants for themselves or their children? Why is it the Deaf community and its culture have no corresponding "Blind community" or "Blind culture"?

Other Important Senses

For humans, the major senses are seeing and hearing. We depend on them, particularly for communication. Our brains give these two senses priority in the allocation of cortical tissue. But extraordinary happenings are hidden within our four other senses: touch, taste, smell, and our sense of body position and movement. Sharks and dogs rely on their extraordinary sense of smell, aided by large brain areas devoted to smell. Without our own senses of touch, taste, and smell, and body motion and position, we humans would also be seriously handicapped, and our capacities for enjoying the world would be devastatingly diminished.

Touch

The precious sense of touch
As William James wrote in his *Principles of Psychology* (1890), "Touch is both the alpha and omega of affection."

Bruce Ayres/Stone/Getty Images

Objective 17 | Describe the sense of touch.

If you had to lose one sense, which would you prefer it to be? If you could have only one, which would you want?

Although not the first sense to come to mind, touch could be our priority sense. Right from the start, touch is essential to our development. Infant rats deprived of their mothers' grooming touch produce less growth hormone and have a lower metabolic rate—a good way to keep alive until the mother returns, but a reaction that stunts growth if prolonged. Infant monkeys allowed to see, hear, and smell—but not touch—their mothers become desperately unhappy; those separated by a screen with holes that allow touching are much less miserable. As we noted in Chapter 3, premature babies gain weight faster and go home sooner if they are stimulated by hand massage. As lovers, we yearn to touch—to kiss, to stroke, to snuggle.

Humorist Dave Barry may be right to jest that your skin "keeps people from seeing the inside of your body, which is repulsive, and it prevents your organs from falling onto the ground." But skin does much more. Our "sense of touch" is actually a mix of at least four distinct skin senses—pressure, warmth, cold, and pain. Within the skin are different types of specialized nerve endings. Touching various spots on the skin with a soft hair, a warm or cool wire, and the point of a pin reveals that some spots are especially sensitive to pressure, others to warmth, others to cold, still others to pain. Does that mean that each nerve ending is a receptor for one of the basic skin senses, much as the eye's cone receptors correspond to light's basic colors?

Surprisingly, there is no simple relationship between what we feel at a given spot and the type of specialized nerve ending found there. Only pressure has identifiable receptors. Other skin sensations are variations of the basic four (pressure, warmth, cold [either very low or very high temperatures], and pain):

- Stroking adjacent pressure spots creates a tickle.
- Repeated gentle stroking of a pain spot creates an itching sensation.
- Touching adjacent cold and pressure spots triggers a sense of wetness, which you can experience by touching dry, cold metal.
- Stimulating nearby cold and warmth spots produces the sensation of hot (**FIGURE 5.27**).

FIGURE 5.27
Warm + cold = hot
When ice-cold water passes through one coil and comfortably warm water through another, we perceive the combined sensation as burning hot.

Touch sensations involve more than tactile stimulation, however. A self-produced tickle produces less somatosensory cortex activation than the same tickle would from something or someone else (Blakemore & others, 1998). (The brain is wise enough to be most sensitive to unexpected stimulation.) The top-down influence on touch sensation also is illustrated by the rubber-hand illusion. Imagine yourself looking at a realistic-looking fake rubber hand while your own real hand is hidden (**FIGURE 5.28**). If an experimenter simultaneously touches your fake and real hands, you likely will perceive the rubber hand as your own hand and sense it being touched.

Dierdre Desmond

FIGURE 5.28
The rubber-hand illusion
When Dublin researcher Deirdre Desmond simultaneously touches a volunteer's real and fake hands, the volunteer feels as though the seen fake hand is her own.

A pain-free, problematic life
Ashlyn Blocker (right), shown here with her mother and sister, has a rare genetic disorder. She feels neither pain nor extreme hot and cold. She must frequently be checked for accidentally self-inflicted injuries that she herself cannot feel. "Some people would say [that feeling no pain is] a good thing," says her mother. "But no, it's not. Pain's there for a reason. It lets your body know something's wrong and it needs to be fixed. I'd give anything for her to feel pain" (quoted by Bynum, 2004).

"When belly with bad pains doth swell, It matters naught what else goes well."

Sadi, *The Gulistan*, 1258

Pain

OBJECTIVE **18** | State the purpose of pain, and describe the biopsychosocial approach to pain.

Be thankful for occasional pain. Pain is your body's way of telling you something has gone wrong. Drawing your attention to a burn, a break, or a rupture, it tells you to change your behavior immediately. The rare people born without the ability to feel pain may experience severe injury without ever being alerted by pain's danger signals. Usually, they die by early adulthood. Without the discomfort that makes us occasionally shift position, their joints fail from excess strain, and without the warnings of pain, the effects of unchecked infections and injuries accumulate (Neese, 1991).

More numerous are those who live with chronic pain, which is rather like an alarm that won't shut off. For those with illness-related hyperalgesia, an extreme sensitivity to something that others would find only mildly painful, the sensory receptors and brain work together to make life miserable (Brune & Handwerker, 2004; Wiertelak & others, 1994). The suffering of such people, and of those with persistent or recurring backaches, arthritis, headaches, and cancer-related pain, prompts two questions: What is pain? How might we control it?

Biological, Psychological, and Social-Cultural Influences on Pain Our pain experiences vary widely, depending on our physiology, our experiences and attention, and our surrounding culture (**FIGURE 5.29**). Pain is a property not only of the senses—of the region where we feel it—but of our brain and our expectations as well. Carrie Armel and Vilayanur Ramachandran (2003) cleverly illustrated this point when they bent a finger slightly backwards on the unseen hands of 16 volunteers, while simultaneously "hurting" (severely bending) a finger on a fake rubber hand. The volunteers felt as if their real finger was being twisted, and they responded with increased skin perspiration.

Consider, too, people's experiences of phantom sensations. As the dreamer may see with eyes closed and the listener may hear a ringing during utter silence, so some

FIGURE 5.29
Biopsychosocial perspective on pain
Our experience of pain is much more than neural messages sent to the brain.

7 in 10 amputees may feel pain or movement in nonexistent limbs, notes psychologist Robert Melzack (1992, 1993). (An amputee may also try to step off a bed onto a phantom limb or to lift a cup with a phantom hand.) Even those born without a limb sometimes perceive sensations from the absent arm or leg. The brain, Melzack (1998) surmises, comes prepared to anticipate "that it will be getting information from a body that has limbs."

These *phantom limb sensations* indicate that with pain, as with sights and sounds, the brain can misinterpret the spontaneous central nervous system activity that occurs in the absence of normal sensory input. A similar phenomenon occurs with other senses. People, especially those with hearing loss, often experience the sound of silence: phantom sounds—a ringing-in-the-ears sensation known as *tinnitus*. People who lose vision to glaucoma, cataracts, diabetes, or macular degeneration sometimes experience phantom sights—nonthreatening hallucinations (Ramachandran & Blakeslee, 1998). (As she became legally blind, my clear-thinking mother-in-law would occasionally see silent visitors to her room doing strange things like walking on the back of her couch.) Nerve damage in the taste system can similarly produce taste phantoms, such as ice water seeming sickeningly sweet (Goode, 1999). Others have experienced phantom smells, such as nonexistent rotten food. The moral: We see, hear, taste, smell, and feel with our brain, which can sense even without functioning senses. Pain-producing brain activity may be triggered with or without sensory input, says Melzack (1999). A brain in a jar could conceivably experience pain and other sensory experiences. No brain, no pain.

Unlike vision, however, the pain system is not located in a simple neural cord running from a sensing device to a definable area in the brain. Moreover, there is no one type of stimulus that triggers pain (as light triggers vision), and there are no special receptors (like the retina's rods and cones) for pain. In fact, at low intensities, the stimuli that produce pain also cause other sensations, including warmth or coolness, smoothness or roughness.

Although no theory of pain explains all the available findings, Melzack and biologist Patrick Wall's (1965, 1983) classic **gate-control theory** still provides a useful model. Melzack and Wall theorized that the spinal cord contains a neurological "gate" that either blocks pain signals or allows them to pass on to the brain. The spinal cord contains small nerve fibers that conduct most pain signals, and larger fibers that conduct most other sensory signals. When tissue is injured, the small fibers activate and open the neural gate, and you feel pain. Large-fiber activity closes the pain gate, turning pain off.

Thus, one way to treat chronic pain is to stimulate (by massage, by electric stimulation, or by acupuncture) "gate-closing" activity in the large neural fibers (Wall, 2000). Rubbing the area around your stubbed toe will create competing stimulation that will block some of the pain messages. Some people with arthritis wear a small, portable electrical stimulation unit next to a painful area. When the unit stimulates nerves in the area, the person feels a vibrating sensation rather than pain (Murphy, 1982).

Melzack and Wall noted that the pain gate can also be closed by information from the brain. These brain-to-spinal-cord messages help explain some striking psychological influences on pain. When we are distracted from pain and soothed by the release of endorphins, our experience of pain may be greatly diminished. Sports injuries may go unnoticed until the after-game shower. During a 1989 basketball game, Ohio State University player Jay Burson broke his neck—and kept playing.

■ **gate-control theory** the theory that the spinal cord contains a neurological "gate" that blocks pain signals or allows them to pass on to the brain. The "gate" is opened by the activity of pain signals traveling up small nerve fibers and is closed by activity in larger fibers or by information coming from the brain.

Seeking relief
This acupuncturist is attempting to help this woman gain relief from back pain by using needles on points of the patient's hand.

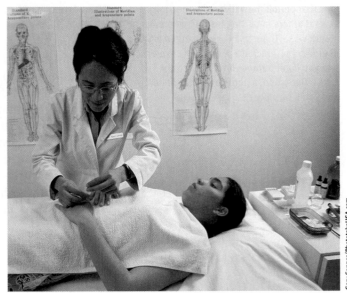

Gary Conner/PhototakeUSA.com

"Pain is increased by attending to it."
Charles Darwin, *Expression of Emotions in Man and Animals*, 1872

People who carry a gene that boosts the availability of the body's natural painkillers, the endorphins, are less bothered by pain, and their brains are less responsive to it (Zubieta & others, 2003).

René Descartes' idea, proposed more than three centuries ago, was wrong. Pain is not merely a physical phenomenon of injured nerves sending impulses to the brain—like pulling on a rope to ring a bell. The brain creates pain. People perceive more pain and endure it less, when others also seem to be experiencing pain (Symbaluk & others, 1997). And when feeling empathy for another's pain, a person's own brain activity may partly mirror that of the other's brain in pain (Singer & others, 2004). This phenomenon may help explain apparent social influences on pain, as when pockets of Australian keyboard operators during the mid-1980s suffered outbreaks of severe pain during typing or other repetitive work—without any discernible physical abnormalities (Gawande, 1998). Sometimes the pain in sprain is mainly in the brain.

Both photos: David Willey

**Pain perception:
A cool look at a hot topic**
At the University of Pittsburgh, Johnstown, physicist David Willey used eight cords of wood to construct the world's longest firewalk. After explaining heat-diffusion principles that permit firewalking, he then joined several others in putting his feet where his mouth was. (Think of a cake baking in a 350-degree oven. Touch the aluminum cake tin and you'll get burned; briefly touch the cake—like wood, a poor conductor of heat—and you'll be okay.)

There is also more to our *memories* of pain than the pain we experienced. In experiments, and after medical procedures, people overlook a pain's duration. Their memory snapshots instead record its peak moment and how much pain they felt at the end. Daniel Kahneman and his co-researchers (1993) discovered this when they asked people to immerse one hand in painfully cold water for 60 seconds, and then the other hand in the same painfully cold water for 60 seconds followed by a slightly less painful 30 seconds more. Curiously, when asked which trial they would prefer to repeat, most preferred the longer trial, with more net pain—but less pain at the end. For medical personnel, the implication is clear: It is better to taper down a painful procedure than to switch it off abruptly. In one experiment, a physician did this for some patients undergoing colon exams—lengthening the discomfort by a minute, but lessening its intensity (Kahneman, 1999). Although this extended milder discomfort added to the net pain experience, patients experiencing this taper-down treatment later recalled the exam as less painful than those whose pain ended abruptly. In a parallel phenomenon, people rate an imagined terrible life with a moderately bad year added on as better than a terrible life that ends abruptly without the moderately bad year. And they rate an imagined wonderful life that ends abruptly as better than one with added mildly pleasant years (Diener & others, 2001).

Pain Control If pain is where body meets mind—if it is indeed a physical and a psychological phenomenon—then it should be treatable both physically and psychologically. Depending on the type of symptoms, pain control clinics select one or more therapies from a list that includes drugs, surgery, acupuncture, electrical stimulation, massage, exercise, hypnosis, relaxation training, and thought distraction. Even an inert placebo can help, by dampening the brain's responses to painful experiences—mimicking analgesic drugs (Wager & others, 2004).

The Lamaze method of childbirth combines relaxation (through deep breathing and muscle relaxation), counterstimulation (through gentle massage), and distraction (through focusing attention on, say, a pleasant photograph). Distracting people with pleasant images ("Think of a warm, comfortable environment") or drawing their attention away from the painful stimulation ("Count backward by 3's") is an especially effective way to increase pain tolerance (Fernandez & Turk, 1989; McCaul & Malott, 1984).

The principle works in health care situations. A well-trained nurse may distract needle-shy patients by chatting with them and asking them to look away when inserting the needle. A pleasing view may similarly relax and distract. In examining the records of one Pennsylvania hospital, Roger Ulrich (1984) discovered that surgery patients assigned to rooms looking out on trees required less pain medication and had shorter stays than those assigned to identical rooms overlooking a brick wall. For burn victims receiving excruciating wound care, an even more effective distraction comes from immersion in a computer-generated 3-D world (**FIGURE 5.30**). Functional MRI scans reveal that playing in the virtual reality reduces the brain's pain-related activity (Hoffman, 2004). Because pain is in the brain, diverting the brain's attention may bring relief.

Although Lamaze training reduces labor pain, most Lamaze patients request a local anesthetic during labor. Some—having expected a "natural, painless birth"—feel needless guilt and failure. Pain researcher Ronald Melzack therefore advocates—as does the Lamaze program itself—childbirth training that prepares a woman "to cope with an event which is often extremely painful and, at the same time, one of the most fulfilling peak experiences in her life" (Melzack, 1984).

FIGURE 5.30
Virtual-reality pain control
For burn victims undergoing painful skin repair, an illusory virtual reality can powerfully distract attention, thus reducing pain and the brain's response to painful stimulation, as shown by these MRI scans.

Image by Todd Richards and Aric Bills, U.W., ©Hunter Hoffman, www.vrpain.com

Taste

OBJECTIVE **19** | Describe the sense of taste, and explain the principle of sensory interaction.

Like touch, our sense of taste involves several basic sensations. Until recently, taste's sensations were thought to be sweet, sour, salty, and bitter (McBurney & Gent, 1979), with all other taste sensations stemming from mixtures of these four. Then, as investigators searched for specialized nerve fibers for the four taste sensations, they encountered a receptor for what we now know is a fifth—the meaty taste of *umami*, best experienced as the flavor enhancer monosodium glutamate (Chaudhari & others, 2000; Nelson & others, 2001; Smith & Margolskee, 2001).

■ **sensory interaction** the principle that one sense may influence another, as when the smell of food influences its taste.

Taste exists for more than our pleasure. Pleasureful tastes attract us to energy-rich foods that enabled our ancestors' survival. Aversive tastes deter us from new foods that might be toxic. Two- to six-year-old children are typically fussy eaters, especially when offered new meats or bitter-tasting vegetables, such as spinach and brussels sprouts (Cooke & others, 2003). There is biological wisdom behind this picky eating. Meat and plant toxins were both potentially dangerous sources of food poisoning for our ancestors, especially for children. Given repeated small tastes of disliked new foods, today's children will, however, typically begin to accept them (Wardle & others, 2003).

Taste is a chemical sense. Inside each little bump on the top and sides of your tongue are 200 or more taste buds, each containing a pore that catches food chemicals. These molecules are sensed by 50 to 100 taste receptor cells that project antennalike hairs into the pore. Some of these receptors respond mostly to sweet-tasting molecules, others to salty- , sour-, or bitter-tasting ones. It doesn't take much to trigger a response that alerts the temporal lobe. If a stream of water is pumped across your tongue, the addition of a concentrated salty or sweet taste for but one-tenth of a second will get your attention (Kelling & Halpern, 1983). When a friend asks for "just a taste" of your soft drink, you can squeeze off the straw after a mere fraction of a second.

Taste receptors reproduce themselves every week or two, so if you burn your tongue with hot food it hardly matters. However, as you grow older, the number of taste buds decreases, as does taste sensitivity (Cowart, 1981). (No wonder adults enjoy strong-tasting foods that children resist.) Smoking and alcohol use accelerate the decline in taste buds and sensitivities.

Taste researcher Linda Bartoshuk (1993) offers other fascinating facts about taste:

- Our emotional responses to taste are hard-wired. Put a sweet or bitter substance on a newborn's tongue and the baby's tongue and face react like an adult's.
- People without tongues can still taste—through receptors in the back and on the roof of the mouth.
- If you lose taste sensation from one side of your tongue, you probably won't notice. That's because the other side will become correspondingly supersensitive. Also, the brain doesn't localize taste well: Although the middle of the tongue has few taste receptors, we perceive taste as coming from the whole tongue.
- We can neither taste nor smell most nutrients—fat, protein, starch, and food vitamins. (Sugar is an exception.) But we do quickly learn a liking or aversion to the taste and smell of other food components that prove nutritious or sickening (see page 322).

Taste buds are certainly essential for taste, but there's more to taste than meets the tongue. Hold your nose, close your eyes, and have someone feed you various foods. A slice of apple may be indistinguishable from a chunk of raw potato; a piece of steak may taste like cardboard; without their smells, a cold cup of coffee may be hard to distinguish from a glass of red wine. To savor a taste, we normally breathe the aroma through our nose—which is why eating is not much fun when you have a bad cold, and why people who lose their sense of smell may think they have also lost their sense of taste. Smell not only adds to our perception of taste, it also changes it: A drink's strawberry odor enhances our perception of its sweetness. This is **sensory interaction** at work—the principle that one sense may influence another. Smell plus texture plus taste equals flavor.

Sensory interaction can also influence what we hear. If we *see* a speaker saying one syllable while *hearing* another, we may perceive a third syllable that blends both inputs. Seeing the mouth movements for *ga* while hearing *ba* we may perceive *da*—a phenomenon known as the *McGurk effect,* after its discoverers, psychologist Harry McGurk and his assistant John MacDonald (1976).

Sensory interaction

When a hard-of-hearing listener *sees* an animated face forming words being spoken at the other end of a phone line, the words become easier to understand (Knight, 2004).

Courtesy of RNID www.rnid.org.uk

Much the same is true with vision and touch. Sensory interaction underlies the rubber hand illusion, where vision influences the sense of touch. In detecting events, the brain can combine simultaneous visual and touch signals, thanks to neurons projecting from the somatosensory cortex back to the visual cortex (Macaluso & others, 2000).

So, the senses interact: Seeing, hearing, touching, tasting, and smelling are not totally separate channels. In interpreting the world, the brain blends their inputs. In a few select individuals, the senses become joined in a phenomenon called *synaesthesia*, where one sort of sensation (such as hearing sound) produces another (such as seeing color). Thus hearing music or seeing a specific number may activate color-sensitive cortex regions and trigger a sensation of color (Hubbard & others, 2005). Seeing the number *3* may evoke a taste sensation (Ward, 2003).

Smell

OBJECTIVE 20 | Describe the sense of smell, and explain why specific odors so easily trigger memories.

Inhale, exhale. Inhale, exhale. Breaths come in pairs—except at two moments: birth and death. Each day, you inhale and exhale nearly 20,000 breaths of life-sustaining air, bathing your nostrils in a stream of scent-laden molecules. The resulting experiences of smell *(olfaction)* are strikingly intimate: You inhale something of whatever or whoever it is you smell.

Like taste, smell is a chemical sense. We smell something when molecules of a substance carried in the air reach a tiny cluster of 5 million receptor cells at the top of each nasal cavity (**FIGURE 5.31**). These olfactory receptor cells, waving like

FIGURE 5.31
The sense of smell
If you are to smell a flower, airborne molecules of its fragrance must reach receptors at the top of your nose. Sniffing swirls air up to the receptors, enhancing the aroma. The receptor cells send messages to the brain's olfactory bulb, and then onward to the temporal lobe's primary smell cortex and to the parts of the limbic system involved in memory and emotion.

sea anemones on a reef, respond selectively—to the aroma of a cake baking, to a wisp of smoke, to a friend's fragrance. Instantly they alert the brain through their axon fibers.

Even nursing infants and their mothers have a literal chemistry to their relationship. They quickly learn to recognize each other's scents (McCarthy, 1986). Aided by smell, a mother fur seal returning to a beach crowded with pups will find her own. Our own sense of smell is less impressive than the acuteness of our seeing and hearing. Looking out across a garden we see its forms and colors in exquisite detail and hear a variety of birds singing, yet we smell little of it without sticking our nose into the blossoms.

Unlike light, which can be separated into its spectral colors, an odor cannot be separated into more elemental odors. The olfaction system has no parallel to the retina, which detects myriad colors with sensory cells dedicated to red, green, or blue. Olfactory receptors recognize odors individually.

Odor molecules come in many shapes and sizes—so many, in fact, that it takes many different receptors to detect them. A large family of genes design the 350 or so receptor proteins that recognize particular odor molecules (Miller, 2004). Richard Axel and Linda Buck (1991) discovered (in work for which they received a 2004 Nobel Prize) that these receptor proteins are embedded on the surface of nasal cavity neurons. As a key slips into a lock, so odor molecules slip into these receptors. Yet we seem not to have a distinct receptor for each detectable odor. This suggests that some odors trigger a combination of receptors, whose activity the olfactory cortex interprets. As the alphabet's 26 letters can combine to form many words, so odor molecules bind to different receptor arrays, producing the 10,000 odors we can detect (Malnic & others, 1999). It is the combinations of olfactory receptors that allow us to distinguish the aromas of fresh-brewed and hours-old coffee.

The ability to identify scents peaks in early adulthood and gradually declines thereafter (**FIGURE 5.32**). Despite our skill at discriminating scents, we aren't nearly so good at describing them. Words more readily portray the sound of coffee brewing than its aroma. Compared with how we experience and remember sights and sounds, smells are almost primitive and certainly harder to describe and recall (Richardson & Zucco, 1989; Zucco, 2003).

As any dog or cat with a good nose could tell us, we each have our own identifiable chemical signature. (One noteworthy exception: A dog will follow the tracks of one identical twin as though they had been made by the other [Thomas, 1974].) Animals that have many times more olfactory receptors than we do also use their sense of smell to communicate and to navigate. Long before the shark can see its prey, or the moth its

Humans have 10 to 20 million olfactory receptors. A bloodhound has some 200 million (Herz, 2001).

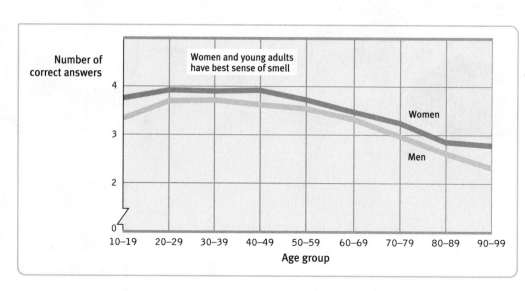

FIGURE 5.32
Age, sex, and sense of smell
Among the 1.2 million people who responded to a *National Geographic* scratch and sniff survey, women and younger adults most successfully identified six sample odors (from Wysocki & Gilbert, 1989). Smokers and people with Alzheimer's, Parkinson's, or alcoholism typically experience a diminished sense of smell (Doty, 2001).

mate, odors direct their way. Migrating salmon follow faint olfactory cues back to their home stream. If exposed in a hatchery to one of two odorant chemicals, they will, when returning two years later, seek whichever stream near their release site is spiked with the familiar smell (Barinaga, 1999). For humans, too, the attractiveness of smells depends on learned associations (Herz, 2001). Babies do not come with a built-in preference for the smell of their mother's breast, but as they nurse their preference builds.

Odors also have the power to evoke memories and feelings (**FIGURE 5.33**). A hotline runs between the brain area that gets information from the nose and the brain's ancient limbic centers associated with memory and emotion. Smell is primitive. Eons before the elaborate analytical areas of our cerebral cortex had fully evolved, our mammalian ancestors sniffed for food—and for predators.

Laboratory studies confirm that, though it's difficult to recall odors by name, we do indeed have a remarkable capacity to recognize long-forgotten odors and their associated personal episodes (Engen, 1987; Schab, 1991). Odors can evoke unpleasant emotions. Rachel Herz and her colleagues (2004) frustrated Brown University students with a rigged computer game in a scented room. Later, if exposed to the same odor while working on a verbal task, their frustration was rekindled and they gave up sooner than students exposed to a different odor or no odor. Pleasant odors can evoke pleasant memories (Ehrlichman & Halpern, 1988). The smell of the sea, the scent of a perfume, or an aroma of a favorite relative's kitchen can bring to mind a happy time. In *Remembrance of Things Past,* the French novelist Marcel Proust described how the aroma and flavor of a bit of cake soaked in tea resurrected long-forgotten memories of his aunt's bedroom in the old family house. "The smell and taste of things," he noted, "bears unfaltering, in the tiny and almost impalpable drop of their essence, the vast structure of recollection."

Such is the power of an odor to switch on memories and to retrieve associated emotions. It's a phenomenon understood by the British travel agent chain Lunn Poly. To evoke memories of lounging on sunny, warm beaches, the company has piped the aroma of coconut suntan oil into its shops (Fracassini, 2000).

Body Position and Movement

OBJECTIVE **21** | Distinguish between kinesthesis and the vestibular sense.

With only the five familiar senses we have so far considered, we could not put food in our mouths, stand up, or reach out and touch someone. We would be helpless. To know just how to move your arms to grasp someone's hand, you need a sixth sense. You need to know the current position of your arms and hands and then be aware of their changing positions as you move them. For you to take just one step requires feedback from, and instructions to, some 200 muscles. The computations our brain must perform for sensorimotor coordination dwarf even those involved in reasoning. We now have computers that can "play" championship chess, but we're a long way from computer-driven robots that can play tennis with Serena Williams, much less dust the house.

We come equipped with millions of position and motion sensors. They are all over our body—in the muscles, tendons, and joints—and they are continually providing information to our brain. If we twist our wrists one degree, the sensors immediately report it. This sense of our body parts' position and movement is **kinesthesis.**

One can momentarily imagine being blind or deaf. Close your eyes, plug your ears, and experience the dark stillness. But what would it be like to live without touch or kinesthesis—without, therefore, being able to sense the positions of your limbs when awakening during the night? Ian Waterman of Hampshire, England, knows. In 1972, at age 19, Waterman contracted a rare viral infection that destroyed the nerves that

FIGURE 5.33
The olfactory brain
Information from the taste buds (orange arrow) travels to an area of the temporal lobe not far from where the brain receives olfactory information, which interacts with taste. The brain's circuitry for smell (red arrow) also connects with areas involved in memory storage, which helps explain why a smell can trigger a memory explosion.

Impress your friends with your new word for the day: People unable to see are said to experience blindness. People unable to hear experience deafness. People unable to smell experience *anosmia*.

■ **kinesthesis** [kin-ehs-THEE-sehs] the system for sensing the position and movement of individual body parts.

■ **vestibular sense** the sense of body movement and position, including the sense of balance.

The intricate vestibular sense
Thank your inner ears for the information that enables your brain to monitor your body's position.

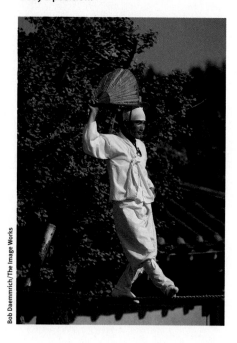

Bob Daemmrich/The Image Works

enabled his sense of light touch and of body position and movement. People with this condition report feeling disembodied, as though their body is dead, not real, not theirs (Sacks, 1985). With prolonged practice Waterman has learned to walk and eat—by visually focusing on his limbs and directing them accordingly. But if the lights go out, he crumples to the floor (Azar, 1998). Even for the rest of us, vision interacts with kinesthesis. Stand with your right heel in front of your left toes. Easy. Now close your eyes and you will probably wobble.

A companion **vestibular sense** monitors the head's (and thus the body's) position and movement. The biological gyroscopes for this sense of equilibrium are in the inner ear. The *semicircular canals,* which look like a three-dimensional pretzel (Figure 5.24a, page 217), and the *vestibular sacs,* which connect the canals with the cochlea, contain fluid that moves when the head rotates or tilts. This movement stimulates hairlike receptors, which send messages to the cerebellum at the back of the brain, thus enabling you to sense your body position and to maintain your balance.

If you twirl around and then come to an abrupt halt, neither the fluid in your semicircular canals nor your kinesthetic receptors will immediately return to their neutral state. The aftereffect fools your dizzy brain with the sensation that you're still spinning. This illustrates a principle that underlies the next chapter's discussion of perceptual illusions: Mechanisms that normally give us an accurate experience of the world can, under special conditions, fool us. Understanding how we get fooled provides clues to how our perceptual system works.

In this chapter we have taken a bottom-up look at how we experience the world, starting with how our ingenious sensory receptors transduce physical energy into neural messages sent to our brain. We've also taken a top-down look at how our mind shapes our experiences. Pain, for example, is a response to information traveling both up the spinal cord's small nerves and down from what our mind is paying attention to. Our experiences are in the brain—so much so that the brain can choose how to interpret neural activity, or may even conjure up perceived sights, sounds, and pains without any external stimulation. Sensation and perception are different aspects of one whole fabric—how we experience the world around us.

>> LEARNING OUTCOMES

Other Important Senses

OBJECTIVE 17 | Describe the sense of touch.
Our sense of touch is actually four senses—*pressure, warmth, cold,* and *pain*—that combine to produce other sensations, such as "hot." Of these, only pressure has specialized receptors.

OBJECTIVE 18 | State the purpose of pain, and describe the biopsychosocial perspective on pain.
Pain is an alarm system that draws our attention to some physical problem. One theory of pain is that a "gate" in the spinal cord either opens to permit pain signals traveling up small nerve fibers to reach the brain, or closes to prevent their passage. The biopsychosocial perspective views a person's experience of pain as the sum of three sets of forces: biological influences, such as nerve fibers sending messages to the brain; psychological influences, such as the situation and our past experiences; and social-cultural influences, such as cultural expectations and the presence of observers. Treatments to control pain often combine physiological and psychological elements.

OBJECTIVE 19 | Describe the sense of taste, and explain the principle of sensory interaction.
Taste, a chemical sense, is a composite of five basic sensations—*sweet, sour, salty, bitter,* and *umami*—and of the aromas that interact with information from the taste buds. Taste buds on the top and sides of the tongue and in the back and on the roof of the mouth contain taste receptor cells. These cells send information to an area of the temporal lobe near the area where olfactory information is received. The influence of smell on our sense of taste is an example of sensory interaction, the ability of one sense to influence another.

OBJECTIVE 20 | Describe the sense of smell, and explain why specific odors so easily trigger memories.
Smell is a chemical sense, but there are no basic sensations for smell, as there are for touch and taste. Unlike the retina's receptor cells that sense color by breaking it into

component parts, the 5 million olfactory receptor cells, with their approximately 350 different receptor proteins, recognize individual odor molecules. The receptor cells send messages to the brain's olfactory bulb, then to the temporal lobe and to parts of the limbic system. Some odors trigger a combination of receptors. An odor's ability to spontaneously evoke memories and feelings is due in part to the close connections between brain areas that process smell and those involved in memory storage.

OBJECTIVE 21 | Distinguish between kinesthesis and the vestibular sense.

By means of millions of position and motion sensors all over our body, our *kinesthetic* sense monitors the position and movement of our individual body parts. Our vestibular sense relies on semicircular canals and vestibular sacs in the inner ear to sense our head's—and thus our whole body's—position and movement, letting us maintain our balance.

ASK YOURSELF: Can you recall a time when, with your attention focused on some activity, you felt no pain from a wound or injury?

REVIEW CHAPTER 5 : Sensation

Test Yourself

1. What is the rough distinction between sensation and perception?
2. What is the rapid sequence of events that occurs when you see and recognize someone you know?
3. In a nutshell, how do we transform sound waves into perceived sound?
4. What does the biopsychosocial perspective on pain teach us?
5. How does our system for sensing smell differ from our sensory systems for vision, touch, and taste?

Answers to the Test Yourself questions can be found in Appendix B at the end of the book.

Terms and Concepts to Remember

sensation, p. 197
perception, p. 197
bottom-up processing, p. 197
top-down processing, p. 197
psychophysics, p. 199
absolute threshold, p. 199
signal detection theory, p. 199
subliminal, p. 200
priming, p. 200
difference threshold, p. 201
Weber's law, p. 202
sensory adaptation, p. 202
transduction, p. 204
wavelength, p. 204
hue, p. 205
intensity, p. 205
pupil, p. 205

iris, p. 205
lens, p. 205
accommodation, p. 205
retina, p. 205
acuity, p. 206
nearsightedness, p. 206
farsightedness, p. 206
rods, p. 206
cones, p. 206
optic nerve, p. 207
blind spot, p. 207
fovea, p. 207
feature detectors, p. 209
parallel processing, p. 210
Young-Helmholtz trichromatic (three-color) theory, p. 212
opponent-process theory, p. 213

color constancy, p. 214
audition, p. 215
frequency, p. 216
pitch, p. 216
middle ear, p. 217
cochlea [KOHK-lee-uh], p. 217
inner ear, p. 217
place theory, p. 219
frequency theory, p. 219
conduction hearing loss, p. 220
sensorineural hearing loss, p. 220
cochlear implant, p. 221
gate-control theory, p. 227
sensory interaction, p. 230
kinesthesis [kin-ehs-THEE-sehs], p. 233
vestibular sense, p. 234

WEB

 To continue your study and review of Sensation, visit this book's Web site at www.worthpublishers.com/myers. You will find practice tests, review activities, and many interesting articles and Web links for more information on topics related to Sensation.

ANOTHER VOICE ON: PERCEPTION

JIM KNIPFEL, FROM *SLACKJAW*, 2000

Despite the training, and the past injuries and humiliations, I found it difficult to get into the habit of pulling my cane out when I needed it. I can handle this, I would think when confronted with a darkened street. I continued thinking that way until I got into trouble again.

I was stumbling home late one night, my vision even blurrier than normal. I was proud of myself after slowing down enough to maneuver without incident for a bunch of voices blocking the sidewalk. I was proud of myself for maintaining my balance after hooking my leg on a gate someone had left open. Pride was what

kept me from pulling the cane out. I could handle things just fine without any props to declare my cripplehood to the world. Then I stepped on something.

The dog—it sounded like a big dog, too—let out a yelp and jerked its leg from beneath my shoe.

"Christ, didn't you see it?" an old man, the dog's owner, shouted at me.

I stopped, thought about my situation, then turned in the direction of the voice. "Jeez, I'm very sorry . . . fact is, I didn't see it."

"It's a big damn dog!"

"I'm sure it is. I'm sorry. Y'see, this is

my fault, see, I have"—I flipped my bag open and reached inside—"I have this red-and-white cane here that I really should be using." I took the cane out and held it for the man to see. "I'm blind, sir. I didn't see the dog, and it was my fault."

"Oh my God, I'm sorry." The anger was gone from his voice, and he touched my arm lightly. "I . . . I didn't know."

"It's okay. There's no way you could have known. If I'd been using the cane the way I was supposed to, you would have, and this wouldn't have happened."

"I'm so sorry." He started to cry, quietly.

6: Perception

Meriwether Lewis, leader of the nineteenth-century Lewis and Clark expedition, was exploring ahead of his group. Startled by an aggressive grizzly bear charging out of the bush, Lewis jumped into a river to escape, and the bear withdrew. While traveling the 12 miles back to his group, the shaken Lewis found himself perceiving other animals as threatening, and he preemptively shot several. "It now seemed to me that all the beasts of the neighborhood had made a league to destroy me" (Larsen, 2004). Primed by his frightening encounter, Lewis was perceiving the world differently.

Two centuries later, Amadou Diallo, an unarmed West African immigrant, was approached by four New York City police officers on the stoop of his Bronx apartment complex. As he pulled his wallet and identification out of his pocket, the officers—apparently feeling threatened by their own previous encounters—mistook his wallet for a gun. Diallo, a street vendor, died in a hail of 41 bullets.

Some 2400 years ago, Plato rightly discerned the principle that these cases illustrate—that we perceive objects through our senses, with our mind. To construct the outside world inside our heads we must detect physical energy from the environment (bottom-up) and then encode it as neural signals (a process traditionally called *sensation*). We must also select, organize, and interpret (top-down) our sensations (a process traditionally called *perception*). We not only sense raw sights and sounds, tastes and smells, we *perceive*. We hear not just a mix of pitches and rhythms but a child's cry, the traffic's hum, a symphony's crescendo. Our perceptions are affected by the biology of our sensory systems, but also by our previous experiences (a bear attack) and cultural expectations (police officers are trained to expect and cope with "action"). In transforming sensations into perceptions, *we* create the meaning.

Selective Attention

OBJECTIVE 1 | Describe the interplay between attention and perception.

Perceptions come to us moment by moment, one perception vanishing as the next appears. Note how the Necker cube in **FIGURE 6.1** evokes more than one perception. The circles can be organized into several coherent images, each equally plausible, and your mind switches back and forth from one to the next. You *know* that alternative interpretations of this figure are possible, but you can consciously experience only one at any moment. This illustrates an important principle: Our conscious attention is *selective*.

Selective attention means that at any moment our awareness focuses, like a flashlight beam, on only a limited aspect of all that we experience. Indeed, a *very* limited aspect: By one estimate, our five senses take in 11,000,000 bits

FIGURE 6.1
Selective attention
What do you see: circles with white lines, or a cube? If you stare at the cube, you may notice that it reverses location, moving the tiny X in the center from the front edge to the back. At times the cube may seem to float in front of the page, with circles behind it; other times the circles may become holes in the page through which the cube appears, as though it were floating behind the page. Because attention is selective, you see only one interpretation at a time. (From Bradley & others, 1976.)

■ **selective attention** the focusing of conscious awareness on a particular stimulus, as in the cocktail party effect.

■ **inattentional blindness** failing to see visible objects when our attention is directed elsewhere.

of information per second, of which we consciously process about 40 (Wilson, 2002). Yet we intuitively make great use of the other 10,999,960 bits. Until reading this sentence, you have been unaware that your shoes are pressing against your feet or that your nose is in your line of vision. Now, suddenly, your attentional spotlight shifts. Your feet feel encased, your nose stubbornly intrudes on the page before you. While attending to these words, you've also been blocking from awareness information coming from your peripheral vision. But you can change that. While staring at the X below, notice what surrounds the book (the edges of the page, your desktop, and so forth).

X

Another example of selective attention, the *cocktail party effect*, is your ability to attend to only one voice among many (though let another voice speak your name and your cognitive radar will instantly bring that voice into consciousness). This focused listening comes at a cost. Imagine hearing two conversations over a headset, one in each ear, and being asked to repeat the message in your left ear while it is spoken. When paying attention to what is being said in your left ear, you won't perceive what is said in your right. Asked later what language your right ear heard, you may draw a blank (though you could report the speaker's gender and loudness).

At the level of conscious awareness, our attention is divided. Talk while driving and your attention will shift back and forth from the road to the phone. That explains why drivers typically stop talking when demanding situations require their full attention. The process of switching attentional gears also costs a bit of time, especially when shifting to complex tasks (Rubenstein & others, 2001). But even shifting from cell-phone talking to a driving crisis can entail a slight delay in coping. In University of Utah driving-simulation experiments, students conversing on cell phones were slower to detect and respond to traffic signals, billboards, and other cars (Strayer & Johnston, 2001; Strayer & others, 2003). Some experienced airline pilots, while attending to data displayed on a flight simulator's console and windshield, have similarly failed to notice visible airplanes blocking their landing path (Haines, 1991).

From the immense array of visual stimuli constantly before us, we select just a few to process. Ulric Neisser (1979) and Robert Becklen and Daniel Cervone (1983) demonstrated this dramatically. They showed people a one-minute videotape in which the images of three men in black shirts tossing a basketball were superimposed over the images of three men in white shirts doing the same thing. They asked the viewers to press a key every time the black-shirted players passed the ball. Midway through the tape, a young woman carrying an umbrella sauntered across the screen. Most had focused their attention so completely on the black-shirted players that they failed to notice the woman. When the researchers replayed the tape for them, they were astonished to see her. In a recent repeat of the experiment, smart-aleck researchers Daniel Simons and Christopher Chabris (1999) sent a gorilla-suited assistant through the swirl of players (**FIGURE 6.2**). During its 5- to 9-second cameo appearance, the gorilla paused to thump its chest. Still, half the conscientious pass-counting participants exhibited **inattentional blindness.** They failed to see it.

Driven to distraction
In one driving-simulation experiment, students whose attention was diverted by cell-phone conversation (rather than merely listening to a radio) missed twice as many traffic signals as did those not talking on the phone.

In other experiments, people also exhibit a remarkable lack of awareness of happenings in their visual environment. After a brief visual interruption, a big Coke bottle may disappear from the scene, a railing may rise, clothing color may change, and, more often than not, viewers don't notice (Resnick & others, 1997; Simons, 1996; Simons & Ambinder, 2005). This form of inattentional blindness, also

FIGURE 6.2
Gorillas in our midst
When attending to one task (counting basketball passes by one of the three-person teams) about half the viewers display inattentional blindness by failing to notice a clearly visible gorilla passing through.

called *change blindness*, has occurred among people giving directions to a construction worker who, unnoticed by two-thirds of them, is replaced by another construction worker (**FIGURE 6.3**). Out of sight, out of mind. *Change deafness* can also occur. In one experiment, 40 percent of people focused on repeating a list of sometimes challenging words failed to notice a change in the person speaking (Vitevitch, 2003).

FIGURE 6.3
Change blindness
While a man (wearing glasses) provides directions to a construction worker, two experimenters rudely pass between them carrying a door. During this interruption, the original construction worker switches places with a different person wearing different colored clothing. Most people, focused on their direction giving, do not notice the switch. (From Daniel Simons.)

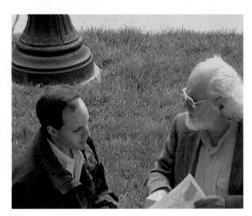

An equally astonishing form of inattentional blindness is the phenomenon of *choice blindness* discovered by a Swedish research team. Petter Johansson and his colleagues (2005) showed 120 volunteers two female faces for 2 to 5 or more seconds and asked them which they thought was more attractive. They then put the photos face down and handed them the one they had chosen, inviting them to explain their choice. On 3 of 15 occasions, the tricky researchers used sleight-of-hand to switch the photos—showing them the face they had *not* chosen. Not only did the people seldom notice the deception (on only 13 percent of the switches), they readily explained why they preferred the face they had actually rejected. "I chose her because she smiled," said one person (after picking the solemn-faced one). When asked after the experiment whether, in a "hypothetical experiment," they would notice such a switch, 84 percent insisted they would. They exhibit a blindness to the phenomenon that the researchers call (can you see the twinkle in their eyes?) *choice-blindness blindness*.

Yet some stimuli are so powerful that we experience *pop-out*, when a strikingly distinct stimulus, such as the only smiling face in **FIGURE 6.4** draws our eye. We don't choose to attend to these stimuli; they demand our attention. Meriwether Lewis couldn't have missed the attacking bear.

FIGURE 6.4
The pop-out phenomenon

>> LEARNING OUTCOMES

Selective Attention

OBJECTIVE 1 | **Describe the interplay between attention and perception.**

In a process traditionally known as sensation, our senses of vision, hearing, taste, smell, and touch detect physical energy from the environment and encode it as neural signals. Aided by knowledge and expectations, our brain perceives meaning in these signals. We selectively attend to, and process, a limited number of the data bombarding our senses and block out the others. This focused attention can result in inattentional or change blindness, and even choice blindness.

ASK YOURSELF: Can you recall a recent time when, your attention focused on one thing, you were oblivious to something else (perhaps to pain, to someone's approach, or to background music)?

Perceptual Illusions

OBJECTIVE 2 | Explain how illusions help us to understand some of the ways we organize stimuli into meaningful perceptions.

Perceptual illusions have long fascinated scientists: Why, even when we know better, do we see illusions? Illusions reveal the ways we normally organize and interpret our sensations. Illusions illuminate. Consider six such perceptual illusions:

Illusion 1 Below is an adaptation of a classic illusion created in 1889 by Franz Müller-Lyer. Does either line segment—AB or BC—appear longer? To most people the two segments appear to be the same length. Surprise! They are not. As your ruler can verify, line AB is more than one-fourth longer than line BC. Why did your eyes deceive you? (On page 251 you will discover one explanation.)

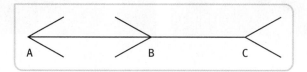

Illusion 2 Below we have two unretouched photos of the same two girls, in the same room. The camera shows you these scenes much as you would see them if you were viewing the room through a peephole. Why do the girls seem to change size when they switch places? (Page 252 will reveal why.)

Both photos: S. Schwartzenberg/The Exploratorium

Rick Friedman/Black Star

Illusion 3 Is the St. Louis Gateway Arch—the world's largest human-made illusion—taller than it is wide? Or wider than it is tall? To most it appears taller. In truth, its height and width are equal. Once again, seeing is deceiving. Why? (On page 247 we will meet this phenomenon again.)

Illusion 4 Here is another brain construction of virtual reality, described in 1935 by Hans Wallach. Do you see, below, a glowing blue worm curving through the black lines? The illusory worm is merely the short blue lines of the left figure with black lines added. Anything else you perceive is a product of your "creative genius" (Hoffman, 1998). (See the discussion of grouping principles on pages 243–244.)

© 1981, by permission of Christoph Redies and Lothar Spillmann and Pion Limited, London

Illusion 5 The real creators of virtual reality are not software developers, but the brains that developers trick into constructing virtual realities. Donald Hoffman's (1998) ripple is a flat, two-dimensional drawing. But can you perceive it as flat? Not easily. Your brain will persist in creating a ripple that is not there. And it will construe it quite differently if you turn the book upside down. The ripple illusion is in part an assumption about light sources, as you will see on page 248.

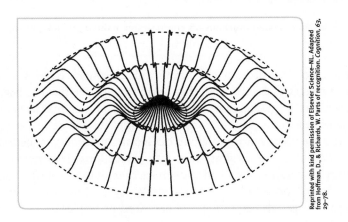

Reprinted with kind permission of Elsevier Science—NL. Adapted from Hoffman, D., & Richards, W. Parts of recognition. Cognition, 63, 29–78.

" Has your visual system gone off the deep end? It constructs from whole cloth a ripple in space and then proceeds to embellish it with mutable parts. Shall we henceforth distrust the witness of vision, knowing now its penchant to perjure?"
Donald Hoffman, *Visual Intelligence*, 1998

Illusion 6 Illusions occur with the other senses, too, as the German psychologist Wilhelm Wundt pointed out more than a century ago. Wundt was puzzled by people's hearing the steady beat of a metronome or clock as if it were a repeating rhythm of two, three, or four beats. Rather than hearing an unaccented click-click-click-click, one might, for example, hear CLICK-click CLICK-click. Although a steady beat strikes the ear, each listener unconsciously shapes an auditory pattern. What perceptual principle is at work here? (See page 253.)

Psychology's emphasis on *visual* illusions reflects vision's preeminence among our senses. When vision competes with other senses, vision usually wins—a phenomenon called **visual capture.** If the sound of a movie comes from a projector behind us, we nevertheless perceive it as coming from the screen, where we *see* the actors talking (much as we perceive a voice from a ventriloquist's dummy). While watching a roller coaster ride on a wraparound movie screen, we may brace ourselves, though our other senses tell us we're not moving. In each case, vision *captures* the other senses.

Hearing can also capture another sense. Kirsten Hötting and Brigitte Röder (2004) invited volunteers to count mechanical touches of their fingers while also hearing multiple tones. When one touch was accompanied by more than one tone, people often reported perceiving more than a single touch. There is more to touch than meets the skin.

>> LEARNING OUTCOMES

Perceptual Illusions

OBJECTIVE 2 | **Explain how illusions help us to understand some of the ways we organize stimuli into meaningful perceptions.**

Perceptual illusions fascinate psychologists because they reveal how we normally organize and interpret sensations. When visual and other sensory information conflict, our brain usually resolves the disagreement by accepting the visual data, a tendency known as *visual capture.* In contests between hearing and touch, hearing may dominate.

ASK YOURSELF: **Have you ever watched a movie where spoken words and people's facial expressions were out of sync? Which did you think needed to be adjusted—the visual image you were seeing, or the sounds you were hearing?**

Perceptual Organization

OBJECTIVE 3 | Describe Gestalt psychology's contribution to our understanding of perception.

■ **visual capture** the tendency for vision to dominate the other senses.

■ **gestalt** an organized whole. Gestalt psychologists emphasized our tendency to integrate pieces of information into meaningful wholes.

■ **figure-ground** the organization of the visual field into objects (the *figures*) that stand out from their surroundings (the *ground*).

■ **grouping** the perceptual tendency to organize stimuli into coherent groups.

To transform sensory information into meaningful perceptions, we must organize it: We must perceive objects as distinct from their surroundings, see them as having a meaningful and constant form, and discern their distance and motion. The brain's rules for constructing perceptions explain some of the puzzling illusions we've considered.

Early in the twentieth century, a group of German psychologists became intrigued with how the mind organizes sensations into perceptions. They noticed that when given a cluster of sensations, we tend to organize them into a **gestalt,** a German word meaning a "form" or a "whole." The Gestalt psychologists provided compelling demonstrations of gestalt perception and described principles by which we organize our sensations into perceptions. For example, look again at Figure 6.1 on page 237.

Note that the individual elements of the figure are really nothing but eight blue circles, each containing three converging white lines. When we view them all together, however, we see a *whole*, a form, a Necker cube.

The Gestalt psychologists were fond of saying that in perception the whole may exceed the sum of its parts. Combine sodium, a corrosive metal, with chlorine, a poisonous gas, and something very different emerges—table salt. Likewise, a unique perceived form emerges from a stimulus' components (Rock & Palmer, 1990). The police officers' perception of Amadou Diallo was very different from his neighbors'—who would not have perceived a threat in the same scene.

Our yen for assembling visual features into complete forms involves bottom-up processing, starting with entry-level sensory analysis, as well as top-down processing that uses our experiences and expectations to interpret those sensations. But the more we learn about this information-processing system, the fuzzier the distinction grows between *sensation* and *perception*. Sensation is not just bottom-up processing, and perception is not just top-down processing. Sensation and perception blend into one continuous process, progressing upward from specialized detector cells and downward from our assumptions.

As you read further about the Gestalt psychologists' organizational principles, keep in mind the fundamental truth they illustrate: Our brains do more than merely register information about the world. Perception is not just opening a shutter and letting a picture print itself on the brain. We constantly filter sensory information and infer perceptions in ways that make sense to us. Mind matters.

Form Perception

OBJECTIVE 4 | Explain the figure-ground relationship, and identify principles of perceptual grouping in form perception.

Imagine designing a video/computer system that, like your eye/brain system, can recognize faces at a glance. What abilities does it need?

Figure and Ground

To start with, the system needs to recognize the faces as distinct from their backgrounds. Likewise, our first perceptual task is to perceive any object, called the figure, as distinct from its surroundings, called the ground. Among the voices you hear at a party, the one you attend to becomes the figure; all others, part of the ground. As you read, the words are the figure; the white paper, the ground. In **FIGURE 6.5**, the **figure-ground** relationship continually reverses—but always we organize the stimulus into a figure seen against a ground. Such reversible figure-and-ground illustrations demonstrate again that the same stimulus can trigger more than one perception.

FIGURE 6.5
Reversible figure and ground

Grouping

Having discriminated figure from ground, we (and our video/computer system) now have to organize the figure into a meaningful form. Some basic features of a scene—such as color, movement, and light/dark contrast—we process instantly and automatically (Treisman, 1987). To bring order and form to these basic sensations, our minds follow certain rules for **grouping** stimuli together (**FIGURE 6.6**, page 244). These rules, identified by the Gestalt psychologists and applied even by infants, illustrate the idea that the perceived whole differs from the sum of its parts (Quinn & others, 2002; Rock & Palmer, 1990):

FIGURE 6.6
Organizing stimuli into groups
We could perceive the stimuli shown here in many ways, yet people everywhere see them similarly. The Gestalt psychologists believed this shows that the brain follows rules to order sensory information into wholes.

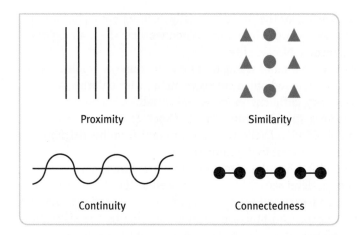

Proximity We group nearby figures together. We see not six separate lines, but three sets of two lines.

Similarity We group together figures that are similar to each other. We see the triangles and circles as vertical columns of similar shapes, not as horizontal rows of dissimilar shapes.

Continuity We perceive smooth, continuous patterns rather than discontinuous ones. This pattern could be a series of alternating semicircles, but we perceive it as two continuous lines—one wavy, one straight.

Connectedness Because they are uniform and linked, we perceive the two dots and the line between them as a single unit.

Enrico Feroelt

FIGURE 6.7
Grouping principles
What's the secret to this impossible doghouse? You probably perceive this doghouse as a gestalt—a whole (though impossible) structure. Actually, your brain imposes this sense of wholeness on the picture. As the photo on page 253 shows, Gestalt grouping principles such as closure and continuity are at work here.

Photo by Walter Wick. Reprinted from GAMES Magazine. © 1983 PCS Games Limited Partnership.

Closure We fill in gaps to create a complete, whole object. Thus we assume that the circles (above) are complete but partially blocked by the (illusory) triangle. Add nothing more than little line segments that close off the circles and now your brain stops constructing a triangle.

Usually, these grouping principles help us construct reality. Sometimes, however, they lead us astray, as with our perception of the neon worm in Illusion 4, page 241, or when we look at the doghouse in **FIGURE 6.7**.

Depth Perception

OBJECTIVE **5** | Explain the importance of depth perception, and discuss the contribution of visual cliff research to our understanding of this ability.

Two-dimensional images fall on our retinas, yet we somehow organize three-dimensional perceptions. Seeing objects in three dimensions, called **depth perception,** enables us to estimate their distance from us. At a glance, we estimate the distance of an oncoming car or the height of a house. This ability is partly innate. Eleanor Gibson and Richard Walk (1960) discovered this using a miniature cliff with a drop-off covered by sturdy glass. Gibson's inspiration for these experiments occurred while she was picnicking on the rim of the Grand Canyon. She wondered: Would a toddler peering over the rim perceive the dangerous drop-off and draw back?

Back in their Cornell University laboratory, Gibson and Walk placed 6- to 14-month-old infants on the edge of a safe canyon—a **visual cliff** (FIGURE 6.8). Their mothers then coaxed them to crawl out onto the glass. Most refused to do so, indicating that they could perceive depth. Perhaps by crawling age the infants had *learned* to perceive depth. Yet newborn animals with virtually no visual experience—including young kittens, a day-old goat, and newly hatched chicks—respond similarly.

■ **depth perception** the ability to see objects in three dimensions although the images that strike the retina are two-dimensional; allows us to judge distance.

■ **visual cliff** a laboratory device for testing depth perception in infants and young animals.

■ **binocular cues** depth cues, such as retinal disparity and convergence, that depend on the use of two eyes.

FIGURE 6.8
Visual cliff

Eleanor Gibson and Richard Walk devised this miniature cliff with a glass-covered drop-off to determine whether crawling infants and newborn animals can perceive depth. Even when coaxed, infants are reluctant to venture onto the glass over the cliff.

Each species, by the time it is mobile, has the perceptual abilities it needs. What is more, by 3 months of age, infants are using Gestalt perception principles, by looking more at novel groupings of objects (Quinn & others, 2002). But if biological maturation predisposes our wariness of heights, experience amplifies it. Infants' wariness increases with their experiences of crawling, no matter when they begin to crawl.

How do we do it? How do we transform two differing two-dimensional retinal images into a single three-dimensional perception? The process begins with depth cues, some that depend on the use of two eyes, and others that are available to each eye separately.

Binocular Cues

OBJECTIVE **6** | Describe two binocular cues for perceiving depth, and explain how they help the brain to compute distance.

Try this: With both eyes open, hold two pens or pencils in front of you and touch their tips together. Now do so with one eye closed. With one eye the task becomes noticeably more difficult, demonstrating the importance of **binocular cues** in judging the distance of nearby objects. Two eyes are better than one.

FIGURE 6.9
The floating finger sausage
Hold your two index fingers about 5 inches in front of your eyes, with their tips half an inch apart. Now look beyond them and note the weird result. Move your fingers out farther and the retinal disparity—and the finger sausage—will shrink.

Because our eyes are about 2½ inches apart, our retinas receive slightly different images of the world. When the brain compares these two images, the difference between them—their **retinal disparity**—provides an important cue to the relative distance of different objects. When you hold your finger directly in front of your nose, your retinas receive quite different views. (You can see this if you close one eye and then the other, or create a finger sausage as in **FIGURE 6.9**.) At a greater distance—say, when you hold your finger at arm's length—the disparity is smaller.

The creators of three-dimensional (3-D) movies simulate or exaggerate retinal disparity by photographing a scene with two cameras placed a few inches apart (a feature we might want to build into our seeing computer). When we view the movie through spectacles that allow the left eye to see only the image from the left camera and the right eye only the image from the right camera, the 3-D effect mimics normal retinal disparity. Similarly, twin cameras in airplanes can take photos of terrain for integration into 3-D maps.

Another binocular cue to distance is **convergence,** a neuromuscular cue caused by the eyes' greater inward turn when they view a near object. The brain notes the angle of convergence, then computes whether you are focusing on this printed page or on something else across the room. The greater the inward strain, the closer the object.

Monocular Cues

OBJECTIVE **7** | Explain how monocular cues differ from binocular cues, and describe several monocular cues for perceiving depth.

How do we judge whether a person is 10 or 100 meters away? In both cases, the retinal disparity and convergence while looking straight ahead are slight. At such distances we depend on **monocular cues** (available to each eye separately), such as the following:

Relative size If we assume that two objects are similar in size, we perceive the one that casts the smaller retinal image as farther away. To a driver, distant pedestrians appear smaller, which also means that small-looking pedestrians (children) may sometimes be misperceived as more distant than they are (Stewart, 2000).

Interposition If one object partially blocks our view of another, we perceive it as closer. The painting at the top of page 247 purposely confuses figure and ground by interposition.

Relative size
(providing *most* people a cue to distance)

Rene Magritte, *The Blank Signature*, oil on canvas, National Gallery of Art, Washington. Collection of Mr. and Mrs. Paul Mellon. Photo by Richard Carafelli.

Interposition

Relative clarity Because light from distant objects passes through more atmosphere, we perceive hazy objects as farther away than sharp, clear objects. In fog or snow, the car in front of you may therefore seem farther away than it is.

Texture gradient A gradual change from a coarse, distinct texture to a fine, indistinct texture signals increasing distance. Objects far away appear smaller and more densely packed.

Relative height We perceive objects higher in our field of vision as farther away. Because we perceive the lower part of a figure-ground illustration as closer, we perceive it as figure (Vecera & others, 2002). Invert the illustration below (right) and the black becomes ground, like a night sky.

Relative height may contribute to the illusion that vertical dimensions are longer than identical horizontal dimensions (as we saw in Illusion 3, page 241, the St. Louis Gateway Arch). No wonder people pour less juice when given a tall, thin glass rather than a short, wide glass (Wansink & van Ittersum, 2003). A tall glass looks as though it has more liquid than it actually does. Is the vertical line in the diagram below (left) longer, shorter, or equal in length to the horizontal line? Measure and see.

© Erich Lessing/Art Resource, NY

Texture gradient
Here, artist Victor Vaserly used texture gradient to depict depth.

Relative height

Image courtesy Shaun P. Vecera, Ph.D., adapted from stimuli that appeared in Vecera et al., 2002

Figure this
Thanks to relative height, lower objects seem closer—and thus are usually perceived as figure.

Relative motion

→ Direction of passenger's motion

Fixation point

Relative motion (motion parallax) As we move, objects that are actually stable may appear to move. If while riding on a bus you fix your gaze on some object—say, a house—the objects closer than the house (the fixation point) appear to move backward. The nearer the object is to you, the faster it seems to move.

Objects beyond the fixation point appear to move with you, and the farther away those objects are, the faster they will move. Your brain uses these speed and direction clues to compute the objects' relative distances.

Linear perspective Parallel lines, such as railroad tracks, appear to converge with distance. The more the lines converge, the greater their perceived distance. Linear perspective can contribute to rail-crossing accidents by leading people to overestimate a train's distance (Leibowitz, 1985).

Light and shadow Nearby objects reflect more light to our eyes. Given two identical objects, the dimmer one seems farther away. This illusion can also contribute to accidents, as when a fog-shrouded vehicle, or one with only its parking lights on, seems farther away than it is. Shading, too, produces a sense of depth consistent with the assumed light source. (Recall the ripples of Illusion 5, on page 241.) Invert the illustration below and the hollow becomes a hill, because our brain follows a simple rule that works well on Planet Earth: *Assume that light comes from above.*

THE FREIGHT ELEVATOR FOR THE MAN WHO HAS EVERYTHING

Linear perspective

Light and shadow

FIGURE 6.10
Perspective techniques
By the time that "Bristol, Broad Quay" was painted (c. 1730, Anonymous), techniques for depicting three dimensions on a flat surface were well established. Note the effective use of distance cues such as texture gradient, interposition, linear perspective, and relative size and height.

Artists use monocular cues to convey depth on a flat canvas (**FIGURE 6.10**). To you and me, the drawing in **FIGURE 6.11** clearly indicates that the elephant is far away, rather than about to be speared—which is how it was perceived a half-century ago by many South African Bantus who had minimal experience with photos and drawings (Deregowski, 1972; Hudson, 1960).

FIGURE 6.11
What's for dinner?
Monocular depth cues such as relative size and distance indicate to people familiar with artistic and photographic use of such cues that it's *not* the elephant. (From Deregowski, 1972.)

Motion Perception

OBJECTIVE **8** | State the basic assumption we make in our perceptions of motion, and explain how these perceptions can be deceiving.

Imagine that you could perceive the world as having color, form, and depth but that you could not see motion. Not only would you be unable to bike or drive, you might even have trouble writing, eating, and walking.

Fortunately, you can perceive motion (sometimes, as in the drawing of the pendulum on page 236, even when there is none). Normally your brain computes motion based partly on its assumption that shrinking objects are retreating (not getting smaller) and enlarging objects are approaching. But you are imperfect at motion perception. Large objects, such as trains, appear to move more slowly than smaller objects, such as cars moving at the same speed. (Perhaps at an airport you've noticed that jumbo jets seem to land more slowly than little jets going the same speed or slower.)

To catch a fly ball, softball or cricket players (unlike drivers) *want* to achieve a collision—with the ball that's flying their way. To accomplish that, they follow a simple rule: By keeping the ball at a constant angle of gaze, a fielder will run through the point of its return as it arrives (McBeath & others, 1995). A dog catching a Frisbee does the same (Shaffer & others, 2004).

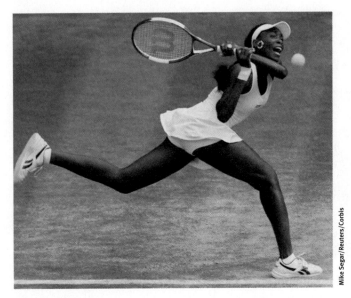

As film animation artists know well, the brain will also perceive continuous movement in a rapid series of slightly varying images (a phenomenon called *stroboscopic movement*). A motion picture creates this illusion by flashing 24 still pictures each second. The motion we see is not in the film, which merely presents a superfast slide show. The motion is constructed in our heads.

Marquees and holiday lights create another illusion of movement using the **phi phenomenon.** When two adjacent stationary lights blink on and off in quick succession, we perceive a single light moving back and forth between them. Lighted signs exploit the phi phenomenon with a succession of lights that creates the impression of, say, a moving arrow. This reinforces a fundamental lesson: Perception is not merely projecting the world onto our brain. Rather, sensations are disassembled into information bits that the brain then reassembles into its own functional model of the external world. *Our brain constructs our perceptions.*

Computing motion
Venus Williams' brain automatically uses available cues to compute motion.

■ **phi phenomenon** an illusion of movement created when two or more adjacent lights blink on and off in quick succession.

■ **perceptual constancy** perceiving objects as unchanging (having consistent lightness, color, shape, and size) even as illumination and retinal images change.

Perceptual Constancy

OBJECTIVE **9** | Explain the importance of perceptual constancy.

So far, we have noted that our video/computer system must first perceive objects as we do—as having a distinct form, location, and perhaps motion. Its next task is even more challenging: to recognize the object without being deceived by changes in its shape, size, brightness, or color. **Perceptual constancy** enables us to perceive an object as unchanging despite a changing stimulus. Thanks to this top-down process, we can identify things regardless of the angle, distance, and illumination by which we view them. You glance at someone ahead of you on the sidewalk and instantly recognize a classmate. In less time than it takes to draw a breath, information reaching your eyes has been sent to your brain, where work teams comprising millions of neurons have extracted the essential features, compared them with stored images, and identified the person. Replicating this human perceptual feat, which has intrigued perception researchers for decades, provides a monumental challenge for our perceiving computer.

FIGURE 6.12
Perceiving shape
Do the tops of these tables have different dimensions? They appear to. But—believe it or not—they are identical. (Measure and see.) With both tables we adjust our perceptions relative to our viewing angle.

Shape and Size Constancies

OBJECTIVE **10** | Describe the shape and size constancies, and explain how our expectations about perceived size and distance contribute to some visual illusions.

Sometimes an object whose actual shape cannot change *seems* to change shape with the angle of our view (**FIGURE 6.12**). More often, thanks to *shape constancy,* we perceive the form of familiar objects as constant even while our retinal images of them change. When a door opens, it casts a changing shape on our retinas, yet we still manage to perceive the door as having a constant doorlike shape (**FIGURE 6.13**).

Thanks to *size constancy* we perceive objects as having a constant size, even while our distance from them varies. Size constancy leads us to perceive a car as large enough to carry people, even when we see its tiny image from two blocks away. This illustrates the

FIGURE 6.13
Shape constancy
A door casts an increasingly trapezoidal image on our retinas as it opens, yet we still perceive it as rectangular.

close connection between an object's perceived *distance* and perceived *size*. Perceiving an object's distance gives us cues to its size. Likewise, knowing its general size—that the object is, say, a car—provides us with cues to its distance.

Size-Distance Relationship It is a marvel how effortlessly size perception occurs. Given an object's perceived distance and the size of its image on our retinas, we instantly and unconsciously infer the object's size. Although the monsters in **FIGURE 6.14a** cast the same retinal images, the linear perspective tells our brain that the monster in pursuit is farther away. We therefore perceive it as larger.

This interplay between perceived size and perceived distance helps explain several well-known illusions. For example, can you imagine why the Moon looks up to 50 percent larger near the horizon than when high in the sky? For at least 22 centuries, scholars have wondered and have argued about reasons for the *Moon illusion* (Hershenson, 1989). One reason is that cues to objects' distances at the horizon make the Moon behind them seem farther away than the Moon high in the night sky (Kaufman & Kaufman, 2000). Thus, the horizon Moon—like the distant monster in Figure 6.14a and the distant bar in the *Ponzo illusion* in Figure 6.14b—seems larger. Take away these distance cues—by looking at the horizon Moon (or each monster or each bar) through a paper tube—and the object immediately shrinks.

The size-distance relationship helps us understand two illusions demonstrated earlier. Illusion 1, the Müller-Lyer illusion concerning the lengths of straight lines between arrow tips, has been the subject of more than 1250 scientific publications, yet psychologists still debate its explanation. One is that our experience with the corners of rooms or buildings prompts us to interpret the vertical line on the ticket booth in **FIGURE 6.15** as closer to us and therefore shorter, and the same-length vertical line by the door as farther away and therefore longer. Thus, what appears as an illusion when isolated in a line drawing actually enables correct depth perception in our three-dimensional world.

From Shepard, 1990.

Alan Choisnet/The Image Bank

(a)   (b)

FIGURE 6.14
The interplay between perceived size and distance

(a) The monocular cues for distance (such as linear perspective and relative height) make the pursuing monster look larger than the pursued. It isn't.
(b) This visual trick, called the Ponzo illusion, is based on the same principle as the fleeing monsters. The two red bars cast identical-sized images on our retinas. But experience tells us that a more distant object can create the same-sized image as a nearer one only if it is actually larger. As a result, we perceive the bar that seems farther away as larger.

FIGURE 6.15
The Müller-Lyer illusion

Richard L. Gregory (1968) suggested that the corners in our rectangularly carpentered world teach us to interpret "outward" or "inward" pointing arrowheads at the ends of a line as a cue to the line's distance from us and so to its length. The red line defined by the corner at the ticket booth looks shorter than the red line defined by the room corner. But if you measure them, you will see that both are the same length.

Culture and perception

Rural Africans who did not live in an environment of constructed rectangular buildings—such as people in South African Zulu round houses shown here—were less vulnerable to the Müller-Lyer illusion.

Ed Kashi / Corbis

Experience supports this theory. People have been more susceptible to the Müller-Lyer illusion if, unlike some mid–twentieth-century rural Africans, they have lived in a carpentered world of rectangular shapes (Segall & others, 1990). The phenomenon reflects cultural experience, not race. Africans who live in cities are more vulnerable to the illusion than are their rural counterparts in uncarpentered environments. Our experience in rectangular contexts helps us construct our perceptions, top-down.

Size-distance relationships also explain Illusion 2, page 240, the shrinking and growing girls. As **FIGURE 6.16** reveals, the room is distorted. Viewed with one eye through a peephole, its trapezoidal walls produce the same images as those of a normal rectangular room viewed with both eyes. Presented with the camera's one-eyed view, the brain makes the reasonable assumption that the room *is* normal and that each of the girls is therefore the same distance from us. And given the different sizes of the images on the retina, our brain ends up calculating that the girls are very different in size.

Our occasional misperceptions reveal the workings of our normally effective perceptual processes. The perceived relationship between distance and size is generally valid, but under special circumstances it can lead us astray—as when helping to create the Moon illusion, the Müller-Lyer illusion, and the distorted-room illusion.

FIGURE 6.16

The illusion of the shrinking and growing girls

This distorted room, designed by Adelbert Ames, appears to have a normal rectangular shape when viewed through a peephole with one eye. The girl in the near corner appears disproportionately large because we judge her size based on the false assumption that she is the same distance away as the girl in the far corner.

S. Schwartzenberg /The Exploratorium

Lightness Constancy

OBJECTIVE 11 | Discuss lightness constancy and its similarity to color constancy.

White paper reflects 90 percent of the light falling on it; black paper, only 10 percent. In sunlight a black paper may reflect 100 times more light than does a white paper viewed indoors, but it still looks black (McBurney & Collings, 1984). This il-lustrates *lightness constancy* (also called *brightness constancy*); we per-ceive an object as having a constant lightness even while its illumination varies. Perceived lightness de-pends on *relative luminance*—the amount of light an object reflects relative to its sur-roundings. If you view sunlit black paper through a narrow tube so nothing else is vis-ible, it may look gray, because in bright sun-shine it reflects a fair amount of light. View it without the tube and it is again black, be-cause it reflects much less light than the ob-

Courtesy Edward Adelson

jects around it. The phenomenon is similar to that of *color constancy* (pages 213–214). As light changes, a red apple in a fruit bowl retains its redness, because our brain com-putes the light reflected by any object relative to its surrounding objects.

Perceived lightness stays roughly constant, given an unchanging context. But what happens when the surrounding context changes? As **FIGURE 6.17** shows, the visual system computes brightness and color relative to surrounding objects. Thus, perceived lightness changes with context.

Form perception, depth perception, motion perception, and perceptual constancy illuminate how we organize our visual experiences. Perceptual organization applies to other senses, too. It explains why we group a clock's steady clicking into patterns (Il-lusion 6, page 242). Listening to an unfamiliar language, we have trouble hearing where one word stops and the next one begins. Listening to our own language, we au-tomatically hear distinct words. This, too, is a form of perceptual organization. But it is more, for we even organize a string of letters—THEDOGATEMEAT—into words that make an intelligible phrase, more likely "The dog ate meat" than "The do gate me at" (McBurney & Collings, 1984). This process involves not only organization but inter-pretation—discerning meaning in what we perceive.

FIGURE 6.17
Brightness contrast
Squares A and B are identical in color, believe it or not. (If you don't believe me, photocopy the illustration, cut out the squares, and compare.) But we perceive B as lighter.

Photo by Walter Wick. Reprinted from GAMES Magazine. © 1983 PCS Games Limited Partnership.

The solution
Another view of the impossible doghouse in Figure 6.7 (page 244) reveals the secrets of this illusion. From the photo angle in Figure 6.7, the grouping principle of closure leads us to perceive the boards as continuous.

>> Learning Outcomes

Perceptual Organization

OBJECTIVE 3 | Describe Gestalt psychology's contribution to our understanding of perception.
Gestalt psychologists searched for rules by which the brain organizes fragments of sensory data into gestalts (from the German word for "whole"), or meaningful forms. In pointing out that the whole is more than the sum of its parts, these researchers showed that we constantly filter sensory information and infer perceptions in ways that make sense to us. This truth remains valid, even though contemporary research demonstrates that sensation and perception are parts of a continuous information pro-cessing system, involving both bottom-up and top-down processing.

OBJECTIVE 4 | Explain the figure-ground relationship, and identify principles of perceptual grouping in form perception.
To recognize an object, we must first perceive it (see it as a figure) as distinct from its surroundings (the ground). We bring order and form to stimuli by organizing them into meaningful groups, following the rules of proximity, similar-ity, continuity, connectedness, and closure.

OBJECTIVE 5 | Explain the importance of depth perception, and dis-cuss the contribution of visual cliff research to our understanding of this ability.
Depth perception is our ability to see objects in three di-mensions, even though our retinas receive two-dimensional images. Without depth perception, we would be unable to judge

distance, height, or depth. The visual cliff research with 6- to 14-month-olds demonstrated that depth perception is in part innate. Many species perceive the world in three dimensions at, or very soon after, birth.

OBJECTIVE 6 | **Describe two binocular cues for perceiving depth, and explain how they help the brain to compute distance.**
Binocular cues are depth cues that rely on information from both eyes. In the retinal disparity cue, the brain computes the relative distance of an object by comparing the slightly different images the object casts on our two retinas. The greater the difference, the closer the object must be. In the convergence cue, the brain calculates the degree of neuromuscular strain when our two eyes turn inward to look at a nearby object. The greater the strain (or the angle of convergence), the closer the object.

OBJECTIVE 7 | **Explain how monocular cues differ from binocular cues, and describe several monocular cues for perceiving depth.**
Monocular cues let us judge depth using information transmitted by only one eye; binocular cues require information from both eyes. Monocular cues include

- *relative size* (smaller is more distant).
- *interposition* (an object that blocks another is closer than the blocked object).
- *relative clarity* (a hazy object is farther away than an object seen clearly).
- *texture gradient* (when texture changes, coarse distinct objects are close and fine indistinct objects are distant).
- *relative height* (objects higher in our field of vision are farther away).
- *relative motion* or *motion parallax* (when you are moving, objects closer than a fixation point appear to move backward—the nearer the object, the faster it moves; objects beyond the fixation point appear to move with you).
- *linear perspective* (the more two parallel lines converge, the farther away they are).
- *light and shadow* (nearby objects reflect more light than faraway objects).

OBJECTIVE 8 | **State the basic assumption we make in our perceptions of motion, and explain how these perceptions can be deceiving.**
As objects move across or toward our retinas, our basic assumption is that shrinking objects are retreating, and enlarging objects are approaching. But our perception of motion is not always trustworthy. We may miscalculate the speed of movement of large objects or objects picked up by our peripheral vision. A quick succession of images on the retina can create an illusion of movement, as in stroboscopic movement (triggered by a rapid series of slightly varying images) or the phi phenomenon (triggered by the rapid on-off blinking of two adjacent stationary lights).

OBJECTIVE 9 | **Explain the importance of perceptual constancy.**
Perceptual constancy is necessary in vision to recognize an object, regardless of its changing angle, distance, or illumination. Because of this ability, we perceive objects as having unchanging characteristics despite the changing images they cast on our retinas.

OBJECTIVE 10 | **Describe the shape and size constancies, and explain how our expectations about perceived size and distance contribute to some visual illusions.**
Shape constancy is our ability to perceive familiar objects (such as an opening door) as unchanging in shape, and *size constancy* is perceiving objects as unchanging in size, despite the changing images they cast on our retinas. There is a close relationship between perceived size and perceived distance. Knowing an object's size gives us clues to its distance; knowing its distance gives clues about its size. This interplay sometimes misleads us, as when we misread monocular distance cues and reach the wrong conclusions, as in the Moon, Ponzo, and Müller-Lyer illusions.

OBJECTIVE 11 | **Discuss lightness constancy and its similarity to color constancy.**
Lightness (or *brightness*) *constancy* is our ability to perceive an object as having a constant lightness even when its illumination—the light cast upon it—changes. *Color constancy* enables us to perceive the color of an object as unchanging even when its illumination changes. In both cases, the brain perceives the quality (lightness or color) relative to surrounding objects.

ASK YOURSELF: **Try drawing a realistic depiction of the scene from your window. How many monocular cues will you use in your drawing?**

Perceptual Interpretation

Philosophers have debated whether our perceptual ability should be credited to our nature or our nurture. To what extent do we *learn* to perceive? German philosopher Immanuel Kant (1724-1804) maintained that knowledge comes from our *inborn* ways of organizing sensory experiences. Indeed, we come equipped to process sensory information. But British philosopher John Locke (1632-1704) argued that through our experiences we also *learn* to perceive the world. Indeed, we learn to link an object's distance with its size. So, just how important is experience? How radically does it shape our perceptual interpretations?

Sensory Deprivation and Restored Vision

OBJECTIVE 12 | Describe the contribution of restored-vision and sensory deprivation research in our understanding of the nature-nurture interplay in our perceptions.

Writing to John Locke, William Molyneux wondered whether "a man *born* blind, and now adult, taught by his *touch* to distinguish between a cube and a sphere" could, if made to see, visually distinguish the two. Locke's answer was no, because the man would never have *learned* to see the difference.

Molyneux' hypothetical case has since been put to the test with a few dozen adults who, though blind from birth, have gained sight (Gregory, 1978; von Senden, 1932). Most had been born with cataracts—clouded lenses that allowed them to see only diffused light, rather as you or I might see a diffuse fog through a Ping-Pong ball sliced in half. When their cataracts were surgically removed, the patients could distinguish figure from ground and could sense colors—suggesting that these aspects of perception are innate. But much as Locke supposed, the formerly blind patients often could not recognize by sight objects that were familiar by touch.

You and I perceive and recognize individual faces as a whole. Show us the same top half of a face paired with two different bottom halves (as in **FIGURE 6.18**), and the identical top halves will seem different. People deprived of visual experience during infancy surpass the rest of us at recognizing that the top halves are the same, because they didn't learn to process faces as a whole (Le Grand & others, 2004). For example, one 43-year-old man, whose sight was recently restored after 40 years of blindness, could associate people with distinct features ("Mary's the one with red hair") but could not instantly recognize a face. He also lacked perceptual constancy: As people walk away from him they seem to be shrinking in size (Bower, 2003). Vision, such cases make clear, is partly an acquired sense.

Seeking to gain more control than is provided by clinical cases, researchers have conducted Molyneux' imaginary experiment with infant kittens and monkeys. In one experiment, they outfitted them with goggles through which the animals could see only diffuse, unpatterned light (Wiesel, 1982). After infancy, when their goggles were removed, these animals exhibited perceptual limitations much like those of humans born with cataracts. They could distinguish color and brightness, but not the form of a circle

> "Let us then suppose the mind to be, as we say, white paper void of all characters, without any ideas: How comes it to be furnished? . . . To this I answer, in one word, from EXPERIENCE."
>
> John Locke, *An Essay Concerning Human Understanding*, 1690

Courtesy of Richard LeGrand

FIGURE 6.18
Perceiving composite faces
To most people, the top halves of these two faces, created by Richard Le Grand and his colleagues (2004), look different. Actually, they are the same, though paired with two different lower face halves. People deprived of visual experience early in life have more difficulty perceiving whole faces, which ironically enables their superiority at recognizing that the top halves of these faces are identical.

Learning to see

At age 3, Mike May lost his vision in an explosion. On March 7, 2000, after a new cornea restored vision to his right eye, he got his first look at his wife and children. Alas, although signals were reaching his long dormant visual cortex, it lacked the experience to interpret them. Faces, apart from features such as hair, were not recognizable. Expressions eluded him. Yet he can see an object in motion and is gradually learning to navigate his world and to marvel at such things as dust floating in sunlight (Abrams, 2002).

from that of a square. Their eyes had not degenerated; their retinas still relayed signals to their visual cortex. But lacking stimulation, the cortical cells had not developed normal connections. Thus, the animals remained functionally blind to shape.

In both humans and animals, a similar period of sensory restriction does no permanent harm if it occurs later in life. Cover the eye of an animal for several months during adulthood, and its vision will be unaffected after the eye patch is removed. Remove cataracts that develop after early childhood, and a human, too, will enjoy normal vision. The effects of visual experiences during infancy in cats, monkeys, and humans suggest there is a *critical period* (page 156) for normal sensory and perceptual development. Experience guides, sustains, and maintains the brain's neural organization.

Human infants born today with an opaque lens (cataract) will typically have corrective surgery within a few months. The brain network responsible for the corrected eye then rapidly develops, enabling improved visual acuity with as little as one hour's visual experience (Maurer & others, 1999). Congenitally deaf kittens and infants given cochlear implants exhibit a similar "awakening" of the pertinent brain area (Klinke & others, 1999; Sirenteanu, 1999). Nurture sculpts what nature has endowed.

Experiments on perceptual limitations and advantages produced by early sensory deprivation provide a partial answer to our question about experience, which we also debated in Chapters 3 and 4: Does the effect of early experience last a lifetime? For some aspects of visual perception, the answer is clearly yes: "Use it *soon* or lose it." We retain the imprint of early visual experiences far into the future.

Perceptual Adaptation

OBJECTIVE 13 | Explain how the research on distorting goggles increases our understanding of the adaptability of perception.

Given a new pair of glasses, we may feel slightly disoriented, even dizzy. Within a day or two, we adjust. Our **perceptual adaptation** to changed visual input makes the world seem normal again. But imagine a far more dramatic new pair of glasses—one that shifts the apparent location of objects 40 degrees to the left. When you first put them on and toss a ball to a friend, it sails off to the left. Walking forward to shake hands with the person, you veer to the left.

Perceptual adaptation

"Oops, missed," thinks researcher Hubert Dolezal as he views the world through inverting goggles. Yet, believe it or not, kittens, monkeys, and humans can adapt to an inverted world.

Could you adapt to this distorted world? Chicks cannot. When fitted with such lenses, they continue to peck where food grains *seem* to be (Hess, 1956; Rossi, 1968). But we humans adapt to distorting lenses quickly. Within a few minutes your throws would again be accurate, your stride on target. Remove the lenses and you would experience an aftereffect: At first your throws would err in the *opposite* direction, sailing off to the right; but again, within minutes you would readapt.

Indeed, given an even more radical pair of glasses—one that literally turns the world upside down—you could still adapt. Psychologist George Stratton (1896) experienced this when he invented, and for eight days wore, optical headgear that flipped left to right *and* up to down, making him the first person to experience a right-side-up retinal image while standing upright. The ground was up, the sky was down.

At first, Stratton felt disoriented. When he wanted to walk, he found himself searching for his feet, which were now "up." Eating was nearly impossible. He became nauseated and depressed. But Stratton persisted, and by the eighth day he could comfortably reach for something in the right direction and walk without bumping into things. When Stratton finally removed the headgear, he readapted quickly.

Later experiments replicated Stratton's experience (Dolezal, 1982; Kohler, 1962). After a period of adjustment, people wearing the optical gear have even been able to ride a motorcycle, ski the Alps, and fly an airplane. Did all these people adjust by perceptually converting their strange worlds to "normal" views? No. Actually, the world around them still seemed above their heads or on the wrong side of them. But by actively moving about in these topsy-turvy worlds, they adapted to the context and learned to coordinate their movements.

Perceptual Set

OBJECTIVE 14 | Define *perceptual set*, and explain how it influences what we do or do not perceive.

As everyone knows, to see is to believe. As we also know, but less fully appreciate, to believe is to see. Our experiences, assumptions, and expectations may give us a **perceptual set,** or mental predisposition, that greatly influences what we perceive (top-down). People perceive an adult-child pair as looking more alike when told they are parent and child (Bressan & Dal Martello, 2002). And consider: Is the image in the center picture of **FIGURE 6.19** a man playing a saxophone or a woman's face? What we see in such a drawing can be influenced by first looking at either of the two unambiguous versions (Boring, 1930).

From Shepard, 1990.

Once we have formed a wrong idea about reality, we have more difficulty seeing the truth. Even scientists, striving for objectivity, perceive reality through the lenses of their theories. When first viewing the "canals" on Mars through telescopes, some people perceived them as the product of intelligent life. They were—but the intelligence was on the viewing end of the telescope.

Everyday examples of perceptual set abound. In 1972, a British newspaper published genuine, unretouched photographs of a "monster" in Scotland's Loch Ness—"the most amazing pictures ever taken," stated the paper. If this information creates in you the same perceptual set it did in most of the paper's readers, you, too, will see the monster in the photo reproduced in **FIGURE 6.20a** (page 258). But when Steuart Campbell (1986) approached the photos with a different perceptual set, he saw a curved tree trunk—very likely the same tree trunk others had seen in the water the day the photo was shot. Moreover, with this different perceptual set, you may now notice that the object is floating motionless, without any rippling water or wake around it—hardly what we would expect of a lively monster. Apparently aided by perceptual set, thousands of others have marveled at a face on the Moon, Mother Teresa on a cinnamon bun, and Jesus on a pancake.

Perceptual set can also influence what we hear. Consider the kindly airline pilot who, on a takeoff run, looked over at his depressed co-pilot and said, "Cheer up." The co-pilot heard the usual "Gear up" and promptly raised the wheels—before they left

■ **perceptual adaptation** in vision, the ability to adjust to an artificially displaced or even inverted visual field.

■ **perceptual set** a mental predisposition to perceive one thing and not another.

FIGURE 6.19
Perceptual set
What do you see in the center picture: a male saxophonist or a woman's face? Glancing first at one of the two unambiguous versions of the picture is likely to influence your interpretation.

" The temptation to form premature theories upon insufficient data is the bane of our profession."
Sherlock Holmes, in Arthur Conan Doyle's *The Valley of Fear*, 1914

When shown the phrase:
Mary had a
a little lamb
many people perceive what they expect, and miss the repeated word. Did you?

FIGURE 6.20
Believing is seeing
What do you perceive in these photos? (a) Is this Nessie, the Loch Ness monster, or a log? (b) Are these flying saucers or clouds? We often perceive what we expect to see.

(a)

(b)

the ground (Reason & Mycielska, 1982). Clearly, much of what we perceive comes not just from the world "out there" but also from what's behind our eyes and between our ears.

What determines our perceptual set? Through experience we form concepts, or *schemas*, that organize and interpret unfamiliar information. Our preexisting schemas for male saxophonists and women's faces, for monsters and tree trunks, for airplane lights and UFOs all influence how we interpret ambiguous sensations with top-down processing. Confronted with an ambiguous moving object in the sky, different people may therefore apply different schemas: "It's a bird." "It's a plane." "It's Superman!"

Children's drawings give us a way to glimpse their developing perceptual schemas. A preschooler can draw circles and angled lines but cannot combine them to create an elaborate human figure. The child's difficulty is not clumsiness. A right-handed adult asked to draw with the left hand will create an awkward drawing, but it will be unlike the child's drawing in **FIGURE 6.21**. Part of the difference lies in the challenge for children to represent visually what they see. The main difference, however, lies in the child's simplified schema for essential human characteristics. To 3- and 4-year-olds, a face is a more important human feature than a body. From ages 3 to 8, children's schemas for bodies become more elaborate, and so do their drawings.

Our schemas for faces prime us to see facial patterns even in random configurations, such as the lunar landscape. Kieran Lee, Graham Byatt, and Gillian Rhodes (2000) demonstrated how we recognize people by facial features that cartoonists can caricature.

FIGURE 6.21
Schemas
Children's drawings reflect their schemas of reality, as well as their abilities to represent what they see. This drawing by 4-year-old Anna illustrates that the face has far greater importance than the body in young children's schemas of essential human characteristics.

Anticaricature   Actual   Caricature

FIGURE 6.22
Recognizing faces
When briefly flashed, a caricature of Arnold Schwarzenegger was more accurately recognized than Schwarzenegger himself. Ditto for other familiar male faces.

For but a fraction of a second they showed University of Western Australia students three versions of familiar faces—the actual face, a computer-created caricature that accentuated the differences between this face and the average face, and an "anticaricature" that muted the distinctive features. As **FIGURE 6.22** shows, the students more accurately recognized the caricatured faces than the actual ones. A caricatured Arnold Schwarzenegger is more recognizably Schwarzenegger than Schwarzenegger himself!

FIGURE 6.23
Aye for an eye
Christopher Tyler (1998) discovered that artists, when trying to capture a sense of the person, consciously or unconsciously place one eye on the painting's centerline.

Peter Thompson (1980) at the University of York discovered that our face recognition is especially attuned to the expressive eyes and mouth. Portrait artists seem to understand this. Two-thirds of portraits sampled from the last five centuries have an eye at or within 5 percent of the painting's exact centerline (**FIGURE 6.23**). We are so attuned to eyes that we have trouble imagining what Madonna's inverted eyes and mouth will look like when we turn her face upright (**FIGURE 6.24**).

FIGURE 6.24
Face schemas
Which of these is the real Madonna? Slowly rotate the page to find out. As you do so, you will reach a point where you suddenly cannot assimilate her mouth and eyes into your schema for faces.

Context Effects

OBJECTIVE 15 | Explain why the same stimulus can evoke different perceptions in different contexts.

A given stimulus may trigger radically different perceptions, partly because of our differing schemas, but also because of the immediate context. Some examples:

- Imagine hearing a noise interrupted by the words "eel is on the wagon." Likely, you would actually perceive the first word as *wheel*. Given "eel is on the orange," you would hear *peel*. This curious phenomenon, discovered by Richard Warren, suggests that the brain can work backward in time to allow a later stimulus to determine how we perceive an earlier one. The context creates an expectation that, top-down, influences our perception as we match our bottom-up signal against it (Grossberg, 1995).
- Did the pursuing monster in Figure 6.14a on page 251 look aggressive? Did the identical pursued one seem frightened? If so, you experienced a context effect.
- Is the "magician's cabinet" in **FIGURE 6.25** sitting on the floor or hanging from the ceiling? How we perceive it depends on the context defined by the rabbits.

FIGURE 6.25
Context effects: The magician's cabinet
Is the box in the far left frame lying on the floor or hanging from the ceiling? What about the one on the far right? In each case, the context defined by the inquisitive rabbits guides our perceptions. From Shepard, 1990.

Soviet film director Lew Kulechov believed that skilled directors evoke emotion in an audience by defining a context in which viewers interpret an actor's expressions. He once produced three short films, each depicting one of three contexts, followed by identical clips of an actor with a neutral expression (Wallbott, 1988). Shown a film of a dead woman, viewers of the clip were struck by the actor's sadness. Shown a dish of soup, viewers judged the actor thoughtful. Shown a playing child, viewers said the actor appeared happy. Even hearing sad rather than happy music can predispose people to perceive a sad meaning in spoken homophonic words—*mourning* rather than *morning*, *die* rather than *dye*, *pain* rather than *pane* (Halberstadt & others, 1995).

Culture and context effects
What is above the woman's head? In one study, nearly all the East Africans who were questioned said the woman was balancing a metal box or can on her head and that the family was sitting under a tree. Westerners, for whom corners and boxlike architecture are more common, were more likely to perceive the family as being indoors, with the woman sitting under a window. (Adapted from Gregory & Gombrich, 1973.)

cathy® by Cathy Guisewite

Given a perceptual set—"this is a girl"—people see a more feminine baby.

Emotional contexts also color our social perceptions. Spouses who feel loved and appreciated perceive less threat in stressful marital events—"He's just having a bad day" (Murray & others, 2003). If told a soccer team has a history of aggressive behavior, professional referees will assign more penalty cards after watching videotaped fouls (Jones & others, 2002). Lee Ross invites us to recall our own perceptions in different contexts: "Ever notice that when you're driving you hate pedestrians, the way they saunter through the crosswalk, almost daring you to hit them, but when you're walking you hate drivers?" (Jaffe, 2004).

The effects of perceptual set and context show how experience helps us construct perception. "We hear and apprehend only what we already half know," said Thoreau. In everyday life, for example, stereotypes about gender (another instance of perceptual set) can color the perception. Without the obvious cues of pink or blue, people will struggle over whether to call the new baby "he" or "she." But told an infant is "David," people (especially children) may perceive "him" as bigger and stronger than if the same infant is called "Diana" (Stern & Karraker, 1989). Some differences, it seems, exist merely in the eyes of their beholders.

To return to the question "Is perception innate or learned?" we can answer: It's both. The river of perception is fed by two streams: sensation and cognition. And that is why we need multiple levels of analysis (**FIGURE 6.26**). "Simple" perceptions are the brain's creative products.

"Have you ever noticed that anyone driving slower than you is an idiot, and anyone going faster is a maniac?"
George Carlin, *George Carlin on Campus*, 1984

Biological influences:
• entry-level sensory analysis
• unlearned visual phenomena
• critical period for sensory development

Psychological influences:
• selective attention
• learned schemas
• Gestalt principles
• emotional context effects
• perceptual set

Perception: Our version of reality

Social-cultural influences:
• cultural assumptions and expectations
• physical context effects

FIGURE 6.26
Perception is a biopsychosocial phenomenon
Psychologists study how we perceive with different levels of analysis, from the biological to the social-cultural.

Perception and the Human Factor

OBJECTIVE 16 | Describe the role human factors psychologists play in creating user-friendly machines and work settings.

I love my new bedside clock-radio, though I struggle to remember which buttons are Snooze, Alarm Off, and Radio On. Our stove is also wonderful, except for the moments I spend puzzling over which control works which burner. The push-bar doors on our campus buildings are sturdy, though occasionally frustrating when I push the wrong end. The extra buttons on my phone are handy, though when transferring a call I still must look up which buttons to press.

Human factors psychologists help to design appliances, machines, and work settings that fit our natural perceptions. Psychologist Donald Norman (1988) suggests how simple design changes could reduce some of our frustrations. For example, by exploiting "natural mapping," we could design stove controls that require no labels (**FIGURE 6.27**, page 262). ATM machines are internally more complex than VCRs ever were, yet, thanks to human factors psychologists working with engineers, ATMs are easier to operate. TiVo has solved the TV recording problem with a simple point-and-click menu system ("record that one").

■ **human factors psychology** a branch of psychology that explores how people and machines interact and how machines and physical environments can be made safe and easy to use.

(a) **(b)**

FIGURE 6.27
Natural mapping
(a) With traditionally positioned stove controls, a person must read the labels to figure out which knob works which burner. (b) By positioning the controls in a natural map, which the brain understands at a glance, we can eliminate the need to ponder written instructions just to boil water.

Norman (2001), who hosts a Web site (jnd.org) on designing equipment to fit people, bemoaned the complexity of assembling his new high-definition TV, receiver, speakers, digital recorder, DVD player, VCR, and seven remotes into a usable home theater system. "I was VP of Advanced Technology at Apple," says Norman, an MIT alumnus with a Ph.D. "I can program dozens of computers in dozens of languages. I understand television, really, I do. . . . It doesn't matter: I am overwhelmed." If only the makers of home entertainment equipment would minimize cords and cables by bundling audio, visual, control, and power lines into a single cable. If only a single control could operate a point-and-click menu. If only engineers would routinely work with human factors psychologists to test their designs and instructions on real people.

Technology developers often suffer the "curse of knowledge," which leads them to mistakenly assume that others share their expertise—that what's clear to them will similarly be clear to others (Camerer & others, 1989; Nickerson, 1999). (Recall from Chapter 1 that once we know an anagram's solution—WREAT is WATER—it seems that it should be obvious to others, too.) When you know a thing, it's hard to mentally simulate what it's like not to know.

Understanding human factors can do more than enable us to design for reduced frustration; it can help avoid disaster. Two-thirds of commercial air accidents, for example, have been caused by human error (Nickerson, 1998). After beginning commercial flights in the late 1960s, the Boeing 727 was involved in several landing accidents caused by pilot error. Psychologist Conrad Kraft (1978) noted a common setting for these accidents: All took place at night, and all involved landing short of the runway after crossing a dark stretch of water or unilluminated ground. Kraft reasoned that, beyond the runway, city lights would project a larger retinal image if on a rising terrain. This would make the ground seem farther away than it was. By re-creating these conditions in flight simulations, Kraft discovered that pilots were deceived into thinking they were flying higher than their actual altitudes (**FIGURE 6.28**). Aided by

FIGURE 6.28
The human factor in misperception
Lacking distance cues when approaching a runway from over a dark surface, pilots simulating a night landing tended to fly too low. (From Kraft, 1978.)

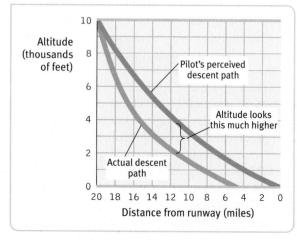

Kraft's finding, the airlines began requiring the co-pilot to monitor the altimeter—calling out altitudes during the descent—and the accidents diminished.

Later Boeing psychologists worked on other human factors problems (Murray, 1998): How should airlines best train and manage mechanics to reduce the maintenance errors that underlie about 50 percent of flight delays and 15 percent of accidents? What illumination and typeface would make on-screen flight data easiest to read? How would warning messages be most effectively worded—as an action statement ("Pull Up") rather than a problem statement ("Ground Proximity")?

In studying human factors issues, psychologists' most powerful tool is research. If an organization wonders what sort of Web design (emphasizing content? speed? graphics?) would most effectively draw in visitors and entice them to return, the psychologist will want to test responses to several alternatives. If NASA (National Aeronautics and Space Administration) wonders what sort of spacecraft design would best facilitate sleeping, work, and morale, their human factors psychologists will want to test the alternatives (**FIGURE 6.29**).

Consider, finally, the available "assistive listening" technologies in various auditoriums, places of worship, and theaters. One technology, commonly available in the United States, requires people with hearing loss to use a headset attached to a pocket-sized receiver that detects infrared or FM signals from the room's sound system. The well-meaning people who design, purchase, and install these systems correctly understand that the technology puts sound directly into the user's ears. Alas, few people with hearing loss undergo the hassle and embarrassment of locating, requesting, wearing, and returning a conspicuous headset. Most such units therefore sit in closets. Britain, the Scandinavian countries, and Australia have instead installed "loop systems" that broadcast customized sound directly through a person's own hearing aid. When suitably equipped, a discrete touch of a switch can transform hearing aids into in-the-ear loudspeakers. A loop system (a special amplifier attached to a wire encircling an audience) can also work in homes, enabling TV sound or phone conversation to broadcast directly through hearing aids (see www.hearingloop.org). When offered convenient, inconspicuous, personalized sound, many more people elect to use assistive listening.

The point to remember: Designers and engineers should consider the human factor, by designing things to fit people, being mindful of the curse of knowledge, and user-testing their inventions before production and distribution.

Courtesy of NASA

FIGURE 6.29

How not to go mad while going to Mars
Future astronauts headed to Mars will be confined in conditions of monotony, stress, and weightlessness for months on end. To help design and evaluate a workable human environment, such as for this Transit Habitation (Transhab) Module, NASA engages human factors psychologists (Weed, 2001; Wichman, 1992).

>> LEARNING OUTCOMES

Perceptual Interpretation

OBJECTIVE **12** | **Describe the contribution of restored-vision and sensory deprivation research in our understanding of the nature-nurture interplay in our perceptions.**

If all aspects of visual perception were entirely inborn, people who were born blind but regained sight after surgery should have normal visual perception. They do not. After cataract surgery, for example, adults who had been blind from birth are able to distinguish figure from ground and to perceive colors, but they lack the experience to recognize shapes, forms, and complete faces. Further evidence comes from animals reared with severely restricted visual input, who suffered enduring visual handicaps when their visual exposure was returned to normal. Clinical and experimental evidence

indicates that there is a critical period for some aspects of sensory and perceptual development. Without the stimulation provided by early visual experiences, the brain's neural organization does not develop normally.

OBJECTIVE **13** | **Explain how the research on distorting goggles increases our understanding of the adaptability of perception.**

When people are given glasses that shift the world slightly to the left or right, or even turn it upside down, they are initially disoriented, but they manage to adapt to their new context and, with practice, to move about with ease. This research demonstrates our ability to adjust to an artificially altered visual field and coordinate our movements in response to that new world.

OBJECTIVE **14** | Define *perceptual set,* and explain how it influences what we do or do not perceive.

Perceptual set is a mental predisposition that functions as a lens through which we perceive the world. Once again, nature and nurture interact: Our sensory input bounces off our experiences, learned assumptions, and beliefs. Because our learned concepts (schemas) prime us to organize and interpret ambiguous stimuli in certain ways, our perceptions reflect our version of reality. Thus, some of us "see" monsters, faces, and UFOs or "hear" messages that others do not.

OBJECTIVE **15** | Explain why the same stimulus can evoke different perceptions in different contexts.

In perceiving a given stimulus that we could interpret by means of several different schemas, we scan the immediate context for information. Context creates expectations that guide our perceptions. Emotional context can color our interpretation of other people's behaviors—and our own. Perceptual set and context effects interact to help us construct our perceptions.

OBJECTIVE **16** | Describe the role human factors psychologists play in creating user-friendly machines and work settings.

Human factors psychologists encourage developers and designers to consider human perceptual abilities, to avoid the *curse of knowledge* (the mistaken assumption that others share our expertise and will behave as we would), and to schedule user-testing to reveal perception-based problems before production and distribution. Human factors psychologists have contributed to improved safety in air and space travel; better-designed appliances, equipment, and workplaces; and easier-to-use assistive listening.

ASK YOURSELF: **Can you recall a time when your expectations have predisposed how you perceived a person (or group of people)?**

Is There Extrasensory Perception?

OBJECTIVE **17** | Identify the three most testable forms of ESP, and explain why most research psychologists remain skeptical of ESP claims.

Can we perceive only what we sense? Or, without sensory input, are we capable of **extrasensory perception (ESP)?** Are there indeed people—any people—who can read minds, see through walls, or foretell the future? Five British universities have **parapsychology** units staffed by Ph.D. graduates of Edinburgh University's parapsychology program (Turpin, 2005). Sweden's Lund University, the Netherlands' Utrecht University, and Australia's University of Adelaide also have added faculty chairs or research units for parapsychology. But other research psychologists and scientists—including 96 percent of the scientists in the U.S. National Academy of Sciences—are skeptical (McConnell, 1991). If ESP is real, we would need to overturn the scientific understanding that we are creatures whose minds are tied to our physical brains and whose perceptual experiences of the world are built of sensations. Sometimes new evidence does overturn our scientific preconceptions. Science, as we will see throughout this book, offers us various surprises—about the extent of the unconscious mind, about the effects of emotion on health, about what heals and what doesn't, and much more. Before we evaluate claims of ESP, let's review them.

SNAPSHOTS

Thank you for calling the Psychic Hotline. How can I help you?

You tell me...

© Jason Love

(c) Love 650

■ **extrasensory perception (ESP)** the controversial claim that perception can occur apart from sensory input. Said to include *telepathy, clairvoyance,* and *precognition.*

■ **parapsychology** the study of paranormal phenomena, including ESP and psychokinesis.

Claims of ESP

Claims of paranormal phenomena include astrological predictions, psychic healing, communication with the dead, and out-of-body experiences. But the most testable and (for a perception chapter) most relevant claims are for three varieties of ESP:

Telepathy, or mind-to-mind communication—one person sending thoughts to another or perceiving another's thoughts.

Clairvoyance, or perceiving remote events, such as sensing that a friend's house is on fire.

Precognition, or perceiving future events, such as a political leader's death or a sporting event's outcome.

Closely linked with these are claims of *psychokinesis*, or "mind over matter," such as levitating a table or influencing the roll of a die (**FIGURE 6.30**). (The claim is illustrated by the wry request, "Will all those who believe in psychokinesis please raise my hand?")

FIGURE 6.30
Parapsychological concepts

```
        Purported paranormal
            phenomena
              ("Psi")
                |
        ┌───────┴───────┐
       ESP             PK
   Extrasensory   Psychokinesis
   perception
        |
  ┌─────┼─────────────┐
Telepathy  Clairvoyance  Precognition
```

Premonitions or Pretensions?

Can psychics see into the future? Although one might wish for a psychic stock forecaster, the tallied forecasts of "leading psychics" reveal meager accuracy. No greedy—or charitable—psychic has been able to predict the outcome of a lottery jackpot, or to make billions on the stock market. During the 1990s, tabloid psychics were all wrong in predicting surprising events. (Madonna did not become a gospel singer, the Statue of Liberty did not lose both its arms in a terrorist blast, Queen Elizabeth did not abdicate her throne to enter a convent.) And the new-century psychics missed the big-news events such as the Florida presidential ballot controversy, the whereabouts and capture of Saddam Hussein, and the horror of 9/11. (Where were the precogs on 9/10 when we needed them?) Gene Emery (2004), who has tracked annual psychic forecasts for 26 years, reports that almost never have unusual predictions come true and virtually never have psychics anticipated any of the year's headline events.

Analyses of psychic visions offered to police departments reveal that these, too, are no more accurate than guesses made by others (Reiser, 1982). Psychics working with the police do, however, generate hundreds of predictions. This increases the odds of an occasional correct guess, which psychics can then report to the media. Moreover, vague predictions can later be interpreted ("retrofitted") to match events that provide a perceptual set for interpreting them. Nostradamus, a sixteenth-century French psychic, explained in an unguarded moment that his ambiguous prophecies "could not possibly be understood till they were interpreted after the event and by it."

Police departments are wise to all this. When Jane Ayers Sweat and Mark Durm (1993) asked the police departments of America's 50 largest cities whether they ever used psychics, 65 percent said they never had. Of those that had, not one had found it helpful.

> "A person who talks a lot is sometimes right."
>
> Spanish proverb

Which supposed psychic ability does Psychic Pizza claim?

Thousands of psychics reportedly overwhelmed police with mispredictions of the whereabouts of Washington, D.C., intern Chandra Levy, whose body was discovered by a jogger on a wooded hill a year after her disappearance (Radford, 2002).

Are the spontaneous "visions" of everyday people any more accurate? Consider our dreams. Do they foretell the future, as about half of university students have believed (Messer & Griggs, 1989)? Or do they only seem to do so because we are more likely to recall or reconstruct dreams that seem to have come true? Two Harvard psychologists (Murray & Wheeler, 1937) tested the prophetic power of dreams after aviator Charles Lindbergh's baby son was kidnapped and murdered in 1932, but before the body was discovered. When the researchers invited the public to report their dreams about the child, 1300 visionaries submitted dream reports. How many accurately envisioned the child dead? Five percent. And how many also correctly anticipated the body's location—buried among trees? Only 4 of the 1300. Although this number was surely no better than chance, to those 4 dreamers the accuracy of their *apparent* precognitions must have seemed uncanny.

Throughout the day, each of us imagines many events. Given the billions of events in the world each day, and given enough days, some stunning coincidences are sure to occur. By one careful estimate, chance alone would predict that more than a thousand times a day someone on Earth will think of someone and then within the ensuing five minutes will learn of the person's death (Charpak & Broch, 2004). With enough time or people, the improbable becomes inevitable.

That has been the experience of comics writer John Byrne (2003). Six months after his Spider-Man story about a New York blackout appeared, New York suffered its massive blackout. A subsequent Spider-Man storyline involved a major earthquake in Japan "and again," he recalls, "the real thing happened in the month the issue hit the stands." Later, when working on a Superman comic book, he "had the Man of Steel fly to the rescue when disaster beset the NASA space shuttle. The *Challenger* tragedy happened almost immediately thereafter" (with time for the issue to be redrawn). "Most recently, and [most chillingly], came when I was writing and drawing Wonder Woman and did a story in which the title character was killed as a prelude to her becoming a goddess." The issue cover "was done as a newspaper front page, with the headline 'Princess Diana Dies.' (Diana is Wonder Woman's real name.) That issue went on sale on a Thursday. The following Saturday . . . I don't have to tell you, do I?"

Putting ESP to Experimental Test

In the past, there have been all kinds of strange ideas—that bumps on the head reveal character traits, that bloodletting is a cure-all, that each sperm cell contains a miniature person. When faced with such claims—or with claims of mind reading or out-of-body travel or communication with the dead—how can we separate bizarre ideas from those that sound bizarre but are true? At the heart of science is a simple answer: *Test them to see if they work.* If they do, so much the better for the ideas. If they don't, so much the better for our skepticism.

This scientific attitude has led both believers and skeptics to agree that what parapsychology needs to give it credibility is a reproducible phenomenon and a theory to explain it. Parapsychologist Rhea White (1998) acknowledges that "the image of parapsychology that comes to my mind, based on nearly 44 years in the field, is that of a small airplane [that] has been perpetually taxiing down the runway of the Empirical Science Airport since 1882 . . . its movement punctuated occasionally by lifting a few feet off the ground only to bump back down on the tarmac once again. It has never taken off for any sustained flight."

> "Things that happen by chance are events in search of causes."
>
> K. C. Cole, *The Universe and the Teacup*, 1998

> "At the heart of science is an essential tension between two seemingly contradictory attitudes—an openness to new ideas, no matter how bizarre or counterintuitive they may be, and the most ruthless skeptical scrutiny of all ideas, old and new."
>
> Carl Sagan (1987)

Courtesy of Claire Cole

Testing psychic powers in the British population
Hertfordshire University psychologist Richard Wiseman created a "mind machine" to see if people can influence or predict a coin toss. Using a touch-sensitive screen, visitors to festivals around the country were given four attempts to call heads or tails. Using a random-number generator, a computer then decided the outcome. When the experiment concluded in January 2000, nearly 28,000 people had predicted 110,972 tosses—with 49.8 percent correct.

Seeking a reproducible phenomenon, how might we test ESP claims in a controlled experiment? An experiment differs from a staged demonstration. In the laboratory, the experimenter controls what the "psychic" sees and hears. On stage, the psychic controls what the audience sees and hears. Time and again, skeptics note, so-called psychics have exploited unquestioning audiences with mind-blowing performances in which they *appeared* to communicate with the spirits of the dead, read minds, or levitate objects—only to have it revealed that their acts were nothing more than the illusions of stage magicians.

The search for a valid and reliable test of ESP has resulted in thousands of experiments. One controlled procedure has invited "senders" to telepathically transmit one of four visual images to "receivers" deprived of sensation in a nearby chamber (Bem & Honorton, 1994). The result? A reported 32 percent accurate response rate, surpassing the chance rate of 25 percent. But follow-up studies have (depending on who was summarizing the results) failed to replicate the phenomenon or produced mixed results (Bem & others, 2001; Milton & Wiseman, 2002; Storm, 2000, 2003).

One skeptic, magician James Randi, has a longstanding offer—now U.S. $1 million—"to anyone who proves a genuine psychic power under proper observing conditions" (Randi, 1999). French, Australian, and Indian groups have parallel offers of up to 200,000 euros to anyone with demonstrable paranormal abilities (CFI, 2003). And $50 million was available for information leading to Osama bin Laden's capture. Large as these sums are, the scientific seal of approval would be worth far more to anyone whose claims could be authenticated. To refute those who say there is no ESP, one need only produce a single person who can demonstrate a single, reproducible ESP phenomenon. (To refute those who say pigs can't talk would take but one talking pig.) So far, no such person has emerged. Randi's offer has been publicized for three decades and dozens of people have been tested, sometimes under the scrutiny of an independent panel of judges. Still, nothing.

Why, then, are so many people predisposed to believe that ESP exists? In part, such beliefs may stem from understandable misperceptions, misinterpretations, and selective recall. But some people also have an unsatisfied hunger for wonderment, an itch to experience the magical. In Britain and the United States, the founders of

"A psychic is an actor playing the role of a psychic."

Psychologist-magician Daryl Bem (1984)

"People's desire to believe in the paranormal is stronger than all the evidence that it does not exist."

Susan Blackmore, "Blackmore's first law," 2004

parapsychology were mostly people who, having lost their religious faith, began searching for a scientific basis for believing in the meaning of life and in life after death (Alcock, 1985; Beloff, 1985). In the upheaval after the collapse of autocratic rule in Russia, there came an "avalanche of the mystical, occult, and pseudoscientific" (Kapitza, 1991). In Russia as elsewhere, "extrasensorial" healers and seers have fascinated the awestruck public. "Many people," declared a statement by 32 leading Russian scientists in 1999, "believe in clairvoyance, astrology, and other superstitions to compensate for the psychological discomforts of our time."

To feel awe and to gain a deep reverence for life, we need look no further than our own perceptual system and its capacity for organizing formless nerve impulses into colorful sights, vivid sounds, and evocative smells. As Shakespeare's Hamlet recognized, "There are more things in Heaven and Earth, Horatio, than are dreamt of in your philosophy." Within our ordinary perceptual experiences lies much that is truly extraordinary—surely much more than has so far been dreamt of in our psychology. A century of research has revealed many of the secrets of sensation and perception, yet for future generations of researchers there remain profound and genuine mysteries to solve.

> "So, how *does* the mind work? I don't know. You don't know. Pinker doesn't know. And, I rather suspect, such is the current state of the art, that if God were to tell us, we wouldn't understand."
>
> Jerry Fodor, "Reply to Steven Pinker," 2005

We have now examined the first steps in our processing of information, from receiving sensory input to constructing meaningful perceptions. But our skull's 3-pound information-processing system does much more: Under the influence of sleep, hypnosis, or drugs, it will construct unreal images (Chapter 7). It learns from our experiences, recalling them long afterward (Chapters 8 and 9). It thinks and makes plans (Chapters 10 and 11). Between our sensing and acting lies an unimaginably complex information system that, more than ever, beckons explorers of our mind's inner space.

>> LEARNING OUTCOMES

Is There Extrasensory Perception?

OBJECTIVE 17 | **Identify the three most testable forms of ESP, and explain why most research psychologists remain skeptical of ESP claims.**

ESP (extrasensory perception) is one form of purported paranormal phenomena. (Another form is psychokinesis [PK].) The three most testable forms of ESP are telepathy (mind-to-mind communication), clairvoyance (perceiving remote events), and precognition (perceiving future events). Most research psychologists' skepticism focuses on two points. First, to believe in ESP, you must believe the brain is capable of perceiving without sensory input. Second (and most important in terms of critical inquiry), parapsychologists have been unable to replicate (reproduce) ESP phenomena under controlled conditions.

ASK YOURSELF: Have you ever had an ESP experience? Can you think of an explanation other than ESP for that experience?

REVIEW CHAPTER 6: Perception

Test Yourself

1. Your friend insists that he *did* call you to dinner as you intently watched TV. What principle explains your not perceiving him?

2. How does the study of illusions inform our understanding of normal perceptions?

3. What do we mean when we say that, in perception, the whole is greater than the sum of its parts?

4. What type of evidence shows that, indeed, "there is more to perception than meets the senses"?

5. What psychic ability is being claimed by the sports channel in the cartoon to the right?

Answers to the Test Yourself questions can be found in Appendix B at the end of the book.

The Quigmans by Buddy Hickerson; © 1990, Los Angeles Times Syndicate. Reprinted with permission.

Terms and Concepts to Remember

selective attention, p. 237

inattentional blindness, p. 238

visual capture, p. 242

gestalt, p. 242

figure-ground, p. 243

grouping, p. 243

depth perception, p. 245

visual cliff, p. 245

binocular cues, p. 245

retinal disparity, p. 246

convergence, p. 246

monocular cues, p. 246

phi phenomenon, p. 250

perceptual constancy, p. 250

perceptual adaptation, p. 256

perceptual set, p. 257

human factors psychology, p. 261

extrasensory perception (ESP), p. 264

parapsychology, p. 264

WEB

 To continue your study and review of Perception, visit this book's Web site at www.worthpublishers.com/myers. You will find practice tests, review activities, and many interesting articles and Web links for more information on topics related to Perception.

Another Voice On: States of Consciousness

Faiz Ahmed Faiz (Pakistan) (1911–1984), From "A Prison Daybreak," *Rebel's Silhouette*

Night wasn't over when the moon stood
  beside my bed
and said, "You've drunk your sleep to the
  dregs,
your share of that wine is finished for this
  night."

My eyes tore themselves from a dream of
  passion–
they said farewell to my lover's image, still
lingering in the night's stagnant waters
that were spread, like a sheet, over the
  earth.

Silver whirlpools began their dervish
  dance
as lotuses of stars fell from the moon's
  hands.
Some sank. Some rose to the surface,
floated, and opened their petals.
Night and daybreak had fallen
  desperately
into each other's arms.

7 : States of Consciousness

> "Neither [psychologist] Steve Pinker nor I can explain human subjective consciousness. . . . We don't understand it."
> Evolutionary biologist Richard Dawkins (1999)

> "Psychology must discard all reference to consciousness."
> Behaviorist John B. Watson (1913)

Now playing at an inner theater near you: the premiere showing of a sleeping person's vivid dream. This never-before-seen mental movie features captivating characters wrapped in a plot so original and unlikely, yet so intricate and so seemingly real, that the viewer later marvels at its creation.

Waking from a troubling dream, wrenched by its emotions, who among us has not wondered about this weird state of consciousness? How does our brain so creatively, colorfully, and completely construct this alternative, conscious world? In the shadowland between our dreaming and waking consciousness, we may even wonder for a moment which is real. And what shall we make of other altered states of consciousness, such as hypnosis, drug-altered hallucinations, and near-death visions?

But first questions first: What is consciousness? In every science there are concepts so fundamental they are nearly impossible to define. Biologists agree on what is alive but not on precisely what life is. In physics, matter and energy elude simple definition. To psychologists, consciousness is similarly a fundamental yet slippery concept.

Consciousness and Information Processing

OBJECTIVE 1 | Discuss the history of psychology's study of consciousness, and contrast conscious and unconscious information processing.

Psychologists have long explored consciousness, at first eagerly, then warily, and now with renewed vigor. At its beginning, *psychology* was "the description and explanation of states of consciousness" (Ladd, 1887). But the difficulty of scientifically studying consciousness led many psychologists during the first half of the last century to turn to direct observations of behavior—an approach favored by an emerging school of psychology called *behaviorism* (page 316). By the 1960s, psychology no longer defined itself as the study of consciousness or "mental life" but rather as the science of behavior. Psychology had nearly lost consciousness. Consciousness was viewed as resembling a car's speedometer: "It doesn't make the car go, it just reflects what's happening" (Seligman, 1991, p. 24).

After 1960, mental concepts began to reenter psychology. Advances in neuroscience made it possible to relate brain activity to various mental states—waking, sleeping, dreaming. Researchers began studying consciousness altered by hypnosis and drugs. Psychologists of all persuasions were affirming the importance of mental processes (cognition). Psychology was regaining consciousness.

For most psychologists today, **consciousness** is our awareness of ourselves and our environment. Consciousness brings varied information to the surface, enabling us to reflect and plan. When we learn a complex concept or behavior—say, driving a car—consciousness focuses our concentration on the car and the traffic. This awareness varies with our attentional spotlight. With practice, driving becomes automatic and no longer requires our undivided attention—freeing our consciousness to focus on other things. If I ask you to pay attention to the weight of your body pressing on your buttocks as you sit reading, you will momentarily stop reading.

Conscious awareness enables us to exert voluntary control and to communicate our mental states to others, yet consciousness is but the tip of the information-processing

■ **consciousness** our awareness of ourselves and our environment.

271

States of consciousness

In addition to normal, waking awareness, consciousness comes to us in altered states, note Dieter Vaitl and colleagues (2005), including daydreaming, sleeping, meditating, and drug-induced hallucinating.

Some occur spontaneously	Daydreaming	Drowsiness	Dreaming
Some are physiologically induced	Hallucinations	Orgasm	Food or oxygen starvation
Some are psychologically induced	Sensory deprivation	Hypnosis	Meditation

iceberg. Research reported throughout this book reveals that we process a great deal of information outside our awareness. We register and react to stimuli we do not consciously perceive. We perform well-learned tasks automatically, as when keyboarding without attending to where the letters are. We change our attitudes and reconstruct our memories with no awareness of doing so. When we meet people, we instantly and unconsciously react to their gender, age, and appearance, and *then* become aware of our response.

Beneath the surface, unconscious information processing occurs simultaneously on many parallel tracks. When we look at a bird flying, we are consciously aware of the result of our cognitive processing ("It's a hummingbird!") but not of our subprocessing of the bird's color, form, movement, distance, and identity.

According to one theory, when reverberating brain activity among interconnected brain areas crosses a threshold of intensity, it triggers consciousness (Sergent & Dehaene, 2004). Stephen Kosslyn and Olivier Koenig (1992) suggest that brain events are to consciousness what a guitar's individual notes are to a chord. As a chord emerges from the interaction of different notes, so consciousness emerges from the interaction of individual brain events.

Today's neuroscientists are identifying neurological activity linked with consciousness. In some provocative experiments, Benjamin Libet (1985, 2004) observed that we experience the chord an instant *after* all the notes are present, so consciousness is known to lag behind the brain events that evoke it. For example, when you move a wrist at will, you consciously experience the decision to move about 0.2 seconds before the actual movement. No surprise there. But your brain waves jump about 0.35 seconds ahead of your conscious perception of the decision (**FIGURE 7.1**)! Thus, before you become aware of it, your brain seems headed toward your decision to move your wrist. Likewise, if asked to press a button when you feel a tap, you can respond in 1/10th of a second—less time than it takes to become conscious that you have responded (Wegner, 2002). The startling conclusion from these experiments is that consciousness sometimes arrives late to the decision-making party.

Unlike the processing of unconscious information, which occurs simultaneously on multiple parallel tracks, conscious processing takes place in sequence (serially). Consciousness is relatively slow and has limited capacity but is skilled at solving novel problems. It is like a chief executive, whose many assistants automatically take care of routine business. Traveling a familiar route, your hands and feet do the driving while your mind is elsewhere. Running on automatic pilot allows consciousness—the mind's CEO—to monitor the whole system and deal with new challenges.

FIGURE 7.1
Is the brain ahead of the mind?
In research by Benjamin Libet, unconscious brain activity precedes conscious awareness of a simple decision preceding an action. A person watches a computer clock that sweeps a revolution every 2.56 seconds, and notes the time at which she decides to move her wrist. About one-third of a second before the person decides to move, brain wave activity jumps, indicating a "readiness potential" to move. Thus, watching a slow motion replay, the researchers can predict when the person is about to decide to move (following which the wrist does move).

Novel tasks require our conscious attention. Try this: If you are right-handed, you can move your right foot in a smooth counterclockwise circle, and you can write the number 3 repeatedly with your right hand—but probably not at the same time. (If you are musically inclined, try something equally difficult: Tap a steady three times with your left hand while tapping four times with your right hand.) Both tasks require conscious attention, which can be in only one place at a time. If time is nature's way of keeping everything from happening at once, then consciousness is nature's way of keeping us from thinking and doing everything at once.

>> LEARNING OUTCOMES

Consciousness and Information Processing

OBJECTIVE 1 | Discuss the history of psychology's study of consciousness, and contrast conscious and unconscious information processing.

Consciousness, currently defined as our awareness of ourselves and our environment, occurs in the normal states of seeing and hearing, reasoning and remembering, but also in the altered consciousness of sleep, hypnotic states, and chemically induced hallucinations. Psychology began as the study of consciousness, then, under the behaviorists, turned to the study of observable behavior. Under the impact of discoveries in neuroscience and cognitive psychology, the scientific investigation of states of mind is again one of psychology's pursuits.

We process information on two levels. Our conscious processing is serial and relatively slow, but this focused state of awareness enables us to perform voluntary acts, solve novel problems, and communicate with others. In unconscious processing, we perform familiar tasks automatically, and our sensory systems and neural pathways register stimuli rapidly and simultaneously on multiple tracks (parallel processing).

ASK YOURSELF: Have you ever wondered how horses, dogs, and cats experience the world? Do you think they are consciously aware? If yes, are they also aware of being aware of the world?

> "I love to sleep. Do you? Isn't it great? It really is the best of both worlds. You get to be alive and unconscious."
>
> Comedian Rita Rudner, 1993

Sleep and Dreams

Sleep—the irresistible tempter to whom we inevitably succumb. Sleep—the equalizer of presidents and peasants. Sleep—sweet, renewing, mysterious sleep. Sleep's age-old mysteries have intrigued scientists for centuries.

Now, some of these mysteries are being solved. In laboratories throughout the world, thousands have slept attached to recording devices while others observe. By recording sleepers' brain waves and muscle movements, and by observing and waking them from time to time, the sleep watchers glimpse things that a thousand years of common sense never told us. Perhaps you can anticipate some of their discoveries. Are the following statements true or false?

1. When people dream of performing some activity, their limbs often move in concert with the dream (page 278).
2. Older adults sleep more than young adults (Figure 7.10, p. 288).
3. Sleepwalkers are acting out their dreams (page 277).
4. Sleep experts recommend treating insomnia with an occasional sleeping pill (page 283).
5. Some people dream every night; others seldom dream (page 278).

All these statements (adapted from Palladino & Carducci, 1983) are false. To see why, read on.

Biological Rhythms

OBJECTIVE 2 | Distinguish four types of biological rhythms, and give an example of each.

Like the ocean, life has its rhythmic tides. Over varying time periods our bodies fluctuate, and with them our minds. These **biological rhythms,** controlled by internal "biological clocks," include

- ***Annual cycles*** On an annual cycle, geese migrate, grizzly bears hibernate, and humans may experience seasonal variations in appetite, sleep length, and moods. For some people, especially in far northern regions, a depressed mood during winter's dark months may define a *seasonal affective disorder*.
- ***Twenty-eight–day cycles*** The female menstrual cycle averages 28 days. Does that cycle cause fluctuating moods? Many believe it indeed does, but some research psychologists are skeptical (**FIGURE 7.2**).

> "When a man can't explain a woman's actions, the first thing he thinks about is the condition of her uterus."
>
> Clare Boothe Luce, *Slam the Door Softly,* 1970

FIGURE 7.2
Menstruation, actual mood, and perceived mood
Cathy McFarland and her colleagues (1989) found that Ontario women's daily mood reports did not vary across their menstrual cycle. Yet they *perceived* that their moods were generally worse just before and after menstruation and better at others times of the cycle.

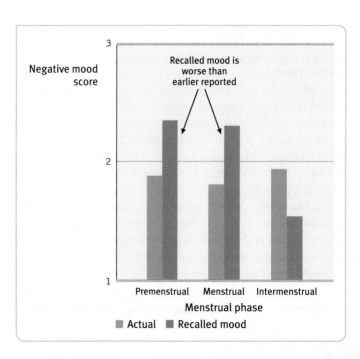

- *Twenty-four–hour cycles* Humans experience 24-hour cycles of varying alertness, body temperature, and growth hormone secretion. And not just humans. All mammals and birds sleep (Siegel, 2002).
- *Ninety-minute cycles* This chapter explores how we move through various stages of sleep in 90-minute cycles. Curiously, small animals have shorter sleep cycles (rats, 9 minutes; cats and dogs, 25 minutes) than big animals (elephants, 100+ minutes) (Hobson, 1989; Morrison, 2003).

> ■ **biological rhythms** periodic physiological fluctuations.
>
> ■ **circadian** [ser-KAY-dee-an] **rhythm** the biological clock; regular bodily rhythms (for example, of temperature and wakefulness) that occur on a 24-hour cycle.
>
> Dolphins can sleep while moving.

The Rhythm of Sleep

Let's look more closely at two of those biological rhythms—our 24-hour biological clock and our 90-minute sleep cycle.

Circadian Rhythm

OBJECTIVE 3 | Describe the cycle of our circadian rhythm, and identify some events that can disrupt this biological clock.

The rhythm of the day parallels the rhythm of life—from our waking to a new day's birth to our nightly return to what Shakespeare called "death's counterfeit." Our bodies roughly synchronize with the 24-hour cycle of day and night through a biological clock called the **circadian rhythm** (from the Latin *circa,* "about," and *diem,* "day"). Our body temperature rises as morning approaches, peaks during the day, dips for a time in early afternoon (when many people take siestas), and then begins to drop again before we go to sleep. Awake at 4:00 A.M., body depressed, we may fret over concerns: Does a lovers' spat signal a split? Does a child's moodiness mean more trouble ahead? By midday, our body energized, we fret less. Pulling an all-nighter, we feel groggiest about 4:00 A.M., and then we get a second wind after our normal wake-up time arrives.

Recent evidence suggests that thinking is sharpest and memory most accurate when people are at their daily peak in circadian arousal. With age, we tend to shift from being evening-energized "owls" to being morning-loving "larks." Most university students are owls (May & Hasher, 1998); their performance typically improves across the day. Most older adults are larks, with their performance declining as the day wears on. In retirement homes, all is quiet by mid-evening; in university dorms, the day is far from over. The transition from sleeping later to sleeping earlier begins about age 20—though slightly earlier for women, who also enter puberty earlier and stop growing earlier than men (Roenneberg & others, 2004).

A transcontinental flight disrupts our circadian rhythm and we experience jet lag, mainly because we are awake when our circadian rhythm cries "Sleep!" Studies in the laboratory and with shift workers reveal that bright light helps reset our biological clocks (Czeisler & others, 1986, 1989; Eastman & others, 1995). Thus, to speed the resetting of your biological clock after a long flight, spend the first day outdoors. Bright light in the morning facilitates awakening (and protects against depression). Bright light at night helps delay sleep (Oren & Terman, 1998).

Light tweaks the circadian clock by activating light-sensitive retinal proteins. These proteins trigger signals to the brain's *suprachiasmatic nucleus*—a pair of pinhead-sized clusters of 20,000 cells that control the circadian clock (Foster, 2004). It does so partly by causing the brain's pineal gland to decrease (in the morning) or increase (in the evening) its production of the sleep-inducing hormone *melatonin* (**FIGURE 7.3**). The longer we are awake, the more our active brain produces

FIGURE 7.3
The biological clock
Light striking the retina causes the suprachiasmatic nucleus (a tiny neural center in the hypothalamus) to alter the production of biologically active substances, such as melatonin production by the pineal gland.

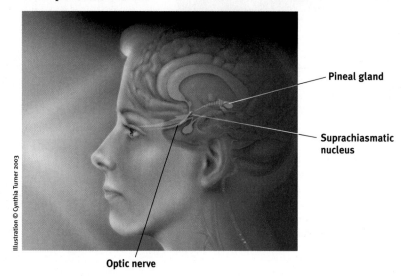

Pineal gland

Suprachiasmatic nucleus

Optic nerve

Illustration © Cynthia Turner 2003

and accumulates the chemical *adenosine,* which inhibits certain neurons, making us sleepy. (Caffeine blocks adenosine's activity.) During sleep, adenosine concentration declines (Porkka-Heiskanen & others, 1997).

We can unwittingly reset our biological clocks by adjusting our sleep schedules. If we stay up late and sleep in on weekends, we may end up with "Sunday night insomnia" and "Monday morning blues." Those who sleep till noon on Sunday and then go to bed just 11 hours later in preparation for the new workweek often find sleep elusive. They are like New Yorkers whose biology is on California time, or like someone who has just flown east from Perth to Sydney.

Curiously—given that our ancestors' body clocks were attuned to the rising and setting sun of the 24-hour day—many of today's young adults adopt something closer to a 25-hour day, by staying up too late to get 8 hours of sleep. For this, we can thank (or blame) Thomas Edison, inventor of the light bulb. Being bathed in light, even in a cave, is like traveling one time zone west—it nudges our 24-hour biological clock back (Czeisler & others, 1999; Dement, 1999). This helps explain why rotating shift workers and store clerks servicing a 24/7 culture adapt better to progressively later shifts than to earlier ones, and why until our later years we must discipline ourselves to go to bed on time and force ourselves to get up. Most animals, too, when placed under unnatural constant illumination will exceed a 24-hour day. Artificial light delays sleep.

> If our natural circadian rhythm were attuned to a 23-hour cycle, would we instead need to discipline ourselves to stay up later at night and sleep in longer in the morning? Do older adults, who typically prefer earlier waking and bedtime than university students, have a shorter circadian rhythm?

Sleep Stages

OBJECTIVE 4 | List the stages of the sleep cycle, and explain how they differ.

As sleep overtakes us and different parts of the cortex stop communicating, consciousness fades (Massimini & others, 2005). But the still-active sleeping brain does not emit a constant dial tone, for there is also a biological rhythm during sleep. About every 90 minutes we pass through a cycle of five distinct sleep stages. This elementary fact apparently was unknown until 8-year-old Armond Aserinsky went to bed one night in 1952. His father, Eugene, a University of Chicago graduate student, needed to test an electroencephalograph he had been repairing during the day (Aserinsky, 1988; Seligman & Yellen, 1987). He placed electrodes near Armond's eyes to record the rolling eye movements believed to occur during sleep. Before long, the machine went wild, tracing deep zigzags on the graph paper. Aserinsky thought the machine was still broken. But as the night proceeded, the activity periodically recurred. This indicated, Aserinsky finally realized, fast, jerky eye movements accompanied by energetic brain activity. When he awakened Armond during one such episode, the boy reported he was having a dream. Aserinsky had discovered what we now know as **REM sleep** (rapid *eye movement* sleep).

To find out if similar cycles occur during adult sleep, Nathaniel Kleitman (1960) and Aserinsky pioneered procedures that have now been used with thousands of volunteers. To appreciate both their methods and findings, imagine yourself as a participant. As the hour grows late, you begin to fight sleepiness and yawn in response to reduced brain metabolism. Yawning stretches your neck muscles and increases your heart rate, which increases your alertness (Moorcroft, 2003). When you are ready for bed, the researcher tapes electrodes to your scalp (to detect your brain waves), just outside the corners of your eyes (to detect eye movements), and on your chin (to detect muscle tension) (**FIGURE 7.4**). Other devices allow

FIGURE 7.4
Measuring sleep activity
Sleep researchers measure brain-wave activity, eye movements, and muscle tension by electrodes that pick up weak electrical signals from the brain, eye, and facial muscles. (From Dement, 1978.)

Left eye movements

Right eye movements

EMG (muscle tension)

EEG (brain waves)

Hank Morgan/Rainbow

the researcher to record your heart rate, your respiration rate, and the degree of your genital arousal.

When you are in bed with your eyes closed, the researcher in the next room sees on the EEG the relatively slow **alpha waves** of your awake but relaxed state (**FIGURE 7.5**). As you adapt to all this equipment and grow tired, you slip into **sleep**. Sleep is a state we do not know we are in until we leave it. Our dive into sleep—marked by the slowed breathing and the irregular brain waves of Stage 1—happens in an unremembered moment (**FIGURE 7.6**).

In one of his 15,000 sleep research participants, William Dement (1999) observed the moment the perceptual door between the brain and outside world slammed shut. Dement asked this sleep-deprived young man, lying on his back with eyelids taped open, to press a button every time a strobe light flashed in his eyes (averaging about every 6 seconds). After a few minutes the subject missed one. Asked why, he said, "Because there was no flash." But there was a flash—which he missed because (as his brain activity revealed) he had fallen asleep for 2 seconds. Unaware that he had done so, he had missed not only the flash 6 inches from his nose but also the abrupt moment of his entry into sleep.

During this brief Stage 1 sleep you may experience fantastic images, resembling **hallucinations**—sensory experiences that occur without a sensory stimulus. You may have a sensation of falling (at which moment your body may suddenly jerk) or of floating weightlessly. Such *hypnagogic* sensations may later be incorporated into memories. People who claim to have been abducted by aliens—often shortly after getting into bed—commonly recall being floated off their beds.

Soon, you relax more deeply and begin about 20 minutes of Stage 2 sleep, characterized by the periodic appearance of *sleep spindles*—bursts of rapid, rhythmic brain-wave activity. Although you can still be awakened without too much difficulty during this phase, you are now clearly asleep. Sleeptalking—usually garbled or nonsensical—can occur during this or any other sleep stage (Mahowald & Ettinger, 1990).

Then for the next few minutes you go through the transitional Stage 3 to the deep sleep of Stage 4. First in Stage 3, and increasingly in Stage 4, your brain emits large, slow **delta waves.** These two *slow-wave sleep* stages last for about 30 minutes, during which you are hard to awaken. Curiously, it is at the end of the deep sleep of Stage 4 that children may wet the bed or begin walking in their sleep. About 20 percent of 3- to 12-year-olds have at least one episode of sleepwalking, usually lasting 2 to 10 minutes; some 5 percent have repeated episodes (Giles & others, 1994).

Even when you are deeply asleep, your brain somehow processes certain stimuli. You move around on your bed, but you manage not to fall out of it. If you sleep with your babies, you will not roll over and suffocate them (assuming you are not intoxicated). The occasional roar of passing vehicles may leave deep sleep undisturbed, but the cry from a baby's nursery quickly interrupts it. So does the sound of your name—a stimulus our

FIGURE 7.5
Brain waves and sleep stages
The regular alpha waves of an awake, relaxed state are quite different from the slower, larger delta waves of deep Stage 4 sleep. Although the rapid REM sleep waves resemble the near-waking Stage 1 sleep waves, the body is more aroused during REM sleep than during Stage 1 sleep. (From Dement, 1978.)

■ **REM sleep** rapid eye movement sleep, a recurring sleep stage during which vivid dreams commonly occur. Also known as *paradoxical sleep*, because the muscles are relaxed (except for minor twitches) but other body systems are active.

■ **alpha waves** the relatively slow brain waves of a relaxed, awake state.

■ **sleep** periodic, natural, reversible loss of consciousness—as distinct from unconsciousness resulting from a coma, general anesthesia, or hibernation. (Adapted from Dement, 1999.)

■ **hallucinations** false sensory experiences, such as seeing something in the absence of an external visual stimulus.

■ **delta waves** the large, slow brain waves associated with deep sleep.

FIGURE 7.6
The moment of sleep
We seem unaware of the moment we fall into sleep, but someone eavesdropping on our brain waves could tell. (From Dement, 1999.)

"Boy are my eyes tired! I had REM sleep all night long."

Question: **Does eating spicy foods cause one to dream more?**
Answer: **Any food that causes you to awaken more increases your chance of *recalling* a dream (Moorcroft, 2003).**

selective attention is ever alert for. EEG recordings confirm that the brain's auditory cortex responds to sound stimuli even during sleep (Kutas, 1990). All this reminds us of one of this book's basic lessons: *We process most information outside our conscious awareness.*

About an hour after you first fall asleep, a strange thing happens. Rather than continuing in deep slumber, you ascend from your initial sleep dive. Returning through Stage 3 and Stage 2 (where you spend about half your night), you enter the most intriguing sleep phase of all—REM sleep (**FIGURE 7.7**). For about 10 minutes, your brain waves become rapid and saw-toothed, more like those of the nearly awake Stage 1 sleep. But unlike Stage 1 sleep, during REM sleep your heart rate rises, your breathing becomes rapid and irregular, and every half-minute or so your eyes dart around in a momentary burst of activity behind closed lids. Because anyone watching a sleeper's eyes can notice these REM bursts, it is amazing that science was ignorant of REM sleep until 1952.

Except during very scary dreams, your genitals become aroused during REM sleep, and you have an erection or increased vaginal lubrication and clitoral engorgement, regardless of whether the dream's content is sexual (Karacan & others, 1966). The phenomenon has been studied mostly in men, from whom measurements are more easily recorded and for whom the common "morning erection" stems from the night's last REM period, often just before waking. In young men, sleep-related erections outlast REM periods, lasting 30 to 45 minutes on average (Karacan & others, 1983; Schiavi & Schreiner-Engel, 1988). A typical 25-year-old man therefore has an erection during nearly half his night's sleep, a 65-year-old man for one-quarter. Many men troubled by *erectile dysfunction* (impotence) have morning erections, suggesting that the problem is not between their legs.

Although your brain's motor cortex is active during REM sleep, your brainstem blocks its messages, leaving your muscles relaxed—so relaxed that, except for an occasional finger, toe, or facial twitch, you are essentially paralyzed. (That explains why horses, which spend 92 percent of each day standing and can sleep standing, must lie down for REM sleep [Morrison, 2003].) Moreover, you cannot easily be awakened. Thus, REM sleep is sometimes called *paradoxical* sleep; the body is internally aroused and externally calm.

More intriguing than the paradoxical nature of REM sleep is what the rapid eye movements announce: the beginning of a dream. Even those who claim they never dream will, more than 80 percent of the time, recall a dream after being awakened during REM sleep. Unlike the fleeting images of Stage 1 sleep ("I was thinking about my exam today," or "I was trying to borrow something from someone"), REM sleep dreams are often emotional, usually storylike, and more richly hallucinatory:

FIGURE 7.7
The stages in a typical night's sleep

Most people pass through the five-stage sleep cycle (graph a) several times, with the periods of Stage 4 sleep and then Stage 3 sleep diminishing and REM sleep periods increasing in duration. Graph b plots this increasing REM sleep and decreasing deep sleep based on data from 30 young adults. (From Cartwright, 1978; Webb, 1992.)

Some sleep deeply, some not
The fluctuating sleep cycle enables safe sleep for these soldiers on the battlefield. One benefit of communal sleeping is that someone will probably be awake or easily roused in the event of a threat during the night.

My husband and I were at some friends' house, but our friends weren't there. Their TV had been left on, but otherwise it was very quiet. After we wandered around for a while, their dogs finally noticed us and barked and growled loudly, with bared teeth.

PET scans of sleeping people's brains (if sleepy enough, you, too, could sleep while lying in a brain-scanning machine) show that visual and auditory brain areas are relatively active during REM sleep and inactive during other sleep stages (Fosse & others, 2001).

Are the eye movements linked to a dream's visual aspects? Is the dreamer "watching" the dream as if it were a private movie projected in the mind's inner theater? Most researchers believe that is not the case: Darting eyes, like the occasional twitching of muscles, seem merely to reflect the overflow of the dreamer's active nervous system (Chase & Morales, 1983).

The sleep cycle repeats itself about every 90 minutes. As the night wears on, deep Stage 4 sleep gets progressively briefer and then disappears. The REM sleep period gets longer (see Figure 7.7b). By morning, 20 to 25 percent of our average night's sleep—some 100 minutes—has been REM sleep. Thirty-seven percent of people report rarely or never having dreams "that you can remember the next morning" (Moore, 2004). Unknown to those people, they spend about 600 hours a year experiencing some 1500 dreams, or more than 100,000 dreams over a typical lifetime—dreams swallowed by the night but never acted out, thanks to REM's protective paralysis.

Fantasy-prone people are especially likely to recall dreams from the previous night (Watson, 2003).

People rarely snore during dreams. When REM starts, snoring stops.

Why Do We Sleep?

OBJECTIVE 5 | Explain why sleep patterns and duration vary from person to person.

The idea that "everyone needs 8 hours of sleep" is untrue. Newborns spend nearly two-thirds of their day asleep, most adults no more than one-third. Age-related differences in average time spent sleeping are rivaled by differences in the normal amount of sleep among individuals at any age. Some people thrive with fewer than 6 hours of sleep per night; others regularly sleep 9 hours or more. Such sleep patterns may be genetically influenced. When Wilse Webb and Scott Campbell (1983) checked the pattern and duration of sleep among fraternal and identical twins, only the identical twins were strikingly similar.

Sleep patterns are also culturally influenced. Because of modern light bulbs, shift work, and social diversions, people in industrialized nations sleep less than they did a century ago. People who would have gone to bed at 9:00 P.M. are now up until 11:00 P.M. Thomas Edison (1948, pp. 52, 178) was pleased to accept credit for this. For him, less sleep meant more productive time and greater opportunities:

> When I went through Switzerland in a motor-car, so that I could visit little towns and villages, I noted the effect of artificial light on the inhabitants. Where water power and electric light had been developed, everyone seemed normally intelligent.

Gallup poll:
"Usually, how many hours sleep do you get at night?"

5 or less	16%
6	27
7	28
8	28

2001 average = 6.7 hours
1942 average = 7.6 hours

In 1989, Michael Doucette was named America's Safest Driving Teen. In 1990, while driving home from college, he fell asleep at the wheel and collided with an oncoming car, killing both himself and the other driver. Michael's driving instructor later acknowledged never having mentioned sleep deprivation and drowsy driving (Dement, 1999).

Sleepless and suffering
This fatigued, sleep-deprived person may also experience a depressed immune system, impaired concentration, and greater vulnerability to accidents.

" Tiger Woods said that one of the best things about his choice to leave Stanford for the professional golf circuit was that he could now get enough sleep."
Stanford sleep researcher William Dement, 1997

To test whether you are one of the many sleep-deprived students, see **Table 7.1**, page 282.

In a 2001 Gallup poll, 61 percent of men, but only 47 percent of women, said they got enough sleep.

When these appliances did not exist, and the natives went to bed with the chickens, staying there till daylight, they were far less intelligent.

Allowed to sleep unhindered, most humans will sleep at least 9 hours a night, reports Stanley Coren (1996). With that much sleep, we do not become groggy. We awake refreshed, sustain better moods, and perform more efficient and accurate work than do those who get less sleep. With a succession of 5-hour nights, however, we accumulate a sleep debt that is not paid off by one 10-hour sleep—which explains why we can feel sleepy even after a long sleep. "The brain keeps an accurate count of sleep debt for at least two weeks," says William Dement (1999, p. 64). Deprived of sleep, we also begin to feel terrible, as our bodies yearn for sleep. Try to stay awake and eventually we will lose. In the tiredness battle, sleep always wins.

Obviously, then, we need sleep. Sleep commands roughly one-third of our lives—some 25 years, on average. But why? It seems an easy question to answer: Just keep people awake for several days and note how they deteriorate. If you were a volunteer in such an experiment, how do you think it would affect your body and mind?

Of course, you would become terribly drowsy at times—especially during the hours when your biological clock programs you to sleep. But could a lack of sleep physically damage you? Would it noticeably alter your biochemistry or body organs? Would you become emotionally disturbed? Mentally disoriented?

The Effects of Sleep Deprivation

OBJECTIVE 6 | Discuss several risks associated with sleep deprivation.

Good news! Psychologists have discovered a treatment that strengthens memory, increases concentration, boosts mood, moderates hunger and obesity, fortifies the disease-fighting immune system, and lessens the risk of fatal accidents. Moreover, while supplies last, it's available free!

Even better news: The treatment feels good, it can be self-administered, and the supplies are limitless. If you are a typical university-age student, often going to bed near 2:00 A.M. and dragged out of bed six hours later by the dreaded alarm, the treatment is simple: Each night just add an hour to your sleep.

A major effect of lessened sleep is not only sleepiness but a general malaise (Mikulincer & others, 1989). People today more than ever suffer from sleep patterns that thwart their having an energized feeling of well-being. Teenagers typically need 8 or 9 hours of sleep, but they now average less than 7 hours, which is nearly 2 hours less sleep a night than their counterparts of 80 years ago (Holden, 1993; Maas, 1999). Many fill this need by using their first class for an early siesta and after-lunch study hall for a slumber party. When the going gets boring, the students start snoring. Even when awake, students often function below their peak. And they know it: Four in five American teens and three in five 18- to 29-year-olds wish they could get more sleep on weekdays (Mason, 2003, 2005).

At Stanford University, William Dement (1997) reports, 80 percent of students are "dangerously sleep deprived." Such individuals "are at high risk for some sort of accident. . . . Sleep deprivation [entails] difficulty studying, diminished productivity, tendency to make mistakes, irritability, fatigue." A large sleep debt "makes you stupid," says Dement (1999, p. 231). But let's put this positively: To manage your life with enough sleep to awaken naturally and well rested is to be more alert, productive, healthy, and happy. For teens, that's easier said than done. The one who staggers glumly out of bed in response to an unwelcome alarm, yawns through morning classes, and feels half-depressed much of the day may be energized at 11 P.M. and mindless of the next day's looming sleepiness (Carskadon, 2002).

In experiments, the U.S. Navy and the National Institutes of Health have paid volunteers to spend 14 hours daily in bed for at least a week. For the first few days, the volunteers in both experiments averaged 12 hours sleep a day or more, apparently paying off a sleep debt that averaged 25 to 30 hours. That accomplished, they then settled back to 7.5 to 9 hours of sleep a night and, with no sleep debt, felt energized and happier. "What this means to me," reflected Dement (1999, p. 72) "is that millions of us are living a less than optimal life and performing at a less than optimal level, impaired by an amount of sleep debt that we're not even aware we carry." When Daniel Kahneman and his colleagues (2004) invited 909 working women to report on their daily moods, they were struck by what mattered little, such as money (so long as they were not battling poverty) and job security, and what mattered a lot—less time pressure at work and a good night's sleep. In a Gallup survey (Mason, 2005), 63 percent of adults who report getting the sleep they need also report being "very satisfied" with their personal life (as do only 36 percent of those needing more sleep).

As a demonstration of the costs of sleep deprivation, Stanley Coren capitalized on what is, for many North Americans, a semi-annual sleep-manipulation experiment—the "spring forward" to "daylight savings" time and "fall backward" to "standard" time. Searching millions of records, he found that in both Canada and the United States, accidents increase immediately after the shortened sleep associated with the spring time change. In Canada, for example, traffic accidents during 1991 and 1992 were 7 percent higher on the Monday after the spring time change than on the Monday before, and they were 7 percent *lower* on the Monday following the extra sleep bestowed by the fall time change (**FIGURE 7.8**).

Similar effects were seen in accident patterns in the United States, though with more effect in the spring than fall. Coren (1996) speculates that we lose more sleep at the spring shift than we gain in the fall.

Sleep deprivation experiments reveal slowed reaction times and increased errors on visual tasks similar to those involved in airport baggage screening, performing surgery, and reading X-rays (Horowitz & others, 2003). And sleep deprivation can be devastating for driving and piloting. Some 30 percent of Australian highway deaths occur when drivers fall asleep on long, monotonous roads (Maas, 1999). Driver fatigue similarly contributes to an estimated 20 percent of American traffic accidents (Brody, 2002). "Rest. That's what I need is rest," said Eastern Airlines Captain James Reeves to the control tower on a September 1974 morning—30 minutes before crashing his airliner at low altitude, killing the crew and all 68 passengers (Moorcroft, 1993). Consider also the 1989 *Exxon Valdez* oil spill; Union Carbide's 1984 Bhopal, India, disaster; and the 1979 Three Mile Island and 1986 Chernobyl nuclear accidents—they all occurred after midnight, when operators in charge were likely to be drowsiest. Severely sleep-deprived, the *Exxon Valdez* mate at the helm was unresponsive to clear signals to turn his vessel back into the shipping lanes.

Sleep loss also affects us in more subtle ways, including suppression of the disease-fighting immune system (Beardsley, 1996; Irwin & others, 1994). Sleep deprivation suppresses immune cells that fight off viral infections and cancer, which helps explain why people who sleep 7 to 8 hours a night tend to outlive those who are chronically sleep deprived, and why older adults who have no difficulty falling or staying asleep tend to live longer (Dement, 1999; Dew & others, 2003). When infections do set in, we typically sleep more, boosting

> "Drowsiness is red alert!"
> William Dement, *The Promise of Sleep*, 1999

FIGURE 7.8

Canadian traffic accidents, 1991 and 1992

On the Monday after the spring time change, when people lose one hour of sleep, accidents increased as compared with the Monday before. In the fall, traffic accidents normally increase because of greater snow, ice, and darkness, but they diminish after the time change. (Adapted from Coren, 1996.)

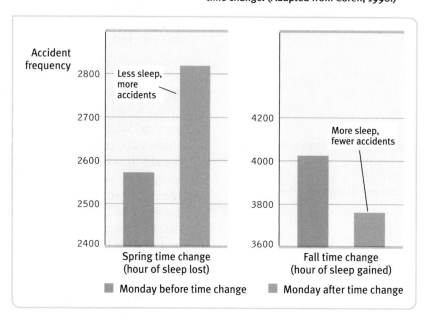

TABLE 7.1

ARE YOU SLEEP DEPRIVED?

Cornell University psychologist James Maas reports that most college students suffer the consequences of sleeping less than they should. To see if you are in that group, answer the following true-false questions:

True	False	
☐	☐	1. I need an alarm clock in order to wake up at the appropriate time.
☐	☐	2. It's a struggle for me to get out of bed in the morning.
☐	☐	3. Weekday mornings I hit the snooze bar several times to get more sleep.
☐	☐	4. I feel tired, irritable, and stressed out during the week.
☐	☐	5. I have trouble concentrating and remembering.
☐	☐	6. I feel slow with critical thinking, problem solving, and being creative.
☐	☐	7. I often fall asleep watching TV.
☐	☐	8. I often fall asleep in boring meetings or lectures or in warm rooms.
☐	☐	9. I often fall asleep after heavy meals or after a low dose of alcohol.
☐	☐	10. I often fall asleep while relaxing after dinner.
☐	☐	11. I often fall asleep within five minutes of getting into bed.
☐	☐	12. I often feel drowsy while driving.
☐	☐	13. I often sleep extra hours on weekend mornings.
☐	☐	14. I often need a nap to get through the day.
☐	☐	15. I have dark circles around my eyes.

If you answered "true" to three or more items, you probably are not getting enough sleep. To determine your sleep needs, Maas recommends that you "go to bed 15 minutes earlier than usual every night for the next week—and continue this practice by adding 15 more minutes each week—until you wake without an alarm clock and feel alert all day." (Quiz reprinted with permission from James B. Maas, *Power sleep: The revolutionary program that prepares your mind and body for peak performance* [New York: HarperCollins, 1999].)

our immune cells. Chronic sleep debt also alters metabolic and hormonal functioning in ways that mimic aging and are conducive to obesity, hypertension, and memory impairment (Spiegel & others, 1999; Taheri, 2004). Other effects include irritability, slowed performance, and impaired creativity, concentration, and communication (Harrison & Horne, 2000). When sleepy frontal lobes confront an unexpected situation, misfortune often results.

Sleep Theories

OBJECTIVE 7 | Identify four theories of why we sleep.

So, nature charges us for our sleep debt. But why do we have this need for sleep?

We have very few answers, but sleep may have evolved for four reasons: First, sleep *protects*. When darkness precluded our ancestors' hunting and food gathering and made travel treacherous, they were better off asleep in a cave, out of harm's way. Our distant ancestors who didn't try to navigate around rocks and cliffs at night were more likely to leave descendants. Our sleep suits our ecological niche. Animals with the most need to graze and the least ability to hide tend to sleep less. Elephants and horses sleep 3 to 4 hours a day, gorillas 12 hours, and cats 14 hours. For bats and eastern chipmunks, both of which sleep 20 hours, to live is hardly more than to eat and to sleep (Moorcroft, 2003).

Second, sleep helps us recuperate. It helps *restore and repair* brain tissue. Bats and other animals with high waking metabolism burn a lot of calories, producing a lot of molecules, called free radicals, that are toxic to neurons. Sleeping a lot gives resting neurons time to repair themselves, while allowing unused connections to weaken

"Sleep faster, we need the pillows."
Yiddish proverb

"Corduroy pillows make headlines."
Anonymous

(Siegel, 2003). Think of it this way: When consciousness leaves your house, brain construction workers come in for a makeover.

But sleep is not just for keeping us safe and for repairing our brain. Sleep is also for *remembering*. New research reveals that sleep restores and rebuilds our fading memories of the day's experiences. People trained to perform tasks recall them better after a night's sleep than after several hours awake (Fenn & others, 2003). And in both humans and rats, neural activity during slow-wave sleep reenacts and promotes recall of prior novel experiences (Peigneux & others, 2004; Ribeiro & others, 2004). Sleep also feeds creative thinking. After working on a task, then sleeping on it, people solve problems more insightfully than do those who stay awake (Wagner & others, 2004).

Finally, sleep may play a role in the *growth* process. During deep sleep, the pituitary gland releases a growth hormone. As adults grow older, they release less of this hormone, and they spend less time in deep sleep (Pekkanen, 1982). These discoveries are beginning to solve the ongoing riddle of sleep.

Sleep Disorders

OBJECTIVE 8 | Identify the major sleep disorders.

No matter what their normal need for sleep, some 10 to 15 percent of adults complain of **insomnia**—persistent problems in falling or staying asleep. True insomnia is not the occasional inability to sleep that we experience when anxious or excited. For any stressed organism, being vigilant is natural and adaptive. A personal conflict during the day often means a fitful sleep that night (Brisette & Cohen, 2002). Moreover, from middle age on, sleep is seldom uninterrupted. Being occasionally awakened becomes the norm, not something to fret over or treat with medication.

Some people fret unnecessarily about their sleep (Coren, 1996). In laboratory studies, insomnia complainers do get less sleep than others, but they typically overestimate—by about double—how long it took them to fall asleep. They also underestimate by nearly half how long they actually slept. Even if we have been awake only an hour or two, we may *think* we have had very little sleep, because it's the waking part we remember. When researchers awaken people repeatedly during the night, some, after quickly falling back to sleep, recall having slept soundly.

The most common quick fixes for true insomnia—sleeping pills and alcohol—can aggravate the problem. Alcohol and some sleep medications reduce REM sleep and can leave a person with next-day blahs. Relying on such, a person may need increasing doses to get an effect. Then, when the drug is discontinued, the insomnia can worsen.

Scientists are searching for natural chemicals that are abundant during sleep, hoping they might be synthesized as a sleep aid without side effects. In the meantime, sleep experts offer other natural alternatives:

- Relax before bedtime, using dimmer light.
- Avoid caffeine (this includes chocolate) after late afternoon, and avoid rich foods before bedtime. A glass of milk may help. (Milk provides raw materials for the manufacture of serotonin, a neurotransmitter that facilitates sleep.)
- Sleep on a regular schedule (rise at the same time even after a restless night) and avoid naps. A regular sleep schedule boosts daytime alertness, too, as shown in an experiment in which University of Arizona students averaged 7.5 hours of sleep a night on either a varying or consistent schedule (Manber & others, 1996).
- Exercise regularly but not in the late evening (late afternoon is best).
- Reassure yourself that a temporary loss of sleep causes no great harm, certainly nothing worth losing sleep over. "Sleep is like love or happiness," notes Wilse Webb (1992, p. 170). "If you pursue it too ardently it will elude you."

■ insomnia recurring problems in falling or staying asleep.

> "The lion and the lamb shall lie down together, but the lamb will not be very sleepy."
> Woody Allen, in the movie *Love and Death*, 1975

> "In 1757 Benjamin Franklin gave us the axiom, 'Early to bed, early to rise, makes a man healthy, wealthy, and wise.' It would be more accurate to say 'consistently to bed and consistently to rise . . .'"
> James B. Maas, *Power Sleep*, 1999

Stress robs sleep
Urban police officers, especially those under stress, report poorer sleep quality and less sleep than average (Neylan & others, 2002).

■ **narcolepsy** a sleep disorder characterized by uncontrollable sleep attacks. The sufferer may lapse directly into REM sleep, often at inopportune times.

■ **sleep apnea** a sleep disorder characterized by temporary cessations of breathing during sleep and repeated momentary awakenings.

■ **night terrors** a sleep disorder characterized by high arousal and an appearance of being terrified; unlike nightmares, night terrors occur during Stage 4 sleep, within two or three hours of falling asleep, and are seldom remembered.

Imagine observing a person with narcolepsy in medieval times. Might such symptoms and their associated hallucinations have seemed like demon possession?

- Hide the clock face so you aren't tempted to check it repeatedly.
- If nothing else works, aim for less sleep; go to bed later or get up earlier.

Rarer but also more troublesome than insomnia are the sleep disorders narcolepsy and sleep apnea. People who suffer **narcolepsy** (from *narco,* "numbness," and *lepsy,* "seizure") experience periodic, overwhelming sleepiness. This usually lasts less than 5 minutes, but sometimes occurs at the most inopportune times, perhaps just after taking a terrific swing at a softball or when laughing loudly, shouting angrily, or having sex (Dement, 1978, 1999). In severe cases, the person may collapse directly into a brief period of REM sleep, with its accompanying loss of muscular tension.

Those who suffer from narcolepsy—1 in 2000 people, estimates the Stanford University Center for Narcolepsy (2002)—must live with extra caution. As a traffic menace, "snoozing is second only to boozing," says the American Sleep Disorders Association, and those with narcolepsy are especially at risk (Aldrich, 1989). Curiously, studies in Canada, France, and the United States have found that September babies are at 37 percent less than average risk for narcolepsy, and March babies 45 percent more so (Dauvilliers & others, 2003; Picchioni & others, 2004). Perhaps, researchers speculate, the March risk relates to the fall cold and flu season, which occurs during the critical second trimester of fetal development.

At the century's end, researchers discovered a gene causing narcolepsy in dogs (Lin & others, 1999; Taheri, 2004). Genes help sculpt the brain, and neuroscientists are searching the brain for abnormalities linked with narcolepsy. One team of researchers discovered a relative absence of a hypothalamic neural center that produces *hypocretin,* an alerting neurotransmitter (Taheri & others, 2002; Thannickal & others, 2000). Narcolepsy, it is now clear, is a brain disease; it is not just "in your mind." And this gives hope that narcolepsy might be effectively relieved by a drug that mimics the missing hypocretin and can sneak through the blood-brain barrier (Fujiki & others, 2003; Siegel, 2000). In the meantime, physicians are prescribing other drugs to relieve narcolepsy's sleepiness in humans.

Another sleep disorder—**sleep apnea**—leaves millions of people (mostly overweight men) tired and sometimes irritable during the day and therefore, like those who suffer narcolepsy, at increased risk of traffic accidents (Teran-Santos & others, 1999). The National Institutes of Health reports that 1 person in 20 suffers from this condition, which was unknown before modern sleep research. They intermittently stop breathing during sleep. (*Apnea* means "with no breath.") After an airless minute or so, decreased blood oxygen arouses the sleeper to awaken and snort in air for a few seconds. The process can repeat more than 400 times a night, depriving the person of slow-wave sleep. Apart from complaints of sleepiness and irritability during the day—and their mates' complaints about their loud "snoring"—apnea sufferers are often unaware of their disorder. (The next morning they have no recall of these episodes.)

As the number of obese people in the United States has increased, so has sleep apnea. Anyone who snores at night, who feels tired during the day, and who possibly has high blood pressure as well (putting them at risk for a stroke or heart attack), should be checked for apnea (Dement, 1999). For serious cases, physicians often give the sleeper a masklike device with an air pump that keeps the airway open and breathing regular. If one doesn't mind looking a little goofy in the dark (imagine a snorkeler at a slumber party), the treatment is often effective.

Unlike sleep apnea, **night terrors** target mostly children, who may sit up or walk around, talk incoherently, experience a doubling of heart and breathing rates, and appear terrified (Hartmann, 1981). They seldom wake up fully during an episode and recall little or nothing the next morning—at most, a fleeting, frightening image. Night terrors are not nightmares (which, like other dreams, typically occur during early morning REM sleep); night terrors usually occur during the first few hours of Stage 4 (**FIGURE 7.9**).

Did Brahms need his own lullabies? Cranky, overweight, and nap-prone, Johannes Brahms exhibited common symptoms of sleep apnea (Margolis, 2000).

Archivo Iconografico, S.A./Corbis

FIGURE 7.9
Night terrors and nightmares
Night terrors occur within two or three hours of falling asleep, during Stage 4 sleep. Nightmares occur toward morning, during REM sleep. (From Hartmann, 1984.)

Children also are most prone to sleepwalking—another Stage 4 sleep disorder—and to sleeptalking, conditions that run in families. Finnish twin studies reveal that occasional childhood sleepwalking occurs for about one-third of those with a sleepwalking fraternal twin and half of those with a sleepwalking identical twin. The same is true for sleeptalking (Hublin & others, 1997, 1998). Sleepwalking is usually harmless and unrecalled the next morning. Sleepwalkers typically return to bed on their own or are guided there by a family member. Young children, who have the deepest and lengthiest Stage 4 sleep, are the most likely to experience both night terrors and sleepwalking. As we grow older and deep Stage 4 sleep diminishes, so do night terrors and sleepwalking. After age 40, sleepwalking is rare.

Dreams

Discovering the link between REM sleep and dreaming opened a new era in dream research. Instead of relying on someone's hazy recall hours or days after having a dream, researchers could catch dreams as they happened. They could awaken people during or within 3 minutes after a REM sleep period and hear a vivid account.

What Do We Dream?

OBJECTIVE 9 | Describe the most common content of dreams.

REM **dreams**—"hallucinations of the sleeping mind"—are vivid, emotional, and bizarre. They are unlike daydreams, which tend to involve the familiar details of our lives—perhaps imagining an alternative approach to something we have to do, or picturing ourselves explaining to an instructor why a paper will be late, or replaying in our minds personal encounters that we relish or regret. The dreams of REM sleep are so vivid we may confuse them with reality. Awakening from a nightmare, a 4-year-old may complain of a bear in the house.

Occasionally, we may be sufficiently aware during a dream to wonder whether we are, in fact, dreaming. When experiencing such *lucid dreams,* some people are able to test their state of consciousness. If they can perform some absurd act, such as floating in the air, then they know they are dreaming.

Would you suppose that people dream if blind from birth? Studies of blind people in France, Hungary, Egypt, and the United States all found them dreaming of using

> "I do not believe that I am now dreaming, but I cannot prove that I am not."
> Philosopher Bertrand Russell (1872–1970)

■ **dream** a sequence of images, emotions, and thoughts passing through a sleeping person's mind. Dreams are notable for their hallucinatory imagery, discontinuities, and incongruities, and for the dreamer's delusional acceptance of the content and later difficulties remembering it.

■ **manifest content** according to Freud, the remembered story line of a dream (as distinct from its latent, or hidden, content).

■ **latent content** according to Freud, the underlying meaning of a dream (as distinct from its manifest content). Freud believed that a dream's latent content functions as a safety valve.

A popular sleep myth: If you dream you are falling and hit the ground (or if you dream of dying), you die. (Unfortunately, those who could confirm these ideas are not around to do so. Some people, however, have had such dreams and are alive to report them.)

" For what one has dwelt on by day, these things are seen in visions of the night."
Menander of Athens (342–292 B.C.), *Fragments*

their nonvisual senses—hearing, touching, smelling, tasting (Buquet, 1988; Taha, 1972; Vekassy, 1977). Yet even congenitally blind people can experience visual images in dreams (Bértolo & others, 2003).

We spend six years of our life in dreams, many of which are anything but sweet. For both women and men, 8 in 10 dreams are marked by negative emotions (Domhoff, 1999). People commonly dream of repeatedly failing in an attempt to do something; of being attacked, pursued, or rejected; or of experiencing misfortune (Hall & others, 1982). When awakened during REM sleep, people report dreams with sexual imagery less often than you might think. In one study, only 1 in 10 dreams among young men and 1 in 30 among young women had sexual overtones (Domhoff, 1996). More commonly, we dream of events in our daily lives, a meeting at work, taking an exam, or relating to a family member or friend. Across the world, people of all ages show an unexplainable gender difference in dream content. Women dream of males and females equally often, whereas 65 percent of the characters in men's dreams are males. No one is sure why (Hall, 1984).

The story line of our dreams—what Sigmund Freud called their **manifest content**—sometimes incorporates traces of previous days' experiences and preoccupations (De Koninck, 2000):

- After suffering a trauma, people commonly report nightmares.
- Robert Stickgold and his colleagues (2000) had people play the computer game "Tetris" for seven hours and then repeatedly awakened them during their first hour of sleep; three-fourths reported experiencing images of the game's falling blocks.
- People in hunter-gatherer societies often dream of animals; urban Japanese rarely do (Mestel, 1997).

The sensory stimuli of our sleeping environment may also intrude. A particular odor or the telephone's ringing may be instantly and ingeniously woven into the dream story. In a classic experiment, William Dement and Edward Wolpert (1958) lightly sprayed cold water on dreamers' faces. Compared with sleepers who did not get the cold-water treatment, these people were more likely to dream about water—about a waterfall, a leaky roof, or even about being sprayed by someone. Even while in REM sleep, focused on internal stimuli, we maintain some awareness of changes in our external environment.

So, could we learn a foreign language by listening to tapes while we sleep? If only it were so easy. While sleeping we can learn to associate a sound with a mild electric shock (and to react to the sound accordingly). But we do not remember taped information played while we are soundly asleep (Eich, 1990; Wyatt & Bootzin, 1994). In fact, anything that happens during the 5 minutes just before we fall asleep is typically lost from memory (Roth & others, 1988). This explains why sleep apnea patients, who repeatedly awaken with a gasp and then immediately fall back to sleep, do not recall the episodes. It also explains why dreams that momentarily awaken us are mostly forgotten by morning. To remember a dream, get up and stay awake for a few minutes.

Why Do We Dream?

OBJECTIVE 10 | Compare the major perspectives on why we dream.

Dream theorists have proposed several possible explanations of why we dream, including these:

To satisfy our own wishes. In his landmark book *The Interpretation of Dreams*, published in 1900, Freud offered what he thought was "the most valuable of all the discoveries it has been my good fortune to make." He argued that by fulfilling wishes, a dream provides a psychic safety valve that discharges otherwise unacceptable feelings. According to Freud, a dream's manifest, or apparent, content is a censored, symbolic version of its **latent content,** which consists of unconscious drives and wishes that would be threatening if expressed directly. Although most dreams have no overt sexual imagery, Freud nevertheless believed that most adult dreams can be "traced back by analysis to *erotic wishes*." Thus, a gun might be a disguised representation of a penis.

Freud considered dreams the key to understanding our inner conflicts. However, his critics say it is time to wake up from Freud's dream theory, which is a scientific nightmare. Based on the accumulated science, "there is no reason to believe any of Freud's specific claims about dreams and their purposes," notes dream researcher William Domhoff (2000). Some contend that even if dreams are symbolic, they could be interpreted any way one wished. Others maintain that dreams hide nothing. A dream about a gun is a dream about a gun. Legend has it that even Freud, who loved to smoke cigars, remarked that "sometimes, a cigar is just a cigar."

To file away memories. Freud's wish-fulfillment theory of dreams has in large part given way to other theories. Researchers who see dreams as *information processing* believe that dreams may help sift, sort, and fix the day's experiences in our memory. We have known for some time that REM sleep facilitates memory (McGrath & Cohen, 1978). In experiments, people have heard unusual phrases or learned to find hidden visual images before bedtime. If awakened every time they began REM sleep, they remembered less the next morning than if awakened during other sleep stages (Empson & Clarke, 1970; Karni & Sagi, 1994).

Moreover, it's true that people tested the next day generally improved on a learned task after a night of memory consolidation. But even after two nights of recovery sleep, those deprived of both slow-wave and REM sleep didn't do as well as those who slept undisturbed on their new learning (Stickgold & others, 2000, 2001).

Other studies confirm that we experience REM sleep, in part, to remember. The brain regions that buzz as rats learn to navigate a maze, or as people learn to perform a visual-discrimination task, buzz again later during REM sleep (Louie & Wilson, 2001; Maquet, 2001). So precise were the activity patterns that the scientists could tell where in the maze the rat would be if awake. Deep, slow-wave sleep, it seems, helps stabilize our memories of experiences. And REM sleep helps convert memories into long-term learning.

So, a night of solid sleep (and dreaming) has an important place in our lives: To sleep, perchance to remember. This is important news for teens and college students, researcher Robert Stickgold (2000) believes. Many students suffer from a kind of sleep bulimia, binge-sleeping on the weekend. "But if you don't get good sleep and enough sleep after you learn new stuff, you won't integrate it effectively into your memories," Stickgold notes. That may help explain why high-achieving secondary students with high grades average 25 minutes more sleep a night and go to bed 40 minutes earlier than their lower-achieving classmates (Wolfson & Carskadon, 1998).

To develop and preserve neural pathways. Dreams may also serve a *physiological function.* Perhaps dreams—or the associated brain activity of REM sleep—provide the

"When people interpret [a dream] as if it were meaningful and then sell those interpretations, it's quackery."

Sleep researcher J. Allan Hobson (1995)

Rapid eye movements also stir the liquid behind the cornea; this delivers fresh oxygen to corneal cells, preventing their suffocation.

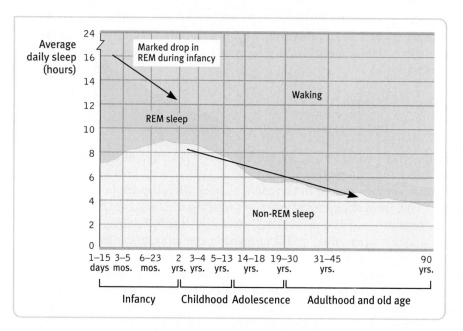

FIGURE 7.10
Sleep across the life span
As we age, our sleep patterns change. During our first few months, we spend progressively less time in REM sleep. During our first 20 years, we spend progressively less time asleep. (Adapted from Snyder & Scott, 1972.)

■ **REM rebound** the tendency for REM sleep to increase following REM sleep deprivation (created by repeated awakenings during REM sleep).

sleeping brain with periodic stimulation. As you may recall from Chapter 2, stimulating experiences develop and preserve the brain's neural pathways. This theory makes sense from a developmental point of view. Infants, whose neural networks are fast developing, spend a great deal of time in REM sleep (**FIGURE 7.10**).

To make sense of neural static. Other physiological theories propose that dreams erupt from neural activity that spreads upward from the brainstem (Antrobus, 1991; Hobson, 2003, 2004). According to one version—the *activation-synthesis* theory—this neural activity is random, and dreams are the brain's attempt to make sense of it. Much as a neurosurgeon can produce hallucinations by stimulating different parts of a patient's cortex, so can stimulation originating within the brain. These internal stimuli activate brain areas that process visual images, but not the visual cortex area, which receives raw input from the eyes. As Freud might have expected, PET scans of sleeping people also reveal increased activity in the emotion-related limbic system (in the amygdala) during REM sleep. In contrast, frontal lobe regions responsible for inhibition and logical thinking seem to idle, which may explain why our dreams are less inhibited than we are (Maquet & others, 1996). Add the limbic system's emotional tone to the brain's visual bursts and—voilà!—we dream. Damage either the limbic system or the visual centers active during dreaming, and dreaming itself may be impaired (Domhoff, 2003).

To reflect cognitive development. Some dream researchers dispute both the Freudian and activation-synthesis theories, preferring instead to see dreams as part of brain maturation and cognitive development. For example, prior to age 9, children's dreams seem more like a slide show and less like an active story in which the dreamer is an actor (Domhoff, 2003; Foulkes, 1999). Dreams also overlap with waking cognition, note those who favor a cognitive theory of dreams. Dreams feature coherent speech. They draw on our concepts and knowledge. And they share some commonalities with the mind's occasional flights during waking reverie. Moreover, some dream images appear outside REM sleep, when brainstem activation is minimal. **TABLE 7.2** compares major dream theories.

There is one thing dream theorists agree on: We *need* REM sleep. Deprived of it by repeatedly being awakened, people return more and more quickly to the REM stage after falling back to sleep. When finally allowed to sleep undisturbed, they literally sleep like babies—with increased REM sleep, a phenomenon called **REM rebound.** Withdrawing REM-suppressing sleeping medications also increases REM sleep, but with accompanying nightmares.

TABLE 7.2

DREAM THEORIES

Theory	Explanation	Critical Considerations
Freud's wish-fulfillment	Dreams provide a "psychic safety valve"—expressing otherwise unacceptable feelings; contain manifest (remembered) content and a deeper layer of latent content—a hidden meaning.	Lacks any scientific support; dreams may be interpreted in many different ways.
Information-processing	Dreams help us sort out the day's events and consolidate our memories.	But why do we sometimes dream about things we have not experienced?
Physiological function	Regular brain stimulation from REM sleep may help develop and preserve neural pathways.	This may be true, but it does not explain why we experience *meaningful* dreams.
Activation-synthesis	REM sleep triggers neural activity that evokes random visual memories, which our sleeping brain weaves into stories.	The individual's brain is weaving the stories, which still tells us something about the dreamer.
Cognitive theory	Dream content reflects dreamers' cognitive development—their knowledge and understanding.	Does not address the neuroscience of dreams.

Most other mammals also experience REM sleep and REM rebound. Animals' need for REM sleep suggests that its causes and functions are deeply biological. That REM sleep occurs in mammals—and not in animals such as fish, whose behavior is less influenced by learning—also fits the information-processing theory of dreams. All of this reminds us once again of a basic lesson: *Biological and psychological explanations of behavior are partners, not competitors.*

But if dreams lack the disguised meanings that Freud supposed and instead serve physiological functions and extend normal cognition, are they therefore psychologically meaningless? Not necessarily. Every psychologically meaningful experience involves an active brain. Moreover, say advocates of dream reflection, dreams may be akin to abstract art—amenable to more than one meaningful interpretation, and illuminating to ponder.

> "Those dreams that on the silent night intrude, and with false flitting shapes our minds delude . . . are mere productions of the brain. And fools consult interpreters in vain."
>
> Jonathan Swift, "On Dreams," 1727

>> LEARNING OUTCOMES

Sleep and Dreams

OBJECTIVE 2 | Distinguish four types of biological rhythms, and give an example of each.

Our internal "biological clocks" create periodic physiological fluctuations. These cycles occur annually (as in seasonal variations in appetite and mood), every 28 days (as in women's menstrual periods), every 24 hours (as in daily cycles of alertness), and every 90 minutes (as in human sleep stages).

OBJECTIVE 3 | Describe the cycle of our circadian rhythm, and identify some events that can disrupt this biological clock.

The circadian rhythm's 24-hour cycle regulates our daily schedule of sleeping and waking. This cycle is in part a response to light striking the retina, signaling the suprachiasmatic nucleus in the hypothalamus to trigger alterations in the level of biochemical substances, including decreased output of sleep-inducing melatonin by the pineal gland. Time changes, long flights, shifts in sleep schedules, and exposure to bright light can reset this biological clock.

OBJECTIVE 4 | List the stages of the sleep cycle, and explain how they differ.

The cycle of five sleep stages totals about 90 minutes. Leaving the alpha waves of the awake, relaxed stage, we descend into transitional Stage 1 sleep, often with the sensation of falling or floating. Stage 2 sleep (the stage in which we spend the most time) follows about 20 minutes later, with its characteristic sleep spindles. Then follow Stages 3 and 4, together lasting about 30 minutes with large, slow delta waves. Reversing course, we retrace our path through these stages—with one difference: About an hour after falling asleep, we begin approximately 10 minutes of REM (rapid eye movement) sleep, in which most dreaming occurs. In this fifth stage (also known as *paradoxical sleep*), we are internally aroused but outwardly paralyzed. As this up-and-down cycle repeats during a normal night's sleep, periods of Stage 4 and then Stage 3 sleep progressively shorten and dreaming REM sleep lengthens.

OBJECTIVE 5 | **Explain why sleep patterns and duration vary from person to person.**

Most people, if allowed to sleep as long as they want, will average about 9 hours. But sleep is affected by age—newborns, for example, sleep twice as much as adults. People also differ in their individual sleep requirements, and twin studies indicate these differences may be partly genetic. Cultural expectations about "the perfect sleep" also help determine the amount of sleep we feel is adequate.

OBJECTIVE 6 | **Discuss several risks associated with sleep deprivation.**

Sleep deprivation puts people at risk not only for fatigue, but also for a depressed immune system; impaired concentration, creativity, and communication; irritability; and slowed performance (with greater vulnerability to accidents). Chronic sleep deprivation can alter metabolic and hormonal functioning, creating conditions that may contribute to obesity, hypertension, and memory impairment.

OBJECTIVE 7 | **Identify four theories of why we sleep.**

Sleep may have played a protective role in human evolution by keeping people safe during potentially dangerous periods. Sleep gives the brain time to heal, as it restores and repairs damaged neurons. During sleep, we restore and rebuild memories of the day's experiences, and a good night's sleep promotes insightful problem-solving the next day. Sleep also encourages growth; the pituitary gland secretes a growth hormone in Stage 4 sleep.

OBJECTIVE 8 | **Identify the major sleep disorders.**

The disorders of sleep include insomnia (recurring wakefulness), narcolepsy (sudden uncontrollable sleepiness or lapsing into REM sleep), sleep apnea (the stopping of breathing while asleep), night terrors (high arousal and the appearance of being terrified), sleepwalking, and sleeptalking. Sleep apnea mainly targets overweight men. Children are most prone to night terrors, sleepwalking, and sleeptalking.

OBJECTIVE 9 | **Describe the most common content of dreams.**

We usually dream of ordinary events and everyday experiences, 80 percent of them involving some anxiety or misfortune. Fewer than 10 percent of dreams (and less among women) have any sexual content. Most dreams occur during REM sleep; those that happen during non-REM sleep tend to be vague fleeting images.

OBJECTIVE 10 | **Compare the major perspectives on why we dream.**

(1) Freud believed that dreams provide a safety valve, because their manifest content (or story line) is a censored version of latent content (some underlying meaning that gratifies our unconscious wishes). (2) The information-processing perspective on dreaming is that dreams help us sort out the day's experiences and fix them in memory. (3) Other physiological theories of dreaming propose that REM-induced regular brain stimulation helps develop and preserve neural pathways in the brain. (4) The activation-synthesis explanation of dreaming is that REM sleep triggers impulses in the visual cortex, evoking random visual images that our brain tries to weave into a story line. (5) The brain-maturation/cognitive-development perspective believes dreams represent the dreamer's level of development, knowledge, and understanding. Despite their differences, most sleep theorists agree that REM sleep and its associated dreams serve an important function, as shown by the REM rebound that occurs following REM deprivation.

ASK YOURSELF: **In some countries, such as Britain, the school day for teenagers runs from about 9:00 A.M. to 4:00 P.M. In other countries, such as the United States, the teen school day often runs from 8:00 A.M. to 3:00 P.M., or even 7:30 A.M. to 2:30 P.M. Early to rise isn't making kids wise, say critics—it's making them sleepy. For optimal alertness and well-being, teens need 8 to 9 hours of sleep a night. So, should early-start schools move to a later start time, even if it requires buying more buses or switching start times with elementary schools? Or is this impractical, and would it do little to remedy the tired-teen problem?**

Hypnosis

OBJECTIVE 11 | Define *hypnosis*, and note some similarities between the behavior of hypnotized people and that of motivated unhypnotized people.

Imagine you are about to be hypnotized. The hypnotist invites you to sit back, fix your gaze on a spot high on the wall, and relax. In a quiet, low voice the hypnotist suggests, "Your eyes are growing tired. . . . Your eyelids are becoming heavy . . . now heavier and heavier. . . . They are beginning to close. . . . You are becoming more deeply relaxed. . . . Your breathing is now deep and regular. . . . Your muscles are becoming more and more relaxed. Your whole body is beginning to feel like lead."

After a few minutes of this hypnotic induction, you may experience **hypnosis.** When the hypnotist suggests, "Your eyelids are shutting so tight that you cannot open them even if you try," it may indeed seem beyond your control to open your eyelids. Told to forget the number 6, you may be puzzled when you count 11 fingers on your hands. Invited to smell a sensuous perfume that is actually ammonia, you may linger delightedly over its

■ **hypnosis** a social interaction in which one person (the hypnotist) suggests to another (the subject) that certain perceptions, feelings, thoughts, or behaviors will spontaneously occur.

pungent odor. Told that you cannot see a certain object, such as a chair, you may indeed report that it is not there, although you manage to avoid the chair when walking around.

Although hypnotic techniques have been used since antiquity, credit for their modern popularity goes to an Austrian physician, Anton Mesmer (1734-1815), who mistakenly thought he had discovered an "animal magnetism." With great flourish, Mesmer passed magnets over the bodies of ailing people, some of whom would lapse into a trancelike ("mesmerized") state, then awaken much improved. A French commission chaired by Benjamin Franklin found no evidence of animal magnetism and attributed Mesmer's "cures" to "mere imagination." Thus, hypnosis—or mesmerism, as it was then called—became linked with quackery.

Also working against the respectability of hypnosis were the grand claims made by its practitioners. Supposedly, mesmerized people could see with the back of their head, perceive others' internal organs, and communicate with the dead. Researchers now agree that hypnotized people can perform no such feats. In experiments, the strength, stamina, learning, and perceptual abilities of those under hypnosis are like those of motivated unhypnotized people (Druckman & Bjork, 1994). Hypnotized people may surprise you by, say, extending their arms for 6 minutes—but unhypnotized people can also do this and other amazing feats (**FIGURE 7.11**).

Before considering whether the hypnotic state is actually an *altered* state of consciousness, let's first consider some areas of general agreement.

Facts and Falsehoods

OBJECTIVE 12 | Discuss the characteristics of people who are susceptible to hypnosis, and evaluate claims that hypnosis can influence people's memory, will, health, and perception of pain.

Those who study hypnosis agree that its power resides not in the hypnotist but in the subject's openness to suggestion (Bowers, 1984). Hypnotists have no magical mind-control power; they merely engage people's ability to focus on certain images or behaviors. But what powers does this openness to suggestion have?

Can Anyone Experience Hypnosis?

To some extent, nearly everyone is suggestible. When people standing upright with their eyes closed are told repeatedly that they are swaying back and forth, most will indeed sway a little. In fact, postural sway is one of the items on the Stanford Hypnotic Susceptibility Scale that assesses a person's hypnotizability. The people who respond to such suggestions without hypnosis are the people who respond with hypnosis (Kirsch & Braffman, 2001). During hypnosis, a hypnotist gives a brief hypnotic induction and then presents a series of suggested experiences that range from easy (one's outstretched arms will move together) to difficult (with eyes open, one will see a nonexistent person).

Those who are highly hypnotizable—say, the 20 percent who can carry out a suggestion not to smell or react to a bottle of ammonia held under the nose—frequently become deeply absorbed in imaginative activities (Barnier & McConkey, 2004; Silva & Kirsch, 1992). Typically, they have rich fantasy lives and easily become absorbed in the imaginary events of a novel or movie. (Perhaps you can recall being riveted by a movie into a trance-like state that had you oblivious to people or noise surrounding you.) Many researchers refer to hypnotic "susceptibility" as hypnotic *ability*—the ability to focus attention totally on a task, to become imaginatively absorbed in it, to entertain fanciful possibilities.

Actually, anyone who can turn attention inward and imagine is able to experience some degree of hypnosis—because that's what hypnosis is. And virtually anyone will experience hypnotic responsiveness if led to *expect* it. Imagine being asked to stare at a high spot and then hearing that "your eyes are growing tired . . . your eyelids are becoming heavy." With such strain, anyone's eyes would get tired. (Try

FIGURE 7.11
The "amazing" hypnotized "human plank"
Actually, unhypnotized people can also perform this feat.

looking up for 30 seconds.) But if the hypnotist is successful, you will attribute your heavy eyelids to the hypnotist's abilities and then become more open to the suggestions that follow.

Can Hypnosis Enhance Recall of Forgotten Events?

Can hypnotic procedures enable people to recall kindergarten classmates? To retrieve forgotten or suppressed details of a crime? Should testimony obtained under hypnosis be admissible in court?

Most people believe (wrongly, as Chapter 9 will explain) that our experiences are all "in there," that everything that happens to us gets recorded in our brains and can be recalled if only we are able to break through our own defenses (Loftus, 1980). In one community survey, 3 in 4 people agreed with the inaccurate statement that hypnosis enables people to "recover accurate memories as far back as birth" (Johnson & Hauck, 1999). But 60 years of research dispute such claims of *age regression*—the supposed ability to relive childhood experiences. Age-regressed people act as they *believe* children would, but they typically miss the mark by outperforming real children of the specified age (Silverman & Retzlaff, 1986). They may, for example, *feel* childlike and print much as they know a 6-year-old would. But they sometimes do so with perfect spelling and typically without any change in their adult brain waves, reflexes, and perceptions.

Researchers have also found that "hypnotically refreshed" memories combine fact with fiction. Without either person being aware of what is going on, the hypnotist's hints—"Did you hear loud noises?"—can plant ideas that become the subject's pseudomemory. Thus, American, Australian, and British courts increasingly ban testimony from witnesses who have been hypnotized (Druckman & Bjork, 1994; Gibson, 1995; McConkey, 1995).

Striking examples of memories created under hypnosis come from the tens of thousands of people who since 1980 have reported being abducted by UFOs, abused in satanic cults, or adored during a past life. Studies reveal that most reports of UFOs have come from people who are predisposed to believe in aliens, are highly hypnotizable, and have undergone hypnosis (Newman & Baumeister, 1996; Nickell, 1996).

Can Hypnosis Force People to Act Against Their Will?

Researchers Martin Orne and Frederick Evans (1965) demonstrated that hypnotized people *could* be induced to perform an apparently dangerous act. The participants followed a request to dip one hand briefly into fuming "acid," then throw the "acid" in a research assistant's face. When interviewed a day later, they exhibited no memory of their acts and emphatically denied they would ever follow orders to commit such an act.

Had hypnosis given the hypnotist a special power to control these people against their will? To find out, Orne and Evans unleashed that enemy of so many illusory beliefs—the control group: Orne asked some other people to *pretend* they were hypnotized. The laboratory experimenter, unaware that those in the control group had not been hypnotized, treated all participants the same. The result? All the *unhypnotized* participants (perhaps believing that the laboratory context assured safety) performed the same acts as those who were hypnotized.

Such studies illustrate a principle that Chapter 18 emphasizes: An authoritative person in a legitimate context can induce people—hypnotized or not—to perform some unlikely acts. Hypnosis researcher Spanos (1982) put it directly: "The overt behaviors of hypnotic subjects are well within normal limits."

Can Hypnosis Be Therapeutic?

Hypnotherapists do nothing magical. They simply try to help patients harness their own healing powers (Baker, 1987). **Posthypnotic suggestions** have helped alleviate headaches, asthma, and stress-related skin disorders. One woman, who for more than 20 years suffered from open sores all over her body, was asked to imagine

"Hypnosis is not a psychological truth serum and to regard it as such has been a source of considerable mischief."

Researcher Kenneth Bowers (1987)

See Chapter 9 for a more detailed discussion of how people may construct false memories.

"It wasn't what I expected. But facts are facts, and if one is proved to be wrong, one must just be humble about it and start again."

Agatha Christie's Miss Marple

herself swimming in shimmering, sunlit liquids that would cleanse her skin, and to experience her skin as smooth and unblemished. Within three months her sores had disappeared (Bowers, 1984).

In one statistical digest of 18 studies, the average client whose therapy was supplemented with hypnosis showed greater improvement than 70 percent of other therapy patients (Kirsch & others, 1995, 1996). Hypnosis seemed especially helpful for treatment of obesity. However, drug, alcohol, and smoking addictions do not respond well to hypnosis (Nash, 2001). In controlled studies, hypnosis speeds the disappearance of warts, but so do the same positive suggestions given without hypnosis (Spanos, 1991, 1996).

Can Hypnosis Alleviate Pain?

Yes, hypnosis *can* relieve pain (Druckman & Bjork, 1994; Patterson, 2004). When unhypnotized people put their arms in an ice bath, they feel intense pain within 25 seconds. When hypnotized people do the same after being given suggestions to feel no pain, they indeed report feeling little pain. As some dentists know, even light hypnosis can reduce fear, and thus hypersensitivity to pain. And nearly 10 percent of us can become so deeply hypnotized that even major surgery can be performed without anesthesia. Half of us can gain at least some pain relief from hypnosis. In surgical experiments, hypnotized patients have required less medication, recovered sooner, and left the hospital earlier than unhypnotized controls, thanks to the inhibition of pain-related brain activity (Lang & others, 2000; Patterson & Jensen, 2003).

How can this be? One theory of hypnotic pain relief finds the answer in **dissociation,** a split between different levels of consciousness. Hypnosis, it suggests, dissociates the sensation of the pain stimulus (of which the subject is still aware) from the emotional suffering that defines our experience of pain. The ice water therefore feels cold—very cold—but not painful.

Another theory proposes that hypnotic pain relief results from selective attention, as when an injured athlete, caught up in the competition, feels little or no pain until the game ends. Support for this view comes from several studies showing that hypnosis relieves pain—for example, the pain women experience during childbirth—no better than does merely relaxing and distracting people (Chaves, 1989; D'Eon, 1989).

Both views of pain assume that at some level a hypnotized person does experience the pain stimulus. Indeed, people who report feeling no pain nevertheless may respond with a pounding heart to electric shock or a surgeon's knife. Similar disparities between self-reports and behavior occur with hearing. Following a suggestion that they are deaf, hypnotized people will deny being able to hear their own voices. But when they hear their voice over a headset with a half-second delay, the supposedly unheard delayed feedback disrupts their ability to speak fluently. Although these individuals *report* perceiving no pain or sound, the stimuli have quite obviously registered within their sensory systems. PET scans reveal that hypnosis reduces brain activity in a region that processes painful stimuli, but not in the sensory cortex that receives the raw sensory input (Rainville & others, 1997). Hypnosis does *not* block sensory input, but it may block our *attention* to those stimuli.

The unanswered question of how hypnosis relieves pain—by *dissociating* the pain sensation from conscious awareness, or merely by focusing *attention* on other things—brings us to the basic issue: Is hypnosis a unique psychological state?

■ **posthypnotic suggestion** a suggestion, made during a hypnosis session, to be carried out after the subject is no longer hypnotized; used by some clinicians to help control undesired symptoms and behaviors.

■ **dissociation** a split in consciousness, which allows some thoughts and behaviors to occur simultaneously with others.

David Young-Wolff/PhotoEdit, Inc.

The Lamaze method of childbirth
Like hypnosis, the Lamaze method uses breathing and concentration techniques that draw attention away from pain. Women for whom the method works tend to have high hypnotic ability (Venn, 1986).

Demonstrating the "hidden observer"
A hypnotized woman being tested by Ernest Hilgard exhibits no pain when her arm is placed in an ice bath. But asked to press a key if some part of her feels the pain, she does so. To Hilgard, this suggested that hypnosis divides consciousness into one part that is unaware of pain and another part—a "hidden observer"—that is aware of it.

> "The total possible consciousness may be split into parts which co-exist but mutually ignore each other."
>
> William James, *Principles of Psychology*, 1890

Is Hypnosis an Altered State of Consciousness?

OBJECTIVE **13** | Give arguments for and against hypnosis as an altered state of consciousness.

We have seen that hypnosis involves heightened suggestibility. We have also seen that hypnotic procedures do not endow a person with special powers. But they can sometimes help a person overcome psychologically influenced ailments or cope with pain. So, just what is hypnosis?

Hypnosis as a Social Phenomenon

Some skeptics believe that hypnotic phenomena may reflect the workings of normal consciousness and the power of social influence (Lynn & others, 1990; Spanos & Coe, 1992). In Chapter 6 we saw how powerfully our interpretations influence ordinary perceptions. Especially in the case of pain, for which the effects of hypnosis seem most dramatic, our attention guides our perceptions.

No one is proposing that people are consciously faking hypnosis. Rather, like actors who get caught up in their roles, they begin to feel and behave in ways appropriate to the role of "good hypnotic subjects." The more they like and trust the hypnotist and feel motivated to demonstrate hypnotic behavior, the more they allow that person to direct their attention and fantasies (Gfeller & others, 1987). "The hypnotist's ideas become the subject's thoughts," explains Theodore Barber (2000), "and the subject's thoughts produce the hypnotic experiences and behaviors." If told later to scratch their ear when they hear the word *psychology,* subjects will likely do so only if they think the experiment is still under way (and scratching is therefore expected). If an experimenter eliminates the motivation for their acting hypnotized—by stating that hypnosis reveals their "gullibility"—subjects become unresponsive.

Based on such findings, advocates of the *social influence theory* contend that hypnotic phenomena are *not* unique to hypnosis. They argue that hypnotic phenomena—like the behaviors associated with other supposed altered states, such as dissociative identity disorder (page 656) and spirit or demon possession—are an extension of everyday social behavior (Spanos, 1994, 1996). Hypnotic subjects may simply be imaginative actors caught up in playing the role of hypnotic subject.

Hypnosis as Divided Consciousness

Most hypnosis researchers grant that normal social and cognitive processes play a part in hypnosis, but they nevertheless believe hypnosis is more than trying to be a "good subject." For one thing, hypnotized subjects will *sometimes* carry out suggested behaviors on cue, even when they believe no one is watching (Perugini & others, 1998). Moreover, many practitioners remain convinced that certain phenomena *are* unique to hypnosis, which is accompanied by distinctive brain activity. In one experiment, when deeply hypnotized people were asked to imagine a color, areas of their brain lit up as if they were really seeing the color. What would only be mere imagination in the unhypnotized state had become—to the hypnotized person's brain—a compelling hallucination (Kosslyn & others, 2000).

To famed researcher Ernest Hilgard (1986, 1992), hypnosis involved not only social influence but also a special state of dissociated (divided) consciousness (**FIGURE 7.12**). Hilgard viewed hypnotic dissociation as a vivid form of everyday mind splits. Putting a child to bed, we might read *Goodnight Moon* for the fourteenth time while mentally organizing a busy schedule for the next day. With practice, you could read and comprehend a short story while copying dictated words, much as you can doodle while listening to a lecture or finish typing a sentence while starting a conversation, or as a skilled pianist can talk to an audience while playing a familiar piece (Hirst & others, 1978).

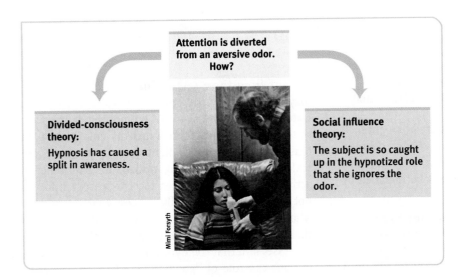

Attention is diverted from an aversive odor. How?

Divided-consciousness theory:

Hypnosis has caused a split in awareness.

Social influence theory:

The subject is so caught up in the hypnotized role that she ignores the odor.

Mimi Forsyth

FIGURE 7.12

Explaining hypnosis

How can she do it? How can this hypnotized young woman in Ernest Hilgard's lab show no reaction to the terrible smell of ammonia? Divided-consciousness theory and social influence theory offer possible explanations.

Although the divided-consciousness theory of hypnosis is controversial, this much seems clear: You and I process much information without conscious awareness. In hypnosis as in life, *much of our behavior occurs on autopilot*. Thus, when hypnotized people write answers to questions about one topic while talking or reading about a different topic, they display an accentuated form of normal dissociation of cognition from behavior. So, when today's researchers refer to a "hypnotic state," note Irving Kirsch and Steven Jay Lynn (1995, 1998a,b), they merely refer to the subjective experience of hypnosis, not to a unique trance state.

Without doubt, there is much more to thinking and acting than we are conscious of. Our information processing, which starts with selective attention, *is* divided into simultaneous conscious and subconscious realms.

But still, there is also little doubt that social influences do play an important role in hypnosis. So, might the two views—social influence and divided consciousness—be bridged? Researchers John Kihlstrom and Kevin McConkey (1990) believe there is no contradiction between the two approaches, which are converging toward a "unified account of hypnosis." Hypnosis, they suggest, is an extension *both* of normal principles of social influence *and* of everyday dissociations between our conscious awareness and our automatic behaviors. Today's hypnosis researchers are therefore moving beyond the "hypnosis is social influence" versus "hypnosis is divided consciousness" debate (Killeen & Nash, 2003; Woody & McConkey, 2003). Using various levels of analysis, they are exploring how brain activity, attention, and social influences affect hypnotic phenomena (**FIGURE 7.13**).

Biological influences:
• distinctive brain activity
• nonconscious information processing

Psychological influences:
• focused attention
• expectations
• heightened suggestibility
• dissociation between normal sensations and conscious awareness

Hypnosis

Social-cultural influences:
• presence of an authoritative person in legitimate context
• role-playing "good subject"

FIGURE 7.13

Levels of analysis for hypnosis

Using a biopsychosocial approach, researchers explore hypnosis from complementary perspectives.

›› LEARNING OUTCOMES

Hypnosis

OBJECTIVE 11 | **Define** *hypnosis,* **and note some similarities between the behavior of hypnotized people and that of motivated unhypnotized people.**

Psychologists now agree that hypnosis is a state of heightened suggestibility to which people are subject in varying degrees. Research indicates that the strength, stamina, learning, and perceptual abilities of hypnotized people may be matched by those of motivated unhypnotized people.

OBJECTIVE 12 | **Discuss the characteristics of people who are susceptible to hypnosis, and evaluate claims that hypnosis can influence people's memory, will, health, and perception of pain.**

Highly hypnotizable people can focus attention totally on a task, become imaginatively absorbed in it, and entertain fanciful possibilities. Hypnosis does not enhance recall of forgotten events and may evoke false memories. Hypnotized people, like unhypnotized people, may perform unlikely acts when told to do so by an authoritative person. Posthypnotic suggestions have helped people harness their own healing powers to reduce headaches and other disorders but have not been effective in treating addictions. Hypnosis can contribute to significant pain relief.

OBJECTIVE 13 | **Give arguments for and against hypnosis as an altered state of consciousness.**

The belief that hypnosis produces a dissociation—a split—between normal sensations and conscious awareness gains support from three sets of findings. (1) Hypnotized people may carry out posthypnotic suggestions when no one is watching. (2) Brain scans of hypnotized people told to "see" things that are not there (such as color) show activity in brain areas that usually light up only when we are sensing real stimuli. (3) People hypnotized for pain relief may show activity in brain areas that receive sensory information but not in areas that normally process that information. Those who reject the hypnosis-as-altered-consciousness view believe that hypnosis is a by-product of normal social and cognitive processes and that the hypnotized person is unknowingly acting out the role of "good subject." In one experiment supporting this interpretation, researchers tell hypnotized people that hypnosis reveals their gullibility and the participants stop responding as directed. Contemporary researchers are intrigued by the puzzle of how brain activity, attention, and social influences interact to create hypnotic phenomena.

ASK YOURSELF: **Two examples of dissociated consciousness are talking while typing, and thinking about something else while reading a child a bedtime story. Can you think of another time when you have experienced dissociated consciousness?**

Drugs and Consciousness

OBJECTIVE 14 | Define *psychoactive drug.*

There is controversy about whether hypnosis uniquely alters consciousness, but there is little dispute that drugs do. **Psychoactive drugs** are chemicals that change perceptions and moods. Let's imagine a day in the life of a legal-drug user. It begins with a wake-up latté. By midday, several cigarettes have calmed frazzled nerves before an appointment at the plastic surgeon's office for Botox injections to smooth wrinkles. A diet pill before dinner helps stem the appetite, and its stimulating effects can later be partially offset with a glass of wine and two Tylenol PMs. And if performance needs enhancing, there are beta blockers for onstage performers, Viagra for middle-aged men, hormone-delivering "libido patches" for middle-aged women, and Adderall for students hoping to focus their concentration. Before drifting off into REM-depressed sleep, our hypothetical drug user is dismayed by a news report of "rising drug abuse."

Dependence and Addiction

OBJECTIVE 15 | Discuss the nature of drug dependence, and identify three common misconceptions about addiction.

Why is it that a person who rarely drinks alcohol might get tipsy on one can of beer, but an experienced drinker may not get tipsy until the second six-pack (**FIGURE 7.14**)? Con-

© 1992 by Sidney Harris.

"Just tell me where you kids got the idea to take so many drugs."

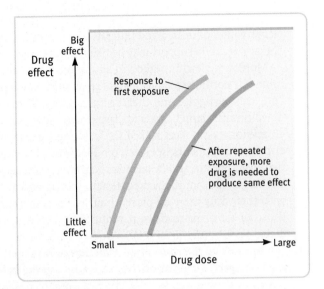

FIGURE 7.14
Drug tolerance
With repeated exposure to a psychoactive drug, the drug's effect lessens. Thus, it takes bigger doses to get the desired effect.

tinued use of alcohol and other psychoactive drugs produces **tolerance:** The user experiences *neuroadaptation* (the brain adapts its chemistry to offset the drug effect). Thus, the user requires larger and larger doses to experience the drug's effect. Ironically, despite the connotations of alcohol "tolerance," alcoholics' brains, hearts, and livers suffer damage from the excessive alcohol they are "tolerating."

Users who stop taking psychoactive drugs may experience the undesirable side effects of **withdrawal.** As the body responds to the drug's absence, the user may feel physical pain and intense cravings, indicating a **physical dependence** on the drug. People can also develop **psychological dependence,** particularly for stress-relieving drugs. Although such drugs may not be physically addictive, they nevertheless become an important part of the user's life, often as a way of relieving negative emotions. With either physical or psychological dependence, the user's primary focus may become obtaining and using the drug.

Misconceptions About Addiction

An **addiction** is a craving for a substance despite adverse consequences and often with physical symptoms such as aches, nausea, and distress following sudden withdrawal. In recent pop psychology, the supposedly irresistible seduction of addiction has been extended to cover many behaviors formerly considered bad habits or even sins. Has the concept been stretched too far? Are addictions as irresistible as commonly believed? Many drug researchers believe the following three myths about addiction are *false:*

1. ***Addictive drugs quickly corrupt; for example, morphine taken to control pain is powerfully addictive and often leads to heroin abuse.*** After taking a psychoactive drug, some people—perhaps 10 percent—do indeed have a hard time using it in moderation or stopping altogether. However, there are many more controlled, occasional users than addicts of drugs such as alcohol and marijuana (Gazzaniga, 1988; Siegel, 1990). "Even for a very addictive drug like cocaine, only 15 to 16 percent of people become addicted within 10 years of first use," report Terry Robinson and Kent Berridge (2003). Much the same is true for rats, only some of which become compulsively addicted to cocaine, even to the point of enduring foot shock to self-administer the drug (Deroche-Garmonet & others, 2004).

   Moreover, people typically don't become addicted when using drugs medically. Those given morphine to control pain rarely develop the cravings of the addict who uses morphine as a mood-altering drug (Melzack, 1990).

2. ***Addictions cannot be overcome voluntarily; therapy is required.*** Some addicts do benefit from treatment programs. Alcoholics Anonymous, for example, has supported many people in overcoming their alcohol dependence. But critics say that the

■ **psychoactive drug** a chemical substance that alters perceptions and mood.

■ **tolerance** the diminishing effect with regular use of the same dose of a drug, requiring the user to take larger and larger doses before experiencing the drug's effect.

■ **withdrawal** the discomfort and distress that follow discontinuing the use of an addictive drug.

■ **physical dependence** a physiological need for a drug, marked by unpleasant withdrawal symptoms when the drug is discontinued.

■ **psychological dependence** a psychological need to use a drug, such as to relieve negative emotions.

■ **addiction** compulsive drug craving and use.

The odds of getting hooked after trying various drugs:

Drug	Percent
Marijuana:	9 percent
Alcohol:	15 percent
Cocaine:	17 percent
Heroin:	23 percent
Tobacco:	32 percent

Source: National Academy of Science, Institute of Medicine (Brody, 2003).

recovery rates of treated and untreated groups differ less than one might suppose. Therapy or group support may be helpful, but people often recover on their own.

Moreover, viewing addiction as a disease, as diabetes is a disease, can undermine self-confidence and the will to change cravings that, without treatment, "one cannot fight." And that, critics say, would be unfortunate, for many people do voluntarily stop using addictive drugs, without treatment. Most of America's 41 million ex-smokers kicked the habit on their own (usually after prior failed efforts or treatments; see Chapter 14). Half of the U.S. soldiers in Vietnam tried heroin or opium, and 20 percent became regular users (Robins & others, 1974). Yet, removed from the war's stressful setting and all the stimulus cues associated with their drug use (the place, the friends, the circumstances), only 7 percent of those whose urine revealed narcotic use when leaving Vietnam became readdicted back home.

3. *We can extend the concept of addiction to cover not just drug dependencies, but a whole spectrum of repetitive, pleasure-seeking behaviors.* We can, and we have, but should we? The addiction-as-disease-needing-treatment idea has been suggested for a host of driven behaviors, including overeating, shopping, exercise, sex, gambling, and work. Initially, we may use the term metaphorically ("I'm a science fiction addict"), but if we begin taking the metaphor as reality, addiction can become an all-purpose excuse. Those who embezzle to feed their "gambling addiction," surf the Web half the night to satisfy their "Internet addiction," or abuse or betray to indulge their "sex addiction" can then explain away their behavior as an illness.

Sometimes, though, behaviors such as gambling or cybersex do become compulsive and dysfunctional, much like abusive drug taking (Griffiths, 2001). Is there justification for stretching the addiction concept to cover certain social behaviors? Debates over the addiction-as-disease model continue.

Psychoactive Drugs

OBJECTIVE 16 | Name the main categories of psychoactive drugs, and list three ways these substances can interfere with neurotransmission in the brain.

There are at least three categories of psychoactive drugs: *depressants, stimulants,* and *hallucinogens.* Drugs in all three categories do their work at the brain's synapses, by stimulating, inhibiting, or mimicking the activity of neurotransmitters, the brain's chemical messengers. But our expectations also play a role in the way these drugs affect us.

Depressants

OBJECTIVE 17 | Explain how depressants affect nervous system activity and behavior, and summarize the findings on alcohol use and abuse.

Depressants are drugs such as alcohol, barbiturates (tranquilizers), and opiates that calm neural activity and slow body functions.

Alcohol True or false? In large amounts, alcohol is a depressant; in small amounts, it is a stimulant.

False. Small doses of "spirits" may, indeed, enliven a drinker, but they do so by slowing brain activity that controls judgment and inhibitions. When provoked, people under alcohol's influence respond more aggressively than usual. If asked to help, people under alcohol's influence respond more willingly than usual. Thus, alcohol is an equal-opportunity drug: It increases harmful tendencies—as when sexually coercive college men lower their dates' sexual inhibitions by getting them to drink (Abbey, 1991; Mosher & Anderson, 1986). And it increases helpful tendencies—as when tipsy

---

"That is not one of the seven habits of highly effective people."

A University of Illinois campus survey showed that before sexual assaults, 80 percent of the male assailants and 70 percent of the female victims had been drinking (Camper, 1990). Another survey of 89,874 American collegians found alcohol or drugs involved in 79 percent of unwanted sexual intercourse experiences (Presley & others, 1997).

restaurant patrons leave extravagant tips (M. Lynn, 1988). *The urges you would feel if sober are the ones you will more likely act upon if intoxicated.*

Low doses of alcohol relax the drinker by slowing sympathetic nervous system activity. With larger doses, alcohol can become a staggering problem: Reactions slow, speech slurs, skilled performance deteriorates. Paired with sleep deprivation, alcohol becomes a potent sedative. (Although either sleep deprivation or drinking can put a driver at risk, their combination is deadlier yet.) These physical effects, combined with lowered inhibitions, contribute to alcohol's worst consequences—the several hundred thousand lives claimed worldwide each year in alcohol-related accidents and violent crime. Car accidents occur despite most drinkers' belief (when sober) that driving while under the influence of alcohol is wrong and despite their insisting that they would not do so. Yet as their blood-alcohol level rises, people's moral judgments become less mature, their qualms about drinking and driving lessen—and virtually all will drive home from a bar, even if given a breathalyzer test and told they are intoxicated (Denton & Krebs, 1990; MacDonald & others, 1995).

Alcohol also disrupts the processing of recent experiences into long-term memories. Thus, the day after being intoxicated, heavy drinkers may not recall people they met the night before or what they said or did. Blackouts after drinking result partly from the way alcohol suppresses REM sleep, which helps fix the day's experiences into permanent memories. Prolonged and excessive drinking can also affect cognition by shrinking the brain, which MRI scans show is especially striking in women (**FIGURE 7.15**), who have less of a stomach enzyme that digests alcohol (Wuethrich, 2001). Girls and young women can also become addicted more quickly than boys and young men, and they suffer lung, brain, and liver damage at less extreme consumption levels (CASA, 2003).

Alcohol not only impairs judgment and memory, it also reduces self-awareness (Hull & others, 1986). Compared with people who feel good about themselves, those who want to suppress their awareness of failures or shortcomings are more likely to drink. Losing a business deal, a game, or a romance will sometimes elicit a drinking binge.

Alcohol focuses one's attention on the immediate situation and away from any future consequences to oneself. This facilitates following urges that a person might otherwise resist (Steele & Josephs, 1990). In surveys, over half of rapists acknowledge drinking before committing their offense (Seto & Barbaree, 1995). The effect reaches onto college campuses. Sexually active university students are less likely to use condoms in a sexually stimulating context when intoxicated (MacDonald & others, 1996, 2000). University women under alcohol's influence find an attractive but sexually promiscuous man a more appealing potential date than they do when sober. It seems, surmise Sheila Murphy and her colleagues (1998), "that when people have been drinking, the restraining forces of reason may weaken and yield under the pressure of their desires."

■ **depressants** drugs (such as alcohol, barbiturates, and opiates) that reduce neural activity and slow body functions.

FIGURE 7.15
Alcoholism shrinks the brain
MRI scans show brain shrinkage in women with alcoholism (left) compared with women in a control group (right).

Scan of woman with alcoholism   Scan of woman without alcoholism

Daniel Hommer, NIAAA, NIH, HHS

Facts: College and university students drink more alcohol than their nonstudent peers, and they spend more on alcohol than on books and other beverages combined. Fraternity and sorority members drink three times as much as other students (Atwell, 1986; Malloy & others, 1994; Slutske, 2005). Although few university students believe they have an alcohol problem, many meet the criteria for alcohol abuse (Marlatt, 1991). As students mature with age, they drink less.

Dangerous disinhibition
Alcohol consumption leads to feelings of invincibility, which become especially dangerous behind the wheel of a car, such as this one totaled by a teenage drunk driver. This Colorado University Alcohol Awareness Week exhibit prompted many students to post their own anti-drinking pledges (white flags).

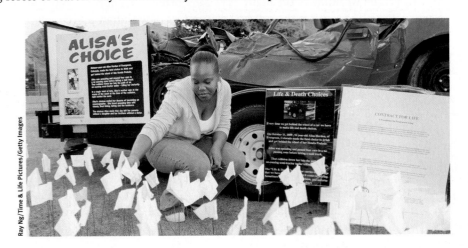

Ray Ng/Time & Life Pictures/Getty Images

Fact: In a Harvard School of Public Health survey of 18,000 students at 140 colleges and universities, almost 9 in 10 students reported abuse by intoxicated peers, including sleep and study interruption, insults, sexual advances, and property damage (Wechsler & others, 1994). In a follow-up survey, 44 percent of students admitted binge drinking within the previous two weeks (Wechsler & others, 2002).

Fact: Drinking annually contributes to 1400 American college student deaths, 70,000 sexual assaults, and 500,000 injuries (Hingson & others, 2002).

Fact: Alcohol kills more people than all illegal drugs combined. So does tobacco (Siegel, 1990).

■ **barbiturates** drugs that depress the activity of the central nervous system, reducing anxiety but impairing memory and judgment.

■ **opiates** opium and its derivatives, such as morphine and heroin; they depress neural activity, temporarily lessening pain and anxiety.

■ **stimulants** drugs (such as caffeine, nicotine, and the more powerful amphetamines, cocaine, and Ecstasy) that excite neural activity and speed up body functions.

■ **amphetamines** drugs that stimulate neural activity, causing speeded-up body functions and associated energy and mood changes.

■ **methamphetamine** a powerfully addictive drug that stimulates the central nervous system, with speeded-up body functions and associated energy and mood changes; over time, appears to reduce baseline dopamine levels.

Dramatic drug-induced decline
This woman's methamphetamine addiction led to obvious physical changes. Her decline is evident in these two photos, taken at age 36 (left) and, after four years of addiction, at age 40 (right).

National Pictures/Topham/The Image Works

As with other psychoactive drugs, alcohol's behavioral effects stem not only from its alteration of brain chemistry but also from the user's expectations. Many studies have found that when people *believe* that alcohol affects social behavior in certain ways, and *believe,* rightly or wrongly, that they have been drinking alcohol, they will behave accordingly (Leigh, 1989). For example, people become more responsive to sexual stimuli if they *believe* alcohol promotes arousal and *believe* they have been drinking. For some people, reported Jay Hull and Charles Bond (1986), alcohol serves "as an excuse to become sexually aroused."

Consider one such experiment by David Abrams and Terence Wilson (1983). They gave Rutgers University men who volunteered for a study on "alcohol and sexual stimulation" either an alcoholic or a nonalcoholic drink. (Both drinks had a strong taste that masked any alcohol.) In each group, half the participants thought they were drinking alcohol and half thought they were not. After being shown an erotic movie clip, the men who *thought* they had consumed alcohol were more likely to report having strong sexual fantasies and feeling guilt-free. Being able to *attribute* their sexual responses to alcohol released their inhibitions—whether they actually had drunk alcohol or not. If, as commonly believed, liquor is the quicker pick-her-upper, the effect lies partly in that powerful sex organ, the mind.

This research illustrates how different levels of analysis explain behavior: A drug's overall effect depends not only on its biological effects, but also on the psychology of the user's expectations, which vary with cultures (Ward, 1994). If one culture assumes that a particular drug produces euphoria (or aggression or sexual arousal) and another does not, each culture may find its expectations fulfilled.

Barbiturates The **barbiturate** drugs, or *tranquilizers,* mimic the effects of alcohol. Because they depress nervous system activity, barbiturates such as Nembutal, Seconal, and Amytal are sometimes prescribed to induce sleep or reduce anxiety. In larger doses, they can lead to impaired memory and judgment. In combination with alcohol—as when people take a sleeping pill after an evening of heavy drinking—the total depressive effect on body functions can be lethal. With sufficient doses, barbiturates by themselves can also cause death, which makes them the drugs often chosen by those attempting suicide.

Opiates The **opiates**—opium and its derivatives, morphine and heroin—also depress neural functioning. The pupils constrict, the breathing slows, and the user becomes lethargic. For a few hours, blissful pleasure replaces pain and anxiety. But for short-term pleasure one pays a long-term price, which for the heroin user is the gnawing craving for another fix, the need for progressively larger doses, the week-long physical anguish of withdrawal, and for some, the ultimate price—death by overdose.

The pathway to addiction is treacherous. When repeatedly flooded with an artificial opiate, the brain eventually stops producing its own opiates, the endorphins. If the drug is then withdrawn, the brain lacks the normal level of these painkilling neurotransmitters. The result is the extreme discomfort of withdrawal.

Stimulants

OBJECTIVE **18** | Identify the major stimulants, and explain how they affect neural activity and behavior.

Stimulants temporarily excite neural activity and arouse body functions. People use these substances to stay awake, lose weight, or boost mood or athletic performance. The most widely used are caffeine, nicotine, the **amphetamines,** and the even more powerful cocaine, Ecstasy, and **methamphetamine** ("speed"), the latter of which is related to its parent drug, amphetamine (NIDA, 2002, 2005). All strong stimulants increase heart and breathing rates and cause pupils to dilate, appetite to diminish (because blood sugar increases), and energy and self-confidence to rise. But methamphetamine has even greater effects, which can include eight hours or so of heightened energy and euphoria (related to its triggering the release of dopamine).

As with other drugs, the benefits of stimulants come with a price. Stimulants—including coffee and caffeinated sodas—can be addictive and may induce an aftermath crash into fatigue, headaches, irritability, and depression (Silverman & others, 1992). Methamphetamine is highly addictive, and its aftereffects may include irritability, insomnia, hypertension, seizures, periods of disorientation, and occasional violent behavior. Over time, methamphetamine also appears to reduce baseline dopamine levels, leaving the user with permanently depressed functioning.

Cocaine In national surveys, 5 percent of American high school seniors and 5 percent of British 18- to 24-year olds reported having tried cocaine during the past year (Home Office, 2003; Johnston & others, 2005). Nearly half of the drug-using seniors had smoked *crack,* a potent form of cocaine. Cocaine addiction is a fast track from euphoria to crash. When extracted cocaine is sniffed ("snorted"), and especially when injected or smoked ("free-based"), it enters the bloodstream quickly. The result: a "rush" of euphoria that lasts 15 to 30 minutes. Because the rush depletes the brain's supply of the neurotransmitters dopamine, serotonin, and norepinephrine, a crash of agitated depression occurs as the drug's effect wears off (**FIGURE 7.16**). Crack works even faster and produces a briefer but more intense high, a more intense crash, and a craving for more crack, which wanes after several hours but then returns several days later (Gawin, 1991).

Many regular cocaine users become addicted. Monkeys have become so strongly addicted that they will press a lever more than 12,000 times to gain each cocaine injection (Siegel, 1990). Human and animal cocaine users may experience emotional disturbance, suspiciousness, convulsions, cardiac arrest, or respiratory failure. In situations that trigger aggression, ingesting cocaine may increase aggressive

Courtesy of Frank Flavin

Wake me up
Drive-through espresso stands are thriving in many places, including Anchorage, where sleepy patrons seek out a caffeinated boost to get them through the dark winter days.

The recipe for Coca-Cola originally included an extract of the coca plant, creating a cocaine tonic for tired elderly people. Between 1896 and 1905, Coke was indeed "the real thing."

"Cocaine makes you a new man. And the first thing that new man wants is more cocaine."

Comedian George Carlin

FIGURE 7.16
Cocaine euphoria and crash

(a)
Neurotransmitters carry a message from a sending neuron across a synapse to receptor sites on a receiving neuron.

(b)
The sending neuron normally reabsorbs excess neurotransmitter molecules, a process called reuptake.

(c)
By binding to the sites that normally reabsorb neurotransmitter molecules, cocaine blocks reuptake of dopamine, norepinephrine, and serotonin (Ray & Ksir, 1990). The extra neurotransmitter molecules therefore remain in the synapse, intensifying their normal mood-altering effects and producing a euphoric rush. When the cocaine level drops, the absence of these neurotransmitters produces a crash.

The hug drug
MDMA, known as Ecstasy, produces a euphoric high and feelings of intimacy. But repeated use destroys serotonin-producing neurons and may permanently deflate mood and impair memory.

FIGURE 7.17
Hallucination-like patterns
Geometric forms, similar to those experienced by drug users during drug-induced hallucinations, can be seen in the embroidery of the Huichol. These Mexican Indians used peyote, from which the hallucinogen mescaline derives.

reactions. Caged rats fight when given foot shocks, and they fight even more when given cocaine and foot shocks. Likewise, humans who have ingested high-dose cocaine impose higher shock levels on a presumed opponent in a laboratory experiment than do those who have received a placebo (Licata & others, 1993).

As with all psychoactive drugs, cocaine's psychological effects depend not only on the dosage and form in which one takes the drug but also on one's expectations, one's personality, and the situation. Given a placebo, cocaine users who *think* they are taking cocaine often have a cocainelike experience (Van Dyke & Byck, 1982).

Ecstasy **Ecstasy,** a street name for MDMA (methylenedioxymethamphetamine), is both a stimulant and a mild hallucinogen. As an amphetamine derivative, it triggers the release of the neurotransmitter dopamine. But its major effect is to release stored serotonin and to block its reabsorption, thus prolonging serotonin's feel-good flood (Braun, 2001). (As we will see in Chapter 17, some antidepressant drugs more moderately elevate serotonin, by blocking its reabsorption.) During the late 1990s, Ecstasy became a fast-growing "club drug" commonly taken at night clubs and all-night raves (Landry, 2002). Beginning about a half-hour after taking an Ecstasy pill, and for the next three to four hours, users commonly experience emotional elevation and, given a social context, feelings of connectedness with those around them ("I love everyone").

There are, however, reasons not to be ecstatic about Ecstasy. One immediate effect is dehydration and, when combined with prolonged dancing, the risk of severe overheating, increased blood pressure, and death. One long-term effect of repeated leeching of brain serotonin is damage to serotonin-producing neurons, leading to reduced serotonin levels and increased risk of permanently depressed mood (Croft & others, 2001; McCann & others, 2001; Roiser & others, 2005). Other research reveals that Ecstasy interferes with serotonin's control of the circadian clock (explaining the drug's disruption of sleep), suppresses the disease-fighting immune system, and impairs memory and other cognitive functions (Biello & Dafters, 2001; Pacifici & others, 2001; Reneman & others, 2001). Ecstasy delights for the night but dispirits the morrow.

Hallucinogens

OBJECTIVE 19 | Describe the physiological and psychological effects of hallucinogens, and summarize the effects of LSD and marijuana.

Hallucinogens distort perceptions and evoke sensory images in the absence of sensory input (which is why these drugs are also called *psychedelics,* meaning "mind-manifesting"). Some are natural substances, such as the mild hallucinogen marijuana. Others are synthetic, the best known of which are LSD and MDMA (Ecstasy).

LSD In 1943, chemist Albert Hofmann, the creator of **LSD** (lysergic acid diethylamide) took the first "acid trip." After accidentally ingesting some of the chemical, Hofmann reported that he "perceived an uninterrupted stream of fantastic pictures, extraordinary shapes with intense, kaleidoscopic play of colors" (Siegel, 1984). LSD and other powerful hallucinogens are chemically similar to (and therefore block the actions of) a subtype of the neurotransmitter serotonin (Jacobs, 1987).

The emotions of an LSD trip vary from euphoria to detachment to panic. As with all drug use, a person's current mood and expectations color the LSD experience. Despite emotional variations, the resulting perceptual distortions and hallucinations have commonalities. Psychologist Ronald Siegel (1982) reports that whether you provoke your brain to hallucinate by loss of oxygen, extreme sensory deprivation, or drugs, "it will hallucinate in basically the same way." The experience typically begins with simple geometric forms, such as a lattice, a cobweb, or a spiral (**FIGURE 7.17**). The next phase consists of more meaningful images; some may be superimposed on a tunnel or funnel, others may be replays of past emotional experiences. When the hallucinogenic experience peaks, people frequently feel separated from their bodies and experience dreamlike scenes as though they were real—so real that users may become panic-stricken or harm themselves.

Marijuana Marijuana consists of the leaves and flowers of the hemp plant, which for 5000 years has been cultivated for its fiber. Marijuana's major active ingredient is **THC** (delta-9-tetrahydrocannabinol). Whether smoked or eaten, THC produces a mix of effects that makes the drug difficult to classify. (Smoking gets the drug into the brain in about 7 seconds, producing a greater effect than does eating the drug, which causes its peak concentration to be reached at a slower, unpredictable rate.) Like alcohol, marijuana relaxes, disinhibits, and may produce a euphoric high. But marijuana also acts as a mild hallucinogen by amplifying sensitivity to colors, sounds, tastes, and smells.

As with other drugs, the marijuana user's experience varies, depending on the situation. If the person feels anxious or depressed, taking the drug may intensify these feelings. And the more one uses it, the greater one's risk of anxiety, depression, or even schizophrenia, even after controlling for other drug use and personal traits (Arseneault & others, 2002; Patton & others, 2002; Zammit & others, 2002). Daily use bodes worse than infrequent use.

In other situations, using marijuana can be not only pleasurable but therapeutic. For those who suffer the pain, nausea, and severe weight loss associated with AIDS, marijuana may spell relief (Watson & others, 2000). (For a time, marijuana was also used to control nausea from chemotherapy and pain from glaucoma, but more effective medications are now available.) Marijuana's therapeutic uses have motivated legislation legalizing the drug for such patients. To avoid the toxicity of marijuana smoke—which, like cigarette smoke, can cause cancer, lung damage, and pregnancy complications—the Institute of Medicine recommends that medical users deliver the THC with a medical inhaler.

The National Academy of Sciences (1982, 1999) and National Institute on Drug Abuse (2004) research reviews have identified other not-so-pleasant marijuana consequences. Like alcohol, marijuana impairs the motor coordination, perceptual skills, and reaction time necessary for safely operating an automobile or other machine. "THC causes animals to misjudge events," reports Ronald Siegel (1990, p. 163). "Pigeons wait too long to respond to buzzers or lights that tell them food is available for brief periods; and rats turn the wrong way in mazes." Marijuana also disrupts memory formation and interferes with immediate recall of information learned only a few minutes before. Such cognitive effects outlast the period of smoking (Pope & Yurgelun-Todd, 1996; Smith, 1995).

Scientists have shed light on marijuana's cognitive, mood, and motor effects with the discovery of concentrations of THC-sensitive receptors in the brain's frontal lobes, limbic system, and motor cortex (Iversen, 2000). Recall from Chapter 2 that the 1970s discovery of the receptors for morphine led to the discovery of morphine-like neurotransmitters (the endorphins). Similarly, the discovery of "cannabinoid receptors" has led to the follow-up discovery of naturally occurring THC-like molecules that bind with cannabinoid receptors, perhaps helping to control pain.

Unlike alcohol, which the body eliminates within hours, THC and its by-products linger in the body for a month or more. Thus, contrary to the usual tolerance phenomenon, regular users may achieve a high with smaller amounts of the drug than occasional users would need to get the same effect.

Despite their differences, the psychoactive drugs summarized in **TABLE 7.3** (page 304) share a common feature: They trigger negative aftereffects that offset their immediate positive effects. The aftereffects illustrate a more general principle: Emotions tend to produce opposing emotions, which linger after the original emotions disappear. With repetition, the opposing emotions grow stronger. This

■ **Ecstasy (MDMA)** a synthetic stimulant and mild hallucinogen. Produces euphoria and social intimacy, but with short-term health risks and longer-term harm to serotonin-producing neurons and to mood and cognition.

■ **hallucinogens** psychedelic ("mind-manifesting") drugs, such as LSD, that distort perceptions and evoke sensory images in the absence of sensory input.

■ **LSD** a powerful hallucinogenic drug; also known as *acid* (*lysergic acid diethylamide*).

■ **THC** the major active ingredient in marijuana; triggers a variety of effects, including mild hallucinations.

TABLE 7.3

A GUIDE TO SELECTED PSYCHOACTIVE DRUGS

Drug	Type	Pleasurable Effects	Adverse Effects
Alcohol	Depressant	Initial high followed by relaxation and disinhibition	Depression, memory loss, organ damage, impaired reactions
Heroin	Depressant	Rush of euphoria, relief from pain	Depressed physiology, agonizing withdrawal
Caffeine	Stimulant	Increased alertness and wakefulness	Anxiety, restlessness, and insomnia in high doses; uncomfortable withdrawal
Methamphet-amine ("speed," "ice")	Stimulant	Euphoria, alertness, energy	Irritability, insomnia, hypertension, seizures
Cocaine	Stimulant	Rush of euphoria, confidence, energy	Cardiovascular stress, suspiciousness, depressive crash
Nicotine	Stimulant	Arousal and relaxation, sense of well-being	Heart disease, cancer (from tars)
Ecstasy (MDMA)	Stimulant; mild hallucinogen	Emotional elevation, disinhibition	Dehydration, overheating, and depressed mood, cognitive, and immune functioning
Marijuana	Mild hallucinogen	Enhanced sensation, relief of pain, distortion of time, relaxation	Impaired learning and memory, increased risk of psychological disorders, lung damage from smoke

> "How strange would appear to be this thing that men call pleasure! And how curiously it is related to what is thought to be its opposite, pain! . . . Wherever the one is found, the other follows up behind."
>
> Plato, *Phaedo*, fourth century B.C.

emotions-trigger-opposing-emotions principle parallels that of drug-induced pleasures; the pleasures wane as the drug exacts its compensatory price. That helps explain both tolerance and withdrawal. As the opposing, negative aftereffects get stronger, it takes larger and larger doses to produce the desired high (tolerance), causing the aftereffects to worsen in the drug's absence (withdrawal). This in turn creates a need to switch off the withdrawal symptoms by taking yet more of the drug.

Influences on Drug Use

OBJECTIVE 20 | Discuss the biological, psychological, and social-cultural factors that contribute to drug use.

Drug use by North American youth increased during the 1970s. Then, with increased drug education and a more realistic and deglamorized media depiction of taking drugs, drug use declined sharply. After the early 1990s, the cultural antidrug voice softened, and drugs for a time were again glamorized in some music and films. Consider some marijuana-related trends:

- In the University of Michigan's annual survey of 15,000 U.S. high school seniors, the proportion who believe there is "great risk" in regular marijuana use rose from 35 percent in 1978 to 79 percent in 1991, then retreated to 55 percent in 2004 (Johnston & others, 2005).
- After peaking in 1978, marijuana use by U.S. high school seniors declined through 1992, then rose, but has recently been tapering off (**FIGURE 7.18**).
- In the UCLA/American Council on Education annual survey of new college and university students, support for the legalization of marijuana dropped from 53 percent in 1977 to 17 percent in 1989; support rebounded to 40 percent in 2002 (Astin & others, 1997; Sax & others, 2002).

Similar ups and downs in attitude and usage since the late 1970s appear in Canadian and British surveys (Conner & McMillan, 1999; Smart & others, 1991). A 2003 survey of 100,000 teens in 35 European countries found that marijuana use in the prior 30

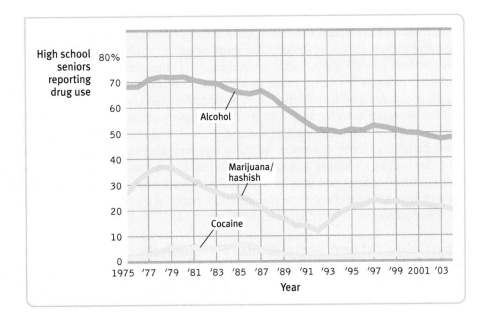

FIGURE 7.18
Trends in drug use
The percentage of U.S. high school seniors who report having used alcohol, marijuana, or cocaine during the past 30 days declined from the late 1970s to 1992, when it partially rebounded for a few years. (From Johnston & others, 2005.)

days ranged from zero to 1 percent in Romania and Sweden to 20 to 22 percent in Britain, Switzerland, and France (ESPAD, 2003).

In Britain, where 23 percent of teens acknowledge having been drunk three or more times in the last 30 days, new efforts seek to contain alcohol abuse and associated violence include eliminating traditional pub closing times. Studies also reveal a changing national attitude toward alcohol in the United States. The number of new U.S. collegians who reported abstaining from drinking beer during the preceding year has nearly doubled, from 25 percent in 1981 to 46 percent in 2004. Four in 10 Americans declare themselves "total abstainer[s]" (Gallup, 2002). Hard liquor consumption per person dropped 60 percent from 1977 to 1997 (Nephew & others, 1999). When the alcohol industry started substituting wine coolers for wine and nonalcoholic beer for alcoholic, it was clear that attitudes were changing.

For some adolescents, occasional drug use represents seeking a thrill. Why, though, do other adolescents become regular drug users? In search of answers, researchers have engaged biological, psychological, and cultural levels of analysis.

Biological Influences

Some people may be biologically vulnerable to alcohol. For example, evidence accumulates that heredity influences some aspects of alcohol abuse problems, especially those appearing by early adulthood (Crabbe, 2002):

- Adopted individuals are more susceptible to alcoholism if one or both biological parents have a history of alcoholism.
- Having an identical rather than fraternal twin with alcoholism puts one at increased risk for alcohol problems (Kendler & others, 2002). (Identical twins more than fraternal twins also resemble one another in marijuana use.)
- Boys who at age 6 are excitable, impulsive, and fearless (genetically influenced traits) are more likely as teens to smoke, drink, and use other drugs (Masse & Tremblay, 1997).
- Researchers have bred rats and mice that prefer alcoholic drinks to water. One such strain has reduced levels of the brain chemical NPY; mice engineered to overproduce NPY are very sensitive to alcohol's sedating effect and drink little.
- Molecular geneticists have identified genes that are more common among people and animals predisposed to alcoholism. These genes may, for example, produce deficiencies in the brain's natural dopamine reward system.

Such findings have fueled the search for a better understanding of genetic and biochemical influences on addiction. The most extensive study yet—a $25 million, 5-year analysis of 600 people with alcoholism, and their relatives—is under way. If biological markers for being prone to addiction can be found, then perhaps young people at risk for specific addictions can be identified and counseled.

One biological basis for addiction is a brain pleasure pathway, the *dopamine reward circuit*. Addictive chemicals such as cocaine, alcohol, and heroin commandeer the reward circuit and boost its activity. But with repeated use come changes. As tolerance develops, a drug no longer lifts one from normal to euphoria; it merely lifts the circuit out of depression and back to normal. Today's scientists are exploring the cellular and molecular details of these changes, with hopes of eventual new treatments for addiction's compulsive cravings (Nestler & Malenka, 2004; Redish, 2004).

Psychological and Social-Cultural Influences

Psychological and social-cultural influences may also contribute to drug use (**FIGURE 7.19**). Relatively drug-free small towns and rural areas constrain any genetic predisposition to drug use, report Lisa Legrand and her colleagues (2005). For those whose genetic predispositions nudge them toward substance use, "cities offer more opportunities" and less supervision. In their studies of youth and young adults, Michael Newcomb and L. L. Harlow (1986) found that one psychological factor is the feeling that one's life is meaningless and directionless, a common feeling among school dropouts who subsist without job skills, without privilege, and with little hope. When young unmarried adults leave home, alcohol and other drug use increases; when they marry and have children, it decreases (Bachman & others, 1997). Yet the ups and downs of marijuana usage over time seem due not to youth becoming more rebellious (which they have not). What predicts usage is instead the ups and downs in how risky the young people perceive regular marijuana use to be (**FIGURE 7.20**).

Other studies reveal that heavy users of alcohol, marijuana, and cocaine often have experienced significant stress or failure and are depressed. Girls with a history of depression, eating disorders, or sexual or physical abuse are at risk for substance addiction, as are girls in times of school or neighborhood transition (CASA, 2003; Logan & others, 2002). Monkeys, too, end up with a taste for alcohol when stressed by permanent separation from their mothers at birth (Small, 2002). By temporarily dulling the pain of self-awareness, alcohol may offer a way to avoid having to cope with depression, anger, anxiety, or insomnia. The relief may be temporary, but as

Warning signs of alcoholism

- Drinking binges
- Regretting things done or said when drunk
- Feeling low or guilty after drinking
- Failing to honor a resolve to drink less
- Drinking to alleviate depression or anxiety
- Avoiding family or friends when drinking

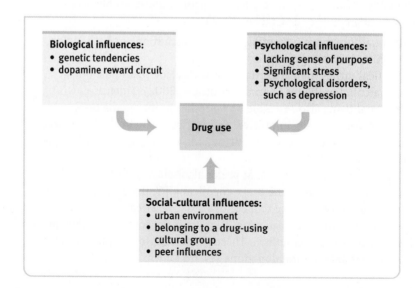

FIGURE 7.19
Levels of analysis for drug use
The biopsychosocial approach enables researchers to investigate drug use from complementary perspectives.

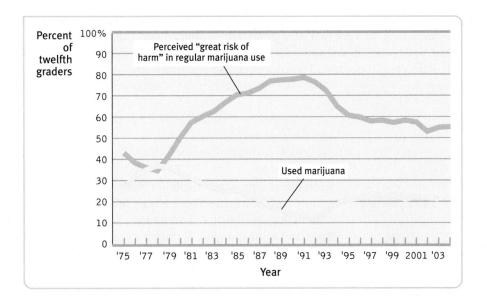

FIGURE 7.20
Perceived marijuana risk and actual use
As the percentage of U.S. twelfth graders perceiving a "great risk" in regular marijuana use increases, the percentage having used it in the previous 30 days decreases. (Data from Johnston & others, 2005.)

Chapter 8 explains, behavior is often controlled more by its immediate consequences than by its later ones.

Especially for teenagers, drug use can also have social roots, evident in differing rates of drug use across cultural and ethnic groups. In the United States, alcohol and other drug addiction rates are extremely low among the Amish, Mennonites, Mormons, and Orthodox Jews (Trimble, 1994). Independent government studies of drug use in households nationwide and among high schoolers in all regions of the United States reveal that African-American teens have sharply lower rates of drinking, smoking, and cocaine use (Bass & Kane-Williams, 1993; ISR, 2003; Kann & others, 1993).

Peer culture is a major social influence. By their words and examples, peers influence attitudes about drugs. They also throw the parties and provide the drugs. If an adolescent's friends use drugs, the odds are that he or she will, too. If the friends do not, the opportunity may not even arise.

Peer influence is not just a matter of what friends do and say but also of what adolescents *believe* their friends are doing and favoring. Young adolescents consume more alcohol when, as often happens, they overestimate their friends' use (Aas & Klepp, 1992; Graham & others, 1991). In one survey of sixth graders in 22 U.S. states, 14 percent believed their friends had smoked marijuana, though only 4 percent acknowledged doing so (Wren, 1999). At the university level, drinking dominates social occasions partly because students overestimate their fellow students' enthusiasm for alcohol (Prentice & Miller, 1993; Self, 1994). Thinking that few students share their concerns about the risks associated with alcohol, most students surrender to the perceived norm.

People are more likely to stop using drugs if their beginning use was influenced by their peers (Kandel & Raveis, 1989). When friends stop or the social network changes, they typically stop. As noted earlier, most soldiers who became drug-addicted while in Vietnam ceased their drug use after returning home. Teenagers who come from happy families and do well in school tend not to use drugs, largely because they rarely associate with those who do (Oetting & Beauvais, 1987, 1990). As always with correlations, the traffic between friends' and one's own drug use may be two-way: Our friends influence us, but we also select as friends those who share our likes and dislikes.

The findings suggest three possible channels of influence for drug prevention and treatment programs: (1) education about the long-term costs of a drug's temporary pleasures, (2) efforts to boost people's self-esteem and purpose in life, and (3) attempts to modify peer associations or to "inoculate" youth against peer pressures by training them in refusal skills. People rarely abuse drugs if they understand the

In the real world, alcohol accounts for one-sixth or less of beverage use. In television's world, drinking alcohol occurs more often than the combined drinking of coffee, tea, soft drinks, and water (Gerbner, 1990).

Annual Beer and Wine Consumption, Liters per Person

	Beer	Wine
France	41	67
Germany	143	25
Italy	23	57
New Zealand	110	15
Australia	102	19
United Kingdom	106	12
United States	87	7
Sweden	59	12

Source: *Australian Social Trends*, 1995.

"Humorist Dave Barry (1995) recalling why he smoked his first cigarette the summer he turned 15: "Arguments against smoking: 'It's a repulsive addiction that slowly but surely turns you into a gasping, gray-skinned, tumor-ridden invalid, hacking up brownish gobs of toxic waste from your one remaining lung.' Arguments for smoking: 'Other teen-agers are doing it.' Case closed! Let's light up!"

physical and psychological costs, feel good about themselves and the direction their lives are taking, and are in a peer group that disapproves of using drugs. These educational, psychological, and social factors help explain why 42 percent of American high school dropouts, but only 15 percent of college graduates, smoke (Ladd, 1998).

>> LEARNING OUTCOMES

Drugs and Consciousness

OBJECTIVE 14 | **Define *psychoactive drug*.**

A *psychoactive drug* is a chemical substance that alters perceptions and mood.

OBJECTIVE 15 | **Discuss the nature of drug dependence, and identify three common misconceptions about addiction.**

Psychoactive drugs alter perceptions and moods. Continued use of these drugs produces tolerance (requiring larger doses to achieve the same effect) and may lead to physical or psychological dependence. Addiction is compulsive drug craving and use. Three common misconceptions about addiction are that (1) addictive drugs quickly corrupt; (2) therapy is always required to overcome addiction; and (3) the concept of addiction can meaningfully be extended beyond chemical dependence to a wide range of other behaviors.

OBJECTIVE 16 | **Name the main categories of psychoactive drugs, and list three ways these substances can interfere with neurotransmission in the brain.**

Depressants, stimulants, and hallucinogens are the three main categories of psychoactive drugs. These substances interfere with neurotransmission by stimulating, inhibiting, or mimicking the activity of chemical messengers (neurotransmitters) at synapses in the brain. The effects of psychoactive drugs also depend on the user's expectations.

OBJECTIVE 17 | **Explain how depressants affect nervous system activity and behavior, and summarize the findings on alcohol use and abuse.**

Depressants, such as alcohol, barbiturates, and the opiates, reduce neural activity and slow body functions. Alcohol is a disinhibitor. It increases the likelihood that we will act on impulses—harmful or helpful—that we might not express in the absence of alcohol. It also slows nervous system activity, impairs judgment, reduces self-awareness, and disrupts memory processes by suppressing REM sleep. If people believe they have consumed alcoholic beverages, they will behave accordingly and explain their behavior as alcohol-induced.

OBJECTIVE 18 | **Identify the major stimulants, and explain how they affect neural activity and behavior.**

Stimulants—caffeine, nicotine, the amphetamines, cocaine, and Ecstasy—excite neural activity and speed up body functions. Methamphetamine is highly addictive, and continued use may permanently reduce dopamine production. Cocaine blocks the reuptake of dopamine, norepinephrine, and serotonin at synapses in the brain and gives users a 15- to 30-minute rush of intense high feelings, followed by a crash. Cocaine is highly addictive, and its risks include cardiovascular stress and suspiciousness. Ecstasy is a combined stimulant and mild hallucinogen. By releasing serotonin and blocking its reuptake at synapses, Ecstasy produces a euphoric high and feelings of intimacy. Its repeated use may suppress the immune system, disrupt the circadian clock, destroy serotonin-producing neurons, and permanently damage mood and memory. Combined with physical activity, it can cause dehydration, leading to potentially fatal overheating.

OBJECTIVE 19 | **Describe the physiological and psychological effects of hallucinogens, and summarize the effects of LSD and marijuana.**

Hallucinogens, such as LSD and marijuana, distort perceptions and evoke sensory images in the absence of sensory input. LSD is chemically similar to one type of serotonin. The user's mood and expectations influence the effects of LSD, but common components are hallucinations and emotions varying from euphoria to panic. Marijuana's main active ingredient, THC, triggers a variety of effects, including disinhibition, a euphoric high, feelings of relaxation, relief from pain, and intense sensitivity to colors, sounds, tastes, and smells. It may also amplify feelings of anxiety or depression, impair motor coordination and reaction time, disrupt memory formation, and—because of the inhaled smoke in which it travels—damage lung tissue.

OBJECTIVE 20 | **Discuss the biological, psychological, and social-cultural factors that contribute to drug use.**

Psychological factors (such as stress, depression, and hopelessness) and social factors (such as peer pressure) combine to lead many people to experiment with—and sometimes become dependent on—drugs. Cultural and ethnic groups have differing rates of drug use. Twin and adoption studies, as well as animal and molecular genetic studies, indicate that some people are biologically more likely to become dependent on drugs such as alcohol. Each of these influences—biological, psychological, and social-cultural—offers a possible path for drug prevention and treatment programs.

ASK YOURSELF: Drinking dominates university parties when students overestimate other students' enthusiasm for alcohol. Do you think such misperceptions exist on your campus? How might you find out?

Near-Death Experiences

OBJECTIVE **21** | Describe the near-death experience and the controversy over whether it provides evidence for a mind-body dualism.

A man . . . hears himself pronounced dead by his doctor. He begins to hear an uncomfortable noise, a loud ringing or buzzing, and at the same time feels himself moving very rapidly through a long dark tunnel. After this, he suddenly finds himself outside of his own physical body . . . and sees his own body from a distance, as though he is a spectator. . . . Soon other things begin to happen. Others come to meet and to help him. He glimpses the spirits of relatives and friends who have already died, and a loving, warm spirit of a kind he has never encountered before—a being of light—appears before him. . . . He is overwhelmed by intense feelings of joy, love, and peace. Despite his attitude, though, he somehow reunites with his physical body and lives. (Moody, 1976, pp. 23, 24)

This is a composite description of a **near-death experience.** In studies of those who have come close to death through cardiac arrest, or other physical traumas, 12 to 40 percent recalled a near-death experience (Gallup, 1982; Ring, 1980; Schnaper, 1980; Van Lommel & others, 2001).

Did the description of the near-death experience sound familiar? The parallels with Ronald Siegel's (1977) descriptions of the typical hallucinogenic experience are striking: replay of old memories, out-of-body sensations, and visions of tunnels or funnels and bright lights or beings of light (**FIGURE 7.21**). Patients who have experienced temporal lobe seizures have also reported profound mystical experiences, sometimes similar to those of near-death experiences. When researchers stimulated the crucial temporal lobe area of one such patient, she reported a sensation of "floating" near the ceiling and seeing herself, from above, lying in bed (Blanke & others, 2002, 2004). Solitary sailors and polar explorers have had out-of-body sensations while enduring monotony, isolation, and cold (Suedfeld & Mocellin, 1987). Oxygen deprivation can produce such hallucinations, complete with tunnel vision (Woerlee, 2004). As oxygen deprivation turns off the brain's inhibitory cells, neural activity increases in the visual cortex, noted Susan Blackmore (1991, 1993). The result is a growing patch of light, which looks much like what you would see as you moved through a tunnel. The near-death experience, argued Siegel (1980), is best understood as "hallucinatory activity of the brain."

Some near-death investigators object. People who have experienced both hallucinations and the near-death phenomenon typically deny their similarity. Moreover, a near-death experience may change people in ways that a drug trip doesn't. Those who have been "embraced by the light" may become kinder, more spiritual, more believing in life after death. And they tend to handle stress well, often by taking the bull by the horns rather than becoming traumatized (Britton & Bootzin, 2004). Skeptics reply that these effects stem from the death-related context of the experience. When near

"My entire vision for the future passed before my eyes."

FIGURE 7.21
Near-death vision or hallucination?
Psychologist Ronald Siegel (1977) reported that people under the influence of hallucinogenic drugs often see "a bright light in the center of the field of vision. . . . The location of this point of light create[s] a tunnel-like perspective."

■ **near-death experience** an altered state of consciousness reported after a close brush with death (such as through cardiac arrest); often similar to drug-induced hallucinations.

THE FAR SIDE® BY GARY LARSON

Before

After

And then suddenly I saw this bright light at the end of a tunnel!

> "The mind seems to act independently of the brain in the same sense that a programmer acts independently of his computer."
>
> Neuroscientist Wilder Penfield, 1975

> "You, your joys and sorrows, your memories and your ambitions, your sense of personal identity and free will, are in fact no more than the behavior of a vast assembly of nerve cells and their associated molecules. As Lewis Carroll's Alice might have phrased it, 'You're nothing but a pack of neurons.'"
>
> Geneticist Sir Francis Crick, *The Astonishing Hypothesis*, 1994

death, people worldwide sometimes report visions of another world, though the content of that vision often depends on the culture (Kellehear, 1996).

The controversy over interpreting near-death experiences raises a basic mind-body issue: Is the mind immaterial? Can it exist separate from the body? **Dualists** answer yes. They believe that the mind and body are interacting but distinct entities—the mind nonphysical, the body physical. As Socrates says in Plato's *Phaedo*, "Does not death mean that the body comes to exist by itself, separated from the soul, and that the soul exists by herself, separated from the body? What is death but that?" For Socrates, for the 84 percent of Americans who believe in the "survival of the soul after death," and for those today who believe that near-death experiences are proof of immortality, death is not really the death of the person (Taylor, 2003). Death is instead a person's liberation from the bodily prison, an occasion for rejoicing.

Monists deny the separation of mind and body. They contend that mind and body are different aspects of the same thing. The mind is what the brain does. In the Western world, monists include both scientists who assume the inseparability of mind and brain and theologians who affirm an afterlife that involves some form of bodily resurrection. Such monists generally believe that life is embodied, that death is real, and that without bodies we truly are nobodies.

As debates over the significance of dreams, fantasy, hypnotic states, drug-induced hallucinations, and near-death experiences illustrate, science informs our wondering about human consciousness and human nature. Although there remain questions that it cannot answer, science nevertheless helps fashion our image of who we are—of our human potentials and our human limits.

>> LEARNING OUTCOMES

Near-Death Experiences

OBJECTIVE 21 | Describe the near-death experience and the controversy over whether it provides evidence for a mind-body dualism.

About one-third of those who have survived a brush with death, such as through cardiac arrest, later recall visionary near-death experiences. These sometimes involve out-of-body sensations and seeing or traveling toward a bright light. Dualists interpret these experiences as evidence of human immortality. Monists point out that reports of such experiences closely parallel reports of hallucinations and may be products of a brain under stress.

ASK YOURSELF: Does your understanding of mind-brain science and your personal philosophy or faith incline you toward dualism or monism?

▪ **dualism** the presumption that mind and body are two distinct entities that interact.

▪ **monism** the presumption that mind and body are different aspects of the same thing.

REVIEW CHAPTER 7: **States of Consciousness**

Test Yourself

1. During psychology's history, what were the ups and downs of "consciousness"?

2. Are you getting enough sleep? What might you ask yourself to answer this question?

3. When is the use of hypnosis potentially harmful, and when can hypnosis be used to help?

4. A U.S. government survey of 27,616 current or former alcohol drinkers found that 40 percent of those who began drinking before age 15 grew dependent on alcohol. The same was true of only 10 percent of those who first imbibed at ages 21 or 22 (Grant & Dawson, 1998). What possible explanations might there be for this correlation between early use and later abuse?

5. In what ways are near-death experiences similar to drug-induced hallucinations?

Answers to the Test Yourself questions can be found in Appendix B at the end of the book.

Terms and Concepts to Remember

consciousness, p. 271

biological rhythms, p. 274

circadian [ser-KAY-dee-an] rhythm, p. 275

REM sleep, p. 276

alpha waves, p. 277

sleep, p. 277

hallucinations, p. 277

delta waves, p. 277

insomnia, p. 283

narcolepsy, p. 284

sleep apnea, p. 284

night terrors, p. 284

dream, p. 285

manifest content, p. 286

latent content, p. 287

REM rebound, p. 288

hypnosis, p. 290

posthypnotic suggestion, p. 292

dissociation, p. 293

psychoactive drug, p. 296

tolerance, p. 297

withdrawal, p. 297

physical dependence, p. 297

psychological dependence, p. 297

addiction, p. 297

depressants, p. 298

barbiturates, p. 300

opiates, p. 300

stimulants, p. 300

amphetamines, p. 300

methamphetamines, p. 300

Ecstasy (MDMA), p. 302

hallucinogens, p. 302

LSD, p. 302

THC, p. 303

near-death experience, p. 309

dualism, p. 310

monism, p. 310

WEB

 To continue your study and review of States of Consciousness, visit this book's Web site atwww.worthpublishers.com/myers. You will find practice tests, review activities, and many interesting articles and Web links for more information on topics related to States of Consciousness.

ANOTHER VOICE ON: LEARNING

SHERMAN ALEXIE (b. 1966), FROM "SUPERMAN AND ME"

I learned to read with a *Superman* comic book. Simple enough, I suppose. . . . I was three years old, a Spokane Indian boy living with his family on the Spokane Indian Reservation in eastern Washington state. . . .

This might be an interesting story all by itself. A little Indian boy teaches himself to read at an early age and advances quickly. He reads *Grapes of Wrath* in kindergarten when other children are struggling through Dick and Jane. If he'd been anything but an Indian boy living on the reservation, he might have been called a prodigy. But he is an Indian boy living on the reservation, and is simply an oddity. . . .

I refused to fail. I was smart. I was arrogant. I was lucky . . . I read anything that had words and paragraphs. I read with equal parts joy and desperation. I loved those books, but I also knew that love had only one purpose. I was trying to save my life.

8: Learning

> "Learning is the eye of the mind."
> Thomas Drake, *Bibliotheca Scholastica Instructissima*, 1633

■ **learning** a relatively permanent change in an organism's behavior due to experience.

OBJECTIVE **1** | Define *learning*, and identify two forms of learning.

When a chinook salmon first emerges from its egg in a stream's gravel bed, its genes provide most of the behavioral instructions it needs for life. It knows instinctively how and where to swim, what to eat, and how to protect itself from predators. Following a built-in plan, the young salmon soon begins its trek to the sea. After some four years in the ocean, the mature salmon returns to its birthplace. It navigates hundreds of miles to the mouth of its home river and then, guided by the scent of its home stream, begins an upstream odyssey to its ancestral spawning ground. Once there, the salmon seeks out the exact conditions of temperature, gravel, and water flow that will facilitate its breeding. It then mates and, its life mission accomplished, dies.

Unlike the salmon, we are not born with a genetic blueprint for life. Much of what we do we learn from experience. Although we struggle to find the life direction a salmon is born with, our learning gives us more flexibility. We can learn how to build grass huts or snow shelters, submarines or space stations, and thereby adapt to almost any environment. Indeed, nature's most important gift to us may be our *adaptability*—our capacity to learn new behaviors that enable us to cope with changing circumstances.

Learning breeds hope. What is learnable we can potentially teach—a fact that encourages parents, educators, coaches, and animal trainers. What has been learned we can potentially change by new learning—an assumption that underlies counseling, psychotherapy, and rehabilitation programs. No matter how unhappy, unsuccessful, or unloving we are, that need not be the end of our story.

No topic is closer to the heart of psychology than **learning,** *a relatively permanent change in an organism's behavior due to experience.* In earlier chapters we considered the learning of visual perceptions, of moral ideas, of a drug's expected effect. In later chapters we will consider how learning shapes our thought and language, our motivations and emotions, our personalities and attitudes. This chapter examines some of the processes of learning.

"Actually, sex just isn't that important to me."

© 1984 by Sidney Harris, *American Scientist Magazine.*

How Do We Learn?

More than 200 years ago, philosophers such as John Locke and David Hume echoed Aristotle's conclusion from 2000 years earlier: We learn by association. Our minds naturally connect events that occur in sequence. If, after seeing and smelling freshly baked bread, you eat some and find it satisfying, then the next time you see and smell fresh bread, your experience will lead you to expect that eating it will be satisfying again. And if

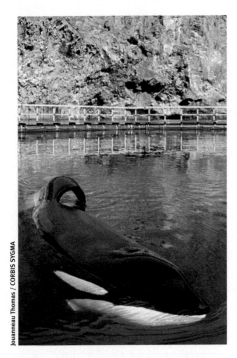

Nature without appropriate nurture
Keiko—the killer whale of *Free Willy* fame—had all the right genes for being dropped right back into his Icelandic home waters. But lacking life experience, he required caregivers to his life's end in a Norwegian fjord.

Most of us would be unable to name the order of the songs on our favorite CD. Yet hearing the end of one piece cues (by association) an anticipation of the next. Likewise, when singing your national anthem, you associate the end of each line with the beginning of the next. (Pick a line out of the middle and notice how much harder it is to recall the *previous* line.)

you associate a sound with a frightening consequence, then your fear may be aroused by the sound itself. As one 4-year-old exclaimed after watching a TV character get mugged, "If I had heard that music, I wouldn't have gone around the corner!" (Wells, 1981).

Simpler animals can learn simple associations. When disturbed by a squirt of water, the sea snail *Aplysia* will protectively withdraw its gill. If the squirts continue, as happens naturally in choppy water, the withdrawal response diminishes. (The snail's response *habituates*.) But if the sea snail repeatedly receives an electric shock just after being squirted, its withdrawal response to the squirt instead becomes stronger. The animal relates the squirt to the impending shock. Complex animals can learn more response-outcome associations. Seals in an aquarium will repeat behaviors, such as slapping and barking, that prompt people to toss them a herring.

By linking two events that occur close together, both the sea snail and the seals exhibit **associative learning.** The sea snail associates the squirt with impending shock; the seals associate slapping and barking with receiving a herring. In both cases, the animals learned something important to their survival: to predict the immediate future.

The significance of an animal's learning is illustrated by the challenges captive-bred animals face when introduced to the wild. After being bred and raised in captivity, 11 Mexican gray wolves—extinct in the United States since 1977—were released in Arizona's Apache National Forest in 1998. Eight months later, the lone survivor of this initial effort was recaptured. The pen-reared wolves had learned how to hunt—and to move 100 feet away from people—but had not learned to run from a human with a gun. The gray wolves' experience is not unusual. Of 145 documented reintroductions of 115 species in the twentieth century, only 11 percent produced self-sustaining populations in the wild. Successful adaptation requires both nature (the needed genetic predispositions) and nurture (a history of appropriate learning).

Conditioning is the process of learning associations. In *classical conditioning,* we learn to associate two stimuli and thus to anticipate events. We learn that a flash of lightning signals an impending crack of thunder, and so we start to brace ourselves when lightning flashes nearby (**FIGURE 8.1**).

In *operant conditioning,* we learn to associate a response (our behavior) and its consequence and thus to repeat acts followed by good results (**FIGURE 8.2**) and avoid acts followed by bad results.

To simplify, we will consider these two types of associative learning separately. Often, though, they occur together in the same situation. A clever Japanese rancher reportedly herds cattle by outfitting them with electronic pagers, which he calls from his cell phone. After a week of training, the animals learn to associate two stimuli—the beep on their pager and the arrival of food (classical conditioning). But they also learn to associate their hustling to the food trough with the pleasure of eating (operant conditioning).

The concept of association by conditioning, however, provokes questions: What principles influence the learning and the loss of associations? How can these principles be applied? And what really are the associations: Does the beep on a steer's pager evoke a mental

Two related events:

Stimulus 1:
Lightning

+

Stimulus 2:
Thunder

Result after repetition:

Stimulus:
We see
lightning

Response:
We wince,
anticipating
thunder

FIGURE 8.1
Classical conditioning

(a) Response: balancing a ball

(b) Consequence: receiving food

(c) Behavior strengthened

FIGURE 8.2
Operant conditioning

representation of food, to which the steer responds by coming to the trough? Or does it make little sense to explain conditioned associations in terms of cognitive processes? (In Chapter 9, Memory, we will see how the brain stores and retrieves learning.)

Conditioning is not the only form of learning. Through *observational learning,* we learn from others' experiences and examples. Complex animals, such as chimpanzees, sometimes learn behaviors merely by observing others perform them. If one animal watches another learn to solve a puzzle that gains a food reward, the observing animal may perform the trick more quickly.

By conditioning and by observation we humans learn and adapt to our environments. We learn to expect and prepare for significant events such as food or pain (classical conditioning). We also learn to repeat acts that bring good results and to avoid acts that bring bad results (operant conditioning). By watching others we learn new behaviors (observational learning). And through language we also learn things we have neither experienced nor observed.

>> LEARNING OUTCOMES

How Do We Learn?

OBJECTIVE **1** | Define *learning,* and identify two forms of learning.

Learning is a relatively permanent change in an organism's behavior due to experience. In *associative learning,* we learn to associate two stimuli (as in classical conditioning) or a response and its consequences (as in operant conditioning). In *observational learning,* we learn by watching others' experiences and examples.

ASK YOURSELF: Can you remember some example from your childhood of learning through classical conditioning—perhaps salivating at the sound or smell of some delicious food cooking in your family kitchen? Can you remember an example of operant conditioning, when you repeated (or decided not to repeat) a behavior because you liked (or hated) its consequences? Can you recall watching someone else perform some act and later repeating or avoiding that act?

Classical Conditioning

OBJECTIVE **2** | Define *classical conditioning* and *behaviorism,* and describe the basic components of classical conditioning.

Although the idea of learning associations had long generated philosophical discussion, only in the early twentieth century did psychology's most famous research verify it. For many people, the name Ivan Pavlov (1849–1936) rings a bell. His experiments are classics, and the phenomenon he explored we justly call **classical conditioning.**

■ **associative learning** learning that certain events occur together. The events may be two stimuli (as in classical conditioning) or a response and its consequences (as in operant conditioning).

■ **classical conditioning** a type of learning in which an organism comes to associate stimuli. A neutral stimulus that signals an unconditioned stimulus (US) begins to produce a response that anticipates and prepares for the unconditioned stimulus. Also called *Pavlovian* or *respondent conditioning.*

■ **behaviorism** the view that psychology (1) should be an objective science that (2) studies behavior without reference to mental processes. Most research psychologists today agree with (1) but not with (2).

■ **unconditioned response (UR)** in classical conditioning, the unlearned, naturally occurring response to the unconditioned stimulus (US), such as salivation when food is in the mouth.

■ **unconditioned stimulus (US)** in classical conditioning, a stimulus that unconditionally—naturally and automatically—triggers a response.

■ **conditioned response (CR)** in classical conditioning, the learned response to a previously neutral (but now conditioned) stimulus (CS).

■ **conditioned stimulus (CS)** in classical conditioning, an originally irrelevant stimulus that, after association with an unconditioned stimulus (US), comes to trigger a conditioned response.

Ivan Pavlov

"Experimental investigation . . . should lay a solid foundation for a future true science of psychology" (1927).

Pavlov's work also laid the foundation for many of psychologist John B. Watson's ideas. In searching for laws underlying learning, Watson (1913) urged his colleagues to discard reference to inner thoughts, feelings, and motives. The science of psychology should instead study how organisms respond to stimuli in their environments, said Watson. "Its theoretical goal is the prediction and control of behavior. Introspection forms no essential part of its methods." Simply said, psychology should be an objective science based on *observable behavior*. This view, which influenced North American psychology during the first half of the twentieth century, Watson called **behaviorism.** Watson and Pavlov shared both a disdain for "mentalistic" concepts such as consciousness and a belief that the basic laws of learning were the same for all animals—whether dogs or humans. Although today's researchers generally agree that psychology should study mental processes, they would also agree that classical conditioning is a basic form of learning by which all organisms adapt to their environment.

Pavlov's Experiments

Pavlov was driven by a lifelong passion for research. After setting aside his initial plan to follow his father into the Russian Orthodox priesthood, Pavlov received a medical degree at age 33 and spent the next two decades studying the digestive system. This work earned him Russia's first Nobel Prize in 1904. But it was his novel experiments on learning, to which he devoted the last three decades of his life, that earned this feisty scientist his place in history.

Pavlov's new direction came when his creative mind seized on an incidental finding. After studying salivary secretion in dogs, he knew that when he put food in a dog's mouth the animal would invariably salivate. He also noticed that when he worked with the same dog repeatedly, the dog began salivating to stimuli associated with food—the mere sight of the food, the food dish, the presence of the person who regularly brought the food, or even the sound of that person's approaching footsteps. Because these "psychic secretions" interfered with his experiments on digestion, Pavlov considered them an annoyance—until he realized they pointed to a simple but important form of learning. From that time on, Pavlov studied learning, which he hoped might enable him to better understand the brain's workings.

At first, Pavlov and his assistants tried to imagine what the dog was thinking and feeling as it drooled in anticipation of the food. This only led them into fruitless debates. So to explore the phenomenon more objectively, they experimented. To eliminate the possible influence of extraneous stimuli, they isolated the dog in a small room, secured it in a harness, and attached a device that diverted its saliva to a measuring instrument. From an adjacent room they could present food—at first by sliding in a food bowl, later by blowing meat powder into the dog's mouth at a precise moment. They then paired various neutral stimuli—something the dog could see or hear—with food in the dog's mouth. If the neutral stimulus regularly signaled the arrival of food, would the dog associate the two stimuli? If so, would it begin salivating to the neutral stimulus in anticipation of the food?

The answers proved to be yes and yes. Just before placing food in the dog's mouth to produce salivation, Pavlov sounded a tone. After several pairings of tone and food, the dog began salivating to the tone alone, in anticipation of the meat powder. Using this procedure, Pavlov conditioned dogs to salivate to other stimuli—a buzzer, a light, a touch on the leg, even the sight of a circle. It works with people, too. When Jay Gottfried and his colleagues (2003) showed some hungry young Londoners abstract figures before exposing them to the aroma of peanut butter or vanilla, their brains soon were responding in anticipation to the abstract images alone.

BEFORE CONDITIONING

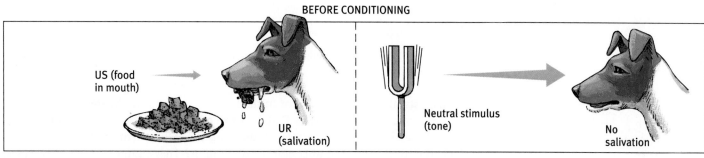

An unconditioned stimulus (US) produces an unconditioned response (UR).

A neutral stimulus produces no salivation response.

DURING CONDITIONING

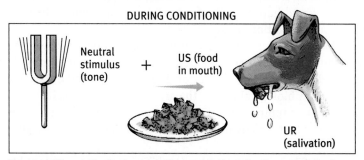

The unconditioned stimulus is repeatedly presented just after the neutral stimulus. The unconditioned stimulus continues to produce an unconditioned response.

AFTER CONDITIONING

The neutral stimulus alone now produces a conditioned response (CR), thereby becoming a conditioned stimulus (CS).

FIGURE 8.3
Pavlov's classic experiment
Pavlov presented a neutral stimulus (a tone) just before an unconditioned stimulus (food in mouth). The neutral stimulus then became a conditioned stimulus, producing a conditioned response.

Because salivation in response to food in the mouth was unlearned, Pavlov called it an **unconditioned response (UR).** Food in the mouth automatically, *unconditionally,* triggers a dog's salivary reflex (**FIGURE 8.3**). Thus, Pavlov called the food stimulus an **unconditioned stimulus (US).**

Salivation in response to the tone was *conditional* upon the dog's learning the association between the tone and the food. One translation of Pavlov therefore calls the salivation the *conditional reflex* (Todes, 1997). Today we call this learned response the **conditioned response (CR).** The previously irrelevant tone stimulus that now triggered the conditional salivation we call the **conditioned stimulus (CS).** It's easy to distinguish these two kinds of stimuli and responses. Just remember: conditioned = learned; *un*conditioned = *un*learned.

A second example, drawn from more recent experiments, may help. An experimenter sounds a tone just before delivering an air puff to your eye. After several repetitions, you blink to the tone alone. What is the US? The UR? The CS? The CR?[1]

If Pavlov's demonstration of associative learning was so simple, what did he do for the next three decades? What discoveries did his research factory publish in his 532 papers on salivary conditioning (Windholz, 1997)? He and his associates explored the causes and effects of classical conditioning. Their experiments identified five major conditioning processes: *acquisition, extinction, spontaneous recovery, generalization,* and *discrimination.*

PEANUTS

[1]US=air puff; UR=blink to air puff; CS=tone; CR=blink to tone

Acquisition

OBJECTIVE 3 | Describe the timing requirements for the initial learning of a stimulus-response relationship.

To understand the **acquisition,** or initial learning, of the stimulus-response relationship, Pavlov and his associates first had to confront the question of timing: How much time should elapse between presenting the neutral stimulus (the tone, the light, the touch) and the unconditioned stimulus? They found that, in most cases, the answer was not much. With many species and procedures, half a second works well. What do you suppose would happen if the food (US) appeared *before* the tone (CS) rather than after? Would conditioning occur?

Not likely. Although there are exceptions, conditioning seldom occurs when the CS follows the US. This finding fits the presumption that classical conditioning is biologically adaptive. It helps organisms *prepare* for good or bad events. Pavlov's tone (CS) signals an important biological event—the arrival of food (US). To a deer in the forest, the sound of a snapping twig (CS) may come to signal a predator (US). If the good or bad event had already occurred, the CS would not likely signal anything significant.

Michael Domjan (1992, 1994, 2005) showed how the CS signals an important biological event by conditioning the sexual arousal of male Japanese quail. Just before presenting an approachable female, the researchers turned on a red light. Over time, with the red light continuing to herald a female's impending arrival, it caused the male quail to become excited (and to copulate with her more quickly when she arrived). Moreover, the male quail developed a preference for their cage's red-light district. Exposure to sexually conditioned stimuli also caused them to release more semen and sperm (Domjan & others, 1998). All in all, the quail's capacity for classical conditioning gives it a reproductive edge. This illustrates the larger lesson that conditioning serves a function: It helps an animal survive and reproduce—by responding to cues that help it gain food, avoid dangers, defeat rivals, locate mates, and produce offspring (Hollis, 1997).

In humans, too, objects, smells, and sights associated with sexual pleasure—even a geometric figure in one experiment—can become conditioned stimuli for sexual arousal (Byrne, 1982). Psychologist Michael Tirrell (1990) recalls: "My first girlfriend loved onions, so I came to associate onion breath with kissing. Before long, onion breath sent tingles up and down my spine. Oh what a feeling!" (*Questions:* What is the unconditioned stimulus here? What is the conditioned response? See **FIGURE 8.4.**)

Check yourself: If the aroma of cake baking sets your mouth to watering, what is the US? The CS? The CR? (See page 321.)

Remember:
US = Unconditioned Stimulus
UR = Unconditioned Response
CS = Conditioned Stimulus
CR = Conditioned Response

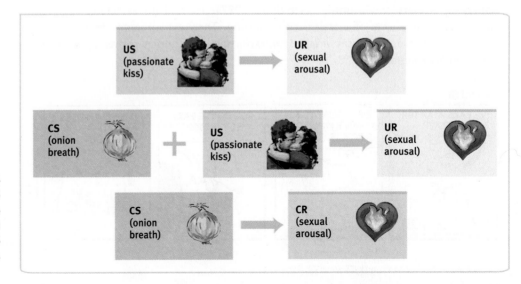

FIGURE 8.4
An unexpected CS
Onion breath does not usually produce sexual arousal. But when repeatedly paired with a passionate kiss, it can become a CS and do just that.

Associations, even associations not consciously noticed, can also give rise to attitudes (De Houwer & others, 2001). Michael Olson and Russell Fazio (2001) discovered this when they classically conditioned people's attitudes toward little-known Pokemon characters. The participants, playing the role of a security guard monitoring a video screen, were shown a stream of words, images, and Pokemon characters; they were told to respond to one target Pokemon character by pressing a button. Unnoticed by the participants, when two other Pokemon characters appeared on the screen one was consistently associated with various positive words and images (such as *awesome* or a hot fudge sundae) and the other with negative words and images (such as *awful* or a cockroach). Afterward, asked to evaluate all Pokemon characters, people preferred those associated with the positive stimuli. Without any conscious memory for the pairings, the participants had formed gut-level positive or negative attitudes.

Extinction and Spontaneous Recovery

OBJECTIVE 4 | Summarize the processes of extinction, spontaneous recovery, generalization, and discrimination.

After conditioning, what happens if the CS occurs repeatedly without the US? Will the CS continue to elicit the CR? Pavlov found that when he sounded the tone again and again without presenting food, the dogs salivated less and less. Their declining salivation illustrates **extinction,** the diminished responding that occurs when the CS (tone) no longer signals an impending US (food).

Pavlov found, however, that if he allowed several hours to elapse before sounding the tone again, the salivation to the tone would reappear spontaneously (**FIGURE 8.5**). This **spontaneous recovery**—the reappearance of a (weakened) CR after a pause—suggested to Pavlov that extinction was suppressing the CR rather than eliminating it.

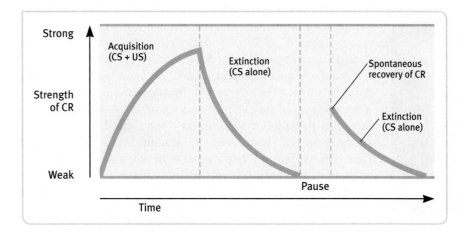

FIGURE 8.5

Idealized curve of acquisition, extinction, and spontaneous recovery
The rising curve shows that the CR rapidly grows stronger as the CS and US are repeatedly paired (acquisition), then weakens as the CS is presented alone (extinction). After a pause, the CR reappears (spontaneous recovery).

- **acquisition** the initial stage in classical conditioning; the phase associating a neutral stimulus with an unconditioned stimulus so that the neutral stimulus comes to elicit a conditioned response. In operant conditioning, the strengthening of a reinforced response.

- **extinction** the diminishing of a conditioned response; occurs in classical conditioning when an unconditioned stimulus (US) does not follow a conditioned stimulus (CS); occurs in operant conditioning when a response is no longer reinforced.

- **spontaneous recovery** the reappearance, after a pause, of an extinguished conditioned response.

After breaking up with his fire-breathing heartthrob, Tirrell also experienced extinction and spontaneous recovery. He recalls that "the smell of onion breath (CS), no longer paired with the kissing (US), lost its ability to shiver my timbers. Occasionally, though, after not sensing the aroma for a long while, smelling onion breath awakens a small version of the emotional response I once felt."

Generalization

Pavlov and his students noticed that a dog conditioned to the sound of one tone also responded somewhat to the sound of a different tone never paired with food. Likewise, a dog conditioned to salivate when rubbed would also salivate somewhat when

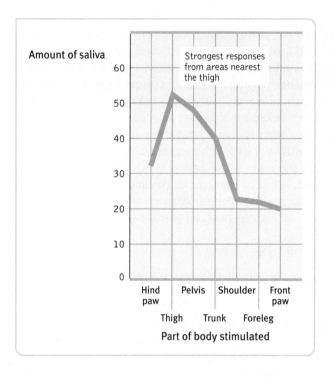

FIGURE 8.6

Generalization

Pavlov demonstrated generalization by attaching miniature vibrators to various parts of a dog's body. After conditioning salivation to stimulation of the thigh, he stimulated other areas. The closer a stimulated spot was to the thigh, the stronger the conditioned response. (From Pavlov, 1927.)

Why child abuse puts children at risk
Seth Pollak (University of Wisconsin-Madison) reports that abused children's sensitized brains react more strongly to angry faces. This generalized anxiety response may help explain their greater risk of psychological disorder.

scratched (Windholz, 1989) or when stimulated on a different body part (**FIGURE 8.6**). This tendency to respond to stimuli similar to the CS is called **generalization.**

Generalization can be adaptive, as when toddlers taught to fear moving cars in the street respond similarly to trucks and motorcycles. So automatic is generalization that one Argentine writer who underwent torture still recoils with fear when he sees black shoes—his first glimpse of his torturers when they approached his cell. Generalization has been brought to the laboratory in studies comparing abused with nonabused children. Shown an angry face on a computer screen, abused children's brain-wave responses are dramatically stronger and longer lasting (Pollak & others, 1998).

Because of generalization, stimuli that are similar to naturally disgusting or appealing objects will, by association, evoke some disgust or liking. Normally desirable foods, such as fudge, are unappealing when presented in a disgusting form, as when shaped to resemble dog feces (Rozin & others, 1986). We perceive adults with childlike facial features (round face, large forehead, small chin, large eyes) as having childlike warmth, submissiveness, and naiveté (Berry & McArthur, 1986). In both cases, people's emotional reactions to one stimulus generalize to similar stimuli.

Discrimination

OBJECTIVE 5 | Discuss the survival value of generalization and discrimination.

■ **generalization** the tendency, once a response has been conditioned, for stimuli similar to the conditioned stimulus to elicit similar responses.

■ **discrimination** in classical conditioning, the learned ability to distinguish between a conditioned stimulus and stimuli that do not signal an unconditioned stimulus.

Pavlov's dogs also learned to respond to the sound of a particular tone and *not* to other tones. **Discrimination** is the learned ability to *distinguish* between a conditioned stimulus (which predicts the US) and other irrelevant stimuli. Like generalization, discrimination has survival value. Slightly different stimuli are at times followed by vastly different consequences. Being able to recognize these differences is adaptive. Confronted by a pit bull, your heart may race; confronted by a golden retriever, it probably will not.

Extending Pavlov's Understanding

Pavlov's and Watson's disdain for "mentalistic" concepts such as consciousness has given way to a growing realization that they underestimated the importance of *cognitive processes* (thoughts, perceptions, expectations) and *biological constraints* on an organism's learning capacity.

Cognitive Processes

OBJECTIVE 6 | Discuss the importance of cognitive processes in classical conditioning.

The early behaviorists believed that the learned behaviors of various organisms could be reduced to mindless mechanisms. Any presumption of cognition in rats and dogs therefore struck many psychologists as unnecessary. No longer. Robert Rescorla and Allan Wagner (1972) argued that when two significant events occur close together in time, an animal learns the *predictability* of the second event. If a shock always is preceded by a tone, and then sometimes also by a light that accompanies the tone, a rat will react with fear to the tone but not to the light. Although the light is always followed by the shock, it adds no new information; the tone better predicts impending shock. The more predictable the association, the stronger the conditioned response. It's as if the animal learns an *expectancy*, an awareness of how likely it is that the US will occur. Classical conditioning "is not a stupid process by which the organism willy-nilly forms associations between any two stimuli that happen to occur," added Rescorla (1988).

This principle helps explain why classical conditioning treatments that ignore cognition often have limited success. For example, people receiving therapy for alcoholism sometimes are given alcohol spiked with a nauseating drug. Will they then associate alcohol with sickness? If classical conditioning were merely a matter of "stamping in" stimulus associations, we might hope so, and to some extent this does occur (as we will see on page 693). However, those receiving the drink are aware that they can blame their nausea on the drug, not on the alcohol. This cognition often weakens the association between alcohol and feeling sick. So, even in classical conditioning, it is, especially with humans, not only the simple CS–US association but also the thought that counts.

Biological Predispositions

OBJECTIVE 7 | Describe some of the ways that biological predispositions can affect learning by classical conditioning.

Ever since Charles Darwin, scientists have assumed that all animals share a common evolutionary history and resulting commonalities in their makeup and functioning. Pavlov and Watson, for example, believed the basic laws of learning were essentially similar in all animals. So it should make little difference whether one studied pigeons or people. Moreover, it seemed that any natural response could be conditioned to any neutral stimulus. As learning researcher Gregory Kimble proclaimed in 1956, "Just about any activity of which the organism is capable can be conditioned and . . . these responses can be conditioned to any stimulus that the organism can perceive" (p. 195).

Twenty-five years later, Kimble (1981) humbly acknowledged that "half a thousand" scientific reports had proven him wrong. More than the early behaviorists realized, an animal's capacity for conditioning is constrained by its biology. Each species' predispositions prepare it to learn the associations that enhance its survival. Environments are not the whole story.

John Garcia was among those who challenged the prevailing idea that any associations can be learned equally well. While researching the effects of radiation on

Stimulus generalization

S Gross

"I don't care if she's a tape dispenser. I love her."

"All brains are, in essence, anticipation machines."

Daniel C. Dennett, *Consciousness Explained*, 1991

Answer to questions on page 318: The cake (and its taste) are the US. The associated aroma is the CS. Salivation to the aroma is the CR.

John Garcia

As the laboring son of California farmworkers, Garcia attended school only in the off-season during his early childhood years. After entering junior college in his late twenties, and earning his Ph.D. in his late forties, he received the American Psychological Association's Distinguished Scientific Contribution Award "for his highly original, pioneering research in conditioning and learning." He was also elected to the National Academy of Sciences.

Courtesy of John Garcia

Colin Young-Wolff / Photo Edit Inc.

Taste aversion

If you became violently ill after eating mussels, you probably would have a hard time eating them again. Their smell and taste would have become a CS for nausea. This learning occurs readily because our biology prepares us to learn taste aversions to toxic foods.

"Once bitten, twice shy."

G. F. Northall, *Folk-Phrases*, 1894

laboratory animals, Garcia and Robert Koelling (1966) noticed that rats began to avoid drinking water from the plastic bottles in radiation chambers. They wondered whether classical conditioning might be the culprit. Might the rats have linked the plastic-tasting water (a CS) to the sickness (UR) triggered by the radiation (US)?

To test their hunch, Garcia and Koelling gave the rats a particular taste, sight, or sound (CS) and later also gave them radiation or drugs (US) that led to nausea and vomiting (UR). Two startling findings emerged: First, even if sickened as late as several hours after tasting a particular novel flavor, the rats thereafter avoided that flavor. This appeared to violate the notion that for conditioning to occur, the US must immediately follow the CS.

Second, the sickened rats developed aversions to tastes but not to sights or sounds. This contradicted the behaviorists' idea that any perceivable stimulus could serve as a CS. But it made adaptive sense, because for rats the easiest way to identify tainted food is to taste it. (If sickened after sampling a new food, they thereafter avoid the food—which makes it difficult to eradicate a population of "bait-shy" rats by poisoning.) Birds, which hunt by sight, appear biologically primed to develop aversions to the *sight* of tainted food (Nicolaus & others, 1983). And remember those Japanese quail that were conditioned to get excited by a red light that signaled a receptive female's arrival? Michael Domjan and his colleagues (2004) report that such conditioning is even speedier, stronger, and more durable when the CS is "ecologically relevant"—something similar to stimuli associated with sexual activity in the natural environment, such as the stuffed head of a female quail. In the real world, observes Domjan (2005), conditioned stimuli have a natural association with the unconditioned stimuli they predict. No wonder organisms are predisposed to learn those associations.

Humans, too, seem biologically prepared to learn some things rather than others. If you become violently ill four hours after eating contaminated mussels, you will probably develop an aversion to the taste of mussels but not to the sight of the associated restaurant, its plates, the people you were with, or the music you heard there. Similarly, we more easily learn to fear snakes and spiders than to fear flowers (Cook & others, 1986). Again, it makes sense: Such animals harm us more frequently than do flowers.

All these cases support Darwin's principle that natural selection favors traits that aid survival. Nature prepares the members of each species to learn those things crucial to their survival. Someone who readily learns a taste aversion is unlikely to eat the same toxic food again and is more likely to survive and leave descendants. Indeed, all sorts of bad feelings, from nausea to anxiety to pain, serve good purposes. Like the low-oil light on a car dashboard, each alerts the body to a threat (Neese, 1991).

The German philosopher Arthur Schopenhauer (1788–1860) once said that important ideas are first ridiculed, then attacked, and finally taken for granted. So it was with Garcia's findings on taste aversion. At first, the leading journals refused to publish his work. The findings were impossible, said some critics. But as often happens in science, Garcia and Koelling's provocative research stimulated new experiments, which confirmed the surprising findings and extended them to other species. In one well-known study, coyotes and wolves that were tempted into eating sheep carcasses laced with a sickening poison developed an aversion to sheep meat (Gustavson & others, 1974, 1976). Two wolves later penned with a live sheep seemed actually to fear it.

Such research suggests possible humane ways for controlling predators and agricultural pests. This is but one instance in which psychological research that began with the discomfort of some laboratory animals enhanced the welfare of many more animals. In this case, the research saved the sheep from the coyotes. The coyotes in turn were saved from angry ranchers and farmers who, with their livestock no longer endangered, were less adamant about destroying the coyotes. Later experiments revealed that conditioned taste aversion could successfully prevent baboons from raiding African gardens, raccoons from attacking chickens, and ravens and crows from feeding on crane eggs—all while preserving predators who occupy an important ecological niche (Garcia & Gustavson, 1997).

The discovery of biological constraints affirms the value of different levels of analysis (including the biological and cognitive) when seeking to understand phenomena such as learning. It also affirms a deep principle: *Learning enables animals to adapt to their environments.* Adaptation shows us why animals would be responsive to stimuli that announce significant events, such as food or pain. And it helps us understand why animals are generally predisposed to associate a CS with a US that follows predictably and immediately: Causes often immediately precede effects.

Adaptation also sheds light on exceptions, such as the taste-aversion finding. In this case, effect need not follow cause immediately—poisoned food usually causes sickness quite a while after the food has been eaten. Similarly, when chemotherapy triggers nausea and vomiting more than an hour following treatment, cancer patients often develop classically conditioned nausea to stimuli associated with taking the drug (**FIGURE 8.7**). After four or five treatments, the patients may react with anxiety and anticipatory nausea to the sights, sounds, and smells associated with the clinic (Hall, 1997). Merely returning to the clinic's waiting room or seeing the nurses can provoke these feelings (Burish & Carey, 1986; Davey, 1992). (Under normal circumstances, such revulsion to sickening stimuli is adaptive.) The conditioned stimuli elicit the associated nausea.

FIGURE 8.7
Nausea conditioning in cancer patients

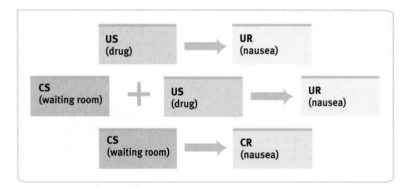

Pavlov's Legacy

OBJECTIVE 8 | Summarize Pavlov's contribution to our understanding of learning.

What, then, remains of Pavlov's ideas about conditioning? A great deal. All the researchers we have met so far in this chapter agree that classical conditioning is a basic form of learning. Judged by today's knowledge of cognitive processes and biological predispositions, Pavlov's ideas were incomplete. But if we see further than Pavlov did, it is because we stand on his shoulders.

Why does Pavlov's work remain so important? If he had taught us only that old dogs can learn new tricks, his experiments would long ago have been forgotten. Why should anyone care that a dog can be conditioned to salivate at the sound of a tone? The importance lies first in this finding: Many other responses to many other stimuli can be classically conditioned in many other organisms—in fact, in every species tested, from earthworms to fish to dogs to monkeys to people (Schwartz, 1984). Thus, classical conditioning is one way that virtually all organisms learn to adapt to their environment.

Second, Pavlov showed us how a process such as learning can be studied objectively. Pavlov was proud that his methods involved virtually no subjective judgments or guesses about what went on in the dogs' minds. The salivary response is an overt behavior measurable in cubic centimeters of saliva. Pavlov's success therefore suggested a scientific model for how the young discipline of psychology might proceed—by isolating the elementary building blocks of complex behaviors and studying them with objective laboratory procedures.

> "[Psychology's] factual and theoretical developments in this century—which have changed the study of mind and behavior as radically as genetics changed the study of heredity—have all been the product of objective analysis—that is to say, behavioristic analysis."
>
> Psychologist Donald Hebb (1980)

Applications of Classical Conditioning

OBJECTIVE 9 | Describe some uses of classical conditioning to improve human health and well-being.

Other chapters in this text—on consciousness, motivation, emotion, health, psychological disorders, and therapy—show how Pavlov's principles of classical conditioning apply to human health and well-being. Some examples:

- Former crack cocaine users often feel a craving when they again encounter cues (people, places) associated with previous highs. Thus, drug counselors advise addicts to steer clear of settings and paraphernalia associated with the euphoria of previous drug use (page 298).
- Counselors sometimes provide people who abuse alcohol with aversive experiences that may partly reverse their positive associations with alcohol (page 693).
- Classical conditioning even works on the body's disease-fighting immune system. When a particular taste accompanies a drug that influences immune responses, the taste by itself may come to produce an immune response (page 560).

Pavlov's work also provided a basis for John Watson's (1913) idea that human emotions and behavior, though biologically influenced, are mainly a bundle of conditioned responses. In one famous study, Watson and Rosalie Rayner (1920; Harris, 1979) showed how specific fears might be conditioned. Their subject was an 11-month-old infant named Albert. Like most infants, "Little Albert" feared loud noises but not white rats. Watson and Rayner presented him with a white rat and, as he reached to touch it, struck a hammer against a steel bar just behind his head. After seven repetitions of seeing the rat and then hearing the frightening noise, Albert burst into tears at the mere sight of the rat (an ethically troublesome study by today's standards). What is more, five days later Albert showed generalization of his conditioned response by reacting with fear to a rabbit, a dog, and a sealskin coat, but not to dissimilar objects such as toys.

In Watson and Rayner's experiment, what was the US? The UR? The CS? The CR? (See page 328.)

John B. Watson

Watson (1924) admitted to "going beyond my facts" when offering his famous boast: "Give me a dozen healthy infants, well-formed, and my own specified world to bring them up in and I'll guarantee to take any one at random and train him to become any type of specialist I might select—doctor, lawyer, artist, merchant-chief, and, yes, even beggar-man and thief, regardless of his talents, penchants, tendencies, abilities, vocations, and race of his ancestors."

Brown Brothers

Although Little Albert's fate is unknown, Watson's is not. After losing his professorship at Johns Hopkins University over an affair with Rayner (whom he later married), he became the J. Walter Thompson advertising agency's resident psychologist. There he used his knowledge of associative learning to conceive many successful campaigns, including one for Maxwell House that helped make the "coffee break" an American custom (Hunt, 1993).

Some psychologists, noting that Albert's fear wasn't learned quickly, had difficulty repeating Watson and Rayner's findings with other children. Nevertheless, Little Albert's case has had legendary significance for many psychologists. Some have wondered if each of us might not be a walking repository of conditioned emotions (see Close-Up on the aftermath of rape). Might our worst emotions be controlled by the application of extinction procedures or by conditioning new responses to emotion-arousing stimuli? One therapist told a patient, who for 30 years had feared going into an elevator alone, to force himself to enter 20 elevators a day. Within 10 days, his fear nearly vanished (Ellis & Becker, 1982). In Chapter 17 we will see more examples of how psychologists use behavioral techniques to treat emotional disorders.

CLOSE-UP:

TRAUMA AS CLASSICAL CONDITIONING

"A burnt child dreads the fire," says a medieval proverb. Experiments with dogs reveal that, indeed, if a painful stimulus is sufficiently powerful, a single event is sometimes enough to traumatize the animal when it again faces the situation. The human counterparts to these experiments can be tragic, as illustrated by one woman's experience of being attacked and raped, and conditioned to a period of fear. Her fear (CR) was most powerfully associated with particular locations and people (CS), but it generalized to other places and people. Note, too, how her traumatic experience robbed her of the normally relaxing associations with such stimuli as home and bed.

Four months ago I was raped. In the middle of the night I awoke to the sound of someone outside my bedroom. Thinking my housemate was coming home, I called out her name. Someone began walking slowly toward me, and then I realized. I screamed and fought, but there were two of them. One held my legs, while the other put a hand over my mouth and a knife to my throat and said, "Shut up, bitch, or we'll kill you." Never have I been so terrified and helpless. They both raped me, one brutally. As they then searched my room for money and valuables, my housemate came home. They brought her into my room, raped her, and left us both tied up on my bed.

We never slept another night in that apartment. We were too terrified. Still, when I go to bed at night—always with the bedroom light left on—the memory of them entering my room repeats itself endlessly. I was an independent person who had lived alone or with other women for four years; now I can't even think about spending a night alone. When I drive by our old apartment, or when I have to go into an empty house, my heart pounds and I sweat. I am afraid of strangers, especially men, and the more they resemble my attackers the more I fear them. My housemate shares many of my fears and is frightened when entering our new apartment. I'm afraid to stay in the same town, I'm afraid it will happen again, I'm afraid to go to bed. I dread falling asleep.

Eleven years later this woman could report—as do many trauma victims (Gluhoski & Wortman, 1996)—that her conditioned fears had mostly extinguished:

The frequency and intensity of my fears have subsided. Still, I remain cautious about personal safety and occasionally have nightmares about my experience. But more important is my renewed ability to laugh, love, and trust—both old friends and new. Life is once again joyful. I have survived.

(*From personal correspondence, with permission.*)

>> LEARNING OUTCOMES

Classical Conditioning

OBJECTIVE **2** | Define *classical conditioning* and *behaviorism*, and describe the basic components of classical conditioning.

Classical conditioning is a type of learning in which an organism comes to associate stimuli. Pavlov's work on classical conditioning laid the foundation for *behaviorism*, the view that psychology should be an objective science that studies behavior without reference to mental processes. In classical conditioning, a *UR* is an event that occurs naturally (such as salivation), in response to some stimulus. A *US* is something that naturally and automatically (without learning) triggers the unlearned response (as food in the mouth triggers salivation). A *CS* in classical conditioning is an originally neutral stimulus (such as a bell) that, through learning, comes to be associated with some unlearned response (salivating). A *CR* is the learned response (salivating) to the originally neutral but now conditioned stimulus.

OBJECTIVE **3** | Describe the timing requirements for the initial learning of a stimulus-response relationship.

Classical conditioning occurs most readily when a CS is presented just before (ideally, about a half-second before) a US, preparing the organism for the upcoming event. This finding supports the view that classical conditioning is biologically adaptive.

OBJECTIVE **4** | Summarize the processes of extinction, spontaneous recovery, generalization, and discrimination.

In classical conditioning, *extinction* is diminished responding when the CS no longer signals an impending US. *Spontaneous recovery* is the appearance of a formerly extinguished response, following a rest period. *Generalization* is the tendency to respond to stimuli that are similar to a CS. *Discrimination* is the learned ability to distinguish between a CS and other irrelevant stimuli.

OBJECTIVE 5 | **Discuss the survival value of generalization and discrimination.**

Generalization (our tendency to respond to stimuli similar to a CS) has survival value because it lets us extend a learned response to other stimuli in a given category—as in fleeing from all dangerous animals. *Discrimination* (our learned ability to distinguish between a CS and other irrelevant stimuli) also has survival value because it lets us limit our learned responses to appropriate stimuli—as in fleeing from a rampaging lion but not from a playful kitten.

OBJECTIVE 6 | **Discuss the importance of cognitive processes in classical conditioning.**

The early behaviorists' optimism that learning principles would generalize from one response to another and from one species to another has given way to the understanding that conditioning principles are influenced by our thoughts, perceptions, and expectations. In classical conditioning, humans and other animals learn when to "expect" a US, and their awareness of the link between stimuli and responses can weaken associations.

OBJECTIVE 7 | **Describe some of the ways that biological predispositions can affect learning by classical conditioning.**

Early behaviorists believed that any natural response could be conditioned to any neutral stimulus in any living organism.

Learning theorists have abandoned this belief. Each species is biologically prepared to learn associations—such as humans' fear of spiders and snakes, or rats' aversion to tastes associated with nausea—that enhance its survival. Outside the laboratory, a CS tends to have a natural association with the US it predicts.

OBJECTIVE 8 | **Summarize Pavlov's contribution to our understanding of learning.**

Pavlov taught us that significant psychological phenomena can be studied objectively, and that conditioning principles have important applications, such as by suggesting how some fears are learned and can be treated. He also demonstrated that principles of learning apply across species, although later research modified this finding somewhat by showing that in many species cognition and biological predispositions place some limits on associative learning.

OBJECTIVE 9 | **Describe some uses of classical conditioning to improve human health and well-being.**

Classical conditioning techniques are used in treatment programs for those recovering from alcohol and other drug abuse and to condition more appropriate responses in therapy for emotional disorders. The body's immune system also appears to respond to classical conditioning.

ASK YOURSELF: How have your emotions or behaviors been classically conditioned?

Operant Conditioning

OBJECTIVE 10 | Identify the two major characteristics that distinguish classical conditioning from operant conditioning.

■ **operant conditioning** a type of learning in which behavior is strengthened if followed by a reinforcer or diminished if followed by a punisher.

■ **respondent behavior** behavior that occurs as an automatic response to some stimulus; Skinner's term for behavior learned through classical conditioning.

■ **operant behavior** behavior that operates on the environment, producing consequences.

■ **law of effect** Thorndike's principle that behaviors followed by favorable consequences become more likely, and that behaviors followed by unfavorable consequences become less likely.

■ **operant chamber** a chamber also known as a *Skinner box*, containing a bar or key that an animal can manipulate to obtain a food or water reinforcer, with attached devices to record the animal's rate of bar pressing or key pecking. Used in operant conditioning research.

It's one thing to classically condition an animal to salivate at the sound of a tone, or a child to fear cars in the street. In each case, the organism associates stimuli it does not control. It's something else to teach an elephant to walk on its hind legs or a child to say *please*. Another type of associative learning—**operant conditioning**—explains and trains such behaviors. Organisms associate their own actions with consequences. Behaviors followed by reinforcers increase; those followed by punishers decrease.

Both classical and operant conditioning involve acquisition, extinction, spontaneous recovery, generalization, and discrimination. Yet their difference is straightforward: Classical conditioning forms associations between stimuli (a CS and the US it signals). It also involves **respondent behavior**—behavior that occurs as an *automatic* response to some stimulus (such as salivating in response to meat powder and later in response to a tone). Operant conditioning involves **operant behavior,** so-called because the behavior *operates* on the environment to *produce* rewarding or punishing stimuli. We can therefore distinguish classical from operant conditioning by asking: *Is the organism learning associations between events that it doesn't control (classical conditioning)? Or is it learning associations between its behavior and resulting events (operant conditioning)?*

Skinner's Experiments

OBJECTIVE **11** | State Thorndike's law of effect, and explain its connection to Skinner's research on operant conditioning.

B. F. Skinner (1904–1990) was a college English major and an aspiring writer who, seeking a new direction, entered graduate school in psychology. He went on to become modern behaviorism's most influential and controversial figure. Skinner's work elaborated a simple fact of life that psychologist Edward L. Thorndike (1874–1949) called the **law of effect:** *Rewarded behavior is likely to recur* (**FIGURE 8.8**).

Time required to escape (seconds) / Successive trials in the puzzle box

FIGURE 8.8
Cat in a puzzle box

Thorndike (1898) used a fish reward to entice cats to find their way out of a puzzle box (right) through a series of maneuvers. The cats' performance tended to improve with successive trials (left), illustrating Thorndike's *law of effect*. (Adapted from Thorndike, 1898.)

Yale University Library

Using Thorndike's law of effect as a starting point, Skinner developed a "behavioral technology" that revealed principles of behavior control. These principles also enabled him to teach pigeons such unpigeonlike behaviors as walking in a figure 8, playing Ping-Pong, and keeping a missile on course by pecking at a target on a screen.

For his pioneering studies with rats (and later with pigeons), Skinner designed an **operant chamber,** popularly known as a *Skinner box* (**FIGURE 8.9**). The box has a bar or key that an animal presses or pecks to release a reward of food or water, and a device that records these responses. Operant conditioning experiments have done far more than teach us how to pull habits out of a rat. They have explored the precise conditions that foster efficient and enduring learning.

Charlotte van Oyen Witvliet

The law of effect at Stingray City

For 35 years, Cayman Islands fishing crews have gathered conch and cleaned them over this barrier reef. Stingrays gradually became accustomed to these yummy treats. Noticing the rays congregating, scuba divers then began feeding the increasingly friendly rays by hand. Today, tourists can do the same and can even pet the rays as they graze past them.

Walter Dawn/Photo Researchers, Inc.

From *The Essentials of Conditioning and Learning,* 3rd Edition by Michael P. Domjan, 2005. Used with permission by Thomson Learning, Wadsworth Division.

Light / Speaker / Water / Lever / Dispenser

FIGURE **8.9**
A Skinner box

Inside the box, the rat presses a bar for a food reward. Outside, a measuring device records the animal's accumulated responses.

Shaping rats to save lives
A Gambian giant pouched rat, having been shaped to sniff out land mines, receives a banana after successfully locating a mine during training in Mozambique.

Khamis Ramadhan / Panapress / Getty Images

Answer to question on page 324: The US was the loud noise; the UR was the startled fear response; the CS was the rat; the CR was fear.

Shaping Behavior

OBJECTIVE **12** | Describe the shaping procedure, and explain how it can increase our understanding of what animals and babies can discriminate.

In his experiments, Skinner used **shaping,** a procedure in which *reinforcers,* such as food, gradually guide an animal's actions toward a desired behavior. Imagine that you wanted to condition a hungry rat to press a bar. After observing how the animal naturally behaves before training, you would build on its existing behaviors. You might give the rat a food reward each time it approaches the bar. Once the rat is approaching regularly, you would require it to move closer before rewarding it, then closer still. Finally, you would require it to touch the bar before you gave it the food. With this method of *successive approximations,* you reward responses that are ever-closer to the final desired behavior, and you ignore all other responses. By making rewards contingent on desired behaviors, researchers and animal trainers gradually shape complex behaviors.

By shaping nonverbal organisms to discriminate between stimuli, a psychologist can also determine what they perceive. Can a dog distinguish colors? Can a baby discriminate sounds? If we can shape them to respond to one stimulus and not to another, then obviously they can perceive the difference. Experiments show that some animals are remarkably capable of forming concepts; they demonstrate this by discriminating between classes of events or objects. If an experimenter reinforces a pigeon for pecking after seeing a human face, but not after seeing other images, the pigeon will learn to recognize human faces (Herrnstein & Loveland, 1964). In this experiment, a face is a *discriminative stimulus;* like a green traffic light, it signals that a response will be reinforced. After being trained to discriminate among flowers, people, cars, and chairs, pigeons can usually identify in which of these categories a new pictured object belongs (Bhatt & others, 1988; Wasserman, 1993). With training, pigeons have even been taught to discriminate between Bach's music and Stravinsky's (Porter & Neuringer, 1984).

In everyday life, too, we continually reward and shape the behavior of others, said Skinner, but we often do so unintentionally. Sometimes we unthinkingly reward behaviors we find annoying. Billy's whining, for example, annoys his mystified parents, but look how they typically deal with Billy:

Billy: *Could you tie my shoes?*
Father: *(Continues reading paper.)*
Billy: *Dad, I need my shoes tied.*
Father: *Uh, yeah, just a minute.*
Billy: *DAAAAD! TIE MY SHOES!*
Father: *How many times have I told you not to whine? Now, which shoe do we do first?*

A discriminating creature
University of Windsor psychologist Dale Woodyard uses a food reward to train this manatee to discriminate between objects of different shapes, colors, and sizes. A manatee can remember such responses for a year or more.

Fred Bavendam/Peter Arnold, Inc.

HI AND LOIS

Billy's whining is reinforced, because he gets something desirable—his dad's attention. Dad's response is reinforced because it gets rid of something aversive—Billy's whining.

Or consider a teacher who pastes gold stars on a wall chart after the names of children scoring 100 percent on spelling tests. All children take the same tests. As everyone can then see, some children, the academic all-stars, easily get 100 percent. The others get no stars. The teacher would be better advised to apply the principles of operant conditioning—to reinforce all spellers for gradual improvements (successive approximations toward perfect spelling of words they find challenging).

Types of Reinforcers

OBJECTIVE **13** | Compare positive and negative reinforcement, and give one example each of a primary reinforcer, a conditioned reinforcer, an immediate reinforcer, and a delayed reinforcer.

People often refer rather loosely to the power of "rewards." This idea gains a more precise meaning in Skinner's concept of **reinforcement:** any event that strengthens, or increases the frequency of, a preceding response. A *positive* reinforcer may be a tangible reward. It may be praise or attention. Or it may be an activity—being able to borrow the car when the dishes are done, or to have a break after an hour of study.

Most people think of reinforcers as rewards. Actually, anything that serves to increase behavior is a reinforcer—even being yelled at, if yelling *increases* a child's offending behavior. Reinforcers vary with circumstances. What's reinforcing to one person (rock concert tickets) may not be to another. What's reinforcing in one situation (food when hungry) may not be in another.

There are two basic kinds of reinforcement (**TABLE 8.1**). One type (**positive reinforcement**) strengthens a response by *presenting* a typically pleasurable stimulus after a response. Food is a positive reinforcer for hungry animals; attention, approval, and money are positive reinforcers for most people. The other type (**negative reinforcement**) strengthens a response by reducing or *removing* an aversive (undesirable) stimulus. Taking aspirin may relieve a headache. Pushing the snooze button silences an annoying alarm. Dragging on a cigarette will reduce a nicotine addict's pangs. All these consequences provide negative reinforcement and increase the likelihood that the behavior will be repeated. For drug addicts, the negative reinforcement of escaping withdrawal pangs becomes compelling (Baker & others, 2004). When someone stops nagging or whining, that, too, is a negative reinforcer. (Note that contrary to popular usage, negative reinforcement is *not* punishment; rather, it *removes* a punishing aversive event.)

So imagine a worried student who, after goofing off and getting a bad exam grade, studies harder for the next exam. The student's studying may be reinforced by reduced anxiety (negative reinforcement) and by a better grade (positive reinforcement). Whether it works by giving something desirable or by reducing something aversive, *reinforcement is any consequence that strengthens behavior.*

■ **shaping** an operant conditioning procedure in which reinforcers guide behavior toward closer and closer approximations of the desired behavior.

■ **reinforcer** in operant conditioning, any event that *strengthens* the behavior it follows.

■ **positive reinforcement** increasing behaviors by presenting positive stimuli, such as food. A positive reinforcer is any stimulus that, when *presented* after a response, strengthens the response.

■ **negative reinforcement** increasing behaviors by stopping or reducing negative stimuli, such as shock. A negative reinforcer is any stimulus that, when *removed* after a response, strengthens the response. (Note: negative reinforcement is *not* punishment.)

Positive reinforcement
A heat lamp positively reinforces this Taronga Zoo meerkat's behavior during a cold snap in Sydney, Australia.

TABLE 8.1

WAYS TO INCREASE BEHAVIOR

Operant Conditioning Term	Description	Possible Examples
Positive reinforcement	*Add* a desirable stimulus	Getting a a hug; receiving a paycheck
Negative reinforcement	*Remove* an aversive stimulus	Fastening seatbelt to turn off beeping

primary reinforcer an innately reinforcing stimulus, such as one that satisfies a biological need.

conditioned reinforcer a stimulus that gains its reinforcing power through its association with a primary reinforcer; also known as *secondary reinforcer.*

continuous reinforcement reinforcing the desired response every time it occurs.

partial (intermittent) reinforcement reinforcing a response only part of the time; results in slower acquisition of a response but much greater resistance to extinction than does continuous reinforcement.

fixed-ratio schedule in operant conditioning, a reinforcement schedule that reinforces a response only after a specified number of responses.

Primary and Conditioned Reinforcers **Primary reinforcers**—getting food when hungry or being relieved of electric shock—are innately satisfying. **Conditioned reinforcers,** also called *secondary reinforcers,* are learned. They get their power through their association with primary reinforcers. If a rat in a Skinner box learns that a light reliably signals that food is coming, the rat will work to turn on the light. The light has become a secondary reinforcer associated with food. Our lives are filled with secondary reinforcers—money, good grades, a pleasant tone of voice, a word of praise—each of which has been linked with more basic rewards. Secondary reinforcers greatly enhance our ability to influence one another.

Immediate and Delayed Reinforcers Let's return to the imaginary shaping experiment in which you were conditioning a rat to press a bar. Before performing this "wanted" behavior, the hungry rat will engage in a sequence of "unwanted" behaviors—scratching, sniffing, and moving around. When the food reinforcer immediately follows one of these behaviors, that response becomes more likely to recur. If the rat presses the bar, but you are distracted and delay the reinforcer for longer than 30 seconds, the rat will not learn to press the bar. Other incidental behaviors will intervene and be reinforced.

Unlike rats, humans do respond to reinforcers that are greatly delayed: the paycheck at the end of the week, the good grade at the end of the semester, the trophy at the end of the season. Indeed, to function effectively we must learn to postpone immediate rewards for greater long-term rewards. In laboratory testing, some 4-year-olds show an ability to delay gratification; in choosing a candy, they would rather have a big reward tomorrow than a small one right now. As they mature, these children tend to become socially competent and high achieving (Mischel & others, 1989). A big step toward maturity—and toward gaining the most satisfying life—is learning to delay gratification, to control one's impulses in order to achieve more valued rewards (Logue, 1998a,b).

But to our detriment, small but immediate consequences (the enjoyment of watching late-night TV, for example) are sometimes more alluring than big but delayed consequences (tomorrow's sluggishness). Smokers, alcoholics, and other drug users may know that their immediate pleasure—the kick that often comes within seconds—is more than offset by future ill effects, such as cancer in 30 years or a hangover in the morning. Still, immediate reinforcement prevails, and drugs such as nicotine and cocaine that provide the biggest kick are the most strongly addictive (Marlatt, 1991). And for many teens, the immediate gratification of risky, unprotected sex in passionate moments prevails over the delayed gratifications of safe sex or saved sex (Loewenstein & Furstenberg, 1991). Likewise, the immediate rewards of today's gas-guzzling vehicles prevail over the bigger consequences of tomorrow's global warming, rising seas, and extreme weather.

"Oh, not bad. The light comes on, I press the bar, they write me a check. How about you?"

Reinforcement Schedules

OBJECTIVE 14 | Discuss the strengths and weaknesses of continuous and partial (intermittent) reinforcement schedules, and identify four schedules of partial reinforcement.

So far, most of our examples assume **continuous reinforcement:** The desired response is reinforced every time it occurs. Under such conditions, learning occurs rapidly. But extinction also occurs rapidly. When the reinforcement stops—when we disconnect the food delivery chute—the rat soon stops pressing the bar. If a normally dependable candy machine fails to deliver a chocolate bar twice in a row, we stop putting money into it (although a week later we may exhibit spontaneous recovery by trying again).

" The charm of fishing is that it is the pursuit of what is elusive but attainable, a perpetual series of occasions for hope."
Scottish author John Buchan (1875–1940)

Real life often does not provide continuous reinforcement. A salesperson does not make a sale with every pitch, nor does an angler get a bite with every cast. But they persist because their efforts have occasionally been rewarded. Researchers have explored several **partial (intermittent) reinforcement** schedules, in which responses are sometimes reinforced, sometimes not (Nevin, 1988). Initial learning is typically slower with intermittent reinforcement, which makes continuous reinforcement preferable until a behavior is mastered. But intermittent reinforcement produces greater persistence—greater *resistance to extinction*—than is found with continuous reinforcement. Imagine a pigeon that has learned to peck a key to obtain food. When the experimenter gradually phases out the delivery of food until it occurs only rarely and unpredictably, pigeons may peck 150,000 times without a reward (Skinner, 1953). With intermittent reinforcement, hope springs eternal.

Corresponding human examples come readily to mind:

- New York City's computer-controlled traffic lights made most of the city's 3250 pedestrian traffic-signal buttons at intersections obsolete. Yet occasionally, usually coincidentally, pedestrians are reinforced with a "Walk" light soon after pressing the button. So the mostly futile button pressing continues.
- Slot machines reward gamblers occasionally and unpredictably. This intermittent reinforcement affects them much as it affects pigeons: They keep trying, sometimes interminably.
- There is also a valuable lesson here for parents. *Occasionally* giving in to children's demanding tantrums for the sake of peace and quiet intermittently reinforces the tantrums. That is the very best procedure for making a behavior persist.

Skinner (1961) and his collaborators compared four schedules of partial reinforcement. Some are rigidly fixed, some unpredictably variable.

Fixed-ratio schedules reinforce behavior after a set number of responses. Like people paid on a piecework basis—say, for every 30 pieces—laboratory animals may be reinforced on a fixed ratio of, say, one reinforcer for every 30 responses. Once conditioned, the animal will pause only briefly after a reinforcer and will then return to a high rate of responding (**FIGURE 8.10**).

In operant conditioning, *acquisition* is the strengthening of a reinforced response. *Extinction* occurs when a response is no longer reinforced. *Generalization* occurs when an organism's response to similar stimuli is also reinforced. *Discrimination* occurs when an organism learns that certain responses, but not others, will be rewarded.

Remember whining Billy on page 328? In that example, which behavior was positively reinforced and which was negatively reinforced? See page 333 for the answer.

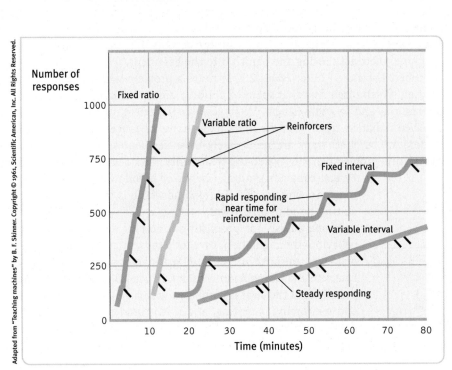

FIGURE 8.10

Intermittent reinforcement schedules
Skinner's laboratory pigeons produced these response patterns to each of four reinforcement schedules. (Reinforcers are indicated by diagonal marks.) For people, as for pigeons, reinforcement linked to number of responses (a ratio schedule) produces a higher response rate than reinforcement linked to amount of time elapsed (an interval schedule). But the predictability of the reward also matters. An unpredictable (variable) schedule produces more consistent responding than does a predictable (fixed) schedule.

Variable-ratio schedules provide reinforcers after an unpredictable number of responses. This is what slot-machine players and fly-casting anglers experience—unpredictable reinforcement—and what makes gambling and fly fishing so hard to extinguish. Like the fixed-ratio schedule, the variable-ratio schedule produces high rates of responding, because reinforcers increase as the number of responses increases.

Fixed-interval schedules reinforce the first response after a fixed time period. Like people checking more frequently for the mail as the delivery time approaches, or checking to see if the Jell-O is set, pigeons on a fixed-interval schedule peck a key more frequently as the anticipated time for reward draws near, producing a choppy stop-start pattern (see Figure 8.10, page 331) rather than a steady rate of response.

Variable-interval schedules reinforce the first response after *varying* time intervals. Like the "You've got mail" that finally rewards persistence in rechecking for e-mail, variable-interval schedules tend to produce slow, steady responding. This makes sense, because there is no knowing when the waiting will be over.

Animal behaviors differ, yet Skinner (1956) contended that these reinforcement principles of operant conditioning are universal. It matters little, he said, what response, what reinforcer, or what species you use. The effect of a given reinforcement schedule is pretty much the same: "Pigeon, rat, monkey, which is which? It doesn't matter. . . . Behavior shows astonishingly similar properties."

Door-to-door salespeople are reinforced by which schedule? People checking the oven to see if the cookies are done are on which schedule? Airline frequent-flyer programs that offer a free flight after every 25,000 miles of travel use which reinforcement schedule? (See page 335.)

Punishment

OBJECTIVE 15 | Discuss the ways negative punishment, positive punishment, and negative reinforcement differ, and list some drawbacks of punishment as a behavior-control technique.

The effect of **punishment** is opposite to that of reinforcement. Reinforcement increases a behavior; punishment decreases it. Thus, a punisher is any consequence that *decreases* the frequency of a preceding behavior, usually by administering an undesirable consequence or withdrawing a desirable one (see **TABLE 8.2**). Swift and sure punishers can powerfully restrain unwanted behavior. The rat that is shocked after touching a forbidden object and the child who loses a treat after running into the street will learn not to repeat the behavior. Some punishments, though unintentional, are nevertheless quite effective: A dog that has learned to come running at the sound of the electric can opener will stop coming if its master starts running the machine to attract the dog and banish it to the basement.

Robert Larzelere (1996, 2000, 2004) notes a problem with human punishment studies, which often find that spanked children are at increased risk for aggression, depression, and low self-esteem. Well, yes, says Larzelere, just as people who have received radiation treatments are more likely to die of cancer, and people who have undergone psychotherapy are more likely to suffer depression—because they had preexisting problems that triggered the treatments. Physical punishment is followed by bad behavior. And bad behavior is followed by physical punishment. So which is the chicken and which is the egg? The correlation doesn't hand us an answer.

If one adjusts for preexisting cancer or depression—or antisocial behavior—then radiation, psychotherapy, or an occasional single swat or two to misbehaving 2- to 6-year-olds looks more effective, note Larzelere and Diana Baumrind and her co-authors (2002). That is especially so if the swat is combined with a generous dose of reasoning and reinforcing parenting, and if it is used only as a backup to enhance the effectiveness of milder disciplinary tactics such as reasoning and time-out.

TABLE 8.2

WAYS TO DECREASE BEHAVIOR

Type of Punisher	Description	Possible Examples
Positive punishment	Administer an aversive stimulus	Spanking; a parking ticket
Negative punishment	Withdraw a desirable stimulus	Time-out from privileges (such as time with friends); revoked driver's license

Nevertheless, say advocates of nonviolent parenting, physical punishment has drawbacks (Gershoff, 2002; Marshall, 2002). Punished behavior is not forgotten; it is suppressed. This temporary suppression may (negatively) reinforce the parents' punishing behavior. The child swears, the parent swats, the parent hears no more swearing from the child, and the parent feels the punishment was successful in stopping the behavior. No wonder spanking is a hit with so many U.S. parents of 3- and 4-year-olds—more than 9 in 10 of whom acknowledge spanking their children (Kazdin & Benjet, 2003).

But was the punishment effective? If the punishment is avoidable, the punished behavior may reappear in safe settings. The child may simply learn discrimination: It's not okay to swear around the house, but it is okay to swear elsewhere. The driver who gets a speeding ticket may buy a radar detector and speed freely when no radar patrol is around.

Physical punishment may increase aggressiveness by demonstrating that aggression is a way to cope with problems. This helps explain why so many aggressive delinquents and abusive parents come from abusive families (Straus & Gelles, 1980; Straus & others, 1997). Moreover, punishment can create fear; the person receiving the punishment may associate the fear not only with the undesirable behavior but also with the person who administers it or with the situation in which it occurs. Thus, a child may come to fear the punitive teacher and want to avoid school. Worse, when punishments are unpredictable and inescapable, both animals and people may develop the sense that events are beyond their control. As a result, they may come to feel helpless and depressed. For these reasons, most European countries have banned hitting children in schools and child-care institutions (Leach, 1993, 1994). Eleven countries, including those in Scandinavia, have further outlawed hitting by parents, thereby extending to children the same legal protection given to spouses (EPOCH, 2000).

Even though punishment suppresses unwanted behavior, it often does not guide one toward more desirable behavior. Punishment tells you what *not* to do; reinforcement tells you what *to* do. Thus, punishment combined with reinforcement is usually more effective than punishment alone. This approach has been used to change self-destructive behaviors by children who bite themselves or bang their heads. They may be mildly punished (say, with a squirt of water in the face) whenever they bite themselves, but also rewarded with positive attention and food when they behave well. The approach also works in the classroom. The teacher whose feedback on a paper says "No, but try this . . ." and "Yes, that's it!" reduces unwanted behavior by reinforcing alternative behaviors.

Parents of delinquent youth often lack this awareness of how to reinforce desirable behavior without screaming or hitting (Patterson & others, 1982). Training programs for such parents help them reframe contingencies from dire threats to positive incentives—from "You clean up your room this minute or no dinner!" to "You're welcome at the dinner table after you get your room cleaned up." When you stop to think about it, many threats of punishment are just as forceful, and perhaps more effective, if rephrased positively. Thus, "If you don't get your homework done, there'll be no car" would better be phrased as . . .

What punishment often teaches, said Skinner, is how to avoid it. Most psychologists now favor an emphasis on reinforcement: Notice people doing something right and affirm them for it.

Extending Skinner's Understanding

Skinner granted the existence of private thought processes and the biological underpinnings of behavior. Nevertheless, many psychologists criticized him for discounting the importance of these processes and predispositions.

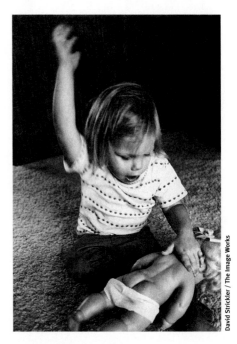

David Strickler / The Image Works

Children see, children do?
Children who often experience physical punishment tend to display more aggression.

Answer to question on page 331: Billy's whining was *positively* reinforced, because Billy got something desirable—his father's attention. His dad's response to the whining (doing what Billy wanted) was *negatively* reinforced, because it got rid of Billy's annoying whining.

■ **variable-ratio schedule** in operant conditioning, a reinforcement schedule that reinforces a response after an unpredictable number of responses.

■ **fixed-interval schedule** in operant conditioning, a reinforcement schedule that reinforces a response only after a specified time has elapsed.

■ **variable-interval schedule** in operant conditioning, a reinforcement schedule that reinforces a response at unpredictable time intervals.

■ **punishment** an event that *decreases* the behavior that it follows.

■ **cognitive map** a mental representation of the layout of one's environment. For example, after exploring a maze, rats act as if they have learned a cognitive map of it.

■ **latent learning** learning that occurs but is not apparent until there is an incentive to demonstrate it.

■ **intrinsic motivation** a desire to perform a behavior for its own sake.

■ **extrinsic motivation** a desire to perform a behavior due to promised rewards or threats of punishment.

For more information on animal behavior, see books by (I am not making this up) Robin Fox and Lionel Tiger.

Cognition and Operant Conditioning

OBJECTIVE **16** | Explain how latent learning and the effect of external rewards demonstrate that cognitive processing is an important part of learning.

A mere eight days before dying of leukemia, Skinner (1990) stood before the American Psychological Association convention for one final critique of "cognitive science," which he viewed as a throwback to early twentieth-century introspectionism. Skinner died resisting the growing belief that cognitive processes—thoughts, perceptions, expectations—have a necessary place in the science of psychology and even in our understanding of conditioning. (He regarded thoughts and emotions as behaviors that follow the same laws as other behaviors.) Yet we have seen several hints that cognitive processes might be at work in operant learning. For example, animals on a fixed-interval reinforcement schedule respond more and more frequently as the time approaches when a response will produce a reinforcer. The animals behave as if they expected that repeating the response would soon produce the reward. (To a strict behaviorist, however, talk of "expectations" is unnecessary; it is enough to say that when responses are reinforced under certain conditions they recur when those conditions recur.)

Latent Learning Evidence of cognitive processes has also come from studying rats in mazes. Rats exploring a maze, with no obvious reward, are like people sightseeing in a new town. The rats seem to develop a **cognitive map,** a mental representation of the maze. When an experimenter then places a reward in the maze's goal box, the rats very quickly perform as well as rats that have been reinforced with food for running the maze (**FIGURE 8.11**).

During their explorations, the rats seemingly experience **latent learning**—learning that becomes apparent only when there is some incentive to demonstrate it. Children, too, may learn from watching a parent, but demonstrate the learning much later when needed. The conclusion: There is more to learning than associating a response with a consequence. There is also cognition. In Chapter 10 we will encounter more striking evidence of animals' cognitive abilities in solving problems and in using aspects of language.

FIGURE 8.11
Latent learning
Animals, like people, can learn from experience, with or without reinforcement. After exploring a maze for 10 days, rats received a food reward at the end of the maze. They quickly demonstrated their prior learning of the maze—by immediately doing as well as (and even better than) rats that had been reinforced for running the maze. (From Tolman & Honzik, 1930.)

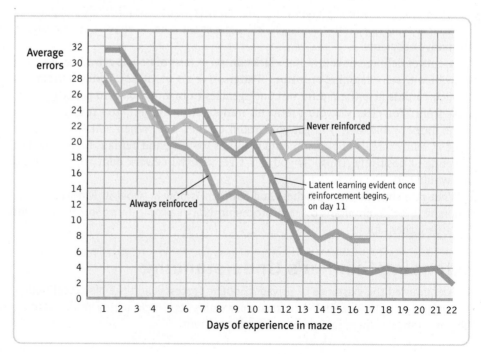

Intrinsic Motivation The cognitive perspective has also led to an important quali-fication concerning the power of rewards: Unnecessary rewards sometimes carry hid-den costs. Most people think that offering tangible rewards will boost anyone's interest in an activity (Boggiano & others, 1987). Actually, promising children a re-ward for a task they already enjoy can backfire. In experiments, children promised a payoff for playing with an interesting puzzle or toy later play with the toy less than do children who are not paid to play (Deci & others, 1999; Tang & Hall, 1995). It is as if the children think, "If I have to be bribed into doing this, then it must not be worth doing for its own sake."

Excessive rewards can undermine **intrinsic motivation**—the desire to perform a behavior effectively and for its own sake. Intrinsically motivated people work and play in search of enjoyment, interest, self-expression, or challenge. **Extrinsic motivation** is the desire to behave in certain ways to receive external rewards or avoid threatened punishment. If youth sports coaches aim to promote enduring interest in an activity, and not just to pressure players into win-ning, they should focus on the intrinsic joy of play and reaching one's potential, note motivation researchers Edward Deci and Richard Ryan (1985, 1992, 2000).

"Bathroom? Sure, it's just down the hall to the left, jog right, left, another left, straight past two more lefts, then right, and it's at the end of the third corridor on your right."

To sense the difference between extrinsic and intrinsic motivation, you might reflect on your own current experience. Are you feeling pressured to get this reading fin-ished before a deadline? Worried about your course grade? Eager for rewards that depend on your doing well? If yes, then you are extrinsically motivated (as, to some ex-tent, almost all students must be). Are you also finding the course material interest-ing? Does learning it make you feel more competent? If there were no grade at stake, might you be curious enough to want to learn the material for its own sake? If yes, intrinsic motivation also fuels your efforts.

Jack Smith/AP World Wide Photos

Answer to question on page 332: Door-to-door salespeople are reinforced on a variable-ratio schedule (after varying numbers of rings). Cookie checkers are reinforced on a fixed-interval schedule. Frequent-flyer programs use a fixed-ratio schedule.

Tiger Woods' intrinsic motivation
"I remember a daily ritual that we had: I would call Pop at work to ask if I could practice with him. He would always pause a second or two, keeping me in suspense, but he'd always say yes. . . . In his own way, he was teaching me initiative. You see, he never pushed me to play" (quoted in *USA Weekend,* 1997).

A person's interest often survives when a reward is used neither to bribe nor to control but to signal a job well done, as in a "most improved player" award (Boggiano & others, 1985). If a reward boosts your feeling of competence after doing good work, your enjoyment of the task may increase. Rewards, rightly administered, can motivate high performance and creativity (Eisenberger & Rhoades, 2001; Henderlong & Lep-per, 2002). And extrinsic rewards (such as good scholarships, admissions, and jobs that often follow good grades) are here to stay.

Biological Predispositions

OBJECTIVE **17** | Explain how biological predispositions place limits on what can be achieved through operant conditioning.

As with classical conditioning, an animal's natural predispositions constrain its ca-pacity for operant conditioning. When you reinforce a hamster's behavior with food, you can easily condition it to dig or to rear up, because these are among the animal's natural behaviors when searching for food. But it is difficult to use food as a rein-forcer to shape other hamster behaviors, such as face washing, that aren't normally associated with food or hunger (Shettleworth, 1973). Similarly, pigeons easily learn to flap their wings to avoid being shocked, and to peck to obtain food, because fleeing

"Never try to teach a pig to sing. It wastes your time and annoys the pig."
Mark Twain (1835–1910)

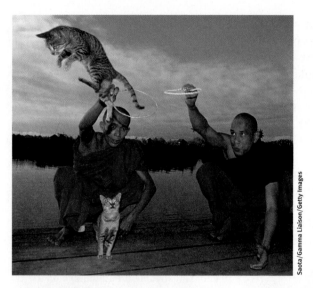

Saota/Gamma Liaison/Getty Images

Natural athletes
Animals can most easily learn and retain behaviors that draw on their biological predispositions, such as cats' inborn tendency to leap high and land on their feet.

with their wings and eating with their beaks are natural behaviors for them. However, pigeons have a hard time learning to peck to avoid a shock, or to flap their wings to obtain food (Foree & LoLordo, 1973). The principle: Biological constraints predispose organisms to learn associations that are naturally adaptive.

Skinner's former associates Keller Breland and Marian Breland (1961) observed biological predispositions while using operant procedures to train animals for circuses, TV shows, and movies. The Brelands had originally assumed that operant principles would work on almost any response that any animal could make. But after training 6000 animals of 38 different species, from chickens to whales, they concluded that biological predispositions were more important than they had supposed. In one act, they trained pigs to pick up large wooden "dollars" and deposit them in a piggy bank. After learning this behavior, however, the animals began to drift back to their natural ways. They would drop the coin, push it with their snouts as pigs are prone to do, pick it up again, and then repeat the sequence—delaying their food reinforcer. As this "instinctive drift" illustrates, "misbehaviors" occurred as the animals reverted to their biologically predisposed patterns.

Skinner's Legacy

OBJECTIVE 18 | Describe the controversy over Skinner's views of human behavior.

B. F. Skinner was one of the most controversial intellectual figures of the late twentieth century. He stirred a hornet's nest by repeatedly insisting that external influences (not internal thoughts and feelings) shape behavior and by urging the use of operant principles to influence people's behavior at school, work, and home. To help or manage people effectively, Skinner said, we should worry less about their illusions of freedom and dignity. Recognizing that behavior is shaped by its consequences, we should, he argued, administer rewards in ways that promote more desirable behavior.

Skinner's critics objected, saying that he dehumanized people by neglecting their personal freedom and by seeking to control their actions. Skinner's reply: People's behavior is already haphazardly controlled by external consequences, so why not administer those consequences for human betterment? In place of the punishments used in homes, schools, and prisons, would not reinforcers be more humanitarian? And if it is humbling to think that we are shaped by our histories, this very idea also gives us hope that we can shape our future.

Applications of Operant Conditioning

OBJECTIVE 19 | Describe some ways to apply operant conditioning principles at school, in sports, at work, and at home.

In later chapters we will see how psychologists apply operant conditioning principles to help people moderate high blood pressure or gain social skills. Reinforcement technologies are also at work in schools, sports, workplaces, and homes (Flora, 2004).

At School A generation ago, Skinner and others advocated the use of teaching machines and textbooks that would shape learning in small steps and provide immediate reinforcement for correct responses. Such machines and texts, they said, would revolutionize education and free teachers to concentrate on their students' special needs.

B. F. Skinner

"I am sometimes asked, 'Do you think of yourself as you think of the organisms you study?' The answer is yes. So far as I know, my behavior at any given moment has been nothing more than the product of my genetic endowment, my personal history, and the current setting" (1983).

Falk/Photo Researchers, Inc.

To envision Skinner's idea, imagine two math teachers, each with a class of academically diverse students. Teacher A gives the whole class the same math lesson, knowing that some students will readily understand the concepts and that others will be frustrated. With so many different children, how can one teacher guide them individually? The whiz kids breeze through unchallenged; the slower learners

Computer-assisted learning
Computers have helped realize Skinner's goal of individually paced instruction with immediate feedback.

experience failure. Faced with a similar class, Teacher B paces the material according to each student's rate of learning and provides prompt feedback with positive reinforcement to both slow and fast learners. Does the individualized instruction of Teacher B seem unrealistic?

Although the predicted education revolution has not occurred, to the end of his life Skinner (1986, 1988, 1989) believed the ideal was achievable. "Good instruction demands two things," he said. "Students must be told immediately whether what they do is right or wrong and, when right, they must be directed to the step to be taken next." Computers were his final hope. For reading and math drills, the computer could be Teacher B—pacing material according to the student's rate of learning, quizzing the student to find gaps in understanding, providing immediate feedback, and keeping flawless records for the supervising teacher. Today's interactive student software, Web-based learning, and on-line testing bring us closer than ever before to achieving Skinner's ideal.

In Sports Reinforcement principles can enhance athletic performance as well. Again, the key is to shape behavior, by first reinforcing small successes and then gradually increasing the challenge. Thomas Simek and Richard O'Brien (1981, 1988) applied these principles to teaching golf and baseball by starting with easily reinforced responses. Golf students learn putting by starting with very short putts. As they build mastery, they eventually step back farther and farther. Likewise, novice batters begin with half swings at an oversized ball pitched from 10 feet away, giving them the immediate pleasure of smacking the ball. As the hitters' confidence builds with their success and they achieve mastery at each level, the pitcher gradually moves back—to 15, then 22, 30, and 40.5 feet—and eventually introduces a standard baseball. Compared with children taught by conventional methods, those trained by this behavioral method show, in both testing and game situations, faster improvement in their skill.

At Work Believing reinforcers influence productivity, business managers have capitalized on psychological research. Many companies now enable their employees to share profits and to participate in company ownership. When workers' productivity boosts rewards for everyone, their motivation, morale, and cooperative spirit often increase (Deutsch, 1991). Reinforcement for a job well done is especially effective in boosting productivity when the desired performance is *well-defined and achievable*. The message for managers? Reward specific behaviors, not vaguely defined merit. Even criticism triggers the least resentment and the greatest performance boost when specific and considerate (Baron, 1988).

It is also wise to make the reinforcement *immediate*. When IBM legend Thomas Watson observed an achievement, he would write the employee a check on the spot (Peters & Waterman, 1982). But rewards need not be material, nor should they be so substantial that they become political and a source of discouragement to those who don't receive them. An effective manager may simply walk the floor and sincerely affirm people for good work, or write notes of appreciation for a completed project. As Skinner said, "How much richer would the whole world be if the reinforcers in daily life were more effectively contingent on productive work?"

At Home Many economists and psychologists believe people's spending behavior is controlled by its consequences (its costs and benefits). Compared with people who rent apartments in buildings where energy costs are paid by the landlord, those who live in comparable buildings but pay their own utility bills (therefore reaping the rewards of their own savings) use about 20 percent less energy. Similarly, those on an "energy diet" for their home electricity are helped by receiving frequent feedback showing current usage compared with past consumption (Darley & others, 1979). In homes, as elsewhere, immediate consequences most effectively influence behavior. Al Gore (1992, p. 348) suggested how U.S. tax policies might harness the power of consequences:

> There is an economic rule of thumb: Whatever we tax, we tend to get less of; whatever we subsidize, we tend to get more of. Currently, we tax work and we subsidize the depletion of natural resources—and both policies have contributed to high unemployment and the waste of natural resources. What if we lowered the tax on work and simultaneously raised it on the burning of fossil fuels?

Parents can also take helpful advantage of operant conditioning. Parent-training researchers Michelle Wierson and Rex Forehand (1994) remind us that when parents say "get ready for bed" and then cave in to protests or defiance, they reinforce such behaviors. Eventually, exasperated, they may yell at their child or gesture menacingly, at which point the child's fearful compliance in turn reinforces the parents' angry behavior. Over time, a destructive parent-child relationship develops. To disrupt this cycle, Wierson and Forehand offer these tips:

- Give children attention and other reinforcers when they are behaving *well*. Target a specific behavior, reward it, and watch it increase.
- Ignore whining. If whining has triggered attention in the past, it may temporarily increase when ignored. Over time, if not reinforced, it will diminish.
- When children misbehave or are defiant, do not yell at or hit them. Simply explain the misbehavior and give them a time-out—for a specific time remove them from any reinforcing surroundings.

Finally, we can use operant conditioning on ourselves, by reinforcing our most desired behaviors and extinguishing those undesired. To take charge of your own behavior, psychologists suggest taking these steps:

1. *State your goal*—to stop smoking, eat less, or study or exercise more—in measurable terms, and make your intention public. You might, for example, aim to boost your study time by an hour a day and announce that goal to some supportive friends.
2. *Monitor* how often you engage in the behavior you wish to promote. You might log your current study time, noting under what conditions you do and don't study. (When I began writing textbooks, I logged how I spent my time throughout each day and was astonished to discover how much time I was wasting.)
3. *Reinforce* the desired behavior. To increase your study time, allow yourself a snack (or some other reinforcing activity) only after specified periods of study. Agree with your friends that you will join them for weekend activities only if you have met your realistic weekly studying goal.
4. *Reduce the incentives* gradually, as your new behaviors become more habitual, while giving yourself a mental pat on the back.

"I wrote another five hundred words. Can I have another cookie?"

Contrasting Classical and Operant Conditioning

OBJECTIVE 20 | Identify the major similarities and differences between classical and operant conditioning.

Both classical and operant conditioning are forms of associative learning, and both involve acquisition, extinction, spontaneous recovery, generalization, and discrimination. The similarities are sufficient to make some researchers wonder if a single stimulus-response learning process might explain them both (Donahoe & Vegas, 2004). Their procedural difference is this: Through classical (Pavlovian) conditioning, an organism associates different stimuli that it does not control and responds automatically (respondent behaviors). Through operant conditioning, an organism associates its operant behaviors—those that act on its environment to produce rewarding or punishing stimuli—with their consequences. Cognitive processes and biological predispositions influence both classical and operant conditioning (**TABLE 8.3**).

" O! This learning, what a thing it is."
William Shakespeare, *The Taming of the Shrew*, 1597

TABLE 8.3

COMPARISON OF CLASSICAL AND OPERANT CONDITIONING

	Classical Conditioning	Operant Conditioning
Response	Involuntary, automatic.	Voluntary, operates on environment.
Acquisition	Associating events; CS announces US.	Associating response with a consequence (reinforcer or punisher).
Extinction	CR decreases when CS is repeatedly presented alone.	Responding decreases when reinforcement stops.
Cognitive processes	Organisms develop expectation that CS signals the arrival of US.	Organisms develop expectation that a response will be reinforced or punished; they also exhibit latent learning, without reinforcement.
Biological predispositions	Natural predispositions constrain what stimuli and responses can easily be associated.	Organisms best learn behaviors similar to their natural behaviors; unnatural behaviors instinctively drift back toward natural ones.

>> LEARNING OUTCOMES

Operant Conditioning

OBJECTIVE 10 | **Identify the two major characteristics that distinguish classical conditioning from operant conditioning.**
In *classical conditioning,* the organism forms associations between behaviors it does not control; this form of conditioning involves *respondent behavior* (automatic responses to some stimulus). In *operant conditioning,* the organism learns associations between its own behavior and resulting events; this form of conditioning involves *operant behavior* (behavior that operates on the environment, producing consequences).

OBJECTIVE 11 | **State Thorndike's law of effect, and explain its connection to Skinner's research on operant conditioning.**
Thorndike's law of effect asserts that rewarded behavior is likely

to recur. Using this as his starting point, Skinner devoted his life to exploring the principles and conditions of learning through operant conditioning.

OBJECTIVE 12 | **Describe the shaping procedure, and explain how it can increase our understanding of what animals and babies can discriminate.**
In shaping, we use reinforcers to guide a person's or an animal's behavior toward a desired goal. Building on existing behaviors, we reward successive approximations to some desired behavior. Because nonverbal animals and babies can respond only to what they perceive, their reactions demonstrate which events they can discriminate.

OBJECTIVE 13 | **Compare positive and negative reinforcement, and give one example each of a primary reinforcer, a conditioned reinforcer, an immediate reinforcer, and a delayed reinforcer.**

Positive reinforcement *adds* something *desirable* to increase the frequency of a behavior. Negative reinforcement *removes* something *undesirable* to increase the frequency of a behavior. *Primary reinforcers* (such as receiving food when hungry or having nausea end during an illness) are innately satisfying—no learning is required. *Conditioned* (or secondary) *reinforcers* (such as cash) are satisfying because we have learned to associate them with more basic rewards (such as the food or medicine we buy with them). *Immediate reinforcers* (such as the nicotine addict's cigarette) offer immediate payback; *delayed reinforcers* (such as a weekly paycheck) require the ability to delay gratification.

OBJECTIVE 14 | **Discuss the strengths and weaknesses of continuous and partial (intermittent) reinforcement schedules, and identify four schedules of partial reinforcement.**

In *continuous reinforcement* (reinforcing desired responses every time they occur), learning is rapid, but so is extinction if rewards cease. Continuous reinforcement is preferable until a behavior is learned. In *partial reinforcement* (reinforcing responses only part of the time), initial learning is slower, but the behavior is much more resistant to extinction. Reinforcement schedules may vary according to the number of responses rewarded or the time gap between responses. *Fixed-ratio schedules* offer rewards after a set number of responses; *variable-ratio schedules,* after an unpredictable number. *Fixed-interval schedules* offer rewards after set time periods; *variable-interval schedules,* after unpredictable time periods.

OBJECTIVE 15 | **Discuss the ways negative punishment, positive punishment, and negative reinforcement differ, and list some drawbacks of punishment as a behavior-control technique.**

Both positive punishment (*administering* an undesirable consequence, such as spanking) and negative punishment (*withdrawing* something desirable, such as taking away a favorite toy) attempt to *decrease* the frequency of a behavior (a child's disobedience). Negative reinforcement (such as taking aspirin) removes something undesirable (such as a headache) to *increase* the frequency of a behavior. Punishment's undesirable side effects may include suppressing rather than changing unwanted behaviors, teaching aggression, creating fear, and encouraging discrimination (so that the undesirable behavior appears when the punisher is not present), and fostering depression and feelings of helplessness.

OBJECTIVE 16 | **Explain how latent learning and the effect of external rewards demonstrate that cognitive processing is an important part of learning.**

Latent learning, as shown in rats' learning of cognitive maps or children's delayed imitation of others' behavior, indicates that we can learn from experience, without apparent reinforcement. An external reward's ability to undermine our interest and pleasure in an activity weakens the idea that behaviors that are rewarded will increase in frequency.

OBJECTIVE 17 | **Explain how biological predispositions place limits on what can be achieved through operant conditioning.**

Biological constraints predispose organisms to learn associations that are naturally adaptive. Training that attempts to override these tendencies will probably not endure because the animals will revert to their biologically predisposed patterns.

OBJECTIVE 18 | **Describe the controversy over Skinner's views of human behavior.**

Many psychologists criticized Skinner for underestimating the importance of cognition and biological constraints on learning. They also engaged in a vigorous intellectual debate with him over the nature of human freedom and the strategies and ethics of managing people.

OBJECTIVE 19 | **Describe some ways to apply operant conditioning principles at school, in sports, at work, and at home.**

In school, teachers can use shaping techniques to guide students' behaviors. Interactive software and Web sites can provide immediate feedback to students. In sports, coaches can build players' skills and self-confidence by rewarding small improvements. At work, managers can boost productivity and morale by rewarding well-defined and achievable behaviors. At home, we can control our energy usage by comparing recent consumption with past consumption. Parents can reward behaviors they consider desirable, but not those that are undesirable. Individually, we can reinforce our own desired behaviors and extinguish undesirable ones by stating our goals, monitoring the frequency of desired behaviors, and cutting back on incentives as behaviors become habitual.

OBJECTIVE 20 | **Identify the major similarities and differences between classical and operant conditioning.**

Classical and operant conditioning are similar in being forms of associative learning. Both also involve acquisition, extinction, spontaneous recovery, generalization, and discrimination. And both are influenced—and sometimes constrained—by cognitive processes and biological predispositions. These two forms of learning differ in an important way. In classical conditioning, an organism associates different stimuli that it does not control and responds automatically (respondent behaviors). In operant conditioning, an organism associates its own behaviors with their consequences (see Table 8.3 on page 339 for other details).

ASK YOURSELF: Can you recall a time when a teacher, coach, family member, or employer helped you learn something by shaping your behavior in little steps until you achieved your goal?

Learning by Observation

OBJECTIVE 21 | Describe the process of observational learning, and explain the importance of the discovery of mirror neurons.

From drooling dogs, running rats, and pecking pigeons we have learned much about the basic processes of learning. But conditioning principles alone do not tell us the whole story. Among higher animals, especially humans, learning need not occur through direct experience. **Observational learning,** in which we observe and imitate others, also plays a big part. A child who sees his big sister burn her fingers on the stove has thereby learned not to touch it.

The process of observing and imitating a specific behavior is often called **modeling.** We learn all kinds of social behaviors by observing and imitating models. Lord Chesterfield (1694–1773) had the idea: "We are, in truth, more than half what we are by imitation."

We can glimpse the roots of observational learning in other species. Rats, pigeons, crows, and gorillas all observe others and learn (Byrne & Russon, 1998; Dugatkin, 2002). So do monkeys. Shortly after a fight, stumptail macaque monkeys often reconcile with one another by approaching their opponent and making friendly contact. Rhesus macaque monkeys rarely make up quickly—unless they grow up with forgiving older stumptails. Then, more often than not, their fights, too, are quickly followed by reconciliation (de Waal & Johanowicz, 1993). Monkey see, monkey do (**FIGURE 8.12**).

Imitation is all the more striking in humans. As we noted in Chapter 3, so many of our ideas, fashions, and habits travel by imitation that these transmitted cultural elements now have a name: *memes.* We humans are the supreme meme machines, notes Susan Blackmore (1999, 2000). Our catch-phrases, hem lengths, ceremonies, foods, traditions, vices, and fads (think Harry Potter) all spread by one person copying another.

Neuroscientists have discovered **mirror neurons** (in a frontal-lobe area adjacent to the brain's motor cortex) that provide a neural basis for observational learning. When a monkey performs a task such as grasping, holding, or tearing, these neurons fire (Rizzolatti & others, 2002). But they also fire when the monkey observes another monkey performing the same task. When one monkey sees, these neurons will mirror what another monkey does.

> "Children need models more than they need critics."
>
> Joseph Joubert, *Pensées*, 1842

■ **observational learning** learning by observing others.

■ **modeling** the process of observing and imitating a specific behavior.

■ **mirror neurons** frontal lobe neurons that fire when performing certain actions or when observing another doing so. The brain's mirroring of another's action may enable imitation, language learning, and empathy.

©Herb Terrace

©Herb Terrace

FIGURE 8.12
Cognitive imitation
When Monkey A, on the left, sees Monkey B touch four pictures on a display screen in a certain order to gain a banana, Monkey A learns to imitate that order, even when shown a different configuration (Subiaul & others, 2004).

Monkey A's screen   Monkey B's screen

It's not just monkey business. PET scans reveal that humans, too, have mirror neurons in this brain area, which also serves language. Human mirror neurons help children learn by observation how to mime lip and tongue movements when forming new words. Mirror neurons also help give rise to children's empathy and to their ability to infer another's mental state (an ability known as *theory of mind;* see page 151). As adults, we often feel what another feels, and we find it harder to frown when viewing a smile than when viewing a frown (Dimberg & others, 2000, 2002). Seeing a loved one's pain, it's not just our faces that mirror their emotion, but also our brains. As **FIGURE 8.13** shows, the pain imagined by an empathic romantic partner triggers some of the same brain activity experienced by the one actually having the pain (Singer & others, 2004).

FIGURE 8.13
Experienced and imagined pain in the brain
Brain activity related to actual pain (left) is mirrored in the brain of an observing loved one. Empathy in the brain involves emotional brain areas, but not the somatosensory cortex, which receives the physical pain input.

Reprinted with permission from The American Association for the Advancement of Science, Subiaul et al., Science 305:407-410 (2004) ©2004 AAAS.

Meltzoff, A. N. (1988). Imitation of televised models by infants. Child Development, 59, 1221–1229. Photos courtesy of A. N. Meltzoff and M. Hanuk.

FIGURE 8.14
Learning from observation
This 14-month-old boy in Andrew Meltzoff's laboratory is imitating behavior he has seen on TV. In the top photo the infant leans forward and carefully watches the adult pull apart a toy. In the middle photo he has been given the toy. In the bottom photo he pulls the toy apart, imitating what he has seen the adult do.

The imitation of models shapes even very young children's behavior. Shortly after birth, an infant may imitate an adult who sticks out his tongue. By 9 months, infants will imitate novel play behaviors. And by age 14 months (**FIGURE 8.14**), children will imitate acts modeled on television (Meltzoff, 1988; Meltzoff & Moore, 1989, 1997). To persuade children to smoke, simply expose them to parents, older youth, and attractive media models who smoke. To encourage children to read, read to them and surround them with books and people who read. To increase the odds of your children practicing your religion, worship and attend other religious activities with them. Children see, children do.

Bandura's Experiments

OBJECTIVE 22 | Describe Bandura's findings on what determines whether we will imitate a model.

Picture this scene from a famous experiment devised by Albert Bandura, the pioneering researcher of observational learning (Bandura & others, 1961). A preschool child is at work on a drawing. An adult in another part of the room is working with some Tinkertoys. The adult then gets up and for nearly 10 minutes pounds, kicks, and throws a large inflated Bobo doll around the room, while yelling such remarks as, "Sock him in the nose. . . . Hit him down. . . . Kick him."

After observing this outburst, the child is taken to another room where there are many appealing toys. Soon the experimenter interrupts the child's play and explains that she has decided to save these good toys "for the other children." She now takes the frustrated child to an adjacent room containing a few toys, including a Bobo doll. Left alone, what does the child do?

Compared with children not exposed to the adult model, those who observed the model's aggressive outburst were much more likely to lash out at the doll. Apparently, observing the adult model beating up the doll lowered their inhibitions. But something more than lowered inhibitions was at work, for the children also imitated the very acts they had observed and used the very words they had heard.

What determines whether we will imitate a model? Bandura believes part of the answer is reinforcements and punishments—those received by the model as well as by the imitator. We look and we learn. By looking, we learn to anticipate a behavior's consequences in situations like those we are observing. We are especially likely to imitate people we perceive as similar to ourselves, as successful, or as admirable.

Albert Bandura

"The Bobo doll follows me wherever I go. The photographs are published in every introductory psychology text and virtually every undergraduate takes introductory psychology. I recently checked into a Washington hotel. The clerk at the desk asked, 'Aren't you the psychologist who did the Bobo doll experiment?' I answered, 'I am afraid that will be my legacy.' He replied, 'That deserves an upgrade. I will put you in a suite in the quiet part of the hotel' " (2005).

Applications of Observational Learning

The bad news from Bandura's studies is that antisocial models—in one's family or neighborhood, or on TV—may have antisocial effects. In the first eight days after the 1999 Columbine High School massacre, every U.S. state except Vermont had to deal with copycat threats or incidents. Pennsylvania alone had 60 threats of school violence (Cooper, 1999). By watching TV programs, children may "learn" that physical intimidation is an effective way to control others, that free and easy sex brings pleasure without later misery or disease, or that men are supposed to be tough and women gentle.

Observational learning also helps us understand how abusive parents might have aggressive children, and why many men who beat their wives had wife-battering fathers (Stith & others, 2000). The lessons we learn as children are not easily unlearned as adults, and they are sometimes visited on future generations. Critics note that the intergenerational transmission of abuse could be genetic. But with monkeys we know it can be environmental. In study after study, young monkeys that received high levels of aggression when reared apart from their mothers grew up to be perpetrators of aggression (Chamove, 1980).

Positive Observational Learning

OBJECTIVE 23 | Discuss the impact of prosocial modeling.

The good news is that **prosocial** (positive, helpful) models can have prosocial effects. People who exemplify nonviolent, helpful behavior can prompt similar behavior in others. India's Mahatma Gandhi and America's Martin Luther King, Jr., both drew on the power of modeling, making nonviolent action a powerful force for social

■ **prosocial behavior** positive, constructive, helpful behavior. The opposite of antisocial behavior.

Bob Daemmrich/The Image Works

A model grandma
This boy is learning to cook by observing his grandmother. As the sixteenth-century proverb states, "Example is better than precept."

"The problem with television is that the people must sit and keep their eyes glued to a screen: The average American family hasn't time for it. Therefore the showmen are convinced that . . . television will never be a serious competitor of [radio] broadcasting."

New York Times, 1939

TV's greatest effect may stem from what it displaces. Children and adults who spend four hours a day watching TV spend four fewer hours in active pursuits—talking, studying, playing, reading, or socializing with friends. What would you have done with your extra time if you had never watched TV, and how might you therefore be different?

change in both countries. Parents are also powerful models. European Christians who risked their lives to rescue Jews from the Nazis usually had a close relationship with at least one parent who modeled a strong moral or humanitarian concern; this was also true for U.S. civil rights activists in the 1960s (London, 1970; Oliner & Oliner, 1988). The observational learning of morality begins early. Socially responsive toddlers who readily imitate their parents tend to become preschoolers with a strong internalized conscience (Forman & others, 2004).

Models are most effective when their actions and words are consistent. Sometimes, however, models say one thing and do another. Many parents seem to operate according to the principle "Do as I *say,* not as I do." Experiments suggest that children learn to do both (Rice & Grusec, 1975; Rushton, 1975). Exposed to a hypocrite, they tend to imitate the hypocrisy by doing what the model did and saying what the model said.

Television and Observational Learning

OBJECTIVE 24 | Explain why correlations cannot prove that watching violent TV causes violent behavior, and cite some experimental evidence that helps demonstrate a cause-effect link.

Wherever television exists, it becomes the source of much observational learning. During their first 18 years, most children in developed countries spend more time watching TV than they spend in school. In Australia, 99.2 percent of households have television and 56 percent have multiple sets (Trewin, 2001). In the United States, where 9 in 10 teens watch TV daily, someone who lives to 75 will have spent 9 years staring at the tube (Gallup, 2002; Kubey & Csikszentmihalyi, 2002). Two-thirds of U.S. homes have three or more sets, which helps explain why parents' reports of what their children watch hardly correlate with children's reports of what they watch (Donnerstein, 1998).

In urban homes across the world, including those of South America and Asia, television is now commonplace. With more than a billion TV sets now in homes worldwide, CNN reaching 150 countries, and MTV broadcasting in 17 languages, television has created a global pop culture (Gunderson, 2001; Lippman, 1992). One can watch American programs in Perth or Prague and catch the latest rock videos from Newfoundland to the tiny Himalayan kingdom of Bhutan, where television was introduced in 1999 and soon began influencing speech and children's behavior (Keys, 2001).

Does the reel world reflect the real world? Our data are limited because funding for ongoing media monitoring by social scientists waned after the early 1990s. But on evening dramas broadcast in the United States during the 1980s and early 1990s and often exported to the rest of the world, only one-third of the characters were women. Fewer than 3 percent were visibly old. One percent were Hispanic. Only 1 in 10 was married (Gerbner, 1993). U.S. network programs have offered about 3 violent acts per hour during prime time, and 18 per hour during children's Saturday morning programs (Gerbner & others, 1994). Unlike the real world, where 87 percent of crimes are nonviolent, in TV's world of "reality-based" police shows, 13 percent of crimes are nonviolent (Oliver, 1994).

Television viewers are learning about life from a rather peculiar storyteller, one who reflects the culture's mythology but not its reality. During the late twentieth century, the average child viewed some 8000 TV murders and 100,000 other acts of violence before finishing elementary school (Huston & others, 1992). If one includes cable programming and video rentals, the violence numbers escalate. (Popular rental films like *Die Hard 1,* with its 264 deaths, are much more violent than major network programs.) An analysis of more than 3000 network and cable programs aired during 1996/1997 revealed that nearly 6 in 10 featured violence, that 74 percent of the violence went unpunished, that 58 percent did not show the victims' pain, and that nearly half the incidents involved "justified" violence and nearly half involved an attractive perpetrator. These conditions define the recipe for the violence-viewing effect described below (Donnerstein, 1998).

Do you think viewing televised aggression influences some people to commit aggression? Was the judge who in 1993 tried two British 10-year-olds for their murder of a 2-year-old right to suspect that one possible influence was the aggressors' exposure to "violent video films"? Were the American media right to think that the teen assassins who killed 13 of their Columbine High School classmates had been influenced by repeated viewings of *Natural Born Killers* and by frequently playing splatter games such as *Doom*? To answer similar questions, researchers have conducted both correlational and experimental studies (Anderson & others, 2003).

Correlational studies do link violence viewing with violent behavior.

- The more hours elementary school children spend engaged with media violence (via television, videos, and video games), the more often they get in fights when restudied two to six months later (**FIGURE 8.15**).
- The more hours children spend watching violent programs, the more at risk they also are for aggression and crime as teens and adults (Eron, 1987; Turner & others, 1986). One study compared 16- and 22-year-olds who had watched less than an hour of TV daily at age 14 with those who had watched more than three hours. The heavy viewer group committed five times as many aggressive acts.
- In the United States and Canada, homicide rates doubled between 1957 and 1974, coinciding with the introduction and spread of TV. Moreover, census regions that were late in acquiring TV service had their homicide rate jump correspondingly later.
- White South Africans were first introduced to TV in 1975. A similar near-doubling of the homicide rate began after 1975 (Centerwall, 1989).

"There is absolutely no doubt," concluded the American Psychological Association Commission on Violence and Youth, "that higher levels of viewing violence on television are correlated with increased acceptance of aggressive attitudes and increased aggressive behavior" (Gentry & Eron, 1993).

But as we know from Chapter 1, correlation does not imply causation. So these correlational studies do not prove that viewing violence *causes* aggression (Freedman, 1988; McGuire, 1986). Maybe aggressive children prefer violent programs. Maybe children of neglectful or abusive parents are both more aggressive and more often left in front of the TV. Maybe violent programs simply reflect, rather than affect, violent trends.

To pin down causation, experimenters have randomly assigned some viewers to view violence and others to view entertaining nonviolence. Does viewing cruelty prepare people, when irritated, to react more cruelly? To some extent, it does. "The consensus among most of the research community," reported the National Institute of Mental Health (1982), "is that violence on television does lead to aggressive behavior by children and teenagers who watch the programs." This is especially so when an attractive person commits seemingly justified, realistic violence that goes unpunished and causes no visible pain or harm (Donnerstein, 1998).

The violence effect seems to stem from a combination of factors including *imitation* (Geen & Thomas, 1986). As we noted earlier, children as young as 14 months will imitate acts they observe on TV. One research team observed a sevenfold increase in violent play immediately after children viewed the "Power Rangers" (Boyatzis &

FIGURE 8.15
Media violence viewing predicts future aggressive behavior
In a study of more than 400 third to fifth graders, Douglas Gentile and his colleagues (2004) reported increased aggression in those heavily exposed to violent television, videos, and video games. The data shown here were adjusted for the children's preexisting differences in hostility and aggression.

> "Thirty seconds worth of glorification of a soap bar sells soap. Twenty-five minutes worth of glorification of violence sells violence."
>
> U.S. Senator Paul Simon, Remarks to the Communitarian Network, 1993

Gallup surveys asked American teens (Mazzuca, 2002): "Do you feel there is too much violence in the movies, or not?"
1977: 42 percent said yes.
1999: 23 percent said yes.

Violence viewing leads to violent play Research has shown that viewing media violence does lead to increased expression of aggression in the viewers, as with these boys imitating pro wrestlers.

others, 1995). Boys often precisely imitated the characters' flying karate kicks and other violent acts.

Prolonged exposure to violence also *desensitizes* viewers; they become more indifferent to it when later viewing a brawl, whether on TV or in real life (Rule & Ferguson, 1986). While spending three evenings watching sexually violent movies, male viewers in one experiment became progressively less bothered by the rapes and slashings. Compared with research participants who did not watch these films, they later expressed less sympathy for domestic violence victims, and they rated the victims' injuries as less severe (Mullin & Linz, 1995).

Indeed, suggested Edward Donnerstein and his co-researchers (1987), an evil psychologist could hardly imagine a better way to make people indifferent to brutality than to expose them to a graded series of scenes, from fights to killings to the mutilations in slasher movies. Watching cruelty fosters indifference.

Our knowledge of learning principles comes from the work of thousands of investigators. This chapter has focused on the ideas of a few pioneers—Pavlov, Watson, Skinner, and Bandura. They illustrate the impact that can result from single-minded devotion to a few well-defined problems and ideas. These researchers defined the issues and impressed on us the importance of learning. As their legacy demonstrates, intellectual history is often made by people who risk going to extremes in pushing ideas to their limits (Simonton, 2000).

"Don't you understand? This is life, this is what is happening. We can't switch to another channel."

>> LEARNING OUTCOMES

Learning by Observation

OBJECTIVE 21 | Describe the process of observational learning, and explain the importance of the discovery of mirror neurons.
In *observational learning*, we observe and imitate others. *Mirror neurons,* located in the brain's frontal lobes, demonstrate a neural basis for observational learning. They fire when we perform certain actions (such as responding to pain or moving our mouth to form words), or when we observe someone else performing those actions.

OBJECTIVE 22 | Describe Bandura's findings on what determines whether we will imitate a model.
Bandura and others demonstrated that we are likely to imitate actions that go unpunished. And we tend to imitate models we perceive as similar to us, successful, or admirable.

OBJECTIVE 23 | Discuss the impact of prosocial modeling.
Research shows that children tend to imitate what a model does and says, whether the behavior is prosocial (positive, constructive, and helpful) or antisocial. If a model's actions and words are inconsistent, children may imitate the hypocrisy they observe.

OBJECTIVE 24 | Explain why correlations cannot prove that watching violent TV causes violent behavior, and cite some experimental evidence that helps demonstrate a cause-effect link.
Correlations show relationships, but not the direction of influence. Correlational studies show that violence viewing and violent behavior are linked, but they do not prove that watching violent TV causes children to become violent. Children who behave violently may enjoy watching violence on TV, or some third factor may cause children both to behave violently and to prefer watching violent programs. To prove cause and effect, researchers have designed experiments in which some participants view violence and others do not. Later, given an opportunity to express violence (in rough play or verbal responses to videos), the people who viewed violence tend to be more aggressive and less sympathetic. Two factors—imitation and desensitization—seem to contribute to the violence effect.

ASK YOURSELF: Who has been a significant role model for you? For whom are you a model?

REVIEW CHAPTER 8: **Learning**

Test Yourself

1. As we develop we learn cues that lead us to expect and prepare for good and bad events. We learn to repeat behaviors that bring rewards. And we watch others and learn. What do psychologists call these three types of learning?

2. In slasher movies, sexually arousing images of women are sometimes paired with violence against women. Based on classical conditioning principles, what might be an effect of this pairing?

3. *Positive reinforcement, negative reinforcement,* and *punishment* are tricky concepts for many students. Can you fit the right term in the four boxes in this table? I'll do the first one (positive reinforcement) for you.

Type of Stimulus	Give It	Take It Away
Desired (for example, a compliment):	Positive reinforcement	
Undesired/aversive (for example, an insult):		

4. Jason's parents and older friends all smoke, but they advise him not to. Juan's parents and friends don't smoke, but they say nothing to deter him from doing so. Will Jason or Juan be more likely to start smoking?

Answers to the Test Yourself questions can be found in Appendix B at the end of the book.

Terms and Concepts to Remember

learning, p. 313
associative learning, p. 314
classical conditioning, p. 315
behaviorism, p. 316
unconditioned response (UR), p. 317
unconditioned stimulus (US), p. 317
conditioned response (CR), p. 317
conditioned stimulus (CS), p. 317
acquisition, p. 318
extinction, p. 319
spontaneous recovery, p. 319
generalization, p. 320
discrimination, p. 320
operant conditioning, p. 326

respondent behavior, p. 326
operant behavior, p. 326
law of effect, p. 327
operant chamber, p. 327
shaping, p. 328
reinforcer, p. 329
positive reinforcement, p. 329
negative reinforcement, p. 329
primary reinforcer, p. 330
conditioned reinforcer (*secondary reinforcer*), p. 330
continuous reinforcement, p. 330
partial (intermittent) reinforcement, p. 331

fixed-ratio schedule, p. 331
variable-ratio schedule, p. 332
fixed-interval schedule, p. 332
variable-interval schedule, p. 332
punishment, p. 332
cognitive map, p. 334
latent learning, p. 334
intrinsic motivation, p. 335
extrinsic motivation, p. 335
observational learning, p. 341
modeling, p. 341
mirror neurons, p. 341
prosocial behavior, p. 343

WEB

 To continue your study and review of Learning, visit this book's Web site at **www.worthpublishers.com/myers.** You will find practice tests, review activities, and many interesting articles and Web links for more information on topics related to Learning.

9: Memory

An event is such a little piece of time and space, leaving only a mindglow behind like the tail of a shooting star. For lack of a better word, we call that scintillation memory.

Diane Ackerman, *An Alchemy of Mind, 2004*

Be thankful for memory. We take it for granted, except when it malfunctions. But it is our memory, notes Rebecca Rupp (1998, p. xvii), that "allows us to recognize friends, neighbors, and acquaintances and call them by their names; to knit, type, drive, and play the piano; to speak English, Spanish, or Mandarin Chinese." It is our memory that accounts for time and defines our life. It is our memory that enables us to sing our national anthem, find our way home, and locate the food and water we need for survival. It is our shared memories that bind us together as Irish or Aussies, as Serbs or Albanians. And it is our memories that occasionally pit us against those whose offenses we cannot forget.

"Waiter, I'd like to order, unless I've eaten, in which case bring me the check."

In large part, you are what you remember. Without memory, there would be no savoring joyful moments past, no guilt or anger over painful recollections. You would instead live in an enduring present. Each moment would be fresh. But each person would be a stranger, every language foreign, every task—dressing, cooking, biking—a novel challenge. You would even be a stranger to yourself, lacking that continuous sense of self that extends from your distant past to your momentary present. Memory researcher James McGaugh (2003) suggested, "If you lose the ability to recall your old memories then you have no life. You might as well be a rutabaga or a cabbage."

The Phenomenon of Memory

OBJECTIVE 1 | Define *memory*, and explain how flashbulb memories differ from other memories.

Your memory is your mind's storehouse, the reservoir of your accumulated learning. To the Roman statesman Cicero, memory was "the treasury and guardian of all things." To a psychologist, **memory** is any indication that learning has persisted over time. It is our ability to store and retrieve information.

Studying memory's extremes has helped researchers understand how memory works. Some studies have explored the roots and fruits of memory loss. At age 92, my father suffered a small stroke that had but one peculiar effect. His genial personality

■ **memory** the persistence of learning over time through the storage and retrieval of information.

MR. TOTAL RECALL

Which is more important—your experiences or your memories of them?

False flashbulb memory
After the second plane hit the World Trade Center on 9/11, U.S. President George W. Bush's chief of staff, Andrew Card, whispered the news to him in a Florida classroom. But what about the first attack? Three months later, when asked how he had heard about the first attack, the president recalled "sitting outside the classroom waiting to go in, and I saw an airplane hit the tower—the TV was obviously on, and I used to fly myself, and I said, 'There's one terrible pilot.' And, I said, 'It must have been a horrible accident.'" But no one saw it on live TV, nor was there at that time any available footage of the first plane crashing (Paltrow, 2004). Hearing the story, some people perceived a blatant lie or even a conspiracy. But as psychologist Daniel Greenberg (2004) later noted, "we need only consider the frailty of human memory. . . . President Bush appears to be suffering from a near-textbook case of false recall."

was intact. He was as mobile as before. He knew us and while poring over family photo albums could reminisce in detail about his past. But he had lost most of his ability to lay down new memories of conversations and everyday episodes. He could not tell me what day of the week it was. Told repeatedly of his brother-in-law's death, he expressed surprise each time he heard the news.

At the other extreme are some people who would be medal winners in a memory Olympics, such as Russian journalist Shereshevskii, or S, as psychologist Alexander Luria (1968) called him. S's memory not only allowed him merely to listen while other reporters were scribbling notes, it also earned him a place in virtually every modern book on memory. You and I can repeat back a string of about 7 digits—almost surely no more than 9. S could repeat up to 70 digits or words, provided they were read about 3 seconds apart in an otherwise silent room. Moreover, he could recall them backward as easily as forward. His accuracy was unerring, even when he was asked to recall a list as much as 15 years later, after having memorized hundreds of other lists. "Yes, yes," he might recall. "This was a series you gave me once when we were in your apartment. . . . You were sitting at the table and I in the rocking chair. . . . You were wearing a gray suit and you looked at me like this. . . ."

Do S's memory feats make your own memory seem feeble? If so, consider your own pretty staggering capacity for remembering countless voices, sounds, and songs; tastes, smells, and textures; faces, places, and happenings. Imagine viewing more than 2500 slides of faces and places, for only 10 seconds each. Later you see 280 of these slides one at a time, paired with a previously unseen slide. If you are like the participants in this experiment by Ralph Haber (1970), you would recognize 90 percent of those you saw before.

Your memory capacity is perhaps most apparent in your recall of unique and highly emotional moments in your past. One of my vivid memories is of my only hit in an entire season of Little League baseball. Perhaps yours is of a car accident, your first romantic kiss, your first day as an immigrant in a new country, or your surroundings when you heard some tragic news. Most Americans over 55 feel sure of exactly what they were doing when they heard the news of President Kennedy's assassination (Brown & Kulik, 1982). Seven months and even four years after Princess Diana's death, most British people could still recall their exact whereabouts on hearing that news (Kvavilashvili & others, 2003; Wynn & Gilhooly, 1999). Six decades after the Nazi invasion of Denmark, few younger Danish adults displayed any knowledge of the details of invasion day. But Danes over 72 years remembered. Seven in ten even recalled the day's weather (Berntsen & Thomsen, 2005). And you perhaps recall where you first heard the news on 9/11—that September day in 2001

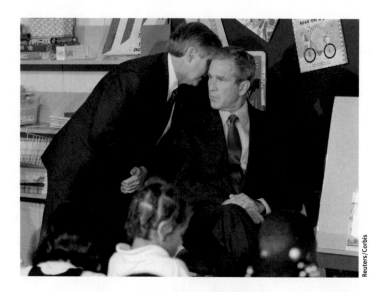

that was, said the next morning's *New York Times,* "one of those moments in which history splits and we define the world as 'before and after.'" This perceived clarity for our memories of surprising, significant events leads some psychologists to call them **flashbulb memories.** It's as if the brain commands, "Capture this!" But like other memories, our flashbulb memories can err (Talarico & others, 2003).

Why can even our flashbulb memories sometimes prove dead wrong? How do we accomplish other memory feats? How can we remember things we have not thought about for years, yet forget the name of someone we met a minute ago? How are memories stored in our brains? How can two people's memories of the same event be so different? Why will you be likely later in this chapter to misrecall this sentence: *"The angry rioter threw the rock at the window"*? How can we improve our memories? These will be among the questions we consider as we review more than a century of research on memory.

Information Processing

OBJECTIVE **2** | Describe Atkinson-Shiffrin's classic three-stage processing model of memory, and explain how the contemporary model of working memory differs.

To think about memory, we first need a model of how it works. Building a memory is in some ways like my information processing in creating this book. For each edition, I first glimpse countless items of information, including some 100,000 journal article titles. Most of it I ignore, but some things merit temporary storage in my briefcase for more detailed processing later. Most of these items I eventually discard. The rest—typically about 3000 articles and news items—gets organized and filed for long-term storage. Later, I retrieve this information and draw from it as I spin the story of today's psychology. Very important current events jump into my long-term mental storage, from which I draw fresh examples of psychology in everyday life. In forming memories, you, too, must select, process, store, and retrieve information. You process information not only in the "cramming" you do to study in your courses, but also in the skills you learn and in your processing of countless daily events.

In some ways, our memory is like a computer's information-processing system. To remember any event, we must *get information into our brain* (**encoding**), *retain* that information (**storage**), and later *get it back out* (**retrieval**). Consider how a computer *encodes, stores,* and *retrieves* information. First, it translates input (keystrokes) into an electronic language, much as the brain encodes sensory information into a neural language. The computer permanently stores vast amounts of information on a disk, from which it can later be retrieved.

Like all analogies, the computer model has its limits. Our memories are less literal and more fragile than a computer's. Moreover, most computers process information speedily but sequentially, even while alternating between tasks. The brain is slower but does many things at once—in parallel.

Psychologists have proposed several information-processing models of memory. Richard Atkinson and Richard Shiffrin's classic *three-stage processing* model of memory (1968) suggests that we form memories through three stages. Atkinson and Shiffrin proposed that we first record to-be-remembered information as a fleeting **sensory memory,** from which it is processed into a **short-term memory** bin, where we encode it through rehearsal for **long-term memory** and later retrieval. This three-step process, though historically important and helpfully simple, is limited and fallible. Some information, as we will see, skips the first two stages and is processed into long-term memory automatically—without our conscious awareness. In addition, we now realize that because we are bombarded daily with sensory information, we cannot possibly focus on everything at once. Instead, we shine the flashlight beam of our attention on certain incoming stimuli—often novel or important

- **flashbulb memory** a clear memory of an emotionally significant moment or event.

- **encoding** the processing of information into the memory system—for example, by extracting meaning.

- **storage** the retention of encoded information over time.

- **retrieval** the process of getting information out of memory storage.

- **sensory memory** the immediate, very brief recording of sensory information in the memory system.

- **short-term memory** activated memory that holds a few items briefly, such as the seven digits of a phone number while dialing, before the information is stored or forgotten.

- **long-term memory** the relatively permanent and limitless storehouse of the memory system. Includes knowledge, skills, and experiences.

THE FAR SIDE BY GARY LARSON

More facts of nature: All forest animals, to this very day, remember exactly where they were and what they were doing when they heard that Bambi's mother had been shot.

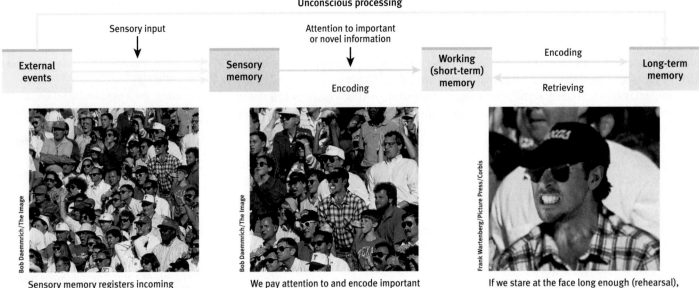

Unconscious processing

Sensory input

Attention to important
or novel information

Encoding

| External events | | Sensory memory | | Working (short-term) memory | | Long-term memory |

Encoding

Encoding

Retrieving

Sensory memory registers incoming information, allowing your brain to capture for a fleeting moment a sea of faces.

We pay attention to and encode important or novel stimuli—in this case an angry face in the crowd.

If we stare at the face long enough (rehearsal), or if we're sufficiently disturbed by it (it's deemed "important"), we will encode it for long-term storage, and we may, an hour later, be able to call up an image of the face.

FIGURE 9.1

A modified three-stage processing model of memory

Today's researchers recognize other ways long-term memories form. For example, as we will see, some information slips into long-term memory via a "back door," without our having consciously attended to it. And we have learned that short-term memory is more than passive rehearsal; it is better termed *working memory* to recognize the active processing that occurs there.

stimuli. These incoming stimuli, along with information we retrieve from our long-term memory, become conscious short-term memories in a temporary construction zone. This zone is a work site where we rehearse and manipulate information (Engle, 2002). But unlike brick-and-mortar work sites, the content of **working memory** quickly fades unless we keep using or rehearsing it. It is here that we actively associate new and old information and solve problems. This chapter's modified version of the three-stage processing model of memory incorporates this important working-memory concept (**FIGURE 9.1**).

Working memory includes both auditory and visual-spatial elements, coordinated by a *central executive* processor (**FIGURE 9.2**) (Baddeley, 1992, 2001, 2002). These separate

FIGURE 9.2

Working memory

Alan Baddeley's (1998, 2001, 2002) model of working memory, simplified here, contains auditory and visual-spatial processors, which are managed by a central executive. Information enters working memory from long-term storage or from immediate experience. The episodic buffer helps the central executive integrate input in a way we can comprehend.

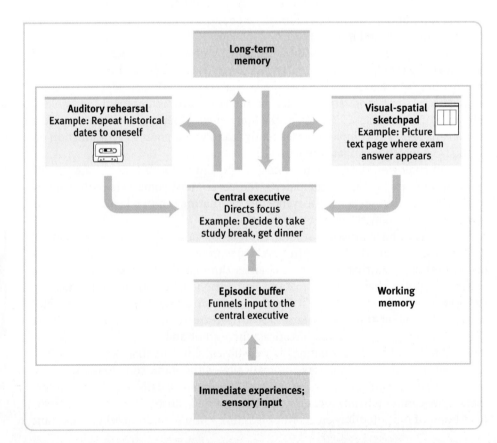

mental subsystems allow us to process images and words simultaneously. This explains why we can talk (verbal processing) while driving (visual-spatial processing). And working memory's limited capacity explains why it is so difficult to try to remember the melody for one song while we are listening to another. Brain activity underlies these working memory components (Jonides & others, 2005). Brain scans show that the frontal lobes are active when the central executive focuses on complex thinking, and that the parietal and temporal lobe areas that help us process auditory and visual information also are active when such information is in our working memory.

>> LEARNING OUTCOMES

The Phenomenon of Memory

OBJECTIVE 1 | Define *memory,* and explain how flashbulb memories differ from other memories.
Memory is the persistence of learning over time, through the storage and retrieval of information. *Flashbulb memories,* which are attached to emotionally significant moments or events, differ from most other memories in their striking clarity.

OBJECTIVE 2 | Describe Atkinson-Shiffrin's classic three-stage processing model of memory, and explain how the contemporary model of working memory differs.
The Atkinson-Shiffrin classic three-stage model of memory suggests that we (1) register fleeting *sensory memories,* some of which are (2) processed into on-screen *short-term* memories, a tiny fraction of which are (3) encoded for *long-term memory* and, possibly, later retrieval. In pointing out the limits of this model, contemporary memory researchers note that we register some information automatically, bypassing the first two stages. And they prefer the term *working memory* (rather than *short-term memory*) because it emphasizes a more active role in this second processing stage, where we rehearse and manipulate information, associating new stimuli with older stored memories. The working-memory model includes visual-spatial and auditory subsystems, coordinated by a central executive processor that focuses attention where needed.

ASK YOURSELF: **What flashbulb memory do you have for an emotion-laden experience in your past?**

Encoding: Getting Information In

How does sensory information, once registered, get encoded and transferred into the memory system? What types of information do we absorb unconsciously? What types require conscious processing?

How We Encode

Some information, such as the route you walked to your last class, you process with great ease, freeing your memory system to focus on less familiar events. But to retain novel information, such as a friend's new cell-phone number, you need to pay attention and try hard.

Automatic Processing

OBJECTIVE 3 | Describe the types of information we encode automatically.

With little or no effort, you absorb an enormous amount of information. For example, without conscious effort you **automatically process** information about

- *space.* While reading your textbook, you often encode the place on a page where certain material appears; later, when struggling to recall the information, you may visualize its location.

■ **working memory** a newer understanding of short-term memory that involves conscious, active processing of incoming auditory and visual-spatial information, and of information retrieved from long-term memory.

■ **automatic processing** unconscious encoding of incidental information, such as space, time, and frequency, and of well-learned information, such as word meanings.

■ **effortful processing** encoding that requires attention and conscious effort.

■ **rehearsal** the conscious repetition of information, either to maintain it in consciousness or to encode it for storage.

■ **spacing effect** the tendency for distributed study or practice to yield better long-term retention than is achieved through massed study or practice.

- *time.* While going about your day, you unintentionally note the sequence of the day's events. Later, when you realize that you left your coat somewhere, you re-create the sequence of what you did that day and retrace your steps.
- *frequency.* You effortlessly keep track of how many times things happen, thus enabling you to realize "this is the third time I've run into her today."

Thanks to our brain's capacity for parallel processing, all of this processing and more goes on without our needing to pay attention to it. Automatic processing occurs so effortlessly that it is difficult to shut off. When you see words in your native language, such as on the side of a delivery truck, you cannot help but register their meanings.

Some forms of processing require attention and effort when we first perform them, but with experience and practice become automatic. When learning to read, you at first sounded out individual letters to figure out what words they made. With effort, you plodded slowly through a mere 20 to 50 words on a page. Now, however, after years of practice, you can read quickly and effortlessly. Imagine now learning to read reversed sentences like this:

.citamotua emoceb nac gnissecorp luftroffE

At first, this requires effort. But after enough practice, tasks like this can be performed much more automatically. We have developed many of our skills in this way: learning to drive, rollerblade, or find our way around town.

Effortful Processing

OBJECTIVE 4 | Contrast effortful processing with automatic processing, and discuss the next-in-line effect, the spacing effect, and the serial position effect.

We encode and retain vast amounts of information automatically, but we remember other types of information, such as this chapter's concepts, only with effort and attention (**FIGURE 9.3**). **Effortful processing** often produces durable and accessible memories.

When learning novel information such as names, we can boost our memory through **rehearsal,** or conscious repetition. This was shown long ago by the pioneering researcher of verbal memory, German philosopher Hermann Ebbinghaus (1850–1909). Ebbinghaus was to the study of memory what Ivan Pavlov was to the study of conditioning. Ebbinghaus became impatient with philosophical speculations about memory and decided to study it scientifically. To do so, he chose to study his own learning and forgetting of novel verbal materials.

Ebbinghaus needed to find verbal material that was not familiar. His solution was to form a list of all possible nonsense syllables created by sandwiching a vowel between two consonants. Then, for a particular experiment, he would randomly select a sample of the syllables. To get a feel for how Ebbinghaus tested himself, rapidly read aloud, eight times over, the following list (from Baddeley, 1982). Then try to recall the items:

JIH, BAZ, FUB, YOX, SUJ, XIR, DAX, LEQ, VUM, PID, KEL, WAV, TUV, ZOF, GEK, HIW.

The day after learning such a list, Ebbinghaus could recall few of the syllables. But were they entirely forgotten? As **FIGURE 9.4** portrays, the more frequently he repeated the list aloud on day 1, the fewer repetitions he required to relearn the list on day 2. Here, then, was a simple beginning principle: *The amount remembered depends on the time spent learning.* Even after we learn material, additional rehearsal (*overlearning*) increases retention.

FIGURE 9.3
Automatic versus effortful processing Some information, such as where you ate dinner yesterday, you process automatically. Other information, such as this chapter's concepts, requires effort to encode and remember.

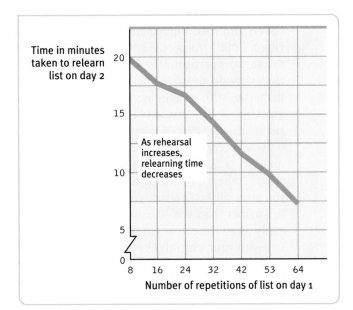

FIGURE 9.4
Ebbinghaus' retention curve
Ebbinghaus found that the more times he practiced a list of nonsense syllables on day 1, the fewer repetitions he required to relearn it on day 2. Said simply, the more time we spend learning novel information, the more we retain. (From Baddeley, 1982.)

The point to remember is that for novel verbal information, practice—effortful processing—does indeed make perfect. And that helps us understand some other interesting phenomena:

- The *next-in-line effect*: When people go around a circle saying words or their names, and attempting to remember what was said by the others, their poorest memories are for what was said by the person just before them (Bond & others, 1991; Brenner, 1973). When we are next in line, we focus on our own performance and often fail to process the last person's words.
- Information presented in the seconds just before sleep is seldom remembered (Wyatt & Bootzin, 1994). When our consciousness fades before we've processed the information, all is lost. Information presented in the *hour* before sleep, as we will see (page 380), is well remembered.
- Taped information played during sleep is registered by the ears but is not remembered (Wood & others, 1992). Without opportunity for rehearsal, "sleep learning" doesn't occur. We also retain information better when our rehearsal is distributed over time (as when learning classmates' names), a phenomenon called the **spacing effect** (Bjork, 1999; Dempster, 1988).

In a 9-year experiment, Harry Bahrick and three of his family members (1993) practiced foreign language word translations for a given number of times, at intervals ranging from 14 to 56 days. Their consistent finding: The longer the space between practice sessions, the better their retention up to 5 years later. Reflecting on the spacing effect, Bahrick saw a practical implication: Restudying material for comprehensive final exams, capstone review courses, and senior examinations will enhance lifelong retention. Spreading out learning—over a semester or a year, rather than over shorter terms—should also help. To paraphrase Ebbinghaus (1885), those who learn quickly also forget quickly. It is another point to remember: Spaced study beats cramming.

To memorize such things as a phone number, "expanding" spaced rehearsal works well. Thomas Landauer (2001) explains: "Rehearse the name or number you are trying to memorize, wait a few seconds, rehearse again, wait a little longer, rehearse again, then wait longer still and rehearse yet again. The waits should be as long as possible without losing the information."

A phenomenon you have surely experienced further illustrates the benefits of rehearsal. Experimenters have shown people a list of items (words, names, dates, even

"He should test his memory by reciting the verses."

Abdur-Rahman Abdul Khaliq,
"Memorizing the Quran"

"The mind is slow in unlearning what it has been long in learning."

Roman philosopher Seneca (4 B.C.–A.D. 65)

FIGURE 9.5
The serial position effect
After being presented with a list of words or names, as Spain's King Juan Carlos I is in this greeting line, people immediately recall the last items well (perhaps because they are still "on-screen"), and quite often the first few items nearly as well. But later they recall the first items best. (From Craik & Watkins, 1973.)

Here is another sentence I will ask you about later: The fish attacked the swimmer.

odors) and then immediately asked them to recall the items in any order (Reed, 2000). As people struggle to recall the list, they often demonstrate the **serial position effect:** They remember the last and first items better than they do those in the middle (**FIGURE 9.5**). Perhaps because the last items are still in working memory, people briefly recall them especially quickly and well. But after a delay—after they shift their attention from the last items—their recall is best for the first items.

As an everyday parallel, imagine it's your first day in a new job, and your manager is introducing you to your co-workers. As you meet each one, you repeat (rehearse) all their names, starting from the beginning. By the time you meet the last person, you will have spent more time rehearsing the earlier names than the later ones; thus, the next day you will probably more easily recall the earlier names. Also, learning the first few names may interfere with your learning the later ones.

But sometimes merely repeating information, such as the new phone number we are about to dial, is not enough to store it for later recall (Craik & Watkins, 1973; Greene, 1987). How, then, do we encode information for processing into long-term memory? Processing our sensory input is like sorting through the day's mail. Some items we instantly discard. Others we process more thoughtfully: We open, read, and retain them. Our memory system processes information by encoding its significant features.

What We Encode

We process information in three key ways—by encoding its meaning, by encoding its image, and by mentally organizing it. To some extent, we do these things automatically. But in each case, there are effortful strategies for enhancing memory.

Encoding Meaning

OBJECTIVE 5 | Compare the benefits of visual, acoustic, and semantic encoding in remembering verbal information, and describe a memory-enhancing strategy related to the self-reference effect.

When processing verbal information for storage, we usually encode its meaning, associating it with what we already know or imagine. Whether we hear "eye-screem" as "ice cream" or "I scream" depends on how the context and our experience guide us to interpret and encode the sounds. (Remember, our working memories interact with our long-term memories.)

Can you repeat the sentence about the rioter (from page 351)? ("The angry rioter threw . . .") Perhaps, like the subjects in an experiment by William Brewer (1977), you recalled the rioter sentence by the meaning you encoded when you read it (for example, "The angry rioter threw the rock *through* the window") and not as it was written ("The angry rioter threw the rock *at* the window"). As such recall indicates, we tend not to remember things exactly as they were. Rather, *we remember what we encoded.* Studying for an exam, you may remember your lecture notes rather than the lecture itself. Gordon Bower and Daniel Morrow (1990) liken our minds to theater directors who, given a raw script, imagine a finished stage production. Asked later to recall what we heard or read, we recall not the literal text but the mental model we constructed from it.

What kind of encoding do you think yields the best memory of verbal information? **Visual encoding** of images? **Acoustic encoding** of sounds? **Semantic encoding** of meaning? Each has its own brain system (Poldrack & Wagner, 2004). And each can help. For example, acoustic encoding enhances the memorability and seeming truth of rhyming aphorisms. "What sobriety conceals, alcohol reveals" seems more accurate than "what sobriety conceals, alcohol unmasks" (McGlone & Tofighbakhsh, 2000). Attorney Johnnie Cochran's celebrated plea to O. J. Simpson's jury— "If the glove doesn't fit, you must acquit"—was also more easily remembered than had Cochran said, "If the glove doesn't fit, you must find him not guilty!"

To compare visual, acoustic, and semantic encoding, Fergus Craik and Endel Tulving (1975) flashed a word at people. Then they asked a question that required the people to process the words (1) visually (the appearance of the letters), (2) acoustically (the sound of the words), or (3) semantically (the meaning of the words). To experience the task yourself, rapidly answer the following questions:

Sample Questions to Elicit Processing	Word Flashed	Yes	No
1. Is the word in capital letters?	chair	___	___
2. Does the word rhyme with train?	BRAIN	___	___
3. Would the word fit in this sentence:			
The girl put the _____ on the table.	gun	___	___

Which type of processing would best prepare you to recognize the words at a later time? In Craik and Tulving's experiment, the deeper, semantic encoding—question 3—yielded much better memory than the "shallow processing" elicited by question 2 and especially by question 1 (**FIGURE 9.6**).

But given too raw a script, we have trouble creating a mental model. Put yourself in the place of the students who John Bransford and Marcia Johnson (1972) asked to remember the following recorded passage:

> The procedure is actually quite simple. First you arrange things into different groups. Of course, one pile may be sufficient depending on how much there is to do. . . . After the procedure is completed one arranges the materials into different groups again. Then they can be put into their appropriate places. Eventually they will be used once more and the whole cycle will then have to be repeated. However, that is part of life.

When the students heard the paragraph you have just read, without a meaningful context, they remembered little of it. When told that the paragraph was about washing clothes (something meaningful to them), they remembered much more of it—as you probably could now after rereading it.

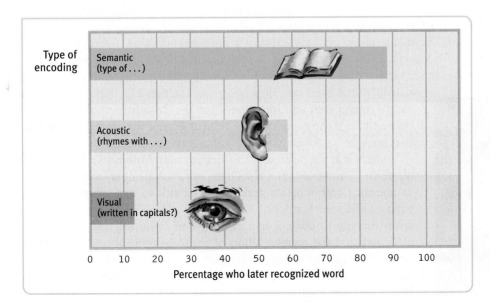

Type of encoding

Semantic (type of . . .)

Acoustic (rhymes with . . .)

Visual (written in capitals?)

0 10 20 30 40 50 60 70 80 90 100

Percentage who later recognized word

FIGURE 9.6
Levels of processing
Processing a word deeply—by its meaning (semantic encoding)—produces better recognition of it at a later time than does shallow processing by attending to its appearance or sound. (From Craik & Tulving, 1975.)

■ **serial position effect** our tendency to recall best the last and first items in a list.
■ **visual encoding** the encoding of picture images.
■ **acoustic encoding** the encoding of sound, especially the sound of words.
■ **semantic encoding** the encoding of meaning, including the meaning of words.

How many *F*s are in the following sentence?
FINISHED FILES ARE THE RESULTS OF YEARS OF SCIENTIFIC STUDY COMBINED WITH THE EXPERIENCE OF YEARS. (See page 360.)

■ **imagery** mental pictures; a powerful aid to effortful processing, especially when combined with semantic encoding.

■ **mnemonics** [nih-MON-iks] memory aids, especially those techniques that use vivid imagery and organizational devices.

■ **chunking** organizing items into familiar, manageable units; often occurs automatically.

> "Among the things which greatly aid the process of memorization is understanding the verses that one has memorized and knowing their relationship and link, one to another."
>
> Abdur-Rahman Abdul Khaliq,
> "Memorizing the Quran"

> "A thing when heard, remember, strikes less keen on the spectator's mind than when 'tis seen."
>
> Horace, *Ars Poetica*, 8 B.C.

The imagery principle

Plastic surgery researcher Darrick Antell observes that "you can talk until you're blue in the face about all the health hazards" of tanning and smoking. But show people photos of identical twins, only one of whom has aged under the influence of tanning and smoking, and they will learn and remember. Sixty-year-old Gay Black, left, was an avid tanner and onetime smoker, unlike her younger-looking identical twin, Gwen Sirota, right.

Such research suggests the benefits of rephrasing what we read and hear into meaningful terms. From his experiments on himself, Ebbinghaus estimated that, compared with learning nonsense material, learning meaningful material required one-tenth the effort. As memory researcher Wayne Wickelgren (1977, p. 346) noted, "The time you spend thinking about material you are reading and relating it to previously stored material is about the most useful thing you can do in learning any new subject matter." Thus, the amount remembered depends both on the time spent learning and on what we do while learning.

We have especially good recall for information we can relate to ourselves. Asked how well certain adjectives describe someone else, we often forget them; asked how well the adjectives describe ourselves, we remember the words well—a phenomenon called the *self-reference effect* (Symons & Johnson, 1997). So, you will profit from taking time to find personal meaning in what you are studying (for example, by taking the time to answer the Ask Yourself questions found at the end of each Learning Outcomes section in this book). Information deemed "relevant to me" is processed more deeply and remains more accessible.

Visual Encoding

OBJECTIVE 6 | Explain how encoding imagery aids effortful processing, and describe some memory-enhancing strategies that use visual encoding.

Why is it that we struggle to remember formulas, definitions, and dates, yet we can easily remember where we were yesterday, who was with us, where we sat, and what we wore? One difference relates to the greater ease of remembering mental pictures. Our earliest memories—probably of something that happened at age 3 or 4—involve visual **imagery.** Researchers have also documented that we remember concrete words that lend themselves to visual mental images better than we remember abstract, low-imagery words. (When I quiz you later, which three of these words—*typewriter, void, cigarette, inherent, fire, process*—will you most likely recall?) Similarly, you probably still recall the sentence about the rock-throwing rioter, not only because of the meaning you encoded, but also because the sentence lent itself to a visual image. Memory for concrete nouns is aided by encoding them *both* semantically and visually (Marschark & others, 1987; Paivio, 1986). Two codes are better than one.

Thanks to the durability of our most vivid images, we sometimes recall our experiences with mental snapshots of their best or worst moments. Thus, the best moment of a pleasure or joy, and the worst moment of a pain or frustration, often colors our memories (Fredrickson & Kahneman, 1993). Recalling the high points while forgetting the mundane moments may explain a phenomenon that Terrence Mitchell, Leigh Thompson, Erika Peterson, and Randy Cronk (1997) call *rosy retrospection:* People tend to recall events such as a camping holiday more positively than they evaluated them at the time. They remember their visit to Disney World less for the muggy heat and long lines than for the surroundings, food, and rides. And it is the experience we remember, not the experience we had, that predicts our future choices (Wirtz & others, 2003).

Imagery is at the heart of many memory aids. **Mnemonic** (nih-MON-ik) devices (so named after the Greek word for memory) were developed by ancient Greek scholars and orators as aids to remembering lengthy passages and speeches. Using the "method of loci," they imagined themselves moving through a familiar series of locations, associating each place with a visual representation of the to-be-remembered topic. Then, when speaking, the orator would mentally revisit each location and retrieve the associated image. A modern study of star performers in the World Memory Championships showed them not to have exceptional intelligence, but rather to be superior at using spatial mnemonic strategies (Maguire & others, 2003).

Other mnemonic devices involve both acoustic and visual codes. For example, the "peg-word" system requires that you first memorize a jingle: *"One is a bun; two is a shoe; three is a tree; four is a door; five is a hive; six is sticks; seven is heaven; eight is a gate; nine is swine; ten is a hen."* Without much effort, you will soon be able to count by peg-words instead of numbers: bun, shoe, tree . . . and then to visually associate the peg-words with to-be-remembered items. Now you are ready to challenge anyone to give you a grocery list to remember. Carrots? Imagine them stuck into a bun. Milk? Fill the shoe with it. Paper towels? Drape them over the tree branch. Think

"bun, shoe, tree" and you see their associated images: carrots, milk, paper towels. With few errors (Bugelski & others, 1968), you will be able to recall the items in any order and to name any given item. Such mnemonic systems are used by memory whizzes who repeat long lists of names and objects, and they can also help you.

Organizing Information for Encoding

OBJECTIVE 7 | Discuss the use of chunking and hierarchies in effortful processing.

Meaning and imagery enhance our memory partly by helping us organize information. When Bransford and Johnson's laundry paragraph (page 357) became meaningful, we could mentally organize its sentences into a sequence. Mnemonic devices help organize material for our later retrieval.

Chunking To experience the importance of organization, glance for a few seconds at row 1 of **FIGURE 9.7**, then look away and try to reproduce what you saw. Impossible, yes? But you can easily reproduce the second row, which is no less complex. Similarly, you will probably find row 4 much easier to remember than row 3, although both contain the same letters. And you could remember the sixth cluster more easily than the fifth, although both contain the same words.

As this demonstrates, we more easily recall information when we can organize it into meaningful units, or chunks. **Chunking** occurs so naturally that we take it for granted. If you are a native English speaker, you can reproduce perfectly the 150 or so line segments that make up the words in the three phrases of item 6 in Figure 9.7. It would astonish someone unfamiliar with the language.

SALLY FORTH

IS THIS CAMPING TRIP ONE OF THOSE SPECIAL TIMES YOU'RE ALWAYS SAYING I'LL WANT TO SHARE SOMEDAY WITH MY KIDS, MOM?

YES, HILARY, THIS IS WHAT FAMILY IS ALL ABOUT, SHARING SPECIAL TIMES TOGETHER.

OK, I'LL TELL THEM. I JUST HOPE I CAN DO IT WITH A STRAIGHT FACE.

DON'T WORRY, THIS TRIP STEEPED IN A FEW YEARS WILL BECOME ONE OF THE BEST MEMORIES OF YOUR LIFE.

Rosy retrospection
A happy fact of life: For most people, the negative emotion recalled from bad events fades more rapidly than the positive emotion recalled from good events (Walker & others, 2003).

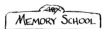

MNEMONICS

"You simply associate each number with a word, such as 'table' and 3,476,029."

1. ◁⊃ꓛꔪ⋃IИꓓ
2. K L C I S N E
3. KLCISNE NVESE YNA NI CSTTIH TNDO
4. NICKELS SEVEN ANY IN STITCH DONT
5. NICKELS SEVEN ANY IN STITCH DONT SAVES AGO A SCORE TIME AND NINE WOODEN FOUR YEARS TAKE
6. DONT TAKE ANY WOODEN NICKELS FOUR SCORE AND SEVEN YEARS AGO A STITCH IN TIME SAVES NINE

FIGURE 9.7
Effects of chunking on memory
When we organize information into meaningful units, such as letters, words, and phrases, we recall it more easily. (From Hintzman, 1978.)

FIGURE 9.8
An example of chunking—
for those who read Chinese
After looking at these characters, can you reproduce them exactly? If so, you are literate in Chinese.

春
夏
秋
冬

Memory researchers agree that Canada's postal codes, with alternating numbers and letters, are especially hard to memorize (Hebert, 2001). A1C 5S7 would be more easily remembered if chunked by letters and numbers, as ACS 157.

Answer to question on page 357: Partly because your initial processing of the letters was primarily acoustic rather than visual, you probably missed some of the six *F*s, especially those that sound like a *V* rather than an *F*.

In the discussion of encoding imagery, on page 358, I gave you six words and told you I would quiz you about them later. How many of these words can you now recall? Of these, how many are high-imagery words? How many are low-imagery?

I am similarly awed at the ability of someone literate in Chinese to glance at **FIGURE 9.8** and then to reproduce all of the strokes; or of a chess master who, after a 5-second look at the board during a game, can recall the exact positions of most of the pieces (Chase & Simon, 1973); or of a varsity basketball player who, given a 4-second glance at a basketball play, can recall the positions of the players (Allard & Burnett, 1985). We all remember information best when we can organize it into personally meaningful arrangements.

Chunking also aids our recall of unfamiliar material. One mnemonic technique organizes it into a more familiar form by encoding the first letters of to-be-remembered words as sentences or as words (called *acronyms*). Want to remember the colors of the rainbow in order of wavelength? Think of the mnemonic ROY G. BIV (red, orange, yellow, green, blue, indigo, violet). Should you ever need to recall the names of North America's five Great Lakes, just remember HOMES (Huron, Ontario, Michigan, Erie, Superior).

With chunking, you can increase your recall of digits, too. An impossible string of 16 numbers—1-4-9-2-1-7-7-6-1-8-1-2-1-9-4-1—becomes easy for an American when chunked into 1492, 1776, 1812, 1941 (as would 1066, 1688, 1815, and 1914 for those familiar with British history). After more than 200 hours of practice in the laboratory of Anders Ericsson and William Chase (1982), two Carnegie-Mellon University students even managed to increase their memory span from the typical 7 digits to more than 80. In another testing session, student Dario Donatelli heard the researcher read one digit per second in a monotonous voice: "1518593765502157841665850612094885686772731418186105462974801294974965928." Motionless while learning the numbers, Donatelli then sprang alive. He whispered numbers, rubbed his chin, tapped his feet, counted on his fingers, and ran his hands through his hair. "Okay," he announced almost 2 minutes later. "The first set is 1518. Then 5937. . . ." He repeated all 73 digits, in groups of 3 and 4.

How did he do it? By increasing the capacity of his working memory? No. When asked to remember letters, Donatelli fell back to about a seven-item capacity. Rather, he had developed a sophisticated strategy for number chunking. "First set was a 3-mile time," reported Donatelli, an All-American cross-country runner. "Second set was a 10-mile time. Then a mile. Half-mile. Two-mile time. An age. . . . Two mile. Age. Age. Age. Two-mile. . . ." (Wells, 1983).

Hierarchies For Donatelli to reach his peak—106 digits—he retrieved the chunks of numbers by clustering them as a hierarchy (Waldrop, 1987). First came "three groups of four," he might think, and so forth. When people develop expertise in an area, they process information not only in chunks but also in hierarchies composed of a few broad concepts divided and subdivided into narrower concepts and facts. By organizing knowledge in hierarchies, we retrieve information efficiently. This chapter therefore aims not only to teach you the elementary facts of memory but also to help you organize these facts around broad principles, such as encoding; subprinciples, such as automatic and effortful processing; and still more specific concepts, such as meaning, imagery, and organization (**FIGURE 9.9**).

Gordon Bower and his colleagues (1969) demonstrated the benefits of hierarchical organization. They presented words either randomly or grouped into categories. When the words were organized into groups, recall was two to three times better. Such results show the benefits of organizing what you study—of giving special attention to chapter outlines, headings, Objectives, Learning Outcomes, and Test Questions. If you can master a chapter's concepts within their overall organization, your recall should be effective at test time. Taking lecture and text notes in outline format—a type of hierarchical organization—may also prove helpful.

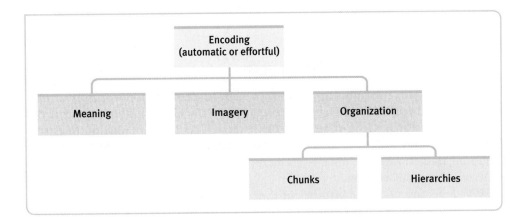

>> Learning Outcomes

Encoding: Getting Information In

OBJECTIVE 3 | Describe the types of information we encode automatically.

We unconsciously and automatically encode incidental information, such as space, time, and frequency. We also register well-learned information, such as words in our native language, by this form of processing.

OBJECTIVE 4 | Contrast effortful processing with automatic processing, and discuss the next-in-line effect, the spacing effect, and the serial position effect.

Automatic processing happens unconsciously, as we absorb information (space, time, frequency, well-learned material) in our environment. *Effortful processing* (of meaning, imagery, organization) requires conscious attention and deliberate effort (rehearsal). The *next-in-line effect* is our tendency to forget (through failure to encode) what the person ahead of us in line has said because we are focusing on what we will say in our upcoming turn. The *spacing effect* is our tendency to retain information more easily if we practice it repeatedly over time (spaced study) than if we practice it in one long session (cramming). The *serial position effect* is our tendency to recall the first and last items in a long list (such as a grocery list) more easily than we recall the intervening items.

OBJECTIVE 5 | Compare the benefits of visual, acoustic, and semantic encoding in remembering verbal information, and describe a memory-enhancing strategy related to the self-reference effect.

Visual encoding (of picture images) and *acoustic encoding* (of sounds, especially of words) are shallower forms of processing than is *semantic encoding* (of meaning). We process verbal information best when we encode it semantically, especially if we apply the self-reference effect, making information "relevant to me."

OBJECTIVE 6 | Explain how encoding imagery aids effortful processing, and describe some memory-enhancing strategies that use visual encoding.

Encoding imagery aids effortful processing because vivid images are very memorable. We tend to remember concrete nouns better than abstract nouns because, for example, we can associate both an image and a meaning with *gorilla*, but only a meaning with *process*. Many *mnemonic devices* (memory strategies or aids) rely on imagery. Others trap items in memory by combining visual encoding (imagining a series of vivid images) and acoustic encoding (a memorable rhyme).

OBJECTIVE 7 | Discuss the use of chunking and hierarchies in effortful processing.

We remember organized information better than we do random data, and chunking and hierarchies are two ways to organize information. In *chunking*, we cluster information into familiar, manageable units, such as words into sentences. In *hierarchies*, we process information by dividing it into logical levels, beginning with the most general and moving to the most specific.

ASK YOURSELF: Can you think of three ways to employ the principles in this section to improve your own learning and retention of important things?

Storage: Retaining Information

At the heart of memory is storage. If you later recall something you experienced, you must, somehow, have stored and retrieved it. Anything stored in long-term memory lies dormant, waiting to be reconstructed by a cue. What is our temporary and our long-term memory storage capacity? Let's start with the first memory store noted in the three-stage processing model (Figure 9.1)—our fleeting sensory memory.

FIGURE 9.10

Momentary photographic memory
When George Sperling flashed a group of letters similar to this for 1/20th of a second, people could recall only about half of the letters. But when signaled to recall a particular row immediately after the letters had disappeared, they could do so with near-perfect accuracy.

■ **iconic memory** a momentary sensory memory of visual stimuli; a photographic or picture-image memory lasting no more than a few tenths of a second.

■ **echoic memory** a momentary sensory memory of auditory stimuli; if attention is elsewhere, sounds and words can still be recalled within 3 or 4 seconds.

Sensory Memory

OBJECTIVE **8** | Contrast two types of sensory memory.

Consider what one intriguing memory experiment revealed about our sensory memory—the initial recording of sensory information in the memory system. As part of his doctoral research, George Sperling (1960) showed people three rows of three letters each for only 1/20th of a second (**FIGURE 9.10**). It was harder than reading by lightning flashes. After the nine letters disappeared from the screen, people could recall only about half of them.

Was it because they had insufficient time to glimpse them? No, Sperling cleverly demonstrated that even at faster than lightning-flash speed, people actually *can* see and recall all the letters, but only momentarily. Rather than ask them to recall all nine letters at once, Sperling sounded a high, medium, or low tone immediately *after* flashing the nine letters. This cue directed participants to report only the letters of the top, middle, or bottom row, respectively. Now they rarely missed a letter, showing that all nine letters were momentarily available for recall.

Sperling's experiment revealed that we have a fleeting photographic memory called **iconic memory.** For an instant, our eyes register an exact representation of a scene and we can recall any part of it in amazing detail—but only for a few tenths of a second. If Sperling delayed the tone signal by more than half a second, the iconic memory was gone and participants once again recalled only about half the letters. Your visual screen clears quickly, as it must, so that new images can be superimposed over old ones.

We also have an impeccable, though fleeting, sensory memory for auditory stimuli, called **echoic memory** (Cowan, 1988; Lu & others, 1992). If partially interpreted, an auditory echo lingers for 3 or 4 seconds. Picture yourself in conversation, as your attention veers to the TV. If your mildly irked conversational partner tests your attention by asking, "What did I just say?" you can recover the last few words from your mind's echo chamber.

Working/Short-Term Memory

OBJECTIVE **9** | Describe the duration and working capacity of short-term memory.

Among the vast amounts of information registered by our sensory memory, we illuminate some with our attentional flashlight. We also retrieve information from long-term storage for "on-screen" display. But unless our working memory meaningfully encodes or rehearses that information, it quickly disappears from our short-term store. During your finger's trip from phone book to phone, your memory of a telephone number may evaporate.

To find out how quickly a short-term memory will disappear, Lloyd Peterson and Margaret Peterson (1959) asked people to remember three-consonant groups, such as *CHJ*. To prevent rehearsal of the letters, the researchers asked participants, for example, to start at 100 and count aloud backwards by threes. After 3 seconds, people recalled the letters only about half the time; after 12 seconds, they seldom recalled them at all (**FIGURE 9.11**). Without active processing, short-term memories have a limited life.

Short-term memory is limited not only in duration but also in capacity. As noted earlier, our short-term memory typically stores just seven or so bits of information (give or take two). George Miller (1956) enshrined this recall capacity as the *Magical Number Seven, plus or minus two*. Not surprisingly, when some phone companies

FIGURE 9.11

Short-term memory decay
Unless rehearsed, verbal information may be quickly forgotten. (From Peterson & Peterson, 1959.)

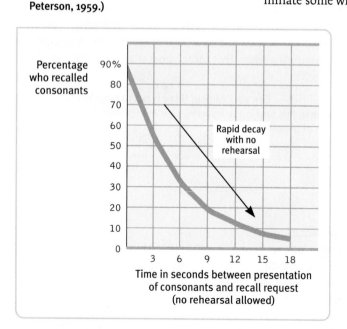

Percentage who recalled consonants

Rapid decay with no rehearsal

Time in seconds between presentation of consonants and recall request (no rehearsal allowed)

began requiring all callers to dial a three-digit area code in addition to a seven-digit number, many people reported trouble retaining the just-looked-up number.

Our short-term recall is slightly better for random digits (as in a phone number) than for random letters, which sometimes have similar sounds. It is slightly better for what we hear than for what we see. Both children and adults have short-term recall for roughly as many words as they can speak in 2 seconds (Cowan, 1994; Hulme & Tordoff, 1989). With information chunks (for example, letters meaningfully grouped as ABC, BBC, FBI, KGB, CIA) and without rehearsal, the average person retains only about four chunks in short-term memory (Cowan, 2001). Suppressing rehearsal by saying "the the the" while hearing random digits also reduces memory to about four items. The basic principle: At any given moment, we can consciously process only a very limited amount of information.

Long-Term Memory

OBJECTIVE **10** | Describe the capacity and duration of long-term memory.

In Arthur Conan Doyle's *A Study in Scarlet,* Sherlock Holmes offers a popular theory of memory capacity:

> I consider that a man's brain originally is like a little empty attic, and you have to stock it with such furniture as you choose. . . . It is a mistake to think that that little room has elastic walls and can distend to any extent. Depend upon it, there comes a time when for every addition of knowledge you forget something that you knew before.

Contrary to Holmes' belief, our capacity for storing long-term memories is essentially limitless. By one careful estimate, the average adult has about a billion bits of information in memory and a storage capacity that will accommodate probably a thousand to a million times that amount (Landauer, 1986). Given the number of brain synapses, one computer engineering group estimated that "the total memory capacity of computers all over the world is far less than that of a single

R. J. Erwin/Photo Researchers

brain" (Wang & others, 2003). Although even a single laptop beats our brain's capacity to remember literal text (What was that definition of negative reinforcement?), this much is sure: Our brains are *not* like attics, which once filled can store more items only if we discard old ones.

The point is vividly illustrated by those who have performed phenomenal memory feats (**TABLE 9.1**, on page 364). Consider the 1990s tests of psychologist Rajan Mahadevan's memory. Give him a block of 10 digits from the first 30,000 or so digits of pi and, after a few moments of mental searching for the string, he would pick up the series from there, firing numbers like a machine gun (Delaney & others, 1999; Thompson & others, 1993). He could also repeat 50 random digits—backwards. It is not a genetic gift, he said; anyone could learn to do it. But given the genetic influence on so many human traits, and knowing that Rajan's father memorized Shakespeare's complete works, one wonders. So how does he do it? As with other psychological phenomena, researchers study memory using different levels of analysis, including the biological.

The Magical Number Seven has become psychology's contribution to an intriguing list of magic sevens—the seven wonders of the world, the seven seas, the seven deadly sins, the seven primary colors, the seven musical scale notes, the seven days of the week—seven magical sevens.

Clark's Nutcracker
Among animals, one contender for champion memorist would be a mere birdbrain—the Clark's Nutcracker—which during winter and early spring can locate up to 6000 caches of buried pine seeds (Shettleworth, 1993).

Pi in the sky: As this book went to press, the world record for memorizing pi was held by Japan's Akira Haraguchi, who in 2005 recited the first 83,431 digits correctly (BBC, 2005).

TABLE 9.1

WORLD MEMORY CHAMPIONSHIP RECORDS

From world memory competition, here are some current records, as of 2005:

Contest	Description	Record
Speed cards	Shortest time to memorize a shuffled pack of 52 playing cards	33 seconds
One-hour cards	Most cards memorized in one hour (52 points for every pack correct; 26 points if 1 mistake)	1170 cards
Speed numbers	Most random digits memorized in 5 minutes	324 digits
Names and faces	Most first and last names memorized in 15 minutes after being shown with faces (1 point for every correctly spelled first or last name; 1/2 point for every phonetically correct but incorrectly spelled name)	167.5 names
Binary digits	Most binary digits (101101, etc.) memorized in 30 minutes when presented in rows of 30 digits	3705

Sources: usamemoriad.com and worldmemorychampionship.com

Storing Memories in the Brain

I marveled at my aging mother-in-law, a retired pianist and organist. At age 88 her blind eyes could no longer read music. But let her sit at a keyboard and she would flawlessly play any of hundreds of hymns, including ones she had not thought of for 20 years. Where did her brain store those thousands of sequenced notes?

For a time, some memory researchers believed that brain stimulation during surgery provided evidence that our whole past, not just well-practiced music, is "in there," in complete detail, just waiting to be relived. To predict possible side effects of brain surgery, Wilder Penfield (1969) electrically stimulated different cortical regions of his patients' brains while they were wide awake. When his patients occasionally reported hearing things, such as a "mother calling her little boy," Penfield assumed he was activating long-lost experiences etched permanently on the brain. Analysis of these famous reports by Elizabeth Loftus and Geoffrey Loftus (1980) revealed that these reports were extremely rare, occurring in only a handful of Penfield's 1100 stimulated patients. Furthermore, the flashbacks appear to have been invented, not relived. (People would recall being in locations they had never visited.)

Psychologist Karl Lashley (1950) provided further evidence that memories do not reside in single, specific spots. He trained rats to solve a maze, then cut out pieces of their cortexes and retested their memory. Alas, no matter what small cortical section he removed, the rats retained at least a partial memory of how to solve the maze.

So, despite the brain's vast storage capacity, we do not seem to store most information with the exactness of a tape recorder. Rather, memory researchers argue, forgetting occurs as new experiences interfere with our retrieval (pages 379–380) and as the physical memory trace decays. But what is the *memory trace*?

Could the physical memory trace be rooted in the brain's ongoing electrical activity? If so, then temporarily shutting down that activity should eliminate them, much as a dead battery will eliminate the settings on a car radio. Testing that idea, Ralph Gerard (1953) first trained hamsters to turn right or left to get food, and then lowered their body temperature until the brains' electrical activity ceased. When the hamsters were revived and their brains were active again, would they remember which way to turn? Yes. Their long-term memories survived the electrical blackout. In commenting on the elusiveness of the memory trace, one memory researcher, with tongue only

"Our memories are flexible and superimposable, a panoramic blackboard with an endless supply of chalk and erasers."
Elizabeth Loftus and Katherine Ketcham, *The Myth of Repressed Memory*, 1994

Electroconvulsive therapy (ECT) for depression disrupts memory for recent experience but leaves most memory intact (see Chapter 17).

■ **long-term potentiation (LTP)** an increase in a synapse's firing potential after brief, rapid stimulation. Believed to be a neural basis for learning and memory.

partly in cheek, said, "I must admit that memories are more of a spiritual than a physical reality. When you try to touch them, they turn to mist and disappear" (Loftus & Ketcham, 1994, p. 4). To know how our brain stores and effortlessly retrieves a flood of details "defies comprehension," said one awestruck neuroscientist (Doty, 1998).

Recently, the search for the physical basis of memory—for information incarnated in matter—has focused on the synapses.

Synaptic Changes

OBJECTIVE 11 | Discuss the synaptic changes that accompany memory formation and storage.

Neuroscientists are expanding the search for the location of memories by exploring changes within and between single neurons. Memories begin as impulses whizzing through brain circuits, somehow leaving permanent neural traces. Where does the neural change occur? The available clues point to the synapses—the sites where nerve cells communicate with one another through their neurotransmitter messengers. Recall from Chapter 3 how experience modifies the brain's neural networks. Given increased activity in a particular pathway, neural interconnections form or strengthen.

Eric Kandel and James Schwartz (1982) observed changes in the sending neurons of a simple animal, the California sea snail, *Aplysia*. Its mere 20,000 or so nerve cells are unusually large and accessible, enabling the researchers to observe synaptic changes during learning. Chapter 8 noted how the sea snail can be classically conditioned (with electric shock) to reflexively withdraw its gills when squirted with water, much as a shell-shocked soldier jumps at the sound of a snapping twig. By observing the snails' neural connections before and after conditioning, Kandel and Schwartz pinpointed changes. When learning occurs, the snail releases more of the neurotransmitter *serotonin* at certain synapses. These synapses then become more efficient at transmitting signals.

Increased synaptic efficiency makes for more efficient neural circuits. In experiments, rapidly stimulating certain memory-circuit connections has increased their sensitivity for hours or even weeks to come. The sending neuron now needs less prompting to release its neurotransmitter, and the receiving neuron's receptor sites may increase (**FIGURE 9.12**). This prolonged strengthening of potential neural firing, called **long-term potentiation (LTP),** a term coined by Gary Lynch (2002) and others, provides a neural basis for learning and remembering associations. We know now that drugs that block LTP interfere with learning (Lynch & Staubli, 1991). Mutant mice engineered to lack an enzyme needed for LTP can't learn their way out of a maze (Silva & others, 1992). And rats given a drug that enhances LTP will learn a maze with half the usual number of mistakes (Service, 1994).

Kandel, Lynch, and several other memory-biology explorers have each helped found pharmaceutical companies that are competing to develop and test memory-boosting drugs (*Economist,* 2004; Marshall, 2004). At least 40 "cognitive enhancers" are currently in some phase of development or clinical trial. Their target market includes millions of people with Alzheimer's disease, millions more with "mild cognitive impairment" that often becomes Alzheimer's, and countless millions who would love to turn back the clock on age-related memory decline. From shrinking memories perhaps will come bulging profits.

One approach is developing drugs that boost production of the protein CREB, which can switch genes off or on. Remember: Genes code the production of protein

Aplysia
The much-studied California sea snail has increased our understanding of the neural basis of learning.

> "The biology of the mind will be as scientifically important to this [new] century as the biology of the gene [was] to the twentieth century."
>
> Eric Kandel, acceptance remarks for the 2000 Nobel prize

FIGURE 9.12
Doubled receptor sites
Electron microscope images show just one receptor site (gray) reaching toward a sending neuron before long-term potentiation (top) and two afterward (bottom). A doubling of the receptor sites means that the receiving neuron has increased sensitivity for detecting the presence of the neurotransmitter molecules that may be released by the sending neuron. (From Toni & others, 1999.)

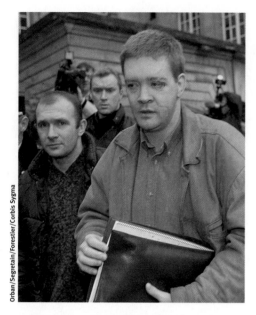

Disrupted memory consolidation
After suffering a concussion in the accident that killed Princess Diana, her bodyguard, Trevor Rees-Jones (right), had no memory for the accident or the minutes before it (Riccio & others, 2003).

molecules. With repeated neural firing, a nerve cell's genes produce synapse-strengthening proteins, enabling long-term memories to form (Fields, 2005). Boosting CREB production might lead to increased production of proteins that help reshape synapses and consolidate a short-term memory into a long-term memory. Sea slugs, mice, and fruit flies with enhanced CREB production have displayed enhanced memories. Another approach is developing drugs that boost glutamate, a brain neurotransmitter that enhances synaptic communication (LTP). Whether such drugs can boost memory without nasty side effects and without cluttering our minds with trivia best forgotten remains to be seen. In the meantime, one effective, safe, and free memory enhancer is already available on college campuses: study followed by adequate sleep! (See pages 280 and 283.)

After long-term potentiation has occurred, passing an electric current through the brain won't disrupt old memories. But the current will wipe out very recent memories. Such is the experience both of laboratory animals and of depressed people given electroconvulsive therapy. A blow to the head can do the same. Like sleepers who can't remember what they heard just before losing consciousness, football players and boxers momentarily knocked unconscious typically have no memory of events just before the knock-out (Yarnell & Lynch, 1970). The information in short-term memory before the blow did not have time to consolidate into long-term memory.

Stress Hormones and Memory

OBJECTIVE 12 | Discuss some ways stress hormones can affect memory.

The stress hormones that humans and animals produce when excited or stressed make more glucose energy available to fuel brain activity, signaling the brain that something important has happened. Moreover, the amygdala, two emotion-processing clusters in the limbic system, boost activity in the brain's memory-forming areas (Dolcos & others, 2004; Hamann & others, 2002). The result? Arousal can sear certain events into the brain, while disrupting memory for neutral events around the same time (Birnbaum & others, 2004; Strange & Dolan, 2004).

The point to remember, according to James McGaugh (1994, 2003), is that "stronger emotional experiences make for stronger, more reliable memories." After traumatic experiences—a wartime ambush, a house fire, a rape—vivid recollections of the horrific event may intrude again and again. It is as if they were burned in.

Conversely, weaker emotion means weaker memories. People given a drug that blocks the effects of stress hormones will later have more trouble remembering the details of an upsetting story (Cahill, 1994). That connection is appreciated by those working to develop an optimum drug that, when taken after a traumatic experience, might blunt intrusive memories.

Severe stress sears in memories
Significantly stressful events, such as the tragic tsunami that struck Southeast Asia in late 2004, may be an indelible part of the memories of those who experience them.

Emotion-triggered hormonal changes help explain why we long remember exciting or shocking events, such as our first kiss, an earthquake, or 9/11. People who experienced the 1989 San Francisco earthquake had perfect recall a year and a half later of where they were and what they were doing (as they had recorded within a day or two of the quake). Others' memories for the circumstances under which they merely *heard* about the quake were more prone to errors (Neisser & others, 1991; Palmer & others, 1991). (A second important reason for the durability of dramatic experiences is our reliving and rehearsing them—as did most people who experienced the earthquake and told their stories to countless others.)

There are, however, limits to stress-enhanced remembering. As Chapter 14 explains, when *prolonged*—as in sustained abuse or combat—stress can act like acid, corroding neural connections and shrinking a brain area (the hippocampus) that is vital for laying down memories. Moreover, when sudden stress hormones are flowing, older memories may be blocked. It is true for rats trying to find their way to a hidden target (de Quervain & others, 1998). And it is true for those of us whose minds have gone blank while speaking in public.

Storing Implicit and Explicit Memories

OBJECTIVE 13 | Distinguish between implicit and explicit memory, and identify the main brain structure associated with each.

A memory-to-be enters the cortex through the senses, then wends its way into the brain's depths. Precisely where it goes depends on the type of information, as dramatically illustrated by those who, as in the case of my father mentioned earlier, suffer from a type of **amnesia** in which they are unable to form new memories.

Neurologist Oliver Sacks (1985, pp. 26–27) describes one such patient, Jimmie, who had brain damage. Jimmie had no memories—thus, no sense of elapsed time—beyond his injury in 1945. Asked in 1975 to name the U.S. President, he replied, "FDR's dead. Truman's at the helm."

When Jimmie gave his age as 19, Sacks set a mirror before him: "Look in the mirror and tell me what you see. Is that a 19-year-old looking out from the mirror?"

Jimmie turned ashen, gripped the chair, cursed, then became frantic: "What's going on? What's happened to me? Is this a nightmare? Am I crazy? Is this a joke?" When his attention was diverted to some children playing baseball, his panic ended, the dreadful mirror forgotten.

Sacks showed Jimmie a photo from *National Geographic*. "What is this?" he asked.
"It's the Moon," Jimmie replied.
"No, it's not," Sacks answered. "It's a picture of the Earth taken from the Moon."
"Doc, you're kidding? Someone would've had to get a camera up there!"
"Naturally."
"Hell! You're joking—how the hell would you do that?" Jimmie's wonder was that of a bright young man from 60 years ago reacting with amazement to his travel back to the future.

Careful testing of these unique people reveals something even stranger: Although incapable of recalling new facts or anything they have done recently, Jimmie and others with similar conditions can learn. Shown hard-to-find figures in pictures (in the *Where's Waldo?* series), they can quickly spot them again later. They can learn to read mirror-image writing or do a jigsaw puzzle, and they have even been taught complicated job skills (Schacter, 1992, 1996; Xu & Corkin, 2001). They can be classically conditioned. However, *they do all these things with no awareness of having learned them.*

These amnesia victims are in some ways like people with brain damage who cannot consciously recognize faces but whose physiological responses to familiar faces reveal an implicit (unconscious) recognition. Their behaviors challenge the idea that memory is a single, unified, conscious system. Instead, we seem to have two memory systems operating in tandem (**FIGURE 9.13,** page 368). Whatever has destroyed *conscious* recall in these individuals with amnesia has not destroyed their *unconscious* capacity for learning. They can learn *how* to do something—called **implicit memory** (*procedural memory*). But they may not know and declare *that* they know—called **explicit memory** (*declarative memory*).

Having read a story once, they will read it faster a second time, showing implicit memory. But there will be no explicit memory, for they cannot recall having seen the story before. If repeatedly shown the word *perfume,* they will not recall having seen it. But if asked the first word that comes to mind in response to the letters *per,* they say *perfume,* readily displaying their learning. Performing such tasks, even Alzheimer's patients,

---

■ **amnesia** the loss of memory.

■ **implicit memory** retention independent of conscious recollection. (Also called *procedural memory.*)

■ **explicit memory** memory of facts and experiences that one can consciously know and "declare." (Also called *declarative memory.*)

FIGURE 9.13
Memory subsystems
We process and store our explicit and implicit memories separately. Thus, one may lose explicit memory (becoming amnesic), yet display implicit memory for material one cannot consciously recall.

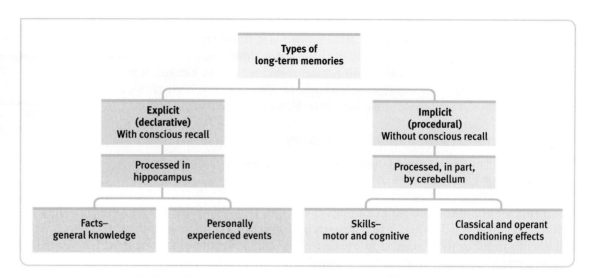

Types of long-term memories

Explicit (declarative)
With conscious recall

Implicit (procedural)
Without conscious recall

Processed in hippocampus

Processed, in part, by cerebellum

Facts— general knowledge

Personally experienced events

Skills— motor and cognitive

Classical and operant conditioning effects

The two-track memory system reinforces an important principle introduced in Chapter 5's description of parallel processing: Mental feats such as vision, thinking, and memory may seem to be single abilities, but they are not. Rather, we split information into different components for separate and simultaneous processing.

"[Brain-scanning] technologies are revolutionizing the study of the brain and mind in the same way that the telescope revolutionized the study of the heavens."

Endel Tulving (1996)

FIGURE 9.14
The hippocampus
Explicit memories for facts and episodes are processed in the hippocampus and fed to other brain regions for storage.

Hippocampus

whose explicit memories for people and events are lost, display an ability to form new implicit memories (Lustig & Buckner, 2004). They retain their new learning but do not explicitly recall it.

The Hippocampus One way to discover how memory works is to study its malfunctions. For example, these remarkable stories provoke us to wonder: Do our explicit and implicit memory systems involve separate brain regions? Scans of the brain in action, and autopsies of people who had amnesia, reveal that new explicit memories of names, images, and events are laid down via the **hippocampus** (**FIGURE 9.14**), a neural center in the limbic system. When brain scans capture the brain forming a memory, they reveal activity in the hippocampus as well as in certain areas of the frontal lobes (Wagner & others, 1998). The hippocampus again lights up on a PET scan when people recall words (using explicit memory) (Squire, 1992).

Damage to the hippocampus disrupts some types of memory. Chickadees and other birds can store food in hundreds of places and return to these unmarked caches months later, but not if their hippocampus has been removed (Sherry & Vaccarino, 1989). Like the cortex, the hippocampus is lateralized. (You've got two of them, one just above each ear and about an inch and a half straight in.) Damage to the left or right hippocampus seems to produce different results. Patients with left-hippocampus damage have trouble remembering verbal information, but they have no trouble recalling visual designs and locations. For those with right-hippocampus damage, the problem is reversed (Schacter, 1996).

New research also pinpoints the functions of different hippocampus subregions. One part is active as people learn to associate names with faces (Zeineh & others, 2003). Another part is active as memory whizzes engage in spatial mnemonics (Maguire & others, 2003b). The rear area, which processes spatial memory, also grows bigger the longer a London cabbie has been navigating the maze of city streets (Maguire & others, 2003a).

Monkeys and people who lose their hippocampus to surgery or disease also lose most of their recall for things learned during the preceding month, though their older memories remain intact (Bayley & others, 2005; McGaugh, 2000). The longer the hippocampus and its pathway to the cortex are left intact after training, the smaller the memory deficit (Remondes & Schuman, 2004). The hippocampus seems to act as a loading dock where the brain registers and temporarily stores the elements of a remembered episode—its smell, feel, sound, and location. But then, like older files shifted to a basement storeroom, memories migrate for storage elsewhere. The hippocampus is active during slow-wave sleep, as memories are processed and filed for later retrieval. The greater the hippocampus activity during sleep after a training experience, the better the next day's memory (Peigneux & others, 2004).

Our brain's librarian assigns different information to different regions. Brain scans reveal that, once stored, our mental encores of past experience activate various parts of the frontal and temporal lobes (Fink & others, 1996; Gabrieli & others, 1996; Markowitsch, 1995). Calling up a telephone number and holding it in working memory activates a region of the left frontal cortex; calling up a party scene would more likely activate a region of the right hemisphere.

There is no longer any doubt: Our memories are not in one place. Many brain regions are active as we encode, store, and retrieve different kinds of information. Savoring that memory of a successful performance requires a mental symphony conductor that retrieves snippets from various cortical storage sites and integrates them with the emotional associations provided by your amygdala. Amnesia patients may retain the distributed fragments of a memory—the sight, sound, smell, objects, people, actions, and emotions. But the connections that enable the patients to reassemble the fragments into an explicit memory of an event may be lost.

The Cerebellum Although your hippocampus is a temporary processing site for your explicit memories, you could lose it and still lay down memories for skills and conditioned associations. Implicit memories require fewer connections among cortical storage areas, so people with hippocampal damage may retain those memories (Paller, 2004). Joseph LeDoux (1996) recounts the story of a brain-damaged patient whose amnesia left her unable to recognize her physician as, each day, he shook her hand and introduced himself. One day, after reaching for his hand, she yanked hers back, for the physician had pricked her with a tack in his palm. The next time he returned to introduce himself she refused to shake his hand but couldn't explain why. Having been classically conditioned, she just wouldn't do it.

The cerebellum, the brain region extending out from the rear of the brainstem, plays a key role in forming and storing the implicit memories created by classical conditioning. Humans with a damaged cerebellum are incapable of developing certain conditioned reflexes, such as associating a tone with an impending puff of air—and thus blinking in anticipation of the puff (Daum & Schugens, 1996; Green & Woodruff-Pak, 2000). By methodically disrupting the function of different pathways in the cortex and cerebellum of rabbits, Richard Thompson, David Krupa, and Judith Thompson showed that rabbits will also fail to learn a conditioned eye-blink response when the cerebellum is temporarily deactivated during training (Krupa & others, 1993; Steinmetz, 1999). Implicit memory formation needs the cerebellum.

Our dual explicit-implicit memory system helps explain infantile amnesia: The reactions and skills we learned during infancy reach far into our future, yet as adults we recall nothing (explicitly) of our first three years. Our conscious minds are blank, not only because we index so much of our explicit memory by words that nonspeaking children have not learned, but also because the hippocampus is one of the last brain structures to mature.

■ **hippocampus** a neural center that is located in the limbic system and helps process explicit memories for storage.

>> **LEARNING OUTCOMES**

Storage: Retaining Information

OBJECTIVE **8** | **Contrast two types of sensory memory.**

As information enters the memory system through our senses, we register and store visual images via *iconic memory,* in which picture images last no more than a few tenths of a second. We register and store sounds via *echoic memory,* where echoes of auditory stimuli may linger as long as 3 or 4 seconds.

OBJECTIVE **9** | **Describe the duration and working capacity of short-term memory.**

At any given time, we can focus on and process only about seven items of information (either new or retrieved from our memory store). Without rehearsal, information disappears within seconds from short-term memory and is forgotten.

OBJECTIVE 10 | **Describe the capacity and duration of long-term memory.**

Our capacity for storing information permanently in long-term memory is essentially unlimited.

OBJECTIVE 11 | **Discuss the synaptic changes that accompany memory formation and storage.**

Contemporary researchers are focusing on memory-related changes within and between single neurons. As experience strengthens the pathways between neurons, synapses transmit signals more efficiently. In a process known as *long-term potentiation (LTP)*, sending neurons in these pathways release neurotransmitters more quickly, and receiving neurons may develop additional receptors, increasing their ability to detect the incoming neurotransmitters. LTP appears to be the neural basis for learning and memory.

OBJECTIVE 12 | **Discuss some ways stress hormones can affect memory.**

By enabling the production of extra glucose (which fuels brain activity), stress hormones alert the brain to important events. The amygdala, an emotion-processing structure in the brain's limbic system, arouses brain areas that process emotion. These emotion-triggered hormonal changes may produce indelible memories.

OBJECTIVE 13 | **Distinguish between implicit and explicit memory, and identify the main brain structure associated with each.**

We are often not aware of our *implicit (procedural) memories*—our memory of our own skills and operantly and classically conditioned responses. These memories are processed in part by the cerebellum, near the brainstem. We consciously recall our *explicit (declarative) memories*—our general knowledge, specific facts, and personally experienced events. Explicit memories are processed in various subregions of the hippocampus (a neural center in the limbic system) and sent for storage in other areas in the brain. The implicit and explicit memory systems are independent. Damage to the hippocampus may destroy the ability to consciously recall memories, without destroying skills or classically conditioned responses.

ASK YOURSELF: Can you name an instance where stress has helped you remember something, and another instance where stress has interfered with remembering something?

■ **recall** a measure of memory in which the person must retrieve information learned earlier, as on a fill-in-the-blank test.

■ **recognition** a measure of memory in which the person need only identify items previously learned, as on a multiple-choice test.

■ **relearning** a memory measure that assesses the amount of time saved when learning material for a second time.

Remembering things past

Even if Oprah Winfrey and Brad Pitt had not become famous, their high school class-mates would most likely still recognize their yearbook photos.

Retrieval: Getting Information Out

OBJECTIVE 14 | Contrast the recall, recognition, and relearning measures of memory.

To remember an event requires not only getting it in (encoding) and retaining it (storage), but also getting it out. To most people, memory is **recall,** the ability to retrieve information not in conscious awareness. To a psychologist, memory is any sign that something learned has been retained. So *recognizing* or more quickly *relearning* information also indicates memory.

Long after you cannot recall most of the people in your high school graduating class, you may still be able to **recognize** their yearbook pictures from a photographic lineup and pick their names from a list of names. Harry Bahrick and his colleagues (1975) reported that people who had graduated 25 years earlier could not *recall* many of their old classmates, but they could *recognize* 90 percent of their pictures and names. If you are like most students, you, too, could likely recognize more names of the Seven Dwarfs than you could recall (Miserandino, 1991).

Our speed at **relearning** can also reveal memory. If you once learned something and then forgot it, you probably will relearn it more quickly than you originally learned it. When you study for a final exam or resurrect a language used in early childhood, the relearning is easier. Tests of recognition and of time spent relearning reveal that we remember more than we can recall.

Our recognition memory is impressively quick and vast. "Is your friend wearing a new or old outfit?" "Old." "Is this five-second movie clip from a film you've ever seen?" "Yes." "Have you ever before seen this person—this minor variation on the same old human features (two eyes, one nose, and so on)?" "No." Before the mouth can form our answer to any of millions of such questions, the mind knows, and knows that it knows.

CLOSE-UP:

RETRIEVING PASSWORDS

There's something that you need lots of, and that your grandparents at your age didn't: passwords. To log into your e-mail, retrieve your voice mail, draw cash from a machine, access your phone card, use the copy machine, or persuade the keypad to open the building door, you need to remember your password. A typical introductory psychology student faces eight demands for passwords, report Alan Brown and his colleagues (2004).

With so many passwords needed, what's a person to do? Memory researcher Henry Roediger takes a simple approach to storing all the important phone, PIN, and code numbers in his life: "I have a sheet in my shirt pocket with all the numbers I need," says Roediger (2001), adding that he can't mentally store them all, so why bother? Other strategies may help those who do not want to lose their PINS in the wash. First, duplicate. The average student uses four different passwords to meet those eight needs. Second, harness retrieval cues. Surveys in Britain and the United States reveal that about half of our passwords harness a familiar name or date. Others often involve familiar phone or identification numbers.

For on-line banking or other situations where security is essential, use a mix of letters and numbers, advise Brown and his colleagues. After composing such a password, rehearse it, then rehearse it a day later, and continue rehearsing at increasing intervals. In such ways, long-term memories will form and be retrievable at the cash and copy machines.

Retrieval Cues

OBJECTIVE 15 | Explain how retrieval cues help us access stored memories, and describe the process of priming.

Imagine a spider suspended in the middle of her web, held up by the many strands extending outward from her in all directions to different points (perhaps a window sill, a tree branch, a leaf on a shrub). If you were to trace a pathway to the spider, you would first need to create a path from one of these anchor points and then follow the strand attached to that point down into the web.

The process of retrieving a memory follows a similar principle, because memories are held in storage by a web of associations, each piece of information interconnected with others. When you encode into memory a target piece of information, such as the name of the person sitting next to you in class, you associate with it other bits of information about your surroundings, mood, seating position, and so on. These other bits of information are like tags, hints, or identifying marks on the target information. They act as *retrieval cues,* anchor points you can use to access the target information when you want to retrieve it later. The more retrieval cues you have, the better your chances of finding a route to the suspended memory (see Close-Up: Retrieving Passwords).

Do you recall the gist of the second sentence I asked you to remember (on page 356)? If not, does the word *shark* serve as a retrieval cue? Experiments show that *shark* (likely what you visualized) more readily retrieves the image you stored than does the sentence's actual word, *fish* (Anderson & others, 1976).

Mnemonic devices provide us with handy retrieval cues: ROY G. BIV; HOMES; bun, shoe, tree. But the best retrieval cues come from the associations formed at the time we encode a memory, and those cues can be experiences as well as words. Tastes, smells, and sights often evoke our recall of associated episodes. To call up visual cues when trying to recall something, we may mentally place ourselves in the original context. For British theologian John Hull (1990, p. 174) this became difficult after losing his sight. On one occasion when his wife asked him what he had done that day he had difficulty recalling. "I knew I had been somewhere, and had done particular things with certain people, but where? I could

Multiple-choice questions test our
a. recall.
b. recognition.
c. relearning.

Fill-in-the-blank questions test our
_____. (See page 375 for answers to these questions.)

> "Memory is not like a container that gradually fills up; it is more like a tree growing hooks onto which memories are hung."
> Peter Russell, *The Brain Book*, 1979

"Let me refresh your memory. It was the night before Christmas and all through the house not a creature was stirring until you landed a sled, drawn by reindeer, on the plaintiff's home, causing extensive damage to the roof and chimney."

not put the conversations I had had into a context. There was no background, no features against which to identify the place. Normally, the memories of people you have spoken to during the day are stored in frames which include the background."

To retrieve a specific memory from the web of associations, you first need to activate one of the strands that leads to it, a process called **priming.** Philosopher-psychologist William James referred to priming as the "wakening of associations." Often our associations are activated, or primed, without our awareness. As **FIGURE 9.15** indicates, seeing or hearing the word *rabbit* primes associations with *hare* even though we may not recall having seen or heard *rabbit*.

FIGURE 9.15
Priming—awakening associations
After seeing or hearing *rabbit,* we are later more likely to spell the spoken word as *h-a-r-e.* The spreading of associations unconsciously activates related associations. This phenomenon is called priming. (Adapted from Bower, 1986.)

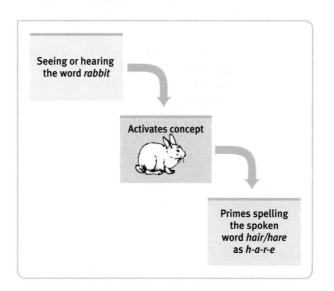

Priming is often "memoryless memory"—memory without explicit remembering, invisible memory. If, walking down a hallway, you see a poster of a missing child, you will then unconsciously be primed to interpret an ambiguous adult-child interaction as a possible kidnapping (James, 1986). Although you don't consciously remember the poster, it predisposes your interpretation. (As we saw in Chapter 5, even subliminal stimuli can briefly prime responses to later stimuli.)

Ask a friend two rapid-fire questions: (a) How do you pronounce the word spelled by the letters *s-h-o-p*? (b) What do you do when you come to a green light? If your friend answers "stop" to the second question, you have demonstrated priming.

Context Effects

OBJECTIVE 16 | Cite some ways that context can affect retrieval.

Putting yourself back in the context where you experienced something can prime your memory retrieval. Duncan Godden and Alan Baddeley (1975) discovered this when they had scuba divers listen to a list of words in two different settings, either 10 feet underwater or sitting on the beach. As **FIGURE 9.16** illustrates, the divers recalled more words when they were retested in the same place.

Consider this scenario: While making notes in this book, you realize you need to sharpen your pencil. You get up and walk downstairs. When you get there, however, you cannot remember why you came. After trying to recall your purpose, you give up and return to your desk. As soon as you sit down to work again, it hits you: "I wanted to sharpen this pencil!" What happens to create this frustrating experience? In one context (desk, reading psychology), it occurs to you that you want the pencil sharpened. When you get up and go downstairs, you move into a different context where you have few cues to lead you to the thought that brought you there. When you give up and go back to your desk, you are back in the context in which you encoded the thought ("This pencil is dull").

■ **priming** the activation, often unconsciously, of particular associations in memory. Ask a friend two rapid-fire questions: (a) How do you pronounce the word spelled by the letters *s-h-o-p*? (b) What do you do when you come to a green light? If your friend answers "stop" to the second question, you have demonstrated priming.

■ **déjà vu** that eerie sense that "I've experienced this before." Cues from the current situation may subconsciously trigger retrieval of an earlier experience.

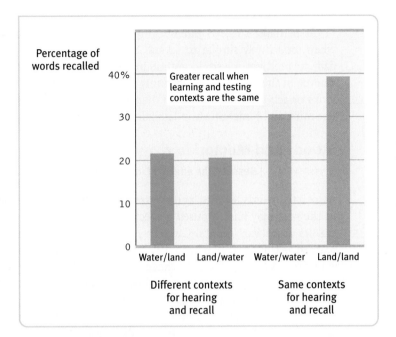

Percentage of
words recalled

40%

Greater recall when
learning and testing
contexts are the same

30

20

10

0

Water/land   Land/water   Water/water   Land/land

Different contexts
for hearing
and recall

Same contexts
for hearing
and recall

FIGURE **9.16**

The effects of context on memory
Words heard underwater are best recalled
underwater; words heard on land are best
recalled on land. (Adapted from Godden &
Baddeley, 1975.)

Fred McConnaughey/Photo Researchers

You have probably experienced similar context effects. You return to where you
once lived or to the school you once attended and are flooded with retrieval cues and
memories. Even taking an exam in the same room where you are taught may help a
little. In several experiments, Carolyn Rovee-Collier (1993) found that a familiar
context activates memories even in 3-month-olds. After infants learned that kicking
a crib mobile would make it move (via a connecting ribbon from the ankle), the infants kicked more when tested again in the same crib with the same bumper than
when in a different context (**FIGURE 9.17**).

Sometimes, being in a context similar to one we've been in before may trigger the
experience of **déjà vu** (French for "already seen")—that eerie sense that "I've been
in this exact situation before." This fleeting experience happens most commonly to
well-educated, imaginative young adults, especially when tired or stressed (Brown,
2003, 2004). The two-thirds of people who report having experienced déjà vu
(McAneny, 1996) often wonder, "How could I recognize a situation I'm experiencing for the first time?" Those who suppose a paranormal explanation may think of
reincarnation ("I must have experienced this in a previous life") or precognition
("I viewed this scene in my mind before experiencing it").

Posing the question differently ("Why
do I feel as if I recognize this situation?"),
we can see how our memory system might
produce déjà vu (Alcock, 1981). If we have
previously been in a similar situation, the
current situation may be loaded with cues
that unconsciously retrieve the earlier experience. (We take in and retain vast
amounts of information while hardly
noticing and often forgetting where it
came from.) Thus, if in a similar context
you see a stranger who looks and walks
like one of your friends, the similarity may
give rise to an eerie feeling of recognition.
Having awakened a shadow of that earlier
experience, you may think, "I've seen that
person in this situation before."

Courtesy of Carolyn Rovee-Collier, Rutgers University

" Do you ever get that strange feeling of
vujà dé? Not déjà vu; vujà dé. It's the distinct sense that, somehow, something just
happened that has never happened
before. Nothing seems familiar. And then
suddenly the feeling is gone. Vujà dé."

George Carlin, *Funny Times*, December 2001

FIGURE 9.17

Familiar context activates memory
After learning to move a mobile by kicking,
infants had their learning reactivated most
strongly when retested in the same rather
than a different context. (From Butler &
Rovee-Collier, 1989.)

"When a feeling was there, they felt as if it would never go; when it was gone, they felt as if it had never been; when it returned, they felt as if it had never gone."

George MacDonald, *What's Mine's Mine*, 1886

CALLAHAN

"I wonder if you'd mind giving me directions. I've never been sober in this part of town before."

Mood and memory
Elated, we remember other happy times and expect more such times. Mood serves as a retrieval cue, activating other memories associated with the same emotion. These memories help sustain the current mood.

Or perhaps, suggests James Lampinen (2002), a situation seems familiar when moderately similar to several events. Imagine you briefly encounter my dad, my brothers, my sister, my children, and a few weeks later meet me. Perhaps you might think, "I've been with this guy before." Although no one in my family looks or acts just like me (lucky them), their looks and gestures are somewhat like mine and I might form a "global match" to what you had experienced.

Moods and Memories

OBJECTIVE 17 | Describe the effects of internal states on retrieval.

Associated words, events, and contexts are not the only retrieval cues. Events in the past may have aroused a specific *emotion* that later can prime us to recall its associated events. Cognitive psychologist Gordon Bower (1983) explained it this way: "An emotion is like a library room into which we place memory records. We best retrieve those records by returning to that emotional room." What we learn in one state—be it joyful or sad, drunk or sober—is sometimes more easily recalled when we are again in that state, a subtle phenomenon called *state-dependent memory*. What people learn when depressed or drunk they don't recall well in *any* state (depression disrupts encoding and alcohol disrupts storage). But they recall it slightly better when again depressed or drunk. Someone who hides money when drunk may forget the location until drunk again.

Our moods similarly bias our memories. We seem to associate good or bad events with their accompanying emotions, which become retrieval cues (Fiedler & others, 2001). Thus, our memories are somewhat **mood-congruent.** Being depressed sours memories by priming negative associations, which we then use to explain our current mood. If put in a buoyant mood—whether under hypnosis or just by the day's events (a World Cup soccer victory for the German participants in one study)—people recall the world through rose-colored glasses (DeSteno & others, 2000; Forgas & others, 1984; Schwarz & others, 1987). They judge themselves competent and effective, other people benevolent, happy events more likely.

Knowing this connection, we should not be surprised that in some studies *currently* depressed people recall their parents as rejecting, punitive, and guilt-promoting, whereas *formerly* depressed people describe their parents much as do those who have never suffered depression (Lewinsohn & Rosenbaum, 1987; Lewis, 1992). No wonder Robert Bornstein and others (1991) report that adolescents' ratings of parental warmth give little clue to how the same adolescents will rate their parents six weeks later. When teenagers are down, their parents seem inhuman; as their mood brightens, their parents morph from devils into angels. You and I may nod our heads knowingly. Yet, in a good or bad mood, we persist in attributing to reality our own changing judgments and memories.

Moods also influence how we *interpret* other people's behavior. Being mindful of our feelings can help us correct for the mood bias (McFarland & others, 2003). Still, the phenomenon is hard to resist. In a bad mood we read someone's look as a glare; in a good mood we encode the same look as interest. How we perceive the world depends on our mood. Passions exaggerate.

Your mood's effect on retrieval helps explain why moods persist. When happy, you recall happy events and therefore see the world as a happy place, which helps prolong the good mood. When depressed, you recall sad events, which darkens your interpretations of current events. As we will see in Chapter 16, this process can maintain a vicious cycle of depression.

■ **mood-congruent memory** the tendency to recall experiences that are consistent with one's current good or bad mood.

Answers to questions on page 371: Multiple-choice questions test recognition. Fill-in-the-blank questions test recall.

>> LEARNING OUTCOMES

Retrieval: Getting Information Out

OBJECTIVE 14 | **Contrast recall, recognition, and relearning measures of memory.**

Recall is the ability to *retrieve* information not in conscious awareness; a fill-in-the-blank question tests recall. *Recognition* is the ability to *identify* items previously learned; a multiple-choice question tests recognition. *Relearning* is the ability to *master* previously stored information more quickly than you originally learned it.

OBJECTIVE 15 | **Explain how retrieval cues help us access stored memories, and describe the process of priming.**

Retrieval cues are bits of related information we encode while processing a target piece of information. These bits are linked in some way to the context of the target, and they become a part of a web of stored associations. When one of these associated bits catches our attention, it is as though we are pulling on a strand in the web of associations, retrieving the target information into our conscious awareness. This process of activating associations (often unconsciously) is *priming*.

OBJECTIVE 16 | **Cite some ways that context can affect retrieval.**

The context in which we originally experienced an event or encoded a thought can flood our memories with retrieval cues, leading us to the target memory. If we are in a different context that is very similar to the original one, we may experience déjà vu as many of these cues return and trick us into unconsciously retrieving the target memory.

OBJECTIVE 17 | **Describe the effects of internal states on retrieval.**

Specific states or emotions can prime us to recall events associated with those states or emotions. While in a good mood, we tend to retrieve memories consistent—or congruent—with that happy state. When depressed, we more easily recall negative memories. Moods also prime us to interpret others' behavior in ways consistent with our emotions.

ASK YOURSELF: **What sort of mood have you been in lately? How has your mood colored your memories, perceptions, and expectations?**

Forgetting

OBJECTIVE 18 | Explain why we should value our ability to forget, and distinguish three general ways our memory fails us.

Amid all the applause for memory—all the efforts to understand it, all the books on how to improve it—have any voices been heard in praise of forgetting? William James (1890, p. 680) was such a voice: "If we remembered everything, we should on most occasions be as ill off as if we remembered nothing." To discard the clutter of useless or out-of-date information—where we parked the car yesterday, a friend's old phone number, restaurant orders already cooked and served—is surely a blessing. The Russian memory whiz S, whom we met at the beginning of this chapter, was haunted by his junk heap of memories. They dominated his consciousness. He had difficulty thinking abstractly—generalizing, organizing, evaluating. A good memory is helpful, but so is the ability to forget. If a memory-enhancing pill becomes available, it had better not be too effective.

" Happiness is nothing more than health and a poor memory."
Physician Albert Schweitzer (1875–1965)

Cellist Yo-Yo Ma forgot his 266-year-old, $2.5 million cello in a New York taxi. (He later recovered it.)

More often, however, our memory dismays and frustrates us. Memories are quirky. My own memory can easily call up such episodes as that wonderful first kiss with the woman I love or trivial facts like the air mileage from London to Detroit. Then it abandons me when I'm trying to recall that new colleague's name or where I left my sunglasses, and discover that I have failed to encode, store, or retrieve the information. Memory researcher Daniel Schacter (1999) enumerates seven ways our memories fail us—the seven sins of memory, he calls them:

Three sins of forgetting:

- *Absent-mindedness*—inattention to details produces encoding failure (our mind is elsewhere as we lay down the car keys).
- *Transience*—storage decay over time (after we part ways with former classmates, unused information fades).
- *Blocking*—inaccessibility of stored information (seeing an old classmate, we may feel the name on the tip of our tongue, but we experience retrieval failure—we cannot get it out).

Three sins of distortion:

- *Misattribution*—confusing the source of information (putting words in someone else's mouth or remembering a movie scene as an actual happening).
- *Suggestibility*—the lingering effects of misinformation (a leading question—"Did Mr. Jones touch your private parts?"—later becomes a young child's false memory).
- *Bias*—belief-colored recollections (a friend's current feelings toward her fiancé may color her recalled initial feelings).

One sin of intrusion:

- *Persistence*—unwanted memories (being haunted by images of a sexual assault).

Let's first consider the sins of forgetting, then those of distortion and intrusion.

"Amnesia seeps into the crevices of our brains, and amnesia heals."
Joyce Carol Oates, "Words Fail, Memory Blurs, Life Wins," 2001

Encoding Failure

OBJECTIVE 19 | Discuss the role of encoding failure in forgetting.

We cannot remember what we fail to encode, because the information never enters long-term memory (**FIGURE 9.18**). And as our "change blindness" (page 239) demonstrates, much of what we sense we never notice. Age can affect encoding efficiency. The same brain areas that jump into action when young adults are encoding new information are less responsive among older adults. This slower encoding helps explain age-related memory decline (Grady & others, 1995). (As Chapter 4 noted, older people tend to *recall* less than younger adults do, but they usually remember as well as younger people when given reminders or a recognition test.)

But no matter how young we are, we selectively attend to few of the myriad sights and sounds continually bombarding us. Consider something you have looked at countless times: What letters accompany the number 5 on your telephone? For most of us, the question is surprisingly difficult.

"Each of us finds that in [our] own life every moment of time is completely filled. [We are] bombarded every second by sensations, emotions, thoughts . . . nine-tenths of which [we] must simply ignore. The past [is] a roaring cataract of billions upon billions of such moments: Any one of them too complex to grasp in its entirety, and the aggregate beyond all imagination. . . . At every tick of the clock, in every inhabited part of the world, an unimaginable richness and variety of 'history' falls off the world into total oblivion."
English novelist-critic C. S. Lewis (1967)

FIGURE 9.18
Forgetting as encoding failure
We cannot remember what we have not encoded.

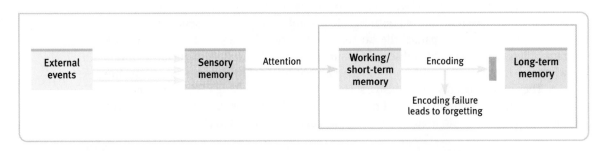

External events → Sensory memory → (Attention) → Working/short-term memory → (Encoding) → Long-term memory

Encoding failure leads to forgetting

Here's another example of encoding failure. If you live in North America, Britain, or Australia, you have looked at thousands of pennies in your lifetime. You can surely recall their color and size, but can you recall what the side with the head looks like? If not, let's make the memory test easier: If you are familiar with U.S. coins, can you recognize the real thing in **FIGURE 9.19**? Most people cannot (Nickerson & Adams, 1979). Of the eight critical features (Lincoln's head, date, "In God we trust," and so on), the average person spontaneously remembers only three. Likewise, few British people can draw from memory the one-pence coin (Richardson, 1993). The details of a penny are not very meaningful—nor are they essential for distinguishing pennies from other coins—and few of us have made the effort to encode them. As we noted earlier, we encode some information—where we had dinner yesterday—automatically; other types of information—like the concepts in this chapter—require effortful processing. Without effort, many memories never form.

Storage Decay

OBJECTIVE **20** | Discuss the concept of storage decay, and describe Ebbinghaus' forgetting curve.

Even after encoding something well, we sometimes later forget it. To study the durability of our stored memories, Ebbinghaus (1885) learned more lists of nonsense syllables and measured how much he retained when relearning each list, from 20 minutes to 30 days later. His famous *forgetting curve* (**FIGURE 9.20**) indicates that much of what we learn we may indeed quickly forget. Later experiments made the forgetting curve into one of psychology's laws: The course of forgetting is initially rapid, then levels off with time (Wixted & Ebbesen, 1991).

Harry Bahrick (1984) extended Ebbinghaus' finding. He examined the forgetting curve for Spanish vocabulary learned in school. Compared with those just completing a high school or college Spanish course, people who had been out of school for 3 years had forgotten much of what they had learned (**FIGURE 9.21**, page 378). However, after

FIGURE 9.19
Test your memory
Which one of these pennies is the real thing? (If you live outside the United States, try drawing one of your own country's coins.) (From Nickerson & Adams, 1979.) (See page 378.)

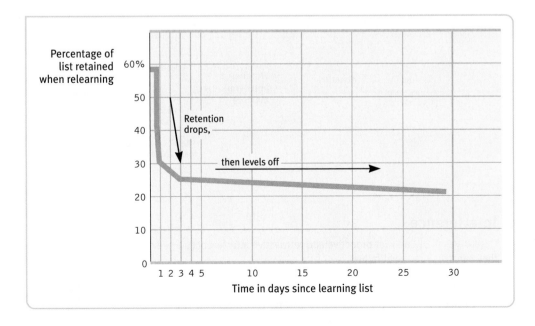

FIGURE 9.20
Ebbinghaus' forgetting curve
After learning lists of nonsense syllables, Ebbinghaus studied how much he retained up to 30 days later. He found that memory for novel information fades quickly, then levels out. (Adapted from Ebbinghaus, 1885.)

Andrew Holbrooke/Corbis

FIGURE 9.21
The forgetting curve for Spanish learned in school
Compared with people just completing a Spanish course, those 3 years out of the course remembered much less. Compared with the 3-year group, however, those who studied Spanish even longer ago did not forget much more. (Adapted from Bahrick, 1984.)

Answer to question on page 377: The first penny (a) is the real penny.

Deaf persons fluent in sign language experience a parallel "tip of the fingers" phenomenon (Thompson & others, 2005).

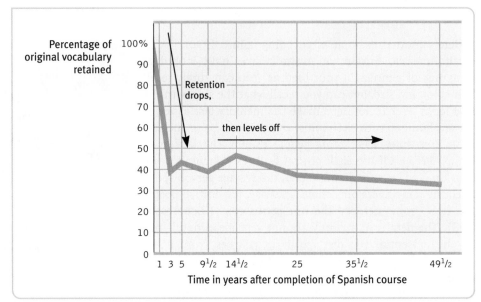

Percentage of original vocabulary retained — Retention drops, then levels off — Time in years after completion of Spanish course

roughly 3 years, their forgetting leveled off; what people remembered then, they still remembered 25 and more years later, even if they had not used their Spanish at all.

One explanation for these forgetting curves is a gradual fading of the physical memory trace. As we are learning more about the physical storage of memory, we are better understanding how memory storage can decay. But memories also fade because of the accumulation of other learning that disrupts our retrieval.

Retrieval Failure

We have seen that forgotten events are like books you can't find in your campus library—some because they were never acquired (not encoded), others because they were discarded (stored memories decay).

But there is a third possibility: Even if the book is stored and available, it may be inaccessible. Perhaps you lack the information needed to look it up and retrieve it. Information sometimes gets into our brain and, though we know it is there, we cannot get it out (**FIGURE 9.22**). A name may lie poised on the tip of the tongue, waiting to be retrieved. Given retrieval cues ("It begins with an *M*"), we may easily retrieve an elusive memory. Retrieval problems contribute to older adults' occasional memory failures. Forgetting is often not memories discarded but memories unretrieved.

FIGURE 9.22
Retrieval failure
We store in long-term memory what's important to us or what we've rehearsed. But sometimes even stored information cannot be accessed, which leads to forgetting.

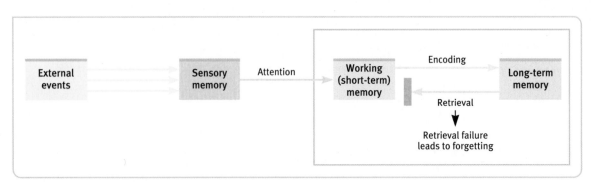

Interference

OBJECTIVE 21 | Contrast proactive and retroactive interference, and explain how they can cause retrieval failure.

Learning some items may interfere with retrieving others, especially when the items are similar. If someone gives you a phone number, you may be able to recall it later.

But if two more people give you their numbers, each successive number will be more difficult to recall. Likewise, if you buy a new combination lock or get a new phone number, your memory of the old one may interfere. Such **proactive** (*forward-acting*) **interference** occurs when something you learned earlier disrupts your recall of something you experience later. As you collect more and more information, your mental attic never fills, but it certainly gets cluttered.

Benton Underwood (1957) found that those who learn different lists of words on successive days have more and more difficulty remembering each new list the next day. This proactive interference explains why Ebbinghaus, after memorizing countless lists of nonsense syllables during his career, could remember only about one-fourth of a new list of syllables on the day after he learned it—far fewer than you as a novice could remember after learning a single list.

Retroactive (*backward-acting*) **interference** occurs when new information makes it harder to recall something you learned earlier (**FIGURE 9.23**). For example, learning new students' names typically interferes with a teacher's recall of the names of previous students. It is rather like a second stone tossed in a pond, disrupting the waves rippling out from a first.

You can minimize retroactive interference by reducing the number of interfering events—say, by going for a walk or to sleep shortly after learning new information. Researchers John Jenkins and Karl Dallenbach (1924) discovered the sleep benefit in a now-classic experiment. Day after day, two people each learned some nonsense syllables, then tried to recall them after up to eight hours of being awake or asleep at night.

■ **proactive interference** the disruptive effect of prior learning on the recall of new information.

■ **retroactive interference** the disruptive effect of new learning on the recall of old information.

FIGURE 9.23
Proactive and retroactive interference

French, learned beforehand, interferes proactively

Study French — papier livre plume école

Study Spanish — papel libro pluma escuela

proactive interference

Spanish, learned afterward, interferes retroactively

Study French — papier livre plume école

Study Spanish — papel libro pluma escuela

retroactive interference

Spanish 101 Mid-term exam

French 101 Mid-term exam

FIGURE **9.24**
Retroactive interference
More forgetting occurred when a person stayed awake and experienced other new material. (From Jenkins & Dallenbach, 1924.)

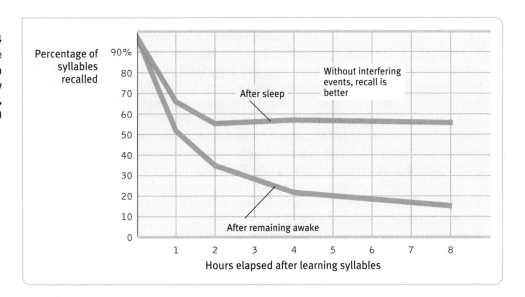

■ **repression** in psychoanalytic theory, the basic defense mechanism that banishes from consciousness anxiety-arousing thoughts, feelings, and memories.

As **FIGURE 9.24** shows, forgetting occurred more rapidly after being awake and involved with other activities. The investigators surmised that "forgetting is not so much a matter of the decay of old impressions and associations as it is a matter of interference, inhibition, or obliteration of the old by the new" (1924, p. 612). Later experiments have confirmed the benefits of sleep and found that the hour before a night's sleep (but not the minute before sleep) is a good time to commit information to memory (Benson & Feinberg, 1977; Fowler & others, 1973; Nesca & Koulack, 1994).

Interference is an important cause of forgetting, and may explain why ads viewed during violent or sexual TV programs are so forgettable (Bushman & Bonacci, 2002). But we should not overstate the point. Sometimes old information can facilitate our learning of new information. Knowing Latin may help us to learn French—a phenomenon called *positive transfer*. It is when old and new information compete with each other that interference occurs.

Motivated Forgetting

OBJECTIVE **22** | Summarize Freud's concept of repression, and state whether this view is reflected in current memory research.

The huge cookie jar in our kitchen was jammed with freshly baked chocolate chip cookies. Still more were cooling across racks on the counter. Twenty-four hours later, not a crumb was left. Who had taken them? During that time, my wife, three children, and I were the only people in the house. So while memories were still fresh, I conducted a little memory test. Andy acknowledged wolfing down as many as 20. Peter admitted eating 15. Laura guessed she had stuffed her then-6-year-old body with 15 cookies. My wife, Carol, recalled eating 6, and I remembered consuming 15 and taking 18 more to the office. We sheepishly accepted responsibility for 89 cookies. Still, we had not come close; there had been 160.

In experiments that parallel the cookie-memory phenomenon, Michael Ross and his colleagues (1981) found that people unknowingly revise their own histories. After Ross persuaded a group of people that frequently brushing their teeth is desirable, they (more than other people) recalled having frequently brushed their teeth in the last two weeks. Having taken a highly touted study skills course, students later inflated their estimates of self-improvement. By *de*flating their evaluations of their previous study habits, they convinced themselves that they had really benefited (Conway & Ross, 1984). To remember our past is often to revise it.

Why do our memories fail us? Why did my family and I not encode, store, and retrieve the actual number of cookies each of us ate? As **FIGURE 9.25** reminds us, we

"[It is] necessary to remember that events happened in the desired manner. And if it is necessary to rearrange one's memories . . . then it is necessary to forget that one has done so. The trick of doing this can be learned like any other mental technique. . . . It is called doublethink."

George Orwell, *Nineteen Eighty-Four*, 1948

automatically encode sensory information in amazing detail. So was it a storage problem? Might our memories of cookies, like Ebbinghaus' memory of nonsense syllables, have vanished almost as fast as the cookies themselves? Or might the information still be intact but irretrievable because it would be embarrassing to remember?[1]

With his concept of **repression,** Sigmund Freud proposed that our memory systems do indeed self-censor painful information. To protect our self-concept and to minimize anxiety, we supposedly repress painful memories. But the submerged memory lingers, said Freud, and with patience and effort may be retrieved by some later cue or during therapy. One reported case involved a woman with an intense, unexplained fear of running water. One day an aunt solved the mystery. She whispered, "I have never told." The words relit a blown-out candle in the mind; they cued the woman's memory of an incident when, as a disobedient young child, she wandered away from a family picnic and became trapped under a waterfall—until being rescued by her aunt, who promised not to tell her parents (Kihlstrom, 1990). Such stories have fed the now-common belief, shared by 9 in 10 university students, that "memories for painful experiences are sometimes pushed into unconsciousness" (Brown & others, 1996). Repression was central to Freud's psychology and became part of psychology's lore. Most everyone believes it. Therapists often assume it. Yet increasing numbers of memory researchers think repression rarely, if ever, occurs. Earlier we noted that emotions and associated stress hormones *strengthen* memories. But what about horrible happenings? Do people typically have trouble remembering traumatic experiences, or trouble forgetting them? Stay tuned.

[1]One of my cookie-scarfing sons, on reading this in his father's textbook years later, confessed that he had fibbed "a little."

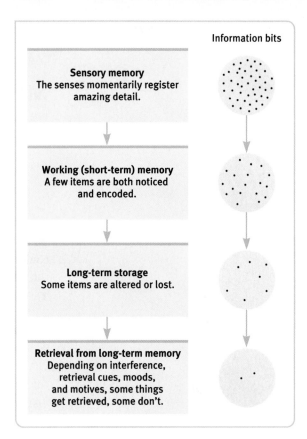

FIGURE 9.25
When do we forget?
Forgetting can occur at any memory stage. As we process information, we filter, alter, or lose much of it.

>> LEARNING OUTCOMES

Forgetting

OBJECTIVE 18 | **Explain why we should value our ability to forget, and distinguish three general ways our memory fails us.**
Without an ability to forget, we would be overwhelmed by out-of-date and irrelevant information. Our memory can fail us through *forgetting* (absent-mindedness, transience, and blocking), through *distortion* (misattribution, suggestibility, and bias), and through *intrusion* (persistence of unwanted memories).

OBJECTIVE 19 | **Discuss the role of encoding failure in forgetting.**
What we encode (whether automatically or through effortful processing) is only a very limited portion of the sensory stimuli around us. And as we age, our encoding grows slower and less efficient. Without encoding, information does not enter our long-term memory store and cannot be retrieved.

OBJECTIVE 20 | **Discuss the concept of storage decay, and describe Ebbinghaus' forgetting curve.**
Encoded memories may fade after storage. From his research on learning and retention, Ebbinghaus determined that the course of forgetting is initially rapid, then levels off with time; this principle became known as the forgetting curve.

OBJECTIVE 21 | **Contrast proactive and retroactive interference, and explain how they can cause retrieval failure.**
One way retrieval failure happens is when old and new information compete for retrieval. In *proactive interference,* something we learned in the past (a friend's old phone number) interferes with our ability to recall something we have recently learned (the friend's new number). In *retroactive interference,* something we have recently learned (vocabulary in this semester's Spanish course) interferes with something we learned in the past (vocabulary in last year's French course).

OBJECTIVE 22 | **Summarize Freud's concept of repression, and state whether this view is reflected in current memory research.**
Freud believed that we banish from conscious thought anxiety-arousing thoughts, feelings, and memories—a concept he called *repression.* In his view, this motivated forgetting submerges memories but leaves them available for later retrieval under the right conditions. Memory researchers tend to believe that repression rarely occurs.

ASK YOURSELF: Most people, especially as they grow older, wish for a better memory. Is that true of you? Or do you more often wish you could discard old memories?

Memory Construction

Picture yourself having this experience:

> You go to a fancy restaurant for dinner. You are seated at a table with a white tablecloth. You study the menu. You tell the server you want prime rib, medium rare, a baked potato with sour cream, and a salad with blue cheese dressing. You also order some red wine from the wine list. A few minutes later the server returns with your salad. Later the rest of the meal arrives. You enjoy it all, except the prime rib is a bit overdone.

Were I immediately to quiz you on this paragraph (adapted from Hyde, 1983), you could surely retrieve considerable detail. For example, without looking back, answer the following questions:

1. What kind of salad dressing did you order?
2. Was the tablecloth red checked?
3. What did you order to drink?
4. Did the server give you a menu?

You were probably able to recall exactly what you ordered, and maybe even the color of the tablecloth. We do have an enormous capacity for storing and reproducing the incidental details of our daily experience. But did the server give you a menu? Not in the paragraph given. Nevertheless, many answer yes. We often construct our memories as we encode them, and we may also alter our memories as we withdraw them from our memory bank. Like a scientist who infers a dinosaur's appearance from its remains, we infer our past from stored information plus what we now assume. By filtering information and filling in missing pieces, your schema for restaurants directed your memory construction.

Misinformation and Imagination Effects

OBJECTIVE 23 | Explain how misinformation and imagination can distort our memory of an event.

In more than 200 experiments, involving more than 20,000 people, Elizabeth Loftus has shown how eyewitnesses similarly reconstruct their memories when questioned. In one classic experiment with John Palmer, Loftus showed people a film of a traffic accident and then quizzed them about what they saw (Loftus & Palmer, 1974). Those asked, "How fast were the cars going when they *smashed* into each other?" gave higher speed estimates than those asked, "How fast were the cars going when they *hit* each other?" A week later, the researchers asked the viewers if they recalled seeing any broken glass. Compared with those asked the question with *hit*, those who had heard *smashed* were more than twice as likely to say they had seen broken glass (**FIGURE 9.26**). In fact, the film showed no broken glass.

FIGURE 9.26
Memory construction
When people who had seen the film of a car accident were later asked a leading question, they recalled a more serious accident than they had witnessed. (From Loftus, 1979.)

Depiction of actual accident

Memory construction

Leading question:
"About how fast were the cars going when they *smashed* into each other?"

DOONESBURY

By Garry Trudeau
DOONESBURY © 1994 G. B. Trudeau. Reprinted with permission of UNIVERSAL PRESS SYNDICATE.

In many follow-up experiments around the world, people have witnessed an event, received or not received misleading information about it, and then taken a memory test. The repeated result is a **misinformation effect:** After exposure to subtle misinformation, many people misremember. They have misrecalled a yield (give way) sign as a stop sign, hammers as screwdrivers, Coke cans as peanut cans, *Vogue* magazine as *Mademoiselle,* "Dr. Henderson" as "Dr. Davidson," breakfast cereal as eggs, and a clean-shaven man as a man with a mustache (Loftus & others, 1992). As a memory fades with time following an event, the injection of misinformation becomes easier (Loftus, 1992).

So unwitting is the misinformation effect that people later find it nearly impossible to discriminate between their memories of real and suggested events (Schooler & others, 1986). As we recount an experience, we fill in memory gaps with plausible guesses and assumptions. After more retellings, we often recall the guessed details, which have now been absorbed into our memories, as if we had actually observed them (Roediger & others, 1993). Others' vivid retelling of an event may also implant false memories.

Even repeatedly *imagining* nonexistent actions and events can create false memories. In one laboratory experiment, students who repeatedly imagined simple acts such as breaking a toothpick or picking up a stapler later experienced "imagination inflation"; they were more likely to think they had actually done such things during the experiment's first phase (Goff & Roediger, 1998). Two other experiments invited American and British university students to imagine certain childhood events, such as breaking a window with their hand or having a nurse remove a skin sample from their little finger. In both, one-fourth came to recall that the imagined event really happened (Garry & others, 1996; Mazzoni & Memon, 2003). Imagination inflation occurs partly because visualizing something and actually perceiving it activate similar brain areas (Gonsalves & others, 2004).

Imagined events later seem more familiar, and familiar things seem more real. Thus the more vividly people can imagine things, the more likely they are to inflate their imaginations into memories (Loftus, 2001; Porter & others, 2000). People who believe they have been abducted by aliens for medical exams on spaceships tend to have powerful imaginations and, in memory tests, to be more susceptible to false memories (Clancy & others, 2002). Those who believe they have recovered memories of childhood sexual abuse likewise tend to have vivid imaginations and to score high on false memory tests (Clancy & others, 2000; McNally, 2003).

"Memory is insubstantial. Things keep replacing it. Your batch of snapshots will both fix and ruin your memory.... You can't remember anything from your trip except the wretched collection of snapshots."

Annie Dillard, "To Fashion a Text," 1988

■ **misinformation effect** incorporating misleading information into one's memory of an event.

■ **source amnesia** attributing to the wrong source an event we have experienced, heard about, read about, or imagined. (Also called *source misattribution*.) Source amnesia, along with the misinformation effect, is at the heart of many false memories.

" It isn't so astonishing, the number of things I can remember, as the number of things I can remember that aren't so."

Mark Twain (1835–1910)

Authors and songwriters sometimes suffer source amnesia. They think an idea came from their own creative imagination, when in fact they are unintentionally plagiarizing something they earlier read or heard.

To see how far the mind's search for a fact will go in creating a fiction, Richard Wiseman and his University of Hertfordshire colleagues (1999) staged eight seances, each attended by 25 curious people. During the supposed seance, the medium—actually a professional actor and magician—asked everyone to concentrate on the moving table. Although it never moved, he suggested that it had: "That's good. Lift the table up. That's good. Keep concentrating. Keep the table in the air." When questioned two weeks later, 34 percent of the participants recalled having actually seen the table levitate.

We psychologists are not immune to memory construction. The psychologist Jean Piaget was startled as an adult to learn that his vivid, detailed memory of his nursemaid's thwarting his kidnapping was utterly false. Piaget apparently constructed the memory from the many retellings of the story he had heard (which his nursemaid, after undergoing a religious conversion, later confessed to have been false).

Source Amnesia

OBJECTIVE 24 | Describe source amnesia's contribution to false memories.

Piaget remembered, but attributed his memory to the wrong sources (to his own experience rather than to his nursemaid's stories). When we encode memories, we distribute different aspects of them to different parts of the brain. Among the frailest parts of a memory is its source. Thus, we may recognize someone but have no idea where we have seen the person. Or we imagine or dream an event and later are unsure whether it really happened. Or we may hear something and later recall seeing it (Henkel & others, 2000). In all these cases, we retain the image, but not the context in which we acquired it.

Debra Poole and Stephen Lindsay (1995, 2001, 2002) replicated Piaget's **source amnesia** (also called *source misattribution*). They had preschoolers interact with "Mr. Science," who engaged them in demonstrations such as blowing up a balloon with baking soda and vinegar. Three months later, their parents on three successive days read them a story about themselves and Mr. Science. The stories described some things they had experienced and some they had not. When asked by a new interviewer what Mr. Science had done with them—"Did Mr. Science have a machine with ropes to pull?"—4 in 10 children spontaneously recalled Mr. Science doing things that were only in the story.

Discerning True and False Memories

OBJECTIVE 25 | List some differences and similarities between true and false memories.

Because memory is reconstruction as well as reproduction, we can't be sure whether a memory is real by how real it feels. Much as perceptual illusions may seem like real perceptions, unreal memories feel like real memories.

Indeed, note today's researchers, memories are akin to perceptions—perceptions of the past (Koriat & others, 2000). And as Jamin Halberstadt and Paula Niedenthal (2001) show, people's initial interpretations influence their perceptual memories. They invited New Zealand university students to view morphed faces that expressed a mix of emotions, such as happiness and anger (**FIGURE 9.27a**), and to imagine and explain "why this person is feeling angry [or happy]." A half-hour later, the researchers asked the students to view a computer video showing a morphed transition from the angry to happy face, and to slide a bar to change the face's expression until it matched the expression they had seen earlier (**FIGURE 9.27b**). Students who had explained anger ("This woman is angry because her best friend has cheated on her with

(a)   (b)

© Simon Niedenthal

FIGURE 9.27
Our assumptions alter our perceptual memories
Researchers showed people faces with computer-blended expressions, such as the angry/happy face in (a), then asked them to explain why the person was either angry or happy. Those asked to explain an "angry" expression later (when sliding a bar on a morphing movie to identify the earlier-seen face) remembered an angrier face, such as the one shown in (b).

her boyfriend") recalled the face as angrier than did those who had explained happiness ("This woman is very happy that everyone remembered her birthday").

We also cannot judge a memory's reality by its persistence. Memory researchers Charles Brainerd and Valerie Reyna (Brainerd & others, 1995, 1998, 2002) note that memories we derive from experience have more detail than memories we derive from imagination. Memories of imagined experiences are more restricted to the *gist* of the supposed event—the meanings and feelings we associate with it. Because gist memories are durable, children's false memories sometimes outlast their true memories, especially as children mature and become better able to process the gist (Brainerd & Poole, 1997). And when therapists or investigators ask for the gist rather than the details, they run a greater risk of eliciting false memories.

False memories created by suggested misinformation and misattributed sources may *feel* as real as true memories and may be very persistent. Imagine that I were to read aloud a list of words such as *candy, sugar, honey,* and *taste.* Later, I ask you to recognize the presented words from a larger list. If you are at all like the people tested by Henry Roediger and Kathleen McDermott (1995), you would err three out of four times—by falsely remembering a nonpresented similar word such as *sweet.* We more easily remember the gist than the words themselves.

In experiments on eyewitness testimony, researchers have repeatedly found that the most confident and consistent eyewitnesses are the most persuasive; however, they often are not the most accurate. Eyewitnesses, whether right or wrong, express roughly similar self-assurance (Bothwell & others, 1987; Cutler & Penrod, 1989; Wells & Murray, 1984).

Memory construction helps explain why "hypnotically refreshed" memories of crimes so easily incorporate errors, some of which originate with the hypnotist's leading questions ("Did you hear loud noises?"). It explains why dating partners who fall in love *over*estimate their first impressions of one another ("It was love at first sight"), while those who break up *under*estimate their earlier liking ("We never really clicked") (McFarland & Ross, 1987). And it explains why people who are asked how they felt 10 years ago about marijuana or gender issues recall attitudes closer to their current views than to the views they actually reported a decade earlier (Markus, 1986).

One research team interviewed 73 ninth-grade boys and then reinterviewed them 35 years later. When asked to recall how they had reported their attitudes, activities, and experiences, most men recalled statements that matched their actual prior responses at a rate no better than chance. One in three now remembered receiving physical punishment, though as ninth-graders 82 percent said they had (Offer & others, 2000). As George Vaillant (1977, p. 197) noted after following adult lives through time, "It is all too common for caterpillars to become butterflies and then to maintain that in their youth they had been little butterflies. Maturation makes liars of us all."

Older adults' susceptibility to suggested false memories makes them vulnerable to scams, as when a repairman overcharges by falsely claiming "I told you it would cost *X* and you agreed to pay" (Jacoby & others, 2005).

"Memory isn't like reading a book; it's more like writing a book from fragmentary notes."
Psychologist John F. Kihlstrom (1994)

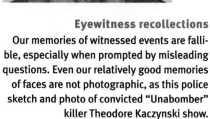

Eyewitness recollections
Our memories of witnessed events are fallible, especially when prompted by misleading
questions. Even our relatively good memories
of faces are not photographic, as this police
sketch and photo of convicted "Unabomber"
killer Theodore Kaczynski show.

Australian psychologist Donald Thompson found his
own work on memory distortion ironically haunting him
when authorities brought him in for questioning about a
rape. Although he was a near-perfect match to the victim's
memory of the rapist, he had an airtight alibi. Just before
the rape occurred, Thompson was being interviewed on live
television. He could not possibly have made it to the crime
scene. Then it came to light that the victim had been watching the interview—ironically about face recognition—and
had experienced source amnesia, confusing her memories
of Thompson with those of the rapist (Schacter, 1996).

Recognizing that the misinformation effect can occur as
police and attorneys ask questions framed by their own understandings of an event, Ronald Fisher, Edward Geiselman, and their colleagues
(1987, 1992) train police interviewers to ask less suggestive, more effective questions.
To activate retrieval cues, the detective first asks witnesses to visualize the scene—the
weather, time of day, lighting, sounds, smells, positions of objects, and their mood.
Then the witness tells in detail, and without interruption, every point recalled, no
matter how trivial. Only then does the detective ask evocative follow-up questions:
"Was there anything unusual about the person's appearance or clothing?" When this
cognitive interview technique is used, Fisher and Geiselman report, accurate recall increases by some 50 percent.

Children's Eyewitness Recall

OBJECTIVE 26 | Give arguments supporting and rejecting the position that very
young children's reports of abuse are reliable.

If memories can be sincere, yet sincerely wrong, might children's recollections of sexual abuse be prone to err? Who is most often victimized—abused children whose recollections are disbelieved or falsely accused adults whose reputations are ruined?

At issue is the reliability of children's reports. As we have seen, interviewers who
ask leading questions can plant false memories. We also know that although children
are sometimes accurate eyewitnesses in criminal cases, they tend to be suggestible.
Many young children have falsely reported that a nurse had licked their knee, a man
had put "something yucky" in their mouth, their doctor had put a stick in their genitals, and someone had touched their private parts. When suggestive interview techniques are added, most preschoolers and many older children can be induced to
report false events, such as seeing a thief steal food in their day-care center (Bruck &
Ceci, 1999, 2004).

Nevertheless, if questioned about their experiences in neutral words they understand, children often accurately recall what happened and who did it (Goodman &
others, 1990; Howe, 1997; Pipe, 1996). When the cognitive interview described earlier
is used, even 4- to 5-year-old children produce more accurate recall (Holliday &
Albon, 2004; Pipe & others, 2004). Children are especially accurate when involved
adults have not talked with them prior to the interview and when their disclosure is
made in a first interview with a neutral person who asks nonleading questions.

Studies of children's recollections of physical examinations illustrate both their
reasonable accuracy and occasional lapses. Lynne Baker-Ward and her colleagues
(1993) tested children's memories with general questions ("Tell me what the doctor
did to check you") and specific questions ("Did the doctor shine a light in your
eyes?"). Three to six weeks after the exam, 3-year-olds recalled about 60 percent and
7-year-olds about 90 percent of what the doctor did. Asked about things that didn't

happen ("Did the doctor cut your hair?" "Did the nurse sit on top of you?"), 3-year-olds gave wrong answers nearly 30 percent of the time; 7-year-olds erred only about 15 percent of the time.

Stephen Ceci (1993) thinks "it would be truly awful to ever lose sight of the enormity of child abuse." Yet Ceci and Maggie Bruck's (1993a, 1995) studies of children's memories have sensitized them to children's suggestibility. In one study, they asked 3-year-olds to show on anatomically correct dolls where a pediatrician had touched them. Fifty-five percent of the children who had not received genital examinations pointed to either genital or anal areas.

In another study, Ceci and Bruck had a child choose a card from a deck of possible happenings and an adult then read from the card. For example, "Think real hard, and tell me if this ever happened to you. Can you remember going to the hospital with a mousetrap on your finger?" After 10 weekly interviews, with the same adult repeatedly asking children to think about several real and fictitious events, a new adult asked the same question. The stunning result: 58 percent of preschoolers produced false (often vivid) stories regarding one or more events they had never experienced, as this little boy did (Ceci & others, 1994):

> My brother Colin was trying to get Blowtorch [an action figure] from me, and I wouldn't let him take it from me, so he pushed me into the wood pile where the mousetrap was. And then my finger got caught in it. And then we went to the hospital, and my mommy, daddy, and Colin drove me there, to the hospital in our van, because it was far away. And the doctor put a bandage on this finger.

Given such detailed stories, professional psychologists who specialize in interviewing children were often fooled. They could not reliably separate real memories from false ones. Nor could the children themselves. The above child, reminded that his parents had told him several times that the mousetrap incident never happened—that he had imagined it—protested, "But it really did happen. I remember it!"

"[The] research leads me to worry about the possibility of false allegations. It is not a tribute to one's scientific integrity to walk down the middle of the road if the data are more to one side."

Stephen Ceci (1993)

Repressed or Constructed Memories of Abuse?

OBJECTIVE 27 | Discuss the controversy over reports of repressed and recovered memories of childhood sexual abuse.

During the 1990s, psychology's most intense controversy—the "memory wars"—concerned claims of repressed and recovered memories of childhood sexual abuse. During 2002, such claims surfaced again amid seemingly more credible accusations of sexual abuse by some priests. Are clinicians who have guided people in "recovering" memories of childhood abuse triggering false memories that damage innocent adults, or are they uncovering the truth?

Some therapists have reasoned with patients that "people who've been abused often have your symptoms, so you probably were abused. Let's see if, aided by hypnosis or drugs, or helped to dig back and visualize your trauma, you can recover it." In one American survey, the average therapist estimated that 11 percent of the population—some 34 million people—have repressed memories of childhood sexual abuse (Kamena, 1998). In another survey, of British and American doctoral-level therapists, 7 in 10 said they had used techniques such as hypnosis or drugs to help clients recover suspected repressed memories of childhood sexual abuse (Poole & others, 1995).

As we might expect from the research on source amnesia and the misinformation effect, many patients exposed to such techniques do form an image of a threatening person. With further visualization, the image grows more vivid, leaving the patient stunned, angry, and ready to confront or sue the equally stunned and devastated parent, relative, or clergy member. As the therapist has predicted, the presumed abuser then vigorously denies the accusation. One woman in her thirty-second therapy session recalled that her father had abused her at age 15 months. After such aided recall, actress Roseanne Barr (1991) claimed to have recovered memories of sexual abuse beginning in infancy.

Without questioning the professionalism of most therapists, skeptics compare the uncorroborated accusations suggested by some therapists to a 1990s reenactment of the Salem witch trials. Clinicians who use "memory work" techniques such as "guided imagery," hypnosis, and dream analysis to recover memories "are nothing more than merchants of mental chaos, and, in fact, constitute a blight on the entire field of psychotherapy," charged some scientific critics (Loftus & others, 1995). Irate clinicians counter that those who dispute recovered memories of abuse add to abused people's trauma and play into the hands of child molesters.

In an effort to find a sensible common ground that might resolve this ideological battle, study panels have been convened and public statements made by the American Medical, American Psychological, and American Psychiatric Associations; the Australian Psychological Society; the British Psychological Society; and the Canadian Psychiatric Association. Those committed to protecting abused children and those committed to protecting wrongly accused adults agree on the following:

- *Injustice happens.* Some innocent people have been falsely convicted. Some guilty people have evaded responsibility by casting doubt on their truth-telling accusers.

- *Incest and other sexual abuse happen.* And it happens more often than we once supposed. There is no characteristic "survivor syndrome" (Kendall-Tackett & others, 1993). However, sexual abuse can leave its victims predisposed to problems ranging from sexual dysfunction to depression.

- *Forgetting happens.* Many of the abused were either very young when abused or may not have understood the meaning of their experience—circumstances under which forgetting is "utterly common." Forgetting isolated past events, both negative and positive, is an ordinary part of everyday life.

- *Recovered memories are commonplace.* Cued by a remark or an experience, we recover memories of long-forgotten events, both pleasant and unpleasant. What is debated is whether the unconscious mind sometimes forcibly represses painful experiences and, if so, whether these can be retrieved by certain therapist-aided techniques.

- *Memories "recovered" under hypnosis or the influence of drugs are especially unreliable.* "Age-regressed" hypnotized subjects incorporate suggestions into their memories, even memories of "past lives."

- *Memories of things happening before age 3 are also unreliable.* People do not reliably recall happenings of any sort from their first 3 years—a phenomenon called *infantile amnesia.* Most psychologists—including most clinical and counseling psychologists—therefore are skeptical of "recovered" memories of abuse during infancy (Gore-Felton & others, 2000; Knapp & Vande Creek, 2000). The older a child's age when suffering sexual abuse, and the more severe it was, the more likely it is to be remembered (Goodman & others, 2003).

- *Memories, whether real or false, can be emotionally upsetting.* If a false memory of abuse becomes a real part of one's history, both the accuser and the accused may suffer. What was born of mere suggestion can, like an actual trauma, become a stinging memory that may drive bodily stress (McNally, 2003). People knocked unconscious by unremembered accidents sometimes later develop stress disorders when haunted by memories constructed from photos, news reports, and friends' accounts (Bryant, 2001).

To more closely approximate therapist-aided recall, Elizabeth Loftus and her colleagues (1996) have experimentally implanted false memories of childhood traumas.

"When memories are 'recovered' after long periods of amnesia, particularly when extraordinary means were used to secure the recovery of memory, there is a high probability that the memories are false."
Royal College of Psychiatrists Working Group on Reported Recovered Memories of Child Sexual Abuse (Brandon & others, 1998)

In one study, she had a trusted family member recall for a teenager three real childhood experiences and a false one—a vivid account of the child's being lost for an extended time in a shopping mall at age 5 until being rescued by an elderly person. Two days later, one participant, Chris, said, "That day I was so scared that I would never see my family

TODAY'S SPECIAL GUEST

BRUNDAGE MORNALD, OF BATTLE CREEK, MONTANA

UNDER HYPNOSIS, MR. MORNALD RECOVERED LONG-BURIED MEMORIES OF A PERFECTLY NORMAL, HAPPY CHILDHOOD.

again." Two days after that, he began to visualize the flannel shirt, bald head, and glasses of the old man who supposedly had found him. Told the story was made up, Chris was incredulous: "I thought I remembered being lost . . . and looking around for the guys. I do remember that, and then crying, and Mom coming up and saying, 'Where were you? Don't you . . . ever do that again.'" In other experiments, a third of participants have become wrongly convinced that they almost drowned as a child, and about half were led to falsely recall an awful experience, such as a vicious animal attack (Heaps & Nash, 2001; Porter & others, 1999).

Such is the memory construction process by which people can recall being abducted by UFOs, victimized by a satanic cult, molested in a crib, or living a past life. Thousands of reasonable, normally functioning human beings, notes Loftus, "speak in terror-stricken voices about their experience aboard flying saucers. They *remember*, clearly and vividly, being abducted by aliens" (Loftus & Ketcham, 1994, p. 66).

Loftus knows firsthand the phenomenon she studies. At a family reunion, an uncle told her that at age 14, she found her mother's drowned body. Shocked, she denied it. But the uncle was adamant, and over the next three days she began to wonder if *she* had a repressed memory. "Maybe that's why I'm so obsessed with this topic." As the now-upset Loftus pondered her uncle's suggestion, she "recovered" an image of her mother lying in the pool, face down, and of herself finding the body. "I started putting everything into place. Maybe that's why I'm such a workaholic. Maybe that's why I'm so emotional when I think about her even though she died in 1959."

Then her brother called and said there had been a mistake. Her uncle now remembered what other relatives also confirmed. Aunt Pearl, not Loftus, had found the body (Loftus & Ketcham, 1994; Monaghan, 1992).

But then again, Loftus also knows firsthand the reality of sexual abuse. A male baby-sitter molested her when she was 6 years old. She has not forgotten. And that makes her wary of those whom she sees as trivializing real abuse by suggesting and seeking out uncorroborated traumatic experiences, then accepting them uncritically as fact. The enemies of the truly victimized are not only those who prey and those who deny, she says, but those whose writings and allegations "are bound to lead to an increased likelihood that society in general will disbelieve the genuine cases of childhood sexual abuse that truly deserve our sustained attention" (Loftus, 1993).

So, does repression of threatening memories ever occur? Or is this concept—the cornerstone of Freud's theory and of so much popular psychology—misleading? In Chapter 15, we will return to this hotly debated issue. As we will see, this much now appears certain: The most common response to a traumatic experience (witnessing a parent's murder, experiencing the horrors of a Nazi death camp, being terrorized by a hijacker or a rapist, escaping the collapsing World Trade

Although scorned by some trauma therapists, Loftus has been elected president of the science-oriented American Psychological Society, awarded psychology's biggest prize ($200,000), and elected to the U.S. National Academy of Sciences and the Royal Society of Edinburgh.

Elizabeth Loftus

"The research findings for which I am being honored now generated a level of hostility and opposition I could never have foreseen. People wrote threatening letters, warning me that my reputation and even my safety were in jeopardy if I continued along these lines. At some universities, armed guards were provided to accompany me during speeches." Elizabeth Loftus, on receiving the American Psychological Society's William James Fellow Award, 2001

Don Shrubshell

" Horror sears memory, leaving . . . the consuming memories of atrocity."

Robert Kraft, *Memory Perceived: Recalling the Holocaust*, 2002

Center towers, surviving the Asian tsunami) is not banishment of the experience into the unconscious. Rather, such experiences are typically etched on the mind as vivid, persistent, haunting memories. Playwright Eugene O'Neill understood. As one of the characters in his *Strange Interlude* (1928) exclaimed, "The devil! . . . what beastly incidents our memories insist on cherishing!"

>> LEARNING OUTCOMES

Memory Construction

OBJECTIVE 23 | **Explain how misinformation and imagination can distort our memory of an event.**

Memories are not stored or retrieved as exact copies of our experiences. Rather, we construct our memories, using both stored and new information. If children or adults are subtly exposed to misinformation after an event, or if they repeatedly imagine and rehearse an event that never occurred, they may incorporate the misleading details into their memory of what actually happened. Memory is thus best understood not only as a cognitive and a biological phenomenon, but also as a social-cultural phenomenon (see **FIGURE 9.28**).

FIGURE 9.28
Levels of analysis for the study of memory
As with other psychological phenomena, memory is fruitfully studied at biological, psychological, and social-cultural levels.

OBJECTIVE 24 | **Describe source amnesia's contribution to false memories.**

When we process memories, we encode and store various aspects of them in different locations in the brain. In reassembling

a memory during retrieval, we may successfully retrieve something we have heard, read, or imagined, but attribute it to the wrong source. Source amnesia is one of two main components of false memories. (The other is the misinformation effect.)

OBJECTIVE 25 | **List some differences and similarities between true and false memories.**

False memories feel like true memories and are equally durable, so neither the sincerity nor the longevity of a memory signifies it is real. True memories contain more details than imagined ones, which tend to be the gist of an event—the meaning and feelings associated with it.

OBJECTIVE 26 | **Give arguments supporting and rejecting the position that very young children's reports of abuse are reliable.**

A supporting argument: Even very young children can accurately recall events (and the people involved) if a neutral person talks with them in words they can understand, asks nonleading questions, and uses the cognitive interview technique. *A rejecting argument:* Preschoolers are more suggestible than older children or adults, and they can be induced, through suggestive questions, to report false events.

OBJECTIVE 27 | **Discuss the controversy over reports of repressed and recovered memories of childhood sexual abuse.**

Psychologists motivated to protect abused children and wrongly accused adults tend to agree on seven points: (1) Innocent people have been falsely convicted of abuse that never happened, and true abusers have used the controversy over recovered memories to avoid punishment. (2) Incest and abuse happen, and they can leave lasting scars. (3) Forgetting isolated past events, either good or bad, is an everyday occurrence for all of us. (4) Recovering good or bad memories, triggered by some memory cue, is commonplace, but memory researchers question whether we forcibly repress memories, in Freud's sense, to avoid anxiety or pain. (5) Memories obtained under the influence of hypnosis or drugs are unreliable. (6) Infantile amnesia—the inability to recall memories from the first three years of life—makes recovery of very early childhood memories unlikely. (7) Both real and false memories cause suffering and can lead to stress disorders.

ASK YOURSELF: **Could you be an impartial jury member in a trial of a parent accused of sexual abuse based on a recovered memory, or of a therapist being sued for creating a false memory of abuse?**

Improving Memory

OBJECTIVE **28** | Explain how an understanding of memory can contribute to effective study techniques.

To recap the chapter, let's consider how we might apply memory principles. What can we do in everyday situations to better remember a person's name, or even the material of this chapter?

Now and then we are dismayed at our forgetfulness—at our embarrassing inability to recall someone's name, at forgetting to bring up a point in conversation, at forgetting to bring along something important, at finding ourselves standing in a room unable to recall why we are there (Herrmann, 1982). Is there anything we can do to minimize such misdeeds of our memory system? Much as biology benefits medicine and botany benefits agriculture, so can the psychology of memory benefit education. Sprinkled throughout this chapter and summarized here for easy reference are concrete suggestions for improving memory. The SQ3R—*Survey, Question, Read, Rehearse, Review*—study technique introduced in the Prologue incorporates several of these strategies.

Study repeatedly to boost long-term recall. Overlearn. To learn a name, say it to yourself after being introduced; wait a few seconds and say it again; wait longer and say it again. To learn a concept, provide yourself with many separate study sessions: Take advantage of life's little intervals—riding on the bus, walking across campus, waiting for class to start.

Spend more time rehearsing or actively thinking about the material. New memories are weak; exercise them and they will strengthen. Speed-reading (skimming) complex material—with minimal rehearsal—yields little retention. Rehearsal and critical reflection help more. It pays to study actively!

Make the material personally meaningful. To build a network of retrieval cues, take thorough text and class notes in your own words. Answer the Ask Yourself questions (at the end of each section) to apply the concepts to your own life. Mindlessly repeating someone else's words is relatively ineffective. It is better to form images, understand and organize information, relate the material to what you already know or have experienced, and put it in your own words. Without such cues, you may find yourself stuck when a question uses phrasing different from the rote forms you memorized. To increase retrieval cues, form as many associations as possible.

To remember a list of unfamiliar items, use mnemonic devices. Associate items with peg-words. Make up a story that incorporates vivid images of the items. Chunk information into acronyms.

Refresh your memory by activating retrieval cues. Mentally re-create the situation and the mood in which the original learning occurred. Return to the same location. Jog your memory by allowing one thought to cue the next.

Recall events while they are fresh, before you encounter possible misinformation. If you are an eyewitness to an important event, record your memory before allowing others to suggest what may have occurred.

Minimize interference. Study before sleeping. Do not schedule back-to-back study times for topics that are likely to interfere with each other, such as Spanish and French.

Test your own knowledge, both to rehearse it and to help determine what you do not yet know. If you must recall information later, do not be lulled into overconfidence by your ability to recognize it. Test your recall using the learning objectives. Outline sections on a blank page. Define terms and concepts listed at each chapter's end before turning back to their definitions. Take practice tests

"I have discovered that it is of some use when you lie in bed at night and gaze into the darkness to repeat in your mind the things you have been studying. Not only does it help the understanding, but also the memory."

Leonardo da Vinci (1452–1519)

"Knit each new thing on to some acquisition already there."

William James, *Principles of Psychology*, 1890

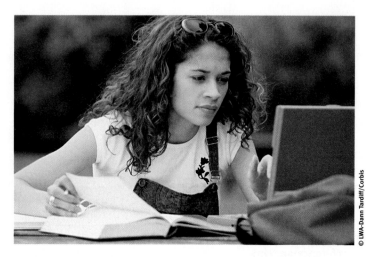

Thinking and memory
Most of what we know is not the result of efforts to memorize. We learn because we're curious and because we spend time thinking about our experiences. Actively thinking as we read, by rehearsing and relating ideas, yields the best retention.

(see the Test Yourself questions on the final page of each chapter). The study guides that accompany many texts, including this one, are a good source for such tests.

Without self-testing, one can easily become overconfident, as John Shaughnessy and Eugene Zechmeister (1992) found in an experiment with two groups of students. A "reread group" repeatedly read dozens of factual statements, then judged the likelihood that they would remember each fact, and finally were tested on their recall. Students in this group felt fairly confident of their knowledge, even on the questions they later missed. Students in a "practice test group" also read the statements, but they then spent the rest of the time responding to tests that required them to retrieve the facts. Compared with the "reread" group, the practice-test group did just as well on the final recall test. What is more, they could better discriminate what they did and did not know. It is clear that self-testing enhances recall and can help you to know what you know—and thus enables you to focus your study time on what you do not yet know. As former British Prime Minister Benjamin Disraeli once said, "To be conscious that you are ignorant is a great step to knowledge."

>> LEARNING OUTCOMES

Improving Memory

OBJECTIVE 28 | Explain how an understanding of memory can contribute to effective study techniques.

The psychology of memory suggests concrete strategies for improving memory. These include scheduling spaced study times; actively rehearsing information to be learned; aiding encoding by making well-organized, vivid, and personally meaningful associations; using mnemonic techniques; returning to contexts and moods that are rich with associations; recording memories before misinformation can corrupt them; minimizing interference; and self-testing to rehearse information and find gaps in your memory.

ASK YOURSELF: Which of the study and memory strategies suggested in this section will work best for you?

REVIEW CHAPTER 9: **Memory**

Test Yourself

1. Memory includes (in alphabetical order) long-term memory, sensory memory, and working/short-term memory. What's the correct order of these three memory stores?

2. What would be the most effective strategy to learn and retain a list of names of key historical figures for a week? For a year?

3. Your friend tells you that her father experienced brain damage in an accident. She wonders if psychology can explain why he can still play checkers very well but has a hard time holding a sensible conversation. What can you tell her?

4. What is priming?

5. Can you offer an example of proactive interference?

6. What—given the commonality of source amnesia—might life be like if we remembered all our waking experiences and all our dreams?

7. What are the recommended memory strategies you just read about? (One advised rehearsing to-be-remembered material. What were the others?)

Answers to the Test Yourself questions can be found in Appendix B at the end of the book.

Terms and Concepts to Remember

memory, p. 349
flashbulb memory, p. 351
encoding, p. 351
storage, p. 351
retrieval, p. 351
sensory memory, p. 351
short-term memory, p. 351
long-term memory, p. 351
working memory, p. 352
automatic processing, p. 353
effortful processing, p. 354
rehearsal, p. 354
spacing effect, p. 355

serial position effect, p. 356
visual encoding, p. 356
acoustic encoding, p. 356
semantic encoding, p. 356
imagery, p. 358
mnemonics [nih-MON-iks], p. 358
chunking, p. 359
iconic memory, p. 362
echoic memory, p. 362
long-term potentiation (LTP), p. 365
amnesia, p. 367
implicit memory, p. 367
explicit memory, p. 367

hippocampus, p. 368
recall, p. 370
recognition, p. 370
relearning, p. 370
priming, p. 372
déjà vu, p. 373
mood-congruent memory, p. 374
proactive interference, p. 379
retroactive interference, p. 379
repression, p. 381
misinformation effect, p. 383
source amnesia, p. 384

WEB

> To continue your study and review of Memory, visit this book's Web site at www.worthpublishers.com/myers. You will find practice tests, review activities, and many interesting articles and Web links for more information on topics related to Memory.

ANOTHER VOICE ON: THINKING AND LANGUAGE

ALLISON JOSEPH (b. 1967), FROM "ON BEING TOLD I DON'T SPEAK LIKE A BLACK PERSON," 1999

Now I realize there's nothing
more personal than speech,
that I don't have to defend
how I speak, how any person,
black, white, chooses to speak.
Let us speak. Let us talk
with the sounds of our mothers

and fathers still reverberating
in our minds, wherever our mothers
or fathers come from:
Arkansas, Belize, Alabama,
Brazil, Aruba, Arizona.
Let us simply speak
to one another,

listen and prize the inflections,
never assuming how any person will
    sound
until his mouth opens, until her
mouth opens, greetings welcome
in any language.

10: Thinking and Language

Throughout history, we humans have both deplored our foolishness and celebrated our wisdom. The poet T. S. Eliot was struck by "the hollow men . . . Headpiece filled with straw." But Shakespeare's Hamlet extolled the human species as "noble in reason! . . . infinite in faculties! . . . in apprehension how like a god!" In the preceding chapters, we have likewise marveled both at our capabilities and at our propensity to err.

We have studied the human brain—3 pounds of wet tissue the size of a small cabbage, yet containing circuitry more complex than the planet's telephone networks. We have appreciated the competence of newborn infants. We have relished the human sensory system, which disassembles visual stimuli into millions of nerve impulses, distributes them for parallel processing, and then reassembles them into clear and colorful perceived images. We have pondered our memory's seemingly limitless capacity and the ease with which we process information, consciously and unconsciously. Little wonder that our species has had the collective genius to invent the camera, the car, and the computer; to unlock the atom and crack the genetic code; to travel out to space and into the oceans' depths.

Yet we have also seen that our species is kin to the other animals, influenced by the same principles that produce learning in rats and pigeons. As one pundit said, echoing Pavlov, "how like a dog!" We have noted that we assimilate reality into our preconceptions and succumb to perceptual illusions. We have seen how easily we deceive ourselves about pseudopsychic claims, hypnotic feats, and false memories.

In this chapter, we encounter further instances of these two images of the human condition—the rational and the irrational. We will see how we form concepts, solve problems, and make judgments. We will look at our flair for language and ask whether our species alone has this capability. In the end, we will reflect on how deserving we are of our name, *Homo sapiens*—wise human.

Thinking

OBJECTIVE **1** | Define *cognition.*

As we think, we form concepts that organize our world, we solve problems, and we make efficient decisions and judgments. While doing so, what strategies do we typically use? What biases put us at risk for error?

Previous chapters explained how we receive, perceive, store, and retrieve information. Now we consider how our cognitive system uses this information. Thinking, or **cognition,** refers to all the mental activities associated with processing, understanding, remembering, and communicating. *Cognitive psychologists* study these mental activities, including the logical and sometimes illogical ways in which we create concepts, solve problems, make decisions, and form judgments.

■ **cognition** the mental activities associated with thinking, knowing, remembering, and communicating.

"Attention, everyone! I'd like to introduce the newest member of our family."

Concepts

OBJECTIVE **2** |Describe the roles of categories, hierarchies, definitions, and prototypes in concept formation.

To think about the countless events, objects, and people in our world, we simplify things. We form **concepts**—mental groupings of similar objects, events, and people. The concept *chair* includes a variety of items—a baby's high chair, a reclining chair, the chairs around a dining room table, a dentist's chair—all of which are for sitting. Chairs vary, but it is their common features that define the concept of *chair*.

Imagine life without concepts. We would need a different name for every object and idea. We could not ask a child to "throw the ball" because there would be no concept of *ball* (or *throw*). Instead of saying, "They were angry," we would have to describe facial expressions, vocal intensities, gestures, and words. Such concepts as *ball* and *angry* provide us with much information without much cognitive effort.

To simplify things further, we organize concepts into category *hierarchies* (**FIGURE 10.1**). Cab drivers organize their cities into geographical sectors, which subdivide into neighborhoods and again into blocks. Once our categories exist, we use them efficiently. Shown a bird, car, or food, people need no more time to identify an item's category than to perceive that something is there. "As soon as you know it is there, you know what it is," report Kalanit Grill-Spector and Nancy Kanwisher (2005).

We form some concepts by *definition*. Told the rule that a triangle has three sides, we thereafter classify all three-sided geometric forms as triangles. More often, however, we form our concepts by developing **prototypes**—a mental image or best example that incorporates all the features we associate with a category (Rosch, 1978). The more closely something matches our prototype of a concept, the more readily we recognize it as an example of the concept. A robin and a goose both satisfy our definition

FIGURE 10.1
Category hierarchy
Organizing our mental categories into hierarchies helps us think about them.

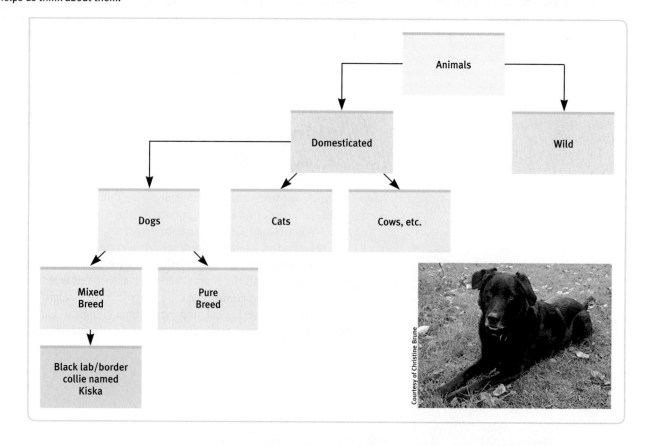

of *bird:* a two-footed animal that has wings and feathers and hatches from an egg. Yet people agree more quickly that "a robin is a bird" than that "a goose is a bird." For most of us, the robin, with its smaller beak and overall size, and its easier flight, is the birdier bird; it more closely resembles our bird prototype.

Once we place an item in a category, our memory for it later shifts toward the category prototype. Olivier Corneille and his colleagues (2004) found memory shifts after showing Belgian students ethnically mixed faces. For example, when shown a face that was a blend of 70 percent of the features of a Caucasian person and 30 percent of an Asian person, people categorized the face as Caucasian and later recalled having seen a more prototypically Caucasian person. (They were more likely to recall an 80 percent Caucasian face than the 70 percent Caucasian they actually saw.) If shown a 70 percent Asian face, they later recalled a more prototypically Asian face (**FIGURE 10.2**). A follow-up study found the phenomenon with gender as well. For example, those shown 70 percent male faces categorized them as male (no surprise there), and then later misrecalled them as even more prototypically male (Huart & others, 2005).

Move away from our prototypes, and categories may have fuzzy boundaries. Is a whale a mammal? Is a tomato a fruit? Is a 17-year-old female a girl or a woman? Are penguins and kiwis birds? Because these nonflying creatures fail to match our prototype, we are slower to recognize them as birds. Similarly, we are slow to perceive an illness when our symptoms don't fit one of our disease prototypes (Bishop, 1991). People whose heart attack symptoms (shortness of breath, exhaustion, a dull weight in the chest) don't match their prototype of a heart attack (sharp chest pain) may not seek help. And when discrimination doesn't fit our prejudice prototypes—of White against Black, male against female, young against old—we often fail to notice it. People more easily detect male prejudice against females than female against males or female against females (Inman & Baron, 1996; Marti & others, 2000).

A bird and a . . . ?
If asked to imagine a bird, most people quickly come up with a mental picture that is something like this American robin. It takes them a bit longer to conceptualize a penguin as a bird because it doesn't match their prototype of a small, feathered, flying creature.

FIGURE 10.2
Face categorization influences our recollection
For example, shown a face that was 70 percent Caucasian, people tended to classify the person as Caucasian and to recollect the face as more Caucasian than it was. (From Corneille & others, 2004.)

| 90% CA | 80% CA | 70% CA | 60% CA | 50%/50% | 60% AS | 70% AS | 80% AS | 90% AS |

Solving Problems

OBJECTIVE **3** | Compare algorithms and heuristics as problem-solving strategies, and explain how insight differs from both of them.

One tribute to our rationality is our ability to form and use concepts. Another is our skill at solving problems as we cope with novel situations. What's the best route around this traffic jam? How shall we respond to a friend's criticism? How can we get into the house when we've lost our keys?

Some problems we solve through trial and error. Thomas Edison tried thousands of light bulb filaments before stumbling upon one that worked. For other problems, we may follow an **algorithm,** a step-by-step procedure that guarantees a solution.

■ **concept** a mental grouping of similar objects, events, ideas, or people.

■ **prototype** a mental image or best example of a category. Matching new items to the prototype provides a quick and easy method for including items in a category (as when comparing feathered creatures to a prototypical bird, such as a robin).

■ **algorithm** a methodical, logical rule or procedure that guarantees solving a particular problem. Contrasts with the usually speedier—but also more error-prone—use of *heuristics.*

Heuristic searching
To search for guava juice you could search every supermarket aisle (an algorithm) or check the bottled beverage, natural foods, and produce sections (heuristics). The heuristic approach is often speedier, but an algorithmic search guarantees you will find it eventually.

Told to find another word using all the letters in *SPLOYOCHYG*, we could try each letter in each position, but generating and examining the 907,200 resulting permutations would be exasperating. Because step-by-step algorithms can be laborious (well-suited to computers), we often solve problems with simple strategies called **heuristics.** Thus, in rearranging the letters of *SPLOYOCHYG*, we might exclude letter combinations such as two *Y*'s together. By using heuristics to reduce the number of options, and then applying trial and error, you may hit upon the answer (page 404).

Sometimes we are unaware of using any problem-solving strategy; the answer just comes to us. We can all recall occasions when we puzzled over a problem. Then, suddenly, the pieces fell together and we perceived the solution. Such sudden flashes of inspiration we call **insight.** Ten-year-old Johnny Appleton displayed insight in solving a problem that had stumped construction workers: how to rescue a young robin that had fallen into a narrow 30-inch-deep hole in a cement-block wall. Johnny's solution: to slowly pour in sand, giving the bird enough time to keep its feet on top of the constantly rising sand (Ruchlis, 1990).

A team of researchers, including psychologists Mark Jung-Beeman, John Kounios, and Edward Bowden (2004), have identified brain activity associated with sudden flashes of insight. They gave people sets of three words, such as *pine, crab, sauce,* and asked them to think of another word that could form a compound word or phrase with each. Participants pressed a button when they achieved the solution (in this case: *apple*). About half the solutions were by a sudden Aha! insight. The researchers mapped either the location of the brain's associated neural activity (using fMRI scans) or its electrical signature (using an EEG). When the solutions occurred with sudden insight, both methods showed a burst of activity in the right temporal lobe, just above the ear (**FIGURE 10.3**). One type of brain activity, which seemingly corresponded to the unconscious processing popping into a conscious insight, preceded the button pressing by about 0.3 second.

Insight provides a sense of satisfaction. After solving a difficult problem or discovering how to resolve a conflict, we feel happy. The joy of a joke may similarly lie in our capacity for insight—our sudden comprehension of an unexpected ending or a double meaning, as illustrated in the two jokes rated funniest (among 2 million ratings of 40,000 submitted jokes) in an Internet humor study co-sponsored by Richard Wiseman (2002) and the British Association for the Advancement of Science. First, the runner-up:

Sherlock Holmes and Dr. Watson are going camping. They pitch their tent under the stars and go to sleep. Sometime in the middle of the night Holmes wakes Watson up.

ALICE, I'VE NOTICED A DISTURBING PATTERN. YOUR SOLUTIONS TO PROBLEMS ARE ALWAYS THE THINGS YOU TRY LAST.

FIGURE 10.3
The Aha! moment
A burst of right temporal lobe activity accompanies insight solutions to word problems.

Holmes: "Watson, look up at the stars, and tell me what you deduce."

Watson: "I see millions of stars and even if a few of those have planets, it's quite likely there are some planets like Earth, and if there are a few planets like Earth out there, there might also be life. What does it tell you, Holmes?"

Holmes: "Watson, you idiot, somebody has stolen our tent!"

And roll the drums for the winner:

> A couple of New Jersey hunters are out in the woods when one of them falls to the ground. He doesn't seem to be breathing, his eyes are rolled back in his head. The other guy whips out his cell phone and calls the emergency services. He gasps to the operator: "My friend is dead! What can I do?" The operator, in a calm, soothing voice says: "Just take it easy. I can help. First, let's make sure he's dead." There is a silence, then a shot is heard. The guy's voice comes back on the line: "OK, now what?"

Obstacles to Problem Solving

OBJECTIVE 4 | Contrast confirmation bias and fixation, and explain how they can interfere with effective problem solving.

Inventive as we can be in solving problems, the correct answer may elude us. Two cognitive tendencies—*confirmation bias* and *fixation*—often lead us astray.

Confirmation Bias A major obstacle to problem solving is our eagerness to search for information that confirms our ideas, a phenomenon known as **confirmation bias.** Peter Wason (1960) demonstrated this tendency by giving British university students the three-number sequence 2-4-6 and asking them to guess the rule he had used to devise the series. (The rule was simple: any three ascending numbers.) Before submitting their answers, the students generated their own sets of three numbers, and each time Wason told them whether their sets conformed to his rule. Once they had done enough testing to feel *certain* they had the rule, they were to announce it. The result? Seldom right but never in doubt. Most of Wason's students convinced themselves of a wrong rule. Typically, they formed a wrong idea ("Maybe it's counting by twos") and then searched only for confirming evidence (by testing 6-8-10, 100-102-104, and so forth).

Such experiments reveal that we seek evidence verifying our ideas more eagerly than we seek evidence that might refute them (Klayman & Ha, 1987; Skov & Sherman, 1986). Business managers, for example, are more likely to follow the successful careers of those they once hired than to track the achievements of those they rejected, leading them to confirm their own perceived hiring ability. "Ordinary people," said Wason (1981), "evade facts, become inconsistent, or systematically defend themselves against the threat of new information relevant to the issue."

The results of doing so sometimes are momentous. The United States launched its war against Iraq on the assumption that Saddam Hussein possessed weapons of mass destruction (WMD) that posed an immediate threat. When that assumption turned out to be false, flaws in the judgment process identified by the bipartisan U.S. Senate Select Committee on Intelligence (2004) included confirmation bias. Administration analysts "had a tendency to accept information which supported [their presumptions] . . . more readily than information which contradicted" them. Sources denying such weapons were deemed "either lying or not knowledgeable about Iraq's problems, while those sources who reported ongoing WMD activities were seen as having provided valuable information."

Fixation Try your hand at these two classic brainteasers:

- Arrange the six matches shown in **FIGURE 10.4** so they will form four equilateral triangles.
- How can you use the box of matches, thumbtacks, and candle shown in **FIGURE 10.5** (page 400) to mount the candle on a bulletin board? (Read on after trying these problems.)

■ **heuristic** a simple thinking strategy that often allows us to make judgments and solve problems efficiently; usually speedier but also more error-prone than *algorithms*.

■ **insight** a sudden and often novel realization of the solution to a problem; it contrasts with strategy-based solutions.

■ **confirmation bias** a tendency to search for information that confirms one's preconceptions.

" The human understanding, when any proposition has been once laid down . . . forces everything else to add fresh support and confirmation."

Francis Bacon, *Novum Organum*, 1620

FIGURE 10.4

The matchstick problem

How would you arrange six matches to form four equilateral triangles?

FIGURE 10.5
The candle-mounting problem
Using these materials, how would you mount the candle on a bulletin board? (From Duncker, 1945.)

FIGURE 10.6
Solution to the matchstick problem
To solve this problem, you must break the fixation of limiting your considerations to two-dimensional solutions.

Fixation—the inability to see a problem from a fresh perspective—is a true impediment to problem solving. Once we incorrectly represent the problem, it's hard to restructure how we approach it. If your attempts to solve the matchstick problem were fixated on two-dimensional solutions, then the three-dimensional solution shown in **FIGURE 10.6** will have eluded you.

Two examples of fixation are *mental set* and *functional fixedness*. As a perceptual set predisposes what we perceive, a **mental set** predisposes how we think. Mental set refers to our tendency to approach a problem with the mindset of what has worked for us previously. Indeed, solutions that worked in the past often do work on new problems. Consider:

Given the sequence O-T-T-F-?-?-?, what are the final three letters?

Most people have difficulty recognizing that the three final letters are *F*(ive), *S*(ix), and *S*(even). But solving this problem may make the next one easier:

Given the sequence J-F-M-A-?-?-?, what are the final three letters? (If you don't get this one, ask yourself what month it is.)

Sometimes, however, our mental set based on what worked in the past precludes our finding a new solution to a new problem. Our mental set from past experience with matchsticks predisposes our arranging them in two dimensions.

Another type of fixation—our tendency to think of only the familiar functions for objects, without imagining alternative uses—goes by the awkward but appropriate label **functional fixedness.** A person may ransack the house for a screwdriver when a dime would have turned the screw. Perhaps you experienced functional fixedness when you tried to solve the candle-mounting problem. If you thought of the matchbox as having only the function of holding matches, you may have overlooked its use shown in **FIGURE 10.7** (page 402). Perceiving and relating familiar things in new ways is part of creativity. Much as stereotypes constrain our perception of people (we may forget that firefighters are also first aid experts and may be good cooks), so fixation constrains our perceptions of objects. Both stereotypes and fixation limit our thinking.

Mental set
The mental set created by reading the first door may predispose how one reads the second door.

Making Decisions and Forming Judgments

When making each day's hundreds of judgments and decisions—Is it worth the bother to take an umbrella? Can I trust this person? Should I shoot the basketball or pass to the player who's hot?—we seldom take the time and effort to reason systematically. We just follow our intuition. After interviewing policymakers in government, business, and education, social psychologist Irving Janis (1986) concluded that they "often do not use a reflective problem-solving approach. How do they usually arrive at their decisions? If you ask, they are likely to tell you . . . they do it mostly by *the seat of their pants.*"

Using and Misusing Heuristics

OBJECTIVE **5** | Contrast the representativeness and availability heuristics, and explain how they can cause us to underestimate or ignore important information.

Those mental shortcuts we call heuristics often do help us make reasonable seat-of-the-pants decisions. When quick action is needed, analysis can mean paralysis. Thanks to the mind's automatic information processing, intuitive judgments are instantaneous. But the price we sometimes pay for this efficiency—quick but bad judgments—can be costly. To gain an idea of how heuristics determine our intuitive judgments—and how they occasionally lead even the smartest people into dumb decisions—consider two heuristics identified by cognitive psychologists Amos Tversky and Daniel Kahneman (1974): *representativeness* and *availability*.

■ **fixation** the inability to see a problem from a new perspective; an impediment to problem solving.

■ **mental set** a tendency to approach a problem in a particular way, often a way that has been successful in the past.

■ **functional fixedness** the tendency to think of things only in terms of their usual functions; an impediment to problem solving.

■ **representativeness heuristic** judging the likelihood of things in terms of how well they seem to represent, or match, particular prototypes; may lead one to ignore other relevant information.

Amos Tversky, 1937–1996

Daniel Kahneman

" In creating these problems, we didn't set out to fool people. All our problems fooled us, too."

Amos Tversky (1985)

" Intuitive thinking [is] fine most of the time. . . . But sometimes that habit of mind gets us in trouble."

Nobel laureate Daniel Kahneman (2005)

The Representativeness Heuristic To judge the likelihood of things in terms of how well they represent particular prototypes is to use the **representativeness heuristic.** To illustrate, consider:

> A stranger tells you about a person who is short, slim, and likes to read poetry, and then asks you to guess whether this person is more likely to be a professor of classics at an Ivy League university or a truck driver (adapted from Nisbett & Ross, 1980). Which would be the better guess?

If you are like most people, you answered "professor" because the description seems more *representative* of Ivy League scholars than of truck drivers. The representativeness heuristic enabled you to make a snap judgment. But it also led you to ignore other relevant information. When I help people think through this question, the conversation goes something like this:

Question: First, let's figure out how many professors fit the description. How many Ivy League universities do you suppose there are?

Answer: Oh, about 10, I suppose.

" The information-processing shortcuts—called heuristics—which are normally both highly efficient and immensely time-saving in day-to-day situations, work systematically against us in the marketplace. . . . The tendency to underestimate or altogether ignore past probabilities in making a decision is undoubtedly the most significant problem of intuitive predictions."

David Dreman, *Contrarian Investment Strategy: The Psychology of Stock Market Success*, 1979

FIGURE 10.7
Solution to the candle-mounting problem
Solving this problem requires recognizing that a box need not always serve as a container. (From Duncker, 1945.)

"The problem is I can't tell the difference between a deeply wise, intuitive nudge from the Universe and one of my own bone-headed ideas!"

Based on the roughly 10-million-to-1 odds against a bet's winning a state Lotto jackpot, one's chances are not much better than the odds of being struck by lightning. If you are an average British citizen and you place a bet in the National Lottery, the odds of your dying during the 20-minute National Lottery draw program on television are several times greater than the odds of your winning (*Chance News,* 1999).

Question:	How many classics professors would you guess there are at each?
Answer:	Maybe 4.
Question:	Okay, that's 40 Ivy League classics professors. What fraction of these are short and slim?
Answer:	Let's say half.
Question:	And, of these 20, how many like to read poetry?
Answer:	I'd say half—10 professors.
Question:	Okay, now let's figure how many truck drivers fit the description. How many truck drivers do you suppose there are?
Answer:	Maybe 400,000.
Question:	What fraction are short and slim?
Answer:	Not many—perhaps 1 in 8.
Question:	Of these 50,000, what percentage like to read poetry?
Answer:	Truck drivers who like poetry? Maybe 1 in 100—oh, oh, I can see where this is going—that leaves me with 500 short, slim, poetry-reading truck drivers.
Comment:	Yup. So, although the person I've described may be much more representative of classics professors than of truck drivers, this person is still (even if we accept your stereotypes) 50 times more likely to be a truck driver than a classics professor.

The representativeness heuristic influences many of our daily decisions. To judge the likelihood of something, we intuitively compare it with our mental representation of that category—of, say, what truck drivers are like. If the two match, that fact usually overrides other considerations of statistics or logic.

The Availability Heuristic The **availability heuristic** operates when we base our judgments on how mentally available information is. If instances of an event are easily available—if they come to mind quickly and with little effort—we presume such events are common. The faster people can remember an instance of some event ("a broken promise"), the more they expect it to recur (MacLeod & Campbell, 1992). Cognitively available events *are* more likely to recur—but not always. To see this, make a guess: Does the letter *k* appear more often as the first or third letter in English usage?

Because words beginning with *k* come to mind more easily than words having *k* as their third letter, most people guess that *k* occurs more frequently as the first letter. Actually, *k* is much more likely to appear as the third letter. So far in this chapter, words such as *know, kingdom,* and *kin* are outnumbered 50 to 15 by words such as *make, likely, asked,* and *acknowledged.*

Why does the availability heuristic lead us astray? Anything that increases the ease of our retrieving information can increase its perceived availability. Many factors enable information to "pop into mind." These include how recently you heard about it, its distinctiveness, and its concreteness. Thus, an event's availability to our memory need not indicate its likelihood in reality.

The judgmental errors influenced by the availability heuristic are not always harmless. A lot of important decisions involve judgments of risk (See Thinking Critically About: The Fear Factor, page 404.) Whether we favor using nuclear power or burning coal to produce energy depends partly on our judgments of their risks to our health, our air, and our climate. Our efforts to prevent various deadly diseases depend on our judgments of the likelihood of their occurrence. Our choice to buy or not to buy a lottery ticket depends on our hunch of the odds of striking it rich. Casinos entice us to gamble by signaling even small wins with bells and lights—making them vividly memorable—while keeping big losses soundlessly invisible. In such ways, hucksters can manipulate the intuitive hopes and fears of anyone naive about statistics.

The availability heuristic also affects our social judgments, as Ruth Hamill and her co-workers demonstrated (1980). They presented people with a single, vivid case of welfare abuse, in which a long-term welfare recipient had several unruly children.

Statistically, this case was exceptional: Most people who received welfare did so for four years or less (Duncan & others, 1988). Yet when the statistical reality was pitted against the single vivid case, the memorable case had greater influence on people's opinions about welfare recipients.

Overconfidence

OBJECTIVE 6 | Describe the drawbacks and advantages of overconfidence in decision making.

Our use of intuitive heuristics when forming judgments, our eagerness to confirm the beliefs we already hold, and our knack for explaining away failures combine to create **overconfidence,** a tendency to overestimate the accuracy of our knowledge and judgments. Across various tasks, people overestimate what their performance was, is, or will be (Metcalfe, 1998).

In a classic study of overconfidence, Kahneman and Tversky (1979) asked people to answer obscure factual questions with a wide enough range to surely include the actual answer. The questions had this format: "I feel 98 percent certain that the population of New Zealand is more than _____ but less than _____." Nearly one-third of the time, people's estimates, made with 98 percent confidence, failed to include the correct answer (4.1 million as of 2006, in this instance). Although very sure of themselves, they were often wrong. Warning people against overconfidence doesn't much reduce overconfidence.

People are also more confident than correct when answering such questions as, "Is absinthe a liqueur or a precious stone?" (It's a licorice-flavored liqueur.) On questions where only 60 percent of people answer correctly, respondents typically feel 75 percent confident. Even when people feel 100 percent certain of their answers to such questions, they err about 15 percent of the time (Fischhoff & others, 1977).

Overconfidence plagues decisions outside the laboratory, too. It was an overconfident Hitler who invaded Russia, an overconfident Lyndon Johnson who waged war with North Vietnam, an overconfident George W. Bush who marched into Iraq to eliminate supposed weapons of mass destruction. On a smaller scale, stockbrokers and investment managers market their services with confidence that they can outperform the market average in picking stocks, despite overwhelming evidence to the contrary (Malkiel, 2004). A purchase of stock X, recommended by a broker who judges this to be the time to buy, is usually balanced by a sale made by someone who judges this to be the time to sell. Despite their confidence, buyer and seller cannot both be right.

Students, too, are routinely overconfident about how quickly they can do assignments and write papers, report Roger Buehler and his colleagues (1994). They typically expect to finish projects ahead of schedule. But in fact, the projects generally get finished after about twice the number of days they predicted. Although we know we have often underestimated completion times, we remain overly confident of our next prediction. Moreover, presuming how much we're going to get done, we also overestimate our future free time (Zauberman, 2005). We expect to be experiencing more free time a month from today than today. So we say yes to requests for our future time, only to discover it's just as busy.

Failing to appreciate one's potential for error when making military, economic, or political judgments can have devastating consequences, but so can a lack of self-confidence. Overconfidence does have adaptive value. People who err on the side of overconfidence live more happily, find it easier to make tough decisions, and seem more credible (Baumeister, 1989; Taylor, 1989). Moreover, if given prompt and clear feedback on the accuracy of their judgments—as weather forecasters are after each day's predictions—people soon learn to assess their accuracy more realistically (Fischhoff, 1982). The wisdom to know when we know a thing and when we do not is born of experience.

> "The human understanding is most excited by that which strikes and enters the mind at once and suddenly, and by which the imagination is immediately filled and inflated. It then begins almost imperceptibly to conceive and suppose that everything is similar to the few objects which have taken possession of the mind."
> Francis Bacon, *Novum Organum*, 1620

■ **availability heuristic** estimating the likelihood of events based on their availability in memory; if instances come readily to mind (perhaps because of their vividness), we presume such events are common.

■ **overconfidence** the tendency to be more confident than correct—to overestimate the accuracy of one's beliefs and judgments.

> "Don't believe everything you think."
> Bumper sticker

Predict your own behavior
When will you finish reading this chapter?

> "When you know a thing, to hold that you know it; and when you do not know a thing, to allow that you do not know it; this is knowledge."
> Confucius (551–479 B.C.), *Analects*

THE FEAR FACTOR—
DO WE FEAR THE RIGHT THINGS?

"Most people reason dramatically, not quantitatively," said Oliver Wendell Holmes. Especially since 9/11, many people fear flying more than driving. Yet National Safety Council (2005) data reveal that between 2000 and 2002, Americans were—mile for mile— 39.5 times more likely to die in an automobile crash than on a commercial flight. In a late-2001 essay, I calculated that if—because of 9/11—we flew 20 percent less and instead drove half those unflown miles, about 800 more people would die in traffic accidents in the year after 9/11 (Myers, 2001). When German psychologist Gerd Gigerenzer (2004) later checked this estimate against accident data (why didn't I think of this?), he found that the last three months

of 2001 indeed produced significantly more U.S. traffic fatalities than the average for those months in the previous five years (**FIGURE 10.8**). Long after 9/11, the dead terrorists were still killing Americans. As air travel gradually recovered during 2002, 2003, and 2004, U.S. commercial flights carried nearly 2 billion passengers, with only 34 deaths—none on a major airline big jet (Miller, 2005). Meanwhile, 128,000 Americans died in traffic accidents.

Why do we fear the wrong things? Why do we fear terrorism more than accidents—which kill nearly as many per *week* in just the United States as did terrorism with its 2527 worldwide deaths in all of the 1990s (Johnson, 2001)? Even with the horror of 9/11, more

Americans in 2001 died of food poisoning (which scares few) than of terrorism (which scares many). And why do so many smokers (whose habit shortens their lives, on average, by about five years) fret before flying (which, averaged across people, shortens life by one day)?

Psychological science has identified four influences on our intuitions about risk. First, we fear *what*

FIGURE 10.8
Still killing Americans
Images of 9/11 etched a sharper image in our minds than did the millions of fatality-free flights on U.S. airlines during 2002 and after. Such dramatic events, being readily available to memory, shape our perceptions of risk. In the three months after 2001, those faulty perceptions led more people to travel, and some to die, by car. (Adapted from Gigerenzer, 2004.)

AP/Wide World Photos

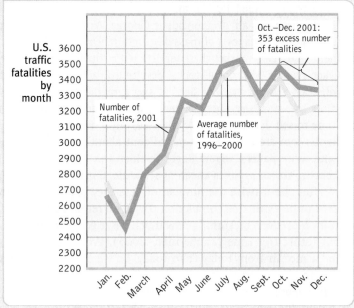

U.S. traffic fatalities by month

3600
3500
3400
3300
3200
3100
3000
2900
2800
2700
2600
2500
2400
2300
2200

Jan. Feb. March April May June July Aug. Sept. Oct. Nov. Dec.

Oct.–Dec. 2001: 353 excess number of fatalities

Number of fatalities, 2001

Average number of fatalities, 1996–2000

Answer to SPLOYOCHYG anagram on page 398: PSYCHOLOGY.

our ancestral history has prepared us to fear. Human emotions were road tested in the Stone Age. Yesterday's risks prepare us to fear snakes, lizards, and spiders (although all three combined now kill virtually no one in developed countries). And they prepare us to fear confinement and heights, and therefore flying.

Second, we fear *what we cannot control*. Driving we control, flying we do not.

Third, we fear *what is immediate*. Threats related to flying are mostly telescoped into the moments of takeoff and landing, while the dangers of driving are diffused across many moments to come, each trivially dangerous. Teens are often indifferent to smoking's toxicity because they live more for the present than for the distant future.

Fourth, we fear *what is most readily available in memory*. Horrific images of United Flight 175 slicing into the World Trade Center form indelible memories. And powerful, available memories serve as our measuring rods as we intuitively judge risks. Thousands of safe car trips (for those who have survived to read this) have extinguished our anxieties about driving.

Vivid events also distort our comprehension of risks and probable outcomes. We comprehend Andrew "Jack" Whittaker's winning $315 million in a 2002 Powerball lottery. We do not comprehend each of the more than 560 million losing players who undramatically enabled his jackpot. We comprehend those 9/11 flights that ended in the deaths of 266 passengers

Ian Berry/Magnum Photos

Dramatic deaths in bunches breed concern and fear

The memorable South Asian tsunami that killed some 300,000 people stirred an outpouring of concern and new tsunami-warning technology. Meanwhile, a "silent tsunami" of poverty-related malaria was killing about that many of the world's children every couple months, noted Jeffrey Sachs, the head of a United Nations project aiming to cut extreme poverty in half by 2015 (Dugger, 2005).

and crew. We do not comprehend the vast numbers of accident-free flights—16 *million* consecutive fatality-free takeoffs and landings during one stretch of the 1990s (Tolchin, 1994). Dramatic outcomes capture our attention; probabilities we hardly grasp. The result: We overvalue lottery tickets, overestimate flight risk, and underestimate the dangers of driving.

We fear too much those things that have killed people dramatically, in bunches, and recently, and we fear too little those threats that will claim lives undramatically, one by one, and in the distant future. If a single 747 were taken down by a rocket-propelled grenade, the horror would be seared upon our minds. But as Bill Gates has noted, each year a half-million children worldwide—the equivalent of four 747s full of children every day—die quietly, one by one, from rotavirus, and we hear nothing of it (Glass, 2004).

We must "learn to protect ourselves and our families against future terrorist attacks," warns a U.S. Department of Homeland Security ad that has appeared periodically in my local newspapers. The ad advises us on the food supplies, duct tape, and battery-powered radios we'll need if "there's a terrorist attack on your city." With 4 in 10 Americans being at least somewhat worried "that you or someone in your family will become a victim of terrorism," the "Be afraid!" message—be afraid not just of a terrorist attack on somebody somewhere, but of one on you and your place—has been heard (Carroll, 2005).

The point to remember: It is perfectly normal to fear purposeful violence from those who hate us. When terrorists strike again, we will all recoil in horror. But smart thinkers will also want to check their fears against facts and to resist those who serve their own purposes by cultivating a culture of fear. By so doing, we can take away the terrorists' most omnipresent weapon: exaggerated fear.

"This CD player costs less than players selling for twice as much."

Framing Decisions

OBJECTIVE **7** | Describe how others can use framing to elicit from us the answers they want.

A further test of rationality is whether the same issue, presented in two different but logically equivalent ways, will elicit the same answer. For example, one surgeon tells someone that 10 percent of people die while undergoing a particular surgery. Another tells someone that 90 percent survive. The information is the same. The effect is not. To both patients and physicians, the risk seems greater to those who hear that 10 percent will die (Marteau, 1989; McNeil & others, 1988; Rothman & Salovey, 1997).

The way we present an issue is called **framing,** and its effects are sometimes striking. Consumers respond more positively to ground beef described as "75 percent lean" rather than "25 percent fat" (Levin & Gaeth, 1988; Sanford & others, 2002). Nine in 10 college students rate a condom as effective if it has a supposed "95 percent success rate" in stopping the AIDS virus; only 4 in 10 think it successful when given a "5 percent failure rate" (Linville & others, 1992). And people express more surprise when a "1 in 20" event happens than when an equivalent "10 in 200" event happens (Denes-Raj & others, 1995). To scare people, frame risks as numbers, not percentages. People told that a chemical exposure is projected to kill 10 of every 10 million people (imagine 10 dead people!) feel more frightened than if told the fatality risk is an infinitesimal .000001 (Kraus & others, 1992).

Consider how the framing effect influences economic and business decisions. Merchants mark up their "regular prices" to appear to offer huge savings on "sale prices." A $100 coat marked down from $150 by Store X can seem like a better deal than the same coat priced regularly at $100 by Store Y (Urbany & others, 1988). My dentist doesn't charge more if we pay later, though she does offer a 5 percent discount for immediate cash payment. She, like thousands of other service providers, knows to frame the price difference as a "cash discount" rather than a "credit-card surcharge."

That our judgments can flip-flop so dramatically is startling. It suggests that our judgments and decisions may not be well reasoned, and that those who understand the power of framing can use it to influence important decisions—for example, by framing survey questions to support or reject a particular viewpoint.

Belief Bias

OBJECTIVE **8** | Explain how our preexisting beliefs can distort our logic.

We have seen that part of psychology's thinking about thinking emphasizes that we are prone to bias as we seek confirmation of our hunches, rely on efficient but fallible heuristics, display overconfidence, and fall prey to the effects of framing. But would logic help us escape the bias inflicted by our beliefs?

Logic does help, but we still find it easier to accept conclusions that agree with our opinions. Consider this logical argument:

> *Premise 1:* Some communists are golfers.
> *Premise 2:* All golfers are Marxists.
> *Conclusion:* Some communists are Marxists.

In experiments, nearly everyone correctly recognized that the conclusion logically follows from the premises (Oakhill & others, 1989). But now consider this argument:

> *Premise 1:* Some communists are golfers.
> *Premise 2:* All golfers are capitalists.
> *Conclusion:* Some communists are capitalists.

■ **framing** the way an issue is posed; how an issue is framed can significantly affect decisions and judgments.

■ **belief bias** the tendency for one's preexisting beliefs to distort logical reasoning, sometimes by making invalid conclusions seem valid, or valid conclusions seem invalid.

■ **belief perseverance** clinging to one's initial conceptions after the basis on which they were formed has been discredited.

Many people had a harder time seeing that, given the premises, this conclusion is equally valid. Judge this next conclusion for yourself (adapted from Hunt, 1982):

> *Premise 1:* Democrats support free speech.
> *Premise 2:* Dictators are not democrats.
> *Conclusion:* Dictators do not support free speech.

If that conclusion seems logical, you are experiencing **belief bias**—the tendency for our beliefs to distort our logic (Oakhill & others, 1990). (Premise 1 did not exclude the possibility that others, even dictators, can believe in free speech.) Consider another set of statements with *identical form and logic* and note how much easier it feels to refute the conclusion:

> *Premise 1:* Robins have feathers.
> *Premise 2:* Chickens are not robins.
> *Conclusion:* Chickens do not have feathers.

Thus, belief bias: We more easily see the illogic of conclusions that run counter to our beliefs than of those that agree with our beliefs.

The Belief Perseverance Phenomenon

OBJECTIVE 9 | Describe the remedy for the belief perseverance phenomenon.

An additional source of irrationality is **belief perseverance,** our tendency to cling to our beliefs in the face of contrary evidence. Belief perseverance often fuels social conflict. Charles Lord and his colleagues (1979) revealed how this happens when they studied people with opposing views of capital punishment. Those on both sides studied two supposedly new research findings, one supporting and the other refuting the claim that the death penalty deters crime. Each side was more impressed by the study that supported its own beliefs, and each readily disputed the other study. Thus, showing the pro– and anti–capital-punishment groups the *same* mixed evidence actually *increased* their disagreement.

If you want to rein in the belief perseverance phenomenon, a simple remedy exists: *Consider the opposite.* When Lord and his colleagues (1984) repeated the capital-punishment study, they asked some of their participants to be "as *objective* and *unbiased* as possible." The plea did nothing to reduce the biased evaluation of evidence. They asked another group to consider "whether you would have made the same high or low evaluations had exactly the same study produced results on the *other* side of the issue." Having imagined and pondered *opposite* findings, these people became much less biased in their evaluations of the evidence.

The more we come to appreciate why our beliefs might be true, the more tightly we cling to them. Once people have explained to themselves why they believe a child is "gifted" or "learning disabled," or why candidate X or Y will be more likely to preserve peace, or why company Z is a stock worth owning, they tend to ignore the evidence that undermines that belief. Prejudice persists. Once beliefs form and get justified, it takes more compelling evidence to change them than it did to create them.

The Perils and Powers of Intuition

OBJECTIVE 10 | Describe the smart thinker's reaction to using intuition to solve problems.

We have seen how our irrational thinking can plague our efforts to solve problems, make wise decisions, form valid judgments, and reason logically. Moreover, these perils of intuition appear even when people are offered extra pay for thinking smart, even when they are asked to justify their answers, and even when they are

"God is love.
Love is blind.
Ray Charles is blind.
Ray Charles is God."
Anonymous graffiti

"Once you have a belief, it influences how you perceive all other relevant information. Once you see a country as hostile, you are likely to interpret ambiguous actions on their part as signifying their hostility."
Political scientist Robert Jervis (1985)

"To begin with, it was only tentatively that I put forward the views I have developed . . . but in the course of time they have gained such a hold upon me that I can no longer think in any other way."
Sigmund Freud,
Civilization and Its Discontents, 1930

"I'm happy to say that my final judgment of a case is almost always consistent with my prejudgment of the case."

expert physicians or clinicians (Shafir & LeBoeuf, 2002). From this we might conclude that our heads are indeed filled with straw. All in all, these and many other findings (see **TABLE 10.1**) suggest "bleak implications for human rationality" (Nisbett & Borgida, 1975).

Truths often come in complementary pairs. It is true that unchecked intuition is perilous. But today's cognitive scientists also are revealing intuition's powers. Our cognition, for the most part, is wonderfully efficient and effective. Its instant, intuitive reactions enable us to react quickly and *usually* adaptively (see Table 10.1 for a synopsis of examples from throughout this book). Experienced nurses, firefighters, art critics, car mechanics, hockey players, and you, for anything in which you develop expertise, learn to size up many a situation in an eye blink.

In showing how everyday heuristics usually make us smart (and only sometimes make us dumb), Gerd Gigerenzer (2004) asked both American and German university students, "Which city has more inhabitants: San Diego or San Antonio?" Sixty-two percent of the Americans, after thinking a moment, guessed right: San Diego. In Germany, where many people have not heard of San Antonio (apologies to our Texas friends), students used a fast and frugal intuitive heuristic: Pick the one you recognize. With less knowledge but an adaptive heuristic, 100 percent of Gigerenzer's German respondents answered correctly.

TABLE 10.1

INTUITION'S PERILS AND POWERS (TEXT CHAPTER NUMBERS FOLLOW)

Intuition's Dozen Deadly Sins	Evidence of Intuition's Powers
• *Hindsight bias*—looking back on events, we falsely surmise that we knew it all along. (1)	• *Blindsight*—brain-damaged persons' "sight unseen" as their bodies react to things and faces not consciously recognized. (2)
• *Illusory correlation*—intuitively perceiving a relationship where none exists. (1)	• *Right-brain thinking*—split-brain persons displaying knowledge they cannot verbalize. (2)
• *Memory construction*—influenced by our present moods and by misinformation, we may form false memories. (9)	• *Infants' intuitive learning*—of language and physics. (4)
• *Representativeness and availability*—fast and frugal heuristics become quick and dirty when leading us into illogical and incorrect judgments. (10)	• *Moral intuition*—quick gut feelings that precede moral reasoning. (4)
• *Overconfidence*—our intuitive assessments of our own knowledge are often more confident than correct. (1,10)	• *Divided attention and priming*—unattended information processed by the mind's downstairs radar watchers. (5, 9)
• *Belief perseverance and confirmation bias*—thanks partly to our preference for confirming information, beliefs are often resilient, even after their foundation is discredited. (1,10)	• *Everyday perception*—the instant parallel processing and integration of complex information streams. (5)
• *Framing*—judgments flip-flop, depending on how the same issue or information is posed. (10)	• *Automatic processing*—the cognitive autopilot that guides us through most of life. (various)
• *Interviewer illusion*—inflated confidence in one's discernment based on interview alone. (12)	• *Implicit memory*—learning *how* to do something without knowing *that* one knows. (9)
• *Mispredicting our own feelings*—we often mispredict the intensity and duration of our emotions. (13)	• *Heuristics*—those fast and frugal mental shortcuts that normally serve us well enough. (10)
• *Self-serving bias*—in various ways, we exhibit inflated self-assessments. (15)	• *Intuitive expertise*—phenomena of nonconscious learning, expert learning, and physical genius. (10, 11, 15)
• *Fundamental attribution error*—overly attributing others' behavior to their dispositions by discounting unnoticed situational forces. (18)	• *Creativity*—the sometimes-spontaneous appearance of novel and valuable ideas. (11)
• *Mispredicting our own behavior*—our intuitive self-predictions often go astray. (18)	• *Social and emotional intelligence*—the intuitive know-how to comprehend and manage ourselves in social situations and to perceive and express emotions. (11)
	• *The wisdom of the body*—when instant responses are needed, the brain's emotional pathways bypass the cortex; hunches sometimes precede rational understanding. (13)
	• *Thin slices*—detecting traits from mere seconds of behavior. (15)
	• *Dual attitude system*—as we have two ways of knowing (unconscious and conscious) and two ways of remembering (implicit and explicit), we also have gut-level and rational attitude responses. (18)

Intuition is huge. More than we realize, thinking occurs off-screen, with the results occasionally displayed on-screen. Intuition is adaptive. It feeds our expertise, our creativity, our love, and our spirituality. And intuition, smart intuition, is born of experience. Chess masters can look at a board and intuitively know the right move. Playing "blitz chess," where every move is made after barely more than a glance, they display a hardly diminished skill (Burns, 2004). At every moment, skilled violin players know, without thinking, just where to place the bow, at what angle, with what pressure. Experienced chicken sexers can tell you a chick's sex at a glance, yet cannot tell you how they do it. In each case, the immediate insight describes acquired, speedy expertise that feels like instant intuition. Intuition is recognition, observed Nobel laureate psychologist-economist Herbert Simon (2001). It is analysis "frozen into habit."

Jean-Philippe Ksiazek/AFP

Chick sexing
When acquired expertise becomes an automatic habit, as it is for experienced chick sexers, it feels like intuition. At a glance, they just know.

Mindful of intuition's perils and powers, smart thinkers will welcome their intuitions but also check them against available evidence. Our gut intuitions are terrific at some things, such as instantly reading emotions in others' faces, but not so good at others, such as assessing risks. Wisdom comes with knowing the difference.

>> LEARNING OUTCOMES

Thinking

OBJECTIVE 1 | Define *cognition*.
Cognition is a term covering all the mental activities associated with thinking, knowing, remembering, and communicating.

OBJECTIVE 2 | Describe the roles of categories, hierarchies, definitions, and prototypes in concept formation.
We use concepts to simplify and order the world around us. We divide clusters of objects, events, ideas, or people into *categories* based on their similarities. In creating *hierarchies,* we subdivide these categories into smaller and more detailed units. We form other concepts, such as triangles, by *definition* (three-sided objects). But we form most concepts around *prototypes,* or best examples of a category. Matching objects and ideas against prototypes is an efficient way of making snap judgments about what belongs in a specific category.

OBJECTIVE 3 | Compare algorithms and heuristics as problem-solving strategies, and explain how insight differs from both of them.
An *algorithm* is a time-consuming but thorough set of rules or procedures (such as a recipe for cookies, or a step-by-step description for evacuating a building during a fire) that guarantees a solution to a problem. A *heuristic* is a simpler thinking strategy (such as running for an exit if you smell heavy smoke) that may allow us to solve problems quickly, but sometimes leads us to incorrect solutions. *Insight* differs from both because it is not a strategy-based solution, but rather an Aha! reaction—a sudden flash of inspiration that solves a problem.

OBJECTIVE 4 | Contrast the confirmation bias and fixation, and explain how they can interfere with effective problem solving.
The *confirmation bias* predisposes us to verify rather than challenge our hypotheses. *Fixation,* such as mental set and functional fixedness, may leave us doggedly pursuing one line of reasoning and prevent us from taking the fresh perspective that would let us solve the problem.

OBJECTIVE 5 | Contrast the representativeness and availability heuristics, and explain how they can cause us to underestimate or ignore important information.
The *representativeness heuristic* leads us to judge the likelihood of things in terms of how they represent our prototype for a group of items. The *availability heuristic* leads us to judge the likelihood of things based on how vivid they are or how readily they come to mind. Either of these two thinking shortcuts can cause us to ignore important information or to underestimate the chances of something happening.

OBJECTIVE 6 | Describe the drawbacks and advantages of overconfidence in decision making.
The main drawback of overconfidence is that our tendencies to seek confirmation of our hypotheses and to use quick and easy heuristics can blind us to our vulnerability to error—a fault that can be tragic if we are in a position of responsibility. But on a personal level, overconfident people tend to live happier lives, make difficult decisions more easily, and seem more credible.

OBJECTIVE **7** | **Describe how others can use framing to elicit from us the answers they want.**

An issue can be presented (or *framed*) in different but equally logical ways, but the subtle wording can nudge us in the direction the questioner wants us to take. (Consider, for example, "Do you think people should be free to smoke in public places?" versus "Do you think smokers should have the right to expose the lungs of nonsmokers to second-hand smoke?")

OBJECTIVE **8** | **Explain how our preexisting beliefs can distort our logic.**

We tend to judge conclusions that agree with our beliefs as more logical than those that do not match our beliefs. This *belief bias* can lead us to accept invalid conclusions and reject valid ones.

OBJECTIVE **9** | **Describe the remedy for the belief perseverance phenomenon.**

Belief perseverance is clinging to our ideas because the explanation we once accepted as valid lingers in our mind even after it has been discredited. The best remedy for this form of bias is making the effort to consider evidence supporting the opposite position.

OBJECTIVE **10** | **Describe the smart thinker's reaction to using intuition to solve problems.**

Although it sometimes leads us astray, human intuition can be remarkably efficient and adaptive, giving us instant help when we need it. As we gain expertise in a field, for example, we grow adept at making quick, shrewd judgments. Smart thinkers will welcome their intuitions but check them against available evidence, hoping to avoid overconfidence and biased and illogical thinking.

ASK YOURSELF: People's perceptions of risk, often biased by vivid images from movies or the news, are surprisingly unrelated to actual risks. (People may hide in the basement during thunderstorms but fail to buckle their seat belts in the car.) What are the things you fear? Are some of those fears out of proportion to statistical risk? Are you failing, in other areas of your life, to take reasonable precautions?

Language

The most tangible indication of our thinking power is **language**—our spoken, written, or signed words and the ways we combine them as we think and communicate. Humans have long and proudly proclaimed that language sets us above all other animals. "When we study human language," asserted linguist Noam Chomsky (1972), "we are approaching what some might call the 'human essence,' the qualities of mind that are, so far as we know, unique" to humans. To cognitive scientist Steven Pinker (1990), language is "the jewel in the crown of cognition."

Imagine an alien species that could pass thoughts from one head to another merely by pulsating air molecules in the space between them. Perhaps these weird creatures could inhabit a future Spielberg movie? Actually, we are those creatures! When we speak, our brain and voice box conjure up air pressure waves that we send banging against another's ear drum—enabling us to transfer thoughts from our brain into theirs. As Pinker (1998) notes, we sometimes sit for hours "listening to other people make noise as they exhale, because those hisses and squeaks contain *information*." And thanks to all those funny sounds created in our heads from the air pressure waves we send out, adds Bernard Guerin (2003), we get people's attention, we get them to do things, and we maintain relationships.

When the human vocal tract evolved the ability to utter vowels, our capacity for language exploded, catapulting our species forward (Diamond, 1989). Whether spoken, written, or signed, language enables us not only to communicate but to transmit civilization's accumulated knowledge across generations. Monkeys mostly know what they see. Thanks to language, we know much that we've never seen.

Language Structure

OBJECTIVE **11** | Describe the basic structural units of a language.

Consider how we might go about inventing a language. For a spoken language, we would need three building blocks. First, we would need a set of basic sounds, which linguists call **phonemes.** To say *bat* we utter the phoneme sounds *b, a,* and *t. Chat* also

---

■ **language** our spoken, written, or signed words and the ways we combine them to communicate meaning.

■ **phoneme** in a language, the smallest distinctive sound unit.

■ **morpheme** in a language, the smallest unit that carries meaning; may be a word or a part of a word (such as a prefix).

■ **grammar** in a language, a system of rules that enables us to communicate with and understand others.

■ **semantics** the set of rules by which we derive meaning from morphemes, words, and sentences in a given language; also, the study of meaning.

■ **syntax** the rules for combining words into grammatically sensible sentences in a given language.

has three phonemes—*ch, a,* and *t.* Languages have varying numbers of phonemes. English has about 40; other languages have anywhere from half to more than twice that many. Linguists surveying nearly 500 languages have identified 869 different phonemes in human speech (Holt, 2002; Maddieson, 1984).

Changes in phonemes produce changes in meaning. In English, varying the vowel sound between *b* and *t* creates 12 different meanings: *bait, bat, beat/beet, bet, bit, bite, boat, boot, bought, bout,* and *but* (Fromkin & Rodman, 1983). Generally, though, consonant phonemes carry more information than do vowel phonemes. The treth ef thes stetement shed be evedent frem thes bref demenstretien.

People who grow up learning one set of phonemes usually have difficulty pronouncing those of another language. The native English speaker may smile at the native German speaker's difficulties with the *th* sound, which can make *this* sound like *dis.* But the German speaker smiles back at the problems English speakers have rolling the German *r* or pronouncing the breathy *ch* in *Ich,* the German word for *I.*

Sign language also has phonemelike building blocks defined by hand shapes and movements. Like speakers, native signers of one of the 200+ sign languages may have difficulty with the phonemes of another. Chinese native signers who come to America and learn sign usually sign with an accent, notes researcher Ursula Bellugi (1994).

But sounds alone do not make a language. The second building block is the **morpheme,** the smallest unit of language that carries meaning. In English, a few morphemes are also phonemes—the personal pronoun *I* and the article *a,* for instance. But most morphemes are combinations of two or more phonemes. Some, like *bat,* are words, but others are only parts of words. Morphemes include prefixes and suffixes, such as the *pre-* in *preview* or the *-ed* that shows past tense. *Undesirables* has four morphemes—*un-desir-able-s*—each of which adds to the word's total meaning.

Finally, our new language must have a **grammar,** a system of rules (*semantics* and *syntax*) in a given language that enables us to communicate with and understand others. **Semantics** is the set of rules we use to derive meaning from morphemes, words, and even sentences. In English, for example, a semantic rule tells us that adding *-ed* to *laugh* means that it happened in the past. **Syntax** refers to the rules we use to order words into sentences. One rule of English syntax says that adjectives usually come before nouns, so we say *white house.* Spanish adjectives usually come after nouns, so a Spanish speaker says *casa blanca.* The English rules of syntax allow the sentence *They are hunting dogs.* Given the context, semantics will tell us whether it refers to dogs that seek animals or people who seek dogs.

In all 6000 human languages, the grammar is intricately complex. "There are 'stone age' societies," says Steven Pinker (1995), "but they do not have 'stone age' languages." Contrary to the illusion that less-educated people speak ungrammatically, they simply speak a different dialect. To a linguist, "ain't got none" is grammatically equal to "doesn't have any." (It has the same syntax.)

Note, however, that language becomes more complex as you move from phoneme to morpheme to word to sentence. In English, the relatively small number of 40 or so phonemes can be combined to form more than 100,000 morphemes, which alone or in combination produce the 616,500 word forms in the *Oxford English Dictionary* (including 290,500 main entries such as *meat* and 326,000 subentries such as *meat eater*). We can then use these words to create an infinite number of sentences, most of which (like this one) are original. Like life itself constructed from the genetic code's simple alphabet, language is complexity built of simplicity. I know that you can know why I worry that you think this sentence is starting to get too complex, but that complexity—and our capacity to communicate and comprehend it—is what distinguishes human language capacity (Hauser & others, 2002).

M. & E. Bernheim/Woodfin Camp & Associates

Language transmits culture
The actual words and grammar may differ from culture to culture, but every society has a history it transmits in story form to its children. Here, a group of Ivory Coast boys listens as an elder retells a tribal legend.

How many morphemes are in the word *cats*? How many phonemes? (See page 413.)

From *The Wall Street Journal*—permission Cartoon Features Syndicate.

"Let me get this straight now. Is what you want to build a jean factory or a gene factory?"

A cultural universal: In every language, the commonest words are the shortest. As a word or phrase is used more and more, it often gets shortened. *Television* becomes *TV, compact disc* becomes *CD, electronic mail* becomes *e-mail* (Triandis, 1994).

Language Development

Make a quick guess: How many words did you learn in one average day during the years between your first birthday and your high school graduation?

The average secondary school graduate knows some 60,000 words (Bloom, 2000). That averages (after age 1) to nearly 3500 words learned each year, or 10 each day! How you did it—how the 3500 words a year you learned could so far outnumber the roughly 200 words a year that your schoolteachers consciously taught you—is one of the great human wonders.

Before children can add 2 + 2, they are creating their own original and grammatically appropriate sentences. Most parents would have trouble stating the rules of syntax. Yet their preschoolers comprehend and speak with a facility that puts to shame a college student struggling to learn a foreign language or a scientist struggling to simulate natural language on a computer. But you, too, have an astonishing facility for language. With remarkable efficiency, you can selectively sample the tens of thousands of words in your memory, effortlessly combine them on the fly with near-perfect syntax, and spew them out three words a second (Vigliocco & Hartsuiker, 2002). It is amazing, given how many ways there are to mess up. You also adapt your language to your social context. You know your culture's rules for speaking and listening, such as how far apart to stand and how to take turns in conversation. Language is a social dance. So, how did your language ability unfold, and how can we explain it?

When Do We Learn Language?

OBJECTIVE **12** | Trace the course of language acquisition from the babbling stage through the two-word stage.

Children's language development mirrors language structure—it moves from simplicity to complexity. Infants start without language (*in fantis* means "not speaking"). Yet by 4 months of age, babies can read lips and discriminate speech sounds. They prefer to look at a face that matches a sound, so we know they can recognize that *ah* comes from wide open lips and *ee* from a mouth with corners pulled back (Kuhl & Meltzoff, 1982). This marks the beginning of the development of babies' *receptive language,* their ability to comprehend speech. Babies' receptive language abilities begin to mature before their *productive language,* their ability to produce words.

Around 4 months of age, babies enter a **babbling stage** in which they spontaneously utter a variety of sounds, such as *ah-goo*. Babbling is not an imitation of adult speech, for it includes sounds from various languages, even sounds that do not occur in the household's language. From this early babbling, a listener could not identify an infant as being, say, French, Korean, or Ethiopian. Deaf infants who observe their Deaf parents signing begin to babble more with their hands (Petitto & Marentette, 1991). It seems, then, that before nurture molds our speech, nature enables a wide range of possible phonemes. Many of these natural babbling sounds are consonant-vowel pairs formed by simply bunching the tongue in front of the mouth (*da-da, na-na, ta-ta*) or by opening and closing the lips (*ma-ma*), both of which babies do naturally for feeding (MacNeilage & Davis, 2000).

Eventually our babbling comes to resemble the characteristic sounds and intonations of our household language. By the time infants are about 10 months old, their babbling has changed so that a trained ear can identify the language of the household (de Boysson-Bardies & others, 1989). Phoneme sounds outside the infant's native tongue begin to disappear, as does the ability to discriminate those sounds.

Without exposure to other languages, we become functionally deaf to speech sounds outside our native languages (Pallier & others, 2001). Thus, by adulthood those who speak only English cannot discriminate certain Japanese phonemes within speech. Nor can Japanese adults with no training in English distinguish between the

---

Although you probably know about 80,000 words, you use only 150 words for about half of what you say.

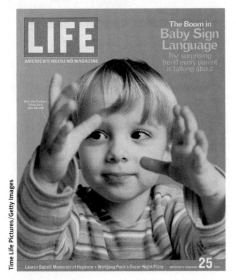

Time Life Pictures/Getty Images

Signs of the times
In an effort to help reduce communication frustration in children before they have fully developed their speaking skills, many hearing parents of hearing children are teaching their children sign language (or supporting their preschool teachers who do so).

■ **babbling stage** beginning at about 4 months, the stage of speech development in which the infant spontaneously utters various sounds at first unrelated to the household language.

■ **one-word stage** the stage in speech development, from about age 1 to 2, during which a child speaks mostly in single words.

■ **two-word stage** beginning about age 2, the stage in speech development during which a child speaks mostly two-word statements.

■ **telegraphic speech** early speech stage in which a child speaks like a telegram—"go car"—using mostly nouns and verbs and omitting auxiliary words.

English *r* and *l*. Thus (believe it or not), *la-la-ra-ra* may sound like the same repeated syllable to a Japanese adult. This makes life challenging for the Japanese tourist who is told the train station is "just after the next light." The next what? After the street veering right, or farther down, after the traffic light?

Around the first birthday (the exact age varies from child to child), most children enter the **one-word stage.** They have already learned that sounds carry meanings, and if repeatedly trained to associate, say, *fish* with a picture of a fish, one-year-olds will look at a fish when a researcher says "Fish, fish! Look at the fish!" (Schafer, 2005). These one-year-olds also begin to use sounds to communicate meaning. Their first words usually contain only one syllable—*ma* or *da,* for instance—and may be barely recognizable. But family members quickly learn to understand the infant's language, and gradually it conforms more and more to the family's language. At this one-word stage, an inflected word may equal a sentence. "Doggy!" may mean "Look at the dog out there!"

Children typically use more and more single words during the second year. At about 18 months, their word learning expands from a word per week to a word per day. Before their second birthday, they usually enter the **two-word stage,** when they start uttering two-word sentences (**TABLE 10.2**). Language at this stage is characterized by **telegraphic speech:** Like telegrams (TERMS ACCEPTED. SEND MONEY), this early form of speech contains mostly nouns and verbs (*Want juice*). Also like telegrams, it follows rules of syntax; the words are in a sensible order. The English-speaking child typically says adjectives before nouns—*big doggy* rather than *doggy big*.

There seems to be no "three-word stage." Once children move out of the two-word stage, they quickly begin uttering longer phrases (Fromkin & Rodman, 1983). Although the sentences may still resemble a telegraphed message (*Mommy get ball*), they continue to follow the rules of syntax. By early elementary school, children understand complex sentences and begin to enjoy the humor conveyed by double meanings: "You never starve in the desert because of all the sand-which-is there."

"Got idea. Talk better. Combine words. Make sentences."

Explaining Language Development

OBJECTIVE 13 | Discuss Skinner's and Chomsky's contributions to the nature-nurture debate over how children acquire language, and explain why statistical learning and critical periods are important concepts in children's language learning.

Those who study language acquisition inevitably wonder how we do it. Attempts to answer this question have sparked a spirited intellectual controversy. The controversy parallels the debate we noted in Chapter 8 over the behaviorist view of the malleable organism versus the view that each organism comes biologically prepared to learn certain associations. The nature-nurture debate surfaces again and, here as elsewhere, appreciation for innate predisposition and the nature-nature interaction has grown.

Skinner: Operant Learning Behaviorist B. F. Skinner (1957) believed that we can explain language development with familiar learning principles, such as association (of the sights of things with the sounds of words); imitation (of the words and syntax modeled by others); and reinforcement (with success, smiles, and hugs when the child says something right). Thus, Skinner (1985) argued, babies learn to talk in many of the same ways that animals learn to peck keys and press bars: "Verbal behavior evidently came into existence when, through a critical step in the evolution of the human species, the vocal musculature became susceptible to operant conditioning."

TABLE 10.2

SUMMARY OF LANGUAGE DEVELOPMENT

Month (approximate)	Stage
4	Babbles many speech sounds.
10	Babbling resembles household language.
12	One-word stage.
24	Two-word, telegraphic speech.
24+	Language develops rapidly into complete sentences.

Answer to question on page 411: Two morphemes—*cat* and *s*, and four phonemes—*c, a, t,* and *s*.

What happens when there is minimal reinforcement for speaking, as is often the case with hearing children of Deaf parents? Their exposure to spoken language, much of it via television, is more passive, and they learn spoken language more slowly. But they learn to sign on a normal time frame (Messer, 2000).

Chomsky: Inborn Universal Grammar Linguist Noam Chomsky (1959, 1987) thinks Skinner's ideas were naive. Surely, Chomsky has said, a Martian scientist observing children in a single-language community would conclude that language is almost entirely inborn. But it isn't. Children do learn their environment's language. However, they acquire untaught words and grammar at a rate too extraordinary to be explained solely by learning principles. They generate all sorts of sentences they have never heard, sometimes with novel errors. (No parent teaches the sentence, "I hate you, Daddy.") Children begin using morphemes in a predictable order. English-speakers begin adding -*ing* to words. Then they start using the prepositions *in* and *on.* Then come *a* and *the,* followed by *is* (Brown, 1973). There are 3,628,800 ways to arrange this sentence's 10 words. Only a handful of them make any sense. Yet any 4-year-old could pick them out from among the 3,628,700+ nonsensical orderings.

Moreover, many of the errors young children make result from *overgeneralizing* logical grammatical rules, such as adding -*ed* to make the past tense (from de Cuevas, 1990):

Child: My teacher holded the baby rabbits and we petted them.
Mother: Did you say your teacher held the baby rabbits?
Child: Yes.
Mother: Did you say she held them tightly?
Child: No, she holded them loosely.

Chomsky (1987) likened the behaviorist view of how language develops to filling a bottle with water. The behaviorists, he believed, oversimplified. Developing language is not just being "filled up" with the right kinds of experiences. Chomsky instead has viewed language development much like "helping a flower to grow in its own way." Language will naturally occur, given adequate nurture; it just "happens to the child." He has contended that all human languages have the same grammatical building blocks, such as nouns and verbs, subjects and objects, negations and questions. Thus, there is a sort of *universal grammar* that underlies all human language. As Steven Pinker (2002) points out, there are no other conceivable ways to power a communication system.

Our 6000 human languages are, therefore, dialects of this universal grammar for which our brains are prewired (Baker, 2001). Thus, we learn readily the specific grammar of whatever language we experience, whether spoken or signed (Bavelier & others, 2003). And no matter what that language is, we start speaking mostly in nouns (*kitty, da-da*) rather than verbs and adjectives (Bornstein & others, 2004). It happens so naturally—as naturally as birds learning to fly—that training hardly helps. Expose children to language and they will soak it up. Raise them in isolation, and they will develop without language. If not exposed to language, a *group* of children will, however, make up their own. Without exposure to language, deaf children, too, will over time create their own with gestures, complete with grammar (Sandler & others, 2005).

Chomsky maintains that our capacity for developing language is natural and quick because we come equipped with a sort of switch box—a *language acquisition device*—already in place. It is as if the switches need to be turned either "on" or "off" for us to understand and produce language. As we hear language, the switches get set for the language we are to learn.

Over time we grasp specific phonemes, morphemes, words, and sentences, and the rules by which we can combine them. These make up what Chomsky calls the *surface structure* of a language, which will vary from one human language to another. For instance, English-speaking children learn to put the object

---

Slightly more than half the world's 6000 languages are spoken by fewer than 10,000 people. And slightly more than half the world's population speaks one of the top 20 languages (Gibbs, 2002).

Creating a language
Brought together as if on a desert island (actually a school), Nicaragua's young deaf children over time drew upon sign gestures from their own home to create their own Nicaraguan Sign Language, complete with words and intricate grammar. Our biological predisposition for language does not create language in a vacuum. But activated by a social context, nature and nurture work creatively together (Osborne, 1999; Senghas & Coppola, 2001).

Susan Meiselas/Magnum Photos

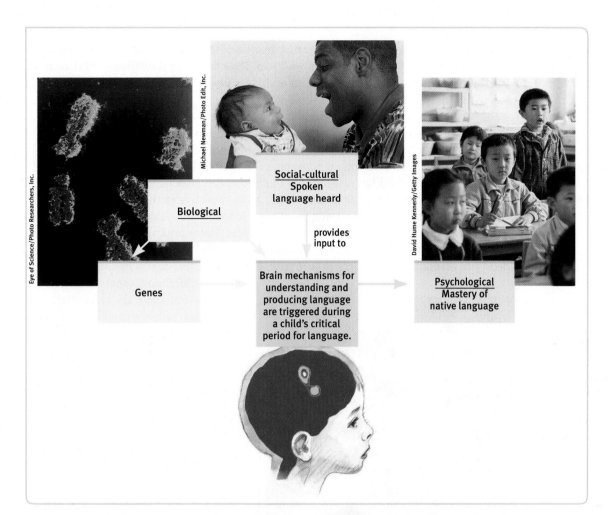

FIGURE 10.9
Levels of understanding language development
Genes design the mechanisms for a language, and experience modifies the brain. Grow up in Paris and you will speak French (environment matters), but not if you are a cat (genes matter).

Biological

Genes

Social-cultural
Spoken language heard

provides input to

Brain mechanisms for understanding and producing language are triggered during a child's critical period for language.

Psychological
Mastery of native language

of a sentence last ("She ate an apple"). Japanese-speaking children learn to put the object before the verb ("She an apple ate"). While deciphering our language's surface structure we also learn to discern its meanings, which Chomsky calls its *deep structure.* In the English and Japanese examples above, the same deep structure is being conveyed through different surface structures. "Mario is easy to please" and "Mario is eager to please" have the same surface structure but different deep structures. (The first can be restructured to "It is easy to please Mario" but not the second.) According to Chomsky, then, it is as if we are born with the hardware and an operating system for language, and our linguistic experiences write the software (**FIGURE 10.9**).

Cognitive Scientists: Statistical Learning and Critical Periods Human infants display a remarkable ability to learn statistical aspects of human speech. When you or I listen to an unfamiliar language, the syllables all run together. Someone unfamiliar with English might, for example, hear *United Nations* as "Uneye Tednay Shuns." Well before our first birthday, our brains were discerning word breaks by statistically analyzing which syllables, as in "hap-py-ba-by," most often go together. Jenny Saffran and her colleagues (1996) showed this by exposing 8-month-old infants to a computer voice speaking an unbroken, monotone string of nonsense syllables (*bidakupadotigolabubidaku . . .*). After just two minutes of exposure, the infants were able to recognize (as indicated by their attention) three-syllable sequences that appeared repeatedly. Others have found infants as young as 6 months able to similarly segment speech (Bortfield & others, 2005).

Follow-up research offers further testimony to infants' surprising knack for soaking up language. For example, 7-month-old infants can learn simple sentence structures. After repeatedly hearing syllable sequences that follow one rule, such as *ga-ti-ga* and

Brain scans reveal a difference in how the brain records a second language learned early versus a second language learned later in life. Adults who learned a second language early in life use the *same* patch of frontal lobe tissue when recounting an event in either the native or the second language. Those who learned their second tongue after childhood display activity in an *adjacent* brain area while using their second language (Kim & others, 1997).

li-na-li (an ABA pattern), they listen longer to syllables in a different sequence, such as *wo-fe-fe* (an ABB pattern) rather than *wo-fe-wo*. Their detecting the difference between the two patterns suggests that babies come with a built-in readiness to learn grammatical rules (Marcus & others, 1999).

But are we capable of performing this same feat of statistical analysis throughout our life span? Many researchers believe not. Childhood seems to represent a *critical period* for mastering certain aspects of language. Those who learn a second language as adults usually speak it with the accent of their first language. (But people who often overhear a second language during childhood can later learn to speak it with a more nativelike accent [Au & others, 2002].) Do they master the foreign grammar better than the accent? To find out, Jacqueline Johnson and Elissa Newport (1991) gave Korean and Chinese immigrants to the United States an English grammar test, requiring them to identify each of 276 sentences ("Yesterday the hunter shoots a deer") as grammatically correct or incorrect. Some of the test-takers had immigrated

Little statistician
Human infants come with a remarkable capacity to statistically analyze language and discern words and grammatical rules. This is a tribute to both nature and nurture—to our biological machinery for learning language.

in early childhood, others as adults. Regardless of their age at immigration, each had been in the United States for approximately 10 years. Nevertheless, as **FIGURE 10.10** reveals, those who learned their second language early learned it best. Chomsky would say that once the grammar switches are thrown during a child's developing years, mastering another grammar becomes more difficult. It is not impossible, but the older the age at which one emigrates to a new country, the harder it is to learn its language (Hakuta & others, 2003). During

"Childhood is the time for language, no doubt about it. Young children, the younger the better, are good at it; it is child's play. It is a onetime gift to the species."

Lewis Thomas, *The Fragile Species*, 1992

childhood and early adolescence, your language acquisition system pretty well mastered grammar and accent, and ever since it has been inclined to rest on its laurels.

As a flower's growth will be stunted without nourishment, so, too, will children become linguistically stunted if isolated from language during the critical period for

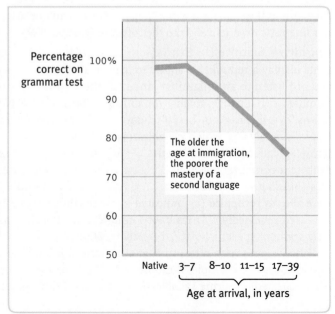

FIGURE 10.10
New language learning gets harder with age
Although there is no sharply defined critical period for second language learning, young children have a greater readiness to learn language than older children and adults. Ten years after coming to the United States, Asian immigrants took a grammar test. Those who arrived before age 8 understood American English grammar as well as native speakers did. Those who arrived later did not. (From Johnson & Newport, 1991.)

Percentage correct on grammar test

The older the age at immigration, the poorer the mastery of a second language

Native   3–7   8–10   11–15   17–39
Age at arrival, in years

its acquisition. The window for learning language is wide open in our early years, then, after age 7, it gradually closes. The impact of early experience is evident in studies of deaf children receiving cochlear implants. Implants by age 2 lead to better oral speech than implants after age 4 (Greers, 2004).

Hearing children of hearing-speaking parents, and deaf children of deaf-signing parents have much in common. As noted earlier, both groups babble as infants— hearing children by repeating sounds, deaf children by repeating elementary sign gestures. Both groups develop vocabularies at comparable rates (Bavelier & others, 2003). For both groups, later-than-usual exposure to language (at age 2 or 3) unleashes their brain's idle language capacity, producing a rush of language. But consider the 90+ percent of deaf children born to hearing-nonsigning parents. These children typically do not experience language during their early years. Compared with children exposed to sign language from birth, those who learn to sign as teens or adults are like immigrants who learn English after childhood. They can master the basic words and learn to order them, but they never become as fluent as native signers in producing and comprehending subtle grammatical differences (Newport, 1990). Moreover, the late-learners show less brain activity in right hemisphere regions that are active as native signers read sign language (Newman & others, 2002).

Those not exposed to either a spoken or a signed language during their early years lose their ability to master *any* language. Natively deaf children who learn sign language after age 9 never learn it as well as those who become deaf at age 9 after learning English. They also never learn English as well as other natively deaf children who learned sign in infancy (Mayberry & others, 2002). The striking conclusion: When a young brain does not learn any language, its language-learning capacity never fully develops.

To summarize, children's genes design complex brain wiring that prepares them to learn language as they interact with their caregivers. Skinner's emphasis on learning helps explain how infants acquire their language as they interact with others. (So does infants' ability to learn statistical probabilities in speech.) Chomsky's emphasis on our built-in readiness to learn grammar rules helps explain why preschoolers acquire language so readily and use grammar so well. Once again, we see biology and experience working together.

Returning to our debate about how deserving we are of our name *Homo sapiens,* let's pause to issue an interim report card. On decision making and judgment, our error-prone species might rate a C+. On problem solving, where humans are inventive yet vulnerable to fixation, we would probably receive better marks, perhaps a B. On cognitive efficiency, our fallible but quick heuristics earn us an A. And when it comes to learning and using language, the awestruck experts would surely award the human species an A+.

No means no—no matter how you say it!
Deaf children of deaf-signing parents and hearing children of hearing parents have much in common. They develop language skills at about the same rate, and they are equally effective at opposing parental wishes and demanding their way.

>> Learning Outcomes

Language

Objective 11 | Describe the basic structural units of a language.
All languages have the same basic structural units. *Phonemes* are the basic units of sound in a language. *Morphemes* are the elementary units of meaning; some (such as *I*) are words, but most are elements such as prefixes (*anti-*) or suffixes *(-ing)*. *Grammar* is the system of rules (mental rules, not those taught in English classes) that enable us to communicate and understand others. *Semantics,* which is part of grammar, is a set of rules for deriving meaning in a given language. *Syntax,* also a part of grammar, is a set of rules for ordering words into sentences.

Objective 12 | Trace the course of language acquisition from the babbling stage through the two-word stage.
At about 4 months of age, infants babble, making a wide range of sounds found in languages located all over the world. By about 10 months, their babbling contains only the sounds found in their household language. Around 12 months of age, babies speak in single words. This one-word stage evolves into two-word (telegraphic) utterances before their second birthday. Shortly after that, children begin speaking in full sentences. The timing of these stages varies a little from one child to another, but all children follow this sequence.

OBJECTIVE **13** | Discuss Skinner's and Chomsky's contributions to the nature-nurture debate over how children acquire language, and explain why statistical learning and critical periods are important concepts in children's language and learning.

Behaviorist B. F. Skinner (representing the nurture side of the language-development debate) proposed that we learn language by the familiar principles of association (of sights of things with sounds of words), imitation (of words and syntax modeled by others), and reinforcement (with smiles and hugs after saying something right). Challenging this claim, linguist Noam Chomsky (representing the nature position) argues that we are born with a language acquisition device that biologically prepares us to learn language. He cites as evidence the species-wide presence of language and its underlying universal grammar; children's amazing rate of acquiring vocabulary; and the uniform sequence of the stages of language development. *Statistical learning* is the ability to detect speech patterns (such as syllable breaks). Childhood is a *critical period* for learning spoken and signed language: Children who do not learn language during this early period lose their ability to fully master language.

ASK YOURSELF: **There has been controversy at some universities about allowing fluency in sign language to fulfill a second-language requirement for an undergraduate degree. What is your opinion?**

■ **linguistic determinism** Whorf's hypothesis that language determines the way we think.

Thinking and Language

Thinking and language intricately intertwine. Asking which comes first is one of psychology's chicken-and-egg questions. Do our ideas come first and we wait for words to name them? Or are our thoughts conceived in words and therefore unthinkable without them?

Language Influences Thinking

OBJECTIVE **14** | Summarize Whorf's linguistic determinism hypothesis, and comment on its standing in contemporary psychology.

Linguist Benjamin Lee Whorf contended that language determines the way we think. According to Whorf's (1956) **linguistic determinism** hypothesis, different languages impose different conceptions of reality: "Language itself shapes a man's basic ideas." The Hopi, Whorf noted, have no past tense for their verbs. Therefore, he contended, a Hopi could not so readily *think* about the past.

Whorf's hypothesis would probably not occur to people who speak only one language and view that language as simply a vehicle for thought. But to those who speak two dissimilar languages, such as English and Japanese, it seems obvious that a person thinks differently in different languages (Brown, 1986). Unlike English, which has a rich vocabulary for self-focused emotions such as anger, Japanese has more words for interpersonal emotions such as sympathy (Markus & Kitayama, 1991). Many bilinguals report that they have a different sense of self, depending on which language they are using (Matsumoto, 1994). After emigrating from Asia to North America, bilinguals may even reveal different personalities when taking the same personality test in their two languages (Dinges & Hull, 1992).

Michael Ross, Elaine Xun, and Anne Wilson (2002) demonstrated this by inviting China-born, bilingual University of Waterloo students to describe themselves in English or Chinese. When describing themselves in English, their self-descriptions were typically Canadian: They expressed mostly positive self-statements and moods. When responding in Chinese, they were typically Chinese: They reported more agreement with Chinese values and roughly equal positive and negative self-statements and moods. Their language use seemed to shape how they thought of themselves.

Learn a language and you learn about a culture. When a language becomes extinct—the likely fate of most of the world's 6000 remaining languages—the world

Before reading on, illustrate this idea: "The girl pushes the boy." Now see the margin note on page 420.

loses the culture and thinking that hang on that language. "To destroy a people, destroy their language," observed poet Joy Harjo.

To say that language *determines* the way we think is much too strong. A Papua New Guinean without our words for shapes and colors nevertheless perceives them much as we do (Rosch, 1974). Yet our words do *influence* what we think (Hardin & Banaji, 1993; Özgen, 2004). In Brazil, the isolated Piraha tribespeople have words for the numbers "1" and "2," but numbers above that are simply "many." Thus if shown seven nuts in a row, they find it very difficult to lay out the same number from their own pile (Gordon, 2004). Whether living in Britain, New Guinea, or Namibia, people also use their language when classifying and remembering colors (Davidoff, 2004; Roberson & others, 2004). If English is your native language, imagine that while viewing three colors you called two of them "yellow" and one of them "blue." Later you would likely see and recall the yellows as being more similar. People in Papua New Guinea's Berinmo tribe, which has words for two different shades of yellow, would better recall the distinctions between the two yellows. On the color spectrum, blue blends into green. But we find it relatively easy to distinguish two colors that are on either side of the dividing line between what we call "blue" and "green." Given the same degree of difference on the color spectrum (**FIGURE 10.11**), two different "blues" (or two different "greens") are, when given the same names, harder to distinguish (Özgen, 2004). The perceived difference grows when we assign different names to colors.

Given the subtle influence of words on thinking, we do well to choose our words carefully. Does referring to women as *girls*—as in "girls' night out"—assume women's lower status? What about the generic use of the pronoun *he*? Does it make any difference whether I write, "A child learns language as *he* interacts with *his* caregivers" or "Children learn language as *they* interact with *their* caregivers"? Some argue it makes no difference because every reader knows "the masculine gender shall be deemed and taken to include females" (as the British Parliament declared in 1850).

But many studies have found that when hearing the generic *he* (as in "the artist and his work") people are more likely to picture a male (Henley, 1989; Ng, 1990). Consider, too, that people use generic pronouns selectively, as in "the doctor . . . he" and "the secretary . . . she" (MacKay, 1983). If *he* and *his* were truly gender-free, we shouldn't skip a beat when hearing that "man, like other mammals, nurses his young."

To expand language is to expand the ability to think. In young children, thinking develops hand in hand with language (Gopnik & Meltzoff, 1986). Indeed, it is very difficult to think about or conceptualize certain abstract ideas (commitment, freedom, or rhyming) without language! And what is true for preschoolers is true for everyone: *It pays to increase your word power.* That's why most textbooks, including this one, introduce new words—to teach new ideas and new ways of thinking.

Increasing word power through sign language has had great benefits for deaf people, who for thousands of years were viewed by the hearing community as incompetent to inherit property, marry, be educated, or have challenging work (Sacks, 1990).

> " Language is not a straight jacket."
> Psychologist Lila Gleitman, American Association for the Advancement of Science Convention, 2002

> " All words are pegs to hang ideas on."
> Henry Ward Beecher, *Proverbs from Plymouth Pulpit*, 1887

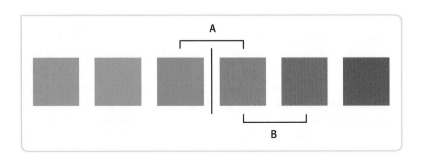

FIGURE 10.11
Language and perception
Emre Özgen (2004) reports that when shown equally different colors, those that carry different names seem more different. Thus the "green" and "blue" in contrast A may appear to differ more than the two similarly different blues in contrast B.

A safe sign

We have outfielder William Hoy to thank for baseball sign language. The first deaf player to join the major leagues (1892), he invented hand signals for "Strike!" "Safe!" (shown here) and "Yerr Out!" (Pollard, 1992). Such gestures worked so well that referees in all sports now use invented signs, and fans are fluent in sports sign language.

Many native English speakers, including most Americans, are monolingual. Most humans are bilingual or multilingual. Does monolingualism limit people's ability to comprehend the thinking of other cultures?

How did you illustrate "the girl pushes the boy" (page 418)? Anne Maass and Aurore Russo (2003) report that people whose language reads from left to right mostly position the pushing girl on the left. Those who speak Arabic, a language that reads from right to left, mostly place her on the right.

Deaf people's competency is clear when they are exposed to signing as preschoolers and then schooled in their own language. Children of signing Deaf parents develop native sign fluency, and they outperform non-fluent deaf children on measures of intelligence and academic achievement (Isham & Kamin, 1993).

Increased word power helps explain what McGill University researcher Wallace Lambert (1992; Lambert & others, 1993) calls the *bilingual advantage*. Bilingual children, who learn to inhibit one language while using their other language, are also better able to inhibit their attention to irrelevant information. If asked to say whether a sentence is grammatically correct ("Why is the cat barking so loudly?") they can more efficiently focus on the grammar alone (Bialystok, 2001).

Lambert helped devise a Canadian program that immerses English-speaking children in French. (From 1981 to 1999, the number of non-Quebec Canadian children immersed in French rose from 65,000 to 280,000 [Commissioner, 1999].) For most of their first three years in school, the English-speaking children are taught entirely in French, and thereafter gradually shift by the end of their schooling to classes mostly in English. Not surprisingly, the children attain a natural French fluency unrivaled by other methods of language teaching. Moreover, compared with similarly capable children in control conditions, they do so without detriment to their English fluency, and with increased aptitude scores, math scores, and appreciation for French-Canadian culture (Genesee & Gándara, 1999).

So, for English-speaking Canadians, immersion followed by bilingual education pays dividends. Does bilingual education for children in a linguistic minority also pay dividends? Advocates of "English-only" education doubt it. They argue that bilingual programs are expensive, ineffective, and detrimental to non–English-speaking children's assimilation into their English-based cultures (Porter, 1998). But some researchers disagree (August & Hakuta, 1998; Padilla & Benavides, 1992; Thomas & Collier, 1998). Children in "two-way" schools where they, together with English-speaking children, experience half their classes in English and half in their native language, tend to develop higher self-esteem than do non–English-speaking children dropped into English-only schools. They drop out less frequently. And they eventually attain higher levels of academic achievement and English proficiency.

Whether we are deaf or hearing, language transforms experience. Language connects us to the past and the future. Language fuels our imagination. Language links us to one another.

Thinking in Images

OBJECTIVE 15 | Discuss the value of thinking in images.

When you are alone, do you talk to yourself? Is "thinking" simply conversing with yourself? Without a doubt, words convey ideas. But aren't there times when ideas precede words? To turn on the cold water in your bathroom, in which direction do you turn the handle? To answer this question, you probably thought not in words but with procedural memory—a mental picture of how you do it. Indeed, we often think in images. Artists think in images. So do composers, poets, mathematicians, athletes, and scientists. Albert Einstein reported that he achieved some of his greatest insights through visual images and later put them into words.

FIGURE 10.12
The power of imagination
Imagining a physical activity triggers action in the same brain areas that are triggered when actually performing that activity. These MRIs show a person imagining the experience of pain, which activates some of the same areas in the brain as the actual experience of pain.

Pianist Liu Chi Kung showed the value of thinking in images. One year after placing second in the 1958 Tchaikovsky piano competition, Liu was imprisoned during China's cultural revolution. Soon after his release, after seven years without touching a piano, he was back on tour, the critics judging his musicianship better than ever. How did he continue to develop without practice? "I did practice," said Liu, "every day. I rehearsed every piece I had ever played, note by note, in my mind" (Garfield, 1986). For someone who has learned a skill, such as ballet dancing, even just watching the activity will activate the brain's internal simulation of it, reports one British research team after collecting fMRI scans as people watched videos (Calvo-Merino & others, 2004).

For Olympic athletes, "mental practice has become a standard part of training," reports Richard Suinn (1997). In a laboratory test, Georgia Nigro (1984) demonstrated the wisdom of such practice. She had people actually throw darts 24 times at a target, then had half the people throw 24 darts mentally, and, finally, had everyone throw another 24 darts. Only those who had rehearsed the throws showed any improvement. Brain-imaging studies, such as the one shown in **FIGURE 10.12,** indicate that mentally simulating an action activates neural networks that are also active when performing the action (Grèzes & Decety, 2001).

Young figure skaters have exhibited similar improvement in their performance ratings for jumps and spins following mental practice while listening to their skating music (Garza & Feltz, 1998). One experiment on mental practice and basketball foul shooting tracked the University of Tennessee women's team over 35 games (Savoy & Beitel, 1996). During that time, the team's free-throw shooting increased from approximately 52 percent in games following standard physical practice to some 65 percent after mental practice. Players had repeatedly imagined making foul shots under various conditions, including being "trash-talked" by their opposition. In a dramatic conclusion, Tennessee won the national championship game in overtime, thanks in part to their foul shooting.

Mental rehearsal can also help you achieve an academic goal. In one study, Shelley Taylor and her UCLA colleagues (1998) engaged introductory psychology students who were a week away from facing a midterm exam. Some were told to visualize themselves scanning the posted grade list, seeing their A, beaming with joy, and feeling proud. Repeating this *outcome simulation* 5 minutes each day until the exam had little effect, adding only 2 points to their exam scores, compared with scores of student counterparts not engaging in any mental simulation. But the researchers had another group visualize themselves effectively studying—reading the chapters, going over notes, eliminating distractions, declining an offer to go out. Repeating this *process simulation* for 5 minutes each day had a beneficial effect. Compared with the control students, this second group began studying sooner, spent more time at it, and beat the others' average by 8 points. From such experiments, the researchers conclude that it is better to spend your fantasy time planning how to get somewhere than to dwell on the imagined destination.

A thoughtful art
Playing the piano engages thinking without language. In the absence of a piano, mental practice can sustain one's skill.

The interplay of thought and language
The traffic runs both ways between thinking and language. Thinking affects our language, which affects our thought.

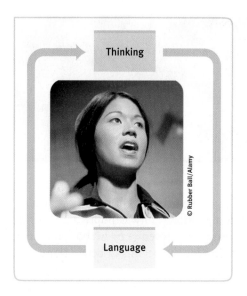

Thinking

Language

© Rubber Ball/Alamy

More evidence of thinking without language comes from evidence seen in earlier chapters of our information processing outside of consciousness. Inside the ever-active brain, many streams of activity flow in parallel, function automatically, are remembered implicitly, and only occasionally surface as conscious words. "Thinking lite," this unconscious processing has been called—"one-fourth the effort of regular thinking." So, yes, there is thinking, much thinking, without language.

What, then, should we say about the relationship between thinking and language? As we have seen, language does influence our thinking. But if thinking did not also affect language, there would never be any new words. And new words and new combinations of old words express new ideas. The basketball term *slam dunk* was coined after the act itself had become fairly common. So, let us say that *thinking affects our language, which then affects our thought.*

Psychological research on thinking and language mirrors the mixed views of our species by those in fields such as literature and religion. The human mind is simultaneously capable of striking intellectual failures and of striking intellectual power. Misjudgments are common and can have disastrous consequences. So we do well to appreciate our capacity for error. Yet our efficient heuristics often serve us well. Moreover, our ingenuity at problem solving and our extraordinary power of language mark humankind as almost "infinite in faculties."

>> LEARNING OUTCOMES

Thinking and Language

OBJECTIVE 14 | Summarize Whorf's linguistic determinism hypothesis, and comment on its standing in contemporary psychology.

Although the linguistic determinism hypothesis suggested that language *determines* thought, it is more accurate to say that language *influences* thought. Words convey ideas, and research on people who are bilingual demonstrates that different languages embody different ways of thinking. Studies of the effects of the generic pronoun *he* show that subtle prejudices can be conveyed by the words we choose to express our everyday thoughts. Some evidence indicates that vocabulary enrichment, particularly immersion in bilingual education, can enhance thinking.

OBJECTIVE 15 | Discuss the value of thinking in images.

We often think in images when we use procedural memory—our unconscious memory system for motor and cognitive skills and conditioned associations. Researchers have found that thinking in images is especially useful for mentally practicing upcoming events and can actually increase our skills.

ASK YOURSELF: Do you use certain words or gestures that only your family or closest circle of friends would understand? Can you envision using these words or gestures to construct a language, as the Nicaraguan children did in building their version of sign?

Animal Thinking and Language

If in our use of language we humans are, as the psalmist long ago rhapsodized, "little lower than God," where do other animals fit in the scheme of things? Are they "little lower than human"? Do animals—in some sense we can identify with—think? Do they even exhibit language?

Do Animals Think?

OBJECTIVE **16** | List five cognitive skills shared by the great apes and humans.

Animals, especially the great apes, display remarkable capacities for thinking. They can, for example, form concepts. After monkeys learn to classify cats and dogs, certain frontal lobe neurons in their brains fire in response to new "catlike" images, others to new "doglike" images (Freedman & others, 2001). Pigeons—mere birdbrains—can sort objects according to their similarity. Shown pictures of cars, cats, chairs, and flowers, they readily learn to identify the categories. Shown a picture of a never-before-seen chair, the pigeon will reliably peck a key that represents "chairs" (Wasserman, 1995).

We also are not the only creatures to display insight. Psychologist Wolfgang Köhler (1925) observed apparent insight while studying chimpanzees placed on an island off the coast of Africa. In one experiment with a caged chimp named Sultan, Köhler placed a piece of fruit and a long stick well beyond reach, and a short stick inside the cage. Spying the short stick, Sultan grabbed it and tried to reach the fruit. But by design, the stick was too short. After several unsuccessful attempts, Sultan dropped the stick and paused to survey the situation. Then suddenly, as if thinking "Aha!" he jumped up, seized the short stick again, and used it to pull in the longer stick—which he then used to reach the fruit. Sultan's actions displayed animal cognition, claimed Köhler, and showed that there is more to learning than conditioning.

Thanks to problem solving shaped by reinforcement, forest-dwelling chimpanzees have become natural tool users (Boesch-Achermann & Boesch, 1993). They select appropriate branches or stones to use as hammers in cracking nuts. They also break off a reed or a stick, strip the twigs and leaves, carry it to a termite mound, fish for termites by twisting it just so, and then carefully remove it without scraping off many termites. They even select different tools for different purposes, including a heavy stick to puncture holes and a light, flexible stick for fishing (Sanz & others, 2004). One anthropologist, trying to mimic the chimpanzee's deft termite fishing, failed miserably.

Researchers have found at least 39 local customs related to chimp tool use, grooming, and courtship (Whiten & Boesch, 2001). One group may slurp ants directly from the stick, while another group plucks them off individually. One group may break nuts with a stone hammer, another with a wooden hammer. Such group differences,

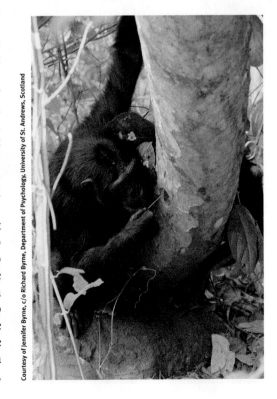

Courtesy of Jennifer Byrne, c/o Richard Byrne, Department of Psychology, University of St. Andrews, Scotland

Chimpanzee inventiveness
A wild chimpanzee shows ingenuity by using a stick to fish for ants living in the tree. Crows, too, have been observed to fashion a twig into a tool that can poke out insect larvae (Emery & Clayton, 2004).

Chimpanzee culture
On the western bank of one Ivory Coast river, a mother uses a stone hammer to open a nut while a youngster watches. On the river's other side, a few miles away, chimps have not learned this trick.

Michael Nichols/National Geographic Image Collection

along with differing dialects and hunting styles, seem not to be genetic. Rather, they are the chimpanzee equivalent of cultural diversity. Like humans, chimpanzees—often younger ones—invent customs and pass them on to their peers and offspring. So do orangutans (van Schaik & others, 2003). And so do at least one group of Australian dolphins, which has learned to break off sponges and wear them on their snouts while probing the sea floor for fish (Krützen & others, 2005).

If primates can form concepts, exhibit insight, use tools, and transmit cultural innovations, do they have what Chapter 4 called a "theory of mind"? Can they infer mental states in themselves and their peers? Chimps are not humans, Daniel Povinelli and Jesse Bering (2002) remind us. When choosing who should retrieve food for them, humans prefer someone who has witnessed it being hidden. Chimps do not. Chimps and orangutans have, however, been observed using mirrors to inspect themselves and touching a colored spot that a researcher has dabbed on their face (Gallup, 1998). Dolphins, too, pause by a mirror to examine ink marks placed on their bodies (Reiss & Marino, 2001).

Copyright Amanda K. Coakes

Cultural transmission in dolphins
This bottlenose dolphin in Shark Bay, Western Australia, is among a small group that has learned to use marine sponges as foraging tools.

As we noted in Chapter 1, chimps and baboons have also been observed using deception, as when a young baboon feigns having been attacked as a seeming tactic for getting its mother to drive a competing baboon away from its food. Do such observations indicate that primates are capable of self-recognition and of comprehending

Smart bird brain
Alex, an African gray parrot trained and tested by University of Arizona professor Irene Pepperberg (2002), displays numerical competence when shown novel assortments of objects. Asked, for example, "How many red blocks?" or "How many green balls?" Alex, with a brain the size of a walnut, answers correctly more than 80 percent of the time.

William Munoz

others' perceptions? Many researchers think so. After reviewing great apes' capacity for reasoning, self-recognition, empathy, imitation, and understanding another's mind, Thomas Suddendorf and Andrew Whiten (2001) estimate their mental accomplishments as "very similar to that observed in 2-year-old humans."

Do Animals Exhibit Language?

OBJECTIVE **17** | Outline the arguments for and against the idea that animals and humans share the capacity for language.

Without doubt, animals communicate. Vervet monkeys have different alarm cries for different predators: a barking call for a leopard, a cough for an eagle, and a chuttering for a snake. Hearing the leopard alarm, other vervets climb the nearest tree. Hearing the eagle alarm, they rush into the bushes. Hearing the snake chutter, they stand up and scan the ground (Byrne, 1991). Whales also communicate, with clicks and wails. Honeybees do a dance that informs other bees of the direction and distance of the food source.

Comprehending canine
Rico, a border collie with a 200-word vocabulary, can infer that an unfamiliar sound refers to a novel object.

And then there is Rico the border collie. He knows 200 items by name and can fetch any one of them (among a group of 10 items, and even when he can hear but cannot see his owner). Moreover, reports a team of psychologists at Leipzig's Max-Planck Institute, if asked to retrieve a novel toy with a name he has never heard, Rico will pick out the novel item from among a group of familiar items (Kaminski & others, 2004). And four weeks later, if this item is placed among other novel and familiar items, Rico, when hearing that novel word for the second time, will as often as not retrieve the object. Without question, such feats show animals' comprehension and communication. But is this language?

The Case of the Apes

The greatest challenge to humanity's claim to be the only language-using species has come from reports of apes that "talk" with people. Genetically speaking, our closest relatives are the chimpanzees, and the chimpanzees' closest relatives are not other apes, but us (Sagan & Druyan, 1992). Knowing that chimpanzees could not vocalize more than a few words, University of Nevada researchers Allen Gardner and Beatrix Gardner (1969) tried to teach sign language words to a chimpanzee named Washoe, as though she were a deaf human child. After four years, Washoe could use 132 signs. At age 32, Washoe had a vocabulary of 181 signs (Sanz & others, 1998). The Gardners' announcement of the success of their efforts aroused enormous scientific and public interest. One *New York Times* reporter, having learned sign language from his deaf parents, visited Washoe and exclaimed, "Suddenly I realized I was conversing with a member of another species in my native tongue."

Human language may have evolved from gestured communications (Corballis, 2002, 2003). If so, it is no wonder that our ape relatives have produced many gestured words but few spoken words. It is no wonder that gestures survive as part of people's speech (even when talking on the phone!). It is no wonder that signing so

Seeing a doll floating in her water, Washoe signed, "Baby in my drink."

Gestured communication
For hearing people, today's gestures may be less central to communication than for those who first used hand signals. Yet gestures remain naturally associated with spontaneous speech, especially speech that has spatial content.

Gesture researcher Robert Krauss (1998) recalls his grandfather telling of two men walking on a bitter winter day. One chattered away while the second nodded, saying nothing. "Schmuel, why aren't you saying anything?" the first friend finally wondered. "Because," replied Schmuel, "I forgot my gloves."

readily develops among Deaf people as an alternative to speech. It is no wonder that congenitally blind people produce gestures similar to those of sighted people, even if they believe the listener is also blind (Iverson & Goldin-Meadow, 1998). It is no wonder that prohibiting gestures disrupts speech that has spatial content (for example, describing an apartment layout). And it's therefore no wonder that gesturing lightens the cognitive load carried by speech. People told not to gesture put more effort into communicating with words alone, and are less able to remember recently learned information, such as lists of words or numbers (Goldin-Meadow & others, 2001). For both humans and apes, communication entails gestures.

Further evidence of gestured "ape language" surfaced during the 1970s. Usually apes sign just single words such as "that" or "gimme" (Bowman, 2003). But sometimes they have strung signs together to form intelligible sentences. Washoe signed, "You me go out, please." Apes even appeared to combine words creatively. Washoe designated a swan as a "water bird." Koko, a gorilla trained by Francine Patterson (1978), reportedly described a long-nosed Pinocchio doll as an "elephant baby." Lana, a "talking" chimpanzee that punches a crude computer keyboard which translates her entries into English, wanted her trainer's orange. She had no word for *orange*, but she did know her colors and the word for *apple*, so she improvised: "?Tim give apple which-is orange" (Rumbaugh, 1977).

As reports of ape language accumulated, it seemed that they might indeed be "little lower than human." Granted, their vocabularies and sentences are simple, rather like those of a 2-year-old child. Yet the apes do seem to share what we humans have considered our unique ability.

But Can Apes Really Talk?

By the late 1970s, fascination with "talking apes" turned toward cynicism: Were the chimps language champs or were the researchers chumps? The ape language researchers were making monkeys of themselves, said the skeptics, who raised the following arguments:

- Apes gain their limited vocabularies only with great difficulty. They are hardly like speaking or signing children, who effortlessly soak up dozens of new words a week (Wynn, 2004). Saying that apes can learn language because they can sign words is like saying humans can fly because they can jump.
- Chimpanzees can make signs or push buttons in sequence to get a reward, just as Moscow circus bears can learn to ride unicycles. But pigeons, too, can peck a sequence of keys to get grain (Straub & others, 1979). No one says the pigeon is "talking."
- Apes can certainly use symbols meaningfully. But "Give orange me give eat orange me eat orange . . ." is a far cry from the exquisite syntax of a 3-year-old (Anderson, 2004; Pinker, 1995). To the child, "you tickle" and "tickle you" communicate different ideas. A chimpanzee, lacking human syntax, might sign the phrases interchangeably.

"Although humans make sounds with their mouths and occasionally look at each other, there is no solid evidence that they actually communicate with each other."

- After training a chimp he named Nim Chimsky, Herbert Terrace (1979) concluded that much of chimpanzees' signing is nothing more than apes aping their trainers' signs and learning that certain arm movements produce rewards.
- Presented with ambiguous information, people, thanks to their "perceptual set," tend to see what they want or expect to see. Interpreting chimpanzee signs as language may be little more than the trainers' wishful thinking, claimed Terrace. (When Washoe signed *water bird*, she perhaps was separately naming *water* and *bird*.)

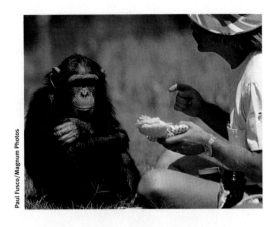

Paul Fusco/Magnum Photos

But is this language?
Chimpanzees' ability to express themselves in American Sign Language (ASL) raises questions about the very nature of language. Here, the trainer is asking, "What is this?" The sign in response is "Baby." Does the response constitute language?

"Chimps do not develop language," concludes Steven Pinker (1995). "But that is no shame on them; humans would surely do no better if trained to hoot and shriek like chimps, to perform the waggle-dance of the bee, or any of the other wonderful feats in nature's talent show."

In science as in politics, controversy can stimulate progress. The provocative claim that "apes share our capacity for language" and the skeptical rejoinder that "apes no use language" (as Washoe might have put it) have moved psychologists toward a greater appreciation of both apes' remarkable abilities and our own (Friend, 2004; Rumbaugh & Washburn, 2003). Everyone agrees: Humans alone possess language, if by the term we mean verbal or signed expression of complex grammar. If we mean, more simply, the ability to communicate through a meaningful sequence of symbols, then apes are indeed capable of language.

Although chimpanzees do not have our facility for language, their abilities to think and communicate continue to impress their trainers. After her second infant died, a depressed Washoe repeatedly asked, "Baby?" and became withdrawn when told, "Baby dead, baby gone, baby finished." Two weeks later, caretaker-researcher Roger Fouts (1992, 1997) had better news for Washoe: "I have baby for you." Washoe reacted to the signed news with instant excitement, her hair on end, swaggering and panting while signing over and again, "Baby, my baby." When Fouts then introduced the foster infant, Loulis, it took several hours for them to warm to each other, whereupon Washoe broke the ice by signing, "Come baby" and cuddling Loulis. In the months that followed, Loulis picked up 68 signs simply by observing Washoe and three other language-trained chimps.

> "[Our] view that [we are] unique from all other forms of animal life is being jarred to the core."
> Duane Rumbaugh and Sue Savage-Rumbaugh (1978)

Moreover, Washoe, Loulis, and the others now sign spontaneously. They ask one another to *chase, tickle, hug, come,* or *groom.* People who sign can actually eavesdrop on these chimp-to-chimp conversations with near-perfect agreement about what the chimps are saying, 90 percent of which pertains to social interaction, reassurance, or play (Fouts & Bodamer, 1987). The chimps are even modestly bilingual; they can translate spoken English words into signs (Shaw, 1989–1990).

More stunning is the claim by Sue Savage-Rumbaugh and her colleagues (1993) that pygmy chimpanzees can learn to comprehend the semantic nuances of spoken English. Kanzi, a pygmy chimpanzee with the seeming grammatical abilities of a human 2-year-old, happened onto language while observing his adoptive mother during language training. Kanzi has behaved intelligently whether asked, "Can you show me the light?" or "Can you bring me the [flash]light?" or "Can you turn the light on?" Kanzi also knows the spoken words *snake, bite,* and *dog.* Given stuffed animals and asked—for the

"He says he wants a lawyer."

Copyright of Great Ape Trust of Iowa.

Another "talking" chimpanzee
Sue Savage-Rumbaugh trains Kanzi, a
very smart pygmy chimpanzee.

What time is it now? On page 403, did
you underestimate or overestimate how
quickly you would finish the chapter?

first time—to "make the dog bite the snake," he put the snake to the dog's mouth. If
Kanzi "had a vocal tract, he would be talking," exclaimed Duane Rumbaugh (1994).
For chimps as for humans, early life is a critical time for learning language. If raised
without early exposure to speech or word symbols, the chimps are unable as adults to
gain language competence (Rumbaugh & Savage-Rumbaugh, 1994).

Believing that animals could not think, Descartes and other philosophers argued
that they were living robots without any moral rights. Animals, it has been said at one
time or another, cannot plan, conceptualize, count, use tools, show compassion, or
use language (Thorpe, 1974). Today, we know better. Animal researchers have shown
us that primates exhibit insight, show family loyalty, communicate with one another,
display altruism, transmit cultural patterns across generations, and comprehend the
syntax of human speech. Accepting and working out the moral implications of all
this is an unfinished task for our own thinking species.

>> LEARNING OUTCOMES

Animal Thinking and Language

OBJECTIVE 16 | **List five cognitive skills shared by the great apes and humans.**
Both humans and the great apes form concepts, display insight, use and create tools,
transmit cultural innovations, and have a theory of mind (including the capacity for
reasoning, self-recognition, empathy, imitation, and understanding another's mind).

OBJECTIVE 17 | **Outline the arguments for and against the idea that animals and humans
share the capacity for language.**
Bees dance to communicate the direction and distance of food, parrots sort items by
number, and dogs comprehend and respond to complicated human commands. Several species of apes have learned to communicate with humans by signing or by pushing buttons wired to a computer. These apes have developed vocabularies of hundreds
of words, have communicated by stringing these words together, and have taught
their skills to younger animals, who—like humans—tend to acquire the skills most
easily and thoroughly if taught them at a very young age. Nevertheless, research reveals an important difference between apes' and humans' facilities with language:
Only humans can master the verbal or signed expression of complex rules of syntax.

ASK YOURSELF: Can you think of a time when you felt an animal was communicating with
you? How might you put such intuition to a test?

REVIEW CHAPTER 10: Thinking and Language

Test Yourself

1. The availability heuristic is a quick-and-easy but sometimes misleading guide to judging reality. What is the availability heuristic?

2. If children are not yet speaking, is there any reason to think they would benefit from parents and other caregivers reading to them?

3. To say that "words are the mother of ideas" assumes the truth of what concept?

4. If your dog barks at a stranger at the front door, does this qualify as language? What if the dog yips in a telltale way to let you know she needs to go out?

Answers to the Test Yourself questions can be found in Appendix B at the end of the book.

Terms and Concepts to Remember

cognition, p. 395

concept, p. 396

prototype, p. 396

algorithm, p. 397

heuristic, p. 398

insight, p. 398

confirmation bias, p. 399

fixation, p. 400

mental set, p. 400

functional fixedness, p. 400

representativeness heuristic, p. 401

availability heuristic, p. 402

overconfidence, p. 403

framing, p. 406

belief bias, p. 407

belief perseverance, p. 407

language, p. 410

phoneme, p. 410

morpheme, p. 411

grammar, p. 411

semantics, p. 411

syntax, p. 411

babbling stage, p. 412

one-word stage, p. 413

two-word stage, p. 413

telegraphic speech, p. 413

linguistic determinism, p. 418

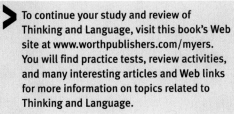

WEB

> To continue your study and review of Thinking and Language, visit this book's Web site at www.worthpublishers.com/myers. You will find practice tests, review activities, and many interesting articles and Web links for more information on topics related to Thinking and Language.

ANOTHER VOICE ON: INTELLIGENCE

WILL COFFEY, FROM "TWO LOVES," (IN *I THOUGHT MY FATHER WAS GOD AND OTHER TRUE TALES FROM NPR'S NATIONAL STORY PROJECT*)

In October 1977 I was twelve years old and nuts for both baseball and Colby (our swaggering, sophisticated black cat). One afternoon, those two loves collided eerily.

Having tired of pitching tennis balls against the wall behind our driveway, I hoisted my Wiffle bat and began driving my four or five Spaldings back and forth across the yard. One by one, the balls became snared in the limbs of an old pear tree. Soon I was down to one surviving tennis ball—which finally surrendered to the same fate. At this point, I was very dismayed. I knew I couldn't quite climb that tree. I began heaving my Jim O'Toole-model glove at the balls. The glove got stuck. I resorted to chucking my flimsy bat at the balls. The bat got stuck. Before I had a chance to lose my sneakers, Colby swayed upon the scene. He sat briefly, head cocked, studying my helplessness. My hero then resolutely scaled the tree, expertly negotiating its far reaches to locate and deftly swat at each hostage sporting good. Moments later, the last one successfully tumbled into my disbelieving grasp.

11 : Intelligence

New York Times *interviewer Deborah Solomon, 2004:* "What is your IQ?"
Physicist Stephen Hawking: "I have no idea. People who boast about their IQ are losers."

■ **intelligence** mental quality consisting of the ability to learn from experience, solve problems, and use knowledge to adapt to new situations.

Three huge controversies have sparked recent debate in and beyond psychology. First is the "memory war," over whether traumatic experiences are repressed and can later be recovered, with therapeutic benefit (Chapters 9 and 15). The second great controversy is the "gender war," over the extent to which nature and nurture shape our behaviors as men and women (Chapters 3 and 18). In this chapter, we focus on the "intelligence war": Does each of us have an inborn general mental capacity (intelligence), and can we quantify this capacity as a meaningful number?

School boards, courts, scientists, and clinicians debate the usefulness and fairness of tests that attempt to assess people's mental abilities, assign them a score, and compare them with the scores of others. Should we use such tests to rank people, to admit them to a particular college, to hire them for a particular job, to diagnose them with a particular psychological disorder? First, we'd better ask some more basic questions: What *is* intelligence? How can we best assess it? To what extent does it result from heredity rather than environment? What do test score differences among individuals and groups really mean? Is intelligence testing a constructive way to guide people toward suitable opportunities? Or is it a potent, discriminatory weapon camouflaged as science? This chapter aims to offer you some answers, and also to remind you that there are a variety of mental gifts and that the recipe for high achievement in any field blends talent and grit.

What Is Intelligence?

OBJECTIVE 1 | Discuss the difficulty of defining *intelligence,* and explain what it means to "reify intelligence."

Psychologists debate: Should we consider intelligence as one aptitude or many? As linked to cognitive speed? As neurologically measurable? Yet, intelligence experts do agree on this: Intelligence is a concept and not a "thing." When we refer to someone's "IQ" (short for *intelligence quotient*) as if it were a fixed and objectively real trait like height, we commit a reasoning error called *reification*—viewing an abstract, immaterial concept as if it were a concrete thing. To reify is to invent a concept, give it a name, and then convince ourselves that such a thing objectively exists in the world. When someone says, "She has an IQ of 120," they are reifying IQ; they are imagining IQ to be a thing one *has,* rather than a score once obtained on a particular *intelligence test.* One should say, "Her score on the intelligence test was 120."

Intelligence is a socially constructed concept. Cultures deem "intelligent" whatever attributes enable success in those cultures (Sternberg & Kaufman, 1998). In the Amazon rain forest, intelligence may be a gift for discerning which native herbs effectively treat particular diseases. In Western countries, it may be superior performance on cognitive tasks. In each context, **intelligence** is the ability to learn from experience, solve problems, and use knowledge to adapt to new situations. In research studies, *intelligence* is whatever intelligence tests measure, which historically, as we will see, has tended to be school smarts.

Despite this general agreement, two controversies remain:

1. Is intelligence a single overall ability or several specific abilities?
2. With the tools neuroscience now offers, can we locate and measure intelligence within the brain?

431

Is Intelligence One General Ability or Several Specific Abilities?

You probably know some people with talents in science, others who excel at the humanities, and still others gifted in athletics, art, music, or dance. You may also know a talented artist who is dumbfounded by the simplest mathematical problems, or a brilliant math student with little aptitude for literary discussion. Perhaps you have wondered whether people's mental abilities are too diverse to justify labeling them with the single word *intelligence* or quantifying them with a number from some single scale. How might you test this idea?

General Intelligence

OBJECTIVE 2 | Present arguments for and against considering intelligence as one general mental ability.

To find out whether there might be a general ability factor that runs throughout our specific mental abilities, psychologists study how individual abilities relate to one another. The statistical procedure **factor analysis** enables researchers to identify clusters of test items that measure a common ability. For example, people who do well on vocabulary items often do well on paragraph comprehension, a cluster that helps define a verbal intelligence factor. Other clusters include a spatial ability factor and a reasoning ability factor.

Charles Spearman (1863–1945), who helped develop factor analysis, believed there is also a **general intelligence,** or **g,** factor that underlies the various clusters. Spearman granted that people often have special abilities that stand out. But he also noted that those who score high on one factor, such as verbal intelligence, typically score higher than average on other factors, such as spatial or reasoning ability. So there is at least a tendency for different abilities to come in the same package. Spearman believed that this commonality, the *g* factor, underlies all of our intelligent behavior, from navigating the sea to excelling in school.

This idea of a general mental capacity expressed by a single intelligence score was controversial in Spearman's day, and it remains so in our own. One of Spearman's early opponents was L. L. Thurstone (1887–1955). Thurstone gave 56 different tests to people and mathematically identified seven clusters of *primary mental abilities* (word fluency, verbal comprehension, spatial ability, perceptual speed, numerical

" *g* is one of the most reliable and valid measures in the behavioral domain . . . and it predicts important social outcomes such as educational and occupational levels far better than any other trait."

Behavior geneticist Robert Plomin (1999)

Athleticism, like intelligence, is many things
Some coaches have therefore encouraged players, such as this baseball player and golfer, to develop efficient movement as well as endurance, speed, and quickness by taking Pilates classes.

ability, inductive reasoning, and memory). Thurstone did not rank his subjects on a single scale of general aptitude. But when other investigators studied the profiles of his subjects, they detected a small tendency for those who excelled in one of the seven clusters to score well on the others. So, they concluded, there was still some evidence of a *g* factor.

We might, then, liken mental abilities to physical abilities. Athleticism is not one thing but many. The ability to run fast is distinct from the strength needed for power lifting, which is distinct from the eye-hand coordination required to throw a ball on target. A champion weightlifter rarely has the potential to be a skilled ice skater. Yet there remains some tendency for good things to come packaged together—for running speed and throwing accuracy to correlate, thanks to general athletic ability. Similarly, intelligence involves several distinct abilities, which correlate enough to define a small general intelligence factor.

Satoshi Kanazawa (2004) argues that general intelligence evolved as a form of intelligence that helps people solve novel problems—how to stop a fire from spreading, how to find food during a drought, how to reunite with one's band on the other side of a flooded river. More common problems, such as how to mate or how to read strangers' faces or how to find one's way back to camp, require a different sort of intelligence. In fact, general intelligence scores *do* correlate with ability to solve various novel problems (like those found in academic and many vocational situations) but do *not* much correlate with individuals' skills in "evolutionarily familiar" situations—such as marrying and parenting, forming close friendships, displaying social competence, and navigating without maps.

Contemporary Intelligence Theories

OBJECTIVE 3 | Compare Gardner's and Sternberg's theories of intelligence.

Since the mid-1980s some psychologists have sought to extend the definition of intelligence beyond Spearman's and Thurstone's academic smarts.

Multiple Intelligences Howard Gardner (1983, 1999) supports Thurstone's idea that intelligence comes in different packages. He notes that brain damage may diminish one type of ability but not others. He observes that different abilities enabled our ancestors to cope with different environmental challenges (finding their way home, reading others' emotions, solving problems). And he studies people with exceptional abilities, including those who excel in only one. People with **savant syndrome,** for example, often score low on intelligence tests but have an island of brilliance—some incredible ability, as in computation, drawing, or musical memory (Treffert & Wallace, 2002). Some have virtually no language ability, yet are able to compute numbers

■ **factor analysis** a statistical procedure that identifies clusters of related items (called *factors*) on a test; used to identify different dimensions of performance that underlie one's total score.

■ **general intelligence (*g*)** a general intelligence factor that according to Spearman and others underlies specific mental abilities and is therefore measured by every task on an intelligence test.

■ **savant syndrome** a condition in which a person otherwise limited in mental ability has an exceptional specific skill, such as in computation or drawing.

Islands of genius: Savant syndrome Matt Savage (left), a 13-year-old with autism, is also an award-winning jazz pianist. Matt has his own band—the Matt Savage Trio. Kim Peek (middle), the inspiration for the character Raymond Babbit in the movie *Rain Man*, depends on his father for many of his daily needs. Yet Peek knows more than 7600 books by heart, as well as all U.S. area codes, Zip codes, and TV stations. Alonzo Clemons (right), despite a developmental disability, can create perfect replicas of any animal he briefly sees. His bronze figures have earned him a national reputation.

Courtesy of Diane and Matt Savage

Ethan Hill

Ethan Hill

as quickly and accurately as an electronic calculator, or identify almost instantly the day of the week that corresponds to any given date in history (Miller, 1999). About 4 in 5 people with this syndrome are males, and many also have autism, a developmental disorder afflicting more males than females. With or without savant syndrome, people with autism may excel in some areas, such as math, and fail at other tasks, such as reading facial expressions.

Using such evidence, Gardner argues that we do not have *an* intelligence, but instead have *multiple* intelligences, each relatively independent of the others. In addition to the verbal and mathematical aptitudes assessed by standard tests, he identifies distinct aptitudes for musical accomplishment, for spatially analyzing the visual world, for mastering movement skills (as in dance), and for insightfully understanding ourselves, others, and our natural environment (**TABLE 11.1**).

According to Gardner (1998), the computer programmer, the poet, the street-smart adolescent who becomes a crafty executive, and the point guard on the basketball team exhibit different kinds of intelligence. He notes,

> If a person is strong (or weak) in telling stories, solving mathematical proofs, navigating around unfamiliar terrain, learning an unfamiliar song, mastering a new game that entails dexterity, understanding others, or understanding himself, one simply does not know whether comparable strengths (or weaknesses) will be found in other areas.

A general intelligence score is therefore like the overall rating of a city—which doesn't give you much specific information about its schools, streets, or nightlife.

Wouldn't it be wonderful if the world were so just, responds intelligence researcher Sandra Scarr (1989), that being weak in any area would often be compensated by genius in some other area? Alas, the world is not just, for there remains some tendency for different skills to correlate. For example, people with mental disadvantages often have lesser physical abilities as well; Special Olympics gives them and others a chance to enjoy fair competition. Moreover, in one digest of 127 studies, an academic intelligence score that predicted graduate school success also predicted later job success (Kuncel & others, 2004). General intelligence scores likewise predict performance on various complex tasks and in various jobs;

Gardner (1998) also speculates about a ninth possible intelligence—*existential intelligence*—the ability "to ponder large questions about life, death, existence."

TABLE 11.1

GARDNER'S EIGHT INTELLIGENCES

Aptitude	Exemplar
1. Linguistic	T. S. Eliot, poet
2. Logical-mathematical	Albert Einstein, scientist
3. Musical	Igor Stravinsky, composer
4. Spatial	Pablo Picasso, artist
5. Bodily-kinesthetic	Martha Graham, dancer
6. Intrapersonal (self)	Sigmund Freud, psychiatrist
7. Interpersonal (other people)	Mahatma Gandhi, leader
8. Naturalist	Charles Darwin, naturalist

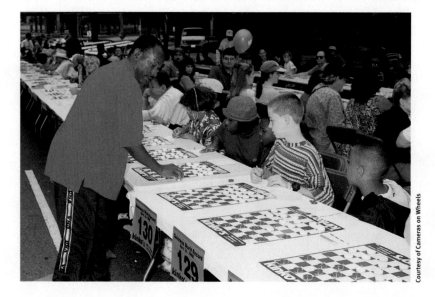

Spatial intelligence genius
In 1998, World Checkers Champion Ron "Suki" King of Barbados set a new record by simultaneously playing 385 players in 3 hours and 44 minutes. Thus, while his opponents often had hours to plot their game moves, King could only devote about 35 seconds to each game. Yet he still managed to win all 385 games!

Courtesy of Cameras on Wheels

g matters (Gottfredson, 2002a,b, 2003a,b; Reeve & Hakel, 2002). It even matters for longevity. In studies controlling for income and education differences, the 11-year-old test-takers who scored low on an intelligence test in 1932 had in their adult years shorter average life spans and a higher likelihood of dying from lung cancer and cardiovascular diseases than did their higher-scoring counterparts (Hart & others, 2003; Whalley & Deary, 2001).

Gardner's critics have pointed out that, without tests for measuring all these intelligences, it is difficult to research his theory. Critics also question whether it really makes sense to lump all sorts of abilities under the concept of intelligence. Intelligence is *mental* ability, they say. The abilities we can manage without, as in music and athletics, are better considered *talents* than the more crucial verbal and reasoning skills. If people lack physical talent, do we consider them as lacking in *intelligence?* Gardner counters that all forms of intelligence have intrinsic value—it is one's culture and context that place greater value on some capacities than on others. Indeed, definitions of intelligence—whether the traditional predictor of school achievement or a broader definition—tend to express what people value in a human being.

Aspects of Successful Intelligence Robert Sternberg (1985, 1999, 2003) agrees with Gardner's idea of multiple intelligences, but his *triarchic theory* (from *triarchy*—"a country under three rulers") distinguishes three, not eight, intelligences:

- *Analytical (academic problem-solving) intelligence*—assessed by intelligence tests, which present well-defined problems having a single right answer.
- *Creative intelligence*—demonstrated in reacting adaptively to novel situations and generating novel ideas.
- *Practical intelligence*—often required for everyday tasks, which are frequently ill-defined, with multiple solutions.

Traditional intelligence tests assess academic intelligence. They predict school grades reasonably well but predict vocational success more modestly. People who demonstrate keen practical intelligence may or may not have distinguished themselves in school. Managerial success, for example, depends less on the academic abilities assessed by an intelligence test score (assuming the score is average or above) than on a shrewd ability to manage oneself, one's tasks, and other people.

Sternberg and Richard Wagner's (1993, 1995) test of practical managerial intelligence measures whether test-takers know how to write effective memos, how to motivate people, when to delegate tasks and responsibilities, how to read people, and how to promote their own careers. Business executives who score high on this test tend to earn higher salaries and receive better performance ratings than do those who score low. In a similar finding, Stephen Ceci and Jeffrey Liker (1986) reported that racetrack fans' expertise in handicapping horses—a practical but complex cognitive task—was unrelated to their intelligence test scores.

Although Sternberg (1998, 1999) and Gardner (1998) differ on specific points, they agree that multiple abilities can contribute to life success. (Neither candidate in the 2000 U.S. presidential election had scored exceptionally high on college entrance aptitude tests, notes Sternberg [2000], yet both, after college, have been successful.) They also agree that the differing varieties of giftedness add spice to life and challenges for education. Under Gardner's or Sternberg's influence, many teachers have been trained to appreciate the varieties of ability and to apply multiple intelligence theory in their classrooms.

Some critics contend that Sternberg's proposed three intelligences are not as independent of one another as he thinks, and actually share an underlying general intelligence (Brody, 2003). Much as the idea of practical intelligence appeals to the popular idea that "everyone can be smart in some way," argues Linda Gottfredson (2003a,b), "no one has yet demonstrated that practical intelligence . . . is even

> "You have to be careful, if you're good at something, to make sure you don't think you're good at other things that you aren't necessarily so good at. . . . Because I've been very successful at [software development] people come in and expect that I have wisdom about topics that I don't."
>
> Bill Gates (1998)

Street smarts
This child selling candy on the streets of Manaus, Brazil, is developing practical intelligence at a very young age.

TABLE 11.2

COMPARING THEORIES OF INTELLIGENCE

Theory	Summary	Strengths	Other Considerations
Spearman's general intelligence (*g*)	A basic intelligence predicts our abilities in varied academic areas.	Different abilities, such as verbal and spatial, do have some tendency to correlate.	Human abilities are too diverse to be encapsulated by a single general intelligence factor.
Thurstone's primary mental abilities	Our intelligence may be broken down into seven factors: word fluency, verbal comprehension, spatial ability, perceptual speed, numerical ability, inductive reasoning, and memory.	A single *g* score is not as informative as scores for seven primary mental abilities.	Even Thurstone's seven mental abilities show a tendency to cluster, suggesting an underlying *g* factor.
Gardner's multiple intelligences	Our abilities are best classified into eight independent intelligences, which include a broad range of skills beyond traditional school smarts.	Intelligence is more than just verbal and mathematical skills. Other abilities are equally important to our human adaptability.	Should all of our abilities be considered *intelligences?* Shouldn't some of them be called less vital *talents* instead?
Sternberg's triarchic	Our intelligence is best classified into three areas that predict our real-world success: analytical, creative, and practical.	These three facets may be reliably measured.	1. These three facets may be less independent than Sternberg thought and may actually share an underlying *g* factor. 2. Additional testing is needed to determine whether these facets can reliably predict success.

© Maya Goded/Magnum Photos

Hands-on healing
Success for this folk healer in Peru may have less to do with general intelligence than with knowledge about his medicinal plants and an understanding of the people he is helping.

■ **emotional intelligence** the ability to perceive, understand, manage, and use emotions.

a useful concept." What predicts successful job performance is not so much practical intelligence, she contends, as general intelligence, personality, and motivation. Actually, replies Sternberg (2003), studies from Kenyan villages to rural Alaska show that *g* measures fail to tap important ability domains, and that the triarchic understanding of intelligence helps "pave the way for subsequent generations of better theories." (**TABLE 11.2** summarizes the four main theories discussed in this chapter.) As Sternberg understands, no one's ideas are the final word; today's best theories are often developed into or replaced by tomorrow's better ideas. So stay tuned.

Emotional Intelligence

OBJECTIVE 4 | Describe the four aspects of emotional intelligence, and discuss criticisms of this concept.

Also distinct from academic intelligence is what Nancy Cantor and John Kihlstrom (1987) first called *social intelligence*—the know-how involved in comprehending social situations and managing oneself successfully. Consistent with this distinction between academic and social intelligence is the repeated finding that college grades only modestly predict later work achievement (Bretz, 1989; Dye & Reck, 1989).

Seymour Epstein and Petra Meier (1989) have wondered why high-aptitude people are "not, by a wide margin, more effective . . . in achieving better marriages, in successfully raising their children, and in achieving better mental and physical well-being." The answer may lie in part in a critical part of social intelligence, which Peter Salovey and John Mayer (1990; Salovey & others, 2002) call **emotional intelligence**—the ability to perceive, understand, manage, and use emotions. One study, led by emotion researcher Carroll Izard (2001), assessed 5-year-olds' ability to recognize and label facial emotions. Even after controlling for verbal aptitude and temperament, researchers found that the 5-year-olds who had most accurately discerned emotions became 9-year-olds who easily made friends, cooperated with the teacher, and effectively managed their emotions.

Emotionally intelligent people are self-aware. Mayer, Salovey, and David Caruso (2002; Grewal & Salovey, 2005) have developed an emotional intelligence test to assess both overall emotional intelligence and its four components—the ability to *perceive* emotions (to recognize them in faces, music, and stories), to *understand* emotions (to predict them and how they change and blend), to *manage* emotions (to know how to express them in varied situations), and to *use* emotions to enable adaptive or creative thinking. In both the United States and Germany, those scoring high on managing emotions enjoy higher-quality interactions with friends of both sexes (Lopes & others, 2004). They avoid being hijacked by overwhelming depression, anxiety, or anger. Their empathy enables them to read others' emotions and to handle those emotions skillfully, knowing what to say to a grieving friend, how to encourage colleagues, and how to manage conflicts well. Across 69 studies in many countries, those scoring high in emotional intelligence also have exhibited modestly better job performance (Van Rooy & Viswesvaran, 2004). They can delay gratification in pursuit of long-range rewards, rather than being overtaken by immediate impulses. Simply said, they are emotionally smart, and thus they often succeed in career, marriage, and parenting situations where academically smarter (but emotionally less intelligent) people fail.

In extreme cases, brain damage may diminish emotional intelligence while leaving general intelligence intact. Antonio Damasio, a University of Iowa neuroscientist known for his registry of more than 2000 brain-damaged patients, tells of Elliot, a man with normal intelligence and memory. Since removal of a brain tumor, Elliot has lived without emotion. "I never saw a tinge of emotion in my many hours of conversation with him," Damasio (1994) reported, "no sadness, no impatience, no frustration." Shown disturbing pictures of injured people, destroyed communities, and natural disasters, Elliot shows—and realizes he feels—no emotion. Like Data, the human-appearing android of *Star Trek: The Next Generation,* he knows but he cannot feel. Unable to intuitively adjust his behavior in response to others' feelings, Elliot lost his job. He went bankrupt. His marriage collapsed. He remarried and divorced again. At last report, he was dependent on custodial care from a sibling and a disability check.

Some scholars, however—including even multiple-intelligence man Howard Gardner (1999)—are concerned that concepts such as "emotional intelligence" stretch *intelligence* too far. It is wise to stretch the concept to include our processing not only of words, numbers, and logic, but also of space, music, and information about ourselves and others, says Gardner. But let us also, he says, respect emotional sensitivity, creativity, and motivation as important but different. Stretch a word to include everything we prize and it will lose its meaning.

In defense of academic smarts—the *g* factor—researchers point to studies in which traditional intelligence scores *do* predict both occupational status and job performance (Brody, 1997; Schmidt & Hunter, 1998). For example, intelligence matters most in mentally demanding jobs. Meteorology more than meter reading requires intelligence to excel. However, once admitted to a vocation, those who become highly successful have other traits as well—they are conscientious, well-connected, and doggedly energetic. Thus, high intelligence does more to get you into a profession (via the schools and training programs that take you there) than it does to make you successful once there. The recipe for success combines talent with grit. Anders Ericsson (2002; Ericsson & Lehmann, 1996) reports a common ingredient of expert performance in chess, dancing, sports, computer programming, music, and medicine: "about 10 years of intense, daily practice."

So, the academic aptitude tapped by intelligence tests is indeed important. Yet our competence in everyday living requires much that traditional intelligence tests do not measure.

"You're wise, but you lack tree smarts."

"I worry about [intelligence] definitions that collapse assessments of our cognitive powers with statements about the kind of human beings we favor."

Howard Gardner, "Rethinking the Concept of Intelligence," 2000

Emotional intelligence
Success in the real world is affected not just by book smarts, but also by our ability to perceive, understand, and express emotions. These prison inmates are trying to learn those traits by participating in a role-playing, parent-training program sponsored by Girl Scouts Beyond Bars.

■ **creativity** the ability to produce novel and valuable ideas.

Intelligence and Creativity

OBJECTIVE 5 | Identify the factors associated with creativity, and describe the relationship between creativity and intelligence.

Pierre de Fermat, a seventeenth-century mischievous genius, challenged mathematicians of his day to match his solutions to various number theory problems. He offered his most famous challenge—his so-called last theorem, after mathematicians solved all his others. This problem baffled the greatest mathematical minds, even after a $2 million prize (in today's dollars) was offered in 1908 to whoever first created a proof.

Like countless others, Princeton mathematician Andrew Wiles had pondered the problem for more than 30 years and had come to the brink of a solution. Then, one morning, out of the blue, the "incredible revelation"—the fix to the one remaining difficulty—struck him. "It was so indescribably beautiful; it was so simple and so elegant. I couldn't understand how I'd missed it and I just stared at it in disbelief for 20 minutes. Then during the day I walked around the department, and I'd keep coming back to my desk looking to see if it was still there. It was still there. I couldn't contain myself, I was so excited. It was the most important moment of my working life" (Singh, 1997, p. 25).

Wiles' incredible moment illustrates **creativity**—the ability to produce ideas that are both novel and valuable. Studies of intelligence and creativity suggest that a certain level of aptitude is necessary but not sufficient for creativity. In general, people who do well on intelligence tests also do well on creativity tests ("How many uses can you think of for a brick?"). But beyond a certain level—a score of about 120—the correlation between intelligence scores and creativity shrivels. Exceptionally creative architects, mathematicians, scientists, and engineers usually score no higher on intelligence tests than do their less creative peers (MacKinnon & Hall, 1972; Simonton, 2000). So clearly there is more to creativity than what intelligence tests reveal. Indeed, the brain areas supporting the *convergent thinking* tested by intelligence tests (which demand a single correct answer) differ from those supporting the *divergent thinking* that imagines multiple possible answers to a problem (such as words beginning with the letter *s*). Injury to the left parietal lobe damages the convergent thinking required by intelligence test scores and for school success. Injury to certain areas of the frontal lobes can leave reading, writing, and arithmetic skills intact but destroy imagination (Kolb & Whishaw, 2006).

Studies of creative people suggest five components of creativity beyond a minimal level of aptitude (Sternberg, 1988; Sternberg & Lubart, 1991, 1992):

1. *Expertise* is a well-developed base of knowledge. "Chance favors only the prepared mind," observed Louis Pasteur. The more ideas, images, and phrases we have available through our accumulated learning, the more chances we have to

After picking up a Nobel Prize in Stockholm, physicist Richard Feynman stopped in Queens, New York, to look at his high school record. "My grades were not as good as I remembered," he reported, "and my IQ was [a good, though unexceptional] 124" (Faber, 1987).

Imaginative thinking

Cartoonists often display creativity as they see things in new ways or make unusual connections.

© 1991 Leigh Rubin. Creator's Syndicate Inc.

FURIOUS GEORGE

© 2000 Jack Duffy

Reprinted with permission of Paul Soderblom.

Everyone held up their crackers as David threw the cheese log into the ceiling fan.

combine these mental building blocks in novel ways. Wiles' well-developed base of knowledge put the needed theorems and methods at his disposal.

2. **Imaginative thinking skills** provide the ability to see things in novel ways, to recognize patterns, to make connections. Having mastered a problem's basic elements, we redefine or explore it in a new way. Copernicus first developed expertise regarding the solar system and its planets and then creatively defined the system as revolving around the Sun, not the Earth. Wiles' imaginative solution combined two important but incomplete solutions.

3. **A venturesome personality** tolerates ambiguity and risk, perseveres in overcoming obstacles, and seeks new experiences rather than following the pack. Inventors, for example, have a willingness to persist after failures. Thomas Edison tried countless substances for his light bulb filament. Wiles said he labored in isolation from the mathematics community partly to stay focused and avoid distraction.

4. **Intrinsic motivation** is creativity's fourth component. As psychologist Teresa Amabile points out, "People will be most creative when they feel motivated primarily by the interest, enjoyment, satisfaction, and challenge of the work itself—rather than by external pressures" (Amabile & Hennessey, 1992). Creative people focus not so much on extrinsic motivators—meeting deadlines, impressing people, or making money—as on the intrinsic pleasure and challenge of their work. Asked how he solved such difficult scientific problems, Isaac Newton reportedly answered, "By thinking about them all the time." Wiles concurred: "I was so obsessed by this problem that for eight years I was thinking about it all the time—when I woke up in the morning to when I went to sleep at night" (Singh & Riber, 1997).

5. **A creative environment** sparks, supports, and refines creative ideas. After studying the careers of 2026 prominent scientists and inventors, Dean Keith Simonton (1992) noted that the most eminent among them were in fact not lone geniuses. Rather they were mentored, challenged, and supported by their relationships with colleagues. Such people often have the emotional intelligence needed to network effectively with peers. Even Wiles stood on the shoulders of others and wrestled his problem with the collaboration of a former student.

Amabile's (1983, 1987) experiments demonstrated that creative environments also free people from concern about social approval. In one experiment, she asked college students to make paper collages, telling half beforehand that experts would evaluate their work. Students, unaware that their work would be evaluated, produced collages that judges rated as more creative. Unworried about being evaluated, they felt freer to be creative.

Managers wanting to foster innovation at work should keep the intrinsic motivation principle in mind, observed Amabile (1988). They should set employees to work on what naturally interests them. And they can emulate managers who have successfully nurtured creativity—by providing their subordinates with time, freedom, and support to attain set goals. The 3M company, with an Eleventh Commandment of "Thou shalt not kill a new product idea," encouraged researchers to spend 15 percent of their time pursuing creative projects that have no immediate payoff. This creativity-nurturing environment produced such products as the now-commonplace Post-it notes (Kreitner, 1992).

> "If you would allow me any talent, it's simply this: I can, for whatever reason, reach down into my own brain, feel around in all the mush, find and extract something from my persona, and then graft it onto an idea."
>
> Cartoonist Gary Larson, *The Complete Far Side*, 2003

Is Intelligence Neurologically Measurable?

OBJECTIVE 6 | Describe the relationship between intelligence and brain anatomy.

Using today's neuroscience tools, might we link differences in people's intelligence test performance to dissimilarities in the heart of smarts—the brain? Might we anticipate a future brain test of intelligence?

A sperm whale's brain is about 6 times heavier than your brain.

Recall from Chapter 1 that the lowest correlation, –1.0, represents perfect disagreement between two sets of scores—as one score goes up, the other goes down. A correlation of zero represents no association. The highest correlation, +1.0, represents perfect agreement—as the first score goes up, so does the second.

FIGURE 11.1

Gray matter matters

A frontal view of the brain shows some of the areas where gray matter is concentrated in people with high intelligence scores, and where *g* therefore may be concentrated. (From Haier & others, 2004.)

" I am, somehow, less interested in the weight and convolutions of Einstein's brain than in the near certainty that people of equal talent have lived and died in cotton fields and sweatshops."

Stephen Jay Gould , *The Panda's Thumb*, 1980

Brain Anatomy

After the brilliant English poet Lord Byron died in 1824, doctors discovered that his brain was a massive 5 pounds. Three years later, Beethoven died and his brain was found to have exceptionally numerous and deep convolutions. Such observations set brain scientists off studying the brains of other geniuses at their wits' end (Burrell, 2005). Do people with big brains have big smarts?

Alas, some geniuses had small brains, and some dim-witted criminals had brains like those of scientists. More recent studies that directly measure brain volume using MRI scans do reveal correlations of about +.40 between brain size (adjusted for body size) and intelligence score (Gignac & others, 2003; Rushton & Ankney, 1996). Moreover, as adults age, brain size and nonverbal intelligence test scores fall in concert (Bigler & others, 1995).

If intelligence does modestly correlate with brain size, the cause could be differing genes, nutrition, environmental stimulation, some combination of these, or perhaps something else. Recall from earlier chapters that experience alters the brain. Rats raised in a stimulating rather than deprived environment develop thicker, heavier cortexes. And learning leaves detectable traces in the brain's neural connections. "Intelligence is due to the development of neural connections in response to the environment," notes University of Sydney psychologist Dennis Garlick (2003).

Postmortem brain analyses reveal that highly educated people die with more synapses—17 percent more in one study—than their less-educated counterparts (Orlovskaya & others, 1999). This does not tell us whether people grow synapses with education, or people with more synapses seek more education (or both). But other evidence suggests that highly intelligent people differ in their *neural plasticity*—their ability during childhood and adolescence to adapt and grow neural connections in response to their environment (Garlick, 2002, 2003).

Efforts to link brain structure with cognition continue. One research team, led by psychologist Richard Haier (2004), correlated intelligence scores from 47 adult volunteers with scans that measured their volume of gray matter (neural bodies) and white matter (axons and dendrites) in various brain regions. Higher intelligence scores were linked with more gray matter in some specific areas known to be involved in memory, attention, and language (**FIGURE 11.1**).

With the brains of 91 Canadians as a comparison base, Sandra Witelson and her colleagues (1999) seized an opportunity to study Einstein's brain. Although not notably heavier or larger in total size than the typical Canadian's brain, Einstein's brain was 15 percent larger in the parietal lobe's lower region—which just happens to be a center for processing mathematical and spatial information. Certain other areas were a tad smaller than average. With different mental functions competing for the brain's real estate, these observations may offer a clue to why Einstein, like some other great physicists such as Richard Feynman and Edward Teller, was slow in learning to talk (Pinker, 1999).

Brain Function

OBJECTIVE 7 | Discuss findings on the correlations between perceptual speed, neural processing speed, and intelligence.

Even if the modest correlations between brain anatomy and intelligence prove reliable, they only begin to explain intelligence differences. Searching for other explanations, neuroscientists are studying the brain's functioning.

As people contemplate a variety of questions like those found on intelligence tests, a frontal lobe area just above the outer edge of the eyebrows becomes especially active—in the left brain for verbal questions, and on both sides for spatial questions (Duncan & others, 2000). Information from various brain areas seems to converge in this spot, suggesting to researcher John Duncan (2000) that it may be a "global workspace for organizing and coordinating information" and that some people may be "blessed with a workspace that functions very, very well."

Are more intelligent people literally more quick-witted, much as today's speedy computer chips enable more powerful computing than did their predecessors? On some tasks they seem to be. Earl Hunt (1983) found that verbal intelligence scores are predictable from the speed with which people retrieve information from memory. Those who recognize quickly that *sink* and *wink* are different words, or that *A* and *a* share the same name, tend to score high in verbal ability. Extremely precocious 12- to 14-year-old college students are especially quick in responding to such tasks (Jensen, 1989). To try to define "quick-wittedness," researchers are taking a close look at speed of perception and speed of neural processing of information.

Perceptual Speed Across many studies, the correlation between intelligence score and the speed of taking in perceptual information tends to be about +.4 to +.5 (Deary & Der, 2005; Grudnik & Kranzler, 2001). A typical experiment flashes an incomplete stimulus, as in **FIGURE 11.2,** then another image that overrides the lingering afterimage of the incomplete stimulus. The researcher then asks participants whether the long side appeared on the right or left. How much stimulus inspection time does one need to answer correctly 80 percent of the time? Perhaps .01 second? Or .02 second? Those who perceive quickly tend to score somewhat higher on intelligence tests, particularly on tests based on perceptual rather than verbal problem solving.

Neurological Speed Do the quicker processing and perceptions of highly intelligent people reflect greater neural processing speed? Repeated studies have found that their brain waves register a simple stimulus (such as a flash of light or a tone beep) more quickly and with greater complexity (Caryl, 1994; Deary & Caryl, 1993; Reed & Jensen, 1992). The evoked brain response also tends to be slightly faster when people with high rather than low intelligence scores perform a simple task, such as pushing a button when an *X* appears on a screen (McGarry-Roberts & others, 1992).

Neural processing speed on a simple task seems far removed from the untimed responses to complex intelligence test items, such as "In what way are *wool* and *cotton* alike?" As yet, notes intelligence expert Nathan Brody (1992, 2001), we have no firm understanding of *why* fast reactions on simple tasks should predict intelligence test performance, though he suspects they reflect one's "core information processing ability." Philip Vernon (1983) has speculated that "faster cognitive processing may allow more information to be acquired." Perhaps people who more quickly process information accumulate more information—about wool, cotton, and millions of other things.

The neurological approach to understanding intelligence (and so many other things in psychology) is currently in its heyday. Will this new research reduce what we now call the *g* factor to simple measures of underlying brain activity? Or are these efforts totally wrongheaded because what we call intelligence is not a single general trait but several culturally adaptive skills? The controversies surrounding the nature of intelligence are a long way from resolution.

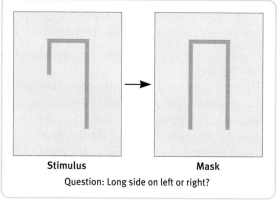

FIGURE 11.2
An inspection time task
A stimulus is flashed before being overridden by a masking image. How long would you need to glimpse the stimulus at the left to answer the question? People who can perceive the stimulus very quickly tend to score somewhat higher on intelligence tests. (Adapted from Deary & Stough, 1996.)

Stimulus — Mask
Question: Long side on left or right?

>> LEARNING OUTCOMES

What Is Intelligence?

OBJECTIVE 1 | **Discuss the difficulty of defining** *intelligence*, **and explain what it means to "reify intelligence."**
Intelligence is a socially constructed concept that differs from culture to culture. The two big controversies in current research on intelligence are (1) whether it is one overall ability or many, and (2) whether neuroscientists can locate and measure intelligence within the brain. To *reify* intelligence is to treat it as though it were a real object, not an abstract concept. Most psychologists now define *intelligence* as the ability to learn from experience, solve problems, and adapt to new situations.

OBJECTIVE 2 | **Present arguments for and against considering intelligence as one general mental ability.**
Arguments for considering intelligence as a general mental ability underlying all specific mental abilities are based in part on factor analysis. This statistical procedure has been used to show that mental abilities tend to form clusters, and that people tend to show about the same level of competence in all abilities in the cluster. In the mid-twentieth century, Charles Spearman (a developer of factor analysis) named this common level of intelligence the *g* factor. Some psychologists today agree with Spear-

man's idea that we have a common level of intelligence that can predict our abilities in all other academic areas.

OBJECTIVE 3 | Compare Gardner's and Sternberg's theories of intelligence.

Howard Gardner disputes the idea of one general intelligence. He proposes eight independent intelligences: *linguistic* (word smarts), *logical-mathematical* (number smarts), *musical* (music smarts), *spatial* (space smarts), *bodily-kinesthetic* (body smarts), *intrapersonal* (self smarts), *interpersonal* (people smarts), and *natural* (nature smarts). Robert Sternberg's triarchic theory proposes only three intelligences: *analytical* (academic problem solving), *creative,* and *practical* intelligences. (For more on the single-intelligence/multiple intelligences debate, see Table 11.2 on page 436.)

OBJECTIVE 4 | Describe the four aspects of emotional intelligence, and discuss criticisms of this concept.

The four components of emotional intelligence are the ability to *perceive* emotions (to recognize them in faces, music, and stories), to *understand* emotions (to predict them and how they change and blend), to *manage* emotions (to know how to express them in varied situations), and to *use* emotions. Critics of the idea of emotional intelligence question whether we stretch the idea of intelligence too far when we apply it to emotions.

OBJECTIVE 5 | Identify the factors associated with creativity, and describe the relationship between creativity and intelligence.

Creativity is the ability to produce novel and valuable ideas. It correlates somewhat with intelligence, but beyond a score of 120, that correlation dwindles. It also correlates with expertise, imaginative thinking skills, a venturesome personality, intrinsic motivation, and the support offered by a creative environment. Different brain areas are active when we engage in convergent thinking (the type required for intelligence test solutions) and divergent thinking (the type required for multiple imaginative solutions).

OBJECTIVE 6 | Describe the relationship between intelligence and brain anatomy.

Recent studies indicate some correlation (about +.40) between brain size (adjusted for body size) and intelligence score. The brain's tendency to decrease in size during late adulthood, as nonverbal intelligence test scores also decrease, supports this idea to some extent. And autopsies of some highly educated people revealed above-average volumes of synapses and gray matter. But the direction of the relationship is not clear. Larger brain size may enable greater intelligence; greater intelligence may lead to experiences that exercise the brain and build more connections, thus increasing its size; or some third factor may be at work.

OBJECTIVE 7 | Discuss findings on the correlations between perceptual speed, neural processing speed, and intelligence.

Studies of brain functioning show that people who score high on intelligence tests tend also to retrieve information from memory more quickly, and to perceive stimuli faster than others. These differences are reflected in neurological studies that show faster brain response times.

ASK YOURSELF: The modern concept of multiple intelligences (as proposed by Gardner and Sternberg) assumes that the analytical word smarts and number smarts measured by traditional intelligence tests are important abilities but that other abilities are also important. Different people have different gifts. What are yours?

Assessing Intelligence

OBJECTIVE 8 | Define *intelligence test* and discuss the history of intelligence testing.

How do we assess intelligence? Movie hero Forrest Gump's answer, "Stupid is as stupid does," catches the spirit of psychology's simplest answer: Intelligent is as intelligent does on an IQ test. In other words, *intelligence* is whatever **intelligence tests** measure. So, what are these tests, and what makes a test credible? Answering those questions begins with a look at why psychologists created tests of mental abilities and how they have used those tests.

■ **intelligence test** a method for assessing an individual's mental aptitudes and comparing them with those of others, using numerical scores.

■ **mental age** a measure of intelligence test performance devised by Binet; the chronological age that most typically corresponds to a given level of performance. Thus, a child who does as well as the average 8-year-old is said to have a mental age of 8.

■ **Stanford-Binet** the widely used American revision (by Terman at Stanford University) of Binet's original intelligence test.

The Origins of Intelligence Testing

Some societies concern themselves with promoting the collective welfare of the family, community, and society. Other societies emphasize individual opportunity. Plato, a pioneer of the individualist tradition, wrote more than 2000 years ago in *The Republic* that "no two persons are born exactly alike; but each differs from the other in natural endowments, one being suited for one occupation and the other for another." As heirs to Plato's individualism, people in Western societies have pondered how and why individuals differ in mental ability.

Western attempts to assess such differences began in earnest about a century ago. The historical story of intelligence testing illustrates an important lesson: Although science itself strives for objectivity, individual scientists are affected by their own assumptions and attitudes.

Alfred Binet: Predicting School Achievement

The modern intelligence-testing movement began at the turn of the twentieth century when France passed a law requiring that all children attend school. Teachers soon faced an overwhelming range of individual differences. Some children, including many newcomers to Paris, seemed incapable of benefiting from the regular school curriculum and in need of special classes. But how could the schools objectively identify children with special needs?

The French government hesitated to trust teachers' subjective judgments of children's learning potential. Academic slowness might merely reflect inadequate prior education. Also, teachers might prejudge children on the basis of their social backgrounds. To minimize bias, France's minister of public education in 1904 commissioned Alfred Binet (1857–1911) and others to study the problem.

Binet and his collaborator, Théodore Simon, began by assuming that all children follow the same course of intellectual development but that some develop more rapidly. On tests, therefore, a "dull" child should perform as does a typical younger child, and a "bright" child as does a typical older child.

Binet and Simon set out to measure what came to be called a child's **mental age,** the chronological age typical of a given level of performance. The average 9-year-old has a mental age of 9. Children with below-average mental ages, such as 9-year-olds who perform at the level of a typical 7-year-old, would struggle with schoolwork considered normal for their age.

To measure mental age, Binet and Simon theorized that mental aptitude, like athletic aptitude, is a general capacity that shows up in various ways. They then developed varied reasoning and problem-solving questions that might predict school achievement, and they tried many of them with Binet's two daughters. By then testing "bright" and "backward" Parisian schoolchildren on these questions, Binet and Simon succeeded: They found items that did predict how well the children would handle schoolwork.

Note that Binet and Simon made no assumptions concerning *why* a particular child was slow, average, or precocious. Binet personally leaned toward an environmental explanation. To raise the capacities of low-scoring children, he recommended "mental orthopedics" that would train them to develop their attention span and self-discipline. He refused to speculate about what the test was actually measuring, and insisted that it did not measure inborn intelligence as a meter stick measures height. Rather, the test had a single practical purpose: to identify French schoolchildren needing special attention. Binet hoped his test would be used to improve children's education, but he also feared it would be used to label children and limit their opportunities (Gould, 1981).

Lewis Terman: The Innate IQ

Binet might have been dismayed to discover that the test he designed as a practical guide for identifying slow learners in need of special help would soon be used as a numerical measure of inherited intelligence. After Binet's death in 1911, Stanford University professor Lewis Terman (1877–1956) attempted to use Binet's test but found that the Paris-developed age norms worked poorly with California schoolchildren. So Terman adapted some of Binet's original items, added others, established new age norms, and extended the upper end of the test's range from teenagers to "superior adults." Terman gave his revision the name it retains today—the **Stanford-Binet.**

National Library of Medicine

Alfred Binet
"The scale, properly speaking, does not permit the measure of intelligence, because intellectual qualities . . . cannot be measured as linear surfaces are measured" (Binet & Simon, 1905).

"The IQ test was invented to predict academic performance, nothing else. If we wanted something that would predict life success, we'd have to invent another test completely."
Social psychologist Robert Zajonc (1984b)

Lewis Terman
"The children of successful and cultured parents test higher than children from wretched and ignorant homes for the simple reason that their heredity is better" (1916, p. 115).

News Service, Stanford University

Mrs. Randolph takes mother's pride too far.

From such tests, German psychologist William Stern derived the famous **intelligence quotient,** or **IQ.** The IQ was simply a person's mental age divided by chronological age and multiplied by 100 to get rid of the decimal point:

$$IQ = \frac{\text{mental age}}{\text{chronological age}} \times 100$$

Thus, an average child, whose mental and chronological ages are the same, has an IQ of 100. But an 8-year-old who answers questions as would a typical 10-year-old has an IQ of 125.

Most current intelligence tests, including the Stanford-Binet, no longer compute an IQ. The original IQ formula works fairly well for children but not for adults. (Should a 40-year-old who does as well on the test as an average 20-year-old be assigned an IQ of only 50?) Today's intelligence tests therefore produce a mental ability score based on the test-taker's performance *relative to the average performance of others the same age.* As on the original Stanford-Binet, current tests define this score so that 100 is average, with about two-thirds of all people scoring between 85 and 115. Although there is no longer any intelligence *quotient,* the term "IQ" still lingers in everyday vocabulary as a shorthand expression for "intelligence test score."

Terman promoted the widespread use of intelligence testing. His motive was to "take account of the inequalities of children in original endowment" by assessing their "vocational fitness." In sympathy with eugenics—a much-criticized nineteenth-century movement that proposed measuring human traits and using the results to encourage only smart and fit people to reproduce—Terman (1916, pp. 91–92) envisioned that the use of intelligence tests would "ultimately result in curtailing the reproduction of feeble-mindedness and in the elimination of an enormous amount of crime, pauperism, and industrial inefficiency" (p. 7).

With Terman's help, the U.S. government developed new tests to evaluate newly arriving immigrants and 1.7 million World War I army recruits—the world's first mass administration of an intelligence test. To some psychologists, the results indicated the inferiority of people not sharing their Anglo-Saxon heritage. Such findings were part of the cultural climate that led to a 1924 immigration law, which reduced immigration quotas for Southern and Eastern Europe to less than a fifth of those for Northern and Western Europe.

Binet probably would have been horrified that his test was adapted and used to draw such conclusions. Indeed, such sweeping judgments did become an embarrassment to most of those who championed testing. Even Terman, for instance, came to appreciate that test scores reflect not only people's innate mental abilities but also their education and their familiarity with the culture assumed by the test. Nevertheless, abuses of the early intelligence tests serve to remind us that science can be value-laden. Behind a screen of scientific objectivity, ideology sometimes lurks.

> "Science must be understood as a social phenomenon, a gutsy, human enterprise, not the work of robots programmed to collect pure information."
>
> Stephen Jay Gould (1981)

Modern Tests of Mental Abilities

OBJECTIVE 9 | Distinguish between aptitude and achievement tests, and describe modern tests of mental abilities such as the WAIS.

By this point in your life, you've faced dozens of ability tests: school tests of basic reading and math skills, course examinations, intelligence tests, driver's license examinations, and college and university entrance examinations, to name just a few. Psychologists classify such tests as either **aptitude tests,** intended to *predict* your ability to learn a new skill, or **achievement tests,** intended to *reflect* what you have learned. Thus, a college entrance exam, which seeks to predict your ability to do college work, is an aptitude test—a "thinly disguised intelligence test," says Howard Gardner (1999). Indeed, report Meredith Frey and Douglas Detterman (2004), total

■ **intelligence quotient (IQ)** defined originally as the ratio of mental age (*ma*) to chronological age (*ca*) multiplied by 100 (thus, IQ = *ma/ca* x 100). On contemporary intelligence tests, the average performance for a given age is assigned a score of 100.

■ **aptitude test** a test designed to predict a person's future performance; *aptitude* is the capacity to learn.

■ **achievement test** a test designed to assess what a person has learned.

■ **Wechsler Adult Intelligence Scale (WAIS)** the WAIS is the most widely used intelligence test; contains verbal and performance (nonverbal) subtests.

FIGURE 11.3
Close cousins: Aptitude and intelligence scores
A scatterplot shows the close correlation between intelligence scores and verbal and quantitative SAT scores. (From Frey and Detterman, 2004.)

scores on the U.S. SAT (Scholastic Assessment Test; formerly called the U.S. Scholastic Aptitude Test) correlated +.82 with general intelligence scores in a national sample of 14- to 21-year-olds (**FIGURE 11.3**). Exams covering what you have learned in this course are achievement tests.

Actually, the differences between aptitude tests and achievement tests are not so clear-cut. Your *achieved* vocabulary influences your score on most aptitude tests. Similarly, your *aptitudes* for learning and test-taking influence your grades on achievement tests. Most tests, whether labeled aptitude or achievement, assess both ability and its development. Practically speaking, however, aptitude tests predict future performance and achievement tests assess current performance.

As a 6-year-old Romanian, David Wechsler arrived just ahead of other Eastern European immigrants who, during the early 1900s, took the Stanford-Binet test and were believed by some to be "feeble-minded." Many years later, Wechsler, then a psychologist, created what is now the most widely used intelligence test, the **Wechsler Adult Intelligence Scale (WAIS).** After creating the WAIS, Wechsler developed the *Wechsler Intelligence Scale for Children (WISC)* for school-age children, and still later a test for preschool children. As illustrated in **FIGURE 11.4,** on page 446, the WAIS consists of 11 subtests. It yields not only an overall intelligence score, as does the Stanford-Binet, but also separate scores for verbal comprehension, perceptual organization, working memory, and processing speed. Striking differences among these scores alert the examiner to possible learning problems or brain disorders. For example, a verbal comprehension score much lower than the same person's other scores might indicate a reading or language disability. Comparing scores can also help a psychologist or psychiatrist to establish a rehabilitation plan for patients who have suffered a stroke or brain injury. In addition, the tests provide clues to cognitive strengths that a teacher, employer, or therapist might build upon.

Lew Merrim/Photo Researchers, Inc.

Matching patterns
Block design puzzles test the ability to analyze patterns. Wechsler's individually administered intelligence test comes in forms suited for adults (WAIS) and children (WISC).

VERBAL

General Information
What day of the year is Independence Day?

Similarities
In what way are *wool* and *cotton* alike?

Arithmetic Reasoning
If eggs cost 60 cents a dozen, what does 1 egg cost?

Vocabulary
Tell me the meaning of corrupt.

Comprehension
Why do people buy fire insurance?

Digit Span
Listen carefully, and when I am through, say the numbers right after me.

> 7   3   4   1   8   6

Now I am going to say some more numbers, but I want you to say them backward.

> 3   8   4   1   6

PERFORMANCE

Picture Completion
I am going to show you a picture with an important part missing. Tell me what is missing.

Picture Arrangement
The pictures below tell a story. Put them in the right order to tell the story.

Block Design
Using the four blocks, make one just like this.

Object Assembly
If these pieces are put together correctly, they will make something. Go ahead and put them together as quickly as you can.

Digit-Symbol Substitution

Thorndike et al., Measurement and evaluation in psychology and education, 5e, © 1990. Published by Prentice Hall.

Getty Images/Stockdisc

FIGURE 11.4
Sample items from the Wechsler Adult Intelligence Scale (WAIS) subtests
(Adapted from Thorndike & Hagen, 1997.)

■ **standardization** defining meaningful scores by comparison with the performance of a pretested standardization group.

■ **normal curve** the symmetrical bell-shaped curve that describes the distribution of many physical and psychological attributes. Most scores fall near the average, and fewer and fewer scores lie near the extremes.

Principles of Test Construction

To be widely accepted, psychological tests must meet three criteria: They must be *standardized, reliable,* and *valid.* The Stanford-Binet and Wechsler tests meet these requirements.

Standardization

OBJECTIVE 10 | Discuss the importance of standardizing psychological tests, and describe the distribution of scores in a normal curve.

The number of questions you answer correctly on an intelligence test would tell us almost nothing. To evaluate your performance, we need a basis for comparing it with others' performance. To enable meaningful comparisons, test-makers first give the test to a representative sample of people. When individuals later take the test following the same procedures, their scores can be compared with the standards defined by the sample. Recall that Lewis Terman and his colleagues recognized that items developed for Parisians did not provide a satisfactory standard for evaluating Americans. They revised the test and recalibrated the new version by testing 2300 native-born, white Americans of differing socioeconomic levels. Ironically, they then used this standard to evaluate nonwhite American and immigrant groups (Van Leeuwen, 1982). The process of defining meaningful scores relative to a pretested group is called **standardization.**

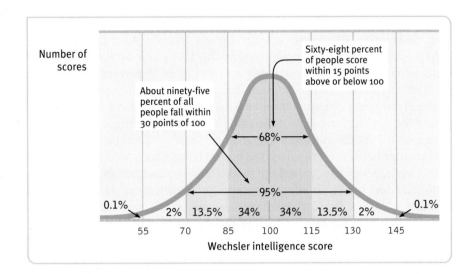

FIGURE 11.5
The normal curve

Scores on aptitude tests tend to form a normal, or bell-shaped, curve around an average score. For the Wechsler scale, for example, the average score is 100.

Standardized test results typically form a *normal distribution,* a bell-shaped pattern of scores that forms the **normal curve** (**FIGURE 11.5**). No matter what we measure—people's heights, weights, or mental aptitudes—scores often form a roughly symmetrical, bell-shaped distribution clustered around the average. On an intelligence test, we call this average score 100. As we move out from the average (toward either extreme), we find fewer and fewer people. Within each age group, the Stanford-Binet and the Wechsler tests assign any person a score according to how much that person's performance deviates above or below the average. As Figure 11.5 shows, a performance higher than all but 2 percent of all scores earns an intelligence score of 130. A raw score that is comparably *below* 98 percent of all the scores earns an intelligence score of 70.

To keep the average score near 100, the Stanford-Binet and the Wechsler scales are periodically restandardized. If you took the WAIS Third Edition recently, your performance was compared with a standardization sample who took the test during 1996, not to David Wechsler's initial 1930s sample. If you compared the performance of the most recent standardization sample with that of the 1930s sample, do you suppose you would find rising or declining test performance? Amazingly—given that college entrance aptitude scores were dropping during the 1960s and 1970s—intelligence test performance has been *improving.* This worldwide phenomenon is called the *Flynn effect* in honor of New Zealand researcher James Flynn (1987, 1999), who first calculated its magnitude. As **FIGURE 11.6** indicates, the average person's intelligence test

FIGURE 11.6
Getting smarter?

In every country studied, intelligence test performance rose during the twentieth century, as shown here with American Wechsler and Stanford-Binet test performance between 1918 and 1989. In Britain, test scores have risen 27 points since 1942. (From Hogan, 1995.)

score 80 years ago was—by today's standard—only a 76! Such rising performance has been observed in 20 countries, from Canada to rural Australia (Daley & others, 2003). Although the gains slowed during the 1990s and may now have ceased, the increase seems real and is now widely accepted as an important phenomenon (Sundet & others, 2004; Teasdale & Owen, 2000).

The Flynn effect's cause is a mystery (Neisser, 1997a, 1998). Does it result from greater test sophistication? (But the gains began before testing was widespread.) Better nutrition? As the nutrition explanation would predict, people have gotten not only smarter but taller. Moreover, the increases have been greatest at the lowest economic levels, which have gained the most from improved nutrition (Colom & others, 2005). Or does the Flynn effect stem from more education? More stimulating environments? Less childhood disease? Smaller families and more parental investment?

Regardless of what combination of factors explains the rise in intelligence test scores, the phenomenon counters one concern of some hereditarians—that the higher twentieth-century birthrates among those with lower scores would shove human intelligence scores downward. Seeking to explain the rising scores and mindful of global mixing, one scholar has even speculated about the influence of a genetic phenomenon comparable to "hybrid vigor," which occurs in agriculture when crossbreeding produces corn or livestock superior to the parent plants or animals (Mingroni, 2004).

Reliability

OBJECTIVE 11 | Explain what it means to say a test is *reliable*.

Comparing your test scores to those of the standardizing group still won't tell us much about you unless the test has **reliability.** A good test must yield dependably consistent scores. To check a test's reliability, researchers retest people using either the same test or another form of it. If the two scores generally agree, or *correlate,* the test is reliable. As an alternative, the researcher may split a test in half and see whether scores derived from odd and even questions agree. Assuming that one's basic ability has not changed between two adjacent testings, any score difference reflects "error" variation related to such things as luck, fatigue, and anxiety.

The higher the correlation between the *test-retest* or the *split-half* scores, the higher the test's reliability. The tests we have considered so far—the Stanford-Binet, the WAIS, and the WISC—all have reliabilities of about +.9, which is very high. When retested, people's scores generally match their first score closely.

Validity

OBJECTIVE 12 | Explain what it means to say a test is *valid*, and describe two types of validity.

High reliability does not ensure a test's **validity**—the extent to which the test actually measures what it is supposed to measure or predicts what it is supposed to predict. If you use an inaccurate tape measure to measure people's heights, your height report would have high reliability (consistency) but low validity. It is enough for some tests that they have **content validity,** meaning the test taps the pertinent behavior. The road test for a driver's license has content validity because it samples the tasks a driver routinely faces. Course exams have content validity if they assess one's mastery of a representative sample of course material.

Other tests are evaluated in terms of how well they agree with some **criterion,** an independent measure of what the test aims to assess. For some tests, the criterion is future performance. For example, aptitude tests must have **predictive validity,** which means they predict future achievement.

■ **reliability** the extent to which a test yields consistent results, as assessed by the consistency of scores on two halves of the test, on alternate forms of the test, or on retesting.

■ **validity** the extent to which a test measures or predicts what it is supposed to. (See also *content validity* and *predictive validity*.)

■ **content validity** the extent to which a test samples the behavior that is of interest (such as a driving test that samples driving tasks).

■ **criterion** the behavior (such as future college grades) that a test (such as the SAT) is designed to predict; thus, the measure used in defining whether the test has predictive validity.

■ **predictive validity** the success with which a test predicts the behavior it is designed to predict; it is assessed by computing the correlation between test scores and the criterion behavior. (Also called *criterion-related validity*.)

FIGURE 11.7
Diminishing predictive power
Let's imagine a correlation between football linemen's body weight and their success on the field. Note how insignificant the relationship becomes when we narrow the range of weight to 260 to 300 pounds. As the range of data under consideration narrows, its predictive power diminishes.

Are general aptitude tests as predictive as they are reliable? As critics are fond of noting, the answer is plainly no. The predictive power of aptitude tests is fairly strong in the early school years, but later it weakens. Academic aptitude test scores are reasonably good predictors of achievement for children ages 6 to 12, where the correlation between intelligence score and school performance is about +.60 (Jensen, 1980). The SAT, used in the United States as a college entrance exam, is less successful in predicting first-year college performance; here, the correlation is less than +.50 (Willingham & others, 1990). By the time we get to the U.S. Graduate Record Examination (GRE; an aptitude test similar to the SAT but for those applying to graduate school), the correlation with graduate school performance is an even more modest +.30 (GRE, 1990).

Why does the predictive power of aptitude scores diminish as students move up the educational ladder? Consider a parallel situation: Among all American or Canadian football linemen, body weight correlates with success. A 300-pound player tends to overwhelm a 200-pound opponent. But within the narrow 260- to 300-pound range typically found at the professional level, the correlation between weight and success becomes negligible (**FIGURE 11.7**). The narrower the *range* of weights, the lower the predictive power of body weight becomes. If an elite university takes only those students who have very high aptitude scores, those scores cannot possibly predict much. This will be true even if the test has excellent predictive validity with a more diverse sample of students. So, when we validate a test using a wide range of people but then use it with a restricted range of people, it loses much of its predictive validity.

>> Learning Outcomes

Assessing Intelligence

OBJECTIVE **8** | Define *intelligence test* and discuss the history of intelligence testing.

Psychologists define *intelligence test* as a method for assessing an individual's mental aptitudes and comparing them with those of others, using numerical scores. More than a century ago in France, Alfred Binet and his collaborator Théodore Simon started the modern intelligence-testing movement by developing questions that helped predict children's future progress in the Paris school system. Lewis Terman of Stanford University revised Binet's work for use in the United States. Terman believed his Stanford-Binet could help guide people toward appropriate opportunities, but more than Binet, he believed intelligence is inherited. During the early twentieth century, intelligence tests were, regrettably, sometimes used to "document" assumptions about the innate inferiority of certain ethnic and immigrant groups. Intelligence test scores have been expressed as an *intelligence quotient (IQ)*, established by dividing mental age by chronological age times 100.

OBJECTIVE 9 | Distinguish between aptitude and achievement tests, and describe modern tests of mental abilities, such as the WAIS.

Aptitude tests are designed to predict what you *can learn*. *Achievement tests* are designed to assess what you *have learned*. The *WAIS (Wechsler Adult Intelligence Scale)*, an aptitude test, is the most widely used intelligence test for adults. Two similar Wechsler scales are designed to test intelligence in preschool and older children. The SAT is an aptitude test, and in one study, test-takers' total SAT scores and their score on a test of general intelligence correlated at a very high level: +.82.

OBJECTIVE 10 | Discuss the importance of standardizing psychological tests, and describe the distribution of scores in a normal curve.

Standardizing a test is the process of administering the test to a representative sample of future test-takers in order to establish a basis for meaningful comparisons of scores. The distribution of many physical and psychological attributes forms a *normal curve* (also known as a *bell-shaped curve*)—a roughly symmetrical shape in which most scores cluster around an average, and increasingly fewer are distributed at the extremes. Intelligence test scores form such a curve, but in the past six decades, the average score has risen 27 points—a phenomenon known as the Flynn effect.

OBJECTIVE 11 | Explain what it means to say that a test is reliable.

A test is *reliable* when it yields consistent results. To establish reliability, researchers compare the consistency of test-takers' scores on two halves of the test, alternate forms of the test, or retests on the same test. A test can be reliable but not valid.

OBJECTIVE 12 | Explain what it means to say a test is valid, and describe two types of validity.

A *valid* test measures or predicts what it is supposed to. *Content validity* is the extent to which a test samples the pertinent behavior (as a driving test measures driving ability). *Predictive validity* is the extent to which the test predicts a behavior it is designed to predict (aptitude tests have predictive ability if they can predict future achievements).

ASK YOURSELF: Are you working to the potential reflected in your college entrance exam scores? What, other than your aptitude, is affecting your college performance?

The Dynamics of Intelligence

We now can address some age-old questions about the dynamics of human intelligence—about its stability over the life span, and about the extremes of intelligence.

Stability or Change?

OBJECTIVE 13 | Describe the stability of intelligence scores over the life span.

If we retested people periodically throughout their lives, would their intelligence scores be stable? Chapter 4 explored the stability of mental abilities in later life. What about the stability of intelligence scores early in life?

Developmental researchers have left few stones unturned in their search for indicators of infants' later intelligence. Unable to talk with infants, they have assessed what they can observe—everything from birth weight, to whether the third toe was longer than the second, to age of sitting up alone. None of these measures provides any useful prediction of intelligence scores at much later ages (Bell & Waldrop, 1989; Broman, 1989). Perhaps, as developmental psychologist Nancy Bayley reflected in 1949, "we have not yet found the right tests." Someday, she speculated, we might find "infant behaviors which are characteristic of underlying intellectual functions" and which will predict later intelligence. Some studies have found that 2- to 7-month-old babies who quickly grow bored with a picture—who, given a choice, prefer to look at a new one—score higher on tests of brain speed and intelligence up to 11 years later, but the prediction is crude (Kavšek, 2004; Tasbihsazan & others, 2003).

So, new parents who are wondering about their baby's intelligence and anxiously comparing their baby to others can relax. Except for extremely impaired or very precocious children, casual observation and intelligence tests before age 3 predict children's future aptitudes only minimally (Humphreys & Davey, 1988). For example, children who are early talkers—speaking in sentences typical of 3-year-olds by age 20 months—are *not* especially likely to be reading by age 4½ (Crain-Thoreson & Dale, 1992). (A better predictor of early reading is having parents who have read lots of stories to their child.) As noted earlier, even Albert Einstein was slow in learning to talk (Quasha, 1980).

By age 4, however, children's performance on intelligence tests begins to predict their adolescent and adult scores. Moreover, high-scoring adolescents tend to have been early readers. One study surveyed the parents of 187 American seventh- and eighth-graders who had taken a college aptitude test as part of a seven-state talent search and had scored considerably higher than most high school seniors. If their parents' memories can be trusted, more than half of this precocious group of adolescents began reading by age 4 and more than 80 percent were reading by age 5 (Van Tassel-Baska, 1983). Not surprisingly, then, intelligence tests given 5-year-olds begin to predict school achievement (Tramontana & others, 1988).

After about age 7, intelligence test scores, though certainly not fixed, stabilize (Bloom, 1964). Thus, the consistency of scores over time increases with the age of the child. The remarkable stability of aptitude scores by late adolescence is seen in a U.S. Educational Testing Service study of 23,000 students who took the SAT and then later took the GRE (Angoff, 1988). On either test, verbal scores correlated only modestly with math scores—revealing that these two aptitudes are distinct. Yet scores on the SAT verbal test correlated +.86 with the scores on the GRE verbal tests taken four to five years later. An equally astonishing +.86 correlation occurred between the two math tests. Given the time lapse and differing educational experiences of these 23,000 students, the stability of their aptitude scores is remarkable.

Ian Deary and his colleagues (2004) recently set a record for long-term follow-up. When the intelligence test administered to 11-year-old Scots in 1932 was readministered to 542 survivors as turn-of-the-millennium 80-year-olds, the correlation between the two sets of scores—after some 70 years of varied life experiences—was striking (**FIGURE 11.8**). High-scoring 11-year-olds also were more likely to be living independently as 77-year-olds and less likely to have suffered late-onset Alzheimer's

> " My dear Adele, I am 4 years old and I can read any English book. I can say all the Latin Substantives and Adjectives and active verbs besides 52 lines of Latin poetry."
> Francis Galton, Letter to his sister, 1827

Ironically, SAT and GRE scores correlate better with each other than either does with its intended criterion, school achievement. Thus, their reliability far exceeds their predictive validity. If either test was much affected by coaching, luck, or how one feels on the test day (as so many people believe), such reliability would be impossible.

FIGURE 11.8
Intelligence endures
When Ian Deary and his colleagues (2004) gave 80-year-old Scots an intelligence test they had taken as 11-year-olds, their scores across seven decades correlated +.66.

Greenlar/The Image Works

A young man with Down syndrome
In the past, people with this condition were often institutionalized. Today, with a supportive family environment and special education, many people with Down syndrome learn to care for themselves and hold a job.

disease (Starr & others, 2000; Whalley & others, 2000). Another study that followed 93 nuns confirmed that those exhibiting less verbal ability in written essays when entering their convent in their teens were more at risk for Alzheimer's disease after age 75 (Snowdon & others, 1996).

Extremes of Intelligence

OBJECTIVE 14 | Discuss the two extremes of the normal distribution of intelligence.

One way to glimpse the validity and significance of any test is to compare people who score at the two extremes of the normal curve. The two groups should differ noticeably, and they do.

The Low Extreme

At one extreme of the normal curve are those whose intelligence test scores fall at 70 or below. To be labeled as having **mental retardation,** a child must have both a low test score and difficulty adapting to the normal demands of independent living. Only about 1 percent of the population meets both criteria, with males outnumbering females by 50 percent (American Psychiatric Association, 1994). As **TABLE 11.3** indicates, most individuals with mental retardation can, with support, live in mainstream society.

Mental retardation sometimes has a known physical cause. **Down syndrome,** for example, is a disorder of varying severity caused by an extra chromosome 21 in the person's genetic makeup.

During the last two centuries, the pendulum of opinion about how best to care for people with mental retardation has made a complete swing. Until the mid-nineteenth century, they were cared for at home. Many of those with the most severe disabilities died, but people with milder forms of retardation often found a place in a farm-based society. Then, residential schools for slow learners were established. By the twentieth century, many of these institutions had become warehouses, providing residents little attention, no privacy, and no hope. Parents often were told to separate themselves permanently from their impaired child before they became attached.

TABLE 11.3

DEGREES OF MENTAL RETARDATION

Level	Approximate Intelligence Scores	Percentage of Persons with Retardation	Adaptation to Demands of Life
Mild	50–70	85%	May learn academic skills up to sixth-grade level. Adults may, with assistance, achieve self-supporting social and vocational skills.
Moderate	35–50	10%	May progress to second-grade level academically. Adults may contribute to their own support by laboring in sheltered workshops.
Severe	20–35	3–4%	May learn to talk and to perform simple work tasks under close supervision but are generally unable to profit from vocational training.
Profound	Below 20	1–2%	Require constant aid and supervision.

Source: Reprinted with permission from the *Diagnostic and Statistical Manual of Mental Disorders*, Fourth Edition, text revision. Copyright 2000 American Psychiatric Association.

In the last half of the twentieth century, the pendulum swung back to normalization—encouraging people to live in their own communities as normally as their functioning permits. Children with mild retardation are educated in less restrictive environments, and many are integrated, or *mainstreamed,* into regular classrooms. Most grow up with their own families, then move into a protected living arrangement, such as a group home. The hope, and often the reality, is a happier and more dignified life.

But think about another reason people diagnosed with mild retardation—those just below the 70 score used to define retardation with an intelligence test—might be better able to live independently today than many decades ago. Recall that, thanks to the Flynn effect, the tests have been periodically restandardized. When that has happened, individuals who scored near 70 suddenly lose about 6 IQ points, and the number of people diagnosed with retardation suddenly jumps (Kanaya & others, 2003). Two people with the same ability level could now be classified differently, depending on when they were tested. With the new norms, more people suddenly become eligible for special education, and for Social Security payments for those with a mental disability, and in the United States (one of only a few countries with the death penalty) fewer for execution. (The U.S. Supreme Court ruled in 2002 that the execution of people with mental retardation is "cruel and unusual punishment.") For people near that score of 70, intelligence testing can be high stakes.

The High Extreme

In one famous project begun in 1921, Lewis Terman studied more than 1500 California schoolchildren with IQ scores over 135. Contrary to the popular notion that intellectually gifted children are frequently maladjusted because they are "in a different world" from their nongifted peers, Terman's high-scoring children, like those in later studies, were healthy, well-adjusted, and unusually successful academically (Lubinski & Benbow, 2000; Stanley, 1997). When restudied over the next seven decades, most people in Terman's group had attained high levels of education (Austin & others, 2002; Holahan & Sears, 1995). They included many doctors, lawyers, professors, scientists, and writers, but no Nobel Prize winners. (Terman did test one future Nobel laureate in physics but excluded him from the gifted sample because his measured IQ wasn't high enough [Cassandro & Simonton, 2003].)

These whiz kids remind one of Jean Piaget, who by age 7 was devoting his free time to studying birds, fossils, and machines; who by 15 began publishing scientific articles on mollusks; and who later went on to become the twentieth century's most famous developmental psychologist (Hunt, 1993). Children with extraordinary academic gifts are sometimes more isolated, introverted, and in their own worlds (Winner, 2000). But most thrive.

There are critics who question many of the assumptions of currently popular "gifted child" programs, such as the belief that only 3 to 5 percent of children are gifted and that it pays to identify and "track" these special few—segregating them in special classes and giving them academic enrichment not available to the other 95 percent. Critics note that tracking by aptitude sometimes creates a self-fulfilling prophecy: Those implicitly labeled "ungifted" can be influenced to become so (Lipsey & Wilson, 1993; Slavin & Braddock, 1993). Denying lower-ability students opportunities for enriched education can widen the achievement gap between ability groups and increase their social isolation from one another—one reason there is no tracking in the elementary schools of Japan and China (Carnegie, 1989; Stevenson & Lee, 1990). Because minority and low-income youth are more often placed in lower academic groups, tracking can also promote segregation and prejudice—hardly, note critics, a healthy preparation for working and living in a multicultural society.

■ **mental retardation** a condition of limited mental ability, indicated by an intelligence score of 70 or below and difficulty in adapting to the demands of life; varies from mild to profound.

■ **Down syndrome** a condition of retardation and associated physical disorders caused by an extra chromosome in one's genetic makeup.

"Joining Mensa means that you are a genius. . . . I worried about the arbitrary 132 cutoff point, until I met someone with an IQ of 131 and, honestly, he was a bit slow on the uptake."

Steve Martin, 1997

The extremes of intelligence
Sho Yano was playing Mozart by age 4, aced the SAT at age 8, and graduated *summa cum laude* from Loyola University at age 12, at which age he began combined Ph.D.–M.D. studies at the University of Chicago.

AP Photo/Anne Ryan

"Alpha children wear grey. They work much harder than we do, because they're so frightfully clever. I'm really awfully glad I'm a Beta, because I don't work so hard. And then we are much better than the Gammas and Deltas. Gammas are stupid."

Aldous Huxley, *Brave New World*, 1932

Critics and proponents of gifted education do, however, agree on this: Children have differing gifts. Some are especially good at math, others at verbal reasoning, others at art, still others at social leadership. Educating children as if all were alike is as naive as assuming that giftedness is something, like blue eyes, that you either have or do not have. One need not hang labels on children to affirm their special talents and to challenge them all at the frontiers of their own ability and understanding. By providing "appropriate developmental placement" suited to each child's talents, we can promote both equity and excellence for all (Colangelo & others, 2004; Lubinski & Benbow, 2000; Sternberg & Grigorenko, 2000).

>> LEARNING OUTCOMES

The Dynamics of Intelligence

OBJECTIVE 13 | Discuss the stability of intelligence scores over the life span.
The stability of intelligence test scores increases with age. By age 4, scores fluctuate somewhat but begin to predict adolescent and adult scores. At about age 7, scores become fairly stable and consistent.

OBJECTIVE 14 | Discuss the two extremes of the normal distribution of intelligence.
If an intelligence test is valid, the two groups of people falling at the extremes of the normal curve should be significantly different, and they are. Those with scores below 70, the cut-off mark for the diagnosis of mental retardation, vary in their abilities, from near-normal, to (at the very lowest scoring levels) requiring constant aid and supervision. Down syndrome is a form of retardation with a physical cause—an extra copy of chromosome 21. High-scoring people, contrary to popular myths, tend to be healthy, well-adjusted, and unusually successful academically. Schools sometimes "track" such children, separating them from those with lower scores. Such programs can become self-fulfilling prophecies as children live up to—or down to—others' perceptions of their ability.

ASK YOURSELF: How do you feel about mainstreaming children of all ability levels in the same classroom? What evidence are you using to support your view?

Genetic and Environmental Influences on Intelligence

Intelligence runs in families. But why? Are our intellectual abilities mostly inherited? Or are they molded by our environment?

Few issues arouse such passion or have such serious political implications. Consider: If we mainly inherit our differing mental abilities, and if success reflects those abilities, then people's socioeconomic standing will correspond to their inborn differences. This could lead to those on top believing their intellectual birthright justifies their social positions.

But if mental abilities are primarily nurtured by the environments that raise and inform us, then children from disadvantaged environments can expect to lead disadvantaged lives. In this case, people's standing will result from their unequal opportunities.

For now, as best we can, let us set aside such political implications and examine the evidence.

Genetic Influences

OBJECTIVE 15 | Discuss the evidence for the genetic contribution to individual intelligence, and explain what psychologists mean by the heritability of intelligence.

Do people who share the same genes also share comparable mental abilities? As you can see from **FIGURE 11.9,** which summarizes many studies, the answer is clearly yes. In support of the genetic contribution to intelligence, researchers cite three sets of findings:

- Across studies of 10,000 twins, the intelligence test scores of identical twins reared together are virtually as similar as those of the same person taking the same test twice (Lykken, 1999; Plomin, 2001). (The scores of fraternal twins, who typically share only half their genes, are much less similar.) Likewise, the test scores of identical twins reared separately are similar enough to lead twin researcher Thomas Bouchard (1996) to estimate that "about 70 percent" of intelligence score variation "can be attributed to genetic variation." Other researchers have offered estimates from 50 to 75 percent (Devlin & others, 1997; Neisser & others, 1996; Plomin, 2003).
- Brain scans reveal that identical twins have very similar gray matter volume. Moreover, unlike fraternal twins, their brains are virtually the same in areas associated with verbal and spatial intelligence (Thompson & others, 2001).
- Are there genes for genius? Comparisons of the genes of people of high versus average intelligence have produced slow progress in identifying the many genes that contribute to cognitive ability (Plomin, 2003). By inserting an extra gene into fertilized mouse eggs, researchers have, however, produced smarter mice—mice that excel at learning and remembering the location of a hidden underwater platform or at recognizing cues that signal impending shock (Tsien, 2000). The gene helps create a neural receptor involved in memory.

But there is also some evidence pointing to an effect of environment. Fraternal twins, who are genetically no more alike than any other siblings—but who are treated more alike because they are the same age—tend to score more alike than other siblings.

Seeking to disentangle genes and environment, researchers have also asked whether adopted children and their siblings, thanks to their shared environment, share similar

" There are more studies addressing the genetics of *g* than any other human characteristic."

Robert Plomin (1999)

Smart scientist, smart mouse
Working with Ya-Ping Tang and others, Princeton University biologist Joe Z. Tsien genetically engineered a strain of smart mice. Such work may shed new light on the biology of human intelligence.

Courtesy of Laura Pedrick

FIGURE 11.9
Intelligence: Nature and nurture
The most genetically similar people have the most similar intelligence scores. Remember: 1.0 indicates a perfect correlation; zero indicates no correlation at all. (Data from McGue & others, 1993.)

Digital Vision/Getty Images

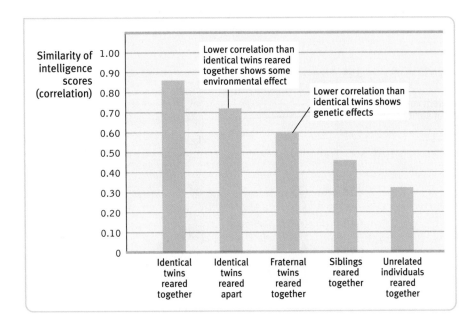

Similarity of intelligence scores (correlation)

- Identical twins reared together
- Identical twins reared apart — Lower correlation than identical twins reared together shows some environmental effect
- Fraternal twins reared together — Lower correlation than identical twins shows genetic effects
- Siblings reared together
- Unrelated individuals reared together

"I told my parents that if grades were so important they should have paid for a smarter egg donor."

aptitudes. During childhood, the intelligence test scores of adoptive siblings correlate modestly. Researchers have also compared the intelligence test scores of adopted children with those of (a) their biological parents, the providers of their genes, and (b) their adoptive parents, the providers of their home environment. Over time, adopted children accumulate experience in their differing adoptive families. So would you expect the family environment effect to grow with age and the genetic legacy effect to shrink?

If you would, behavior geneticists have a surprise for you. With age, mental similarities between adopted children and their adoptive families disappear as parental influence wanes; by adulthood, the correlation is roughly zero (McGue & others, 1993). As we accumulate life experience, genetic influences—not environmental ones—become more apparent (Bouchard, 1995, 1996a). Adopted children's intelligence scores become more like those of their biological parents (**FIGURE 11.10**), and identical twins' similarities continue or increase into their eighties (McClearn & others, 1997; Plomin & others, 1997).

Recall from Chapter 3 the meaning of *heritability*. To say that the heritability of intelligence—the variation in intelligence test scores attributable to genetic factors—is 50 percent (or a tad more) does *not* mean that your genes are responsible for 50 percent of *your* intelligence and your environment for the rest. It means that we can attribute to heredity 50 percent *of the variation in intelligence* (among those studied). This point is so often misunderstood that I repeat: We can never say what percentage of an *individual's* intelligence is inherited. Heritability refers instead to the extent to which *differences among people* are attributable to genes. Heritability *never* pertains to an individual, only to why people differ.

Even this conclusion must be qualified, because heritability can vary from study to study. For example, environmental differences are more predictive of intelligence scores among children of less-educated parents—among whom family environments may vary widely (Rowe & others, 1999). Recall from Chapter 3 Mark Twain's proposal to raise boys in barrels to age 12, feeding them through a hole. Given the boys' equal environments, differences in their individual intelligence test scores at age 12 could be explained only by their heredity. Thus, heritability for their differences would be nearly 100 percent. But if we raise people with similar heredities in drastically different

A check on your understanding of heritability: If environments become more equal, the heritability of intelligence would
a. increase.
b. decrease.
c. be unchanged.
(See page 458.)

FIGURE 11.10
Who do adopted children resemble?
As the years went by in their adoptive families, children's verbal ability scores became modestly more like their *biological* parents' scores. (Adapted from Plomin & DeFries, 1998.)

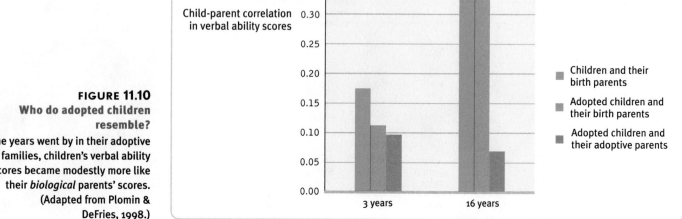

Child-parent correlation in verbal ability scores

■ Children and their birth parents
■ Adopted children and their birth parents
■ Adopted children and their adoptive parents

environments (barrels versus advantaged homes), the environment effect will be greater, and heritability—differences due to genes—will therefore be lower. In a world of clones, heritability would be zero.

Remember, too, that genes and environment correlate. If you are just slightly taller and quicker than others, notes James Flynn (2003), you will more likely be picked for a basketball team, will play more, and will get more coaching. The same would be true for your separated identical twin—who might, *not just for genetic reasons,* also come to excel at basketball. Likewise, students with a natural aptitude for mathematics are more likely to select math courses in high school and later to score well on math aptitude tests—thanks *both* to their natural math aptitude *and* to their math experience. If you have a slight genetically disposed intelligence edge, you will more likely stay in school, read books, and ask questions—all of which will amplify your cognitive brain power. Thanks to such gene-environment correlation, modest genetic advantages can be socially multiplied into big performance advantages. Our genes shape the experiences that shape us.

"Selective breeding has given me an aptitude for the law, but I still love fetching a dead duck out of freezing water."

Environmental Influences

OBJECTIVE **16** | Discuss the evidence for environmental influences on individual intelligence.

Genes make a difference. Even if we were all raised in the same intellectually stimulating environment, we would have differing aptitudes. But we have also seen that, even when explaining the similarities of identical twins, heredity does not tell the whole story. In ways sometimes predisposed by our genes, our life experiences matter.

Human environments are rarely as impoverished as the dark and barren cages inhabited by deprived rats that develop thinner-than-normal brain cortexes (see Chapter 3). Yet severe life experiences do leave footprints on the brain.

Early Intervention Effects

In a destitute Iranian orphanage, J. McVicker Hunt (1982) observed the dramatic effects of early experiences and demonstrated the impact of early intervention. The typical child Hunt observed there could not sit up unassisted at age 2 or walk at age 4. The little care the infants received was not in response to their crying, cooing, or other behaviors, so the children developed little sense of personal control over their environment. They were instead becoming passive "glum lumps." Extreme deprivation was bludgeoning native intelligence.

Aware of the benefits of responsive caregiving, Hunt began a program of "tutored human enrichment." He trained caregivers to play vocal games with the infants. They first imitated the babies' babbling. Then they led the babies in vocal follow-the-leader by shifting from one familiar sound to another. Then they began to teach sounds from the Persian language.

The results were dramatic. By 22 months of age, all 11 infants who received these language-fostering experiences could name more than 50 objects and body parts. So charming had the infants become that most were adopted—an unprecedented success for the orphanage.

Hunt's findings testify to the importance of environment. Severe disadvantage takes a toll (Ramey & Ramey, 1992). Unlike children of affluence, siblings within impoverished families have more similar intelligence scores (Turkheimer & others, 2003). This indicates that among the poor, environmental conditions can override genetic differences. One study of 1450 Virginia schools found that schools with lots of poverty-level children often had less-qualified teachers. And even after controlling for poverty, less-qualified teachers predicted lower achievement scores (Tuerk, 2005).

Devastating neglect
Romanian orphans who had minimal interaction with caregivers, such as this child in the Lagunul Pentro Copii orphanage in 1990, suffered delayed development.

" There is a large body of evidence indicating that there is little if anything to be gained by exposing middle-class children to early education."

Developmental psychologist
Edward F. Zigler (1987)

Getting a head start

To increase readiness for schoolwork and expand children's notions of where school might lead them, Project Head Start offers educational activities. Here children in a classroom learn about colors, and children on a field trip prepare for the annual Head Start parade in Boston.

Answer to question on page 456: Heritability—variation explained by genetic influences—will *increase* as environmental variation decreases.

Malnutrition can also influence cognitive development. When the infant malnutrition associated with severe poverty is relieved with nutritional supplements, poverty's effect on physical and cognitive development lessens (Brown & Pollitt, 1996). And improving nutrition helps explain the rising intelligence scores across generations.

Do such findings indicate a way to "give your child a superior intellect"? Some popular books claim that with intensive preschool training such is possible. But most experts are doubtful (Bruer, 1999). Although malnutrition, sensory deprivation, and social isolation can retard normal brain development, the difference between normal and "enriched" environments matters less. There is no environmental recipe for superbabies, beyond normal exposure to sights, sounds, and speech. Sandra Scarr's (1984) verdict still is widely shared: "Parents who are very concerned about providing special educational lessons for their babies are wasting their time."

Hunt would probably have agreed with Scarr that extra instruction has little effect on the intellectual development of children from stimulating environments. But he was optimistic when it came to children from disadvantaged environments. Indeed, his 1961 book, *Intelligence and Experience*, helped launch Project Head Start in 1965. Head Start, a U.S. government-funded preschool program, serves more than 900,000 children, most of whom come from families below the poverty level (Head Start, 2005). It aims to enhance children's chances for success in school and beyond by boosting their cognitive and social skills.

Does it succeed? Researchers study Head Start and other preschool programs by comparing children who experience the program with their counterparts who don't. Quality programs, offering individual attention, increase children's school readiness, which decreases their likelihood of repeating a grade or being placed in special education. Generally, the aptitude benefits dissipate over time (reminding us that life experience *after* Head Start matters, too). Psychologist Edward Zigler, the program's first director, nevertheless believes there are long-term benefits (Ripple & Zigler, 2003; Zigler & Styfco, 2001). High-quality preschool programs can provide at least a small boost to emotional intelligence—creating better attitudes toward learning and reducing school dropouts and criminality (Reynolds & others, 2001).

Schooling Effects

Schooling itself is an intervention that pays dividends reflected in intelligence scores. Stephen Ceci and Wendy Williams (1997) have amassed evidence that schooling and intelligence contribute to each other (and that both enhance later income). High intelligence is conducive to prolonged schooling. But intelligence scores tend to rise during the school year and drop over the summer months and when schooling is discontinued. Completing high school elevates intelligence scores over those obtained by comparable children who leave school early. The Flynn effect of rising IQ scores is probably partly due to increasing years of schooling over the last half-century—and to the more stimulating home environments provided by today's better-educated parents.

Group Differences in Intelligence Test Scores

If there were no group differences in aptitude scores, psychologists could politely debate hereditary and environmental influences in their ivory towers. But there are group differences. What are they? And what shall we make of them?

Ethnic Similarities and Differences

OBJECTIVE **17** | Describe ethnic similarities and differences in intelligence test scores, and discuss some genetic and environmental factors that might explain them.

Fueling this discussion are two disturbing but agreed-upon facts:

- Racial groups differ in their average scores on intelligence tests.
- High-scoring people (and groups) are more likely to attain high levels of education and income.

A statement by 52 intelligence researchers explained: "The bell curve for Whites is centered roughly around IQ 100; the bell curve for American Blacks roughly around 85; and those for different subgroups of Hispanics roughly midway between those for Whites and Blacks" (Avery & others, 1994). Comparable results come from other academic aptitude tests, such as the SAT. In recent years, the Black-White difference has diminished somewhat, and among children has dropped to 10 points in some studies (Neisser & others, 1996). Yet the test score gap stubbornly persists.

There are differences among other groups as well. European New Zealanders outscore native Maori New Zealanders. Israeli Jews outscore Israeli Arabs. Most Japanese outscore the stigmatized Japanese minority, the Burakumin. And those who can hear outscore those born deaf (Braden, 1994; Steele, 1990; Zeidner, 1990).

Everyone further agrees that such *group* differences provide little basis for judging individuals. Women outlive men by six years, but knowing someone's sex doesn't tell us with any precision how long that person will live. Even Charles Murray and Richard Herrnstein (1994), whose writings drew attention to Black-White differences, reminded us that "millions of Blacks have higher IQs than the average White."

Swedes and Bantus differ in complexion and language. That first factor is genetic, the second environmental. So what about intelligence scores?

As we have seen, heredity contributes to individual differences in intelligence. Does that mean it also contributes to group differences? Some psychologists believe it does, perhaps because of the world's differing climates and survival challenges (Herrnstein & Murray, 1994; Lynn, 1991, 2001; Rushton, 1998, 2003).

But we have also seen that group differences in a heritable trait may be entirely environmental, as in our earlier barrel-versus-home-reared boys example. Consider one of nature's experiments: Allow some children to grow up hearing their culture's dominant language, while others, born deaf, do not. Then give them an intelligence test rooted in that language, and (no surprise) those with expertise in the test's language will score highest. Although individual performance differences may be substantially genetic, the group difference is not (**FIGURE 11.11** on page 460).

Consider: If each identical twin were exactly as tall as his or her co-twin, heritability would be 100 percent. Imagine that we then separated some young twins and gave only half of them a nutritious diet, and that the well-nourished twins all grew to be exactly 3 inches taller than their counterparts—an environmental effect comparable to that actually observed in both Britain and America, where adolescents are several

Since 1850, the average Dutch man has grown from 5 feet 4 inches to today's 5 feet 10 inches (Bogin, 1998).

In prosperous country X everyone eats all they want. In country Y the rich are well fed, but the semistarved poor are often thin. In which country will the heritability of body weight be greater? (See page 461.)

FIGURE 11.11
Group differences and environmental impact
Even if the variation between members within a group reflects genetic differences, the average difference between groups may be wholly due to the environment. Imagine that seeds from the same mixture are sown in poor and fertile soil. Although height differences within each window box will be genetic, the height difference between the two groups will be environmental. (From Lewontin, 1976.)

inches taller than their counterparts were a half-century ago (Angoff, 1987; Lynn, 1987). What would the heritability of height now be for our well-nourished twins? Still 100 percent, because the variation in height within the group would remain entirely predictable from the heights of their malnourished identical siblings. So even perfect heritability within groups would not eliminate the possibility of a strong environmental impact on the group differences.

Might the racial gap be similarly environmental? Consider:

Genetics research reveals that under the skin, the races are remarkably alike (Cavalli-Sforza & others, 1994; Lewontin, 1982). Individual differences within a race are much greater than differences between races. The average genetic difference between two Icelandic villagers or between two Kenyans greatly exceeds the group difference between Icelanders and Kenyans. Moreover, looks can deceive. Light-skinned Europeans and dark-skinned Africans are genetically closer than are dark-skinned Africans and dark-skinned Aboriginal Australians.

Race is not a neatly defined biological category. Some scholars argue that there is a reality to race, noting that there are genetic markers for race and that medical risks vary by race. Your vulnerability to skin cancer depends on both sun exposure and who your ancestors were. Behavioral traits may also vary by race. "No runner of Asian or European descent—a majority of the world's population—has broken 10 seconds in the 100-meter dash, but dozens of runners of West African descent have done so," observes psychologist David Rowe (2005). Many more social scientists, though, see race primarily as a social construction without well-defined physical boundaries (Helms & others, 2005; Smedley & Smedley, 2005; Sternberg & others, 2005). People with varying ancestry may categorize themselves in the same race. Moreover, with increasingly mixed ancestries, more and more people defy neat racial categorization. (What race is Tiger Woods?)

Asian students outperform North American students on math achievement and aptitude tests. But this difference appears to be a recent phenomenon and may reflect conscientiousness more than competence. Asian students also attend school 30 percent more days per year and spend much more time in and out of school studying math (Geary & others, 1996; Larson & Verma, 1999; Stevenson, 1992).

Nature's own morphing
Nature draws no sharp boundaries between races, which blend gradually one into the next around the Earth. Thanks to the human urge to classify, however, people socially define themselves in racial categories, which become catch-all labels for physical features, social identity, and nationality.
© Paul Almasy/Corbis; © Rob Howard/ Corbis; © Barbara Bannister; Gallo Images/ Corbis; © David Turnley/Corbis; © Dave Bartruff/Corbis; © Haruyoshi Yamaguchi/Corbis; © Richard T. Nowitz/Corbis; © Owen Franken/Corbis; © Paul Almasy/Corbis; © John-Francis Bourke/zefa/Corbis

The intelligence test performance of today's better-fed, better-educated, and more test-prepared population exceeds that of the 1930s population (the Flynn effect, on page 447)—by the same margin that the intelligence test score of the average White today exceeds that of the average Black. No one attributes the generational group difference to genetics.

White and black infants have scored equally well on an infant intelligence measure (preference for looking at novel stimuli—a crude predictor of future intelligence scores [Fagan, 1992]).

In different eras, different ethnic groups have experienced golden ages—periods of remarkable achievement. Twenty-five-hundred years ago it was the Greeks and the Egyptians, then the Romans; in the eighth and ninth centuries, genius seemed to reside in the Arab world; 500 years ago it was the Aztec Indians and the peoples of Northern Europe. Today, people marvel at Asians' technological genius. Cultures rise and fall over centuries; genes do not. That fact makes it difficult to attribute a natural superiority to any race.

Moreover, consider the striking results of a national study that looked back over the mental test performances of white and black young adults after graduation from college. From eighth grade through the early high school years, the average aptitude score of the white students increased, while those of the black students decreased—creating a gap that reached its widest point at about the time that high school students take college admissions tests. But during college, the black students' scores increased "more than four times as much" as those of their white counterparts, thus greatly *decreasing* the aptitude gap. "It is not surprising," concluded researcher Joel Myerson and his colleagues (1998), "that as black and white students complete more grades in high school environments that differ in quality, the gap in cognitive test scores widens. At the college level, however, where black and white students are exposed to educational environments of comparable quality . . . many Blacks are able to make remarkable gains, closing the gap in test scores."

The culture of scholarship
The children of Indochinese refugee families studied by Nathan Caplan, Marcella Choy, and James Whitmore (1992) typically excel in school. On weekday nights after dinner, the family clears the table and begins homework. Family cooperation is valued, and older siblings help younger ones.

"Do not obtain your slaves from Britain, because they are so stupid and so utterly incapable of being taught."
Cicero, 106–43 B.C.

"African-Americans, from a condition of mass illiteracy 50 years ago, are now among the most educated groups of people in the world, with median years of schooling and college completion rates higher than those of most European nations."
Sociologist Orlando Patterson, *The Ordeal of Integration*, 1997

Gender Similarities and Differences

OBJECTIVE 18 | Describe gender differences in abilities.

In science, as in everyday life, differences, not similarities, excite interest. Compared with the anatomical and physiological similarities between men and women, our sex differences are relatively minor. Yet it is the differences we find exciting. Similarly, in the psychological domain, gender similarities vastly outnumber gender differences, but most people find differences more newsworthy.

Spelling Girls are better spellers: At the end of high school in the United States, only 30 percent of males spell better than the average female (Lubinski & Benbow, 1992). Through 2004, of the 80 U.S. national spelling bee champions, 42 were girls.

Verbal ability Girls are more verbally fluent and more capable of remembering words. And among nearly 200,000 students taking Germany's Test for Medical Studies, young women year after year have surpassed men in remembering facts from short medical cases (Stumpf & Jackson, 1994). (My wife, who remembers many of my experiences for me, tells me that if she died I'd be a man without a past.)

Answer to question on page 459: Heritability—differences due to genes—will be greater in country X, where environmental differences in nutrition are minimal.

Despite the gender equivalence in intelligence test scores, males are more likely than females to overestimate their own test scores. Both males and females tend to rate their father's scores higher than their mother's, their brothers' scores higher than their sisters', and their sons' scores higher than their daughters' (Furnham, 2001; Furnham & others, 2002a,b, 2004a,b,c).

FIGURE 11.12
Gender and variability
When nearly 80,000 Scottish 11-year-olds were administered an intelligence test in 1932, the average IQ scores for girls (100.6) and boys (100.5) were virtually identical. But boys were modestly overrepresented at the low and high extremes. (Adapted from Deary & others, 2003.)

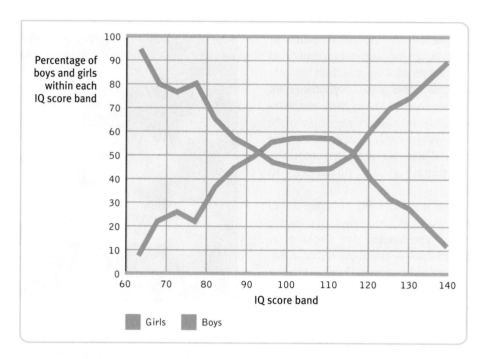

Nonverbal memory Girls have the edge on boys at locating objects (Halpern, 2000). In studies of more than 100,000 American adolescents, girls also modestly surpassed boys in memory for picture associations (Hedges & Nowell, 1995).

Sensation Girls are more sensitive to touch, taste, and odor. (See, for example, page 232.)

Underachievement Boys outnumber girls at the low extremes and therefore in special education classes (Kleinfeld, 1998; **FIGURE 11.12**). Boys tend to talk later and to stutter more often. In remedial reading classes, boys outnumber girls three to one (Finucci & Childs, 1981). Among U.S. high school underachievers, boys outnumber girls by two to one (McCall & others, 1992).

Math and spatial aptitudes In U.S. schools, the average girl's math scores typically equal or surpass the average boy's (ETS, 1992; Kimball, 1989). And on math tests given to more than 3 million representatively sampled people in 100 independent studies, males and females obtained nearly identical average scores (Hyde & others, 1990). But again—despite greater diversity within the genders than between them—group differences make the news. Although females have an edge in math computation, males in 20 of 21 countries scored higher in math problem solving

World math Olympics champs
After outscoring 350,000 of their U.S. peers, these boys all had perfect scores in competition with math whizzes from 68 other countries.

(Bronner, 1998; Hedges & Nowell, 1995). Male U.S. high school seniors, for example, have averaged 45 points higher on the 200- to 800-point SAT math test (literally meaning that they averaged 4 more correct answers on the 60-question test).

The score differences are sharpest at the extremes. Among 12- to 14-year-olds scoring extremely high on SAT math, boys have outnumbered girls 13 to 1, and within that precocious group the boys more often went on to earn a degree in the inorganic sciences and engineering (Benbow & others, 2000). In the United States, males also have an edge in the annual physics and computer science Advanced Placement exams (Stumpf & Stanley, 1998). And in other Western countries, virtually all math prodigies participating in the International Mathematics Olympiad have been males. More female math prodigies have, however, reached the top levels in non-Western countries such as China (Halpern, 1991).

The average male edge seems most reliable in tests like the one shown in **FIGURE 11.13,** which involves speedily rotating three-dimensional objects in one's mind (Collins & Kimura, 1997; Halpern, 2000). Such spatial ability helps when fitting suitcases into a car trunk, playing chess, or doing certain types of geometry problems.

Working from an evolutionary perspective, David Geary (1995, 1996) and Irwin Silverman and his colleagues (1992, 1998) speculate that skills in navigating within three-dimensional space helped our ancestral fathers in tracking their prey and making their way home. In contrast, the survival of our ancestral mothers was enhanced by keen memory for the location of edible plants—a legacy that lives today in women's superior memory for objects and their location.

Do natural sex differences therefore explain why most mathematicians and more than 9 in 10 rated chess players and American architects, engineers, and mapmakers are men? Or why the world chess body has found it necessary to hold separate competitions for men and women? In 2005, Harvard president Lawrence Summers caused an uproar when wondering aloud whether the underrepresentation of women in top math and science positions might suggest not only the influence of socialization but also a gender difference in innate abilities.

Exposure to high levels of male sex hormones during the prenatal period does enhance spatial abilities (Berenbaum & others, 1995). Moreover, argues evolutionary psychologist Steven Pinker (2005), there do appear to be biological as well as social influences on gender differences in life priorities (women's greater interest in people versus men's in money and things), in risk-taking (with men more reckless), and in math reasoning and spatial abilities. Such differences are, he notes, observed across cultures, stable over time, observed in genetic boys raised as girls, and influenced by prenatal hormones.

Actually, replied Elizabeth Spelke (2005), it oversimplifies to say that women have more verbal ability and men more math ability. Women excel at verbal fluency, men at verbal analogies. Women excel at rapid math calculations, men at rapid math reasoning.

In the first 56 years of the college Putnam Mathematical Competition, all of the nearly 300 awardees were men (Arenson, 1997). In 1997, a woman broke the male grip by joining 5 men in the winner's circle. In 1998 Melanie Wood became the first female member of a U.S. math Olympics team (Shulman, 2000). Her training began at an early age: When mall-shopping with her then-4-year-old daughter, Melanie's mother would alleviate her child's boredom by giving her linear equations to solve.

AP Photo/Paul Sakuma

Nature or nurture?

At this 2005 Google Inc.-sponsored computer coding competition, programmers competed for cash prizes and possible jobs. What do you think accounted for the fact that only one of the 100 finalists was female?

Which two circles contain a configuration of blocks identical to the one in the circle at the left?

Standard

Responses

FIGURE 11.13

The mental rotation test

This is a test of spatial abilities. Which two responses show a different view of the standard? (From Vandenberg & Kuse, 1978.) (See page 465 for answers.)

Women excel at remembering objects' spatial positions, men at remembering geometric layouts. And as Summers' other critics emphasized, social expectations and divergent opportunities do shape boys' and girls' interests and abilities (Crawford & others, 1995; Eccles & others, 1990). The male edge in math problem solving grows with age, becoming detectable only after elementary school. Traditionally, math and science have been considered masculine subjects. Many parents send their sons to computer camps and give their daughters more encouragement in English. But as more and more girls are encouraged to develop their abilities in math and science, the gender gap is narrowing (Nowell & Hedges, 1998). In some fields, including psychology, women now earn most of the Ph.D.s. Yet, notes Diane Halpern (2005) with a twinkle in her eye, "no one has asked if men have the innate ability to succeed in those academic disciplines where *they* are underrepresented."

Emotion-detecting ability Recall that part of emotional intelligence is empathic accuracy in reading others' emotions. Some of us are more sensitive to emotional cues. Robert Rosenthal, Judith Hall, and their colleagues (1979; McClure, 2000) demonstrated this by showing hundreds of people brief film clips of portions of a person's emotionally expressive face or body, sometimes with a garbled voice added. For example, after showing a 2-second scene revealing only the face of an upset woman, the researchers asked whether the woman was criticizing someone for being late or was talking about her divorce. Rosenthal and Hall found that some people are much better emotion detectors than others are, and that women are better at it than men.

Some psychologists speculate that women's ability to detect emotions helped our ancestral mothers read emotions in their infants and would-be lovers, which may in turn have fueled cultural tendencies to encourage women's empathic skills. Such skills may, as noted in Chapter 4, explain women's somewhat greater responsiveness in both positive and negative emotional situations.

The Question of Bias

OBJECTIVE 19 | Discuss whether intelligence tests are biased, and describe the stereotype threat phenomenon.

Knowing there are group differences in intelligence test scores leads us to wonder whether intelligence tests are biased. The answer depends on which of two very different definitions of *bias* are used, and on an understanding of stereotypes.

Two Meanings of Bias

If a test detects not only innate differences in intelligence but also performance differences caused by cultural experiences (as when little David Wechsler scored low), it may be considered biased. In this popular sense, everyone agrees that intelligence tests are biased. An intelligence test measures your developed abilities, which reflect, in part, your education and experiences.

You may have read examples of intelligence test items that make middle-class assumptions (for example, that a cup goes with a saucer, or, as in one of the sample test items from the WAIS [Figure 11.4, page 446], that people buy insurance to protect the value of their homes and possessions). Do such items bias the test against those who do not use saucers or do not have enough possessions to make the cost of insurance relevant? Could such questions explain racial differences in test performance? If so, are tests a vehicle for discrimination, consigning potentially capable children to dead-end classes and jobs?

Defenders of aptitude testing note that racial group differences are at least as great on nonverbal items, such as counting digits backward (Jensen, 1983, 1998). Moreover, they add, blaming the test for a group's lower scores is like blaming a messenger for bad news. Why blame the tests for exposing unequal experiences and opportunities? If, because of malnutrition, people were to suffer stunted growth, would you blame the measuring stick that reveals it? If unequal past experiences predict unequal future achievements, a valid aptitude test will detect such inequalities.

The *scientific* meaning of bias, however, is different. It hinges on whether a test is less valid for some groups than for others—whether it predicts future behavior only for some groups of test-takers. For example, if the U.S. SAT accurately predicted the college achievement of women but not that of men, then the test would be biased. The near-consensus among psychologists, as summarized by the U.S. National Research Council's Committee on Ability Testing and the American Psychological Association's Task Force on Intelligence, is that the major U.S. aptitude tests are *not* biased in this statistical meaning of the term (Neisser & others, 1996; Wigdor & Garner, 1982). The predictive validity of the SAT or of a standard intelligence test is roughly the same for women and men, for Blacks and Whites, and for rich and poor. If an intelligence test score of 95 predicts slightly below average grades, the rough prediction usually applies equally to both genders and all ethnic and economic groups.

Stereotype Threat

To predict school performance accurately, an aptitude test must mirror any gender or racial bias in school teaching and testing. Among students given a difficult math test by Steven Spencer and his colleagues (1997), men outperformed equally capable women—except when the women had been led to expect that women usually do as well as men on the test. Otherwise, the women apparently felt apprehensive, which affected their performance. Claude Steele, Steven Spencer, and Joshua Aronson (2002) have observed the same self-fulfilling effect of negative racial stereotypes. They found this **stereotype threat** phenomenon in black students' verbal aptitude scores, which were lower when they took tests under conditions designed to make black students feel threatened. Stereotype threat also explains why women have scored higher on math tests when no male test-takers were in the group, and why Blacks have scored higher when tested by Blacks than when tested by Whites (Danso & Esses, 2001; Inzlicht & Ben-Zeev, 2000).

Steele (1995, 1997) concluded that if you tell students they probably won't succeed (as remedial "minority support" programs often do), this stereotype will eventually erode their performance both on aptitude tests and in school. Over time, such students may "disidentify" with school achievement. They may detach their self-esteem from academics and look for self-esteem elsewhere—which might help explain why minority students tend to underachieve relative to their abilities. Indeed, as African-American boys progress from eighth to twelfth grade, the disconnect between their grades and their self-esteem becomes pronounced (Osborne, 1997). Minority students in university programs that challenge them to believe in their potential have produced markedly higher grades and had lower dropout rates.

What then can we realistically conclude about aptitude tests and bias? The tests do seem biased (appropriately so, some would say) in one sense—sensitivity to performance differences caused by cultural experience. But they are not biased in the scientific sense of making valid statistical predictions for different groups.

Bottom line: Are the tests discriminatory? Again, the answer can be yes or no. In one sense, yes, their purpose is to discriminate—to distinguish among individuals. In another sense, their purpose is to reduce discrimination by reducing reliance on subjective criteria for school and job placement—criteria such as whom you know, what you look like, or how much the interviewer likes "your kind of person." Civil service aptitude tests, for example, were devised to discriminate more fairly and objectively, by reducing the political, racial, and ethnic discrimination that preceded their use. Banning aptitude tests would lead those who decide on jobs and admissions to rely more on other considerations, such as their personal opinions.

■ **stereotype threat** a self-confirming concern that one will be evaluated based on a negative stereotype.

"Math class is tough!"
"Teen talk" talking Barbie doll (introduced February 1992, recalled October 1992)

Answers to the mental rotation test on page 463: the first and fourth alternatives.

Untestable compassion

Intelligence test scores are only one part of the picture of a whole person. They don't measure the abilities, talent, and commitment of, for example, people who devote their lives to helping others.

J. Griffin/The Image Works

"Almost all the joyful things of life are outside the measure of IQ tests."

Madeleine L'Engle, *A Circle of Quiet*, 1972

Perhaps, then, our aim should be threefold. First, we should realize the benefits Alfred Binet foresaw for tests of mental abilities—to enable schools to recognize who might profit most from early intervention. Second, we must remain alert to Binet's fear that intelligence test scores may be misinterpreted as literal measures of a person's worth and fixed potential. And finally, we must remember that *intelligence test scores reflect only one aspect of personal competence*. Our practical intelligence and emotional intelligence matter, too, as do other forms of talent and character. The competence that general intelligence tests sample is important; it helps enable success in some life paths. But it is far from all-important. The carpenter's spatial ability differs from the programmer's logical ability, which differs from the poet's verbal ability. Because there are many ways of being successful, our differences are variations of human adaptability.

>> LEARNING OUTCOMES

Genetic and Environmental Influences on Intelligence

OBJECTIVE 15 | Discuss the evidence for the genetic contribution to individual intelligence, and explain what psychologists mean by the heritability of intelligence.

Studies of twins, family members, and adopted children together support the idea that there is a significant genetic contribution to intelligence scores. The most genetically similar people have the most similar scores, ranging from about +.85 for identical twins raised together, to about +.33 for unrelated individuals raised together. No "genius gene" has been discovered yet, but the search is under way. *Heritability of intelligence* refers to the extent to which variation in intelligence test scores in a *group of people* being studied is attributable to genetic factors. Heritability never applies to an individual's intelligence, but only to differences among people.

OBJECTIVE 16 | Discuss the evidence for environmental influences on individual intelligence.

Studies of twins, family members, and adopted children also provide evidence of environmental influence on intelligence. The intelligence test scores of fraternal twins raised together are more similar than those of other siblings, and the scores of identical twins raised apart are less similar (though still very highly correlated) than the scores of identical twins raised together. Other studies, of children reared in extremely impoverished, enriched, or culturally different environments, indicate that life experiences significantly influence intelligence test performance.

OBJECTIVE 17 | Describe ethnic similarities and differences in intelligence test scores, and discuss some genetic and environmental factors that might explain them.

As a group, white Americans tend to have an average intelligence test score about 8 to 15 points higher than their Hispanic or African-American counterparts. This gap has dropped recently among children. The evidence suggests that environmental differences are largely responsible for these group differences. Six points were considered in this chapter. (1) The races are remarkably alike genetically. (2) Race is a socially, not biologically, defined category. (3) Asian students outperform North American students on math achievement and aptitude tests. (4) Intelligence test performance of today's better-fed, better-educated, and more test-prepared population exceeds that of the 1930s population, by the same margin that the score of the average White today exceeds that of the average Black. (5) White and black infants tend to score equally well on tests predicting future intelligence. (6) In different eras, different ethnic groups have experienced periods of remarkable achievement.

OBJECTIVE 18 | Describe gender differences in abilities.

This chapter considered seven ways that males and females differ in their abilities. (1) Girls are better spellers. (2) Girls are more verbally fluent and can remember more words. (3) Girls are better at locating objects. (4) Girls are more sensitive to touch, taste, and color. (5) Boys outnumber girls in counts of underachievement. (6) Boys outperform girls at math problem solving, though girls outperform boys in math computation. (7) Women detect emotions more easily than men do.

OBJECTIVE 19 | Discuss whether intelligence tests are biased, and describe the stereotype threat phenomenon.

Aptitude tests aim to predict how well a test-taker will perform in a given situation. So they are necessarily biased in the sense that they are sensitive to performance differences caused by cultural experience. But *bias* can also mean what psychologists commonly mean by the term—that a biased test predicts less accurately for one group than for another. In this sense of the term, most experts do not consider the major aptitude tests to be significantly biased. *Stereotype threat* is a self-confirming concern that one will be evaluated based on a negative stereotype. This phenomenon appears in some instances in intelligence testing among African-Americans and among women of all colors.

ASK YOURSELF: How have genetic and environmental influences shaped *your* intelligence?

REVIEW CHAPTER 11: Intelligence

Test Yourself

1. Joseph is a student at Harvard Law School. He carries a straight-A average, writes a small column for the *Harvard Law Review,* and will be working for a Supreme Court justice the year after he graduates. Joseph's grandmother, Judith, is very proud of her grandson and says he is way more intelligent than she ever was. But Joseph is also very proud of Judith: As a young woman, Judith was imprisoned by the Nazis. When the war ended, she walked out of Germany, made contact with an agency helping refugees, traveled to the United States, and began a new life here as an assistant chef in her cousin's restaurant. According to the definition of intelligence in this chapter, is Joseph the only intelligent person in this story? Why or why not?

2. What was the purpose of Binet's pioneering intelligence test?

3. The Smiths have enrolled their 2-year-old son in a special program that promises to assess his IQ and, if he places in the top 5 percent of test-takers, to create a plan that will guarantee his admission to a top university at age 18. Why is this endeavor of questionable value?

4. As society succeeds in creating equality of opportunity, it will also increase the heritability of ability. The heritability of intelligence scores will be greater in a society marked by equal opportunity than in a society of peasants and aristocrats. Why?

Answers to the Test Yourself questions can be found in Appendix B at the end of the book.

Terms and Concepts to Remember

intelligence, p. 431

factor analysis, p. 432

general intelligence (*g*), p. 432

savant syndrome, p. 433

emotional intelligence, p. 436

creativity, p. 438

intelligence test, p. 442

mental age, p. 443

Stanford-Binet, p. 443

intelligence quotient (IQ), p. 444

aptitude test, p. 444

achievement test, p. 444

Wechsler Adult Intelligence Scale (WAIS), p. 445

standardization, p. 446

normal curve, p. 447

reliability, p. 448

validity, p. 448

content validity, p. 448

criterion, p. 448

predictive validity, p. 448

mental retardation, p. 452

Down syndrome, p. 452

stereotype threat, p. 465

WEB

> To continue your study and review of Intelligence, visit this book's Web site at www.worthpublishers.com/myers. You will find practice tests, review activities, and many interesting articles and Web links for more information on topics related to Intelligence.

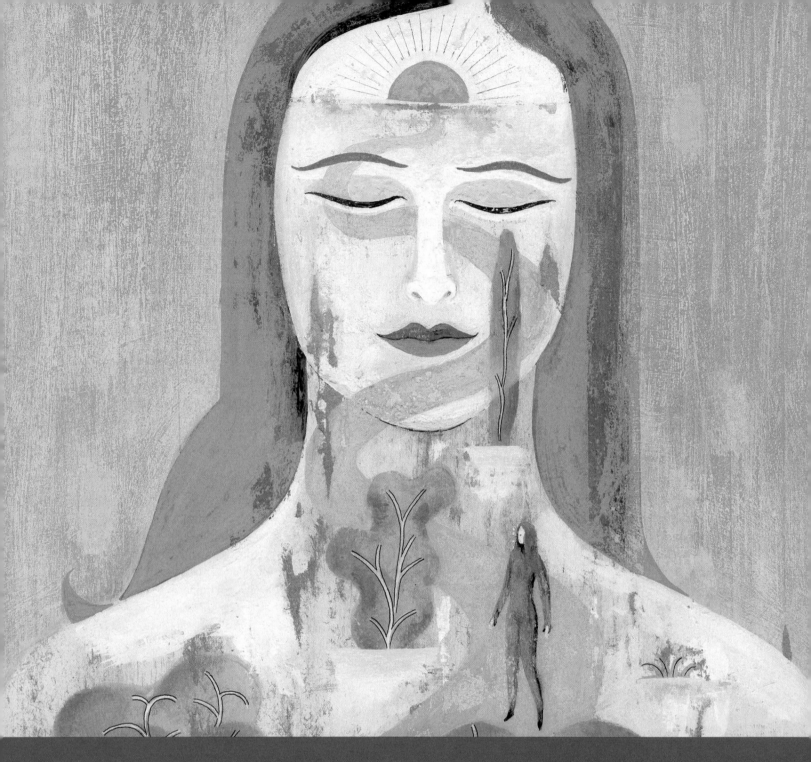

YANN MARTEL, FROM *THE LIFE OF PI*, 2000

As the cartons of survival rations diminished, I reduced my intake, holding myself to only two biscuits every eight hours. I was continuously hungry. I thought about food obsessively. The less I had to eat, the larger became the portions I dreamed of. My fantasy meals grew to be the size of India. A Ganges of dhal soup. Hot chapattis the size of Rajasthan. Bowls of rice as big as Uttar Pradesh. Sambars to flood all of Tali Nadu. Ice cream heaped as high as the Himalayas. My dreaming became quite expert: All ingredients for my dishes were always in fresh and plentiful supply; the oven or frying pan was always at just the right temperature; the proportion of things was always bang on; nothing was ever burnt or undercooked, nothing too hot or too cold. Every meal was simply perfect—only just beyond the reach of my hands.

By the time the last of the biscuits had disappeared, anything was good to eat, no matter the taste. I could put anything in my mouth, chew it, and swallow it— delicious, foul, or plain—so long as it wasn't salty. My body developed a revulsion for salt that I still experience to this day.

12 : Motivation and Work

"What's my motivation?" the actor asks the director. In our everyday conversation, "What motivated you to do *that*?" is a way of asking "What *caused* your behavior?" To psychologists, a *motivation* is a need or desire that *energizes* behavior and *directs* it toward a goal. Experienced mountaineer Aron Ralston understands the extent to which motivation can energize and direct behavior. Having bagged nearly all of Colorado's tallest peaks, many of them solo and in winter, Ralston, on a Saturday spring morning in 2003, ventured to do some solo canyon hiking that seemed so risk-free he did not bother to tell anyone where he was going. In Utah's narrow Bluejohn Canyon, just 150 yards above his final rappel, he was climbing over an 800-pound rock when it shifted and pinned his right wrist and arm. He was, as the title of his recent book says, caught *Between a Rock and a Hard Place*.

Realizing no one would be rescuing him, Ralston tried with all his might to dislodge the rock. Then with his dull pocket knife he tried chipping away at the rock. When that, too, failed, he rigged up ropes to lift the rock. Alas, nothing worked. Hour after hour, then cold night after cold night, he was stuck. By Tuesday, he had run out of food and water. On Wednesday, as thirst and hunger gnawed, he began saving and sipping his own urine. Using his video recorder, he said his good-byes to family and friends, for whom he now felt intense love: "So again love to everyone. Bring love and peace and happiness and beautiful lives into the world in my honor. Thank you. Love you."

On Thursday, surprised to find himself still alive, Ralston had a seemingly divine insight into his reproductive future, a vision of a preschool boy being scooped up by a one-armed man. With this inspiration, he summoned his remaining strength and his enormous will to live and, over the next hour, willfully broke his bones and then proceeded to use that dull knife to cut off his arm. The moment after putting on a tourniquet, chopping the last piece of skin, and breaking free—and before rappelling with his bleeding half-arm down a 65-foot cliff and hiking 5 miles till finding someone—he was, in his own words, "just reeling with this euphoria . . . having been dead and standing in my grave, leaving my last will and testament, etching 'Rest in peace' on the wall, all of that, gone and then replaced with having my life again. It was undoubtedly the sweetest moment that I will ever experience" (Ralston, 2004).

Aron Ralston's thirst and hunger, his sense of belonging to others, and his underlying will to live and become a father highlight motivation's energizing and directing power. In this chapter we explore how such motives arise from the interplay between nature (the physiological "push") and nurture (the cognitive and cultural "pulls").

Motivation personified
Aron Ralston's motivation to live and belong energized and directed his sacrificing half of his arm.

AP Photo / Rocky Mountain News, Judy Walgren

"What do you think . . . should we get started on that motivation research or not?"

Perspectives on Motivation

OBJECTIVE 1 | Define *motivation* as psychologists use the term today, and name four perspectives useful for studying motivated behaviors.

We have seen that psychologists today define **motivation** as a need or desire that energizes and directs behavior. Let's step back now and consider four perspectives psychologists have used in their attempt to understand motivated behaviors. These include instinct theory (now replaced by the evolutionary perspective), drive-reduction theory (emphasizing the interaction between inner pushes and external pulls), and arousal theory (emphasizing the urge for an optimum level of stimulation). The fourth perspective, Abraham Maslow's hierarchy of needs, describes how some motives are, if unsatisfied, more basic and compelling than others.

Instincts and Evolutionary Psychology

OBJECTIVE 2 | Discuss the similarities and differences between instinct theory and the evolutionary perspective.

Early in the twentieth century, as the influence of Charles Darwin's evolutionary theory grew, it became fashionable to classify all sorts of behaviors as instincts. If people criticized themselves, it was because of their "self-abasement instinct." If they boasted, it reflected their "self-assertion instinct." After scanning 500 books, one sociologist compiled a list of 5759 supposed human instincts! Before long, this fad for naming instincts collapsed under its own weight. Rather than *explaining* human behaviors, the early instinct theorists were simply *naming* them. It was like "explaining" a bright child's low grades by labeling the child an "underachiever." To name a behavior is *not* to explain it.

To qualify as an **instinct,** a complex behavior must have a fixed pattern throughout a species and be unlearned (Tinbergen, 1951). Such behaviors are common in other species (recall imprinting in birds in Chapter 4 and the return of salmon to their birthplace in Chapter 8). Human behavior, too, exhibits certain innate tendencies, including simple fixed patterns such as an infant's rooting and sucking. Most psychologists, though, view human behavior as directed by physiological needs *and* by psychological wants.

Although instinct theory failed to explain human motives, the underlying assumption that genes predispose species-typical behavior remains as strong as ever. We saw

Same motive, different wiring
The more complex the nervous system, the more adaptable the organism. Both the woman and the weaverbird satisfy their need for shelter in ways that reflect their inherited capacities. The woman's behavior is flexible; she can learn whatever skills she needs to build a house. The bird's behavior pattern is fixed; it can build only this kind of nest.

this in Chapter 3's explanation of our human similarities. We saw this again in Chapter 8's discussion of animals' biological predispositions to learn certain behaviors. And we will see this in later discussions of how evolution might influence our phobias, our helping behaviors, and our romantic attractions.

Drives and Incentives

OBJECTIVE 3 | Explain how drive-reduction theory views human motivation.

When the original instinct theory of motivation collapsed, it was replaced by **drive-reduction theory**—the idea that a physiological need creates an aroused state that *drives* the organism to reduce the need by, say, eating or drinking. With few exceptions, when a physiological need increases, so does a psychological drive—an aroused, motivated state.

The physiological aim of drive reduction is **homeostasis**—the maintenance of a steady internal state. An example of homeostasis (literally "staying the same") is the body's temperature-regulation system, which works like a thermostat. Both systems operate through feedback loops: Sensors feed room temperature to a control device. If the room temperature cools, the control device switches on the furnace. Likewise, if our body temperature cools, blood vessels constrict to conserve warmth, and we feel driven to put on more clothes or seek a warmer environment. Similarly, if the water level in our cells drops, sensors detect our need for water and we feel thirsty **(FIGURE 12.1).**

Not only are we *pushed* by our "need" to reduce drives, we also are *pulled* by **incentives**—positive or negative stimuli that lure or repel us. This is one way our individual learning histories influence our motives. Depending on our learning, the aroma of good food, whether fresh roasted peanuts or toasted ants, can motivate our behavior. So can the sight of someone we find attractive or the threat of disapproval from family or friends.

When there is both a need and an incentive, we feel strongly driven. The food-deprived person who smells baking bread feels a strong hunger drive. In the presence of that drive, the baking bread becomes a compelling incentive. For each motive, we can therefore ask, "How is it pushed by our inborn physiological needs and pulled by incentives in the environment?"

FIGURE 12.1
Drive-reduction theory

- **motivation** a need or desire that energizes and directs behavior.

- **instinct** a complex behavior that is rigidly patterned throughout a species and is unlearned.

- **drive-reduction theory** the idea that a physiological need creates an aroused tension state (a drive) that motivates an organism to satisfy the need.

- **homeostasis** a tendency to maintain a balanced or constant internal state; the regulation of any aspect of body chemistry, such as blood glucose, around a particular level.

- **incentive** a positive or negative environmental stimulus that motivates behavior.

Optimum Arousal

OBJECTIVE 4 | Discuss the contribution of arousal theory to the study of motivation.

We are much more than homeostatic systems, however. Some motivated behaviors actually *increase* arousal. Well-fed animals will leave their shelter to explore, seemingly in the absence of any need-based drive. From taking such risks, animals gain information and resources (Renner, 1992).

Curiosity drives monkeys to monkey around trying to figure out how to unlock a latch that opens nothing or how to open a window that allows them to see outside their room (Butler, 1954). It drives the 9-month-old infant who investigates every accessible corner of the house. It drives the scientists whose work this text discusses. And it drives explorers and adventurers such as Aron Ralston. Asked why he wanted to climb Mount Everest, George Mallory answered, "Because it is there." Those who, like Mallory and Ralston, enjoy high arousal are most likely to enjoy intense music, novel foods, and risky behaviors (Zuckerman, 1979).

Driven by curiosity
Baby monkeys and small children are fascinated by things they've never handled before. Their drive to explore the relatively unfamiliar is one of several motives that do not fill any immediate physiological need.

So, human motivation aims not to eliminate arousal but to seek optimum levels of arousal. Having all our biological needs satisfied, we feel driven to experience stimulation. Lacking stimulation, we feel bored and look for a way to increase arousal to some optimum level. However, with too much stimulation comes stress, and we then look for a way to decrease arousal.

A Hierarchy of Motives

OBJECTIVE 5 | Describe Maslow's hierarchy of needs.

Some needs take priority over others. At this moment, with your needs for air and water satisfied, other motives—such as your desire to achieve—are energizing and directing your behavior. Let your need for water go unsatisfied and your thirst will preoccupy you. Just ask Aron Ralston. But if you were deprived of air, your thirst would disappear.

Abraham Maslow (1970) described these priorities as a **hierarchy of needs (FIGURE 12.2).** At the base of this pyramid are our physiological needs, such as those for food and water. Only if these needs are met are we prompted to meet our need for safety, and then to satisfy the uniquely human needs to give and receive love and to enjoy self-esteem. Beyond this, said Maslow (1971), lies the highest of human needs: to actualize one's full potential. (More on self-esteem and self-actualization in Chapter 15.)

Maslow's hierarchy is somewhat arbitrary; the order of such needs is not universally fixed. People have starved themselves to make a political statement. Nevertheless, the

FIGURE 12.2
Maslow's hierarchy of needs
Once our lower-level needs are met, we are prompted to satisfy our higher-level needs. While struggling to meet their basic needs for water, food, safe shelter, and medical attention, these survivors of the 2005 New Orleans hurricane were probably not immediately concerned with the higher-level needs on Maslow's hierarchy, such as esteem and self-actualization. (From Maslow, 1970.)

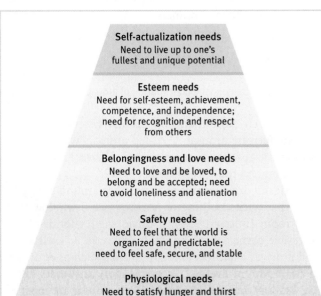

Self-actualization needs
Need to live up to one's fullest and unique potential

Esteem needs
Need for self-esteem, achievement, competence, and independence; need for recognition and respect from others

Belongingness and love needs
Need to love and be loved, to belong and be accepted; need to avoid loneliness and alienation

Safety needs
Need to feel that the world is organized and predictable; need to feel safe, secure, and stable

Physiological needs
Need to satisfy hunger and thirst

simple idea that some motives are more compelling than others provides a framework for thinking about motivation, and life-satisfaction surveys in 39 nations support this basic idea (Oishi & others, 1999). In poorer nations that lack easy access to money and the food and shelter it buys, financial satisfaction more strongly predicts subjective well-being. In wealthy nations, where most are able to meet basic needs, home-life satisfaction is a better predictor. Self-esteem matters most in individualist nations, whose citizens tend to focus more on personal achievements than on family and community identity.

Let's now consider four representative motives, beginning at the basic, physiological level with hunger and working up through sexual motivation to the higher-level needs to belong and to achieve. At each level, we shall see how environmental factors interact with what is physiologically given.

■ **hierarchy of needs** Maslow's pyramid of human needs, beginning at the base with physiological needs that must first be satisfied before higher-level safety needs and then psychological needs become active.

"Hunger is the most urgent form of poverty."

Alliance to End Hunger, 2002

>> LEARNING OUTCOMES

Perspectives on Motivation

OBJECTIVE **1** | **Define** *motivation* **as psychologists use the term today, and name four perspectives useful for studying motivated behavior.**
Psychologists define *motivation* as the energizing and directing of behavior. The four perspectives discussed in this chapter are the *instinct/evolutionary, drive-reduction, arousal,* and *hierarchy of needs* perspectives.

OBJECTIVE **2** | **Discuss the similarities and differences between instinct theory and the evolutionary perspective.**
Instincts are rigidly patterned, complex behaviors found throughout a species, such as the nest-building behaviors of species of birds. Early instinct theorists, influenced by Darwin's theory of natural selection, tried to classify human behaviors as though they were propelled by such instincts. When it became clear that they were naming, not explaining, behaviors, this approach fell into disfavor. The underlying idea—that genes predispose species-typical behavior—is, however, still influential in *evolutionary psychology,* which studies behaviors in search of their adaptive functions.

OBJECTIVE **3** | **Explain how drive-reduction theory views human motivation.**
Drive-reduction theory proposes that physiological needs (hunger, thirst) create aroused psychological states that drive us (motivate us) to reduce or satisfy those needs (by eating, drinking). The physiological aim of drive reduction is internal stability, or *homeostasis.* We are most strongly driven when

pushed by our need to reduce a drive (such as satisfying hunger), and also pulled by an external incentive (the smell of cooking food, for example). Depending on our personal and cultural histories, we will respond more to some stimuli (for example, raw oysters) than to others.

OBJECTIVE **4** | **Discuss the contribution of arousal theory to the study of motivation.**
Not all behaviors reduce immediate physiological needs or tension states. *Arousal theory* helps explain the motivation for these behaviors. Curiosity-driven behaviors, for example, suggest that too little as well as too much stimulation can motivate people to seek an optimum level of arousal.

OBJECTIVE **5** | **Describe Maslow's hierarchy of needs.**
Maslow's hierarchy of needs proposes a pyramid-shaped sequence in which lower-level needs, such as hunger and thirst, are more compelling than higher-level needs, such as the need to love, to belong, or to be respected. Although critics note that Maslow's sequence of needs is not universal, his hierarchy provides a framework for thinking about motivated behaviors.

ASK YOURSELF: Consider your own experiences with Maslow's hierarchy of needs. Have you ever experienced true hunger or thirst that displaced your concern for other, higher-level needs? Do you usually feel safe? Loved? Confident? How often do you feel you are able to address what Maslow called your "self-actualization" needs?

Hunger

A vivid demonstration of the supremacy of physiological needs came from starvation experiences in World War II prison camps. David Mandel (1983), a Nazi concentration camp survivor, recalled how a starving "father and son would fight over a piece of bread. Like dogs." One father, whose 20-year-old son stole his bread from under his pillow while he slept, went into a deep depression, asking over and over how his son could do such a thing. The next day the father died. "Hunger does something to you that's hard to describe," Mandel explained.

To learn more about the results of semistarvation, scientist Ancel Keys and his colleagues (1950) fed 36 male volunteers—all conscientious objectors to the war—just

"Never get a tattoo when you're drunk and hungry."

enough to maintain their initial weight. Then, for six months, they cut this food level in half. The effects soon became visible. Without thinking about it, the men began conserving energy; they appeared listless and apathetic. Their body weights dropped rapidly, eventually stabilizing at about 25 percent below their starting weights. But the psychological effects were especially dramatic. Consistent with Maslow's idea of a needs hierarchy, the men became obsessed with food. They talked food. They daydreamed food. They collected recipes, read cookbooks, and feasted their eyes on delectable forbidden foods. At the same time, they lost interest in sex and social activities. They became preoccupied with their unfulfilled basic need. As one participant reported, "If we see a show, the most interesting part of it is contained in scenes where people are eating. I couldn't laugh at the funniest picture in the world, and love scenes are completely dull."

> "Nobody wants to kiss when they are hungry."
>
> Dorothea Dix, 1801–1887

The Physiology of Hunger

OBJECTIVE 6 | Describe the physiological determinants of hunger.

Keys' semistarved volunteers felt their hunger in response to a homeostatic system designed to maintain normal body weight and an adequate nutrient supply. But what precisely triggers hunger? Is it the pangs of an empty stomach? That is how it feels. And so it seemed after A. L. Washburn, working with Walter Cannon (Cannon & Washburn, 1912), intentionally swallowed a balloon. When inflated in his stomach, the balloon transmitted his stomach contractions to a recording device **(FIGURE 12.3)**. While his stomach was being monitored, Washburn pressed a key each time he felt hungry. The discovery: Washburn was indeed having stomach contractions whenever he felt hungry.

Washburn swallows balloon, which measures stomach contractions.

Washburn presses key each time he feels hungry.

Stomach contractions

Hunger pangs

0 1 2 3 4 5 6 7 8 9 10
Time in minutes

FIGURE 12.3
Monitoring stomach contractions
Using this procedure, Washburn showed that stomach contractions (transmitted by the stomach balloon) accompany our feelings of hunger (indicated by a key press). (From Cannon, 1929.)

Would hunger persist without stomach pangs? Researchers answered that question early in the twentieth century, when they removed some rats' stomachs and attached their esophagi to their small intestines (Tsang, 1938). Did the rats continue to eat? Indeed they did. Some hunger persists similarly in humans whose ulcerated or cancerous stomachs have been removed. You and I can feel some hunger even on a full stomach. So can animals that fill their stomachs by eating low-calorie food; they will eat more than animals that consume a less-filling, high-calorie diet (McHugh & Moran, 1978).

If the pangs of an empty stomach are not the only source of hunger, what else matters? Body chemicals and brain states offer some insights.

Body Chemistry and the Brain

People and other animals automatically regulate their caloric intake to prevent energy deficits and maintain a stable body weight. This suggests that the body is somehow, somewhere, keeping tabs on its available resources. One such resource is the blood sugar **glucose.** Increases in the hormone *insulin* (secreted by the pancreas) diminish blood glucose, partly by converting it to stored fat. Your body is normally adept at maintaining its blood glucose level. But if that level drops, your hunger increases.

You do not consciously feel this change in your blood chemistry. Rather, your brain is automatically monitoring your body's internal state. Signals from your stomach, intestines, and liver (indicating whether glucose is being deposited or withdrawn) all signal your brain to motivate eating or not. But where in the brain are these messages integrated? During the 1940s and 1950s, researchers located hunger controls within the hypothalamus, a small but complex neural traffic intersection buried deep in the brain **(FIGURE 12.4).**

Actually, two distinct hypothalamic centers help control eating. Experiments during the 1960s suggested that activity along the sides of the hypothalamus (the *lateral hypothalamus*) brings on hunger. When electrically stimulated there, well-fed animals would begin to eat; when the area was destroyed, even starving animals had no interest in food. Late-twentieth-century research helped explain this behavior. If a rat is deprived of food and its blood sugar levels wane, the lateral hypothalamus will churn out the hunger-triggering hormone *orexin*. When given orexin, rats become ravenously hungry (Sakurai & others, 1998).

Activity in the second center—the lower mid-hypothalamus (the *ventromedial hypothalamus*)—depresses hunger. Stimulate this area and an animal will stop eating; destroy it and the animal's stomach and intestines will process food more rapidly, causing it to become ex-

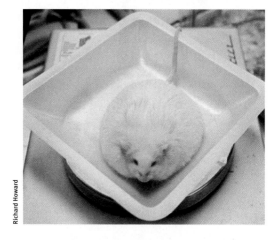

tremely fat (Duggan & Booth, 1986; Hoebel & Teitelbaum, 1966). After these mid-hypothalamus lesions, rats eat more often, produce more fat, and use less fat for energy, rather like a miser who runs every bit of extra money to the bank and resists taking any out (Pinel, 1993). This discovery also explains why some patients with tumors near the base of the brain (in what we now realize is the hypothalamus) eat excessively and become very overweight (Miller, 1995).

■ **glucose** the form of sugar that circulates in the blood and provides the major source of energy for body tissues. When its level is low, we feel hunger.

"The full person does not understand the needs of the hungry."

Irish proverb

FIGURE 12.4
The hypothalamus
As we saw in Chapter 2, the hypothalamus (colored red) performs various body maintenance functions, including control of hunger. Blood vessels supply the hypothalamus, enabling it to respond to our current blood chemistry as well as to incoming neural information about the body's state.

Evidence for the brain's control of eating
A lesion near the middle (ventromedial) area of the hypothalamus caused this rat's weight to triple.

"To put it simply, PYY is the fullness hormone and ghrelin is the hunger hormone."

Hunger researcher Stephen R. Bloom (2002)

Over the next 40 years you will eat about 20 tons of food. If during those years you increase your daily intake by just .01 ounce more than required for your energy needs, you will gain 24 pounds (Martin & others, 1991).

The hypothalamus monitors levels of the body's appetite hormones **(FIGURE 12.5).** One interesting line of research is focusing on *ghrelin,* a hunger-arousing hormone secreted by an empty stomach. When people with severe obesity undergo bypass surgery that seals off part of the stomach, the remaining stomach then produces much less ghrelin, and their appetite lessens (Lemonick, 2002).

Experimental manipulation of appetite hormones has raised hopes for an appetite-reducing medication. Such a pill might counteract the body's hunger-producing chemicals, such as ghrelin, and hunger-dampening chemicals such as *leptin,* which is secreted by fat cells. Or perhaps it might increase levels of *PYY,* a digestive hormone that *suppresses* appetite. The recent ups and downs of excitement over PYY illustrate the intense search for a substance that might someday be a treatment, if not a magic bullet, for obesity. The initial report that PYY suppresses appetite in mice was followed by a skeptical statement from 12 laboratories reporting a big fat disappointment: The PYY finding did not replicate. But a few months later, this was followed by newer studies using different methods that *did* find at least a temporary appetite-suppressing effect (Gura, 2004).

An older hunger theory proposes that manipulating the lateral and ventromedial hypothalamus alters the body's "weight thermostat," predisposing us to keep our body at a particular weight level, called its **set point** (Keesey & Corbett, 1983). When semistarved rats fall below their normal weight, biological pressures act to restore the lost weight: Hunger increases and energy expenditure decreases. If body weight rises—as happens when rats are force-fed—hunger decreases and energy expenditure increases. This stable weight toward which semistarved and overstuffed rats return is their set point. In rats and humans, heredity influences body type and set point.

Human bodies regulate weight through the control of food intake, energy output, and **basal metabolic rate**—the rate of energy expenditure for maintaining basic body functions when the body is at rest. By the end of their 24 weeks of semistarvation, the men who participated in Key's experiment had stabilized at three-quarters of their normal weight—while eating half of what they previously did. The stabilization resulted from reduced energy expenditure, achieved partly by physical lethargy and partly by a 29 percent drop in their basal metabolic rate. In a reverse experiment—in which volunteers were overfed 1000 calories a day for eight weeks—those who gained the least weight tended to spend the extra caloric energy by fidgeting more (Levine & others, 1999). Under normal circumstances, those who fidget most (and burn more calories) weigh less than more inactive obese people, report James Levine and his colleagues (2005). (The researchers outfitted people with undergarments that for 10 days monitored their movements every half second.)

Some researchers, however, doubt that the body has a precise set point that drives hunger. They believe that slow, sustained changes in body weight can, for example, alter one's set point. This casts doubt on the idea that our bodies have a preset tendency to maintain optimum weight (Assanand & others, 1998). Psychological factors also sometimes drive our feelings of hunger. Given unlimited access to a wide variety of tasty foods, people and other animals

FIGURE 12.5
The appetite hormones
Insulin: Hormone secreted by pancreas; controls blood glucose.
Leptin: Protein secreted by fat cells; when abundant, causes brain to increase metabolism and decrease hunger.
Orexin: Hunger-triggering hormone secreted by hypothalamus.
Ghrelin: Hormone secreted by empty stomach; sends "I'm hungry" signals to the brain.
PYY: Digestive tract hormone; sends "I'm *not* hungry" signals to the brain.

tend to overeat and gain weight. For all these reasons, some researchers have abandoned the idea of a biologically fixed *set point*. They prefer the term *settling point* to indicate the level at which a person's weight settles in response to caloric intake and expenditure (which is influenced by environment as well as biology).

The Psychology of Hunger

OBJECTIVE 7 | Discuss psychological and cultural influences on hunger.

Our eagerness to eat is indeed pushed by our physiological state—our body chemistry and hypothalamic activity. Yet there is more to hunger than meets the stomach. This was strikingly apparent when Paul Rozin and his trickster colleagues (1998) tested two patients with amnesia who had no memory for events occurring more than a minute ago. If, 20 minutes after eating a normal lunch, the patients were offered another, both readily consumed it . . . and usually a third meal offered 20 minutes after the second was finished. This suggests that part of knowing when to eat is our memory of our last meal. As time accumulates since we last ate, we anticipate eating again and start feeling hungry.

Taste Preference: Biology or Culture?

Body chemistry and environmental factors together influence not only when we feel hunger, but what we feel hungry for—our taste preference. When feeling tense or depressed, do you crave starchy, carbohydrate-laden foods? Carbohydrates help boost levels of the neurotransmitter serotonin, which has calming effects.

Our preferences for sweet and salty tastes are genetic and universal. Other taste preferences are conditioned, as when people given highly salted foods develop a liking for excess salt (Beauchamp, 1987), or when people develop an aversion to a food eaten before becoming violently ill. (The frequency of children's illnesses provides many chances for them to learn food aversions.)

Culture affects taste, too. Bedouins enjoy eating the eye of a camel, which most North Americans would find repulsive. Similarly, most North Americans and Europeans shun dog, rat, and horse meat, all of which are prized elsewhere.

Our natural wariness of things unfamiliar extends to novel foods (especially novel animal-based rather than vegetarian foods). In experiments, people have tried novel fruit drinks or ethnic foods. With repeated exposure, their appreciation for the new taste typically increases; moreover, exposure to one set of novel foods increases our willingness to try another (Pliner, 1982; Pliner & others, 1993). Rats, too, tend to avoid unfamiliar foods (Sclafani, 1995). This *neophobia* surely was adaptive for our ancestors, protecting them from potentially toxic substances.

■ **set point** the point at which an individual's "weight thermostat" is supposedly set. When the body falls below this weight, an increase in hunger and a lowered metabolic rate may act to restore the lost weight.

■ **basal metabolic rate** the body's resting rate of energy expenditure.

Richard Olsenius/Black Star

Victor Englebert

An acquired taste
For Alaskan natives (left), but not for most other North Americans, whale blubber is a tasty treat. For these Campa Indians in Peru (right), roasted ants are similarly delicious. People everywhere learn to enjoy the fatty, bitter, or irritating foods prescribed by their culture.

FIGURE 12.6
Hot cultures like hot spices
Countries with hot climates, in which food historically spoiled more quickly, feature recipes with more bacteria-inhibiting spices (Sherman & Flaxman, 2001). India averages nearly 10 spices per meat recipe, Finland 2 spices.

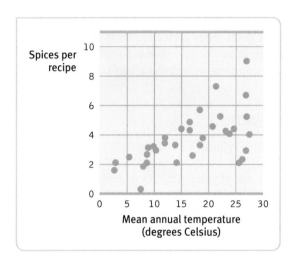

Other taste preferences are also adaptive. For example, the spices most commonly used in the recipes of hot climates, where food—especially meat—spoils more quickly, inhibit the growth of bacteria **(FIGURE 12.6)**. Pregnancy-related nausea is another example of adaptive taste preferences. Food aversions stemming from this nausea peak about the tenth week, when the developing embryo is most vulnerable to toxins.

Eating Disorders

OBJECTIVE 8 | Explain how the eating disorders anorexia nervosa and bulimia nervosa demonstrate the influence of psychological forces on physiologically motivated behaviors.

Psychological influences on eating behavior are strikingly evident when a motive for abnormal thinness overwhelms normal homeostatic pressures. Two such eating disorders are anorexia nervosa and bulimia.

Anorexia nervosa always begins as a weight-loss diet. People with this disorder drop significantly below normal weight (typically, by 15 percent or more) yet feel fat and remain obsessed with losing weight. Even when emaciated, the person—usually an adolescent and 9 times out of 10 a female—continues to limit food intake.

Bulimia nervosa nearly always begins after a dieter has broken diet restrictions and gorged. Those with bulimia have repeated episodes of overeating followed by compensatory vomiting, laxative use, fasting, or excessive exercise. Most binge-purge eaters are women in their late teens or early twenties. They eat the way some people with alcoholism drink—in spurts, sometimes influenced by friends who are bingeing (Crandall, 1988). Preoccupied with food (craving sweet and high-fat foods), and fearful of becoming overweight, people with bulimia experience bouts of depression and anxiety, most severe during and following binges (Hinz & Williamson, 1987; Johnson & others, 2002). About half of those with anorexia also display the binge-purge-depression symptoms of bulimia. Unlike anorexia, bulimia is marked by weight fluctuations within or above normal ranges, making the condition easy to hide.

Dying to be thin
Anorexia was identified and named in the 1870s, when it appeared among affluent adolescent girls (Brumberg, 2000). This 1930s photo illustrates the physical condition (left). Many modern-day celebrities have struggled publicly with eating disorders, including millionaire teen actress Mary-Kate Olsen (right).

Eating disorders do *not* provide (as some have speculated) a telltale sign of childhood sexual abuse (Smolak & Murnen, 2002; Stice, 2002). Families may provide a fertile ground for the growth of eating disorders in another way, however. Mothers of girls with eating disorders are themselves often focused on their own weight and on their daughters' weight and appearance (Pike & Rodin, 1991). The families of bulimia patients have a higher-than-usual incidence of childhood obesity and negative self-evaluation (Jacobi & others, 2004). Anorexia patients also tend to have low self-evaluations and often come from families that are competitive, high-achieving, and protective (Pate & others, 1992; Yates, 1989, 1990). Sufferers set perfectionist standards, fret about falling short of expectations, and are intensely concerned with how others perceive them (Polivy & Herman, 2002; Striegel-Moore & others, 1993). Some of these factors also predict teen boys' pursuit of unrealistic muscularity (Ricciardelli & McCabe, 2004).

Genetics, too, may influence susceptibility to eating disorders. If twins are identical rather than fraternal, the chances of the other twin's sharing the disorder are somewhat greater (Fairburn & others, 1999; Kaplan, 2004). Evolution may have predisposed such genes, suggests Shan Guisinger (2004). Faced with famine, our ancestors who denied their starvation and became hyperactive rather than hunkering down may have been more likely to search for food.

There is, however, a cultural explanation for the fact that anorexia and bulimia occur mostly in women and mostly in weight-conscious cultures. Body ideals vary across culture and time. In India, women students rate their ideals as close to their actual shape. In much of Africa—where thinness can signal poverty, AIDS, and hunger, and the prosperous are plump—bigger is better (Knickmeyer, 2001). In Western cultures, however, the rise in eating disorders over the last 50 years has coincided with a dramatic increase in women having a poor body image, according to a recent analysis of 222 studies of 141,000 people (Feingold & Mazzella, 1998).

Other research confirms that those vulnerable to eating disorders are those who most idealize thinness and have the greatest body dissatisfaction (Stice, 2002; Thompson & Stice, 2001; Vohs & others, 2001). Not surprisingly, those people are most often women. In one national survey, nearly one-half of U.S. women reported feeling negative about their appearance and preoccupied with being or becoming overweight (Cash & Henry, 1995). And in a turn-of-the-century British survey of 3500 bank and university staff, men were more likely to *be* overweight and women were more likely to *perceive* themselves as overweight (Emslie & others, 2001).

Similar gender differences appeared in an experiment led by Barbara Fredrickson (1998), who had University of Michigan men and women put on a sweater or a swim suit and complete a math test while alone in a changing room. For the women but not the men, wearing the swimsuit triggered self-consciousness and shame that disrupted their math performance. In one informal survey with 60,000 respondents, 9 in 10 women said they would rather have a perfect body than have a mate with a perfect body; 6 of 10 men preferred the reverse (Lever, 2003).

Part of the cultural pressure is surely transmitted by the "thin-ideal" exemplified in fashion magazines, advertisements, and even in some toys. What do you suppose happens when young women repeatedly encounter doctored magazine images of fashion models, who appear to be unnaturally thin (Tovee & others, 1997)? Eric Stice and Heather Shaw (1994) and Heidi Posavac and colleagues (1998) report that women often feel ashamed, depressed, and dissatisfied with their own bodies—the very attitudes that predispose eating disorders. When Stice and his colleagues (2001) gave some adolescent girls (but not others) a 15-month subscription to a teen fashion magazine (*Seventeen*), vulnerable girls (who were already dissatisfied, idealizing thinness, and lacking social support) exhibited increased body dissatisfaction and eating disorder

■ **anorexia nervosa** an eating disorder in which a normal-weight person (usually an adolescent female) diets and becomes significantly (15 percent or more) underweight, yet, still feeling fat, continues to starve.

■ **bulimia nervosa** an eating disorder characterized by episodes of overeating, usually of high-calorie foods, followed by vomiting, laxative use, fasting, or excessive exercise.

"Thanks, but we don't eat."

> Diana remained throughout a very insecure person at heart, almost childlike in her desire to do good for others, so she could release herself from deep feelings of unworthiness, of which her eating disorders were merely a symptom."
>
> Charles, Ninth Earl of Spencer, eulogizing his sister Princess Diana, 1997

"Gee, I had no idea you were married to a supermodel."

FIGURE 12.7

Levels of analysis for our hunger motivation

Clearly, we are biologically driven to eat, yet psychological and social-cultural factors strongly influence what, when, and how much we eat.

> "Why do women have such low self-esteem? There are many complex psychological and societal reasons, by which I mean Barbie."
>
> Dave Barry, 1999

tendencies. But even ultra-thin models do not reflect the impossible standard of the classic Barbie doll. Adjusted to a height of 5 feet 7 inches, her 32–16–29 figure (in centimeters, 82 bust, 41 waist, and 73 hips) defines a body shape approximated by fewer than 1 in 100,000 women (Norton & others, 1996).

It seems clear that the sickness of today's eating disorders lies not just within the victims but also within our weight-obsessed culture—a culture that says, in countless ways, "Fat is bad," that motivates millions of women to be "always dieting," and that encourages eating binges by pressuring women to live in a constant state of semistarvation. As compelling as our biological motives are, eating behavior is clearly also affected by psychological and social-cultural factors **(FIGURE 12.7)**.

>> LEARNING OUTCOMES

Hunger

OBJECTIVE 6 | **Describe the physiological determinants of hunger.**
Washburn and Cannon showed that hunger's inner push corresponds to the stomach's contractions, but hunger has other causes. Variations in body chemistry that influence our feelings of hunger include those of *insulin* (secreted by the pancreas; controls blood glucose), *leptin* (secreted by fat cells; signals brain to increase metabolism and decrease hunger), *orexin* (secreted by the hypothalamus; triggers hunger), *ghrelin* (secreted by empty stomach; sends hunger signals to brain), and *PYY* (secreted by digestive tract; sends not-hungry signals to brain). All this information is integrated in two areas of the hypothalamus, which regulates the body's weight by affecting our feelings of hunger and satiety. Researchers differ on whether the body has a precise set point (a biologically fixed tendency to maintain an optimum weight) or a settling point (an environmentally and biologically influenced level at which weight settles in response to caloric intake and output).

OBJECTIVE 7 | **Discuss psychological and cultural influences on hunger.**
Our hunger is influenced not only by our physical state but also by our memory of when we last ate and our expectation of when we should eat again. And although we humans as a species prefer certain tastes (such as sweet and salty), we learn to satisfy those preferences with specific foods eaten in

the context of our families and our culture. Some of our taste preferences, such as the avoidance of new foods or of foods that have made us ill, have survival value.

OBJECTIVE 8 | **Explain how the eating disorders anorexia nervosa and bulimia nervosa demonstrate the influence of psychological forces on physiologically motivated behaviors.**
In the past half-century, a dramatic increase in poor body image has coincided with a rise in eating disorders among women in Western cultures. In both anorexia and bulimia, psychological factors, such as challenging family settings and weight-obsessed societal pressures, apparently overwhelm the homeostatic drive to maintain a balanced internal state. People with *anorexia nervosa* (usually adolescent females) starve themselves but continue to diet because they view themselves as fat; those with *bulimia nervosa* (primarily females in their teens and twenties) binge and purge in secret. In addition to cultural pressures, low self-esteem and negative emotions seem to interact with stressful life experiences to produce these disorders. Twin research also indicates, however, that these eating disorders may have a genetic component.

ASK YOURSELF: Do you feel in touch with your body's hunger signals? Do you eat when your body needs food? Or do you tend to be more externally influenced by enticing foods even when you're full?

Sexual Motivation

Sex is part of life. Had this not been so for all your ancestors, you would not be reading this book. Sexual motivation is nature's clever way of making people procreate, thus enabling our species' survival. When two people feel attracted, they hardly stop to think of themselves as guided by their genes. As the pleasure we take in eating is nature's inventive method of getting our body nourishment, so the pleasure of sex is our genes' way of preserving and spreading themselves.

Our first descriptions of sexual behavior in the United States came from Indiana University biologist Alfred Kinsey and his colleagues (1948, 1953). Unable to answer his students' questions about people's sexual practices, Kinsey set out to find some answers. His controversial research was shocking to a 1940s audience. Social scientists were quick to point out what Kinsey readily acknowledged—that his nonrandom sample contained an overrepresentation of well-educated white urbanites. Nevertheless, his statistics-laden volumes became bestsellers. Here readers learned the surprising news that most of the men and nearly half the women reported having had premarital sexual intercourse; that most women and virtually all men reported having masturbated; and that women who reported masturbating to orgasm before marriage seldom had difficulties experiencing orgasm after marriage. Kinsey's books also revealed enormously varied sexual behavior, some men and women saying they had never had an orgasm and others reporting they had four or more a day. For those who evaluate themselves by comparisons with others, Kinsey's nonrandom sample—and other more reliable findings showing wide variations in "normal" sexual behavior around the world—are reassuring. Given the range of sex drives and the variety of sexual behaviors, our own sexual interests probably fall well within the definition of "normal."

The Physiology of Sex

Like hunger, sexual arousal depends on the interplay of internal and external stimuli. To understand sexual motivation, we must consider both.

The Sexual Response Cycle

OBJECTIVE 9 | Describe the human sexual response cycle, and discuss some causes of sexual disorders.

The headlines created by Kinsey's 1940s surveys reappeared in the 1960s after other scientists recorded the physiological responses of volunteers who masturbated or had intercourse. With the help of 382 female and 312 male volunteers—a somewhat atypical sample, consisting only of people able and willing to display arousal and orgasm while being observed in a laboratory—gynecologist-obstetrician William Masters and his collaborator Virginia Johnson (1966) monitored or filmed more than 10,000 sexual "cycles."

Their description of the **sexual response cycle** identified four stages, similar in men and women. During the initial *excitement phase,* the genital areas become engorged with blood, a woman's vagina expands and secretes lubricant, and her breasts and nipples may enlarge.

In the *plateau phase,* excitement peaks as breathing, pulse, and blood pressure rates continue to increase. The penis becomes fully engorged and some fluid—frequently containing enough live sperm to enable conception—may appear at its tip. Vaginal secretion continues to increase, the clitoris retracts, and orgasm feels imminent.

Masters and Johnson observed muscle contractions all over the body during *orgasm;* these were accompanied by further increases in breathing, pulse, and blood pressure rates. A woman's arousal and orgasm facilitate conception by helping propel semen from the penis, positioning the uterus to receive sperm, and drawing the sperm further inward. A woman's orgasm therefore not only reinforces intercourse, which is essential

> "Maybe...it starts with a kiss."
> Prenatal photographer Lennart Nilsson, answering
> the question "When does life begin?"

In one British survey, of the 18,876 people contacted, 1 percent were reportedly asexual, having "never felt sexually attracted to anyone at all" (Bogaert, 2004).

"I love the idea of there being two sexes, don't you?"

■ **sexual response cycle** the four stages of sexual responding described by Masters and Johnson—excitement, plateau, orgasm, and resolution.

A nonsmoking 50-year-old male has about a 1-in-a-million chance of a heart attack during any hour. This increases to merely 2-in-a-million during the hour following sex (with no increase for those who exercise regularly). Compared with risks associated with heavy exertion or anger (see Chapter 14), this risk seems not worth losing sleep (or sex) over (Muller & others, 1996).

to natural reproduction, it also increases retention of deposited sperm (Furlow & Thornhill, 1996). In the excitement of the moment, men and women are hardly aware of all this as their rhythmic genital contractions create a pleasurable feeling of sexual release.

The feeling apparently is much the same for both sexes. In one study, a panel of experts could not reliably distinguish between descriptions of orgasm written by men and those written by women (Vance & Wagner, 1976). University of Groningen neuroscientist Gerg Holstege and his colleagues (2003a,b) understand why. They discovered that when men and women undergo PET scans while having orgasms, the same subcortical brain regions glow. And when people who are passionately in love undergo fMRI scans while viewing photos of their beloved or of a stranger, men's and women's brain responses to their partner are pretty similar (Fisher & others, 2002).

After orgasm, the body gradually returns to its unaroused state as the engorged genital blood vessels release their accumulated blood—relatively quickly if orgasm has occurred, relatively slowly otherwise. (It's like the nasal tickle that goes away rapidly if you have sneezed, slowly otherwise.) During this *resolution phase,* the male enters a **refractory period,** lasting from a few minutes to a day or more, during which he is incapable of another orgasm. The female's much shorter refractory period may enable her to have another orgasm if restimulated during or soon after resolution.

Masters and Johnson sought not only to describe the human sexual response cycle but also to understand and treat the inability to complete it. **Sexual disorders** are problems that consistently impair sexual functioning. Some involve sexual motivation, especially lack of sexual energy and arousability. Others include, for men, *premature ejaculation* and *erectile dysfunction* (inability to have or maintain an erection), and, for women, *orgasmic disorder* (infrequently or never experiencing orgasm).

What causes such problems? The idea that personality disorders are to blame has been largely discounted. Most women who experience sexual distress relate it to their emotional relationship with the partner during sex, not to physical aspects of the activity (Bancroft & others, 2003). Men or women with sexual disorders can often be helped by receiving behaviorally oriented therapy where, for example, men may learn ways to control their urge to ejaculate, and women are trained to bring themselves to orgasm. Starting with the introduction of Viagra in 1998, erectile disorder has been routinely treated by taking a pill.

Hormones and Sexual Behavior

OBJECTIVE 10 | Discuss the impact of hormones on sexual motivation and behavior.

Sex hormones have two effects: They direct the physical development of male and female sex characteristics, and (especially in nonhuman animals) they activate sexual behavior. In most mammals, nature neatly synchronizes sex with fertility. The female becomes sexually receptive ("in heat") when production of the female hormone **estrogen** peaks at ovulation. In experiments, researchers can stimulate receptivity by injecting female animals with estrogen. Male hormone levels are more constant, and researchers cannot so easily manipulate the sexual behavior of male animals with hormones (Feder, 1984). Nevertheless, castrated male rats—having lost their testes, which manufacture the male sex hormone **testosterone**—gradually lose much of their interest in receptive females. They gradually regain it if injected with testosterone.

In humans, hormones more loosely influence sexual behavior, although sexual desire rises slightly at ovulation among women with mates (Pillsworth & others, 2004). One study invited partnered women who were not at risk for pregnancy to keep a diary of their sexual activity. (These women were either

"Fill'er up with testosterone."

using intrauterine devices or had undergone surgery to prevent pregnancy.) On the days around ovulation, intercourse was 24 percent more frequent (Wilcox & others, 2004). But women's sexuality also differs from that of other mammalian females in being more responsive to testosterone level than to estrogen level (Meston & Frohlich, 2000; Reichman, 1998). If a woman's natural testosterone level drops, as happens with removal of the ovaries or adrenal glands, her sexual interest may wane. But testosterone-replacement therapy can often restore diminished sexual appetite, as it did for 549 naturally menopausal women who found that a testosterone-replacement patch restored sexual activity, arousal, and pleasure more than did a placebo (Davis & others, 2003; Kroll & others, 2004).

In men, normal fluctuations in testosterone levels, from man to man and hour to hour, have little effect on sexual drive (Byrne, 1982). Indeed, fluctuations in male hormones are partly a *response* to sexual stimulation. When James Dabbs and his colleagues (1987, 2000) had heterosexual male collegians converse separately with another male student and with a female student, the men's testosterone levels rose with the social arousal, but especially after talking with the female. Thus, sexual arousal can be a cause as well as a consequence of increased testosterone levels.

Although normal short-term hormonal changes have little effect on men's and women's desire, large hormonal shifts over the life span have a greater effect. A person's interest in dating and sexual stimulation usually increases with the pubertal surge in sex hormones, as happens with male testosterone levels during puberty.

If the hormonal surge is precluded—as it was during the 1600s and 1700s for prepubertal boys who were castrated to preserve their soprano voices for Italian opera— the normal development of sex characteristics and sexual desire does not occur (Peschel & Peschel, 1987). Among adult men who suffer castration, sex drive typically falls as testosterone levels decline (Hucker & Bain, 1990). Male sex offenders similarly lose much of their sexual urge when voluntarily taking Depo-Provera, a drug that reduces testosterone level to that of a prepubertal boy (Money & others, 1983). In later life, as sex hormone levels decline, the frequency of sexual fantasies and intercourse declines as well (Leitenberg & Henning, 1995). For men with abnormally low testosterone levels, testosterone-replacement therapy often increases sexual desire and also energy and vitality (Yates, 2000).

To summarize: We might compare human sex hormones, especially testosterone, to the fuel in a car. Without fuel, a car will not run. But if the fuel level is minimally adequate, adding more fuel to the gas tank won't change how the car runs. The analogy is imperfect, because the interaction between hormones and sexual motivation is two-way. However, the analogy correctly suggests that biology is a necessary but not sufficient explanation of human sexual behavior. The hormonal fuel is essential, but so are the psychological stimuli that turn on the engine, keep it running, and shift it into high gear.

The Psychology of Sex

OBJECTIVE **11** | Describe the role of external stimuli and fantasies in sexual motivation and behavior.

Hunger and sex are different sorts of motivations. Hunger responds to a *need*. If we do not eat, we die. Sex is not in this sense a need. If we do not have sex, we may feel like dying, but we do not. Nevertheless, there are similarities between hunger and sexual motivation. Both depend on internal physiological factors. And both are influenced by external and imagined stimuli, as well as cultural expectations **(FIGURE 12.8)**.

■ **refractory period** a resting period after orgasm, during which a man cannot achieve another orgasm.

■ **sexual disorder** a problem that consistently impairs sexual arousal or functioning.

■ **estrogen** a sex hormone, secreted in greater amounts by females than by males. In nonhuman female mammals, estrogen levels peak during ovulation, promoting sexual receptivity.

■ **testosterone** the most important of the male sex hormones. Both males and females have it, but the additional testosterone in males stimulates the growth of the male sex organs in the fetus and the development of the male sex characteristics during puberty.

FIGURE 12.8
Levels of analysis for sexual motivation
Compared with our motivation for eating, our sexual motivation is less influenced by biological factors. Psychological and social-cultural factors play a bigger role.

Biological influences:
• sexual maturity
• sex hormones, especially testosterone
• sexual orientation

Psychological influences:
• exposure to stimulating conditions
• sexual fantasies

Sexual motivation

Social-cultural influences:
• family and society values
• religious and personal values
• cultural expectations

"Ours is a society which stimulates interest in sex by constant titillation. . . . Cinema, television, and all the formidable array of our marketing technology project our very effective forms of titillation and our prejudices about man as a sexy animal into every corner of every hovel in the world."

Germaine Greer, 1984

External Stimuli

Many studies confirm that men become aroused when they see, hear, or read erotic material. Surprising to many (because sexually explicit materials are sold mostly to men) is that most women—at least the less-inhibited women who volunteer to participate in such studies—report or exhibit nearly as much arousal to the same stimuli (Heiman, 1975; Stockton & Murnen, 1992). (Their brains do, however, respond differently, with fMRI scans revealing a more active amygdala in men viewing erotica [Hamann & others, 2004].)

People may find such arousal either pleasing or disturbing. (Those who find it disturbing often limit their exposure to such materials, just as those wishing to control hunger limit their exposure to tempting cues.) With repeated exposure, the emotional response to any erotic stimulus often *habituates* (lessens). During the 1920s, when Western women's hemlines first reached the knee, an exposed leg was a mildly erotic stimulus, as were modest (by today's standards) two-piece swimsuits and movie scenes of a mere kiss.

Can sexually explicit material have adverse effects? Research indicates that it can. Depictions of women being sexually coerced—and enjoying it—tend to increase viewers' acceptance of the false idea that women enjoy rape and tend to increase male viewers' willingness to hurt women (Malamuth & Check, 1981; Zillmann, 1989). Images of sexually attractive women and men may also lead people to devalue their own partners and relationships. After male collegians watch TV or magazine depictions of sexually attractive women, they often find an average woman, or their own girlfriends or wives, less attractive (Kenrick & Gutierres, 1980; Kenrick & others, 1989; Weaver & others, 1984). Viewing X-rated sex films similarly tends to diminish people's satisfaction with their own sexual partners (Zillmann, 1989). Some sex researchers suspect that reading or watching erotica may create expectations that few men and women can fulfill.

Sexually explicit TV programs also divert attention from TV ads, making the ads more forgettable. Ads embedded in nonsexual and nonviolent programs more often produce memory for the products (Bushman & Bonacci, 2002).

Imagined Stimuli

The brain, it has been said, is our most significant sex organ. The stimuli inside our heads—our imagination—can influence sexual arousal and desire. People who, because of a spinal cord injury, have no genital sensation, can still feel sexual desire (Willmuth, 1987). Consider, too, the erotic potential of dreams. Sleep researchers have discovered that genital arousal accompanies all types of dreams, even though most dreams have no sexual content. But in nearly all men and some 40 percent of women (Wells, 1986), dreams sometimes do contain sexual imagery that leads to orgasm. In men, nighttime orgasm and nocturnal emissions ("wet dreams") are more likely when orgasm has not occurred recently.

Wide-awake people become sexually aroused not only by memories of prior sexual activities but also by fantasies. In one survey of masturbation-related fantasies (Hunt, 1974), 19 percent of women and 10 percent of men reported imagining being taken by someone overwhelmed with desire for them. Fantasy is not reality, however. To paraphrase Susan Brownmiller (1975), there's a big difference between fantasizing that Brad Pitt just won't take no for an answer and having a hostile stranger actually force himself on you. (See pages 753–754 for a discussion of the *rape myth*.)

"There is no difference between being raped and being run over by a truck except that afterward men ask if you enjoyed it."

Marge Piercy, "Rape Poem," 1976

About 95 percent of both men and women say they have had sexual fantasies. But men (whether gay or straight) fantasize about sex more often, more physically, and less romantically—and prefer less personal and faster-paced sex content in books and videos (Leitenberg & Henning, 1995). Fantasizing about sex does *not* indicate a sexual problem or dissatisfaction. If anything, sexually active people have more sexual fantasies.

Adolescent Sexuality

OBJECTIVE 12 | Discuss some of the forces that influence teen pregnancy and teen attitudes toward contraception.

Adolescents' physical maturation fosters a sexual dimension to their emerging identity. Yet sexual expression varies dramatically with time and culture. Among American women born before 1900, a mere 3 percent had experienced premarital sex by age 18 (Smith, 1998). In the United States today, about half of ninth- to twelfth-graders report having had sexual intercourse, as do 42 percent of Canadian 16-year-olds (Boroditsky & others, 1995; CDC, 2004). Teen intercourse rates are higher in Western Europe but much lower in Arab and Asian countries and among North Americans of Asian descent (McLaughlin & others, 1997). In one survey, only 2.5 percent of 4688 unmarried Chinese students entering Hong Kong's six universities reported having had sexual intercourse (Meston & others, 1996).

An increase in teen sexual activity in Western countries led to a twentieth-century increase in the adolescent pregnancy rate. The often-impoverished futures of teen mothers and of children in father-absent homes have in turn prompted new research on teen sexuality, adolescents' use of contraceptives, and teens' risk of contracting *sexually transmitted infections* (STIs).

Teen Pregnancy

Compared with European teens, American teens have lower rates of intercourse, but they also have lower rates of contraceptive use and thus higher rates of teen pregnancy and abortion (Call & others, 2002). (Only one-third of sexually active male teens use condoms consistently [Sonenstein, 1992]). Why?

Ignorance Half of sexually active Canadian teen girls have mistaken ideas about which birth control methods will protect them from pregnancy and STIs (Immen, 1995). Most teens also overestimate their peers' sexual activity, and that misperception may influence their own behavior (Child Trends, 2001).

Guilt related to sexual activity In one survey, 72 percent of 12- to 17-year-old American girls who have had sex said they regretted it (Reuters, 2000). Sexual inhibitions can reduce sexual activity, but they may also reduce attempts at birth control if passion overwhelms intentions (Gerrard & Luus, 1995). Not wanting to appear deliberately sexual or promiscuous, teens may hesitate to carry and produce a condom. The result may be conception.

Minimal communication about birth control Many teenagers are uncomfortable discussing contraception with their parents, partners, and peers (Kotva & Schneider, 1990; Milan & Kilmann, 1987). Teens who talk freely with friends or parents and are in an exclusive relationship with a partner with whom they communicate openly are more likely to use contraceptives.

Alcohol use Sexually active teens are typically alcohol-using teens (Albert & others, 2003; National Research Council, 1987), and those who use alcohol prior to sex are less likely to use condoms (Kotchick & others, 2001). By depressing the brain centers that control judgment, inhibition, and self-awareness, alcohol tends to break down normal restraints, a phenomenon well known to sexually coercive males (page 299).

"Will your child learn to multiply before she learns to subtract?"
Anti–teen-pregnancy poster, Children's Defense Fund

"Condoms should be used on every conceivable occasion."
Anonymous

" All of us who make motion pictures are teachers, teachers with very loud voices."
Film producer George Lucas, Academy Award ceremonies, 1992

Mass media norms of unprotected promiscuity An average hour of prime-time television on the three major U.S. networks contains approximately 15 sexual acts, words, and innuendos. Nearly all of these instances involve unmarried partners, about half have no prior romantic relationship or have just met, and few communicate any concern for birth control or STIs (Brown & others, 2002; Kunkel, 2001; Sapolsky & Tabarlet, 1991). TV and movie portrayals of unsafe sex without consequence, contends Planned Parenthood, amounts to a campaign of sex disinformation.

Sexually Transmitted Infections

OBJECTIVE 13 | Describe trends in the spread of sexually transmitted infections.

Unprotected sex has led to increased rates of STIs (also called *STD* for *sexually transmitted disease*). Two-thirds of new infections occur in persons under 25 (ASHA, 2003). Teenage girls, because of their less mature biological development and lower levels of protective antibodies, seem especially vulnerable to STIs (Guttmacher, 1994; Morell, 1995). To comprehend the mathematics of sexually transmitted infection, imagine this scenario: Over the course of a year, Pat has sex with 9 people, each of whom over the same period has sex with 9 other people, who in turn have sex with 9 others. How many "phantom" sex partners (past partners of partners) will Pat have? Laura Brannon and Timothy Brock (1994) report that the actual number—511—is more than five times the estimate given by the average student.

Given these odds, the rapid spread of STIs is not surprising. Condoms offer no protection against certain skin-to-skin STIs—notably the human papilloma virus, which is responsible for most genital cancers (Medical Institute, 1994; NIH, 2001). Condoms do, however, reduce tenfold the risk of contracting HIV (human immunodeficiency virus—the virus that causes AIDS) from an infected partner (Pinkerton & Abramson, 1997).

One response to these facts of life has been a greater emphasis on teen abstinence within some comprehensive sex education programs. A National Longitudinal Study of Adolescent Health among 12,000 teens found several predictors of sexual restraint:

High intelligence Teens with high rather than average intelligence test scores more often delay sex, evidently because they appreciate possible negative consequences and are more focused on future achievement than on here-and-now pleasures (Halpern & others, 2000).

Religiosity Actively religious teens and adults more often reserve sex for marital commitment (Rostosky & others, 2004; Smith, 1998).

Father presence In studies that followed hundreds of New Zealand and U.S. girls from age 5 to 18, a father's absence was linked to sexual activity before age 16 and teen pregnancy (Ellis & others, 2003). These associations held even after adjusting for other adverse influences such as poverty.

Participation in service learning programs In several experiments, teens who volunteer as tutors or teachers' aides or take part in community projects have lower pregnancy rates than other comparable teens randomly assigned to control conditions (Kirby, 2002; O'Donnell & others, 2002). Researchers are unsure why. Does service learning promote a sense of personal competence, control, and responsibility? Does it encourage more future-oriented thinking? Or does it simply reduce opportunities for unprotected sex?

In recent history, the pendulum of sexual values has swung from the European eroticism of the early 1800s to the conservative Victorian era of the late 1800s, from the libertine flapper era of the 1920s to the family values period of the 1950s. The pendulum may have begun a new swing toward commitment in the twenty-first century, with declining teen birth rates since 1991, and virgins (54 percent in 2002) now outnumbering nonvirgins (46 percent) among U.S. 15- to 19-year-olds (CDC, 2004; Mohn & others, 2003).

Sexual Orientation

OBJECTIVE 14 | Summarize current views on the number of people whose sexual orientation is homosexual, and discuss the research on environmental and biological influences on sexual orientation.

To motivate is to energize and direct behavior. So far, we have considered the energizing of sexual motivation but not its direction. We express the direction of our sexual interest in our **sexual orientation**—our enduring sexual attraction toward members of our own sex (homosexual orientation) or the other sex (heterosexual orientation). Cultures vary in their attitudes toward homosexuality. But as far as we know, all cultures in all times have been predominantly heterosexual (Bullough, 1990). Whether a culture condemns or accepts homosexuality, heterosexuality prevails and homosexuality survives.

Gay men and lesbians often recall childhood play preferences like those of the other sex (Bailey & Zucker, 1995). But most homosexual people report not becoming aware of same-sex attraction until during or shortly after puberty, and not thinking of themselves as gay or lesbian until around age 20 (Garnets & Kimmel, 1990).

Sexual Orientation Statistics

How many people are exclusively homosexual? Until recently, the popular press assumed a homosexuality rate of 10 percent. In a 2002 Gallup survey, the average American estimated that 21 percent of men are gay and 22 percent of women are lesbian (Robinson, 2002). But in both Europe and the United States, more than a dozen national surveys in the early 1990s explored sexual orientation, using methods that protected the respondent's anonymity. Their results agree in suggesting that a more accurate figure is about 3 or 4 percent of men and 1 or 2 percent of women (Laumann & others, 1994; National Center for Health Statistics, 1991; Smith, 1998). Estimates derived from the sex of unmarried partners reported in the 2000 U.S. Census suggest that 2.5 percent of the population is gay or lesbian (Tarmann, 2002). Fewer than 1 percent of survey respondents—for example, 12 people out of 7076 Dutch adults in one recent survey (Sandfort & others, 2001)—reported being actively bisexual. (Studies indicate that men who describe themselves as bisexual tend to respond like homosexual men; they typically have genital arousal to same-sex erotic stimuli [Rieger & others, 2005].) In the Dutch study, a larger number of adults reported having had an isolated homosexual experience. And most people report having had an occasional homosexual fantasy. Health experts find it helpful to know sexual statistics, but numbers do not decide issues of human rights.

What does it feel like to be homosexual in a heterosexual culture? If you are heterosexual, one way to understand is to imagine how you would feel if you were ostracized or fired for openly admitting or displaying your feelings toward someone of the other sex; if you overheard people making crude jokes about heterosexual people; if most movies, TV shows, and advertisements portrayed (or implied) homosexuality; and if your family members were pleading with you to change your heterosexual lifestyle and to enter into a homosexual marriage.

Facing such reactions, homosexual people often struggle with their sexual orientation. They may at first try to ignore or deny their desires, hoping they will go away.

■ **sexual orientation** an enduring sexual attraction toward members of either one's own sex (homosexual orientation) or the other sex (heterosexual orientation).

" It has been maintained for years that we each use only about 10 percent of our brain capacity; that the condom failure rate is 10 percent; and until just last year, that 10 percent of Americans are homosexual. Such statistics are partly artifacts, I suspect, of our decimal system; in a base 12 system, we'd no doubt show a similar affinity for statistics that were multiples of 8.333 percent."

John Allen Paulos, "Counting on Dyscalculia," 1993

Personal values affect sexual orientation less than they affect other forms of sexual behavior. Compared with people who rarely attend religious services, for example, those who attend regularly are one-third as likely to have cohabited before marriage, and they report having had many fewer sex partners. But (if male) they are just as likely to be homosexual (Smith, 1998).

But they don't. Then they may try to change, through psychotherapy, willpower, or prayer. But the feelings typically persist, as do those of heterosexual people—who are similarly incapable of becoming homosexual (Haldeman, 1994, 2002; Myers & Scanzoni, 2005). Most of today's psychologists therefore view sexual orientation as neither willfully chosen nor willfully changed. Sexual orientation in some ways is like handedness: Most people are one way, some the other. A very few are truly ambidextrous. Regardless, the way one is endures.

Women's sexual orientation tends to be less strongly felt and potentially more fluid and changeable than men's (Diamond, 2000, 2003; Peplau & Garnets, 2000). Men's lesser sexual variability is apparent in many ways, notes Roy Baumeister (2000). Across time, across cultures, across situations, and across differing levels of education, religiosity, and peer influence, adult women's sexual drive and interests are more flexible and varying than are adult men's. Women, more than men, for example, prefer to alternate periods of high sexual activity with periods of almost none, and are somewhat more likely than men to feel bisexual attractions. Baumeister calls this phenomenon the gender difference in *erotic plasticity*.

Gays and lesbians suffer elevated rates of depression and risk of suicide attempts, which researchers suspect result from their experiences with bullying, harassment, and discrimination (Sandfort & others, 2001; Warner & others, 2004). Most people, whether straight or gay, accept their orientation—by electing celibacy, by engaging in promiscuous sex (a choice more commonly made by gay men than by lesbian women), or by entering into a committed, long-term love relationship (a choice more often made by lesbians than by gays) (Kulkin & others, 2000; Peplau, 1982; Remafedi, 1999; Weinberg & Williams, 1974). Mental health professionals are now more accepting of clients' sexual orientation. The American Psychiatric Association dropped homosexuality from its list of "mental illnesses" in 1973, as did the World Health Organization in 1993, and Japan's and China's psychiatric associations in 1995 and 2001.

Origins of Sexual Orientation

Note that the scientific question is not "What causes homosexuality?" (or "What causes heterosexuality?") but "What causes differing sexual orientation?" In pursuit of answers, psychological science compares the backgrounds and physiology of people whose sexual orientations *differ*.

If our sexual orientation is indeed something we do not choose and seemingly cannot change, then where do these preferences come from? How do we move toward either a heterosexual or a homosexual orientation? See if you can anticipate the consensus that has emerged from hundreds of research studies by responding yes or no to the following questions:

1. Is homosexuality linked with problems in a child's relationships with parents, such as with a domineering mother and an ineffectual father, or a possessive mother and a hostile father?
2. Does homosexuality involve a fear or hatred of people of the other gender, leading individuals to direct their sexual desires toward members of their own sex?
3. Is sexual orientation linked with levels of sex hormones currently in the blood?
4. As children, were many homosexuals molested, seduced, or otherwise sexually victimized by an adult homosexual?

The answer to all these questions appears to be no (Storms, 1983). Consider the findings of lengthy Kinsey Institute interviews with nearly 1000 homosexuals and 500 heterosexuals (Bell & others, 1981; Hammersmith, 1982). The investigators assessed nearly every imaginable psychological cause of homosexuality—parental relationships, childhood sexual experiences, peer relationships, dating experiences. Their findings: Homosexuals were no more likely than heterosexuals to have been smothered by maternal love, neglected by their father, or sexually abused. And consider this: If "distant fathers" were more likely to produce homosexual sons, then shouldn't boys growing up in father-absent homes more often be gay? (They are not.) And shouldn't the rising number of such homes have led to a noticeable increase in the gay population? (It has not.)

Homosexual people do, however, appear more often in certain populations. One study (Ludwig, 1995) of the biographies of 1004 eminent people found homosexual and bisexual people overrepresented (11 percent of the sample), especially among poets (24 percent), fiction writers (21 percent), and artists and musicians (15 percent). Men who have older brothers are also somewhat more likely to be gay, report Ray Blanchard (1997, 2001) and Anthony Bogaert (2003). Assuming the odds of homosexuality are roughly 3 percent among first sons, they rise to about 4 percent among second sons, 5 percent or a little more for third sons, and so on for each additional older brother. The reason for this curious phenomenon—the *fraternal birth-order effect*—is unclear. Blanchard suspects a defensive maternal immune response to foreign substances produced by male fetuses. The maternal antibodies may become stronger after each pregnancy with a male fetus and may prevent the fetus' brain from developing in a male-typical pattern. Women with older sisters, and women who were womb-mates of twin brothers, exhibit no such sibling effect (Rose & others, 2002).

So, what else might influence sexual orientation? One theory proposes that people develop same-sex erotic attachments if segregated by gender at the time their sex drive matures (Storms, 1981). Indeed, gay men tend to recall going through puberty somewhat earlier, when peers are more likely to be all males (Bogaert & others, 2002). But even in a tribal culture in which homosexual behavior is expected of all boys before marriage, heterosexuality prevails (Money, 1987). (As this illustrates, homosexual *behavior* does not always indicate a homosexual *orientation*.)

The bottom line from a half-century's theory and research: If there are environmental factors that influence sexual orientation, we do not yet know what they are. This reality has motivated researchers to consider more carefully the possible biological influences on orientation, including evidence of homosexuality in the animal world, and the influences of differing brain centers, genetics, and prenatal hormone exposure.

Erick has two moms
Maria Christina Vlassidis (left) and Marie Tatro (center), who are lesbians, tell playmates of their son Erick, 8, that they are both his moms. Both women attend school conferences and support other aspects of his life. Studies suggest that being reared by lesbian or gay parents does not appreciably affect a child's sexual orientation.

Same-Sex Attraction in Animals At Coney Island's New York Aquarium, Wendell and Cass spent several years as devoted same-sex partners. So, also, are the Central Park Zoo penguins Silo and Roy. Biologist Bruce Bagermihl (1999) identifies several hundred species in which at least occasional same-sex relations have been observed. Grizzlies, gorillas, monkeys, flamingos, and owls are all on the long list. Among rams, for example, some 6 to 10 percent—to sheep-breeding ranchers, the "duds"—display same-sex attraction by shunning ewes and seeking to mount other males (Perkins & Fitzgerald, 1997). So, some degree of homosexuality seems to be a natural part of the animal world as well.

"Gay" penguins
New York Aquarium penguins Wendell and Cass have company in the animal kingdom.

The Brain and Sexual Orientation Researcher Simon LeVay (1991) studied sections of the hypothalamus taken from deceased heterosexual and homosexual people. As a gay scientist, LeVay wanted to do "something connected with my gay identity." He knew he had to avoid biasing the results, so he did the study *blind,* without knowing which donors were gay. For nine months he peered through his microscope at a cell cluster he thought might be important. Then one morning, LeVay sat down and broke the codes. His discovery: The cell cluster was reliably larger in heterosexual men than in women and homosexual men. As the brain difference became apparent, LeVay said (1994), "I was almost in a state of shock. . . . I took a walk by myself on the cliffs over the ocean. I sat for half an hour just thinking what this might mean."

It should not surprise us that brains differ with sexual orientation. Remember our maxim: *Everything psychological is simultaneously biological.* The critical question is, when did the brain difference begin? At conception? In the womb? During childhood or adolescence? Did experience produce the difference? Or did genes or prenatal hormones (or genes via prenatal hormones)?

LeVay does not view this neural center as a sexual orientation center; rather, he sees it as an important part of the neural pathway engaged in sexual behavior. He acknowledges that sexual behavior patterns may influence the brain's anatomy. In fish, birds, rats, and humans, brain structures vary with experience—including sexual experience, reports sex researcher Marc Breedlove (1997). But LeVay believes it more likely that brain anatomy influences sexual orientation. His hunch seems confirmed by the discovery of a similar hypothalamic difference between the 6 to 10 percent of male sheep that display same-sex attraction and the 90+ percent attracted to females (Larkin & others, 2002; Roselli & others, 2002). Moreover, report University of London psychologists Qazi Rahman and Glenn Wilson (2003), "The neuroanatomical correlates of male homosexuality differentiate very early postnatally, if not prenatally."

A functional hypothalamus difference surfaced in recent reports of brain responses to hormone-derived sexual scents. Swedish researchers (Savic & others, 2005) reported that when straight women are given a whiff of a scent derived from men's sweat, their hypothalamus lights up in an area governing sexual arousal. Gay men's brains responded similarly to the men's scent, but straight men's brains showed the arousal response only to a female hormone derivative. It's not surprising, then, that another research team has since reported that gays and lesbians differ from their straight counterparts in their preferences for sex-related sweat odors (Martins & others, 2005). Odors taken from gay men, for example, are liked by other gay men but not by heterosexual men.

Laura Allen and Roger Gorski (1992) also concluded that brain anatomy influences sexual orientation after discovering that a section of the anterior commissure (the fibers that, like the corpus callosum, connect right and left hemispheres) is one-third larger in homosexual men than in heterosexual men. "The emerging neuroanatomical picture," noted Brian Gladue (1994), "is that, in some brain areas, homosexual men are more likely to have female-typical neuroanatomy than are heterosexual men."

Genes and Sexual Orientation There is evidence to suggest a genetic influence on sexual orientation. "First, homosexuality does appear to run in families," note Brian Mustanski and Michael Bailey (2003). "Second, twin studies have established that genes play a substantial role in explaining individual differences in sexual orientation." Although results vary, an identical twin is somewhat more likely than a fraternal twin to share a co-twin's homosexual orientation. However, in many identical twin pairs (especially female twins), the twin and co-twin's orientations differ, indicating that other factors besides genes are at work. And third, experimenters have, by genetic manipulations, managed to create female fruit flies that during courtship act like males (pursuing other females) and males that act like females (Demir & Dickson, 2005). "We have shown that a single gene in the fruit fly is sufficient to determine all aspects of the flies' sexual orientation and behavior," explained Barry Dickson (2005).

But why, many people wonder, would "gay genes" exist? Given that same-sex couples cannot naturally reproduce, how could genes that predispose homosexuality have survived in the human gene pool? Researchers have speculated about possible reasons. Perhaps, for example, kin selection is at work. Recall from Chapter 3 the evolutionary psychology reminder that many of our genes also reside in our biological relatives. Perhaps, then, gay people's genes live on through their supporting the survival and reproductive success of their nieces, nephews, and other relatives (who also carry many of the same genes). Or perhaps maternal genetics are at work. A recent Italian study (Camperio-Ciani & others, 2004) confirms what others have found—that homosexual men have more homosexual relatives on their mother's side than on their father's.

"Gay men simply don't have the brain cells to be attracted to women."
Simon LeVay, *The Sexual Brain*, 1993

"Studies indicate that male homosexuality is more likely to be transmitted from the mother's side of the family."
Robert Plomin, John DeFries, Gerald McClearn, and Michael Rutter, *Behavioral Genetics*, 1997

It also finds that, compared with the maternal relatives of heterosexual men, the maternal relatives of homosexual men produce more offspring. Perhaps, surmised the researchers, genes that convey a reproductive advantage in mothers and aunts somehow influence the sexual orientation of their sons and nephews.

Prenatal Hormones and Sexual Orientation There are elevated rates of homosexual orientation in identical *and* fraternal twins, which suggests that not just shared genetics but also a shared prenatal environment may be a factor. In animals and some exceptional human cases, abnormal prenatal hormone conditions have altered a fetus' sexual orientation. German researcher Gunter Dorner (1976, 1988) pioneered this research by manipulating a fetal rat's exposure to male hormones, thereby "inverting" its sexual orientation. Similarly, when pregnant sheep are injected with testosterone during a critical period of fetal development, their female offspring will later show homosexual behavior (Money, 1987).

In humans, a critical period for the brain's neural-hormonal control system may exist between the middle of the second and fifth months after conception (Ellis & Ames, 1987; Gladue, 1990; Meyer-Bahlburg, 1995). Exposure to the hormone levels typically experienced by female fetuses during this time appears to predispose the person (whether female or male) to be attracted to males in later life.

Some research reveals that homosexual individuals of both sexes have many traits that are intermediate between heterosexual females and males **(TABLE 12.1)**. For example, in some (but not all) studies, gay men have had fingerprint patterns rather like those of heterosexual women (Mustanski & others, 2002; Sanders & others, 2002). Most people have more fingerprint ridges on their right hand than on their left. Jeff Hall and Doreen Kimura (1994) first observed that this difference was greater for heterosexual males than for females and gay males. Given that fingerprint ridges are complete by the sixteenth fetal week, the researchers suspected the difference was due to prenatal hormones. Prenatal hormones also are a possible explanation for why data from 20 studies revealed that "homosexual participants had 39 percent greater odds of being non–right-handed" (Lalumière & others, 2000).

> Genetic study of sexual orientation: Are you in (or do you know of) a family with two or more gay brothers? If so, a nationwide study being conducted by a Chicago-area university research team welcomes your visit to www.gaybros.com.

> "Were it not for delicately balanced combinations of genetic, neurological, hormonal, and environmental factors, largely occurring prior to birth, each and every one of us would be homosexual."
>
> Lee Ellis and M. Ashley Ames (1987)

TABLE 12.1

BIOLOGICAL CORRELATES OF SEXUAL ORIENTATION

On average (the evidence is strongest for males), various biological and behavioral traits of gays and lesbians fall between those of straight men and straight women. Tentative findings—some in need of replication—include these:

Brain differences
- One hypothalamic cell cluster is larger in straight men than in women and gay men; same difference is found in male sheep displaying other-sex versus same-sex attraction.
- Anterior commissure is larger in gay men than in women or straight men.
- Gay men's hypothalamus reacts as does a woman's to the smell of sex-related hormones.

Genetic influences
- Shared sexual orientation is higher among identical twins than among fraternal twins.
- Sexual attraction in fruit flies can be genetically manipulated.

Prenatal hormonal influences
- Altered prenatal hormone exposure may lead to homosexuality in humans and other animals.
- Men with several older brothers are more likely to be gay.

These brain differences and genetic and prenatal influences may contribute to observed gay-straight differences in
- spatial abilities.
- fingerprint ridge counts.
- auditory system development.
- handedness.
- occupational preferences.
- relative finger lengths.
- gender nonconformity.
- age of onset of puberty in males.
- male body size.
- sleep length.

Gay more than straight men express interest in occupations that attract many women, such as decorator, florist, and flight attendant (Lippa, 2002). (Given that some 96 percent of men are not gay, most men in such occupations may nevertheless be straight.)

"Evidence suggesting that biology plays an important role in the development of male and female sexual orientation is rapidly increasing."

Scott L. Hershberger (2001)

FIGURE 12.9
Spatial abilities and sexual orientation
Which of the four figures can be rotated to match the target figure at the top? Straight males tend to find this an easier task than do straight females, with gays and lesbians intermediate. (From Rahman, Wilson, & Abrahams, 2004, with 60 people tested in each group.)

Lesbians likewise have some male-typical traits. For example, their cochlea and hearing system develop in a way that is intermediate between those of heterosexual females and heterosexual males, and which seems attributable to prenatal hormonal influence (McFadden, 2002).

Another striking illustration of gay-straight differences appears in studies showing that homosexual men's spatial abilities resemble those typical of heterosexual women (Cohen, 2002; Gladue, 1994; McCormick & Witelson, 1991; Sanders & Wright, 1997). On mental rotation tasks such as the one illustrated in **FIGURE 12.9,** for example, heterosexual men tend to outscore women. A study by Qazi Rahman and colleagues (2003) found that, as on a number of other measures, the scores of both homosexual males and females fall between those of heterosexual males and heterosexual females.

Because the physiological evidence is preliminary and controversial, some scientists remain skeptical. Rather than specifying sexual orientation, they suggest, biological factors may predispose a temperament that influences sexuality "in the context of individual learning and experience" (Byne & Parsons, 1993). Daryl Bem (1996, 1998, 2000) has theorized that genes code for prenatal hormones and brain anatomy, which predispose *temperaments* that lead children to prefer gender-typical or gender-atypical activities and friends. These preferences may later lead children to feel attracted to whichever sex feels different from their own. The dissimilar-seeming sex (whether or not it conforms to one's own anatomy) becomes associated with anxiety and other forms of arousal, which are eventually transformed into romantic arousal. The exotic becomes erotic.

Regardless of the process, the consistency of the genetic, prenatal, and brain findings has swung the pendulum toward a biological explanation of sexual orientation (Rahman & Wilson, 2003). Nature more than nurture, most psychiatrists now believe, predisposes orientation (Vreeland & others, 1995). This helps explain why sexual orientation is so difficult to change.

Still, some people wonder: Should the cause of sexual orientation matter? Perhaps it shouldn't, but people's assumptions matter. Those who believe, as do 40 percent of Americans (up from 13 percent in 1977 [Gallup, 2002]) and most gays and lesbians, that sexual orientation is biologically disposed, express more accepting attitudes toward homosexual people (Allen & others, 1996; Furnham & Taylor, 1990; Kaiser, 2001; Whitley, 1990). Consider:

- Between 1977 and 2002, American Gallup surveys found that support for equal job rights for gays and lesbians rose from 56 to 85 percent, and agreement that "homosexuality should be an acceptable alternative life-style" rose from 34 to 52 percent.
- In Canadian Gallup surveys between 1992 and 2001, support for same-sex marriages nearly doubled—from 24 to 46 percent (Mazzuca, 2002), and will likely rise further, now that Canada has begun allowing same-sex marriage.
- Acceptance is most common among women, among those with a gay or lesbian friend or relative, and among younger adults (Altmeyer, 2001; Herek & Capitanio, 1996; Kaiser, 2001; Kite & Whitley, 1996; Whitley, 2002). In 2001 surveys by the Gallup Organization and by the Kaiser Family Foundation, 60 to 65 percent of 18- to 29-year-olds supported gay/lesbian marriage or legal relationships—double the support expressed by those 65 and older (Carlson, 2002; Kaiser, 2001). Moreover, among entering collegians, support for laws prohibiting homosexual relationships has plummeted since 1987 **(FIGURE 12.10).**

These dramatic attitude shifts do not represent a liberalization of all sex-related attitudes. For example, in periodic U.S. national surveys, agreement that extramarital sex is "always wrong" *increased* from 69.6 percent in 1973 to 79.4 percent in 2000 (NORC, 2002).

To gay and lesbian activists, the new biological research is a double-edged sword (Diamond, 1993). If sexual orientation, like skin color and sex, is genetically influenced, that offers a further rationale for civil rights protection. Moreover, it may alleviate parents' concerns about their children being unduly influenced by gay teachers and role models. It does, however, raise the troubling possibility that genetic markers of sexual orientation could someday be identified through fetal testing, and a fetus could be aborted simply for being predisposed to an unwanted orientation.

Sex and Human Values

OBJECTIVE **15** | Discuss the place of values in sex research.

Recognizing that values are both personal and cultural, most sex researchers and educators strive to keep their writings on sexuality value-free.

But can the study of sexual behavior and what motivates it ever be free of values? The very words we use to describe behavior often reflect our personal values, as when sex researchers label sexually restrained individuals as "erotophobic" and as having "high sex guilt." Whether we label sexual acts we do not practice as "perversions," "deviations," or part of an "alternative sexual life-style" depends on our attitude toward the behaviors. Labels describe, but they also evaluate.

Sex education separated from the context of human values may also give some students the idea that sexual intercourse is simply a recreational activity. Diana Baumrind (1982), a University of California child-rearing expert, has observed that an implication that adults are neutral about adolescent sexual activity is unfortunate, because "promiscuous recreational sex poses certain psychological, social, health, and moral problems that must be faced realistically."

Perhaps we can agree that the knowledge provided by sex research is preferable to ignorance, and yet also agree that researchers' values should be stated openly, enabling us to debate them and to reflect on our own values. We should remember that scientific research on sexual motivation does not aim to define the personal meaning of sex in our own lives. You could know every available fact about sex— that the initial spasms of male and female orgasm come at 0.8-second intervals, that the female nipples expand 10 millimeters at the peak of sexual arousal, that systolic blood pressure rises some 60 points and the respiration rate to 40 breaths per minute—but fail to understand the human significance of sexual intimacy.

Surely one significance of sexual intimacy is its expression of our profoundly social nature. Sex is a socially significant act. Men and women can achieve orgasm alone, yet most people find greater satisfaction while embracing their loved one. There is a yearning for closeness in sexual motivation. Sex at its human best is life-uniting and love-renewing.

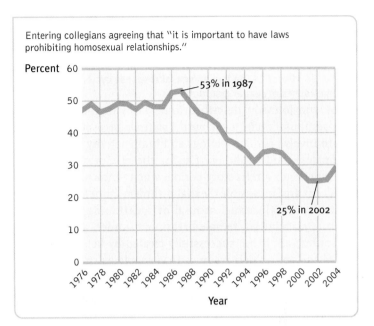

Entering collegians agreeing that "it is important to have laws prohibiting homosexual relationships."

53% in 1987

25% in 2002

FIGURE 12.10
Changing attitudes
(Source: Annual UCLA/American Council on Education surveys of some 7 million entering collegians.)

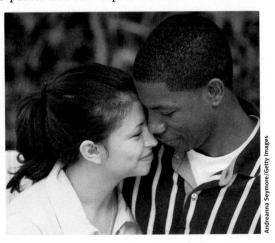

Andreanna Seymore/Getty Images

A sharing of love
For most adults, a sexual relationship fulfills not only a biological motive, but a social need for intimacy.

>> Learning Outcomes

Sexual Motivation

OBJECTIVE 9 | **Describe the human sexual response cycle, and discuss some causes of sexual disorders.**

Masters and Johnson described four stages in the human sexual response cycle: *excitement, plateau, orgasm* (which seems to involve similar feelings and brain activity in males and females), and *resolution*. During the resolution phase, males experience a refractory period, when renewed arousal and orgasm are impossible. Sexual disorders (problems that consistently impair sexual arousal or functioning, such as premature ejaculation, female orgasmic disorder, and erectile disorder) are being successfully treated by behaviorally oriented therapy, which assumes that people learn and can modify their sexual responses, or with drug therapy.

OBJECTIVE 10 | **Discuss the impact of hormones on sexual motivation and behavior.**

The sex hormones *testosterone* and *estrogen* are present in both males and females, but males have a higher level of testosterone and females a higher level of estrogen. These hormones help our bodies develop and function as either male or female. In nonhuman animals, they also help stimulate sexual activity. Assuming a normal level is present, hormones have a looser influence on human sexual behavior, though desire does rise slightly at ovulation among women with mates. Unlike other mammalian females, women's sexuality is more responsive to testosterone level than to estrogen level. Short-term shifts in testosterone level are normal in men.

OBJECTIVE 11 | **Describe the role of external stimuli and fantasies on sexual motivation and behavior.**

Erotic material and other external stimuli can trigger sexual arousal in both men and women, although the activated brain areas differ somewhat. Sexually explicit material may lead people to perceive their partners as comparatively less appealing and to devalue their relationships. Sexually coercive material tends to increase viewers' acceptance of rape and violence toward women. In combination with the internal hormonal push and the external pull of sexual stimuli, fantasies (imagined stimuli) influence sexual arousal.

OBJECTIVE 12 | **Discuss some of the forces that influence teen pregnancy and teen attitudes toward contraception.**

Adolescents' physical maturation fosters a sexual dimension to their emerging identity, but rates of teen intercourse vary from culture to culture. In the twentieth century, increased teen sexual activity in North America was reflected in increased rates of adolescent pregnancies. Factors contributing to teen pregnancy include ignorance of the potential conse-quences of sexual activity; guilt related to sexual activity; minimal communication about contraception with parents, partners, and peers; alcohol use; and mass media norms of unprotected promiscuity.

OBJECTIVE 13 | **Describe trends in the spread of sexually transmitted infections.**

STIs—*sexually transmitted infections,* such as the human papilloma virus, AIDS, and others—have spread rapidly. People under the age of 25 account for two-thirds of such infections, and teen girls seem especially vulnerable because of their less mature bodies and lower levels of protective antibodies. Attempts to protect teens through comprehensive sex-education programs include a greater emphasis on teen abstinence. High intelligence, religiosity, father presence, and participation in service learning programs tend to be predictors of teen sexual restraint.

OBJECTIVE 14 | **Summarize current views on the number of people whose sexual orientation is homosexual, and discuss the research on environmental and biological influences on sexual orientation.**

Studies indicate that about 3 or 4 percent of men and 1 or 2 percent of women are homosexual, and that sexual orientation is enduring. Research does not support cause-effect links between homosexuality and any of the following: a child's relationships with parents, father-absent homes, fear or hatred of people of the other gender, childhood sexual experiences, peer relationships, or dating experiences. Evidence supporting the likelihood of a biological component of homosexuality is found in studies of same-sex behavior in several hundred species, straight-gay differences in body and brain characteristics, genetic studies of family members and twins, and the effect of exposure to certain hormones during critical periods of prenatal development. The increasing public perception that sexual orientation is biologically influenced is reflected in increasing acceptance of gays and lesbians and their relationships.

OBJECTIVE 15 | **Discuss the place of values in sex research.**

Scientific research on sexual motivation does not attempt to define the personal meaning of sex in our lives, but sex research and education are not value-free. Some say that researchers and educators should therefore openly acknowledge their sex-related values, recognizing the emotional significance of sexual expression.

ASK YOURSELF: What do you think would be an effective strategy for reducing teen pregnancy?

The Need to Belong

OBJECTIVE 16 | Describe the adaptive value of social attachments, and identify both healthy and unhealthy consequences of our need to belong.

Separated from friends or family—isolated in prison, alone at a new school, living in a foreign land—most people feel keenly their lost connections with important others. We are what Aristotle called *the social animal.* "Without friends," wrote Aristotle in his *Nichomachean Ethics,* "no one would choose to live, though he had all other goods." We have a need to affiliate with others, even to become strongly attached to certain others in enduring, close relationships. Human beings, contended the personality theorist Alfred Adler, have an "urge to community" (Ferguson, 1989). Roy Baumeister and Mark Leary (1995) have assembled evidence for this deep *need to belong.*

Aiding Survival Social bonds boosted our ancestors' survival rate. By keeping children close to their caregivers, attachments served as a powerful survival impulse. As adults, those who formed attachments were more likely to come together to reproduce and to stay together to nurture their offspring to maturity. To be "wretched" literally means, in its Middle English origin (*wrecche*), to be without kin nearby.

Cooperation in groups also enhanced survival. In solo combat, our ancestors were not the toughest predators. But as hunters they learned that six hands were better than two. And as foragers, they gained protection from predators and enemies by traveling in groups. Those who felt a need to belong survived and reproduced most successfully, and their genes now predominate. We are innately social creatures. People in every society on Earth belong to groups (and, as Chapter 18 explains, prefer and favor "us" over "them").

Wanting to Belong The need to belong colors our thoughts and emotions. We spend a great deal of time thinking about actual and hoped-for relationships. When relationships form, we often feel joy. Falling in mutual love, people have been known to feel their cheeks ache from their irrepressible grins. Asked, "What is necessary for your happiness?" or "What is it that makes your life meaningful?" most people mention—before anything else—close, satisfying relationships with family, friends, or romantic partners (Berscheid, 1985). Happiness hits close to home.

Pause a moment to consider: What was your most satisfying moment in the past week? Kennon Sheldon and his colleagues (2001) asked that question of American and South Korean collegians, then asked them to rate how much this peak experience had satisfied various needs. In both countries, the satisfaction of self-esteem and relatedness-belonging needs were the top two contributors to the peak moment. Another study found that *very* happy university students are not distinguished by their money but by their "rich and satisfying close relationships" (Diener & Seligman, 2002). The need to belong runs deeper, it seems, than any need to be rich.

South Africans have a word for these human bonds that define us all. *Ubuntu* (oo-BOON-too), explains Desmond

Separation amplifies the felt need to belong
In the film *Cast Away* Chuck Noland (played by Tom Hanks) combats social starvation by talking with his girlfriend's snapshot and a volleyball he named Wilson.

20TH Century Fox/Dreamworks/The Kobal Collection

Tutu (1999), expresses the fact that "my humanity is caught up, is inextricably bound up, in yours." A Zulu maxim captures the idea: *Umuntu ngumuntu ngabantu*— "a person is a person through other persons."

Acting to Increase Social Acceptance   When we feel included, accepted, and loved by those important to us, our self-esteem rides high. Indeed, say Mark Leary and his colleagues (1998), self-esteem is a gauge of how valued and accepted we feel. Much of our social behavior therefore aims to increase our belonging—our social acceptance and inclusion. To avoid rejection, we generally conform to group standards and seek to make favorable impressions (more on this in Chapter 18). To win friendship and esteem, we monitor our behavior, hoping to create the right impressions. Seeking love and belonging, we spend billions on clothes, cosmetics, and diet and fitness aids—all motivated by our quest for acceptance.

Like sexual motivation, which feeds both love and exploitation, the need to belong feeds both deep attachments and menacing threats. Out of our need to define a "we" come loving families, faithful friendships, and team spirit, but also teen gangs, ethnic rivalries, and fanatic nationalism.

Maintaining Relationships   For most of us, familiarity breeds liking, not contempt. We resist breaking social bonds. Thrown together at school, at summer camp, on a vacation cruise, people resist the group's dissolution. Hoping to maintain our relationships, we promise to call, to write, to come back for reunions. Parting, we feel distress. Attachments can even keep people in abusive relationships if the fear of being alone seems worse than the pain of emotional or physical abuse. Even when bad relationships break, people suffer. In one 16-nation survey, separated and divorced people were only half as likely as married people to say they were "very happy" (Inglehart, 1990). After such separations, feelings of loneliness and anger—and sometimes even a strange desire to be near the former partner—are commonplace.

The fear of being alone has some basis in reality. Children who move through a series of foster homes, with repeated disruption of budding attachments, may come to have difficulty forming deep attachments. And children reared in institutions without a sense of belonging to anyone, or locked away at home under extreme neglect, become pathetic creatures—withdrawn, frightened, speechless.

When something threatens or dissolves our social ties, negative emotions—anxiety, loneliness, jealousy, guilt—overwhelm us. The bereaved often feel life is empty, pointless. Even the first weeks living on a college campus away from home can be distressing. For immigrants and refugees who move alone to new places, the stress and loneliness can be depressing. But if feelings of acceptance and connection build, so do self-esteem, positive feelings, and desires to help rather than hurt others (Buckley & Leary, 2001). After years of placing individual refugee and immigrant families in isolated communities, U.S. policies today encourage *chain migration* (Pipher, 2002). The second refugee Sudanese family settling in a town generally has an easier adjustment than the first.

The Pain of Ostracism   Sometimes, though, the need to belong is denied. Perhaps you can recall such a time, when you felt excluded or ignored or shunned. Perhaps you received the silent treatment. Perhaps others avoided you, or averted their eyes in your presence, or even mocked you behind your back.

The need to connect

Six days a week, women from the Philippines work as "domestic helpers" in 154,000 Hong Kong households. On Sundays, they throng to the central business district to picnic, dance, sing, talk, and laugh. "Humanity could stage no greater display of happiness," reported one observer (*Economist*, 2001).

AP/Wide World Photos

Social psychologist Kipling Williams (2002) and his colleagues have studied such experiences of *ostracism*—of social exclusion—in both natural and laboratory settings. Worldwide, humans use ostracism to control social behavior, with punishing effects. For children, even a brief time-out in isolation can be punishing. For adults, ostracism can be even more painful. Exile, imprisonment, and solitary confinement are progressively more severe forms of punishment. Even to be shunned—given the cold shoulder or the silent treatment, with others' eyes avoiding yours—is to have one's need to belong threatened, observe Kipling Williams and Lisa Zadro (2001). "It's the meanest thing you can do to someone, especially if you know they can't fight back. I never should have been born," said Lea, a lifelong victim of the silent treatment by her mother and grandmother. Like Lea, people often respond to social ostracism with depressed moods, initial efforts to restore their acceptance, and then withdrawal. "I came home every night and cried. I lost 25 pounds, had no self-esteem and felt that I wasn't worthy," reported Richard, after two years of silent treatment by his employer.

Social exclusion fosters freaking out Most socially excluded teens do not commit violence, but some do. Charles "Andy" Williams, described by a classmate as someone his peers derided as "freak, dork, nerd, stuff like that," went on a shooting spree at his suburban California high school, killing 2 and wounding 13 (Bowles & Kasindorf, 2001).

Williams and his colleagues were surprised to discover a toll even from "cyberostracism" by strangers. (Perhaps you can recall the feeling from being ignored in a chat room or having an e-mail go unanswered.) Such ostracism, they discovered, elicits increased activity in a brain area, the *anterior cingulate cortex*, that also activates in response to physical pain (Eisenberger & others, 2003). Psychologically, too, we experience social pain with the same emotional unpleasantness that marks physical pain (MacDonald & Leary, 2005). To experience ostracism is to experience real pain. And pain, whatever its source, focuses our attention and motivates corrective action.

If rejected and unable to remedy the situation, people sometimes turn nasty. In a series of studies, Jean Twenge and her collaborators (2001, 2002; Baumeister & others, 2002) either told people (based on a personality test) that they were "the type likely to end up alone later in life" or that others whom they had met didn't want them in a group that was forming. The researchers told other participants that they would have "rewarding relationships throughout life" or that "everyone chose you as someone they'd like to work with." Those excluded became much more likely to engage in self-defeating behaviors and underperform on aptitude tests. They also exhibited more antisocial behavior, such as disparaging or aggressing against (with a blast of noise) those who had insulted them. "If intelligent, well-adjusted, successful university students can turn aggressive in response to a small laboratory experience of social exclusion," noted the research team, "it is disturbing to imagine the aggressive tendencies that might arise from a series of important rejections or chronic exclusion from desired groups in actual social life."

Fortifying Health Do you have close friends—people with whom you freely disclose your ups and downs? As we shall see in Chapter 13, people who have close friends tend to be happier. As we shall see in Chapter 14, people who feel supported by close relationships also live with better health and at lower risk for psychological disorder and premature death than do those who lack social support. Married people, for example, are less at risk for depression, suicide, and early death than are unattached people. All this evidence affirms Baumeister and Leary's (1995) contention that "human beings are fundamentally and pervasively motivated by a need to belong."

■ **flow** a completely involved, focused state of consciousness, with diminished awareness of self and time, resulting from optimal engagement of one's skills.

■ **industrial-organizational (I/O) psychology** the application of psychological concepts and methods to optimizing human behavior in workplaces.

■ **personnel psychology** a subfield of I/O psychology that focuses on employee recruitment, selection, placement, training, appraisal, and development.

■ **organizational psychology** a subfield of I/O psychology that examines organizational influences on worker satisfaction and productivity and facilitates organizational change.

Sometimes, notes Gene Weingarten (2002), a humor writer knows "when to just get out of the way." Here are some sample job titles from the U.S. Department of Labor *Dictionary of Occupational Titles*: Animal impersonator, human projectile, banana ripening-room supervisor, impregnator, impregnator helper, dope sprayer, finger waver, rug scratcher, egg smeller, bottom buffer, cookie breaker, brain picker, hand pouncer, bosom presser, mother repairer, and breaker repairer.

>> LEARNING OUTCOMES

The Need to Belong

OBJECTIVE 16 | **Describe the adaptive value of social attachments, and identify both healthy and unhealthy consequences of our need to belong.**

Our need to *affiliate*—to feel connected and identified with others—boosted our ancestors' chances for survival, which may explain why humans in every society live in groups. The need to belong appears when people seek social acceptance, work to maintain relationships (or mourn their loss), and feel the joy of love (or the gloom of loneliness). *Ostracized*—excluded or shunned by others—people suffer from stress and depression—a real pain that increases activity in the same brain areas that respond to physical pain. When socially secure in their friendships, families, or marriages, people tend to be healthier and to have lower levels of depression, suicide, and early death. When socially excluded, they may engage in self-defeating behaviors (performing below their ability) or in antisocial behaviors.

ASK YOURSELF: **Have there been times when you felt "out of the loop" with family and friends, or even ostracized by them? How did you respond?**

Motivation at Work

OBJECTIVE 17 | Discuss the importance of flow, and identify the three subfields of industrial-organizational psychology.

The healthy life, said Sigmund Freud, is filled by love and by work. For most of us, work is life's biggest single waking activity. To live is to work. Work helps satisfy several levels of need identified in Maslow's pyramid of needs. Work supports us. Work connects us. Work defines us. Meeting someone for the first time, and wondering "Who are you?" we may ask, "So, what do you do?"

If we feel dissatisfied with our work-related pay, relationships, or identity, we may change where or for whom we work, as 16 percent of Australians did in just the year 2000 (Trewin, 2001). Most people therefore have neither a single vocation nor a predictable career path. Two decades from now, most of you reading this book will be doing work you cannot now imagine. To prepare you and others for this unknown future, many colleges and universities focus less on training your job skills and more on enlarging your capacities for understanding, thinking, and communicating in any work environment.

Amy Wrzensniewski and her colleagues (1997, 2001) have identified person-to-person variations in people's attitudes toward their work. Across various occupations, some people view their work as a *job*, a necessary way to make money but not a positive and fulfilling activity. Others view their work as a *career*, an opportunity to advance from one position to a better position. The rest—those who view their work as a *calling*, a fulfilling and socially useful activity—report the highest satisfaction with their work and their lives.

This finding would not surprise Mihaly Csikszentmihalyi (1990, 1999), who has observed that people's quality of life increases when they are purposefully engaged. Between the anxiety of being overwhelmed and stressed, and the apathy of being underwhelmed and bored, lies a zone in which people experience **flow.** Csikszentmihalyi (chick-SENT-me-hi) formulated the flow concept after studying artists who spent hour after hour painting or sculpting with enormous concentration. Immersed in a project, they worked as if nothing else mattered, and then promptly forgot about it once they finished. The artists seemed driven less by the external rewards of producing art—money, praise, promotion—than by the intrinsic rewards of creating the work. Recognizing that e-mail and other Internet-related distractions can disrupt such flow, Microsoft is developing an *attentional user interface* that aims to "detect when users are available for communication, or when the user is in a state of flow" (Ullman, 2005).

Csikszentmihalyi's later observations—of dancers, chess players, surgeons, writers, parents, mountain climbers, sailors, and farmers; of Australians, North Americans, Koreans, Japanese, and Italians; of people from their teens to their golden years—confirmed an overriding principle: It's exhilarating to flow with an activity that fully engages our skills. Flow experiences boost our sense of self-esteem, competence, and well-being. When the researchers beeped people at random intervals and asked them to report what they were doing and how much they were enjoying themselves, those who were vegetating usually reported little sense of flow and little satisfaction. People reported more positive feelings when interrupted while doing something active, something that engaged their skills, be it play or work. And other research (Inglehart, 1990) indicates that in almost every industrialized nation, people have reported markedly lower well-being if unemployed **(FIGURE 12.11)**. Idleness may sound like bliss, but purposeful work enriches our lives.

In industrialized nations, work has been changing, from farming to manufacturing to "knowledge work." More and more work is *outsourced* to temporary employees and consultants who communicate electronically from virtual workplaces in remote locations. (This book and its teaching package are developed and produced by a team of people in a dozen cities, from Alaska to Florida.) As work changes, will our attitudes toward our work also change? Will our satisfaction with work increase or decrease? Will the *psychological contract*—the subjective sense of mutual obligations between workers and employers—become more or less trusting and secure? These are among the questions that fascinate psychologists who study work-related behavior.

Industrial-organizational (I/O) psychology is a fast-growing profession that applies psychology's principles to the workplace (see Close-Up: I/O Psychology at Work, page 500). In Chapter 6, we encountered one of its subfields: *human factors psychology,* which explores how machines and environments can be optimally designed to fit human abilities. Here we consider two other subfields: **personnel psychology,** which applies psychology's methods and principles to selecting and evaluating workers, and **organizational psychology,** which considers how work environments and management styles influence worker motivation, satisfaction, and productivity. Personnel psychologists match people with jobs, by identifying and placing well-suited candidates. Organizational psychologists modify jobs and supervision in ways that boost morale and productivity.

Have you ever noticed that when you are immersed in an activity, time flies? and that when you are watching the clock, it seems to move more slowly? French researchers have confirmed that the more we attend to an event's duration, the longer it seems to last (Couli & others, 2004).

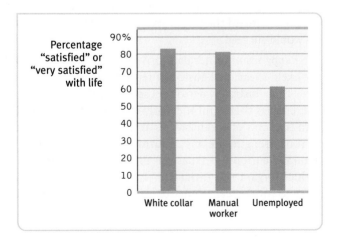

FIGURE 12.11
The bane of unemployment
To want work but not have it is to feel less satisfied with life. Data from 169,776 adults in 16 nations (Inglehart, 1990).

CLOSE-UP:

I/O PSYCHOLOGY AT WORK

As scientists, consultants, and management professionals, industrial-organizational psychologists are found working in varied areas:

PERSONNEL PSYCHOLOGY

Selecting and placing employees
- Developing and validating assessment tools for selecting, placing and promoting workers
- Analyzing job content
- Optimizing worker placement

Training and developing employees
- Identifying needs
- Designing training programs
- Evaluating training programs

Appraising performance
- Developing criteria
- Measuring individual performance
- Measuring organizational performance

ORGANIZATIONAL PSYCHOLOGY

Developing organizations
- Analyzing organizational structures
- Maximizing worker satisfaction and productivity
- Facilitating organizational change

Enhancing quality of worklife
- Expanding individual productivity
- Identifying elements of satisfaction
- Redesigning jobs

HUMAN FACTORS (ENGINEERING) PSYCHOLOGY
- Designing optimum work environments
- Optimizing person-machine interactions
- Developing systems technologies

Adapted from the Society of Industrial and Organizational Psychology (siop.org)

Personnel Psychology

OBJECTIVE 18 | Describe how personnel psychologists help organizations with employee selection, work placement, and performance appraisal.

Psychologists can assist organizations at various stages of selecting and assessing employees. They may help identify needed job skills, decide upon selection methods, recruit and evaluate applicants, introduce and train new employees, and appraise their performance.

Harnessing Strengths

As a new AT&T human resource executive, psychologist Mary Tenopyr (1997) was assigned to solve a problem: Customer service representatives were failing at a high rate. After concluding that many of the hires were ill-matched to the demands of their new job, Tenopyr developed a new selection instrument:

1. She asked new applicants to respond to various questions (without as yet making any use of their responses).
2. She followed up later to assess which of the applicants excelled on the job.
3. She identified the individual items on the earlier test that best predicted who would succeed.

The happy result of her data-driven work was a new test that enabled AT&T to identify likely-to-succeed customer representatives.

As this illustrates, personnel selection aims to match people's strengths with work that enables them and their organizations to flourish. Marry the strengths of people with the tasks of organizations and the result is often prosperity and profit.

Your strengths are any enduring qualities that can be productively applied. Are you naturally curious? Persuasive? Charming? Persistent? Competitive? Analytical? Empathic? Organized? Articulate? Neat? Mechanical? Any such trait, if matched with suitable work, can function as a strength. (See Close-Up: Discovering Your Strengths.)

Artistic strengths

At age 21, Henri Matisse was a sickly and often depressed lawyer's clerk. When his mother gave him a box of paints to cheer him up one day, he felt the darkness lift and his energy surge. He began to fill his days with painting and drawing and went on to art school and a life as one of the world's great painters. For Matisse, doing art felt like "a comfortable armchair." That is how exercising our strengths often feels.

© CNAC/MNAM/Dist. Réunion des Musées Nationaux/Art Resource, NY

CLOSE-UP:

DISCOVERING YOUR STRENGTHS

You can use some of the techniques personnel psychologists have developed to identify your own strengths and pinpoint types of work that will likely prove satisfying and successful. Buckingham and Clifton (2001) have suggested asking yourself:

- What activities give me pleasure? (Bringing order out of chaos? Playing host? Helping others? Challenging sloppy thinking?)
- What activities leave me wondering, "When can I do this again?" (Rather than "When will this be over?")
- What sort of challenges do I relish? (And which do I dread?)
- What sorts of tasks do I learn easily? (And which do I struggle with?)

Some people find themselves in flow—their skills engaged and time flying—when teaching or selling or writing or cleaning or consoling or creating or repairing. If an activity feels good, if it comes easily, if you look forward to it, then look deeper and see your strengths at work.

Satisfied and successful people devote far less time to correcting their deficiencies than to accentuating their strengths. Top performers are "rarely well rounded," Buckingham and Clifton found (p. 26). Instead, they have sharpened their existing skills.

Given the persistence of our traits and temperaments, we should focus not on our deficiencies, but rather on identifying and employing our talents. Better to recognize the activities we quickly learn and become absorbed in—and to further develop those strengths—than to sign up for assertiveness training if shy, for public speaking courses if nervous and soft-spoken, or for drawing classes if we express our artistic side in stick figures.

As Robert Louise Stevenson said in *Of Men and Books* (1882), "To be what we are, and to become what we are capable of becoming, is the only end of life."

Marcus Buckingham and Donald Clifton (2001) argued that the first step to a stronger organization is instituting a strengths-based selection system. Thus, as a manager, you would first identify a group of the most effective people in any role—the ones you would want to hire more of—and compare their strengths with those of a group of the least effective people in that role. In defining these groups, you would try to measure performance as objectively as possible. In one Gallup study of more than 5000 telecommunications customer-service representatives, those evaluated most favorably by their managers were strong in "harmony" and "responsibility," while those actually rated most effective by customers were strong in energy, assertiveness, and eagerness to learn. So, for example, if you needed to hire new people in software development, and you had discovered that your best software developers are analytical, disciplined, and eager to learn, you would focus employment ads less on experience than on the identified strengths: "Do you take a logical and systematic approach to problem solving [analytical]? Are you a perfectionist who strives for timely completion of your projects [disciplined]? Do you want to learn to use Java, C++, and PHP [eager to learn]? If you can say yes to these questions, then please call. . . ."

Identifying people's strengths and matching strengths to work is a first step toward workplace effectiveness. Personnel managers use various tools to assess applicants' strengths and decide who is best-suited to the job. In Chapter 11, we saw how psychologists assess candidates using ability tests. And in Chapter 15, we will explore personality tests and "assessment centers" that enable observations of behaviors on simulated job tasks. For now, let's consider the job interview.

Do Interviews Predict Performance? Interviewers tend to feel confident in their ability to predict long-term job performance from an unstructured, get-acquainted interview. What's therefore shocking is how error-prone those predictions are. Whether predicting job or graduate school success, interviewers' judgments are weak predictors. From their review of 85 years of personnel-selection research, I/O psychologists Frank Schmidt and John Hunter (1998; Schmidt, 2002) determined that for all but less-skilled jobs, general mental ability best predicts on-the-job performance. Subjective overall evaluations from informal interviews are more useful than handwriting analysis (which is worthless). But informal interviews are less informative than aptitude tests, work samples, job knowledge tests, and past job performance. If there's a contest between what our gut tells us about someone and what test scores, work samples, and past performance tell us, we should distrust our gut.

The Interviewer Illusion Interviewers often overrate their discernment, a phenomenon psychologist Richard Nisbett (1987) has labeled the *interviewer illusion*. "I have excellent interviewing skills, and so don't need reference checking as much as someone who doesn't have my ability to read people," is a comment sometimes heard by I/O consultants. Four factors explain this gap between interviewers' intuition and the resulting reality:

- *Interviews disclose the interviewee's good intentions, which are less revealing than habitual behaviors* (Ouellette & Wood, 1998). Intentions matter. People can change. But the best predictor of the person we will be is the person we have been. Wherever we go, we take ourselves along.
- *Interviewers more often follow the successful careers of those they have hired than the successful careers of those they have rejected and lost track of.* This missing feedback prevents interviewers from getting a reality check on their hiring ability.
- *Interviewers presume that people are what they seem to be in the interview situation.* As Chapter 18 explains, we discount the enormous influence of varying situations and mistakenly presume, when meeting others, that what we see is what we will get. But mountains of research on everything from chattiness to conscientiousness reveals that how we behave reflects not only our enduring traits, but the details of the particular situation (wanting to impress in a job interview).
- *Interviewers' preconceptions and moods color how they perceive interviewees' responses* (Cable & Gilovich, 1998; Macan & Dipboye, 1994). If interviewers instantly like a person who perhaps is similar to themselves, they may interpret the person's assertiveness as indicating "confidence" rather than "arrogance." If told certain applicants have been prescreened, interviewers are disposed to judge them more favorably.

An unstructured interview does provide a sense of someone's personality—their expressiveness, warmth, and verbal ability, for example. But this information reveals less about the person's behavior toward others in different situations than most people suppose. Hoping to improve prediction and selection, personnel psychologists have put people in simulated work situations (see pages 629–630), scoured sources for information on past performance, aggregated evaluations from multiple interviews, administered tests, and developed job-specific interviews.

Structured Interviews Unlike casual conversation aimed at getting a feel for someone, **structured interviews** offer a disciplined method of collecting information. A personnel psychologist may analyze a job, script questions, and train interviewers. The interviewers then put the same questions, in the same order, to all applicants, and rate each applicant on established scales.

In an *unstructured* interview, someone might ask, "How organized are you?" "How well do you get along with people?" or "How do you handle stress?" Street-smart applicants know how to score high: "Although I sometimes drive myself too hard, I handle stress by prioritizing and delegating, and by making sure I leave time for sleep and exercise."

By contrast, structured interviews pinpoint strengths (attitudes, behaviors, knowledge, and skills) that distinguish high performers in a particular line of work. The process includes specifying job-specific situations and asking candidates to explain how they would handle them, and how they handled similar situations in their prior employment. "Tell me about a time when you were caught between conflicting demands, without time to accomplish both. How did you handle that?"

> "Between the idea and reality . . . falls the shadow."
>
> T. S. Eliot, *The Hollow Men*, 1925

■ **structured interviews** interview process that asks the same job-relevant questions of all applicants, each of whom is rated on established scales.

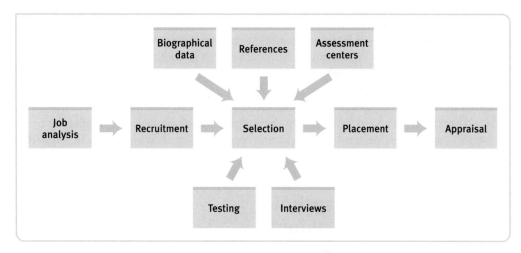

FIGURE 12.12
Personnel psychologists' tasks
Personnel psychologists consult in human resource activities, from job definition to employee appraisal.

To reduce memory distortions and bias, the interviewer takes notes and makes ratings as the interview proceeds and avoids irrelevant and follow-up questions. The structured interview therefore feels less warm, but that can be explained to the applicant: "This conversation won't typify how we relate to each other in this organization."

A review of 150 findings revealed that structured interviews had double the predictive accuracy of unstructured seat-of-the-pants interviews (Schmidt & Hunter, 1998; Wiesner & Cronshaw, 1988). Thanks partly to its greater reliability and partly to its job-analysis focus, the predictive power of one structured interview is roughly equal to that of the average judgment from three or four unstructured interviews (Huffcutt & others, 2001; Schmidt & Zimmerman, 2004).

If, instead, we let our intuitions bias the hiring process, notes Malcolm Gladwell (2000), then "all we will have done is replace the old-boy network, where you hired your nephew, with the new-boy network, where you hire whoever impressed you most when you shook his hand. Social progress, unless we're careful, can merely be the means by which we replace the obviously arbitrary with the not so obviously arbitrary."

To recap, personnel psychologists assist organizations in analyzing jobs, recruiting well-suited applicants, selecting and placing employees, and appraising their performance **(FIGURE 12.12)**—the topic we turn to next.

Appraising Performance

Performance appraisal serves organizational purposes: It helps decide who to retain, how to appropriately reward and pay people, and how to better harness employee strengths, sometimes with job shifts or promotions. Performance appraisal also serves individual purposes: Feedback affirms workers' strengths and helps motivate needed improvements.

Performance appraisal methods include

- *checklists* on which supervisors simply check behaviors that describe the worker ("always attends to customers' needs," "takes long breaks").
- *graphic rating scales* on which a supervisor checks the extent to which a worker is dependable, productive, and so forth.
- *behavior rating scales* on which a supervisor checks behaviors that best describe a worker's performance. If rating the extent to which a worker "follows procedures," the supervisor might mark the employee somewhere between "often takes shortcuts" and "always follows established procedures" (Levy, 2003).

In some organizations, performance feedback comes not only from supervisors but also from all organizational levels. If you join an organization that practices *360-degree feedback* **(FIGURE 12.13)** you will rate yourself, your manager, and your other colleagues, and you will be rated by your manager, other colleagues, and customers (Green, 2002). The net result is often more open communication and more complete appraisal.

FIGURE 12.13
360-degree feedback
With multisource 360-degree feedback, one's knowledge, skills, and behaviors are rated by self and surrounding others. Professors, for example, may be rated by their department chairs, their students, and their colleagues. After receiving all these ratings, professors discuss the 360-degree feedback with their department chair.

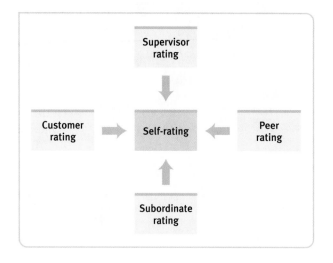

■ **achievement motivation** a desire for significant accomplishment: for mastery of things, people, or ideas; for attaining a high standard.

Performance appraisal, like other social judgments, is vulnerable to bias (Murphy & Cleveland, 1995). *Halo errors* occur when one's overall evaluation of an employee, or of a trait such as their friendliness, biases ratings of their specific work-related behaviors, such as their reliability. *Leniency* and *severity errors* reflect evaluators' tendencies to be either too easy or too harsh on everyone. *Recency errors* occur when raters focus only on easily remembered recent behavior. By encouraging multiple raters and developing objective, job-relevant performance measures, personnel psychologists seek to support their organizations while also helping employees perceive the appraisal process as fair.

Organizational Psychology: Motivating Achievement

OBJECTIVE 19 | Define *achievement motivation,* and explain why organizations would employ an I/O psychologist to help motivate employees and foster employee satisfaction.

The appraisal of work and the matching of talents to work matter, but so does overall motivation. Before considering how organizational psychologists assist with efforts to motivate employees and keep them engaged, let's take a closer look at why any employee might want to pursue high standards or difficult goals.

Think of someone you know who strives to succeed by excelling at any task where evaluation is possible. Now think of someone who is less driven. Psychologist Henry Murray (1938) defined the first person's **achievement motivation** as a desire for significant accomplishment, for mastering skills or ideas, for control, and for rapidly attaining a high standard.

As you might expect from their persistence and eagerness for realistic challenges, people with high achievement motivation do achieve more. One study followed the lives of 1528 California children whose intelligence test scores were in the top 1 percent. Forty years later, when researchers compared those who were most and least successful professionally, they found a motivational difference. Those most successful were more ambitious, energetic, and persistent. As children, they had more active hobbies. As adults, they participated in more groups and favored being a sports participant to being a spectator (Goleman, 1980). In other studies of both secondary school and university students, self-discipline has been a better predictor of school performance, attendance, and graduation honors than intelligence scores have been. "Discipline outdoes talent," concluded researchers Angela Duckworth and Martin Seligman (2005). By their early twenties, for example, top violinists have accumulated some 10,000 lifetime practice hours—double the practice time of other violin students aiming to be teachers (Ericsson & others, 1993, 2001). From his studies, Herbert Simon (1998), a psychologist who won the Nobel Prize for economics, estimates that world-class experts in a field typically have invested "at least 10 years of hard work—say, 40 hours a week for 50 weeks a year."

Similarly, a study of outstanding scholars, athletes, and artists found that all were highly motivated and self-disciplined, willing to dedicate hours every day to the pursuit of their goals (Bloom, 1985). These superstar achievers were distinguished not so much by their extraordinary natural talent as by their extraordinary daily discipline. Great achievement, it seems, mixes a teaspoon of inspiration with a gallon of perspiration.

What distinguishes extremely successful individuals from their equally talented peers, note Duckworth and Seligman, is *grit*—passionate dedication to an ambitious, long-term goal. Although intelligence is distributed like a bell curve, achievements are not. That tells us that achievement involves much more than raw ability. And that is why organizational psychologists seek ways to engage and motivate ordinary people doing ordinary jobs.

Disciplined motivation feeds achievement

Aware that he was far behind other students when beginning his graduate education in psychology, B. F. Skinner devised a daily discipline of rising at 6:00 A.M., studying until breakfast, then going to classes, labs, and the library. After dinner he studied some more, leaving no more than 15 unscheduled minutes each day, and later continued a disciplined daily routine as he became one of the twentieth century's most influential psychologists.

Ken Heyman/Woodfin Camp & Associates

Satisfaction and Engagement

Because work is such a big part of life, employee satisfaction is a priority concern for I/O psychologists. Satisfaction with work feeds satisfaction with life (see Close-Up: Doing Well While Doing Good, page 506). Moreover, decreased job stress feeds improved health (Chapter 14).

Does employee satisfaction also contribute to successful organizations? Positive moods at work do contribute to creativity, persistence, and helpfulness (Brief & Weiss, 2002). But are engaged, happy workers also less often absent? Less likely to quit? Less prone to theft? More punctual? More productive? Conclusive evidence of satisfaction's benefits is, some have said, the holy grail of I/O psychology. Statistical digests of prior research have found a modest positive correlation between individual job satisfaction and performance (Judge & others, 2001; Parker & others, 2003). In one recent analysis of 4500 employees at 42 British manufacturing companies, the most productive workers tended to be those in satisfying work environments (Patterson & others, 2004).

In the United States, the *Fortune* "100 Best Companies to Work For" have also produced markedly higher than average returns for their investors (Fulmer & others, 2003). Other positive data come from the biggest-ever study, a recent analysis of Gallup data from more than 198,000 employees **(TABLE 12.2)** in nearly 8000 business units of 36 large companies (including some 1100 bank branches, 1200 stores, and 4200 teams or departments). James Harter, Frank Schmidt, and Theodore Hayes (2002) explored correlations between various measures of organizational success and *employee engagement*—the extent of workers' involvement, satisfaction, and enthusiasm. They found that engaged workers know what's expected

Capital-Journal/David Eulitt/AP/Wide World Photos

Engaged employees facilitate organizational success

Best Buy's 400 electronic goods stores have nearly identical product layout and operations manuals. Yet some stores have much more engaged employees—and more profitable performance. The store with the highest worker-engagement scores is in the top tenth of stores in having profits beyond budget. And the store with the least-engaged employees is in the bottom tenth (Buckingham, 2001).

TABLE 12.2

THE GALLUP WORKPLACE AUDIT

Overall satisfaction—On a 5-point scale, where 5 is extremely satisfied and 1 is extremely dissatisfied, how satisfied are you with *(name of company)* as a place to work? _____

On a scale of 1 to 5, where 1 is strongly disagree and 5 is strongly agree, please indicate your agreement with the following items.

1. I know what is expected from me at work.

2. I have the materials and equipment I need to do my work right.

3. At work, I have the opportunity to do what I do best every day.

4. In the last seven days, I have received recognition or praise for doing good work.

5. My supervisor, or someone at work, seems to care about me as a person.

6. There is someone at work who encourages my development.

7. At work, my opinions seem to count.

8. The mission/purpose of my company makes me feel my job is important.

9. My associates (fellow employees) are committed to doing quality work.

10. I have a best friend at work.

11. In the last six months, someone at work has talked to me about my progress.

12. This last year, I have had opportunities at work to learn and grow.

Note: These statements are proprietary and copyrighted by The Gallup Organization. They may not be printed or reproduced in any manner without the written consent of The Gallup Organization. Reprinted here by permission.

CLOSE-UP:

DOING WELL WHILE DOING GOOD: "THE GREAT EXPERIMENT"

At the end of the 1700s, the more than 1000 workers in the cotton mill at New Lanark, Scotland—many of them children drawn from Glasgow's poorhouses—worked 13-hour days and lived in grim conditions, with education and sanitation neglected, theft and drunkenness commonplace, and most families occupying just one room.

On a visit to Glasgow, Welsh-born Robert Owen—an idealistic young cotton-mill manager—chanced to meet and fall in love with the mill owner's daughter. After their marriage, Owen, with several partners, purchased the mill and on the first day of the 1800s took control as its manager. Before long, he began what he said was "the most important experiment for the happiness of the human race that had yet been instituted at any time in any part of the world" (Owen, 1814). The exploitation of child and adult labor was, he observed, producing unhappy and inefficient workers. Believing that better working and living conditions could pay economic dividends, he undertook (with some resistance from his partners, whom he ultimately bought out) numerous innovations: a nursery for preschool children, education (with encouragement rather than corporal punishment), Sundays off, health care, paid sick days, unemployment pay for days when the mill could not operate, and a company store selling goods at reduced prices.

Owen also innovated a goals and worker-assessment program that included detailed records of daily productivity and costs. By each employee's workstation, one of four colored boards indicated that person's performance for the previous day. Owen could walk through the mill and at a glance see how individuals were performing. There was, he said, "no beating, no abusive language. . . . I merely looked at the person and then at the color. . . . I could at once see by the expression [which color] was shown."

The commercial success that followed was essential to sustaining what became a movement toward humanitarian reforms. By 1816, with decades of profitability still ahead, Owen believed he had demonstrated "that society may be formed so as to exist without crime, without poverty, with health greatly improved, with little if any misery, and with intelligence and happiness increased a hundredfold." Although his Utopian vision has not been fulfilled, Owen's great experiment did lay the groundwork for employment practices that have today become accepted in much of the world.

Courtesy of New Lanark World Heritage Site

The great experiment
New Lanark Mills, which today are preserved as a World Heritage Site (www.newlanark.org), provided an influential demonstration of how industries could do well while doing good. In its heyday, New Lanark was visited by many European royals and reformers who came to observe its vibrant workforce and prosperous business.

Three types of employees (Crabtree, 2005):
Engaged: working with passion and feeling a profound connection to their company or organization.
Not-engaged: putting in the time, but investing little passion or energy into their work.
Actively disengaged: unhappy workers undermining what their colleagues accomplish.

of them, have what they need to do their work, feel fulfilled in their work, have regular opportunities to do what they do best, perceive that they are part of something significant, and have opportunities to learn and develop. They also found that business units with engaged employees have more loyal customers, less turnover, higher productivity, and greater profits: "Business units above the median on employee engagement had a 70 percent higher success rate than those below the median." Business units in the top quarter on employee engagement averaged about $100,000 more in monthly revenue. A separate analysis for a company with 275 retail stores found that annual turnover was 55 percent among stores whose employee engagement was in the top quarter, and 75 percent among stores with employees in the bottom quarter (Harter, 2000).

Managing Well

OBJECTIVE 20 | Describe some effective management techniques.

Every leader dreams of managing in ways that enhance people's satisfaction, engagement, and productivity and their organization's success. Effective leaders harness job-relevant strengths, set goals, and choose an appropriate leadership style.

Harnessing Job-Relevant Strengths "The major challenge for CEOs over the next 20 years will be the effective deployment of human assets," observes Marcus Buckingham (2001). That challenge is "about psychology. It's about getting [individuals] to be more productive, more focused, more fulfilled than [they were] yesterday." To do so, he and others maintain, effective leaders want first to select the right people. Then, they aim to discern their employees' natural talents, adjust their work roles to suit their talents, and develop those talents into great strengths (FIGURE 12.14). For example, should every college professor at a given school be expected to teach the same load, advise the same number of students, serve on the same number of committees, and engage in the same amount of research? Or should each job description be tailored to harness a specific person's unique strengths?

Managers who excel spend less time trying to instill talents that are not there and more time developing and drawing out what is there. Kenneth Tucker (2002) notes that great managers

- start by helping people identify and measure their talents.
- match tasks to talents and then give people freedom to do what they do best.
- care how their people feel about their work.
- reinforce positive behaviors through recognition and reward.

Thus, rather than focusing on weaknesses and packing people off to training seminars to fix those problems, good managers focus training time on educating people about their strengths and building upon them (which means not promoting people into roles ill-suited to their strengths).

Celebrating engaged and productive employees in every organizational role builds upon a basic principle of operant conditioning (Chapter 8): To teach a behavior, catch a person doing something right and reinforce it. These principles also apply to reinforcing employees. It sounds simple, but many managers are like parents who,

FIGURE 12.14
On the right path
The Gallup Organization path to organizational success (adapted from Fleming, 2001).

Positive coaching
Larry Brown, an adviser to "The Positive Coaching Alliance," has been observed during practices to offer his players 4 to 5 positive comments for every negative comment (Insana, 2005). In 2004, his underdog Detroit Pistons won the National Basketball Association championship.

■ **task leadership** goal-oriented leadership that sets standards, organizes work, and focuses attention on goals.

■ **social leadership** group-oriented leadership that builds teamwork, mediates conflict, and offers support.

when a child returns home with perfect scores, except for that one troublesome biology class, focus on the biology score and ignore the rest. "Sixty-five percent of Americans received NO praise or recognition in the workplace last year," reported the Gallup Organization (2004).

Setting Specific, Challenging Goals In study after study, people merely asked to do their best do not do so. But more specific, challenging goals do motivate higher achievement, especially when combined with progress reports (Locke & Latham, 2002). Specific, measurable objectives, such as "finish gathering information for the history paper by Friday," serve to direct attention, promote effort, motivate persistence, and stimulate creative strategies. When people share in setting a goal and find the goal challenging yet attainable, reaching it boosts their self-evaluation (White & others, 1995). Moreover, when people state not only goals but also *implementation intentions*—action plans that specify when, where, and how they will march toward achieving those goals—they become more focused in their work and on-time completion becomes more likely (Burgess & others, 2004; Koestner & others, 2002; Koole & Spijker, 2000). (Before beginning each new edition of this book, my editor, my associates, and I *manage by objectives*—we agree on target dates for the completion of each chapter draft.) So, to motivate high productivity, effective leaders work with people to define explicit goals, elicit commitments to implementation plans, and provide feedback on progress.

Choosing an Appropriate Leadership Style Leadership varies from a boss-focused directive style to a democratic style that empowers workers in setting goals and strategies. Which works best may depend on the situation and the leader. The best leadership style for leading a discussion may not be the best style for leading troops on a charge (Fiedler, 1981). Moreover, different leaders are suited to different styles. Some excel at **task leadership**—setting standards, organizing work, and focusing attention on goals. Being goal-oriented, task leaders are good at keeping a group centered on its mission. Typically, they have a directive style, which can work well if the leader is bright enough to give good orders (Fiedler, 1987).

Other managers excel at **social leadership**—mediating conflicts and building high-achieving teams (Evans & Dion, 1991). Social leaders often have a democratic style: They delegate authority and welcome the participation of team members. Many experiments show that social leadership is good for morale. Subordinates usually feel more satisfied and motivated when they can participate in decision making (Burger, 1987; Spector, 1986).

Because effective leadership styles vary with the situation and the person, the once-popular *great person theory of leadership*—that all great leaders share certain traits—now seems overstated. But a leader's personality does matter. Effective leaders of laboratory groups, work teams, and large corporations tend to exude a self-confident *charisma* (House & Singh, 1987; Shamir & others, 1993). Their charisma is a mix of a *vision* of some goal, an ability to *communicate* it clearly and simply, and enough optimism and faith in their group to *inspire* others to follow. In one study of 50 Dutch companies, the highest morale was at those firms with chief executives who most inspired their colleagues "to transcend their own self-interests for the sake of the collective" (de Hoogh & others, 2004). Leadership of this kind—*transformational leadership*—motivates others to identify with and commit themselves to the group's mission. Transformational leaders, many of whom are natural extraverts, articulate high standards, inspire people to share their vision, and offer personal attention (Bono & Judge, 2004). The frequent result is more engaged, trusting, and effective workers (Turner & others, 2002).

Peter Smith and Monir Tayeb (1989) compiled data from studies in India, Taiwan, and Iran indicating that effective managers—whether in coal mines, banks, or government offices—often exhibit a high degree of *both* task and social leadership. As achievement-minded people, effective managers certainly care about how well work is done, yet at the same time they are sensitive to their subordinates' needs. In one national survey of American workers, those in family-friendly organizations offering flexible-time hours reported feeling greater loyalty to their employers (Roehling & others, 2001).

Many successful businesses have also increased employee participation in making decisions, a management style common in Sweden and Japan and increasingly elsewhere (Naylor, 1990; Sundstrom & others, 1990). Although managers often think better of work they have directly supervised, studies reveal a *voice effect*: If given a chance to voice their opinion during a decision-making process, people will respond more positively to the decision (van den Bos & Spruijt, 2002). And as we noted earlier, positive engaged employees are a mark of thriving organizations.

The rags-to-riches Harley-Davidson story illustrates the potential of inviting workers to participate in decision making (Teerlink & Ozley, 2000). In 1987, the struggling company began transforming its *command-and-control* management process to a *joint-vision process*. The aim: "To push decision-making, planning, and strategizing from a handful of people at the top, down throughout the organization. We wanted

> "Good leaders don't ask more than their constituents can give, but they often ask—and get—more than their constituents intended to give or thought it was possible to give."
>
> John W. Gardner, *Excellence*, 1984

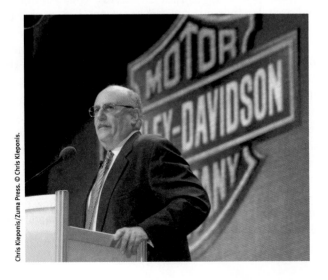

Sharing vision and decisions
As CEO, Jeffrey Bleustein helped Harley-Davidson thrive, in part by replacing the organization's command-and-control management style with one based on companywide consensus planning and decision making.

all the employees to think every day about how to improve the company," reported CEO Jeffrey Bleustein (2002). In the mid-1990s, Harley signed a cooperative agreement with its unions that included them "in decision-making in virtually every aspect of the business." Consensus decision-making can take longer, but "when the decision is made, it gets implemented quickly and the commitment is by the group," says Bleustein. The result has been more engaged workers and also more satisfied stockholders. Every $1 of Harley-Davidson stock purchased at the beginning of 1988 was worth $125 by mid-2005.

In this chapter we have seen that identifiable physiological mechanisms drive some motives, such as hunger (though learned tastes and cultural expectations matter, too). Other motives, such as achievement at work, are more obviously driven by psychological factors, such as an intrinsic quest for mastery and the external rewards of recognition. What unifies all motives is their common effect: the energizing and directing of behavior.

>> LEARNING OUTCOMES

Motivation at Work

OBJECTIVE 17 | **Discuss the importance of flow, and identify the three subfields of industrial-organizational psychology.**

People may view their work as a job, a career, or a calling. Those in the last group report the highest satisfaction—a feeling consistent with *flow*, the involved focused state of consciousness in which we have a diminished awareness of ourselves and of passing time. *Industrial-organizational (I/O) psychology* studies behavior in the workplace through the three subfields of *personnel psychology, organizational psychology,* and *human factors psychology* (discussed in Chapter 6).

OBJECTIVE 18 | **Describe how personnel psychologists help organizations with employee selection, work placement, and performance appraisal.**

Personnel psychologists work with organizations to devise selection methods for new employees, recruit and evaluate applicants, design and evaluate training programs, identify people's strengths, analyze job content, and appraise individual and organizational performance. Subjective interviews lead to quickly formed impressions, but they tend to foster the *interviewer illusion*—a feeling of overconfidence in one's intuitive ability to predict employee success. Structured interviews (which pinpoint job-relevant strengths) are better predictors because they reduce interviewers' memory distortions and biases. Checklists, graphic rating scales, and behavior rating scales are useful performance appraisal methods. Forms of bias that can affect performance appraisal are *halo errors* (judgments based on personal qualities rather than on-the-job behavior), *leniency or severity errors* (blanket judgments treating everyone too kindly or harshly), and *recency errors* (judgments based on easily remembered recent behavior).

OBJECTIVE 19 | **Define *achievement motivation,* and explain why organizations would employ an I/O psychologist to help motivate employees and foster employee satisfaction.**

Achievement motivation is the desire for significant accomplishment; for mastery of things, people, or ideas; and for attaining a high standard. Organizations turn to I/O psychologists because research shows that the most productive and engaged workers are those working in satisfying environments. Employee satisfaction also tends to translate into higher profits, higher productivity, lower turnover, and more loyal customers.

OBJECTIVE 20 | **Describe some effective management techniques.**

Effective managers focus their training on people's strengths, rather than on weak areas that may never advance to the point where they can contribute to the organization's success. They attempt to "catch the employee doing something right" and reward that behavior. Effective managers also work with employees to set specific, challenging, and measurable objectives and to outline detailed paths to achieving those goals. Leadership style should be appropriate for the people and goals involved. *Task leadership* sets standards, organizes work, and focuses attention on goals. *Social leadership* builds teamwork, mediates conflict, and offers support. Managers' personalities do matter, and some may be better suited to one leadership style than to the other, or to a combination of the two.

ASK YOURSELF: **Are you highly motivated, or not highly motivated, to achieve in school? How has this affected your academic success? How might you improve upon your own achievement levels?**

REVIEW CHAPTER 12: Motivation and Work

Test Yourself

1. While on a long road trip, you suddenly feel very lonely and want to pull over and call a loved one. But the dark, deserted stretch of road is intimidating, so you keep on driving. What motivational perspective would most easily explain this behavior and why?

2. You are traveling and have not eaten anything in eight hours. As your long-awaited favorite dish is placed in front of you, your mouth waters. Even imagining this may set your mouth to watering. What triggers this anticipatory drooling?

3. How might drive-reduction theory, arousal theory, and the evolutionary perspective explain our sexual motivation?

4. How might drive-reduction theory, arousal theory, and the evolutionary perspective explain our affiliation needs?

5. A human resources director explains to you that "I don't bother with tests or references. I can pick employees by my gut." Based on I/O research, what concerns does this raise?

Answers to the Test Yourself questions can be found in Appendix B at the end of the book.

Terms and Concepts to Remember

motivation, p. 470

instinct, p. 470

drive-reduction theory, p. 471

homeostasis, p. 471

incentive, p. 471

hierarchy of needs, p. 472

glucose, p. 475

set point, p. 476

basal metabolic rate, p. 476

anorexia nervosa, p. 478

bulimia nervosa, p. 478

sexual response cycle, p. 481

refractory period, p. 482

sexual disorder, p. 482

estrogen, p. 482

testosterone, p. 482

sexual orientation, p. 487

flow, p. 498

industrial-organizational psychology, p. 499

personnel psychology, p. 499

organizational psychology, p. 499

structured interviews, p. 502

achievement motivation, p. 504

task leadership, p. 508

social leadership, p. 508

WEB

> To continue your study and review of Motivation and Work, visit this book's Web site at www.worthpublishers.com/myers. You will find practice tests, review activities, and many interesting articles and Web links for more information on topics related to Motivation and Work.

ANOTHER VOICE ON: EMOTION

ADMIRAL DENNIS BLAIR, COMMANDER OF U.S. PACIFIC FORCES (USCINCPAC),
REMARKS AT PACIFIC ISLANDS CONFERENCE OF LEADERS, JANUARY 31, 2001, EAST-WEST CENTER, HONOLULU

On a recent trip to one of your beautiful islands . . . , I had the opportunity to take a break and go fishing, and I overheard a conversation between a Harvard businessman on vacation, and one of the local fishermen. The fisherman had a small boat with several large yellowfin tuna. . . . The businessman complimented the man on the quality of his fish, and asked how long it took to catch them. The fisherman replied only a little while. The businessman asked . . . why didn't he stay out longer and catch more fish? The fisherman said he had enough to support his family's immediate needs.

The businessman then asked, "But what do you do with the rest of your time?"

The fisherman said, "I sleep late, fish a little, play with my children, take a nap with my wife, stroll into the village each evening where I drink a beer and play the ukelele with my friends. I have a full and wonderful life."

The businessman scoffed, "I'm a Harvard MBA, and I could help you. You should spend more time fishing, and with the proceeds, you could buy a bigger boat. With the money from the bigger boat, you could buy several boats. Eventually, you'd own a fleet of fishing boats . . . . You'd make millions of dollars!"

"But what then?" asked the fisherman.

The businessman said, "Then you could retire—move to a small fishing village where you could sleep late . . . fish a little . . . play with your kids . . . take a nap with your wife . . . stroll down to the village in the evenings . . . where you could drink a beer . . . and play the ukelele with your friends!"

13 : Emotion

No one needs to tell you that feelings add color to your life, or that in times of stress they can disrupt your life or save it. Of all the species, we seem the most emotional (Hebb, 1980). More often than any other creature, we express fear, anger, sadness, joy, and love.

We all can recall times when we have been overcome with emotion. I retain a flashbulb memory for the day I went to a huge store to drop off film and brought along Peter, my toddler first-born child. As I set Peter down on his feet and prepared to complete the paperwork, a passerby warned, "You'd better be careful or you'll lose that boy!" Not more than a few breaths later, after dropping the film in the slot, I turned and found no Peter beside me.

With mild anxiety, I peered around one end of the counter. No Peter in sight. With slightly more anxiety, I peered around the other end. No Peter there, either. Now, with my heart accelerating, I circled the neighboring counters. Still no Peter anywhere. As anxiety turned to panic, I began racing up and down the store aisles. He was nowhere to be found. Apprised of my alarm, the store manager used the public-address system to ask customers to assist in looking for a missing child. Soon after, I passed the customer who had warned me. "I told you that you were going to lose him!" he said scornfully. With visions of kidnapping (strangers routinely adored that beautiful child), I braced for the possibility that my negligence had caused me to lose what I loved above all else, and—dread of all dreads—that I might have to return home and face my wife without our only child.

But then, as I passed the customer service counter yet again, there he was, having been found and returned by some obliging customer! In an instant, the arousal of dread spilled into the elation of ecstasy. Clutching my son, with tears suddenly flowing, I found myself unable to speak my thanks and stumbled out of the store awash in joy.

Where do such emotions come from? Why do we have them? What are they made of? Emotions are our body's adaptive response. They exist not to give us interesting experiences but to enhance our survival. When we face challenges, emotions focus our attention and energize our action. Our heart races. Our pace quickens. All our senses go on high alert. Receiving unexpected good news, we may find our eyes tearing. We raise our hands triumphantly. We feel exuberance and a newfound confidence.

In this chapter, we consider psychology's understanding of our emotion-related feelings, thoughts, and actions. And we'll take a close look at fear, anger, and happiness.

Theories of Emotion

OBJECTIVE 1 | Identify the three components of emotions, and contrast the James-Lange, Cannon-Bard, and two-factor theories of emotion.

As my anguished search for Peter illustrates, **emotions** are a mix of (1) physiological arousal (heart pounding), (2) expressive behaviors (quickened pace), and (3) conscious experience, including thoughts (is this a kidnapping?) and feelings (a sense of fear, and later joy). The puzzle for psychologists has been figuring out how these three pieces fit together.

■ **emotion** a response of the whole organism, involving (1) physiological arousal, (2) expressive behaviors, and (3) conscious experience.

Not only emotion, but most psychological phenomena (vision, sleep, memory, sex, and so forth) can be approached these three ways—physiologically, behaviorally, and cognitively.

There are two controversies over the interplay of our physiology, expressions, and experience in emotions. The first, a chicken-and-egg debate, is old: Does your physiological arousal precede or follow your emotional experience? (Did I first notice my heart racing and my faster step, and then feel anxious dread about losing Peter? Or did my sense of fear come first, stirring my heart and legs to respond?) The second controversy concerns the interaction between thinking and feeling: Does cognition always precede emotion? (Was I required to make a conscious appraisal of the kidnapping threat before I could react emotionally?)

Common sense tells most of us that we cry because we are sad, lash out because we are angry, tremble because we are afraid. First comes conscious awareness, then the physiological trimmings. But to pioneering psychologist William James, this commonsense view of emotion was 180 degrees out of line. According to James, "We feel sorry because we cry, angry because we strike, afraid because we tremble" (1890, p. 1066). Perhaps you can recall a time when your car skidded on slick pavement. As it careened crazily you hit your brakes and regained control. Just after the fishtail ended, you noticed your racing heart and *then,* shaking with fright, you felt the whoosh of emotion. Your feeling of fear *followed* your body's response. James' idea, also proposed by Danish physiologist Carl Lange, is called the **James-Lange theory.**

The James-Lange theory struck U.S. physiologist Walter Cannon (1871–1943) as implausible. Cannon thought the body's responses were not distinct enough to evoke the different emotions. Does a racing heart signal fear, anger, or love? Also, changes in heart rate, perspiration, and body temperature seemed too slow to trigger sudden emotion. Cannon, and later another physiologist, Philip Bard, concluded that physiological arousal and our emotional experience occur simultaneously: The emotion-triggering stimulus is routed simultaneously to the brain's cortex, causing the subjective awareness of emotion, and to the sympathetic nervous system, causing the body's arousal. This **Cannon-Bard theory** implies that your heart begins pounding *as* you experience fear; one does not cause the other.

The joys of friendship
According to the James-Lange theory, we don't just smile because we share a friend's joy. We also share the joy because we are smiling with them.

Let's check your understanding of the James-Lange and Cannon-Bard theories. Imagine that your brain could not sense your heart pounding or your stomach churning. According to each theory, how would this affect your experienced emotions?

Cannon and Bard would have expected you to experience emotions normally, because they believed emotions occur separately from (though simultaneously with) the body's arousal. James and Lange would have expected greatly diminished emotions because they believed that to experience emotion you must first perceive your body's arousal.

Stanley Schachter and Jerome Singer (1962) proposed a third theory: that our physiology and our cognitions—perceptions, memories, and interpretations—together create emotion. In their **two-factor theory,** emotions therefore have two ingredients: physical arousal and a cognitive label **(FIGURE 13.1)**. Like James and Lange, Schachter and Singer presumed that our experience of emotion grows from our awareness of our body's arousal. Yet like Cannon and Bard, Schachter and Singer also believed that emotions are physiologically similar. Thus, in their view, an emotional experience requires a conscious interpretation of the arousal.

To assess the James-Lange, Cannon-Bard, and two factor theories, we'll consider in the next section the answers researchers have gleaned to three questions:

- Does physiological arousal always precede emotional experience?
- Are different emotions marked by distinct physiological responses?
- What is the connection between what we *think* and how we *feel*?

■ **James-Lange theory** the theory that our experience of emotion is our awareness of our physiological responses to emotion-arousing stimuli.

■ **Cannon-Bard theory** the theory that an emotion-arousing stimulus simultaneously triggers (1) physiological responses and (2) the subjective experience of emotion.

■ **two-factor theory** Schachter-Singer's theory that to experience emotion one must (1) be physically aroused and (2) cognitively label the arousal.

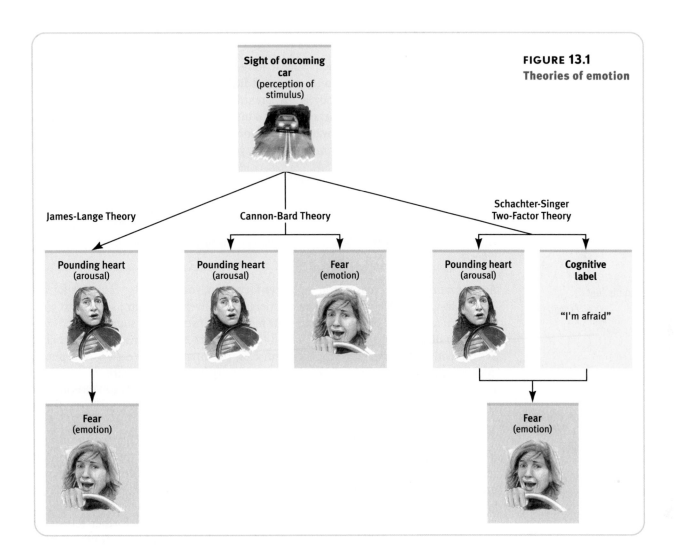

FIGURE 13.1
Theories of emotion

>> LEARNING OUTCOMES

Theories of Emotion

OBJECTIVE **1** | Identify the three components of emotions, and contrast the James-Lange, Cannon-Bard, and two-factor theories of emotion.

The three components of emotion are (1) physiological arousal, (2) expressive behaviors, and (3) conscious experience. William James and Carl Lange proposed that we feel emotion *after* we notice our physiological responses. Walter Cannon and Philip Bard believed that we feel emotion *at the same time* that our bodies respond. Stanley Schachter and Jerome Singer's two-factor theory of emotion focused on the interplay of thinking and feeling, not on the timing of feelings. They proposed that emotions have two components, physical arousal and a cognitive label.

ASK YOURSELF: Can you remember a time when you began to feel upset or uneasy and only later labeled those feelings?

Embodied Emotion

Whether you are eagerly anticipating a long-awaited vacation, falling in love, or grieving the death of a loved one, you need little convincing that emotions involve the body. Feeling without a body is like breathing without lungs. Some physical responses are easy to notice, others—many taking place at the level of neurons in your brain—happen without your awareness. As you hear a motorcycle slowing down behind you on a dark street, your muscles tense, your stomach develops butterflies, your mouth becomes dry.

Emotions and the Autonomic Nervous System

OBJECTIVE 2 | Describe the role of the autonomic nervous system during emotional arousal.

"Fear lends wings to his feet."
Virgil, *Aeneid*, 19 B.C.

As your *autonomic nervous system* mobilizes for action, your body also responds for action in less noticeable ways. To provide energy, your liver pours extra sugar into your bloodstream. To help burn the sugar, your respiration increases to supply needed oxygen. Your digestion slows, diverting blood from your internal organs to your muscles. With blood sugar driven into the large muscles, running becomes easier. Your pupils dilate, letting in more light. To cool your stirred-up body, you perspire. If wounded, your blood would clot more quickly. After your next crisis, think of this: Without any conscious effort, your body's response to danger was wonderfully coordinated and adaptive—preparing you to fight or flee.

One explanation of sudden death caused by a voodoo "curse" is that the terrified person's parasympathetic nervous system, which calms the body, overreacts to the extreme arousal by slowing the heart to a stop (Seligman, 1974).

As we learned in Chapter 2, the autonomic nervous system controls our arousal **(FIGURE 13.2)**. Its *sympathetic division* directs the adrenal glands atop the kidneys to release the stress hormones epinephrine (adrenaline) and norepinephrine (noradrenaline). This hormonal surge increases heart rate, blood pressure, and blood sugar levels. When the crisis passes, the parasympathetic neural centers become active, calming the body. Even after the *parasympathetic division* inhibits further release of stress hormones, those already in the bloodstream linger awhile, so arousal diminishes gradually.

FIGURE 13.2
Emotional arousal
Emotional arousal involves autonomic nervous system activation.

Sympathetic division (arousing)	Autonomic Nervous System Controls Physiological Arousal	Parasympathetic division (calming)
Pupils dilate	EYES	Pupils contract
Decreases	SALIVATION	Increases
Perspires	SKIN	Dries
Increases	RESPIRATION	Decreases
Accelerates	HEART	Slows
Inhibits	DIGESTION	Activates
Secrete stress hormones	ADRENAL GLANDS	Decrease secretion of stress hormones

Arousal and Performance

OBJECTIVE 3 | Discuss the relationship between arousal and performance.

Prolonged physical arousal, produced by sustained stress, taxes the body (more on this in Chapter 17). Yet in many situations arousal is adaptive. Too little arousal (say, sleepiness) can be as disruptive as extremely high levels. When you're taking an exam, it pays to be moderately aroused—alert but not trembling with nervousness.

Although we usually perform best when we feel moderately aroused, the level of arousal for optimal performance varies for different tasks. With easy or well-learned tasks, peak performance comes with relatively high arousal. With more difficult or unrehearsed tasks, optimal arousal is somewhat lower **(FIGURE 13.3)**. Runners, who are performing a well-learned task, usually achieve their peak performances when highly aroused by competition. Basketball players shooting free throws—a less automatic skill—may not perform quite as well if a packed fieldhouse makes them hyperaroused (Sokoll & Mynatt, 1984). Likewise, students who feel great anxiety during exams perform more poorly than those equally able but more confident. Teaching anxious students how to relax before an exam often enables them to perform better (Hembree, 1988).

FIGURE 13.3
Arousal and performance
Performance peaks at lower levels of arousal for difficult tasks, and at higher levels for easy or well-learned tasks.

Physiological Similarities Among Specific Emotions

OBJECTIVE 4 | Name three emotions that involve similar physiological arousal.

Imagine conducting an experiment measuring the physiological responses of emotion. In each of four rooms, you have someone watching a movie: In the first, the person is viewing a horror show; in the second, an anger-provoking film; in the third, a sexually arousing film; in the fourth, an utterly boring movie. From the control center you monitor each person's physiological responses, measuring perspiration, breathing, and heart rates. Do you think you could tell who is frightened? Who is angry? Who is sexually aroused? Who is bored?

With training, you could probably pick out the bored viewer. But discerning physiological differences among fear, anger, and sexual arousal would be much more difficult (Cacioppo & others, 1997; Zillmann, 1986).

To you and me, sexual arousal, fear, and anger nevertheless *feel* different. If sexually stimulated, you will experience a genital response. If afraid, you may feel a clutching, sinking sensation in your chest and a knot in your stomach. If angry, you may feel "hot under the collar" and experience a pressing inner tension. And, despite similar arousal, fear and anger not only feel different,

> "No one ever told me that grief felt so much like fear. I am not afraid, but the sensation is like being afraid. The same fluttering in the stomach, the same restlessness, the yawning. I keep on swallowing."
> C. S. Lewis, *A Grief Observed*, 1961

M. Grecco/Stock, Boston

Emotional arousal
Elated excitement and panicky fear involve similar physiological arousal. That allows us to flip rapidly between the two emotions.

they also *look* different. People may appear "paralyzed with fear" or "ready to explode." So, does research pinpoint any distinct physiological or brain pattern indicators of each emotion? Sometimes. Read on.

Physiological Differences Among Specific Emotions

OBJECTIVE 5 | Describe some physiological and brain pattern indicators of specific emotions.

The finger temperatures and hormone secretions that accompany fear and rage do sometimes differ (Ax, 1953; Levenson, 1992). And, though fear and joy can prompt similar increased heart rate, they stimulate different facial muscles. During fear, brow muscles tense. During joy, muscles in the cheek and under the eye pull into a smile (Witvliet & Vrana, 1995).

Emotions differ much more in the brain circuits they use (Kalin, 1993; Panksepp, 1982). Observers watching (and subtly mimicking) fearful faces show more amygdala brain activity than do those watching angry faces (Whalen & others, 2001). You may recall the power of the amygdala from Chapter 2, where we saw that stimulating one area of a cat's amygdala makes it pull back in terror at the sight of a mouse. Stimulate another amygdala area and the cat will look enraged—pupils dilated, fur and tail erect, claws out, hissing furiously.

Emotions also activate different areas of the brain's cortex. Experiencing negative emotions such as disgust, people show more activity in the right prefrontal cortex than in the left. Depression-prone people, and those with generally negative personalities also show more right frontal activity (Harmon-Jones, Abramson, & others, 2002). One man, having lost part of his right frontal lobe in brain surgery, became (his not-unhappy wife reported) less irritable and more affectionate (Goleman, 1995). My father, after a right-hemisphere stroke at age 92, lived the last two years of his life with happy gratitude and nary a complaint or negative emotion.

When people experience positive moods—when they are enthusiastic, energized, and happy—brain scans and EEG recordings reveal more left frontal lobe activity. People with positive personalities—exuberant infants and alert, energetic, and persistently goal-directed adults—also show more activity in the left frontal lobe than in the right (Davidson, 2000, 2003; Urry & others, 2004). Indeed, the more a person's baseline frontal lobe activity tilts left, the more upbeat the person typically is. (When you're happy and you know it, your brain will surely show it.)

The left frontal lobe's rich supply of dopamine receptors may help explain why a peppy left hemisphere predicts a perky disposition. A neural pathway that increases dopamine levels runs from the frontal lobes to a nearby cluster of neurons, the *nucleus accumbens*. This small region lights up when people experience natural or drug-induced pleasures. In case studies, electrical stimulation of the nucleus accumbens of depressed patients has triggered smiling, laughter, and giddy euphoria (Okun & others, 2004).

To return to our assessment of the James-Lange, Cannon-Bard, and two-factor theories of emotion, we have seen that emotions as varied as fear, joy, and anger involve a similar general autonomic arousal (as in similar heart rate). But we have also seen that real, if subtle, physiological and brain differences help explain why we experience them so differently. As long as the evidence suggested that our physiological reactions to different emotions were much the same, the James-Lange assumption that we experience our emotions through differing body states seemed improbable. But this new evidence showing subtle physiological distinctions among the emotions makes the James-Lange theory plausible.

In 1966, a young man named Charles Whitman killed his wife and mother and then climbed to the top of a tower at the University of Texas and shot 38 people. An autopsy later revealed a tumor pressing against his amygdala, which may have contributed to his violence.

Given the physical indicators of emotion, might we, like Pinocchio, give some telltale sign whenever we lie? See Thinking Critically About: Lie Detection on page 520.

The James-Lange theory also finds support in observations of people with severed spinal cords. Psychologist George Hohmann (1966) interviewed 25 soldiers who suffered such injuries in World War II. He asked them to recall emotion-arousing incidents that occurred before and after their spinal injuries. Those with lower-spine injuries, who had lost sensation only in their legs, reported little change in their emotions. Those who could feel nothing below the neck reported a considerable decrease in emotional intensity (as James and Lange would have expected). The anger, as one man confessed, "just doesn't have the heat to it that it used to. It's a mental kind of anger." But emotions expressed mostly in body areas above the neck are felt more intensely by those with high spinal-cord injury. Virtually all the men Hohmann interviewed reported increases in weeping, lumps in the throat, and getting choked up when saying good-bye, worshipping, or watching a touching movie.

Such evidence has breathed new life into the James-Lange theory and has led some researchers to view feelings as "mostly shadows" of our bodily responses and behaviors (Damasio, 2003). But most researchers agree with Cannon and Bard that our experienced emotions also involve cognition (Averill, 1993). Whether we fear the man behind us on the dark street depends entirely on whether we interpret his actions as threatening or friendly. So, with James and Lange we can say that our body's reactions are an important ingredient of emotion. And with Cannon and Bard we can say that there is more to the experience of emotion than reading our body's responses.

"Every moment is more intense."
Christopher Reeve (1952–2004) after his paralysis

Cognition and Emotion

What is the connection between what we *think* and how we *feel*? Which is the chicken and which the egg?

We know that our emotions affect our thinking. When we *feel* like singing "Oh, what a beautiful morning!" we *see* the world and the people around us as wonderful. If the following day we find ourselves singing the blues, we perceive the same world and the same people as less than wonderful.

Can we experience emotion apart from thinking? Or do we become what we think? The issue has practical implications for self-improvement. Can we change our emotions by changing our thinking?

Cognition Can Define Emotion

OBJECTIVE 6 | Explain how the spillover effect influences our experience of emotions.

Sometimes our arousal response to one event spills over into our response to the next event. Imagine arriving home after an invigorating run and finding a message that you got a longed-for job. With arousal lingering from the run, would you feel more elated than if you received this news after awakening from a nap?

To find out whether this *spillover effect* exists, Stanley Schachter and Jerome Singer (1962) aroused college men with injections of the hormone epinephrine. Picture yourself as one of their participants: After receiving the injection, you go to a waiting room, where you find yourself with another person (actually an accomplice of the experimenters) who is acting either euphoric or irritated. As you observe this person, you begin to feel your heart race, your body flush, and your breathing become more rapid. If told to expect these effects from the injection, what would you feel? Schachter's and Singer's volunteers felt little emotion—because they attributed their arousal to the drug. But if told the injection would produce no effects, what would

The spillover effect
Arousal from a soccer match (top photo) or a political protest (bottom photo) can fuel anger, which can descend into rioting or other violent confrontations.

LIE DETECTION

The creators and users of the *lie detector,* or **polygraph** have believed that our physical indicators of emotion can provide a telltale equivalent of Pinocchio's nose. Polygraphs do not literally detect lies, and their accuracy has been increasingly questioned as our understanding of physiological measures of emotion has grown.

Rather, they measure several physical responses that accompany emotion, such as changes in breathing, cardiovascular activity, and perspiration. While you try to relax, an examiner monitors these responses as you answer questions. Some items, called control questions, aim to make anyone a little nervous. If asked, "In the last 20 years, have you ever taken something that didn't belong to you?" many people will tell a white lie and say no, causing arousal the polygraph will detect. If your physiological reactions to critical questions ("Did you ever steal anything from your previous employer?") are weaker than to control questions, the examiner infers you are telling the truth. The assumption has been that only a thief becomes agitated when denying a theft.

Can polygraph tests like this identify liars?

To learn more, read on.

But there are two problems: First, as you have seen, our physiological arousal is much the same from one emotion to another—anxiety, irritation, and guilt all prompt similar physiological reactivity. Second, these tests err about one-third of the time, especially when innocent people respond with heightened tension to the accusations implied by the relevant questions **(FIGURE 13.4)**. Many rape victims, for example, "fail" lie detector tests when reacting emotionally while telling the truth about their assailant (Lykken, 1991). Good advice, then, would be never to take a lie detector test if you are innocent.

A 2002 U.S. National Academy of Sciences report noted that "no spy has ever been caught [by] using the polygraph." It is not for lack of trying. The FBI, CIA, and Departments of Defense and Energy in the United States have spent millions of dollars testing tens of thousands of employees. Meanwhile Aldrich Ames, who enjoyed an unexplained lavish life-style as a Russian spy within the CIA, went undetected. Ames "took scores of polygraph tests and passed them all," notes Robert Park (1999). "Nobody thought to investigate the source of his sudden wealth—after all, he was passing the lie detector tests." The truth is, lie detectors can lie.

In a recent survey, more than 9 in 10 psychophysiologists and research psychologists agreed that savvy criminals and spies could beat the test by augmenting their arousal to control questions, such as by biting their tongues (Iacono & Lykken, 1997). Serial rapist and killer Gary Ridgway, who admitted to 48 Seattle-area murders ("I killed so many women I have a hard time keeping them straight"), was an

■ **polygraph** a machine, commonly used in attempts to detect lies, that measures several of the physiological responses accompanying emotion (such as perspiration and cardiovascular and breathing changes).

you feel? Perhaps you would react, as another group of participants did, by "catching" the apparent emotion of the person you are with—becoming happy if the accomplice is acting euphoric, and testy if the accomplice is acting irritated.

This discovery—that a stirred-up state can be experienced as one emotion or another very different one, depending on how we interpret and label it—has been replicated in dozens of experiments. Insult people who have just been aroused by pedaling an exercise bike or watching rock videos and they will find it easy to misattribute their arousal to the provocation. Their feelings of anger will be greater than those of people who were similarly provoked but not previously aroused. Likewise, sexually aroused people react with more hostility in anger-provoking situations. And, vice versa—the arousal that lingers after an intense argument or a frightening experience may intensify sexual passion (Palace, 1995). Just as the Schachter-Singer two-factor theory predicts, arousal + label = emotion. As we have seen, emotional arousal is not as undifferentiated as Schachter and Singer believed. But arousal—from emotions as diverse as anger, fear, and sexual excitement—can indeed spill from one emotion to another (Reisenzein, 1983; Sinclair & others, 1994; Zillmann, 1986). *The point to remember:* Arousal fuels emotion; cognition channels it.

early suspect but had been cleared after passing a polygraph test (Johnson, 2003).

A more effective approach to lie detection uses the *guilty knowledge test,* which assesses a suspect's physiological responses to crime-scene details known only to the police and the guilty person (Ben-Shakhar & Elaad, 2003). If a camera and computer had been stolen, for example, presumably only one guilty of the crime would react strongly to the specific brand name of these items. Given enough such specific probes, an innocent person will seldom be wrongly accused.

Several twenty-first century research teams are exploring new ways to nab liars. Some are developing computer software that compares the language of truth-tellers and liars (who use fewer first-person pronouns and more negative-emotion words). Other software analyzes facial microexpressions linked with lying (Adelson, 2004; Newman & others, 2003). Psychologist Paul

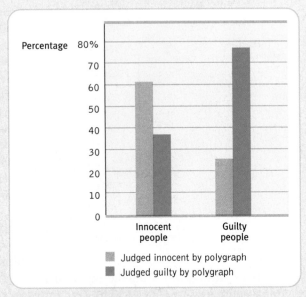

FIGURE 13.4

How often do lie detectors lie?
Benjamin Kleinmuntz and Julian Szucko (1984) had polygraph experts study the polygraph data of 50 theft suspects who later confessed to being guilty and 50 suspects whose innocence was later established by someone's confession. Had the polygraph experts been the judges, more than one-third of the innocent would have been declared guilty, and almost one-fourth of the guilty would have been declared innocent.

Ekman (2003) runs training seminars that teach law enforcement officers to detect the fleeting signals of deceit in facial expressions (see page 527).

Other researchers are going straight to the seat of deceit—the brain. EEG recordings have revealed a brain wave that indicates familiarity with a crime scene, and fMRI scans have shown liars' brains lighting up in places that honest people's brains do not (Faro & others, 2004; Farwell & Smith, 2001; Langleben & others, 2002, 2005). Given the cumbersome and expensive nature of such assessments, researchers are also testing a portable "near-infrared light" that similarly detects brain blood-flow patterns associated with lying (Izzetoglu & others, 2003). Pinocchio's giveaway signal of lying may be not the length of his nose, but rather the telltale activity in places such as his left frontal lobe and anterior cingulate cortex. Skeptics, however, note that we are a long way from commercial reality (Illes, 2004).

Cognition Does Not Always Precede Emotion

OBJECTIVE **7** | Distinguish the two alternative pathways that sensory stimuli may travel when triggering an emotional response.

To experience an emotion, must we first label our arousal? Sometimes we experience unlabeled emotion. Imagine receiving some unsettling news. There's a deadline you've forgotten about, or you discover that you've hurt someone's feelings. As the ongoing conversation distracts your attention, you lose awareness of the bad news. Yet as its bodily effects linger, the now-unlabeled feeling still churns. You feel a little bad. You know there's a reason. But for the moment you can't put your finger on it. Robert Zajonc (pronounced ZI-yence; 1980, 1984a) has contended that we actually have many emotional reactions apart from, or even before, our interpretations of a situation. In earlier chapters, we noted that when people repeatedly view stimuli flashed too briefly for them to perceive and recall, they nevertheless come to prefer those stimuli. Without being consciously aware of having seen the stimuli, they rather like them. A subliminally flashed smiling or angry face can also prime us to

Can you recall liking something or someone immediately, without knowing why?

(a) The speedy low road

(b) The thinking high road

FIGURE 13.5

The brain's shortcut for emotions
Sensory input may be routed (a) directly to the amygdala (via the thalamus) for an instant emotional reaction and (b) to the cortex for analysis.

The amygdala, notes biologist Robert Sapolsky (2003), "is also central to aggression, underlining the fact that aggression can be rooted in fear—an observation that can explain much sociopolitical behavior."

"Oh! ye'll take the high road and I'll take the low road, And I'll be in Scotland afore ye."
Bonnie Banks O' Loch Lomond

feel better or worse about a follow-up stimulus (Murphy & others, 1995). In one set of experiments, thirsty people drank about 50 percent more fruit-flavored drink after viewing a subliminally flashed (thus unperceived) happy rather than neutral face (Berridge & Winkielman, 2003). If flashed an angry face, they drank substantially less. Research on neurological processes shows how we can experience emotion unconsciously, before cognition.

Like speedy reflexes that operate apart from the brain's thinking cortex, some emotions take the "low road," via neural pathways that bypass the cortex (which offers the alternative "high road" pathway). One low-road pathway runs from the eye or ear via the thalamus to the *amygdala,* an emotional control center **(FIGURE 13.5)**. This amygdala shortcut, bypassing the cortex, enables our greased-lightning emotional response before our intellect intervenes. So speedy is the amygdala response that we may be unaware of what's transpired (Dimberg & others, 2000). In one fascinating experiment, Paul Whalen and his colleagues (2004) used fMRI scans to observe the amygdala's response to subliminally presented fearful eyes **(FIGURE 13.6)**. Compared with a control condition that presented the whites of happy eyes, the fearful eyes triggered increased amygdala activity (despite no one's being aware of seeing them).

The amygdala sends more neural projections up to the cortex than it receives back. This makes it easier for our feelings to hijack our thinking than for our thinking to rule our feelings, note Joseph LeDoux and Jorge Armony (1999). In the forest, we jump at the sound of rustling bushes nearby, leaving the cortex to decide later whether the sound was made by a predator or just the wind. Such an experience supports Zajonc's belief that *some* of our emotional reactions involve no deliberate thinking and that cognition is not always necessary for emotion. The heart is not always subject to the mind.

Emotion researcher Richard Lazarus (1991, 1998) conceded that our brains process and react to vast amounts of information without our conscious awareness, and he willingly granted that some emotional responses do not require *conscious*

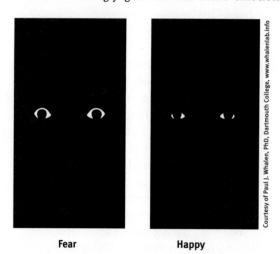

FIGURE 13.6
The brain's sensitivity to threats
Even when fearful eyes (left) were flashed too briefly for people to consciously perceive them, fMRI scans revealed that their hypervigilant amygdala was alerted (Whalen & others, 2004).

Fear

Happy

Courtesy of Paul J. Whalen, PhD, Dartmouth College, www.whalenlab.info

thinking. But, he noted, even instantaneously felt emotions require some sort of cognitive appraisal of the situation; otherwise, how would we *know* what we are reacting to? The appraisal may be effortless and we may not be conscious of it, but it is still a mental function. Emotions arise when we *appraise* an event as beneficial or harmful to our well-being, whether we truly know it is or not. We appraise the sound of the rustling bushes as the presence of a threat. Later, we learn that it was "just the wind."

Complex emotions such as guilt, happiness, and love most clearly arise from our interpretations and expectations. Highly emotional people are intense partly because of their interpretations. They may *personalize* events as being somehow directed at them, and they may *generalize* their experiences by blowing single incidents out of proportion (Larsen & others, 1987). We may attribute a bad exam grade to an unfair exam and feel angry, to our own inability and feel depressed, or to lack of preparation and feel accepting (Weiner, 1985).

To sum up, as Zajonc and LeDoux have demonstrated, some emotional responses—especially simple likes, dislikes, and fears—involve no conscious thinking **(FIGURE 13.7)**. We may fear the spider, even if we "know" it is harmless. Such responses are difficult to alter by changing our thinking.

Other emotions—including moods such as depression and complex feelings such as hatred and love—are, as Lazarus, Schachter, and Singer predicted, greatly affected by our interpretations, memories, and expectations. For these emotions, as you will see in Chapter 16, learning to *think* more positively about ourselves and the world around us helps us *feel* better.

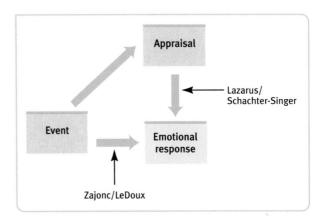

FIGURE 13.7

Two routes to emotion

Zajonc and LeDoux emphasize that some emotional responses are immediate, before any conscious appraisal. Lazarus, Schachter, and Singer emphasized that our appraisal and labeling of events also determines our emotional responses.

>> Learning Outcomes

Embodied Emotion

OBJECTIVE 2 | Describe the role of the autonomic nervous system during emotional arousal.

The autonomic nervous system (ANS) controls arousal. Its sympathetic division mobilizes us for action by directing adrenals to release stress hormones, which in turn increase heart rate, blood pressure, and blood sugar levels, and by triggering other defensive physical reactions. The parasympathetic division calms us after a crisis has passed, though arousal diminishes gradually.

OBJECTIVE 3 | Discuss the relationship between arousal and performance.

Very high or very low arousal can be disruptive. We perform best when arousal is moderate, though this varies with the difficulty of the task. For easy or well-learned tasks, best performance is linked to high arousal. For difficult tasks, performance peaks at lower levels.

OBJECTIVE 4 | Name three emotions that involve similar physiological arousal.

We display similar physiological arousal during fear, anger, and sexual arousal. Observers would have trouble discerning these states from measuring physiological responses alone, but our emotional experiences (and sometimes our facial expressions) differ during these three states.

OBJECTIVE 5 | Describe some physiological and brain pattern indicators of specific emotions.

Using sophisticated equipment, researchers have found linkages between some emotions and minute movements of muscles in the brow (during fear) and cheeks (during joy) and under the eyes (during joy). Brain scans also show increased activity in the amygdala during fear. Differences also appear in the brain's cortical areas. Negative emotions (disgust, for example) trigger more activity in the right prefrontal cortex, whereas positive moods (enthusiasm, for example) register in the left frontal lobe, which has a rich supply of dopamine receptors.

OBJECTIVE 6 | Explain how the spillover effect influences our experience of emotions.

The *spillover effect* occurs when our arousal from one event influences our response to other events. Although not completely undifferentiated, emotional arousal is sometimes general enough to require us to define the emotion we are experiencing. Arousal fuels emotion; cognition channels it.

OBJECTIVE 7 | Distinguish the two alternative pathways that sensory stimuli may travel when triggering an emotional response.

Emotional responses are immediate when sensory input goes directly to the amygdala via the thalamus, bypassing the cortex, triggering a rapid reaction that is often outside our conscious awareness. Responses to complex emotions (such as guilt, happiness, and love) require interpretation and are routed along the slower route to the cortex for analysis.

ASK YOURSELF: Can you think of a recent time when you noticed your body's reactions to an emotionally charged situation, such as a difficult social setting or perhaps even a test or game you were worrying about in advance? Did you perceive the situation as a challenge or a threat? How well did you do?

Expressed Emotion

There is a simpler method of deciphering people's emotions: We read their bodies, listen to their tone of voice, and study their faces. People's expressive behavior reveals their emotion. Does this nonverbal language vary with culture, or is it universal? And do our expressions influence our experienced emotions?

Nonverbal Communication

OBJECTIVE 8 | Describe some of the factors that affect our ability to decipher nonverbal cues.

All of us communicate nonverbally as well as verbally. To Westerners, a firm handshake immediately conveys an outgoing, expressive personality (Chaplin & others, 2000). With a gaze, an averted glance, or a stare we can communicate intimacy, submission, or dominance (Kleinke, 1986). Among those passionately in love, gazing into one another's eyes is typically prolonged and mutual (Rubin, 1970). Joan Kellerman, James Lewis, and James Laird (1989) wondered if intimate gazes would stir such feelings between strangers. To find out, they asked unacquainted male-female pairs to gaze intently for two minutes either at one another's hands or into one another's eyes. After separating, the eye-gazers reported feeling a tingle of attraction and affection. What if you do not want people to know how you feel, or if you do not even want to feel that way in the first place? Can we suppress our emotional expressions? Sometimes. But as Jane Richards and James Gross (2000) discovered, suppressing expression comes at a cost. Compared with those who simply watched a distressing film, those who diverted mental energy and attention into suppressing their emotional expressions remembered its details less well.

Most of us are good enough at reading nonverbal cues to decipher the emotions in an old silent film. We are especially good at detecting nonverbal threats. When hearing emotions conveyed in another language, people most readily detect anger (Scherer & others, 2001). When viewing subliminally flashed words, we more often sense the presence of a negative word, such as *snake* or *bomb* (Dijksterhuis & Aarts, 2003). In a crowd of faces, a single angry face **(FIGURE 13.8)** will "pop out" faster than a single happy one (Fox & others, 2000; Hansen & Hansen, 1988).

By exposing different parts of emotion-laden faces, Robert Kestenbaum (1992) discovered that we read fear and anger mostly from the eyes, and happiness from the mouth. Fleeting *changes* in expression also help us read a face (Ambadar & others, 2005). Some of us are more sensitive than others to such cues. Robert Rosenthal, Judith

"Your face, my thane, is as a book where men may read strange matters."
Lady Macbeth to her husband, in William Shakespeare's *Macbeth*

Injected as part of the war on wrinkles, Botox paralyzes facial muscles that create wrinkles, allowing the overlying skin to relax and smooth. By erasing the subtle expressions of frown lines or twinkling eyes, might this cosmetic procedure hide subtle emotions?

FIGURE 13.8
Radar for threats: An angry face pops out
Our emotion-detecting radar excels at detecting threats, and thus an angry face. Using stimuli such as these, Arne Öhman and his Stockholm colleagues (2001) found that people more speedily detect an angry face than a happy one. In other "Where's Waldo?"-like experiments, people more readily spotted images of threat-relevant snakes than of flowers (Öhman & others, 2001).

Used by permission of S. D. Pollak, D. J. Kistler and the National Academy of Sciences

FIGURE 13.9

Experience influences how we perceive emotions

Shown one of the morphed middle faces, evenly mixing fear or sadness with anger, physically abused children were more likely than nonabused children to perceive the face as angry (Pollak & Kistler, 2002; Pollak & Tolley-Schell, 2003).

Hall, and their colleagues (1979) discovered this by showing hundreds of people brief film clips of portions of a person's emotionally expressive face or body, sometimes accompanied by a garbled voice. For example, after a 2-second scene revealing only the face of an upset woman, the researchers would ask whether the woman was criticizing someone for being late or was talking about her divorce. Rosenthal and Hall reported that, given such "thin slices," some people are much better than others at detecting emotion. Introverts tend to do better at reading others' emotions, although extraverts are themselves easier to read (Ambady & others, 1995).

Experience can sensitize us to particular emotions. Shown a series of faces that morphed from sadness or fear to anger, physically abused children are much quicker than other children to see anger **(FIGURE 13.9)**. Shown a face that is 60 percent fear and 40 percent anger, they are as likely to perceive anger as fear. Their perceptions become sensitively attuned to glimmers of danger signals that nonabused children miss.

Gender, Emotion, and Nonverbal Behavior

OBJECTIVE 9 | Describe some gender differences in perceiving and communicating emotions.

Is women's intuition, as so many believe, superior to men's? Consider: As Jackie Larsen left her Grand Marais, Minnesota, church prayer group one April 2001 morning, she encountered Christopher Bono, a clean-cut, well-mannered youth. Bono's car had broken down, and he said he was looking for a ride to meet friends in Thunder Bay. When Bono later appeared in Larsen's shop, where she had promised to help him phone his friends, she felt a pain in her stomach. Intuitively sensing that something was very wrong with this young man, she insisted that they talk outside on the sidewalk. "I said, 'I am a mother and I have to talk to you like a mother. . . . I can tell by your manners that you have a nice mother.'" At the mention of his mother, Bono's eyes fixed on her. "I don't know where my mother is," he said.

As the conversation ended, Larsen directed Bono back to the church to meet the pastor. She also called the police and suggested that they trace his license plates. The car was registered to his mother in southern Illinois. When police went to her apartment, they found blood all over and Lucia Bono dead in the bathtub. Christopher Bono, 16, was charged with first-degree murder (Biggs, 2001).

Was it a coincidence that Larsen, who saw through Bono's calm exterior, was a woman? Some psychologists would say no. In her analysis of 125 studies of sensitivity to nonverbal cues, Judith Hall (1984, 1987) discerned that women generally surpass men at reading people's emotional cues. Women's nonverbal sensitivity also gives them an edge in spotting lies (DePaulo, 1994). And women have surpassed men in discerning whether a male-female couple is a genuine romantic couple or a posed phony couple, and in discerning which of two people in a photo is the other's supervisor (Barnes & Sternberg, 1989).

Women's nonverbal sensitivity helps explain their greater emotional literacy. Invited by Lisa Feldman Barrett and her colleagues (2000) to describe how they would feel in certain situations, men described simpler emotional reactions. You might like to try this yourself: Ask some people how they might feel when saying good-bye to

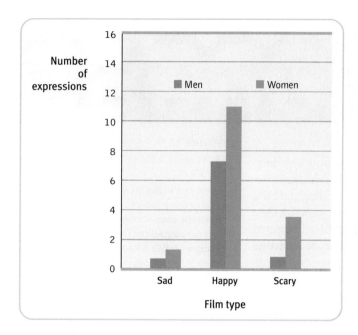

FIGURE 13.10

Gender and expressiveness

Although male and female students did not differ dramatically in self-reported emotions or physiological responses while viewing emotional films, the women's faces *showed* much more emotion. (From Kring & Gordon, 1998.)

friends after graduation. Barrett's work suggests you are more likely to hear men say, simply, "I'll feel bad," and to hear women express more complex emotions: "It will be bittersweet; I'll feel both happy and sad."

Women's skill at decoding others' emotions may also contribute to their greater emotional responsiveness in both positive and negative situations (Grossman & Wood, 1993; Sprecher & Sedikides, 1993; Stoppard & Gruchy, 1993). In studies of 23,000 people from 26 cultures around the world, women more than men reported themselves open to feelings (Costa & others, 2001). That helps explain the extremely strong perception that emotionality is "more true of women"—a perception expressed by nearly 100 percent of 18- to 29-year-old Americans (Newport, 2001).

When surveyed, women are also far more likely than men to describe themselves as empathic. If you have *empathy*, you identify with others and imagine what it must be like to walk in their shoes. You rejoice with those who rejoice and weep with those who weep. Physiological measures of empathy, such as one's heart rate while seeing another's distress, reveal a much smaller gender gap than is reported in surveys (Eisenberg & Lennon, 1983). Nevertheless, females are more likely to *express* empathy—to cry and to report distress when observing someone in distress. Ann Kring and Albert Gordon (1998) observed this gender difference in videotapes of men and women students watching film clips that were sad (children with a dying parent), happy (slapstick comedy), or frightening (a man nearly falling off the ledge of a tall building). As **FIGURE 13.10** shows, the women reacted more visibly to each film type. Women also tend to experience emotional events (such as viewing pictures of mutilation) more deeply—with more brain activation in areas sensitive to emotion—and then to remember the scenes better three weeks later (Canli & others, 2002).

In another exploration of gender and facial expression, Harold Hill and Alan Johnston (2001) animated an image of an average head with expressions (smirks, head tosses, raised eyebrows) that had been digitally captured from the faces of London University students as they read a joke. Despite having no anatomical clues to gender, observers could usually detect gender in the telltale expressions.

Gender differences also appear in the emotions women and men express best. After asking students to recall and talk about times when they were happy, sad, and angry, Erik Coats and Robert Feldman (1996) showed silent 5-second videos of the students' recollections to other participants acting as judges. Nearly two-thirds of the time, the judges correctly discerned women's recall of being happy, but they were able to spot happy recollections less than half the time when observing men. Men, however, slightly surpassed women in conveying their anger.

Detecting and Computing Emotion

OBJECTIVE 10 | Discuss the research on reading and misreading facial and behavioral indicators of emotion.

Hard-to-control facial muscles reveal signs of emotions you may be trying to conceal. Lifting just the inner part of your eyebrows, which few people do consciously, reveals distress or worry. Eyebrows raised and pulled together signal fear. Activated muscles under the eyes and raised cheeks suggest a natural smile. A feigned smile, such as one we make for a photographer, often continues for more than 4 or 5 seconds. Most authentic expressions have faded by that time. Feigned smiles are also switched on and off more abruptly than is a genuine happy smile (Bugental, 1986).

Most people find it difficult to detect deceiving expressions. In one digest of 186 studies of discerning lies from truths, people were just 54 percent accurate—barely better than a coin toss (Bond & DePaulo, 2005). Can we learn how to better detect deceit? Paul Ekman and Maureen O'Sullivan (1991) found that by teaching researchers to watch for telltale signs of lying, such as a rise in voice pitch, they could boost accuracy rates. They had university students watch either a nature film or an upsetting gruesome film. Regardless, the students were instructed to talk and act as if they were watching and enjoying the nature film. Training enabled the researchers to discern lying versus truth-telling with 86 percent accuracy. Using our intuition, could the rest of us do as well? Not likely. Ekman and O'Sullivan challenged 39 college students, 67 psychiatrists, 110 court judges, 126 police officers, and 90 federal polygraphers to spot the liars. All five groups' guesses were, as we noted from other research, near chance (50 percent). Only a sixth group of experienced crowd-scanners—U.S. Secret Service agents—beat chance. But even they were only 64 percent correct.

In a follow-up study, the Ekman team (1999) found three more groups of skilled lie-catchers. When viewing videotapes of people stating their opinions—or the opposite of their opinions—on issues such as the death penalty, federal law officers (mostly CIA agents) spotted the liars 73 percent of the time. Clinical psychologists interested in lying research did so 68 percent of the time, and street-smart Los Angeles County sheriff's interrogators scored an almost equal 67 percent. Experienced British police interrogators exhibit similar accuracy (Mann & others, 2004). With experience—trained intuition—people can often catch the liar's leaking microexpressions of guilt, despair, and fear.

When people aren't seeking to deceive us, we do much better. As we noted earlier, our brains are rather amazing detectors of subtle expressions. Elisha Babad, Frank Bernieri, and Robert Rosenthal (1991) discovered just *how* amazing after videotaping teachers talking to unseen schoolchildren. A mere 10-second clip of either the teacher's voice or face provided enough clues for both young and old viewers to determine whether the teacher liked and admired the child he or she was addressing. Teachers may think they can conceal their feelings and stay objective, but their students can sense what their expressive tones and gestures reveal.

The growing awareness that we communicate through the body's silent language has led to studies of how job applicants and interviewers communicate (or miscommunicate) nonverbally. Popular guidebooks and articles offer advice on how to interpret nonverbal signals when negotiating a business deal, selling a product, or flirting. It pays to be able to read feelings that leak through via subtle facial expressions, body movements, and postures. Fidgeting, for example, may reveal anxiety or boredom. More specific interpretations of postures and gestures are risky, because different expressions may convey the same emotion: Either a cold stare or the avoidance of eye contact may signify hostility. And a single gesture can convey very different emotions: Folded arms, for example, can signify either irritation or relaxation.

Such gestures, facial expressions, and tones of voice are all absent in computer-based communication. E-mail communications sometimes include sideways *emoticons*, such as ;-) for a knowing wink and :-(for a frown. But e-mail letters and Internet discussions otherwise lack nonverbal cues to status, personality, and age. Nobody knows what you look or sound like, or anything about your background; you are judged solely on your

Which of Paul Ekman's smiles is feigned, which natural? The smile on the right engages the facial muscles of a natural smile.

A silent language of emotion Hindu classic dance uses the face and body to effectively convey 10 different emotions (Hejmadi & others, 2000).

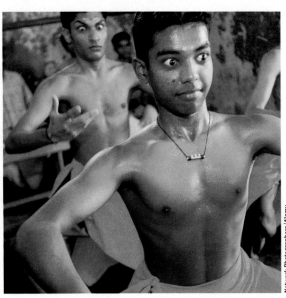

words. When first meeting an e-mail pen pal face to face, people are often surprised at the person they encounter.

It's also easy to misread e-mailed communications, where the absence of expressive e-motion can make for ambiguous emotion. So can the absence of those vocal nuances by which we signal that a statement is serious, kidding, or sarcastic. Research by Justin Kruger and his colleagues (1999) shows that communicators often think their "just kidding" intent is equally clear, whether e-mailed or spoken. But they commonly exhibit egocentrism by not foreseeing misinterpretations in the absence of nonverbal cues.

Culture and Emotional Expression

OBJECTIVE 11 | Discuss the culture-specific and culturally universal aspects of emotional expression, and explain how emotional expressions could enhance survival.

The meaning of gestures varies with the culture. Some years ago, psychologist Otto Klineberg (1938) observed that in Chinese literature people clapped their hands to express worry or disappointment, laughed a great "Ho-Ho" to express anger, and stuck out their tongues to show surprise. Similarly, the North American "thumbs up" and "A-OK" signs would be insults in certain other cultures. (When former U.S. President Richard Nixon made the latter sign in Brazil, he didn't realize he was saying "Let's have sex.") Just how important cultural definitions of gestures can be was demonstrated in 1968, when North Korea publicized photos of supposedly happy officers from a captured U.S. Navy spy ship. In the photo, three of the men raised their middle fingers; they had told captors it was a "Hawaiian good luck sign" (Fleming & Scott, 1991).

Do facial expressions also have different meanings in different cultures? To find out, two investigative teams—one led by Paul Ekman, Wallace Friesen, and others (1975, 1987, 1994), the other by Carroll Izard (1977, 1994)—showed photographs of different facial expressions to people in different parts of the world and asked them to guess the emotion. You can try this matching task yourself by pairing the six emotions with the six faces of **FIGURE 13.11.**

Regardless of your cultural background, you probably did pretty well. A smile's a smile the world around. Ditto for anger, and to a lesser extent the other basic expressions (Elfenbein & Ambady, 1999). (There is no culture where people frown when they are happy.) Despite some differences, cultures and languages share many similarities in the ways they categorize emotions—as anger, fear, and so on.

FIGURE 13.11
Culture-specific or culturally universal expressions?
As people of differing cultures and races, do our faces speak differing languages? Which face expresses disgust? Anger? Fear? Happiness? Sadness? Surprise? The answers are on page 531. (From Matsumoto and Ekman, 1989.)

Ekman & Matsumoto, Japanese and Caucasian Facial Expression of Emotion

Do people from different cultures share these similarities because they share experiences, such as American movies, the BBC, and CNN? Apparently not. Ekman and his team asked isolated people in New Guinea to display various emotions in response to such statements as, "Pretend your child has died." When the researchers showed videotapes of the New Guineans' facial reactions to North American collegians, the students read them easily.

Facial expressions do contain some nonverbal accents that provide clues to one's culture (Marsh & others, 2003). So it is not surprising that data from 182 studies show slightly enhanced accuracy when people judge emotions from their own culture (Elfenbein & Ambady, 2002, 2003a,b). Still, the telltale signs of emotion generally cross cultures.

Children's facial expressions—even those of blind children who have never seen a face—are also universal (Eibl-Eibesfeldt, 1971). People blind from birth spontaneously exhibit the common facial expressions associated with such emotions as joy, sadness, fear, and anger (Galati & others, 1997). The world over, children cry when distressed, shake their heads when defiant, and smile when they are happy.

The discovery that facial muscles speak a fairly universal language would not have surprised pioneering emotion researcher Charles Darwin (1809–1882). He speculated that in prehistoric times, before our ancestors communicated in words, their ability to convey threats, greetings, and submission with facial expressions helped them survive. That shared heritage, he believed, is why all humans express the basic emotions with similar facial expressions. A sneer, for example, retains elements of an animal's baring its teeth in a snarl.

Smiles, too, are social phenomena as well as emotional reflexes. Bowlers don't smile when they score a strike—they smile when they turn to face their companions (Jones & others, 1991; Kraut & Johnston, 1979). Even euphoric winners of Olympic gold medals typically don't smile when they are awaiting their ceremony but do when interacting with officials and facing the crowd and cameras (Fernández-Dols & Ruiz-Belda, 1995).

It has also been adaptive for us to interpret faces in particular contexts. (Recall the aggressive or frightened monster from page 251.) People judge an angry face set in a frightening situation as afraid. They judge a fearful face set in a painful situation as pained (Carroll & Russell, 1996). Movie directors harness this phenomenon by creating contexts and soundtracks that amplify our perceptions of particular emotions.

Emotional expressions may enhance our survival in other ways, too. Surprise raises the eyebrows and widens the eyes, enabling us to take in more information. Disgust wrinkles the nose, closing it from foul odors.

Although cultures share a universal facial language for basic emotions, they differ in how much emotion they express. In cultures that encourage individuality, as in Western Europe, Australia, New Zealand, and North America, emotional displays often are intense and prolonged. People focus on their own goals and attitudes and express themselves accordingly. Watching a film of someone's hand being cut, Americans grimace (whether alone or with other viewers). Japanese viewers hide their emotions when in the presence of others (Triandis, 1994). Cultural differences exist both between and within nations. The Irish and their Irish-American descendants tend to be more expressive than Scandinavians and their Scandinavian-American descendants (Tsai & Chentsova-Dutton, 2003). And that reminds us of a familiar lesson: Like most psychological events, emotion is best understood not only as a biological and cognitive phenomenon, but also as a social-cultural phenomenon (**FIGURE 13.12**).

> " For news of the heart, ask the face."
> Guinean proverb

While weightless, astronauts' fluids move toward their upper body and their faces become puffy. This makes nonverbal communication more difficult, increasing the risks of misunderstanding, especially among multinational crews (Gelman, 1989).

FIGURE 13.12

Levels of analysis for the study of emotion

As with other psychological phenomena, researchers explore emotion at biological, psychological, and social-cultural levels.

Biological influences:
• physiological arousal
• evolutionary adaptiveness
• response pathways in the brain
• spillover effect

Psychological influences:
• cognitive labeling
• gender differences

Emotion

Social-cultural influences:
• expressiveness
• presence of others
• cultural expectations

The Effects of Facial Expressions

OBJECTIVE 12 | Discuss the facial feedback and behavior feedback phenomena, and give an example of each.

As William James struggled with feelings of depression and grief, he came to believe that we can control emotions by going "through the outward movements" of any emotion we want to experience. "To feel cheerful," he advised, "sit up cheerfully, look around cheerfully, and act as if cheerfulness were already there."

Recent findings concerning the emotional effects of facial expressions are precisely what James might have predicted. Expressions not only communicate emotion, they also amplify and regulate it. In his 1872 book, *The Expression of the Emotions in Man and Animals,* Darwin contended that "the free expression by outward signs of an emotion intensifies it. . . . He who gives way to violent gestures will increase his rage."

Was Darwin right? I was driving in my car one day when the song "Put On a Happy Face" came on the radio. How phony, I thought. But I tested Darwin's hypothesis anyway, as you can, too. Fake a big grin. Now scowl. Can you feel the "smile therapy" difference?

Participants in dozens of experiments have felt a difference. For example, James Laird and his colleagues (1974, 1984, 1989) subtly induced students to make a frowning expression by asking them to "contract these muscles" and "pull your brows together" (supposedly to help the researchers attach facial electrodes). The results? The students reported feeling a little angry. Students similarly induced to smile felt happier, found cartoons funnier, and recalled happier memories than did the frowners. People instructed to mold their faces in ways that express other basic emotions also experienced those emotions. For example, they reported feeling more fear than anger, disgust, or sadness when made to construct a fearful expression: "Raise your eyebrows. And open your eyes wide. Move your whole head back, so that your chin is tucked in a little bit, and let your mouth relax and hang open a little" (Duclos & others, 1989). The face is more than a billboard that displays our feelings; it also feeds our feelings.

In the absence of competing emotions, this *facial feedback* effect is subtle yet detectable. Consider these findings:

- If manipulated into furrowing their brows **(FIGURE 13.13),** people feel sadder while looking at sad photos.
- Saying the phonemes *e* and *ah,* which activate smiling muscles, puts people— believe it or not—in a better mood than saying the German *ü* (rather like saying the English *e* and *u* together), which activates muscles associated with negative emotions (Zajonc & others, 1989).
- Just activating one of the smiling muscles by holding a pen in the teeth (rather than with the lips, which activates a frowning muscle) is enough to make cartoons seem more amusing (Strack & others, 1988). A heartier smile— made not just with the mouth but with raised cheeks that crinkle the eyes—

enhances positive feelings even more when you are reacting to something pleasant or funny (Soussignan, 2001). Looking at yourself in a mirror further amplifies the effect (Kleinke & others, 1998). Smile warmly on the outside and you feel better on the inside. Scowl and the whole world seems to scowl back.

FIGURE 13.13

How to make people frown without telling them to frown

Randy Larsen, Margaret Kasimatis, and Kurt Frey's (1992) solution: Attach two golf tees above the eyebrows and ask people to make the tee tips touch. Research participants felt sad while viewing scenes of war, sickness, and starvation, and even sadder with their "sad face" muscles activated.

Courtesy of Louis Schakel/Michael Kausman/The New York Times Pictures

Sara Snodgrass and her associates (1986) observed the *behavior feedback* phenomenon with walking. You can duplicate the participants' experience: Walk for a few minutes while taking short, shuffling steps, keeping your eyes downcast. Now walk around taking long strides, with your arms swinging and your eyes looking straight ahead. Can you feel your mood shift? Going through the motions awakens the emotions.

Better yet, report William Flack and his team (1999), manipulate *both* face and posture. To generate an angry feeling, for example, follow the instructions they gave their research participants:

> Push your eyebrows together and down. Clench your teeth tightly and push your lips together. Put your feet flat on the floor directly below your knees, and put your forearms and elbows on the arms of the chair. Now clench your fists tightly and lean your upper body slightly forward.

But let's leave you feeling happier:

> Push the corners of your mouth up and back, letting your mouth open a little. Sit up as straight as you can in your chair. Put your hands at the ends of the armrests, and make sure that your legs are straight in front of you, knees bent, and feet right below your knees.

If assuming emotional expressions and postures triggers a feeling, then would imitating others' expressions help us feel what they are feeling? Again, the laboratory evidence is supportive. Kathleen Burns Vaughn and John Lanzetta (1981) asked some students but not others to make a pained expression whenever an electric shock was apparently delivered to someone they were watching. With each apparent shock, the grimacing observers perspired more and had a faster heart rate than observers who didn't imitate the expression. Just seeing a loved one wince at a light electrical shock also activates a pain-related brain region. This suggests a neural basis for empathy—for literally feeling the other's pain (Singer & others, 2004). So one small way to become more empathic—to feel what others feel—is to let your own face mimic the other person's expression. Acting as another acts helps us feel what another feels. Indeed, natural mimicry of others' emotions helps explain why emotions are contagious (Dimberg & others, 2000; Newmann & Strack, 2000).

Answers to the questions in Figure 13.11 (page 528): From left to right, top to bottom: happiness, surprise, fear, sadness, anger, disgust.

>> LEARNING OUTCOMES

Expressed Emotion

OBJECTIVE 8 | **Describe some of the factors that affect our ability to decipher nonverbal cues.**

Most people can detect nonverbal cues, and we are especially sensitive to nonverbal threats. Experience contributes to our sensitivity to cues, as studies of abused children show.

OBJECTIVE 9 | **Describe some gender differences in perceiving and communicating emotions.**

Women generally are better than men at reading people's emotional cues, including those displayed during deception. Women also give more detailed descriptions of their emotional reactions, more readily describe themselves as emotional, and express empathy more often, in words and in their facial expressions. Women surpass men in conveying happiness, but men communicate anger better.

OBJECTIVE 10 | **Discuss the research on reading and misreading facial and behavioral indicators of emotion.**

Facial muscles reveal signs of emotion. But lie detection methods based on facial expressions don't yet exist, and most of us have difficulty detecting expressions of deceit. The absence of verbal or emotional cues in e-mails deprives us of an important source of information.

OBJECTIVE 11 | **Discuss the culture-specific and culturally universal aspects of emotional expression, and explain how emotional expressions could enhance survival.**

The meaning of gestures varies with culture, but many facial expressions, such as those of happiness and fear, are found all over the world (and among children blind from birth), indicating that these expressions are culturally universal aspects of emotion. Cultures differ, however, in the amount of emotional expression they consider acceptable. In prelinguistic, prehistoric times, emotional expressions could have enhanced survival by enabling communication of threats, greetings, and submission. Some emotional expressions help us to take in more sensory information or to avoid taking in toxic substances.

OBJECTIVE 12 | **Discuss the facial feedback and behavior feedback phenomena, and give an example of each.**

The *facial feedback hypothesis* proposes that expressions amplify our emotions by activating muscles associated with specific states, and the muscles signal the body to respond as though we were experiencing those states. Thus, when we simulate the facial expressions normally associated with happiness, we may feel happier. Similarly, the *behavior feedback hypothesis* assumes that if we move our body as we would when experiencing some emotion (shuffling along with downcast eyes, as when sad), we are likely to feel that emotion to some degree.

ASK YOURSELF: **Can you think of one situation in which you would like to change the way you feel, and create a simple plan for doing so? For instance, if you would like to feel more cheerful on your way to class tomorrow morning rather than dragging yourself there, you might try walking briskly—with head held high and a pleasant expression on your face.**

Experienced Emotion

OBJECTIVE 13 | Name several basic emotions, and describe two dimensions psychologists use to differentiate emotions.

How many distinct emotions are there? Carroll Izard (1977) isolated 10 such basic emotions (joy, interest-excitement, surprise, sadness, anger, disgust, contempt, fear, shame, and guilt), most of which are present in infancy **(FIGURE 13.14)**. Jessica Tracey and Richard Robins (2004) believe that pride is also a distinct emotion, signaled by a small smile, head slightly tilted back, and an open posture. And Phillip Shaver and his colleagues (1996) believe that love, too, may be a basic emotion. But Izard has argued that other emotions are combinations of these 10. Love, he says, is a mixture of joy and interest-excitement.

The ingredients of emotion include not only physiology and expressive behavior but also our conscious experience. We sometimes experience feelings as "obscure and

FIGURE 13.14
Infants' naturally occurring emotions
To identify the emotions present from birth, Carroll Izard analyzed the facial expressions of very young infants.

(a) Joy (mouth forming smile, cheeks lifted, twinkle in eye)

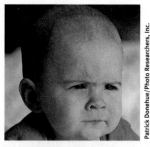

(b) Anger (brows drawn together and downward, eyes fixed, mouth squarish)

(c) Interest (brows raised or knitted, mouth softly rounded, lips may be pursed)

(d) Disgust (nose wrinkled, upper lip raised, tongue pushed outward)

(e) Surprise (brows raised, eyes widened, mouth rounded in oval shape)

(f) Sadness (brow's inner corner raised, mouth corners drawn down)

(g) Fear (brows level, drawn in and up, eyelids lifted, mouth corners retracted) confused," noted Benjamin Constant de Rebecque in 1816. To cut through the obscurity, psychologists have asked people to describe their emotions. Varied people, including Estonians, Poles, Greeks, Chinese, and Canadians, place emotions along the two dimensions illustrated in **FIGURE 13.15**—pleasant (or positive) versus unpleasant (or negative) *valence* and low versus high *arousal* (Russell & Carroll, 1999a,b; Russell & others, 1989; Watson & others, 1999).

Successful Olympic gymnasts and high-performing students taking exams label arousal as energizing, as giving them an edge (Raglin, 1992). For them arousal has positive valence, while for those suffering stage fright it has negative valence. Experienced professors and public speakers similarly welcome prelecture arousal as meaning they are "up" or "on" rather than flat. On the valence and arousal dimensions, terrified is more frightened (more unpleasant and aroused) than afraid, enraged is angrier than angry, delighted is happier than happy.

Let's take a closer look at three of these emotions: fear, anger, and happiness. What functions do they serve? What influences our experience of each?

Fear

Fear can be poisonous. It can torment us, rob us of sleep, and preoccupy our thinking. People can be literally scared to death. Fear can also be contagious. In 1903, someone yelled "Fire!" as a fire broke out in Chicago's Iroquois Theater. Eddie Foy, the comedian on stage at the time, tried to reassure the crowd by calling out, "Don't get excited. There's no danger. Take it easy!" Alas, the crowd panicked. During the 10 minutes it took the fire department to arrive and quickly extinguish the flames, more than 500 people perished, most of them trampled or smothered in a stampede. Bodies were piled 7 or 8 feet deep in the stairways, and many of the faces bore heel marks (Brown, 1965).

More often, fear is adaptive. It's an alarm system that prepares our bodies to flee from danger. Fear of real or imagined enemies binds people together as families, tribes, and nations. Fear of injury can protect us from harm. Fear of punishment or retaliation can constrain us from harming one another. Fear helps us focus on a problem and rehearse coping strategies.

Learning Fear

OBJECTIVE 14 | State two ways we learn our fears.

People can be afraid of almost anything—"afraid of truth, afraid of fortune, afraid of death, and afraid of each other," observed Ralph Waldo Emerson. Why so many fears? Recall from Chapter 8 that infants come to fear furry objects associated with frightening noises. Child development researchers now know that when infants begin to crawl, they learn from their falls and near-falls—and become increasingly afraid of heights (Campos & others, 1992). Through such conditioning, the short list of naturally painful and frightening events can multiply into a long list of human fears—fear of driving or flying, fear of mice or cockroaches, fear of closed or open spaces, fear of failure or of success, fear of another race or nation.

Learning by observation extends the list. Susan Mineka (1985) sought to explain why nearly all monkeys reared in the wild fear snakes, yet lab-reared monkeys do not.

FIGURE 13.15
Two dimensions of emotion
James Russell, David Watson, Auke Tellegen, and others describe emotions as variations on two dimensions—arousal (low versus high) and valence (pleasant versus unpleasant feeling).

Surely, most wild monkeys do not actually suffer snake bites. Do they learn their fear through observation? To find out, Mineka experimented with six monkeys reared in the wild (all strongly fearful of snakes) and their lab-reared offspring (virtually none of which feared snakes). After repeatedly observing their parents or peers refusing to reach for food in the presence of a snake, the younger monkeys developed a similar strong fear of snakes. When retested three months later, their learned fear persisted, suggesting that our fears may reflect not only our own past traumas but also the fears we learn from our parents and friends.

It did not take direct experience for people to become more fearful after observing the trauma of 9/11. Within New York City, a school system study found tens of thousands of children experiencing nightmares and fears of public places (Goodnough, 2002). Nationally, women responded to the attacks with greater fear, men with greater anger (Lerner & others, 2002). Four weeks after the attack, 27 percent of women and 10 percent of men reported being afraid to fly (ICR, 2001).

The Biology of Fear

OBJECTIVE **15** | Discuss some of the biological components of fear.

We may be biologically prepared to learn some fears more quickly than others. Monkeys learn to fear snakes even by watching videotapes of monkeys reacting fearfully to a snake; but they *don't* learn to fear flowers when video splicing transposes the seemingly feared stimulus into a flower (Cook & Mineka, 1991). We humans quickly learn to fear snakes, spiders, and cliffs—fears that probably helped our ancestors survive (Öhman & Mineka, 2003). But our Stone Age fears leave us unprepared for high-tech dangers—cars, electricity, bombs, and global warming—all of which are now far more dangerous (Lumsden & Wilson, 1983; McNally, 1987).

One key to fear learning lies in the amygdala, that limbic system neural center deep in the brain **(FIGURE 13.16)**. The amygdala plays a key role in associating various emotions, including fear, with certain situations (Barinaga, 1992b). Rabbits learn to react with fear to a tone that predicts an impending small shock—unless their amygdala is damaged. If rats have their amygdala deactivated by a drug that blocks the strengthening of neural connections, they, too, show no fear learning. The amygdala receives input from regions such as the *anterior cingulate cortex,* a higher-level center for processing emotion. And it sends output to all the parts of the brain that produce the bodily symptoms of extreme fear, such as diarrhea and shortness of breath.

FIGURE 13.16
The amygdala—a neural key to fear learning
Nerves running out from these knots of neural tissue, one on either side of the brain's center, carry messages that control heart rate, sweating, stress hormones, attention, and other engines that rev up in threatening situations.

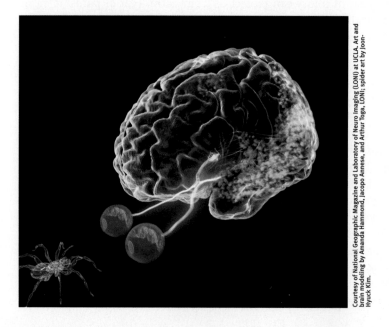

Courtesy of National Geographic Magazine and Laboratory of Neuro Imaging (LONI) at UCLA. Art and brain modeling by Amanda Hammond, Jacopo Annese, and Arthur Toga, LONI; spider art by Joon-Hyuck Kim.

The amygdala is similarly involved in human fears. If an experimenter repeatedly blasts people with a blaring horn after showing a blue slide, they will begin to react emotionally to the slide (as measured by their perspiring skin conducting electricity). If they have suffered damage to the nearby hippocampus, they still show the emotional reaction but won't be able to remember why. If they have suffered amygdala damage, they will remember the conditioning but will show no emotional effect of it (Schacter, 1996).

Researchers have been mapping these circuits, showing which activate as humans and other animals learn fears. If people are subjected to an aversive sound while viewing faces, amygdala fear pathways will become active on future viewings of the face (Buchel & others, 1998; Morris & others, 1998). Patients who have lost use of the amygdala are unusually trusting of scary-looking people (Adolphs & others, 1998).

Of course, there are people whose fears seem to fall outside the average range. Some, with *phobias,* have intense fears of specific objects (such as bugs) or situations (such as public speaking) that disrupt their ability to cope. They may be very fearful of threatening or embarrassing situations. To be ever-attentive to potential threats is to be chronically anxious (Mineka & Sutton, 1992). But others—courageous heroes and remorseless criminals—are less fearful than most of us. Astronauts and adventurers who have "the right stuff"—who can keep their wits and function coolly and effectively in times of severe stress—seem to thrive on risk. So, too, do con artists and killers who charm their intended victims without a hint of nervousness. In laboratory tests, they exhibit little fear of a tone that predictably precedes a painful electric shock.

Experience helps shape such fearfulness or fearlessness, but so do our genes. (Recall from Chapter 3 that genes influence our temperament—our emotional reactivity.) Among identical twins, one twin's level of fearfulness is similar to the other's—even when they have been reared separately (Lykken, 1982). Scientists have isolated a gene that influences the amygdala's response to frightening situations (Hariri & others, 2002). People with a short version of this gene have less of a protein that speeds the re-uptake of the neurotransmitter serotonin. With more serotonin available to activate their amygdala neurons, people with this short gene exhibit a revved-up amygdala response to frightening pictures.

Hard-wired fears
Entertainment businesses exploit our survival circuits. Although we can *know* that amusement park deaths are extremely rare, our fear alarm system nevertheless gives us an adrenaline rush and sweaty palms during a free-flying fair ride.

Chapters 16 and 17 discuss how such phobias develop and are treated.

Anger

OBJECTIVE 16 | Identify some common triggers and consequences of anger, and assess the catharsis hypothesis.

Anger, the sages have said, is "a short madness" (Horace, 65–8 B.C.) that "carries the mind away" (Virgil, 70–19 B.C.) and can be "many times more hurtful than the injury that caused it" (Thomas Fuller, 1654–1734). But they have also said, "noble anger" (William Shakespeare, 1564–1616) "makes any coward brave" (Cato, 234–149 B.C.) and "brings back . . . strength" (Virgil).

What makes us angry? To find out, James Averill (1983) asked people to recall or keep careful records of their experiences with anger. Most reported becoming at least mildly angry several times a week, some several times a day. The anger was often a response to friends' or loved ones' perceived misdeeds and was especially common when another person's act seemed willful, unjustified, and avoidable. But blameless annoyances—foul odors, high temperatures, a traffic jam, aches and pains—also have the power to make us angry (Berkowitz, 1990).

What do we do with our anger? And what *should* we do with our anger? In a Gallup survey of teens, boys more than girls reported walking away from the situation or working it off with exercise; girls more often reported talking with a friend, listening to music, or writing (Ray, 2005).

> " Anger will never disappear so long as thoughts of resentment are cherished in the mind."
>
> The Buddha, 500 B.C.

"I thought it would be nice if we had a forum where we could get together and have screaming tantrums."

When anger fuels physically or verbally aggressive acts we later regret, it becomes maladaptive. Anger also primes prejudice, and after 9/11 Americans who responded with anger more than fear also displayed intolerance for immigrants and Muslims (DeSteno & others, 2004; Skitka & others, 2004). And anger can harm us—chronic hostility is linked to heart disease (page 556). But controlled expressions of anger are more adaptive than either hostile outbursts or pent-up angry feelings. Participants in Averill's research recalled that when they were angry they often reacted assertively rather than hurtfully. Their anger frequently led them to talk things over with the offender, thereby lessening the aggravation.

Popular books and articles on aggression at times advise that even releasing angry feelings as hostile outbursts can be better than internalizing them. When irritated, should we lash out at the offender? Was Ann Landers (1969) right that "youngsters should be taught to vent their anger"? Are "recovery" therapists right in encouraging us to rage at our dead parents, imaginatively curse the boss, or confront our childhood abuser?

Such encouragement to vent our rage is typical in individualized cultures, but it would seldom be heard in cultures where people's identity is centered more on the group. People who keenly sense their *inter*dependence see anger as a threat to group harmony (Markus & Kitayama, 1991). In Tahiti, for instance, people learn to be considerate and gentle. In Japan, from infancy on, anger expressions are less common than in Western cultures.

The Western "vent your anger" advice presumes that through aggressive action or fantasy we can achieve emotional release, or **catharsis.** Experimenters report that *sometimes* when people retaliate against a provoker, they may indeed calm down. But this tends to be true only *if* their counterattack is directed against the provoker, *if* their retaliation seems justifiable, and *if* their target is not intimidating (Geen & Quanty, 1977; Hokanson & Edelman, 1966). In short, expressing anger can be *temporarily* calming *if* it does not leave us feeling guilty or anxious.

However, despite the afterglow—people sometimes feel better for hours afterward—catharsis usually fails to cleanse one's rage. More often, expressing anger breeds more anger. For one thing, it may provoke further retaliation, thus escalating a minor conflict into a major confrontation. For another, expressing anger can magnify anger. (Recall the behavior feedback research: Acting angry can make us feel angrier.) Ebbe Ebbesen and his colleagues (1975) saw this when they interviewed 100 frustrated engineers and technicians just laid off by an aerospace company. They asked some of the workers questions that released hostility, such as, "What instances can you think of where the company has not been fair with you?" When these people later filled out a questionnaire that assessed their attitudes toward the company, did this opportunity to "drain off" their hostility reduce it? Quite the contrary. Compared with those who had not vented their anger, those who had let it all out exhibited *more* hostility. Even when provoked people hit a punching bag *believing* it will be cathartic, the effect is the opposite—leading them to exhibit *more* cruelty (Bushman & others, 1999). And when they wallop a punching bag while ruminating about the person who angered them, they become even more aggressive when given a chance for revenge. "Venting to reduce anger is like using gasoline to put out a fire," concluded the researcher, Brad Bushman (2002).

Ironically, when angry outbursts do temporarily calm us, they may be reinforcing and therefore habit forming. If stressed managers find they can drain off some of their tension by berating an employee, then the next time they feel irritated and tense they may be more likely to explode again. Think about it: The next time you are angry you are likely to do whatever has relieved your anger in the past.

What, then, is the best way to handle our anger? Experts offer two suggestions. First, wait. You can bring down the level of physiological arousal of anger by waiting.

SIX CHIX

The catharsis myth: Is it true?

"It is true of the body as of arrows," noted Carol Tavris (1982), "what goes up must come down. Any emotional arousal will simmer down if you just wait long enough." Second, deal with anger in a way that involves neither being chronically angry over every little annoyance nor passively sulking, merely rehearsing your reasons for your anger. Ruminating inwardly about the causes of your anger serves only to increase it (Rusting & Nolen-Hoeksema, 1998). Don't join those who stifle their feelings over a series of provocations and then suddenly overreact to a single incident (Baumeister & others, 1990). Calm yourself in other ways, such as by exercising, playing an instrument, or talking it through with a friend.

Anger does communicate strength and competence (Tiedens, 2001). It can benefit a relationship when it expresses a grievance in ways that promote reconciliation rather than retaliation. Civility means not only keeping silent about trivial irritations but also communicating important ones clearly and assertively. A nonaccusing statement of feeling—perhaps letting one's housemate know that "I get irritated when you leave your dirty dishes for me to clean up"—can help resolve the conflicts that cause anger.

What if someone else's behavior really hurts you? Research suggests that the age-old response of forgiveness may be what the doctor ordered. Without letting the offender off the hook or inviting further harm, forgiveness releases anger and can calm the body. To explore the bodily effects of forgiveness, Charlotte Witvliet and her co-researchers (2001) invited college students to recall an incident where someone had hurt them. As the students mentally rehearsed forgiveness, their negative feelings—and their perspiration, blood pressure, heart rate, and facial tension—all were lower than when they rehearsed their grudges.

A cool culture
Domestic violence is rare in Micronesia. This photo of community life on Pulap Island suggests one possible reason: Family life takes place in the open on this island. Relatives and neighbors who witness angry outbursts can step in before the emotion escalates into child, spouse, or elder abuse.

Happiness

OBJECTIVE **17** | Describe how the feel-good, do-good phenomenon works, and discuss the importance of research on subjective well-being.

"How to gain, how to keep, how to recover happiness is in fact for most men at all times the secret motive for all they do," observed William James (1902, p. 76). People everywhere—in 48 countries on six continents in one study—also desire happiness for their children (Diener & Lucas, 2004). Understandably so, for one's state of happiness or unhappiness colors everything. People who are happy perceive the world as safer, make decisions more easily, rate job applicants more favorably, are more cooperative, and live healthier and more energized and satisfied lives (Lyukomirsky & others, 2005; Myers, 1993). When your mood is gloomy and your thinking preoccupied, life as a whole seems depressing. Let your mood brighten and your thinking broadens and becomes more playful and creative (Fredrickson, 2002, 2003). Your relationships, your self-image, and your hopes for the future also seem more promising. Positive emotions fuel upward spirals.

Moreover—and this is one of psychology's most consistent findings—when we feel happy we are more willing to help others. In study after study, a mood-boosting experience (finding money, succeeding on a challenging task, recalling a happy event) has made people more likely to give money, pick up someone's dropped papers, volunteer time, and do other good deeds. Psychologists call it the **feel-good, do-good phenomenon** (Salovey, 1990). Happiness doesn't just feel good, it does good. (Doing good also promotes good feeling, a phenomenon harnessed by some happiness coaches and instructors as they assign people to perform a daily "random act of kindness" and to record the results.)

■ **catharsis** emotional release. In psychology, the catharsis hypothesis maintains that "releasing" aggressive energy (through action or fantasy) relieves aggressive urges.

■ **feel-good, do-good phenomenon** people's tendency to be helpful when already in a good mood.

Human resilience

Seven weeks after her 1994 wedding, Anna Putt of South Midlands, England, shown here with her husband, Des, suffered a brain-stem stroke that left her "locked-in." For months afterward, she recalls, "I was paralyzed from the neck down and was unable to communicate. These were VERY frightening times. But with encouragement from family, friends, faith, and medical staff, I tried to keep positive." In the ensuing three years, she became able to "talk" (by nodding at letters), to steer an electric wheelchair with her head, and to use a computer (by nodding while wearing spectacles that guide a cursor). Despite her paralysis, she reports that "I enjoy going out in the fresh air. My motto is 'Don't look back, move forward.' God would not want me to stop trying and I have no intention of doing so. Life is what you make of it!"

FIGURE 13.17

Moods across the day

When psychologist David Watson (2000) sampled nearly 4500 mood reports from 150 people, he found this pattern of variation from the average levels of positive and negative emotions.

Despite the significance of happiness, psychology throughout its history has more often focused on negative emotions. Since 1887, *Psychological Abstracts* (a guide to psychology's literature) has included, as of this writing, 12,876 articles mentioning anger, 82,297 mentioning anxiety, and 103,840 mentioning depression. For every 17 articles on these topics, only one dealt with the positive emotions of joy (1450), life satisfaction (5263), or happiness (4727). There is, of course, good reason to focus on negative emotions; they can make our lives miserable and drive us to seek help. But researchers are becoming increasingly interested in **subjective well-being,** assessed either as feelings of happiness (sometimes defined as a high ratio of positive to negative feelings) or as a sense of satisfaction with life. A new *positive psychology* is on the rise (see page 628).

On this subject, as on so many others, whatever psychological research reveals will have been anticipated by someone. We have inherited many contradictory maxims concerning happiness: that it comes from knowing the truth, or from preserving illusions; from living for the present, or from living for the future; from being with others, or from living in peaceful solitude (Tatarkiewicz, 1976). The list goes on, making the scientific task clear: to ask which of these competing ideas fit reality. Sifting the actual predictors of happiness from the plausible hunches requires research.

The Short Life of Emotional Ups and Downs

OBJECTIVE **18** | Discuss some of the daily and longer-term variations in the duration of emotions.

In their happiness research, psychologists have studied influences on both our temporary moods and our long-term life satisfaction. When studying people's hour-by-hour moods, David Watson (2000) and Daniel Kahneman and his colleagues (2004) discovered that positive emotion rises over the early to middle part of most days **(FIGURE 13.17).** Studying people's reports of day-to-day moods confirms that stressful events—an argument, a sick child, a car problem—trigger bad moods. No surprise there. But by the next day, the gloom nearly always lifts (Affleck & others, 1994; Bolger & others, 1989; Stone & Neale, 1984). If anything, people tend to rebound from bad days to a *better*-than-usual good mood the following day. When in a bad mood, can you usually depend on rebounding within a day or two? Are your times of elation similarly hard to sustain? Over the long run, our emotional ups and downs tend to balance.

Apart from prolonged grief over the loss of a loved one or lingering anxiety after a trauma (such as child abuse, rape, or the terrors of war), even tragedy is not permanently depressing. Learning that one is HIV-positive is devastating. But after five weeks of adapting to the grim news, those who tested positive felt less emotionally distraught than they had expected (Sieff & others, 1999). Kidney dialysis patients recognize that their health is relatively poor, yet in their moment-to-moment experiences they report being just as happy as healthy nonpatients (Riis & others, 2005). People who become blind or paralyzed also usually recover near-normal levels of day-to-day happiness (Gerhart & others, 1994; Myers, 1993). Among a sample of Germans incapacitated by ALS (amyotrophic lateral sclerosis, a progressive neurological disease that leads to paralysis), a striking 85 percent rated their quality of life as "satisfactory," "good," or "very good." Moreover, their ratings were not much affected by whether they were or were not on ventilators or feeding tubes (Kübler & others, 2005). "If you are a paraplegic," explains Daniel Kahneman (2005), "you will gradually start thinking of other things, and the more time you spend thinking of other things the less miserable you are going to be." A major disability often leaves people somewhat less happy than the average person (Lucas, 2005). Yet they reportedly express considerably more happiness than able-bodied people with depression (Schwartz & Estrin, 2004; Kübler & others, 2005). Even patients "locked-in" a motionless body "rarely want to die," report Eimar Smith and Mark Delargy (2005), which "counters a popular misconception that such patients would have been better off dead."

In less life-threatening contexts, the pattern continues. Faculty members up for tenure expect their lives would be deflated by a negative decision. Actually, 5 to 10 years later, those denied are not noticeably less happy than those who were awarded tenure, report Daniel Gilbert and colleagues (1998). The same is true of romantic breakups, which feel devastating. The surprising reality: *We overestimate the duration of emotions and underestimate our capacity to adapt.*

Wealth and Well-Being

OBJECTIVE 19 | Summarize the findings on the relationship between affluence and happiness.

The emotional impact of dramatically positive events also dissipates sooner than we might expect. Once their rush of euphoria wears off, state lottery winners typically find their overall happiness unchanged (Brickman & others, 1978). Other research confirms that there is much more to well-being than being well-off. Many people (including most German citizens, and most new American collegians, as **FIGURE 13.18** suggests) believe they would be happier if they had more money (Csikszentmihalyi, 1999).

They probably would be—temporarily. Consider:

- Within most affluent countries, people with lots of money are somewhat happier than those who struggle to afford life's basic needs (Di Tella & others, 2001).
- People in rich countries are also somewhat happier than those in poor countries (Steel & Ones, 2002).
- Those who have experienced a recent windfall from a lottery, an inheritance, or a surging economy typically feel some elation (Diener & Oishi, 2000; Gardner & Oswald, 2001). *Losing* money has even more emotional impact (Hobfoll & others, 2003; Kahneman & Tversky, 1979). This illustrates a basic principle, note Roy Baumeister and his colleagues (2001): "Bad is stronger than good." Losses loom larger than gains, cruel words linger longer than kind ones, a bad reputation is more easily acquired than a good one, and pain produces misery more than health produces joy.

■ **subjective well-being** self-perceived happiness or satisfaction with life. Used along with measures of objective well-being (for example, physical and economic indicators) to evaluate people's quality of life.

" Weeping may tarry for the night, but joy comes with the morning."

Psalms 30:5

" I have a 'fortune cookie maxim' that I'm very proud of: Nothing in life is quite as important as you think it is while you are thinking about it. So, nothing will ever make you as happy as you think it will."

Nobel Laureate psychologist Daniel Kahneman, Gallup interview, "What Were They Thinking?" 2005

FIGURE 13.18

The changing materialism of entering college students

From 1970 through most of the 1980s, annual surveys of more than 200,000 entering U.S. college students revealed an increasing desire for wealth. (From *The American Freshman* surveys, UCLA, 1966 to 2005.)

"Money won't make you happy, Waldron. So instead of a raise, I'm giving a Prozac."

"Australians are three times richer than their parents and grandparents were in the 1950s, but they are not happier."

A Manifesto for Well-Being, 2005

Yet in the long run, increased affluence hardly affects happiness. Even in Calcutta and Pakistani slums, people "are more satisfied than one might expect" (Biswas-Diener & Diener, 2001; Suhail & Chaudry, 2004). Wealth is like health: Its utter absence can breed misery, yet having it is no guarantee of happiness. Growing up poor puts one at risk for certain problems, but so does growing up rich. Children of affluence are at greater-than-normal risk for substance abuse, anxiety, and depression (Luthar & Latendresse, 2005). What matters more than money (assuming one can afford life's necessities with a sense of security) is how you feel about what you have. Those who live with a sense of gratitude—or who cultivate their gratitude by each day writing down what they are grateful for—enjoy greater happiness (McCullough & others, 2004; Watkins, 2004).

Most people agree that money can't buy happiness, but they do believe that a *little* more money would make them a *little* more happy, secure, and comfortable. So, over time, does our happiness grow, little by little, with our paychecks? If his government achieves its 4 percent economic growth-rate goal, noted Australian researcher Richard Eckersley (2001), its people will be twice as rich in 20 years, "and 10 times richer than we were 100 years ago. Can we be sure that this increasing wealth creation is beneficial to personal and social well-being?"

No, we cannot. During the last four decades, the average U.S. citizen's buying power more than doubled. The 1957 after-tax income, inflated to 1995 dollars, was $8500 per person; by 2005, thanks partly to the rich getting richer and to women's increasing employment, it was well above $20,000. Did this more-than-doubled wealth—enabling twice as many cars per person, not to mention iPods, laptops, and camera cell phones—also buy more happiness? Are those of us who enjoy the abundance of the affluent Western world happier with its little levers we can adjust to heat and cool our homes to precisely the desired degree, to release clean water for a warm shower or a cold drink, and to microwave our plentiful food? As **FIGURE 13.19** shows,

FIGURE 13.19

Does money buy happiness?
It surely helps us to avoid certain types of pain. Yet, though buying power has almost tripled since the 1950s, the average American's reported happiness has remained almost unchanged. (Happiness data from National Opinion Research Center surveys; income data from *Historical Statistics of the United States* and *Economic Indicators*.)

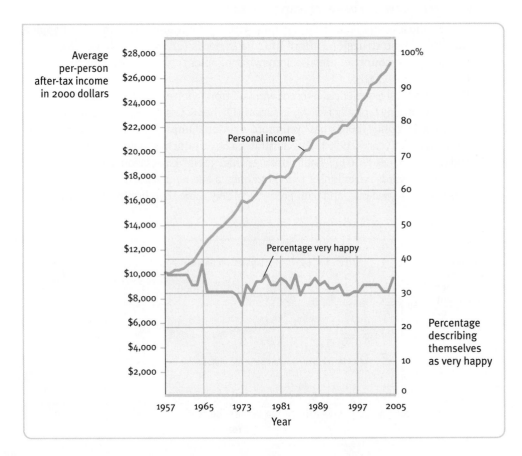

the average American, though certainly richer, is not a bit happier. In 1957, some 35 percent said they were "very happy," as did slightly fewer—34 percent—in 2004.

Indeed, if we can judge from statistics—including doubled divorce and teen suicide rates, and mushrooming depression—contemporary Americans seem to be more often miserable. Much the same has been true of the European countries, Australia, and Japan: In these countries, people enjoy better nutrition, health care, education, and science, and they are somewhat happier than those in very poor countries (Diener & Biswas-Diener, 2002; Eckersley, 2000). Yet their increasing real incomes have *not* produced increasing happiness. Such findings lob a bombshell at modern materialism: *Economic growth in affluent countries has provided no apparent boost to morale or social well-being.*

The wealthier-but-no-happier phenomenon even appears in China, which in the decade after 1994 enjoyed a dramatic economic advance. Average household incomes more than doubled, enabling households with a color TV to soar from 40 to 82 percent, those with a landline phone to jump from 10 to 63 percent, and those with cell phones to skyrocket from near zero to 48 percent. Despite this dramatic growth in income and consumption, nationwide Gallup surveys revealed that the proportion of Chinese expressing satisfaction with their lives simultaneously *declined* (Burkholder, 2005a,b). Moreover, the better-off urban Chinese were more likely to feel dissatisfaction than were the poorer rural Chinese. And in the latest World Values Surveys of well-being in 82 countries, the happiest two—Puerto Rico and Mexico—were far from the richest (though the unhappiest, mostly in Eastern Europe, were economically stressed—see **TABLE 13.1**).

Equally interesting are studies showing that individuals who strive hardest for wealth tend to live with lower well-being, a finding that "comes through very strongly in every culture I've looked at," reports Richard Ryan (1999). This is especially so for those seeking money to prove themselves, gain power, or show off rather than support their families (Srivastava & others, 2001). Ryan's collaborator, Tim Kasser (2000, 2002), concludes from their studies that those who instead strive for "intimacy, personal growth, and contribution to the community" experience a higher quality of life. This echoes an earlier finding by H. W. Perkins (1991): Among 800 college alumni surveyed, those preferring a high income and occupational success and prestige to having very close friends and a close marriage were twice as likely as their former classmates to describe themselves as "fairly" or "very" *un*happy. A similar correlation appears among 7167 college students surveyed in 41 countries. Those who value love more than money report much higher satisfaction with life than do their money-hungry peers **(FIGURE 13.20).**

If we are both richer and healthier, but no happier, than our grandparents were at our age, should our national priorities focus more on advancing psychological well-being? In Bhutan, says King Jigme Singye Wangchuk, "gross national happiness is more important than gross national product." Bhutan's prime minister frames his annual report in terms of Bhutan's

> "Americans say that money doesn't bring happiness. But it helps you to live with misery in comfort."
>
> Farah Pahlavi, exiled widow of the wealthy Shah of Iran, 2004

TABLE 13.1

SUBJECTIVE WELL-BEING (COMBINED HAPPINESS AND SATISFACTION) IN 82 SOCIETIES

The Top 10	The Bottom 10
1. Puerto Rico	73. Bulgaria
2. Mexico	74. Belarus
3. Denmark	75. Georgia
4. Ireland	76. Romania
5. Iceland	77. Moldova
6. Switzerland	78. Russia
7. Northern Ireland	79. Armenia
8. Colombia	80. Ukraine
9. Netherlands	81. Zimbabwe
10. Canada	82. Indonesia

(The United States and Australia were in a virtual tie for fifteenth place.)

Source: Ronald Inglehart and others (2004)

FIGURE 13.20

Values and life satisfaction

Among college and university students worldwide, those who report high life satisfaction give priority to love over money. (From Diener & Oishi, 2000.)

"But on the positive side, money can't buy happiness—so who cares?"

" No happiness lasts for long."

Seneca, *Agamemnon*, A.D. 60

" Continued pleasures wear off. . . . Pleasure is always contingent upon change and disappears with continuous satisfaction."

Dutch psychologist Nico Frijda (1988)

four pillars of progress toward national happiness: "The promotion of equitable and sustainable socio-economic development, preservation and promotion of cultural values, conservation of the natural environment, and establishment of good governance" (Esty, 2004). Ed Diener and Martin Seligman (2004) have proposed ways in which the U.S. Census Bureau and other national organizations might measure national well-being. "If high well-being is the overarching goal of all nations, national indicators of well-being are crucial to assessing the impact of national and corporate policies," they note.

Two Psychological Phenomena: Adaptation and Comparison

OBJECTIVE **20** | Describe how adaptation and relative deprivation affect our appraisals of our achievements.

Two psychological principles explain why, for all but the very poor, more money buys no more than a temporary surge of happiness and why our emotions seem attached to elastic bands that pull us back from highs or lows. In its own way, each principle suggests that happiness is relative.

Happiness and Prior Experience The **adaptation-level phenomenon** describes our tendency to judge various stimuli relative to those we have previously experienced. As psychologist Harry Helson (1898–1977) explained, we adjust our *neutral* levels—the points at which sounds seem neither loud nor soft, temperatures neither hot nor cold, events neither pleasant nor unpleasant—based on our experience. We then notice and react to variations up or down from these levels.

Thus, if our current condition—our income, academic average, or social prestige—increases, we feel an initial surge of pleasure. We then adapt to this new level of achievement, come to consider it as normal, and require something even better to give us another surge of happiness. From my childhood, I can recall the thrill of watching my family's first 12-inch, black-and-white TV. Now, if the color goes out on

HI & LOIS

our 27-inch TV, I feel deprived. Having adapted upward, I perceive as negative what I once experienced as positive. *The point to remember:* Satisfaction and dissatisfaction, success and failure—all are relative to our recent experience. Satisfaction, as Ryan (1999) says, "has a short half-life."

So, could we ever create a permanent social paradise? Social psychologist Donald Campbell (1975) answered no: If you woke up tomorrow to your utopia—perhaps a world with no bills, no ills, perfect scores, someone who loves you unreservedly—you would feel euphoric, for a time. But then you would gradually recalibrate your adaptation level. Before long you would again sometimes feel gratified (when achievements surpass expectations), sometimes feel deprived (when they fall below), and sometimes feel neutral. That helps explain why material wants can be insatiable—why many a child "needs" just one more Nintendo game. When the victor belongs to the spoils and the possessor is possessed by possessions, adaptation level has run amuck.

"Shortly after I realized I had plenty, I realized there was plenty more."

Seeking happiness through material achievement requires an ever-increasing abundance of things (which means depletion of the Earth's resources). At the end of his *Chronicles of Narnia,* C. S. Lewis depicts heaven as a place where good things do continually increase, where life is a never-ending story "in which every chapter is better than the one before." Here on Earth the unavoidable ups and downs of real life preclude a perpetual high.

Happiness and Others' Attainments Happiness is relative not only to our past experience but also to our comparisons with others (Lyubomirsky, 2001). We are always comparing ourselves with others. And whether we feel good or bad depends on who those others are. We are slow-witted or clumsy only when others are smart or agile.

Two examples: To explain the frustration expressed by U.S. Air Corps soldiers during World War II, researchers formulated the concept of **relative deprivation**—the sense that we are worse off than others with whom we compare ourselves. Despite a relatively rapid promotion rate for the group, many soldiers were frustrated about their own promotion rates (Merton & Kitt, 1950). Apparently, seeing so many others being promoted inflated the soldiers' expectations. And when expectations soar above attainments, the result is disappointment. Alex Rodriguez's $252 million, 10-year baseball contract surely made him temporarily happy, but it also diminished other star players' satisfaction with their lesser, multimillion-dollar contracts. Likewise, the economic surge that has made some urban Chinese newly affluent may have fueled among others a sense of relative deprivation.

Such comparisons help us understand why the middle- and upper-income people in a given country, who can compare themselves with the relatively poor, tend to be slightly more satisfied with life than their less fortunate compatriots. Nevertheless, once people reach a moderate income level, further increases do little to increase their happiness. Why? Because as people climb the ladder of success they mostly compare themselves with peers who are at or above their current level (Gruder, 1977; Suls & Tesch, 1978). "Beggars do not envy millionaires, though of course they will envy other beggars who are more successful," noted Bertrand Russell (1930, p. 90). Thus, "Napoleon envied Caesar, Caesar envied Alexander, and Alexander, I daresay, envied Hercules, who never existed. You cannot, therefore, get away from envy by means of success alone, for there will always be in history or legend some person even more successful than you are" (pp. 68–69).

Just as comparing ourselves with those who are better off creates envy, so counting our blessings as we compare ourselves with those less well off boosts our contentment. Marshall Dermer and his colleagues (1979) demonstrated this by asking University of Wisconsin-Milwaukee women to study others' deprivation and suffering. After viewing vivid depictions of how grim life was in Milwaukee in 1900, or after imagining and then writing about various personal tragedies, such as being burned and disfigured, the women expressed greater satisfaction with their own lives. Similarly, when mildly depressed people read about someone who is even more depressed, they feel somewhat better (Gibbons, 1986). "I cried because I had no shoes," states a Persian saying, "until I met a man who had no feet."

Predictors of Happiness

OBJECTIVE **21** | Summarize the ways that we can influence our own levels of happiness.

If, as the adaptation-level phenomenon implies, our emotions tend to balance around normal, why do some people seem so filled with joy and others so gloomy day after day? What makes one person normally happy and another less so? The answers vary somewhat by culture. Self-esteem matters more to individualistic Westerners,

> "The mind of every man, in a longer or shorter time, returns to its natural and usual state of tranquility. In prosperity, after a certain time, it falls back to that state; in adversity, after a certain time, it rises up to it."
> Adam Smith, *The Theory of Moral Sentiments,* 1759

> "I have also learned why people work so hard to succeed: It is because they envy the things their neighbors have. But it is useless. It is like chasing the wind. . . . It is better to have only a little, with peace of mind, than be busy all the time with both hands, trying to catch the wind."
> Ecclesiastes 4:4

> "Our poverty became a reality. Not because of our having less, but by our neighbors having more."
> Will Campbell, *Brother to a Dragonfly,* 1977

The effect of comparison with others helps explain why students of a given level of academic ability tend to have a higher academic self-concept if they attend a school where most other students are not exceptionally able (Marsh & Parker, 1984). If you were near the top of your high school class, you might feel inferior upon entering a college where everyone was near the top of their class.

■ **adaptation-level phenomenon** our tendency to form judgments (of sounds, of lights, of income) relative to a neutral level defined by our prior experience.

■ **relative deprivation** the perception that one is worse off relative to those with whom one compares oneself.

TABLE 13.2

HAPPINESS IS . . .

Researchers Have Found That Happy People Tend To	However, Happiness Seems Not Much Related to Other Factors, Such As
Have high self-esteem (in individualistic countries).	Age.
Be optimistic, outgoing, and agreeable.	Gender (women are more often depressed, but also more often joyful).
Have close friendships or a satisfying marriage.	Education levels.
Have work and leisure that engage their skills.	Parenthood (having children or not).
Have a meaningful religious faith.	Physical attractiveness.
Sleep well and exercise.	

Source: Summarized from DeNeve & Cooper (1998), Diener & others (2003), Lucas & others (2004), Myers (1993, 2000), and Myers & Diener (1995, 1996).

social acceptance matters more to those in communal cultures (Diener & others, 2003). But across many countries, research does reveal several predictors of happiness **(TABLE 13.2).**

Although tasks and relationships affect our happiness, genes matter, too. From their study of 254 identical and fraternal twins, David Lykken and Auke Tellegen (1996) estimated that 50 percent of the difference among people's happiness ratings is heritable. Even identical twins raised apart are often similarly happy. Depending on our outlook and recent experiences,

"Researchers say I'm not happier for being richer, but do you know how much researchers make?"

our happiness seems to fluctuate around our "happiness set point," which disposes some people to be ever upbeat and others more negative. But when researchers have followed thousands of lives over two decades, they observe that people's satisfaction with life is not fixed (Fujita & Diener, 2005; Mroczek & Spiro, 2005). Satisfaction may rise or fall, and happiness can be influenced by factors that are under our control. (See Close-Up: How to Be Happier.)

Our studies of happiness, regardless of their source and duration, remind us that emotions combine physiological activation (left hemisphere especially), expressive behaviors (huge smile), and conscious experience, including thoughts (I was so ready for that test) and feelings (pride, satisfaction). Fear, anger, happiness, and so much else have this in common: They are biopsychosocial phenomena. Our genetic predispositions, brain activity, outlooks, experiences, relationships, and cultures jointly form us.

Studies of chimpanzees in zoos reveal that happiness in chimpanzees, as rated by 200 employees, is also genetically influenced (Weiss & others, 2000, 2002).

"I could cry when I think of the years I wasted accumulating money, only to learn that my cheerful disposition is genetic."

CLOSE-UP:

HOW TO BE HAPPIER

Happiness, like cholesterol level, is a genetically influenced trait. Yet as cholesterol is also influenced by diet and exercise, so our happiness is to some extent under our personal control. Here are some research-based suggestions for improving your mood and increasing your satisfaction with life.

1. *Realize that enduring happiness doesn't come from financial success.* People adapt to changing circumstances—even to wealth or a disability. Thus wealth is like health: Its utter absence breeds misery, but having it (or any circumstance we long for) doesn't guarantee happiness.

2. *Take control of your time.* Happy people feel in control of their lives, often aided by mastering their use of time. It helps to set goals and break them into daily aims. Although we often overestimate how much we will accomplish in any given day (leaving us frustrated), we generally *underestimate* how much we can accomplish in a year, given just a little progress every day.

3. *Act happy.* We can sometimes act ourselves into a frame of mind. Manipulated into a smiling expression, people feel better; when they scowl, the whole world seems to scowl back. So put on a happy face. Talk *as if* you feel positive self-esteem, are optimistic, and are outgoing. Going through the motions can trigger the emotions.

4. *Seek work and leisure that engage your skills.* Happy people often are in a zone called "flow"—absorbed in a task that challenges them without overwhelming them. The most expensive forms of leisure (sitting on a yacht) often provide less flow experience than gardening, socializing, or craft work.

5. *Join the "movement" movement.* An avalanche of research reveals that aerobic exercise not only promotes health and energy, it also is an antidote for mild depression and anxiety. Sound minds reside in sound bodies. Off your duffs, couch potatoes.

6. *Give your body the sleep it wants.* Happy people live active vigorous lives yet reserve time for renewing sleep and solitude. Many people suffer from sleep debt, with resulting fatigue, diminished alertness, and gloomy moods.

7. *Give priority to close relationships.* Intimate friendships with those who care deeply about you can help you weather difficult times. Confiding is good for soul and body. Resolve to nurture your closest relationships: to *not* take those closest to you for granted, to display to them the sort of kindness that you display to others, to affirm them, to play together and share together.

8. *Focus beyond self.* Reach out to those in need. Happiness increases helpfulness (those who feel good do good). But doing good also makes one feel good.

9. *Be grateful.* People who keep a gratitude journal—who pause each day to reflect on some positive aspect of their lives (their health, friends, family, freedom, education, senses, natural surroundings, and so on) experience heightened well-being.

10. *Nurture your spiritual self.* For many people, faith provides a support community, a reason to focus beyond self, and a sense of purpose and hope. That helps explain why people active in faith communities report greater than average happiness and often cope well with crisis.

Digested from David G. Myers, *The Pursuit of Happiness* (Avon Books)

>> LEARNING OUTCOMES

Experienced Emotion

OBJECTIVE 13 | **Name several basic emotions, and describe two dimensions psychologists use to differentiate emotions.**

Carroll Izard's research found the 10 basic emotions of joy, interest-excitement, surprise, sadness, anger, disgust, contempt, fear, shame, and guilt. Some psychologists believe that pride and love may also be basic emotions. Emotions can be placed along two basic dimensions: *arousal* (high versus low) and *valence* (pleasant, or positive, versus unpleasant, or negative).

OBJECTIVE 14 | **State two ways we learn our fears.**

What we learn through experience best explains the variety of human fears. We learn specific fears through *conditioning* (associating emotions with specific situations) and through *observational learning* (watching others display fear in response to certain events or surroundings).

OBJECTIVE 15 | **Discuss some of the biological components of fear.**
We are biologically prepared to learn some fears (snakes, spiders, heights) but not others (fast driving, bombs, electricity). The amygdala plays a key role in fear learning, associating fear with specific situations. The amygdala receives information from cortical areas that process emotion, and it sends information to other areas that produce the bodily symptoms of fear. People differ in the extent to which they are fearful or fearless, and part of that difference is genetic.

OBJECTIVE 16 | **Identify some common triggers and consequences of anger, and assess the catharsis hypothesis.**
Frustrating or insulting actions we interpret as willful, unjustified, and avoidable may evoke anger. Research does not support the *catharsis hypothesis*—the idea that releasing negative energy will calm aggressive tendencies. Venting rage may calm us temporarily, but in the long run it does not reduce anger and may actually amplify it. Anger is better handled by waiting until the level of physical arousal diminishes, calming oneself, and expressing grievances in ways that promote reconciliation rather than retaliation. When reconciliation fails, forgiveness can reduce one's anger and its physical symptoms.

OBJECTIVE 17 | **Describe how the feel-good, do-good phenomenon works, and discuss the importance of research on subjective well-being.**
The *feel-good, do-good phenomenon* is our increased willingness to help others when we are in a good mood. Research in positive psychology is currently exploring the causes and consequences of subjective well-being (self-perceived happiness or satisfaction with life), supplementing psychology's traditional focus on negative emotions.

OBJECTIVE 18 | **Discuss some of the daily and longer-term variations in the duration of emotions.**
Negative emotion is highest just after we wake up and before we go to sleep. Positive emotion rises gradually, peaking about seven hours after we rise, then falls gradually. The moods triggered by the day's good or bad events seldom last beyond that day. Even significant bad events, such as a serious illness, seldom destroy happiness for long, although we tend to underestimate our capacity to adapt.

OBJECTIVE 19 | **Summarize the findings on the relationship between affluence and happiness.**
At a basic level, money helps us avoid pain by enabling better nutrition, health care, education, and science, and these in turn increase happiness. Increases in wealth can also increase happiness in the short term. But in the longer term, research does not show an increase in happiness accompanying affluence at either the individual or national level.

OBJECTIVE 20 | **Describe how adaptation and relative deprivation affect our appraisals of our achievements.**
The *adaptation-level phenomenon* is our tendency to assess stimuli (including material possessions) by contrasting them with a neutral level that changes with our experience. The *relative-deprivation principle* is our perception that we are less well off than others with whom we compare ourselves. Thus, happiness is relative to both our past experience and our comparisons with others.

OBJECTIVE 21 | **Summarize the ways that we can influence our own levels of happiness.**
Happiness is in part genetically influenced, and in part under our own control. Research-based suggestions for improving our own happiness are (1) realizing that enduring happiness doesn't come from financial success; (2) taking control of one's time; (3) acting happy; (4) seeking work and leisure that engage one's skills; (5) exercising regularly; (6) getting adequate sleep; (7) giving priority to close relationships; (8) focusing beyond oneself; (9) being grateful for what we have; and (10) nurturing our spiritual selves.

ASK YOURSELF: **If we learn our emotional responses, we may be able to learn new responses to replace old ones. Would you like to change any of your emotional responses? Do you feel you are too easily provoked to anger or fear, for instance? How might you go about changing your behavior or your thinking in order to change your emotional reactions?**

REVIEW CHAPTER 13 : Emotion

Test Yourself

1. Christine is holding her 8-month-old baby when a fierce dog appears out of nowhere and, with teeth bared, leaps for the baby's face. Christine immediately ducks for cover to protect the baby, screams at the dog, then notices that her heart is banging in her chest and she's broken out in a cold sweat. How would the James-Lange, Cannon-Bard, and two-factor theories explain Christine's emotional reaction?

2. How do the two divisions of the autonomic nervous system help us respond to and recover from a crisis, and why is this relevant to the study of emotions?

3. Who tends to express more emotion—men or women? How do we know the answer to that question?

4. What things do (and do not) predict self-reported happiness?

Answers to the Test Yourself questions can be found in Appendix B at the end of the book.

Terms and Concepts to Remember

emotion, p. 513

James-Lange theory, p. 514

Cannon-Bard theory, p. 514

two-factor theory, p. 514

polygraph, p. 520

catharsis, p. 536

feel-good, do-good phenomenon, p. 537

subjective well-being, p. 538

adaptation-level phenomenon, p. 542

relative deprivation, p. 543

WEB

To continue your study and review of Emotion, visit this book's Web site at www.worthpublishers.com/myers. You will find practice tests, review activities, and many interesting articles and Web links for more information on topics related to Emotion.

ANOTHER VOICE ON: STRESS AND HEALTH

AUDRE LORDE (1934–1992), "LATER," FROM *THE CANCER JOURNALS*, 1980

October 5, 1978

If I said this all didn't matter I would be lying. I see this as a serious break in my work/living, but also as a serious chance to learn something that I can share for use. And I mourn the women who limit their loss to the physical loss alone, who do not move into the whole terrible meaning of mortality as both weapon and power. After all, what could we possibly be afraid of after having admitted to ourselves that we had dealt face to face with death and not embraced it? For once we accept the actual existence of our dying, who can ever have power over us again? Now I am anxious for more living—to sample and partake of the sweetness of each moment . . .

14 : Stress and Health

OBJECTIVE 1 | Identify some behavior-related causes of illness and death, and describe health psychology's contribution to the field of behavioral medicine.

No one needs to be told that psychological states cause physical reactions. Nervous about an important encounter, we feel stomach butterflies. Anxious over speaking in public, we frequent the bathroom. Smoldering over a conflict with a family member, we get a splitting headache.

If such stress endures, it may also bring on (in those physiologically predisposed) skin rashes, asthma attacks, or high blood pressure. This mind-body connection was strikingly apparent in an inadvertent experiment conducted by British Airways on an April 23, 1999, flight from San Francisco to London. Three hours after takeoff, a mistakenly played message told passengers the plane was about to crash into the sea. Although the flight crew immediately recognized the error and tried to calm the terrified passengers, several required medical assistance (Associated Press, 1999).

Prolonged stress—together with unhealthy behaviors—can increase our risk for today's four leading causes of serious illness and death: heart disease, cancer, stroke, and chronic lung disease (**FIGURE 14.1**, page 550). Centers for Disease Control researchers have attributed half of the deaths in the United States to people's behavior—to cigarette smoking, alcohol abuse, unprotected sex, ignoring doctors' orders, insufficient exercise, illicit drugs, and poor nutrition (Mokdad & others, 2004). Modify these behavioral sources of illness and we might lessen suffering, increase life expectancy, and enhance quality of life. To pursue these goals, psychologists and physicians created the interdisciplinary field of **behavioral medicine,** integrating behavioral and medical knowledge.

Health psychology provides psychology's contribution to behavioral medicine. Its numbers include many of the 3900 psychologists who were recently counted on the faculties of Canadian and U.S. medical schools (Williams & Kohut, 1999). In the early 1950s, the average medical school had 2 faculty psychologists; at the century's end, each averaged about 30 (Sheridan, 1999).

For psychologists, health is more than "merely the slowest possible rate at which one can die" (Prairie Home Companion, 1999). Health psychologists ask: How do our emotions and personality influence our risk of disease? (More on personality in Chapter 15.) What attitudes and behaviors help prevent illness and promote health and well-being? How do our perceptions of a situation determine the stress we feel? How can we reduce or control stress?

Stress and Illness

Walking along the path toward his mountain campsite, Karl hears a rustle at his feet. As he glimpses a rattlesnake, his body mobilizes: His muscles tense, his adrenaline flows, his heart pounds, and he flees, racing to the security of camp. Once there, Karl's muscles gradually relax and his heart rate and breathing ease.

At about the same time, Karen leaves her suburban apartment and, delayed by road construction, arrives at the parking lot of the commuter train station just in time to see the 8:05 pull away. Catching the next train, she arrives in the city late and elbows

■ **behavioral medicine** an interdisciplinary field that integrates behavioral and medical knowledge and applies that knowledge to health and disease.

■ **health psychology** a subfield of psychology that provides psychology's contribution to behavioral medicine.

FIGURE 14.1
The four leading causes of death in the United States in 1900 and 2000
With the conquering of the major infectious diseases, diseases influenced by behavior have now emerged as the major causes of death. The story is much the same in Canada, Australia, New Zealand, and most European countries. (From National Center for Health Statistics, *World Health Statistics Annual*, and Statistics Canada, 2002.)

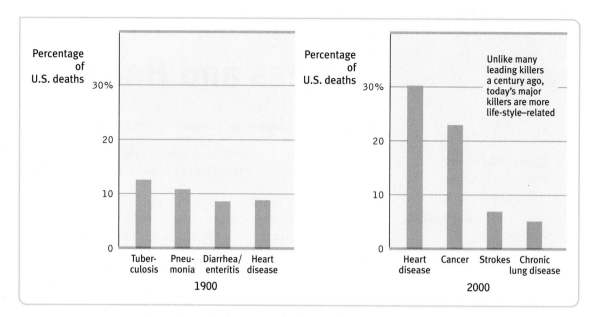

her way through crowds of rush-hour pedestrians. Once at her bank office, she apologizes to her first client, who wonders where Karen has been and why his quarterly investment report is not ready. Karen does her best to mollify the client. Afterward, she notices her tense muscles, clenched teeth, and churning stomach.

Karl's response to stress saved his life; Karen's, if chronic, could increase her risk of serious illness or stress-linked health problems. Moreover, feeling under pressure, she might sleep and exercise less and smoke and drink more, further endangering her long-term health.

Stress and Stressors

OBJECTIVE **2** | Discuss the role of appraisal in the way we respond to stressful events.

Four in 10 people frequently report experiencing stress (Saad, 2001). What are they talking about? Stress is a slippery concept. It sometimes describes threats or challenges ("Karen was under a lot of stress"), other times our responses ("When Karl saw the rattler, he experienced acute stress"). Karen's missed train was a *stressor,* Karl's physical and emotional responses were a *stress reaction,* and the process by which Karen and Karl related to their environments was *stress.*

Thus, **stress** is not just a stimulus or a response. It is the process by which we appraise and cope with environmental threats and challenges (**FIGURE 14.2**). Stress arises less from events themselves than from how we appraise them (Lazarus, 1998). One person, alone in a house, dismisses its creaking sounds and experiences no stress; someone else suspects an intruder and becomes alarmed. One person regards a new job as a welcome challenge; someone else appraises it as risking failure.

When short-lived, or when perceived as challenges, stressors can have positive effects. A momentary stress can mobilize the immune system for fending off infections and healing wounds (Segerstrom & Miller, 2004). Stress also arouses and motivates us to conquer problems. Championship athletes, successful entertainers, and great teachers and leaders all thrive and excel when aroused by a challenge (Blascovich & others, 2004). Having conquered cancer or rebounded from a lost job, some people emerge with stronger self-esteem and a deepened spirituality and sense of purpose. Indeed, some stress early in life is conducive to later emotional resilience and physical growth (Landauer & Whiting, 1979). Adversity can beget growth. The Chinese character for *crisis,* note Virginia O'Leary and Jeannette Ickovics (1995), combines the symbols for *danger* and *opportunity.*

■ **stress** the process by which we perceive and respond to certain events, called *stressors,* that we appraise as threatening or challenging.

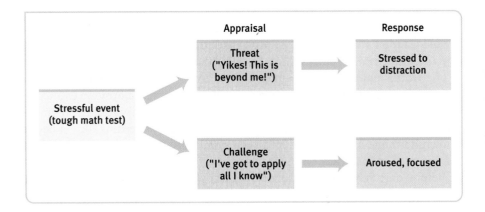

Stressful event (tough math test) → Appraisal:

Threat ("Yikes! This is beyond me!") → Response: Stressed to distraction

Challenge ("I've got to apply all I know") → Response: Aroused, focused

FIGURE 14.2
Stress appraisal
The events of our lives flow through a psychological filter. How we appraise an event influences how much stress we experience and how effectively we respond.

But stressors can also threaten us. And experiencing severe or prolonged stress may harm us. Children's physiological responses to severe child abuse put them at later risk of chronic disease (Repetti & others, 2002). Those who had post-traumatic stress reactions to heavy combat in the Vietnam War went on to suffer greatly elevated rates of circulatory, digestive, respiratory, and infectious diseases (Boscarino, 1997).

The Stress Response System

OBJECTIVE 3 | Describe the dual-track system by which our body responds to stress, and identify the three phases of the general adaptation syndrome.

Medical interest in stress dates back to Hippocrates (460–377 B.C.). But it was not until the 1920s that physiologist Walter Cannon (1929) confirmed that the stress response is part of a unified mind-body system. He observed that extreme cold, lack of oxygen, and emotion-arousing incidents all trigger an outpouring of the stress hormones epinephrine and norepinephrine from the adrenal glands. As we saw in Chapter 13's discussion of emotional arousal, this is but one part of the sympathetic nervous system's response. When alerted by any of a number of brain pathways, the sympathetic nervous system increases heart rate and respiration, diverts blood from digestion to the skeletal muscles, dulls pain, and releases sugar and fat from the body's stores—all to prepare the body for the wonderfully adaptive response that Cannon called *fight or flight*.

Since Cannon's time, physiologists have identified an additional stress response system. On orders from the cerebral cortex (via the hypothalamus and pituitary gland), the outer part of the adrenal glands secretes *glucocorticoid* stress hormones such as *cortisol*. The two stress hormone systems work at different speeds, explains biologist Robert Sapolsky (2003): "In a fight-or-flight scenario, epinephrine is the one handing out guns; glucocorticoids are the ones drawing up blueprints for new aircraft carriers needed for the war effort" (**FIGURE 14.3**).

There are alternatives to fight-or-flight. One is a common response to the stress of a loved one's death: Withdraw. Pull back. Conserve energy. Another, especially common among women, report Shelley Taylor and her colleagues (2000), is to seek and give support: "Tend and befriend."

FIGURE 14.3
Two-track stress response system
Our body responds to stress with a two-track system. (1) The sympathetic nervous system prompts the release of the stress hormones epinephrine and norepinephrine from nerve endings in the *inner* part of the adrenal glands. (2) The cerebral cortex, by way of the hypothalamus and pituitary gland, directs the release of glucocorticoid stress hormones from the *outer* part of the adrenal glands. Both systems trigger fight-or-flight physiological effects in our bodies, such as faster breathing and tense muscles.

(2) Cerebral cortex orchestrates release of glucocorticoids

Cerebral cortex (perceives stressor)

Hypothalamus

Amygdala

Pituitary gland

(1) Sympathetic nervous system triggers release of epinephrine and norepinephrine.

Arteries widen

Lungs work faster

Heart beats faster

Muscles tense

Adrenal glands release hormones

Stomach, digestion shuts down

■ **general adaptation syndrome (GAS)**
Selye's concept of the body's adaptive response to stress in three stages—alarm, resistance, exhaustion.

Canadian scientist Hans Selye's (1936, 1976) 40 years of research on stress extended Cannon's findings and helped make stress a major concept in both psychology and medicine. The story of how Selye arrived at his concept of the stress response is one worth remembering in times of intellectual discouragement. Hoping to discover a new sex hormone, Selye injected rats with ovarian hormone extract. He detected three effects: enlargement of the adrenal cortex, shrinkage of the thymus gland (which contains disease-fighting white blood cells), and bleeding ulcers. Because no known hormone had ever produced such symptoms, Selye was elated: "At the age of 28, I seemed to be already on the track of a new hormone."

Before long, Selye's elation turned to disappointment. When he injected the rats with other fluids, he observed the same effects: adrenal enlargement, thymus shrinkage, and bleeding ulcers. Alas, he concluded, the effects were *not* due to a new hormone:

> All my dreams of discovering a new hormone were shattered. All the time and all the materials that went into this long study were wasted. . . . I became so depressed that for a few days I could not do any work at all. I just sat in my laboratory, brooding. . . . The ensuing period of introverted contemplation turned out to be the decisive factor in my whole career; it pointed the way for all my subsequent work. . . . As I repetitiously continued to go over my ill-fated experiments and their possible interpretation, it suddenly struck me that one could look at them from an entirely different angle. If there was such a thing as a single nonspecific reaction of the body to damage of any kind, . . . the general medical implications of the syndrome would be enormous! (1976, pp. 24–26)

To verify his hunch, Selye studied animals' reactions to various other stressors, such as electric shock, surgical trauma, and immobilizing restraint. He discovered that the body's adaptive response to stress was so general—like a single burglar alarm that sounds no matter what intrudes—that he called it the **general adaptation syndrome (GAS)**.

Selye saw the GAS as having three phases (**FIGURE 14.4**). Let's say you suffer a physical or emotional trauma. In Phase 1, you experience an *alarm reaction* due to the sudden activation of your sympathetic nervous system. Your heart rate zooms. Blood is diverted to your skeletal muscles. You feel the faintness of shock. With your resources mobilized, you are now ready to fight the challenge during Phase 2, *resistance*.

FIGURE 14.4
Selye's general adaptation syndrome
This girl being carried to freedom and medical attention managed to escape her terrorist captors in a 2004, three-day Chechnya school holdup. After such a trauma, the body enters an alarm phase of temporary shock. From this it rebounds, as stress resistance rises. If the stress is prolonged, as it was for the 400 school hostages and their waiting loved ones, wear and tear may lead to exhaustion.

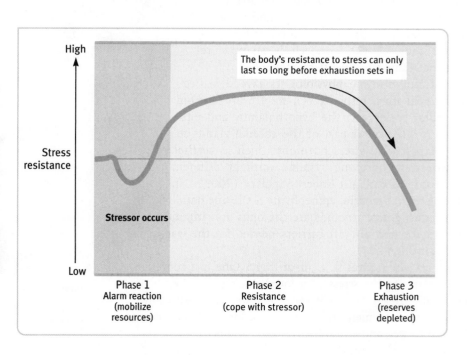

High

The body's resistance to stress can only last so long before exhaustion sets in

Stress resistance

Stressor occurs

Low

Phase 1
Alarm reaction
(mobilize resources)

Phase 2
Resistance
(cope with stressor)

Phase 3
Exhaustion
(reserves depleted)

Your temperature, blood pressure, and respiration remain high, and there is a sudden outpouring of hormones. If persistent, the stress may eventually deplete your body's reserves during Phase 3, *exhaustion*. With exhaustion, you are more vulnerable to illness or even, in extreme cases, collapse and death.

Few medical experts today quarrel with Selye's basic point: Although the human body comes designed to cope with temporary stress, prolonged stress can produce physical deterioration. In one recent study, women who suffered enduring stress as caregivers for children with serious disorders displayed a symptom that is a normal part of the aging process—shorter bits of DNA at the ends of their chromosomes (Epel & others, 2004). When these DNA pieces, called *telomeres,* get too short, the cell can no longer divide, and it ultimately dies. The most stressed women had cells that looked a decade older than their chronological age, which may help explain why severe stress seems to age people. Even fearful, easily stressed rats have been found to die sooner (after about 600 days) than their more confident siblings, which average 700-day life spans (Cavigelli & McClintock, 2004).

Other studies have taken MRI brain scans of people who have experienced a prolonged flood of stress hormones, due to sustained child abuse, combat, or an endocrine disease (Sapolsky, 1999). Most have a shrunken *hippocampus,* the inner brain structure vital to laying down explicit (declarative) memories. In animals, too, various stresses—being subordinate in a group, being physically restrained, being isolated—can cause hippocampal tissue to shrink (McEwen, 1998, 2002). Such findings serve as further incentives to today's health psychologists, as they ask, What causes stress? And how does stress affect us?

Stressful Life Events

OBJECTIVE **4** | Discuss the health consequences of catastrophes, significant life changes, and daily hassles.

Research has focused on our responses to three types of stressors: catastrophes, significant life changes, and daily hassles.

Catastrophes Catastrophes are unpredictable large-scale events, such as war and natural disasters, that nearly everyone appraises as threatening. Although people often provide one another with aid as well as comfort after such events, the health consequences can be significant. In the three weeks after the 9/11 terrorist attacks, two-thirds of Americans surveyed by University of Michigan researchers said they were having some trouble concentrating and sleeping (Wahlberg, 2001). In another national survey, New Yorkers were especially likely to report such symptoms (NSF, 2001). Sleeping pill prescriptions rose by a reported 28 percent in the New York area (HMHL, 2002).

Do other community disasters usually produce effects this great? After digesting data from 52 studies of catastrophic floods, hurricanes, and fires, Anthony Rubonis and Leonard Bickman (1991) found the typical effect more modest but nonetheless genuine. In disaster's wake, rates of psychological disorders such as depression and anxiety rose an average 17 percent. Refugees fleeing their homeland also suffer increased rates of psychological disorder. Their stress stems from the trauma of uprooting and family separation, and from the challenges of adjusting to a foreign culture's new language, ethnicity, climate, and social norms (Pipher, 2002; Williams & Berry, 1991).

Toxic stress

On the day of its 1994 earthquake, Los Angeles experienced a fivefold increase in sudden-death heart attacks—especially in the first two hours after the quake and near its epicenter. Physical exertion (running, lifting debris) was a factor in only 13 percent of the deaths, leaving stress as the likely trigger for the others (Muller & Verier, 1996).

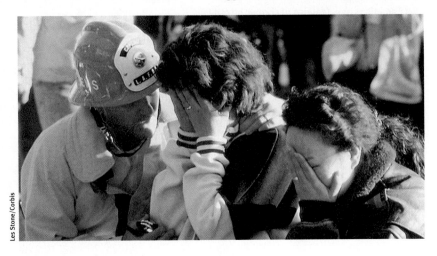

Les Stone/Corbis

■ **coronary heart disease** the clogging of the vessels that nourish the heart muscle; the leading cause of death in many developed countries

■ **Type A** Friedman and Rosenman's term for competitive, hard-driving, impatient, verbally aggressive, and anger-prone people.

■ **Type B** Friedman and Rosenman's term for easygoing, relaxed people.

"It's not the large things that send a man to the madhouse . . . no, it's the continuing series of small tragedies . . . not the death of his love but the shoelace that snaps with no time left."

Charles Bukowski, cited by Lazarus in Wallis, 1983

Significant Life Changes The second type of life-event stressor is a significant personal life change—leaving home, the death of a loved one, the loss of a job, a marriage, a divorce. Life transitions and insecurities are often keenly felt during young adulthood. That helps explain why, when 15,000 Canadian adults were asked whether "You are trying to take on too many things at once," responses indicated highest stress levels among the youngest adults (**FIGURE 14.5**). The same is true of Americans: Half of adults under age 50 report "frequent" stress, as do fewer than 30 percent of those over 50 (Saad, 2001).

Some psychologists study the health effects of life changes by following people over time to see if such events precede illnesses. Others compare the life changes recalled by those who have or have not suffered a specific health problem, such as a heart attack. A review of these studies commissioned by the U.S. National Academy of Sciences revealed that people recently widowed, fired, or divorced are more vulnerable to disease (Dohrenwend & others, 1982). A Finnish study of 96,000 widowed people confirmed the phenomenon: Their risk of death doubled in the week following their partner's death (Kaprio & others, 1987). Experiencing a cluster of crises puts one even more at risk.

Daily Hassles As we noted in Chapter 13, our happiness stems less from enduring good fortune than from our response to daily events—a perfect exam score, a gratifying e-mail, your team's winning the big game.

This principle works for negative events, too. Everyday annoyances—rush-hour traffic, aggravating housemates, long lines at the store, too many things to do, e-mail spam, and obnoxious cell-phone talkers—may be the most significant sources of stress (Kohn & Macdonald, 1992; Lazarus, 1990; Ruffin, 1993). Although some people can simply shrug off such hassles, others are "driven up the wall" by them.

Over time, these little stressors can add up and take a toll on our health and well-being. Hypertension (high blood pressure) rates are high among residents of urban ghettos, where the stresses that accompany poverty, unemployment, solo parenting, and overcrowding are part of daily life for some people. And these daily pressures may be compounded by racism, which—like other stressors—can have both psychological and physical consequences. Thinking that some of the people you encounter each day will distrust you, dislike you, or doubt your abilities makes daily life stressful. Rodney Clark and his colleagues (1999) found that this stress took a toll on the health of many African-Americans, driving up blood pressure levels.

FIGURE 14.5
Chronic stress, by age
As Canadians age, feelings of chronic stress tend to subside. (Data from Statistics Canada, 1999.)

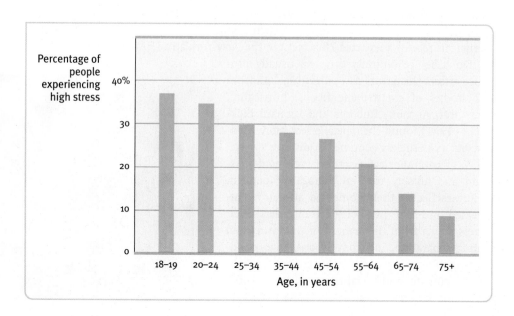

Stress and the Heart

OBJECTIVE 5 | Discuss the role of stress in causing coronary heart disease, and contrast Type A and Type B personalities.

Elevated blood pressure is just one of the factors that increase the risk of **coronary heart disease,** the closing of the vessels that nourish the heart muscle. Although infrequent before 1900, this condition became by the 1950s North America's leading cause of death, and it remains so today. In addition to hypertension and a family history of the disease, many behavioral and physiological factors—smoking, obesity, a high-fat diet, physical inactivity, and an elevated cholesterol level—increase the risk of heart disease. The psychological factors of stress and personality also play a big role.

In 1956, cardiologists Meyer Friedman, Ray Rosenman, and their colleagues stumbled upon an indication of how big that role is (Friedman & Ulmer, 1984). While studying the eating behavior of San Francisco Junior League women and their husbands, Friedman and Rosenman discovered that the women consumed as much cholesterol and fat as their husbands did, yet they were far less susceptible to heart disease. Was it because of their female sex hormones? No, the researchers surmised, because African-American women (with the same sex hormones but facing more stress than the white Junior Leaguers) were as prone to heart disease as their husbands.

The Junior League president thought she knew the answer: "It's the stress they have to face in their businesses, day in, day out," she said sadly. "Why, when my husband comes home at night, it takes at least one martini just to unclench his jaws."

To test the idea that stress increases vulnerability to heart disease, Friedman and Rosenman measured the blood cholesterol level and clotting speed of 40 tax accountants. From January through March, both of these coronary warning indicators were completely normal. Then, as the accountants began scrambling to finish their clients' tax returns before the April 15 filing deadline, their cholesterol and clotting measures rose to dangerous levels. In May and June, with the deadline past, the measures returned to normal. The researchers' hunch had paid off: Stress predicted heart attack risk.

The stage was set for Friedman and Rosenman's classic nine-year study of more than 3000 healthy men aged 35 to 59. At the start of the study, they interviewed each man for 15 minutes about his work and eating habits. During the interview, they noted the man's manner of talking and other behavioral patterns. Those who seemed the most reactive, competitive, hard-driving, impatient, time-conscious, supermotivated, verbally aggressive, and easily angered they called **Type A.** The roughly equal number who were more easygoing they called **Type B.** Which group do you suppose turned out to be the most coronary-prone?

By the time the study was complete, 257 men had suffered heart attacks; 69 percent of them were Type A. Moreover, not one of the "pure" Type Bs—the most mellow and laid-back of their group—had suffered a heart attack.

As often happens in science, this exciting discovery provoked enormous public interest. But after the honeymoon period, in which the finding seemed definitive and revolutionary, other researchers began asking: Is the finding reliable? If so, what is the toxic component of the Type A profile: Time-consciousness? Competitiveness? Anger?

In relaxed situations, the arousal of Type As and Type Bs is no different. But when harassed, given a challenge, or threatened with a loss of control, Type A individuals are more physiologically reactive. Their hormonal secretions, pulse rate, and blood pressure soar, while Type Bs remain calm (Lyness, 1993). For example, when Redford Williams (1989) asked Duke University men to do simple math problems (with a prize for the fastest), the Type A students' stress-hormone levels rose to more than double those of their Type B classmates. These hormones accelerate the buildup of

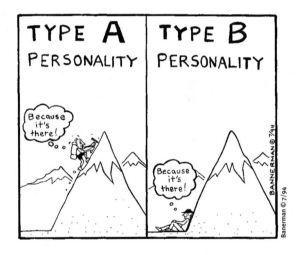

In both India and America, Type A bus drivers are literally hard-driving: They brake, pass, and honk their horns more often than their more easygoing Type B colleagues (Evans & others, 1987).

■ **psychophysiological illness** literally, "mind-body" illness; any stress-related physical illness, such as hypertension and some headaches. *Note:* This is distinct from *hypochondriasis*—misinterpreting normal physical sensations as symptoms of a disease.

■ **lymphocytes** the two types of white blood cells that are part of the body's immune system: *B lymphocytes* form in the *b*one marrow and release antibodies that fight bacterial infections; *T lymphocytes* form in the *t*hymus and other lymphatic tissue and attack cancer cells, viruses, and foreign substances.

❝The fire you kindle for your enemy often burns you more than him."

Chinese proverb

❝A cheerful heart is a good medicine, but a downcast spirit dries up the bones."

Proverbs 17:22

plaque (scarlike masses formed by cholesterol deposits) on the artery walls. And that produces atherosclerosis ("hardening" of the arteries), high blood pressure, and increased risk of strokes and heart attacks (Schneiderman & others, 1989).

These findings suggest that reactive Type A individuals are more often "combat ready." When harassed or challenged, their active sympathetic nervous system redistributes bloodflow to the muscles and away from internal organs such as the liver, which removes cholesterol and fat from the blood. Thus, their blood may contain excess cholesterol and fat that later get deposited around the heart. Further stress—sometimes conflicts brought on by their own abrasiveness—may trigger the altered heart rhythms that, in those with weakened hearts, can cause sudden death (Kamarck & Jennings, 1991). In important ways, the hearts and minds of people interact.

More recent research has revealed that Type A's toxic core is negative emotions—especially the anger associated with an aggressively reactive temperament (Smith & Ruiz, 2002; Williams, 1993). The effect of an anger-prone personality appears most noticeably in studies in which interviewers assess verbal assertiveness and emotional intensity. (If you pause in the middle of a sentence, an intense, anger-prone person may jump in and finish it for you.) Among young and middle-aged adults, those who react with anger over little things are the most coronary-prone. One study followed 13,000 middle-aged people for five years. Among those with normal blood pressure, people who had scored high on anger were three times more likely to have had heart attacks, even after researchers controlled for smoking and weight (Williams & others, 2000). Another study followed 1055 male medical students over an average of 36 years. Those who had reported being hot-tempered were five times more likely to have had a heart attack by age 55 (Chang & others, 2002). As Charles Spielberger and Perry London (1982) put it, rage "seems to lash back and strike us in the heart muscle."

Pessimism seems to be similarly toxic. Laura Kubzansky and her colleagues (2001) studied 1306 initially healthy men who a decade earlier had scored as optimists, pessimists, or neither. Over the decade, pessimists were more than twice as likely as optimists to develop heart disease, even after other risk factors such as smoking had been ruled out (**FIGURE 14.6**).

Depression, too, can be lethal. The accumulated evidence from 57 studies suggests that "depression substantially increases the risk of death, especially death by unnatural causes and cardiovascular disease" (Wulsin & others, 1999). One study of 7406 women age 67 or older found that among those with no depressive symptoms, 7 percent died within six years, as did 24 percent of those with six or more depressive symptoms (Whooley & Browner, 1998). In the years following a heart attack, people with high scores for depression are four times likelier than their low-scoring counterparts to develop further heart problems (Frasure-Smith & others, 2005). Depression is disheartening.

FIGURE 14.6
Pessimism and heart disease
A Harvard School of Public Health team found pessimistic adult men at doubled risk of developing heart disease over a 10-year period. (From Kubzansky & others, 2001.)

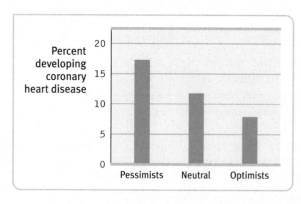

Stress and Susceptibility to Disease

OBJECTIVE 6 | Distinguish between a psychophysiological illness and hypochondriasis.

Not so long ago, the term *psychosomatic* described psychologically caused physical symptoms. To laypeople, the term implied that the symptoms were unreal—"merely" psychosomatic. To avoid such connotations and to better describe the genuine physiological effects of psychological states, most experts today refer instead to stress-related **psychophysiological illnesses,** such as hypertension and some headaches. Let's take a closer look at some ways stress also affects our resistance to disease.

Stress and the Immune System

OBJECTIVE 7 | Describe the effect of stress on immune system functioning.

Hundreds of new experiments reveal the nervous and endocrine systems' influence on the immune system (Sternberg, 2001). Your immune system is a complex surveillance system that defends your body by isolating and destroying bacteria, viruses, and other foreign substances. This system includes two types of white blood cells, called **lymphocytes.** *B lymphocytes* form in the bone marrow and release antibodies that fight bacterial infections. *T lymphocytes* form in the thymus and other lymphatic tissue and attack cancer cells, viruses, and foreign substances—even "good" ones, such as transplanted organs. Another agent of the immune system is the *macrophage* ("big eater"), which identifies, pursues, and ingests harmful invaders (**FIGURE 14.7**). Age, nutrition, genetics, body temperature, and stress all influence the immune system's activity.

FIGURE 14.7
The immune system in action
A large macrophage (at top) is about to trap and ingest a tiny bacterium (lower right). Macrophages constantly patrol our bodies in search of invaders—such as this *Escherichia coli* bacterium—and debris, such as worn-out red blood cells.

Your immune system can err in two directions. Responding too strongly, it may attack the body's own tissues, causing arthritis or an allergic reaction. Underreacting, it may allow a dormant herpes virus to erupt or cancer cells to multiply. Women are immunologically stronger than men (Morell, 1995), making them less susceptible to infections. But this very strength also makes them more susceptible to self-attacking diseases, such as lupus and multiple sclerosis.

Your immune system is not a headless horseman. The brain regulates the secretion of stress hormones, which suppress the disease-fighting lymphocytes. Thus, when animals are physically restrained, given unavoidable electric shocks, or subjected to noise, crowding, cold water, social defeat, or maternal separation, their immune systems become less active (Maier & others, 1994). One study monitored immune responses in 43 monkeys over six months (Cohen & others, 1992). Twenty-one were stressed by being housed with new roommates—three or four new monkeys—each month. (To empathize with the monkeys, recall the stress of leaving home to attend school or summer camp, and imagine having to repeat this experience monthly.) Compared with monkeys left in stable groups, the socially disrupted monkeys experienced weakened immune systems. Stress similarly depresses the immune system of humans. Consider:

" In the eyes of God or biology or what have you, it is just very important to have women."

Immunologist Normal Talal (1995)

- Surgical wounds heal more slowly in stressed animals and humans. In one experiment, dental students received *punch wounds* (precise small holes punched in the skin). Compared with wounds placed during summer vacation, those placed three days before a major exam healed 40 percent more slowly. In fact, report Janice Kiecolt-Glaser and her co-researchers (1998), "no student healed as rapidly during this stressful period as during vacation."

- In another experiment, 47 percent of participants living stress-filled lives developed colds after a virus was dropped in their noses, as did only 27 percent of those living relatively free of stress (**FIGURE 14.8**). In follow-up research, the happiest and most relaxed people were likewise markedly less vulnerable to an experimentally delivered cold virus (Cohen & others, 2003).

- Data combined from 23 studies reveal that family caregivers of people with dementia exhibit a 15 percent below-normal immune antibody response and a 23 percent increase in stress hormones (Vitaliano & others, 2003). Other data, assembled from 293 studies, confirm that chronic stress causes wear and tear on the immune system (Segerstrom & Miller, 2004).

FIGURE 14.8
Stress and colds
In an experiment by Sheldon Cohen and colleagues (1991), people with the highest life stress scores were also most vulnerable when exposed to an experimentally delivered cold virus.

"When the heart is at ease, the body is healthy."

Chinese proverb

- Managing stress may be life-sustaining. The one personality trait shared by 169 centenarians (people over 100) was their ability to manage stress well (Perls & others, 1999).

The stress effect on immunity makes physiological sense (Maier & others, 1994). It takes energy to fight infections, produce inflammations, and maintain fevers. Thus, when diseased, our bodies reduce muscular energy output by inactivity and increased sleep. But stress creates a competing energy need. Stress triggers an aroused fight-or-flight response, diverting energy from the disease-fighting system to the muscles and brain, rendering us more vulnerable to illness. The bottom line: Stress does not make us sick, but it does restrain our immune functioning, making us more vulnerable to foreign invaders.

Stress and AIDS

OBJECTIVE 8 | Discuss the findings on the link between stress and AIDS.

AIDS has become the world's fourth leading cause of death and the number one killer in Africa. AIDS, as its name tells us, is an immune disorder—an *acquired immune deficiency syndrome* caused by the *human immunodeficiency virus (HIV)*, which is spread by the exchange of bodily fluids, primarily semen and blood. If a disease spread by human contact kills slowly, as does HIV, it ironically can be lethal to more people: Those who carry the disease have time to spread it, often without realizing they are infected. When the HIV infection manifests itself as AIDS, some years after the initial infection, the person has difficulty fighting off other diseases, such as pneumonia. Worldwide, reports the United Nations, more than 25 million people have died of AIDS, including 3.1 million in 2005 (UNAIDS, 2005). (In the United States, where "only" a half-million of these fatalities have occurred, AIDS has killed more people than did combat in all the twentieth-century wars.) In 2005, some 40 million—half of them women—were infected with HIV, often without their awareness (UNAIDS, 2005). In Africa, which is ground zero for AIDS, UNAIDS (2005) warns, more than 80 million AIDS deaths are possible by 2025.

In North America and Western Europe, 75 percent of people with AIDS are men. In Sub-Saharan Africa, 60 percent of people with AIDS are women (and among 15- to 24-year-olds, 75% are women). Girls' thin layer of cervical cells makes them especially vulnerable (Altman, 2004; UNAIDS, 2005).

So if stress serves to suppress immune functioning, could it also exacerbate the course of AIDS? Researchers have found that stress and negative emotions do correlate with a progression from HIV infection to AIDS and with the speed of decline in those infected (Bower & others, 1998; Kiecolt-Glaser & Glaser, 1995; Leserman & others, 1999). HIV-infected men faced with stressful life circumstances, such as the loss of a partner, exhibit somewhat greater immune suppression and a faster disease progression.

Would efforts to reduce stress help control the disease? Although the benefits are small compared with available drug treatments, the answer appears again to be yes.

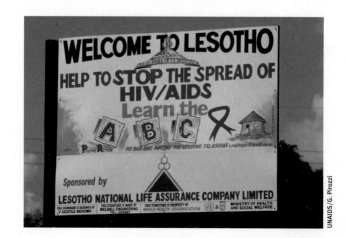

Africa is ground zero for AIDS
In Lesotho and elsewhere, the "ABC" Campaign—Abstinence, Be Faithful, and use Condoms—is a key part of prevention efforts.

Educational initiatives, bereavement support groups, cognitive therapy, and exercise programs that reduce distress have all had positive consequences for HIV-positive individuals (Baum & Posluszny, 1999; Schneiderman, 1999). Better yet is preventing HIV infection, which is the focus of many educational programs, such as the ABC (abstinence, being faithful, condom use) program used in many countries, with notable success in Uganda (Altman, 2004; USAID, 2004).

Stress and Cancer

OBJECTIVE 9 | Discuss the findings on the link between stress and cancer.

Stress and negative emotions have also been linked to cancer's rate of progression. To explore a possible connection between stress and cancer, experimenters have implanted tumor cells into rodents or given them *carcinogens* (cancer-producing substances). Those rodents also exposed to uncontrollable stress, such as inescapable shocks, were more prone to cancer (Sklar & Anisman, 1981). In rodents with immune systems weakened by stress, tumors developed sooner and grew larger.

Some investigators have reported that people are at increased risk for cancer within a year after experiencing depression, helplessness, or bereavement. One large Swedish study revealed that people with a history of workplace stress had 5.5 times greater risk of colon cancer than those who reported no such problems, a difference not attributable to differing age, smoking, drinking, or physical characteristics (Courtney & others, 1993). Other researchers have found no link between stress and human cancer (Edelman & Kidman, 1997; Fox, 1998; Petticrew & others, 1999, 2002). Concentration camp survivors and former prisoners of war, for example, have not exhibited elevated cancer rates.

One danger in hyping reports on attitudes and cancer is that some patients may be led to blame themselves for their illness—"If only I had been more expressive, relaxed, and hopeful." A corollary danger is a "wellness macho" among the healthy, who take credit for their "healthy character" and lay a guilt trip on the ill: "She has cancer? That's what you get for holding your feelings in and being so nice." Dying thus becomes the ultimate failure.

The emerging view seems to be that stress does not create cancer cells. At worst, it may affect their growth by weakening the body's natural defenses against a few proliferating, malignant cells. Although a relaxed, hopeful state may enhance these defenses, we should be aware of the thin line that divides science from wishful thinking. The powerful biological processes at work in advanced cancer or AIDS are not likely to be derailed by avoiding stress or maintaining a relaxed but determined spirit (Anderson, 2002; Kessler & others, 1991).

> "I didn't give myself cancer."
> Mayor Barbara Boggs Sigmund, 1939–1990, Princeton, New Jersey

When organic causes of illness are unknown, it is tempting to invent psychological explanations. Before the germ that causes tuberculosis was discovered, personality explanations of TB were popular (Sontag, 1978).

Conditioning the Immune System

OBJECTIVE 10 | Describe the impact of learning on immune system functioning.

A seasonal allergy sufferer sees a flower on a restaurant table and, not realizing it is plastic, begins to sneeze. Such experiences hint that stress is not the only psychological influence on the body's ailments. Simple classical conditioning may be an added influence. This raises an intriguing question: If conditioning affects the body's overt physiological responses, might it affect the immune system as well?

Psychologist Robert Ader and immunologist Nicholas Cohen (1985) discovered that the answer is yes. Ader came upon this discovery while researching taste aversion in rats. He paired the rats' drinking of saccharin-sweetened water with injections of a drug that suppresses immune functioning. After repeated pairings, sweetened water alone triggered immune suppression, as if the drug had been given (**FIGURE 14.9** on page 560). Such conditioned immune suppression can triple an animal's likelihood of growing a tumor when fed a carcinogen (Blom & others, 1995).

FIGURE 14.9
The conditioning of immune suppression
After Ader and Cohen (1985) associated sweetened water with a drug that causes immune suppression in rats, the inert substance alone triggered the conditioned immune response.

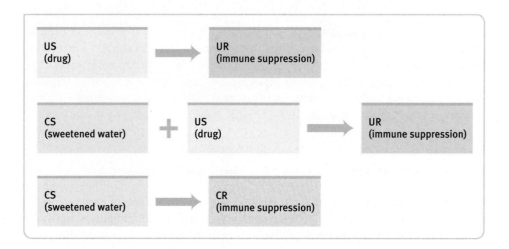

Many questions about the role of the immune system and ways to harness its healing potential remain unanswered. If it is possible to condition the immune system's suppression, should it not also be possible to condition its enhancement? Might this be one way in which *placebos*—treatments that have no biochemical effect—sometimes promote healing? Might negative beliefs—expecting the worst—have an opposite ("nocebo") effect, as people get what they expect? Although results have been mixed, researchers are hoping to answer such questions (Hróbjartsson & Gøtzsche, 2001).

For now, we can view the stress effect on our disease resistance as a price we pay for the benefits of stress (**FIGURE 14.10**). Stress invigorates our lives by arousing and motivating us. An unstressed life would hardly be challenging or productive. Moreover, it pays to spend our resources in fighting or fleeing an external threat. But we do so at the cost of diminished resources for fighting internal threats to health. When the stress is momentary, the cost is negligible. When uncontrollable aggravations persist, the cost may become considerable.

This behavioral medicine research provides yet another reminder of one of contemporary psychology's overriding themes: *Mind and body interact; everything psychological is simultaneously physiological.* Psychological states are physiological events that influence other parts of our physiological system. Just pausing to *think* about biting into an orange section—the sweet, tangy juice from the pulpy fruit flooding across your tongue—can trigger salivation. As the Indian sage Santi Parva recognized more than 4000 years ago, "Mental disorders arise from physical causes, and likewise physical disorders arise from mental causes." There is an interplay between our heads and our health. We are biopsychosocial systems.

FIGURE 14.10
Stress can have a variety of health-related consequences
This is especially so when experienced by "disease-prone" angry, depressed, or anxious persons.

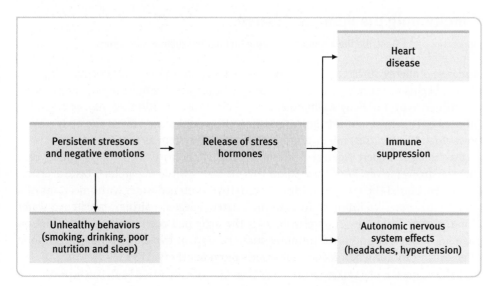

Stress and Illness

OBJECTIVE 1 | Identify some behavior-related causes of illness and death, and describe health psychology's contribution to the field of behavioral medicine.

Our behaviors, such as smoking, regular exercise, nutrition, and exposure to prolonged stress, can affect our susceptibility to heart disease, cancer, stroke, and chronic lung diseases (currently the four leading causes of death), as well as making us more vulnerable to high blood pressure, skin rashes, and other illnesses. The field of behavioral medicine is based on the understanding that mind and body interact. Within that field, health psychology studies the ways our attitudes, emotions, behaviors, and personality influence our health, well-being, and risk of disease.

OBJECTIVE 2 | Discuss the role of appraisal in the way we respond to stressful events.

Stress is not an action or a condition; instead, it is the *process* by which we respond to stressful events (stressors). An important part of that process is our appraisal of an event as threatening, challenging, or unimportant. Our appraisals help determine whether our response will be healthy feelings of energized and directed arousal, or overwhelming feelings of distress.

OBJECTIVE 3 | Describe the dual-track system by which our body responds to stress, and identify the three phases of the general adaptation syndrome.

Our response to stress is a prime example of mind-body interaction. The first (and faster) track of the stress-response system is the fight-or-flight response, identified by Walter Cannon, in which the sympathetic nervous system responds to a stressor on several fronts: The inner parts of the adrenal glands pour out epinephrine and norepinephrine, heart and respiration rates increase, blood flows away from digestive organs and toward skeletal muscles, sensations of pain diminish, and the body releases stored sugar and fat. On the slower track of the system, the cerebral cortex, perceiving a stressor, stimulates the hypothalamus and the pituitary gland to trigger the release of glucocorticoid stress hormones, such as cortisol, from the outer part of the adrenals. The three stages of the general adaptation syndrome, Hans Selye's concept of the body's response to stress, are alarm (temporary shock state in which the body mobilizes resources), resistance (period of coping with the stressor), and exhaustion (depletion of reserves following prolonged stress).

OBJECTIVE 4 | Discuss the health consequences of catastrophes, significant life changes, and daily hassles.

Large-scale catastrophic events can increase depression and anxiety and cause problems with concentrating and sleeping. Significant personal life events, such as losses (death of a loved one, a divorce, losing a job) or even changes (marriage, leaving home) may leave people vulnerable to disease. But daily hassles—the continuing series of small, everyday stressors—are the most significant sources of stress for most people and can damage health (by, for example, raising blood pressure) and well-being.

OBJECTIVE 5 | Discuss the role of stress in causing coronary heart disease, and contrast Type A and Type B personalities.

Stress can increase the risk of coronary heart disease. The vital link in this stress-disease path is negative emotions—depression, pessimism, but especially anger. The Friedman-Rosenman study, the first to show the anger–heart-disease link, contrasted Type A personalities (competitive, hard-driving, impatient, and anger-prone) with Type B personalities (easygoing and relaxed). Under stress, Type A people are physiologically more reactive, with an outpouring of hormones that accelerate the buildup of plaque on artery walls, leading to high blood pressure and increased risk of strokes and heart attacks.

OBJECTIVE 6 | Distinguish between a psychophysiological illness and hypochondriasis.

Psychologists use the term *psychophysiological illness* to describe stress-related physical illnesses, such as hypertension (high blood pressure) and some headaches. These real illnesses differ from *hypochondriasis,* or misinterpreting normal physical sensations as symptoms of a disease.

OBJECTIVE 7 | Describe the effect of stress on immune system functioning.

The immune system's B lymphocytes (formed in bone marrow) release antibodies that fight bacterial infections. The T lymphocytes (formed in the thymus and lymphatic tissue) fight cancer cells, viruses, and foreign substances. Other immune-system agents, the macrophages, ingest harmful invaders, worn-out cells, and other internal debris. Stress does not directly cause disease, but when energy is diverted away from immune system activities and redirected toward the stress-response system, we become more vulnerable to infections and disease.

OBJECTIVE 8 | Discuss the findings on the link between stress and AIDS.

AIDS is caused by the HIV virus, not by stress. But stress and negative emotions may accelerate the progression from viral infection to actual AIDS. HIV-positive individuals benefit more from drug treatments, but programs that reduce stress do seem to help somewhat.

OBJECTIVE 9 | Discuss the findings on the link between stress and cancer.

Stress does not create cancer cells. Researchers disagree on whether stress influences the disease's progression, but they do agree that avoiding stress and maintaining a hopeful and determined attitude cannot reverse the destructive processes under way in advanced cancer.

OBJECTIVE 10 | Describe the impact of learning on immune system functioning.

Researchers have conditioned immune system suppression in laboratory experiments. Encouraged by these results, others are working on ways to condition immune-system enhancement.

ASK YOURSELF: What are the stresses of your own life? How intensely do you respond to them? Are there changes you could make to avoid the persistent stressors in your life?

■ **coping** alleviating stress using emotional, cognitive, or behavioral methods.

■ **problem-focused coping** attempting to alleviate stress directly—by changing the stressor or the way we interact with that stressor.

■ **emotion-focused coping** attempting to alleviate stress by avoiding or ignoring a stressor and attending to emotional needs related to one's stress reaction.

Promoting Health

Promoting health begins with implementing strategies that prevent illness and enhance wellness. Traditionally, people have thought about their health only when something goes wrong—visiting a physician for diagnosis and treatment. That, say health psychologists, is like ignoring a car's maintenance and going to a mechanic only when the car breaks down. Now that we realize that our attitudes and behaviors affect our health, attention is turning to health maintenance—ways of coping with stress, preventing illness, and promoting well-being.

Coping With Stress

OBJECTIVE 11 | Contrast problem-focused coping and emotion-focused coping.

Stressors are unavoidable. This fact, coupled with the growing awareness that persistent stress correlates with heart disease, lowered immunity, and other bodily ailments, gives us a clear message. We need to learn to **cope** with the stress in our lives by finding emotional, cognitive, or behavioral ways to alleviate it. We address some stressors directly, with **problem-focused coping.** For example, if our impatience leads to a family fight, we may go directly to that family member to work things out. If, despite our best efforts, we cannot get along with that family member, we may also incorporate an **emotion-focused strategy,** such as reaching out to friends to help address our own emotional needs.

We tend to use problem-focused strategies when we feel a sense of control over a situation and think we can change the circumstances, or at least change ourselves to more capably deal with the circumstances. We turn to emotion-focused strategies when we cannot—or *believe* we cannot—change a situation. Sometimes these strategies are movements toward better long-term health, as when we attempt to gain emotional distance from a damaging, discontinued relationship or keep busy with active hobbies to avoid thinking about an old addiction. Emotion-focused strategies can be nonadaptive, however, as when students worried about not keeping up with the reading in class go out to party to get it off their mind. Sometimes a problem-focused strategy (catching up with the reading) more effectively reduces stress and promotes long-term health and satisfaction.

Several factors affect our ability to cope successfully, including our feelings of personal control, our explanatory style, and our supportive connections.

Perceived Control

OBJECTIVE 12 | Describe how a perceived lack of control can affect health.

If two rats receive simultaneous shocks, but one can turn a wheel to stop the shocks, the helpless rat becomes more susceptible to ulcers and lowered immunity to disease (Laudenslager & Reite, 1984) (**FIGURE 14.11**). In humans, too, uncontrollable threats trigger the strongest stress responses (Dickerson & Kemeny, 2004). For example, a bacterial infection often combines with uncontrollable stress to produce the most severe ulcers (Overmier & Murison, 1997). To cure the ulcer, kill the bug with antibiotics and control the acid secretions with reduced stress.

Perceiving a loss of control, we become vulnerable to ill health. Elderly nursing home residents who have little perceived control over their activities tend to decline faster and die sooner than do those given more control over their activities (Rodin, 1986). Workers given control over their work environment—by being able to adjust office furnishings and control interruptions and distractions—also experience less stress (O'Neill, 1993). This helps explain why British civil service workers at the executive grades outlive those at clerical or laboring grades, and why Finnish workers with

"Executive" rat   "Subordinate" rat   Control rat

To shock control   To shock source   No connection to shock source

FIGURE 14.11
Health consequences of a loss of control
The "executive" rat at the left can switch off the tail shock by turning the wheel. Because it has control over the shock, it is no more likely to develop ulcers than is the unshocked control rat on the right. The "sub-ordinate" rat in the center receives the same shocks as the executive rat, but with no control over the shocks, it is more likely to develop ulcers. (Adapted from Weiss, 1977.)

low job stress are less than half as likely to die of cardiovascular disease (strokes or heart disease) as those with a demanding job and little control. The more control workers have, the longer they live (Bosma & others, 1997, 1998; Kivimaki & others, 2002; Marmot & others, 1997).

Control may also help explain a well-established link between economic status and longevity. In one study of 843 grave markers in an old graveyard in Glasgow, Scotland, those with the costliest, highest pillars (indicating the most affluence) tended to live the longest (Carroll & others, 1994). Likewise, Scottish regions with the least overcrowding and unemployment have the greatest longevity. There and elsewhere, high economic status predicts a lower risk of heart and respiratory diseases (Sapolsky, 2005). Wealthy predicts healthy among children, too (Chen, 2004). With higher economic status comes lower risks of infant mortality, low birth weight, smoking, and violence. Even among other primates, those at the bottom of the social pecking order are more likely than their higher-status companions to become sick when exposed to a coldlike virus (Cohen & others, 1997). But for those high-status baboons and monkeys who frequently have to physically defend their dominant position, high-status also entails stress (Sapolsky, 2005).

Why does perceived loss of control predict health problems? Animal studies show—and human studies confirm—that losing control provokes an outpouring of stress hormones. When rats cannot control shock or when primates or humans feel unable to control their environment, stress hormone levels rise, blood pressure increases, and immune responses drop (Rodin, 1986; Sapolsky, 2005). Captive animals therefore experience more stress and are more vulnerable to disease than are wild animals (Roberts, 1988). The crowding that occurs in high-density neighborhoods, prisons, and college dorms is another source of diminished feelings of control—and of elevated levels of stress hormones and blood pressure (Fleming & others, 1987; Ostfeld & others, 1987).

Explanatory Style

OBJECTIVE **13** | Discuss the links among explanatory style, stress, and health.

Another influence on our coping with stress is whether our basic outlook is optimistic or pessimistic. Psychologists Michael Scheier and Charles Carver (1992) report that optimists—people who agree with statements such as, "In uncertain times, I usually expect the best"—perceive more control, cope better with stressful events, and enjoy better health. During the last month of a semester, students previously identified as optimistic report less fatigue and fewer coughs, aches, and pains. And during

Friendships are good medicine
Several long-term studies of thousands of people have found that individuals with close supportive relationships are less likely than socially isolated people to die prematurely.

"There ain't much fun in medicine, but there's a heck of a lot of medicine in fun."
Humorist Josh Billings, 1818–1885

the stressful first few weeks of law school, those who are optimistic ("It's unlikely that I will fail") enjoy better moods and stronger infection-thwarting immune systems (Segerstrom & others, 1998). Optimists also respond to stress with smaller increases in blood pressure, and they recover more quickly from heart bypass surgery.

One study that followed 2428 middle-aged Finnish men for up to 10 years discovered that the number of deaths among men with a bleak, hopeless outlook was more than double that found among their optimistic counterparts. Another study asked 795 Americans aged 64 to 79 years if they were "hopeful about the future." When the researchers checked up on these folks about five years later, 29 percent of those answering "No" had died—more than double the 11 percent of deaths among those who said "Yes" (Stern & others, 2001). Mayo Clinic research similarly finds that optimists tend to outlive pessimists (Maruta & others, 2002).

Those with a hopeful outlook live longer. At least that was so among 180 Catholic nuns who at about 22 years of age wrote brief autobiographies. Despite living thereafter with similar life-styles and status, those who had expressed happiness, love, and other positive feelings lived an average seven years longer than their more dour counterparts (Danner & others, 2001). By age 80, some 54 percent of those expressing few positive emotions had died, as had only 24 percent of the most positive-spirited.

Those who manage to find humor in life's daily events also seem to benefit. Laughter arouses us, massages muscles, and then leaves us feeling relaxed (Robinson, 1983). There is not yet enough consistent evidence to suggest that "laughter is the best medicine" (Martin, 2001, 2002). But some recent studies suggest that mirthful humor (not hostile sarcasm) may defuse stress and strengthen immune activity (Berk & others, 2001; Kimata, 2001). People who laugh a lot also have exhibited a lower incidence of heart disease (Clark & others, 2001). In one experiment, laughter in response to a hilarious movie clip caused the blood vessels' inner lining to respond with improved tone and increased blood flow, the opposite of what happened after people viewed a stressful movie clip (Miller, 2005). Perhaps future experiments will show that, indeed, those who laugh, last.

Social Support

OBJECTIVE **14** | Describe some of the ways that social support acts as a stress buffer.

Social support also matters. Consider Linda and Emily. When interviewed for a study conducted by UCLA social psychologist Shelley Taylor (1989), both Los Angeles women had married, raised three children, suffered comparable breast tumors, and recovered from surgery and six months of chemotherapy. But there was a difference. Linda, a widow in her early fifties, was living alone, her children scattered in Atlanta, Boston, and Europe. "She had become odd in ways that people sometimes do when they are isolated," reported Taylor. "Having no one with whom to share her thoughts on a daily basis, she unloaded them somewhat inappropriately with strangers, including our interviewer."

Interviewing Emily was difficult in a different way. Phone calls interrupted. Her children, all living nearby, were in and out of the house, dropping things off with a quick kiss. Her husband called from his office for a brief chat. Two dogs roamed the house, greeting visitors enthusiastically. All in all, Emily "seemed a serene and contented person, basking in the warmth of her family."

Three years later, the researchers tried to reinterview the women. Linda, they learned, had died two years before. Emily was still lovingly supported by her family and friends and was as happy and healthy as ever.

CLOSE-UP:

PETS ARE FRIENDS, TOO

Jonathan Cavendish /Corbis

Have you ever wished for a friend who would love you just as you are, who is nonjudgmental, and who is always there for you, no matter your mood? For many tens of millions of people that friend exists, and it is a loyal dog or a friendly cat.

Many people describe their pet as a cherished family member who helps them feel calm, happy, and valued. Can pets also help people handle stress? If so, might pets have a healing power? From her review of research, Karen Allen (2003) reports that, yes, pets have been found to increase the odds of survival after a heart attack, to relieve depression among AIDS patients, and to lower the level of blood lipids that contribute to cardiovascular risk. As nursing pioneer Florence Nightingale (1860) foresaw, "A small pet animal is often an excellent companion for the sick." Allen reports from her own research that women's blood pressure rises as they struggle with challenging math problems in the presence of a best friend or even a spouse, but much less so when accompanied by their dog.

So would pets be good medicine for people who do not have pets? To find out, Allen studied a group of stockbrokers who lived alone, described their work as stressful, and had high blood pressure. She randomly selected half to adopt an animal shelter cat or dog. When later facing stress, these new pet owners exhibited less than half the blood pressure increase of their counterparts without pets. The effect was greatest for those with few social contacts or friends. Her conclusion: For lowering blood pressure, pets are no substitute for effective drugs and exercise, but they are, for those who enjoy animals and live alone, a healthy pleasure.

Pet Ownership Statistics (in millions)

	Dogs	Cats
Australia	4.0	3.5
Canada	3.5	4.5
United States	65	75
United Kingdom	6.1	7.5

Sources: petnet.com.au, Statistics Canada, U.S. Humane Society, U.K. Cats Protection League

No two cancers are identical, so we cannot be certain that different social situations led to Linda's and Emily's fates. But they do illustrate a conclusion drawn from several large studies: Social support—feeling liked, affirmed, and encouraged by intimate friends and family—promotes not only happiness, but also health. Humans aren't the only source of stress-buffering comfort. After stressful events, Medicare patients who have a dog or other companionable pet are less likely to visit their doctor (Siegel, 1990). (See Close-Up: Pets Are Friends, Too.)

Relationships can sometimes be stressful, especially in crowded living conditions lacking privacy (Evans & others, 1989). "Hell is others," wrote Jean-Paul Sartre. Peter Warr and Roy Payne (1982) asked a representative sample of British adults what, if anything, had emotionally strained them the day before. Their most frequent answer? "Family."

But asked what prompted yesterday's times of pleasure, the same British sample, by an even larger margin, again answered, "Family." For most of us, family relationships provide not only our greatest heartaches (even when well-meaning, family intrusions can be stressful) but also our greatest comfort and joy. Moreover, seven massive investigations, each following thousands of people for several years, revealed that close relationships predict health. Compared with those having few social ties, people are less likely to die prematurely if supported by close relationships with friends, family, fellow workers, members of a faith community, or other support groups (Cohen, 1988; House & others, 1988; Nelson, 1988). Leukemia and heart disease patients also have enjoyed markedly increased survival rates if married or supported by family or friends (Case & others, 1992; Colon & others, 1991; Williams & others, 1992).

Carefully controlled studies indicate that married people live longer, healthier lives than the unmarried (Murray, 2000; Wilson & Oswald, 2002). The National Center for

> "Woe to one who is alone and falls and does not have another to help."
>
> Ecclesiastes 4:10

Health Statistics (2004) reports that regardless of people's age, sex, race, and income, they tend to be healthier if married. Married folks experience less pain from headaches and backaches, suffer less stress, drink and smoke less, and, despite being slightly more overweight, are generally healthier. A seven-decades-long Harvard study found that a good marriage at age 50 predicts healthy aging better than does a low cholesterol level at 50 (Vaillant, 2002). But marital functioning also matters. Conflict-laden marriages are not conducive to health; positive, happy, supportive ones are (Kiecolt-Glaser & Newton, 2001). One five-year study following 1532 older married adults found it was even better to give than to receive. After controlling for preexisting health and personality differences, researchers observed a markedly lower risk of dying during the five-year period among those who frequently reached out to help friends and neighbors and who made their spouse feel loved and cared for (Brown & others, 2003).

How can we explain this link between social support and health? Is it just that healthy people are more likely to support others and to marry and stay married? Actually, the research suggests that people with supportive friends and marriage partners eat better, exercise more, sleep better, and smoke less, and therefore cope with stress more effectively (Helgeson & others, 1998).

Environments that support our need to belong also foster stronger immune functioning. Given ample social support, spouses of cancer patients exhibit stronger immune functioning (Baron & others, 1990). Social ties and positive sociability even confer resistance to cold viruses. Sheldon Cohen and his colleagues (1997, 2004) demonstrated this by putting 276 healthy volunteers in quarantine for five days after administering nasal drops laden with a cold virus, and then repeating the experiment with 334 more volunteers. (In both experiments, the volunteers were paid $800 each to endure this experience.) The cold fact is that the effect of social ties is nothing to sneeze at. Age, race, sex, smoking, and other health habits being equal, those with the most social ties were least likely to catch a cold and they produced less mucus. More sociability meant less susceptibility. More than 50 studies further reveal that social support calms the cardiovascular system, lowering blood pressure and stress hormones (Uchino & others, 1996, 1999).

> "I get by with a little help from my friends."
>
> John Lennon and Paul McCartney, *Sgt. Pepper's Lonely Hearts Club Band*, 1967

Close relationships also provide the opportunity to *confide* painful feelings, a social support component that has now been extensively studied. In one study, health psychologists James Pennebaker and Robin O'Heeron (1984) contacted the surviving spouses of people who had committed suicide or died in car accidents. Those who bore their grief alone had more health problems than those who could express it openly. Talking about our troubles can be "open heart therapy."

Older people, many of whom have lost a spouse and close friends, are somewhat less likely to enjoy such confiding (**FIGURE 14.12**), and suppressing emotions is sometimes detrimental to our physical health. When Pennebaker surveyed more than 700 undergraduate women, he found that about 1 in 12 reported a traumatic sexual experience in childhood. Compared with women who had experienced nonsexual traumas, such as parental death or divorce, the sexually abused women—especially those who had kept their secret to themselves—reported more headaches and stomach ailments. Another study, of 437 Australian ambulance drivers, confirmed the ill effects of suppressing one's emotions after witnessing traumas (Wastell, 2002).

Actively suppressing thoughts can cause them to bubble up intrusively, preoccupying the person (Wegner, 1990). (In the next five seconds, please *do not* picture a white bear.) Disclosing suppressed thoughts may stop the cycle. In a simulated confessional, Pennebaker asked volunteers to share with a hidden experimenter some upsetting events that had been preying on their minds. He asked some of the volunteers to describe a trivial event before they divulged the troubling one. Physiological measures revealed that their bodies remained tense the whole time they talked about the trivial event; they relaxed only when they later confided the cause of their turmoil.

■ **aerobic exercise** sustained exercise that increases heart and lung fitness; may also alleviate depression and anxiety.

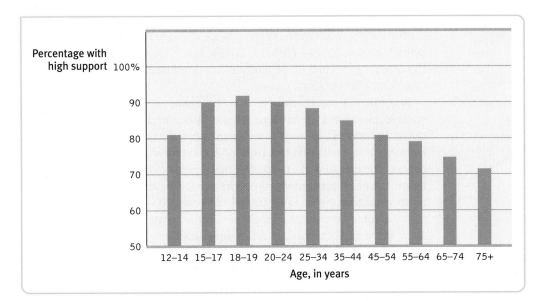

Percentage with high support

FIGURE 14.12
Social support across the life span
Do you have someone you can confide in? Someone to count on in a crisis? Someone to count on for advice? Someone who makes you feel loved and cared for? In a national health survey, 9 in 10 young adult Canadians, but only 7 in 10 over the age of 75, indicated high social support by answering yes to all four questions. (Data from Statistics Canada, 1999, p. 133.)

Writing about personal traumas in a diary can also help (Hemenover, 2003; Lyubomirsky & others, 2006). When volunteers in one experiment did this, they had fewer health problems during the ensuing four to six months (Pennebaker, 1990). As one participant explained, "Although I have not talked with anyone about what I wrote, I was finally able to deal with it, work through the pain instead of trying to block it out. Now it doesn't hurt to think about it."

Pennebaker and his colleagues (1989) also invited 33 Holocaust survivors to spend two hours recalling their experiences. Many did so in intimate detail never before disclosed. In the weeks following, most watched a videotape of their recollections and showed it to family and friends. Those who were most self-disclosing had the most improved health 14 months later. Talking about a stressful event can temporarily arouse people, but in the long run it calms them (Mendolia & Kleck, 1993). Confiding is good for the soul.

Managing Stress

Having a sense of control, developing a more optimistic explanatory style, and building our base of social support can help us *experience* less stress and thus improve our health. But sometimes we cannot alleviate stress and simply need to *manage* our stress in a healthful way. Aerobic exercise, biofeedback, relaxation, meditation, and spirituality may help us gather inner strength and lessen stress.

Aerobic Exercise

OBJECTIVE 15 | Discuss the advantages of aerobic exercise as a technique for managing stress and fostering well-being.

Aerobic exercise is sustained exercise that increases heart and lung fitness. Jogging, swimming and biking are common examples. Such exercise strengthens the body. Does it also boost the spirit?

Exercise and Mood Many studies suggest that aerobic exercise can reduce stress, depression, and anxiety. For example, 3 in 10 American and Canadian, and 2 in 10 British people who do aerobic exercise three times a week or more also manage stressful events better, exhibit more self-confidence, feel more vigor, and feel depressed and fatigued less often than those who exercise less (McMurray, 2004). In a 2002

"Is there anyone here who specializes in stress management?"

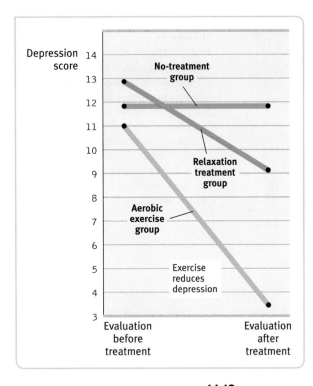

FIGURE 14.13

Aerobic exercise and depression
Mildly depressed college women who participated in an aerobic exercise program showed markedly reduced depression, compared with those who did relaxation exercises or received no treatment. (From McCann & Holmes, 1984.)

Gallup survey, nonexercisers were twice as likely as exercisers to report being "not too happy" (Brooks, 2002). But if we state this observation the other way around—that stressed and depressed people exercise less—cause and effect become unclear.

Experiments have resolved this ambiguity by randomly assigning stressed, depressed, or anxious people either to aerobic exercise or to other treatments. In one such experiment, Lisa McCann and David Holmes (1984) assigned one third of a group of mildly depressed female college students to a program of aerobic exercise and another third to a treatment of relaxation exercises; the remaining third, a control group, received no treatment. As **FIGURE 14.13** shows, 10 weeks later the women in the aerobic exercise program reported the greatest decrease in depression. Many of them had, quite literally, run away from their troubles. Vigorous exercise provides a "substantial" immediate mood boost, reports David Watson (2000) from his monitoring of university students. Even a 10-minute walk stimulates two hours of increased well-being by raising energy levels and lowering tension (Thayer, 1987, 1993).

More than 150 other studies confirm that exercise reduces depression and anxiety and is therefore a useful adjunct to antidepressant drugs and psychotherapy (Arent & others, 2000; Berger & Motl, 2000; Dunn & others, 2005). Not only is exercise about as effective as drugs, some research suggests it better prevents symptom recurrence (Babyak & others, 2000; Salmon, 2001). Researchers are now wondering *why* aerobic exercise alleviates negative emotions. They know that exercise:

- orders up mood-boosting chemicals from our body's internal pharmacy—neurotransmitters such as norepinephrine, serotonin, and the endorphins (Jacobs, 1994; Salmon, 2001).
- modestly enhances cognitive abilities, such as memory (Etnier & others, 1997).
- promotes the growth of new brain cells in mice exercising daily on a running-wheel regimen (Kempermann & Gage, 1999).

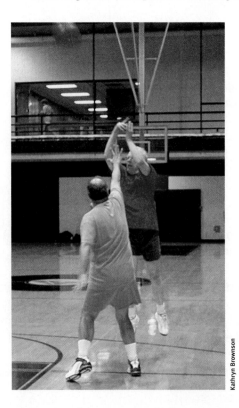

The mood boost
When one's energy or spirits are sagging, few things reboot the day better than exercising (as I can vouch from my daily noontime basketball). Aerobic exercise appears to counteract depression partly by increasing arousal (replacing depression's low-arousal state) and by doing naturally what Prozac does—increasing the brain's serotonin activity.

Perhaps the emotional benefits of exercise are also a side effect of increased warmth and body arousal (counteracting depression's low arousal state), or of the muscle relaxation and sounder sleep that occur afterward. Or perhaps a sense of accomplishment and an improved physique enhance one's emotional state.

Exercise and Health Other research reveals that exercise not only boosts our mood, but also strengthens the heart, increases blood flow, keeps blood vessels open, and lowers both blood pressure and the blood pressure reaction to stress (Ford, 2002; Manson, 2002). And being physically healthy may make us stronger and better able to manage our stress. Compared with inactive adults, people who exercise suffer half as many heart attacks (Powell & others, 1987). Exercise makes the muscles hungry for the "bad fats" that, if not used by the muscles, contribute to clogged arteries (Barinaga, 1997). One study following adult Finnish twins for nearly 20 years revealed that, other things being equal, occasional exercise reduced the risk of death by 29 percent, compared with no exercise. Daily conditioning exercise reduced death risk by 43 percent (Kujala & others, 1998).

The genes passed down to us from our distant ancestors were those that enabled the physical activity essential to hunting, foraging, and farming. In muscle cells, those genes, when activated by exercise, respond by producing proteins. In the modern inactive person, note biologists Frank Booth and Darrell Neufer (2005), these genes produce lower quantities of proteins and leave us susceptible to more than 20 chronic diseases, such as type-2 diabetes, cardiovascular disease, and cancer. Inactivity is thus potentially toxic.

By one estimate, moderate exercise adds two years to one's expected life. "Perhaps God does not subtract the time spent exercising from your allotted time on Earth," jests Martin Seligman (1994, p. 193).

Biofeedback, Relaxation, and Meditation

OBJECTIVE 16 | Compare the benefits of biofeedback and relaxation training as stress-management techniques, and discuss meditation as a relaxation technique.

Knowing the damaging effects of stress, could we train people to bring their heart rate and blood pressure under conscious control? When a few psychologists started experimenting with this idea, many of their colleagues thought them foolish. After all, these functions are controlled by the autonomic ("involuntary") nervous system. Then, in the late 1960s, experiments by respected psychologists made the skeptics wonder. Neal Miller, for one, found that rats could modify their heartbeat if given pleasurable brain stimulation when their heartbeat increased or decreased. Later research revealed that some paralyzed humans could also learn to control their blood pressure (Miller & Brucker, 1979).

Miller was experimenting with **biofeedback,** a system of recording, amplifying, and feeding back information about subtle physiological responses. Biofeedback instruments mirror the results of a person's own efforts, thereby allowing the person to learn techniques for controlling a particular physiological response (**FIGURE 14.14**).

After a decade of study, however, researchers decided the initial claims for biofeedback were overblown and oversold (Miller, 1985). A 1995 National Institutes of Health panel declared that biofeedback works best on tension headaches. Many have since turned to alternative medicine (see Thinking Critically About: Alternative Medicine—New Ways to Health, or Old Snake Oil? on page 570) in search of quick relief from stress and illnesses, but simple methods of relaxation, which require no expensive equipment, produce many of the same results biofeedback once promised.

Sixty studies find that relaxation procedures can help alleviate headaches, hypertension, anxiety, and insomnia (Stetter & Kupper, 2002). Such findings would not surprise Meyer Friedman and his colleagues. To find out whether teaching Type A heart attack victims to relax might reduce their risk of another attack, the researchers randomly assigned hundreds of middle-aged, male heart-attack survivors to one of two groups. The first group received standard advice from cardiologists concerning medications, diet, and exercise habits. The second group received similar advice plus continuing counseling on modifying their life-styles—how to slow down and relax by walking, talking, and eating more slowly; by smiling at others

biofeedback a system for electronically recording, amplifying, and feeding back information regarding a subtle physiological state, such as blood pressure or muscle tension.

System receives signal — Amplifies signal — Processes signal

Displays signal

Feedback

Patient observes signal

FIGURE 14.14
Biofeedback systems Biofeedback systems— such as this one, which records tension in the forehead muscle of a headache sufferer— allow people to monitor their subtle physiological responses. As this man relaxes his forehead muscle, the pointer on the display screen (or a tone) may go lower.

ALTERNATIVE MEDICINE—NEW WAYS TO HEALTH, OR OLD SNAKE OIL?

One health care growth market is **complementary and alternative medicine**, which encompasses such methods as acupuncture, massage therapy, homeopathy, spiritual healing, herbal remedies, chiropractic, and aromatherapy. In Germany, herbal remedies and homeopathy are enormously popular. In China, herbal therapies have long flourished, as have acupuncture and acupressure therapies that claim to correct "imbalances of energy flow" (called *Qi* or *Chi*) at identifiable points close to the skin. Andrew Weil's many books on alternative medicine have sold millions of copies, putting him on the cover of *Time* magazine. Facing political pressure to explore such things, the U.S. National Institutes of Health established the National Center for Complementary and Alternative Medicine, which the center defines as health care treatments not taught widely in medical schools, not usually reimbursed by insurance companies, and not used in hospitals (**TABLE 14.1**).

So what shall we make of alternative medicine? Some aspects, such as life-style changes and stress management, have acknowledged validity. Do the other aspects offer, as some believe, a new medical paradigm? Or do they represent, as others maintain, a retreat from rationality and science?

Supporters of alternative medicine offer inspirational cases, such as these from Andrew Weil's books (Relman, 1998):

- A young woman diagnosed with bone cancer starts a vigorous exercise program (biking 500 miles and running 60 miles weekly), becomes vegetarian (consuming fresh fruit, juices, and whole grains), and shucks the alleged cancer.
- A woman uses "respiratory biofeedback" to end her Parkinson's-induced seizures.
- A man with scleroderma, a progressive and fatal disease of the skin and internal organs, cures himself with vinegar, lemons, aloe vera juice, and vitamin E.

Critics point out that people consult physicians for diagnosable, curable diseases and employ alternative medicine when they are either incurably ill or well but feeling subpar. Thus, an otherwise healthy person with a cold may try an herbal remedy and then credit the subsequent return to good health to alternative medicine, rather than to the body's natural return to normal. (Of course, the same may happen when people take traditional medicine for a cold.) Alternative medicine will seem especially effective with cyclical diseases, such as arthritis and allergies, as people seek therapy during the downturn and presume its effectiveness during the ensuing upturn. Add to this the healing power of belief—the placebo effect—plus the natural disappearance (*spontaneous remission*) of many diseases, and alternative medicine practices are bound to seem effective, whether they are or not. One study of 302 migraine headache patients in Germany found that 51 percent of those receiving acupuncture treatment found relief, as did only 15 percent of those in a waiting list control group. But among a third group that received "sham acupuncture" (needles inserted at nonacupuncture points), 53 percent enjoyed relief. Such results, the investigators suspected, may indicate "a powerful placebo effect" (Linde & others, 2005).

The National Council Against Health Fraud and the editors of leading medical journals and of the *Scientific Review of Alternative Medicine* doubt the efficacy of alternative medicine therapies. "After more than ten years and $200 million," contends Kimball Atwood (2003), government-funded alternative medicine research "has not demonstrated efficacy" for any of the alternative medicine treatments studied.

Sickness is the manifestation of evil in the body."

Andrew Weil, Health and Healing, 1998

and laughing at themselves; by admitting mistakes; by taking time to enjoy life; and by renewing their religious faith. As **FIGURE 14.15** on page 572 indicates, during the ensuing three years, the second group experienced half as many repeat heart attacks as the first group. This, wrote the exuberant Friedman, is an unprecedented, spectacular reduction in heart-attack recurrence. A smaller-scale British study similarly divided heart-attack–prone people into control and life-style modification groups (Eysenck & Grossarth-Maticek, 1991). During the next 13 years, it also found a 50 percent reduction in death rate among those trained to alter their thinking and life-style.

TABLE 14.1

SUBFIELDS OF ALTERNATIVE MEDICINE

Alternative systems of medical practice	Health care ranging from self-care following popular beliefs to treatments based on alternative traditions or practices
Bioelectromagnetic applications	The study of how living organisms interact with electromagnetic (EM) fields
Diet, nutrition, life-style changes	The knowledge of how to prevent illness, maintain health, and reverse the effects of chronic disease through dietary or nutritional intervention
Herbal medicine	Employing plant and plant products from folk medicine traditions for pharmacological use
Manual healing	Using touch and manipulation with the hands as a diagnostic and therapeutic tool
Mind-body control	Exploring the mind's capacity to affect the body, based on traditional medical systems that make use of the interconnectedness of mind and body
Pharmacological and biological treatments	Drugs and vaccines not yet accepted by mainstream medicine

Source: Offered without endorsement by the National Center for Complementary and Alternative Medicine (nccam.nih.gov)

> "In God we trust. All others must have data."
> George Lundberg, Editor, Journal of the American Medical Association, 1998

In November 1998, the *Journal of the American Medical Association* published seven new alternative medicine research studies. Three explored treatments that proved useless (chiropractic manipulation for tension headaches, a popular herb for weight loss, and acupuncture to control nerve pain caused by HIV). Four other treatments, however—an herb mixture for inflammatory bowel syndrome, an herbal remedy for bladder problems, yoga for carpal tunnel syndrome pain, and a Chinese method for inducing fetuses in the breech position to turn—showed some benefits. As always, the way to discern what works and what does not is to experiment: Randomly assign patients to receive the therapy or a placebo control. Then ask the critical question: When neither the therapist nor the patient knows who is getting the real therapy, is the real therapy effective?

Much of today's mainstream medicine began as yesterday's alternative medicine. Natural botanical life has given us digitalis (from purple foxglove), morphine (from the opium poppy), and penicillin (from penicillium mold). In each case, the active ingredient was verified in controlled trials. We have medical and public health science to thank for the antibiotics, vaccines, surgical procedures, sanitation, and emergency medicine that helped lengthen our life expectancy by three decades during the last century. If you have acute chest pain, find a lump in your chest, cough up blood, or develop a high fever, you would do well to seek out someone trained in medical science—someone undergirded by research on what treatments really work best for what ailments at what doses for what lengths of time.

Indeed, said *New England Journal of Medicine* editors Marcia Angell and Jerome Kassirer (1998), "There cannot be two kinds of medicine—conventional and alternative. There is only medicine that has been adequately tested and medicine that has not, medicine that works and medicine that may or may not work. Once a treatment has been tested rigorously, it no longer matters whether it was considered alternative at the outset."

■ **complementary and alternative medicine** Unproven health care treatments not taught widely in medical schools, not used in hospitals, and not usually reimbursed by insurance companies.

Cardiologist Herbert Benson (1996) became intrigued with meditative relaxation when he found that experienced meditators could decrease their blood pressure, heart rate, and oxygen consumption and raise their fingertip temperature. You can experience the essence of this *relaxation response,* as Benson calls it, right now: Assume a comfortable position, breathe deeply, and relax your muscles from foot to face. Now, close your eyes and focus on a single word or a phrase. (About 80 percent of Benson's patients choose to focus on a favorite prayer.) When other thoughts intrude, let them drift away as you silently repeat your phrase continually for 10 to 20 minutes. Tibetan Buddhists deep in meditation and Franciscan nuns

Meditation is a modern phenomenon with a long history: "Sit down alone and in silence. Lower your head, shut your eyes, breathe out gently, and imagine yourself looking into your own heart. . . . As you breathe out, say 'Lord Jesus Christ, have mercy on me.' . . . Try to put all other thoughts aside. Be calm, be patient, and repeat the process very frequently" (Gregory of Sinai, died 1346).

FIGURE 14.15
Recurrent heart attacks and life-style modification
The San Francisco Recurrent Coronary Prevention Project offered counseling from a cardiologist to survivors of heart attacks. Those who were also guided in modifying their Type A life-style suffered fewer repeat heart attacks. (From Friedman & Ulmer, 1984.)

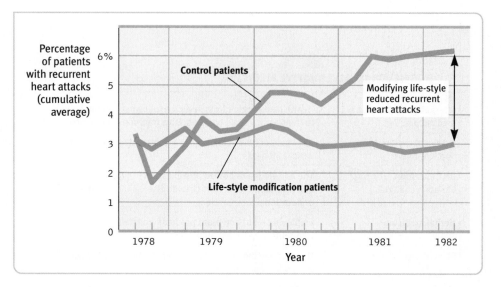

deep in centering prayer report a diminished sense of self, space, and time. Brain scans reveal the neural footprints of such spiritual feelings during these mystical experiences: A part of the parietal lobe that tracks where we are in space is less active than usual, and a frontal lobe area involved in focused attention is more active (Newberg & D'Aquili, 2001).

Psychologist Richard Davidson reports that Buddhist monks who are experienced in meditation display elevated levels of the left frontal lobe activity associated with positive emotions. To explore whether such activity is a *result* of meditation, Davidson and his colleagues (2003) ran baseline brain scans of all volunteers and then randomly assigned them either to a control group or to an eight-week course in "mindfulness meditation." Compared with both the control group and their own baseline, the meditation participants exhibited noticeably more left-hemisphere activity, and also improved immune functioning, after the training. Such effects may help explain the astonishing results of a study that randomly assigned 73 residents of homes for the elderly either to daily meditation or to none. After three years, one-fourth of the nonmeditators had died, but all the meditators were still alive (Alexander & others, 1989). A more recent study found that hypertension patients assigned to meditation training had (compared with other treatment groups) a 30 percent lower cardiovascular death rate over the ensuing 19-year study period (Schneider & others, 2005).

Spirituality and Faith Communities

OBJECTIVE **17** | Discuss the correlation between religiosity and longevity, and offer some possible explanations for this link.

As humans suffered ills and sought healing throughout history, two healing traditions—religion and medicine—have joined hands in caring for them. Often those hands belonged to the same person—the spiritual leader was also the healer. Maimonides was a twelfth-century rabbi and a renowned physician. Hospitals, which were first established in monasteries and then spread by missionaries, often carry the names of saints or faith communities.

As medical science matured, healing and religion diverged. Rather than asking God to spare their children from smallpox, people were able to vaccinate them. Rather than seeking a spiritual healer when burning with bacterial fever, they were able to use antibiotics. Recently, however, religion and healing are converging once again:

- Of America's 135 medical schools, 101 offered spirituality and health courses in 2005, up from 5 in 1992 (Koenig, 2002; Puchalski, 2005).
- Since 1995, Harvard Medical School has annually attracted 1000 to 2000 health professionals to its Spirituality and Healing in Medicine conferences.
- Duke University has established a Center for Spirituality, Theology, and Health.
- A Yankelovich survey (1997) found 94 percent of U.S. HMO professionals and 99 percent of family physicians agreeing that "personal prayer, meditation, or other spiritual and religious practices" can enhance medical treatment.
- Booksellers are featuring such titles as *The Healing Power of Faith* (Simon & Schuster, 1999), *Religion and Health* (Oxford University Press, 2000), and *Faith, Medicine, and Science* (Haworth, 2005).

Is there fire underneath all this smoke? More than a thousand studies have sought to correlate the *faith factor* with health and healing. For example, Jeremy Kark and his colleagues (1996) compared the death rates for 3900 Israelis either in one of 11 religiously orthodox or in one of 11 matched, nonreligious collective settlements (kibbutz communities). The researchers reported that over a 16-year period, "belonging to a religious collective was associated with a strong protective effect" not explained by age or economic differences. In every age group, religious community members were about half as likely to have died as were their nonreligious counterparts. This is roughly comparable to the gender difference in mortality.

In response to such findings, Richard Sloan and his skeptical colleagues (1999, 2000, 2002, 2005) remind us that mere correlations can leave many factors uncontrolled. Consider one obvious possibility: Women are more religiously active than men, and women outlive men. So perhaps religious involvement is merely an expression of the gender effect on longevity.

However, several new studies find the religiosity-longevity correlation among men alone, and even more strongly among women (McCullough & others, 2000, 2005). One study that followed 5286 Californians over 28 years found that, after controlling for age, gender, ethnicity, and education, frequent religious attenders were 36 percent less likely to have died in any year (**FIGURE 14.16**).

A U.S. National Health Interview Survey (Hummer & others, 1999) followed 21,204 people over 8 years. After controlling for age, sex, race, and region, researchers found that nonattenders were 1.87 times more likely to have died than were those attending more than weekly. This translated into a life expectancy at age 20 of 83 years for frequent attenders and 75 years for infrequent attenders (**FIGURE 14.17** on page 574).

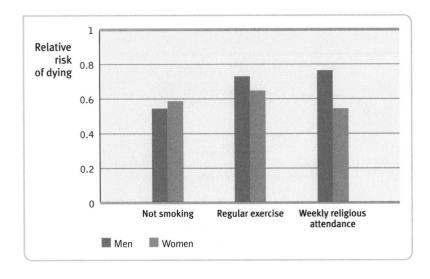

FIGURE 14.16
Predictors of mortality: not smoking, frequent exercise, and regular religious attendance
Epidemiologist William Strawbridge and his co-workers (1997, 1999; Oman & others, 2002) followed 5286 Alameda, California, adults over 28 years. After adjusting for age and education, the researchers found that not smoking, regular exercise, and religious attendance all predicted a lowered risk of death in any given year. Women attending weekly religious services, for example, were only 54 percent as likely to die in a typical study year as were nonattenders.

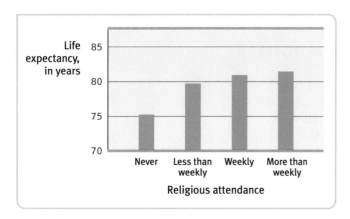

FIGURE 14.17
Religious attendance and life expectancy
In a national health survey financed by the U.S. Centers for Disease Control and Prevention, religiously active people had longer life expectancies. (Data from Hummer & others, 1999.)

These correlational findings do not indicate that nonattenders who start attending services and change nothing else will live 8 years longer. But they do indicate that as a *predictor* of health and longevity, religious involvement rivals nonsmoking and exercise effects. Such findings demand explanation. Can you imagine what intervening variables might account for the correlation?

First, religiously active people have healthier life-styles; for example, they smoke and drink less (Lyons, 2002; Strawbridge & others, 2001). Health-oriented, vegetarian Seventh Day Adventists have a longer-than-usual life expectancy (Berkel & de Waard, 1983). Religiously orthodox Israelis eat less fat than do their nonreligious compatriots. But such differences are not great enough to explain the dramatically reduced mortality in the religious kibbutzim, argued the Israeli researchers. In the recent American studies, too, about 75 percent of the longevity difference remains after controlling for unhealthy behaviors such as inactivity and smoking (Musick & others, 1999).

Social support is another variable that helps explain the faith factor (George & others, 2002). For Judaism, Christianity, and Islam, faith is not solo spirituality but a communal experience that helps satisfy the need to belong. The more than 350,000 faith communities in North America and the millions more elsewhere provide support networks for their active participants—people who are there for one another when misfortune strikes. Moreover, religion encourages another predictor of health and longevity—marriage. In the religious kibbutzim, for example, divorce has been almost nonexistent.

But even after controlling for gender, unhealthy behaviors, social ties, and preexisting health problems, the mortality studies find much of the mortality reduction remaining (George & others, 2000; Powell & others, 2003). Researchers therefore speculate that a third set of intervening variables is the stress protection and enhanced well-being associated with a coherent worldview, a sense of hope for the long-term future, feelings of ultimate acceptance, and the relaxed meditation of prayer or Sabbath observance (**FIGURE 14.18**). These variables might also help to explain other recent findings among the religiously active, such as healthier immune functioning and fewer hospital admissions and, for AIDS patients, fewer stress hormones and longer survival (Ironson & others, 2002; Koenig & Larson, 1998; Lutgendorf & others, 2004).

Although the religion-health correlation is yet to be fully explained, Harold Pincus (1997), deputy medical director of the American Psychiatric Association,

FIGURE 14.18
Possible explanations for the correlation between religious involvement and health/longevity

FIGURE 14.19
Managing stress
Life events can be debilitating or not. It all depends on how we appraise them and whether the stresses are buffered by a stress-resistant disposition, healthy habits, enduring social support, and spiritual engagement.

John David Mercer/The Gamma Liason Network

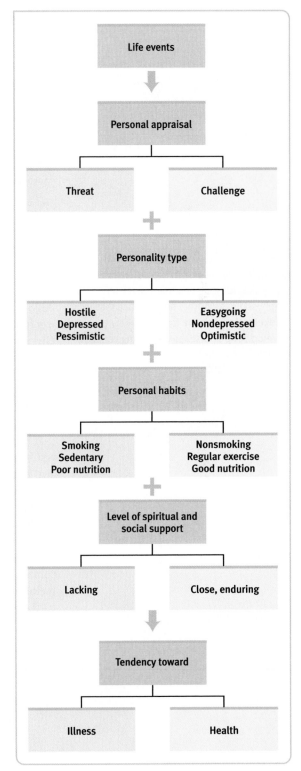

believes these findings "have made clear that anyone involved in providing health care services . . . cannot ignore . . . the important connections between spirituality, religion, and health."

Let's summarize: Sustained emotional reactions to stressful events can be debilitating. However, we can cope with stressors by problem-solving or emotional coping, and we can manage stress by making ourselves emotionally and physically stronger (**FIGURE 14.19**).

Modifying Illness-Related Behaviors

Researchers are persuaded that health-promotion programs would cost far less than many countries now spend to treat diseases (**TABLE 14.2**, page 576). (U.S. Bureau of the Census, 2004). Moreover, among patients visiting their primary care physicians with such typical complaints as fatigue, headache, chest or abdominal pain, dizziness, constipation, and insomnia, fewer than 20 percent have a clear organic problem (Kroenke & Mangelsdorff, 1989). Medical researchers presume many of the rest involve *psychosocial factors*. It is clear that even modestly successful health-promotion programs could save more money than they cost.

What makes health-promoting programs successful? Let's take a closer look at smoking, nutrition, and weight control.

The Risks of Smoking

OBJECTIVE 18 | Explain why people smoke.

Imagine that cigarettes were harmless—except, once in every 25,000 packs, an occasional innocent-looking one is filled with dynamite instead of tobacco. Not such a bad risk of having your head blown off. But with 250 million packs a day consumed worldwide, we could expect more than 10,000 gruesome daily deaths (more than three times the 9/11 fatalities each and every day)—surely enough to have cigarettes banned everywhere.[1]

---

[1] This analogy, adapted here with world-based numbers, was suggested by mathematician Sam Saunders, as reported by K. C. Cole (1998).

TABLE 14.2

HEALTH-CARE COSTS AND LONGEVITY

More than health-care expenditures are at issue when it comes to predicting longevity—one measure of a nation's overall health.

	Health Care as Percentage of GDP (gross domestic product)	Life Expectancy (in years) for Those Born in 2003
United States	14%	77.1
United Kingdom	8%	78.2
Canada	9%	79.8
Australia	9%	80.1

Source: U.S. Bureau of the Census, 2004

> "There is an overwhelming medical and scientific consensus that cigarette smoking causes lung cancer, heart disease, emphysema, and other serious diseases in smokers. Smokers are far more likely to develop serious diseases, like lung cancer, than nonsmokers."
>
> Philip Morris Companies Inc., 1999

The lost lives from these dynamite-loaded cigarettes approximate those from today's actual cigarettes. Each year throughout the world, tobacco kills nearly 5 million of its 1.3 billion customers, reports the World Health Organization ([WHO] 2005). (Imagine the outrage if terrorists took down an equivalent of 25 loaded jumbo jets today, let alone tomorrow and every day thereafter.) And the worst is yet to come. Given present trends, according to the WHO, the death rate will soon grow to 10 million annually, meaning that *half a billion* (say that number slowly) people alive today will be killed by tobacco (Lopez, 1999). A teen-to-the-grave smoker has a 50 percent chance of dying from the habit, and the death is often agonizing and premature, as the Philip Morris company acknowledged in 2001. Responding to Czech Republic complaints about the health-care costs of tobacco, Philip Morris reassured the Czechs that there was actually a net "health-care cost savings due to early mortality" and the resulting savings on pensions and elderly housing (Herbert, 2001). Smoke a cigarette and nature will charge you 12 minutes—ironically, just about the length of time you spend smoking it (*Discover*, 1996). Eliminating smoking would increase life expectancy more than any other preventive measure (**FIGURE 14.20**).

The risks of smoking are hardly well-guarded secrets. Indeed, reports the World Health Organization (2005), "evidence shows that smoking harms nearly every organ of the body." The type of smoker who doesn't know about smoking's hazards, comic Dave Barry notes, is the "type of smoker whose brain has been removed with a melon scoop." The "Smoking Can Be Harmful to Your Health" warning is on every pack sold in the United States, and 97 percent of Americans believe that smoking is

FIGURE 14.20
Premature deaths per 100,000 Canadians who were smoking by age 15 Smoking-related early deaths will eventually claim nine times more Canadian teen smokers than will suicide, car accidents, AIDS, and homicide combined (Statistics Canada, 1999).

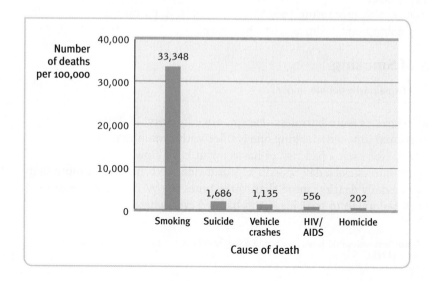

harmful (Blizzard, 2004). In Canada, 97 percent of adults and teens agree that smoking is associated with lung cancer, and nearly as many acknowledge smoking's links with respiratory ailments and heart disease (Statistics Canada, 1999).

Nevertheless, the statistics of smoking risks fail to persuade many teens (which brings to mind Joseph Stalin's reputed saying, "A single death is a tragedy; a million deaths is a statistic"). Asked to consider a 16-year-old smoker, 4 in 10 adolescent smokers agree that "although smoking may eventually harm this person's health, the very next single cigarette he/she smokes will probably not cause any harm" (Slovic, 2000). (The next one and the next and the next also, individually, do not matter; but the 300,000 smoked before age 60 by today's pack-a-day teens do, of course.)

Nonsmokers not only live healthier, they live happier. Smoking correlates with higher rates of depression, chronic disabilities, and divorce (Doherty & Doherty, 1998; Vita & others, 1998). For example, nondepressed teens who smoke suffer a quadrupled risk of developing depression (Goodman, 2000). Healthy living seems to add both years to life and life to years.

When and Why Do People Start Smoking?

Smoking is a *pediatric disease*. It usually begins during early adolescence and is especially common among those who get low grades, who drop out of school, who feel less competent and in control of their future, and whose friends, parents, and siblings smoke (Chassin & others, 1987; Schulenberg & others, 1994). If you are in college or university, and if by now the cigarette manufacturers haven't attracted your business, they almost surely never will.

We learn behaviors through the models we imitate and the social rewards we receive, which largely explains an adolescent's vulnerability to the allure of smoking. Adolescents are self-conscious and often think the world is watching their every move. So, they may begin smoking to imitate cool models, to get the social reward of being accepted by other smokers, and to project a mature image (Covington & Omelich, 1988). Cigarette companies, mindful that people decide on smoking and establish their brand loyalty during their teens, have effectively modeled smoking with themes that appeal to youths: independence, adventure-seeking, social approval, sophistication. Typically, teens who start smoking also have friends who smoke, who suggest its pleasures, and who offer them cigarettes (Eiser, 1985; Evans & others, 1988; Rose & others, 1999). Among teens whose parents and best friends are nonsmokers, the smoking rate is close to zero (Moss & others, 1992, and see **FIGURE 14.21**).

SNAPSHOTS

A correlation–causation question: Does the close link between teen smoking and friends' smoking reflect peer influence? Teens seeking similar friends? Or both?

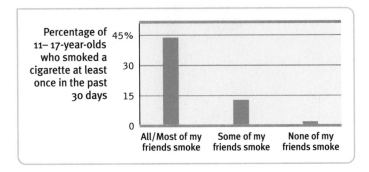

FIGURE 14.21
Peer influence
Kids don't smoke if their friends don't (Philip Morris, 2003).

Russel Einhorn/The Gamma Liaison Network

Nic-a-teen

Aware that virtually all smokers start as teenagers—and that sales would plummet if no teens were enticed to smoke—cigarette companies target teens. By portraying tough, appealing, socially adept smokers, they entice teens to imitate. They are supported by the resurgence of Hollywood's modeling of smoking. With such stars as Vanessa Williams, Gwyneth Paltrow, Sharon Stone, Julia Roberts, Brad Pitt, Jim Carrey, Bruce Willis, and Arnold Schwarzenegger all looking cool or rebellious while dragging on a cigarette or cigar, teens in the mid-1990s were getting the message and becoming addicted in increasing numbers.

> "A cigarette in the hands of a Hollywood star on screen is a gun aimed at a 12- or 14-year-old."
>
> Screenwriter Joe Eszterhas, 2002

After smoking's toxicity became known, smoking in movies declined to about once every 12 minutes, on average, during the 1970s and 1980s, but then returned to about every 4 minutes during the 1990s (Brody, 2001). Smoking was modeled in films for teens, and by popular stars such as Julia Roberts, Gwyneth Paltrow, Jim Carrey, and Brad Pitt. Moreover, the more teens watch smoking in films, the more likely they are to experiment with tobacco (Dalton & others, 2002). Joe Eszterhas (2002), a screenwriter for 14 of the recent movies that often glamorized smoking, and a throat-cancer patient after a lifetime of smoking, says, "I find it hard to forgive myself. I have been an accomplice to the murders of untold numbers of human beings. . . . I don't wish my fate upon anyone in Hollywood, but I beg that Hollywood stop imposing it upon millions of others."

Why Do People Not Stop Smoking? Once addicted to nicotine we find it very hard to quit. Tobacco products are as addictive as heroin and cocaine. Indeed, some who have kicked the heroin habit have been unable to also stop smoking. Surveys in Britain and the United States show that at least one in three of those who try cigarettes become hooked—a higher addiction rate than for heroin and cocaine (Anthony & others, 1994; Heishman & others, 1997).

As with other addictions, a smoker becomes *dependent;* each year fewer than one of every seven smokers who want to quit will do so. A smoker also develops *tolerance,* eventually needing larger and larger doses to get the same effect. A sad irony is that those who are initially most sensitive to nicotine—and most likely to feel sick or dizzy on first smoking—tend to develop a tolerance quickly and to become most strongly addicted (Pomerleau & others, 1993). Quitting causes *nicotine-withdrawal* symptoms, including craving, insomnia, anxiety, and irritability. And all it takes to relieve these aversive states is a cigarette—a portable nicotine dispenser.

As with all addictive drugs, nicotine use is not only compulsive and mood-altering, it is also reinforcing. Smoking delivers its hit of nicotine within 7 seconds, triggering the release of epinephrine and norepinephrine, which in turn diminish appetite and boost alertness and mental efficiency (**FIGURE 14.22**). At the same time, nicotine stimulates the central nervous system to release neurotransmitters that calm anxiety and reduce sensitivity to pain. For example, nicotine stimulates dopamine, and, like heroin and morphine, stimulates opioid release (Nowak, 1994; Scott & others, 2004). These rewards keep people smoking even when they wish they could stop (as do four in five smokers)—indeed, even when they know they are committing

Asked "If you had to do it all over again, would you start smoking?" more than 85 percent of adult smokers answer No (Slovic & others, 2002).

1. Arouses the brain to a state of increased alertness

2. Increases heart rate and blood pressure

3. At high levels, relaxes muscles and triggers the release of endorphins, natural opiates that may reduce stress

4. Reduces circulation to extremities

5. Suppresses appetite for carbohydrates

FIGURE 14.22
Where there's smoke . . . :
The physiological effects of nicotine
Nicotine reaches the brain within 7 seconds, twice as fast as intravenous heroin. Within minutes, the amount in the blood soars.

slow-motion suicide (Saad, 2002). Even if given low-nicotine cigarettes, smokers end up smoking more of them to maintain a roughly constant level of nicotine in the blood.

Consistent with the biopsychosocial perspective, genes influence one's propensity to cigarette addiction (**FIGURE 14.23**). A meta-analysis of twin studies indicates a 60 percent heritability (Heath & Madden, 1995). Two recent studies have further discovered that smokers and nonsmokers tend to differ in a gene that influences responses to the neurotransmitter dopamine (Lerman & others, 1999; Sabol & others, 1999).

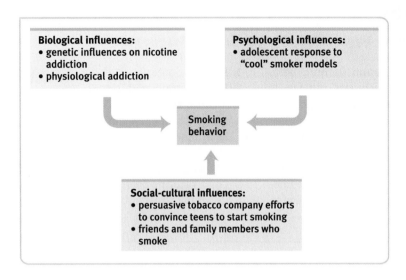

FIGURE 14.23
Biopsychosocial approach to studying smoking behavior

Helping Smokers Quit

OBJECTIVE 19 | Discuss ways of helping smokers to quit smoking—or preventing young people from ever starting.

The efforts to help people stop smoking include public health warnings, counseling, drug treatments, hypnosis, aversive conditioning (for example, having people sicken themselves by rapidly smoking cigarette after cigarette), operant conditioning, cognitive therapy, and support groups. The good news is that these treatments are often effective in the short run. But the bad news is that all but one-fifth of the participants eventually succumb to the habit again (Schelling, 1992). For those quitting solo, the odds are even lower. With a pack of cigarettes seldom more than minutes away, a single moment of weakness, often while experiencing stress or a negative mood, can be enough to break the resolve (Kassel & others, 2003).

Better news comes from a Centers for Disease Control report that half of Americans who have ever smoked have quit. More than 90 percent did so on their own, often after repeated attempts. For those who endure, the acute craving and withdrawal symptoms gradually dissipate over the ensuing six months (Ward & others, 1997). Because so many people have stopped or not started smoking, the percentage of American, Canadian, and British smokers has dropped sharply over the last 30 years (**FIGURE 14.24**). By 2004, 6 in 10 survey respondents in America, 7 in 10 in Britain, and almost 8 in 10 in Canada favored bans on workplace and restaurant smoking (Mason, 2004). And in 2005, the World Health Organization announced that 57 countries (including Australia, Britain, and Canada, but not the United States) had committed themselves to a global tobacco treaty that ensures strong tobacco warnings and bans on tobacco advertising, promotion, and sponsorship.

Still, among high school dropouts and those of lower socioeconomic levels, smoking rates remain high. It's among college students and graduates that smoking has become gauche rather than cool. In the United States, Canada, and Britain, smoking has become rare among the highly educated or in the upper socioeconomic level, but two to three times as common among the least educated (Halsey & Webb, 2000; Statistics Canada, 1999). The drop has been most pronounced

> " To cease smoking is the easiest thing I ever did; I ought to know because I've done it a thousand times."
>
> Mark Twain, 1835–1910

FIGURE 14.24
Smoking trends
Gallup surveys reveal sharp drops in population smoking rates in Canada, the United States, and Britain since 1974 (McMurray, 2004).

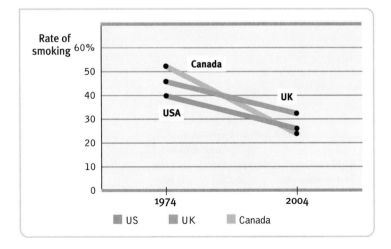

CLOSE-UP:

FOR THOSE WHO WANT TO STOP SMOKING

Most smokers want to quit, and nearly half try each year, but fewer than one in seven succeed permanently, reports an expert panel appointed by the U.S. Agency for Health Care Policy and Research. The panel's smoking-cessation guidelines do, however, offer some helpful pointers (Wetter & others, 1998).

1. Set a quit date.
2. Inform family and friends.
3. Remove all cigarettes.
4. Review things you learned from previous attempts to quit and anticipate challenges.
5. Use a nicotine patch or gum.
6. Be totally abstinent—not even a single puff.

7. Abstain from or greatly limit alcohol (which facilitates relapse).
8. If other smokers live or work with you, quit together.
9. Avoid places where others are likely to smoke.
10. Exercise. In controlled experiments, quitters assigned to regular exercise had higher success rates (Bock & others, 1999).

"There's no shooting—we just make you keep smoking."

in the male smoking rate, which now barely exceeds that of women. Thanks in part to such trends, the death rate due to coronary heart disease has declined by about 30 percent since the mid-1960s. Smoking-related cancer deaths have also been declining, especially among men (Wingo & others, 1999). If you, or someone you love, would like to stop smoking, see the Close-Up: For Those Who Want to Stop Smoking.

Smoking rebounded among U.S. teens during the mid-1990s, before falling again (**FIGURE 14.25**). A similar 1990s comeback occurred among Canadian teens (Brooke, 2000). And despite the declining cigarette sales among educated Western adults and new cigarette advertising restrictions, per-person cigarette consumption is near an all-time high worldwide.

Smoking has skyrocketed in Asia. In China, where most men but no more than 1 in 10 women smoke and where one-third of men are destined to be killed by tobacco, cigarette consumption soared from 100 billion cigarettes a year in the early 1950s to 1.8 trillion at the century's end (Cheng, 1999; Schwartz & Pomfret, 1998). In Japan, 35 percent (50 percent of men) are smokers (Coleman, 1997). Countries such as Kenya and Zimbabwe, with their relatively low per-person consumption rates, are prime targets for British and U.S. tobacco companies, which are putting hundreds of millions of unsuspecting people at risk for ill health and premature death. The World Health Organization has predicted that in the next three decades, 70 percent of tobacco-related deaths will occur in developing countries where many people are unaware of the dangers of smoking (Lopez, 1999; Schwartz & Pomfret, 1999).

FIGURE 14.25
The ups and downs of U.S. teen smoking
Adult smoking has dropped sharply over the last quarter-century, especially among educated people. But smoking made a temporary comeback among U.S. teens in the 1990s as Hollywood modeled smoking. (Data from Johnston & others, 2005.)

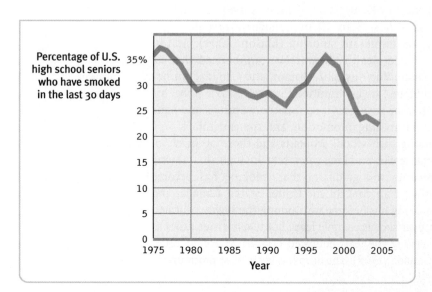

How Can We Prevent Smoking? It is vastly easier never to begin smoking than, once addicted, to stop. Social psychological analyses of why adolescents start smoking, have helped generate curricular programs teachers can implement easily and inexpensively. According to a National Cancer Institute panel, the key ingredients of such programs are

- information about the effects of smoking.
- information about peer, parent, and media influences.
- training in refusal skills, through modeling and role playing.

The informational ingredients can also be offered through the mass media, which Australia has effectively used to discourage smoking across educational levels (Macaskill & others, 1992). In 1998, Florida initiated a massive youth-oriented media campaign to reduce the allure of smoking, and by early 1999, the number of 12- to 14-year-olds who reported smoking had dropped 19 percent from that of the previous year (*MMWR*, 1999).

There is one other way to discourage smoking: Make it more immediately costly. Recall from Chapter 8 that the most effective rewards and punishments are immediate. When the delayed rewards of exercise compete with the immediate discomfort of doing so, the immediate consequences may win out. Likewise, even *knowing* that in the long run smoking is often suicidal, many continue to smoke. If we could only raise the immediate costs, consumption would surely decline. The U.S. Centers for Disease Control (Brown & others, 1993) reports that raising cigarette taxes (and therefore prices) cuts consumption by about 4 percent for each 10 percent rise. The effect is doubly great among smokers in developing countries and among teenagers—the age when 90 percent of smokers start their habit (de Beyer, 2005). Many U.S. states sharply increased cigarette taxes—producing a 70 percent cigarette price increase between 1997 and 2001—and, sure enough, teen smoking began declining, especially in states also having vigorous smoking-prevention programs (Manning, 2002; Robison & Mason, 2002).

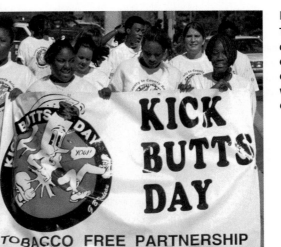

Effective prevention
The state of Florida directed a huge, youth-oriented anti-smoking campaign in 1998, which had reduced rates of smoking by 1999.

Paul J. Millette/Palm Beach Post

Obesity and Weight Control

OBJECTIVE 20 | Discuss the adaptive advantages and modern-day disadvantages of a body that stores fat.

Why do some people gain weight while others eat the same amount and seldom add a pound? And why do so few overweight people win the battle of the bulge? Is there weight-loss hope for the 65 percent of Americans who, according to the Centers for Disease Control, are overweight?

Our bodies store fat for good reasons. Fat is an ideal form of stored energy—a high-calorie fuel reserve to carry the body through periods when food is scarce—a common occurrence in the feast-or-famine existence of our prehistoric ancestors. (Think of that spare tire around the middle as an energy storehouse—biology's counterpart to a hiker's waist-borne snack pack.) No wonder that in most developing societies today, as in Europe in earlier centuries—in fact, wherever people face famine—obesity signals affluence and social status (Furnham & Baguma, 1994).

In those parts of the world where food and sweets are now abundantly available, the rule that once served our hungry distant ancestors (When you find energy-rich fat or sugar, eat it!) has become dysfunctional. Being slightly overweight poses

Cultures without a thin-ideal for women are also cultures without eating disorders. Ghanians, for example, idealize a larger body size than do Americans—and experience fewer eating disorders (Cogan & others, 1996). The same is true of African-American women compared with European-American women (Parker & others, 1995).

Rubens' *The Garden of Love*
In other times and places, plumper bodies have been idealized. When food is scarce, plump seems beautiful; where food is plentiful, slender seems beautiful.

The Garden of Love (detail), Peter Paul Rubens, The Prado, Madrid/The Bridgeman Art Library/Superstock

Yearly health care expenditures per U.S. woman, age 35 to 44 (Wee & others, 2005). As economist Paul Krugman (2005) says, "Fat is a fiscal issue."

Normal weight:	$2127
BMIs 25 to 29.9:	$2358
BMIs 30 to 34.9:	$2873
BMIs 35 to 39.9:	$3058
BMIs 40 and up:	$3506

only modest health risks (Gibbs, 2005). Fitness matters more than being a little overweight. But significant obesity (**FIGURE 14.26**), especially among children, increases the risk of diabetes, high blood pressure, heart disease, gallstones, arthritis, and certain types of cancer, thus shortening life expectancy (Olshansky & others, 2005). The risks are greater for apple-shaped people who carry their weight in pot bellies than for pear-shaped people with ample hips and thighs (Greenwood, 1989). New research also has linked women's obesity to their risk of late-life Alzheimer's disease and brain tissue loss (Gustafson & others, 2003, 2004).

Not surprisingly, then, one study (Calle & others, 1999) that followed more than 1 million Americans over 14 years revealed that being significantly overweight can cut life short (**FIGURE 14.27**). Those overweight at age 40 die three years earlier than their slim counterparts, reports another long-term study (Peeters & others, 2003). The death rate is especially high among very overweight men. Understandably, in 2004 the U.S. Medicare system began recognizing obesity as an illness.

FIGURE 14.26
Obesity measured as body mass index (BMI)
U.S. government guidelines encourage a body mass index (BMI) under 25. The World Health Organization and many countries define obesity as a BMI of 30 or more. The shading in this graph is based on BMI measurements for these heights and weights. BMI is calculated by using the following formula:

$$\frac{\text{Weight in kg (pounds} \times .45)}{\text{Squared height in meters (inches} \div 39.4)^2} = \text{BMI}$$

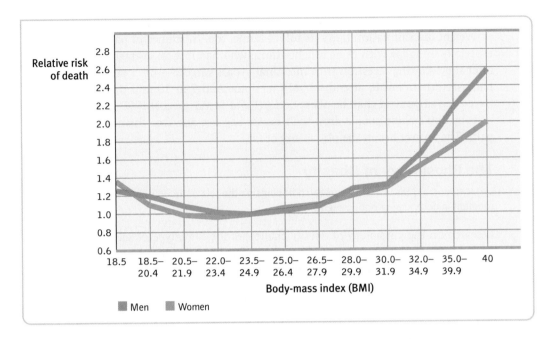

FIGURE **14.27**
Obesity and mortality
Relative risk of death among healthy nonsmokers rises with extremely high or low body mass index. (Data from 14-year study of 1.05 million Americans, Calle & others, 1999.)

The Social Effects of Obesity

OBJECTIVE **21** | Describe some of the social effects of obesity.

Obesity can also be socially toxic, by affecting both how you are treated and how you feel about yourself. Obese people know the stereotype: slow, lazy, and sloppy (Crandall, 1994, 1995; Ryckman & others, 1989). Many people see obesity as a matter of choice or as evidence of a lack of self-discipline or a personality problem—a maladjusted way of reducing anxiety, dealing with guilt, or gratifying an "oral fixation." Widen people's images on a video monitor (making them look fatter) and observers suddenly rate them as less sincere, less friendly, meaner, and more obnoxious (Gardner & Tockerman, 1994). The social effects of obesity were clear in a study that followed 370 obese 16- to 24-year-old women (Gortmaker & others, 1993). When restudied seven years later, two-thirds of the women were still obese. They also were making less money—$7000 a year less—than an equally intelligent comparison group of some 5000 nonobese women. And they were less likely to be married. In personal ads, men often state their preference for, and women often advertise, slimness (Miller & others, 2000; Smith & others, 1990).

In one clever experiment, Regina Pingitore and her colleagues (1994) demonstrated weight discrimination. They videotaped mock job interviews in which professional actors appeared as either normal-weight or overweight applicants. In one condition, actors wore makeup and prostheses that made them look 30 pounds heavier. When appearing overweight, the same person, using the same lines, intonation, and gestures, was rated less worthy of hiring. The weight bias was especially strong against women applicants (**FIGURE 14.28**). Other studies reveal that weight discrimination, though hardly discussed, is greater than race and gender discrimination. It occurs at every stage of the employment cycle—hiring, placement, promotion, compensation, discipline, and discharge (Roehling, 1999). Experiments show that anti-fat prejudice even extends to applicants who are *seen* with an obese person (Hebl & Mannix, 2003).

"The [obesity lawsuit] bill says, 'Don't run off and file a lawsuit if you are fat.' It says, 'Look in the mirror because you're the one to blame.'"

U.S. Representative F. James Sensenbrenner, 2004

FIGURE **14.28**
Gender and weight discrimination
When women applicants were made to look overweight, university students were less willing to think they would hire them. Among men applicants, weight mattered less. (Data from Pingitore & others, 1994.)

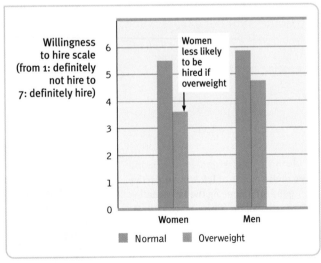

Weight discrimination takes its toll at home, too. In studies of patients who were especially unhappy with their weight—those who had lost an average of 100 pounds after short-cutting digestion with intestinal bypass surgery—4 in 5 said their children had asked them not to attend school functions. And 9 in 10 said they would rather have a leg amputated than be obese again (Rand & Macgregor, 1990, 1991).

Why don't obese people drop their excess baggage and free themselves of all this pain? The answer lies in the physiology of fat.

The Physiology of Obesity

OBJECTIVE 22 | Discuss some research findings on the role of heredity and environment in determining body weight.

Research on the physiology of obesity challenges the stereotype of severely overweight people being weak-willed gluttons. First, consider the arithmetic of weight gain: People get fat by consuming more calories than they expend. The energy equivalent of a pound of fat is 3500 calories; therefore, dieters have been told they will lose a pound for every 3500-calorie reduction in their diet. Surprise: This conclusion is false. Why? Read on.

Fat Cells The immediate determinants of body fat are the size and number of fat cells. A typical adult has 30 to 40 billion of these miniature fuel tanks, half of which lie near the skin's surface. A fat cell can vary from relatively empty, like a deflated balloon, to overly full. In an obese person, fat cells may swell to two or three times their normal size and then divide or trigger nearby immature fat cells to divide—resulting in up to 75 billion fat cells (Hirsch, 2003). Once the number of fat cells increases—due to genetic predisposition, early childhood eating patterns, or adult overeating—it never decreases (**FIGURE 14.29**). On a diet, fat cells may shrink, but they never disappear (Sjöstrum, 1980).

Never obese

Obese

Reduced obese

FIGURE 14.29
Fat cells
We store energy in fat cells, which become larger and more numerous if we are obese, and smaller (but still more numerous) if we then lose weight. (Adapted from Jules Hirsch, 2003.)

Set Points and Metabolism Once we become fat, we require less food to maintain our weight than we did to attain it. Why? Because compared with other tissue, fat has a lower metabolic rate—it takes less food energy to maintain. The "weight thermostat" of an obese person's body is set to maintain body weight within a higher-than-average range. When weight drops below this *set-point* (often considered a *settling-point* range of weight rather than a precise number of pounds), the person's hunger increases and metabolism decreases. Thus, the body adapts to starvation by burning off fewer calories, and to extra calories by burning off more.

In a classic month-long experiment (Bray, 1969), obese patients whose daily food intake was reduced from 3500 to 450 calories lost only 6 percent of their weight—partly because their bodies reacted as though they were being starved—their metabolic rates dropped about 15 percent (**FIGURE 14.30**). That is why reducing your food intake by 3500 calories may not reduce your weight by 1 pound. That is also why further weight loss comes slowly following the rapid losses during the initial three weeks or so of a rigorous diet. And that is why amounts of food that worked to maintain weight before a diet began may increase it when a diet ends—the body is still conserving energy.

Individual differences in resting metabolism also explain why two people of the same height, age, and activity level can maintain the same weight, even if one of them eats much less than the other does. Lean people are naturally disposed to fidget and move about more than are energy-conserving overweight people

Fat-signaling hormone
The obese mouse at left has a defective gene for producing the fat-signaling hormone, leptin. When the genetically similar mouse at right was treated with leptin, it shed 40 percent of its body weight.

Courtesy of John Soltis, The Rockefeller University, New York, NY

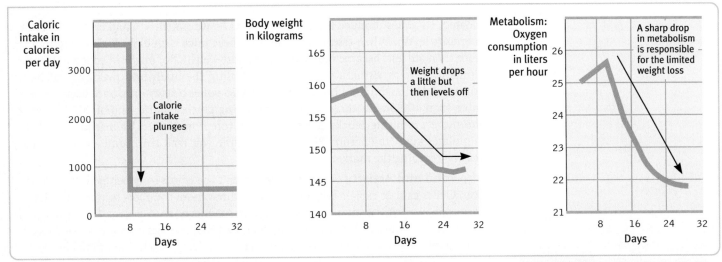

After seven days on a 3500-calorie diet, six obese patients were given only 450 calories a day for the next 24 days.

Caloric intake in calories per day — Calorie intake plunges

Body weight in kilograms — Weight drops a little but then levels off

Metabolism: Oxygen consumption in liters per hour — A sharp drop in metabolism is responsible for the limited weight loss

who tend to sit still longer (Levine & others, 2005). Most overweight people are just normal people whose bodies predispose them to weigh more. This appears true despite findings that people—obese people, especially—tend to overestimate their physical activity and underestimate their caloric intake (Brownell & Wadden, 1992; Lichtman & others, 1992).

The Genetic Factor Studies reveal a genetic influence on body weight. Consider:

- Despite shared family meals, adoptive siblings' body weights are uncorrelated with one another or with those of their adoptive parents. Rather, people's weights resemble those of their biological parents (Grilo & Pogue-Geile, 1991).
- Identical twins have closely similar weights, even when reared apart (Plomin & others, 1997; Stunkard & others, 1990). Across studies, their weight correlates +.74. The much lower +.32 correlation among fraternal twins suggests that genes explain two-thirds of our varying body mass (Maes & others, 1997). Being overweight is therefore *not* simply a matter of scarfing too many hot fudge sundaes. And losing weight is not merely a matter of mind over platter.
- Given an obese parent, a boy is three times, and a girl six times, more likely to be obese than their counterparts with normal-weight parents (Carrière, 2003).

So, the specifics of our genes predispose the size of our jeans. But the genetic influence is surely complex, with different genes, like differing band members, making music by playing together. Some genes might influence when our intestines signal "full," with others dictating how efficiently we burn calories or convert extra calories to fat, and still others prompting us to fidget or sit still. But recent experiments do detail one genetic mechanism for weight control. As a normal mouse's fat cells become

FIGURE 14.30

The effects of a severe diet on obese patients' body weight and metabolism
After seven days on a 3500-calorie diet, six obese patients were given only 450 calories a day for the next 24 days. Body weight declined only 6 percent and then leveled off, because metabolism dropped about 15 percent. (From Bray, 1969.)

Survival of the fattest

bloated, its genes produce the protein leptin. As we noted in Chapter 12, the brain monitors leptin. When researchers injected obese mice with daily doses of leptin, the mice then ate less, became more active, and lost weight. So, might injections of leptin similarly serve as virtual fat for humans, fooling the brain into making a fat body trimmer? Although initial hopes for this magic-bullet obesity drug have been dashed, more than 100 obesity drugs were in the testing pipeline at the end of 2004. One of the more promising blocks the same brain receptors tickled by marijuana, which stimulates appetite (*Science,* 2004). By the time you read this, some of these drugs may be reaching the market.

The Food and Activity Factors Genes aren't the whole story behind obesity, however. Genes cannot explain why obesity is six times more common in women in lower socioeconomic classes, more common among Americans than among Europeans, and more common among Americans today than in 1900, and less common among recent immigrants (Goel & others, 2004). Western cultures have become like animal feedlots—places where farmers fatten animals by restricting their exercise and offering abundant fattening food. In a massive long-term study of 50,000 nurses, researchers found—even after controlling for exercise, smoking, age, and diet—each two-hour increase in daily TV watching predicted a 23 percent obesity increase and a 7 percent diabetes increase (Hu & others, 2003). Among Ontario's Old Order Amish, where farming and gardening is labor intensive and pedometers reveal that men walk nine miles a day and women seven miles, the obesity rate is one-seventh the U.S. rate (Bassett & others, 2004). People living in walking-dependent communities such as Manhattan tend to weigh less than more sedentary folks in car-dependent suburbs (Ewing & others, 2003).

Lack of exercise and high-calorie foods are compounded by larger serving sizes (Double Whoppers) and a tripled percentage of meals eaten at fast-food restaurants since 1997 (Farley & Cohen, 2001). Compared with 1971, today's women are eating 300 more calories a day and today's men nearly 200 more (O'Connor, 2004). For example, on most North American college campuses, yesterday's cafeteria line with limited choices has been replaced by today's food buffet, with multiple serving stations offering all-you-can-eat entrees and make-your-own waffles washed down with limitless soft drinks (Brody, 2003). For many, the understandable result is the "freshman 15." And compared with their counterparts in the early 1900s, people are eating a higher-fat, higher-sugar diet, expending fewer calories, and suffering higher rates of diabetes at younger ages (Brody, 2003; Thompson, 1998). Taken together, Big Macs, sugar-laden soft drinks, inactivity, and tobacco form a weapon of mass destruction. Obese smokers die, on average, 13.5 years sooner than their normal-weight nonsmoking neighbors (Peeters & others, 2003).

Your parents and grandparents at age 30 likely weighed less than you did or will. Since 1960, the average American has grown one inch and gained 23 pounds (**TABLE 14.3**). In Britain, the average woman's dress size has increased from size 12 in 1951 to size 16 today; just since 1980, adult obesity rates have nearly tripled, to 21 percent

In Gallup surveys from 1990 to 2001, the average American's reported body weight rose 10 pounds (Saad, 2002). That comes to a collective weight gain of well over a billion pounds. The extra 10 pounds per person cost airlines $275 million in 2000 to burn the extra fuel needed to lift that weight (Dannenberg & others, 2004).

TABLE 14.3

AVERAGE U.S. BODY WEIGHT (POUNDS), 1960 TO 2002

	1960–1962	1971–1974	1988–1994	1999–2002
19-year-olds				
Men	–	160	161	172
Women	–	131	139	149
20- to 74-year-olds				
Men	166	173	182	189
Women	140	144	153	163

Source: Centers for Disease Control and Prevention report by C. L. Ogden & others (2004).

(Hawkes, 2002; Merriman, 1999). And over the last 40 years, as health experts have cajoled Americans to lose weight, the adult obesity rate has more than doubled to over 30 percent (CDC, 2004; and see **FIGURE 14.31**). Just since 1986, the number of obese Americans who were more than 100 pounds overweight has quadrupled (Sturm, 2003).

And so it goes, pretty much everywhere this book is being read. World-wide, 60 percent of people are overweight, estimates the World Health Organization (Booth & Neufer, 2005). Australia, similar to Britain and America, classifies some 60 percent of its population as overweight or obese (Australian Bureau of Statistics; Halsey & Webb, 2000; Healey, 2004). In Canada, the proportion of people classified as overweight has increased by 60 percent since 1985 (Statistics Canada, 1999). Commenting on a reported tripling of child obesity over the past 15 years, Canadian National Institute of Nutrition president, Anne Kennedy, noted, "The trend is mimicking the United States. We're five years behind, but catching up" (Krauss, 2002).

The "bottom" line: New stadiums, theaters, and subway cars are offering wider seats to accommodate this population growth (Hampson, 2000). The Washington State Ferries abandoned its 50-year-old standard of 18 inches per person. "Eighteen-inch butts are a thing of the past," explained a spokesperson (Shepherd, 1999). New York City, facing a large problem with Big Apple bottoms, has mostly replaced its 17.5-inch bucket-style subway seats with bucketless seats (Hampson, 2000). In the end, today's people need more room.

Note how these findings reinforce a familiar lesson from our earlier study of intelligence: There can be high levels of heritability (genetic influence on individual differences) without heredity explaining group differences. Genes mostly determine why one person today is heavier than another. Environment mostly determines why people today are heavier than their counterparts 50 years ago.

Losing Weight

OBJECTIVE **23** | Discuss the chances of success for an overweight person who wants to lose weight.

Perhaps you are shaking your head: "Slim chance we have of becoming and staying thin. If we lose weight on a diet, our metabolism slows and our hungry fat cells cry out, 'Feed me!' We're fated for fat!" Indeed, the condition of an obese person's body reduced to average weight is much like that of a semistarved body. Held under normal set point, each body "thinks" it is starving. Having lost weight, formerly obese people look normal, but their fat cells may be abnormally small, their metabolism slowed, and their minds obsessed with food.

All this explains why, short of drastic surgery to tie off part of the stomach and small intestine, most people who succeed on a weight-loss program eventually regain most of the weight (Garner & Wooley, 1991; Jeffery & others, 2000). (Millions of people can vouch that it is possible to lose weight; they have done it lots of times.) Some people do manage to keep pounds off, especially with programs that modify their life-style and ongoing eating behavior. But for most people, the only long-term result of this losing battle is a thinner wallet.

Yet, the battle of the bulge rages on as intensely as ever, and it is most intense among those with two X chromosomes. Fighting obesity is an enormous business. Americans spend $40 billion a year on diet foods and drinks (Kolata, 2004). Two-thirds of women and half of men say they want to lose weight, about half of those women and men say they are "seriously trying" (Moore, 2003). Asked if they would rather "be five years younger or weigh 15 pounds less," 29 percent of men and 48 percent of women said they would prefer losing the weight (*Responsive Community*, 1996).

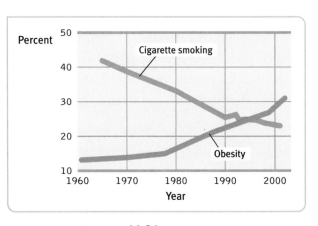

FIGURE 14.31
Trading risks
As smoking, which kills some 400,000 Americans a year, has been dropping, obesity, which also contributes to many deaths, has been increasing. (Source: Centers for Disease Control and Prevention.)

" We've been active in this field for 35 years, and our enthusiasm for dieting, especially dieting based on unrealistic expectations, has not yet been kindled."
University of Toronto researchers C. Peter Herman and Janet Polivy (2003)

"It works as well as most other diet plans....
I've lost over $200 in less than three weeks."

With fat cells, set points, metabolism, and genetic factors all tirelessly conspiring against shedding excess pounds, what advice can psychology offer? For some helpful hints, see Close-Up: For Those Who Want to Lose Weight.

Psychologist Kelly Brownell (2002) proposes altering the environments that put people at risk for obesity.

- Slap an extra tax on calorie-laden junk food and soft drinks. We're reducing smoking with increased cigarette taxes. Why not, for the same reason, institute a "Twinkie Tax"?
- Use the revenues to subsidize healthy foods and to finance health-supportive nutritional advertising.
- Establish a fast-food–free zone around schools.
- Ban the advertising of junk foods to kids.
- Encourage activity by designing communities with walks, bike paths, and residences near workplaces.

Although mindful that preserving weight loss is a constant challenge, Stanley Schachter (1982) was less pessimistic than most of today's obesity researchers about the dieter's chances of success. He recognized the overwhelming rate of failure among those in structured weight-loss programs, but he also noted that these people are a special group who probably have been unable to help themselves. Moreover, the failure rates recorded for these programs are based on single attempts at weight loss. Perhaps when people try repeatedly to lose weight, more of them do eventually succeed. When Schachter interviewed people, he found that one-fourth had at one time been significantly overweight and had tried to slim down. Of these, 6 out of 10 had *succeeded*: They weighed at least 10 percent less than their maximum prediet weight (an average loss of 35 pounds) and were no longer obese. A 1993 survey of 90,000 *Consumer Reports* readers found 25 percent of dieters claiming an enduring weight loss. Aided by media publicity, the National Weight Control Registry has identified more than 4000 people who have maintained significant weight loss for at least one year and are being studied over time. On average, these people have lost 60 pounds and kept it off for five years, virtually always with continued diet and exercise.

These findings hint that prospects for losing weight may be somewhat brighter than the dismal conclusions drawn from following patients who undergo a single weight-loss program. If all this has a familiar ring, recall that stop-smoking programs tend to be (1) effective in the short run and (2) ineffective in the long run, but that (3) many people are former smokers.

There is another option for overweight people, and one chosen by 13 percent of the people Schachter interviewed: to accept one's weight. We all do well to note that researchers have *not* identified guilt, hostility, oral fixation, or any similar personality maladjustment as causes of obesity. Nor is obesity simply a matter of a lack of willpower. Dieters are more likely to binge when under stress or after breaking their diets, which may be largely a consequence of their constant dieting. Indeed, the relentless pursuit of thinness puts people at risk not only for binge eating and food obsession, but also for weight fluctuations, malnutrition, smoking, depression, and harmful side effects of weight-loss drugs (Cogan & Ernsberger, 1999).

A hard-won success story
Tammy and Jeffrey Munson—two volunteers in the National Weight Control Registry—shown before and after she lost 147 pounds and he lost 100 pounds.

Joe R. Liuzzo

CLOSE-UP:

FOR THOSE WHO WANT TO LOSE WEIGHT

People struggling with obesity are well advised to seek medical evaluation and guidance. For others who wish to take off a few pounds, researchers have offered these tips.

Begin only if you feel motivated and self-disciplined. For most people, permanent weight loss requires making a career of staying thin—a lifelong change in eating habits combined with gradually increased exercise.

Minimize exposure to tempting food cues. Keep tempting foods out of the house or out of sight. Go to the supermarket only on a full stomach, and avoid the sweets and chips aisles. Eat simple meals, with only a few different foods; given more variety, people consume more (Raynor & Epstein, 2001).

Take steps to boost your metabolism. Inactive people are often overweight **(FIGURE 14.32)**. One of the few predictors of successful long-term weight loss is exercise, both during and after changing your eating patterns (Jeffery & others, 2000; McGuire & others, 1999; Wadden & others, 1998). Exercise, such as brisk walking, running, and swimming, not only empties fat cells, builds muscle, and makes you feel better, it also temporarily speeds up metabolism and can help lower your set point (Bennett, 1995; Kolata, 1987; Thompson & others, 1982). Even brief bouts of exercise—four 10-minute walks a day—provide benefits (Jakicic & others, 1999). Lack of exercise helps explain why many fail to lose weight permanently. In a Centers for Disease Control study of 107,000 adults, only one in five of those trying to lose weight were following the government recommendation to both count calories and exercise 150 minutes weekly (Serdula & others, 1999).

Be realistic and moderate. Being moderately heavy is less risky than being extremely thin (Ernsberger & Koletsky, 1999). Permanent weight loss is not easy. Set a realistic goal and take it gradually. "A reasonable time line for a 10 percent reduction in body weight is six months," advises the National Institutes of Health (1998).

Eat healthy foods. Whole grains, fruits, vegetables, and healthy fats such as those found in olive oil and fish help regulate appetite and artery-clogging cholesterol (Taubes, 2001, 2002). Better crispy greens than Krispy Kremes.

Don't starve all day and eat one big meal at night. This eating pattern, common among overweight people, slows metabolism. Moreover, those who eat a balanced breakfast are, by late morning, more alert and less fatigued (Spring & others, 1992).

Beware of the binge. Among people who consciously restrain their eating, drinking alcohol or feeling anxious or depressed can unleash the urge to eat (Herman & Polivy, 1980). So can being distracted from monitoring your eating (Ward & Mann, 2000). (Ever notice that you eat more when out with friends?) Once the diet is broken, the person often thinks "what the heck" and then binges (Polivy & Herman, 1985, 1987). A lapse need not become a full collapse: Remember, most people occasionally lapse. Remind yourself that you've succeeded before, and continue with your plan, which may require lifelong self-control.

"I looked at you and thought, I bet this man runs marathons."

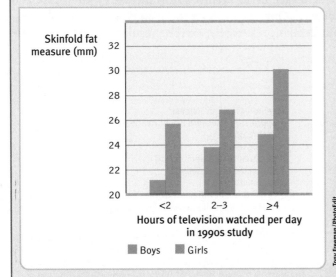

Tony Freeman/PhotoEdit

FIGURE 14.32
American idle: Couch potatoes beware—TV watching correlates with obesity

In a 1980s study of 6671 young people 12 to 17 years old, and in a 1990s follow-up study of 4063 individuals 8 to 16 years old, obesity was more common among those who watched the most television (Andersen & others, 1998; Dietz & Gortmaker, 1985). Of course, overweight people may avoid activity, preferring to sit and watch TV. But the association between TV watching and obesity remained when many other factors were controlled, suggesting that inactivity and snacking while watching TV do contribute to obesity. Also, as life-styles have become more sedentary and TV watching has increased, so has the percentage of overweight people in Britain, North America, and elsewhere. When California children were placed in a TV-reduction educational program, they watched less—and lost weight (Robinson, 1999).

"Fat is not a four-letter word," proclaims the National Association to Advance Fat Acceptance, so "a waist is a terrible thing to mind." Such statements discount the health risks linked with significant obesity, but they do convey a valid point: It is surely better to accept oneself as a bit heavy than to diet and binge and feel continually out of control and guilty. Fans loved Oprah Winfrey before she lost 67 pounds. They loved her after she put them back on. They loved her when she shed them again. And they will love her still, chubby or not.

While working to clarify the precise relationships among diet, behavior, and health (**FIGURE 14.33**), health psychologists continue their efforts to persuade us to adopt healthier life-styles. Such persuasion is a challenge. Happy people tend to see themselves as relatively invulnerable to health problems, especially those that might arise from their own actions (Salovey & Birnbaum, 1989; Weinstein, 1987). They also typically believe their own life-style is healthier than other people's—that they drink less alcohol, consume less fat and cholesterol, and get more exercise. Often they are fooling themselves. Most smokers—even most of those who have smoked for 20 years or tried quitting 10 or more times—think they will successfully quit within the next year (Slovic, 2001). Few young adults expect to gain weight, yet most do. When buying clothes, we prefer snug fits over loose fits, telling ourselves we will soon be taking off a few pounds. (Store clerks never hear, "I'll take that sweater in an extra large, because people my age usually put on more weight.")

Furthermore, many individuals who admit to risky behaviors will deny that the behaviors actually make them personally more vulnerable to illness or injury. Unlike people who are told they have normal blood pressure, those told they have high blood pressure tend to dismiss its seriousness (Croyle & Ditto, 1990). And smokers may delude themselves by saying that their exercising counteracts smoking's effects.

Because of our tendency to deny health risks, the first hurdle health-promotion programs must surmount is to get us to realize our vulnerability to stress- and behavior-related health problems. Only then will we make an effort to control stress, stop smoking, moderate our drinking, eat wisely, exercise regularly, and even buckle our seat belts.

"Fat! So?"

Popular T-shirt at the 1999 convention of the National Association to Advance Fat Acceptance

FIGURE 14.33
A biopsychosocial approach to health

Biological influences:
• genetic predisposition toward physiological reactivity, disease, addiction, depression, and other health problems

Psychological influences:
• appraising stressors as challenges or threats
• coping ability
• personality (resilient or not)
• optimistic or pessimistic explanatory style
• healthful or harmful behaviors (exercise, nutrition, smoking)
• personal control and other previous experiences
• spirituality

Health

Social-cultural influences:
• environmental stressors
• cultural influences on eating, smoking, and other behaviors
• social support
• available medical support

>> LEARNING OUTCOMES

Promoting Health

OBJECTIVE 11 | Contrast problem-focused coping and emotion-focused coping.

When we use problem-focused coping, we attempt to reduce stress directly by changing the events that trigger stress reactions or by changing the way we react to those events. We tend to use emotion-focused coping (putting distance between ourselves and a stressor, or attending to our own emotional needs) when we believe—rightly or wrongly—that we cannot change a stressful situation.

OBJECTIVE 12 | Describe how a perceived lack of control can affect health.

A perceived lack of control has been associated with higher than normal susceptibility to bacterial infections, cardiovascular disease, and, possibly, a shorter life span due to elevated levels of stress hormones and diminished immune system responses.

OBJECTIVE 13 | Discuss the links among explanatory style, stress, and health.

Compared with people with a pessimistic explanatory style, optimists tend to feel they have more control over stressors, cope better with stressful events, enjoy better moods, have stronger immune systems, and live longer than pessimists. Laughter (but not sarcasm) may reduce stress and strengthen the immune system.

OBJECTIVE 14 | Describe some of the ways that social support acts as a stress buffer.

Supportive family members, marriage partners, close friends, and companionable pets help people cope with stressful events. Social support fosters stronger immune functioning, calms the cardiovascular system, and lowers blood pressure.

OBJECTIVE 15 | Discuss the advantages of aerobic exercise as a technique for managing stress and fostering well-being.

Stress-management programs often include aerobic exercise (sustained exercise that increases heart and lung fitness), which raises energy levels, increases self-confidence, lowers tension, and may alleviate depression and anxiety. Studies have linked aerobic exercise to lowered blood pressure, increased arousal, higher levels of neurotransmitters that boost moods (such as norepinephrine, serotonin, and the endorphins), enhanced cognitive abilities, and (in mice) the growth of new brain cells.

OBJECTIVE 16 | Compare the benefits of biofeedback and relaxation training as stress-management techniques, and discuss meditation as a relaxation technique.

Biofeedback techniques have helped people control tension headaches, but simple relaxation exercises have been equally effective in combating hypertension, anxiety, and insomnia, and in lowering rates of recurring heart attacks. Some have searched for relief from stress and illnesses in complementary and alternative medicine. Studies of people while meditating have shown increased left frontal lobe activity and improved immune functioning, compared with their counterparts in control groups.

OBJECTIVE 17 | Discuss the correlation between religiosity and longevity, and offer some possible explanations for this link.

Regular religious attendance has been a reliable predictor of a longer life span. Researchers trying to determine the cause-effect relationship have isolated three intervening variables: (1) Religiously active people have healthy lifestyles (smoking and drinking less, for example). (2) Faith communities often function as social support networks and often encourage marriage (which, when happy, is associated with better health and longer life span). (3) Religious attendance—with its accompanying coherent worldview, sense of hope for the future, feelings of acceptance, and relaxed meditative state—may enhance feelings of positive emotions (such as hope and optimism) and decrease feelings of stress and anxiety.

OBJECTIVE 18 | Explain why people smoke.

Smoking's allure for teens comes in part from social rewards—identifying with or being accepted by "cool" people. Depending on their genetic inheritance, one in three early smokers will develop a physiological addiction to nicotine, as hard to break as an addiction to heroin or cocaine. By triggering a release of epinephrine, norepinephine, dopamine, and the opioids, nicotine takes away unpleasant cravings and delivers rewards.

OBJECTIVE 19 | Discuss ways of helping smokers to quit smoking—or preventing young people from ever starting.

Many approaches offer short-term quitting help for smokers, but long-term rates are less successful. Helpful pointers for quitting include setting a quit date, informing family and friends of the decision, removing all cigarettes, reviewing successful strategies learned in previous attempts, using a nicotine patch or gum, abstaining totally from smoking, abstaining from alcohol, avoiding places where others are likely to smoke, and exercising. Programs that successfully discourage young people from smoking (1) provide information about the effects of smoking; (2) educate young people about the influence of peers, parents, and the media; and (3) use modeling and role playing to train young people in refusal skills. Raising taxes on cigarettes also effectively cuts consumption.

OBJECTIVE 20 | **Discuss the adaptive advantages and modern-day disadvantages of a body that stores fat.**

Fat is a concentrated fuel reserve, and a body that can store this reserve can use it during times of famine. But this tendency, which was adaptive for our ancestors who gathered and hunted their food, is maladaptive for modern humans in a world of easily accessible food. Combined with a lack of exercise, the abundance of high-calorie food has led to high rates of obesity (defined as a body mass index of 30 or more), with increased risks of diabetes, high blood pressure, heart disease, gallstones, arthritis, sleep disorders, and certain types of cancer.

OBJECTIVE 21 | **Describe some of the social effects of obesity.**

Obesity threatens psychological well-being as well as physical health. Obese people, particularly obese women, encounter weight discrimination when seeking employment (where they encounter bias in hiring, placement, promotion, compensation, discipline, and discharge), searching for a romantic relationship, and interacting with family (bias sometimes extends to those seen with an obese person).

OBJECTIVE 22 | **Discuss some research findings on the role of heredity and environment in determining body weight.**

Studies of twins and adopted children indicate that being overweight is at least in part an inherited trait. But genes influence body weight—they don't determine it. For example, some people are genetically predisposed to have more fat cells and larger fat cells than others, but in an obese person, the original fat cells double or triple in size and then divide (or trigger nearby immature fat cells to divide), which is an irreversible environmental effect. Individuals also differ in their resting metabolic rates, but once someone gains weight in the form of fat tissue, less energy is needed to maintain that tissue than is needed to maintain muscle tissue. Environmental factors, such as frequently eating high-calorie foods and living a sedentary life, also matter, as comparisons of similar people from different generations or different locations indicate. Genes mostly determine why one man is heavier than another, but environment mostly determines why the same man is heavier than his grandfather was at the same age.

OBJECTIVE 23 | **Discuss the chances of success for an overweight person who wants to lose weight.**

Participants in structured weight-loss programs do experience a very high rate of failure, but these individuals may represent a group at especially high risk (they may have been unable to help themselves before joining the program). Moreover, surveys indicate that 25 to 60 percent of people who were once significantly overweight have successfully lost weight and kept it off for at least one year, and some for five years. Some overweight people, realizing that obesity is not a matter of willpower, choose to accept their weight. Others who want to lose weight can improve their chances: Begin a weight-loss program only when feeling motivated and self-disciplined; minimize exposure to tempting food cues; boost energy expenditure through exercise; set realistic and moderate goals; eat healthy foods; space small meals throughout the day; and forgive yourself (rather than giving up) if you have a lapse, remembering that occasional lapses will occur when you are making a lifelong change in eating patterns.

ASK YOURSELF: **To promote health by discouraging smoking, many governments now heavily tax cigarettes. Would you concur with the suggestion of Kelly Brownell (1997), director of Yale's Center for Eating and Weight Disorders, to slap a similar tax on unhealthy foods to decrease their consumption? Explain your perspective on this issue.**

REVIEW CHAPTER 14: **Stress and Health**

Test Yourself

1. What are the basic links in our stress response system?

2. Nonsmokers, this chapter reports, are less likely to become depressed and get divorced. What type of research finding is this, and what explanations might it have?

Answers to the Test Yourself questions can be found in Appendix B at the end of the book.

Terms and Concepts to Remember

behavioral medicine, p. 549

health psychology, p. 549

stress, p. 550

general adaptation syndrome (GAS), p. 552

coronary heart disease, p. 555

Type A, p. 555

Type B, p. 555

psychophysiological illness, p. 556

lymphocytes, p. 557

coping, p. 562

problem-focused coping, p. 562

emotion-focused coping, p. 562

aerobic exercise, p. 567

biofeedback, p. 569

complementary and alternative medicine, p. 570

WEB

To continue your study and review of Stress and Health, visit this book's Web site at www.worthpublishers.com/myers. You will find practice tests, review activities, and many interesting articles and Web links for more information on topics related to Stress and Health.

ANOTHER VOICE ON: PERSONALITY

JAMES BALDWIN (1924–1987), FROM "SONNY'S BLUES," 1957, *GOING TO MEET THE MAN*

So, we drove along, between the green of the park and the stony, lifeless elegance of hotels and apartment buildings, toward the vivid, killing streets of our childhood. These streets hadn't changed, though housing projects jutted up out of them now like rocks in the middle of a boiling sea. Most of the houses in which we had grown up had vanished. . . . Houses exactly like the houses of our past yet dominated the landscape, boys exactly like the boys we once had been found themselves smothering in these houses, came down into the streets for light and air and found themselves encircled by disaster. Some escaped the trap, most didn't. Those who got out always left something of themselves behind, as some animals amputate a leg and leave it in the trap. It might be said, perhaps, that I had escaped, after all, I was a school teacher, or that Sonny had, he hadn't lived in Harlem for years. Yet, as the cab moved uptown through streets which seemed, with a rush, to darken with dark people, . . . it came to me that what we both were seeking through our separate cab windows was that part of ourselves which had been left behind. It's always at the hour of trouble and confrontation that the missing member aches.

15 : Personality

■ **personality** an individual's characteristic pattern of thinking, feeling, and acting.

OBJECTIVE 1 | Define *personality*.

Lord of the Rings hobbit-hero Frodo Baggins knew that throughout his harrowing journey there was one who would never fail him—his loyal and ever-cheerful companion, Sam Gamgee. Even before they left their beloved hometown, Frodo warned Sam that the journey would not be easy:

> "It is going to be very dangerous, Sam. It is already dangerous. Most likely neither of us will come back."
>
> "If you don't come back, sir, then I shan't, that's certain," said Sam. "[The Elves told me] 'Don't you leave him!' Leave him! I said. I never mean to. I am going with him, if he climbs to the Moon; and if any of those Black Riders try to stop him, they'll have Sam Gamgee to reckon with." (Tolkien, *The Fellowship of the Ring*, p. 96)

And so they did! Later in the story, when it became clear that Frodo had to venture into the dreaded land of Mordor without the rest of the company, it was Sam who insisted he would accompany Frodo, come what may. It was Sam who lifted Frodo's flagging spirits with songs and stories from their boyhood, and Sam upon whom Frodo leaned when he could barely take another step. When Frodo was overcome by the evil of the ring he bore, it was Sam who saved Frodo from completely succumbing to it. And in the end, it was Sam who enabled Frodo to successfully reach the end of his journey. Sam Gamgee—the cheerful, conscientious, emotionally stable optimist—never faltered in his faithfulness or his belief that they could overcome the threatening darkness.

J. R. R. Tolkien's character Sam Gamgee, as he appears and reappears throughout the trilogy, exhibits the distinctiveness and consistency that define **personality**—an individual's characteristic pattern of thinking, feeling, and acting. The preceding chapters have emphasized our similarity—how we all develop, perceive, learn, remember, think, and feel. This chapter emphasizes our individuality.

> "There is no man who is not, at each moment, what he has been and what he will be."
>
> Oscar Wilde, 1854–1900

Much of this book deals with personality. In earlier chapters, we considered biological influences on personality, personality development across the life span, and personality-related aspects of learning, motivation, emotion, and health. In later chapters we will study disorders of personality and social influences on personality.

In this chapter we begin with two grand theories—historically significant perspectives that helped establish the field of personality psychology, raised key issues still being addressed in today's research and clinical work, and became part of our cultural legacy.

- Sigmund Freud's *psychoanalytic* theory proposed that childhood sexuality and unconscious motivations influence personality.
- The *humanistic* approach focused on our inner capacities for growth and self-fulfillment.

These historic theories, which offer sweeping perspectives on human nature, are complemented by what this chapter goes on to explore: today's more focused and down-to-earth scientific research of specific aspects of personality.

Today's personality researchers engage in focused analyses of the basic dimensions of personality and their impact on behavior; on the biological roots of these basic dimensions; on the interaction of persons and environments; and on studies of self-esteem, self-serving bias, and cultural influences on one's sense of self. Along the way, we'll survey some contemporary findings about the unconscious mind—findings that probably would have surprised Freud himself.

>> LEARNING OUTCOMES

Personality

OBJECTIVE 1 | Define *personality*.

Psychologists define *personality* as an individual's characteristic pattern of thinking, feeling, and acting. The early grand theories of personality tried to explain human nature, but current theories tend to focus on specific aspects of personality, such as our traits, uniqueness, sense of personal control, and concept of self.

ASK YOURSELF: **How would you describe *your* personality? What characteristics make up your typical patterns of thinking, feeling, and acting?**

The Psychoanalytic Perspective

OBJECTIVE 2 | Explain how Freud's experiences in private practice led to his theory of psychoanalysis.

"Sigmund Freud has left an important—and I believe indelible—mark on human self-understanding," observes Drew Westen (1998). Others disagree, noting that Freud's current influence in psychological science has diminished (Robins & others, 1999). But love him or hate him, Freud has profoundly influenced Western culture. Ask 100 people on the street to name a notable deceased psychologist, suggests Keith Stanovich (1996, p. 1), and "Freud would be the winner hands down." In the popular mind, he is to psychology's history what Elvis is to rock music's history. Freud's influence lingers in literary and film interpretation, psychiatry, and clinical psychology. So, who was this early personality theorist, and what did he teach?

Long before entering the University of Vienna in 1873, a youthful Sigmund Freud showed signs of independence and brilliance. He had a prodigious memory and so loved reading plays, poetry, and philosophy that he once ran up a bookstore debt beyond his means. As a teen he often took his evening meal in his tiny bedroom in order to lose no time from his studies.

Sigmund Freud, 1856–1939
"I was the only worker in a new field."

Freud went to medical school and after graduation set up a private practice, specializing in nervous disorders. Before long, however, he faced patients whose disorders made no neurological sense. For example, a patient might have lost all feeling in a hand—yet there is no sensory nerve that, if damaged, would numb the entire hand and nothing else. Freud's search for a cause for such disorders set his mind running. His views, which evolved as he treated patients and analyzed himself, eventually filled 24 volumes published between 1888 and 1939. Following his first solo book, *The Interpretation of Dreams* (1900), his ideas gradually began to attract both dedicated followers and intense criticism. For now, let's reserve judgment on Freud's theory and instead try to see things as he did. It is impossible to summarize 24 volumes in these few pages, but we can highlight Freud's *psychoanalytic theory*—the first comprehensive theory of personality, which included ideas about an unconscious region of the mind, psychosexual stages, and defense mechanisms for holding anxiety at bay.

Exploring the Unconscious

OBJECTIVE **3** | Discuss Freud's view of the mind as an iceberg, and explain how he used this image to represent conscious and unconscious regions of the mind.

Might some neurological disorders have psychological rather than physiological causes? Observing patients led Freud to his "discovery" of the unconscious. He decided that the peculiar loss of feeling in one's hand might be caused by a fear of touching one's genitals; that unexplained blindness or deafness might be caused by not wanting to see or hear something that aroused intense anxiety. Initially, Freud thought hypnosis might unlock the door to the unconscious, but patients displayed an uneven capacity for hypnosis. He then turned to **free association**—in which he merely told the patient to relax and say whatever came to mind, no matter how embarrassing or trivial. Freud assumed that a line of mental dominoes had fallen from his patients' distant past to their troubled present. Free association, he believed, allowed him to retrace that line, following a chain of thought leading into the patient's unconscious, where painful unconscious memories, often from childhood, could be retrieved and released. Freud called his theory of personality and the associated treatment techniques **psychoanalysis.**

Basic to Freud's theory was his belief that the mind is like an iceberg—mostly hidden (**FIGURE 15.1**). Our conscious awareness is the part of the iceberg that floats above the surface. Below the surface is the much larger, **unconscious** region containing thoughts, wishes, feelings, and memories, of which we are unaware. Some of these thoughts we store temporarily in a *preconscious* area, from which we can retrieve them into conscious awareness. Of greater interest to Freud was the mass of unacceptable passions and thoughts that he believed we *repress,* or forcibly block from our consciousness because they would be too unsettling to acknowledge. Freud believed that, although we are not consciously aware of them, these troublesome feelings and ideas powerfully influence us, sometimes gaining expression in disguised forms—the work we choose, the beliefs we hold, our daily habits, our troubling symptoms.

For Freud the determinist, nothing was ever accidental. He believed he could glimpse the unconscious seeping not only into people's free associations, beliefs, habits, and symptoms but also into slips of the tongue and pen. He illustrated with a financially stressed patient who, not wanting any large pills, said, "Please do not give

■ **free association** in psychoanalysis, a method of exploring the unconscious in which the person relaxes and says whatever comes to mind, no matter how trivial or embarrassing.

■ **psychoanalysis** Freud's theory of personality that attributes thoughts and actions to unconscious motives and conflicts; the techniques used in treating psychological disorders by seeking to expose and interpret unconscious tensions.

■ **unconscious** according to Freud, a reservoir of mostly unacceptable thoughts, wishes, feelings, and memories. According to contemporary psychologists, information processing of which we are unaware.

"Good morning, beheaded—uh, I mean beloved."

"I know how hard it is for you to put food on your family."

George W. Bush, 2000

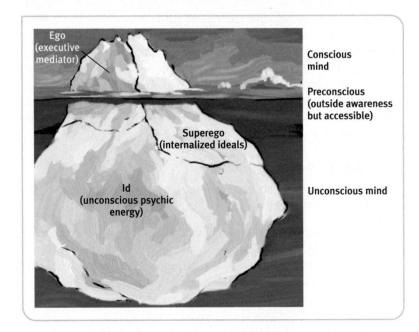

FIGURE 15.1
Freud's idea of the mind's structure
Consciousness is like an iceberg's visible tip. Note that the id is totally unconscious, but ego and superego operate both consciously and unconsciously. (Adapted from Freud, 1933, p. 111.)

■ **id** contains a reservoir of unconscious psychic energy that, according to Freud, strives to satisfy basic sexual and aggressive drives. The id operates on the pleasure principle, demanding immediate gratification.

■ **ego** the largely conscious, "executive" part of personality that, according to Freud, mediates among the demands of the id, superego, and reality. The ego operates on the *reality principle*, satisfying the id's desires in ways that will realistically bring pleasure rather than pain.

■ **superego** the part of personality that, according to Freud, represents internalized ideals and provides standards for judgment (the conscience) and for future aspirations.

■ **psychosexual stages** the childhood stages of development (oral, anal, phallic, latency, genital) during which, according to Freud, the id's pleasure-seeking energies focus on distinct erogenous zones.

■ **Oedipus** [ED-uh-puss] **complex** according to Freud, a boy's sexual desires toward his mother and feelings of jealousy and hatred for the rival father.

■ **identification** the process by which, according to Freud, children incorporate their parents' values into their developing superegos.

■ **fixation** according to Freud, a lingering focus of pleasure-seeking energies at an earlier psychosexual stage, in which conflicts were unresolved.

"Fifty is plenty."   "Hundred and fifty."

The ego struggles to reconcile the demands of superego and id, said Freud.

me any bills, because I cannot swallow them." Similarly, Freud viewed jokes as expressions of repressed sexual and aggressive tendencies, and dreams as the "royal road to the unconscious." The remembered content of dreams (their *manifest content*) he believed to be a censored expression of the dreamer's unconscious wishes (the dream's *latent content*). In his analysis of dreams, Freud searched for the nature of patients' inner conflicts and their release from inner tensions.

Personality Structure

OBJECTIVE 4 | Describe Freud's view of personality structure, and discuss the interactions of the id, ego, and superego.

In Freud's view, human personality—including its emotions and strivings—arises from a conflict between our aggressive, pleasure-seeking biological impulses and the internalized social restraints against them. Freud believed personality is the result of our efforts to resolve this basic conflict—to express these impulses in ways that bring satisfaction without also bringing guilt or punishment. To understand the mind's dynamics during this conflict, Freud proposed three interacting systems: the *id, ego,* and *superego* (see Figure 15.1 on page 597.)

The **id** has a reservoir of unconscious psychic energy constantly striving to satisfy basic drives to survive, reproduce, and aggress. The id operates on the *pleasure principle:* If not constrained by reality, it seeks immediate gratification. To envision an id-dominated person, think of newborn infants, crying out for satisfaction the moment they feel a need, caring nothing for the outside world's conditions and demands. Or think of people with a present rather than future time perspective—those who often use tobacco, alcohol, and other drugs, and would sooner party now than sacrifice today's pleasure for future success and happiness (Keough & others, 1999).

As the **ego** develops, the young child learns to cope with the real world. The ego, operating on the *reality principle,* seeks to gratify the id's impulses in realistic ways that will bring long-term pleasure rather than pain or destruction. (Imagine what would happen if, lacking an ego, we expressed our unrestrained sexual or aggressive impulses whenever we felt them.) The ego contains our partly conscious perceptions, thoughts, judgments, and memories.

Beginning around age 4 or 5, Freud theorized, a child's ego recognizes the demands of the newly emerging **superego,** the voice of conscience that forces the ego to consider not only the real but the ideal, and that focuses solely on how one *ought* to behave. The superego strives for perfection, judging actions and producing positive feelings of pride or negative feelings of guilt. Someone with an exceptionally strong superego may be virtuous yet, ironically, guilt-ridden; another with a weak superego may be wantonly self-indulgent and remorseless.

Because the superego's demands often oppose the id's, the ego struggles to reconcile the two. It is the personality "executive," mediating the impulsive demands of the id, the restraining demands of the superego, and the real-life demands of the external world. If chaste Jane feels sexually attracted to John she may satisfy both id and superego by joining a volunteer organization to which John belongs.

Personality Development

OBJECTIVE 5 | Identify Freud's psychosexual stages of development, and describe the effects of fixation on behavior.

Analysis of his patients' histories convinced Freud that personality forms during life's first few years. Again and again his patients' symptoms seemed rooted in unresolved conflicts from early childhood. He concluded that children pass through a series of **psychosexual stages,** during which the id's pleasure-seeking energies focus on distinct pleasure-sensitive areas of the body called *erogenous zones* (**TABLE 15.1**).

TABLE 15.1

FREUD'S PSYCHOSEXUAL STAGES

Stage	Focus
Oral (0–18 months)	Pleasure centers on the mouth—sucking, biting, chewing
Anal (18–36 months)	Pleasure focuses on bowel and bladder elimination; coping with demands for control
Phallic (3–6 years)	Pleasure zone is the genitals; coping with incestuous sexual feelings
Latency (6 to puberty)	Dormant sexual feelings
Genital (puberty on)	Maturation of sexual interests

Freud believed that during the *phallic stage* boys seek genital stimulation, and they develop both unconscious sexual desires for their mother and jealousy and hatred for their father, whom they consider a rival. Given these feelings, boys supposedly also feel guilt and a lurking fear of punishment, perhaps by castration, from their father. Freud called this collection of feelings the **Oedipus complex** after the Greek legend of Oedipus, who unknowingly killed his father and married his mother. Some psychoanalysts in Freud's era believed that girls experienced a parallel *Electra complex*. Freud's own thinking seemed to vary on this issue.

Children eventually cope with threatening feelings, said Freud, by repressing them and by identifying with (trying to become like) the rival parent. It's as though something inside the child decides, "If you can't beat 'em [the parent of the same sex], join 'em." Through this **identification** process, children's superegos gain strength as they incorporate many of their parents' values. Freud believed that identification with the same-sex parent provides what psychologists now call our *gender identity*—our sense of being male or female. This illustrates what both Freud and today's *object relations theorists* have presumed: that our early childhood relations with parents, caregivers, and everything else influences our developing identity, personality, and frailties.

In Freud's view, conflicts unresolved during earlier psychosexual stages could surface as maladaptive behavior in the adult years. At any point in the oral, anal, or phallic stages, strong conflict could lock, or **fixate,** the person's pleasure-seeking energies in that stage. A person who had been either orally overindulged or deprived (perhaps by abrupt, early weaning) might fixate at the oral stage, for example. This orally fixated adult could exhibit either passive dependence (like that of a nursing infant) or an exaggerated denial of this dependence—perhaps by acting tough and uttering biting sarcasm. Or the person might continue to seek oral gratification by smoking and eating excessively. In such ways, Freud suggested, the twig of personality is bent at an early age.

Defense Mechanisms

OBJECTIVE 6 | Describe the function of defense mechanisms, and identify six of them.

Anxiety, said Freud, is the price we pay for civilization. As members of social groups, we must control our sexual and aggressive impulses, not act them out. But sometimes the ego fears losing control of this inner war between the demands of the id and the superego, and the result is a dark cloud of unfocused anxiety, which leaves us feeling unsettled but unsure why.

Identification
Freud believed that children cope with threatening feelings of competition with their same-sex parent by identifying with that parent.

"Oh, for goodness' sake! Smoke!"

Freud proposed that the ego protects itself with **defense mechanisms,** tactics that reduce or redirect anxiety by distorting reality. Here are six examples.

- **Repression** banishes anxiety-arousing thoughts and feelings from consciousness. According to Freud, *repression underlies all the other defense mechanisms,* each of which disguises threatening impulses and keeps them from reaching consciousness. Freud believed that repression explains why we do not remember our childhood lust for our parent of the other sex. However, he also believed that repression is often incomplete, that repressed urges seep out in dream symbols and slips of the tongue.

- **Regression** allows us to retreat to an earlier, more infantile stage of development. Facing the anxious first days of school, a child may regress to the oral comfort of thumb-sucking. Juvenile monkeys, when anxious, retreat to infantile clinging to their mothers or to one another (Suomi, 1987). Even homesick new college students may long for the security and comfort of home.

- In **reaction formation,** the ego unconsciously makes unacceptable impulses look like their opposites. En route to consciousness, the unacceptable proposition "I hate him" becomes "I love him." Timidity becomes daring. Feelings of inadequacy become bravado.

- **Projection** disguises threatening impulses by attributing them to others. Thus, "He doesn't trust me" may be a projection of the actual feeling "I don't trust him" or "I don't trust myself." An El Salvadoran saying captures the idea: "The thief thinks everyone else is a thief."

- **Rationalization** occurs when we unconsciously generate self-justifying explanations to hide from ourselves the real reasons for our actions. Thus, habitual drinkers may say they drink with their friends "just to be sociable." Students who fail to study may rationalize, "All work and no play makes Jack [or Jill] a dull person."

- **Displacement** diverts sexual or aggressive impulses toward an object or person that is psychologically more acceptable than the one that aroused the feelings. Children who fear expressing anger against their parents may displace it by kicking the family pet. Students upset over an exam may snap at a roommate.

Note that all these defense mechanisms function indirectly and unconsciously. They reduce anxiety by disguising our threatening impulses. Just as the body unconsciously defends itself against disease, so also, believed Freud, does the ego unconsciously defend itself against anxiety.

■ **defense mechanisms** in psychoanalytic theory, the ego's protective methods of reducing anxiety by unconsciously distorting reality.

■ **repression** in psychoanalytic theory, the basic defense mechanism that banishes anxiety-arousing thoughts, feelings, and memories from consciousness.

■ **regression** psychoanalytic defense mechanism in which an individual faced with anxiety retreats to a more infantile psychosexual stage, where some psychic energy remains fixated.

Regression
Faced with a mild stressor, children and young monkeys will regress, retreating to the comfort of earlier behaviors.

The Neo-Freudian and Psychodynamic Theorists

OBJECTIVE 7 | Contrast the views of the neo-Freudians and psychodynamic theorists with Freud's original theory.

Freud's writings were controversial, but they soon attracted followers, mostly young, ambitious physicians who formed an inner circle around their strong-minded leader. These pioneering psychoanalysts and others, whom we now call *neo-Freudians,* accepted Freud's basic ideas: the personality structures of id, ego, and superego; the importance of the unconscious; the shaping of personality in childhood; and the dynamics of anxiety and the defense mechanisms. But they veered away from Freud in two important ways. First, they placed more emphasis on the conscious mind's role in interpreting experience and in coping with the environment. And second, they doubted that sex and aggression were all-consuming motivations. Instead, they tended to emphasize loftier motives and social interactions. The following examples illustrate.

Alfred Adler and Karen Horney [HORN-eye] agreed with Freud that childhood is important. But they believed that childhood *social,* not sexual, tensions are crucial for personality formation. Adler (who had proposed the still-popular idea of the *inferiority complex*) himself struggled to overcome childhood illnesses and accidents, and he believed that much of our behavior is driven by efforts to conquer childhood feelings of inferiority, feelings that trigger our strivings for superiority and power. Horney said childhood anxiety, caused by the dependent child's sense of helplessness, triggers our desire for love and security. Horney countered Freud's assumptions that women have weak superegos and suffer "penis envy," and she attempted to balance the bias she detected in this masculine view of psychology.

Unlike other neo-Freudians, Carl Jung—Freud's disciple-turned-dissenter—placed less emphasis on social factors and agreed with Freud that the unconscious exerts a powerful influence. But to Jung (pronounced Yoong), the unconscious contains more than our repressed thoughts and feelings. He believed we also have a **collective unconscious,** a common reservoir of images derived from our species' universal experiences. Jung said that the collective unconscious explains why, for many people, spiritual concerns are deeply rooted and why people in different cultures share certain myths and images, such as mother as a symbol of nurturance. (Today's psychologists discount the idea of inherited experiences. But many do believe that our shared evolutionary history shaped some universal dispositions.)

■ **reaction formation** psychoanalytic defense mechanism by which the ego unconsciously switches unacceptable impulses into their opposites. Thus, people may express feelings that are the opposite of their anxiety-arousing unconscious feelings.

■ **projection** psychoanalytic defense mechanism by which people disguise their own threatening impulses by attributing them to others.

■ **rationalization** defense mechanism that offers self-justifying explanations in place of the real, more threatening, unconscious reasons for one's actions.

■ **displacement** psychoanalytic defense mechanism that shifts sexual or aggressive impulses toward a more acceptable or less threatening object or person, as when redirecting anger toward a safer outlet.

■ **collective unconscious** Carl Jung's concept of a shared, inherited reservoir of memory traces from our species' history.

" The female . . . acknowledges the fact of her castration, and with it, too, the superiority of the male and her own inferiority; but she rebels against this unwelcome state of affairs."

Sigmund Freud, *Female Sexuality*, 1931

Alfred Adler
"The individual feels at home in life and feels his existence to be worthwhile just so far as he is useful to others and is overcoming feelings of inferiority" (*Problems of Neurosis*, 1964).

Karen Horney
"The view that women are infantile and emotional creatures, and as such, incapable of responsibility and independence is the work of the masculine tendency to lower women's self-respect" (*Feminine Psychology*, 1932).

Carl Jung
"We can keep from a child all knowledge of earlier myths, but we cannot take from him the need for mythology" (*Symbols of Transformation*, 1912).

■ **projective test** a personality test, such as the Rorschach or TAT, that provides ambiguous stimuli designed to trigger projection of one's inner dynamics.

■ **Thematic Apperception Test (TAT)** a projective test in which people express their inner feelings and interests through the stories they make up about ambiguous scenes.

■ **Rorschach inkblot test** the most widely used projective test, a set of 10 inkblots, designed by Hermann Rorschach; seeks to identify people's inner feelings by analyzing their interpretations of the blots.

"We don't see things as they are; we see things as we are."

The Talmud

FIGURE 15.2
The TAT
This clinician presumes that the hopes, fears, and interests expressed in this boy's descriptions of a series of ambiguous pictures in the Thematic Apperception Test (TAT) are projections of his inner feelings.

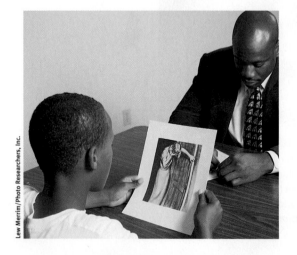

Freud died in 1939. Since then, some of his ideas have been incorporated into *psychodynamic theory*. "Most contemporary dynamic theorists and therapists are not wedded to the idea that sex is the basis of personality," notes Drew Westen (1996). They "do not talk about ids and egos, and do not go around classifying their patients as oral, anal, or phallic characters." What they do assume, with Freud, is that much of our mental life is unconscious, that we often struggle with inner conflicts among our wishes, fears, and values, and that childhood shapes our personalities and ways of becoming attached to others. For example, Freud's idea that early childhood experiences with caregivers were key to the developing personality laid the groundwork for later theory and research on infant attachment and on its long-term consequences (see Chapter 4).

Assessing Unconscious Processes

OBJECTIVE 8 | Describe two projective tests used to assess personality, and discuss some criticisms of them.

Those who study personality or provide therapy need ways to evaluate personality characteristics. Methods of assessment differ because they are tailored to different personality theories. So what might be the tool of choice for clinicians working in the Freudian tradition?

Evaluating personality from this perspective would require a road into the unconscious mind, which contains residues from early childhood experiences. (Recall that Freud believed free association and dream interpretation could reveal the unconscious.) Objective assessment tools, such as agree-disagree or true-false questionnaires would be inadequate because they would merely tap the conscious surface. The tool of choice would be a sort of psychological x-ray—a test that sees through our surface pretensions and reveals our hidden conflicts and impulses.

Projective tests aim to provide such a view by presenting an ambiguous stimulus and then asking test-takers to describe it or tell a story about it. The stimulus has no inherent significance, so any meaning people read into it presumably is a projection of their interests and conflicts. Henry Murray (1933) demonstrated a possible basis for such a test at a party hosted by his 11-year-old daughter. Murray engaged the children in a frightening game called "Murder." When shown some photographs after the game, the children perceived the photos as more malicious than they had before the game. These children, it seemed to Murray, had *projected* their inner feelings into the pictures. A few years later, Murray introduced the **Thematic Apperception Test (TAT),** in which people view ambiguous pictures and then make up stories about them (**FIGURE 15.2**). One use of storytelling has been to assess achievement motivation. Shown a daydreaming boy, those who imagine he is fantasizing about an achievement are presumed to be projecting their own goals. "As a rule," said Murray, "the subject leaves the test happily unaware that he has presented the psychologist with what amounts to an x-ray of his inner self" (quoted by Talbot, 1999).

Other projective tests ask test-takers to draw a person, to complete sentences ("My mother . . ."), or to provide the first word that comes to mind after the examiner says a test word. Most widely used is the famous **Rorschach inkblot test,** introduced in 1921 by Swiss psychiatrist Hermann Rorschach [ROAR-shock]. The test assumes that what we see in its 10 inkblots reflects our inner feelings and conflicts (**FIGURE 15.3**). If we see predatory animals or weapons, the examiner may infer we have aggressive tendencies.

Is this a reasonable assumption? If so, can a psychologist use the Rorschach to understand one's personality and diagnose an emotional disorder? Recall from Chapter 11's discussion of intelligence tests that the two primary criteria of a good test are *reliability* (consistency of results) and *validity* (predicting what it's supposed to). On those criteria, how good is the Rorschach?

By the second half of the twentieth century, critics had pointed out that no universally accepted system existed for scoring and interpreting the Rohrschach tests (Sechrest & others, 1998). Two raters who had been trained in different scoring systems would display only minimal agreement on the results of a given test. Nor was the test very successful at predicting behavior or at discriminating between groups (for example, identifying who is suicidal and who is not). The Rorschach is not an emotional MRI.

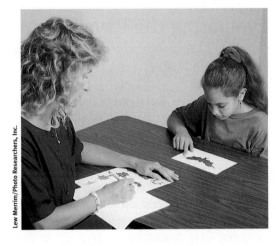

Lew Merrim/Photo Researchers, Inc.

FIGURE 15.3
The Rorschach test
In this projective test, people tell what they see in a series of symmetrical inkblots. Some who use this test are confident that the interpretation of ambiguous stimuli will reveal unconscious aspects of the test-taker's personality. Others use it as an icebreaker or to supplement other information.

With all the criticisms, the Rorschach remains "simultaneously, the most cherished and the most reviled of all psychological assessment tools" (Hunsley & Bailey, 1999). Clinicians—82 percent of whom report administering it at least occasionally—often cherish the Rorschach (Watkins & others, 1995; Lilienfeld & others, 2000). Some offer judges Rorschach-based assessments of criminals' violence potential. Other clinicians view it as a diagnostic tool, a source of suggestive leads, or an icebreaker and a revealing interview technique. Edward Aronow and his colleagues (1995) report the example of a woman who found "four pink geese" in a Rorschach card, and then, under prompting, recalled that her uncle, a farmer, had molested her, that he had four daughters, and that his white geese became pink when slaughtered. There is now a research-based, computer-aided coding and interpretation tool that aims to improve agreement among raters and enhance the test's validity (Erdberg, 1990; Exner, 2003). For example, a person seeing lots of reflections in the blots, treating them much like a mirror, would indicate self-centeredness. The Society for Personality Assessment acknowledges that one should not "use Rorschach findings alone to draw a legal conclusion" or to decide whether, for example, child sexual abuse has occurred. But the society contends that "the Rorschach possesses documented reliability and validity" and that its use in personality assessment is "appropriate and justified."

But the evidence is insufficient to its revilers, who argue that the test has very limited validity and who note that inkblot assessments diagnose many normal adults as pathological (Wood & others, 2003, 2006). They argue that only a few of the many Rorschach-derived scores, such as ones for hostility and anxiety, have demonstrated validity. Other critics find "no scientific basis for justifying the use of Rorschach scales in psychological assessments" (Hunsley & Bailey, 1999) and even propose a moratorium on its clinical and forensic use (Garb & others, 2005). "If psychologists used tea leaves instead of the Rorschach, we'd probably be better off," suggests psychologist-critic James Wood (2003), "because then, at least, no one would take the results seriously."

Alternative projective assessment techniques, such as the TAT and the Draw-a-Person test fare little better, conclude Scott Lilienfeld, James Wood, and Howard Garb (2001). "Even seasoned professionals," they warn, "can be fooled by their intuitions and their faith in tools that lack strong evidence of effectiveness. When a substantial body of research demonstrates that old intuitions are wrong, it is time to adopt new ways of thinking." Freud himself probably would have been uncomfortable with trying to diagnose patients based on tests and would have been more interested in the therapist–patient interactions that take place during the test.

"If a professional psychologist is 'evaluating' you in a situation in which you are at risk and asks you for responses to ink blots . . . walk out of that psychologist's office."
Robyn Dawes, *House of Cards: Psychology and Psychotherapy Based on Myth*, 1994

© 1983 by Sidney Harris; American Scientist Magazine.

"The forward thrust of the antlers shows a determined personality, yet the small sun indicates a lack of self-confidence. . . ."

"The Rorschach Inkblot Test has been resoundingly discredited . . . I call it the Dracula of psychological tests, because no one has been able to drive a stake through the cursed thing's heart."
Carol Tavris, "Mind Games: Psychological Warfare Between Therapists and Scientists," 2003

"Dawkins' law of adversarial debate: "When two incompatible beliefs are advocated with equal intensity, the truth does not lie half way between them."
Richard Dawkins, 2004

Evaluating the Psychoanalytic Perspective

OBJECTIVE 9 | Summarize psychology's current assessment of Freud's theory of psychoanalysis.

Contradictory Evidence from Modern Research

We critique Freud from an early twenty-first-century perspective, a perspective that itself will be subject to revision. Freud did not have access to neurotransmitter or DNA studies, or to all that we have since learned about human development, thinking, and emotion. Thus, to criticize his theories by comparing them with current concepts, some say, is like comparing Henry Ford's Model T with today's Mustang.

But Freud's admirers and his critics agree that recent research contradicts many of his specific ideas. Today's developmental psychologists see our development as lifelong, not fixed in childhood. They doubt that infants' neural networks are mature enough to sustain as much emotional trauma as Freud assumed. Some think Freud overestimated parental influence and underestimated peer influence (and abuse). They also doubt that conscience and gender identity form as the child resolves the Oedipus complex at age 5 or 6. We gain our gender identity earlier and become strongly masculine or feminine even without a same-sex parent present. And they note that Freud's ideas about childhood sexuality arose from his rejection of stories of childhood sexual abuse told by his female patients—stories that some scholars believe he suggested, coerced, or later misremembered and then attributed to their own childhood sexual wishes and conflicts (Esterson, 2001; Powell & Boer, 1994). Today, we understand how Freud's questioning might have created false memories, and we also know that childhood sexual abuse does happen.

As we saw in Chapter 7, new ideas about why we dream dispute Freud's belief that dreams disguise and fulfill wishes. And slips of the tongue can be explained as competition between similar verbal choices in our memory network. Someone who says "I don't want to do that—it's a lot of brothel" may simply be blending *bother* and *trouble* (Foss & Hakes, 1978). Researchers find little support for Freud's idea that defense mechanisms disguise sexual and aggressive impulses (though our cognitive gymnastics do indeed work to protect our self-esteem). History also has failed to support another of Freud's ideas—that suppressed sexuality causes psychological disorders. From Freud's time to ours, sexual inhibition has diminished; psychological disorders have not.

Is Repression a Myth?

Freud's entire psychoanalytic theory rests on his assumption that the human mind often *represses* painful experiences, banishing them into the unconscious until, with the help of a guide, we somehow uncover them, finding them intact, like long-lost books in a dusty attic. Recover and resolve the painful repressed memories of our childhood and emotional healing would follow. Under Freud's influence, repression became a widely accepted concept, used to explain hypnotic phenomena, psychological disorders, and apparent lost and recovered memories of childhood traumas (Cheit, 1998). In one survey, 88 percent of university students believed that painful experiences commonly get pushed out of awareness and into the unconscious (Garry & others, 1994).

Actually, contend many of today's researchers, repression, if it ever occurs, is a rare mental response to terrible trauma. "Repression folklore is . . . partly refuted, partly untested, and partly untestable," says Elizabeth Loftus (1995). Consider: If the human mind indeed commonly banishes painful experiences, how do we explain these odd findings?

- Shouldn't we expect children who have witnessed a parent's murder to repress the experience? A study of sixteen 5- to 10-year-old children who had this horrific experience found that not one repressed the memory (Malmquist, 1986).

> "Many aspects of Freudian theory are indeed out of date, and they should be: Freud died in 1939, and he has been slow to undertake further revisions."
>
> Psychologist Drew Westen (1998)

> "I remember your name perfectly but I just can't think of your face."
>
> Oxford professor W. A. Spooner, 1844–1930, famous for his linguistic flip-flops *(spoonerisms)*. Spooner rebuked one student for "fighting a liar in the quadrangle" and another who "hissed my mystery lecture," adding "You have tasted two worms."

- Shouldn't survivors of Nazi death camps have banished the atrocities from consciousness? With rare exceptions, they remember all too well—although many do benefit from disclosing and talking through their experiences (Helmreich, 1992, 1994; Pennebaker, 1990).
- Shouldn't battle-scarred veterans suffer amnesia for their worst experiences? In one neurological unit in a British hospital, 35 percent of military patients arrived with amnesia after severe combat during World War II (Arrigo & Pezdek, 1997; Karon & Widener, 1997, 1998). But such cases often appear to be either concussion-related or a *false amnesia* tactic for escaping intolerable situations (Holmes, 1990, 1994). Folklore regarding recovered battlefield memories is either unconfirmed or related to therapists' use of suggestive techniques.

There are exceptions—one death camp survivor reportedly forgot for more than 30 years the snatching and shooting of her infant son (Kraft, 1996). Some researchers believe that extreme, prolonged stress, such as the stress some severely abused children experience, might disrupt memory by damaging the hippocampus (Schacter, 1996). But the far more common reality is that high stress (and associated stress hormones) enhances memory (see Chapter 9, Memory). Powerfully negative emotional events are therefore remembered well (Alexander & others, 2005; Shobe & Kihlstrom, 1997).

In fact, too well: Traumatic events, such as rape and torture, haunt survivors, who experience unwanted flashbacks. They are seared onto the soul. "You see the babies," said Holocaust survivor Sally H. (1979). "You see the screaming mothers. You see hanging people. You sit and you see that face there. It's something you don't forget."

The Modern Unconscious Mind

Freud was right about at least one thing: We indeed have limited access to all that goes on in our minds (Erdelyi, 1985, 1988; Kihlstrom, 1990). In fact, our capacity for unconscious learning is quite sophisticated. Pawel Lewicki and his colleagues (1992, 1997) at the University of Tulsa's Nonconscious Information Processing Laboratory discovered that people's nonconscious learning can anticipate patterns "too complex and too confusing to be consciously noticed." In one study, some students watched (others did not) as the numeral 6 jumped around a computer screen from quadrant to quadrant. Although the movement seemed to be in random order—no one consciously detected any rule—it was based on a complex, hidden pattern. And those who had seen the earlier presentations were quicker to find the next 6 when it was hidden among a screen full of numbers. Without knowing how they did it, their ability to track the number from one quadrant to another was improving. When the number's movement became truly random, their performance declined.

Lewicki repeated the experiment with his quick-witted psychology professor colleagues, who knew he was studying nonconscious learning. They, too, gained speed in locating the target's next position, and they, too, did not know why. When the experimenters switched to a random sequence and performance declined, the professors conjectured reasons for the decline (threatening subliminal messages, perhaps?). To students who had displayed nonconscious learning, Lewicki even offered $100 if they could uncover the hidden pattern. Some spent hours trying to decipher the sequence. None succeeded.

Other researchers have confirmed the reality of nonconscious *implicit learning* (Fletcher & others, 2005; Frensch & Rünger, 2003). Such experiments point to a vast realm of out-of-sight information. Nevertheless, the "iceberg" notion held by today's research psychologists differs from Freud's—so much so, argues Anthony Greenwald (1992), that it is time to abandon Freud's view of the unconscious. As we saw in earlier chapters, many now think of the unconscious not as seething passions

> " Warning. Despite 70 years of research, there is no objective evidence to support the concept of repression."
>
> Psychologist David S. Holmes (1994)

> " During the Holocaust, many children . . . were forced to endure the unendurable. For those who continue to suffer [the] pain is still present, many years later, as real as it was on the day it occurred."
>
> Eric Zillmer, Molly Harrower, Barry Ritzler, and Robert Archer, *The Quest for the Nazi Personality*, 1995

and repressive censoring but as cooler information processing that occurs without our awareness. To these researchers, the unconscious also involves

- the schemas that automatically control our perceptions and interpretations (Chapter 6).
- the priming by stimuli to which we have not consciously attended (Chapters 5 and 9).
- the right-hemisphere activity that enables the split-brain patient's left hand to carry out an instruction the patient cannot verbalize (Chapter 2).
- the parallel processing of different aspects of vision and thinking (Chapters 5 and 10).
- the implicit memories that operate without conscious recall, even among those with amnesia (Chapter 9).
- the emotions that activate instantly, before conscious analysis (Chapter 13).
- the self-concept and stereotypes that automatically and unconsciously influence how we process information about ourselves and others (Chapter 18).

More than we realize, we fly on autopilot. Our lives are guided by off-screen, out-of-sight, nonconscious information processing. The nonconscious mind is huge. This understanding of nonconscious information processing is more like the pre-Freudian view of an underground stream of thought from which spontaneous creative ideas surface.

Recent history has supported Freud's idea that we defend ourselves against anxiety. Again, however, the contemporary idea differs from Freud's. Jeff Greenberg, Sheldon Solomon, and Tom Pyszczynski (1997) believe that one source of anxiety is "the terror resulting from our awareness of vulnerability and death." More than 130 studies testing their **terror-management theory** show that thinking about one's mortality—for example, by writing a short essay on dying and its associated emotions—provokes enough anxiety to intensify prejudices. Death anxiety motivates contempt for others and esteem for oneself.

Faced with a threatening world, people act not only to enhance their self-esteem but also to adhere more strongly to worldviews that answer questions about life's meaning. Moreover, they cleave to close relationships (Mikulincer & others, 2003). The events of 9/11—a striking experience of the terror of death—led trapped World Trade Center occupants to spend their last moments calling loved ones, and led most Americans to reach out to family and friends.

Recent research has also provided some support for Freud's idea of defense mechanisms (even if they don't work exactly as Freud supposed). For example, Roy Baumeister and his colleagues (1998) found that people tend to see their foibles and attitudes in others, a phenomenon that Freud called projection and that today's researchers call the *false consensus effect,* the tendency to overestimate the extent to which others share our beliefs and behaviors. People who cheat on their taxes or break speed limits tend to think many others do likewise. People falsely told they are high in repressed anger or dishonesty tend more to see such in others (Schimel & others, 2003). Moreover, when trying to suppress thinking about our own faults we become more likely to see them in others (Newman & others, 1997). Supportive evidence is, however, meager for other defenses, such as displacement, that are tied to instinctual energy. More evidence exists for defenses, such as reaction formation, that defend self-esteem. Defense mechanisms, Baumeister concludes, are motivated less by the seething impulses that Freud presumed than by our need to protect our self-image.

Freud's Ideas as Scientific Theory

Psychologists also criticize Freud's theory for its scientific shortcomings. Recall from Chapter 1 that good scientific theories explain observations and offer testable hypotheses. Freud's theory rests on few objective observations and parts of it offer few hypotheses to verify or reject. (For Freud, his own recollections and interpretations of patients' free associations, dreams, and slips were evidence enough.)

"Two passengers leaned against the ship's rail and stared at the sea. 'There sure is a lot of water in the ocean,' said one. 'Yes,' answered his friend, 'we've only seen the top of it.'"

Psychologist George A. Miller (1962)

"I don't want to attain immortality through my work; I want to attain immortality by not dying."

Woody Allen

■ **terror-management theory** proposes that faith in one's worldview and the pursuit of self-esteem provide protection against a deeply rooted fear of death.

What is the most serious problem with Freud's theory? It offers after-the-fact explanations of any characteristic (of one person's smoking, another's fear of horses, another's sexual orientation) yet fails to *predict* such behaviors and traits. If you feel angry at your mother's death, you illustrate his theory because "your unresolved childhood dependency needs are threatened." If you do not feel angry, you again illustrate his theory because "you are repressing your anger." That, said Calvin Hall and Gardner Lindzey (1978, p. 68), "is like betting on a horse after the race has been run." A good theory makes testable predictions.

For such reasons, some of Freud's critics offer harsh words. They see a decaying Freudian edifice built on the swamplands of childhood sexuality, repression, dream analysis, and after-the-fact speculation. "When we stand on [Freud's] shoulders, we only discover that we're looking further in the wrong direction," says John Kihlstrom (1997). Freud's most searing critic, Frederick Crews (1998), likens Freud to Peter Sellers' bumbling Inspector Clouseau, albeit with a unique talent for bamboozling an entire century. What is original about Freud's ideas is not good, and what is good is not original (the unconscious mind is an idea that dates back to Plato).

So, should psychology post a "Do Not Resuscitate" order on this old theory? Freud's supporters object. To criticize Freudian theory for not making testable predictions is, they say, like criticizing baseball for not being an aerobic exercise, something it was never intended to be. Freud never claimed that psychoanalysis was predictive science. He merely claimed that, looking back, psychoanalysts could find meaning in our state of mind (Rieff, 1979).

Freud's supporters also note that some of his ideas *are* enduring. It was Freud who drew our attention to the unconscious and the irrational, to our self-protective defenses, to the importance of human sexuality, and to the tension between our biological impulses and our social well-being. It was Freud who challenged our self-righteousness, punctured our pretensions, and reminded us of our potential for evil.

In science, Darwin's legacy lives while Freud's is waning (Bornstein, 2001). In the popular culture, Freud's legacy lives on. Some ideas that many people assume to be true—that childhood experiences mold personality, that dreams have meaning, that many behaviors have disguised motives—are part of that legacy. His early twentieth-century concepts penetrate our twenty-first-century language. Without realizing their source, we may speak of *ego, repression, projection, complex* (as in "inferiority complex"), *sibling rivalry, Freudian slips,* and *fixation.* "Freud's premises may have undergone a steady decline in currency within academia for many years," noted Martin Seligman (1994), "but Hollywood, the talk shows, many therapists, and the general public still love them."

> We are arguing like a man who should say, 'If there were an invisible cat in that chair, the chair would look empty; but the chair does look empty; therefore there is an invisible cat in it.'"
>
> C. S. Lewis, *Four Loves*, 1958

>> LEARNING OUTCOMES

The Psychoanalytic Perspective

OBJECTIVE 2 | **Explain how Freud's experiences in private practice led to his theory of psychoanalysis.**

As a physician specializing in nervous disorders, Freud encountered patients whose complaints could not be explained in terms of purely physical causes. His attempt to understand these conditions led to his theory of psychoanalysis, the first comprehensive theory of personality.

OBJECTIVE 3 | **Discuss Freud's view of the mind as an iceberg, and explain how he used this image to represent conscious and unconscious regions of the mind.**

Freud compared the human mind to an iceberg because he believed that most of the mind—the *unconscious*—is hidden from view (as most of an iceberg is hidden below water) because we repress the thoughts, wishes, feelings, and memories that create feelings of anxiety. In his view, this repression is never fully successful, and the troublesome thoughts and feelings express themselves in disguised forms unless we retrieve them into conscious awareness and free ourselves from the tensions they create. He sought to analyze these unconscious dynamics through *free association* and *dream interpretation*.

OBJECTIVE 4 | **Describe Freud's view of personality structure, and discuss the interactions of the id, ego, and superego.**

Freud saw personality as the product of a conflict between our biological impulses and our internalized social restraints on these impulses. The players in this conflict are three interacting systems: the id, the ego, and the superego. The *id*, which wants immediate gratification, operates in the unconscious and attempts to satisfy basic sexual and aggressive drives. The *superego*, our internalized set of ideals, is the voice of our conscience, judging our actions and producing feelings of pride or guilt. Between them is the *ego*, the largely conscious, reality-oriented executive that attempts to reconcile the impulses of the id with the demands of the superego and those of the external world.

OBJECTIVE 5 | **Identify Freud's psychosexual stages of development, and describe the effects of fixation on behavior.**

Freud believed that children develop through psychosexual stages—oral, anal, phallic, latency, and genital—in which the id is focused on a particular erogenous zone. During the phallic stage, for example, boys may desire their mother and fear punishment for these feelings from their father—a set of reactions Freud called the Oedipus complex. A person who fails to resolve the conflicts associated with a psychosexual stage may remain locked into, or fixated at, that stage. The person's personality will show the symptoms of this fixation in maladaptive behavior focused on the erogenous zone dominant at that stage.

OBJECTIVE 6 | **Describe the function of defense mechanisms, and identify six of them.**

Freud believed the ego uses defense mechanisms to protect itself from anxiety, which arises as a byproduct of the conflict between the competing demands of the id and the superego. The basic defense mechanism, according to Freud, is *repression* (banishing troublesome ideas and feelings into the unconscious); others include *regression* (retreating to an infantile stage), *reaction formation* (transforming unacceptable impulses into their acceptable opposites), *projection* (attributing one's own unacceptable impulses to others), *rationalization* (explaining one's behavior in terms of self-justifying motives rather than unacceptable ones), and *displacement* (focusing sexual or aggressive impulses on someone who is more acceptable than the person who aroused the emotion).

OBJECTIVE 7 | **Contrast the views of the neo-Freudians and psychodynamic theorists with Freud's original theory.**

The *neo-Freudians* accepted Freud's basic ideas (the id-ego-superego structure, the importance of the unconscious, the shaping of personality in childhood, and the dynamics of anxiety and the defense mechanisms). But they also argued that we have motives other than sex and aggression, and that the ego's conscious control is greater than Freud supposed. Alfred Adler (who coined the term *inferiority complex*) and Karen Horney (who refuted Freud's view of the inferiority of women) argued that social, not sexual, tensions are critical in personality formation. Carl Jung proposed a human collective unconscious containing memory traces from our species' history.

Contemporary *psychodynamic* theorists and therapists refute some aspects of Freud's theory, such as the idea that sexual tensions are central to personality formation. They share with Freud the view that much of our mental life is unconscious, that childhood shapes our personality and attachment styles, and that we experience inner conflicts among our wishes, fears, and values.

OBJECTIVE 8 | **Describe two projective tests used to assess personality, and discuss some criticisms of them.**

The *Thematic Apperception Test (TAT)* is a series of ambiguous pictures used to elicit a story in which test-takers express their own inner feelings and interests. Users of the *Rorschach inkblots*, the most widely used projective test, ask people to interpret a series of inkblots, again on the assumption that test-takers will reveal hidden feelings. Neither of these tests is noted for reliability (consistency of results) or validity (predicting what it's supposed to predict).

OBJECTIVE **9** | **Summarize psychology's current assessment of Freud's theory of psychoanalysis.**

Recent research has contradicted many of Freud's basic ideas, including the overriding importance of childhood experiences, degree of parental influence, timing of gender-identity formation, importance of sexuality during childhood, existence of hidden content in dreams, and frequency of repressed memories. Critics note that Freud's ideas are not verifiable by scientific methods, and that his theory offers only after-the-fact explanations. Freud's supporters reply that Freud viewed psychoanalysis as a way to find meaning in our existence, not as a predictive science. Freud drew psychology's attention to the unconscious and to the struggle to cope with anxiety. Although contemporary research fails to support Freud's view of the unconscious mind as a reservoir of repressed thoughts and emotions, findings throughout this text indicate that a vast amount of unconscious information processing occurs without our awareness. Current research does not support the concept of defense mechanisms closely tied to defense of the unconscious. It does support some defenses that protect self-esteem, such as reaction formation, the false-consensus effect (similar to Freud's projection mechanism), and terror management (warding off fears of death by pursuit of self-esteem or faith in one's worldview). Finally, Freud is credited with focusing attention on the conflict between biological impulses and social restraints. And without question, his cultural impact has been enormous.

ASK YOURSELF: **What understanding and impressions of Freud did you bring to this chapter? Have they changed in any way after reading this section?**

The Humanistic Perspective

By the 1960s, some personality psychologists had become discontented with Freud's negativity and the mechanistic psychology of B. F. Skinner's behaviorism. In contrast to Freud's study of the base motives of "sick" people, these *humanistic psychologists* focused on the ways "healthy" people strive for self-determination and self-realization. In contrast to behaviorism's scientific objectivity, they studied people through their own self-reported experiences and feelings.

Two pioneering theorists—Abraham Maslow (1908–1970) and Carl Rogers (1902–1987)—offered a *third-force perspective* that emphasized human potential and seeing the world through the person's (not the researcher's) eyes.

■ **self-actualization** according to Maslow, the ultimate psychological need that arises after basic physical and psychological needs are met and self-esteem is achieved; the motivation to fulfill one's potential.

Abraham Maslow's Self-Actualizing Person

OBJECTIVE **10** | Summarize Abraham Maslow's concept of self-actualization, and explain how his ideas illustrate the humanistic perpective.

Maslow proposed that we are motivated by a hierarchy of needs (page 472). If our physiological needs are met, we become concerned with personal safety; if we achieve a sense of security, we then seek to love, to be loved, and to love ourselves; with our love needs satisfied, we seek self-esteem. Having achieved self-esteem, we ultimately seek **self-actualization,** the process of fulfilling our potential.

Maslow (1970) developed his ideas by studying healthy, creative people rather than troubled clinical cases. He based his description of self-actualization on a study of those who seemed notable for their rich and productive lives—among them, Abraham Lincoln, Thomas Jefferson, and Eleanor Roosevelt. Maslow reported that these people shared certain characteristics: They were self-aware and self-accepting, open and spontaneous, loving and caring, and not paralyzed by others' opinions. Secure in their sense of who they were, their interests were problem-centered rather than self-centered. They focused their energies on a particular task, one they often regarded as their mission in life. Most enjoyed a few deep relationships rather than many superficial ones. Many had been moved by spiritual or personal *peak experiences* that surpassed ordinary consciousness.

Abraham Maslow

"Any theory of motivation that is worthy of attention must deal with the highest capacities of the healthy and strong person as well as with the defensive maneuvers of crippled spirits" (*Motivation and Personality*, 1970).

Ted Polumbaum/Time Pix/Getty Images

The picture of empathy
Being open and sharing confidences is easier when the listener shows real understanding. Within such relationships people can relax and fully express their true selves.

These, said Maslow, are mature adult qualities, ones found in those who have learned enough about life to be compassionate, to have outgrown their mixed feelings toward their parents, to have found their calling, to have "acquired enough courage to be unpopular, to be unashamed about being openly virtuous, etc." Maslow's work with college students led him to speculate that those likely to become self-actualizing adults were likable, caring, "privately affectionate to those of their elders who deserve it," and "secretly uneasy about the cruelty, meanness, and mob spirit so often found in young people."

Carl Rogers' Person-Centered Perspective

OBJECTIVE 11 | Discuss Carl Rogers' person-centered perspective, and explain the importance of unconditional positive regard.

Fellow humanistic psychologist Carl Rogers agreed with much of Maslow's thinking. Rogers believed that people are basically good and are endowed with self-actualizing tendencies. Unless thwarted by an environment that inhibits growth, each of us is like an acorn, primed for growth and fulfillment. Rogers (1980) believed that a growth-promoting climate required three conditions—genuineness, acceptance, and empathy.

According to Rogers, people nurture our growth by being *genuine*—by being open with their own feelings, dropping their facades, and being transparent and self-disclosing.

People also nurture our growth by being *accepting*—by offering us what Rogers called **unconditional positive regard.** This is an attitude of grace, an attitude that values us even knowing our failings. It is a profound relief to drop our pretenses, confess our worst feelings, and discover that we are still accepted. In a good marriage, a close family, or an intimate friendship, we are free to be spontaneous without fearing the loss of others' esteem.

Finally, people nurture our growth by being *empathic*—by sharing and mirroring our feelings and reflecting our meanings. "Rarely do we listen with real understanding, true empathy," said Rogers. "Yet listening, of this very special kind, is one of the most potent forces for change that I know."

Genuineness, acceptance, and empathy are the water, sun, and nutrients that enable people to grow like vigorous oak trees, according to Rogers. For "as persons are accepted and prized, they tend to develop a more caring attitude toward themselves" (Rogers, 1980, p. 116). As persons are empathically heard, "it becomes possible for them to listen more accurately to the flow of inner experiencings."

Rogers believed that genuineness, acceptance, and empathy nurture growth not only in the relationship between therapist and client but also between parent and child, leader and group, teacher and student, administrator and staff member—in fact, between any two human beings.

For Maslow, and even more for Rogers, a central feature of personality is one's **self-concept**—all the thoughts and feelings we have in response to the question, "Who am I?" If our self-concept is positive, we tend to act and perceive the world positively. If it is negative—if in our own eyes we fall far short of our *ideal self*—said Rogers, we feel dissatisfied and unhappy. A worthwhile goal for therapists, parents, teachers, and friends is therefore, he said, to help others know, accept, and be true to themselves.

Assessing the Self

OBJECTIVE 12 | Explain how humanistic psychologists assessed personality.

Humanistic psychologists sometimes assessed personality by asking people to fill out questionnaires that would evaluate self-concept. One questionnaire, inspired by Carl Rogers, asked people to describe themselves both as they would *ideally* like to be and as they *actually* are. When the ideal and the actual self are nearly alike, said Rogers,

"Just remember, son, it doesn't matter whether you win or lose—unless you want Daddy's love."

A father *not* offering unconditional positive regard.

the self-concept is positive. Assessing his clients' personal growth during therapy, he looked for successively closer ratings of actual and ideal self.

Some humanistic psychologists believed that any standardized assessment of personality, even a questionnaire, is depersonalizing. Rather than forcing the person to respond to narrow categories, these humanistic psychologists presumed that interviews and intimate conversation would provide a better understanding of each person's unique experiences.

Evaluating the Humanistic Perspective

OBJECTIVE **13** | State the major criticisms of the humanistic perspective on personality.

One thing said of Freud can also be said of the humanistic psychologists: Their impact has been pervasive. Their ideas have influenced counseling, education, child-rearing, and management.

They have also influenced—sometimes in ways they did not intend—much of today's popular psychology. Many people have absorbed Maslow's and Rogers' ideas—that a positive self-concept is the key to happiness and success, that acceptance and empathy help nurture positive feelings about oneself, and that people are basically good and capable of self-improvement. One study found that, by a four-to-one margin, Americans believe "human nature is basically good" rather than "fundamentally perverse and corrupt" (NORC, 1985). Humanistic psychologists can also take satisfaction in the changed response to one item on the MMPI (the most widely used personality test): Among those in the 1930s normal standardization sample, only 9 percent agreed that "I am an important person"; by the mid-1980s, more than half agreed (Holden, 1986b). Responding to a 1989 Gallup poll, 85 percent of Americans rated "having a good self-image or self-respect" as *very* important; 0 percent rated it unimportant. And 89 percent of people responding to a 1992 *Newsweek* Gallup poll rated self-esteem as very important for "motivating a person to work hard and succeed." Humanistic psychology's message has been heard.

Perhaps one reason that message has been so well received is that its emphasis on the individual self reflects and reinforces Western cultural values. Movie plots feature rugged individualists who, true to themselves, buck social convention or take the law into their own hands. Popular songs have proclaimed "I Did It My Way" and reminded us that to love yourself is "The Greatest Love of All" (Schoeneman, 1994).

The prominence of the humanistic perspective set off a backlash of criticism. First, said the critics, its concepts are vague and subjective. Consider the description of self-actualizing people as open, spontaneous, loving, self-accepting, and productive. Is this a scientific description? Isn't it merely a description of Maslow's personal values and ideals? Maslow, noted M. Brewster Smith (1978), offered impressions of his own personal heroes. Imagine another theorist who began with a different set of heroes—perhaps Napoleon, Alexander the Great, and John D. Rockefeller, Sr. This theorist would likely describe self-actualizing people as "undeterred by the needs of others," "motivated to achieve," and "obsessed with power."

Critics also objected to the idea that, as Carl Rogers put it, "The only question which matters is, 'Am I living in a way which is deeply satisfying to me, and which truly expresses me?'" (quoted by Wallach & Wallach, 1985). The individualism encouraged by humanistic psychology—trusting and acting on one's feelings, being true to oneself, fulfilling oneself—can, the critics have said, lead to self-indulgence, selfishness, and an erosion of moral restraints (Campbell & Specht, 1985; Wallach & Wallach, 1983). Indeed, it is those who focus beyond themselves who are most likely to experience social support, to enjoy life, and to cope effectively with stress (Crandall, 1984).

Humanistic psychologists have countered that a secure, nondefensive self-acceptance is actually the first step toward loving others. Indeed, people who feel intrinsically liked

"We do pretty well when you stop to think that people are basically good."

and accepted—for who they are, not just for their achievements—exhibit less-defensive attitudes (Schimel & others, 2001).

A final accusation leveled against humanistic psychology is that it fails to appreciate the reality of our human capacity for evil. Faced with global warming, overpopulation, terrorism, and the spread of nuclear weapons, we may become apathetic from either of two rationalizations. One is a naive optimism that denies the threat ("People are basically good; everything will work out;"). The other is a dark despair ("It's hopeless; why try?"). Action requires enough realism to fuel concern and enough optimism to provide hope. Humanistic psychology, say the critics, encourages the needed hope but not the equally necessary realism about evil.

Even within humanistic psychology there has been debate over whether people are basically good. Carl Rogers clearly thought so. Although aware of the "incredible amount" of cruel, destructive behavior in the world, he did "not find that this evil is inherent in human nature." He stated that he had never known an individual who—given growth-promoting conditions—had chosen "the cruel or destructive path" (Rogers, 1981). Evil, in his view, springs not from human nature but from toxic cultural influences, including "the constricting, destructive influence of our educational system, the injustice of our distribution of wealth, [and] our cultivated prejudices against individuals who are different."

Fellow humanistic psychologist Rollo May dissented. Of course the cultural context matters, he said. But "who makes up the culture except persons like you and me? The culture is evil as well as good because we, the human beings who constitute it, are evil as well as good." May agreed with the critics who saw people joining the humanistic movement as seekers of "a community of like-minded persons who also are playing possum to the evils about us." Accepting the reality of human evil requires "the age-old religious truths of mercy and forgiveness," he said, "and it leaves no place for self-righteousness" (May, 1982).

>> LEARNING OUTCOMES

The Humanistic Perspective

OBJECTIVE 10 | Summarize Abraham Maslow's concept of self-actualization, and explain how his ideas illustrate the humanistic perspective.

Maslow proposed a hierarchy of needs, ranging from the most basic physiological needs to the ultimate need for self-actualization. He believed that after fulfilling other needs (physiological; safety; belongingness and love; self-esteem), people will be motivated to achieve their highest potential. He arrived at his description of a self-actualized person by studying, and summarizing the qualities of, healthy and creative people who had lived exemplary lives. Maslow typifies humanistic psychology's attempt to turn psychology's attention from baser motives and environmental conditioning to the growth potential of healthy people, believed to be basically good.

OBJECTIVE 11 | Discuss Carl Rogers' person-centered perspective, and explain the importance of unconditional positive regard.

Like Maslow, Rogers believed that unless thwarted by their environment, people will grow and realize their self-actualizing tendencies. We can promote others' growth toward a deeper self-awareness and a more realistic and positive self-concept by being genuine, accepting, and empathic. Part of being accepting, he believed, is unconditional positive regard—an attitude of total acceptance toward the other person. In Rogers' view, a central feature of personality is our self-concept, our thoughts and feelings in response to the question "Who am I?"

OBJECTIVE 12 | Explain how humanistic psychologists assessed personality.

Some humanistic psychologists assessed personality through questionnaires on which people reported their self-concept, for example, by comparing their actual self with their ideal self. Others believed that we could understand a person's subjective personal experiences only through interviews and intimate conversations.

OBJECTIVE 13 | State the major criticisms of the humanistic perspective on personality.

Humanistic psychology helped to renew psychology's interest in the self. Nevertheless, its critics have complained that humanistic psychology's concepts were vague and subjective, its values individualist and self-centered, and its assumptions naively optimistic.

ASK YOURSELF: Have you had someone in your life who accepted you unconditionally? Do you think this person helped you to know yourself better and to develop a better image of yourself?

The Trait Perspective

OBJECTIVE 14 | Cite the main difference between the trait and psychoanalytic perspectives on personality.

■ **trait** a characteristic pattern of behavior or a disposition to feel and act, as assessed by self-report inventories and peer reports.

Trait researchers attempt to define personality in terms of stable and enduring behavior patterns, such as Sam Gamgee's loyalty and optimism. The trait perspective can be traced in part to a remarkable meeting in 1919, when Gordon Allport, a curious 22-year-old psychology student, interviewed Sigmund Freud in Vienna. Allport soon discovered just how preoccupied the founder of psychoanalysis was with finding hidden motives.

> Soon after I had entered the famous red burlap room with pictures of dreams on the wall, he summoned me to his inner office. He did not speak to me but sat in expectant silence, for me to state my mission. I was not prepared for silence and had to think fast to find a suitable conversational gambit. I told him of an episode on the tram car on my way to his office. A small boy about 4 years of age had displayed a conspicuous dirt phobia. He kept saying to his mother, "I don't want to sit there . . . don't let that dirty man sit beside me." To him everything was *schmutzig* (filthy). His mother was a well-starched *Hausfrau,* so dominant and purposive looking that I thought the cause and effect apparent.
>
> When I finished my story Freud fixed his kindly therapeutic eyes upon me and said, "And was that little boy you?" Flabbergasted and feeling a bit guilty, I contrived to change the subject. While Freud's misunderstanding of my motivation was amusing, it also started a deep train of thought (1967, pp. 7–8).

That train of thought ultimately led Allport to do what Freud did not do—to describe personality in terms of fundamental **traits**—people's characteristic behaviors and conscious motives (such as the professional curiosity that actually motivated Allport to see Freud). Meeting Freud, said Allport, "taught me that [psychoanalysis], for all its merits, may plunge too deep, and that psychologists would do well to give full recognition to manifest motives before probing the unconscious." Allport came to define personality in terms of identifiable behavior patterns. He was concerned less with *explaining* individual traits than with *describing* them. How, then, can theorists use traits to describe and classify personalities? One way is describing people using broad personality "types" that signal one's most noteworthy trait and its associated characteristics. An analogy may help. Imagine that you want to describe and classify apples. Someone might correctly say that every apple is unique. Still, you might find it useful to begin by classifying apples as distinct *types*—Granny Smith, McIntosh, Red or Golden Delicious, and so forth. That is precisely how the ancient Greeks described personality—by classifying people according to four types. Depending on which of one's bodily "humors," or fluids they believed to predominate, they declared people melancholic (depressed), sanguine (cheerful), phlegmatic (unemotional), or choleric (irritable).

A more recent classification, written by Isabel Briggs Myers (1987) and her mother, Kathleen Briggs, attempts to sort people according to Carl Jung's personality types, based on their responses to 126 questions. The *Myers-Briggs Type Indicator,* which has been taken by 2.5 million Americans a year and used by 89 of the 100 largest corporations, is quite simple (Gladwell, 2004). It offers choices, such as "Do you usually value sentiment more than logic, or value logic more than sentiment?" Then it counts the test-taker's preferences, labels them as indicating, say, a "feeling" or "thinking" type, and feeds them back to the person in complimentary terms. Feeling types, for example, are told they are sensitive to values and "sympathetic, appreciative, and tactful"; thinking types are told they "prefer an objective standard of truth" and are "good at analyzing." (Every type has its strengths, so everyone gets flattered.)

Most people agree with their announced type profile. It mirrors their declared preferences and leaves them feeling good. They may also accept their label as a basis for being matched with work partners and tasks that supposedly suit their temperaments. A National Research Council report noted, however, that despite the test's popularity in business and career counseling, its initial use outran research on its value as a predictor of job performance, and "the popularity of this instrument in the absence of proven scientific worth is troublesome" (Druckman & Bjork, 1991, p. 101; see also Pittenger, 1993). Since those cautionary words, research on the Myers-Briggs has been accumulating, thanks to periodicals such as the *Journal of Psychological Type*.

Exploring Traits

OBJECTIVE **15** | Describe some of the ways psychologists have attempted to compile a list of basic personality traits.

Classifying people as one or another distinct personality type fails to capture their full individuality. We are each a unique complex of multiple traits. So how else could we describe our personalities? To return to our apple analogy, we might describe an apple by placing it along several trait dimensions—relatively large or small, red or yellow, sweet or sour. By placing people on several trait dimensions simultaneously, psychologists can describe countless individual personality variations. (Remember from Chapter 5 that variations on just three color dimensions—hue, saturation, and brightness—create many thousands of colors.)

What trait dimensions describe personality? If you had an upcoming blind date, what personality traits might give you an accurate sense of the person? Allport and his associate H. S. Odbert (1936) literally counted all the words in an unabridged dictionary with which one could describe people. How many were there? Almost 18,000! How, then, could psychologists condense the list to a manageable number of basic traits?

Chris Rock: the extravert
Trait labels such as *extraversion* can describe our temperament and typical behaviors.

Factor Analysis

One way has been to propose traits, such as anxiety, that some theory regards as basic. A newer technique is *factor analysis*, the statistical procedure described in Chapter 11 to identify clusters of test items that tap basic components of intelligence (such as spatial ability or verbal skill). Imagine that people who describe themselves as outgoing also tend to say that they like excitement and practical jokes and dislike quiet reading. Such a statistically correlated cluster of behaviors reflects a basic factor, or trait—in this case, *extraversion*.

British psychologists Hans Eysenck and Sybil Eysenck [EYE-zink] believed that we can reduce many of our normal individual variations to two or three dimensions, including *extraversion-introversion* and *emotional stability-instability* (**FIGURE 15.4**). People in 35 countries around the world, from China to Uganda to Russia, have taken the *Eysenck Personality Questionnaire,* and when their answers are analyzed, the extraversion and emotionality factors inevitably emerged as basic personality dimensions (Eysenck, 1990, 1992). The Eysencks believed that these factors are genetically influenced and recent research supports this belief.

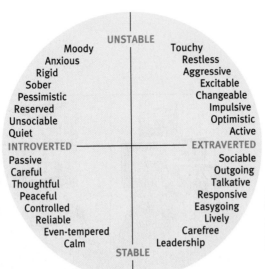

UNSTABLE

| INTROVERTED | | EXTRAVERTED |

Moody — Touchy
Anxious — Restless
Rigid — Aggressive
Sober — Excitable
Pessimistic — Changeable
Reserved — Impulsive
Unsociable — Optimistic
Quiet — Active

Passive — Sociable
Careful — Outgoing
Thoughtful — Talkative
Peaceful — Responsive
Controlled — Easygoing
Reliable — Lively
Even-tempered — Carefree
Calm — Leadership

STABLE

FIGURE 15.4
Two personality factors
Mapmakers can tell us a lot by using two axes (north-south and east-west). Hans Eysenck and Sybil Eysenck use two primary personality factors—extraversion-introversion and stability-instability—as axes for describing personality variation. Varying combinations define other, more specific traits. (From Eysenck & Eysenck, 1963.)

Biology and Personality

Brain-activity scans of extraverts add to the growing list of traits and mental states that have been explored with brain-imaging procedures. (At this writing, that list includes intelligence, impulsivity, addictive cravings, sexual attraction, aggressiveness, empathy, spiritual experience, and even racial and political attitudes [Olson, 2005]). Such studies indicate that extraverts seek stimulation because their normal *brain arousal* is relatively low. For example, PET scans show that a frontal lobe area involved in behavior inhibition is less active in extraverts than in introverts (Johnson & others, 1999).

Our biology influences our personality in other ways as well. Our *genes* have much to say about the *temperament*—our emotional reactivity (see Chapter 3)—and the behavioral style that help define our personality. Jerome Kagan, for example, attributes differences in children's shyness and inhibition to their *autonomic nervous system* reactivity. Given a reactive autonomic nervous system, we respond to stress with greater anxiety and inhibition. The fearless, curious child may become the rock-climbing or fast-driving adult. And, as you may recall from the twin and adoption studies in Chapter 3, personality forms under the influence of genes.

That fact of life also appears in animal personalities. Samuel Gosling and his colleagues (2003) report that personality differences among dogs (in energy, affection, reactivity, and curious intelligence) are as evident, and as consistently judged, as personality differences among humans. Even birds have stable personalities. Among a European relative of the chickadee, bold birds more quickly inspect new objects and explore trees (Groothuis & Carere, 2005; Verbeek & others, 1994). By selective breeding, researchers can produce bold or shy birds. Both have their place in natural history. In lean years, bold birds are more likely to find food; in abundant years, shy birds feed with less risk.

Assessing Traits

OBJECTIVE 16 | Explain how psychologists use personality inventories to assess traits, and discuss the most widely used personality inventory.

If stable and enduring traits guide our actions, can we devise valid and reliable tests of them? Several trait assessment techniques exist. Some profile a person's behavior patterns—often providing quick assessments of a single trait, such as extraversion, anxiety, or self-esteem. **Personality inventories**—longer questionnaires covering a wide range of feelings and behaviors—are designed to assess several traits at once.

■ **personality inventory** a questionnaire (often with true-false or agree-disagree items) on which people respond to items designed to gauge a wide range of feelings and behaviors; used to assess selected personality traits.

HOW TO BE A "SUCCESSFUL" ASTROLOGER OR PALM READER

Can we discern people's traits from the alignment of the stars and planets at the time of their birth? From their handwriting? From lines on their palms?

Astronomers scoff at the naiveté of astrology—the constellations have shifted in the millennia since astrologers formulated their predictions (Kelly, 1997, 1998). Humorists mock it: "No offense," writes Dave Barry, "but if you take the horoscope seriously your frontal lobes are the size of Raisinets." Psychologists instead ask questions: Does it work? Can astrologers surpass chance when given someone's birth date and asked to identify the person from a short lineup of different personality descriptions? Can people pick out their own horoscopes from a lineup of horoscopes?

The consistent answers have been: No, no, and no (British Psychological Society, 1993; Carlson, 1985; Kelly, 1997). Graphologists, who make predictions from handwriting samples, have similarly been found to do no better than chance when trying to discern people's occupations from examining several pages of their handwriting (Beyerstein & Beyerstein, 1992; Dean & others, 1992). Nevertheless, graphologists—and introductory psychology students—will often *perceive* correlations between personality and handwriting even where there are none (King & Koehler, 2000).

If all these perceived correlations evaporate under close scrutiny, how do astrologers and the like persuade thousands of newspapers and millions of people worldwide to buy their advice? Ray Hyman (1981),

palm reader turned research psychologist, has revealed the suckering methods of astrologers, palm readers, and crystal-ball gazers.

Their first technique, the "stock spiel," builds on the observation that each of us is in some ways like no one else and in other ways just like everyone. That some things are true of us all enables the "seer" to offer statements that seem impressively accurate: "I sense that you worry about things more than you let on, even to your best friends." A number of such generally true statements can be combined into a personality description. Imagine that you take a personality test and then receive the following character sketch:

You have a strong need for other people to like and to admire you. You have a tendency to be critical of your-

self. . . . You pride yourself on being an independent thinker and do not accept other opinions without satisfactory proof. You have found it unwise to be too frank in revealing yourself to others. At times you are extraverted, affable, sociable; at other times you are introverted, wary, and reserved. Some of your aspirations tend to be pretty unrealistic (Davies, 1997; Forer, 1949).

In experiments, college students have received stock assessments like this one, drawn from statements in a newsstand astrology book. When they think the bogus, generic feedback was prepared just for them and when it is favorable, they nearly always rate the description as either

■ **Minnesota Multiphasic Personality Inventory (MMPI)** the most widely researched and clinically used of all personality tests. Originally developed to identify emotional disorders (still considered its most appropriate use), this test is now used for many other screening purposes.

The most extensively researched personality inventory is the **Minnesota Multiphasic Personality Inventory (MMPI).** Although it assesses "abnormal" personality tendencies rather than normal personality traits, the MMPI illustrates a good way of developing a personality inventory. One of its creators, Starke Hathaway (1960), compared his effort to that of Alfred Binet. Binet, as you may recall from Chapter 11, "good" or "excellent" (Davies, 1997). Even skeptics of astrology, when given a flattering description attributed to an astrologer, begin to think that "maybe there's something to this astrology stuff after all" (Glick & others, 1989). An astrologer, it has been said, is someone "prepared to tell you what you think of yourself" (Jones, 2000).

French psychologist Michael Gauguelin had similar results when he placed an ad in a Paris newspaper offering a free personal horoscope. Ninety-four percent of those receiving the horoscope praised the description as accurate. Whose horoscope had they all actually received? That of France's Dr. Petiot, a notorious mass murderer (Kurtz, 1983). This acceptance of stock, positive descriptions is called the *Barnum effect*, named in honor of master showman P. T. Barnum's dictum, "There's a sucker born every minute."

A second technique used by seers is to "read" our clothing, physical features, nonverbal gestures, and reactions to what they are saying. Imagine yourself as the character reader visited by a young woman in her late twenties or early thirties. Hyman described the woman as "wearing expensive jewelry, a wedding band, and a black dress of cheap material. The observant reader noted that she was wearing shoes which were advertised for people with foot trouble." Do these clues suggest anything?

Drawing on these observations, the character reader proceeded to amaze his client with his insights. He assumed the woman had come

to see him, as did most of his female customers, because of a love or financial problem. The black dress and the wedding band led him to reason that her husband had died recently. The expensive jewelry suggested she had been financially comfortable during the marriage, but the cheap dress suggested her husband's death had left

"Madame Zelinski can provide an even more accurate reading with your date of birth and Social Security number."

her impoverished. The therapeutic shoes signified she was now on her feet more than she had been used to, implying that she had been working to support herself since her husband's death. Based on these insights, the reader correctly guessed that the woman was wondering if she should remarry in hope of ending her economic hardship. No wonder, say the skeptics, that when mediums cannot see the person who has come to them, their clients cannot recognize the reading that was meant for them from among other readings (O'Keeffe & Wiseman, 2005).

If you are not as shrewd as this character reader, Hyman says it hardly matters. If people seek you out for a reading, start with some safe sympathy: "I sense you're having some problems lately. You seem unsure what to do. I get the feeling another person is involved." Then tell them what they want to hear. Memorize some Barnum statements from astrology and fortune-telling manuals and use them liberally. Tell people it is their responsibility to cooperate by relating your message to their specific experiences. Later they will recall that you predicted those specific details. Phrase statements as questions, and when you detect a positive response assert the statement strongly. Finally, be a good listener, and later, in different words, reveal to people what they earlier revealed to you. If you dupe them, they will come.

Better yet, beware of those who, by exploiting people with these techniques, are fortune takers rather than fortune tellers.

---

developed the first intelligence test by selecting items that discriminated children who would have trouble progressing normally in French schools. The MMPI items, too, were **empirically derived.** That is, from a large pool of items, Hathaway and his colleagues selected those on which particular diagnostic groups differed. They then grouped the questions into 10 clinical scales.

■ **empirically derived test** a test (such as the MMPI) developed by testing a pool of items and then selecting those that discriminate between groups.

Hathaway and others initially gave hundreds of true-false statements ("No one seems to understand me"; "I get all the sympathy I should"; "I like poetry") to groups of psychologically disordered patients and to "normal" people. They retained any statement— no matter how silly it sounded—on which the patient group's answer differed from that of the normal group. "Nothing in the newspaper interests me except the comics" may seem senseless, but it just so happened that depressed people were more likely to answer "true." (Nevertheless, people have had fun spoofing the MMPI with their own mock items: "Weeping brings tears to my eyes," "Frantic screams make me nervous," and "I stay in the bathtub until I look like a raisin" [Frankel & others, 1983].) Today's MMPI-2 also has newer scales assessing, for instance, work attitudes, family problems, and anger.

In contrast to the subjectivity of most projective tests favored by psychoanalysts, personality inventories are scored objectively—so objectively that a computer can administer and score them. (The computer can also provide descriptions of people who previously responded similarly.) Objectivity does not, however, guarantee validity. For example, individuals taking the MMPI for employment purposes can give socially desirable answers to create a good impression. But in so doing they may also score high on a "lie scale" that assesses faking (as when people respond "false" to a universally true statement such as "I get angry sometimes"). For better or worse, the objectivity of the MMPI contributes to its popularity and to its translation into more than 100 languages.

The Big Five Factors

OBJECTIVE 17 | Identify the Big Five personality factors, and discuss some of the strengths of this approach to studying personality.

Today's trait researchers believe that earlier trait dimensions, such as the Eysencks' introverted-extraverted and unstable-stable dimensions, are important. But they do not tell the whole story. A slightly expanded set of factors—dubbed the *Big Five*—does a better job (John & Srivastava, 1999; McCrae & Costa, 1999). If a test specifies where you are on the five dimensions (conscientiousness, agreeableness, neuroticism, openness, and extraversion; see **TABLE 15.2**), it has said much of what there is to say about your personality. Around the world, people describe others in terms roughly consistent with this list.

TABLE 15.2

THE "BIG FIVE" PERSONALITY FACTORS

(*Memory tip*: Picturing a **CANOE** will help you recall these.)

Trait Dimension	Endpoints of the Dimension		
Conscientiousness	Organized	⟷	Disorganized
	Careful	⟷	Careless
	Disciplined	⟷	Impulsive
Agreeableness	Soft-hearted	⟷	Ruthless
	Trusting	⟷	Suspicious
	Helpful	⟷	Uncooperative
Neuroticism (emotional stability vs. instability)	Calm	⟷	Anxious
	Secure	⟷	Insecure
	Self-satisfied	⟷	Self-pitying
Openness	Imaginative	⟷	Practical
	Preference for variety	⟷	Preference for routine
	Independent	⟷	Conforming
Extraversion	Sociable	⟷	Retiring
	Fun-loving	⟷	Sober
	Affectionate	⟷	Reserved

Source: Adapted from McCrae & Costa (1986, p. 1002).

But the Big Five is not the last word: Other factor analysis researchers and theorists wonder whether we should add dimensions such as self-consciousness, masculinity-femininity, intellect-imagination, religiosity, or positive-negative emotion (Ashton & others, 2004). For now, though, the winning number in the personality lottery is five. The Big Five—today's "common currency for personality psychology" (Funder, 2001)—has been the most active personality research topic since the early 1990s and is currently our best approximation of the basic trait dimensions (Endler & Speer, 1998).

The recent wave of Big Five research explores various questions:

- *How stable are these traits?* In adulthood, the Big Five traits are quite stable, with some tendencies (emotional instability, extraversion, and openness) waning a bit in the decades after college, and others (agreeableness and conscientiousness) rising (McCrae & others, 1999; Vaidya & others, 2002). Conscientiousness increases the most during people's twenties, as people mature and learn to manage their jobs and relationships. Agreeableness increases the most during people's thirties and continues to increase through their sixties (Srivastava & others, 2003).

- *How heritable are they?* Heritability of individual differences varies with the diversity of people studied, but it generally runs 50 percent or a tad more for each dimension (Loehlin & others, 1998).

- *How well do they apply to various cultures?* The Big Five dimensions describe personality in various cultures reasonably well (McCrae, 2001; Paunonen & others, 2000). "Features of personality traits are common to all human groups," infer Robert McCrae and 79 co-researchers (2005) from their recent 50-culture study.

- *Do the Big Five traits predict other personal attributes?* Yes again. Two examples: Highly conscientious people are more likely to be morning types (sometimes called "larks"); evening types ("owls") are marginally more extraverted (Jackson & Gerard, 1996). When one's partner scores lower on agreeableness, stability, and openness, marital and sexual satisfaction may suffer (Botwin & others, 1997; Donnellan & others, 2004).

By exploring such questions, Big Five research has sustained trait psychology and renewed appreciation for the importance of personality.

Evaluating the Trait Perspective

Are our personality traits stable and enduring? Or does our behavior depend on where and with whom we find ourselves? J. R. R. Tolkien created characters, like the loyal Sam Gamgee, whose personality traits were consistent across various times and places. The Italian playwright Luigi Pirandello had a different view. For him, personality was ever-changing, tailored to the particular role or situation. In one of Pirandello's plays, Lamberto Laudisi describes himself: "I am really what you take me to be; though, my dear madam, that does not prevent me from also being really what your husband, my sister, my niece, and Signora Cini take me to be—because they also are absolutely right!" To which Signora Sirelli responds, "In other words you are a different person for each of us."

The Person-Situation Controversy

OBJECTIVE 18 | Summarize the person-situation controversy, and explain its importance as a commentary on the trait perspective.

Who, then, typifies human personality, Tolkien's consistent Sam Gamgee or Pirandello's inconsistent Laudisi? Both. Our behavior is influenced by the interaction of our inner disposition with our environment. Still, the question lingers: Which is *more* important? Are we *more* as Tolkien or as Pirandello imagined us to be?

> "There is as much difference between us and ourselves, as between us and others."
> Michel de Montaigne, *Essays*, 1588

Roughly speaking, the temporary, external influences on behavior are the focus of social psychology, and the enduring, inner influences are the focus of personality psychology. In actuality, behavior always depends on the interaction of persons with situations.

Change and consistency can co-exist. If all people were to become somewhat less shy with age, there would be personality change, but also relative stability and predictability.

"Mr. Coughlin over there was the founder of one of the first motorcycle gangs."

When we explore this *person-situation controversy,* we look for genuine personality traits that persist over time *and* across situations. Are some people dependably conscientious and others unreliable, some cheerful and others dour, some friendly and outgoing and others shy? If we are to consider friendliness a trait, friendly people must act friendly at different times and places. Do they? In Chapter 4, we considered research that has followed lives through time. We noted that some scholars (especially those who study infants) are impressed with personality change; others are struck by personality stability during adulthood. As **FIGURE 15.5** illustrates, data from 152 long-term studies reveal that personality trait scores are positively correlated with scores obtained seven years later, and that as people grow older their personality stabilizes. Interests may change—the avid collector of tropical fish may become the avid gardener. Careers may change—the determined salesperson may become a determined social worker. Relationships may change—the hostile spouse may start over with a new partner. But most people recognize their traits as their own, note Robert McCrae and Paul Costa (1994), "and it is well that they do. A person's recognition of the inevitability of his or her one and only personality is . . . the culminating wisdom of a lifetime." So most people—including most psychologists—would probably side with Tolkien's assumption of stability of personality traits.

But the consistency of specific *behaviors* from one situation to the next is another matter. As Walter Mischel (1968, 1984, 2004) has pointed out, people do not act with predictable consistency. Mischel's studies of college students' conscientiousness revealed but a modest relationship between a student's being conscientious on one occasion (say, showing up for class on time) and being similarly conscientious on another occasion (say, turning in assignments on time). Pirandello would not have been surprised. If you've noticed how outgoing you are in some situations and how reserved you are in others, perhaps you're not surprised either (though for certain traits, Mischel reports, you may accurately assess yourself as more consistent).

This inconsistency in behaviors also makes personality test scores weak predictors of behaviors. People's scores on an extraversion test, for example, do not neatly predict how sociable they actually will be on any given occasion. If we remember such results, says Mischel, we will be more cautious about labeling and pigeonholing individuals. We will be more restrained when asked to predict whether someone is likely to violate parole, commit suicide, or be an effective employee. Years in advance, science can tell us the phase of the moon for any given date. A day in advance, meteorologists can often predict the weather. But we are much further from being able to predict how *you* will feel and act tomorrow.

In defense of traits, Seymour Epstein (1983a,b) maintained that trying to predict a specific act on the basis of a personality test result is like trying to predict your answer to a specific aptitude question on the basis of an intelligence test result. Your answer to

FIGURE 15.5
Personality stability
With age, personality traits become more stable, as reflected in the correlation of trait scores with follow-up scores seven years later. (Data from Roberts & DelVecchio, 2000).

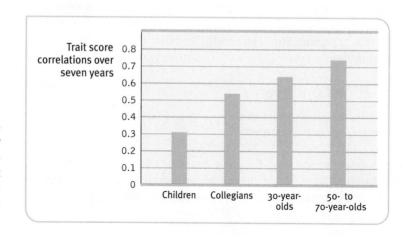

any given question is unpredictable because it depends on so many variables (your intelligence, yes, but also your reading of the question, your momentary concentration, luck). Your *average* accuracy over many questions on several tests is more predictable. Similarly, people's *average* outgoingness, happiness, or carelessness over *many* situations is predictable, Epstein observed. When rating someone's shyness or agreeableness, this consistency enables people who know someone well to agree (Kenrick & Funder, 1988). As our best friends can verify, we *do* have personality traits—genetically influenced traits, we now know.

Moreover, our traits are socially significant. They influence our health, our thinking, and our job performance (Deary & Matthews, 1993; Hogan, 1998). Our traits even lurk, report Samuel Gosling and his colleagues in a series of studies, in our

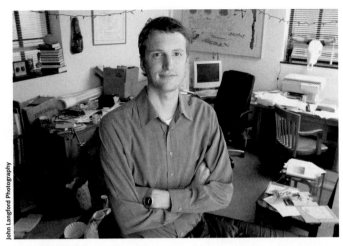

Our spaces express our personalities
Even at "zero acquaintance," people can discern something of others' personality from glimpsing their Web site, dorm room, or office. So, what is your read on University of Texas researcher Samuel Gosling?

- *music preferences.* Classical, jazz, blues, and folk music lovers tend to be open to experience and verbally intelligent; country, pop, and religious music lovers tend to be cheerful, outgoing, and conscientious (Rentfrow & Gosling, 2003).
- *dorm rooms and offices.* Our personal spaces display our identity and leave a behavioral residue (in our scattered laundry or neat desktop). And that helps explain why just a few minutes' inspection of our living and working spaces can enable someone to assess with reasonable accuracy our conscientiousness, our openness to new experience, and even our emotional stability (Gosling & others, 2002).
- *personal Web sites.* Is a personal Web site also a canvas for self-expression? Or is it an opportunity for people to present themselves in false or misleading ways? It's more the former, report Simine Vazire and Gosling (2004). Visitors to personal Web sites quickly gain important clues to the owner's extraversion, conscientiousness, and openness to experience.

The bottom line: Traits exist. We differ. And our differences matter.

Consistency of Expressive Style

OBJECTIVE 19 | Explain why psychologists are interested in the consistency of the trait of expressiveness.

In unfamiliar, formal situations—perhaps as a guest in the home of a person from another culture—our traits may remain hidden as we attend carefully to social cues. In familiar, informal situations—just hanging out with friends—we feel less constrained, allowing our traits to emerge (Buss, 1989). In these informal situations, our expressive styles—our animation, manner of speaking, and gestures—are impressively consistent. Thus, we often form lasting impressions within a few moments of meeting someone. Nalini Ambady and Robert Rosenthal (1992, 1993) videotaped 13 Harvard University graduate students teaching undergraduate courses. Observers then viewed three *thin slices* of each teacher's behavior—mere 10-second clips from the beginning, middle, and end of a class—and rated each teacher's level of confidence, activeness, warmth, and so forth. These behavior ratings, based on 30 *seconds* of teaching from an entire semester, predicted amazingly well the teacher's average student ratings at the semester's end. Observing even thinner slices—three 2-second clips—yielded ratings that still correlated as high as +.72 with the student evaluations. Some people's first impressions, derived from expressive behavior, predicted other people's lasting impressions!

Mere glimpses of someone's behavior can be revealing because of the potency of traits such as expressiveness. In a study of physician malpractice suits, Ambady and her colleagues (2002) filtered four 10-second slices of surgeon-patient conversation, rendering the speech unintelligible while preserving its intonation, pitch, and rhythm.

From those remaining clues, listeners were able to sense the surgeons' warmth, hostility, and dominance and to accurately assess which of them had been sued. Knowing nothing of a surgeon's skill or even what was being said, listeners could nonetheless derive from the tone of voice a feeling for whether the doctor was being empathic or overbearing, and that was enough to help predict the patients' responses.

Some people are naturally expressive (and therefore talented at pantomime and charades); others are less expressive (and therefore better poker players). To evaluate people's voluntary control over their expressiveness, Bella DePaulo and her colleagues (1992) asked people to *act* as expressive or inhibited as possible while stating opinions. Their remarkable findings: Inexpressive people, even when feigning expressiveness, were less expressive than expressive people acting naturally. Similarly, expressive people, even when trying to seem inhibited, were less inhibited than inexpressive people acting naturally. It's hard to be someone you're not, or not to be what you are.

The irrepressibility of expressiveness explains why we can size up how outgoing someone is within seconds. Picture this experiment by Maurice Levesque and David Kenny (1993). They seated groups of four university women around a table and asked each woman merely to state her name, year in school, hometown, and college residence. Judging from just these few seconds of verbal and nonverbal behavior, the women were then to guess one another's talkativeness. (How do you think you would do in guessing someone's talkativeness, based on such a small glimpse of their behavior?) When later correlated with how talkative each woman actually was during a series of one-on-one videotaped conversations, the snap judgments proved reasonably accurate. So did the judgments of Peter Borkenau and his co-workers (2004), who videotaped German adults as they engaged in varied behaviors, from making up a story to reading short sentences to introducing someone. Despite situational variations in behavior, personality came shining through. Someone who seemed smart or outgoing in one situation tended to seem (to someone else) smart or outgoing in another. When we judge an expressive trait such as outgoingness, thin slices of behavior can be revealing.

To sum up, we can say that at any moment the immediate situation powerfully influences a person's behavior, especially when the situation makes clear demands. We can better predict drivers' behavior at traffic lights from knowing the color of the lights than from knowing the drivers' personalities. Thus, professors may perceive certain students as subdued (based on their classroom behavior), but friends may perceive them as pretty wild (based on their party behavior). Averaging our behavior across many occasions does, however, reveal distinct personality traits. Moreover, we can, in a flash, perceive individual differences in some traits, such as expressiveness.

>> LEARNING OUTCOMES

The Trait Perspective

OBJECTIVE **14** | **Cite the main difference between the trait and psychoanalytic perspectives on personality.**

Rather than explain personality in terms of childhood sexuality and unconscious motivations, as Freud did, trait researchers have attempted to describe personality in terms of stable and enduring behavior patterns, or predispositions to feel and act. Some psychologists also have attempted to use dominant traits to describe personality "types."

OBJECTIVE **15** | **Describe some of the ways psychologists have attempted to compile a list of basic personality traits.**

Trait researchers attempt to describe personality by placing individuals at points on several trait dimensions simultaneously. Some have attempted to isolate important dimensions of personality by using *factor analysis*. Hans Eysenck and Sybil Eysenck proposed that two primary, genetically influenced dimensions (extraversion-introversion and emotional stability-instability) will explain normal individual variations. Brain-activity scans do indicate that extraverts and introverts differ in their level of brain arousal. Jerome Kagan believes that heredity, by influencing autonomic nervous system reactivity, also influences temperament and behavioral style, which help define personality.

OBJECTIVE **16** | Explain how psychologists use personality inventories to assess traits, and discuss the most widely used personality inventory.

Personality inventories are questionnaires on which people respond to items designed to gauge a wide range of feelings and behaviors. The MMPI-2 is the most widely used personality inventory. Items on the MMPI are empirically derived, and the tests are objectively scored. Objectivity does not, however, guarantee *validity* (measuring what it is supposed to measure), and people may answer MMPI questions in ways that are socially appropriate but not truthful.

OBJECTIVE **17** | Identify the Big Five personality factors, and discuss some of the strengths of this approach to studying personality.

The Big Five personality factors are *conscientiousness, agreeableness, neuroticism, openness,* and *extraversion.* These traits appear to be stable in adulthood, substantially heritable, applicable to all cultures, and good predictors of other personal attributes. Locating an individual on these five dimensions currently offers the most comprehensive picture of personality.

OBJECTIVE **18** | Summarize the person-situation controversy, and explain its importance as a commentary on the trait perspective.

Critics of the trait perspective point out that although people's general traits may persist over time, their specific behavior varies from situation to situation as their inner disposition interacts with a particular environment. Thus, traits are not good predictors of behavior. Trait theorists reply that despite these variations, a person's *average* behavior across many different situations tends to be fairly consistent.

OBJECTIVE **19** | Explain why psychologists are interested in the consistency of the trait of expressiveness.

Expressive styles—animation, manner of speaking, and gestures—demonstrate how consistent traits can be, despite situational variations in behavior. Observers have been able to judge expressiveness in video snippets as short as 2 seconds long. We have little voluntary control over our expressiveness.

ASK YOURSELF: Where would you place yourself on the five personality dimensions—stability, extraversion, openness, agreeableness, and conscientiousness? Where would your family and friends place you?

The Social-Cognitive Perspective

OBJECTIVE **20** | Describe the social-cognitive perspective, and explain how reciprocal determinism illustrates that perspective.

Today's psychological science, as we have noted so often, views persons as biopsychosocial organisms. As we have just noted, people's biologically influenced psychological traits interact with their situations. The **social-cognitive perspective** on personality proposed by Albert Bandura (1986, 2001, 2005)—emphasizes the interaction of persons and their situations. Much as nature and nurture always work together, so do persons and their situations.

Like learning theorists, social-cognitive theorists believe we learn many of our behaviors either through conditioning or by observing others and modeling our behavior after theirs. (That is the "social" part.) They also emphasize the importance of mental processes: What we *think* about our situations affects our behavior. (That is the "cognitive" part.) Instead of focusing solely on how our environment *controls* us (behaviorism), social-cognitive theorists focus on how we and our environment *interact:* How do we interpret and respond to external events? How do our schemas, our memories, and our expectations influence our behavior patterns?

Reciprocal Influences

Bandura (1986) called the process of interacting with our environment **reciprocal determinism.** "Behavior, internal personal factors, and environmental influences," he said, "all operate as interlocking determinants of each other" (**FIGURE 15.6,** page 624). For example, children's TV-viewing habits (past behavior) influence their viewing preferences (internal factor), which influence how television (environmental factor) affects their current behavior. The influences are mutual.

Consider three specific ways in which individuals and environments interact:

1. ***Different people choose different environments.*** The school you attend, the reading you do, the television programs you watch, the music you listen to, the

■ **social-cognitive perspective** views behavior as influenced by the interaction between persons (and their thinking) and their social context.

■ **reciprocal determinism** the interacting influences between personality and environmental factors.

624

FIGURE 15.6
Reciprocal determinism
The social-cognitive perspective proposes that our personalities are shaped by the interaction of personal/cognitive factors (our feelings and thoughts), our environment, and our behaviors.

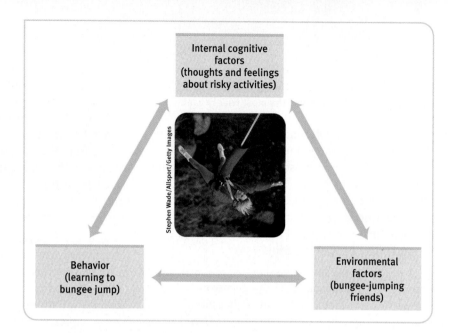

friends you associate with—all are part of an environment you have chosen, based partly on your dispositions (Ickes & others, 1997). *You choose your environment and it then shapes you.*

2. ***Our personalities shape how we interpret and react to events.*** Anxious people, for example, are attuned to potentially threatening events (Eysenck & others, 1987). Thus, they perceive the world as threatening, and they react accordingly.

3. ***Our personalities help create situations to which we react.*** Many experiments reveal that how we view and treat people influences how they in turn treat us. If we expect someone to be angry with us, we may give the person a cold shoulder, touching off the very anger we expect. If we have an easygoing, positive disposition, we will likely enjoy close, supportive friendships (Donnellan & others, 2005; Kendler, 1997).

In such ways, we are both the products and the architects of our environments.

If all this has a familiar ring, it may be because it parallels and reinforces a pervasive theme in psychology and in this book: *Behavior emerges from the interplay of external and internal influences.* Boiling water turns an egg hard and a potato soft. A threatening environment turns one person into a hero, another into a scoundrel. *At every moment,* our behavior is influenced by our biology, our social experiences, and our cognition and personality. And that, again, is why psychology benefits from these multiple levels of analysis (**FIGURE 15.7**).

FIGURE 15.7
The biopsychosocial approach to the study of personality
As with other psychological phenomena, personality is fruitfully studied at multiple levels.

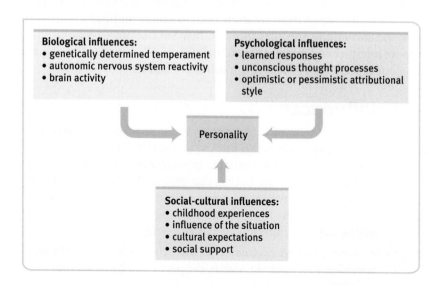

Personal Control

OBJECTIVE **21** | Discuss the effects of a perception of internal or external control, and describe the concept of learned helplessness.

In studying how we interact with our environment, social-cognitive psychologists emphasize our sense of **personal control**—whether we learn to see ourselves as controlling, or as controlled by, our environment. Psychologists have two basic ways to study the effect of personal control (or any personality factor). One: *Correlate* people's feelings of control with their behaviors and achievements. Two: *Experiment,* by raising or lowering people's sense of control and noting the effects. Let's take these one at a time.

Internal Versus External Locus of Control

Consider your own feelings of control. Do you believe that your life is beyond your control? That the world is run by a few powerful people? That getting a good job depends mainly on being in the right place at the right time? Or do you more strongly believe that what happens to you is your own doing? That the average person can influence government decisions? That being a success is a matter of hard work, not luck?

Hundreds of studies have compared people who differ in their perceptions of control. On the one side are those who have what psychologist Julian Rotter called an **external locus of control**—the perception that chance or outside forces determine their fate. On the other are those who perceive an **internal locus of control** and believe that to a great extent they control their own destiny. In study after study, "internals" achieve more in school, act more independently, enjoy better health, and feel less depressed than do "externals" (Lachman & Weaver, 1998; Lefcourt, 1982; Presson & Benassi, 1996). Moreover, they are better able to delay gratification and cope with various stresses, including marital problems (Miller & others, 1986).

Self-control—the ability to control impulses and delay gratification—in turn predicts good adjustment, better grades, and social success, report June Tangney and her colleagues (2004). University students who plan their day's activities and then live out their day as planned are also at low risk for depression (Nezlek, 2001).

None of us experiences unvarying self-control. Self-control requires attention and energy. Like a muscle, self-control temporarily weakens after an exertion, replenishes with rest, and becomes stronger with exercise, report Roy Baumeister and Julia Exline (2000). Exercising willpower depletes mental energy. In one experiment, hungry people's resisting temptations to eat chocolate chip cookies led to their giving up sooner on a tedious task.

Learned Helplessness Versus Personal Control

People who feel helpless and oppressed often perceive control as external. This perception may then deepen their feelings of resignation. In fact, this is precisely what researcher Martin Seligman (1975, 1991) and others found in experiments with both animals and people. Dogs strapped in a harness and given repeated shocks, with no opportunity to avoid them, learned a sense of helplessness. Later placed in another situation where they *could* escape the punishment by simply leaping a hurdle, the dogs cowered as if without hope. People, too, when repeatedly faced with traumatic events over which they have no control, come to feel helpless, hopeless, and depressed. Psychologists call this passive resignation **learned helplessness** (**FIGURE 15.8**). In contrast, animals able to escape the shocks in the first situation learned personal control and easily escaped the shocks in the new situation.

■ **personal control** our sense of controlling our environment rather than feeling helpless.

■ **external locus of control** the perception that chance or outside forces beyond one's personal control determine one's fate.

■ **internal locus of control** the perception that one controls one's own fate.

■ **learned helplessness** the hopelessness and passive resignation an animal or human learns when unable to avoid repeated aversive events.

FIGURE 15.8
Learned helplessness
When animals and people experience no control over repeated bad events, they often learn helplessness.

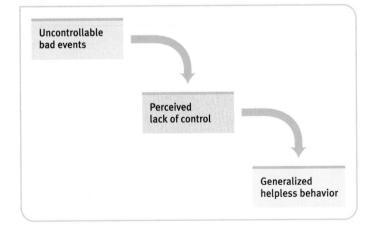

Uncontrollable bad events

Perceived lack of control

Generalized helpless behavior

Happy are those who choose their own path
These happy East Berliners, crossing over to West Berlin after the wall came down in 1989, seem to personify this sentiment, from the Roman philosopher Seneca.

Peter Turnley/Corbis

Part of the shock we feel in an unfamiliar culture comes from a diminished sense of control when unsure how people in the new environment will respond (Triandis, 1994). Similarly, people given little control over their world in prisons, factories, colleges, and nursing homes experience lower morale and increased stress. Measures that increase control—allowing prisoners to move chairs and control room lights and the TV, having workers participate in decision making, offering nursing home patients choices about their environment—noticeably improve health and morale (Miller & Monge, 1986; Ruback & others, 1986; Wener & others, 1987). In one famous study of nursing home patients, 93 percent of those encouraged to exert more control became more alert, active, and happy (Rodin, 1986). As researcher Ellen Langer (1983, p. 291) concluded, "perceived control is basic to human functioning." She recommended that "for the young and old alike," it is important that we create environments that enhance our sense of control and personal efficacy. No wonder so many people like their iPods and TiVos, which give them control of the content and timing of their entertainment.

The verdict of these studies is reassuring: Under conditions of personal freedom and empowerment, people thrive. Small wonder that the citizens of stable democracies report higher levels of happiness (Inglehart, 1990). Shortly before the democratic revolution in the former East Germany, psychologists Gabriele Oettingen and Martin Seligman (1990) studied the telltale body language of working-class men in East and West Berlin bars. Compared with their counterparts on the other side of the Wall, the empowered West Berliners much more often laughed, sat upright rather than slumped, and had upward- rather than downward-turned mouths.

Since these data were gathered, democracy movements have increased the personal control enjoyed by many Eastern Europeans. Not so for American collegians, who report feeling more and more *external* control. "The average college student in 2002 had a more external locus of control than 80 percent of college students in the early 1960s," report Jean Twenge and her collaborators (2004).

Some freedom and control is better than none, notes Barry Schwartz (2000, 2004). But does ever-increasing choice breed ever-happier lives? Apparently not. Schwartz notes that the "excess of freedom" in today's Western cultures contributes to decreasing life satisfaction, increased depression, and sometimes paralysis. (One reason I haven't replaced my rusty 12-year-old car is my dread of sorting through all the choices.) Increased consumer choices have not been an unmixed blessing. After choosing among 30 brands of jam or chocolate, people express less satisfaction than those choosing among a half-dozen options (Iyengar & Lepper, 2000). This *tyranny of choice* brings information overload and a greater likelihood that we will feel regret over some of the unchosen options.

RUBES

Creators Syndicate, Inc. © Leigh Rubin

YOU SEEM TO HAVE TROUBLE ACCEPTING RESPONSIBILITY.

IT'S MY PARENTS' FAULT.

7-6   Creators Syndicate, Inc.
© 1993 Leigh Rubin!

Optimism Versus Pessimism

OBJECTIVE **22** | Discuss the link between performance and optimistic or pessimistic attributional style, and contrast positive psychology with humanistic psychology.

One measure of how helpless or effective you feel is where you stand on optimism-pessimism. How do you characteristically explain negative and positive events? Perhaps you have known students whose *attributional style* is negative—who attribute poor performance to their lack of ability ("I can't do this") or to situations enduringly beyond their control ("There is nothing I can do about it"). Such students are more likely to persist in getting low grades than are students who adopt the more hopeful attitude that effort, good study habits, and self-discipline can make a difference (Noel & others, 1987; Peterson & Barrett, 1987). Although mere fantasies tend not to fuel motivation and success, realistic positive expectations do (Oettingen & Mayer, 2002).

In their study of professional achievement, Seligman and Peter Schulman (1986) compared sales made by new life insurance representatives who were more or less optimistic in their outlooks. Those who put an optimistic spin on their setbacks—seeing them as flukes or as a means to learning a new approach—sold more policies during their first year and were half as likely to quit as were their more pessimistic peers. Seligman's finding came to life for him when Bob Dell, one of the optimistic recruits who began selling for Metropolitan Life after taking Seligman's optimism test, later dialed him up and sold him a policy.

Health, too, benefits from a basic optimism. As we saw in Chapter 14, a depressed hopelessness dampens the body's disease-fighting immune system. In repeated studies, optimists have outlived pessimists or lived with fewer illnesses. Such studies helped point Seligman toward proposing a more positive psychology (see Close-Up on page 628).

If positive thinking in the face of adversity pays dividends, so, too, can a dash of realism (Schneider, 2001). Self-disparaging explanations of past failures can depress ambition, but realistic anxiety over possible *future* failures can fuel energetic efforts to avoid the dreaded fate (Norem, 2001; Goodhart, 1986; Showers, 1992). If concerned about bombing the upcoming exam, students may study thoroughly and outperform their equally able but more confident peers. Edward Chang (2001) reports that, compared with European-American students, Asian-American students express somewhat greater pessimism—which he suspects helps explain their impressive academic achievements. Success requires enough optimism to provide hope and enough pessimism to prevent complacency.

Excessive optimism can blind us to real risks. Neil Weinstein (1980, 1982, 1996) has shown how our natural positive-thinking bias can promote "an unrealistic optimism about future life events." Most college students perceive themselves as less likely than their average classmate to develop drinking problems, drop out of school, or have a heart attack by age 40. Most late adolescents see themselves as much less vulnerable than their peers to the AIDS virus (Abrams, 1991).

Our natural positive-thinking bias does seem to vanish, however, when we are bracing ourselves for feedback, such as exam results (Taylor & Shepperd, 1998). (Have you ever noticed that, as a game nears its end, the outcome seems more in doubt when your team is ahead than when it is behind?) Positive illusions also vanish after a traumatic personal experience—as they did for California victims of a catastrophic earthquake, who had to give up their illusions of being less vulnerable than others to earthquakes (Helweg-Larsen, 1999).

Given illusory optimism, documented in some 200 research reports, people may fail to take sensible precautions. Most young Americans know that roughly half of U.S. marriages end in divorce, but they are confident that *theirs* will not (Lehman & Nisbett, 1985). Most cigarette smokers smoke high-tar brands, but only 17 percent believe their brand has a more hazardous tar level than most others (Segerstrom &

"We just haven't been flapping them hard enough."

Positive expectations often motivate eventual success.

> " O God, give us grace to accept with serenity the things that cannot be changed, courage to change the things which should be changed, and the wisdom to distinguish the one from the other."
> Reinhold Niebuhr, "The Serenity Prayer," 1943

> " I didn't think it could happen to me."
> Earvin "Magic" Johnson, *My Life*, 1993
> (after contracting HIV)

CLOSE-UP:

TOWARD A MORE POSITIVE PSYCHOLOGY

During its first century, psychology understandably focused much of its attention on understanding and alleviating negative states. We have studied abuse and anxiety, depression and disease, prejudice and poverty. As Chapter 13 noted, articles on selected negative emotions since 1887 have outnumbered those on positive emotions by 17 to 1.

In ages past, notes 1998 American Psychological Association president Martin Seligman (2002), times of relative peace and prosperity have enabled cultures to turn their attention from repairing weakness and damage to promoting "the highest qualities of life." Prosperous fifth-century Athens nurtured philosophy and democracy. Flourishing fifteenth-century Florence nurtured great art. Victorian England, flush with the bounty of the British empire, nurtured honor, discipline, and duty. In this millennium, Seligman believes, thriving Western cultures have a parallel opportunity to create, as a "humane, scientific monument," a more **positive psychology**— a psychology concerned not only with weakness and damage but also with strength and virtue. Thanks to his own leadership and to some $30 million in new funding, the new positive psychology movement is gaining strength (Seligman, 2004).

Positive psychology shares with humanistic psychology an interest in advancing human fulfillment, but its methodology is scientific. From these roots have grown not only the new

Courtesy of Martin E.P. Seligman, Ph.D. Director, Positive Psychology Center/University of Pennsylvania

Martin E. P. Seligman

"The main purpose of a positive psychology is to measure, understand, and then build the human strengths and the civic virtues."

studies of happiness (Chapter 13) and health (Chapter 14), but also the shift in emphasis from learned helplessness and depression to optimism and thriving. "Positive psychology," say Seligman and colleagues (2005) "is an umbrella term for the study of positive emotions, positive character traits, and enabling institutions."

Taken together, satisfaction with the past, happiness with the present, and optimism about the future define the movement's first pillar: *positive emotions*. Happiness, Seligman argues, is a by-product of a pleasant, engaged, and meaningful life.

Positive psychology is about building not just a pleasant life, says Seligman, but also a *good life* that engages one's skills, and a *meaningful life* that points beyond oneself.

Thus, the second pillar, *positive character*, focuses on exploring and enhancing virtues such as creativity, courage, compassion, integrity, self-control, leadership, wisdom, and spirituality. Current research examines the roots and fruits of such virtues, sometimes by studying individuals who exemplify them in extraordinary ways.

The third pillar, *positive groups, communities, and cultures*, seeks to foster a positive social ecology, including healthy families, communal neighborhoods, effective schools, socially responsible media, and civil dialogue.

Will psychology have a more positive mission in this century? Without slighting the need to repair damage and cure disease, positive psychology's proponents hope so. With *American Psychologist* and *British Psychologist* special issues devoted to positive psychology, with new books (*Authentic Happiness*, 2002; *A Psychology of Human Strengths*, 2003; *Character Strengths and Virtues*, 2004), with 150 networked scientists worldwide working in 50 research groups, and with prizes, research awards, summer institutes, and a new graduate program promoting positive psychology scholarship, these psychologists have reason to be positive.

■ **positive psychology** the scientific study of optimal human functioning; aims to discover and promote strengths and virtues that enable individuals and communities to thrive.

others, 1993). Compared with other women at their university, sexually active undergraduate women—especially those who do *not* consistently use effective contraception—perceive themselves as *less* vulnerable to unwanted pregnancy (Burger & Burns, 1988). Those who optimistically venture into ill-fated relationships, deny the effects of smoking, or engage in unprotected sex remind us that, like pride, blind optimism may go before a fall.

Ironically, people often are most overconfident when most incompetent. That's because it often takes competence to recognize competence, note Justin Kruger and David Dunning (1999). They found that most students scoring at the low end of tests

"Ignorance more freely begets confidence than does knowledge."

Charles Darwin, *The Descent of Man*, 1871

DOONESBURY

of grammar and logic believed they had scored in the top half. If you do not know what good grammar is, you may be unaware that your grammar is poor. This "ignorance of one's own incompetence" phenomenon has a parallel, as I can vouch, in hard-of-hearing persons' difficulty recognizing their own hearing loss. We're not so much "in denial" as we are simply unaware of what we don't hear. If I fail to hear my friend calling my name, the friend notices my inattention. But for me it's a nonevent. I hear what I hear—which, to me, seems pretty normal.

The difficulty in recognizing one's own incompetence helps explain why so many low-scoring students are dumbfounded after doing badly on an exam. If you don't know all the Scrabble word possibilities you've overlooked, you may feel pretty smart—until someone points them out. As Deanna Caputo and Dunning (2005) demonstrate in experiments that re-create this phenomenon, our ignorance of what we don't know helps sustain our confidence in our own abilities.

Assessing Behavior in Situations

OBJECTIVE **23** | Explain why social-cognitive researchers assess behavior in realistic situations.

Social-cognitive psychologists explore how people interact with situations. To predict behavior, they often observe behavior in realistic situations.

The idea, though effective, is not new. One ambitious example was the U.S. Army's World War II strategy for assessing candidates for spy missions. Rather than using paper-and-pencil tests, army psychologists subjected the candidates to simulated undercover conditions. They tested their ability to handle stress, solve problems, maintain leadership, and withstand intense interrogation without blowing their covers. Although time-consuming and expensive, this assessment of behavior in a realistic situation helped predict later success on actual spy missions (OSS Assessment Staff, 1948).

Military and educational organizations and many Fortune 500 companies are adopting similar strategies in their evaluations of hundreds of thousands of people each year in assessment centers (Bray & others, 1991, 1997; Spychalski & others, 1997). AT&T has observed prospective managers doing simulated managerial work. Many colleges assess potential faculty members' teaching abilities by observing them teach, and assess graduate students' potentials via internships and student teaching.

> "The living-room [Scrabble] player is lucky. . . . He has no idea how miserably he fails with almost every turn, how many possible words or optimal plays slip by unnoticed."
>
> Stefan Fatsis, *Word Freak*, 2001

Assessing behavior in situations

Reality TV shows may take "show me" job interviews to the extreme, but they do illustrate a valid point. Seeing how a potential employee behaves in a job-relevant situation helps predict job performance.

© NBC/ Courtesy Everett Collection

Armies assess their soldiers by observing them during military exercises. Most American cities with populations of 50,000 or more use assessment centers in evaluating police and fire officers (Lowry, 1997).

These procedures exploit the principle that the best means of predicting future behavior is neither a personality test nor an interviewer's intuition. Rather, it is the person's past behavior patterns in similar situations (Mischel, 1981; Ouellette & Wood, 1998; Schmidt & Hunter, 1998).

A *New York Times* analysis of 100 rampage murders over the last half-century revealed that 55 of the killers had regularly exploded in anger and 63 had threatened violence (Goodstein & Glaberson, 2000). Most didn't, out of the blue, "just snap."

As long as the situation and the person remain much the same, the best predictor of future job performance is past job performance; the best predictor of future grades is past grades; the best predictor of future aggressiveness is past aggressiveness; the best predictor of drug use in young adulthood is drug use in high school. If you can't check the person's past behavior, the next-best thing is to create an assessment situation that simulates the task so you can see how the person handles it.

Evaluating the Social-Cognitive Perspective

OBJECTIVE 24 | State the major criticism of the social-cognitive perspective.

The social-cognitive perspective on personality sensitizes researchers to how situations affect, and are affected by, individuals. More than other perspectives, it builds from psychological research on learning and cognition.

Critics charge that the social-cognitive perspective focuses so much on the situation that it fails to appreciate the person's inner traits. Where is the person in this view of personality, ask the dissenters (Carlson, 1984), and where are human emotions? True, the situation does guide our behavior. But, say the critics, in many instances our unconscious motives, our emotions, and our pervasive traits shine through. Personality traits have been shown to predict behavior at work, love, and play. Our biologically influenced traits really do matter. Consider Percy Ray Pridgen and Charles Gill. Each faced the same situation: They had jointly won a $90 million lottery jackpot (Harriston, 1993). When Pridgen learned of the winning numbers, he began trembling uncontrollably, huddled with a friend behind a bathroom door while confirming the win, then sobbed. When Gill heard the news, he told his wife and then went to sleep.

>> LEARNING OUTCOMES

The Social-Cognitive Perspective

OBJECTIVE 20 | Describe the social-cognitive perspective, and explain how reciprocal determinism illustrates that perspective.

Reciprocal determinism is a term applied to the interacting influences between personality and environmental factors. This interaction is central to the social-cognitive perspective, which applies principles of learning (through conditioning and observation) and cognition (our thinking about our situations) to the study of personality. Interactions between individuals and environments occur, for example, when we choose an environment that then shapes us, when our personality shapes how we interpret and react to events, and when our personality helps create situations to which we react.

OBJECTIVE 21 | **Discuss the effects of a perception of internal or external control, and describe the concept of learned helplessness.**

People with an *internal locus of control* (who believe they control their own destiny) tend to experience higher school achievement, better health, less depression, and greater self-control than those with an *external locus of control* (who believe forces beyond their control determine their fate). *Learned helplessness* is an acquired response of hopelessness and passive resignation that animals and humans display after repeated exposure to traumatic events they cannot control. Environments that increase people's feelings of control can boost morale and empower people. Ever-increasing personal freedom, however, in the form of a wealth of consumer choices, can result in a *tyranny of choices* that can decrease life satisfaction, increase depression, and lead to feelings of paralysis.

OBJECTIVE 22 | **Discuss the link between performance and optimistic or pessimistic attributional style, and contrast positive psychology with humanistic psychology.**

An optimistic or pessimistic *attributional style*—your way of explaining events—can be a window revealing how effective or helpless you feel. Students who express an attitude of hopeful optimism tend to get better grades than those who have a negative attributional style. But excessive optimism can foster feelings of invincibility that expose us to unnecessary risks.

Positive psychology, like humanistic psychology, attempts to foster human fulfillment. But it differs from humanistic psychology in its scientific methods. The three goals of positive psychology are studying and fostering positive subjective well-being; positive character; and positive groups, communities, and cultures.

OBJECTIVE 23 | **Explain why social-cognitive researchers assess behavior in realistic situations.**

Social-cognitive researchers are interested in how people's behaviors and beliefs affect, and are affected by, their surroundings. They observe people in realistic situations because they have found that the best way to predict someone's behavior in a given situation is to observe that person's behavior pattern in similar situations.

OBJECTIVE 24 | **State the major criticism of the social-cognitive perspective.**

Critics fault the social-cognitive perspective for focusing so much on the situation that it loses sight of the person. They maintain that this perspective slights the importance of unconscious dynamics, emotions, and biologically influenced traits.

ASK YOURSELF: **Are you a pessimist? Do you readily catastrophize, have low expectations, and attribute bad events to your inability or to circumstances beyond your control? Or are you an optimist, perhaps even someone who frequently exhibits "illusory optimism"? How did either tendency influence your choice of school or major?**

Exploring the Self

OBJECTIVE 25 | Explain why psychology has generated so much research on the self, and give three examples of current research on the self.

Psychology's concern with people's sense of self dates back at least to William James, who devoted more than 100 pages of his 1890 *Principles of Psychology* to the topic. By 1943, Gordon Allport lamented that the self had become "lost to view." Although humanistic psychology's emphasis on the self did not instigate much scientific research, it did help renew the concept of self and keep it alive. Now, more than a century after James, the self is one of Western psychology's most vigorously researched topics. Every year, new studies galore appear on self-esteem, self-disclosure, self-awareness, self-schemas, self-monitoring, and so forth—more than 220,000 articles in all since 1967. Underlying this research is an assumption that the self, as organizer of our thoughts, feelings, and actions, is a pivotal center of personality.

One example of thinking about self is the concept of *possible selves* put forth by Hazel Markus and her colleagues (Cross & Markus, 1991; Markus & Nurius, 1986). Your possible selves include your visions of the self you dream of becoming—the rich self, the successful self, the loved and admired self. They also include the self you fear becoming—the unemployed self, the lonely self, the academically failed self. Such possible selves motivate us by laying out specific goals and calling forth the energy to work toward them. University of Michigan students in a combined

"The first step to better times is to imagine them."

Chinese fortune cookie

Possible selves

By giving them a chance to try out many possible selves, pretend games offer children important opportunities to grow emotionally, socially, and cognitively. This young boy may or may not grow up to be a physician, but playing adult roles will certainly bear fruit in terms of an expanded vision of what he might become.

undergraduate/medical school program earn higher grades if they undergo the program with a clear vision of themselves as successful doctors. Dreams do often give birth to achievements.

Our self-focused perspective may motivate us, but it can also lead us to presume too readily that others are noticing and evaluating us. Thomas Gilovich (1996) demonstrated this **spotlight effect** by having individual Cornell University students don Barry Manilow T-shirts before entering a room with other students. Feeling self-conscious, the T-shirt wearers guessed that nearly half of their peers would take note of the shirt as they walked in. In reality, only 23 percent did. This absence of attention applies not only to our dorky clothes and bad hair but also to our nervousness, irritation, or attraction: Fewer people notice than we presume (Gilovich & Savitsky, 1999). Others are also less aware than we suppose of the variability—the ups and downs—of our appearance and performance (Gilovich & others, 2002). Even after a blunder (setting off a library alarm, showing up for dinner in the wrong clothes), we stick out like a sore thumb less than we imagine (Savitsky & others, 2001). Knowing about the spotlight effect can be empowering. Help public speakers to understand that their natural nervousness is not so apparent to their audience and their speaking performance improves (Savitsky & Gilovich, 2003).

Self-focus affects our recall, too, but in a more constructive way: We remember information better if we encode it in terms of ourselves. Tory Higgins and John Bargh (1987) demonstrated this *self-reference* phenomenon by asking people to consider whether some specific words such as *friendly* described them, and whether the words described someone else. The participants better recalled words they had considered in relation to themselves.

The Benefits of Self-Esteem

OBJECTIVE **26** | Give two alternative explanations for the positive correlation between low self-esteem and personal problems.

How we feel about ourselves is also important. High **self-esteem**—a feeling of self-worth—pays dividends. People who feel good about themselves (who strongly agree with self-affirming questionnaire statements) have fewer sleepless nights, succumb less easily to pressures to conform, are more persistent at difficult tasks, are less shy and lonely, and are just plain happier (Crocker & Wolfe, 1999; Leary, 1999; Murray & others, 2002; Watson & others, 2002). Give high–self-esteem people happy news, and they are more likely than low–self-esteem people to savor it rather than dampen it (Wood & others, 2003).

Those whose self-esteem is low do not necessarily see themselves as worthless or wicked, but they seldom say good things about themselves. Low self-esteem often co-exists with unhappiness and despair, as psychotherapy researcher Hans Strupp (1982) noted: "As soon as one listens to a patient's story, one encounters unhappiness, frustration, and despair. . . . Basic to all these difficulties are impairments in self-acceptance and self-esteem." When low self-esteem signals social rejection, it may aid survival—by motivating people to behave in ways that restore their inclusion within a supportive group (Leary & others, 1995).

The correlational links between low self-esteem and personal problems have other possible interpretations. Psychologists Roy Baumeister and colleagues (2003, 2005), William Damon (1995), Robyn Dawes (1994), Mark Leary (1999), and Martin Seligman (1994, 2002) all doubt that high self-esteem is really "the armor that protects kids" from life's problems. Maybe self-esteem simply reflects reality. Maybe feeling good *follows* doing well. Maybe it's a side effect of meeting challenges and surmounting difficulties. Maybe self-esteem is a gauge that reads out the state of our relationships with others. If so, isn't pushing the gauge artificially higher akin to forcing a car's low

Dear diary, Sorry to bother you again.

LOW SELF-ESTEEM

fuel gauge to display "full"? And if problems and failures cause low self-esteem, won't the best boost therefore come not so much from our repeatedly telling children how wonderful they are as from their own effective coping and hard-won achievements?

However, experiments do reveal an *effect* of low self-esteem. Temporarily deflate people's self-image (say, by telling them they did poorly on an aptitude test or by disparaging their personality) and they will be more likely to disparage others or to express heightened racial prejudice (Ybarra, 1999). Those who are negative about themselves also tend to be thin-skinned and judgmental (Baumgardner & others, 1989; Pelham, 1993). Some "love their neighbors as themselves"; others loathe their neighbors as themselves. In experiments, those made to feel insecure often become excessively critical, as if to impress others with their own brilliance (Amabile, 1983). Such findings are consistent with Maslow's and Rogers' presumptions that a healthy self-image pays dividends. Accept yourself and you'll find it easier to accept others. Disparage yourself and you will be prone to the floccinaucinihilipilification[1] of others. Said more simply, people who are down on themselves tend to be down on other things and people.

Culture and Self-Esteem

OBJECTIVE 27 | Discuss some ways that people maintain their self-esteem under conditions of discrimination or low status.

Is it true, as so many assume, that ethnic minorities, people with disabilities, and women live lives handicapped by impoverished self-esteem? The accumulated evidence says no. The National Institute of Mental Health's 1980s study of *Psychiatric Disorders in America* found rates of depression and alcoholism among African- and Hispanic-Americans roughly comparable with those of other Americans (if anything, America's ethnic minorities suffered slightly less depression. More recently, 261 comparisons of more than half a million people have revealed slightly *higher* self-esteem scores for black than for white children, adolescents, and young adults (Gray-Little & Hafdahl, 2000; Twenge & Crocker, 2002).

Some people wonder: How can this be? Some members of stigmatized groups (people of color, those with disabilities, women) have faced discrimination and lower status, yet, according to Jennifer Crocker and Brenda Major (1989), they maintain their self-esteem in three ways:

- They value the things at which they excel.
- They attribute problems to prejudice.
- They do as everyone does—they compare themselves to those in their own group.

These findings help us understand why, despite the realities of prejudice, such groups report levels of happiness roughly comparable to others.

Self-Serving Bias

OBJECTIVE 28 | Discuss self-serving bias, and contrast defensive and secure self-esteem.

Carl Rogers (1958) once objected to the religious doctrine that humanity's problems arise from excessive self-love, or pride. He noted that most people he had known "despise themselves, regard themselves as worthless and unlovable." Mark Twain had a similar idea: "No man, deep down in the privacy of his heart, has any considerable respect for himself."

> "There's a lot of talk about self-esteem these days. It seems pretty basic to me. If you want to feel proud of yourself, you've got to do things you can be proud of."
>
> Oseola McCarty, Mississippi washerwoman, after donating $150,000 to the University of Southern Mississippi

■ **spotlight effect** overestimating others' noticing and evaluating our appearance, performance, and blunders (as if we presume a spotlight shines on us).

■ **self-esteem** one's feelings of high or low self-worth.

---

[1] I couldn't resist throwing that in. But don't worry, you won't be tested on *floccinaucinihilipilification*, which is the act of estimating something as worthless (and was the longest nontechnical word in the first edition of the *Oxford English Dictionary*).

PEANUTS

Actually, most of us have a good reputation with ourselves. In studies of self-esteem, even those who score low respond in the midrange of possible scores. (A low–self-esteem person responds to statements such as "I have good ideas" with qualifying adjectives such as *somewhat* or *sometimes*.) Moreover, one of psychology's most provocative and firmly established recent conclusions concerns our potent **self-serving bias**—our readiness to perceive ourselves favorably (Mezulis & others, 2004; Myers, 2005). Consider these findings:

People accept more responsibility for good deeds than for bad, and for successes than for failures. Athletes often privately credit their victories to their own prowess and their losses to bad breaks, lousy officiating, or the other team's exceptional performance. After receiving poor grades on an exam, most students in a half-dozen studies criticized the exam, not themselves. On insurance forms, drivers have explained accidents in such words as: "An invisible car came out of nowhere, struck my car, and vanished." "As I reached an intersection, a hedge sprang up, obscuring my vision, and I did not see the other car." "A pedestrian hit me and went under my car." The question "What have I done to deserve this?" is one we usually ask of our troubles, not our successes—those, we assume we deserve.

Most people see themselves as better than average. This is true for nearly any subjective and socially desirable dimension. In national surveys, most business executives say they are more ethical than their average counterpart. In several studies, 90 percent of business managers and more than 90 percent of college professors rated their performance as superior to that of their average peer. In Australia, 86 percent of people rate their job performance as above average, and only 1 percent as below average. The phenomenon, which reflects the overestimation of self rather than the underestimation of others (Epley & Dunning, 2000), is less striking in Asia, where people value modesty. Yet self-serving biases have been observed worldwide: among Dutch, Australian, and Chinese students; Japanese drivers; Indian Hindus; and French people of most walks of life. Ironically, people even see themselves as more immune than others to self-serving bias (Pronin & others, 2002). The world, it seems, is Garrison Keillor's Lake Wobegon writ large—a place where "all the women are strong, all the men are good-looking, and all the children are above average."

And who is at least "somewhat likely" to go to heaven? Of Americans surveyed by *U.S. News* (1997), 19 percent thought O. J. Simpson would make it. They were more optimistic about Bill Clinton (52 percent), Princess Diana (60 percent), and Michael Jordan (65 percent). The public figure closest to a perceived heavenly shoo-in was Mother Teresa (79 percent). But she was topped by the survey's respondents, 87 percent of whom believed *they* themselves were destined for eternal bliss.

Self-serving bias flies in the face of pop psychology. "All of us have inferiority complexes," wrote John Powell (1989, p. 15). "Those who seem not to have such a complex are only pretending." But additional findings remove any doubts (Myers, 2005):

- We remember and justify our past actions in self-enhancing ways.
- We exhibit an inflated confidence in our beliefs and judgments.

"To love oneself is the beginning of a life-long romance."

Oscar Wilde, *An Ideal Husband*, 1895

Three in four pet owners believe their pet is smarter than average (Nier, 2004).

"The [self-]portraits that we actually believe, when we are given freedom to voice them, are dramatically more positive than reality can sustain."

Shelley Taylor, *Positive Illusions*, 1989

- We overestimate how desirably *we* would act in situations where most people behave less than admirably.
- We often seek out favorable, self-enhancing information.
- We are quicker to believe flattering descriptions of ourselves than unflattering ones, and we are impressed with psychological tests that make us look good.
- We shore up our self-image by overestimating the commonality of our foibles and by *under*estimating the commonality of our strengths.
- We exhibit group pride—a tendency to see our group (our school, our country, our race) as superior.

Moreover, pride does often go before a fall. Self-serving perceptions underlie conflicts ranging from blaming one's spouse for marital discord to arrogantly promoting one's own ethnic superiority. "Aryan pride" fueled Nazi atrocities. No wonder religion and literature so often warn against the perils of excessive pride.

Finding their self-esteem threatened, people with large egos may do more than put others down; they may react violently. Among children, the recipe for frequent fighting mixes high self-esteem with social rejection. The most aggressive children tend to have high self-regard that gets punctured by other kids' dislike (van Boxtel, 2004). An adolescent or adult with a swelled head that gets deflated by insult is potentially dangerous. Brad Bushman and Roy Baumeister (1998) experimented with this "dark side of high self-esteem." They had 540 undergraduate volunteers write a paragraph, in response to which another supposed student gave them either praise ("Great essay!") or stinging criticism ("One of the worst essays I have read!"). Then the essay writers played a reaction-time game against the other student. After wins, they could assault their opponent with noise of any intensity for any duration.

Can you anticipate the result? After criticism, those with unrealistically high self-esteem were "exceptionally aggressive." They delivered three times the auditory torture of those with normal self-esteem. Threatened egotism, more than low self-esteem, it seems, predisposes aggression. "Encouraging people to feel good about themselves when they haven't earned it" poses problems, Baumeister (2001) concludes. "Conceited, self-important individuals turn nasty toward those who puncture their bubbles of self-love."

Despite the demonstrated perils of pride, many people reject the idea of self-serving bias, insisting it overlooks those who feel worthless and unlovable and seem to despise themselves. If self-serving bias prevails, why do so many people disparage themselves? For three reasons: Sometimes self-directed put-downs are *subtly strategic:* They elicit reassuring strokes. Saying "No one likes me" may at least elicit "But not everyone has met you!" Other times, such as before a game or an exam, self-disparaging comments *prepare us for possible failure.* The coach who extols the superior strength of the upcoming opponent makes a loss understandable, a victory noteworthy. And finally, self-disparagement also frequently pertains to one's *old self.* People are much more critical of their distant past selves than of their current selves—even when they have not changed (Wilson & Ross, 2001). "At 18, I was a jerk; today I'm more sensitive." In their own eyes, chumps yesterday, champs today.

Even so, it's true: All of us some of the time, and some of us much of the time, *do* feel inferior—especially when we compare ourselves with those who are a step or two higher on the ladder of status, looks, income, or ability. The deeper and more frequently we have such feelings, the more unhappy, even depressed, we are. But for most people, thinking has a naturally positive bias.

While recognizing the dark side of self-serving bias and self-esteem, some researchers prefer isolating the effects of two types of self-esteem—defensive and secure (Jordan & others, 2003; Kernis, 2003; Ryan & Deci, 2004). *Defensive self-esteem* is fragile. It focuses on sustaining itself, which makes failures and criticism feel threatening. Such egotism exposes one to perceived threats, which feed

■ **self-serving bias** a readiness to perceive oneself favorably

"The enthusiastic claims of the self-esteem movement mostly range from fantasy to hogwash. The effects of self-esteem are small, limited, and not all good."

Roy Baumeister (1996)

> "If you compare yourself with others, you may become vain and bitter; for always there will be greater and lesser persons than yourself."
>
> Max Ehrmann, "Desiderata," 1927

anger and disorder, note Jennifer Crocker and Lora Park (2004). Thus, like low self-esteem, defensive self-esteem correlates with aggressive and antisocial behavior (Donnellan & others, 2005). *Secure self-esteem* is less fragile, because it is less contingent on external evaluations. To feel accepted for who we are, and not for our looks, wealth, or acclaim, relieves pressures to succeed and enables us to focus beyond ourselves. By losing ourselves in relationships and purposes larger than self, Crocker and Park add, we may achieve a more secure self-esteem and greater quality of life.

Recognizing both the perils of self-righteousness and the dividends of secure self-esteem, psychologists Baumeister (1989), Jonathan Brown (1991), and Shelley Taylor (1989; Taylor & others, 2003) have all suggested that humans function best with modest self-enhancing illusions. Like the Japanese and European magnetic levitation trains, Brown notes, we function optimally when riding just off the rails—not so high that we gyrate and crash, yet not so in touch that we grind to a halt.

>> Learning Outcomes

Exploring the Self

OBJECTIVE 25 | Explain why psychology has generated so much research on the self, and give three examples of current research on the self.

Psychological research on the self has been accumulating for more than a century. Many psychologists view the self—the organizer of our thoughts, feelings and actions—as a critical part of personality. One recent example of research on the self is the study of the influence of possible selves, the visions of the selves we dream of becoming or fear we may become. Another example is the concept of the spotlight effect, the assumption that we overestimate the extent to which others notice and evaluate our appearance, performance, and blunders. A third example is the self-reference effect, the ability to better recall information if we relate it to our own person or life.

OBJECTIVE 26 | Give two alternative explanations for the positive correlation between low self-esteem and personal problems.

Abraham Maslow and Carl Rogers argued that a healthy self-image (high self-esteem) pays dividends in a personally fulfilling and successful life, and some experiments have shown the destructive power of a negative self-image. But other psychologists have proposed an alternative explanation of the link between low self-esteem and personal problems—that self-esteem, low or high, reflects reality, that it is a side effect of one's success or failure in meeting challenges and surmounting difficulties. In this view, the best boost to self-esteem would be helping children meet challenges, not rewarding them despite their failures.

OBJECTIVE 27 | Discuss some ways that people maintain their self-esteem under conditions of discrimination or low status.

Studies show that under conditions of discrimination or low status, people—often those of color, those with disabilities, and women—maintain their self-esteem by valuing the things at which they excel, by attributing problems to prejudice, and by comparing themselves with people in similar positions.

OBJECTIVE 28 | Discuss self-serving bias, and contrast defensive and secure self-esteem.

The *self-serving bias* (our readiness to perceive ourselves favorably) includes our tendencies (1) to more readily accept responsibility for good deeds and for successes than for bad deeds and failures, and (2) to see ourselves as better than average. *Defensive self-esteem* is fragile and takes the form of egotism focused on sustaining itself at any cost. *Secure self-esteem* is less fragile and less dependent on external evaluations.

ASK YOURSELF: What possible future selves do you envision? To what extent do these imagined selves motivate you now?

REVIEW CHAPTER 15: **Personality**

Test Yourself

1. What, according to Freud, were some of the important defense mechanisms, and what do they defend against? How many of these find support in modern research?

2. What does it mean to be "empathic"? To be "self-actualized"?

3. How many trait dimensions are currently used to describe personality, and what are those dimensions?

4. How do learned helplessness and optimism influence behavior?

5. In a 1997 Gallup poll, white Americans estimated 44 percent of their fellow white Americans to be high in prejudice (scoring them 5 or higher on a 10-point scale). How many rated themselves similarly high in prejudice? Just 14 percent. What phenomenon does this illustrate?

Answers to the Test Yourself questions can be found in Appendix B at the end of the book.

Terms and Concepts to Remember

personality, p. 595
free association, p. 597
psychoanalysis, p. 597
unconscious, p. 597
id, p. 598
ego, p. 598
superego, p. 598
psychosexual stages, p. 598
Oedipus [ED-uh-puss] complex, p. 599
identification, p. 599
fixation, p. 599
defense mechanisms, p. 600
repression, p. 600
regression, p. 600

reaction formation, p. 600
projection, p. 600
rationalization, p. 600
displacement, p. 600
collective unconscious, p. 601
projective test, p. 602
Thematic Apperception Test (TAT), p. 602
Rorschach inkblot test, p. 602
terror-management theory, p. 606
self-actualization, p. 609
unconditional positive regard, p. 610
self-concept, p. 610
trait, p. 613
personality inventory, p. 615

Minnesota Multiphasic Personality Inventory (MMPI), p. 616
empirically derived test, p. 617
social-cognitive perspective, p. 623
reciprocal determinism, p. 623
personal control, p. 625
external locus of control, p. 625
internal locus of control, p. 625
learned helplessness, p. 625
positive psychology, p. 628
spotlight effect, p. 632
self-esteem, p. 632
self-serving bias, p. 634

WEB

> To continue your study and review of Personality, visit this book's Web site at www.worthpublishers.com/myers. You will find practice tests, review activities, and many interesting articles and Web links for more information on topics related to Personality.

ANOTHER VOICE ON: PSYCHOLOGICAL DISORDERS

CHRISTINE LINCOLN (b. 1966), FROM "SAP RISING"

We share the story about the women called maniacs. Women who lived a long time ago. They were just country women, really, who got tired of cookin' and cleanin', takin' care of their husband and chirrun. Got tired of everybody else usin' up what was supposed to be their lives.

So they met in the woods one night and had this dance. When the men found out, they got angry and tried to put an end to their women's foolishness. But they couldn't. The women rebelled. Started gatherin' every night. Before long, the men started callin' the women crazy, and

started treatin' them like they was, until the women began to believe it. Why is it when a man wants to be free, he's just being a man, but when a woman wants to live life from the position of the birds, the first thing folks say is that she's crazy?

16: Psychological Disorders

I felt the need to clean my room at home in Indianapolis every Sunday and would spend four to five hours at it. I would take every book out of the bookcase, dust and put it back. At the time I loved doing it. Then I didn't want to do it anymore, but I couldn't stop. The clothes in my closet hung exactly two fingers apart. . . . I made a ritual of touching the wall in my bedroom before I went out because something bad would happen if I didn't do it the right way. I had a constant anxiety about it as a kid, and it made me think for the first time that I might be nuts.

> Marc, diagnosed with
> obsessive-compulsive disorder
> (from Summers, 1996)

Whenever I get depressed it's because I've lost a sense of self. I can't find reasons to like myself. I think I'm ugly. I think no one likes me. . . . I become grumpy and short-tempered. Nobody wants to be around me. I'm left alone. Being alone confirms that I am ugly and not worth being with. I think I'm responsible for everything that goes wrong.

> Greta, diagnosed with depression
> (from Thorne, 1993, p. 21)

Voices, like the roar of a crowd came. I felt like Jesus; I was being crucified. It was dark. I just continued to huddle under the blanket, feeling weak, laid bare and defenseless in a cruel world I could no longer understand.

> Stuart, diagnosed with schizophrenia
> (from Emmons & others, 1997)

People are fascinated by the exceptional, the unusual, the abnormal. "The sun shines and warms and lights us and we have no curiosity to know why this is so," observed Ralph Waldo Emerson, "but we ask the reason of all evil, of pain, and hunger, and [unusual] people." But why such fascination with disturbed people? Do we see in them something of ourselves? At various moments, all of us feel, think, or act the way disturbed people do much of the time. We, too, get anxious, depressed, withdrawn, suspicious, or deluded, just less intensely and more briefly. It's no wonder then that studying psychological disorders may at times evoke an eerie sense of self-recognition, one that illuminates the dynamics of our own personality. "To study the abnormal is the best way of understanding the normal," proposed William James (1842–1910).

Another reason for our curiosity is that so many of us have felt, either personally or through friends or family members, the bewilderment and pain of a psychological disorder that may bring unexplained physical symptoms, irrational fears, or a feeling that life is not worth living.

> "We are all mad at some time or another."
> Battista Mantuanus, *Eclogues*, 1500

No known culture is free of the two terrible maladies this chapter examines in depth—depression and schizophrenia (Castillo, 1997; Draguns, 1990a,b, 1997). Some 450 million people worldwide suffer psychological disorders, according to the World Health Organization (WHO, 2004). The WHO also reports that, worldwide, mental disorders have accounted for 15.4 percent of the years of life lost due to death

■ **psychological disorder** deviant, distressful, and dysfunctional behavior patterns.

■ **attention-deficit hyperactivity disorder (ADHD)** a psychological disorder marked by the appearance by age 7 of one or more of three key symptoms: extreme inattention, hyperactivity, and impulsivity.

or disability—scoring slightly below cardiovascular conditions and slightly above cancer (Murray & Lopez, 1996). As members of the human family, few of us go through life unacquainted with the reality of psychological disturbance.

Perspectives on Psychological Disorders

Most people would agree that someone who is too depressed to get out of bed for weeks at a time has a psychological disorder. But what about those who, having experienced a loss, are unable to resume their usual social activities? Where should we draw the line between sadness and depression? Between zany creativity and bizarre irrationality? Between normality and abnormality? Let's start with these questions:

- How should we *define* psychological disorders?
- How should we *understand* disorders—as sicknesses that need to be diagnosed and cured, or as natural responses to a troubling environment?
- How should we *classify* psychological disorders? And can we do so in a way that allows us to help people without stigmatizing them with *labels?*

Defining Psychological Disorders

OBJECTIVE 1 | Identify the criteria for judging whether behavior is psychologically disordered.

Mental health workers view **psychological disorders** as persistently harmful thoughts, feelings, and actions. When behavior is *deviant, distressful,* and *dysfunctional,* psychiatrists and psychologists label it disordered (Comer, 2004).

Being different (deviant) from most other people in one's culture is *part* of what it takes to define a psychological disorder. As the reclusive poet Emily Dickinson observed in 1862,

> Assent—and you are sane—
> Demur—you're straightaway dangerous—
> and handled with a Chain.

Standards for deviant behavior vary by culture and context. In some cultures, people routinely behave in ways (such as going about naked) that in other cultures would be grounds for arrest. In at least one cultural context—wartime—even mass killing may be viewed as normal and even heroic. Stuart claimed to hear voices and people presumed he was deranged. But others may claim to talk with the dead and not be seen as disordered because enough people find them rational (Friedrich, 1987).

Standards for deviance also vary with time. From 1952 through December 9, 1973, homosexuality was classified as an illness. By day's end on December 10, it was not. The American Psychiatric Association had dropped homosexuality as a disorder because more and more of its members no longer viewed being gay as a psychological problem. (Later research has revealed that the stigma and stresses associated with being gay do, however, increase the risk of mental health problems [Meyer, 2003].) In this new century, controversy swirls over the frequent diagnosing of children with *attention-deficit hyperactivity disorder* (see Thinking Critically About: ADHD—Pathologizing Rambunctiousness or Genuine Disorder?).

But there is more to a disorder than being deviant. Olympic gold medalists deviate from the norm in their physical abilities, and society honors them. To be considered disordered, deviant behavior must also cause the person *distress.* Marc, Greta, and Stuart were all clearly distressed by their behaviors.

Culture and normality
Men of the Wodaabe tribe put on elaborate makeup and costumes to attract women. In Western society, the same behavior would break behavioral norms and might be judged abnormal.

Carol Beckwith

ADHD—PATHOLOGIZING RAMBUNCTIOUSNESS OR GENUINE DISORDER?

Eight-year-old Todd has always been energetic. At home, he darts from one activity to the next, rarely settling down to read a book or focus on play. At meals, he chatters away and often answers questions before they are fully asked. At play, he is reckless and overreacts to playmates who bump into him or take one of his toys. At school, his exasperated teacher complains that fidgety Todd won't listen or follow instructions and just can't seem to stay seated and do his lessons.

If taken to a psychologist or psychiatrist for an evaluation, Todd is much more likely today than two decades ago to be diagnosed with **attention-deficit hyperactivity disorder (ADHD).** According to the National Institute of Mental Health (2003), ADHD plagues some 4 percent of children who display one or more of its three key symptoms:

- *Inattention*—distractibility, forgetfulness, disorganization
- *Hyperactivity*—fidgeting, restlessness and not staying seated at school, excessive talking
- *Impulsivity*—difficulty taking turns, interrupting, blurting out answers while questions are being asked

To skeptics, being distractible, fidgety, and impulsive sounds like a "disorder" caused by a single genetic variation: a Y chromosome. And sure enough, ADHD is diagnosed two to three times more often in boys than in girls. Does energetic child + boring school = ADHD overdiagnosis? Is the label being applied to healthy schoolchildren who, in more natural outdoor environments, would seem perfectly normal?

Skeptics think so. In the decade after 1987, they note, the proportion of American children being

treated for ADHD nearly quadrupled (Olfson & others, 2003). By 2005, a Gallup survey of 13- to 17-year-olds found that 10 percent reported taking prescribed medication for ADHD (Mason, 2005). In some places, the diagnosis is commonplace, in others it is rare. Toddlers who watch lots of TV are, at age 7, more likely than average to display ADHD symptoms (Christakis & others, 2004). Some teachers refer lots of kids for ADHD assessment, others none. ADHD rates have varied by a factor of 10 in different counties of New York State (Carlson, 2000). Adults, too, now willingly accept the ADHD diagnosis for themselves and, contend the skeptics, find it a handy excuse for their past school failures, vocational difficulties, and lack of self-discipline.

Although acknowledging the diagnostic subjectivity and inconsistency—ADHD is not as objectively defined as is a broken arm—the World Federation for Mental Health (2005) has declared that "there is strong agreement among the international scientific community that ADHD is a real neurobiological disorder whose existence should no longer be debated." ADHD, agrees the National Institute of Mental Health (1999, 2003) is heritable. It is also marked in neuroimaging studies by telltale brain activity, notes a consensus statement by 75 researchers (Barkley & others, 2002). It is *not* caused by too much sugar or poor schools. It often coexists with a learning disorder or with defiant and temper-prone behavior. It is treatable with nonaddictive medications such as Ritalin and Adderall, which are stimulants but help calm the hyperactivity and increase a person's ability to sit and focus on a task. Psychological therapies, such as those focused on shaping behaviors

in the classroom and at home, have also helped address the distress of ADHD. And its more frequent diagnosis today may reflect increased awareness of the disorder, especially in areas where the diagnosis is more common.

New research is seeking a more objective assessment of ADHD. Measures include a physical measure of fidgeting, an eye-tracking device that measures ability to focus on and follow spots of light, and more detailed brain imaging (Ashtari & others, 2004; Pavlidis, 2005; Teicher, 2002). Recognizing that about 80 percent of children medicated for ADHD still require medication as teens, as do 50 percent or more as adults, other researchers are exploring the long-term effects of taking stimulant drugs. People appear to tolerate long-term stimulant use with no increased risk of substance abuse (Biederman & others, 1999), but other possible effects are being investigated. In one study, rats were given prolonged exposure to Ritalin early in life, at a dosage comparable to that commonly prescribed for children. When the drug was withdrawn later in life, the rats (compared with others in a control group) were more prone to depressive symptoms and to giving up quickly when facing challenging tasks (Carlezon & others, 2003).

The bottom line: Extreme inattention, hyperactivity, and impulsivity can derail social, academic, and vocational achievements, and these symptoms can be treated with stimulant drugs. But the debate continues over whether normal rambunctiousness is too often diagnosed as a psychiatric disorder, and whether there is a cost to the long-term use of stimulant drugs in treating ADHD.

■ **medical model** the concept that diseases have physical causes that can be diagnosed, treated, and, in most cases, cured. When applied to psychological disorders, the medical model assumes that these *mental illnesses* can be diagnosed on the basis of their symptoms and cured through therapy, which may include treatment in a psychiatric hospital.

Deviant and distressful behaviors are more likely to be considered disordered when also judged *dysfunctional*. For example, Marc's distracting obsessive behaviors interfered with his work and leisure. By this measuring stick, even typical behaviors, such as the occasional despondency that many college students feel, may signal a psychological disorder *if* they become disabling. Dysfunction is key to defining a disorder: An intense fear of spiders may be deviant, but if it doesn't impair your life it is not a disorder.

Disordered behavior may also be dangerous. If Greta's depression deepens and she develops suicidal thoughts, she may be considered a danger to herself.

Understanding Psychological Disorders

OBJECTIVE 2 | Contrast the medical model of psychological disorders with the biopsychosocial approach to disordered behavior.

To explain puzzling behavior, people in earlier times often presumed that strange forces—the movements of the stars, godlike powers, or evil spirits—were at work. "The devil made him do it," you might have said had you lived during the Middle Ages. The cure might have been to get rid of the evil force—by placating the great powers or exorcising the demon. Until the last two centuries, "mad" people were sometimes caged in zoolike conditions or given "therapies" appropriate to a demon: beatings, burning, or castration. In other times, therapy might have included pulling teeth, removing lengths of intestines, cauterizing the clitoris, or receiving transfusions of animal blood (Farina, 1982).

The Medical Model

In opposition to this brutal treatment, reformers such as Philippe Pinel (1745-1826) in France insisted that madness was not demon possession but a sickness of the mind caused by severe stresses and inhumane conditions. For Pinel and other reformers, "moral treatment" included boosting patients' morale by unchaining them and talking with them, and by replacing brutality with gentleness, isolation with activity, and filth with clean air and sunshine.

When physicians later discovered that syphilis infects the brain and distorts the mind, health reformers and medical workers refocused on physical causes for mental disorders and treatments that would cure them. By the 1800s, the assumption of this **medical model**—that psychological disorders are sicknesses—provided the impetus for further reform as hospitals replaced asylums. Today, the medical perspective is

John W. Verano

Yesterday's "therapy"
In other times and places, psychologically disordered people sometimes received brutal treatments, including the *trephination* evident in this Stone Age skull. Such skull holes may have been drilled in an attempt to release evil spirits and cure those with mental disorders. This patient may or may not have survived the "cure."

"Moral treatment"
Under Philippe Pinel's influence, hospitals sometimes sponsored patient dances, such as the "Lunatic Ball" depicted in this painting by George Bellows (*Dance in a Madhouse*).

George Wesley Bellows, *Dance in a Madhouse*, 1907. © 1997 The Art Institute of Chicago

recognizable in the terminology of the mental *health* movement: A mental *illness* (also called a psycho*pathology*) needs to be *diagnosed* on the basis of its *symptoms* and *cured* through *therapy,* which may include *treatment* in a psychiatric *hospital.*

The medical perspective has gained credibility from recent discoveries. As we will see, genetically influenced abnormalities in brain structure and biochemistry contribute to a number of disorders. "Mental illnesses are diagnosable disorders of the brain," declared a U.S. White House fact sheet on mental illness (1999). Two of the most troubling, depression and schizophrenia, often are treated medically. But as we will see, psychological factors, such as traumatic stress, also play an important role.

The Biopsychosocial Approach

Today's psychologists contend that *all* behavior, whether called normal or disordered, arises from the interaction of nature (genetic and physiological factors) and nurture (past and present experiences). To presume that a person is "mentally ill" attributes the condition solely to an internal problem—to a "sickness" that must be found and cured. But maybe there is no deep, internal problem. Maybe instead there is a growth-blocking difficulty in the person's environment, in the person's current interpretations of events, or in the person's bad habits and poor social skills.

Evidence of environmental effects comes from links between disorder and culture. As we noted earlier, some major disorders, such as depression and schizophrenia, occur worldwide. From Asia to Africa and across the Americas, schizophrenia symptoms often include irrationality and incoherent speech (Brislin, 1993; Draguns, 1990b). Other disorders are culture-bound (Beardsley, 1994; Castillo, 1997). Different cultures have different sources of stress, and they produce different ways of coping. Anorexia nervosa and bulimia, for example, are eating disorders that occur mostly in Western cultures (pages 478–480). *Susto,* marked by severe anxiety, restlessness, and a fear of black magic, is found in Latin America. *Taijin-kyofusho,* which combines social anxiety about one's appearance with a readiness to blush and a fear of eye contact, appears in Japan. Such disorders may share an underlying dynamic (such as anxiety) while differing in the symptoms (an eating problem or a type of fear) manifested in a particular culture.

Today, most mental health workers assume that disorders are influenced by genetic predispositions and physiological states; by inner psychological dynamics; and by social and cultural circumstances. To get the whole picture, we need to use the biopsychosocial approach (**FIGURE 16.1**), which recognizes that mind and body are inseparable. Negative emotions contribute to physical illness, and physical abnormalities contribute to emotional malaise. We are mind embodied.

> "Who in the rainbow can draw the line where the violet tint ends and the orange tint begins? Distinctly we see the difference of the colors, but where exactly does the one first blendingly enter into the other? So with sanity and insanity?"
> Herman Melville, *Billy Budd, Sailor,* 1924

> "It's no measure of health to be well adjusted to a profoundly sick society."
> Krishnamurti, 1895–1986

Biological influences:
• evolution
• individual genes
• brain structure and chemistry

Psychological influences:
• stress
• trauma
• learned helplessness
• mood-related perceptions and memories

Psychological disorder

Social-cultural influences:
• roles
• expectations
• definitions of *normality* and *disorder*

FIGURE 16.1
The biopsychosocial approach to psychological disorders
Today's psychology studies how biological, psychological, and social-cultural factors interact to produce specific psychological disorders.

■ **DSM-IV** the American Psychiatric Association's *Diagnostic and Statistical Manual of Mental Disorders* (Fourth Edition), a widely used system for classifying psychological disorders. Presently distributed in an updated "text revision" (DSM-IV-TR).

Classifying Psychological Disorders

OBJECTIVE 3 | Describe the goals and content of the DSM-IV.

In biology and the other sciences, classification creates order. To classify an animal as a mammal says a great deal—that it is warm-blooded, has hair or fur, and nourishes its young with milk. In psychiatry and psychology, too, classification orders and describes symptoms. To classify a person's disorder as "schizophrenia" suggests that the person talks incoherently, hallucinates or has delusions (bizarre beliefs), shows either little emotion or inappropriate emotion, or is socially withdrawn. "Schizophrenia" provides a handy shorthand for describing a complex disorder.

In psychiatry and psychology, diagnostic classification aims not only to describe a disorder but also to predict its future course, imply appropriate treatment, and stimulate research into its causes. Indeed, to study a disorder we must first name and describe it. A current authoritative scheme for classifying psychological disorders is the American Psychiatric Association's *Diagnostic and Statistical Manual of Mental Disorders* (Fourth Edition), nicknamed **DSM-IV.** This 1994 volume, now updated as a 2000 "text revision" (DSM-IV-TR), will be more substantially revised as DSM-V, to appear about 2011. (A book of case illustrations accompanying DSM-IV provides the basis for much of this chapter.) DSM-IV was developed in coordination with the tenth edition of the World Health Organization's *International Classification of Diseases* (ICD-10), which covers both medical and psychological disorders.

The very idea of "diagnosing" people's problems in terms of their "symptoms" presumes a mental "illness." As a result, some practitioners are not enthralled with this medical terminology, but most find the classification to be a helpful and practical tool. It is also financially necessary: Most North American health insurance companies require an ICD diagnosis before they will pay for therapy.

DSM-IV defines a diagnostic process and 16 clinical syndromes (**TABLE 16.1**). Without presuming to explain their causes, it describes various disorders and lists their prevalence. To be helpful and useful, DSM-IV categories and diagnostic guidelines must be reliable, and they are. If one psychiatrist or psychologist diagnoses someone as having, say, catatonic schizophrenia, the chances are good that another mental health worker will independently give the same diagnosis. Following these guidelines, clinicians answer a series of objective questions about observable behaviors, such as, "Is the person afraid to leave home?" In one study, 16 psychologists used this structured-interview procedure to diagnose 75 psychiatric patients as suffering from (1) depression, (2) generalized anxiety, or (3) some other disorder (Riskind & others, 1987). Without knowing the first psychologist's diagnosis, another psychologist viewed a videotape of each interview and offered a second opinion. For 83 percent of the patients, the two opinions agreed.

Some critics have faulted the manual for casting too wide a net and bringing "almost any kind of behavior within the compass of psychiatry" (Eysenck & others, 1983). These critics point to behaviors ranging from irrational fear of humiliation and embarrassment (social phobia) to persistently breaking rules at home or school (conduct disorder). As the number of disorder categories has swelled (from 60 in the 1950s' DSM to 400 in today's), so has the number of adults who meet the criteria for at least one of them—nearly 30 percent in one recent year, according to a U.S. survey (Regier & others, 1998). As a complement to the DSM, some psychologists are offering a manual of human strengths and virtues (see Close-Up: The "un-DSM": A Diagnostic Manual of Human Strengths, page 646).

"I'm always like this, and my family was wondering if you could prescribe a mild depressant."

TABLE **16.1**

HOW ARE PSYCHOLOGICAL DISORDERS DIAGNOSED?

Based on assessments, interviews, and observations, many clinicians diagnose by answering the following questions from the five levels, or *axes,* of the DSM-IV-TR. (Parenthetical page references refer to this text.)

Axis I Is a *Clinical Syndrome* present?
Using specifically defined criteria, clinicians may select none, one, or more syndromes from the following list:

- Disorders usually first diagnosed in infancy, childhood, and adolescence
- Delirium, dementia, amnesia, and other cognitive disorders (Chapters 4 and 9)
- Mental disorders due to a general medical condition
- Substance-related disorders (Chapter 7)
- Schizophrenia and other psychotic disorders (page 669)
- Mood disorders (page 658)
- Anxiety disorders (page 649)
- Somatoform disorders
- Factitious disorders (intentionally feigned)
- Dissociative disorders (page 656)
- Eating disorders (Chapter 12)
- Sexual disorders and gender identity disorder (Chapter 12)
- Sleep disorders (Chapter 7)
- Impulse-control disorders not classified elsewhere
- Adjustment disorders
- Other conditions that may be a focus of clinical attention

Axis II Is a *Personality Disorder* (page 667) or *Mental Retardation* (Chapter 11) present?
Clinicians may or may not also select one of these two conditions.

Axis III Is a *General Medical Condition,* such as diabetes, hypertension, or arthritis, also present?

Axis IV Are *Psychosocial or Environmental Problems,* such as school or housing issues, also present?

Axis V What is the *Global Assessment* of this person's functioning?
Clinicians assign a code from 0–100. For example:

91–100 Superior functioning in a wide range of activities; life's problems never seem to get out of hand; is sought out by others because of his or her many positive qualities. No symptoms.
51–60 Moderate symptoms (for example, flat affect or occasional panic attacks) or moderate difficulty in social, occupational, or school functioning (for example, few friends, or conflicts with peers or co-workers).
1–10 Persistent danger of severely hurting self or others (for example, recurrent violence) or persistent inability to maintain minimal personal hygiene or serious suicidal act with clear expectation of death.

Labeling Psychological Disorders

OBJECTIVE 4 | Discuss the potential dangers and benefits of using diagnostic labels.

The DSM has other critics who register a more fundamental complaint—that these labels are at best arbitrary and at worst value judgments masquerading as science. Once we label a person, we view that person differently (Farina, 1982). Labels create preconceptions that guide our perceptions and our interpretations. It is better, some clinicians say, to study the roots of specific symptoms, such as distorted thoughts or perceptions, than to study catchall categories, such as "schizophrenia" (Persons, 1986).

In the most controversial demonstration of the biasing power of diagnostic labels, David Rosenhan (1973) and seven others went to mental hospital admissions offices, complaining of "hearing voices" that were saying "empty," "hollow," and "thud." Apart from this complaint and giving false names and occupations, they answered questions truthfully. All eight were diagnosed as mentally ill.

That these normal people were misdiagnosed is unsurprising. As one psychiatrist noted, if someone swallowed blood, went to an emergency room, and spat it up,

"One of the unpardonable sins, in the eyes of most people, is for a man to go about unlabeled. The world regards such a person as the police do an unmuzzled dog, not under proper control."

T. H. Huxley, *Evolution and Ethics*, 1893

CLOSE-UP:

THE "UN-DSM": A DIAGNOSTIC MANUAL OF HUMAN STRENGTHS

One facet of the fast-expanding positive psychology movement (page 628) is an effort, led by psychologists Christopher Peterson and Martin Seligman (2004), to create a classification system for human strengths and virtues. A manual that orders and defines harmful dysfunctions has been helpful, these researchers note. Why not also have a companion manual that would similarly order and define our human strengths—the thinking-feeling-action tendencies that contribute to the *good* life, for self and others?

Like the DSM-IV, *The Values in Action Classification of Strengths* draws insights from many researchers in proposing a common vocabulary that lends itself to cross-cultural understanding and to the budding science of strengths. Also like the DSM, the strengths manual offers assessment strategies and questionnaires that help researchers assess six clusters of 24 strengths:

Wisdom and Knowledge
- curiosity
- love of learning
- critical judgment and open-mindedness
- creativity
- perspective (wisdom)

Courage (overcoming opposition)
- bravery/valor
- industry and perseverance
- integrity and honesty
- vitality (zest and enthusiasm)

Love
- kindness
- intimate attachment
- social intelligence

Justice
- citizenship and teamwork
- fairness and equity
- leadership

Temperance
- humility
- self-control

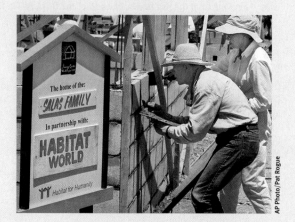

Building strengths
In their work for Habitat for Humanity, former U.S. President Jimmy Carter and First Lady Rosalynn Carter model strengths related to love and justice.

- prudence and caution
- forgiveness and mercy

Transcendence
- appreciation of beauty, awe/wonder
- gratitude
- hope and optimism
- playfulness and humor
- spirituality and purpose

Labeling effect

Seeing *Asylum* on the shirts of this baseball team (from the State Homeopathic Asylum for the Insane in Middletown, New York), most observers of this 1890s photo will comment on the players' apparent depression or confusion. Actually, all the players were from the asylum's staff.

would we fault the doctor for diagnosing a bleeding ulcer? What followed the diagnosis *was* startling. Until being released (an average of 19 days later), the "patients" exhibited no further symptoms. Yet the clinicians were able to "discover" the causes of their disorders, such as reacting to mixed emotions about a parent, after analyzing their (quite normal) life histories. Even the routine behavior of taking notes was misinterpreted as a symptom.

Other studies confirm that labels affect how we perceive people. Ellen Langer and her colleagues (1974, 1980) had people watch a videotaped interview. Some were told the interviewee was normal (a job applicant). Others were told the person was out of the ordinary (a psychiatric or cancer patient). Those who watched unlabeled interviewees perceived them as normal; those who watched supposed patients perceived them as "different from most people." Therapists who thought they were evaluating a psychiatric patient perceived the interviewee as "frightened of his own aggressive impulses," a "passive, dependent type," and so forth. A label can, as Rosenhan discovered, have "a life and an influence of its own." (See Thinking Critically About: Insanity and Responsibility.)

INSANITY AND RESPONSIBILITY

My brain . . . my genes . . . my bad up-bringing made me do it. Such defenses were anticipated by Shakespeare's *Hamlet*. If I wrong someone when not myself, he explained, "then Hamlet does it not, Hamlet denies it. Who does it then? His madness." Such is the essence of a legal insanity defense, created in 1843 after a deluded Scots-man tried to shoot the prime minister (who he thought was persecuting him) but killed an assistant by mistake. Like U.S. President Reagan's near-assassin, John Hinckley, Scots-man Daniel M'Naughten was sent to a mental hospital rather than to prison.

In both cases, the public was out-raged. "Hinckley Insane, Public Mad," declared one headline. And they were mad again when a de-ranged Jeffrey Dahmer in 1991 ad-mitted murdering 15 young men and eating parts of their bodies. They were mad in 1998 when 15-year-old Kip Kinkel, driven by "those voices in my head," killed his parents and 2 fellow Springfield, Oregon, students and wounded 25 others. And they were mad in 2002 when Andrea Yates, after being taken off her anti-psychotic medication, was tried in Texas for drowning her five children. All of these people were sent to jails, not hospitals, following their arrests.

These cases are not uncommon. A 1999 U.S. Justice Department study found that 283,000 jail and prison inmates had severe mental disorders. This is about 16 percent of the U.S. inmate population and considerably more than the 183,000 psychiatric inpatients in all types of U.S. hospitals (Bureau of the Cen-sus, 2004; Butterfield, 1999). Many

people who have been executed or are on death row have been limited by mental retardation or motivated by delusional voices. Larry Robison (1999) was twice hospitalized for paranoid schizophrenia, as were his

Elaine Thompson/AP Photo

Jail or hospital?

Unabomber Theodore Kaczynski lived in a shack for some 20 years, rarely bathed, sent bombs to strangers (killing 3 and injuring 23), and was diagnosed by his state-appointed psychiatrist with paranoid schiz-ophrenia. One of his early letter bombs was addressed to the author of what was, at the time, psychology's most widely studied text. (The bomb was opened by his assis-tant, who recovered from injuries.) Should Kaczynski be jailed as a criminal or hospi-talized (but also confined) as mentally ill?

brother, sister, uncle, and grandfa-ther. When denied further treat-ment after insurance coverage ran out, Robison was discharged, killed five people, and was executed by the state of Texas. Four years later, an-other murderer with schizophrenia, Charles Singleton, was executed by the State of Arkansas after being forcibly medicated with antipsy-chotic drugs—in order to make him mentally competent, so that he could then be put to death.

Whom should we hold responsi-ble? The people who commit such rare but terrible crimes or the "mad-ness" that clouds their vision? Should we treat or should we punish executives who sexually harass their employees and then claim to have a sexual disorder? If a perpetrator's re-volting crime is taken to indicate a disorder, does this create a social basis for evading responsibility (like the person who, having killed his parents, demands mercy because he is an orphan)? Some in Britain be-lieved that is what happened when Brian Blackwell was allowed to plead guilty to a reduced charge of manslaughter after brutally killing his parents. Should he be credited with diminished responsibility be-cause of his "narcissistic personality disorder," as the judicial system agreed, or was the disorder more a description than an explanation of his criminal behavior (*Psychologist*, 2005)? This much seems likely: If some superpsychologist were to un-derstand the biological and environ-mental basis for everything—from generosity to vandalism—society would still wish to hold people re-sponsible for their actions.

The stigmatizing power of labels was illustrated when a female associate of psychol-ogist Stewart Page (1977) called 180 people in Toronto who were advertising furnished rooms for rent. When she merely asked if the room was still available, the answer was nearly always yes. When she instead said she was about to be released from a mental hospital, the answer three times out of four was no (as it was when she said she was

Coping With Disorder

"The only way I knew how to deal with it was to write a song about it," musician Billy Joe Armstrong of Green Day explained, referring to his song "Basket Case," which chronicles a personal struggle with anxiety disorders.

calling for her brother who was about to be released from jail). Some who said no room was available were later called by a second person who simply asked if the room was still available. Nearly always it was. Surveys in Western Europe have uncovered similar attitudes toward those labeled mentally ill. As we are coming to understand that many psychological disorders are diseases of the brain, not failures of character, the stigma seems to be lifting (Solomon, 1996). Public figures are feeling freer to "come out" and speak with candor about their struggles with disorders such as depression. And the more often people have contact with mental health patients, the more accepting their attitudes are (Kolodziej & Johnson, 1996).

But stereotypes linger. This is hardly surprising, given media images of psychological disorders. Movies sometimes offer reasonably accurate and sympathetic portrayals of disorders, as in the portrayal of mathematician John Nash's schizophrenia in *A Beautiful Mind*. But too often they stereotype mental health patients as homicidal (Hannibal Lecter in *Silence of the Lambs*) or as freaks (Hyler & others, 1991; Wahl, 1992). People with schizophrenia are more likely than others to commit violent crime, especially if they also abuse alcohol (Citrome & Volavka, 1999; Tiihonen & others, 1997). However, at least 9 in 10 people with disorders are *not* dangerous; instead, they are anxious, depressed, or withdrawn. And *if* they steer clear of alcohol and drugs, those released from mental hospitals are no more prone to violence than are their neighbors (Steadman & others, 1998). Indeed, reports the U.S. Surgeon General's Office (1999, p. 7), "There is very little risk of violence or harm to a stranger from casual contact with an individual who has a mental disorder." (In fact, people with psychological disorders are more likely to be victims of violence, rather than perpetrators [Marley & Bulia, 2001].)

Not only can labels bias perceptions, they can also change reality. When teachers are told certain students are "gifted," when students expect someone to be "hostile," or when interviewers check to see whether someone is "extraverted," they may act in ways that elicit the very behavior expected (Snyder, 1984). Someone who was led to think you are nasty may treat you coldly, leading you to respond as a mean-spirited person would. Labels can serve as self-fulfilling prophecies.

But let us remember the benefits of diagnostic labels. Mental health professionals use labels to communicate about their cases, to comprehend the underlying causes, and to discern effective treatment programs.

>> LEARNING OUTCOMES

Perspectives on Psychological Disorders

OBJECTIVE **1** | **Identify the criteria for judging whether behavior is psychologically disordered.**

Psychologists and psychiatrists consider behavior disordered when it is deviant, distressful, and dysfunctional. The definition of *deviant* varies with context and culture. It also varies with time; for example, some children who might have been judged rambunctious a few decades ago now are being diagnosed with attention-deficit hyperactivity disorder.

OBJECTIVE **2** | **Contrast the medical model of psychological disorders with the biopsychosocial approach to disordered behavior.**

The medical model assumes that psychological disorders are mental illnesses that can be diagnosed on the basis of their symptoms and cured through therapy, sometimes in a hospital. The biopsychosocial approach assumes that disordered behavior, like other behavior, arises from genetic predispositions and physiological states; inner psychological dynamics; and social-cultural circumstances.

OBJECTIVE **3** | **Describe the goals and content of the DSM-IV.**

The American Psychiatric Association's *Diagnostic and Statistical Manual of Mental Disorders,* Fourth Edition (DSM-IV), currently describes 400 disorders and their prevalence. The manual defines a structured interview technique that clinicians can use to reach a diagnosis. They answer objective questions, posed at five different levels, or axes, about the individual's observable behaviors. The reliability of the classification is sufficiently high. DSM diagnoses are developed in coordination with International Classification of Diseases (ICD).

OBJECTIVE 4 | **Discuss the potential dangers and benefits of using diagnostic labels.**

Critics of the DSM-IV argue that diagnostic labels can stigmatize a person by biasing others' interpretations and perceptions of past and present behaviors and by affecting the ways people react to the labeled person. The benefits of diagnostic labels are that they help mental health professionals communicate with one another about care and therapy, and they establish a common vocabulary for the exchange of ideas among researchers working on causes and treatments of disorders. Most health insurance policies in North America require an ICD diagnosis before they will pay for therapy. One label, "insanity"—used in some legal defenses—raises moral and ethical questions about how a society should treat people who have disorders and have committed crimes.

ASK YOURSELF: **How would you draw the line between sending disturbed criminals to prisons or to mental hospitals? Would the person's history (for example, having suffered child abuse) influence your decisions?**

Anxiety Disorders

OBJECTIVE 5 | Define *anxiety disorders,* and explain how these conditions differ from normal feelings of stress, tension, or uneasiness.

Anxiety is part of life. Speaking in front of a class, peering down from a ledge, or waiting to play in a big game, any one of us might feel anxious. At times many of us feel enough anxiety that we fail to make eye contact or we avoid talking to someone— "shyness," we call it. Fortunately for most of us, our uneasiness is not intense and persistent. If it becomes so, we may have one of the **anxiety disorders,** marked by distressing, persistent anxiety or maladaptive behaviors that reduce anxiety. In this section we focus on four anxiety disorders:

- *Generalized anxiety disorder,* in which a person is unexplainably and continually tense and uneasy
- *Panic disorder,* in which a person experiences sudden episodes of intense dread
- *Phobias,* in which a person feels irrationally and intensely afraid of a specific object or situation
- *Obsessive-compulsive disorder,* in which a person is troubled by repetitive thoughts or actions

Generalized Anxiety Disorder and Panic Disorder

OBJECTIVE 6 | Contrast the symptoms of generalized anxiety disorder and panic disorder.

Tom, a 27-year-old electrician, complains of dizziness, sweating palms, heart palpitations, and ringing in his ears. He feels edgy and sometimes finds himself shaking. With reasonable success he hides his symptoms from his family and co-workers. Nevertheless, he has had few social contacts since the symptoms began two years ago. He occasionally has to leave work. His family doctor and a neurologist can find no physical problem.

Tom's unfocused, out-of-control, negative feelings suggest **generalized anxiety disorder.** The symptoms of this disorder are commonplace; their persistence is not. People with this condition (two-thirds are women), are continually tense and jittery, worried about various bad things that might happen, and plagued by muscular tension, agitation, and sleeplessness. The tension and apprehension may leak out through furrowed brows, twitching eyelids, trembling, perspiration, or fidgeting.

■ **anxiety disorders** psychological disorders characterized by distressing, persistent anxiety or maladaptive behaviors that reduce anxiety.

■ **generalized anxiety disorder** an anxiety disorder in which a person is continually tense, apprehensive, and in a state of autonomic nervous system arousal.

Gender and anxiety: Eight months after 9/11, more U.S. women (34 percent) than men (19 percent) told Gallup (2002) they were still less willing than before 9/11 to go into skyscrapers, or fly on planes. In early 2003, more women (57 percent) than men (36 percent) were "somewhat worried" about becoming a terrorist victim (Jones, 2003).

■ **panic disorder** an anxiety disorder marked by unpredictable minutes-long episodes of intense dread in which a person experiences terror and accompanying chest pain, choking, or other frightening sensations.

■ **phobia** an anxiety disorder marked by a persistent, irrational fear and avoidance of a specific object or situation.

Concentration is difficult, as attention switches from worry to worry. One of the worst characteristics of generalized anxiety disorder is that the person cannot identify, and therefore cannot deal with or avoid, its cause. To use Freud's term, the anxiety is *free-floating*. Generalized anxiety disorder is often accompanied by depression, but even without depression it tends to be disabling (Hunt & others, 2004) and may lead to physical problems, such as ulcers and high blood pressure.

Panic disorder is to anxiety what a tornado is to a windy day. It strikes suddenly, wreaks havoc, and disappears. For the 1 person in 75 with this disorder, anxiety suddenly escalates into a terrifying *panic attack*—a minutes-long episode of intense fear that something horrible is about to happen. Heart palpitations, shortness of breath, choking sensations, trembling, or dizziness typically accompany the panic, which may be misperceived as a heart attack or other serious physical ailment. Smokers have a two- to fourfold risk of a first-time panic attack (Breslau & Klein, 1999; Goodwin & Hamilton, 2002; Insensee & others, 2003). Because nicotine is a stimulant, lighting up doesn't lighten up.

One woman recalled suddenly feeling "hot and as though I couldn't breathe. My heart was racing and I started to sweat and tremble and I was sure I was going to faint. Then my fingers started to feel numb and tingly and things seemed unreal. It was so bad I wondered if I was dying and asked my husband to take me to the emergency room. By the time we got there (about 10 minutes) the worst of the attack was over and I just felt washed out" (Greist & others, 1986). So unpredictable and frightening is this false-alarm experience that after several attacks, people come to fear the fear itself and to avoid situations where the panic has struck before.

Agoraphobia is fear or avoidance of situations in which escape might be difficult or help unavailable when panic strikes. Given such fear, people may avoid being outside the home, in a crowd, on a bus, or even on an elevator. After spending five years sailing the world, Charles Darwin began suffering panic disorder at age 28. Because of the attacks, he moved to the country, avoided social gatherings, and traveled only in his wife's company. But the relative seclusion did free him to focus on developing his evolutionary theory. "Even ill health," he reflected, "has saved me from the distraction of society and its amusements" (quoted in Ma, 1997).

Phobias

OBJECTIVE 7 | Explain how a phobia differs from the fears we all experience.

Phobias *focus* anxiety on a specific object, activity, or situation. (**FIGURE 16.2** ranks some common and less common fears and phobias.) A phobia is an irrational fear that disrupts behavior. Many people accept and live with this common psychological

FIGURE 16.2
Some common and uncommon fears
This national interview study identified the commonality of various fears. A strong fear becomes a phobia if it provokes a compelling but irrational desire to avoid the dreaded object or situation.
(From Curtis & others, 1998.)

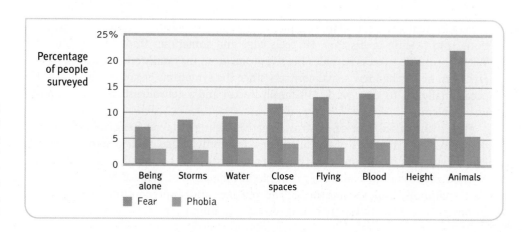

disorder, but some specific phobias can lead to incapacitating efforts to avoid the feared situation. Marilyn, a 28-year-old homemaker, is otherwise healthy and happy, but she so fears thunderstorms that she feels anxious as soon as a weather forecaster mentions possible storms later in the week. If her husband is away and a storm is forecast, she may stay with a close relative. During a storm, she hides from windows and buries her head to avoid seeing the lightning.

Other people suffer from irrational fears of specific animals, insects, heights, blood, or tunnels. Often they avoid the stimulus that arouses the fear, hiding during thunderstorms or avoiding high places. Potentially embarrassing social situations are difficult for those with a *social phobia,* an intense fear of being scrutinized by others. The anxious person may avoid speaking up, eating out, or going to parties—or will sweat, tremble, or have diarrhea when doing so. Social phobia is shyness taken to an extreme.

■ **obsessive-compulsive disorder (OCD)** an anxiety disorder characterized by unwanted repetitive thoughts (obsessions) and/or actions (compulsions).

Obsessive-Compulsive Disorder

OBJECTIVE **8** | Describe the symptoms of obsessive-compulsive disorder.

As with generalized anxiety and phobias, we can see aspects of our own behavior in **obsessive-compulsive disorder (OCD).** We may at times be obsessed with senseless or offensive thoughts that will not go away. Or we may engage in compulsive behaviors, rigidly checking, ordering, and cleaning before guests arrive, or lining up books and pencils "just so" before studying.

Obsessive thoughts and compulsive behaviors cross the fine line between normality and disorder when they become so persistent that they interfere with everyday living and cause the person distress. Checking to see that the door is locked is normal; checking 10 times is not. Washing your hands is normal; washing so often that your skin becomes raw is not. (**TABLE 16.2** offers more examples.) At some time during their lives, often during their late teens or twenties, 2 to 3 percent of people cross that line from normal preoccupations and fussiness to debilitating disorder (Karno & others, 1988). The obsessive thoughts become so haunting, the compulsive rituals so senselessly time-consuming, that effective functioning becomes impossible.

One such person was billionaire aviator Howard Hughes. Hughes compulsively dictated the same phrases over and over again. Under stress, he developed a phobic fear of germs, which led to compulsive behaviors. Hughes became reclusive and insisted his assistants carry out elaborate hand-washing rituals and wear white gloves when handling any document he would later touch. He ordered tape around doors and windows and forbade his staff to touch or even look at him. "Everybody carries germs around with them," he explained. "I want to live longer than my parents, so I avoid germs" (Fowler, 1986).

Snapshots

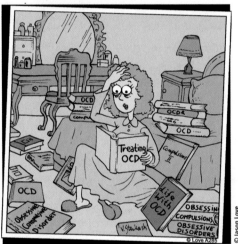

Obsessing about obsessive-compulsive disorder.

TABLE 16.2

COMMON OBSESSIONS AND COMPULSIONS AMONG CHILDREN AND ADOLESCENTS WITH OBSESSIVE-COMPULSIVE DISORDER

Thought or Behavior	Percentage Reporting Symptom
Obsessions (repetitive thoughts)	
Concern with dirt, germs, or toxins	40
Something terrible happening (fire, death, illness)	24
Symmetry, order, or exactness	17
Compulsions (repetitive behaviors)	
Excessive hand washing, bathing, tooth brushing, or grooming	85
Repeating rituals (in/out of a door, up/down from a chair)	51
Checking doors, locks, appliances, car brake, homework	46

Source: Adapted from Rapoport, 1989.

Warner Bros./The Kobal Collection

The Aviator

Howard Hughes, and his lifelong struggles with obsessive-compulsive disorder, were portrayed in this 2004 film starring Leonardo DiCaprio.

Although Hughes' symptoms worsened with age, older people are less often plagued by obsessive-compulsive disorder than are teens and young adults (Samuels & Nestadt, 1997). A 40-year follow-up study of 144 Swedish people diagnosed around 1950 found that, for most, the obsessions and compulsions had gradually lessened, though only 1 in 5 had completely recovered (Skoog & Skoog, 1999).

Post-Traumatic Stress Disorder

OBJECTIVE 9 | Describe the symptoms of post-traumatic stress disorder, and discuss survivor resiliency.

During the Iraq war, Jack's platoon was repeatedly under fire. In one ambush, his closest friend was killed while Jack stood a few feet away. Jack himself killed someone in an assault. Years later, images of these events intrude on him as flashbacks and nightmares. He still jumps at the sound of a firecracker or the backfire of a car. When annoyed by his family or friends, he lashes out in ways he seldom did before Iraq. To calm his continuing anxiety, he drinks more than he should.

Traumatic stress—experiencing or witnessing severely threatening, uncontrollable events with a sense of fear, helplessness, or horror—can produce **post-traumatic stress disorder (PTSD),** characterized by lingering symptoms including haunting memories and nightmares, a numbed social withdrawal, jumpy anxiety, and insomnia (Goodman & others, 1993; Kessler, 2000; Wilson & others, 1988). The more frequent and severe the assault experiences are, the more adverse the long-term outcomes tend to be (Golding, 1999). A sensitive limbic system that floods the body with stress hormones also increases vulnerability (Ozer & Weiss, 2004).

Many combat veterans, accident and disaster survivors, and sexual assault victims, including an estimated two-thirds of prostitutes, have experienced the symptoms of PTSD (Brewin & others, 1999; Farley & others, 1998; Taylor & others, 1998). After witnessing atrocities or living in life-threatening circumstances, children of the world's war zones and violent neighborhoods show similar symptoms (Garbarino, 1991, 1992). Their sense of basic trust erodes; many experience fearful wariness, troubled sleep, nightmares, and a sense of hopelessness about their future. This *learned helplessness* on the part of children who have repeatedly suffered abuse appears to make them more vulnerable to post-traumatic stress if assaulted as adults (Mineka & Zinbarg, 1996). Stretch a metal spring and it will snap back—unless stretched too far.

To pin down the frequency of PTSD, the U.S. Centers for Disease Control (1988) compared 7000 Vietnam combat veterans with 7000 noncombat veterans who served during the same years. Combat stress more than doubled a veteran's risk of alcohol abuse, depression, or anxiety. On average, 15 percent of all Vietnam veterans reported PTSD symptoms, but this rate was halved among those who had never seen combat and tripled among those who had experienced heavy combat. And among soldiers held captive in Vietnam, the more torture they suffered, the greater its psychological toll (Mollica & others, 1998). In the more recent Iraq war, one in six U.S. combat infantry has also reported symptoms of PTSD, depression, or severe anxiety in the months after returning home (Hoge & others, 2004).

Civilians, too, exhibit a stress *dose-response relationship.* PTSD rates vary from 4 percent among those who have experienced a natural disaster, to up to 50 percent among those who have been kidnapped, held captive, tortured, or raped (Brewin & others, 2000; Brody, 2000; Kessler, 2000). The greater one's emotional distress during a trauma, the higher the risk for post-traumatic symptoms (Ozer & others, 2003).

A month after the 9/11 terrorist attacks, a survey of Manhattan residents indicated that 8.5 percent were suffering PTSD, most as a result of the attack (Galea &

■ **post-traumatic stress disorder (PTSD)** an anxiety disorder characterized by haunting memories, nightmares, social withdrawal, jumpy anxiety, and/or insomnia that lingers for four weeks or more after a traumatic experience.

others, 2002). Among those living near the World Trade Center, 20 percent reported such telltale signs as nightmares, severe anxiety, and fear of public places (Susser & others, 2002).

Some psychologists, however, believe that PTSD is overdiagnosed, due partly to a broadening definition of *trauma* (which originally meant direct exposure to serious threat, such as combat or rape [McNally, 2003]). PTSD is actually infrequent, say the critics, and no good purpose is served by pathologizing normal stress reactions (Wakefield & Spitzer, 2002). "Debriefing" survivors right after a trauma by getting them to revisit the experience and vent emotions has actually proven generally ineffective and sometimes harmful (McNally & others, 2003; Rose & others, 2003). Sometimes reliving the trauma exacerbates one's emotions.

Researchers also point to the impressive *survivor resiliency* most people display (Bonanno, 2004, 2005). About half of adults experience at least one traumatic event in their lifetime, but only about 1 in 10 women and 1 in 20 men develop PTSD (Ozer & Weiss, 2004). More than 9 in 10 New Yorkers, although understandably stunned and grief-stricken by 9/11, did *not* respond pathologically, and by the following January the stress symptoms of the rest had mostly subsided (Galea & others, 2002). Similarly, most combat-stressed veterans and most political dissidents who survive dozens of episodes of torture do *not* later exhibit PTSD (Mineka & Zinbarg, 1996).

Toxic trauma
Stressed soldiers, such as these in Northern Ireland, are at risk for PTSD.

Psychologist Peter Suedfeld (1998, 2000), who as a boy survived the Holocaust under conditions of privation while his mother died in Auschwitz, has documented the resilience of Holocaust survivors, most of whom have lived productive lives. The successes of southeast Asians who escaped war and emigrated to America in small boats further testify to the "hardiness and resilience of the survivors," notes Suedfeld. "It is not always true that 'What doesn't kill you makes you stronger,' but it is often true; and, in addition, what doesn't kill you may reveal to you just how strong you really are."

Indeed, suffering can lead to what Richard Tedeschi and Lawrence Calhoun (2004) call *post-traumatic growth*. Tedeschi and Calhoun have found that the struggle with challenging crises often leads people later to report an increased appreciation for life, more meaningful relationships, increased personal strength, changed priorities, and a richer spiritual life. An ancient idea common to Judaism, Christianity, Hinduism, Buddhism, and Islam—that suffering has transformative power—is, they say, borne out in the lives of cancer survivors who take fresh delight in their children and the joy of each new day, and even of bereaved people who report gaining new sensitivities. Reflecting on his son's death, Rabbi Harold Kushner (1986) observed that "I am a more sensitive person, a more effective pastor, a more sympathetic counselor because of Aaron's life and death than I would ever have been without it," though adding that, even so, "I would give up all of those gains in a second if I could have my son back."

Explaining Anxiety Disorders

OBJECTIVE 10 | Discuss the contributions of the learning and biological perspectives to our understanding of the development of anxiety disorders.

Anxiety is both a feeling and a cognition—a doubt-laden appraisal of one's safety or social skill. How do these anxious feelings and cognitions arise? Sigmund Freud's psychoanalytic theory proposed that, beginning in childhood, people repress intolerable

John Coletti/Stock, Boston

An emotional high

Although we humans seem biologically predisposed to fear heights—certainly an adaptive response—this construction worker seems fearless. The biological perspective helps us understand why most people would be terrified in this situation.

impulses, ideas, and feelings and that this submerged mental energy sometimes produces mystifying symptoms such as anxiety. Many of today's psychologists have turned to two contemporary perspectives—learning and biological—for a more complete understanding.

The Learning Perspective

Fear Conditioning When bad events happen unpredictably and uncontrollably, anxiety often develops (Chorpita & Barlow, 1998). Researchers have linked general anxiety with classical conditioning of fear. In the laboratory, they have created chronically anxious, ulcer-prone rats by giving them unpredictable electric shocks (Schwartz, 1984). Like assault victims who report feeling anxious when entering their old neighborhoods, the rats become apprehensive in their lab environment. For many victims of PTSD, anxiety swells with any reminder of their trauma. Such experiences might help explain why anxious people are hyperattentive to possible threats, and how panic-prone people come to associate anxiety with certain cues (Bouton & others, 2001; Mineka & Zinbarg, 1996). In one survey, 58 percent of those with social phobia experienced their disorder after a traumatic event (Ost & Hugdahl, 1981).

Recall from Chapter 8 that dogs learn to fear neutral stimuli associated with shock, that infants come to fear furry objects associated with frightening noises, and that adults can become terrified of incidental stimuli linked with traumatic experiences. As infants become mobile they experience falls and near-falls—and become increasingly afraid of heights (Campos & others, 1992). Conditioned fears may remain long after we have forgotten the experiences that produced them (Jacobs & Nadel, 1985).

Through such conditioning, the short list of naturally painful and frightening events can multiply into a long list of human fears. My car was once struck by another whose driver missed a stop sign. For months afterward, I felt a twinge of unease when any car approached from a side street. Marilyn's phobia may have been similarly conditioned during a terrifying or painful experience associated with a thunderstorm. Two specific learning processes that might have contributed to her anxiety are stimulus generalization and reinforcement.

Stimulus generalization occurs, for example, when a person fears heights after a fall and later develops a fear of flying in an airplane without ever having flown. Once phobias and compulsions arise, *reinforcement* helps maintain them. Avoiding or escaping the feared situation reduces anxiety, thus reinforcing the phobic behavior. Feeling anxious or fearing a panic attack, a person may go inside and be reinforced by calmed anxiety (Antony & others, 1992). Compulsive behaviors similarly reduce anxiety. If washing your hands relieves your feelings of unease, you may wash your hands again when the feelings return.

Observational Learning We might also learn fear through observational learning—by observing others' fears. As we saw in Chapter 13, wild monkeys transmit their fear of snakes to their watchful offspring. Human parents similarly transmit fears to their children. Moreover, just observing someone receiving a mild electric shock after a conditioned stimulus produces fear learning similar to that produced by direct experience (Olsson & Phelps, 2004).

The Biological Perspective

There is, however, more to anxiety than simple conditioning or observational learning, as evident from how few people develop lasting phobias after suffering traumas. The biological perspective can broaden our understanding of anxiety disorders. It cannot explain the sharp increase in the anxiety levels of both children and college students over the last half-century, which appears related to such things as fraying social support accompanying family breakup (Twenge, 2000). But the biological perspective does help explain why we learn some fears more readily and why some individuals are more vulnerable.

Natural Selection We humans seem biologically prepared to fear threats faced by our ancestors. Most of our phobias focus on such objects: spiders, snakes, and other animals; closed spaces and heights; storms and darkness. (Those fearless about these occasional threats were less likely to survive and leave descendants.) It is easy to condition but hard to extinguish fears of such stimuli (Davey, 1995; Öhman, 1986). Many of our modern fears may also have an evolutionary explanation. For example, a fear of flying may also come from our biological past, which predisposes us to fear confinement and heights.

Moreover, consider what people tend *not* to learn to fear. World War II air raids produced remarkably few lasting phobias. As the air blitzes continued, the British, Japanese, and German populations became not more panicked, but rather more indifferent to planes outside of their immediate neighborhood (Mineka & Zinbarg, 1996). Evolution has not prepared us to fear bombs dropping from the sky.

Just as our phobias focus on dangers faced by our ancestors, our compulsive acts typically exaggerate behaviors that contributed to our species' survival. Grooming gone wild becomes hair pulling. Washing up becomes ritual hand washing. Checking territorial boundaries becomes checking and rechecking an already locked door (Rapoport, 1989).

Genes Some people more than others seem genetically predisposed to particular fears and high anxiety. Pair a traumatic event with a sensitive, high-strung temperament and the result may be a new phobia. Among monkeys, fearfulness runs in families. Individual monkeys react more strongly to stress if their close biological relatives are anxiously reactive (Suomi, 1986). The power of genes appears in studies of humans, too. Vulnerability to anxiety disorder rises when the afflicted relative is an identical twin (Barlow, 1988; Hettema & others, 2001; Kendler & others, 1992, 1999, 2002a,b). Identical twins often develop similar phobias, in some cases even when raised separately (Carey, 1990; Eckert & others, 1981). One pair of 35-year-old female identical twins independently developed claustrophobia. They also became so afraid of water that each would gingerly wade backward into the ocean, and then only up to the knees.

The Brain Generalized anxiety, panic attacks, and even obsessions and compulsions are biologically measurable as an overarousal of brain areas involved in impulse control and habitual behaviors. Brain scans of people with obsessive-compulsive disorder reveal elevated activity in specific brain areas associated with behaviors such as compulsive hand washing, checking, ordering, or hoarding (Mataix-Cols & others, 2004, 2005). As **FIGURE 16.3** shows, the *anterior cingulate cortex,* a brain region that monitors our actions and checks for errors, seems especially likely to be hyperactive in those with OCD (Ursu & others, 2003). When the disordered brain detects that something is amiss, it seems to generate a mental hiccup of repeating thoughts or actions (Gehring & others, 2000).

Fear-learning experiences can traumatize the brain, by creating fear circuits within the amygdala (Armony & others, 1998). Some antidepressant drugs dampen this fear-circuit activity and its associated obsessive-compulsive behavior. All in all, it is clear that biology is part of anxiety.

S. Ursu, V. A. Stenger, M. K. Shear, M. R. Jones, & C. S. Carter (2003). Overactive action monitoring in obsessive-compulsive disorder. *Psychological Science, 14,* 347–353.

FIGURE 16.3
An obsessive-compulsive brain
Neuroscientist Stefan Ursu and his colleagues (2003) used functional magnetic resonance imaging (fMRI) scans to compare the brains of those with and without OCD as they engaged in a challenging cognitive task. The fMRI scans showed elevated activity in the anterior cingulate cortex of those with OCD.

THINKING CRITICALLY ABOUT:

DISSOCIATION AND MULTIPLE PERSONALITIES

OBJECTIVE 11 | Describe the symptoms of dissociative disorders, and explain why some critics are skeptical about dissociative identity disorder.

Among the most bewildering disorders are the rare **dissociative disorders,** in which a person appears to experience a sudden loss of memory or change in identity. When a situation becomes overwhelmingly stressful, people are said to dissociate themselves from it. Their conscious awareness becomes separated from painful memories, thoughts, and feelings. (Note that this explanation presumes the existence of repressed memories, which have recently been questioned, as discussed in Chapters 9 and 15.)

Certain symptoms of dissociation are not so rare. Now and then, many people may have a sense of being unreal, of being separated from their body, of watching themselves as if in a movie. Sometimes we may say, "I was not myself at the time." Perhaps you can recall getting in your car and driving to some unintended location while your mind was preoccupied elsewhere. Facing trauma, such detachment may actually protect a person from being overwhelmed by emotion. Only when such experiences are severe and prolonged do they suggest a dissociative disorder.

The king of dissociative disorders is the presumed massive dissociation of self from ordinary consciousness in those with **dissociative identity disorder (DID).** These people are said to have two or more distinct identities that alternately control the person's behavior, with memory impairment across the different personality states. The person with this disorder may be prim and proper one moment and loud and flirtatious the next. Each personality has its own voice and mannerisms, and the original one typically denies any awareness of the other(s).

Although people diagnosed as having multiple personalities are usually not violent, there have been cases in which the person reportedly became dissociated into a "good" and a "bad" (or aggressive) personality—a modest version of the Dr. Jekyll/Mr. Hyde split immortalized in Robert Louis Stevenson's story. One unusual case involved Kenneth Bianchi, who was on trial for the "Hillside Strangler" rapes and murders of 10 California women. During a hypnosis session with Bianchi, psychologist John Watkins (1984) "called forth" a hidden personality: "I've talked a bit to Ken, but I think that perhaps there might be another part of Ken that I haven't talked to, another part that maybe feels somewhat differently from the part that I've talked to. . . . Would you talk with me, Part, by saying, 'I'm here'?" Bianchi answered "Yes" and then claimed to be "Steve."

When speaking as Steve, Bianchi stated that he hated Ken because Ken was nice and that he (Steve), aided by a cousin, had murdered women. He also claimed that Ken knew nothing about his existence and that Ken was innocent of the murders. Was Bianchi's second personality a ruse, simply a way of disavowing responsibility for his actions? Indeed, Bianchi—a practiced liar who had read about multiple personality in psychology books—was later convicted.

Exploring our capacity for personality shifts, Nicholas Spanos (1986, 1994, 1996) asked college students to

Multiple personalities
Chris Sizemore's story, *The Three Faces of Eve,* gave early visibility to what is now called *dissociative identity disorder.*

Lois Bernstein/Gamma Liaison

pretend they were accused murderers being examined by a psychiatrist. When given the same hypnotic treatment Bianchi received, most spontaneously expressed a second personality. This discovery made Spanos wonder: Are dissociative identities simply a more extreme version of our normal human capacity to vary the "selves" we present—as when we might display a goofy, loud self while hanging out with friends, and a subdued, respectful self around grandparents? Are clinicians who discover multiple personalities merely triggering role-playing by fantasy-prone people? If so, can such people then convince themselves of the authenticity of their own role enactments? Are they like actors, who commonly report "losing themselves" in their roles? (Recall from Chapter 7 that Spanos also raised these questions about the hypnotic state. Given that most DID patients are highly hypnotizable, whatever explains one condition—dissociation or role playing—may help explain the other.)

Pretense may become reality."

—Chinese proverb

Those who accept DID as a genuine disorder find support in the distinct brain and body states associated with differing personalities (Putnam, 1991). Handedness, too, sometimes switches with personality (Henninger, 1992). Subtle memories of one personality's experience sometimes fail to transfer to another personality (Eich & others, 1997). In one study, ophthalmologists detected shifting visual acuity and eye-muscle balance as patients switched personalities. These changes did not occur among control subjects trying to simulate DID (Miller & others, 1991).

Skeptics nevertheless find it suspicious that the disorder became so popular in the late twentieth century. In North America, the number of diagnoses exploded from only 2 reported cases per decade from 1930 to 1960, to more than 20,000 in the 1980s—when the DSM contained the first formal code for this disorder (McHugh, 1995a). The average number of displayed personalities also mushroomed—from 3 to 12 per patient (Goff & Simms, 1993). How could such a dramatic disorder have gone unnoticed for so long? Many clinicians have never encountered a case of DID, and the disorder is much less prevalent outside North

"Would it be possible to speak with the personality that pays the bills?"

America, although in other cultures some people are said to be "possessed" by an alien spirit (Aldridge-Morris, 1989; Kluft, 1991). In Britain, the diagnosis—which some consider "a wacky American fad" (Cohen, 1995)—is rare. In India and Japan, it is essentially nonexistent.

To skeptics, these findings point to a cultural phenomenon—a disorder created by therapists in a particular social context (Merskey, 1992). Patients do not enter therapy saying "Allow me to introduce myselves." Rather, note skeptics, some therapists go fishing for multiple personalities: "Have you ever felt like another part of you does things you can't control? Does this part of you have a name? Can I talk to the angry part of you?" Once patients permit a therapist to talk, by name, "to the part of you that says those angry things" they have begun acting out the fantasy. The result may be a real phenomenon, which vulnerable patients may experience as another self. Yet, say skeptics, "It is no coincidence," that multiple personality studies began among practitioners of hypnosis and that symptoms are most dramatic *after* beginning therapy (Goff, 1993; Piper, 1998).

With the dissociative disorders, as with the anxiety disorders, both psychoanalytic and learning perspectives see the symptoms as ways of dealing with anxiety. Psychoanalysts see them as defenses against the anxiety caused by the eruption of unacceptable impulses; a wanton second personality enables the discharge of forbidden impulses. Learning theorists see dissociative disorders as behaviors reinforced by anxiety reduction.

Others view dissociative disorders as post-traumatic disorders—a natural, protective response to

Though this be madness, yet there is method in 't."
—William Shakespeare, *Hamlet*, 1600

"histories of childhood trauma" (Putnam, 1995). Researchers debate whether most DID patients suffered physical, sexual, or emotional abuse as children (Gleaves, 1996; Kihlstrom, 2005; Lilienfeld & others, 1999). One study of 12 murderers diagnosed with DID did find that 11 of them had suffered severe, torturous child abuse (Lewis & others, 1997). One was set afire by his parents. Another was used in child pornography and was scarred from being made to sit on a stove burner. Perhaps, then, multiple personalities are the desperate efforts of the traumatized to detach from a horrific existence.

But then why, wonder the skeptics, did the children of the Holocaust, after enduring boxcars, concentration camps, and their parents' murders, not develop DID? Can the condition sometimes be contrived by fantasy-prone, emotionally vulnerable people, and constructed out of the therapist-patient interaction? If so, predicts psychiatrist Paul McHugh (1995b), "this epidemic will end in the way that the witch craze ended in Salem. The [multiple personality phenomenon] will be seen as manufactured."

■ **dissociative disorders** disorders in which conscious awareness becomes separated (dissociated) from previous memories, thoughts, and feelings.

■ **dissociative identity disorder (DID)** a rare dissociative disorder in which a person exhibits two or more distinct and alternating personalities. Also called *multiple personality disorder*.

>> LEARNING OUTCOMES

Anxiety Disorders and Dissociative Disorders

OBJECTIVE 5 | Define *anxiety disorders,* and explain how these conditions differ from normal feelings of stress, tension, or uneasiness.

Anxiety is part of our everyday experience. It is classified as a psychological disorder only when it becomes distressing or persistent or is characterized by maladaptive behaviors intended to reduce it.

OBJECTIVE 6 | Contrast the symptoms of generalized anxiety disorder and panic disorder.

People with *generalized anxiety disorder* (two-thirds of whom are women) feel persistently and uncontrollably tense and apprehensive and are in a state of autonomic nervous system arousal. They are unable to identify, or avoid, the cause of these feelings. People with *panic disorder* experience periodic minutes-long episodes of intense dread, which may include feelings of terror, chest pains, choking, or other frightening sensations. Anxiety is a component of both disorders, but the reactions in panic disorder are more extreme and may cause people to avoid situations where they have had panic attacks.

OBJECTIVE 7 | Explain how a phobia differs from the fears we all experience.

Phobias differ from normal fears in their extremity and their potential effect on behavior. People with a *phobia* experience such persistent and irrational fears that they may be incapacitated by their attempts to avoid a specific object, animal, or situation.

OBJECTIVE 8 | Describe the symptoms of obsessive-compulsive disorder.

Persistent and repetitive thoughts and actions that characterize *obsessive-compulsive disorder* interfere with everyday living and cause the person distress. The *obsession* (the repetitive thought) may, for example, be a concern with dirt, germs, or toxins; the *compulsion* (the repetitive action) may, for example, be excessive hand washing, bathing, or some other form of grooming.

OBJECTIVE 9 | Describe the symptoms of post-traumatic stress disorder, and discuss survivor resiliency.

Four or more weeks of haunting memories, nightmares, social withdrawal, jumpy anxiety, and sleep problems are symptoms of *PTSD* (*post-traumatic stress disorder*). These symptoms appear following some traumatic event or events the individual witnessed or experienced but could not control. Some people are more resilient than others. On average, only about 10 percent of women and 20 percent of men react to trauma by developing PTSD at some point in their lifetime. For those who survive the trauma, the experience can lead to a period of growth.

OBJECTIVE 10 | Discuss the contributions of the learning and biological perspectives to our understanding of the development of anxiety disorders.

Those working from the *learning perspective* view anxiety disorders as a product of fear conditioning, stimulus generalization, reinforcement of fearful behaviors, and observational learning of others' fear. Those working from the *biological perspective* consider the role that fears of life-threatening animals, objects, or situations played in natural selection and evolution; the genetic inheritance of a high level of emotional reactivity; and abnormal responses in the brain's fear circuits.

OBJECTIVE 11 | Describe the symptoms of dissociative disorders, and explain why some critics are skeptical about dissociative identity disorder.

Dissociative disorders are conditions in which conscious awareness seems to become separated from previous memories, thoughts, and feelings. The most famous dissociative disorder is *dissociative identity disorder,* commonly known as multiple personality disorder. Critics note that this diagnosis increased dramatically in the late twentieth century, that it is not found in many countries and is very rare in others, and that it may reflect role-playing by people who are very open to therapists' suggestions. Some view this disorder as a manifestation of feelings of anxiety, or as a response learned when behaviors are reinforced by reductions in feelings of anxiety.

ASK YOURSELF: Can you recall a fear that you have learned? What role, if any, was played by fear conditioning and by observational learning?

Mood Disorders

OBJECTIVE 12 | Define *mood disorders,* and contrast major depressive disorder and bipolar disorder.

■ **mood disorders** psychological disorders characterized by emotional extremes. See *major depressive disorder, mania,* and *bipolar disorder.*

The emotional extremes of **mood disorders** come in two principal forms: (1) *major depressive disorder,* in which the person experiences prolonged hopelessness and lethargy until usually rebounding to normality, and (2) *bipolar disorder* (formerly called *manic depressive disorder*), in which the person alternates between depression and *mania,* an overexcited, hyperactive state.

Major Depressive Disorder

Perhaps you know what depression feels like. If you are like most college students, at some time during this year—more likely the dark months of winter than the bright days of summer—you will probably experience a few of the symptoms of depression. You may feel deeply discouraged about the future, dissatisfied with your life, or isolated from others. You may lack the energy to get things done or even to force yourself out of bed; be unable to concentrate, eat, or sleep normally; or even wonder if you would be better off dead. Perhaps academic success came easily to you in high school, and now you find that disappointing grades jeopardize your goals. Maybe social stresses, such as feeling you don't belong or the breakup of a romance, have plunged you into despair. And maybe brooding has at times only worsened your self-torment.

You are not alone. Depression is the "common cold" of psychological disorders—an expression that effectively describes its pervasiveness but not its seriousness. Although phobias are more common, depression is the number one reason people seek mental health services. Moreover, it is the leading cause of disability worldwide (WHO, 2002). In any given year a depressive episode plagues 5.8 percent of men and 9.5 percent of women, reports the World Health Organization.

As anxiety is a response to the threat of future loss, depression is often a response to past and current loss. To feel bad in reaction to profoundly sad events (such as the death of a loved one) is to be in touch with reality. In such times, depression is like a car's low-oil-pressure light—a signal that warns us to stop and take protective measures. Recall that, biologically speaking, life's purpose is not happiness but survival and reproduction. To this end, coughing, vomiting, and various forms of pain protect the body from dangerous toxins. Similarly, depression is a sort of psychic hibernation: It slows us down, defuses aggression, and restrains risk taking (Allen & Badcock, 2003). To grind temporarily to a halt and ruminate, as depressed people do, is to reassess one's life when feeling threatened, and to redirect energy in more promising ways. From this perspective, there is sense to suffering.

But when does this response become seriously maladaptive? The line separating life's normal "downs" from major depression is difficult to draw. Joy, contentment, sadness, and despair are different points on a continuum, points at which any of us may be found at any given moment.

Major depressive disorder occurs when signs of depression (including lethargy, feelings of worthlessness, or loss of interest in family, friends, and activities) last two weeks or more and are not caused by drugs or a medical condition. The difference between a blue mood after bad news and a mood disorder is like the difference between gasping for breath for a few minutes after a hard run and being chronically short of breath. To sense what major depression feels like, suggest some clinicians, imagine combining the anguish of grief with the sluggishness of jet lag.

Between the temporary blue moods we all experience and the crushing impact of major depression is a condition called *dysthymic disorder*—a down-in-the-dumps mood that fills most of the day, nearly every day, for two years or more. Although less disabled than people with major depressions, those with dysthymic disorder tend to experience chronic low energy and self-esteem, have difficulty concentrating or making decisions, and sleep and eat too much or too little.

Bipolar Disorder

With or without therapy, episodes of major depression usually end, and people temporarily or permanently return to their previous behavior patterns. However, some people rebound to, or sometimes start with, the opposite emotional extreme—the euphoric, hyperactive, wildly optimistic state of **mania.** If depression is living in slow motion, mania is fast forward. Alternation between depression and mania signals **bipolar disorder.** During the manic phase of bipolar disorder, the person is typically overtalkative,

For some people, recurring depression during winter's dark months constitutes a seasonal affective disorder. For others, winter darkness means more blue moods. When asked "Have you cried today?" Americans answered "yes" more often in the winter:

	Percentage answering yes	
	Men	Women
August	4%	7%
December	8%	21%

*Source: Time/*CNN survey, 1994

"Depression . . . is well adapted to make a creature guard itself against any great or sudden evil."
Charles Darwin, *The Life and Letters of Charles Darwin*, 1887

"My life had come to a sudden stop. I was able to breathe, to eat, to drink, to sleep. I could not, indeed, help doing so; but there was no real life in me."
Leo Tolstoy, *My Confession*, 1887

■ **major depressive disorder** a mood disorder in which a person experiences, in the absence of drugs or a medical condition, two or more weeks of significantly depressed moods, feelings of worthlessness, and diminished interest or pleasure in most activities.

■ **mania** a mood disorder marked by a hyperactive, wildly optimistic state.

■ **bipolar disorder** a mood disorder in which the person alternates between the hopelessness and lethargy of depression and the overexcited state of mania. (Formerly called manic-depressive disorder.)

Creativity and bipolar disorders
History has given us many creative artists, composers, and writers with bipolar disorder, including (left to right) Walt Whitman, Virginia Woolf, Samuel Clemens (Mark Twain), and Ernest Hemingway.

"All the people in history, literature, art, whom I most admire: Mozart, Shakespeare, Homer, El Greco, St. John, Chekhov, Gregory of Nyssa, Dostoevsky, Emily Brontë: not one of them would qualify for a mental-health certificate."

Madeleine L'Engle, *A Circle of Quiet*, 1972

overactive, and elated (though easily irritated if crossed); has little need for sleep; and shows fewer sexual inhibitions. Speech is loud, flighty, and hard to interrupt.

One of mania's maladaptive symptoms is grandiose optimism and self-esteem, which may lead to reckless investments, spending sprees, and unsafe sex. Although people in a manic state find advice irritating, they need protection from their own poor judgment. In milder forms, however, the energy and free-flowing thinking of mania can fuel creativity. History offers many examples of creative bipolar people, from Walt Whitman and Ernest Hemingway to actress Margot Kidder. Bipolar disorder is especially common among creative artists and poets (Jamison, 1993, 1995; Kaufman & Baer, 2002). George Frideric Handel (1685–1759), who many believe suffered a mild form of bipolar disorder, composed his nearly four-hour-long *Messiah* during three weeks of intense, creative energy (Keynes, 1980). Robert Schumann composed 51 musical works during two years of mania (1840 and 1849) and none during 1844, when he was severely depressed (Slater & Meyer, 1959). Creative professionals who rely on precision and logic (architects, designers, journalists) less often suffer bipolar disorder than those who rely on emotional expression and vivid imagery (poets, novelists, entertainers), reports Arnold Ludwig (1995).

It is as true of emotions as of everything else: What goes up comes down. Before long, the elated mood either returns to normal or plunges into a depression. Though as maladaptive as major depression, bipolar disorder is much less common. Unlike major depression, it afflicts as many men as women.

Explaining Mood Disorders

OBJECTIVE 13 | Discuss the facts that an acceptable theory of depression must explain.

Because depression profoundly affects so many people, it understandably has been the subject of thousands of studies. Psychologists are working to develop a theory of mood disorders that will suggest more effective ways to treat and prevent them. Researcher Peter Lewinsohn and his colleagues (1985, 1998) summarized the facts that any theory of depression must explain. Among them are the following:

- **Many behavioral and cognitive changes accompany depression.** Depressed people are inactive and feel unmotivated. They are sensitive to negative happenings, expect negative outcomes, and more often recall negative information. In a depressed mood, we expect our team to lose, our grades to fall, our love to fail. When the depression lifts, these behavioral and cognitive accompaniments disappear. Nearly half the time, depressed people also exhibit symptoms of another disorder, such as anxiety or substance abuse.
- **Depression is widespread.** Its commonality suggests that its causes, too, must be common.
- **Compared with men, women are nearly twice as vulnerable to major depression** (**FIGURE 16.4**). In general, women are most vulnerable to disorders involving internalized states, such as depression, anxiety, and inhibited sexual desire. Men's

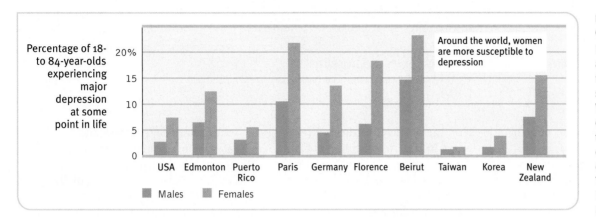

FIGURE 16.4
Gender and depression
Interviews with 38,000 adults in 10 countries confirm what many smaller studies have found: Women's risk of major depression is nearly double that of men's. Lifetime risk of depression also varies by culture—from 1.5 percent in Taiwan to 19 percent in Beirut. (Data from Weissman & others, 1996.)

disorders tend to be more external—alcohol abuse, antisocial conduct, lack of impulse control. When women get sad they often get sadder than men do. When men get mad, they often get madder than women do.

- *Most major depressive episodes self-terminate.* Therapy tends to speed recovery, yet most people suffering major depression eventually return to normal even without professional help. The plague of depression comes and, a few weeks or months later, it usually goes, though it sometimes recurs later.
- *Stressful events related to work, marriage, and close relationships often precede depression.* A family member's death, a job loss, a marital crisis, or a physical assault increase one's risk of depression. If stress-related anxiety is a "crackling, menacing brushfire," notes biologist Robert Sapolsky (2003), "depression is a suffocating heavy blanket thrown on top of it." One study followed 2000 people over time. It found that the risk of the onset of depression in the ensuing month ranged from less than 1 percent among those who had experienced no stressful life event to 24 percent among those with three such events (Kendler, 1998). The early loss of a parent due to death or separation also increases later vulnerability to depression (Agid & others, 1999).
- *With each new generation, the rate of depression is increasing, and the disorder is striking earlier (now often in the late teens).* This is true not only in Canada and the United States but also in Germany, Italy, France, Lebanon, New Zealand, Taiwan, and Puerto Rico (Cross-National Collaborative Group, 1992). In Australia, 12 percent of adolescents interviewed reported symptoms of depression. Most hid it from their parents; almost 90 percent of their parents perceived their depressed teen as *not* suffering depression (Sawyer & others, 2000). In North America, today's young adults are three times as likely as their grandparents to report having recently—or ever—suffered depression (despite the grandparents' many more years of being at risk). Asked "Have you ever felt that you were going to have a nervous breakdown?" 17 percent of Americans said "yes" in 1957, as did 24 percent in 1996 (Swindle & others, 2000). The increase appears partly authentic, but may also reflect today's young adults' greater willingness to disclose depression, as well as our tendency to forget many negative experiences over time.

About 50 percent of those who recover from depression will suffer another episode within two years. Recovery is more likely to be permanent the later the first episode strikes, the longer the person stays well, the fewer the previous episodes, the less stress experienced, and the more social support received (Belsher & Costello, 1988; Fergusson & Woodward, 2002; Kendler & others, 2001).

"I see depression as the plague of the modern era."
Lewis Judd, former chief, National Institute of Mental Health, 2000

Down Came the Rain
Actress Brooke Shields chronicled her disabling postpartum depression in this 2005 book.

CLOSE-UP:

SUICIDE

"But life, being weary of these worldly bars, Never lacks power to dismiss itself."
—William Shakespeare, *Julius Caesar,* 1599

Each year some 1 million despairing people worldwide will say no to life by electing a permanent solution to what may be a temporary problem (Mann, 2003; WHO, 2004). Comparing the suicide rates of different groups, researcher have found

- *national differences:* The suicide rates of England, Italy, and Spain are little more than half those of Canada, Australia, and the United States; Austria and Finnish suicide rates are about double (WHO, 2002a). Within Europe, the most suicide-prone people (Lithuanians) have been 15 times more likely to kill themselves than the least (Portuguese).
- *racial differences:* White Americans are nearly twice as likely as black Americans to kill themselves (NIMH, 2002).
- *gender differences:* Women are much more likely than men to attempt suicide. But men are two to four times more likely (depending

on the country) to succeed (**FIGURE 16.5**). (An exception is China, where women account for most suicides [WHO, 2002c]). Men are more likely to use lethal methods, such as firing a bullet into the head, the method of choice in 6 of 10 U.S. suicides. The more lethal a suicide attempt, the more depressed the frontal lobe's serotonin-based activity often is (Mann, 2003).

- *age differences and trends:* The suicide rate surges among older men (Figure 16.5). Across the Western world, suicide rates have also surged since 1960 among older teens, especially males (Eckersley & Dear, 2002). For American, Australian, British, Canadian, and New Zealand 15- to 25-year-olds, suicide rates all doubled or more than doubled in the 30 years after 1960, paralleling the increasing late-teen and early-twenties rates of anxiety and depression.

- *other group differences:* Suicide rates are much higher among the rich, the nonreligious, and those who are single, widowed, or divorced (Hoyer & Lund, 1993; Stack, 1992; Stengel, 1981). In both the United States and Australia, the teen suicide surge was almost entirely among males (Hassan & Carr, 1989). Gay and lesbian youth much more often suffer distress and attempt suicide than do their heterosexual peers (Goldfried, 2001).

Those who have been depressed have at least five times the general population's risk of suicide (Bostwick & Pankratz, 2000), but people seldom commit suicide while in the depths of depression, when energy and initiative are lacking. It is when they begin to rebound and become capable of following through that the risk increases. Teenage suicides may follow a traumatic event, such as a romantic breakup or a guilt-provoking antisocial

As you might expect, researchers understand and interpret these facts in ways that reflect their different perspectives. Psychoanalytic theory, applying Freud's ideas about the importance of early childhood experiences and unconscious impulses, suggested that depression occurs when significant losses evoke feelings associated with losses experienced in childhood. Loss of a romantic relationship or a job might evoke feelings associated with the loss of the intimate relationship with one's mother, for example. Alternatively, unresolved anger toward one's parents might be turned inward against the self. Today's biopsychosocial perspective is broadening our understanding with biological and cognitive explanations.

The Biological Perspective

OBJECTIVE 14 | Summarize the contributions of the biological perspective to the study of depression, and discuss the link between suicide and depression.

Most recent mental health research dollars have funded explorations of biological influences on mood disorders. Depression is a whole-body disorder. It involves genetic predispositions, biochemical imbalances, negative thoughts, and melancholy mood.

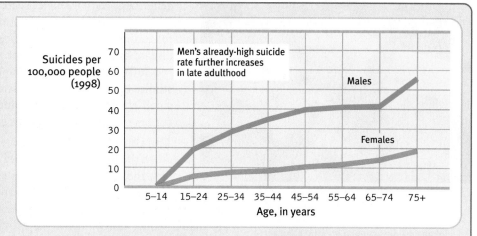

FIGURE 16.5
Suicide rates by gender and age
Worldwide suicide rates are higher among males than among females. The highest rates of all are found among older men. (From WHO, 2002a.)

act; they are often linked with drug and alcohol abuse (Fowler & others, 1986; Kolata, 1986). Compared with people who suffer no disorder, those addicted to alcohol are roughly 100 times more likely to commit suicide; some 3 percent of them do (Murphy & Wetzel, 1990). Even among those who have attempted suicide, those who abuse alcohol are five times more likely than others to kill themselves eventually (Beck & Steer, 1989).

Social suggestion may trigger the final act. Following highly publicized suicides and TV programs featuring suicide, known suicides increase. So do fatal auto "accidents" and private airplane crashes (page 732).

Suicide is not necessarily an act of hostility or revenge. The elderly sometimes choose death as an alternative to current or future suffering.

In people of all ages, suicide may be a way of switching off unendurable pain and relieving the perceived burden on family members (Joiner & others, 2002; Shneidman, 1987).

In retrospect, families and friends may recall signs that they believe should have forewarned them—verbal hints, giving possessions away, or withdrawal and preoccupation with death. But few who talk of suicide or think suicidal thoughts (a number that includes one-third of all adolescents and college students) actually attempt suicide, and few of those who

attempt it complete the act (Yip, 1998). The United States, for example, records about 30,000 suicides annually, but a half-million emergency room visits for attempted suicide (Surgeon General, 1999). One-third of those who kill themselves have tried to kill themselves previously. Most who do commit suicide have talked of it, and anyone who does threaten suicide is at least sending a signal of being desperate or feeling despondent. So, if a friend talks suicide, it's important to listen and to direct the friend to professional help.

Genetic Influences We have long known that mood disorders run in families. The risk of major depression and bipolar disorder increases if you have a depressed parent or sibling (Sullivan & others, 2000). If one identical twin is diagnosed with major depressive disorder, the chances are about 1 in 2 that at some time the other twin will be, too. If one identical twin has bipolar disorder, the chances are 7 in 10 that the other twin will at some point be diagnosed similarly. Among fraternal twins, the corresponding odds are just under 2 in 10 (Tsuang & Faraone, 1990). The greater similarity of identical twins' depressive tendencies also occurs among twins reared apart (DiLalla & others, 1996). Moreover, adopted people who suffer a mood disorder often have close biological relatives who suffer mood disorders, become dependent on alcohol, or commit suicide (Wender & others, 1986). (Close-Up: Suicide reports other research findings on suicide.)

A search for the genes that put people at risk for depression is now under way. To tease out which genes are implicated, researchers use *linkage analysis*. First, they find families that have had the disorder across several generations. Then they draw blood from both affected and unaffected family members and examine their DNA, looking for differences. Linkage analysis points us to a chromosome neighborhood,

Gene-hunters' pursuit of bipolar-DNA links

Linkage studies seek to identify aberrant genes in family members suffering the disorder. These Pennsylvania Amish family members—an isolated population sharing a common life-style and some vulnerability to the disorder—have been among the volunteer participants.

note behavior genetics researchers Robert Plomin and Peter McGuffin (2003); "a house-to-house search is then needed to find the culprit gene." *Association studies* search for correlations between more specific DNA variation and a population trait. One such DNA variation occurs, for example, in about 40 percent of people with late-onset Alzheimer's disease and about 15 percent of those without Alzheimer's (Plomin & McGuffin, 2003). The anticipated outcome of linkage and association studies in research on depression is a complex picture: Many genes have small effects that can combine with one another and with nongenetic factors to put some people at greater risk.

The Depressed Brain Genes act by directing biochemical events that, down the line, influence behavior. The biochemical key is neurotransmitters, those messenger molecules that shuttle signals between nerve cells.

Norepinephrine, a neurotransmitter that increases arousal and boosts mood, is scarce during depression and overabundant during mania. (Drugs that alleviate mania reduce norepinephrine.) Most people with a history of depression also have a history of habitual smoking. This may indicate an attempt to self-medicate with inhaled nicotine, which can temporarily increase norepinephrine and boost mood (HMHL, 2002).

A second neurotransmitter, *serotonin,* is also scarce during depression. Drugs that relieve depression tend to increase norepinephrine or serotonin supplies by blocking either their reuptake (as Prozac, Zoloft, and Paxil do with serotonin) or their chemical breakdown. Repetitive physical exercise, such as jogging, reduces depression as it increases serotonin (Jacobs, 1994).

Some of the genes under scrutiny provide codes for neurotransmitter systems such as serotonin (Plomin & McGuffin, 2003). One large study identified New Zealand young adults who had experienced several major stresses, such as a relationship breakup or a family death. These stressed individuals were much more likely to suffer depression if they carried a variation of a gene that codes for a protein that controls serotonin activity (Caspi & others, 2003). As we have seen so often throughout this book, genes and environments—nature and nurture—interact to form us.

People with depression have also recently been observed to have lower levels in their diet and blood of a "good" fat, *omega-3 fatty acid,* believed to enhance brain function (Edwards & others, 1998; Maes & others, 1999). Countries such as Japan, where people eat omega-3–rich fish, tend to have low depression rates (Hibbeln, 1998). Future research may determine whether eating more fish, walnuts, and other foods rich in omega-3 supports mental health.

Using modern scanning machines, researchers are also spotting neurological signs of depression. In many recent studies, the brain shows less activity during periods of depression, indicating a slowed-down state, and more activity during periods of mania (**FIGURE 16.6**). The left frontal lobe, which is active during positive emotions, is likely to be inactive during depressed states (Davidson & others, 2002). In

FIGURE 16.6
The ups and downs of bipolar disorder
PET scans show that brain energy consumption rises and falls with the patient's emotional switches. Red areas are where the brain rapidly consumes glucose.

 Depressed state (May 17)

 Manic state (May 18)

 Depressed state (May 27)

one study of people with severe depression, MRI scans found their frontal lobes 7 percent smaller than normal (Coffey & others, 1993). The *hippocampus,* a memory-processing center linked with the brain's emotional circuitry, is vulnerable to stress-related damage. By boosting serotonin, which stimulates hippocampus neuron growth, antidepressant drugs may promote recovery from depression (Jacobs & others, 2000).

The Social-Cognitive Perspective

OBJECTIVE 15 | Summarize the contributions of the social-cognitive perspective to the study of depression, and describe the events in the cycle of depression.

Some people slide into depression for no obvious reason, even when life has been going well. But as we have noted, biological risk factors can predispose psychological reactions to stressful experiences (**FIGURE 16.7**). And the mind's negative thoughts somehow influence biological events that in a vicious cycle amplify depressing thoughts.

Depressed people view life through dark glasses. Their intensely negative assumptions about themselves, their situation, and their future lead them to magnify bad experiences and minimize good ones. Listen to Norman, a Canadian college professor, recalling his depression:

> I [despaired] of ever being human again. I honestly felt subhuman, lower than the lowest vermin. Furthermore, I was self-deprecatory and could not understand why anyone would want to associate with me, let alone love me. . . . I was positive that I was a fraud and a phony and that I didn't deserve my Ph.D. I didn't deserve to have tenure; I didn't deserve to be a Full Professor. . . . I didn't deserve the research grants I had been awarded; I couldn't understand how I had written books and journal articles. . . . I must have conned a lot of people. (Endler, 1982, pp. 45–49)

Research reveals how *self-defeating beliefs* and a *negative explanatory style* feed depression's vicious cycle.

Negative Thoughts and Negative Moods Interact Self-defeating beliefs may arise from *learned helplessness.* As we saw in Chapter 15, both dogs and humans act depressed, passive, and withdrawn after experiencing uncontrollable painful events. Gender differences in uncontrollable stress help explain why, beginning in their early teens, women are nearly twice as vulnerable to depression (Kessler, 2001). Women

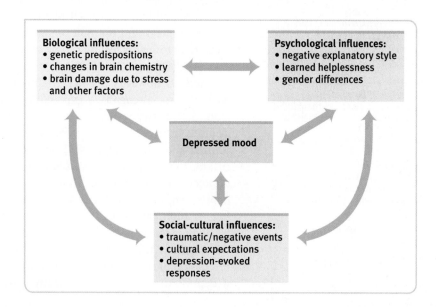

FIGURE 16.7
Biopsychosocial approach to depression
Seriously depressed moods result from a combination of factors, which affect each other. Altering any one component can alter the others.

more often than men have been abused or made to feel helpless, and they may respond more strongly to stress (Hankin & Abramson 2001; Mazure & others, 2002; Nolen-Hoeksema, 2001, 2003). Thirty-six percent of women and 16 percent of men entering American colleges feel "frequently overwhelmed by all I have to do" (Sax & others, 2004). (Men report spending more of their time in "light anxiety" activities such as sports, TV watching, and partying, possibly avoiding activities that might make them feel overwhelmed.)

But why do life's unavoidable failures lead some people and not others to become depressed? The difference lies partly with people's explanatory style. We have some choice of whom or what to blame for our failures. If you fail a test and blame yourself, you may feel stupid and depressed. If you externalize the blame—perhaps attributing your failure to an unfair test—you are more likely to feel angry.

Depressed people tend to explain bad events in terms that are stable ("It's going to last forever"), global ("It's going to affect everything I do"), and internal ("It's all my fault") (**FIGURE 16.8**). Lyn Abramson, Gerald Metalsky, and Lauren Alloy (1989) theorized that the result of these pessimistic, overgeneralized, self-blaming attributions is a depressing sense of hopelessness. If you tend to see bad grades, social rejection, and work problems as inevitable and your own fault, and if you ruminate about such things, then when bad things happen you will probably experience the blues.

What might you expect of new college students who are not depressed but do exhibit a pessimistic explanatory style (some of whom are about to complete Seligman's depression recipe: pessimism encountering failure)? Lauren Alloy and her collaborators (1999) monitored Temple University and University of Wisconsin students every 6 weeks for 2.5 years. Among those identified as having pessimistic thinking styles, 17 percent had a first episode of major depression, as did only 1 percent of those who began college with optimistic thinking styles. Follow-up research has found that students who exhibit optimism as they begin college develop more social support, which contributes to a lowered risk of depression (Brissette & others, 2002).

Martin Seligman (1991, 1995) argues that depression is common among young Westerners because of epidemic hopelessness stemming from the rise of individualism and the decline of commitment to religion and family. When facing failure or rejection, contends Seligman, the self-focused individual takes on personal responsibility for problems and has nothing to fall back on for hope. In non-Western cultures, where close-knit relationships and cooperation are the norm, major depression is less common and less tied to self-blame over personal failure. In Japan, for example, depressed people instead tend to report feeling shame over letting others down (Draguns, 1990a).

There is, however, a chicken-and-egg problem with the social-cognitive explanation of depression. Self-defeating beliefs, negative attributions, and self-blame surely do support depression. Peter Barnett and Ian Gotlib (1988) note that such cognitions *coincide* with a depressed mood and are *indicators* of depression. But do they *cause* depression, any more than a speedometer's reading 70 mph causes a car's speed? Before or after being depressed, people's thoughts are less negative. Perhaps this is because, as we noted in our discussion of state-dependent memory (page 375), a depressed mood triggers negative thoughts. If

> "I have learned to accept my mistakes by referring them to a personal history which was not of my making."
>
> B. F. Skinner (1983)

FIGURE 16.8
Explanatory style and depression

PEANUTS

Reprinted by permission of United Feature Syndicate, Inc.

Might Charlie Brown be helped by an optimism-training program?

you temporarily put people in a bad or sad mood, their memories, judgments, and expectations suddenly become more pessimistic.

Joseph Forgas and his associates (1984) provided a striking demonstration of the mood effect. First, they videotaped people talking to each other. The next day, they put those participants in a good or bad mood via hypnosis and had them watch the videotape of themselves. The happy participants detected in their screen selves more positive than negative behaviors; the unhappy participants more often saw themselves behaving negatively. Thus, even when watching themselves on videotape, mildly depressed people judge themselves more negatively.

Depression's Vicious Cycle "A recipe for severe depression is preexisting pessimism encountering failure," notes Martin Seligman (1991, p. 78). Depression, as we have seen, is often brought on by stressful experiences—losing a job, getting divorced or rejected, suffering physical trauma—anything that disrupts your sense of who you are and why you are a worthy human being. We have also seen that depression can be adaptive, a time for lying low and gaining insights that can later lead to more effective strategies for interacting with the world. But depression-prone people respond to bad events in an especially self-focused, self-blaming way (Mor & Winquist, 2002; Pyszczynski & others, 1991; Wood & others, 1990a,b). Their self-esteem fluctuates more rapidly up with boosts and down with threats (Butler & others, 1994). When down, their brooding amplifies their negative feelings, which in turn trigger depression's other cognitive and behavioral symptoms.

This cycle also helps explain women's doubled risk of depression. When trouble strikes, men tend to act, women tend to think—and often to *overthink,* as Susan Nolen-Hoeksema (2003) describes their rumination. Women often have vivid recall for both wonderful and horrid experiences; men more vaguely recall such experiences (Seidletz & Diener, 1998). This gender difference in emotional memory may feed women's greater rumination over negative events and explain why fewer men than women reported being "frequently overwhelmed on entering college."

None of us is immune to the dejection, diminished self-esteem, and negative thinking brought on by rejection or defeat. As Edward Hirt and his colleagues (1992) demonstrated, even small losses can temporarily sour our thinking. They studied some avid Indiana University basketball fans who seemed to regard the team as an extension of themselves. After the fans watched their team lose or win, the researchers asked them to predict the team's future performance and their own. After a loss, the morose fans offered bleaker assessments not only of the team's future, but also of their own likely performance at throwing darts, solving anagrams, and getting a date. When things aren't going our way, it may seem as though they never will.

But being withdrawn, self-focused, and complaining can elicit rejection (Furr & Funder, 1998; Gotlib & Hammen, 1992). In one study, researchers Stephen Strack and James Coyne (1983) noted that "depressed persons induced hostility, depression, and anxiety in others and got rejected. Their guesses that they were not accepted were not a matter of cognitive distortion." Weary of the person's fatigue, hopeless attitude, and lethargy, a spouse may threaten to leave or a boss may begin to question the person's competence. Indeed, people in the throes of depression are at high risk for

> "Man never reasons so much and becomes so introspective as when he suffers, since he is anxious to get at the cause of his sufferings."
>
> Luigi Pirandello, *Six Characters in Search of an Author,* 1922

Susan Nolen-Hoeksema

"This epidemic of morbid meditation is a disease that women suffer much more than men. Women can ruminate about anything and everything—our appearance, our families, our career, our health." (*Women Who Think Too Much: How to Break Free of Overthinking and Reclaim Your Life,* 2003)

Michael Marsland

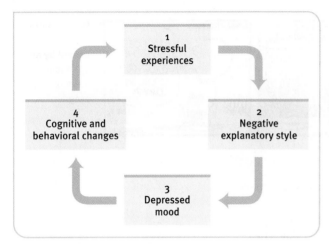

FIGURE 16.9
The vicious cycle of depressed thinking
Cognitive therapists attempt to break this cycle, as we will see in Chapter 17, by changing the way depressed people process events. Psychiatrists attempt to alter with medication the biological roots of persistently depressed moods.

divorce, job loss, and other stressful life events. (This provides another example of genetic–environmental interaction: People genetically disposed to depression more often experience depressing events.) The losses and stress only serve to compound the original depression. Rejection and depression feed each other. Misery may love another's company, but company does not love another's misery.

We can now assemble some of the pieces of the depression puzzle (**FIGURE 16.9**): (1) Negative, stressful events interpreted through (2) a ruminating, pessimistic explanatory style create (3) a hopeless, depressed state that (4) hampers the way the person thinks and acts. This, in turn, fuels (1) negative experiences such as rejection.

It is a cycle we can all recognize. Bad moods feed on themselves: When we *feel* down, we *think* negatively and remember bad experiences. On the brighter side, we can break the cycle of depression at any of these points—by moving to a different environment, by reversing our self-blame and negative attributions, by turning our attention outward, or by engaging in more pleasant activities and more competent behavior.

Winston Churchill called depression a "black dog" that periodically hounded him. Poet Emily Dickinson was so afraid of bursting into tears in public that she spent much of her adult life in seclusion (Patterson, 1951). Abraham Lincoln was so withdrawn and brooding as a young man that his friends feared he might take his own life (Kline, 1974). As each of these lives reminds us, people can and do struggle through depression. Most regain their capacity to love, to work, and even to succeed at the highest levels.

>> LEARNING OUTCOMES

Mood Disorders

OBJECTIVE 12 | Define *mood disorders,* and contrast major depressive disorder and bipolar disorder.

Mood disorders are characterized by emotional extremes. A person with *major depressive disorder* experiences two or more weeks of seriously depressed moods and feelings of worthlessness, takes little interest in most activities, and derives little pleasure from them. These feelings are not caused by drugs or a medical condition. Although less disabling, *dysthymic disorder* is marked by two years of chronic low energy and poor self-esteem. People with *bipolar disorder* alternate between depression and mania, a hyperactive and wildly optimistic impulsive state. Major depressive disorder is much more common than is bipolar disorder.

OBJECTIVE 13 | Discuss the facts that an acceptable theory of depression must explain.

An acceptable theory of depression must account for the many behavioral and cognitive changes that accompany depression; its widespread occurrence; women's greater susceptibility to the disorder; the tendency of depressive episodes to self-terminate; the link between stressful events and the onset of depression; and the increasing rates and earlier onset of depression.

OBJECTIVE 14 | Summarize the contributions of the biological perspective to the study of depression, and discuss the link between suicide and depression.

The biological perspective on depression focuses on genetic influences, in part through *linkage analysis* and *association studies.* Researchers working from this perspective also study abnormalities in brain structure and function, including those found in neurotransmitter systems. Their work has shown that a predisposition to depression does run in some families, that the neurotransmitters norepinephrine and serotonin are scarce during depression, that activity in the left frontal lobes is slowed during depression, and that stress-related damage to the hippocampus increases the risk of depression. Despair drives some people to suicide, and the risk is greatest when their energy returns as the depression begins to lift.

OBJECTIVE 15 | **Summarize the contributions of the social-cognitive perspective to the study of depression, and describe the events in the cycle of depression.**

The social-cognitive perspective has drawn attention to the power of self-defeating beliefs (arising in part from learned helplessness), and negative explanatory styles that view bad events as stable, global, and internally caused. Critics note that these characteristics may coincide with depression but not cause it. The cycle of depression consists of (1) negative stressful events (2) interpreted through a pessimistic explanatory style, creating a (3) hopeless depressed state, which (4) hampers the way the person thinks and acts, fueling more negative stressful events, such as rejection.

ASK YOURSELF: **Has your entry into college life been a challenging time for you? What advice would you have for future collegians?**

Schizophrenia

If depression is the common cold of psychological disorders, chronic schizophrenia is the cancer. Nearly 1 in 100 people will develop schizophrenia, joining the estimated 24 million across the world who suffer one of humanity's most dreaded disorders (WHO, 2002d). It typically strikes as young people are maturing into adulthood, it knows no national boundaries, and it affects both males and females—though men tend to be struck earlier, more severely, and slightly more often (Aleman & others, 2003).

Symptoms of Schizophrenia

OBJECTIVE 16 | Describe the symptoms of schizophrenia, and differentiate delusions and hallucinations.

Literally translated, **schizophrenia** means "split mind." It refers not to a multiple-personality split but rather to a split from reality that shows itself in disorganized thinking, disturbed perceptions, and inappropriate emotions and actions.

Disorganized Thinking

Imagine trying to communicate with Maxine, a young woman whose thoughts spill out in no logical order. Her biographer, Susan Sheehan (1982, p. 25), observed her saying aloud to no one in particular, "This morning, when I was at Hillside [Hospital], I was making a movie. I was surrounded by movie stars . . . I'm Mary Poppins. Is this room painted blue to get me upset? My grandmother died four weeks after my eighteenth birthday."

As this strange monologue illustrates, the thinking of a person with schizophrenia is fragmented, bizarre, and distorted by false beliefs, called **delusions** ("I'm Mary Poppins"). Those with *paranoid* tendencies are particularly prone to delusions of persecution. Jumping from one idea to another may occur even within sentences, creating a

■ **schizophrenia** a group of severe disorders characterized by disorganized and delusional thinking, disturbed perceptions, and inappropriate emotions and actions.

■ **delusions** false beliefs, often of persecution or grandeur, that may accompany psychotic disorders.

August Natterer, *Witch's Head.* The Prinzhorn Collection, University of Heidelberg

L. Berthold, *Untitled.* The Prinzhorn Collection, University of Heidelberg

Photos of paintings by Krannert Museum, University of Illinois at Urbana-Champaign

sort of "word salad." One young man begged for "a little more allegro in the treatment," and suggested that "liberationary movement with a view to the widening of the horizon" will "ergo extort some wit in lectures."

Many psychologists believe disorganized thoughts result from a breakdown in selective attention. Recall from Chapter 6 that we normally have a remarkable capacity for selective attention—for, say, giving our undivided attention to one voice at a party while filtering out competing sensory stimuli. Those with schizophrenia cannot do this. Thus, an irrelevant stimulus or an extraneous part of the preceding thought easily distracts them. Minute stimuli, such as the grooves on a brick or the inflections of a voice, may distract their attention from the whole scene or from the speaker's meaning. As one former patient recalled, "What had happened to me . . . was a breakdown in the filter, and a hodge-podge of unrelated stimuli were distracting me from things which should have had my undivided attention" (MacDonald, 1960, p. 218). This selective attention difficulty is but one of dozens of cognitive differences associated with schizophrenia. Others range from deficiencies in working memory to the ability to smoothly follow a swinging pendulum with the eyes, a task that requires the coordination of several brain regions (Heinrichs, 2005).

Disturbed Perceptions

A person with schizophrenia may perceive things that are not there. Such *hallucinations* (sensory experiences without sensory stimulation) are usually auditory and often take the form of voices making insulting statements or giving orders. The voices may tell the patient that she is bad or that she must burn herself with a cigarette lighter. Less commonly, people see, feel, taste, or smell things that are not there. Hallucinations have been compared to dreams breaking into waking consciousness. When the unreal seems real, the resulting perceptions are at best bizarre, at worst terrifying.

Inappropriate Emotions and Actions

The emotions of schizophrenia are often utterly inappropriate. Maxine's emotions seemed split off from reality. She laughed after recalling her grandmother's death. On occasion, she became angry for no apparent reason or cried when others laughed. Other victims of schizophrenia sometimes lapse into *flat affect,* a zombielike state of apparent apathy.

Motor behavior may also be inappropriate. The person may perform senseless, compulsive acts, such as continually rocking or rubbing an arm. Those who exhibit *catatonia* may remain motionless for hours on end and then become agitated.

As you can imagine, such disorganized thinking, disturbed perceptions, and inappropriate emotions and actions profoundly disrupt social relationships and make it difficult to hold a job. During their most severe periods, people with schizophrenia live in a private inner world, preoccupied with illogical ideas and unreal images. Given a supportive environment, some eventually recover to enjoy a normal life or experience bouts of schizophrenia only intermittently. Others remain socially withdrawn and isolated throughout much of their lives, and their frequent hospitalizations help explain why many countries devote about 2 percent of their national health budget to care and treatment of those with schizophrenia (Knapp & others, 2004).

Subtypes of Schizophrenia

OBJECTIVE **17** | Distinguish the five subtypes of schizophrenia, and contrast chronic and acute schizophrenia.

We have thus far described schizophrenia as if it were a single disorder. Actually, it is a cluster of disorders. The subtypes share some common features, but they also have some distinguishing symptoms (**TABLE 16.3**). Schizophrenia patients with *positive symptoms* may experience hallucinations, talk in disorganized and deluded ways, and exhibit inappropriate laughter, tears, or rage. Those with *negative symptoms* have toneless voices, expressionless faces, or mute and rigid bodies. Thus, positive symptoms are the *presence* of inappropriate behaviors, and negative symptoms are the *absence* of appropriate behaviors. Because schizophrenia is a cluster of disorders, these varied symptoms could have more than one cause.

Sometimes, as in the case of Maxine, schizophrenia develops gradually, emerging from a long history of social inadequacy (which helps explain why those predisposed to schizophrenia often end up in the lower socioeconomic levels, or even homeless). Other times it appears suddenly, seemingly as a reaction to stress. One rule holds true around the world (World Health Organization, 1979): When schizophrenia is a slow-developing process (called *chronic,* or *process,* schizophrenia), recovery is doubtful. When a previously well-adjusted person develops schizophrenia rapidly (called *acute,* or *reactive,* schizophrenia) in reaction to particular life stresses, recovery is much more likely. Those with chronic schizophrenia often exhibit the negative symptom of withdrawal. Men, whose schizophrenia develops on average four years earlier than women's, more often exhibit negative symptoms and chronic schizophrenia (Räsänen & others, 2000). The outlook is better for those with positive symptoms—they more often have a reactive condition that responds to drug therapy (Fenton & Mc-Glashan, 1991, 1994; Fowles, 1992).

"When someone asks me to explain schizophrenia I tell them, you know how sometimes in your dreams you are in them yourself and some of them feel like real nightmares? My schizophrenia was like I was walking through a dream. But everything around me was real. At times, today's world seems so boring and I wonder if I would like to step back into the schizophrenic dream, but then I remember all the scary and horrifying experiences."

Stuart Emmons, with Craig Geisler, Kalman J. Kaplan, and Martin Harrow, *Living With Schizophrenia*, 1997

TABLE 16.3

SUBTYPES OF SCHIZOPHRENIA

Paranoid:	Preoccupation with delusions or hallucinations, often with themes of persecution or grandiosity
Disorganized:	Disorganized speech or behavior, or flat or inappropriate emotion
Catatonic:	Immobility (or excessive, purposeless movement), extreme negativism, and/or parrotlike repeating of another's speech or movements
Undifferentiated:	Many and varied symptoms
Residual:	Withdrawal, after hallucinations and delusions have disappeared

Understanding Schizophrenia

Schizophrenia is not only the most dreaded psychological disorder but also one of the most heavily researched. Most of the new research studies link it with brain abnormalities and genetic predispositions. Schizophrenia is a disease of the brain exhibited in symptoms of the mind.

Brain Abnormalities

OBJECTIVE 18 | Outline some abnormal brain chemistry, functions, and structures associated with schizophrenia, and discuss the possible link between prenatal viral infections and schizophrenia.

Might imbalances in brain chemistry underlie schizophrenia? Scientists have long known that strange behavior can have strange chemical causes. The saying "mad as a hatter" refers to the psychological deterioration of British hatmakers whose brains, it was later discovered, were slowly poisoned as they moistened the brims of mercury-laden felt hats with their lips (Smith, 1983). As we saw on page 302, scientists are clarifying the mechanism by which chemicals such as LSD produce hallucinations. These discoveries hint that schizophrenia symptoms might have a biochemical key.

Dopamine Overactivity Researchers discovered one such key when they examined schizophrenia patients' brains after death, and found an excess of receptors for *dopamine*—a sixfold excess for the so-called D4 dopamine receptor (Seeman & others, 1993; Wong & others, 1986). They speculate that such a high level may intensify brain signals in schizophrenia, creating positive symptoms such as hallucinations and paranoia. As we might therefore expect, drugs that block dopamine receptors often lessen these symptoms; drugs that increase dopamine levels, such as amphetamines and cocaine, sometimes intensify them (Swerdlow & Koob, 1987). Dopamine overactivity may underlie patients' overreactions to irrelevant external and internal stimuli.

Dopamine-blocking drugs have little effect on persistent negative symptoms of withdrawal. Researchers are now exploring another neurotransmitter, *glutamate,* which directs neurons to pass along an impulse. Impaired glutamate activity appears to be another source of schizophrenia symptoms (Javitt & Coyle, 2004). Drugs that interfere with glutamate receptors can produce schizophrenialike negative symptoms. Moreover, medications that neutralize the effect of such street drugs also seem to alleviate negative symptoms (HMHL, 2001).

Abnormal Brain Activity and Anatomy Modern brain-scanning techniques reveal that many people with chronic schizophrenia have abnormal activity in multiple brain areas. Some have abnormally low brain activity in the frontal lobes, which are critical for reasoning, planning, and problem solving (Morey & others, 2005; Pettegrew & others, 1993; Resnick, 1992). People diagnosed with schizophrenia also display a noticeable decline in the brain waves that reflect synchronized neural firing in the frontal lobes (Spencer & others, 2004; Symond & others, 2005). Out-of-sync neurons may disrupt the integrated functioning of neural networks, possibly contributing to schizophrenia symptoms.

One study took PET scans of brain activity while people were hallucinating (Silbersweig & others, 1995). When participants heard a voice or saw something, their brains became vigorously active in several core regions, including the thalamus, a structure deep in the brain that filters incoming sensory signals and transmits them to the cortex. Another PET scan study of people with paranoia found increased activity in a fear-processing center, the amygdala (Epstein & others, 1998).

Many studies have found enlarged, fluid-filled areas and a corresponding shrinkage of cerebral tissue in people with schizophrenia (Wright & others, 2000), and one study even found such abnormalities in the brains of people who would *later* develop

About 60 percent of schizophrenia patients smoke, often heavily. Nicotine apparently stimulates certain brain receptors, which helps focus attention (Javitt & Coyle, 2004).

Studying the neurophysiology of schizophrenia
Psychiatrist E. Fuller Torrey is collecting the brains of hundreds of those who died as young adults and suffered disorders such as schizophrenia and bipolar disorder. Torrey is making tissue samples available to researchers worldwide.

Chris Usher

Tissue loss in normal adolescents

Tissue loss in adolescents with schizophrenia

Average annual loss

0%
-1%
-2%
-3%
-4%
-5%

Paul Thompson and Arthur W. Toga, UCLA Laboratory of Neuro Imaging and Judith L. Rapoport, National Institute of Mental Health

FIGURE 16.10
Schizophrenia and the shrinking brain.
Among adolescents who suffer a relatively rare childhood-onset schizophrenia, MRI scans by Paul Thompson and his colleagues (2001) revealed a much-greater-than-normal loss of cerebral cortex tissue between the ages of 13 and 18.

this disorder (Pantelis & others, 2002). The greater the shrinkage, the more severe the thought disorder (Collinson & others, 2003; Nelson & others, 1998; Shenton, 1992). One smaller-than-normal area is the cortex (**FIGURE 16.10**). Another is the thalamus, which may explain why people with schizophrenia have difficulty filtering sensory input and focusing attention (Andreasen & others, 1994). The bottom line of various studies, reports Nancy Andreasen (1997, 2001), is that schizophrenia involves not one isolated brain abnormality but problems with several brain regions and their interconnections.

Naturally, scientists wonder what causes these abnormalities. One possibility is some problem during prenatal development or delivery. Low birth weight and birth complications such as oxygen deprivation are known risk factors for schizophrenia (Buka & others, 1999; Zornberg & others, 2000). Famine is also a suspect. People conceived during the peak of the Dutch wartime famine later displayed a doubled rate of schizophrenia, as did those conceived during a 1959–1961 famine in eastern China (St. Clair & others, 2005; Susser & others, 1996).

Maternal Virus During Midpregnancy Another possible culprit is a midpregnancy viral infection that impairs fetal brain development. Can you imagine some ways to test this fetal-virus idea? Scientists exploring this possibility have asked the following questions:

- *Are people at increased risk of schizophrenia if, during the middle of their fetal development, their country experienced a flu epidemic?* The repeated answer is yes (Mednick & others, 1994; Murray & others, 1992; Wright & others, 1995).

- *Are people born in densely populated areas, where viral diseases spread more readily, at greater risk for schizophrenia?* The answer, confirmed in a study of 1.75 million Danes, is yes (Jablensky, 1999; Mortensen & others, 1999).

- *Are those born during the winter and spring months—after the fall-winter flu season—also at increased risk?* The answer is again yes, at 5 to 8 percent increased risk (Torrey & others, 1997, 2002).

- *In the Southern Hemisphere, where the seasons are the reverse of the Northern Hemisphere, are the months of above-average schizophrenia births similarly reversed?* Again, the answer is yes, though somewhat less so. In Australia, for example, people born between August and October are at greater risk—unless they migrated from the Northern Hemisphere, in which case their risk is greater if they were born between January and March (McGrath & others, 1995, 1999).

- *Are mothers who report being sick with influenza during pregnancy more likely to bear children who develop schizophrenia?* In one study of nearly 8000 women, the answer was yes. The schizophrenia risk increased from the customary 1 percent risk to about 2 percent—but only for infections during the second trimester (Brown & others, 2000).

• *Does blood drawn from pregnant women whose offspring develop schizophrenia show higher-than-normal levels of antibodies that suggest a viral infection?* In one study of 27 women whose children later developed schizophrenia, the answer was yes (Buka & others, 2001). One huge California study collected blood samples from some 20,000 pregnant women during the 1950s and 1960s, some of whose offspring were later diagnosed with schizophrenia. When antibodies in the blood indicated the mother was exposed to influenza during the first half of the pregnancy, the risk of the child's developing schizophrenia tripled. Flu during the second half of the pregnancy produced no such increase (Brown & others, 2004).

Schizophrenia has other causes (as genetics research makes plain). Moreover, the children of some 98 percent of women who catch the flu during their second trimester of pregnancy do *not* develop schizophrenia. Nevertheless, these converging lines of evidence suggest that prenatal viral infections play a contributing role. They also strengthen the U.S. Centers for Disease Control (2003) recommendation that "women who will be more than three months pregnant during the flu season" have a flu shot.

Why might a second-trimester maternal flu bout put fetuses at risk? Is it the virus itself? The mother's immune response to it? Medications taken? (Wyatt & others, 2001). Does the infection weaken the brain's supportive glial cells, leading to reduced synaptic connections (Moises & others, 2002)? In time, answers may become available.

Genetic Factors

OBJECTIVE 19 | Discuss the evidence for a genetic contribution to the development of schizophrenia.

Might people also inherit a predisposition to certain brain abnormalities? The evidence strongly suggests that, yes, some do. The nearly 1-in-100 odds of any person's being diagnosed with schizophrenia become about 1 in 10 among those whose sibling or parent has the disorder, and close to 1 in 2 if the affected sibling is an identical twin (**FIGURE 16.11**). Although there are barely more than a dozen such known cases, it appears that an identical twin of a person with schizophrenia retains that 1-in-2 chance when the twins are reared apart (Plomin & others, 1997).

Even with identical twins, there may be a prenatal environmental component. About two-thirds of identical twins share the same placenta and blood. (They usually also have opposite handedness to their co-twin.) If an identical twin has schizophrenia, the co-twin's chances of being similarly afflicted are 6 in 10 if they shared a single placenta, but only 1 in 10 if the twins had separate placentas (Davis & others, 1995a,b; Phelps & others, 1997). Twins who share a placenta are more likely to experience the same prenatal viruses. So it is possible that shared germs as well as shared genes produce identical twin similarities.

Adoption studies, however, confirm that the genetic link is real (Gottesman, 1991). Children adopted by someone who develops schizophrenia seldom "catch" the disorder. Rather, adopted children have an elevated risk if a biological parent is diagnosed with schizophrenia. One intriguing study of 87,907 Israelis also found that the older the biological father—and thus the more opportunities for the DNA in his sperm cells to have mutated—the greater the risk of offspring with schizophrenia (Malaspina & others, 2001).

Schizophrenia in identical twins

When twins differ, only the one afflicted with schizophrenia typically has enlarged, fluid-filled cranial cavities (right) (Suddath & others, 1990). The difference between the twins implies some nongenetic factor, such as a virus, is also at work.

No schizophrenia

Schizophrenia

Both photos: Courtesy of Daniel R. Weinberger, M.D., NIH–NIMH/NSC

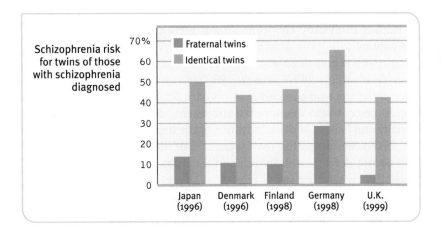

Schizophrenia risk for twins of those with schizophrenia diagnosed

FIGURE 16.11
Risk of developing schizophrenia
The lifetime risk of developing schizophrenia varies with one's genetic relatedness to someone having this disorder. Across countries, barely more than 1 in 10 fraternal twins, but some 5 in 10 identical twins, share a schizophrenia diagnosis. (Adapted from Gottesman, 2001.)

With the genetic factor established, researchers are now sleuthing specific genes that, in some combination, might predispose schizophrenia-inducing brain abnormalities (Callicott & others, 2005; Egan & others, 2004). (It is not our genes but our brains that directly control our behavior.) Some of these genes provide the code for proteins involved in the brain's neurotransmission (including one that breaks down dopamine). Other important genes appear to code for proteins used to make the myelin that coats brain cells and influences their impulse transmission. Despite tantalizing findings, the culprit genes have proven elusive. The genetic contribution to schizophrenia is beyond question. But the genetic role is not as straightforward as the inheritance of eye color. A complex disorder such as schizophrenia is surely influenced by multiple genes with small effects.

Also remember that half the twins who share identical genes with a schizophrenia victim do *not* develop the disorder. Thus, behavior geneticists Susan Nicol and Irving Gottesman (1983) concluded that some people "have a genetic predisposition to the disorder but that this predisposition by itself is not sufficient for the development of schizophrenia." Other factors—including the prenatal viral infections, nutritional deprivation, and oxygen deprivation at birth mentioned earlier—may be ingredients for the disease.

Our knowledge of human genetics and of genetic influences on maladies such as schizophrenia is exploding, thanks partly to millions of new National Institute of Mental Health dollars focused on solving the schizophrenia riddle. So, can scientists develop genetic tests that reveal who is at risk? If so, will people in the future subject their embryos to genetic testing (and gene repair or abortion) if they are at risk for this or some other psychological or physical malady? Might they take their egg and sperm to the genetics lab for screening before combining them to produce an embryo? Or will children be tested for genetic risks and given appropriate preventive treatments? In this brave new twenty-first-century world, such questions await answers.

Psychological Factors

OBJECTIVE 20 | Describe some psychological factors that may be early warning signs of schizophrenia in children.

If genetically predisposed physiological abnormalities do not, by themselves, cause schizophrenia, neither do prenatal and psychological factors alone. It remains true, as Nicol and Gottesman (1983) noted more than two decades ago, that "no environmental causes have been discovered that will invariably, or even with moderate probability, produce schizophrenia in persons who are not related to" a person with schizophrenia. Psychologists long ago ceased blaming parents; no longer do they attribute schizophrenia to cold and capricious "refrigerator mothers."

The Genain quadruplets

The odds of any four people picked at random all being diagnosed with schizophrenia are 1 in 100 million. But genetically identical sisters Nora, Iris, Myra, and Hester Genain all have the disease. Two of the sisters have more severe forms of the disorder than the others, suggesting the influence of environmental as well as biological factors.

Hoping to identify environmental triggers of schizophrenia, several investigators are now following the development of "high-risk" children, such as those born to a parent with schizophrenia or exposed to prenatal risks (Freedman & others, 1998; Olin & Mednick, 1996; Susser, 1999). One study followed 163 teens and early-twenties adults who had two relatives with schizophrenia. During the 2½-year study, the 20 percent who developed schizophrenia displayed some tendency to withdraw socially and behave oddly in advance of the onset of the disorder (Johnstone & others, 2005). By comparing the experiences of high-risk and low-risk children who do and do not develop schizophrenia, researchers have so far pinpointed the following possible early warning signs:

- A mother whose schizophrenia was severe and long-lasting
- Birth complications, often involving oxygen deprivation and low birth weight
- Separation from parents
- Short attention span and poor muscle coordination
- Disruptive or withdrawn behavior
- Emotional unpredictability
- Poor peer relations and solo play

Most of us can relate more easily to the ups and downs of mood disorders than to the strange thoughts, perceptions, and behaviors of schizophrenia. Sometimes our thoughts do jump around, but we do not talk nonsensically. Occasionally we feel unjustly suspicious of someone, but we do not fear that the world is plotting against us. Often our perceptions err, but rarely do we see or hear things that are not there. We have felt regret after laughing at someone's misfortune, but we rarely giggle in response to bad news. At times we just want to be alone, but we do not live in social isolation. However, millions of people around the world do talk strangely, suffer delusions, hear nonexistent voices, see things that are not there, laugh or cry at inappropriate times, or withdraw into private imaginary worlds. The quest to solve the cruel puzzle of schizophrenia therefore continues, and more vigorously than ever.

>> LEARNING OUTCOMES

Schizophrenia

OBJECTIVE 16 | **Describe the symptoms of schizophrenia, and differentiate delusions and hallucinations.**

Schizophrenia is a group of disorders that typically strike during late adolescence, affect men very slightly more than women, and seem to occur in all cultures. Symptoms of schizophrenia are disorganized and delusional thinking (which may stem from a breakdown of selective attention), disturbed perceptions, and inappropriate emotions and actions. *Delusions* are false beliefs; *hallucinations* are sensory experiences without sensory stimulation.

OBJECTIVE 17 | **Distinguish the five subtypes of schizophrenia, and contrast chronic and acute schizophrenia.**

The subtypes of schizophrenia are *paranoid* (preoccupation with delusions or hallucinations, often of persecution or grandiosity), *disorganized* (disorganized speech or behavior, or flat affect or inappropriate emotions), *catatonic* (immobility, extreme negativism, and/or parrotlike repetition of another's speech or movements), *undifferentiated* (varied

symptoms), and *residual* (withdrawal following hallucinations and delusions). *Chronic* (or *process*) *schizophrenia* emerges gradually, is often associated with negative symptoms (absence of appropriate behaviors), and carries a low chance of recovery. *Acute* (or *reactive*) schizophrenia develops rapidly (often in response to stress) in a previously well-adjusted person, may be associated with positive symptoms (presence of inappropriate behaviors), and carries a greater chance of recovery.

OBJECTIVE 18 | **Outline some abnormal brain chemistry, functions, and structures associated with schizophrenia, and discuss the possible link between prenatal viral infections and schizophrenia.**

People with schizophrenia have increased receptors for the neurotransmitter dopamine, which may intensify the positive symptoms of schizophrenia. Research is under way on a possible link between negative symptoms and impaired glutamate activity. Brain abnormalities associated with schizophrenia include enlarged, fluid-filled cerebral cavities and corresponding decreases in the cortex. Brain scans reveal abnormal activity in the frontal lobes, thalamus, and amygdala. Malfunctions in multiple brain regions and their connections apparently interact to produce the symptoms of schizophrenia. Research support is mounting for the causal effects of a virus suffered in mid-pregnancy.

OBJECTIVE 19 | **Discuss the evidence for a genetic contribution to the development of schizophrenia.**

The odds of developing schizophrenia are approximately 1 in 100 in the general population; 1 in 10 if a family member has it; and 1 in 2 if an identical twin has the disorder. Adoption studies show that an adopted child's chances of developing the disorder are greater if the biological parents have schizophrenia, but not if the adopted parents have it. But 50 percent of those whose identical twins have schizophrenia do not develop the condition themselves, demonstrating that genetics is not the sole cause of this disorder.

OBJECTIVE 20 | **Describe some psychological factors that may be early warning signs of schizophrenia in children.**

No environmental event can by itself trigger schizophrenia, though some things may trigger the disorder in those genetically predisposed to it. Research has identified some early warning signs of schizophrenia, including a mother whose schizophrenia was severe and long-lasting; birth complications; separation from parents; short attention span and poor muscle coordination; disruptive or withdrawn behavior; emotional unpredictability; and poor peer relations and solo play.

ASK YOURSELF: Civil libertarians defend the right of schizophrenia patients not to be hospitalized against their will. E. Fuller Torrey (1998), a psychiatrist who views schizophrenia as a brain disorder, objects: "If a person with Alzheimer's wanted to go outside with no shoes in the winter, we wouldn't say, 'That's fine, he should have free choice.'" Do you think patients with schizophrenia should be hospitalized and treated against their will? Or do they always have the right to live free, even if under bridges or in shelters?

Personality Disorders

OBJECTIVE 21 | Contrast the three clusters of personality disorders, and describe the behaviors and brain activity associated with antisocial personality disorder.

Some maladaptive behavior patterns impair people's social functioning without anxiety, depression, or delusions. These disruptive patterns, called **personality disorders,** are inflexible and enduring patterns of behavior that impair one's social functioning. One cluster of disorders expresses anxiety, such as a fearful sensitivity to rejection that predisposes the withdrawn *avoidant personality disorder*. A second cluster expresses eccentric behaviors, such as the emotionless disengagement of the *schizoid personality disorder*.

A third cluster exhibits dramatic or impulsive behaviors. A person with a *histrionic personality disorder* displays shallow, attention-getting emotions and goes to great lengths to gain others' praise and reassurance. Those with self-focused *narcissistic personality disorder* exaggerate their own importance, aided by success fantasies. They find criticism hard to accept, often reacting with rage or shame. Those with *borderline personality disorder* have an unstable identity, unstable relationships, and unstable and impulsive emotions. If personality is one's enduring pattern of thinking, feeling, and acting, then a markedly unstable sense of self defines a *borderline personality*.

Antisocial personality? Dennis Rader, known as the "BTK killer" in Kansas, was convicted in 2005 of killing 10 people over a 30-year span. Rader exhibited the extreme lack of conscience that marks antisocial personality disorder.

EPA/Jeff Tuttle/Landov

■ **personality disorders** psychological disorders characterized by inflexible and enduring behavior patterns that impair social functioning.

■ **antisocial personality disorder** a personality disorder in which the person (usually a man) exhibits a lack of conscience for wrongdoing, even toward friends and family members. May be aggressive and ruthless or a clever con artist.

Antisocial Personality Disorder

The most troubling and heavily researched personality disorder is the **antisocial personality disorder.** The person (formerly called a *sociopath* or a *psychopath*) is typically a male whose lack of conscience becomes plain before age 15, as he begins to lie, steal, fight, or display unrestrained sexual behavior (Cale & Lilienfeld, 2002).

Adrenaline excretion (ng/min.)

Those with criminal convictions have lower levels of arousal

Nonstressful situation

Stressful situation

■ No criminal conviction
■ Criminal conviction

FIGURE 16.12
Cold-blooded arousability and risk of crime
Levels of the stress hormone adrenaline were measured in two groups of 13-year-old Swedish boys. In both stressful and nonstressful situations, those who were later convicted of a crime (as 18- to 26-year-olds) showed relatively low arousal. (From Magnusson, 1990.)

FIGURE 16.13
Murderous minds
PET scans illustrate reduced activation (less red and yellow) in a murderer's frontal cortex—a brain area that helps brake impulsive, aggressive behavior. (From Raine, 1999.)

Normal

Murderer

About half of such children become antisocial adults—unable to keep a job, irresponsible as a spouse and parent, and assaultive or otherwise criminal (Farrington, 1991). When the antisocial personality combines a keen intelligence with amorality, the result may be a charming and clever con artist—or worse.

Despite their antisocial behavior, most criminals do not fit the description of antisocial personality disorder. Why? Because most criminals actually show responsible concern for their friends and family members. Antisocial personalities feel and fear little, and in extreme cases, the results can be horrifyingly tragic. Henry Lee Lucas reported that at age 13 he strangled a woman who refused to have sex with him. He at one time confessed to having bludgeoned, suffocated, stabbed, shot, or mutilated some 360 women, men, and children during his 32 years of crime. During the last 6 years of his reign of terror, Lucas teamed with Elwood Toole, who reportedly slaughtered about 50 people he "didn't think was worth living anyhow." It ended when Lucas confessed to stabbing and dismembering his 15-year-old common-law wife, who was Toole's niece.

The antisocial personality expresses little regret over violating others' rights. "Once I've done a crime, I just forget it," said Lucas. Toole was equally matter-of-fact: "I think of killing like smoking a cigarette, like another habit" (Darrach & Norris, 1984).

Understanding Antisocial Personality Disorder

As with mood disorders and schizophrenia, the antisocial personality disorder is woven of both biological and psychological strands. No single gene codes for a complex behavior such as crime, but twin and adoption studies reveal that biological relatives of those with antisocial and unemotional tendencies are at increased risk for antisocial behavior (Rhee & Waldman, 2002; Viding & others, 2005). Their genetic vulnerability appears as a fearless approach to life. When they await aversive events, such as electric shocks or loud noises, they show little autonomic nervous system arousal (Hare, 1975). Even as youngsters, before committing any crime, they react with lower levels of stress hormones than do others their age (**FIGURE 16.12**).

Some studies have detected the early signs of antisocial behavior in children as young as ages 3 to 6 (Caspi & others, 1996; Tremblay & others, 1994). Boys who later became aggressive or antisocial adolescents tended, as young children, to have been impulsive, uninhibited, unconcerned with social rewards, and low in anxiety. If channeled in more productive directions, such fearlessness may lead to courageous heroism, adventurism, or star-level athleticism (Poulton & Milne, 2002). Lacking a sense of social responsibility, the same disposition produces a cool con artist or killer (Lykken, 1995).

Genetic influences help wire the brain. Adrian Raine (1999) compared PET scans of 41 murderers' brains with those from people of similar age and sex. Raine found reduced activity in the murderers' frontal lobes, an area of the cortex that helps control impulses (**FIGURE 16.13**). This reduction was especially apparent in those who murdered impulsively. In a follow-up study, Raine and his team (2000) found that violent repeat offenders had 11 percent less frontal lobe tissue than normal. This helps explain why people with antisocial personality disorder exhibit marked deficits in frontal lobe cognitive functions, such as planning, organization, and inhibition (Morgan & Lilienfeld, 2000).

Perhaps a biologically based fearlessness, as well as early environment, helps explain the reunion of long-separated sisters Joyce Lott, 27, and Mary Jones, 29—in a South Carolina prison where both were sent on drug charges. After a newspaper story about their reunion, their long-lost half-brother Frank Strickland called. He explained it would be a while before he could come see them—because he, too, was in jail, on drug, burglary, and larceny charges (Shepherd & others, 1990).

Genetics alone is hardly the whole story of antisocial crime, however. Relative to 1960, the average American in 1995 (before the late 1990s crime decline) was twice as likely to be murdered, four times as likely to report being raped, four times as likely to report being robbed, and five times as likely to report being assaulted (FBI, *Uniform Crime Reports*). Violent crime was also surging in other Western nations. Yet the human gene pool had hardly changed. Or consider the British social experiment begun in 1787, exiling 160,000 criminals to Australia. The descendants of these exiles, carrying their ancestors' supposed "criminal genes," have helped create a civilized democracy whose crime rate is similar to Britain's. Genetic predispositions do put some individuals more at risk for antisocial conduct than others; biological as well as environmental influences explain why 5 to 6 percent of offenders commit 50 to 60 percent of crimes (Lyman, 1996). But we must look to sociocultural factors to explain the modern epidemic of violence.

A study of criminal tendencies among young Danish men illustrates the usefulness of a complete biopsychosocial approach. A research team led by Adrian Raine (1996) checked criminal records on nearly 400 men at ages 20 to 22, knowing that all had experienced either biological risk factors at birth, such as premature birth, or had come from family backgrounds marked by poverty and family instability. The researchers compared each of these groups with a *biosocial* group whose lives were marked by *both* the biological and social risk factors. The biosocial group had double the risk of committing crime (**FIGURE 16.14**). In one quarter-century study that followed 1037 children, two combined factors predicted antisocial problems: childhood maltreatment and a gene that altered neurotransmitter balance (Caspi & others, 2002). Neither "bad" genes nor a "bad" environment alone predisposed later antisocial behavior; rather, genes predisposed some children to be more sensitive to maltreatment. Within "genetically vulnerable segments of the population," environmental influences matter (Moffitt, 2005). With antisocial behavior, as with so much else, nature and nurture interact.

FIGURE 16.14
Biopsychosocial roots of crime
Danish male babies whose backgrounds were marked *both* by obstetrical complications and social stresses associated with poverty were twice as likely to be criminal offenders by ages 20 to 22 as those in either the biological or social risk groups. (From Raine & others, 1996.)

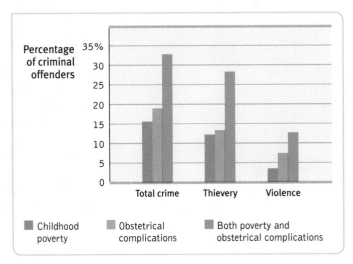

>> Learning Outcomes

Personality Disorders

OBJECTIVE 21 | Contrast the three clusters of personality disorders, and describe the behaviors and brain activity associated with antisocial personality disorder.

Personality disorders are inflexible and enduring patterns of behavior that impair social functioning. The main component of the first cluster is *anxiety;* of the second cluster, *eccentric behaviors;* of the third cluster, *dramatic or impulsive behaviors. Antisocial personality disorder* is characterized by a lack of conscience and, sometimes, aggressive and ruthless behavior. Brain scans of some murderers with this disorder have shown reduced activity in the frontal lobes, an area of control for impulsive, aggressive behavior. There is no gene for antisocial personality disorder, though genetic predisposition may interact with environmental influences to produce it.

ASK YOURSELF: How would you evaluate the relative contributions of nature and nurture to antisocial personality disorder?

Rates of Psychological Disorders

OBJECTIVE 22 | Discuss the prevalence of psychological disorders, and summarize the findings on the link between poverty and serious psychological disorders.

Does a full moon trigger "madness" in some people? James Rotton and I. W. Kelly (1985) examined data from 37 studies that related lunar phase to crime, homicides, crisis calls, and mental hospital admissions. Their conclusion: There is virtually no evidence of "moon madness." Nor does lunar phase correlate with suicides, assaults, emergency room visits, or traffic disasters (Martin & others, 1992; Raison & others, 1999).

How prevalent are the various disorders? Who is most vulnerable to them? At what times of life? To answer such questions, various countries have conducted lengthy, structured interviews with representative samples of thousands of their citizens. After asking hundreds of questions that probed for symptoms—"Has there ever been a period of two weeks or more when you felt like you wanted to die?"—the researchers have estimated the current, prior year, and lifetime prevalence of various disorders.

How many people suffer, or have suffered, a psychological disorder? More than most of us suppose:

- Summarizing a U.S. National Institute of Mental Health interview study and a follow-up survey, William Narrow and his colleagues (2002) estimated that 1 in 7 Americans had suffered a clinically significant mental disorder during the prior year (**TABLE 16.4**).
- Britain's Office of National Statistics (2002) recently reported a similar 1-in-6 disorder rate.
- An Australian government survey of 10,600 adults found that in any 12 months, slightly less than 1 in 6 "have a mental disorder" (Andrews & others, 1999). Another Australian government study of 4500 children and adolescents concluded that 1 in 7 had "mental health problems" (Sawyer & others, 2000).
- A twenty-first-century World Health Organization (2004) study—based on 90-minute interviews of 60,463 people—estimated the number of prior-year mental disorders in 20 countries. As **FIGURE 16.15** displays, the lowest rate of reported mental disorders was in Shanghai, the highest rate in the United States. Moreover, when people immigrate to the United States from Mexico and elsewhere, their mental health and their children's declines as they assimilate over time. For example, compared with people who have recently immigrated from Mexico, Mexican-Americans born in the United States are at greater risk of mental disorder (Grant & others, 2004; Vega & others, 1998).

TABLE 16.4

PERCENTAGE OF AMERICANS WHO HAVE EXPERIENCED SELECTED PSYCHOLOGICAL DISORDERS IN THE PRIOR YEAR

Disorder	Percentage
Alcohol abuse	5.2
Generalized anxiety	4.0
Phobias	7.8
Obsessive-compulsive disorder	2.1
Mood disorder	5.1
Schizophrenia	1.0
Antisocial personality	1.5
Any mental disorder	14.9

(Some people experience two or more of these disorders, such as depression and alcohol abuse, simultaneously.)

Source: Data from Narrow & others, 2002.

One predictor of mental disorder is poverty. The incidence of serious psychological disorders is doubly high among those below the poverty line (Centers for Disease Control, 1992). Like so many other correlations, the poverty-disorder association raises a chicken-and-egg question: Does poverty cause disorders? Or do disorders cause poverty? It is both, though the answer varies with the disorder. Schizophrenia understandably leads to poverty. Yet the stresses and demoralization of poverty can also precipitate disorders, especially depression in women and substance abuse in men (Dohrenwend & others, 1992). In one natural experiment on the poverty-pathology link, researchers tracked rates of behavior problems in North Carolina Native American children as economic development enabled a dramatic reduction in their community's poverty rate. As the study began, children of poverty exhibited more deviant and aggressive behaviors. After four years, children whose families had moved above the poverty line exhibited a 40 percent decrease in the behavior problems, while those who continued in their previous positions below or above the poverty line exhibited no change (Costello & others, 2003).

As **TABLE 16.5** indicates, there is a wide range of risk and protective factors for mental disorders. Those who experience a psychological disorder usually do so by early adulthood. "Over 75 percent of our sample with any disorder had experienced its first symptoms by age 24," reported Robins and Regier (1991, p. 331). The symptoms

TABLE 16.5

RISK AND PROTECTIVE FACTORS FOR MENTAL DISORDERS

Risk Factors	Protective Factors
Academic failure	Aerobic exercise
Birth complications	Community offering empowerment, opportunity, and security
Caring for chronically ill or patients with dementia	Economic independence
Child abuse and neglect	Feelings of security
Chronic insomnia	Feelings of mastery and control
Chronic pain	Good parenting
Family disorganization or conflict	Literacy
Low birth weight	Positive attachment and early bonding
Low socioeconomic status	Positive parent-child relationships
Medical illness	Problem-solving skills
Neurochemical imbalance	Resilient coping with stress and adversity
Parental mental illness	Self-esteem
Parental substance abuse	Social and work skills
Personal loss and bereavement	Social support from family and friends
Poor work skills and habits	
Reading disabilities	
Sensory disabilities	
Social incompetence	
Stressful life events	
Substance abuse	
Trauma experiences	

Source: World Health Organization (2004a,b)

FIGURE 16.15

Prevalence of mental disorders during prior year

From World Health Organization (2004) interviews in 20 countries.

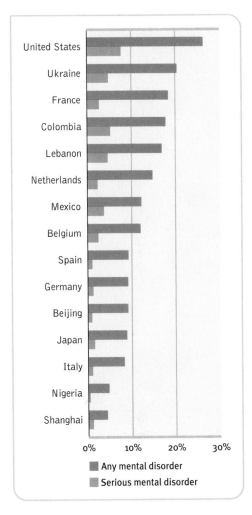

■ Any mental disorder
■ Serious mental disorder

of antisocial personality disorder and of phobias are among the earliest to appear, at a median age of 8 and 10, respectively. Symptoms of alcohol abuse, obsessive-compulsive disorder, bipolar disorder, and schizophrenia appear at a median age near 20. Major depression often hits somewhat later, at a median age of 25. Such findings make clear the need for research and treatment to help the growing number of people, especially teenagers and young adults, who suffer the bewilderment and pain of a psychological disorder.

Although mindful of the pain, we can also be encouraged by the many successful people—including Leonardo da Vinci, Isaac Newton, and Leo Tolstoy—who pursued brilliant careers while enduring psychological difficulties. The bewilderment, fear, and sorrow caused by psychological disorders are real. But, as Chapter 17 shows, hope, too, is real.

>> LEARNING OUTCOMES

Rates of Psychological Disorders

OBJECTIVE 22 | Discuss the prevalence of psychological disorders, and summarize the findings on the link between poverty and serious psychological disorders.

Research indicates that about 1 in 6 people has, or has had, a psychological disorder, usually by early adulthood. Poverty is a predictor of mental illness. Conditions and experiences associated with poverty contribute to the development of mental disorders, but the converse is also true. Some mental disorders, such as schizophrenia, can drive people into poverty.

ASK YOURSELF: Do you have a family member or friend who has experienced a psychological disorder? If so, has anything you have read in this chapter increased your understanding of the challenges that person has been facing?

REVIEW CHAPTER 16: Psychological Disorders

Test Yourself

1. What is the biopsychosocial perspective, and why is it important in our understanding of psychological disorders?

2. How do generalized anxiety disorder, phobias, and obsessive-compulsive disorder differ?

3. What does it mean to say that "depression is the common cold of psychological disorders?

4. What are the five subtypes of schizophrenia?

5. Is antisocial personality disorder an inherited condition?

6. Does poverty cause psychological disorder? Explain.

Answers to the Test Yourself questions can be found in Appendix B at the end of the book.

Terms and Concepts to Remember

psychological disorder, p. 640

attention-deficit hyperactivity disorder (ADHD), p. 641

medical model, p. 642

DSM-IV, p. 644

anxiety disorders, p. 649

generalized anxiety disorder, p. 649

panic disorder, p. 650

phobia, p. 650

obsessive-compulsive disorder (OCD), p. 651

post-traumatic stress disorder (PTSD), p. 652

dissociative disorders, p. 656

dissociative identity disorder (DID), p. 656

mood disorders, p. 658

major depressive disorder, p. 659

mania, p. 659

bipolar disorder, p. 659

schizophrenia, p. 669

delusions, p. 669

personality disorders, p. 677

antisocial personality disorder, p. 677

WEB

 To continue your study and review of Psychological Disorders, visit this book's Web site at www.worthpublishers.com/myers. You will find practice tests, review activities, and many interesting articles and Web links for more information on topics related to Psychological Disorders.

▌ ANOTHER VOICE ON: THERAPY

▌ JACK RIDL (b. 1944) FROM "THE HEALERS," POEMS FROM *THE SAME GHOST AND BETWEEN*

My father guessed at work.
He gave me things to do.
We strangled weeds from the flower bed,
Washed the car,
Walked the dog.

My mother guessed at a mother's love.
She went back to tucking sheets
Around me as I lay awake in bed.
She pulled her fingers through my hair.
She turned away. She held me.

My good friend guessed at leaving town.
So we lugged gravel, grinding gears
Up and down the western Pennsylvania
   hills.
We'd raise the bed and listen
To the gravel rush into a silent pile.

My preacher guessed at God.
He knew my answer; spread my sin;
Prayed; asked me to pray;
Sprinkled oil on my head;
Pronounced me of this world.

My doctor guessed at shock.
Strapped me down.
Hooked electrodes to my head.
Baptized me with volts.

I guessed at empty space
And all the breath
That I could spill to fill it up.

17 : Therapy

OBJECTIVE **1** | Discuss some ways that *psychotherapy, biomedical therapy,* and an *eclectic approach* to therapy differ.

Today we comprehend deep outer space and can state with certainty the chemical composition of Jupiter's atmosphere. But in understanding and treating the disturbances of deep inner space—the psychological disorders described in Chapter 16—we are only beginning to make real progress. In the 2200 years since Eratosthenes correctly estimated the Earth's circumference, we have charted the heavens, explored our solar system, reconstructed the basic history of life, cracked the genetic code, and eliminated or found cures for all sorts of diseases. Meanwhile, we have treated psychological disorders with a bewildering variety of harsh and gentle methods: by cutting holes in the head and by giving warm baths and massages; by restraining, bleeding, or "beating the devil" out of people; by placing them in sunny, serene environments; by administering drugs and electric shocks; and by talking—talking about childhood experiences, about current feelings, about maladaptive thoughts and behaviors.

The transition from brutal to gentler treatments occurred thanks to the efforts of reformers such as Philippe Pinel in France and Dorothea Dix in the United States, Canada, and Scotland. Both advocated constructing mental hospitals to offer more humane methods of treatment. As we shall see, however, the introduction of therapeutic drugs and community-based treatment programs has largely emptied mental health hospitals since the mid-1950s.

Mental health therapies can be classified into two main categories: the psychological therapies and the biomedical therapies.

Today, the favored treatment depends on both the disorder and the therapist's viewpoint. Psychological disorders that researchers believe are learned, such as phobias, will likely be treated with psychological therapy, or **psychotherapy**—"a planned, emotionally charged, confiding interaction between a trained, socially sanctioned healer and a sufferer" (Frank, 1982).

The history of treatment
The engraving (right) by William Hogarth (1697–1764) of London's St. Mary of Bethlehem hospital (commonly called Bedlam) depicts the treatment of mental disorders in the eighteenth century. Visitors paid to gawk at the patients as if they were viewing zoo animals. The chair on the left was designed by Benjamin Rush (1746–1813) "for the benefit of maniacal patients." Rush, a founder of the movement for more humane treatment of the mentally ill, believed they required restraint to regain their sensibilities.

Dorothea Dix (1802–1887)
"I . . . call your attention to the state of the Insane Persons confined within this Commonwealth, in cages."

Biologically rooted disorders, such as schizophrenia, are likely to be treated with **biomedical therapy**—a prescribed medication or medical procedure that acts directly on the patient's nervous system.

Of course, many psychological disorders are also responses to social conditions, so therapists may be interested in improving an unhealthy environment as well. Children of poverty, for example, are at risk for conduct disorder; children of affluence are at risk for eating disorders.

Depending on the client and the problem, some therapists—particularly the many using a biopsychosocial approach—draw from a variety of techniques. Indeed, half of all psychotherapists have described themselves as taking an **eclectic approach,** by using a blend of therapies (Beitman & others, 1989; Castonguay & Goldfried, 1994). Closely related to eclecticism is *psychotherapy integration*. Rather than picking and choosing methods, integration advocates aim to combine them into a single, coherent system.

>> LEARNING OUTCOMES

OBJECTIVE 1 | **Discuss some ways that *psychotherapy, biomedical therapy,* and an *eclectic approach* to therapy differ.**

Psychotherapy is an emotionally charged, confiding interaction between a trained therapist and someone suffering from psychological difficulties. The *biomedical therapies* are prescribed medications or medical procedures that act directly on a patient's nervous system. An *eclectic approach* to psychotherapy uses techniques from various forms of therapy; psychotherapy integration attempts to combine a selection of assorted techniques into a single, coherent system.

The Psychological Therapies

Among the dozens of types of psychotherapy, we will look at only the most influential. Each is built on one or more of psychology's major theories: psychoanalytic, humanistic, behavioral, and cognitive. We will also consider the use of some of these techniques in groups.

Psychoanalysis

OBJECTIVE 2 | Define *psychoanalysis,* and discuss the aims of this form of therapy.

Although few clinicians today practice therapy as Sigmund Freud did, many of his techniques and assumptions survive, especially in the *psychodynamic therapies* (see page 688). Freudian terminology has also crept into our modern vocabulary. Freud's **psychoanalysis** was the first of the psychological therapies.

Aims

In Chapter 15 we noted that Freud assumed that many psychological problems are fueled by childhood's residue of repressed impulses and conflicts. Psychoanalysts try to bring these repressed feelings into conscious awareness where the patient can deal with them. By gaining insight into the origins of the disorder—by fulfilling the ancient imperative to "know thyself" in a deep way—patients work through the buried feelings and take responsibility for their own growth. Psychoanalytic theory presumes that healthier, less anxious living becomes possible when people release the energy they had previously devoted to id-ego-superego conflicts.

■ **psychotherapy** an emotionally charged, confiding interaction between a trained therapist and someone who suffers from psychological difficulties.

■ **biomedical therapy** prescribed medications or medical procedures that act directly on the patient's nervous system.

■ **eclectic approach** an approach to psychotherapy that, depending on the client's problems, uses techniques from various forms of therapy.

■ **psychoanalysis** Sigmund Freud's therapeutic technique. Freud believed the patient's free associations, resistances, dreams, and transferences—and the therapist's interpretations of them—released previously repressed feelings, allowing the patient to gain self-insight.

■ **resistance** in psychoanalysis, the blocking from consciousness of anxiety-laden material.

■ **interpretation** in psychoanalysis, the analyst's noting supposed dream meanings, resistances, and other significant behaviors and events in order to promote insight.

■ **transference** in psychoanalysis, the patient's transfer to the analyst of emotions linked with other relationships (such as love or hatred for a parent).

Freud's consulting room
Freud's office was rich with antiquities from around the world, including artwork related to his ideas about unconscious motives. His famous couch, piled high with pillows, placed patients in a comfortable reclining position facing away from him to help them focus inward.

Methods

OBJECTIVE 3 | Describe some of the methods used in psychoanalysis, and list some criticisms of this form of therapy.

Psychoanalysis is historical reconstruction. It aims to unearth the past in hope of unmasking the present. But how?

When Freud discarded hypnosis as unreliable, he turned to *free association*. Imagine yourself as a patient using free association. First, you relax, perhaps by lying on a couch. To help you focus attention on your own thoughts and feelings, the psychoanalyst may sit out of your line of vision. You say aloud whatever comes to your mind from moment to moment, which may be a childhood memory, a dream, or a recent experience. It sounds easy, but soon you notice how often you edit your thoughts as you speak, omitting what seems trivial, irrelevant, or shameful. Even in the safe presence of the analyst, you may pause momentarily before uttering an embarrassing thought. You may make a joking remark or change the subject to something less threatening. Sometimes your mind goes blank or you find yourself unable to remember important details.

To the psychoanalyst, these blocks in the flow of your free associations indicate **resistance.** They hint that anxiety lurks and you are defending against sensitive material. The analyst will want to make you aware of your resistances and then **interpret** their meaning, providing *insight* into your underlying wishes, feelings, and conflicts. This interpretation—of, say, your not wanting to talk about your mother—may, if offered at the right moment, illuminate what you are avoiding and demonstrate how this resistance fits with other pieces of your psychological puzzle.

Freud believed that another clue to unconscious conflicts is your dreams' *latent content*—their underlying but censored meaning. Thus, after inviting you to report a dream, the analyst may offer a dream analysis, suggesting its meaning.

During many such sessions you will probably disclose to your analyst more of yourself than you have ever revealed to anyone else. Because psychoanalytic theory emphasizes the formative power of childhood experiences, much of what you reveal will pertain to your earliest memories. You may find yourself experiencing strong positive or negative feelings for your analyst. Freud would say you are **transferring** to the analyst your strongest feelings from earlier relationships with family members or other important people. Analysts and other therapists believe that transference exposes feelings that a person has previously defended against, such as dependency or mingled love and anger, giving you a belated chance to work through them with your analyst's help. But psychoanalysis is not just about excavating your childhood past. By examining your feelings toward the analyst you may also gain insight into your current relationships.

Critics point out that psychoanalysts' interpretations are hard to refute because they cannot be proven or disproven, a criticism psychoanalysts

" I haven't seen my analyst in 200 years. He was a strict Freudian. If I'd been going all this time, I'd probably almost be cured by now."

Woody Allen, after awakening from suspended animation in the movie *Sleeper*

"In the mental-health profession, we try to avoid negative labels, like 'a hundred and fifty bucks an hour—that's *crazy*!' or 'three fifty-minute sessions a week—that's *insane*!'"

acknowledge. But they insist that interpretations often are a great help to patients. Psychoanalysis is therapy, not science.

Traditional psychoanalysis takes time, up to several years of several sessions a week, and it is expensive. (Three times a week for just two years at more than $100 per hour comes to at least $30,000.) This helps explain why, outside of France, Germany, Quebec, and New York City, relatively few therapists offer it (Goode, 2003). Indeed, in the United States, managed health care has severely limited the types and length of mental health services that may be covered by insurance. This has contributed to a trend toward much shorter treatment periods and many fewer instances of in-patient care.

Psychodynamic Therapy

OBJECTIVE 4 | Contrast psychodynamic therapy and interpersonal therapy with traditional psychoanalysis.

Michael Newman/PhotoEdit, Inc.

Face-to-face therapy

In this type of therapy session, the couch has disappeared. But the influence of psychoanalytic theory may not have, especially if the therapist probes for the origin of the patient's symptoms by seeking information from the patient's childhood.

Influenced by Freud, *psychodynamic* therapists try to understand a patient's current symptoms by focusing on themes across important relationships, including childhood experiences and the therapist relationship. They also help the person explore and gain perspective on defended-against thoughts and feelings. But these therapists may talk to the patient face to face (rather than out of the line of vision), once a week (rather than several times weekly), and for only a few weeks or months (rather than several years).

No brief excerpt can exemplify the way psychodynamic therapy interprets a patient's conflict. But we can illustrate psychodynamic therapists' goal of enabling insight by looking for common, recurring themes, especially in relationships. In the following interaction, therapist David Malan responds to all he has heard from a depressed patient by suggesting insights into her problems. Note how Malan interprets the woman's earlier remarks (when she did most of the talking) and suggests that her relationship with him reveals a characteristic pattern of behavior (1978, pp. 133–134).

Malan: *I get the feeling that you're the sort of person who needs to keep active. If you don't keep active, then something goes wrong. Is that true?*

Patient: *Yes.*

Malan: *I get a second feeling about you and that is that you must, underneath all this, have an awful lot of very strong and upsetting feelings. Somehow they're there but you aren't really quite in touch with them. Isn't this right? I feel you've been like that as long as you can remember.*

Patient: *For quite a few years, whenever I really sat down and thought about it I got depressed, so I tried not to think about it.*

Malan: *You see, you've established a pattern, haven't you? You're even like that here with me, because in spite of the fact that you're in some trouble and you feel that the bottom is falling out of your world, the way you're telling me this is just as if there wasn't anything wrong.*

Interpersonal psychotherapy, a brief (12- to 16-session) variation of psychodynamic therapy, has been effective in treating depression (Weissman, 1999). Interpersonal psychotherapy aims to help people gain insight into the roots of their difficulties, but its goal is symptom relief in the here and now, not overall personality change. Rather than focusing mostly on undoing past hurts and offering interpretations, the therapist focuses primarily on current relationships and on helping people improve their relationship skills.

The case of Anna (not her real name), a 34-year-old married professional, illustrates these goals. Five months after receiving a promotion, with accompanying increased responsibilities and longer hours, Anna experienced increased tensions with her husband

"You say, 'Off with her head' but what I'm hearing is, 'I feel neglected.'"

over his wish for a second child. She began feeling depressed, had trouble sleeping, became irritable, and was gaining weight. A typical psychodynamic therapist might have helped Anna gain insight into her angry impulses and her defenses against anger. An interpersonal therapist similarly wanted Anna to gain these insights, but also engaged her thinking on more immediate issues—how she could balance work and home, resolve the dispute with her husband, and express her emotions more effectively (Markowitz & others, 1998).

Humanistic Therapies

OBJECTIVE 5 | Identify the basic characteristics of the humanistic therapies, and describe the specific goals and techniques of Carl Rogers' client-centered therapy.

The humanistic perspective (Chapter 15) has emphasized people's inherent potential for self-fulfillment. Not surprisingly, humanistic therapists aim to boost self-fulfillment by helping people grow in self-awareness and self-acceptance. Like psychoanalytic therapies, humanistic therapies attempt to reduce the conflicts that are impeding natural developmental growth. But unlike many psychoanalytic therapists, humanistic therapists tend to focus on

- the *present* and *future* more than the past. They explore feelings as they occur, rather than achieving insights into the childhood origins of the feelings.
- *conscious* rather than unconscious thoughts.
- taking immediate *responsibility* for one's feelings and actions, rather than uncovering hidden determinants.
- promoting growth instead of curing illness. Thus, those in therapy became "clients" rather than "patients" (a label change that many therapists have followed).

One widely used humanistic technique has been Carl Rogers' (1961, 1980) **client-centered therapy.** A client-centered therapist focuses on the person's conscious self-perceptions rather than on the therapist's own interpretations. The therapist listens, without judging or interpreting, and refrains from directing the client toward certain insights, a strategy labeled *nondirective therapy*.

Believing that most people already possess the resources for growth, Rogers encouraged therapists to exhibit *genuineness, acceptance,* and *empathy*. When therapists drop their facades and genuinely express their true feelings, when they enable their clients to feel unconditionally accepted, and when they empathically sense and reflect their clients' feelings, the clients may deepen their self-understanding and self-acceptance (Hill & Nakayama, 2000). As Rogers (1980, p. 10) explained,

> Hearing has consequences. When I truly hear a person and the meanings that are important to him at that moment, hearing not simply his words, but him, and when I let him know that I have heard his own private personal meanings, many things happen. There is first of all a grateful look. He feels released. He wants to tell me more about his world. He surges forth in a new sense of freedom. He becomes more open to the process of change.
>
> I have often noticed that the more deeply I hear the meanings of the person, the more there is that happens. Almost always, when a person realizes he has been deeply heard, his eyes moisten. I think in some real sense he is weeping for joy. It is as though he were saying, "Thank God, somebody heard me. Someone knows what it's like to be me."

■ **client-centered therapy** a humanistic therapy, developed by Carl Rogers, in which the therapist uses techniques such as active listening within a genuine, accepting, empathic environment to facilitate clients' growth. (Also called *person-centered therapy*.)

Active listening
Carl Rogers (right) empathized with a client during this group therapy session.

Michael Rougier/*Life* Magazine © Time Warner, Inc.

❝ We have two ears and one mouth that we may listen the more and talk the less.❞
Zeno, 335–263 B.C., *Diogenes Laertius*

"Hearing" refers to Rogers' technique of **active listening**—echoing, restating, and seeking clarification of what the person expresses (verbally or nonverbally) and acknowledging the expressed feelings. Active listening is now an accepted part of therapeutic counseling practices in many schools, colleges, and clinics. The counselor listens attentively and interrupts only to restate and confirm the client's feelings, to accept what the client is expressing, or to seek clarification. The following brief excerpt between Rogers and a male client illustrates how he sought to provide a psychological mirror that would help clients see themselves more clearly.

Client: *I just ain't no good to nobody, never was, and never will be.*

Rogers: *Feeling that now, hm? That you're just no good to yourself, no good to anybody. Never will be any good to anybody. Just that you're completely worthless, huh?—Those really are lousy feelings. Just feel that you're no good at all, hm?*

Client: *Yeah.* (Muttering in low, discouraged voice) *That's what this guy I went to town with just the other day told me.*

Rogers: *This guy that you went to town with really told you that you were no good? Is that what you're saying? Did I get that right?*

Client: *M-hm.*

Rogers: *I guess the meaning of that if I get it right is that here's somebody that—meant something to you and what does he think of you? Why, he's told you that he thinks you're no good at all. And that just really knocks the props out from under you.* (Client weeps quietly.) *It just brings the tears.* (Silence of 20 seconds)

Client: (Rather defiantly) *I don't care though.*

Rogers: *You tell yourself you don't care at all, but somehow I guess some part of you cares because some part of you weeps over it.* (Meador & Rogers, 1984, p. 167)

Can a therapist be a perfect mirror, without selecting and interpreting what is reflected? Rogers conceded that one cannot be *totally* nondirective. Nevertheless, he believed that the therapist's most important contribution is to accept and understand the client. Given a nonjudgmental, grace-filled environment that provides *unconditional positive regard*, people may accept even their worst traits and feel valued and whole.

If you want to listen more actively in your own relationships, three hints may help:

1. *Paraphrase.* Check your understandings by summarizing the speaker's words in your own words.
2. *Invite clarification.* "What might be an example of that?" may encourage the speaker to say more.
3. *Reflect feelings.* "It sounds frustrating" might mirror what you're sensing from the speaker's body language and intensity.

Behavior Therapies

OBJECTIVE 6 | Explain how the basic assumption of behavior therapy differs from those of traditional psychoanalytic and humanistic therapies.

The therapies we have considered so far assume that many psychological problems diminish as self-awareness grows. Traditional psychoanalysts expect problems to subside as people gain insight into their unresolved and unconscious tensions. Humanistic therapists expect problems to abate as people get in touch with their feelings. Behavior therapists, however, doubt the healing power of self-awareness. They assume problem behaviors *are* the problems. For example, you can become aware of why you are highly anxious during exams and still be anxious. **Behavior therapy** applies learning principles to eliminate a troubling behavior. To treat phobias or sexual disorders, behavior

■ **active listening** empathic listening in which the listener echoes, restates, and clarifies. A feature of Rogers' client-centered therapy.

■ **behavior therapy** therapy that applies learning principles to the elimination of unwanted behaviors.

■ **counterconditioning** a behavior therapy procedure that conditions new responses to stimuli that trigger unwanted behaviors; based on classical conditioning. Includes *exposure therapy* and *aversive conditioning*.

■ **exposure therapies** behavioral techniques, such as systematic desensitization, that treat anxieties by exposing people (in imagination or actuality) to the things they fear and avoid.

therapists do not delve deeply below the surface looking for inner causes. They view maladaptive symptoms, such as anxiety, as learned behaviors that can be replaced with constructive behaviors.

Classical Conditioning Techniques

OBJECTIVE 7 | Define *counterconditioning*, and describe the techniques used in exposure therapies and aversive conditioning.

One cluster of behavior therapies derives from principles developed in Pavlov's early-twentieth-century conditioning experiments (pages 315–317). As Pavlov and others showed, we learn various behaviors and emotions through classical conditioning. So, are maladaptive symptoms examples of conditioned responses? If so, might reconditioning be a solution? Learning theorist O. H. Mowrer developed one such conditioning therapy for chronic bed-wetters. The child sleeps on a liquid-sensitive pad connected to an alarm. Moisture on the pad triggers the alarm, waking the child. With sufficient repetition, this association of urinary relaxation with waking up stops the bed-wetting. In three out of four cases the treatment is effective, and the success provides a boost to the child's self-image (Christophersen & Edwards, 1992; Houts & others, 1994).

What might a psychoanalyst say about this therapy for bed-wetting? How might a behavior therapist reply?

Another example: If a claustrophobic fear of elevators is a learned aversion to the stimulus of being in a confined space, then might one unlearn the fear by counterconditioning the fear response? **Counterconditioning** pairs the trigger stimulus with a new response that is incompatible with fear. And indeed, behavior therapists have successfully counterconditioned this fear by repeatedly pairing the enclosed space of the elevator with a relaxed response may displace the fear response. In such therapy, two specific counterconditioning techniques—*exposure therapies* and *aversive conditioning* may be used.

Exposure Therapies Picture this scene reported in 1924 by Mary Cover Jones, an associate of the behaviorist John B. Watson: Three-year-old Peter is petrified of rabbits and other furry objects. (Unlike Little Albert's laboratory-conditioned fear of white rats, described in Chapter 8, Peter's fear arose during the course of his life at home and is more intense.) Jones aims to replace Peter's fear of rabbits with a conditioned response that is incompatible with fear. Her strategy is to associate the fear-evoking rabbit with the pleasurable, relaxed response associated with eating.

As Peter begins his midafternoon snack, Jones introduces a caged rabbit on the other side of the huge room. Peter, eagerly munching away on his crackers and drinking his milk, hardly notices. On succeeding days, she gradually moves the rabbit closer and closer. Within two months, Peter is tolerating the rabbit in his lap, even stroking it while he eats. Moreover, his fear of other furry objects subsides as well, having been "countered," or replaced, by a relaxed state that cannot coexist with fear (Fisher, 1984; Jones, 1924).

Unfortunately for those who might have been helped by her counterconditioning procedures, Jones' story of Peter and the rabbit did not immediately become part of psychology's lore. It was not until more than 30 years later that psychiatrist Joseph Wolpe (1958; Wolpe & Plaud, 1997) refined Jones' technique into what has become the most widely used method of behavior therapy: **exposure therapies,** which expose people to what they normally avoid. As people can habituate to the sound of a train passing their new apartment, so, with repeated exposure, can they become less anxiously responsive to things that once petrified them (Deacon & Abramowitz, 2004).

Hoping to fly free of fear
Some airlines offer programs that ease fear of flying through education and gradual exposure to simulated and actual air travel. Here a pilot explains the functions of the cockpit equipment to participants.

Professor Gallagher and his controversial technique of simultaneously confronting the fear of heights, snakes, and the dark.

Virtual reality exposure therapy
Within the confines of a room, virtual reality technology exposes people to vivid simulations of feared stimuli, such as a plane's takeoff.

One widely used exposure therapy is **systematic desensitization.** Wolpe assumed, as did Jones, that you cannot be simultaneously anxious and relaxed. Therefore, if you can repeatedly relax when facing anxiety-provoking stimuli, you can gradually eliminate your anxiety. The trick is to proceed gradually.

Let's see how this might work with a common phobia. Imagine yourself afraid of public speaking. A behavior therapist might first ask for your help in constructing a hierarchy of anxiety-triggering speaking situations. Your anxiety hierarchy could range from mildly anxiety-provoking situations, such as speaking up in a small group of friends, to panic-provoking situations, such as having to address a large audience.

Using *progressive relaxation,* the therapist trains you to relax one muscle group after another, until you achieve a drowsy state of complete relaxation and comfort. Then the therapist asks you to imagine, with your eyes closed, a mildly anxiety-arousing situation: You are having coffee with a group of friends and are trying to decide whether to speak up. If imagining the scene causes you to feel any anxiety, you signal your tension by raising your finger, and the therapist instructs you to switch off the mental image and go back to deep relaxation. This imagined scene is repeatedly paired with relaxation until you feel no trace of anxiety.

The therapist progresses up the constructed anxiety hierarchy, using the relaxed state to desensitize you to each imagined situation. After several sessions, you practice what you had imagined in actual situations, beginning with relatively easy tasks and gradually moving to more anxiety-filled ones. Conquering your anxiety in an actual situation, not just in your imagination, raises your self-confidence (Foa & Kozak, 1986; Williams, 1987). Eventually, you may even become a confident public speaker.

When the anxiety-arousing situation is too expensive, difficult, or embarrassing to re-create, **virtual reality exposure therapy** offers an efficient middle ground. Wearing a head-mounted display unit that projects a three-dimensional virtual world, you would view a lifelike series of scenes. As your head turns, motion sensors adjust the scene. Experiments led by several research teams have treated people who fear flying, fear heights, fear particular animals, and fear public speaking (Gershon & others, 2002; Rothbaum & others, 2002). People who fear flying, for example, can peer out a virtual window of a simulated plane, feel vibrations, and hear the engine roar as the plane taxis down the runway and takes off. In initial experiments, those experiencing virtual reality exposure therapy have had greater relief from their fears—in real life—than have those in control groups (Hoffman, 2004; Krijn & others, 2004).

Aversive Conditioning In systematic desensitization, the goal is substituting a positive (relaxed) response for a negative (fearful) response to a *harmless* stimulus. In **aversive conditioning,** the goal is substituting a negative (aversive) response for a positive response to a *harmful* stimulus (such as alcohol). Thus, aversive conditioning is the reverse of systematic desensitization—it seeks to condition an aversion to something the client *should* avoid.

The procedure is simple: It associates the unwanted behavior with unpleasant feelings. To treat nail biting, one can paint the fingernails with a yucky-tasting nail polish (Baskind, 1997). To treat alcoholism, an aversion therapist offers the client appealing drinks laced with a drug that produces severe nausea. By linking alcohol with violent nausea (recall the taste-aversion experiments with rats and coyotes in Chapter 8), the therapist seeks to transform the person's reaction to alcohol from positive to negative (**FIGURE 17.1**).

Does aversive conditioning work? In the short run it may. Arthur Wiens and Carol Menustik (1983) studied 685 patients with alcoholism who completed an aversion therapy program at a Portland, Oregon, hospital. One year later, after returning for several booster treatments of alcohol-sickness pairings, 63 percent were still successfully abstaining. But after three years, only 33 percent had remained abstinent.

The problem, as we saw in Chapter 8, is that cognition influences conditioning. People know that outside the therapist's office they can drink without fear of nau-

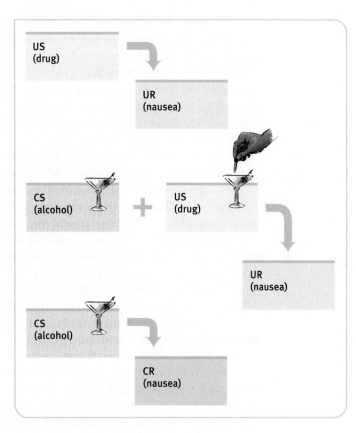

FIGURE 17.1
Aversion therapy for alcoholism
After repeatedly imbibing an alcoholic drink mixed with a drug that produces severe nausea, some people with a history of alcohol abuse develop at least a temporary conditioned aversion to alcohol.

sea. Their ability to discriminate between the aversive conditioning situation and all other situations can limit the treatment's effectiveness. Thus, aversive conditioning is often used in combination with other treatments.

Operant Conditioning

OBJECTIVE **8** | State the main premise of therapy based on operant conditioning principles, and describe the views of proponents and critics of behavior modification.

Recall from Chapter 8 that voluntary behaviors are strongly influenced by their consequences. This simple fact enables behavior therapists to practice *behavior modification*— to reinforce desired behaviors and to withhold reinforcement for undesired behaviors or to punish them. Using operant conditioning to solve specific behavior problems has raised hopes for some cases thought to be hopeless. Children with mental retardation have been taught to care for themselves. Socially withdrawn children with autism have learned to interact. People with schizophrenia have been helped to behave more rationally in their hospital ward. In such cases, therapists use positive reinforcers to shape behavior in the step-by-step manner described on pages 328–329.

In extreme cases, treatment must be intensive. In one study, 19 withdrawn, uncommunicative 3-year-olds with autism participated in a 2-year program in which their parents spent 40 hours each week attempting to shape their behavior (Lovaas, 1987). The combination of positively reinforcing desired behaviors and ignoring or punishing aggressive and self-abusive behaviors worked wonders for some. By first grade, 9 of the 19 children were functioning successfully in school and exhibiting normal intelligence. In a group of 40 comparable children who did not undergo this treatment, only one showed similar improvement.

Rewards used to modify behavior vary. For some people, the reinforcing power of attention or praise is sufficient. Others require concrete rewards, such as food. In institutional settings, therapists may create a **token economy.** When people display

■ **systematic desensitization** a type of counterconditioning that associates a pleasant relaxed state with gradually increasing anxiety-triggering stimuli. Commonly used to treat phobias.

■ **virtual reality exposure therapy** An anxiety treatment that progressively exposes people to simulations of their greatest fears, such as airplane flying, spiders, or public speaking.

■ **aversive conditioning** a type of counterconditioning that associates an unpleasant state (such as nausea) with an unwanted behavior (such as drinking alcohol).

■ **token economy** an operant conditioning procedure in which people earn a token of some sort for exhibiting a desired behavior and can later exchange the tokens for various privileges or treats.

appropriate behavior, such as getting out of bed, washing, dressing, eating, talking coherently, cleaning up their rooms, or playing cooperatively, they receive a token or plastic coin as a positive reinforcer. Later, they can exchange their accumulated tokens for various rewards, such as candy, watching television, trips to town, or better living quarters. Token economies have been successfully applied in various settings (homes, classrooms, hospitals, institutions for the delinquent) and among members of various populations (including disturbed children and people with schizophrenia and other mental disabilities).

Critics of behavior modification express two concerns. The first is practical: What happens when the reinforcers stop, as when the person leaves the institution? Could the person become so dependent on extrinsic rewards that the appropriate behaviors quickly disappear? If so, how can therapists make the appropriate behaviors durable? Proponents of behavior modification respond that they may wean patients from the tokens by shifting them toward other rewards, such as social approval, more typical of life outside the institution. They may also train people to behave in ways that are intrinsically rewarding. For example, as a withdrawn person becomes more socially competent, the intrinsic satisfactions of social interaction may help the person maintain the behavior.

The second concern is ethical: Is it right for one human to control another's behavior? Those who set up token economies may deprive people of something they desire and then decide which behaviors they will reinforce. To critics, the whole behavior modification process has an authoritarian taint. So why not reinforce adaptive behavior instead? They argue that treatment with positive rewards is more humane than being institutionalized or punished, and that the right to effective treatment and to an improved life justifies temporary deprivation. Advocates reply that some clients request the therapy. Moreover, control already exists; rewards and punishers are already maintaining destructive behavior patterns.

Cognitive Therapies

OBJECTIVE 9 | Contrast cognitive therapy and cognitive-behavior therapy, and give some examples of cognitive therapy for depression.

We have seen how behavior therapists treat specific fears and problem behaviors. But how do they deal with major depression? Or with general anxiety, in which anxiety has no focus and developing a hierarchy of anxiety-triggering situations is difficult? Behavior therapists treating these less clearly defined psychological problems have had help from the same *cognitive revolution* that has profoundly changed other areas of psychology during the last five decades.

Cognitive therapy for eating disorders aided by journaling
Cognitive therapists guide people toward new ways of explaining their good and bad experiences. By recording each day's positive events, and how one enabled them, for example, people may become more mindful of their self-control.

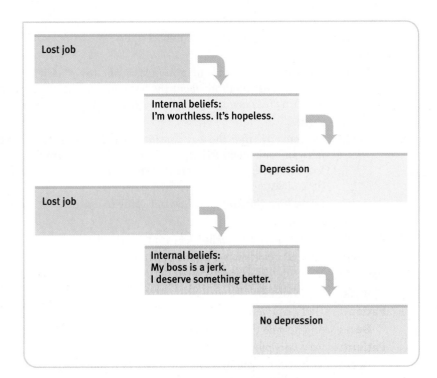

FIGURE 17.2
A cognitive perspective on psychological disorders
The person's emotional reactions are produced not directly by the event but by the person's thoughts in response to the event.

The **cognitive therapies** assume that our thinking colors our feelings (**FIGURE 17.2**), that between the event and our response lies the mind. Self-blaming and overgeneralized explanations of bad events are often an integral part of the vicious cycle of depression (see Chapter 16). The person experiencing depression interprets a suggestion as criticism, disagreement as dislike, praise as flattery, friendliness as pity. Ruminating on such thoughts sustains the bad mood. If depressed thinking patterns can be learned, then surely they can be replaced. Cognitive therapists therefore try in various ways to teach people new, more constructive ways of thinking. If people are miserable, they can be helped to change their minds.

> "Life does not consist mainly, or even largely, of facts and happenings. It consists mainly of the storm of thoughts that are forever blowing through one's mind."
> Mark Twain, 1835–1910

Cognitive Therapy for Depression

Cognitive therapist Aaron Beck was originally trained in Freudian techniques. As Beck analyzed the dreams of people with depression, he found recurring negative themes of loss, rejection, and abandonment that extended into their waking thoughts. Such negativity even extends into therapy, as clients recall and rehearse their failings and worst impulses (Kelly, 2000). So with cognitive therapy Beck and his colleagues (1979) instead have sought to reverse clients' catastrophizing beliefs about themselves, their situations, and their futures. With gentle questioning that aims to help people discover their irrationalities, they persuade depressed people to take off the dark glasses through which they view life (Beck & others, 1979, pp. 145–146):

Patient: *I agree with the descriptions of me but I guess I don't agree that the way I think makes me depressed.*

Beck: *How do you understand it?*

Patient: *I get depressed when things go wrong. Like when I fail a test.*

Beck: *How can failing a test make you depressed?*

Patient: *Well, if I fail I'll never get into law school.*

Beck: *So failing the test means a lot to you. But if failing a test could drive people into clinical depression, wouldn't you expect everyone who failed the test to have a depression? . . . Did everyone who failed get depressed enough to require treatment?*

Patient: *No, but it depends on how important the test was to the person.*

■ **cognitive therapy** therapy that teaches people new, more adaptive ways of thinking and acting; based on the assumption that thoughts intervene between events and our emotional reactions.

Beck: *Right, and who decides the importance?*

Patient: *I do.*

Beck: *And so, what we have to examine is your way of viewing the test (or the way that you think about the test) and how it affects your chances of getting into law school. Do you agree?*

Patient: *Right.*

Beck: *Do you agree that the way you interpret the results of the test will affect you? You might feel depressed, you might have trouble sleeping, not feel like eating, and you might even wonder if you should drop out of the course.*

Patient: *I have been thinking that I wasn't going to make it. Yes, I agree.*

Beck: *Now what did failing mean?*

Patient: *(tearful) That I couldn't get into law school.*

Beck: *And what does that mean to you?*

Patient: *That I'm just not smart enough.*

Beck: *Anything else?*

Patient: *That I can never be happy.*

Beck: *And how do these thoughts make you feel?*

Patient: *Very unhappy.*

Beck: *So it is the meaning of failing a test that makes you very unhappy. In fact, believing that you can never be happy is a powerful factor in producing unhappiness. So, you get yourself into a trap—by definition, failure to get into law school equals "I can never be happy."*

Another variety of cognitive therapy builds on the finding that depressed people do not exhibit the self-serving bias common in nondepressed people (page 666). Instead, they often attribute their failures to themselves and attribute their successes to external circumstances. Thus, Adele Rabin and her colleagues (1986) explained to 235 depressed adults the advantages of interpreting events as nondepressed people do. She then trained the participants to reform their habitually negative patterns of thinking and labeling. For example, she had them record each day's positive events and write down how they contributed to each. Compared with people who remained on a waiting list for therapy for depression, those who went through the positive-thinking exercises found their depression dropped dramatically (**FIGURE 17.3**). The more people change their negative thinking styles, the more their mood lifts (Seligman, 1991).

Here is another example: We often think in words. Therefore, getting people to change what they say to themselves is an effective way to change their thinking. Perhaps you can identify with the anxious students who before an exam make matters worse with self-defeating thoughts: "This exam's probably going to be impossible. All these other students seem so relaxed and confident. I wish I were better prepared. Anyhow, I'm so nervous I'll forget everything." To change such negative self-talk, Donald Meichenbaum (1977, 1985) has offered *stress inoculation training,* teaching people to restructure their thinking in stressful situations. Sometimes it may be enough simply to say more positive things to oneself: "Relax. The exam may be hard, but it will be hard for everyone else, too. I studied harder than most people. Besides, I don't need a perfect score to get a good grade." In experiments, depression-prone children and college students exhibit a halved rate of future depression after being trained to dispute their negative thoughts (Seligman, 2002). To a great extent, it *is* the thought that counts.

Knowing that there is two-way traffic between depressed mood and negative thinking, the Penn Optimism Program reached out to 9- to 13-year-old children targeted as at risk for depression. The program puts children through 12 small-group sessions, each lasting two hours, in which they learn to tune into their thoughts when facing tough situa-

FIGURE 17.3

Cognitive therapy for depression

Participants in a program that trained them to think more as nondepressed people do—noticing and taking personal credit for good events and not taking blame for, or overgeneralizing from, bad events—experienced dramatic declines in depression. (From Rabin & others, 1986.)

PEANUTS

tions and to imagine alternatives to negative thoughts. The leader might, for example, present a cartoon depicting a child being called a name and invite the children to brainstorm positive ways to cope. In early experiments, the training halved the proportion of children suffering depression for up to two ensuing years (Gillham & others, 1995).

Cognitive therapists often combine the reversal of self-defeating thinking with efforts to modify behavior. This integrated therapy, called **cognitive-behavior therapy,** aims to alter the way people act (behavior therapy) and to alter the way they think (cognitive therapy). It seeks to make people aware of their irrational negative thinking, to replace it with new ways of thinking, *and* to practice the more positive approach in everyday settings.

In one study, for example, people with obsessive-compulsive behaviors learned to relabel their compulsive thoughts (Schwartz & others, 1996). Feeling the urge to wash their hands again, they would tell themselves, "I'm having a compulsive urge," and attribute it to their brain's abnormal activity, as shown in PET scans. Instead of giving in to the urge, they then engaged for 15 minutes in an enjoyable, alternative behavior, such as practicing an instrument, taking a walk, or gardening. This helped "unstick" the brain by shifting attention and engaging other parts of the brain. For two or three months, the weekly therapy sessions continued, with relabeling and refocusing practice at home. By the study's end, most participants' symptoms had diminished and their PET scans revealed normalized brain activity.

Group and Family Therapies

OBJECTIVE **10** | Discuss the rationale and benefits of group therapy, including family therapy.

Except for traditional psychoanalysis, the therapies we have considered may also occur in therapist-led small groups. Group therapy does not provide the same degree of therapist involvement with each client; however, it saves therapists' time and clients' money—and it often is no less effective than individual therapy (Fuhriman & Burlingame, 1994). Therapists frequently suggest group therapy for people experiencing family conflicts or those whose behavior is distressing to others. For up to 90 minutes a week, the therapist guides the interactions of 6 to 10 people as they engage issues and react to one another.

Group sessions also offer a unique benefit: The social context allows people both to discover that others have problems similar to their own and to receive feedback as they try out new ways of behaving. It can be a relief to find that you are not alone—to learn that others, despite their apparent composure, share your problems and your troublesome feelings. It can also be reassuring to hear that you yourself look poised even though you feel anxious and self-conscious.

One special type of group interaction, **family therapy,** assumes that no person is an island, that we live and grow in relation to others, especially our families. We struggle to differentiate ourselves from our families, but we also need to connect with them emotionally. Some of our problem behaviors arise from the tension between these two tendencies, which can create family stress. Clients often come to therapists seeking help in their relationships with family members.

■ **cognitive-behavior therapy** a popular integrated therapy that combines cognitive therapy (changing self-defeating thinking) with behavior therapy (changing behavior).

■ **family therapy** therapy that treats the family as a system. Views an individual's unwanted behaviors as influenced by or directed at other family members; attempts to guide family members toward positive relationships and improved communication.

Group therapy

This counselor works with troubled teens in groups, which enables the youths to feel less alone in their troubles and enables the counselor to assist more teens at lower cost.

With an estimated 1.8 million members worldwide, AA is said to be "the largest organization on Earth that nobody wanted to join" (Finlay, 2000).

Unlike most psychotherapy, which focuses on what happens inside the person's own skin, family therapists work with family groups to heal relationships and to mobilize family resources. Their aim is to help family members discover the role they play within their family's social system. A child's rebellion, for example, affects and is affected by other family tensions. Family therapists also attempt—usually with some success, research suggests (Hazelrigg & others, 1987; Shadish & others, 1993)—to open up communication within the family or to help family members discover new ways of preventing or resolving conflicts.

A wide range of people participate in self-help and support groups (Yalom, 1985). One analysis (Davison & others, 2000) of on-line support groups and more than 14,000 self-help groups reports that most support groups focus on stigmatized or hard-to-discuss illnesses. AIDS patients are 250 times more likely than hypertension patients to be in support groups. Those struggling with anorexia and alcoholism often join groups; those with migraines and ulcers do not. People with hearing loss have national organizations with local chapters; people with vision loss more often cope without such.

The grandparent of support groups, Alcoholics Anonymous (AA), reportedly has 87,000 groups worldwide (McKillop & others, 2003). Its famous 12-step strategy, emulated by many other self-help groups, asks members to admit their powerlessness, to seek help from a higher power and from one another, and (the twelfth step) to take the message to others in need of it. In one eight-year, $27 million investigation, people seeking treatment for alcoholism reduced their drinking sharply, although so did those assigned to cognitive-behavior therapy or to a "motivational therapy" (Project Match, 1997). The more AA meetings patients attend, the greater their alcohol abstinence. In one study of 2300 veterans who sought alcoholism treatment, a high level of AA involvement was followed by diminished alcohol problems (McKellar & others, 2003).

In an individualistic age, with more and more people living alone or feeling isolated, the popularity of support groups—for the addicted, the bereaved, the divorced, or simply those seeking fellowship and growth—seems to reflect a longing for community and connectedness. More than 100 million Americans belong to small religious, interest, or self-help groups that meet regularly—and 9 in 10 report that group members "support each other emotionally" (Gallup, 1994).

>> LEARNING OUTCOMES

The Psychological Therapies

OBJECTIVE 2 | Define *psychoanalysis*, and discuss the aims of this form of therapy.

Psychoanalysis is Sigmund Freud's therapeutic technique of using a patient's free associations, resistances, dreams, and transferences, and the therapist's interpretations of them, to help the person release previously repressed feelings and gain insight into current conflicts. Clinicians working from the psychoanalytic perspective try to help people gain insight into the unconscious origins of their disorders, work through the accompanying feelings, and take responsibility for their own growth.

OBJECTIVE 3 | Describe some of the methods used in psychoanalysis, and list some criticisms of this form of therapy.

Psychoanalysts may ask patients to *free associate* (saying aloud anything that comes to mind) and watch for pauses or diver-

sions that may indicate *resistance* (the defensive blocking from consciousness of anxiety-laden material). Analysts may offer patients their interpretations of these instances of resistance, of dreams, and of other behaviors, such as *transference* (transferring to the therapist the strong feelings harbored against a family member or other significant person). Critics note that traditional psychoanalysis has relied on after-the-fact interpretations and repressed memories, and that it is time-consuming and very costly.

OBJECTIVE 4 | Contrast psychodynamic therapy and interpersonal therapy with traditional psychoanalysis.

Psychodynamic therapy was influenced by traditional psychoanalysis but is briefer and less expensive. A psychodynamic therapist attempts to focus on and conceptualize a patient's current conflicts and defenses by searching for themes common to many past and present important relationships, including (but not limited to) childhood experiences and interactions with the therapist. *Interpersonal therapy* (a brief 12- to 16-session form of psychodynamic therapy) focuses primarily on relieving current symptoms (such as depression) rather than on an intensive interpretation of the origins of unconscious conflicts.

OBJECTIVE 5 | **Identify the basic characteristics of the humanistic therapies, and describe the specific goals and techniques of Carl Rogers' client-centered therapy.**

Humanistic therapists focus on clients' present and future experiences, on conscious rather than unconscious thoughts, and on taking responsibility for one's feelings and actions. One of the most famous humanistic therapies was Carl Rogers' *client-centered therapy.* Rogers proposed that therapists' most important contributions are to function as a psychological mirror for the client through active listening, and to provide an environment of unconditional positive regard, characterized by genuineness, acceptance, and empathy. In this growth-fostering environment, Rogers believed, clients would increase their own self-understanding and self-acceptance.

OBJECTIVE 6 | **Explain how the basic assumption of behavior therapy differs from those of traditional psychoanalytic and humanistic therapies.**

To help people alleviate current conflicts and problems, traditional psychoanalytic therapists attempt to explain the origin of behaviors, and humanistic therapists attempt to promote self-acceptance and self-awareness. Behavior therapists assume the problem behaviors *are* the problem, and they attempt to change them through new learning.

OBJECTIVE 7 | **Define *counterconditioning*, and describe the techniques used in exposure therapies and aversive conditioning.**

Counterconditioning uses classical conditioning techniques to pair new responses with old stimuli that have triggered maladaptive behaviors. *Exposure therapies* (including systematic desensitization and virtual reality exposure therapy) train people to relax (a response that cannot co-exist with fear) and then gradually but repeatedly expose them to the things they fear and avoid. Exposure therapies try to substitute a positive response (relaxation) for a negative one (fear). *Aversive conditioning* uses counterconditioning techniques to pair an unpleasant state with an unwanted behavior. Aversive conditioning tries to substitute a negative response (such as nausea) for a positive one (pleasure) to a harmful stimulus (alcohol).

OBJECTIVE 8 | **State the main premise of therapy based on operant conditioning principles, and describe the views of proponents and critics of behavior modification.**

Operant conditioning therapies are based on the principle that voluntary behaviors are strongly influenced by their consequences. *Behavior modification* procedures thus enforce desired behaviors and withhold reinforcement for, or punish, undesired behaviors. Therapists sometimes create *token economies,* in which people receive tokens for exhibiting a desired behavior and can later trade the tokens for a privilege or treat. Critics object (1) on the practical grounds that these behaviors may disappear when the tokens are discontinued, and (2) on the ethical grounds that it is not right to control other people's behavior. Proponents counter with the arguments that (1) social or intrinsic rewards can replace the tokens and continue to be reinforcing, and (2) reinforcing adaptive behavior is justified because, with or without behavior modification, rewards and punishers will always control people's behavior.

OBJECTIVE 9 | **Contrast cognitive therapy and cognitive-behavior therapy, and give some examples of cognitive therapy for depression.**

Cognitive therapy attempts to teach people to think in more adaptive ways, on the assumption that thoughts intervene between an event and our emotional reactions to it. *Cognitive-behavior therapy* attempts to teach people to think in more adaptive ways but also to practice their new ways of thinking in everyday life. In Aaron Beck's cognitive therapy for depression, therapists try to change self-defeating thinking by training clients to look at themselves in new, more positive ways. In *stress inoculation training,* another form of cognitive therapy, people with depression learn to dispute their negative thoughts and to restructure their thinking in stressful situations. Depressed people also work to establish the attribution style of nondepressed people (taking credit for good events and not taking blame for, or overgeneralizing from, bad events).

OBJECTIVE 10 | **Discuss the rationale and benefits of group therapy, including family therapy.**

In groups normally consisting of 6 to 9 people, therapists may be less involved with each member, but the (on average) 90-minute session can help more people and cost less per person than individual therapy would. Clients may benefit from knowing others have similar problems and from getting feedback and reassurance. Most forms of therapy can be adapted to a group setting. *Family therapy* views a family as an interactive system and attempts to help members discover the roles they play and to learn to communicate more openly and directly. Millions of people participate in self-help and support groups, such as Alcoholics Anonymous.

ASK YOURSELF: Without trying to play therapist, how might you use the helping principles discussed in this chapter with a friend who is anxious?

Evaluating Psychotherapies

Advice columnist Ann Landers frequently advised her troubled letter writers to get professional help. One response urged the writer "not to give up. Hang in there until you find [a psychotherapist] who fills the bill. It's worth the effort." On the same day, she advised a second letter writer, "There are many excellent mental health facilities in your city. I urge you to make an appointment at once" (Farina & Fisher, 1982). Many share Ann Landers' confidence in psychotherapy's effectiveness.

Before 1950, the primary mental health providers were psychiatrists. Since then, demand has outgrown the psychiatric profession, and now most psychotherapy is done by clinical and counseling psychologists; clinical social workers; pastoral, marital, abuse, and school counselors; and psychiatric nurses. Thus, in addition to 55,000 clinical psychiatrists and 95,000 doctoral-level clinical psychologists in the United States, there are a quarter million other licensed therapists, many with social work training (Glenn, 2003). Much therapy is done through community mental health programs, which provide outpatient therapy, crisis phone lines, and halfway houses for those making the transition from hospitalization to independent living. With such an enormous outlay of time, money, effort, and hope, it is important to ask: Is the faith that Ann Landers and millions of others worldwide place in these therapists justified? And was the *Wall Street Journal* (1999) therefore wrong to suppose that including psychotherapy in health insurance plans would lead to "endless payments for dubious benefits of apparently marginal problems"?

Is Psychotherapy Effective?

The question, though simply put, is not simply answered. For one thing, measuring therapy's effectiveness is not like taking your body's temperature to see if your fever has gone away. If you and I were to undergo psychotherapy, how would we gauge its effectiveness? By how we feel about our progress? How our therapist feels about it? How our friends and family feel about it? How our behavior has changed?

Clients' Perceptions

OBJECTIVE 11 | Explain why clients tend to overestimate the effectiveness of psychotherapy.

If clients' testimonials were the only measuring stick, we could strongly affirm the effectiveness of psychotherapy. When 2900 *Consumer Reports* readers (1995; Kotkin & others, 1996; Seligman, 1995) related their experiences with mental health professionals, 89 percent said they were at least "fairly well satisfied." Among those who recalled feeling *fair* or *very poor* when beginning therapy, 9 in 10 now were feeling *very good, good,* or at least *so-so.* We have their word for it—and who should know better?

We should not dismiss these testimonials lightly. People enter therapy because they are suffering, and most leave feeling better about themselves. But there are several reasons why client testimonials do not persuade psychotherapy's skeptics:

- ***People often enter therapy in crisis.*** When, with the normal ebb and flow of events, the crisis passes, people may attribute their improvement to the therapy.
- ***Clients may need to believe the therapy was worth the effort.*** To admit investing time and money in something ineffective is like admitting to having one's car serviced repeatedly by a mechanic who never fixes it. Self-justification is a powerful human motive.
- ***Clients generally speak kindly of their therapists.*** Even if the clients' problems remain, say the critics, "they work hard to find something positive to say. The therapist had been very understanding, the client had gained a new perspective, he learned to communicate better, his mind was eased, anything at all so as not to have to say treatment was a failure" (Zilbergeld, 1983, p. 117).

Testimonials can be misleading. As earlier chapters document, we are prone to selective and biased recall and to making judgments that confirm our beliefs. Consider a massive experiment with over 500 Massachusetts boys, aged 5 to 13 years, many of whom seemed bound for delinquency. By the toss of a coin, half the boys were assigned to a five-year treatment program. Counselors visited the treated boys twice a month. The boys participated in community programs such as the Boy Scouts. As the need arose, they received academic tutoring, medical attention, and family assistance. Some 30 years after the end of the program, Joan McCord (1978, 1979) located 97 percent of the participants. To assess the treatment's impact, she sent them questionnaires and checked public records from courts, mental hospitals, and other sources.

Assessing the treatment program with client testimonials yielded encouraging results. Many of the men offered glowing reports. Some noted that had it not been for their counselors, "I would probably be in jail," "My life would have gone the other way," or "I think I would have ended up in a life of crime." The court records offered apparent support for these testimonials. Even among the "difficult" boys in the program, *66 percent* had no official juvenile crime record.

But recall psychology's most powerful tool for sorting reality from wishful thinking: the *control group*. For every boy who was counseled, there was a similar boy in a control group who was not. McCord tracked down these untreated people and found that among the predelinquent boys in the control group, *70 percent* had no juvenile record. Moreover, on some measures, such as a record of having committed a second crime, alcoholic tendencies, death rate, and job satisfaction, the untreated men exhibited slightly *fewer* problems. The glowing testimonials of those treated had been unintentionally deceiving.

This shocking finding—that testimonials can badly mislead—was confirmed in the 1990s. Delinquent boys put through "Scared Straight" programs (visiting jails, being taunted by prison inmates) said they were now more likely to be law-abiding. But they weren't. Compared with those not assigned to Scared Straight, boys who were in the program became *more* likely to commit new offenses (Dishion & others, 1999; Petrosino & others, 2000). Testimonials can and do mislead.

Clinicians' Perceptions

OBJECTIVE 12 | Give some reasons why clinicians tend to overestimate the effectiveness of psychotherapy, and describe two phenomena that contribute to clients' and clinicians' misperceptions in this area.

If clinicians' perceptions accurately reflected therapeutic effectiveness, we would have even more reason to celebrate. Case studies of successful treatment abound. Furthermore, every therapist treasures compliments from clients as they say good-bye or later express their gratitude. The problem is that clients justify entering psychotherapy by emphasizing their unhappiness, justify leaving therapy by emphasizing their well-being, and stay in touch only if satisfied. Therapists are aware of failures, but they are mostly the failures of *other* therapists—those whose clients, having experienced only temporary relief, are now seeking a new therapist for their recurring problems. Thus, the same person with the same recurring difficulty—the same old anxieties, depression, or marital difficulty—may be a "success" story in several therapists' files.

Because people enter therapy when they are extremely unhappy, and usually leave when they are less extremely unhappy, most therapists, like most clients, testify to therapy's success—regardless of the treatment (see Thinking Critically About: "Regressing" From Unusual to Usual on page 702). Although "treatments" have varied widely, from chains to counseling, every generation views its own approach as enlightened.

THINKING CRITICALLY ABOUT

"REGRESSING" FROM UNUSUAL TO USUAL

Clients' and therapists' perceptions of therapy's effectiveness are vulnerable to inflation from two phenomena. One is the *placebo effect*—the power of *belief* in a treatment. As we saw in Chapter 1, an inert placebo is often used as a control treatment in drug experiments. If you *think* a treatment is going to be effective, it just may be (thanks to the healing power of your positive expectation).

The second phenomenon is **regression toward the mean**—the tendency for unusual events (or emotions) to "regress" (return) toward their average state. Thus, extraordinary happenings (feeling low) tend to be followed by more ordinary ones (a return to our more usual state). Because we returned to that more usual state, anything we tried in the interim may seem to

> The real purpose of [the] scientific method is to make sure Nature hasn't misled you into thinking you know something that you actually don't."
>
> Robert Pirsig, *Zen and the Art of Motorcycle Maintenance*, 1974

have been effective. Indeed, when things hit bottom, whatever we try—going to a psychotherapist, starting yoga, doing aerobic exercise—is more likely to be followed by improvement than by further descent.

The point may seem obvious, yet we regularly miss it: We sometimes attribute what may be a normal regression (the expected return to normal) to something we have done. Consider:

- Students who score much lower or higher on an exam than they usually do are likely, when retested, to return toward their average.
- Unusual ESP subjects who defy chance when first tested nearly always lose their "psychic powers" when retested (a phenomenon parapsychologists have called the "decline effect").
- Coaches often yell at their players after an unusually bad first half. They may then feel rewarded for having done so when the team's performance improves (returns to normal) during the second half.

Once you become sensitized to it, you see regression everywhere."
Psychologist Daniel Kahneman (1985)

- Scientists who win a Nobel Prize—an extraordinary accomplishment—almost always experience diminished accomplishments thereafter, leading some to believe that winning a Nobel hinders creativity.

In each case, the cause-effect link may be genuine. More likely, however, is that each is an instance of the natural tendency for behavior to regress from the unusual to the more usual. And this defines a task for therapy-efficacy research: discerning whether troubled people's improvement following a particular therapy exceeds what we could expect from the placebo and regression effects, as shown in control groups not receiving the treatment.

■ **regression toward the mean** the tendency for extremes of unusual scores to fall back (regress) toward their average.

Outcome Research

OBJECTIVE 13 | Describe the importance of outcome studies in judging the effectiveness of psychotherapies, and discuss some of these findings.

How, then, can we objectively measure the effectiveness of psychotherapy? What types of people and problems are best helped, and by what type of psychotherapy? The questions have both academic and personal relevance. If you or someone you care about feels anxious or depressed, or suffers some psychological disorder, it is crucial for you to understand the likelihood of psychotherapy's being of help.

In hopes of better assessing psychotherapy's effectiveness, psychologists have turned to controlled research studies. Similar research in the 1800s transformed medicine from concocted treatments (bleeding, purging, infusions of plant and metal substances) into a science. The transformation occurred when skeptical physicians began to realize that many patients got better on their own, that most of the fashionable treatments were doing no good, and that sorting fact from superstition required following illnesses closely—with and without a particular treatment. Typhoid fever patients, for example, often improved after being bled, convincing most physicians that the treatment worked. Not until a control group was given mere bed rest—and 70 percent were observed to improve after five weeks of fever—did physicians learn, to their shock, that this treatment was worthless (Thomas, 1992).

■ **meta-analysis** a procedure for statistically combining the results of many different research studies.

In psychology, the opening challenge in what became a spirited debate over such research was issued by British psychologist Hans Eysenck (1952). He summarized studies showing that two-thirds of those suffering nonpsychotic disorders improve markedly after undergoing psychotherapy. To this day, no one disputes that optimistic estimate.

So why then are we still debating psychotherapy's effectiveness? Because Eysenck also reported similar improvement among *untreated* persons, such as those who were on waiting lists. With or without psychotherapy, he said, roughly two-thirds improved noticeably. Time was a great healer.

The avalanche of criticism prompted by Eysenck's conclusions revealed shortcomings in his analyses. Also, in 1952 Eysenck could find only 24 studies of psychotherapy outcomes to analyze. Today, there are hundreds. The best of these *randomized clinical trials* randomly assign people on a waiting list to therapy or to no therapy. Afterward, researchers evaluate everyone, using tests and the reports of friends and family or of psychologists who don't know whether therapy was given. The results of many such studies are then digested by a technique called **meta-analysis,** a procedure for statistically combining the conclusions of a large number of different studies as if the results had come from one huge study with thousands of participants. Simply said, meta-analyses give us the bottom-line results of lots of studies.

In the first of more than five dozen meta-analyses of psychotherapy outcome studies, Mary Lee Smith and her colleagues (1980) combined the results of 475 investigations. For psychotherapists, the welcome result was that "the evidence overwhelmingly supports the efficacy of psychotherapy" (p. 183). **FIGURE 17.4** depicts their finding—that the average therapy client ends up better off than 80 percent of the untreated individuals on waiting lists. The claim is more modest than it first appears—by definition, about 50 percent of untreated people also are better off than the average untreated person. Nevertheless, Smith and her collaborators exulted that "psychotherapy benefits people of all ages as reliably as schooling educates them, medicine cures them, or business turns a profit" (p. 183).

Newer research summaries confirm that psychotherapy works (Kopta & others, 1999; Shadish & others, 2000). In one ambitious study, the National Institute of Mental Health compared three depression treatments: cognitive therapy, interpersonal therapy, and a standard drug therapy. Twenty-eight experienced therapists at research sites in Norman, Oklahoma; Washington, DC; and Pittsburgh, Pennsylvania, were trained in one of the three methods and randomly assigned their share of the 239 participants suffering from depression. Clients in all three groups improved more than did those in a control group who received merely an inert medication and supportive attention, encouragement, and advice. Among people who completed a full 16-week treatment program, the depression had lifted for slightly more than half of those in each treatment group—but for only 29 percent of those in the control group (Elkin & others, 1989). This verdict echoes the results of the earlier outcome studies: *Those not undergoing therapy often improve, but those undergoing therapy are more likely to improve.*

Psychotherapy is also cost-effective when compared with the greater costs of medical care for psychologically related complaints. When people seek psychological treatment, their search for medical treatment drops—by 16 percent in one digest of 91 studies (Chiles & others, 1999).

The annual cost of psychological disorders and substance abuse—including crime, accidents, lost work, and treatment—is staggering.

> "Fortunately, [psycho]analysis is not the only way to resolve inner conflicts. Life itself still remains a very effective therapist."
>
> Karen Horney, *Our Inner Conflicts*, 1945

FIGURE 17.4
Treatment versus no treatment
These two normal distribution curves based on data from 475 studies show the improvement of untreated people and psychotherapy clients. The outcome for the average therapy client surpassed that for 80 percent of the untreated people. (Adapted from Smith & others, 1980.)

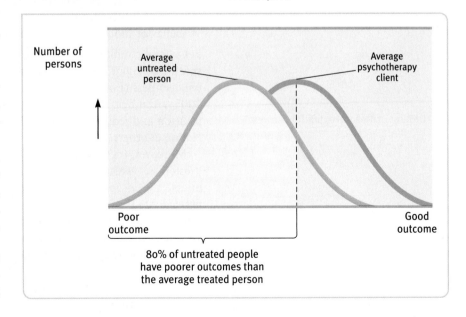

Number of persons

Average untreated person

Average psychotherapy client

Poor outcome

Good outcome

80% of untreated people have poorer outcomes than the average treated person

Thus, just as an investment in prenatal and well-baby care *reduces* long-term costs, so will an investment in almost any effective treatment for psychological problems. Anything that boosts employees' psychological well-being will reduce medical costs, improve work efficiency, and diminish absenteeism. Studies by health insurers show that mental health treatment can more than pay for itself with reduced medical costs (American Psychological Association, 1991).

But note that the claim—that psychotherapy, *on average,* is somewhat effective—refers to no one therapy in particular. It is like saying, "Surgery is somewhat effective," or reassuring lung-cancer patients that "on average," medical treatment of health problems is effective. What people want to know is not the average effectiveness of all therapy but the particular effectiveness of a treatment for their specific problems.

The Relative Effectiveness of Different Therapies

OBJECTIVE 14 | Summarize the findings on which psychotherapies are most effective for specific disorders.

> "Whatever differences in treatment efficacy exist, they appear to be extremely small, at best."
>
> Bruce Wampold and colleagues (1997)

So what can we tell people considering therapy, and those paying for it, about *which* psychotherapy will be most effective for their problem? Despite claims of superiority by advocates of different types of therapy, the meta-analysis conducted by Mary Lee Smith and her colleagues (1977, 1980) revealed no one type of therapy as generally superior. *Consumer Reports* readers, too, were equally satisfied, no matter what type of therapy they received and whether treated by a psychiatrist, psychologist, or social worker (Seligman, 1995). Moreover—and more astonishing—the group or individual context of the therapy made no discernible difference, nor did the level of training and experience of the therapist. Now, more than two decades after Smith's analysis, newer evidence indicates little if any connection between clinicians' experience, training, supervision, and licensing and their clients' outcomes (Bickman, 1999; Luborsky & others, 2002). Was the dodo bird in *Alice in Wonderland* right: "Everyone has won and all must have prizes"?

A Society of Clinical Psychology task force is answering that question by identifying treatments shown to be beneficial in controlled treatment studies (Chambless & others, 1997; Norcross, 2002). The task force has pinpointed some elements of effective therapy, such as empathy. And it offers lists of *empirically supported therapies,* including, for example,

- cognitive therapy, interpersonal therapy, and behavior therapy for depression.
- cognitive therapy, exposure therapy, and stress inoculation training for anxiety.
- cognitive-behavior therapy for bulimia.
- behavior modification for bed wetting.

Behavioral conditioning therapies have also achieved especially favorable results with specific behavior problems such as phobias, compulsions, marital problems, and sexual disorders (Bowers & Clum, 1988; Hunsley & DiGiulio, 2002; Shadish & Baldwin, 2005). And new studies confirm cognitive therapy's effectiveness in coping with depression and reducing suicide risk (Brown & others, 2005; DeRubeis & others, 2005; Hollon & others, 2005).

> "Different sores have different salves."
>
> English proverb

Moreover, therapy is most effective when the problem is clear-cut (Singer, 1981; Westen & Morrison, 2001). Those who experience phobias or panic, who are unassertive, or who are frustrated by sexual performance problems can hope for improvement. Those who suffer less-focused problems, such as depression and anxiety, usually benefit in the short term but often relapse later. Those who have chronic schizophrenia or who wish to change their whole personality are unlikely to benefit from psychotherapy alone (Zilbergeld, 1983). The more specific the problem, the greater the hope.

Meanwhile, controversy continues—some call it today's civil war in psychology—over the extent to which science should guide both clinical practice and the willingness of health care providers and insurers to pay for psychotherapy. On the one side are science-oriented psychologists working to extend the list of evidence-based practice, with well-defined and validated therapies for various disorders. On the other side are those who view therapy as more art than science, not something amenable to describing in a manual or testing in an experiment. People are too complex and therapy too intuitive for a cookie-cutter approach, say the nonscientist therapists. But by basing practice on evidence and making mental health professionals accountable for effectiveness, say the science-oriented clinicians, therapy stands to gain credibility. Moreover, the public will be protected from pseudotherapies, and therapists will be protected from accusations of sounding like snake-oil salesmen—"Trust me, I know it works, I've seen it work."

Evaluating Alternative Therapies

OBJECTIVE 15 | Evaluate the effectiveness of eye movement desensitization and reprocessing (EMDR) and light exposure therapies.

The tendency of abnormal states of mind to "regress" to normal, combined with the placebo effect, creates fertile soil for pseudotherapies. Bolstered by anecdotes, heralded by the media, praised on the Internet, alternative therapies can spread like wildfire. Princess Diana typified the modern fascination with alternative healers by seeking out spiritualists, a hypnotherapist, an "anger-release" therapist, reflexologists, aromatherapists, colonic irrigationists, and a "mind-body" therapist (Smith, 1999). She had much company. In one national survey, 57 percent of those with a history of anxiety attacks and 54 percent of those with a history of depression had used alternative treatments such as herbal medicine, massage, and spiritual healing (Kessler & others, 2001).

What can we say of such alternative therapies? Testimonials aside—every therapy, whether effective or not, will *seem* effective to some—what does the evidence say? Which are empirically validated?

About most, there is no evidence, because their proponents and devotees feel no need for controlled research. For them, personal experience is evidence enough. So which therapies do get systematically evaluated? To gauge scientific versus popular interest in various treatments and assessment techniques, clinical researcher Scott Lilienfeld (1998) suggests comparing the number of times each is mentioned in electronic searches of psychology's scientific literature and on unfiltered Web sources. As **TABLE 17.1** shows, some topics exist almost exclusively on the Web.

In earlier chapters, we critically evaluated alternative therapies such as subliminal self-help tapes, recovery of supposedly repressed memories, and hypnosis. Let's now consider two more. As we do, remember that sifting sense from nonsense requires the scientific attitude: being skeptical but not cynical, open to surprises but not gullible.

TABLE 17.1

COMPARISON OF SCIENTIFIC PSYCHOLOGY CITATIONS AND UNFILTERED WEB SITES

Topic	Psychology Journal Citations*	Web Sites**	Ratio
Systematic desensitization	2,301	56,800	1 to 25
Therapeutic touch	94	383,000	1 to 4,074
St. John's wort (herbal remedy)	200	2,590,000	1 to 12,950
Enneagram (personality typing)	32	775,000	1 to 24,218

*Using PsycINFO, January 2006
**Using Google, January 2006

Eye Movement Desensitization and Reprocessing (EMDR)

Walking in a park one day, Francine Shapiro (1989) observed that anxious thoughts vanished as her eyes spontaneously darted about. From this experience she developed a novel anxiety treatment: *eye movement desensitization and reprocessing (EMDR)*. While people imagined traumatic scenes, Shapiro triggered eye movements by waving her finger in front of their eyes, supposedly enabling them to unlock and reprocess previously frozen trauma memories. She tried this on 22 people haunted by old traumatic memories, and all reported marked reductions in their distress after just one therapeutic session. This extraordinary result evoked an enormous response from mental health professionals, 40,000 of whom from 52 countries have undergone training (EMDR, 2002). Not since the similarly charismatic Franz Anton Mesmer introduced *animal magnetism* (hypnosis) more than two centuries ago (also after feeling inspired by an outdoor experience) has a new therapy attracted so many devotees so quickly.

Does it work? For 84 to 100 percent of single-trauma victims participating in four recent studies, the answer is yes, reports Shapiro (1999, 2002). (When EMDR did not fare well in other trials, Shapiro argued that the therapists were not properly trained.) Moreover, the treatment need take no more than three 90-minute sessions. The Society of Clinical Psychology task force on empirically validated treatments acknowledges that the treatment is "probably efficacious" for the treatment of nonmilitary posttraumatic stress disorder (Chambless & others, 1997). Encouraged by their seeming successes, EMDR therapists are now applying the technique to other anxiety disorders, such as panic disorder, and, with Shapiro's (1995, 2002) encouragement, to a wide range of complaints, including pain, grief, paranoid schizophrenia, rage, and guilt.

EMDR is a therapy that thousands adore, and thousands more dismiss as a sham—"an excellent vehicle for illustrating the differences between scientific and pseudoscientific therapy techniques," suggest James Herbert and seven others (2000). Why, wondered skeptics, should rapidly moving one's eyes while recalling traumas be therapeutic? Indeed, eye movements, it seems, are not the therapeutic ingredient. When researchers tested the therapy without the eye movements—with finger tapping, for example, or with eyes fixed straight ahead while the therapist's finger wagged—the therapeutic results were the same (Devilly, 2003). What is therapeutic, the skeptics suspect, is the combination of exposure therapy—repeatedly reliving traumatic memories in a safe and reassuring context—and a robust placebo effect. Had Mesmer's pseudotherapy been compared with no treatment at all, notes Richard McNally (1999), it, too (thanks to the healing power of positive belief), could have been found "probably efficacious."

> "Meta-analyses [indicate that EMDR is] just as effective with fixed eyes. If that conclusion is right, what's useful in the therapy (chiefly behavioral desensitization) is not new, and what's new is superfluous."
>
> *Harvard Mental Health Letter*, 2002

Light therapy

To counteract winter depression, some people spend time each morning in front of a box emitting intense light that mimics natural outdoor light.

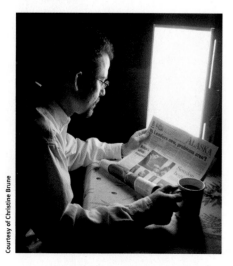

Light Exposure Therapy

Have you ever found yourself oversleeping, gaining weight, and feeling lethargic during the dark mornings and overcast days of winter? For some people, especially women and those living far from the equator, the wintertime blahs constitute a form of depression known as *seasonal affective disorder,* for which the appropriate acronym is SAD. To counteract these dark spirits, National Institute of Mental Health researchers in the early 1980s had a bright idea: Give SAD people a timed daily dose of intense light. When clinical experience indicated that light exposure could also relieve symptoms associated with wintertime depression, manufacturers produced light boxes that can now be rented or purchased from health supply and lighting stores.

Is this another placebo effect, attributable to people's expectations? Recent studies shed light on this therapy. One exposed some people with SAD to 90 minutes of bright light and others to a sham placebo treatment—a hissing "negative ion generator" about which the staff expressed similar enthusiasm (but which, unknown to the participants, was not turned on). After four weeks of exposure, 61 percent of those exposed to morning light had greatly improved, as had 50 percent of those exposed to evening light and 32 percent of those exposed to the placebo treatment (Eastman &

others, 1998). Two other studies found that 30 minutes of light exposure produced relief for more than half the people receiving morning light therapy and for one-third receiving evening light therapy (Terman & Terman, 1998, 2001). From 20 carefully controlled trials we have a verdict (Golden & others, 2005): For many people, morning bright light does indeed dim SAD symptoms.

Commonalities Among Psychotherapies

OBJECTIVE 16 | Describe the three benefits attributed to all psychotherapies.

Good therapists may have differing perspectives, yet share much in common, including compassion, sensitivity, and empathy. Jerome Frank (1982), Marvin Goldfried (Goldfried & Padawer, 1982), Hans Strupp (1986), and Bruce Wampold (2001) studied the common ingredients of various therapies and suggest they all offer at least three benefits: hope for demoralized people; a new perspective on oneself and the world; and an empathic, trusting, caring relationship. These nonspecific factors aren't all that therapy offers, but they are important (Barker & others, 1988; Jones & others, 1988; Roberts & others, 1993). They are part of what the growing numbers of self-help and support groups offer their members. And they have been part of what traditional healers offer (Jackson, 1992). Healers—special people to whom others disclose their suffering—have for centuries listened in order to understand and to empathize, reassure, advise, console, interpret, or explain.

Hope for Demoralized People

People who seek therapy typically feel anxious, depressed, devoid of self-esteem, and incapable of turning things around. What any therapy offers is the expectation that, with commitment from the therapy seeker, things can and will get better. Apart from the particular therapeutic technique, this belief may itself function as a placebo, promoting improved morale, new feelings of self-efficacy, and diminished symptoms (Prioleau & others, 1983). Similar effects have been found in psychotherapy experiments in which the placebo treatment was listening to inspirational tapes or taking a fake pill.

The finding from meta-analyses that improvement is greater for placebo-treated people than for untreated people (although not as great as for those receiving actual psychotherapy) suggests that one reason therapies help is that they offer hope. Said another way, therapy outcomes vary with the attitude of the person seeking help—the person's motivation, confidence, and commitment. Each therapy, in its individual way, may harness the person's own healing powers. And that, says psychiatrist Jerome Frank, helps us understand why all sorts of treatments—including some folk healing rites that are powerless apart from the participants' belief—may in their own time and place produce cures.

A New Perspective

Every therapy offers people a plausible explanation of their symptoms and an alternative way of looking at themselves or responding to their world. Therapy can offer new experiences as well, ones that help people change their behaviors and their views of themselves. Armed with a believable fresh perspective, they may approach life with a new attitude.

An Empathic, Trusting, Caring Relationship

To say that all therapies are about equally effective is not to say all *therapists* are equally effective. Regardless of their therapeutic technique, effective therapists are empathic people who seek to understand another's experience; who communicate their care and

"I utilize the best from Freud, the best from Jung, and the best from my Uncle Marty, a very smart fellow."

© 1994 by Sidney Harris—"Stress Test," Rutgers University Press.

A caring relationship
Effective therapists form a bond of trust with their patients.

concern to the client; and who earn the client's trust and respect through respectful listening, reassurance, and advice. In a National Institute of Mental Health depression-treatment study, the most effective therapists were those who were perceived as most empathic and caring and who established the closest therapeutic bonds with their clients (Blatt & others, 1996). In another study, Marvin Goldfried and his associates (1998) analyzed taped therapy sessions from 36 recognized master therapists. Some were cognitive-behavior therapists, others were psychodynamic-interpersonal therapists. Regardless, the striking finding was how *similar* the therapists were during the parts of their sessions they considered most significant. At key moments, the empathic therapists of both persuasions would help clients evaluate themselves, link one aspect of their life with another, and gain insight into their interactions with others. Indeed, some believe warmth and empathy are hallmarks of healers everywhere, whether psychiatrists, witch doctors, or shamans (Torrey, 1986). The emotional bond between therapist and client—the *therapeutic alliance*—is a key aspect of effective therapy (Klein & others, 2003; Wampold, 2001).

That all therapies offer *hope* through a *fresh perspective* offered by a *caring person* is supported by a meta-analysis of 39 studies. Each study compared treatment offered by professional therapists with treatment offered by laypeople: friendly professors, people who had had a few hours' training in empathic listening skills, and college students supervised by a professional clinician. The result? The *paraprofessionals,* as these and other briefly trained people are called, typically proved as effective as the professionals (Christensen & Jacobson, 1994). Although most of the problems they treated were mild, the trained paraprofessionals were—believe it or not—as effective as professionals even when dealing with more disturbed adults, such as those diagnosed with serious depression.

To recap, people who seek help usually improve. So do many of those who do not undergo psychotherapy, and that is a tribute to our human resourcefulness and our capacity to care for one another. Nevertheless, though the therapist's orientation and experience appear not to matter much, people who receive some psychotherapy usually improve more than those who do not. People with clear-cut, specific problems tend to improve the most.

Part of what all therapies offer is hope, a fresh way of looking at life, and an empathic, caring relationship. That may explain why the empathy and friendly counsel of paraprofessionals are often as helpful as professional psychotherapy. And that may also explain why people who feel supported by close relationships—who enjoy the fellowship and friendship of caring people—are less likely to need or seek therapy (Frank, 1982; O'Connor & Brown, 1984).

Culture and Values in Psychotherapy

OBJECTIVE **17** | Discuss the role of values and cultural differences in the therapeutic process.

All therapies offer hope, and nearly all therapists attempt to enhance their clients' sensitivity, openness, personal responsibility, and sense of purpose (Jensen & Bergin, 1988). But on certain matters of moral and cultural diversity, therapists may differ from one another and from their clients (Kelly, 1990). In Canada and the United States, for example, about 1 person in 25 is a self-proclaimed atheist or agnostic, as are (depending on the survey) one-fifth to one-half of psychiatrists and clinical psychologists (Gallup, 1993; Lukoff & others, 1992). In Britain, two-thirds of psychiatrists say they are atheists (Neeleman & Persaud, 1995). That raises an intriguing issue: What values prevail in psychotherapy? What values *should* prevail? Should it matter that highly religious people prefer religiously similar therapists (Worthington & others, 1996)?

CLOSE-UP:

A CONSUMER'S GUIDE TO PSYCHOTHERAPISTS

Life for everyone is marked by a mix of serenity and stress, blessing and bereavement, good moods and bad. So, when should a person seek the help of a mental health professional? When troubling thoughts and emotions interfere with your normal living, you might consider talking to a professional. The American Psychological Association offers these common trouble signals:

- Feelings of hopelessness
- Deep and lasting depression
- Self-destructive behavior, such as alcohol and drug abuse
- Disruptive fears
- Sudden mood shifts
- Thoughts of suicide
- Compulsive rituals, such as hand washing
- Sexual difficulties

In looking for a therapist, you may want to have a preliminary consultation with two or three. You can describe your problem and learn each therapist's treatment approach. You can ask questions about the therapist's values, credentials (**TABLE 17.2**), and fees. And, knowing the importance of the emotional bond between therapist and client, you can assess your own feelings about each of them.

TABLE 17.2

THERAPISTS AND THEIR TRAINING

Type	Description
Counselors	Marriage and family counselors specialize in problems arising from family relations. Pastoral counselors provide counseling to countless people. Abuse counselors work with substance abusers and with spouse and child abusers and their victims.
Clinical or psychiatric social workers	A two-year master of social work graduate program plus post-graduate supervision prepares some social workers to offer psychotherapy, mostly to people with everyday personal and family problems. About half have earned the National Association of Social Workers' designation of clinical social worker.
Clinical psychologists	Most are psychologists with a Ph.D. or Psy.D. and expertise in research, assessment, and therapy, supplemented by a supervised internship and, often, post-doctoral training. About half work in agencies and institutions, half in private practice.
Psychiatrists	Psychiatrists are physicians who specialize in the treatment of psychological disorders. Not all psychiatrists have had extensive training in psychotherapy, but as M.D.s they can prescribe medications. Thus, they tend to see those with the most serious problems. Many have their own private practice.

Albert Ellis, a well-known therapist, and Allen Bergin, co-editor of the *Handbook of Psychotherapy and Behavior Change,* illustrate how sharply values can differ. Ellis (1980) assumes that "no one and nothing is supreme," that "self-gratification" should be encouraged, and that "unequivocal love, commitment, service, and . . . fidelity to any interpersonal commitment, especially marriage, leads to harmful consequences." Bergin (1980) assumes the opposite—that "because God is supreme, humility and the acceptance of divine authority are virtues," that "self-control and committed love and self-sacrifice are to be encouraged," and that "infidelity to any interpersonal commitment, especially marriage, leads to harmful consequences." Bergin and Ellis disagree more radically than most therapists on what values are healthiest. In so doing, however, they illustrate what they agree on: that psychotherapists' personal beliefs and values influence their practice. Knowing that clients tend to adopt their therapists' values (Worthington & others, 1996), Bergin and Ellis also agree that therapists should divulge their values more openly. (For those thinking about seeking therapy, Close-Up: A Consumer's Guide to Psychotherapists offers some tips on when to seek help and how to start your search for a therapist with values and goals similar to yours.)

Value differences also can become significant when a therapist from one culture meets a client from another. In North America, Europe, and Australia, for example, most therapists reflect their culture's individualism, which often gives priority to personal desires and identity. Clients who are immigrants from Asian countries, which expect people to be more mindful of

Changing in China

These men are listening sympathetically to fellow patients, many of whom are HIV positive, at a support group meeting at a drug rehabilitation center in southwest China.

Michael Reynolds/EPA/SIPA

others' expectations, may have trouble relating to therapies that require them to think only of their own well-being. Such differences help explain the reluctance of some minority populations to use mental health services (Sue, 1990). In one experiment, Asian-American clients matched with counselors who shared their cultural values (rather than mismatched with those who didn't) perceived more counselor empathy and felt more alliance with the counselor (Kim & others, 2005). Recognizing that therapists and clients may differ in their values, communication styles, and language, many therapy training programs now provide training in cultural sensitivity and recruit members of underrepresented cultural groups.

>> LEARNING OUTCOMES

Evaluating Psychotherapies

OBJECTIVE 11 | Explain why clients tend to overestimate the effectiveness of psychotherapy.

Clients judge psychotherapy to be effective for three reasons: They tend to enter therapy in crisis, they need to believe their time and expense justified, and they try to find something positive to say when asked to evaluate their therapist. But research has not generally upheld clients' estimates of therapy's effectiveness.

OBJECTIVE 12 | Give some reasons why clinicians tend to overestimate the effectiveness of psychotherapy, and describe two phenomena that contribute to clients' and clinicians' misperceptions in this area.

Clients enter therapy when they are unhappy, leave it when they are less unhappy, and stay in touch only if satisfied with the treatment they received. So clinicians are mostly aware of other therapists' failures, not their own. Both the *placebo effect* (the belief a treatment will work) and *regression toward the mean* (the tendency for extreme or unusual scores to fall back toward the mean) contribute to clients' and clinicians' misperceptions of the effectiveness of psychotherapy.

OBJECTIVE 13 | Describe the importance of outcome studies in judging the effectiveness of psychotherapies, and discuss some of these findings.

Outcome studies are randomized clinical trials in which people on a waiting list receive therapy or no therapy. Statistical digests (*meta-analyses*) of hundreds of these studies reveal that (1) people who remain untreated often improve, but (2) those who receive psychotherapy are more likely to improve, and (3) people who receive psychological treatment spend less time and money later seeking other medical treatment, compared with their counterparts on waiting lists.

OBJECTIVE 14 | Summarize the findings on which psychotherapies are most effective for specific disorders.

Meta-analyses indicate that no one type of therapy is most effective overall, nor is there any connection between effectiveness and a therapist's training, experience, supervision, or licensing. Some therapies are particularly well-suited to specific disorders, such as cognitive, interpersonal, and behavior therapies for depression; cognitive, exposure, and stress-inoculation therapies for anxiety; cognitive-behavior therapy for bulimia; behavior modification for bed wetting; and behavior conditioning therapies for phobias, compulsions, and sexual disorders. The more specific the problem, the greater the chances for effective treatment. Debate continues over the extent to which clinical practice should be based on scientific evidence or intuitive responses.

OBJECTIVE 15 | Evaluate the effectiveness of eye movement desensitization and reprocessing (EMDR) and light exposure therapies.

In *EMDR* therapy, a therapist attempts to unlock and reprocess previously frozen traumatic memories by waving a finger in front of the eyes of a person imagining traumatic scenes. EMDR has not held up under scientific testing, and its modest successes may be attributable to the placebo effect. In people with *seasonal affective disorder,* a form of depression linked to periods of decreased sunlight, *light exposure therapy* (exposure to daily timed doses of light that mimics outdoor light) has been proven effective by scientific research.

OBJECTIVE 16 | Describe the three benefits attributed to all psychotherapies.

All types of psychotherapy seem to offer new hope for demoralized people, a fresh perspective, and an empathic, trusting, caring relationship. The *therapeutic alliance*—the emotional bond between therapist and client—is an important part of effective therapy and may help explain why some paraprofessionals can be as helpful as professional psychotherapists.

OBJECTIVE 17 | Discuss the role of values and cultural differences in the therapeutic process.

Psychotherapists may differ from each other and from clients in personal beliefs, values, and cultural background. Such differences can affect the formation of a bond between therapist and client. People searching for a therapist should have preliminary consultations with two or three to gain an understanding of the therapists' values, credentials, and fees, and to find someone with whom they feel comfortable.

ASK YOURSELF: Can you think of a time when your positive expectations for improvement may have been self-fulfilling?

The Biomedical Therapies

Psychotherapy is one way to treat psychological disorders. The other, often used with serious disorders, is *biomedical therapy*—physically changing the brain's functioning by altering its chemistry with drugs, overloading its circuits with electroconvulsive shock, using magnetic impulses to stimulate or dampen its activity, or altering its circuits through psychosurgery.

Drug Therapies

OBJECTIVE 18 | Define *psychopharmacology,* and explain how double-blind studies help researchers evaluate a drug's effectiveness.

By far the most widely used biomedical treatments today are the drug therapies. Since the 1950s, discoveries in **psychopharmacology** (the study of drug effects on mind and behavior) have revolutionized the treatment of people with severe disorders, liberating hundreds of thousands from hospital confinement. Thanks to drug therapy—and to efforts to minimize involuntary hospitalization and to support people with community mental health programs—the resident population of U.S. state and county mental hospitals is a fraction of what it was a half-century ago (**FIGURE 17.5**). For some unable to care for themselves, however, release from hospitals has meant homelessness, not liberation.

"The mentally ill were out of the hospital, but in many cases they were simply out on the streets, less agitated but lost, still disabled but now uncared for."

Lewis Thomas, *Late Night Thoughts on Listening to Mahler's Ninth Symphony*, 1983

FIGURE 17.5
The emptying of U.S. mental hospitals
After the widespread introduction of antipsychotic drugs, starting in about 1955, the number of residents in state and county mental hospitals declined sharply. But in the rush to deinstitutionalize the mentally ill, many people who were ill-equipped to care for themselves were left homeless on city streets. (Data from the National Institute of Mental Health and Bureau of the Census, 2004.)

Almost any new treatment, including drug therapy, is greeted by an initial wave of enthusiasm as many people apparently improve. But that enthusiasm often diminishes after researchers subtract the rates of (1) normal recovery among untreated persons and (2) recovery due to the placebo effect, which arises from the positive expectations of patients and mental health workers alike. So, to evaluate the effectiveness of any new drug, researchers use the *double-blind technique.* Half the patients receive the drug, the other half a similar-appearing placebo. Neither the staff nor the patients know who gets which. The good news: In double-blind studies, several types of drugs have proven useful in treating psychological disorders.

Antipsychotic Drugs

OBJECTIVE 19 | Describe the characteristics of antipsychotic drugs, and discuss their use in treating schizophrenia.

The revolution in drug therapy for psychological disorders began with the accidental discovery that certain drugs, used for other medical purposes, calmed psychotic patients. These *antipsychotic* drugs, such as chlorpromazine (sold as Thorazine),

■ **psychopharmacology** the study of the effects of drugs on mind and behavior.

dampened responsiveness to irrelevant stimuli. Thus they provided the most help to schizophrenia patients experiencing positive symptoms, such as auditory hallucinations and paranoia (Lehman & others, 1998; Lenzenweger & others, 1989). Patients exhibiting negative symptoms, such as apathy and withdrawal, often do not respond well to these antipsychotic drugs. A newer drug, clozapine (marketed since 1989 as Clozaril), does sometimes enable "awakenings" in such people. It also sometimes helps those who have positive symptoms but have not responded to other drugs. Those who take clozapine must have regular blood tests because in 1 percent of cases, it has a toxic effect on white blood cells.

The molecules of antipsychotic drugs are similar enough to molecules of the neurotransmitter dopamine to occupy its receptor sites and block its activity (Pickar & others, 1984; Taubes, 1994). (Clozapine blocks serotonin activity as well.) The finding that most antipsychotic drugs block dopamine receptors reinforces the idea that an overactive dopamine system contributes to schizophrenia.

Antipsychotics are powerful drugs. The first-generation dopamine-blocking drugs (such as Thorazine), which target D2 dopamine receptors, can produce sluggishness, tremors, and twitches similar to those of Parkinson's disease, which is marked by too little dopamine (Kaplan & Saddock, 1989). Long-term use of these medications can also produce **tardive dyskinesia,** a neurotoxic effect, involving involuntary movements of the facial muscles (such as grimacing), tongue, and limbs. In contrast, *new-generation antipsychotic drugs* (such as clozapine, Risperdal, and Zyprexa), which target D1 dopamine receptors, have fewer such side effects. However, these newer medications appear hardly more effective and seem to increase the risk of obesity and diabetes (Leberman & others, 2005). Another complication with both generations of these medications is that one person's effective dose may be another person's overdose or underdose. Only by carefully monitoring the dosage and its effects can psychiatrist and patient tread the fine line between symptom relief and extremely unpleasant side effects. But with the appropriate dosage, combined with life-skills programs and family support, hundreds of thousands of people with schizophrenia who had been consigned to the back wards of mental hospitals have returned to work and to near-normal lives, and relapse rates have been reduced (Leucht & others, 2003).

Antianxiety Drugs

OBJECTIVE **20** | Describe the characteristics of antianxiety drugs.

Like alcohol, *antianxiety* agents, such as Xanax or Ativan, depress central nervous system activity (and so should not be used in combination with alcohol). Used in combination with psychological therapy, an antianxiety drug can help a person learn to cope with frightening situations and fear-triggering stimuli.

The criticism sometimes made of the behavior therapies—that they reduce symptoms without resolving underlying problems—is also made of antianxiety drugs. Unlike the behavior therapies, however, these substances may be used as an ongoing treatment. "Popping a Xanax" at the first sign of tension can produce psychological dependence; the immediate relief reinforces a person's tendency to take drugs when anxious. Antianxiety drugs can also cause physiological dependence. When heavy users stop taking them, they may experience withdrawal symptoms, such as increased anxiety and insomnia.

Over the dozen years at the end of the twentieth century, the rate of outpatient treatment for anxiety disorders nearly doubled. The proportion of patients receiving medication during that time increased from 52 to 70 percent (Olfson & others, 2004). And the new standard drug treatment for anxiety disorders? Antidepressants.

Perhaps you can guess an occasional side effect of L-dopa, a drug that raises dopamine levels for Parkinson's patients: hallucinations.

■ **tardive dyskinesia** involuntary movements of the facial muscles, tongue, and limbs; a possible neurotoxic side effect of long-term use of antipsychotic drugs that target D2 dopamine receptors.

Antidepressant Drugs

OBJECTIVE **21** | Describe the characteristics of antidepressant drugs, and discuss their use in treating specific disorders.

As the antianxiety drugs can calm people down from a state of anxiety, the *antidepressants* sometimes lift people up from a state of depression. (Their name is a bit of a misnomer now that these drugs are increasingly being used to successfully treat anxiety disorders such as obsessive-compulsive disorder.) This class of drugs works by increasing the availability of norepinephrine or serotonin, neurotransmitters that elevate arousal and mood and appear scarce during depression. Fluoxetine, which tens of million of users worldwide have known as Prozac, partially blocks the reabsorption and removal of serotonin from synapses (**FIGURE 17.6**). Because they slow the synaptic vacuuming up of serotonin, Prozac, and its cousins Zoloft and Paxil, are called *selective-serotonin-reuptake-inhibitors (SSRIs)*. Other dual-action antidepressants work by blocking the reabsorption or breakdown of both norepinephrine and serotonin. Though no less effective, the dual-action drugs have more potential side effects, such as dry mouth, weight gain, hypertension, or dizzy spells (Anderson, 2000; Mulrow, 1999). Administering them by means of a patch, bypassing the intestines and liver, helps reduce such side effects (Bodkin & Amsterdam, 2002).

The greater popularity of SSRI drugs helps explain why 89 percent of patients diagnosed with depression in 2001 received medication from their physicians, up from 70 percent in 1987, the year before SSRIs were introduced (Olfson & others, 2003; Stafford & others, 2001). And that, plus increasing numbers seeking help for depression and anxiety, helps explain a reported tripling in the total number of antidepressant prescriptions since 1992 (Goode, 2002). The drugs account for most of the $19.5 billion in worldwide antidepressant sales in 2000 (Sherman, 2004).

Be advised: Patients with depression who begin taking antidepressants do not wake up the next day singing "Oh, what a beautiful morning!" Although the influence of antidepressants on neurotransmission does occur within hours, their full psychological effect often requires four weeks. One possible reason for the delayed effect is that increased serotonin seems to promote *neurogenesis*—the birth of new brain cells, perhaps reversing stress-induced loss of neurons (Jacobs; 2004; Santarelli & others, 2003).

Antidepressant drugs are not the only way to give the body a lift. Aerobic exercise, which helps calm people who feel anxious and energize those who feel depressed, does about as much good for some people with mild to moderate depression, and has

One side effect of SSRI drugs can be decreased sexual appetite, which has led to their occasional prescription to control sexual behavior (Slater, 2000).

On U.S. college campuses, the 9 percent of counseling center visitors taking psychiatric medication in 1994 nearly tripled, to 24.5 percent in 2004 (Duenwald, 2004).

FIGURE 17.6
Biology of antidepressants
Shown here is the action of Prozac, which partially blocks the reuptake of serotonin.

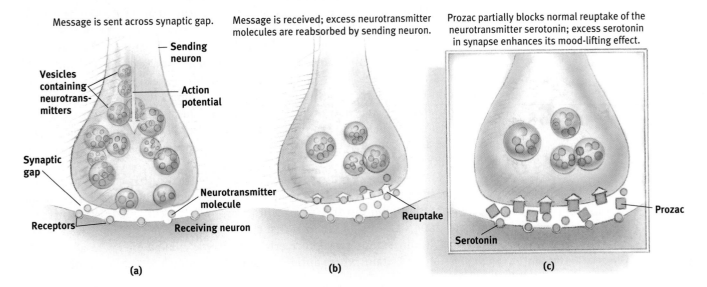

(a) Message is sent across synaptic gap. — Sending neuron, Vesicles containing neurotransmitters, Action potential, Synaptic gap, Neurotransmitter molecule, Receptors, Receiving neuron

(b) Message is received; excess neurotransmitter molecules are reabsorbed by sending neuron. — Reuptake

(c) Prozac partially blocks normal reuptake of the neurotransmitter serotonin; excess serotonin in synapse enhances its mood-lifting effect. — Prozac, Serotonin

"If this doesn't help you don't worry, it's a placebo."

"No twisted thought without a twisted molecule."

Attributed to psychologist Ralph Gerard

"I think the dosage needs adjusting. I'm not nearly as happy as the people in the ads."

additional positive side effects (see pages 567–568). Cognitive therapy, by helping people reverse their habitual negative thinking style, can boost the drug-aided relief from depression and reduce the post-treatment risk of relapse (Hollon & others, 2002; Keller & others, 2000). Better yet, some studies suggest, is to attack depression from both above and below (Goldapple & others, 2004; TADS, 2004). Use antidepressant drugs (which work, bottom-up, on the emotion-forming limbic system) in conjunction with cognitive behavior therapy (which works, top-down, starting with changed frontal lobe activity).

Everyone agrees that people with depression often improve after a month on antidepressants. But after allowing for natural recovery (the regression to normal called *spontaneous recovery*) and the placebo effect, how big is the drug effect? Not big, report Irving Kirsch and his colleagues (1998, 2002) from their analyses of double-blind clinical trials: Placebos produced improvement comparable to 75 percent or so of the active drug's effect. Another research team analyzed data from 45 studies. Given antidepressants, 41 percent of participants improved; given placebos, 31 percent improved (Khan & others, 2000). Moreover, Kirsch reports, some of the 25 percent difference between the active drug and the placebo in the double-blind trials seems due to an additional placebo effect derived from the drug's side effects, which raise people's expectations because they know they're getting an active drug. Placebos that mimic the side effects of antidepressants are nearly as effective as the drugs themselves (Fisher & Greenberg, 1997).

Many who have witnessed or experienced the healing power of antidepressants question these findings. "It would be very miraculous if all the people I've seen getting better were getting better only by virtue of placebo," said the National Institute of Mental Health's director, Steven Hyman (1999). But this much seems assured: Our expectations have surprisingly powerful effects not only on our perceptions and our responses to alcohol, hypnosis, and sexual situations (as we saw in earlier chapters), but also on our biology and well-being (Kirsch & Lynn, 1999). The mind matters.

Skeptics of the biomedical therapies are unsurprised. Yesterday, says neuroscientist Elliot Valenstein (1998), we blamed mothers and sought to heal their children's inner wounds. Today, hardly wiser, we blame brain chemistry and circuitry and pump in "molecules of the mind." But our knowledge of the biochemical roots of disorder and recovery is elementary, he contends. Psychotherapeutic drugs are not "'smart missiles' that can correct the precise biochemical error responsible for each mental illness" without side effects (1998, p. 5). The chemistry, brain circuitry, and life experiences that underlie behavior are too complex for that.

Although the effects of drug therapy are less exciting than many TV ads suggest, they also are less frightening than other stories have warned. Some people taking Prozac, for example, have committed suicide, but their numbers seem fewer than we would expect from the millions of people with depression who are now taking the medication. Prozac users who commit suicide are like cellular phone users who get brain cancer. Given the millions of people taking Prozac and using cellular phones, alarming anecdotes tell us nothing. The question critical thinkers want answered is this: Do these groups suffer an elevated *rate* of suicide and brain cancer? The answer in each case appears to be no (Paulos, 1995; Tollefson & others, 1993, 1994).

The suicide-risk concern resurfaced in the early twenty-first century with studies indicating that children and adults are at a temporary heightened risk of suicide just after beginning drug treatment (Wessely & Kerwin, 2004; Whittington & others, 2004). One explanation is that the drugs reduce one's lethargy before they lift one's feelings, thus giving formerly inert people enough energy to act on their depression. In Britain, where antidepressant prescriptions for children rose 70 percent from 1992 through 2001, the Department of Health warned against treating mild childhood depression with antidepressant drugs (Alvarez, 2004). In the United States, the Food and Drug Administration began requiring a warning label—that the drugs can cause suicidal behavior in children and teens. But other recent studies indicate that the long-term increase in antidepressant use correlates with a *decline* in the adolescent suicide rate (Grunebaum & others, 2004; Olfson & others, 2003). In U.S. Zip Code areas where antidepressant use increased during the 1990s, teen suicide was most likely to decrease. Such studies suggest that perhaps antidepressants increase suicide risk in the short run, but lower it in the long run.

Mood-Stabilizing Medications

OBJECTIVE 22 | Describe the use and effects of mood-stabilizing medications.

In addition to antipsychotic, antianxiety, and antidepressant drugs, psychiatrists have *mood-stabilizing drugs* in their arsenal. The simple salt *lithium* can be an effective mood stabilizer for those suffering the manic-depressive swings of bipolar disorder. Australian physician John Cade discovered this in the 1940s when he administered lithium to a patient with severe mania. Although his reason for doing so was misguided—he thought lithium had calmed excitable guinea pigs when actually it had made them sick—Cade found that in less than a week the patient became perfectly well (Snyder, 1986). With continued lithium use, emotional highs and lows typically stabilize. After suffering mood swings for years, about 7 in 10 people with bipolar disorder benefit from a long-term daily dose of this cheap salt (Solomon & others, 1995). Their risk of suicide is but one-sixth that of bipolar patients not taking lithium (Tondo & others, 1997). Although we do not fully understand why, lithium works. And so does Depakote, a drug originally used to treat epilepsy and more recently found effective in the control of manic episodes associated with bipolar disorder.

"First of all I think you should know that last quarter's sales figures are interfering with my mood-stabilizing drugs."

Brain Stimulation
Electroconvulsive Therapy

OBJECTIVE 23 | Describe the use of electroconvulsive therapy in treating severe depression, and discuss some possible alternatives to ECT.

A more controversial brain manipulation occurs through shock treatment, or **electroconvulsive therapy (ECT).** When ECT was first introduced in 1938, the wideawake patient was strapped to a table and jolted with roughly 100 volts of electricity to the brain, producing racking convulsions and brief unconsciousness. ECT therefore gained a barbaric image, one that lingers still. Today, however, patients first receive a general anesthetic so they are not conscious, and a muscle relaxant to prevent injury from convulsions. Then a psychiatrist momentarily electrically shocks the unconscious patient's brain. Within 30 minutes, the patient awakens and remembers nothing of the treatment or of the hours preceding it (**FIGURE 17.7**, page 716).

Psychiatrists usually limit ECT to treatment of severe depression. (It tends to be ineffective in treating other psychological disorders.) After three such sessions each week for two to four weeks, 80 percent or more of people receiving ECT improve markedly, showing some memory loss for the treatment period but no discernible brain damage (Bergsholm & others, 1989; Coffey, 1993). "A miracle had happened in two weeks," reported noted research psychologist Norman Endler (1982) after ECT alleviated his deep depression. Study after study confirms that ECT is an effective

The medical use of electricity is an ancient practice. Physicians treated the Roman Emperor Claudius (10 B.C.–A.D. 54) for headaches by pressing electric eels to his temples.

■ **electroconvulsive therapy (ECT)** a biomedical therapy for severely depressed patients in which a brief electric current is sent through the brain of an anesthetized patient.

FIGURE 17.7
Electroconvulsive therapy
Although ECT is controversial, it is the preferred treatment for depression that does not respond to drug therapy.

treatment for severe depression in patients who have not responded to drug therapy (Consensus Conference, 1985; UK ECT Review Group, 2003). By 2001, confidence in ECT had further increased, with a *JAMA* (*Journal of the American Medical Association*) editorial concluding that "the results of ECT in treating severe depression are among the most positive treatment effects in all of medicine" (Glass, 2001).

How does ECT work? After more than 50 years, no one knows for sure. One recipient likened ECT to the smallpox vaccine, which was saving lives before we knew how it worked. Perhaps the shock-induced seizures cause the brain to react by calming neural centers where overactivity produces depression.

ECT reduces suicidal thoughts and is credited with saving many from suicide (Kellner & others, 2005). It is now administered with briefer pulses that disrupt memory less (Fink, 1998; Kho & others, 2003). Yet its Frankensteinlike image continues. No matter how impressive the results, the idea of electrically shocking people into convulsions still strikes many as barbaric, especially given our ignorance about why ECT works. Moreover, ECT-treated patients, like other patients with a history of depression, are vulnerable to relapse. Nevertheless, electroconvulsive therapy is, in the minds of many psychiatrists and patients, a lesser evil than severe depression's misery, anguish, and risk of suicide.

Alternatives to ECT

Hopes are now rising for gentler alternatives for jump-starting the depressed brain. Some patients with chronic depression have found relief through a chest implant that intermittently stimulates the vagus nerve, which sends signals to the brain's mood-related limbic system (Marangell & others, 2002; Rush & others, 2005). In another study of six patients who had failed to respond even to ECT, four gained "striking and sustained remission of depression" following stimulation through electrodes planted deep in their brains (Mayberg & others, 2005). The stimulation served to reduce activity in a region that is hyperactive in depression, and patients immediately experienced such impressions as a "disappearance of the void" and a sense of "connectedness." This finding will surely inspire further experiments to test the possibility of a brain pacemaker that can buzz people out of depression.

Depressed moods also seem to improve when repeated pulses surge through a magnetic coil held close to a person's skull (**FIGURE 17.8**). Unlike deep brain stimulation, the magnetic energy penetrates only to the brain's surface (though tests are under way with a higher energy field that penetrates more deeply). The painless procedure—called **repetitive transcranial magnetic stimulation (rTMS)**—is performed on wide-awake patients for 20 to 30 minutes for two to four weeks. Unlike ECT, the rTMS procedure produces no seizures, memory loss, or other side effects.

In one double-blind experiment, 67 Israelis with major depression were randomly assigned to two groups (Klein & others, 1999). One group received daily stimulations over a two-week period, while the other received sham treatments (without magnetic stimulation). At the end of the two weeks, half of the stimulated patients showed at least a 50 percent improvement in their scores on a depression scale, as did only a quarter of the placebo group. Newer studies confirmed the therapeutic effect, which inspired the beginning in 2005 of two large, multilocation clinical experiments on rTMS (Cohen & others, 2004; Janicak, 2005; Martin & others, 2003). One possible

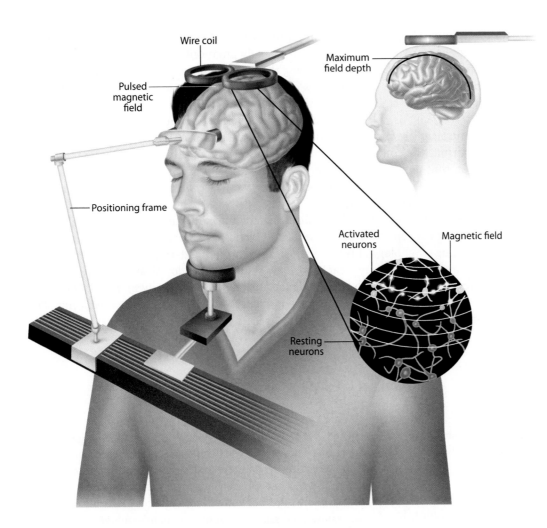

FIGURE 17.8
Magnets for the mind
Repetitive transcranial magnetic stimulation (rTMS) sends a painless magnetic field through the skull to the cortical surface, where pulses can be used to stimulate or dampen activity in various areas (from George, 2003).

explanation of this effect is that the stimulation energizes depressed patients' relatively inactive left frontal lobe (Helmuth, 2001). When repeatedly stimulated, nerve cells can form functioning circuits through a process that Chapter 9 called long-term potentiation (LTP). Before long, conclusive data from the clinical experiments should become available, indicating whether magnetic stimulation is, indeed, a valuable new treatment for depression.

Psychosurgery

OBJECTIVE 24 | Summarize the history of the psychosurgical procedure known as a lobotomy, and discuss the use of psychosurgery today.

Because its effects are irreversible, **psychosurgery**—surgery that removes or destroys brain tissue—is the most drastic and the least-used biomedical intervention for changing behavior. In the 1930s, Portuguese physician Egas Moniz developed what became the best-known psychosurgical operation: the **lobotomy.** Moniz found that cutting the nerves connecting the frontal lobes with the emotion-controlling centers of the inner brain calmed uncontrollably emotional and violent patients. After shocking the patient into a coma, a neurosurgeon would hammer an icepicklike instrument through each eye socket into the brain, then wiggle it to sever connections running up to the frontal lobes. The whole procedure was crude but easy and inexpensive, and it took only about 10 minutes. During the 1940s and 1950s, tens of thousands of severely disturbed people were "lobotomized," and Moniz was honored with a Nobel Prize (Valenstein, 1986).

■ **repetitive transcranial magnetic stimulation (rTMS)** the application of repeated pulses of magnetic energy to the brain; used to stimulate or suppress brain activity.

■ **psychosurgery** surgery that removes or destroys brain tissue in an effort to change behavior.

■ **lobotomy** a now-rare psychosurgical procedure once used to calm uncontrollably emotional or violent patients. The procedure cut the nerves that connect the frontal lobes to the emotion-controlling centers of the inner brain.

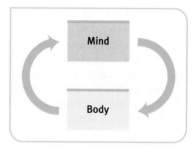

Mind-body interaction
The biomedical therapies assume that mind and body are a unit: Affect one and you will affect the other.

Although the intention was simply to disconnect emotion from thought, the effect was often more drastic: The lobotomy usually produced a permanently lethargic, immature, impulsive personality. During the 1950s, after some 35,000 people had been lobotomized in the United States alone, calming drugs became available and psychosurgery was largely abandoned. Today, lobotomies are history and other psychosurgery is used only in extreme cases. For example, if a patient suffers uncontrollable seizures, surgeons can deactivate the specific nerve clusters that cause or transmit the convulsions. MRI-guided precision surgery is also occasionally done to cut the circuits involved in severe obsessive-compulsive disorder (Sachdev & Sachdev, 1997). Because these procedures are irreversible, however, neurosurgeons perform them only as a last resort.

The effectiveness of the biomedical therapies reminds us of a fundamental lesson: We find it convenient to talk of separate psychological and biological influences, but everything psychological is also biological. Every thought and feeling depends on the functioning brain. Every creative idea, every moment of joy or anger, every period of depression emerges from the electrochemical activity of the living brain. The influence is two-way: When psychotherapy relieves obsessive-compulsive behavior, PET scans reveal a calmer brain (Schwartz & others, 1996).

>> LEARNING OUTCOMES

The Biomedical Therapies

OBJECTIVE 18 | **Define** *psychopharmacology,* **and explain how double-blind studies help researchers evaluate a drug's effectiveness.**

Psychopharmacology is the study of drug effects on mind and behavior. Since the 1950s, drug therapy has been used extensively to treat psychological disorders. *Double-blind studies,* in which neither the medical staff nor the patient knows whether the patient is taking the real drug or a placebo, eliminate the bias that can result from clinicians' and patients' expectations of improvement.

OBJECTIVE 19 | **Describe the characteristics of antipsychotic drugs, and discuss their use in treating schizophrenia.**

The antipsychotic drugs dampen responsiveness to irrelevant stimuli, and they have been used effectively to treat schizophrenia accompanied by positive symptoms (the presence of hallucinations and delusions). Dosage varies from person to person. The first-generation antipsychotic drugs, which block D2 (dopamine) receptors, can produce *tardive dyskinesia,* (involuntary movements of facial muscles, the tongue, and arms and legs). The second-generation of antipsychotics, which target D1 receptors, can affect metabolism, increasing the risk of obesity and diabetes.

OBJECTIVE 20 | **Describe the characteristics of antianxiety drugs.**

The antianxiety drugs depress central nervous system activity. They are often used in combination with psychotherapy for treatment of anxiety disorders. Antianxiety drugs can be psychologically and physically addictive.

OBJECTIVE 21 | **Describe the characteristics of antidepressant drugs, and discuss their use in treating specific disorders.**

Antidepressant drugs increase the availability of norepinephrine or serotonin, which elevate arousal and mood. Antidepressants like Prozac, which block the reuptake of serotonin, are known as *selective-serotonin-reuptake-inhibitors (SSRIs).* Dual-action antidepressants block the reuptake or absorption of both norepinephrine and serotonin, but they have a greater risk of side effects. Antidepressants are used to treat depression (often in combination with cognitive therapy) and the anxiety disorders. Antidepressants begin to influence neurotransmitter systems almost immediately, but their full psychological effects may not appear until weeks later. The suicide risk for those taking these drugs may have been overestimated.

OBJECTIVE 22 | **Describe the use and effects of mood-stabilizing medications.**

A few drugs, such as *lithium* for bipolar disorder, have proven very effective in stabilizing moods. Researchers do not yet understand how these medications work.

OBJECTIVE 23 | **Describe the use of electroconvulsive therapy in treating severe depression, and discuss some possible alternatives to ECT.**

ECT is a biomedical therapy in which a brief electric current is sent through the brain of an anesthetized patient. Although controversial, ECT remains an effective, last-resort treatment for many people with severe depression (it is ineffective in treating other disorders) who have not responded to drug therapy. How ECT works is unknown. Depression has also been alleviated by some implanted devices that stimulate parts of the brain or the vagus nerve sending signals to the limbic system. Following early reports of success, large clinical trials are under way to study repetitive transcranial magnetic stimulation (rTMS). In this painless procedure, pulses of magnetic energy sent through the skull to the surface of the cortex stimulate or dampen activity in various areas of the brain.

OBJECTIVE **24** | **Summarize the history of the psychosurgical procedure known as a lobotomy, and discuss the use of psychosurgery today.**

Lobotomy was a crude procedure in which surgical instruments inserted through a patient's eye sockets were used to sever connections running to the frontal lobes of the brain. The intent was to calm uncontrollably emotional or violent patients, but instead it usually created lethargy and an impulsive personality. This surgery disappeared in the 1950s, when its harmful effects became known and new and effective drug treatments were introduced. Today, neurosurgeons rarely perform brain surgery to treat psychological disorders. Even when MRI-guided precision surgery is considered for exceptional, life-threatening conditions, it is a treatment of last resort because its effects are irreversible.

ASK YOURSELF: **Have your feelings about therapy changed since you entered this course? If so, in what ways?**

Preventing Psychological Disorders

OBJECTIVE **25** | Explain the rationale of preventive mental health programs.

Psychotherapies and biomedical therapies tend to locate the cause of psychological disorders within the person with the disorder. We infer that people who act cruelly must be cruel and that people who act "crazy" must be "sick." We attach labels to such people, thereby distinguishing them from "normal" folks. It follows, then, that we try to treat "abnormal" people by giving them insight into their problems, by changing their thinking, and/or by helping them gain control with drugs.

There is an alternative viewpoint: We could interpret many psychological disorders as understandable responses to a disturbing and stressful society. According to this view, it is not just the person who needs treatment, but also the person's social context. Better to prevent a problem by reforming a sick situation and by developing people's coping competencies than to wait for a problem to arise and then treat it.

A story about the rescue of a drowning person from a rushing river illustrates this viewpoint: Having successfully administered first aid to the first victim, the rescuer spots another struggling person and pulls her out, too. After a half-dozen repetitions, the rescuer suddenly turns and starts running away while the river sweeps yet another floundering person into view. "Aren't you going to rescue that fellow?" asks a bystander. "Heck no," the rescuer replies. "I'm going upstream to find out what's pushing all these people in."

Preventive mental health is upstream work. It seeks to prevent psychological casualties by identifying and alleviating the conditions that cause them. George Albee (1986) believes there is abundant evidence that poverty, meaningless work, constant criticism, unemployment, racism, and sexism undermine people's sense of competence, personal control, and self-esteem. Such stresses increase their risk of depression, alcoholism, and suicide.

Albee contends that we who care about preventing psychological casualties should therefore support programs that alleviate poverty, discrimination, and other demoralizing situations. We eliminated smallpox not by treating the afflicted but by inoculating the unafflicted. We conquered yellow fever by controlling mosquitoes. Prevention of psychological problems means empowering those who have learned an attitude of helplessness, changing environments that breed loneliness, renewing the disintegrating family, and bolstering parents' and teachers' skills at nurturing children's achievements and resulting self-esteem. Indeed, "Everything aimed at improving the

> "It is better to prevent than to cure."
> Peruvian folk wisdom

FIGURE 17.9
A biopsychosocial approach to therapy
Effective treatment of psychological disorders requires considering all possible influences—biological, psychological, and social-cultural—that may be contributing to a problem.

Biological considerations:
Biomedical techniques, including drug therapy, ECT, and rTMS (and on very rare occasion, psychosurgery) may be used to correct malfunctioning brain circuitry. *For example, a patient diagnosed with bipolar disorder (with moods swinging from depression to mania) might be given a prescription for drugs that would reduce her dramatic mood swings.*

Psychological considerations:
Therapy may help clients gain insight into patterns of thinking and behaving that are causing them distress and leading to dysfunction. *The client with bipolar disorder might be helped to recognize the patterns of relationship damage caused by her mood swings and to develop ways to improve her relationships with family and friends.*

Successful intervention

Social-cultural considerations:
Therapy can help people relearn more adaptive responses to the social and cultural influences in their environment. To be effective, all types of psychotherapy need to be sensitive to cultural differences in the clients being treated. *The client with bipolar disorder might be trained to recognize the settings and symptoms of her mood swings and to respond in ways that help her retain a healthier balance.*

human condition, at making life more fulfilling and meaningful, may be considered part of primary prevention of mental or emotional disturbance" (Kessler & Albee, 1975, p. 557). That includes the cognitive training that promotes positive thinking in children at risk for depression (see pages 696–697).

There is, however, more to the story of psychological disorders than toxic environments and pessimism. Anxiety disorders, major depression, bipolar disorder, and schizophrenia are in part biological events. Yet Albee reminds us again of one of this book's themes: *A human being is an integrated biopsychosocial system* (**FIGURE 17.9**). For years we have trusted our bodies to physicians and our minds to psychiatrists and psychologists. That neat separation no longer seems valid. Stress affects body chemistry and health. And chemical imbalances, whatever their cause, can produce schizophrenia and depression. *"Mens sana in corpore sano,"* says an ancient Latin adage: "A healthy mind in a healthy body."

> "Mental disorders arise from physical ones, and likewise physical disorders arise from mental ones."
>
> *The Mahabharata,* C. A.D. 200

>> LEARNING OUTCOMES

Preventing Psychological Disorders

OBJECTIVE **25** | **Explain the rationale of preventive mental health programs.**
Advocates of preventive mental health argue that many psychological disorders could be prevented. Their aim is to change oppressive, esteem-destroying environments into more benevolent, nurturing environments that foster individual growth and self-confidence.

ASK YOURSELF: Can you think of a specific way that improving the environment in your own community might prevent some psychological disorders among its residents?

REVIEW CHAPTER 17 : **Therapy**

Test Yourself

1. What is the major distinction between the underlying assumption in psychoanalytic and humanistic therapies and the underlying assumption in behavior therapies?

2. How does the placebo effect bias clients' appraisals of the effectiveness of psychotherapies?

3. How do researchers evaluate the effectiveness of particular drug therapies?

4. What are the influences to keep in mind for successful therapeutic intervention?

Answers to the Test Yourself questions can be found in Appendix B at the end of the book.

Terms and Concepts to Remember

psychotherapy, p. 685

biomedical therapy, p. 686

eclectic approach, p. 686

psychoanalysis, p. 686

resistance, p. 687

interpretation, p. 687

transference, p. 687

client-centered therapy, p. 689

active listening, p. 690

behavior therapy, p. 690

counterconditioning, p. 691

exposure therapies, p. 691

systematic desensitization, p. 692

virtual reality exposure therapy, p. 692

aversive conditioning, p. 692

token economy, p. 693

cognitive therapy, p. 695

cognitive-behavior therapy, p. 697

family therapy, p. 697

regression toward the mean, p. 702

meta-analysis, p. 703

psychopharmacology, p. 711

tardive dyskinesia, p. 712

electroconvulsive therapy (ECT), p. 715

repetitive transcranial magnetic stimulation (rTMS), p. 716

psychosurgery, p. 717

lobotomy, p. 717

WEB

> To continue your study and review of Therapy, visit this book's Web site at www.worthpublishers.com/myers. You will find practice tests, review activities, and many interesting articles and Web links for more information on topics related to Therapy.

SEKOU SUNDIATA (b. 1948), "BLINK YOUR EYES," 1995, *THE BLUE ONENESS DREAMS*

I could wake up in the morning
without a warning
and my world could change:

blink your eyes.
All depends, all depends on the skin,
all depends on the skin you're living in.

18: Social Psychology

OBJECTIVE 1 | Describe the three main focuses of social psychology.

On September 11, 2001, shortly after terrorists flew hijacked planes into the World Trade Center, I spoke by phone with my daughter, Laura. She was on the street in her Manhattan neighborhood, describing the tumultuous scene, when suddenly she yelled, "Oh my gosh! Oh my gosh!" as the second massive tower collapsed before her eyes. By almost anyone's definition, this catastrophic violence—accomplished by a mere 19 men with box cutters—was an evil act, to which the communal response was fear mixed with anger. A bully's single kick that collapses a nearly finished sandcastle triggers both fright and outrage. Likewise, for millions of stunned Americans, 9/11 evoked anxiety about what might come next and a lust for revenge.

But the cataclysm also triggered an outpouring of love and compassion. From around the country and the world, money and countless truckloads of food, clothing, and teddy bears—more than New Yorkers could possibly use—poured in. People in Toledo, Fargo, and Stockholm wept for those who wept. There on 6th Avenue and 24th Street, strangers hugged and talked, trying to make sense of senseless destruction. Although few transfusions would be needed, willing donors formed long lines at blood banks. "Everywhere I go I see concern," Laura wrote that evening.

> I see compassion. I see people with many differences united. I don't see violence. I don't see impatience. I don't see cruelty. Except when I look at that cloud of smoke, a constant backdrop all day. People are helping each other. People are desperate to do whatever they can.
>
> In the midst of this nightmare, I am utterly filled with love for the people of this city. It is incredible to witness their response. I am covered in goose bumps. My faith in humanity rises over that cloud and I see goodness and respect.

We watch and we wonder: What drives people to feel such hatred and to destroy so many innocent lives? And what motivates the heroic altruism of those who died trying to save others and of the many more who reached out to those coping with loss?

As the 9/11 horror so compellingly demonstrates, we are social animals. Depending on who or what influences our thinking, we may assume the best or the worst in others. And depending on our attitudes, we may approach them with closed fists or open arms.

"We cannot live for ourselves alone," remarked the novelist Herman Melville. "Our lives are connected by a thousand invisible threads." **Social psychologists** explore these connections by scientifically studying how we *think about, influence,* and *relate to* one another.

Social Thinking

Especially when the unexpected occurs, we analyze why people act as they do. Does her warmth reflect romantic interest, or is that how she relates to everyone? Does his absenteeism signify illness? Laziness? A stressful work atmosphere? Was the horror of 9/11 the work of crazed evil people, or of ordinary people corrupted by life events?

■ **social psychology** the scientific study of how we think about, influence, and relate to one another.

723

■ **attribution theory** suggests how we explain someone's behavior—by crediting either the situation or the person's disposition.

■ **fundamental attribution error** the tendency for observers, when analyzing another's behavior, to underestimate the impact of the situation and to overestimate the impact of personal disposition.

Attributing Behavior to Persons or to Situations

OBJECTIVE **2** | Contrast dispositional and situational attributions, and explain how the fundamental attribution error can affect our analyses of behavior.

After studying how people explain others' behavior, Fritz Heider (1958) proposed an **attribution theory.** Heider noted that people usually attribute others' behavior either to their internal dispositions or to their external situations. A teacher, for example, may wonder whether a child's hostility reflects an aggressive personality (*a dispositional attribution*) or a reaction to stress or abuse (*a situational attribution*).

In class, we notice that Juliette seldom talks; over coffee, Jack talks nonstop. Attributing their behaviors to their personal dispositions, we decide Juliette is shy and Jack is outgoing. Because people do have enduring personality traits, such attributions are sometimes valid. However, we often fall prey to the **fundamental attribution error,** by overestimating the influence of personality and underestimating the influence of situations. In class, Jack may be as quiet as Juliette. Catch Juliette at a party and you may hardly recognize your quiet classmate.

An experiment by David Napolitan and George Goethals (1979) illustrates the phenomenon. They had Williams College students talk, one at a time, with a young woman who acted either aloof and critical or warm and friendly. Beforehand, they told half the students the woman's behavior would be spontaneous. They told the other half the truth—that she had been instructed to *act* friendly (or unfriendly). What do you suppose was the effect of being told the truth?

There was no effect. The students disregarded the information. If the woman acted friendly, they inferred she really was a warm person. If she acted unfriendly, they inferred she really was a cold person. In other words, they attributed her behavior to her personal disposition *even when told that her behavior was situational*—that she was merely acting that way for the purposes of the experiment. Although the fundamental attribution error occurs in all cultures studied, this tendency to attribute behavior to people's dispositions runs especially strong in individualistic Western countries. In East Asian cultures, for example, people are more sensitive to the power of the situation (Masuda & Kitayama, 2004).

As with other biases (such as the self-serving bias discussed in Chapter 15), people see themselves as less susceptible than others to the phenomenon (Pronin & others, 2004). The fundamental attribution error is almost irresistible, though. In a high school play, I saw a talented 16-year-old convincingly play the part of a bitter old woman—so convincingly that, although I reminded myself of the fundamental attribution error, I still assumed that the young actress was typecast because she was well-suited for the part. Meeting her later at a cast party, I discovered she actually had a very pleasant disposition. I then remembered that several months earlier I had seen her play the part of a charming 10-year-old in *The Sound of Music*.

The fundamental attribution error

If our new colleague at work acts grouchy, we may infer that she's a grouchy person, discounting her having lost sleep over a family worry, having a flat tire on the way to work, and being unable to find a parking place.

B. Busco/The Image Bank/Getty Images

You, too, have surely committed the fundamental attribution error. In judging whether your psychology instructor is shy or outgoing, you have perhaps by now inferred that he or she has an outgoing personality. But you know your instructor only from the classroom, a situation that demands outgoing behavior. Catch the instructor in a different situation and you might be surprised (as some of my students have been when confronting me in a pick-up basketball game). Outside their assigned roles, professors seem less professorial, presidents less presidential, servants less servile.

The instructor, on the other hand, observes his or her own behavior in many different situations—in the classroom, in meetings, at home—and so might say, "Me, outgoing? It all depends on the situation. In class or with good friends, yes, I'm outgoing. But at conventions I'm really rather shy." So, when explaining *our own* behavior, or the behavior of those we know well and see in varied situations, we are sensitive to how behavior changes with the situations (Idson & Mischel, 2001).

When explaining *others'* behavior, particularly the behavior of strangers we have observed in only one type of situation, we often commit the fundamental attribution error: We disregard the situation and leap to unwarranted conclusions about their personality traits. Many people initially assumed that Nazi death camp commanders exhibited consistently vile behavior. Actually, many were unremarkable men who went home after the day's brutality and relaxed with a good book and the strains of classical music. Many of us initially assumed the 9/11 terrorists were obviously crazy, when actually they went unnoticed in their neighborhoods, health clubs, and favorite restaurants.

Researchers who have reversed the perspectives of actor and observer—by having each view a videotape replay of the situation from the other's perspective—have also reversed the attributions (Lassiter & Irvine, 1986; Storms, 1973). Seeing the world from the actor's perspective, the observers better appreciate the situation. Taking the observer's point of view, the actors better appreciate their own personal style.

The Effects of Attribution

In everyday life we often struggle to explain others' actions. A jury must decide whether a shooting was malicious or in self-defense. An interviewer must judge whether the applicant's geniality is genuine. When we make such judgments, our attributions—either to the person or to the situation—have important consequences (Fincham & Bradbury, 1993; Fletcher & others, 1990). Happily married couples attribute a spouse's tart-tongued remark to a temporary situation ("She must have had a bad day at work"). Unhappily married persons attribute the same remark to a mean disposition ("Why did I marry such a hostile person?").

Or consider the political effects of attribution: How do you explain poverty or unemployment? Researchers in Britain, India, Australia, and the United States (Furnham, 1982; Pandey & others, 1982; Wagstaff, 1982; Zucker & Weiner, 1993) report that political conservatives tend to attribute such social problems to the personal dispositions of the poor and unemployed themselves: "People generally get what they deserve. Those who don't work are often freeloaders. Anybody who takes the initiative can still get ahead." "Society is not to blame for crime, criminals are," said one conservative U.S. presidential candidate (Dole, 1996). Political liberals (and social scientists) are more likely to blame past and present situations: "If you or I had to live with the same poor education, lack of opportunity, and discrimination, would we be any better off?" To understand and prevent terrorism, they say, consider the situations that breed terrorists. Better to drain the swamps than swat the mosquitoes.

Recall from Chapter 15 that personality psychologists study the enduring, inner determinants of behavior that help to explain why *different people* act differently in a given situation. Social psychologists study the social influences that help explain why the same person will act differently in *different situations*.

" Calling [9/11] *senseless, mindless, insane*, or the work of *madmen* is wrong . . . [it] fails to adopt the perspective of the perpetrators, as an act with a clearly defined purpose that we must understand in order to challenge it most effectively."

Psychologist Philip G. Zimbardo, "Fighting Terrorism by Understanding Man's Capacity for Evil," September 16, 2001

"Otis, shout at that man to pull himself together."

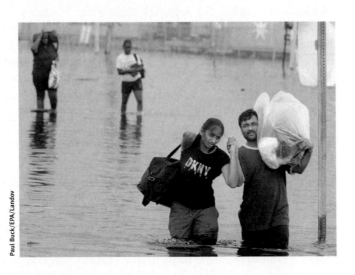

Paul Buck/EPA/Landov

An attribution question
Some people blamed the New Orleans residents for not evacuating before the predicted Hurricane Katrina. Others attributed their inaction to the situation—to their not having cars or not being offered bus transportation.

FIGURE 18.1
Attributions and reactions
How we explain someone's behavior affects how we react to it.

Negative behavior

Situational attribution
"Maybe that driver is ill."

Tolerant reaction
(proceed cautiously, allow driver a wide berth)

Dispositional attribution
"Crazy driver!"

Unfavorable reaction
(speed up and race past the other driver, craning to give a dirty look)

Managers also have to make attributions. In evaluating employees, they are likely to attribute poor performance to personal factors, such as low ability or lack of motivation. But remember the actor's viewpoint: Workers doing poorly on a job recognize situational influences, such as inadequate supplies, poor working conditions, difficult co-workers, or impossible demands (Rice, 1985).

The point to remember: Our attributions—to individuals' dispositions or to their situations—have real consequences (**FIGURE 18.1**).

Attitudes and Actions

OBJECTIVE 3 | Define *attitude*.

Attitudes are feelings, based on our beliefs, that predispose our reactions to objects, people, and events. If we *believe* someone is mean, we may *feel* dislike for the person and *act* unfriendly. "Change the way people think," said South African civil rights martyr Steve Biko, "and things will never be the same." Such is the power of persuasion.

Attitudes Can Affect Actions

OBJECTIVE 4 | Describe the conditions under which attitudes can affect actions.

Our attitudes predict our behavior imperfectly because other factors, including the external situation, also influence behavior. Strong social pressures can weaken the attitude-behavior connection (Wallace & others, 2005). For example, the American public's overwhelming support for President George W. Bush's preparation to attack Iraq motivated Democratic leaders to vote to support Bush's war plan, despite their private reservations (Nagourney, 2002). Nevertheless, attitudes may indeed affect behavior when other influences are minimal, when the attitude is specific to the behavior, and when we are keenly aware of our attitudes.

Actions Can Affect Attitudes

OBJECTIVE 5 | Explain how the foot-in-the-door phenomenon, role-playing, and cognitive dissonance illustrate the influence of actions on attitudes.

Now consider a more surprising principle: Not only will people sometimes stand up for what they believe, they will also come to believe in what they have stood up for. Many streams of evidence confirm that *attitudes follow behavior* (**FIGURE 18.2**).

■ **attitude** feelings, often based on our beliefs, that predispose us to respond in a particular way to objects, people, and events.

■ **foot-in-the-door phenomenon** the tendency for people who have first agreed to a small request to comply later with a larger request.

The Foot-in-the-Door Phenomenon Convincing people to act against their beliefs can affect their attitude. During the Korean War, many captured U.S. soldiers were imprisoned in war camps run by Chinese communists. Without using brutality, the captors secured the collaboration of hundreds of their prisoners in various activities. Some merely ran errands or accepted favors. Others made radio appeals and false confessions. Still others informed on fellow prisoners and divulged military information. When the war ended, 21 prisoners chose to stay with the communists. More returned home "brainwashed"—convinced that communism was a good thing for Asia.

A key ingredient of the Chinese "thought-control" program was its effective use of the **foot-in-the-door phenomenon**—a tendency for people who agree to a small action to comply later with a larger one. The Chinese began with harmless requests but gradually escalated their demands on the prisoners (Schein, 1956). Having "trained" the prisoners to speak or write trivial statements, the communists then asked them to copy or create something more important, noting, perhaps, the flaws of capitalism. Then, perhaps to gain privileges, the prisoners participated in group discussions, wrote self-criticisms, or uttered public confessions. After doing so, they often adjusted their beliefs toward consistency with their public acts.

The point is simple, says Robert Cialdini (1993): To get people to agree to something big, "start small and build." And be wary of those who would exploit you with the tactic. This chicken-and-egg spiral, of actions-feeding-attitudes-feeding-actions, enables behavior to escalate. A trivial act makes the next act easier. Succumb to a temptation and you will find the next temptation harder to resist.

Dozens of experiments have simulated part of the war prisoners' experience by coaxing people into acting against their attitudes or violating their moral standards. The nearly inevitable result: Doing becomes believing. When people are induced to harm an innocent victim—by making nasty comments or delivering electric shocks—they then begin to disparage their victim. If induced to speak or write on behalf of a position they have qualms about, they begin to believe their own words.

Fortunately, the attitudes-follow-behavior principle works as well for good deeds as for bad. The foot-in-the-door tactic has helped boost charitable contributions, blood donations, and product sales. In one experiment, researchers posing as safe-driving volunteers asked Californians to permit the installation of a large, poorly lettered "Drive Carefully" sign in their front yards. Only 17 percent consented. They approached other home owners with a small request first: Would they display a 3-inch-high "Be a Safe Driver" sign? Nearly all readily agreed. When reapproached two weeks later to allow the large, ugly sign in their front yards, 76 percent consented (Freedman & Fraser, 1966).

Racial attitudes likewise follow behavior. In the years immediately following the introduction of school desegregation in the United States and the passage of the Civil Rights Act of 1964, white Americans expressed diminishing racial prejudice. And as Americans in different regions came to act more alike—thanks to more uniform national standards against discrimination—they began to think more alike. Experiments confirm the observation: Moral action strengthens moral convictions.

Role-Playing Affects Attitudes When you adopt a new role—when you become a college student, marry, or begin a new job—you strive to follow the social prescriptions. At first, your behaviors may feel phony, because you are *acting* a role. The first weeks in the military feel artificial—as if one is pretending to be a soldier. The first weeks of a marriage may feel like "playing house." Before long, however, what began as play-acting in the theater of life becomes *you*.

Researchers have confirmed this effect by assessing people's attitudes before and after they adopt a new role, sometimes in laboratory situations, sometimes in every-

FIGURE 18.2
Attitudes follow behavior
Cooperative actions, such as those performed by people on sports teams, feed mutual liking. Such attitudes, in turn, promote positive behavior.

"If the King destroys a man, that's proof to the King it must have been a bad man."
Thomas Cromwell, in Robert Bolt's *A Man for All Seasons*, 1960

The power of the situation
In Philip Zimbardo's Stanford Prison simulation, a toxic situation triggered degrading behaviors among those assigned to the guard role.

Philip G. Zimbardo, Inc.

"Fake it until you make it."
Alcoholics Anonymous saying

■ **cognitive dissonance theory** the theory that we act to reduce the discomfort (dissonance) we feel when two of our thoughts (cognitions) are inconsistent. For example, when our awareness of our attitudes and of our actions clash, we can reduce the resulting dissonance by changing our attitudes.

day situations, such as before and after taking a job. In one well-known laboratory study, male college students volunteered to spend time in a simulated prison devised by psychologist Philip Zimbardo (1972). Some he randomly designated as guards; he gave them uniforms, billy clubs, and whistles and instructed them to enforce certain rules. The remainder became prisoners; they were locked in barren cells and forced to wear humiliating outfits. After a day or two in which the volunteers self-consciously "played" their roles, the simulation became real—too real. Most of the guards developed disparaging attitudes, and some devised cruel and degrading routines. One by one, the prisoners broke down, rebelled, or became passively resigned, causing Zimbardo to call off the study after only six days. More recently, similar situations have played themselves out in the real world—as in Iraq at the Abu Ghraib Prison (see Close-Up).

Greece's military junta during the early 1970s took advantage of the effects of role playing to train men to become torturers (Staub, 1989). The men's indoctrination into their roles occurred in small steps. First, the trainee stood guard outside the interrogation cells—the "foot in the door." Next, he stood guard inside. Only then was he ready to become actively involved in the questioning and torture. As the nineteenth-century writer Nathaniel Hawthorne noted, "No man, for any considerable period, can wear one face to himself and another to the multitude without finally getting bewildered as to which may be true." What we do, we gradually become.

Cognitive Dissonance: Relief from Tension So far we have seen that actions can affect attitudes, sometimes turning prisoners into collaborators, doubters into believers, mere acquaintances into friends, and compliant guards into abusers. But why? One explanation is that when we become aware that our attitudes and actions don't coincide, we experience tension, or *cognitive dissonance*. To relieve this tension, according to the **cognitive dissonance theory** proposed by Leon Festinger, we often bring our attitudes into line with our actions. It is as if we rationalize, "If I chose to do it (or say it), I must believe in it." The less coerced and more responsible we feel for a troubling act, the more dissonance we feel. The more dissonance we feel, the more motivated we are to find consistency, such as changing our attitudes to help justify the act.

The U.S. invasion of Iraq was mainly premised on the presumed threat of Saddam Hussein's weapons of mass destruction (WMD). As the war began, only 38 percent of Americans surveyed said the war was justified even if Iraq did not have WMD (Gallup, 2003), and nearly 80 percent believed such weapons would be found (Duffy, 2003; Newport & others, 2003). When no WMD were found, many

CLOSE-UP:

ABU GHRAIB PRISON: AN "ATROCITY-PRODUCING SITUATION"?

As the first photos emerged in 2004 from Iraq's Abu Ghraib Prison, the civilized world was shocked. The photos showed U.S. military guards stripping prisoners naked, placing hoods on them, stacking them in piles, prodding them with electricity, taunting them with attack dogs, and subjecting them to sleep deprivation, humiliation, and extreme stress. Was the problem, as so many people initially supposed, a few bad apples—irresponsible or even sadistic guards? That was the U.S. Army's seeming verdict when it court-martialed and imprisoned some of the guards, and then cleared four of the five top commanding officers responsible for Abu Ghraib's policies and operations. The lower-level military guards were "sick bastards," explained the defense attorney for one of the commanding officers (Tarbert, 2004).

Many social psychologists, however, reminded us that a toxic situation can make even good apples go bad (Fiske &

Originally published in the *New Yorker*

Bad apples or bad barrels?
Both the Stanford Prison Experiment in 1972 and the real-life Abu Ghraib Prison fiasco in 2004 were powerfully toxic situations, contends social psychologist Philip Zimbardo.

others, 2004). "When ordinary people are put in a novel, evil place, such as most prisons, Situations Win, People Lose," offered Philip Zimbardo (2004),

adding, "That is true for the majority of people in all the relevant social psychological research done over the past 40 years."

Consider the situation, explains Zimbardo. The guards, some of them model soldier-reservists with no prior criminal or sadistic history, were exhausted from working 12-hour shifts, seven days a week, for more than a month at a time. They were dealing with an enemy, and their prejudices were heightened by fears of lethal attacks and by the violent deaths of many fellow soldiers. They were put in an understaffed guard role, given minimal training and oversight, and encouraged to "soften up" for interrogation detainees who had been denied access to the Red Cross. "When you put that set of horrendous work conditions and external factors together, it creates an evil barrel. You could put virtually anybody in it and you're going to get this kind of evil behavior" (Zimbardo, 2005).

Americans felt dissonance, which was heightened by their awareness of the war's financial and human costs, by scenes of chaos in Iraq, and by inflamed anti-American and pro-terrorist sentiments in some parts of the world.

To reduce dissonance, some people revised their memories of the main rationale for going to war, which now became liberating an oppressed people and promoting democracy in the Middle East. Before long, the once-minority opinion became the majority view: 58 percent of Americans said they supported the war even if there were no WMD (Gallup, 2003). "Whether or not they find weapons of mass destruction doesn't matter," explained Republican pollster Frank Luntz (2003), "because the rationale for the war changed." It was not until late 2004, when hopes for a flourishing peace waned, that Americans' support for the war dropped below 50 percent.

Dozens of experiments have explored cognitive dissonance by making people feel responsible for behavior that is inconsistent with their attitudes and that has foreseeable consequences. As a subject in one of these experiments, you might agree for a measly $2 to

© The New Yorker Collection, 2004, Robert Mankoff from cartoonbank.com. All Rights Reserved.

"Look, I have my misgivings, too, but what choice do we have except stay the course?"

help a researcher by writing an essay that supports something you don't believe in (perhaps a tuition increase). Feeling responsible for the statements (which are not consistent with your attitudes), you would probably feel dissonance, especially if you thought an administrator would be reading your essay. How could you reduce the uncomfortable dissonance? One way would be to start believing your phony words. Your pretense would become your reality.

The attitudes-follow-behavior principle has another heartening implication: Although we cannot directly control all our feelings, we can influence them by altering our behavior. (Recall from Chapter 13 the emotional effects of facial expressions and of body postures.) If we are down in the dumps, we can do as cognitive therapists advise and talk in more positive, self-accepting ways with fewer self–put-downs. If we are unloving, we can become more loving by behaving as if we were so—by doing thoughtful things, expressing affection, giving affirmation. "Assume a virtue, if you have it not," says Hamlet to his mother. "For use can almost change the stamp of nature." *The point to remember:* Evil acts shape the self. But so do acts of good will. Act as though you like someone, and you soon will. Changing our behavior can change how we think about others and how we feel about ourselves.

> "Sit all day in a moping posture, sigh, and reply to everything with a dismal voice, and your melancholy lingers. . . . If we wish to conquer undesirable emotional tendencies in ourselves, we must . . . go through the outward movements of those contrary dispositions which we prefer to cultivate."
>
> William James, *Principles of Psychology*, 1890

>> Learning Outcomes

Social Thinking

Objective 1 | Describe the three main focuses of social psychology.

Social psychology focuses on three broad topics: how people think about, influence, and relate to one another.

Objective 2 | Contrast dispositional and situational attributions, and explain how the fundamental attribution error can affect our analyses of behavior.

We usually rely on *situational attributions,* stressing the influence of external events, to explain our own behavior (and often the behavior of those we know well and see in many different contexts). But in explaining the actions of people we do not know well, we often resort to *dispositional attributions,* assuming they behave as they do because of their personal traits. This *fundamental attribution error* (overestimating the influence of personal factors and underestimating the effect of context) can introduce inaccuracies into judgments we make about others.

Objective 3 | Define *attitude.*

Attitudes are positive, negative, or mixed feelings, based on our beliefs, that predispose us to respond in a particular way to objects, people, and events.

Objective 4 | Describe the conditions under which attitudes can affect actions.

Our attitudes are most likely to affect our behavior when social influences are minimal, the attitude is specific to the behavior, and we are very aware of the attitude.

Objective 5 | Explain how the foot-in-the-door phenomenon, role-playing, and cognitive dissonance illustrate the influence of actions on attitudes.

The *foot-in-the-door phenomenon* describes people's willingness to agree to a large request after having agreed to a related small request. In *role-playing* studies, such as Philip Zimbardo's prison experiment, people who behaved in certain ways in scripted scenarios have adopted attitudes in keeping with those roles. Leon Festinger's *cognitive dissonance theory* proposes that we feel uncomfortable when we act in ways that conflict with our feelings and beliefs, and we reduce this discomfort by revising our attitudes to align them more closely with our behavior. In all three instances, attitudes adapt to behavior, rather than drive it.

ASK YOURSELF: Do you have an attitude or tendency you would like to change? Using the attitudes-follow-behavior principle, how might you go about changing that attitude?

Social Influence

Social psychology's great lesson is the enormous power of social influence. This influence can be seen in our conformity, our compliance, and our group behavior. Suicides, bomb threats, airplane hijackings, and UFO sightings all have a curious tendency to come in clusters. On campus, blue jeans are the dress code; on New

York's Wall Street or London's Bond Street, dress suits are the norm. When we know how to act, how to groom, how to talk, life functions smoothly. Armed with principles of social influence, advertisers, fund-raisers, and campaign workers aim to sway our decisions to buy, to donate, to vote. Isolated with others who share their grievances, dissenters may gradually become rebels, and rebels may become terrorists. Let's examine the pull of these social strings. How strong are they? How do they operate?

Conformity and Obedience

OBJECTIVE **6** | Describe the chameleon effect, and give an example of it.

Behavior is contagious.

- One person laughs, coughs, or yawns, and others in the group soon do the same. Chimps, too, are more likely to yawn after observing another chimp yawn (Anderson & others, 2004)
- A cluster of people stand gazing upward, and passersby pause to do likewise.
- Bartenders and street musicians know to "seed" their tip containers with money to suggest that others have given.
- "Sickness" can also be psychologically contagious. In the anxious 9/11 aftermath, more than two dozen elementary and middle schools had outbreaks of children reporting red rashes, sometimes causing parents to wonder whether biological terrorism was at work (Talbot, 2002). Some cases may have been stress-related, but mostly, said health experts, people were just noticing normal early acne, insect bites, eczema, and dry skin from overheated classrooms.

We are natural mimics—an effect Tanya Chartrand and John Bargh (1999) call the *chameleon effect*. Unconsciously mimicking others' expressions, postures, and voice tones helps us feel what they are feeling. This helps explain why we feel happier around happy people than around depressed ones, and why studies of groups of British nurses and accountants reveal *mood linkage*—sharing up and down moods (Totterdell & others, 1998). Just hearing someone reading a neutral text in either a happy- or sad-sounding voice creates "mood contagion" in listeners (Neumann & Strack, 2000).

Chartrand and Bargh demonstrated the chameleon effect when they had students work in a room alongside a confederate working for the experimenter. Sometimes the confederates rubbed their face; on other occasions, they shook their foot. Sure enough, participants tended to rub their own face when they were with the face-rubbing person and shake their own foot when they were with the foot-shaking person. Such automatic mimicry is part of empathy. The most empathic people mimic—and are liked—the most. And those most eager to fit in with a group seem intuitively to know this, for they are especially prone to nonconscious mimicry (Lakin & Chartrand, 2003).

Niche conformity
Are these students asserting their individuality or identifying themselves with others of the same microculture?

NON SEQUITUR   by WILEY

■ **conformity** adjusting one's behavior or thinking to coincide with a group standard.

■ **normative social influence** influence resulting from a person's desire to gain approval or avoid disapproval.

■ **informational social influence** influence resulting from one's willingness to accept others' opinions about reality.

Sometimes the effects of suggestibility are more serious. In the eight days following the 1999 shooting rampage at Colorado's Columbine High School, every U.S. state except Vermont experienced threats of copycat violence. Pennsylvania alone recorded 60 such threats (Cooper, 1999). Sociologist David Phillips and his colleagues (1985, 1989) found that suicides, too, sometimes increase following a highly publicized suicide. In the wake of Marilyn Monroe's suicide on August 6, 1962, the number of suicides in the United States exceeded the usual August count by 200. Although not all studies have confirmed the copycat suicide phenomenon, suicides have sometimes occurred in local clusters. Within an 18-day span, one 1500-student high school recorded 2 completed suicides, 7 attempted suicides, and 23 students with suicidal thoughts. Within a one-year period, one London psychiatric unit experienced 14 patient suicides (Joiner, 1999).

What causes suicide clusters? Do people act similarly because of their influence on one another? Or because they are simultaneously exposed to the same events and conditions? Seeking answers, social psychologists have conducted experiments on group pressure and conformity.

Group Pressure and Conformity

OBJECTIVE 7 | Discuss Asch's experiments on conformity, and distinguish between normative and informational social influence.

Suggestibility is a subtle type of **conformity**—adjusting our behavior or thinking toward some group standard. To study conformity, Solomon Asch (1955) devised a simple test. As a participant in the study, you arrive at the experiment location in time to take a seat at a table where five people are already seated. The experimenter asks which of three comparison lines is identical to a standard line (**FIGURE 18.3**). You see clearly that the answer is Line 2 and await your turn to say so after the others. Your boredom with this experiment begins to show when the next set of lines proves equally easy.

Now comes the third trial, and the correct answer seems just as clear-cut, but the first person gives what strikes you as a wrong answer: "Line 3." When the second person and then the third and fourth give the same wrong answer, you sit up straight and squint. When the fifth person agrees with the first four, you feel your heart begin to pound. The experimenter then looks to you for your answer. Torn between the unanimity of your five fellow respondents and the evidence of your own eyes, you feel tense and much less sure of yourself than you were moments ago. You hesitate before answering, wondering whether you should suffer the discomfort of being the oddball. What answer do you give?

In the experiments conducted by Asch and others after him, thousands of college students have experienced this conflict. Answering such questions alone, they erred less than 1 percent of the time. But the odds were quite different when several others—confederates working for the experimenter—answered incorrectly. Asch reports that

FIGURE 18.3

Asch's conformity experiments
Which of the three comparison lines is equal to the standard line? What do you suppose most people would say after hearing five others say, "Line 3"? In this photo from one of Asch's experiments, the student in the center shows the severe discomfort that comes from disagreeing with the responses of other group members (in this case, confederates of the experimenter).

Standard line   Comparison lines

William Vandivert/*Scientific American*

more than one-third of the time, these "intelligent and well-meaning" college-student participants were then "willing to call white black" by going along with the group.

Conditions That Strengthen Conformity Asch's procedure became the model for later investigations. Although experiments have not always found so much conformity, they do reveal that conformity increases when

- one is made to feel incompetent or insecure.
- the group has at least three people.
- the group is unanimous. (The dissent of just one other person greatly increases social courage.)
- one admires the group's status and attractiveness.
- one has made no prior commitment to any response.
- others in the group observe one's behavior.
- one's culture strongly encourages respect for social standards.

Thus, we might predict the behavior of Austin, an enthusiastic but insecure new fraternity member: Noting that the 40 other members appear unanimous in their plans for a fund-raiser, Austin is unlikely to voice his dissent.

Reasons for Conforming Fish swim in schools. Birds fly in flocks. And humans, too, tend to go with their group, to think what it thinks and do what it does. But why? Why do we clap when others clap, eat as others eat, believe what others believe, even see what others see? Frequently, it is to avoid rejection or to gain social approval. In such cases, we are responding to what social psychologists call **normative social influence.** We are sensitive to social norms—understood rules for accepted and expected behavior—because the price we pay for being different may be severe.

Marco Lokar knows. During the 1991 Persian Gulf War, Lokar, an Italian, was the only Seton Hall University basketball player who chose not to display an American flag on his uniform. As the team traveled, the fans' abusive responses to his nonconforming behavior became unbearable, so he left the team and returned to Italy. Tony Smith also knows. In 2003, when the Manhattanville College basketball player likewise dissented from the impending war with Iraq—by turning sideways and not looking at the flag during the pregame national anthem—similar outrage resulted. In one game at another college, students stood and chanted "Leave the country!"

Respecting norms is not the only reason we conform: Groups may provide valuable information, and only an uncommonly stubborn person will *never* listen to others. When we accept others' opinions about reality, we are responding to **informational social influence.** "Those who never retract their opinions love themselves more than they love truth," observed the eighteenth-century French essayist, Joseph Joubert. As Rebecca Denton demonstrated in 2004, sometimes it pays to assume others are right and to follow their lead. Denton set a record for the furthest distance driven on the wrong side of a British divided highway—30 miles, with only one minor sideswipe, before the Welsh motorway ran out and police were able to puncture her tires. Denton later explained that she thought the hundreds of other drivers coming at her were all on the wrong side of the road (Woolcock, 2004).

Robert Baron and his colleagues (1996) cleverly demonstrated our openness to informational influence on tough, important judgments. They modernized the Asch experiment by showing University of Iowa students a slide of a stimulus person, followed by a slide of a four-person lineup (**FIGURE 18.4**, page 734). Their experiment made the task either easy (viewing the lineup for five seconds) or difficult (viewing the lineup for but half a second). It also led them to think their judgments as either unimportant (just a preliminary test of some eyewitness identification procedures) or as important (establishing norms for an actual police procedure, with a U.S. $20 award to the most accurate participants). When the accuracy of their judgments seemed important, people rarely conformed when the task was easy, but they conformed half the time when the task was difficult. If we are unsure of what is right, and if being right matters, we are receptive to others' opinions.

> "Have you ever noticed how one example—good or bad—can prompt others to follow? How one illegally parked car can give permission for others to do likewise? How one racial joke can fuel another?"
>
> Marian Wright Edelman, *The Measure of Our Success*, 1992

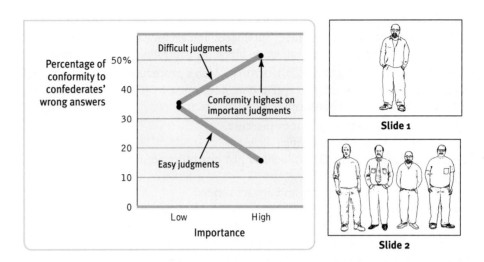

FIGURE 18.4
Informational influence
Sample task: After seeing Slides 1 and 2, participants judged which person in Slide 2 was the same as the person in Slide 1. (From Baron, Vandello, & Brunsman, 1996.)

Our view of social influence as bad or good depends on our values. When influence supports what we approve, we applaud those who are "open-minded" and "sensitive" enough to be "responsive." When influence supports what we disapprove, we scorn the "submissive conformity" of those who comply with others' wishes. As we saw in Chapter 3, cultures vary in the extent to which they value individualism or collectivism. Western Europeans and people in most English-speaking countries tend to prize individualism more than conformity and obedience. These values are reflected in social influence experiments that have been conducted in 17 countries: In individualist cultures, conformity rates are lower (Bond & Smith, 1996).

Obedience

OBJECTIVE 8 | Describe Milgram's experiments on obedience, and outline the conditions in which obedience was highest.

Social psychologist Stanley Milgram (1963, 1974) knew that people often comply with social pressures. But how would they respond to outright commands? To find out, he undertook what have become social psychology's most famous and controversial experiments. Imagine yourself as one of the nearly 1000 participants in Milgram's 20 experiments.

Responding to an advertisement, you come to Yale University's psychology department to participate in an experiment. Professor Milgram's assistant explains that the study concerns the effect of punishment on learning. You and another person draw slips from a hat to see who will be the "teacher" (which your slip says) and who will be the "learner." The learner is then led to an adjoining room and strapped into a chair that is wired through the wall to an electric shock machine. You sit in front of the machine, which has switches labeled with voltages. Your task: to teach and then test the learner on a list of word pairs. You are to punish the learner for wrong answers by delivering brief electric shocks, beginning with a switch labeled "15 Volts—Slight Shock." After each of the learner's errors, you are to move up to the next higher voltage. With each flick of a switch, lights flash, relay switches click on, and an electric buzzing fills the air.

If you comply with the experimenter's instructions, you hear the learner grunt when you flick the third, fourth, and fifth switches. After you activate the eighth switch (labeled "120 Volts—Moderate Shock"), the learner shouts that the shocks are painful. After the tenth switch ("150 Volts—Strong Shock"), he cries, "Get me out of here! I won't be in the experiment anymore! I refuse to go on!" When you hear these pleas, you draw back. But the experimenter prods you: "Please continue—the experiment requires that you continue." If you still resist, he insists, "It is absolutely essential that you continue," or "You have no other choice, you *must* go on."

Stanley Milgram (1933–1984)
The late social psychologist's obedience experiments now "belong to the self-understanding of literate people in our age" (Sabini, 1986).

If you obey, you hear the learner's protests escalate to shrieks of agony as you continue to raise the shock level with each succeeding error. After the 330-volt level, the learner refuses to answer and soon falls silent. Still, the experimenter pushes you toward the final, 450-volt switch, ordering you to ask the questions and, if no correct answer is given, to administer the next shock level.

How far do you think you would follow the experimenter's commands? In a survey Milgram conducted before the experiment, most people declared they would stop playing such a sadistic-seeming role soon after the learner first indicated pain and certainly before he shrieked in agony. This also was the prediction made by each of 40 psychiatrists whom Milgram asked to guess the outcome. When Milgram actually conducted the experiment with men aged 20 to 50, he was astonished to find that 63 percent complied fully—right up to the last switch. Ten later studies that included women found women's compliance rates were similar to men's (Blass, 1999).

Did the "teachers" figure out the hoax—that no shock was being delivered? Did they correctly guess the learner was a confederate who only pretended to feel the shocks? Did they realize the experiment was really testing their willingness to comply with commands to inflict punishment? No, the teachers typically displayed genuine distress: They perspired, trembled, laughed nervously, and bit their lips.

Milgram's use of deception and stress triggered a debate over his research ethics. In his own defense, Milgram pointed out that, after the participants learned of the deception and actual research purposes, virtually none regretted taking part (though perhaps by then the participants had reduced their dissonance). When 40 of the "teachers" who had agonized most were later interviewed by a psychiatrist, none appeared to be suffering emotional aftereffects. All in all, said Milgram, the experiments provoked less enduring stress than university students experience when facing and failing big exams (Blass, 1996).

Wondering whether the participants obeyed because the learners' protests were not convincing, Milgram repeated the experiment, with 40 new teachers. This time his confederate mentioned a "slight heart condition" while being strapped into the chair, and then he complained and screamed more intensely as the shocks became more punishing. Still, 65 percent of the new teachers complied fully (**FIGURE 18.5**).

FIGURE 18.5
Milgram's follow-up obedience experiment

In a repeat of the earlier experiment, 65 percent of the adult male "teachers" fully obeyed the experimenter's commands to continue. They did so despite the "learner's" earlier mention of a heart condition and despite hearing cries of protest after 150 volts and agonized protests after 330 volts. (Data from Milgram, 1974.)

"**Drive off the cliff, James, I want to commit suicide.**"

In later experiments, Milgram discovered that subtle details of a situation powerfully influence people. When he varied the social conditions, the proportion of fully compliant participants varied from 0 to 93 percent. Obedience was highest when

- the person giving the orders was close at hand and was perceived to be a legitimate authority figure. (Such was the case in 2005 when Temple University's basketball coach sent a 250-pound bench player, Nehemiah Ingram, into a game with instructions to commit "hard fouls." Following orders, Ingram fouled out in four minutes after breaking an opposing player's right arm.)
- the authority figure was supported by a prestigious institution. Compliance was somewhat lower when Milgram dissociated his experiments from Yale University.
- the victim was depersonalized or at a distance, even in another room. (Similarly, in combat with an enemy they can see, many soldiers either do not fire their rifles or do not aim them properly. Such refusals to kill are rare among those who operate the more distant weapons of artillery or aircraft [Padgett, 1989].)
- there were no role models for defiance; that is, no other participants were seen disobeying the experimenter.

The power of legitimate, close-at-hand authorities is dramatically apparent in stories of those who complied with orders to carry out the atrocities of the Holocaust, and those who didn't. Obedience alone does not explain the Holocaust; anti-Semitic ideology produced eager killers as well (Mastroianni, 2002). But obedience was a factor. In the summer of 1942 nearly 500 middle-aged German reserve police officers were dispatched to Jozefow, Poland, in German-occupied territory. On July 13, the group's visibly upset commander informed his recruits, mostly family men, that they had been ordered to round up the village's Jews, who were said to be aiding the enemy. Able-bodied men were to be sent to work camps, and all the rest were to be shot on the spot. Given a chance to refuse participation in the executions, only about a dozen immediately did so. Within 17 hours, the remaining 485 officers killed 1500 helpless women, children, and elderly by shooting them in the back of the head as they lay face down. Hearing the pleadings of the victims, and seeing the gruesome results, some 20 percent of the officers did eventually dissent, managing either to miss their victims or to wander away and hide until the slaughter was over (Browning, 1992). But in real life, as in Milgram's experiments, the disobedient were the minority.

Another story was being played out in the French village of Le Chambon, where French Jews destined for deportation to Germany were being sheltered by villagers who openly defied orders to cooperate with the "New Order." The villagers' ancestors had themselves been persecuted and their pastors had been teaching them to "resist whenever our adversaries will demand of us obedience contrary to the orders of the

Standing up for democracy
Some individuals—roughly one in three in Milgram's experiments—resist social coercion, as did this unarmed man in Beijing, by single-handedly challenging an advancing line of tanks the day after the 1989 Tiananmen Square student uprising was suppressed.

Gospel" (Rochat, 1993). Ordered by police to give a list of sheltered Jews, the head pastor modeled defiance: "I don't know of Jews, I only know of human beings." Without realizing how long and terrible the war would be, or how much punishment and poverty they would suffer, the resisters made an initial commitment to resist. Supported by their beliefs, their role models, their interaction with one another, and their own initial acts, they remained defiant to the war's end.

Lessons From the Conformity and Obedience Studies

OBJECTIVE 9 | Explain how the conformity and obedience studies can help us understand our susceptibility to social influence.

What do the Asch and Milgram experiments teach us about ourselves? How does judging the length of a line or flicking a shock switch relate to everyday social behavior? Recall from Chapter 1 that psychological experiments aim not to re-create the literal behaviors of everyday life but to capture and explore the underlying processes that shape those behaviors. Asch and Milgram devised experiments in which the participants had to choose between adhering to their own standards and being responsive to others, a dilemma we all face frequently.

In Milgram's experiments, participants were also torn between what they should respond to—the pleas of the victim or the orders of the experimenter. Their moral sense warned them not to harm another, yet it also prompted them to obey the experimenter and to be a good research participant. With kindness and obedience on a collision course, obedience usually won.

Such experiments demonstrate that strong social influences can make people conform to falsehoods or capitulate to cruelty. "The most fundamental lesson of our study," Milgram noted, is that "ordinary people, simply doing their jobs, and without any particular hostility on their part, can become agents in a terrible destructive process" (1974, p. 6). Milgram did not entrap his "teachers" by asking them first to zap "learners" with enough electricity to make their hair stand on end. Rather, he exploited the foot-in-the-door effect, beginning with a little tickle of electricity and escalating step by step. In the minds of those throwing the switches, the small action became justified, making the next act tolerable. In Jozefow, in Le Chambon, and in Milgram's experiments, those who resisted usually did so early. After the first acts of compliance or resistance, attitudes began to follow and justify behavior.

So it happens when people succumb, gradually, to evil. In any society, great evils sometimes grow out of people's compliance with lesser evils. The Nazi leaders suspected that most German civil servants would resist shooting or gassing Jews directly, but they found them surprisingly willing to handle the paperwork of the Holocaust (Silver & Geller, 1978). Likewise, when Milgram asked 40 men to administer the learning test while someone else did the shocking, 93 percent complied. Contrary to images of devilish villains, evil does not require monstrous characters; all it takes is ordinary people corrupted by an evil situation—ordinary soldiers who follow orders to torture prisoners, ordinary students who follow orders to haze initiates into their group, ordinary employees who follow orders to produce and market harmful products. Before leading the 9/11 attacks, Mohamed Atta reportedly was a sane, rational person who had been a "good boy" and an excellent student from a close-knit family—not someone who fits our image of evil monster.

> "I was only following orders."
>
> Adolf Eichmann, Director of Nazi deportation of Jews to concentration camps

> "The normal reaction to an abnormal situation is abnormal behavior."
>
> James Waller, *Becoming Evil: How Ordinary People Commit Genocide and Mass Killing*, 2002

Group Influence

How do groups affect our behavior? To find out, social psychologists study the various influences that operate in the simplest of groups—one person in the presence of another—and those that operate in more complex groups, such as families, teams, and committees.

Social facilitation

Skilled athletes often find they are "on" before an audience. What they do well, they do even better when people are watching.

Individual Behavior in the Presence of Others

OBJECTIVE 10 | Describe the conditions in which the presence of others is likely to result in social facilitation, social loafing, or deindividuation.

Appropriately, social psychology's first experiments focused on the simplest of all questions about social behavior: How are we influenced by the mere presence of others—by people watching us or joining us in various activities?

Social Facilitation Having noticed that cyclists' racing times were faster when they competed against each other than when they competed with a clock, Norman Triplett (1898) hypothesized that the presence of others boosts performance. To test his hypothesis, Triplett had adolescents wind a fishing reel as rapidly as possible. He discovered that they wound the reel faster in the presence of someone doing the same thing. This phenomenon of stronger performance in others' presence is called **social facilitation.** For example, after a light turns green, drivers take about 15 percent less time to travel the first 100 yards when another car is beside them at the intersection than when they are alone (Towler, 1986).

But now things get tricky. On tougher tasks (learning nonsense syllables or solving complex multiplication problems), people perform *less* well when observers or others working on the same task are present. Further studies revealed why the presence of others sometimes helps and sometimes hinders performance (Guerin, 1986; Zajonc, 1965). When others observe us, we become aroused. This arousal strengthens the most *likely* response—the correct one on an easy task, an incorrect one on a difficult task. Thus, when we are being observed, we perform well-learned tasks more quickly and accurately, and unmastered tasks less quickly and accurately. James Michaels and his associates (1982) found that expert pool players who made 71 percent of their shots when alone made 80 percent when four people came to watch them. Poor shooters, who made 36 percent of their shots when alone, made only 25 percent when watched. The energizing effect of an enthusiastic audience probably contributes to the home advantage enjoyed by various sports teams. Studies of more than 80,000 college and professional athletic events in Canada, the United States, and England reveal that home teams win about 6 in 10 games (somewhat fewer for baseball and football, somewhat more for basketball and soccer—see **TABLE 18.1**).

The point to remember: What you do well, you are likely to do even better in front of an audience, especially a friendly audience; what you normally find difficult may seem all but impossible when you are being watched.

Social facilitation also helps explain a funny effect of crowding: Comedy records that are mildly amusing to people in an uncrowded room seem funnier in a densely packed room (Aiello & others, 1983; Freedman & Perlick, 1979). As comedians and actors know, a "good house" is a full one. The arousal triggered by crowding amplifies other reactions, too. If sitting close to one another, participants in experiments like a friendly person even more, an unfriendly person even less (Schiffenbauer & Schiavo, 1976; Storms & Thomas, 1977). The practical lesson: If choosing a room for a class or setting up chairs for a gathering, have barely enough seating.

Social Loafing Social facilitation experiments test the effect of others' presence on performance on an individual task, such as shooting pool. But what happens to performance when people perform the task as a group? In a team tug-of-war, for example, do you suppose the effort a person puts forth would be more than, less than, or the same as the effort he or she would exert in a one-on-one tug-of-war? To find out, Alan Ingham and his fellow researchers (1974) asked blindfolded University of Massachusetts students to "pull as hard as you can" on a rope. When Ingham fooled the students into believing three others were also pulling behind them, they exerted only 82 percent as much effort as when they knew they were pulling alone.

TABLE 18.1

HOME ADVANTAGE IN MAJOR TEAM SPORTS

Sport	Games Studied	Home Team Winning Percentage
Baseball	23,034	53.5%
Football	2,592	57.3
Ice hockey	4,322	61.1
Basketball	13,596	64.4
Soccer	37,202	69.0

From Courneya & Carron, 1992

To describe this diminished effort, Bibb Latané (1981; Jackson & Williams, 1988) coined the term **social loafing.** In 78 experiments conducted in the United States, India, Thailand, Japan, China, and Taiwan, social loafing occurred on various tasks, though it was especially common among men in individualistic cultures (Karau & Williams, 1993). In one of Latané's experiments, blindfolded people seated in a group clapped or shouted as loud as they could while listening through headphones to the sound of loud clapping or shouting. When told they were doing it with the others, the participants produced about one-third less noise than when they thought their individual efforts were identifiable.

Why this social loafing? First, people acting as part of a group feel less accountable and therefore worry less about what others think. Second, they may view their contribution as dispensable (Harkins & Szymanski, 1989; Kerr & Bruun, 1983). As many leaders of organizations know—and as you have perhaps observed on student group assignments—if group members share equally in the benefits regardless of how much they contribute, some may slack off. Unless highly motivated and identified with their group, they may free-ride on the other group members' efforts.

Deindividuation So, the presence of others can arouse people (as in the social facilitation experiments) or can diminish their feelings of responsibility (as in the social loafing experiments). But sometimes the presence of others both arouses people *and* diminishes their sense of responsibility. The result can be uninhibited behavior ranging from a food fight in the dining hall or screaming at a basketball referee to vandalism or rioting. Abandoning normal restraints to the power of the group is termed **deindividuation.** To be deindividuated is to be less self-conscious and less restrained when in a group situation.

Deindividuation often occurs when group participation makes people feel aroused and anonymous. In one experiment, New York University women dressed in depersonalizing Ku Klux Klan-style hoods delivered twice as much electric shock to a victim as did identifiable women (Zimbardo, 1970). (As in all such experiments, the "victim" did not actually receive the shocks.) Similarly, tribal warriors who depersonalize themselves with face paints or masks are more likely than those with exposed faces to kill, torture, or mutilate captured enemies (Watson, 1973). Whether in a mob, at a rock concert, at a ballgame, or at worship, to lose self-consciousness (to become deindividuated) is to become more responsive to the group experience.

Effects of Group Interaction

OBJECTIVE 11 | Discuss how group interaction can facilitate group polarization and groupthink.

We have examined the conditions under which being in the *presence* of others can

- motivate people to exert themselves or tempt them to free-ride on the efforts of others.
- make easy tasks easier and difficult tasks harder.
- enhance humor or fuel mob violence.

Research shows that *interacting* with others can similarly have both bad and good effects.

Group Polarization Educational researchers have noted that, over time, initial differences between groups of college students tend to grow. If the first-year students at College X tend to be more intellectually oriented than those at College Y, that difference will probably be amplified by the time they are seniors. Similarly, if the political conservatism of students who join fraternities and sororities is greater than that of students who do not, the gap in the political attitudes of the two groups will probably widen as they progress through college (Wilson & others, 1975). Likewise, notes Eleanor Maccoby (2002) from her decades of observing gender development, girls talk more intimately than boys do and play and fantasize less aggressively—and these gender differences widen over time as they interact mostly with their own gender.

> **social facilitation** stronger responses on simple or well-learned tasks in the presence of others.
>
> **social loafing** the tendency for people in a group to exert less effort when pooling their efforts toward attaining a common goal than when individually accountable.
>
> **deindividuation** the loss of self-awareness and self-restraint occurring in group situations that foster arousal and anonymity.

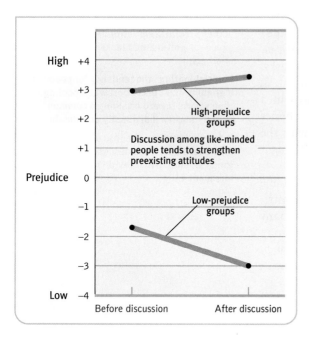

FIGURE 18.6
Group polarization
If a group is like-minded, discussion strengthens its prevailing opinions. Talking over racial issues increased prejudice in a high-prejudice group of high school students and decreased it in a low-prejudice group (Myers & Bishop, 1970).

> "One's impulse to blow the whistle on this nonsense was simply undone by the circumstances of the discussion."
>
> Arthur M. Schlesinger, Jr., *A Thousand Days*, 1965

This enhancement of a group's prevailing tendencies—called **group polarization**—occurs when people within a group discuss an idea that most of them either favor or oppose. Group polarization can have beneficial results, as when it amplifies a sought-after spiritual awareness or reinforces the resolve of those in a self-help group, or strengthens feelings of tolerance in a low-prejudice group. But it can also have dire consequences. George Bishop and I discovered that when high-prejudice students discussed racial issues, they became *more* prejudiced (**FIGURE 18.6**). (Low-prejudice students became even more accepting.) The experiment's ideological separation and polarization finds a seeming parallel in the growing polarization of American politics. The percentage of landslide counties—voting 60 percent or more for one presidential candidate—increased from 26 percent in 1976 to 48 percent in 2004 (Bishop, 2004). More and more, people are living near and learning from others who think as they do.

The polarizing effect of interaction among the like-minded applies not only to U.S. "red" and "blue" states, but also to suicide terrorists. After analyzing terrorist organizations around the world, psychologists Clark McCauley and Mary Segal (1987; McCauley, 2002) noted that the terrorist mentality does not erupt suddenly. Rather, it usually arises among people who get together because of a grievance and then become more and more extreme as they interact in isolation from any moderating influences. Increasingly, group members (who may be isolated with other "brothers" and "sisters" in camps) categorize the world as "us" and "them" (Moghaddam, 2005; Qirko, 2004). Suicide terrorism virtually never is done on a personal whim, reports researcher Ariel Merari (2002).

The Internet provides a medium for group polarization. Its tens of thousands of virtual groups enable bereaved parents, peacemakers, and teachers to find solace and support from kindred spirits. But the Internet also enables people who share interests in government cover-ups, extraterrestrial visitors, white supremacy, or citizen militias to find one another and to find support for their shared suspicions (McKenna & Bargh, 1998).

Groupthink   Does group interaction ever distort important decisions? Social psychologist Irving Janis began to think so as he read historian Arthur M. Schlesinger, Jr.'s account of how President John F. Kennedy and his advisers blundered into an ill-fated plan to invade Cuba with 1400 CIA-trained Cuban exiles. When the invaders were easily captured and soon linked to the U.S. government, Kennedy wondered in hindsight, "How could we have been so stupid?"

To find out, Janis (1982) studied the decision-making procedures that led to the fiasco. He discovered that the soaring morale of the recently elected president and his advisers fostered undue confidence in the plan. To preserve the good group feeling, any dissenting views were suppressed or self-censored, especially after President Kennedy voiced his enthusiasm for the scheme. Since no one spoke strongly against the idea, everyone assumed consensus support. To describe this harmonious but unrealistic group thinking, Janis coined the term **groupthink.**

Janis and others then examined other historical fiascos—the failure to anticipate the 1941 Japanese attack on Pearl Harbor, the escalation of the Vietnam War, the U.S. Watergate cover-up, the Chernobyl nuclear reactor accident (Reason, 1987), and the U.S. space shuttle *Challenger* explosion (Esser & Lindoerfer, 1989). They discovered that in these cases, too, groupthink was fed by overconfidence, conformity, self-justification, and group polarization.

Groupthink surfaced again, reported the U.S. Senate Intelligence Committee (2004), when "personnel involved in the Iraq WMD issue demonstrated several aspects of groupthink: examining few alternatives, selective gathering of information, pressure to conform within the group or withhold criticism, and collective rationalization." This groupthink led analysts to "interpret ambiguous evidence as conclusively indicative of a WMD program as well as ignore or minimize evidence that Iraq did not have [WMD] programs."

Despite such fiascos and tragedies, two heads are better than one in solving some types of problems. Knowing this, Janis also studied instances in which U.S. presidents and their advisers collectively made good decisions, such as when the Truman administration formulated the Marshall Plan, which offered assistance to Europe after World War II, and when the Kennedy administration worked to keep the Soviets from installing missiles in Cuba. In such instances—and in the business world, too, Janis believed—groupthink is prevented when a leader welcomes various opinions, invites experts' critiques of developing plans, and assigns people to identify possible problems. Just as the suppression of dissent bends a group toward bad decisions, so open debate often shapes good ones. None of us is as smart as all of us.

The Power of Individuals

OBJECTIVE 12 | Identify the characteristic common to minority positions that sway majorities.

In affirming the power of social influence, we must not overlook our power as individuals. *Social control* (the power of the situation) and *personal control* (the power of the individual) interact. People aren't billiard balls. When feeling pressured, we may react by doing the opposite of what is expected, thereby reasserting our sense of freedom (Brehm & Brehm, 1981).

Such was the experience of three individual soldiers at the Abu Ghraib prison (O'Connor, 2004). Lt. David Sutton put an end to one incident, which he reported to his commanders. Navy dog-handler William Kimbro refused pressure to participate in improper interrogations using his attack dogs. Specialist Joseph Darby brought visual images of the horrors into the light of day, providing incontestable evidence of the atrocities. Each risked ridicule or even court-martial for not following orders.

As these three soldiers discovered, committed individuals can sway the majority and make social history. Were this not so, communism would have remained an obscure theory, Christianity would be a small Middle Eastern sect, and Rosa Parks' refusal to sit at the back of the bus would not have ignited the civil rights movement. Technological history, too, is often made by innovative minorities who overcome the majority's resistance to change. To many, the railroad was a nonsensical idea; some farmers even feared that train noise would prevent hens from laying eggs. People derided Robert Fulton's steamboat as "Fulton's Folly." As Fulton later said, "Never did a single encouraging remark, a bright hope, a warm wish, cross my path." Much the same reaction greeted the printing press, the telegraph, the incandescent lamp, and the typewriter (Cantril & Bumstead, 1960).

European social psychologists have sought to better understand *minority influence*—the power of one or two individuals to sway majorities (Moscovici, 1985). They investigated groups in which one or two individuals consistently expressed a controversial attitude or an unusual perceptual judgment. They repeatedly found that a minority that unswervingly holds to its position is far more successful in swaying the majority than is a minority that waffles. Holding consistently to a minority opinion will not make you popular, but it may make you influential. This is especially so if your self-confidence stimulates others to consider why you react as you do. Although people often follow the majority view publicly, they may privately develop sympathy for the minority view. Even when a minority's influence is not yet visible, it may be persuading some members of the majority to rethink their views (Wood & others, 1994). The powers of social influence are enormous, but so are the powers of the committed individual.

■ **group polarization** the enhancement of a group's prevailing inclinations through discussion within the group.

■ **groupthink** the mode of thinking that occurs when the desire for harmony in a decision-making group overrides a realistic appraisal of alternatives.

> "Truth springs from argument among friends."
>
> Philosopher David Hume, 1711–1776

Gandhi

As the life of Mahatma Gandhi powerfully testifies, a consistent and persistent minority voice can sometimes sway the majority. The nonviolent appeals and fasts of the Hindu nationalist and spiritual leader were instrumental in winning India's independence from Britain in 1947.

Margaret Bourke-White/Life Magazine. © 1946 Time Warner, Inc.

>> LEARNING OUTCOMES

Social Influence

OBJECTIVE 6 | **Describe the chameleon effect, and give an example of it.**

The *chameleon effect* is our tendency to unconsciously mimic those around us, as when we yawn when others yawn, or pick up the mood of a happy or sad person. Automatic mimicry is an ingredient in the ability to empathize with others.

OBJECTIVE 7 | **Discuss Asch's experiments on conformity, and distinguish between normative and informational social influence.**

Solomon Asch found that people will conform to a group's judgment even when it is clearly incorrect. Conformity increases when we feel incompetent or insecure, admire the group's status and attractiveness, have made no prior commitment to a response, are being observed by members of the group, come from a culture that strongly encourages respect for group standards, and are in a group with at least three members, all unanimous in their decision. We may conform either to gain social approval (*normative social influence*) or because we welcome the information that others provide (*informational social influence*). We are most open to informational social influence if we are unsure of what is right and being right matters.

OBJECTIVE 8 | **Describe Milgram's experiments on obedience, and outline the conditions in which obedience was highest.**

In Stanley Milgram's experiments, people torn between obeying an experimenter and responding to another's pleas to stop the shocks usually chose to obey orders, even though obedience supposedly meant harming the other person. People were most likely to obey when the person giving orders was nearby and was perceived as a legitimate authority figure; when the person giving orders was supported by a prestigious institution; when the victim was depersonalized or at a distance; and when no other person modeled defiance by disobeying.

OBJECTIVE 9 | **Explain how the conformity and obedience studies can help us understand our susceptibility to social influence.**

In the conformity studies, randomly chosen ordinary people conformed in spite of their own beliefs. In the obedience studies, randomly chosen ordinary people obeyed instructions to deliver punishments that, if real, would have harmed total strangers. People who resisted instructions did so early; after that, attitudes followed behavior. If we learn from these experiments the underlying processes that can shape our behavior, we may be less susceptible to powerful social influences in real-life situations in which we must choose between adhering to our own standards or being responsive to others.

OBJECTIVE 10 | **Describe the conditions in which the presence of others is likely to result in social facilitation, social loafing, or deindividuation.**

The presence of either observers or co-actors boosts arousal, strengthening our most likely response. This *social facilitation* tends to increase performance on easy or well-learned tasks but decrease it on difficult or newly learned ones. The presence of others pooling their efforts toward a group goal can decrease performance when *social loafing* occurs, as some individuals ride free on the efforts of others. *Deindividuation*, a psychological state in which people become less self-aware and self-restrained, may result when a group experience arouses people and makes them feel anonymous.

OBJECTIVE 11 | **Discuss how group interaction can facilitate group polarization and groupthink.**

Within groups, discussions among like-minded members often produce *group polarization*, an enhancement of the group's prevailing opinions. This process fosters *groupthink*, as groups pressure members to conform, suppress dissenting information, and fail to consider alternatives. To prevent groupthink, leaders can welcome a variety of opinions, invite experts' critiques, and assign people to identify possible problems in developing plans.

OBJECTIVE 12 | **Identify the characteristic common to minority positions that sway majorities.**

Minorities that successfully sway group opinions usually express their views consistently.

ASK YOURSELF: What two examples of social influence have you experienced this week? (Remember, influence may be informational.)

Social Relations

We have sampled how we *think* about and *influence* one another. Now we come to social psychology's third focus—how we *relate* to one another. What causes us to harm or to help or to fall in love? How can we transform the closed fists of aggression into the open arms of compassion? We will ponder the bad and the good: from prejudice and aggression to attraction, altruism, and peacemaking.

Prejudice

OBJECTIVE **13** | Identify the three components of prejudice.

Prejudice means "prejudgment." It is an unjustifiable and usually negative attitude toward a group—often a different cultural, ethnic, or gender group. Like all attitudes, **prejudice** is a mixture of *beliefs* (called **stereotypes**), *emotions* (hostility, envy, or fear), and predispositions to *action* (to discriminate). To *believe* that overweight people are gluttonous, to *feel* antipathy for an overweight person, and to be hesitant to hire or date an overweight person is to be prejudiced. Prejudice is a negative *attitude;* **discrimination** is a negative *behavior.*

Like other forms of prejudgment, prejudices are schemas that influence how we notice and interpret events. In one 1970s study, most white participants perceived a white man shoving a black man as "horsing around." When they saw a black man shove a white man, they interpreted the act as "violent" (Duncan, 1976). Our preconceived ideas about people bias our impressions of their behavior. Prejudgments color perceptions.

How Prejudiced Are People?

OBJECTIVE **14** | Contrast overt and subtle forms of prejudice, and give examples of each.

To learn about levels of prejudice, we can assess what people say and what they do. To judge by what Americans say, gender and racial attitudes have changed dramatically in the last half-century. The one-third of Americans who in 1937 said they would vote for a qualified woman whom their party nominated for president soared to 87 percent in 2003 (Jones & Moore, 2003). Support for all forms of racial contact, including interracial marriage (**FIGURE 18.7**), has also dramatically increased. Nearly everyone agrees that children of all races should attend the same schools and that women and men should receive the same pay for the same job.

Yet as overt prejudice wanes, subtle prejudice lingers. Despite increased verbal support for interracial marriage, many people admit that in socially intimate settings (dating, dancing, marrying) they would feel uncomfortable with someone of another race. And in Western Europe, where many "guest workers" and refugees settled at the end of the twentieth century, "modern prejudice"—rejecting immigrant minorities as job applicants for supposedly nonracial reasons—has been replacing blatant prejudice (Jackson & others, 2001; Pettigrew, 1998). A slew of recent experiments illustrate that prejudice can be not only subtle but also automatic and unconscious (see Close-Up: Automatic Prejudice, page 744).

■ prejudice an unjustifiable (and usually negative) attitude toward a group and its members. Prejudice generally involves stereotyped beliefs, negative feelings, and a predisposition to discriminatory action.

■ stereotype a generalized (sometimes accurate but often overgeneralized) belief about a group of people.

■ discrimination unjustifiable negative behavior toward a group or its members.

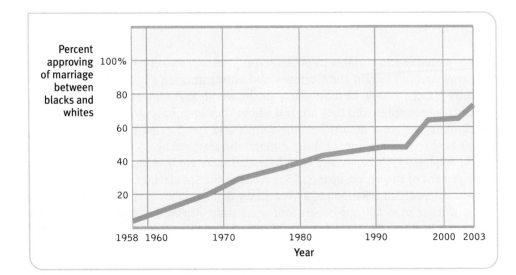

FIGURE 18.7
Prejudice over time
Americans' approval of interracial marriage has soared over the past half-century. (Gallup surveys reported by Ludwig, 2004.)

CLOSE-UP:

AUTOMATIC PREJUDICE

As we have seen throughout this book, we process information on two levels: conscious and unconscious. To some extent, our thinking, our memories, and our attitudes are *explicit*—on the radar screen of our awareness. And to an even greater extent, today's researchers believe, they are *implicit*—below the radar, out-of-sight. Modern studies of implicit, automatic attitudes indicate that prejudice is often more of an unthinking knee-jerk response than a decision. Consider these findings on U.S. racial prejudice:

Implicit racial associations Anthony Greenwald and his colleagues (1998) showed that even people who deny harboring racial prejudice may carry negative associations. For example, 9 in 10 white respondents took longer to identify pleasant words (such as *peace* and *paradise*) as "good" when good was presented with black rather than white faces. Moreover, report Kurt Hugenberg and Galen Bodenhausen (2003), people who displayed the most *implicit prejudice* on this test also were the quickest to perceive anger and apparent threat in black faces.

Unconscious patronization Kent Harber (1998) asked white university women to evaluate a flawed essay said to be written by a black or a white fellow student. When they believed the writer was black, the women gave markedly *higher* ratings and never expressed the harsh criticisms they assigned to white-authored essays, such as "When I read college work this bad I just want to lay my head down on the table and cry." Did the evaluators calibrate their evaluations to their racial stereotypes, Harber wondered, leading them to patronize the black writers with less exacting standards? If used in real-world evaluations, such low expectations and the resulting "inflated praise and insufficient criticism" could hinder minority student achievement. (To preclude such bias, many teachers read essays while "blind" to their authors.)

Race-influenced perceptions Two research teams were curious about the shooting of an unarmed man in the doorway of his Bronx apartment building by officers who mistook his wallet for a gun. Each research team reenacted the situation, asking people to press buttons quickly to "shoot" or not shoot men who suddenly appeared on screen holding either a gun or a harmless object such as a flashlight or bottle (Correll & others, 2002; Greenwald & others, 2003). People (both Blacks and Whites, in one of the studies) more often mistakenly shot targets who were black.

Seeing black Several studies show that the more a person's features are perceived as typical of their racial category, the more likely they are to elicit race-based responding (Maddox, 2004). In one study of 182 police officers, Jennifer Eberhardt and her collaborators (2004) found that "black faces looked more criminal to police officers; the more black, the more criminal."

Reflexive bodily responses Today's biopsychosocial approach has stimulated neuroscience studies that measure people's instant responses to viewing white and black faces. These studies have detected implicit prejudice in people's facial-muscle responses and in the activation of their amygdala, an emotion-processing center (Cunningham & others, 2004; Eberhardt, 2005; Vanman & others, 2004). Even people who consciously express little prejudice may give off telltale signals as their body responds selectively to another's race.

If your own gut check sometimes reveals feelings you would rather not have about other people, be assured that you are not alone. It is what we do with our feelings that matters. By monitoring our feelings and actions, and by replacing old habits with new ones based on new friendships, we can free ourselves from prejudice.

But prejudice still surfaces in public settings. In a 2004 survey of Europeans, 6 in 10 people in both Britain and Germany said immigrants are a bad influence on their country (Lester, 2004). In most places in the world, gays and lesbians cannot comfortably acknowledge who they are and whom they love. In several U.S. states where black motorists are a minority of the drivers and speeders on interstate highways, they have been the majority of those stopped and searched by state police (Lamberth, 1998; Staples, 1999a,b). In one New Jersey turnpike study, African-Americans were 13.5 percent of the car occupants, 15 percent of the speeders, and 35 percent of the drivers stopped. Elmo Randolph, a New Jersey dentist, knew it all along. After being stopped more than 100 times over four years while driving his gold BMW from his home to his office, Dr. Randolph, guilty of nothing more than "driving while black," sold the car.

> "Unhappily the world has yet to learn how to live with diversity."
> Pope John Paul II, Address to the United Nations, 1995

Gender prejudice and discrimination persist, too. Despite gender equality in intelligence scores, people tend to perceive their fathers as more intelligent than their mothers (Furnham & Rawles, 1995). In Saudi Arabia, women are not allowed to drive. In Western countries, we pay more to those (usually men) who drive machines that take care of our streets than to those (usually women) who take care of our children. Worldwide, women are more likely to live in poverty (Lipps, 1999), and their 69 percent literacy rate is well below men's 83 percent (PRB, 2002).

Female infants are no longer left out on a hillside to die of exposure, as was the practice in ancient Greece. Yet even today boys are often valued more than their sisters. During the 1970s Bangladesh famine, preschool girls were more malnourished than boys were, and in many developing countries death rates are higher for girls than for boys (Bairagi, 1987). With testing that enables sex-selective abortions, several south Asian countries, including certain regions of China and India, have experienced a shortfall in female births. Natural female mortality and the normal 105-to-100 male-to-female birth ratio hardly explains the world's estimated 101 million (say that number slowly) "missing women" (Sen, 2003). In 2005, China announced that the newborn sex ratio had reached 119 boys for every 100 girls (Yardley, 2005). With demographic predictions of 40 million Chinese bachelors unable to find mates, China has declared that sex-selective abortions—gender genocide—are now a criminal offense.

Suppose that you could only have one child. Would you prefer that it be a boy or a girl? When Gallup asked that question of Americans, two-thirds expressed a gender preference, and for two-thirds of those—in 2003 as in 1941—it was for a boy (Lyons, 2003). But the news isn't all bad for girls and women. Most people *feel* more positively about women in general than they do about men (Eagly, 1994; Haddock & Zanna, 1994). People worldwide see women as having some traits, such as nurturance, sensitivity, and less aggressiveness, that most people prefer (Glick & others, 2004; Swim, 1994). That may explain why women tend to like women more than men like men (Rudman & Goodwin, 2004). And perhaps that is also why people prefer slightly feminized computer-generated faces—men's and women's—to slightly masculinized faces. Researcher David Perrett and his colleagues (1998) speculate that a slightly feminized male face connotes kindness, cooperativeness, and other traits of a good father. When the British Broadcasting Company invited 18,000 women to guess which of the men in **FIGURE 18.8** was most likely to place a personal ad seeking a "special lady to love and cherish forever," 66 percent guessed the slightly feminized face (b).

FIGURE 18.8
Who do you like best?
Which one placed an ad seeking a special lady to love and cherish forever? (See page 748.)

(a)   (b)

Professor Dave Perrett, St. Andrews University

Social Roots of Prejudice

OBJECTIVE **15** | Discuss the social factors that contribute to prejudice.

Why does prejudice arise? Inequalities, social divisions, and emotional scapegoating are partly responsible.

Social Inequalities When some people have money, power, and prestige and others do not, the "haves" usually develop attitudes that justify things as they are. In the extreme case, slave owners perceived slaves as innately lazy, ignorant, and irresponsible—as having the very traits that "justified" enslaving them. More commonly, women are perceived as unassertive but sensitive and therefore suited for the caretaking tasks they have traditionally performed (Hoffman & Hurst, 1990). In short, prejudice rationalizes inequalities.

Discrimination also increases prejudice through the reactions it provokes in its victims. In his classic 1954 book, *The Nature of Prejudice*, Gordon Allport noted

The ingroup
Scotland's famed "Tartan Army" football fans, shown here during a match against archrival England, share a social identity that defines "us" (the Scottish ingroup) and "them" (the English outgroup).

Mike Hewitt/Getty Images

that being a victim of discrimination can produce either self-blame or anger. Both reactions may create new grounds for prejudice through the classic *blame-the-victim* dynamic. If the circumstances of poverty breed a higher crime rate, someone can then use the higher crime rate to justify continuing the discrimination against those who live in poverty.

Us and Them: Ingroup and Outgroup Thanks to our ancestral need to belong, we are a group-bound species. We cheer for our groups, kill for them, die for them. Indeed, we define who we are—our identities—partly in terms of our groups. Australian psychologists John Turner (1987) and Michael Hogg (1996) note that through our *social identities* we associate ourselves with certain groups and contrast ourselves with others. When Ian identifies himself as a man, an Aussie, a Labourite, a University of Sydney student, a Catholic, and a MacGregor, he knows who he is, and so do we.

The social definition of who you are also implies who you are not. Mentally drawing a circle that defines "us" (the **ingroup**) excludes "them" (the **outgroup**). Such group identifications typically promote an **ingroup bias**—a favoring of one's own group. Even arbitrarily creating an us-them distinction—by grouping people with the toss of a coin—leads people to show favoritism to their own group when dividing any rewards (Tajfel, 1982; Wilder, 1981).

> "You cannot oppress people for over three centuries and then say it is all over and expect them to put on suits and ties and [be] attaché-carrying citizens and go to work on Wall Street."
>
> Shelby Steele, "The New Segregation," 1992

French fury
Members of France's marginalized ethnic groups reached the tipping point for tolerance in 2005, when they began destructive rioting.

Eric Travers/EPA/Landov

The urge to distinguish enemies from friends and to have one's group be dominant predisposes prejudice against strangers (Whitley, 1999). To Greeks of the classical era, all non-Greeks were "barbarians." Most children believe their own school is better than the other schools in town. Many high school students form cliques—jocks, goths, skaters, gangsters, freaks, geeks—and disparage those outside their group. Even chimpanzees have been seen to wipe clean the spot where they were touched by a chimp from another group (Goodall, 1986).

Emotional Roots of Prejudice

OBJECTIVE 16 | Explain how scapegoating illustrates the emotional component of prejudice.

Prejudice springs not only from the divisions of society but also from the passions of the heart. Facing the terror of death tends to heighten patriotism and produce loathing and aggression toward "them"—those who threaten one's worldview (Pyszczynski & others, 2002). Recalling such terror may alter attitudes, as happened to participants when Mark Landau and eight others (2004) reminded them of their own mortality or of the terror of 9/11. This reminder of terror led to their expressing increased support for President Bush (a phenomenon harnessed by the president's 2004 campaign).

Prejudice may also express anger: When things go wrong, finding someone to blame can provide a target, a scapegoat, for one's anger. In the late 1600s, New England settlers, after suffering devastating losses at the hands of Native Americans and their French allies, lashed out by hanging people as supposed witches (Norton, 2002). Following 9/11, some outraged people lashed out at innocent Arab-Americans, about whom negative stereotypes blossomed. Calls to eliminate Saddam Hussein, whom Americans had been grudgingly tolerating, also increased. "Fear and anger create aggression, and aggression against citizens of different ethnicity or race creates racism and, in turn, new forms of terrorism," noted Philip Zimbardo (2001).

Evidence for this **scapegoat theory** of prejudice comes from high prejudice levels among economically frustrated people and from experiments in which a temporary frustration intensifies prejudice. In experiments, students who experience failure or are made to feel insecure will often restore their self-esteem by disparaging a rival school or another person (Cialdini & Richardson, 1980; Crocker & others, 1987). To boost our own sense of status, it helps to have others to denigrate. That is why a rival's misfortune sometimes provides a twinge of pleasure. By contrast, those made to feel loved and supported become more open to and accepting of others who differ (Mikulincer & Shaver, 2001).

Cognitive Roots of Prejudice

OBJECTIVE 17 | Cite four ways that cognitive processes help create and maintain prejudice.

Prejudice springs from the divisions of society, the passions of the heart, and also from the mind's natural workings. Stereotyped beliefs are a by-product of how we cognitively simplify the world.

Categorization One way we simplify our world is to categorize. A chemist categorizes molecules as organic and inorganic. A mental health professional categorizes psychological disorders by types. In categorizing people into groups, however, we often stereotype them, biasing our per-

> "All good people agree,
> And all good people say
> All nice people, like us, are We
> And everyone else is They.
> But if you cross over the sea
> Instead of over the way
> You may end by (think of it)
> Looking on We
> As only a sort of They."
>
> Rudyard Kipling, "We and They," 1926

> "If the Tiber reaches the walls, if the Nile does not rise to the fields, if the sky doesn't move or the Earth does, if there is famine, if there is plague, the cry is at once: 'The Christians to the lion!'"
>
> Tertullian, *Apologeticus*, A.D. 197

■ **ingroup** "Us"—people with whom one shares a common identity.

■ **outgroup** "Them"—those perceived as different or apart from one's ingroup.

■ **ingroup bias** the tendency to favor one's own group.

■ **scapegoat theory** the theory that prejudice offers an outlet for anger by providing someone to blame.

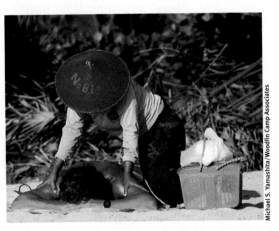

Michael S. Yamashita/Woodfin Camp Associates

Do people of another race look alike?
Foreign sunbathers on Bali's beaches may think they do. Balinese masseuses wear identifying numbers on their hats, enabling visitors to recognize them easily.

ceptions of their diversity. We recognize how greatly we differ from other individuals in our groups. But we overestimate the similarity of those within other groups. "They"—the members of some other group—seem to look and act alike, but "we" are diverse (Bothwell & others, 1989). To those in one ethnic group, members of another often seem more alike in appearance, personality, and attitudes than they are. With experience, however, people get better at recognizing individual faces from another group. For example, people of European descent more accurately identify individual African faces if they have watched a great deal of basketball on television, exposing them to many African-heritage faces (Li & others, 1996).

Vivid Cases   As we saw in Chapter 10, we often judge the frequency of events by instances that readily come to mind. In a classic experiment, Myron Rothbart and his colleagues (1978) demonstrated this ability to overgeneralize from vivid, memorable cases. They divided University of Oregon student volunteers into two groups, then showed them information about 50 men. The first group's list included 10 men arrested for nonviolent crimes, such as forgery. The second group's list included 10 men arrested for violent crimes, such as assault. Later when both groups recalled how many men on their list had committed any sort of crime, the second group overestimated the number. Vivid (violent) cases are readily available to our memory and therefore influence our judgments of a group (**FIGURE 18.9**).

FIGURE 18.9
Vivid cases feed stereotypes
The 9/11 Muslim terrorists created, in many minds, an exaggerated stereotype of Muslims as terror-prone. Actually, reported a National Research Council panel on terrorism, when offering the inexact illustration at right, most terrorists are not Muslim and "the vast majority of Islamic people have no connection with and do not sympathize with terrorism" (Smelser & Mitchell, 2002).

Islam   Terrorism

The Just-World Phenomenon   As we noted earlier, people often justify their prejudice by blaming its victims. Bystanders, too, may blame victims by assuming the world is just and therefore "people get what they deserve." In experiments, merely observing someone receive painful shocks has led many people to think less of the victim (Lerner, 1980). This **just-world phenomenon** reflects an idea we commonly teach our children—that good is rewarded and evil is punished. From this it is but a short leap to assume that those who succeed must be good and those who suffer must be bad. Such reasoning enables the rich to see both their own wealth and the poor's misfortune as justly deserved. As one German civilian is said to have remarked when visiting the Bergen-Belsen concentration camp shortly after World War II, "What terrible criminals these prisoners must have been to receive such treatment."

Hindsight bias is also at work here (Carli & Leonard, 1989). Have you ever heard people say that rape victims, abused spouses, or people with AIDS got what they deserved? In some countries, women who have been raped have been sentenced to severe punishment for having violated a law against adultery (Mydans, 2002). An experiment by Ronnie Janoff-Bulman and her collaborators (1985) illustrates this phenomenon of blaming the victim. When given a detailed account of a date that ended with the woman's being raped, people perceived the woman's behavior as at least partly to blame. In hindsight, they thought, "She should have known better." (Blaming the victim also serves to reassure people that it couldn't happen to them.) Others, given the same account with the rape ending deleted, did not perceive the woman's behavior as inviting rape.

THERE IS NO JUSTICE IN THE WORLD.

THERE IS SOME JUSTICE IN THE WORLD.

THE WORLD IS JUST.

Aggression

OBJECTIVE 18 | Explain how psychology's definition of *aggression* differs from everyday usage.

The most destructive force in our social relations is aggression. In psychology, *aggression* has a more precise meaning than it does in everyday usage. The assertive, persistent salesperson is not aggressive. Nor is the dentist who makes you wince with pain. But the person who passes along a vicious rumor about you, the person who verbally assaults you, and the attacker who mugs you are aggressive. In psychology, **aggression** is any physical or verbal behavior intended to hurt or destroy, whether done reactively out of hostility or proactively as a calculated means to an end. Thus, murders and assaults that occurred as hostile outbursts are aggression. So were the 110 million war-related deaths that took place during the last century, many of which were cool and calculated.

Aggression research affirms that behavior emerges from the interaction of biology and experience. For a gun to fire, the trigger must be pulled; with some people, as with hair-trigger guns, it doesn't take much to trip an explosion. Let us look first at biological factors that influence our thresholds for aggressive behavior, then at the psychological factors that pull the trigger.

The Biology of Aggression

OBJECTIVE 19 | Describe three levels of biological influences on aggression.

Aggression varies too widely from culture to culture, era to era, and person to person to be considered an unlearned instinct. But biology does *influence* aggression. Stimuli that trigger aggressive behavior operate through our biological system. We can look for biological influences at three levels—genetic, neural, and biochemical. Our genes engineer our individual nervous systems, which operate electrochemically.

Genetic Influences Animals have been bred for aggressiveness—sometimes for sport, sometimes for research. Twin studies suggest that genes influence human aggression as well (Miles & Carey, 1997; Rowe & others, 1999). If one identical twin admits to "having a violent temper," the other twin will often independently admit the same. Fraternal twins are much less likely to respond similarly. Researchers are now searching for genetic markers found in those who commit the most violence. (One is already well known and is carried by half the human race: the Y chromosome.)

Neural Influences Animal and human brains have neural systems that, when stimulated, either inhibit or produce aggressive behavior (Moyer, 1983). Consider:

- The domineering leader of a caged monkey colony had a radio-controlled electrode implanted in a brain area that, when stimulated, inhibits aggression. When researchers placed the button that activated the electrode in the colony's cage, one small monkey learned to push it every time the boss became threatening.
- A mild-mannered woman had an electrode implanted in her brain's limbic system (in the amygdala) by neurosurgeons seeking to diagnose a disorder. Because the brain has no sensory receptors, she was unable to feel the stimulation. But at the flick of a switch she snarled, "Take my blood pressure. Take it now," then stood up and began to strike the doctor.
- Intensive evaluation of 15 death-row inmates revealed that all 15 had suffered a severe head injury. Although most neurologically impaired people are not violent, researcher Dorothy Lewis and her colleagues (1986) inferred that unrecognized neurological disorders may be one ingredient in the violence recipe. Other studies of violent criminals have revealed diminished activity in the frontal lobes, which play an important role in controlling impulses (Amen & others, 1996; Davidson & others, 2000; Raine, 1999).

In the last 25 years in the United States, guns have caused some 800,000 suicidal, homicidal, and accidental deaths. Compared with people of the same sex, race, age, and neighborhood, those who keep a gun in the home (ironically, often for protection) are nearly three times more likely to be murdered in the home—nearly always by a family member or close acquaintance. For every self-defense use of a gun in the home, there are 4 unintentional shootings, 7 criminal assaults or homicides, and 11 attempted or completed suicides (Kellermann & others, 1993, 1997, 1998).

■ **just-world phenomenon** the tendency of people to believe the world is just and that people therefore get what they deserve and deserve what they get.

■ **aggression** any physical or verbal behavior intended to hurt or destroy.

"It's a guy thing."

" We could avoid two-thirds of all crime simply by putting all able-bodied young men in cryogenic sleep from the age of 12 through 28."

David T. Lykken, *The Antisocial Personalities*, 1995

So, does the brain have a "violence center" that produces aggression when stimulated? Actually, no one spot in the brain controls aggression, because aggression is a complex behavior that occurs in particular contexts. Rather, the brain has neural systems that *facilitate* aggression, given provocation. And it has a frontal lobe system for inhibiting aggression, making aggression more likely if this system is damaged, inactive, disconnected, or not yet fully mature.

Biochemical Influences Hormones, alcohol, and other substances in the blood influence the neural systems that control aggression. A raging bull will become a gentle Ferdinand when castration reduces its testosterone level. The same is true of castrated mice. When injected with testosterone, the castrated mice once again become aggressive.

Although humans are less sensitive to hormonal changes, violent criminals tend to be muscular young males with lower-than-average intelligence scores, low levels of the neurotransmitter serotonin, and higher-than-average testosterone levels (Dabbs & others, 2001a; Pendick, 1994). Drugs that sharply reduce their testosterone levels also subdue their aggressive tendencies. High testosterone correlates with irritability, low tolerance for frustration, assertiveness, and impulsiveness—qualities that predispose somewhat more aggressive responses to provocation (Dabbs & others, 2001b; Harris, 1999). Among both teenage boys and adult men, high testosterone levels correlate with delinquency, hard drug use, and aggressive-bullying responses to frustration (Berman & others, 1993; Dabbs & Morris, 1990; Olweus & others, 1988). With age, testosterone levels—and aggressiveness—diminish.

The traffic between hormones and behavior is two-way. Testosterone heightens dominance and aggressiveness. But dominating behavior also boosts testosterone levels (Mazur & Booth, 1998). One study measured testosterone levels in the saliva of male college basketball fans before and after a big game. Testosterone levels swelled among the victorious fans and sank among the dejected ones (Bernhardt & others, 1998).

For both biological and psychological reasons, alcohol unleashes aggressive responses to frustration (Bushman, 1993; Ito & others, 1996; Taylor & Chermack, 1993). (Just *thinking* you've imbibed alcohol has some effect; but so, too, does unknowingly ingesting alcohol slipped into a drink.) Police data and prison surveys reinforce conclusions drawn from experiments on alcohol and aggression. Aggression-prone people are more likely to drink and to become violent when intoxicated (White & others, 1993). People who have been drinking commit 4 in 10 violent crimes and 3 in 4 acts of spousal abuse (Greenfeld, 1998).

A lean, mean fighting machine—the testosterone-laden female hyena The hyena's unusual embryology pumps testosterone into female fetuses. The result is revved-up young female hyenas who seem born to fight.

The Psychology of Aggression

OBJECTIVE 20 | Outline four psychological triggers of aggression.

Biological factors influence the ease with which aggression is triggered. But what psychological factors pull the trigger?

Aversive Events Although suffering sometimes builds character, it may also bring out the worst in us. Studies in which animals or humans experience unpleasant events reveal that those made miserable often make others miserable (Berkowitz, 1983, 1989).

Being blocked short of a goal also increases people's readiness to aggress. This phenomenon is called the **frustration-aggression principle:** Frustration creates anger, which may in some people generate aggression, especially in the presence of an aggressive cue, such as a gun. Recall that organisms often respond to stress with a *fight-or-flight reaction*. After the frustration and stress of 9/11, Americans responded with a readiness to fight. Terrorism similarly may spring from a desire for revenge, sometimes after a friend or family member has been killed or injured.

Like frustration, other aversive stimuli—physical pain, personal insults, foul odors, hot temperatures, cigarette smoke, and a host of others—can also evoke hostility. For example, violent crime and spousal abuse rates are higher during hotter years, seasons, months, and days (**FIGURE 18.10**). When people are hotter than usual, they think, feel, and act more aggressively. From the available data, Craig Anderson and his colleagues (2000) project that, other things being equal, global warming of 4 degrees Fahrenheit (about 2 degrees centigrade) would induce more than 50,000 additional assaults and murders in the United States alone.

Ostracism, as we noted in Chapter 12, can also be a real pain. In a series of studies, Jean Twenge and her collaborators (2001, 2002, 2003) told some people that others whom they had met didn't want them in their group, or that a personality test indicated they "were likely to end up alone later in life." Those led to feel socially excluded were later more likely to disparage or even deliver a blast of noise to someone who insulted them. This rejection-induced aggression brings to mind various North American and European school shootings, committed by youth who had been shunned and mocked by peers. Other studies confirm that rejection often intensifies aggression (Catanese & Tice, 2005; Gaertner & Iuzzini, 2005).

Jeff Kowalsky/EPA/Landov

Recipe for aggression
When Indiana Pacers' Ron Artest attacked Detroit Pistons basketball fans, many influences appeared to create the perfect storm for aggression. The young male Pacer players, who were dominating the Pistons, were likely flush with testosterone. The Pistons' frustration had led one of its players to aggressively shove Artest. The high arousal level of the players and of the frustrated fans (many of whom were disinhibited by alcohol consumption) was easily channeled into aggression when one deindividuated fan threw a cup of beer at Artest.

■ **frustration-aggression principle** the principle that frustration—the blocking of an attempt to achieve some goal—creates anger, which can generate aggression.

FIGURE 18.10

Uncomfortably hot weather and aggressive reactions
Between 1980 and 1982 in Houston, murders and rapes were more common on days over 91 degrees Fahrenheit (33 degrees centigrade), as shown in the graph. This finding is consistent with those from laboratory experiments in which people working in a hot room react to provocations with greater hostility. (From Anderson & Anderson, 1984.)

Learning That Aggression Is Rewarding Aggression may be a natural response to aversive events, but learning can alter natural reactions. Animals naturally eat when they are hungry. But if appropriately rewarded or punished, they can be taught either to overeat or to starve.

Our reactions are more likely to be aggressive in situations where experience has taught us that aggression pays. Children whose aggression successfully intimidates other children may become more aggressive. Animals that have successfully fought to get food or mates become increasingly ferocious.

Different cultures model, reinforce, and evoke different tendencies toward violence. For example, crime rates are higher (and average happiness is lower) in countries marked by a great disparity between rich and poor (Triandis, 1994). Richard Nisbett and Dov Cohen (1996) show how violence can vary by culture within a country. They analyzed violence among white Americans in southern U.S. towns settled by Scots-Irish herders whose tradition emphasized "manly honor," the use of arms to protect one's flock, and a history of coercive slavery. Their cultural descendants have triple the homicide rates and are more supportive of physically punishing children, of warfare initiatives, and of uncontrolled gun ownership than are their white counterparts in New England towns settled by Puritan, Quaker, and Dutch farmer-artisans.

Social influence also appears in high violence rates among cultures and families that experience minimal father care (Triandis, 1994). For example, the U.S. Bureau of Justice Statistics has reported that 70 percent of imprisoned juveniles did not grow up with two parents (Beck & others, 1988). (An absent parent is usually a father.) The correlation between father absence and violence in the United States holds for all races, income levels, and locations (Myers, 2000).

It is important, however, to note how many individuals are leading gentle, even heroic lives amid social stresses, reminding us again that individuals differ. The person matters. That people differ over time and place reminds us that environments differ. Yesterday's plundering Vikings have become today's peace-promoting Scandinavians. Situations matter. Like all behavior, aggression arises from the interaction of persons and situations.

Once established, however, aggressive behavior patterns are difficult to change. To foster a kinder, gentler world we had best model and reward sensitivity and cooperation from an early age, perhaps by training parents to discipline without modeling violence. Modeling violence—screaming and hitting—is precisely what exasperated parents often do. Parents of delinquent youngsters typically discipline with beatings, thus modeling aggression as a method of dealing with problems (Patterson & others, 1982, 1992). They also frequently cave into (reward) their children's tears and temper tantrums.

Parent-training programs advise a more positive approach. They encourage parents to reinforce desirable behaviors and to frame statements positively ("When you finish loading the dishwasher you can go play," rather than "If you don't load the dishwasher, there'll be no playing"). One *aggression-replacement program* that brought down re-arrest rates of juvenile offenders and gang members taught the youths and their parents communication skills, trained them in how to control anger, and encouraged more thoughtful moral reasoning (Goldstein & others, 1998).

Observing Models of Aggression Parents are hardly the only aggression models. As we noted in Chapter 8, observing TV violence tends to desensitize people to cruelty and prime them to respond aggressively when provoked. Does this media effect extend to sexual violence?

A woman's risk of rape has varied across cultures and times and was greater at the last century's end than half a century previous (Koss & others, 1994; Tjaden & Thoennes, 2000). In surveys, about one-fifth of women have reported that a man has forced them to do something sexually, about one-half have reported some form of unwanted sexual coercion, and most have reported experiencing verbal sexual harassment (Craig & others, 1989; Laumann & others, 1994; Sandberg & others, 1985). Similar levels of sexual coercion have been found in Canadian, Australian, and New Zealand surveys (Koss & others, 1994; Patton & Mannison, 1995).

What factors might explain this increased sexual aggression? Alcohol consumption—often linked with aggression—has not increased. We do know that sexually coercive men typically are sexually promiscuous and hostile in their relationships with women (**FIGURE 18.11**). Might changes in the media have contributed to such tendencies?

Coinciding with the increase in sexual aggression was the rise of the home video business, giving easier access to R-rated "slasher films" and X-rated films. Content analyses reveal that most X-rated films depict quick, casual sex between strangers, but that scenes of rape and sexual exploitation of women by men are also common (Cowan & others, 1988; NCTV, 1987; Yang & Linz, 1990). In just the United States, video, pay-per-view, and Internet pornography have combined to create a $10 billion- to $14-billion business—a bigger business than professional football, basketball, and baseball, put together," noted the *New York Times* (Rich, 2001). In one survey of collegians, 10 percent of women and 28.4 percent of men acknowledged accessing sexually explicit material on the Internet more often than "rarely" (Goodson & others, 2001). Although the explosion in Internet pornography has not been accompanied by a further increase in reported rapes, researchers nevertheless wonder whether images of sexual exploitation influence sexual aggression.

Rape scenes often portray the victim at first fleeing and resisting her attacker, but then becoming aroused and finally driven to ecstasy. In less graphic form, the same unrealistic script—she resists, he persists, she melts—is commonplace on TV and in romance novels. In *Gone With the Wind,* Scarlett O'Hara is carried to bed screaming and wakes up singing. Most rapists accept this *rape myth*—the idea that some women invite or enjoy rape and get "swept away" while being "taken" (Brinson, 1992). (In actuality, rape is traumatic, and it frequently harms women's reproductive and sexual health [Golding, 1996].)

When interviewed, Canadian and U.S. sex offenders (rapists, child molesters, and serial killers) do report a greater-than-usual appetite for sexually explicit and sexually violent materials—materials typically labeled as pornography (Marshall, 1989; Ressler & others, 1988; Oddone-Paolucci & others, 2000). For example, the Los Angeles Police Department has reported that pornography was "conspicuously present" in 62 percent of its extrafamilial child sexual abuse cases during the 1980s (Bennett, 1991). But are the sexual offenders merely, as sex researcher John Money (1988) suspected, using pornography "as an alibi to explain to themselves and their captors what otherwise is inexplicable"?

Laboratory experiments reveal that repeatedly watching X-rated films (even if nonviolent) later makes one's own partner seem less attractive (page 484), makes a woman's friendliness seem more sexual, and makes sexual aggression seem less serious (Harris, 1994). In one such experiment, Dolf Zillmann and Jennings Bryant (1984) showed undergraduates six brief, sexually explicit films each week for six weeks. A control group viewed nonerotic films during the same six-week period. Three weeks later, both groups read a newspaper report about a man convicted but not yet sentenced for raping a hitchhiker. When asked to suggest an appropriate prison term, those who had viewed sexually explicit films recommended sentences half as long as those recommended by the control group.

Experiments cannot elicit actual sexual violence, but they can assess a man's willingness to hurt a woman. Often the research gauges the effect of violent versus nonviolent erotic films on men's willingness to deliver supposed electric shocks to women who had earlier provoked the men. These experiments suggest that it's not the eroticism but rather the depictions of sexual *violence* (whether in R-rated slasher films or X-rated films) that most directly affect men's acceptance and performance of

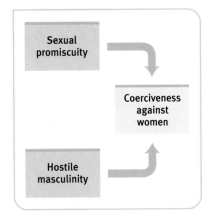

FIGURE 18.11
Men who sexually coerce women
The recipe for coercion against women combines an impersonal approach to sex with a hostile masculinity. (Adapted from Malamuth, 1996.)

Pornography means different things to different people. Following Webster's dictionary, some define pornography as erotic depictions intended to excite sexual arousal. Others define it as sexual materials that exploit, degrade, or subordinate women.

In follow-up studies, Zillmann (1989) found that after massive exposure to X-rated sexual films, men and women became more accepting of extramarital sex, of women's sexual submission to men, and of a man's seducing a 12-year-old girl. As people heavily exposed to televised crime perceive the world as more dangerous, so people heavily exposed to pornography see the world as more sexual.

As U.S. First Lady, Hillary Rodham Clinton voiced concerns shared by many when she worried about media models of an "impulsive sexuality" that encourage uncommitted sex (a predictor of sexual violence) and father-absent families (a predictor of juvenile violence).

" What we're trying to do is raise the level of awareness of violence against women and pornography to at least the level of awareness of racist and Ku Klux Klan literature."

Gloria Steinem (1988)

Densensitizing people to violence

Mark C. Burnett/Stock, Boston

aggression against women. A conference of 21 social scientists, including many of the researchers who conducted these experiments, produced a consensus (Surgeon General, 1986): "Pornography that portrays sexual aggression as pleasurable for the victim increases the acceptance of the use of coercion in sexual relations." Contrary to much popular opinion, viewing such depictions does not provide an outlet for bottled-up impulses. Rather, "in laboratory studies measuring short-term effects, exposure to violent pornography increases punitive behavior toward women."

Acquiring Social Scripts   Significant behaviors, such as violence, usually have many determinants, making any single explanation an oversimplification. Asking what causes violence is therefore like asking what causes cancer. Those who study the effects of asbestos exposure on cancer rates may remind us that asbestos is indeed a cancer cause, albeit only one among many. Likewise, report Neil Malamuth and his colleagues (1991, 1995), several factors can create a predisposition to sexual violence. They include the media but also dominance motives, disinhibition by alcohol, and a history of child abuse. Still, if media depictions of violence can disinhibit and desensitize; if viewing sexual violence fosters hostile, domineering attitudes and behaviors; and if viewing pornography leads viewers to trivialize rape, devalue their partners, and engage in uncommitted sex, then media influence is not a minor issue.

Social psychologists attribute the media's influence partly to the *social scripts* (mental tapes for how to act, provided by our culture) they portray. When we find ourselves in new situations, uncertain how to act, we rely on social scripts. After so many action films, youngsters may acquire a script that gets played when they face real-life conflicts. Challenged, they may "act like a man" by intimidating or eliminating the threat. Likewise, after viewing multiple sexual innuendoes and acts in most prime-time TV hours—often involving impulsive or short-term relationships—youths may acquire sexual scripts they later enact in real-life relationships (Kunkel & others, 2001; Sapolsky & Tabarlet, 1991).

Might public consciousness be raised by making people aware of the information you have just been reading (see Close-Up: Parallels Between Smoking Effects and Media Violence Effects)? In the 1940s, movies often depicted African-Americans as childlike superstitious buffoons. Today, we would not tolerate such images. In the 1960s and 1970s, some rock music and movies glamorized drug use. Responding to a tidal change in cultural attitudes, the entertainment industry now more often portrays the dark side of drug use. In response to growing public concern about violence in the media, television violence levels declined in the early 1990s (Gerbner & others, 1993). The growing sensitivity to violence has raised hopes that entertainers, producers, and audiences might someday look back with embarrassment on the days when movies "entertained" people with scenes of torture, mutilation, and sexual coercion.

Do Video Games Teach or Release Violence?

OBJECTIVE 21 | Discuss the effects of violent video games on social attitudes and behavior.

Violent video games became an issue for public debate after teen assassins in Paducah, Kentucky; Littleton, Colorado; and more than a dozen other places seemed to mimic the carnage in the splatter games they had so often played (Anderson, 2004a). In 2002, two Grand Rapids, Michigan, teens and a man in his early twenties spent part of a night drinking beer and playing Grand Theft Auto III, using cars to run down simulated pedestrians, then beating them with fists, leaving a bloody body behind (Kolker, 2002). Then they went driving on a real drive, spotted a 38-year-old man on a bicycle, ran him down with their car, got out, stomped and punched him, and returned home to play the game some more. (The man, a father of three, died six days later.)

PARALLELS BETWEEN SMOKING EFFECTS AND MEDIA VIOLENCE EFFECTS

Researchers Brad Bushman and Craig Anderson (2001) note that the correlation between viewing violence and behaving aggressively nearly equals the correlation between smoking and lung cancer. They also note other parallels:

1. Not everyone who smokes gets lung cancer.
2. Smoking is only one cause of lung cancer, although an important one.
3. The first cigarette can nauseate, but the sickening effect lessens with repetition.
4. The short-term effect of one cigarette is minor and dissipates within an hour or so.

5. The long-term, cumulative effect of smoking can be severe.

6. Corporate interests have denied the smoking–lung cancer link.

1. Not everyone who watches violence becomes aggressive.
2. Viewing violence is only one cause of aggression, although an important one.
3. The first violence exposure can upset, but the upset lessens with repetition.
4. One violent TV program can prime aggressive thoughts and behaviors, but the effect dissipates within an hour or so.
5. The long-term, cumulative effect of viewing violence is increased likelihood of habitual aggression.
6. Corporate interests have denied the viewing violence–aggression link.

When youths play such games, do they learn social scripts? Interactive games transport the player into their own vivid reality. When youths play Grand Theft Auto: San Andreas, they can carjack vehicles; run down pedestrians; do drive-by shootings; pick up a prostitute, have sex with her, and then kill her. What scripts are being learned?

Most abused children don't become abusive adults. And most youths who spend hundreds of hours in these mass murder simulators won't become teen assassins. Still, we wonder: If passively viewing violence elevates aggressive responses to provocation and lowers sensitivity to cruelty, what will be the effect of actively role-playing aggression? Although very few will commit slaughter, how many will become desensitized to violence and more open to violent acts?

Thirty-eight recent studies of more than 7000 people offer some answers (Anderson & others, 2004). Mary Ballard and Rose Wiest (1998) observed a rising level of arousal and feelings of hostility in college men as they played Mortal Kombat. Other studies have found that video games can prime aggressive thoughts and increase aggression. Consider this report from Craig Anderson and Karen Dill (2000): University men who have spent the most hours playing violent video games tend to be the most physically aggressive (for example, to acknowledge having hit or attacked someone else). In one experiment, people randomly assigned to play a game involving bloody murders with groaning victims (rather than to play nonviolent Myst) became more hostile. On a follow-up task, they also were more likely to blast intense noise at a fellow student.

Studies of young adolescents by Douglas Gentile and his co-researchers (2004) further reveal that kids who play a lot of violent video games see the world as more hostile, get into more arguments and fights, and get worse grades (those hours aren't spent reading or studying). Ah, but is this merely because naturally hostile kids are drawn to such games? No, says Gentile. Even among violent-game players who scored low in hostility, the 38 percent who had been in fights was nearly 10 times the 4 percent involved in fights among their nongaming counterparts. Moreover, over time, the nongamers become more likely to have fights only if they start playing the violent games. Anderson (2004a) believes that, due partly to the more repetitive and active participation of game

> "It'll be like the LA riots, the Oklahoma bombing, WWI, Vietnam, Duke, and Doom all mixed together."
> Journal entry by Columbine killer Eric Harris, 1998

> "We are what we repeatedly do."
> Aristotle

> "Absent the combination of extremely violent video games and these boys' incredibly deep involvement . . . this massacre would not have occurred."
> Lawsuit against video game makers by Columbine victims' families, 2001

Biological influences:	Psychological influences:
• genetic influences	• dominating behavior (which boosts testosterone levels in the blood)
• biochemical influences, such as testosterone and alcohol	• believing you've drunk alcohol (whether you actually have or not)
• neural influences, such as severe head injuries	• frustration
	• aggressive role models
	• rewards for aggressive behavior

Aggressive behavior

Social-cultural influences:
• deindividuation from being in a crowd
• challenging environmental factors, such as crowding, heat, and direct provocations
• parental models of aggression
• minimal father involvement
• being rejected from a group
• exposure to violent media

FIGURE 18.12
Biopsychosocial understanding of aggression
Many factors contribute to aggressive behavior, but there are many ways to combat these influences, including learning anger management and communication skills, and avoiding violent media and video games.

play, violent video games have even greater effects "than the well-documented effects of exposure to violent television and movies."

Although much remains to be learned, these studies again disconfirm the *catharsis hypothesis*—the idea that we feel better if we "blow off steam" by venting our emotions (Chapter 13). Playing violent video games *increases* aggressive thoughts, emotions, and behaviors. One video game company's CEO rationalizes that we are "violent by nature [and] need release valves." "It's a way to process violent feelings and anxieties through a fantasy medium," adds a prominent civil liberties lawyer in explaining her hunch that playing violent games calms violent tendencies (Heins, 2004). Actually, expressing anger breeds more anger, and practicing violence breeds more violence. Tomorrow's games may have even greater effects. Social psychologists Susan Persky and Jim Blascovich (2005) created a violent video game for students to play on either a desktop computer or by putting on a headset and stepping into a virtual reality. As they predicted, the virtual reality more dramatically heightened aggressive feelings and behavior during and after the play.

To sum up, research reveals biological, psychological, and social influences on aggressive behavior. Like so much else, aggression is a biopsychosocial phenomenon (**FIGURE 18.12**).

Conflict

OBJECTIVE **22** | Explain how social traps and mirror-image perceptions fuel social conflict.

We live in surprising times. With astonishing speed, late-twentieth-century democratic movements swept away totalitarian rule in Eastern European countries, and hopes for a new world order displaced the Cold War chill. And yet, the twenty-first century began with terrorist acts and war, and the world continued to spend $2 billion every day for arms and armies—money that could have been used for housing, nutrition, education, and health. Knowing that wars begin in human minds, psychologists have wondered: What in the human mind causes destructive conflict? How might the perceived threats of social diversity be replaced by a spirit of cooperation?

To a social psychologist, a **conflict** is a seeming incompatibility of actions, goals, or ideas. The elements of conflict are much the same at all levels, from nations at war, to cultural disputes within a society, to individuals in a marital dispute. In each situation, people become enmeshed in a potentially destructive social process that can produce results no one wants. Among the destructive processes are social traps and distorted perceptions.

Social Traps

In some situations, we support our collective well-being by pursuing our personal interests. As capitalist Adam Smith wrote in *The Wealth of Nations* (1776), "It is not from the benevolence of the butcher, the brewer, or the baker that we expect our dinner, but from their regard to their own interest." In other situations, we harm our collective well-being by pursuing our personal interests. Such situations are **social traps.**

■ **conflict** a perceived incompatibility of actions, goals, or ideas.

■ **social trap** a situation in which the conflicting parties, by each rationally pursuing their self-interest, become caught in mutually destructive behavior.

Consider the simple game matrix in **FIGURE 18.13**, which is similar to those used in experiments with countless thousands of people. In this game, both sides can win or both can lose, depending on the players' individual choices. Pretend you are Person 1, and that you and Person 2 will each receive the amount shown after you separately choose either *A* or *B*. (You might invite someone to look at the matrix with you and take the role of Person 2.) Which do you choose—*A* or *B*?

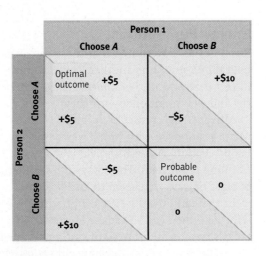

FIGURE 18.13

Social-trap game matrix

By pursuing our self-interest and not trusting others, we can end up losers. To illustrate this, imagine playing the game to the left. The pink triangles show the outcomes for Person 1, which depend on the choices made by both players. If you were Person 1, would you choose *A* or *B*? (This game is called a *non-zero-sum game* because the outcomes need not add up to zero; both sides can win or both can lose.)

As you ponder the game, you will discover that you and Person 2 are caught in a dilemma. If you both choose *A*, you both benefit, making $5 each. Neither of you benefits if you both choose *B*, for neither of you makes anything. Nevertheless, on any single trial you serve your own interests if you choose *B*: You can't lose, and you might make $10. But the same is true for the other person. Hence, the social trap: As long as you both pursue your own immediate best interest and choose *B*, you will both end up with nothing—the typical result—when you could have made $5.

Many real-life situations similarly pit our individual interests against our communal well-being. Individual whalers reasoned that the few whales they took would not threaten the species and that if they didn't take them other whalers would anyway. The result: Some species of whales became endangered. The individual car owner and home owner reasons, "It would cost me comfort or money to buy a more fuel-efficient car and furnace. Besides, the fossil fuels I burn don't noticeably add to the greenhouse gases." When enough others reason similarly, the collective result threatens disaster—global warming and the threat of rising seas and more extreme weather.

Social traps challenge us to find ways of reconciling our right to pursue our personal well-being with our responsibility for the well-being of all. Psychologists are therefore exploring ways to convince people to cooperate for their mutual betterment—through agreed-upon *regulations,* through better *communication,* and through promoting *awareness* of our responsibilities toward community, nation, and the whole of humanity (Dawes, 1980, Linder, 1982, Sato, 1987). Under such conditions, people more often cooperate, whether it be in playing a laboratory game or the real game of life.

Not in my ocean!

Many people support alternative energy sources, including windmills. But proposals to construct windmill farms in real-world neighborhoods elicit less support. One such proposal, for locating windmills off the coast of Massachusetts' Nantucket Island, has produced heated debate over the future benefits of clean energy versus the costs of altering treasured ocean views and, possibly, migratory bird routes.

Enemy Perceptions

Psychologists have noted that those in conflict have a curious tendency to form diabolical images of one another. These distorted images are ironically similar, so similar in fact that we call them *mirror-image perceptions:* As we see "them"—as untrustworthy and evil intentioned—so "they" see us. Each demonizes the other.

Mirror-image perceptions often feed a vicious cycle of hostility. If Juan believes Maria is annoyed with him, he may snub her, causing her to act in ways that justify his perception. As with individuals, so with countries. Perceptions can become self-fulfilling prophecies. They may confirm themselves by influencing the other country to react in ways that seem to justify them.

In the early twenty-first century, many Americans came to loathe Saddam Hussein. Like the "evil" Saddam Hussein, declared George W. Bush (2001), "some of today's tyrants are gripped by an implacable hatred of the United States of America. They hate our friends, they hate our values, they hate democracy and freedom and individual liberty. Many care little for the lives of their own people." Hussein (2002) reciprocated the perception, seeing the United States as "an evil tyrant" that, with Satan as its protector, lusted for oil and aggressively attacked those who "defend what is right."

The point is not that truth must lie midway between two such views (one may be more accurate). The point is that enemy perceptions often form mirror images. Moreover, as enemies change, so do perceptions. In American minds and media, the "bloodthirsty, cruel, treacherous" Japanese of World War II later became our "intelligent, hardworking, self-disciplined, resourceful allies" (Gallup, 1972).

Attraction

Pause a moment and think about your relationships with two people—a close friend, and someone who stirs in you feelings of romantic love. What is the psychological chemistry that binds us together in these special sorts of attachments that help us cope with all other relationships? Social psychology suggests some answers.

The Psychology of Attraction

OBJECTIVE 23 | Describe the influence of proximity, physical attractiveness, and similarity on interpersonal attraction.

We endlessly wonder how we can win others' affection and what makes our own affections flourish or fade. Does familiarity breed contempt, or does it intensify our affection? Do birds of a feather flock together, or do opposites attract? Is beauty only skin deep, or does attractiveness matter greatly? Consider three ingredients of our liking for one another: proximity, physical attractiveness, and similarity.

Proximity   Before friendships become close, they must begin. *Proximity*—geographic nearness—is friendship's most powerful predictor. Proximity provides opportunities for aggression, but much more often it breeds liking. Study after study reveals that people are most likely to like, and even to marry, those who live in the same neighborhood, who sit nearby in class, who work in the same office, who share the same parking lot, who eat in the same dining hall. Look around.

Why is proximity so conducive to liking? Obviously, part of the answer is the greater availability of those we often meet. But there is more to it than that. For one thing, repeated exposure to novel stimuli—be they nonsense syllables, musical selections, geometric figures, Chinese characters, human faces, or the letters of our own name—increases our liking for them (Moreland & Zajonc, 1982; Zajonc, 2001; Nuttin, 1987). People are even somewhat more likely to marry someone whose first or last name resembles their own (Jones & others, 2004).

■ **mere exposure effect** the phenomenon that repeated exposure to novel stimuli increases liking of them.

This phenomenon, exploited by advertisers, we call the **mere exposure effect.** Within certain limits (Bornstein, 1989, 1999), familiarity breeds fondness. Richard Moreland and Scott Beach (1992) demonstrated this by having four equally attractive women silently attend a 200-student class for zero, 5, 10, or 15 class sessions. At the end of the course, students were shown slides of each woman and asked to rate each one's attractiveness. The most attractive? The ones they'd seen most often. The phenomenon will come as no surprise to the young Taiwanese man who wrote more than 700 letters to his girlfriend, urging her to marry him. She did marry—the mail carrier (Steinberg, 1993).

Familiarity breeds acceptance
When this rare white penguin was born in the Sydney, Australia, zoo, his tuxedoed peers ostracized him. Zookeepers thought they would need to dye him black to gain acceptance. But after three weeks of contact, the other penguins came to accept him.

No face is more familiar than one's own. And that explains why, when Lisa DeBruine (2002) had McMaster University students play a social trap–type game with a supposed other player, they were more trusting and cooperative when the other person's image had some features of their own face morphed into it. In me I trust. In a follow-up study, DeBruine (2004) found that men also *liked* other men (and women liked other women) whose faces incorporated some morphed features of their own.

The mere exposure effect
The mere exposure effect applies even to ourselves. Because the human face is not perfectly symmetrical, the face we see in the mirror is not the same as the one our friends see. Most of us prefer the familiar mirror image, while our friends like the reverse (Mita & others, 1977). The Prime Minister Junichiro Koizumi known to the Japanese people is shown at left. The person Koizumi sees in the mirror each morning is shown at right, and that's the photo he would probably prefer.

For our ancestors, the mere exposure phenomenon was adaptive. What was familiar was generally safe and approachable. What was unfamiliar was more often dangerous and threatening. Robert Zajonc (1998) concludes that evolution has hard-wired into us the tendency to bond with those who are familiar and to be wary of those who are unfamiliar. Gut-level prejudice against those culturally different may thus be a primitive, automatic emotional response (Devine, 1995).

Physical Attractiveness Once proximity affords you contact, what most affects your first impressions: The person's sincerity? Intelligence? Personality? Hundreds of experiments reveal that it is something far more superficial: Appearance. For people taught that "beauty is only skin deep" and that "appearances can be deceiving," the power of physical attractiveness is unnerving. In one early study, Elaine Hatfield and her co-workers (Walster & others, 1966) randomly matched new University of Minnesota students for a Welcome Week dance. Before the dance, each student took a battery of personality and aptitude tests. On the night of the blind date, the couples danced and talked for more than two hours and then took a brief intermission to rate their dates. What determined whether they liked each other? As far as the researchers could determine, only one thing mattered: Physical attractiveness (which had been rated by the researchers beforehand). Both the men and the women liked good-looking dates best. Although women are more likely than men to *say* that another's looks don't affect them, a man's looks do affect women's behavior (Feingold, 1990; Sprecher, 1989; Woll, 1986).

"I'm going to have to recuse myself."

"Personal beauty is a greater recommendation than any letter of introduction."
Aristotle, *Apothegems*, 330 B.C.

"Love comes in at the eye."
William Butler Yeats, "A Drinking Song," 1909

Good looks help people get good jobs
In the 2004 presidential election, many Americans found the face on the left more likeable and trustworthy.

Percentage of Men and Women Who "Constantly Think About Their Looks"

	Men	Women
Canada	18%	20%
United States	17	27
Mexico	40	45
Venezuela	47	65

From Roper Starch survey, reported by McCool (1999).

When Neanderthals fall in love.

New York Times columnist Maureen Dowd on liposuction (January 19, 2000): "Women in the 50's vacuumed. Women in the 00's *are* vacuumed. Our Hoovers have turned on us!"

People's physical attractiveness has wide-ranging effects. It predicts their frequency of dating, their feelings of popularity, and others' initial impressions of their personalities. We perceive attractive people to be healthier, happier, more sensitive, more successful, and more socially skilled, though not more honest or compassionate (Eagly & others, 1991; Feingold, 1992; Hatfield & Sprecher, 1986). Attractive, well-dressed people are more likely to make a favorable impression on potential employers and to enjoy occupational success (Cash & Janda, 1984; Langlois & others, 2000; Solomon, 1987). Income analyses show a penalty for plainness or obesity and a premium for beauty (Engemann & Owyang, 2005).

An analysis of 100 top-grossing films since 1940 found that attractive characters were portrayed as morally superior to unattractive characters (Smith & others, 1999). But Hollywood modeling doesn't explain why, to judge from their gazing times, even babies prefer attractive over unattractive faces (Langlois & others, 1987). So do some blind people, discovered University of Birmingham professor John Hull (1990, p. 23) after going blind. A colleague's remarking on a woman's beauty would strangely affect his feelings. He finds this "deplorable . . . but I still feel it. . . . What can it matter to me what sighted men think of women . . . yet I do care what sighted men think, and I do not seem able to throw off this prejudice."

The importance of looks seems unfair and unenlightened. Why should it matter? Two thousand years ago the Roman statesman Cicero felt the same way: "The final good and the supreme duty of the wise person is to resist appearance." Cicero might be reassured by two other findings about attractiveness.

First, people's attractiveness is surprisingly unrelated to their self-esteem and happiness (Diener & others, 1995; Major & others, 1984). One reason may be that, except after comparing themselves with superattractive people, few people (thanks, perhaps, to the mere exposure effect) view themselves as unattractive (Thornton & Moore, 1993). Another reason is that strikingly attractive people are sometimes suspicious that praise for their work may simply be a reaction to their looks. When less attractive people are praised, they are more likely to accept it as sincere (Berscheid, 1981).

Cicero might also find comfort in knowing that attractiveness judgments are relative. The standards by which judges crown Miss Universe hardly apply to the whole planet. Rather, beauty is in the eye of the culture—beauty standards reflect one's place and time. Hoping to look attractive, people in different cultures have pierced their noses, lengthened their necks, bound their feet, and dyed or painted their skin and hair. They have gorged themselves to achieve a full figure or liposuctioned fat to achieve a slim one, applied chemicals hoping to rid themselves of unwanted hair or to regrow wanted hair, strapped on leather garments to make their breasts seem smaller or surgically filled their breasts with silicone and put on Wonder Bras to make them

Extreme makeover
In affluent, beauty-conscious cultures, increasing numbers of people, such as this woman from the American TV show *Extreme Makeover,* have turned to cosmetic surgery to improve their looks. If money were no concern, might you ever do the same?

look bigger. In North America, the ultra-thin ideal of the Roaring Twenties gave way to the soft, voluptuous Marilyn Monroe ideal of the 1950s, only to be replaced by today's lean yet busty ideal. Americans now spend more on beauty supplies than on education and social services combined and, when still not satisfied, undergo millions of cosmetic medical treatments each year, including plastic surgery, Botox skin smoothing, teeth-capping or whitening, and laser hair removal (Wall, 2002). But the beauty race is like the arms race, with the result that since 1970 more and more women have become *un*happy with their appearance (Feingold & Mazella, 1998).

Some aspects of attractiveness, however, do cross place and time (Cunningham & others, 1995; Langlois & others, 2000). As we noted in Chapter 3, men in 37 cultures, from Australia to Zambia, judge women as more attractive if they have a youthful appearance. Women feel attracted to healthy-looking men, but especially to those who seem mature, dominant, and affluent.

People everywhere also seem to prefer physical features—noses, legs, physiques—that are neither unusually large nor small. An averaged face is attractive (**FIGURE 18.14**). In one clever demonstration of this, Judith Langlois and Lori Roggman (1990) digitized the faces of up to 32 college students and used a computer to average them. Students judged the averaged, composite faces as more attractive than 96 percent of the individual faces. One reason is that averaged faces are symmetrical, and people with symmetrical faces and bodies are more sexually attractive (Rhodes & others, 1999; Singh, 1995; Thornhill & Gangestad, 1994). Merge either half of your face with its mirror image and your symmetrical new face would boost your attractiveness a notch.

In the eye of the beholder
Conceptions of attractiveness vary by culture. Moreover, the current concept of attractiveness in Kenya, Morocco, and Scandinavia may well change in the future.

FIGURE 18.14
Average is attractive
Which of these faces offered by University of St. Andrews psychologist David Perrett (2002) is most attractive? Most people say it's the face on the right—of a nonexistent person that is the average composite of these three plus 57 other actual faces.

Beauty grows with mere exposure
Herman Miller, Inc.'s famed Aeron chair initially received high comfort ratings but abysmal beauty ratings. To some it looked like "lawn furniture" or "a giant prehistoric insect" (Gladwell, 2005). But then, with design awards, media visibility, and imitators, the ugly duckling came to be the company's best-selling chair ever and to be seen as beautiful. With people, too, beauty lies partly in the beholder's eye and can grow with exposure.

AP Photo/ Herman Miller Inc.

> "Love has ever in view the absolute loveliness of that which it beholds."
>
> George MacDonald, *Unspoken Sermons*, 1867

Cultural standards aside, attractiveness also depends on our feelings about the person. In a Rodgers and Hammerstein musical, Prince Charming asks Cinderella, "Do I love you because you're beautiful, or are you beautiful because I love you?" Chances are it's both. As we see our loved ones again and again, their physical imperfections grow less noticeable and their attractiveness grows more apparent (Beaman & Klentz, 1983; Gross & Crofton, 1977). Shakespeare said it in *A Midsummer Night's Dream:* "Love looks not with the eyes, but with the mind." Come to love someone and watch beauty grow.

Similarity Let's say that proximity has brought you into contact with someone and that your appearance has made a favorable first impression. What now influences whether acquaintances develop into friends? For example, as you get to know someone better, is the chemistry better if you are opposites or if you are alike?

It makes a good story—extremely different types living in harmonious union: Rat, Mole, and Badger in *The Wind in the Willows,* Frog and Toad in Arnold Lobel's books. The stories delight us by expressing what we seldom experience, for we tend *not* to like dissimilar people (Rosenbaum, 1986). In real life, opposites retract. Birds that flock together usually *are* of a feather. Friends and couples are far more likely to share common attitudes, beliefs, and interests (and, for that matter, age, religion, race, education, intelligence, smoking behavior, and economic status) than are randomly paired people. Much as you and I may dismiss such differences, seeing ourselves as one human family in a global village, we can't hang out with 6 billion people. Moreover, the more alike people are, the more their liking endures (Byrne, 1971). Journalist Walter Lippmann was right to suppose that love is best sustained "when the lovers love many things together, and not merely each other." That is also the assumption of one psychologist-founded Internet dating site, which claims to use the similarities that mark happy couples to match singles, some 10,000 of whom are known to have married (Carter & Snow, 2004; Warren, 2005). Similarity breeds content.

Proximity, attractiveness, and similarity are not the only determinants of attraction. We also like those who like us, especially when our self-image is low. When we believe someone likes us, we respond to them more warmly, which leads them to like us even more (Curtis & Miller, 1986). To be liked is powerfully rewarding.

Indeed, a simple *reward theory of attraction*—that we will like those whose behavior is rewarding to us and that we will continue relationships that offer more rewards than costs—can explain all the findings we have considered so far. When a person lives or works in close proximity with someone else, it costs less time and effort to develop the friendship and enjoy its benefits. Attractive people are aesthetically pleasing, and associating with them can be socially rewarding. Those with similar views reward us by validating our own.

"I can't wait to see what you're like online."

© The New Yorker Collection, 2005, Paul Noth from cartoonbank.com. All Rights Reserved.

Romantic Love

OBJECTIVE **24** | Describe the effect of physical arousal on passionate love, and identify two predictors of enduring companionate love.

Occasionally, people move quickly from initial impressions, to friendship, to the more intense, complex, and mysterious state of romantic love. Elaine Hatfield (1988) distinguishes two types of love: temporary passionate love and a more enduring companionate love.

HI & LOIS

Reprinted with special permission of King Features Syndicate.

Passionate Love Noting that arousal is a key ingredient of **passionate love,** Hatfield suggests that the two-factor theory of emotion (page 513) can help us understand this intense positive absorption in another. The theory assumes that (1) emotions have two ingredients—physical arousal plus cognitive appraisal—and that (2) arousal from any source can enhance one emotion or another, depending on how we interpret and label the arousal.

In tests of this theory, college men have been aroused by fright, by running in place, by viewing erotic materials, or by listening to humorous or repulsive monologues. They were then introduced to an attractive woman and asked to rate her (or their girlfriend). Unlike unaroused men, those who were stirred up attributed some of their arousal to the woman or girlfriend and felt more attracted to her (Carducci & others, 1978; Dermer & Pyszczynski, 1978; White & Kight, 1984).

Outside the laboratory, Donald Dutton and Arthur Aron (1974, 1989) went to two bridges across British Columbia's rocky Capilano River. One, a swaying footbridge, was 230 feet above the rocks; the other was low and solid. An attractive young female accomplice intercepted men coming off each bridge, sought their help in filling out a short questionnaire, and then offered her phone number in case they wanted to hear more about her project. Far more of those who had just crossed the high bridge—which left their hearts pounding—accepted the number and later called the woman. To be revved up and to associate some of that arousal with a desirable person is to feel the pull of passion. Adrenaline makes the heart grow fonder.

Companionate Love Although the spark of romantic love often endures, the intense absorption in the other, the thrill of the romance, the giddy "floating on a cloud" feeling typically fades. Does this mean the French are correct in saying that "love makes the time pass and time makes love pass"? Or can friendship and commitment keep a relationship going after the passion cools? In Leo Tolstoy's *Family Happiness,* a young woman walks with a man she loves and realizes "that from that day he was mine, and I should never lose him now." Later, after their marriage, she reflects while sitting at home that their romantic courtship has been replaced by something quieter and more secure. "That day ended the romance of our marriage," she explains. "The old feeling became a precious irrecoverable remembrance; but a new feeling of love for my children and the father of my children laid the foundation of a new life and a quite different happiness; and that life and happiness have lasted to the present time."

Hatfield agrees, noting that as love matures it becomes a steadier **companionate love**—a deep, affectionate attachment. There may be adaptive wisdom to this change from passion to affection. Passionate love often produces children, whose survival is aided by the parents' waning obsession with one another. Social psychologist Ellen Berscheid and her colleagues (1984) noted that the failure to appreciate passionate love's limited half-life can doom a relationship: "If the inevitable odds against eternal passionate love in a relationship were better understood, more people might choose to be satisfied with the quieter feelings of satisfaction and contentment." Indeed, recognizing the short duration of passionate love, some societies have deemed

❝When two people are under the influence of the most violent, most insane, most delusive, and most transient of passions, they are required to swear that they will remain in that excited, abnormal, and exhausting condition continuously until death do them part.❞

George Bernard Shaw, "Getting Married," 1908

■ **passionate love** an aroused state of intense positive absorption in another, usually present at the beginning of a love relationship.

■ **companionate love** the deep affectionate attachment we feel for those with whom our lives are intertwined.

Sometimes passionate love becomes enduring companionate love, sometimes not (invert the picture)
What, in addition to similar attitudes and interests, predicts long-term loving attachment?

MATRIMONY

COURTSHIP

Courtship and Matrimony (from the collection of Werner Nekes)

"When a match has equal partners then I fear not."

Aeschylus, *Prometheus Bound*, 478 B.C.

such feelings an irrational reason for marrying. Better, such cultures say, to choose (or have someone choose for you) a partner with a compatible background and interests. Non-Western cultures, where people rate love less important for marriage, do have lower divorce rates (Levine & others, 1995).

One key to a gratifying and enduring relationship is **equity:** Both partners receive in proportion to what they give. When equity exists—when both partners freely give and receive, when they share decision making—their chances for sustained and satisfying companionate love are good (Gray-Little & Burks, 1983; Van Yperen & Buunk, 1990). Mutually sharing self and possessions, giving and getting emotional support, promoting and caring about one another's welfare are at the core of every type of loving relationship (Sternberg & Grajek, 1984). It's true for lovers, for parent and child, and for intimate friends.

Another vital ingredient of loving relationships is **self-disclosure,** the revealing of intimate details about ourselves—our likes and dislikes, our dreams and worries, our proud and shameful moments. "When I am with my friend," noted the Roman statesman Seneca, "me thinks I am alone, and as much at liberty to speak anything as to think it." Self-disclosure breeds liking, and liking breeds self-disclosure (Collins & Miller, 1994). As one person reveals a little, the other reciprocates, the first then reveals more, and on and on, as friends or lovers move to deeper intimacy. Each increase in intimacy rekindles passion (Baumeister & Bratslavsky, 1999).

One experiment marched pairs of volunteer students through 45 minutes of increasingly self-disclosing conversation—from "When did you last sing to yourself" to "When did you last cry in front of another person? By yourself?" By the experiment's end, those experiencing the escalating intimacy felt remarkably close to their conversation partner, much closer than others who had spent the time with small-talk questions, such as "What was your high school like?" (Aron & others, 1997). Given self-disclosing intimacy plus mutually supportive equality, the odds favor enduring companionate love.

Altruism

OBJECTIVE 25 | Define *altruism*, and give an example.

Carl Wilkens, a Seventh Day Adventist missionary, was living with his family in Kigali, Rwanda, when Hutu militia began to slaughter the Tutsi in 1994. The U.S. government, church leaders, and friends all implored Wilkens to leave. He refused. After evacuating his family, and even after every other American had left Kigali, he alone stayed and contested the 800,000-person genocide. When the militia came to kill him and his Tutsi servants, his Hutu neighbors deterred them. Despite repeated death threats, he spent his days risking roadblocks to take food and water to orphanages and to negotiate, plead, and bully his way through the bloodshed, saving lives time and again. "It just seemed the right thing to do," he later explained (Kristof, 2004). Elsewhere in Kigali, Paul Rusesabagina, a Hutu married to a Tutsi and the acting manager of a luxury hotel, was sheltering more than 1200 terrified Tutsis and moderate Hutus.

■ **equity** a condition in which people receive from a relationship in proportion to what they give to it.

■ **self-disclosure** revealing intimate aspects of oneself to others.

■ **altruism** unselfish regard for the welfare of others.

When international peacemakers abandoned the city and hostile militia threatened his guests in the "Hotel Rwanda" (as it became called in a 2004 movie), the courageous Rusesabagina began cashing in past favors, bribing the militia, and telephoning influential persons abroad to bring pressure on local authorities, thereby sparing the lives of the hotel's occupants from the surrounding chaos.

Such selfless goodness exemplifies **altruism**—the unselfish regard for the welfare of others. Altruism became a major concern of social psychologists after an especially vile act of sexual violence. On March 13, 1964, a stalker repeatedly stabbed Kitty Genovese, then raped her as she lay dying outside her Queens, New York, apartment at 3:30 A.M. "Oh, my God, he stabbed me!" Genovese screamed into the early morning stillness. "Please help me!" Windows opened and lights went on as 38 of her neighbors heard her screams. Her attacker fled and then returned to stab her eight more times and rape her again. Not until he had fled for good did anyone so much as call the police, at 3:50 A.M.

> "Probably no single incident has caused social psychologists to pay as much attention to an aspect of social behavior as Kitty Genovese's murder."
>
> R. Lance Shotland (1984)

Bystander Intervention

OBJECTIVE 26 | Describe the steps in the decision-making process involved in bystander intervention.

Reflecting on the Genovese murder and other such tragedies, most commentators were outraged by the bystanders' "apathy" and "indifference." Rather than blaming the onlookers, social psychologists John Darley and Bibb Latané (1968b) attributed their inaction to an important situational factor—the presence of others. Given certain circumstances, they suspected, most of us might behave similarly.

After staging emergencies under various conditions, Darley and Latané assembled their findings into a decision scheme: We will help only if the situation enables us first to *notice* the incident, then to *interpret* it as an emergency, and finally to *assume responsibility* for helping (**FIGURE 18.15**). At each step, the presence of other bystanders turns people away from the path that leads to helping. In the laboratory and on the street, people in a group of strangers are more likely than solitary individuals to keep their eyes focused on what they themselves are doing or where they are going. If they notice an unusual situation, they may infer from the blasé reactions of the other passersby that the situation is not an emergency. "The person lying on the sidewalk must be drunk," they think, and move on.

But sometimes, as with the Genovese murder, the emergency is unambiguous and people still fail to help. The witnesses looking out through their windows noticed the incident, correctly interpreted the emergency, and yet failed to assume responsibility. Why? To find out, Darley and Latané (1968a) simulated a physical emergency in their laboratory. University students participated in a discussion over an intercom. Each student was in a separate cubicle, and only the person whose microphone was switched on could be heard. One of the students was an accomplice of the experimenters. When his turn came, he made sounds as though he were having an epileptic seizure and called for help.

FIGURE 18.15
The decision-making process for bystander intervention
Before helping, one must first notice an emergency, then correctly interpret it, and then feel responsible. (From Darley & Latané, 1968b.)

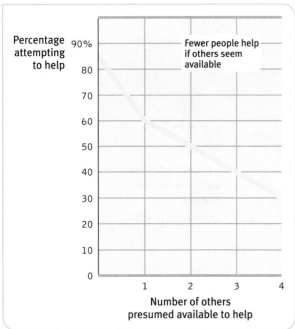

FIGURE 18.16

Responses to a simulated physical emergency

When people thought they alone heard the calls for help from a person they believed to be having an epileptic seizure, they usually helped. But when they thought four others were also hearing the calls, fewer than a third responded. (From Darley & Latané, 1968a.)

❝ Oh, make us happy and you make us good!"

Robert Browning, *The Ring and the Book*, 1868

How did the other students react? As **FIGURE 18.16** shows, those who believed only they could hear the victim—and therefore thought they bore total responsibility for helping him—usually went to his aid. Those who thought others also could hear were more likely to react as did Kitty Genovese's neighbors. When more people shared responsibility for helping—when there was diffusion of responsibility—any single listener was less likely to help.

In hundreds of additional experiments, psychologists have studied the factors that influence bystanders' willingness to relay an emergency phone call, aid a stranded motorist, donate blood, pick up dropped books, contribute money, and give time. For example, Latané, James Dabbs (1975), and 145 collaborators took 1497 elevator rides in three cities and "accidentally" dropped coins or pencils in front of 4813 fellow passengers. The women coin droppers were more likely to receive help than were the men—a gender difference often reported by other researchers (Eagly & Crowley, 1986). But the major finding was the **bystander effect**—any particular bystander was less likely to give aid with other bystanders present. When alone with the person in need, 40 percent helped; in the presence of five other bystanders, only 20 percent helped.

From their observations of behavior in tens of thousands of such "emergencies," altruism researchers have discerned some additional patterns. The *best* odds of our helping someone occur when

- the victim appears to need and deserve help.
- the victim is in some way similar to us.
- we have just observed someone else being helpful.
- we are not in a hurry.
- we are in a small town or rural area.
- we are feeling guilty.
- we are focused on others and not preoccupied.
- we are in a good mood.

This last result, that happy people are helpful people, is one of the most consistent findings in all of psychology. No matter how people are cheered—whether by being made to feel successful and intelligent, by thinking happy thoughts, by finding money, or even by receiving a posthypnotic suggestion—they become more generous and more eager to help (Carlson & others, 1988).

The Norms for Helping

OBJECTIVE *27* | Explain altruistic behavior from the perspective of social exchange theory and social norms.

Why do we help? One widely held view is that self-interest underlies all human interactions, that our constant goal is to maximize rewards and minimize costs. Accountants call it cost-benefit analysis. Philosophers call it utilitarianism. Social psychologists call it **social exchange theory.** If you are pondering whether to donate blood, you may weigh the costs of doing so (time, discomfort, and anxiety) against the benefits (reduced guilt, social approval, good feelings). If you anticipate rewards from helping that exceed the costs, you help.

But why do we leave tips for people we will never see again and give directions to strangers? In part because we have been socialized to do so, through norms that prescribe how we *ought* to behave, often to our mutual benefit. Through socialization, we learn the **reciprocity norm,** the expectation that we should return help, not harm, to those who have helped us. In our relations with others of similar status, the reciprocity norm compels us to give (in favors, gifts, or social invitations) about as much as we receive. We also learn a **social-responsibility norm:** that we should help those who need our help—young children and others who cannot give as much as they receive—even if the costs outweigh the benefits. In repeated Gallup surveys, people who each week attend religious services often exhibit the social responsibility norm: They report volunteering more than twice as many hours in helping the poor and infirm than do those who rarely or never attend religious services (Hodgkinson & Weitzman, 1992; Independent Sector, 2002). They also give away three times as much money.

Peacemaking

OBJECTIVE 28 | Discuss effective ways of encouraging peaceful cooperation and reducing social conflict.

How can we make peace? Can cooperation, communication, and conciliation transform the antagonisms fed by prejudice and conflicts into attitudes that promote peace? Research indicates that in some cases, they can.

Cooperation

Does it help to put two conflicting parties into close contact? It depends. When such contact is noncompetitive and between parties with equal status, such as fellow store clerks, it may help. Initially prejudiced co-workers of different races have, in such circumstances, usually come to accept one another. Among North Americans and Europeans, friendly contact with ethnic minorities has led to less prejudice (Pettigrew, 1969, 2004). However, mere contact is not always enough. In most desegregated schools, ethnic groups resegregate themselves in the lunchrooms and on the school grounds (Clack & others, 2005; Schofield, 1986). People in each group often think that they would welcome more contact with the other group, but they assume the other group does not reciprocate the wish (Shelton & Richeson, 2005). "I don't reach out to them, because I don't want to be rebuffed; they don't reach out to me, because they're just not interested." When such mirror-image misperceptions are corrected, friendships may then form and prejudices melt.

To see if enemies could overcome their differences, researcher Muzafer Sherif (1966) first instigated conflict. He placed 22 Oklahoma City boys in two separate areas of a Boy Scout camp. He then put the two groups through a series of competitive activities, with prizes going to the victors. Before long, each group became intensely proud of itself and hostile to the other group's "sneaky," "smart-alecky stinkers." Food wars broke out during meals. Cabins were ransacked. Fistfights had to be broken up by members of the camp staff. When Sherif brought the two groups together, they avoided one another, except to taunt and threaten.

Nevertheless, within a few days Sherif transformed these young enemies into jovial comrades. He gave them **superordinate goals**—shared goals that overrode their differences and that could be achieved only through cooperation. A planned disruption of the camp water supply necessitated that all 22 boys work together to restore water. Renting a movie in those pre-VCR days required their pooled resources. A stalled truck needed the combined force of all the boys pulling and pushing together to get it moving. Having used isolation and competition to make strangers into enemies, Sherif used shared predicaments and goals to reconcile the enemies and make them friends. What reduced conflict was not mere contact, but *cooperative* contact.

A shared predicament—a fearsome external threat and a superordinate desire to overcome it—likewise had a powerfully unifying effect in the weeks after 9/11. Nothing breeds solidarity quite like a common enemy. As suicide attacks in Israel can unify partisan Jews, and as Israeli military attacks on Palestinians can unify diverse Muslims, so

■ **bystander effect** the tendency for any given bystander to be less likely to give aid if other bystanders are present.

■ **social exchange theory** the theory that our social behavior is an exchange process, the aim of which is to maximize benefits and minimize costs.

■ **reciprocity norm** an expectation that people will help, not hurt, those who have helped them.

■ **social-responsibility norm** an expectation that people will help those dependent upon them.

■ **superordinate goals** shared goals that override differences among people and require their cooperation.

" You cannot shake hands with a clenched fist."

Indira Gandhi, 1971

Americans immediately felt that "we" were under attack. Gallup-surveyed approval of "our President" shot up from 51 percent the week before the attack to a highest-ever level of 90 percent 10 days after, just surpassing the previous approval-rating record of 89 percent enjoyed by his father, George Bush, at the climax of the 1991 Persian Gulf War (Newport, 2002). In chat groups and everyday speech, even the word *we* (relative to *I*) surged in the immediate aftermath (Pennebaker, 2002).

John Dovidio and Samuel Gaertner (1999) report that cooperation has especially positive effects when it leads people to define a new, inclusive group that dissolves their former subgroups. Seat the members of two groups not on opposite sides, but alternately around the table. Give them a new, shared name. Have them work together. Such experiences change "us and them" into "we." Those once perceived as being in another group now are seen as part of one's own group. One 18-year-old New Jersey man would not be surprised. After 9/11, he explained a shift in his social identity: "I just thought of myself as black. But now I feel like I'm an American, more than ever" (Sengupta, 2001). In one experiment by Dovidio and his colleagues (2004), white Americans who read a newspaper article about a terrorist threat against all Americans subsequently expressed reduced prejudice against African-Americans.

During the 1970s, several teams of educational researchers simultaneously wondered: If cooperative contacts between members of rival groups encourage positive attitudes, could we apply this principle in multicultural schools? Could we promote interracial friendships by replacing competitive classroom situations with cooperative ones? And could cooperative learning maintain or even enhance student achievement? Many experiments confirm that in all three cases, the answer is yes (Johnson & Johnson, 1989, 1994; Slavin & others, 2003). Members of interracial groups who work together on projects and play together on athletic teams typically come to feel friendly toward those of the other race. So do those who engage in cooperative classroom learning. So encouraging are these results that thousands of teachers have introduced interracial cooperative learning into their classrooms. Working with fellow students in all their diversity sets the stage, declared the Carnegie Council on Adolescent Development (1989), for "adult work life and for citizenship in a multicultural society."

The power of cooperative activity to make friends of former enemies has led psychologists to urge increased international exchange and cooperation (Klineberg, 1984). As we engage in mutually beneficial trade, as we work to protect our common destiny on this fragile planet, and as we become more aware that our hopes and fears are shared, we can change misperceptions that lead to fragmentation and conflict into a solidarity based on common interests.

Working toward shared goals enables diverse peoples to discover unity in their common values and superordinate identity. "Common values," are what we need, declared the chair of Britain's Commission for Racial Equality as ethnic tensions recently flared (Phillips, 2004). And today's Rwandan government policy proclaims, "There is no ethnicity here. We are all Rwandan," as it seeks to resolve historic animosities between Tutsis and Hutus (Lacey, 2004). Western democracies have largely been spared ethnic tribal warfare because their different racial groups share so many of the very same goals, notes sociologist Amitai Etzioni (1999). In the United States, these shared goals include fair treatment for all, higher moral standards, and a wish that all high school graduates "understand the common history and ideas that tie all Americans together." Although diversity commands attention, we are—as working toward shared goals reminds us—more alike than different.

> "Most of us have overlapping identities which unite us with very different groups. We *can* love what we are, without hating what—and who—we are *not*. We can thrive in our own tradition, even as we learn from others."
>
> U.N. Secretary General Kofi Annan, Nobel Prize Lecture, 2001

> "I am prepared this day to declare myself a citizen of the world, and to invite everyone everywhere to embrace this broader vision of our interdependent world, our common quest for justice, and ultimately for Peace on Earth."
>
> Father Theodore Hesburgh, *The Human Imperative*, 1974

Superordinate goals override differences
Cooperative efforts to achieve shared goals are an effective way to break down social barriers.

Syracuse Newspapers / The Image Works

Communication

In the social-trap game we considered earlier, distrusting people pursue their individual interests as a defense against exploitation. But when they are allowed to discuss the dilemma and negotiate, cooperation increases (Jorgenson & Papciak, 1981).

When real-life conflicts become intense, a third-party mediator—a marriage counselor, labor mediator, diplomat, community volunteer—may likewise facilitate much-needed communication (Rubin & others, 1994). Mediators help each party to voice its viewpoint and to understand the other's. By leading each side to think about the other's underlying needs and goals, the mediator aims to replace a competitive *win-lose* orientation with a cooperative *win-win* orientation that aims at a mutually beneficial resolution. A classic example: Two friends, after quarreling over an orange, agreed to split it. One squeezed his half for juice. The other used the peel from her half to make a cake. If only the two had understood each other's motives, they could have hit on the win-win solution of one having all the juice, the other all the peel.

Such understanding and cooperative resolution is most needed, yet least likely, in times of anger or crisis (Bodenhausen & others, 1994; Tetlock, 1988). When conflicts intensify, images become more stereotyped, communication more difficult, and judgments more rigid.

Conciliation

When tension and suspicion peak, cooperation and communication may become impossible. Each party is likely to threaten, coerce, or retaliate. In the weeks before the Persian Gulf War, President George Bush threatened, in the full glare of publicity, to "kick Saddam's ass." Saddam Hussein communicated in kind, threatening to make Americans "swim in their own blood."

Under such conditions, is there an alternative to war or surrender? Social psychologist Charles Osgood (1962, 1980) has advocated a strategy of "Graduated and Reciprocated Initiatives in Tension-Reduction," nicknamed **GRIT.** In applying GRIT, one side first announces its recognition of mutual interests and its intent to reduce tensions. It then initiates one or more small, conciliatory acts. Without weakening one's retaliatory capability, this modest beginning opens the door for reciprocation by the other party. Should the enemy respond with hostility, one reciprocates in kind. But so, too, with any conciliatory response. Thus, President Kennedy's gesture of stopping atmospheric nuclear tests began a series of reciprocated conciliatory acts that culminated in the 1993 atmospheric test-ban treaty.

In laboratory experiments, GRIT has been the most effective strategy known for increasing trust and cooperation (Lindskold, 1978; Lindskold & Hans, 1988). Even during intense personal conflict, when communication has been nonexistent, a small conciliatory gesture—a smile, a touch, a word of apology—may work wonders. Conciliations allow both parties to begin edging down the tension ladder to a safer rung where communication and mutual understanding can begin.

And how good that such can happen, for civilization advances not by cultural isolation—maintaining walls around ethnic enclaves—but by tapping the knowledge, the skills, and the arts that are each culture's legacy to the whole human race. Thomas Sowell (1991) observed that, thanks to cultural sharing, every modern society is enriched by a cultural mix. We have China to thank for paper and printing, and for the magnetic compass that opened the great explorations. We have Egypt to thank for trigonometry. We have the Islamic world and India's Hindus to thank for our Arabic numerals.

"To begin with, I would like to express my sincere thanks and deep appreciation for the opportunity to meet with you. While there are still profound differences between us, I think the very fact of my presence here today is a major breakthrough."

While celebrating and claiming these diverse cultural legacies, we can also welcome the enrichment of today's social diversity. We can view ourselves as instruments in a human orchestra. And we can therefore affirm our own culture's heritage while building bridges of communication, understanding, and cooperation across cultural traditions as we think about, influence, and relate to one another.

>> LEARNING OUTCOMES

Social Relations

OBJECTIVE 13 | **Identify the three components of prejudice.**

Prejudice is an attitude composed of *beliefs, emotions,* and *predispositions to action.* The beliefs are frequently *stereotypes* (sometimes accurate but often overgeneralized beliefs). The emotions are most often negative, and the action is usually *discrimination* (unjustifiable negative behavior).

OBJECTIVE 14 | **Contrast overt and subtle forms of prejudice, and give examples of each.**

Overt prejudice, such as denying a particular ethnic group the right to vote, is discrimination that *explicitly* (openly and consciously) expresses negative beliefs and emotions. *Subtle prejudice,* such as feeling fearful in the presence of a stranger with a particular ethnic background, is an *implicit* (often unconscious) expression of negative beliefs and emotions.

OBJECTIVE 15 | **Discuss the social factors that contribute to prejudice.**

One social factor contributing to prejudice is *inequality* (unequal distribution of money, power, and prestige) within a group; in such conditions, the "haves" usually develop negative attitudes toward the "have-nots" to justify their more privileged positions. Definitions of *social identity* ("we" the ingroup versus "they" the outgroup) are another source of prejudice because they promote ingroup bias (a tendency to favor one's own group) and discrimination.

OBJECTIVE 16 | **Explain how scapegoating illustrates the emotional component of prejudice.**

Troubled times, especially those that remind us of our own mortality, produce feelings of fear and anger. As in-group loyalty and out-group prejudice intensify, people may search for a *scapegoat*—someone to blame for the troubling event. Such denigrating of despised others can boost in-group members' self-esteem.

OBJECTIVE 17 | **Cite four ways that cognitive processes help create and maintain prejudice.**

We simplify the world around us by *creating categories,* but when we categorize people, we often stereotype them, overgeneralizing their characteristics and underestimating their differences. We also tend to judge the frequency of events by *vivid cases* (violence, for example) that come to mind more readily than the long string of less vivid events involving the same group. We may justify people's less-privileged or punished position by the *just-world phenomenon,* assuming that the world is just and people get what they deserve. *Hindsight bias* (the tendency to believe, after learning an outcome, that we would have predicted it beforehand) may contribute to this tendency to blame the victim.

OBJECTIVE 18 | **Explain how psychology's definition of *aggression* differs from everyday usage.**

Psychology's definition of *aggression* is "any physical or verbal behavior intended to harm or destroy." This is more precise than the everyday definition of aggression and includes behaviors (such as killing in combat) that might not be included in everyday usage.

OBJECTIVE 19 | **Describe three levels of biological influences on aggression.**

Psychologists dismiss the idea that aggression is instinctual and confirm that it results from an interaction between biology and experience. *Genes* influence aggression, for example by influencing our temperament. Experiments stimulating portions of the brain (such as the amygdala and frontal lobes) demonstrate that the brain has *neural systems* that facilitate or inhibit aggression. Studies of the effect of hormones (such as testosterone), alcohol (which releases inhibitions), and other substances show that *biochemical influences* also contribute to aggression.

OBJECTIVE 20 | **Outline four psychological triggers of aggression.**

Biological conditions set the threshold for aggressiveness, but psychological factors trigger aggressive behaviors. *Aversive events* (such as environmental conditions or social rejection) can create frustration, leading to feelings of anger and hostility. *Reinforcement for aggressive behavior* (such as gaining a treat from another student by bullying) can establish learned patterns of aggression that are difficult to change. People can also learn aggression and become desensitized to violence by *observing models act aggressively* in person (watching violence within the family or neighborhood, for example) or in the media (watching violence or sexual aggression on TV or in movies). Media depictions of violence can trigger aggression in another way: by providing *social scripts* (culturally sanctioned ways of acting in a given situation).

OBJECTIVE 21 | **Discuss the effects of violent video games on social attitudes and behavior.**

Violent video games can heighten aggressive behavior by providing social scripts and opportunities to observe modeled aggression and to role-play aggression. Playing these games can increase arousal and feelings of hostility; prime aggressive thoughts and increase aggression; and (in adolescents) lead to increased participation in arguments and fights and falling grades. Virtual reality games may heighten these effects.

OBJECTIVE 22 | **Explain how social traps and mirror-image perceptions fuel social conflict.**

Social conflicts are situations in which people perceive their actions, goals, or ideas to be incompatible. In social traps, two or more individuals engage in mutually destructive behavior by rationally pursuing their own personal interests without regard for the well-being of others. Helping people to agree on regulations, communicate better, and be more aware of responsibilities toward others can foster cooperation and avoid social traps. People in conflict tend to perceive the worst in each other, producing mirror-images of identical demons. The perceptions can become self-fulfilling prophecies, triggering reactions that confirm the images.

OBJECTIVE 23 | **Describe the influence of proximity, physical attractiveness, and similarity on interpersonal attraction.**

Proximity—geographical nearness—promotes attraction, in part because it increases the opportunities for interaction and in part because of the mere exposure effect (repeated exposure to novel stimuli enhances liking). *Physical attractiveness* also increases opportunities for interaction. People prefer being with attractive people and perceive them as healthier, happier, more sensitive, more successful, and more socially skilled. Judgments of attractiveness vary by culture, and as time goes by we find those we care about to be more attractive. *Similarity of attitudes and interests* greatly increases liking after people make it past the first impression. The reward theory of attraction states that we tend to like people whose behavior is rewarding to us, and we will continue relationships that offer more rewards than costs.

OBJECTIVE 24 | **Describe the effect of physical arousal on passionate love, and identify two predictors of enduring companionate love.**

Associating arousal with a desirable person is a key ingredient of *passionate love,* the intense absorption we cognitively label as love. Passionate love often matures into the deep affectionate attachment of *companionate love.* This transition is most likely in relationships characterized by *equality* and *intimate self-disclosure.*

OBJECTIVE 25 | **Define *altruism,* and give an example.**

Altruism is the unselfish regard for the welfare of others. Examples of altruism include helping victims of a natural disaster, giving blood, or donating to local food pantries with no expectation of personal reward.

OBJECTIVE 26 | **Describe the steps in the decision-making process involved in bystander intervention.**

The *bystander effect* is the tendency, identified by John Darley and Bibb Latané, for any given observer to be less likely to help if others are present. To offer help, a person must notice the incident, interpret it as an emergency, and assume responsibility for offering help. Diffusion of responsibility lowers the likelihood of helping. Odds of helping are highest when the victim is similar to us and appears to need and deserve help, and when we observe others helping, are feeling guilty, are not in a hurry or preoccupied, are in a small town or rural area, and are in a good mood.

OBJECTIVE 27 | **Explain altruistic behavior from the perspective of social exchange theory and social norms.**

Social exchange theory proposes that our social behaviors—even altruistic, helpful acts—are based on self-interest: maximizing our benefits (which may include our own good feelings) and minimizing our costs. *Social norms* influence altruistic behaviors by telling us how we *should* behave. The *reciprocity norm* is the expectation that we will help those who help us, and the *social-responsibility norm* is the expectation that we will help those who are dependent on us.

OBJECTIVE 28 | **Discuss effective ways of encouraging peaceful cooperation and reducing social conflict.**

Friendly contact between prejudiced people can change attitudes. But social conflict is most likely to be reduced when the circumstances favor cooperation to achieve superordinate goals (especially if subgroups disappear), understanding through communication (sometimes with the help of a third party), and reciprocated conciliatory gestures (such as the GRIT strategy).

ASK YOURSELF: Do you regret not getting along with some friend or family members? How might you go about reconciling that relationship?

REVIEW CHAPTER 18: **Social Psychology**

Test Yourself

1. Driving to school one wintry day, Marco narrowly misses a car that slides through a red light. "Slow down! What a terrible driver," he thinks to himself. Moments later, Marco himself slips through an intersection and yelps, "Wow! These roads are awful. The city snow plows need to get out here." What social psychology principle has Marco just demonstrated? Explain.

2. You are organizing a Town Hall–style meeting of fiercely competitive political candidates. To add to the fun, friends have suggested handing out masks of the candidates' faces for supporters to wear. What phenomenon might these masks engage?

3. Why didn't anybody help Kitty Genovese? What social relations principle did this incident illustrate?

Answers to the Test Yourself questions can be found in Appendix B at the end of the book.

Terms and Concepts to Remember

social psychology, p. 723

attribution theory, p. 724

fundamental attribution error, p. 724

attitude, p. 726

foot-in-the-door phenomenon, p. 727

cognitive dissonance theory, p. 728

conformity, p. 732

normative social influence, p. 733

informational social influence, p. 733

social facilitation, p. 738

social loafing, p. 739

deindividuation, p. 739

group polarization, p. 740

groupthink, p. 740

prejudice, p. 743

stereotype, p. 743

discrimination, p. 743

ingroup, p. 746

outgroup, p. 746

ingroup bias, p. 746

scapegoat theory, p. 747

just-world phenomenon, p. 748

aggression, p. 749

frustration-aggression principle, p. 751

conflict, p. 756

social trap, p. 756

mere exposure effect, p. 759

passionate love, p. 763

companionate love, p. 763

equity, p. 764

self-disclosure, p. 764

altruism, p. 765

bystander effect, p. 766

social exchange theory, p. 766

reciprocity norm, p. 766

social-responsibility norm, p. 767

superordinate goals, p. 767

GRIT, p. 769

WEB

 To continue your study and review of Social Psychology, visit this book's Web site at www.worthpublishers.com/myers. You will find practice tests, review activities, and many interesting articles and Web links for more information on topics related to Social Psychology.

Careers in Psychology

Jennifer Lento
University of San Diego

What can you do with a degree in psychology? Lots!

As a psychology major, you will graduate with a scientific mindset and an awareness of basic principles of human behavior (biological mechanisms, development, cognition, psychological disorders, social interaction). This background will prepare you for success in many areas, including business, helping professions, health services, marketing, law, sales, and teaching. You may even go on to graduate school for specialized training to become a psychology professional. This appendix describes the various levels of psychology education and some jobs available at those levels; psychology's specialized subfields; and ways you can improve your chances of admission to graduate school.[1]

Preparing for a Career in Psychology

Psychology is the second most popular major in the United States, second only to business (*Princeton Review,* 2005). More than 70,000 psychology majors graduate from U.S. colleges and universities each year. An undergraduate degree in psychology can prepare you for a broad array of jobs after graduation. For other jobs, you will need a graduate degree.

The Bachelor's Degree

Psychology majors graduate with a valuable skill set that increases their marketability in many fields. About 42 percent of U.S. psychology majors go on to graduate school in psychology (Fogg, Harrington, & Harrington, 2004). What happens to the rest? Most work in for-profit organizations after graduation, especially in management, sales, and administration. **TABLE A.1** shows the top 10 occupations that employ people with a bachelor's degree in psychology.

Clearly, psychology majors are marketable beyond the boundaries of psychology. Their sought-after skills and abilities include an ability to work and get along with others, a desire and willingness to learn new skills, adaptability to changing situations, and good critical-thinking and problem-solving skills (Landrum, 2001). There are some things that all psychology majors can do to maximize success in the job market.

---

[1]Although this text covers the world of psychology for students in many countries, this appendix draws primarily from available U.S. data. Its description of psychology's subfields and its suggestions for preparing to enter the profession are, however, also applicable in many other countries.

TABLE A.1

TOP 10 U.S. OCCUPATIONS THAT EMPLOY PEOPLE WITH A BACHELOR'S DEGREE IN PSYCHOLOGY

1. Top- and mid-level managers, executives, administrators
2. Sales occupations, including retail
3. Social workers
4. Other management-related occupations
5. Personnel, training, labor relations specialists
6. Other administrative (record clerks, telephone operators)
7. Insurance, securities, real estate, business services
8. Other marketing and sales occupations
9. Registered nurses, pharmacists, therapists, physician assistants
10. Accountants, auditors, other financial specialists

Source: Fogg, Harrington, & Harrington (2004).

Employers that hire people with only a bachelor's degree tend to favor individuals with positive explanatory styles and practical experience as well as a good education (Cannon, 2005). Betsy Morgan and Ann Korschgen (1998) offer the following helpful tips for increasing your chances of getting a job after graduation:

1. Get to know your instructors.
2. Take courses that support your interests.
3. Familiarize yourself with available resources, such as campus career services and alumni.
4. Participate in at least one internship experience.
5. Volunteer some of your time and talent to campus or community organizations, such as Psi Chi (the national honor society in psychology) or your school's psychology club.

Postgraduate Degrees

A graduate degree in psychology will give you proficiency in an area of psychological specialization. According to the U.S. Bureau of Labor Statistics (2004), psychologists with advanced degrees held approximately 139,000 jobs in 2000. Such jobs are expected to increase 21 to 35 percent (depending on the subfield of psychology) through 2012 because of the need for psychological services in a variety of settings. The work settings for psychologists vary somewhat by type of graduate degree. As shown in **FIGURE A.1,** psychologists with a doctorate work primarily in universities and colleges; most people with a master's degree work in other educational institutions (such as elementary and middle schools) and in for-profit companies. Among those seeking advanced training in psychology in the United States, 29 percent earn a master's degree, 7 percent earn a doctoral degree, and 6 percent earn some other professional degree (e.g., law or health professions) (Fogg, Harrington, & Harrington, 2004).

The Master's Degree

A master's degree in psychology requires at least two years of full-time graduate study in a specific subfield of psychology. In addition to specialized course work in psychology, requirements usually include practical experience in an applied setting and/or a master's thesis reporting on an original research project. You might acquire a master's degree to do specialized work in psychology. As a graduate with a master's degree,

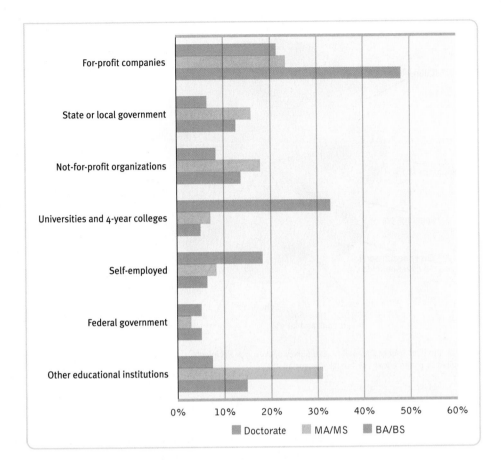

FIGURE A.1
Work settings for psychology-degree recipients
(Fogg, Harrington, & Harrington, 2004)

you might handle research and data collection and analysis in a university, government, or private industry setting. You might work under the supervision of a psychologist with a doctorate, providing some clinical service such as therapy or testing. Or you might find a job in the health, government, industry, or education fields. You might also acquire a master's degree as a stepping stone for more advanced study in a doctoral program in psychology, which will considerably expand the number of employment opportunities available to you (Super & Super, 2001).

Doctoral Degrees

You will probably need five to seven years of graduate study in a specific subfield of psychology to get your doctoral degree. The *doctor of philosophy (Ph.D.)* in psychology culminates in a *dissertation* (an extensive research paper you will be required to defend orally) based on original research. Courses in quantitative research methods, which include the use of computer-based analysis, are an important part of graduate study and are necessary to complete the dissertation. The *doctor of psychology (Psy.D.)* may be based on clinical (therapeutic) work and examinations rather than a dissertation. If you pursue clinical and counseling psychology programs, you should expect at least a one-year internship in addition to the regular course work, clinical practice, and research.

FIGURE A.2 lists by subfield the Ph.D.s earned in the United States in a recent year. Clinical psychology is the most popular specialty area among holders of doctorates in psychology. The largest employment growth areas for doctoral graduates have been in the for-profit and self-employment sectors, including health services providers, industrial/organizational psychology, and educational psychology. About one-third of doctoral-level psychologists are employed in academic settings (Fogg, Harrington, & Harrington, 2004).

FIGURE A.2
U.S. Ph.D.s by subfield, 2001

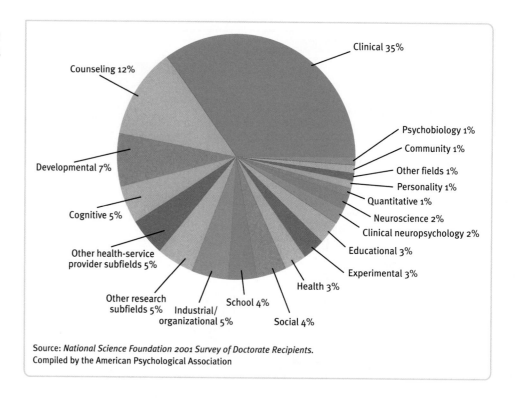

Source: *National Science Foundation 2001 Survey of Doctorate Recipients.*
Compiled by the American Psychological Association

Prescription privileges

Many psychologists would like the opportunity to prescribe psychotropic medicines in order to expand the scope of clinical practice and to meet the need for psychiatric services in many parts of the United States. Psychologists in the U.S. military and in the states of New Mexico and Louisiana currently have prescription privileges.

In 2001, a total of 73 percent of new doctoral respondents and 55 percent of new master's respondents indicated that their primary occupational position was their first choice. Most new graduates with a master's degree or a Ph.D. are fairly satisfied with their current positions overall in terms of salary, benefits, opportunities for personal development, supervisors, colleagues, and working conditions (Kohout & Wicherski, 2004; Singleton, Tate, & Kohout, 2003).

Subfields of Psychology

If you are like most psychology students, you may be unaware of the wide variety of specialties and work settings available in psychology (Terre & Stoddart, 2000). To date, the American Psychological Association (APA) has 53 divisions (**TABLE A.2**). The following paragraphs (arranged alphabetically) describe some careers in the main specialty areas of psychology, most of which require a graduate degree in psychology.

Clinical psychologists promote psychological health in individuals, groups, and organizations. Some clinical psychologists specialize in specific psychological disorders. Others treat a range of disorders, from adjustment difficulties to severe psychopathology. Clinical psychologists might engage in research, teaching, assessment, and consultation. Some hold workshops and lectures on psychological issues for other professionals or for the public. Clinical psychologists work in a variety of settings, including private practice, mental health service organizations, schools, universities, industries, legal systems, medical systems, counseling centers, government agencies, and military services.

To become a clinical psychologist, you will need to earn a doctorate from a clinical psychology program. The APA sets the standards for clinical psychology graduate programs, offering *accreditation* (official recognition) to those who meet their standards. Unlike practitioners in most other subfields of psychology, clinical psychologists must, in all U.S. states, obtain a license to offer services such as therapy and testing.

Tom Stewart/Corbis

TABLE A.2

APA DIVISIONS BY NUMBER AND NAME

1. Society for General Psychology
2. Society for the Teaching of Psychology
3. Experimental Psychology
4. *There is no Division 4.*
5. Evaluation, Measurement, and Statistics
6. Behavioral Neuroscience and Comparative Psychology
7. Developmental Psychology
8. Society for Personality and Social Psychology
9. Society for the Psychological Study of Social Issues (SPSSI)
10. Society for the Psychology of Aesthetics, Creativity, and the Arts
11. *There is no Division 11.*
12. Society of Clinical Psychology
13. Society of Consulting Psychology
14. Society for Industrial and Organizational Psychology
15. Educational Psychology
16. School Psychology
17. Society of Counseling Psychology
18. Psychologists in Public Service
19. Society for Military Psychology
20. Adult Development and Aging
21. Applied Experimental and Engineering Psychology
22. Rehabilitation Psychology
23. Society for Consumer Psychology
24. Society for Theoretical and Philosophical Psychology
25. Behavior Analysis
26. Society for the History of Psychology
27. Society for Community Research and Action: Division of Community Psychology
28. Psychopharmacology and Substance Abuse
29. Psychotherapy
30. Society of Psychological Hypnosis
31. State, Provincial, and Territorial Psychological Association Affairs
32. Humanistic Psychology
33. Mental Retardation and Developmental Disabilities
34. Population and Environmental Psychology
35. Society for the Psychology of Women
36. Psychology of Religion
37. Child, Youth, and Family Services
38. Health Psychology
39. Psychoanalysis
40. Clinical Neuropsychology
41. American Psychology-Law Society
42. Psychologists in Independent Practice
43. Family Psychology
44. Society for the Psychological Study of Lesbian, Gay, and Bisexual Issues
45. Society for the Psychological Study of Ethnic Minority Issues
46. Media Psychology
47. Exercise and Sport Psychology
48. Society for the Study of Peace, Conflict, and Violence: Peace Psychology Division
49. Group Psychology and Group Psychotherapy
50. Addictions
51. Society for the Psychological Study of Men and Masculinity
52. International Psychology
53. Society of Clinical Child and Adolescent Psychology
54. Society of Pediatric Psychology
55. American Society for the Advancement of Pharmacotherapy

Source: American Psychological Association

Karen Moskowitz/Getty Images

Cognitive consulting
Cognitive psychologists may advise businesses on how to operate more effectively by understanding the human factors involved.

Cognitive psychologists primarily do research to add to psychology's store of knowledge. Cognitive psychologists study thought processes and focus on such topics as perception, language, attention, problem solving, memory, judgment and decision making, forgetting, and intelligence. Recent areas of research interest include designing computer-based models of thought processes and identifying biological correlates of cognition. As a cognitive psychologist, you might work as a professor, industrial consultant, or human factors specialist in an educational or business setting.

Community psychologists move beyond focusing on specific individuals or families and deal with broad problems of mental health in community settings. These psychologists believe that human behavior is powerfully influenced by the interaction between people and their physical, social, political, and economic environments. They seek to improve individual functioning by enhancing environmental settings that promote psychological health. Community psychologists focus on prevention, promotion of positive mental health, and crisis intervention, with special attention to the problems of underserved groups and ethnic minorities. As a community psychologist, your work settings could include federal, state, and local departments of mental health, corrections, and welfare. You might conduct research or help evaluate research in health service settings, serve as an independent consultant for a private or government agency, or teach and consult as a college or university faculty member.

Counseling psychologists help people adjust to life transitions or make life-style changes. This field is very similar to clinical psychology, except that counseling psychologists typically help people with adjustment problems rather than severe psychopathology. Like clinical psychologists, counseling psychologists conduct therapy and provide assessments to individuals and groups. As a counseling psychologist, you would emphasize your clients' strengths, helping clients cope during a transitional time using their own skills, interests, and abilities. You might find yourself working in an academic setting as a faculty member or administrator or in a university counseling center, community mental health center, business, or private practice. As with clinical psychology, you will need to obtain a state license to provide counseling services to the public.

Developmental psychologists conduct research in age-related behavioral changes and apply their scientific knowledge to educational, child care, policy, and related settings. As a developmental psychologist, you would investigate change across a broad range of topics, including the biological, social, psychological, and cognitive aspects of development. Developmental psychology informs a number of applied fields, including educational psychology, school psychology, child psychopathology, and gerontology. You will probably specialize in behavior during infancy, childhood, adolescence, or middle or late adulthood. Your work setting could be an educational institution, day-care center, youth group program, or senior center.

Educational psychologists study the relationship between learning and our physical and social environments. They study the psychological processes involved in learning and develop strategies for enhancing the learning process. As an educational psychologist, you might work in a university—in a psychology department or a school of education. You might conduct basic research on topics related to learning or develop innovative methods of teaching to enhance the learning process. You might be employed by a school or government agency or charged with designing and implementing effective employee-training programs in a business setting.

Experimental or *research psychologists* are a diverse group of scientists who investigate a variety of basic behavioral processes in research involving humans and/or other animals. Prominent areas of study in experimental research include motivation, thought, attention, learning, memory, perception, and language. As an experimental psychologist, you would most likely work in an academic setting, teaching courses and supervising students' research in addition to conducting your own research. Or you might be employed by a research institution, business, industry affiliate, or government agency.

Health psychologists are researchers and practitioners concerned with psychology's contribution to promoting health and preventing disease. As applied psychologists or clinicians, they may help individuals lead healthier lives by designing, conducting, and evaluating programs to stop smoking, lose weight, improve sleep, or prevent the spread of sexually transmitted diseases. As researchers and clinicians, they identify conditions and practices associated with health and illness to help create effective interventions. In public service, health psychologists study and work to improve government policies and health-care systems. As a health psychologist, you could be employed in a hospital, medical school, rehabilitation center, public health agency, college or university, or, if you are also a clinical psychologist, in private practice.

Forensic psychologists apply psychological principles to legal issues. They conduct research on the interface of law and psychology, help to create public policies related to mental health, and help law-enforcement agencies in criminal investigations. They also provide therapy and assessment to assist the legal community. Some forensic psychologists hold law degrees and provide clients with legal services as well. Although most forensic psychologists are clinical psychologists, they might have expertise in other areas of psychology, such as social or cognitive psychology. As a forensic psychologist, you might work in a university psychology department, law school, research organization, community mental health agency, law-enforcement agency, court, or correctional setting.

Industrial/organizational (I/O) psychologists study the relationship between people and their working environments. They may develop new ways to increase productivity, improve personnel selection, or promote job satisfaction in a business setting. Their interests include organizational structure and change, consumer behavior, and personnel selection and training. As an I/O psychologist, you might conduct workplace training or provide organizational analysis and development. You may find yourself working in business, industry, the government, or a college or university. Or you may be self-employed as a consultant or work for a management counseling firm.

Neuropsychologists investigate the relationship between neurological processes (structure and function of the brain) and behavior. As a neuropsychologist you might assess, diagnose, or treat disorders related to the central nervous system, such as Alzheimer's disease or stroke. If you are a *clinical neuropsychologist*, you might work in the neurology, neurosurgery, or psychiatric unit of a hospital. Neuropsychologists also work in academic settings, where they conduct research and teach.

Psychometric and *quantitative psychologists* study the methods and techniques used to acquire psychological knowledge. A psychometrician may update existing neurocognitive or personality tests or devise new tests for use in clinical and school settings or in business and industry. These psychologists also administer, score, and interpret such tests. Quantitative psychologists collaborate with researchers to design, analyze, and interpret the results of research programs. As a psychometric or quantitative psychologist, you will need to be well trained in research methods, statistics, and computer technology. You will most likely be employed by a university or college, testing company, private research firm, or government agency.

Rehabilitation psychologists are researchers and practitioners who work with people who have lost optimal functioning after an accident, illness, or other event. As a rehabilitation psychologist, you would probably work in a medical rehabilitation institution or hospital. You might also work in a medical school, university, state or federal vocational rehabilitation agency, or in private practice serving people with physical disabilities.

AP Photo/Jennifer Graylock

Criminal profiling
On the popular TV show *Law and Order, Special Victims Unit*, Dr. George Huang (played by B.D. Wong) is an FBI agent and psychiatrist who uses his background in forensic psychology to conduct criminal investigations.

School psychologists are involved in the assessment of and intervention for children in educational settings. They diagnose and treat cognitive, social, and emotional problems that may negatively influence children's learning or overall functioning at school. As a school psychologist, you would collaborate with teachers, parents, and administrators, making recommendations to improve student learning. You would work in an academic setting, a mental health clinic, a federal or state government agency, a child guidance center, or a behavioral research laboratory.

Social psychologists are interested in our interactions with others. Social psychologists study how our beliefs, feelings, and behaviors are affected by and influence other people. They study topics such as attitudes, aggression, prejudice, interpersonal attraction, group behavior, and leadership. As a social psychologist, you might work in organizational consultation, marketing research, or other applied psychology fields. You would probably also be a college or university faculty member. Some social psychologists work for hospitals, federal agencies, or businesses performing applied research.

Sports psychologists are interested in how participation in sports and other physical activities can enhance personal development and well-being throughout the life span. As a sports psychologist, you would study the psychological factors that influence, and are influenced by, participation in sports and other physical activities, and you would apply this knowledge to everyday settings. You would most likely work as part of a team or organization, but you might also work in a private capacity.

Preparing Early for Graduate Study in Psychology

Competition for the openings for advanced degrees in psychology is keen. If you choose to go to graduate school, there a number of things you can do now to maximize your chances of gaining admission to the school of your choice.

If possible, begin preparing during your first year on campus to maximize opportunities and obtain the experience needed to gain admission to a competitive program. Kristy Arnold and Kelly Horrigan (2002) offer a number of suggestions to facilitate this process:

1. *Network.* Get to know faculty members and the psychology department by attending activities and meetings. Become involved in psychology clubs and in Psi Chi, the national honor society in psychology. These meetings connect students with similar interests and expose them to a broader study of the field.

2. *Become actively involved in research as early as possible.* Start by doing simple tasks such as data entry and data collection, and over time you will be prepared to conduct your own research project under the supervision of a research mentor.

3. *Volunteer or get a job in a psychology-related field.* Getting involved will show your willingness to apply psychological concepts to real-world settings. Further, it will showcase your ability to juggle a number of tasks successfully, such as work and school—an important skill for graduate school success.

4. *Maintain good grades.* Demonstrate the ability to do well in graduate school by demonstrating successful completion of challenging courses, especially those related to your interests in graduate school. (See pages 15–16 and 391–392 for tips on how to do well in this and other courses and how to improve your retention of the information you are learning.)

Membership benefits

Members of the Psi Chi Honor Society, such as those meeting here, enjoy educational and professional benefits. They may attend special Psi Chi sessions at psychological conventions, apply for research grants and awards, and read about research advances in the society's journal *Eye on Psi Chi.*

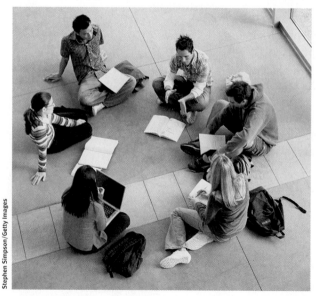

Stephen Simpson/Getty Images

In your junior year, you should begin studying for the Graduate Record Exam (GRE), the standardized test that applicants to graduate school must complete. If you start preparing early, you will be ready for success in your graduate school application and study.

So, the next time someone asks you what you will do with your psychology degree, tell them you have a lot of options. You might use your acquired skills and understanding to get a job and succeed in any number of fields, or you might pursue graduate school and then career opportunities in psychology or other associated professions. In any case, what you have learned about behavior and mental processes will surely enrich your life (Hammer, 2003).

For More Information

American Psychological Association (2003). *Careers for the twenty-first century.* Washington, DC.

American Psychological Association (2005). *Graduate study in psychology.* Washington, DC.

Appleby, D. C. (2002). *The savvy psychology major.* Dubuque, IA: Kendall/Hunt.

Arnold, K., & Horrigan, K. (2002). Gaining admission into the graduate program of your choice. *Eye on Psi Chi,* 30-33.

Actkinson, T. R. (2000). Master's and myths. *Eye on Psi Chi, 4,* 19-25.

Aubrecht, L. (2001). What can you do with a BA in psychology? *Eye on Psi Chi, 5,* 29-31.

Huss, M. (1996). Secrets to standing out from the pile: Getting into graduate school. *Psi Chi Newsletter,* 6-7.

Lammers, B. (2000). Quick tips for applying to graduate school in psychology. *Eye on Psi Chi, 4,* 40-42.

Landrum, E. (2001). I'm getting my bachelor's degree in psychology. What can I do with it? *Eye on Psi Chi, 6,* 22-24.

Morgan, B., & Korschgen, A. (2001). Psychology career exploration made easy. *Eye on Psi Chi,* 35-36.

Sternberg, R. (Ed.) (2002). *Career paths in psychology: Where your degree can take you.* Washington, DC: APA.

Answers to *Test Yourself* Questions

PROLOGUE
The Story of Psychology

1. What events defined the founding of scientific psychology?

ANSWER: The most outstanding event defining the founding of scientific psychology was Wilhelm Wundt's opening of the University of Leipzig psychology laboratory in 1879. The new science of psychology was soon organized into different schools of thought, including structuralism (founded by Edward Bradford Titchener, using introspection to explore the elemental structure of the human mind) and functionalism (founded by William James, focusing on how mental and behavioral processes enable organisms to adapt, survive, and flourish). James also wrote an important psychology textbook, completed in 1890.

2. What are psychology's major levels of analysis?

ANSWER: Psychology's three major levels of analysis are the biological, psychological, and social-cultural. The complementary insights of psychologists studying behavior and mental processes from the neuroscience, evolutionary, behavior genetics, psychodynamic, behavioral, cognitive, and social-cultural perspectives offer a richer understanding than could usually be gained from any one viewpoint alone.

CHAPTER 1
Thinking Critically With Psychological Science

1. What is the scientific attitude, and why is it important for critical thinking?

ANSWER: The scientific attitude combines *skeptical* testing of various claims and ideas with *humility* about ones' own unexamined presumptions. Examining assumptions, searching for hidden values, evaluating evidence, and assessing conclusions are essential parts of critical thinking.

2. What are the strengths and weaknesses of the three different methods psychologists use to describe behavior—case studies, surveys, and naturalistic observation?

ANSWER: *Case studies* offer in-depth insights that may offer clues to what's true of others—or may, if the case is atypical, mislead. *Surveys* can accurately reveal the tendencies of large populations. But if the questions are leading, or if nonrandom samples are queried, the results can again mislead us. *Naturalistic observation* enables study of behavior undisturbed by researchers. But the lack of control may leave cause and effect ambiguous.

3. Here are some recently reported correlations, with interpretations drawn by journalists. Further research, often including experiments, has clarified cause and effect in each case. Knowing just these correlations, can you come up with other possible explanations for each of these?

   a. Alcohol use is associated with violence. (One interpretation: Drinking triggers or unleashes aggressive behavior.)

   b. Educated people live longer, on average, than less-educated people. (One interpretation: Education lengthens life and enhances health.)

   c. Teens engaged in team sports are less likely to use drugs, smoke, have sex, carry weapons, and eat junk food than are teens who do not engage in team sports. (One interpretation: Team sports encourage healthy living.)

   d. Adolescents who frequently see smoking in movies are more likely to smoke. (One interpretation: Movie stars' behavior influences impressionable teens.)

   ANSWER:

   a. Perhaps anger triggers drinking, or perhaps the same genes or rearing predispose both drinking and aggression. (Here researchers have learned that drinking does indeed trigger aggressive behavior.)

   b. Perhaps richer people can afford more education *and* better health care. (Research supports *this* conclusion.)

   c. Perhaps some third factor explains this correlation—teens who use drugs, smoke, have sex, carry weapons, and eat junk food may be "loners" who do not enjoy playing on any team.

   d. Perhaps adolescents who smoke and attend movies frequently have less parental supervision and more access to spending money than other adolescents.

4. Why, when testing a new drug for blood pressure, would we learn more about its effectiveness from giving it to half of the participants in a group of 1000 than to all 1000 participants?

   ANSWER: To determine whether this drug is medically effective, we must compare its effect on those randomly assigned to receive it (the experimental condition) with those who receive a placebo (the control condition). The only difference between the groups is whether they received the actual drug. So, if blood pressure is lower in the experimental group, then we know that the drug itself has produced this effect, not just the participants' knowledge that they are being treated (placebo effect).

5. Consider a question posed by Christopher Jepson, David Krantz, and Richard Nisbett (1983) to University of Michigan introductory psychology students:

   The registrar's office at the University of Michigan has found that usually about 100 students in Arts and Sciences have perfect marks at the end of their first term at the University. However, only about 10 to 15 students graduate with perfect marks. What do you think is the most likely explanation for the fact that there are more perfect marks after one term than at graduation?

   ANSWER: Most students in the study came up with plausible causes for the drop in marks, such as, "Students tend to work harder at the beginning of their college careers than toward the end." Fewer than a third recognized the statistical phenomenon clearly at work: Averages based on fewer courses are more variable, which guarantees a greater number of extremely low and high marks at the end of the first term.

6. How are human and animal research subjects protected?

   ANSWER: Animal protection legislation, laboratory regulation and inspection, and local ethics committees serve to protect human and animal welfare.

CHAPTER 2
Neuroscience and Behavior

1. How do neurons communicate with one another?

   ANSWER: A neuron fires when excitatory inputs exceed inhibitory inputs by a sufficient threshold. When the resulting impulse reaches the axon's end, it triggers the release of chemical neurotransmitters. After crossing a tiny gap, these molecules activate receptor sites on neighboring neurons. So, the brief answer to how neurons communicate with one another is *chemically*.

2. **How does information flow through your nervous system as you pick up a fork? Can you summarize this process?**

   ANSWER: Your central nervous system's hungry brain activates and guides the muscles of your arm and hand via your peripheral nervous system's motor neurons. As you pick up the fork, your brain processes the information from your sensory nervous system, enabling it to continue to guide the fork to your mouth. The functional circle starts with sensory input, continues with interneuron processing by the central nervous system, and finishes with motor output.

3. **Why is the pituitary gland called the "master gland"?**

   ANSWER: The pituitary gland, responding to signals from the hypothalamus, releases hormones that act as triggers. In response, other endocrine glands release their own hormones, which in turn influence brain and behavior.

4. **Within what brain region would damage be most likely to disrupt your ability to skip rope? Your ability to sense tastes or sounds? In what brain region would damage perhaps leave you in a coma? Without the very breath and heartbeat of life?**

   ANSWER: These regions are, respectively, the *cerebellum*, the *thalamus*, the *reticular formation*, and the *medulla*. These questions assess your understanding of the essential functions of the lower-level brain areas.

5. **As you look straight ahead, how is the visual information sent to your two brain hemispheres?**

   ANSWER: Each of your eyes receives sensory information from your left and right visual fields. Each eye sends information (via your optic nerves) from the left half of your field of vision to the visual area of your right hemisphere. Each eye also sends information from the right half of your field of vision to the visual area of your left hemisphere. Assuming your corpus callosum is intact, each hemisphere quickly transmits the data it receives to the opposite hemisphere.

CHAPTER 3
Nature, Nurture, and Human Diversity

1. **What is *heritability*?**

   ANSWER: *Heritability* is the proportion of variation among individuals that we can attribute to genes. Note: Heritability is *not* the extent to which an *individual's* traits are genetically determined. Rather, it is the extent to which variation *among* individuals is due to their differing genes. For any trait, heritability can vary, depending on the population and range of environments studied.

2. **What are the three main criticisms of the evolutionary explanation of human sexuality?**

   ANSWER: Critics of the evolutionary explanation of human sexuality point out that (1) it starts with an effect and works backward to propose an explanation; (2) unethical and immoral men could use such explanations to rationalize their behavior toward women; and (3) this explanation overlooks the effects of cultural expectations and socialization.

3. **To predict whether a teenager smokes, ask how many of the teen's friends smoke. One explanation for this correlation is peer influence. What's another?**

   ANSWER: There may also be a *selection effect*. Adolescents tend to sort themselves into likeminded groups—the jocks, the geeks, the druggies, and so forth. Those who smoke may similarly seek out other teenagers who also smoke.

4. **How do individualist and collectivist cultures differ?**

   ANSWER: A culture that favors individualism gives priority to personal goals over group goals; people in that culture will tend to define their identity in terms of their own personal attributes. A culture that favors collectivism gives priority to group goals over individual goals; people in collectivist cultures tend to define their identity in terms of group identifications. Cultures vary in the extent to which they favor individualism or collectivism.

5. **What are gender roles, and what do their variations tell us about our human capacity for learning and adaptation?**

ANSWER: *Gender roles* are social rules or norms for accepted and expected behavior for females and males. The norms associated with various roles, including gender roles, vary widely in different cultural contexts, which is proof that we are very capable of learning and adapting to the social demands of different environments.

CHAPTER 4
Developing Through the Life Span

1. **Your friend—a heavy smoker—hopes to become pregnant soon and has stopped smoking. Why is this a good idea? What negative effects does smoking during pregnancy have on the fetus?**

ANSWER: If a woman smokes during her pregnancy, the fetus may receive fewer nutrients and be born underweight and at risk for health problems. Your friend is wise to quit smoking before there is a chance that the pregnancy has begun. The most harmful effects of teratogens, such as cigarette smoke, occur during the first trimester of pregnancy—often before a woman even knows she is pregnant.

2. **Use Piaget's first three stages of cognitive development to explain why young children are *not* just miniature adults in the way they think.**

ANSWER: Infants in the *sensorimotor stage* tend to be focused only on their own perceptions of the world and may, for example, be unaware that objects continue to exist when unseen. A *preoperational* child is still egocentric and incapable of appreciating simple logic, such as the reversibility of operations. A preteen in the *concrete operational stage* is beginning to think logically about concrete events but not about abstract concepts.

3. **How has the transition from childhood to adulthood changed in Western cultures in the last 100 years?**

ANSWER: In the last 100 years, the transition to adulthood has started earlier and lasted longer, so that adolescence has lengthened from a period of about 7 years in 1890 to about 12 years in the 1990s.

4. **Research has shown that living together before marriage predicts an increased likelihood of future divorce. Can you imagine two possible explanations for this correlation?**

ANSWER: William Axinn and Arland Thornton (1992) report data that support two explanations. (1) The first explanation is an example of a *selection effect*—our tendency to seek out others who are similar to us. Cohabitation attracts people who are more open to terminating unsatisfying relationships. People who cohabit bring a more individualistic ethic to marriage, are more likely to see close relationships as temporary and fragile, are more accepting of divorce, and are about three times more likely after marriage to have an affair (Forste & Tanfer, 1996). (2) Axinn and Thornton's second explanation illustrates the *causal effect* of the experience of cohabitation. Over time, those who cohabit tend to become more approving of dissolving an unfulfilling union. This divorce-accepting attitude increases the odds of later divorce.

5. **What findings in psychology support the stage theory of development and the idea of stability in personality across the life span? What findings challenge these ideas?**

ANSWER: Stage theory is supported by the work of Piaget (cognitive development), Kohlberg (moral development), and Erikson (psychosocial development), but it is challenged by findings that change is more gradual and less culturally universal than these theorists supposed. Some traits, such as temperament, do exhibit remarkable stability across many years. But we do change in other ways, such as in our social attitudes, especially during life's early years.

CHAPTER 5
Sensation

1. What is the rough distinction between sensation and perception?

ANSWER: *Sensation* is the bottom-up process by which the physical sensory system receives and represents stimuli. *Perception* is the top-down mental process of organizing and interpreting sensory input. But in our everyday experiences, sensation and perception are different aspects of one continuous process.

2. What is the rapid sequence of events that occurs when you see and recognize someone you know?

ANSWER: Light waves reflect off the person and travel into your eye, where the rods and cones convert the light waves' energy into neural impulses sent to your brain. Your brain then processes the subdimensions of this visual input—including color, depth, movement, and form—separately but simultaneously, and integrates this information (along with previously stored information) into a conscious perception of the person you know.

3. In a nutshell, how do we transform sound waves into perceived sound?

ANSWER: A simple figure offers a synopsis:

4. What does the biopsychosocial perspective on pain teach us?

ANSWER: Considering the biological, psychological, and social-cultural influences on the perception of pain teaches us that our experience of pain is much more than neural messages sent to the brain.

5. How does our system for sensing smell differ from our sensory systems for vision, touch, and taste?

ANSWER: We have three types of color receptors, four basic touch senses, and five taste sensations. But we have no basic smell receptors. Instead, 350 receptor proteins, individually and in combination, recognize some 10,000 discernible odors.

CHAPTER 6
Perception

1. Your friend insists that he *did* call you to dinner as you intently watched TV. What principle explains your not perceiving him?

ANSWER: This example illustrates *selective attention*—focusing conscious awareness on a particular stimulus. Your not perceiving the voice probably indicates that you were selectively focusing your attention on the TV.

2. How does the study of illusions inform our understanding of normal perceptions?

ANSWER: Perceptual illusions reveal the ways we organize and interpret sensory information. Our occasional misperceptions demonstrate the workings of our normally

And, as you already know, the Lakers will win tomorrow 98-93. Stay tuned for next week's scores, even though you already know those too, right HERE on ESP-N, the Psychic Sports Channel!

The Quigmans by Buddy Hickerson; © 1990, Los Angeles Times Syndicate. Reprinted with permission.

effective perceptual processes. For example, the perceived relationship between distance and size is generally valid, but under special circumstances it can lead us astray—as when it helps create the Moon illusion.

3. What do we mean when we say that, in perception, the whole is greater than the sum of its parts?

ANSWER: Gestalt psychologists used this saying to describe our perceptual tendency to organize clusters of sensations into meaningful forms or coherent groups.

4. What type of evidence shows that, indeed, "there is more to perception than meets the senses"?

ANSWER: We construct our perceptions based on both sensory input and—experiments show—on our assumptions, expectations, schemas, and perceptual sets, often influenced by the surrounding context.

5. What psychic ability is being claimed by the sports channel in the cartoon at left?

ANSWER: The psychic sports channel claims precognition—the ability to foresee future events.

CHAPTER 7
States of Consciousness

1. During psychology's history, what were the ups and downs of "consciousness"?

ANSWER: Psychology began as the study of consciousness, but during the behaviorist era (for much of the first half of the twentieth century) psychologists focused on observations of behavior. After 1960, driven by discoveries in cognitive psychology and neuroscience, the study of consciousness (our awareness of ourselves and our environment) reemerged as a major topic in psychology.

2. Are you getting enough sleep? What might you ask yourself to answer this question?

ANSWER: You could start with the true/false questions in James Mass' sleep deprivation quiz on page 282. Also, William Dement (1999, p. 73) invites you to consider these questions: "How often do you think about taking a quick snooze? How often do you rub your eyes and yawn during the day? How often do you feel like you really need some coffee?" Dement concludes that "each of these is a warning of a sleep debt that you ignore at your peril."

3. When is the use of hypnosis potentially harmful, and when can hypnosis be used to help?

ANSWER: Hypnosis is potentially harmful when some therapists, seeking to "hypnotically refresh" memories, plant false memories. But posthypnotic suggestions have helped alleviate some ailments, and hypnosis can also help control pain.

4. A U.S. government survey of 27,616 current or former alcohol drinkers found that 40 percent of those who began drinking before age 15 grew dependent on alcohol. The same was true of only 10 percent of those who first imbibed at ages 21 or 22 (Grant & Dawson, 1998). What possible explanations might there be for this correlation between early use and later abuse?

ANSWER: Possible explanations include (1) a biological predisposition to both early use and later abuse, (2) brain changes and taste preferences induced by early use, and (3) enduring habits, attitudes, activities, and/or peer relationships that are conducive to alcohol use.

5. In what ways are near-death experiences similar to drug-induced hallucinations?

ANSWER: Reports of near-death experiences and drug-induced hallucinations feature similar experiences: replay of old memories, out-of-body sensations, and visions of tunnels or funnels of bright light or beings of light.

CHAPTER 8
Learning

1. As we develop we learn cues that lead us to expect and prepare for good and bad events. We learn to repeat behaviors that bring rewards. And we watch others and learn. What do psychologists call these three types of learning?

ANSWER: Through *classical conditioning,* we learn cues that lead us to expect and prepare for good and bad events. Through *operant conditioning,* we learn to repeat behaviors that bring rewards. Through *observational learning,* we watch others and learn.

2. **In slasher movies, sexually arousing images of women are sometimes paired with violence against women. Based on classical conditioning principles, what might be an effect of this pairing?**

ANSWER: If viewing an attractive nude or semi-nude woman (a US) elicits sexual arousal (a UR), then pairing the US with a new stimulus (violence) could turn the violence into a conditioned stimulus (CS) that also becomes sexually arousing, a conditioned response (CR).

3. ***Positive reinforcement, negative reinforcement,*** **and** ***punishment*** **are tricky concepts for many students. Can you fit the right term in the four boxes in this table? (The first one— positive reinforcement—was done for you on page 347).**

Type of Stimulus	Give It	Take It Away
Desired (for example, a compliment):	*Positive reinforcement*	*Punishment (e.g., time-out)*
Undesired/aversive (for example, an insult):	*Punishment*	*Negative reinforcement*

4. **Jason's parents and older friends all smoke, but they advise him not to. Juan's parents and friends don't smoke, but they say nothing to deter him from doing so. Will Jason or Juan be more likely to start smoking?**

ANSWER: Although both saying and doing can influence people, experiments suggest that children more often do as others do and say as they say. Generalizing this finding to smoking, we can expect that Jason will be more likely to start smoking.

CHAPTER 9
Memory

1. **Memory includes (in alphabetical order) long-term memory, sensory memory, and working/short-term memory. What's the correct order of these three memory stores?**

ANSWER: Sensory memory, working/short-term memory, long-term memory.

2. **What would be the most effective strategy to learn and retain a list of names of key historical figures for a week? For a year?**

ANSWER: For a week: Make the names personally meaningful. For a year: Overlearn the list and space out rehearsals over the course of several weeks.

3. **Your friend tells you that her father experienced brain damage in an accident. She wonders if psychology can explain why he can still play checkers very well but has a hard time holding a sensible conversation. What can you tell her?**

ANSWER: Our *explicit* (declarable) memories differ from our *implicit* memories of skills and procedures, such as checkers. Our implicit memories are processed by more ancient brain areas, which apparently escaped damage during the accident.

4. **What is priming?**

ANSWER: *Priming* is the activation (often without our awareness) of associations. Seeing a gun, for example, might temporarily predispose someone to interpret an ambiguous face as threatening or to recall a boss as nasty. Although the person might not consciously remember the gun, it may prime how that individual interprets or recalls events.

5. **Can you offer an example of proactive interference?**

ANSWER: *Proactive* (forward-acting) interference occurs when earlier learning disrupts your recall of a later experience. Proactive interference has occurred if learning the names of new classmates in your first class makes it more difficult to learn the new names in your second class.

6. **What—given the commonality of source amnesia—might life be like if we remembered all our waking experiences and all our dreams?**

ANSWER: Real experiences would be confused with those we dreamed. When meeting someone, we might therefore be unsure whether we were reacting to something they previously did or to something we dreamed they did. William Dement (1999, p. 298) thinks this "would put a great burden on your sanity. . . . I truly believe that the wall of memory is a blessed protection."

7. **What are the recommended memory strategies you just read about? (One advised rehearsing to-be-remembered material. What were the others?)**

ANSWER: Study repeatedly to boost long-term recall. Spend more time rehearsing or actively thinking about the material. Make the material personally meaningful. To remember a list of unfamiliar items, use mnemonic devices. Refresh your memory by activating retrieval cues. Recall events while they are fresh, before you encounter possible misinformation. Minimize interference. Test your own knowledge, both to rehearse it and to help determine what you do not yet know.

CHAPTER 10
Thinking and Language

1. **The availability heuristic is a quick-and-easy but sometimes misleading guide to judging reality. What is the availability heuristic?**

ANSWER: The *availability heuristic* is our tendency to judge the likelihood of an event by how easily we can recall instances of it. Like all heuristics, this guide is efficient. But it can mislead, as it does when we attempt to judge various risks (for example, of plane travel).

2. **If children are not yet speaking, is there any reason to think they would benefit from parents and other caregivers reading to them?**

ANSWER: Indeed there is, because well before age 1 children are learning to detect words among the stream of spoken sounds and to discern grammatical rules. Before age 1, they also are babbling with the phonemes of their own language. More than many parents realize, their infants are soaking up language. As researcher Peter Jusczyk reminds us, "Little ears are listening."

3. **To say that "words are the mother of ideas" assumes the truth of what concept?**

ANSWER: This phrase supports the linguistic determinism hypothesis, which asserts that language determines thought. Research indicates that this position is too extreme, but language does *influence* what we perceive and think.

4. **If your dog barks at a stranger at the front door, does this qualify as *language*? What if the dog yips in a telltale way to let you know she needs to go out?**

ANSWER: These are definitely communications. But if language consists of words and the grammatical rules we use to combine them to communicate meaning, few scientists would label a dog's barking and yipping as language.

CHAPTER 11
Intelligence

1. **Joseph is a student at Harvard Law School. He carries a straight-A average, writes a small column for the *Harvard Law Review*, and will be working for a Supreme Court justice the year after he graduates. Joseph's grandmother, Judith, is very proud of her grandson and says he is way more intelligent than she ever was. But Joseph is also very proud of Judith: As a young woman, Judith was imprisoned by the Nazis. When the war ended, she walked out of Germany, made contact with an agency helping refugees, traveled to the United States, and began a new life here as an assistant chef in her cousin's restaurant. According to the definition of intelligence in this chapter, is Joseph the only intelligent person in this story? Why or why not?**

ANSWER: Joseph is not the only intelligent person in this story. *Intelligence* is the ability to learn from experience, solve problems, and use knowledge to adapt to new situations. Judith certainly fits this description, given all that she accomplished after her release.

2. **What was the purpose of Binet's pioneering intelligence test?**

   ANSWER: Binet's original test was designed to predict school achievement.

3. **The Smiths have enrolled their 2-year-old son in a special program that promises to assess his IQ and, if he places in the top 5 percent of test-takers, to create a plan that will guarantee his admission to a top university at age 18. Why is this endeavor of questionable value?**

   ANSWER: The Smiths would be wasting their time and money. Two years is too young an age for reliably predicting future intelligence.

4. **As society succeeds in creating equality of opportunity, it will also increase the heritability of ability. The heritability of intelligence scores will be greater in a society marked by equal opportunity than in a society of peasants and aristocrats. Why?**

   ANSWER: Perfect environmental equality would create 100 percent heritability—because genes alone would account for any remaining human differences.

CHAPTER 12
Motivation and Work

1. **While on a long road trip, you suddenly feel very lonely and want to pull over and call a loved one. But the dark, deserted stretch of road is intimidating, so you keep on driving. What motivational perspective would most easily explain this behavior and why?**

   ANSWER: *Drive-reduction theory*—the idea that physical needs create an aroused state that drives us to reduce the need—helps explain your behavior.

2. **You are traveling and have not eaten anything in eight hours. As your long-awaited favorite dish is placed in front of you, your mouth waters. Even imagining this may set your mouth to watering. What triggers this anticipatory drooling?**

   ANSWER: You, like Pavlov's dogs, have learned through *classical conditioning* to respond to the cues—the sight and aroma—that signal the food about to enter your mouth. Both *physiological cues* (eight hours of deprivation have left you with low blood sugar) and *psychological cues* (the anticipation of the tasty meal) have heightened your experienced hunger.

3. **How might drive-reduction theory, arousal theory, and the evolutionary perspective explain our sexual motivation?**

   ANSWER: Drive-reduction theory could imply that hormonal influences create a driven (physiologically aroused) state that compels us to reduce the drive. Arousal theory could add that people sometimes *seek* the pleasure and stimulation of arousal. Evolutionary psychologists would remind us that those motivated to have sex were more likely to leave descendants—us—than others who lacked sexual motivation.

4. **How might drive-reduction theory, arousal theory, and the evolutionary perspective explain our affiliation needs?**

   ANSWER: Drive-reduction theory might say that being threatened and afraid drive us to find safety in the company of others (thus reducing our aroused state). Arousal theory reminds us that we welcome optimal levels of arousal, and that the presence of others is arousing. Evolutionary psychologists have noted that our ancestors hunted and survived threats as group-dwelling creatures. In numbers there were food and safety. As their descendants, we therefore are disposed to live in groups, connected to supportive others.

5. **A human resources director explains to you that "I don't bother with tests or references. I can pick employees by my gut." Based on I/O research, what concerns does this raise?**

   ANSWER: Personnel interviewers feel very confident in their ability to predict long-term job performance from informal interviews. Unfortunately, this ability goes astray so often that I/O psychologists have labeled the gap between interviewers' intuition and workplace reality the *interviewer illusion*. Four factors contribute: (1) interviews disclose prospective workers' good intentions, not their habitual behaviors; (2) interviewers tend to track the successful careers of those they hire, not the successful careers of those they reject; (3) interviewers presume people are what they seem to be in interviews; and (4) interviewers' preconceptions and moods color how they perceive interviewees' responses.

CHAPTER 13
Emotion

1. **Christine is holding her 8-month-old baby when a fierce dog appears out of nowhere and, with teeth bared, leaps for the baby's face. Christine immediately ducks for cover to protect the baby, screams at the dog, then notices that her heart is banging in her chest and she's broken out in a cold sweat. How would the James-Lange, Cannon-Bard, and two-factor theories explain Christine's emotional reaction?**

   ANSWER: The James-Lange theory would say that Christine's emotional reaction consists of her awareness of her physiological responses to the dog attack. The Cannon-Bard theory would say that her fear experience happened simultaneously with her physiological arousal. Schacter's two-factor theory would presume that her emotional reaction stemmed from her interpreting and labeling the arousal.

2. **How do the two divisions of the autonomic nervous system help us respond to and recover from a crisis, and why is this relevant to the study of emotions?**

   ANSWER: The sympathetic division of the ANS arouses us in a crisis, and the parasympathetic division of the ANS calms us when the crisis has passed. Researchers study these physiological responses, in combination with brain pattern indicators, to reach a more complete understanding of the feeling component of emotions.

3. **Who tends to express more emotion—men or women? How do we know the answer to that question?**

   ANSWER: Women tend to surpass men not only as emotion detectors but also at expressing certain emotions (though men have slightly surpassed women in conveying anger). Researchers discovered this by showing people brief, silent clips of men's and women's faces expressing various emotions and by observing who is most skilled at reading and sending emotions.

4. **What things do (and do not) predict self-reported happiness?**

   ANSWER: People's age, gender, education level, parenthood, and physical attractiveness are not closely related to their happiness. Predictors of happiness include high self-esteem; optimism and an agreeable, outgoing personality; close friendships or a satisfying marriage; satisfying work and leisure activities; a meaningful religious faith; and adequate sleep and exercise.

CHAPTER 14
Stress and Health

1. **What are the basic links in our stress response system?**

   ANSWER: When alerted to a threat (to negative, uncontrollable events), our sympathetic nervous system arouses us. Heart rate and respiration increase. Blood is diverted from digestion to the skeletal muscles. The body releases sugar and fat to prepare for fight or flight. Simultaneously, the brain (via the hypothalamus and adjacent pituitary gland) orders the adrenal glands to secrete the stress hormone cortisol. The system is wonderfully adaptive. But if stress is continuous, health consequences and exhaustion may result.

2. **Nonsmokers, this chapter reports, are less likely to become depressed and get divorced. What type of research finding is this, and what explanations might it have?**

   ANSWER: This is a correlational finding. Like other correlational findings, it can be interpreted in several ways:

   - Not smoking may be just one part of a generally healthy life-style that includes healthy emotions and relationships.

   - Depressed people and those with troubled relationships may be drawn to smoking.

   - Smoking, depression, and divorce may share common roots. Perhaps certain genes predispose a temperament that is prone to smoking, depression, and divorce. Or perhaps a certain upbringing or peer environment is conducive to smoking, depression, and divorce.

CHAPTER 15
Personality

1. What, according to Freud, were some of the important defense mechanisms, and what do they defend against? How many of these find support in modern research?

ANSWER: Freud believed repression to be the basic defense mechanism. Others include regression, reaction formation, projection, rationalization, and displacement. All supposedly serve to reduce anxiety. Modern research supports the phenomenon Freud called *projection* and current researchers call the *false consensus effect*. Some evidence also supports self-esteem defenses, such as reaction formation. But there is little support for the others.

2. What does it mean to be "empathic"? To be "self-actualized"?

ANSWER: To be *empathic* is to share and mirror another person's feelings. Carl Rogers believed that people nurture growth in others by being empathic. Abraham Maslow viewed *self-actualization* as the ultimate psychological need—the motivation to fulfill one's potential.

3. How many trait dimensions are currently used to describe personality, and what are those dimensions?

ANSWER: "The Big Five" trait dimensions—*emotional stability, extraversion, openness, agreeableness,* and *conscientiousness*—provide a reasonably complete personality description.

4. How do learned helplessness and optimism influence behavior?

ANSWER: Learned helplessness produces passive resignation after organisms find themselves unable to avoid aversive events. Nursing homes, prisons, colleges, and autocratic companies and countries have all been observed to produce symptoms of learned helplessness. Optimism has the opposite effect, leading to better moods, more persistence, and better health. Excessive optimism, however, can expose us to risks.

5. In a 1997 Gallup poll, white Americans estimated 44 percent of their fellow white Americans to be high in prejudice (scoring them 5 or higher on a 10-point scale). How many rated themselves similarly high in prejudice? Just 14 percent. What phenomenon does this illustrate?

ANSWER: This illustrates the general tendency to see oneself as superior to the average other, which is one example of the *self-serving bias*.

CHAPTER 16
Psychological Disorders

1. What is the biopsychosocial approach, and why is it important in our understanding of psychological disorders?

ANSWER: This contemporary approach assumes that biological, psychological, and social-cultural influences combine to produce psychological disorders. Genes matter. The brain matters. Inner thoughts and feelings matter. Social and cultural influences matter. To get the whole integrated picture, a biopsychosocial perspective helps.

2. How do generalized anxiety disorder, phobias, and obsessive-compulsive disorder differ?

ANSWER: *Generalized anxiety disorder* is unfocused tension, apprehension, and arousal. *Phobias* focus anxiety on specific feared objects or situations. *Obsessive-compulsive disorders* express anxiety through unwanted repetitive thoughts (obsessions) or actions (compulsions).

3. What does it mean to say that "depression is the common cold of psychological disorders"?

ANSWER: Saying that "depression is the common cold of psychological disorders" is a quick way to state that this serious disorder is the most common condition in those seeking mental health treatment—with almost 6 percent of men and nearly 10 percent of women reporting a depressive episode each year. Worldwide, depression is the leading cause of disability.

4. **What are the five subtypes of schizophrenia?**

    ANSWER: They are *paranoid* (marked by delusions or hallucinations), *disorganized* (disorganized speech, flat emotion), *catatonic* (immobility or repetitive purposeless movements), *undifferentiated* (varied symptoms), and *residual* (withdrawal, after hallucinations and delusions have disappeared).

5. **Is antisocial personality disorder an inherited condition?**

    ANSWER: *Antisocial personality disorder*—in which a person exhibits a lack of conscience for wrongdoing—seems to have both biological and psychological components. Twin and adoption studies show that biological relatives of people with this disorder are at increased risk for antisocial behavior. But the tendency to be fearless, when combined with a sense of social responsibility, can lead to heroism, adventurism, or athletic success.

6. **Does poverty cause psychological disorder? Explain.**

    ANSWER: Poverty-related stresses can indeed help trigger disorders. But disabling disorders can also contribute to poverty. Thus, poverty and disorder are often a chicken-and-egg situation, and it's hard to know which came first.

CHAPTER 17
Therapy

1. **What is the major distinction between the underlying assumption in psychoanalytic and humanistic therapies and the underlying assumption in behavior therapies?**

    ANSWER: Psychoanalytic and humanistic therapies seek to relieve problems by providing insight into their origins. Behavior therapies assume the problem behavior *is* the problem and treat it directly, paying less attention to its origins.

2. **How does the placebo effect bias clients' appraisals of the effectiveness of psychotherapies?**

    ANSWER: The *placebo effect* is the healing power of *belief* in a treatment. Patients who expect a treatment to be effective, may believe it was.

3. **How do researchers evaluate the effectiveness of particular drug therapies?**

    ANSWER: Ideally, researchers assign people to treatment and no-treatment conditions to see if those who receive therapy improve more than those who don't. In many studies, the no-treatment comparison includes a placebo condition, which allows a double-blind controlled study. If neither the therapist nor the client knows for sure whether the client has received the experimental treatment (for example, a drug), then any difference between the treated and untreated groups will reflect the treatment's actual effect.

4. **What are the influences to keep in mind for successful therapeutic intervention?**

    ANSWER: Successful therapeutic intervention—or prevention—can intervene at many different levels because biological, psychological, and social-cultural influences can combine and interact to produce psychological disorders. Bodily (for example, neurochemical) imbalances can affect mental states, and both biochemical and mental states may be affected by environmental conditions.

CHAPTER 18
Social Psychology

1. **Driving to school one wintry day, Marco narrowly misses a car that slides through a red light. "Slow down! What a terrible driver," he thinks to himself. Moments later, Marco himself slips through an intersection and yelps, "Wow! These roads are awful. The city snow plows need to get out here." What social psychology principle has Marco just demonstrated? Explain.**

    ANSWER: By attributing the other person's behavior to the person ("he's a terrible driver") and his own to the situation ("these roads are awful"), Marco has exhibited the *fundamental attribution error*.

2. **You are organizing a Town Hall–style meeting of fiercely competitive political candidates. To add to the fun, friends have suggested handing out masks of the candidates' faces for supporters to wear. What phenomenon might these masks engage?**

   ANSWER: The anonymity provided by the masks, combined with the arousal of the contentious setting, might create *deindividuation* (lessened self-awareness and self-restraint).

3. **Why didn't anybody help Kitty Genovese? What social relations principle did this incident illustrate?**

   ANSWER: The incident illustrated the *bystander effect.* In the presence of others, an individual is less likely to notice a situation, correctly interpret it as an emergency, and then take responsibility for offering help. Many of Kitty Genovese's neighbors noticed the situation and recognized it as an emergency but they apparently assumed others would help, and they did not feel responsible for offering help.

GLOSSARY

absolute threshold the minimum stimulation needed to detect a particular stimulus 50 percent of the time. (p. 199)

accommodation adapting one's current understandings (schemas) to incorporate new information. (p. 148)

accommodation the process by which the eye's lens changes shape to focus near or far objects on the retina. (p. 205)

acetylcholine [ah-seat-el-KO-leen] **(ACh)** a neurotransmitter that enables learning and memory and also triggers muscle contraction. (p. 58)

achievement motivation a desire for significant accomplishment: for mastery of things, people, or ideas; for attaining a high standard. (p. 504)

achievement test a test designed to assess what a person has learned. (p. 444)

acoustic encoding the encoding of sound, especially the sound of words. (p. 356)

acquisition the initial stage in classical conditioning; the phase associating a neutral stimulus with an unconditioned stimulus so that the neutral stimulus comes to elicit a conditioned response. In operant conditioning, the strengthening of a reinforced response. (p. 318)

action potential a neural impulse; a brief electrical charge that travels down an axon. The action potential is generated by the movement of positively charged atoms in and out of channels in the axon's membrane. (p. 55)

active listening empathic listening in which the listener echoes, restates, and clarifies. A feature of Rogers' client-centered therapy. (p. 689)

acuity the sharpness of vision. (p. 206)

adaptation-level phenomenon our tendency to form judgments (of sounds, of lights, of income) relative to a neutral level defined by our prior experience. (p. 542)

addiction compulsive drug craving and use. (p. 297)

adolescence the transition period from childhood to adulthood, extending from puberty to independence. (p. 164)

adrenal [ah-DREEN-el] **glands** a pair of endocrine glands just above the kidneys. The adrenals secrete the hormones epinephrine (adrenaline) and norepinephrine (noradrenaline), which help to arouse the body in times of stress. (p. 66)

aerobic exercise sustained exercise that increases heart and lung fitness; may also alleviate depression and anxiety. (p. 567)

aggression any physical or verbal behavior intended to hurt or destroy. (pp. 127, 749)

algorithm a methodical, logical rule or procedure that guarantees solving a particular problem. Contrasts with the usually speedier—but also more error-prone—use of *heuristics*. (p. 397)

alpha waves the relatively slow brain waves of a relaxed, awake state. (p. 277)

altruism unselfish regard for the welfare of others. (p. 765)

Alzheimer's disease a progressive and irreversible brain disorder characterized by gradual deterioration of memory, reasoning, language, and, finally, physical functioning. (p. 180)

amnesia the loss of memory. (p. 367)

amphetamines drugs that stimulate neural activity, causing speeded-up body functions and associated energy and mood changes. (p. 300)

amygdala [uh-MIG-duh-la] two lima bean-sized neural clusters that are components of the limbic system and are linked to emotion. (p. 72)

anorexia nervosa an eating disorder in which a normal-weight person (usually an adolescent female) diets and becomes significantly (15 percent or more) underweight, yet, still feeling fat, continues to starve. (p. 478)

antisocial personality disorder a personality disorder in which the person (usually a man) exhibits a lack of conscience for wrong-doing, even toward friends and family members. May be aggressive and ruthless or a clever con artist. (p. 677)

anxiety disorders psychological disorders characterized by distressing, persistent anxiety or maladaptive behaviors that reduce anxiety. (p. 649)

aphasia impairment of language, usually caused by left hemisphere damage either to Broca's area (impairing speaking) or to Wernicke's area (impairing understanding). (p. 80)

applied research scientific study that aims to solve practical problems. (p. 13)

aptitude test a test designed to predict a person's future performance; *aptitude* is the capacity to learn. (p. 444)

assimilation interpreting one's new experience in terms of one's existing schemas. (p. 148)

association areas areas of the cerebral cortex that are not involved in primary motor or sensory functions; rather, they are involved in higher mental functions such as learning, remembering, thinking, and speaking. (p. 79)

associative learning learning that certain events occur together. The events may be two stimuli (as in classical conditioning) or a response and its consequences (as in operant conditioning). (p. 314)

attachment an emotional tie with another person; shown in young children by their seeking closeness to the caregiver and showing distress on separation. (p. 155)

attention-deficit hyperactivity disorder (ADHD) a psychological disorder marked by the appearance by age 7 of one or more of three key symptoms: extreme inattention, hyperactivity, and impulsivity. (p. 641)

attitude feelings, often based on our beliefs, that predispose us to respond in a particular way to objects, people, and events. (p. 726)

attribution theory suggests how we explain someone's behavior—by crediting either the situation or the person's disposition. (p. 724)

audition the sense or act of hearing. (p. 215)

autism a disorder that appears in childhood and is marked by deficient communication, social interaction, and understanding of others' states of mind. (p. 152)

automatic processing unconscious encoding of incidental information, such as space, time, and frequency, and of well-learned information, such as word meanings. (p. 353)

autonomic [aw-tuh-NAHM-ik] **nervous system** the part of the peripheral nervous system that controls the glands and the muscles of the internal organs (such as the heart). Its sympathetic division arouses; its parasympathetic division calms. (p. 62)

availability heuristic estimating the likelihood of events based on their availability in memory; if instances come readily to mind (perhaps because of their vividness), we presume such events are common. (p. 402)

aversive conditioning a type of counterconditioning that associates an unpleasant state (such as nausea) with an unwanted behavior (such as drinking alcohol). (p. 692)

axon the extension of a neuron, ending in branching terminal fibers, through which messages pass to other neurons or to muscles or glands. (p. 55)

babbling stage at about 4 months, the stage of speech development in which the infant spontaneously utters various sounds at first unrelated to the household language. (p. 412)

barbiturates drugs that depress the activity of the central nervous system, reducing anxiety but impairing memory and judgment. (p. 300)

basal metabolic rate the body's resting rate of energy expenditure. (p. 476)

basic research pure science that aims to increase the scientific knowledge base. (p. 12)

basic trust according to Erik Erikson, a sense that the world is predictable and trustworthy; said to be formed during infancy by appropriate experiences with responsive caregivers. (p. 158)

behavior genetics the study of the relative power and limits of genetic and environmental influences on behavior. (p. 96)

behavior therapy therapy that applies learning principles to the elimination of unwanted behaviors. (p. 690)

behavioral medicine an interdisciplinary field that integrates behavioral and medical knowledge and applies that knowledge to health and disease. (p. 549)

behaviorism the view that psychology (1) should be an objective science that (2) studies behavior without reference to mental processes. Most research psychologists today agree with (1) but not with (2). (p. 316)

belief bias the tendency for one's preexisting beliefs to distort logical reasoning, sometimes by making invalid conclusions seem valid, or valid conclusions seem invalid. (p. 407)

belief perseverance clinging to one's initial conceptions after the basis on which they were formed has been discredited. (p. 407)

binocular cues depth cues, such as retinal disparity and convergence, that depend on the use of two eyes. (p. 245)

biofeedback a system for electronically recording, amplifying, and feeding back information regarding a subtle physiological state, such as blood pressure or muscle tension. (p. 569)

biological psychology a branch of psychology concerned with the links between biology and behavior. (Some biological psychologists call themselves *behavioral neuroscientists, neuropsychologists, behavior geneticists, physiological psychologists,* or *biopsychologists.*) (p. 54)

biological rhythms periodic physiological fluctuations. (p. 274)

biomedical therapy prescribed medications or medical procedures that act directly on the patient's nervous system. (p. 686)

biopsychosocial approach an integrated perspective that incorporates biological, psychological, and social-cultural levels of analysis. (p. 10)

bipolar disorder a mood disorder in which the person alternates between the hopelessness and lethargy of depression and the overexcited state of mania. (Formerly called manic-depressive disorder.) (p. 659)

blind spot the point at which the optic nerve leaves the eye, creating a "blind" spot because no receptor cells are located there. (p. 207)

bottom-up processing analysis that begins with the sensory receptors and works up to the brain's integration of sensory information. (p. 197)

brainstem the oldest part and central core of the brain, beginning where the spinal cord swells as it enters the skull; the brainstem is responsible for automatic survival functions. (p. 71)

Broca's area controls language expression—an area of the frontal lobe, usually in the left hemisphere, that directs the muscle movements involved in speech. (p. 81)

bulimia nervosa an eating disorder characterized by episodes of overeating, usually of high-calorie foods, followed by vomiting, laxative use, fasting, or excessive exercise. (p. 478)

bystander effect the tendency for any given bystander to be less likely to give aid if other bystanders are present. (p. 766)

Cannon-Bard theory the theory that an emotion-arousing stimulus simultaneously triggers (1) physiological responses and (2) the subjective experience of emotion. (p. 514)

case study an observation technique in which one person is studied in depth in the hope of revealing universal principles. (p. 26)

catharsis emotional release. In psychology, the catharsis hypothesis maintains that "releasing" aggressive energy (through action or fantasy) relieves aggressive urges. (p. 536)

central nervous system (CNS) the brain and spinal cord. (p. 61)

cerebellum [sehr-uh-BELL-um] the "little brain" attached to the rear of the brainstem; its functions include processing sensory input and coordinating movement output and balance. (p. 72)

cerebral [seh-REE-bruhl] **cortex** the intricate fabric of interconnected neural cells that covers the cerebral hemispheres; the body's ultimate control and information-processing center. (p. 74)

chromosomes threadlike structures made of DNA molecules that contain the genes. (p. 96)

chunking organizing items into familiar, manageable units; often occurs automatically. (p. 359)

circadian [ser-KAY-dee-an] **rhythm** the biological clock; regular bodily rhythms (for example, of temperature and wakefulness) that occur on a 24-hour cycle. (p. 275)

classical conditioning a type of learning in which an organism comes to associate stimuli. A neutral stimulus that signals an unconditioned stimulus (US) begins to produce a response that anticipates and prepares for the unconditioned stimulus. Also called *Pavlovian* or *respondent conditioning.* (p. 315)

client-centered therapy a humanistic therapy, developed by Carl Rogers, in which the therapist uses techniques such as active listening within a genuine, accepting, empathic environment to facilitate clients' growth. (Also called *person-centered therapy*.) (p. 689)

clinical psychology a branch of psychology that studies, assesses, and treats people with psychological disorders. (p. 13)

cochlea [KOHK-lee-uh] a coiled, bony, fluid-filled tube in the inner ear through which sound waves trigger nerve impulses. (p. 217)

cochlear implant a device for converting sounds into electrical signals and stimulating the auditory nerve through electrodes threaded into the cochlea (p. 221)

cognition all the mental activities associated with thinking, knowing, remembering, and communicating. (pp. 148, 395)

cognitive-behavior therapy a popular integrated therapy that combines cognitive therapy (changing self-defeating thinking) with behavior therapy (changing behavior). (p. 697)

cognitive dissonance theory the theory that we act to reduce the discomfort (dissonance) we feel when two of our thoughts (cognitions) are inconsistent. For example, when our awareness of our attitudes and of our actions clash, we can reduce the resulting dissonance by changing our attitudes. (p. 728)

cognitive map a mental representation of the layout of one's environment. For example, after exploring a maze, rats act as if they have learned a cognitive map of it. (p. 334)

cognitive therapy therapy that teaches people new, more adaptive ways of thinking and acting; based on the assumption that thoughts intervene between events and our emotional reactions. (p. 695)

collective unconscious Carl Jung's concept of a shared, inherited reservoir of memory traces from our species' history. (p. 601)

collectivism giving priority to the goals of one's group (often one's extended family or work group) and defining one's identity accordingly. (p. 121)

color constancy perceiving familiar objects as having consistent color, even if changing illumination alters the wavelengths reflected by the object. (p. 214)

companionate love the deep affectionate attachment we feel for those with whom our lives are intertwined. (p. 763)

complementary and alternative medicine Unproven health care treatments not taught widely in medical schools, not used in hospitals, and not usually reimbursed by insurance companies. (p. 570)

concept a mental grouping of similar objects, events, ideas, or people. (p. 396)

concrete operational stage in Piaget's theory, the stage of cognitive development (from about 6 or 7 to 11 years of age) during which children gain the mental operations that enable them to think logically about concrete events. (p. 153)

conditioned reinforcer a stimulus that gains its reinforcing power through its association with a primary reinforcer; also known as *secondary reinforcer*. (p. 330)

conditioned response (CR) in classical conditioning, the learned response to a previously neutral (but now conditioned) stimulus (CS). (p. 317)

conditioned stimulus (CS) in classical conditioning, an originally irrelevant stimulus that, after association with an unconditioned stimulus (US), comes to trigger a conditioned response. (p. 317)

conduction hearing loss hearing loss caused by damage to the mechanical system that conducts sound waves to the cochlea. (p. 220)

cones retinal receptor cells that are concentrated near the center of the retina and that function in daylight or in well-lit conditions. The cones detect fine detail and give rise to color sensations. (p. 206)

confirmation bias a tendency to search for information that confirms one's preconceptions. (p. 399)

conflict a perceived incompatibility of actions, goals, or ideas. (p. 756)

conformity adjusting one's behavior or thinking to coincide with a group standard. (p. 732)

consciousness our awareness of ourselves and our environment. (p. 271)

conservation the principle (which Piaget believed to be a part of concrete operational reasoning) that properties such as mass, volume, and number remain the same despite changes in the forms of objects. (p. 150)

content validity the extent to which a test samples the behavior that is of interest (such as a driving test that samples driving tasks). (p. 448)

continuous reinforcement reinforcing the desired response every time it occurs. (p. 330)

control condition the condition of an experiment that contrasts with the experimental condition and serves as a comparison for evaluating the effect of the treatment. (p. 37)

convergence a binocular cue for perceiving depth; the extent to which the eyes converge inward when looking at an object. The greater the inward strain, the closer the object. (p. 246)

coping alleviating stress using emotional, cognitive, or behavioral methods. (p. 562)

coronary heart disease the clogging of the vessels that nourish the heart muscle; the leading cause of death in many developed countries. (p. 555)

corpus callosum [KOR-pus kah-LOW-sum] the large band of neural fibers connecting the two brain hemispheres and carrying messages between them. (p. 84)

correlation a measure of the extent to which two factors vary together, and thus of how well either factor predicts the other. The *correlation coefficient* is the mathematical expression of the relationship, ranging from −1 to +1. (p. 30)

counseling psychology a branch of psychology that assists people with problems in living (often related to school, work, or marriage) and in achieving greater well-being. (p. 13)

counterconditioning a behavior therapy procedure that conditions new responses to stimuli that trigger unwanted behaviors; based on classical conditioning. Includes *exposure therapies* and *aversive conditioning*. (p. 691)

creativity the ability to produce novel and valuable ideas. (p. 438)

criterion the behavior (such as future college grades) that a test (such as the SAT) is designed to predict; thus, the measure used in defining whether the test has predictive validity. (p. 448)

critical period an optimal period shortly after birth when an organism's exposure to certain stimuli or experiences produces proper development. (p. 156)

critical thinking thinking that does not blindly accept arguments and conclusions. Rather, it examines assumptions, discerns hidden values, evaluates evidence, and assesses conclusions. (p. 24)

cross-sectional study a study in which people of different ages are compared with one another. (p. 183)

crystallized intelligence one's accumulated knowledge and verbal skills; tends to increase with age. (p. 184)

culture the enduring behaviors, ideas, attitudes, and traditions shared by a large group of people and transmitted from one generation to the next. (pp. 45, 119)

defense mechanisms in psychoanalytic theory, the ego's protective methods of reducing anxiety by unconsciously distorting reality. (p. 600)

deindividuation the loss of self-awareness and self-restraint occurring in group situations that foster arousal and anonymity. (p. 739)

déjà vu that eerie sense that "I've experienced this before." Cues from the current situation may subconsciously trigger retrieval of an earlier experience. (p. 373)

delta waves the large, slow brain waves associated with deep sleep. (p. 277)

delusions false beliefs, often of persecution or grandeur, that may accompany psychotic disorders. (p. 669)

dendrite the bushy, branching extensions of a neuron that receive messages and conduct impulses toward the cell body. (p. 55)

dependent variable the outcome factor; the variable that may change in response to manipulations of the independent variable. (p. 38)

depressants drugs (such as alcohol, barbiturates, and opiates) that reduce neural activity and slow body functions. (p. 298)

depth perception the ability to see objects in three dimensions although the images that strike the retina are two-dimensional; allows us to judge distance. (p. 245)

developmental psychology a branch of psychology that studies physical, cognitive, and social change throughout the life span. (p. 139)

difference threshold the minimum difference between two stimuli required for detection 50 percent of the time. We experience the difference threshold as a just noticeable difference. (Also called *just noticeable difference* or *jnd.*) (p. 201)

discrimination in classical conditioning, the learned ability to distinguish between a conditioned stimulus and stimuli that do not signal an unconditioned stimulus. (p. 320)

discrimination unjustifiable negative behavior toward a group or its members. (p. 743)

displacement psychoanalytic defense mechanism that shifts sexual or aggressive impulses toward a more acceptable or less threatening object or person, as when redirecting anger toward a safer outlet. (p. 600)

dissociation a split in consciousness, which allows some thoughts and behaviors to occur simultaneously with others. (p. 293)

dissociative disorders disorders in which conscious awareness becomes separated (dissociated) from previous memories, thoughts, and feelings. (p. 656)

dissociative identity disorder (DID) a rare dissociative disorder in which a person exhibits two or more distinct and alternating personalities. Also called *multiple personality disorder.* (p. 656)

DNA (deoxyribonucleic acid) a complex molecule containing the genetic information that makes up the chromosomes. (p. 96)

double-blind procedure an experimental procedure in which both the research participants and the research staff are ignorant (blind) about whether the research participants have received the treatment or a placebo. Commonly used in drug-evaluation studies. (p. 37)

Down syndrome a condition of retardation and associated physical disorders caused by an extra chromosome in one's genetic makeup. (p. 452)

dream a sequence of images, emotions, and thoughts passing through a sleeping person's mind. Dreams are notable for their hallucinatory imagery, discontinuities, and incongruities, and for the dreamer's delusional acceptance of the content and later difficulties remembering it. (p. 285)

drive-reduction theory the idea that a physiological need creates an aroused tension state (a drive) that motivates an organism to satisfy the need. (p. 471)

DSM-IV the American Psychiatric Association's *Diagnostic and Statistical Manual of Mental Disorders* (Fourth Edition), a widely used system for classifying psychological disorders. Presently distributed in an updated "text revision" (DSM-IV-TR). (p. 644)

dualism the presumption that mind and body are two distinct entities that interact. (p. 310)

echoic memory a momentary sensory memory of auditory stimuli; if attention is elsewhere, sounds and words can still be recalled within 3 or 4 seconds. (p. 362)

eclectic approach an approach to psychotherapy that, depending on the client's problems, uses techniques from various forms of therapy. (p. 686)

Ecstasy (MDMA) a synthetic stimulant and mild hallucinogen. Produces euphoria and social intimacy, but with short-term health risks and longer-term harm to serotonin-producing neurons and to mood and cognition. (p. 302)

effortful processing encoding that requires attention and conscious effort. (p. 354)

ego the largely conscious, "executive" part of personality that, according to Freud, mediates among the demands of the id, superego, and reality. The ego operates on the *reality principle*, satisfying the id's desires in ways that will realistically bring pleasure rather than pain. (p. 598)

egocentrism in Piaget's theory, the preoperational child's difficulty in taking another's point of view. (p. 150)

electroconvulsive therapy (ECT) a biomedical therapy for severely depressed patients in which a brief electric current is sent through the brain of an anesthetized patient. (p. 715)

electroencephalogram (EEG) an amplified recording of the waves of electrical activity that sweep across the brain's surface. These waves are measured by electrodes placed on the scalp. (p. 68)

embryo the developing human organism from about 2 weeks after fertilization through the second month. (p. 141)

emotion a response of the whole organism, involving (1) physiological arousal, (2) expressive behaviors, and (3) conscious experience. (p. 513)

emotion-focused coping attempting to alleviate stress by avoiding or ignoring a stressor and attending to emotional needs related to one's stress reaction. (p. 562)

emotional intelligence the ability to perceive, understand, manage, and use emotions. (p. 436)

empirically derived test a test (such as the MMPI) developed by testing a pool of items and then selecting those that discriminate between groups. (p. 617)

empiricism the view that (a) knowledge comes from experience via the senses, and (b) science flourishes through observation and experiment. (p. 3)

encoding the processing of information into the memory system—for example, by extracting meaning. (p. 351)

endocrine [EN-duh-krin] **system** the body's "slow" chemical communication system; a set of glands that secrete hormones into the bloodstream. (p. 65)

endorphins [en-DOR-fins] "morphine within"—natural, opiatelike neurotransmitters linked to pain control and to pleasure. (p. 59)

environment every nongenetic influence, from prenatal nutrition to the people and things around us. (p. 96)

equity a condition in which people receive from a relationship in proportion to what they give to it. (p. 764)

estrogen a sex hormone, secreted in greater amounts by females than by males. In nonhuman female mammals, estrogen levels peak during ovulation, promoting sexual receptivity. (p. 482)

evolutionary psychology the study of the evolution of behavior and the mind, using principles of natural selection. (p. 107)

experiment a research method in which an investigator manipulates one or more factors (independent variables) to observe the effect on some behavior or mental process (the dependent variable). By random assignment of participants, the experimenter aims to control other relevant factors. (p. 36)

experimental condition the condition of an experiment that exposes participants to the treatment, that is, to one version of the independent variable. (p. 37)

explicit memory memory of facts and experiences that one can consciously know and "declare." (Also called *declarative memory.*) (p. 367)

exposure therapies behavioral techniques, such as systematic desensitization, that treat anxieties by exposing people (in imagination or actuality) to the things they fear and avoid. (p. 691)

external locus of control the perception that chance or outside forces beyond one's personal control determine one's fate. (p. 625)

extinction the diminishing of a conditioned response; occurs in classical conditioning when an unconditioned stimulus (US) does not follow a conditioned stimulus (CS); occurs in operant conditioning when a response is no longer reinforced. (p. 319)

extrasensory perception (ESP) the controversial claim that perception can occur apart from sensory input. Said to include *telepathy, clairvoyance,* and *precognition.* (p. 264)

extrinsic motivation a desire to perform a behavior due to promised rewards or threats of punishment. (p. 335)

factor analysis a statistical procedure that identifies clusters of related items (called *factors*) on a test; used to identify different dimensions of performance that underlie one's total score. (p. 432)

false consensus effect the tendency to overestimate the extent to which others share our beliefs and behaviors. (p. 28)

family therapy therapy that treats the family as a system. Views an individual's unwanted behaviors as influenced by or directed at other family members; attempts to guide family members toward positive relationships and improved communication. (p. 697)

farsightedness a condition in which faraway objects are seen more clearly than near objects because the image of near objects is focused behind the retina. (p. 206)

feature detectors nerve cells in the brain that respond to specific features of the stimulus, such as shape, angle, or movement. (p. 209)

feel-good, do-good phenomenon people's tendency to be helpful when already in a good mood. (p. 537)

fetal alcohol syndrome (FAS) physical and cognitive abnormalities in children caused by a pregnant woman's heavy drinking. In severe cases, symptoms include noticeable facial misproportions. (p. 142)

fetus the developing human organism from 9 weeks after conception to birth. (p. 141)

figure-ground the organization of the visual field into objects (the *figures*) that stand out from their surroundings (the *ground*). (p. 243)

fixation according to Freud, a lingering focus of pleasure-seeking energies at an earlier psychosexual stage in which conflicts were unresolved. (p. 599)

fixation the inability to see a problem from a new perspective; an impediment to problem solving. (p. 400)

fixed-interval schedule in operant conditioning, a reinforcement schedule that reinforces a response only after a specified time has elapsed. (p. 332)

fixed-ratio schedule in operant conditioning, a reinforcement schedule that reinforces a response only after a specified number of responses. (p. 331)

flashbulb memory a clear memory of an emotionally significant moment or event. (p. 351)

flow a completely involved, focused state of consciousness, with diminished awareness of self and time, resulting from optimal engagement of one's skills. (p. 498)

fluid intelligence one's ability to reason speedily and abstractly; tends to decrease during late adulthood. (p. 184)

fMRI (functional magnetic resonance imaging) a technique for revealing blood flow and, therefore, brain activity by comparing successive MRI scans. MRI scans show brain anatomy; fMRI scans show brain function. (p. 69)

foot-in-the-door phenomenon the tendency for people who have first agreed to a small request to comply later with a larger request. (p. 727)

formal operational stage in Piaget's theory, the stage of cognitive development (normally beginning about age 12) during which people begin to think logically about abstract concepts. (p. 154)

fovea the central focal point in the retina, around which the eye's cones cluster. (p. 207)

framing the way an issue is posed; how an issue is framed can significantly affect decisions and judgments. (p. 406)

fraternal twins twins who develop from separate fertilized eggs. They are genetically no closer than brothers and sisters, but they share a fetal environment. (p. 78)

free association in psychoanalysis, a method of exploring the unconscious in which the person relaxes and says whatever comes to mind, no matter how trivial or embarrassing. (p. 597)

frequency the number of complete wavelengths that pass a point in a given time (for example, per second). (p. 216)

frequency theory in hearing, the theory that the rate of nerve impulses traveling up the auditory nerve matches the frequency of a tone, thus enabling us to sense its pitch. (p. 219)

frontal lobes the portion of the cerebral cortex lying just behind the forehead; involved in speaking and muscle movements and in making plans and judgments. (p. 76)

frustration-aggression principle the principle that frustration—the blocking of an attempt to achieve some goal—creates anger, which can generate aggression. (p. 751)

functional fixedness the tendency to think of things only in terms of their usual functions; an impediment to problem solving. (p. 400)

functionalism a school of psychology that focused on how mental and behavioral processes function—how they enable the organism to adapt, survive, and flourish. (p. 5)

fundamental attribution error the tendency for observers, when analyzing another's behavior, to underestimate the impact of the situation and to overestimate the impact of personal disposition. (p. 724)

gate-control theory the theory that the spinal cord contains a neurological "gate" that blocks pain signals or allows them to pass on to the brain. The "gate" is opened by the activity of pain signals traveling up small nerve fibers and is closed by activity in larger fibers or by information coming from the brain. (p. 227)

gender in psychology, the biologically and socially influenced characteristics by which people define *male* and *female*. (p. 110)

gender-typing the acquisition of a traditional masculine or feminine role. (p. 132)

gender identity one's sense of being male or female. (p. 132)

gender role a set of expected behaviors for males and for females. (p. 131)

gender schema theory the theory that children learn from their cultures a concept of what it means to be male and female and that they adjust their behavior accordingly. (p. 132)

general adaptation syndrome (GAS) Selye's concept of the body's adaptive response to stress in three stages—alarm, resistance, exhaustion. (p. 552)

general intelligence (g) a general intelligence factor that according to Spearman and others underlies specific mental abilities and is therefore measured by every task on an intelligence test. (p. 432)

generalization the tendency, once a response has been conditioned, for stimuli similar to the conditioned stimulus to elicit similar responses. (p. 320)

generalized anxiety disorder an anxiety disorder in which a person is continually tense, apprehensive, and in a state of autonomic nervous system arousal. (p. 649)

genes the biochemical units of heredity that make up the chromosomes; a segment of DNA capable of synthesizing a protein. (p. 96)

genome the complete instructions for making an organism, consisting of all the genetic material in that organism's chromosomes. (p. 96)

gestalt an organized whole. Gestalt psychologists emphasized our tendency to integrate pieces of information into meaningful wholes. (p. 242)

glial cells (glia) cells in the nervous system that support, nourish, and protect neurons. (p. 75)

glucose the form of sugar that circulates in the blood and provides the major source of energy for body tissues. When its level is low, we feel hunger. (p. 475)

grammar in a language, a system of rules that enables us to communicate with and understand others. (p. 411)

GRIT Graduated and Reciprocated Initiatives in Tension-Reduction—strategy designed to decrease international tensions. (p. 769)

group polarization the enhancement of a group's prevailing inclinations through discussion within the group. (p. 740)

grouping the perceptual tendency to organize stimuli into coherent groups. (p. 243)

groupthink the mode of thinking that occurs when the desire for harmony in a decision-making group overrides a realistic appraisal of alternatives. (p. 740)

habituation decreasing responsiveness with repeated stimulation. As infants gain familiarity with repeated exposure to a visual stimulus, their interest wanes and they look away sooner. (p. 143)

hallucinations false sensory experiences, such as seeing something in the absence of an external visual stimulus. (p. 277)

hallucinogens psychedelic ("mind-manifesting") drugs, such as LSD, that distort perceptions and evoke sensory images in the absence of sensory input. (p. 302)

health psychology a subfield of psychology that provides psychology's contribution to behavioral medicine. (p. 549)

heritability the proportion of variation among individuals that we can attribute to genes. The heritability of a trait may vary, depending on the range of populations and environments studied. (p. 102)

heuristic a simple thinking strategy that often allows us to make judgments and solve problems efficiently; usually speedier but also more error-prone than *algorithms*. (p. 398)

hierarchy of needs Maslow's pyramid of human needs, beginning at the base with physiological needs that must first be satisfied before higher-level safety needs and then psychological needs become active. (p. 472)

hindsight bias the tendency to believe, after learning an outcome, that one would have foreseen it. (Also known as the I-knew-it-all-along phenomenon.) (p. 20)

hippocampus a neural center located in the limbic system that helps process explicit memories for storage. (p. 368)

homeostasis a tendency to maintain a balanced or constant internal state; the regulation of any aspect of body chemistry, such as blood glucose, around a particular level. (p. 471)

hormones chemical messengers, mostly those manufactured by the endocrine glands, that are produced in one tissue and affect another. (p. 65)

hue the dimension of color that is determined by the wavelength of light; what we know as the color names *blue, green,* and so forth. (p. 205)

human factors psychology a branch of psychology that explores how people and machines interact and how machines and physical environments can be made safe and easy to use. (p. 261)

humanistic psychology historically significant perspective that emphasized the growth potential of healthy people; used personalized methods to study personality in hopes of fostering personal growth. (p. 7)

hypnosis a social interaction in which one person (the hypnotist) suggests to another (the subject) that certain perceptions, feelings, thoughts, or behaviors will spontaneously occur. (p. 290)

hypothalamus [hi-po-THAL-uh-muss] a neural structure lying below (*hypo*) the thalamus; it directs several maintenance activities (eating, drinking, body temperature), helps govern the endocrine system via the pituitary gland, and is linked to emotion. (p. 73)

hypothesis a testable prediction, often implied by a theory. (p. 25)

iconic memory a momentary sensory memory of visual stimuli; a photographic or picture-image memory lasting no more than a few tenths of a second. (p. 362)

id contains a reservoir of unconscious psychic energy that, according to Freud, strives to satisfy basic sexual and aggressive drives. The id operates on the pleasure principle, demanding immediate gratification. (p. 598)

identical twins twins who develop from a single fertilized egg that splits in two, creating two genetically identical organisms. (p. 97)

identification the process by which, according to Freud, children incorporate their parents' values into their developing superegos. (p. 599)

identity one's sense of self; according to Erikson, the adolescent's task is to solidify a sense of self by testing and integrating various roles. (p. 171)

illusory correlation the perception of a relationship where none exists. (p. 33)

imagery mental pictures; a powerful aid to effortful processing, especially when combined with semantic encoding. (p. 358)

implicit memory retention independent of conscious recollection. (Also called *procedural memory*.) (p. 367)

imprinting the process by which certain animals form attachments during a critical period very early in life. (p. 156)

inattentional blindness failing to see visible objects when our attention is directed elsewhere. (p. 238)

incentive a positive or negative environmental stimulus that motivates behavior. (p. 471)

independent variable the experimental factor that is manipulated; the variable whose effect is being studied. (p. 38)

individualism giving priority to one's own goals over group goals, and defining one's identity in terms of personal attributes rather than group identifications. (p. 121)

industrial-organizational (I/O) psychology the application of psychological concepts and methods to optimizing human behavior in workplaces. (p. 499)

informational social influence influence resulting from one's willingness to accept others' opinions about reality. (p. 733)

ingroup "Us"—people with whom one shares a common identity. (p. 746)

ingroup bias the tendency to favor one's own group. (p. 746)

inner ear the innermost part of the ear, containing the cochlea, semicircular canals, and vestibular sacs (p. 217)

insight a sudden and often novel realization of the solution to a problem; it contrasts with strategy-based solutions. (p. 398)

insomnia recurring problems in falling or staying asleep. (p. 283)

instinct a complex behavior that is rigidly patterned throughout a species and is unlearned. (p. 470)

intelligence mental quality consisting of the ability to learn from experience, solve problems, and use knowledge to adapt to new situations. (p. 431)

intelligence quotient (IQ) defined originally as the ratio of mental age (*ma*) to chronological age (*ca*) multiplied by 100 (thus, IQ = *ma/ca* × 100). On contemporary intelligence tests, the average performance for a given age is assigned a score of 100. (p. 444)

intelligence test a method for assessing an individual's mental aptitudes and comparing them with those of others, using numerical scores. (p. 442)

intensity the amount of energy in a light or sound wave, which we perceive as brightness or loudness, as determined by the wave's amplitude. (p. 205)

interaction the effect of one factor (such as environment) depends on another factor (such as heredity). (p. 105)

internal locus of control the perception that one controls one's own fate. (p. 625)

interneurons central nervous system neurons that internally communicate and intervene between the sensory inputs and motor outputs. (p. 62)

interpretation in psychoanalysis, the analyst's noting supposed dream meanings, resistances, and other significant behaviors and events in order to promote insight. (p. 687)

intimacy in Erikson's theory, the ability to form close, loving relationships; a primary developmental task in late adolescence and early adulthood. (p. 172)

intrinsic motivation a desire to perform a behavior for its own sake. (p. 335)

iris a ring of muscle tissue that forms the colored portion of the eye around the pupil and controls the size of the pupil opening. (p. 205)

James-Lange theory the theory that our experience of emotion is our awareness of our physiological responses to emotion-arousing stimuli. (p. 514)

just-world phenomenon the tendency of people to believe the world is just and that people therefore get what they deserve and deserve what they get. (p. 748)

kinesthesis [kin-ehs-THEE-sehs] the system for sensing the position and movement of individual body parts. (p. 233)

language our spoken, written, or signed words and the ways we combine them to communicate meaning. (p. 410)

latent content according to Freud, the underlying meaning of a dream (as distinct from its manifest content). Freud believed that a dream's latent content functions as a safety valve. (p. 287)

latent learning learning that occurs but is not apparent until there is an incentive to demonstrate it. (p. 334)

law of effect Thorndike's principle that behaviors followed by favorable consequences become more likely, and that behaviors followed by unfavorable consequences become less likely. (p. 327)

learned helplessness the hopelessness and passive resignation an animal or human learns when unable to avoid repeated aversive events. (p. 625)

learning a relatively permanent change in an organism's behavior due to experience. (p. 313)

lens the transparent structure behind the pupil that changes shape to help focus images on the retina. (p. 205)

lesion [LEE-zhuhn] tissue destruction. A brain lesion is a naturally or experimentally caused destruction of brain tissue. (p. 68)

levels of analysis the differing complementary views, from biological to psychological to social-cultural, for analyzing any given phenomenon. (p. 10)

limbic system a doughnut-shaped system of neural structures at the border of the brainstem and cerebral hemispheres; associated with emotions such as fear and aggression and drives such as those for food and sex. Includes the hippocampus, amygdala, and hypothalamus. (p. 72)

linguistic determinism Whorf's hypothesis that language determines the way we think. (p. 418)

lobotomy a now-rare psychosurgical procedure once used to calm uncontrollably emotional or violent patients. The procedure cut the nerves that connect the frontal lobes to the emotion-controlling centers of the inner brain. (p. 717)

long-term memory the relatively permanent and limitless storehouse of the memory system. Includes knowledge, skills, and experiences. (p. 351)

long-term potentiation (LTP) an increase in a synapse's firing potential after brief, rapid stimulation. Believed to be a neural basis for learning and memory. (p. 365)

longitudinal study research in which the same people are restudied and retested over a long period. (p. 183)

LSD a powerful hallucinogenic drug; also known as *acid* (*lysergic acid diethylamide*). (p. 302)

lymphocytes the two types of white blood cells that are part of the body's immune system: *B lymphocytes* form in the *bone marrow* and release antibodies that fight bacterial infections; *T lymphocytes* form in the *thymus* and other lymphatic tissue and attack cancer cells, viruses, and foreign substances. (p. 557)

major depressive disorder a mood disorder in which a person experiences, in the absence of drugs or a medical condition, two or more weeks of significantly depressed moods, feelings of worthlessness, and diminished interest or pleasure in most activities. (p. 659)

mania a mood disorder marked by a hyperactive, wildly optimistic state. (p. 659)

manifest content according to Freud, the remembered story line of a dream (as distinct from its latent, or hidden, content). (p. 286)

maturation biological growth processes that enable orderly changes in behavior, relatively uninfluenced by experience. (p. 145)

mean the arithmetic average of a distribution, obtained by adding the scores and then dividing by the number of scores. (p. 41)

median the middle score in a distribution; half the scores are above it and half are below it. (p. 41)

medical model the concept that diseases have physical causes that can be diagnosed, treated, and, in most cases, cured. When applied to psychological disorders, the medical model assumes that these *mental illnesses* can be diagnosed on the basis of their symptoms and cured through therapy, which may include treatment in a psychiatric hospital. (p. 642)

medulla [muh-DUL-uh] the base of the brainstem; controls heartbeat and breathing. (p. 71)

memory the persistence of learning over time through the storage and retrieval of information. (p. 349)

menarche [meh-NAR-key] the first menstrual period. (p. 166)

menopause the time of natural cessation of menstruation; also refers to the biological changes a woman experiences as her ability to reproduce declines. (p. 176)

mental age a measure of intelligence test performance devised by Binet; the chronological age that most typically corresponds to a given level of performance. Thus, a child who does as well as the average 8-year-old is said to have a mental age of 8. (p. 443)

mental retardation a condition of limited mental ability, indicated by an intelligence score of 70 or below and difficulty in adapting to the demands of life; varies from mild to profound. (p. 452)

mental set a tendency to approach a problem in a particular way, often a way that has been successful in the past. (p. 400)

mere exposure effect the phenomenon that repeated exposure to novel stimuli increases liking of them. (p. 759)

meta-analysis a procedure for statistically combining the results of many different research studies. (p. 703)

methamphetamine a powerfully addictive drug that stimulates the central nervous system, with speeded-up body functions and associated energy and mood changes; over time, appears to reduce baseline dopamine levels. (p. 300)

middle ear the chamber between the eardrum and cochlea containing three tiny bones (hammer, anvil, and stirrup) that concentrate the vibrations of the eardrum on the cochlea's oval window. (p. 217)

Minnesota Multiphasic Personality Inventory (MMPI) the most widely researched and clinically used of all personality tests. Originally developed to identify emotional disorders (still considered its most appropriate use), this test is now used for many other screening purposes. (p. 616)

mirror neurons frontal lobe neurons that fire when performing certain actions or when observing another doing so. The brain's mirroring of another's action may enable imitation, language learning, and empathy. (p. 341)

misinformation effect incorporating misleading information into one's memory of an event. (p. 383)

mnemonics [nih-MON-iks] memory aids, especially those techniques that use vivid imagery and organizational devices. (p. 358)

mode the most frequently occurring score(s) in a distribution. (p. 41)

modeling the process of observing and imitating a specific behavior. (p. 341)

molecular genetics the subfield of biology that studies the molecular structure and function of genes. (p. 105)

monism the presumption that mind and body are different aspects of the same thing. (p. 310)

monocular cues depth cues, such as interposition and linear perspective, available to either eye alone. (p. 246)

mood-congruent memory the tendency to recall experiences that are consistent with one's current good or bad mood. (p. 374)

mood disorders psychological disorders characterized by emotional extremes. See *major depressive disorder, mania,* and *bipolar disorder.* (p. 658)

morpheme in a language, the smallest unit that carries meaning; may be a word or a part of a word (such as a prefix). (p. 411)

motivation a need or desire that energizes and directs behavior. (p. 470)

motor cortex an area at the rear of the frontal lobes that controls voluntary movements. (p. 77)

motor neurons neurons that carry outgoing information from the central nervous system to the muscles and glands. (p. 62)

MRI (magnetic resonance imaging) a technique that uses magnetic fields and radio waves to produce computer-generated images that distinguish among different types of soft tissue; allows us to see structures within the brain. (p. 69)

mutation a random error in gene replication that leads to a change. (p. 108)

myelin [MY-uh-lin] **sheath** a layer of fatty tissue segmentally encasing the fibers of many neurons; enables vastly greater transmission speed of neural impulses as the impulse hops from one node to the next. (p. 55)

narcolepsy a sleep disorder characterized by uncontrollable sleep attacks. The sufferer may lapse directly into REM sleep, often at inopportune times. (p. 284)

natural selection the principle that, among the range of inherited trait variations, those that lead to increased reproduction and survival will most likely be passed on to succeeding generations. (pp. 9, 108)

naturalistic observation observing and recording behavior in naturally occurring situations without trying to manipulate and control the situation. (p. 29)

nature-nurture issue the longstanding controversy over the relative contributions that genes and experience make to the development of psychological traits and behaviors. (p. 9)

near-death experience an altered state of consciousness reported after a close brush with death (such as through cardiac arrest); often similar to drug-induced hallucinations. (p. 309)

nearsightedness a condition in which nearby objects are seen more clearly than distant objects because distant objects focus in front of the retina. (p. 206)

negative reinforcement increasing behaviors by stopping or reducing negative stimuli, such as shock. A negative reinforcer is any stimulus that, when *removed* after a response, strengthens the response. (*Note:* Negative reinforcement is *not* punishment.) (p. 329)

nerves neural "cables" containing many axons. These bundled axons, which are part of the peripheral nervous system, connect the central nervous system with muscles, glands, and sense organs. (p. 62)

nervous system the body's speedy, electrochemical communication network, consisting of all the nerve cells of the peripheral and central nervous systems. (p. 61)

neural networks interconnected neural cells. With experience, networks can learn, as feedback strengthens or inhibits connections that produce certain results. Computer simulations of neural networks show analogous learning. (p. 64)

neuron a nerve cell; the basic building block of the nervous system. (p. 55)

neurotransmitters chemical messengers that traverse the synaptic gaps between neurons. When released by the sending neuron, neurotransmitters travel across the synapse and bind to receptor sites on the receiving neuron, thereby influencing whether that neuron will generate a neural impulse. (p. 57)

night terrors a sleep disorder characterized by high arousal and an appearance of being terrified; unlike nightmares, night terrors occur during Stage 4 sleep, within two or three hours of falling asleep, and are seldom remembered. (p. 284)

norm an understood rule for accepted and expected behavior. Norms prescribe "proper" behavior. (p. 120)

normal curve the symmetrical bell-shaped curve that describes the distribution of many physical and psychological attributes. Most scores fall near the average, and fewer and fewer scores lie near the extremes. (p. 447)

normative social influence influence resulting from a person's desire to gain approval or avoid disapproval. (p. 733)

object permanence the awareness that things continue to exist even when not perceived. (p. 149)

observational learning learning by observing others. (p. 341)

obsessive-compulsive disorder (OCD) an anxiety disorder characterized by unwanted repetitive thoughts (obsessions) and/or actions (compulsions). (p. 651)

occipital [ahk-SIP-uh-tuhl] **lobes** the portion of the cerebral cortex lying at the back of the head; includes the visual areas, which receive visual information from the opposite visual field. (p. 76)

Oedipus [ED-uh-puss] **complex** according to Freud, a boy's sexual desires toward his mother and feelings of jealousy and hatred for the rival father. (p. 599)

one-word stage the stage in speech development, from about age 1 to 2, during which a child speaks mostly in single words. (p. 413)

operant behavior behavior that operates on the environment, producing consequences. (p. 326)

operant chamber a chamber also known as a *Skinner box*, containing a bar or key that an animal can manipulate to obtain a food or water reinforcer, with attached devices to record the animal's rate of bar pressing or key pecking. Used in operant conditioning research. (p. 327)

operant conditioning a type of learning in which behavior is strengthened if followed by a reinforcer or diminished if followed by a punisher. (p. 326)

operational definition a statement of the procedures (operations) used to define research variables. For example, *human intelligence* may be operationally defined as what an intelligence test measures. (p. 25)

opiates opium and its derivatives, such as morphine and heroin; they depress neural activity, temporarily lessening pain and anxiety. (p. 300)

opponent-process theory the theory that opposing retinal processes (red-green, yellow-blue, white-black) enable color vision. For example, some cells are stimulated by green and inhibited by red; others are stimulated by red and inhibited by green. (p. 213)

optic nerve the nerve that carries neural impulses from the eye to the brain. (p. 207)

organizational psychology a subfield of I/O psychology that examines organizational influences on worker satisfaction and productivity and facilitates organizational change. (p. 499)

outgroup "Them"—those perceived as different or apart from one's ingroup. (p. 746)

overconfidence the tendency to be more confident than correct—to overestimate the accuracy of one's beliefs and judgments. (p. 403)

panic disorder an anxiety disorder marked by unpredictable minutes-long episodes of intense dread in which a person experiences terror and accompanying chest pain, choking, or other frightening sensations. (p. 650)

parallel processing the processing of several aspects of a problem simultaneously; the brain's natural mode of information processing for many functions, including vision. Contrasts with the step-by-step (serial) processing of most computers and of conscious problem solving. (p. 210)

parapsychology the study of paranormal phenomena, including ESP and psychokinesis. (p. 264)

parasympathetic nervous system the division of the autonomic nervous system that calms the body, conserving its energy. (p. 62)

parietal [puh-RYE-uh-tuhl] **lobes** the portion of the cerebral cortex lying at the top of the head and toward the rear; receives sensory input for touch and body position. (p. 76)

partial (intermittent) reinforcement reinforcing a response only part of the time; results in slower acquisition of a response but much greater resistance to extinction than does continuous reinforcement. (p. 331)

passionate love an aroused state of intense positive absorption in another, usually present at the beginning of a love relationship. (p. 763)

perception the process of organizing and interpreting sensory information, enabling us to recognize meaningful objects and events. (p. 197)

perceptual adaptation in vision, the ability to adjust to an artificially displaced or even inverted visual field. (p. 256)

perceptual constancy perceiving objects as unchanging (having consistent lightness, color, shape, and size) even as illumination and retinal images change. (p. 250)

perceptual set a mental predisposition to perceive one thing and not another. (p. 257)

peripheral nervous system (PNS) the sensory and motor neurons that connect the central nervous system (CNS) to the rest of the body. (p. 61)

personal control our sense of controlling our environment rather than feeling helpless. (p. 625)

personal space the buffer zone we like to maintain around our bodies. (p. 120)

personality an individual's characteristic pattern of thinking, feeling, and acting. (p. 595)

personality disorders psychological disorders characterized by inflexible and enduring behavior patterns that impair social functioning. (p. 677)

personality inventory a questionnaire (often with true-false or agree-disagree items) on which people respond to items designed to gauge a wide range of feelings and behaviors; used to assess selected personality traits. (p. 615)

personnel psychology a subfield of I/O psychology that focuses on employee recruitment, selection, placement, training, appraisal, and development. (p. 499)

PET (positron emission tomography) scan a visual display of brain activity that detects where a radioactive form of glucose goes while the brain performs a given task. (p. 69)

phi phenomenon an illusion of movement created when two or more adjacent lights blink on and off in quick succession. (p. 250)

phobia an anxiety disorder marked by a persistent, irrational fear and avoidance of a specific object or situation. (p. 650)

phoneme in a language, the smallest distinctive sound unit. (p. 410)

physical dependence a physiological need for a drug, marked by unpleasant withdrawal symptoms when the drug is discontinued. (p. 297)

pitch a tone's experienced highness or lowness; depends on frequency. (p. 216)

pituitary gland the endocrine system's most influential gland. Under the influence of the hypothalamus, the pituitary regulates growth and controls other endocrine glands. (p. 66)

place theory in hearing, the theory that links the pitch we hear with the place where the cochlea's membrane is stimulated. (p. 219)

placebo [pluh-SEE-bo; Latin for "I shall please"] **effect** experimental results caused by expectations alone; any effect on behavior caused by the administration of an inert substance or condition, which is assumed to be an active agent. (p. 37)

plasticity the brain's capacity for modification, as evident in brain reorganization following damage (especially in children) and in experiments on the effects of experience on brain development. (p. 82)

polygraph a machine, commonly used in attempts to detect lies, that measures several of the physiological responses accompanying emotion (such as perspiration and cardiovascular and breathing changes). (p. 520)

population all the cases in a group, from which samples may be drawn for a study. (*Note:* Except for national studies, this does not refer to a country's whole population.) (p. 28)

positive psychology the scientific study of optimal human functioning; aims to discover and promote strengths and virtues that enable individuals and communities to thrive. (p. 628)

positive reinforcement increasing behaviors by presenting positive stimuli, such as food. A positive reinforcer is any stimulus that, when *presented* after a response, strengthens the response. (p. 329)

post-traumatic stress disorder (PTSD) an anxiety disorder characterized by haunting memories, nightmares, social withdrawal, jumpy anxiety, and/or insomnia that lingers for four weeks or more after a traumatic experience. (p. 652)

posthypnotic suggestion a suggestion, made during a hypnosis session, to be carried out after the subject is no longer hypnotized; used by some clinicians to help control undesired symptoms and behaviors. (p. 292)

predictive validity the success with which a test predicts the behavior it is designed to predict; it is assessed by computing the correlation between test scores and the criterion behavior. (Also called *criterion-related validity*.) (p. 448)

prejudice an unjustifiable (and usually negative) attitude toward a group and its members. Prejudice generally involves stereotyped beliefs, negative feelings, and a predisposition to discriminatory action. (p. 743)

preoperational stage in Piaget's theory, the stage (from about 2 to 6 or 7 years of age) during which a child learns to use language but does not yet comprehend the mental operations of concrete logic. (p. 150)

primary reinforcer an innately reinforcing stimulus, such as one that satisfies a biological need. (p. 330)

primary sex characteristics the body structures (ovaries, testes, and external genitalia) that make sexual reproduction possible. (p. 165)

priming the activation, often unconsciously, of certain associations, thus predisposing one's perception, memory, or response. (pp. 200, 372)

proactive interference the disruptive effect of prior learning on the recall of new information. (p. 379)

problem-focused coping attempting to alleviate stress directly—by changing the stressor or the way we interact with that stressor. (p. 562)

projection psychoanalytic defense mechanism by which people disguise their own threatening impulses by attributing them to others. (p. 600)

projective test a personality test, such as the Rorschach or TAT, that provides ambiguous stimuli designed to trigger projection of one's inner dynamics. (p. 602)

prosocial behavior positive, constructive, helpful behavior. The opposite of antisocial behavior. (p. 343)

prototype a mental image or best example of a category. Matching new items to the prototype provides a quick and easy method for including items in a category (as when comparing feathered creatures to a prototypical bird, such as a robin). (p. 396)

psychiatry a branch of medicine dealing with psychological disorders; practiced by physicians who sometimes provide medical (for example, drug) treatments as well as psychological therapy. (p. 13)

psychoactive drug a chemical substance that alters perceptions and mood. (p. 296)

psychoanalysis Freud's theory of personality and therapeutic technique that attributes thoughts and actions to unconscious motives and conflicts. Freud believed the patient's free associations, resistances, dreams, and transferences—and the therapist's interpretations of them—released previously repressed feelings, allowing the patient to gain self-insight. (pp. 597, 686)

psychological dependence a psychological need to use a drug, such as to relieve negative emotions. (p. 297)

psychological disorder deviant, distressful, and dysfunctional behavior patterns. (p. 640)

psychology the scientific study of behavior and mental processes. (p. 2)

psychopharmacology the study of the effects of drugs on mind and behavior. (p. 711)

psychophysics the study of relationships between the physical characteristics of stimuli, such as their intensity, and our psychological experience of them. (p. 199)

psychophysiological illness literally, "mind-body" illness; any stress-related physical illness, such as hypertension and some headaches. *Note:* This is distinct from *hypochondriasis*—misinterpreting normal physical sensations as symptoms of a disease. (p. 556)

psychosexual stages the childhood stages of development (oral, anal, phallic, latency, genital) during which, according to Freud, the id's pleasure-seeking energies focus on distinct erogenous zones. (p. 598)

psychosurgery surgery that removes or destroys brain tissue in an effort to change behavior. (p. 717)

psychotherapy an emotionally charged, confiding interaction between a trained therapist and someone who suffers from psychological difficulties. (p. 685)

puberty the period of sexual maturation, during which a person becomes capable of reproducing. (p. 165)

punishment an event that *decreases* the behavior that it follows. (p. 332)

pupil the adjustable opening in the center of the eye through which light enters. (p. 205)

random assignment assigning participants to experimental and control conditions by chance, thus minimizing preexisting differences between those assigned to the different groups. (p. 37)

random sample a sample that fairly represents a population because each member has an equal chance of inclusion. (p. 28)

range the difference between the highest and lowest scores in a distribution. (p. 42)

rationalization defense mechanism that offers self-justifying explanations in place of the real, more threatening, unconscious reasons for one's actions. (p. 600)

reaction formation psychoanalytic defense mechanism by which the ego unconsciously switches unacceptable impulses into their opposites. Thus, people may express feelings that are the opposite of their anxiety-arousing unconscious feelings. (p. 600)

recall a measure of memory in which the person must retrieve information learned earlier, as on a fill-in-the-blank test. (p. 370)

reciprocal determinism the interacting influences between personality and environmental factors. (p. 623)

reciprocity norm an expectation that people will help, not hurt, those who have helped them. (p. 766)

recognition a measure of memory in which the person need only identify items previously learned, as on a multiple-choice test. (p. 370)

reflex a simple, automatic, inborn response to a sensory stimulus, such as the knee-jerk response. (p. 63)

refractory period a resting period after orgasm, during which a man cannot achieve another orgasm. (p. 482)

regression psychoanalytic defense mechanism in which an individual faced with anxiety retreats to a more infantile psychosexual stage, where some psychic energy remains fixated. (p. 600)

regression toward the mean the tendency for extremes of unusual scores to fall back (regress) toward their average. (p. 702)

rehearsal the conscious repetition of information, either to maintain it in consciousness or to encode it for storage. (p. 354)

reinforcer in operant conditioning, any event that *strengthens* the behavior it follows. (p. 329)

relative deprivation the perception that one is worse off relative to those with whom one compares oneself. (p. 343)

relearning a memory measure that assesses the amount of time saved when learning material for a second time. (p. 370)

reliability the extent to which a test yields consistent results, as assessed by the consistency of scores on two halves of the test, on alternate forms of the test, or on retesting. (p. 448)

REM rebound the tendency for REM sleep to increase following REM sleep deprivation (created by repeated awakenings during REM sleep). (p. 288)

REM sleep rapid eye movement sleep, a recurring sleep stage during which vivid dreams commonly occur. Also known as *paradoxical sleep,* because the muscles are relaxed (except for minor twitches) but other body systems are active. (p. 276)

repetitive transcranial magnetic stimulation (rTMS) the application of repeated pulses of magnetic energy to the brain; used to stimulate or suppress brain activity. (p. 716)

replication repeating the essence of a research study, usually with different participants in different situations, to see whether the basic finding extends to other participants and circumstances. (p. 25)

representativeness heuristic judging the likelihood of things in terms of how well they seem to represent, or match, particular prototypes; may lead one to ignore other relevant information. (p. 401)

repression in psychoanalytic theory, the basic defense mechanism that banishes anxiety-arousing thoughts, feelings, and memories from consciousness. (pp. 381, 600)

resistance in psychoanalysis, the blocking from consciousness of anxiety-laden material. (p. 687)

respondent behavior behavior that occurs as an automatic response to some stimulus; Skinner's term for behavior learned through classical conditioning. (p. 326)

reticular formation a nerve network in the brainstem that plays an important role in controlling arousal. (p. 71)

retina the light-sensitive inner surface of the eye, containing the receptor rods and cones plus layers of neurons that begin the processing of visual information. (p. 205)

retinal disparity a binocular cue for perceiving depth: By comparing images from the two eyeballs, the brain computes distance—the greater the disparity (difference) between the two images, the closer the object. (p. 246)

retrieval the process of getting information out of memory storage. (p. 351)

retroactive interference the disruptive effect of new learning on the recall of old information. (p. 379)

rods retinal receptors that detect black, white, and gray; necessary for peripheral and twilight vision, when cones don't respond. (p. 206)

role a set of expectations (norms) about a social position, defining how those in the position ought to behave. (p. 131)

rooting reflex a baby's tendency, when touched on the cheek, to turn toward the touch, open the mouth, and search for the nipple. (p. 142)

Rorschach inkblot test the most widely used projective test, a set of 10 inkblots, designed by Hermann Rorschach; seeks to identify people's inner feelings by analyzing their interpretations of the blots. (p. 602)

savant syndrome a condition in which a person otherwise limited in mental ability has an exceptional specific skill, such as in computation or drawing. (p. 433)

scapegoat theory the theory that prejudice offers an outlet for anger by providing someone to blame. (p. 747)

scatterplot a graphed cluster of dots, each of which represents the values of two variables. The slope of the points suggests the direction of the relationship between the two variables. The amount of scatter suggests the strength of the correlation (little scatter indicates high correlation). (Also called a *scattergram* or *scatter diagram*.) (p. 31)

schema a concept or framework that organizes and interprets information. (p. 147)

schizophrenia a group of severe disorders characterized by disorganized and delusional thinking, disturbed perceptions, and inappropriate emotions and actions. (p. 669)

secondary sex characteristics nonreproductive sexual characteristics, such as female breasts and hips, male voice quality, and body hair. (p. 165)

selective attention the focusing of conscious awareness on a particular stimulus, as in the cocktail party effect. (p. 237)

self-actualization according to Maslow, the ultimate psychological need that arises after basic physical and psychological needs are met and self-esteem is achieved; the motivation to fulfill one's potential. (p. 609)

self-concept (1) a sense of one's identity and personal worth. (2) all our thoughts and feelings about ourselves, in answer to the question, "Who am I?" (pp. 161, 610)

self-disclosure revealing intimate aspects of oneself to others. (p. 764)

self-esteem one's feelings of high or low self-worth. (p. 632)

self-serving bias a readiness to perceive oneself favorably (p. 634)

semantic encoding the encoding of meaning, including the meaning of words. (p. 356)

semantics the set of rules by which we derive meaning from morphemes, words, and sentences in a given language; also, the study of meaning. (p. 411)

sensation the process by which our sensory receptors and nervous system receive and represent stimulus energies from our environment. (p. 197)

sensorimotor stage in Piaget's theory, the stage (from birth to about 2 years of age) during which infants know the world mostly in terms of their sensory impressions and motor activities. (p. 149)

sensorineural hearing loss hearing loss caused by damage to the cochlea's receptor cells or to the auditory nerves; also called *nerve deafness*. (p. 220)

sensory adaptation diminished sensitivity as a consequence of constant stimulation. (p. 202)

sensory cortex the area at the front of the parietal lobes that registers and processes body touch and movement sensations. (p. 78)

sensory interaction the principle that one sense may influence another, as when the smell of food influences its taste. (p. 230)

sensory memory the immediate, very brieg recording of sensory information in the memory system. (p. 351)

sensory neurons neurons that carry incoming information from the sense receptors to the central nervous system. (p. 62)

serial position effect our tendency to recall best the last and first items in a list. (p. 356)

set point the point at which an individual's "weight thermostat" is supposedly set. When the body falls below this weight, an increase in hunger and a lowered metabolic rate may act to restore the lost weight. (p. 476)

sexual disorder a problem that consistently impairs sexual arousal or functioning. (p. 482)

sexual orientation an enduring sexual attraction toward members of either one's own sex (homosexual orientation) or the other sex (heterosexual orientation). (p. 487)

sexual response cycle the four stages of sexual responding described by Masters and Johnson—excitement, plateau, orgasm, and resolution. (p. 481)

shaping an operant conditioning procedure in which reinforcers guide behavior toward closer and closer approximations of the desired behavior. (p. 328)

short-term memory activated memory that holds a few items briefly, such as the seven digits of a phone number while dialing, before the information is stored or forgotten. (p. 351)

signal detection theory a theory predicting how and when we detect the presence of a faint stimulus ("signal") amid background stimulation ("noise"). Assumes there is no single absolute threshold and detection depends partly on a person's experience, expectations, motivation, and level of fatigue. (p. 199)

sleep periodic, natural, reversible loss of consciousness—as distinct from unconsciousness resulting from a coma, general anesthesia, or hibernation. (Adapted from Dement, 1999.) (p. 277)

sleep apnea a sleep disorder characterized by temporary cessations of breathing during sleep and repeated momentary awakenings. (p. 284)

social-cognitive perspective views behavior as influenced by the interaction between persons (and their thinking) and their social context. (p. 623)

social-responsibility norm an expectation that people will help those dependent upon them. (p. 767)

social clock the culturally preferred timing of social events such as marriage, parenthood, and retirement. (p. 186)

social exchange theory the theory that our social behavior is an exchange process, the aim of which is to maximize benefits and minimize costs. (p. 766)

social facilitation stronger responses on simple or well-learned tasks in the presence of others. (p. 738)

social leadership group-oriented leadership that builds teamwork, mediates conflict, and offers support. (p. 508)

social learning theory the theory that we learn social behavior by observing and imitating and by being rewarded or punished. (p. 132)

social loafing the tendency for people in a group to exert less effort when pooling their efforts toward attaining a common goal than when individually accountable. (p. 739)

social psychology the scientific study of how we think about, influence, and relate to one another. (p. 723)

social trap a situation in which the conflicting parties, by each rationally pursuing their self-interest, become caught in mutually destructive behavior. (p. 756)

somatic nervous system the division of the peripheral nervous system that controls the body's skeletal muscles. Also called the *skeletal nervous system*. (p. 62)

source amnesia attributing to the wrong source an event we have experienced, heard about, read about, or imagined. (Also called *source misattribution*.) Source amnesia, along with the misinformation effect, is at the heart of many false memories. (p. 384)

spacing effect the tendency for distributed study or practice to yield better long-term retention than is achieved through massed study or practice. (p. 355)

split brain a condition in which the two hemispheres of the brain are isolated by cutting the connecting fibers (mainly those of the corpus callosum) between them. (p. 84)

spontaneous recovery the reappearance, after a pause, of an extinguished conditioned response. (p. 319)

spotlight effect overestimating others' noticing and evaluating our appearance, performance, and blunders (as if we presume a spotlight shines on us). (p. 632)

standard deviation a computed measure of how much scores vary around the mean score. (p. 42)

standardization defining meaningful scores by comparison with the performance of a pretested standardization group. (p. 446)

Stanford-Binet the widely used American revision (by Terman at Stanford University) of Binet's original intelligence test. (p. 443)

statistical significance a statistical statement of how likely it is that an obtained result occurred by chance. (p. 43)

stereotype a generalized (sometimes accurate but often overgeneralized) belief about a group of people. (p. 743)

stereotype threat a self-confirming concern that one will be evaluated based on a negative stereotype. (p. 465)

stimulants drugs (such as caffeine, nicotine, and the more powerful amphetamines, cocaine, and Ecstasy) that excite neural activity and speed up body functions. (p. 300)

storage the retention of encoded information over time. (p. 351)

stranger anxiety the fear of strangers that infants commonly display, beginning by about 8 months of age. (p. 155)

structuralism an early school of psychology that used introspection to explore the elemental structure of the human mind. (p. 4)

stress the process by which we perceive and respond to certain events, called *stressors*, that we appraise as threatening or challenging. (p. 550)

structured interviews interview process that asks the same job-relevant questions of all applicants, each of whom is rated on established scales. (p. 502)

subjective well-being self-perceived happiness or satisfaction with life. Used along with measures of objective well-being (for example, physical and economic indicators) to evaluate people's quality of life. (p. 538)

subliminal below one's absolute threshold for conscious awareness. (p. 200)

superego the part of personality that, according to Freud, represents internalized ideals and provides standards for judgment (the conscience) and for future aspirations. (p. 598)

superordinate goals shared goals that override differences among people and require their cooperation. (p. 767)

survey a technique for ascertaining the self-reported attitudes or behaviors of people, usually by questioning a representative, random sample of them. (p. 27)

sympathetic nervous system the division of the autonomic nervous system that arouses the body, mobilizing its energy in stressful situations. (p. 62)

synapse [SIN-aps] the junction between the axon tip of the sending neuron and the dendrite or cell body of the receiving neuron. The tiny gap at this junction is called the *synaptic gap* or *cleft*. (p. 57)

syntax the rules for combining words into grammatically sensible sentences in a given language. (p. 411)

systematic desensitization a type of counterconditioning that associates a pleasant relaxed state with gradually increasing anxiety-triggering stimuli. Commonly used to treat phobias. (p. 692)

tardive dyskinesia involuntary movements of the facial muscles, tongue, and limbs; a possible neurotoxic side effect of long-term use of antipsychotic drugs that target D2 dopamine receptors. (p. 712)

task leadership goal-oriented leadership that sets standards, organizes work, and focuses attention on goals. (p. 508)

telegraphic speech early speech stage in which a child speaks like a telegram—"go car"—using mostly nouns and verbs and omitting auxiliary words. (p. 413)

temperament a person's characteristic emotional reactivity and intensity. (p. 102)

temporal lobes the portion of the cerebral cortex lying roughly above the ears; includes the auditory areas, each of which receives auditory information primarily from the opposite ear. (p. 76)

teratogens agents, such as chemicals and viruses, that can reach the embryo or fetus during prenatal development and cause harm. (p. 141)

terror-management theory proposes that faith in one's worldview and the pursuit of self-esteem provide protection against a deeply rooted fear of death. (p. 606)

testosterone the most important of the male sex hormones. Both males and females have it, but the additional testosterone in males stimulates the growth of the male sex organs in the fetus and the development of the male sex characteristics during puberty. (pp. 130, 482)

thalamus [THAL-uh-muss] the brain's sensory switchboard, located on top of the brainstem; it directs messages to the sensory receiving areas in the cortex and transmits replies to the cerebellum and medulla. (p. 72)

THC the major active ingredient in marijuana; triggers a variety of effects, including mild hallucinations. (p. 303)

Thematic Apperception Test (TAT) a projective test in which people express their inner feelings and interests through the stories they make up about ambiguous scenes. (p. 602)

theory an explanation using an integrated set of principles that organizes and predicts observations. (p. 24)

theory of mind people's ideas about their own and others' mental states—about their feelings, perceptions, and thoughts and the behavior these might predict. (p. 151)

threshold the level of stimulation required to trigger a neural impulse. (p. 56)

token economy an operant conditioning procedure in which people earn a token of some sort for exhibiting a desired behavior and can later exchange the tokens for various privileges or treats. (p. 693)

tolerance the diminishing effect with regular use of the same dose of a drug, requiring the user to take larger and larger doses before experiencing the drug's effect. (p. 297)

top-down processing information processing guided by higher-level mental processes, as when we construct perceptions drawing on our experience and expectations. (p. 197)

trait a characteristic pattern of behavior or a disposition to feel and act, as assessed by self-report inventories and peer reports. (p. 613)

transduction conversion of one form of energy into another. In sensation, the transforming of stimulus energies, such as sights, sounds, and smells, into neural impulses our brains can interpret. (p. 204)

transference in psychoanalysis, the patient's transfer to the analyst of emotions linked with other relationships (such as love or hatred for a parent). (p. 687)

two-factor theory Schachter-Singer's theory that to experience emotion one must (1) be physically aroused and (2) cognitively label the arousal. (p. 514)

two-word stage beginning about age 2, the stage in speech development during which a child speaks mostly two-word statements. (p. 413)

Type A Friedman and Rosenman's term for competitive, hard-driving, impatient, verbally aggressive, and anger-prone people. (p. 555)

Type B Friedman and Rosenman's term for easygoing, relaxed people. (p. 555)

unconditional positive regard according to Rogers, an attitude of total acceptance toward another person. (p. 610)

unconditioned response (UR) in classical conditioning, the unlearned, naturally occurring response to the unconditioned stimulus (US), such as salivation when food is in the mouth. (p. 317)

unconditioned stimulus (US) in classical conditioning, a stimulus that unconditionally—naturally and automatically—triggers a response. (p. 317)

unconscious according to Freud, a reservoir of mostly unacceptable thoughts, wishes, feelings, and memories. According to contemporary psychologists, information processing of which we are unaware. (p. 597)

validity the extent to which a test measures or predicts what it is supposed to. (See also *content validity* and *predictive validity*.) (p. 448)

variable-interval schedule in operant conditioning, a reinforcement schedule that reinforces a response at unpredictable time intervals. (p. 332)

variable-ratio schedule in operant conditioning, a reinforcement schedule that reinforces a response after an unpredictable number of responses. (p. 332)

vestibular sense the sense of body movement and position, including the sense of balance. (p. 234)

virtual reality exposure therapy An anxiety treatment that progressively exposes people to simulations of their greatest fears, such as airplane flying, spiders, or public speaking. (p. 692)

visual capture the tendency for vision to dominate the other senses. (p. 242)

visual cliff a laboratory device for testing depth perception in infants and young animals. (p. 245)

visual encoding the encoding of picture images. (p. 356)

wavelength the distance from the peak of one light or sound wave to the peak of the next. Electromagnetic wavelengths vary from the short blips of cosmic rays to the long pulses of radio transmission. (p. 204)

Weber's law the principle that, to be perceived as different, two stimuli must differ by a constant minimum percentage (rather than a constant amount). (p. 202)

Wechsler Adult Intelligence Scale (WAIS) the WAIS is the most widely used intelligence test; contains verbal and performance (nonverbal) subtests. (p. 445)

Wernicke's area controls language reception—a brain area involved in language comprehension and expression; usually in the left temporal lobe. (p. 81)

withdrawal the discomfort and distress that follow discontinuing the use of an addictive drug. (p. 297)

working memory a newer understanding of short-term memory that involves conscious, active processing of incoming auditory and visual-spatial information, and of information retrieved from long-term memory. (p. 352)

X chromosome the sex chromosome found in both men and women. Females have two X chromosomes; males have one. An X chromosome from each parent produces a female child. (p. 129)

Y chromosome the sex chromosome found only in males. When paired with an X chromosome from the mother, it produces a male child. (p. 129)

Young-Helmholtz trichromatic (three-color) theory the theory that the retina contains three different color receptors—one most sensitive to red, one to green, one to blue—which when stimulated in combination can produce the perception of any color. (p. 212)

zygote the fertilized egg; it enters a 2-week period of rapid cell division and develops into an embryo. (p. 140)

REFERENCES

Aas, H., & Klepp, K-I. (1992). Adolescents' alcohol use related to perceived norms. *Scandinavian Journal of Psychology, 33,* 315–325. (p. 307)

Abbey, A. (1987). Misperceptions of friendly behavior as sexual interest: A survey of naturally occurring incidents. *Psychology of Women Quarterly, 11,* 173–194. (p. 110)

Abbey, A. (1991). Acquaintance rape and alcohol consumption on college campuses: How are they linked? *Journal of American College Health, 39,* 165–169. (p. 297)

Abbott, R. D., White, L. R., Ross, G. W., Masaki, K. H., Curb, J. D., & Petrovitch, H. (2004). Walking and dementia in physically capable elderly men. *Journal of the American Medical Association, 292,* 1447–1453. (p. 181)

Abrams, D. (1991). AIDS: What young people believe and what they do. Paper presented at the British Association for the Advancement of Science conference. (p. 627)

Abrams, D. B., & Wilson, G. T. (1983). Alcohol, sexual arousal, and self-control. *Journal of Personality and Social Psychology, 45,* 188–198. (p. 300)

Abrams, M. (2002, June). Sight unseen—Restoring a blind man's vision is now a real possibility through stem-cell surgery. But even perfect eyes cannot see unless the brain has been taught to use them. *Discover, 23,* 54–60. (p. 256)

Abramson, L. Y., Metalsky, G. I., & Alloy, L. B. (1989). Hopelessness depression: A theory-based subtype. *Psychological Review, 96,* 358–372. (p. 666)

Ackerman, D. (2004). *An alchemy of mind: The marvel and mystery of the brain.* New York: Scribner. (pp. 57, 67)

Adelmann, P. K., Antonucci, T. C., Crohan, S. F., & Coleman, L. M. (1989). Empty nest, cohort, and employment in the well-being of midlife women. *Sex Roles, 20,* 173–189. (p. 188)

Adelson, R. (2004, August). Detecting deception. *APA Monitor,* pp. 70–73. (p. 521)

Ader, R., & Cohen, N. (1985). CNS-immune system interactions: Conditioning phenomena. *Behavioral and Brain Sciences, 8,* 379–394. (p. 560)

Adolphs, R., Tranel, D., & Damasio, A. R. (1998). The human amygdala in social judgment. *Nature, 393,* 470–474. (p. 535)

Affleck, G., Tennen, H., Urrows, S., & Higgins, P. (1994). Person and contextual features of daily stress reactivity: Individual differences in relations of undesirable daily events with mood disturbance and chronic pain intensity. *Journal of Personality and Social Psychology, 66,* 329–340. (p. 538)

Aggleton, J. P., Kentridge, R. W., & Neave, N. J. (1993). Evidence for longevity differences between left handed and right handed men: An archival study of cricketers. *Journal of Epidemiology and Community Health, 47,* 206–209. (p. 90)

Agid, O., Shapira, B., Zislin, J., Ritsner, M., Hanin, B., Murad, H., Troudart, T., Bloch, M., Heresco-Levy, U., & Lerer, B. (1999). Environment and vulnerability to major psychiatric illness: A case control study of early parental loss in major depression, bipolar disorder and schizophrenia. *Molecular Psychiatry, 4,* 163–172. (p. 661)

Agnati, L. F., Bjelke, B., & Fuxe, K. (1992). Volume transmission in the brain. *American Scientist, 80,* 362–373. (p. 67)

Aiello, J. R., Thompson, D. D., & Brodzinsky, D. M. (1983). How funny is crowding anyway? Effects of room size, group size, and the introduction of humor. *Basic and Applied Social Psychology, 4,* 193–207. (p. 738)

Ainsworth, M. D. S. (1973). The development of infant-mother attachment. In B. Caldwell & H. Ricciuti (Eds.), *Review of child development research* (Vol. 3). Chicago: University of Chicago Press. (p. 156)

Ainsworth, M. D. S. (1979). Infant-mother attachment. *American Psychologist, 34,* 932–937. (p. 156)

Ainsworth, M. D. S. (1989). Attachments beyond infancy. *American Psychologist, 44,* 709–716. (p. 156)

Albee, G. W. (1986). Toward a just society: Lessons from observations on the primary prevention of psychopathology. *American Psychologist, 41,* 891–898. (p. 719)

Albert, B., Brown, S., & Flanigan, C. M. (Eds.) (2003). *14 and younger: The sexual behavior of young adolescents.* Washington, DC: National Campaign to Prevent Teen Pregnancy. (p. 485)

Alcock, J. E. (1981). *Parapsychology: Science or magic?* Oxford: Pergamon. (p. 373)

Alcock, J. E. (1985, Spring). Parapsychology: The "spiritual" science. *Free Inquiry,* pp. 25–35. (pp. 267–268)

Aldrich, M. S. (1989). Automobile accidents in patients with sleep disorders. *Sleep, 12,* 487–494. (p. 283)

Aldridge-Morris, R. (1989). *Multiple personality: An exercise in deception.* Hillsdale, NJ: Erlbaum. (p. 657)

Aleman, A., Kahn, R. S., & Selten, J-P. (2003). Sex differences in the risk of schizophrenia: Evidence from meta-analysis. *Archives of General Psychiatry, 60,* 565–571. (p. 669)

Alexander, C. N., Langer, E. J., Newman, R. I., Chandler, H. M., & Davies, J. L. (1989). Transcendental meditation, mindfulness, and longevity: An experimental study with the elderly. *Journal of Personality and Social Psychology, 57,* 950–964. (p. 572)

Alexander, K. W., Quas, J. A., Goodman, G. S., Ghetti, S., Edelstein, R. S., Redlich, A. D., Cordon, I. M., & Jones, D. P. H. (2005). Traumatic impact predicts long-term memory for documented child sexual abuse. *Psychological Science, 16,* 33–40. (p. 605)

Allard, F., & Burnett, N. (1985). Skill in sport. *Canadian Journal of Psychology, 39,* 294–312. (p. 360)

Allen, J. B., Repinski, D. J., Ballard, J. C., & Griffin, B. W. (1996). Beliefs about the etiology of homosexuality may influence attitudes toward homosexuals. Paper presented to the American Psychological Society convention. (p. 492)

Allen, K. (2003). Are pets a healthy pleasure? The influence of pets on blood pressure. *Current Directions in Psychological Science, 12,* 236–239. (p. 568)

Allen, L. S., & Gorski, R. A. (1992). Sexual orientation and the size of the anterior commisure in the human brain. *Proceedings of the National Academy of Sciences, 89,* 7199–7202. (p. 490)

Allen, N. B., & Badcock, P. B. T. (2003). The social risk hypothesis of depressed mood: Evolutionary, psychosocial, and neurobiological perspectives. *Psychological Bulletin, 129,* 887–913. (p. 659)

Alloy, L. B., Abramson, L. Y., Whitehouse, W. G., Hogan, M. E., Tashman, N. A., Steinberg, D. L., Rose, D. T., & Donovan, P. (1999). Depressogenic cognitive styles: Predictive validity, information processing and personality characteristics, and developmental origins. *Behaviour Research and Therapy, 37,* 503–531. (p. 666)

Allport, G. W. (1954). *The nature of prejudice.* New York: Addison-Wesley. (pp. 27, 746)

Allport, G. W. (1967). Gordon W. Allport. In E. G. Boring & G. Lindzey (Eds.), *A history of psychology in autobiography* (Vol. V). New York: Appleton-Century-Crofts. (p. 613)

Allport, G. W., & Odbert, H. S. (1936). Trait-names: A psycho-lexical study. *Psychological Monographs, 47*(1). (p. 614)

Altman, L. K. (2004, November 24). Female cases of HIV found rising worldwide. *New York Times* (www.nytimes.com). (p. 559)

Altmeyer, B. (2001). Changes in attitudes toward homosexuals. *Journal of Homosexuality, 42,* 63-75. (p. 492)

Alvarez, L. (2004, December 21). Therapy? or pills? A quandary in Britain. *New York Times* (www.nytimes.com). (p. 715)

Alwin, D. F. (1990). Historical changes in parental orientations to children. In N. Mandell (Ed.), *Sociological studies of child development* (Vol. 3). Greenwich, CT: JAI Press. (p. 124)

Amabile, T. M. (1983). *The social psychology of creativity.* New York: Springer-Verlag. (pp. 429, 633)

Amabile, T. M. (1987). The motivation to be creative. In S. Isaksen (Ed.), *Frontiers in creativity: Beyond the basics.* Buffalo, NY: Bearly Limited. (p. 439)

Amabile, T. M. (1988). From individual creativity to organizational innovation. In K. Gronhaug & G. Kaufmann (Eds.), *Innovation: A crossdisciplinary perspective.* Oslo: Norwegian University Press. (p. 439)

Amabile, T. M., & Hennessey, B. A. (1992). The motivation for creativity in children. In A. K. Boggiano & T. S. Pittman (Eds.), *Achievement and motivation: A social-developmental perspective.* New York: Cambridge University Press. (p. 439)

Ambadar, Z., Schooler, J. W., & Cohn, J. F. (2005). Deciphering the enigmatic face: The importance of facial dynamics in interpreting subtle facial expressions. *Psychological Science, 16,* 403-410. (p. 524)

Ambady, N., Hallahan, M., & Rosenthal, R. (1995). On judging and being judged accurately in zero-acquaintance situations. *Journal of Personality and Social Psychology, 69,* 518-529. (p. 525)

Ambady, N., LaPlante, D., Nguyen. T., Rosenthal, R., & Levinson, W. (2002). Surgeon's tone of voice: A clue to malpractice history. *Surgery, 132,* 5-9. (p. 621)

Ambady, N., & Rosenthal, R. (1992). Thin slices of expressive behavior as predictors of interpersonal consequences: A meta-analysis. *Psychological Bulletin, 111,* 256-274. (p. 621)

Ambady, N., & Rosenthal, R. (1993). Half a minute: Predicting teacher evaluations from thin slices of nonverbal behavior and physical attractiveness. *Journal of Personality and Social Psychology, 64,* 431-441. (p. 621)

Amedi, A., Floel, A., Knect, S., Zohary, E., & Cohen, L. (2004). Transcranial magnetic stimulation of the occipital pole interferes with verbal processing in blind subjects. *Nature Neuroscience, 7,* 1266-1270. (p. 83)

Amen, D. G., Stubblefield, M., Carmichael, B., & Thisted, R. (1996). Brain SPECT findings and aggressiveness. *Annals of Clinical Psychiatry, 8,* 129-137. (p. 749)

American Enterprise (1992, January/February). Women, men, marriages & ministers. p.106. (p. 123)

American Psychiatric Association. (1994). *Diagnostic and statistical manual of mental disorders (Fourth Edition).* Washington, DC: American Psychiatric Press. (p. 452)

American Psychological Association. (1991). Medical cost offset. Washington, DC: American Psychological Association Practice Directorate. (pp. 703-704)

American Psychological Association. (1992). Ethical principles of psychologists and code of conduct. *American Psychologist, 47,* 1597-1611. (p. 48)

American Psychological Association. (2002). *Ethical principles of psychologists and code of conduct.* Washington, DC: American Psychological Association. (p. 48)

American Psychological Association. (2003). *Careers for the twenty-first century.* Washington, DC: Author. (pp. A-9, 13)

American Psychological Association. (2004). Roper v. Simmons. Synopsis at http://www.apa.org/psyclaw/roper-v-simmons.html. (p. 167)

American Psychological Association. (2005). *Graduate study in psychology.* Washington, DC: Author. (p. A-9)

Andersen, R. E., Crespo, C. J., Bartlett, S. J., Cheskin, L. J., & Pratt, M. (1998). Relationship of physical activity and television watching with body weight and level of fatness among children. *Journal of the American Medical Association, 279,* 938-942. (p. 590)

Andersen, S. M. (1998). Service Learning: A National Strategy for Youth Development. A position paper issued by the Task Force on Education Policy. Washington, DC: Institute for Communitarian Policy Studies, George Washington University. (p. 170)

Anderson, A. K., & Phelps, E. A. (2000). Expression without recognition: Contributions of the human amygdala to emotional communication. *Psychological Science, 11,* 106-111. (p. 73)

Anderson, B. L. (2002). Biobehavioral outcomes following psychological interventions for cancer patients. *Journal of Consulting and Clinical Psychology, 70,* 590-610. (p. 560)

Anderson, C. A. (2004a). An update on the effects of playing violent video games. *Journal of Adolescence, 27,* 113-122. (pp. 754, 755-756)

Anderson, C. A., & Anderson, D. C. (1984). Ambient temperature and violent crime: Tests of the linear and curvilinear hypotheses. *Journal of Personality and Social Psychology, 46,* 91-97. (p. 751)

Anderson, C. A., Anderson, K. B., Dorr, N., DeNeve, K. M., & Flanagan, M. (2000). Temperature and aggression. In M. P. Zanna (Ed.), *Advances in Experimental Social Psychology.* San Diego: Academic Press. (p. 751)

Anderson, C. A., Berkowitz, L., Donnerstein, E., Huesmann, L. R., Johnson, J. D., Linz, D., Malamuth, N. M., & Wartella, E. (2003). The influence of media violence on youth. *Psychological Science in the Public Interest, 4*(3), 81-110. (p. 345)

Anderson, C. A., Carnagey, N. L., Flanagan, M., Benjamin, A. J. ,Jr., Eubanks, J., & Valentine, J. C. (2004). Violent video games: Specific effects of violent content on aggressive thoughts and behavior. *Advances in Experimental Social Psychology, 36,* 199-249. (p. 755)

Anderson, C. A., & Dill, K. E. (2000). Video games and aggressive thoughts, feelings, and behavior in the laboratory and in life. *Journal of Personality and Social Psychology, 78,* 772-790. (p. 755)

Anderson, C. A., Lindsay, J. J., & Bushman, B. J. (1999). Research in the psychological laboratory: Truth or triviality? *Current Directions in Psychological Science, 8,* 3-9. (p. 45)

Anderson, I. M. (2000). Selective serotonin reuptake inhibitors versus tricyclic antidepressants: A meta-analysis of efficacy and tolerability. *Journal of Affective Disorders, 58,* 19-36. (p. 713)

Anderson, J. R., Myowa-Yamakoshi, M., & Matsuzawa, T. (2004). Contagious yawning in chimpanzees. *Biology Letters, 271,* S468-S470. (p. 731)

Anderson, R. C., Pichert, J. W., Goetz, E. T., Schallert, D. L., Stevens, K. V., & Trollip, S. R. (1976). Instantiation of general terms. *Journal of Verbal Learning and Verbal Behavior, 15,* 667-679. (p. 371)

Anderson, S. R. (2004). *Doctor Dolittle's delusion: Animals and the uniqueness of human language.* New Haven: Yale University Press. (p. 426)

Andreasen, N. C. (1997). Linking mind and brain in the study of mental illnesses: A project for a scientific psychopathology. *Science, 275,* 1586-1593. (p. 673)

Andreasen, N. C. (2001). *Brave new brain: Conquering mental illness in the era of the genome.* New York: Oxford University Press. (p. 673)

Andreasen, N. C., Arndt, S., Swayze, V., II, Cizadlo, T., & Flaum, M. (1994). Thalamic abnormalities in schizophrenia visualized through magnetic resonance image averaging. *Science, 266,* 294-298. (p. 673)

Andrews, G., Hall, W., Teesson, M., & Henderson, S. (1999, April). *The mental health of Australians.* Canberra: Mental Health Branch, Commonwealth Department of Health and Aged Care. (p. 680)

Angell, M., & Kassirer, J. P. (1998). Alternative medicine: The risks of untested and unregulated remedies. *New England Journal of Medicine, 17,* 839-841. (p. 581)

Angelsen, N. K., Vik, T., Jacobsen, G., & Bakketeig, L. S. (2001). Breast feeding and cognitive development at age 1 and 5 years. *Archives of Disease in Childhood, 85,* 183-188. (p. 36)

Angoff, W. H. (1987). The nature-nurture debate, aptitudes, and group differences. Presidential address to American Psychological Association Division 5. (p. 460)

Angoff, W. H. (1988, Winter). A philosophical discussion: The issues of test and item bias. *ETS Developments*, pp. 10–11. (p. 451)

Anthony, J. C., Warner, L. A., & Kessler, R. C. (1994). Comparative epidemiology of dependence on tobacco, alcohol, controlled substances, and inhalants: Basic findings from the national comorbidity survey. *Experimental and Clinical Psychopharmacology, 2,* 244–268. (p. 577)

Antony, M. M., Brown, T. A., & Barlow, D. H. (1992). Current perspectives on panic and panic disorder. *Current Directions in Psychological Science, 1,* 79–82. (p. 654)

Antrobus, J. (1991). Dreaming: Cognitive processes during cortical activation and high afferent thresholds. *Psychological Review, 98,* 96–121. (p. 288)

APA. (2003, November). *Psychology careers for the twenty-first century.* Washington, DC: American Psychological Association. (p. A-9)

Appleby, D. C. (2002). *The savvy psychology major.* Dubuque, IA: Kendall/Hunt. (p. A-9)

Archer, J. (2004). Sex differences in aggression in real-world settings: A meta-analytic review. *Review of General Psychology, 8,* 291–322. (p. 127)

Arendt, H. (1963). *Eichmann in Jerusalem: A report on the banality of evil.* New York: Viking Press. (p. 170)

Arenson, K. W. (1997, May 4). Romanian woman breaks male grip on top math prize. *New York Times* News Service (in *Grand Rapids Press,* p. A7). (p. 463)

Arent, S. M., Landers, D. M., & Etnier, J. L. (2000). The effects of exercise on mood in older adults: A meta-analytic review. *Journal of Aging and Physical Activity, 8,* 407–430. (p. 569)

Aries, E. (1987). Gender and communication. In P. Shaver & C. Henrick (Eds.), *Review of Personality and Social Psychology, 7,* 149–176. (p. 127)

Armel, K. C., & Ramachandran, V. S. (2003). Projecting sensations to external objects: Evidence from skin conductance response. *Proceedings of the Royal Society of London. Series B. Biological Sciences, 270,* 1499–1506. (p. 226)

Armony, J. L., Quirk, G. J., & LeDoux, J. E. (1998). Differential effects of amygdala lesions on early and late plastic components of auditory cortex spike trains during fear conditioning. *Journal of Neuroscience, 18,* 2592–2601. (p. 655)

Arnett, J. J. (1999). Adolescent storm and stress, reconsidered. *American Psychologist, 54,* 317–326. (p. 165)

Arnett, J. J. (2000). Emerging adulthood: A theory of development from the late teens through the twenties. *American Psychologist, 55,* 469–480. (p. 174)

Arnold, K., & Horrigan, K. (2002). Gaining admission into the graduate program of your choice. *Eye on Psi Chi,* 30–33. (pp. A-8, A-9)

Aron, A., Melinat, E., Aron, E. N., Vallone, R. D., & Bator, R. J. (1997). The experimental generation of interpersonal closeness: A procedure and some preliminary findings. *Personality and Social Psychology Bulletin, 23,* 363–377. (p. 764)

Aronow, E., Reznikoff, M., & Moreland, K. (1995). The Rorschach: Projective technique or psychometric test? *Journal of Personality Assessment, 64,* 213–228. (p. 603)

Aronson, E. (2001, April 13). Newsworthy violence. E-mail to SPSP discussion list, drawing from *Nobody Left to Hate.* New York: Freeman, 2000. (p. 173)

Arrigo, J. M., & Pezdek, K. (1997). Lessons from the study of psychogenic amnesia. *Current Directions in Psychology, 6,* 148–152. (p. 605)

Arseneault, L., Cannon, M., Poulton, R., Murray, R., Caspi, A., & Moffitt, T. E. (2002). Cannabis use in adolescence and risk for adult psychosis: Longitudinal prospective study. *British Medical Journal, 325,* 1212–1213. (p. 303)

Asch, S. E. (1955). Opinions and social pressure. *Scientific American, 193,* 31–35. (p. 732)

Aserinsky, E. (1988, January 17). Personal communication. (p. 276)

ASHA. (2003). STD statistics. American Social Health Association (www.ashastd.org/stdfaqs/statistics.html). (p. 486)

Ashtari, M., Kumra, S., Clarke, T., Ardekani, B., Bhaskar, S., & Rhinewine, J. (2004, November 29). Diffusion tensor imaging of children with attention deficit/hyperactivity disorder. Paper presented to the Radiological Society of North America convention. (p. 641)

Ashton, M. C., Lee, K., & Goldberg, L. R. (2004). A hierarchical analysis of 1,710 English personality-descriptive adjectives. *Journal of Personality and Social Psychology, 87,* 707–721. (p. 619)

Assanand, S., Pinel, J. P. J., & Lehman, D. R. (1998). Personal theories of hunger and eating. *Journal of Applied Social Psychology, 28,* 998–1015. (p. 476)

Associated Press. (1999, April 26). Airline passengers mistakenly told plane would crash. *Grand Rapids Press,* p. A3. (p. 549)

Astin, A. W., Parrott, S. A., Korn, W. S., & Sax, L. J. (1997). *The American freshman: Thirty year trends, 1966-1996.* Los Angeles, CA: Higher Education Research Institute, UCLA. (p. 304)

Atkinson, R. (1988). *The teenage world: Adolescent self-image in ten countries.* New York: Plenum Press. (p. 122)

Atkinson, R. C., & Schiffrin, R. M. (1968). Human memory: A control system and its control processes. In K. Spence (Ed.), *The psychology of learning and motivation* (Vol. 2). New York: Academic Press. (p. 351)

Atkinson, T. (2000). Master's and myths. *Eye on Psi Chi,* 19–25. (p. A-9)

Atwell, R. H. (1986, July 28). Drugs on campus: A perspective. *Higher Education & National Affairs,* p. 5. (p. 299)

Atwood, K. C., IV (2003, September/October). The ongoing problem with the National Center for Complementary and Alternative Medicine. *Skeptical Inquirer,* pp. 23–29. (p. 580)

Au, T. K., Knightly, L. M., Jun, S-A., & Oh, J. S. (2002). Overhearing a language during childhood. *Psychological Science, 13,* 238–242. (p. 416)

Aubrecht, L. (2001). What can you do with a BA in psychology? *Eye on Psi Chi,* 29–31. (p. A-9)

August, D., & Hakuta, K. (Ed.), *Educating language-minority children.* Washington, DC: National Academy of Sciences. (p. 420)

Austin, E. J., Deary, I. J., Whiteman, M. C., Fowkes, F. G. R., Pedersen, N. L., Rabbitt, P., Bent, N., & McInnes, L. (2002). Relationships between ability and personality: Does intelligence contribute positively to personal and social adjustment? *Personality and Individual Differences, 32,* 1391–1411. (p. 453)

Australian Bureau of Statistics. (1999). *Australia now—A statistical profile: Health—overweight and obesity* (www.abs.gov.au). (p. 587)

Australian Social Trends, (1995). Health risk factors: Alcohol use. Australian Bureau of Statistics, 4102. (p. 307)

Averill, J. R. (1983). Studies on anger and aggression: Implications for theories of emotion. *American Psychologist, 38,* 1145–1160. (p. 535)

Averill, J. R. (1993). William James's other theory of emotion. In M. E. Donnelly (Ed.), *Reinterpreting the legacy of William James.* Washington, DC: American Psychological Association. (p. 519)

Avery, R. D., & others. (1994, December 13). Mainstream science on intelligence. *Wall Street Journal,* p. A-18. (p. 459)

Avis, N. E. (2003). Depression during the menopausal transition. *Psychology of Women Quarterly, 27,* 91–100. (p. 176)

Ax, A. F. (1953). The physiological differentiation of fear and anger in humans. *Psychosomatic Medicine, 15,* 433–442. (p. 518)

Azar, B. (1998, June). Why can't this man feel whether or not he's standing up? *APA Monitor* (www.apa.org/monitor/jun98/touch.html). (p. 234)

Babad, E., Bernieri, F., & Rosenthal, R. (1991). Students as judges of teachers' verbal and nonverbal behavior. *American Educational Research Journal, 28,* 211–234. (p. 527)

Babyak, M., Blumenthal, J. A., Herman, S., Khatri, P., Doraiswamy, M., Moore, K., Craighead, W. W., Baldewics, T. T., & Krishnan, K. R. (2000). Exercise treatment for major depression: Maintenance of therapeutic benefit at ten months. *Psychosomatic Medicine, 62,* 633–638. (p. 569)

Bachman, J., Wadsworth, K., O'Malley, P., Johnston, L., & Schulenberg, J. (1997). *Smoking, drinking, and drug use in young adulthood: The impact of new freedoms and new responsibilities.* Mahwah, NJ: Erlbaum. (p. 306)

Backman, L., & Dixon, R. A. (1992). Psychological compensation: A theoretical framework. *Psychological Bulletin, 112,* 259–283. (p. 223)

Backus, J. (1977). *The acoustical foundations of music* (2nd ed.). New York: Norton. (p. 218)

Baddeley, A. (1992). Working memory. *Science, 255,* 556–569. (p. 352)

Baddeley, A. (1998). *Human memory: Theory and practice, revised edition.* Boston: Allyn and Bacon. (p. 352)

Baddeley, A. D. (1982). *Your memory: A user's guide.* New York: Macmillan. (p. 354)

Baddeley, A. D. (2001). Is working memory still working? *American Psychologist, 56,* 849–864. (p. 348, 352)

Baddeley, A. D. (2002, June). Is working memory still working? *European Psychologist, 7,* 85–97. (p. 352)

Bagemihl, B. (1999). *Biological exuberance: Animal homosexuality and natural diversity.* New York: St. Martins. (p. 489)

Bahrick, H. P. (1984). Semantic memory content in permastore: 50 years of memory for Spanish learned in school. *Journal of Experimental Psychology: General, 111,* 1–29. (pp. 377–378)

Bahrick, H. P., Bahrick, L. E., Bahrick, A. S., & Bahrick, P. E. (1993). Maintenance of foreign language vocabulary and the spacing effect. *Psychological Science, 4,* 316–321. (p. 355)

Bahrick, H. P., Bahrick, P. O., & Wittlinger, R. P. (1975). Fifty years of memory for names and faces: A cross-sectional approach. *Journal of Experimental Psychology: General, 104,* 54–75. (p. 370)

Bailey, J. M., Gaulin, S., Agyei, Y., & Gladue, B. A. (1994). Effects of gender and sexual orientation on evolutionary relevant aspects of human mating psychology. *Journal of Personality and Social Psychology, 66,* 1081–1093. (p. 110)

Bailey, J. M., Kirk, K. M., Zhu, G., Dunne, M. P., & Martin, N. G. (2000). Do individual differences in sociosexuality represent genetic or environmentally contingent strategies? Evidence from the Australian twin registry. *Journal of Personality and Social Psychology, 78,* 537–545. (p. 110)

Bailey, J. M., & Zucker, K. J. (1995). Childhood sex-typed behavior and sexual orientation: A conceptual analysis and quantitative review. *Developmental Psychology, 31,* 43–55. (p. 487)

Baillargeon, R. (1995). A model of physical reasoning in infancy. In C. Rovee-Collier & L. P. Lipsitt (Eds.), *Advances in infancy research* (Vol. 9). Stamford, CT: Ablex. (p. 149)

Baillargeon, R. (1998). Infants' understanding of the physical world. In M. Sabourin, F. I. M. Craik, & M. Roberts (Eds.), *Advances in psychological science, Vol. 2: Biological and cognitive aspects.* Hove, England: Psychology Press. (p. 149)

Baillargeon, R. (2004). Infants' physical world. *Current Directions in Psychological Science, 13,* 89–94. (p. 149)

Bairagi, R. (1987). Food crises and female children in rural Bangladesh. *Social Science, 72,* 48–51. (p. 745)

Baker, E. L. (1987). The state of the art of clinical hypnosis. *International Journal of Clinical and Experimental Hypnosis, 35,* 203–214. (p. 292)

Baker, M. C. (2001). *The atoms of language: The mind's hidden rules of grammar.* New York: Basic Books. (p. 414)

Baker, T. B., Piper, M. E., McCarthy, D. E., Majeskie, M. R., & Fiore, M. C. (2004). Addiction motivation reformulated: An affective processing model of negative reinforcement. *Psychological Review, 111,* 33–51. (p. 329)

Baker-Ward, L., Gordon, B. N., Ornstein, P. A., Larus, D. M., & Clubb, P. A. (1993). Young children's long-term retention of a pediatric examination. *Child Development, 64,* 1519–1533. (p. 386)

Bakermans-Kranenburg, M. J., van Ijzendoorn, M. H., & Juffer, F. (2003). Less is more: Meta-analyses of sensitivity and attachment interventions in early childhood. *Psychological Bulletin, 129,* 195–215. (p. 157)

Ballard, M. E., & Wiest, J. R. (1998). Mortal Kombat: The effects of violent videogame play on males' hostility and cardiovascular responding. *Journal of Applied Social Psychology, 26,* 717–730. (p. 755)

Baltes, P. B. (1993). The aging mind: Potential and limits. *The Gerontologist, 33,* 580–594. (p. 184)

Baltes, P. B. (1994). Life-span developmental psychology: On the overall landscape of human development. Invited address, American Psychological Association convention. (p. 184)

Baltes, P. B., & Baltes, M. M. (1999, September-October). Harvesting the fruits of age: Growing older, growing wise. *Science and the Spirit,* pp. 11–14. (p. 184)

Bancroft, J., Loftus, J., & Long, J. S. (2003). Distress about sex: A national survey of women in heterosexual relationships. *Archives of Sexual Behavior, 32,* 193–208. (p. 482)

Bandura, A. (1982). The psychology of chance encounters and life paths. *American Psychologist, 37,* 747–755. (p. 186)

Bandura, A. (1986). *Social foundations of thought and action: A social-cognitive theory.* Englewood Cliffs, NJ: Prentice-Hall. (p. 623)

Bandura, A. (2001). Social cognitive theory: An agentic perspective. *Annual Review of Psychology, 52,* 1–26. (p. 623)

Bandura, A. (2005). The evolution of social cognitive theory. In K. G. Smith & M. A. Hitt (Eds.), *Great minds in management: The process of theory development.* Oxford: Oxford University Press. (pp. 343, 623)

Bandura, A., Ross, D., & Ross, S. A. (1961). Transmission of aggression through imitation of aggressive models. *Journal of Abnormal and Social Psychology, 63,* 575–582. (p. 343)

Barber, T. X. (2000). A deeper understanding of hypnosis: Its secrets, its nature, its essence. *American Journal of Clinical Hypnosis, 42,* 208–272. (p. 294)

Barbour, D. L., & Wang, X. (2003). Contrast tuning in auditory cortex. *Science, 299,* 1073–1075. (p. 220)

Barinaga, M. (1991). How long is the human life-span? *Science, 254,* 936–938. (p. 178)

Barinaga, M. (1992a). The brain remaps its own contours. *Science, 258,* 216–218. (p. 83)

Barinaga, M. (1992b). How scary things get that way. *Science, 258,* 887–888. (p. 534)

Barinaga, M. (1997). Visual system provides clues to how the brain perceives. *Science, 275,* 1583–1585. (p. 210)

Barinaga, M. (1999). Salmon follow watery odors home. *Science, 286,* 705–706. (p. 233)

Barinaga, M. B. (1997). How exercise works its magic. *Science, 276,* 1325. (p. 570)

Barker, S. L., Funk, S. C., & Houston, B. K. (1988). Psychological treatment versus nonspecific factors: A meta-analysis of conditions that engender comparable expectations for improvement. *Clinical Psychology Review, 8,* 579–594. (p. 707)

Barkley, R. A., & 74 others (2002). International consensus statement (January 2002). *Clinical Child and Family Psychology Review, 5,* 2. (p. 641)

Barlow, D. H. (1988). *Anxiety and its disorders: The nature and treatment of anxiety and panic.* New York: Guilford. (p. 655)

Barnes, M. L., & Sternberg, R. J. (1989). Social intelligence and decoding of nonverbal cues. *Intelligence, 13,* 263–287. (p. 525)

Barnett, P. A., & Gotlib, I. H. (1988). Psychosocial functioning and depression: Distinguishing among antecedents, concomitants, and consequences. *Psychological Bulletin, 104,* 97–126. (p. 666)

Barnier, A. J., & McConkey, K. M. (2004). Defining and identifying the highly hypnotizable person. In M. Heap, R. J. Brown, & D. A. Oakley (Eds.), *High hypnotisability: Theoretical, experimental and clinical issues.* London: Brunner-Routledge. (p. 291)

Baron, R. A. (1988). Negative effects of destructive criticism: Impact on conflict, self-efficacy, and task performance. *Journal of Applied Psychology, 73,* 199–207. (p. 337)

Baron, R. S., Cutrona, C. E., Hicklin, D., Russell, D. W., & Lubaroff, D. M. (1990). Social support and immune function among spouses of cancer patients. *Journal of Personality and Social Psychology, 59,* 344–352. (p. 566)

Baron, R. S., Vandello, J. A., & Brunsman, B. (1996). The forgotten variable in conformity research: Impact of task importance on social influence. *Journal of Personality and Social Psychology, 71,* 915–927. (pp. 733, 734)

Baron-Cohen, S. (2004). *The essential difference: Men, women, and the extreme male brain.* London: Penguin Books. (p. 152)

Baron-Cohen, S. (2005, April 6 and May 19). The assortative mating theory: A talk with Simon Baron-Cohen. *The Edge* (www.edge.org). (p. 152)

Baron-Cohen, S., Leslie, A. M., & Frith, U. (1985). Does the autistic child have a "theory of mind"? *Cognition, 21,* 37–46. (p. 151)

Barr, R. (1991, October). In *The Evening Standard,* 9. (p. 388)

Barrett, L. F., Lane, R. D., Sechrest, L., & Schwartz, G. E. (2000). Sex differences in emotional awareness. *Personality and Social Psychology Bulletin, 26,* 1027–1035. (p. 525)

Barry, D. (1995, September 17). Teen smokers, too, get cool, toxic, waste-blackened lungs. *Asbury Park Press,* p. D3. (p. 307)

Barry, D. (1996, August 11). The power to embarrass (syndicated column). (p. 165)

Bartoshuk, L. M. (1993). The wisdom of the body: Using case studies to teach sensation and perception. Paper presented to the National Institute on the Teaching of Psychology, St. Petersburg Beach, Florida. (p. 230)

Baruch, G. K., & Barnett, R. (1986). Role quality, multiple role involvement, and psychological well-being in midlife women. *Journal of Personality and Social Psychology, 51,* 578–585. (p. 189)

Bashore, T. R., Ridderinkhof, K. R., & van der Molen, M. W. (1997). The decline of cognitive processing speed in old age. *Current Directions in Psychological Science, 6,* 163–169. (p. 179)

Baskind, D. E. (1997, December 14). Personal communication, from Delta College. (p. 692)

Bass, L. E., & Kane-Williams, E. (1993). Stereotype or reality: Another look at alcohol and drug use among African American children. U.S. Department of Health and Human Services, *Public Health Reports, 108* (Supplement 1), 78–84. (p. 307)

Bassett, D. R., Schneider, P. L., & Huntington, G. E. (2004). Physical activity in an Old Order Amish community. *Medicine and Science in Sports and Exercise, 36,* 79–85. (p. 587)

Bat-Chava, Y. (1993). Antecedents of self-esteem in deaf people: A meta-analytic review. *Rehabilitation Psychology, 38*(4), 221–234. (p. 222)

Bat-Chava, Y. (1994). Group identification and self-esteem of deaf adults. *Personality and Social Psychology Bulletin, 20,* 494–502. (p. 222)

Bauer, P. J. (2002). Long-term recall memory: Behavioral and neuro-developmental changes in the first 2 years of life. *Current Directions in Psychology, 11,* 137–141. (p. 146)

Baum, A., & Posluszny, D. M. (1999). Health psychology: Mapping biobehavioral contributions to health and illness. *Annual Review of Psychology, 50,* 137–163. (p. 559)

Baumeister, R. (2005). *The cultural animal: Human nature, meaning, and social life.* New York: Oxford University Press. (p. 119)

Baumeister, R. F. (1989). The optimal margin of illusion. *Journal of Social and Clinical Psychology, 8,* 176–189. (pp. 403, 636)

Baumeister, R. F. (1996). Should schools try to boost self-esteem? Beware the dark side. *American Educator, 20,* 14019, 43. (p. 635)

Baumeister, R. F. (2000). Gender differences in erotic plasticity: The female sex drive as socially flexible and responsive. *Psychological Bulletin, 126,* 347–374. (p. 488)

Baumeister, R. F. (2001, April). Violent pride: Do people turn violent because of self-hate, or self-love? *Scientific American,* pp. 96–101. (pp. 539, 635)

Baumeister, R. F., & Bratslavsky, E. (1999). Passion, intimacy, and time: Passionate love as a function of change in intimacy. *Personality and social Psychology Review, 3,* 49–67. (p. 764)

Baumeister, R. F., Bratslavsky, E., Finkenauer, C. & others. (2001). Bad is stronger than good. *Review of General Psychology, 5,* 323–370. (p. 539)

Baumeister, R. F., Campbell, J., Krueger, J. I., & Vohs, K. D. (2003). Does high self-esteem cause better performance, interpersonal success, happiness, or healthier lifestyles? *Psychological Science in the Public Interest, 4*(1), 1–44. (p. 632)

Baumeister, R. F., Campbell, J. D., Krueger, J. I., & Vohs, K. D. (2005, January). Exploding the self-esteem myth. *Scientific American,* pp. 84–91. (p. 632)

Baumeister, R. F., Catanese, K. R., & Vohs, K. D. (2001). Is there a gender difference in strength of sex drive? Theoretical views, conceptual distinctions, and a review of relevant evidence. *Personality and Social Psychology Review, 5,* 242–273. (p. 110)

Baumeister, R. F., Dale, K., & Sommer, K. L. (1998). Freudian defense mechanisms and empirical findings in modern personality and social psychology: Reaction formation, projection, displacement, undoing, isolation, sublimation, and denial. *Journal of Personality, 66,* 1081–1125. (p. 606)

Baumeister, R. F., & Exline, J. J. (2000). Self-control, morality, and human strength. *Journal of Social and Clinical Psychology, 19,* 29–42. (p. 625)

Baumeister, R. F., & Leary, M. R. (1995). The need to belong: Desire for interpersonal attachments as a fundamental human motivation. *Psychological Bulletin, 117,* 497–529. (pp. 495, 497)

Baumeister, R. F., Stillwell, A., & Wotman, S. R. (1990). Victim and perpetrator accounts of interpersonal conflict: Autobiographical narratives about anger. *Journal of Personality and Social Psychology, 59,* 994–1005. (p. 537)

Baumeister, R. F., & Tice, D. M. (1986). How adolescence became the struggle for self: A historical transformation of psychological development. In J. Suls & A. G. Greenwald (Eds.), *Psychological perspectives on the self* (Vol. 3). Hillsdale, NJ: Erlbaum. (p. 173)

Baumeister, R. F., Twenge, J. M., & Nuss, C. K. (2002). Effects of social exclusion on cognitive processes: Anticipated aloneness reduces intelligent thought. *Journal of Personality and Social Psychology, 83,* 817–827. (p. 497)

Baumgardner, A. H., Kaufman, C. M., & Levy, P. E. (1989). Regulating affect interpersonally: When low esteem leads to greater enhancement. *Journal of Personality and Social Psychology, 56,* 907–921. (p. 633)

Baumrind, D. (1982). Adolescent sexuality: Comment on Williams' and Silka's comments on Baumrind. *American Psychologist, 37,* 1402–1403. (p. 493)

Baumrind, D. (1996). The discipline controversy revisited. *Family Relations, 45,* 405–414. (p. 162)

Baumrind, D., Larzelere, R. E., & Cowan, P. A. (2002). Ordinary physical punishment: Is it harmful? Comment on Gershoff (2002). *Psychological Bulletin, 128,* 602–611. (p. 332)

Bavelier, D., Newport, E. L., & Supalla, T. (2003). Children need natural languages, signed or spoken. *Cerebrum, 5*(1), 19–32. (pp. 414, 417)

Bavelier, D., Tomann, A., Hutton, C., Mitchell, T., Corina, D., Liu, G., & Neville, H. (2000). Visual attention to the periphery is enhanced in congenitally deaf individuals. *Journal of Neuroscience, 20,* 1–6. (p. 82)

Bayley, P. J., Gold, J. J., Hopkins, R. O., & Squire, L. R. (2005). The neuroanatomy of remote memory. *Neuron, 46,* 799–810. (p. 368)

BBC. (2005, July). Japanese breaks pi memory record. http://news.bbc.co.uk/2/hi/asia-pacific/4644103.stm. (p. 363)

Beaman, A. L., & Klentz, B. (1983). The supposed physical attractiveness bias against supporters of the women's movement: A meta-analysis. *Personality and Social Psychology Bulletin, 9,* 544–550. (p. 762)

Beardsley, L. M. (1994). Medical diagnosis and treatment across cultures. In W. J. Lonner & R. Malpass (Eds.), *Psychology and culture.* Boston: Allyn & Bacon. (p. 642)

Beardsley, T. (1996, July). Waking up. *Scientific American,* pp. 14, 18. (p. 281)

Beauchamp, G. K. (1987). The human preference for excess salt. *American Scientist, 75,* 27–33. (p. 477)

Beck, A. J., Kline, S. A., & Greenfeld, L. A. (1988). Survey of youth in custody, 1987. U.S. Department of Justice, Bureau of Justice Statistics Special Report. (p. 752)

Beck, A. T., Rush, A. J., Shaw, B. F., & Emery, G. (1979). *Cognitive therapy of depression.* New York: Guilford Press. (p. 695)

Beck, A. T., & Steer, R. A. (1989). Clinical predictors of eventual suicide: A 5- to 10-year prospective study of suicide attempters. *Journal of Affective Disorders, 17,* 203–209. (p. 663)

Becklen, R., & Cervone, D. (1983). Selective looking and the noticing of unexpected events. *Memory and Cognition, 11,* 601–608. (p. 238)

Beckman, M. (2004). Crime, culpability, and the adolescent brain. *Science, 305,* 596–599. (p. 167)

Beeman, M. J., & Chiarello, C. (1998). Complementary right- and left-hemisphere language comprehension. *Current Directions in Psychological Science, 7,* 2–8. (p. 88)

Beitman, B. D., Goldfried, M. R., & Norcross, J. C. (1989). The movement toward integrating the psychotherapies: An overview. *American Journal of Psychiatry, 146,* 138–147. (p. 686)

Bell, A. P., Weinberg, M. S., & Hammersmith, S. K. (1981). *Sexual preference: Its development in men and women.* Bloomington: Indiana University Press. (p. 488)

Bell, R. Q., & Waldrop, M. F. (1989). Achievement and cognitive correlates of minor physical anomalies in early development. In M. G. Bornstein & N. A. Krasnegor (Eds.), *Stability and continuity in mental development: Behavioral and biological perspectives.* Hillsdale, NJ: Erlbaum. (p. 450)

Bellugi, U. (1994, August). Quoted in P. Radetsky, Silence, signs, and wonder. *Discover,* pp. 60–68. (p. 411)

Beloff, J. (1985, Spring). Science, religion and the paranormal. *Free Inquiry,* pp. 36–41 (p. 268)

Belsher, G., & Costello, C. G. (1988). Relapse after recovery from unipolar depression: A critical review. *Psychological Bulletin, 104,* 84–96. (p. 661)

Belsky, J. (1990). Parental and nonparental child care and children's socioemotional development: A decade in review. *Journal of Marriage and the Family, 52,* 885–903. (p. 160)

Belsky, J. (2003). The politicized science of day care: A personal and professional odyssey. *Family Policy Review 1(2),* 23–40. (p. 160)

Bem, D. J. (1984). Quoted in *The Skeptical Inquirer, 8,* 194. (p. 267)

Bem, D. J. (1996). Exotic becomes erotic: A developmental theory of sexual orientation. *Psychological Review, 103,* 320–335. (p. 492)

Bem, D. J. (1998). Is EBE theory supported by the evidence? Is it androcentric? A reply to Peplau et al. (1998). *Psychological Review, 105,* 395–398. (p. 492)

Bem, D. J. (2000). Exotic becomes erotic: Interpreting the biological correlates of sexual orientation. *Archives of Sexual Behavior, 29,* 531–548. (p. 492)

Bem, D. J., & Honorton, C. (1994). Does psi exist? Replicable evidence for an anomalous process of information transfer. *Psychological Bulletin, 115,* 4–18. (p. 267)

Bem, D. J., Palmer, J., & Broughton, R. S. (2001). Updating the Ganzfeld database: A victim of its own success? *Journal of Parapsychology, 65,* 207–218. (p. 267)

Bem, S. L. (1987). Masculinity and femininity exist only in the mind of the perceiver. In J. M. Reinisch, L. A. Rosenblum, & S. A. Sanders (Eds.), *Masculinity/femininity: Basic perspectives.* New York: Oxford University Press. (p. 132)

Bem, S. L. (1993). *The lenses of gender.* New Haven: Yale University Press. (p. 132)

Ben-Shakhar, G., & Elaad, E. (2003). The validity of psychophysiological detection of information with the guilt knowledge test: A meta-analytic review. *Journal of Applied Psychology, 88,* 131–151. (p. 521)

Benbow, C. P., Lubinski, D., Shea, D. L., & Eftekhari-Sanjani, H. (2000). Sex differences in mathematical reasoning ability at age 13: Their status 20 years later. *Psychological Science, 11,* 474–2000. (p. 463)

Bennett, R. (1991, February). Pornography and extrafamilial child sexual abuse: Examining the relationship. Unpublished manuscript, Los Angeles Police Department Sexually Exploited Child Unit. (p. 753)

Bennett, W. I. (1995). Beyond overeating. *New England Journal of Medicine, 332,* 673–674. (p. 590)

Benson, H. (1996). *Timeless healing: The power and biology of belief.* New York: Scribner. (p. 571)

Benson, K., & Feinberg, I. (1977). The beneficial effect of sleep in an extended Jenkins and Dallenbach paradigm. *Psychophysiology, 14,* 375–384. (p. 380)

Benson, P. L. (1992, Spring). Patterns of religious development in adolescence and adulthood. *PIRI Newsletter,* 2–9. (p. 128)

Benson, P. L., Sharma, A. R., & Roehlkepartain, E. C. (1994). *Growing up adopted: A portrait of adolescents and their families.* Minneapolis: Search Institute. (p. 101)

Berenbaum, S. A., & Bailey, J. M. (2003). Effects on gender identity of prenatal androgens and genital appearance: Evidence from girls with congenital adrenal hyperplasia. *Journal of Clinical Endocrinology and Metabolism, 88,* 1102–1106. (p. 130)

Berenbaum, S. A., & Hines, M. (1992). Early androgens are related to childhood sex-typed toy preferences. *Psychological Science, 3,* 203–206. (p. 130)

Berenbaum, S. A., Korman, K., & Leveroni, C. (1995). Early hormones and sex differences in cognitive abilities. *Learning and Individual Differences, 7,* 303–321. (p. 463)

Berger, B. G., & Motl, R. W. (2000). Exercise and mood: A selective review and synthesis of research employing the profile of mood states. *Journal of Applied Sports Psychology, 12,* 69–92. (p. 569)

Bergin, A. E. (1980). Psychotherapy and religious values. *Journal of Consulting and Clinical Psychology, 48,* 95–105. (p. 709)

Bergsholm, P., Larsen, J. L., Rosendahl, K., & Holsten, F. (1989). Electroconvulsive therapy and cerebral computed tomography. *Acta Psychiatrica Scandinavia, 80,* 566–572. (p. 715)

Berk, L. E. (1994, November). Why children talk to themselves. *Scientific American,* pp. 78–83. (p. 153)

Berk, L. S., Felten, D. L., Tan, S. A., Bittman, B. B., & Westengard, J. (2001). Modulation of neuroimmune parameters during the eustress of humor-associated mirthful laughter. *Alternative Therapies, 7,* 62–76. (p. 565)

Berkel, J., & de Waard, F. (1983). Mortality pattern and life expectancy of Seventh Day Adventists in the Netherlands. *International Journal of epidemiology, 12,* 455–459. (p. 573)

Berkowitz, L. (1983). Aversively stimulated aggression: Some parallels and differences in research with animals and humans. *American Psychologist, 38,* 1135–1144. (p. 751)

Berkowitz, L. (1989). Frustration-aggression hypothesis: Examination and reformulation. *Psychological Bulletin, 106,* 59–73. (p. 751)

Berkowitz, L. (1990). On the formation and regulation of anger and aggression: A cognitive-neoassociationistic analysis. *American Psychologist, 45,* 494–503. (p. 535)

Berman, M., Gladue, B., & Taylor, S. (1993). The effects of hormones, Type A behavior pattern, and provocation on aggression in men. *Motivation and Emotion, 17,* 125–138. (p. 750)

Berndt, T. J. (1992). Friendship and friends' influence in adolescence. *Current Directions in Psychological Science, 1,* 156–159. (p. 129)

Bernhardt, P. C., Dabbs, J. M., Jr., Fielden, J. A., & Lutter, C. D. (1998). Testosterone changes during vicarious experiences of winning and losing among fans at sporting events. *Physiology and Behavior, 65,* 59–62. (p. 750)

Bernstein, D. M., Atance, C., Loftus, G. R., & Meltzoff, A. (2004). We saw it all along: Visual hindsight bias in children and adults. *Psychological Science, 15,* 264–267. (p. 21)

Bernstsen, D., & Thomsen, D. K. (2005). Personal memories for remote historical events: Accuracy and clarity of flashbulb memories related to World War II. *Journal of Experimental Psychology: General, 134,* 242–257. (p. 350)

Berridge, K. C., & Winkielman, P. (2003). What is an unconscious emotion? (The case of unconscious "liking"). *Cognition and Emotion, 17,* 181–211. (p. 522)

Berry, D. S., & McArthur, L. Z. (1986). Perceiving character in faces: The impact of age-related craniofacial changes on social perception. *Psychological Bulletin, 100*, 3–18. (p. 320)

Berscheid, E. (1981). An overview of the psychological effects of physical attractiveness and some comments upon the psychological effects of knowledge of the effects of physical attractiveness. In G. W. Lucker, K. Ribbens, & J. A. McNamara (Eds.), *Psychological aspects of facial form (Craniofacial growth series)*. Ann Arbor: Center for Human Growth and Development, University of Michigan. (p. 760)

Berscheid, E. (1985). Interpersonal attraction. In G. Lindzey & E. Aronson (Eds.), *The handbook of social psychology*. New York: Random House. (p. 495)

Berscheid, E., Gangestad, S. W., & Kulakowski, D. (1984). Emotion in close relationships: Implications for relationship counseling. In S. D. Brown & R. W. Lent (Eds.), *Handbook of counseling psychology*. New York: Wiley. (p. 763)

Bértolo, H., Paiva, T., Pessoa, L., Mestre, T., Marques, R., & Santos, R. (2003). Visual dream content, graphical representation and EEG alpha activity in congenitally blind subjects. *Cognitive Brain Research, 15*, 277–284. (p. 286)

Besson, M., Faita, F., Peretz, I., Bonnel, A.-M., & Requin, J. (1998). Singing in the brain: Independence of lyrics and tunes. *Psychological Science, 9*, 494–498. (p. 77)

Bettencourt, B. A., & Dorr, N. (1997). Collective self-esteem as a mediator of the relationship between allocentrism and subjective well-being. *Personality and Social Psychology Bulletin, 23*, 955–964. (p. 122)

Bettencourt, B. A., & Kernahan, C. (1997). A meta-analysis of aggression in the presence of violent cues: Effects of gender differences and aversive provocation. *Aggressive Behavior, 23*, pp. 447–457. (p. 127)

Beyerstein, B., & Beyerstein, D. (Eds.) (1992). *The write stuff: Evaluations of graphology*. Buffalo, NY: Prometheus Books. (p. 616)

Bhatt, R. S., Wasserman, E. A., Reynolds, W. F., Jr., & Knauss, K. S. (1988). Conceptual behavior in pigeons: Categorization of both familiar and novel examples from four classes of natural and artificial stimuli. *Journal of Experimental Psychology: Animal Behavior Processes, 14*, 219–234. (p. 328)

Bialystok, E. (2001). *Bilingualism in development, language, literacy, and cognition*. New York: Cambridge University Press. (p. 420)

Bickman, L. (1999). Practice makes perfect and other myths about mental health services. *American Psychologist, 54*, 965–978. (p. 704)

Biederman, J., Wilens, T., Mick, E., Spencer, T., & Faraone, S. V. (1999). Pharmacotherapy of Attention-Deficit/Hyperactivity Disorder reduces risk for substance use disorder. *Pediatrics, 104*, 1–5. (p. 641)

Biello, S. M., & Dafters, R. I. (2001). MDMA and fenfluramine alter the response of the circadian clock to a serotonin agonist in vitro. *Brain Research, 920*, 202–209. (p. 302)

Biggs, V. (2001, April 13). Murder suspect captured in Grand Marais. *Cook County News-Herald*. (p. 525)

Bigler, E. D., Johnson, S. C., Jackson, C., & Blatter, D. D. (1995). Aging, brain size, and IQ. *Intelligence, 21*, 109–119. (p. 440)

Binet, A., & Simon, T. (1905; reprinted 1916). New methods for the diagnosis of the intellectual level of subnormals. In A. Binet & T. Simon, *The development of intelligence in children*. Baltimore: Williams & Wilkins. (p. 443)

Birch, S. A. J. (2005). When knowledge is a curse: Children's and adults' reasoning about mental states. *Current Directions in Psychological Science, 14*, 25–29. (p. 151)

Birnbaum, S. G., Yuan, P. X., Wang, M., Vijayraghavan, S., Bloom, A. K., Davis, D. J., Gobeski, K. T., Sweatt, J. D., Manhi, H. K., & Arnsten, A. F. T. (2004). Protein kinase C overactivity impairs prefrontal cortical regulation of working memory. *Science, 306*, 882–884. (p. 366)

Bishop, B. (2004, November 22). Personal correspondence, and earlier articles on "The great divide" in the *Austin Statesman*. (p. 740)

Bishop, G. D. (1991). Understanding the understanding of illness: Lay disease representations. In J. A. Skelton & R. T. Croyle (Eds.), *Mental representation in health and illness*. New York: Springer-Verlag. (p. 397)

Biswas-Diener, R., & Diener, E. (2001). Making the best of a bad situation: Satisfaction in the slums of Calcutta. *Social Indicators Research, 55*, 329–352. (p. 540)

Bjork, R. A. (1999). Assessing our own competence: Heuristics and illusions. In D. Gopher & A. Koriat (Eds.), *Attention and performance XVII. Cognitive regulation of performance: Interaction of theory and application*. Cambridge, MA: MIT Press. (p. 355)

Bjork, R. A. (2000, July/August). Toward one world of psychological science. *APS Observer*, p. 3. (p. 8)

Bjorklund, D. F., & Green, B. L. (1992). The adaptive nature of cognitive immaturity. *American Psychologist, 47*, 46–54. (p. 154)

Blackmore, S. (1991, Fall). Near-death experiences: In or out of the body? *Skeptical Inquirer*, pp. 34–45. (p. 309)

Blackmore, S. (1993). *Dying to live*. Amherst, NY: Prometheus Books. (p. 309)

Blackmore, S. (1999). *The meme machine*. Oxford: Oxford University Press. (p. 341)

Blackmore, S. (2000, October). The power of memes. *Scientific American*, pp. 63–73. (p. 341)

Blakemore, S-J., Wolpert, D. M., & Frith, C. D. (1998). Central cancellation of self-produced tickle sensation. *Nature Neuroscience, 1*, 635–640. (p. 225)

Blakeslee, S. (2005, February 8). Focus narrows in search for autism's cause. *New York Times* (www.nytimes.com). (p. 152)

Blanchard, R. (1997). Birth order and sibling sex ratio in homosexual versus heterosexual males and females. *Annual Review of Sex Research, 8*, 27–67. (p. 489)

Blanchard, R. (2001). Fraternal birth order and the maternal immunie hypothesis of male homosexuality. *Hormones and Behavior, 40*, 105–114. (p. 489)

Blanke, O., Landis, T., & Spinelli, L. (2004). Out-of-body experience and autoscopy of neurological origin. *Brain: Journal of Neurology, 127*, 243–258. (p. 309)

Blanke, O., Ortigue, S., Landis, T., & Seeck, M. (2002). Stimulating illusory own-body perceptions. *Nature, 419*, 269–270. (p. 309)

Blankenburg, F., Taskin, B., Ruben, J., Moosmann, M., Ritter, P., Curio, G., & Villringer, A. (2003). Imperceptive stimuli and sensory processing impediment. *Science, 299*, 1864. (p. 201)

Blascovich, J., Seery, M. D., Mugridge, C. A., Norris, R. K., & Weisbuch, M. (2004). Predicting athletic performance from cardiovascular indexes of challenge and threat. *Journal of Experimental Social Psychology, 40*, 683–688. (p. 551)

Blass, T. (1996). Stanley Milgram: A life of inventiveness and controversy. In G. A. Kimble, C. A. Boneau, & M. Wertheimer (Eds.), *Portraits of pioneers in psychology* (Vol. II). Washington, DC and Mahwah, NJ: American Psychological Association and Lawrence Erlbaum Publishers. (p. 735)

Blass, T. (1999). The Milgram paradigm after 35 years: Some things we now know about obedience to authority. *Journal of Applied Social Psychology, 29*, 955–978. (p. 735)

Blatt, S. J., Sanislow, C. A., III, Zuroff, D. C., & Pilkonis, P. (1996). Characteristics of effective therapists: Further analyses of data from the National Institute of Mental Health Treatment of Depression Collaborative Research Program. *Journal of Consulting and clinical Psychology, 64*, 1276–1284. (p. 708)

Bleustein, J. (2002, June 15). Quoted in "Harley retooled," by S. S. Smith, *American Way Magazine*. (p. 510)

Blizzard, R. (2004, August 31). Smoking: Will education overpower addiction? Gallup Poll (www.gallup.com). (p. 575)

Blom, J. M. C., Tamarkin, L., Shiber, J. R., & Nelson, R. J. (1995). Learned immunosuppression is associated with an increased risk of chemically-induced tumors. *Neuroimmunomodulation, 2*, 92–99. (p. 560)

Bloom, B. J. (1964). *Stability and change in human characteristics*. New York: Wiley. (p. 451)

Bloom, B. S. (Ed.). (1985). *Developing talent in young people*. New York: Ballantine. (p. 504)

Bloom, F. E. (1993, January/February). What's new in neurotransmitters. *BrainWork*, pp. 7–9. (p. 58)

Bloom, P. (2000). *How children learn the meanings of words.* Cambridge, MA: MIT Press. (p. 412)

Bloom, S. R. (2002, September/October). Quoted in Researchers identify natural appetite suppressant. *Brain Work.* (p. 476)

Blum, K., Cull, J. G., Braverman, E. R., & Comings, D. E. (1996). Reward deficiency syndrome. *American Scientist, 84,* 132–145. (p. 74)

Boahen, K. (2005, May). Neuromorphic microchips. *Scientific American,* pp. 56–63. (p. 221)

Bock, B. C., Marcus, B. H., King. T. E., Borrelli, B., & Roberts, M. R. (1999). Exercise effects on withdrawal and mood among women attempting smoking cessation. *Addictive Behavior, 24,* 399–410. (p. 579)

Bodenhausen, G. V., Sheppard, L. A., & Kramer, G. P. (1994). Negative affect and social judgment: The differential impact of anger and sadness. *European Journal of Social Psychology, 24,* 45–62. (p. 769)

Bodkin, J. A., & Amsterdam, J. D. (2002). Transdermal selegiline in major depression: A double-blind, placebo-controlled, parallel-group study in outpatients. *American Journal of Psychiatry, 159,* 1869–1875. (p. 713)

Boehm, K. E., Schondel, C. K., Marlowe, A. L., & Manke-Mitchell, L. (1999). Teens' concerns: A national evaluation. *Adolescence, 34,* 523–528. (p. 172)

Boesch-Achermann, H., & Boesch, C. (1993). Tool use in wild chimpanzees: New light from dark forests. *Current Directions in Psychological Science, 2,* 18–21. (p. 423)

Bogaert, A. F. (2003). Number of older brothers and sexual orientation: New texts and the attraction/behavior distinction in two national probability samples. *Journal of Personality and Social Psychology, 84,* 644–652. (p. 489)

Bogaert, A. F. (2004). Asexuality: Prevalence and associated factors in a national probability sample. *Journal of Sex Research, 41,* 279–287. (p. 481)

Bogaert, A. F., Friesen, C., & Klentrou, P. (2002). Age of puberty and sexual orientation in a national probability sample. *Archives of Sexual Behavior, 31,* 73–81. (p. 489)

Boggiano, A. K., Barrett, M., Weiher, A. W., McClelland, G. H., & Lusk, C. M. (1987). Use of the maximal-operant principle to motivate children's intrinsic interest. *Journal of Personality and Social Psychology, 53,* 866–879. (p. 335)

Boggiano, A. K., Harackiewicz, J. M., Bessette, M. M., & Main, D. S. (1985). Increasing children's interest through performance-contingent reward. *Social Cognition, 3,* 400–411. (p. 335)

Bogin, B. (1998, February). The tall and the short of it (range of height in humans demonstrates plasticity of human species). *Discover.* (p. 459)

Bohman, M., & Sigvardsson, S. (1990). Outcome in adoption: Lessons from longitudinal studies. In D. Brodzinsky & M. Schechter (Eds.), *The psychology of adoption.* New York: Oxford University Press. (p. 101)

Bolger, N., DeLongis, A., Kessler, R. C., & Schilling, E. A. (1989). Effects of daily stress on negative mood. *Journal of Personality and Social Psychology, 57,* 808–818. (p. 538)

Bonanno, G. A. (2001). Grief and emotion: Experience, expression, and dissociation. In M. Stroebe, W. Stroebe, R. O. Hansson, & H. Schut (Eds.), *New handbook of bereavement: Consciousness, coping, and care.* Cambridge: Cambridge University Press. (p. 191)

Bonanno, G. A. (2004). Loss, trauma, and human resilience: Have we underestimated the human capacity to thrive after extremely aversive events? *American Psychologist, 59,* 20–28. (pp. 191, 653)

Bonanno, G. A. (2005). Adult resilience to potential trauma. *Current Directions in Psychological Science, 14,* 135–137. (p. 653)

Bonanno, G. A., & Kaltman, S. (1999). Toward an integrative perspective on bereavement. *Psychological Bulletin, 125,* 760–777. (p. 191)

Bond, C. F., Jr., & DePaulo, B. M. (in press). Accuracy of deception judgments. Unpublished manuscript, Texas Christian University. (p. 527)

Bond, C. F., Jr., Pitre, U., & Van Leeuwen, M. D. (1991). Encoding operations and the next-in-line effect. *Personality and Social Psychology Bulletin, 17,* 435–441. (p. 355)

Bond, M. H. (1988). Finding universal dimensions of individual variation in multi-cultural studies of values: The Rokeach and Chinese values surveys. *Journal of Personality and Social Psychology, 55,* 1009–1015. (p. 122)

Bond, R., & Smith, P. B. (1996). Culture and conformity: A meta-analysis of studies using Asch's (1952b, 1956) line judgment task. *Psychological Bulletin, 119,* 111–137. (p. 734)

Boneva, B. S., & Frieze, I. H. (2001). Toward a concept of a migrant personality. *Journal of Social Issues, 57,* 477–491. (p. 122)

Bono, J. E., & Judge, T. A. (2004). Personality and transformational and transactional leadership: A meta-analysis. *Journal of Applied Psychology, 89,* 901–910. (p. 509)

Bookheimer, S. H., Strojwas, M. H., Cohen, M. S., Saunders, A. M., Pericak-Vance, M. A., Mazziotta, J. C., & Small, G. W. (2000). Patterns of brain activation in people at risk for Alzheimer's disease. *New England Journal of Medicine, 343,* 450–456. (p. 181)

Booth, F. W., & Neufer, P. D. (2005). Exercise controls gene expression. *American Scientist, 93,* 28–35. (pp. 570, 587)

Boring, E. G. (1930). A new ambiguous figure. *American Journal of Psychology, 42,* 444–445. (p. 257)

Borkenau, P., Mauer, N., Riemann, R., Spinath, F. M., & Angleitner, A. (2004). Thin slices of behavior as cues of personality and intelligence. *Journal of Personality and Social Psychology, 86,* 599–614. (p. 622)

Bornstein, M. H., Cote, L. R., Maital, S., Painter, K., Park, S-Y., Pascual, L., Pecheux, M-G., Ruel, J., Venute, P., & Vyt, A. (2004). Cross-linguistic analysis of vocabulary in young children: Spanish, Dutch, French, Hebrew, Italian, Korean, and American English. *Child Development, 75,* 1115–1139. (p. 414)

Bornstein, M. H., Tal, J., Rahn, C., Galperin, C. Z., Pecheux, M-G., Lamour, M., Toda, S., Azuma, H., Ogino, M., & Tamis-LeMonda, C. S. (1992a). Functional analysis of the contents of maternal speech to infants of 5 and 13 months in four cultures: Argentina, France, Japan, and the United States. *Developmental Psychology, 28,* 593–603. (p. 125)

Bornstein, M. H., Tamis-LeMonda, C. S., Tal, J., Ludemann, P., Toda, S., Rahn, C. W., Pecheux, M-G., Azuma, H., Vardi, D. (1992b). Maternal responsiveness to infants in three societies: The United States, France, and Japan. *Child Development, 63,* 808–821. (p. 125)

Bornstein, R. F. (1989). Exposure and affect: Overview and meta-analysis of research, 1968–1987. *Psychological Bulletin, 106,* 265–289. (pp. 156, 759)

Bornstein, R. F. (1999). Source amnesia, misattribution, and the power of unconscious perceptions and memories. *Psychoanalytic Psychology, 16,* 155–178. (p. 759)

Bornstein, R. F. (2001). The impending death of psychoanalysis. *Psychoanalytic Psychology, 18,* 3–20. (p. 607)

Bornstein, R. F., Galley, D. J., Leone, D. R., & Kale, A. R. (1991). The temporal stability of ratings of parents: Test-retest reliability and influence of parental contact. *Journal of Social Behavior and Personality, 6,* 641–649. (p. 374)

Boroditsky, R., Fisher, W., & Sand, M. (1995, July). Teenagers and contraception. Section of The Canadian contraception study. *Journal of the Society of Obstetricians and Gynaecologists of Canada,* Special Supplement, pp. 22–25. (p. 485)

Bortfeld, H., Morgan, J. L., Golinkoff, R. M., & Rathbun, K. (2005). Mommy and me: Familiar names help launch babies into speech-stream segmentation. *Psychological Science, 16,* 298–304. (p. 415)

Boscarino, J. A. (1997). Diseases among men 20 years after exposure to severe stress: Implications for clinical research and medical care. *Psychosomatic Medicine, 59,* 605–614. (p. 551)

Bosma, H., Marmot, M. G., Hemingway, H., Nicolson, A. C., Brunner, E., & Stansfeld, S. A. (1997). Low job control and risk of coronary heart disease in Whitehall II (prospective cohort) study. *British Medical Journal, 314,* 558–565. (p. 564)

Bosma, H., Peter, R., Siegrist, J., & Marmot, M. (1998). Two alternative job stress models and the risk of coronary heart disease. *American Journal of Public Health, 88,* 68–74. (p. 564)

Bostwick, J. M., & Pankratz, V. S. (2000). Affective disorders and suicide risk: A re-examination. *American Journal of Psychiatry, 157*, 1925–1932. (p. 662)

Bosworth, R. G., & Dobkins, K. R. (1999). Left-hemisphere dominance for motion processing in deaf signers. *Psychological Science, 10*, 256–262. (p. 83)

Bothwell, R. K., Brigham, J. C., & Malpass, R. S. (1989). Cross-racial identification. *Personality and Social Psychology Bulletin, 15*, 19–25. (p. 747)

Bothwell, R. K., Deffenbacher, K. A., & Brigham, J. C. (1987). Correlation of eyewitness accuracy and confidence: Optimality hypothesis revised. *Journal of Applied Psychology, 72*, 691–695. (p. 385)

Botwin, M. D., Buss, D. M., & Shackelford, T. K. (1997). Personality and mate preferences: Five factors in mate selection and marital satisfaction. *Journal of Personality, 65*, 107–136. (p. 619)

Bouchard, T. J., Jr. (1981, December 6). Interview on *Nova: Twins* [program broadcast by the Public Broadcasting Service]. (p. 100)

Bouchard, T. J., Jr. (1995). Longitudinal studies of personality and intelligence: A behavior genetic and evolutionary psychology perspective. In D. H. Saklofske & M. Zeidner (Eds.), *International handbook of personality and intelligence.* New York: Plenum. (p. 456)

Bouchard, T. J., Jr. (1996a). IQ similarity in twins reared apart: Finding and responses to critics. In R. Sternberg & C. Grigorenko (Eds.), *Intelligence: Heredity and environment.* New York: Cambridge University Press. (pp. 455, 456)

Bouchard, T. J., Jr. (1996b). Behavior genetic studies of intelligence, yesterday and today: The long journey from plausibility to proof. *Journal of Biosocial Science, 28*, 527–555. (p. 456)

Bouchard, T. J., Jr. (2004). Genetic influence on human psychological traits. *Current Directions in Psychological Science, 13*, 148–151. (p. 98)

Bouchard, T. J., Jr., & McGue, M. (1990). Genetic and rearing environmental influences on adult personality: An analysis of adopted twins reared apart. *Journal of Personality, 58*, 263. (p. 100)

Bouton, M. E., Mineka, S., & Barlow, D. H. (2001). A modern learning theory perspective on the etiology of panic disorder. *Psychological Review, 108*, 4–32. (p. 654)

Bowden, E. M., & Beeman, M. J. (1998). Getting the right idea: Semantic activation in the right hemisphere may help solve insight problems. *Psychological Science, 9*, 435–440. (p. 88)

Bower, B. (2003, November 22). Vision seekers. *Science News, 164*, pp. 331, 332. (p. 255)

Bower, G. H. (1983). Affect and cognition. *Philosophical Transaction: Royal Society of London, Series B, 302*, 387–402. (p. 374)

Bower, G. H. (1986). Prime time in cognitive psychology. In P. Eelen (Ed.), *Cognitive research and behavior therapy: Beyond the conditioning paradigm.* Amsterdam: North Holland Publishers. (p. 372)

Bower, G. H., Clark, M. C., Lesgold, A. M., & Winzenz, D. (1969). Hierarchical retrieval schemes in recall of categorized word lists. *Journal of Verbal Learning and Verbal Behavior, 8*, 323–343. (p. 360)

Bower, G. H., & Morrow, D. G. (1990). Mental models in narrative comprehension. *Science, 247*, 44–48. (p. 356)

Bower, J. E., Kemeny, M. E., Taylor, S. E., & Fahey, J. L. (1998). Cognitive processing, discovery of meaning, CD4 decline, and AIDS-related mortality among bereaved HIV-seropositive men. *Journal of Consulting and Clinical Psychology, 66*, 979–986. (p. 559)

Bower, J. M., & Parsons, L. M. (2003, August). Rethinking the "lesser brain." *Scientific American*, pp. 50–57. (p. 72)

Bowers, K. S. (1984). Hypnosis. In N. Endler & J. M. Hunt (Eds.), *Personality and behavioral disorders* (2nd ed.). New York: Wiley. (pp. 291, 293)

Bowers, K. S. (1987, July). Personal communication. (p. 292)

Bowers, T. G., & Clum, G. A. (1988). Relative contribution of specific and nonspecific treatment effects: Meta-analysis of placebo-controlled behavior therapy research. *Psychological Bulletin, 103*, 315–323. (p. 704)

Bowlby, J. (1973). *Separation: Anxiety and anger.* New York: Basic Books. (p. 159)

Bowles, S., & Kasindorf, M. (2001, March 6). Friends tell of picked-on but 'normal' kid. *USA Today*, p. 4A. (p. 497)

Bowman, H. (2003, Fall). Interactions between chimpanzees and their human caregivers in captive settings: The effects of gestural communication on reciprocity. *Friends of Washoe, 25*(1), 7–16. (p. 426)

Boyatzis, C. J., Matillo, G. M., & Nesbitt, K. M. (1995). Effects of the `Mighty Morphin Power Rangers' on children's aggression with peers. *Child Study Journal, 25*, 45–55. (pp. 345–346)

Boynton, R. M. (1979). *Human color vision.* New York: Holt, Rinehart & Winston. (p. 213)

Braden, J. P. (1994). *Deafness, deprivation, and IQ.* New York: Plenum. (pp. 222, 459)

Bradley, D. R., Dumais, S. T., & Petry, H. M. (1976). Reply to Cavonius. *Nature, 261*, 78. (p. 237)

Bradshaw, J. (1990). *Homecoming: Reclaiming and championing your inner child.* New York: Bantam Books. (p. 116)

Brainerd, C. J. (1996). Piaget: A centennial celebration. *Psychological Science, 7*, 191–195. (p. 147)

Brainerd, C. J., & Poole, D. A. (1997). Long-term survival of children's memories: A review. *Learning and Individual Differences, 9*, 125–151. (p. 385)

Brainerd, C. J., & Reyna, V. F. (1998). When things that were never experienced are easier to "remember" than things that were. *Psychological Science, 9*, 484–489. (p. 385)

Brainerd, C. J., & Reyna, V. F. (2002). Fuzzy-trace theory and false memory. *Current Directions in Psychological Science, 11*, 164–169. (p. 385)

Brainerd, C. J., Reyna, V. F., & Brandse, E. (1995). Are children's false memories more persistent than their true memories? *Psychological Science, 6*, 359–364. (p. 385)

Brandon, S., Boakes, J., Glaser, D., & Green, R. (1998). Recovered memories of childhood sexual abuse: Implications for clinical practice. *British Journal of Psychiatry, 172*, 294–307. (p. 388)

Brannon, L. A., & Brock, T. C. (1994). Perilous underestimation of sex partners' sexual histories in calculating personal AIDS risk. Paper presented to the American Psychological Society convention. (p. 486)

Bransford, J. D., & Johnson, M. K. (1972). Contextual prerequisites for understanding: Some investigations of comprehension and recall. *Journal of Verbal Learning and Verbal Behavior, 11*, 717–726. (p. 357)

Braun, S. (1996). New experiments underscore warnings on maternal drinking. *Science, 273*, 738–739. (p. 142)

Braun, S. (2001, Spring). Seeking insight by prescription. *Cerebrum*, pp. 10–21. (p. 302)

Bray, D. W., & Byham, W. C. (1991, Winter). Assessment centers and their derivatives. *Journal of Continuing Higher Education*, pp. 8–11. (p. 629)

Bray, D. W., Byham, W. (1997). Insights into the history and future of assessment centers: An interview with Dr. Douglas W. Bray and Dr. William Byham. *Journal of Social Behavior and Personality, 12*, 3–12. (p. 629)

Bray, G. A. (1969). Effect of caloric restriction on energy expenditure in obese patients. *Lancet, 2*, 397–398. (p. 585)

Brayne, C., Spiegelhalter, D. J., Dufouil, C., Chi, L-Y., Dening, T. R., Paykel, E. S., O'Connor, D. W., Ahmed, A., McGee, M. A., & Huppert, F. A. (1999). Estimating the true extent of cognitive decline in the old old. *Journal of the American Geriatrics Society, 47*, 1283–1288. (p. 184)

Breedlove, S. M. (1997). Sex on the brain. *Nature, 389*, 801. (p. 490)

Brehm, S., & Brehm, J. W. (1981). *Psychological reactance: A theory of freedom and control.* New York: Academic Press. (p. 741)

Breland, K., & Breland, M. (1961). The misbehavior of organisms. *American Psychologist, 16*, 661–664. (p. 336)

Brenner, M. (1973). The next-in-line effect. *Journal of Verbal Learning and Verbal Behavior, 12*, 320–323. (p. 355)

Breslau, N., & Klein, D. F. (1999). Smoking and panic attacks: An epidemiologic investigation. *Archives of General Psychiatry, 56*, 1141–1147. (p. 650)

Bressan, P., & Dal Martello, M. F. (2002). Talis pater, talis filius: Perceived resemblance and the belief in genetic relatedness. *Psychological Science, 13*, 213–218. (p. 257)

Bretz, R. D. (1989). College grade point average as a predictor of adult success: A meta-analytic review and some additional evidence. *Public Personnel Management, 18,* 11–22. (p. 436)

Brewer, C. L. (1990). Personal correspondence. (p. 104)

Brewer, C. L. (1996). Personal communication. (p. 10)

Brewer, W. F. (1977). Memory for the pragmatic implications of sentences. *Memory & Cognition, 5,* 673–678. (p. 356)

Brewin, C. R., Andrews, B., Rose, S., & Kirk, M. (1999). Acute stress disorder and posttraumatic stress disorder in victims of violent crime. *American Journal of Psychiatry, 156,* 360–366. (p. 652)

Brewin, C. R., Andrews, B., & Valentine, J. D. (2000). Meta-analysis of risk factors for posttraumatic stress disorder in trauma-exposed adults. *Journal of Consulting and Clinical Psychology, 68,* 748–766. (p. 652)

Brickman, P., Coates, D., & Janoff-Bulman, R. J. (1978). Lottery winners and accident victims: Is happiness relative? *Journal of Personality and Social Psychology, 36,* 917–927. (p. 539)

Brief, A. P., & Weiss, H. M. (2002). Organizational behavior: Affect in the workplace. *Annual Review of Psychology, 53,* 279–307. (p. 505)

Brinson, S. L. (1992). The use and opposition of rape myths in prime-time television dramas. *Sex Roles, 27,* 359–375. (p. 753)

Briscoe, D. (1997, February 16). Women lawmakers still not in charge. Associated Press (in *Grand Rapids Press,* p. A23). (p. 131)

Brislin, R. (1993). *Understanding culture's influence on behavior.* Fort Worth, TX: Harcourt Brace. (p. 643)

Brislin, R. W. (1988). Increasing awareness of class, ethnicity, culture, and race by expanding on students' own experiences. In I. Cohen (Ed.), *The G. Stanley Hall Lecture Series.* Washington, DC: American Psychological Association. (p. 119)

Brissette, I., & Cohen, S. (2002). The contribution of individual differences in hostility to the associations between daily interpersonal conflict, affect, and sleep. *Personality and Social Psychology Bulletin, 28,* 1265–1274. (p. 283)

Brissette, I., Scheier, M. F., & Carver, C. S. (2002). The role of optimism in social network development, coping, and psychological adjustment during a life transition. *Journal of Personality and Social Psychology, 82,* 102–111. (p. 666)

British Psychological Society. (1993). Ethical principles for conducting research with human participants. *The Psychologist: Bulletin of the British Psychological Society, 6,* 33–36. (pp. 48, 616)

Britton, W. B., & Bootzin, R. R. (2004). Near-death experiences and the temporal lobe. *Psychological Science, 15,* 254–258. (p. 309)

Broadbent, D. E. (1978). The current state of noise research: Reply to Poulton. *Psychological Bulletin, 85,* 1052–1067. (p. 218)

Brody, J. E. (1999, November 30). Yesterday's precocious puberty is norm today. *New York Times* (www.nytimes.com). (p. 165)

Brody, J. E. (2000, March 21). When post-traumatic stress grips youth. *New York Times* (www.nytimes.com). (p. 652)

Brody, J. E. (2001, December 11). An old enemy, smoking, hangs tough. *New York Times* (www.nytimes.com). (p. 576)

Brody, J. E. (2002, November 26). When the eyelids snap shut at 65 miles an hour. *New York Times* (www.nytimes.com). (p. 281)

Brody, J. E. (2003, August 19). Skipping a college course: Weight gain 101. *New York Times* (www.nytimes.com). (p. 587)

Brody, J. E. (2003, September). Addiction: A brain ailment, not a moral lapse. *New York Times* (www.nytimes.com). (pp. 297, 435)

Brody, J. E. (2003, December 23). Stampede of diabetes as U.S. races to obesity. *New York Times* (www.nytimes.com). (p. 587)

Brody, N. (1992). *Intelligence,* 2nd ed. San Diego: Academic Press. (p. 441)

Brody, N. (1997). Dispositional paradigms: Comment on Eysenck (1997) and the biosocial science of individual differences. *Journal of Personality and Social Psychology, 73*(6), 1242–1245. (p. 437)

Brody, N. (2001). Inspection time: Past, present, and future. *Intelligence, 29,* 537–541. (p. 441)

Brody, N. (2003). Construct validation of the Sternberg Triarchic Abilities Test: Comment and reanalysis. *Intelligence, 31,* 319–329. (p. 435)

Brodzinsky, D. M., & Schechter, M. D. (Eds.) (1990). *The psychology of adoption.* New York: Oxford University Press. (p. 101)

Broman, S. H. (1989). Infant physical status and later cognitive development. In M. G. Bornstein & N. A. Krasnegor (Eds.), *Stability and continuity in mental development: Behavioral and biological perspectives.* Hillsdale, NJ: Erlbaum. (p. 450)

Bronner, E. (1998, February 25). U.S. high school seniors among worst in math and science. *New York Times* (www.nytimes.com). (pp. 462–463)

Brooke, J. (2000, January 20). Canada proposes scaring smokers with pictures on the pack. *New York Times* (www.nytimes.com) (p. 579)

Brooks, D. (2005, April 28). Mourning Mother Russia. *New York Times* (www.nytimes.com). (p. 178)

Brooks, D. J. (2002, October 8). Running down the road to happiness. *Gallup Tuesday Briefing* (www.gallup.com). (pp. 568–569)

Brooks, G. (1960). "The Bean Eaters," *The World of Gwendolyn Brooks,* Harper & Row. (p. 348)

Brown, A. S. (2003). A review of the déjà vu experience. *Psychological Bulletin, 129,* 394–413. (p. 373)

Brown, A. S. (2004). *The déjà vu experience.* East Sussex, England: Psychology Press. (p. 373)

Brown, A. S., Begg, M. D., Gravenstein, S., Schaefer, C. A., Wyatt, R. J., Bresnahan, M., Babulas, V. P., & Susser, E. S. (2004). Serologic evidence of prenatal influenza in the etiology of schizophrenia. *Archives of General Psychiatry, 61,* 774–780. (p. 674)

Brown, A. S., Bracken, E., Zoccoli, S., & Douglas, K. (2004). Generating and remembering passwords. *Applied Cognitive Psychology, 18,* 641–651. (p. 371)

Brown, A. S., Schaefer, C. A., Wyatt, R. J., Goetz, R., Begg, M. D., Gorman, J. M., & Susser, E. S. (2000). Maternal exposure to respiratory infections and adult schizophrenia spectrum disorders: A prospective birth cohort study. *Schizophrenia Bulletin, 26,* 287–295. (p. 674)

Brown, E. L., & Deffenbacher, K. (1979). *Perception and the senses.* New York: Oxford University Press. (p. 219)

Brown, G. K., Ten Have, T., Henriques, G. R., Xie, S. X., Hollander, J. E., & Beck, A. T. (2005). Cognitive therapy for the prevention of suicide attempts. *JAMA: Journal of the American Medical Association, 294,* 563–570. (p. 704)

Brown, J. D. (1991). Accuracy and bias in self-knowledge. In C. R. Snyder & D. F. Forsyth (Eds.), *Handbook of social and clinical psychology: The health perspective.* New York: Pergamon Press. (p. 636)

Brown, J. D., Steele, J. R., & Walsh-Childers, K. (2002). Sexual teens, sexual media: Investigating media's influence on adolescent sexuality. Mahwah, NJ: Erlbaum. (p. 486)

Brown, J. L., & Pollitt, E. (1996, February). Malnutrition, poverty and intellectual development. *Scientific American,* pp. 38–43. (p. 458)

Brown, L. R., Kane, H., & Ayres, E. (1993). *Vital signs 1993: The trends that are shaping our future.* New York: Norton. (p. 582)

Brown, R. (1965). *Social psychology.* New York: Free Press. (p. 533)

Brown, R. (1973). *A first language: The early stages.* Cambridge, MA: Harvard University Press. (p. 414)

Brown, R. (1986). Linguistic relativity. In S. H. Hulse & B. F. Green, Jr. (Eds.), *One hundred years of psychological research in America.* Baltimore: Johns Hopkins University Press. (p. 418)

Brown, R., & Kulik, J. (1982). Flashbulb memories. In U. Neisser (Ed.), *Memory observed.* San Francisco: Freeman. (p. 350)

Brown, S. L., Nesse, R. M., Vinokur, A. D., & Smith, D. M. (2003). Providing social support may be more beneficial than receiving it: Results from a prospective study of mortality. *Psychological Science, 14,* 320–327. (p. 566)

Brown, S. W., Garry, M., Loftus, E., Silver, B., DuBois, K., & DuBreuil, S. (1996). People's beliefs about memory: Why don't we have better memories? Paper presented at the American Psychological Society convention. (p. 381)

Brownell, K. D. (1997, March). We must be more militant about food. *APA Monitor*, p. 48. (p. 593)

Brownell, K. D. (2002). Public policy and the prevention of obesity. In C. G. Fairburn & K. D. Brownell (Eds.), *Eating disorders and obesity: A comprehensive handbook* (2nd ed.). New York: Guilford. (pp. 588–589)

Brownell, K. D., & Wadden, T. A. (1992). Etiology and treatment of obesity: Understanding a serious, prevalent, and refractory disorder. *Journal of Consulting and Clinical Psychology, 60,* 505–517. (p. 586)

Browning, C. (1992). *Ordinary men: Reserve police battalion 101 and the final solution in Poland.* New York: HarperCollins. (p. 736)

Brownmiller, S. (1975). *Against our will: Men, women, and rape.* New York: Simon and Schuster. (p. 484)

Bruce, D., Dolan, A., & Phillips-Grant, K. (2000). On the transition from childhood amnesia to the recall of personal memories. *Psychological Science, 11,* 360–364. (p. 146)

Bruck, M., & Ceci, S. (2004). Forensic developmental psychology: Unveiling four common misconceptions. *Current Directions in Psychological Science, 15,* 229–232. (p. 386)

Bruck, M., & Ceci, S. J. (1999). The suggestibility of children's memory. *Annual Review of Psychology, 50,* 419–439. (p. 386)

Bruer, J. T. (1999). *The myth of the first three years: A new understanding of early brain development and lifelong learning.* New York: Free Press. (p. 458)

Brumberg, J. J. (2000). *Fasting girls: The history of anorexia nervosa.* New York: Vintage. (p. 478)

Brune, K., & Handwerker, H. (2004). *Hyperalgesia: Molecular mechanisms and clinical implications.* Special issue of *Progress in Pain Research and Management, 30.* Seattle, WA: International Association for the Study of Pain, IASP Press. (p. 226)

Bryant, R. A. (2001). Posttraumatic stress disorder and traumatic brain injury: Can they co-exist? *Clinical Psychology Review, 21,* 931–948. (p. 388)

Buchel, C., Morris, J., Dolan, R. J., & Friston, K. J. (1998). Brain systems mediating aversive conditioning: An event-related fMRI study. *Neuron, 20,* 947–957. (p. 535)

Buck, L., & Axel, R. (1991). A novel multigene family may encode odorant receptors: A molecular basis for odor recognition. *Cell, 65,* 175–187. (p. 232)

Buckingham, M. (2001, August). Quoted by P. LaBarre, "Marcus Buckingham thinks your boss has an attitude problem." *The Magazine* (fastcompany.com/online/49/buckingham.html). (pp. 505, 507)

Buckingham, M., & Clifton, D. O. (2001). *Now, discover your strengths.* New York: Free Press. (p. 501)

Buckley, K. E., & Leary, M. R. (2001). Perceived acceptance as a predictor of social, emotional, and academic outcomes. Paper presented at the Society of Personality and Social Psychology annual convention. (p. 496)

Buehler, R., Griffin, D., & Ross, M. (1994). Exploring the "planning fallacy": Why people underestimate their task completion times. *Journal of Personality and Social Psychology, 67,* 366–381. (p. 403)

Bugelski, B. R., Kidd, E., & Segmen, J. (1968). Image as a mediator in one-trial paired-associate learning. *Journal of Experimental Psychology, 76,* 69–73. (p. 359)

Bugental, D. B. (1986). Unmasking the "polite smile": Situational and personal determinants of managed affect in adult-child interaction. *Personality and Social Psychology Bulletin, 12,* 7–16. (p. 527)

Buka, S. L., Goldstein, J. M., Seidman, L. J., Zornberg, G., Donatelli, J-A. A., Denny, L. R., & Tsuang, M. T. (1999). Prenatal complications, genetic vulnerability, and schizophrenia: The New England longitudinal studies of schizophrenia. *Psychiatric Annals, 29,* 151–156. (p. 673)

Buka, S. L., Tsuang, M. T., Torrey, E. F., Klebanoff, M. A., Wagner, R. L., & Yolken, R. H. (2001). Maternal infections and subsequent psychosis among offspring. *Archives of General Psychiatry, 58,* 1032–1037. (p. 674)

Bullough, V. (1990). The Kinsey scale in historical perspective. In D. P. McWhirter, S. A. Sanders, & J. M. Reinisch (Eds.), *Homosexuality/heterosexuality: Concepts of sexual orientation.* New York: Oxford University Press. (p. 487)

Buquet, R. (1988). Le reve et les deficients visuels (Dreams and the visually-impaired). *Psychanalyse-a-l'Universite, 13,* 319–327. (p. 286)

Bureau of Labor Statistics. (2004, September 14). American time-user survey summary. Washington, DC: United States Department of Labor (www.bls.gov). (pp. A–2, 131)

Bureau of Labor Statistics, U.S. Department of Labor. (2004–2005). Occupational Outlook Handbook, 2004–05 Edition. (p. A–2)

Bureau of the Census. (2004). *Statistical abstract of the United States 2004.* Washington, DC: U.S. Government Printing Office. (pp. 187, 575, 576, 647, 711)

Bureau of the Census. (2004). *Statistical abstract of the United States 2004.* Washington, DC: U.S. Government Printing Office. (pp. 575, 576, 647)

Burger, J. M. (1987). Increased performance with increased personal control: A self-presentation interpretation. *Journal of Experimental Social Psychology, 23,* 350–360. (p. 508)

Burger, J. M., & Burns, L. (1988). The illusion of unique invulnerability and the use of effective contraception. *Personality and Social Psychology Bulletin, 14,* 264–270. (p. 628)

Burgess, M., Enzle, M. E., & Schmaltz, R. (2004). Defeating the potentially deleterious effects of externally imposed deadlines: Practitioners' rules-of-thumb. *Personality and Social Psychology Bulletin, 30,* 868–877. (p. 508)

Buri, J. R., Louiselle, P. A., Misukanis, T. M., & Mueller, R. A. (1988). Effects of parental authoritarianism and authoritativeness on self-esteem. *Personality and Social Psychology Bulletin, 14,* 271–282. (p. 162)

Burish, T. G., & Carey, M. P. (1986). Conditioned aversive responses in cancer chemotherapy patients: Theoretical and developmental analysis. *Journal of Counseling and Clinical Psychology, 54,* 593–600. (p. 323)

Burke, D. M., & Shafto, M. A. (2004). Aging and language production. *Current Directions in Psychological Science, 13,* 21–24. (p. 182)

Burkholder, R. (2005a, January 11). Chinese far wealthier than a decade ago—but are they happier? *Gallup Poll News Service* (www.gallup.com). (p. 182)

Burkholder, R. (2005b, January 18). China's citizens optimistic, yet not entirely satisfied. *Gallup Poll News Service* (www.gallup.com). (p. 541)

Burns, B. C. (2004). The effects of speed on skilled chess performance. *Psychological Science, 15,* 442–447. (p. 409)

Burns, B. D. (2004). Heuristics as beliefs and as behaviors: The adaptiveness of the "hot hand." *Cognitive Psychology, 48,* 295–331. (p. 409)

Burrell, B. (2005). *Postcards from the brain museum: The improbable search for meaning in the matter of famous minds.* New York: Broadway Books. (p. 440)

Burt, D. M., & Perrett, D. I. (1995). Perception of age in adult Caucasian male faces: Computer graphic manipulation of shape and colour information. *Proceedings of the Royal Society, 259,* 137–143. (p. 177)

Bush, G. W. (2001, May 1). Speech to the National Defense University, Washington, DC. (p. 758)

Bushman, B. J. (1993). Human aggression while under the influence of alcohol and other drugs: An integrative research review. *Current Directions in Psychological Science, 2,* 148–152. (p. 750)

Bushman, B. J. (2002). Does venting anger feed or extinguish the flame? Catharsis, rumination, distraction, anger, and aggressive responding. *Personality and Social Psychology Bulletin, 28,* 724–731. (p. 536)

Bushman, B. J., & Anderson, C. A. (2001). Media violence and the American public: Scientific facts versus media misinformation. *American Psychologist, 56,* 477–489. (p. 755)

Bushman, B. J., & Baumeister, R. F. (1998). Threatened egotism, narcissism, self-esteem, and direct and displaced aggression: Does self-love or self-hate lead to violence? *Journal of Personality and Social Psychology, 75,* 219–229. (p. 635)

Bushman, B. J., Baumeister, R. F., & Stack, A. D. (1999). Catharsis, aggression, and persuasive influence: Self-fulfilling or self-defeating prophecies? *Journal of Personality and Social Psychology, 76,* 367–376. (p. 536)

Bushman, B. J., & Bonaci, A. M. (2002). Violence and sex impair memory for television ads. *Journal of Applied Psychology, 87,* 557–564. (pp. 380, 484)

Busnel, M. C., Granier-Deferre, C., & Lecanuet, J. P. (1992, October). Fetal audition. *New York Academy of Sciences, 662,* 118-134. (p. 141)

Buss, A. H. (1989). Personality as traits. *American Psychologist, 44,* 1378-1388. (p. 621)

Buss, D. M. (1991). Evolutionary personality psychology. *Annual Review of Psychology, 42,* 459-491. (p. 103)

Buss, D. M. (1994). The strategies of human mating: People worldwide are attracted to the same qualities in the opposite sex. *American Scientist, 82,* 238-249. (p. 112)

Buss, D. M. (1995). Evolutionary psychology: A new paradigm for psychological science. *Psychological Inquiry, 6,* 1-30. (p. 111)

Buss, D. M. (1996). Sexual conflict: Evolutionary insights into feminism and the "battle of the sexes." In D. M. Buss & N. M. Malamuth (Eds.), *Sex, power, conflict: Evolutionary and feminist perspectives.* New York: Oxford University Press. (p. 111)

Butler, A. C., Hokanson, J. E., & Flynn, H. A. (1994). A comparison of self-esteem lability and low trait self-esteem as vulnerability factors for depression. *Journal of Personality and Social Psychology, 66,* 166-177. (p. 667)

Butler, J., & Rovee-Collier, C. (1989). Contextual gating of memory retrieval. *Developmental Psychobiology, 22,* 533-552. (p. 373)

Butler, R. A. (1954, February). Curiosity in monkeys. *Scientific American,* pp. 70-75. (p. 471)

Butterfield, F. (1999, July 12). Experts say study confirms prison's new role as mental hospital. *New York Times* (www.nytimes.com). (p. 648)

Butterworth, G. (1992). Origins of self-perception in infancy. *Psychological Inquiry, 3,* 103-111. (p. 161)

Byne, W., & Parsons, B. (1993). Human sexual orientation: The biologic theories reappraised. *Archives of General Psychiatry, 50,* 228-239. (p. 492)

Bynum, R. (2004, November 1). Associated Press article. (p. 226)

Byrne, D. (1971). *The attraction paradigm.* New York: Academic Press. (p. 762)

Byrne, D. (1982). Predicting human sexual behavior. In A. G. Kraut (Ed.), *The G. Stanley Hall Lecture Series* (Vol. 2). Washington, DC: American Psychological Association. (pp. 318, 483)

Byrne, J. (2003, September 21). From correspondence reported by Michael Shermer, "E-Skeptic for September 21, 2003, from The Skeptics Society. (p. 266)

Byrne, R. W. (1991, May/June). Brute intellect. *The Sciences,* pp. 42-47. (p. 425)

Byrne, R. W., & Russon, A. E. (1998). Learning by imitation: A hierarchical approach. *Behavioral and Brain Sciences, 21,* 667-721. (p. 341)

Byrnes, J. P., Miller, D. C., & Schafer, W. C. (1999). Gender differences in risk taking: A meta-analysis. *Psychological Bulletin 125,* 367-383. (p. 111)

Cable, D. M., & Gilovich, T. (1998). Looked over or overlooked? Prescreening decisions and postinterview evaluations. *Journal of Personality and Social Psychology, 83,* 501-508. (p. 502)

Cacioppo, J. T., Berntson, G. G., Klein, D. J., & Poehlmann, K. M. (1997). The psychophysiology of emotion across the lifespan. *Annual Review of Gerontology and Geriatrics, 17,* 27. (p. 517)

Cahill, L. (1994). (Beta)-adrenergic activation and memory for emotional events. *Nature, 371,* 702-704. (p. 366)

Cahill, L. (2005, May). His brain, her brain. *Scientific American,* pp. 40-47. (p. 130)

Cale, E. M., Lilienfeld, S. O. (2002). Sex differences in psychopathy and antisocial personality disorder: A review and integration. *Clinical Psychology Review, 22,* 1179-1207. (p. 677)

Call, K. T., Riedel, A. A., Hein, K., McLoyd, V., Petersen, A., & Kipke, M. (2002). Adolescent health and well-being in the twenty-first century: A global perspective. *Journal of Research on Adolescence, 12,* 69-98. (p. 485)

Callaghan, T., Rochat, P., Lillard, A., Claux, M. L., Odden, H., Itakura, S., Tapanya, S., & Singh, S. (2005). Synchrony in the onset of mental-state reasoning. *Psychological Science, 16,* 378-384. (p. 151)

Calle, E. E., Thun, M. J., Petrelli, J. M., Rodriguez, C., & Health, C. W., Jr. (1999). Body-mass index and mortality in a prospective cohort of U.S. adults. *New England Journal of Medicine, 341,* 1097-1105. (pp. 583-584)

Callicott, J. H., & 11 others (2005). Variation in DISC1 affects hippocampal structure and function and increased risk for schizophrenia. *Proceedings of the National Academy of Sciences, 102,* 8627-8632. (p. 675)

Calvin, W. H. (1996). *The cerebral code: Thinking a thought in the mosaics of the mind.* Cambridge, MA: MIT Press. (p. 76)

Calvo-Merino, B., Glaser, D. E., Grèzes, J., Passingham, R. E., & Haggard, P. (2004). Action observation and acquired motor skills: An fMRI study with expert dancers. *Cerebral Cortex, 15,* 1243-1249. (p. 421)

Camerer, C. F., Loewenstein, G., & Weber, M. (1989). The curse of knowledge in economic settings: An experimental analysis. *Journal of Political Economy, 97,* 1232-1254. (p. 262)

Campbell, D. T. (1975). On the conflicts between biological and social evolution and between psychology and moral tradition. *American Psychologist, 30,* 1103-1126. (p. 542)

Campbell, D. T., & Specht, J. C. (1985). Altruism: Biology, culture, and religion. *Journal of Social and Clinical Psychology, 3*(1), 33-42. (p. 611)

Campbell, S. (1986). *The Loch Ness Monster: The evidence.* Willingborough, Northamptonshire, U.K.: Acquarian Press. (p. 257)

Camper, J. (1990, February 7). Drop pompom squad, U. of I. rape study says. *Chicago Tribune,* p. 1. (p. 298)

Camperio-Ciani, A., Corna, F., & Capiluppi, C. (2004). Evidence for maternally inherited factors favouring male homosexuality and promoting female fecundity. *Proceedings of the Royal Society of London B, 271,* 2217-2221. (p. 490)

Campos, J. J., Bertenthal, B. I., & Kermoian, R. (1992). Early experience and emotional development: The emergence of wariness and heights. *Psychological Science, 3,* 61-64. (pp. 533, 654)

Canli, T., Desmond, J. E., Zhao, Z., & Gabrieli, J. D. E. (2002). Sex differences in the neural basis of emotional memories. *Proceedings of the National Academy of Sciences, 99,* 10789-10794. (p. 526)

Cannon, J. (2005). Career planning and opportunities: The bachelor's degree in psychology. *Eye on Psi Chi, 26-28.* (p. A-2)

Cannon, W. B. (1929). *Bodily changes in pain, hunger, fear, and rage.* New York: Branford. (pp. 474, 551)

Cannon, W. B., & Washburn, A. (1912). An explanation of hunger. *American Journal of Physiology, 29,* 441-454. (p. 474)

Cantor, N., & Kihlstrom, J. F. (1987). *Personality and social intelligence.* Englewood Cliffs, NJ: Prentice-Hall. (p. 436)

Cantril, H., & Bumstead, C. H. (1960). *Reflections on the human venture.* New York: New York University Press. (p. 741)

Caplan, N., Choy, M. H., & Whitmore, J. K. (1992, February). Indochinese refugee families and academic achievement. *Scientific American,* pp. 36-42. (pp. 117, 461)

Caputo, D., & Dunning, D. (2005). What you don't know: The role played by errors of omission in imperfect self-assessments. *Journal of Experimental Social Psychology,* 488-505. (p. 629)

Carducci, B. J., Cosby, P. C., & Ward, D. D. (1978). Sexual arousal and interpersonal evaluations. *Journal of Experimental Social Psychology, 14,* 449-457. (p. 763)

Carey, G. (1990). Genes, fears, phobias, and phobic disorders. *Journal of Counseling and Development, 68,* 628-632. (p. 655)

Carlezon, W. A., Jr., Mague, S. D., & Andersen, S. L. (2003). Enduring behavioral effects of early exposure to methylphenidate in rats. *Biological Psychiatry, 54,* 1330-1337. (p. 640)

Carli, L. L., & Leonard, J. B. (1989). The effect of hindsight on victim derogation. *Journal of Social and Clinical Psychology, 8,* 331-343. (p. 748)

Carlson, C. L. (2000). ADHD is overdiagnosed. In R. L. Atkinson, R. C. Atkinson, E. E. Smith, D. J. Bem, & S. Nolen-Hoeksema (Eds.), *Hilgard's introduction to psychology, Thirteenth edition.* Fort Worth: Harcourt. (p. 641)

Carlson, D. K. (2002, February 19). Acceptance of homosexuality: A youth movement. The Gallup Organization (www.gallup.com/poll/tb/educaYouth/200220219.asp). (p. 492)

Carlson, M. (1995, August 29). Quoted by S. Blakeslee, In brain's early growth, timetable may be crucial. *New York Times*, pp. C1, C3. (p. 158)

Carlson, M., Charlin, V., & Miller, N. (1988). Positive mood and helping behavior: A test of six hypotheses. *Journal of Personality and Social Psychology, 55*, 211–229. (p. 766)

Carlson, R. (1984). What's social about social psychology? Where's the person in personality research? *Journal of Personality and Social Psychology, 47*, 1304–1309. (p. 630)

Carlson, S. (1985). A double-blind test of astrology. *Nature, 318*, 419–425. (p. 616)

Carnegie Council on Adolescent Development. (1989, June). *Turning points: Preparing American youth for the 21st century.* (The report of the Task Force on Education of Young Adolescents.) New York: Carnegie Corporation. (pp. 453, 768)

Carrière, G. (2003). Parent and child factors associated with youth obesity. *Statistics Canada, Catalogue 82-003, Supplement to Health Reports, 2003.* (p. 586)

Carroll, D., Davey Smith, G., & Bennett, P. (1994, March). Health and socio-economic status. *The Psychologist*, pp. 122–125. (p. 564)

Carroll, J. (2005, January 14). Terrorism concerns fade. *The Gallup Organization* (www.gallup.com). (p. 405)

Carroll, J. M., & Russell, J. A. (1996). Do facial expressions signal specific emotions? Judging emotion from the face in context. *Journal of Personality and Social Psychology, 70*, 205–218. (p. 529)

Carskadon, M. (2002). *Adolescent sleep patterns: Biological, social, and psychological influences.* New York: Cambridge University Press. (p. 280)

Carter, R. (1998). *Mapping the mind.* Berkeley, CA: University of California Press. (p. 58)

Carter, S., & Snow, C. (2004, May). Helping singles enter better marriages using predictive models of marital success. Presented to the American Psychological Society convention. (p. 762)

Cartwright, R. D. (1978). *A primer on sleep and dreaming.* Reading, MA: Addison-Wesley. (p. 278)

Caryl, P. G. (1994). Early event-related potentials correlate with inspection time and intelligence. *Intelligence, 18*, 15–46. (p. 441)

CASA. (2003). *The formative years: Pathways to substance abuse among girls and young women ages 8–22.* New York, NY: National Center on Addiction and Substance Use, Columbia University. (pp. 299, 306)

Case, R. B., Moss, A. J., Case, N., McDermott, M., & Eberly, S. (1992). Living alone after myocardial infarction: Impact on prognosis. *Journal of the American Medical Association, 267*, 515–519. (p. 566)

Cash, T., & Janda, L. H. (1984, December). The eye of the beholder. *Psychology Today*, pp. 46–52. (p. 760)

Cash, T. F., & Henry, P. E. (1995). Women's body images: The results of a national survey in the U.S.A. *Sex Roles, 33*, 19–28. (p. 479)

Caspi, A. (2000). The child is father of the man: Personality continuities from childhood to adulthood. *Journal of Personality and Social Psychology, 78*, 158–172. (p. 102)

Caspi, A., Harrington, H., Milne, B., Amell, J. W., Theodore, R. F., & Moffitt, T. E. (2003). Children's behavioral styles at age 3 are linked to their adult personality traits at age 26. *Journal of Personality, 71*, 496–513. (p. 194)

Caspi, A., McClay, J., Moffitt, T., Mill, J., Martin, J., Craig, I. W., Taylor, A., & Poulton, R. (2002). Role of genotype in the cycle of violence in maltreated children. *Science, 297*, 851–854. (p. 679)

Caspi, A., Moffitt, T. E., Newman, D. L., & Silva, P. A. (1996). Behavioral observations at age 3 years predict adult psychiatric disorders: Longitudinal evidence from a birth cohort. *Archives of General Psychiatry, 53*, 1033–1039. (p. 678)

Caspi, A., Sugden, K., Moffitt, T. E., Taylor, A., Craig, I. W., Harrington, H. L., McClay, J., Mill, J., Martin, J., Braithwaite, A., & Poulton, R. (2003). Influence of life stress on depression: Moderation by a polymorphism in the 5-HTT gene. *Science, 30*, 386–389. (p. 664)

Cassandro, V. J., & Simonton, D. K. (2003). Creativity and genius. In C. L. M. Keyes & J. Haidt (Eds.), *Flourishing: Positive psychology and the life well-lived.* Washington, DC: American Psychological Association. (p. 453)

Cassidy, J., & Shaver, P. R. (1999). *Handbook of attachment.* New York: Guilford. (p. 156)

Castillo, R. J. (1997). *Culture and mental illness: A client-centered approach.* Pacific Grove, CA: Brooks/Cole. (pp. 639, 643)

Castonguay, L. G., & Goldfried, M. R. (1994). Psychotherapy integration: An idea whose time has come. *Applied & Preventive Psychology, 3*, 159–172. (p. 686)

Catanese, K. R., & Tice, D. M. (2005). The effect of rejection on anti-social behaviors: Social exclusion produces aggressive behaviors. In K. D. Williams, J. P. Forgas, & W. Von Hippel (Eds.), *The social outcast: Ostracism, social exclusion, rejection, and bullying.* New York: Psychology Press. (p. 751)

Cattell, R. B. (1963). Theory of fluid and crystallized intelligence: A critical experiment. *Journal of Educational Psychology, 54*, 1–22. (p. 184)

Cavalli-Sforza, L., Menozzi, P., & Piazza, A. (1994). *The history and geography of human genes.* Princeton, NJ: Princeton University Press. (p. 460)

Cavigelli, S. A., & McClintock, M. K. (2003). Fear of novelty in infant rats predicts adult corticosterone dynamics and an early death. *Proceedings of the National Academy of Sciences, 100*, 16131–16136. (p. 553)

CDC. (2004). Teenagers in the United States: Sexual activity, contraceptive use, and childbearing, 2002. A fact sheet for series 23, number 24. DHHS Publication (PHS) 2005–1976. (pp. 485, 487)

CDC. (2004, December 16). Prevalence of overweight and obesity among adults: United States, 1999–2002. Centers for Disease Control and Prevention, National Center for Health Statistics (www.cdc.gov). (p. 587)

Ceci, S. J. (1993). Cognitive and social factors in children's testimony. Master Lecture, American Psychological Association convention. (p. 387)

Ceci, S. J., & Bruck, M. (1993). Child witnesses: Translating research into policy. *Social Policy Report* (Society for Research in Child Development), *7*(3), 1–30. (p. 387)

Ceci, S. J., & Bruck, M. (1995). *Jeopardy in the courtroom: A scientific analysis of children's testimony.* Washington, DC: American Psychological Association. (p. 387)

Ceci, S. J., Huffman, M. L. C., Smith, E., & Loftus, E. F. (1994). Repeatedly thinking about a non-event: Source misattributions among preschoolers. *Consciousness and Cognition, 3*, 388–407. (p. 387)

Ceci, S. J., & Liker, J. K. (1986). A day at the races: A study of IQ, expertise, and cognitive complexity. *Journal of Experimental Psychology: General, 115*, 255–266. (p. 435)

Ceci, S. J., & Williams, W. M. (1997). Schooling, intelligence, and income. *American Psychologist, 52*, 1051–1058. (p. 458)

Centers for Disease Control. (1992, September 16). Serious mental illness and disability in the adult household population: United States, 1989. *Advance Data* No. 218 from *Vital and Health Statistics*, National Center for Health Statistics. (p. 681)

Centers for Disease Control. (2003). Who should get a flu shot (influenza vaccine). National Center for Infectious Diseases (http://www.cdc.gov/ncidod/diseases/flu/who.htm). (p. 674)

Centers for Disease Control Vietnam Experience Study. (1988). Health status of Vietnam veterans. *Journal of the American Medical Association, 259*, 2701–2709. (p. 652)

Centerwall, B. S. (1989). Exposure to television as a risk factor for violence. *American Journal of Epidemiology, 129*, 643–652. (p. 345)

Cerella, J. (1985). Information processing rates in the elderly. *Psychological Bulletin, 98*, 67–83. (p. 179)

CFI. (2003, July). International developments. *Report.* Amherst, NY: Center for Inquiry International. (p. 267)

Chambless, D. L., Baker, M. J., Baucom, D. H., Beutler, L. E., Calhoun, K. S., Crits-Christoph, P., Daiuto, A., DeRubeis, R., Detweiler, J., Haaga, D. A. F., Johnson, S. B., McCurry, S., Mueser, K. T., Pope, K. S., Sanderson, W. C., Shoham, V., Stickle, T., Williams, D. A., & Woody, S. R. (1997). Update on empirically validated therapies, II. *The Clinical Psychologist, 51*(1), 3–16. (pp. 704, 706)

Chamove, A. S. (1980). Nongenetic induction of acquired levels of aggression. *Journal of Abnormal Psychology, 89*, 469–488. (p. 343)

Chance News (1999, July 15). National Lottery and death rates. From *Daily Express*, 13 August 1998. (p. 402)

Chang, E. C. (2001). Cultural influences on optimism and pessimism: Differences in Western and Eastern construals of the self. In E. C. Chang (Ed.), *Optimism and pessimism*. Washington, DC: APA Books. (p. 627)

Chang, P. P., Ford, D. E., Meoni, L. A., Wang, N-Y., & Klag, M. J. (2002). Anger in young men and subsequent premature cardiovascular disease: The precursors study. *Archives of Internal Medicine, 162*, 901–906. (p. 556)

Chaplin, W. F., Phillips, J. B., Brown, J. D., Clanton, N. R., & Stein, J. L. (2000). Handshaking, gender, personality, and first impressions. *Journal of Personality and Social Psychology, 79*, 110–117. (p. 524)

Charles, S. T., Reynolds, C. A., & Gatz, M. (2001). Age-related differences and change in positive and negative affect over 23 years. *Journal of Personality and Social Psychology, 80*, 136–151. (p. 189)

Charpak, G., & Broch, H. (2004). *Debunked! ESP, telekinesis, and other pseudoscience*. Baltimore, MD: Johns Hopkins University Press. (p. 266)

Chartrand, T. L., & Bargh, J. A. (1999). The chameleon effect: The perception-behavior link and social interaction. *Journal of Personality and Social Psychology, 76*, 893–910. (p. 731)

Chase, M. H., & Morales, F. R. (1983). Subthreshold excitatory activity and motorneuron discharge during REM periods of active sleep. *Science, 221*, 1195–1198. (p. 279)

Chase, W. G., & Simon, H. A. (1973). Perception in chess. *Cognitive Psychology, 4*, 55–81. (p. 360)

Chase-Lansdale, P. L., Moffitt, R. A., Lohman, B. J., Cherlin, A. J., Coley, R. L., Pittman, L. D., Roff, J., & Votruba-Drzal, E. (2003). Mothers' transitions from welfare to work and the well-being of preschoolers and adolescents. *Science, 299*, 1548–1552. (p. 160)

Chassin, L., Presson, C. C., Sherman, S. J., & McGrew, J. (1987). The changing smoking environment for middle and high school students: 1980–1983. *Journal of Behavioral Medicine, 10*, 581–593. (p. 576)

Chaudhari, N., Landin, A. M., & Roper, S. D. (2000). A metabotropic glutamate receptor variant functions as a taste receptor. *Nature Neuroscience, 3*, 113–119. (p. 229)

Chaves, J. F. (1989). Hypnotic control of clinical pain. In N. P. Spanos & J. F. Chaves (Eds.), *Hypnosis: The cognitive-behavioral perspective*. Buffalo, NY: Prometheus Books. (p. 293)

Cheek, J. M., & Melchior, L. A. (1990). Shyness, self-esteem, and self-consciousness. In H. Leitenberg (Ed.), *Handbook of social and evaluation anxiety*. New York: Plenum. (p. 122)

Cheit, R. E. (1998). Consider this, skeptics of recovered memory. *Ethics & Behavior, 8*, 141–160. (p. 604)

Chen, E. (2004). Why socioeconomic status affects the health of children: A psychosocial perspective. *Current Directions in Psychological Science, 13*, 112–115. (p. 564)

Cheng, C. (2001). Assessing coping flexibility in real-life and laboratory settings: A multimethod approach. *Journal of Personality and Social Psychology, 80*, 814–833. (p. 45)

Cheng, T. O. (1999). Teenage smoking in China. *Journal of Adolescence, 22*, 607–620. (p. 579)

Chess, S., & Thomas, A. (1987). *Know your child: An authoritative guide for today's parents*. New York: Basic Books. (pp. 102, 157)

Child Trends. (2001, August). Facts at a glance. (www.childtrends.org). (p. 485)

Chiles, J. A., Lambert, M. J., & Hatch, A. L. (1999). The impact of psychological interventions on medical cost offset: A meta-analytic review. *Clinical Psychology: Science and Practice, 6*, 204–220. (p. 703)

Chisholm, K. (1998). A three year follow-up of attachment and indiscriminate friendliness in children adopted from Romanian orphanages. *Child Development, 69*, 1092–1106. (p. 158)

Choi, I., & Choi, Y. (2002). Culture and self-concept flexibility. *Personality and Social Psychology Bulletin, 28*, 1508–1517. (p. 122)

Chomsky, N. (1959). Review of B. F. Skinner's *Verbal behavior. Language, 35*, 26–58. (p. 414)

Chomsky, N. (1972). *Language and mind*. New York: Harcourt Brace Jovanovich. (p. 410)

Chomsky, N. (1987). Language in a psychological setting. Sophia Linguistic Working Papers in Linguistics, No. 22, Sophia University, Tokyo. (p. 414)

Chorpita, B. F., & Barlow, D. H. (1998). The development of anxiety: The role of control in the early environment. *Psychological Bulletin, 124*, 3–21. (p. 654)

Christakis, D. S., Zimmerman, F. J., DiGiuseppe, D. L., & McCarty, C. A. (2004). Early television exposure and subsequent attentional problems in children. *Pediatrics, 113*, 708–713. (p. 641)

Christensen, A., & Jacobson, N. S. (1994). Who (or what) can do psychotherapy: The status and challenge of nonprofessional therapies. *Psychological Science, 5*, 8–14. (p. 708)

Christophersen, E. R., & Edwards, K. J. (1992). Treatment of elimination disorders: State of the art 1991. *Applied & Preventive Psychology, 1*, 15–22. (p. 691)

Chugani, H. T., & Phelps, M. E. (1986). Maturational changes in cerebral function in infants determined by [18]FDG Positron Emission Tomography. *Science, 231*, 840–843. (p. 145)

CIA. (2005). Life expectancy at birth. *The world fact book*. www.cia.gov. (p. 178)

Cialdini, R. B. (1993). *Influence: Science and practice* (3rd ed.). New York: HarperCollins. (p. 727)

Cialdini, R. B., & Richardson, K. D. (1980). Two indirect tactics of image management: Basking and blasting. *Journal of Personality and Social Psychology, 39*, 406–415. (p. 747)

Citrome, L., & Volavka, J. (1999). Schizophrenia: Violence and comorbidity. *Current Opinion in Psychiatry, 12*, 47–51. (p. 647)

Clack, B., Dixon, J., & Tredoux, C. (2005). Eating together apart: Patterns of segregation in a multi-ethnic cafeteria. *Journal of Community and Applied Social Psychology, 15*, 1–16. (p. 767)

Clancy, S. A., McNally, R. J., Schachter, D. L., Lenzenweger, M. F., & Pitman, R. K. (2002). Memory distortion in people reporting abduction by aliens. *Journal of Abnormal Psychology, 111*, 455–461. (p. 383)

Clancy, S. A., Schacter, D. L., McNally, R. J., & Pitman, R. K. (2000). False recognition in women reporting recovered memories of sexual abuse. *Psychological Science, 11*, 26–31. (p. 383)

Clark, A., Seidler, A., & Miller, M. (2001). Inverse association between sense of humor and coronary heart disease. *International Journal of Cardiology, 80*, 87–88. (p. 565)

Clark, K. B., Chein, I., & Cook, S. W. (1952; reprinted 2004). The effects of segregation and the consequences of desegregation: A (September 1952) social science statement in the *Brown v Board of Education of Topeka* Supreme Court Case. *American Psychologist, 59*, 495–501. (p. 50)

Clark, K. B., & Clark, M. P. (1947). Racial identification and preference in Negro children. In T. M.. Newcomb and E. L. Hartley (Eds.), *Readings in social psychology*. New York: Holt. (p. 50)

Clark, R., Anderson, N. B., Clark, V. R., & Williams, D. R. (1999). Racism as a stressor for African Americans: A biopsychosocial model. *American Psychologist, 54*, 805–816. (p. 555)

Clark, R. D. (1990, May). The impact of AIDS on gender differences in willingness to engage in casual sex. *Journal of Applied Social Psychology, 20*, 771–782. (p. 110)

Clark, R. D., III, & Hatfield, E. (1989). Gender differences in willingness to engage in casual sex. *Journal of Psychology and Human Sexuality, 2,* 39–55. (p. 110)

Coats, E. J., & Feldman, R. S. (1996). Gender differences in nonverbal correlates of social status. *Personality and Social Psychology Bulletin, 22,* 1014–1022. (p. 526)

Cofer, J. O., (1993). *The Latin Deli,* New York: W. W. Norton and Company. (p. 94)

Coffey, C. E. (Ed.) (1993). *Clinical science of electroconvulsive therapy.* Washington, DC: American Psychiatric Press. (p. 715)

Coffey, C. E., Lucke, J. F. , Saxton, J. A., Ratcliff, G., Unitas, L. J., Billig, B., & Bryan, R. N. (1998). Sex differences in brain aging: A quantitative magnetic resonance imagine study. *Archives of Neurology, 55,* 169–179. (p. 180)

Coffey, C. E., Wilkinson, W. E., Weiner, R. D., Parashos, I. A., Djang, W. T., Webb, M. C., Figiel, G. S., & Spritzer, C. E. (1993). Quantitative cerebral anatomy in depression: A controlled magnetic resonance imaging study. *Archives of General Psychiatry, 50,* 7–16. (p. 665)

Cogan, J. C., Bhalla, S. K., Sefa-Dedeh, A., & Rothblum, E. D. (1996). A comparison study of United States and African students on perceptions of obesity and thinness. *Journal of Cross-Cultural Psychology, 27,* 98–113. (p. 582)

Cogan, J. C., & Ernsberger, P. (1999). Dieting, weight, and health: Reconceptualizing research and policy. *Journal of Social Issues, 55,* 187–205. (p. 589)

Cohen, D. (1995, June 17). Now we are one, or two, or three. *New Scientist,* pp. 14–15. (p. 657)

Cohen, G., Conway, M. A., & Maylor, E. A. (1994, September). Flashbulb memories in older adults. *Psychology & Aging, 9(3),* 454–463. (p. 182)

Cohen, H., Kaplan, Z., Kotler, M., Kouperman, I., Moisa, R., & Grisaru, N. (2005). Repetitive transcranial magnetic stimulation of the right dorsolaterial prefrontal cortex in posttraumatic stress disorder: A double-blind, placebo-controlled study. *American Journal of Psychiatry, 16,* 515–524. (p. 716)

Cohen, K. M. (2002). Relationships among childhood sex-atypical behavior, spatial ability, handedness, and sexual orientation in men. *Archives of Sexual Behavior, 31,* 129–143. (p. 492)

Cohen, S. (1988). Psychosocial models of the role of social support in the etiology of physical disease. *Health Psychology, 7,* 269–297. (p. 566)

Cohen, S. (2004). Social relationships and health. *American Psychologist, 59,* 676–684. (p. 566)

Cohen, S., Doyle, W. J., Skoner, D. P., Rabin, B. S., & Gwaltney, J. M., Jr. (1997). Social ties and susceptibility to the common cold. *Journal of the American Medical Association, 277,* 1940–1944. (p. 566)

Cohen, S., Doyle, W. J., Turner, R., Alper, C. M., & Skoner, D. P. (2003). Sociability and susceptibility to the common cold. *Psychological Science, 14,* 389–395. (p. 558)

Cohen, S., Kaplan, J. R., Cunnick, J. E., Manuck, S. B., & Rabin, B. S. (1992). Chronic social stress, affiliation, and cellular immune response in nonhuman primates. *Psychological Science, 3,* 301–304. (p. 557)

Cohen, S., Line, S., Manuck, S. B., Rabin, B. S., Heise, E. R., & Kaplan, J. R. (1997). Chronic social stress, social status, and susceptibility to upper respiratory infections in nonhuman primates. *Psychosomatic Medicine, 59,* 213–221. (p. 564)

Cohen, S., Tyrrell, D. A. J., & Smith, A. P. (1991). Psychological stress and susceptibility to the common cold. *New England Journal of Medicine, 325,* 606–612. (p. 558)

Colangelo, N., Assouline, S. G., & Gross, M. U. M. (2004). *A nation deceived: How schools hold back America's brightest students,* Volumes I and II. *The Templeton National Report on Acceleration.* Iowa City, IA: College of Education, University of Iowa. (p. 454)

Colapinto, J. (2000). *As nature made him: The boy who was raised as a girl.* New York: HarperCollins. (p. 130)

Colarelli, S. M., & Dettman, J. R. (2003). Intuitive evolutionary perspectives in marketing. *Psychology and Marketing, 20,* 837–865. (p. 109)

Colarelli, S. M., Spranger, J. L., & Hechanova, M. R. (2005). Women, power, and sex composition in small groups: An evolutionary perspective. *Journal of Organizational Behavior,* in press. (p. 127)

Colcombe, S., & Kramer, A. F. (2003). Fitness effects on the cognitive function of older adults: A meta-analytic study. *Psychological Science, 14,* 125–130. (p. 180)

Colcombe, S. J., Kramer, A. F., Erickson, K. I., Scalf, P., McAuley, E., Cohen, N. J., Webb, A., Jerome, G. J., Marquex, D. X., & Elavsky, S. (2004). Cardiovascular fitness, cortical plasticity, and aging. *Proceedings of the National Academy of Sciences, 101,* 3316–3321. (p. 180)

Cole, K. C. (1998). *The universe and the teacup: The mathematics of truth and beauty.* New York: Harcourt Brace. (p. 575)

Coleman, J. (1997, June 30). Cigarette industry thriving in Japan. Associated Press (in *Grand Rapids Press,* p. A14). (pp. 579–580)

Coleman, J. C. (1980). *The nature of adolescence.* London: Methuen. (p. 165)

Coleman, P. D., & Flood, D. G. (1986). Dendritic proliferation in the aging brain as a compensatory repair mechanism. In D. F. Swaab, E. Fliers, M. Mirmiram, W. A. Van Gool, & F. Van Haaren (Eds.), *Progress in brain research* (Vol. 20). New York: Elsevier. (p. 180)

Collins, D. W., & Kimura, D. (1997). A large sex difference on a two-dimensional mental rotation task. *Behavioral Neuroscience, 111,* 845–849. (p. 463)

Collins, N. L., & Miller, L. C. (1994). Self-disclosure and liking: A meta-analytic review. *Psychological Bulletin, 116,* 457–475. (p. 764)

Collins, R. L., Elliott, M. N., Berry, S. H., Danouse, D. E., Kunkel, D., Hunter, S. B., & Miu, A. (2004). Watching sex on television predicts adolescent initiation of sexual behavior. *Pediatrics, 114,* 280–289. (p. 31)

Collins, W. A., Maccoby, E. E., Steinberg, L., Hetherington, E. M., & Bornstein, M. H. (2000). Contemporary research on parenting: The case for nature and nurture. *American Psychologist, 55,* 218–232. (p. 117)

Collinson, S. L., MacKay, C. E., James, A. C., Quested, D. J., Phillips, T., Roberts, N., & Crow, T. J. (2003). Brain volume, asymmetry and intellectual impairment in relation to sex in early-onset schizophrenia. *British Journal of Psychiatry, 183,* 114–120. (p. 673)

Colom, R., Lluis-Font, J. M., & Andrés-Pueyo, A. (2005). The generational intelligence gains are caused by decreasing variance in the lower half of the distribution: Supporting evidence for the nutrition hypothesis. *Intelligence, 33,* 83–91. (p. 448)

Colombo, J. (1982). The critical period concept: Research, methodology, and theoretical issues. *Psychological Bulletin, 91,* 260–275. (p. 156)

Colon, E. A., Callies, A. L., Popkin, M. K., & McGlave, P. B. (1991). Depressed mood and other variables related to bone marrow transplantation survival in acute leukemia. *Psychosomatics, 32,* 420–425. (p. 566)

Comer, R. J. (2004). *Abrtormal psychology.* New York: Worth Publishers. (p. 640)

Commissioner of Official Languages. (1999). *Annual Report 1998.* Minister of Public Works and Government Services Canada, Cat. No. SF1-1998. (p. 420)

Conner, M., & McMillan, B. (1999). Interaction effects in the theory of planned behaviour: Studying cannabis use. *British Journal of Social Psychology, 38,* 195–222. (p. 304)

Consensus Conference. (1985). Electroconvulsive therapy. *Journal of the American Medical Association, 254,* 2103–2108. (pp. 715–716)

Consumer Reports. (1995, November). Does therapy help? Pp. 734–739. (p. 700)

Conway, M., & Ross, M. (1984). Getting what you want by revising what you had. *Journal of Personality and Social Psychology, 47,* 738–748. (p. 380)

Conway, M. A., Wang, Q., Hanyu, K., & Haque, S. (2005). A cross-cultural investigation of autobiographical memory. On the universality and cultural variation of the reminiscence bump. *Journal of Cross-Cultural Psychology, 36,* 739–749. (p. 181)

Cook, E. W., III, Hodes, R. L., & Lang, P. J. (1986). Preparedness and phobia: Effects of stimulus content on human visceral conditioning. *Journal of Abnormal Psychology, 95,* 195–207. (p. 322)

Cook, M., & Mineka, S. (1991). Selective associations in the origins of phobic fears and their implications for behavior therapy. In P. Martin (Ed.), *Handbook of behavior therapy and psychological science: An integrative approach.* New York: Pergamon Press. (p. 534)

Cooke, L. J., Wardle, J., & Gibson, E. L. (2003). Relationship between parental report of food neophobia and everyday food consumption in 2–6-year-old children. *Appetite, 41,* 205–206. (p. 230)

Cooper, K. J. (1999, May 1). This time, copycat wave is broader. *Washington Post* (www.washingtonpost.com). (pp. 343, 732)

Coopersmith, S. (1967). *The antecedents of self-esteem.* San Francisco: Freeman. (p. 162)

Corballis, M. C. (1989). Laterality and human evolution. *Psychological Review, 96,* 492–505. (p. 88)

Corballis, M. C. (2002). *From hand to mouth: The origins of language.* Princeton: Princeton University Press. (p. 425)

Corballis, M. C. (2003). From mouth to hand: Gesture, speech, and the evolution of right-handedness. *Behavioral and Brain Sciences, 26,* 199–260. (p. 425)

Coren, S. (1993a). Failure to find statistical significance in left-handedness and pathology studies: A forgotten consideration. *Bulletin of the Psychonomic Society, 31,* 443–446. (p. 89)

Coren, S. (1993b). *The left-hander syndrome: The causes and consequences of left-handedness.* New York: Vintage Books. (pp. 87, 89, 91)

Coren, S. (1996). *Sleep thieves: An eye-opening exploration into the science and mysteries of sleep.* New York: Free Press. (pp. 280, 281, 283)

Corey, D. P., & 15 others (2004). TRPA1 is a candidate for the mechanosensitive transduction channel of vertebrate hair cells. *Nature* (advance online publication, October 13, at www.nature.com). (p. 218)

Corina, D. P. (1998). The processing of sign language: Evidence from aphasia. In B. Stemmer & H. A. Whittaker (Eds.), *Handbook of neurolinguistics.* San Diego: Academic Press. (p. 88)

Corina, D. P., Vaid, J., & Bellugi, U. (1992). The linguistic basis of left hemisphere specialization. *Science, 255,* 1258–1260. (p. 88)

Corneille, O., Huart, J., Becquart, E., & Brédart, S. (2004). When memory shifts toward more typical category exemplars: Accentuation effects in the recollection of ethnically ambiguous faces. *Journal of Personality and Social Psychology, 86,* 236–250. (p. 397)

Correll, J., Park, B., Judd, C. M., & Wittenbrink, B. (2002). The police officer's dilemma: Using ethnicity to disambiguate potentially threatening individuals. *Journal of Personality and Social Psychology, 83,* 1314–1329. (p. 744)

Costa, P. T., Jr., Terracciano, A., & McCrae, R. R. (2001). Gender differences in personality traits across cultures: Robust and surprising findings. *Journal of Personality and Social Psychology, 81,* 322–331. (p. 526)

Costa, P. T., Jr., Zonderman, A. B., McCrae, R. R., Cornoni-Huntley, J., Locke, B. Z., & Barbano, H. E. (1987). Longitudinal analyses of psychological well-being in a national sample: Stability of mean levels. *Journal of Gerontology, 42,* 50–55. (p. 190)

Costanzo, M. (1997). *Just revenge: Costs and consequences of the death penalty.* New York: St. Martins. (p. 50)

Costello, E. J., Compton, S. N., Keeler, G., & Angold, A. (2003). Relationships between poverty and psychopathology: A natural experiment. *Journal of the American Medical Association, 290,* 2023–2029. (pp. 31, 681)

Coughlin, J. F., Mohyde, M., D'Ambrosio, L. A., & Gilbert, J. (2004). Who drives older driver decisions? Cambridge, MA: MIT Age Lab. (p. 180)

Coull, J. T., Vidal, F., Nazarian, B., & Macar, F. (2004). Functional anatomy of the attentional modulation of time estimation. *Science, 303,* 1506–1508. (p. 499)

Courage, M. L., & Howe, M. L. (2002). From infant to child: The dynamics of cognitive change in the second year of life. *Psychological Bulletin, 128,* 250–277. (p. 161)

Courneya, K. S., & Carron, A. V. (1992). The home advantage in sports competitions: A literature review. *Journal of Sport and Exercise Psychology, 14,* 13–27. (p. 738)

Courtney, J. G., Longnecker, M. P., Theorell, T., & de Verdier, M. G. (1993). Stressful life events and the risk of colorectal cancer. *Epidemiology, 4,* 407–414. (p. 559)

Cousins, N. (1989). *Head first: The biology of hope.* New York: Dutton. (p. 122)

Covington, M. V., & Omelich, C. L. (1988). I can resist anything but temptation: Adolescent expectations for smoking cigarettes. *Journal of Applied Social Psychology, 18,* 203–227. (p. 576)

Cowan, G., Lee, C., Levy, D., & Snyder, D. (1988). Dominance and inequality in X-rated videocassettes. *Psychology of Women Quarterly, 12,* 299–311. (p. 753)

Cowan, N. (1988). Evolving conceptions of memory storage, selective attention, and their mutual constraints within the human information-processing system. *Psychological Bulletin, 104,* 163–191. (p. 362)

Cowan, N. (1994). Mechanisms of verbal short-term memory. *Current Directions in Psychological Science, 3,* 185–189. (p. 363)

Cowan, N. (2001). The magical number 4 in short-term memory: A reconsideration of mental storage capacity. *Behavioral and Brain Sciences, 24,* 87–185. (p. 363)

Cowart, B. J. (1981). Development of taste perception in humans: Sensitivity and preference throughout the life span. *Psychological Bulletin, 90,* 43–73. (p. 230)

Crabbe, J. C. (2002). Genetic contributions to addiction. *Annual Review of Psychology, 53,* 435–462. (p. 305)

Crabtree, S. (2002, January 22). Gender roles reflected in teen tech use. *Gallup Tuesday Briefing* (www.gallup.com). (p. 128)

Crabtree, S. (2005, January 13). Engagement keeps the doctor away. *Gallup Management Journal* (gmj.gallup.com). (p. 506)

Craig, M. E., Kalichman, S. C., & Follingstad, D. R. (1989). Verbal coercive sexual behavior among college students. *Archives of Sexual Behavior, 18,* 421–434. (pp. 752–753)

Craik, F. I. M. (1986). A functional account of age differences in memory. In F. Klix & H. Hagendorf (Eds.), *Human memory and cognitive capabilities.* Amsterdam: Elsevier. (p. 183)

Craik, F. I. M., & Tulving, E. (1975). Depth of processing and the retention of words in episodic memory. *Journal of Experimental Psychology: General, 104,* 268–294. (p. 357)

Craik, F. I. M., & Watkins, M. J. (1973). The role of rehearsal in short-term memory. *Journal of Verbal Learning and Verbal Behavior, 12,* 599–607. (p. 356)

Crain-Thoreson, C., & Dale, P. S. (1992). Do early talkers become early readers? Linguistic precocity, preschool language, and emergent literacy. *Developmental Psychology, 28,* 421–429. (p. 451)

Crandall, C. S. (1988). Social contagion of binge eating. *Journal of Personality and Social Psychology, 55,* 588–598. (p. 478)

Crandall, C. S. (1994). Prejudice against fat people: Ideology and self-interest. *Journal of Personality and Social Psychology, 66,* 882–894. (p. 583)

Crandall, C. S. (1995). Do parents discriminate against their heavyweight daughters? *Personality and Social Psychology Bulletin, 21,* 724–735. (p. 583)

Crandall, J. E. (1984). Social interest as a moderator of life stress. *Journal of Personality and Social Psychology, 47,* 164–174. (p. 611)

Crawford, M., Chaffin, R., & Fitton, L. (1995). *Learning and Individual Differences, 7,* 341–362. (p. 464)

Crews, F. (Ed.) (1998). *Unauthorized Freud: Doubters confront a legend.* New York: Viking. (p. 607)

Crocker, J., & Major, B. (1989). Social stigma and self-esteem: The self-protective properties of stigma," *Psychological Review, 89,* 608–630. (p. 633)

Crocker, J., & Park, L. E. (2004). The costly pursuit of self-esteem. *Psychological Bulletin, 130,* 392–414. (p. 636)

Crocker, J., Thompson, L. L., McGraw, K. M., & Ingerman, C. (1987). Downward comparison, prejudice, and evaluation of others: Effects of self-esteem and threat. *Journal of Personality and Social Psychology, 52,* 907–916. (p. 747)

Crocker, J., & Wolfe, C. (1999). Rescuing self-esteem: A contingencies of worth perspective. Unpublished manuscript, University of Michigan. (p. 632)

Croft, R. J., Klugman, A., Baldeweg, T., & Gruzelier, J. H. (2001). Electrophysiological evidence of serotonergic impairment in long-term MDMA ("Ecstasy") users. *American Journal of Psychiatry, 158,* 1687-1692. (p. 302)

Crombie, A. C. (1964, May). Early concepts of the senses and the mind. *Scientific American,* pp. 108-116. (p. 206)

Crook, T. H., & West, R. L. (1990). Name recall performance across the adult life-span. *British Journal of Psychology, 81,* 335-340. (p. 181)

Cross, S., & Markus, H. (1991). Possible selves across the life span. *Human Development, 34,* 230-255. (p. 631)

Cross-National Collaborative Group. (1992). The changing rate of major depression. *Journal of the American Medical Association, 268,* 3098-3105. (p. 661)

Crossen, C. (1994). *Tainted truth: The manipulation of fact in America.* New York: Simon & Schuster. (p. 40)

Crowell, J. A., & Waters, E. (1994). Bowlby's theory grown up: The role of attachment in adult love relationships. *Psychological Inquiry, 5,* 1-22. (p. 156)

Croyle, R. T., & Ditto, P. H. (1990). Illness cognition and behavior: An experimental approach. *Journal of Behavioral Medicine, 13,* 31-52. (p. 591)

Csikszentmihalyi, M. (1990). *Flow: The psychology of optimal experience.* New York: Harper & Row. (p. 498)

Csikszentmihalyi, M. (1999). If we are so rich, why aren't we happy? *American Psychologist, 54,* 821-827. (pp. 498, 539)

Csikszentmihalyi, M., & Hunter, J. (2003). Happiness in everyday life: The uses of experience sampling. *Journal of Happiness Studies, 4,* 185-199. (p. 172)

Csikszentmihalyi, M., & Larson, R. (1984). *Being adolescent: Conflict and growth in the teenage years.* New York: Basic Books. (p. 190)

Cunningham, M. R., & others. (2005). "Their ideas of beauty are, on the whole, the same as ours": Consistency and variability in the cross-cultural perception of female physical attractiveness. *Journal of Personality and Social Psychology, 68,* 261-279. (p. 761)

Cunningham, W. A., Johnson, M. K., Raye, C. L., Gatenby, J. C., Gore, J. C., & Banaji, M. R. (2004). Separable neural components in the processing of Black and White faces. *Psychological Science, 15,* 806-813. (p. 744)

Curtis, G. C., Magee, W. J., Eaton, W. W., Wittchen, H-U., & Kessler, R. C. (1998). Specific fears and phobias: Epidemiology and classification. *British Journal of Psychiatry, 173,* 212-217. (p. 650)

Curtis, R. C., & Miller, K. (1986). Believing another likes or dislikes you: Behaviors making the beliefs come true. *Journal of Personality and Social Psychology, 51,* 284-290. (p. 762)

Cutler, B. L., & Penrod, S. D. (1989). Forensically relevant moderators of the relation between eyewitness identification accuracy and confidence. *Journal of Applied Psychology, 74,* 650-652. (p. 385)

Czeisler, C. A., Allan, J. S., Strogatz, S. H., Ronda, J. M., Sanchez, R., Rios, C. D., Freitag, W. O., Richardson, G. S., & Kronauer, R. E. (1986). Bright light resets the human circadian pacemaker independent of the timing of the sleep-wake cycle. *Science, 233,* 667-671. (p. 275)

Czeisler, C. A., Duffy, J. F., Shanahan, T. L., Brown, E. N., Mitchell, J. F., Rimmer, D. W., Ronda, J. M., Silva, E. J., Allan, J. S., Emens, J. S., Dijk, D-J., & Kronauer, R. E. (1999). Stability, precision, and near-24-hour period of the human circadian pacemaker. *Science, 284,* 2177-2181. (p. 276)

Czeisler, C. A., Kronauer, R. E., Allan, J. S., & Duffy, J. F. (1989). Bright light induction of strong (type O) resetting of the human circadian pacemaker. *Science, 244,* 1328-1333. (p. 9)

Dabbs, J. M., Jr. (2000). Heroes, rogues, and lovers: Testosterone and behavior. New York: McGraw-Hill. (p. 483)

Dabbs, J. M., Jr., Bernieri, F. J., Strong, R. K., Campo, R., & Milun, R. (2001b). Going on stage: Testosterone in greetings and meetings. *Journal of Research in Personality, 35,* 27-40. (p. 750)

Dabbs, J. M., Jr., & Morris, R. (1990). Testosterone, social class, and antisocial behavior in a sample of 4,462 men. *Psychological Science, 1,* 209-211. (p. 750)

Dabbs, J. M., Jr., Riad, J. K., & Chance, S. E. (2001a). Testosterone and ruthless homicide. *Personality and Individual Differences, 31,* 599-603. (p. 750)

Dabbs, J. M., Jr., Ruback, R. B., & Besch, N. F. (1987). Male saliva testosterone following conversations with male and female partners. Paper presented at the American Psychological Association convention. (p. 483)

Daley, T. C., Whaley, S. E., Sigman, M. D., Espinosa, M. P., & Neumann, C. (2003). IQ on the rise: The Flynn effect in rural Kenyan children. *Psychological Science, 14,* 215-219. (p. 448)

Dalton, M. A., Ahrens, M. B., Sargent, J. D., Mott, L. A., Beach, M. L., Tickle, J. J., & Heatherton, T. F. (2002). Relation between parental restrictions on movies and adolescent use of tobacco and alcohol. *Effective Clinical Practice, 5,* 1-9. (p. 576)

Damasio, A. (2003). *Looking for Spinoza: Joy, sorrow, and the feeling brain.* New York: Harcourt. (p. 519)

Damasio, A. R. (1994). *Descartes error: Emotion, reason, and the human brain.* New York: Grossett/Putnam & Sons. (p. 437)

Damasio, H., Grabowski, T., Frank, R., Galaburda, A. M., & Damasio, A. R. (1994). The return of Phineas Gage: Clues about the brain from the skull of a famous patient. *Science, 264,* 1102-1105. (p. 80)

Damon, W. (1995). *Greater expectations: Overcoming the culture of indulgence in America's homes and schools.* New York: Free Press. (pp. 147, 632)

Damon, W., & Hart, D. (1982). The development of self-understanding from infancy through adolescence. *Child Development, 53,* 841-864. (p. 161)

Damon, W., & Hart, D. (1988). *Self-understanding in childhood and adolescence.* Cambridge: Cambridge University Press. (p. 161)

Damon, W., Menon, J., & Bronk, K. (2003). The development of purpose during adolescence. *Applied Developmental Science, 7,* 119-128. (p. 171)

Dannenberg, A. L., Burton, D., & Jackson, R. J. (2004). Economic and environmental costs of obesity: The impact on airlines. *American Journal of Preventive Medicine, 27,* 264. (p. 587)

Danner, D. D., Snowdon, D. A., & Friesen, W. V. (2001). Positive emotions in early life and longevity: Findings from the Nun Study. *Journal of Personality and Social Psychology, 80,* 804-813. (p. 565)

Danso, H., & Esses, V. (2001). Black experimenters and the intellectual test performance of white participants: The tables are turned. *Journal of Experimental Social Psychology, 37,* 158-165. (p. 465)

Darley, J. M., & Latané, B. (1968a). Bystander intervention in emergencies: Diffusion of responsibility. *Journal of Personality and Social Psychology, 8,* 377-383. (p. 765)

Darley, J. M., & Latané, B. (1968b, December). When will people help in a crisis? *Psychology Today,* pp. 54-57, 70-71. (p. 765)

Darley, J. M., Seligman, C., & Becker, L. J. (1979, April). The lesson of twin rivers: Feedback works. *Psychology Today,* pp. 16, 23-24. (p. 338)

Darrach, B., & Norris, J. (1984, August). An American tragedy. *Life,* pp. 58-74. (p. 678)

Daum, I., & Schugens, M. M. (1996). On the cerebellum and classical conditioning. *Psychological Science, 5,* 58-61. (p. 369)

Dauvilliers, Y., Carlander, B., Moinari, N., Desautels, A., Okun, M., Tafti, M., Montplaisir, J., Mignot, E., & Billard, M. (2003). Month of birth as a risk factor for narcolepsy. *Sleep, 26,* 663-665. (p. 284)

Davey, G. C. L. (1992). Classical conditioning and the acquisition of human fears and phobias: A review and synthesis of the literature. *Advances in Behavior Research and Therapy, 14,* 29-66. (p. 323)

Davey, G. C. L. (1995). Preparedness and phobias: Specific evolved associations or a generalized expectancy bias? *Behavioral and Brain Sciences, 18,* 289-297. (p. 655)

Davidoff, J. (2004). Coloured thinking. *The Psychologist, 17,* 570-572. (p. 419)

Davidson, R. (2000). Affective style, psychopathology, and resilience: Brain mechanisms and plasticity. *American Psychologist, 55,* 1196-1209. (p. 518)

Davidson, R. J. (2003). Affective neuroscience and psychophysiology: Toward a synthesis. *Psychophysiology, 40,* 655-665. (p. 518)

Davidson, R. J., Kabat-Zinn, J., Schumacher, J., Rosenkranz, M., Muller, D., Santorelli, S. F., Urbanowski, F., Harrington, A., Bonus, K., & Sheridan, J. F. (2003). Alterations in brain and immune function produced by mindfulness meditation. *Psychosomatic Medicine, 65,* 564-570. (p. 571)

Davidson, R. J., Pizzagalli, D., Nitschke, J. B., & Putnam, K. (2002). Depression: Perspectives from affective neuroscience. *Annual Review of Psychology, 53,* 545-574. (p. 665)

Davidson, R. J., Putnam, K. M., & Larson, C. L. (2000). Dysfunction in the neural circuitry of emotion regulation—a possible prelude to violence. *Science, 289,* 591-594. (p. 749)

Davies, D. R., Matthews, G., & Wong, C. S. K. (1991). Aging and work. *International Review of Industrial and Organizational Psychology, 6,* 149-211. (p. 186)

Davies, M. F. (1997). Positive test strategies and confirmatory retrieval processes in the evaluation of personality feedback. *Journal of Personality and Social Psychology, 73,* 574-583. (pp. 616-617)

Davies, P. (1992). *The mind of God: The scientific basis for a rational world.* New York: Simon & Schuster. (p. 135)

Davies, P. (1999). *The fifth miracle: The search for the origin and meaning of life.* New York: Simon & Schuster. (p. 135)

Davies, P. (2004, April 14). Into the 21st century. *Metaviews* (www.metanexus.net). (p. 136)

Davis, B. E., Moon, R. Y., Sachs, H. C., & Ottolini, M. C. (1998). Effects of sleep position on infant motor development. *Pediatrics, 102,* 1135-1140. (p. 145)

Davis, J. O., & Phelps, J. A. (1995a). Twins with schizophrenia: Genes or germs? *Schizophrenia Bulletin, 21,* 13-18. (pp. 114, 674)

Davis, J. O., Phelps, J. A., & Bracha, H. S. (1995b). Prenatal development of monozygotic twins and concordance for schizophrenia. *Schizophrenia Bulletin, 21,* 357-366. (pp. 114, 624)

Davis, S., Rees, M., Ribot, J., Moufarege, A., Rodenberg, C., & Purdie, D. (2003). Efficacy and safety of testosterone patches for the treatment of low sexual desire in surgically menopausal women. Presented to the American Society for Reproductive Medicine, San Antonio, October 11-15. (p. 483)

Davison, K. P., Pennebaker, J. W., & Dickerson, S. S. (2000). Who talks? The social psychology of illness support groups. *American Psychologist, 55,* 205-217. (p. 698)

Dawes, R. M. (1980). Social dilemmas. *Annual Review of Psychology, 31,* 169-193. (p. 757)

Dawes, R. M. (1994). *House of cards: Psychology and psychotherapy built on myth.* New York: Free Press. (p. 632)

Dawkins, R. (1998). *Unweaving the rainbow.* Boston: Houghton Mifflin. (p. 135)

Dawkins, R. (1999, April 8). Is science killing the soul (a discussion with Richard Dawkins and Steven Pinker). www.edge.org (p. 271)

Dawson, N. V., Arkes, H. R., Siciliano, C., Blinkhorn, R., Lakshmanan, M., & Petrelli, M. (1988). Hindsight bias: An impediment to accurate probability estimation in clinicopathologic conferences. *Medical Decision Making, 8,* 259-264. (p. 20)

Deacon, B. J., & Abramowitz, J. S. (2004). Cognitive and behavioral treatments for anxiety disorders: A review of meta-analytic findings. *Journal of Clinical Psychology, 60,* 429-441. (p. 691)

Dean, G. A., Kelly, I. W., Saklofske, D. H., & Furnham, A. (1992). Graphology and human judgment. In B. Beyerstein & D. Beyerstein (Eds.), *The write stuff: Evaluations of graphology.* Buffalo, NY: Prometheus Books. (p. 616)

Deary, I. J., & Caryl, P. G. (1993). Intelligence, EEG and evoked potentials. In P. A. Vernon (Ed.), *Biological approaches to the study of human intelligence.* Norwood, NJ: Ablex. (p. 441)

Deary, I. J., & Der, G. (2005). Reaction time explains IQ's association with death. *Psychological Science, 16,* 64-69. (p. 441)

Deary, I. J., & Matthews, G. (1993). Personality traits are alive and well. *The Psychologist: Bulletin of the British Psychological Society, 6,* 299-311. (p. 621)

Deary, I. J., & Stough, C. (1997). Looking down on human intelligence. *American Psychologist, 52,* 1148-1149. (p. 441)

Deary, I. J., Thorpe, G., Wilson, V., Starr, J. M., & Whalley, L. J. (2003). Population sex differences in IQ at age 11: The Scottish mental survey 1932. *Intelligence, 31,* 533-541. (p. 462)

Deary, I. J., Whiteman, M. C., Starr, J. M., Whalley, L. J., & Fox, H. C. (2004). The impact of childhood intelligence on later life: Following up the Scottish mental surveys of 1932 and 1947. *Journal of Personality and Social Psychology, 86,* 130-147. (p. 451)

de Beyer, J. (1999). Why is tobacco control a public health priority around the world? Washington, DC: World Bank. (p. 582)

de Beyer, J. (2005, February 4). Tobacco: How trade policy affects health. Annual Conference: Health in Foreign Policy. Panel II: Global Commerce and Health. (p. 581)

de Boysson-Bardies, B., Halle, P., Sagart, L., & Durand, C. (1989). A cross linguistic investigation of vowel formats in babbling. *Journal of Child Language, 16,* 1-17. (p. 412)

DeBruine, L. M. (2002). Facial resemblance enhances trust. *Proceedings of the Royal Society of London, 269,* 1307-1312. (p. 759)

DeBruine, L. M. (2004). Facial resemblance increases the attractiveness of same-sex faces more than other-sex faces. *Proceedings of the Royal Society of London B, 271,* 2085-2090. (p. 759)

DeCasper, A. J., Lecanuet, J-P., Busnel, M-C., & others. (1994). Fetal reactions to recurrent maternal speech. *Infant Behavior and Development, 17,* 159-164. (p. 141)

DeCasper, A. J., & Prescott, P. A. (1984). Human newborns' perception of male voices: Preference, discrimination and reinforcing value. *Developmental Psychobiology, 17,* 481-491. (p. 141)

DeCasper, A. J., & Spence, M. J. (1986). Prenatal maternal speech influences newborns' perception of speech sounds. *Infant Behavior and Development, 9,* 133-150. (p. 141)

Deci, E. L., Koestner, R., & Ryan, R. M. (1999, November). A meta-analytic review of experiments examining the effects of extrinsic rewards on intrinsic motivation. *Psychological Bulletin, 125(6),* 627-668. (p. 335)

Deci, E. L., & Ryan, R. M. (1985). *Intrinsic motivation and self-determination in human behavior.* New York: Plenum Press. (p. 335)

Deci, E. L., & Ryan, R. M. (1992). The initiation and regulation of intrinsically motivated learning and achievement. In A. K. Boggiano & T. S. Pittman (Eds.), *Achievement and motivation: A social-developmental perspective.* New York: Cambridge University Press. (p. 335)

Deci, E. L., & Ryan, R. M. (2000). The "what" and "why" of goal pursuits: Human needs and the self-determination of behavior. *Psychological Inquiry, 11,* 227-268. (p. 335)

de Courten-Myers, G. (2005, February 4). Personal correspondence (estimating total brain neurons, extrapolating from her carefully estimated 20 to 23 billion cortical neurons). (p. 64)

de Courten-Myers, G. M. (2002, May 9). Personal correspondence. (pp. 75, 144)

de Cuevas, J. (1990, September-October). "No, she holded them loosely." *Harvard Magazine,* pp. 60-67. (p. 414)

de Hoogh, A. H. B., den Hartog, D. N., Koopman, P. L., Thierry, H., van den Berg, P. T., van der Weide, J. G., & Wilderom, C. P. M. (2004). Charismatic leadership, environmental dynamism, and performance. *European Journal of Work and Organisational Psychology, 13,* 447-471. (p. 509)

De Houwer, J., Thomas, S., & Baeyens, F. (2001). Associative learning of likes and dislikes: A review of 25 years of research on human evaluative conditioning. *Psychological Bulletin, 127,* 853-869. (p. 319)

De Koninck, J. (2000). Waking experiences and dreaming. In M. Kryger, T. Roth, & W. Dement (Eds.), *Principles and practice of sleep medicine, 3rd ed.* Philadelphia: Saunders. (p. 286)

Delaney, P. F., Ericsson, K. A., Weaver, G. E., & Mahadevan, S. (1999). Accounts of the memorist Rajan's exceptional performance: Comparing three theoretical proposals. Paper presented to the American Psychological Society convention. (p. 363)

Delgado, J. M. R. (1969). *Physical control of the mind: Toward a psychocivilized society.* New York: Harper & Row. (p. 78)

DeLoache, J. S. (1995). Early understanding and use of symbols: The model model. *Current Directions in Psychological Science, 4,* 109–113. (p. 150)

DeLoache, J. S., & Brown, A. L. (1987, October-December). Differences in the memory-based searching of delayed and normally developing young children. *Intelligence, 11*(4), 277–289. (p. 150)

DeLoache, J. S., Uttal, D. H., & Rosengren, K. S. (2004). Scale errors offer evidence for a perception-action dissociation early in life. *Science, 304,* 1027–1029. (p. 147)

Dement, W. (1997, September). What all undergraduates should know about how their sleeping lives affect their waking lives. Stanford University: www.leland.stanford.edu/~dement/sleepless.html (p. 279)

Dement, W. C. (1978). *Some must watch while some must sleep.* New York: Norton. (pp. 276, 277, 284)

Dement, W. C. (1999). *The promise of sleep.* New York: Delacorte Press. (pp. 276, 277, 280–281, 284)

Dement, W. C., & Wolpert, E. A. (1958). The relation of eye movements, body mobility, and external stimuli to dream content. *Journal of Experimental Psychology, 55,* 543–553. (p. 286)

Demir, E., & Dickson, B. J. (2005). *Fruitless* splicing specifies male courtship behavior in *Drosophila. Cell, 121,* 785–794. (p. 490)

Dempster, F. N. (1988). The spacing effect: A case study in the failure to apply the results of psychological research. *American Psychologist, 43,* 627–634. (p. 355)

Denes-Raj, V., Epstein, S., & Cole, J. (1995). The generality of the ratio-bias phenomenon. *Personality and Social Psychology Bulletin, 21,* 1083–1092. (p. 406)

DeNeve, K. M., & Cooper, H. (1998). The happy personality: A meta-analysis of 137 personality traits and subjective well-being. *Psychological Bulletin, 124,* 197–229. (p. 544)

Dennerstein, L., Dudley, E., Guthrie, J., & Barrett-Connor, E. (2000). Life satisfaction, symptoms, and the menopausal transition. *Medscape Women's Health, 5*(4) (www.medscape.com). (p. 176)

Dennett, D. (1996, September 9). Quoted by Ian Parker, Richard Dawkins' evolution. *The New Yorker,* pp. 41–45. (p. 9)

Denton, K., & Krebs, D. (1990). From the scene to the crime: The effect of alcohol and social context on moral judgment. *Journal of Personality and Social Psychology, 59,* 242–248. (p. 299)

D'Eon, J. L. (1989). Hypnosis in the control of labor pain. In N. P. Spanos & J. F. Chaves (Eds.), *Hypnosis: The cognitive-behavioral perspective.* Buffalo, NY: Prometheus Books. (p. 293)

DePaulo, B. M. (1994). Spotting lies: Can humans learn to do better? *Current Directions in Psychological Science 3,* 83–86. (p. 525)

DePaulo, B. M., Blank, A. L., Swaim, G. W., & Hairfield, J. G. (1992). Expressiveness and expressive control. *Personality and Social Psychology Bulletin, 18,* 276–285. (p. 622)

De Quervain, D. J.-F., Roozendaal, B., & McGaugh, J. L. (1998). Stress and glucocorticoids impair retrieval of long-term spatial memory. *Nature, 394,* 787–790. (p. 367)

Deregowski, J. (1972, November). Pictorial perception and culture. *Scientific American,* pp. 82–88. (pp. 249, 603)

Dermer, M., Cohen, S. J., Jacobsen, E., & Anderson, E. A. (1979). Evaluative judgments of aspects of life as a function of vicarious exposure to hedonic extremes. *Journal of Personality and Social Psychology, 37,* 247–260. (p. 543)

Dermer, M., & Pyszczynski, T. A. (1978). Effects of erotica upon men's loving and liking responses for women they love. *Journal of Personality and Social Psychology, 36,* 1302–1309. (p. 763)

Deroche-Garmonet, V., Belin, D., & Piazza, P. V. (2004). Evidence for addiction-like behavior in the rat. *Science, 305,* 1014–1017. (p. 297)

DeRubeis, R. J., & 10 others, (2005). Cognitive therapy vs. medications in the treatment of moderate to severe depression. *Archives of General Psychiatry, 62,* 409–416. (p. 704)

DeSteno, D., Dasgupta, N., Bartlett, M. Y., & Cajdric, A. (2004). Prejudice from thin air: The effect of emotion on automatic intergroup attitudes. *Psychological Science, 15,* 319–324. (p. 536)

DeSteno, D., Petty, R. E., Wegener, D. T., & Rucker, D. D. (2000). Beyond valence in the perception of likelihood: The role of emotion specificity. *Journal of Personality and Social Psychology, 78,* 397–416. (p. 374)

Deutsch, J. A. (1972, July). Brain reward: ESP and ecstasy. *Psychology Today,* 46–48. (p. 74)

Deutsch, M. (1991). Egalitarianism in the laboratory and at work. In R. Vermunt & H. Steensma (Eds.), *Social justice in human relations.* New York: Plenum. (p. 337)

DeValois, R. L., & DeValois, K. K. (1975). Neural coding of color. In E. C. Carterette & M. P. Friedman (Eds.), *Handbook of perception: Vol. V. Seeing.* New York: Academic Press. (p. 213)

Devilly, G. J. (2003). Eye movement desensitization and reprocessing: A chronology of its development and scientific standing. *Scientific Review of Mental Health Practice, 1,* 113–118. (p. 706)

Devine, P. G. (1995). Prejudice and outgroup perception. In A. Tesser (Ed.), *Advanced social psychology.* New York: McGraw-Hill. (p. 759)

Devlin, B., Daniels, M., & Roeder, K. (1997). The heritability of IQ. *Nature, 388,* 468–471. (p. 445)

Dew, M. A., Hoch, C. C., Buysse, D. J., Monk, T. H., Begley, A. E., Houck, P. R., Hall, M., Kupfer, D. J., Reynolds, C. F., III (2003). Healthy older adults' sleep predicts all-cause mortality at 4 to 19 years of follow-up. *Psychosomatic Medicine, 65,* 63–73. (p. 281)

de Waal, F. B. M. (1999, December). The end of nature versus nurture. *Scientific American,* pp. 94–99. (p. 130)

de Waal, F. B. M., Dindo, M., Freeman, C. A., & Hall, M. J. (2005). The monkey in the mirror: Hardly a stranger. *Proceedings of the National Academy of Sciences, 102,* 11140–11147. (p. 161)

de Waal, F. B. M., & Johanowicz, D. L. (1993). Modification of reconciliation behavior through social experience: An experiment with two macaque species. *Child Development, 64,* 897–908. (p. 341)

De Wolff, M. S., & van IJzendoorn, M. H. (1997). Sensitivity and attachment: A meta-analysis of parental antecedents of infant attachment. *Child Development, 68,* 571–591. (p. 157)

Dey, E. L., Astin, A. W., & Korn, W. S. (1991). *The American freshman: Twenty-five year trends.* Los Angeles: Higher Education Research Institute, UCLA. (p. 132)

Dhawan, N., Roseman, I. J., Naidu, R. K., Thapa, K., & Rettek, S. I. (1995). Self-concepts across two cultures: India and the United States. *Journal of Cross-Cultural Psychology, 26,* 606–621. (p. 122)

Diaconis, P. (2002, August 11). Quoted by L. Belkin, The odds of that. *New York Times* (www.nytimes.com). (p. 35)

Diaconis, P., & Mosteller, F. (1989). Methods for studying coincidences. *Journal of the American Statistical Association, 84,* 853–861. (p. 35)

Diamond, J. (1989, May). The great leap forward. *Discover,* pp. 50–60. (p. 410)

Diamond, J. (2001, February). A tale of two reputations: Why we revere Darwin and give Freud a hard time. *Natural History,* pp. 20–24. (p. 109)

Diamond, L. M. (2000). Sexual identity, attractions, and behavior among young sexual-minority women over a 2-year period. *Developmental Psychology, 36,* 241–250. (p. 488)

Diamond, L. M. (2003). Was it a phase? Young women's relinquishment of lesbian/bisexual identities over a 5-year period. *Journal of Personality and Social Psychology, 84,* 352–364. (p. 488)

Diamond, R. (1993). Genetics and male sexual orientation (letter). *Science, 261*, 1258. (p. 493)

Dickerson, S. S., & Kemeny, M. E. (2004). Acute stressors and cortisol responses: A theoretical integration and synthesis of laboratory research. *Psychological Bulletin, 130*, 355–391. (p. 563)

Dickson, B. (2005, June 3). Quoted in E. Rosenthal, For fruit flies, gene shift tilts sex orientation. *New York Times* (www.nytimes.com). (p. 490)

Diener, E., & Biswas-Diener, R. (2002). Will money increase subjective well-being? A literature review and guide to needed research. *Social Indicators Research, 57*, 119–169. (p. 541)

Diener, E., Diener, M., & Diener, C. (1995). Factors predicting the subjective well-being of nations. *Journal of Personality and Social Psychology, 69*, 851–864. (p. 123)

Diener, E., Emmons, R. A., & Sandvik, E. (1986). The dual nature of happiness: Independence of positive and negative moods. Unpublished manuscript, University of Illinois. (p. 190)

Diener, E., & Oishi, S. (2000). Money and happiness: Income and subjective well-being across nations. In E. Diener & E. M. Suh (Eds.), *Subjective well-being across cultures*. Cambridge, MA: MIT Press. (pp. 539, 541)

Diener, E., Oishi, S., & Lucas, R. E. (2003). Personality, culture, and subjective well-being: Emotional and cognitive evaluations of life. *Annual Review of Psychology, 54*, 403–425. (p. 544)

Diener, E., & Seligman, M. E. P. (2002). Very happy people. *Psychological Science, 13*, 81–84. (p. 495)

Diener, E., & Seligman, M. E. P. (2004). Beyond money: Toward an economy of well-being. *Psychological Science in the Public Interest, 5*, 1–31. (p. 542)

Diener, E., Wirtz, D., & Oishi, S. (2001). End effects of rated life quality: The James Dean effect. *Psychological Science, 12*, 124–128. (p. 228)

Diener, E., Wolsic, B., & Fujita, F. (1995). Physical attractiveness and subjective well-being. *Journal of Personality and Social Psychology, 69*, 120–129. (p. 760)

Diener, M. L., & Lucas, R. E. (2004). Adults' desires for children's emotions across 48 countries: Associations with individual and national characteristics. *Journal of Cross-Cultural Psychology, 35*, 525–547. (p. 537)

Dietz, W. H., Jr., & Gortmaker, S. L. (1985). Do we fatten our children at the television set? Obesity and television viewing in children and adolescents. *Pediatrics, 75*, 807–812. (p. 590)

Dijksterhuis, A., & Aarts, H. (2003). On wildebeests and humans: The preferential detection of negative stimuli. *Psychological Science, 14*, 14–18. (p. 524)

DiLalla, D. L., Carey, G., Gottesman, I. I., & Bouchard, T. J., Jr. (1996). Heritability of MMPI personality indicators of psychopathology in twins reared apart. *Journal of Abnormal Psychology, 105*, 491–499. (pp. 100, 663)

Dimberg, U., Thunberg, M., & Elmehed, K. (2000). Unconscious facial reactions to emotional facial expressions. *Psychological Science, 11*, 86–89. (pp. 342, 531, 552)

Dimberg, U., Thunberg, M., & Grunedal, S. (2002). Facial reactions to emotional stimuli: Automatically controlled emotional responses. *Cognition and Emotion, 16*, 449–472. (p. 342)

Dindia, K., & Allen, M. (1992). Sex differences in self-disclosure: A meta-analysis. *Psychological Bulletin, 112*, 106–124. (p. 129)

Dinges, N. G., & Hull, P. (1992). Personality, culture, and international studies. In D. Lieberman (Ed.), *Revealing the world: An interdisciplinary reader for international studies*. Dubuque, IA: Kendall-Hunt. (p. 418)

Dion, K. K., & Dion, K. L. (1993). Individualistic and collectivistic perspectives on gender and the cultural context of love and intimacy. *Journal of Social Issues, 49*, 53–69. (p. 123)

Dion, K. K., & Dion, K. L. (2001). Gender and cultural adaptation in immigrant families. *Journal of Social Issues, 57*, 511–521. (p. 132)

DiPietro, J. A. (2004). The role of prenatal maternal stress in child development. *Current Directions in Psychological Science, 13*, 71–74. (p. 142)

Discover (1996, May). A fistful of risks. Pp. 82–83. (p. 575)

Dishion, T. J., McCord, J., & Poulin, F. (1999). When interventions harm: Peer groups and problem behavior. *American Psychologist, 54*, 755–764. (p. 702)

Di Tella, R., MacCulloch, R. J., & Oswald, A. J. (2001). The macroeconomics of happiness. Warwick Economic Research Paper No. 615, Department of Economics, University of Warwick. (p. 539)

Doherty, E. W., & Doherty, W. J. (1998). Smoke gets in your eyes: Cigarette smoking and divorce in a national sample of American adults. *Families, Systems, and Health, 16*, 393–400. (p. 576)

Dohrenwend, B. P., Levav, I., Shrout, P. E., Schwartz, S., Naveh, G., Link, B. G., Skodol, A. E., & Stueve, A. (1992). Socioeconomic status and psychiatric disorders: The causation-selection issue. *Science, 255*, 946–952. (p. 681)

Dohrenwend, B., Pearlin, L., Clayton, P., Hamburg, B., Dohrenwend, B. P., Riley, M., & Rose, R. (1982). Report on stress and life events. In G. R. Elliott & C. Eisdorfer (Eds.), *Stress and human health: Analysis and implications of research* (A study by the Institute of Medicine/National Academy of Sciences). New York: Springer. (p. 554)

Dolan, R. J. (1999). On the neurology of morals. *Nature Neuroscience, 2*, 927–929. (p. 80)

Dolcos, F., LaBar, K. S., & Cabeza, R. (2004). Interaction between the amygdala and the medial temporal lobe memory system predicts better memory for emotional events. *Neuron, 42*, 855–863. (p. 366)

Dole, R. (1996, April 20). Quoted by M. Duffy, Look who's talking. *Time*, p. 48. (p. 725)

Dolezal, H. (1982). *Living in a world transformed*. New York: Academic Press. (p. 257)

Domhoff, G. W. (1996). *Finding meaning in dreams: A quantitative approach*. New York: Plenum. (p. 286)

Domhoff, G. W. (1999). New directions in the study of dream content using the Hall and Van de Castle coding system. *Dreaming, 9*, 115–137. (p. 286)

Domhoff, G. W. (2000). Moving Dream Theory Beyond Freud and Jung. Paper presented to the symposium "Beyond Freud and Jung?" Graduate Theological Union, Berkeley, CA, 9/23/2000. (p. 287)

Domhoff, G. W. (2003). *The scientific study of dreams: Neural networks, cognitive development, and content analysis*. Washington, DC: APA Books. (p. 288)

Domjan, M. (1992). Adult learning and mate choice: Possibilities and experimental evidence. *American Zoologist, 32*, 48–61. (p. 318)

Domjan, M. (1994). Formulation of a behavior system for sexual conditioning. *Psychonomic Bulletin & Review, 1*, 421–428. (p. 318)

Domjan, M. (2005). Pavlovian conditioning: A functional perspective. *Annual Review of Psychology, 56*. (pp. 318, 322)

Domjan, M., Blesbois, E., & Williams, J. (1998). The adaptive significance of sexual conditioning: Pavlovian control of sperm release. *Psychological Science, 9*, 411–415. (p. 318)

Domjan, M., Cusato, B., & Krause, M. (2004). Learning with arbitrary versus ecological conditioned stimuli: Evidence from sexual conditioning. *Psychonomic Bulletin & Review, 11*, 232–246. (p. 322)

Donahoe, J. W., & Vegas, R. (2004). Pavlovian conditioning: The CS-UR relation. *Journal of Experimental Psychology: Animal Behavior, 30*, 17–33. (p. 339)

Donnellan, M. B., Conger, R. D., & Bryant, C. M. (2004). The Big Five and enduring marriages. *Journal of Research in Personality, 38*, 481–504. (p. 619)

Donnellan, M. B., Trzesniewski, K. H., Robins, R. W., Moffitt, T. E., & Caspi, A. (2005). Low self-esteem is related to aggression, antisocial behavior, and delinquency. *Psychological Science, 16*, 328–335. (pp. 619, 636)

Donnerstein, E. (1998). Why do we have those new ratings on television. Invited address to the National Institute on the Teaching of Psychology. (pp. 344, 345)

Donnerstein, E., Linz, D., & Penrod, S. (1987). *The question of pornography*. New York: Free Press. (p. 346)

Dorman, M. F., & Wilson, B. S. (2004). The design and function of cochlear implants. *American Scientist, 92*, 436–445. (p. 221)

Dorner, G. (1976). *Hormones and brain differentiation.* Amsterdam: Elsevier Scientific. (p. 491)

Dorner, G. (1988). Neuroendocrine response to estrogen and brain differentiation in heterosexuals, homosexuals, and transsexuals. *Archives of Sexual Behavior, 17,* 57–75. (p. 491)

Dorozyaski, A. (1993, January/February). Maternal alcoholism: Grapes of wrath. *Psychology Today,* p. 18. (p. 142)

Dorris, M. (1989). *The Broken Cord.* New York: HarperCollins. (p. 142)

Doty, R. L. (2001). Olfaction. *Annual Review of Psychology, 52,* 423–452. (p. 232)

Doty, R. L., Shaman, P., Applebaum, S. L., Giberson, R., Siksorski, L., & Rosenberg, L. (1984). Smell identification ability: Changes with age. *Science, 226,* 1441–1443. (p. 179)

Doty, R. W. (1998). The five mysteries of the mind, and their consequences. *Neuropsychologia, 36,* 1069–1076. (p. 365)

Dovidio, J. F., & Gaertner, S. L. (1999). Reducing prejudice: Combating intergroup biases. *Current Directions in Psychological Science, 8,* 101–105. (p. 768)

Dovidio, J. F., ten Vergert, M., Stewart, T. L., Gaertner, S. L., Johnson, J. D., Esses, V. M., Riek, B. M., & Pearson, A. R. (2004). Perspective and prejudice: Antecedents and mediating mechanisms. *Personality and Social Psychology Bulletin, 30,* 1537–1549. (p. 768)

Downing, P. E., Jiang, Y., & Shuman, M. (2001). A cortical area selective for visual processing of the human body. *Science, 293,* 2470–2473. (p. 209)

Doyle, R. (2005, March). Gay and lesbian census. *Scientific American,* p. 28. (p. 110)

Draguns, J. G. (1990a). Normal and abnormal behavior in cross-cultural perspective: Specifying the nature of their relationship. *Nebraska Symposium on Motivation 1989, 37,* 235–277. (pp. 639, 666)

Draguns, J. G. (1990b). Applications of cross-cultural psychology in the field of mental health. In R. W. Brislin (Ed.), *Applied cross-cultural psychology.* Newbury Park, CA: Sage. (pp. 639, 643)

Draguns, J. G. (1997). Abnormal behavior patterns across cultures: Implications for counseling and psychotherapy. *International Journal of Intercultural Relations, 21,* 213–248. (p. 639)

Druckman, D., & Bjork, R. A. (1991). *In the mind's eye: Enhancing human performance.* National Academy Press: Washington, DC. (p. 614)

Druckman, D., & Bjork, R. A. (Eds.) (1994). *Learning, remembering, believing: Enhancing human performance.* Washington, DC: National Academy Press. (pp. 291, 292, 293)

Drugger, C. W. (2005, January 18). U.N. proposes doubling of aid to cut poverty. *New York Times* (www.nytimes.com). (p. 405)

Duckworth, A. L., & Seligman, M. E. P. (2005). Discipline outdoes talent: Self-discipline predicts academic performance in adolescents. *Psychological Science, 12,* 939–944. (p. 504)

Duclos, S. E., Laird, J. D., Sexter, M., Stern, L., & Van Lighten, O. (1989). Emotion-specific effects of facial expressions and postures on emotional experience. *Journal of Personality and Social Psychology, 57,* 100–108. (p. 530)

Duenwald, M. (2004, October 26). The dorms may be great, but how's the counseling? *New York Times* (www.nytimes.com). (p. 713)

Duffy, M. (2003, June 9). Weapons of mass disappearance. *Time,* pp. 28–33. (pp. 728–739)

Dugatkin, L. A. (2002, Winter). Watching culture shape even guppy love. *Cerebrum,* pp. 51–66. (p. 341)

Duggan, J. P., & Booth, D. A. (1986). Obesity, overeating, and rapid gastric emptying in rats with ventromedial hypothalamic lesions. *Science, 231,* 609–611. (p. 475)

Duncan, B. L. (1976). Differential social perception and attribution of intergroup violence: Testing the lower limits of stereotyping of blacks. *Journal of Personality and Social Psychology, 34,* 590–598. (p. 743)

Duncan, G. J., Hill, M. S., & Hoffman, S. D. (1988). Welfare dependence within and across generations. *Science, 239,* 467–471. (pp. 402–403)

Duncan, J. (2000, July 21). Quoted by N. Angier, Study finds region of brain may be key problem solver. *New York Times* (www.nytimes.com). (p. 440)

Duncan, J., Seitz, R. J., Kolodny, J., Bor, D., Herzog, H., Ahmed, A., Newell, F. N., & Emslie, H. (2000). A neural basis of general intelligence. *Science, 289,* 457–460. (p. 440)

Duncker, K. (1945). On problem solving. *Psychological Monographs, 58* (Whole no. 270). (pp. 400, 402)

Dunn, A. L., Trivedi, M. H., Kampert, J. B., Clark, C. G., & Chambliss, H. O. (2005). Exercise treatment for depression: Efficacy and dose response. *American Journal of Preventive Medicine, 28,* 1–8. (p. 569)

Dunson, D. B., Colombo, B., & Baird, D. D. (2002). Changes with age in the level and duration of fertility in the menstrual cycle. *Human Reproduction, 17,* 1399–1403. (p. 176)

Durston, S., Hulshoff, P., Hilleke, E., Casey, B. J., Giedd, J. N., Buitelaar, J. K., & van Engeland, H. (2001). Anatomical MRI of the developing human brain: What have we learned? *Journal of the American Academy of Child and Adolescent Psychiatry, 40,* 1012–1020. (p. 166)

Dush, C. M. K, Cohan, C. L., & Amato, P. R. (2003). The relationship between cohabitation and marital quality and stability: Change across cohorts? *Journal of Marriage and Family, 65,* 539–549. (p. 187)

Dutton, D. G., & Aron, A. (1989). Romantic attraction and generalized liking for others who are sources of conflict-based arousal. *Canadian Journal of Behavioural Sciences, 21,* 246–257. (p. 763)

Dutton, D. G., & Aron, A. P. (1974). Some evidence for heightened sexual attraction under conditions of high anxiety. *Journal of Personality and Social Psychology, 30,* 510–517. (p. 763)

Dye, D. A., & Reck, M. (1989). College grade point average as a predictor of adult success: A reply. *Public Personnel Management, 18,* 235–241. (p. 436)

Eagly, A. (1994). Are people prejudiced against women? Donald Campbell Award invited address, American Psychological Association convention. (p. 745)

Eagly, A. H., Ashmore, R. D., Makhijani, M. G., & Kennedy, L. C. (1991). What is beautiful is good, but . . .: A meta-analytic review of research on the physical attractiveness stereotype. *Psychological Bulletin, 110,* 109–128. (p. 760)

Eagly, A. H., & Crowley, M. (1986). Gender and helping behavior: A meta-analytic review of the social psychological literature. *Psychological Bulletin, 100,* 283–308. (p. 766)

Eagly, A. H., & Johnson, B. T. (1990). Gender and leadership style: A meta-analysis. *Psychological Bulletin, 108,* 233–256. (p. 127)

Eagly, A. H., & Wood, W. (1999). The origins of sex differences in human behavior: Evolved dispositions versus social roles. *American Psychologist, 54,* 408–423. (p. 112)

Eastman, C. L., Boulos, Z., Terman, M., Campbell, S. S., Dijk, D-J., & Lewy, A. J. (1995). Light treatment for sleep disorders: Consensus report. VI. Shift work. *Journal of Biological Rhythms, 10,* 157–164. (p. 275)

Eastman, C. L., Young, M. A., Fogg, L. F., Liu, L., & Meaden, P. M. (1998). Bright light treatment of winter depression: A placebo-controlled trial. *Archives of General Psychiatry, 55,* 883–889. (pp. 706–707)

Ebbesen, E. B., Duncan, B., & Konecni, V. J. (1975). Effects of content of verbal aggression on future verbal aggression: A field experiment. *Journal of Experimental Social Psychology, 11,* 192–204. (p. 536)

Ebbinghaus, H. (1885). *Über das Gedachtnis.* Leipzig: Duncker & Humblot. Cited in R. Klatzky (1980), *Human memory: Structures and processes.* San Francisco: Freeman. (p. 355)

Ebbinghaus, H. (1885/1964). *Memory: A contribution to experimental psychology* (tr. by H. A. Ruger & C. E. Bussenius). New York: Dover. (p. 377)

Eberhardt, J. L. (2005). Imaging race. *American Psychologist, 60,* 181–190. (p. 744)

Eberhardt, J. L., Goff, P. A., Purdie, V. J., & Davies, P. G. (2004). Seeing Black: Race, crime, and visual processing. *Journal of Personality and Social Psychology, 87,* 876–893. (p. 744)

Eccles, J. S., Jacobs, J. E., & Harold, R. D. (1990). Gender role stereotypes, expectancy effects, and parents' socialization of gender differences. *Journal of Social Issues, 46,* 183–201. (p. 464)

Eckensberger, L. H. (1994). Moral development and its measurement across cultures. In W. J. Lonner & R. Malpass (Eds.), *Psychology and culture.* Boston: Allyn and Bacon. (p. 168)

Eckersley, R. (2000). The mixed blessings of material progress: Diminishing returns in the pursuit of happiness. *Journal of Happiness Studies, 1,* 267–292. (p. 541)

Eckersley, R. (2001, March 23). Wealthier, but poorer for all that. *The Australian,* p. 13. (p. 540)

Eckersley, R., & Dear, K. (2002). Correlates of youth suicide. *Social Science and Medicine, 55,* 1891–1935. (p. 662)

Eckert, E. D., Heston, L. L., & Bouchard, T. J., Jr. (1981). MZ twins reared apart: Preliminary findings of psychiatric disturbances and traits. In L. Gedda, P. Paris, & W. D. Nance (Eds.), *Twin research: Vol. 3. Pt. B. Intelligence, personality, and development.* New York: Alan Liss. (p. 655)

Ecklund-Flores, L. (1992). The infant as a model for the teaching of introductory psychology. Paper presented to the American Psychological Association annual convention. (p. 141)

Economist. (2001, December 20). An anthropology of happiness. *The Economist* (www.economist.com/world/asia). (p. 496)

Economist. (2004, September 16). Supercharging the brain (www.economist.co.uk). (p. 365)

Edelman, S., & Kidman, A. D. (1997). Mind and cancer: Is there a relationship? A review of the evidence. *Australian Psychologist, 32,* 1–7. (p. 559)

Edison, T. A. (1948). *The diary and sundry observations of Thomas Alva Edison,* edited by D. D. Runes. New York: Philosophical Library. Cited by S. Coren (1996). *Sleep Thieves.* New York: Free Press. (p. 279)

Edwards, C. P. (1981). The comparative study of the development of moral judgment and reasoning. In R. H. Munroe, R. L. Munroe, & B. B. Whiting (Eds.), *Handbook of cross-cultural human development.* New York: Garland Press. (p. 168)

Edwards, C. P. (1982). Moral development in comparative cultural perspective. In D. A. Wagner & H. W. Stevenson (Eds.), *Cultural perspectives on child development.* San Francisco: Freeman. (p. 168)

Edwards, R., Peet, M., Shay, J., & Horrobin, D. (1998). Omega-3 polyunsaturated fatty acid levels in the diet and in red blood cell membranes of depressed patients. *Journal of Affective Disorders, 48,* 149–155. (p. 664)

Egan, M. F., & 16 others (2004). Variation in *GRM3* affects cognition, prefrontal glutamate, and risk for schizophrenia. *Proceedings of the National Academy of Sciences, 101,* 12604–12609. (p. 675)

Ehrhardt, A. A. (1987). A transactional perspective on the development of gender differences. In J. M. Reinisch, L. A. Rosenblum, & S. A. Sanders (Eds.), *Masculinity/femininity: Basic perspectives.* New York: Oxford University Press. (p. 130)

Ehrlichman, H., & Halpern, J. N. (1988). Affect and memory: Effects of pleasant and unpleasant odors on retrieval of happy and unhappy memories. *Journal of Personality and Social Psychology, 55,* 769–779. (p. 233)

Eibl-Eibesfeldt, I. (1971). *Love and hate: The natural history of behavior patterns.* New York: Holt, Rinehart & Winston. (p. 529)

Eich, E. (1990). Learning during sleep. In R. B. Bootzin, J. F. Kihlstrom, & D. L. Schacter (Eds.), *Sleep and cognition.* Washington, DC: American Psychological Association. (p. 286)

Eich, E., Macaulay, D., Loewenstein, R. J., & Dihle, P. H. (1997). Memory, amnesia, and dissociative identity disorder. *Psychological Science, 8,* 417–422. (p. 697)

Einstein, G. O., & McDaniel, M. A. (1990). Normal aging and prospective memory. *Journal of Experimental Psychology: Learning, Memory, and Cognition, 16,* 717–726. (p. 182)

Einstein, G. O., McDaniel, M. A., Richardson, S. L., Guynn, M. J., & Cunfer, A. R. (1995). Aging and prospective memory: Examining the influences of self-initiated retrieval processes. *Journal of Experimental Psychology: Learning, Memory, and Cognition, 21,* 996–1007. (p. 182)

Einstein, G. O., McDaniel, M. A., Smith, R. E., & Shaw, P. (1998). Habitual prospective memory and aging: Remembering intentions and forgetting actions. *Psychological Science, 9,* 284–288. (p. 182)

Eisenberg, N., Cumberland A., & Spinrad, T. L. (1998a). Parental socialization of emotion. *Psychological Inquiry, 9,* 241–271. (p. 117)

Eisenberg, N., & Lennon, R. (1983). Sex differences in empathy and related capacities. *Psychological Bulletin, 94,* 100–131. (p. 526)

Eisenberg, N., Spinrad, T. L., & Cumberland, A. (1998b). The socialization of emotion: Reply to commentaries. *Psychological Inquiry, 9,* 317–333. (p. 117)

Eisenberger, N. I., Lieberman, M. D., & Williams, K. D. (2003). Does rejection hurt? An fMRI study of social exclusion. *Science, 302,* 290–292. (p. 497)

Eisenberger, R., & Rhoades, L. (2001). Incremental effects of reward on creativity. *Journal of Personality and Social Psychology, 81,* 728–741. (p. 335)

Eiser, J. R. (1985). Smoking: The social learning of an addiction. *Journal of Social and Clinical Psychology, 3,* 446–457. (p. 576)

Ekman, P. (1994). Strong evidence for universals in facial expressions: A reply to Russell's mistaken critique. *Psychological Bulletin, 115,* 268–287. (p. 528)

Ekman, P. (2003). *Emotions revealed: Recognizing faces and feelings to improve communication and emotional life.* New York: Times Books. (p. 521)

Ekman, P., Friesen, W. V., O'Sullivan, M., Chan, A., Diacoyanni-Tarlatzis, I., Heider, K., Krause, R., LeCompte, W. A., Pitcairn, T., Ricci-Bitti, P. E., Scherer, K., Tomita, M., & Tzavaras, A. (1987). Universals and cultural differences in the judgments of facial expressions of emotion. *Journal of Personality and Social Psychology, 53,* 712–717. (p. 528)

Ekman, P., & O'Sullivan, M. (1991). Who can catch a liar? *American Psychologist, 46,* 913–920. (p. 527)

Ekman, P., O'Sullivan, M. O., & Frank, M. G. (1999). A few can catch a liar. *Psychological Science, 10,* 263–266. (p. 527)

Elbert, T., Pantev, C., Wienbruch, C., Rockstroh, B., & Taub, E. (1995). Increased cortical representation of the fingers of the left hand in string players. *Science, 270,* 305–307. (p. 115)

Elfenbein, H. A., & Ambady, N. (1999). Does it take one to know one? A meta-analysis of the universality and cultural specificity of emotion recognition. Unpublished manuscript, Harvard University. (p. 528)

Elfenbein, H. A., & Ambady, N. (2002). On the universality and cultural specificity of emotion recognition: A meta-analysis. *Psychological Bulletin, 128,* 203–235. (p. 529)

Elfenbein, H. A., & Ambady, N. (2003a). When familiarity breeds accuracy: Cultural exposure and facial emotion recognition. *Journal of Personality and Social Psychology, 85,* 276–290. (p. 529)

Elfenbein, H. A., & Ambady, N. (2003b). Universals and cultural differences in recognizing emotions. *Current Directions in Psychological Science, 12,* 159–164. (p. 529)

Elkin, I., Shea, T., Watkins, J. T., Imber, S. D., Sotsky, S. M., Collins, J. F., Glass, D. R., Pilkonis, P. A., Leber, W. R., Docherty, J. P., Fiester, S. J., & Parloff, M. B. (1989). National Institute of Mental Health treatment of depression collaborative research program. *Archives of General Psychiatry, 46,* 971–983. (p. 703)

Elkind, D. (1970). The origins of religion in the child. *Review of Religious Research, 12,* 35–42. (pp. 167–168)

Elkind, D. (1978). *The child's reality: Three developmental themes.* Hillsdale, NJ: Erlbaum. (p. 167)

Ellis, A. (1980). Psychotherapy and atheistic values: A response to A. E. Bergin's "Psychotherapy and religious values." *Journal of Consulting and Clinical Psychology, 48,* 635–639. (p. 709)

Ellis, A., & Becker, I. M. (1982). *A guide to personal happiness.* North Hollywood, CA: Wilshire Book Co. (p. 324)

Ellis, B. J. (2004). Timing of pubertal maturation in girls: An integrated life history approach. *Psychological Bulletin, 130,* 920–958. (p. 173)

Ellis, B. J., Bates, J. E., Dodge, K. A., Fergusson, D. M., John, H. L., Pettit, G. S., & Woodward, L. (2003). Does father absence place daughters at special risk for early sexual activity and teenage pregnancy? *Child Development, 74*, 801–821. (p. 486)

Ellis, L., & Ames, M. A. (1987). Neurohormonal functioning and sexual orientation: A theory of homosexuality-heterosexuality. *Psychological Bulletin, 101*, 233–258. (p. 491)

Emde, R. N., Plomin, R., Robinson, J., Corley, R., DeFries, J., Fulker, D. W., Reznick, J. S., Campos, J., Kagan, J., & Zahn-Waxler, C. (1992). Temperament, emotion, and cognition at fourteen months: The MacArthur Longitudinal Twin Study. *Child Development, 63*, 1437–1455. (p. 102)

EMDR. (2002, September 19). Description for professionals. (www.emdr.org). (p. 706)

Emerging Trends. (1997, September). Teens turn more to parents than friends on whether to attend church. Princeton, NJ: Princeton Religion Research Center, p. 5. (p. 173)

Emery, G. (2004). Psychic predictions 2004. Committee for the Scientific Investigation of Claims of the Paranormal (www.csicop.org). (p. 265)

Emery, N. J., & Clayton, N. S. (2004). The mentality of crows: Convergent evolution of intelligence in corvids and apes. *Science, 306*, 1903–1907. (p. 423)

Emmons, S., Geisler, C., Kaplan, K. J., & Harrow, M. (1997). *Living with schizophrenia*. Muncie, IN: Taylor and Francis (Accelerated Development). (p. 639)

Emmorey, K., Allen, J. S., Bruss, J., Schenker, N., & Damasio, H. (2003). A morphometric analysis of auditory brain regions in congenitally deaf adults. *Proceedings of the National Academy of Sciences, 100*, 10049–10054. (p. 223)

Empson, J. A. C., & Clarke, P. R. F. (1970). Rapid eye movements and remembering. *Nature, 227*, 287–288. (p. 286)

Emslie, C., Hunt, K., & Macintyre, S. (2001). Perceptions of body image among working men and women. *Journal of Epidemiology and Community Health, 55*, 406–407. (p. 479)

Endler, N. S. (1982). *Holiday of darkness: A psychologist's personal journey out of his depression*. New York: Wiley. (pp. 665, 715)

Endler, N. S., & Speer, R. L. (1998). Personality psychology: Research trends for 1993–1995. *Journal of Personality, 66*, 621–669. (p. 619)

Engemann, K. M., & Owyang, M. T. (2005, April). So much for that merit raise: The link between wages and appearance. *Regional Economist* (www.stlouisfed.org). (p. 760)

Engen, T. (1987). Remembering odors and their names. *American Scientist, 75*, 497–503. (p. 233)

Engle, R. W. (2002). Working memory capacity as executive attention. *Current Directions in Psychological Science, 11*, 19–23. (p. 352)

Epel, E. S., Blackburn, E. H., Lin, J., Dhabhar, F. S., Adler, N. E., Morrow, J. D., & Cawthon, R. M. (2004). Accelerated telomere shortening in response to life stress. *Proceedings of the National Academy of Sciences, 101*, 17312–17315. (p. 553)

Epley, N., & Dunning, D. (2000). Feeling "holier than thou": Are self-serving assessments produced by errors in self- or social prediction? *Journal of Personality and Social Psychology, 79*, 861–875. (p. 634)

Epley, N., Keysar, B., Van Boven, L., & Gilovich, T. (2004). Perspective taking as egocentric anchoring and adjustment. *Journal of Personality and Social Psychology, 87*, 327–339. (p. 151)

EPOCH. (2000). *Legal reforms: Corporal punishment of children in the family* (www.stophitting.com/laws/legalReform.php). (p. 333)

Epstein, J., Stern, E., & Silbersweig, D. (1998). Mesolimbic activity associated with psychosis in schizophrenia: Symptom-specific PET studies. In J. F. McGinty (Ed.), *Advancing from the ventral striatum to the extended amygdala: Implications for neuropsychiatry and drug use: In honor of Lennart Heimer*. *Annals of the New York Academy of Sciences, 877*, 562–574. (p. 672)

Epstein, S. (1983a). Aggregation and beyond: Some basic issues on the prediction of behavior. *Journal of Personality, 51*, 360–392. (pp. 620–621)

Epstein, S. (1983b). The stability of behavior across time and situations. In R. Zucker, J. Aronoff, & A. I. Rabin (Eds.), *Personality and the prediction of behavior*. San Diego: Academic Press. (pp. 620–621)

Epstein, S., & Meier, P. (1989). Constructive thinking: A broad coping variable with specific components. *Journal of Personality and Social Psychology, 57*, 332–350. (p. 436)

Erdberg, P. (1990). Rorschach assessment. In G. Goldstein & M. Hersen (Eds.), *Handbook of psychological assessment*, 2nd ed. New York: Pergamon. (p. 603)

Erdelyi, M. H. (1985). *Psychoanalysis: Freud's cognitive psychology*. New York: Freeman. (p. 605)

Erdelyi, M. H. (1988). Repression, reconstruction, and defense: History and integration of the psychoanalytic and experimental frameworks. In J. Singer (Ed.), *Repression: Defense mechanism and cognitive style*. Chicago: University of Chicago Press. (p. 605)

Erel, O., & Burman, B. (1995). Interrelatedness of marital relations and parent-child relations: A meta-analytic review. *Psychological Bulletin, 118*, 108–132. (p. 188)

Erel, O., Oberman, Y., & Yirmiya, N. (2000). Maternal versus nonmaternal care and seven domains of children's development. *Psychological Bulletin, 126*, 727–747. (p. 160)

Erickson, M. F., & Aird, E. G. (2005). *The motherhood study: Fresh insights on mothers' attitudes and concerns*. New York: The Motherhood Project, Institute for American Values. (p. 187)

Ericsson, K. A. (2001). Attaining excellence through deliberate practice: Insights from the study of expert performance. In M. Ferrari (Ed.), *The pursuit of excellence in education*. Hillsdale, NJ: Erlbaum. (p. 504)

Ericsson, K. A. (2002). Attaining excellence through deliberate practice: Insights from the study of expert performance. In C. Desforges & R. Fox (Eds.), *Teaching and learning: The essential readings*. Malden, MA: Blackwell Publishers. (p. 437)

Ericsson, K. A., & Chase, W. G. (1982). Exceptional memory. *American Scientist, 70*, 607–615. (p. 360)

Ericsson, K. A., Krampe, R. T., & Heizman, S. (1993). Can we create gifted people? In G. R. Bock & K. Ackrill (Eds.), *Ciba Foundation Symposium 178: The origins and development of high ability*. New York: Wiley. Cited by M. J. A. Howe, J. W. Davison, & J. A. Sioboda (1998). Innate talents: Reality or myth? *Behavioral and Brain Sciences, 21*, 399–442. (p. 504)

Ericsson, K. A., & Lehmann, A. C. (1996). Expert and exceptional performance: Evidence of maximal adaptations to task constraints. *Annual Review of Psychology, 47*, 273–305. (p. 437)

Erikson, E. H. (1963). *Childhood and society*. New York: Norton. (p. 170)

Erikson, E. H. (1983, June). A conversation with Erikson (by E. Hall). *Psychology Today*, pp. 22–30. (p. 158)

Ernsberger, P., & Koletsky, R. J. (1999). Biomedical rationale for a wellness approach to obesity: An alternative to a focus on weight loss. *Journal of Social Issues, 55*, 221–260. (p. 590)

Eron, L. D. (1987). The development of aggressive behavior from the perspective of a developing behaviorism. *American Psychologist, 42*, 435–442. (p. 345)

ESPAD. (2003). Summary of the 2003 findings. European School Survey Project on Alcohol and Other Drugs (www.espad.org). (p. 305)

Esser, J. K., & Lindoerfer, J. S. (1989). Groupthink and the space shuttle *Challenger* accident: Toward a quantitative case analysis. *Journal of Behavioral Decision Making, 2*, 167–177. (p. 740)

Esterson, A. (2001). The mythologizing of psychoanalytic history: Deception and self-deception in Freud's accounts of the seduction theory episode. *History of Psychiatry, 12*, 329–352. (p. 604)

Esty, A. (2004). The new wealth of nations. *American Scientist, 92*, 513. (p. 542)

Eszterhas, J. (2002, August 9). Hollywood's responsibility for smoking deaths. *New York Times* (www.nytimes.com). (p. 576)

Etcoff, N. L., Ekman, P., Magee, J. J., & Frank, M. G. (2000). Lie detection and language comprehension. *Nature, 405*, 139. (p. 223)

Etnier, J. L., Salazar, W., Landers, D. M., Petruzzello, S. J., Han, M., & Nowell, P. (1997). The influence of physical fitness and exercise upon cognitive functioning: A meta-analysis. *Journal of Sport & Exercise Psychology, 19*, 249–277. (p. 569)

ETS. (1992). Three reports shed new light on gender differences in testing. *ETS Developments, 37*(3), 4-7. (p. 462)

Etzioni, A. (1999). The monochrome society. *The Public Interest, 137* (Fall), 42-55. (p. 768)

Evans, C. R., & Dion, K. L. (1991). Group cohesion and performance: A meta-analysis. *Small Group Research, 22,* 175-186. (p. 508)

Evans, G. W. (2004). The environment of childhood poverty. *American Psychologist, 59,* 77-92. (p. 160)

Evans, G. W., Hygge, S., & Bullinger, M. (1995). Chronic noise and psychological stress. *Psychological Science, 6,* 333-338. (p. 218)

Evans, G. W., Palsane, M. N., & Carrere, S. (1987). Type A behavior and occupational stress: A cross-cultural study of blue-collar workers. *Journal of Personality and Social Psychology, 52,* 1002-1007. (p. 556)

Evans, G. W., Palsane, M. N., Lepore, S. J., & Martin, J. (1989). Residential density and psychological health: The mediating effects of social support. *Journal of Personality and Social Psychology, 57,* 994-999. (p. 565)

Evans, R. I., Dratt, L. M., Raines, B. E., & Rosenberg, S. S. (1988). Social influences on smoking initiation: Importance of distinguishing descriptive versus mediating process variables. *Journal of Applied Social Psychology, 18,* 925-943. (p. 576)

Ewing, R., Schmid, T., Killingsworth, R., Zlot, A., & Raudenbush, S. (2003). Relationship between urban sprawl and physical activity, obesity, and morbidity. *American Journal of Health Promotion, 18,* 47-57. (p. 587)

Exner, J. E. (2003). *The Rorschach: A comprehensive system,* 4th edition. Hoboken, NJ: Wiley. (p. 603)

Eysenck, H. J. (1952). The effects of psychotherapy: An evaluation. *Journal of Consulting Psychology, 16,* 319-324. (p. 702)

Eysenck, H. J. (1990, April 30). An improvement on personality inventory. *Current Contents: Social and Behavioral Sciences, 22*(18), 20. (p. 614)

Eysenck, H. J. (1992). Four ways five factors are *not* basic. *Personality and Individual Differences, 13,* 667-673. (p. 614)

Eysenck, H. J., & Grossarth-Maticek, R. (1991). Creative novation behaviour therapy as a prophylactic treatment for cancer and coronary heart disease: Part II—Effects of treatment. *Behaviour Research and Therapy, 29,* 17-31. (p. 571)

Eysenck, H. J., Wakefield, J. A., Jr., & Friedman, A. F. (1983). Diagnosis and clinical assessment: The DSM-III. *Annual Review of Psychology, 34,* 167-193. (p. 644)

Eysenck, M. W., MacLeod, C., & Mathews, A. (1987). Cognitive functioning and anxiety. *Psychological Research, 49,* 189-195. (p. 624)

Eysenck, S. B. G., & Eysenck, H. J. (1963). The validity of questionnaire and rating assessments of extraversion and neuroticism, and their factorial stability. *British Journal of Psychology, 54,* 51-62. (p. 615)

Faber, N. (1987, July). Personal glimpse. *Reader's Digest,* p. 34. (p. 438)

Fagan, J. F., III (1992). Intelligence: A theoretical viewpoint. *Current Directions in Psychological Science, 1,* 82-86. (p. 461)

Fairburn, C. G., Cowen, P. J., & Harrison, P. J. (1999). Twin studies and the etiology of eating disorders. *International Journal of Eating Disorders, 26,* 349-358. (p. 479)

Fantz, R. L. (1961, May). The origin of form perception. *Scientific American,* pp. 66-72. (p. 143)

Farah, M. J., Rabinowitz, C., Quinn, G. E., & Liu, G. T. (2000). Early commitment of neural substrates for face recognition. *Cognitive Neuropsychology, 17,* 117-124. (p. 82)

Farina, A. (1982). The stigma of mental disorders. In A. G. Miller (Ed.), *In the eye of the beholder.* New York: Praeger. (p. 645)

Farina, A., & Fisher, J. D. (1982). Beliefs about mental disorders: Findings and implications. In G. Weary & H. L. Mirels (Eds.), *Integrations of clinical and social psychology.* New York: Oxford University Press. (pp. 642, 700)

Farley, M, Baral, I., Kiremire, M., & Sezgin, U. (1998). Prostitution in five countries: Violence and post-traumatic stress disorder. *Feminism and Psychology, 8,* 405-426. (p. 652)

Farley, T., & Cohen, D. (2001, December). Fixing a fat nation. *Washington Monthly* (www.washingtonmonthly.com/features/2001/0112.farley.cohen.html). (p. 587)

Faro, S. (2004). Presentation to the Radiological Society of North America, Chicago. (p. 521)

Farrington, D. P. (1991). Antisocial personality from childhood to adulthood. *The Psychologist: Bulletin of the British Psychological Society, 4,* 389-394. (p. 678)

Farwell, L. A., & Smith, S. S. (2001). Using brain MERMER testing to detect concealed knowledge despite efforts to conceal. *Journal of Forensic Sciences, 46* (1), 1-9. (p. 521)

FBI. (2004). Crime in the United States 2003, Five-Year Arrest Trends by Sex, 1999-2003. Table 35. (p. 127)

Feder, H. H. (1984). Hormones and sexual behavior. *Annual Review of Psychology, 35,* 165-200. (p. 482)

Feeney, J. A., & Noller, P. (1990). Attachment style as a predictor of adult romantic relationships. *Journal of Personality and Social Psychology, 58,* 281-291. (p. 158)

Feigenson, L., Carey, S., & Spelke, E. (2002). Infants' discrimination of number vs. continuous extent. *Cognitive psychology, 44,* 33-66. (p. 149)

Feingold, A. (1990). Gender differences in effects of physical attractiveness on romantic attraction: A comparison across five research paradigms. *Journal of Personality and Social Psychology, 59,* 981-993. (p. 759)

Feingold, A. (1992). Good-looking people are not what we think. *Psychological Bulletin, 111,* 304-341. (p. 760)

Feingold, A., & Mazzella, R. (1998). Gender differences in body image are increasing. *Psychological Science, 9,* 190-195. (pp. 479, 761)

Feminist Psychologist. (2002, Winter). Justice for Mary Whiton Calkins, p. 11. (p. 6)

Fenn, K. M., Nusbaum, H. C., & Margoliash, D. (2003). Consolidation during sleep of perceptual learning of spoken language. *Nature, 425,* 614-616. (p. 283)

Fenton, W. S., & McGlashan, T. H. (1991). Natural history of schizophrenia subtypes: II. Positive and negative symptoms and long-term course. *Archives of General Psychiatry, 48,* 978-986. (p. 671)

Fenton, W. S., & McGlashan, T. H. (1994). Antecedents, symptom progression, and long-term outcome of the deficit syndrome in schizophrenia. *American Journal of Psychiatry, 151,* 351-356. (p. 671)

Ferguson, E. D. (1989). Adler's motivational theory: An historical perspective on belonging and the fundamental human striving. *Individual Psychology, 45,* 354-361. (p. 495)

Fergusson, D. M., & Woodward, L. G. (2002). Mental health, educational, and social role outcomes of adolescents with depression. *Archives of General Psychiatry, 59,* 225-231. (p. 661)

Fernandez, E., & Turk, D. C. (1989). The utility of cognitive coping strategies for altering pain perception: A meta-analysis. *Pain, 38,* 123-135. (p. 229)

Fernández-Ballesteros, R., & Caprara, M. (2003). Psychology of aging in Europe. *European Psychologist, 8,* 129-130. (p. 178)

Ferris, C. F. (1996, March). The rage of innocents. *The Sciences,* pp. 22-26. (p. 159)

Fiedler, F. E. (1981). Leadership effectiveness. *American Behavioral Scientist, 24,* 619-632. (p. 508)

Fiedler, F. E. (1987, September). When to lead, when to stand back. *Psychology Today,* pp. 26-27. (p. 508)

Fiedler, K., Nickel, S., Muehlfriedel, T., & Unkelbach, C. (2001). Is mood congruency an effect of genuine memory or response bias? *Journal of Experimental Social Psychology, 37,* 201-214. (p. 374)

Field, T. (1996). Attachment and separation in young children. *Annual Review of Psychology, 47,* 541-561. (p. 161)

Field, T. (2001). Massage therapy facilitates weight gain in preterm infants. *Current Directions in Psychological Science, 10,* 51-54. (p. 115)

Field, T., Hernandez-Reif, M., Diego, M., Feijo, L., Vera, Y., & Gil, K. (2004). Massage therapy by parents improves early growth and development. *Infant Behaviour and Development, 27,* 435-442. (p. 115)

Fields, R. D. (2004, April). The other half of the brain. *Scientific American,* pp. 54-61. (p. 76)

Fields, R. D. (2005, February). Making memories stick. *Scientific American,* pp. 75-81. (p. 366)

Fincham, F. D., & Bradbury, T. N. (1993). Marital satisfaction, depression, and attributions: A longitudinal analysis. *Journal of Personality and Social Psychology, 64,* 442-452. (p. 725)

Fink, G. R., Markowitsch, H. J., Reinkemeier, M., Bruckbauer, T., Kessler, J., & Heiss, W-D. (1996). Cerebral representation of one's own past: Neural networks involved in autobiographical memory. *Journal of Neuroscience, 16,* 4275-4282. (p. 369)

Fink, M. (1998). ECT and managed care. *Journal Watch Psychiatry, 4,* 73, 76. (p. 716)

Finkel, L. H., & Sajda, P. (1994). Constructing visual perception. *American Scientist, 82,* 224-237. (p. 210)

Finlay, S. W. (2000). Influence of Carl Jung and William James on the origin of alcoholics anonymous. *Review of General Psychology, 4,* 3-12. (p. 698)

Finney, E. M., Fine, I., & Dobkins, K. R. (2001). Visual stimuli activate auditory cortex in the deaf. *Nature Neuroscience, 4,* 1171-1173. (p. 223)

Finucci, J. M., & Childs, B. (1981). Are there really more dyslexic boys than girls? In A. Ansara, N. Geschwind, A. Galaburda, M. Albert, & N. Gartrell (Eds.), *Sex differences in dyslexia.* Towson, MD: The Orton Dyslexia Society. (p. 462)

Fischhoff, B. (1982). Debiasing. In D. Kahneman, P. Slovic, & A. Tversky (Eds.), *Judgment under uncertainty: Heuristics and biases.* New York: Cambridge University Press. (p. 403)

Fischhoff, B., Slovic, P., & Lichtenstein, S. (1977). Knowing with certainty: The appropriateness of extreme confidence. *Journal of Experimental Psychology: Human Perception and Performance, 3,* 552-564. (p. 403)

Fisher, H. E. (1993, March/April). After all, maybe it's biology. *Psychology Today,* pp. 40-45. (p. 187)

Fisher, H. E., Aron, A., Mashek, D., Li, H., & Brown, L. L. (2002). Defining the brain systems of lust, romantic attraction, and attachment. *Archives of Sexual Behavior, 31,* 413-419. (p. 482)

Fisher, H. T. (1984). Little Albert and Little Peter. *Bulletin of the British Psychological Society, 37,* 269. (p. 691)

Fisher, R. P., & Geiselman, R. E. (1992). *Memory-enhancing techniques for investigative interviewing: The cognitive interview.* Springfield, IL: Charles C. Thomas. (p. 386)

Fisher, R. P., Geiselman, R. E., & Raymond, D. S. (1987). Critical analysis of police interview techniques. *Journal of Police Science and Administration, 15,* 177-185. (p. 386)

Fisher, S., & Greenberg, R. (Eds.) (1997). *From placebo to panacea: Putting psychiatric drugs to the test.* New York: Wiley. (p. 714)

Fiske, S. T., Harris, L. T., & Cuddy, A. J. C. (2004). Why ordinary people torture enemy prisoners. *Science, 306,* 1482-1483. (p. 729)

Flack, W. F., Jr., Laird, J. D., & Cavallaro, L. A. (1999). Separate and combined effects of facial expressions and bodily postures on emotional feelings. *European Journal of Social Psychology, 29,* 203-217. (p. 531)

Flavell, J. H., Flavell, E. R., & Green, F. L. (2001). Development of children's understanding of connections between thinking and feeling. *Psychological Science, 12,* 430-432. (p. 151)

Fleming, I., Baum, A., & Weiss, L. (1987). Social density and perceived control as mediator of crowding stress in high-density residential neighborhoods. *Journal of Personality and Social Psychology, 52,* 899-906. (p. 564)

Fleming, J. H. (2001, Winter/Spring). Introduction to the special issue on linkage analysis. *The Gallup Research Journal,* pp. i-vi. (p. 507)

Fleming, J. H., & Scott, B. A. (1991). The costs of confession: The Persian Gulf War POW tapes in historical and theoretical perspective. *Contemporary Social Psychology, 15,* 127-138. (p. 528)

Fletcher, G. J. O., Fitness, J., & Blampied, N. M. (1990). The link between attributions and happiness in close relationships: The roles of depression and explanatory style. *Journal of Social and Clinical Psychology, 9,* 243-255. (p. 725)

Fletcher, P. C., Zafiris, O., Frith, C. D., Honey, R. A. E., Corlett, P. R., Zilles, K., & Fink, G. R. (2005). On the benefits of not trying: Brain activity and connectivity reflecting the interactions of explicit and implicit sequence learning. *Cerebral Cortex, 7,* 1002-1015. (p. 605)

Flora, S. R. (2004). *The power of reinforcement.* Albany, NJ: SUNY Press. (p. 336)

Flouri, E., & Buchanan, A. (2004). Early father's and mother's involvement and child's later educational outcomes. *British Journal of Educational Psychology, 74,* 141-153. (p. 157)

Flynn, J. R. (1987). Massive IQ gains in 14 nations: What IQ tests really measure. *Psychological Bulletin, 101,* 171-191. (p. 447)

Flynn, J. R. (1999). Searching for justice: The discovery of IQ gains over time. *American Psychologist, 54,* 5-20. (p. 447)

Flynn, J. R. (2003). Movies about intelligence: The limitations of *g. Current Directions in Psychological Science, 12,* 95-99. (p. 457)

Foa, E. B., & Kozak, M. J. (1986). Emotional processing of fear: Exposure to corrective information. *Psychological Bulletin, 99,* 20-35. (p. 692)

Fogg, N. P., Harrington P. E., & Harrington T. F. (1999). *The College Majors Handbook.* Indianapolis, IN: JIST Works, Inc. (pp. A-1, A-2, A-3)

Fong, G. T., Frantz, D. H., & Nisbett, R. E. (1986). The effects of statistical training on thinking about everyday problems. *Cognitive Psychology, 18,* 253-292. (p. 44)

Ford, E. S. (2002). Does exercise reduce inflammation? Physical activity and C-reactive protein among U.S. adults. *Epidemiology, 13,* 561-569. (p. 570)

Foree, D. D., & LoLordo, V. M. (1973). Attention in the pigeon: Differential effects of food-getting versus shock-avoidance procedures. *Journal of Comparative and Physiological Psychology, 85,* 551-558. (p. 336)

Forer, B. R. (1949). The fallacy of personal validation: A classroom demonstration of gullibility. *Journal of Abnormal and Social Psychology, 44,* 118-123. (p. 616)

Forgas, J. P., Bower, G. H., & Krantz, S. E. (1984). The influence of mood on perceptions of social interactions. *Journal of Experimental Social Psychology, 20,* 497-513. (pp. 374, 667)

Forge, A., Li, L., Corwin, J. T., & Nevill, G. (1993). Ultrastructural evidence for hair cell regeneration in the mammalian inner ear. *Science, 259,* 1616-1619. (p. 221)

Forman, D. R., Aksan, N., & Kochanska, G. (2004). Toddlers' responsive imitation predicts preschool-age conscience. *Psychological Science, 15,* 699-704. (p. 344)

Foss, D. J., & Hakes, D. T. (1978). *Psycholinguistics: An introduction to the psychology of language.* Englewood Cliffs, NJ: Prentice-Hall. (p. 584)

Fosse, R., Stickgold, R., & Hobson, J. A. (2001). Brain-mind states: Reciprocal variation in thoughts and hallucinations. *Psychological Science, 12,* 30-36. (p. 279)

Foster, J. D., Campbell, W. K., & Twenge, J. M. (2003). Individual differences in narcissism: Inflated self-views across the lifespan and around the world. *Journal of Research in Personality, 37,* 469-486. (p. 123)

Foster, R. G. (2004). Are we trying to banish biological time? *Cerebrum, 6*(2), 7-26. (p. 275)

Foulkes, D. (1999). *Children's dreaming and the development of consciousness.* Cambridge, MA: Harvard University Press. (p. 288)

Fouts, R. (1997). *Next of kin: What chimpanzees have taught me about who we are.* New York: Morrow. (p. 427)

Fouts, R. S. (1992). Transmission of a human gestural language in a chimpanzee mother-infant relationship. *Friends of Washoe, 12/13,* pp. 2-8. (p. 427)

Fouts, R. S., & Bodamer, M. (1987). Preliminary report to the National Geographic Society on: "Chimpanzee intrapersonal signing." *Friends of Washoe, 7*(1), 4-12. (p. 428)

Fowler, M. J., Sullivan, M. J., & Ekstrand, B. R. (1973). Sleep and memory. *Science, 179*, 302–304. (p. 380)

Fowler, R. C., Rich, C. L., & Young, D. (1986). San Diego suicide study: II. Substance abuse in young cases. *Archives of General Psychiatry, 43*, 962–965. (pp. 662–663)

Fowler, R. D. (1986, May). Howard Hughes: A psychological autopsy. *Psychology Today*, pp. 22–33. (p. 651)

Fowles, D. C. (1992). Schizophrenia: Diathesis-stress revisited. *Annual Review of Psychology, 43*, 303–336. (p. 671)

Fox, B. H. (1998). Psychosocial factors in cancer incidence and prognosis. In P. M. Cinciripini & others (Eds.), *Psychological and behavioral factors in cancer risk*. New York: Oxford University Press. (p. 559)

Fox, E., Lester, V., Russo, R., Bowles, R. J., Pichler, A., & Dutton, K. (2000). Facial expression of emotion: Are angry faces detected more efficiently? *Cognition and Emotion, 14*, 61–92. (p. 524)

Fox, J. L. (1984). The brain's dynamic way of keeping in touch. *Science, 225*, 820–821. (p. 83)

Fox, N. C., Crum, W. R., Scahill, R. I., Stevens, J. M., Janssen, J. C., Rossor, M. N. (2001). Imaging of onset and progression of Alzheimer's disease with voxel-compression mapping of serial magnetic resonance images. *Lancet, 358*, 201–205. (p. 181)

Fozard, J. L., & Popkin, S. J. (1978). Optimizing adult development: Ends and means of an applied psychology of aging. *American Psychologist, 33*, 975–989. (p. 178)

Fracassini, C. (2000, August 27). Holidaymakers led by the nose in sales quest. *Scotland on Sunday*. (p. 233)

Fraley, R. C. (2002). Attachment stability from infancy to adulthood: Meta-analysis and dynamic modeling of developmental mechanisms. *Personality and Social Psychology Review, 6*, 123–151. (p. 158)

Francis, D., Diorio, J., Liu, D., & Meaney, M. J. (1999). Nongenomic transmission across generations of maternal behavior and stress responses in the rat. *Science, 286*, 1155–1158. (p. 156)

Frank, J. D. (1982). Therapeutic components shared by all psychotherapies. In J. H. Harvey & M. M. Parks (Eds.), *The Master Lecture Series: Vol. 1. Psychotherapy research and behavior change*. Washington, DC: American Psychological Association. (pp. 685, 707, 708)

Frank, R. (1999). *Luxury fever: Why money fails to satisfy in an era of excess*. New York: Free Press. (p. 121)

Frank, S. J. (1988). Young adults' perceptions of their relationships with their parents: Individual differences in connectedness, competence, and emotional autonomy. *Developmental Psychology, 24*, 729–737. (p. 173)

Frankel, A., Strange, D. R., & Schoonover, R. (1983). CRAP: Consumer rated assessment procedure. In G. H. Scherr & R. Liebmann-Smith (Eds.), *The best of The Journal of Irreproducible Results*. New York: Workman Publishing. (p. 618)

Frankenburg, W., Dodds, J., Archer, P., Shapiro, H., & Bresnick, B. (1992). The Denver II: A major revision and restandardization of the Denver Developmental Screening Test. *Pediatrics, 89*, 91–97. (p. 145)

Franz, E. A., Waldie, K. E., & Smith, M. J. (2000). The effect of callosotomy on novel versus familiar bimanual actions: A neural dissociation between controlled and automatic processes? *Psychological Science, 11*, 82–85. (p. 85)

Frasure-Smith, N., & Lespérance, F. (2005). Depression and coronary heart disease: Complex synergism of mind, body, and environment. *Current Directions in Psychological Science, 14*, 39–43. (p. 556)

Fredrickson, B. L. (2002). Positive emotions. In C. R. Snyder & S. J. Lopez (Eds.), *Handbook of positive psychology*. New York: Oxford. (p. 537)

Fredrickson, B. L. (2003). The value of positive emotions. *American Scientist, 91*, 330–335. (p. 537)

Fredrickson, B. L., & Kahneman, D. (1993). Duration neglect in retrospective evaluations of affective episodes. *Journal of Personality and Social Psychology, 65*, 45–55. (p. 358)

Fredrickson, B. L., Roberts, T-A., Noll, S. M., Quinn, D. M., & Twenge, J. M. (1998). That swimsuit becomes you: Sex differences in self-objectification, restrained eating, and math performance. *Journal of Personality and Social Psychology, 75*, 269–284. (p. 479)

Freedman, D. J., Riesenhuber, M., Poggio, T., & Miller, E. K. (2001). Categorical representation of visual stimuli in the primate prefrontal cortex. *Science, 291*, 312–316. (p. 423)

Freedman, J. L. (1978). *Happy people*. San Diego: Harcourt Brace Jovanovich. (p. 189)

Freedman, J. L. (1988). Television violence and aggression: What the evidence shows. In S. Oskamp (Ed.), *Television as a social issue*. Newbury Park, CA: Sage. (p. 345)

Freedman, J. L., & Fraser, S. C. (1966). Compliance without pressure: The foot-in-the-door technique. *Journal of Personality and Social Psychology, 4*, 195–202. (p. 727)

Freedman, J. L., & Perlick, D. (1979). Crowding, contagion, and laughter. *Journal of Experimental Social Psychology, 15*, 295–303. (p. 738)

Freedman, L. R., Rock, D., Roberts, S. A., Cornblatt, B. A., & Erlenmeyer-Kimling, L. (1998). The New York high-risk project: Attention, anhedonia and social outcome. *Schizophrenia Research, 30*, 1–9. (p. 676)

Freeman, W. J. (1991, February). The physiology of perception. *Scientific American*, pp. 78–85. (p. 215)

Frensch, P. A., & Rünger, D. (2003). Implicit learning. *Current Directions in Psychological Science, 12*, 13–18. (p. 605)

Freud, S. (1933). *New introductory lectures on psychoanalysis*. New York: Carlton House. (p. 598)

Freud, S. (1935; reprinted 1960). *A general introduction to psychoanalysis*. New York: Washington Square Press. (pp. 186–187)

Frey, M. C., & Detterman, D. K. (2004). Scholastic assessment or *g*? The relationship between the Scholastic Assessment Test and general cognitive ability. *Psychological Science, 15*, 373–378. (pp. 444–445)

Freyd, J. J., Putnam, F. W., Lyon, T. D., Becker-Blease, K. A., Cheit, R. E., Siegel, N. B., & Pezdek, K. (2005). The science of child sexual abuse. *Science, 308*, 501. (p. 159)

Friedman, M., & Ulmer, D. (1984). *Treating Type A behavior—and your heart*. New York: Knopf. (pp. 555, 570–571)

Friedrich, O. (1987, December 7). New age harmonies. *Time*, pp. 62–72. (p. 640)

Friend, T. (2004). *Animal talk: Breaking the codes of animal language*. New York: Free Press. (p. 427)

Frith, U., & Frith, C. (2001). The biological basis of social interaction. *Current Directions in Psychological Science, 10*, 151–155. (p. 152)

Fritsch, G., & Hitzig, E. (1870; reprinted 1960). On the electrical excitability of the cerebrum. In G. Von Bonin (Trans.), *Some papers on the cerebral cortex*. Springfield, IL: Charles C. Thomas. (p. 77)

Fromkin, V., & Rodman, R. (1983). *An introduction to language* (3rd ed.). New York: Holt, Rinehart & Winston. (pp. 411, 413)

Fry, A. F., & Hale, S. (1996). Processing speed, working memory, and fluid intelligence: Evidence for a developmental cascade. *Psychological Science, 7*, 237–241. (p. 179)

Fuhriman, A., & Burlingame, G. M. (1994). Group psychotherapy: Research and practice. In A. Fuhriman & G. M. Burlingame (Eds.), *Handbook of group psychotherapy*. New York: Wiley. (p. 697)

Fujiki, N., Yoshida, Y., Ripley, B., Mignot, E., & Nishino, S. (2003). Effects of IV and ICV hypocretin-1 (Orexin A) in hypocretin receptor-2 gene mutated narcoleptic dogs and IV hypocretin-1 replacement therapy in a hypocretin-ligand-deficient narcoleptic dog. *Sleep, 26*, 953–959. (p. 284)

Fujita, F., & Diener, E. (2005). Life satisfaction set point: Stability and change. *Journal of Personality and Social Psychology, 88*, 158–164. (p. 544)

Fuller, M. J., & Downs, A. C. (1990). Spermarche is a salient biological marker in men's development. Poster presented at the American Psychological Society convention. (p. 166)

Fulmer, I. S., Gerhart, B., & Scott, K. S. (2003). Are the 100 best better? An empirical investigation fo the relationship between being a "great place to work" and firm performance. *Personnel Psychology, 56*, 965–993. (p. 505)

Funder, D. C. (2001). Personality. *Annual Review of Psychology, 52*, 197–221. (p. 619)

Funder, D. C., & Block, J. (1989). The role of ego-control, ego-resiliency, and IQ in delay of gratification in adolescence. *Journal of Personality and Social Psychology, 57*, 1041–1050. (p. 170)

Furlow, F. B., & Thornhill, R. (1996, January/February). The orgasm wars. *Psychology Today*, pp. 42–46. (p. 482)

Furnham, A. (1982). Explanations for unemployment in Britain. *European Journal of Social Psychology, 12*, 335–352. (p. 725)

Furnham, A. (2001). Self-estimates of intelligence: Culture and gender difference in self and other estimates of both general (g) and multiple intelligences. *Personality and Individual Differences, 31*, 1381–1405. (p. 461)

Furnham, A., & Baguma, P. (1994). Cross-cultural differences in the evaluation of male and female body shapes. *International Journal of Eating Disorders, 15*, 81–89. (p. 582)

Furnham, A., Callahan, I., & Akande, D. (2004). Self-estimates of intelligence: A study in two African countries. *Journal of Psychology, 138*, 265–285. (p. 461)

Furnham, A., Callahan, I., & Rawles, R. (2003). Adults' knowledge of general psychology. *European Psychologist, 8*, 101–116. (p. 21)

Furnham, A., Hosoe, T., & Tang, T. L-P. (2002a). Male hubris and female humility? A cross-cultural study of ratings of self, parental, and sibling multiple intelligence in American, Britain, and Japan. *Intelligence, 30*, 101–115. (p. 461)

Furnham, A., & Mottabu, R. (2004). Sex and culture differences in the estimates of general and multiple intelligence: A study comparing British and Egyptian students. *Individual Differences Research, 3*, 82–96. (p. 461)

Furnham, A., & Rawles, R. (1995). Sex differences in the estimation of intelligence. *Journal of Social Behavior and Personality, 10*, 741–748. (p. 745)

Furnham, A., Reeves, E., & Bughani, S. (2002b). Parents think their sons are brighter than their daughters: Sex differences in parental self-estimations and estimations of their children's multiple intelligences. *Journal of Genetic Psychology, 163*, 24–39. (p. 461)

Furnham, A., & Taylor, L. (1990). Lay theories of homosexuality: Aetiology, behaviours, and `cures.' *British Journal of Social Psychology, 29*, 135–147. (p. 492)

Furnham, A., & Thomas, C. (2004). Parents' gender and personality and estimates of their own and their children's intelligence. *Personality and Individual Differences, 37*, 887–903. (p. 461)

Furr, R. M., & Funder, D. C. (1998). A multimodal analysis of personal negativity. *Journal of Personality and Social Psychology, 74*, 1580–1591. (p. 667)

Gabbay, F. H. (1992). Behavior-genetic strategies in the study of emotion. *Psychological Science, 3*, 50–55. (p. 102)

Gabrieli, J. D. E., Desmond, J. E., Demb, J. E., Wagner, A. D., Stone, M. V., Vaidya, C. J., & Glover, G. H. (1996). Functional magnetic resonance imaging of semantic memory processes in the frontal lobes. *Psychological Science, 7*, 278–283. (p. 368)

Gaertner, L., & Iuzzini, J. (2005). Rejection and entitativity: A synergistic model of mass violence. In K. D. Williams, J. P. Forgas, & W. von Hippel (Eds.). *The social outcast: Ostracism, social exclusion, rejection, and bullying.* New York: Psychology Press. (p. 751)

Gage, F. H. (2003, September). Repair yourself. *Scientific American*, pp. 46–53. (p. 83)

Galambos, N. L. (1992). Parent-adolescent relations. *Current Directions in Psychological Science, 1*, 146–149. (p. 172)

Galanter, E. (1962). Contemporary psychophysics. In R. Brown, E. Galanter, E. H. Hess, & G. Mandler (Eds.), *New directions in psychology.* New York: Holt Rinehart, & Winston. (p. 199)

Galati, D., Scherer, K. R., & Ricci-Bitti, P. E. (1997). Voluntary facial expression of emotion: Comparing congenitally blind with normally sighted encoders. *Journal of Personality and Social Psychology, 73*, 1363–1379. (p. 529)

Galea, S., Boscarino, J., Resnick, H., & Vlahov, D. (2002). Mental health in New York City after the September 11 terrorist attacks: Results from two population surveys. Chapter 7. In *Mental-Health, United States, 2001*, R. W. Manderscheid, & M. J. Henderson (Eds.). Washington, DC: Superintendent of Documents, U.S. Government Printing Office. (p. 653)

Gallup. (2002, February 21). Homosexual relations. The Gallup Organization (www.gallup.com/poll/topics/homosexual.asp). (p. 492)

Gallup. (2002, June 11). Poll insights: The gender gap—post Sept. 11th fear. The Gallup Organization (www.gallup.com/poll/pollInsights). (p. 649)

Gallup. (2002). Alcohol and drinking (results of November 8–11, 2001 survey) (www.gallup.com/poll/topics/alcohol.asp). (p. 305)

Gallup. (2005, May 5). The gender gap: President Bush's handling of Iraq. The Gallup Poll (www.gallup.com). (p. 127)

Gallup, G., Jr. (1982). *Adventures in immortality.* New York: McGraw-Hill. (p. 309)

Gallup, G., Jr. (1998). Can animals empathize? *Scientific American, 4*, 66. (p. 424)

Gallup, G., Jr. (2002, April 30). Education and youth. *Gallup Tuesday Briefing* (www.gallup.com/poll/tb/educaYouth/20020430.asp). (p. 344)

Gallup, G. G., Jr., & Suarez, S. D. (1986). Self-awareness and the emergence of mind in humans and other primates. In J. Suls & A. G. Greenwald (Eds.), *Psychological perspectives on the self* (Vol. 3.). Hillsdale, NJ: Erlbaum. (p. 161)

Gallup, G. H. (1972). *The Gallup poll: Public opinion 1935–1971* (Vol. 3). New York: Random House. (p. 758)

Gallup, G. H., Jr. (1994, October). Millions finding care and support in small groups. *Emerging Trends*, pp. 2–5. (p. 698)

Gallup Organization. (1993). Other hemispheres may think our religion is alien and exotic. *PRRC Emerging Trends, 15*, 1–3. (p. 708)

Gallup Organization. (2003, July 8). American public opinion about Iraq. Gallup Poll News Service (www.gallup.com) (p. 728)

Gallup Organization. (2004, August 16). 65% of Americans receive NO praise or recognition in the workplace. E-mail from Tom Rath: bucketbook@gallup.com. (p. 508)

Gangestad, S. W., & Simpson, J. A. (2000). The evolution of human mating: Trade-offs and strategic pluralism. *Behavioral and Brain Sciences, 23*. (p. 111)

Garb, H. N., Wood, J. M., Lilienfeld, S. O., & Nezworski, M. T. (2005). Roots of the Rorschach controversy. *Clinical Psychology Review, 25*, 97–118. (p. 603)

Garbarino, J., Dubrow, N., & Kostelny, K. (1992). *Children in danger: Coping with the consequences of community violence.* San Francisco: Jossey-Bass Inc. (p. 652)

Garbarino, J., Kostelny, K., & Dubrow, N. (1991). What children can tell us about living in danger. *American Psychologist, 46*, 376–383. (p. 652)

Garcia, J., & Gustavson, A. R. (1997, January). Carl R. Gustavson (1946-1996): Pioneering wildlife psychologist. *APS Observer*, pp. 34–35. (p. 323)

Garcia, J., & Koelling, R. A. (1966). Relation of cue to consequence in avoidance learning. *Psychonomic Science, 4*, 123–124. (p. 322)

Gardner, H. (1983). *Frames of mind: The theory of multiple intelligences.* New York: Basic Books. (p. 433)

Gardner, H. (1998, March 19). An intelligent way to progress. *The Independent* (London), p. E4. (pp. 118, 435)

Gardner, H. (1998, November 5). Do parents count? *New York Review of Books* (www.nybooks.com). (p. 434)

Gardner, H. (1999, February). Who owns intelligence? *Atlantic Monthly*, pp. 67–76. (pp. 437, 444)

Gardner, H. (1999). *Multiple views of multiple intelligence.* New York: Basic Books. (p. 433)

Gardner, J., & Oswald, A. (2001). Does money buy happiness? A longitudinal study using data on windfalls. Working paper, Department of Economics, Cambridge University. (p. 539)

Gardner, R. A., & Gardner, B. I. (1969). Teaching sign language to a chimpanzee. *Science, 165,* 664–672. (p. 425)

Gardner, R. M., & Tockerman, Y. R. (1994). A computer-TV video methodology for investigating the influence of somatotype on perceived personality traits. *Journal of Social Behavior and Personality, 9,* 555–563. (pp. 583–584)

Garfield, C. (1986). *Peak performers: The new heroes of American business.* New York: Morrow. (p. 421)

Garlick, D. (2002). Understanding the nature of the general factor of intelligence: The role of individual differences in neural plasticity as an explanatory mechanism. *Psychological Review, 109,* 116–136. (p. 440)

Garlick, D. (2003). Integrating brain science research with intelligence research. *Current Directions in Psychological Science, 12,* 185–189. (p. 440)

Garner, D. M., & Wooley, S. C. (1991). Confronting the failure of behavioral and dietary treatments for obesity. *Clinical Psychology Review, 11,* 729–780. (p. 588)

Garnets, L., & Kimmel, D. (1990). Lesbian and gay dimensions in the psychological study of human diversity. Master lecture, American Psychological Association convention. (p. 487)

Garry, M., & Loftus, E. F., & Brown, S. W. (1994). Memory: A river runs through it. *Consciousness and Cognition, 3,* 438–451. (p. 604)

Garry, M., Manning, C. G., Loftus, E. F., & Sherman, S. J. (1996). Imagination inflation: Imagining a childhood event inflates confidence that it occurred. *Psychonomic Bulletin & Review, 3,* 208–214. (p. 383)

Garza, D. L., & Feltz, D. L. (1998). Effects of selected mental practice on performance, self-efficacy, and competition confidence of figure skaters. *The Sports Psychologist, 12,* 1–15. (p. 421)

Gates, G. A., & Miyamoto, R. T. (2003). Cochlear implants. *New England Journal of Medicine, 349,* 421–423. (p. 221)

Gates, W. (1998, July 20). Charity begins when I'm ready (interview). *Fortune* (www.pathfinder.com/fortune/1998/980720/bil7.html). (p. 435)

Gawande, A. (1998, September 21). The pain perplex. *The New Yorker,* pp. 86–94. (p. 228)

Gawin, F. H. (1991). Cocaine addiction: Psychology and neurophysiology. *Science, 251,* 1580–1586. (p. 301)

Gazzaniga, M. S. (1967, August). The split brain in man. *Scientific American,* pp. 24–29. (p. 84)

Gazzaniga, M. S. (1983). Right hemisphere language following brain bisection: A 20-year perspective. *American Psychologist, 38,* 525–537. (p. 85)

Gazzaniga, M. S. (1988). Organization of the human brain. *Science, 245,* 947–952. (p. 297)

Gazzaniga, M. S. (1992). *Nature's mind: The biological roots of thinking, emotions, sexuality, language, and intelligence.* New York: Basic Books. (p. 117)

Gazzaniga, M. S. (1997). Brain, drugs, and society. *Science, 275,* 459. (p. 289)

Geary, D. C. (1995). Sexual selection and sex differences in spatial cognition. *Learning and Individual Differences, 7,* 289–301. (p. 463)

Geary, D. C. (1996). Sexual selection and sex differences in mathematical abilities. *Behavioral and Brain Sciences, 19,* 229–247. (p. 463)

Geary, D. C. (1998). *Male, female: The evolution of human sex differences.* Washington, DC: American Psychological Association. (p. 111)

Geary, D. C., Salthouse, T. A., Chen, G-P., & Fan, L. (1996). Are East Asian versus American differences in arithmetical ability a recent phenomenon? *Developmental Psychology, 32,* 254–262. (p. 460)

Geen, R. G., & Quanty, M. B. (1977). The catharsis of aggression: An evaluation of a hypothesis. In L. Berkowitz (Ed.), *Advances in experimental social psychology* (Vol. 10). New York: Academic Press. (p. 536)

Geen, R. G., & Thomas, S. L. (1986). The immediate effects of media violence on behavior. *Journal of Social Issues, 42*(3), 7–28. (p. 345)

Gehring, W. J., Wimke, J., & Nisenson, L. G. (2000). Action monitoring dysfunction in obsessive-compulsive disorder. *Psychological Science, 11*(1), 1–6. (p. 655)

Geldard, F. A. (1972). *The human senses* (2nd ed.). New York: Wiley. (p. 212)

Gelman, D. (1989, May 15). Voyages to the unknown. *Newsweek,* pp. 66–69. (p. 529)

Genesee, F., & Gándara, P. (1999). Bilingual education programs: A cross-national perspective. *Journal of Social Issues, 55,* 665–685. (p. 420)

Genevro, J. L. (2003). *Report on bereavement and grief research.* Washington, DC: Center for the Advancement of Health. (p. 191)

Genovese, J. E. C. (2004). The ten percent solution. *Skeptic, 10*(4), 55–57. (p. 40)

Gentile, D. A., Lynch, P. J., Linder, J. R., & Walsh, D. A. (2004). The effects of violent video game habits on adolescent hostility, aggressive behaviors, and school performance. *Journal of Adolescence, 27,* 5–22. (p. 755)

Gentile, D. A., Walsh, D. A., Ellison, P. R., Fox, M., & Cameron, J. (2004). Media violence as a risk factor for children: A longitudinal study. Paper presented at the American Psychological Society Convention. (p. 755)

Gentry, J., & Eron, L. D. (1993). American Psychological Association Commission on Violence and Youth. *American Psychological Association, 48,* 89. (p. 345)

George, L. K., Ellison, C. G., & Larson, D. B. (2002). Explaining the relationships between religious involvement and health. *Psychological Inquiry, 13,* 190–200. (p. 573)

George, L. K., Larson, D. B., Koenig, H. G., & McCullough, M. E. (2000). Spirituality and health: What we know, what we need to know. *Journal of Social and Clinical Psychology, 19,* 102–116. (p. 573)

George, M. S. (2003, September). Stimulating the brain. *Scientific American,* pp. 67–73. (p. 717)

Gerard, R. W. (1953, September). What is memory? *Scientific American,* pp. 118–126. (p. 364)

Gerbner, G. (1990). Stories that hurt: Tobacco, alcohol, and other drugs in the mass media. In H. Resnik (Ed.), *Youth and drugs: Society's mixed messages.* Rockville, MD: Office for Substance Abuse Prevention, U.S. Department of Health and Human Services. (p. 307)

Gerbner, G. (1993, June). Women and minorities on television: A study in casting and fate. A report to the Screen Actors Guild and the American Federation of Radio and Television Artists. (p. 344)

Gerbner, G., Gross, L., Morgan, M., & Signorielli, N. (1994). Growing up with television: The cultivation perspective. In J. Bryant, & D. Zillman (Eds.), *Media Effects: Advances in theory and research* (pp. 17–41). Hillsdale, NJ: Erlbaum. (p. 344)

Gerbner, G., Morgan, M., & Signorielli, N. (1993). Television violence profile No. 16: The turning point from research to action. Annenberg School for Communication, University of Pennsylvania. (p. 754)

Gerhart, K. A., Koziol-McLain, J., Lowenstein, S. R., & Whiteneck, G. G. (1994). Quality of life following spinal cord injury: Knowledge and attitudes of emergency care providers. *Annals of Emergency Medicine, 23,* 807–812. (p. 538)

Gerrard, M., & Luus, C. A. E. (1995). Judgments of vulnerability to pregnancy: The role of risk factors and individual differences. *Personality and Social Psychology Bulletin, 21,* 160–171. (p. 485)

Gershoff, E. T. (2002). Parental corporal punishment and associated child behaviors and experiences: A meta-analytic and theoretical review. *Psychological Bulletin, 128,* 539–579. (p. 333)

Gershon, J., Anderson, P., Graap, K., Zimand, E., Hodges, L., & Rothbaum, B. O. (2002). Virtual reality exposure therapy in the treatment of anxiety disorders, *Scientific Review of Mental Health Practice, 1,* 76–81. (p. 692)

Geschwind, N. (1979, September). Specializations of the human brain. *Scientific American,* pp. 180–199. (p. 81)

Geschwind, N., & Behan, P. O. (1984). Laterality, hormones, and immunity. In N. Geschwind & A. M. Galaburda (Eds.), *Cerebral dominance: The biological foundations.* Cambridge, MA: Harvard University Press. (p. 88)

Gfeller, J. D., Lynn, S. J., & Pribble, W. E. (1987). Enhancing hypnotic susceptibility: Interpersonal and rapport factors. *Journal of Personality and Social Psychology, 52*, 586–595. (p. 294)

Gibbons, F. X. (1986). Social comparison and depression: Company's effect on misery. *Journal of Personality and Social Psychology, 51*, 140–148. (p. 543)

Gibbs, W. W. (1996, June). Mind readings. *Scientific American*, pp. 34–36. (p. 78)

Gibbs, W. W. (2002, August). Saving dying languages. *Scientific American*, pp. 79–85. (p. 414)

Gibbs, W. W. (2005, June). Obesity: An overblown epidemic? *Scientific American*, pp. 70–77. (pp. 582–583)

Gibson, E. J., & Walk, R. D. (1960, April). The "visual cliff." *Scientific American*, pp. 64–71. (p. 245)

Gibson, H. B. (1995, April). Recovered memories. *The Psychologist*, pp. 153–154. (p. 292)

Gigerenzer, G. (2004). Dread risk, September 11, and fatal traffic accidents. *Psychological Science, 15*, 286–287. (p. 404)

Gigerenzer, G. (2004). Fast and frugal heuristics: The tools of bounded rationality. In D. Koehler & N. Harvey (Eds.), *Handbook of judgment and decision making*. Oxford, UK: Blackwell. (p. 408)

Gignac, G., Vernon, P. A., & Wickett, J. C. (2003). Factors influencing the relationship between brain size and intelligence. In H. Nyborg, *The scientific study of general intelligence*. Amsterdam: Pergamon. (p. 440)

Gilbert, D. T., Pelham, B. W., & Krull, D. S. (2003). The psychology of good ideas. *Psychological Inquiry, 14*, 258–260. (p. 21)

Gilbert, D. T., Pinel, E. C., Wilson, T. D., Blumberg, S. J., & Wheatley, T. P. (1998). Immune neglect: A source of durability bias in affective forecasting. *Journal of Personality and Social Psychology, 75*, 617–638. (p. 539)

Giles, D. E., Dahl, R. E., & Coble, P. A. (1994). Childbearing, developmental, and familial aspects of sleep. In J. M. Oldham & M. B. Riba (Eds.), *Review of Psychiatry*, (Vol. 13). Washington, DC: American Psychiatric Press. (p. 277)

Gillham, J. E., Reivich, K. J., Jaycox, L. H., & Seligman, M. E. P. (1995). Preventing depressive symptoms in schoolchildren: Two year follow-up. *Psychological Science, 6*, 343–351. (pp. 696–697)

Gilligan, C. (1982). *In a different voice: Psychological theory and women's development*. Cambridge, MA: Harvard University Press. (p. 128)

Gilligan, C., Lyons, N. P., & Hanmer, T. J. (Eds.). (1990). *Making connections: The relational worlds of adolescent girls at Emma Willard School*. Cambridge, MA: Harvard University Press. (p. 128)

Gilovich, T. (1991). *How we know what isn't so: The fallibility of human reason in everyday life*. New York: Free Press. (pp. 22, 33–34)

Gilovich, T. D. (1996). The spotlight effect: Exaggerated impressions of the self as a social stimulus. Unpublished manuscript, Cornell University. (p. 632)

Gilovich, T., Kruger, J., & Medvec, V. H. (2002). The spotlight effect revisited: Overestimating the manifest variability of our actions and appearance. *Journal of Experimental Social Psychology, 38*, 93–99. (p. 632)

Gilovich, T., & Medvec, V. H. (1995). The experience of regret: What, when, and why. *Psychological Review, 102*, 379–395. (p. 189)

Gilovich, T., & Savitsky, K. (1999). The spotlight effect and the illusion of transparency: Egocentric assessments of how we are seen by others. *Current Directions in Psychological Science, 8*, 165–168. (p. 632)

Gilovich, T., Vallone, R., & Tversky, A. (1985). The hot hand in basketball: On the misperception of random sequences. *Cognitive Psychology, 17*, 295–314. (p. 35)

Gingerich, O. (1999, February 6). Is there a role for natural theology today? *The Real Issue* (www.origins.org/real/n9501/natural.html). (p. 136)

Giuliano, T. A., Barnes, L. C., Fiala, S. E., & Davis D. M. (1998a). An empirical investigation of male answer syndrome. Paper presented at the Southwestern Psychological Association convention. (p. 128)

Giuliano, T. A., Fiala, S. E., Davis, D. M., Barnes, L. C., & Patrick, E. C. (1998b). The reluctance to admit "I don't know": Exploring "male answer syndrome." Paper presented to the American Psychological Society convention. (p. 128)

Gladue, B. A. (1990). Hormones and neuroendocrine factors in atypical human sexual behavior. In J. R. Feierman (Ed.), *Pedophilia: Biosocial dimensions*. New York: Springer-Verlag. (p. 491)

Gladue, B. A. (1994). The biopsychology of sexual orientation. *Current Directions in Psychological Science, 3*, 150–154. (pp. 490, 492)

Gladwell, M. (2000, May 9). The new-boy network: What do job interviews really tell us? *New Yorker*, pp. 68–86. (p. 503)

Gladwell, M. (2004, September 20). Personality plus. *New Yorker*, pp. 42–48. (p. 613)

Gladwell, M. (2005). *Blink: The power of thinking without thinking*. New York: Little Brown. (p. 762)

Glass, D. C., & Singer, J. E. (1972). *Urban stress*. New York: Academic Press. (p. 218)

Glass, R. I. (2004). Perceived threats and real killers. *Science, 304*, 927. (p. 405)

Glass, R. M. (2001). Electroconvulsive therapy: Time to bring it out of the shadows. *Journal of the American Medical Association, 285*, 1346–1348. (p. 716)

Glater, J. D. (2001, March 26). Women are close to being majority of law students. *New York Times* (www.nytimes.com). (p. 131)

Gleaves, D. H. (1996). The sociocognitive model of dissociative identity disorder: A reexamination of the evidence. *Psychological Bulletin, 120*, 42–59. (p. 657)

Glenn, N. D. (1975). Psychological well-being in the postparental stage: Some evidence from national surveys. *Journal of Marriage and the Family, 37*, 105–110. (p. 188)

Glick, P., & 15 others (2004). Bad but bold: Ambivalent attitudes toward men predict gender inequality in 16 nations. *Journal of Personality and Social Psychology, 86*, 713–728. (p. 745)

Glick, P., Gottesman, D., & Jolton, J. (1989). The fault is not in the stars: Susceptibility of skeptics and believers in astrology to the Barnum effect. *Personality and Social Psychology Bulletin, 15*, 572–583. (p. 617)

Gluhoski, V. L., & Wortman, C. B. (1996). The impact of trauma on world views. *Journal of Social and Clinical Psychology, 15*, 417–429. (p. 325)

Godden, D. R., & Baddeley, A. D. (1975). Context-dependent memory in two natural environments: On land and underwater. *British Journal of Psychology, 66*, 325–331. (pp. 372–373)

Goel, M. S., McCarthy, E. P., Phillips, R. S., & Wee, C. C. (2004). Obesity among U.S. immigrant subgroups by duration of residence. *Journal of the American Medical Association, 292*, 2860–2867. (p. 587)

Goel, V., & Dolan, R. J. (2001). The functional anatomy of humor: Segregating cognitive and affective components. *Nature Neuroscience, 4*, 237–238. (p. 82)

Goff, D. C. (1993). Reply to Dr. Armstrong. *Journal of Nervous and Mental Disease, 181*, 604–605. (p. 657)

Goff, D. C., & Simms, C. A. (1993). Has multiple personality disorder remained consistent over time? *Journal of Nervous and Mental Disease, 181*, 595–600. (p. 657)

Goff, L. M., & Roediger, III, H. L. (1998). Imagination inflation for action events: Repeated imaginings lead to illusory recollections. *Memory and Cognition, 26*, 20–33. (p. 383)

Gold, M., & Yanof, D. S. (1985). Mothers, daughters, and girlfriends. *Journal of Personality and Social Psychology, 49*, 654–659. (p. 172)

Goldapple, K., Segal, Z., Garson, C., Lau, M., Bieling, P., Kennedy, S., & Mayberg, H. (2004). Modulation of cortical-limbic pathways in major depression. *Archives of General Psychiatry, 61*, 34–41. (p. 714)

Golden, R. N., Gaynes, B. N., Ekstrom, R. D., Hamer, R. M., Jacobsen, F. M., Suppes, T., Wisner, K. L., & Nemeroff, C. B. (2005). The efficacy of light therapy in the treatment of mood disorders: A review and meta-analysis of the evidence. *American Journal of Psychiatry, 162*, 656–662. (p. 707)

Goldfried, M. R. (2001). Integrating gay, lesbian, and bisexual issues into mainstream psychology. *American Psychologist, 56*, 977–988. (p. 662)

Goldfried, M. R., & Padawer, W. (1982). Current status and future directions in psychotherapy. In M. R. Goldfried (Ed.), *Converging themes in psychotherapy: Trends in psychodynamic, humanistic, and behavioral practice.* New York: Springer. (p. 707)

Goldfried, M. R., Raue, P. J., & Castonguay, L. G. (1998). The therapeutic focus in significant sessions of master therapists: A comparison of cognitive-behavioral and psychodynamic-interpersonal interventions. *Journal of Consulting and Clinical Psychology, 66,* 803–810. (p. 708)

Goldin-Meadow, S., Nusbaum, H., Kelly, S. D., & Wagner, S. (2001). Explaining math: Gesturing lightens the load. *Psychological Science, 12,* 516–522. (p. 426)

Golding, J. M. (1996). Sexual assault history and women's reproductive and sexual health. *Psychology of Women Quarterly, 20,* 101–121. (p. 753)

Golding, J. M. (1999). Sexual-assault history and the long-term physical health problems: Evidence from clinical and population epidemiology. *Current Directions in Psychological Science, 8,* 191–194. (p. 652)

Goldstein, A. P., Glick, B., & Gibbs, J. C. (1998). *Aggression replacement training: A comprehensive intervention for aggressive youth* (rev. ed.). Champaign, IL: Research Press. (p. 752)

Goldstein, I. (2000, August). Male sexual circuitry. *Scientific American,* pp. 70–75. (p. 64)

Goldstein, I., Lue, T. F., Padma-Nathan, H., Rosen, R. C., Steers, W. D., & Wicker, P. A. (1998). Oral sildenafil in the treatment of erectile dysfunction. *New England Journal of Medicine, 338,* 1397–1404. (p. 38)

Goleman, D. (1980, February). 1,528 little geniuses and how they grew. *Psychology Today,* pp. 28–53. (p. 504)

Goleman, D. (1995). *Emotional intelligence.* New York: Bantam. (p. 518)

Gonsalves, B., Reber, P. J., Gitelman, D. R., Parrish, T. B., Mesulam, M-M., & Paller, K. A. (2004). Neural evidence that vivid imagining can lead to false remembering. *Psychological Science, 15,* 655–659. (p. 383)

Goodall, J. (1968). The behaviour of free-living chimpanzees in the Gombe Stream Reserve. *Animal Behaviour Monographs, 1,* 161–311. (p. 116)

Goodall, J. (1986). *The chimpanzees of Gombe: Patterns of behavior.* Cambridge, MA: Harvard University Press. (p. 747)

Goodall, J. (1998). Learning from the chimpanzees: A message humans can understand. *Science, 282,* 2184–2185. (p. 29)

Goodchilds, J. (1987). Quoted by Carol Tavris, Old age is not what it used to be. *The New York Times Magazine: Good Health Magazine,* September 27, pp. 24–25, 91–92. (p. 176)

Goode, E. (1999, February 16). Tales of midlife crisis found greatly exaggerated. *New York Times* (www.nytimes.com). (p. 176)

Goode, E. (1999, April 13). If things taste bad, 'phantoms' may be at work. *New York Times* (www.nytimes.com). (p. 227)

Goode, E. (2002, June 30). Antidepressants life clouds, but lose 'miracle drug' label. *New York Times* (www.nytimes.com). (p. 713)

Goode, E. (2003, January 28). Even in the age of Prozac, some still prefer the couch. *New York Times* (www.nytimes.com). (p. 687)

Goodhart, D. E. (1986). The effects of positive and negative thinking on performance in an achievement situation. *Journal of Personality and Social Psychology, 51,* 117–124. (p. 627)

Goodman, E. (2000). Depressive symptoms and cigarette smoking among teens. *Pediatrics, 106,* 4. 748–756. (p. 577)

Goodman, G. S., Ghetti, S., Quas, J. A., Edelstein, R. S., Alexander, K. W., Redlich, A. D., Cordon, I. M., & Jones, D. P. H. (2003). A prospective study of memory for child sexual abuse: New findings relevant to the repressed-memory controversy. *Psychological Science, 14,* 113–118. (p. 388)

Goodman, G. S., Rudy, L., Bottoms, B. L., & Aman, B. (1990). Children's concerns and memory: Issues of ecological validity in the study of children's eyewitness testimony. In R. Fivush & J. A. Hudson (Eds.), *Knowing and remembering in young children.* New York: Cambridge University Press. (p. 386)

Goodman, L. A., Koss, M. P., & Russo, N. F. (1993). Violence against women: Mental health effects. Part II. Conceptualizations of posttraumatic stress. *Applied & Preventive Psychology, 2,* 123–130. (p. 652)

Goodnough, A. (2002, May 2). Post-9/11 pain found to linger in young minds. *New York Times* (www.nytimes.com). (p. 534)

Goodson, P., McCormick, D., & Evans, A. (2001). Searching for sexually explicit materials on the Internet: An exploratory study of college students' behavior and attitudes. *Archives of Sexual Behavior, 30,* 101–118. (p. 753)

Goodstein, L., & Glaberson, W. (2000, April 9). The well-marked roads to homicidal rage. *New York Times* (www.nytimes.com). (p. 630)

Goodwin, F. K., & Morrison, A. R. (1999). Scientists in bunkers: How appeasement of animal rights activism has failed. *Cerebrum, 1*(2), 50–62. (p. 47)

Goodwin, R., & Hamilton, S. P. (2002). Cigarette smoking and panic: The role of neuroticism. *American Journal of Psychiatry, 159,* 1208–1213. (p. 650)

Gopnik, A., & Meltzoff, A. N. (1986). Relations between semantic and cognitive development in the one-word stage: The specificity hypothesis. *Child Development, 57,* 1040–1053. (p. 419)

Goranson, R. E. (1978). *The hindsight effect in problem solving.* Unpublished manuscript, cited by G. Wood (1984), Research methodology: A decision-making perspective. In A. M. Rogers & C. J. Scheirer (Eds.), *The G. Stanley Hall Lecture Series* (Vol. 4). Washington, DC: American Psychological Association. (p. 22)

Gordon, P. (2004). Numerical cognition without words: Evidence from Amazonia. *Science, 306,* 496–499. (p. 419)

Gore, A., Jr. (1992). *Earth in the balance: Ecology and the human spirit.* Boston: Houghton-Mifflin. (p. 338)

Gore-Felton, C., Koopman, C., Thoresen, C., Arnow, B., Bridges, E., & Spiegel, D. (2000). Psychologists' beliefs and clinical characteristics: Judging the veracity of childhood sexual abuse memories. *Professional Psychology: Research and Practice, 31,* 372–377. (p. 388)

Gortmaker, S. L., Must, A., Perrin, J. M., Sobol, A. M., & Dietz, W. H. (1993). Social and economic consequences of overweight in adolescence and young adulthood. *New England Journal of Medicine, 329,* 1008–1012. (p. 584)

Gosling, S. D., Ko, S. J., Mannarelli, T., & Morris, M. E. (2002). A room with a cue: Personality judgments based on offices and bedrooms. *Journal of Personality and Social Psychology, 82,* 379–398. (p. 621)

Gosling, S. D., Kwan, V. S. Y., & John, O. P. (2003). A dog's got personality: A cross-species comparative approach to personality judgments in dogs and humans. *Journal of Personality and Social Psychology, 85,* 1161–1169. (p. 615)

Gotlib, I. H., & Hammen, C. L. (1992). *Psychological aspects of depression: Toward a cognitive-interpersonal integration.* New York: Wiley. (p. 667)

Gottesman, I. I. (1991). *Schizophrenia genesis: The origins of madness.* New York: Freeman. (pp. 674–675)

Gottesman, I. I. (2001). Psychopathology through a life span—genetic prism. *American Psychologist, 56,* 867–881. (p. 675)

Gottfredson, L. S. (2002a). Where and why g matters: Not a mystery. *Human Performance, 15,* 25–46. (p. 435)

Gottfredson, L. S. (2002b). g: Highly general and highly practical. In R. J. Sternberg & E. L. Grigorenko (Eds.), *The general factor of intelligence: How general is it?* Mahwah, NJ: Erlbaum. (p. 435)

Gottfredson, L. S. (2003a). Dissecting practical intelligence theory: Its claims and evidence. *Intelligence, 31,* 343–397. (p. 435)

Gottfredson, L. S. (2003b). On Sternberg's "Reply to Gottfredson." *Intelligence, 31,* 415–424. (p. 435)

Gottfried, J. A., O'Doherty, J., & Dolan, R. J. (2003). Encoding predictive reward value in human amygdala and orbitofrontal cortex. *Science, 301,* 1104–1108. (p. 316)

Gottman, J., with Silver N. (1994). *Why marriages succeed or fail.* New York: Simon & Schuster. (p. 188)

Gougoux, F., Zatorre, R., Lassonde, M., Voss, P., & Lepore, F. (2005). A functional neuroimaging study of sound localization: Visual cortex activity predicts performance in early-blind individuals. *PloS Biology, 3*(2): e27. (p. 223)

Gould, E., Reeves, A. J., Graziano, M. S. A., & Gross, C. G. (1999). Neurogenesis in the neocortex of adult primates. *Science, 286,* 548–552. (p. 83)

Gould, S. J. (1981). *The mismeasure of man.* New York: Norton. (pp. 443–444)

Gould, S. J. (1997, June 12). Darwinian fundamentalism. *The New York Review of Books, XLIV*(10), 34–37. (p. 112)

Grady, C. L., & McIntosh, A. R., Horwitz, B., Maisog, J. M., Ungeleider, L. G., Mentis, M. J., Pietrini, P., Schapiro, M. B., & Haxby, J. V. (1995). Age-related reductions in human recognition memory due to impaired encoding. *Science, 269,* 218–221. (p. 376)

Graf, P. (1990). Life-span changes in implicit and explicit memory. *Bulletin of the Psychonomic Society, 28,* 353–358. (p. 182)

Graham, J. W., Marks, G., & Hansen, W. B. (1991). Social influence processes affecting adolescent substance use. *Journal of Applied Psychology, 76,* 291–298. (p. 307)

Grant, B. F., & Dawson, D. A. (1998). Age of onset of drug use and its association with DSM-IV drug abuse and dependence: Results from the national Longitudinal Alcohol Epidemiologic Survey. *Journal of Substance Abuse, 10,* 163–173. (p. 311)

Grant, B. F., Stinson, F. S., Hasin, D. S., Dawson, D. A., Chou, S. P., & Anderson, K. (2004). Immigration and lifetime prevalence of DSM-IV psychiatric disorders among Mexican Americans and non-Hispanic Whites in the United States. *Archives of General Psychiatry, 61,* 1226–1233. (p. 680)

Gray-Little, B., & Burks, N. (1983). Power and satisfaction in marriage: A review and critique. *Psychological Bulletin, 93,* 513–538. (p. 764)

Gray-Little, B., & Hafdahl, A. R. (2000). Factors influencing racial comparisons of self-esteem: A quantitative review. *Psychological Bulletin, 126,* 26–54. (p. 633)

GRE. (1990). *GRE guide to the use of the Graduate Record Examinations Program.* Princeton, NJ: Graduate Record Examinations Board, Educational Testing Service. (p. 449)

Green, B. (2002). Listening to leaders: Feedback on 360-degree feedback one year later. *Organizational Development Journal, 20,* 8–16. (p. 503)

Green, C. S., & Bavelier, D. (2003). Action video game modifies visual selective attention. *Nature, 423,* 534–537. (p. 200)

Green, J. T., & Woodruff-Pak, D. S. (2000). Eyeblink classical conditioning: Hippocampal formation is for neutral stimulus associations as cerebellum is for association-response. *Psychological Bulletin, 126,* 138–158. (p. 369)

Greenberg, D. L. (2004). President Bush's false 'flashbulb' memory of 9/11/01. *Applied Cognitive Psychology, 18,* 363–370. (p. 350)

Greenberg, J., Solomon, S., & Pyszczynski, T. (1997). Terror management theory of self-esteem and cultural worldviews: Empirical assessments and conceptual refinements. *Advances in Social Psychology, 29,* 61–142. (p. 606)

Greene, J., Sommerville, R. B., Nystrom, L. E., Darley, J. M., & Cohen, J. D. (2001). An fMRI investigation of emotional engagement in moral judgment. *Science, 293,* 2105. (pp. 169–170)

Greene, R. L. (1987). Effects of maintenance rehearsal on human memory. *Psychological Bulletin, 102,* 403–413. (p. 356)

Greenfeld, L. A. (1998). *Alcohol and crime: An analysis of national data on the prevalence of alcohol involvement in crime.* Washington, DC: Document NCJ-168632, Bureau of Justice Statistics (www.ojp.usdoj.gov/bjs). (p. 750)

Greenough, W. T., Black, J. E., & Wallace, C. S. (1987). Experience and brain development. *Child Development, 58,* 539–559. (p. 115)

Greenwald, A. G. (1992). New look 3: Unconscious cognition reclaimed. *American Psychologist, 47,* 766–779. (p. 605)

Greenwald, A. G. (1992). Subliminal semantic activation and subliminal snake oil. Paper presented to the American Psychological Association Convention, Washington, DC. (p. 201)

Greenwald, A. G., McGhee, D. E., & Schwartz, J. L. K. (1998). Measuring individual differences in implicit cognition: The implicit association test. *Journal of Personality and Social Psychology, 74,* 1464–1480. (p. 744)

Greenwald, A. G., Oakes, M. A., & Hoffman, H. (2003). Targets of discrimination: Effects of race on responses to weapons holders. *Journal of Experimental Social Psychology, 39,* 399. (p. 744)

Greenwald, A. G., Spangenberg, E. R., Pratkanis, A. R., & Eskenazi, J. (1991). Double-blind tests of subliminal self-help audiotapes. *Psychological Science, 2,* 119–122. (p. 201)

Greenwood, M. R. C. (1989). Sexual dimorphism and obesity. In A. J. Stunkard & A. Baum (Eds.). *Perspectives in behavioral medicine: Eating, sleeping, and sex.* Hillsdale, NJ: Erlbaum. (p. 583)

Greers, A. E. (2004). Speech, language, and reading skills after early cochlear implantation. *Archives of Otolaryngology—Head & Neck Surgery, 130,* 634–638. (p. 417)

Gregory, R. L. (November, 1968). Visual illusions. *Scientific American, 219*(5), 66–76. (p. 251)

Gregory, R. L. (1978). *Eye and brain: The psychology of seeing* (3rd ed.). New York: McGraw-Hill. (p. 255)

Gregory, R. L., & Gombrich, E. H. (Eds.). (1973). *Illusion in nature and art.* New York: Charles Scribner's Sons. (p. 260)

Greif, E. B., & Ulman, K. J. (1982). The psychological impact of menarche on early adolescent females: A review of the literature. *Child Development, 53,* 1413–1430. (p. 166)

Greist, J. H., Jefferson, J. W., & Marks, I. M. (1986). *Anxiety and its treatment: Help is available.* Washington, DC: American Psychiatric Press. (p. 650)

Grewal, D., & Salovey, P. (2005). Feeling smart: The science of emotional intelligence. *American Scientist, 93,* 330–339. (p. 436)

Grèzes, J., & Decety, J. (2001). Function anatomy of execution, mental simulation, observation, and verb generation of actions: A meta-analysis. *Human Brain Mapping, 12,* 1–19. (p. 421)

Griffiths, M. (2001). Sex on the Internet: Observations and implications for Internet sex addiction. *Journal of Sex Research, 38,* 333–342. (p. 298)

Grill-Spector, K., & Kanwisher, N. (2005). Visual recognition: As soon as you know it is there, you know what it is. *Psychological Science, 16,* 152–160. (p. 396)

Grilo, C. M., & Pogue-Geile, M. F. (1991). The nature of environmental influences on weight and obesity: A behavior genetic analysis. *Psychological Bulletin, 110,* 520–537. (p. 586)

Grobstein, C. (1979, June). External human fertilization. *Scientific American,* pp. 57–67. (p. 140)

Groothuis, T. G. G., & Carere, C. (2005). Avian personalities: Characterization and epigenesis. *Neuroscience and Biobehavioral Reviews, 29,* 137–150. (p. 615)

Gross, A. E., & Crofton, C. (1977). What is good is beautiful. *Sociometry, 40,* 85–90. (p. 762)

Grossberg, S. (1995). The attentive brain. *American Scientist, 83,* 438–449. (p. 260)

Grossman, M., & Wood, W. (1993). Sex differences in intensity of emotional experience: A social role interpretation. *Journal of Personality and Social Psychology, 65,* 1010–1022. (p. 526)

Gruder, C. L. (1977). Choice of comparison persons in evaluating oneself. In J. M. Suls & R. L. Miller (Eds.), *Social comparison processes.* New York: Hemisphere. (p. 543)

Grudnik, J., & Kranzler, J. H. (2001). Meta-analysis of the relationship between intelligence and inspection time. *Intelligence, 13,* 523–537. (p. 441)

Grunebaum, M. F., Ellis, S. P., Li, S., O(quendo, M. A., Mann, J. J. (2004). Antidepressants and suicide risk in the United States, 1985–1999. *Journal of Clinical Psychiatry, 65,* 1456–1462. (p. 715)

Guerin, B. (1986). Mere presence effects in humans: A review. *Journal of Personality and Social Psychology, 22,* 38–77. (p. 738)

Guerin, B. (2003). Language use as social strategy: A review and an analytic framework for the social sciences. *Review of General Psychology, 7,* 251–298. (p. 410)

Guilbault, R. L., Bryant, F. B., Brockway, J. H., & Posavac, E. J. (2004). A meta-analysis of research on hindsight bias. *Basic and Applied Social Psychology, 26,* 103–117. (p. 21)

Guisinger, S. (2004). Adapted to flee famine: Adding an evolutionary perspective on anorexia nervosa. *Psychological Review, 110,* 745–761. (p. 479)

Gundersen, E. (2001, August 1). MTV is a many splintered thing. *USA Today,* pp. D1, D2. (p. 344)

Güntürkün, O. (2003). Adult persistence of head-turning asymmetry. *Nature, 421,* 711. (p. 88)

Gura, T. (2004). New data on appetite-suppressing peptide challenges critics. *Science, 306,* 1453–1454. (p. 476)

Gustafson, D., Lissner, L., Bengtsson, C., Björkelund, C., & Skoog, I. (2004). A 24-year follow-up of body mass index and cerebral atrophy. *Neurology, 63,* 1876–1881. (p. 583)

Gustafson, D., Rothenberg, E., Blennow, K., Steen, B., & Skoog, I. (2003). An 18-year follow-up of overweight and risk of Alzheimer disease. *Archives of Internal Medicine, 163,* 1524–1528. (pp. 181, 583)

Gustavson, C. R., Garcia, J., Hankins, W. G., & Rusiniak, K. W. (1974). Coyote predation control by aversive conditioning. *Science, 184,* 581–583. (p. 322)

Gustavson, C. R., Kelly, D. J., & Sweeney, M. (1976). Prey-lithium aversions I: Coyotes and wolves. *Behavioral Biology, 17,* 61–72. (p. 322)

Guttmacher Institute. (1994). *Sex and America's teenagers.* New York: Alan Guttmacher Institute. (p. 486)

Guttmacher Institute. (2000). *Fulfilling the promise: Public policy and U.S. family planning clinics.* New York: Alan Guttmacher Institute. (p. 173)

H., Sally (1979, August). Videotape recording number T-3, Fortunoff Video Archive of Holocaust Testimonies. New Haven, CT: Yale University Library. (p. 605)

Haber, R. N. (1970, May). How we remember what we see. *Scientific American,* pp. 104–112. (p. 350)

Haddock, G., & Zanna, M. P. (1994). Preferring "housewives" to "feminists." *Psychology of Women Quarterly, 18,* 25–52. (p. 745)

Haidt, J. (2000). The positive emotion of elevation. *Prevention and Treatment, 3,* article 3 (journals.apa.org/prevention/volume3). (p. 169)

Haidt, J. (2001). The emotional dog and its rational tail: A social intuitionist approach to moral judgment. *Psychological Review, 108,* 814–834. (p. 169)

Haidt, J. (2002). The moral emotions. In R. J. Davidson, K. Scherer, & H. H. Goldsmith (Eds.), *Handbook of Affective Sciences.* New York: Oxford University Press. (p. 169)

Haier, R. J., Jung, R. E., Yeo, R. A., Head, K., & Alkire, M. T. (2004). Structural brain variation and general intelligence. *NeuroImage, 23,* 425–433. (p. 440)

Haines, R. F. (1991). A breakdown in simultaneous information processing. In G. Obrecht & L. W. Stark (Eds.), *Presbyopia research.* New York: Plenum Press. (p. 238)

Hakuta, K., Bialystok, E., & Wiley, E. (2003). Critical evidence: A test of the critical-period hypothesis for second-language acquisition. *Psychological Science, 14,* 31–38. (p. 416)

Halberstadt, J. B., & Niedenthal, P. M. (2001). Effects of emotion concepts on perceptual memory for emotional expressions. *Journal of Personality and Social Psychology, 81,* 587–598. (p. 384)

Halberstadt, J. B., Niedenthal, P. M., & Kushner, J. (1995). Resolution of lexical ambiguity by emotional state. *Psychological Science, 6,* 278–281. (p. 260)

Haldeman, D. C. (1994). The practice and ethics of sexual orientation conversion therapy. *Journal of Consulting and Clinical Psychology, 62,* 221–227. (p. 488)

Haldeman, D. C. (2002). Gay rights, patient rights: The implications of sexual orientation conversion therapy. *Professional Psychology: Research and Practice, 33,* 260–264. (p. 488)

Hall, C. S. (1984). "A ubiquitous sex difference in dreams" revisited. *Journal of Personality and Social Psychology, 46,* 1109–1117. (p. 286)

Hall, C. S., Dornhoff, W., Blick, K. A., & Weesner, K. E. (1982). The dreams of college men and women in 1950 and 1980: A comparison of dream contents and sex differences. *Sleep, 5,* 188–194. (p. 286)

Hall, C. S., & Lindzey, G. (1978). *Theories of personality* (2nd ed.). New York: Wiley. (p. 607)

Hall, G. (1997). Context aversion, Pavlovian conditioning, and the psychological side effects of chemotherapy. *European Psychologist, 2,* 118–124. (p. 323)

Hall, G. S. (1904). *Adolescence: Its psychology and its relations to physiology, anthropology, sex, crime, religion and education* (Vol. I). New York: Appleton-Century-Crofts. (p. 165)

Hall, J. A. (1984). *Nonverbal sex differences: Communication accuracy and expressive style.* Baltimore: Johns Hopkins University Press. (p. 525)

Hall, J. A. (1987). On explaining gender differences: The case of nonverbal communication. In P. Shaver & C. Hendrick (Eds.), *Review of Personality and Social Psychology, 7,* 177–200. (pp. 127, 525)

Hall, J. A. Y., & Kimura, D. (1994). Dermatoglyphic assymetry and sexual orientation in men. *Behavioral Neuroscience, 108,* 1203–1206. (p. 491)

Hall, J. G. (2003). Twinning. *Lancet, 362,* 735–743. (p. 98)

Hall, S. S. (2004, May). The good egg. *Discover,* pp. 30–39. (p. 140)

Halpern, C. T., Joyner, K., Udry, J. R., & Suchindran, C. (2000). Smart teens don't have sex (or kiss much either). *Journal of Adolescent Health, 26,* 213–225. (p. 486)

Halpern, D. F. (1991). Cognitive sex differences: Why diversity is a critical research issue. Paper presented to the American Psychological Association convention. (p. 463)

Halpern, D. F. (2000). *Sex-related ability differences: Changing perspectives, changing minds.* Mahwah, NJ: Erlbaum. (pp. 462, 463)

Halpern, D. F. (2005, May 20). Response to Drs. Pinker and Spelke. www.edge.org. (p. 464)

Halpern, D. F., & Coren, S. (1988). Do right-handers live longer? *Nature, 333,* 213. (p. 88)

Halpern, D. F., & Coren, S. (1990). Laterality and longevity: Is left-handedness associated with a younger age at death? In S. Coren (Ed.), *Left-handedness: Behavioral implications and anomalies.* Amsterdam: North-Holland. (p. 89)

Halpern, D. F., & Coren, S. (1991). Lateral preference and life span. *New England Journal of Medicine, 324,* 998. (p. 89)

Halpern, D. F., & Coren, S. (1993). Left-handedness and life span: A reply to Harris. *Psychological Bulletin, 114,* 235–241. (p. 89)

Halpern, D. F., Gilbert, R., & Coren, S. (1996). PC or not-PC? Contemporary challenges to unpopular research. *Journal of Social Distress and the Homeless, 5,* 251–271. (p. 90)

Halsey, A. H., & Webb, J. (2000). *Twentieth-century British social trends.* Basingstoke: Macmillan. (pp. 579, 587)

Hamann, S., Herman, R. A., Nolan, C. L., & Wallen, K. (2004). Men and women differ in amygdala response to visual sexual stimuli. *Nature Neuroscience, 7,* 411–416. (p. 484)

Hamann, S., Monarch, E. S., & Goldstein, F. C. (2002). Impaired fear conditioning in Alzheimer's disease. *Neuropsychologica, 40,* 1187–1195. (p. 366)

Hamill, R., Wilson, T. D., & Nisbett, R. E. (1980). Insensitivity to sample bias: Generalizing from atypical cases. *Journal of Personality and Social Psychology, 39,* 578–589. (p. 402)

Hamilton, G. (2001, July 11). Family sues Coca-Cola over son's death. *National Post.* (p. 721)

Hamilton, R. H. (2000, November). Increased prevalence of absolute pitch in blind musicians (Abstract 739.13). Society for Neuroscience meeting, New Orleans. (p. 223)

Hammer, E. (2003). How lucky you are to be a psychology major. *Eye on Psi Chi,* 4–5. (p. A-9)

Hammersmith, S. K. (1982, August). *Sexual preference: An empirical study from the Alfred C. Kinsey Institute for Sex Research.* Paper presented at the meeting of the American Psychological Association, Washington, DC. (p. 488)

Hampson, R. (2000, April 10). In the end, people just need more room. *USA Today,* p. 19A. (p. 588)

Haney, C., & Logan, D. D. (1994). Broken promise: The Supreme Court's response to social science research on capital punishment. *Journal of Social Issues, 50,* 75–101. (p. 50)

Hankin, B. L., & Abramson, L. Y. (2001). Development of gender differences in depression: An elaborated cognitive vulnerability-transactional stress theory. *Psychological Bulletin, 127,* 773–796. (p. 666)

Hansen, C. H., & Hansen, R. D. (1988). Finding the face-in-the-crowd: An anger superiority effect. *Journal of Personality and Social Psychology, 54,* 917–924. (p. 524)

Harber, K. D. (1998), Feedback to minorities: Evidence of a positive bias. *Journal of Personality and Social Psychology, 74,* 622–628. (p. 744)

Hardin, C., & Banaji, M. R. (1993). The influence of language on thought. *Social Cognition, 11,* 277–308. (p. 419)

Hare, R. D. (1975). Psychophysiological studies of psychopathy. In D. C. Fowles (Ed.), *Clinical applications of psychophysiology.* New York: Columbia University Press. (p. 678)

Hariri, A. R., Mattay, V. S., Tessitore, A., Kolachana, B., Fera, F., Goldman, D., Egan, M. F., & Weinberger, D. R. (2002). Serotonin transporter genetic variation and the response of the human amygdala. *Science, 297,* 400–403. (p. 535)

Harkins, S. G., & Szymanski, K. (1989). Social loafing and group evaluation. *Journal of Personality and Social Psychology, 56,* 934–941. (p. 739)

Harlow, H. F., Harlow, M. K., & Suomi, S. J. (1971). From thought to therapy: Lessons from a primate laboratory. *American Scientist, 59,* 538–549. (p. 155)

Harlow, R. E., & Cantor, N. (1996). Still participating after all these years: A study of life task participation in later life. *Journal of Personality and Social Psychology, 71,* 1235–1249. (p. 190)

Harmon-Jones, E., Abramson, L. Y., Sigelman, J., Bohlig, A., Hogan, M. E., & Harmon-Jones, C. (2002). Proneness to hypomania/mania symptoms or depression symptoms and asymmetrical frontal cortical responses to an anger-evoking event. *Journal of Personality and Social Psychology, 82,* 610–618. (p. 518)

Harris, B. (1979). Whatever happened to Little Albert? *American Psychologist, 34,* 151–160. (p. 324)

Harris, J. A. (1999). Review and methodological considerations in research on testosterone and aggression. *Aggression and Violent Behavior, 4,* 273–291. (p. 750)

Harris, J. R. (1998). *The nurture assumption.* New York: Free Press. (pp. 101, 157)

Harris, J. R. (2000b). Socialization, personality development, and the child's environments: Comment on Vandell (2000). *Developmental Psychology, 36,* 711–723. (p. 118)

Harris, J. R. (2006). *No two are alike: Human nature and human individuality.* New York: Norton. (p. 100)

Harris, L. J. (1993). Do left-handers die sooner than right-handers? Commentary on Coren and Halpern's (1991) "Left-handedness: A marker for decreased survival fitness." *Psychological Bulletin, 114,* 203–234. (p. 90)

Harris, R. J. (1994). The impact of sexually explicit media. In J. Brant & D. Zillmann (Eds.), *Media effects: Advances in theory and research.* Hillsdale, NJ: Erlbaum. (p. 753)

Harrison, Y., & Horne, J. A. (2000). The impact of sleep deprivation on decision making: A review. *Journal of Experimental Psychology: Applied, 6,* 236–249. (p. 281)

Harriston, K. A. (1993, December 24). 1 shakes, 1 snoozes; both win $45 million. *Washington Post* release (in *Tacoma News Tribune,* pp. 630)

Hart, C. L., Taylor, M. D., Smith, G. D., Whalley, L. J., Starr, J. M., Hole, D. J., Wilson, V., & Deary, I. J. (2003). Childhood IQ, social class, deprivation, and their relationships with mortality and morbidity risk in later life: Prospective observational study linking the Scottish Mental Survey 1932 and the Midspan Studies. *Psychosomatic Medicine, 65,* 877–883. (p. 435)

Hart, D. (1988). The development of personal identity in adolescence: A philosophical dilemma approach. *Merrill-Palmer Quarterly, 34,* 105–114. (p. 171)

Harter, J. K. (2000, Winter/Spring). The linkage of employee perceptions to outcomes in a retail environment—cause and effect? *Gallup Research Journal,* pp. 25–38. (p. 506)

Harter, J. K., Schmidt, F. L., & Hayes, T. L. (2002). Business-unit-level relationship between employee satisfaction, employee engagement, and business outcomes: A meta-analysis. *Journal of Applied Psychology, 87,* 268–279. (p. 505)

Hartmann, E. (1981, April). The strangest sleep disorder. *Psychology Today,* pp. 14, 16, 18. (p. 284)

Hartmann, E. (1984). *The nightmare: The psychology and biology of terrifying dreams.* New York: Basic Books. (p. 285)

Harvey, F. (2002, February). Surrounded by sound. *Scientific American,* pp. 94–95. (p. 220)

Hassan, R., & Carr, J. (1989). Changing patterns of suicide in Australia. *Australian and New Zealand Journal of Psychiatry, 23,* 226–234. (p. 662)

Hatfield, E. (1988). Passionate and companionate love. In R. J. Sternberg & M. L. Barnes (Eds.), *The psychology of love.* New Haven: Yale University Press. (p. 762)

Hatfield, E., & Sprecher, S. (1986). *Mirror, mirror . . . The importance of looks in everyday life.* Albany: State University of New York Press. (p. 760)

Hathaway, S. R. (1960). *An MMPI Handbook* (Vol. 1, Foreword). Minneapolis: University of Minnesota Press. (Revised edition, 1972). (pp. 616–618)

Hauser, M. D., Chomsky, N., & Fitch, W. T. (2002). The faculty of language: What is it, who has it, and how did it evolve? *Science, 298,* 1569–1579. (p. 411)

Hawkes, N. (2002, September 10). Fat children may die before their parents (report on presentation to the British Association for the Advancement of Science). *Times of London,* p. 3. (p. 587)

Haxby, J. V. (2001, July 7). Quoted by B. Bower, Faces of perception. *Science News,* pp. 10–12. See also J. V. Haxby, M. I. Gobbini, M. L. Furey, A. Ishai, J. L. Schouten & P. Pietrini, Distributed and overlapping representations of faces and objects in ventral temporal cortex. *Science, 293,* 2425–2430. (p. 209)

Hayne, H. (2004). Infant memory development: Implications for childhood amnesia. *Developmental Review, 24,* 33–73. (p. 146)

Hazan, C., & Shaver, P. R. (1994). Attachment as an organizational framework for research on close relationships. *Psychological Inquiry, 5,* 1–22. (p. 160)

Hazelrigg, M. D., Cooper, H. M., & Borduin, C. M. (1987). Evaluating the effectiveness of family therapies: An integrative review and analysis. *Psychological Bulletin, 101,* 428–442. (p. 698)

Head Start. (2005). Head Start program fact sheet. www.acf.hhs.gov/programs/hsb/research/2005.htm (p. 458)

Healey, J. (2004). *Overweight and obesity.* Thirroul, NSW, Australia: Spinney Press. (p. 587)

Heaps, C. M., & Nash, M. (2001). Comparing recollective experience in true and false autobiographical memories. *Journal of Experimental Psychology: Learning, Memory, and Cognition, 27,* 920–930. (p. 389)

Heath, A. C., & Madden, P. A. F. (1995). Genetic influences on smoking behavior. In J. R. Turner & L. R. Cardon (Eds.), *Behavior genetic approaches in behavioral medicine.* New York: Plenum Press, 45–66. (p. 578)

Hebb, D. O. (1980). *Essay on mind.* Hillsdale, NJ: Erlbaum. 9–16. (p. 513)

Hebert, R. (2001, September). Doing a number on memory. *APS Observer,* pp. 1, 7–11. (p. 360)

Hebl, M. R., & Mannix, L. M. (2003). The weight of obesity in evaluating others: A mere proximity effect. *Personality and Social Psychology Bulletin, 29,* 28–38. (p. 584)

Hedges, L. V., & Nowell, A. (1995). Sex differences in mental test scores, variability, and numbers of high-scoring individuals. *Science, 269,* 41–45. (pp. 462, 463)

Heider, F. (1958). *The psychology of interpersonal relations.* New York: Wiley. (p. 724)

Heiman, J. R. (1975, April). The physiology of erotica: Women's sexual arousal. *Psychology Today,* 90–94. (p. 484)

Heinrichs, R. W. (2005). The primacy of cognition in schizophrenia. *American Psychologist, 60,* 229–242. (p. 670)

Heins, M. (2004, December 14). Quoted by B. Kloza, Violent Christmas games. *ScienCentralNews* (www.sciencecentral.com). (p. 756)

Heishman, S. J., Kozlowski, L. T., & Henningfield, J. E. (1997). Nicotine addiction: Implications for public health policy. *Journal of Social Issues, 53,* 13–33. (p. 577)

Hejmadi, A., Davidson, R. J., & Rozin, P. (2000). Exploring Hindu Indian emotion expressions: Evidence for accurate recognition by Americans and Indians. *Psychological Science, 11,* 183–187. (p. 527)

Helgeson, V. S., Cohen, S., & Fritz, H. L. (1998). Social ties and cancer. In P. M. Cinciripini & others (Eds.), *Psychological and behavioral factors in cancer risk.* New York: Oxford University Press. (p. 566)

Heller, W. (1990, May/June). Of one mind: Second thoughts about the brain's dual nature. *The Sciences,* pp. 38–44. (p. 88)

Helmreich, W. B. (1992). *Against all odds: Holocaust survivors and the successful lives they made in America.* New York: Simon & Schuster. (pp. 159, 605)

Helmreich, W. B. (1994). Personal correspondence. Department of Sociology, City University of New York. (p. 605)

Helms, J. E., Jernigan, M., & Mascher, J. (2005). The meaning of race in psychology and how to change it: A methodological perspective. *American Psychologist, 60,* 27–36. (p. 460)

Helmuth, L. (2001). Boosting brain activity from the outside in. *Science, 292,* 1284–1286. (pp. 716–717)

Helweg-Larsen, M. (1999). (The lack of) optimistic biases in response to the 1994 Northridge earthquake: The role of personal experience. *Basic and Applied Social Psychology, 21,* 119–129. (p. 627)

Hembree, R. (1988). Correlates, causes, effects, and treatment of test anxiety. *Review of Educational Research, 58,* 47–77. (p. 517)

Hemenover, S. H. (2003). The good, the bad, and the healthy: Impacts of emotional disclosure of trauma on resilient self-concept and psychological distress. *Personality and Social Psychology Bulletin, 29,* 1236–1244. (p. 567)

Henderlong, J., & Lepper, M. R. (2002). The effects of praise on children's intrinsic motivation: A review and synthesis. *Psychological Bulletin, 128,* 774–795. (p. 335)

Henkel, L. A., Franklin, N., & Johnson, M. K. (2000, March). Cross-modal source monitoring confusions between perceived and imagined events. *Journal of Experimental Psychology: Learning, Memory, & Cognition, 26,* 321–335. (p. 384)

Henley, N. M. (1989). Molehill or mountain? What we know and don't know about sex bias in language. In M. Crawford & M. Gentry (Eds.), *Gender and thought: Psychological perspectives.* New York: Springer-Verlag. (p. 419)

Henninger, P. (1992). Conditional handedness: Handedness changes in multiple personality disordered subject reflect shift in hemispheric dominance. *Consciousness and Cognition, 1,* 265–287. (p. 657)

Henry, J. D., MacLeod, M. S., Phillips, L. H., & Crawford, J. R. (2004). A meta-analytic review of prospective memory and aging. *Psychology and Aging, 19,* 27–39. (p. 182)

Hepper, P. G., Shahidullah, S., & White, R. (1990). Origins of fetal handedness. *Nature, 347,* 431. (p. 88)

Hepper, P. G., Wells, D. L., & Lynch, C. (2004). Prenatal thumb sucking is related to postnatal handedness. *Neuropsychologia, 43,* 313–315. (p. 88)

Herbert, B. (2001, July 23). Economics 202 at Big Tobacco U. *New York Times* (www.nytimes.com). (p. 575)

Herbert, J. D., Lilienfeld, S. O., Lohr, J. M., Montgomery, R. W., O'Donohue, W. T., Rosen, G. M., & Tolin, D. F. (2000). Science and pseudoscience in the development of eye movement desensitization and re-

processing: Implications for clinical psychology. *Clinical Psychology Review, 20,* 945–971. (p. 706)

Herek, G. M., & Capitanio, J. P. (1996). "Some of my best friends": Intergroup contact, concealable stigma, and heterosexuals' attitudes toward gay men and lesbians. *Personality and Social Psychology Bulletin, 22,* 412–424. (p. 492)

HERI. (2005, April 13). Spirituality in higher education: A national study of college students' search for meaning and purpose. Press release from Higher Education Research Institute, UCLA. (p. 171)

Herman, C. P., & Polivy, J. (1980). Restrained eating. In A. J. Stunkard (Ed.), *Obesity.* Philadelphia: Saunders. (p. 590)

Herman, C. P., & Polivy, J. (2003). Realistic and unrealistic self-change efforts. *American Psychologist, 58,* 823. (p. 588)

Herman-Giddens, M. E., Wang, L., & Koch, G. (2001). Secondary sexual characteristics in boys: Estimates from the National Health and Nutrition Examination Survey III, 1988–1994. *Archives of Pediatrics and Adolescent Medicine, 155,* 1022–1028. (p. 165)

Herrmann, D. (1982). Know thy memory: The use of questionnaires to assess and study memory. *Psychological Bulletin, 92,* 434–452. (p. 391)

Herrnstein, R. J., & Loveland, D. H. (1964). Complex visual concept in the pigeon. *Science, 146,* 549–551. (p. 328)

Hershenson, M. (1989). *The moon illusion.* Hillsdale, NJ: Erlbaum. (p. 251)

Hertenstein, M. J. (2002). Touch: Its communicative functions in infancy. *Human Development, 45,* 70–94. (p. 155)

Herz, R. S. (2001). Ah sweet skunk! Why we like or dislike what we smell. *Cerebrum, 3*(4), 31–47. (pp. 232, 233)

Herz, R. S., Schankler, C., & Beland, S. (2004). Olfaction, emotion and associative learning: Effects on motivated behavior. *Motivation and Emotion, 28*(4), 363–383. (p. 233)

Hess, E. H. (1956, July). Space perception in the chick. *Scientific American,* pp. 71–80. (p. 256)

Hettema, J. M., Neale, M. C., & Kendler, K. S. (2001). A review and meta-analysis of the genetic epidemiology of anxiety disorders. *American Journal of Psychiatry, 158,* 1568–1578. (p. 655)

Hewlett, B. S. (1991). *Intimate fathers: The nature and context of Aka Pygmy.* Ann Arbor: University of Michigan Press. (p. 157)

Hibbeln, J. R. (1998). Fish consumption and major depression. *Lancet, 351,* 1213. (p. 664)

Hickok, G., Bellugi, U., & Klima, E. S. (2001, June). Sign language in the brain. *Scientific American,* pp. 58–65. (p. 88)

Higgins, E. T., & Bargh, J. A. (1987). Social cognition and social perception. *Annual Review of Psychology, 38,* 369–425. (p. 632)

Hilgard, E. R. (1986). *Divided consciousness: Multiple controls in human thought and action.* New York: Wiley. (p. 294)

Hilgard, E. R. (1992). Dissociation and theories of hypnosis. In E. Fromm & M. R. Nash (Eds.), *Contemporary hypnosis research.* New York: Guilford. (p. 294)

Hill, C. E., & Nakayama, E. Y. (2000). Client-centered therapy: Where has it been and where is it going? A comment on Hathaway. *Journal of Clinical Psychology, 56,* 961–875. (p. 689)

Hill, H., & Johnston, A. (2001). Categorizing sex and identity from the biological motion of faces. *Current Biology, 11,* 880–885. (p. 526)

Hines, M. (2004). *Brain gender.* New York: Oxford University Press. (p. 130)

Hines, M., & Green, R. (1991). Human hormonal and neural correlates of sex-typed behaviors. *Review of Psychiatry, 10,* 536–555. (p. 130)

Hingson, R. W., Heeren, T., Zakocs, R. C., Kopstein, A., & Wechsler, H. (2002). Magnitude of alcohol-related mortality and morbidity among U.S. college students ages 18–24. *Journal of Studies on Alcohol, 63,* 136–144. (p. 300)

Hintzman, D. L. (1978). *The psychology of learning and memory.* San Francisco: Freeman. (p. 359)

Hinz, L. D., & Williamson, D. A. (1987). Bulimia and depression: A review of the affective variant hypothesis. *Psychological Bulletin, 102,* 150–158. (p. 478)

Hirsch, J. (2003). Obesity: Matter over mind? *Cerebrum, 5*(1), 7–18. (p. 585)

Hirst, W., Neisser, U., & Spelke, E. (1978, June). Divided attention. *Human Nature*, pp. 54–61. (p. 294)

Hirt, E. R., Zillmann, D., Erickson, G. A., & Kennedy, C. (1992). Costs and benefits of allegiance: Changes in fans' self-ascribed competencies after team victory versus defeat. *Journal of Personality and Social Psychology, 63*, 724–738. (p. 667)

HMHL. (2001, February). How schizophrenia develops: New evidence and new ideas. *Harvard Mental Health Letter*, pp. 1–4. (p. 672)

HMHL. (2002, January). Disaster and trauma. *Harvard Mental Health Letter*, pp. 1–5. (p. 554)

HMHL. (2002, August). Smoking and depression. *Harvard Mental Health Letter*, pp. 6–7. (p. 664)

Hobfoll, S. E., Johnson, R. J., Ennis, E., & Jackson, A. P. (2003). Resource loss, resource gain, and emotional outcomes among inner city women. *Journal of Personality, 84*, 632–643. (p. 539)

Hobson, J. A. (1989). *Sleep.* New York: Scientific American Library. (p. 275)

Hobson, J. A. (1995, September). Quoted by C. H. Colt, The power of dreams. *Life*, pp. 36–49. (p. 287)

Hobson, J. A. (2003). *Dreaming: An introduction to the science of sleep.* New York: Oxford. (p. 288)

Hobson, J. A. (2004). *13 dreams Freud never had: The new mind science.* New York: Pi Press. (p. 288)

Hodgkinson, V. A., & Weitzman, M. S. (1992). *Giving and volunteering in the United States.* Washington, DC: Independent Sector. (p. 767)

Hoebel, B. G., & Teitelbaum, P. (1966). Effects of forcefeeding and starvation on food intake and body weight in a rat with ventromedial hypothalamic lesions. *Journal of Comparative and Physiological Psychology, 61*, 189–193. (p. 475)

Hoffman, C., & Hurst, N. (1990). Gender stereotypes: Perception or rationalization? *Journal of Personality and Social Psychology, 58*, 197–208. (p. 746)

Hoffman, D. D. (1998). *Visual intelligence: How we create what we see.* New York: Norton. (pp. 210, 241)

Hoffman, H. G. (2004, August). Virtual-reality therapy. *Scientific American*, pp. 58–65. (pp. 229, 692)

Hofstede, G. (1980). *Culture's consequences: International differences in work-related values.* Beverly Hills: Sage. (p. 122)

Hogan, J. (1995, November). Get smart, take a test. *Scientific American*, pp. 12, 14. (p. 447)

Hogan, R. (1998). Reinventing personality. *Journal of Social and Clinical Psychology, 17*, 1–10. (p. 621)

Hoge, C. W., Castro, C. A., Messer, S. C., McGurk, D., Cotting, D. I., & Koffman, R. L. (2004). Combat duty in Iraq and Afghanistan, mental health problems, and barriers to care. *New England Journal of Medicine, 35*, 13–22. (p. 652)

Hogg, M. A. (1996). Intragroup processes, group structure and social identity. In W. P. Robinson (Ed.), *Social groups and identities: Developing the legacy of Henri Tajfel.* Oxford: Butterworth Heinemann. (p. 746)

Hohmann, G. W. (1966). Some effects of spinal cord lesions on experienced emotional feelings. *Psychophysiology, 3*, 143–156. (p. 519)

Hokanson, J. E., & Edelman, R. (1966). Effects of three social responses on vascular processes. *Journal of Personality and Social Psychology, 3*, 442–447. (p. 536)

Holahan, C. K., & Sears, R. R. (1995). *The gifted group in later maturity.* Stanford, CA: Stanford University Press. (p. 453)

Holden, C. (1980a). Identical twins reared apart. *Science, 207*, 1323–1325. (p. 99)

Holden, C. (1980b, November). Twins reunited. *Science, 80*, 55–59. (p. 99)

Holden, C. (1986b). Researchers grapple with problems of updating classic psychological test. *Science, 233*, 1249–1251. (p. 611)

Holden, C. (1993). Wake-up call for sleep research. *Science, 259*, 305. (p. 280)

Holden, C. (2003). Deconstructing schizophrenia. *Science, 299*, 333–335. (p. 647)

Holden, G. W., & Miller, P. C. (1999). Enduring and different: A meta-analysis of the similarity in parents' child rearing. *Psychological Bulletin, 125*, 223–254. (p. 162)

Holliday, R. E., & Albon, A. J. (2004). Minimizing misinformation effects in young children with cognitive interview mnemonics. *Applied Cognitive Psychology, 18*, 263–281. (p. 386)

Hollis, K. L. (1997). Contemporary research on Pavlovian conditioning: A "new" functional analysis. *American Psychologist, 52*, 956–965. (p. 318)

Hollon, S. D., & 10 others (2005). Prevention of relapse following cognitive therapy vs. medications in moderate to severe depression. *Archives of General Psychiatry, 62*, 417–422. (p. 704).

Hollon, S. D., Thase, M. E., & Markowitz, J. C. (2002). Treatment and prevention of depression. *Psychological Science in the Public Interest, 3*, 39–77. (p. 714)

Holloway, K. (2000, June 22). Among the deaf, sign language faces a challenge. *New York Times* (www.nytimes.com). (p. 221)

Holmes, D. (1990). The evidence for repression: An examination of sixty years of research. In J. Singer (Ed.), *Repression and dissociation: Implications for personality theory, psychopathology, and health.* Chicago: University of Chicago Press. (p. 605)

Holmes, D. S. (1994). Is there evidence for repression? No. (Unexpurgated version on an article which was rewritten by the *Harvard Mental Health Letter* and published as "Is there evidence for repression? Doubtful," June, 1994, pp. 4–6.) (p. 605)

Holstege, G., Georgiadis, J. R., Paans, A. M. J., Meiners, L. C., van der Graaf, F. H. C. E., & Reinders, A. A. T. S. (2003). Brain activation during male ejaculation. *Journal of Neuroscience, 23*, 9185–9193. (p. 482)

Holstege, G., Reinders, A. A. T., Paans, A. M. J., Meiners, L. C., Pruim, J., & Georgiadis, J. R. (2003). Brain activation during female sexual orgasm. Program No. 727.7. Washington, DC: Society for Neuroscience. (p. 482)

Holt, L. (2002, August). Reported in "Sounds of speech," p. 26, and in personal correspondence, July 18, 2002. (p. 411)

Holzman, P. S., & Matthysse, S. (1990). The genetics of schizophrenia: A review. *Psychological Science, 1*, 279–286. (p. 202)

Home Office. (2003). Prevalence of drug use: Key findings from the 2002/2003 British Crime Survey. London: Research, Development and Statistics Directorate, Home Office. (p. 301)

Hooper, J., & Teresi, D. (1986). *The three-pound universe.* New York: Macmillan. (p. 74)

Hooykaas, R. (1972). *Religion and the rise of modern science.* Grand Rapids, MI: Eerdmans. (p. 23)

Hopkins, W. D., Russell, J., Freeman, H., Buehler, N., Reynolds, E., & Schapiro, S. J. (2005). The distribution and development of handedness for manual gestures in captive chimpanzees (*Pan troglodytes*). *Psychological Science, 16*, 487–493. (p. 88)

Horn, J. L. (1982). The aging of human abilities. In J. Wolman (Ed.), *Handbook of developmental psychology.* Englewood Cliffs, NJ: Prentice-Hall. (p. 184)

Horowitz, T. S., Cade, B. E., Wolfe, J. M., & Czeisler, C. A. (2003). Searching night and day: A dissociation of effects of circadian phase and time awake on visual selective attention and vigilance. *Psychological Science, 14*, 549–557. (p. 281)

Horwood, L. J., & Fergusson, D. M. (1998). Breastfeeding and later cognitive and academic outcomes. *Pediatrics, 101*(1). (p. 31)

Hötting, K, & Röder, B. (2004). Hearing cheats touch, but less in congenitally blind than in sighted individuals. *Psychological Science, 15*, 60–64. (p. 242)

House, J. S., Landis, K. R., & Umberson, D. (1988). Social relationships and health. *Science, 241*, 540–545. (p. 566)

House, R. J., & Singh, J. V. (1987). Organizational behavior: Some new directions for I/O psychology. *Annual Review of Psychology, 38,* 669–718. (p. 509)

Houts, A. C., Berman, J. S., & Abramson, H. (1994). Effectiveness of psychological and pharmacological treatments for nocturnal enuresis. *Journal of Consulting and Clinical Psychology, 62,* 737–745. (p. 691)

Howe, M. L. (1997). Children's memory for traumatic experiences. *Learning and Individual Differences, 9,* 153–174. (p. 386)

Howe, M. L. (2003). Memories from the cradle. *Current Directions in Psychological Science, 12,* 62–65. (p. 146)

Hoyer, G., & Lund, E. (1993). Suicide among women related to number of children in marriage. *Archives of General Psychiatry, 50,* 134–137. (p. 662)

Hróbjartsson, A., & Gøtzsche, P. C. (2001). Is the placebo powerless? An analysis of clinical trials comparing placebo with no treatment. *New England Journal of Medicine, 344,* 1594–602. (p. 560)

Hu, F. B., Li, T. Y., Colditz, G. A., Willett, W. C., & Manson, J. E. (2003). Television watching and other sedentary behaviors in relation to risk of obesity and type 2 diabetes mellitus in women. *Journal of the American Medical Association, 289,* 1785–1791. (p. 587)

Huart, J., Corneille, O., & Becquart, E. (2005). Face-based categorization, context-based categorization, and distortions in the recollection of gender ambiguous faces. *Journal of Experimental Social Psychology, 41,* 598–608. (p. 397)

Hubbard, E. M., Arman, A. C., Ramachandran, V. S., & Boynton, G. M. (2005). Individual differences among grapheme-color synesthetes: Brain-behavior correlations. *Neuron, 45,* 975–985. (p. 231)

Hubel, D. H. (1979, September). The brain. *Scientific American,* pp. 45–53. (p. 202)

Hubel, D. H., & Wiesel, T. N. (1979, September). Brian mechanisms of vision. *Scientific American,* pp. 150–162. (p. 209)

Hublin, C., Kaprio, J., Partinen, M., Heikkila, K., & Koskenvuo, M. (1997). Prevalence and genetics of sleepwalking—A population-based twin study. *Neurology, 48,* 177–181. (p. 285)

Hublin, C., Kaprio, J., Partinen, M., & Koskenvuo, M. (1998). Sleeptalking in twins: Epidemiology and psychiatric comorbidity. *Behavior Genetics, 28,* 289–298. (p. 285)

Hucker, S. J., & Bain, J. (1990). Androgenic hormones and sexual assault. In W. Marshall, R. Law, & H. Barbaree (Eds.), *The handbook on sexual assault.* New York: Plenum. (p. 483)

Hudson, W. (1960). Pictorial depth perception in sub-cultural groups in Africa. *Journal of Social Psychology, 52,* 183–208. (p. 249)

Huffcutt, A. I., Conway, J. M., Roth, P. L., & Stone, N. J. (2001). Identification and meta-analytic assessment of psychological constructs measured in employment interviews. *Journal of Applied Psychology, 86,* 897–913. (p. 503)

Hugenberg, K., & Bodenhausen, G. V. (2003). Facing prejudice: Implicit prejudice and the perception of facial threat. *Psychological Science, 14,* 640–643. (p. 744)

Hughes, H. C. (1999). *Sensory exotica: A world beyond human experience.* Cambridge, MA: MIT Press. (p. 199)

Hugick, L. (1989, July). Women play the leading role in keeping modern families close. *Gallup Report,* No. 286, pp. 27–34. (p. 128)

Huizink, A. C., Mulder, E. J. H., & Buitelaar, J. K. (2004). Prenatal stress and risk for psychopathology: Specific effects or indication of general susceptibility? *Psychological Bulletin, 130,* 115–142. (p. 142)

Hull, J. G., & Bond, C. F., Jr. (1986). Social and behavioral consequences of alcohol consumption and expectancy: A meta-analysis. *Psychological Bulletin, 99,* 347–360. (p. 300)

Hull, J. G., Young, R. D., & Jouriles, E. (1986). Applications of the self-awareness model of alcohol consumption: Predicting patterns of use and abuse. *Journal of Personality and Social Psychology, 51,* 790–796. (p. 299)

Hull, J. M. (1990). *Touching the rock: An experience of blindness.* New York: Vintage Books. (pp. 371, 760)

Hulme, C., & Tordoff, V. (1989). Working memory development: The effects of speech rate, word length, and acoustic similarity on serial recall. *Journal of Experimental Child Psychology, 47,* 72–87. (p. 363)

Hummer, R. A., Rogers, R. G., Nam, C. B., & Ellison, C. G. (1999). Religious involvement and U.S. adult mortality. *Demography, 36,* 273–285. (p. 573)

Humphreys, L. G., & Davey, T. C. (1988). Continuity in intellectual growth from 12 months to 9 years. *Intelligence, 12,* 183–197. (p. 451)

Hunsley, J., & Bailey, J. M. (1999). The clinical utility of the Rorschach: Unfulfilled promises and an uncertain future. *Psychological Assessment, 11*(3), 266–277. (p. 603)

Hunsley, J., & Di Giulio, G. (2002). Dodo bird, phoenix, or urban legend? The question of psychotherapy equivalence. *Scientific Review of Mental Health Practice, 1,* 11–22. (p. 704)

Hunt, C., Slade, T., & Andrews, G. (2004). Generalized anxiety disorder and major depressive disorder comorbidity in the National Survey of Mental Health and Well-Being. *Depression and Anxiety, 20,* 23–31. (p. 650)

Hunt, E. (1983). On the nature of intelligence. *Science, 219,* 141–146. (p. 441)

Hunt, J. M. (1982). Toward equalizing the developmental opportunities of infants and preschool children. *Journal of Social Issues, 38*(4), 163–191. (p. 457)

Hunt, M. (1974). *Sexual behavior in the 1970s.* Chicago: Playboy Press. (p. 484)

Hunt, M. (1982). *The universe within.* New York: Simon and Schuster. (p. 407)

Hunt, M. (1990). *The compassionate beast: What science is discovering about the humane side of humankind.* New York: William Morrow. (p. 14)

Hunt, M. (1993). *The story of psychology.* New York: Doubleday. (pp. 3, 5, 6, 171, 453)

Hunter, J. E. (1997). Needed: A ban on the significance test. *Psychological Science, 8,* 3–7. (p. 43)

Hunter, S., & Sundel, M. (Eds.). (1989). *Midlife myths: Issues, findings, and practice implications.* Newbury Park, CA: Sage. (p. 186)

Huss, M. (1996). Secrets to standing out from the pile: Getting into graduate school. *Psi Chi Newsletter,* 6–7. (p. A-9)

Hussein, S. (2002, July 17 and August 28). Speeches to the Iraqi people as reported by various media. (p. 758)

Huston, A. C., & Aronson, S. R. (2005). Mothers' time with infant and time in employment as predictors of mother-child relationships and children's early development. *Child Development, 76,* 467–482. (p. 160)

Huston, A. C., Donnerstein, E., Fairchild, H., Feshbach, N. D., Katz, P. A., & Murray, J. P. (1992). *Big world, small screen: The role of television in American society.* Lincoln, NE: University of Nebraska Press. (p. 344)

Hyde, J. S. (1983, November). *Bem's gender schema theory.* Paper presented at GLCA Women's Studies Conference, Rochester, IN. (p. 382)

Hyde, J. S., Fennema, E., & Lamon, S. J. (1990). Gender differences in mathematics performance: A meta-analysis. *Psychological Bulletin, 107,* 139–155. (p. 462)

Hygge, S., Evans, G. W., & Bullinger, M. (2002). A prospective study of some effects of aircraft noise on cognitive performance in schoolchildren. *Psychological Science, 13,* 469–474. (p. 218)

Hyler, S., Gabbard, G. O., & Schneider, I. (1991). Homicidal maniacs and narcissistic parasites: Stigmatization of mentally ill persons in the movies. *Hospital and Community Psychiatry, 42,* 1044–1048. (p. 647)

Hyman, R. (1981). Cold reading: How to convince strangers that you know all about them. In K. Frazier (Ed.), *Paranormal borderlands of science.* Buffalo, NY: Prometheus. (p. 616)

Hyman, S. (1999). Quoted by M. Enserink, Can the placebo be the cure? *Science, 284,* 238–240. (p. 714)

Iacono, W. G., & Lykken, D. T. (1997). The validity of the lie detector: Two surveys of scientific opinion. *Journal of Applied Psychology, 82,* 426–433. (p. 520)

Ickes, W., Snyder, M., & Garcia, S. (1997). Personality influences on the choice of situations. In R. Hogan, J. Johnson, & S. Briggs (Eds.). *Handbook of Personality Psychology.* San Diego, CA: Academic Press. (p. 624)

ICR. (2001, October 12). Women fear flying; pill sales rise (survey by ICR of Media, PA). Associated Press (in *Grand Rapids Press*), p. A3. (p. 534)

Idson, L. C., & Mischel, W. (2001). The personality of familiar and significant people: The lay perceiver as a social-cognitive theorist. *Journal of Personality and Social Psychology, 80,* 585–596. (p. 725)

Ikonomidou, C., Bittigau, P., Ishimaru, M. J., Wozniak, D. F., Koch, C., Genz, K., Price, M. T., Stefovska, V., Hoerster, F., Tenkova, T., Dikranian, K., & Olney, J. W. (2000). Ethanol-induced apoptotic neurodegeneration and fetal alcohol syndrome. *Science, 287,* 1056–1060. (p. 142)

Illes, J. (2004, Fall). A fish story? Brain maps, lie detection, and personhood. *Cerebrum,* pp. 73–80. (p. 521)

Immen, W. (1995, July 16). Canadians ignore 'safe sex' warning. *Toronto Globe and Mail* (in *Grand Rapids Press*, p. A22). (p. 485)

Independent Sector. (2002). *Faith and philanthropy: The connection between charitable giving behavior and giving to religion.* Washington, DC: Independent Sector. (p. 767)

Ingham, A. G., Levinger, G., Graves, J., & Peckham, V. (1974). The Ringelmann effect: Studies of group size and group performance. *Journal of Experimental Social Psychology, 10,* 371–384. (p. 738)

Inglehart, R. (1990). *Culture shift in advanced industrial society.* Princeton, NJ: Princeton University Press. (pp. 189, 496, 499, 626)

Inglehart, R., Basañez, M., Diez-Medrano, J., Halman, L., & Luijkx, R. (Eds.). (2004). *Human beliefs and values: A sourcebook based on the 1999–2001 values surveys.* Mexico City: Siglo XXI. (p. 541)

Ingram, V. (2003). Alzheimer's disease. *American Scientist, 91,* 312–321. (p. 181)

Inman, M. L., & Baron, R. S. (1996). Influence of prototypes on perceptions of prejudice. *Journal of Personality and Social Psychology, 70,* 727–739. (p. 397)

Insana, R. (2005, February 21). Coach says honey gets better results than vinegar (interview with Larry Brown). *USA Today,* p. 4B. (p. 507)

Inzlicht, M., & Ben-Zeev, T. (2000). A threatening intellectual environment: Why females are susceptible to experiencing problem-solving deficits in the presence of males. *Psychological Science, 11,* 365–371. (p. 465)

IPU. (2005). Women in national parliaments: Situation as of 28 February 2005. Inter-Parliamentary Union (www.ipu.org). (p. 128)

Ireland, T. O., Smith, C. A., & Thornberry, T. P. (2002). Developmental issues in the impact of child maltreatment on later delinquency and drug use. *Criminology, 40,* 359–399. (p. 159)

Ironson, G., Solomon, G. F., Balbin, E. G., O'Cleirigh, C., George, A., Kumar, M., Larson, D., & Woods, T. E. (2002). The Ironson-Woods spiritual/religiousness index is associated with long survival, health behaviors, less distress, and low cortisol in people with HIV/AIDS. *Annals of Behavioral Medicine, 24,* 34–48. (p. 574)

Irwin, M., Mascovich, A., Gillin, J. C., Willoughby, R., Pike, J., & Smith, T. L. (1994). Partial sleep deprivation reduces natural killer cell activity in humans. *Psychosomatic Medicine, 56,* 493–498. (p. 281)

Isensee, B., Wittchen, H-U., Stein, M. B., Hofler, M., & Lieb, R. (2003). Smoking increases the risk of panic: Findings from a prospective community study. *Archives of General Psychiatry, 60,* 692–700. (p. 650)

Isham, W. P., & Kamin, L. J. (1993). Blackness, deafness, IQ, and *g. Intelligence, 17,* 37–46. (p. 420)

ISR. (2003, Spring). Drug use: Religion plays role for White as well as Black teens (data from 70,000 seniors surveyed 1997–2001, *ISR Monitoring the Future Study*). Ann Arbor, MI: Institute for Social Research Newsletter, University of Michigan. (p. 307)

Ito, T. A., Miller, N., & Pollock, V. E. (1996). Alcohol and aggression: A meta-analysis on the moderating effects of inhibitory cues, triggering events, and self-focused attention. *Psychological Bulletin, 120,* 60–82. (p. 750)

Iversen, L. L. (2000). *The science of marijuana.* New York: Oxford. (p. 303)

Iverson, J. M., & Goldin-Meadow, S. (1998). Why people gesture when they speak. *Nature, 396,* 228. (p. 426)

Iyengar, S. S., & Lepper, M. R. (2000). When choice is demotivating: Can one desire too much of a good thing? *Journal of Personality and Social Psychology, 79,* 995–1006. (p. 626)

Iyer, P. (1993, April). The soul of an intercontinental wanderer. *Harper's, 286,* 13–17. (p. 119)

Izard, C., Fine, S., Schultz, D., Mostow, A., Ackerman, B., & Younstrom, E. (2001). Emotion knowledge as a predictor of social behavior and academic competence in children at risk. *Psychological Science, 12,* 18–23. (p. 436)

Izard, C. E. (1977). *Human emotions.* New York: Plenum Press. (p. 528, 532)

Izzetoglu, K., Yurtsever, G., Bozkurt, A., Yazici, B., Bunce, S., Pourrezaei, K., Onaral, B. (2003). NIR spectroscopy measurements of cognitive load elicited by GKT and target categorization. System Sciences, Proceedings of the 36th Hawaii International Conference on System Sciences, 129–134. (p. 521)

Jablensky, A. (1999). Schizophrenia: Epidemiology. *Current Opinion in Psychiatry, 12,* 19–28. (p. 673)

Jackson, J. M., & Williams, K. D. (1988). Social loafing: A review and theoretical analysis. Unpublished manuscript, Fordham University. (p. 739)

Jackson, J. S., Brown, K. T., Brown, T. N., & Marks, B. (2001). Contemporary immigration policy orientations among dominant-group members in western Europe. *Journal of Social Issues, 57,* 431–456. (p. 743)

Jackson, L. A., & Gerard, D. A. (1996). Diurnal types, the "Big Five" personality factors and other personal characteristics. *Journal of Social Behavior and Personality, 11,* 273–283. (p. 619)

Jackson, S. W. (1992). The listening healer in the history of psychological healing. *American Journal Psychiatry, 149,* 1623–1632. (p. 707)

Jacobe, D. (2003, December 2). Why the gender gap in investor optimism? Gallup Poll Tuesday Briefing (www.gallup.com). (p. 111)

Jacobi, C., Hayward, C., deZwaan, M., Kraemer, H. C., & Agras, W. S. (2004). Coming to terms with risk factors for eating disorders: Application of risk terminology and suggestions for a general taxonomy. *Psychological Bulletin, 130,* 19–65. (p. 479)

Jacobs, B. L. (1987). How hallucinogenic drugs work. *American Scientist, 75,* 386–392. (p. 302)

Jacobs, B. L. (1994). Serotonin, motor activity, and depression-related disorders. *American Scientist, 82,* 456–463. (pp. 569, 664)

Jacobs, B. L. (2004). Depression: The brain finally gets into the act. *Current Directions in Psychological Science, 13,* 103–106. (pp. 713–714)

Jacobs, B., van Praag, H., & Gage, F. H. (2000). Adult brain neurogenesis and psychiatry: A novel theory of depression. *Molecular Psychiatry, 5,* 262–269. (p. 665)

Jacobs, W. J., & Nadel, L. (1985). Stress-induced recovery of fears and phobias. *Psychological Bulletin, 92,* 512–531. (p. 654)

Jacoby, L. L., Bishara, A. J., Hessels, S., & Toth, J. P. (2005). Aging, subjective experience, and cognitive control: Dramatic false remembering by older adults. *Journal of Experimental Psychology: General, 154,* 131–148. (p. 385)

Jaffe, E. (2004, October). Peace in the Middle East may be impossible: Lee D. Ross on naive realism and conflict resolution. *APS Observer,* pp. 9–11. (p. 261)

Jakicic, J. M., Winters, C., Lang, W., & Wing R. R. (1999). Effects of intermittent exercise and use of home exercise equipment on adherence, weight loss, and fitness in overweight women. *Journal of the American Medical Association, 282,* 1554–1560. (p. 590)

James, K. (1986). Priming and social categorizational factors: Impact on awareness of emergency situations. *Personality and Social Psychology Bulletin, 12,* 462–467. (p. 372)

James, W. (1890). *The principles of psychology* (Vol. 2). New York: Holt. (pp. 63, 224, 375)

James, W. (1902; reprinted 1958). *Varieties of religious experience.* New York: Mentor Books. (p. 537)

Jameson, D. (1985). Opponent-colors theory in light of physiological findings. In D. Ottoson & S. Zeki (Eds.), *Central and peripheral mechanisms of color vision.* New York: Macmillan. (p. 214)

Jamison, K. R. (1993). *Touched with fire: Manic-depressive illness and the artistic temperament.* New York: Free Press. (p. 660)

Jamison, K. R. (1995, February). Manic-depressive illness and creativity. *Scientific American,* pp. 62-67. (p. 660)

Janicak, P. G. (2005). Treating psychiatric disorders using transcranial magnetic stimulation. *Psychiatric Annals, 35,* 102-108. (p. 716)

Janis, I. L. (1982). *Groupthink: Psychological studies of policy decisions and fiascoes.* Boston: Houghton Mifflin. (p. 740)

Janis, I. L. (1986). Problems of international crisis management in the nuclear age. *Journal of Social Issues, 42*(2), 201-220. (p. 401)

Janoff-Bulman, R., Timko, C., & Carli, L. L. (1985). Cognitive biases in blaming the victim. *Journal of Experimental Social Psychology, 21,* 161-177. (p. 748)

Javitt, D. C., & Coyle, J. T. (2004, January). Decoding schizophrenia. *Scientific American,* pp. 48-55. (p. 672)

Jeffery, R. W., Drewnowski, A., Epstein, L. H., Stunkard, A. J., Wilson, G. T., Wing, R. R., & Hill, D. R. (2000). Long-term maintenance of weight loss: Current status. *Health Psychology, 19,* No. 1 (Supplement), 5-16. (pp. 588, 590)

Jenkins, J. G., & Dallenbach, K. M. (1924). Obliviscence during sleep and waking. *American Journal of Psychology, 35,* 605-612. (pp. 379-380)

Jenkins, J. M., & Astington, J. W. (1996). Cognitive factors and family structure associated with theory of mind development in young children. *Developmental Psychology, 32,* 70-78. (p. 151)

Jensen, A. R. (1980). *Bias in mental testing.* New York: The Free Press. (p. 449)

Jensen, A. R. (1983, August). The nature of the black-white difference on various psychometric tests: Spearman's hypothesis. Paper presented at the meeting of the American Psychological Association, Anaheim, CA. (p. 464)

Jensen, A. R. (1989). New findings on the intellectually gifted. *New Horizons, 30,* 73-80. (p. 441)

Jensen, A. R. (1998). *The g factor: The science of mental ability.* Westport, CT: Praeger/Greenwood. (p. 464)

Jensen, J. P., & Bergin, A. E. (1988). Mental health values of professional therapists: A national interdisciplinary survey. *Professional Psychology: Research and Practice, 19,* 290-297. (p. 708)

Jepson, C., Krantz, D. H., & Nisbett, R. E. (1983). Inductive reasoning: Competence or skill. *The Behavioral and Brain Sciences, 3,* 494-501. (p. 51)

Jervis, R. (1985, April 2). Quoted in D. Goleman, Political forces come under new scrutiny of psychology. *The New York Times,* pp. C1, C4. (p. 407)

Jing, H. (1999, Summer). China faces myriad psychological challenges of modernization. *Psychology International* (APA newsletter), p. 7. (p. 8)

Johansson, P., Hall, L., Sikström, S., & Olsson, A. (2005). Failure to detect mismatches between intention and outcome in a simple decision task. *Science, 310,* 116-119. (p. 239)

John, O. P., & Srivastava, S. (1999). The Big Five trait taxonomy: History, measurement, and theoretical perspectives. In L. A. Pervin & O. P. John (Eds.), *Handbook of personality: Theory and research.* New York: Guilford. (p. 618)

Johnson, C. B., Stockdale, M. S., & Saal, F. E. (1991). Persistence of men's misperceptions of friendly cues across a variety of interpersonal encounters. *Psychology of Women Quarterly, 15,* 463-475. (p. 110)

Johnson, D. F. (1997, Winter). Margaret Floy Washburn. *Psychology of Women Newsletter,* pp. 17, 22. (p. 6)

Johnson, D. L., Wiebe, J. S., Gold, S. M., Andreasen, N. C., Hichwa, R. D., Watkins, G. L., & Ponto, L. L. B. (1999). Cerebral blood flow and personality: A Positron Emission Tomography study. *American Journal of Psychiatry, 156,* 252-257. (p. 615)

Johnson, D. W., & Johnson, R. T. (1989). *Cooperation and competition: Theory and research.* Edina, MN: Interaction Book. (p. 768)

Johnson, D. W., & Johnson, R. T. (1994). Constructive conflict in the schools. *Journal of Social Issues, 50*(1), 117-137. (p. 768)

Johnson, G. (2002, July 14). To err is human. *New York Times* (www.nytimes.com). (p. 397)

Johnson, G. (2003, November 5). Suspect admits 48 Seattle-area killings. Associated Press release. (p. 521)

Johnson, J. G., Cohen, P., Kotler, L., Kasen, S., & Brook, J. S. (2002). Psychiatric disorders associated with risk for the development of eating disorders during adolescence and early adulthood. *Journal of Consulting and Clinical Psychology, 70,* 1119-1128. (p. 478)

Johnson, J. S., & Newport, E. L. (1991). Critical period effects on universal properties of language: The status of subjacency in the acquisition of a second language. *Cognition, 39,* 215-258. (p. 416)

Johnson, L. C. (2001, July 10). The declining terrorist threat. *New York Times* (www.nytimes.com). (p. 404)

Johnson, M. E., & Hauck, C. (1999). Beliefs and opinions about hypnosis held by the general public: A systematic evaluation. *American Journal of Clinical Hypnosis, 42,* 10-20. (p. 292)

Johnson, M. H. (1992). Imprinting and the development of face recognition: From chick to man. *Current Directions in Psychological Science, 1,* 52-55. (p. 156)

Johnson, M. H., & Morton, J. (1991). *Biology and cognitive development: The case of face recognition.* Oxford: Blackwell Publishing. (p. 143)

Johnson, W., McGue, M., & Krueger, R. F. (2005). Personality stability in late adulthood: A behavioral genetic analysis. *Journal of Personality, 73,* 523-552. (p. 194)

Johnston, L. D., O'Malley, P. M., Bachman, J. G., & Schulenberg, J. E. (2005). *Monitoring the future: National results on adolescent drug use: Overview of key findings, 2004.* Bethesda, MD: National Institute on Drug Abuse. (pp. 301, 307)

Johnston, L. D., O'Malley, P. M., Bachman, J. G., & Schulenberg, J. E. (2005). *Teen drug use down but progress halts among youngest teens.* University of Michigan News and Information Services: Ann Arbor, MI. www.monitoringthefuture.org. (pp. 304-305)

Johnstone, E. C., Ebmeier, K. P., Miller, P., Owens, D. G. C., & Lawrie, S. M. (2005). Predicting schizophrenia: Findings from the Edinburgh High-Risk Study. *British Journal of Psychiatry, 186,* 18-25. (p. 676)

Joiner, T. E., Jr. (1999). The clustering and contagion of suicide. *Current Directions in Psychological Science, 8,* 89-92. (p. 732)

Joiner, T. E., Pettit, J. W., Walker, R. L., Voelz, Z. R., Cruz, J., Rudd, M. D., & Lester, D. (2002). Perceived burdensomeness and suicidality: Two studies on the suicide notes of those attempting and those completing suicide. *Journal of Social and Clinical Psychology, 21,* 531-545. (p. 663)

Jones, E. E., Cumming, J. D., & Horowitz, M. J. (1988). Another look at the nonspecific hypothesis of therapeutic effectiveness. *Journal of Consulting and Clinical Psychology, 56,* 48-55. (p. 707)

Jones, J. M. (2003, February 12). Fear of terrorism increases amidst latest warning. *Gallup News Service* (www.gallup.com/releases/pr030212.asp). (pp. 617, 649)

Jones, J. M., & Moore, D. W. (2003, June 17). Generational differences in support for a woman president. The Gallup Organization (www.gallup.com). (p. 743)

Jones, J. T., Pelham, B. W., Carvallo, M., & Mirenberg, M. C. (2004). How do I love thee? Let me count the Js: Implicit egotism and interpersonal attraction. *Journal of Personality and Social Psychology, 87,* 665-683. (p. 758)

Jones, L. (2000, December). Skeptics New Year quiz. *Skeptical Briefs,* p. 11. (p. 597)

Jones, M. C. (1924). A laboratory study of fear: The case of Peter. *Journal of Genetic Psychology, 31,* 308-315. (p. 691)

Jones, M. V., Paull, G. C., & Erskine, J. (2002). The impact of a team's aggressive reputation on the decisions of association football referees. *Journal of Sports Sciences, 20,* 991-1000. (p. 261)

Jones, S. S., Collins, K., & Hong, H-W. (1991). An audience effect on smile production in 10-month-old infants. *Psychological Science, 2*, 45-49. (p. 529)

Jones, W. H., Carpenter, B. N., & Quintana, D. (1985). Personality and interpersonal predictors of loneliness in two cultures. *Journal of Personality and Social Psychology, 48*, 1503-1511. (p. 46)

Jonides, J., Lacey, S. C., & Nee, D. E. (2005). Processes of working memory in mind and brain. *Psychological Science, 14*, 2-5. (p. 353)

Jordan, C. H., Spencer, S. J., Zanna, M. P., Hoshino-Browne, E., & Correll, J. (2003). Secure and defensive high self-esteem. *Journal of Personality and Social Psychology, 85*, 969-978. (pp. 635-636)

Jorgenson, D. O., & Papciak, A. S. (1981). The effects of communication, resource feedback, and identifiability on behavior in a simulated commons. *Journal of Experimental Social Psychology, 17*, 373-385. (p. 769)

Joseph, J. (2001). Separated twins and the genetics of personality differences: A critique. *American Journal of Psychology, 114*, 1-30. (p. 100)

Judge, T. A., Thoresen, C. J., Bono, J. E., & Patton, G. K. (2001). The job satisfaction/job performance relationship: A qualitative and quantitative review. *Psychological Bulletin, 127*, 376-407. (p. 505)

Jung-Beeman, M., Bowden, E. M., Haberman, J., Frymiare, J. L., Arambel-Liu, S., Greenblatt, R., Reber, P. J., & Kounios, J. (2004). Neural activity when people solve verbal problems with insight. *PloS Biology* 2(4): e111. (p. 398)

Kagan, J. (1976). Emergent themes in human development. *American Scientist, 64*, 186-196. (p. 158)

Kagan, J. (1984). *The nature of the child.* New York: Basic Books. (p. 155)

Kagan, J. (1990). Interview with M. V. Ellis & E. S. Robbins, In Celebration of nature: A dialogue with Jerome Kagan. *Journal of Counseling and Development, 68*, 623-627. (p. 102)

Kagan, J. (1995). On attachment. *Harvard Review of Psychiatry, 3*, 104-106. (p. 156)

Kagan, J. (1998). *Three seductive ideas.* Cambridge, MA: Harvard University Press. (pp. 91, 194)

Kagan, J., Arcus, D., Snidman, N., Feng, W. Y., Hendler, J., & Greene, S. (1994). Reactivity in infants: A cross-national comparison. *Developmental Psychology, 30*, 342-345. (p. 102)

Kagan, J., Lapidus, D. R., & Moore, M. (December, 1978). Infant antecedents of cognitive functioning: A longitudinal study. *Child Development, 49*(4), 1005-1023. (p. 194)

Kagan, J., & Snidman, N. (2004). *The long shadow of temperament.* Cambridge, MA: Belknap Press. (p. 102)

Kagan, J., Snidman, N., & Arcus, D. M. (1992). Initial reactions to unfamiliarity. *Current Directions in Psychological Science, 1*, 171-174. (p. 102)

Kahneman, D. (1985, June). Quoted by K. McKean, Decisions, decisions. *Discover*, pp. 22-31. (p. 701)

Kahneman, D. (1999). Assessments of objective happiness: A bottom-up approach. In D. Kahneman, E. Diener, & N. Schwartz (Eds.), *Understanding well-being: Scientific perspectives on enjoyment and suffering.* New York: Russell Sage Foundation. (p. 228)

Kahneman, D. (2005, January 13). What were they thinking? Q&A with Daniel Kahneman. *Gallup Management Journal* (gmj.gallup.com). (p. 401)

Kahneman, D. (2005, February 10). Are you happy now? *Gallup Management Journal* interview (www.gmj.gallup.com). (p. 401)

Kahneman, D., Fredrickson, B. L., Schreiber, C. A., & Redelmeier, D. A. (1993). When more pain is preferred to less: Adding a better end. *Psychological Science, 4*, 401-405. (p. 228)

Kahneman, D., Krueger, A. B., Schkade, D. A., Schwarz, N., & Stone, A. A. (2004). A survey method for characterizing daily life experience: The day reconstruction method. *Science, 306*, 1776-1780. (pp. 281, 538)

Kahneman, D., & Tversky, A. (1972). Subjective probability: A judgment of representativeness. *Cognitive Psychology, 3*, 430-454. (p. 34)

Kahneman, D., & Tversky, A. (1979). Intuitive prediction: Biases and corrective procedures. *Management Science, 12*, 313-327. (pp. 403, 539)

Kail, R. (1991). Developmental change in speed of processing during childhood and adolescence. *Psychological Bulletin, 109*, 490-501. (p. 179)

Kaiser (2001). Inside-out: A report on the experiences of lesbians, gays and bisexuals in America and the public's views on issues and policies related to sexual orientation. The Henry J. Kaiser Foundation (www.kff.org). (p. 492)

Kaiser Family Foundation. (2003, October 28). New study finds children age zero to six spend as much time with TV, computers and video games as playing outside. www.kff.org/entmedia/entmedia102803nr.cfm (p. 31)

Kalff, A. C., Kroes, M., Vles, J. S. H., Hendriksen, J. G. M., Feron, F. J. M., Steyaert, J., van Zeban, T. M. C. B., Jolles, J., & van Os, J. (2001). Neighbourhood level and individual level SES effects on child problem behaviour: a multilevel analysis. *Journal of Epidemiology and Community Health, 55*, 246-250. (p. 118)

Kalin, N. H. (1993, May). The neurobiology of fear. *Scientific American,* pp. 94-101. (p. 518)

Kamarck, T., & Jennings, J. R. (1991). Biobehavioral factors in sudden cardiac death. *Psychological Bulletin, 109*, 42-75. (p. 556)

Kamena, M. (1998). Repressed/false childhood sexual abuse memories: A survey of therapists. Paper presented to the Sexual Abuse memories Symposium at the American Psychological Association convention. (p. 387)

Kaminski, J., Cali, J., & Fischer, J. (2004). Word learning in a domestic dog: Evidence for "fast mapping." *Science, 304*, 1682-1683. (p. 425)

Kanaya, T., Scullin, M. H., & Ceci, S. J. (2003). The Flynn effect and U.S. policies: The impact of rising IQ scores on American society via mental retardation diagnoses. *American Psychologist, 58*, 778-790. (p. 453)

Kanazawa, S. (2004). General intelligence as a domain-specific adaptation. *Psychological Review, 111*, 512-523. (p. 433)

Kandel, D. B., & Raveis, V. H. (1989). Cessation of illicit drug use in young adulthood. *Archives of General Psychiatry, 46*, 109-116. (p. 307)

Kandel, E. R., & Schwartz, J. H. (1982). Molecular biology of learning: Modulation of transmitter release. *Science, 218*, 433-443. (p. 365)

Kann, L., Warren, W., Collins, J. L., Ross, J., Collins, B., Kolbe, L. J. (1993). Results from the national school-based 1991 Youth Risk Behavior Survey and progress toward achieving related health objectives for the nation. U.S. Department of Health and Human Services, *Public Health Reports, 108* (Supplement 1), 47-55. (p. 307)

Kapitza, S. (1991, August). Antiscience trends in the U.S.S.R. *Scientific American,* pp. 32-38. (p. 268)

Kaplan, A. (2004). Exploring the gene-environment nexus in anorexia, bulimia. *Psychiatric Times, 21* (www.psychiatrictimes.com/p040801b.html). (p. 479)

Kaplan, H. I., & Saddock, B. J. (Eds.). (1989). *Comprehensive textbook of psychiatry, V.* Baltimore, MD: Williams and Wilkins. (p. 712)

Kaprio, J., Koskenvuo, M., & Rita, H. (1987). Mortality after bereavement: A prospective study of 95,647 widowed persons. *American Journal of Public Health, 77*, 283-287. (p. 554)

Karacan, I., Aslan, C., & Hirshkowitz, M. (1983). Erectile mechanisms in man. *Science, 220*, 1080-1082. (p. 278)

Karacan, I., Goodenough, D. R., Shapiro, A., & Starker, S. (1966). Erection cycle during sleep in relation to dream anxiety. *Archives of General Psychiatry, 15*, 183-189. (p. 278)

Karau, S. J., & Williams, K. D. (1993). Social loafing: A meta-analytic review and theoretical integration. *Journal of Personality and Social Psychology, 65*, 681-706. (p. 739)

Kark, J. D., Shemi, G., Friedlander, Y., Martin, O., Manor, O., & Blondheim, S. H. (1996). Does religious observance promote health? Mortality in secular vs. religious kibbutzim in Israel. *American Journal of Public Health, 86*, 341-346. (p. 572)

Karni, A., Meyer, G., Rey-Hipolito, C., Jezzard, P., Adams, M. M., Turner, R., & Ungerleider, L. G. (1998). The acquisition of skilled motor performance: Fast and slow experience-driven changes in primary motor cortex. *Proceedings of the National Academy of Sciences, 95,* 861–868. (p. 116)

Karni, A., & Sagi, D. (1994). Dependence on REM sleep for overnight improvement of perceptual skills. *Science, 265,* 679–682. (p. 286)

Karno, M., Golding, J. M., Sorenson, S. B., & Burnam, A. (1988). The epidemiology of obsessive-compulsive disorder in five US communities. *Archives of General Psychiatry, 45,* 1094–1099. (p. 651)

Karon, P. B., & Widener, A. (1998). Repressed memories: The real story. *Professional Psychology: Research and Practice, 29,* 482–487. (p. 605)

Karon, P. B., & Widener, A. J. (1997). Repressed memories and World War II: Lest we forget. *Professional Psychology: Research and Practice, 28,* 338–340. (p. 605)

Kashima, Y., Siegal, M., Tanaka, K., & Kashima, E. S. (1992). Do people believe behaviours are consistent with attitudes? Towards a cultural psychology of attribution processes. *British Journal of Social Psychology, 31,* 111–124. (p. 122)

Kassel, J. D., Stroud, L. R., & Paronis, C. A. (2003). Smoking, stress, and negative affect: Correlation, causation, and context across stages of smoking. *Psychological Bulletin, 129,* 270–304. (p. 578)

Kasser, T. (2000). Two version of the American dream: Which goals and values make for a high quality of life? In E. Diener (Ed.), *Advances in quality of life theory and research.* Dordrecth, Netherlands: Kluwer. (p. 541)

Kasser, T. (2002). *The high price of materialism.* Cambridge, MA: MIT Press. (p. 541)

Kaufman, J. C., & Baer, J. (2002). I bask in dreams of suicide: Mental illness, poetry, and women. *Review of General Psychology, 6,* 271–286. (p. 660)

Kaufman, J., & Zigler, E. (1987). Do abused children become abusive parents? *American Journal of Orthopsychiatry, 57,* 186–192. (p. 159)

Kaufman, L., & Kaufman, J. H. (2000). Explaining the moon illusion. *Proceedings of the National Academy of Sciences, 97,* 500–505. (p. 251)

Kavšek, M. (2004). Predicting later IQ from infant visual habituation and dishabituation: A meta-analysis. *Journal of Applied Developmental Psychology, 25,* 369–393. (p. 450)

Kazdin, A. E., & Benjet, C. (2003). Spanking children: Evidence and issues. *Current Directions in Psychological Science, 12,* 99–103. (p. 333)

Keenan, J. P., Nelson, A., O'Connor, M., & Pascual-Leone, A. (2001). Self-recognition and the right hemisphere. *Nature, 409,* 305. (p. 86)

Keesey, R. E., & Corbett, S. W. (1983). Metabolic defense of the body weight set-point. In A. J. Stunkard & E. Stellar (Eds.), *Eating and its disorders.* New York: Raven Press. (p. 476)

Kellehear, A. (1996). *Experiences near death: Beyond medicine and religion.* New York: Oxford University Press. (p. 310)

Keller, H. (2003). "Before the Soul Dawn," *The World I Live In,* New York Review Books. (p. 196)

Keller, M. B., McCullough, J. P., Klein, D. N., Arnow, B., Dunner, D. L., Gelenberg, A. J., Markowitz, J. C., Nemeroff, C. B., Russell, J. M., Thase, M. E., Trivedi, M. H., & Zajecka J. (2000), A comparison of nefazodone, the cognitive behavioral-analysis system of psychotherapy, and their combination for the treatment of chronic depression. *New England Journal of Medicine, 342,* 1462–1470. (p. 714)

Kellerman, J., Lewis, J., & Laird, J. D. (1989). Looking and loving: The effects of mutual gaze on feelings of romantic love. *Journal of Research in Personality, 23,* 145–161. (p. 524)

Kellermann, A. L. (1997). Comment: Gunsmoke—changing public attitudes toward smoking and firearms. *American Journal of Public Health, 87,* 910–913. (p. 749)

Kellermann, A. L., Rivara, F. P., Rushforth, N. B., Banton, H. G., Feay, D. T., Francisco, J. T., Locci, A. B., Prodzinski, J., Hackman, B. B., & Somes, G. (1993). Gun ownership as a risk factor for homicide in the home. *New England Journal of Medicine, 329,* 1084–1091. (p. 749)

Kellermann, A. L., Somes, G. Rivara, F. P., Lee, R. K., & Banton, J. G. (1998). Injuries and deaths due to firearms in the home. *Journal of Trauma, 45,* 263–267. (p. 749)

Kelley, J., & De Graaf, N. D. (1997). National context, parental socialization, and religious belief: Results from 15 nations, *American Sociological Review, 62,* 639–659. (p. 101)

Kelling, S. T., & Halpern, B. P. (1983). Taste flashes: Reaction times, intensity, and quality. *Science, 219,* 412–414. (p. 230)

Kellner, C. H., & 15 others (2005). Relief of expressed suicidal intent by ECT: A consortium for research in ECT study. *American Journal of Psychiatry, 162,* 977–982. (p. 716)

Kelly, A. E. (2000). Helping construct desirable identities: A self-presentational view of psychotherapy. *Psychological Bulletin, 126,* 475–494. (p. 695)

Kelly, I. W. (1997). Modern astrology: A critique. *Psychological Reports, 81,* 1035–1066. (p. 616)

Kelly, I. W. (1998). Why astrology doesn't work. *Psychological Reports, 82,* 527–546. (p. 616)

Kelly, T. A. (1990). The role of values in psychotherapy: A critical review of process and outcome effects. *Clinical Psychology Review, 10,* 171–186. (p. 708)

Kempe, R. S., & Kempe, C. C. (1978). *Child abuse.* Cambridge, MA: Harvard University Press. (p. 158)

Kempermann, G., & Gage, F. H. (1999, May). New nerve cells for the adult brain. *Scientific American,* pp. 48–53. (pp. 83, 569)

Kempermann, G., Kuhn, H. G., & Gage, F. H. (May, 1998). *Journal of Neuroscience, 18(9),* 3206–3212. (p. 180)

Kendall-Tackett, K. A., Williams, L. M., & Finkelhor, D. (1993). Impact of sexual abuse on children: A review and synthesis of recent empirical studies. *Psychological Bulletin, 113,* 164–180. (pp. 159, 388)

Kendler, K. S. (1996). Parenting: A genetic-epidemiologic perspective. *The American Journal of Psychiatry, 153,* 11–20. (p. 162)

Kendler, K. S. (1997). Social support: A genetic-epidemiologic analysis. *American Journal of Psychiatry, 154,* 1398–1404. (p. 624)

Kendler, K. S. (1998, January). Major depression and the environment: A psychiatric genetic perspective. *Pharmacopsychiatry, 31(1),* 5–9. (p. 661)

Kendler, K. S., Jacobson, K. C., Myers, J., & Prescott, C. A. (2002a). Sex differences in genetic and environmental risk factors for irrational fears and phobias. *Psychological Medicine, 32,* 209–217. (p. 655)

Kendler, K. S., Karkowski, L. M., & Prescott, C. A. (1999). Fears and phobias: Reliability and heritability. *Psychological Medicine, 29,* 539–553. (p. 655)

Kendler, K. S., Myers, J., & Prescott, C. A. (2002b). The etiology of phobias: An evaluation of the stress-diathesis model. *Archives of General Psychiatry, 59,* 242–248. (p. 655)

Kendler, K. S., Neale, M. C., Kessler, R. C., Heath, A. C., & Eaves, L. J. (1992). Generalized anxiety disorder in women: A population-based twin study. *Archives of General Psychiatry, 49,* 267–272. (p. 655)

Kendler, K. S., Neale, M. C., Thornton, L. M., Aggen, S. H., Gilman, S. E., & Kessler, R. C. (2002). Cannabis use in the last year in a U.S. national sample of twin and sibling pairs. *Psychological Medicine, 32,* 551–554. (p. 305)

Kendler, K. S., Thornton, L. M., & Gardner, C. O. (2001). Genetic risk, number of previous depressive episodes, and stressful life events in predicting onset of major depression. *American Journal of Psychiatry, 158,* 582–586. (p. 661)

Kendler, K. S., Thornton, L. M., Gilman, S. E., & Kessler, R. C. (2000). Sexual orientation in a U.S. national sample of twin and nontwin sibling pairs. *American Journal of Psychiatry, 157,* 1843–1846. (p. 159)

Kennedy, S., & Over, R. (1990). Psychophysiological assessment of male sexual arousal following spinal cord injury. *Archives of Sexual Behavior, 19,* 15–27. (p. 64)

Kenrick, D. T., & Funder, D. C. (1988). Profiting from controversy: Lessons from the person-situation debate. *American Psychologist, 43,* 23–34. (p. 621)

Kenrick, D. T., & Gutierres, S. E. (1980). Contrast effects and judgments of physical attractiveness: When beauty becomes a social problem. *Journal of Personality and Social Psychology, 38,* 131–140. (p. 484)

Kenrick, D. T., Gutierres, S. E., & Goldberg, L. L. (1989). Influence of popular erotica on judgments of strangers and mates. *Journal of Experimental Social Psychology, 25,* 159-167. (p. 484)

Kenrick, D. T., & Trost, M. R. (1987). A biosocial theory of heterosexual relationships. In K. Kelly (Ed.), *Females, males, and sexuality.* Albany: State University of New York Press. (p. 111)

Keough, K. A., Zimbardo, P. G., & Boyd, J. N. (1999). Who's smoking, drinking, and using drugs? Time perspective as a predictor of substance use. *Basic and Applied Social Psychology, 2,* 149-164. (p. 598)

Kernis, M. H. (2003). Toward a conceptualization of optimal self-esteem. *Psychological Inquiry, 14,* 1-26. (pp. 635-636)

Kerr, N. L., & Bruun, S. E. (1983). Dispensability of member effort and group motivation losses: Free-rider effects. *Journal of Personality and Social Psychology, 44,* 78-94. (p. 739)

Kessler, M., & Albee, G. (1975). Primary prevention. *Annual Review of Psychology, 26,* 557-591. (p. 720)

Kessler, R. C. (2000). Posttraumatic stress disorder: The burden to the individual and to society. *Journal of Clinical Psychiatry, 61*(suppl. 5), 4-12. (pp. 652, 653)

Kessler, R. C. (2001). Epidemiology of women and depression. *Journal of Affective Disorders, 74,* 5-13. (p. 665)

Kessler, R. C., Foster, C., Joseph, J., Ostrow, D., Wortman, C., Phair, J., & Chmiel, J. (1991). Stressful life events and symptom onset in HIV infection. *American Journal of Psychiatry, 148,* 733-738. (p. 560)

Kessler, R. C., Soukup, J., Davis, R. B., Foster, D. F., Wilkey, S. A., Van Rompay, M. I., & Eisenberg, D. M. (2001). The use of complementary and alternative therapies to treat anxiety and depression in the United States. *American Journal of Psychiatry, 158,* 289-294. (p. 705)

Kestenbaum, R. (1992). Feeling happy versus feeling good: The processing of discrete and global categories of emotional expressions by children and adults. *Developmental Psychology, 28,* 1132-1142. (p. 524)

Keynes, M. (1980, December 20/27). Handel's illnesses. *The Lancet,* pp. 1354-1355. (p. 660)

Keys, A., Brozek, J., Henschel, A., Mickelsen, O., & Taylor, H. L. (1950). *The biology of human starvation.* Minneapolis: University of Minnesota Press. (p. 473)

Keys, L. (2001, May 27). Once isolated nation falls for TV. Associated Press (*Grand Rapids Press,* p. A14). (p. 344)

Khan, A., Warner, H. A., & Brown, W. A. (2000). Symptom reduction and suicide risk inpatients treated with placebo in antidepressant clinical trials. *Archives of General Psychiatry, 57,* 311-317. (p. 714)

Kho, K. H., van Vreeswijk, M. F., Simpson, S., & Zwinderman, A. H. (2003). A meta-analysis of electroconvulsive therapy efficacy in depression. *Journal of ECT, 19,* 139-147. (p. 716)

Kiecolt-Glaser, J. K., & Glaser, R. (1995). Psychoneuroimmunology and health consequences: Data and shared mechanisms. *Psychosomatic Medicine, 57,* 269-274. (p. 559)

Kiecolt-Glaser, J. K., & Newton, T. L. (2001). Marriage and health: His and hers. *Psychological Bulletin, 127,* 472-503. (p. 566)

Kiecolt-Glaser, J. K., Page, G. G., Marucha, P. T., MacCallum, R. C., & Glaser, R. (1998). Psychological influences on surgical recovery: Perspectives from psychoneuroimmunology. *American Psychologist, 53,* 1209-1218. (p. 558)

Kihlstrom, J. F. (1985). Hypnosis. *Annual Review of Psychology, 36,* 385-418. (p. 286)

Kihlstrom, J. F. (1990). Awareness, the psychological unconscious, and the self. Address to the American Psychological Association convention. (p. 381)

Kihlstrom, J. F. (1990). The psychological unconscious. In L. A. Pervin (Ed.), *Handbook of personality: Theory and research.* New York: Guilford Press. (p. 605)

Kihlstrom, J. F. (1994). The social construction of memory. Paper presented at the American Psychological Society convention. (p. 385)

Kihlstrom, J. F. (1997, November 11). Freud as giant pioneer on whose shoulders we should stand. Social Psychology listserv posting (spsp@stolaf.edu). (p. 607)

Kihlstrom, J. F. (2005). Dissociative disorders. *Annual Review of Clinical Psychology, 1,* 227-253. (p. 657)

Kihlstrom, J. F., & McConkey, K. M. (1990). William James and hypnosis: A centennial reflection. *Psychological Science, 1,* 174-177. (p. 295)

Killeen, P. R., & Nash, M. R. (2003). The four causes of hypnosis. *Internal Journal of Clinical and Experimental Hypnosis, 51,* 195-231. (p. 295)

Kim, B. S. K., Ng, G. F., & Ahn, A. J. (2005). Effects of client expectation for counseling success, client-counselor worldview match, and client adherence to Asian and European American cultural values on counseling process with Asian Americans. *Journal of Counseling Psychology, 52,* 67-76. (p. 710)

Kim, H., & Markus, H. R. (1999). Deviance or uniqueness, harmony or conformity? A cultural analysis. *Journal of Personality and Social Psychology, 77,* 785-800. (p. 123)

Kim, K. H. S., Relkin, N. R., Lee, K-M., & Hirsch, J. (1997). Distinct cortical areas associated with native and second languages. *Nature, 388,* 171-174. (p. 416)

Kim, Y., & Lee, S-H. (1994). The Confucian model of morality, justice, selfhood and society: Implications for modern society. In *The universal and particular natures of Confucianism.* The Academy of Korean Studies. (p. 123)

Kimata, H. (2001). Effect of humor on allergen-induced wheal reactions. *Journal of the American Medical Association, 285,* 737. (p. 565)

Kimball, M. M. (1989). A new perspective on women's math achievement. *Psychological Bulletin, 105,* 198-214. (p. 462)

Kimble, G. A. (1956). *Principles of general psychology.* New York: Ronald. (p. 321)

Kimble, G. A. (1981). *Biological and cognitive constraints on learning.* Washington, DC: American Psychological Association. (p. 321)

King, R. N., & Koehler, D. J. (2000). Illusory correlations in graphological interference. *Journal of Experimental Psychology: Applied, 6,* 336-348. (p. 616)

Kinnier, R. T., & Metha, A. T. (1989). Regrets and priorities at three stages of life. *Counseling and Values, 33,* 182-193. (p. 189)

Kinsey, A. C., Pomeroy, W., & Martin, C. (1948). *Sexual behavior in the human male.* Philadelphia: Saunders. (p. 481)

Kinsey, A. C., Pomeroy, W., Martin, C., & Gebhard, P. (1953). *Sexual behavior in the human female.* Philadelphia: Saunders. (p. 481)

Kirby, D. (2002). Effective approaches to reducing adolescent unprotected sex, pregnancy, and childbearing. *Journal of Sex Research, 39,* 51-57. (p. 486)

Kirkpatrick, L. (1999). Attachment and religious representations and behavior. In J. Cassidy & P. R. Shaver (Eds.), *Handbook of attachment.* New York: Guilford. (p. 156)

Kirsch, I. (1996). Hypnotic enhancement of cognitive-behavioral weight loss treatments: Another meta-reanalysis. *Journal of Consulting and Clinical Psychology, 64,* 517-519. (p. 293)

Kirsch, I., & Braffman, W. (2001). Imaginative suggestibility and hypnotizability. *Current Directions in Psychological Science, 10,* 57-61. (p. 291)

Kirsch, I., & Lynn, S. J. (1995). The altered state of hypnosis. *American Psychologist, 50,* 846-858. (p. 295)

Kirsch, I., & Lynn, S. J. (1998a). Dissociation theories of hypnosis. *Psychological Bulletin, 123,* 100-115. (p. 295)

Kirsch, I., & Lynn, S. J. (1998b). Social-cognitive alternatives to dissociation theories of hypnotic induction. *Review of General Psychology, 2,* 66-80. (p. 295)

Kirsch, I., & Lynn, S. J. (1999). Automaticity in clinical psychology. *American Psychologist, 54,* 504-515. (p. 714)

Kirsch, I., Montgomery, G., & Sapirstein, G. (1995). Hypnosis as an adjunct to cognitive-behavioral psychotherapy: A meta-analysis. *Journal of Consulting and Clinical Psychology, 63,* 214-220. (p. 293)

Kirsch, I., Moore, T. J., Scoboria, A., & Nicholls, S. S. (2002, July 15). New study finds little difference between effects of antidepressants and placebo. *Prevention and Treatment* (journals.apa.org/prevention). (p. 714)

Kirsch, I., & Sapirstein, G. (1998). Listening to Prozac but hearing placebo: A meta-analysis of antidepressant medication. *Prevention and Treatment, 1*, posted June 26 at (journals.apa.org/prevention/volume1). (pp. 37, 714)

Kisor, H. (1990). *What's that pig outdoors.* New York: Hill and Wang. (p. 222)

Kitayama, S., & Markus, H. R. (2000). The pursuit of happiness and the realization of sympathy: Cultural patterns of self, social relations, and well-being. In E. Diener & E. M. Suh (Eds.), *Subjective well-being across cultures.* Cambridge, MA: MIT Press. (p. 123)

Kite, M. E., & Whitley, B. E., Jr. (1996). Sex differences in attitudes toward homosexual persons, behaviors, and civil rights: A meta-analysis. *Personality and Social Psychology Bulletin, 22*, 336-353. (p. 492)

Kivimaki, M., Leino-Arjas, P., Luukkonen, R., Rihimaki, H., & Kirjonen, J. (2002). Work stress and risk of cardiovascular mortality: Prospective cohort study of industrial employees. *British Medical Journal, 325*, 857. (p. 564)

Klayman, J., & Ha, Y-W. (1987). Confirmation, disconfirmation, and information in hypothesis testing. *Psychological Review, 94*, 211-228. (p. 399)

Klein, D. N., & 16 others (2003). Therapeutic alliance in depression treatment: Controlling for prior change and patient characteristics. *Journal of Consulting and Clinical Psychology, 71*, 997-1006. (p. 708)

Klein, E., Kreinin, I., Chistyakov, A., Koren, D., Mecz, L., Marmur, S., Ben-Shachar, D., & Feinsod, M. (1999). Therapeutic efficacy of right prefrontal slow repetitive transcranial magnetic stimulation in major depression. *Archives of General Psychiatry, 56*, 315-320. (p. 716)

Klein, S. B., & Kihlstrom, J. F. (1998). On bridging the gap between social-personality psychology and neuropsychology. *Personality and Social Psychology Review, 2*, 228-242. (p. 152)

Kleinfeld, J. (1998). The myth that schools shortchange girls: Social science in the service of deception. Washington, DC: Women's Freedom Network. Available from ERIC, Document ED423210, and via www.uaf.edu/northern/schools/myth.html (p. 462)

Kleinke, C. L., Peterson, T. R., & Rutledge, T. R. (1998). Effects of self-generated facial expressions on mood. *Journal of Personality and Social Psychology, 74*, 272-279. (p. 530)

Kleinmuntz, B., & Szucko, J. J. (1984). A field study of the fallibility of polygraph lie detection. *Nature, 308*, 449-450. (p. 521)

Kleitman, N. (1960, November). Patterns of dreaming. *Scientific American,* pp. 82-88. (p. 276)

Klemm, W. R. (1990). Historical and introductory perspectives on brainstem-mediated behaviors. In W. R. Klemm & R. P. Vertes (Eds.), *Brainstem mechanisms of behavior.* New York: Wiley. (p. 71)

Kline, D., & Schieber, F. (1985). Vision and aging. In J. E. Birren & K. W. Schaie (Eds.), *Handbook of the psychology of aging.* New York: Van Nostrand Reinhold. (p. 178-179)

Kline, G. H., Stanley, S. M., Markman, J. H., Olmos-Gallo, P. A., St. Peters, M., Whitton, S. W., & Prado, L. M. (2004). Timing is everything: Pre-engagement cohabitation and increased risk for poor marital outcomes. *Journal of Family Psychology, 18*, 311-318. (p. 187)

Kline, N. S. (1974). *From sad to glad.* New York: Ballantine Books. (p. 668)

Klineberg, O. (1938). Emotional expression in Chinese literature. *Journal of Abnormal and Social Psychology, 33*, 517-520. (p. 528)

Klineberg, O. (1984). Public opinion and nuclear war. *American Psychologist, 39*, 1245-1253. (p. 768)

Klinke, R., Kral, A., Heid, S., Tillein, J., & Hartmann, R. (1999). Recruitment of the auditory cortex in congenitally deaf cats by long-term cochlear electrostimulation. *Science, 285*, 1729-1733. (p. 256)

Kluft, R. P. (1991). Multiple personality disorder. In A. Tasman & S. M. Goldfinger (Eds.), *Review of Psychiatry,* (Vol. 10). Washington, DC: American Psychiatric Press. (p. 657)

Klüver, H., & Bucy, P. C. (1939). Preliminary analysis of functions of the temporal lobes in monkeys. *Archives of Neurology and Psychiatry, 42*, 979-1000. (p. 72)

Knapp, M., Mangalore, R., & Simon, J. (2004). The global costs of schizophrenia. *Schizophrenia Bulletin, 30*, 279-293. (p. 671)

Knapp, S., & VandeCreek, L. (2000, August). Recovered memories of childhood abuse: Is there an underlying professional consensus? *Professional Psychology: Research and Practice, 31*, 365-371. (p. 388)

Knecht, S., Floeel, A., Draeger, B., Breitenstein, C., Sommer, J., Henningsen, H., Ringelstein, E. F., & Pascual-Leone, A. (2002). Degree of language lateralization determines susceptibility to unilateral brain lesions. *Nature Neuroscience, 5*, 695-699. (p. 86)

Knickmeyer, E. (2001, August 7). In Africa, big is definitely better. Associated Press (*Seattle Times,* p. A7). (p. 479)

Knight, W. (2004, August 2). Animated face helps deaf with phone chat. *NewScientist.com.* (p. 230)

Koenig, H. (2002, October 9). Personal communication, from Director of Center for the Study of Religion/Spirituality and Health, Duke University. (p. 572)

Koenig, H. G., & Larson, D. B. (1998). Use of hospital services, religious attendance, and religious affiliation. *Southern Medical Journal, 91*, 925-932. (p. 574)

Koenig, L. B., McGue, M., Krueger, R. F., & Bouchard, T. J., Jr. (2005). Genetic and environmental influences on religiousness: Findings for retrospective and current religiousness ratings. *Journal of Personality, 73*, 471-488. (p. 101)

Koestner, R., Lekes, N., Powers, T. A., & Chicoine, E. (2002). Attaining personal goals: Self-concordance plus implementation intentions equals success. *Journal of Personality and Social Psychology, 83*, 231-244. (p. 508)

Kohlberg, L. (1981). *The philosophy of moral development: Essays on moral development* (Vol. I). San Francisco: Harper & Row. (p. 168)

Kohlberg, L. (1984). *The psychology of moral development: Essays on moral development* (Vol. II). San Francisco: Harper & Row. (p. 168)

Kohler, I. (1962, May). Experiments with goggles. *Scientific American,* pp. 62-72. (p. 257)

Köhler, W. (1925; reprinted 1957). *The mentality of apes.* London: Pelican. (p. 423)

Kohn, P. M., & Macdonald, J. E. (1992). The survey of recent life experiences: A decontaminated hassles scale for adults. *Journal of Behavioral Medicine, 15*, 221-236. (pp. 554-555)

Kohout, J., & Wicherski, M. (2004). *2001 Doctorate employment survey,* Washington, DC: American Psychological Association. (p. A-4)

Kolata, G. (1986). Youth suicide: New research focuses on a growing social problem. *Science, 233*, 839-841. (p. 663)

Kolata, G. (1987). Metabolic catch-22 of exercise regimens. *Science, 236*, 146-147. (p. 590)

Kolata, G. (2004, September 30). Health and money issues arise over who pays for weight loss. *New York Times* (www.nytimes.com). (p. 588)

Kolb, B. (1989). Brain development, plasticity, and behavior. *American Psychologist, 44*, 1203-1212. (p. 83)

Kolb, B., & Whishaw, I. Q. (1998). Brain plasticity and behavior. *Annual Review of Psychology, 49*, 43-64. (p. 115)

Kolb, B., & Whishaw, I. Q. (2006). *An introduction to brain and behavior,* 2nd edition. *New York: Worth Publishers.* (p. 438)

Kolker, K. (2002, December 8). Video violence disturbs some; others scoff at influence. *Grand Rapids Press,* pp. A1, A12. (p. 754)

Kolodziej, M. E., & Johnson, B. T. (1996). Interpersonal contact and acceptance of persons with psychiatric disorders: A research synthesis. *Journal of Consulting and Clinical Psychology, 64*, 1387-1396. (p. 647)

Konishi, M. (1993, April). Listening with two ears. *Scientific American,* pp. 66-73. (p. 220)

Koole, S., & Spijker, M. (2000). Overcoming the planning fallacy through willpower: Effects of implementation intentions on actual and predicted task-completion times. *European Journal of Social Psychology, 30*, 873-888. (p. 508)

Kopta, S. M., Lueger, R. J., Saunders, S. M., & Howard, K. I. (1999). Individual psychotherapy outcome and process research: Challenges leading to greater turmoil or a positive transition? *Annual Review of Psychology, 30,* 441-469. (p. 703)

Koriat, A., Goldsmith, M., & Pansky, A. (2000). Toward a psychology of memory accuracy. *Annual Review of Psychology, 51,* pp. 481-537. (p. 384)

Koss, M. P., Heise, L., & Russo, N. P. (1994). The global health burden of rape. *Psychology of Women Quarterly, 18,* 509-537. (pp. 752, 753)

Kosslyn, S. M., & Koenig, O. (1992). *Wet mind: The new cognitive neuroscience.* New York: Free Press. (pp. 64, 210, 272)

Kosslyn, S. M., Thompson, W. L., Costantini-Ferrando, M. F., Alpert, N. M., & Spiegel, D. (2000). Hypnotic visual illusion alters color processing in the brain. *American Journal of Psychiatry, 157,* 1279-1284. (p. 294)

Kotchick, B. A., Shaffer, A., & Forehand, R. (2001). Adolescent sexual risk behavior: A multi-system perspective. *Clinical Psychology Review, 21,* 493-519. (p. 485)

Kotkin, M., Daviet, C., & Gurin, J. (1996). The *Consumer Reports* mental health survey. *American Psychologist, 51,* 1080-1082. (p. 700)

Kotva, H. J., & Schneider, H. G. (1990). Those "talks"—general and sexual communication between mothers and daughters. *Journal of Social Behavior and Personality, 5,* 603-613. (p. 485)

Kraft, C. (1978). A psychophysical approach to air safety: Simulator studies of visual illusions in night approaches. In H. L. Pick, H. W. Leibowitz, J. E. Singer, A. Steinschneider, & H. W. Stevenson (Eds.), *Psychology: From research to practice.* New York: Plenum Press. (pp. 262-263)

Kraft, R. (1996, December 2, and 1994, July 20). Personal correspondence (from Otterbein College) regarding Holocaust memories. (p. 605)

Kraus, N., Malmfors, T., & Slovic, P. (1992). Intuitive toxicology: Expert and lay judgments of chemical risks. *Risk Analysis, 12,* 215-232. (p. 406)

Krauss, C. (2002, August 11). A well-rounded Canada. *New York Times* (in *Grand Rapids Press,* p. E5). (p. 588)

Krauss, R. M. (1998). Why do we gesture when we speak? *Current Directions in Psychology, 7,* 54-60. (p. 426)

Kraut, R. E., & Johnston, R. E. (1979). Social and emotional messages of smiling: An ethological approach. *Journal of Personality and Social Psychology, 37,* 1539-1553. (p. 529)

KRC Research & Consulting. (2001, August 7). Memory isn't quite what it used to be (survey for General Nutrition Centers). *USA Today,* p. D1. (p. 182)

Krebs, D. L., & Van Hesteren, F. (1994). The development of altruism: Toward an integrative model. *Developmental Review, 14,* 103-158. (p. 168)

Kreitner, R. (1992). *Management,* 5th ed. Boston: Houghton Mifflin. (p. 439)

Krijn, M., Emmelkamp, P. M. G., Olafsson, R. P., & Biemond, R. (2004). Virtual reality exposure therapy of anxiety disorders: A review. *Clinical Psychology Review, 24,* 259-281. (p. 692)

Kring, A. M., & Gordon, A. H. (1998). Sex differences in emotion: Expression, experience, and physiology. *Journal of Personality and Social Psychology, 74,* 686-703. (p. 526)

Kristof, N. D. (2004, July 21). Saying no to killers. *New York Times* (www.nytimes.com). (p. 764)

Kroenke, K., & Mangelsdorff, A. D. (1989). Common symptoms in ambulatory care: Incidence, evaluation, therapy, and outcome. *American Journal of Medicine, 86,* 262-266. (p. 575)

Kroll, R., Danis, S., Moreau, M., Waldbaum, A., Shifren, J., & Wekselman, K. (2004). Testosterone transdermal patch (TPP) significantly improved sexual function in naturally menopausal women in a large Phase III study. Presented to the American Society of Reproductive Medicine annual meeting, Philadelphia, October. (p. 483)

Krosnick, J. A., & Alwin, D. F. (1989). Aging and susceptibility to attitude change. *Journal of Personality and Social Psychology, 57,* 416-425. (p. 194)

Krosnick, J. A., Betz, A. L., Jussim, L. J., & Lynn, A. R. (1992). Subliminal conditioning of attitudes. *Personality and Social Psychology Bulletin, 18,* 152-162. (p. 200)

Kruger, J., & Dunning, D. (1999). Unskilled and unaware of it: How difficulties in recognizing one's own incompetence lead to inflated self-assessments. *Journal of Personality and Social Psychology, 77,* 1121-1134. (pp. 628-629)

Kruger, J., Epley, N., & Gilovich, T. (1999). Egocentrism over email. Paper presented to the American Psychological Society meeting. (p. 528)

Krugman, P. (2003, September 14). The tax-cut con. *New York Times* (www.nytimes.com). (p. 41)

Krugman, P. (2005, July 4). Girth of a nation. *New York Times* (www.nytimes.com). (p. 583)

Krupa, D. J., Thompson, J. K., & Thompson, R. F. (1993). Localization of a memory trace in the mammalian brain. *Science, 260,* 989-991. (p. 369)

Krützen, M., Mann, J., Heithaus, M. R., Connor, R. C., Bejder, L., & Sherwin,, W. B. (2005). Cultural transmission of tool use in bottlenose dolphins. *Proceedings of the National Academy of Sciences, 102,* 8939-8943. (p. 424)

Kubey, R., & Csikszentmihalyi, M. (2002, February). Television addiction is no mere metaphor. *Scientific American,* pp. 74-80. (p. 344)

Kübler, A., Winter, S., Ludolph, A. C., Hautzinger, M., & Birbaumer, N. (2005). Severity of depressive symptoms and quality of life in patients with amyotrophic lateral sclerosis. *Neurorehabilitation and Neural Repair, 19*(3), 182-193. (p. 539)

Kubzansky, L. D., Sparrow, D., Vokanas, P., Kawachi, I. (2001). Is the glass half empty or half full? A prospective study of optimism and coronary heart disease in the normative aging study. *Psychosomatic Medicine, 63,* 910-916. (p. 556)

Kuhl, P. K., & Meltzoff, A. N. (1982). The bimodal perception of speech in infancy. *Science, 218,* 1138-1141. (p. 412)

Kujala, U. M., Kaprio, J., Sarna, S., & Koskenvuo, M. (1998). Relationship of leisure-time physical activity and mortality: The Finnish twin cohort. *Journal of the American Medical Association, 279,* 440-444. (p. 570)

Kulkin, H. S., Chauvin, E. A., & Percle, G. A. (2000). Suicide among gay and lesbian adolescents and young adults: A review of the literature. *Journal of Homosexuality, 40,* 1-29. (p. 488)

Kuncel, N. R., Nezlett, S. A., & Ones, D. S. (2004). Academic performance, career potential, creativity, and job performance: Can one construct predict them all? *Journal of Personality and Social Psychology, 86,* 148-161. (p. 434)

Kunkel, D. (2001, February 4). *Sex on TV.* Menlo Park, CA: Henry J. Kaiser Family Foundation (www.kff.org). (p. 486)

Kunkel, D., Cope-Farrar, K., Biely, E., Farinola, W. J. M., & Donnerstein, E. (2001). *Sex on TV (2): A biennial report to the Kaiser Family Foundation.* Menlo Park, CA: Kaiser Family Foundation. (p. 754)

Kurtz, P. (1983, Spring). Stars, planets, and people. *The Skeptical Inquirer,* pp. 65-68. (p. 617)

Kushner, H. (1986). Quoted by J. Viorst, *Necessary losses.* New York: Fawcett, p. 295. (p. 653)

Kutas, M. (1990). Event-related brain potential (ERP) studies of cognition during sleep: Is it more than a dream? In R. R. Bootzin, J. F. Kihlstrom, & D. Schacter (Eds.), *Sleep and cognition.* Washington, DC: American Psychological Association. (p. 278)

Kvavilashvili, L., Mirani, J., Schlagman, S., & Kornbrot, D. E. (2003). Comparing flashbulb memories of September 11 and the death of Princess Diana: Effects of time delays and nationality. *Applied Cognitive Psychology, 17,* 1017-1031. (p. 350)

Labouvie-Vief, G., & Schell, D. A. (1982). Learning and memory in later life. In B. B. Wolman (Ed.), *Handbook of developmental psychology.* Englewood Cliffs, NJ: Prentice-Hall. (p. 182)

Lacayo, R. (1995, June 12). Violent reaction. *Time,* pp. 25-39. (p. 28)

Lacey, M. (2004. April 9). A decade after massacres, Rwanda outlaws ethnicity. *New York Times* (www.nytimes.com). (p. 768)

Lachman, M. E. (2004). Development in midlife. *Annual Review of Psychology, 55,* 305-331. (p. 186)

Lachman, M. E., & Weaver, S. L. (1998). The sense of control as a moderator of social class differences in health and well-being. *Journal of Personality and Social Psychology, 74,* 763–773. (p. 625)

Ladd, E. C. (1998, August/September). The tobacco bill and American public opinion. *The Public Perspective,* pp. 5–19. (p. 307)

Ladd, G. T. (1887). *Elements of physiological psychology.* New York: Scribner's. (p. 271)

Laird, J. D. (1974). Self-attribution of emotion: The effects of expressive behavior on the quality of emotional experience. *Journal of Personality and Social Psychology, 29,* 475–486. (p. 530)

Laird, J. D. (1984). The real role of facial response in the experience of emotion: A reply to Tourangeau and Ellsworth, and others. *Journal of Personality and Social Psychology, 47,* 909–917. (p. 530)

Laird, J. D., Cuniff, M., Sheehan, K., Shulman, D., & Strum, G. (1989). Emotion specific effects of facial expressions on memory for life events. *Journal of Social Behavior and Personality, 4,* 87–98. (p. 530)

Lakin, J. L., & Chartrand, T. L. (2003). Using nonconscious behavioral mimicry to create affiliation and rapport. *Psychological Science, 14,* 334–339. (p. 731)

Lalumière, M. L., Blanchard, R., & Zucker, K. J. (2000). Sexual orientation and handedness in men and women: A meta-analysis. *Psychological Bulletin, 126,* 575–592. (p. 491)

Lambert, W. E. (1992). Challenging established views on social issues: The power and limitations of research. *American Psychologist, 47,* 533–542. (p. 420)

Lambert, W. E., Genesee, F., Holobow, N., & Chartrand, L. (1993). Bilingual education for majority English-speaking children. *European Journal of Psychology of Education, 8,* 3–22. (p. 420)

Lamberth, J. (1998, August 6). Driving while black: A statistician proves that prejudice still rules the road. *Washington Post,* p. C1. (p. 744)

Lammers, W. (2000). Quick tips for applying to graduate school in psychology. *Eye on Psi Chi, 4*(3), 40–42. (p. A-9)

Lampinen, J. M. (2002). What exactly is déjà vu? *Scientific American* (scieam.com/askexpert/biology/biology63). (p. 374)

Landau, M. J., Solomon, S., Greenberg, J., Cohen, F., Pyszczynski, T., Arndt, J., Miller, C. H., Ogilvie, D. M., & Cook, A. (2004). Deliver us from evil: The effects of mortality salience and reminders of 9/11 on support for President George W. Bush. *Personality and Social Psychology Bulletin, 30,* 1136–1150. (p. 747)

Landauer, T. (2001, September). Quoted by R. Herbert, You must remember this. *APS Observer,* p. 11. (p. 355)

Landauer, T. K. (1986). How much do people remember? Some estimates of the quantity of learned information in long-term memory. *Cognitive Science, 10,* 477–493. (p. 363)

Landauer, T. K., & Whiting, J. W. M. (1979). Correlates and consequences of stress in infancy. In R. Munroe, B. Munroe & B. Whiting (Eds.), *Handbook of Cross-Cultural Human Development.* New York: Garland. (p. 551)

Landers, A. (1969, April 8). Syndicated newspaper column. Cited by L. Berkowitz, The case for bottling up rage. *Psychology Today,* September, 1973, pp. 24–31. (p. 536)

Landrum, E. (2001). I'm getting my bachelor's degree in psychology. What can I do with it? *Eye on Psi Chi,* 22–24. (pp. A-1, A-9)

Landry, M. J. (2002). MDMA: A review of epidemiologic data. *Journal of Psychoactive Drugs, 34,* 163–169. (p. 302)

Lang, E. V., Benotsch, E. G., Fick, L. J., Lutgendorf, S., Berbaum, M. L., Logan, H., & Spiegel, D. (2000). Adjunctive non-pharmacological analgesia for invasive medical procedures: A randomised trial. *Lancet, 355,* 1486–1490. (p. 293)

Langer, E. J. (1983). *The psychology of control.* Beverly Hills, CA: Sage. (p. 626)

Langer, E. J., & Abelson, R. P. (1974). A patient by any other name . . . : Clinician group differences in labeling bias. *Journal of Consulting and Clinical Psychology, 42,* 4–9. (p. 646)

Langer, E. J., & Imber, L. (1980). The role of mindlessness in the perception of deviance. *Journal of Personality and Social Psychology, 39,* 360–367. (p. 646)

Langleben, D. D., Schroeder, L., Maldjian, J. A., Gur, R. C., McDonald, S., Ragland, J. D., O'Brien, C. P., & Childress, A. R. (2002). Brain activity during simulated deception: An event-related functional magnetic resonance study. *NeuroImage, 15,* 727–732. (pp. 70, 521)

Langlois, J. H., Kalakanis, L., Rubenstein, A. J., Larson, A., Hallam, M., & Smoot, M. (2000). Maxims or myths of beauty? A meta-analytic and theoretical review. *Psychological Bulletin, 126,* 390–423. (pp. 760, 761)

Langlois, J. H., & Roggman, L. A. (1990). Attractive faces are only average. *Psychological Science, 1,* 115–121. (p. 761)

Langlois, J. H., Roggman, L. A., Casey, R. J., Ritter, J. M., Rieser-Danner, L. A., & Jenkins, V. Y. (1987). Infant preferences for attractive faces: Rudiments of a stereotype? *Developmental Psychology, 23,* 363–369. (p. 760)

Larkin, K., Resko, J. A., Stormshak, F., Stellflug, J. N., & Roselli, C. E. (2002). Neuroanatomical correlates of sex and sexual partner preference in sheep. Society for Neuroscience convention. (p. 490)

Larrance, D. T., & Twentyman, C. T. (1983). Maternal attributions and child abuse. *Journal of Abnormal Psychology, 92,* 449–457. (p. 151)

Larsen, R. J. (2004). Emotion and cognition: The case of automatic vigilance. *Psychological Science Agenda, 18* (www.apa.org/science/psa/sb-larsenprt.html). (p. 237)

Larsen, R. J., & Diener, E. (1987). Affect intensity as an individual difference characteristic: A review. *Journal of Research in Personality, 21,* 1–39. (p. 102)

Larsen, R. J., Diener, E., & Cropanzano, R. S. (1987). Cognitive operations associated with individual differences in affect intensity. *Journal of Personality and Social Psychology, 53,* 767–774. (p. 523)

Larsen, R. J., Kasimatis, M., & Frey, K. (1992). Facilitating the furrowed brow: An unobtrusive test of the facial feedback hypothesis applied to unpleasant affect. *Cognition and Emotion, 6,* 321–338. (p. 530)

Larson, R. W. (2001). How U.S. children and adolescents spend time: What it does (and doesn't) tell us about their development. *Current Directions in Psychological Science, 10,* 160–164. (p. 172)

Larson, R. W., & Verma, S. (1999). How children and adolescents spend time across the world: Work, play, and developmental opportunities. *Psychological Bulletin, 125,* 701–736. (p. 460)

Larzelere, R. E. (1996). A review of the outcomes of parental use of nonabusive or customary physical punishment. *Pediatrics, 78,* 824–828. (p. 332)

Larzelere, R. E. (1999). The intervention selection bias. Unpublished manuscript. Boys Town, NE: Boys Town. (p. 328)

Larzelere, R. E. (2000). Child outcomes of non-abusive and customary physical punishment by parents: An updated literature review. *Clinical Child and Family Psychology Review, 3,* 199–221. (p. 332)

Larzelere, R. E., Kuhn, B. R., & Johnson, B. (2004). The intervention selection bias: An underrecognized confound in intervention research. *Psychological Bulletin, 130,* 289–303. (p. 332)

Lashley, K. S. (1950). In search of the engram. In *Symposium of the Society for Experimental Biology* (Vol. 4). New York: Cambridge University Press. (p. 364)

Lassiter, G. D., & Irvine, A. A. (1986). Video-taped confessions: The impact of camera point of view on judgments of coercion. *Journal of Personality and Social Psychology, 16,* 268–276. (p. 725)

Latané, B. (1981). The psychology of social impact. *American Psychologist, 36,* 343–356. (p. 739)

Latané, B., & Dabbs, J. M., Jr. (1975). Sex, group size and helping in three cities. *Sociometry, 38,* 180–194. (p. 766)

Laudenslager, M. L., & Reite, M. L. (1984). Losses and separations: Immunological consequences and health implications. *Review of Personality and Social Psychology, 5,* 285–312. (p. 563)

Laumann, E. O., Gagnon, J. H., Michael, R. T., & Michaels, S. (1994). *The social organization of sexuality: Sexual practices in the United States.* Chicago: University of Chicago Press. (pp. 110, 486, 753)

Lazarus, R. S. (1990). Theory-based stress measurement. *Psychological Inquiry, 1*, 3–13. (pp. 554–555)

Lazarus, R. S. (1991). Progress on a cognitive-motivational-relational theory of emotion. *American Psychologist, 46*, 352–367. (p. 522)

Lazarus. R. S. (1998). *Fifty years of the research and theory of R. S. Lazarus: An analysis of historical and perennial issues.* Mahwah, NJ: Erlbaum. (pp. 550, 522)

Lea, S. E. G. (2000). Towards an ethical use of animals. *The Psychologist, 13*, 556–557. (p. 48)

Leach, P. (1993). Should parents hit their children? *The Psychologist: Bulletin of the British Psychological Society, 6*, 216–220. (p. 333)

Leach, P. (1994). *Children first.* New York: Knopf. (p. 333)

Leary, M. R. (1999). The social and psychological importance of self-esteem. In R. M. Kowalski & M. R. Leary (Eds.), *The social psychology of emotional and behavioral problems.* Washington, DC: APA Books. (p. 632)

Leary, M. R., Haupt, A. L., Strausser, K. S., & Chokel, J. T. (1998). Calibrating the sociometer: The relationship between interpersonal appraisals and state self-esteem. *Journal of Personality and Social Psychology, 74*, 1290–1299. (p. 496)

Leary, M. R., Schreindorfer, L. S., & Haupt, A. L. (1995). The role of low self-esteem in emotional and behavioral problems: Why is low self-esteem dysfunctional? *Journal of Social and Clinical Psychology, 14*, 297–314. (p. 632)

Leary, W. E. (1998, September 28). Older people enjoy sex, survey says. *New York Times* (www.nytimes.com). (p. 177)

LeDoux, J. (1996). *The emotional brain: The mysterious underpinnings of emotional life.* New York: Simon & Schuster. (p. 369)

LeDoux, J. E. (2002). *The synaptic self.* London: Macmillan. (p. 63)

LeDoux, J. E., & Armony, J. (1999). Can neurobiology tell us anything about human feelings? In D. Kahneman, E. Diener, & N. Schwartz (Eds.), *Well-being: The foundations of hedonic psychology.* New York: Sage. (p. 522)

Lee, K., Byatt, G., & Rhodes, G. (2000). Caricature effects, distinctiveness, and identification: Testing the face-space framework. *Psychological Science, 11*, 379–385. (pp. 258–259)

Lefcourt, H. M. (1982). *Locus of control: Current trends in theory and research.* Hillsdale, NJ: Erlbaum. (p. 625)

Legrand, L. N., Iacono, W. G., & McGue, M. (2005). Predicting addiction. *American Scientist, 93*, 140–147. (pp. 98, 306)

Le Grand, R., Mondloch, C. J., Maurer, D., & Brent, H. P. (2004). Impairment in holistic face processing following early visual deprivation. *Psychological Science, 15*, 762–768. (p. 255)

Lehman, A. F., Steinwachs, D. M., Dixon, L. B., Goldman, H. H., Osher, F., Postrado, L., Scott, J. E., Thompson, J. W., Fahey, M., Fischer, P., Kasper, J. A., Lyles, A., Skinner, E. A., Buchanan, R., Carpenter, W. T., Jr., Levine, J., McGlynn, E. A., Rosenheck, R., & Zito, J. (1998). Translating research into practice: The schizophrenia patient outcomes research team (PORT) treatment recommendations. *Schizophrenia Bulletin, 24*, 1–10. (p. 712)

Lehman, D. R., Lempert, R. O., & Nisbett, R. E. (1988). The effects of graduate training on reasoning: Formal discipline and thinking about everyday-life events. *American Psychologist, 43*, 431–442. (p. 44)

Lehman, D. R., & Nisbett, R. E. (1985). Effects of higher education on inductive reasoning. Unpublished manuscript, University of Michigan. (p. 627)

Lehman, D. R., Wortman, C. B., & Williams, A. F. (1987). Long-term effects of losing a spouse or child in a motor vehicle crash. *Journal of Personality and Social Psychology, 52*, 218–231. (p. 190)

Leibowitz, H. W. (1985). Grade crossing accidents and human factors engineering. *American Scientist, 73*, 558–562. (p. 248)

Leigh, B. C. (1989). In search of the seven dwarves: Issues of measurement and meaning in alcohol expectancy research. *Psychological Bulletin, 105*, 361–373. (p. 300)

Leitenberg, H., & Henning, K. (1995). Sexual fantasy. *Psychological Bulletin, 117*, 469–496. (pp. 483, 485)

Lemonick, M. D. (2002, June 3). Lean and hungrier. *Time,* p. 54. (p. 476)

L'Engle, M. (1972). *A wind in the door.* Bantam Doubleday Dell Books for Young Readers. (p. 20)

Lennox, B. R., Bert, S., Park, G., Jones, P. B., & Morris, P. G. (1999). Spatial and temporal mapping of neural activity associated with auditory hallucinations. *Lancet, 353*, 644. (p. 79)

Lenzenweger, M. F., Dworkin, R. H., & Wethington, E. (1989). Models of positive and negative symptoms in schizophrenia: An empirical evaluation of latent structures. *Journal of Abnormal Psychology, 98*, 62–70. (p. 712)

Leonhardt, D. (2004, August 17). Top athletes may be running into a tall hurdle: Themselves. *New York Times* (www.nytimes.com). (p. 127)

Lerman, C., Caporaso, N. E., Audrain, J., Main, D., Bowman, E. D., Lockshin, B., Boyd, N. R., & Shields, P. G. (1999). Evidence suggesting the role of specific genetic factors in cigarette smoking. *Health Psychology, 18*, 14–20. (p. 578)

Lerner, J. S, Gonzalez, R. M., Small, D. A., & Fischhoff, B. (2002). Effects of Fear and Anger on Perceived Risks of Terrorism: A National Field Experiment. *Psychological Science, 14*(2), 144–150. (p. 534)

Lerner, M. J. (1980). *The belief in a just world: A fundamental delusion.* New York: Plenum Press. (p. 748)

Leserman, J., Jackson, E. D., Petitto, J. M., Golden, R. N., Silva, S. G., Perkins, D. O., Cai, J., Folds, J. D., & Evans, D. L. (1999). Progression to AIDS: The effects of stress, depressive symptoms, and social support. *Psychosomatic Medicine, 61*, 397–406. (p. 559)

Lessard, N., Pare, M., Lepore, F., & Lassonde, M. (1998). Early-blind human subjects localize sound sources better than sighted subjects. *Nature, 395*, 278–280. (p. 223)

Lester, W. (2004, May 26). AP polls: Nations value immigrant workers. Associated Press release. (p. 744)

Leucht, S., Barnes, T. R. E., Kissling, W., Engel, R. R., Correll, C., & Kane, J. M. (2003). Relapse prevention in schizophrenia with new-generation antipsychotics: A systematic review and exploratory meta-analysis of randomized, controlled trials. *American Journal of Psychiatry, 160*, 1209–1222. (p. 712)

LeVay, S. (1991). A difference in hypothalamic structure between heterosexual and homosexual men. *Science, 253*, 1034–1037. (p. 489)

LeVay, S. (1994, March). Quoted in D. Nimmons, Sex and the brain. *Discover,* pp. 64–71. (p. 489)

Levenson, R. W. (1992). Autonomic nervous system differences among emotions. *Psychological Science, 3*, 23–27. (p. 518)

Leventhal, T., & Brooks-Gunn, J. (2000). The neighborhoods they live in: The effects of neighborhood residence on child and adolescent outcomes. *Psychological Bulletin, 126*, 309–337. (p. 118)

Lever, J. (2003, November 11). Personal correspondence reporting data responses volunteered to *Elle/MSNBC.com* survey of weight perceptions. (p. 479)

Levesque, M. J., & Kenny, D. A. (1993). Accuracy of behavioral predictions at zero acquaintance: A social relations analysis. *Journal of Personality and Social Psychology, 65*, 1178–1187. (p. 622)

Levin, I. P., & Gaeth, G. J. (1988). How consumers are affected by the framing of attribute information before and after consuming the product. *Journal of Consumer Research, 15*, 374–378. (p. 406)

Levine, J. A., Eberhardt, N. L., & Jensen, M. D. (1999). Role of nonexercise activity thermogenesis in resistance to fat gain in humans. *Science, 283*, 212–214. (p. 476)

Levine, J. A., Lanningham-Foster, L. M., McCrady, S. K., Krizan, A. C., Olson, L. R., Kane, P. H., Jensen, M. D., & Clark, M. M. (2005). Interindividual variation in posture allocation: Possible role in human obesity. *Science, 307*, 584–586. (pp. 476, 586)

Levine, R., Sato, S., Hashimoto, T., & Verma, J. (1995). Love and marriage in eleven cultures. *Journal of Cross-Cultural Psychology, 26*, 554–571. (p. 764)

Levine, R. V., & Norenzayan, A. (1999). The pace of life in 31 countries. *Journal of Cross-Cultural Psychology, 30*, 178–205. (pp. 30, 121)

Levy, B., & Langer, E. (1992). Avoidance of the memory loss stereotype: Enhanced memory among the elderly deaf. American Psychological Association convention, Washington, DC. (p. 223)

Levy, P. E. (2003). *Industrial/organizational psychology: Understanding the workplace.* Boston: Houghton Mifflin. (p. 503)

Lewicki, P., Hill, T., & Czyzewska, M. (1992). Nonconscious acquisition of information. *American Psychologist, 47,* 796–801. (p. 605)

Lewicki, P., Hill, T., & Czyzewska, M. (1997). Hidden covariation detection: A fundamental and ubiquitous phenomenon. *Journal of Experimental Psychology: Learning, Memory, and Cognition, 23,* 221–228. (p. 605)

Lewinsohn, P. M., Hoberman, H., Teri, L., & Hautziner, M. (1985). An integrative theory of depression. In S. Reiss & R. Bootzin (Eds.), *Theoretical issues in behavior therapy.* Orlando, FL: Academic Press. (p. 660)

Lewinsohn, P. M., Rohde, P., & Seeley, J. R. (1998). Major depressive disorder in older adolescents: Prevalence, risk factors, and clinical implications. *Clinical Psychology Review, 18,* 765–794. (p. 660)

Lewinsohn, P. M., & Rosenbaum, M. (1987). Recall of parental behavior by acute depressives, remitted depressives, and nondepressives. *Journal of Personality and Social Psychology, 52,* 611–619. (p. 374)

Lewis, C. S. (1960). *Mere Christianity.* New York: Macmillan. (p. 5)

Lewis, C. S. (1967). *Christian reflections.* Grand Rapids, MI: Eerdmans. (p. 376)

Lewis, D. O., Pincus, J. H., Bard, B., Richardson, E., Prichep, L. S., Feldman, M., & Yeager, C. (1988). Neuropsychiatric, psychoeducational, and family characteristics of 14 juveniles condemned to death in the United States. *American Journal of Psychiatry, 145,* 584–589. (p. 158)

Lewis, D. O., Pincus, J. H., Feldman, M., Jackson, L., & Bard, B. (1986). Psychiatric, neurological, and psychoeducational characteristics of 15 death row inmates in the United States. *American Journal of Psychiatry, 143,* 838–845. (p. 749)

Lewis, D. O., Yeager, C. A., Swica, Y., Pincus, J. H., & Lewis, M. (1997). Objective documentation of child abuse and dissociation in 12 murderers with dissociative identity disorder. *American Journal of Psychiatry, 154,* 1703–1710. (p. 657)

Lewis, M. (1992). Commentary. *Human Development, 35,* 44–51. (p. 374)

Lewontin, R. (1976). Race and intelligence. In N. J. Block & G. Dworkin (Eds.), *The IQ controversy: Critical readings.* New York: Pantheon. (p. 460)

Lewontin, R. (1982). *Human diversity.* New York: Scientific American Library. (pp. 109, 460)

Li, J. C., Dunning, D., & Malpass, R. L. (1996). Cross-racial identification among European-Americans Basketball fandom and the contact hypothesis. Unpublished manuscript, Cornell University. (p. 748)

Li, J., Laursen, T. M., Precht, D. H., Olsen, J., & Mortensen, P. B. (2005). Hospitalization for mental illness among parents after the death of a child. *New England Journal of Medicine, 352,* 1190–1196. (p. 190)

Libet, B. (1985). Unconscious cerebral initiative and the role of conscious will in voluntary action. *Behavioral and Brain Sciences, 12,* 181–187. (p. 272)

Libet, B. (2004). Mind time: The temporal factor in consciousness. Cambridge, MA: Harvard University Press. (p. 272)

Licata, A., Taylor, S., Berman, M., & Cranston, J. (1993). Effects of cocaine on human aggression. *Pharmacology Biochemistry and Behavior, 45,* 549–552. (p. 302)

Lichtman, S. W., Pisarska, K., Berman, E. R., Pestone, M., Dowling, H., Offenbacher, E., Weisel, H., Heshka, S., Matthews, D. E., & Heymsfield, S. B. (1992). Discrepancy between self-reported and actual caloric intake and exercise in obese subjects. *New England Journal of Medicine, 327,* 1893–1898. (p. 586)

Lieberman, J. A., & 11 others (2005). Effectiveness of antipsychotic drugs in patients with chronic schizophrenia. *New England Journal of Medicine, 353,* 1209–1223. (p. 712)

Lilienfeld, S. O. (1998). Pseudoscience in contemporary clinical psychology: What it is and what we can do about it. *The Clinical Psychologist, 51*(4), 3–5. (p. 705)

Lilienfeld, S. O., Lynn, S. J., Kirsch, I., Chaves, J. F., Sarbin, T. R., Ganaway, G. K., & Powell, R. A. (1999). Dissociative identity disorder and the sociocognitive model: Recalling the lessons of the past. *Psychological Bulletin, 125,* 507–523. (p. 657)

Lilienfeld, S. O., Wood, J. M., & Garb, H. N. (2000). The scientific status of projective techniques. *Psychological Science in the Public Interest, 1,* 27–66. (p. 603)

Lilienfeld, S. O., Wood, J. M., & Garb, H. N. (2001, May). What's wrong with this picture? *Scientific American,* pp. 81–87. (p. 603)

Lin, L., Faraco, J., Li, R., Kadotani, H., Rogers, W., Lin, X., Qiu, X., de Jong, P. J., Nishino, S., & Mignot E. (1999). The sleep disorder canine narcolepsy is caused by a mutation in the hypocretin (orexin) receptor 2 gene. *Cell, 98,* 365–376. (p. 284)

Lincoln, C. (2001). *Sap Rising,* Pantheon Books. (p. 638)

Linde, K., & 10 others (2005). Acupuncture for patients with migraine: A randomized controlled trial. *Journal of the American Medical Association, 293,* 2118–2125. (p. 580)

Linder, D. (1982). Social trap analogs: The tragedy of the commons in the laboratory. In V. J. Derlega & J. Grzelak (Eds.), *Cooperative and helping behavior: Theories and research.* New York: Academic Press. (p. 757)

Lindskold, S. (1978). Trust development, the GRIT proposal, and the effects of conciliatory acts on conflict and cooperation. *Psychological Bulletin, 85,* 772–793. (p. 769)

Lindskold, S., & Han, G. (1988). GRIT as a foundation for integrative bargaining. *Personality and Social Psychology Bulletin, 14,* 335–345. (p. 769)

Linville, P. W., Fischer, G. W., & Fischhoff, B. (1992). AIDS risk perceptions and decision biases. In J. B. Pryor & G. D. Reeder (Eds.), *The social psychology of HIV infection.* Hillsdale, NJ: Erlbaum. (p. 406)

Lippa, R. A. (2002). Gender-related traits of heterosexual and homosexual men and women. *Archives of Sexual Behavior, 31,* 83–98. (p. 492)

Lippman, J. (1992, October 25). Global village is characterized by a television in every home. *Los Angeles Times* Syndicate (in *Grand Rapids Press,* p. F9). (p. 344)

Lipps, H. M. (1999). *A new psychology of women: Gender, culture, and ethnicity.* Mountain View, CA: Mayfield Publishing. (p. 745)

Lipsey, M. W., & Wilson, D. B. (1993). The efficacy of psychological, educational, and behavioral treatment: Confirmation from meta-analyses. *American Psychologist, 48,* 1181–1209. (p. 453)

Lipsitt, L. P. (2003). Crib death: A biobehavioral phenomenon? *Current Directions in Psychological Science, 12,* 164–170. (p. 145)

Lipton, J. S., & Spelke, E. S. (2003). Origins of number sense: Large-number discrimination in human infants. *Psychological Science, 14,* 296–401. (p. 149)

Livingstone, M., & Hubel, D. (1988). Segregation of form, color, movement, and depth: Anatomy, physiology, and perception. *Science, 240,* 740–749. (p. 210)

Lock, M. (1998). Menopause: Lessons from anthropology. *Psychosomatic Medicine, 60,* 410–419. (p. 176)

Locke, E. A., & Latham, G. P. (2002). Building a practically useful theory of goal setting and task motivation. *American Psychologist, 57,* 705–717. (p. 508)

Loehlin, J. C., McCrae, R. R., & Costa, P. T., Jr. (1998). Heritabilities of common and measure-specific components of the Big Five personality factors. *Journal of Research in Personality, 32,* 431–453. (p. 619)

Loehlin, J. C., & Nichols, R. C. (1976). *Heredity, environment, and personality.* Austin: University of Texas Press. (p. 98)

Loewenstein, G., & Furstenberg, F. (1991). Is teenage sexual behavior rational? *Journal of Applied Social Psychology, 21,* 957–986. (p. 330)

Loftus, E. F. (1979). The malleability of human memory. *American Scientist, 67,* 313–320. (p. 382)

Loftus, E. (1995, March/April). Remembering dangerously. *Skeptical Inquirer,* pp. 20–29. (p. 604)

Loftus, E. F. (1980). *Memory: Surprising new insights into how we remember and why we forget.* Reading, MA: Addison-Wesley. (p. 292)

Loftus, E. F. (1993). The reality of repressed memories. *American Psychologist, 48,* 518–537. (p. 389)

Loftus, E. F. (2001, November). Imagining the past. *The Psychologist, 14,* 584–587. (p. 383)

Loftus, E. F., Coan, J., & Pickrell, J. E. (1996). Manufacturing false memories using bits of reality. In L. Reder (Ed.), *Implicit memory and metacognition.* Mahway, NJ: Erlbaum. (p. 388)

Loftus, E. F., & Kaufman, L. (1992). Why do traumatic experiences sometimes produce good memory (flashbulbs) and sometimes no memory (repression)? In E. Winograd & U. Neisser (Eds.), *Affect and accuracy in recall: Studies of "flashbulb" memories.* New York: Cambridge University Press. (p. 146)

Loftus, E. F., & Ketcham, K. (1994). *The myth of repressed memory.* New York: St. Martin's Press. (pp. 365, 389)

Loftus, E. F., Levidow, B., & Duensing, S. (1992). Who remembers best? Individual differences in memory for events that occurred in a science museum. *Applied Cognitive Psychology, 6,* 93–107. (p. 383)

Loftus, E. F., & Loftus, G. R. (1980). On the permanence of stored information in the human brain. *American Psychologist, 35,* 409–420. (p. 364)

Loftus, E. F., Milo, E. M., & Paddock, J. R. (1995). The accidental executioner: Why psychotherapy must be informed by science. *The Counseling Psychologist, 23,* 300–309. (p. 388)

Loftus, E. F., & Palmer, J. C. (October, 1974). Reconstruction of automobile destruction: An example of the interaction between language and memory. *Journal of Verbal Learning & Verbal Behavior, 13(5),* 585–589. (p. 382)

Loftus, G. R. (1992). When a lie becomes memory's truth: Memory distortion after exposure to misinformation. *Current Directions in Psychological Science, 1,* 121–123. (p. 383)

Logan, T. K., Walker, R., Cole, J., & Leukefeld, C. (2002). Victimization and substance abuse among women: Contributing factors, interventions, and implications. *Review of General Psychology, 6,* 325–397. (p. 306)

Logothetis, N. K., & Schall, J. D. (1989). Neuronal correlates of subjective visual perception. *Science, 245,* 761–763. (p. 210)

Logue, A. W. (1998a). Laboratory research on self-control: Applications to administration. *Review of General Psychology, 2,* 221–238. (p. 330)

Logue, A. W. (1998b). Self-control. In W. T. O'Donohue, (Ed.), *Learning and behavior therapy.* Boston, MA: Allyn & Bacon. (p. 330)

London, P. (1970). The rescuers: Motivational hypotheses about Christians who saved Jews from the Nazis. In J. Macaulay & L. Berkowitz (Eds.), *Altruism and helping behavior.* New York: Academic Press. (p. 344)

Looy, H. (2001). Sex differences: Evolved, constructed, and designed. *Journal of Psychology and Theology, 29,* 301–313. (p. 112)

Lopes, P. N., Brackett, M. A., Nezlek, J. B., Sch_tz, A., Sellin, Il, & Salovey, P. (2004). Emotional intelligence and social interaction. *Personality and Social Psychology Bulletin, 30,* 1018–1034. (p. 437)

Lopez, A. D. (1999). Measuring the health hazards of tobacco: Commentary. *Bulletin of the World Health Organization, 77(1),* 82–83. (pp. 575, 580)

Lopez, D. J. (2002, January/February). Snaring the fowler: Mark Twain debunks phrenology. *Skeptical Inquirer* (www.csicop.org). (p. 54)

Lord, C. G., Lepper, M. R., & Preston, E. (1984). Considering the opposite: A corrective strategy for social judgment. *Journal of Personality and Social Psychology, 47,* 1231–1247. (p. 407)

Lord, C. G., Ross, L., & Lepper, M. (1979). Biased assimilation and attitude polarization: The effects of prior theories on subsequently considered evidence. *Journal of Personality and Social Psychology, 37,* 2098–2109. (p. 407)

Lorenz, K. (1937). The companion in the bird's world. *Auk, 54,* 245–273. (p. 156)

Los Angeles Times (1998, 14 March). Daughters give birth on same day, p. A15. (p. 35)

Louie, K., & Wilson, M. A. (2001). Temporally structured replay of awake hippocampal ensemble activity during rapid eye movement sleep. *Neuron, 29,* 145–156. (p. 287)

Lourenco, O., & Machado, A. (1996). In defense of Piaget's theory: A reply to 10 common criticisms. *Psychological Review, 103,* 143–164. (p. 154)

Lovaas, O. I. (1987). Behavioral treatment and normal educational and intellectual functioning in young autistic children. *Journal of Consulting and Clinical Psychology, 55,* 3–9. (p. 693)

Love, J. M., & 13 others (2003). Child care quality matters: How conclusions may vary with context. *Child Development, 74,* 1021–1033. (p. 160)

Love, S. M. (2002, July 16). Preventive medicine, properly practiced. *New York Times* (www.nytimes.com). (p. 38)

Lowry, P. E. (1997). The assessment center process: New directions. *Journal of Social Behavior and Personality, 12,* 53–62. (p. 630)

Lu, Z.-L., Williamson, S. J., & Kaufman, L. (1992). Behavioral lifetime of human auditory sensory memory predicted by physiological measures. *Science, 258,* 1668–1670. (p. 362)

Lubinski, D., & Benbow, C. P. (1992). Gender differences in abilities and preferences among the gifted: Implications for the math-science pipeline. *Current Directions in Psychological Science, 1,* 61–66. (p. 461)

Lubinski, D., & Benbow, C. P. (2000). States of excellence. *American Psychologist,* 137–150. (pp. 453, 454)

Luborsky, L., Rosenthal, R., Diguer, L., Andrusyna, T. P., Berman, J. S., Levitt, J. T., Seligman, D. A., & Krause, E. D. (2002). The dodo bird verdict is alive and well—mostly. *Clinical Psychology: Science and Practice, 9,* 2–34. (p. 704)

Lucas, A., Morley, R., Cole, T. J., Lister, G., & Leeson-Payne, C. (1992). Breast milk and subsequent intelligence quotient in children born preterm. *Lancet, 339,* 261–264. (p. 36)

Lucas, R. E. (2005). Long-term disability has lasting effects on subjective well-being: Evidence from two nationally representative longitudinal studies. Unpublished manuscript, Michigan State University. (p. 539)

Lucas, R. E., Clark, A. E., Georgellis, Y., & Diener, E. (2003). Re-examining adaptation and the setpoint model of happiness: Reactions to changes in marital status. *Journal of Personality and Social Psychology, 84,* 527–539. (Figure courtesy of R. E. Lucas.) (p. 191)

Lucas, R. E., Clark, A. E., Georgellis, Y., & Diener, E. (2004). Unemployment alters the set point for life satisfaction. *Psychological Science, 15,* 8–13. (p. 544)

Ludwig, A. M. (1995). *The price of greatness: Resolving the creativity and madness controversy.* New York: Guilford Press. (pp. 489, 660)

Ludwig, J. (2004, June 1). Acceptance of interracial marriage at record high. Gallup Poll Tuesday Briefing (www.gallup.com). (p. 743)

Lukoff, D., Lu, F., & Turner, R. (1992). Toward a more culturally sensitive DSM-IV: Psychoreligious and psychospiritual problems. *Journal of Nervous and Mental Disease, 180,* 673–682. (p. 708)

Lumsden, C. J., & Wilson, E. O. (1983). *Promethean fire: Reflections on the origin of mind.* Cambridge, MA: Harvard University Press. (p. 534)

Luntz, F. (2003, June 10). Quoted by T. Raum, "Bush insists banned weapons will be found." Associated Press (story.news.yahoo.com). (p. 729)

Luria, A. M. (1968). In L. Solotaroff (Trans.), *The mind of a mnemonist.* New York: Basic Books. (p. 350)

Lustig, C., & Buckner, R. L. (2004). Preserved neural correlates of priming in old age and dementia. *Neuron, 42,* 865–875. (p. 729)

Lutgendorf, S. K., Russell, D., Ullrich, P., Harris, T. B., & Wallace, R. (2004). Religious participation, Interleukin-6, and mortality in older adults. *Health Psychology, 23,* 465–475. (p. 574)

Luthar, S. S., & Latendresse, S. J. (2005). Children of the affluent: Challenges to well-being. *Current Directions in Psychological Science, 14,* 49–53. (p. 540)

Lykken, D. T. (1982, September). Fearlessness: Its carefree charm and deadly risks. *Psychology Today,* pp. 20–28. (p. 535)

Lykken, D. T. (1991). Science, lies, and controversy: An epitaph for the polygraph. Invited address upon receipt of the Senior Career Award for

Distinguished Contribution to Psychology in the Public Interest, American Psychological Association convention. (p. 520)

Lykken, D. T. (1995). *The antisocial personalities.* Hillsdale, NJ: Erlbaum. (p. 678)

Lykken, D. T. (1999). *Happiness.* New York: Golden Books. (pp. 184, 455)

Lykken, D. T. (2001). Happiness—stuck with what you've got? *The Psychologist, 14,* 470–473. (p. 101)

Lykken, D. T., & Tellegen, A. (1993) Is human mating adventitious or the result of lawful choice? A twin study of mate selection. *Journal of Personality and Social Psychology, 65,* 56–68. (p. 186)

Lykken, D. T., & Tellegen, A. (1996). Happiness is a stochastic phenomenon. *Psychological Science, 7,* 186–189. (p. 544)

Lyman, D. R. (1996). Early identification of chronic offenders: Who is the fledgling psychopath? *Psychological Bulletin, 120,* 209–234. (p. 679)

Lynch, G. (2002). Memory enhancement: The search for mechanism-based drugs. *Nature Neuroscience, 5* (suppl.), 1035–1038. (p. 365)

Lynch, G., & Staubli, U. (1991). Possible contributions of long-term potentiation to the encoding and organization of memory. *Brain Research Reviews, 16,* 204–206. (p. 365)

Lyness, S. A. (1993). Predictors of differences between Type A and B individuals in heart rate and blood pressure reactivity. *Psychological Bulletin, 114,* 266–295. (p. 556)

Lynn, M. (1988). The effects of alcohol consumption on restaurant tipping. *Personality and Social Psychology Bulletin, 14,* 87–91. (p. 299)

Lynn, R. (1987). Japan: Land of the rising IQ. A reply to Flynn. *Bulletin of the British Psychological Society, 40,* 464–468. (p. 460)

Lynn, R. (1991, Fall/Winter). The evolution of racial differences in intelligence. *The Mankind Quarterly, 32,* 99–145. (p. 459)

Lynn, R. (2001). *Eugenics: A reassessment.* Westport, CT: Praeger/Greenwood. (p. 459)

Lynn, S. J., Rhue, J. W., & Weekes, J. R. (1990). Hypnotic involuntariness: A social cognitive analysis. *Psychological Review, 97,* 169–184. (p. 294)

Lyons, L. (2002, June 25). Are spiritual teens healthier? *Gallup Tuesday Briefing,* Gallup Organization (www.gallup.com/poll/tb/religValue/20020625b.asp). (p. 573)

Lyons, L. (2003, September 23). Oh, boy: Americans still prefer sons. *Gallup Poll Tuesday Briefing* (www.gallup.com). (p. 745)

Lyons, L. (2004, February 3). Growing up lonely: Examining teen alienation. Gallup Poll Tuesday Briefing (www.gallup.com). (p. 171)

Lyons, L. (2005, January 4). Teens stay true to parents' political perspectives. Gallup Poll News Service (www.gallup.com). (p. 173)

Lytton, H., & Romney, D. M. (1991). Parents' differential socialization of boys and girls: A meta-analysis. *Psychological Bulletin, 109,* 267–296. (p. 132)

Lyubomirsky, S. (2001). Why are some people happier than others? The role of cognitive and motivational processes in well-being. *American Psychologist, 56,* 239–249. (p. 543)

Lyubomirsky, S., King, L., & Diener, E. (2005). The benefits of frequent positive affect: Does happiness lead to success? *Psychological Bulletin, 131,* 803–855. (p. 537)

Lyubomirsky, S., Sousa, L., & Dickerhoof, R. (2006). The costs and benefits of writing, talking, and thinking about life's triumphs and defeats. *Journal of Personality and Social Psychology,* in press. (p. 567)

Ma, L. (1997, September). On the origin of Darwin's ills. *Discover,* p. 27. (p. 650)

Maas, J. B. (1999). *Power sleep. The revolutionary program that prepares your mind for peak performance.* New York: HarperCollins. (pp. 280, 281, 282)

Maass, A., & Russo, A. (2003). Directional bias in the mental representation of spatial events: Nature or culture? *Psychological Science, 14,* 296–301. (p. 420)

Macaluso, E., Frith, C. D., & Driver, J. (2000). Modulation of human visual cortex by crossmodal spatial attention. *Science, 289,* 1206–1208. (p. 231)

Macan, T. H., & Dipboye, R. L. (1994). The effects of the application on processing of information from the employment interview. *Journal of Applied Social Psychology, 24,* 1291. (p. 502)

Macaskill, P., Pierce, J. P., Simpson, J. M., & Lyle, D. M. (1992). Mass media-led antismoking campaign can remove the education gap in quitting behavior. *American Journal of Public Health, 82,* 96–98. (p. 581)

Maccoby, E. (1980). *Social development: Psychological growth and the parent-child relationship.* New York: Harcourt Brace Jovanovich. (p. 161)

Maccoby, E. E. (1990). Gender and relationships: A developmental account. *American Psychologist, 45,* 513–520. (p. 128)

Maccoby, E. E. (1995). Divorce and custody: The rights, needs, and obligations of mothers, fathers, and children. *Nebraska Symposium on Motivation, 42,* 135–172. (p. 131)

Maccoby, E. E. (1998). *The paradox of gender.* Cambridge, MA: Harvard University Press. (p. 128)

Maccoby, E. E. (2002). Gender and group process: A developmental perspective. *Current Directions in Psychological Science, 11,* 54–58. (p. 739)

Maccoby, E. E. (2003, July 22). In Susan Gilbert, Turning a mass of data on child care into advice for parents. *New York Times* (www.nytimes.com). (p. 160)

MacDonald, G., & Leary, M. R. (2005). Why does social exclusion hurt? The relationship between social and physical pain. *Psychological Bulletin, 131,* 202–223. (p. 497)

MacDonald, N. (1960). Living with schizophrenia. *Canadian Medical Association Journal, 82,* 218–221. (p. 670)

MacDonald, T. K., Fong, G. T., Zanna, M. P., & Martineau, A. M. (2000). Alcohol myopia and condom use: Can alcohol intoxication be associated with more prudent behavior? *Journal of Personality and Social Psychology, 78,* 605–619. (p. 299)

MacDonald, T. K., Zanna, M. P., & Fong, G. T. (1995). Decision making in altered states: Effects of alcohol on attitudes toward drinking and driving. *Journal of Personality and Social Psychology, 68,* 973–985. (p. 299)

MacDonald, T. K., Zanna, M. P., & Fong, G. T. (1996). Why common sense goes out the window: The effects of alcohol on intentions to use condoms. *Personality and Social Psychology Bulletin, 22,* 763–775. (p. 299)

Macfarlane, J. W. (1964). Perspectives on personality consistency and change from the guidance study. *Vita Humana, 7,* 115–126. (pp. 165)

MacFarlane, A. (1978, February). What a baby knows. *Human Nature,* pp. 74–81. (p. 143)

MacKay, D. G. (1983). Prescriptive grammar and the pronoun problem. In B. Thorne, C. Kramarae, & N. Henley (Eds.), *Language, gender and society.* Rowley, MA: Newbury House. (p. 419)

MacKinnon, D. W., & Hall, W. B. (1972). Intelligence and creativity. In *Proceedings, XVIIth International Congress of Applied Psychology* (Vol. 2). Brussels: Editest. (p. 438)

MacLeod, C., & Campbell, L. (1992). Memory accessibility and probability judgments: An experimental evaluation of the availability heuristic. *Journal of Personality and Social Psychology, 63,* 890–902. (p. 402)

MacNeilage, P. F., & Davis, B. L. (2000). On the origin of internal structure of word forms. *Science, 288,* 527–531. (p. 412)

Maddieson, I. (1984). *Patterns of sounds.* Cambridge: Cambridge University Press. (p. 411)

Maddox, K. B. (2004). Perspectives on racial phenotypicality bias. *Personality and Social Psychology Review, 8,* 383–401. (p. 744)

Maes, H. H. M., Neale, M. C., & Eaves, L. J. (1997). Genetic and environmental factors in relative body weight and human adiposity. *Behavior Genetics, 27,* 325–351. (p. 586)

Maes, M., Armand, C., Delanghe, J., Altamura, C., Neels, H., & Meltzer, H. Y. (1999). Lowered omega3 polyunsaturated fatty acids in serum phospholipids and cholesteryl esters of depressed patients. *Psychiatry Residency, 85,* 275–291. (p. 664)

Maestripieri, D. (2003). Similarities in affiliation and aggression between cross-fostered rhesus macaque females and their biological mothers. *Developmental Psychobiology, 43,* 321-327. (p. 101)

Magnusson, D. (1990). Personality research—challenges for the future. *European Journal of Personality, 4,* 1-17. (p. 678)

Maguire, E. A., Spiers, H. J., Good, C. D., Hartley, T., Frackowiak, R. S. J., & Burgess, N. (2003). Navigation expertise and the human hippocampus: A structural brain imaging analysis. *Hippocampus, 13,* 250-259. (pp. 359, 368)

Maguire, E. A., Valentine, E. R., Wilding, J. M., & Kapur, N. (2003b). Routes to remembering: The brains behind superior memory. *Nature Neuroscience, 6,* 90-95. (p. 368)

Mahowald, M. W., & Ettinger, M. G. (1990). Things that go bump in the night: The parsomias revisited. *Journal of Clinical Neurophysiology, 7,* 119-143. (p. 277)

Maier, S. F., Watkins, L. R., & Fleshner, M. (1994). Psychoneuroimmunology: The interface between behavior, brain, and immunity. *American Psychologist, 49,* 1004-1017. (pp. 557, 558)

Major, B., Carrington, P. I., & Carnevale, P. J. D. (1984). Physical attractiveness and self-esteem: Attribution for praise from an other-sex evaluator. *Personality and Social Psychology Bulletin, 10,* 43-50. (p. 760)

Major, B., Schmidlin, A. M., & Williams, L. (1990). Gender patterns in social touch: The impact of setting and age. *Journal of Personality and Social Psychology, 58,* 634-643. (p. 127)

Malamuth, N. M. (1996). Sexually explicit media, gender differences, and evolutionary theory. *Journal of Communication, 46,* 8-31. (p. 753)

Malamuth, N. M., & Check, J. V. P. (1981). The effects of media exposure on acceptance of violence against women: A field experiment. *Journal of Research in Personality, 15,* 436-446. (p. 484)

Malamuth, N. M., Linz, D., Heavey, C. L., Barnes, G., & Acker, M. (1995). Using the confluence model of sexual aggression to predict men's conflict with women: A 10-year follow-up study. *Journal of Personality and Social Psychology, 69,* 353-369. (p. 754)

Malamuth, N. M., Sockloskie, R. J., Koss, M. P., & Tanaka, J. S. (1991). Characteristics of aggressors against women: Testing a model using a national sample of college students. *Journal of Consulting and Clinical Psychology, 59,* 670-681. (p. 754)

Malan, D. H. (1978). "The case of the secretary with the violent father." In H. Davanloo (Ed.), *Basic principles and techniques in short-term dynamic psychotherapy.* New York: Spectrum. (p. 688)

Malaspina, D., Harlap, S., Fennig, S., Heiman, D., Nahon, D., Feldman, D., & Susser, E. S. (2001). Advancing paternal age and the risk of schizophrenia. *Archives of General Psychiatry, 58,* 361-367. (p. 674)

Malinosky-Rummell, R., & Hansen, D. J. (1993). Long-term consequences of childhood physical abuse. *Psychological Bulletin, 114,* 68-79. (p. 158)

Malkiel, B. (2004). *A random walk down Wall Street* (8th ed.). New York: Norton. (p. 403)

Malkiel, B. G. (1989). Is the stock market efficient? *Science, 243,* 1313-1318. (p. 35)

Malkiel, B. G. (1995, June). Returns from investing in equity mutual funds 1971 to 1991. *Journal of Finance,* pp. 549-572. (p. 35)

Malloy, E. A. (1994, June 7). Report of the Commission on Substance Abuse at Colleges and Universities, reported by *Associated Press.* (p. 299)

Malmquist, C. P. (1986). Children who witness parental murder: Posttraumatic aspects. *Journal of the American Academy of Child Psychiatry, 25,* 320-325. (p. 605)

Malnic, B., Hirono, J., Sato, T., & Buck, L. B. (1999). Combinatorial receptor codes for odors. *Cell, 96,* 713-723. (p. 232)

Manber, R., Bootzin, R. R., Acebo, C., & Carskadon, M. A. (1996). The effects of regularizing sleep-wake schedules on daytime sleepiness. *Sleep, 19,* 432-441. (p. 283)

Mandel, D. (1983, March 13). One man's holocaust: Part II. The story of David Mandel's journey through hell as told to David Kagan. *Wonderland Magazine* (Grand Rapids Press), pp. 2-7. (p. 473)

Mann, J. J. (2003). Neurobiology of suicidal behaviour. *Nature Reviews Neuroscience, 4,* 819-828. (p. 662)

Mann, S., Vrij, A., & Bull, R. (2004). Detecting true lies: Police officers' ability to detect suspects' lies. *Journal of Applied Psychology, 89,* 137-149. (p. 527)

Manning, A. (2002, May 17). Teenage smoking rates drop. *USA Today* (story.news.yahoo.com). (p. 582)

Manson, J. E. (2002). Walking compared with vigorous exercise for the prevention of cardiovascular events in women. *New England Journal of Medicine, 347,* 716-725. (p. 570)

Maquet, P. (2001). The role of sleep in learning and memory. *Science, 294,* 1048-1052. (p. 287)

Maquet, P., Peters, J-M., Aerts, J., Delfiore, G., Degueldre, C., Luxen, A., & Franck, G. (1996). Functional neuroanatomy of human rapid-eye-movement sleep and dreaming. *Nature, 383,* 163-166. (p. 288)

Marangell, L. B., Rush, A. J., George, M. S., Sackeim, H. A., Johnson, C. R., Husain, M. M., Nahas, Z., & Lisanby, S. H. (2002). Vagus nerve stimulation (VNS) for major depressive episodes: One year outcomes. *Biological Psychiatry, 51,* 280-287. (p. 716)

Marcus, G. (2004). *The birth of the mind: How a tiny number of genes creates the complexity of human thought.* New York: Basic Books. (p. 103)

Marcus, G. F., Vijayan, S., Rao, S. B., & Vishton, P. M. (1999). Rule learning by seven-month-old infants. *Science, 283,* 77-80. (p. 416)

Margolis, M. L. (2000). Brahms' lullaby revisited: Did the composer have obstructive sleep apnea? *Chest, 118,* 210-213. (p. 284)

Marino, L. A., Reiss, D., & Gallup, G. G., Jr. (1994). Mirror self-recognition in bottlenose dolphins: Implications for comparative investigations of highly dissimilar species. In S. P. Parker, R. Mitchell, & M. Boccia (Eds.), *Self-awareness in animals and humans: Developmental perspectives.* New York: Cambridge University Press. (p. 161)

Mark, V., & Ervin, F. (1970). *Violence and the brain.* New York: Harper & Row. (p. 73)

Markowitsch, H. J. (1995). Which brain regions are critically involved in the retrieval of old episodic memory? *Brain Research Reviews, 21,* 117-127. (p. 369)

Markowitz, J. C., Svartberg, M., & Swartz, H. A. (1998). Is IPT time-limited psychodynamic psychotherapy? *Journal of Psychotherapy Practice and Research, 7,* 185-195. (p. 688)

Markus, G. B. (1986). Stability and change in political attitudes: Observe, recall, and "explain." *Political Behavior, 8,* 21-44. (p. 385)

Markus, H. (2001, October 7). Culture and the good life. Address to the Positive Psychology Summit conference, Washington, DC. (p. 123)

Markus, H., & Kitayama, S. (1991). Culture and the self: Implications for cognition, emotion, and motivation. *Psychological Review, 98,* 224-253. (pp. 122, 419, 536)

Markus, H., & Nurius, P. (1986). Possible selves. *American Psychologist, 41,* 954-969. (p. 631)

Marlatt, G. A. (1991). Substance abuse: Etiology, prevention, and treatment issues. Master lecture, American Psychological Association convention. (pp. 299, 330)

Marley, J., & Bulia, S. (2001). Crimes against people with mental illness: Types, perpetrators and influencing factors. *Social Work, 46,* 115-124. (p. 647)

Marmot, M. G., Bosma, H., Hemingway, H., Brunner, E., & Stansfeld, S. (1997). Contribution fo job control and other risk factors to social variations in coronary heart disease incidents. *Lancet, 350,* 235-239. (p. 564)

Marr, D. (1982). *Vision.* San Francisco: W. H. Freeman. (p. 210)

Marschark, M., Richman, C. L., Yuille, J. C., & Hunt, R. R. (1987). The role of imagery in memory: On shared and distinctive information. *Psychological Bulletin, 102,* 28-41. (p. 358)

Marsh, A. A., Elfenbein, H. A., & Ambady, N. (2003). Nonverbal "accents": Cultural differences in facial expressions of emotion. *Psychological Science, 14,* 373-376. (p. 529)

Marsh, H. W., & Parker, J. W. (1984). Determinants of student self-concept: Is it better to be a relatively large fish in a small pond even if you don't learn to swim as well? *Journal of Personality and Social Psychology, 47,* 213–231. (p. 543)

Marshall, E. (2004). A star-studded search for memory-enhancing drugs. *Science, 304,* 36–38. (p. 365)

Marshall, M. J. (2002). *Why spanking doesn't work.* Springville, UT: Bonneville Books. (p. 333)

Marshall, W. L. (1989). Pornography and sex offenders. In D. Zillmann & J. Bryant (Eds.), *Pornography: Research advances and policy considerations.* Hillsdale, NJ: Erlbaum. (p. 753)

Marteau, T. M. (1989). Framing of information: Its influences upon decisions of doctors and patients. *British Journal of Social Psychology, 28,* 89–94. (p. 406)

Marti, M. W., Robier, D. M., & Baron, R. S. (2000). Right before our eyes: The failure to recognize non-prototypical forms of prejudice. *Group Processes and Intergroup Relations, 3,* 403–418. (p. 397)

Martin, A., Wiggs, C. L., Ungerleider, L. G., & Haxby, J. V. (1996). Neural correlates of category-specific knowledge. *Nature, 379,* 649–652. (p. 69)

Martin, C. L., & Ruble, D. (2004). Children's search for gender cues. *Current Directions in Psychological Science, 13,* 67–70. (p. 716)

Martin, C. L., Ruble, D. N., & Szkrybalo, J. (2002). Cognitive theories of early gender development. *Psychological Bulletin, 128,* 903–933. (p. 132)

Martin, J. L. R., Barbanojh, M. J., Schlaepfer, T. E., Thompson, E., Perez, V., & Kulisevsky, J. (2005). Repetitive transcranial magnetic stimulation for the treatment of depression: Systematic review and meta-analysis. *British Journal of Psychiatry, 182,* 480–491. (p. 716)

Martin, R. A. (2001). Humor, laughter, and physical health: Methodological issues and research findings. *Psychological Bulletin, 127,* 504–519. (p. 565)

Martin, R. A. (2002). Is laughter the best medicine? Humor, laughter, and physical health. *Current Directions in Psychological Science, 11,* 216–220. (p. 565)

Martin, R. J., White, B. D., & Hulsey, M. G. (1991). The regulation of body weight. *American Scientist, 79,* 528–541. (p. 476)

Martin, S. J., Kelly, I. W., & Saklofske, D. H. (1992). Suicide and lunar cycles: A critical review over 28 years. *Psychological Reports, 71,* 787–795. (p. 680)

Martins, Y., Preti, G., Crabtree, C. R., & Wysocki, C. J. (2005). Preference for human body odors is influenced by gender and sexual orientation. *Psychological Science, 16,* 694–701. (p. 490)

Maruta, T., Colligan, R. C., Malinchoc, M., & Offord, K. P. (2002). Optimists vs. pessimists: Survival rate among medical patients over a 30-year period. *Mayo Clinic Proceedings, 75,* 140–143. (p. 565)

Marx, J. (2005). Preventing Alzheimer's: A lifelong commitment? *Science, 309,* 864–866. (p. 181)

Maslow, A. H. (1970). *Motivation and personality* (2nd ed.). New York: Harper & Row. (pp. 472, 609)

Maslow, A. H. (1971). *The farther reaches of human nature.* New York: Viking Press. (p. 472)

Mason, C., & Kandel, E. R. (1991). Central visual pathways. In E. R. Kandel, J. H. Schwartz, & T. M. Jessell (Eds.), *Principles of neural science* (3rd ed.). New York: Elsevier. (p. 62)

Mason, H. (2003, March 25). Wake up, sleepy teen. *Gallup Poll Tuesday Briefing* (www.gallup.com). (p. 280)

Mason, H. (2003, September 2). Americans, Britons at odds on animal testing. Gallup Poll News Service (www.gallup.com). (p. 47)

Mason, H. (2004, September 28). Support for smoking bans smoldering in Britain, Canada. *Gallup Poll* (www.gallup.com). (p. 578)

Mason, H. (2005, January 25). Who dreams, perchance to sleep? Gallup Poll News Service (www.gallup.com). (pp. 280, 281)

Mason, H. (2005, February 22). How many teens are on mood medication? The Gallup Organization (www.gallup.com). (pp. 280, 281, 641, 578)

Mason, R. A., & Just, M. A. (2004). How the brain processes causal inferences in text. *Psychological Science, 15,* 1–7. (p. 88)

Masse, L. C., & Tremblay, R. E. (1997). Behavior of boys in kindergarten and the onset of substance use during adolescence. *Archives of General Psychiatry, 54,* 62–68. (p. 305)

Massimini, M., Ferrarelli, F., Huber, R., Esser, S. K., Singh, H., & Tononi, G. (2005). Breakdown of cortical effective connectivity during sleep. *Science, 309,* 2228–2232. (p. 276)

Masten, A. S. (2001). Ordinary magic: Resilience processes in development. *American Psychologist, 56,* 227–238. (p. 159)

Masters, W. H., & Johnson, V. E. (1966). *Human sexual response.* Boston: Little, Brown. (p. 481)

Masuda, T., & Kitayama, S. (2005). Perceiver-induced constraint and attitude attribution in Japan and the US: A case for the cultural dependence of the correspondence bias. *Journal of Experimental Social Psychology, 40,* 409–416. (p. 724)

Mataix-Cols, D., Rosario-Campos, M. C., & Leckman, J. F. (2005). A multidimensional model of obsessive-compulsive disorder. *American Journal of Psychiatry, 162,* 228–238. (p. 655)

Mataix-Cols, D., Wooderson, S., Lawrence, N., Brammer, M. J., Speckens, A., & Phillips, M. L. (2004). Distinct neural correlates of washing, checking, and hoarding symptom dimensions in obsessive-compulsive disorder. *Archives of General Psychiatry, 61,* 564–576. (p. 655)

Mather, M., Canli, T., English, T., Whitfield, S., Wais, P., Ochsner, K., Gabrieli, J. D. E., & Carstensen, L. L. (2004). Amygdala responses to emotionally valenced stimuli in older and younger adults. *Psychological Science, 15,* 259–263. (p. 189)

Mather, M., & Carstensen, L. L. (2003). Aging and attentional biases for emotional faces. *Psychological Science, 14,* 409–415. (p. 189)

Matsumoto, D. (1994). *People: Psychology from a cultural perspective.* Pacific Grove, CA: Brooks/Cole. (p. 418)

Matsumoto, D., & Ekman, P. (1989). American-Japanese cultural differences in intensity ratings of facial expressions of emotion. *Motivation and Emotion, 13,* 143–157. (p. 528)

Matsumoto, D., Kudoh, T., Scherer, K., & Wallbott, H. (1988). Antecedents of and reactions to emotions in the United States and Japan. *Journal of Cross-Cultural Psychology, 19,* 267–286. (p. 516)

Maurer, D., Lewis, T. L., Brent, H. P., & Levin, A. V. (1999). Rapid improvement in the acuity of infants after visual input. *Science, 286,* 108–110. (p. 256)

Maurer, D., & Maurer, C. (1988). *The world of the newborn.* New York: Basic Books. (p. 143)

May, C., & Hasher, L. (1998). Synchrony effects in inhibitory control over thought and action. *Journal of Experimental Psychology: Human Perception and Performance, 24,* 363–380. (p. 275)

May, C. P., Hasher, L., & Stoltzfus, E. R. (1993). Optimal time of day and the magnitude of age differences in memory. *Psychological Science, 4,* 326–330. (p. 182)

May, R. (1982). The problem of evil: An open letter to Carl Rogers. *Journal of Humanistic Psychology, 22,* 10–21. (p. 611)

Mayberg, H. S., Lozano, A. M., Voon, V., McNeely, H. E., Seminowicz, D., Hamani, C., Schwalb, J. M., & Kennedy, S. H. (2005). Deep brain stimulation for treatment-resistant depression. *Neuron, 45,* 651–660. (p. 716)

Mayberry, R. I., Lock, E., & Kazmi, H. (2002). Linguistic ability and early language exposure. *Nature, 417,* 38. (p. 417)

Mayer, J. D. Salovey, P., & Caruso, D. (2002). *The Mayer-Salovey-Caruso emotional intelligence test (MSCEIT).* Toronto: Multi-Health Systems, Inc. (p. 436)

Mazur, A., & Booth, A. (1998). Testosterone and dominance in men. *Behavioral and Brain Sciences, 21,* 353–363. (p. 750)

Mazure, C., Keita, G., & Blehar, M. (2002). *Summit on women and depression: Proceedings and recommendations.* Washington, DC: American Psychological Association (www.apa.org/pi/wpo/women&depression.pdf). (p. 666)

Mazzoni, G., & Memon, A. (2003). Imagination can create false autobiographical memories. *Psychological Science, 14,* 186–188. (p. 383)

Mazzuca, J. (2002, July 2). Same-sex parenting: Does public back Rosie? The Gallup Organization (www.gallup.com/poll/tb/religValue/20020702.asp). (p. 492)

Mazzuca, J. (2002, August 20). Teens shrug off movie sex and violence. *Gallup Tuesday Briefing* (www.gallup.com/poll/tb/educayouth/20020820b.asp). (p. 345)

McAneny, L. (1996, September). Large majority think government conceals information about UFO's. *Gallup Poll Monthly,* pp. 23–26. (p. 373)

McBeath, M. K., Shaffer, D. M., & Kaiser, M. K. (1995). How baseball outfielders determine where to run to catch fly balls. *Science, 268,* 569–572. (p. 249)

McBurney, D. H. (1996). *How to think like a psychologist: Critical thinking in psychology.* Upper Saddle River, NJ: Prentice-Hall. (p. 80)

McBurney, D. H., & Collings, V. B. (1984). *Introduction to sensation and perception* (2nd ed.). Englewood Cliffs, NJ: Prentice-Hall. (p. 253)

McBurney, D. H., & Gent, J. F. (1979). On the nature of taste qualities. *Psychological Bulletin, 86,* 151–167. (p. 229)

McCall, R. B., Evahn, C., & Kratzer, L. (1992). *High school underachievers.* Newbury Park, CA: Sage. (p. 462)

McCann, I. L., & Holmes, D. S. (1984). Influence of aerobic exercise on depression. *Journal of Personality and Social Psychology, 46,* 1142–1147. (p. 569)

McCann, U. D., Eligulashvili, V., & Ricaurte, G. A. (2001). (+-)3,4-Methylenedioxymethamphetamine ('Ecstasy')-induced serotonin neurotoxicity: Clinical studies. *Neuropsychobiology, 42,* 11–16. (p. 302)

McCarthy, P. (1986, July). Scent: The tie that binds? *Psychology Today,* pp. 6, 10. (p. 232)

McCarthy, T. (2001, July 30). Why can't we be friends? *Time,* pp. 34–41. (p. 393)

McCaul, K. D., & Malott, J. M. (1984). Distraction and coping with pain. *Psychological Bulletin, 95,* 516–533. (p. 229)

McCauley, C. R. (2002). Psychological issues in understanding terrorism and the response to terrorism. In C. E. Stout (Ed.), *The psychology of terrorism,* Vol. 3. Westport, CT: Praeger/Greenwood. (p. 740)

McCauley, C. R., & Segal, M. E. (1987). Social psychology of terrorist groups. In C. Hendrick (Ed.), *Group processes and intergroup relations.* Beverly Hills, CA: Sage. (p. 740)

McClearn, G. E., Johansson, B., Berg, S., Pedersen, N. L., Ahern, F., Petrill, S. A., & Plomin, R. (1997). Substantial genetic influence on cognitive abilities in twins 80 or more years old. *Science, 276,* 1560–1563. (p. 456)

McClintock, M. K., & Herdt, G. (December, 1996). Rethinking puberty: The development of sexual attraction. *Current Directions in Psychological Science, 5*(6), 178–183. (p. 165)

McClure, E. B. (2000). A meta-analytic review of sex differences in facial expression processing and their development in infants, children, and adolescents. *Psychological Bulletin, 126,* 424–453. (p. 464)

McClure, S. M., Laibson, D. I., Loewenstein, G., & Cohen, J. D. (2004). Separate neural systems value immediate and delayed monetary rewards. *Science, 306,* 503–507. (pp. 166–167)

McConkey, K. M. (1995). Hypnosis, memory, and the ethics of uncertainty. *Australian Psychologist, 30,* 1–10. (p. 292)

McConnell, R. A. (1991). National Academy of Sciences opinion on parapsychology. *Journal of the American Society for Psychical Research, 85,* 333–365. (p. 264)

McCool, G. (1999, October 26). Mirror-gazing Venezuelans top of vanity stakes. *Toronto Star* (via web.lexis-nexis.com). (p. 760)

McCord, J. (1978). A thirty-year follow-up on treatment effects. *American Psychologist, 33,* 284–289. (pp. 701–702)

McCord, J. (1979). Following up on Cambridge-Somerville. *American Psychologist, 34,* 727. (pp. 701–702)

McCormick, C. M., & Witelson, S. F. (1991). A cognitive profile of homosexual men compared to heterosexual men and women. *Psychoneuroendocrinology, 16,* 459–473. (p. 492)

McCrae, R. R. (2001). Trait psychology and culture. *Journal of Personality, 69,* 819–846. (p. 619)

McCrae, R. R., & Costa, P. T., Jr. (1986). Clinical assessment can benefit from recent advances in personality psychology. *American Psychologist, 41,* 1001–1003. (p. 618)

McCrae, R. R., & Costa, P. T., Jr. (1990). *Personality in adulthood.* New York: Guilford. (p. 186)

McCrae, R. R., & Costa, P. T., Jr. (1994). The stability of personality: Observations and evaluations. *Current Directions in Psychological Science, 3,* 173–175. (pp. 194, 620)

McCrae, R. R., & Costa, P. T., Jr. (1999). A five-factor theory of personality. In L. A. Pervin & O. P. John (Eds.), *Handbook of personality: Theory and research.* New York: Guilford. (p. 618)

McCrae, R. R., Costa, P. T., Jr., de Lirna, M. P., Simoes, A., Ostendorf, F., Angleitner, A., Marusic, I., Bratko, D., Caprara, G. V., Barbaranelli, C., Chae, J-H., & Piedmont, R. L. (1999). Age differences in personality across the adult life span: Parallels in five cultures. *Developmental Psychology, 35,* 466–477. (p. 619)

McCrae, R. R., Costa, P. T., Jr., Ostendorf, F., Angleitner, A., Hrebickova, M., Avia, M. D., Sanz, J., Sanchez-Bernardos, M. L., Kusdil, M. E., Woodfield, R., Saunders, P. R., & Smith, P. B. (2000). Nature over nurture: Temperament, personality, and life span development. *Journal of Personality and Social Psychology, 78,* 173–186. (p. 102)

McCrae, R. R., Terracciano, A., & 78 others (2005). Universal features of personality traits from the observer's perspective: Data from 50 cultures. *Journal of Personality and Social Psychology, 88,* 547–561. (p. 619)

McCrink, K., & Wynn, K. (2004). Large-number addition and subtraction by 9-month-old infants. *Psychological Science, 15,* 776–781. (p. 149)

McCullough, M. E., Hoyt, W. T., Larson, D. B., Koenig, H. G., & Thoresen, C. (2000). Religious involvement and mortality: A meta-analytic review. *Health Psychology, 19,* 211–222. (p. 572)

McCullough, M. E., & Laurenceau, J-P. (2005). Religiousness and the trajectory of self-rated health across adulthood. *Personality and Social Psychology Bulletin, 31,* 560–573. (p. 572)

McCullough, M. E., Tsang, J-A., & Emmons, R. A. (2004). Gratitude in intermediate affective terrain: Links of grateful moods to individual differences and daily emotional experience. *Journal of Personality and Social Psychology, 86,* 295–309. (p. 540)

McEwen, B. S. (1998). Protective and damaging effects of stress mediators. *Seminars in Medicine of the Beth Israel Deaconess Medical Center, 338,* 171–179. (p. 553)

McEwen, B. S. (2002). Sex, stress and the hippocampus: Allostasis, allostatic load and the aging process. *Neurobiology of Aging, 23,* 921–939. (p. 553)

McFadden, D. (2002). Masculinization effects in the auditory system. *Archives of Sexual Behavior, 31,* 99–111. (p. 492)

McFarland, C., & Ross, M. (1987). The relation between current impressions and memories of self and dating partners. *Psychological Bulletin, 13,* 228–238. (p. 385)

McFarland, C., Ross, M., & DeVourville, N. (1989). Women's theories of menstruation and biases in recall of menstrual symptoms. *Journal of Personality and Social Psychology, 57,* 522–531. (p. 274)

McFarland, C., White, K., & Newth, S. (2003). Mood acknowledgment and correction for the mood-congruency bias in social judgment. *Journal of Experimental Social Psychology, 39,* 483–491. (p. 375)

McGarry-Roberts, P. A., Stelmack, R. M., & Campbell, K. B. (1992). Intelligence, reaction time, and event-related potentials. *Intelligence, 16,* 289–313. (p. 441)

McGaugh, J. I. (2003). *Memory and emotion: The making of lasting memories.* New York: Columbia University Press. (pp. 349, 366)

McGaugh, J. L. (1994). Quoted by B. Bower, Stress hormones hike emotional memories. *Science News, 146,* p. 262. (p. 366)

McGaugh, J. L. (2000). Memory—a century of consolidation. *Science, 287,* 248–251. (p. 368)

McGhee, P. E. (June, 1976). Children's appreciation of humor: A test of the cognitive congruency principle. *Child Development, 47(2),* 420–426. (p. 153)

McGlone, M. S., & Tofighbakhsh, J. (2000). Birds of a feather flock conjointly (?): Rhyme as reason in aphorisms. *Psychological Science, 11,* 424–428. (p. 357)

McGrath, J. J., & Welham, J. L. (1999). Season of birth and schizophrenia: A systematic review and meta-analysis of data from the Southern hemisphere. *Schizophrenia Research, 35,* 237–242. (p. 673)

McGrath, J., Welham, J., & Pemberton, M. (1995). Month of birth, hemisphere of birth and schizophrenia. *British Journal of Psychiatry, 167,* 783–785. (p. 673)

McGrath, M. J., & Cohen, D. B. (1978). REM sleep facilitation of adaptive waking behavior: A review of the literature. *Psychological Bulletin, 85,* 24–57. (p. 287)

McGregor, D. (1960). *The human side of enterprise.* New York: McGraw-Hill. (p. 495)

McGue, M., & Bouchard, T. J., Jr. (1998). Genetic and environmental influences on human behavioral differences. *Annual Review of Neuroscience, 21,* 1–24. (p. 100)

McGue, M., Bouchard, T. J., Jr., Iacono, W. G., & Lykken, D. T. (1993). Behavioral genetics of cognitive ability: A life-span perspective. In R. Plomin & G. E. McClearn (Eds.), *Nature, nurture and psychology.* Washington, DC: American Psychological Association. (pp. 455–456)

McGue, M., & Lykken, D. T. (1992). Genetic influence on risk of divorce. *Psychological Science, 3,* 368–373. (p. 98)

McGuire, M. T., Wing, R. R., Klem, M. L., Lang, W., & Hill, J. O. (1999). What predicts weight regain in a group of successful weight losers? *Journal of Consulting and Clinical Psychology, 67,* 177–185. (p. 590)

McGuire, W. J. (1986). The myth of massive media impact: Savings and salvagings. In G. Comstock (Ed.), *Public communication and behavior.* Orlando, FL: Academic Press. (p. 345)

McGuire, W. J., McGuire, C. V., Child, P., & Fujioka, T. (1978). Salience of ethnicity in the spontaneous self-concept as a function of one's ethnic distinctiveness in the social environment. *Journal of Personality and Social Psychology, 36,* 511–520. (p. 127)

McGurk, H., & MacDonald, J. (1976). Hearing lips and seeing voices. *Nature, 264,* 746–748. (p. 230)

McHugh, P. R. (1995a). Witches, multiple personalities, and other psychiatric artifacts. *Nature Medicine, 1(2),* 110–114. (p. 657)

McHugh, P. R. (1995b). Resolved: Multiple personality disorder is an individually and socially created artifact. *Journal of the American Academy of Child and Adolescent Psychiatry, 34,* 957–959. (p. 657)

McHugh, P. R., & Moran, T. H. (1978). Accuracy of the regulation of caloric ingestion in the rhesus monkey. *American Journal of Physiology, 235,* R29–34. (p. 475)

McKellar, J., Stewart, E., & Humphreys, K. (2003). Alcoholics Anonymous involvement and positive alcohol-related outcomes: Cause, consequence, or just a correlate? A prospective 2-year study of 2,319 alcohol-dependent men. *Journal of Consulting and Clinical Psychology, 71,* 302–308. (p. 698)

McKenna, K. Y. A., & Bargh, J. A. (1998). Coming out in the age of the Internet: Identity "demarginalization" through virtual group participation. *Journal of Personality and Social Psychology, 75,* 681–694. (p. 740)

McKillop, J., Lisman, S. A., Weinstein, A., & Rosenbaum, D. (2003). Controversial treatments for alcoholism. In S. O. Lilienfeld, S. J. Lynn, & J. M. Lohr (Eds.), *Science and pseudoscience in clinical psychology.* New York: Guilford Press. (p. 698)

McLaughlin, C. S., Chen, C., Greenberger, E., & Biermeier, C. (1997). Family, peer, and individual correlates of sexual experience among Caucasian and Asian American late adolescents. Journal of Personality and Social Psychology, *Journal of Research on Adolescence, 7,* 33–53. (p. 485)

McMurray, C. (2004, January 13). U.S., Canada, Britain: Who's getting in shape? *Gallup Poll Tuesday Briefing* (www.gallup.com). (p. 568)

McMurray, C. (2004, February 24). Current smoking trends in U.S., Canada, Britain. *Gallup Poll Tuesday Briefing* (www.gallup.com). (p. 578)

McNally, R. J. (1987). Preparedness and phobias: A review. *Psychological Bulletin, 101,* 283–303. (p. 534)

McNally, R. J. (1999). EMDR and Mesmerism: A comparative historical analysis. *Journal of Anxiety Disorders, 13,* 225–236. (p. 706)

McNally, R. J. (2003). *Remembering trauma.* Cambridge, MA: Harvard University Press. (pp. 383, 388, 653)

McNally, R. J., Bryant, R. A., & Ehlers, A. (2003). Does early psychological intervention promote recovery from posttraumatic stress? *Psychological Science in the Public Interest, 4,* 45–79. (p. 653)

McNeil, B. J., Pauker, S. G., & Tversky, A. (1988). On the framing of medical decisions. In D. E. Bell, H. Raiffa, & A. Tversky (Eds.), *Decision making: Descriptive, normative, and prescriptive interactions.* New York: Cambridge, 1988. (p. 406)

Meador, B. D., & Rogers, C. R. (1984). Person-centered therapy. In R. J. Corsini (Ed.), *Current psychotherapies* (3rd ed.). Itasca, IL: Peacock. (p. 690)

Medical Institute for Sexual Health. (1994, April). Condoms ineffective against human papilloma virus. *Sexual Health Update, 2.* (p. 486)

Medland, S. E., Perelle, I., De Monte, V., & Ehrman, L. (2004). Effects of culture, sex, and age on the distribution of handedness: An evaluation of the sensitivity of three measures of handedness. *Laterality: Asymmetries of Body, Brain, and Cognition, 9,* 287–297. (p. 88)

Mednick, S. A., Huttunen, M. O., & Machon, R. A. (1994). Prenatal influenza infections and adult schizophrenia. *Schizophrenia Bulletin, 20,* 263–267. (p. 673)

Mehl, M. R., & Pennebaker, J. W. (2003). The sounds of social life: A psychometric analysis of students' daily social environments and natural conversations. *Journal of Personality and Social Psychology, 84,* 857–870. (p. 29)

Meichenbaum, D. (1977). *Cognitive-behavior modification: An integrative approach.* New York: Plenum Press. (p. 696)

Meichenbaum, D. (1985). *Stress inoculation training.* New York: Pergamon. (p. 696)

Meier, R. P. (1991). Language acquisition by deaf children. *American Scientist, 79,* 60–70. (pp. 218, 407)

Meltzoff, A. N. (1988). Infant imitation after a 1-week delay: Long-term memory for novel acts and multiple stimuli. *Developmental Psychology, 24,* 470–476. (p. 342)

Meltzoff, A. N., & Moore, M. K. (1989). Imitation in newborn infants: Exploring the range of gestures imitated and the underlying mechanisms. *Developmental Psychology, 25,* 954–962. (p. 342)

Meltzoff, A. N., & Moore, M. K. (1997). Explaining facial imitation: A theoretical model. *Early Development and Parenting, 6,* 179–192. (p. 342)

Melzack, R. (1984). The myth of painless childbirth. *Pain, 19,* 321–337. (p. 229)

Melzack, R. (1990, February). The tragedy of needless pain. *Scientific American,* pp. 27–33. (p. 297)

Melzack, R. (1992, April). Phantom limbs. *Scientific American,* pp. 120–126. (p. 227)

Melzack, R. (1993). Distinguished contribution series. *Canadian Journal of Experimental Psychology, 47,* 615–629. (p. 227)

Melzack, R. (1998, February). Quoted in Phantom limbs. *Discover,* p. 20. (p. 227)

Melzack, R. (1999). Pain and Stress: A new perspective. In R. J. Gatchel, & D. C. Turk (Eds.), *Psychosocial factors in pain: Critical perspectives.* New York: Guilford Press. (p. 227)

Melzack, R., & Wall, P. D. (1965). Pain mechanisms: A new theory. *Science, 150,* 971-979. (p. 227)

Melzack, R., & Wall, P. D. (1983). *The challenge of pain.* New York: Basic Books. (p. 227)

Mendolia, M., & Kleck, R. E. (1993). Effects of talking about a stressful event on arousal: Does what we talk about make a difference? *Journal of Personality and Social Psychology, 64,* 283-292. (p. 567)

Merari, A. (2002). Explaining suicidal terrorism: Theories versus empirical evidence. Invited address to the American Psychological Association. (p. 740)

Merriman, J. (1999, May 13). These pounds aren't sterling. *Reuters* (www.abcnews.go.com). (p. 587)

Merskey, H. (1992). The manufacture of personalities: The production of multiple personality disorder. *British Journal of Psychiatry, 160,* 327-340. (p. 657)

Merton, R. K. (1938; reprinted 1970). *Science, technology and society in seventeenth-century England.* New York: Fertig. (p. 23)

Merton, R. K., & Kitt, A. S. (1950). Contributions to the theory of reference group behavior. In R. K. Merton & P. F. Lazarsfeld (Eds.), *Continuities in social research: Studies in the scope and method of the American soldier.* Glencoe, IL: Free Press. (p. 543)

Messer, D. (2000). Language acquisition. *The Psychologist, 13,* 138-143. (p. 414)

Messer, W. S., & Griggs, R. A. (1989). Student belief and involvement in the paranormal and performance in introductory psychology. *Teaching of Psychology, 16,* 187-191. (p. 266)

Mestel, R. (1997, April 26). Get real, Siggi. *New Scientist* (www.newscientist.com/ns/970426/siggi.html). (p. 286)

Meston, C. M., & Frohlich, P. F. (2000). The neurobiology of sexual function. *Archives of General Psychiatry, 57,* 1012-1030. (p. 483)

Meston, C. M., Trapnell, P. D., & Gorzalka, B. B. (1996). Ethnic and gender differences in sexuality: Variations in sexual behavior between Asian and non-Asian university students. *Archives of Sexual Behavior, 25,* 33-72. (p. 485)

Metcalfe, J. (1998). Cognitive optimism: Self-deception or memory-based processing heuristics. *Personality and Social Psychology Review, 2,* 100-110. (p. 403)

Meyer, I. H. (2003). Prejudice, social stress, and mental health in lesbian, gay, and bisexual populations: Conceptual issues and research evidence. *Psychological Bulletin, 129,* 674-697. (p. 640)

Meyer-Bahlburg, H. F. L. (1995). Psychoneuroendocrinology and sexual pleasure: The aspect of sexual orientation. In P. R. Abramson & S. D. Pinkerton (Eds.), *Sexual nature/sexual culture.* Chicago: University of Chicago Press. (p. 491)

Mezulis, A. M., Abramson, L. Y., Hyde, J. S., & Hankin, B. L. (2004). Is there a universal positivity bias in attributions? A meta-analytic review of individual, developmental, and cultural differences in the self-serving attributional bias. *Psychological Bulletin, 130,* 711-747. (p. 634)

Michaels, J. W., Bloomel, J. M., Brocato, R. M., Linkous, R. A., & Rowe, J. S. (1982). Social facilitation and inhibition in a natural setting. *Replications in Social Psychology, 2,* 21-24. (p. 738)

Michel, G. F. (1981). Right-handedness: A consequence of infant supine head-orientation preference? *Science, 212,* 685-687. (p. 88)

Middlebrooks, J. C., & Green, D. M. (1991). Sound localization by human listeners. *Annual Review of Psychology, 42,* 135-159. (p. 219)

Mikkelsen, T. S., & 66 others (2005). Initial sequence of the chimpanzee genome and comparison with the human genome. *Nature, 437,* 69-87. (p. 96)

Mikulincer, M., Babkoff, H., Caspy, T., & Sing, H. (1989). The effects of 72 hours of sleep loss on psychological variables. *British Journal of Psychology, 80,* 145-162. (p. 280)

Mikulincer, M., Florian, V., & Hirschberger, G. (2003). The existential function of close relationships: Introducing death into the science of love. *Personality and Social Psychology Review, 7,* 20-40. (p. 606)

Mikulincer, M., & Shaver, P. R. (2001). Attachment theory and intergroup bias: Evidence that priming the secure base schema attenuates negative reactions to our-groups. *Journal of Personality and Social Psychology, 81,* 97-115. (p. 747)

Mikulincer, M., & Shaver, P. R. (2005). Attachment theory and emotions in close relationships: Exploring the attachment-related dynamics of emotional reactions to relational events. *Personal Relationships, 12,* 149-168. (p. 158)

Milan, R. J., Jr., & Kilmann, P. R. (1987). Interpersonal factors in premarital contraception. *Journal of Sex Research, 23,* 289-321. (p. 485)

Miles, D. R., & Carey, G. (1997). Genetic and environmental architecture of human aggression. *Journal of Personality and Social Psychology, 72,* 207-217. (p. 749)

Milgram, S. (1963). Behavioral study of obedience. *Journal of Abnormal & Social Psychology, 67*(4), 371-378. (p. 734)

Milgram, S. (1974). *Obedience to authority.* New York: Harper & Row. (pp. 734, 735)

Miller, E. J., Smith, J. E., & Trembath, D. L. (2000). The "skinny" on body size requests in personal ads. *Sex Roles, 43,* 129-141. (p. 584)

Miller, G. (2004). Axel, Buck share award for deciphering how the nose knows. *Science, 306,* 207. (p. 232)

Miller, G. A. (1956). The magical number seven, plus or minus two: Some limits on our capacity for processing information. *Psychological Review, 63,* 81-97. (p. 362)

Miller, G. A. (1962). *Psychology: The science of mental life.* New York: Harper & Row. (p. 606)

Miller, J. G., & Bersoff, D. M. (1995). Development in the context of everyday family relationships: Culture, interpersonal morality and adaptation. In M. Killen and D. Hart (Eds.), *Morality in everyday life: A developmental perspective.* New York: Cambridge University Press. (p. 168)

Miller, K. I., & Monge, P. R. (1986). Participation, satisfaction, and productivity: A meta-analytic review. *Academy of Management Journal, 29,* 727-753. (p. 626)

Miller, L. (2005, January 4). U.S. airlines have 34 deaths in 3 years. Associated Press. (p. 404)

Miller, L. C., Putcha-Bhagavatula, A., & Pedersen, W. C. (2002). Men's and women's mating preferences: Distinct evolutionary mechanisms? *Current Directions in Psychological Science, 11,* 88-93. (p. 112)

Miller, L. K. (1999). The Savant Syndrome: Intellectual impairment and exceptional skill. *Psychological Bulletin, 125,* 31-46. (p. 434)

Miller, M. (2005, March 7). Effects of laughter and mental stress on endothelial function: Potential impact of entertainment. Paper presented to the Scientific Session of the American College of Cardiology, Orlando. (p. 565)

Miller, N. E. (1985, February). Rx: biofeedback. *Psychology Today,* pp. 54-59. (p. 570)

Miller, N. E. (1995). Clinical-experimental interactions in the development of neuroscience: A primer for nonspecialists and lessons for young scientists. *American Psychologist, 50,* 901-911. (p. 475)

Miller, N. E., & Brucker, B. S. (1979). A learned visceral response apparently independent of skeletal ones in patients paralyzed by spinal lesions. In N. Birbaumer & H. D. Kimmel (Eds.), *Biofeedback and self-regulation.* Hillsdale, NJ: Erlbaum. (p. 570)

Miller, P. A., Eisenberg, N., Fabes, R. A., & Shell, R. (1996). Relations of moral reasoning and vicarious emotion to young children's prosocial behavior toward peers and adults. *Developmental Psychology, 32,* 210-219. (p. 168)

Miller, P. C., Lefcourt, H. M., Holmes, J. G., Ware, E. E., & Saleh, W. E. (1986). Marital locus of control and marital problem solving. *Journal of Personality and Social Psychology, 51,* 161-169. (p. 625)

Miller, S. D., Blackburn, T., Scholes, G., White, G. L., & Mamalis, N. (1991). Optical differences in multiple personality disorder: A second look. *Journal of Nervous and Mental Disease, 179,* 132-135. (p. 657)

Mills, M., & Melhuish, E. (1974). Recognition of mother's voice in early infancy. *Nature, 252,* 123-124. (p. 143)

Milner, D. A. (2003). Visual awareness and the primate brain. In M. A. Jeeves (Ed.), *Human nature.* London: Routledge. (p. 211)

Milton, J., & Wiseman, R. (2001). Does psi exist? Reply to Storm and Ertel (2001). *Psychological Bulletin, 127,* 434–438. (p. 267)

Milton, J., & Wiseman, R. (2002). A response to Storm and Ertel (2002). *Journal of Parapsychology, 66,* 183–185. (p. 267)

Mineka, S. (1985). The frightful complexity of the origins of fears. In F. R. Brush & J. B. Overmier (Eds.), *Affect, conditioning and cognition: Essays on the determinants of behavior.* Hillsdale, NJ: Erlbaum. (p. 533)

Mineka, S., & Suomi, S. J. (1978). Social separation in monkeys. *Psychological Bulletin, 85,* 1376–1400. (p. 159)

Mineka, S., & Sutton, S. K. (1992). Cognitive biases and the emotional disorders. *Psychological Science, 3,* 65–69. (p. 535)

Mineka, S., & Zinbarg, R. (1996). Conditioning and ethological models of anxiety disorders: Stress-in-dynamic-context anxiety models. In D. Hope (Ed.), *Perspectives on anxiety, panic, and fear. Nebraska symposium on motivation.* Lincoln, NE: University of Nebraska Press. (pp. 633, 654, 655)

Miner-Rubino, K., & Winter, D. G., & Stewart, A. J. (2004). Gender, social class, and the subjective experience of aging: Self-perceived personality change from early adulthood to late midlife. *Personality and Social Psychology Bulletin, 30,* 1599–1610. (p. 189)

Mingroni, M. A. (2004). The secular rise in IQ: Giving heterosis a closer look. *Intelligence, 32,* 65–83. (p. 448)

Mirescu, C., Peters, J. D., & Gould, E. (2004). Early life experience alters response of adult neurogenesis to stress. *Nature Neuroscience, 7,* 841–846. (p. 159)

Mischel, W. (1968). *Personality and assessment.* New York: Wiley. (p. 620)

Mischel, W. (1981). Current issues and challenges in personality. In L. T. Benjamin, Jr. (Ed.), *The G. Stanley Hall Lecture Series* (Vol. 1). Washington, DC: American Psychological Association. (p. 630)

Mischel, W. (1984). Convergences and challenges in the search for consistency. *American Psychologist, 39,* 351–364. (p. 620)

Mischel, W. (2004). Toward an integrative science of the person. *Annual Review of Psychology, 55,* 1–22. (p. 620)

Mischel, W., Shoda, Y., & Peake, P. K. (1988). The nature of adolescent competencies predicted by preschool delay of gratification. *Journal of Personality and Social Psychology, 54,* 687–696. (p. 170)

Mischel, W., Shoda, Y., & Rodriguez, M. L. (1989). Delay of gratification in children. *Science, 244,* 933–938. (pp. 170, 330)

Miserandino, M. (1991). Memory and the seven dwarfs. *Teaching of Psychology, 18,* 169–171. (p. 370)

Mita, T. H., Dermer, M., & Knight, J. (1977). Reversed facial images and the mere-exposure hypothesis. *Journal of Personality and Social Psychology, 35,* 597–601. (p. 759)

Mitchell, T. R., Thompson, L., Peterson, E., & Cronk, R. (1997). Temporal adjustments in the evaluation of events: The "rosy view." *Journal of Experimental Social Psychology, 33,* 421–448. (p. 358)

MMWR. (1999, April 2). Tobacco use among middle and high school students—Florida, 1998 and 1999. *Morbidity and Mortality Weekly Report, 48,* 248–253. (pp. 571–582)

Moffitt, T. E. (2005). The new look of behavioral genetics in developmental psychopathology: Gene-environment interplay in antisocial behaviors. *Psychological Bulletin, 131,* 533–554. (p. 679)

Moffitt, T. E., Caspi, A., Harrington, H., & Milne, B. J. (2002). Males on the life-course-persistent and adolescence-limited antisocial pathways: Follow-up at age 26 years. *Development and Psychopathology, 14,* 179–207. (p. 194)

Moghaddam, F. M. (2005). The staircase to terrorism: A psychological exploration. *American Psychologist, 60,* 161–169. (p. 740)

Mohn, J. K., Tingle, L. R., & Finger, R. (2003). An analysis of the causes of the decline in non-marital birth and pregnancy rates for teens from 1991 to 1995. *Adolescent and Family Health, 3,* 39–47. (p. 487)

Moises, H. W., Zoega, T., & Gottesman, I. I. (2002, 3 July). The glial growth factors deficiency and synaptic destabilization hypothesis of schizophrenia. *BMC Psychiatry, 2*(8) (www.biomedcentral.com/1471-244X/2/8). (p. 674)

Mokdad, A. H., Marks, J. S., Stroup, D. F., & Gerberding, J. L. (2004). Actual causes of death in the United States, 2000. *Journal of the American Medical Association, 291,* 1238–1245. (p. 549)

Mollica, R. F., McInnes, K., Pham, T., Fawzi, M. C. S., Murphy, E., & Lin, L. (1998). The dose-effect relationships between torture and psychiatric symptoms in Vietnamese ex-political detainees and a comparison group. *Journal of Nervous and Mental Diseases, 186,* 543–553. (p. 652)

Monaghan, P. (1992, September 23). Professor of psychology stokes a controversy on the reliability and repression of memory. *Chronicle of Higher Education,* pp. A9–A10. (p. 389)

Mondloch, C. J., Lewis, T. L., Budreau, D. R., Maurer, D., Dannemiller, J. L., Stephens, B. R., & Kleiner-Gathercoal, K. A. (1999). Face perception during early infancy. *Psychological Science, 10,* 419–422. (p. 143)

Money, J. (1987). Sin, sickness, or status? Homosexual gender identity and psychoneuroendocrinology. *American Psychologist, 42,* 384–399. (pp. 489, 491)

Money, J. (1988). *Gay, straight, and in-between.* New York: Oxford University Press. (p. 753)

Money, J., Berlin, F. S., Falck, A., & Stein, M. (1983). *Antiandrogenic and counseling treatment of sex offenders.* Baltimore: Department of Psychiatry and Behavioral Sciences, The Johns Hopkins University School of Medicine. (p. 483)

Moody, R. (1976). *Life after life.* Harrisburg, PA: Stackpole Books. (p. 309)

Mook, D. G. (1983). In defense of external invalidity. *American Psychologist, 38,* 379–387. (p. 45)

Moorcroft, W. (1993). *Sleep, dreaming, and sleep disorders: An introduction* (2nd ed.). Landam, MD: University Press of America. (p. 281)

Moorcroft, W. H. (2003). *Understanding sleep and dreaming.* New York: Kluwer/Plenum. (pp. 276, 282)

Moore, D. W. (2003, November 23). Many Americans deluding themselves about weight. *Gallup Poll* (poll.gallup.com). (p. 588)

Moore, D. W. (2004, December 17). Sweet dreams go with a good night's sleep. Gallup News Service (www.gallup.com). (p. 279)

Mor, N., & Winquist, J. (2002). Self-focused attention and negative affect: A meta-analysis. *Psychological Bulletin, 128,* 638–662. (p. 667)

Moreland, R. L., & Beach, S. R. (1992). Exposure effects in the classroom: The development of affinity among students. *Journal of Experimental Social Psychology, 28,* 255–276. (p. 759)

Moreland, R. L., & Zajonc, R. B. (1982). Exposure effects in person perception: Familiarity, similarity, and attraction. *Journal of Experimental Social Psychology, 18,* 395–415. (p. 758)

Morell, V. (1995). Attacking the causes of "silent" infertility. *Science, 269,* 775–776. (p. 557)

Morell, V. (1995). Zeroing in on how hormones affect the immune system. *Science, 269,* 773–775. (p. 486)

Morelli, G. A., Rogoff, B., Oppenheim, D., & Goldsmith, D. (1992). Cultural variation in infants' sleeping arrangements: Questions of independence. *Developmental Psychology, 26,* 604–613. (p. 124)

Morey, R. A., Inan, S., Mitchell, T. V., Perkins, D. O., Lieberman, J. A., & Belger, A. (2005). Imaging frontostriatal function in ultra-high-risk, early, and chronic schizophrenia during executive processing. *Archives of General Psychiatry, 62,* 254–262. (p. 672)

Morgan, A. B., & Lilienfeld, S. O. (2000). A meta-analytic review of the relation between antisocial behavior and neuropsychological measures of executive function. *Clinical Psychology Review, 20,* 113–136. (p. 678)

Morgan, B., & Korschgen, A. (2001). Psychology career exploration made easy. *Eye on Psi Chi, 35*–36. (p. A-2)

Morin, R., & Brossard, M. A. (1997, March 4). Communication breakdown on drugs. *Washington Post,* pp. A1, A6. (p. 172)

Morris, J. S., Ohman, A., & Dolan, R. (1998). Conscious and unconscious emotional learning in the human amygdala. *Nature, 393,* 467–470. (p. 535)

Morrison, A. R. (2003). The brain on night shift. *Cerebrum, 5*(3), 23-36. (pp. 275, 278)

Mortensen, E. L., Michaelsen, K. F., Sanders, S. A., & Reinisch, J. M. (2002). The association between duration of breastfeeding and adult intelligence. *Journal of the American Medical Association, 287,* 2365-2371. (p. 36)

Mortensen, P. B. (1999). Effects of family history and place and season of birth on the risk of schizophrenia. *New England Journal of Medicine, 340,* 603-608. (p. 673)

Moruzzi, G., & Magoun, H. W. (1949). Brain stem reticular formation and activation of the EEG. *Electroencephalography and Clinical Neurophysiology, 1,* 455-473. (p. 71)

Moscovici, S. (1985). Social influence and conformity. In G. Lindzey & E. Aronson (Eds.), *The handbook of social psychology* (3rd ed). Hillsdale, N.J.: Erlbaum. (p. 741)

Moser, P. W. (1987, May). Are cats smart? Yes, at being cats. *Discover,* pp. 77-88. (p. 208)

Mosher, D. L., & Anderson, R. D. (1986). Macho personality, sexual aggression, and reactions to guided imagery of realistic rape. *Journal of Research in Personality, 20,* 77-94. (p. 297)

Moss, A. J., Allen, K. F., Giovino, G. A., & Mills, S. L. (1992, December 2). Recent trends in adolescent smoking, smoking-update correlates, and expectations about the future. *Advance Data* No. 221 (from Vital and Health Statistics of the Centers for Disease Control and Prevention). (p. 576)

Moss, H. A., & Susman, E. J. (1980). Longitudinal study of personality development. In O. G. Brim, Jr., & J. Kagan (Eds.), *Constancy and change in human development.* Cambridge, MA: Harvard University Press. (p. 194)

Moyer, K. E. (1983). The physiology of motivation: Aggression as a model. In C. J. Scheier & A. M. Rogers (Eds.), *G. Stanley Hall Lecture Series* (Vol. 3). Washington, DC: American Psychological Association. (p. 749)

Mroczek, D. K. (2001). Age and emotion in adulthood. *Current Directions in Psychological Science, 10,* 87-90. (p. 189)

Mroczek, D. K., & Kolarz, D. M. (1998). The effect of age on positive and negative affect: A developmental perspective on happiness. *Journal of Personality and Social Psychology, 75,* 1333-1349. (p. 186)

Mroczek, D. K., & Spiro, A., III (2005). Change in life satisfaction during adulthood: Findings from the Veterans Affairs normative aging study. *Journal of Personality and Social Psychology, 88,* 189-202. (p. 544)

Muhlnickel, W. (1998). Article on tinnitus processing in the brain *Proceedings of the National Academy of Sciences, 95,* 10340-10343. (p. 79)

Muller, J. E., Mittleman, M. A., Maclure, M., Sherwood, J. B., & Tofler, G. H. (1996). Triggering myocardial infarction by sexual activity. *Journal of the American Medical Association, 275,* 1405-1409. (p. 482)

Muller, J. E., & Verrier, R. L. (1996). Triggering of sudden death—Lessons from an earthquake. *New England Journal of Medicine, 334,* 461. (p. 553)

Mullin, C. R., & Linz, D. (1995). Desensitization and resensitization to violence against women: Effects of exposure to sexually violent films on judgments of domestic violence victims. *Journal of Personality and Social Psychology, 69,* 449-459. (p. 346)

Mulrow, C. D. (1999, March). Treatment of depression—newer pharmacotherapies, summary. *Evidence Report/Technology Assessment, 7.* Agency for Health Care Policy and Research, Rockville, MD. (http://www.ahrq.gov/clinic/deprsumm.htm). (p. 713)

Murphy, G. E., & Wetzel, R. D. (1990). The lifetime risk of suicide in alcoholism. *Archives of General Psychiatry, 47,* 383-392. (p. 663)

Murphy, K. R., & Cleveland, J. N. (1995). *Understanding performance appraisal: Social, organizational, and goal-based perspectives.* Thousand Oaks, CA: Sage. (p. 504)

Murphy, S. T., Monahan, J. L., & Miller, L. C. (1998). Inference under the influence: The impact of alcohol and inhibition conflict on women's sexual decision making. *Personality and Social Psychology Bulletin, 24,* 517-528. (p. 299)

Murphy, S. T., Monahan, J. L., & Zajonc, R. B. (1995). Additivity of nonconscious affect: Combined effects of priming and exposure. *Journal of Personality and Social Psychology, 69,* 589-602. (p. 522)

Murphy, T. N. (1982). Pain: Its assessment and management. In R. J. Gatchel, A. Baum, & J. E. Singer (Eds.), *Handbook of psychology and health: Vol. I. Clinical psychology and behavioral medicine: Overlapping disciplines.* Hillsdale, NJ: Erlbaum. (p. 227)

Murray, B. (1998, May). Psychology is key to airline safety at Boeing. *The APA Monitor,* p. 36. (p. 263)

Murray, C., & Herrnstein, R. J. (1994, October 31). Race, genes and I.Q.—An apologia. *New Republic,* pp. 27-37. (p. 459)

Murray, C. J., & Lopez, A. D. (Eds.) (1996). *The global burden of disease: A comprehensive assessment of mortality and disability from diseases, injuries, and risk factors in 1990 and projected to 2020.* Cambridge, MA: Harvard University Press. (p. 640)

Murray, H. (1938). *Explorations in personality.* New York: Oxford University Press. (p. 504)

Murray, H. A. (1933). The effect of fear upon estimates of the maliciousness of other personalities. *Journal of Social Psychology, 4,* 310-329. (p. 602)

Murray, H. A., & Wheeler, D. R. (1937). A note on the possible clairvoyance of dreams. *Journal of Psychology, 3,* 309-313. (p. 266)

Murray, J. E. (2000). Marital protection and marital selection: Evidence from a historical-prospective sample of American men. *Demography, 37,* 511-521. (p. 566)

Murray, R., Jones, P., O'Callaghan, E., Takei, N., & Sham, P. (1992). Genes, viruses, and neurodevelopmental schizophrenia. *Journal of Psychiatric Research, 26,* 225-235. (p. 673)

Murray, S. L., Bellavia, G. M., Rose, P., & Griffin, D. W. (2003). Once hurt, twice hurtful: How perceived regard regulates daily marital interactions. *Journal of Personality and Social Psychology, 84,* 126-147. (p. 261)

Murray, S. L., Rose, P., Bellavia, G. M., Holmes, J. G., & Kusche, A. G. (2002). When rejection stings: How self-esteem constrains relationship-enhancement processes. *Journal of Personality and Social Psychology, 83,* 556-573. (p. 632)

Musallam, S., Corneil, B. D., Greger, B., Scherberger, H., & Andersen, R. A. (2004). Cognitive control signals for neural prosthetics. *Science, 305,* 258-262. (p. 78)

Musick, M. A., Herzog, A. R., & House, J. S. (1999). Volunteering and mortality among older adults: Findings from a national sample. *Journals of Gerontology, 54B,* 173-180. (p. 573)

Mustanski, B. S., & Bailey, J. M. (2003). A therapist's guide to the genetics of human sexual orientation," *Sexual and Relationship Therapy 18,* 1468-1479. (p. 490)

Mustanski, B. S., Bailey, J. M., & Kaspar, S. (2002). Dermatoglyphics, handedness, sex, and sexual orientation. *Archives of Sexual Behavior, 31,* 113-122. (p. 491)

Mydans, S. (2002, May 17). In Pakistan, rape victims are the 'criminals.' *New York Times* (www.nytimes.com). (p. 748)

Myers, D. G. (1993). *The pursuit of happiness.* New York: Avon Books. (pp. 537, 538, 544)

Myers, D. G. (2000). *The American paradox: Spiritual hunger in an age of plenty.* New Haven: Yale University Press. (pp. 121, 544, 752)

Myers, D. G. (2001, December). Do we fear the right things? *American Psychological Society Observer,* p. 3. (p. 404)

Myers, D. G. (2002). *Intuition: Its powers and perils.* New Haven: Yale University Press. (pp. 5, 35, 111, 201)

Myers, D. G. (2005). *Social psychology,* 8th edition. New York: McGraw-Hill. (p. 634)

Myers, D. G., & Bishop, G. D. (1970). Discussion effects on racial attitudes. *Science, 169,* 78-779. (p. 740)

Myers, D. G., & Diener, E. (1995). Who is happy? *Psychological Science, 6,* 10-19. (p. 544)

Myers, D. G., & Diener, E. (1996, May). The pursuit of happiness. *Scientific American,* p. 544)

Myers, D. G., & Scanzoni, L. D. (2005). *What God has joined together? A Christian case for gay marriage.* San Francisco: HarperSanFrancisco. (pp. 187, 488)

Myers, I. B. (1987). *Introduction to type: A description of the theory and applications of the Myers-Briggs Type Indicator.* Palo Alto, CA: Consulting Psychologists Press. (p. 613)

Myerson, J., Rank, M. R., Raines, F. Q., & Schnitzler, M. A. (1998). Race and general cognitive ability: The myth of diminishing returns to education. *Psychological Science, 9,* 139–142. (p. 461)

Nagourney, A. (2002, September 25). For remarks on Iraq, Gore gets praise and scorn. *New York Times* (www.nytimes.com). (p. 726)

Napolitan, D. A., & Goethals, G. R. (1979). The attribution of friendliness. *Journal of Experimental Social Psychology, 15,* 105–113. (p. 724)

Narrow, W. E., Rae, D. S., Robins, L. N., & Regier, D. A. (2002). Revised prevalence estimates of mental disorders in the United States. *Archives of General Psychiatry, 59,* 115–123. (p. 680)

Nash, M. R. (2001, July). The truth and the hype of hypnosis. *Scientific American,* pp. 47–55. (p. 293)

National Academy of Sciences. (1999). *Marijuana and medicine: Assessing the science base* (by J. A. Benson, Jr. & S. J. Watson, Jr.). Washington, DC: National Academy Press. (p. 303)

National Academy of Sciences. (2001). *Exploring the biological contributions to human health: Does sex matter?* Washington, DC: Institute of Medicine, National Academy Press. (p. 130)

National Academy of Sciences. (2002). *The polygraph and lie detection.* Washington, DC: Committee to Review the Scientific Evidence on the Polygraph, National Research Council. (p. 303)

National Academy of Sciences, Institute of Medicine. (1982). *Marijuana and health.* Washington, DC: National Academic Press. (p. 303)

National Center for Health Statistics. (1990). *Health, United States, 1989.* Washington, DC: U.S. Department of Health and Human Services. (pp. 179, 486)

National Center for Health Statistics. (1991). Family structure and children's health: United States, 1988, *Vital and Health Statistics, Series 10, No. 178,* CHHS Publication No. PHS 91-1506 by Deborah A. Dawson. (p. 487)

National Center for Health Statistics. (1992, May). *Health United States 1991.* Hyattsville, MD: Department of Health and Human Services Pub. No. (PHS) 92-1232, Table 27. (p. 178)

National Center for Health Statistics. (2002, September 16). Deaths: Leading Causes for 2000. *National Vital Statistics Reports, 50,* 16. Hyattsville, MD: National Center for Health Statistics. (p. 550)

National Center for Health Statistics. (2004, December 15). Marital status and health: United States, 1999–2002 (by Charlotte A. Schoenborn). *Advance Data from Vital and Human Statistics,* number 351. Centers for Disease Control and Prevention. (p. 566)

National Institute of Mental Health. (1982). *Television and behavior: Ten years of scientific progress and implications for the eighties.* Washington, DC: U. S. Government Printing Office. (p. 345)

National Institute of Mental Health. (1999). *ADHD: Attention deficit hyperactivity disorder.* Bethesda, MD: National Institute of Health Publication No 96-3572, 1994, update July 1, 1999. (p. 641)

National Institute of Mental Health. (2003). *Attention deficit hyperactivity disorder.* Bethesda, MD: National Institute of Mental Health. (p. 641)

National Institute on Drug Abuse. (2004). NIDA InfoFacts: Marijuana. www.nida.nih.gov/Infofax/marijuana.html. (p. 303)

National Institutes of Health. (1998). Clinical guidelines on the identification evaluation and treatment of overweight and obesity in adults. Executive summary, Obesity Education Initiative, National Heart, Lung, and Blood Institute. (p. 590)

National Research Council. (1987). *Risking the future: Adolescent sexuality, pregnancy, and childbearing.* Washington, DC: National Academy Press. (p. 485)

National Research Council. (1990). *Human factors research needs for an aging population.* Washington, DC: National Academy Press. (p. 178)

National Safety Council. (2005, October 3). Passenger deaths and death rates, from *Injury Facts* (via correspondence with Kevin T. Fearn, Research & Statistical Services Department). (p. 404)

Naylor, T. H. (1990). Redefining corporate motivation, Swedish style. *Christian Century, 107,* 566–570. (p. 509)

NCTV News. (1987, July-August). More research links harmful effects to non-violent porn, p. 12. (p. 753)

Neeleman, J., & Persaud, R. (1995). Why do psychiatrists neglect religion? *British Journal of Medical Psychology, 68,* 169–178. (p. 708)

Neese, R. M. (1991, November/December). What good is feeling bad? The evolutionary benefits of psychic pain. *The Sciences,* pp. 30–37. (pp. 226, 322)

Neisser, U. (1979). The control of information pickup in selective looking. In A. D. Pick (Ed.), *Perception and its development: A tribute to Eleanor J. Gibson.* Hillsdale, NJ: Erlbaum. (p. 238)

Neisser, U. (1997). The ecological study of memory. *Philosophical Transactions of the Royal Society of London, 352,* 1697–1701. (p. 448)

Neisser, U. (1998). *The rising curve: Long-term gains in IQ and related measures.* Washington, DC: American Psychological Association. (p. 448)

Neisser, U., Boodoo, G., Bouchard, T. J., Jr., Boykin, A. W., Brody, N., Ceci, S. J., Halpern, D. F., Loehlin, J. C., Perloff, R., Sternberg, R. J., & Urbina, S. (1996). Intelligence: Knowns and unknowns. *American Psychologist, 51,* 77–101. (pp. 455, 459, 465)

Neisser, U., Winograd, E., & Weldon, M. S. (1991). Remembering the earthquake: "What I experienced" vs. "How I heard the news." Paper presented to the Psychonomic Society convention. (p. 366)

Neitz, J., Geist, T., & Jacobs, G. H. (1989). Color vision in the dog. *Visual Neuroscience, 3,* 119–125. (p. 213)

Nell, V. (2002). Why young men drive dangerously: Implications for injury prevention. *Current Directions in Psychological Science, 11,* 75–79. (p. 111)

Nelson, E. C., Heath, A. C., Madden, P. A. F., Cooper, M. L., Dinwiddie, S. H., Bucholtz, K. K., Glowinski, A., McLaughlin, T., Dunne, M. P., Statham, D. J., & Martin, N. G. (2002). Association between self-reported childhood sexual abuse and adverse psychosocial outcomes. *Archives of General Psychiatry, 59,* 139–145. (p. 159)

Nelson, G., Hoon, M. A., Chandrashekar, J., Zhang, Y., Ryba, N. J., Nicholas, J. P., & Zuker, C. S. (2001). Mammalian sweet taste receptors. *Cell, 106,* 381–390. (p. 229)

Nelson, M. D., Saykin, A. J., Flashman, L. A., & Riordan, H. J. (1998). Hippocampal volume reduction in schizophrenia as assessed by magnetic resonance imaging. *Archives of General Psychiatry, 55,* 433–440. (p. 673)

Nelson, N. (1988). *A meta-analysis of the life-event/health paradigm: The influence of social support.* Philadelphia: Temple University Ph.D. dissertation. (p. 566)

Nephew, T. M., Williams, G. D., Stinson, F. S., Nguyen, K., & Dufour, M. C. (1999). Surveillance report #51: Apparent per capita alcohol consumption: National, state, and regional trends, 1977–1997. Bethesda, MD: National Institute on Alcohol Abuse and Alcoholism. (p. 305)

Nesca, M., & Koulack, D. (1994). Recognition memory, sleep and circadian rhythms. *Canadian Journal of Experimental Psychology, 48,* 359–379. (p. 380)

Nestler, E. J., & Malenka, R. C. (2004, March). The addicted brain. *Scientific American,* pp. 79–83. (p. 306)

Neubauer, P. B., & Neubauer, A. (1990). *Nature's thumbprint: The new genetics of personality.* Reading, MA: Addison-Wesley. (p. 116)

Neugarten, B. L., Wood, V., Kraines, R. J., & Loomis, B. (1963). Women's attitudes toward the menopause. *Vita Humana, 6,* 140–151. (p. 176)

Neumann, R., & Strack, F. (2000). "Mood contagion": The automatic transfer of mood between persons. *Journal of Personality and Social Psychology, 79,* 211–223. (p. 731)

Nevin, J. A. (1988). Behavioral momentum and the partial reinforcement effect. *Psychological Bulletin, 103,* 44–56. (p. 331)

Newberg, A., & D'Aquili, E. (2001). *Why God won't go away: Brain science and the biology of belief*. New York: Simon and Schuster. (p. 571)

Newcomb, M. D., & Harlow, L. L. (1986). Life events and substance use among adolescents: Mediating effects of perceived loss of control and meaninglessness in life. *Journal of Personality and Social Psychology, 51*, 564–577. (p. 306)

Newcombe, N. S., Drummey, A. B., Fox, N. A., Lie, E., & Ottinger-Alberts, W. (2000). Remembering early childhood: How much, how, and why (or why not). *Current Directions in Psychological Science, 9*, 55–58. (p. 146)

Newman, A. J., Bavelier, D., Corina, D., Jezzard, P., & Neville, H. J. (2002). A critical period for right hemisphere recruitment in American Sign Language processing. *Nature Neuroscience, 5*, 76–80. (p. 417)

Newman, L. S., & Baumeister, R. F. (1996). Toward an explanation of the UFO abduction phenomenon: Hypnotic, elaboration, extraterrestrial sadomasochism, and spurious memories. *Psychological Inquiry, 7*, 99–126. (p. 292)

Newman, L. S., Duff, K. J., & Baumeister, R. F. (1997). A new look at defensive projection: Thought suppression, accessibility, and biased person perception. *Journal of Personality and Social Psychology, 72*, 980–1001. (p. 606)

Newman, L. S., & Ruble, D. N. (1988). Stability and change in self-understanding: The early elementary school years. *Early Child Development and Care, 40*, 77–99. (p. 161)

Newman, M. L., Pennebaker, J. W., Berry, D. S., & Richards, J. M. (2003). Lying words: Predicting deception from linguistic style. *Personality and Social Psychology Bulletin, 29*, 665–675. (p. 521)

Newport, E. L. (1990). Maturational constraints on language learning. *Cognitive Science, 14*, 11–28. (p. 417)

Newport, F. (2001, February). Americans see women as emotional and affectionate, men as more aggressive. *The Gallup Poll Monthly*, pp. 34–38. (p. 526)

Newport, F. (2002, July 29). Bush job approval update. Gallup News Service (www.gallup.com/poll/releases/pr020729.asp). (p. 768)

Newport, F., Moore, D. W., Jones, J. M., & Saad, L. (2003, March 21). Special release: American opinion on the war. *Gallup Poll Tuesday Briefing* (www.gallup.com). (p. 729)

Newton, I. (1704). *Opticks, or a treatise of the reflections, refractions, inflections & colours of light*. Oxford, England Whittlesey House, McGraw-Hill, 1931. (p. 212).

Neylan, T. C., Metzler, T. J., Best, S. R., Weiss, D. S., Fagan, J. A., Liberman, A., Rogers, C., Vedantham, K., Brunet, A., Lipsey, T. L., & Marmar, C. R. (2002). Critical incident exposure and sleep quality in police officers. *Psychosomatic Medicine, 64*, 345–352. (p. 283)

Nezlek, J. B. (2001). Daily psychological adjustment and the planfulness of day-to-day behavior. *Journal of Social and Clinical Psychology, 20*, 452–475. (p. 625)

Ng, S. H. (1990). Androcentric coding of *man* and *his* in memory by language users. *Journal of Experimental Social Psychology, 26*, 455–464. (p. 419)

NHTSA. (2000). Traffic safety facts 1999: Older population. Washington, DC: National Highway Traffic Safety Administration (National Transportation Library: www.ntl.bts.gov). (p. 179)

Niccols, G. A. (1994). Fetal alcohol syndrome: Implications for psychologists. *Clinical Psychology Review, 14*, 91–111. (p. 142)

NICHHD Early Child Care Research Network. (2002). Structure/process/outcome: Direct and indirect effects of caregiving quality on young children's development. *Psychological Science, 13*, 199–206. (p. 160)

NICHHD Early Child Care Research Network. (2003). Does amount of time spent in child care predict socioemotional adjustment during the transition to kindergarten? *Child Development, 74*, 976–1005. (p. 160)

Nickell, J. (1996, May/June). A study of fantasy proneness in the thirteen cases of alleged encounters in John Mack's *Abduction*. *Skeptical Inquirer*, pp. 18–20, 54. (p. 292)

Nickerson, R. S. (1998). Applied experimental psychology. *Applied Psychology: An International Review, 47*, 155–173. (p. 262)

Nickerson, R. S. (1999). How we know—and sometimes misjudge—what others know: Imputing one's own knowledge to others. *Psychological Bulletin, 125*, 737–759. (p. 262)

Nickerson, R. S., & Adams, M. J. (1979). Long-term memory for a common object. *Cognitive Psychology, 11*, 287–307. (p. 377)

Nicol, S. E., & Gottesman, I. I. (1983). Clues to the genetics and neurobiology of schizophrenia. *American Scientist, 71*, 398–404. (p. 675)

Nicolaus, L. K., Cassel, J. F., Carlson, R. B., & Gustavson, C. R. (1983). Taste-aversion conditioning of crows to control predation on eggs. *Science, 220*, 212–214. (p. 322)

Nicolelis, M. A. L., & Chapin, J. K. (2002, October). Controlling robots with the mind. *Scientific American*, pp. 46–53. (p. 78)

NIDA. (2002). Methamphetamine abuse and addiction. *Research Report Series*. National Institute on Drug Abuse, NIH Publication Number 02–4210. (p. 300)

NIDA. (2005, May). Methamphetamine. *NIDA Info Facts*. National Institute on Drug Abuse. (p. 300)

Nier, J. A. (2004). Why does the "above average effect" exist? Demonstrating idiosyncratic trait definition. *Teaching of Psychology, 31*, 53–54. (p. 634)

Nightingale, F. (1860/1969). *Notes on nursing*. Mineola, NY: Dover. (p. 568)

Nigro, G. (1984). Cited by U. Neisser, The role of invariant structures in the control of movement. In M. Frese & J. Sabini (Eds.), *Goal directed behavior: The concept of action in psychology*. Hillsdale, NJ: Erlbaum. (p. 421)

NIH. (2001, July 20). Workshop summary: Scientific evidence on condom effectiveness for sexually transmitted disease (STD) prevention. Bethesda: National Institute of Allergy and Infectious Diseases, National Institutes of Health. (p. 486)

NIMH. (2002, April 26). U.S. suicide rates by age, gender, and racial group. National Institute of Mental Health (www.nimh.nih.gov/research/suichart.cfm). (p. 662)

Nisbett, R. E. (1987). Lay personality theory: Its nature, origin, and utility. In N. E. Grunberg, R. E. Nisbett, & others, *A distinctive approach to psychological research: The influence of Stanley Schachter* (Hillsdale, NJ: 1987). (p. 502)

Nisbett, R. E., & Borgida, E. (1975). Attribution and the psychology of prediction. *Journal of Personality and Social Psychology, 32*, 932–943. (p. 408)

Nisbett, R. E., & Cohen, D. (1996). *Culture of honor: The psychology of violence in the South*. Boulder, CO: Westview Press. (p. 752)

Nisbett, R. E., & Ross, L. (1980). *Human inference: Strategies and shortcomings of social judgment*. Englewood Cliffs, NJ: Prentice-Hall. (p. 401)

Noel, J. G., Forsyth, D. R., & Kelley, K. N. (1987). Improving the performance of failing students by overcoming their self-serving attributional biases. *Basic and Applied Social Psychology, 8*, 151–162. (p. 627)

Nolen-Hoeksema, S. (2001). Gender differences in depression. *Current Directions in Psychological Science, 10*, 173–176. (p. 666)

Nolen-Hoeksema, S. (2003). *Women who think too much: How to break free of overthinking and reclaim your life*. New York: Holt. (pp. 666, 667)

Nolen-Hoeksema, S., & Larson, J. (1999). *Coping with loss*. Mahwah, NJ: Erlbaum. (p. 191)

NORC (National Opinion Research Center). (1985, October/November). Images of the world. *Public Opinion*, p. 38. (p. 611)

NORC (National Opinion Research Center). (2002). Percent saying sex with person other than spouse is always or almost always wrong. National Opinion Research Center General Social Survey of 2000 (www.csa.berkeley.edu:7502). (p. 492)

Norcross, J. C. (Ed.). (2002). *Psychotherapy relationships that work: Therapist contributions and responsiveness to patient needs*. New York: Oxford University Press. (p. 704)

Norem, J. K. (2001). *The positive power of negative thinking: Using defensive pessimism to harness anxiety and perform at your peak*. Basic Books. (p. 627)

Norman, D. A. (1988). *The psychology of everyday things*. New York: Basic Books. (p. 261)

Norman, D. A. (2001). The perils of home theater (www.jnd.org/dn.mss/ProblemsOfHomeTheater.html). (p. 262)

Noroozian, M., Lofti, J., Gassemzadeh, H., Emami, H., & Mehrabi, Y. (2003). Academic achievement and learning abilities in left-handers: Guilt or gift? *Cortex, 38,* 779–785. (p. 88)

Norton, K. L., Olds, T. S., Olive, S., & Dank, S. (1996). Ken and Barbie at life size. *Sex Roles, 34,* 287–294. (p. 480)

Norton, M. B. (2002, October 31). *They called it witchcraft. New York Times* (www.nytimes.com). (p. 747)

Nowak, R. (1994). Nicotine scrutinized as FDA seeks to regulate cigarettes. *Science, 263,* 1555–1556. (p. 577)

Nowell, A., & Hedges, L. V. (1998). Trends in gender differences in academic achievement from 1960 to 1994: An analysis of differences in mean, variance, and extreme scores. *Sex Roles, 39,* 21–43. (p. 464)

NSF. (2001, October 24). Public bounces back after Sept. 11 attacks, national study shows. *NSF News,* National Science Foundation (www.nsf.gov/od/lpa/news/press/ol/pr0185.htm). (pp. 553–554)

Nuttin, J. M., Jr. (1987). Affective consequences of mere ownership: The name letter effect in twelve European languages. *European Journal of Social Psychology, 17,* 381–402. (p. 758)

Oakhill, J., Garnham, A., & Johnson-Laird, P. N. (1990). Belief bias effects in syllogistic reasoning. In D. J. Gilhooly, M. T. G. Keane, R. H. Logie, & G. Erdos (Eds.), *Lines of thinking* (Vol. 1). Chichester, England: Wiley. (p. 407)

Oakhill, J. V., Johnson-Laird, P. N., & Garnham, A. (1989). Believability and syllogistic reasoning. *Cognition, 31,* 117–140. (p. 406)

O'Connor, A. (2004, February 6). Study details 30-year increase in calorie consumption. *New York Times* (www.nytimes.com). (p. 587)

O'Connor, A. (2004, May 14). Pressure to go along with abuse is strong, but some soldiers find strength to refuse. *New York Times* (www.nytimes.com). (p. 741)

O'Connor, P., & Brown, G. W. (1984). Supportive relationships: Fact or fancy? *Journal of Social and Personal Relationships, 1,* 159–175. (p. 708)

Oddone-Paolucci, E., Genuis, M., & Violato, C. (2000). A meta-analysis of the published research on the effects of pornography. In C. Violato, E. Oddone-Paolucci, & M. Genuis (Eds.), *The changing family and child development.* Aldershot, England: Ashgate. (p. 753)

O'Donnell, L., Stueve, A., O'Donnell, C., Duran, R., San Doval, A., Wilson, R. F., Haber, D., Perry, E., & Pleck, J. H. (2002). Long-term reduction in sexual initiation and sexual activity among urban middle schoolers in the reach for health service learning program. *Journal of Adolescent Health, 31,* 93–100. (p. 486)

Oetting, E. R., & Beauvais, F. (1987). Peer cluster theory, socialization characteristics, and adolescent drug use: A path analysis. *Journal of Counseling Psychology, 34,* 205–213. (p. 307)

Oetting, E. R., & Beauvais, F. (1990). Adolescent drug use: Findings of national and local surveys. *Journal of Social and Personal Relationships, 1,* 159–175. (p. 307)

Oettingen, G., & Mayer, D. (2002). The motivating function of thinking about the future: Expectations versus fantasies. *Journal of Personality and Social Psychology, 83,* 1198–1212. (p. 627)

Oettingen, G., & Seligman, M. E. P. (1990). Pessimism and behavioural signs of depression in East versus West Berlin. *European Journal of Social Psychology, 20,* 207–220. (p. 626)

Offer, D., Kaiz, M., Howard, K. I., & Bennett, E. S. (2000). The altering of reported experiences. *Journal of the American Academy of Child and Adolescent Psychiatry, 39,* pp. 735–742. (p. 385)

Offer, D., Ostrov, E., Howard, K. I., & Atkinson, R. (1988). *The teenage world: Adolescents' self-image in ten countries.* New York: Plenum. (p. 172)

Office of National Statistics. (2002). *The social and economic circumstances of adults with mental disorders* (report based on the analysis of the ONS Survey of Psychiatric Morbidity Among Adults in Great Britain carried out in 2000). Norwich: HMSO. (p. 680)

Ogden, C. L., Fryar, C. D., Carroll, M. D., & Flegal, K. M. (2004, October 27). Mean body weight, heights, and body mass index, Unites States 1960–2002. *Advance Data from Vital and Health Statistics,* No. 347. (p. 587)

Öhman, A. (1986). Face the beast and fear the face: Animal and social fears as prototypes for evolutionary analyses of emotion. *Psychophysiology, 23,* 123–145. (p. 655)

Öhman, A., Lundqvist, D., & Esteves, F. (2001). The face in the crowd revisited: A threat advantage with schematic stimuli. *Journal of Personality and Social Psychology, 80,* 381–396. (p. 524)

Öhman, A., & Mineka, S. (2003). The malicious serpent: Snakes as a prototypical stimulus for an evolved module of fear. *Current Directions in Psychological Science, 12,* 5–9. (p. 534)

Oishi, S., Diener, E. F., Lucas, R. E., & Suh, E. M. (1999). Cross-cultural variations in predictors of life satisfaction: Perspectives from needs and values. *Personality and Social Psychology Bulletin, 25,* 980–990. (p. 473)

O'Keeffe, C., & Wiseman, R. (2005). Testing alleged mediumship: Methods and results. *British Journal of Psychology, 96,* 165–179. (p. 617)

Okun, M. S., & 12 others (2004). What's in a "smile?" Intra-operative observations of contralateral smiles induced by deep brain stimulation. *Neurocase, 10,* 271–279. (p. 518)

Olds, J. (1958). Self-stimulation of the brain. *Science, 127,* 315–324. (p. 74)

Olds, J. (1975). Mapping the mind onto the brain. In F. G. Worden, J. P. Swazey, & G. Adelman (Eds.), *The neurosciences: Paths of discovery.* Cambridge, MA: MIT Press. (p. 74)

Olds, J., & Milner, P. (1954). Positive reinforcement produced by electrical stimulation of the septal area and other regions of rat brain. *Journal of Comparative and Physiological Psychology, 47,* 419–427. (p. 74)

O'Leary, V. E., & Ickovics, J. R. (1995). Resilience and thriving in response to challenge: An opportunity for a paradigm shift in women's health. *Women's Health: Research on Gender, Behavior, and Policy, 1,* 121–142. (p. 551)

Olfson, M., Gameroff, M. J., Marcus, S. C., & Jensen, P. S. (2003). National trends in the treatment of attention deficit hyperactivity disorder. *American Journal of Psychiatry, 160,* 1071–1077. (p. 641)

Olfson, M., Marcus, S. C., Wan, G. J., & Geissler, E. C. (2004). National trends in the outpatient treatment of anxiety disorders. *Journal of Clinical Psychiatry, 65,* 1166–1173. (p. 712)

Olfson, M., Shaffer, D., Marcus, S. C., & Greenberg, T. (2003). Relationship between antidepressant medication treatment and suicide in adolescents. *Archives of General Psychiatry, 60,* 978–982. (pp. 713, 715)

Olin, S. S., & Mednick, S. A. (1996). Risk factors of psychosis: Identifying vulnerable populations premorbidly. *Schizophrenia Bulletin, 22,* 223–240. (p. 676)

Oliner, S. P., & Oliner, P. M. (1988). *The altruistic personality: Rescuers of Jews in Nazi Europe.* New York: Free Press. (p. 344)

Oliver, M. B. (1994). Portrayals of crime, race, and aggression in "reality-based" police shows: A content analysis. *Journal of Broadcasting and Electronic Media, 38,* 179–192. (p. 344)

Olshansky, S. J., Carnes, B. A., & Cassel, C. K. (1993, April). The aging of the human species. *Scientific American,* pp. 46–52. (p. 178)

Olshansky, S. J., Passaro, D. J., Hershow, R. C., Layden, J., Carnes, B. A., Brody, J., Hayflick, L., Butler, R. N., Allison, D. B., & Ludwig, D. S. (2005). A potential decline in life expectancy in the United States in the 21st century. *New England Journal of Medicine, 352,* 1138–1145. (p. 583)

Olson, M. A., & Fazio, R. H. (2001). Implicit attitude formation through classical conditioning. *Psychological Science, 12,* 413–417. (p. 319)

Olson, S. (2005). Brain scans raise privacy concerns. *Science, 307,* 1548–1550. (p. 615)

Olsson, A., & Phelps, E. A. (2004). Learned fear of "unseen" faces after Pavlovian, observational, and instructed fear. *Psychological Science, 15,* 822–828. (p. 654)

Olweus, D., Mattsson, A., Schalling, D., & Low, H. (1988). Circulating testosterone levels and aggression in adolescent males: A causal analysis. *Psychosomatic Medicine, 50,* 261–272. (p. 750)

Oman, D., Kurata, J. H., Strawbridge, W. J., & Cohen, R. D. (2002). Religious attendance and cause of death over 31 years. *International Journal of Psychiatry in Medicine, 32,* 69–89. (p. 573)

O'Neil, J. (2002, September 3). Vital Signs: Behavior: Parent smoking and teenage sex. *New York Times.* (p. 33)

O'Neill, M. J. (1993). The relationship between privacy, control, and stress responses in office workers. Paper presented to the Human Factors and Ergonomics Society convention. (p. 564)

Oren, D. A., & Terman, M. (1998). Tweaking the human circadian clock with light. *Science, 279,* 333–334. (p. 275)

Orlovskaya, D. D., Uranova, N. A., Zimina, I. S., Kolomeets, N. S., Vikhreva, O. V., Rachmanova, V. I., Black, J. E., Klintsova, A. Y., & Greenough, W. T. (1999). Effect of professional status on the number of synapses per neuron in the prefrontal cortex of normal human and schizophrenic brain. *Society for Neuroscience Abstracts,* 329.11, 25, 818, 1999. (p. 440)

Orne, M. T., & Evans, F. J. (1965). Social control in the psychological experiment: Antisocial behavior and hypnosis. *Journal of Personality and Social Psychology, 1,* 189–200. (p. 292)

Osborne, J. W. (1997). Race and academic disidentification. *Journal of Educational Psychology, 89,* 728–735. (p. 465)

Osborne, L. (1999, October 27). A linguistic big bang. *New York Times Magazine* (www.nytimes.com). (p. 414)

Osgood, C. E. (1962). *An alternative to war or surrender.* Urbana: University of Illinois Press. (p. 769)

Osgood, C. E. (1980). GRIT: A strategy for survival in mankind's nuclear age? Paper presented at the Pugwash Conference on New Directions in Disarmament. (p. 769)

OSS Assessment Staff. (1948). *The assessment of men.* New York: Rinehart. (p. 629)

Ost, L. G., & Hugdahl, K. (1981). Acquisition of phobias and anxiety response patterns in clinical patients. *Behaviour Research and Therapy, 16,* 439–447. (p. 654)

Ostfeld, A. M., Kasl, S. V., D'Atri, D. A., & Fitzgerald, E. F. (1987). *Stress, crowding, and blood pressure in prison.* Hillsdale, NJ: Erlbaum. (p. 564)

Ouellette, J. A., & Wood, W. (1998). Habit and intention in everyday life: The multiple processes by which past behavior predicts future behavior. *Psychological Bulletin, 124,* 54–74. (pp. 502, 630)

Overmier, J. B., & Murison, R. (1997). Animal models reveal the "psych" in the psychosomatics of peptic ulcers. *Current Directions in Psychological Science, 6,* 180–184. (p. 563)

Owen, R. (1814). First essay in *New view of society or the formation of character.* Quoted in *The story of New Lanark.* New Lanark Mills, Lanark, Scotland: New Lanark Conservation Trust, 1993. (p. 506)

Oxfam (2005, March 26). Three months on: New figures show tsunami may have killed up to four times as many women as men. Oxfam Press Release (www.oxfam.org.uk). (p. 131)

Oyserman, D., Coon, H. M., & Kemmelmeier, M. (2002a). Rethinking individualism and collectivism: Evaluation of theoretical assumptions and meta-analyses. *Psychological Bulletin, 128,* 3–72. (p. 122)

Oyserman, D., Kemmelmeier, M., & Coon, H. M. (2002b). Cultural psychology, a new look: Reply to Bond (2002), Fiske (2002), Kitayama (2002), and Miller (2002). *Psychological Bulletin, 128,* 110–117. (p. 122)

Ozer, E. J., Best, S. R., Lipsey, T. L., & Weiss, D. S. (2003). Predictors of posttraumatic stress disorder and symptoms in adults: A meta-analysis. *Psychological Bulletin, 129,* 52–73. (p. 653)

Ozer, E. J., & Weiss, D. S. (2004). Who develops posttraumatic stress disorder. *Current Directions in Psychological Science, 13,* 169–172. (pp. 652, 653)

Özgen, E. (2004). Language, learning, and color perception. *Current Directions in Psychological Science, 13,* 95–98. (p. 419)

Pacifici, R., Zuccaro, P., Farre, M., Pichini, S., Di Carlo, S., Roset, P. N., Ortuno, J., Pujadas, M., Bacosi, A., Menoyo, E., Segura, J., & de la Torre, R. (2001). Effects of repeated doses of MDMA ("Ecstasy") on cell-mediated immune response in humans. *Life Sciences, 69,* 2931–2941. (p. 302)

Padgett, V. R. (1989). Predicting organizational violence: An application of 11 powerful principles of obedience. Paper presented to the American Psychological Association convention. (p. 736)

Padilla, R. V., & Benavides, A. H. (Eds.) (1992). *Critical perspectives on bilingual education research.* Tempe, AZ: Bilingual Press. (p. 420)

Page, S. (1977). Effects of the mental illness label in attempts to obtain accommodation. *Canadian Journal of Behavioral Science, 9,* 84–90. (p. 646)

Paikoff, R. L., & Brooks-Gunn, J. (1991). Do parent-child relationships change during puberty? *Psychological Bulletin, 110,* 47–66. (p. 172)

Paivio, A. (1986). *Mental representations: A dual coding approach.* New York: Oxford University Press. (p. 358)

Palace, E. M. (1995). Modification of dysfunctional patterns of sexual response through autonomic arousal and false physiological feedback. *Journal of Consulting and Clinical Psychology, 63,* 604–615. (p. 520)

Palladino, J. J., & Carducci, B. J. (1983). "Things that go bump in the night": Students' knowledge of sleep and dreams. Paper presented at the meeting of the Southeastern Psychological Association. (p. 274)

Paller, K. A. (2004). Electrical signals of memory and of the awareness of remembering. *Current Directions in Psychological Science, 13,* 49–55. (p. 369)

Pallier, C., Colomé, A., & Sebastián-Gallés, N. (2001). The influence of native-language phonology on lexical access: Exemplar-based versus abstract lexical entries. *Psychological Science, 12,* 445–448. (p. 412)

Palmer, S., Schreiber, C., & Box, C. (1991). Remembering the earthquake: "Flashbulb" memory for experienced vs. reported events. Paper presented to the Psychonomic Society convention. (p. 366)

Paltrow, S. J. (2004, March 22). Detailed picture of U.S. actions on Sept. 22 remains elusive. *Wall Street Journal,* pp. A1, A9. (p. 350)

Pandey, J., Sinha, Y., Prakash, A., & Tripathi, R. C. (1982). Right-left political ideologies and attribution of the causes of poverty. *European Journal of Social Psychology, 12,* 327–331. (p. 725)

Panksepp, J. (1982). Toward a general psychobiological theory of emotions. *Behavioral and Brain Sciences, 5,* 407–467. (p. 518)

Pantelis, C., Velakoulis, D., McGorry, P. D., Wood, S. J., Suckling, J., Phillips, L. J., Yung, A. R., Bullmore, E. T., Brewer, W., Soulsby, B., Desmond, P., & McGuire, P. K. (2002). Neuroanatomical abnormalities before and after onset of psychosis: A cross-sectional and longitudinal MRI comparison. *The Lancet,* published online at image.thelancet.com/extras/01art9092web.pdf. (p. 673)

Pantev, C., Oostenveld, R., Engelien, A., Ross, B., Roberts, L. R., & Hoke, M. (1998). Increased auditory cortical representation in musicians. *Nature, 392,* 811–814. (p. 82)

Parducci, A. (1995). *Happiness, pleasure, and judgment: The contextual theory and its applications.* Hillsdale, NJ: Erlbaum. (p. 526)

Park, D. C., Lautenschlager, G., Hedden, T., Davidson, N. S., Smith, A. D., & Smith, P. K. (2002). Models of visuospatial and verbal memory across the adult life span. *Psychology and Aging, 17,* 299–320. (pp. 184–185)

Park, R. L. (1999). Liars never break a sweat. *New York Times,* July 12, 1999 (www.nytimes.com). (p. 520)

Parker, C. P., Baltes, B. B., Young, S. A., Huff, J. W., Altmann, R. A., LaCost, H. A., & Roberts, J. E. (2003). Relationships between psychological climate perceptions and work outcomes: A meta-analytic review. *Journal of Organizational Behavior, 24,* 389–416. (p. 505)

Parker, S., Nichter, M., Nichter, M., & Vuckovic, N. (1995). Body image and weight concerns among African American and white adolescent females: Differences that make a difference. *Human Organization, 54,* 103–114. (p. 582)

Passell, P. (1993, March 9). Like a new drug, social programs are put to the test. *New York Times,* pp. C1, C10. (p. 38)

Pate, J. E., Pumariega, A. J., Hester, C., & Garner, D. M. (1992). Cross-cultural patterns in eating disorders: A review. *Journal of the American Academy of Child and Adolescent Psychiatry, 31,* 802–809. (p. 479)

Patoine, B. (2005, January-February). Imagine that! Neural prosthetics harness thoughts to control computers and robotics. *Brain Work*, pp. 1–3. (p. 78)

Patterson, D. R. (2004). Treating pain with hypnosis. *Current Directions in Psychological Science, 13*,, 252–255. (p. 293)

Patterson, D. R., & Jensen, M. (2003). Hypnosis for clinical pain control. *Psychological Bulletin, 129,* 495–521. (p. 293)

Patterson, F. (1978, October). Conversations with a gorilla. *National Geographic*, pp. 438–465. (p. 426)

Patterson, G. R., Chamberlain, P., & Reid, J. B. (1982). A comparative evaluation of parent training procedures. *Behavior Therapy, 13,* 638–650. (pp. 333, 752)

Patterson, G. R., Reid, J. B., & Dishion, T. J. (1992). *Antisocial boys.* Eugene, OR: Castalia. (p. 752)

Patterson, M., Warr, P., & West, M. (2004). Organizational climate and company productivity: The role of employee affect and employee level. *Journal of Occupational and Organizational Psychology, 77,* 193–216. (pp. 293, 505)

Patterson, R. (1951). *The riddle of Emily Dickinson.* Boston: Houghton Mifflin. (p. 668)

Patton, G. C., Coffey, C., Carlin, J. B., Degenhardt, L., Lynskey, M., & Hall, W. (2002). Cannabis use and mental health of young people: Cohort study. *British Medical Journal, 325,* 1195–1198. (p. 303)

Patton, W., & Mannison, M. (1995). Sexual coercion in dating situations among university students: Preliminary Australian data. *Australian Journal of Psychology, 47,* 66–72. (p. 753)

Paulesu, E., Demonet, J-F., Fazio, F., McCrory, E., Chanoine, V., Brunswick, N., Cappa, S. F., Cossu, G., Habib, M., Frith, C. D., & Frith, U. (2001). Dyslexia: Cultural diversity and biological unity. *Science, 291,* 2165–2167. (p. 46)

Paulos, J. A. (1995). *A mathematician reads the newspaper.* New York: Basic Books. (p. 714)

Paunonen, S. V., Zeidner, M., Engvik, H. A., Oosterveld, P., & Maliphant, R. (2000). The nonverbal assessment of personality in five cultures. *Journal of Cross-Cultural Psychology, 31,* 220–239. (p. 619)

Paus, T., Zijdenbos, A., Worsley, K., Collins, D. L., Blumenthal, J., Giedd, J. N., Rapoport, J. L., & Evans, A. C. (1999) Structural maturation of neural pathways in children and adolescents: In vivo study. *Science, 283,* 1908–1911. (p. 145)

Pavlidis, G. T. (2005, January 17). Eye movements can diagnose preschoolers at high risk for attention deficit/hyperactivity disorder (ADHD). Press release, Brunel University (www.brunel.ac.uk). (p. 641)

Pavlov, I. (1927). *Conditioned reflexes: An investigation of the physiological activity of the cerebral cortex.* Oxford: Oxford University Press. (p. 320)

Pedersen, N. L., Plomin, R., McClearn, G. E., & Friberg, L. (1988). Neuroticism, extraversion, and related traits in adult twins reared apart and reared together. *Journal of Personality and Social Psychology, 55,* 950–957. (p. 100)

Peeters, A., Barendregt, J. J., Willekens, F., Mackenbach, J. P., & Mamum, A. A. (2003). Obesity in adulthood and its consequences for life expectancy: A life-table analysis. *Annals of Internal Medicine, 138,* 24–32. (pp. 583, 587)

Peigneux, P., Laureys, S., Fuchs, S., Collette, F., Perrin, F., Reggers, J., Phillips, C., Degueldre, C., Del Fiore, G., Aerts, J., Luxen, A., & Maquet, P. (2004). Are spatial memories strengthened in the human hippocampus during slow wave sleep? *Neuron, 44,* 535–545. (pp. 283, 268)

Pekkanen, J. (1982, June). Why do we sleep? *Science, 82,* p. 86. (p. 283)

Pelham, B. W. (1993). On the highly positive thoughts of the highly depressed. In R. F. Baumeister (Ed.), *Self-esteem: The puzzle of low self-regard.* New York: Plenum. (p. 633)

Pendick, D. (1994, January/February). The mind of violence. *Brain Work: The Neuroscience Newsletter,* pp. 1–3, 5. (p. 750)

Penfield, W. (1969). Consciousness, memory, and man's conditioned reflexes. In K. Pigram (Ed.), *On the biology of learning.* New York: Harcourt, Brace & World. (p. 364)

Penhune, V. B., Cismaru, R., Dorsaint-Pierre, R., Petitto, L-A., & Zatorre, R. J. (2003). The morphometry of auditory cortex in the congenitally deaf measured using MRI. *NeuroImage, 20,* 1215–1225. (p. 223)

Pennebaker, J. (1990). *Opening up: The healing power of confiding in others.* New York: William Morrow. (pp. 567, 605)

Pennebaker, J. W. (2002, January 28). Personal communication. (p. 768)

Pennebaker, J. W., Barger, S. D., & Tiebout, J. (1989). Disclosure of traumas and health among Holocaust survivors. *Psychosomatic Medicine, 51,* 577–589. (p. 567)

Pennebaker, J. W., & O'Heeron, R. C. (1984). Confiding in others and illness rate among spouses of suicide and accidental death victims. *Journal of Abnormal Psychology, 93,* 473–476. (pp. 566–567)

Pennebaker, J. W., & Stone, L. D. (2003). Words of wisdom: Language use over the life span. *Journal of Personality and Social Psychology, 85,* 291–301. (p. 189)

Peplau, L. A. (1982). Research on homosexual couples: An overview. *Journal of Homosexuality, 8*(2), 3–8. (p. 488)

Peplau, L. A., & Garnets, L. D. (2000). A new paradigm for understanding women's sexuality and sexual orientation. *Journal of Social Issues, 56,* 329–350. (p. 488)

Pepperberg, I. M. (2002). Cognitive and communicative abilities of grey parrots. *Current Directions in Psychological Science, 11,* 83–87. (p. 424)

Perkins, A., & Fitzgerald, J. A. (1997). Sexual orientation in domestic rams: Some biological and social correlates. In L. Ellis and L. Ebertz (Eds.), *Sexual orientation: Toward biological understanding.* Westport, CT: Praeger Publishers. (p. 489)

Perkins, H. W. (1991). Religious commitment, Yuppie values, and well-being in post-collegiate life. *Review of Religious Research, 32,* 244–251. (p. 541)

Perlmutter, M. (1983). Learning and memory through adulthood. In M. W. Riley, B. B. Hess, & K. Bond (Eds.), *Aging in society: Selected reviews of recent research.* Hillsdale, NJ: Erlbaum. (p. 182)

Perls, T., & Silver, M. H., with Lauerman, J. F. (1999). *Living to 100: Lessons in living to your maximum potential.* Thorndike, ME: Thorndike Press. (p. 558)

Perrett, D. (2002, October 1). Perception laboratory, Department of Psychology, University of St. Andrews, Scotland (www.perception.st-and.ac.uk). (p. 761)

Perrett, D. I., Harries, M., Misflin, A. J., & Chitty, A. J. (1988). Three stages in the classification of body movements by visual neurons. In H. B. Barlow, C. Blakemore, & M. Weston Smith (Eds.), *Images and understanding.* Cambridge: Cambridge University Press. (p. 209)

Perrett, D. I., Hietanen, J. K., Oram, M. W., & Benson, P. J. (1992). Organization and functions of cells responsive to faces in the temporal cortex. *Philosophical Transactions of the Royal Society of London: Series B, 335,* 23–30. (p. 209)

Perrett, D. I., Lee, K. J., Penton-Voak, I., Rowland, D., Yoshikawa, S., Burt, D. M., Henzi, S. P., Castles, D. L., Akamatsu, S. (1998, August). Effects of sexual dimorphism on facial attractiveness. *Nature, 394,* 884–887. (p. 745)

Perrett, D. I., May, K. A., & Yoshikawa, S. (1994). Facial shape and judgments of female attractiveness. *Nature, 368,* 239–242. (p. 209)

Persky, S., & Blascovich, J. (2005). Consequences of playing violent video games in immersive virtual environments, In A. Axelsson & Ralph Schroeder (Eds.). *Work and Play in Shared Virtual Environments.* New York: Springer. (p. 756)

Persons, J. B. (1986). The advantages of studying psychological phenomena rather than psychiatric diagnoses. *American Psychologist, 41,* 1252–1260. (p. 645)

Pert, C. (1986). Quoted in J. Hooper & D. Teresi, *The three-pound universe.* New York: Macmillan. (p. 74)

Pert, C. B. (1986, Summer). The wisdom of the receptors: Neuropeptides, the emotions, and bodymind. *Advances* (Institute for the Advancement of Health), *3,* 8–16. (p. 67)

Pert, C. B., & Snyder, S. H. (1973). Opiate receptor: Demonstration in nervous tissue. *Science, 179,* 1011–1014. (p. 59)

Perugini, E. M., Kirsch, I., Allen, S. T., Coldwell, E., Meredith, J., Montgomery, G. H., & Sheehan, J. (1998). Surreptitious observation of responses to hypnotically suggested hallucinations: A test of the compliance hypothesis. *International Journal of Clinical and Experimental Hypnosis, 46,* 191–203. (p. 294)

Peschel, E. R., & Peschel, R. E. (1987). Medical insights into the castrati in opera. *American Scientist, 75,* 578–583. (p. 483)

Peters, T. J., & Waterman, R. H., Jr. (1982). *In search of excellence: Lessons from America's best-run companies.* New York: Harper & Row. (p. 337)

Peterson, C., & Barrett, L. C. (1987). Explanatory style and academic performance among university freshmen. *Journal of Personality and Social Psychology, 53,* 603–607. (p. 627)

Peterson, C., Peterson, J., & Skevington, S. (1986). Heated argument and adolescent development. *Journal of Social and Personal Relationships, 3,* 229–240. (p. 168)

Peterson, C., & Seligman, M. E. P. (2004). *Character strengths and virtues: A handbook and classification.* New York: Oxford. (p. 646)

Peterson, C. C., & Siegal, M. (1999). Representing inner worlds: Theory of mind in autistic, deaf, and normal hearing children. *Psychological Science, 10,* 126–129. (p. 152)

Peterson, L. R., & Peterson, M. J. (1959). Short-term retention of individual verbal items. *Journal of Experimental Psychology, 58,* 193–198. (p. 362)

Petitto, L. A., & Marentette, P. F. (1991). Babbling in the manual mode: Evidence for the ontogeny of language. *Science, 251,* 1493–1496. (p. 412)

Petrosino, A., Turpin-Petrosino, C., & Finckenauer, J. O. (2000). Well-meaning programs can have harmful effects! Lessons from experiments of programs such as Scared Straight. *Crime and Delinquency, 46,* 354–379. (p. 702)

Pettegrew, J. W., Keshavan, M. S., & Minshew, N. J. (1993). 31P nuclear magnetic resonance spectroscopy: Neurodevelopment and schizophrenia. *Schizophrenia Bulletin, 19,* 35–53. (p. 672)

Petticrew, C., Bell, R., & Hunter, D. (2002). Influence of psychological coping on survival and recurrence in people with cancer: Systematic review. *British Medical Journal, 325,* 1066. (p. 559)

Petticrew, M., Fraser, J. M., & Regan, M. F. (1999). Adverse life events and risk of breast cancer: A meta-analysis. *British Journal of Health Psychology, 4,* 1–17. (p. 559)

Pettigrew, T. F. (1969). Racially separate or together? *Journal of Social Issues, 25,* 43–69. (p. 767)

Pettigrew, T. F. (1998). Reactions toward the new minorities of western Europe. *Annual Review of Sociology, 24,* 77–103. (p. 743)

Pettigrew, T. F. (2004). Justice deferred a half century after Brown v. Board of Education. *American Psychologist, 59,* 521–529. (p. 767)

Pew. (2003). Views of a changing world 2003. The Pew Global Attitudes Project. Washington, DC: Pew Research Center for the People and the Press (http://people-press.org/reports/pdf/185.pdf). (p. 131)

Phelps, J. A., Davis J. O., & Schartz, K. M. (1997). Nature, nurture, and twin research strategies. *Current Directions in Psychological Science 6,* 117–120. (pp. 114, 674)

Philip Morris. (2003). Philip Morris USA youth smoking prevention. Teenage attitudes and behavior study, 2002. In "Raising kids who don't smoke," vol. 1(2). (p. 577)

Phillips, D. P. (1985). Natural experiments on the effects of mass media violence on fatal aggression: Strengths and weaknesses of a new approach. In L. Berkowitz (Ed.), *Advances in experimental social psychology* (Vol. 19). Orlando, FL: Academic Press. (p. 732)

Phillips, D. P., Carstensen, L. L., & Paight, D. J. (1989). Effects of mass media news stories on suicide, with new evidence on the role of story content. In D. R. Pfeffer (Ed.), *Suicide among youth: Perspectives on risk and prevention.* Washington, DC: American Psychiatric Press. (p. 732)

Phillips, J. L. (1969). *Origins of intellect: Piaget's theory.* San Francisco: Freeman. (p. 151)

Phillips, T. (2004, April 3). Quoted by T. Baldwin & G. Rozenberg, Britain 'must scrap multiculturalism.' *The Times,* p. 1. (p. 768)

Piaget, J. (1932). *The moral judgment of the child.* New York: Harcourt, Brace & World. (p. 168)

Picchioni, D., Mignot, E. J., & Harsh, J. R. (2004). The month-of-birth pattern in narcolepsy is moderated by cataplexy severity and may be independent of HLA-DQB1*0602. *Sleep, 27,* 1471–1475. (p. 284)

Pickar, D., Labarca, R., Linnoila, M., Roy, A., Hommer, D., Everett, D., & Payl, S. M. (1984). Neuroleptic-induced decrease in plasma homovanillic acid and antipsychotic activity in schizophrenic patients. *Science, 225,* 954–957. (p. 712)

Pike, K. M., & Rodin, J. (1991). Mothers, daughters, and disordered eating. *Journal of Abnormal Psychology, 100,* 198–204. (p. 479)

Piliavin, J. A. (2003). Doing well by doing good: Benefits for the benefactor. In C. L. M. Keyes & J. Haidt (Eds.), *Flourishing: Positive psychology and the life well-lived.* Washington, DC: American Psychological Association. (p. 170)

Pillemer, D. (1998). *Momentous events, vivid memories.* Cambridge: Harvard University Press, 1998. (p. 181)

Pillemer, D. G. (1995). What is remembered about early childhood events? Invited paper presentation to the American Psychological Society convention. (p. 146)

Pillsworth, M. G., Haselton, M. G., & Buss, D. M. (2004). Ovulatory shifts in female desire. *Journal of Sex Research, 41,* 55–65. (p. 482)

Pincus, H. A. (1997) Commentary: Spirituality, religion, and health: Expanding, and using the knowledge base. *Mind/Body Medicine, 2,* 49. (p. 574)

Pinel, J. P. J. (1993). *Biopsychology* (2nd ed). Boston: Allyn & Bacon. (p. 475)

Pingitore, R., Dugoni, B. L., Tindale, R. S., & Spring, B. (1994). Bias against overweight job applicants in a simulated employment interview. *Journal of Applied Psychology, 79,* 909–917. (p. 584)

Pinker, S. (1990, September-October). Quoted by J. de Cuevas, "No, she holded them loosely." *Harvard Magazine,* pp. 60–67. (p. 410)

Pinker, S. (1995). The language instinct. *The General Psychologist, 31,* 63–65. (pp. 411, 426, 427)

Pinker, S. (1998). Words and rules. *Lingua, 106,* 219–242. (p. 401)

Pinker, S. (1999, June 24). His brain measured up. *New York Times* (www.nytimes.com). (p. 440)

Pinker, S. (2002, September 9). A biological understanding of human nature: A talk with Steven Pinker. The Edge Third Culture Mail List (www.edge.org). (pp. 101, 108, 414)

Pinker, S. (2002). *The blank slate.* New York: Viking. (p. 108)

Pinker, S. (2005, April 22). The science of gender and science: A conversation with Elizabeth Spelke. Harvard University (www.edge.org). (p. 463)

Pinkerton, S. D., & Abramson, P. R. (1997). Condoms and the prevention of AIDS. *American Scientist, 85,* 364–373. (p. 486)

Pipe, M-E. (1996). Children's eyewitness memory. *New Zealand Journal of Psychology, 25,* 36–43. (p. 386)

Pipe, M-E., Lamb, M. E., Orbach, Y., & Esplin, P. W. (2004). Recent research on children's testimony about experienced and witnessed events. *Developmental Review, 24,* 440–468. (p. 386)

Piper, A., Jr. (1998, Winter). Multiple personality disorder: Witchcraft survives in the twentieth century. *Skeptical Inquirer,* pp. 44–50. (p. 657)

Pipher, M. (2002). *The middle of everywhere: The world's refugees come to our town.* New York: Harcourt Brace. (pp. 120, 496, 554)

Pittenger, D. J. (1993). The utility of the Myers-Briggs Type Indicator. *Review of Eductional Research, 63,* 467–488. (p. 614)

Pleck, J. H., Sonenstein, F. L., & Ku, L. C. (1993). Masculinity ideology: Its impact on adolescent males' heterosexual relationships. *Journal of Social Issues, 49,* 11–29. (p. 110)

Pliner, P. (1982). The effects of mere exposure on liking for edible substances. *Appetite: Journal for Intake Research, 3,* 283–290. (p. 477)

Pliner, P., & Pelchat, M. L. (1991). Neophobia in humans and the special status of foods of animal origin. *Appetite, 16,* 205–218. (p. 477)

Plomin, R. (1997). Identifying genes for cognitive abilities and disabilities. In R. Sternberg, & E. Grigorenko (Eds.), *Intelligence, heredity, and environment.* New York: Cambridge University Press. (p. 105)

Plomin, R. (1999). Genetics and general cognitive ability. *Nature, 402* (Suppl), C25–C29. (pp. 432, 455)

Plomin, R. (2001). Genetics and behaviour. *The Psychologist, 14,* 134–139. (p. 455)

Plomin, R. (2003). General cognitive ability. In R. Plomin, J. C. DeFries, I. W. Craig, & P. McGuffin (Eds.), *Behavioral genetics in a postgenomic world.* Washington, DC: APA Books. (p. 455)

Plomin, R., & Bergeman, C. S. (1991). The nature of nurture: Genetic influence on "environmental" measures. *Behavioral and Brain Sciences, 14,* 373–427. (p. 105)

Plomin, R., Corley, R., Caspi, A., Fulker, D. W., & DeFries, J. (1998). Adoption results for self-reported personality: Evidence for nonadditive genetic effects? *Journal of Personality and Social Psychology, 75,* 211–219. (p. 100)

Plomin, R., & Crabbe, J. (2000). DNA. *Psychological Bulletin, 126,* 806–828. (pp. 96, 105)

Plomin, R., & Daniels, D. (1987). Why are children in the same family so different from one another? *Behavioral and Brain Sciences, 10,* 1–60. (p. 117)

Plomin, R., & DeFries, J. C. (1998, May). The genetics of cognitive abilities and disabilities. *Scientific American,* pp. 62–69. (p. 456)

Plomin, R., DeFries, J. C., McClearn, G. E., & Rutter, M. (1997). *Behavioral genetics.* New York: Freeman. (pp. 98, 456, 586, 674)

Plomin, R., Fulker, D. W., Corley, R., & DeFries, J. C. (1997). Nature, nurture and cognitive development from 1 to 16 years: A parent-offspring adoption study. *Psychological Science, 8,* 442–447. (p. 108)

Plomin, R., McClearn, G. E., Pedersen, N. L., Nesselroade, J. R., & Bergeman, C. S. (1988). Genetic influence on childhood family environment perceived retrospectively from the last half of the life span. *Developmental Psychology, 24,* 37–45. (p. 105)

Plomin, R., & McGuffin, P. (2003). Psychopathology in the postgenomic era. *Annual Review of Psychology, 54,* 205–228. (p. 664)

Plomin, R., Reiss, D., Hetherington, E. M., & Howe, G. W. (January, 1994). Nature and nurture: Genetic contributions to measures of the family environment. *Developmental Psychology, 30*(1), 32–43. (p. 105)

Plous, S. (1993). Psychological mechanisms in the human use of animals. *Journal of Social Issues, 49*(1), 11–52. (p. 47)

Plous, S., & Herzog, H. A. (2000). Poll shows researchers favor lab animal protection. *Science, 290,* 711. (p. 47)

Poldrack, R. A., & Wagner, A. D. (2004). What can neuroimaging tell us about the mind? *Current Directions in Psychological Science, 13,* 177–181. (p. 356)

Polivy, J., & Herman, C. P. (1985). Dieting and binging: A causal analysis. *American Psychologist, 40,* 193–201. (p. 590)

Polivy, J., & Herman, C. P. (1987). Diagnosis and treatment of normal eating. *Journal of Personality and Social Psychology, 55,* 635–644. (p. 59)

Polivy, J., & Herman, C. P. (2002). Causes of eating disorders. *Annual Review of Psychology, 53,* 187–213. (p. 479)

Pollack, A. (2004, April 13). With tiny brain implants, just thinking may make it so. *New York Times* (www.nytimes.com). (p. 78)

Pollak, S., Cicchetti, D., & Klorman, R. (1998). Stress, memory, and emotion: Developmental considerations from the study of child maltreatment. *Developmental Psychopathology, 10,* 811–828. (p. 320)

Pollak, S. D., & Kistler, D. J. (2002). Early experience is associated with the development of categorical representations for facial expressions of emotion. *Proceedings of the National Academy of Sciences, 99,* 9072–9076. (p. 525)

Pollak, S. D., & Tolley-Schell, S. A. (2003). Selective attention to facial emotion in physically abused children. *Journal of Abnormal Psychology, 112,* 323–328. (p. 525)

Pollard, R. (1992). 100 years in psychology and deafness: A centennial retrospective. Invited address to the American Psychological Association convention, Washington, DC. (p. 420)

Polusny, M. A., & Follette, V. M. (1995). Long-term correlates of child sexual abuse: Theory and review of the empirical literature. *Applied & Preventive Psychology, 4,* 143–166. (p. 159)

Pomerleau, O. F., Collins, A. C., Shiffman, S., & Pomerleau, C. S. (1993). Why some people smoke and others do not: New perspectives. *Journal of Consulting and Clinical Psychology, 61,* 723–731. (p. 577)

Poole, D. A., & Lindsay, D. S. (1995). Interviewing preschoolers: Effects of nonsuggestive techniques, parental coaching and leading questions on reports of nonexperienced events. *Journal of Experimental Child Psychology, 60,* 129–154. (p. 384)

Poole, D. A., & Lindsay, D. S. (2001). Children's eyewitness reports after exposure to misinformation from parents. *Journal of Experimental Psychology: Applied, 7,* 27–50. (p. 384)

Poole, D. A., & Lindsay, D. S. (2002). Reducing child witnesses' false reports of misinformation from parents. *Journal of Experimental Child Psychology, 81,* 117–140. (p. 384)

Poole, D. A., Lindsay, D. S., Memon, A., & Bull, R. (1995). Psychotherapy and the recovery of memories of childhood sexual abuse: U.S. and British practitioners' opinions, practices, and experiences. *Journal of Consulting and Clinical Psychology, 63,* 426–437. (p. 387)

Poon, L. W. (1987). Myths and truisms: Beyond extant analyses of speed of behavior and age. Address to the Eastern Psychological Association convention. (p. 179)

Pope, H. G., & Yurgelun-Todd, D. (1996). The residual cognitive effects of heavy marijuana use in college students. *Journal of the American Medical Association, 275,* 521–527. (p. 303)

Popenoe, D. (1993). The evolution of marriage and the problem of stepfamilies: A biosocial perspective. Paper presented at the National Symposium on Stepfamilies, Pennsylvania State University. (p. 123)

Popenoe, D., & Whitehead, B. D. (2002). *Should We Live Together?,* 2nd Ed. New Brunswick, NJ: The National Marriage Project, Rutgers University. (p. 187)

Porac, C., Coren, S., & Duncan, P. (1980). Life-span age trends in laterality. *Journal of Gerontology, 35,* 715–721. (p. 89)

Poremba, A., & Gabriel, M. (2001). Amygdalar efferents initiate auditory thalamic discriminative training-induced neuronal activity. *Journal of Neuroscience, 21,* 270–278. (p. 73)

Porkka-Heiskanen, T., Strecker, R. E., Thakkar, M., Bjorkum, A. A., Greene, R. W., & McCarley, R. W. (1997). Adenosine: A mediator of the sleep-inducing effects of prolonged wakefulness. *Science, 276,* 1265–1268. (p. 276)

Porter, D., & Neuringer, A. (1984). Music discriminations by pigeons. *Journal of Experimental Psychology: Animal Behavior Processes, 10,* 138–148. (p. 328)

Porter, R. P. (1998). Twisted tongues: The failure of bilingual education. Washington, DC: The Communitarian Network (www.gwu.edu/~ccps/pop_biling.html). (p. 420)

Porter, S., Birt, A. R., Yuille, J. C., & Lehman, D. R. (2000, Nov.). Negotiating false memories: Interviewer and rememberer characteristics relate to memory distortion. *Psychological Science, 11,* 507–510. (p. 383)

Porter, S., Yuille, J. C., & Lehman, D. R. (1999). The nature of real, implanted, and fabricated memories for childhood events: Implications for the recovered memory debate. *Law and Human Behavior, 23,* 517–537. (p. 389)

Posavac, H. D., Posavac, S. S., & Posavac, E. J. (1998). Exposure to media images of female attractiveness and concern with body weight among young women. *Sex Roles, 38,* 187–201. (p. 479)

Posner, M. I., & Carr, T. H. (1992). Lexical access and the brain: Anatomical constraints on cognitive models of word recognition. *American Journal of Psychology, 105,* 1–26. (p. 82)

Poulton, R., & Milne, B. J. (2002). Low fear in childhood is associated with sporting prowess in adolescence and young adulthood. *Behaviour Research and Therapy, 40,* 1191–1197. (p. 678)

Povinelli, D. J., & Bering, J. M. (2002). The mentality of apes revisited. *Current Directions in Psychological Science, 11,* 115–119. (p. 424)

Powell, J. (1989). *Happiness is an inside job.* Valencia, CA: Tabor. (p. 634)

Powell, K. E., Thompson, P. D., Caspersen, C. J., & Kendrick, J. S. (1987). Physical activity and the incidence of coronary heart disease. *Annual Review of Public Health, 8,* 253–287. (p. 570)

Powell, L. H., Schahabi, L., & Thoresen, C. E. (2003). Religion and spirituality: Linkages to physical health. *American Psychologist, 58,* 36–52. (p. 573)

Powell, R. A., & Boer, D. P. (1994). Did Freud mislead patients to confabulate memories of abuse? *Psychological Reports, 74,* 1283–1298. (p. 604)

Prairie Home Companion. (1999). *The Prairie Home Companion's Pretty Good Joke Book* (Vol. 4). St. Paul, MN: Prairie Home Companion. (p. 549)

Pratkanis, A. R. (1992). The cargo-cult science of subliminal persuasion. *Skeptical Inquirer, 16,* 260–272. (p. 200)

Pratkanis, A. R., & Greenwald, A. G. (1988). Recent perspectives on unconscious processing: Still no marketing applications. *Psychology and Marketing, 5,* 337–353. (p. 201)

PRB. (2002). *2002 Women of our World.* Population Reference Bureau (www.prb.org). (p. 745)

PRB. (2004). *2004 world population data sheet.* Washington, DC: Population Reference Bureau. (p. 178)

Prentice, D. A., & Miller, D. T. (1993). Pluralistic ignorance and alcohol use on campus: Some consequences of misperceiving the social norm. *Journal of Personality and Social Psychology, 64,* 243–256. (p. 307)

Presley, C. A., Meilman, P. W., & Lyerla, R. (1997). *Alcohol and drugs on American college campuses: Issues of violence and harrassment.* Carbondale, IL: Core Institute, Southern Illinois University. (p. 297)

Presson, P. K., & Benassi, V. A. (1996). Locus of control orientation and depressive symptomatology: A meta-analysis. *Journal of Social Behavior and Personality, 11,* 201–212. (p. 625)

Pringle, P. J., Geary, M. P., Rodeck, C. H., Kingdom, J. C., Kayamba-Kay's, S., & Hindmarsh, P. C. (2005). The influence of cigarette smoking on antenatal growth, birth size, and the insulin-like growth factor axis. *Journal of Clinical Endocrinology and Metabolism, 90,* 2556–2562. (p. 141)

Prioleau, L., Murdock, M., & Brody, N. (1983). An analysis of psychotherapy versus placebo studies. *The Behavioral and Brain Sciences, 6,* 275–310. (p. 707)

Project Match Research Group. (1997). Matching alcoholism treatments to client heterogeneity: Project MATCH posttreatment drinking outcomes. *Journal of Studies on Alcohol, 58,* 7–29. (p. 698)

Project on Redefining the Meaning and Purpose of Baccalaureate Degrees. (1985). *Integrity in the college curriculum.* Washington, DC: Association of American Colleges. (p. 44)

Pronin, E., Gilovich, T., & Ross, L. (2004). Objectivity in the eye of the beholder: Divergent perceptions of bias in self versus others. *Psychological Review, 111,* 781–799. (p. 724)

Pronin, E., Lin, D. Y., & Ross, L. (2002). The bias blind spot: Perceptions of bias in self versus others. *Personality and Social Psychology Bulletin, 28,* 369–381. (p. 634)

Provine, R. R. (2001). *Laughter: A scientific investigation.* New York: Penguin. (p. 29)

Psychologist (2003, April). Who's the greatest? *The Psychologist, 16,* 17. (p. 154)

Psychologist (2005, August). Description or explanation? *The Psychologist, 18,* 460–461. (p. 648)

Puchalski, C. (2005, March 12). Personal correspondence from Director, George Washington Institute for Spirituality and Health. (p. 572)

Putnam, F. W. (1991). Recent research on multiple personality disorder. *Psychiatric Clinics of North America, 14,* 489–502. (p. 657)

Putnam, F. W. (1995). Rebuttal of Paul McHugh. *Journal of the American Academy of Child and Adolescent Psychiatry, 34,* 963. (p. 657)

Putnam, R. (2000). *Bowling alone.* New York: Simon and Schuster. (p. 121)

Pyszczynski, T., Hamilton, J. C., Greenberg, J., & Becker, S. E. (1991). Self-awareness and psychological dysfunction. In C. R. Snyder & D. O. Forsyth (Eds.), *Handbook of social and clinical psychology: The health perspective.* New York: Pergamon. (p. 667)

Pyszczynski, T. A., Solomon, S., & Greenberg, J. (2002). *In the wake of 9/11: The psychology of terror.* Washington, DC: American Psychological Association. (p. 747)

Qirko, H. N. (2004). "Fictive kin" and suicide terrorism. *Science, 304,* 49–50. (p. 740)

Quasha, S. (1980). *Albert Einstein: An intimate portrait.* New York: Forest. (p. 451)

Quinn, P. C. (2002). Category representation in young infants. *Current Directions in Psychological Science, 11,* 66–70. (p. 143)

Quinn, P. C., Bhatt, R. S., Brush, D., Grimes, A., & Sharpnack, H. (2002). Development of form similarity as a Gestalt grouping principle in infancy. *Psychological Science, 13,* 320–328. (pp. 243, 245)

Quinn, P. J., Williams, G. M., Najman, J. M., Andersen, M. J., & Bor, W. (2001). The effect of breastfeeding on child development at 5 years: A cohort study. *Journal of Pediatrics & Child Health, 3,* 465–469. (p. 36)

Rabin, A. S., Kaslow, N. J., & Rehm, L. P. (1986). Aggregate outcome and follow-up results following self-control therapy for depression. Paper presented at the American Psychological Association convention. (p. 696)

Rabinowicz, T., Dean, D. E., Petetot, J. M., & de Courten-Myers, G. M. (1999). Gender differences in the human cerebral cortex: More neurons in males; more processes in females. *Journal of Child Neurology, 14,* 98–107. (p. 144)

Rabinowicz, T., de Courten-Myers, G. M., Petetot, J. M., Xi, G., & de los Reyes, E. (1996). Human cortex development: Estimates of neuronal numbers indicate major loss late during gestation. *Journal of Neuropathology and Experimental Neurology, 55,* 320–328. (p. 144)

Radford, B. (2002, November/December). Psychics wrong about Chandra Levy. *Skeptical Inquirer,* p. 9. (p. 266)

Raglin, J. S. (1992). Anxiety and sport performance. In J. O. Holloszy (Ed.), *Exercise and sports sciences reviews* (Vol. 20). Baltimore: Williams & Wilkins. (p. 533)

Rahman, Q., & Wilson, G. D. (2003). Born gay? The psychobiology of human sexual orientation. *Personality and Individual Differences, 34,* 1337–1382. (pp. 490, 492)

Rahman, Q., Wilson, G. D., & Abrahams, S. (2003). Biosocial factors, sexual orientation and neurocognitive functioning. *Psychoneuroendocrinology, 29,* 867–881. (p. 492)

Raine, A. (1999). Murderous minds: Can we see the mark of Cain? *Cerebrum: The Dana Forum on Brain Science 1*(1), 15–29. (pp. 678, 749)

Raine, A., Brennan, P., Mednick, B., & Mednick, S. A. (1996). High rates of violence, crime, academic problems, and behavioral problems in males with both early neuromotor deficits and unstable family environments. *Archives of General Psychiatry, 53,* 544–549. (p. 679)

Raine, A., Lencz, T., Bihrle, S., LaCasse, L., & Colletti, P. (2000). Reduced prefrontal gray matter volume and reduced autonomic activity in antisocial personality disorder. *Archives of General Psychiatry, 57,* 119–127. (p. 678)

Rainville, P., Duncan, G. H., Price, D. D., Carrier, B., & Bushnell, M. C. (1997). Pain affect encoded in human anterior cingulate but not somatosensory cortex. *Science, 277,* 968–971. (p. 293)

Raison, C. L., Klein, H. M., & Steckler, M. (1999). The mood and madness reconsidered. *Journal of Affective Disorders, 53,* 99–106. (p. 680)

Ralston, A. (2004). Enough rope. Interview for ABC TV, Australia, by Andrew Denton (www.abc.net.au/enoughrope/stories/s1227885.htm). (p. 469)

Ramachandran, V. S., & Blakeslee, S. (1998). *Phantoms in the brain: Probing the mysteries of the human mind.* New York: Morrow. (pp. 64, 83, 227)

Ramey, S. L., & Ramey, C. T. (1992). Early educational intervention with disadvantaged children—To what effect? *Applied and Preventive Psychology, 1,* 131-140. (p. 457)

Rand, C. S. W., & Macgregor, A. M. C. (1990). Morbidly obese patients' perceptions of social discrimination before and after surgery for obesity. *Southern Medical Journal, 83,* 1390-1395. (p. 584)

Rand, C. S. W., & Macgregor, A. M. C. (1991). Successful weight loss following obesity surgery and perceived liability or morbid obesity. *Internal Journal of Obesity, 15,* 577-579. (p. 584)

Randi, J. (1999, February 4). 2000 Club mailing list e-mail letter. (p. 267)

Rapoport, J. L. (1989, March). The biology of obsessions and compulsions. *Scientific American,* pp. 83-89. (pp. 651, 655)

Räsänen, S., Pakaslahti, A., Syvalahti, E., Jones, P. B., & Isohanni, M. (2000). Sex differences in schizophrenia: A review. *Nordic Journal of Psychiatry, 54,* 37-45. (p. 671)

Ray, J. (2005, April 12). U.S. teens walk away from anger: Boys and girls manage anger differently. The Gallup Organization (www.gallup.com). (p. 535)

Ray, O., & Ksir, C. (1990). *Drugs, society, and human behavior* (5ᵗʰ ed.). St. Louis: Times Mirror/Mosby. (p. 301)

Raynor, H. A., & Epstein, L. H. (2001). Dietary variety, energy regulation, and obesity. *Psychological Bulletin, 127,* 325-341. (p. 590)

Reason, J. (1987). The Chernobyl errors. *Bulletin of the British Psychological Society, 40,* 201-206. (p. 740)

Reason, J., & Mycielska, K. (1982). *Absent-minded? The psychology of mental lapses and everyday errors.* Englewood Cliffs, NJ: Prentice-Hall. (pp. 257-258)

Redelmeier, D. A., & Tversky, D. A. (1996). On the belief that arthritis pain is related to the weather. *Proceedings of the National Academy of Sciences, 93,* 2895-2896. (p. 33)

Redish, A. D. (2004). Addiction as a computational process gone awry. *Science, 306,* 1944-1947. (p. 306)

Reed, P. (2000). Serial position effects in recognition memory for odors. *Journal of Experimental Psychology: Learning, Memory, and Cognition, 26,* 411-422. (p. 356)

Reed, T. E., & Jensen, A. R. (1992). Conduction velocity in a brain nerve pathway of normal adults correlates with intelligence level. *Intelligence, 16,* 259-272. (p. 441)

Reeve, C. L., & Hakel, M. D. (2002). Asking the right questions about *g. Human Performance, 15,* 47-74. (p. 435)

Regier, D. A., Kaelber, C. T., Rae, D. S., Farmer, M. E., Knauper, B., Kessler, R. C., & Norquist, G. S. (1998). Limitations of diagnostic criteria and assessment instruments for mental disorders: Implications for research and policy. *Archives of General Psychiatry, 55,* 109-115. (p. 644)

Reichman, J. (1998). *I'm not in the mood: What every woman should know about improving her libido.* New York: Morrow. (p. 483)

Reiner, W. G., & Gearhart, J. P. (2004). Discordant sexual identity in some genetic males with cloacal exstrophy assigned to female sex at birth. *New England Journal of Medicine, 350,* 333-341. (p. 130)

Reisenzein, R. (1983). The Schachter theory of emotion: Two decades later. *Psychological Bulletin, 94,* 239-264. (p. 520)

Reiser, M. (1982). *Police psychology.* Los Angeles: LEHI. (p. 265)

Reiss, D., & Marino, L. (2001). Mirror self-recognition in the bottlenose dolphin: A case of cognitive convergence. *Proceedings of the National Academy of Sciences, 98,* 5937-5942. (p. 424)

Relman, A. S. (1998, December 14). A trip to stonesville. *New Republic* (www.thenewrepublic.com). (p. 580)

Remafedi, G. (1999). Suicide and sexual orientation: Nearing the end of controversy? *Archives of General Psychiatry, 56,* 885-886. (p. 488)

Remley, A. (1988, October). From obedience to independence. *Psychology Today,* pp. 56-59. (p. 124)

Remondes, M., & Schuman, E. M. (2004). Role for a cortical input to hippocampal area CA1 in the consolidation of a long-term memory. *Nature, 431,* 699-703. (p. 368)

Reneman, L., Lavalaye, J., Schmand, B., De Wolff, F. A., Van Den Brink, W., Den Heeten, G., & Booij, J. (2001). Cortical serotonin transporter density and verbal memory in individuals who stopped using 3, 4-methylenedioxy-methampetamine. *Archives of General Psychiatry, 58,* 901-908. (p. 302)

Renner, M. J. (1992). Curiosity and exploration. In L. R. Squire (Ed.), *Encyclopedia of Learning and Memory.* New York: Macmillan. (p. 471)

Renner, M. J., & Renner, C. H. (1993). Expert and novice intuitive judgments about animal behavior. *Bulletin of the Psychonomic Society, 31,* 551-552. (p. 114)

Renner, M. J., & Rosenzweig, M. R. (1987). *Enriched and impoverished environments: Effects on brain and behavior.* New York: Springer-Verlag. (p. 114)

Rentfrow, P. J., & Gosling, S. D. (2003). The Do Re Mi's of everyday life: The structure and personality correlates of music preferences. *Journal of Personality and Social Psychology, 84,* 1236-1256. (p. 621)

Repetti, R. L., Taylor, S. E., & Seeman, T. E. (2002). Risky families: Family social environments and the mental and physical health of offspring. *Psychological Bulletin, 128,* 330-366. (p. 551)

Rescorla, R. A. (1988, March). Pavlovian conditioning: It's not what you think it is. *American Psychologist, 43,* 151-160. (p. 321)

Rescorla, R. A., & Wagner, A. R. (1972). A theory of Pavlovian conditioning: Variations in the effectiveness of reinforcement and nonreinforcement. In A. H. Black & W. F. Perokasy (Eds.), *Classical conditioning II: Current theory.* New York: Appleton-Century-Crofts. (p. 321)

Resnick, M. D., Bearman, P. S., Blum, R. W., Bauman, K. E., Harris, K. M., Jones, J., Tabor, J., Beuhring, T., Sieving, R., Shew, M., Bearinger, L. H., & Udry, J. R. (1997). Protecting adolescents from harm: Findings from the National Longitudinal Study on Adolescent Health. *Journal of the American Medical Association, 278,* 823-832. (pp. 33, 170, 172)

Resnick, R. A., O'Regan, J. K., & Clark, J. J. (1997). To see or not to see: The need for attention to perceive changes in scenes. *Psychological Science, 8,* 368-373. (p. 239)

Resnick, S. M. (1992). Positron emission tomography in psychiatric illness. *Current Directions in Psychological Science, 1,* 92-98. (p. 672)

Responsive Community. (1996, Fall). Age vs. weight. Page 83 (reported from a *Wall Street Journal* survey). (p. 588)

Ressler, R. K., Burgess, A. W., & Douglas, J. E. (1988). *Sexual homicide patterns.* Boston: Lexington Books. (p. 753)

Reynolds, A. J., Temple, J. A., Robertson, D. L., & Manri, E. A. (2001). Long-term effects of an early childhood intervention on educational achievement and juvenile arrest. *Journal of the American Medical Association, 285,* 2339-2346. (p. 458)

Rhee, S. H., & Waldman, I. D. (2002). Genetic and environmental influences on antisocial behavior: A meta-analysis of twin and adoption studies. *Psychological Bulletin, 128,* 490-529. (p. 678)

Rhodes, G., Sumich, A., & Byatt, G. (1999). Are average facial configurations attractive only because of their symmetry? *Psychological Science, 10,* 52-58. (p. 761)

Rhodes, S. R. (1983). Age-related differences in work attitudes and behavior: A review and conceptual analysis. *Psychological Bulletin, 93,* 328-367. (p. 179)

Rholes, W. S., & Simpson, J. A. (Eds.) (2004). *Adult attachment: Theory, research, and clinical implications.* New York: Guilford. (p. 158)

Ribeior, R., Gervasoni, D., Soares, E. S., Zhou, Y., & Lin S-C., Pantoja, J., Lavine, M., & Nicolelis, M. A. L. (2004). Long-lasting novelty-induced neuronal reverberation during slow-wave sleep in multiple forebrain areas. *PloS Biology, 2*(1), e37 (www.plosbiology.org). (p. 283)

Ricciardelli, L. A., & McCabe, M. P. (2004). A biopsychosocial model of disordered eating and the pursuit of muscularity in adolescent boys. *Psychological Bulletin, 130,* 179-205. (p. 479)

Riccio, D. C., Millin, P. M., & Gisquet-Verrier, P. (2003). Retrograde amnesia: Forgetting back. *Current Directions in Psychological Science, 12,* 41–44. (p. 366)

Rice, B. (1985, September). Performance review: The job nobody likes. *Psychology Today,* pp. 30–36. (p. 726)

Rice, M. E., & Grusec, J. E. (1975). Saying and doing: Effects on observer performance. *Journal of Personality and Social Psychology, 32,* 584–593. (p. 344)

Rich, F. (2001, May 20). Naked capitalists: there's no business like porn business. *New York Times* (www.nytimes.com). (p. 753)

Richards, J. M., & Gross, J. J. (2000). Emotion regulation and memory: The cognitive costs of keeping one's cool. *Journal of Personality and Social Psychology, 79,* 410–424. (p. 524)

Richardson, J. (1993). The curious case of coins: Remembering the appearance of familiar objects. *The Psychologist: Bulletin of the British Psychological Society, 6,* 360–366. (p. 377)

Richardson, J. T. E., & Zucco, G. M. (1989). Cognition and olfaction: A review. *Psychological Bulletin, 105,* 352–360. (p. 232)

Rieff, P. (1979). *Freud: The mind of a moralist* (3rd ed.). Chicago: University of Chicago Press. (p. 607)

Rieger, G., Chivers, M. L., & Bailey, J. M. (2005). Sexual arousal patterns of bisexual men. *Psychological Science, 16,* 579–584. (p. 487)

Riis, J., Loewenstein, G., Baron, J., Jepson, C., Fagerlin, A., & Ubel, P. A. (2005). Ignorance of hedonic adaptation to hemodialysis: A study using ecological momentary assessment. *Journal of Experimental Psychology: General, 134,* 3–9. (p. 538)

Ring, K. (1980). *Life at death: A scientific investigation of the near-death experience.* New York: Coward, McCann & Geoghegan. (p. 309)

Ripple, C. H., & Zigler, E. (2003). Research, policy, and the federal role in prevention initiatives for children. *American Psychologist, 58,* 482–490. (p. 458)

Riskind, J. H., Beck, A. T., Berchick, R. J., Brown, G., & Steer, R. A. (1987). Reliability of DSM-III diagnoses for major depression and generalized anxiety disorder using the structured clinical interview for DSM-III. *Archives of General Psychiatry, 44,* 817–820. (p. 644)

Rizzolatti, G., Fadiga, L., Fogassi, L., & Gallese, V. (2002). From mirror neurons to imitation: Facts and speculations. In A. N. Meltzoff & W. Prinz (Eds.), *The imitative mind: Development, evolution, and brain bases.* Cambridge: Cambridge University Press, 2002. (p. 341)

Roberson, D., Davidoff, J., Davies, I. R. L., & Shapiro, L. R. (2004). The development of color categories in two languages: A longitudinal study. *Journal of Experimental Psychology: General, 133,* 554–571. (p. 419)

Roberts, A. H., Kewman, D. G., Mercier, L., & Hovell, M. (1993). The power of nonspecific effects in healing: Implications for psychosocial and biological treatments. *Clinical Psychology Review, 13,* 375–391. (p. 707)

Roberts, B. W., Caspi, A., & Moffitt, T. E. (2001). The kids are alright: Growth and stability in personality development from adolescence to adulthood. *Journal of Personality and Social Psychology, 81,* 670–683. (p. 194)

Roberts, B. W., Caspi, A., & Moffitt, T. E. (2003). Work experiences and personality development in young adulthood. *Journal of Personality and Social Psychology, 84,* 582–593. (pp. 188, 194)

Roberts, B. W., & DelVecchio, W. F. (2000). The rank-order consistency of personality traits from childhood to old age: A quantitative review of longitudinal studies. *Psychological Bulletin, 126,* 3–25. (p. 620)

Roberts, B. W., O'Donnell, M., & Robins, R. W. (2004). Goal and personality trait development in emerging adulthood. *Journal of Personality and Social Psychology, 87,* 541–550. (p. 194)

Roberts, L. (1988). Beyond Noah's ark: What do we need to know? *Science, 242,* 1247. (p. 564)

Roberts, T-A. (1991). Determinants of gender differences in responsiveness to others' evaluations. *Dissertation Abstracts International, 51*(8-B). (p. 128)

Robins, L. N., Davis, D. H., & Goodwin, D. W. (1974). Drug use by U.S. Army enlisted men in Vietnam: A follow-up on their return home. *American Journal of Epidemiology, 99,* 235–249. (p. 298)

Robins, L., & Regier, D. (Eds.). (1991). *Psychiatric disorders in America.* New York: Free Press. (p. 681)

Robins, R. W., Gosling, S. D., & Craik, K. H. (1999). An empirical analysis of trends in psychology. *American Psychologist, 54,* 117–128. (p. 596)

Robins, R. W., & Trzesniewski, K. H. (2005). Self-esteem development across the lifespan. *Current Directions in Psychological Science, 14*(3), 158–162. (p. 189)

Robins, R. W., Trzesniewski, K. H., Tracy, J. L., Gosling, S. D., & Potter, J. (2002). Global self-esteem across the lifespan. *Psychology and Aging, 17,* 423–434. (p. 171)

Robinson, J. (2002, October 8). What percentage of the population is gay? *Gallup Tuesday Briefing* (www.gallup.com/poll/tb/religValue/20021008b.asp). (p. 487)

Robinson, J. L., Kagan, J., Reznick, J. S., & Corley, R. (1992). The heritability of inhibited and uninhibited behavior: A twin study. *Developmental Psychology, 28,* 1030–1037. (p. 102)

Robinson, T. E., & Berridge, K. C. (2003). Addiction. *Annual Review of Psychology, 54,* 25–53. (p. 297)

Robinson, T. N. (1999). Reducing children's television viewing to prevent obesity. *Journal of the American Medical Association, 282,* 1561–1567. (p. 590)

Robinson, V. M. (1983). Humor and health. In P. E. McGhee & J. H. Goldstein (Eds.), *Handbook of humor research: Vol. II. Applied studies.* New York: Springer-Verlag. (p. 565)

Robison, J., & Mason, H. (2002, July 2). Getting between teens and tobacco. *Gallup Tuesday Briefing,* Gallup Organization (www.gallup.com/poll/tb/healthcare/20020702.asp). (p. 582)

Robison, L. (1999). Why our MENTALLY ILL son is on DEATH ROW. www.swuuc.org/fjuuc/Courier/robison.htm. See also www.larryrobison.org (p. 648)

Rochat, F. (1993). How did they resist authority? Protecting refugees in Le Chambon during World War II. Paper presented at the American Psychological Association convention. (pp. 736–737)

Rock, I., & Palmer, S. (1990, December). The legacy of Gestalt psychology. *Scientific American,* pp. 84–90. (p. 243)

Rodin, J. (1986). Aging and health: Effects of the sense of control. *Science, 233,* 1271–1276. (pp. 563–564, 626)

Rodriguez, E., George, N., Lachaux, J-P., Martinerie, J., Renault, B., & Varela, F. J. (1999). Perception's shadow: Long-distance synchronization of human brain activity. *Nature, 297,* 430–433. (pp. 210, 211)

Roediger, H. (2001, September). Quoted by R. Herbert, Doing a number on memory. *APS Observer,* pp. 1, 7–11. (p. 370)

Roediger, H. L., III, & McDermott, K. B. (1995). Creating false memories: Remembering words not presented in lists. *Journal of Experimental Psychology: Learning, Memory, and Cognition, 21,* 803–814. (p. 385)

Roediger, H. L., III, Wheeler, M. A., & Rajaram, S. (1993). Remembering, knowing, and reconstructing the past. In D. L. Medin (Ed.), *The psychology of learning and motivation: Advances in research and theory* (Vol. 30). Orlando, FL: Academic Press. (p. 383)

Roehling, M. V. (1999). Weight-based discrimination in employment: Psychological and legal aspects. *Personnel Psychology, 52,* 969–1016. (p. 584)

Roehling, M. V. (2000). Weight-based discrimination in employment: psychological and legal aspects. *Personnel Psychology, 52*(4), 969–1016. (p. 584)

Roehling, P. V., Roehling, M. V., & Moen, P. (2001). The relationship between work-life policies and practices and employee loyalty: A life course perspective. *Journal of Family and Economic Issues, 22,* 141–170. (p. 509)

Roenneberg, T., Kuehnle, T., Pramstaller, P. P., Ricken, J., Havel, M., Guth, A., Merrow, M. (2004). A marker for the end of adolescence. *Current Biology, 14,* R1038-9. (p. 275)

Roesser, R. (1998). What you should know about hearing conservation. Better Hearing Institute (www.betterhearing.org). (p. 218)

Rogers, C. R. (1958). Reinhold Niebuhr's *The self and the dramas of history:* A criticism. *Pastoral Psychology, 9,* 15–17. (p. 633)

Rogers, C. R. (1961). *On becoming a person: A therapist's view of psychotherapy.* Boston: Houghton Mifflin. (p. 689)

Rogers, C. R. (1980). *A way of being.* Boston: Houghton Mifflin. (pp. 610, 689)

Rogers, C. R. (1981, Summer). Notes on Rollo May. *Perspectives, 2*(1), p. 16. (p. 611)

Rogers, L. J. (2003, Fall). Seeking the right answers about right brain-left brain. *Cerebrum, 5*(4), 55–68. (p. 86)

Rogers, S. (1992–1993, Winter). How a publicity blitz created the myth of subliminal advertising. *Public Relations Quarterly,* pp. 12–17. (p. 200)

Rogers, S. (1994). Subliminal advertising: Grand scam of the 20th century. Paper presented to the American Academy of Advertising convention. (p. 200)

Rogerson, P. A. (1994). On the relationship between handedness and longevity. *Social Biology, 40,* 283–287. (p. 90)

Rohan, M. J., & Zanna, M. P. (1996). Value transmission in families," in C. Seligman, J. M. Olson, & M. P. Zanna (Eds.), *The psychology of values: The Ontario Symposium* (Vol. 8). Malwah, NJ: Erlbaum. (p. 101)

Rohner, R. P. (1986). *The warmth dimension: Foundations of parental acceptance-rejection theory.* Newbury Park, CA: Sage. (p. 125)

Rohner, R. P., & Veneziano, R. A. (2001). The importance of father love: History and contemporary evidence. *Review of General Psychology, 5,* 382–405. (pp. 157, 162)

Roiser, J. P., Cook, L. J., Cooper, J. D., Rubinsztein, D. C., & Sahakian, B. J. (2005). Association of a functional polymorphism in the serotonin transporter gene with abnormal emotional processing in ecstasy users. *American Journal of Psychiatry, 162,* 609–612. (p. 302)

Rokach, A., Orzeck, T., Moya, M., & Exposito, F. (2002). Causes of loneliness in North America and Spain. *European Psychologist, 7,* 70–79. (p. 46)

Rosch, E. (1974). Linguistic relativity. In A. Silverstein (Ed.), *Human communication: Theoretical perspectives.* New York: Halsted Press. (p. 419)

Rosch, E. (1978). Principles of categorization. In E. Rosch & B. L. Lloyd (Eds.), *Cognition and categorization.* Hillsdale, NJ: Erlbaum. (p. 396)

Rose, J. S., Chassin, L., Presson, C. C., & Sherman, S. J. (1999). Peer influences on adolescent cigarette smoking: A prospective sibling analysis. *Merrill-Palmer Quarterly, 45,* 62–84. (pp. 118, 576)

Rose, R. J., Kaprio, J., Winter, T., Dick, D. M., Viken, R. J., Pulkkinen, L., & Koskenvuo, M. (2002). Femininity and fertility in sisters with twin brothers: Prenatal androgenization? Cross-sex socialization? *Psychological Science, 13,* 263–266. (p. 489)

Rose, R. J., Viken, R. J., Dick, D. M., Bates, J. E., Pulkkinen, L., & Kaprio, J. (2003). It *does* take a village: Nonfamiliar environments and children's behavior. *Psychological Science, 14,* 273–277. (p. 653)

Rose, S. (1999). Precis of *Lifelines: Biology, freedom, determinism. Behavioral and Brain Sciences, 22,* 871–921. (p. 112)

Rose, S., Bisson, J., & Wessely, S. (2003). A systematic review of single-session psychological interventions ('debriefing') following trauma. *Psychotherapy and Psychosomatics, 72,* 176–184. (p. 653)

Roselli, C. E., Resko, J. A., & Stormshak, F. (2002). Hormonal influences on sexual partner preference in rams. *Archives of Sexual Behavior, 31,* 43–9. (p. 490)

Rosenbaum, M. (1986). The repulsion hypothesis: On the nondevelopment of relationships. *Journal of Personality and Social Psychology, 51,* 1156–1166. (p. 762)

Rosenberg, N. A., Pritchard, J. K., Weber, J. L., Cann, H. M., Kidd, K. K., Zhivotosky, L. A., & Feldman, M. W. (2002). Genetic structure of human populations. *Science, 298,* 2381–2385. (p. 109)

Rosenhan, D. L. (1973). On being sane in insane places. *Science, 179,* 250–258. (p. 645)

Rosenthal, R., Hall, J. A., Archer, D., DiMatteo, M. R., & Rogers, P. L. (1979). The PONS test: Measuring sensitivity to nonverbal cues. In S. Weitz (Ed.), *Nonverbal communication* (2nd ed.). New York: Oxford University Press. (pp. 464, 524–525)

Rosenzweig, M. R. (1984). Experience, memory, and the brain. *American Psychologist, 39,* 365–376. (p. 114)

Ross, L., Greene, D., & House, P. (1977). The false consensus effect: An egocentric bias in social perception and attribution process. *Journal of Experimental Social Psychology, 13,* 279–301. (p. 28)

Ross, M., McFarland, C., & Fletcher, G. J. O. (1981). The effect of attitude on the recall of personal histories. *Journal of Personality and Social Psychology, 40,* 627–634. (p. 380)

Ross, M., Xun, W. Q. E., & Wilson, A. E. (2002). Language and the bicultural self. *Personality and Social Psychology Bulletin, 28,* 1040–1050. (p. 418)

Rossi, A. S., & Rossi, P. H. (1993). *Of human bonding: Parent-child relations across the life course.* Hawthorne, NY: Aldine de Gruyter. (p. 129)

Rossi, P. J. (1968). Adaptation and negative after effect to lateral optical displacement in newly hatched chicks. *Science, 160,* 430–432. (p. 256)

Rostosky, S. S., Wilcox, B. L., Wright, M. L. C., & Randall, B. A. (2004). The impact of religiosity on adolescent sexual behavior: A review of the evidence. *Journal of Adolescent Research, 19,* 677–697. (p. 486)

Roth, T., Roehrs, T., Zwyghuizen-Doorenbos, A., Stpeanski, E., & Witting, R. (1988). Sleep and memory. In I. Hindmarch & H. Ott (Eds.), *Benzodiazepine receptor ligans, memory and information processing.* New York: Springer-Verlag. (p. 286)

Rothbart, M., Fulero, S., Jensen, C., Howard, J., & Birrell, P. (1978). From individual to group impressions: Availability heuristics in stereotype formation. *Journal of Experimental Social Psychology, 14,* 237–255. (p. 748)

Rothbart, M. K., Ahadi, S. A., & Evans, D. E. (2000). Temperament and personality: Origins and outcomes. *Journal of Personality and Social Psychology, 78,* 122–135. (p. 102)

Rothbaum, B. O., Hodges, L., Anderson, P. L., Price, L., & Smith, S. (2002). Twelve-month followup of virtual reality and standard exposure therapies for the fear of flying. *Journal of Consulting and Clinical Psychology, 70,* 428–432. (p. 692)

Rothbaum, F., & Tsang, B. Y-P. (1998). Lovesongs in the United States and China: On the nature of romantic love. *Journal of Cross-Cultural Psychology, 29,* 306–319. (p. 123)

Rothman, A. J., & Salovey, P. (1997). Shaping perceptions to motivate healthy behavior: The role of message framing. *Psychological Bulletin, 121,* 3–19. (p. 406)

Rothstein, W. G. (1980). The significance of occupations in work careers: An empirical and theoretical review. *Journal of Vocational Behavior, 17,* 328–343. (p. 189)

Rotton, J., & Kelly, I. W. (1985). Much ado about the full moon: A meta-analysis of lunar-lunacy research. *Psychological Bulletin, 97,* 286–306. (p. 680)

Rovee-Collier, C. (1989). The joy of kicking: Memories, motives, and mobiles. In P. R. Solomon, G. R. Goethals, C. M. Kelley, & B. R. Stephens (Eds.), *Memory: Interdisciplinary approaches.* New York: Springer-Verlag. (p. 146)

Rovee-Collier, C. (1993). The capacity for long-term memory in infancy. *Current Directions in Psychological Science, 2,* 130–135. (p. 373)

Rovee-Collier, C. (1997). Dissociations in infant memory: Rethinking the development of implicit and explicit memory. *Psychological Review, 104,* 467–498. (p. 146)

Rowe, D. C. (1990). As the twig is bent? The myth of child-rearing influences on personality development. *Journal of Counseling and Development, 68,* 606–611. (p. 100)

Rowe, D. C. (2005). Under the skin: On the impartial treatment of genetic and environmental hypotheses of racial differences. *American Psychologist, 60,* 60–70. (p. 460)

Rowe, D. C., Almeida, D. M., & Jacobson, K. C. (1999). School context and genetic influences on aggression in adolescence. *Psychological Science, 10,* 277–280. (p. 749)

Rowe, D. C., Jacobson, K. C., & Van den Oord, E. J. C. G. (1999). Genetic and environmental influences on vocabulary IQ: Parental education level as moderator. *Child Development, 70*(5), 1151–1162. (p. 456)

Rowe, D. C., Vazsonyi, A. T., & Flannery, D. J. (1994). No more than skin deep: Ethnic and racial similarity in developmental process. *Psychological Review, 101*(3), 396. (p. 125)

Rowe, D. C., Vazsonyi, A. T., & Flannery, D. J. (1995). Ethnic and racial similarity in developmental process: A study of academic achievement. *Psychological Science, 6*, 33–38. (p. 125)

Rozin, P., Dow, S., Mosovitch, M., & Rajaram, S. (1998). What causes humans to begin and end a meal? A role for memory for what has been eaten, as evidenced by a study of multiple meal eating in amnesic patients. *Psychological Science, 9*, 392–396. (p. 477)

Rozin, P., Millman, L., & Nemeroff, C. (1986). Operation of the laws of sympathetic magic in disgust and other domains. *Journal of Personality and Social Psychology, 50*, 703–712. (p. 320)

Ruback, R. B., Carr, T. S., & Hopper, C. H. (1986). Perceived control in prison: Its relation to reported crowding, stress, and symptoms. *Journal of Applied Social Psychology, 16*, 375–386. (p. 626)

Rubenstein, J. S., Meyer, D. E., & Evans, J. E. (2001). Executive control of cognitive processes in task switching. *Journal of Experimental Psychology: Human Perception and Performance, 27*, 763–797. (p. 238)

Rubin, D. C., Rahhal, T. A., & Poon, L. W. (1998). Things learned in early adulthood are remembered best. *Memory and Cognition, 26*, 3–19. (p. 181)

Rubin, J. Z., Pruitt, D. G., & Kim, S. H. (1994). *Social conflict: Escalation, stalemate, and settlement.* New York: McGraw-Hill. (p. 769)

Rubin, L. B. (1985). *Just friends: The role of friendship in our lives.* New York: Harper & Row. (p. 129)

Rubin, Z. (1970). Measurement of romantic love. *Journal of Personality and Social Psychology, 16*, 265–273. (p. 524)

Rubonis, A. V., & Bickman, L. (1991). Psychological impairment in the wake of disaster: The disaster-psychopathology relationship. *Psychological Bulletin, 109*, 384–399. (p. 554)

Ruchlis, H. (1990). *Clear thinking: A practical introduction.* Buffalo, NY: Prometheus Books. (p. 398)

Rudman, L. A., & Goodwin, S. A. (2004). Gender differences in automatic in-group bias: Why do women like women more than men like men? *Journal of Personality and Social Psychology, 87*, 494–509. (p. 745)

Ruffin, C. L. (1993). Stress and health—little hassles vs. major life events. *Australian Psychologist, 28*, 201–208. (pp. 554–555)

Rule, B. G., & Ferguson, T. J. (1986). The effects of media violence on attitudes, emotions, and cognitions. *Journal of Social Issues, 42*(3), 29–50. (p. 346)

Rumbaugh, D. M. (1977). *Language learning by a chimpanzee: The Lana project.* New York: Academic Press. (p. 426)

Rumbaugh, D. M. (1994, February 15). Remarks on *Nova: Can chimps talk?* PBS Television. (p. 428)

Rumbaugh, D. M., & Savage-Rumbaugh, S. (1978). Chimpanzee language research: Status and potential. *Behavior Research Methods & Instrumentation, 10*, 119–131. (p. 427)

Rumbaugh, D. M., & Savage-Rumbaugh, S. (1994, January/February). Language and apes. *Psychology Teacher Network*, pp. 2–5, 9. (p. 428)

Rumbaugh, D. M., & Washburn, D. A. (2003). *Intelligence of apes and other rational beings.* New Haven, CT: Yale University Press. (p. 427)

Rupp, R. (1998). *How we remember and why we forget.* New York: Three Rivers Press. (p. 349)

Rush, A. J., & 15 others (2005). Vagus nerve stimulation for treatment-resistant depression: A randomized, controlled acute phase trial. *Biological Psychiatry, 58*, 347–354. (p. 716)

Rushton, J. P. (1975). Generosity in children: Immediate and long-term effects of modeling, preaching, and moral judgment. *Journal of Personality and Social Psychology, 31*, 459–466. (p. 344)

Rushton, J. P. (1998). The "Jensen effect" and the "Spearman-Jensen hypothesis" of black-white IQ differences. *Intelligence, 26*, 217–225. (p. 459)

Rushton, J. P. (2003). Race, brain size, and IQ: The case for consilience. *Behavioral and Brain Sciences, 26*, 648–649. (p. 459)

Rushton, J. P., & Ankney, C. D. (1996). Brain size and cognitive ability: Correlations with age, sex, social class, and race. *Psychonomic Bulletin & Review, 3*, 21–36. (p. 440)

Russell, B. (1930/1985). *The conquest of happiness.* London: Unwin Paperbacks. (p. 543) 527)

Russell, J. A., & Carroll, J. M. (January, 1999A). On the bipolarity of positive and negative affect. *Psychological Bulletin, 125*, 3–30. (p. 533)

Russell, J. A., & Carroll, J. M. (1999B). The phoenix of bipolarity: Reply to Watson and Tellegan (1999). *Psychological Bulletin, 125*, 611–614. (p. 533)

Russell, J. A., Lewicka, M., & Niit, T. (1989). A cross-cultural study of a circumplex model of affect. *Journal of Personality and Social Psychology, 57*, 848–856. (p. 533)

Rusting, C. L., & Nolen-Hoeksema, S. (1998). Regulating responses to anger: Effects of rumination and distraction on angry mood. *Journal of Personality and Social Psychology, 74*, 790–803. (p. 537)

Rutter, M., and the English and Romanian Adoptees (ERA) study team. (1998). Developmental catch-up, and deficit, following adoption after severe global early privation. *Journal of Child Psychology and Psychiatry, 39*, 465–476. (p. 158)

Ryan, L., Hatfield, C., & Hofstetter, M. (2002). Caffeine reduces time-of-day effects on memory performance in older adults. *Psychological Science, 13*, 68–71. (p. 182)

Ryan, R. (1999, February 2). Quoted by Alfie Kohn, In pursuit of affluence, at a high price. *New York Times* (www.nytimes.com). (pp. 541, 542)

Ryan, R. M., & Deci, E. L. (2004). Avoiding death or engaging life as accounts of meaning and culture: Comment on Pyszczynski et al. (2004). *Psychological Bulletin, 130*, 473–477. (pp. 635–636)

Ryckman, R. M., Robbins, M. A., Kaczor, L. M., & Gold J. A. (1989). Male and female raters' stereotyping of male and female physiques. *Personality and Social Psychology Bulletin, 15*, 244–251. (p. 583)

Saad, L. (2001, December 17). Americans' mood: Has Sept. 11 made a difference? Gallup Poll News Service (www.gallup.com/poll/releases/pr011217.asp). (pp. 550, 554)

Saad, L. (2002, July 30). Dieter's dilemma: Bagel or bacon? *Gallup Tuesday Briefing*, Gallup Organization (www.gallup.com/poll/tb/healthcare/20020730.asp). (p. 587)

Saad, L. (2002, November 21). Most smokers wish they could quit. Gallup News Service (www.gallup.com). (p. 577)

Saad, L. (2003, December 9). Religion is very important to majority of Americans. Gallup News Service (www.gallup.com). (pp. 128, 577)

Sabini, J. (1986). Stanley Milgram (1933–1984). *American Psychologist, 41*, 1378–1379. (p. 734)

Sabol, S. Z., Nelson, M. L., Fisher, C., Gunzerath, L., Brody, C. L., Hu, S., Sirota, L. A., Marcus, S. E., Greenberg, B. D., Lucas, F. R., IV, Benjamin, J. Murphy, D. L., & Hamer, D. H. (1999). A genetic association for cigarette smoking behavior. *Health Psychology, 18*, 7–13. (p. 578)

Sachdev, P., & Sachdev, J. (1997). Sixty years of psychosurgery: Its present status and its future. *Australian and New Zealand Journal of Psychiatry, 31*, 457–464. (p. 718)

Sacks, O. (1985). *The man who mistook his wife for a hat.* New York: Summit Books. (pp. 234, 367)

Sacks, O. (1990). *Seeing voices: A journey into the world of the deaf.* New York: HarperCollins. (p. 419)

Sadato, N., Pascual-Leone, A., Grafman, J., Ibanez, V., Deiber, M-P., Dold, G., & Hallett, M. (1996). Activation of the primary visual cortex by Braille reading in blind subjects. *Nature, 380*, 526–528. (p. 83)

Saffran, J. R., Aslin, R. N., & Newport, E. L. (1996). Statistical learning by 8-month-old infants. *Science, 274*, 1926–1928. (p. 415)

Sagan, C. (1979a). *Broca's brain.* New York: Random House. (p. 67)

Sagan, C. (1987, February 1). The fine art of baloney detection. *Parade.* (p. 266)

Sagan, C., & Druyan, A. (1992). *Shadows of forgotten ancestors: A search for who we are.* New York: Random House. (p. 425)

Sage, C., Huang, M., Karimi, K., Gutierrez, G., Vollrath, M. A., Zhang, D-S., Garcia-Anoveros, J., Hinds, P. W., Corwin, J. T., Coren, D. P., & Chen, Z-Y. (2005). Proliferation of functional hair cells in vivo in the absence of the retinoblastoma protein. *Science, 307,* 1114-1118. (p. 221)

Sakurai, T., Amemiya, A., Ishii, M., Matsuzaki, I., Chemelli, R. M., Tanaka, H., Williams, S. C., Richardson, J. A., Kozlowski, G. P., Wilson, S., Arch, J. R. S., Buckingham, R. E., Haynes, A. C., Carr, S. A., Annan, R. S., McNulty, D. E., Liu, W-S., Terrett, J. A., Elshourbagy, N. A., Bergsma, D. J., Yanagisawa, M. (1998). Orexins and orexin receptors: A family of hypothalamic neuropeptides and G protein-coupled receptors that regulate feeding behavior. *Cell, 92,* 573-585. (p. 475)

Salive, M. E., Guralnik, J. M., & Glynn, R. J. (1993). Left-handedness and mortality. *American Journal of Public Health, 83,* 265-267. (pp. 90-91)

Salmon, P. (2001). Effects of physical exercise on anxiety, depression, and sensitivity to stress: A unifying theory. *Clinical Psychology Review, 21,* 33-61. (p. 569)

Salovey, P. (1990, January/February). Interview. *American Scientist,* pp. 25-29. (p. 537)

Salovey, P., & Birnbaum, D. (1989). Influence of mood on health-relevant cognitions. *Journal of Personality and Social Psychology, 57,* 539-551. (p. 591)

Salovey, P., & Mayer, J. D. (1990). Emotional intelligence. *Imagination, Cognition, and Personality, 9,* 185-211. (p. 437)

Salovey, P., Mayer, J. D., & Caruso, D. (2002). The positive psychology of emotional intelligence. In C. R. Snyder & S. J. Lopez (Eds.), *Handbook of positive psychology.* New York: Oxford. (p. 436)

Salthouse, T. A. (2004). What and when of cognitive aging. *Current Directions in Psychological Science, 13,* 140-144. (p. 184)

Sampson, E. E. (2000). Reinterpreting individualism and collectivism: Their religious roots and monologic versus dialogic person–other relationship. *American Psychologist, 55,* 1425-1432. (p. 122)

Samuels, J., & Nestadt, G. (1997). Epidemiology and genetics of obsessive-compulsive disorder. *International Review of Psychiatry, 9,* 61-71. (p. 652)

Samuels, S., & McCabe, G. (1989). Quoted by P. Diaconis & F. Mosteller, Methods for studying coincidences. *Journal of the American Statistical Association, 84,* 853-861. (p. 35)

Sandberg, G. G., Jackson, T. L., & Petretic-Jackson, P. (1985). *Sexual aggression and courtship violence in dating relationships.* Paper presented at the meeting of the Midwestern Psychological Association. (p. 753)

Sanders, G., Sjodin, M., & de Chastelaine, M. (2002). On the elusive nature of sex differences in cognition hormonal influences contributing to within-sex variation. *Archives of Sexual Behavior, 31,* 145-152. (p. 491)

Sanders, G., & Wright, M. (1997). Sexual orientation differences in cerebral asymmetry and in the performance of sexually dimorphic cognitive and motor tasks. *Archives of Sexual Behavior, 26,* 463-479. (p. 492)

Sandfort, T. G. M., de Graaf, R., Bijl, R., & Schnabel, P. (2001). Same-sex sexual behavior and psychiatric disorders. *Archives of General Psychiatry, 58,* 85-91. (pp. 487, 488)

Sandler, W., Meir, I., Padden, C., & Aronoff, M. (2005). The emergence of grammar: Systematic structure in a new language. *Proceedings of the National Academy of Sciences, 102,* 2261-2265. (p. 414)

Sanford, A. J., Fray, N., Stewart, A., & Moxey, L. (2002). Perspective in statements of quantity, with implications for consumer psychology. *Psychological Science, 13,* 130-134. (p. 406)

Santarelli, L., & 11 others (2003). Requirement of hippocampal neurogenesis for the behavioral effects of antidepressants. *Science, 301,* 805-809. (pp. 713-714)

Sanz, C., Blicher, A., Dalke, K., Gratton-Fabri, L., McClure-Richards, T., & Fouts, R. (1998, Winter-Spring). Enrichment object use: Five chimpanzees' use of temporary and semi-permanent enrichment objects. *Friends of Washoe, 19*(1,2), 9-14. (p. 425)

Sanz, C., Morgan, D., Gulick, S. (2004). New insights into chimpanzees, tools, and termites from the Congo Basin. *American Naturalist, 164,* 567-581. (p. 423)

Sapadin, L. A. (1988). Friendship and gender: Perspectives of professional men and women. *Journal of Social and Personal Relationships, 5,* 387-403. (p. 129)

Sapolsky, B. S., & Tabarlet, J. O. (1991). Sex in primetime television: 1979 versus 1989. *Journal of Broadcasting and Electronic Media, 35,* 505-516. (pp. 486, 754)

Sapolsky, R. (1999, March). Stress and your shrinking brain. *Discover,* pp. 116-120. (p. 553)

Sapolsky, R. (2003, September). Taming stress. *Scientific American,* pp. 87-95. (pp. 522, 551, 661)

Sapolsky, R. (2005). The influence of social hierarchy on primate health. *Science, 308,* 648-652. (p. 564)

Sapolsky, R. M., & Finch, C. E. (1991, March/April). On growing old. *The Sciences,* pp. 30-38. (p. 178)

Sato, K. (1987). Distribution of the cost of maintaining common resources. *Journal of Experimental Social Psychology, 23,* 19-31. (p. 757)

Saudino, K. J., Wertz, A. E., Gagne, J. R., & Chawla, S. (2004). Night and day: Are siblings as different in temperament as parents say they are? *Journal of Personality and Social Psychology, 87,* 698-706. (p. 102)

Savage-Rumbaugh, E. S., Murphy, J., Sevcik, R. A., Brakke, K. E., Williams, S. L., & Rumbaugh, D. M., with commentary by Bates, E. (1993). Language comprehension in ape and child. *Monographs of the Society for Research in Child Development, 58* (no. 233), 1-254. (p. 428)

Savic, I., Berglund, H., & Lindstrom, P. (2005). Brain response to putative pheromones in homosexual men. *Proceedings of the National Academy of Sciences, 102,* 7356-7361. (p. 490)

Savitsky, K., Epley, N., & Gilovich, T. (2001). Do others judge us as harshly as we think? Overestimating the impact of our failures, shortcomings, and mishaps. *Journal of Personality and Social Psychology, 81,* 44-56. (p. 632)

Savitsky, K., & Gilovich, T. (2003). The illusion of transparency and the alleviation of speech anxiety. *Journal of Experimental Social Psychology, 39,* 618-625. (p. 632)

Savoy, C., & Beitel, P. (1996). Mental imagery for basketball. *International Journal of Sport Psychology, 27,* 454-462. (p. 421)

Sawyer, M. G., Arney, F. M., Baghurst, P. A., Clark, J. J., Graetz, B. W., Kosky, R. J., Nurcombe, B., Patton, G. C., Prior, M. R., Raphael, B., Rey, J., Whaites, L. C., & Zubrick, S. R. (2000). *The mental health of young people in Australia.* Canberra: Mental Health and Special Programs Branch, Commonwealth Department of Health and Aged Care. (pp. 661, 680)

Sax, L. J., Hurtado, S., Lindholm, J A., Astin, A. W., Korn, W. S., & Mahoney, K. M. (2004). *The American freshman: National norms for Fall, 2004.* Los Angeles: Cooperative Institutional Research Program, UCLA. (pp. 110, 132, 166)

Sax, L. J., Lindholm, J. A., Astin, A. W., Korn, W. S., & Mahoney, K. M. (2002). *The American freshman: National norms for Fall 2002.* Los Angeles, CA: Higher Education Research Institute, UCLA. (p. 304)

Sayre, R. F. (1979). The parents' last lessons. In D. D. Van Tassel (Ed.), *Aging, death, and the completion of being.* Philadelphia: University of Pennsylvania Press. (p. 180)

Sbraga, T. P., & O'Donohue, W. (2003). Post hoc reasoning in possible cases of child sexual abuse: Symptoms of inconclusive origins. *Clinical Psychology: Science and Practice, 10,* 320-334. (p. 159)

Scarborough, E., & Furumoto, L. (1987). *Untold lives: The first generation of American women psychologists.* New York: Columbia University Press. (p. 5-6)

Scarr, S. (1984, May). What's a parent to do? A conversation with E. Hall. *Psychology Today,* pp. 58-63. (p. 458)

Scarr, S. (1986). *Mother care/other care.* New York: Basic Books. (p. 160)

Scarr, S. (1989). Protecting general intelligence: Constructs and consequences for interventions. In R. J. Linn (Ed.), *Intelligence: Measurement, theory, and public policy.* Champaign: University of Illinois Press. (p. 434)

Scarr, S. (1990). Back cover comments on J. Dunn & R. Plomin (1990). *Separate lives: Why siblings are so different.* New York: Basic Books. (p. 105)

Scarr, S. (1993, May/June). Quoted by *Psychology Today*, Nature's thumbprint: So long, superparents, p. 16. (p. 117)

Scarr, S. (1997). Why child care has little impact on most children's development. *Current Directions in Psychological Science, 6*, 143–148. (p. 160)

Schab, F. R. (1991). Odor memory: Taking stock. *Psychological Bulletin, 109*, 242–251. (p. 233)

Schachter, S. (1982). Recidivism and self-cure of smoking and obesity. *American Psychologist, 37*, 436–444. (p. 589)

Schachter, S., & Singer, J. E. (1962). Cognitive, social and physiological determinants of emotional state. *Psychological Review, 69*, 379–399. (pp. 514, 519)

Schacter, D. L. (1992). Understanding implicit memory: A cognitive neuroscience approach. *American Psychologist, 47*, 559–569. (p. 367)

Schacter, D. L. (1996). *Searching for memory: The brain, the mind, and the past.* New York: Basic Books. (pp. 180, 367, 368, 386, 535, 605)

Schacter, D. L. (1999). The seven sins of memory: Insights from psychology and cognitive neuroscience. *American Psychologist, 54*, 182–201. (p. 376)

Schafer, G. (2005). Infants can learn decontextualized words before their first birthday. *Child Development, 76*, 87–96. (p. 413)

Schaie, K. W. (1994). The life course of adult intellectual abilities. *American Psychologist, 49*, 304–313. (p. 183)

Schaie, K. W., & Geiwitz, J. (1982). *Adult development and aging.* Boston: Little, Brown. (p. 183)

Schall, T., & Smith, G. (2000, Fall). Career trajectories in baseball. *Chance*, pp. 35–38. (p. 176)

Scheier, M. F., & Carver, C. S. (1992). Effects of optimism on psychological and physical well-being: Theoretical overview and empirical update. *Cognitive Therapy and Research, 16*, 201–228. (p. 564)

Schein, E. H. (1956). The Chinese indoctrination program for prisoners of war: A study of attempted brainwashing. *Psychiatry, 19*, 149–172. (p. 727)

Schelling, T. C. (1992). Addictive drugs: The cigarette experience. *Science, 255*, 430–433. (p. 578)

Scherer, K. R., Banse, R., & Wallbott, H. G. (2001). Emotion inferences from vocal expression correlate across languages and cultures. *Journal of Cross-Cultural Psychology, 32*, 76–92. (p. 524)

Schiavi, R. C., & Schreiner-Engel, P. (1988). Nocturnal penile tumescence in healthy aging men. *Journal of Gerontology: Medical Sciences, 43*, M146–150. (p. 278)

Schiffenbauer, A., & Schiavo, R. S. (1976). Physical distance and attraction: An intensification effect. *Journal of Experimental Social Psychology, 12*, 274–282. (p. 738)

Schimel, J., Arndt, J., Pyszczynski, T., & Greenberg, J. (2001). Being accepted for who we are: Evidence that social validation of the intrinsic self reduces general defensiveness. *Journal of Personality and Social Psychology, 80*, 35–52. (pp. 611–612)

Schimel, J., Greenberg, J., & Martens, A. (2003). Evidence that projection of a feared trait can serve a defensive function. *Personality and Social Psychology Bulletin, 29*, 969–979. (p. 606)

Schlaug, G., Jancke, L., Huang, Y., & Steinmetz, H. (1995). In vivo evidence of structural brain asymmetry in musicians. *Science, 267*, 699–701. (p. 69)

Schmidt, F. L. (2002). The role of general cognitive ability and job performance: Why there cannot be a debate. *Human Performance, 15*, 187–210. (p. 501)

Schmidt, F. L., & Hunter, J. E. (1998). The validity and utility of selection methods in personnel psychology: Practical and theoretical implications of 85 years of research findings. *Psychological Bulletin, 124*, 262–274. (pp. 437, 501, 503, 630)

Schmidt, F. L., & Zimmerman, R. D. (2004). A counterintuitive hypothesis about employment interview validity and some supporting evidence. *Journal of Applied Psychology, 89*, 553–561. (p. 503)

Schmitt, D. P., & Pilcher, J. J. (2004). Evaluating evidence of psychological adaptation: How do we know one when we see one? *Psychological Science, 15*, 643–649. (p. 109)

Schnaper, N. (1980). Comments germane to the paper entitled "The reality of death experiences" by Ernst Rodin. *Journal of Nervous and Mental Disease, 168*, 268–270. (p. 309)

Schneider, R. H., Alexander, C. N., Staggers, F., Rainforth, M., Salerno, J. W., Hartz, A., Arndt, S., Barnes, V. A., & Nidich, S. (2005). Long-term effects of stress reduction on mortality in persons > or = 55 years of age with systemic hypertension. *American Journal of Cardiology, 95*, 1060–1064. (p. 572)

Schneider, S. L. (2001). In search of realistic optimism: Meaning, knowledge, and warm fuzziness. *American Psychologist, 56*, 250–263. (p. 627)

Schneiderman, N. (1999). Behavioral medicine and the management of HIV/AIDS. *International Journal of Behavioral Medicine, 6*, 3–12. (p. 559)

Schneiderman, N., Chesney, M. A., & Krantz, D. S. (1989). Biobehavioral aspects of cardiovascular disease: Progress and prospects. *Health Psychology, 8*, 649–676. (p. 556)

Schoeneman, T. J. (1994). *Individualism.* In V. S. Ramachandran (Ed.), *Encyclopedia of Human Behavior.* San Diego: Academic Press. (p. 611)

Schofield, J. W. (1986). Black-White contact in desegregated schools. In M. Hewstone & R. Brown (Eds.), *Contact and conflict in intergroup encounters.* Oxford: Basil Blackwell. (p. 767)

Schonfield, D., & Robertson, B. A. (1966). Memory storage and aging. *Canadian Journal of Psychology, 20*, 228–236. (p. 182)

Schooler, J. W., Gerhard, D., & Loftus, E. F. (1986). Qualities of the unreal. *Journal of Experimental Psychology: Learning, Memory, and Cognition, 12*, 171–181. (p. 383)

Schulenberg, J., Bachman, J. G., O'Malley, P. M., & Johnston, L. D. (March, 1994). High school educational success and subsequent substance use: A panel analysis following adolescents into young adulthood. *Journal of Health & Social Behavior, 35*(1), 45–62. (p. 576)

Schuman, H., & Scott, J. (June, 1989). Generations and collective memories. *American Sociological Review, 54*(3), 359–381. (p. 181)

Schwartz, B. (1984). *Psychology of learning and behavior* (2nd ed.). New York: Norton. (pp. 323, 654)

Schwartz, B. (2000). Self-determination: The tyranny of freedom. *American Psychologist, 55*, 79–88. (p. 626)

Schwartz, B. (2004). *The paradox of choice: Why more is less.* New York: Ecco/HarperCollins. (p. 626)

Schwartz, J., & Estrin, J. (2004, November 7). Living for today, locked in a paralyzed body. *New York Times* (www.nytimes.com). (p. 539)

Schwartz, J., & Pomfret, J. (1998, November 20). Smoking-related deaths in China are up sharply. *Washington Post* (www.washingtonpost.com). (p. 580)

Schwartz, J. M., Stoessel, P. W., Baxter, L. R., Jr., Martin, K. M., & Phelps, M. E. (1996). Systematic changes in cerebral glucose metabolic rate after successful behavior modification treatment of obsessive-compulsive disorder. *Archives of General Psychiatry, 53*, 109–113. (pp. 618, 697)

Schwarz, N., Strack, F., Kommer, D., & Wagner, D. (1987). Soccer, rooms, and the quality of your life: Mood effects on judgments of satisfaction with life in general and with specific domains. *European Journal of Social Psychology, 17*, 69–79. (p. 374)

Science (2004). Obesity drugs. *Science, 306*, 2014. (p. 587)

Sclafani, A. (1995). How food preferences are learned: Laboratory animal models. *Proceedings of the Nutrition Society, 54*, 419–427. (p. 477)

Scott, D. J., & others. (2004, November 9). U-M team reports evidence that smoking affects human brain's natural "feel good" chemical system (press release by Kara Gavin). University of Michigan Medical School (www.med.umich.edu). (p. 577)

Scott, W. A., Scott, R., & McCabe, M. (1991). Family relationships and children's personality: A cross-cultural, cross-source comparison. *British Journal of Social Psychology, 30*, 1–20. (p. 125)

Sechrest, L., Stickle, T. R., & Stewart, M. (1998). The role of assessment in clinical psychology. In A. Bellack, M. Hersen (Series eds.) & C. R. Reynolds (Vol. ed.), *Comprehensive clinical psychology: Vol 4: Assessment.* New York: Pergamon. (p. 603)

Seeman, P., Guan, H-C., & Van Tol, H. H. M. (1993). Dopamine D4 receptors elevated in schizophrenia. *Nature, 365,* 441–445. (p. 672)

Segal, N. L. (1999). *Entwined lives: Twins and what they tell us about human behavior.* New York: Dutton. (p. 100)

Segal, N. L. (2000). Virtual twins: New findings on within-family environmental influences on intelligence. *Journal of Educational Psychology, 92,* 442–448. (p. 100)

Segall, M. H., Dasen, P. R., Berry, J. W., & Poortinga, Y. H. (1990). *Human behavior in global perspective: An introduction to cross-cultural psychology.* New York: Pergamon. (pp. 110, 131, 154, 252)

Segerstrom, S. C., McCarthy, W. J., Caskey, N. H., Gross, T. D., & Jarvik, M. E. (1993). Optimistic bias among cigarette smokers. *Journal of Applied Social Psychology, 23,* 1606–1618. (pp. 627–628)

Segerstrom, S. C., Taylor, S. E., Kemeny, M. E., & Fahey, J. L. (1998). Optimism is associated with mood, coping, and immune change in response to stress. *Journal of Personality and Social Psychology, 74,* 1646–1655. (p. 564)

Segerstrom, S., & Miller, G. E. (2004). Psychological stress and the human immune system: A meta-analytic study of 30 years of inquiry. *Psychological Bulletin, 130,* 601–630. (pp. 551, 558)

Seidlitz, L., & Diener, E. (1998). Sex differences in the recall of affective experiences. *Journal of Personality and Social Psychology, 74,* 262–271. (p. 667)

Self, C. E. (1994). *Moral culture and victimization in residence halls.* Dissertation: Thesis (M.A.). Bowling Green University. (p. 307)

Seligman, M. E. P. (1974, May). Submissive death: Giving up on life. *Psychology Today,* pp. 80–85. (p. 516)

Seligman, M. E. P. (1975). *Helplessness: On depression, development and death.* San Francisco: Freeman. (p. 625)

Seligman, M. E. P. (1991). *Learned optimism.* New York: Knopf. (pp. 271, 625, 666, 667, 696)

Seligman, M. E. P. (1994). *What you can change and what you can't.* New York: Knopf. (pp. 570, 607, 632)

Seligman, M. E. P. (1995). The effectiveness of psychotherapy: The *Consumer Reports* study. *American Psychologist, 50,* 965–974. (p. 666, 700, 704)

Seligman, M. E. P. (2002). *Authentic happiness: Using the new positive psychology to realize your potential for lasting fulfillment.* New York: Free Press. (pp. 628, 632, 696)

Seligman, M. E. P. (2004). Eudaemonia, the good life. A talk with Martin Seligman. www.edge.org. (p. 628)

Seligman, M. E. P., & Schulman, P. (1986). Explanatory style as a predictor of productivity and quitting among life insurance sales agents. *Journal of Personality and Social Psychology, 50,* 832–838. (p. 627)

Seligman, M. E. P., Steen, T. A., Park, N., & Peterson, C. (2005). Positive psychology progress: Empirical validation of interventions. *American Psychologist, 60,* 410–421. (p. 628)

Seligman, M. E. P., & Yellen, A. (1987). What is a dream? *Behavior Research and Therapy, 25,* 1–24. (p. 276)

Selye, H. (1936). A syndrome produced by diverse nocuous agents. *Nature, 138,* 32. (pp. 552–553)

Selye, H. (1976). *The stress of life.* New York: McGraw-Hill. (pp. 552–553)

Sen, A. (2003). Missing women—revisited. *British Medical Journal, 327,* 1297–1298. (p. 745)

Senghas, A., & Coppola, M. (2001). Children creating language: How Nicaraguan Sign Language acquired a spatial grammar. *Psychological Science, 12,* 323–328. (p. 414)

Sengupta, S. (2001, October 10). Sept. 11 attack narrows the racial divide. *New York Times* (www.nytimes.com). (p. 768)

Serdula, M. K., Mokdad, A., Williamson, D. F., Galuska, D. A., Mendlein, J. M., & Heath, G. W. (1999). Prevalence of attempting weight loss and strategies for controlling weight. *Journal of the American Medical Association, 282,* 1353–1358. (p. 590)

Sergent, C., & Dehaene, S. (2004). Is consciousness a gradual phenomenon? *Psychological Science, 15,* 720–728. (p. 272)

Serruya, M. D., Hatsopoulos, N. G., Paninski, L., Fellow, M. R., & Donoghue, J. P. (2002). Instant neural control of a movement signal. *Nature, 416,* 141–142. (p. 78)

Service, R. F. (1994). Will a new type of drug make memory-making easier? *Science, 266,* 218–219. (p. 365)

Seto, M. C., & Barbaree, H. E. (1995). The role of alcohol in sexual aggression. *Clinical Psychology Review, 15,* 545–566. (p. 299)

Shadish, W. R., Baldwin, S. A. (2005). Effects of behavioral marital therapy: A meta-analysis of randomized controlled trials. *Journal of Consulting and Clinical Psychology, 73,* 6–14. (p. 704)

Shadish, W. R., Matt, G. E., Navarro, A. M., & Phillips, G. (2000). The effects of psychological therapies under clinically representative conditions: A meta-analysis. *Psychological Bulletin, 126,* 512–529. (p. 703)

Shadish, W. R., Montgomery, L. M., Wilson, P., Wilson, M. R., Bright, I., & Okwumabua, T. (1993). Effects of family and marital psychotherapies: A meta-analysis. *Journal of Consulting and Clinical Psychology, 61,* 992–1002. (p. 698)

Shaffer, D. M., Krauchunas, S. M., Eddy, M., & McBeath, M. K. (2004). How dogs navigate to catch frisbees. *Psychological Science, 15,* 437–441. (p. 249)

Shafir, E., & LeBoeuf, R. A. (2002). Rationality. *Annual Review of Psychology, 53,* 491–517. (pp. 407–408)

Shamir, B., House, R. J., & Arthur, M. B. (1993). The motivational effects of charismatic leadership: A self-concept based theory. *Organizational Science, 4*(4), 577–594. (p. 509)

Shapiro, F. (1989). Efficacy of the eye movement desensitization procedure in the treatment of traumatic memories. *Journal of Traumatic Stress, 2,* 199–223. (p. 706)

Shapiro, F. (1995). *Eye movement desensitization and reprocessing: Basic principles, protocols, and procedures.* New York: Guilford. (p. 706)

Shapiro, F. (1999). Eye movement desensitization and reprocessing (EMDR) and the anxiety disorders: Clinical and research implications of an integrated psychotherapy treatment. *Journal of Anxiety Disorders, 13,* 35–67. (p. 706)

Shapiro, F. (Ed.) (2002). *EMDR as an integrative psychotherapy approach: Experts of diverse orientations explore the paradigm prism.* Washington, DC: APA Books. (p. 706)

Sharma, A. R., McGue, M. K., & Benson, P. L. (1998). The psychological adjustment of United States adopted adolescents and their nonadopted siblings. *Child Development, 69,* 791–802. (p. 101)

Shaughnessy, J., & Zechmeister, E. (1992). Memory monitoring accuracy as influenced by the distribution of retrieval practice. *Bulletin of the Psychonomic Society, 30,* 125–128. (p. 392)

Shaver, P. R., Morgan, H. J., & Wu, S. (1996). Is love a basic emotion? *Personal Relationships, 3,* 81–96. (p. 532)

Shaw, H. L. (1989–90). Comprehension of the spoken word and ASL translation by chimpanzees (Pan troglodytes). *Friends of Washoe, 9*(1/2), 8–19. (p. 428)

Sheehan, S. (1982). *Is there no place on earth for me?* Boston: Houghton Mifflin. (p. 669)

Sheldon, K. M., Elliot, A. J., Kim, Y., & Kasser, T. (2001). What is satisfying about satisfying events? Testing 10 candidate psychological needs. *Journal of Personality and Social Psychology, 80,* 325–339. (p. 495)

Shelton, J. N., & Richeson, J. A. (2005). Intergroup contact and pluralistic ignorance. *Journal of Personality and Social Psychology, 88,* 91–107. (p. 767)

Shenton, M. E. (1992). Abnormalities of the left temporal lobe and thought disorder in schizophrenia: A quantitative magnetic resonance imaging study. *New England Journal of Medicine, 327,* 604–612. (p. 673)

Shepard, R. N. (1990). *Mind sights.* New York: Freeman. (pp. 48, 260)

Shepherd, C. (1997, April). News of the weird. *Funny Times,* p. 15. (p. 99)

Shepherd, C. (1999, June). News of the weird. *Funny Times*, p. 21. (p. 588)

Shepherd, C., Kohut, J. J., & Sweet, R. (1990). *More news of the weird*. New York: Penguin/Plume Books. (p. 679)

Sheridan, E. P. (1999). Psychology's future in medical schools and academic health care centers. *American Psychologist, 54*, 267-271. (p. 549)

Sherif, M. (1966). *In common predicament: Social psychology of intergroup conflict and cooperation*. Boston: Houghton Mifflin. (p. 767)

Sherman, D. (2004, May 30). Doctors peer into brains to gauge antidepressants. Reuters News Service. (p. 713)

Sherman, P. W., & Flaxman, S. M. (2001). Protecting ourselves from food. *American Scientist, 89*, 142-151. (p. 478)

Shermer, M. (1999). *How we believe: The search for God in an age of science*. New York: Freeman. (p. 128)

Sherry, D., & Vaccarino, A. L. (1989). Hippocampus and memory for food caches in black-capped chickadees. *Behavioral Neuroscience, 103*, 308-318. (p. 368)

Shettleworth, S. J. (1973). Food reinforcement and the organization of behavior in golden hamsters. In R. A. Hinde & J. Stevenson-Hinde (Eds.), *Constraints on learning*. London: Academic Press. (p. 335)

Shettleworth, S. J. (1993). Where is the comparison in comparative cognition? Alternative research programs. *Psychological Science, 4*, 179-184. (p. 363)

Shneidman, E. (1987, March). At the point of no return. *Psychology Today*, pp. 54-58. (p. 663)

Shobe, K. K., & Kihlstrom, J. F. (June, 1997). Is traumatic memory special? *Current Directions in Psychological Science, 6*(3), 70-74. (p. 605)

Shotland, R. L. (1984, March 12). Quoted in Maureen Dowd, 20 years after the murder of Kitty Genovese, the question remains: Why? *The New York Times*, p. B1. (p. 765)

Showers, C. (1992). The motivational and emotional consequences of considering positive or negative possibilities for an upcoming event. *Journal of Personality and Social Psychology, 63*, 474-484. (p. 627)

Shulman, P. (2000, June). The girl who loved math. *Discover*, pp. 67-70. (p. 463)

Sieff, E. M., Dawes, R. M., & Loewenstein, G. (1999). Anticipated versus actual reaction to HIV test results. *The American Journal of Psychology, 112*, 297-313. (p. 538)

Siegel, J. (2000, Winter). Recent developments in narcolepsy research: An explanation for patients and the general public. *Narcolepsy Network Newsletter*, pp. 1-2. (p. 284)

Siegel, J. M. (1990). Stressful life events and use of physician services among the elderly: The moderating role of pet ownership. *Journal of Personality and Social Psychology, 58*, 1081-1086. (p. 565)

Siegel, J. M. (2002). Sleep. *Encarta encyclopedia* (www.bol.ucla.edu/~jsiegel/encarta/Article.htm). (p. 274)

Siegel, J. M. (2003, November). Why we sleep. *Scientific American*, pp. 92-97. (p. 283)

Siegel, R. K. (1977, October). Hallucinations. *Scientific American*, pp. 132-140. (p. 309)

Siegel, R. K. (1980). The psychology of life after death. *American Psychologist, 35*, 911-931. (p. 309)

Siegel, R. K. (1982, October). Quoted by J. Hooper, Mind tripping. *Omni*, pp. 72-82, 159-160. (p. 302)

Siegel, R. K. (1984, March 15). Personal communication. (p. 302)

Siegel, R. K. (1990). *Intoxication*. New York: Pocket Books. (pp. 297, 300, 301, 303)

Siegler, R. S., & Ellis, S. (1996). Piaget on childhood. *Psychological Science, 7*, 211-215. (p. 147)

Silberswieg, D. A., Stern, E., Frith, C., Cahill, C., Holmes, A., Grootoonk, S., Seaward, J., McKenna, P., Chua, S. E., Schnorr, L., Jones, T., & Frackowiak, R. S. J. (1995). A functional neuroanatomy of hallucinations in schizophrenia. *Nature, 378*, 176-179. (p. 672)

Silva, A. J., Stevens, C. F., Tonegawa, S., & Wang, Y. (1992). Deficient hippocampal long-term potentiation in alpha-calcium-calmodulin kinase II mutant mice. *Science, 257*, 201-206. (p. 365)

Silva, C. E., & Kirsch, I. (1992). Interpretive sets, expectancy, fantasy proneness, and dissociation as predictors of hypnotic response. *Journal of Personality and Social Psychology, 63*, 847-856. (p. 291)

Silver, M., & Geller, D. (1978). On the irrelevance of evil: The organization and individual action. *Journal of Social Issues, 34*, 125-136. (p. 737)

Silverman, I., & Eals, M. (1992). Sex differences in spatial abilities: Evolutionary theory and data. In J. H. Barkow, L. Cosmides, & J. Tooby (Eds.), *The adapted mind: Evolutionary psychology and the generation of culture*. New York: Oxford University Press. (p. 463)

Silverman, I., & Phillips, K. (1998). The evolutionary psychology of spatial sex differences. In C. Crawford & D. L. Krebs (Eds.), *Handbook of Evolutionary Psychology: Ideas, Issues, and Applications*. Mahwah, NJ: Erlbaum. (p. 463)

Silverman, K., Evans, S. M., Strain, E. C., & Griffiths, R. R. (1992). Withdrawal syndrome after the double-blind cessation of caffeine consumption. *New England Journal of Medicine, 327*, 1109-1114. (p. 301)

Silverman, P. S., & Retzlaff, P. D. (1986). Cognitive stage regression through hypnosis: Are earlier cognitive stages retrievable? *International Journal of Clinical and Experimental Hypnosis, 34*, 192-204. (p. 292)

Simek, T. C., & O'Brien, R. M. (1981). *Total golf: A behavioral approach to lowering your score and getting more out of your game*. Huntington, NY: B-MOD Associates. (p. 337)

Simek, T. C., & O'Brien, R. M. (1988). A chaining-mastery, discrimination training program to teach Little Leaguers to hit a baseball. *Human Performance, 1*, 73-84. (p. 337)

Simon, H. (1998, November 16). Flash of genius (interview with P. E. Ross). *Forbes*, pp. 98-104. (p. 504)

Simon, H. (2001, February). Quoted by A. M. Hayashi, "When to trust your gut." *Harvard Business Review*, pp. 59-65. (p. 409)

Simons, D. J. (1996). In sight, out of mind: When object representations fail. *Psychological Science, 7*, 301-305. (p. 239)

Simons, D. J., & Ambinder, M. S. (2005). Change blindness: Theory and consequences. *Current Directions in Psychological Science, 14*, 44-48. (p. 239)

Simons, D. J., & Chabris, C. F. (1999). Gorillas in our midst: Sustained inattentional blindness for dynamic events. *Perception, 28*, 1059-1074. (p. 238)

Simonton, D. K. (1988). Age and outstanding achievement: What do we know after a century of research? *Psychological Bulletin, 104*, 251-267. (p. 185)

Simonton, D. K. (1990). Creativity in the later years: Optimistic prospects for achievement. *The Gerontologist, 30*, 626-631. (p. 185)

Simonton, D. K. (1992). The social context of career success and course for 2,026 scientists and inventors. *Personality and Social Psychology Bulletin, 18*, 452-463. (p. 439)

Simonton, D. K. (2000). Creativity: Cognitive, personal, developmental, and social aspects. *American Psychologist, 55*, 151-158. (pp. 346, 438)

Sinclair, R. C., Hoffman, C., Mark, M. M., Martin, L. L., & Pickering, T. L. (1994). Construct accessibility and the misattribution of arousal: Schachter and Singer revisited. *Psychological Science, 5*, 15-18. (p. 520)

Singelis, T. M., Bond, M. H., Sharkey, W. F., & Lai, C. S. Y. (1999). Unpackaging culture's influence on self-esteem and embarrassability: The role of self-construals. *Journal of Cross-Cultural Psychology, 30*, 315-341. (p. 122)

Singelis, T. M., & Sharkey, W. F. (1995). Culture, self-construal, and embarrassability. *Cross-Cultural Psychology, 26*, 622-644. (p. 122)

Singer, J. L. (1981). Clinical intervention: New developments in methods and evaluation. In L. T. Benjamin, Jr. (Ed.), *The G. Stanley Hall Lecture Series* (Vol. 1). Washington, DC: American Psychological Association. (p. 704)

Singer, T., Seymour, B., O'Doherty, J., Kaube, H., Dolan, R. J., & Frith, C. (2004). Empathy for pain involves the affective but not sensory components of pain. *Science, 303*, 1157-1162. (pp. 228, 342, 531)

Singh, D. (1993). Adaptive significance of female physical attractiveness: Role of waist-to-hip ratio. *Journal of Personality and Social Psychology, 65,* 293–307. (p. 111)

Singh, D. (1995b). Female health, attractiveness, and desirability for relationships: Role of breast asymmetry and waist-to-hip ratio. *Ethology and Sociobiology, 16,* 465–481. (pp. 111, 761)

Singh, S. (1997). *Fermat's enigma: The epic quest to solve the world's greatest mathematical problem.* New York: Bantam Books. (p. 438)

Singh, S., & Riber, K. A. (1997, November). Fermat's last stand. *Scientific American,* pp. 68–73. (p. 439)

Singleton, D., Tate, A., & Kohout, J. (2003). *2002 Master's, specialist's, and related degrees employment survey.* Washington, DC: American Psychological Association. (p. A-4)

Sipski, M. L., & Alexander, C. J. (1999). Sexual response in women with spinal cord injuries: Implications for our understanding of the able bodied. *Journal of Sex and Marital Therapy, 25,* 11–22. (p. 64)

Sirenteanu, R. (1999). Switching on the infant brain. *Science, 286,* 59, 61. (p. 256)

Sivard, R. L. (1996). *World military and social expenditures 1996,* 16th edition. Washington, DC: World Priorities. (p. 178)

Sjöstrum, L. (1980). Fat cells and body weight. In A. J. Stunkard (Ed.), *Obesity.* Philadelphia: Saunders. (p. 584)

Skinner, B. F. (1953). *Science and human behavior.* New York: Macmillan. (p. 331)

Skinner, B. F. (1956). A case history in scientific method. *American Psychologist, 11,* 221–233. (p. 332)

Skinner, B. F. (1957). *Verbal behavior.* Englewood Cliffs, NJ: Prentice-Hall. (p. 413)

Skinner, B. F. (1961, November). Teaching machines. *Scientific American,* pp. 91–102. (p. 331)

Skinner, B. F. (1983, September). Origins of a behaviorist. *Psychology Today,* pp. 22–33. (pp. 336, 666)

Skinner, B. F. (1985). *Cognitive science and behaviorism.* Unpublished manuscript, Harvard University. (p. 413)

Skinner, B. F. (1986). What is wrong with daily life in the western world? *American Psychologist, 41,* 568–574. (p. 337)

Skinner, B. F. (1988). The school of the future. Address to the American Psychological Association convention. (p. 337)

Skinner, B. F. (1989). Teaching machines. *Science, 243,* 1535. (p. 337)

Skinner, B. F. (1990). Address to the American Psychological Association convention. (p. 334)

Skitka, L. J., Bauman, C. W., & Mullen, E. (2004). Political tolerance and coming to psychological closure following the September 11, 2001, terrorist attacks: An integrative approach. *Personality and Social Psychology Bulletin, 30,* 743–756. (p. 536)

Sklar, L. S., & Anisman, H. (1981). Stress and cancer. *Psychological Bulletin, 89,* 369–406. (p. 559)

Skoog, G., & Skoog, I. (1999). A 40-year follow-up of patients with obsessive-compulsive disorder. *Archives of General Psychiatry, 56,* 121–127. (p. 652)

Skov, R. B., & Sherman, S. J. (1986). Information-gathering processes: Diagnosticity, hypothesis-confirmatory strategies, and perceived hypothesis confirmation. *Journal of Experimental Social Psychology, 22,* 93–121. (p. 399)

Slater, A. (1994, February 15). Personal correspondence. (p. 143)

Slater, E., & Meyer, A. (1959). *Confinia Psychiatra.* Basel: S. Karger AG. (p. 660)

Slater, L. (2000, November 19). How do you cure a sex addict? *New York Times Magazine* (www.nytimes.com). (p. 713)

Slavin, R. E., & Braddock, J. H., III (1993, Summer). Ability grouping: On the wrong track. *The College Board Review,* pp. 11–18. (p. 453)

Slavin, R. E., Hurley, E. A., & Chamberlain, A. (2003). Cooperative learning and achievement: Theory and research. In W. M. Reynolds & G. E.

Miller (Eds.), *Handbook of psychology: Educational psychology,* Vol. 7. New York: Wiley. (p. 768)

Sloan, R. P. (2005). Field analysis of the literature on religion, spirituality, and health. Columbia University (available at www.metanexus.net/tarp). (p. 572)

Sloan, R. P., & Bagiella, E. (2002). Claims about religious involvement and health outcomes. *Annals of Behavioral Medicine, 24,* 14–21. (p. 572)

Sloan, R. P., Bagiella, E., & Powell, T. (1999). Religion, spirituality, and medicine. *Lancet, 353,* 664–667. (p. 572)

Sloan, R. P., Bagiella, E., VandeCreek, L., & Poulos, P. (2000). Should physicians prescribe religious activities? *New England Journal of Medicine, 342,* 1913–1917. (p. 572)

Slovic, P. (2000). What does it mean to know a cumulative risk? Adolescents' perceptions of short-term and long-term consequences of smoking. *Journal of Behavioral Decision Making, 13,* 259–266. (pp. 575–576)

Slovic, P. (2001). Cigarette smokers: Rational actors or rational fools? In P. Slovic (Ed.), *Smoking risk, perception and policy.* Thousand Oaks, CA: Sage. (p. 591)

Slovic, P., Finucane, M., Peters, E., & MacGregor, D. G. (2002). The affect heuristic. In T. Gilovich, D. Griffin, & D. Kahneman (Eds.), *Intuitive judgment: Heuristics and biases.* New York: Cambridge University Press. (p. 577)

Slovic, P., & Fischhoff, B. (1977). On the psychology of experimental surprises. *Journal of Experimental Psychology: Human Perception and Performance, 3,* 544–551. (p. 20)

Slutske, W. S. (2005). Alcohol use disorders among U.S. college students and their non-college-attending peers. *Archives of General Psychiatry, 62,* 321–327. (p. 299)

Small, M. F. (1997). Making connections. *American Scientist, 85,* 502–504. (p. 124)

Small, M. F. (2002, July). What you can learn from drunk monkeys. *Discover,* pp. 40–45. (p. 306)

Smart, R. G., Adlaf, E. M., & Walsh, G. W. (1991). The Ontario student drug use survey: Trends between 1977 and 1991. Toronto: Addiction Research Foundation. (p. 304)

Smedley, A., & Smedley, B. D. (2005). Race as biology is fiction, racism as a social problem is real: Anthropological and historical perspectives on the social construction of race. *American Psychologist, 60,* 16–26. (p. 460)

Smelser, N. J., & Mitchell, F. (Eds.) (2002). *Terrorism: Perspectives from the behavioral and social sciences.* Washington, DC: National Research Council, National Academies Press. (p. 748)

Smith, A. (1983). Personal correspondence. (p. 672)

Smith, D. V., & Margolskee, R. F. (2001, March). Making sense of taste. *Scientific American,* pp. 32–39. (p. 229)

Smith, E., & Delargy, M. (2005). Locked-in syndrome. *British Medical Journal, 330,* 406–409. (pp. 223, 539)

Smith, J. E., Waldorf, V. A., & Trembath, D. L. (1990). "Single white male looking for thin, very attractive . . ." *Sex Roles, 23,* 675–685. (p. 584)

Smith, M. B. (1978). Psychology and values. *Journal of Social Issues, 34,* 181–199. (p. 611)

Smith, M., Franz, E. A., Joy, S. M., & Whitehead, K. (2005). Superior performance of blind compared with sighted individuals on bimanual estimations of object size. *Psychological Science, 16,* 11–14. (p. 223)

Smith, M. L., & Glass, G. V. (1977). Meta-analysis of psychotherapy outcome studies. *American Psychologist, 32,* 752–760. (p. 704)

Smith, M. L., Glass, G. V., & Miller, R. L. (1980). *The benefits of psychotherapy.* Baltimore: Johns Hopkins Press. (pp. 703, 704)

Smith, P. B., & Tayeb, M. (1989). Organizational structure and processes. In M. Bond (Ed.), *The cross-cultural challenge to social psychology.* Newbury Park, CA: Sage. (p. 509)

Smith, P. F. (1995). Cannabis and the brain. *New Zealand Journal of Psychology, 24,* 5–12. (p. 303)

Smith, S. B. (1999). *Diana in search of herself: Portrait of a troubled princess.* New York: Times Books. (p. 705)

Smith, S. M., McIntosh, W. D., & Bazzini, D. G. (1999). Are the beautiful good in Hollywood? An investigation of the beauty-and-goodness stereotype on film. *Basic and Applied Social Psychology, 21,* 69–80. (p. 760)

Smith, T. W. (1998, December). American sexual behavior: Trends, socio-demographic differences, and risk behavior. National Opinion Research Center GSS Topical Report No. 25. (pp. 485, 486, 487, 488)

Smith, T. W., & Ruiz, J. M. (2002). Psychosocial influences on the development and course of coronary heart disease: Current status and implications for research and practice. *Journal of Consulting and Clinical Psychology, 70,* 548–568. (p. 556)

Smolak, L., & Murnen, S. K. (2002). A meta-analytic examination of the relationship between child sexual abuse and eating disorders. *International Journal of Eating Disorders, 31,* 136–150. (p. 479)

Smoreda, Z., & Licoppe, C. (2000). Gender-specific use of the domestic telephone. *Social Psychology Quarterly, 63,* 238–252. (p. 128)

Snarey, J. R. (1985). Cross-cultural universality of social-moral development: A critical review of Kohlbergian research. *Psychological Bulletin, 97,* 202–233. (p. 168)

Snarey, J. R. (1987, June). A question of morality. *Psychology Today,* pp. 6–7. (p. 168)

Snodgrass, S. E., Higgins, J. G., & Todisco, L. (1986). The effects of walking behavior on mood. Paper presented at the American Psychological Association convention. (p. 531)

Snowdon, D. A., Kemper, S. J., Mortimer, J. A., Greiner, L. H., Wekstein, D. R., & Markesbery, W. R. (1996). Linguistic ability in early life and cognitive function and Alzheimer's disease in late life: Finds from the Nun Study. *Journal of the American Medical Association, 275,* 528–532. (p. 452)

Snyder, F., & Scott, J. (1972). The psychophysiology of sleep. In N. S. Greenfield & R. A. Sterbach (Eds.), *Handbook of psychophysiology.* New York: Holt, Rinehart & Winston. (p. 288)

Snyder, M. (1984). When belief creates reality. In L. Berkowitz (Ed.), *Advances in experimental social psychology* (Vol. 18). New York: Academic Press. (p. 647)

Snyder, S. H. (1984). Neurosciences: An integrative discipline. *Science, 225,* 1255–1257. (p. 57)

Snyder, S. H. (1986). *Drugs and the brain.* New York: Scientific American Library. (p. 715)

Society for Personality Assessment. (2005). The status of the Rorschach in clinical and forensic practice: An official statement by The Board of Trustees of the Society for Personality Assessment (www.personality.org). (p. 603)

Sokol, D. K., Moore, C. A., Rose, R. J., Williams, C. J., Reed, T., & Christian, J. C. (1995). Intrapair differences in personality and cognitive ability among young monozygotic twins distinguished by chorion type. *Behavior Genetics, 25,* 457–466. (p. 114)

Sokoll, G. R., & Mynatt, C. R. (1984). *Arousal and free throw shooting.* Paper presented at the meeting of the Midwestern Psychological Association. (p. 517)

Solomon, D. A., Keitner, G. I., Miller, I. W., Shea, M. T., & Keller, M. B. (1995). Course of illness and maintenance treatments for patients with bipolar disorder. *Journal of Clinical Psychiatry, 56,* 5–13. (p. 715)

Solomon, J. (1996, May 20). Breaking the silence. *Newsweek,* pp. 20–22. (p. 647)

Solomon, M. (1987, December). Standard issue. *Psychology Today,* pp. 30–31. (p. 760)

Sommer, R. (1969). *Personal space.* Englewood Cliffs, NJ: Prentice-Hall. (p. 120)

Sonenstein, F. L. (1992). Condom use. *Science, 257,* 861. (p. 485)

Sontag, S. (1978). *Illness as metaphor.* New York: Farrar, Straus, & Giroux. (p. 559)

Soussignan, R. (2001). Duchenne smile, emotional experience, and autonomic reactivity: A test of the facial feedback hypothesis. *Emotion, 2,* 52–74. (p. 530)

Sowell, T. (1991, May/June). Cultural diversity: A world view. *American Enterprise,* pp. 44–55. (p. 769)

Spanos, N. P. (1982). A social psychological approach to hypnotic behavior. In G. Weary & H. L. Mirels (Eds.), *Integrations of clinical and social psychology.* New York: Oxford. (p. 292)

Spanos, N. P. (1986). Hypnosis, nonvolitional responding, and multiple personality: A social psychological perspective. *Progress in Experimental Personality Research, 14,* 1–62. (p. 655)

Spanos, N. P. (1991). Hypnosis, hypnotizability, and hypnotherapy. In C. R. Snyder & D. R. Forsyth (Eds.), *Handbook of social and clinical psychology: The health perspective.* New York: Pergamon Press. (p. 293)

Spanos, N. P. (1994). Multiple identity enactments and multiple personality disorder: A sociocognitive perspective. *Psychological Bulletin, 116,* 143–165. (pp. 294, 656)

Spanos, N. P. (1996). *Multiple identities and false memories: A sociocognitive perspective.* Washington, DC: American Psychological Association Books. (pp. 293, 294, 656)

Spanos, N. P., & Coe, W. C. (1992). A Social-psychological approach to hypnosis. In E. Fromm & M. R. Nash (Eds.), *Contemporary hypnosis research.* New York: Guilford. (p. 294)

Spector, P. E. (1986). Perceived control by employees: A meta-analysis of studies concerning autonomy and participation at work. *Human Relations, 39,* 1005–1016. (p. 508)

Spelke, E. (2005, April 22). The science of gender and science. Harvard University (www.edge.org). (pp. 152, 463)

Spelke, E. S. (2000). Core knowledge. *American Psychologist, 55,* 1233–1243. (p. 149)

Spencer, J., Quinn, P. C., Johnson, M. H., & Karmiloff-Smith, A. (1997). Heads you win, tails you lose: Evidence for young infants categorizing mammals by head and facial attributes. *Early Development & Parenting, 6,* 113–126. (p. 143)

Spencer, K. M., Nestor, P. G., Perlmutter, R., Niznikiewicz, M. A., Klump, M. C., Frumin, M., Shenton, M. E., & McCarley, R. W. (2004). Neural synchrony indexes disordered perception and cognition in schizophrenia. *Proceedings of the National Academy of Sciences, 101,* 17288–17293. (p. 672)

Spencer, S. J., Steele, C. M., & Quinn, D. M. (1997). Stereotype threat and women's math performance. Unpublished manuscript, Hope College. (p. 465)

Sperling, G. (1960). The information available in brief visual presentations. *Psychological Monographs, 74* (Whole No. 498). (p. 362)

Sperry, R. W. (1964). *Problems outstanding in the evolution of brain function.* James Arthur Lecture, American Museum of Natural History, New York. Cited by R. Ornstein (1977), *The psychology of consciousness* (2nd ed.). New York: Harcourt Brace Jovanovich. (p. 85)

Sperry, R. W. (1982). Some effects of disconnecting the cerebral hemispheres. *Science, 217,* 1223–1226. (p. 87)

Sperry, R. W. (1985). Changed concepts of brain and consciousness: Some value implications. *Zygon, 20,* 41–57. (p. 211)

Sperry, R. W. (1992, Summer). Turnabout on consciousness: A mentalist view. *Journal of Mind & Behavior, 13*(3), 259–280. (p. 91)

Spiegel, K., Leproult, R., & Van Cauter, E. (1999). Impact of sleep debt on metabolic and endrocrine function. *Lancet, 354,* 1435–1439. (p. 281)

Spielberger, C., & London, P. (1982). Rage boomerangs. *American Health, 1,* 52–56. (p. 556)

Spradley, J. P., & Phillips, M. (1972). Culture and stress: A quantitative analysis. *American Anthropologist, 74,* 518–529. (p. 121)

Sprecher, S. (1989). The importance to males and females of physical attractiveness, earning potential, and expressiveness in initial attraction. *Sex Roles, 21,* 591–607. (p. 759)

Sprecher, S., & Sedikides, C. (1993). Gender differences in perceptions of emotionality: The case of close heterosexual relationships. *Sex Roles, 28,* 511–530. (p. 526)

Spring, B., Pingitore, R., Bourgeois, M., Kessler, K. H., & Bruckner, E. (1992). The effects and non-effects of skipping breakfast: Results of three studies. Paper presented at the American Psychological Association convention. (p. 590)

Springer, S. P., & Deutsch, G. (1985). *Left brain, right brain.* San Francisco: Freeman. (p. 88)

Spychalski, A., Quinones, M. A., & Gaugler, B. B. (1997). A survey of assessment center practices in the United States. *Personnel Psychology, 50,* 71–90. (p. 629)

Squire, L. R. (1992). Memory and the hippocampus: A synthesis from findings with rats, monkeys, and humans. *Psychological Review, 99,* 195–231. (p. 368)

Srivastava, S., John, O. P., Gosling, S. D., & Potter, J. (2003). Development of personality in early and middle adulthood: Set like plaster or persistent change? *Journal of Personality & Social Psychology, 84,* 1041–1053. (pp. 194, 619)

Srivastava, A., Locke, E. A., & Bartol, K. M. (2001). Money and subject well-being: It's not the money, it's the motives. *Journal of Personality and Social Psychology, 80,* 959–971. (p. 541)

St. Clair, D., Xu, M., Wang, P., Yu, Y., Fang, Y., Zhang, F., Zheng, X., Gu, N., Feng, G., Sham, P., & He, L. (2005). Rates of adult schizophrenia following prenatal exposure to the Chinese famine of 1959–1961. *Journal of the American Medical Association, 294,* 557–562. (p. 673)

Stack, S. (1992). Marriage, family, religion, and suicide. In R. Maris, A. Berman, J. Maltsberger, & R. Yufit (Eds.), *Assessment and prediction of suicide.* New York: Guilford Press. (p. 662)

Stafford, R. S., MacDonald, E. A., & Finkelstein, S. N. (2001). National patterns of medication treatment for depression, 1987 to 2001. *Primary Care Companion Journal of Clinical Psychiatry, 3,* 232–235. (p. 713)

Stanford University Center for Narcolepsy. (2002). Narcolepsy is a serious medical disorder and a key to understanding other sleep disorders (www.med.stanford.edu/school/Psychiatry/narcolepsy). (p. 284)

Stanley, J. C. (1997). Varieties of intellectual talent. *Journal of Creative Behavior, 31,* 93–119. (p. 453)

Stanovich, K. (1996). *How to think straight about psychology.* New York: HarperCollins. (p. 596)

Staples, B. (1999a, May 2). When the 'paranoids' turn out to be right. *New York Times* (www.nytimes.com). (p. 744)

Staples, B. (1999b, May 24). Why 'racial profiling' will be tough to fight. *New York Times* (www.nytimes.com). (p. 744)

Stark, R. (2002). Physiology and faith: Addressing the "universal" gender difference in religious commitment. *Journal for the Scientific Study of Religion, 41,* 495–507. (p. 128)

Stark, R. (2003a). *For the glory of God: How monotheism led to reformations, science, witch-hunts, and the end of slavery.* Princeton, NJ: Princeton University Press. (p. 23)

Stark, R. (2003b, October–November). False conflict: Christianity is not only compatible with science—it created it. *American Enterprise,* pp. 27–33. (p. 23)

Starr, J. M., Deary, I. J., Lemmon, H., & Whalley, L. J. (2000). Mental ability age 11 years and health status age 77 years. *Age and Ageing, 29,* 523–528. (p. 452)

Statistics Canada. (1999). *Statistical report on the health of Canadians.* Prepared by the Federal, Provincial and Territorial Advisory Committee on Population Health for the Meeting of Ministers of Health, Charlottetown, PEI, September 16–17, 1999. (pp. 172, 567, 575, 576, 579, 587)

Statistics Canada. (2002). (www.statcan.ca). (p. 550)

Statistics Canada. (2003). Victims and persons accused of homicide, by age and sex. Table 253-0003. www.statcan.ca (p. 127)

Staub, E. (1989). *The roots of evil: The psychological and cultural sources of genocide.* New York: Cambridge University Press. (p. 728)

Steadman, H. J., Mulvey, E. P., Monahan, J., Robbins, P. C., Appelbaum, P. S., Grisso, T., Roth, L. H., & Silver, E. (1998). Violence by people discharged from acute psychiatric inpatient facilities and by others in the same neighborhoods. *Archives of General Psychiatry, 55,* 393–401. (p. 647)

Steel, P., & Ones, D. S. (2002). Personality and happiness: A national-level analysis. *Journal of Personality and Social Psychology, 83,* 767–781. (p. 539)

Steele, C. (1990, May). A conversation with Claude Steele. *APS Observer,* pp. 11–17. (p. 459)

Steele, C. M. (1995, August 31). Black students live down to expectations. *New York Times.* (p. 465)

Steele, C. M. (1997). A threat in the air: How stereotypes shape intellectual identity and performance. *American Psychologist, 52,* 613–629. (p. 465)

Steele, C. M., & Josephs, R. A. (1990). Alcohol myopia: Its prized and dangerous effects. *American Psychologist, 45,* 921–933. (p. 299)

Steele, C. M., Spencer, S. J., & Aronson, J. (2002). Contending with group image: The psychology of stereotype and social identity threat. *Advances in Experimental Social Psychology, 34,* 379–440. (p. 465)

Steele, J. (2000). Handedness in past human population: Skeletal markers. *Laterality, 5,* 193–220. (p. 88)

Steenhuysen, J. (2002, May 8). Bionic retina gives six patients partial sight. Reuters News Service. (See also www.optobionics.com/artificialretina.htm.) (p. 221)

Steinberg, L. (1987, September). Bound to bicker. *Psychology Today,* pp. 36–39. (p. 172)

Steinberg, L., & Morris, A. S. (2001). Adolescent development. *Annual Review of Psychology, 52,* 83–110. (pp. 162, 166, 172, 173)

Steinberg, L., & Scott, E. S. (2003). Less guilty by reason of adolescence: Developmental immaturity, diminished responsibility, and the juvenile death penalty. *American Psychologist, 58,* 1009–1018. (p. 167)

Steinberg, N. (1993, February). Astonishing love stories (from an earlier United Press International report). *Games,* p. 47. (p. 759)

Steinem, G. (1988). Six great ideas that television is missing. In G. Comstock (Ed.), *Public communication and behavior.* New York: Academic Press. (p. 754)

Steinhauer, J. (1999). More traffic in the double-stroller lane: Twin births surge, and the parents face special, and costly challenges. *New York Times* (www.nytimes.com). (p. 98)

Steinhauer, J. (1999, November 29). Number of twins rises; so does parental stress. *New York Times* (www.nytimes.com). (p. 98)

Steinmetz, J. E. (1999). The localization of a simple type of learning and memory: The cerebellum and classical eyeblink conditioning. *Contemporary Psychology, 7,* 72–77. (p. 369)

Stengel, E. (1981). Suicide. In *The new encyclopaedia britannica, macropaedia* (Vol. 17, pp. 777–782). Chicago: Encyclopaedia Britannica. (p. 662)

Stern, M., & Karraker, K. H. (1989). Sex stereotyping of infants: A review of gender labeling studies. *Sex Roles, 20,* 501–522. (p. 261)

Stern, S. L., Dhanda, R., & Hazuda, H. P. (2001). Hopelessness predicts mortality in older Mexican and European Americans. *Psychosomatic Medicine, 63,* 344–351. (pp. 564–565)

Sternbach, H. (1998). Age-associated testosterone decline in men: Clinical issues for psychiatry. *American Journal of Psychiatry, 155,* 1310–1318. (p. 177)

Sternberg, E. M. (2001). *The balance within: The science connecting health and emotions.* New York: Freeman. (p. 557)

Sternberg, R. (Ed.), (2002). *Career paths in psychology: Where your degree can take you.* Washington, DC: APA. (p. A-9)

Sternberg, R. J. (1985). *Beyond IQ: A triarchic theory of human intelligence.* New York: Cambridge University Press. (p. 435)

Sternberg, R. J. (1988). Applying cognitive theory to the testing and teaching of intelligence. *Applied Cognitive Psychology, 2,* 231–255. (p. 438)

Sternberg, R. J. (1998). Principles of teaching for successful intelligence. *Educational Psychologist, 33,* 65–72. (p. 435)

Sternberg, R. J. (1999). The theory of successful intelligence. *Review of General Psychology, 3,* 292–316. (p. 435)

Sternberg, R. J. (2000). Presidential aptitude in Science. (p. 435)

Sternberg, R. J. (2003). Our research program validating the triarchic theory of successful intelligence: Reply to Gottfredson. *Intelligence, 31,* 399–413. (pp. 435–436)

Sternberg, R. J., & Grajek, S. (1984). The nature of love. *Journal of Personality and Social Psychology, 47,* 312–329. (p. 764)

Sternberg, R. J., & Grigorenko, E. L. (2000). Theme-park psychology: A case study regarding human intelligence and its implications for education. *Educational Psychology Review, 12,* 247–268. (p. 454)

Sternberg, R. J., Grigorenko, E. L., & Kidd, K. K. (2005). Intelligence, race, and genetics. *American Psychologist, 60,* 46–59. (p. 460)

Sternberg, R. J., & Kaufman, J. C. (1998). Human abilities. *Annual Review of Psychology, 49,* 479–502. (p. 431)

Sternberg, R. J., & Lubart, T. I. (1991). An investment theory of creativity and its development. *Human Development,* 1–31. (p. 438)

Sternberg, R. J., & Lubart, T. I. (1992). Buy low and sell high: An investment approach to creativity. *Psychological Science, 1,* 1–5. (p. 438)

Sternberg, R. J., & Wagner, R. K. (1993). The *g*-ocentric view of intelligence and job performance is wrong. *Current Directions in Psychological Science, 2,* 1–5. (p. 435)

Sternberg, R. J., Wagner, R. K., Williams, W. M., & Horvath, J. A. (1995). Testing common sense. *American Psychologist, 50,* 912–927. (p. 435)

Stetter, F., & Kupper, S. (2002). Autogenic training: A meta-analysis of clinical outcome studies. *Applied Psychophysiology and Biofeedback, 27,* 45–98. (p. 570)

Stevenson, H. W. (1992, December). Learning from Asian schools. *Scientific American,* pp. 70–76. (p. 460)

Stevenson, H. W., & Lee, S-Y. (1990). Contexts of achievement: A study of American, Chinese, and Japanese children. *Monographs of the Society for Research in Child Development, 55* (Serial No. 221, Nos. 1–2). (p. 453)

Stewart, B. (2002, April 6). Recall of the wild. *New York Times* (www.nytimes.com). (p. 48)

Stewart, D. (2000, February). Driving the wrong way. *The Psychologist,* pp. 64–65. (p. 246)

Stice, E. (2002). Risk and maintenance factors for eating pathology: A meta-analytic review. *Psychological Bulletin, 128,* 825–848. (p. 479)

Stice, E., & Shaw, H. E. (1994). Adverse effects of the media portrayed thin-ideal on women and linkages to bulimic symptomatology. *Journal of Social and Clinical Psychology, 13,* 288–308. (p. 479)

Stice, E., Spangler, D., & Agras, W. S. (2001). Exposure to media-portrayed thin-ideal images adversely affects vulnerable girls: A longitudinal experiment. *Journal of Social and Clinical Psychology, 20,* 270–288. (p. 479)

Stickgold, R. (2000, March 7). Quoted by S. Blakeslee, For better learning, researchers endorse "sleep on it" adage. *New York Times,* p. F2. (p. 287)

Stickgold, R., Hobson, J. A., Fosse, R., & Fosse, M. (2001). Sleep, learning, and dreams: Off-line memory processing. *Science, 294,* 1052–1057. (p. 287)

Stickgold, R., James, L., & Hobson, J. A. (2000). Visual discrimination learning requires sleep after training. *Nature Neuroscience, 3,* 1237–1238. (p. 287)

Stickgold, R., Malia, A., Maquire, D., Roddenberry, D., & O'Connor, M. (2000, October 13). Replaying the game: Hypnagogic images in normals and amnesics. *Science, 290,* 350–353. (p. 286)

Stipek, D. (1992). The child at school. In M. H. Bornstein & M. E. Lamb (Eds.), *Developmental psychology: An advanced textbook.* Hillsdale, NJ: Erlbaum. (p. 161)

Stith, S. M., Rosen, K. H., Middleton, K. A., Busch, A. L., Lunderberg, K., & Carlton, R. P. (2000). The intergenerational transmission of spouse abuse: A meta-analysis. *Journal of Marriage and the Family, 62,* 640–654. (p. 343)

Stockton, M. C., & Murnen, S. K. (1992). Gender and sexual arousal in response to sexual stimuli: A meta-analytic review. Presented at the American Psychological Society convention. (p. 484)

Stone, A. A., Cox, D. S., Valdimarsdottir, H., Jandor, L., & Neale, J. M. (1987). Evidence that secretory IgA antibody is associated with daily mood. *Journal of Personality and Social Psychology, 52,* 988–993. (p. 538)

Stone, A. A., & Neale, J. M. (1984). Effects of severe daily events on mood. *Journal of Personality and Social Psychology, 46,* 137–144. (p. 538)

Stoolmiller, M. (1999). Implications of the restricted range of family environments for estimates of heritability and nonshared environment in behavior-genetic adoption studies. *Psychological Bulletin, 125,* 392–409. (p. 101)

Stoppard, J. M., & Gruchy, C. D. G. (1993). Gender, context, and expression of positive emotion. *Personality and Social Psychology Bulletin, 19,* 143–150. (p. 526)

Storm, L. (2000). Research note: Replicable evidence of psi: A revision of Milton's (1999) meta-analysis of the ganzfeld data bases. *Journal of Parapsychology, 64,* 411–416. (p. 267)

Storm, L. (2003). Remote viewing by committee: RV using a multiple agent/multiple percipient design. *Journal of Parapsychology, 67,* 325–342. (p. 267)

Storms, M. D. (1973). Videotape and the attribution process: Reversing actors' and observers' points of view. *Journal of Personality and Social Psychology, 27,* 165–175. (p. 725)

Storms, M. D. (1981). A theory of erotic orientation development. *Psychological Review, 88,* 340–353. (p. 489)

Storms, M. D. (1983). *Development of sexual orientation.* Washington, DC: Office of Social and Ethical Responsibility, American Psychological Association. (p. 488)

Storms, M. D., & Thomas, G. C. (1977). Reactions to physical closeness. *Journal of Personality and Social Psychology, 35,* 412–418. (p. 738)

Strack, F., Martin, L., & Stepper, S. (1988). Inhibiting and facilitating conditions of the human smile: A nonobtrusive test of the facial feedback hypothesis. *Journal of Personality and Social Psychology, 54,* 768–777. (p. 530)

Strack, S., & Coyne, J. C. (1983). Social confirmation of dysphoria: Shared and private reactions to depression. *Journal of Personality and Social Behavior, 44,* 798–806. (p. 667)

Strahan, E. J., Spencer, S. J., & Zanna, M. P. (2002). Subliminal priming and persuasion: Striking while the iron is hot. *Journal of Experimental Social Psychology, 38,* 556–568. (p. 201)

Strange, B. A., & Dolan, R. J. (2004). b-Adrenergic modulation of emotional memory-evoked human amygdala and hippocampal responses. *Proceedings of the National Academy of Sciences, 101,* 11454–11458. (p. 366)

Stratton, G. M. (1896). Some preliminary experiments on vision without inversion of the retinal image. *Psychological Review, 3,* 611–617. (p. 256)

Straub, R. O., Seidenberg, M. S., Bever, T. G., & Terrace, H. S. (1979). Serial learning in the pigeon. *Journal of the Experimental Analysis of Behavior, 32,* 137–148. (p. 426)

Straus, M. A., & Gelles, R. J. (1980). *Behind closed doors: Violence in the American family.* New York: Anchor/Doubleday. (p. 333)

Straus, M. A., Sugarman, D. B., & Giles-Sims, J. (1997). Spanking by parents and subsequent antisocial behavior of children. *Archives of Pediatric Adolescent Medicine, 151,* 761–767. (p. 333)

Strawbridge, W. J. (1999). Mortality and religious involvement: A review and critique of the results, the methods, and the measures. Paper presented at a Harvard University conference on religion and health, sponsored by the National Institiue for Healthcare Research and the John Templeton Foundation. (p. 573)

Strawbridge, W. J., Cohen, R. D., & Shema, S. J. (1997). Frequent attendance at religious services and mortality over 28 years. *American Journal of Public Health, 87,* 957–961. (p. 573)

Strawbridge, W. J., Shema, S. J., Cohen, R. D., & Kaplan, G. A. (2001). Religious attendance increases survival by improving and maintaining good health behaviors, mental health, and social relationships. *Annals of Behavioral Medicine, 23,* 68–74. (p. 573)

Strayer, D. L., Drews, F. A., & Johnston, W. A. (2003). Cell phone-induced failures of visual attention during simulated driving. *Journal of Experimental Psychology: Applied, 9*, 23-32. (p. 238)

Strayer, D. L., & Johnston, W. A. (2001). Driven to distraction: Dual-task studies of simulated driving and conversing on a cellular telephone. *Psychological Science, 12*, 462-466. (p. 238)

Streissguth, A. P., Aase, J. M., Clarren, S. K., Randels, S. P., LaDue, R. A., & Smith, D. F. (1991). Fetal alcohol syndrome in adolescents and adults. *Journal of the American Medical Association, 265*, 1961-1967. (p. 142)

Strickland, B. (1992, February 20). Gender differences in health and illness. Sigma Xi national lecture delivered at Hope College. (p. 178)

Striegel-Moore, R. H., Silberstein, L. R., & Rodin, J. (1993). The social self in bulimia nervosa: Public self-consciousness, social anxiety, and perceived fraudulence. *Journal of Abnormal Psychology, 102*, 297-303. (p. 479)

Stroebe, M., Stroebe, W., & Schut, H. (2001). Gender differences in adjustment to bereavement: An empirical and theoretical review. *Review of General Psychology, 5*, 62-83. (p. 191)

Stroebe, M., Stroebe, W., Schut, H., Zech, E., & van den Bout, J. (2002). Does disclosure of emotions facilitate recovery from bereavement? Evidence from two prospective studies. *Journal of Consulting and Clinical Psychology, 70*, 169-178. (p. 191)

Stroebe, W., Schut, H., & Stroebe, M. S. (2005). Grief work, disclosure and counseling: Do they help the bereaved? *Clinical Psychology Review, 25*, 395-414. (p. 191)

Strupp, H. H. (1982). The outcome problem in psychotherapy: Contemporary perspectives. In J. H. Harvey & M. M. Parks (Eds.), *The master lecture series: Vol. 1. Psychotherapy research and behavior change*. Washington, DC: American Psychological Association. (p. 632)

Strupp, H. H. (1986). Psychotherapy: Research, practice, and public policy (How to avoid dead ends). *American Psychologist, 41*, 120-130. (p. 707)

Stumpf, H., & Jackson, D. N. (1994). Gender-related differences in cognitive abilities: Evidence from a medical school admissions testing program. *Personality and Individual Differences, 17*, 335-344. (p. 461)

Stumpf, H., & Stanley, J. C. (1998). Stability and change in gender-related differences on the college board advanced placement and achievement tests. *Current Directions in Psychology, 7*, 192-196. (p. 463)

Stunkard, A. J., Harris, J. R., Pedersen, N. L., & McClearn, G. E. (1990). A separated twin study of the body mass index. *New England Journal of Medicine, 322*, 1483-1487. (p. 586)

Sturm, R. (2003). Increases in clinically severe obesity in the United States, 1986-2000. *Archives of Internal Medicine, 163*, 2146-2148. (p. 587)

Subiaul, F., Cantlon, J. F., Holloway, R. L., & Terrace, H. S. (2004). Cognitive imitation in rhesus macaques. *Science, 305*, 407-410. (p. 341)

Suddath, R. L., Christison, G. W., Torrey, E. F., Casanova, M. F., & Weinberger, D. R. (1990). Anatomical abnormalities in the brains of monozygotic twins discordant for schizophrenia. *New England Journal of Medicine, 322*, 789-794. (p. 675)

Suddendorf, T., & Whiten, A. (2001). Mental evolution and development: Evidence for secondary representation in children, great apes, and other animals. *Psychological Bulletin, 137*, 629-650. (p. 425)

Sue, D. W. (1990). Culture-specific strategies in counseling: A conceptual framework. *Professional Psychology: Research and Practice, 21*, 424-433. (pp. 709-710)

Suedfeld, P. (1998). Homo invictus: The indomitable species. *Canadian Psychology, 38*, 164-173. (p. 653)

Suedfeld, P. (2000). Reverberations of the Holocaust fifty years later: Psychology's contributions to understanding persecution and genocide. *Canadian Psychology, 41*, 1-9. (p. 653)

Suedfeld, P., & Mocellin, J. S. P. (1987). The "sensed presence" in unusual environments. *Environment and Behavior, 19*, 33-52. (p. 309)

Sugita, Y. (2004). Experience in early infancy is indispensable for color perception. *Current Biology. 14*, 1267-1271. (p. 214)

Suhail, K., & Chaudry, H. R. (2004). Predictors of subjective well-being in an Eatern Muslim Cultre. *Journal of Social and Clinical Psychology, 23*, 359. (p. 540)

Suinn, R. M. (1997). Mental practice in sports psychology: Where have we been, Where do we go? *Clinical Psychology: Science and Practice*. (p. 421)

Sullivan, P. F., Neale, M. C., & Kendler, K. S. (2000). Genetic epidemiology of major depression: Review and meta-analysis. *American Journal of Psychiatry, 157*, 1552-1562. (p. 663)

Suls, J. M., & Tesch, F. (1978). Students' preferences for information about their test performance: A social comparison study. *Journal of Experimental Social Psychology, 8*, 189-197. (p. 543)

Summers, M. (1996, December 9). Mister clean. *People Weekly*, pp. 139-142. (p. 639)

Sundet, J. M., Barlaug, D. G., & Torjussen, T. M. (2004). The end of the Flynn effect? A study of secular trends in mean intelligence test scores of Norwegian conscripts during half a century. *Intelligence, 32*, 349-362. (p. 448)

Sundstrom, E., De Meuse, K. P., & Futrell, D. (1990). Work teams: Applications and effectiveness. *American Psychologist, 45*, 120-133. (p. 509)

Suomi, S. J. (1986). Anxiety-like disorders in young nonhuman primates. In R. Gettleman (Ed.), *Anxiety disorders of childhood*. New York: Guilford Press. (p. 655)

Suomi, S. J. (1987). Genetic and maternal contributions to individual differences in rhesus monkey biobehavioral development. In N. A. Krasnegor & others (Eds.), *Perinatal development: A psychobiological perspective*. Orlando, FL: Academic Press. (p. 600)

Super, C., & Super, D. (2001). Education and Training. *Opportunities in psychology careers* (pp. 68-80). Chicago, IL: VGM Career Books. (p. A-3)

Suppes, P. Quoted by R. H. Ennis (1982). Children's ability to handle Piaget's propositional logic: A conceptual critique. In S. Modgil & C. Modgil (Eds.), *Jean Piaget: Consensus and controversy*. New York: Praeger. (p. 154)

Surgeon General. (1986). *The Surgeon General's workshop on pornography and public health*, June 22-24. Report prepared by E. P. Mulvey & J. L. Haugaard and released by Office of the Surgeon General on August 4, 1986. (p. 754)

Surgeon General. (1999). *Mental health: A report of the Surgeon General*. Rockville, MD: U.S. Department of Health and Human Services. (p. 663)

Susser, E. (1999). Life course cohort studies of schizophrenia. *Psychiatric Annals, 29*, 161-165. (p. 676)

Susser, E., Neugenbauer, R., Hoek, H. W., Brown, A. S., Lin, S., Labovitz, D., & Gorman, J. M. (1996). Schizophrenia after prenatal famine. *Archives of General Psychiatry, 53*(1), 25-31 (p. 673)

Susser, E. S., Herman, D. B., & Aaron, B. (2002, August). Combating the terror of terrorism. *Scientific American*, pp. 70-77. (p. 653)

Svirsky, M. A., Robbins, A. M., Kirk, K. I., Pisoni, D. B., & Miyamoto, R. T. (2000). Language development in profoundly deaf children with cochlear implants. *Psychological Science, 11*, 153-158. (p. 221)

Sweat, J. A., & Durm, M. W. (1993). Psychics: Do police departments really use them? *Skeptical Inquirer, 17*, 148-158. (p. 265)

Swerdlow, N. R., & Koob, G. F. (1987). Dopamine, schizophrenia, mania, and depression: Toward a unified hypothesis of cortico-stiato-pallido-thalamic function (with commentary). *Behavioral and Brain Sciences, 10*, 197-246. (p. 672)

Swim, J. K. (1994). Perceived versus meta-analytic effect sizes: An assessment of the accuracy of gender stereotypes. *Journal of Personality and Social Psychology, 66*, 21-36. (p. 745)

Swindle, R., Jr., Heller, K., Bescosolido, B., & Kikuzawa, S. (2000). Responses to nervous breakdowns in America over a 40-year period: Mental health policy implications. *American Psychologist, 55*, 740-749. (p. 661)

Symbaluk, D. G., Heth, C. D., Cameron, J., & Pierce, W. D. (1997). Social modeling, monetary incentives, and pain endurance: The role of self-efficacy and pain perception. *Personality and Social Psychology Bulletin, 23*, 258-269. (p. 228)

Symond, M. B., Harris, A. W. F., Gordon, E., & Williams, L. M. (2005). "Gamma synchrony" in first-episode schizophrenia: A disorder of temporal connectivity? *American Journal of Psychiatry, 162,* 459–465. (p. 672)

Symons, C. S., & Johnson, B. T. (1997). The self-reference effect in memory: A meta-analysis. *Psychological Bulletin, 121*(3), 371–394. (p. 358)

TADS (Treatment for Adolescents with Depression Study Team). (2004). Fluoxetine, cognitive-behavioral therapy, and their combination for adolescents with depression: Treatment for adolescents with depression study (TADS) randomized controlled trial. *Journal of the American Medical Association, 292,* 807–820. (p. 714)

Taha, F. A. (1972). A comparative study of how sighted and blind perceive the manifest content of dreams. *National Review of Social Sciences, 9*(3), 28. (p. 286)

Taheri, S. (2004). The genetics of sleep disorders. *Minerva Medica, 95,* 203–212. (pp. 282, 284)

Taheri, S., Lin, L., Austin, D., Young, T., & Mignot, E. (2004). Short sleep duration is associated with reduced leptin, elevated ghrelin, and increased body mass index. *PloS Medicine, 1*(3), e62 (www.plosmedicine.org). (p. 284)

Taheri, S., Zeitzer, J. M., & Mignot, E. (2002). The role of hypocretins (orexins) in sleep regulation and narcolepsy. *Annual Review of Neuroscience, 25,* 283–313. (p. 284)

Tajfel, H. (Ed.). (1982). *Social identity and intergroup relations.* New York: Cambridge University Press. (p. 746)

Talal, N. (1995). Quoted by V. Morell, Zeroing in on how hormones affect the immune system. *Science, 269,* 773–775. (p. 557)

Talarico, J. M., & Rubin, D. C. (2003). Confidence, not consistency, characterizes flashbulb memories. *Psychological Science, 14,* 455–461. (p. 351)

Talbot, M. (1999, October 31). The Rorschach chronicles. *New York Times* (www.nytimes.com). (p. 602)

Talbot, M. (2002, June 2). Hysteria hysteria. *New York Times* (www.nytimes.com). (p. 731)

Talwar, S. K., Xu, S., Hawley, E. S., Weiss, S. A., Moxon, K. A., & Chapin, J. K. (2002). Rat navigation guided by remote control. *Nature, 417,* 37–38. (p. 74)

Tamres, L. K., Janicki, D., & Helgeson, V. S. (2002). Sex differences in coping behavior: A meta-analytic review and an examination of relative coping. *Personality and Social Psychology Review, 6,* 2–30. (p. 129)

Tang, S-H., & Hall, V. C. (1995). The overjustification effect: A meta-analysis. *Applied Cognitive Psychology, 9,* 365–404. (p. 335)

Tangney, J. P., Baumeister, R. F., & Boone, A. L. (2004). High self-control predicts good adjustment, less pathology, better grades, and interpersonal success. *Journal of Personality, 72,* 271–324. (p. 625)

Tannen, D. (1990). *You just don't understand: Women and men in conversation.* New York: Morrow. (pp. 46, 128)

Tannenbaum, P. (2002, February). Quoted by R. Kubey & M. Csikszentmihalyi, Television addiction is no mere metaphor. *Scientific American,* pp. 74–80. (p. 203)

Tanner, J. M. (1978). *Fetus into man: Physical growth from conception to maturity.* Cambridge, MA: Harvard University Press. (p. 165)

Tarbert, J. (2004, May 14). Bad apples, bad command, or both? Dart Center for Journalism and Trauma (www.dartcenter.org). (p. 729)

Tarmann, A. (2002, May/June). Out of the closet and onto the Census long form. *Population Today, 30,* pp. 1, 6. (p. 487)

Tasbihsazan, R., Nettelbeck, T., & Kirby, N. (2003). Predictive validity of the Fagan Test of Infant Intelligence. *British Journal of Developmental Psychology, 21,* 585–597. (p. 450)

Tatarkiewicz, W. (1976). *Analysis of happiness.* The Hague: Martinus Nijhoff, 1976. (p. 538)

Taubes, G. (1994). Will new dopamine receptors offer a key to schizophrenia? *Science, 265,* 1034–1035. (p. 712)

Taubes, G. (2001). The soft science of dietary fat. *Science, 291,* 2536–2545. (p. 590)

Taubes, G. (2002, July 7). What if it's all been a big fat lie? *New York Times* (www.nytimes.com). (p. 590)

Tavris, C. (1982, November). Anger defused. *Psychology Today,* pp. 25–35. (p. 537)

Taylor, H. (2003, February 26). The religious and other beliefs of Americans 2003. *The Harris Poll #11* (www.harrisinteracctive.com). (p. 310)

Taylor, K. M., Shepperd, J. A. (1998). Bracing for the worst: Severity, testing, and feedback timing as moderators of the optimistic bias. *Personality and Social Psychology Bulletin, 24,* 915–926. (p. 627)

Taylor, S. E. (1989). *Positive illusions.* New York: Basic Books. (pp. 403, 565, 636)

Taylor, S. E. (2002). *The tending instinct: How nurturing is essential to who we are and how we live.* New York: Times Books. (p. 129)

Taylor, S. E., Cousino, L. K., Lewis, B. P., Gruenewald, T. L., Gurung, R. A. R., & Updegraff, J. A. (2000). Biobehavioral responses to stress in females: Tend-and-befriend, not fight-or-flight. *Psychological Review, 107,* 411–430. (p. 552)

Taylor, S. E., Lerner, J. S., Sherman, D. K., Sage, R. M., & McDowell, N. K. (2003). Portrait of the self-enhancer: Well adjusted and well liked or maladjusted and friendless? *Journal of Personality and Social Psychology, 84,* 165–176. (p. 636)

Taylor, S. E., Pham, L. B., Rivkin, I. D., & Armor, D. A. (1998). Harnessing the imagination: Mental simulation, self-regulation, and coping. *American Psychologist, 53,* 429–439. (p. 421)

Taylor, S., Kuch, K., Koch, W. J., Crockett, D. J., & Passey, G. (1998). The structure of posttraumatic stress symptoms. *Journal of Abnormal Psychology, 107,* 154–160. (p. 652)

Taylor, S. P., & Chermack, S. T. (1993). Alcohol, drugs and human physical aggression. *Journal of Studies on Alcohol,* Supplement No. 11, 78–88. (p. 750)

Teasdale, T. W., & Owen, D. R. (2000). Forty-year secular trends in cognitive abilities. *Intelligence, 28,* 115–120. (p. 448)

Tedeschi, R. G., & Calhoun, L. G. (2004). Posttraumatic growth: Conceptual foundations and empirical evidence. *Psychological Inquiry, 15,* 1–18. (p. 653)

Teerlink, R., & Ozley, L. (2000). *More than a motorcycle: The leadership journey at Harley-Davidson.* Cambridge, MA: Harvard Business School Press. (p. 509)

Teghtsoonian, R. (1971). On the exponents in Stevens' law and the constant in Ekinan's law. *Psychological Review, 78,* 71–80. (p. 201)

Teicher, M. (2002). McLean motion and attention test (M-MAT): A new test to diagnose a troubling disorder. *McLean Hospital Annual Report* (www.mclean.harvard.edu). (p. 641)

Teicher, M. H. (2002, March). The neurobiology of child abuse. *Scientific American,* pp. 68–75. (p. 159)

Tenopyr, M. L. (1997). Improving the workplace: Industrial/organizational psychology as a career. In R. J. Sternberg (Ed.), *Career paths in psychology: Where your degree can take you.* Washington, DC: American Psychological Association. (p. 500)

Teran-Santos, J., Jimenez-Gomez, A., & Cordero-Guevara, J. (1999). The association between sleep apnea and the risk of traffic accidents. *New England Journal of Medicine, 340,* 847–851. (p. 284)

Terman, J. S., Terman, M., Lo, E-S., & Cooper, T. B. (2001). Circadian time of morning light administration and therapeutic response in winter depression. *Archives of General Psychiatry, 58,* 69–73. (p. 707)

Terman, L. M. (1916). *The measurement of intelligence.* Boston: Houghton Mifflin. (p. 444)

Terman, M., Terman, J. S., & Ross, D. C. (1998). A controlled trial of timed bright light and negative air ionization for treatment of winter depression. *Archives of General Psychiatry, 55,* 875–882. (p. 707)

Terrace, H. S. (1979, November). How Nim Chimpsky changed my mind. *Psychology Today,* pp. 65–76. (p. 427)

Terre, L., & Stoddart, R. (2000). Cutting edge specialties for graduate study in psychology. *Eye on Psi Chi, 23–26.* (p. A-4)

Tesser, A., Forehand, R., Brody, G., & Long, N. (1989). Conflict: The role of calm and angry parent-child discussion in adolescent development. *Journal of Social and Clinical Psychology, 8,* 317–330. (p. 172)

Tetlock, P. E. (1988). Monitoring the integrative complexity of American and Soviet policy rhetoric: What can be learned? *Journal of Social Issues, 44,* 101–131. (p. 769)

Tetlock, P. E. (1998). Close-call counterfactuals and belief-system defenses: I was not almost wrong but I was almost right. *Journal of Personality and Social Psychology, 75,* 639–652. (p. 22)

Thannickal, T. C., Moore, R. Y., Nienhuis, R., Ramanathan, L., Gulyani, S., Aldrich, M., Cornford, M., & Siegel, J. M. (2000). Reduced number of hypocretin neurons in human narcolepsy. *Neuron, 27,* 469–474. (p. 284)

Thatcher, R. W., Walker, R. A., & Giudice, S. (1987). Human cerebral hemispheres develop at different rates and ages. *Science, 236,* 1110–1113. (pp. 145, 193)

Thayer, R. E. (1987). Energy, tiredness, and tension effects of a sugar snack versus moderate exercise. *Journal of Personality and Social Psychology, 52,* 119–125. (p. 569)

Thayer, R. E. (1993). Mood and behavior (smoking and sugar snacking) following moderate exercise: A partial test of self-regulation theory. *Personality and Individual Differences, 14,* 97–104. (p. 569)

Thomas, A., & Chess, S. (1986). The New York Longitudinal Study: From infancy to early adult life. In R. Plomin & J. Dunn (Eds.), *The study of temperament: Changes, continuities, and challenges.* Hillsdale, NJ: Erlbaum. (p. 194)

Thomas, L. (1974). *The lives of a cell.* New York: Viking Press. (p. 232)

Thomas, L. (1979). *The medusa and the snail.* New York: Viking. (p. 140)

Thomas, L. (1983). *The youngest science: Notes of a medicine watcher.* New York: Viking Press. (p. 59)

Thomas, L. (1992). *The fragile species.* New York : Scribner's. (pp. 135, 702)

Thomas, W. P., & Collier, V. P. (1998). Two languages are better than one. *Educational Leadership, 55,* 23–36. (p. 420)

Thompson, C. P., Frieman, J., & Cowan, T. (1993). Rajan's memory. Paper presented to the American Psychological Society convention. (p. 363)

Thompson, C. P., Vogl, R. J., Walker, W. R., & Wooten, L. (1996). Involuntary memories in depressed and nondepressed individuals. Paper presented to the Psychonomic Society convention. (p. 585)

Thompson, G. (1998, December 14). As obesity in children increases, so do cases of adult-onset diabetes. *New York Times* (www.nytimes.com). (p. 587)

Thompson, J. K., Jarvie, G. J., Lahey, B. B., & Cureton, K. J. (1982). Exercise and obesity: Etiology, physiology, and intervention. *Psychological Bulletin, 91,* 55–79. (p. 590)

Thompson, J. K., & Stice, E. (2001). Thin-ideal internalization: Mounting evidence for a new risk factor for body-image disturbance and eating pathology. *Current Directions in Psychological Science, 10,* 181–183. (p. 479)

Thompson, P. (1980). Margaret Thatcher: A new illusion. *Perception, 9,* 483–484. (p. 259)

Thompson, P. M., Cannon, T. D., Narr, K. L., van Erp, T., Poutanen, V-P., Huttunen, M., Lönnqvist, J., Standerskjöld-Nordenstam, C-G., Kaprio, J., Khaledy, M., Dail, R., Zoumalan, C. I., & Toga, A. W. (2001). Genetic influences on brain structure. *Nature Neuroscience, 4,* 1253–1258. (pp. 455, 673)

Thompson, P. M., Giedd, J. N., Woods, R. P., MacDonald, D., Evans, A. C., & Toga, A. W. (2000). Growth patterns in the developing brain detected by using continuum mechanical tensor maps. *Nature, 404,* 190–193. (p. 145)

Thompson, R., Emmorey, K., & Gollan, T. H. (2005). "Tip of the fingers" experiences by Deaf signers. *Psychological Science, 16,* 856–860. (p. 378)

Thomson, R., & Murachver, T. (2001). Predicting gender from electronic discourse. *British Journal of Social Psychology, 40,* 193–208 (and personal correspondence from T. Murachver, May 23, 2002). (p. 128)

Thorndike, A. L., & Hagen, E. P. (1977). Measurement and evaluation in psychology and education. New York: Macmillan. (p. 446)

Thorndike, E. L. (1898). Animal intelligence: An experimental study of associative processes in animals. *Psychological Review Monograph Supplements, 2,* 4–160. (p. 327)

Thorne, J., with Larry Rothstein (1993). *You are not alone: Words of experience and hope for the journey through depression.* New York: HarperPerennial. (p. 639)

Thornhill, R., & Gangestad, S. W. (1994). Human fluctuating asymmetry and sexual behavior. *Psychological Science, 5,* 297–302. (p. 761)

Thornton, B., & Moore, S. (1993). Physical attractiveness contrast effect: Implications for self-esteem and evaluations of the social self. *Personality and Social Psychology Bulletin, 19,* 474–480. (p. 760)

Thorpe, W. H. (1974). *Animal nature and human nature.* London: Metheun. (p. 428)

Tiedens, L. Z. (2001). Anger and advancement versus sadness and subjugation: The effect of negative emotion expressions on social status conferral. *Journal of Personality and Social Psychology, 80,* 86–94. (p. 537)

Tiihonen, J., Isohanni, M., Rasanen, P, Koiranen, M., & Moring, J. (1997). Specific major mental disorders and criminality: A 26-year prospective study of the 1966 northern Finland birth cohort. *American Journal of Psychiatry, 154,* 840–845. (p. 647)

Tikkanen, T. (2001). Psychology in Europe: A growing profession with high standards and a bright future. *European Psychologist, 6,* 144–146. (p. 8)

Time. (1997, December 22). Greeting card association data, p.19. (p.128)

Tinbergen, N. (1951). *The study of instinct.* Oxford: Clarendon. (p. 470)

Tirrell, M. E. (1990). Personal communication. (p. 318)

Tjaden, P., & Thoennes, N. (2000b). Full report of the prevalence, incidence, and consequences of violence against women: Findings from the National Violence Against Women Survey (NCJ 183781). Washington, DC: U.S. Department of Justice, National Institute of Justice. (p. 752)

Todes, D. P. (1997). From the machine to the ghost within: Pavlov's transition from digestive physiology to conditional reflexes. *American Psychologist, 52,* 947–955. (p. 317)

Tolchin, M. (1994, April 17). Major airlines go two years without a fatality. *New York Times* report (in *Grand Rapids Press,* p. A10). (p. 405)

Tolkien, J. R. R. (1965). *The fellowship of the ring.* Boston: Houghton Mifflin Co. (pp. 595, 619)

Tollefson, G. D., Fawcett, J., Winokur, G., Beasley, C. M., et al. (1993). Evaluation of suicidality during pharmacologic treatment of mood and non-mood disorders. *Annals of Clinical Psychiatry, 5*(4), 209–224. (p. 714)

Tollefson, G. D., Rampey, A. H., Beasley, C. M., & Enas, G. G. (1994). Absence of a relationship between adverse events and suicidality during pharmacotherapy for depression. *Journal of Clinical Psychopharmacology, 14,* 163–169. (p. 714)

Tolman, E. C., & Honzik, C. H. (1930). Introduction and removal of reward, and maze performance in rats. *University of California Publications in Psychology, 4,* 257–275. (p. 334)

Tolstoy, L. (1904). *My confessions.* Boston: Dana Estes. (p. 12)

Tondo, L., Jamison, K. R., & Baldessarini, R. J. (1997). Effect of lithium maintenance on suicidal behavior in major mood disorders. In D. M. Stoff & J. J. Mann (Eds.), *The neurobiology of suicide: From the bench to the clinic.* New York: New York Academy of Sciences. (p. 715)

Toni, N., Buchs, P.-A., Nikonenko, I., Bron, C. R., & Muller, D. (1999). LTP promotes formation of multiple spine synapses between a single axon terminal and a dendrite. *Nature, 402,* 421–42. (p. 365)

Torrey, E. F. (1986). *Witchdoctors and psychiatrists.* New York: Harper & Row. (p. 708)

Torrey, E. F. (1998, February 22). Quoted by M. Winerip, Schizophrenia's most zealous foe. *New York Times Magazine,* pp. 26–28. (p. 653)

Torrey, E. F., & Miller, J. (2002). The invisible plague: The rise of mental illness from 1750 to the present. New Brunswick, NJ: London: Rutgers University Press. (p. 673)

Torrey, E. F., Miller, J., Rawlings, R., & Yolken, R. H. (1997). Seasonality of births in schizophrenia and bipolar disorder: A review of the literature. *Schizophrenia Research, 28,* 1–38. (p. 673)

Totterdell, P., Kellett, S., Briner, R. B., & Teuchmann, K. (1998). Evidence of mood linkage in work groups. *Journal of Personality and Social Psychology, 74,* 1504–1515. (p. 731)

Tovee, M. J., Mason, S. M., Emery, J. L., McCluskey, S. E., & Cohen-Tovee, E. M. (1997). Supermodels: Stick insects or hourglasses? *The Lancet, 350,* 1474–1475. (p. 479)

Towler, G. (1986). From zero to one hundred: Coaction in a natural setting. *Perceptual and Motor Skills, 62,* 377–378. (p. 738)

Tracey, J. L., & Robins, R. W. (2004). Show your pride: Evidence for a discrete emotion expression. *Psychological Science, 15,* 194–197. (p. 532)

Tramontana, M. G., Hooper, S. R., & Selzer, S. C. (1988). Research on the preschool prediction of later academic achievement: A review. *Developmental Review, 8,* 89–146. (p. 451)

Tranel, D., Bechara, A., & Denburg, N. L. (2002). Asymmetric functional roles of right and left ventromedial prefrontal cortices in social conduct, decision-making and emotional processing. *Cortex, 38,* pp. 589–613. (p. 86)

Travis, J. (1994). Glia: The brain's other cells. *Science, 266,* 970–972. (p. 75)

Treffert, D. A., & Wallace, G. L. (2002). Island of genius—The artistic brilliance and dazzling memory that sometimes accompany autism and other disorders hint at how all brains work. *Scientific American, 286,* 76–86. (p. 433)

Treisman, A. (1987). Properties, parts, and objects. In K. R. Boff, L. Kaufman, & J. P. Thomas (Eds.), *Handbook of perception and human performance.* New York: Wiley. (p. 243)

Tremblay, R. E., Pihl, R. O., Vitaro, F., & Dobkin, P. L. (1994). Predicting early onset of male antisocial behavior from preschool behavior. *Archives of General Psychiatry, 51,* 732–739. (p. 678)

Trewin, D. (2001). *Australian social trends 2001.* Canberra: Australian Bureau of Statistics. (pp. 119, 131, 344, 498)

Triandis, H. C. (1981). Some dimensions of intercultural variation and their implications for interpersonal behavior. Paper presented at the American Psychological Association convention. (p. 120)

Triandis, H. C. (1989a). The self and social behavior in differing cultural contexts. *Psychological Review, 96,* 506–520. (p. 122)

Triandis, H. C. (1989b). Cross-cultural studies of individualism and collectivism. In J. J. Berman (Ed.), *Nebraska symposium on motivation 1989* (Vol. 37). Lincoln, NE: University of Nebraska Press. (p. 122)

Triandis, H. C. (1994). *Culture and social behavior.* New York: McGraw-Hill. (pp. 122, 411, 529, 626, 752)

Triandis, H. C., Bontempo, R., Villareal, M. J., Asai, M., & Lucca, N. (1988). Individualism and collectivism: Cross-cultural perspectives on self-ingroup relationships. *Journal of Personality and Social Psychology, 54,* 323–338. (p. 123)

Trickett, P. K., & McBride-Chang, C. (1995). The developmental impact of different forms of child abuse and neglect. *Developmental Review, 15,* 311–337. (p. 159)

Trimble, J. E. (1994). Cultural variations in the use of alcohol and drugs. In W. J. Lonner & R. Malpass (Eds.), *Psychology and culture.* Boston: Allyn & Bacon. (p. 307)

Triplett, N. (1898). The dynamogenic factors in pacemaking and competition. *American Journal of Psychology, 9,* 507–533. (p. 738)

Trolier, T. K., & Hamilton, D. L. (1986). Variables influencing judgments of correlational relations. *Journal of Personality and Social Psychology, 50,* 879–888. (p. 33)

Trut, L. N. (1999). Early canid domestication: The farm-fox experiment. *American Scientist, 87,* 160–169. (p. 108)

Tsai, J. L., & Chentsova-Dutton, Y. (2003). Variation among European Americans in emotional facial expression. *Journal of Cross-Cultural Psychology, 34,* 650–657. (p. 529)

Tsang, Y. C. (1938). Hunger motivation in gastrectomized rats. *Journal of Comparative Psychology, 26,* 1–17. (p. 475)

Tsien, J. Z. (April, 2000). Building a brainier mouse. *Scientific American,* 62–68. (p. 455)

Tsuang, M. T., & Faraone, S. V. (1990). *The genetics of mood disorders.* Baltimore, MD: Johns Hopkins University Press. (p. 663)

Tuber, D. S., Miller, D. D., Caris, K. A., Halter, R., Linden, F., & Hennessy, M. B. (1999). Dogs in animal shelters: Problems, suggestions, and needed expertise. *Psychological Science, 10,* 379–386. (p. 48)

Tucker, K. A. (2002). I believe you can fly. *Gallup Management Journal* (www.gallupjournal.com/CA/st/20020520.asp). (p. 507)

Tuerk, P. W. (2005). Research in the high-stakes era: Achievement, resources, and no child left behind. *Psychological Science, 16,* 419–425. (p. 457)

Tulving, E. (1996, August 18). Quoted in J. Gatehouse, Technology revealing brain's secrets. *Montreal Gazette,* p. A3. (p. 368)

Turkheimer, E., Haley, A., Waldron, M., D'Onofrio, B., & Gottesman, I. I. (2003). Socioeconomic status modifies heritability of IQ in young mothers. *Psychological Science, 14,* 623–628. (p. 457)

Turner, C. W., Hesse, B. W., & Peterson-Lewis, S. (1986). Naturalistic studies of the long-term effects of television violence. *Journal of Social Issues, 42*(3), 7–28. (p. 345)

Turner, J. C. (1987). *Rediscovering the social group: A self-categorization theory.* New York: Basil Blackwell. (p. 746)

Turner, N., Barling, J., & Zacharatos, A. (2002). Positive psychology at work. In C. R. Snyder & S. J. Lopez (Eds.), *The handbook of positive psychology.* New York: Oxford University Press. (p. 509)

Turpin, A. (2005, April 3). The science of psi. *FT Weekend,* pp. W1, W2. (p. 264)

Tutu, D. (1999). *No future without forgiveness.* New York: Doubleday. (p. 495)

Tversky, A. (1985, June). Quoted in K. McKean, Decisions, decisions. *Discover,* pp. 22–31. (p. 401)

Tversky, A., & Kahneman, D. (1974). Judgment under uncertainty: Heuristics and biases. *Science, 185,* 1124–1131. (p. 401)

Twenge, J. M. (1997). Changes in masculine and feminine traits over time: A meta-analysis. *Sex Roles 36*(5–6), 305–325. (p. 135)

Twenge, J. M. (2000). The age of anxiety? Birth cohort change in anxiety and neuroticism, 1952–1993. *Journal of Personality and Social Psychology, 79,* 1007–1021. (p. 654)

Twenge, J. M. (2001). Changes in women's assertiveness in response to status and roles: A cross-temporal meta-analysis, 1931–1993. *Journal of Personality and Social Psychology, 8,* 133–145. (p. 132)

Twenge, J. M., Baumeister, R. F., Tice, D. M., & Stucke, T. S. (2001). If you can't join them, beat them: Effects of social exclusion on aggressive behavior. *Journal of Personality and Social Psychology, 81,* 1058–1069. (pp. 497, 751)

Twenge, J. M., & Campbell, W. K. (2001). Age and birth cohort differences in self-esteem: A cross-temporal meta-analysis. *Personality and Social Psychology Review, 5,* 321–344. (p. 171)

Twenge, J. M., Catanese, K. R., & Baumeister, R. F. (2002). Social exclusion causes self-defeating behavior. *Journal of Personality and Social Psychology, 83,* 606–615. (pp. 497, 751)

Twenge, J. M., Catanese, K. R., & Baumeister, R. F. (2003). Social exclusion and the deconstructed state: Time perception, meaninglessness, lethargy, lack of emotion, and self-awareness. *Journal of Personality and Social Psychology, 85,* 409–423. (p. 497)

Twenge, J. M., & Crocker, J. (2002). Race and self-esteem: Meta-analyses comparing Whites, Blacks, Hispanics, Asians, and American Indians and comment on Gray-Little and Hafdahl (2000). *Psychological Bulletin, 128,* 371–408. (p. 633)

Twenge, J. M., & Nolen-Hoeksema, S. (2002). Age, gender, race, socioeconomic status, and birth cohort differences on the children's depression inventory: A meta-analysis. *Journal of Abnormal Psychology, 111,* 578–588. (p. 171)

Twenge, J. M., Zhang, L., & Im, C. (2004). It's beyond my control: A cross-temporal meta-analysis of increasing externality in locus of control, 1960–2002. *Personality and Social Psychology Review, 8,* 308–319. (p. 626)

Twiss, C., Tabb, S., & Crosby, F. (1989). Affirmative action and aggregate data: The importance of patterns in the perception of discrimination. In F. Blanchard & F. Crosby (Eds.), *Affirmative action: Social psychological perspectives.* New York: Springer-Verlag. (p. 31)

Tyler, C. (1998). An eye-placement principle in 500 years of portraits. San Francisco: Smith-Kettlewell Eye Reseach Institute (http://www.ski.org/CWTyler_lab/ARVO/cwtarvo.html). (p. 259)

Tyler, K. A. (2002). Social and emotional outcomes of childhood sexual abuse: A review of recent research. *Aggression and Violent Behavior, 7,* 567–589. (p. 159)

U.S. News & World Report. (1997, March 31). Oprah: A heavenly body? Survey finds talk-show host a celestial shoo-in. P. 18. (p. 634)

U.S. Senate Select Committee on Intelligence (2004, July 9). *Report of the U.S. Intelligence Community's prewar intelligence assessments on Iraq.* www.gpoaccess.gov/serialset/creports/iraq.html (pp. 25, 399, 740)

Uchino, B. N., Cacioppo, J. T., & Kiecolt-Glaser, J. K. (1996). The relationship between social support and physiological processes: A review with emphasis on underlying mechanisms and implications for health. *Psychological Bulletin, 119,* 488–531. (p. 566)

Uchino, B. N., Uno, D., & Holt-Lunstad, J. (1999). Social support, physiological processes, and health. *Current Directions in Psychological Science, 8,* 145–148. (p. 566)

Udry, J. R. (2000). Biological limits of gender construction. *American Sociological Review, 65,* 443–457. (p. 130)

Uehling, M. C. (1998, August). A brief history of Stephen Hawking. *Biography Magazine,* pp. 61–65, 116–117. (p. 223)

UK ECT Review Group. (2003). Efficacy and safety of electroconvulsive therapy in depressive disorders: A systematic review and meta-analysis. *Lancet, 361,* 799–808. (pp. 715–716)

Ullman, E. (2005, October 19). The boss in the machine. *New York Times* (www.nytimes.com). (p. 499)

Ulrich, R. E. (1991). Animal rights, animal wrongs and the question of balance. *Psychological Science, 2,* 197–201. (p. 47)

Ulrich, R. S. (1984). View through a window may influence recovery from surgery. *Science, 224,* 420–421. (p. 229)

UNAIDS. (2004, July). *UNAIDS 2004 report on the global AIDS epidemic* (www.unaids.org). (p. 190)

UNAIDS. (2004). *AIDS epidemic update 2004.* United Nations (www.unaids.org). (p. 190)

UNAIDS. (2004). Sub-Saharan Africa. Joint United Nations Programme on HIV/AIDS (www.unaids.org). (p. 559)

UNAIDS. (2005). *AIDS epidemic update, December 2005.* United Nations (www.unaids.org). (pp. 190, 559)

UNAIDS. (2005). *AIDS in Africa: Three scenarios to 2025.* United Nations (www.unaids.org). (pp. 190, 559)

UNAIDS. (2005). Epidemiology. Joint United Nations Programme on HIV/AIDS (www.unaids.org). (pp. 190, 559)

Underwood, B. J. (1957). Interference and forgetting. *Psychological Review, 64,* 49–60. (p. 379)

United Nations. (1992). *1991 demographic yearbook.* New York: United Nations. (p. 186)

Urbany, J. E., Bearden, W. O., & Weilbaker, D. C. (1988). The effect of plausible and exaggerated reference prices on consumer perceptions and price search. *Journal of Consumer Research, 15,* 95–110. (p. 406)

Urry, H. L., Nitschke, J. B., Dolski, I., Jackson, D. C., Dalton, K. M., Mueller, C. J., Rosenkranz, M. A., Ryff, C. D., Singer, B. H., & David-

son, R. J. (2004). Making a life worth living: Neural correlates of well-being. *Psychological Science, 15,* 367–372. (p. 518)

Ursu, S., Stenger, V. A., Shear, M. K., Jones, M. R., & Carter, C. S. (2003). Overactive action monitoring in obsessive-compulsive disorder: Evidence from functional magnetic resonance imaging. *Psychological Science, 14,* 347–353. (p. 655)

USAID. (2004, January). The ABCs of HIV prevention. www.usaid.gov. (p. 559)

Vaidya, J. G., Gray, E. K., Haig, J., & Watson, D. (2002). On the temporal stability of personality: Evidence for differential stability and the role of life experiences. *Journal of Personality and Social Psychology, 83,* 1469–1484. (pp. 194, 619)

Vaidya, J. G., Gray, E. K., Haig, J., & Watson, D. (2002). On the temporal stability of personality: Evidence for differential stability and the role of life experiences. *Journal of Personality and Social Psychology, 83,* 1469–1484. (p. 193)

Vaillant, G. E. (1977). *Adaptation to life.* New York: Little, Brown. (p. 385)

Vaillant, G. E. (2002). *Aging well: Surprising guideposts to a happier life from the landmark Harvard study of adult development.* Boston: Little, Brown. (p. 566)

Vaitl, D., & 14 others (2005). Psychobiology of altered states of consciousness. *Psychological Bulletin, 131,* 98–127. (p. 272)

Valenstein, E. (1998). *Blaming the brain: The truth about drugs and mental health.* Free Press. (p. 714)

Valenstein, E. S. (1986). *Great and desperate cures: The rise and decline of psychosurgery.* New York: Basic Books. (pp. 73, 717)

Vallone, R. P., Griffin, D. W., Lin, S., & Ross, L. (1990). Overconfident prediction of future actions and outcomes by self and others. *Journal of Personality and Social Psychology, 58,* 582–592. (p. 22)

van Boxtel, H. W., Orobio de Castro, B., & Goossens, F. A. (2004). High self-perceived social competence in rejected children is related to frequent fighting. *European Journal of Developmental Psychology, 1,* 205–214. (p. 635)

Vance, E. B., & Wagner, N. N. (1976). Written descriptions of orgasm: A study of sex differences. *Archives of Sexual Behavior, 5,* 87–98. (p. 482)

Vandell, D. L. (2000). Parents, peer groups, and other socializing influences. *Developmental Psychology, 36,* 699–710. (p. 117)

Vandello, J. A., & Cohen, D. (1999). Patterns of individualism and collectivism across the United States. *Journal of Personality and Social Psychology, 77,* 279–292. (p. 122)

Vandenberg, S. G., & Kuse, A. R. (1978). Mental rotations: A group test of three-dimensional spatial visualization. *Perceptual and Motor Skills, 47,* 599–604. (p. 463)

van den Boom, D. (1990). Preventive intervention and the quality of mother-infant interaction and infant exploration in irritable infants. In W. Koops, H. J. G. Soppe, J. L. van der Linden, P. C. M. Molenaar, & J. J. F. Schroots (Eds.), *Developmental psychology behind the dikes: An outline of developmental psychology research in The Netherlands.* The Netherlands: Uitgeverij Eburon. Cited by C. Hazan & P. R. Shaver (1994). Deeper into attachment theory. *Psychological Inquiry, 5,* 68–79. (p. 157)

van den Bos, K., & Spruijt, N. (2002). Appropriateness of decisions as a moderator of the psychology of voice. *European Journal of Social Psychology, 32,* 57–72. (p. 509)

VanderStoep, S. W., & Shaughnessy, J. J. (1997). Taking a course in research methods improves reasoning about real-life events. *Teaching of Psychology, 24,* 122–124. (p. 44)

Van Dyke, C., & Byck, R. (1982, March). Cocaine. *Scientific American,* pp. 128–141. (p. 302)

van Engen, M. L., & Willemsen, T. M. (2004). Sex and leadership styles: A meta-analysis of research published in the 1990s. *Psychological Reports, 94,* 3–18. (p. 127)

van IJzendoorn, M. H., & De Wolff, M. S. (1997). In search of the absent father—Meta-analyses of infant-father attachment: A rejoinder to our discussants. *Child Development, 68,* 604–610. (p. 156) van IJzendoorn, M. H., & Kroonenberg, P. M. (1988). Cross-cultural patterns of attachment: A meta-analysis of the strange situation. *Child Development, 59,* 147–156. (p. 156)

Van Leeuwen, M. S. (1978). A cross-cultural examination of psychological differentiation in males and females. *International Journal of Psychology, 13,* 87–122. (p. 131)

Van Leeuwen, M. S. (1982). IQism and the just society: Historical background. *Journal of the American Scientific Affiliation, 34,* 193–201. (p. 446)

van Lommel, P., van Wees, R., Meyers, V., & Elfferich, I. (2001). Near-death experience in survivors of cardiac arrest: A prospective study in the Netherlands. *Lancet, 358,* 2039–2045. (p. 307)

Vanman, E. J., Saltz, J. L., Nathan, L. R., & Warren, J. A. (2004). Racial discrimination by low-prejudiced Whites. *Psychological Science, 15,* 711–714. (p. 744)

Van Praag, H., Schinder, A. F., Christie, B. R., Toni, N., Palmer, T. D., & Gage, F. H. (2002). Neurogenesis: Functional neurons in adult hippocampus. *Nature, 415,* 1030–1034. (p. 83)

Van Rooy, D. L., & Viswesvaran, C. (2004). Emotional intelligence: A meta-analytic investigation of predictive validity and nomological net. *Journal of Vocational Behavior, 65,* 71–95. (p. 437)

van Schaik, C. P., Ancrenaz, M., Borgen, G., Galdikas, B., Knott, C. D., Singleton, I., Suzuki, A., Utami, S. S., & Merrill, M. (2003). Orangutan cultures and the evolution of material culture. *Science, 299,* 102–105. (p. 424)

VanTassel-Baska, J. (1983). Profiles of precocity: The 1982 Midwest Talent Search finalists. *Gifted Child Quarterly, 27,* 139–145. (p. 451)

Van Yperen, N. W., & Buunk, B. P. (1990). A longitudinal study of equity and satisfaction in intimate relationships. *European Journal of Social Psychology, 20,* 287–309. (p. 764)

Vaughn, K. B., & Lanzetta, J. T. (1981). The effect of modification of expressive displays on vicarious emotional arousal. *Journal of Experimental Social Psychology, 17,* 16–30. (p. 530)

Vazire, S., & Gosling, S. D. (2004). e-Perceptions: Personality impressions based on personal websites. *Journal of Personality and Social Psychology, 87,* 123–132. (p. 621)

Vecera, S. P., Vogel, E. K., & Woodman, G. F. (2002). Lower region: A new cue for figure-ground assignment. *Journal of Experimental Psychology: General, 13,* 194–205. (p. 247)

Vega, W. A., Kolody, B., Aguilar-Gaxiola, S., Alderete, E., Catalano, R., & Caraveo-Anduaga, J. (1998). Lifetime prevalence of DSM-III-R psychiatric disorders among urban and rural Mexican Americans in California. *Archives of General Psychiatry, 55,* 771–778. (p. 680)

Vekassy, L. (1977). Dreams of the blind. *Magyar Pszichologiai Szemle, 34,* 478–491. (p. 286)

Vemer, E., Coleman, M., Ganong, L. H., & Cooper, H. (1989). Marital satisfaction in remarriage: A meta-analysis. *Journal of Marriage and the Family, 51,* 713–725. (p. 187)

Venn, J. (1986). Hypnosis and the Lamaze method: A reply to Wideman and Singer. *American Psychologist, 41,* 475–476. (p. 293)

Verbeek, M. E. M., Drent, P. J., & Wiepkema, P. R. (1994). Consistent individual differences in early exploratory behaviour of male great tits. *Animal Behaviour, 48,* 1113–1121. (p. 615)

Verhaeghen, P., & Salthouse, T. A. (1997). Meta-analyses of age-cognition relations in adulthood: Estimates of linear and nonlinear age effects and structural models. *Psychological Bulletin, 122,* 231–249. (p. 179)

Vernon, P. A. (1983). Speed of information processing and general intelligence. *Intelligence, 7,* 53–70. (p. 441)

Viding, E., Blair, R., James, R., Moffitt, T. E., & Plomin, R. (2005). Evidence for substantial genetic risk for psychopathy in 7-year-olds. *Journal of Child Psychology & Psychiatry, 46,* 592–597. (p. 678)

Vigliocco, G., & Hartsuiker, R. J. (2002). The interplay of meaning, sound, and syntax in sentence production. *Psychological Bulletin, 128,* 442–472. (p. 412)

Vining, E. P. G., Freeman, J. M., Pillas, D. J., Uematsu, S., Carson, B. S., Brandt, J., Boatman, D., Pulsifer, M. B., & Zukerberg, A. (1997). Why would you remove half a brain? The outcome of 58 children after hemispherectomy—The Johns Hopkins Experience: 1968 to 1996. *Pediatrics, 100,* 163–171. (p. 83)

Vita, A. J., Terry, R. B., Hubert, H. B., & Fries, J. F. (1998). Aging, health risks, and cumulative disability. *New England Journal of Medicine, 338,* 1035–1041. (p. 576)

Vitaliano, P. P., Zhang, J., & Scanlan, J. M. (2003). Is caregiving hazardous to one's physical health? A meta-analysis. *Psychological Bulletin, 129,* 946–972. (p. 558)

Vitevitch, M. S. (2003). Change deafness: The inability to detect changes between two voices. *Journal of Experimental Psychology: Human Perception and Performance, 29,* 333–342. (p. 239)

Vogel, S. (1999). *The skinny on fat: Our obsession with weight control.* New York: W. H. Freeman. (p. 105)

Vohs, K., Voelz, Z., Pettit, J., Bardone, A., Katz, J., Abramson, L., Heatherton, T., & Joiner, T. (2001). Perfectionism, body dissatisfaction, and self-esteem: An interactive model of bulimic symptom development. *Journal of Social and Clinical Psychology, 20,* 476–497. (p. 479)

Vokey, J. R. (2002). Subliminal messages. In J. R. Vokey and S.W. Allen (Eds.), *Psychological sketches* (6th Edition). Lethbridge, Alberta: Psyence Ink, pp. 223–246. (p. 200)

von Békésy, G. (1957, August). The ear. *Scientific American,* pp. 66–78. (p. 219)

von Senden, M. (1932; reprinted 1960). In P. Heath (Trans.), *Space and sight: The perception of space and shape in the congenitally blind before and after operation.* Glencoe, IL: Free Press. (p. 255)

Vreeland, C. N., Gallagher, B. J., III, & McFalls, J. A., Jr. (1995). The beliefs of members of the American Psychiatric Association on the etiology of male homosexuality: A national survey. *Journal of Psychology, 129,* 507–517. (p. 492)

Wadden, T. A., Vogt, R. A., Foster, G. D., & Anderson, D. A. (1998). Exercise and the maintenance of weight loss: 1-year follow-up of a controlled clinical trial. *Journal of Consulting and Clinical Psychology, 66,* 429–433. (p. 590)

Wager, T. D., Rilling, J. K., Smith, E. E., Sokolik, A., Casey, K. L., Davidson, R. J., Kosslyn, S. M., Rose, R. M., & Cohen, J. D. (2004). Placebo-induced changes in fMRI in the anticipation and experience of pain. *Science, 303,* 1162–1167. (p. 229)

Wagner, A. D., Schacter, D. L., Rotte, M., Koutstaal, W., Maril, A., Dale, A. M., Rosen, B. R., & Buckner, R. L. (1998). Building memories: Remembering and forgetting of verbal experiences as predicted by brain activity. *Science, 281,* 1188–1191. (p. 368)

Wagner, U., Gais, S., Haider, H., Verleger, R., & Born, J. (2004). Sleep inspires insight. *Nature, 427,* 352–355. (p. 283)

Wagstaff, G. (1982). Attitudes to rape: The "just world" strikes again? *Bulletin of the British Psychological Society, 13,* 275–283. (p. 725)

Wahl, O. F. (1992). Mass media images of mental illness: A review of the literature. *Journal of Community Psychology, 20,* 343–352. (p. 647)

Wahlberg, D. (2001, October 11). We're more depressed, patriotic, poll finds. *Grand Rapids Press,* p. A15. (p. 553)

Wakefield, J. C., & Spitzer, R. L. (2002). Lowered estimates—but of what? *Archives of General Psychiatry, 59,* 129–130. (p. 653)

Waldrop, M. M. (1987). The workings of working memory. *Science, 237,* 1564–1567. (p. 360)

Walker, W. R., Skowronski, J. J., Gibbons, J. A., Vogl, R. J., & Thompson, C. P. (2003). On the emotions that accompany autobiographical memories: Dysphoria disrupts the fading affect bias. *Cognition and Emotion, 17,* 703–723. (p. 189)

Walker, W. R., Skowronski, J. J., & Thompson, C. P. (2003). Life is pleasant—and memory helps to keep it that way! *Review of General Psychology, 7,* 203–210. (pp. 189, 359)

Wall, B. (2002, August 24–25). Profit matures along with baby boomers. *International Herald Tribune*, p. 13. (p. 761)

Wall, P. (2000). *Pain: The science of suffering*. New York: Columbia University Press. (p. 227)

Wall Street Journal. (1999, December 17). Money and misery. Editorial, p. A14. (p. 700)

Wallace, D. S., Paulson, R. M., Lord, C. G., & Bond, C. F., Jr. (2005). Which behaviors do attitudes predict? Meta-analyzing the effects of social pressure and perceived difficulty. *Review of General Psychology, 9*(3), 214–227. (p. 726)

Wallach, M. A., & Wallach, L. (1983). *Psychology's sanction for selfishness: The error of egoism in theory and therapy*. New York: Freeman. (p. 611)

Wallach, M. A., & Wallach, L. (1985, February). How psychology sanctions the cult of the self. *Washington Monthly*, pp. 46–56. (p. 611)

Wallbott, H. G. (1988). In and out of context: Influences of facial expression and context information on emotion attributions. *British Journal of Social Psychology, 27*, 357–369. (p. 260)

Wallis, C. (1983, June 6). Stress: Can we cope? *Time*, pp. 48–54. (p. 554)

Walster (Hatfield), E., Aronson, V., Abrahams, D., & Rottman, L. (1966). Importance of physical attractiveness in dating behavior. *Journal of Personality and Social Psychology, 4*, 508–516. (p. 759)

Wampold, B. E. (2001). *The great psychotherapy debate: Models, methods, and findings*. Mahwah, NJ: Erlbaum. (pp. 707, 708)

Wampold, B. E., Mondin, G. W., Moody, M., & Ahn, H. (1997). The flat earth as a metaphor for the evidence for uniform efficacy of bona fide psychotherapies: Reply to Crits-Christoph (1997) and Howard et al. (1997). *Psychological Bulletin, 122*, 226–230. (p. 704)

Wang, Y., Liu, D., & Wang, Y. (2003). Discovering the capacity of human memory. *Brain and Mind, 4*, 189–198. (p. 363)

Wansink, B., & van Ittersum, K. (2003). Bottoms up! The influence of elongation on pouring and consumption volume. *Journal of Consumer Research, 30*, 455–464. (p. 247)

Warchol, M. E., Lambert, P. R., Goldstein, B. J., Forge, A., & Corwin, J. T. (1993). Regenerative proliferation in inner ear sensory epithelia from adult guinea pigs and humans. *Science, 259*, 1619–1622. (p. 221)

Ward, A., & Mann, T. (2000). Don't mind if I do: Disinhibited eating under cognitive load. *Journal of Personality and Social Psychology, 78*, 753–763. (p. 590)

Ward, C. (1994). Culture and altered states of consciousness. In W. J. Lonner & R. Malpass (Eds.), *Psychology and culture*. Boston: Allyn & Bacon. (p. 300)

Ward, J. (2003). State of the art synaesthesia. *The Psychologist, 16*, 196–199. (p. 231)

Ward, K. D., Klesges, R. C., & Halpern, M. T. (1997). Predictors of smoking cessation and state-of-the-art smoking interventions. *Journal of Socies Issues, 53*, 129–145. (p. 578)

Wardle, J., Cooke, L. J., Gibson, L., Sapochnik, M., Sheiham, A., Lawson, M. (2003). Increasing children's acceptance of vegetables; a randomized trial of parent-led exposure. *Appetite, 40*, 155–162. (p. 230)

Warm, J. S., & Dember, W. N. (1986, April). Awake at the switch. *Psychology Today*, pp. 46–53. (p. 200)

Warner, J., McKeown, E., Johnson, K., Ramsay, A., Cort, C., & King, M. (2004). Rates and predictors of mental illness in gay men, lesbians and bisexual men and women. *British Journal of Psychiatry, 185*, 479–485. (p. 488)

Warr, P., & Payne, R. (1982). Experiences of strain and pleasure among British adults. *Social Science and Medicine, 16*, 1691–1697. (p. 565)

Warren, N. C. (2005, March 4). Personal correspondence from founder of eHarmony.com. (p. 762)

Wason, P. C. (1960). On the failure to eliminate hypotheses in a conceptual task. *Quarterly Journal of Experimental Psychology, 12*, 129–140. (p. 399)

Wason, P. C. (1981). The importance of cognitive illusions. *The Behavioral and Brain Sciences, 4*, 356. (p. 399)

Wasserman, E. A. (1993). Comparative cognition: Toward a general understanding of cognition in behavior. *Psychological Science, 4*, 156–161. (p. 328)

Wasserman, E. A. (1995). The conceptual abilities of pigeons. *American Scientist, 83*, 246–255. (p. 423)

Wastell, C. A. (2002). Exposure to trauma: The long-term effects of suppressing emotional reactions. *Journal of Nervous and Mental Disorders, 190*, 839–845. (p. 567)

Watamura, S. E., Donzella, B., Alwin, J., & Gunnar, M. R. (2003). Morning-to-afternoon increases in cortisol concentrations for infants and toddlers at child care: Age differences and behavioral correlates. *Child Development, 74*, 1006–1020. (p. 160)

Waterhouse, R. (1993, July 19). Income for 62 percent is below average pay. *The Independent*, p. 4. (p. 41)

Waterman, A. S. (1988). Identity status theory and Erikson's theory: Commonalities and differences. *Developmental Review, 8*, 185–208. (p. 171)

Watkins, C. E., Campbell, V. L., Nieberding, R., & Hallmark, R. (1995). Contemporary practice of psychological assessment by clinical psychologists. *Professional Psychology: Research and Practice, 26*, 54–60. (p. 603)

Watkins, J. G. (1984). The Bianchi (L. A. Hillside Strangler) case: Sociopath or multiple personality? *International Journal of Clinical and Experimental Hypnosis, 32*, 67–101. (p. 656)

Watkins, L. R. (1994). Acute and conditioned hyperalgesic responses to illness. *Pain, 56*, 227–234. (p. 226)

Watkins, P. C. (2004). Gratitude and subjective well-being. In R. A. Emmons and M. E. McCullough (Eds.), *The psychology of gratitude*. New York: Oxford University Press. (p. 540)

Watson, D. (2000). *Mood and temperament*. New York: Guilford Press. (pp. 538, 569)

Watson, D. (2003). To dream, perchance to remember: Individual differences in dream recall. *Personality and Individual Differences, 34*, 1271–1286. (p. 279)

Watson, D., Suls, J., & Haig, J. (2002). Global self-esteem in relation to structural models of personality and affectivity. *Journal of Personality and Social Psychology, 83*, 185–197. (p. 632)

Watson, D., Wiese, D., Vaidya, J., & Tellegen, A. (1999). The two general activation systems of affect: Structured findings, evolutionary considerations, and psychobiological evidence. *Journal of Personality and Social Psychology, 76*, 820–838. (p. 533)

Watson, J. B. (1913). Psychology as the behaviorist views it. *Psychological Review, 20*, 158–177. (pp. 271, 324)

Watson, J. B. (1924). The unverbalized in human behavior. *Psychological Review, 31*, 339–347. (p. 324)

Watson, J. B., & Rayner, R. (1920). Conditioned emotional reactions. *Journal of Experimental Psychology, 3*, 1–14. (p. 324)

Watson, R. I., Jr. (1973). Investigation into deindividuation using a cross-cultural survey technique. *Journal of Personality and Social Psychology, 25*, 342–345. (p. 739)

Watson, S. J., Benson, J. A., Jr., & Joy, J. E. (2000). NEWS AND VIEWS—Marijuana and medicine: Assessing the science base: A summary of the 1999 Institute of Medicine report. *Archives of General Psychiatry, 57*, 547–553. (p. 303)

Wayment, H. A., & Peplau, L. A. (1995). Social support and well-being among lesbian and heterosexual women: A structural modeling approach. *Personality and Social Psychology Bulletin, 21*, 1189–1199. (p. 187)

Weaver, J. B., Masland, J. L., & Zillmann, D. (1984). Effect of erotica on young men's aesthetic perception of their female sexual partners. *Perceptual and Motor Skills, 58*, 929–930. (p. 484)

Webb, W. B. (1992). *Sleep: The gentle tyrant*. Bolton, MA: Anker Publishing. (pp. 278, 283)

Webb, W. B., & Campbell, S. S. (1983). Relationships in sleep characteristics of identical and fraternal twins. *Archives of General Psychiatry, 40*, 1093–1095. (p. 279)

Wechsler, D. (1972). "Hold" and "Don't Hold" tests. In S. M. Chown (Ed.), *Human aging.* New York: Penguin. (p. 183)

Wechsler, H., Davenport, A., Dowdall, G., Moeykens, B., & Castillo, S. (1994). Health and behavioral consequences of binge drinking in college. *Journal of the American Medical Association, 272,* 1672-1677. (p. 300)

Wechsler, H., Lee, J. E., Kuo, M., Seibring, M., Nelson, T. F., & Lee, H. (2002). Trends in college binge drinking during a period of increased prevention efforts. *Journal of American College Health, 50,* 203-217. (p. 300)

Wee, C. C., Phillips, R. S., Legedza, A. T. R., Davis, R. B., Soukup, J. R., Colditz, G. A., & Hamel, M. B. (2005). Health care expenditures associated with overweight and obesity among US adults: Importance of age and race. *American Journal of Public Health, 95,* 159-165. (p. 583)

Weed, W. S. (2001, May). Can we go to Mars without going crazy? *Discover,* pp. 31-43. (p. 263)

Wegner, D. M. (1990). *White bears and other unwanted thoughts: Suppression, obsession, and the psychology of mental control.* New York: Penguin Books. (p. 567)

Wegner, D. M. (2002). *The illusion of conscious will.* Cambridge, MA: MIT Press. (pp. 86, 272)

Weigel, G. (2005, March-April). Is Europe dying? Notes on a crisis of civilizational morale. *New Atlantic Initiative,* American Enterprise Institute for Public Policy Research (www.aei.org/nai). (p. 178)

Weinberg, M. S., & Williams, C. (1974). *Male homosexuals: Their problems and adaptations.* New York: Oxford University Press. (p. 488)

Weinberger, N. M. (2004, November). Music and the brain. *Scientific American,* pp. 89-95. (p. 77)

Weiner, B. (1985). An attributional theory of achievement motivation and emotion. *Psychological Review, 92,* 548-573. (pp. 504, 523)

Weingarten, G. (2002, March 10). Below the beltway. *Washington Post,* p. WO3. (p. 498)

Weinstein, N. D. (1980). Unrealistic optimism about future life events. *Journal of Personality and Social Psychology, 39,* 806-820. (p. 627)

Weinstein, N. D. (1982). Unrealistic optimism about susceptibility to health problems. *Journal of Behavioral Medicine, 5,* 441-460. (p. 627)

Weinstein, N. D. (1987). Unrealistic optimism about susceptibility to health problems: Conclusions from a community-wide sample. *Journal of Behavioral Medicine, 10,* 481-500. (p. 591)

Weinstein, N. D. (1996, October 4). 1996 optimistic bias bibliography. Distributed via internet (weinstein_c@aesop.rutgers.edu). (p. 627)

Weiskrantz, L. (1986). *Blindsight: A case study and implications.* Oxford, UK: Oxford University Press. (p. 211)

Weiss, A., King, J. E., & Enns, R. M. (2002). Subjective well-being is heritable and genetically correlated with dominance in chimpanzees (*Pan troglodytes*). *Journal of Personality and Social Psychology, 83,* 1141-1149. (p. 544)

Weiss, A., King, J. E., & Figueredo, A. J. (2000). The heritability of personality factors in chimpanzees (*Pan troglodytes*). *Behavior Genetics, 30,* 213-221. (pp. 101, 544)

Weiss, J. M. (1977). Psychological and behavioral influences on gastrointestinal lesions in animal models. In J. D. Maser & M. E. P. Seligman (Eds.), *Psychopathology: Experimental models.* San Francisco: Freeman. (p. 563)

Weissman, M. M. (1999). Interpersonal psychotherapy and the health care scene. In D. S. Janowsky (Ed.), *Psychotherapy indications and outcomes.* Washington, DC: American Psychiatric Press. (p. 688)

Weissman, M. M., Bland, R. C., Canino, G. J., Faravelli, C., Greenwald, S., Hwu, H-G., Joyce, P. R., Karam, E. G., Lee, C-K., Lellouch, J., Lepine, J-P., Newman, S. C., Rubio-Stepic, M., Wells, J. E., Wickramaratne, P. J., Wittchen, H-U., & Yeh, E-K. (1996). Cross-national epidemiology of major depression and bipolar disorder. *Journal of the American Medical Association, 276,* 293-299. (p. 661)

Weisz, J. R., Rothbaum, F. M., & Blackburn, T. C. (1984). Standing out and standing in: The psychology of control in America and Japan. *American Psychologist, 39,* 955-969. (p. 119)

Wellman, H. M., Cross, D., & Watson, J. (2001). Meta-analysis of theory-of-mind development: The truth about false belief. *Child Development, 72,* 655-684. (pp. 151, 152)

Wellman, H. M., & Gelman, S. A. (1992). Cognitive development: Foundational theories of core domains. *Annual Review of Psychology, 43,* 337-375. (p. 149)

Wells, B. L. (1986). Predictors of female nocturnal orgasms: A multivariate analysis. *Journal of Sex Research, 22,* 421-437. (p. 484)

Wells, C. (1983, March). Teaching the brain new tricks. *Esquire,* 49-57. (p. 360)

Wells, G. L. (1981). Lay analyses of causal forces on behavior. In J. Harvey (Ed.), *Cognition, social behavior and the environment.* Hillsdale, NJ: Erlbaum. (p. 314)

Wells, G., & Murray, D. M. (1984). Eyewitness confidence. In G. L. Wells & E. F. Loftus (Eds.), *Eyewitness testimony: Psychological perspectives.* New York: Cambridge University Press. (p. 385)

Wender, P. H., Kety, S. S., Rosenthal, D., Schulsinger, F., Ortmann, J., & Lunde, I. (1986). Psychiatric disorders in the biological and adoptive families of adopted individuals with affective disorders. *Archives of General Psychiatry, 43,* 923-929. (p. 663)

Wener, R., Frazier, W., & Farbstein, J. (1987, June). Building better jails. *Psychology Today,* pp. 40-49. (p. 626)

Wessely, S., & Kerwin, R. (2004). Suicide risk and the SSRIs. *Journal of the American Medical Association, 292,* 379-381. (p. 714)

West, P. D. B., & Evans, E. F. (1990). Early detection of hearing damage in young listeners resulting from exposure to amplified music. *British Journal of Audiology, 24,* 89-103. (p. 218)

Westen, D. (1996). Is Freud really dead? Teaching psychodynamic theory to introductory psychology. Presentation to the Annual Institute on the Teaching of Psychology, St. Petersburg Beach, Florida. (p. 602)

Westen, D. (1998). The scientific legacy of Sigmund Freud: Toward a psychodynamically informed psychological science. *Psychological Bulletin, 124,* 333-371. (pp. 596, 604)

Westen, D., & Morrison, K. (2001). A multidimensional meta-analysis of treatments for depression, panic, and generalized anxiety disorder: An empirical examination of the status of empirically supported therapies. *Journal of Consulting and Clinical Psychology, 69,* 875-899. (p. 704)

Wetter, D. W., Fiore, M. C., Gritz, E. R., Lando, H. A., Stitzer, M. L., Hasselblad, V., & Baker, T. B. (1998). The Agency for Health Care Policy and Research. *Smoking cessation clinical practice guideline: Findings and implications for psychologists. American Psychologist, 53,* 657-669. (p. 579)

Weuve, J., Kang, J. H., Manson, J. E., Breteler, M. M. B., Ware, J. H., & Grodstein, F. (2004). Physical activity, including walking, and cognitive function in older women. *Journal of the American Medical Association, 292,* 1454-1460. (p. 180)

Wever, E. G. (1949). Theory of hearing. New York: Wiley. (p. 220)

Whalen, P. J., Kagan, J., Cook, R. G., Davis, F. C., Kim, H., Polis, S., McLaren, D. G., Somerville, L. H., McLean, A. A., Maxwell, J. S., & Johnstone, T. (2004). Human amygdala responsibility to masked fearful eye whites. *Science, 302,* 2061. (p. 522)

Whalen, P. J., Shin, L. M., McInerney, S. C., Fisher, H., Wright, C. I., & Rauch, S. L. (2001). A functional MRI study of human amygdala responses to facial expressions of fear versus anger. *Emotion, 1,* 70-83. (p. 518)

Whaley, S. E., Sigman, M., Beckwith, L., Cohen, S. E., & Espinosa, M. P. (2002). Infant-caregiver interaction in Kenya and the United States: The importance of multiple caregivers and adequate comparison samples. *Journal of Cross-Cultural Psychology, 33,* 236-247. (p. 161)

Whalley, L. J., & Deary, I. J. (2001). Longitudinal cohort study of childhood IQ and survival up to age 76. *British Medical Journal, 322,* 1-5. (p. 435)

Whalley, L., Starr, J. M. Athawes, R., Hunter, D., Pattie, A., & Deary, I. J. (2000). Childhood mental ability and dementia. *Neurology, 55,* 1455-1459. (p. 452)

Wheelwright, J. (2004, August). Study the clones first. *Discover*, pp. 44–50. (p. 99)

White, G. L., & Kight, T. D. (1984). Misattribution of arousal and attraction: Effects of salience of explanations for arousal. *Journal of Experimental Social Psychology, 20*, 55–64. (p. 763)

White, H. R., Brick, J., & Hansell, S. (1993). A longitudinal investigation of alcohol use and aggression in adolescence. *Journal of Studies on Alcohol*, Supplement No. 11, 62–77. (p. 750)

White House. (1999, June 7). White House fact sheet on myths and facts about mental illness. Washington, DC: White House Press Office. (p. 643)

White, K. M. (1983). Young adults and their parents: Individuation to mutuality. *New Directions for Child Development, 22*, 61–76. (p. 173)

White, L., & Edwards, J. (1990). Emptying the nest and parental well-being: An analysis of national panel data. *American Sociological Review, 55*, 235–242. (p. 188)

White, P. H., Kjelgaard, M. M., & Harkins, S. G. (1995). Testing the contribution of self-evaluation to goal-setting effects. *Journal of Personality and Social Psychology, 69*, 69–79. (p. 508)

White, R. A. (1998). Intuition, heart knowledge, and parapsychology. *Journal of the American Society for Psychical Research, 92*, 158–171. (p. 266)

Whitehead, B. D., & Popenoe, D. (2001). *The state of our unions 2001: The social health of marriage in America*. Rutgers University: The National Marriage Project. (p. 187)

Whiten, A., & Boesch, C. (2001, January). Cultures of chimpanzees. *Scientific American*, pp. 60–67. (p. 423)

Whiten, A., & Byrne, R. W. (1988). Tactical deception in primates. *Behavioral and Brain Sciences, 11*, 233–244, 267–273. (p. 29)

Whiting, B. B., & Edwards, C. P. (1988). *Children of different worlds: The formation of social behavior*. Cambridge, MA: Harvard University Press. (p. 124)

Whitley, B. E., Jr. (1990). The relationships of heterosexuals' attributions for the causes of homosexuality to attitudes toward lesbians and gay men. *Personality and Social Psychology Bulletin, 16*, 369–377. (p. 492)

Whitley, B. E., Jr. (1999). Right-wing authoritarianism, social dominance orientation, and prejudice. *Journal of Personality and Social Psychology, 77*, 126–134. (p. 747)

Whitley, B. E., Jr. (2002). Gender-role variables and attitudes toward homosexuality. *Sex Roles, 45*, 691–720. (p. 492)

Whittington, C. J., Kendall, T., Fonagy, P., Cottrell, D., Cotgrove, A., & Boddington, E. (2004). Selective serotonin reuptake inhibitors in childhood depression: Systematic review of published versus unpublished data. *Lancet, 363*, 1341–1345. (p. 714)

WHO. (2002). The global burden of disease. Geneva: World Health Organization (www.who.int/msa/mnh/ems/dalys/intro.htm). (p. 659)

WHO. (2002a, September 4). Suicide rates. World Health Organization (www5.who.int/mental_health). (pp. 662–663)

WHO. (2002c, December 9). China: WHO lauds launch of nation's first suicide prevent center: Xinhua news. World Health Organization (www5.who.int/mental_health). (p. 662)

WHO. (2002d). Schizophrenia. World Health Organization (www5.who.int/mental_health). (p. 669)

WHO. (2004). Prevalence, severity, and unmet need for treatment of mental disorders in the World Health Organization World Mental Health Surveys. *Journal of the American Medical Association, 291*, 2581–2590. (pp. 639, 662, 680, 681)

WHO. (2005, February 24). Global tobacco treaty enters into force with 57 countries already committed. World Health Organization media centre (www.who.int). (p. 575)

WHO. (2005). Introduction to Health Evidence Network, by G. Thornicroft & M. Tansella. World Health Organization (www.euro.who.int). (p. 575)

Whooley, M. A., & Browner, W. S. (1998). Association between depressive symptoms and mortality in older women. *Archives of Internal Medicine, 158*, 2129–2135. (p. 556)

Whorf, B. L. (1956). Science and linguistics. In J. B. Carroll (Ed.), *Language, thought, and reality: Selected writings of Benjamin Lee Whorf*. Cambridge, MA: MIT Press. (p. 418)

Wichman, H. (1992). *Human factors in the design of spacecraft*. Stony Brook, NY: State University of New York. (p. 263)

Wickelgren, I. (2005). Autistic brains out of sync? *Science, 308*, 1856–1858. (p. 152)

Wickelgren, W. A. (1977). *Learning and memory*. Englewood Cliffs, NJ: Prentice-Hall. (p. 358)

Widom, C. S. (1989a). Does violence beget violence? A critical examination of the literature. *Psychological Bulletin, 106*, 3–28. (p. 159)

Widom, C. S. (1989b). The cycle of violence. *Science, 244*, 160–166. (p. 159)

Wiens, A. N., & Menustik, C. E. (1983). Treatment outcome and patient characteristics in an aversion therapy program for alcoholism. *American Psychologist, 38*, 1089–1096. (p. 693)

Wierson, M., & Forehand, R. (1994). Parent behavioral training for child noncompliance: Rationale, concepts, and effectiveness. *Current Directions in Psychological Science, 3*, 146–149. (p. 338)

Wiertelak, E. P., Smith K. P., Furness, L., Mooney-Heiberger, K., Mayr, T., Maier, S. F., & Watkins, L. R. (1994). Acute and conditioned hyperalgesic responses to illness. *Pain, 56*, 227–234. (p. 226)

Wierzbicki, M. (1993). Psychological adjustment of adoptees: A meta-analysis. *Journal of Clinical Child Psychology, 22*, 447–454. (p. 101)

Wiesel, T. N. (1982). Postnatal development of the visual cortex and the influence of environment. *Nature, 299*, 583–591. (p. 255)

Wiesner, W. H., & Cronshow, S. P. (1988). A meta-analytic investigation of the impact of interview format and degree of structure on the validity of the employment interview. *Journal of Occupational Psychology, 61*, 275–290. (p. 503)

Wigdor, A. K., & Garner, W. R. (1982). *Ability testing: Uses, consequences, and controversies*. Washington, DC: National Academy Press. (p. 465)

Wilcox, A. J., Baird, D. D., Dunson, D. B., McConnaughey, D. R., Kesner, J. S., & Weinberg, C. R. (2004). On the frequency of intercourse around ovulation: Evidence for biological influences. *Human Reproduction, 19*, 1539–1543. (p. 483)

Wilder, D. A. (1981). Perceiving persons as a group: Categorization and intergroup relations. In D. L. Hamilton (Ed.), *Cognitive processes in stereotyping and intergroup behavior*. Hillsdale, NJ: Erlbaum. (p. 746)

Wildman, D. E., Uddin, M., Liu, G., Grossman, L. I., & Goodman, M. (2003). Implications of natural selection in shaping 99.4% nonsynonymous DNA identity between humans and chimpanzees: Enlarging genus *Homo*. *Proceedings of the National Academy of Sciences, 100*, 7181–7188. (p. 97)

Wilford, J. N. (1999, February 9). New findings help balance the cosmological books. *New York Times* (www.nytimes.com). (p.136)

Williams, C. L., & Berry, J. W. (1991). Primary prevention of acculturative stress among refugees. *American Psychologist, 46*, 632–641. (p. 554)

Williams, J. E., & Best, D. L. (1990). *Measuring sex stereotypes: A multination study*. Newbury Park, CA: Sage. (p. 127)

Williams, J. E., Paton, C. C., Siegler, I. C., Eigenbrodt, M. L., Nieto, F. J., & Tyroler, H. A. (2000). Anger proneness predicts coronary heart disease risk: Prospective analysis from the artherosclerosis risk in communities (ARIC) study. *Circulation, 101*, 17, 2034–2040. (p. 556)

Williams, K. D. (2002). *Ostracism: The power of silence*. New York: Guilford. (p. 497)

Williams, K. D., & Zadro, L. (2001). Ostracism: On being ignored, excluded and rejected. In M. Leary (Ed.), *Rejection*. New York: Oxford University Press. (p. 497)

Williams, R. (1989). *The trusting heart: Great news about Type A behavior*. New York: Random House. (p. 556)

Williams, R. (1993). *Anger kills*. New York: Times Books. (p. 556)

Williams, R. B., Barefoot, J. C., Califf, R. M., Haney, T. L., Saunders, W. B., Pryor, D. B., Hlatky, M. A., Siegler, I. C., & Mark, D. B.

(1992). Prognostic importance of social and economic resources among medically treated patients with angiographically documented coronary artery disease. *Journal of the American Medical Association, 267*, 520–524. (p. 566)

Williams, S., & Kohut, J. L. (1999). Psychologists in medical schools in 1997: Research brief. *American Psychologist, 54*, 272–276. (p. 549)

Williams, S. L. (1987). Self-efficacy and mastery-oriented treatment for severe phobias. Paper presented to the American Psychological Association convention. (p. 692)

Willingham, W. W., Lewis, C., Morgan, R., & Ramist, L. (1990). *Predicting college grades: An analysis of institutional trends over two decades.* Princeton: Educational Testing Service. (p. 449)

Willmuth, M. E. (1987). Sexuality after spinal cord injury: A critical review. *Clinical Psychology Review, 7*, 389–412. (p. 484)

Wilson, A. E., & Ross, M. (2001). From chump to champ: People's appraisals of their earlier and present selves. *Journal of Personality and Social Psychology, 80*, 572–584. (p. 635)

Wilson, C. M., & Oswald, A. J. (2002). How does marriage affect physical and psychological health? A survey of the longitudinal evidence. Working paper, University of York and Warwick University. (p. 566)

Wilson, J. P., Harel, Z., & Kahana, B. (1988). *Human adaptation to extreme stress: From the Holocaust to Vietnam.* New York: Plenum Press. (p. 652)

Wilson, R. C., Gaft, J. G., Dienst, E. R., Wood, L., & Bavry, J. L. (1975). *College professors and their impact on students.* New York: Wiley. (p. 739)

Wilson, R. S. (1979). Analysis of longitudinal twin data: Basic model and applications to physical growth measures. *Acta Geneticae medicae et Gemellologiae, 28*, 93–105. (p. 145)

Wilson, R. S., & Bennett, D. A. (2003). Cognitive activity and risk of Alzheimer's disease. *Current Directions in Psychological Science, 12*, 87–91. (p. 181)

Wilson, R. S., & Matheny, A. P., Jr. (1986). Behavior-genetics research in infant temperament: The Louisville twin study. In R. Plomin & J. Dunn (Eds.), *The study of temperament: Changes, continuities, and challenges.* Hillsdale, NJ: Erlbaum. (p. 102)

Wilson, T. D. (2002). *Strangers to ourselves: Discovering the adaptive unconscious.* Cambridge: Harvard University Press. (pp. 86, 238)

Windholz, G. (1989, April–June). The discovery of the principles of reinforcement, extinction, generalization, and differentiation of conditional reflexes in Pavlov's laboratories. *Pavlovian Journal of Biological Science, 26*, 64–74. (p. 320)

Windholz, G. (1997). Ivan P. Pavlov: An overview of his life and psychological work. *American Psychologist, 52*, 941–946. (p. 317)

Wingo, P. A., Ries, L. A. G., Giovino, G. A., Miller, D. S., Rosenberg, H. M., Shopland, D. R., Thun, M. J., & Edwards, B. K. (1999) The annual report to the nation on the status of cancer, 1973–1996, with a special section on lung cancer and tobacco smoking. *Journal of the National Cancer Institute, 91*, 675–690. (p. 579)

Wink, P., & Dillon, M. (2002). Spiritual development across the adult life course: Findings from a longitudinal study. *Journal of Adult Development, 9*, 79–94. (p. 190)

Winner, E. (2000). The origins and ends of giftedness. *American Psychologist, 55*, 159–169. (p. 453)

Wirtz, D., Kruger, J., Scollon, C. N., & Diener, E. (2003). What to do on Spring break? The role of predicted, on-line, and remembered experience in future choice. *Psychological Science, 14*, 520–524. (p. 358)

Wiseman, R. (2002). Laugh Lab—final results. University of Hertfordshire (www.laughlab.co.uk). (p. 398)

Wiseman, R., Jeffreys, C., Smith, M., & Nyman, A. (1999). The psychology of the seance. *The Skeptical Inquirer, 23*(2), 30–33. (p. 384)

Wisman, A., & Goldenberg, J. L. (2005). From the grave to the cradle: Evidence that mortality salience engenders a desire for offspring. *Journal of Personality and Social Psychology, 89*, 46–61. (p. 163)

Witelson, S. F., Kigar, D. L., & Harvey, T. (1999). The exceptional brain of Albert Einstein. *The Lancet, 353*, 2149–2153. (pp. 88, 440)

Witvliet, C. V. O., Ludwig, T., & Vander Laan, K. (2001). Granting forgiveness or harboring grudges: Implications for emotions, physiology, and health. *Psychological Science, 12*, 117–123. (p. 537)

Witvliet, C. V. O., & Vrana, S. R. (1995). Psychophysiological responses as indices of affective dimensions. *Psychophysiology, 32*, 436–443. (p. 518)

Wixted, J. T., & Ebbesen, E. B. (1991). On the form of forgetting. *Psychological Science, 2*, 409–415. (p. 377)

Woehr, D. J., & Cavell, T. A. (1993). Self-report measures of ability, effort, and nonacademic activity as predictors of introductory psychology test scores. *Teaching of Psychology, 20*, 156–160. (p. 16)

Woerlee, G. M. (2004, May/June). Darkness, tunnels, and light. *Skeptical Inquirer*, pp. 28–32. (p. 309)

Wolfson, A. R., & Carskadon, M. A. (1998). Sleep schedules and daytime functioning in adolescents. *Child Development, 69*, 875–887. (p. 287)

Woll, S. (1986). So many to choose from: Decision strategies in videodating. *Journal of Social and Personal Relationships, 3*, 43–52. (p. 759)

Wolpe, J. (1958). *Psychotherapy by reciprocal inhibition.* Stanford, CA: Stanford University Press. (p. 691)

Wolpe, J., & Plaud, J. J. (1997). Pavlov's contributions to behavior therapy: The obvious and the not so obvious. *American Psychologist, 52*, 966–972. (p. 666)

Wong, D. F., Wagner, H. N., Tune, L. E., Dannals, R. F., & others. (1986). Positron emission tomography reveals elevated D_2 dopamine receptors in drug-naive schizophrenics. *Science, 234*, 1588–1593. (p. 672)

Wong, M. M., & Csikszentmihalyi, M. (1991). Affiliation motivation and daily experience: Some issues on gender differences. *Journal of Personality and Social Psychology, 60*, 154–164. (p. 128)

Wood, C. J, & Aggleton, J. P. (1989). Handedness in `fast ball' sports: Do left-handers have an innate advantage? *British Journal of Psychology, 80*, 227–240. (p. 89)

Wood, J. (2003, May 19). Quoted by R. Mestel, Rorschach tested: Blot out the famous method? Some experts say it has no place in psychiatry. *Los Angeles Times* (www.latimes.com). (p. 603)

Wood, J. M., Bootzin, R. R., Kihlstrom, J. F., & Schacter, D. L. (1992). Implicit and explicit memory for verbal information presented during sleep. *Psychological Science, 3*, 236–239. (p. 355)

Wood, J. M., Nezworski, M. T., Garb, H. N., & Lilienfeld, S. O. (2006). The controversy over the Exner Comprehensive System and the Society for Personality Assessment's white paper on the Rorschach. *Independent Practitioner*, in press. (p. 603)

Wood, J. V., Heimpel, S. A., & Michela, J. L. (2003). Savoring versus dampening: Self-esteem differences in regulating positive affect. *Journal of Personality and Social Psychology, 85*, 566–580. (p. 632)

Wood, J. V., Saltzberg, J. A., & Goldsamt, L. A. (1990a). Does affect induce self-focused attention? *Journal of Personality and Social Psychology, 58*, 899–908. (p. 667)

Wood, J. V., Saltzberg, J. A., Neale, J. M., Stone, A. A., & Rachmiel, T. B. (1990b). Self-focused attention, coping responses, and distressed mood in everyday life. *Journal of Personality and Social Psychology, 58*, 1027–1036. (p. 667)

Wood, W. (1987). Meta-analytic review of sex differences in group performance. *Psychological Bulletin, 102*, 53–71. (p. 127)

Wood, W., & Eagly, A. (2002). A cross-cultural analysis of the behavior of women and men: Implications for the origins of sex differences. *Psychological Bulletin, 128*, 699–727. (pp. 112, 127, 129, 135)

Wood, W., Lundgren, S., Ouellette, J. A., Busceme, S., & Blackstone, T. (1994). Minority influence: A meta-analytic review of social influence processes. *Psychological Bulletin, 115*, 323–345. (p. 741)

Woodruff-Pak, D. S. (1989). Aging and intelligence: Changing perspectives in the twentieth century. *Journal of Aging Studies, 3*, 91–118. (p. 183)

Woods, N. F., Dery, G. K., & Most, A. (1983). Recollections of menarche, current menstrual attitudes, and premenstrual symptoms. In S. Golub (Ed.), *Menarche: The transition from girl to woman.* Lexington, MA: Lexington Books. (p. 166)

Woody, E. Z., & McConkey, K. M. (2003). What we don't know about the brain and hypnosis, but need to: A view from the Buckhorn Inn. *International Journal of Clinical and Experimental Hypnosis, 51,* 309–338. (p. 295)

Woolcock, N. (2004, September 3). Driver thought everyone else was on wrong side. *The Times,* p. 22. (p. 733)

World Federation for Mental Health. (2005). ADHD: The hope behind the hype. www.wfmh.org (p. 641)

World Health Organization. (1979). *Schizophrenia: An international follow-up study.* Chicester, England: Wiley. (p. 671)

World Health Organization. (2004a). *Prevention of mental disorders: Effective interventions and policy options. Summary report.* Geneva: World Health Organization, Department of Mental Health and Substance Abuse. (p. 681)

World Health Organization. (2004b). *Promoting mental health: Concepts, emerging evidence, practice. Summary report.* Geneva: World Health Organization, Department of Mental Health and Substance Abuse. (p. 681)

Worobey, J., & Blajda, V. M. (1989). Temperament ratings at 2 weeks, 2 months, and 1 year: Differential stability of activity and emotionality. *Developmental Psychology, 25,* 257–263. (p. 102)

Worthington, E. L., Jr. (1989). Religious faith across the life span: Implications for counseling and research. *The Counseling Psychologist, 17,* 555–612. (pp. 167–168)

Worthington, E. L., Jr., Kurusu, T. A., McCullogh, M. E., & Sandage, S. J. (1996). Empirical research on religion and psychotherapeutic processes and outcomes: A 10-year review and research prospectus. *Psychological Bulletin, 119,* 448–487. (pp. 708, 709)

Wortman, C. B., & Silver, R. C. (1989). The myths of coping with loss. *Journal of Consulting and Clinical Psychology, 57,* 349–357. (p. 191)

Wren, C. S. (1999, April 8). Drug survey of children finds middle school a pivotal time. *New York Times* (www.nytimes.com). (p. 307)

Wright, I. C., Rabe-Hesketh, S., Woodruff, P. W. R., David, A. S., Murray, R. M., & Bullmore, E. T. (2000). Meta-analysis of regional brain volumes in schizophrenia. *American Journal of Psychiatry, 157,* 16–25. (p. 672)

Wright, K. (November, 1996). The Tarzan syndrome. *Discover, 17*(11), 88–94, 96, 98. (p. 161)

Wright, P. H. (1989). Gender differences in adults' same- and cross-gender friendships. In R. G. Adams & R. Blieszner (Eds.), *Older adult friendships: Structure and process.* Newbury Park, CA: Sage. (p. 129)

Wright, P., Takei, N., Rifkin, L., & Murray, R. M. (1995). Maternal influenza, obstetric complications, and schizophrenia. *American Journal of Psychiatry, 152,* 1714–1720. (p. 673)

Wright, R. (1999, January 11). Who gets the good genes? *Time,* p. 67. (p. 106)

Wright, W. (1998). *Born that way: Genes, behavior, personality.* New York: Knopf. (p. 99)

Wrzesniewski, A., & Dutton, J. E. (2001). Crafting a job: Revisioning employees as active crafters of their work. *Academy of Management Review, 26,* 179–201. (p. 498)

Wrzesniewski, A., McCauley, C. R., Rozin, P., & Schwartz, B. (1997). Jobs, careers, and callings: People's relations to their work. *Journal of Research in Personality, 31,* 21–33. (p. 498)

Wuethrich, B. (2001, March). Features—GETTING STUPID—Surprising new neurological behavioral research reveals that teenagers who drink too much may permanently damage their brains and seriously compromise their ability to learn. *Discover, 56,* 56–64. (p. 299)

Wulsin, L. R., Vaillant, G. E., & Wells, V. E. (1999). A systematic review of the mortality of depression. *Psychosomatic Medicine, 61,* 6–17. (p. 556)

Wyatt, J. K., & Bootzin, R. R. (1994). Cognitive processing and sleep: Implications for enhancing job performance. *Human Performance, 7,* 119–139. (pp. 286, 355)

Wyatt, R. J., Henter, I., & Sherman-Elvy, E. (2001). Tantalizing clues to preventing schizophrenia. *Cerebrum: The Dana Forum on Brain Science, 3,* pp. 15–30. (p. 674)

Wynn, K. (1992). Addition and subtraction by human infants. *Nature, 358,* 749–759. (pp. 149, 150)

Wynn, K. (2000). Findings of addition and subtraction in infants are robust and consistent: reply to Wakeley, Rivera, and Langer. *Child Development, 71,* 1535–1536. (p. 149)

Wynn, K., Bloom, P., & Chiang, W-C. (2002). Enumeration of collective entities by 5-month-old infants. *Cognition, 83,* B55-B62. (p. 149)

Wynn, V., & Gilhooly, K. (1999). The veracity of memories for what you were doing and who you were with when you heard of the death of Diana. *British Psychological Society 1999 Proceedings, 71,* p. 47. (p. 350)

Wynne, C. D. L. (2004). *Do animals think?* Princeton, NJ: Princeton University Press. (p. 426)

Wysocki, C. J., & Gilbert, A. N. (1989). *National Geographic* survey: Effects of age are heterogeneous. *Annals of the New York Academy of Sciences, 561,* 12–28. (p. 232)

Xu, Y., & Corkin, S. (2001). H.M. revisits the Tower of Hanoi puzzle. *Neuropsychology, 15,* 69–79. (p. 367)

Yalom, I. D. (1985). *The theory and practice of group psychotherapy* (3rd ed.). New York: Basic Books. (p. 698)

Yang, N., & Linz, D. (1990). Movie ratings and the content of adult videos: The sex-violence ratio. *Journal of Communication, 40*(2), 28–42. (p. 753)

Yankelovich Partners. (1993). *Inside affluent America.* Westport, CT: Yankelovich Partners. (p. 614)

Yankelovich Partners. (1995, May/June). Growing old. *American Enterprise,* p. 108. (p. 175)

Yankelovich Partners. (1997, December 15). Ability of spirituality to help people who are sick. (Press release.) (p. 572)

Yardley, J. (2005, January 31). Fearing future, China starts to give girls their due. *New York Times* (www.nytimes.com). (p. 745)

Yarnell, P. R., & Lynch, S. (1970, April 25). Retrograde memory immediately after concussion. *Lancet,* pp. 863–865. (p. 366)

Yarrow, L. J., Goodwin, M. S., Manheimer, H., & Milowe, I. D. (1973). Infancy experience and cognitive and personality development at ten years. In L. J. Stone, H. T. Smith, & L. B. Murphy (Eds.), *The competent infant.* New York: Basic Books. (p. 159)

Yates, A. (1989). Current perspectives on the eating disorders: I. History, psychological and biological aspects. *Journal of the American Academy of Child and Adolescent Psychiatry, 28,* 813–828. (p. 479)

Yates, A. (1990). Current perspectives on the eating disorders: II. Treatment, outcome, and research directions. *Journal of the American Academy of Child and Adolescent Psychiatry, 29,* 1–9. (p. 479)

Yates, W. R. (2000). Testosterone in psychiatry. *Archives of General Psychiatry, 57,* 155–156. (p. 483)

Ybarra, O. (1999). Misanthropic person memory when the need to self-enhance is absent. *Personality and Social Psychology Bulletin, 25,* 261–269. (p. 633)

Yip, P. S. F. (1998). Age, sex, marital status and suicide: An empirical study of east and west. *Psychological Reports, 82,* 311–322. (p. 663)

Yirmiya, N., Erel, O., Shaken, M., & Solomonica-Levi, D. (1998). Meta-analyses comparing theory of mind abilities of individuals with autism, individuals with mental retardation, and normally developing individuals. *Psychological Bulletin, 124,* 283–307. (p. 152)

Zajonc, R. B. (1965). Social facilitation. *Science, 149,* 269–274. (p. 738)

Zajonc, R. B. (1980). Feeling and thinking: Preferences need no inferences. *American Psychologist, 35,* 151–175. (p. 521)

Zajonc, R. B. (1984a). On the primacy of affect. *American Psychologist, 39,* 117–123. (p. 521)

Zajonc, R. B. (1984b, July 22). Quoted by D. Goleman, Rethinking IQ tests and their value. *The New York Times*, p. D22. (p. 443)

Zajonc, R. B. (1998). Emotions. In D. Gilbert, S. T. Fiske, & G. Lindzey (Eds.), *Handbook of social psychology*, 4th ed. New York: McGraw-Hill. (p. 759)

Zajonc, R. B. (2001). Mere exposure: A gateway to the subliminal. *Current Directions in Psychological Science, 10*, 224–228. (p. 758)

Zajonc, R. B., & Markus, G. B. (1975). Birth order and intellectual development. *Psychological Review, 82*, 74–88. (p. 43)

Zajonc, R. B., Murphy, S. T., & Inglehart, M. (1989). Feeling and facial efference: Implications of the vascular theory of emotions. *Psychological Review, 96*, 395–416. (p. 530)

Zammit, S., Allebeck, P., Andreasson, S., Lundberg, I., & Lewis, G. (2002). Self reported cannabis use as a risk factor for schizophrenia in Swedish conscripts of 1969: Historical cohort study. *British Medical Journal, 325*, 1199. (p. 303)

Zauberman, G., & Lynch, J. G., Jr. (2005). Resource slack and propensity to discount delayed investments of time versus money. *Journal of Experimental Psychology: General, 134*, 23–37. (p. 403)

Zeidner, M. (1990). Perceptions of ethnic group modal intelligence: Reflections of cultural stereotypes or intelligence test scores? *Journal of Cross-Cultural Psychology, 21*, 214–231. (p. 459)

Zeineh, M. M., Engel, S. A., Thompson, P. M., & Bookheimer, S. Y. (2003). Dynamics of the hippocampus during encoding and retrieval of face-name pairs. *Science, 299*, 577–580. (p. 368)

Zigler, E. F. (1987). Formal schooling for four-year-olds? No. *American Psychologist, 42*, 254–260. (p. 457)

Zigler, E., & Styfco, S. J. (2001). Extended childhood intervention prepared children for school and beyond. *Journal of the American Medical Association, 285*, 2378–2380. (p. 458)

Zilbergeld, B. (1983). *The shrinking of America: Myths of psychological change.* Boston: Little, Brown. (pp. 700, 704)

Zillmann, D. (1986). Effects of prolonged consumption of pornography. Background paper for *The Surgeon General's workshop on pornography and public health*, June 22–24. Report prepared by E. P. Mulvey & J. L. Haugaard and released by Office of the Surgeon General on August 4, 1986. (pp. 517, 520)

Zillmann, D. (1989). Effects of prolonged consumption of pornography. In D. Zillmann & J. Bryant (Eds.), *Pornography: Research advances and policy considerations.* Hillsdale, NJ: Erlbaum. (pp. 484, 753)

Zillmann, D., & Bryant, J. (1984). Effects of massive exposure to pornography. In N. Malamuth & E. Donnerstein (Eds.), *Pornography and sexual aggression.* Orlando, FL: Academic Press. (p. 753)

Zimbardo, P. G. (1970). The human choice: Individuation, reason, and order versus deindividuation, impulse, and chaos. In W. J. Arnold & D. Levine (Eds.), *Nebraska Symposium on Motivation, 1969.* Lincoln, NE: University of Nebraska Press. (p. 739)

Zimbardo, P. G. (1972, April). Pathology of imprisonment. *Transaction/Society*, pp. 4–8. (pp. 727–728)

Zimbardo, P. G. (2001, September 16). Fighting terrorism by understanding man's capacity for evil. Op Ed Essay distributed by spsp-discuss@stolaf.edu. (p. 747)

Zimbardo, P. G. (2004, May 25). Journalist interview re: Abu Ghraib prison abuses: Eleven answers to eleven questions. Unpublished manuscript, Stanford University. (p. 729)

Zimbardo, P. G. (2005, January 18). You can't be a sweet cucumber in a vinegar barrel. *The Edge* (www.edge.org). (p. 729)

Zimmer, C. (2003). How the mind reads other minds. *Science, 300*, 1079–1080. (p. 151)

Zornberg, G. L., Buka, S. L., & Tsuang, M. T. (2000). At issue: The problem of obstetrical complications and schizophrenia. *Schizophrenia Bulletin, 26*, 249–256. (p. 672)

Zubieta, J-K., Heitzeg, M. M., Smith, Y. R., Bueller, J. A., Xu, K., Xu, Y., Koeppe, R. A., Stohler, C. S., & Goldman, D. (2003). COMT val[158]met genotype affects μ-opioid neurotransmitter responses to a pain stressor. *Science, 299*, 1240–1243. (p. 228)

Zucco, G. M. (2003). Anomalies in cognition: Olfactory memory. *European Psychologist, 8*, 77–86. (p. 232)

Zucker, G. S., & Weiner, B. (1993). Conservatism and perceptions of poverty: An attributional analysis. *Journal of Applied Social Psychology, 23*, 925–943. (p. 725)

Zuckerman, M. (1979). *Sensation seeking: Beyond the optimal level of arousal.* Hillsdale, NJ: Erlbaum. (p. 471)

NAME INDEX

SUBJECT INDEX

The Story of Psychology: A Timeline   (continued from inside front cover)

1949 In *The Organization of Behavior: A Neuropsychological Theory*, Canadian psychologist Donald O. Hebb outlines a new and influential conceptualization of how the nervous system functions.

1950 Solomon Asch publishes studies of effects of conformity on judgments of line length.

1951 In *Childhood and Society*, Erik Erikson outlines his stages of psychosocial development.

1952 Carl Rogers publishes *Client-Centered Therapy*.

1953 The American Psychiatric Association publishes *Diagnostic and Statistical Manual of Mental Disorders*, an influential book that will be updated periodically.

Eugene Aserinski and Nathaniel Kleitman describe rapid eye movements (REM) that occur during sleep.

Janet Taylor's Manifest Anxiety Scale appears in the *Journal of Abnormal Psychology*.

1954 In *Motivation and Personality*, Abraham Maslow proposes a hierarchy of motives ranging from physiological needs to self-actualization.

James Olds and Peter Milner, McGill University neuropsychologists, describe rewarding effects of electrical stimulation of the hypothalamus in rats.

Gordon Allport publishes *The Nature of Prejudice*.

1956 In his *Psychological Review* article titled "The Magical Number Seven, Plus or Minus Two: Some Limits on Our Capacity for Processing Information," George Miller coins the term *chunk* for memory researchers.

1957 Robert Sears, Eleanor Maccoby, and Harry Levin publish *Patterns of Child Rearing*.

Charles Ferster and B. F. Skinner publish *Schedules of Reinforcement*.

Noam Chomsky's critical review of B. F. Skinner's *Verbal Behavior* appears in the journal *Language*.

Eleanor Gibson and Richard Walk report their research on infants' depth perception in "The Visual Cliff."

Harry Harlow outlines "The Nature of Love," his work on attachment in monkeys.

1959 Lloyd Peterson and Margaret Peterson in the *Journal of Experimental Psychology* article, "Short-Term Retention of Individual Verbal Items," highlight the importance of rehearsal in memory.

John Thibaut and Harold Kelley publish *The Social Psychology of Groups*.

1969 In his APA presidential address, "Psychology as a Means of Promoting Human Welfare," George Miller emphasizes the importance of "giving psychology away."

1971 Kenneth B. Clark becomes the first African-American president of the American Psychological Association.

Albert Bandura publishes *Social Learning Theory*.

Allan Paivio publishes *Imagery and Verbal Processes*.

B. F. Skinner publishes *Beyond Freedom and Dignity*.

1972 Elliot Aronson publishes *The Social Animal*.

Fergus Craik and Robert Lockhart's "Levels of Processing: A Framework for Memory Research" appears in the *Journal of Verbal Learning and Verbal Behavior*.

Robert Rescorla and Allan Wagner publish their associative model of Pavlovian conditioning.

Under the leadership of Derald Sue and Stanley Sue, the Asian-American Psychological Association is founded.

1973 Ethologists Karl von Frisch, Konrad Lorenz, and Nikolaas Tinbergen receive the Nobel Prize for their research on animal behavior.

1974 APA's Division 2 first publishes its journal, *Teaching of Psychology*, with Robert S. Daniel as editor.

Eleanor Maccoby (pictured) and Carol Jacklin publish *The Psychology of Sex Differences*.

1975 Biologist Edward O. Wilson's *Sociobiology* appears; it will be a controversial precursor to evolutionary psychology.

1976 Sandra Wood Scarr and Richard A. Weinberg publish "IQ Test Performance of Black Children Adopted by White Families" in *American Psychologist*.

1978 Psychologist Herbert A. Simon, Carnegie-Mellon University, wins a Nobel Prize for pioneering research on computer simulations of human thinking and problem solving.

1979 James J. Gibson publishes *The Ecological Approach to Visual Perception*.

Elizabeth Loftus publishes *Eyewitness Testimony*.

1981 Ellen Langer is the first woman to be granted tenure in Harvard University's Department of Psychology.

David Hubel and Torsten Wiesel receive a Nobel Prize for research on single-cell recordings that identified feature detector cells in the visual cortex.

Roger Sperry receives a Nobel Prize for research on split-brain patients.

legislature (sometimes called the *president of city council*). And in most towns, the president of city council hails from the majority party. In addition, paid professional positions such as city solicitor (the town's lawyer), town planner, and city engineer are often awarded on the basis of the support of the majority of council. Even though the entire council votes on appointments, the minority party members often defer to the majority, since appointments typically are viewed as a privilege of winning a majority. Other appointments might include positions on voluntary boards such as a town planning or zoning board.

On the state level, the party in government plays a similarly prominent role in organizing government work. Typically, state legislatures are organized around political party. Seating assignments and committee assignments are made by the majority party leadership and are based on a legislator's party affiliation. Figure 8.4 illustrates the partisan breakdown of state legislatures. In each state, the party with a majority (shown in the figure) in the legislature also has a majority on the legislature's committees, which decide the outcome of proposed legislation. Parties moreover are important in the executive branch of state government, since state governors typically appoint party loyalists to key positions in their administrations. Depending on the appointment powers of the governor, which vary from state to state, a governor may also appoint party members to plum assignments on state regulatory boards. In states where the governor appoints the judiciary, the governor also frequently selects judicial nominees from his or her own political party.

Parties perform a similar role in the federal government. Presidents draw from party loyalists to fill cabinet and subcabinet appointments and typically appoint federal judges from their own political party. Congress is organized based on the party affiliation of its members. When representatives or senators refer to a colleague "on the other side of the aisle," they are referring to a member of the other political party, since congressional Democrats and Republicans sit across the aisle from one another. As in state legislatures, the party with the majority in Congress essentially runs the legislative branch. From its ranks comes the congressional leadership, including the Senate Majority Leader, the Speaker of the House of Representatives, and the House Majority Leader (see Chapter 11).

Partisan control

- Democrat
- Republican
- Split
- Non-Partisan

FIGURE 8.4

Partisan Control of State Legislatures Before the Election of 2010

*Republicans control the Montana Senate 27–23, but the House is evenly divided 50–50. Republicans control the Tennessee Senate 19–14, but the House is evenly divided 49–49.

SOURCE: The National Conference of State Legislatures, www.ncsl.org/default.aspx?tabid=16507.

> Speakers of the House of Representatives are members of the party in government. Nancy Pelosi (D-California) served as Speaker from 2007–2011, and was the first woman to serve in that post. John Boehner (R-Ohio) is the current Speaker, elected after the Republican majority took control of the House in 2011.

DIVIDED GOVERNMENT There are limits to a party's power. Probably the most important check comes from the opposition party, which can openly criticize the party in power and aggressively investigate alleged misconduct on the part of its officials. During parts of the Bill Clinton and George W. Bush administrations, for example, the president and the members of Congress functioned with a **divided government,** the situation in which one party controls Congress and the other party, the presidency.[13] Divided government emerged after the 2006 midterm elections, when the Democrats won control of both houses of Congress. Democrats in Congress alleged administration misconduct when it appeared that Bush's attorney general, Alberto Gonzales, dismissed federal prosecutors for political reasons of politics rather than competence.

divided government
the situation that exists when Congress is controlled by one party and the presidency by the other

Political Parties in U.S. History

Modern Americans' divided opinions of political parties would not be surprising to the founders, who viewed political parties with suspicion.[14] Thomas Jefferson said, "If I could not go to heaven but with a party, I would not go there at all." That sentiment was shared by George Washington, who warned of "the baneful effects of the spirit of party."[15] Despite those reservations, political parties began to emerge in the United States during the debate over ratification of the Constitution (with both Washington and Jefferson instrumental in their creation). Those who advocated ratification and a strong central government were called Federalists, and those who opposed ratification and favored states' rights were called Anti-Federalists. Thus began the first party system in the United States. **Party system** refers to the number and competitiveness of political parties in a polity[16]—for example, a government may have a two-party system in which one party is ascending in power. As we will see, the demarcation of party systems typically occurs in hindsight, when social scientists recognize points where there has been a **realignment,** a shift in party allegiances or electoral support.[17]

party system
the categorization of the number and competitiveness of political parties in a polity

realignment
a shift in party allegiances or electoral support

Although these shifting allegiances have played a pivotal role in shaping the context of politics since the country's early days, the founders generally believed that parties threatened the stability of the fledgling democracy.[18] Most thought that political parties enabled individuals and groups to pursue self-serving interests that were often contrary to the common good. Some of the founders argued that parties discouraged independence in thought and action. Some thought that parties exacerbated conflicts and disagreements among the people rather than building consensus. Yet their formation and continued evolution testifies to their important role in achieving political and policy goals for their members.[19]

The First Party System:
The Development of Parties, 1789–1828

In 1788, George Washington was elected president, but the consensus surrounding his election proved short-lived. Washington deeply opposed the idea of political parties and ruled during an era without formal parties. But he recognized that despite his popularity, he needed legislators who would push his initiatives through Congress. Washington's secretary of the treasury and close ally, Alexander Hamilton, gathered legislators into a loosely knit party, the Federalists, that favored a strong national government.

Thomas Jefferson, secretary of state during Washington's first term (1789–1793), feared a strong central government, and he and his backers opposed Hamilton's Federalists. But Jefferson's primary concern was that the new government should succeed, and so despite his opposition, he remained in Washington's cabinet during the president's first term. When Jefferson later resigned his secretarial post, in 1793, many of those who shared his apprehensions about a strong central government remained in Congress.

Although Jefferson lost to Federalist John Adams in the 1796 presidential election, he paved the way for his future electoral success by building a base of support—including partisan groups in the states and newly established political newspapers—that allowed him to get his message out.[20] This direct communication with voters marked a significant step in the civic development of the U.S. electorate. The strategy was effective: Jefferson won election to the presidency in 1800 over Adams, and Adams's defeat marked the end of the Federalist Party. Jefferson was reelected in 1804, and both of his elections demonstrated the important function that political parties would play in elections.[21] His supporters became known as Jeffersonian Republicans; later, Democratic-Republicans. The modern descendants of the Democratic-Republicans today are called Democrats.

The Jeffersonian Republicans' effective campaign tactics of communicating with voters, along with the absence of well-organized opposition, resulted in their continued dominance from 1815 to 1828. Historians call those years the Era of Good Feelings, largely because of the widespread popular support for Democratic-Republican presidents James Madison (1809–1817), James Monroe (1817–1825), and John Quincy Adams (1825–1829).

The Second Party System:
The Democrats' Rise to Power, 1828–1860

By 1828, some dissension among the Jeffersonian Republicans was becoming apparent. Members of the party, including the charismatic military general and politician Andrew Jackson of Tennessee, chafed at the elitism of the party and the era. The Jacksonian Democrats—the name for the new coalition that Jackson formed—emphasized leadership through merit rather than birth.[22] They espoused **populism,** a philosophy supporting the rights and empowerment of the masses, particularly in the area of political participation, and the **spoils system,** in which political supporters were rewarded with jobs (from the phrase "to the victor go the spoils"). The Jacksonian Democrats succeeded in mobilizing the masses, sweeping Jackson to victory in the presidential election of 1828.[23] Political parties had become the medium through which many Americans were politicized, and in 1828, for the first time, more than one million Americans cast their ballots in the presidential contest.

Jackson's populism marked a critical step in opening up the civic life of the polity to many new groups of citizens who had not been involved in politics previously.[24] It redefined not only who was eligible to succeed as political leaders but also who should be eligible to participate in the selection of those leaders. Historian Richard P. McCormick noted that the Jacksonian Democrats extended voting rights to all white adult males, changed the mechanism for selecting presidential electors to popular elections by voters instead of by the state legislatures, and increased the importance of the party convention, in effect giving party members more say in candidates' selection. And although women would not gain the right to vote until 1920, the Jacksonian era saw the formal beginnings of the women's suffrage movement with the formation of the two major women's suffrage organizations and the advent of the Seneca Falls Convention (1848) in support of expanded rights for women.[25]

During the 1830s, southern plantation owners and northern industrialists became concerned about the impact the Democrats' populism would have on economic elites.[26] Their mutual interests crystallized in the formation of the Whig Party in 1836, which succeeded in electing two presidents, William Henry Harrison (succeeded by John Tyler upon his death) and Zachary Taylor.[27] But the era of the Second Party System ultimately was defined by the long-standing effects that Jacksonian principles would have on U.S. politics, namely through the politicization of a previously excluded mass of citizens—many of whom had been initiated into the rites of full citizenship and others of whom had begun the struggle to win their own status as full citizens.[28]

The Third Party System:
The Republicans' Rise to Power, 1860–1896

In the 1850s, slavery became the primary concern for both the Whigs and the Democrats.[29] This highly charged issue divided the Whig Party into proslavery and abolitionist factions, and the party consequently faded away.[30] In its place, a new antislavery party, the Republicans (also called the Grand Old Party, or GOP), took shape in 1854 and gained the support

populism
a philosophy supporting the rights and empowerment of the masses as opposed to elites

spoils system
the practice of rewarding political supporters with jobs

THE CURIOUS EFFECT OF CLEAN LINEN UPON
THE DEMOCRATIC PARTY

POLITICAL INQUIRY

In this cartoon by the famous nineteenth-century caricaturist and cartoonist Thomas Nast, what does the tiger represent? What point is the cartoonist making about the "clean linen" the tiger is wearing?

of abolitionist Whigs and northern Democrats.[31] The victory of the Republican presidential nominee, Abraham Lincoln, in the election of 1860 marked the beginning of a period of dominance of the antislavery Republicans, which continued even after the Civil War.[32] During this time, the Republican Party enjoyed strong support from newly franchised African American voters. Although many African Americans in the South were prevented from exercising their right to vote through threats, intimidation, and tactics such as the white primary (see Chapter 5), African Americans in the North widely voted Republican. They would remain strong supporters of the "party of Lincoln" for decades.

During this time, political parties grew very strong, and political machines came to dominate the political landscape. A **political machine** was both a corrupt and a useful organization that dominated politics around the turn of the twentieth century, particularly in cities. Each political machine was headed by a "boss," whose power rested on a system of patronage. A party leader used **patronage** as a device to reward political supporters—rather than individuals who might demonstrate greater merit or particular competence—with jobs or government contracts. In exchange, those receiving patronage would vote for the party and might be expected to volunteer on a campaign or kick back some of their wages to the party.

Although political machines were known for corruption, they did accomplish some good. Richard Croker was political boss of Tammany Hall, New York City's Democratic Party political machine from 1886 until 1902. He explained: "Think of what New York is and what the people of New York are. One half are of foreign birth. . . . They do not speak our language, they do not know our laws. . . . There is no denying the service which Tammany has rendered to the Republic, there is no such organization for taking hold of the untrained, friendless man and converting him into a citizen. Who else would do it if we did not?"[33]

On that score, Croker was right. At the time, political machines provided the vital service of socializing a generation of immigrants to democracy and to the American way of political life. Some machines, including Tammany Hall, generated widespread political participation, and some allowed the participation of women.[34] Political machines helped integrate immigrants into the social, economic, and political fabric of the United States, usually by awarding jobs for loyalty to the party. And in an era when the federal government had not yet become a large-scale provider of social services, urban political machines also provided a safety net for the injured, the elderly, and widows.

The Fourth Party System: Republican Dominance, 1896–1932

The 1896 presidential election between populist Democrat William Jennings Bryan and Republican William McKinley marked the beginning of a new era in party politics. Bryan appealed widely to Protestants, southerners, midwesterners, and rural dwellers who were suspicious of Catholic, ethnic, working-class immigrants in the urban Northeast. McKinley emphasized economic growth and development and garnered support from industrialists, bankers, and even working-class factory workers, who saw his backing of business as being good for the economy. McKinley won the election handily, his victory ushering in an era of Republican dominance in presidential politics that would last until the election of 1912.

That year, Theodore Roosevelt (who had succeeded McKinley as president in 1901 after the latter's assassination, and who had been elected president as a Republican in 1904) ran in the presidential election as a Progressive. The Progressive Party advocated widespread governmental reform and sought to limit the power of political bosses. The Republicans'

political machine
big-city party organization that exerted control over many aspects of life and lavishly rewarded supporters

patronage
system in which a party leader rewarded political supporters with jobs or government contracts in exchange for their support of the party

split between William Howard Taft's regular Republicans and Roosevelt's Progressives powered Democrat Woodrow Wilson to the presidency with only 42 percent of the popular vote.

As Wilson's Democratic administration ended up enacting many of the Progressive Party's proposals, the power of the urban political machines declined. For example, recorded voter registration and secret ballot laws were passed, the direct party primary was established, and civil service reform was expanded. The national leaders who spearheaded those measures designed them to take political power out of the bosses' hands and give it to the electorate.

After Wilson's two terms, the Republicans continued to enjoy the support of business elites and the industrial working class. They also benefited from the backing of the many African Americans in the northern cities who continued to support the party of Lincoln, and of women voters, many of whom had been activists in the Progressive movement. With this widespread and diverse support, the Republicans retained control of the presidency throughout the 1920s.

The Fifth Party System: Democratic Dominance, 1932–1968

When the stock market crashed in 1929, the economy entered the deep downturn that history remembers as the Great Depression. In the election of 1932, a broad constituency responded to the calls of the Democratic candidate, Franklin D. Roosevelt, for an increased governmental role in promoting the public welfare. Roosevelt pressed tirelessly for a **New Deal** for all Americans, a broad program in which the government would bear the responsibility of providing a "safety net" to protect the most disadvantaged members of society.

A new alignment among American voters swept "FDR" into presidential office. In fact, the **New Deal coalition**—the name for the voting bloc comprising traditional southern Democrats, northern city dwellers (especially immigrants and the poor), Catholics, unionized and blue-collar workers, African Americans, and women—would give Roosevelt the presidency an unprecedented four times.[35]

The era of the Fifth Party System significantly opened up party politics and civic activity to a widening spectrum of Americans. Notably for African Americans and women, Franklin Roosevelt's elections marked the first time that they had been actively courted by political parties, and their new political activism—particularly in the form of voting and political party activities—left them feeling they had a voice in their government.

Vice President Harry Truman assumed the presidency on Roosevelt's death in 1945 and was elected in his own right in 1948, but subsequent Democrats were unable to keep Roosevelt's coalition together. Republican Dwight Eisenhower won the White House in 1952 and again in 1956. And although Democrats John F. Kennedy and Lyndon Johnson held the presidency through most of the 1960s, the events of that decade wreaked havoc on the

Party Politics in Flux

THEN (1889)	NOW (2011)
Powerful political parties were in their heyday, and party bosses ruled the cities with an iron fist.	The era of party politics in the United States is over, according to some scholars.
The patronage system was in high gear, and political parties derived enormous power and loyalty from the recipients of jobs and lucrative contracts.	A merit-based civil service system has largely replaced patronage, and parties are weakened because of a decline in the number of loyal members.
Elected officials toed the party line, because they depended on the party for their office.	Elected officials pride themselves on their "independence" and sometimes owe very little to their political party.

WHAT'S NEXT?

> How are advancing technologies likely to change political parties and their operations in the future? Will these weaken or strengthen the parties? Explain.

> Do you think that the voters who went to the polls in the 2008 primaries and general election remained loyal to their parties in 2010? Why or why not?

> How do parties today help voters evaluate candidates? Will they still perform this function in the future? Will the nature of this process change? Explain.

New Deal
Franklin Roosevelt's broad social welfare program in which the government would bear the responsibility of providing a "safety net" to protect the most disadvantaged members of society

New Deal coalition
the group composed of southern Democrats, northern city dwellers, immigrants, the poor, Catholics, labor union members, blue-collar workers, African Americans, and women that elected FDR to the presidency four times

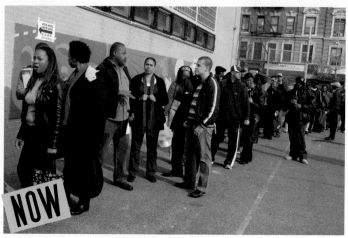

> African American voters were a key constituency in electing both Franklin Roosevelt and Barack Obama to the presidency. Here, voters in New York City's Harlem wait to cast their ballots for President Roosevelt in 1936 and President Obama in 2008.

Democratic Party, with deep divisions opening up over the Vietnam War and civil rights for African Americans.[36]

A New Party System?

Political scientists have sought to determine whether the era that began when Richard Nixon was elected president in 1968 can be considered a separate party system. Barack Obama's election in 2008, particularly his strong support among young and first-time voters, points to a continuation of the trend of Democratic dominance established in the Fifth Party System. But Republican dominance of the presidency since 1968, coupled with increasing support of the Republican Party by southern whites and the increasing activism of conservative Christians in the party, gives support to the claim that a new party system has emerged.

Additional characteristics of this new party system, according to scholars, include *intense party competition,* in which the two major U.S. political parties have been nearly evenly matched and neither one has dominated; and *divided government,* where a president of one party has to deal with a Congress of the other. This fierce partisan competitiveness is clearly apparent in the outcomes of recent national elections. In particular, the 2000 presidential campaign demonstrated the ferocious rivalry of the two parties, with a presidential election so close that the outcome was in question for weeks after the voting had ended. That year, voters also evenly divided the Senate, electing fifty Democrats and fifty Republicans.

Moreover, some scholars see **dealignment,** the phenomenon in which fewer voters support the two major political parties and instead self-identify as independent, as a notable characteristic of this new party system.[37] Others view the increasing trend toward supporting candidates from both parties (**ticket splitting**) or from other parties as evidence of a new party system's emergence.

The period since 1968 has also been characterized by the growing importance of candidate-centered politics. The rise of **candidate committees,** organizations that candidates form to support their individual election as opposed to the party's slate of candidates, is one reflection of how politics has increasingly become candidate-centered. Candidate committees compete with political parties in many arenas. They raise and spend money, organize campaigns, and attempt to mobilize voters. One impact of their enhanced influence has been that elected officials, particularly members of Congress, are less indebted to their parties than in previous eras and thus sometimes demonstrate less loyalty when voting on bills in the legislature.

Some political scientists argue that these characteristics of the new party system demonstrate that the responsible party model (discussed earlier) is not as strong as it once was.

dealignment
the situation in which fewer voters support the two major political parties, instead identifying themselves as independent, or splitting their ticket between candidates from more than one party

ticket splitting
the situation in which voters vote for candidates from more than one party

candidate committees
organizations that candidates form to support their individual election

The rise of candidate committees and the increase in ticket splitting mean that parties are less helpful to voters as they assess candidates, because the differences between Republican and Democratic candidates may dissipate in the face of constituent opinion. Yet most Americans disagree: a recent Gallup poll indicated that nearly two-thirds of those surveyed believe that there are important differences between the Democratic and the Republican parties.[38] And the research of some scholars, including David Karol, Hans Noel, John Zaller, and Marty Cohen, indicates that party elites, including elected officials and former elected officials, have increased their control in selecting party presidential nominees, suggesting a potential revival of the importance of parties as players in politics today.[39]

Two-Party Domination in U.S. Politics

Since the ratification of the Constitution in 1787, the United States has had a two-party system for all but about thirty years in total. This historical record stands in marked contrast to the experience of the many nations that have third parties.[40] A **third party** is a political party organized as opposition or an alternative to the existing parties in a two-party system. Many countries even have *multi*party systems. (See "Global Context" on page 258.)

third party
a party organized as opposition or an alternative to the existing parties in a two-party system

The United States' two-party system has had two contradictory influences on people's civic engagement. On the one hand, the dominance of only two strong political parties through most of American history has made it easy for individuals to find avenues for becoming civically engaged. Further, at various historical points, political parties have worked for the outright extension of political rights to groups that were excluded, although often with the foremost aim of bolstering their core supporters. On the other hand, the dominance of just two political parties that tend to be ideologically moderate discourages the political participation of some people, particularly those who are strongly ideological.

Although the grip of the United States' two-party system is frustrating to people who support a greater diversity of parties, the reasons for the two-party system are numerous and difficult to change.

The Dualist Nature of Most Conflicts

Historically, many issues in the United States have been dualist, or "two-sided." For example, the debate over ratification of the U.S. Constitution found people with two basic opinions. On one side, the Federalists supported ratification of the Constitution, which created a federal government that separated powers among three branches and shared power with state governments. They were opposed by the Anti-Federalists, who campaigned against ratification of the Constitution, supported stronger states' rights, and wanted to see states and individuals enjoy greater protections. This split provided the initial structure for the two-party system, and a multitude of issues followed that format.

Political scientists Seymour Martin Lipset and Stein Rokkan asserted that the dualist nature of voter alignments or cleavages shapes how political parties form. In particular, these alignments or cleavages concern the character of the national fabric (for example, should religious ideals or secular notions prevail?), and they are determined by function (business versus agrarian interests, for example).[41] These cleavages shaped party formation during the nineteenth century, when the dualist nature of conflict continued to be in evidence in public affairs. Some states wanted slavery; other states opposed "the peculiar institution" of human bondage. In some states, commercial and industrial interests dominated; in other states, agricultural interests held the reins of power. Immigrants, often Catholics, controlled the politics of some states, whereas native-born Protestants held sway in others.

"IT JUST WOULDN'T WORK OUT, DEREK. I'M FROM A RED STATE, AND YOU'RE FROM A BLUE STATE."

POLITICAL PARTIES IN NORTHERN IRELAND

Although the functions and the focus of political parties in the United States today are broad and important, it may be hard to envision modern parties as institutions that can change people's everyday lives and alter the course of a nation's history. But that is exactly what happened in the mid-1990s in the six counties that make up Northern Ireland. This region, which was under the rule of the British government, had been racked by violence for decades as Catholic and Protestant paramilitary forces engaged in guerrilla warfare over a deep division among the citizenry: Catholics wanted the counties to be reunited with the Republic of Ireland, but Protestants wanted them to remain part of Great Britain.

> **Will Northern Ireland's bold experiment in governance by party power-sharing succeed?**

Reflecting the varying preferences of the country's voters, Northern Ireland features more than a dozen political parties. Only a subset of those parties enjoys a competitive edge, however, because of their wider support among the people. In the mid-1990s, Gerry Adams and John Hume, the leaders of two of Northern Ireland's most influential political parties, began talks to explore how to end political violence in the provinces once and for all. Gerry Adams's Sinn Fein Party (pronounced "shin fane," meaning "ourselves alone" in Irish) was affiliated with the Provisional Irish Republican Army, the Catholic paramilitary group engaged in violence that sought to end British rule in Northern Ireland. John Hume's Social Democratic and Labour Party, Northern Ireland's largest political party, has a liberal ideology and has always rejected violence as a means of achieving political goals. Over the course of many months that turned into years, Adams and Hume, later joined by Ulster Unionist Party (UUP) leader David Trimble (who negotiated with Adams despite the UUP's fierce commitment to retaining British control in the region), agreed to a six-plank set of principles. Called the Mitchell Principles in honor of then-U.S. senator George Mitchell (D-Maine), who helped to broker the deal, the agreement called for the people of Northern Ireland to decide their political fate democratically and provided for the verifiable disarmament of the paramilitary groups.

The so-called Good Friday agreement was signed by the Irish and British governments and was endorsed by nearly all major political parties in 1998. In May of that year, 71 percent of the voters of Northern Ireland approved the Good Friday agreements, a major step in the Northern Ireland peace process. The way was paved for the election of a devolved Northern Irish Assembly, a legislature that would essentially govern the territory through a power-sharing agreement among the leading political parties. Until March 2007, it appeared that all the negotiations would be undone when Democratic Unionist Party (DUP) leader Ian Paisley refused even to discuss the agreement with Adams or other Sinn Feiners. (The DUP is vehemently anti-Catholic and opposed the Good Friday agreement.) But on March 27, one day before a deadline that would have put Northern Ireland back under British control, Paisley relented and accepted the power-sharing scenario. A new era of devolved democracy thus began in Northern Ireland. By May 2007, a power-sharing agreement covering executive power was established, with Paisley and Sinn Fein's Martin McGuinness holding equal powers. Upon Paisley's retirement in 2008, DUP leader Peter Robinson replaced Paisley, and he and McGuinness continue the power-sharing executive arrangement today.

> As a testament to the power of political parties to shape policy, Northern Ireland First Minister Peter Robinson of the Democratic Unionist Party (second from the right) and Deputy First Minister Martin McGuiness of Sinn Fein (second from the left) attend a 2009 North-South Council meeting along with Minister for Foreign Affairs Michael Martin (left) and Jeffrey Donaldson, DUP member of Parliament (right).

By the twentieth century, the dualist conflict had become more ideological. Some Americans agreed with President Franklin D. Roosevelt's plan to help lift the country out of the Great Depression by significantly increasing the role of government in people's everyday lives. Others opposed this unprecedented expansion of the federal government's power. In later decades, debates over civil rights and women's rights demonstrated the continued dualist nature of conflict in American society and culture.

The Winner-Take-All Electoral System

In almost all U.S. elections, the person with the most votes wins. If a competitor gets just one vote fewer than the victor, he or she wins nothing. If a third party garners a significant proportion of the vote in congressional elections nationwide but does not win the most votes in any given district, the party will not win any seats in Congress.

Compare the **winner-take-all** system with the proportional representation system found in many nations. In a **proportional representation system,** political parties win the number of parliamentary seats equal to the percentage of the vote each party receives. So, for example, if the Green Party were to capture 9 percent of the vote in a country's election, it would get nine seats in a one-hundred-member parliament. In a proportional representation system, the 19 percent of the vote that Reform Party candidate Ross Perot won in the 1992 U.S. presidential election would have given the Reform Party about 85 seats in the House of Representatives!

In nations with proportional representation, third parties (which we consider in more detail later in the chapter) are encouraged because such parties can win a few seats in the legislature and use them to further their cause and broaden their support.[42] In addition, in proportional representation systems, third parties sometimes form a *coalition,* or working union, with a larger party so that the two together can control a majority of a legislature. And so, for example, the Green Party that won nine seats in Parliament in the example mentioned above might form a coalition with another party that had received 42 percent of the vote, together forming a majority government. In this way, a third party can get members appointed to key positions as a reward for forming the coalition. Consequently, societies with proportional representation systems can sometimes be more inclusive of differing points of view because even those winning a small proportion of the vote achieve representation, and that representation can be pivotal in the formation of coalitions.

winner-take-all
electoral system in which the candidate who receives the most votes wins that office, even if that total is not a majority.

proportional representation system
an electoral structure in which political parties win the number of parliamentary seats equal to the percentage of the vote the party receives

Continued Socialization to the Two-Party System

Another reason that the two-party system dominates in the United States is that party identification—like ideology, values, and religious beliefs—is an attribute that often passes down from one generation to the next. Hence many an individual is likely to be a Democrat or a Republican because his or her parents were one or the other. Many people first learn about government and politics at home. Around the dinner table, a child may have heard her parents rail against Barack Obama's health care proposal or criticize George W. Bush's Iraq policy. Having become socialized to their household's political culture, children are likely to mimic their parents' views.

Even children who do not share their parents' political outlook or who grow apart from it over time (as commonly occurs during the college years) have been socialized to the legitimacy of the two-party system—unless, of course, their parents routinely criticized both Democrats and Republicans or voiced dissatisfaction with the two-party system.

Election Laws That Favor the Two-Party System

At both the federal and the state level in the United States, election laws benefit the two major parties because they are usually written by members of one of those parties. Although some local governments mandate nonpartisan elections, in most cities and towns, getting on the ballot typically means simply winning the party's nomination and collecting a state-specified number of signatures of registered party members on a nominating petition. Usually, the party organization will circulate this petition for a candidate. Third parties have a much steeper climb to get their candidates in office. In the 2008 presidential election, candidate Ralph Nader, who ran as an independent, had difficulty just getting his name on the ballot in some states.

Scholars of civic engagement point to the structural impediments to the formation of third parties as key to the low level of civic engagement on the part of individuals who are dissatisfied with the two-party system. Facing seemingly insurmountable structural obstacles to the formation of successful third parties, some Americans shy away from political engagement.

The Two-Party System Today: In Decline or in Resurgence?

Given the various historical changes to the U.S. political party system that we have examined, many political scientists have inquired into what the impact of those changes will be. Do the changes signify an end to party control in American politics? Or can political parties adapt to the altered environment and find new sources of power?

The Party's Over

Some scholars argue that changes in the political environment have rendered today's political parties essentially impotent to fulfill the functions that parties performed during stronger party systems. In 1982, political scientist Gary Orren wrote, "In a world in which political scientists disagree on almost everything, there is remarkable agreement among the political science profession that the strength of American political parties has declined significantly over the past several decades."[43] Although some political scientists would subsequently challenge Orren's perspective, many agreed with him at the time.

These theorists note several key factors that have contributed to party decline. Some argue that the elimination of political patronage through the requirement of civil service qualifications for government employees has significantly hurt parties' ability to reward loyal followers with government jobs. Patronage jobs still exist, but most government positions are now awarded upon an applicant's successful performance on a civil service exam that is designed to measure qualifications based on objective criteria. Whereas the recipients of patronage jobs were among the most loyal party members in previous decades, party loyalty has decreased as political parties have lost a significant amount of control in the awarding of jobs.

Other political scientists emphasize the government's increased role over time in providing social welfare benefits as a contributor to the decline of political parties. Because of President Franklin Roosevelt's New Deal and further expansion of the government's role as the key provider of social services, the parties typically no longer perform that function. Thus changing times have brought the elimination of another source of party loyalty.

primary election
an election in which voters choose the party's candidates who will run in the later general election

Primary elections—elections in which voters choose the party's candidates who will run in the later general election—also have decreased parties' power by taking the control of nominations from party leaders and handing it to voters. In the past, when a party machine anointed nominees at nominating conventions, those nominees became indebted to the party and typically responded with loyalty if they got elected. But today's candidates are less likely to owe their nomination to the party: instead, in many cases they have fought for and won the nomination by taking their campaign directly to primary voters.

Changes in the mass media have also meant a drastically decreased role for political parties. In their heyday, political parties were one of the most important providers of news. Parties published so-called penny papers that reported information to the public. Today, political parties may still provide some information to voters at election time, but most voters rely on other, independent media outlets—newspapers, television, radio, and Internet news sources—rather than exclusively partisan sources.

The rise in candidate-centered campaigns has also weakened political parties. **Candidate-centered campaigns,** in which an individual seeking election, rather than an entire party slate, is the focus, have come about because of changes in the parties' functions, the advent of direct primaries, and trends in the mass media that have shifted the focus to individual office-seekers. Candidate-centered campaigns also must rely more heavily on paid professional campaign workers (instead of party volunteers), making it necessary for contributors to support individual candidates rather than political parties.

These changes in the nature of political parties and in their ability to perform their traditional functions have led some political scientists to conclude that the era of party rule is ending. Other players, they say—including interest groups, candidate-based organizations, and the media—will come to assume the roles traditionally performed by political parties.

candidate-centered campaign
a campaign in which an individual seeking election, rather than an entire party slate, is the focus

The Party's Just Begun

Pointing to the record-breaking turnout in the 2008 presidential primaries, other political scientists strongly disagree that U.S. parties' prime has passed.[44] While conceding that political parties' functions have changed, these theorists observe that parties have proved themselves remarkably adaptable. When the political environment has changed in the past, political parties have responded by assuming different functions or finding new avenues by which to seed party loyalty. According to this view, the parties' ability to rebound is alive and well.

These scholars also argue that the continued dominance in the United States of two political parties—through decades of threats to their survival—has demonstrated a strength and a resilience that are likely to prevail. Today's Republicans, the party of Lincoln, have endured the assassinations of party leaders, the Great Depression, the four-term presidency of popular Democrat Franklin D. Roosevelt, and the Watergate scandal during the Nixon presidency. Today's Democrats are the same party that opposed suffrage for African Americans in the aftermath of the Civil War, and that survived internal divisions over civil rights through the 1960s, to become strong supporters of African American rights in recent decades. The Democrats too have endured assassinations and scandals, and have weathered Republican control of the White House for all but twelve years since 1968. Both political parties have remained remarkably competitive despite the challenges to their success.

Scholars who argue that the two main U.S. political parties are once again rebounding cite the lack of viable alternatives to the two-party system. Yes, third parties have made a mark in recent presidential elections. But the present-day party system has not seen the emergence of a strong, viable third party with a cohesive ideology that has attracted a significant portion of the vote in more than one election. And civic education scholars agree that third parties have served an important function by encouraging the political participation of people who are disenchanted with the current two-party system. They also acknowledge, however, the continued dominance of the two main parties in creating opportunities for civic engagement within communities.

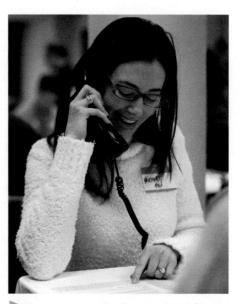

> The party organization consists of both paid staff and party volunteers. Here, Republican party volunteers in Texas make last minute calls to remind supporter to get out and vote in the 2008 election.

Third Parties in the United States

As we have seen, the absence of viable U.S. political parties beyond the Democrats and the Republicans is a source of frustration for some Americans. Despite that frustration, there has been little consensus about whether the Democratic and Republican political parties do an adequate job in representing the American people, as shown in Figure 8.5 on page 262. The figure does not show that, at different times, the proportions of conservatives, liberals, and moderates vary in their likelihood of agreeing that a third party is needed. According to pollsters, this difference may reflect the respondents' opinions of the effectiveness of their party at representing their views. And so, for example, at high points in the

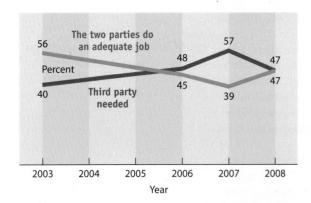

FIGURE 8.5 ■ IS A THIRD PARTY NEEDED?
What trend do the polling data in this figure show? What factors in the political and social environments might explain this trend?

SOURCE: The Gallup Poll, "Public Divided on Need for Third Party," www.gallup .com/poll/110764/Public-Divided-Need-Third-Party.aspx.

George W. Bush presidency, conservatives would have been less likely to say a third party was needed, and the same would hold true for liberals during high points in Barack Obama's presidency.

Because of the differing ideological viewpoints of those who agree a third party is needed, third parties have had little success in contesting elections. In recent times, Ralph Nader was an influential candidate in 2000, not because he netted a sizeable proportion of votes but because the 3 percent that he did win was enough to change the outcome of that razor-close election. Other third-party candidacies have proved influential because of their role in focusing attention—particularly the attention of the victorious candidate—on an issue that might not otherwise have been addressed.[45] Such was the case in 1912 when Progressive Party candidate Theodore Roosevelt ran against Woodrow Wilson. Although he lost the presidency, Roosevelt succeeded in shaping public opinion so that Wilson felt compelled to enact part of the Progressives' national agenda, including sweeping changes to the nation's child labor laws.

One of the most significant obstacles to the formation of a viable third party is that people who are dissatisfied with the two dominant parties fall across the ideological spectrum: some are very liberal; others, quite conservative; still others, moderate. Thus, although many Americans are dissatisfied with the current parties, a third party would have difficulty attracting enough support from among these diversely dissatisfied party members.

Nonetheless, third parties have played, and continue to play, an influential role in American electoral politics. Third parties are particularly effective at encouraging the civic engagement of people who feel that the two dominant parties do not represent their views or do not listen to them. Third parties give such citizens a voice. And even though third parties often do not succeed electorally, their mere presence in the political arena enlivens civic discourse and frequently encourages debate about urgent policy issues that the two major parties ignore or slight.

Types of Third Parties

Third parties have existed in the United States since the early nineteenth century. Over the nation's history, third parties typically have fallen into one of three general categories: issue advocacy parties, ideologically oriented parties, and splinter parties.

ISSUE ADVOCACY PARTIES   Formed to promote a stance on a particular issue, many issue advocacy parties are short-lived. Once the issue is dealt with or fades from popular concern, the mobilizing force behind the party disintegrates. An example is today's Green Party, which promotes environmental protection as a primary issue and also emphasizes human rights, childhood poverty, globalization, health care, and corporate corruption and greed in its party platform. In the 2000 presidential election, the Green Party sought to win 5 percent of the vote for its presidential candidate, Ralph Nader. If the Greens had succeeded, they would have automatically qualified their party for federal matching funds in the 2004 campaign. The Green Party fell short, however, since it captured only 3 percent of the vote. Its share of the vote then dropped sharply in the 2004 presidential election.

IDEOLOGICALLY ORIENTED PARTIES   The agenda of an ideologically oriented party is typically broader than that of an issue-oriented party. Ideologically oriented parties are structured around an *ideology*—a highly organized and coherent framework concerning the nature and role of government in society (see Chapter 6). Such parties have broad views about many different aspects of government. For example, the Libertarian Party, which holds the ideological position that government should not interfere with individuals' social, political, and economic rights, advocates a very limited role for government: no guarantees of minimum wages or other forms of governmental regulation of the economy, including environmental regulation; no governmental interference in individuals' privacy; the legalization of prostitution and drugs; and the elimination of major governmental bureaucracies, including the Central Intelligence Agency, the Internal Revenue Service, and the Federal Bureau of Investigation.

Another ideologically oriented party is the Socialist Party, which lies at the other end of the ideological spectrum from the Libertarian Party. The Socialist Party, formed in 1901, is one of the longest-standing ideologically oriented parties in the United States. Socialists believe that government should play a large role in ensuring economic equality for all people.

SPLINTER PARTIES A splinter party is a political party that breaks off, or "splinters," from one of the two dominant parties. Often a group splinters off because of intra-party (internal, or within the party) disagreement on a particular issue. Though many Tea Party candidates sought election under the Republican Party label in 2010, the sometimes fractured relationship between the activists and more moderate Republicans caused many to wonder if the Tea Party will splinter from the Republican Party. In 1948, a group of southern Democrats who opposed the Democratic Party's support of civil rights for African Americans splintered from the Democratic Party to form the States' Rights Party, which quickly became known as the Dixiecrat Party. The party called itself the States' Rights Party because it claimed that Congress had no power to interfere with the administration of laws made by the states. It used that claim to retain the policies that created a system of racial segregation in the South. Although the States' Rights Party was a separate, formal organization, many southern Democratic elected officials and party leaders who agreed with the States' Rights Party's platform supported its views from within the Democratic Party.

The Impact of Third Parties

Despite the difficulties associated with sustaining support in American electoral politics, third parties have important effects in the political arena. First, although U.S. third parties usually do not win elections, they can influence electoral outcomes. For example, given the closeness of the 2000 presidential race, many Democrats believe that Green Party candidate Ralph Nader caused Democrat Al Gore to lose the election. They reason that Nader voters would have been more likely to vote for the liberal Gore than for the conservative George W. Bush if Nader had not been a candidate. In a state such as Florida where the electorate was evenly divided, Nader's candidacy in fact could have changed the outcome of that state's balloting and thus the results of the national election as well. Of course, many third-party advocates claim that supporters of a third-party candidate may not have voted at all if their party had not been on the ballot. (See "Thinking Critically About Democracy" on page 264.)

Second, third parties provide a release valve for dissatisfied voters. People who are disgruntled with the two major parties can join or form another political party. And although a third party's chances of electoral success are not great, such parties provide a mechanism for like-minded people to come together to try to effect change. Sometimes, these efforts result in a victory, especially on the local level. A well-known third-party victor is Jesse Ventura, a former professional wrestler who was elected governor of Minnesota in 1998 as a candidate of the Reform Party. At the national level, there have been several elections in which third parties were a release valve for discontented voters, as shown in Figure 8.6. In U.S. history, third-party presidential candidates have won more than 10 percent of the vote seven times, the latest being in 1992, when Independent Party candidate H. Ross Perot captured 19 percent of the vote. As the figure illustrates, in five of those seven cases, the incumbent party's presidential nominee lost the presidency. Thus, third parties tend to help the major out-of-power party win election.

Finally, third parties put a variety of issues on the national political agenda. When a third party, especially an issue-oriented third party, draws attention to an issue of

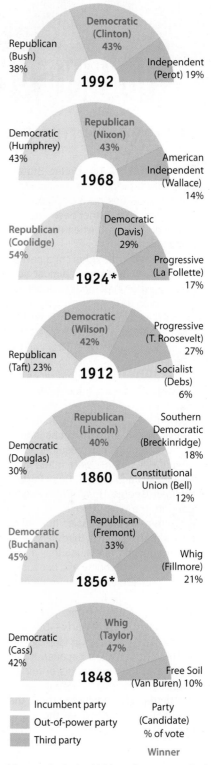

FIGURE 8.6

Third Parties Help the Out-of-Power Party

NOTE: Candidate appears in parentheses; percentage is percentage of vote won by candidate.

ARE THIRD PARTIES BAD FOR THE UNITED STATES?

The Issue: The United States' political culture and electoral structure predispose the country to a two-party system. Historically, two parties have dominated, and when third parties have emerged, they have either been subsumed by the dominant parties or simply disappeared when their primary issue of concern was no longer relevant.

The question of whether third parties are bad or good for American democracy dates back almost as far as the democracy itself. But the question has modern implications. Third-party candidates are often seen as spoilers who siphon off votes from the majority's top candidate and thereby enable the less-favored candidate to win. Many pundits argued that was the case in the 2010 congressional elections, when Tea Party candidates challenged Democrats and Republicans for seats in the U.S. House of Representatives and the U.S. Senate. In some races that year, critics charged that conservative Tea Party candidates who had won primaries against mainstream candidates were weaker general election candidates, and paved the way for some Democratic victories. In other races, Tea Party candidates who ran as independents may have siphoned votes from Republicans, resulting in a stronger Democratic showing. Similar arguments were made in 1992, when pundits charged Reform Party candidate H. Ross Perot with taking votes away from Republican George H. W. Bush and thus ushering Democrat Bill Clinton into the White House.

Do third-party candidacies hurt American democracy by skewing elections away from the third party's major party rival? Or are they good for democracy because they bring out voters who would otherwise have stayed at home and because they help ensure that issues of crucial concern to the electorate get on the national agenda?

Yes: The presence of third-party candidates on a ballot means that the major political party—Democratic or Republican—that is closest to the third party in ideology and in base of support will be hurt. This effect occurs because if the third-party candidate were not on the ballot, many of his or her supporters would vote for the candidate (Democratic or Republican) who is ideologically closest to the third-party candidate. Thus, that major party candidate is at a disadvantage, because the third-party candidate essentially siphons off or splits the vote for the major party candidate. Democ-

racy is subverted, because often a candidate wins who is least appealing to the majority of voters (that is, those who voted for the losing major party candidate and those who voted for the third-party candidate). As a result, people are highly dissatisfied with both the political process and elected officials.

No: Only through third parties and third-party candidacies can voters get the national agenda they desire. In 2010, many citizens wanted issues such as labor law reform and corporate crime to be priorities on the federal policy agenda. Other citizens wanted serious national attention given to tort reform, the elimination of most social welfare benefits, and flat taxes. These issues were not part of the national policy debate between the two major political parties. Without third parties to spearhead such conversations of democracy, many more people will be turned off by and disaffected from the political process.

Other approaches: Third parties are a mixed blessing for the United States. Proponents of third parties are correct in asserting that they provide a safety valve for participation by those dissatisfied with the status quo. Third parties have been effective at getting specific policy concerns on the national agenda, even though frequently that has occurred because one of the major parties co-opts a third party's key issue. But supporters of third parties should realize that the electoral politics in the United States is structured to ensure the perpetuation of the two-party system, and that by supporting a third party candidate, they run the risk of spoiling the chances of their preferred major party candidate.

What do you think?

① Do you think third parties help or hurt American democracy? Why?

② What was the impact of third-party candidates in the 2010 election?

③ What kind of third party do you think would be successful in winning elections?

---

concern, sometimes government officials respond to that concern even if the third party fails in its election bid. In some such cases, the issue has not previously been given priority, and the attention the third party draws to it serves to create a groundswell of political pressure that forces action. In other cases, the policy makers might act to address the issue in order to woo the supporters of the third party who have expressed that particular issue concern.

Historically, the two major parties' co-option of issues that were first promoted by third parties has sometimes contributed to the demise of third parties. For example, as we have seen, the Progressives' presidential candidate, Theodore Roosevelt, lost to Democrat Woodrow Wilson in 1912, but Wilson enacted many elements of the Progressive Party's platform, including antitrust regulations, corporate law reforms, and banking regulations. Lacking a unique platform, and with comparatively little electoral success, the Progressives faded away. More recently, Reform Party candidate H. Ross Perot's activism concerning campaign finance reform eventually led the two major parties to pass the Bipartisan Campaign Finance Reform Act of 2002. The Reform Party's inability to sustain voter support over the long haul is also apparent: after the party's 2000 presidential nominee Pat Buchanan failed to net even 1 percent of the national vote, the party did not nominate a candidate in 2004, instead backing Green Party nominee Ralph Nader.

Tea Party movement
a grassroots, conservative protest movement that opposed recent government actions, including economic stimulus spending and health care reform

New Ideologies, New Technologies: The Parties in the Twenty-First Century

American political parties have changed dramatically in recent years. Global events such as the end of the Cold War, international and domestic terrorism, and the impact of the Internet have partly driven the changes. Within the Republican and Democratic parties, the changes have reflected an ideological shift from an era when a party's defining position was its position on social welfare policy, to a time when foreign policy issues were central, and back again. Today, much emphasis is placed on the differences between the Democrats and the Republicans, but for many citizens there are shades of "purple" between the reds and the blues (see Figure 8.7).

Struggling for the Heart of the Republican Party: Moderates, Neocons, and a Tea Party Movement

In the wake of the inauguration of Barack Obama in January 2009, a grassroots movement began growing in communities across the United States. Outraged by what they saw as excessive spending by the administration and the Democrats in Congress, and particularly incensed during the debates concerning health care reform, conservative activists formed the **Tea Party movement,** a grassroots, conservative protest movement that opposed recent government actions, including economic stimulus spending and health care reform. The moniker is a reference to the colonial era, when colonists dumped tea into Boston Harbor to protest taxes imposed by the British Crown, an action that contributed to the American Revolution.

Though plagued with the growing pains characteristic of virtually any large-scale political movement, Tea Partiers have identified five key principles they believe. These include

In General, Do You Believe …

	YES	NO
That government should play a more active role in ensuring individuals' well being?	☐	☐
That government should actively promote equality in the workplace through affirmative action programs?	☐	☐
That tax cuts are among the best ways to spur economic growth?	☐	☐
That the government should regulate gun ownership?	☐	☐
That U.S.-targeted international terrorism is linked to the Arab-Israeli conflict and that fighting terrorism should include furthering the peace process there?	☐	☐
That the government should promote economic growth and job creation through tax and wage policies that promote domestic job growth and increase workers' salaries?	☐	☐
That marriage should be defined as a heterosexual union?	☐	☐
That women should have the right to an abortion?	☐	☐
That the government should promote economic growth and job creation with tax, legal, and labor policies that businesses advocate?	☐	☐
That the government should aggressively protect the environment, even if it means more government regulations for industries?	☐	☐

FIGURE 8.7

Are You Red, Blue, or Purple? News commentators use *red* and *blue* to refer to Republicans and Democrats, respectively. Although the basis for an individual's political ideology is complex (see Chapter 1), party identification in the United States often reflects differences in viewpoint on several key issues. Do you know what each party stands for? Do you know which party best represents your views? Take this brief quiz to find out which party you lean toward. Of course, before voting for candidates of that party or even counting yourself as a party identifier, you should further investigate the positions of the parties. The Web sites listed at the end of the chapter are a good place to start.

- less government
- fiscal responsibility
- lower taxes
- states' rights
- national security

Activism centering on these principles has involved a variety of tactics. Some, such as the formation of a political action committee that contributes donations to endorsed candidates who espouse the Tea Party's views, are standard for such movements. But other strategies have proven more controversial: the first candidate endorsed by the Tea Party movement was Florida Republican Marco Rubio, who challenged Florida's Republican governor, Charlie Crist, for the GOP nomination for the U.S. Senate. Faced with Rubio's strong challenge and eventually trailing in the polls, Crist effectively conceded the nomination to Rubio and announced his intention to run for the Senate as an Independent candidate.

In another controversial maneuver, a New Jersey branch of the Tea Party movement sued to recall U.S. Senator Robert Menendez because of his support of government-sponsored health care. The lawsuit had national significance because of the Tea Party movement's argument that state election law (which provided for the recall of state elected officials) applied to federal elected officials, including members of the U.S. House and Senate.

Many view the Tea Party as a splinter party, in part a backlash against the neoconservative faction of the Republican party that dominated party politics during the Bush administration. Neoconservatives are less concerned with domestic issues but are frequently defined (and distinguished from other conservatives) by their aggressive foreign policy stance, particularly in defense of Israel.[46] Neoconservatives also advocate for the proactive spread of democracy.

Democrats Today

The Democratic Party today—the party of Barack Obama—is a markedly different party from the Democratic Party President Bill Clinton molded and shaped in the 1990s. When it comes to issues and policy priorities, today's Democrats, under Obama's leadership, more resemble the Democrats of the mid-twentieth century: a party that emphasized a strong role of government. In particular, today's Democrats emphasize the need for government to provide a safety net for its most disadvantaged citizens, particularly during tough economic times. President Obama's priority of reforming health care and his desire to include a public option demonstrates the Democrats' comfort with expanding the role of the federal government. This is contrasted with Democrats during the Clinton era, sometimes called New Democrats, who were less likely to emphasize government solutions to problems, and who, during a healthy economic era, recognized that *globalization*—the continuing integration of world markets for goods, services, and financial capital—was the most significant factor in framing public policy problems and their solutions

But coupled with the Democratic Party's emphasis today on its traditional values, there also is an emphasis and a sophistication when it comes to maximizing the use of new technologies in politics. Indeed, part of President Obama's success has stemmed from the savvy use of technology—from relying on Facebook to mobilize student primary voters in early primary states in 2008 to raising millions online for his general election campaign. And so while the values of today's Democrats resemble those of Presidents Franklin Roosevelt and Lyndon Johnson more closely than those of Bill Clinton, the means by which these values and priorities are communicated is decidedly modern and technologically sophisticated.

Changing Both Parties: New Technologies

The ways in which party members and voters give and get information, as well as the methods by which parties campaign, have changed drastically in recent years. More and more people in the electorate are finding information about issues on the Internet and via their cell phones. For their part, the parties are increasingly using new technologies as tools for reaching loyalists and communicating with potential supporters. Take, for example, the way the president now communicates with the electorate. Using a medium unheard of only a decade ago, President Obama regularly relies on YouTube (his channel is http://www.youtube.com/user/BarackObamadotcom) not just as a means of disseminating information but also as a two-way tool of communicating with Americans. And throughout the 2010 congressional elections, we have seen an ever-expanding use of technology by candidates who tweet supporters, ooVoo their staff, text volunteers, organize through Facebook, and raise money online.

> Twitter offers candidates another means of communicating with their supporters and potential voters. While private individuals use Twitter to send micro-messages about their everyday lives ("standing in line @ bookstore behind a guy named Buster"), candidates can tweet about the everyday lives of their campaigns ("just got Rev. Buster's endorsement").

During the 2008 campaign, both the McCain and the Obama campaigns used their Web sites to plug their supporters into assorted outlets for their interest and activism. Both offered downloadable apps that allowed supporters to link their social-networking pages and to raise funds by linking the campaign site to their own Web sites. Both also hosted a wide variety of ways for individuals to stay connected to the campaigns, including listing candidates' favorites on del.icio.us, links to campaign videos on YouTube and to Facebook and MySpace pages, a Twitter micro-blog through which the campaign sent short, updated communications to instant messaging and e-mail accounts and to the Twitter Web site, and campaign photos available at the flickr Web site.

The Internet has also democratized the party process. Partisan activism is no longer limited to individuals who can attend meetings. Whole new forms of Internet activism have emerged. People with access to the Internet can chat, organize, plan, lobby, raise funds, contribute, and mobilize without leaving their desks.

Today, each party relies heavily on the Internet for communicating with supporters, as, for example, the Democratic Party's blog "Kicking Ass" and the Republican Party's activist arm, "The Digital Brigade," reveal. Each party's Web site gives visitors information and plenty of opportunities to volunteer. Moreover, adopting a strategy first employed by individual candidates, parties are also using the Internet as a fund-raising tool: they solicit contributions via special e-mail accounts and on party Web sites and accept donations through online credit card payments. At the end of this chapter, you will find URLs for the Web sites of the Democratic National Committee, the Republican National Committee, and a nonpartisan organization, where you can explore your own opportunities for Internet activism.

CONCLUSION

THINKING CRITICALLY ABOUT WHAT'S NEXT IN AMERICAN POLITICAL PARTIES

Despite the cynicism with which people often view them, political parties are a vital institution for the civic engagement of Americans and are essential to democracy. For many citizens, political parties are the gateway to political participation. For others, they provide cues that guide decisions at the ballot box. The role of parties in teaching individuals essential skills that may lead to elective office, in recruiting candidates, in contesting elections, and in governing—all these valuable functions often do not get the recognition they deserve.

The two major U.S. political parties have demonstrated enormous adaptability over time. The ability to change in response to constituent demands is a consistent trait of these two dominant parties. The cultural and structural forces that perpetuate the two-party system show little sign of relenting. And although groups such as the Tea Party movement and third parties such as the Green Party provide rich fodder for political pundits who speculate about their importance, in electoral terms third parties have demonstrated very little ability to win elections. Instead, third parties commonly advocate issues that eventually are co-opted by one or both of the major parties, and they sometimes play the role of spoiler in elections. What issues advocated by the Tea Party movement were incorporated into the major party stances in the 2010 elections?

In the future, the parties will be challenged to adapt. In particular, they will need to adjust continually to new circumstances, as technology changes how the party organizations identify, organize, mobilize, and communicate with the party in the electorate, as well as how the party in government governs. The contemporary faces of the two major parties demonstrate their continuing evolution and responsiveness to their identifiers and constituents.

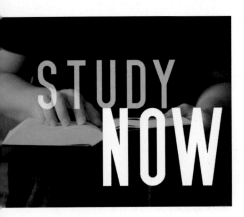

Summary

1. Parties Today and Their Functions

Political parties run candidates in elections in an effort to control government. They advance the cause of civic engagement by facilitating citizens' participation, providing unity and cohesiveness, encouraging civic discourse, and communicating important cues to voters.

2. The Three Faces of Parties

Three spheres of operation of parties are the party in the electorate (the individuals who tend to support a particular party), the party organization (the formal party apparatus), and the party in government (the partisan identification of elected leaders).

3. Political Parties in U.S. History

Political scientists have identified five U.S. party systems. Stretching back to the eighteenth century, these systems describe the evolution of party competition and dominance. Through these party systems, we see the ideological roots and political foundations of the two dominant political parties today.

4. Two-Party Domination in U.S. Politics

Explanations of why two political parties dominate include the ideas that parties reflect the dualist nature of conflict in the United States; that the winner-take-all election system creates a two-party structure; that people are socialized to the two-party system; and that election laws strengthen and perpetuate that structure.

5. The Two-Party System Today: In Decline or in Resurgence?

Some political scientists argue that recent times show a decline in the influence of the two major U.S. parties. As factors, they cite waning constituent loyalty to parties, caused by decreases in patronage, and the advent of direct primaries and candidate-centered campaigns. Other scholars assert that parties are rebounding, and they note parties' adaptability, as well as the lack of viable alternatives to the two major parties.

6. Third Parties in the United States

Third parties, which include issue advocacy parties, ideologically oriented parties, and splinter parties, sometimes act as a spoiler for one of the two major parties. Although third-party candidates typically lose elections, they do succeed in getting various issues on the national agenda.

7. New Ideologies, New Technologies: The Parties in the Twenty-First Century

Neoconservatives and Tea Party activists are important factions within the Republican Party. Whereas neocons are less concerned than traditional Republicans with constraining governmental involvement in domestic policy, Tea Party activists emphasize a staunchly conservative stance on domestic issues. New Democrats shy away from the traditional liberal advocacy of government as the chief solution to social problems and focus on globalization as a determining factor shaping public policy dilemmas and their solutions.

Key Terms

For Review

1. What functions do political parties perform? How do these functions encourage the civic engagement of Americans?

2. What are the three faces of political parties?

3. Explain the development of the five party systems in U.S. history. Why, historically, does the majority change from one party to another?

4. Why do two parties dominate in politics and government in the United States?

5. What are the arguments that political parties are in decline? What do opponents of these arguments contend?

6. What has been the impact of third parties in recent elections?

7. Describe the political philosophy of the neoconservatives, the Tea Party movement, and the New Democrats. How do these factions represent new ways of thinking about politics?

For Critical Thinking and Discussion

1. How were you socialized to the two-party system? Do your views reflect your parents' views? Were third parties even mentioned in your house when you were growing up?

2. What factors explain the demographic bases of the two major parties? How could each party expand its base of support?

3. What impact do you think the neoconservatives, the Tea Party activists, and the New Democrats will have on the two major parties over time? Why?

4. What evidence is there that a new party system is emerging? Do the 2010 election results support the claim that a new party system is taking shape?

5. In what ways beyond those discussed in the chapter might the Internet and other new technologies be used as means of communication between voters and parties? In your view, what are the most important uses for new technologies in partisan politics?

MULTIPLE CHOICE: Choose the lettered item that answers the question correctly.

1. The formal statement of a party's principles and policy objectives is called a
   a. policy memo.
   b. policy manifesto.
   c. platform.
   d. mission statement.

2. Individuals who identify with or tend to support a party are called the
   a. the party in the electorate.
   b. the party organization.
   c. the party in government.
   d. responsible party members.

3. The formal party apparatus, including committees, party leaders, conventions and workers, is called
   a. the party in the electorate.
   b. the party organization.
   c. the party in government.
   d. responsible party members.

4. The situation that exists when Congress is controlled by one party and the presidency by the other is called
   a. party disorganization.
   b. bipartisan camaraderie.
   c. divided government.
   d. executive/legislative split.

5. A philosophy supporting the rights and empowerment of the masses as opposed to elites is called
   a. neoconservatism.   c. New Deal philosophy.
   b. conservatism.   d. populism.

6. A significant shift in party allegiances or electoral support is called
   a. populism.   c. realignment.
   b. dealigment.   d. disalignment.

7. Franklin Roosevelt's broad social welfare program in which the government would bear the responsibility of providing a "safety net" to protect the weakest members of society was called
   a. the New Deal.   c. the War on Poverty.
   b. the Grand Formula.   d. the Social Contract.

8. The situation in which voters vote for candidates from more than one party is called
   a. populism.
   b. dealigment.
   c. realignment.
   d. ticket splitting.

9. An election structure in which political parties win the number of parliamentary seats equal to the percentage of the vote the party receives is called
   a. a first-past-the-post system.
   b. a winner-take-all system.
   c. a proportional representation system.
   d. a two-party system.

10. An election in which voters choose the party's candidates who will run in the later general election is called a
   a. primary election.
   b. recall election.
   c. general election.
   d. referendum election.

FILL IN THE BLANKS.

11. A new, grassroots, conservative protest movement that opposed recent government actions, including economic stimulus spending and health care reform, is called the _____ .

12. Political scientists' view that a function of a party is to offer a clear choice to voters by establishing priorities or policy stances that differ from those of rival parties is called the _____ .

13. The role that the party out of power plays, highlighting its objections to policies and priorities of the government in power, is called the _____ .

14. Organizations that candidates form to support their individual election are called _____ .

15. A campaign in which an individual seeking election, rather than an entire party slate, is the focus in a _____ .

Answers: 1. c; 2. a; 3. b; 4. c; 5. d; 6. c; 7. a; 8. d; 9. c; 10. a; 11. Tea Party movement; 12. responsible party model; 13. loyal opposition; 14. candidate committees; 15. candidate-centered campaign.

Internet Resources

Democratic National Committee
www.democrats.org The Democrats' Web site contains hotlinks for state and local party Web sites and opportunities for volunteering, internships, and employment, as well as party position papers and platforms and candidate information.

Project Vote Smart
www.vote-smart.org This nonpartisan site provides independent, factual information on candidates and elected officials of all political parties.

Republican National Committee
www.gop.com The Republicans' site also has links for state and local party sites and opportunities for volunteering, internships, and employment, as well as party position papers and platforms and candidate information.

The American Presidency Project
www.presidency.ucsb.edu/platforms.php The American Presidency Project Web site at the University of California Santa Barbara provides the party platforms of every party whose presidential candidate received electoral votes.

Internet Activism

The path to becoming a party activist begins on the Internet. Use Figure 8.7 on page 265 to help you determine your own party beliefs. Then, plan on attending a party county committee meeting. If you are a Democrat, go to www.democrats.org, click on "local," and enter your zip code. If you are a Republican go to www.gop.com, click on "our GOP," then click on "states." Enter your state in the "Search community" box and then "view state." If you are interested in volunteering for party activities, be certain to introduce yourself to the party chair and let him or her know that you would like to volunteer.

Recommended Readings

Berlatsky, Noah. *Does the U.S. Two-party System Still Work?* Belmont, CA: Greenhaven Press, 2010. Part of the "At Issue" series, this work examines the effectiveness of the U.S. party system.

Flammang, Janet. *Women's Political Voice.* Philadelphia: Temple University Press, 1997. A well-researched account of women's political participation in general and women's participation in political parties in particular.

Hershey, Marjorie Random. *Party Politics in America,* 14th ed. New York: Longman, 2010. A classic work on American political parties, analyzing the changing roles of parties in the twentieth century and the impact of the campaign finance system on political parties.

Lijphart, Arend. *Electoral Systems and Party Systems: A Study of Twenty-Seven Democracies 1945–1990.* New York: Oxford University Press, 1994. An exploration of the nature of party systems in many industrialized democracies both historically and in modern times.

Pimlott, Jamie Pamelia. *Women and the Democratic Party: The Evolution of EMILY's List.* Amherst, NY: Cambria Press, 2010. This work consists of both descriptive and quantitative analysis of the growth and impact of EMILY's List, the leading fund-raising organization that supports Democratic women candidates.

Rohde, David W. *Parties and Leaders in the Postreform House.* Chicago: University of Chicago Press, 1991. Analyzes the reasons behind the realignment and resurgence of partisanship in Congress during the 1980s.

Schattschneider, E. E. *Party Government.* New York: Rinehart, 1942. A classic work that explains the nature of political parties and their impact on party government.

Movies of Interest

Primary Colors (1998)
Starring John Travolta, and based on the anonymously written book of the same name, this popular movie—a fictionalized account of Bill Clinton's 1992 campaign—provides insight into the primary election season of a presidential nominee.

City Hall (1996)
This film starring Al Pacino and John Cusack shows the workings of a corrupt political machine—and the consequences of that corruption.

Elections, Campaigns, and Voting

THEN

Political party–dominated campaigns and grassroots activism were deciding factors in how people voted.

NOW

Candidate-centered campaigns rely on paid professionals to shape and spin candidates' messages—and on costly media buys to disseminate it.

NEXT

How will new technologies drive and change campaigns?

How will changes in the campaign finance structure affect how campaigns are conducted?

What new faces and voices will determine the campaign environment?

politics, their first thought is often about elections, campaigns, and voting. In the eyes of many of us, these activities are the essence of political participation, because it is through the electoral process that we feel we participate most directly and meaningfully in our democracy. Often viewed as the pinnacle of the democratic experience, the act of voting is the culmination of a wide range of forms of political engagement. In the discussion that follows, we see the interconnectedness of many aspects of political campaigns and elections, including fund-raising, **grassroots organizing,** candidate selection, and voter mobilization. These opportunities for civic participation in the democratic process are present in such a broad variety of forms that they are accessible to everyone who wants to be engaged.

In this chapter, we explore opportunities for—and the value of—citizens' participation in electoral politics; the processes of voting and running for office; and the elements of modern campaigns and elections. We also analyze the factors that determine whether an individual will vote, how voters decide among candidates, and why some people do not vote.

FIRST, we examine *political participation* in the electoral process.

SECOND, we consider the various kinds of *elections in the United States.*

THIRD, we focus on *the act of voting* and the impact that the type of ballot used can have on election outcomes.

FOURTH, we examine the requirements of *running for office* and making *the choice to run.*

FIFTH, we look at *the nature of political campaigns today,* paying particular attention to campaigns' extensive use of professional consultants and deep reliance on electronic media and the Internet.

SIXTH, we survey legislators' efforts at *regulating federal campaign contributions.*

SEVENTH, we probe the long duration and various stages of *presidential campaigns.*

EIGHTH, we look at *who votes*—the factors influencing voter participation.

NINTH, we delve into the question of *how voters decide* on the candidates whom they will endorse at the ballot box.

TENTH, we investigate the many reasons *why some people do not vote,* including factors such as lack of efficacy, voter fatigue, and negative campaigns.

grassroots organizing
tasks that involve direct contact with voters or potential voters.

Political Participation:
Engaging Individuals, Shaping Politics

Elections, campaigns, and voting are fundamental aspects of the civic engagement of Americans and people in other democracies. These activities represent concentrated forms of civic engagement and are important both for the polity as a whole and for the individuals who participate.[1] But intensive political engagement—working on a campaign or running for office, say—rarely represents an individual's first foray into a civically engaged life. Rather, people who are engaged in the political process usually are initiated through smaller, less intensive steps. Perhaps a group of classmates who especially enjoy the political discussions in your American government class might continue their conversations of democracy over a cup of Starbucks after class. Those same classmates might begin regularly reading political blogs and daily newspapers to become better informed about candidates and issues. Some members of the informal group might decide to hear a candidate who is giving a speech on campus—and wind up volunteering on his or her campaign. Political engagement often begins with small steps such as those, but the cumulative results are large: they help to ensure that the government is representative of the people and responsive to their needs. Representative governments, which are the product of individuals' political engagement, tend to be more stable and to make decisions that best reflect the needs and the will of the people who elect them.

Direct forms of political participation such as voting, volunteering on a campaign, and running for office are of keen interest to scholars of civic engagement. Many scholarly analysts have noticed an overall decrease in levels of political participation. As discussed in Chapter 7, political scientist Robert Putnam argues that the United States is seeing a decline in its social capital, the social networks and reciprocal relationships characteristic of a community or a society. These networks are varied and include formal organizations such as clubs, fraternities, sororities, interest groups, and sports teams. But there are also informal networks, such as babysitting co-ops, car pools, and study groups. Putnam details how solitary pursuits such as watching television and using a computer have pervasively replaced group activities related to civic participation.

Some scholars have challenged Putnam's assertion that social capital has declined. They point out that new forms of social capital have arisen in the form of Internet social networks, instant messaging, and Internet activism to replace the traditional social networks that Putnam studied. Despite these differing views, there is consensus that civic participation is essential and that among its most important forms is electoral political participation.

Indeed, elections offer a wealth of opportunities for citizen involvement:

- Members of political parties recruit candidates to run for election.
- Cadres of volunteers organize campaign events, including fund-raisers, rallies, and neighborhood leafleting.
- Phone bank volunteers try to persuade other people to participate in the electoral process—for instance, by giving a campaign contribution, putting a candidate's sign on their lawn, or simply voting for the candidate.
- Other volunteers focus exclusively on **GOTV**—that is, they work to get out the vote. They register voters for both primary and general elections, and they provide absentee ballots to people who are ill or who will be out of town on election day. On Election Day itself, they remind people to vote by phoning them or knocking on their door and asking if they need a ride to the polls.[2]
- Others (who may be paid) volunteer to work at the polls on election day.

Although each volunteer effort plays a part in ensuring the success of a democracy, a key form of political participation is running for office. Electoral contests in which more than one candidate seeks to win office are a fundamental component of a democracy.

> Are more people really "Bowling Alone"? Political scientist Robert Putnam has argued that the United States is experiencing a decline in social capital because its citizens are participating less in civic life. But perhaps Americans are engaged in civic life in very different ways from those of previous generations. Here, a group of Wii bowling enthusiasts compete in a friendly match in an Illinois restaurant.

Elections in the United States

Every state holds at least two types of elections. A *primary election* comes first and determines the party's nominees—those who will run for office. For most political offices, there is little or no competition in the primary election. But in presidential and gubernatorial primary elections, vigorous contention is often the rule, particularly within the out-of-power party. House and Senate primary elections that lack an incumbent candidate (that is, one who has been elected to that office before) are also often highly competitive as many candidates attempt to win their party's nomination.

In a **general election,** the parties' respective nominees run against each other, and voters decide who should hold office, since the person with the most votes wins. (Presidential elections, discussed later in this chapter, are a notable exception.) The degree of competition in general elections depends on a number of factors, including the presence of and the strength of incumbency, the degree of party competition, and the level of the office. In recent times, presidential elections have been brutally competitive, as have been certain gubernatorial races and many congressional contests where no incumbent is seeking reelection. Some communities, particularly big cities, may also experience intense competition for office in general elections.

GOTV
get out the vote

general election
an election that determines which candidates win the offices being sought

Nominations and Primary Elections

In a primary election, voters decide which nominees the political parties should run in the general election. But *which* voters decide varies greatly from state to state. In some states, only registered party members are eligible to vote in primary elections, whereas in other states, any registered voter can vote in any party's primary, and in North Dakota, voters are not even required to register.

In U.S. presidential primaries, voters do not vote directly for the candidate whom they would like their party to nominate. Instead, the popular vote determines which candidate's delegates will attend the party's nominating convention and vote for that party's nominee.

> Chicago police restrained protesters during the 1968 Democratic National Convention by using tear gas, among other methods. As a result of the riots during this convention, sparked by dissatisfaction over the selection of Hubert Humphrey as the nominee by party insiders, the two major U.S. parties made major reforms to the delegate-selection process.

caucus
meeting of party members held to select delegates to the national convention

open primary
a type of primary in which both parties' ballots are available in the voting booth, and voters select one on which to register their preferences

closed primary
a type of primary in which voting in a party's primary is limited to members of that party

Super Tuesday
the Tuesday in early March on which the most primary elections were held, many of them in southern states; provided the basis for Super-Duper Tuesday in 2008

This system of selecting delegates through primary voting is different from the earlier system, when party leaders selected the presidential nominee with little or no input from the rank-and-file party members.

The two major U.S. parties made reforms to the earlier delegate selection process after the 1968 Democratic National Convention in Chicago. Anti-Vietnam War activists outside the convention protested the presumed nomination of Vice President Hubert Humphrey as the Democratic Party's presidential candidate. Humphrey had not won any primaries but was favored among the convention's delegates who had been hand-picked by party leaders. The activists instead supported the candidacy of Senator Eugene McCarthy (D-Minnesota), an outspoken war opponent. The demonstrations turned into riots when Chicago police beat the protesters. The Democratic National Committee, in an attempt to address the concerns of those complaining that they had been excluded from the nomination process, appointed the McGovern-Fraser Commission (named after its cochairs), which recommended a series of reforms to the delegate-selection process.

The reforms, many of which both the Democratic Party and the Republican Party adopted, significantly increased the influence of party voters. Voters could now select delegates to the national conventions, a power previously restricted to the party elite. Party voters today select the delegates at statewide conventions or through primary elections or **caucuses**—meetings of party members held to select delegates to the national convention. The reforms also included provisions that would ensure the selection of a more representative body of delegates, with certain delegate slots set aside for women, minorities, union members, and young party voters. These slots roughly correspond with the proportion of support the party receives from those groups.

When an individual is elected to be a delegate at the national convention, often that delegate has pledged to vote for a specific candidate. That pledge is nonbinding, however, since delegates of a losing candidate often switch their support to the apparent victor.

TYPES OF PRIMARY ELECTIONS In an **open primary** election, any registered voter can vote in any party's primary, as can independent voters not registered with a party. In an open primary, parties' ballots are available in the voting booth, and the voter simply selects privately or publicly one on which to register his or her preferences.

In a **closed primary** election, voting in a party's primary is limited to members of that party. In some states, voters must declare their party affiliation well in advance of the primary election—sometimes as many as sixty days before. In other states, voters can declare their party preference at the polling place on the day of the election. Such restrictions on who can vote in a party's primary originated in the parties' maneuvering to have the strongest candidate nominated. For example, if a popular incumbent president were running unopposed in a primary election, members of the president's party might choose to vote in the other party's primary as a way of scheming to get a weak candidate nominated. A closed primary aims to thwart that strategy.

PRESIDENTIAL PRIMARIES The states determine the timing of primary elections. Historically, states that held their presidential primary earlier in the year had a greater say in determining the nominee than did states with later primaries. The reason is that candidates tended to drop out if they did not win primaries, did not meet media expectations, or ran out of funds. (See "Thinking Critically About Democracy.") In general, past presidential primaries gave great sway to the agricultural states, because many of the more urban states' primaries fell later in the season.

All of that changed in 2007 when, in an attempt to increase their political clout, a number of diverse states banded together to hold their primaries on the same day so that presidential candidates would be forced to address issues of the keenest interest to those states. These states modeled their objective on **Super Tuesday,** the day in early March on which the most presidential primary elections took place, many of them in southern states. Super Tuesday had been the fruit of a successful effort in 1988 by several southern and rural

THINKING CRITICALLY ABOUT DEMOCRACY

SHOULD THE UNITED STATES HAVE A NATIONAL PRIMARY?

The Issue: The party primary process that selects each party's nominee for president was a hot-button issue in the 2008 presidential race. Historically, the primary system focused enormous attention on the states of Iowa, where the first caucus is held, and New Hampshire, where the first party primary takes place. In these states, voters have had the opportunity to gain a deep familiarity with all the candidates seeking the parties' nominations. But critics of the system have charged that these two states' political culture does not reflect the vast majority of Americans. As a result, many of the most populous states moved their primaries to the earliest day allowed by the political parties—in 2008, that day was February 5. Other states, including Pennsylvania, Texas, West Virginia, and Kentucky, held off having their primaries, in the hopes that one state could find itself in the position of kingmaker by bringing one of the party candidates over the top in the needed delegate count. Given this structure, many citizens have asked, "Is this any way to begin electing a president?"

Should states matter when it comes to selecting the parties' nominees? One potential solution to the skewed emphasis on various states is to hold a national primary so that party members throughout the country can choose their nominees on the same day. People have voiced arguments for and against the idea of a national primary.

Yes: Having a national primary will help the parties, because it will ensure that the nominee chosen in each case is the best candidate for the party. With the shift to a national primary, states that currently have late primaries will no longer be forced to accept a nominee chosen by party members who might be very different from themselves. Furthermore, if more people have a say in choosing their party's nominee, voter turnout might rise in both the primary and the general election. Holding a national primary also will shorten the election season, so that voters will be less fatigued by the length of the campaign.

No: The primary system ensures that small, agricultural states have a voice in national politics. In the general election, smaller states are overshadowed because the Electoral College, which is based on state population, determines the winner. The current primary and caucus system enables voters in those states to analyze the candidates thoroughly, without the noise and distraction that would come with a large-scale, media-saturated national primary. And because the voters in states such as Iowa and New Hampshire are, after all, party members, they naturally understand that a large part of their responsibility is to select the nominee best equipped to win the general election.

Other approaches: Some have suggested the idea of holding regional primaries instead of one national primary, with a different region holding its primary election first in each presidential election year so that no region would have the influence that Iowa and New Hampshire now enjoy. Each region would include a mix of large and small states and urban and rural areas. Candidates would need to campaign throughout each region in turn rather than the entire country, thus allowing them to focus their efforts more than they would be able to with one national primary, and with three or four regional primaries, the campaign season would still be shortened significantly, thus eliminating voter fatigue.

What do you think?

① Do you believe that we should have a national primary? Explain.

② What impact would a national primary have on your home state's say in the nomination process? How will small states fare compared with large states? Rural compared with urban?

③ What impact do you think a national primary or regional primaries would have on voter turnout? What effect might either type of primary have on how presidential campaigns are waged? Would money be more or less important? Why?

---

states to hold their primaries on the same day so as to increase their political importance and allow expression of southern voters' political will.[3] But in 2007, the Super Tuesday strategy was challenged by state legislators in some of the most populous states, including California, New York, Illinois, and New Jersey, who sought to have their presidential primaries on the earliest day that national political party rules allowed. In 2008, that day, dubbed "Super-Duper Tuesday" by the media, was February 5. In all, twenty other states jumped on the early-primary bandwagon, with the result that twenty-four states held their primaries and caucuses on February 5, 2008. Under normal circumstances, such a change would have muted the impact of other primaries because the most populous states control an enormous number of delegates to the national conventions, in 2008 that was not the case. That year, the highly competitive Democratic primary between Senator Hillary Clinton (D-New York) and Senator Barack Obama (D-Illinois) meant that states such as New Mexico and Oregon (which had late primaries, in early June) were competitive and received national media coverage.

General Elections

In a general election, voters decide who should hold office from among the candidates determined in the primary election. Most general elections, including presidential elections, are held on the first Tuesday after the first Monday in November. But because the states schedule and oversee elections, you might find that your gubernatorial election, state legislative election, or town council election occurs at a different time of the year.

General elections for Congress and most state legislatures feature a **winner-take-all** system. That is, the candidate who receives the most votes wins that office (even if that total is not a majority, or even if an opponent receives only one vote fewer than the victor). Thus, a member of the U.S. House of Representatives or Senate can be elected with less than a majority of the votes in his or her district, particularly when three or more candidates are seeking that seat.

Because electoral law varies from state to state, and counties and municipalities within those states have their own structures of governance, less common kinds of elections are possible and are used in some locales. For example, some states require a runoff election when no candidate receives the majority of the votes cast. In a **runoff election,** if no candidate receives more than 50 percent of the vote, several of the top vote-getters (usually the top two) run in another, subsequent election. Typically, the field of candidates is winnowed down until one candidate receives the requisite 50 percent plus one vote. Runoff elections often occur in *nonpartisan* municipal elections where candidates do not run on a party label.

Owing to advances in technology, runoff elections can occur immediately in some states when needed. In an **instant runoff election,** a computerized voting machine simulates the elimination of last-place vote-getters. How does this system work? In an instant runoff, voters rank candidates in order of preference (first choice, second choice, and so on). If any candidate garners more than 50 percent of all the first-choice votes, that candidate wins. But if no candidate gets a majority of first-choice votes, the candidate in last place is electronically eliminated. The voting machine computer then recalculates the ballots, using the second-choice vote for those voters who voted for the eliminated last-place finisher; in effect, every voter gets to choose among the candidates remaining on the ballot. This process is repeated until a candidate who receives more than 50 percent of the votes emerges. Today's voting machines allow this process to take place instantly.

Referendum, Initiative, and Recall

Whereas primary elections and general elections select an individual to run for and serve in office, other kinds of elections are held for the purpose of deciding public policy questions. Although no national mechanism allows all Americans to vote for or against a given policy proposal, citizens can directly decide policy questions in their states by referendum or initiative.[4]

A **referendum** is an election in which voters in a state can vote for or against a measure proposed by the state legislature. Frequently, referenda concern matters such as state bond issues, state constitutional amendments, and controversial pieces of legislation. An **initiative,** sometimes called an initiative petition, is a citizen-sponsored proposal that can result in new or amended legislation or a state constitutional amendment. Initiatives differ from referenda in that they are typically propelled to public vote through the efforts of citizens and interest groups.[5] The initiative process usually requires that 10 percent of the number of the voters in the previous election in that state sign a petition agreeing that the **proposition,** or proposed measure, should be placed on the ballot. An example of an initiative is California's Proposition 8, also called the California Marriage Protection Act, which passed

winner-take-all
an electoral system in which the candidate who receives the most votes wins that office, even if that total is not a majority.

runoff election
a follow-up election held when no candidate receives the majority of votes cast in the original election

instant runoff election
a special runoff election in which the computerized voting machine simulates the elimination of last-place vote-getters

referendum
an election in which voters in a state can vote for or against a measure proposed by the state legislature

initiative
a citizen-sponsored proposal that can result in new or amended legislation or a state constitutional amendment

proposition
a proposed measure placed on the ballot in an initiative election

with a majority of votes in the November 2008 state elections. Prop. 8 amended California's state constitution to read "Only a marriage between a man and a woman is valid or recognized in California." As a state constitutional amendment, Prop. 8 had the effect of overturning the California Supreme Court decision stating that same-sex couples have the right to marry. That decision had nullified a previous initiative, Proposition 22, in which a majority of voters had statutorily banned same-sex marriage. The validity of Prop. 8 was the subject of *Perry v. Schwarzenegger*.[6]

A third type of special election, the recall, differs from referenda and initiatives in that it is not concerned with policy-related issues. Rather, the **recall** election allows voters to cut an officeholder's term of office short. Recall elections are typically citizen-sponsored efforts that demonstrate serious dissatisfaction with a particular officeholder. Concerned citizens circulate a petition, and after they gather the required number of signatures, an election is held to determine whether the official should be thrown out of office. In 2010, a federal district court decided that Prop. 8 violated the Due Process and Equal Protection clauses of the Foureenth Amendment. The decision has been stayed pending an appeal to the U.S. Supreme Court.

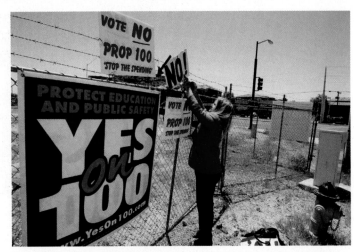

> A proposition is a question placed on a ballot for voters' approval. Arizona's Proposition 100 proposed to increase the state sales tax from 5.6 cents on the dollar to 6.6 cents, for a temporary three years, to raise a projected $1 billion annually. It won passage in May, 2010.

The Act of Voting

The process of voting begins when a voter registers to vote. Voting registration requirements vary greatly from state to state. Some states require registration months in advance of an election; others allow voters to register on the day of voting. In the United States, the voters use an **Australian ballot,** a secret ballot prepared by the government, distributed to all eligible voters, and, when balloting is completed, counted by government officials in an unbiased fashion, without corruption or regard to individual preferences. Because the U.S. Constitution guarantees the states the right to conduct elections, the mechanics and methods of voting vary widely from state to state. Some states use touch-screen technology; others employ computerized ballots or punch cards that are counted by computers. Still other states use traditional lever ballots, in which voters pull a lever to register their vote for a particular candidate. Despite those differences, all ballots are secret ballots.

Although secret ballots are the norm today, that was not always the case. From the days of the early republic through the nineteenth century, many citizens exercised their right to vote using oral votes cast in public or written votes witnessed by others; some made their electoral choices on color-coded ballots prepared by the political parties, which indicated which party the voter was supporting.

recall
a special election in which voters can remove officeholders before their term is over

Australian ballot
a secret ballot prepared by the government, distributed to all eligible voters, and, when balloting is completed, counted by government officials in an unbiased fashion, without corruption or regard to individual preferences

The 2000 Election and Its Impact

In the 2000 presidential election between Democrat Al Gore and Republican George W. Bush, an enormous controversy erupted over the voting in Florida. Because of the closeness of the electoral vote, the outcome of the Florida election turned out to be pivotal. But the tallies in that state's election were in question, not only because of the narrow difference in the number of votes won by each candidate, but also because of the voting process itself. Florida citizens cast their vote on a punch card by poking through a **chad,** a ready-made perforation, near the name of their candidate of choice. Officials then counted the punch card ballots using a computer program that calculated votes by counting the absence of chads. But in the case of the 2000 election, thousands of ballots could not be read by the computer and needed to be counted by hand. This unexpected development put election officials in the difficult, and ultimately deeply controversial, position of gauging "voter intent." If a chad was hanging by one perforation only, did the voter intend to vote for that

chad
a ready-made perforation on a punch card ballot

> The problems with chads: A hanging chad . . . and a pregnant chad.

candidate? What if the chad was "pregnant" (that is, sticking out but not removed; see the photo)? What if the chad was dimpled, and the voter had cast his or her entire ballot by only dimpling the chads?

In the end, the U.S. Supreme Court had the final say. On December 12, 2000, the Court halted the hand counting of ballots in Florida, with the Court's majority ruling that the differing standards of hand counting ballots from one county to the next and the absence of a single judicial officer charged with overseeing the hand counts violated the equal protection clause of the U.S. Constitution. The ruling meant that George W. Bush, who was leading in the count, was certified the winner of the Florida race, thus securing that state's twenty-five Electoral College votes and the presidency of the United States.

Indignation surrounding the 2000 election resulted in federal policy changes to the conduct of elections by the states. The key policy revision came through the passage of the Help America Vote Act of 2002 (HAVA). HAVA allocated $650 million to assist states in changing from punch card ballots to electronic voting systems and set a deadline of 2005 for states to comply, although some states have not yet done so.

Types of Ballots

party-column ballot
a ballot that organizes the candidates by political party

There are two types of ballots most commonly used in general elections in the states today. The first, the **party-column ballot,** organizes the candidates by party, so that all of a given party's candidates for every office are arranged in one column. The opposing party's candidates appear in a different column.

The impact of a party-column ballot is twofold. First, party-column ballots increase voters' tendency to vote the "party line," that is, to vote for every candidate of a given party for every office. In fact, some states provide a party lever, which allows a voter to vote for all of a given party's candidates simply by one pull of a lever or one press of a "vote party" button. Second, because they increase the tendency to vote the party line, party-column ballots also increase the **coattail effect,** the phenomenon whereby *down-ballot candidates* (candidates who are running for lower-level offices, such as city council) benefit from the popularity of a top-of-ticket nominee. Often, the composition of city councils, county legislatures, and even state legislatures changes because of a coattail effect from a popular presidential or gubernatorial candidate. Because party-column ballots strengthen political parties, parties tend to favor this type of ballot, which is the most commonly used ballot in the United States.

coattail effect
the phenomenon by which candidates running for a lower-level office such as city council benefit in an election from the popularity of a top-of-ticket nominee

office-block ballot
a type of ballot that arranges all the candidates for a particular office under the name of that office

Another type of general election ballot is the **office-block ballot,** which arranges all candidates for a particular office under the name of that office. Office-block ballots are more likely to encourage ticket splitting, where voters "split their ticket"—that is, divide their votes—between candidates from different parties.[7] Because office-block ballots deemphasize political parties by breaking up the party line, the parties do not tend to favor them.

Why Ballot Design Matters

The 2000 presidential election voting in Florida provides evidence that not only the voting process but also the design of ballots can make a difference in outcomes. Specifically, with respect to the vote in Florida's Palm Beach County, where voters push a button on their voting machine ballot to register their vote, critics charge that the ballot in use, the *butterfly ballot* (so called because candidates are listed on two "wings" with a common "spine"), was particularly confusing to voters.

Because of the lack of ballot clarity, many Democrats complained that this ballot layout put the Gore/Lieberman ticket at a disadvantage. Although supporters of Reform Party candidate Pat Buchanan in Palm Beach County projected that he should have received at best

1,000 votes there, Buchanan received over 3,400 votes. Many people, including Buchanan himself, believed that these votes were mistakenly cast for him and intended for Al Gore.[8]

In fact, an additional 19,000 votes were nullified in the Palm Beach County election because voters cast *two* votes for president, presumably with balloters realizing too late that they had pushed the wrong button. Buchanan himself addressed this issue, saying, "If the two candidates they pushed were Buchanan and Gore, almost certainly those are Al Gore's votes and not mine. I cannot believe someone would vote for Gore and say, 'I made a mistake, I should have voted for Buchanan.' Maybe a small minority of them would have done that. But I—I've got to think that the vast majority of those [votes] would naturally belong to Al Gore and not to me."[9]

Voting by Mail

One form of voting, **absentee voting,** is a long-standing tradition by which voters cast their ballots in advance by mail when disability, illness, school, work, service in the armed forces, or travel prevents them from casting a ballot in their voting precinct. To cast an absentee ballot, an individual must typically apply (before a specific state-designated deadline) to vote by absentee in the county where he or she usually votes. The superintendent of elections then mails a ballot to the voter, who votes and then mails the ballot back. The absentee ballots are counted and added to the votes cast in the voting precincts. Requirements for absentee ballots vary from state to state. Some states require a legitimate excuse, but increasingly many states accept ballot applications simply because absentee voting is more convenient for the voter.

A relatively recent development is the advent of statewide voting by mail, a practice that states have adopted in an attempt to increase voter participation by making voting more convenient. The first experiment with statewide vote by mail occurred in Oregon in 1996. In a special election there, where officials had predicted a turnout of less than 50 percent, more than 66 percent of voters cast their ballots. This experiment brought another benefit: it saved taxpayers more than $1 million. Oregon decided to continue the practice in the 2000 presidential election, in which voter turnout hit 80 percent, and in the 2004 presidential race, where the turnout approached 85 percent. Oregon has now taken the drastic step of abandoning voting in polling places on Election Day.

There are obvious advantages to voting by mail. As Oregon's experience demonstrates, more people participate when voting becomes easier. Further, increased participation may bring to office candidates who are more representative of the will of the people because more people had a say in their election.

Some scholars, however, have criticized the vote-by-mail trend. One important criticism is that voting by mail means that people vote before the final days of the campaign, thus casting their ballot before some additional last-minute information might be revealed about a candidate. Indeed, some voters may cast their ballots before the political rivals' debates occur or before candidates fully articulate their message. Consider one case in Bainbridge Island, Washington, where it was revealed just days before the election that a candidate for mayor had padded his résumé. By the time the exaggerations came to light, some voters had already cast their ballots by mail.[10]

Voting by mail also increases the chances of vote fraud. Even though states take measures to ensure the principle of "one person, one vote," voting by mail presents opportunities for corruption. Voting at the polls requires a face-to-face encounter, but voting by mail does not, so ballots could be stolen from individuals' mailboxes or intercepted after having been mailed by a voter.

Voting by mail also may eliminate the privacy associated with voting in recent times. With mail balloting, the vote occurs in a less controlled setting, and the voter might feel pressured by others to select a particular candidate. In contrast, booth voting affords privacy and secrecy that go far toward ensuring that the votes cast behind the curtain reflect the individual voter's will.

Finally, voting by mail may undermine feelings of civic engagement by eliminating a source of psychological rewards for voters. Going to a polling place, signing the voting

absentee voting
casting a ballot in advance by mail in situations where illness, travel, or other circumstances prevent voters from voting in their precinct

registry, entering the voting booth, and casting your vote can elicit feelings of patriotism, civic pride, and fulfillment of civic responsibility: the sense that you are doing your duty to help ensure the election of the best-qualified candidates. Although the results may be the same with voting by mail, some evidence suggests that voting by mail does not bring with it the same sense of civic satisfaction that voting at a polling place confers.

Running for Office: The Choice to Run

The reasons that individuals become political candidates vary almost as much as the individuals do. Yet four types of motivation are generally in play when a person decides to declare a candidacy:

- a sense of civic responsibility—the feeling on the candidate's part that he or she bears an obligation to govern
- a sense of party loyalty—of filling the need for parties to run viable candidates
- personal goals, and in particular, interest in electoral politics and officeholding as a career
- interest in increasing the candidate's name recognition and stature in the community, often for business reasons

Some people believe they have an obligation to put their experience, knowledge, and skills to work for the greater good of the community or country. Often these civically motivated people become politically involved out of concerns about specific issues. They might object to a specific policy or want to see the government take action on a given issue. For example, Representative Carolyn McCarthy (D-New York) ran for and won a seat in the House of Representatives after her husband was killed and her son was injured in a mass shooting on the Long Island Railroad. While nursing her adult son's injuries after the senseless tragedy, McCarthy decided to run when her congressman voted to repeal a ban on assault weapons.

Sometimes an individual may choose to run for office out of a sense of party duty. The candidate may run as a "sacrificial lamb" for a seat he or she has little chance of winning, mainly with the intent to ensure that the party offers an alternative to the favored candidate. Or an elected official may decide to run for another office because he or she has the best chance at winning an election and allowing the party to attain control of that office.

Other people are motivated to run for a particular office because of personal goals. Many of these individuals seek elected office as their career. Whereas presidents and governors typically serve no more than eight years, members of Congress, state legislators, county commissioners, and council members often serve for decades. Holding office is what they do—and because of the advantages of incumbency, once elected, many remain in office for years. Other candidates run for office because of political ambitions: a town council member who aspires to serve in the state legislature might run for county commissioner even if she thinks she will not win because she realizes that leading a viable campaign might help her in a later bid for the statehouse.

Finally, some people run for office because of the heightened stature that a candidacy brings to their "regular" careers. Lawyers may run for the state legislature, realtors for the city council, or insurance brokers for county commissioner because a candidacy makes them more successful in their daily occupations. Running for office enhances a person's name recognition so that, for example, the realtor sitting on the city council might get more business because people in the community know his name. Running for office also opens doors to networks of potential business contacts, as many candidates address civic groups and get to know people in the community. These networks can be useful in business as well as politics.

Many candidates, of course, run for office for a combination of reasons. They might believe, for example, that they have a responsibility to serve their country *and* that they have something valuable to contribute.

Formal Eligibility Requirements

Article I of the U.S. Constitution specifies some minimum criteria for those seeking election to federal office:

- President: A candidate for the presidency must be a natural-born citizen. Naturalized citizens, who are born citizens of another country and then choose to become American citizens such as Ileana Ros-Lehtinen (R-Florida), a member of the House of Representatives and a native of Cuba, cannot run for president. Presidential candidates also must be at least 35 years old. The youngest person elected president was the 43-year-old John F. Kennedy, but Theodore Roosevelt, who assumed the presidency after William McKinley's assassination, was the youngest to hold the office, at age 42. A presidential candidate also must have been a resident of the United States for fourteen years by the time of inauguration.
- Vice president: A vice-presidential candidate, like a contender for the presidency, must be a natural-born citizen and must be at least 35 years old; he or she must not be a resident of the same state as the candidate for president with whom he or she will serve. John Breckinridge, elected vice president in 1856 at age 35, was the youngest person to win the office.
- U.S. senator: A candidate for the Senate must have citizen status of at least nine years, must be at least 30 years old when taking office, and must be a resident of the state from which he or she is elected.
- U.S. representative: A candidate for the House of Representatives must be a citizen for at least seven years, must be at least 25 years old when taking office, and must be a resident of the state from which he or she is elected.

Typically, a state's constitution determines the minimal qualifications for the governorship and state legislature, and these vary from state to state. In general, state requirements address the same issues as federal guidelines—citizenship, age, and residency.

Informal Eligibility Requirements

In addition to the legal eligibility requirements prescribed by the federal and state constitutions, informal eligibility criteria—that is, the characteristics that voters expect officeholders to have—help to determine who is qualified to run for a particular office. By and large, the eligibility pool for elected office depends on the office—and so although your car mechanic might be considered a good candidate for your town council, he would not likely meet the informal eligibility criteria to be elected president of the United States.

Generally speaking, the higher and more prestigious the political office, the greater the informal eligibility requirements are. On the local level, particularly in smaller communities, an individual would be considered eligible to run for town council if he or she was liked and respected in the community, had lived in the community long enough to know the voters, and was gainfully employed, a homemaker, or retired.

Farther up the political office ladder, state legislative candidates in most states are expected to have some kind of professional career. Still, there is a great deal of variation from state to state, and certainly nonprofessionals occupy many state legislative seats. State legislatures tend to be dominated by lawyers and business professionals, occupations that offer the prestige to be considered part of the informal eligibility pool and that allow enough flexibility to facilitate campaigning and legislative work.

The informal eligibility requirements for federal office are even more stringent. Voters expect candidates for the House of

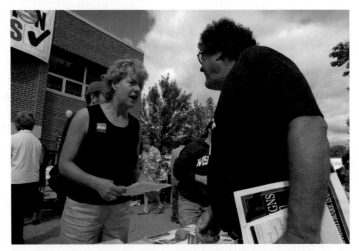

> Informal qualifications for Congress vary according to the political culture in the district. Openly gay members of Congress are a rarity. Representative Tammy Baldwin (D-Wisconsin), the only openly lesbian member of Congress, talks here with a constituent.

Representatives, the U.S. Senate, and the presidency to have higher qualifications than candidates for state and local offices. Among most congressional constituencies, candidates for federal office would be viewed as "qualified" to hold office if they had a college degree, considerable professional and leadership experience, and strong communication skills. But informal qualifications vary according to the political culture in a district, with some districts favoring a particular religious affiliation, ethnicity, or other characteristic. In races for the U.S. Senate and the presidency, the popular press examines the minutest details of candidates' professional and educational background. For example, sometimes it is not enough that candidates are college graduates; where they went to college, whose university is more prestigious, and who had the higher grade point average are all fodder for the media and political pundits.

The Nature of Political Campaigns Today

Campaigns today are different from the campaigns of the 1980s or even the early 1990s. The main reasons for the changes are the professionalization of campaign staffs, the dramatically expanded role of the media and the Internet, and candidates' ever-rising need for funding to keep pace with the unprecedented demands of contemporary campaigning.[11]

The Professionalization of Political Campaigns

One of the most significant changes in the conduct of campaigns is the rise in prominence of **campaign consultants,** paid professionals who specialize in the overall management of political campaigns or an aspect of campaigns, such as fund-raising or advertising. Previously, volunteers who believed in the party's ideals and in the candidate ran most campaigns. Although some volunteers may have been motivated by the expectation that they would personally benefit from the election of their candidate, their efforts focused largely on the election itself—of a single candidate or a slate of candidates.

In contrast, professional consultants dominate modern campaigns for federal offices, many state offices, and some municipal offices. Typically, these advisers receive generous compensation for their services. Although professional consultants may not be as dedicated to a single candidate as earlier grassroots volunteers were, these strategists are typically committed to seeing their candidate elected and often are quite partisan, usually working only for candidates of one party throughout their careers. For example, during the 2008 presidential campaign, Democratic strategist David Axelrod faced a difficult choice in deciding which potential Democratic nominee he would work for: five of the contenders for the nomination—Barack Obama, Hillary Rodham Clinton, John Edwards, Christopher Dodd, and Tom Vilsack—had been past clients of Axelrod.[12] Though he considered sitting 2008 out, Axelrod wound up working for Obama and now serves as Senior Advisor to the President. Similarly, Steve Schmidt, who managed the 2008 McCain-Palin presidential campaign, works exclusively for Republican candidates.

One of the top jobs in a political campaign is that of **campaign manager,** a professional whose duties comprise a variety of strategic and managerial tasks. Among these responsibilities may be the development of the overall **campaign strategy,** the blueprint for the campaign, which includes a budget and fund-raising plan, an advertising strategy, and staffing objectives. Once the campaign strategy is set, the campaign manager often hires and manages the office staff; selects the campaign's theme, colors, and slogan; and shapes the candidate's image. Another crucial campaign professional is the pollster, who conducts focus groups and polls that help develop the campaign strategy by identifying the candidate's strengths and weaknesses and by revealing what voters care about.

Other professionals round out the candidate's team. A **fund-raising consultant** works with the candidate to identify likely contributors and arranges fund-raising events and meetings with donors. Policy directors and public relations consultants help to develop the candidate's stance on crucial issues and to get the candidate's positions out to the voters, and a **media consultant** brings the campaign message to voters by creating handouts and

campaign consultant
paid professional who specializes in the overall management of political campaigns or an aspect of campaigns

campaign manager
a professional whose duties comprise a variety of strategic and managerial tasks, from fund-raising to staffing a campaign

campaign strategy
blueprint for the campaign, including a budget and fund-raising plan, advertising strategy, and staffing plan

fund-raising consultant
a professional who works with candidates to identify likely contributors to the campaign and arrange events and meetings with donors

media consultant
a professional who brings the campaign message to voters by creating handouts and all forms of media ads

brochures, as well as newspaper, radio, and television promotions. Media consultants rely increasingly on the Internet to bring the campaign to voters through e-mail campaigns, Web-based advertising, blogs, and message boards.[13]

Media and New Technologies: Transforming Political Campaigns

Today, with the presence everywhere of the media in all its forms—television, Internet news sites, blogs, Twitter, radio, podcasts, newspapers, magazines—citizens' access to information is unprecedented. Whereas our ancestors had far fewer sources of news—word of mouth and the printed newspaper dominated for most of American history—people today can choose from a wide range of information sources and a bounty of information. Today, twenty-four-hour news channels such as CNN and MSNBC compete with the Internet news outlets, satellite radio programming, and news text messages to grab audience attention. But not all of this bombardment of information is accurate.

Given the abundance of information disseminated today, and in light of its diverse and sometimes questionable sources, engaged citizens have a greater responsibility to be discerning consumers of the news, including coverage of campaigns, voting, and elections. They cannot be passive listeners and spoon-fed watchers of news as it is dished out by daily newspapers, nightly newscasts, and the occasional weekly or monthly periodical. Vivé Griffith at the University of Texas at Austin's Think Democracy Project writes, "The challenge for the contemporary citizen is to be more than an audience member. Voters have unprecedented opportunities to access information and, at the same time, myriad ways to see issues obscured. An informed polity is essential to a democracy, and it can be difficult to sort through whether our media-saturated world ultimately serves to make us more or less informed."[14] We consider media coverage of elections, campaigns, and voting in detail in Chapter 10.

PERSONALITY VERSUS POLICY In sorting through the abundance of "news," citizens must also contend with changes in how information is presented by the media. When news was less available, that is, when TV networks aired a single fifteen-minute nightly news broadcast, the content tended to be policy-oriented and hard-hitting. Today, networks have much more time to fill: in addition to their nightly thirty-minute news broadcasts, most metropolitan areas have an hour and a half of local news in the evening, with two additional half-hour broadcasts in the morning and at noon. This all-day banquet of news programming does not include national morning talk shows such as *Good Morning*

> Recognizing the enormous importance of the national media in helping to deliver his 2008 presidential campaign's message to voters, Republican candidate Senator John McCain (R-Arizona) talks to reporters while riding in his campaign bus, the Straight Talk Express, in New Hampshire.

How Political Campaigns Have Changed in the Past 30 Years

THEN (1980s)	NOW (2011)
Many campaigns were managed and staffed by volunteers.	Campaigns are increasingly managed professionally by "guns for hire" and often have an extensive staff dedicated to strategy setting, fund-raising, and media relations.
Grassroots activism was the norm in all but the largest campaigns.	*Netroots* activism—political activism driven by candidates' Web sites, tweets, blogs, and social-networking sites—uses the Internet as a complement to traditional grassroots campaign efforts.
Money was a crucial consideration in campaigns, but grassroots activism demanded fewer financial resources.	Money rules the day in most campaigns, but technology has the potential to level the campaign playing field.

WHAT'S NEXT?

> How can the Internet change the need for money in political campaigns?

> Given the extent of Web activism during the 2010 campaigns, is there still a role for grassroots activism in future campaigns? Explain.

> Will campaigns continue to be dominated by professional staffers? Why or why not?

America and the *Today Show,* nor does it include evening news magazines such as *60 Minutes, 20/20,* and *48 Hours.* Because of the many (and sometimes endless) hours that networks and twenty-four-hour cable news shows must fill, the focus has shifted more and more from the policy stances of candidates and government officials to the personalities of these individuals. Many Americans are well equipped to describe the personality traits and lifestyle preferences of elected leaders: President Barack Obama's preference for Hawaii beach vacations, his reputation as a strict but loving father, his reliance on his BlackBerry, and his battle with his pack-a-day smoking habit; former President George W. Bush's exercise routine; or former president Bill Clinton's reputation as a fast-food junkie. The reason for this shift is twofold: many viewers enjoy lighter content when watching so much television, and personality-oriented coverage is less likely to offend viewers and advertisers.

Revolutionizing the Campaign: New Technologies

New technologies have dramatically changed the conduct of political campaigns in recent years, and continuing developments promise to force campaigns to continue to evolve and adapt as technology develops new and faster ways to communicate and interact. Through texting, tweeting, and Web-chatting, candidates can use technologies to communicate with voters, mobilize supporters, and interact with the media. The Internet is among the most valuable and powerful new tools used by candidates. It serves as an efficient means by which office seekers can communicate with potential supporters, contributors, and the media. Candidates' Web sites provide a readily available forum where the electorate can find out about candidates' experiences, policy positions, and priorities. This information can be used by voters to make more informed decisions in the voting booth. In addition, the Internet is a powerful fund-raising tool. Indeed, Barack Obama's use of the Internet to raise thousands of small donations in the 2008 Democratic presidential primary was an important part of the formula for his successful campaign. In his twenty-one-month campaign for the presidency, Obama raised a half-billion (yes, billion) dollars. "Three million donors made a total of 6.5 million donations online adding up to more than $500 million. Of those 6.5 million donations, six million were in increments of $100 or less. The average online donation was $80, and the average Obama donor gave more than once."[15] In discussing the growth of campaign fund-raising on the Internet, Eli Pariser, founder of MoveOn.org's Peace Campaign, noted that "candidates are wasting their time with rubber-chicken donors,"[16] an illusion to the donors who contribute to candidates by paying to attend campaign dinners.

Using e-mail and instant messaging, campaigns can communicate quickly with the media, both informing them of positive campaign developments and spinning negative developments in the best possible light for the candidate. Through campaign blogs, candidates can also supplement the information available in more traditional news media outlets. Internet communities and social-networking sites such as Facebook also provide a powerful tool for campaigns and an important mechanism for political engagement for individuals. Some Internet communities may be dedicated to advancing the electoral chances of a candidate for a particular office—and may or may not be sponsored by that candidate. But Internet communities and social-networking sites also provide a forum for average citizens to engage in political discourse, become informed about candidates and issues, and get information that facilitates activism in their communities.

Regulating Federal Campaign Contributions

Money—lots of it—is essential in electoral races today. Money and the modern campaign are inextricably linked because of the importance of costly media advertising in modern campaigns.[17] Federal regulations require any group that contributes to candidates' campaigns to register as a political action committee (PAC), and many interest groups form PACs as one arm of their organization. PACs are a relatively recent phenomenon, but the influence of money in electoral politics goes back a long time, as do the efforts to regulate it.[18] Reformers have attempted to limit the impact of money on political campaigns for almost as long as campaigns have existed.

Those efforts started after a scandal that erupted during the administration of President Warren Harding (1921–1923). In 1921, the president transferred oil reserves at Teapot Dome, Wyoming, from the Department of the Navy to the Department of the Interior. The following year, Harding's secretary of the interior leased the oil fields without competitive bidding. A Senate investigation into the deal revealed that the lessee of the fields had "loaned" the interior secretary more than $100,000 in order to win political influence. The interior secretary was convicted and sentenced to a year in prison and a $100,000 fine. Dubbed the Teapot Dome scandal, this sordid affair led Congress to try to limit influence of money on politics through legislation.

The Federal Corrupt Practices Act of 1925 sought to prevent future wrongdoing. This act aimed to regulate campaign finance by limiting campaign contributions and requiring public disclosure of campaign expenditures, and it was one of the first attempts at campaign finance regulation. But because the act did not include an enforcement mechanism, it was a weak attempt to fight corruption, and candidates found numerous loopholes in the law.

The Political Activities Act of 1939, also known as the Hatch Act, marked another congressional attempt to eliminate political corruption. With the growth of the federal bureaucracy as a result of the New Deal programs of President Franklin D. Roosevelt, several scandals had emerged, demonstrating the problems that could arise when government employees took an active role in politics. The Hatch Act banned partisan political activities by all federal government employees except the president, the vice president, and Senate-confirmed political appointees. The act also sought to regulate the campaign finance system by limiting the amount of money a group could spend on an election and placing a $5,000 cap on contributions from an individual to a campaign committee. Although the Hatch Act was more effective than the Federal Corrupt Practices Act of 1925, it also contained a significant loophole: groups that wanted to spend more than the legislated limit of $3 million simply formed additional groups.

© N. Y. "Tribune."

> A *New York Tribune* cartoon titled "The First Good Laugh They've Had in Years" depicts the Democrats' jubilation over the Teapot Dome Scandal of 1921, which saddled Republicans with a reputation for corruption. The scandal led Congress to try to limit the influence of money on politics.

In 1971, Congress passed the Federal Election Campaign Act (FECA), the most significant attempt at overhauling the nation's campaign finance system. The law was sponsored by Democrats in Congress who were concerned about the enormous fund-raising advantage the Republicans had had during the 1968 presidential election. This law placed considerable limitations on both campaign expenditures and campaign contributions, and it provided for a voluntary tax-return check-off for qualified presidential candidates. This provision enables you, when filling out your federal income tax return, to contribute three dollars, which will go toward the matching funds that qualified presidential candidates receive.

In 1974, FECA was amended to place more stringent limitations on individual contributions and to limit expenditures by PACs, and it revamped the presidential election process by restricting spending and providing public financing for qualified candidates who abided by the limits. The act also required public disclosure of contributions and expenditures by all candidates for federal office. Most important, the act created an enforcement mechanism in the Federal Election Commission, the agency charged with enforcing federal campaign finance laws.

In the subsequent, highly significant Supreme Court case *Buckley v. Valeo* (1976), however, the plaintiffs contended that placing limitations on the amount an individual candidate could spend on his or her own campaign violated First Amendment protections of free speech. The Court agreed, ruling that "the candidate . . . has a First Amendment right to engage in the discussion of public issues and vigorously and tirelessly to advocate his own election."[19] This ruling paved the way for the subsequent explosion in the formation of PACs, by recognizing political expenditures as a protected form of speech and removing limits on overall campaign spending, on personal expenditures by an individual candidate, and on expenditures not coordinated with a candidate's campaign and made by independent interest groups. In its *Buckley* ruling, the Court boldly overturned the limitations on expenditures that to that point had been written into law.

In 2010, the Supreme Court further cleared the way for the increased presence of money in political campaigns by more broadly interpreting First Amendment protections. In *Citizens United v. Federal Election Commission*, the Supreme Court ruled that corporations and labor unions are entitled to the same free speech rights that individuals enjoy, and thus their expenditures to influence the outcome of elections cannot be limited. The controversial 5–4 decision was hailed by conservatives as a recognition of free speech rights and was decried by liberals as an avenue by which corporations could increase their stranglehold on politics and the policy process.

Regulatory Loopholes: Independent Expenditures

independent expenditures
outlays by PACs and others, typically for advertising for or against a candidate, but uncoordinated with a candidate's campaign

When the Supreme Court determined that campaign expenditures constitute free speech for individuals, it uncovered an important loophole in the Federal Election Campaign Act of 1974. Because expenditures are protected from limitations, many PACs now use the so-called independent expenditure loophole to spend unlimited sums for or against political candidates.[20] **Independent expenditures** are outlays, typically for advertising supporting or opposing a candidate, that are uncoordinated with a candidate's campaign. Although PAC contributions to a candidate are limited, a PAC can spend as much as it wants on mailings, television promotions, or other advertisements supporting (or working against) candidates for federal office. This tactic is legal if these expenditures are not coordinated with the candidates' campaigns. Until the Court's ruling in the 2010 *Citizens United* decision, these ads could not "expressly advocate" a candidate by using terms such as "Vote for . . ." or "Elect . . . ,"[21] but those restrictions were eliminated by the Court's decision.

Regulatory Loopholes: Soft Money

Another loophole in the amended Federal Election Campaign Act of 1974 proved important in the 1990s. *Soft money* constitutes contributions to the political parties that are not subject to contribution limits and are designated for use on so-called party-building activities. The soft money loophole allowed donors who had contributed the maximum to federal candidates to give even more money by contributing to the national party committees. The party committees then gave the money to state parties, which subsequently spent the funds on party-building activities under more lenient state regulations. Frequently, such soft money contributions benefited federal candidates by paying for voter registration drives, polls, and general, party-based advertisements. Then, during the 1990s, the political parties began to use soft money for television advertisements that featured the presidential candidates but did not expressly advocate their election. The Bipartisan Campaign Finance Reform Act of 2002 banned soft money contributions to political parties.

The Bipartisan Campaign Finance Reform Act of 2002

Throughout the 1980s and 1990s, campaign finance reform was a perennial topic in presidential campaigns, and candidates roundly criticized the role of "special interests" in politics. But members of Congress had little to gain from reforming the system that had brought them to office. Although various campaign finance proposals were considered, only one passed both the Senate and the House, in 1992, and President George H. W. Bush vetoed it.

Then in 2002, the world's largest energy-trading company and one of the nation's biggest corporations, Enron, collapsed after an internal accounting scandal, leaving in its wake furious stockholders, employees, and retirees whose financial health depended upon the company. Investigations revealed extensive corporate fraud, including accounting improprieties that had enabled corporate leaders to lie about profits and debt. Investigations also revealed that Enron had contributed nearly $4 million to state and federal political parties for "party-building activities" through the soft money loophole. Public indignation at the scandal flared, leading to the passage of the McCain-Feingold Act. This bipartisan campaign reform proposal, named after its two sponsors, Senator John McCain (R-Arizona) and Senator Russell Feingold (D-Wisconsin), had been making its way at a snail's pace through committees before the Enron scandal broke.

The McCain-Feingold Act, formally known as the Bipartisan Campaign Finance Reform Act (BCRA) of 2002, banned nearly all soft money contributions, although PACs can contribute up to $5,000 to state, county, or local parties for voter registration and get-out-the-vote drives. Table 9.1 on page 290 shows that the law also increased individual contribution limitations and regulated some independent expenditure advertising. Although BCRA sought to fix many of the system's problems, some of the remedies remain in dispute.

One aspect of the McCain-Feingold Act became the subject of a series of legal challenges. In 2003, Senator Mitch McConnell (R-Kentucky), an opponent of the act, and a variety of groups affected by the new law (including the National Rifle Association and the California State Democratic Party) filed *McConnell v. the Federal Election Commission.*[22] The suit alleged that McCain-Feingold was a violation of the plaintiffs' First Amendment rights. One aspect of the law to which the groups objected was a ban on independent issue ads (thirty days before a primary election and sixty days before a general election), in which a group purchases advertising targeting a particular candidate for federal office. But the Supreme Court upheld the constitutionality of McCain-Feingold in a 5–4 decision.

Then in 2007, the Court (in another 5–4 decision) did an about-face and created an exception to the ban on issue-based ads. In *Federal Election Commission v. Wisconsin Right to Life, Inc.,*[23] the justices held that advertising within the thirty- and sixty-day window could not be prohibited, thus paving the way for its extensive use in the 2008 presidential race.

Regulatory Loophole: 527s

Another loophole in the campaign finance law became apparent with the emergence of a new form of political group, the so-called 527. Named after the section of the Internal Revenue Service tax code that regulates such organizations, a **527** is a tax-exempt group that raises money for political activities, much like those allowed under the soft money loophole. If a 527 engages only in activities such as voter registration, voter mobilization, and issue advocacy, it does not have to report its activities to the Federal Election Commission, only to the government of the state in which it is located or to the IRS. Disclosure to the FEC is required only if a 527 engages in activities expressly advocating the election or defeat of a federal candidate, or in electioneering communications.

527
a tax-exempt group that raises money for political activities, much like those allowed under the soft money loophole

Campaign Finance Rules Under the Bipartisan Campaign Finance Reform Act, 2010 Cycle

TABLE 9.1

	To Each Candidate or Candidate Committee per Election	To National Party Committee per Calendar Year	To State, District, and Local Party Committee per Calendar Year	To Any Other Political Committee per Calendar Year[1]	Special Limits
Individual may give	$2,400*	$30,400*	$10,000 (combined limit)	$5,000	$115,500* overall biennial limit: • $45,600* to all candidates • $69,900* to all PACs and parties[2]
National Party Committee may give	$5,000	No limit	No limit	$5,000	$42,600* to Senate candidate per campaign[3]
State, District, and Local Party Committee may give	$5,000 (combined limit)	No limit	No limit	$5,000	No limit
PAC (multicandidate)[4] may give	$5,000	$15,000	$5,000 (combined limit)	$5,000	No limit
PAC (not multi-candidate) may give	$2,400*	$30,400*	$10,000 (combined limit)	$5,000	No limit
Authorized Campaign Committee may give	$2,000[5]	No limit	No limit	$5,000	No limit

*These contribution limits are indexed for inflation.

[1]A contribution earmarked for a candidate through a political committee counts against the original contributor's limit for that candidate. In certain circumstances, the contribution may also count against the contributor's limit to the PAC. 11 CFR 110.6. See also 11 CFR 110.1(h).

[2]No more than $45,600 of this amount may be contributed to state and local party committees and PACs.

[3]This limit is shared by the national committee and the national Senate campaign committee.

[4]A multicandidate committee is a political committee with more than fifty contributors which has been registered for at least six months and, with the exception of state party committees, has made contributions to five or more candidates for federal office. 11 CFR 100.5(e)(3).

[5]A federal candidate's authorized committee(s) may contribute no more than $2,000 per election to another federal candidate's authorized committee(s). 11 CFR 102.12(c)(2).

SOURCE: Federal Election Commission, www.fec.gov/ans/answers_general.shtml#How_much_can_I_contribute.

In 2004, two 527s—Swift Boat Veterans and POWs for Truth, which opposed the presidential bid of Senator John Kerry (D-Massachusetts), and MoveOn.org, which opposed President George W. Bush's candidacy—grabbed national attention as each ran television "issue advocacy" advertisements across the country targeting the opposing candidate. Many observers viewed the emergence of these and other 527s as attempts to get around the ban on unlimited soft money contributions to political parties. Campaign finance reform advocates note that several 527s have been partially funded by large contributions from a few wealthy individuals, a claim bolstering the charge that 527s are a way to evade the soft money ban. In 2008, 527s spent about $200 million to influence the outcome of federal elections through voter registration and mobilization efforts and through ads that, though purportedly issue based, typically criticized a candidate's record. In the 2010 elections, 527s spent more than $154 million on federal campaigns.

The Growth of PACs

The year 2010 saw one of the most dramatic episodes in U.S. campaign finance history, with the Supreme Court's decision that corporations and labor unions are entitled to the same First Amendment protections that individuals enjoy. The impact of the *Citizens United*

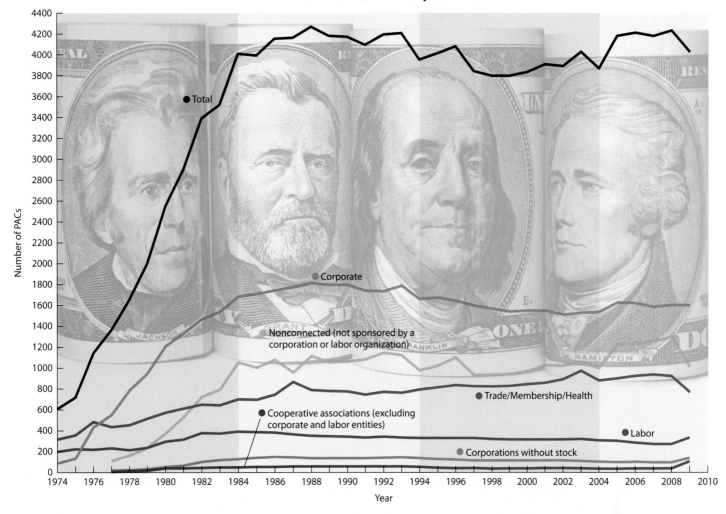

PAC Count, 1974 to present

FIGURE 9.1 ■ **What trends does the figure show with respect to the number of political action committees since 1977? For which groups has the growth in PACs risen most steeply?**

SOURCE: Federal Election Commission, www.fec.gov/press/press2009/20090309PAC.count.shtml.

decision has been a continued expansion of political action committees, as corporations and labor unions now recognize the uncontestable influence that they may have in federal elections. In the 2010 congressional elections, PACs played an important role in creating the most expensive mid-term elections in history.

The last time that the United States saw such an important campaign finance ruling was after *Buckley v. Valeo* in 1976, when the number of political action committees shot up dramatically, as Figure 9.1 demonstrates. The figure shows that the number of corporate PACs alone nearly doubled between 1977 and 1980. Many of those PACs were formed by corporations that do business with the federal government and by associations whose members' livelihoods are significantly affected by federal regulations, including defense contractors, agricultural producers, and government employee unions.

The ballooning of the number of PACs over time is indicative of the increased power that PACs have wielded in campaigns for federal office since 1980, and, in light of the 2010 Supreme Court decision, many campaign finance analysts predict that PACs will continue to increase both in numbers and in influence.

Presidential Campaigns

To many Americans, presidential campaigns epitomize the democratic process. In presidential election years, nonstop campaigning affords ample opportunities for the public to learn about the candidates and their positions. Campaigns also provide avenues for participation by the people—for example, by volunteering in or contributing to candidates' campaigns or even just by debating candidates' views around the water cooler. Although these opportunities for citizen engagement are especially abundant during a presidential election, they arise well before, because potential candidates typically position themselves years in advance of a presidential election to secure their party's nomination and to win the general election.

Party Conventions and the General Election Campaign

As Figure 9.2 illustrates, political parties hold conventions in presidential election years to select their party's nominee for president of the United States. As discussed in Chapter 8 and as reviewed earlier in this chapter, the delegates to the national conventions are chosen by citizens in each state who vote in their party's primary election. After the conventions are over and the nominees have been decided (typically by late August or early September of the election year), the nominees and their vice-presidential running mates begin their general election campaign. Usually, the parties' choice of nominee is a foregone conclusion by the time of the convention. Eligible incumbent presidents (who have served only one term) are nearly always renominated, and the nominee of the opposing party is often determined by the primary results.

FIGURE 9.2

Timeline of Presidential Elections U.S. presidential elections occur every four years; the next one will take place in November 2012.

The Electoral College

The votes tallied on Election Day determine which presidential candidate's slate of electors will cast their ballots, in accordance with state law. There are 538 electors in the Electoral College because the number of electors is based on the number of members of Congress—435 in the House of Representatives, 100 in the Senate—plus 3 electors who represent the District of Columbia. A presidential candidate needs a simple majority of votes (270) to win. Figure 9.3 shows the electoral votes of each state from the 2008 election.

On the Monday following the second Wednesday of December, the slate of electors chosen in each state meets in the state capital and casts their electoral votes. The results are then announced in a joint session of Congress in early January. In most presidential elections, however, the winner is known on election night, because analysts tabulate the outcome in each state and predict the electoral vote. The winner takes the oath of office as president in inaugural ceremonies on January 20. Figure 9.3 shows the electoral votes of each state from the 2008 election.

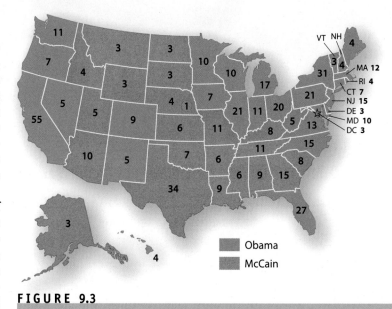

FIGURE 9.3

The 2008 Electoral College Vote In what areas of the country did President Obama get most of his support? Where did John McCain win? Which candidate won the most populous states?

Who Votes? Factors in Voter Participation

Not all people are equally likely to participate in the process of voting for the president or other government officials. Yet of all the forms of political participation, the act of voting has been analyzed perhaps more than any other.[24] (See "Analyzing the Sources" on page 294) Scholars such as Angus Campbell, Philip E. Converse, Warren Miller, and Donald Stokes have examined what factors influence who votes and how voters decide.[25] They and others have analyzed how characteristics such as education level, income, age, race, and the degree of party competitiveness in a given election influence whether a person will vote.[26] Of course, in considering demographic characteristics such as voter age and income level, we must remember that these are merely generalizations.

Education Level— the Number One Predictor of Voting

An individual's level of education is the best predictor of whether that person will vote. Table 9.2 shows that in 2008, less than one-third of U.S. citizens with less than a ninth-grade education were registered to vote, and only 23 percent actually voted. As education increases, so too does the likelihood of voting, with measurable differences even among those who have only attended college, those who have graduated, and those with advanced degrees. Among those with a college or an advanced degree, about three-quarters are registered and have voted.

TABLE 9.2

U.S. Voters' Rate of Registering and Voting by Educational Attainment, 2008

	Total Number (millions)	Percent Registered	Percent Voted
Less than 9th grade	7	30	23
Less than high school graduate	16	43	34
High school graduate or GED	65	60	51
Some college or associate degree	61	72	65
Bachelor's degree	38	76	72
Advanced degree	19	79	76

SOURCE: "Reported Voting and Registration by Educational Attainment: November 2008," www.census.gov/hhes/www/socdemo/voting/publications/p20/2008/tables.html.

ANALYZING THE SOURCES

EXPLORING VOTER TURNOUT IN THE STATES, 2008

STATE	TURNOUT RATE*	STATE	TURNOUT RATE*
United States	61.7%	Missouri	68.1%
Alabama	61.8%	Montana	66.3%
Alaska	68.3%	Nebraska	62.6%
Arizona	56.0%	Nevada	58.6%
Arkansas	53.4%	New Hampshire	71.3%
California	61.7%	New Jersey	66.2%
Colorado	69.8%	New Mexico	60.3%
Connecticut	67.2%	New York	58.0%
Delaware	66.2%	North Carolina	65.8%
District of Columbia	60.7%	North Dakota	65.0%
Florida	67.5%	Ohio	66.7%
Georgia	61.4%	Oklahoma	56.7%
Hawaii	50.5%	Oregon	67.8%
Idaho	63.3%	Pennsylvania	64.2%
Illinois	62.8%	Rhode Island	62.5%
Indiana	59.4%	South Carolina	58.6%
Iowa	69.9%	South Dakota	63.8%
Kansas	62.5%	Tennessee	57.3%
Kentucky	57.9%	Texas	54.7%
Louisiana	62.1%	Utah	53.3%
Maine	71.4%	Vermont	66.7%
Maryland	67.7%	Virginia	67.7%
Massachusetts	66.2%	Washington	67.0%
Michigan	68.9%	West Virginia	50.6%
Minnesota	78.2%	Wisconsin	72.5%
Mississippi	61.0%	Wyoming	65.4%

SOURCE: http://elections.gmu.edu/Turnout_2008G.html. Copyright © Dr. Michael McDonald.

*Turnout rate is the proportion of the voting-eligible population who cast a ballot for the highest office; that is, the vote for the highest office on the ballot (in this case, the presidency) divided by the voting-eligible population.

Evaluating the Evidence

① What states enjoy the highest voter turnout? Do these states share any common characteristics that you are aware of?

② What states have the lowest voter turnout? Do they share any common traits?

③ What is the turnout in your home state? How does it compare with that of neighboring states? Can you think of any reasons for similarities or dissimilarities in the turnout for these states?

The Age Factor

During any presidential campaign, you will hear much about age as a factor in the likelihood of voting. Despite efforts by organizations such as MTV's Rock the Vote, and despite campus-focused initiatives by presidential campaigns, young adults are less likely to vote than Americans who are middle-aged and older, though that figure has increased in re-

FIGURE 9.4 ■ AGE AND VOTING IN THE 2008 PRESIDENTIAL ELECTION For which age group was the percentage of people voting highest? For which age group was the voting percentage lowest? What overall pattern does the graph show? How do you explain it? In 2008, about 53 percent of individuals aged 18 to 29 voted, compared with a national average of 58 percent. Why did the youth vote matter in 2008? Was President Obama's ability to mobilize young voters a phenomenon unique to 2008?

SOURCE: U.S. Census Bureau, www.census.gov/hhes/www/socdemo/voting/publications/p20/2008/tables.html.

Percent voting

Age of voters

18–24	25–34	35–44	45–54	55–64	65–74	75+
44%	49%	55%	63%	68%	70%	66%

cent years.[27] In the 2008 election, we saw that the turnout rate among young Americans—those aged 18 to 29—continued to climb, reaching about 53 percent, the highest turnout rate for voters of that age group since 18-year-olds were first granted the right to vote in 1972. Although the turnout rate may not have broken records, the youth vote was key in President Obama's election: 66 percent of young voters favored Obama. But given the lower turnout among young people in subsequent elections, many wonder if the influence and participation of young voters peaked in 2008. Figure 9.4, which plots the percentage of people in various age groups who voted in the 2008 presidential election, shows a historic trend: as Americans age, they are more likely to vote. Whereas 44 percent of individuals aged 18 to 24 years reported that they had voted, 70 percent of people aged 65 to 74 said that they had. There are numerous reasons why young people do not vote. Among 18- to 24-year-olds, the reason most often cited is that they were too busy or had a schedule conflict, but members of this age group are also more likely to report that they forgot to vote or were out of town. Age also is related to mobility—young people might move when they leave for college or to start a new job, and mobility depresses voter turnout.

Race and Voter Participation

As the 2008 presidential contest demonstrated, race plays a significant role in voter turnout. For decades after the Voting Rights Act of 1965 ensured that African Americans could freely exercise the right to vote, turnout rates among African Americans lagged substantially behind those of non-Hispanic white Americans. Today, however, voter participation among African Americans nearly equals that of whites, as Figure 9.5 indicates. The figure also shows that voting participation among Hispanics and Asian Americans lags behind that of whites and African Americans.

Figure 9.5 shows that the percentage of non-Hispanic whites who reported they voted in the 2008 presidential election was 65 percent, and for African Americans the voting rate was 61 percent. The 2008 election saw increases in the turnout rate among all racial and ethnic groups. Importantly, in addition to increased turnout by African Americans, Barack Obama's candidacy netted him 95 percent of all votes cast by African Americans.

Turnout Rate

White non-Hispanic	African American	Asian-American	Hispanic of any race
65%	61%	32%	32%

FIGURE 9.5 ■ VOTER TURNOUT IN THE 2008 PRESIDENTIAL ELECTION, BY RACE Which demographic group had the highest turnout of the four groups shown? Which had the lowest? Which groups do you believe increased the most in the 2008 election? Why? Looking ahead to the next presidential election in 2012, what do you predict about the voting turnout rates for each of the groups shown?

Income—a Reliable Predictor of Voting

Besides education, income is one of the best predictors of whether an American will vote.[28] Typically in recent years, U.S. citizens with the lowest income level have had voter turnout levels of 50–60 percent, whereas those with the highest income level have had turnout levels above 85 percent.[29] As income increases, so too does the likelihood of voting.

The reasons for the close correlation between income and likelihood of voting are complex.[30] One possibility is that people with lower incomes may have less belief than higher-income earners that the government listens to people like them. Another factor may be that individuals with lower incomes have less leisure time in which to learn about candidates and issues and even to vote. Further, in contrast to the situation in many European democracies, U.S. political parties and political organizations tend not to be highly class based. Whereas European voters are often mobilized—by class-based trade unions and by the parties themselves—to vote on the basis of their economic interests, in the United States, the lowest-income workers are less likely to be members of organized labor unions and thus are less likely to be mobilized to vote on the basis of their own economic interests.

Party Competitiveness and Voter Turnout

Finally, researchers have found that party competitiveness in elections also influences voter turnout.[31] In tight contests, in which either party has a viable chance of winning, voter turnout typically is high because the race generates more voter interest than an election in which the winner is a foregone conclusion. Sometimes turnout is high in competitive elections because voter efficacy is higher—a voter may believe that her vote "counts" more in a close election than in a less competitive race. Voter turnout also runs high in competitive elections because the parties and other campaign organizations work harder to get out the vote when they think they have a chance at winning but know that victory is not guaranteed.

Competitive races also draw increased media attention. A tightly competitive local mayoral race might get greater than usual regional news attention, and a close race for the White House brings nearly nonstop media reports and candidate advertisements. The barrage of media coverage increases public awareness and may also boost voter efficacy by conveying the message that every vote counts.

The impact of this competitiveness can be seen in recent presidential elections. In 2008, about 130 million Americans voted, about 5 million more than the 126 million who voted in 2004. In both elections, the **turnout rate,** the proportion of eligible voters who actually voted, was 64 percent.[32] The 2008 election saw higher turnout rates among those in competitive battleground states, where intense party competition generated turnout. Turnout also was higher among African Americans, Hispanics, and young voters, but lower or flat turnout among other demographic groups offset those increases.

How Voters Decide

When deciding for whom they will vote, some voters evaluate candidates on the basis of their positions on issues and then cast their ballots for those who best represent their views. Called **prospective voting,** this method of candidate evaluation focuses on what the candidates will do in the future. A more common form of candidate evaluation is **retrospective voting,** in which a voter evaluates an incumbent candidate on the basis of whether the incumbent's past decisions and actions are satisfactory to the voter.[33] If they are satisfactory, the voter will likely support the incumbent. If not, the voter will be disposed to support the incumbent's opponent. The prevalence of an incumbency advantage in election outcomes indicates that many voters have a favorable view of the decisions and actions of incumbent candidates for most offices.[34]

The most important factor that plays into how a voter decides on a candidate and perceives specific candidates, however, is the voter's party identification. Other influential de-

turnout rate
the proportion of eligible voters who actually voted

prospective voting
a method of evaluating candidates in which voters focus on candidates' positions on issues important to them and vote for the candidates who best represent their views

retrospective voting
a method of evaluating candidates in which voters evaluate incumbent candidates and decide whether to support them based on their past performance

terminants include those specific to a given election, such as candidates' attributes and the impact of the candidates' campaigns.

Major Factors in Voter Decision Making

The strongest bearing on voter preference is party identification, with about half of all voters basing their candidate choice on which party they identify with. Table 9.3 shows that in the 2008 presidential election, party identification was a potent influence on how voters decided among candidates. As shown in the table, among voters who identified themselves as either Democrats or Republicans, loyalty to their party's candidate was high, with 90 percent of both Democrats and Republicans voting for their party's nominee for president. President Obama's victory came in part because of his support among the nation's independent or unaffiliated voters—those who do not identify themselves as either Democrats or Republicans.

TABLE 9.3

Party Loyalty in the 2008 Presidential Election

	Voting for McCain (%)	Voting for Obama (%)
Democrats	10	90
Independents	45	51
Republicans	90	9

Often a significant determinant in why people vote the way they do, policy priorities are to a certain extent aligned with party identification (or, even more generally, with ideology), because the political parties usually embrace differing viewpoints on issues. National issues that top the list of concerns among voters have remained consistent over many years and include several domestic policy matters, such as the health of the economy, education, crime, health care, and Social Security. Since the terrorist attacks of 2001, homeland security and issues related to terrorism and then the wars in Iraq and Afghanistan have also ranked high in the list of issue concerns on which voters base their vote choices.

But how do voters decide which party and which candidate to support at the polls, based on the issues? First and foremost, an issue must be **salient** to voters—that is, it must resonate with them and reflect something that they care deeply about, an issue they are willing to base their vote on.[35] The ability of voters to cast an issue-based vote increases when candidates differ in their positions on an issue.

salient
having resonance, in relation to a voting issue, reflecting intense interest

Incumbency, the situation of already holding an office or an official position, as we've seen, is also a key factor influencing how people vote. Because an incumbent is a "known commodity" with demonstrated experience to serve in office, voters are much more likely to vote for incumbents than for their challengers. Thus, for most offices, incumbents are much more likely to be reelected than their challengers are to be elected. Indeed, in congressional elections, generally more than 90 percent of incumbent U.S. senators and 95 percent of incumbent members of the House of Representatives win reelection. But incumbency is also an influence in presidential elections, gubernatorial and state legislative elections, and probably even your local city council elections. Incumbents have notable advantages over challengers, namely, greater name recognition, a track record that voters can evaluate, and access to campaign contributions that help get their message out.

incumbency
the situation of already holding the office that is up for reelection

Campaign Influences on Voter Choice

As we have seen, parties and candidates conduct campaigns to influence voters' choices at the polls. Campaigns today vary a great deal in how they are waged. Whereas a candidate for a small town's board of selectmen might knock on the door of every voter in the community, a U.S. Senate or gubernatorial candidate might spend most of his or her time raising money to pay for expensive television and radio advertisements. Generally, the lower the level of office, the greater the likelihood that the candidate will rely on grassroots activism.

Trends in modern campaigns, including a far deeper reliance on paid professional staffers and the prevalence of the media as a tool for communicating with voters, are catapulting the costs of campaigns sky-high. Voter choices are also affected by increasingly negative campaigns, one outcome of the modern political campaigns' reliance on paid professionals. Outside consultants typically have far fewer qualms about "going negative" than do activists in the all-community volunteer-run campaigns that were more typical of earlier times.

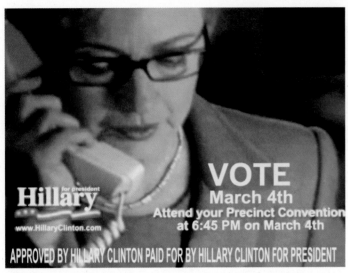

> "Going negative" is a common feature of many modern campaigns. In 2008, as the competition for the Democratic nomination wore on, the campaigns of both Senator Hillary Clinton and Senator Barack Obama became increasingly negative. A widely publicized Clinton ad questioned Senator Obama's foreign policy experience, asking voters to consider who they wanted to answer a 3:00 a.m. phone call at the White House, while their children sleep soundly in their beds.

Consultants use negative campaign tactics for a simple reason: research shows that the approach sways voter opinion.[36] Although the candidates themselves often prefer to accentuate a positive message that highlights their background, experience, and qualifications, paid campaign consultants generally do not hesitate to sling the mud. Once a candidate establishes name recognition and credibility with voters, many consultants believe highlighting the opponent's negative qualities and actions is an effective campaign strategy.

But the impact of negative campaigning is not limited merely to swaying voters from one candidate to another. Research by political scientists shows that negative campaigning can suppress voter turnout in several ways. For example, Shanto Iyengar and Jennifer A. McGrady note that negative advertising may suppress voter turnout among the attacked candidate's supporters.[37] Other political scientists' research shows that negative campaigning undermines the democratic process by decreasing civic engagement among all voters. According to these findings, the electorate becomes disenchanted with the candidates (about whom voters get a barrage of negative information), with the campaigns (because campaigns serve as the primary messengers for delivering negative information about opponents), or with the entire electoral process that facilitates this negativity. Some voters view negative campaigning as being completely at odds with their idealized conception of the democratic process, and this may discourage them from voting.

Why Some People Do Not Vote

Negative campaigning is one reason why some people do not vote, but political scientists have proposed several others. Lack of civic engagement on the part of voters underlies many of these ideas. Other reasons have to do with the nature of campaigns and the structure of elections.

Lack of Efficacy

Some voters do not vote because they do not participate in civic affairs, either locally or at the national level. Many of these nonvoters lack efficacy.[38] They do not believe that the government listens to people like them or that their vote actually matters in determining the outcome of elections and the business of government.[39]

Scholars have determined that individuals who lack efficacy exist across the social and economic spectrums but that poorer people are more likely than better-off individuals to feel that the government does not listen to people like them. Yet although it is a common notion that people are alienated from politics or think that the government does not listen to their concerns, a recent study estimated that only about 9 percent of the U.S. population feels that way.[40] This same survey indicated that people lacking efficacy—a group that the study called the "disaffecteds"—typically had a low level of educational attainment and were less likely to follow current events than more engaged citizens.

Voter Fatigue and Negative Campaigns

Another explanation for why some Americans do not vote stems from the nature of political campaigns. In the United States, campaigns tend to be long-drawn-out affairs. For example, presidential campaigns typically last for more than a year, with some candidates positioning themselves three or four years in advance of an election. Contrast that with many parliamentary systems, including Germany's, in which an election must be held within sixty days of the dissolution of parliament because of a "no confidence" vote of the chancellor (similar to a prime minister). Some scholars say that the lengthiness of the campaigns leads to **voter fatigue,** the condition in which voters simply grow tired of all candidates by the time Election Day arrives, and may thus be less likely to vote.

American journalist and humorist Franklin Adams commented that "elections are won by men and women chiefly because most people vote against somebody rather than for somebody." The prevalence of negative campaigning compounds the impact of voter fatigue. Even the most enthusiastic supporters of a candidate may feel their advocacy withering under the unceasing mudslinging that occurs in many high-level campaigns. And so while evidence shows that negative advertising is effective in swaying voters' opinions, sometimes it also succeeds in suppressing voter turnout by making voters less enthusiastic about voting.

voter fatigue
the condition in which voters grow tired of all candidates by the time Election Day arrives, and may thus be less likely to vote

The Structure of Elections

Political scientists also cite the structure of U.S. elections as a reason why more Americans do not vote. For years, voting rights activists claimed that the registration requirements in many states were too complicated and discouraged people from voting by making it too difficult to register. In 1993, Congress sought to remedy that situation by passing the National Voter Registration Act, frequently called the "Motor Voter" Act, which allows eligible people to register to vote when they apply for a driver's license or enroll in a public assistance program or when they submit the necessary information by mail. Although there was enormous anticipation that the motor voter law would significantly boost voter registration and turnout, in fact its impact has been negligible.

Critics of the structure of elections also point to their frequency. In the United States, the number of elections varies from municipality to municipality, and local government charters may call for more than four elections for municipal offices alone. Although most federal offices require only two elections (a primary and a general), these elections are not always held in conjunction with state, county, and municipal elections.

The timing of elections also affects voter participation. Most general elections are held on a weekday—the first Tuesday after the first Monday in November. Moreover, although states decide when to hold primary elections, state legislative elections, and municipal and school board elections, these elections, too, typically occur on a weekday. Critics say that holding elections on weekends or over a two-day period instead, or establishing a national voting holiday, would increase voter turnout by ensuring that voters had ample opportunity to cast their ballots. (See "Global Context" on page 300.)

The Rational Abstention Thesis

A final explanation as to why some people do not vote is that they make a conscious choice that not voting is a rational, logical action. Called the **rational abstention thesis,** this theory states that some individuals decide that the "costs" of voting—in terms of the time, energy, and inconvenience required to register to vote, to become informed about candidates and elections, and actually to vote—are not worth the effort when compared with the expected "benefits," or what the voters could derive from voting.

In light of these cumulative "costs," it is perhaps surprising that so many people choose to vote.[41] One explanation for why they do is that most voters report that they derive psychological rewards from exercising this citizen's right—feelings of being civically engaged, satisfied, and patriotic. But when the costs associated with voting increase too much, turnout drops; more people choose not to vote when voting becomes too inconvenient. This drop-off occurs, for example, when municipalities shorten voting hours and during inclement weather.

rational abstention thesis
a theory that some individuals decide the costs of voting are not worth the effort when compared to the benefits

The Impact of Nonvoting

From a civic engagement perspective, nonvoting is both a symptom and a result of a lack of civic involvement on the part of individuals.[42] Your roommate might not vote because she is not civically engaged—because she feels that she has little to contribute and that the

ELECTIONS IN INDIA

Although we may think that conducting elections in the United States is a large undertaking, holding elections in India is even more challenging. India is the largest democracy in the world and the second most populous country after China. Thus, the efforts associated with organizing the general election process are enormous.

The Indian Election Commission, an independent committee that is insulated from executive interference, has authority for running elections. The commission's job is to ensure free and fair elections. Since the beginning of India's democracy in 1947, free and fair elections have taken place at regular intervals, as the Indian constitution requires.

Indian elections today constitute the largest elections in human history. Eight hundred thousand polling stations span the country in widely varying climatic and geographic zones, giving accessibility to the vote to more than 668 million people. With such a large electorate, polling for the national elections extends to at least three days.

The entire election process takes five to eight weeks for the national election to the Lok Sabha (the House of the People), the lower house of India's Parliament, and four to six weeks for the state legislative assemblies. Elections begin with the announcement of the election schedule, usually at a press conference a few weeks before the formal election

Should the United States adopt a general election process like India's?

> In the world's most populous democracy, Indian voters in Chandigarh hold their voter identity cards and wait to cast their ballots in the fifth and final phase of country's marathon elections on May 13, 2009.

process begins, and with notifications calling upon the electorate to elect members of the House. Once the notifications are made, candidates can file their nominations. Candidates then get two weeks to campaign before the voting begins.

After the minimum three days set aside for voting, a later date is set for counting the votes, and the election commission compiles a complete list of the House members elected.

For more information on India's Parliament, visit the Parliament of India's Web site: http://rajyasabha.nic.in/. For more information on elections in India, visit www.indian-elections.com/.

government does not listen to "people like her" anyway. But by not voting, she perpetuates this lack of efficacy by remaining outside the process rather than staking a claim to what is rightfully hers: the idea that every individual has the right to a voice in the composition and priorities of the government. Only by becoming civically engaged—learning about the candidates, discussing issues, and voting—can she break the cycle of inefficacy. Voting will make her pay more attention to campaigns, candidates, and issues.

Beyond the effects of nonvoting on individuals, low voter turnout affects the polity. When relatively few people vote in a given election, the outcome is likely to represent the will of only that subset of the electorate who voted. This impact is important: consider that polls indicate that the outcomes of the 2000 and 2004 presidential elections would have been different if voter turnout had been higher. In each of those elections, the Democratic nominee (Al Gore and John Kerry, respectively) was the favored candidate among several groups whose turnout falls below average, including voters under age 24, African American voters, and voters with lower incomes. The process becomes cyclical: these nonvoters who disagree with the outcome conclude that the government does not represent them, feel less efficacious, and are less inclined to vote in the future.

Moreover, some scholars assert that democracies with low voter turnout are more likely to generate threats to their own well-being.[43] In democracies with low turnout, these scholars say, charismatic, popular political figures may rise to power and become authoritarian leaders. Corruption, too, can be a problem in low-turnout democracies where government officials might feel relatively unconcerned about the disapproval of disgruntled constituents.

Other researchers, however, contend that nonvoting is not a big problem, especially in cases where large numbers in the electorate are relatively uninformed about candidates and issues.[44] A number of scholars in this camp argue that participation by the uninformed is undesirable, because it may lead to drastic changes in government. Opponents of this view counter that because of political parties' role in selecting candidates, the menu for voter choice is actually quite limited in most elections. Those who argue that nonvoting does not matter also ignore the fact that voting tends to produce more engaged citizens who, because they vote, feel a duty to be informed and involved.

Other scholars who claim that low voter turnout is not a problem argue that low voting rates are simply a function of people's satisfaction with the status quo: their nonvoting simply means that they do not seek change in government. This argument, however, does not explain why lower turnout is most likely to occur in populations that are least likely to be satisfied with their situation. For example, people with lower incomes are much less likely to vote than those with higher incomes. Whatever the reason—a lack of efficacy as argued by some, satisfaction as argued by others—nonvoters' best chances of having their views reflected in the policy process is to articulate them through voting.

CONCLUSION

THINKING CRITICALLY ABOUT WHAT'S NEXT IN ELECTIONS, CAMPAIGNS, AND VOTING

The nature of political campaigns in the United States has continuously evolved, but the changes in recent decades have been especially dramatic. An era in which political parties and grassroots activism dominated campaigns has given way to the present-day realities where money, media, and mavens of strategy are key forces in shaping campaigns, which have grown increasingly candidate-centered. Prominently driving the changes are the simultaneous *decrease* in political party clout and *increase* in the need for money—money to pay for the small army of professional staffers that run the campaigns; and money to cover the expensive media buys that candidates, especially those running for national and state office, heavily depend on for communicating with the electorate.

Technology offers the potential to bring the politics of electoral campaigns back to the grassroots—now perhaps more appropriately called the netroots. Although campaigns' use of technology certainly is not free, digital communication is cost-effective and rapid. Campaigns' and candidates' option of communicating with voters through mediums such as social-networking sites, YouTube, e-mail, and instant messaging presents an exciting alternative to high-priced "campaigning-as-usual." In what ways did congressional candidates make use of these new media in the 2010 elections? How might the use of these technologies change in the 2012 campaign?

Through the new mediums of communication, there is great potential, too, for the inclusion of a variety of new voices in the political campaigning process. Groups that want to influence campaigns and voters have at their disposal a vast arsenal of new technology that makes such influence possible.

Summary

1. Political Participation: Engaging Individuals, Shaping Polities
Active political engagement benefits both the individual and the polity. When it comes to elections, campaigns, and voting, the opportunities for civic engagement are numerous. Although some civic activities, such as working full-time on a campaign, might represent enormous commitments, others, including casting a ballot and engaging in political discourse, are less time-consuming and are manageable for even the busiest people.

2. Elections in the United States
U.S. elections include the primary election, in which a party's nominee to run in the general election is selected; the general election, in which the winning candidate attains the office being sought; and special-purpose elections such as the initiative, the referendum, and the recall, which are citizen-sponsored efforts to have a greater say in the political process.

3. The Act of Voting
Although all the states rely on the Australian (secret) ballot, the types of ballots used in states vary significantly. The type of ballot can have an impact on election outcomes, as in the 2000 presidential election.

4. Running for Office: The Choice to Run
Most offices have formal eligibility requirements, but there are also more subjective requirements by which voters view candidates as qualified to hold a given office. Often these characteristics have to do with occupation, education, and experience.

5. The Nature of Political Campaigns Today
Today's political campaigns hire a wide variety of professionals who perform the tasks that were once accomplished by volunteer staffs. Office seekers' increasing reliance on electronic media, in particular television, has drastically changed both the ways in which campaigns are conducted and the costs of those campaigns. The widespread use of the Internet, too, continues to alter the nature of campaigns.

6. Regulating Campaign Contributions
Government efforts over the years to regulate campaign contributions have led to laws with numerous loopholes. The latest attempt to curtail the influence of money on politics is the Bipartisan Campaign Finance Reform Act of 2002.

7. Presidential Campaigns
Presidential campaigns are increasing in duration. They begin with the primary process, continue through the national party conventions, proceed to the general election campaign and voting, and end with the Electoral College vote.

8. Who Votes? Factors in Voter Participation
Influences on voter participation include education, age, race, income, and party competitiveness.

9. How Voters Decide
Party identification, policy priorities, incumbency, and campaigns are factors influencing how voters decide for whom to vote.

10. Why Some People Do Not Vote
The many reasons why people don't vote include a lack of efficacy, the impact of voter fatigue and negative campaigns, the structure of elections, and the rational abstention thesis. Whatever the reason, nonvoting has a harmful impact on individuals and the government.

Key Terms

absentee voting 281

Australian ballot 279

campaign consultant 284

campaign manager 284

campaign strategy 284

caucus 276

chad 279

closed primary 276

coattail effect 280

527 289

fund-raising consultant 284

general election 275

GOTV 275

grassroots organizing 274

incumbency 297

independent
   expenditures 288

initiative 278

instant runoff election 278

media consultant 284

office-block ballot 280

open primary 276

party-column ballot 280

proposition 278

prospective voting 296

rational abstention
   thesis 299

recall 279

referendum 278

retrospective voting 296

runoff election 278

salient 297

Super Tuesday 276

turnout rate 296

voter fatigue 299

winner-take-all 278

For Review

1. What are some opportunities for civic engagement related to elections, campaigns, and voting?

2. What are the different kinds of elections in the United States? What is the difference between a primary election and a general election?

3. What is the difference between formal and informal eligibility requirements for political office?

4. Why is regulating campaign finance so difficult? Explain the various efforts to limit the impact of money on campaigns.

5. What factors influence whether a person will vote or not?

6. What factors influence how or for whom an individual will vote?

7. What is the rational abstention thesis? Is it rational? What factors might not be calculated into the costs and benefits of voting?

For Critical Thinking and Discussion

1. Why do formal and informal eligibility requirements for office differ? What are the informal eligibility requirements to run for the state legislature where you live? What are the requirements for the city or town council in your hometown or the community where your school is located? How do these differences reflect the nature of the constituency for the office being sought?

2. How has the increasing cost of political campaigns changed the nature of American politics? Why have costs escalated?

3. What has been the impact of the increasing negativity in American political campaigns?

4. Using the text discussion of factors influencing whether a person votes, assess a classmate's likelihood of voting based solely on those factors. Then ask the person if he or she votes. Was your assessment accurate?

5. In your view, what is the impact of nonvoting?

MULTIPLE CHOICE: Choose the lettered item that answers the question correctly.

1. An election that determines which candidates win the offices being sought is called a(n)
   a. blanket primary.
   b. open primary.
   c. caucus.
   d. general election.

2. A meeting of party members held to select delegates to the national convention is called a(n)
   a. blanket primary.
   b. open primary.
   c. caucus.
   d. general election.

3. A special election in which voters can remove officeholders before their term is over is called a(n)
   a. referendum.   c. recall.
   b. initiative.   d. proposition.

4. An election in which voters in a state can vote for or against a measure proposed by the state legislature is called a(n)
   a. referendum.   c. recall.
   b. initiative.   d. proposition.

5. The phenomenon by which candidates running for lower-level office such as city council benefit in an election from the popularity of a top-of-ticket nominee is called
   a. the petticoat effect.
   b. the bustle effect.
   c. the coattail effect.
   d. the bolster effect.

6. A professional who brings the campaign message to voters by creating all forms of media ads is called a(n)
   a. campaign manager.
   b. fund-raising consultant.
   c. outreach manager.
   d. a media consultant.

7. The proportion of voters who actually voted is called
   a. the turnout rate.
   b. the electoral rate.
   c. the eligibility factor.
   d. the voter sample.

8. Outlays by PACs and others, typically for advertising for or against a candidate but uncoordinated with a candidate's campaign, are called
   a. a soft money expenditure.
   b. an independent expenditure.
   c. a 527 expenditure.
   d. a 626 expenditure.

9. An issue that has resonance and intense interest among voters is said to be
   a. a divide issue.
   b. a fence-sitting issue.
   c. a salient issue.
   d. a litmus-test issue.

10. The condition in which voters grow tired of all candidates by the time Election Day arrives, making them possibly less likely to vote, is called
    a. rational abstention.
    b. absentee voting.
    c. voter ennui.
    d. voter fatigue.

FILL IN THE BLANKS.

11. A follow-up election held when no candidate receives the majority of votes cast in the original election is called a(n) _____ .

12. A special election in which the computerized voter machine simulates the elimination of last-place vote-getters to eventually decide a winner is called a(n) _____ .

13. A measure proposed by voters and placed on the ballot for their approval is called a(n) _____ election.

14. A ballot that organizes the candidates by political party is called a(n) _____ .

15. A(n) _____ is the blueprint for an election campaign, including a budget and fund-raising plan, an advertising strategy, and a staffing plan.

Answers: 1. d; 2. c; 3. c; 4. a; 5. c; 6. d; 7. a; 8. b; 9. c; 10. d; 11. runoff election; 12. instant runoff; 13. initiative; 14. party-column ballot; 15. campaign strategy.

Internet Resources

The Living Room Candidate
www.livingroomcandidate.org   This site, maintained by the Museum of the Moving Image, provides videos of television commercials run by presidential campaigns from 1956 to 2008.

Project Vote Smart
www.vote-smart.org   This nonpartisan Web site provides independent, factual information on election procedures in each state.

Rock the Vote
www.rockthevote.org   This nonprofit, nonpartisan organization encourages political participation by young people and provides resources on policies of interest, as well as voting information.

Vote, Run, Lead
www.voterunlead.org   This is the Web site for an organization that encourages the civic engagement of young women as voters, activists, and candidates for political office.

Internet Activism

Both political parties provide processes for including young people as delegates to their national party conventions every four years, and volunteer opportunities abound at these meetings. To try to become a delegate or a volunteer at the 2012 national party conventions, go to **www.democrats.org** or **www.gop.com**.

Twitter
www.Media Bloggers.org
Follow "electionblogs" to receive coverage of U.S. elections.

YouTube
Watch and analyze the effectiveness of 2010 mid-term campaign commercials on YouTube's thehilldotcom channel (sponsored by The Hill newspaper). **http://www.youtube.com/user/thehilldotcom**.

Facebook
Search "politicians" to see a list of candidates and elected officials you can friend or fan.

Recommended Readings

Abramson, Paul R., John H. Aldrich, and David W. Rohde. *Change and Continuity in the 2008 Elections*. Washington, DC: CQ Press, 2009. The latest in this series of election analyses examines the tactics employed in the 2008 presidential and congressional elections.

Bimber, Bruce, and Richard Davis. *Campaigning Online: The Internet in U.S. Elections*. New York: Oxford University Press, 2003. Describes how voters and political campaigns are increasingly relying on the Internet as a communication, fund-raising, and organizing tool.

Burns, Nancy, Kay Lehman Schlozman, and Sidney Verba. *The Private Roots of Public Action: Gender Equality, and Public Action*. Cambridge, MA: Harvard University Press, 2003. Explores the differences in political participation between men and women.

Faucheux, Ron. *Campaigns and Elections: Winning Elections*. New York: M. Evans and Company, 2003. A collection of the "best of the best" articles from *Campaigns and Elections* magazine; a practical guide to conducting campaigns.

Herrnson, Paul S., Richard G. Niemi, Michael J. Hanmer, Benjamin B. Bederson, and Frederick C. Conrad. *Voting Technology: The Not-So-Simple Act of Casting a Ballot*. Washington, DC: Brookings Institution Press, 2008. Explains the intricacies of voting technology, including the electoral implications of how votes are cast.

Jacobson, Gary C. *The Politics of Congressional Elections*. New York: Longman, 2008. A classic work explaining the process of congressional elections and demonstrating how electoral politics reflects and shapes other basic components of American democracy.

Leighley, Jan. *Strength in Numbers: The Political Mobilization of Racial and Ethnic Minorities*. Princeton, NJ: Princeton University Press, 2001. Examines the factors that influence political participation by African Americans and Hispanic Americans.

Plouffe, David. *The Audacity to Win: The Inside Story and Lessons of Barack Obama's Historic Victory*. New York: Viking Press, 2009. Barack Obama's campaign manager writes a captivating political memoir of the 2008 campaign.

Zukin, Cliff, Scott Keeter, Molly Andolina, Krista Jenkins, and Michael X. Delli Carpini. *A New Engagement? Political Participation, Civic Life, and the Changing American Citizen*. New York: Oxford University Press, 2006. Describes the changing ways in which Americans are participating in the political life of their country and communities.

Movies of Interest

Swing Vote (2008)
Kevin Costner stars in this film in which one man—an average apolitical American—determines the outcome of a presidential election.

Bulworth (1999)
Warren Beatty stars in this offbeat skewering of the impact of money on political campaigns in the United States.

The Candidate (1972)
Robert Redford's character is convinced to run for the Senate on the premise that, with no chance at success, he can say whatever he wants. But success changes him, and his values shift as the prospect of winning becomes apparent.

The Media

THEN

The relationship between the media and consumers was one-way.

NOW

Technology has created a two-way relationship between the media and consumers, involving the exchange of a seemingly limitless amount of information of varying quality.

NEXt

Will the abundance and the reach of the media overload people with information?

Will people select media sources that serve only to confirm their views?

Will the ever-increasing speed and volume of information affect its quality?

PREVIEW

If you are like most Americans

—and indeed like multitudes of people across the globe—the media are a fixture in your daily life. You may wake up to a radio show each morning or read a newspaper over breakfast or while commuting on a bus or train. You may watch televised news stories on the war in Afghanistan in the evening. You may receive real-time news updates on your cell phone, Internet news sites, and Weblogs or tune in to the twenty-four-hour news channels available virtually everywhere. There is no escaping that as a citizen of the twenty-first century, you are bathed in a sea of news and information. Some of what the media offer you is meant to entertain, some is meant to inform, but increasingly the lines between the two have blurred.

No one can dispute that the sheer amount of information and entertainment available courtesy of the media has increased immeasurably over the past few decades. Within a generation, the modern media have transformed American life. Where once people had to seek out news and information, today they are inundated with it, and they must develop the skill to filter the good from the bad.

Although this abundance of information at times may rise to the level of a blitz, information is empowering. It serves as the basis on which people shape well-founded opinions. Those opinions are the building blocks for meaningful civic engagement and political participation. In the discussion that follows, we see how the media continuously shape the ways we receive information and the ways we exercise the rights and privileges of our American democracy.

This chapter focuses on the role of the contemporary U.S. media as both an information source and a conduit through which individuals convey information and opinions to others, and it explores the growing, shifting influence of the media on politics and civic life over time.

FIRST, we examine what *the modern media* are.

SECOND, we consider *the political functions of the media.*

THIRD, we explore *the press and politics,* taking *a historical view.*

FOURTH, we focus on the origins and formats of the first of the electronic media with a look at *the radio and television revolutions.*

FIFTH, we examine the diverse and growing uses of the Internet as *the media revolution continues.*

SIXTH, we ponder charges that the U.S. media are *biased media.* Do most people believe that the media are too liberal or too conservative? Are they right?

SEVENTH, we consider the government's *regulation of the media* and examine how the media's rapidly continuing transformation affects government's ability to regulate new formats of communicating.

The Modern Media

On June 20, 2009, 27-year-old Neda Agha-Soltan was shot to death in the streets of Tehran, Iran, as she was about to join a demonstration to protest the outcome of the Iranian election. Agha-Soltan was killed by a bullet allegedly fired by a member of the Basij, the Iranian paramilitary organization loyal to Iranian President Mahmoud Ahmadinejad. What made Agha-Soltan's death unique was that it became the iconic representation of the antigovernment movement. The murder was captured on a cell phone video camera by a bystander. It was sent to the British newspaper *The Guardian* and to the Voice of America radio network. It was also sent to several individuals, one of whom uploaded the video to Facebook, and then to YouTube. Within hours, it was broadcast on CNN. In 2010, the anonymously recorded video won the prestigious George Polk journalism award for videography. Polk Award curator John Darnton, of the *New York Times,* noted that "this award celebrates the fact that, in today's world, a brave bystander with a cellphone camera can use video-sharing and social networking sites to deliver news."[1]

The Agha-Soltan case demonstrates a tension that now exists in defining the media. Traditionally, we have easily recognized the media: our hometown newspaper, the local television news, and the cable news networks. But defining the media today is trickier: do tweets from your mayor, blogs from your roommate, or Facebook posts from your mom count as media? Although many regard the **media** simply as tools used to store and deliver information or data (in which case, all of the above would be considered media), we must differentiate between media outlets that distribute unverifiable or opinion-based information, and those that disseminate verifiable information.

The media are present in various forms today, including print media such as newspapers and magazines; the electronic media, which traditionally means radio and television; and new media, usually thought of as being those forms associated with the Internet and cellular technology, including Web sites and social-networking sites such as Facebook, Twitter,

media
tools used to store and deliver information or data

and YouTube. In previous eras, media consumers often accepted what was broadcast or printed as fact, but today one must be a critical consumer of information. Just because information appears on a blog, or even hundreds of blogs, it is not necessarily true. How can today's media consumers be certain the information they are receiving is accurate? One good method is by relying on media outlets with a track record of providing solid information and adhering to journalistic standards. Another is to check sources independently: today, the Internet has made it possible to verify some information simply by clicking on a hotlink to the original sources. More and more, news organizations will come to rely on citizen journalists such as the videographer who filmed Agha-Soltan's death, increasing the probability that false information will be widely distributed by unscrupulous individuals. Thus today's media consumers must exercise a high level of caution when reading, listening, or viewing.

> Epitomizing how new technologies have changed the media: a frame grab from a cell-phone video shows a woman identified as Neda Agha-Soltan lying on the ground after getting shot in the chest in Tehran June 20, 2009. The footage, filmed by a citizen journalist, later won the prestigious Polk journalism award for videography.

The Political Functions of the Media

In the United States today, the media in all their forms—including print, television, radio, and the Internet—fulfill several key functions. Much of what the media do revolves around entertaining us, whether that means watching *NCIS* or reading the Sunday funnies. But the media perform important political functions as well and are a vital element of our democracy. Specifically, the media perform the following political functions:

- provide political information
- help us to interpret events and policies and are influential in setting the national policy agenda
- provide a forum for political conversations
- socialize children to the political culture

Providing Information

One long-standing function of the mass media is to serve up a steady diet of news and information to readers, viewers, and listeners. Indeed, the media, particularly the electronic media, are the primary source of information for most individuals. And today, the quantity of information available—on blogs, Web sites, and cable television stations—surpasses the volume available at any other time in history. Coverage includes everything from weather watches, to sports scores, to the latest legislative developments on Capitol Hill, to serious analysis of top domestic policy issues and international problems. From this steady diet arises the problem of information overload—the constant availability of news information to the point of excess, which may cause media consumers to ignore, dismiss, or fail to see the significance of particular events. Media critics especially fault the television networks for injecting entertainment into news shows. They dub this combination **infotainment** (a hybrid of the words *information* and *entertainment*). More recent is the trend of uniting comedy with political content, as in Jon Stewart's *The Daily Show* and Stephen Colbert's *The Colbert Report,* both of which interpret news events with a comedic slant.

infotainment
news shows that combine entertainment and news, a hybrid of the words *information* and *entertainment*

Interpreting Matters of Public Interest and Setting the Public Agenda

Besides reporting information, the media help people to comprehend and interpret matters of public interest and to make informed decisions about public policies. Political scientist Shanto Iyengar asserts that this process often begins with media **framing**—setting a context that helps people understand important events and matters of shared interest.

framing
the process by which the media set a context that helps people understand important events and matters of shared interest

CONFIDENCE IN THE MEDIA

The Gallup Organization has asked the following question in surveys since 1972: "In general, how much trust and confidence do you have in the mass media—such as newspapers, T.V., and radio—when it comes to reporting the news fully, accurately, and fairly: a great deal, a fair amount, not very much, or none at all?"

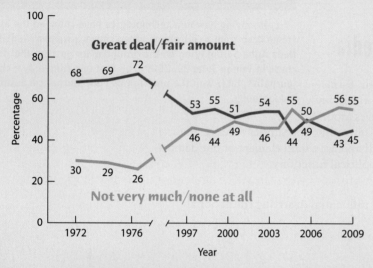

SOURCE: The Gallup Poll, *Media Use and Evaluation*, www.galluppoll.com/poll/1663/Media-Use-Evaluation.aspx.

The line graph illustrates survey respondents' views on that question, showing survey data at various times between May 1972 and September 2009. You can see that considerable changes have occurred in people's assessment of news organizations in this period.

Evaluating the Evidence

① Describe trends during the 1970s in people's confidence in the media, citing specific data from the graph.

② Describe trends since 2001 in people's confidence in the media, citing specific data.

③ What do the latest surveys indicate about respondents' opinions on the issue of confidence in the media?

④ What do the data say about the *overall* trends with regard to people's confidence in the media?

⑤ What factors could have contributed to the changes in people's assessment of the media over time? Explain.

Political scientist Pippa Norris has analyzed the process of framing as it relates to gender. She asserts that gender has become a common frame through which journalists provide context for different kinds of political stories.[2] Norris explains that voters, candidates, public opinion, and issues all may be viewed from a gender-based perspective. For example, in the 2008 presidential campaign, the media initially covered the race for the Democratic nomination by accentuating the gender of Senator Hillary Clinton (D-New York) and played up Clinton's potential to be the first woman president of the United States. Media reporting defined her opponent, Senator Barack Obama, as potentially the first African American president. Similarly, when Senator John McCain announced that Alaska governor Sarah Palin would be his running mate in the 2008 general election campaign, the media emphasized the gendered aspects of her nomination, particularly her role as a mother.

The media also help to shape the **public agenda**—public issues that most demand the attention of government officials. The media commonly influence the setting of the public agenda by **priming**—using their coverage to bring particular policies on issues to the public agenda.

public agenda
the public issues that most demand the attention of government officials

priming
bringing certain policies on issues to the public agenda through media coverage

Providing a Forum for Conversations About Politics

Although the media have provided an often lively forum for conversations about politics, the prominence of this role has reached new heights in the Internet era. Historically, information flowed from the media—which through the years have included everything from the political broadsides and leaflets of colonial times to modern newspapers, radio news, and television programming—to the people. The people then formed opinions based on what they read, heard, and saw. This historical one-way tradition typically featured little give-and-take between media sources and their consumers. A notable exception has been the **letter to the editor,** in which a reader responds to a newspaper story, knowing that the letter might be published in that paper.

The advent of talk radio gave listeners one of their first regular opportunities to express their views publicly. Television took note, and call-in shows such as *Larry King Live* now are common fare on cable television stations.

But no other medium has expanded the ability of people to communicate their views to the degree that the Internet has. David Weinberger, a Democratic marketing consultant and Internet adviser, describes this phenomenon: "Think of it as conversation space. Conversation is the opposite of marketing. It's talking in our own voices about things we want to hear about."[3] Weblogs facilitate this conversation by inviting an ongoing dialogue between the blog hosts and the posters. Discussion boards (even those that are "nonpolitical") are filled with political discussion and opinions. Social-networking sites such as MySpace, Facebook, BlackPlanet, MyBatanga, AsiaAve, and Faithbase allow individuals to share their stories, interests, and political viewpoints.

letter to the editor
a letter in which a reader responds to a story in a newspaper, knowing that the letter might be published in that paper

Socializing Children to Political Culture

The media also socialize new generations to the political culture. For young children, television remains the dominant medium for both entertainment and socialization. TV-viewing toddlers receive regular messages about important cultural values. Shows such as *Sesame Street* and *Barney* send powerful messages about the value of diversity in society. A song such as *Barney*'s "You Are Special" underscores the value of individualism in the culture. Young children's shows also subtly instruct watchers on the value of patriotism and of specific civic behaviors, such as voting.

TV programming for older children similarly takes on political issues. In *Arthur,* the main character comes face-to-face with censorship when adults in his town have the "Scare Your Pants Off" book series removed from the public library, thus providing a concise fifteen-minute lesson on civil liberties issues.

Even television and radio programs not specifically aimed at youth often reinforce democratic principles and practices. What is *American Idol* if not a televised election? And when the tribe speaks on *Survivor,* they do so through the process of voting. Talk radio and television call-in programs rest on the assumption that individuals' opinions matter and that they have the right to voice them. (See "Global Context" on page 312.) These various kinds of programming may not directly spur a particular political behavior on the part of viewers. Nonetheless, television and other forms of media that we often think of as pure entertainment frequently reinforce and legitimize dominant American political values.

> The media socialize individuals to key political values. On shows such as *American Idol,* principles of democracy prevail as viewers vote for their favorite contestant. What are some other popular television shows that reflect society's core political values?

TALK RADIO, SAUDI STYLE—MUBASHER FM

When you think of Saudi Arabia, one thing that probably does not pop into your mind is talk radio. But every Monday night during prime-time hours, radio host Salama al-Zaid takes calls from about twenty listeners, most of whom are seeking help in dealing with the national bureaucracy or lodging complaints of corruption against government officials.

Saudi Arabia, an oil-rich nation bordered by the Persian Gulf on the east and the Red Sea on the west, is a kingdom ruled by King Abdullah and administered primarily through an enormous network of the royal family. The Muslim Shari'a is the basis of the nation's laws, although some secular laws have been enacted in recent years. Women do not have basic rights such as voting and driving. Although the country traditionally has enjoyed a high standard of living, poverty is a growing problem. Restrictions on the media abound, and criticism of the monarchy is especially frowned upon. It is in this environment that Zaid hosts his radio program. *Mubasher FM* ("Live FM" in Arabic) went on the air in 2006.

Zaid claims that King Abdullah views Zaid's program as a useful tool in gauging public opinion. "The media has always been a red line in this country. But the king came and said this is the way to reach the people. And he sent a message to me: 'Keep going,'" explains Zaid, who fully supports the monarchy. Callers to the program get more than a sympathetic ear. Not only do government officials try to rectify problems aired on the program, but also callers sometimes receive an audience with the king, who has issued decrees to address various issues broadcast on *Mubasher FM*.

Zaid is highly critical of corrupt officials, whom he has challenged to phone in and explain their behavior. Moreover, he is not afraid of speaking out on some of the most controversial issues in Saudi society, including those affecting the rights of women. During one program, he took Saudi schools and universities to task for failing to hire qualified women as teachers. Calling on the royal court to address this problem, he complained that "our daughters are being wronged by our universities and places of higher learning."

The optimistic Zaid believes that Saudis are advancing toward being a more open society. He takes heart that people are increasingly willing to come forward and complain about corruption of government officials and unacceptable problems such as the sexual harassment of women. That he must sift through thousands of calls each week indicates a willingness by individuals to voice their complaints without fear of reprisals, and Zaid characterizes that as progress.

> **Can the media open up closed societies?**

> Radio Host Salama al-Zaid.

SOURCE: Hassan M. Fattah, "Challenging Saudi Arabia's Powerful, One Caller at a Time," *New York Times*, May 5, 2007, p. A4.

The Press and Politics: A Historical View

The sheer volume of information available today through the media makes the influence of the media in our times beyond dispute. Historically, too, the media have played an essential role in setting the political agenda and shaping public policy. The power of the media was evident even in pre-Revolutionary times, when, for example, newspaper owners and readers rallied against the Stamp Act's (1765) imposition of taxes on newspapers and other kinds of legal documents. Newspaper publishers sympathetic to the colonists' cause of ejecting Great Britain from American shores used their "power of the pen" to arouse public opinion, and they strongly supported the patriot cause throughout the Revolution. Taking sides in an internal conflict was a new role for the press, one that would sow the seeds of future media influence on the country's domestic and foreign policy. The early history of media development also raised issues that continue to create conflict about the media's role in society.

The Early Role of the Press

Great leaders learned early how intimately their careers were linked to favorable press coverage and influence. From the 1790s to the 1830s, the press served primarily as a vehicle for the leaders of political parties, who expressed their opinions through newspapers known to reflect their particular viewpoints in reporting the news. The circulation of these newspapers was small, but so was their audience; most people could not read and write and did not vote.

By the 1830s, the environment had changed. For openers, the average American was now able to read. New technology made possible the **penny press**—newspapers that sold for a penny. The field of **journalism,** the practice of gathering and reporting events, flourished. Circulation increased, and the working class became interested in what the newspapers had to offer. Another reason newspapers reduced their price was the advent of advertising; newspaper owners figured out that if they sold advertising, they could increase both their profits and their papers' circulation. The 1830s was the first time advertising became part and parcel of the newspaper business, and although pressures from advertisers sometimes affected coverage and editorial opinion, few readers noticed that practice, and even fewer challenged it.

Over time, the influence of advertising grew exponentially. Although today's major newspapers do not openly change their editorial opinions to please their advertisers, occasionally advertisers flex their muscles, as General Motors did when it withdrew its advertising from the *Los Angeles Times* after the newspaper recommended the firing of the company's CEO.[4]

penny press
newspapers that sold for a penny in the 1830s

journalism
the practice of gathering and reporting events

Yellow Journalism and Muckraking

Throughout the last part of the nineteenth century, newspapers competed vigorously with one another for ever-greater shares of readership. Publishers found that stories about sex, gore, violence, and government corruption sold papers faster than reports about garbage collection and school budgets. Well-known publishers William Randolph Hearst and Joseph Pulitzer established their reputations and their fortunes at that time, Hearst with the *New York Journal American* and Pulitzer with the *New York World.* Along with Hearst and Pulitzer at the beginning of the twentieth century came the practice of yellow journalism, so named after the yellow ink used in the "Yellow Kid" cartoons in the *New York World.* The term **yellow journalism** has come to signify an irresponsible, sensationalist approach to news reporting and is used to this day to criticize certain elements of the press.

yellow journalism
irresponsible, sensationalist approach to news reporting, so named after the yellow ink used in the "Yellow Kid" cartoons in the *New York World*

The most famous example of the impact of yellow journalism came with both Hearst's and Pulitzer's support of the United States' entry into the Spanish-American War (1898). This conflict is sometimes referred to as "the newspaper war" because of the major role of the press in President William McKinley's decision to invade Cuba and later the Philippines. Public sentiment in the United States, influenced by reports of Spanish cruelty toward the Cubans during and after the Cuban independence movement, strongly favored Cuba. Hearst and Pulitzer, followed by other newspapers across the country, fanned the flames of war with sensational and lurid anti-Spanish stories, dwelling on the brutality of the Spanish toward Cuban rebels. The precipitating event, the explosion of the U.S. battleship *Maine* in Havana harbor in February 1898, may or may not have been due to a Spanish torpedo according to recent evidence; but press reports, accompanied by the cry "Remember the *Maine*," galvanized the public and Congress. The president responded to

> Yellow journalism can influence the national policy agenda. When the battleship *Maine* exploded in Havana harbor in February 1898, newspaper coverage significantly molded public opinion, and in turn Congress declared war on Spain. Can you think of examples of recent media coverage of events that have influenced public opinion?

the intensifying pressures, and Congress declared war on Spain in April. The press and the public had guided public policy.

Hard on the heels of the Spanish-American "newspaper war" came the era of **muckraking,** an about-face that placed journalists in the heroic role of exposing the dark underbelly of government and industry. The most famous of the muckrakers included Ida Tarbell, who exposed the oil industry in a series of articles running from 1902 to 1904 in *McClure's* magazine; Lincoln Steffens, who published *The Shame of the Cities* in 1904; and Upton Sinclair, whose novel *The Jungle* (1906) revealed the horrors of the meat-processing industry, leading to passage of the Pure Food and Drug Act and later to the establishment of the Food and Drug Administration.[5]

A Widening War for Readership

Yellow journalism died down after World War I, and newspapers entered a period that at least on the surface valued objectivity. Newspapers increasingly found themselves competing with the new media that were just coming into being: radio stations from 1920 to 1950; television from the 1940s to 1980; and from then on, the explosion of the **new media**— cable television, the Internet, blogs, and satellite technology.

This increased competition has had several impacts on the newspaper industry. First, newspaper readership has steadily declined, particularly the audience for local newspapers. For example, Figure 10.1 shows that between 1998 and 2008, the proportion of people who read a local newspaper every day or several times a week decreased from 68 percent to 53 percent. This figure also illustrates that although readership of national newspapers increased slightly after the terrorist strikes of September 11, 2001, since that time readership has ebbed to the same level as before the attacks. Partly as a result of a long-term decline in local newspaper readership, the number of daily newspapers has decreased dramatically, with many cities that used to support three or four "dailies" now typically having only one newspaper. Second, competition has resulted in consolidation of the newspaper industry, so that today a single large parent company typically owns many local newspapers. For example, the Gannett Corporation, which publishes *USA Today,* also publishes numerous daily and weekly newspapers in towns throughout the country. Third, competition has forced nearly every newspaper to offer free online editions. Thus you can receive nearly any newspaper at no cost in your e-mail inbox each morning.

Beyond falling readership, the newspaper industry has changed as society has changed. Large cities are now likely to have smaller weekly publications targeted to specific demographic audiences—gays, women, African Americans, for example— and to publish foreign-language newspapers appealing to such diverse newcomers to the United States as Mexican, Brazilian, Vietnamese, Iranian, Nigerian, and Russian immigrants.

As the industry has changed, so, too, has the human face of the newsrooms. Figure 10.2 shows that in 2009, more than one third of all newsroom supervisors were women, as were more than

FIGURE 10.1

Readership of Local Newspapers Declines, National Newspaper Readership Stagnates

SOURCE: www.gallup.com/poll/1663/Media-Use-Evaluation.aspx.

40 percent of all layout and copy editors and reporters. Those figures reflect the societal changes from the times when "newsmen" were in fact news*men*. Among all positions measured in the annual newsroom census, women were least likely to hold jobs in the visual arts, such as photographer and artist.

Table 10.1 shows another measure of how modern newsrooms have changed along with American society. The table illustrates the proportion of minority journalists working at newspapers in eight circulation categories. From Table 10.1 we can see that minority journalists are much more likely to be employed at larger-circulation newspapers, with minorities constituting one fifth of the journalists at papers having a circulation of 250,000 to 500,000. That proportion is nearly identical at the largest-circulation newspapers and steadily tapers off among newspapers with circulation of less than 250,000.

The Media Go Electronic:
The Radio and Television Revolutions

It is impossible to overemphasize the transformative impact of the early electronic media. From the time of the first U.S. radio broadcasts in the early 1920s, radio allowed listeners to hear news in real time. That immediacy marked a drastic change from the standard, delayed method of receiving news, which was by reading the morning and evening editions of newspapers, plus the occasional "extra edition" published when important breaking news warranted it. Radio also altered the relationship between politicians—particularly presidents—and their constituents, because it enabled listeners to hear the voices of their elected leaders. Television further revolutionized that relationship by making it possible for people to see their leaders (though initially only in black and white).

employment

Supervisors — 65% Men / 35% Women
Copy/layout editors/online producers — 58% / 42%
Reporters — 61% / 39%
Photographers/artists/videographers — 73% / 27%
Total — 63% / 37%

POLITICAL INQUIRY

FIGURE 10.2 ■ NEWSROOM EMPLOYMENT BY GENDER In the past, "newsmen" were in fact news*men*. What does the graph indicate about women's employment in today's newsrooms?

SOURCE: The American Society of Newspaper Editors, "Newsroom Employment Census," Table M, www.asne.org/index.cfm?id=5660.

TABLE 10.1

Minority Journalists as a Percentage of the Professional Workforce of Newspapers in Eight Circulation Categories

NEWSPAPER CIRCULATION	YEAR				
	1980	1992	2000	2005	2009
Over 500,000	7	16	18	18	20
250,001 to 500,000	6	13	18	21	21
100,001 to 250,000	6	10	14	16	17
50,001 to 100,000	6	9	10	12	13
25,001 to 50,000	4	6	8	10	8
10,001 to 25,000	3	6	7	8	6
5,001 to 10,000	2	5	6	6	6
5,000 and under	3	5	6	7	6

SOURCE: The American Society of Newspaper Editors, "Newsroom Employment Census," Table F, www.asne.org/index.cfm?id=5653. Copyright © 2009 The American Society of Newspaper Editors.

How Radio Has Opened Up Political Communication

Radio was the first electronic medium that brought people into direct contact with their leaders. Beginning in the 1920s, radios became a fixture in American living rooms, and families who could not afford a radio of their own would often spend evenings at the homes of friends or neighbors who could.

FDR'S FIRESIDE CHATS   Franklin D. Roosevelt was the first politician to realize the value of radio as a device for political communication—and to exploit that value. As governor of New York (1928–1932), Roosevelt faced a Republican state legislature hostile to many of his liberal social welfare programs. To overcome the opposition, Roosevelt used radio addresses to appeal directly to his constituents, who would then lobby the legislators for his policies. Indeed, after some of Roosevelt's radio addresses, legislative offices were flooded with letters from constituents asking lawmakers to support a particular policy.

By the time Roosevelt became president in 1933, he had grasped the importance of radio as a tool for communicating directly with the people. FDR often began his radio addresses to the country—his **fireside chats**—with the greeting, "Good evening, friends," highlighting the personal relationship he wished to cultivate between himself and his listeners. (You can download many of Roosevelt's fireside chats in MP3 format from the Vincent Voice Library at Michigan State University.) Through the folksy fireside chats, Americans learned about presidential initiatives on the banking crisis, New Deal social welfare programs, the declaration of war on Japan after that nation's attack on Pearl Harbor, and the progress of U.S. forces during World War II. In all, Roosevelt had thirty fireside chats with Americans over his twelve years as president.

During the golden age of radio—the period from the early 1920s through the early 1960s—radio was the dominant form of electronic entertainment. Radio programming included a wide array of shows, from newscasts, to serial dramas, to comedies, to variety shows. Although political and news radio programming remained popular during the 1950s and 1960s, radio generally took a backseat to television during that era.

TALK RADIO: TALKING THE POLITICAL TALK   Radio began to emerge from the shadows of television in the 1970s and 1980s. Those decades brought a renaissance of sorts for radio, as the medium saw tremendous growth in **talk radio**—a format featuring conver-

fireside chats
President Franklin Roosevelt's radio addresses to the country

talk radio
a format featuring conversations and interviews about topics of interest, along with call-ins from listeners

fairness doctrine
requirement that stations provide equal time to all parties regarding important public issues and equal access to airtime to all candidates for public office

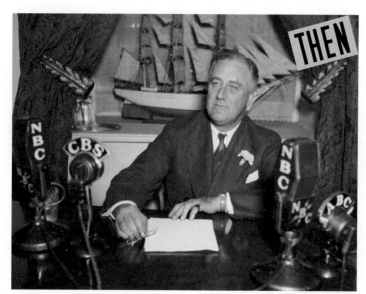

> President Franklin Roosevelt was recognized as a master political communicator. Roosevelt relied on a folksy, conversational tone and the medium of radio to bring his message to the people.

> Some seventy-five years later, another president, Barack Obama, is widely recognized as a skilled political speaker. Unlike FDR, however, Obama uses lofty rhetoric and new technologies to drive his message home. How does a politician's ability to communicate successfully with the people influence his or her governing?

sations and interviews about topics of interest, along with call-ins from listeners. As many AM station owners switched to an all-talk format in those years, music programming migrated to the FM band.

In 1987, the Federal Communications Commission (FCC) repealed the **fairness doctrine,** which had required stations to provide equal time to all sides regarding important public issues and equal access to airtime to all candidates for public office. Since the law's repeal, partisan radio programming has grown dramatically. Today, listeners tend to tune in to radio hosts who share—many say, reinforce—their opinions, and they interact with them through call-in opportunities. Talk radio features numerous well-known personalities, including Rush Limbaugh, Sean Hannity, Mark Levin, and Laura Ingraham, whose shows are also available via the Internet and through podcasts, thus potentially reaching a significantly expanded number of listeners.

Figure 10.3 shows the rise in listenership for talk radio programs since 1995. Daily listenership of such programs nearly doubled between 1995 and 2002, increasing from 12 percent to 22 percent in that time. Since 2002, although daily listnership has dropped, the proportion of people who listen several times a week has held steady at 9 percent.

Talk radio was one of the first forums that allowed media consumers to "talk back" to the host. At its best, talk radio allows for a natural, real-time exchange of information between the host and the audience; at its worst, it has given rise to loud, angry rants and arguments. Scholars widely agree that talk radio programs promote citizen engagement in the form of civic discourse. Recall from earlier chapters that civic discourse means the sharing of viewpoints and the articulation of personal positions on public issues (along with the information gathering and reflective thinking that must accompany that expression). This information sharing is fundamental to a civic society. That is, without informed and shared opinions, people cannot be responsible, politically engaged citizens.

The appeal of talk radio, particularly as broadcast via the Internet, mirrors the allure of Internet blogs. The messages of both media have become highly personal and emotional, targeted to a narrow segment of the public. Conservative radio commentators tend to draw an audience dominated by middle-aged conservative males, while the much smaller liberal market segment tends to draw the coveted younger audience.

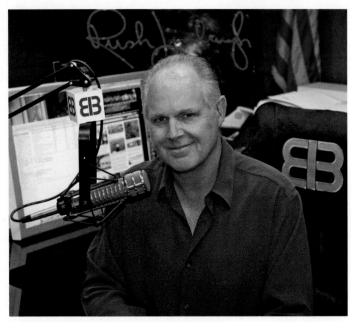

> Although political talk radio programs have been around for decades, technologies such as the Internet and podcasts expand the reach of talk radio hosts such as conservative commentator Rush Limbaugh to a significantly larger audience.

Radio Talk Show Listenership, 1995–2008

Television and the Transformation of Campaigns and Elections

Although radio predates television, TV nonetheless has been the centerpiece of U.S. home entertainment for a long time. Television began to make a mark on the American scene in the 1940s, when small TV sets—their screens flecked with static snowflakes—hit the market. Today, the images we view are crystal clear, as high-definition big-screen

POLITICAL INQUIRY

FIGURE 10.3 ■ **What has been the trend in talk radio listenership since 1995? What factors might explain this trend?**

SOURCE: The Gallup Poll, "Media Use and Evaluation," www.galluppoll.com/content/?ci=1663&pg=1.

TVs increasingly dominate households. Hundreds of channels compete for audience share, ending the previous dominance of the three major networks, ABC, NBC, and CBS.

With all the new competition, network television is rapidly losing viewers. Along with announcing in July 2004 that cable television enjoyed 52 percent of the prime-time TV-viewing audience, Nielsen Media Research, publisher of the famous Nielsen ratings for television shows, reported that network television had just 44 percent (with public television having a 4 percent market share). In addition, total viewership for the television networks had fallen by 41 percent between 1977 and 2003, from 51 million viewers to 30 million.

Figure 10.4 shows the continuation of those changes. Viewership of nightly network news broadcasts on ABC, CBS, and NBC plummeted between 1996 and 2008. In 1996, a large majority of Americans watched a nighttime network news broadcast; by 2008, only 34 percent did, and the number who never watched grew to 23 percent. Compare those figures with the data for the networks' cable news counterparts, where daily viewership has increased by 17 percent in those same years. Among the other categories of TV news (morning shows such as *Good Morning America* and the *Today* show, public television news broadcasts, and local news shows), viewership has essentially stagnated.

As cable news channels such as CNN and Fox News have increased their viewing audience, it is no wonder the word *broadcasting* has spawned the term **narrowcasting**: the practice of aiming political media content at specific segments of the public, divided according to political ideology, party affiliation, or economic interests. This winnowing of audiences has led to **media segmentation,** the breaking down of the media in general according to the specific audiences they target. Examples of segmented media include Black Entertainment Television (BET); the U.S.-based Spanish-language television network Telemundo; and the Lifestyle Network, which includes the Food Network and HGTV. Through media segmentation, advertisers can hone their advertising to the tastes of their targeted market.

Being **telegenic,** or looking good on TV, has become almost mandatory today for serious political candidates. It is unlikely that President William Howard Taft (1909–1913), who weighed over 300 pounds, would ever have been elected if he had been forced to appear on television. Nor would Abraham Lincoln, whose handlers would have marched him straight to a cosmetic surgeon to have the giant mole on his cheek removed. Richard Nixon might have won the presidency in 1960 had it not been for his nervous demeanor and the "five o'clock shadow" on his face that made him look sinister in the first-ever televised presidential candidate debates that year. His opponent, the handsome, relaxed, and articu-

narrowcasting

the practice of aiming media content at specific segments of the public

media segmentation

the breaking down of the media according to the specific audiences they target

telegenic

the quality of looking good on TV

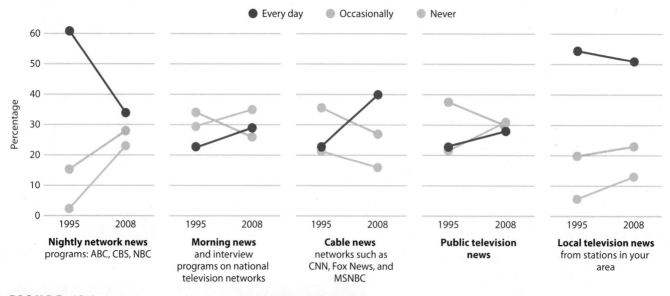

FIGURE 10.4

Where Do Americans Get Their News?

SOURCE: The Gallup Poll, "Media Use and Evaluation," www.gallup.com/poll/1663/Media-Use-Evaluation.aspx.

late John F. Kennedy, won the visual debate hands down, even though in hindsight most analysts agree that Nixon "won" the debate on its verbal merits.

The Media Revolution Continues: The Internet and Cellular Technology

The modern media revolution continued with the birth of the Internet. As a medium of communication, a source of news and information, and a tool for political engagement and grassroots organizing, the Internet has had an incalculable—and a global—impact on the way people interact.

But access to the Internet is not equal, because affluent individuals are more likely than the less affluent to have computers and Internet connections. The term for this unequal access to computer technology is the **digital divide.** Sociologist Mark Wheeler has examined the digital divide, particularly when it comes to high-speed Internet connectivity. He has noted that income and wealth affect individuals' access to high-speed Internet service, even in the world's most affluent democracies.[6]

Yet even for those without computers of their own, the Internet has broadly transformed life in the United States. How the average U.S. citizen is educated, communicates, gets news, shops, receives information about politics, and participates in the political process all have changed because of the Internet. As political scientist Michael Cornfield noted, "I can't think of anything except kissing babies that you can't do online."[7] The influence of the Internet has been both positive and negative, and it continues to evolve.

How the Media Have Shaped Entertainment and the Information Highways

THEN (1960s)	NOW (2011)
Television programming matured and revolutionized how the media entertained and provided information.	The Internet matures and revolutionizes how we are entertained and how we get information.
Television accentuated a new set of candidate qualities—including being telegenic—that had not mattered much in earlier political campaigns.	The Internet accentuates a new set of candidate qualities—including being tech savvy and Net organized—that were unheard of a generation ago.
Communication between the media and voters was one-way: people got information but could not "talk back."	Information flow is two-way, thanks to talk radio and the Internet—including blogs, YouTube, and social-networking sites.

WHAT'S NEXT?

> What new media technologies will shape campaigns and political participation in the future?

> For individuals seeking information about policy issues and political campaigns, what might be the negative consequences of the abundance of information flowing through the electronic media?

> How will technology change political participation in the future?

The Internet and Civic Engagement

Over time, the Internet has transformed the media's function as a conveyor of information and a resource for civic engagement. Communications scholar Howard Rheingold argues that the digital media in particular serve as a key avenue by which young people can use their "public voice" to consume and share information.[8]

THE EVOLUTION OF THE INTERNET In its early years, the Internet functioned in much the same way that traditional media formats such as newspapers and periodicals functioned: it provided a convenient but "one-way" means for people to get information at times determined by the publishers. As **bandwidth**—the amount of data that can travel through a network in a given time period—has increased, so, too, has the sophistication of Web content, as well as the venues and formats that serve as information sources. Today's

digital divide
the inequality of access to computers and Internet connections

bandwidth
the amount of data that can travel through a network in a given time period

news Web sites—including those of all the network and cable news stations, plus sites maintained by Internet service providers such as AOL—give Internet users news stories when they want them instead of at predetermined times. Users can selectively search for specific information about public issues that matter to them, potentially building their knowledge base with a mouse click. Moreover, many contemporary news outlets, including magazines and radio programs, are now making available downloadable podcasts of content that users can view or listen to at their convenience. These podcasts are giving individuals even greater access to information, including reports on social issues, policy initiatives, and politics. Civic participation has been facilitated by the rise of news Web sites and social-networking sites, as well as blogs that allow readers to engage in virtual civic discourse.

THE INTERNET AS A SOURCE OF INFORMATION AND COMMUNITY YouTube provides a compelling example of how the evolving Internet has worked to the benefit of civic engagement. This Web site, which debuted in February 2005, allows individuals to post and watch original videos. The success of the YouTube experiment is inconceivable in the world of the dial-up Internet connection that was the norm just a few years ago. And so, if you want to watch a political advertisement, see congressional testimony, or participate in Citizen Tube (YouTube's video Weblog, or **vblog**), today's technology makes it possible for you to do so in seconds. In fact, President Obama has his own YouTube channel, which broadcasts speeches and press conferences. The interactivity embodied in viewing, commenting, posting, and vblogging has revolutionized civic discourse.

Today's Internet technology also facilitates the formation of virtual communities. These networks of interested participants, though different from their IRL (in real life) counterparts, share features with those real-world groups. Many blogs, for example, have community leaders, regular contributors, expert commentators, and participants with established roles. Blogs promote civic engagement by disseminating information, exposing readers to the viewpoints of others, providing a forum allowing bloggers to share their own views, serving as a venue for the formation of online communities that can foster feelings of efficacy among participants, and channeling activism, both virtual and real.* In short, the Internet has led to the phenomenon of the **prosumer**—the individual who simultaneously consumes information and news and produces information in the form of videos, blogs, and Web sites.

The Internet as a Source of News

The amount of time that Americans spend on the Internet is steadily increasing: in 2005, the average time spent online was three hours daily; it is now over four.[9] Time spent online exceeds the amount of time that people spend consuming other media, including television, radio, and newspaper. Perhaps more important, the number of individuals using the Internet as a source of news continues to increase dramatically. Figure 10.5 shows that in the thirteen-year span from 1995 to 2008, the proportion of Americans who get news from the Internet has grown exponentially. In fact, by 2008 two-thirds of Americans got news from the Internet at least sometimes, and nearly one-third used the Internet as a news source daily. It is no wonder Nielsen TV ratings and newspaper subscriptions have declined.

The adage that a "week is an eternity in politics" has become an understatement in the age of the Internet and the twenty-four-hour news cycle. Things happen in the click of a mouse button, and increasingly politicians are making snap statements in front of ever-present cell phone video cameras and regretting them later.

Such was the case in 2010, when Vice President Joseph Biden used an expletive caught on an open microphone. After introducing President Barack Obama, who had just succeeded in

---

*A note about content: The authors recognize the enormous variation in the quality of information available on the Internet in general and in blogs in particular. So when you are using the Internet as a source of information, a healthy dose of skepticism can be quite useful.

vblog
a video Weblog

prosumers
individuals who simultaneously consume information and news and produce information in the form of videos, blogs, and Web sites

shepherding health care reform through Congress, the vice president turned to the president and said, "This is a big [expletive] deal." Video footage of the gaffe spread like wildfire on the Internet, and more than 1 million people watched a YouTube video of the blunder. In response (and in an effort to control damage), Robert Gibbs, the White House Press Secretary, tweeted, "And yes Mr. Vice President, you're right . . ." on Twitter.

Internet news sites could be doing some things better, though. For example, many news outlets present a news story as either an article or a video, but few major media outlets offer hotlinks to original source data that would aid interested site users in delving more deeply into the story. Instead of a synthesized news article on a Supreme Court decision, for instance, media outlets could provide links to the original opinions on the case as well as links to audio recordings of the arguments before the court, records of lower-court decisions, and briefs filed with the court, supporting or opposing one side or the other, which are available elsewhere online *if* one is willing to search for them. Instead, most outlets offer only broad coverage with links to related stories—an approach that does not make it easy for an individual to research a matter of interest more deeply.

How Often Do You Get News From the Internet?

FIGURE 10.5

Increasing Percentages of Americans Get News from the Internet

SOURCE: The Gallup Poll, "Media Use and Evaluation," www.gallup.com/poll/1663/Media-Use-Evaluation.aspx.

The Internet's Influence on Political Participation and Campaigns

Even more than talk radio, the Internet has made politics participative. People can express their preferences online on issues from health reform to term limits, from income tax credits to repealing the inheritance tax. But besides acting as a gauge for public opinion, the Internet can also be a useful tool for citizens' political activism. The traditional media have not had nearly the impact on political participation that the Internet has had. For example, the left-of-center wing of the Democratic Party has not achieved the same media dominance in radio as the conservative wing of the Republican Party. One radio station targeting liberal listeners, Air America, went on the air in 2004, but it never succeeded in attracting a competitive share of the radio audience and ceased operation early in 2010. What *has* worked in attracting the liberal wing of the youth vote are blogs and Web sites such as www.moveon.org.

USING THE INTERNET TO MOBILIZE VOTERS Jesse Ventura, a professional wrestler who served as the governor of Minnesota from 1999 to 2003, credits the Web for opening up the political process by enabling grassroots mobilization through **e-campaigning,** the practice of mobilizing voters using the Internet, which allowed an outsider like him to be elected governor. Winning half of the under-thirty vote, Ventura conducted a campaign without any physical headquarters—at least at first. Armed with a large e-mail list, he enlisted pledges of support that short-circuited the traditional doorbell ringing and telephone calls that go with the territory when running for office. His tactics gave him the final surge of voters that he needed to win. Ventura's victory testifies to the power of the Internet as a political campaign tool.

During the 2010 mid-term congressional elections, candidates updated their Facebook status and tweeted press releases. E-campaigning became fully integrated into the political communication process. For example. Sen. Pat Toomey (R-PA) tweeted "why Democrats are supporting Pat Toomey." BlogHer.com collected questions from blog readers, then posed those questions to women candidates running for Congress. The responses were then posted on the blog's site. Nearly every candidate boasted a Facebook page, and staffers often jokingly compared the numbers of candidates friends and fans.

e-campaigning
the practice of mobilizing voters using the Internet

The Internet has even changed how candidacies are announced and presidential campaigns unfold. A campaign video of former senator John Edwards announcing his candidacy in New Orleans ran on YouTube, and both Senator Barack Obama and Senator Hillary Rodham Clinton announced their candidacies via their Web sites, followed by the posting of the corresponding videos on YouTube.

HOW THE INTERNET CAN AFFECT A POLITICAL CAMPAIGN

The Internet has also changed the nature of political organizing. On the day that Senator Obama announced his bid for the presidency, Farouk Olu Aregbe, a student government adviser at the University of Missouri, logged on to www.facebook.com and announced the formation of a group called "One Million Strong for Barack." Within a month, Aregbe's Facebook group had over a quarter of a million members, and other Facebook users had formed more than five hundred groups supporting the candidate.

But the rapid expansion of Internet technology has also made it more difficult for presidential campaigns (and administrations) to manage the news.[10]

Today's Blogosphere

Clearly, the widespread use of the Internet has also contributed to the spread of blogs. A

blogosphere
a community, or social network, of bloggers

new language has sprouted to incorporate this development, beginning with **blogosphere**—the community, or social network, of bloggers. Estimates indicate that the number of blogs has doubled every five months since 2003 to a current level of over 50 million individual blogs.[11] As the number has multiplied, their variety and credibility have increased. Bloggers received press credentials at both the Democratic and the Republican conventions in 2008. Traditional television and print media outlets now host blogs as well. Many who read blogs note that they are more up to date than traditional media outlets, and bloggers themselves believe that blogs have influenced and are most likely to continue to influence the field of politics. Figures 10.6 and 10.7 show the results of a Technorati.com poll, in which the majority of bloggers (57 percent) said they thought that bloggers have influenced politics more than any other field. Fifty-one percent also said that they thought blogging will have more impact in the field of politics than in any other field in the next decade.

The blog's rise as a tool of grassroots organizing has given birth to the term **netroots** to describe Net-centered political efforts on behalf of candidates and causes. A blog makes information available to large numbers of users immediately, spreading news and energizing supporters more rapidly than any other medium. It also differs from traditional media in one important way: bloggers make no attempt to be impartial. A blog is an opinion journal, offering a specific perspective and appealing to a specific segment of the public. In that respect, it cannot replace traditional journalism, especially because there is no check on whether the facts it presents are correct. But blogs continue to change the face of political campaigning and grassroots organization—for better and for worse.

netroots
the Internet-centered political efforts on behalf of candidates and causes

> In 2008, bloggers at the national party conventions were granted press credentials. Blogs spread news—though sometimes *inaccurate* news—and opinions very quickly. Their drawbacks aside, blogs have changed the landscape of political campaigning and grassroots organizing.

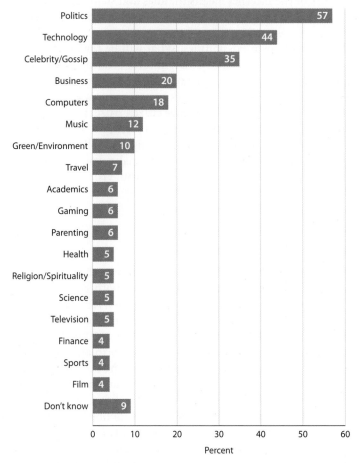

Bloggers believe blogging has influenced politics the most...

Field	Percent
Politics	57
Technology	44
Celebrity/Gossip	35
Business	20
Computers	18
Music	12
Green/Environment	10
Travel	7
Academics	6
Gaming	6
Parenting	6
Health	5
Religion/Spirituality	5
Science	5
Television	5
Finance	4
Sports	4
Film	4
Don't know	9

Percent

FIGURE 10.6

Looking back on the history of blogging so far, what fields do you think it has had the greatest impact on?

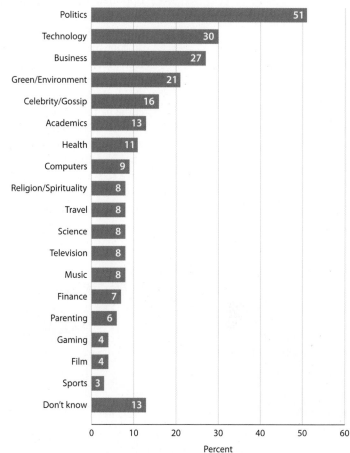

...and will continue to influence politics in the future.

Field	Percent
Politics	51
Technology	30
Business	27
Green/Environment	21
Celebrity/Gossip	16
Academics	13
Health	11
Computers	9
Religion/Spirituality	8
Travel	8
Science	8
Television	8
Music	8
Finance	7
Parenting	6
Gaming	4
Film	4
Sports	3
Don't know	13

Percent

FIGURE 10.7

Looking forward, what fields do you think blogging will have the greatest impact on in the next ten years?

SOURCE: http://technorati.com/blogging/article/day-5-twitter-global-impact-and/page-2/.

Media Convergence

The concept of convergence has taken hold among media observers today. **Convergence** refers to the merging of various forms of media—newspapers, television stations, radio networks, and blogs—under one corporate roof with one set of business and editorial leaders. The emergence of Politico, a multimedia start-up that debuted in Washington, D.C., in January 2007, is an example of this concept come to life. What would have been regarded in the past as a violation of antitrust laws is now considered the wave of the future. Politico's mission is to report on the daily politics on Capitol Hill and in the White House. Politico is a publication of Capital News Corp., which is financed by Allbritton Communications, which used to own a now-defunct newspaper called the *Washington Star*.

convergence

the merging of various forms of media, including newspapers, television stations, radio networks, and blogs, under one corporate roof and one set of business and editorial leaders

The Negative Political Impact of the Internet

The explosion of the Internet in politics has also opened a Pandora's box of problems. One key problem is misinformation. Unlike newspapers, magazines, and television networks, where editors and fact-checkers are responsible for ensuring accuracy, the Internet is almost entirely unmonitored. In political campaigns, misinformation can be devastating.

Another problem is that the Internet has contributed to the decline in civility in political discourse. Some bloggers and anonymous messageboard posters seek to destroy their opponents' reputations. The nature of the Internet means that lies and slanderous accusations can often be leveled with no consequence to the poster. This problem occurs not just in national politics but in community politics as well.

The Internet also poses a host of unknown possibilities. What will be the crossover effects, for example, of such present-day crimes as identity theft and the stealing of social security numbers and state secrets by hackers? Consider the problems of a national election conducted through computer terminals. How would a recount be managed? Would the outcome be fair? Would the losers view it as fair? Would the average citizen trust the results?

And although new communications tools allow politicians substantially to reduce the amount of legwork and "flesh pressing" required in a typical campaign, the absence of such glad-handing could also destroy the flavor of local politics. Politicians would no longer have to stand in front of supermarkets and kiss babies, but neither would the voters be able to get to know the candidates or to probe into their views on the issues.

> New media has changed how politics occurs within societies. During protests in Iran in 2009, the Iranian government restricted reporters covering the events, but both journalists and private citizens used Twitter to post updates about the situation there.

SOURCE: http://travelintoaprworld.files.wordpress.com/2009/06/iran_tweets_0616.jpg.

The Internet and Free Speech

The rise of the Internet has occurred at a pace that has not allowed societies to digest its potential for both good and evil causes in the battle for free speech. Consider, for example, the impact the Internet and cellular technology had in the aftermath of the Iranian elections in the summer of 2009. That year, Web sites, blogs, and cell phones were the primary tools used by pro-democracy activists who disputed the outcome of the Iranian elections, in which President Mahmoud Ahmadinejad claimed victory over opposition candidate Mir-Hossein Mousavi, so that the protests came to be dubbed the "Twitter Revolution." Protesters relied on Twitter, text messages, and social-networking sites to organize rallies. In response, the Iranian government also used technology, including videos recorded on cell phones, to identify and arrest protesters.

But the use of the Internet as a dangerous tool is not limited to Iranian government officials half a world away: in the United States, there are few restrictions on the content that can be posted on the Internet. Thus hate groups throughout the world are able to register their domain name in the United States. These Web sites can be used to spew hatred and organize like-minded individuals.

The danger is that some of these activities might lead to acts of violence, including murder. In spring 2005, U.S. District Court judge Joan Humphrey Lefkow returned home from work to find the murdered bodies of her husband and her mother in the basement of her home on Chicago's North Side. Their killer, an unemployed electrician, had found Judge Lefkow's name and address posted on several hate Web sites, where readers were encouraged to take justice into their own hands. The day after the murders, Bill White, editor of one of the hate sites, posted his approval: "Everyone associated with the Matt Hale trial [over which Judge Lefkow had presided] has deserved assassination for a long time. I don't feel bad that Judge Lefkow's family was murdered. . . . In fact . . . I laughed."[12]

The availability of cheap worldwide communications technology makes the Internet an ideal tool for terrorists and other haters who hide among the world's 1.8 billion users, including about 220 million Americans.[13] The murder of Judge Lefkow's husband and her mother introduced a new dimension to the nation's debate over the limits of free speech. The Internet has allowed extremists to seize on new technologies to spread their messages far more effectively than the soapboxes of earlier days; it also enhances their ability to promote and recruit supporters to their causes.

The United States is wedded to the principle of freedom of speech, refusing to regulate the Internet or any other vehicle of free speech. Throughout the nation's history, speech of all kinds has been protected, with periodic exceptions for sedition in war as well as for child pornography in peacetime. Americans have great tolerance for language and believe that fringe groups can flourish freely in a democracy without risking tears in the fabric of society. But the world has changed since 9/11, and as the threat of terrorism grows, many citizens expect lawmakers to do whatever is necessary—including setting limits on free speech—to curb violence spawned by the prevalence of hate on the Internet.[14]

Biased Media?

A recent joke about how the media will cover the end of the world stereotyped the nation's major newspapers while also emphasizing their importance in reporting world events. As the story goes, the *New York Times* headline would be: "World Ends; Third World Hit Worst." The *Washington Post*'s front page would blare: "World Ends; Unnamed Source Says White House Had Prior Knowledge." In *USA Today*, a newspaper with a huge national and international circulation, the story would be titled "We're Dead; State-by-State Analysis, page 4D; Sports, page 6C." And the *Wall Street Journal*? "World Ends; Stock Market Goes Down."

Media critics today are everywhere. All of them claim that both print and electronic media exhibit bias in their reporting, in their selection of what issues to cover, and in favoring one side of an issue (or one politician) over another. One of the most common complaints is that the media have an ideological bias.

THE QUESTION OF IDEOLOGICAL BIAS A long-standing complaint is that the media—particularly big-city newspapers—evidence a liberal bias. For example, former House majority leader Tom DeLay (R-Texas) protested the liberal leanings of two of the country's major newspapers, the *New York Times* and the *Washington Post*, for running stories about his ethics problems. Those media, he claimed, ignored the same practices when Democrats such as Nancy Pelosi (D-California), then House minority leader, engaged in them. The day after the *New York Times* published an article revealing that DeLay's congressional campaign had paid his wife and daughter more than $500,000 for their services, DeLay lashed out, stating that the article was "just another seedy attempt by the liberal media to embarrass me."

The notion that the media have a liberal bias is an often-heard criticism. In 1964, former president Dwight D. Eisenhower, in his address to the Republican National Convention, condemned a liberal media bias:

> My friends, we are Republicans. If there is any finer word in the field of partisan politics, I have not heard it. So let us particularly [scorn] the divisive efforts of those outside our family, including sensation-seeking columnists and commentators, who couldn't care less about the good of our party.[15]

Many conservatives point to studies indicating that a majority of newsroom reporters identify themselves as liberal or Democrat. Conservatives charge that the ideological bent of the journalists carries through to the topics covered and to the perspectives of the stories. But studies conducted by various political scientists, including C. Richard Hofstetter, Michael J. Robinson, and Margaret A. Sheehan, refute the idea that journalists' personal viewpoints tinge the content of the news in a liberal way.[16] Indeed, studies suggest that most news stories take the form of a debate, with the journalist presenting the various sides of an issue and leaving the conclusion to the reader's interpretation.

Changes in the nature of the mass media have led to increasingly vocal charges, especially by Democratic elected officials, that newer media outlets, particularly talk radio and the blogosphere, are dominated by conservatives.

THE PUBLIC'S VIEW ON MEDIA BIAS   What does the public think about partisan bias? Figure 10.8 shows that when asked the question "In general, do you think the news media are — ?" (the survey rotated the potential responses: "too liberal," "just about right," and "too conservative"), 45 percent responded that they thought the news media were too liberal. Thirty-five percent said they thought the media were "just about right" ideologically, and 15 percent said they believed the news media were too conservative.

Thus more than half (60 percent) of those surveyed believed that the media are biased (either liberally or conservatively). Yet research by William P. Eveland Jr. and Dhavan V. Shah into people's perception of media bias concluded that it is often linked to whether people have conversations with others whose views differ from theirs. When they do not have such dialogues, they are more likely to believe that the media are biased against their view.[17]

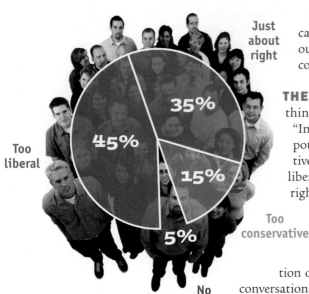

FIGURE 10.8

Public Opinion of Ideological Media Bias

SOURCE: The Gallup Poll, "Media Use and Evaluation," www.gallup.com/poll/1663/Media-Use-Evaluation.aspx.

THE ISSUE OF CORPORATE BIAS   Most professional journalists hold journalistic objectivity to be important, and that principle well serves the interests of the large corporations that dominate the U.S. media industry today. Within the giant media conglomerates, motivated as they are by the drive for profits, there is strong disincentive for ideological bias on the part of their reporters. Newspapers and television stations rely on advertisers, and advertisers want not only to attract the largest number of readers or viewers but also to avoid offending the largest numbers. Thus, given the corporate nature of today's media, neutrality is generally a guiding principle.

Critics on the left, however, argue that these corporate structures create their own bias and that this bias has altered what is considered news and how that news is covered.[18] Corporate bias—and the desire to attract, keep, and please an audience—produces skewed programming. Will corporate conglomerates be willing to report on situations that may put themselves and their advertisers in a negative light? How does the drive for profits influence what is in the news? Are viewers being fed "news" that is not particularly newsworthy? There is no doubt that profits influence the media to cover the kinds of stories that viewers and readers want. In particular, violence dominates most local news programming, so much so that the principle of "if it bleeds, it leads" now extends into the first fifteen minutes of many local news broadcasts. Fires; political, sport, and sex scandals; and celebrity-heavy news are also powerful audience attractors.

"Why don't the media report good news?" is an oft-repeated question from those who feel scarred by bad publicity. Are the media biased in favor of the negative? If the sun comes up in the morning, is that news? In fact, although many individuals bemoan the emphasis on the negative, good news typically does not attract the audience that bad news does.

Regulation of the Media: Is It Necessary?

The framers of the Constitution had to be concerned only with print media when they guaranteed freedom of the press—one of the fundamental liberties they ensured in the Bill of Rights. As the media evolved beyond print into electronic formats, so, too, did thinking about the government's role in regulating the media, especially media outlets such as radio and television stations. But technology has outpaced the ability of the government to regulate certain forms of electronic media, including the Internet and satellite radio services

> Should telecommunications giants such as Verizon and Comcast be allowed to use their market power to control information flowing over the Internet or to favor certain online clients?

such as Sirius XM. Nonetheless, television and regular radio transmissions are still subject to government regulation.

The government regulates and controls the ownership of radio and television stations through the independent regulatory agency known as the Federal Communications Commission (FCC), founded in 1934. Most of the FCC's rules have concerned ownership, such as the number of outlets a network may own.

In 1996, Congress passed the Telecommunications Act, which opened the communications markets to telephone companies. This sweeping law allowed competition in the communications industry. It presented new (often confusing) options for consumers, as individual companies began to offer a suite of services, from local and long-distance telephone service, to Internet access, to cable and satellite television.

With the combination of all of these services under single companies, large corporate conglomerates have increasingly gained control of the media. Firms such as Disney, Viacom, News Corporation, and Time Warner exert a powerful influence over what news the average American sees and reads on a given day. The advent of these media titans has given rise to concerns about whether this type of control will deter balanced reporting of the news and unbiased presentations of issues. In addition, public conversations about our democracy are questioning whether the relative lack of competition (because there are so few competitors) means that a valuable check on what the media do and how they do it has been lost.

Congress is currently considering another question of control over the business of the media. The issue, a controversial one, centers on **Net neutrality**: the idea that Internet traffic—e-mail, Web sites, videos, and phone calls—should flow through the Internet pipeline without interference or discrimination by those who own or are running the pipeline. (See "Thinking Critically About Democracy" on page 328.) *Should* these broadband behemoths be able to use their market power to control information or to favor certain clients online? Critics charge that congressional passage of legislation supporting the service providers would destroy the neutrality and openness of the Internet. Tim Berners-Lee, the inventor of the World Wide Web, says, "The neutral communications medium is essential to our society. . . . It is the basis of democracy, by which a community should decide what to do."[19] Do you agree with Berners-Lee? In what ways would you say that neutral media are the basis of a democracy?

Net neutrality
the idea that Internet traffic—e-mail, Web site content, videos, and phone calls—should flow without interference or discrimination by those who own or run the Internet pipeline

SHOULD CONGRESS REGULATE THE INTERNET INFRASTRUCTURE?

The Issue: The technological revolution has brought on-going, exponential growth in Internet traffic. As rising numbers of people turn to the Internet for more and more uses—from viewing videos online to sending pictures to Grandma, and from buying gifts and personal items to calling friends and relatives—the volume of information that the broadband infrastructure of the Internet must transmit is becoming overwhelming. The owners of that infrastructure—corporate giants such as AT&T, Verizon, and Comcast—seek legislation that would allow them to charge companies that produce high volumes of traffic. In effect, this legislation would set up a two-tiered system of broadband access in which one tier is an "express lane" with tolls, and the other an older, slower lane with free access. One problem is that many of today's services require the faster access to make them effective.

Yes: Congress should regulate the Internet infrastructure. We need a two-tiered system of broadband access. The telecommunications titans in command of the Internet infrastructure argue that to keep up with the increasing demand for broadband space, they will have to expand and improve the system continually. Corporate advocates of a two-tiered system of broadband access are also interested in providing premium-quality broadband service to their own clientele. Thus, for example, Verizon wants to ensure that its Internet subscribers (rather than the subscribers of its competitors) have high-quality access to the broadband infrastructure technology that Verizon owns so that its subscribers do not get caught in an Internet traffic jam.

No: "Fast lane" services are a bad idea, because they would hurt both businesses and consumers. In fact, a broad coalition of businesses and interest groups, including savetheinternet.org, oppose measures that would enable broadband providers to charge for their services. The opposing entities also include firms such as Microsoft, Google, eBay, and Yahoo and powerful citizen organizations such as the American Association of Retired People (AARP). Senator Ron Wyden (D-Oregon) has introduced legislation that would prevent broadband providers from creating for-fee "fast lane" services.

It is the very accessibility of the Internet that has fostered strong business growth. Start-ups such as YouTube and Vonage Internet phone service are examples of ventures that may not have been able to compete and survive in a tiered broadband system. A paying system could also prevent future Internet business development.

Other approaches: Without essential maintenance and expansion, the Internet infrastructure cannot keep up with soaring demand. In addition, the security of the system is crucial to continued business activity and corporate financial growth, as well as to national economic health. Broadband availability is a national security issue because if law enforcers, airports, hospitals, nuclear power plants, and first responders do not have adequate or immediate access to the information they need to perform their jobs, human lives are at risk. Because of these critical financial and security implications, a tax or user fee could be instituted that would pay for Internet infrastructure improvements.

What do you think?

① Do you believe that Congress should reject proposals to create a for-fee fast lane for Internet traffic? If so, why? Or do you think the marketplace should determine which services get faster access to broadband lines? If so, why would the latter be preferable?

② What impact would the creation of a two-tiered Internet structure have on Internet business development? On national security?

③ Should the federal government help to defray the costs of improvements to the Internet infrastructure? Why, or why not?

The surge in the number and the variety of media outlets—along with the changes in the nature of the media and in people's interactions with them—has affected politics and government in many ways. Once defined as a one-way relationship, the relationship between the media and consumers has evolved in unforeseen ways. Even the nature of the "old media" has changed, although many would ask whether the change has been for the better. On the one hand, narrowcasting and the resulting segmentation of media markets, a central feature of media growth, might raise the comfort level of many people, who no longer have to throw soft objects at their television sets in protest but can instead pick and choose what they watch. On the other hand, media segmentation also limits the exposure of many people to new ideas. Like gated communities, segmented media are also segregated media, detached environments that expose people only to viewpoints with which they agree, thus cordoning them off from society and from many of its problems. Segmented media also confuse genuine political participation with mere ranting. After all, sounding off on a radio talk show is much easier and more entertaining than attending a zoning board meeting to fight urban congestion or becoming civically engaged in other ways.

Technology has created a two-way relationship between the media and consumers, involving the exchange of seemingly limitless information in a vast conversation of democracy. The openness and easy accessibility of the new media have led to considerable criticism of them, but the good news is that almost all public—and to a lesser extent, private—institutions have become much more transparent in recent years. Supreme Court justice Louis Brandeis (1856-1941) once said that sunlight was the best disinfectant, that public scrutiny was the best step toward genuine reform. This two-way relationship has also meant that citizens are afforded greater opportunities to use their public voice to influence government and the policies it creates. How can this changing public voice be used in today's political arena?

Can we predict the future of the media by examining the past and the present? Certainly we can foretell increasing transparency because of the pervasive nature of today's media and the steady trend in that direction, but we cannot predict the forms media will take. What we can guarantee is continued change in the forms and usage of media, and steadily increasing access to information. Will this expanding access overload people with information? It appears that many of us are developing new skills to cope with the abundance of information, much in the way that our grandparents may have developed the skill of skimming a newspaper, selecting only those stories that mattered to them. The question remains as to whether we will select only information that confirms what we already think. One trend is clear: the ever-increasing volume of information and the speed of its delivery will yield an abundance of both poor-quality and high-quality information. How can media consumers use the plethora of information to ensure they are receiving verifiable information?

The modern media have opened the door more widely to citizens' direct participation in the democratic process. In light of Americans' high levels of cynicism about their elected leaders, might this powerful new opportunity to be heard make our democracy more participatory than the Constitution's framers ever intended or imagined? Will the availability of the Internet as a forum for citizens and a tool for organizing lead to a meaningful expansion of participation in civic life and in the conversation of democracy? Will citizens use the new technology productively?

STUDY NOW

Summary

1. The Modern Media
Changing technology has meant an overabundance of information, which varies greatly in quality. The modern media is also increasingly reliant on citizen journalists. Both trends mean that consumers of the media must be cautious and consider the sources of information.

2. The Political Functions of the Media
The media perform several key political functions, including disseminating information, helping to interpret matters of public interest and to set the national policy agenda, providing a forum for political conversations, and socializing children to the political culture.

3. The Press and Politics: A Historical View
Since early in American history, the press has played a vital role in shaping the political context. As the format of the media has evolved over the centuries, so has media impact on politics and policy making.

4. The Media Go Electronic: The Radio and Television Revolutions
The advent of the electronic media marked a revolutionary change with respect to the impact of media on politics. Television has altered the nature of politics and campaigning, affecting everything from how campaigns for office are conducted to how candidates look and dress. Talk radio, too, has had a significant impact on politics and government by providing a forum for political discourse that is open to participation by virtually everyone.

5. The Media Revolution Continues: The Internet and Cellular Technology
The Internet has drastically altered the political landscape by making available, in a keystroke, an abundance of information and by serving as a powerful medium for the broad, rapid dissemination of information and opinion. The Internet has changed how political campaigns are conducted, including aspects such as fund-raising, voter mobilization, candidacy announcements, and campaign strategy.

6. A Biased Media?
In considering the question of media bias, we must consider the issues both of content bias and of ideological bias. A frequent complaint is that the media—particularly big-city newspapers—have a liberal bias. However, studies by various political scientists conclude that journalists' personal views do not color news content in a liberal way. This research stresses, rather, that most news stories take the form of a debate that presents the various sides of an issue and leaves the conclusion to the reader's interpretation.

7. Regulation of the Media: Is It Necessary?
The Federal Communications Commission is the government agency charged with regulating radio and TV stations and controlling their ownership. The Telecommunications Act of 1996 allowed competition in the communications industry and presented new options for consumers, as individual companies began to offer a suite of services. With the combination of all these services under single companies, large corporate conglomerates increasingly have gained control of the media. Thus, in an era of new media technologies, the FCC's job has become more complex.

Key Terms

For Review

1. What has been the impact of changing technologies on the type of information available to media consumers?

2. What political functions do the media perform? How have these functions changed over time?

3. Describe the evolution of the press in the United States. How do newspapers today differ from newspapers in earlier centuries?

4. What impact has television had on how people get information? On how political campaigns are waged?

5. How have changes in technology influenced political participation? In particular, what has been the impact of the Internet and blogs?

6. What evidence is there to support claims of media bias? Is all bias ideological?

7. In what specific ways does the government regulate media? What aspects of the media and their coverage does the government not regulate?

For Critical Thinking and Discussion

1. Has the Internet changed how you personally participate in politics? Does virtual activism make real-world activism less likely or more likely? Explain.

2. What do you think are the *most important* functions the media perform? Why? Does the diversity of media outlets hinder the media's ability to serve some of their more traditional functions? Explain.

3. Compare and contrast the penny papers of the nineteenth century with today's blogs. What are the similarities and differences between the two? How will blogs evolve given the evolution of other media forms?

4. Discuss the dangers of the unchecked Internet in the political world. Can these dangers be combated? If so, how?

5. What difficulties are associated with government regulation of the media in an era of cable television, the Internet, and satellite radio?

PRACTICE QUIZ

MULTIPLE CHOICE: Choose the lettered item that answers the question correctly.

1. Merging various media forms (newspapers, television stations, radio networks, and blogs) under one roof is called
   a. networking.
   b. convergence.
   c. media relations.
   d. blogosphere.

2. When it comes to content on the Internet,
   a. all information posted must be verifiable.
   b. all information posted must be opinion.
   c. consumers must exercise caution and consider the source of the information.
   d. citizen journalists do not play a role in providing information.

3. Individuals who simultaneously consume information and news and produce information in the form of videos, blogs, and Web sites are called
   a. bloggers.
   b. net audience.
   c. Web makers.
   d. prosumers.

4. President Franklin Roosevelt's radio addresses to the country were called
   a. great communications.
   b. White House communiqués.
   c. roundtable conversations.
   d. fireside chats.

5. The idea that Internet traffic—e-mails, Web site content, videos, and phone calls—can be transmitted through the Internet pipeline without interference or discrimination by those who own or run the pipeline is called
   a. Net neutrality.
   b. Internet objectivity.
   c. the neutral frontier.
   d. absolute Web domain.

6. The practice of aiming media messages at specific segments of the public is called
   a. limited media.
   b. media messaging.
   c. narrowcasting.
   d. information limitation.

7. The requirement that stations provide equal time to all parties regarding important public issues and equal access to airtime to all candidates for public office is called
   a. Net neutrality.
   b. the limited media.
   c. the fairness doctrine.
   d. information objectivity.

8. The breaking down of the media according to specific audiences they target is called
   a. media segmentation.
   b. media messaging.
   c. narrowcasting.
   d. media categorization.

9. The practice of mobilizing voters using the Internet is called
   a. I-rallying.
   b. e-campaigning.
   c. netroots.
   d. Web mobilization.

10. The inequality of access to computers and Internet connections is called
    a. narrowcasting.
    b. media inequality.
    c. the media class system.
    d. the digital divide.

FILL IN THE BLANKS.

11. Public issues that most demand the attention of government officials are called the _____ .

12. A _____ is a video weblog.

13. The journalists who criticized and exposed corruption in government and industry at the turn of the twentieth century were called _____ .

14. The amount of data that can travel through a network in a given time period is called _____ .

15. A person who looks good on TV is called _____ .

Answers: 1. b, 2. c, 3. d, 4. d, 5. a, 6. c, 7. c, 8. a, 9. b, 10. d, 11. public agenda, 12. vblog, 13. muckrakers, 14. bandwidth, 15. telegenic.

Internet Resources

State of the Media
www.stateofthemedia.org Run by the Project for Excellence in Journalism, this site features an annual report on the media and tracks trends in media usage and confidence in the media.

The Pew Research Center for People and the Press
http://people-press.org This site provides independent research, surveys, data sets, and commentary on the media and issues of media interest.

Media Watch
www.mediawatch.com Visit this site to learn about the initiatives of an activist group that monitors media content and seeks to combat stereotypes and violence in the media.

Internet Activism

Twitter
Follow ReadWriteWeb on Twitter to keep up with one of the most popular technology blog's coverage of the Internet industry.

YouTube
Watch the YouTube video channel Reporter's Center, which teaches aspiring citizen journalists how to cover news events.

Recommended Readings

Arnold, R. Douglas. *Congress, the Press, and Political Accountability.* Princeton, NJ: Princeton University Press, 2004. Analyzes how local newspapers cover members of Congress in their districts throughout a legislative session.

Bennett, W. Lance. *News: The Politics of Illusion.* 7th ed. New York: Longman, 2006. Offers a behind-the-scenes tour of the media in politics while grappling with the question, How well does the news, as the core of the national political information system, serve the needs of democracy?

Cavanaugh, John William. *Media Effects on Voters.* Lanham, MD: University Press of America, 1995. Explores how traditional and new media influence voting choices.

Cook, Timothy E. *Governing with the News: The News Media as a Political Institution.* Chicago: University of Chicago Press, 1998. Examines the media as the "fourth branch" of government, including how the media shape public policy and how policy makers respond to the media's agenda setting.

Crouse, Timothy. *The Boys on the Bus.* New York: Random House, 1973. A classic tale of the presidential campaign press corps.

Graber, Doris. *Media Power and Politics.* Washington, DC: CQ Press, 2006. Analyzes the influence of the media on opinions, elections, and policies, as well as efforts to shape the content and impact of media coverage.

Iyengar, Shanto, and Jennifer A. McGrady. *Media Politics: A Citizen's Guide.* New York: W.W. Norton, 2006. Surveys how politicians use the media to get elected, wield power in office, and achieve policy goals.

Jamieson, Kathleen Hall, and Paul Waldman. *The Press Effect: Politicians, Journalists, and the Stories That Shape the Political World.* Oxford: Oxford University Press, 2003. Demonstrates how the national press molds the news through its reporting, using the examples of the 2000 presidential election, the Supreme Court's decision on the Florida vote that year, and the press's response to national politics after 9/11.

Plissner, Martin. *The Control Room: How Television Calls the Shots in Presidential Elections.* New York: Free Press, 1999. Describes the effect of television news and advertising on presidential elections.

Movies of Interest

Good Night and Good Luck (2005)
Directed by George Clooney, this film tells the story of famed CBS newsman Edward R. Murrow, who takes on Senator Joseph McCarthy and the House Un-American Activities Committee's communist witch hunt during the 1950s despite pressure from corporate sponsors and from McCarthy himself.

Shattered Glass (2003)
Stephen Glass was a staff writer for the *New Republic* and was also freelancing for other prominent publications when it was discovered that he had fabricated stories. This film depicts his career and his downfall.

Veronica Guerin (2003)
Starring Cate Blanchett, this film is based on the true story of Veronica Guerin, a crime reporter for the *Dublin Sunday Independent,* who was murdered in 1996.

Live from Baghdad (2002)
This movie demonstrates the differences in tactics between twenty-four-hour news channels and network news shows, telling the story of CNN's coverage of the U.S. invasion of Iraq in 1990.

All the President's Men (1976)
Starring Dustin Hoffman and Robert Redford, this film, based on Bob Woodward and Carl Bernstein's best-selling book of the same title, tells the saga of the two *Washington Post* reporters' investigation of the Watergate scandal that rocked the Nixon White House.

Network (1976)
Faye Dunaway, Peter Finch, William Holden, and Robert Duvall star in this classic satirizing the nature of newscasting in the 1970s.

Citizen Kane (1941)
This classic, directed by and starring Orson Welles, is Welles's fictionalized version of newspaper scion William Randolph Hearst, who purportedly attempted to halt release of the film.

11

Congress

THEN

The framers granted to Congress certain explicit powers, as well as key implied powers by which the national government strengthened and broadened its authority.

NOW

A much more demographically diverse Congress exercises wide powers, its decision making influenced by shifting constituencies in a fast-growing, fast-changing country.

NEXT

Will technology significantly affect the ability of "average" citizens to influence Congress?

Will the composition and policy making of Congress more broadly reflect the changing face of the United States?

What pressing new issues will Congress be forced to consider?

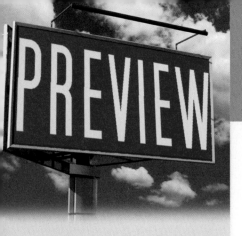

PREVIEW

Congress is an institution shaped

by the people elected to serve there, men and women acting as the trusted representatives of the constituents who voted them into office. Congress and the policies it sets are molded by the times; laws passed in one generation may seem antiquated to the next. And Congress and the policies it creates are influenced by many other factors, including the legislative body's institutional history, the lawmaking process, and the internal and external actors—congressional leaders, political parties, interest groups, the president, staff members, ordinary citizens, and the media, who seek to influence congressional actions.

The Constitution's framers structured the government so that Congress—more so than the two other institutions of the federal government—would be responsive to the needs and the will of the people. In representing their constituents, members of Congress provide an easily accessed point of contact for people to connect with their government and to have their voices heard.

Citizens today have countless opportunities to participate in shaping Congress's agenda and influencing how the members of Congress vote. Individuals and groups of constituents communicate through e-mail, networking sites on the Internet such as Facebook, and telephone, and meet face-to-face with members of Congress on issues that concern them. Constituents meet with congressional staff members for help in understanding how to deal with government bureaucracy. Through congressional campaigns and elections, citizens learn about issues of national importance and can participate in a variety of ways, such as volunteering in support of a candidate's run for office, contributing to the individual's campaign, becoming informed about the candidates and the issues, and casting a ballot on Election Day.

Throughout this chapter, we view Congress through the lens of civic engagement, seeing that Congress—the people's branch of the federal government—though imperfect, is structured to empower citizens to play a role in determining public policy priorities. And ultimately it is the people, through their choices at the ballot box, who decide who the creators of those policies will be.

This chapter provides a foundation for your study of Congress.

FIRST, we examine *the origins of Congress.*

SECOND, we explore the process of *congressional elections.*

THIRD, we consider the *powers of Congress.*

FOURTH, we survey the *functions of Congress,* including representation, policy making, oversight, agenda setting and civic engagement, and management of societal conflict.

FIFTH, we take stock of the similarities and differences between the two chambers of the national legislature as we look at *the House and the Senate compared.*

SIXTH, we focus on how a bill becomes a law by examining *the legislative process.*

SEVENTH, we analyze how the *congressional leadership* affects the legislature's ability to perform its functions.

EIGHTH, we consider *decision making in Congress,* with a particular eye to *the legislative context.*

NINTH, we examine the similarities and differences between *the people and their elected representatives.*

The Origins of Congress

For the United States' founders, creating the national Congress was a crucially important task. Fearful of a powerful executive, but having endured the problems stemming from the weak national government under the Articles of Confederation, the framers of the Constitution believed that the legislature should be the key branch of the newly formed national government. In their vision, the Congress would be the institution responsible for making laws that would create effective public policy. In structuring the Congress, the framers strove to create a legislative branch that was at once powerful enough to govern and to check the power of the president and yet not so powerful that the legislature itself would exercise tyrannical rule. (See "Global Context" for an example of how a different constitution structured Japan's legislature.)

As they debated the shape of the Congress, the Constitution's framers had to balance the desires of representation of two opposing groups. The Constitution created a bicameral, or

GLOBAL CONTEXT

JAPAN'S NATIONAL DIET, 国会

Should the U.S. House of Representatives have the ultimate decision-making power in the event of policy disagreements, like the Japanese Shūgiin?

Much like the United States, Japan has a bicameral legislature. The Japanese call this body the *Kokkai,* or National Diet. Japan's post–World War II constitution created the current legislative structure, which eliminated the power held by the emperor in the previous constitution and granted the legislature the exclusive power to create laws. It also bestowed on the legislature the power to select the country's prime minister.

Japan's lower house, like that of the United States, is the House of Representatives (*Shūgiin*), which has 480 members. Of those members, 300 are elected in district elections, in which the candidate with the most votes wins the seat. If a particular candidate nets 40 percent of the vote and that is more than any other candidate receives, that candidate wins the seat. (There is no minimum percentage of the vote required; the candidate with more votes than anyone else wins.) The remaining 180 seats are elected in a proportional representation system, in which candidates in eleven separate blocs are elected in proportion to the percentage of the votes their party receives. And so, if a particular party receives 10 percent of the votes, they win 18 seats (10 percent of the 180 proportional representation seats).

Japan's upper house, the House of Councilors (*Sangiin*), is the equivalent of the U.S. Senate. Of its 242 members, 146 are elected from districts through a single nontransferable vote system. This means that each voter (in Japan the voting age is 20) may cast a vote for only one candidate and that candidate cannot transfer extra votes to other members of his or her party, but the top several candidates with the most votes win. The other 96 members of the Senate are elected in a proportional representation system, in which rank-ordered candidates are awarded seats based on the percentage of the vote their party receives in national balloting.

If the *Sangiin* and the *Shūgiin* disagree on policy matters such as the ratification of treaties, the national budget, and the designation of the prime minister, the Japanese Constitution grants the ultimate decision-making power to the House of Representatives, the *Shūgiin*. But outside those policy matters, the *Shūgiin* needs a two-thirds majority vote to override action taken by the House of Councilors, or *Sangiin*.

two-house, legislature in which one house, the House of Representatives, would be based on population, and the other chamber, the Senate, would be based on state representation.[1] The constitutionally specified duties of each house of Congress reflect the framers' views of the essential nature of the two chambers and the people who would serve in them.

The House of Representatives, with the smallest constituencies of any federal office (currently about 647,000 people reside in each congressional district), is the chamber closer to the people. As such, the framers intended the House to closely represent the people's views. The Constitution thus requires, for example, that all revenue bills (bills that would impose taxes) must originate in the House of Representatives. In the framers' eyes, unwarranted taxation was an egregious offense. By placing the power to tax in the hands of the members of the House of Representatives—the officials who face more frequent federal elections—the framers sought to avoid the types of unpopular, unfair taxes that had sparked the American Revolution. A short electoral cycle, they reasoned, would allow disfavored politicians to be voted out of office. Like all other bills, revenue bills must be passed in identical form by both the House and the Senate to become law, but requiring revenue bills to originate in the House reflected a victory by the large states at the Constitutional Convention. (Smaller states wanted taxation power to reside with the Senate.)

Although the framers viewed the House as the "people's chamber," they conceived the Senate to be a more elite, more deliberative institution, one not subject to the whims of mass politics like its lower-house counterpart. Today, because of its smaller size and because its members face elections less frequently than House members, the Senate remains a more deliberative body than the House. In addition, because of the specific constitutional duties mandated to the upper house, particularly the requirement that treaties must be ratified in the Senate, many U.S. senators have specialized in U.S. foreign policy issues. (See "The House and the Senate Compared" later in this chapter for further discussion of House-Senate differences.)

The framers' vision was to structure the Congress to embody republican principles, ensuring that in its central policy-making responsibilities, the national legislature would be responsive to the needs and the will of the people. Both historically and continuing in the present day, civically engaged citizens have exerted a strong influence on the outcome of the policy-making process. One important avenue by which individuals influence Congress and its acts is through congressional elections, a topic we now consider.

Congressional Elections

The timetable for congressional elections reflects the framers' views of the differing nature of the House of Representatives and the Senate. House members, as public servants in the legislative body that the framers conceived as closer to the people, are elected every two years, in even-numbered years (2010, 2012, and so on). But the framers also sought to check the power of the people, who they believed could be irrational and unruly, and so members of the Senate originally were chosen by state legislators. Ratification of the Seventeenth Amendment to the Constitution in 1913 shifted the election of senators to popular election within the states. Senators serve six-year terms, which are staggered so that one-third of the Senate is elected every two years. Thus, in any given congressional election year, thirty-three or thirty-four members of the Senate are up for election. Usually, the two senators from a given state will not be elected in the same cycle, unless the death or resignation of a sitting senator requires a special election. As we saw in Chapter 2, the Constitution requires that the number of seats in the House of Representatives awarded to each state be based on that state's population and that each state have two U.S. senators. On average, a successful campaign for a seat in the House of Representatives cost about $1.1 million in 2008. That is a veritable bargain compared with the price tag for a successful bid for the U.S. Senate, which averaged about $5.6 million that year. Compare this with the annual salary of $174,000 that rank-and-file members of the House and the Senate collect.

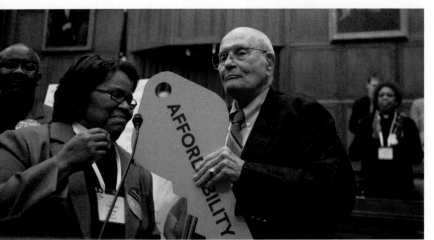

> At 84, Representative John Dingell (D-Michigan), is the longest serving member of the U.S. House of Representatives. Here he accepts a ceremonial key from Deacon Claudia Hollinger of Flint, Michigan, after speaking at the 2010 National Affordability Summit, which brought more than 200 clergy and community leaders together with members of Congress to urge the passage of health care reform. In any election year, about 95 percent of the members of the House of Representatives are reelected. Dingell has been reelected 28 times since his first election in 1955.

Incumbency

The status of already holding office—known as incumbency—strongly influences a candidate's ability to raise money and is probably the most important factor in determining success in a congressional campaign. Indeed, in any election year, about 95 percent of incumbent members of the House of Representatives running for reelection win, and about 93 percent of their Senate counterparts do. These outcomes may indicate what *individual* members of Congress are doing right: representing their own constituencies effec-

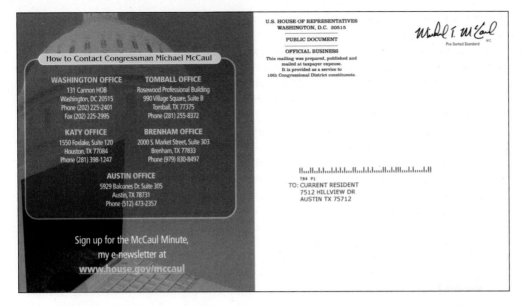

tively, engaging with their constituents, and listening to and addressing their needs. But voters typically think about Congress in terms of *a whole,* rather than individuals, viewing it as a body that is overwhelmingly composed of "other people's" representatives, who do not reflect their views.[2] Thus the voting public frequently attacks Congress as a collective entity.

Why do incumbents so often win reelection? Several factors make it more likely that someone already in office will be returned to that office in a reelection bid:

- **Stronger name recognition.** Having run for election before and served in government, incumbents tend to be better known than challengers.
- **Easier access to media coverage.** Media outlets routinely publicize the activities of elected congressional officials, rationalizing that they are covering the institution of Congress rather than the individuals. Nonincumbent challengers face an uphill battle in trying to get coverage of their campaigns.
- **Franking.** The privilege of sending mail free of charge is known as *franking.* Federal law allows members of Congress free mailings to every household in their state or congressional district. These mailings make it easy for members of Congress to stay in touch with their constituencies throughout their tenure in office.
- **Campaign contributions.** Political action committees and individuals are interested in supporting candidates who will be in a position to help them once the election is over. Because donors are aware of the high reelection rates of incumbent candidates, incumbents garner an enormous proportion of contributions, sometimes as much as 80 percent in any given congressional election year.
- **Casework.** When an incumbent personally helps constituents solve problems with the federal bureaucracy, the resulting loyalty and good-word-of-mouth reputation helps to attract support for that candidate during a run for reelection.

Thus incumbency is a powerful obstacle for outsiders who seek to unseat an elected member of Congress. Despite the incumbency advantage, in each congressional election, many individuals challenge incumbent members of Congress, often doing so knowing that the odds are stacked against them but believing in giving voters a ballot choice. Others run because they seek to bring attention to a particular issue or to shape the policy agenda—or sometimes because they simply underestimate the power of incumbency.

Reapportionment and Redistricting

Sometimes the advantages of incumbency can be diminished, as in election years after reapportionment and redistricting. **Reapportionment** is the reallocation of seats in the House of Representatives on the basis of changes in a state's population since the last

reapportionment
reallocation of seats in the House of Representatives to each state based on changes in the state's population since the last census

redistricting
redrawing of congressional district boundaries within each state, based on the reapportionment from the census

census. Every ten years, in the year ending in zero (2010, 2020, and so on), the federal government counts the number of people in the country as a whole. If the census indicates that a state's population has changed significantly, that state may gain or lose seats in the House of Representatives. **Redistricting,** the redrawing of congressional district boundaries within a state, is based on the reapportionment from the census.

Because the composition of a given congressional district can change as a result of reapportionment and redistricting, this process can mitigate the impact of incumbency. Frequently, the greatest shifts in the composition of the House of Representatives occur in election years ending in 2 (2002, 2012, and so on), when the first elections take place that incorporate the changes from reapportionment and redistricting. As a result of reapportionment in 2002, for example, New York and Pennsylvania each lost two House seats. Five states in the Midwest lost one House seat each, while several states in the South and the Southwest gained seats. Reapportionment and redistricting following the 2010 census does not occur until 2012, but on the basis of U.S. Census Bureau projections, demographers have projected that Texas will probably gain the largest number of House seats, perhaps as many as four, while Arizona and Florida could each gain two additional seats. Other states whose congressional delegations may increase in size include Georgia, Nevada, South Carolina, and Utah, which probably will each gain one seat. States whose slow population growth may mean the loss of one seat include Illinois, Iowa, Louisiana, Massachusetts, Michigan, Minnesota, Missouri, New Jersey, New York, and Pennsylvania, while Ohio could lose two representatives.[3] When a state loses a seat, the result is that an incumbent member of Congress is likely to lose a seat. When a state gains a seat, a new member of Congress can be elected to the open seat.

In some states, the goal of congressional redistricting is to protect House incumbents. The redrawing of congressional boundaries for the purpose of political advantage is a form of **gerrymandering,** the practice of drawing legislative district boundaries to benefit an incumbent, a political party, or some other group. The term was coined in reference to Massachusetts governor Elbridge Gerry after a district shaped like a salamander was created to favor his party in 1811. The illustration shows the first gerrymander.

gerrymandering
the drawing of legislative district boundaries to benefit an incumbent, a political party, or another group

majority-minority district
a legislative district composed of a majority of a given minority community—say, African Americans—the intent of which is to make it likely that a member of that minority will be elected to Congress

Most forms of gerrymandering are legal. The U.S. Supreme Court ruled in 1986 that a gerrymandering plan is unconstitutional only when it eliminates the minority party's influence statewide.[4] Because of the strict standards, only one partisan gerrymandering plan filed after the 1990 census was successfully challenged.

State legislatures have attempted to address the issue of racial imbalance in the House of Representatives by constructing a kind of gerrymander called a majority-minority district. A **majority-minority district** is composed of a majority of a given minority community—say, African Americans—and the creators' intent is to make it likely that a member of that minority will be elected to Congress. The Supreme Court has ruled that such racial gerrymandering is illegal unless the state legislature redrawing the district lines creates majority and minority districts at the expense of other redistricting concerns. Typically, those concerns include preserving the geographic continuity of districts, keeping communities within one legislative district, and reelecting incumbents.

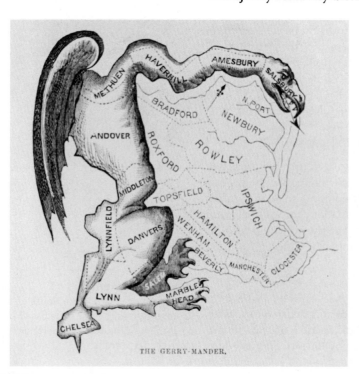

THE GERRY-MANDER.

POLITICAL INQUIRY

> The term *gerrymander* originated from this Gilbert Stuart cartoon of a Massachusetts electoral district. To Stuart, the district looked like a salamander. A friend christened it a "Gerry-mander," after Massachusetts governor Elbridge Gerry, a signer of the Declaration of Independence and the politician who approved redrawing district lines for political advantage. What point does this famous historical cartoon of 1812, representing Massachusetts legislative districts, make about the nature of a gerrymander? What do people today mean when they talk about gerrymandering? What are your own views on the practice?

Powers of Congress

The primary source of congressional authority is the U.S. Constitution. As shown in Table 11.1, the Constitution enumerates to Congress a number of different powers. The nature of these responsibilities reveals that the Constitution is both very specific in describing congressional powers (as in punishing illegal acts on the high seas) and at the same time quite vague (as in its language establishing the federal court system). Many of the specific duties of Congress reflect Americans' bitter experience in the colonial era, in that the framers granted powers to Congress that they did not want to place in the hands of a strong executive. For example, the economic powers granted to Congress, including the ability to tax and spend, to establish tariffs, and to borrow money, all limit the power of the president.

Powers specifically granted to Congress still have a distinct impact on our everyday lives. For example, Congress regulates currency, establishes weights and measures, and administers post offices. As we have seen, the connection between Congress, particularly the House, and the people was crucial to the framers, and so the Constitution requires that all taxation and spending measures originate in the House because the framers believed this chamber would be nearer to the people—and that House members would therefore ensure that the people's will was done.

The Constitution moreover imbues the Congress with an additional source of power, one that has proved very important in the expansion of legislative authority over time. As discussed in Chapter 2, the necessary and proper—or elastic—clause states that the Congress shall have the power to "make all Laws which shall be necessary and proper for carrying into Execution the foregoing powers, and all other Powers vested by this Constitution in the Government of the United States, or in a Department or Officer thereof." This clause has been responsible for

TABLE 11.1

Enumerated Powers of the Congress

JUDICIAL POWERS

Establish the federal court system

Punish counterfeiters

Punish illegal acts on the high seas

ECONOMIC POWERS

Impose taxes

Establish import tariffs

Borrow money

Regulate interstate commerce

Coin and print money, determine the value of currency

NATIONAL SECURITY POWERS

Declare war

Raise and regulate national armed forces

Call up and regulate state national guard

Suppress insurrections

Repel invasions

REGULATORY POWERS

Establish standards of weights and measures

Regulate copyrights and patents

ADMINISTRATIVE POWERS

Establish procedures for naturalizing citizens

Establish post offices

Govern the District of Columbia

> The Constitution's necessary and proper clause has resulted in the expansion of congressional authority into policy areas not specifically mentioned in the Constitution, including health care. Here, Senate Minority Leader Mitch McConnell (left), then-House Minority Leader John Boehner (now Speaker of the House of Representatives, center), and Republican Senator Jon Kyl of Arizona (right), prepare for a 2010 bipartisan summit on health care with President Barack Obama.

Congress's ability to legislate in many matters not described in the enumerated powers. Reforming our nation's health care system, determining the powers of law enforcement in investigating terrorism, and regulating stem cell research are all examples of powers not enumerated in the Constitution but that Congress exercises because of the broad scope of authority provided by the necessary and proper clause.

In addition to the Constitution, Congress derives power from Supreme Court decisions, the media, and the people. Supreme Court decisions often uphold the constitutionality of a law, in a sense verifying Congress's ability to create policy on a given subject. The media grant Congress power by providing members with a forum in which to communicate with constituents, sway public opinion, and create a favorable climate for the passage of legislation. The people are a key source of congressional power through civic participation in the electoral and legislative processes. Citizens communicate their views and priorities to their representatives, who then can claim public support in their endeavors to enact policy.

Functions of Congress

The Constitution is far more explicit in defining the responsibilities of the national legislature than it is in describing the function of the other branches of the government.[5] In its shaping of congressional functions, the Constitution's concerns with limited government, checks and balances, the separation of powers, and the creation of a federal system are all readily apparent.

Representation Comes in Many Forms

In delineating the composition of the federal legislature and the procedures for electing its members, the Constitution shapes the congressional function of representation in several ways. Representation traditionally involves a House or Senate member's articulating and voting for the position that best represents the views of his or her constituents.[6] But sometimes a member of Congress may speak for other constituencies as well. For example, a feminist legislator might "represent" feminists nationwide,[7] just as a gay legislator might "represent" the collective interests of gays across the United States.

Often, Congress's policy-making function is at odds with its representation function. A legislator may be pressured—by his or her political party or own conscience—to vote for a policy that clashes with constituents' interests or views. In representing constituents, legislators frequently follow one of two models of representative behavior.

trustee model
a model of representation in which a member of the House or Senate follows his or her own conscience when deciding issue positions

MODELS OF REPRESENTATION According to the **trustee model** of representation, a member of the House or the Senate follows his or her own conscience when deciding issue positions and determining how to vote. Sometimes a legislator relying on the trustee model will act contrary to the views of his or her constituents. This model was espoused by British political theorist Edmund Burke (1729-1797), who served in Parliament as a representative of Bristol, England. Explaining his conception of representation, Burke emphasized to his constituents, however, that a member of Parliament "is not a member of Bristol, he is a member of Parliament."[8] Burke accordingly argued that a member of Parliament should follow his conscience when making decisions in the legislature: "Your representative owes you, not his industry only, but his judgement [sic]; and he betrays, instead of serving you, if he sacrifices it to your opinion."[9] In this trustee view, a legislator may act in opposition to the clear wishes of his or her constituents, such as in cases where an action is "for their own good" or the good of society.

instructed delegate model
a model of representation in which legislators, as representatives of their constituents, should vote in keeping with the constituents' views, even if those views contradict the legislator's personal views

Another model of representation is the **instructed delegate model,** the idea that a legislator, as a representative of his or her constituents, should vote in keeping with the constituents' views, *even if those views contradict the legislator's personal views.* This model of representation conceives of legislators as the agents of their constituents. A legislator hewing to the instructed delegate model faces a dilemma when his or her constituency is evenly divided on an issue.

Given these two different models of representation, which one do legislators typically follow? Most analyses of representation indicate that legislators are likely to combine the approaches. Specifically, with regard to many important or high-profile issues, legislators act as instructed delegates, whereas for more mundane matters about which their constituents are less likely to be aware or to hold a strong position, they rely on the trustee model.

PORK BARREL AND EARMARKS   Members of Congress also represent their constituencies through pork barrel politics. **Pork barrel** (also called simply *pork*) refers to legislators' appropriations of funds for special projects located within their congressional district. Because pork brings money and jobs to a particular district, legislators who are seeking reelection work aggressively to secure monies for their states or districts—to "bring home the bacon."[10] Members frequently use transportation bills as a means of creating pork barrel projects for their districts. One analysis estimates, for example, that every $1 billion spent on highway and mass transit projects creates about 47,500 jobs, and members of Congress are happy to take credit for the jobs and for highway and mass transit improvements when running for reelection.[11] In 2010, Congress appropriated about $16.5 billion for pork barrel projects. Hawaii received the most pork per capita at $259.78. Wyoming took home the least, $12.28 per capita.[12] Table 11.2 lists the top ten recipients.

Members of Congress also use **earmarks** as a means of representing constituent interests: a designation within a spending bill that provides for a specific expenditure. And so, for example, in 2009 Representative Lynn Woolsey (D-California) helped ensure that the Sonoma County Integrated Emergency Operations Center (EOC) Information and Communication System was granted a $190,000 earmark in the federal budget for police and emergency communications. But many critics of the earmark process complain that earmarks are a way for members of Congress to reward supporters. Sonoma County had spent $320,000 lobbying federal lawmakers.

CASEWORK   A special form of representation called **casework** refers to providing representation in the form of personal aid to a constituent or a group of constituents, typically by getting the government to do something the constituent wants done. Members of Congress and their staffs commonly assist constituents in dealing with bureaucratic agencies. In doing so, they serve in the capacity of an **ombudsperson,** an elected or appointed representative who acts as a citizens' advocate by listening to their needs and investigating their complaints

pork barrel
legislators' appropriations of funds for special projects located within their congressional district

earmark
a designation within a spending bill that provides for a specific expenditure

casework
personal work by a member of Congress on behalf of a constituent or a group of constituents, typically aimed at getting the government to do something the constituent wants done

ombudsperson
a role in which an elected or appointed leader acts as an advocate for citizens by listening to and investigating complaints against a government agency

TABLE 11.2

Top 10 States: Pork per Capita
(National Average: $27.36 per Person)

2010 Rank	State	2010 Pork	Population	Pork/Capita
1	Hawaii	$326,099,850	1,295,178	$251.78
2	North Dakota	$127,743,350	646,844	$197.49
3	West Virginia	$265,728,000	1,819,777	$146.02
4	Alaska	$92,072,850	698,473	$131.82
6	Mississippi	$321,643,000	2,951,996	$108.96
5	South Dakota	$87,874,150	812,383	$108.17
7	Montana	$102,400,450	974,989	$105.03
8	District of Columbia	$62,318,500	599,657	$103.92
9	Vermont	$61,733,280	621,760	$99.29
10	Rhode Island	$71,937,000	1,053,209	$68.30

SOURCE: Citizens Against Government Waste, *2010 Congressional Pig Book Summary*, p. 63, www.cagw.org/assets/pig-book-files/2010/2010-pig-book-summary.pdf.

with respect to a particular government agency. For example, a member of Congress might intervene with the Immigration and Naturalization Service (INS) to request that a constituent's relative in a foreign country be granted a visa to travel to the United States.

According to political scientist Morris Fiorina, casework is a valuable tool for legislators. Fiorina points out that serving constituents is relatively easy for members of Congress, because bureaucrats—who depend on Congress for their funding—typically respond quickly to the requests of legislators.[13] The loyalty derived from assisting constituents is one aspect of the incumbency advantage that makes incumbent members of Congress more likely to be elected than their challengers, who do not enjoy that source of constituent loyalty.

Casework benefits constituents when, for example, a member of Congress's staff works with a local branch of a Veterans' Administration clinic to secure services for a retired veteran, whose family members derive a sense of efficacy—a feeling that they can get things done and that the government works for people like them. They perceive that their individual member of Congress genuinely represents them and protects their interests, with the result that these constituents not only feel engaged but also are likely to advocate for their member's reelection bid.

But casework is not without its costs, as noted by Walter F. Mondale. Mondale, who served as a member of both the House and the Senate, as well as vice president of the United States, warns that casework can take a legislator's time away from his or her legislative responsibilities:

> Good constituent service is, of course, necessary—and honorable—work for any member of Congress and his [sic] staff. Citizens must have somewhere to turn for help when they become victims of government bureaucracy. But constituent service can also be a bottomless pit. The danger is that a member of Congress will end up as little more than an ombudsman between citizens and government agencies. As important as this work is, it takes precious time away from Congress' central responsibilities as both a deliberative and a law-making body.[15]

In describing the constituent service dilemma, Mondale raises questions worthy of citizens' reflection. For example: Is the national interest served when a congressional staff member has to track down your grandma's Social Security check? Does doing so result in a missed opportunity for government officials to create policy with broad, significant implications? And is the use of congressional staff members as ombudspeople a prudent application of taxpayers' money?

Policy Making: A Central Responsibility

Each year, Congress passes laws determining everything from incentives for the creation of alternative energy sources, to what restrictions should govern gun purchases, to what law enforcers can do when they suspect someone of being a terrorist. The Constitution invests Congress with other policy-making powers as well, including the authority to tax and spend, to declare war, to establish courts, and to regulate the armed forces. This policy-making function is the central responsibility that the Congress carries out, and nearly all its other functions are related to its policy-making role. Congressional policy-making power also extends to the operations and priorities of governmental departments and agencies. For example, Congress has directed the State Department to select a domestic secure production facility to create ePassports, next-generation passports with an embedded microchip.

Oversight: A Check on the Executive Branch

In creating a system of checks and balances in the Constitution, the framers established the key congressional function of oversight.[14] **Oversight** is the process by which Congress "checks" the executive branch to ensure that the laws Congress passes are being administered in keeping with legislators' intentions. Congressional oversight is a check on the executive branch because the federal bureaucracy that implements laws is part of the executive branch.

In carrying out their oversight function, members of Congress use a variety of tools, some of which are listed here:

oversight
the process by which the legislative branch "checks" the executive branch to ensure that the laws Congress has passed are being administered in keeping with legislators' intent

- congressional hearings, in which government officials, bureaucrats, and interest groups testify as to how a law or a policy is being implemented and examine the impact of its implementation
- confirmation hearings on presidential appointees to oversee executive departments or governmental agencies
- investigations to determine whether a law or a policy is being implemented the way Congress intended it to be, and inquiries into allegations of wrongdoing by government officials or bureaucrats
- budgetary appropriations that determine funding of an executive department or a government agency

These tools ensure that Congress has some say in how the executive branch administers the laws that Congress creates. Members of Congress increasingly have viewed their role of checking the executive branch as crucially important.

Agenda Setting and Civic Engagement

Congress engages continuously in **agenda setting:** determining which public policy issues the federal legislature should consider.[16] Indeed, political scientists such as Cox and McCubbins assert that agenda setting relieves the pressure parties face in getting their members to vote with the party.[17] At the beginning of a congressional term, House and Senate leaders announce their goals for the coming session. Those goals reflect the issues and positions that predominated during the electoral campaign and that congressional leaders perceive to represent the people's priorities.

In setting the national agenda, Congress serves as a key agent in molding the scope of civic engagement and discourse, as people learn about, discuss, and form positions about issues. Frequently, agenda setting is itself influenced by public discourse, as when constituents complain to a member of Congress about a problem that needs to be solved or when an interest group contacts a legislator about a policy its membership would like to see implemented. For example, in 2010, pressure from gay rights activists led Congress to eliminate the "Don't Ask, Don't Tell" policy on gays in the military as part of a defense spending measure. Though elimination of the policy was narrowly defeated, its inclusion demonstrates how the public shapes the congressional agenda.

> One function of Congress is to provide oversight—to examine how a law or policy is being implemented. Here Toyota President and CEO Akio Toyoda (center) and North American President and CEO Yoshimi Inaba (right) and their official interpreter (left) are sworn in before they testify at the U.S. House of Representatives committee hearing "Toyota Gas Pedals: Is the Public at Risk?" on February, 2010. The hearing focused on the U.S. government's response to the recall of millions of Toyota vehicles due to reports of malfunctioning gas pedals.

agenda setting
determination by Congress of which public issues the government should consider for legislation

Managing Societal Conflict

Congress also has a significant influence in managing the societal conflict inherent in a divided society such as the United States. Some citizens want policies benefiting rural areas, and others give higher priority to urban areas. Some want more money for programs for senior citizens; others seek funding for children's programs. With respect to abortion policy, some people are pro-life, and others are pro-choice. In addition, there are divisions related to social class, race, geography, gender, sexual orientation, religion, and so on. Congress manages these conflicts by representing a wide range of views and interests.

The House and the Senate Compared

Although the House of Representatives and the Senate share numerous functions, the two chambers of Congress differ in significant ways. As President Woodrow Wilson remarked, the "House and Senate are naturally unalike."[18] Constitutionally, the two houses are

Differences Between the House and the Senate

TABLE 11.3

House	Senate
Larger (435 members)	Smaller (100 members)
Shorter electoral cycle (two-year term)	Longer electoral cycle (six-year term)
Narrow constituency (congressional districts)	Broad constituency (states)
Less prestigious	More prestigious
Originates all revenue bills	Ratifies treaties; confirms presidential nominees
Less reliant on staff	More reliant on staff
Power vested in leaders and committee chairs	Power more evenly distributed

bill
a proposed piece of legislation

hopper
a wooden box that sits on a desk at the front of the House of Representatives, into which House members place bills they want to introduce

> California senators must balance the views not only of surfers and Hollywood stars but also of farmers and ranchers. They must take into account the concerns of liberal urban coastal dwellers along with the more conservative views of those who live in the state's heartland to the east, including the significant agricultural interests in those areas. Agribusiness interests and farmers often lobby for government support of irrigation programs, for example. Here, sprinklers irrigate a cotton field at pre-bloom stage.

conceived as unique organizations, and the framers designated their duties to match the strengths and expertise of the people who would come to hold office in each chamber. Table 11.3 highlights these major differences. As discussed earlier in this chapter, the Constitution empowers the House of Representatives, as the legislative body closer to the people, with initiating any bills that result in taxes; whereas it empowers the Senate, as the more deliberative house, to give the president advice and consent on appointments and the ratification of treaties. The differences between the House and the Senate are not limited merely to their functions, however. The electoral and legislative structures are also sources of differences between the two houses.

Each of the 435 current members of the House of Representatives represents a legislative district determined by the reapportionment and redistricting process that occurs every ten years, as described earlier in this chapter. In more populated areas, these congressional districts are often homogeneous, cohesive units in which a House member's constituency is likely to have fairly unified positions on many issues.[19] Senators, however, are elected by the population of an entire state, and although the political culture in some states is somewhat cohesive (for example, Vermont voters are more liberal on most issues than are Kansas voters), in many states there are notable differences in constituents' views, ideology, and policy priorities. For instance, senators Barbara Boxer and Dianne Feinstein both represent the entire state of California, and both are Democrats. Although California is generally viewed as a very liberal political culture, Boxer and Feinstein also must represent the interests of both liberal voters in the western coastal areas of the state and more conservative voters inland to the east. At times, moreover, the interests of a senator's constituents divide over a given issue: in California, for example, environmental activists and fishers have argued against programs that divert water from lakes and streams so that it can be used for irrigation on commercial farms, whereas affluent agribusinesses advocate water diversion. A U.S. senator must balance such conflicting positions when making policy decisions.

The differing length of representatives' and senators' terms of service affects how members of each chamber of Congress relate to their constituents. Given their short two-year terms, members of the House of Representatives naturally are reluctant to defy the will of the electorate on a given issue because of the likelihood that their opposition will be used against them during their reelection campaign. As the framers structured it, the House remains "the people's house," the chamber in which civically engaged individuals can effectively have their interests represented. And although U.S. senators naturally also want to please their constituents, they recognize that voting against their constituents' will on a particular issue might be less significant than such an action would be for a House member, especially if the issue arises early in their term and is not important enough for people to hold against them six years down the road.

The size of the chambers and the length of terms also affect the relative prestige of each chamber. In general, the smaller Senate is considered more prestigious than the House of Representatives, although some individual House members may enjoy more prestige than some senators.

Although the House and the Senate differ in their constitutionally determined duties, both must pass any piece of legislation before it can become law. But the way in which legislation is considered and voted upon differs in each house of Congress.

The larger size of the House of Representatives, with its 435 members, necessitates a more formal legislative structure to prevent unruliness.

The House, for example, generally has more, and more formal, rules guiding debate than the Senate. Despite the differences between the two chambers, the legislative process is remarkably similar in both.

joint referral
the practice, abolished in the 104th Congress, by which a bill could be referred to two different committees for consideration

The Legislative Process

Article I, Section 1, of the Constitution states, "All Legislative Powers herein granted shall be vested in a Congress of the United States, which shall consist of a Senate and House of Representatives." A **bill** is a proposed piece of legislation. As shown in Figure 11.1, every bill must be approved by *both houses* (the House and the Senate) *in identical form.* In general, bills must pass through five steps to become law:

1. **Introduction.** A member of the House of Representatives or the Senate formally proposes the bill.
2. **Committee review.** Subgroups within the House and the Senate, composed of legislators who have expertise in the bill's subject matter, review the bill.
3. **House and Senate approval.** If the bill makes it out of committee, a majority of members in the House and the Senate must approve it.
4. **Conference Committee reconciliation.** The Conference Committee reconciles the bill when different versions have passed in the House and the Senate.
5. **Presidential approval.** If the president signs the bill, it becomes law. But even after this arduous process, a presidential veto can kill the bill.

Introducing a Bill

Bills are introduced differently in each chamber of Congress. In the House of Representatives, a member of a legislator's staff drafts the proposed legislation, and the House member puts the bill into the **hopper,** a wooden box that sits on a desk at the front of the House chamber. Upon introduction, a bill is referred to as "H.R.," meaning House of Representatives, followed by a number that indicates the order in which it was introduced in a given legislative session, for example, "H.R. 207."

In the Senate, the process is less formal. Here, senators can announce proposed legislation to colleagues in a speech on the Senate floor. (See "Analyzing the Sources" on page 348.) Alternatively, a senator can submit a written draft of the proposed legislation to an official known as the Senate clerk, or sometimes a senator will propose legislation simply by offering it as an amendment to an already pending piece of legislation. Once a bill is introduced in the Senate, it is referred to as "S.," or "Senate," followed by its number reflecting the order in which it was introduced in a given legislative session—for example, "S. 711."

Before 1995, a bill introduced in the House of Representatives could be subject to **joint referral,** the practice of referring the bill simultaneously to two different House committees for consideration. But the 104th Congress abolished joint committee referrals. Today, bills introduced in the

POLITICAL INQUIRY

FIGURE 11.1 ■ Where are there similarities between the House and the Senate in the legislative process? How do the Senate and the House resolve differences in versions of a bill passed in each chamber? What outcomes are possible once a bill goes to the president for approval?

The Legislative Process

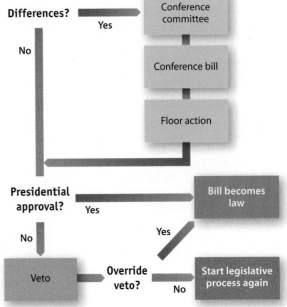

ANALYZING THE SOURCES

NAVIGATING CONGRESS

When we think of Congress, we typically picture the gleaming white dome of the Capitol. This image is appropriate, because the Capitol Rotunda is a highly important place for members of Congress and the people whom they represent. The Capitol is home to the House and Senate chambers where issues are debated on the floor and where votes are cast.

As shown in the map, however, a large part of Congress's work takes place in the office buildings surrounding the rotunda that are considered part of "Capitol Hill." Members of the House of Representatives are typically assigned an office in one of three buildings on the south side of the Capitol Rotunda: the Cannon Office Building, the Longworth Office Building, and the Rayburn Office Building. Senators work out of an office in one of the three office buildings located on the north side of the rotunda: the Russell Office Building, the Dirksen Office Building, and the Hart Office Building. The Cannon and Russell buildings share essentially the same design. The House office buildings are named after former Speakers of the House of Representatives, and the Senate office buildings are named after prominent U.S. senators.

Many of the buildings boast beautiful architecture and amenities such as gymnasiums, post offices, kitchens, and recording studios. In the Rayburn Office Building, members can travel to the Capitol via a subway tunnel with two cars, and pedestrian tunnels join it to the Longworth Building. A double-track subway system connects Dirksen, Russell, and the Capitol, and tunnels beneath the Cannon and Russell buildings connect to the Capitol. Immediately east of the Capitol Rotunda is the Library of Congress, and the U.S. Supreme Court Building sits just south of the Senate office buildings.

Although office space and layout are not something that political scientists typically analyze, the proximity of members of Congress to their office neighbors, along with the common facilities they share, surely has an impact on the legislative process. In the Capitol Hill office buildings, just as in any other kind of office or group setting, senators and representatives of diverse backgrounds become familiar with colleagues whom they see regularly in the hallways, elevators, gyms, kitchens, and subway trains between buildings.

Evaluating the Evidence

① Like a member of Congress, you also have a network of relationships based on your daily activities. What people do you see regularly because of your work or school schedule? What unlikely relationships have you formed because of your daily activities?

② In what ways might the time spent in their Capitol Hill offices and common facilities breed familiarity among federal legislators? What different kinds and backgrounds of people might this daily contact bring together?

③ In what specific ways do you think legislators' interactions in their office buildings might affect their political decision making in the chambers of the House and the Senate?

Legend

HOB: House Office Building
LOC: Library of Congress Building
SOB: Senate Office Building
USBG: United States Botanic Garden

SOURCE: www.aol.gov/cc/cc-map.cfm

House are referred to one committee, called the **lead committee.** Occasionally, when the substance of a bill warrants additional referrals to other committees that also have jurisdiction over the subject of the bill, the bill might be subsequently referred to a second committee.[20] In the Senate, bills typically are referred to only one committee.

The Bill in Committee

After introduction by a member of the House or the Senate, a bill is read into the *Congressional Record,* a formal record of all actions taken by Congress. Because of the large number of bills introduced, both chambers rely on an extensive committee structure that facilitates the consideration of so high a volume of bills.[21] Most bills that are introduced "die" in committee. That is, a committee does not consider the bill (sometimes because the committee does not have the time in a legislative session to take up the measure) or declines to forward the bill to the full chamber.

Each congressional committee and subcommittee is composed of a majority of members of the majority party in that chamber. For example, if 218 or more members (a majority in the House) elected to the House of Representatives are Republicans, then every committee and subcommittee in the House has a majority of Republicans. The parties in each chamber decide members' committee and subcommittee assignments.

Though the selection of committee chairs varies between chambers and parties, committee chairs are often chosen using the **seniority system,** by which the member with the longest continuous tenure on a standing committee receives preference when the committee chooses its chair. The committee chairs run committee meetings and control the flow of work in each committee. Although the seniority system is an institution in Congress, it is an informal system, and seniority does not always determine who will be the committee chair.[22] Chairs are chosen by a secret ballot, and in recent years junior members sometimes have won out over senior committee members.

Standing committees are permanent committees with a defined legislative jurisdiction. The House has twenty-four standing committees, and the Senate has twenty. The House Committee on Homeland Security and the Senate Armed Services Committee are examples of standing committees.

Select committees are specially created to consider a specific policy issue or to address a particular concern. In 2005, the House formed a select committee, the Select Bipartisan Committee to Investigate the Preparation for and Response to Hurricane Katrina, which examined what went wrong in the preparations for and response to that killer storm. Other select committees have focused on such issues as homeland security and terrorism, aging, and transportation.

Joint committees are bicameral committees composed of members of both chambers of Congress. Sometimes these committees offer administrative or managerial guidance of various kinds. For example, one joint committee oversees the presidential inauguration, and another supervises the administration of the Library of Congress.

In addition to the congressional committees, the House has more than ninety subcommittees, and the Senate has sixty-eight. **Subcommittees** typically handle specific areas of the committees' jurisdiction. For example, the House Committee on Foreign Affairs is a standing committee. Within the committee there are seven subcommittees: the Subcommittee on Africa and Global Health; the Subcommittee on Asia, Pacific, and the Global Environment; the Subcommittee on Europe; the Subcommittee on the Middle East and South Asia; the Subcommittee on International Organizations, Human Rights, and Oversight; the Subcommittee on Terrorism, Nonproliferation, and Trade; and the Subcommittee on the Western Hemisphere. Each subcommittee handles bills relevant to its specified jurisdiction.

When a committee or a subcommittee favors a measure, it usually takes four actions:

- **Agency review.** During **agency review,** the committee or subcommittee asks the executive agencies that would administer the law for written comments on the measure.
- **Hearings.** Next the committee or subcommittee holds **hearings** to gather information and views from experts, including interest groups, concerned citizens, and celebrities involved with the issue.

lead committee
the primary committee considering a bill

seniority system
the system in which the member with the longest continuous tenure on a standing committee is given preference when the committee chooses its chair

standing committee
permanent committee in Congress, with a defined legislative jurisdiction

select committee
congressional committee created to consider specific policy issues or address a specific concern

joint committee
bicameral committee composed of members of both chambers of Congress

subcommittee
a subordinate committee in Congress that typically handles specific areas of a standing committee's jurisdiction

agency review
part of the committee or subcommittee process of considering a bill, in which committee members ask executive agencies that would administer the law for written comments on the measure

hearings
sessions held by committees or subcommittees to gather information and views from experts

markup

the process by which members of legislative committees "mark up" a bill with suggested language for changes and amendments

report

a legislative committee's explanation to the full chamber of a bill and its intent

■ **Markup.** During **markup,** the committee "marks up" the bill with suggested language changes and amendments. The committee does not actually alter the bill; rather, members recommend changes to the full chamber. In a typical bill markup, the committee may eliminate a component of the proposal or amend the proposal in some way.

■ **Report.** After agreeing to the wording of the bill, the committee issues a **report** to the full chamber, explaining the bill and its intent. The bill may then be considered by the full chamber.

In the House of Representatives, a special measure known as a **discharge petition** is used to extract a bill from a committee to have it considered by the entire House. A discharge petition requires the signature of a majority (218) of the members of the House.

Debate on the House and Senate Floor

Table 11.4 compares the legislative process in the House and the Senate. For example, if a House bill is "discharged," or makes it out of committee, it then goes to the **Rules Committee,** one of the most important committees in the House, which decides on the length of debate and the scope of amendments that will be allowed on a bill. The Rules Committee sets the structure for the debate that ensues in the full House. For important bills, the Rules Committee tends to set strict limits on the types of amendments that can be attached to a bill. In general, the Rules Committee also establishes limits to floor debate in the House.

The Senate does not have a committee to do the work of the Rules Committee, but the Senate's small size allows members to agree to the terms of debate through **unanimous consent** agreements. Unanimous consent must be just that: every senator needs to agree to the terms of debate (including time limits on debate), and if even one senator objects, unanimous consent does not take effect. Senators do not look favorably on objections to unanimous consent, and so such objections are rare. Objecting to unanimous consent agreements can potentially undermine a senator's ability to get legislation passed by provoking the ire of other senators.

If the Senate does not reach unanimous consent, the possibility of a **filibuster** arises—a procedural move that attempts to halt passage of the bill.[23] Sometimes the mere threat of a filibuster is enough to compel a bill's supporters to alter a bill's content. During a filibuster, a senator can speak for an unlimited time on the Senate floor. Filibustering senators do

discharge petition

a special tactic used to extract a bill from a committee to have it considered by the entire House

Rules Committee

one of the most important committees in the House, which decides the length of debate and the scope of amendments that will be allowed on a bill

unanimous consent

an agreement by every senator to the terms of debate on a given piece of legislation

filibuster

a procedural move by a member of the Senate to attempt to halt passage of or change a bill, during which the senator can speak for an unlimited time on the Senate floor

TABLE 11.4

Differences in the Legislative Process in the House and Senate

House	Senate
Bill introduced by member placing bill in hopper	Bill introduced by member
Relies on Rules Committee to schedule debate on House floor and to establish rules for amendments	Relies on unanimous consent agreements to determine rules for debate and amendments
Has a rule barring nongermane amendments	No rule banning nongermane amendments
Does not allow filibusters	Allows filibusters
Discharge petition can be used to extract a bill from a committee	No discharge petitions allowed

not need to restrict themselves to speaking only on the subject of the bill—they just need to keep talking. Some senators have read the Bible, cookbooks, and even the Nynex Yellow Pages into the *Congressional Record.* In the 1930s, Senator Huey P. Long (D-Louisiana) filibustered many bills, once speaking for fifteen hours to block one that he viewed as "helping the rich get richer and the poor get poorer." Long, viewed as a character by many of his Senate colleagues, was a favorite among visitors to the Senate galleries, where he would entertain onlookers with New Orleans recipes for "pot-likkers" and with his articulations of Shakespeare in a Louisiana drawl. Former Republican South Carolina senator Strom Thurmond holds the Senate record for the longest filibuster. In an attempt to block passage of the Civil Rights Act of 1957, Thurmond filibustered for twenty-four hours and eighteen minutes. A filibuster can end by a vote of **cloture,** in which a supermajority of sixty senators agrees to invoke cloture and end debate. Cloture is initiated if sixteen senators sign a cloture petition. In 2010, when Senator Scott Brown (R-Massachusetts) was elected in a special election to replace the late Democratic senator Edward M. Kennedy, the specter of filibusters in the Senate became more likely as Brown's election as the forty-first Republican in the Senate meant that Democrats had lost the sixty-member filibuster-proof majority they had held.

After a bill is debated by the full chamber, the members vote on it. Before a bill can become law, identical versions of the bill must pass in both the House and the Senate. If only one chamber passes a bill during a congressional term, the bill dies. If both the House and the Senate pass bills on the same topic but with differences between the bills, the bills are then sent to a **conference committee,** a bicameral, bipartisan committee composed of legislators whose job is to reconcile the two versions of the bill. Typically, the legislators appointed to the conference committee will be members of the standing committees that considered the bill in their chambers. After the committee develops a compromise version of the bill, the bill then goes back to both chambers for another vote. If the bill does not pass in both chambers during a congressional term, the bill is dead, although it can be reintroduced in the next session. If both chambers approve the bill, it then goes to the president for signature or veto.

Presidential Action

When both the House and the Senate manage to pass a bill in identical form, it proceeds to the president, who may take one of three actions. First, the president may sign it, in which case the bill becomes a law. Second, the president may choose to do nothing. If the president does nothing and Congress is in session, the bill becomes law after ten days without the president's signature. A president may take this route if he or she does not support the bill but knows that Congress would override a veto. If, however, the Congress has adjourned (that is, the bill was passed at the end of a legislative session), the president may exercise a pocket veto. A **pocket veto** occurs when Congress has adjourned and the president waits ten days without signing the bill; the president effectively "puts the bill in his pocket," and the bill dies. Finally, a president may exercise the executive power of a *veto:* rejecting the bill and returning it to Congress with a message explaining why the bill should not become law. Congress can vote to override the veto by a two-thirds vote in both houses, in which case the bill becomes law. But overriding a presidential veto is a difficult and rare achievement.

Congressional Leadership

The House and the Senate alike choose the majority and minority leaders for their adept negotiating skills, their finely honed ability to guide compromise, and their skills of persuasion. A majority leader nurtures compromise in the legislative process by knowing the members' positions on legislation well enough to recognize which issues are negotiable and which are deal-breakers; by engineering trade-offs between players; and by convincing committee chairs that a negotiated compromise is the best outcome they can expect.

In earlier eras, forceful leaders rose to the position of majority leader in both houses and strongly influenced congressional priorities and legislation.[24] But as political parties

cloture
a procedural move in which a supermajority of sixty senators agrees to end a filibuster

conference committee
a bicameral, bipartisan committee composed of legislators whose job is to reconcile two versions of a bill

pocket veto
a special presidential veto of a bill passed at the conclusion of a legislative session, whereby the president waits ten days without signing the bill, and the bill dies

> Rep. Nancy Pelosi, former Speaker of the House of Representatives, proved to be a lightning rod for critics in the 2010 mid-term elections, with Republican candidates urging voters to "Fire Pelosi" by electing a Republican majority. They did, and John Boehner was selected by the Republican caucus as her replacement.

Speaker of the House
the leader of the House of Representatives, chosen by the majority party

House majority leader
the leader of the majority party, who helps the Speaker develop and implement strategy and works with other members of the House of Representatives

have come to play a less important role in the election of members of the House and the Senate, allegiance to party leaders in these institutions has dwindled.[25] The era has long passed in which individuals could essentially control what Congress did through their assertive personalities.[26] Today's congressional power brokers face members whose loyalty to the party and the leadership is tempered by the need to please constituencies that themselves are less loyal to the parties than in bygone times.[27] Nonetheless, despite the evolution in the role of congressional leader, partisanship remains a strong aspect of congressional politics, particularly since 1994.

Leadership in the House of Representatives

Although Article I, Section 2, of the Constitution states, "The House of Representatives shall choose their Speaker and other Officers," and all members of the House vote for the Speaker, it is really the members of the majority party who select their **Speaker of the House.** Second in the line of presidential succession (after the vice president), the Speaker serves as the presiding officer and manager of the House. In this capacity, the Speaker chairs floor debates, makes majority party committee assignments, assigns members to the powerful Rules Committee, negotiates with members of the minority party and the White House, and guides legislation through the House.[28] But the Speaker is also the leader of his or her party in the House, and a key duty associated with this role is helping party members get reelected. Finally, the Speaker is himself or herself an elected member of the House.

The House leadership—which, in addition to the Speaker, includes the majority leader, the minority leader, and the party whips—is chosen at the beginning of each session of Congress through a conference also known as a *caucus*. During a caucus, all the members of the political party meet and elect their chamber leaders, approve committee assignments, and elect committee chairpersons. Party leaders also may call a party caucus during a legislative session to shore up support on an issue being voted upon or to formulate the party's position on an issue on the agenda.[29] One issue before Congress is the problem of controlling greenhouse gas emissions, which is considered in "Thinking Critically About Democracy."

In 2010, Republicans won a majority in the House of Representatives, ousting Rep. Nancy Pelosi (D-CA), who had served as speaker since 2006. Pelosi proved to be a lightning rod for critics in the 2010 mid-term elections, with Republican candidates urging voters to "Fire Pelosi" by electing a Republican majority. Voters, many of whom objected to President Obama and the Democratic Congress's handling of the economy and health care reform, listened and the Republican majority swept into office.

Pelosi, the first woman to serve as speaker, was an unabashed liberal who had railed against many of the George W. Bush administration's policies during her first two years as speaker. Her posturing resulted in a lack of cooperation by many Republicans in her chamber, and then the loss of the Democratic majority in the 2010 elections paved the way for the election of John Boehner (pronounced BAY-ner) as Speaker of the House.

As speaker, Boehner's priority is repealing the Affordable Healthcare Act, President Obama's healthcare reform package that had been passed during Pelosi's tenure. Boehner, who enjoys respect and loyalty among his colleagues, is also a vocal critic of the Obama administration, much in the way that Pelosi opposed the Bush administration during her tenure. As speaker, Boehner will be forced to herd the various elements of the Republican party in House of Representatives, including those members ascribing the Tea Party positions, to a cohesive position. He will need to unify liberal, moderate, and conservative Republicans, build coalitions composed of representatives from different districts, generations, ethnicities, and sexes. These skills are essential attributes for the Speaker of the House.

The Speaker relies on the **House majority leader** to help develop and implement the majority party's legislative strategy, work with the minority party leadership, and encourage unity among majority party legislators. In this last task, the Speaker and the House

SHOULD CONGRESS LIMIT GREENHOUSE GAS EMISSIONS?

The Issue: One policy issue taken up in several recent sessions of Congress is emissions of carbon dioxide (CO_2), a "greenhouse gas" believed to contribute to global warming. These emissions, produced by public utilities, industries, and motor vehicles' burning of fossil fuels, have been an increasingly hot-button issue since the Democrats took control of Congress in 2006. After former vice president Al Gore won the Nobel Peace Prize for his contributions to raising public awareness about global climate change, many members of Congress felt pressure from their constituents to address the problem of carbon dioxide emissions. Should Congress limit greenhouse gas emissions?

Yes: The United States generates 22 percent of the world's CO_2 emissions, excluding gases that are the by-product of foreign countries' production of goods for U.S. consumption. Given this volume of consumption, Americans should take responsibility for protecting the global environment. Failure to curb greenhouse gas emissions will have terrible long-term consequences for the environmental and the economic health of not only the United States but also the wider world. Failure to reduce CO_2 emissions promotes global warming, resulting in the melting of the polar ice caps, higher tides throughout the world, and drastic changes in weather patterns and ecology, all of which can have a devastating impact on humans' as well as other species' ability to survive and thrive.

No: There is no need to create a massive regulatory structure to compel industry to reduce CO_2 emissions. Some political leaders maintain that carbon dioxide is not a pollutant and does not threaten public health. Furthermore, Senator James Inhofe (R-Oklahoma) has said that global warming is a hoax and has faulted environmental groups for duping the American public.* Forcing regulations on industry will significantly harm the U.S. economy. Regulating CO_2 emissions will drive up costs for gasoline, utilities, and various products we use every day.

Other approaches: Instead of mandating curbs directly, Congress could take a cue from states such as California and use the federal government's role as an energy customer to encourage companies to curb emissions and become more green. For example, it could require national parks or other federally owned properties to purchase electricity from sources that meet certain emissions standards. It should also further encourage the development of alternative, renewable sources of energy—such as wind, solar, and geothermal energy—by continuing to extend tax credits for these promising industries.

What do you think?

① Do you support legislation that would limit industrial output of carbon dioxide? Why or why not?

② What businesses and industries could be hurt by such legislation? Would you be willing to pay more at the pump to curb greenhouse emissions?

③ If limiting the production of greenhouse gases is crucial, what role should other countries play? What are some challenges of getting other countries to reduce their emissions of carbon dioxide?

*www.usatoday.com/news/world/2009-12-13-copenhagen_N.htm?loc=interstitialskip.

---

majority leader are assisted by the **majority whip,** who acts as a go-between with the leadership and the party members in the House. The term *whip* comes from the English hunting term *whipper-in,* a hunter whose job is to keep the foxhounds in the pack and to prevent them from straying during a fox hunt. Similarly, the job of the party whip is to keep party members together, encouraging them to vote with the party on issues and preventing them from straying off into their own positions. The minority party in the House also elects leaders, the **House minority leader** and the **minority whip,** whose jobs mirror those of their majority party colleagues but without the power that comes from holding a majority in the House.

Leadership in the Senate

In the Senate, the vice president of the United States serves as the president of that body, according to the Constitution. But in actual practice, vice presidents preside over the Senate only rarely. Vice presidents, however, have one power in the Senate that, although rarely exercised, is enormously important. If a vote in the upper house of Congress is tied, the

majority whip
a go-between with the majority leadership and party members in the House of Representatives

House minority leader
the leader of the minority party, whose job mirrors that of the majority leader but without the power that comes from holding a majority in the House of Representatives

minority whip
go-between with the minority leadership, whose job mirrors that of the majority whip but without the power that comes from holding a majority in the House of Representatives

vice president breaks the tie. Such a situation occurred in 2005 when Vice President Dick Cheney cast the tie-breaking vote on a major budget bill that slashed federal spending by nearly $40 billion by allowing states to impose new fees on Medicaid recipients, cutting federal funds that enforce child-support regulations, and imposing new federal work requirements on state welfare recipients.

president pro tempore

(also called *president pro tem*) theoretically, the chair of the Senate in the vice president's absence; in reality, an honorary title, with the senator of the majority party having the longest record of continuous service being elected to the position

The majority party in the Senate elects a Senate leader called the **president pro tempore.** Meaning "president for the time," this position is often referred to as "president pro tem." The job of the president pro tem is to chair the Senate in the vice president's absence. Historically, this position has been honorary, with the majority party senator who has the longest record of continuous Senate service being elected to the office. Although the position is honorary, the Senate's president pro tem is third in the line of presidential succession (following the vice president and the Speaker of the House). Following the death of Senator Robert Byrd (D-West Virginia) on June 28, 2010, Senator Daniel Inouye (D-Hawaii) was sworn in as the current president pro tem.

Senate majority leader

the most powerful position in the Senate; the majority leader manages the legislative process and schedules debate on legislation

The real power in the U.S. Senate is held and wielded by the **Senate majority leader,** whose job is to manage the legislative process so that favored bills are passed; to schedule debate on legislation in consultation with his or her counterpart in the minority party, the **Senate minority leader;** and to act as the spokesperson for the majority party in the Senate. The majority and the minority leaders both play crucial roles in ushering bills through the Senate, and the majority leader facilitates the numerous negotiations that arise when senators bargain over the content of a given piece of proposed legislation.[31]

Senate minority leader

the leader of the minority party in the Senate, who works with the majority leader in negotiating legislation

Senate majority leader Harry Reid (D-Nevada) was elected after the Democrats won a majority of seats in the 2006 Senate elections. Reid is a soft-spoken politician who was elected partly because of his talent at building consensus, a necessary skill given his desire to tackle some highly partisan and controversial issues when he assumed his leadership role, including ethics reform, funding for stem cell research, and an increase in the federal minimum wage.

Decision Making in Congress: The Legislative Context

When deciding whether to "toe the party line" on a legislative vote, members of Congress do not operate independently and in isolation. Throughout the legislative process, they face a variety of external pressures that influence their views. Some of these influences are subtle; others are more pronounced. Moreover, the impact of the influence varies according to the timing and type of legislation being considered. For example, political scientist Barry C. Burden has noted that the personal experiences of legislators sometimes have a bearing on their policy stances on issues.[32] Among the most important influences on members of Congress with respect to the legislative process are political parties, members' colleagues and staff, interest groups, the president, and of course their constituents—the people who elected them to serve as their representatives in our system of republican government.

Political Parties and Partisanship in Decision Making

Figure 11.2 shows the party breakdown in Congress since 1985. The data show that 1994 was a pivotal year, ending Democratic control in the House and the Senate. For nearly all of the next twelve years, Republicans retained control over both the House and the Senate. (Re-

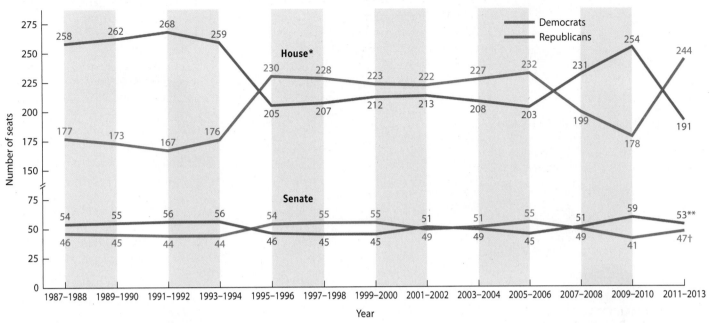

Party Breakdowns in the House and Senate, 1987–2013

* Based on projected outcomes at press time.

** Two Independent members of the Senate typically vote Democratic.

† Sen. Lisa Murkowski appeared to be the winner of Alaska's U.S. Senate election. Murkowski lost a primary to Tea Party candidate Joe Miller, but Murkowski launched a write-in campaign against Miller and Democratic candidate Scott McAdams. At press time, "write-in candidate" (presumed to be Murkowski) held 41 percent of the vote to Miller's 34 percent and McAdams' 24 percent.

POLITICAL INQUIRY

FIGURE 11.2 ■ **What trends does this graph show with respect to party representation in the House of Representatives since 1987? What trends does it indicate for the Senate? Generally speaking, do the patterns for the House resemble those for the Senate?**

publicans lost their narrow majority in the Senate in 2001 when one Republican senator switched parties, but they regained control in the 2002 elections.) But in 2006, the balance of power shifted back to the Democrats, who won majorities in both houses, squeaking out a majority in the Senate with a one-member lead. That year, Democratic candidates benefited from President George W. Bush's unpopularity and public weariness with the war in Iraq. As shown in Figure 11.3 (on page 356), in 2008 the Democrats continued to increase their majorities in both houses, as a result of voters' continuing dislike of Bush's policies, and—for some Democratic congressional candidates—from Barack Obama's coattails. But this trend was reversed in 2010, with Republicans winning a majority of seats in the House of Representatives and increasing their numbers in the U.S. Senate.

The partisan breakdown of Congress is important because most major legislative votes cast are "party votes," meaning that most members of one political party vote one way, and most members of the other party vote the other way. In some cases, this divide is due to the differing ideologies. In other instances, party voting is simply pure partisanship: Democrats vote against something because Republicans vote for it and vice versa. For example, in 2009, when Congress voted to overhaul the nation's health care system, all 60 Democrats in the Senate voted for the bill, and all 39 Republicans voted against it (Senator Jim Bunning, a Republican, did not vote). Similarly, in the House of Representatives, only one of 216 Republicans supported the measure, whereas all 219 Democrats voted for it.

Partisan voting increased after the Watergate scandal in the 1970s and rose again after the 1994 congressional elections, in which Republicans took control of Congress. Partisan voting tends to be particularly acrimonious immediately before congressional and presidential elections. It occurs more often when members are voting on domestic policy issues, such as environmental or economic regulatory policy and entitlement programs, that tend

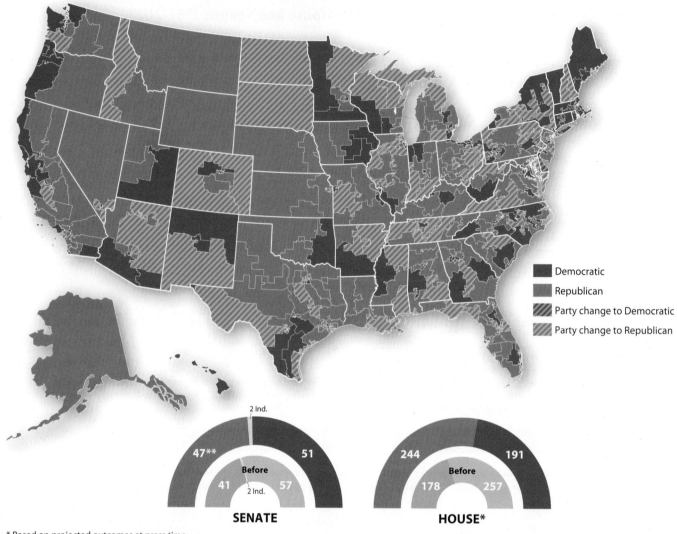

Democratic

Republican

Party change to Democratic

Party change to Republican

2 Ind.

47** · 51

Before

41 · 57
2 Ind.

SENATE

244 · 191

Before

178 · 257

HOUSE*

* Based on projected outcomes at press time.

** Senator Lisa Murkowski appeared to be the winner of Alaska's U.S. Senate election. Murkowski lost a primary to Tea Party candidate Joe Miller, but Murkowski launched a write-in campaign against Miller and Democratic candidate Scott McAdams. At press time, "write-in candidate" (presumed to be Murkowski) held 41 percent of the vote to Miller's 34 percent and McAdams' 24 percent.

FIGURE 11.3 ■ PARTY REPRESENTATION IN THE HOUSE OF REPRESENTATIVES, 2011 How many seats in the house do the Republicans have as a result of the 2010 election? How many seats do the Democrats have? Which party has the majority? Given the party of the president, how do you think the new House composition might affect lawmaking?

to crystallize ideological differences between the parties, as the health care bill did. But often, partisan votes are politically motivated, plain and simple. One of the most partisan votes on record in Congress was the 1998 vote on whether President Bill Clinton should be impeached. In that vote, 98 percent of all members of Congress voted the party line—Republicans for impeachment, Democrats against.

Scholars believe that changes in how congressional district maps are drawn partly explains increased partisan voting in the House of Representatives. In earlier times, redistricting occurred through a simple redrawing of the lines of a congressional district to accommodate population changes. But today, with the widespread use of computer-driven mapmaking technology, congressional seats can be configured to ensure a "safe seat"—one in which the party identification of the majority of a district's voters makes it likely that a candidate from a given party will win election. Sometimes, for example, more than 60 percent of a district's population identifies with one political party. A House member holding a safe seat generally can be partisan with immunity because his or her constituency often agrees with the representative's partisan stance. In contrast, when congressional districts were more competitive, a House member typically would have to temper partisan impulses to placate the sizeable proportion of his or her constituency that identified with the opposing party. Today, that is no longer the case, and it appears that Republicans in the House of Representatives have become more conservative and their Democratic counterparts have become increasingly liberal. Consequently, House members are less likely to compromise or to be moderate in their positions in negotiating issues with the opposition.

Many scholars assert that a similar bifurcation of political ideology has not occurred in the Senate. They claim that because state populations as a whole tend to be more ideologically diverse and less homogeneous than House districts, U.S. senators often must temper their views to reflect the wider range of their constituents' perspectives. Thus senators tend to be more willing to compromise and to take a more moderate stance in negotiating with the opposing party than their House counterparts. Nonetheless, on some issues, other scholars note that the Senate is increasingly dividing along strongly partisan lines.[33] In the 2006 Senate confirmation hearings for Supreme Court nominee Samuel Alito, Democrats opposed Alito's nomination, fearing that the conservative judge would provide the swing vote to overturn the landmark Supreme Court ruling *Roe v. Wade,* which legalized abortion in the United States. In the Senate's vote to confirm Alito, forty out of forty-four Democratic senators voted against Alito's confirmation, whereas all but one of the fifty-four Republicans (Rhode Island senator Lincoln Chafee) voted for Alito's confirmation.

Partisanship in Congress

THEN (1980s)	NOW (2011)
Congress was divided; Democrats controlled the House of Representatives, and Republicans controlled the Senate.	Congress is divided; Republicans control the House of Representatives and Democrats control the Senate.
Although incumbents enjoyed a considerable advantage, many congressional districts were a mix of constituents of both major parties.	Fewer congressional districts are competitive. Many districts are more homogeneous because district boundaries can be drawn with sophisticated computer programs.
Partisan voting was evident, but legislators were often forced to base their positions on constituent preferences in addition to their own party loyalty.	With the advent of less competitive districts, legislators are more partisan than their predecessors.

WHAT'S NEXT?

> Has the outcome of the 2010 elections increased or decreased party tensions, in your view? Why?

> In recent years, partisanship has increased when there has been a president of one party and a Congress of another. Does such a scenario exist today? What implications does that have for the future of partisanship in Congress for the next several years?

> Increases in technological sophistication could make redistricting an even more exact science. What impact would this have on partisanship in Congress?

Colleagues and Staff: Trading Votes and Information

Congressional colleagues provide cues for members of the House and the Senate in their decision making over whether to vote for a pending piece of legislation. Members may seek the opinions of like-minded colleagues in determining how to vote on a proposed bill. In addition, legislators may consult with peers who are policy experts, such as Senator Tom Harkin (D-Iowa) and Senator Mike Enzi (R-Wyoming), both of whom are recognized as health care policy experts.

Members of Congress also engage in **logrolling,** the practice of trading votes between members. Logrolling is a reciprocal tactic by which a member agrees to vote on one piece of legislation in exchange for a colleague's vote on another.

logrolling
the practice in which members of Congress agree to vote for a bill in exchange for their colleague's vote on another bill

attentive public

the segment of voters who pay careful attention to political issues

In addition, House and Senate members rely on their staffs to inform their decision making on legislation.[34] Staff members frequently have policy expertise that can guide a legislator's decision on an upcoming vote. They also figure in the legislative voting process by communicating with legislators about the desires of constituents and interest groups with respect to a pending piece of legislation.

Interest Groups: Influence Through Organization

In various ways, interest groups also influence congressional elections. They can affect electoral outcomes, for example, through an endorsement process by which a group notifies its members that it backs a certain candidate in the hope that members get on the bandwagon and express their support at the polls. In addition, through their political action committees, interest groups make financial contributions to congressional campaigns. And interest groups whose memberships are mobilized to support or oppose a candidate often provide grassroots activists to political campaigns.[35]

As we considered in Chapter 7, interest groups also shape the legislative process. They make their mark by influencing congressional campaigns, by providing information to members of Congress as they try to decide whether to vote for a particular piece of legislation, and by lobbying members of Congress to support or oppose legislation.[36]

TABLE 11.5

Demographic Characteristics of the 111th Congress Compared to the U.S. Population

	House (%)	Senate (%)	Population (%)
PARTY			
Democrat	58	57	34
Republican	42	41	29
Independent Unaffiliated	0	2	37
AVERAGE AGE	57 years	63 years	37 years
SEX			
Male	83	83	49
Female	17	17	51
RACE			
White	85	95	81
Black	9	1	13
Hispanic (any race)	6	1	14
Asian/Pacific Is.	2	2	3.5
Native American	.22	0	0.7
EDUCATION			
Bachelor's degree	94	99	27
Master's degree	20	17	7
Law degree	39	57	1
PhD	6	0	1
MD	4	3	2

SOURCES: Jennifer E. Manning, *Membership in the 111th Congress: A Profile* (Washington, DC: Congressional Research Service), www.senate.gov/CRSReports/crs-publish.cfm?pid=%260BL) PL%3B%3D%0A, U.S. Census Bureau, *The Statistical Abstract of the United States.*

The President's Effect on Decision Making

As we have seen, the president determines whether to sign or to veto legislation that reaches his desk. But often, before a bill reaches the signing stage, the president's position on it carries enough influence to sway members of Congress, particularly members of his political party, to vote for or against the proposed legislation.

The president can compel congressional action on an issue. Consider, for example, the issue of health care. President Obama challenged the Congress in 2009 to reform the nation's health care system, and it was this initiative that spurred Congress to consider overhauling this structure.

Constituents: The Last Word

Of all the players with a voice in the legislative process, congressional constituents—the people whom the members of Congress represent—wield perhaps the strongest, if indirect, influence with respect to congressional decision making. Most members of Congress want to be reelected, and representing constituents' views (and being able to convince voters that their views are represented well) is a major avenue to reelection to Congress. Thus constituents influence the legislative process by ensuring that their representatives in Congress work hard to represent their perspectives and policy interests, whether those concerns are over environmental pollution, crime, or the soaring cost of higher education.

In fact, some research shows that the public's "potential preferences" can motivate legislators to espouse a policy position likely to be embraced by constituents.[37] But other research shows that most voters are not especially vigilant when it comes to monitoring their elected officials in Congress. In fact, only a very small percentage of voters, sometimes called the **attentive public,** pay careful attention to the public policies being debated by Congress and to the votes cast by their representatives and senators. But the fact that the attentive public is a relatively small minority does not mean that votes taken in Congress are insignificant as far as constituents' opinions go. Indeed, if a member of Congress should disregard constituents' views in voting on a major issue, it is quite likely that an opposing candidate or political party will bring this misstep to the public's attention during the individual's next congressional campaign.

The People and Their Elected Representatives

Although members of Congress may make it a priority to represent the viewpoints and interests of their constituents, demographically speaking, they do not represent the American public at large. As Table 11.5 shows, Congress, especially the Senate, is older, whiter, more educated, and more likely to be male than the population as a whole. That said, Congress is not designed to be a perfect sampling of American demographics.[38] It is logical that the leaders of government would more closely resemble individuals who have achieved leadership positions in other realms, such as the corporate world and academia.

Yet importantly, Congress is more diverse today than at any other point in history. Figure 11.4 shows that most states have women as part of their congressional delegation. But the proportion of women in Congress is not nearly equal to their proportion in the national population. In 2010, at least 70 women were elected to the House of Representatives (with the races of four additional women too close to call at press time), including 12 new women.

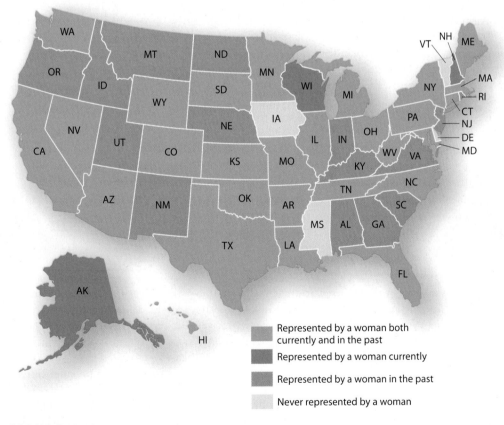

FIGURE 11.4

States Represented by Women in the U.S. Congress

African Americans in the House of Representatives

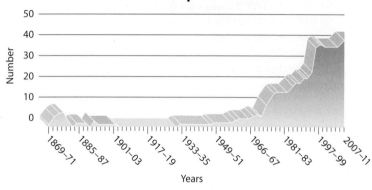

POLITICAL INQUIRY

FIGURE 11.5 ■ What explains the rise in African American representation in the House from 1871 through 1887? Why did blacks' representation fall after 1877? What pattern do you see since the late 1960s, and what political and social changes explain it?

Despite this upward trend, the United States lags behind many industrialized democracies with respect to the proportion of women serving in the national legislature.

Similarly, African Americans have historically been underrepresented in Congress. To date, only five African Americans have served in the Senate, including two, Hiram Revels and Blanche Bruce, who served during the Reconstruction era that followed the Civil War. After Bruce left the Senate in 1881, no other African American would be elected to the Senate until 1967, when Senator Edward Brooke (R-Massachusetts) was elected for one term. More recently, Senator Carol Moseley Braun (D-Illinois) was elected in 1992 and served for one term, and Barack Obama was elected from the state of Illinois in 2004. Today, the only African American in the U.S. Senate is Senator Roland Burris (D-Illinois). Burris's controversial appointment to the Senate seat, formerly held by Barack Obama, came in the wake of a major corruption scandal involving the man who appointed Burris to the seat, then Illinois governor Rod Blagojevich.

Figure 11.5 (on page 360) traces the increasing success of African Americans in getting elected to the House of Representatives. The figure shows that as in the Senate, African Americans' initial service in the House came about in the Reconstruction period. But the successes of that era were short-lived, and the numbers of African Americans in Congress would not match those of the immediate post-Reconstruction period until after the civil rights movement of the 1960s. Today, as in the case of women, more African Americans serve in Congress than at any other point in U.S. history.

Latinos' success at winning election to Congress still drastically lags behind their proportion of the population, with Latinos constituting nearly 14 percent of the population but just 6 percent of the members of the House of Representatives and 1 percent of the Senate. But many states, including New Mexico, California, Texas, and Arizona, are seeing rising numbers of Latinos elected to state legislatures, providing a pool of candidates who could move on to run for Congress. As women, African Americans, and ethnic minorities take up an increasing proportion of the eligibility pool—the group of people deemed qualified for office—diversity in Congress is sure to grow.

CONCLUSION

THINKING CRITICALLY ABOUT WHAT'S NEXT IN CONGRESS

Congress is an ever-evolving institution. The national legislature is shaped by the framers' vision that created it; by the groups and individuals that seek to, and do, influence it; and by the broader electorate who vote for the representatives who serve in it. The Constitution's framers ingeniously created a strong legislative system designed to dominate the national government. In doing so, they simultaneously—and significantly—checked the power of the executive. Do the checks the framers created enable Congress to constrain presidential action today?

The framers ensured that the legislative branch of the federal government would be responsive to changing times. Today, Congress is more demographically diverse than ever before in history. It has also responded to modern challenges by exercising a wider scope of powers, concerned with issues that were unimaginable even two decades ago, let alone more than two centuries ago. Congressional decision making today is influenced by shifting constituencies in a country that is rapidly growing more diverse. How will continued increasing diversity affect congressional decision making in the future?

With Congress well structured to respond to constituents' needs, ongoing technological advances and the spread of cheap technology to more and more citizens mean that members of Congress and their staffs should be increasingly accessible to the people. And representatives' district offices will continue to provide constituents another easily accessed channel through which to convey their needs and interests to their representatives—and through which their representatives, in turn, can monitor the opinions of their constituents so that they may better represent them.

Congress has proved itself to be a remarkably flexible institution, responding to changes in society, shifting constituencies, and increasingly diverse members, particularly in recent times. That Congress will become even more diverse is relatively assured.

Summary

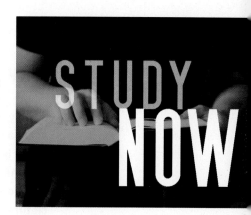

1. The Origins of Congress

The Constitution's framers intended Congress to be the strongest and most important branch of the federal government, a body both representative and deliberative. They structured the national legislature in such a way as to ensure both a check on the power of the executive and a voice for the people. The Constitution provided a flexible framework for the evolution of Congress to meet changing times. That framework continues to this day to shape the structural and procedural differences between the House of Representatives and the Senate, including the two houses' respective sizes, rules, and processes.

2. Congressional Elections

One of the most important factors shaping congressional elections is incumbency, which confers numerous advantages to those already serving in elective office. Congressional elections are also shaped by the processes of reapportionment and redistricting, which occur every ten years.

3. Powers of Congress

The Constitution enumerates certain powers for Congress, including judicial, economic, national security, regulatory, and administrative powers. Other powers of the federal legislature have evolved through national legislators' interpretation of the Constitution's necessary and proper clause, which has been a mechanism for the expansion of congressional authority.

4. Functions of Congress

The primary functions of Congress are public policy making, popular representation, oversight of the executive branch to ensure the proper administration of laws, civic education, and management of societal conflict. In their representation function, members of Congress may follow the instructed delegate model or the trustee model of representation.

5. The House and the Senate Compared

Members of the House of Representatives and the Senate serve different constituencies for different terms of office. House members are elected for a two-year term from a congressional district, and senators serve for a six-year term and represent an entire state. With respect to the legislative structure and environment, the House, with its larger size (435 members today), is more formal, and the Senate (100 members) is less formal.

6. The Legislative Process

A member of the House or the Senate can introduce a bill, the precursor to a law. Once proposed, the bill is then referred to a committee, where it is debated, reviewed, and amended. If it passes out of committee, it is debated by the full chamber; if it passes in both the House and the Senate, the president may sign the bill, veto it, or take no action. By far, most bills introduced do not become law.

7. Congressional Leadership

House leadership consists of the Speaker of the House of Representatives and the House majority and minority leaders, plus the majority and minority whips. In practice, the Senate majority leader wields the power in the upper chamber of the national legislature. Frequently, the skills demonstrated by various leaders in Congress reflect the needs of their chambers—quiet fortitude in some circumstances, adept partisanship in others.

8. Decision Making in Congress: The Legislative Context

Political parties, congressional colleagues, interest groups, the president, and constituent viewpoints all influence members of Congress. In recent years, partisanship has increased in Congress, making legislators' debates more rancorous and divisive.

9. The People and Their Elected Representatives

Although Congress is not demographically representative of the United States, it is more demographically diverse than the leadership structure of other institutions. Nonetheless, Congress is becoming increasingly diverse, with higher proportions of women, African Americans, and Latinos serving today than ever before.

Key Terms

agency review 349
agenda setting 345
attentive public 358
bill 346
casework 343
cloture 351
conference committee 351
discharge petition 350
earmark 343
filibuster 350
gerrymandering 340
hearings 349
hopper 346
House majority leader 352
House minority leader 353

instructed delegate
   model 342
joint committee 349
joint referral 347
lead committee 349
logrolling 357
majority whip 352
majority-minority
   district 340
markup 350
minority whip 353
ombudsperson 343
oversight 344
pocket veto 351
pork barrel 343

president pro tempore 354
reapportionment 339
redistricting 340
report 350
Rules Committee 350
select committee 349
Senate majority leader 354
Senate minority leader 354
seniority system 349
Speaker of the House 352
standing committee 349
subcommittee 349
trustee model 342
unanimous consent 350

For Review

1. Why was Congress created in the way it was?
2. What impact does incumbency have on congressional elections?
3. What is the difference between reapportionment and redistricting?
4. Historically, what has been the impact of the necessary and proper (elastic) clause?
5. Describe the two types of congressional powers.
6. What impact do the constitutionally enumerated duties of the House and the Senate have on the expertise of each chamber?
7. Outline the basic steps of the legislative process.
8. What factors influence the legislative process? How?
9. Why are so many bills introduced but so few passed?
10. How do the qualities of congressional leaders differ today from those needed in earlier eras?
11. Why has party-line voting increased in Congress in recent years?

For Critical Thinking and Discussion

1. If you were serving in Congress, would you tend to follow the instructed delegate model of representation or the trustee model? Why? What might be the likely outcome of your choice?
2. How does the legislative process differ in the House and the Senate? In which chamber is the process more streamlined? More deliberative? Why?
3. What do you and the people you know think about the work and contributions of Congress? Would you give Congress high or low approval ratings as an institution, or something in between? Who is your own congressional representative, and what rating would you give her or him? Why?
4. Log on to the Library of Congress Web site (http://thomas.loc.gov/) and read about issues currently on the floor of the House of Representatives. Can you see the impact of any of the external influences mentioned in this chapter on the legislative process? Describe those influences and discuss how they are shaping the process.
5. Why do you think so few women and racial and ethnic minorities have been elected to Congress? Why is this situation changing? What do you imagine that Congress will look like, demographically speaking, in the year 2050?

MULTIPLE CHOICE: Choose the lettered item that answers the question correctly.

1. Reallocation of seats in the House of Representatives to each state based on changes in the state's population since the last census is called
   a. earmarking.
   b. reapportionment.
   c. gerrymandering.
   d. redistricting.

2. Redrawing congressional district boundaries within each state is called
   a. earmarking.
   b. reapportionment.
   c. gerrymandering.
   d. redistricting.

3. A model of representation that says that a member of Congress should vote for the position that best represents his or her constituents' view even if the legislator does not share those views is called
   a. the instructed delegate model.
   b. the logrolling model.
   c. the trustee model.
   d. the pork barrel model.

4. The process by which the legislative branch checks the executive branch to ensure that the laws Congress passed are being administered in keeping with the legislature's intent is called
   a. oversight.
   b. earmarking.
   c. gerrymandering.
   d. agenda setting.

5. Differences between the House and the Senate do not include
   a. the Senate being more prestigious than the House.
   b. the Senate being larger than the House.
   c. the Senate being more reliant on staff than the House.
   d. the Senate having broader constituencies than the House.

6. A primary committee considering a bill is called
   a. a standing committee.
   b. a subcommittee.
   c. a select committee.
   d. a lead committee.

7. The system in which the member with the longest continuous tenure on a standing committee is given preference when the committee chooses its chair is called
   a. the spoils system.
   b. the patronage system.
   c. the seniority system.
   d. the last man standing principle.

8. A congressional committee created to consider specific policy issues or address a specific concern is called
   a. a standing committee.
   b. a subcommittee.
   c. a select committee.
   d. a joint committee.

9. A special tactic used to extract a bill from a committee to have it considered by the entire House is called
   a. a report.
   b. markup.
   c. filibuster.
   d. a discharge petition.

10. A procedural move in which a supermajority of sixty senators agrees to end a filibuster is called
    a. cloture.
    b. unanimous consent.
    c. a discharge petition.
    d. senatorial courtesy.

FILL IN THE BLANKS.

11. A designation within a spending bill that provides for a specific expenditure is called a(n) _____ .

12. A role in which an elected or appointed leader acts as an advocate for citizens by listening to and investigating complaints about a government agency is called a(n) _____ .

13. A proposed piece of legislation is called a _____ .

14. A legislative committee's explanation to the full chamber of a bill and its intent is called a _____ .

15. _____ is an agreement by every senator to the terms of debate on a given piece of legislation.

RESOURCES FOR RESEARCH AND ACTION

Internet Resources

Congressional Quarterly
www.cq.org *Congressional Quarterly (CQ)* is an important provider of news and analysis for Washington insiders, but its Web site is a subscriber site. Nonetheless, free trial subscriptions are available. Its job opportunities site, www.cq.com/corp/show.do?page=corp_hilljobs, is not password protected.

C-Span
www.c-span.org The cable television network C-Span provides a plethora of information on Congress, including Internet video, audio, and podcast programs of congressional hearings, committee meetings, C-Span video series, and a wide variety of public affairs information.

Library of Congress
http://thomas.loc.gov (note the absence of www) Thomas (named for Thomas Jefferson) is the Web site for the Library of Congress, the most important clearinghouse for information about Congress, legislation, hearings, votes, and other federal matters.

Roll Call
www.rollcall.com This Web site for *Roll Call,* the "newspaper of Capitol Hill since 1955," offers an insider's look at the world of Capitol Hill, including issue analysis, politics, and opinions.

U.S. Senate and U.S. House of Representatives
www.senate.gov and **www.house.gov** These Web sites for the Senate and the House provide information about members of Congress, votes, pending legislation, committees, and session schedules, plus information about the Capitol and information for visitors.

Internet Activism

Twitter
Follow HouseFloor and SenateFloor for congressional proceedings. Go to www.congressional140.com/tweeting.php for a list of all members of Congress on Twitter.

YouTube
YouTube's househub and senatehub channels provide an organized platform for citizens to access YouTube videos from members of Congress.

Recommended Readings

Ahuja, Sunil. *Congress Behaving Badly: The Rise of Partisanship and Incivility and the Death of Public Trust.* Santa Barbara, CA: Praeger, 2008. This analysis examines the causes and the results of increased party cleavages in Congress.

Dodd, Lawrence C., and Bruce J. Oppenheimer. *Congress Reconsidered,* 8th ed. Washington, DC: CQ Press, 2008. The most recent edition of a classic series providing comprehensive coverage of the evolution of the American Congress.

Fenno, Richard F., Jr. *Home Style: House Members in Their Districts.* New York: Longman, 2009. Fenno traveled the United States observing members of Congress at home in their districts and explains how constituent interaction affects congressional decision making.

Loomis, Burdett, and Wendy J. Schiller. *The Contemporary Congress.* Belmont, CA: Wadsworth, 2005. A concise yet comprehensive analysis of Congress, particularly the legislative context that influences the legislative process.

O'Neill, Thomas P. *Man of the House: The Life and Political Memoirs of Speaker Tip O'Neill.* New York: Random House, 1987. The political memoir of a long-term Speaker of the House of Representatives, providing a fascinating glimpse into the "real world" of Capitol Hill politics from the 1960s through the 1980s.

Sulkin, Tracy. *Issue Politics in Congress.* New York: Cambridge University Press, 2005. An examination of the issue of representation through the rubric of issue politics—that is, why legislators adopt the issue stances they do.

Thomas, Sue. *How Women Legislate.* New York: Oxford University Press, 1994. Groundbreaking analysis of the differences and similarities between how men and women approach the task of legislating.

Waxman, Henry. *The Waxman Report: How Congress Really Works.* Amazon Kindle edition, 2009. One of the liberal icons of the U.S. House of Representatives shares experiences from his 35-year tenure in Congress.

Movies of Interest

The Congress (1988)
This Ken Burns documentary provides a fine introduction to the U.S. Congress (both the institution and the Capitol building). Burns traces the history of the institution and the people who have served in it, including nineteenth-century statesmen Henry Clay and Daniel Webster and continuing to Congress's modern leaders.

The Ugly American (1963)
This drama stars Marlon Brando as Harrison Carter MacWhite, who, after surviving an acrimonious Senate confirmation hearing, becomes ambassador to a Southeast Asian nation on the brink of civil war.

Mr. Smith Goes to Washington
(1939) This classic Frank Capra movie features Jimmy Stewart as Jefferson Smith, who, after the death of a senator, is appointed to serve in the U.S. Senate despite his political naïveté. Stewart's depiction of a filibuster informs most Americans' perception of this political maneuver.

CHAPTER

12

The Presidency

THEN

Presidential power grew over the centuries to "imperial" proportions and then ebbed in the late twentieth century in the wake of scandals.

NOW

The power of modern presidents varies, and is affected by congressional actions and public opinion.

NEXT

Will future presidents continue down the path of an imperial presidency?

What checks will constrain future presidents' exercise of power?

How will the relationship between presidents and the people change in the future?

Each presidency is shaped not

only by the person who holds the office but also by the support of constituencies within the public, the support of Congress for presidential policy priorities, and the societal context of the day. Each presidential term can be molded and manipulated in many ways, with the result that one president may appear strong, and the next, weak—or a president may be both effective and ineffectual during the course of just one term. Compare, for example, the early days of Barack Obama's presidency, when he enjoyed strong support for his policy agenda both in the Congress and among the public, with the period leading up to the 2010 midterm congressional elections, when some Democrats in Congress were hesitant to support presidential initiatives because of his lower public approval ratings. In looking at the roles presidents play in conducting their office, as well as the sources of their power, we consider in this chapter why some presidents are more effective than others.

The presidency is constantly evolving. The institution of the presidency that Barack Obama has is not the one that George Washington left behind. In the discussion that follows, we examine the development of the presidency to gain historical perspective on how the individuals who have served as president have changed the nature of the institution over time and what the impacts of those changes are for presidents today.

The presidency has changed in part because of the way this institution—which for many Americans embodies their government—has evolved.[1] We consider that even within this most "imperial" of the American institutions of government, the people play a vital part in determining not only who serves as president but also how effective and successful the president is in exercising the executive power.[2]

Presidential Elections

The relationship between Americans and their president begins well before a president takes the oath of office. In presidential election years, nonstop campaigning provides ample opportunities for the public to learn about presidential candidates and their positions on issues. Campaigns also present many avenues for participation by the people—for example, by volunteering in or contributing to candidates' campaigns or even just by debating candidates' views around the water cooler. Although these opportunities for citizen engagement are especially abundant during a presidential election year, similar chances to get involved arise well before, because potential candidates typically position themselves years in advance of Election Day to secure their party's nomination and to win the general election.

As discussed in Chapter 8, citizens in each state who vote in their party's primary election choose the delegates to the national conventions. After the nominees have been decided, typically by late August, they and their vice-presidential running mates begin their general election campaign. Usually, the parties' choice of nominee is a foregone conclusion by the time of the convention. Eligible incumbent presidents (that is, those who have served only one term) are nearly always renominated, and the nominee of the opposing party is chosen at the National Party Convention, many of the delegates to which are chosen based on the outcome of caucuses and primary elections held in the states.

The votes tallied on Election Day determine which presidential candidate's slate of electors will cast their ballots, in accordance with state law. There are 538 electors in the

SHOULD WE ABOLISH THE ELECTORAL COLLEGE?

The Issue: The 2000 presidential election saw a historically unlikely but obviously possible occurrence: the candidate with the most popular votes, Democrat Al Gore, lost the presidential election to his opponent, Republican George W. Bush. In every other election for federal office, the candidate with the most popular votes wins that seat. But instead of the direct election of the president, the Constitution requires that the president be elected by the Electoral College. Essentially, the winner is determined by the cumulative results of fifty-one separate elections, one conducted in each state plus the District of Columbia, with the number of electoral votes determined in proportion to the size of the state's congressional delegation.

Is the Electoral College system unfair? Should we abolish it?

Yes: The Electoral College is exclusive and undemocratic. The Electoral College system demands that candidates focus nearly exclusively on key swing states that will be pivotal to their election and on populous states that carry the most electoral votes. The system is undemocratic because of its reliance on plurality elections within the states. In a plurality, the candidate with the most votes wins, even if that candidate does not receive a majority of the votes. The ultimate victory in the 2000 presidential election by the candidate (George W. Bush) whom the most people did not prefer highlights the undemocratic nature of the Electoral College. The Electoral College should be abolished.

No: The constitutionally mandated Electoral College system provides a crucial check on what would otherwise be the unchecked will of the people. In structuring the Electoral College as they did, the Constitution's framers devised a way of representing the views of both the *people* who elect the electors and the *states* because of the state-based nature of the elections. Other checks on the will of the people include staggered senatorial elections (in which one-third of that body is elected every two years) and appointed Supreme Court justices, and these are evidence of the framers' view that the will of the people needed to be tempered. If the Electoral College were abolished, the most populous geographical regions would dominate in presidential elections. Urban areas would have tremendous clout in presidential elections, and less densely populated rural areas would be virtually ignored. The current structure strengthens the power of the states and in this way ensures that our federal system remains strong.

Other approaches: Because of the difficulty of abolishing the Electoral College, various schemes have been proposed that would make it almost impossible for the loser of the popular vote to win the presidency, including awarding a state's electoral votes proportionally instead of on a winner-take-all basis, dividing electoral votes by congressional district (currently done in Maine and Nebraska), and awarding extra electoral votes to the winner of the popular vote. Legislation recently passed in Maryland, Hawaii, Illinois, and New Jersey would commit those states' electors to vote for the winner of the popular vote if states representing a 270-vote majority in the Electoral College enact similar legislation.

What do you think?

① Do you think that the Electoral College should be abolished, should remain the same, or should be reformed? Why? If your answer is "should be reformed," what changes would you implement?

② If the Electoral College were abolished, what impact would the change likely have on voters in your home state? Does that scenario influence your view?

③ Americans revere the Constitution as a near-sacred document. Typically, citizens are reluctant to advocate amending the "supreme law of the land." What is your view concerning amending the Constitution?

Electoral College because the number of electors is based on the number of members of Congress—435 in the House of Representatives, 100 in the Senate—plus three electors who represent the people of the District of Columbia. (See "Thinking Critically About Democracy.") A presidential candidate today needs a simple majority of votes (270) to win the presidency. On the Monday following the second Wednesday of December, the slate of electors chosen in each state meets in their respective state capitals and casts their electoral votes. The results are then announced in a joint session of Congress in early January. In most presidential elections, however, the winner is known on election night because analysts tabulate the outcome in each state and predict the electoral vote. The winner takes the oath of office as president in inaugural ceremonies on January 20.

Presidential Roles in the Domestic Sphere

A newly elected president quickly discovers that the presidential office requires the performance of a variety of functions each day. Many of these roles involve leadership in domestic policy issues,[3] whether it is Barack Obama's desire to overhaul health care, George W. Bush's priority of reforming schools, or all presidents' need to keep the economy sound and growing strongly. As leaders in the domestic sphere, presidents must interact with Congress, manage the economy, and serve as the leader of their party.[4]

Chief Legislator

Although the separation of powers precludes the president from actually creating laws, presidents nonetheless have significant legislative power.[5] Presidents can influence Congress by lobbying its members to support or oppose pending legislation and by defining the congressional agenda in the annual presidential State of the Union message, a constitutionally required address to Congress. Presidents also "legislate" when they submit the budget for the entire federal government to Congress annually, although Congress ultimately passes the spending plan.

Today, one of the most important legislative tools at a president's disposal is the authority either to sign legislation into law or to veto it,[6] as described in Chapter 2. Although a veto allows the president to check the power of Congress, it also provides Congress with the opportunity to check presidential power by overriding the veto with a two-thirds majority vote.[7] In giving the president the right to veto laws, the Constitution essentially integrates the executive into the legislative process.[8]

As discussed in Chapter 11, there are several variations on the veto. During a regular legislative session, if the president does not sign or veto a bill within ten days after receiving it from Congress, the bill becomes law even without the president's consent. But if the president receives a congressional bill for his signature and Congress is scheduled to adjourn within ten days, the president can exercise a pocket veto by taking no action at all. Further, during the presidency of Bill Clinton, Congress statutorily equipped the president with a new kind of veto power: the **line-item veto** allowed the president to strike out specific line items on an appropriations bill while allowing the rest of the bill to become law. In 1997, however, the Supreme Court declared the line-item veto unconstitutional, asserting that it violated the separation of powers because the Constitution grants Congress the inherent power to tax and to spend.

Figure 12.1 shows that the use of the veto varies widely from president to president. Modern presidents are generally much more likely to veto legislation than their predecessors were. A primary determinant of whether a president will regularly exercise veto power is whether the president's party has a majority in Congress.

An exception to this trend was the presidency of Franklin D. Roosevelt. As Figure 12.1 shows, during Roosevelt's twelve-year term in the White House, he issued 372 vetoes, or 12 percent of all presidential vetoes. Roosevelt chalked up this exceptional record despite having strong Democratic majorities in Congress throughout his tenure. But Roosevelt used the veto much differently than most presidents do. Because he was such a strong president, he exercised his veto power to prevent the passage of even small pieces of legislation with which he disagreed. Most presidents save the veto for important legislative matters, because they are unwilling to offend members of Congress over smaller laws that they do not favor.

President George W. Bush vetoed relatively few (fifteen) pieces of legislation during his two terms of office. His first veto came in 2006, when a congressionally passed measure that would have eased restrictions on federal funding for stem cell research reached Bush's desk. One explanation for Bush's scant use of vetoes is that while the Republicans controlled Congress, Bush did not need to veto legislation often because he effectively persuaded Congress to act on his legislative priorities. (See "Analyzing the Sources") Indeed, ten of President Bush's eleven successful vetoes occurred after the Democrats took control of Congress in 2006.

But President Bush used a different tactic—the signing statement—to put his mark on the way policies were to be administered during his tenure of office. A presidential **signing**

line-item veto
power of the president to strike out specific line items on an appropriations bill while allowing the rest of the bill to become law; declared unconstitutional by the Supreme Court in 1997

signing statement
a written message that the president issues upon signing a bill into law

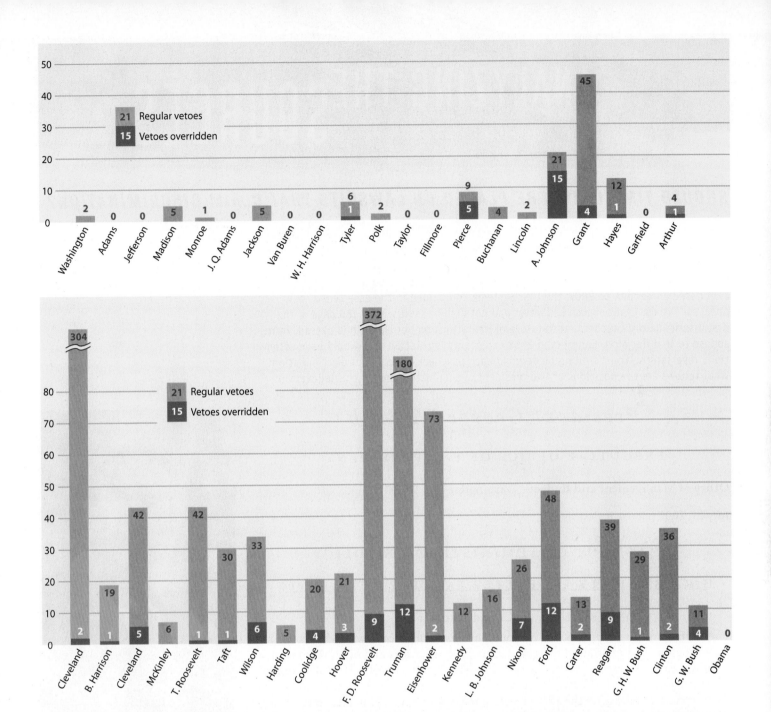

FIGURE 12.1 ■ **PRESIDENTIAL VETOES, 1789–2010** What does this graph generally indicate about the use of the presidential veto over time? What trend is evident in presidents' use of the veto from the administration of Franklin Roosevelt to the present? Why do you think a president is more likely to veto legislation when one party controls Congress and the other controls the presidency?

statement is a written message that the president issues upon signing a bill into law. A presidential signing statement may, for example, direct executive departments in how they should implement a law, taking into account constitutional or political considerations. Controversy arose over the perception that the president used the tool of the signing statement to modify the intent of the laws. Critics, including the American Bar Association, complained that by using signing statements, President Bush was asserting unconstitutional legislative authority, and some critics compared the presidential directives to

SHOULD TIME LIMITS BE PLACED ON LAWSUITS THAT CLAIM DISCRIMINATION?

While planning for her retirement, Lilly Ledbetter learned that during the nearly twenty years she had been a salaried worker in Goodyear Tire Company's Gadsden, Alabama, plant, she had received less pay than had men employed in the same job. In 1998, Ledbetter filed a lawsuit claiming that Goodyear had for years engaged in wage discrimination based on gender. In 2007, the U.S. Supreme Court ruled in the case *Ledbetter v. Goodyear Tire Co.* that because Ledbetter had not filed her suit within 180 days of the first discriminatory paycheck, the statute of limitations on her claims had passed. In response to that decision, Congress in 2008 considered legislation that would have essentially reversed the Court's ruling by defining each paycheck as an act of discrimination. What follows are the positions of two presidential administrations on this legislation:

President George W. Bush

EXECUTIVE OFFICE OF THE PRESIDENT

Office of Management and Budget   Washington, D.C. 20503

July 27, 2007 (House Rules)

STATEMENT OF ADMINISTRATION POLICY

H.R. 2831–LILLY LEDBETTER FAIR PAY ACT OF 2007

(Rep. Miller (D) CA and 31 cosponsors)

The Administration supports our Nation's anti-discrimination laws and is committed to the timely resolution of discrimination claims. For this and other reasons, the Administration strongly opposes the Ledbetter Fair Pay Act of 2007. H.R. 2831 would allow employees to bring a claim of pay or other employment-related discrimination years or even decades after the alleged discrimination occurred. H.R. 2831 constitutes a major change in, and expanded application of, employment discrimination law. The change would serve to impede justice and undermine the important goal of having allegations of discrimination expeditiously resolved. Furthermore, the effective elimination of any statute of limitations in this area would be contrary to the centuries-old notion of a limitations period for all lawsuits. If H.R. 2831 were presented to the President, his senior advisors would recommend that he veto the bill.

. . . H.R. 2831 purports to undo the Supreme Court's decision of May 29, 2007, in *Ledbetter v. Goodyear Tire & Rubber Co.* by permitting pay discrimination claims to be brought within 180 days not of a discriminatory pay decision, which is the rule under current law, but rather within 180 days of receiving any paycheck affected by such a decision, no matter how far in the past the underlying act of discrimination allegedly occurred. As a result, this legislation effectively eliminates any time requirement for filing a claim involving compensation discrimination. Allegations from thirty years ago or more could be resurrected and filed in federal courts. . . .

President Barack Obama

REMARKS BY THE PRESIDENT
UPON SIGNING THE LILLY LEDBETTER BILL
EAST ROOM

January 29, 2009

It's . . . fitting that we're joined today by the woman after whom this bill is named—someone who Michelle and I have had the privilege to get to know ourselves. And it is fitting that we are joined this morning by the first woman Speaker of the House of Representatives, Nancy Pelosi. . . .

Lilly Ledbetter did not set out to be a trailblazer or a household name. She was just a good hard worker who did her job—and she did it well—for nearly two decades before discovering that for years, she was paid less than her male colleagues for doing the very same work. . . .

. . . [S]he set out on a journey that would take more than ten years, take her all the way to the Supreme Court of the United States, and lead to this day and this bill which will help others get the justice that she was denied.

Because while this bill bears her name, Lilly knows that this story isn't just about her. It's the story of women across this country still earning just 78 cents for every dollar men earn—women of color even less—which means that today, in the year 2009, countless women are still losing thousands of dollars in salary, income and retirement savings over the course of a lifetime. . . .

That is what Lilly Ledbetter challenged us to do. And today, I sign this bill not just in her honor, but in the honor of those who came before—women like my grandmother, who worked in a bank all her life, and even after she hit that glass ceiling, kept getting up and giving her best every day, without complaint, because she wanted something better for me and my sister.

And I sign this bill for my daughters, and all those who will come after us, because I want them to grow up in a nation that values their contributions, where there are no limits to their dreams and they have opportunities their mothers and grandmothers never could have imagined. . . .

So thank you, Lilly Ledbetter.

Evaluating the Evidence

① How does the Bush administration shape—and justify—its threatened rejection of the Ledbetter Fair Pay Act? What is your opinion of the argument for vetoing the bill?

② How does the Obama administration frame its advocacy for the Ledbetter Fair Pay Act? What is your opinion of the argument presented in Obama's speech?

③ In his remarks upon signing the bill, President Obama refers to his wife, his grandmother, his daughters, and House Speaker Nancy Pelosi. What is the desired impact of referring to these women in his life in this speech? How might the Bush administration answer this type of appeal?

---

invoking the line-item veto in some pieces of legislation.[9] In all, President Bush issued more than 750 signing statements during his two terms of office.

Chief Economist

Although the Constitution makes no mention of presidential responsibilities with respect to the economy, submitting a budget to Congress reflects what has become another key presidential role: the manager of the economy. Of course, the president does not exert a great deal of control over the enormous national economy, but presidents have numerous tools at their disposal that powerfully influence the country's economic performance. For example, in 2009 President Obama persuaded Congress to pass a $787 billion program intended to stimulate the U.S. economy. Obama's plan came on the heels of Bush administration policies, which urged Congress in 2008 to allocate funds to bail out banking, mortgage, insurance, and financial services corporations that were at risk of failing. By submitting a budget to Congress, presidents shape where federal tax dollars are spent, and

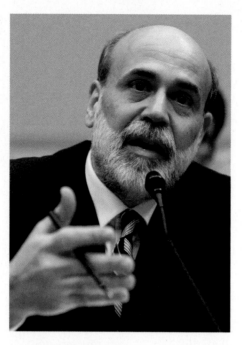

> One way presidents try to affect the nation's economy is through the appointment of the "Fed Chief," who oversees the board that plays a crucial role in managing the economy. Federal Reserve chair Ben Bernanke, who was appointed by President Bush in 2005, was reappointed by President Obama in 2009. Bernanke is frequently called on to testify before Congress on the state of the economy and monetary policy.

thereby set the economic priorities of the legislative agenda. Presidents also help to establish the regulatory and economic environment in which businesses must operate, and in that way they can influence economic growth and employment levels.

Central in presidents' oversight of economic performance is the appointment of the Federal Reserve Board ("the Fed") and its chair, who play a crucial role in managing the economy. The position of Fed chair tends to be less partisan than many other appointments, and a given chair often serves under presidents of both political parties. In 2005, President Bush named Ben Bernanke as Fed chair, replacing Alan Greenspan, who had served for eighteen years under both Democrats and Republicans. President Obama reappointed Bernanke to a second four-year term in 2009, despite criticism that Bernanke was slow to recognize the severity of the economic crisis.[10] But many lauded Obama's reappointment of Bernanke, arguing that appointing a new, inexperienced Fed chair would be destabilizing to already-bruised markets.

The appointment of a Fed chair has a lot to do with consumer confidence, as well as with support from economically influential individuals on Wall Street, including investment bankers, stockbrokers, and mortgage lenders. The fact that reaction to a Fed action (such as increasing the interest rate that banks charge one another for loans, which affects other interest rates charged to private individuals and businesses) can send the stock market plummeting sheds light on why presidential appointments to the Fed are watched so closely.

Party Leader

One of the most important domestic roles for the president is political: the function of party leader. As chief of one of the two main parties, the president is a symbolic leader for the party members and asserts influence in the party's operations by selecting the national party chair and serving as the party's premier fund-raiser. The presidential function of party leader has become even more significant in recent White House administrations, with presidents working ever more aggressively to promote the reelection of candidates from their party by ensuring that enough money is available for their campaigns.

The president also acts as party head in the day-to-day operations of the executive branch, because many of the staff appointments to the White House Office, cabinet, subcabinet, ambassadorships, and judiciary typically come from party ranks. Finally, at the end of a president's term, he likely campaigns on behalf of his party's presidential nominee.

> In the president's role as party leader, President Barack Obama endorsed former U.S. senator Arlen Specter of Pennsylvania. Specter had switched to the Democratic party after serving as a Republican senator for decades to increase his chances of reelection in 2010. Despite the president's endorsement, Specter lost his primary bid.

Presidential Roles in the Foreign Policy Sphere

Presidential responsibilities also extend to setting and executing foreign policy. The president's foreign policy powers are for the most part constitutionally derived.[11] Specifically, the Constitution gives the pres-

GLOBAL CONTEXT

PARLIAMENTARY SYSTEMS

In the many nations of the world that have parliamentary systems, the country's chief executive—the *prime minister* or *premier*—is elected not by the people but by the members of the majority political party in the legislature. Parliamentary systems distinguish between the head of government and the head of state. The *head of government* is the prime minister or premier, the individual who leads the government in its work. The *head of state* is frequently a constitutional monarch whose duties are primarily ceremonial and symbolic. In Great Britain, Prime Minister David Cameron is the head of government, and Queen Elizabeth II is the head of state.

When compared with a presidential system such as that of the United States, parliamentary systems are viewed as being more responsive to the will of the people. Although the people do not directly elect the prime minister, the desire of members of a parliament to serve the needs of their constituents ensures that the prime minister remains responsive as well.

Although the United States' presidential system has not yet produced a woman president, female members of many parliaments around the world have succeeded in getting elected to the chief executive post—prime minister. This is the case even in nations where the political culture places less emphasis on women's equality than Americans do. Women have served as prime minister in Sri Lanka, India, Israel, the Central African Republic, Great Britain, Portugal, Bolivia, Dominica, Norway, Yugoslavia, Netherlands Antilles, New Zealand, Bermuda, Guyana, Bangladesh, Haiti, Turkey, Rwanda, Canada, Burundi, France, Nicaragua, Lithuania, and Pakistan.

Parliamentary systems lack the separation of powers between the legislative and executive branches that characterizes presidential systems. In addition, parliamentary systems are seen as more unstable than presidential systems because the governments they form often depend on coalitions made up of members of two or more parties. When those parties disagree, the coalition sometimes disintegrates.

> ✳ **What are the trade-offs between presidential and parliamentary systems?**

---

ident the authority with which to carry out the roles of chief diplomat and commander in chief of the U.S. armed forces.

Chief Diplomat

Serving in the capacity of chief diplomat, the president (along with advisers) shapes and administers the nation's foreign policy. Supported by a wide array of foreign policy resources, including the State Department, the National Security Council, the Central Intelligence Agency, and the various branches of the U.S. military, the president creates and administers foreign policy. In setting foreign policy, the president can act more unilaterally than with most domestic policies. Members of Congress, who, in reflection of their constituents' main interests, tend to be concerned primarily with domestic policy issues, are much less likely to challenge presidents in the foreign policy arena.

As chief diplomat, the president, in conjunction with his or her staff, negotiates treaties and other international agreements with foreign nations and represents the United States at international summits. The president also has the authority to enter into an **executive agreement,** a kind of international agreement. Executive agreements are based on the constitutional authority vested in the president, and, unlike treaties, they may not be binding on future presidents nor do they require Senate approval.

The Constitution also empowers the president to appoint ambassadors to other nations. As high-ranking diplomats, ambassadors are the official representatives of the United

executive agreement
international agreement between the United States and other nations, not subject to Senate approval and only in effect during the administration of the president who negotiates the agreement

States in their host nation. Ambassadors' duties vary widely, depending upon the locale of their appointment. Some ambassadors play an influential, highly visible role in carrying out U.S. foreign policy, but others remain in the background.

The president, acting in the role of chief diplomat, is the leader of the diplomatic corps. In the capacity of chief diplomat, the president also hosts state dinners at the White House and formally receives the ambassadors of other nations.

Commander in Chief

As commander in chief, the president is the supreme military commander of the U.S. Army, Navy, Air Force, Marines, and Coast Guard. Counseled by advisers, the president decides when to send troops into battle (although only Congress can formally declare war) and sets military strategy in times of both peace and war.[12] Advisers have played an important part in shaping how President Obama carries out the role of commander in chief:

> [C]ircumstances made Obama commander in chief of a nation fighting two wars. Consciously or not, he prepared himself for the transition by his choice of associates. He picked a vice president, Joe Biden, who visited the battlefronts repeatedly as chairman of the Senate Foreign Relations Committee; a secretary of state, Hillary Clinton, who immersed herself in defense issues as a member of the Senate Armed Services Committee; and a defense secretary, Bob Gates, who ran the wars for Bush. Then, most strikingly, as his national security adviser he chose not another of the academics who have customarily filled that role but a very tough retired Marine general, James L. Jones.[13]

Journalist David S. Broder argues that, shaped by the views of his advisers, Barack Obama's actions as commander in chief, including his decision to increase the number of troops in Afghanistan, vary drastically from the positions Obama espoused as a candidate. Broder also cites Obama's opposition to releasing photos of detainees abused in custody and retention of military tribunals as evidence that Obama's positions as commander in chief do not vary drastically from those of his predecessor, George W. Bush.

But a key difference between Obama and Bush has been Obama's position on the "don't ask, don't tell" policy regarding gays in the military. In his January 2010 State of the Union address, President Obama urged Congress to repeal the policy so that gays might serve openly

> In modern times, the president's role as commander in chief is particularly important. In that role, President Barack Obama has had to decide where to send troops, and how many troops should be sent. Here, Obama waves to U.S. troops during a rally at Osan Air Base in Songtan, South Korea.

in the military. But when repealing the measure was proposed as part of a larger defense bill in September, 2010, Senate Democrats failed to win the votes necessary to repeal the policy.

The role of commander in chief is often a difficult one for presidents. In 2009, President Obama announced that he would send an additional 34,000 troops into Afghanistan in an effort to secure the nation so that Afghani forces could retain control of the nation after U.S. forces leave. When asked what the most difficult decision of his presidency had been so far, Obama answered, "Ordering 17,000 additional troops into Afghanistan. There is a sobriety that comes with a decision like that because you have to expect that some of those young men and women are going to be harmed in the theater of war."[14]

Overlap in the Domestic and Foreign Policy Roles: Chief Executive and Chief of State

Some presidential functions overlap the domestic and foreign policy spheres. This spillover notably exists in the president's role as chief executive—in which the president, as head of the executive branch, appoints advisers and staff—and the role of chief of state, the ceremonial function of the president.

Chief Executive

As the nation's leader in domestic and foreign policy initiatives, the president serves as chief executive. In this capacity, the president appoints the *secretaries* (top administrators) of the cabinet—the fifteen departments of the federal government—as well as the heads of other federal government agencies charged with developing and implementing the administration's policy. As chief executive, the president also appoints other staff members and numerous advisers, including staff in the Executive Office of the President. In the capacity of chief executive, the president determines how the bureaucracy will implement the laws Congress has passed and which policies—those concerning education, crime, social welfare, and so on—will be emphasized.[15]

Chief of State

The president's role as chief of state reflects the chief executive's embodiment of the values and ideals of the nation, both within the United States and abroad. The function of chief of state is similar to the ceremonial role played by the constitutional monarch in parliamentary systems such as Great Britain's (see "Global Context" on page 375). In the United States, the role of symbolic leader of the nation enhances the president's image and authority and promotes national unity. We may experience this sense that we are one indivisible nation, for example, when the president, as chief of state, makes a formal state visit to another nation, hosts Olympic medalists at the White House, and visits the sites of national tragedies such as Ground Zero after the terrorist attacks of September 11, 2001.

The President and the Executive Branch

Because daily news reports so often showcase the president acting as head of state and chief diplomat, it is easy to overlook one of the president's primary responsibilities—administering the federal government. As chief executive, the president is constitutionally charged with ensuring that the "laws be faithfully executed." Today, this responsibility means that the president oversees a bureaucracy of more than 4 million government employees, including the members of the military, while presiding over an astonishing annual federal budget of nearly *$4 trillion*. In addition, as we now consider, the president is the leader of the executive branch of government, which includes the vice president, the cabinet, the offices within the White House, and the entire federal bureaucracy.

The Vice President's Role

John Nance Garner, Franklin D. Roosevelt's vice president from 1933 to 1941, vulgarly commented that "the vice presidency isn't worth a pitcher of warm piss."[16] This insider's observation on the vice-presidential office matches the perceptions of many Americans fairly well. But although the media and the public tend to ignore the vice presidency and to marginalize the responsibilities of the second-in-command, vice presidents have an enormously important function. They are first in the line of succession to the presidency if the president should die or become incapacitated. Only eight presidents have died while in office, and although presidential succession may not be the foremost consideration in selecting a running mate for many presidential candidates, it can be an issue. Bill Clinton, in describing his selection of Tennessee senator Al Gore as his running mate, explained that his choice of Gore in part reflected Clinton's belief that Gore would make a good president "if something happened to me."[17]

THE VICE PRESIDENT'S JOB Many vice presidents serve a largely ceremonial function, performing such activities as attending state dinners, visiting foreign nations, and attending the funerals of foreign dignitaries. But vice presidents may have more substantive responsibilities, depending upon their skills and the needs of the administration. Sometimes, for example, a vice president acts as legislative liaison with Congress, particularly if the vice president has more experience in dealing with the legislative branch than the president. Such was the case with Al Gore, who had served eight years in the House of Representatives and eight years in the Senate, whereas the president under whom he served, Bill Clinton, lacked Washington experience. In other instances, vice presidents' policy expertise is a crucial resource for the administration. In the case of Vice President Dick Cheney, experience in foreign policy and national security determined the pivotal role he played in developing the foreign policy of George W. Bush's administration.

Although vice presidents are only "a heartbeat away" from the presidency, their own election to the presidency (should they decide to run) is not ensured when their term as second-in-command has ended. It is true that several vice presidents—among them, George H. W. Bush and Lyndon B. Johnson—have won election to the presidency in their own right; but many other former vice presidents have failed.[18] Notably, Al Gore, Walter Mondale, and Gerald Ford (the vice presidents of Bill Clinton, Jimmy Carter, and Richard Nixon, respectively) all went down to defeat at the polls in their bid for the White House.

balanced ticket
the selection of a running mate who brings diversity of ideology, geographic region, age, gender, race, or ethnicity to the slate

> Presidential candidates often choose a running mate who complements their attributes. Vice President Joe Biden, who served thirty-six years in the U.S. Senate, brought experience to Democratic President Barack Obama's ticket in 2008.

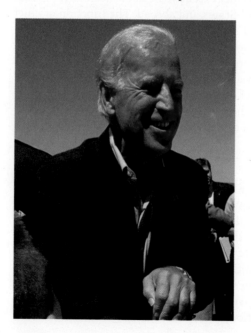

CHOOSING A VICE PRESIDENT In selecting a vice-presidential running mate, presidential candidates weigh several considerations. Would-be presidents strive for a **balanced ticket;** that is, to broaden their appeal to the electorate and increase their chances of getting elected, they select a running mate who brings diversity of ideology, geographic region, age, gender, race, or ethnicity to the slate.

Or they may base their vice-presidential selection on their own shortcomings, whether in policy expertise or in governing experience. For example, as a candidate vying for the presidency against Senator John McCain, an older and respected member of the U.S. Senate, Barack Obama chose Senator Joe Biden, who was thought to complement Obama in terms of age (Biden was 65 years old, compared with Obama's 47); experience (Biden had served in the Senate since 1972, Obama since 2000); and expertise (Biden was chair of the Senate Foreign Relations Committee, Obama had faced criticism in the media about his lack of foreign policy experience). In naming Alaska governor Sarah Palin as his running mate, Senator McCain also sought to bring youth, vigor, and enthusiasm to the Republican ticket to complement his experience and expertise. McCain's selection was also designed to attract the votes of women and cultural conservatives.

The Cabinet

Since George Washington's presidency, every president has depended upon the advice of a **cabinet,** the group of experts chosen by the president to serve as advisers on running the country. These advisers serve as the heads of each of the executive departments. Figure 12.2 shows the fifteen departments of the cabinet. Each cabinet member except the head of the Department of Justice is called the *secretary* of that department. The head of the Department of Justice is called the attorney general.

Figure 12.2 shows cabinet departments and their respective Web sites. President George W. Bush created the newest department, the Department of Homeland Security, in 2002. This department is charged with increasing the nation's preparedness, particularly with respect to catastrophic events such as terrorist attacks and natural disasters. George Washington's cabinet consisted of the heads of only four departments—justice, state, treasury, and war. (The last is now called the Department of Defense.) Subsequent presidents added other departments.

Each president may also designate cabinet rank to other advisers whose agencies are not permanent cabinet departments. Typically, presidents have specified that their national security adviser, director of the Office of Management and Budget, and administrator of the Environmental Protection Agency be included in their administration's cabinet.

Today, presidents and the public scrutinize presidential cabinet appointments to determine whether, in the words of Bill Clinton, they "look like America." As the data in Table 12.1 (see page 381) confirm, this is a relatively new gauge, since only three women and two members of ethnic minority groups had served in presidential cabinets until the Carter administration. Increasingly, however, as the table shows, presidential cabinets have become more diverse, with significant strides made during the Clinton administration.[19] President Clinton became the first president to appoint a woman to any of the "big four" posts when he named Janet Reno attorney general and Madeleine Albright secretary of state. George W. Bush named Colin Powell the first black secretary of state, and when Powell resigned, Bush replaced him with Condoleezza Rice, an African American woman who had served previously as national security adviser. Female members of President Obama's cabinet include Hillary Rodham Clinton as secretary of state; Labor Secretary Hilda Solis, who is Latina; Secretary of Homeland Security Janet Napolitano; Secretary of Health and Human Services Kathleen Sebelius; Environmental Protection Agency Administrator Lisa Jackson, who is African American; and United Nations Ambassador Susan Rice, who is African American. Other African Americans in Obama's cabinet include Attorney General Eric Holder and U.S. Trade Representative Ron Kirk. Latinos also include Interior Secretary Ken Salazar. And three Asian Americans, Secretary of Commerce Gary Locke, Secretary of Veterans' Affairs Eric Shinseki, and Energy secretary Stephen Chu, serve in the Obama cabinet.

The Executive Office of the President

Whereas the cabinet usually functions as an advisory board for the president, the **Executive Office of the President (EOP)** typically is the launch pad for the implementation of policy. The offices, counsils, and boards that compose the EOP help the president to carry out the day-to-day responsibilities of the presidency and similarly assist the First Lady and the vice president in their official activities. The EOP also coordinates policies among different agencies and departments.

Among the EOP offices, several are particularly important, including the White House Office, the National Security Council, the Office of Management and Budget, and the Council

cabinet
the group of experts chosen by the president to serve as advisers on running the country

Executive Office of the President (EOP)
offices, counsils, and boards that help the president to carry out the day-to-day responsibilities of the office

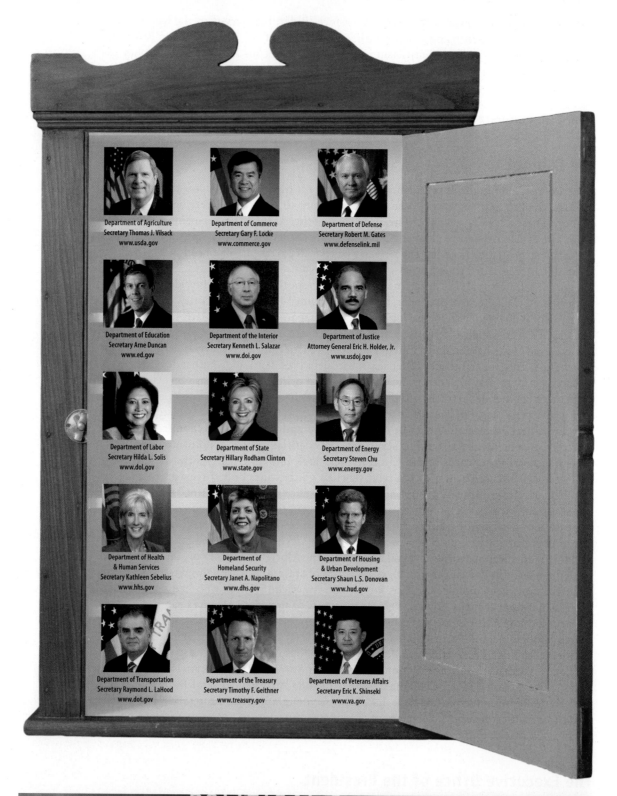

POLITICAL INQUIRY

FIGURE 12.2 ■ **THE DEPARTMENTS OF THE PRESIDENT'S CABINET** The presidential cabinet consists of the heads of the fifteen departments shown in the figure. Which department is concerned with finding alternatives to the use of fossil fuels? Which one addresses the problems of the dedicated service men and women who serve in Afghanistan and Iraq? Which department arose as a result of the 9/11 terrorist strikes?

of Economic Advisers. These offices are crucial not only because of the prominent issues with which they deal but also because of their strong role in developing and implementing policy in these issue areas.[20]

THE WHITE HOUSE OFFICE

Playing a pivotal role in most presidential administrations, the **White House Office (WHO)** staff members develop policies favored by the presidential administration and protect the president's legal and political interests. They research policy and keep the president informed about policy issues on the horizon. WHO staffers also regularly interact with members of Congress, their primary goal being to get presidential policy priorities enacted into law. They strive to ensure that those policies, once passed into law, are administered in keeping with the president's expectations.

Because of the enormous influence of staff members in the White House Office, presidents take pains to ensure their loyalty and trustworthiness. Among the top staff members of the White House Office is the **chief of staff,** who serves as both an adviser to the president and the manager of the WHO. Other staff members with clout include the **press secretary,** the president's spokesperson to the media, and the **White House counsel,** the president's lawyer. The president's secretary and appointments secretary are also influential WHO employees; they act as gatekeepers by controlling access to the president by other staffers and by members of Congress and the cabinet.

NATIONAL SECURITY COUNCIL

The president consults members of the **National Security Council (NSC)** on domestic and foreign matters related to national security. Since its creation in 1947 during the Truman administration,[21] the NSC has advised presidents on key national security and foreign policy decisions and assisted in the implementation of those decisions by coordinating policy administration among different agencies. For example, once the president has decided on a specific policy, the NSC might coordinate its implementation among the Department of State, the Central Intelligence Agency, various branches of the military, and diplomatic officials.

The president officially chairs the National Security Council. Its other regular members include the vice president, the secretary of defense, the secretary of state, the secretary of the treasury, and the assistant to the president for national security affairs, who is responsible for administering the day-to-day operations of the NSC and its staff. Other administration officials serve the NSC in advisory capacities or are invited to meetings when matters concerning their area of expertise are being decided.

OFFICE OF MANAGEMENT AND BUDGET

Once part of the Department of the Treasury, the **Office of Management and Budget** (OMB—originally called the Bureau of the Budget) has been a separate office within the EOP since 1939. Its chief responsibility is to create the president's annual budget, which the president submits to Congress each January. The budget outlines all of the anticipated revenue that the government will receive in

TABLE 12.1

Women and Minorities Appointed to Presidential Cabinets

President	Number of Women* Cabinet Members	Number of Minority** Cabinet Members	Tenure
Obama	7	9	2009–
G. W. Bush	7	10	2001–2009
Clinton	13	11	1993–2001
G. H. W. Bush	4	3	1989–1993
Reagan	4	2	1981–1989
Carter	4	1	1977–1981
Ford	1	1	1974–1977
Nixon	0	0	1969–1974
Johnson	0	1	1963–1969
Kennedy	0	0	1961–1963
Eisenhower	1	0	1953–1961
Truman	0	0	1945–1953
F. Roosevelt	1	0	1933–1945

*Includes cabinet and cabinet-level appointments.
**Includes African American, Latino/a, and Asian Americans.

SOURCES: Brigid C. Harrison, *Women in American Politics: An Introduction* (Belmont, CA: Wadsworth Publishing, 2003); the Center for the American Woman and Politics, *National Information Bank on Women in Public Office,* Eagleton Institute of Politics, Rutgers University; www.whitehouse.gov, and various presidential library Web sites.

White House Office (WHO)
the office that develops policies and protects the president's legal and political interests

chief of staff
among the most important staff members of the WHO; serves as both an adviser to the president and manager of the WHO

press secretary
the president's spokesperson to the media

White House counsel
the president's lawyer

National Security Council (NSC)
consisting of top foreign policy advisers and relevant cabinet officials, this is an arm of the EOP that the president consults on matters of foreign policy and national security

Office of Management and Budget (OMB)
office that creates the president's annual budget

the next year, usually from taxes and fees paid by businesses and individuals. The budget also lists the anticipated expenditures for the coming year, detailing how much money the various departments and agencies in the federal government will have available to spend on salaries, administrative costs, and programs. The OMB is among the president's most important agencies for policy making and policy implementation.

The director of the Office of Management and Budget, a presidential appointee confirmed by the Senate, has a staff of about six hundred career civil servants. In recent decades, the OMB director has figured prominently in presidential administrations and typically has been designated a member of the cabinet. The director's job is complex. He or she interacts intensively with Congress, trying to ensure that the budget that passes resembles the president's proposed budget as closely as possible. The director also lobbies members of Congress with the goal of ensuring that the key provisions of the budget that are important to the president remain intact in the congressionally approved version.

Once Congress approves the budget, the director of the OMB turns attention to its implementation, since it is the job of the OMB staff to manage the budget's execution by federal departments and agencies—to ensure that monies are spent on their designated purposes and that fraud and financial abuse do not occur. This managerial responsibility of the Office of Management and Budget was the reasoning behind the change in the office's name (from the Bureau of the Budget) in 1970.

Presidential Succession

No examination of the executive branch would be complete without considering the question, What happens if the president dies? Presidential succession is determined by the Presidential Succession Law of 1947. But sometimes incapacitation other than death prevents presidents from fulfilling their duties. In such cases, the Twenty-Fifth Amendment, ratified in 1967, determines the course of action.

> When a president dies in office, the line of presidential succession is clear. Crowds watched the funeral procession for President Franklin D. Roosevelt, who died in office in 1945 and was succeeded by his vice president, Harry S. Truman (1945–1953).

When the President Dies in Office

When the president dies, the course of action is clear in most cases: the vice president assumes the presidency. Such was the situation when Harry Truman became president upon Franklin D. Roosevelt's death from natural causes in 1945 and when Lyndon Johnson was sworn in as president after the assassination of John F. Kennedy in 1963. Vice presidents sometimes fill the unexpired term of their president for reasons other than the president's death, as when Gerald Ford acceded to the presidency upon the resignation of Richard Nixon after the Watergate scandal.

The Presidential Succession Law of 1947 determines presidential succession if the vice president also dies or is unable to govern. Table 12.2 shows that after the vice president, the next in line for the presidency is the Speaker of the House of Representatives, then the president pro tem of the Senate, followed by a specified order of the members of the cabinet. Notice that as new cabinet departments have been established, their secretaries have been added to the bottom of the line of succession. As a precaution, at the State of the Union address each year, one cabinet member is chosen not to attend the president's speech before Congress but, rather, to stay behind at the White House. This measure ensures that if a catastrophe should occur in Congress during the address, someone in the line of succession will be able to assume the duties of the president.

When the President Cannot Serve: The Twenty-Fifth Amendment

What happens when a president is alive but unable to carry out the responsibilities of the office? Until the ratification of the Twenty-Fifth Amendment in 1967, the course of action was not clear. Such was the case in 1881, when an assassin shot President James Garfield, and Garfield lived two and a half months before succumbing to his injuries. In another such instance, President Woodrow Wilson was so ill during his last months in office that he was incapacitated. First Lady Edith Wilson assumed some of his responsibilities and decision making. Questions about presidential health also arose toward the end of Franklin D. Roosevelt's tenure; and during the Eisenhower administration, the president authorized Vice President Richard Nixon to determine whether Eisenhower, who was battling a series of illnesses, was competent to govern. President Kennedy, who suffered from a host of physical ailments including severe, chronic back pain and Addison's disease, similarly empowered Vice President Lyndon Johnson: in an informal agreement, the men arranged that if Kennedy was physically unable to communicate with Johnson, Johnson was authorized to assume the presidency.

After Kennedy's assassination, the ratification of the Twenty-Fifth Amendment (1967) finally put codified procedures in place for dealing with an incapacitated president. According to the Twenty-Fifth Amendment, if a president believes he or she is unable to carry out the duties of the office, the president must notify Congress, and the vice president becomes the acting president until the president can resume authority. The amendment would apply in the case when a president is anesthetized for surgery, for example, or perhaps recuperating from a debilitating illness.

In other situations, a president might be incapable of carrying out the duties of office and incapable of notifying Congress. In such a case, the Twenty-Fifth Amendment requires that the vice president and a majority of the cabinet notify Congress, and the vice president becomes the acting president. If a question arises as to whether the president is fit to reassume the duties of office, a two-thirds vote of Congress is required for the acting president to remain.

TABLE 12.2

The Line of Presidential Succession

1. Vice president
2. Speaker of the House of Representatives
3. President pro tem of the Senate
4. Secretary of state
5. Secretary of the treasury
6. Secretary of defense
7. Attorney general
8. Secretary of the interior
9. Secretary of agriculture
10. Secretary of commerce
11. Secretary of labor
12. Secretary of health and human services
13. Secretary of housing and urban development
14. Secretary of transportation
15. Secretary of energy
16. Secretary of education
17. Secretary of veterans affairs
18. Secretary of homeland security

Sources of Presidential Power

The presidency that Barack Obama assumed on January 20, 2009, scarcely resembled George Washington's presidency in the 1790s. From the late eighteenth century to today, the powers of the president have evolved, reflecting the expansion of the federal government, changes in public attitudes about the proper role of government, and the personalities and will of those who have served as president.

In describing the powers that would guide presidents for centuries to come, the framers of the Constitution created a unique office. These visionary authors had lived through a repressive era in which an authoritarian monarch had exercised absolute power. They subsequently had witnessed the new American nation's struggles under the ineffectual Articles of Confederation, in which the federal government had too little power and the states too much. Thus the framers sought to establish an office that would balance the exercise of authority with the preservation of the rights and the will of the people.

Given their colonial experience, it was no surprise that the framers granted the presidents both *expressed powers* and *inherent powers* in the Constitution. Congress grants presidents additional powers, called *statutory powers,* through congressional action. We consider these various powers in this section.

Additional presidential powers have emerged over time. These newer authorities reflect both changes in the institution of the presidency and shifts in popular views on the appropriate role of government and the president. These powers include emergency powers granted in Supreme Court decisions and powers that, though not formalized, are given to presidents by the public through election mandates, presidential popularity, or unified public opinion on a particular issue or course of action.

The Constitution: Expressed Powers

The primary source of presidential power comes from the Constitution in the form of the **expressed powers,** which are those enumerated in the Constitution. Article II, Sections 2 and 3, list the following powers:

expressed powers
presidential powers enumerated in the Constitution

- serve as commander in chief of the armed forces
- appoint heads of the executive departments, ambassadors, Supreme Court justices, people to fill vacancies that occur during the recess of the Senate, and other positions
- pardon crimes, except in cases of impeachment
- enter into treaties, with two-thirds consent of the Senate
- give the State of the Union address to Congress
- convene the Congress
- receive ambassadors of other nations
- commission all officers of the United States

The expressed powers outlined in the Constitution provide a framework for presidential responsibilities and an outline of presidential power. They also shape how presidents themselves develop their authority.

The Constitution: Inherent Powers

take care clause
the constitutional basis for inherent powers, which states that the president "shall take Care that the Laws be faithfully executed"

inherent powers
presidential powers that are implied in the Constitution

One of the principal ways by which the Constitution provides for presidents themselves to assert additional powers, beyond those expressed in the Constitution, is the **take care clause,** which states that "the executive Power shall be vested in a President of the United States of America" and that "he shall take Care that the Laws be faithfully executed." On the basis of that clause, presidents throughout U.S. history have asserted various **inherent powers,** which are powers that are not expressly granted by the Constitution but are inferred.

President Thomas Jefferson exercised inherent powers in his far-reaching Louisiana Purchase in 1803. Jefferson authorized this $15 million purchase of 800,000 square miles of land, even though the Constitution did not authorize any such action on the part of a president. Interestingly, in the civic discourse over the Constitution, Jefferson, an Anti-Federalist, had argued for states' rights and against a strong central government and a powerful presidency. Jefferson had believed that the powers enumerated in the Constitution defined the powers of the government. But Jefferson thought that the purchase of the Louisiana Territory was of crucial strategic and economic importance. He believed that the deal was key to the United States' averting war with France and to securing the port of New Orleans, which was essential for the new American republic's fortunes in trade. Jefferson could not wait for a constitutional amendment to authorize the transaction, and so he forged ahead with the purchase. Congress and many Americans of the day agreed with his actions, and so there were no negative consequences to them.

More recently, in the 1930s, President Franklin D. Roosevelt drew on the inherent powers when he expanded the size of the federal government to administer his New Deal programs, designed to relieve the economic and human distress of the Great Depression. Beginning in 2002, President George W. Bush used the inherent powers when he suspended the civil liberties of foreign nationals being held in a military prison at the U.S. naval base at Guantánamo Bay, Cuba, as part of the administration's war on terror. The individuals at Guantánamo Bay have been detained indefinitely for questioning about their possible terrorist activities. These instances of presidents' exercise of inherent powers generated varying degrees of controversy among Americans of the times.

Statutory Powers

The Constitution's expressed and inherent powers provided a foundation for presidential power that has evolved over time. Those powers have been supplemented by additional powers—**statutory powers**—explicitly granted to presidents by congressional action.

An example of such a grant of statutory powers is the 1996 Line Item Veto Act, discussed earlier, which gave the president the power to strike down specific line items on an appropriations bill while allowing the rest of the bill to become law. As noted, in 1997 the Supreme Court declared the line-item veto unconstitutional on the grounds that the congressional action violated the separation of powers.

statutory powers
powers explicitly granted to presidents by congressional action

Special Presidential Powers

Presidents also have special powers that have evolved from various sources, including the Constitution, Supreme Court decisions, and congressional statutes. These powers, which numerous presidents have exercised, have come to be regarded as accepted powers and privileges of the presidency. They include *executive orders, emergency powers,* and *executive privilege.*

EXECUTIVE ORDERS The president has the power to issue **executive orders** that have the force of law. Executive orders carry the same weight as congressional statutes and have been used in a variety of circumstances to guide the executive branch's administrative functions.[22] In general, executive orders:

executive order
power of the president to issue orders that carry the force of law

- direct the enforcement of congressional statutes or Supreme Court rulings
- enforce specific provisions of the Constitution
- guide the administration of treaties with foreign governments
- create or change the regulatory guidelines or practices of an executive department or agency

Executive orders can be an important strategic tool, because they convey the president's priorities to the bureaucracy that implements the laws. For example, in 1948 President Harry Truman signed Executive Order 9981, which states, "It is hereby declared to be the policy of the President that there shall be equality of treatment and opportunity for all persons in the armed services without regard to race, color, religion, or national origin."[23] This executive order effectively banned segregation in the U.S. military. Why would Truman issue an executive order instead of working for congressional passage of a statute that would desegregate the military? Many analysts think the reason is that Truman, who ardently believed that the military should be desegregated, not only doubted that Congress would pass such a measure but also faced pressure from early civil rights activists who had pledged an African American boycott of military service if the military was not desegregated.

Executive orders have very few limitations and stipulations. One limitation is that presidents cannot use them to create new taxes or appropriate funds, because the Constitution reserves those powers for Congress. But although there are few limitations on executive orders, an order itself is sometimes not sufficient to ensure that the president's will is followed. Take the case of President Obama, who two days into his tenure as president issued an executive order declaring that the detention facilities at Guantánamo Naval Base in Cuba be closed by January 2010. Because of the complexity of the Guantánamo situation—the need to determine the status of all prisoners and to relocate them—the detention facility will remain open until at least 2011.

emergency powers
broad powers exercised by the president during times of national crisis

EMERGENCY POWERS Broad powers that a president exercises during times of national crisis have been invoked by presidents since Abraham Lincoln's claim to **emergency powers** during the Civil War. Lincoln used emergency powers during the war to suspend the civil liberties of alleged agitators, to draft state militia units into national service, and to federalize the governance of southern states after the war.

In 1936, the U.S. Supreme Court acknowledged the existence of presidential emergency powers in *United States v. Curtiss-Wright Export Corp.*[24] In this case, the U.S. government charged the Curtiss-Wright Corporation with conspiring to sell fifteen machine guns to Bolivia, in violation of a joint resolution of Congress and a presidential proclamation. Without congressional approval, President Franklin D. Roosevelt had ordered an embargo on the machine gun shipment. The Court supported Roosevelt's order, ruling that the president's powers, particularly in foreign affairs, are not limited to those powers expressly stated in the Constitution. The justices also stated that the federal government is the primary actor in foreign affairs and that the president in particular has inherent powers related to his constitutional duties in foreign relations.

executive privilege
the right of the chief executive and members of the administration to withhold information from Congress or the courts, or the right to refuse to appear before legislative or judicial bodies

EXECUTIVE PRIVILEGE Presidents also can exercise **executive privilege,** the authority of the president and other executive officials to refuse to disclose information concerning confidential conversations or national security to Congress or the courts. In invoking executive privilege, presidents draw on the idea that the Constitution's framework of separation of powers justifies the withholding of certain information from Congress or the judiciary,[25] a claim initially asserted when George Washington refused to grant Congress access to all documents pertaining to treaty negotiations. Typically, presidents claim executive privilege so they can get advice from aides without fear that such conversations might be made public or scrutinized by members of Congress or the judiciary. Presidents also have invoked executive privilege when negotiating foreign policies with other heads of state, to shield these leaders from having sensitive negotiations examined by the other branches of the federal government.

On occasion, the judicial branch of the federal government has successfully challenged executive privilege. For example, when President Richard Nixon refused to turn over tapes of Oval Office conversations to a special prosecutor investigating the Watergate scandal in 1974, the Supreme Court intervened. In *United States v. Richard M. Nixon,* the Court asserted that although executive privilege does exist, it was not applicable regarding the tapes because President Nixon's claim of executive privilege concerning the tapes was too broad.[26] (See pages 390–391 for more on Watergate.)

More recent cases in which a president has invoked executive privilege are notable. President Bill Clinton attempted to do so to prevent White House aides from testifying before special prosecutor Kenneth Starr during the Monica Lewinsky scandal. (Clinton was accused of having extramarital relations with Lewinsky, a White House intern.) Clinton's maneuver failed, and his aides were compelled to testify. In 2007, President George W. Bush asserted executive authority in a showdown with Congress over the politically motivated firing of nine U.S. attorneys. Bush invoked executive privilege to prevent White House Counsel Harriet Miers and presidential adviser Karl Rove from testifying before Congress. The congressional inquiry continued without Miers's and Rove's testimony, however, and eventually Attorney General Alberto Gonzales stepped down as a result of the scandal.

In general, the courts have allowed executive privilege in cases where a clear issue of separation of powers exists—as with respect to international negotiations and conversations regarding matters of policy or national security. The courts have tended to limit the use of executive privilege when presidents have exercised it in an effort to prevent the revelation of misdeeds by members of the executive branch.

The People as a Source of Presidential Power

One of the most important sources of presidential power today comes from the people. Although one president generally will have the same formal powers as the next, presidents' ability to wield their power, to control the political agenda, and to get things done typically is a function of political skill, charisma, and what political scientist Richard Neustadt has called "the power to persuade."[27]

The President and the Bully Pulpit

Modern presidents work to persuade the public on a virtually continuous basis. They know that if they win popular support for their views and political agenda, they will have an easier time getting their policy priorities through Congress. In their efforts to persuade the people, they exploit the power of their office, using the presidency as a forum from which to speak out on any matter—and to have their views listened to. This ready access to the public ear and broad power of the president to communicate led President Theodore Roosevelt to exclaim, "I have got such a bully pulpit!"[28]

In using their bully pulpit, presidents seek to communicate that their stances on important issues are the right choices and that their actions, particularly controversial decisions, should be supported. Presidents also strive to persuade the public that they are doing a good job on key policy fronts such as economic and foreign policy. Sometimes presidents seek to mobilize the public to take specific actions or to adopt certain beliefs. For example, President Barack Obama attempted to use the bully pulpit to convince the American public that the health care system was in need of reform—and that Congress should enact his proposals to change the system.

The reason why presidents work so tirelessly to win public support for their agenda is that they understand that getting Congress to act on policy priorities, to approve budgets, and to pass favored legislation depends heavily on the perception that the public supports presidential initiatives. Indeed, political scientist Richard Neustadt argues that the modern institution of the presidency is weak and that presidents in fact must rely on public and congressional support in order to enact their agendas.[29] Getting Congress to do what the president wants is more difficult when a president faces a divided government, the situation in which the president belongs to one political party and Congress is controlled by a majority of members of the other party. For example, when the Republicans lost control of both the House and the Senate in the 2006 congressional elections, President Bush's chances of enacting his legislative priorities, such as privatizing Social Security, decreased significantly because the new Democratic majorities in Congress did not share those priorities.

But beyond partisan differences, presidents' ability to get things done in Congress also is a function of their popularity with the people. A popular president can use that clout to persuade members of Congress that his positions are the right ones; an unpopular president will face greater obstacles to having his legislative agenda enacted.

The President and Public Approval

When Barack Obama was sworn in as president, fully 67 percent of the American people approved of the way he was handling his job as president. He enjoyed a strong **honeymoon period,** a time early in a new president's administration characterized by optimistic approval by the public. As his presidency progressed, however, the president's approval rating steadily declined, reaching a low point of 43 percent in August 2010, as shown in Figure 12.3 on page 388. Americans grew increasingly wary of the president's proposal to reform the nation's health care system and increasingly frustrated at the sluggish rate of economic recovery.

The flow and ebb of presidential popularity during the administration of George W. Bush illustrates how essential the people's support is to the success of a chief executive's initiatives. After the September 11, 2001, terrorist attacks and President Bush's rapid and dignified response to them, Bush enjoyed record high approval ratings. **Approval ratings** are the percentage of survey respondents who say that they "approve" or "strongly approve"

honeymoon period
a time early in a new president's administration characterized by optimistic approval by the public

approval ratings
the percentage of survey respondents who say that they "approve" or "strongly approve" of the way the president is doing his job

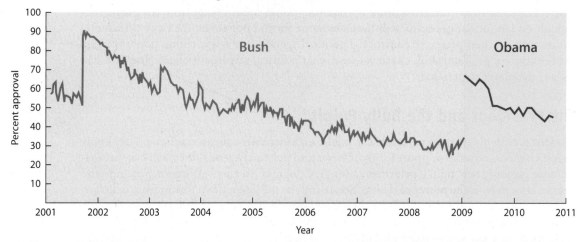

**Job Approval Ratings for Presidents
George W. Bush and Barack Obama**

POLITICAL INQUIRY

FIGURE 12.3 ■ **GEORGE W. BUSH'S APPROVAL RATINGS (2001–2009) COMPARED TO BARACK OBAMA'S APPROVAL RATINGS (2009–2010)** What could cause Obama's approval ratings to reach their former levels? To decline further? How important is the economy in determining his approval ratings? What other issues or circumstances might have an impact on presidential approval ratings in the future?

SOURCE: www.gallup.com/poll/116500/Presidential-Approval-Ratings-George-Bush.aspx; www.gallup.com/poll/113980/Gallup-Daily-Obama-Job-Approval.aspx.

of the way the president is doing his job. Immediately after September 11, President Bush's approval ratings hovered in the high 80s, occasionally reaching 90 percent, meaning that 90 percent of those surveyed indicated that they approved of the way the president was handling his job. (In contrast, the average presidential approval rating since the Franklin D. Roosevelt administration was 56 percent.) During this time, Bush had enormous legislative successes. These included the passage of the USA PATRIOT Act of 2001, which gave law enforcement officers greater authority in handling suspected terrorist acts, and the congressional declaration of a "war on terror." When Bush's popularity subsequently waned because of the people's dissatisfaction with the rate of progress in the war in Iraq, the high number of casualties in the war, and continued weakness in the American economy, so too did support decrease for the continuation of the war, the president's economic policies, and a proposed extension of the USA PATRIOT Act.

In general, presidential approval ratings reveal that some presidents are simply more popular than others. For example, presidents Reagan and Clinton tended to enjoy high approval ratings, with President Clinton's second-term ratings running particularly high, especially in light of the Monica Lewinsky scandal and the subsequent impeachment proceedings against him.

When the United States engages in a short-term military action or is the subject of an attack by terrorists, we see similar peaks of approval ratings, sometimes referred to as the **rally 'round the flag effect.**

A president rarely sustains high public approval continuously. Once achieved, however, high ratings help the chief executive to achieve his goals by demonstrating the people's support of the presidential agenda.[30]

The Media as a Tool of Presidential Influence

Modern presidents rely heavily on the mass media to convey their message to the people. As presidential candidates, they hire media consultants to assist them in preparing for televised debates. Teams of consultants create sophisticated media strategies that aim to integrate the presidential campaign's use of television, radio, and the Internet.

rally 'round the flag effect
peaks in presidential approval ratings during short-term military action

Once a president takes office, the expertise of the White House communications office kicks in to "spin" news in a favorable light for the administration. In particular, the White House communications director forges relationships with the most prominent media outlets by providing access, exclusive interviews, and scoops on breaking stories to reporters considered friendly to the administration. And today, the president relies on YouTube, Facebook, and Twitter to communicate directly with the American people.

Important national speeches and the State of the Union address are televised and made available on YouTube, just as press conferences are. Interestingly, before the advent of television, presidential press conferences occurred more frequently than they do today, providing the best opportunity for the president to "talk to the people" and for reporters and their audiences to learn about presidential priorities.[31]

> Today, the president relies on technology to communicate directly with the American people. On the White House's Online Town Hall Web site, viewers can submit questions to President Obama.

Although the nature of presidential press conferences and other media forums has evolved over time, the mass media have served as a key avenue by which modern presidents have communicated directly to the population at large. And because the nature of the president's relationship with his constituency is constantly evolving, so too is presidential power.

The Evolution of Presidential Power

Although the constitutional powers of the presidency have changed little over time, the power of the presidency has evolved a great deal.[32] In part, this development stems from some presidents' skillful use of powers not granted by the Constitution, such as the powers to persuade and to assert more authority. But the political environment within which presidents have governed has also contributed to the evolution of presidential power.[33]

The history of the early republic saw an incremental expansion of the power of the presidency, whereas the Great Depression of the 1930s and the election of Franklin D. Roosevelt in 1932 spawned an enormous growth of presidential authority.[34] As successor presidents inherited the large bureaucracy that Roosevelt built, presidential powers have further expanded—gradually creating what historian Arthur Schlesinger Jr. has called the "imperial presidency."

Early Presidents and the Scope of Presidential Power

Thomas Jefferson's election to the presidency in 1801 marked one of the earliest expansions of presidential power. Jefferson broadened the powers of the office despite his Anti-Federalist reluctance to delegate too much power to the national government. Jefferson increased presidential power in two significant ways. First, as we have seen, Jefferson established the principle of inherent powers of the presidency by undertaking the Louisiana Purchase. Second, Jefferson's tenure of office witnessed the first time that a president had to act as party leader. Jefferson had no choice but to assume this role: if he had not, he would not have been elected president given the dominance of the Federalist Party during this era (see Chapter 8).

Twenty-five years later, Andrew Jackson would also adopt the role of president-as-party-leader, but he would add a new twist. Jackson's emphasis on *populism,* a political philosophy that emphasizes the needs of the common person, spawned a new source of presidential power, because Jackson was the first president to derive real and significant power from the people. Whereas earlier politics had mostly emphasized the needs of the elite, Jackson's populism mobilized the masses of common people who traditionally had not been civically engaged. This populism augmented the power of the presidency by increasing the popularity of the president and investing him with power that came from the people's goodwill.

In the twentieth century, the nature and scope of presidential power changed as a consequence of the prevailing political environment. One of the most extraordinary shifts in the nature of the presidency occurred during Franklin D. Roosevelt's administration, which lasted from 1932 until his death in 1945. (Roosevelt was elected to an unprecedented four terms; the Twenty-Second Amendment to the Constitution, which allows only two elected presidential terms, was ratified six years after his death.)

Having come to power during the Great Depression, Roosevelt engineered a significant change in the function of the federal government. He called for a New Deal for the American people, a series of social welfare programs that would provide employment for many of the nation's unemployed workers. Roosevelt's New Deal was based on the ideas of economist John Maynard Keynes, who argued for temporary deficit spending by the government (that is, going into debt) to spur the economy during economic downturns.

Roosevelt's primary weapon in his New Deal arsenal was the **Works Progress Administration (WPA),** a federal government program that employed 8.5 million people at a cost of more than $11 million between 1935 and 1943. The idea was that government-funded employment would create economic growth in the private sector because those employed by the government would have the money to buy goods and services, thus creating spiraling demand. The rising demand for goods and services would mean that the private sector could then employ more people, and the cycle of recovery and growth would continue. For example, if during the 1930s, the government employed your great-grandfather to work on a road-building project in his town, he might have put his paycheck toward buying more bread and other baked goods than he previously could have afforded. If enough people in town could have similarly patronized the bakery, then the baker might have had to hire an assistant to keep up with demand, and consequently the assistant would have had money to spend on, say, new shoes for his children. In that way, the increased demand for products and services would continue, creating additional economic growth.

Roosevelt's New Deal was important to the presidency for two reasons. First, it dramatically changed people's views of the role of the federal government. People now tend to think of the federal government as the provider of a "safety net" that protects the most vulnerable citizens—a safeguard that did not exist before the New Deal, when those needing assistance had to rely on the help of family, friends, churches and private charities. Second, this popular perception and the programs that emerged—the Works Progress Administration, unemployment insurance, Social Security—meant that the federal government would have to grow larger in order to administer these programs. As a result, the president's role as chief executive would become much more important to modern presidents than it had been to those who served before Roosevelt.[35]

The Watershed 1970s: The *Pentagon Papers,* Watergate, and the "Imperial Presidency"

Americans' penchant for strong presidents modeled after Roosevelt diminished drastically in the 1970s. In 1971, an employee of the Department of Defense named Daniel Ellsberg leaked a classified, top-secret 7,000-page history of the nation's involvement in and thinking on Vietnam dating from the Truman administration in 1945 to the Nixon administration then installed in the White House. Called the *Pentagon Papers,* the work first appeared as a series of articles in the *New York Times.* When the Nixon administration in 1971 successfully petitioned the Department of Justice to prevent the publication of the remainder of the articles, the *Washington Post* assumed publication of them. When the Department of Justice sued the *Post,* the *Boston Globe* resumed their publication. Two weeks later, in an expedited appeals process, the U.S. Supreme Court ruled in *The New York Times Co. v. The United States* that the government "carries a heavy burden of showing justification for the imposition of such a restraint" and that the government had failed to meet that burden, thus allowing the continued publication of the papers.[36]

Works Progress Administration (WPA)
a New Deal program that employed 8.5 million people at a cost of more than $11 million between 1935 and 1943

> William Frazee, the chief of the presses for the *Washington Post,* makes the victory sign after learning of the Supreme Court's decision allowing newspapers to publish the *Pentagon Papers.* Applause broke out in the press room as the first print run began rolling.

The *Pentagon Papers* tainted the public's view of the presidency. The published work revealed miscalculations by policy makers in presidential administrations from Truman's to Nixon's, as well as arrogance and deception on the part of policy makers, cabinet members, and presidents. Specifically, the *Pentagon Papers* revealed that the federal government had repeatedly lied about or misrepresented the fact of increasing U.S. military involvement in Southeast Asia. In particular, the analysis in the *Pentagon Papers* indicated not only that U.S. marines had conducted offensive military maneuvers well before the public was informed, but also that the U.S. military had engaged in other actions, including air strikes, over Laos and military raids throughout the North Vietnamese coastal regions. The Nixon administration's legal wrangling to prevent release of the *Pentagon Papers* cast a dark cloud over the public's perception of the presidency.

Cynicism about the presidency continued to grow in light of the **Watergate** scandal that took place a year later. In 1972, men affiliated with President Nixon's reelection campaign broke into the headquarters of the Democratic National Committee (located in the Watergate Hotel in Washington, D.C.) to retrieve wiretaps that they had previously installed to monitor their opponents. *Washington Post* reporters Bob Woodward and Carl Bernstein, in a groundbreaking series of stories, traced the burglaries and the subsequent cover-up to high-level officials in the Nixon administration. This crime and the Nixon administration's attempts at cover-ups became known as the Watergate scandal. A Senate investigation revealed that President Nixon had secretly taped conversations in the Oval Office that would shed light on "what the president knew [about the break-in] and when he knew it."[37] Nixon claimed executive privilege and refused to turn the tapes over to a special prosecutor who had been appointed to investigate the scandal. When the U.S. Supreme Court ruled in *United States v. Richard Nixon* that Nixon must provide the tapes to the special prosecutor, one key tape was found to have a gap of almost twenty minutes where someone, reportedly his secretary, Rosemary Woods, had erased part of the recording.

Meanwhile, all the Watergate burglars had pleaded guilty and been sentenced, and only one refused to name the superiors who had orchestrated the break-in. But the testimony of burglar James W. McCord Jr. linked the crime to the Committee to Re-Elect the President (CREEP), Nixon's campaign organization, and to high-ranking Nixon White House officials. The disclosure prompted John Dean, Nixon's White House counsel, to remark, "We have a cancer within, close to the presidency, that is growing."[38] With indictments handed down for many of Nixon's top aides, and with a Senate investigation and a special prosecutor's investigation in progress, the House Judiciary Committee took up the matter of impeachment. The committee handed down three articles of impeachment against Nixon—one for obstruction of justice, a second for abuse of power, and a third for contempt of Congress. When a newly released tape documented that Nixon had planned to block the investigations by having the Federal Bureau of Investigation and the Central Intelligence Agency falsely claim that matters of national security were involved, the tape was referred to as a "smoking gun."[39] Nixon lost the support of his few loyalists in Congress and on August 8, 1974, announced that he would resign from office the following day.

Watergate might seem like a relatively insignificant event in the history of the American presidency, but the impact of the Watergate scandal on the presidency has been enormous. Watergate badly wounded the trust that many Americans held for their president and for their government. Combined with the unpopularity of the Vietnam War and the release of the *Pentagon Papers,* it created a deep cynicism that pervades many Americans' perception of their government even today—a pessimistic attitude that has passed from generation to generation.

Watergate also dramatically demonstrated how enormously the presidency had changed. Modern presidents had supplanted Congress as the center of federal power and in so doing had become too powerful. Historian Arthur Schlesinger Jr. and other presidential scholars have decried the problem of the growth of the executive branch and, in particular, the imperial "courts"—the rising number of Executive Office of the President staff members, many of whom are not subject to Senate confirmation and share a deep loyalty to the person who is president rather than to the institution of the presidency. In juxtaposition with an attitude like that expressed by Richard Nixon in his comment that "when the president does it, that means it is not illegal,"[40] the imperial presidency left much room for abuse.

Watergate
during the Nixon administration, a scandal involving burglaries and the subsequent cover-up by high-level administration officials

Evolution of the Modern Presidency

THEN (1970s)	NOW (2011)
The presidency had become an increasingly powerful institution, shaped by the predecessors of Richard Nixon, who assumed office in 1969.	Congress continues to attempt to "check" the power of modern presidents.
The presidency supplanted Congress as the epicenter of power in the federal government.	Presidential exercise of authority in the foreign policy realm serves to limit Congress's ability to rein in presidential power.
Backlash against abuses of executive power in the Nixon administration paved the way for the election of Jimmy Carter, a comparatively weak president.	Voter backlash against the Obama administration's economic policy propels a Republican majority to the House of Representatives, providing a check on presidential power in the domestic policy realm.

WHAT'S NEXT?

> How do you anticipate that the congressional election of 2010 will further shape the institution of the presidency?

> What public policy issues will likely dominate in the months and years to come? How will these issues influence the ways presidential power is exercised?

The Post-Watergate Presidency

With the election of Jimmy Carter to the White House in 1976, many observers believed that the era of the imperial presidency had passed. Carter, the mild-mannered governor of Georgia and thus a Washington outsider, seemed to be the antidote the nation needed after the display of power-run-amok during Nixon's tenure. But given the significant challenges Carter faced during his term, many people believed that he did not exercise *enough* authority—that he acted weakly when faced with various crises.

Ronald Reagan's election in 1980 in some ways represented a return to a more powerful, "imperial" presidency. Reagan, a former actor, was Hollywood swagger personified, speaking tough talk that many Americans found appealing. His administration was not unlike an imperial court, featuring a group of advisers with deep loyalties to Reagan. Although the era of unchecked presidential power was gone for good, many would argue that the George W. Bush administration was best at re-creating a form of an imperial presidency. Bush was able to exercise strong authority because of the fear created both among the citizenry and in Congress after the September 11, 2001, terror attacks. And given President Bush's activist foreign policy, he exercised great authority in that realm, with Congress having little ability to check him. Ironically, many critics of the Bush administration would assert that he was assisted in creating a modern imperial presidency by many of the same staff members who were part of the Nixon administration. But administration supporters would note that a strong presidency was necessary at this critical juncture in the nation's history.

Impeachment: A Check on Abuses of Presidential Power

impeachment
the power of the House of Representatives to formally accuse the president (and other high-ranking officials, including the vice president and federal judges) of crimes

articles of impeachment
charges against the president during an impeachment

Although presidential powers are flexible and can be shaped by the individuals holding the office, these powers do not go unchecked. One crucial check on presidential power is **impeachment,** the power of the House of Representatives to formally accuse the president (and other high-ranking officials, including the vice president and federal judges) of crimes. The Constitution specifically refers to charges of "Treason, Bribery, or other high Crimes and Misdemeanors," an appropriately vague description of the potential offenses a president could commit. An impeachment can be thought of as an indictment: If a majority of the members of the House of Representatives vote to impeach the president, they forward the charges against the president, called the **articles of impeachment,** to the Senate. The Senate then tries the president and, in the event of conviction for the offenses, determines the penalty. In convicting a president, the Senate has the authority to punish the president by removing him from office.

Although the Senate can force a president to step down, it has never done so in practice, and only two presidents have been impeached by the House of Representatives. The first was Andrew Johnson, who succeeded Abraham Lincoln as president in 1865 upon the latter's assassination. When he assumed the presidency, Johnson faced not only a divided nation but also a government in turmoil. The eleven articles of impeachment against him had to do primarily with his removal of the secretary of war, Edwin Stanton, who was working with Johnson's congressional opponents to undermine Johnson's reconstruction policies in the South. The so-called Radical Republicans in the House believed that Johnson's policies were too moderate, and they sought to treat the Confederate states as conquered territories and to confiscate the land of slaveholders. Those same House members wanted to protect their ally Stanton and prevent him from being removed from office. The Senate ultimately recognized the politically motivated nature of the articles of impeachment against Johnson and acquitted him on all counts.

The most recent occurrence of the impeachment of a president was in 1998, when the House of Representatives approved two articles of impeachment against President Bill Clinton. On the basis of an investigation by a special prosecutor, the House impeached Clinton for lying to a grand jury about his relationship with White House intern Monica Lewinsky and for obstructing justice. The Senate acquitted Clinton on both counts.

During the Watergate scandal that rocked Richard Nixon's presidency, the House Judiciary Committee approved articles of impeachment against the president and sent them to the full House for a vote. Republican members of Congress convinced Nixon that the House would vote to impeach him and that the Senate would convict him and remove him from office. Faced with the inevitable, Nixon became the first president to resign from office before the House could vote to impeach him.

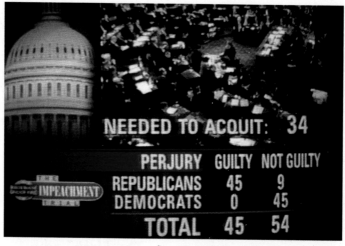

> On the basis of an investigation by special prosecutor Kenneth Starr, the House impeached President Bill Clinton for committing perjury by lying to a grand jury about his relationship with White House intern Monica Lewinsky and for obstructing justice. The Senate voted to acquit Clinton on those perjury charges.

Evaluating Presidential Leadership

In 1998, while President Clinton was mired in impeachment hearings in Congress, his public approval ratings stood at 60 percent. Despite the Monica Lewinsky scandal and the risk that the president might be removed from office for lying about his relationship with the White House intern, a healthy majority of Americans separated Clinton's personal moral failings from his ability to govern successfully.

While a president is in office, people evaluate the president's performance on the basis of specific criteria. These include questions such as these: Does the president prioritize the same issues that I do? Is the president effectively managing the economy? Is the United States respected around the world? Is the president a strong leader, unafraid to exercise power? Does the president have a vision for the nation and for his administration? Is the president able to communicate that vision to the people? If presidents are successful in these areas, they tend to have generally high approval ratings. As we have seen, however, high approval ratings are difficult to sustain over the course of an administration.

In general, the average American's criteria for presidential greatness differ substantially from assessments by scholars of the presidency. The American public at large tends to emphasize recent presidents with strong communication skills, citing Ronald Reagan, John F. Kennedy, and Bill Clinton among the top four presidents in one survey (with Abraham Lincoln number three). Scholarly rankings tend to be more historically inclusive, with George Washington, Abraham Lincoln, Franklin D. Roosevelt, and Thomas Jefferson leading the list of the greatest presidents.

Women in the White House

Of the three branches of government, the executive branch has been the most challenging for women to gain entry into as formal participants. As we saw earlier in this chapter, no woman served as a cabinet member until the twentieth century, and to date, a woman has not been elected president. Yet cabinet positions are not the only place where women's influence in the executive branch has been felt. Historically, the women who have served as First Lady have influenced both presidents and policy.

Some recent First Ladies, among them Nancy Reagan and Hillary Clinton, have exercised undisguised public power. Following President Obama's election, many Americans wondered whether First Lady Michelle Obama would take up the reigns as policy leader, but that has not been the case. And with women becoming an increasing proportion of the pool of candidates deemed eligible to be president, a woman's election to the presidency in the near future becomes nearly assured. Indeed, Senator John McCain's selection of Alaska Governor Sarah Palin was seen by many analysts as an acknowledgment of the importance of women voters and the inevitability of a woman president. As President Richard Nixon remarked, "Certainly in the next 50 years we shall see a woman president, perhaps sooner than you think. A woman can and should be able to do any political job that a man can do."[41]

The First Lady

Much like the presidency itself, the office of the First Lady has been defined by the individuals who have occupied it. That women as different as Barbara Bush, the wife of President George H. W. Bush, and Hillary Clinton, the wife of President Bill Clinton, could consecutively and successfully serve as First Lady demonstrates the open-mindedness with which the American people view the role. First Lady Michelle Obama has shunned the policy-oriented role that Hillary Rodham Clinton forged, though Obama did show her activist side in the aftermath of the devastating earthquake in Haiti in January 2010. By and large, though, Obama has instead preferred to focus on raising the Obamas' young daughters, Malia and Sasha, and on the more ceremonial aspect of serving as First Lady.

Other First Ladies have used their proximity to the chief executive to influence policy concerns more broadly and more forcefully. Some have acted "behind the scenes," as was the case with Edith Wilson, the wife of Woodrow Wilson. Others have taken a more public role. Eleanor Roosevelt, the wife of Franklin D. Roosevelt, fought for many causes during her husband's administration, including human rights and civil rights for African Americans. Hillary Clinton transformed the office of First Lady by serving, at her husband's appointment, as the chair of a presidential task force on health care reform. Her role in the task force, and indeed throughout the Clinton administration, proved to be a lightning rod for critics who thought that a First Lady should not be so prominent. Laura Bush by contrast was a more reserved and less public First Lady.

When a Woman Is Elected President

As First Lady, Barbara Bush speculated about the election of a woman president. She wryly commented, "Somewhere out in this audience may even be someone who will one day follow my footsteps, and preside over the White House as the president's spouse. I wish him well!"[43]

Over a period of time, pollsters have explored the possibility that Americans would vote for a qualified woman for president. Figure 12.4 shows that since 1937, when only 33 percent of Americans said they would cast their presidential ballot for a qualified woman, that figure has steadily risen. By 1999, the number rose to 92 percent of respondents who said they would vote for a female presidential candidate. Yet by 2005, that figure had declined to 89 percent. One explanation for this drop could be that Senator Hillary Clinton was frequently mentioned at the time of the poll as a likely 2008 presidential candidate and that respondents unwilling to support her candidacy responded that they were unwilling to vote for a woman for president.

Though Senator Clinton's bid for the White House was unsuccessful, inevitably, the United States will have to face the issue of the role of the First Gentleman. We can wonder about the dilemmas that might arise for the men who pioneer in this new role. Will the ceremonial functions of the first spouse remain the same? Will the First Gentleman choose the White House china; will he assist in the organization of state dinners and other social functions? Will he work in a private-sector job outside the White House? Will he have a voice in influencing administration policy?

We will learn the answers only when a married woman becomes president. In all likelihood, people's fascination with the role of First Gentleman will wane when the novelty of the office wears off. And similarly to the various interpretations of the role that First Ladies have created, it is likely that the role of First Gentleman will be flexible and adaptable, responding to the inclinations and the personalities of the men who occupy it, as well as to public preferences.

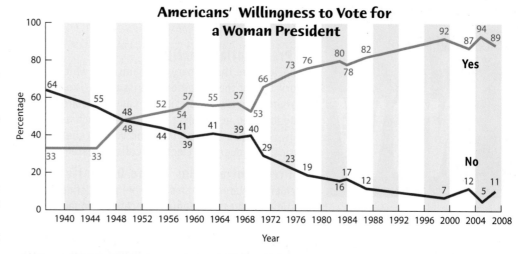

POLITICAL INQUIRY

FIGURE 12.4 ■ **What has been the trend since the late 1930s in the American electorate's willingness to vote for a woman president? What factors do you think explain this shift?**

SOURCE: The Gallup Poll, www.galluppoll.com/content/?ci=8611&pg=1, Please move the entire title "Americans' Willingness..." 1p above the top edge of the vertical blue bars. (To match all other figures of this style.)

WWW.GALLUP.COM/POLL/18937/, and www.gallup.com/poll/26875/
Analysis=Impact=Personal=characteristics=Candidate=Support. aspx.

CONCLUSION

THINKING CRITICALLY ABOUT WHAT'S NEXT IN THE PRESIDENCY

The American presidency is a dynamic institution, one that is molded by the individuals who serve as president and by the American people—by their changing interests, viewpoints, struggles, and needs. The presidency has a symbiotic relationship with the larger culture in which it exists; it is at once shaped by, and shapes, the culture.

The executive branch of the federal government is also flexible, incorporating the needs of diverse constituencies and participants, particularly in recent times. The continued evolution of the presidency as a more diverse institution is relatively assured. How will this evolution take place in the next several decades? In your view, what is the likelihood of a woman being elected president in the next twenty years?

The presidency is a product of both the design of the framers and the desires of the citizenry. As the country's need for stronger presidents has increased, the resources and authorities of presidents have grown to accommodate new powers. But at what point does the presidency become, in the minds of Americans, *too* powerful?

Since the activist administration of Franklin D. Roosevelt, the characterization of the presidency as an "imperial" institution has dogged numerous presidents, most recently former president George W. Bush. Looking ahead, how will the citizens of the future view the scope of presidential power? The answer will depend in large part on the people themselves, particularly those who vote. It will depend on whom citizens elect to the highest office in the land; on how the people's opinions shape (or, in some cases, fail to shape) presidential actions; and on how the people's relationship with their presidents develops. For although the Constitution created a system in which presidential powers can institutionally be checked, the framers did not foresee the most significant checks on modern presidents: the will of the people and a ruthlessly investigatory media, both of which ensure that presidential power is not unrestrained.[44]

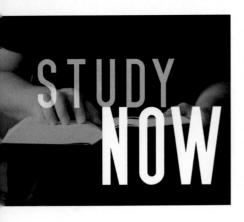

Summary

1. Presidential Elections

Campaigns are the primary mechanism by which candidates for the presidency outline their priorities and their positions on issues. It is during campaigns that the people forge their relationship with the president. Campaigns are key avenues by which individuals can become involved in the electoral process, such as through participating in nominating conventions, voting on Election Day, and voicing their opinions about the formal selection of the president through the Electoral College system.

2. Presidential Roles in the Domestic Sphere

As chief legislator, the president helps to define Congress's agenda through the annual State of the Union address and influences congressional legislation, particularly concerning the federal budget. Presidents also "legislate" when they veto legislation. As chief economist, the president uses a variety of tools, including the federal budget and the appointment of the chair of the Federal Reserve, to shape economic policy. As party leader, the president acts as the chief of his own party and helps party members get elected to federal, state, and local offices.

3. Presidential Roles in the Foreign Policy Sphere

As chief diplomat, the president and his administration shape the foreign policy of the United States. As commander in chief, the president is the leader of all branches of the armed forces.

4. Overlap in the President's Domestic and Foreign Policy Roles

The president's roles of chief executive and chief of state encompass both domestic and foreign policy spheres. The responsibility as chief executive includes the job of chief administrator of the entire executive branch of government, including the cabinet departments. As chief of state, the president is the ceremonial head of state, a function that is carried out by a separate officeholder in many other nations.

5. The President and the Executive Branch

Leading the executive branch of the federal government is among the president's top responsibilities. Key executive branch offices are the vice president, the cabinet, and the Executive Office of the President (EOP). The EOP includes the White House Office, the Office of Management and Budget, the National Security Council, and the Council of Economic Advisers. Each office assists the president in devising and implementing policy.

6. Presidential Succession

A president who dies in office is succeeded by the vice president, the Speaker of the House, the president pro tem of the Senate, and then by a specified order of cabinet officials, according to the Presidential Succession Act of 1947. When a president becomes incapacitated in office, the Twenty-Fifth Amendment to the Constitution prescribes the course of action.

7. Sources of Presidential Power

Article II, Sections 2 and 3, of the U.S. Constitution enumerate the expressed powers of the president. Inherent powers emanate from the "take care" clause of the Constitution and have been asserted by presidents as constitutionally implied. Statutory powers include powers that the Congress grants presidents, and special presidential powers include emergency powers, executive privilege, and the power to issue executive orders.

8. The People as a Source of Presidential Power

Because the people are a major source of presidential power, presidents continuously seek to secure public support. To that end, presidents exploit their easy access to the "bully pulpit" and the media. High public approval ratings can be an important source of presidential power and are of particular help in getting Congress to enact popular presidential proposals.

9. The Evolution of Presidential Power

The presidential powers of George Washington contrast strikingly with the powers of contemporary presidents. Presidential power first expanded during the administration of Thomas Jefferson, and this authority continued to grow through Andrew Jackson's tenure of office. Franklin D. Roosevelt's administration witnessed the greatest expansion in executive power to date, to the point that modern presidencies have been characterized as "imperial presidencies." The Watergate scandal in 1973 significantly damaged the notion of the imperial presidency. Since then, presidents have fought hard to secure the public trust while often facing a media skeptical of their integrity and motivations.

10. Evaluating Presidential Leadership

Scholarly assessments of presidents differ significantly from the views of the general population. Nonacademics tend to name modern presidents who are effective communicators as among the greatest, whereas scholars cite a number of earlier presidents as most effective.

11. Women in the White House

Traditionally, the most prominent role for women in the White House has been that of First Lady. Some First Ladies, among them Eleanor Roosevelt and Hillary Clinton, have been much more powerful and visible public figures than others. As the pool of potential female presidential candidates increases, there is a growing likelihood that a woman will be elected president.

Key Terms

approval ratings 387

articles of impeachment 392

balanced ticket 378

cabinet 379

chief of staff 381

emergency powers 386

executive agreement 375

Executive Office of the
   President (EOP) 379

executive order 385

expressed powers 384

executive privilege 386

honeymoon period 387

impeachment 392

inherent powers 384

line-item veto 370

National Security Council
   (NSC) 381

Office of Management and
   Budget (OMB) 381

press secretary 381

rally 'round the flag effect 388

signing statement 371

statutory powers 385

take care clause 384

Watergate 391

White House counsel 381

White House Office
   (WHO) 381

Works Progress
   Administration (WPA) 390

For Review

1. Explain the process of presidential elections. What role do states play in the process?
2. List the various roles of the president, and provide an example of each.
3. What are the sources of presidential power?
4. How has presidential power evolved over time?
5. Explain the organization and the functions of the Executive Office of the President.
6. Discuss Americans' willingness to vote for a qualified woman for president.

For Critical Thinking and Discussion

1. What do you think are the most important roles for presidents today? Why do these roles matter more than others?
2. Who do you think has been the greatest president in U.S. history? What characteristics do you admire about the president you choose?
3. What factors affect how frequently presidents veto legislation? Does vetoing legislation signify presidential strength or weakness? Explain.
4. What impact did Watergate have on people's perception of the presidency and of government? Have there been lasting effects from this scandal? Explain.
5. Would people you know vote for a woman for president? Which demographic groups do you think would be more willing? Which groups would be less willing? Why?

MULTIPLE CHOICE: Choose the lettered item that answers the question correctly.

1. A written message that the president issues upon signing a bill into law is called
   a. a veto message.
   b. a presidential resolution.
   c. a signing statement.
   d. an executive decree.

2. Appointing the Fed chair and submitting a budget to Congress are part of the president's responsibilities as
   a. party leader.
   b. chief economist.
   c. chief legislator.
   d. chief diplomat.

3. Appointing the cabinet and determining how the bureaucracy will implement the laws are part of the president's responsibilities as
   a. chief executive.
   b. chief economist.
   c. chief legislator.
   d. chief diplomat.

4. The office that develops policies and protects the president's legal and political interests is
   a. the Executive Office of the President.
   b. the Chief Executive's Office.
   c. the Office of Management and Budget.
   d. the White House Office.

5. The office that creates the president's annual budget is
   a. the Executive Office of the President.
   b. the Chief Executive's Office.
   c. the Office of Management and Budget.
   d. the White House Office.

6. Presidential powers that are implied in the Constitution are called
   a. enumerated powers.
   b. inherent powers.
   c. expressed powers.
   d. statutory powers.

7. Presidential powers granted to presidents by congressional action are called
   a. enumerated powers.
   b. inherent powers.
   c. expressed powers.
   d. statutory powers.

8. The right of the president to withhold information from Congress or the courts is called
   a. emergency powers.
   b. executive privilege.
   c. expressed powers.
   d. statutory powers.

9. A time early in a new president's administration characterized by optimistic approval by the public is called
   a. the rose-colored-glasses period.
   b. the honeymoon period.
   c. the benefit-of-the-doubt period.
   d. the goodwill period.

10. During the Nixon administration, a scandal involving burglaries and the subsequent cover-up by high-level administration officials was called
    a. Watergate.
    b. Iran-Contra.
    c. Whitewater.
    d. Newport.

FILL IN THE BLANKS.

11. The _____ is the group of experts chosen by the president to serve as advisers on running the country.

12. The executive staff member who serves as both an adviser to the president and manager of the White House Office is the _____ .

13. The _____ consists of the top foreign policy advisers and relevant cabinet officials who advise the president on matters of foreign policy and national security.

14. The constitutional basis for inherent powers is the _____ .

15. A(n) _____ is the power of the president to issue orders that carry the force of law.

RESOURCES FOR RESEARCH AND ACTION

Internet Resources

270 to Win
www.270towin.com This interactive Web site demonstrates how the Electoral College outcome is determined; users can experiment with altering the results of elections. It also contains past voting information for all states.

Center for the Study of the Presidency
www.thepresidency.org This research center analyzes presidential leadership and offers seminars and symposia for presidential researchers, including the Center Fellows program for undergraduate students.

Presidential Libraries
You can find the Web sites of the libraries of recent presidents, which typically include a wealth of information about individual presidencies and archival resources, by searching "[President's name] Presidential Library."

The White House
www.whitehouse.gov You can visit the White House Web site for information about current issues and news, the text of presidential speeches, links to cabinet departments, the EOP, and information about the First Lady and the vice president.

Internet Activism

Twitter
Follow President Obama's White House spokesman Robert Gibbs on Twitter. Follow: PressSec.

YouTube
Subscribe to the White House's YouTube channel at www.youtube .com/user/whitehouse.

Recommended Readings

Borrelli, MaryAnne. *The President's Cabinet: Gender, Power, and Representation.* Boulder, CO: Lynne Rienner, 2002. Analysis of the evolution of presidential cabinets in terms of gender representation.

Ehrenhalt, Alan. *The United States of Ambition: Politicians, Power and the Pursuit of Office.* New York: Times Books, 1991. Interesting account of the importance of personal drive and ambition in catapulting would-be presidents to the White House.

Halberstam, David. *The Best and the Brightest.* Fawcett Books, 1993. Riveting analysis of how the Kennedy and Johnson administrations entrenched the United States in the war in Vietnam.

Neustadt, Richard E. *Presidential Power and the Modern President.* New York: The Free Press, 1990. Update of the author's classic 1960 volumes, explaining the evolution of power in the modern presidency and probing, in particular, presidents' ability to persuade.

Schlesinger, Arthur M., Jr. *The Imperial Presidency.* Boston: Houghton Mifflin, 1973. Classic volume describing how the presidency has become a rarely checked, "imperial" institution.

Suskind, Ronald. *The Price of Loyalty: George W. Bush, the White House, and the Education of Paul O'Neill.* New York: Simon & Schuster, 2004. Critical account of decision making in the George W. Bush White House.

Woodward, Bob, and Carl Bernstein. *All the President's Men,* 2nd ed. New York: Simon & Schuster, 1994. Classic work that launched investigative journalism, particularly concerning the presidency, in which the authors describe their investigation of the Watergate scandal that led to President Richard Nixon's resignation.

Movies of Interest

Recount (2008)
This movie chronicles the 2000 presidential election, focusing on the controversy surrounding ballot counting in Florida that culminated in the U.S. Supreme Court case *Bush v. Gore.*

Air Force One (1997)
In this suspense thriller, the president of the United States, played by Harrison Ford, is forced to do battle with terrorist hijackers aboard Air Force One.

The American President (1995)
Rob Reiner directed this comedic drama about an unmarried male president (portrayed by Michael Douglas) and a lobbyist (Annette Bening), who fall in love.

All the President's Men (1976)
In this 1976 film adaptation of the book by the same name, Robert Redford and Dustin Hoffman star as *Washington Post* reporters Bob Woodward and Carl Bernstein (respectively), who uncover the details of the Watergate scandal that led to President Nixon's resignation.

In addition, there are numerous biographical movies of American presidents, including many that air on the A&E network's *Biography* series. You can find these programs at www.biography.com.

CHAPTER 13

The Bureaucracy

THEN

The federal bureaucracy under President George Washington had three departments and two offices serving a national population of 4 million.

NOW

Almost 3 million civilian federal bureaucrats—plus 35 to 40 million state, local, private for-profit, and non-profit bureaucrats—serve a national population of over 300 million.

NEXT

Will the bureaucracy remain a target of criticism from citizens, candidates, and elected officials?

Will the best and the brightest respond to the call to serve as a large proportion of federal employees retire in the next decade?

Will the volume of public service outsourced to private organizations continue to increase?

Citizens turn to the government

to solve their problems and provide services. Through policy-making processes, Congress and the president determine which problems the national government will address and what services it will provide. After Congress and the president approve policies, millions of public servants put them into action. The daily implementation of policy by public servants is the key to citizens' satisfaction with government.

President Barack Obama (2009–present) estimated the cost of providing national public services in his proposed 2011 budget to be $3.7 trillion.[1] This staggering sum amounts to $10.2 billion per day, $425 million per hour, or $7 million per minute. Almost 3 million national civilian bureaucrats and 1.5 million military personnel provide public services. Beyond the legions of federal public servants, almost 20 million state and local bureaucrats assist in implementing national public policies. In addition, through grants and contracts with the national government, millions of employees in private for-profit businesses and in nonprofit organizations help to do the work of the national government.

Americans expect these millions of government and nongovernment employees to provide public services and benefits efficiently and effectively. In our democracy, citizens also expect accountability. They want assurance that their tax dollars are spent properly for the public good. But such accountability is hindered by the complexities of public service delivery. Moreover, assessing performance is difficult when the services bureaucrats provide include ensuring justice and domestic tranquility, defending the nation, and promoting the general welfare.

Bureaucrats and Bureaucracy

Most people think of government agencies when they hear the word *bureaucracy,* and they think of government employees when they hear the word *bureaucrat*—and their thoughts are often negative. They typically focus on a large government organization with inefficient, dehumanizing procedures that require tedious paperwork. They visualize long lines at the Department of Motor Vehicles as uncaring workers (who they believe cannot be fired) slowly process mounds of forms.

Taxpayers are not the only people who think and speak negatively of the bureaucracy. Even our presidents—who rely on bureaucrats and bureaucracies to implement their policy promises—historically have not hesitated to criticize bureaucrats. In an April 2009 radio and Internet address, President Barack Obama stated that with the leaders he had placed in the bureaucracy, in the positions of chief performance officer, chief information officer, and chief technology officer, "I am confident that we can break our bad habits, put an end to the mismanagement that has plagued our government and start living within our means."

Are the negative images and the criticisms of bureaucrats and bureaucracies fair? Before we can answer, we must understand who the bureaucrats are, what they are hired to do, and how they are expected to accomplish their work.

Who Are the Bureaucrats?

Who was the last government employee with whom you had a face-to-face interaction? Who was the last government worker to make a decision that directly affected you? Chances are it was not an elected official such as the president or a member of the Senate. It was probably not an appointed federal judge. Rather, the government employees that you (and the people around you) interact with and are affected by on a daily basis are those individuals who are hired into executive branch agencies to implement public policy—that is, **bureaucrats.** Bureaucrats include government employees such as the administrator who reviews college students' Pell Grant applications, the Food and Drug Administration (FDA) inspector who monitors food and drug quality, and the Equal Employment Opportunity Commission (EEOC) lawyer who argues that an employer allowed sexual harassment of its workers. Bureaucrats provide the public services that elected officials authorize, and in doing so they make decisions that affect people daily.

Because elected officials and ordinary citizens perpetually criticize bureaucrats and bureaucracies, individuals working in the national bureaucracy do not take being called a bureaucrat as a compliment. Bureaucrats prefer the term *public servant,* because that phrase captures how they see themselves and their essential job goal.[2] Even as people love to bash bureaucrats, data from the International Social Survey Programme (ISSP) indicate that 63.9 percent of U.S. respondents agreed that "public service" in the United States is "somewhat committed" to serving the people, and an additional 11.6 percent agreed that public service is "very committed" to serving the people.[3] See "Global Context" on page 404 for a cross-national look at citizens' perceptions of the public service commitment of the bureaucracy in their country.

Charles Goodsell, a respected scholar of public administration and public policy, notes that studies show government employees to be very hard workers who are motivated by the recognition of the importance of public service. This public service motivation is distinct from the motivation of private-sector employees, for whom salary levels and shorter work hours provide key incentives.[4] Compared with private-sector employees, public servants have higher levels of formal education, must comply with more stringent codes of behavior, and express a greater concern for serving the public.[5] In addition, government bureaucrats tend to report somewhat higher levels of job satisfaction than do their private sector counterparts.[6]

Very few children say that they want to be bureaucrats. Yet millions do aspire to careers as public servants, including teachers, police officers, lawyers, and health care professionals. National, state, and local governments hire professionals such as these to implement public policy—to do the business of government. Chances are, whatever your major in college, you can get a job as a public servant. In fact, approximately 40 percent of federal civilian public servants and almost 50 percent of both state and local public servants have at least a bachelor's degree. In comparison, only about 25 percent of private-sector workers have at least a bachelor's degree.[7] Figure 13.1 presents a comparison of the distribution of employment by major occupational groups for the federal government and for all industries in the United States.

Joining the 23 million national, state, and local bureaucrats are the so-called **shadow bureaucrats**—employees on the payroll of private for-profit businesses and private nonprofit organizations with government

bureaucrats
people employed in a government executive branch unit to implement public policy; public administrators; public servants

shadow bureaucrats
people hired and paid by private for-profit and nonprofit organizations that implement public policy through a government contract

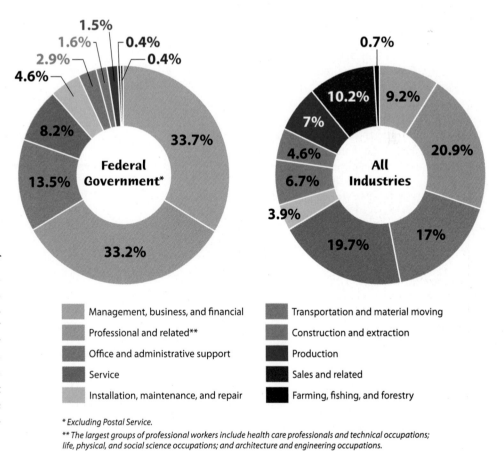

FIGURE 13.1

Percent Distribution of Employment in Federal Government and All Industries by Major Occupational Group in 2008

SOURCE: U.S. Bureau of Labor Statistics, "Career Guide to Industries, 2010–11 Edition," http://data.bls.gov/cgi-bin/print.pl/oco/cg/cgs041.htm.

PUBLIC SERVICE COMMITMENT TO SERVING THE PEOPLE

Criticism of bureaucrats in the private and public sectors is widespread. Yet research by political scientists David J. Houston and Lauren K. Harding reveals that the majority of citizens in European countries, Canada, and the United States think that the public service in their own country is at least somewhat committed to, if not very committed to, serving the people.*

The research results reveal certain patterns. In most countries—the United States being an exception—there is a significant positive correlation between a person's being employed as a public servant himself or herself and thinking that public service is committed to serving the public. In addition, younger and older citizens are generally more likely than middle-aged citizens to perceive that their national bureaucracies have a distinct public service motivation. But most important to thinking that one's national bureaucracy is committed to public service is a person's overall attitudes about government. Citizens with a relatively greater sense that they have the ability to influence government report higher trust in public service, as measured by their belief that the bureaucracy is committed to public service. Moreover, those who think that democracy is working well in their nation are more likely to report that their public servants are committed to serving the public.

So, although bureaucrat-bashing is common, research indicates that at least in the majority of European nations, Canada, and the United States, the majority of people believe that public servants have a public service motivation—in other words, that bureaucrats are committed to serving the public.

COUNTRY	PERCENTAGE OF CITIZENS WHO THINK THE PUBLIC SERVICE IN THEIR COUNTRY IS SOMEWHAT OR VERY COMMITTED TO SERVING THE PEOPLE
Austria	80.3%
Ireland	77.1%
United States	**75.4%**
Switzerland	71.8%
Canada	69.9%
Great Britain	68.9%
Norway	67.9%
Belgium	66.5%
Germany-West	63.9%
Denmark	60.3%
Germany-East	59.5%
Netherlands	56.7%
France	56.1%
Finland	55.6%
Sweden	55.0%
Spain	50.3%
Portugal	39.3%

*David J. Houston and Lauren K. Harding, "Trust in the Public Service: A Cross-National Examination," presented at the 66th Annual National Conference of the Midwest Political Science Association, Chicago, April 3–6, 2008, p. 24.

---

contracting-out
also called *outsourcing* or *privatizing;* a process by which the government contracts with a private for-profit or nonprofit organization to provide public services, such as disaster relief, or resources needed by the government, such as fighter planes

contracts. Through a process of **contracting-out** (also called *outsourcing* or *privatizing*), the government signs work contracts with these organizations to assist in the implementation of national policy. In other words, shadow bureaucrats do the work of government, but they do not receive a government paycheck.

In summary, today, a mix of national, state, and local bureaucrats, as well as shadow bureaucrats, deliver national public services. In addition to having in common the delivery of public services, public and shadow bureaucrats share a similar work environment. That is, they work in bureaucratic organizations.

Bureaucracy: An Organizational Structure

Max Weber (1864–1920), the "father of sociology," coined the word *bureaucracy* to describe large organizations, such as government, with the following features: a division of labor, specialization of job tasks, hiring systems based on worker competency, hierarchy with a vertical chain of command, and standard operating procedures. Weber argued that those features enhance the performance and accountability of large organizations. In our discussion, **bureaucracy** is any organization with a hierarchical structure, although the term is most commonly used to designate a government agency or the collection of all national executive branch organizations.

Organizations with those bureaucratic features are not unique to government. For example, colleges and universities are also bureaucratic organizations. They have a division of labor with specialization of tasks. (Consider the various academic departments, each specializing in a different discipline.) They hire employees (such as professors, computer technicians, and student affairs staff) with the knowledge, skills, and abilities essential to doing their jobs well. Colleges and universities also have a hierarchy with a chain of command (faculty members report to chairpersons, who report to a dean, who reports to the vice president for academic affairs, who reports to the president, who makes final decisions). University employees implement standardized procedures to register students for classes, determine financial aid eligibility, and punish violations of the conduct code.

So, although most people think of government when they hear the word *bureaucracy,* a bureaucracy is *any* organization with Weber's bureaucratic structure. Yet in this chapter, as is appropriate to our study of American government, we focus on the departments and agencies that compose the national government bureaucracy. And even though most people think of government employees when they hear the term *bureaucrat,* nongovernment employees, as we have seen, may also be paid with taxpayer money to serve the public, and so it is appropriate that we consider them, too.

bureaucracy
any organization with a hierarchical structure; most commonly used to designate a government agency or the collection of all national executive branch organizations

Federal Bureaucrats

Political scientists distinguish among national bureaucrats according to several factors, including the process by which they are hired, the procedures by which they can be fired, and the grounds for which they can be fired. On the basis of these factors, we can differentiate among three categories of national civilian bureaucrats: political appointees, civil servants, and senior executive service employees.

Political Appointees

In 1863, President Abraham Lincoln, suffering from smallpox, told his secretary to "send all the office seekers in here. I finally have something I can give to them all." Indeed, before the creation of the civil service system in 1883, presidents had the authority to hire bureaucrats, selecting whomever they wanted and establishing whatever qualifications they desired, in a noncompetitive hiring system known as *patronage.* Under the patronage system, hordes of men seeking government jobs presented themselves to the president after each election.

Every four years, after the presidential election, the federal government publishes the **plum book,** which lists thousands of top jobs in the bureaucracy to which the president will appoint people through the patronage system. As we've seen, there is no standard process for assessing the knowledge, skills, and abilities needed for appointive positions, nor is there open competition for these patronage jobs. Further, because citizens expect presidents to be responsive and accountable to them, and presidents rely on their political appointees to support their efforts to meet those expectations, presidents tend to appoint people who support their policy preferences to these top positions.

Patronage positions come with a downside for the appointees: no job security. The president not only hires but also can fire political appointees at his pleasure. More common than firing is the resignation or retirement of appointees who no longer enjoy presidential approval.

plum book
a publication that lists the top jobs in the bureaucracy to which the president will appoint people through the patronage system

Civil Servants

During the first century of U.S. history, all national bureaucrats got their jobs through patronage. Then in 1883, mobilized by the assassination of President James Garfield (whose brief administration lasted from March to September 1881) by an unsuccessful seeker of a

> This engraving depicts President James Garfield's assassination. Shot in July 1881, Garfield died two and a half months later of a fatal heart attack brought on by his doctors' attempts to find the assassin's bullet in his body.

What was President Garfield's assassin's motivation? How did the tragedy change the process of choosing civil servants?

patronage position, Congress and President Chester Arthur (1881–1885) approved the Pendleton Civil Service Act. This law introduced a merit-based civil service system to the national government. The hiring principles of the **merit-based civil service** system are open competition, competence, and political neutrality. **Civil servants** are bureaucrats hired through the merit-based personnel system. The 1978 Civil Service Reform Act reinforced these merit principles and legislated the right to unionize for many federal civil servants.

OPEN COMPETITION AND COMPETENCE

Today, merit-based civil service jobs, which compose at least 85 percent of the national bureaucracy, are open and accessible to all who wish to compete for a position. The competition requires that candidates prove their competence to do the job (their merit). Jobs covered by the merit-based civil service system are analyzed and ranked on the basis of the knowledge, skills, and abilities needed to do the job competently. A job's rank determines its salary. The pay scales offer equal pay for jobs of equal worth, as determined by the job analysis. (See Table 13.1 for the pay scales and education requirements for white-collar government jobs.)

Several national laws have helped to make today's civil servants, as a group, look more like the U.S. pop-

TABLE 13.1

Education Requirements and Salary Ranges for White-Collar Federal Civil Service Positions* (2009)

Level	Salary Range	Qualifying Education
GS-1	$17,540–21,944	No high school diploma required
GS-2	$19,721–24,815	High school graduation or equivalent
GS-3	$21,517–27,970	One academic year above high school
GS-4	$24, 156–31,401	Two academic years above high school, or associate's degree
GS-5	$27,026–35,135	Four academic years above high school leading to a bachelor's degree, or a bachelor's degree
GS-7	$33,477–43,521	Bachelor's degree with superior academic achievement or one academic year of graduate education or law school
GS-9	$40,949–53,234	Master's (or equivalent graduate degree) or two academic years of progressively higher level graduate education
GS-11	$49,544–64,403	PhD or equivalent degree or three academic years of progressively higher level graduate education
GS-12	$59,383–77,194	Completion of all requirements for a doctoral or equivalent degree (for research positions only)
GS-13	$70,615–91,801	Appropriate specialized experience.
GS-14	$83,445–108,483	Appropriate specialized experience.
GS-15	$98,156–127,604	Appropriate specialized experience.

* Table shows the amount and level of education typically required for each grade for which education alone can be qualifying.

SOURCES: www.opm.gov/flsa/oca/09tables/html/gs.asp (salary data); www.govcentral.com/benefits/articles/1757-what-determines-where-you-stand-on-the-gs-scale (education level data).

ulation at large than they did in the past. Title VII of the 1964 Civil Rights Act, as amended, prohibits employers, including the government, from making personnel decisions based on factors irrelevant to job competence, such as sex, race, color, ethnicity, age, and disabilities that can be reasonably accommodated. The merit principles of the 1978 Civil Service Reform Act (CSRA) reiterate this prohibition against discrimination in personnel practices. The bans against discrimination in Title VII and the CSRA do not apply to the positions of elected officials or political appointees.

Title VI of the 1964 Civil Rights Act prohibits discrimination based on race, color, religion, and ethnicity in educational opportunities offered by institutions receiving federal funding. Title IX, which was added to the act in 1972, extended this prohibition to sex-based discrimination. Enforcement of these laws has increased the diversity of people who are able to gain the education and experience needed to do government jobs competently. The interaction of Titles VI, VII, and IX has fostered greater *descriptive representation* among civil servants than among any other category of government worker. This means that the people serving resemble the larger population whom they serve in demographic characteristics such as race, age, ethnicity, sex, religion, and economic status. "Analyzing the Sources" on page 408 considers the influence these laws have had on the national civil service.

POLITICAL NEUTRALITY Merit-based civil servants cannot be fired merely because someone with different political beliefs is elected or appointed to supervise them. They can be fired for poor quality of work (misfeasance), or for nonperformance of their work (nonfeasance), or for violating the rules or regulations that guide their work (malfeasance). The system thus gives civil servants job protection and does not require them (unlike political appointees) to adhere to the president's policy preferences. Hence the civil service system supports political neutrality to ensure efficient and effective public service delivery.

In 1939, Congress approved the Hatch Act, limiting civil servants' rights to engage in political activity. The rationale behind this law's passage was that if civil servants stayed out of politics, they would be less inclined to allow party loyalty to influence their job performance. Over time, however, civil servants have contested the constitutionality of the legal limits on their political engagement. As a result, the Hatch Act has been modified in the last few decades to loosen the restrictions on civil servants' political activities. This easing of limits on political engagement has allowed civil servants to exercise their First Amendment rights of expression, including political expression, more freely and fully.

CIVIL SERVICE REFORM ACT (1978) "There is widespread criticism of federal government performance. The public suspects that there are too many government workers,

Characteristics of Federal Bureaucrats

THEN (1970)*	NOW (2011)**
30% female	44% female
Average age: 41	Average age: 47
Average length of service: 13 years	Average length of service: 16 years
20% minorities (included "Negroes, American Indians, Orientals, and persons with Spanish surnames")	32% minorities (includes "black, Hispanic, Asian/Pacific Islander, and American Indian/Alaska Native")
80% in white-collar positions	89% in white-collar positions
91% in competitive, civil service positions	72% in competitive, civil service positions

WHAT'S NEXT?

> Will the percentage of female and minority bureaucrats continue to increase? Why or why not?

> Will the percentage of white-collar positions continue to increase with continuing changes in technology? Explain.

> How might the health of the economy affect the retirement decisions of the many bureaucrats who become eligible for retirement in the next few years, and hence affect the average age of bureaucrats as well as the average length of service?

> How will demands for new or expanded government services affect the proportion of white-collar positions in the federal bureaucracy? Explain your answer.

* U.S. Department of Commerce, Bureau of the Census, *Statistical Abstract* 1972.
** Office of Personnel Management, *Federal Civilian Workforce Statistics, The Fact Book* 2007 Edition.

merit-based civil service
a personnel system in which bureaucrats are hired on the basis of the principles of competence, equal opportunity (open competition), and political neutrality; once hired, these civil servants have job protection

civil servants
bureaucrats hired through a merit-based personnel system who have job protection

ANALYZING THE SOURCES

EQUAL EDUCATIONAL AND EMPLOYMENT OPPORTUNITY AND STRATIFIED OCCUPATIONAL SEGREGATION

Laws prohibit race-based and sex-based discrimination in educational and employment opportunities. In addition, affirmative action requires most governments (as employers) and private businesses with government contracts to adopt and implement personnel plans detailing how they will actively recruit qualified women and minorities for open positions.

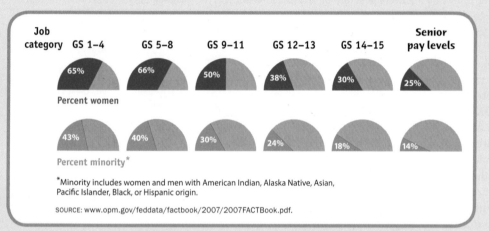

| Job category | GS 1–4 | GS 5–8 | GS 9–11 | GS 12–13 | GS 14–15 | Senior pay levels |

Percent women: 65%, 66%, 50%, 38%, 30%, 25%

Percent minority*: 43%, 40%, 30%, 24%, 18%, 14%

*Minority includes women and men with American Indian, Alaska Native, Asian, Pacific Islander, Black, or Hispanic origin.

SOURCE: www.opm.gov/feddata/factbook/2007/2007FACTBook.pdf.

COLLEGE DEGREES CONFERRED BY SEX AND RACE/ETHNICITY

DEMOGRAPHIC	BACHELOR'S	MASTER'S	DOCTOR'S*
Men	42.5%	41.2%	52.9%
Women	57.5%	58.2%	47.1%
White	70.0%	60.3%	56.2%
Black	8.7%	7.8%	5.1%
Hispanic	6.3%	4.4%	3.2%
Asian/Pacific Islander	6.2%	4.8%	4.9%
Native American	0.7%	0.5%	0.4%

* Doctor's degrees are the highest degree a student can earn for graduate study and include EdD, JD, PhD.
SOURCE: U.S. Department of Education, National Center for Education Statistics, http://nces.ed.gov/fastfacts/display.asp?id=72.

Evaluating the Evidence

① Review the accompanying chart and table. Do equal educational and equal employment laws work? Explain.

② Are there additional data you would want to review before answering question 1? If so, what kind of information would that supplementary data provide? Why?

③ Sex-based and race-based occupational segregation occurs when women and minority men dominate low-paying, low-status jobs and white men dominate high-paying, high-status jobs. Based on the data presented here, does occupational segregation exist in the national civil service? Explain.

that they are underworked, overpaid, and insulated from the consequences of incompetence."[8] With those words, President Jimmy Carter (1977–1981) announced proposed civil service reforms in 1978. The resulting Civil Service Reform Act of 1978 (CSRA) reaffirmed and expanded the merit principles established by the Pendleton Act and reorganized the management of the national civil service. Carter's reforms also eliminated the Civil Service Commission (CSC), the central personnel office created by the Pendleton Act.

Three new independent administrative agencies—the Office of Personnel Management (OPM), the Merit System Protection Board (MSPB), and the Federal Labor Relations Authority (FLRA)—replaced the old Civil Service Commission. Today, the OPM is the central personnel office, responsible for developing and implementing merit-based civil service personnel policies and procedures. The MSPB ensures proper implementation of the merit system. The CSRA also legislated for the collective bargaining rights (unionization rights) of national civil servants and created the FLRA to monitor the relations between unionized bureaucrats and the federal government.

UNIONIZED CIVIL SERVANTS   Twenty-eight percent of U.S. federal civil servants belong to labor unions.[9] The American Federation of Government Employees (AFGE) is the largest such union, representing 600,000 national bureaucrats. The level of union membership varies dramatically from agency to agency. Whereas about 90 percent of U.S. Postal Service employees are union members (not AFGE members but members of one of several unions for postal employees), the level of union membership among bureaucrats in the State Department is close to zero. Part of the explanation for the range of unionization levels across national agencies is the percentage of each agency's workers that is composed of blue-collar workers. In general, blue-collar workers are likelier to be union members than are white-collar workers.

Unionized civil servants have leverage to negotiate certain conditions of work. For example, they may bargain for improved training opportunities and enhanced due process protections in disciplinary matters. National civil service employee unions cannot negotiate salaries or work hours, however. And unlike private-sector unions, national civil servant unions do not have the legal right to strike. The prohibition of strikes by national civil servants is typically justified by the fact that these workers provide essential services that are vital to public safety. A strike by these workers would therefore threaten public safety and health.

THE SENIOR EXECUTIVE SERVICE   One additional CSRA-mandated change to the national bureaucracy was the creation of a new category of civil servant, the **senior executive service (SES)** bureaucrat. SES positions are hybrids of political appointee and civil service positions. The SES includes most of the top managerial, supervisory, and policy positions that are not patronage positions.

senior executive service (SES)
a unique personnel system for top managerial, supervisory, and policy positions offering less job security but higher pay than the merit-based civil service system

> First Lady Michele Obama greets employees at the Department of Housing and Urban Development as she arrives to make remarks. Mrs. Obama visited with public servants from numerous departments and agencies during the first few months of President Barack Obama's administration to thank them for their service to the nation.

At least 90 percent of SES bureaucrats are career civil servants (hired through an open competition based on competence) who have given up some job security for positions with higher pay. These employees can be moved from job to job and from agency to agency (less job security), but they are immune from firing except for proven misfeasance, nonfeasance, or malfeasance. The remaining SES bureaucrats are typically hired from outside the merit-based civil service system. Appointed with approval of the OPM and the White House Office of Presidential Personnel, these SES noncareer bureaucrats do not face open competition and do not have the job protection of merit-based civil servants.[10]

Supplementing the work of national political appointees, civil servants, and SES bureaucrats are armies of state, local, and shadow bureaucrats. The volume of national public policy executed by these non-national bureaucrats has been increasing dramatically since the 1960s because of devolution and a rise in contracting-out.

State, Local, and Shadow Bureaucrats

Today, the overwhelming majority of the almost 20 million state and local bureaucrats, and possibly as many as 15 million shadow bureaucrats, provide various national public services. Through devolution and contracting-out, the national government relies on these non-national bureaucrats to serve the people's daily needs. National bureaucrats monitor these state, local, and shadow bureaucrats' compliance with the rules and regulations that come with devolution and outsourcing.

As you may recall from Chapter 3, devolution is the federal government's shifting of greater responsibility for financing and administering public policies to state and local governments, putting the implementation of national policy in the hands of state and local bureaucrats. Mandates in federal laws require state and local governments to implement national policies. In cases where national law preempts (takes precedence over) state and local law, state and local bureaucrats have to implement federal policy instead of state or local programs. Preemption is common, for example, in the area of environmental protection, where state and local officials must ensure private- and public-sector compliance with federal air, water, and landfill standards.

As we've seen, the national government also contracts with shadow bureaucracies—private for-profit and nonprofit organizations—to provide vital services as well as to produce certain resources needed to serve the public. Outsourcing, for example, includes the federal government's contracting-out with Lockheed Martin and Boeing for the production of defense resources such as helmets, fighter planes, and laser-guided missiles. Traditionally, too, the government undertakes large capital projects such as the construction of roads and government buildings through contracts with private businesses. Further, the federal government outsources medical as well as social research to cure disease and address the ills of society. And through government contracts, the Red Cross has dispensed disaster relief for decades. The federal government's contracts totaled more than $523 billion in its 2009 budget.[11]

The national government expects that contracting-out will reduce the expense of government by eliminating the overhead costs (including employee benefits and basic operating costs) of producing public goods and services. Outsourcing also provides a means by which the government can hire experts and specialists when they are needed and keep them off the payroll at other times. The government can eliminate these contracted personnel and their costs more easily than it can fire civil servants, who have job protection. The expectation is that the private- and nonprofit-sector employees and organizations will be more efficient and effective than government bureaucracies.

Some government contracts and grants-in-aid flow to faith-based organizations (FBOs). This development has sparked concerns about the preservation of the constitutionally mandated separation of church and government. (See "Thinking Critically About Democracy.")

Even with the increased use of state, local, and shadow bureaucrats, the national bureaucracy itself is neither small nor streamlined. It is composed of thousands of bodies with a

SHOULD FAITH-BASED ORGANIZATIONS RECEIVE PUBLIC FUNDING TO DELIVER SOCIAL SERVICES?

The Issue: The federal government provides more than $3 billion of grants-in-aid to thousands of faith-based organizations (FBOs) each year to provide social services. For example, the Young Men's Christian Association (YMCA) and the Salvation Army both receive federal funds to support their housing, counseling, and after-school programs. The amount of public funding going to FBOs has been on the rise since the 1990s. However, the courts have interpreted the First Amendment of the Constitution, which establishes religious freedom, to mean that there must be a separation between religious organizations and government support, including financial support. So the question is, should faith-based organizations be receiving public funds?

Yes: Faith-based hospitals, nursing homes, and children's institutions, as well as the YMCA and the Salvation Army, have received government funds for decades. These FBOs provide vital services to those in need and in some cases do a superior job at distributing these services. People in need of assistance for housing, food, and clothing—and individuals seeking treatment for an addiction—feel more comfortable turning to a familiar local religious organization than to a complex government bureaucracy. In addition, because volunteers compose a large percentage of the FBO labor force, providing social services through FBOs is cheaper than paying government workers.

No: First, it is unconstitutional for the government to support a religion. Providing funding to any FBO flagrantly does exactly this.

Further, we cannot ensure that the FBO employee who has a strong faith will not include religious education or preaching in delivering services. Nor can we prevent such an individual from using a religious test to determine whom he or she will serve. Government bureaucrats who monitor the grant rules will have difficulty ensuring that public money is not supporting religious activities.

Other approaches: The law prohibits FBOs from spending public funds on religious activities. Therefore, FBOs should be required to keep separate accounts for the public funds they receive. Such separate accounts would make it easier to ensure that FBOs are not spending public funds on religious activities.

What do you think?

① Reflecting back on the discussion in Chapter 4 of the First Amendment's religious freedom guarantee, do you think the public funding of social services delivered by faith-based organizations violates the Constitution? Explain.

② Just as opponents of public funding of FBOs claim that FBO employees may push their religious beliefs on clients or use a religious test to deny services to some clients, do you think that some government employees may also behave this way? How might the government prevent such behavior among its bureaucrats as well as publicly funded FBO employees?

---

variety of names and organizational structures. The national bureaucracy, an evolving organism, continues to grow in complexity even as it privatizes and devolves more of its work.

The Evolution and Organization of the Federal Bureaucracy

Four million people resided in the United States in 1789, the year George Washington was sworn in as the first president. Most of them lived off the land and were self-sufficient; they expected few services from the national government. The federal bureaucracy consisted of the Department of War, Department of Foreign Affairs, Treasury Department, Attorney General's Office, and Postal Services Office. Those three departments and two offices handled the core functions demanded of the national government at that time: respectively, providing defense; managing foreign affairs; collecting revenues and paying bills; resolving lawsuits and legal questions; and delivering mail. Initially, other than for military personnel, the work of public servants was mostly clerical in nature.

Today, as the U.S. population tops 300 million, more than 2,000 executive branch units, employing 4 million bureaucrats (2.7 million civilian bureaucrats and about 1.5 million military personnel), implement volumes of national policies. The number of bureaucrats is equal to the nation's population in 1789. Figure 13.2, the organizational chart of the federal government, provides a window on the breadth of the federal bureaucracy today. Figures 13.3 and 13.4 show the growth in size and cost of the national bureaucracy since the 1940s.

Political scientists distinguish among five categories of executive branch organizations based on their structure and the type of work they perform: (1) departments, (2) indepen-

FIGURE 13.2

U.S. Government Organizational Chart

SOURCE: www.gpoaccess.gov/gmanual/browse-gm-08.html.

The Government of the United States

The Constitution

Legislative Branch

The Congress
Senate   House

Architect of the Capitol
United States Botanic Garden
Government Accountability Office
Government Printing Office
Library of Congress
Congressional Budget Office

Executive Branch

The President
The Vice President
Executive Office of the President

White House Office
Office of the Vice President
Council of Economic Advisors
Council on Environmental Quality
National Security Council

Office of Administration
Office of Management and Budget
Office of National Drug Control Policy
Office of Policy Development
Office of Science and Technology Policy
Office of the United States Trade Representative

Judicial Branch

The Supreme Court of the United States

United States Courts of Appeals
United States District Courts
Territorial Courts
United States Court of International Trade
United States Court of Federal Claims
United States Court of Appeals for the Armed Forces
United States Tax Court
United States Court of Appeals for Veterans Claims
Administrative Office of the United States Courts
Federal Judicial Center
United States Sentencing Commission

Department of Agriculture

Department of Commerce

Department of Defense

Department of Education

Department of Energy

Department of Health and Human Services

Department of Homeland Security

Department of Housing and Urban Development

Department of the Interior

Department of Justice

Department of Labor

Department of State

Department of Transportation

Department of the Treasury

Department of Veterans Affairs

Independent Establishments and Government Corporations

African Development Foundation
Broadcasting Board of Governors
Central Intelligence Agency
Commodities Futures Trading Commission
Consumer Product Safety Commission
Corporation for National and Community Service
Defense Nuclear Facilities Safety Board
Environmental Protection Agency
Equal Employment Opportunity Commission
Export-Import Bank of the United States
Farm Credit Administration
Federal Communications Commission
Federal Deposit Insurance Corporation
Federal Election Commission

Federal Housing Finance Board
Federal Labor Relations Authority
Federal Maritime Commission
Federal Mediation and Conciliation Service
Federal Mine Safety and Health Review Commission
Federal Reserve System
Federal Retirement Thrift Investment Board
Federal Trade Commission
General Services Administration
Inter-American Foundation
Merit Systems Protection Board
National Aeronautics and Space Administration
National Archives and Records Administration
National Capital Planning Commission

National Credit Union Administration
National Foundation of the Arts and the Humanities
National Labor Relations Board
National Mediation Board
National Railroad Passenger Corporation (Amtrak)
National Science Foundation
National Transportation Safety Board
Nuclear Regulatory Commission
Occupational Safety and Health Review Commission
Office of the Director of National Intelligence
Office of Government Ethics
Office of Personnel Management
Office of Special Counsel
Overseas Private Investment Corporation

Peace Corps
Pension Benefit Guaranty Corporation
Postal Regulatory Commission
National Railroad Retirement Board
Securities and Exchange Commission
Selective Service System
Small Business Administration
Social Security Administration
Tennessee Valley Authority
Trade and Development Agency
United States Agency for International Development
United States Commission on Civil Rights
United States International Trade Commission
United States Postal Service

Growth in National Civilian Bureaucrats and State and Local Bureaucrats

	Federal bureaucrats (thousands)	State and local bureaucrats (thousands)
1940	1,033 / 1,928	
1945	3,496	3,140
1950	2,052	4,258
1955	2,376	5,054
1960	2,496	6,387
1965	2,496	7,696
1970	2,944	9,822
1975	2,848	11,937
1980	2,821	13,375
1985	3,008	13,519
1990	3,067	15,219
1995	2,858	16,484
2000	2,639	17,925
2005	2,636	19,078
2007	2,636	19,538

POLITICAL INQUIRY

FIGURE 13.3 ■ What has been the trend in the growth of the national civilian bureaucracy since 1965? What has been the pattern for the growth of state and local bureaucracies over the same period? What explains the patterns?

SOURCE: Table 17.5 in *Fiscal Year 2009 Historical Tables*, www.whitehouse.gov/omb/budget/fy2009/pdf/hist.pdf; Statistical Abstracts of the United States, 1941, 1946 1961, 1981.

Growth in Federal Expenditures, 1940–2011

Year	Budget in billions of current dollars (rounded to nearest billion)
1940	$10
1945	$93
1950	$43
1955	$68
1960	$92
1965	$118
1970	$196
1975	$332
1980	$591
1985	$946
1990	$1,253
1995	$1,516
2000	$1,789
2005	$2,472
2011	$3,755 (estimate)

POLITICAL INQUIRY

FIGURE 13.4 ■ What has been the overall trend in the growth of federal government spending since 1940? What would you say about the pattern since 2000? What political factors—domestic and international—explain the trend in federal spending over the past decade?

SOURCE: http://www.whitehouse.gov/sites/default/files/omb/budget/fy2011/assets/tables.pdf.

dent administrative agencies, (3) independent regulatory commissions, (4) government corporations, and (5) agencies in the Executive Office of the President.

Within each category there is much variation in size, structure, and function. When Congress and the president authorize a new policy, they must decide whether they will assign its implementation to an existing agency or create a new agency. If they choose the latter option, they must determine which type of agency to create.

Departments

The Department of Homeland Security, established in 2002, is the newest of fifteen federal **departments,** each responsible for one broadly defined policy area. The president holds the fifteen departments accountable through the appointment of a head official. *Secretary* is the title of this top political appointee in all departments except the Department of Justice, where the head is the attorney general. Although the Senate must confirm them, these top appointees serve at the president's pleasure. In addition to appointing the department secretaries, the president names bureaucrats to positions in several levels of the hierarchy below the secretaries. These political appointees have titles such as *deputy secretary, assistant deputy secretary, agency director,* and *deputy director.* Table 13.2 lists the fifteen departments and gives the number of employees and budget outlay for each in 2008.

department
one of fifteen executive branch units responsible for a broadly defined policy area and whose top administrator (secretary) is appointed by the president, is confirmed by the Senate, and serves at the discretion of the president

Evolution of Federal Government Departments

TABLE 13.2

Department and Year Created	Civilian Employees (July 2008)	Budget Outlay in Billions of Dollars (2008)
State, 1789	35,724	$17.5
Treasury, 1789	112,366	$548.8
Interior, 1849	68,414	$9.9
Justice, 1870 (attorney general's office 1789; department status 1870)	107,790	$26.6
Agriculture, 1889	97,584	$90.8
Commerce, 1913 (separated from Department of Commerce and Labor, which had been created in 1903)	41,217	$7.7
Labor, 1913 (separated from Department of Commerce and Labor, which had been created in 1903)	16,267	$58.8
Defense, 1947 (previously, Department of War, created 1789; Army Department and Navy Department, created 1798)	680,025	$640.5
Housing and Urban Development, 1965	9,559	$49.1
Transportation, 1966	54,547	$70.0
Energy, 1977	14,782	$21.4
Health and Human Services, 1979 (created from Department of Health, Education and Welfare, established in 1953)	62,097	$700.5
Education, 1979 (created from Department of Health, Education and Welfare, established in 1953)	4,281	$66.0
Veterans Affairs, 1988	263,620	$84.8
Homeland Security, 2003	164,592	$40.7

SOURCES: Civil employee statistics from www.opm.gov/feddata/html/2008/july/table3.asp; budget information from www.whitehouse.gov/omb/budget/Historicals/, Table 3.1.

independent administrative agency
an executive branch unit created by Congress and the president that is responsible for a narrowly defined function and whose structure is intended to protect it from partisan politics

Independent Administrative Agencies

Whereas each executive branch department has authority for a broadly defined policy area, a host of **independent administrative agencies** are each responsible for a more narrowly defined function of the national government. Congress and the president create these agencies to fulfill one of several purposes. Some of them, such as the Smithsonian Institution, were established to handle new governmental functions that did not easily fall within the purview of existing departments. Other independent administrative agencies support the work of existing departments and agencies, including recruiting and training employees (Office of Personnel Management) and managing government properties and records (General Services Administration). Still others, such as the National Science Foundation and the National Aeronautics and Space Administration, focus on research and preservation of national resources.

Structurally independent administrative agencies look like cabinet departments, with a single head appointed by the president. However, these agencies are "independent" because Congresses and presidents place them outside of the cabinet departments. In addition, these agencies have a varying level of independence from the president. Some independent administrative agency heads serve fixed terms, making their agencies independent from the president. In other agencies, the heads serve at the pleasure of the president, but the president must have a cause (misconduct or malfeasance) to remove them. In yet other agencies, the president can remove the head without specifying a cause. Although the structures of independent administrative agencies are expected to make them "independent" of patrician politics, ultimately such agencies still need to earn the support of those who authorize the spending of money and who have authority to restructure the agency or its mission—Congress or the president.

Independent Regulatory Commissions

Over time, Congress and presidents have recognized the need for expertise in regulating the country's diverse economic activities and their impact on the overall economy, workers, consumers, and the environment. Acknowledging their own lack of such expertise, they have created numerous **independent regulatory commissions,** bureaucracies outside of the cabinet departments with the authority to develop standards of behavior for specific industries and businesses, to monitor compliance with these standards, and to impose sanctions on those it finds guilty of violating the standards.

Initially, such government regulation centered on *economic regulation*—matters such as setting the prices of goods and services and ensuring competition in the marketplace. The first independent regulatory commission, the Interstate Commerce Commission (ICC, 1887), was set up to oversee the prices and services of the railroad industry. Beginning in the 1960s, Congress turned more in the direction of *social regulation,* establishing regulatory commissions that focused on how business practices affected the environment, and the health and safety of consumers and workers. For example, legislation created the Consumer Product Safety Commission (CPSC) in 1972.

Independent regulatory agencies are under the direction of bipartisan boards whose members do not need to be loyal to the president's preferences. Typically, the president nominates and the Senate confirms an odd number of board members. Board members serve staggered fixed terms. This structure allows the agency to make decisions based on the expertise of its board members, not on the preferences of the president or Congress. Still, the agencies need both presidential and congressional support to survive.

independent regulatory commission
an executive branch unit outside of cabinet departments responsible for developing standards of behavior within specific industries and businesses, monitoring compliance with these standards, and imposing sanctions on violators

Government Corporations

Like private businesses, **government corporations** sell a service or a product; but unlike private businesses, they are government owned. Congress and the president create government corporations when they believe it is in the public interest for the national government to engage in a commercial activity, such as selling stamps to pay for the cost of delivering mail. (In fact, the best-known U.S. government corporation is the United States Postal Service.) Unlike the other categories of bureaucracies, government corporations are expected to make enough money to cover their costs.

A bipartisan board typically directs each government corporation. The president appoints the board members to serve for staggered fixed terms. Typically, the Senate is not

government corporation
an executive branch unit that sells a service and is expected to be financially self-sufficient

required to confirm the board members. Like regulatory commissions and administrative agencies, government corporations are structured to be independent.

Executive Office of the President

By 1939, the national bureaucracy for which the president serves as chief executive officer had grown tremendously in size and diversity of structure and functions. Acknowledging that the president needed help to manage this constellation of departments, independent administrative agencies, independent regulatory commissions, and government corporations, President Franklin Roosevelt (1933–1945) and the Congress created the Executive Office of the President (EOP).

The EOP is composed of dozens of offices and councils that assist the president in managing the complex and sprawling executive branch of the bureaucracy. The EOP has evolved into the locomotive of the national government—the engine driving the development and implementation of presidential policies and programs. The president appoints the top-level bureaucrats in EOP agencies, and the majority of these appointments are not subject to Senate confirmation. The president has the authority to fire these appointees at his pleasure. Therefore the EOP serves the president; it is in fact the presidential bureaucracy. (See Chapter 12 for a detailed discussion of the EOP.)

Hybrids

Although political scientists commonly talk about five categories of bureaucracies, not all bureaucracies fit neatly into a given category. In addition to the five categories of bureaucracy we have considered, the executive branch features hybrid agencies that have characteristics of more than one category. The Food and Drug Administration (FDA) is one such hybrid. The FDA regulates the food and pharmaceutical industries to ensure the safety of food and drugs on the market and hence is a regulatory agency. Yet it is not an independent regulatory commission, because it is housed within the Department of Health and Human Services.

In this section, we took stock of the executive branch organizations in which national bureaucrats implement policy. We next consider the nature of the essential roles bureaucrats play in all stages of public policy.

Federal Bureaucrats' Roles in Public Policy

Although the primary work of bureaucrats is implementation—putting public policy into action—bureaucrats play an active, vital role in all six stages of the public policy cycle. These stages are (1) agenda setting, (2) policy formulation, (3) policy approval, (4) resource allocation, (5) policy implementation, and (6) policy evaluation.

politics-administration dichotomy

the concept that elected government officials, who are accountable to the voters, create and approve public policy, and then competent, politically neutral bureaucrats implement the public policy

According to the **politics-administration dichotomy,** there is a clear line between *politics* (the formulation and approval of public policy, and the allocation of resources to put the policy into effect) and the *administration* of public policy (the real-world implementation of the policy). The dichotomy says that elected officials (whom citizens hold accountable through the ballot box) have authority for politics and that competent bureaucrats (hired through merit-based civil service) have authority for policy administration. Theoretically, this arrangement fosters not only responsive government but also efficient and effective public services.

The politics-administration dichotomy may sound good, but the reality of public policy processes does not allow for such a clean separation between those who "do politics" and those who administer policy. Although bureaucrats are hired to implement policy made by elected officials, those officials tap the expertise of bureaucrats throughout the other five stages of the policy process, allowing bureaucrats to influence and even make policies themselves, as we now shall see.

Agenda Setting

In the first stage of the public policy cycle, elected officials place issues on their agendas to discuss, if not to address by formulating a *policy*—a plan of government action to deal with a particular public concern. Bureaucrats play an instrumental role in setting the policy agenda. Because their focus is to implement public policy at the street level, bureaucrats have a clear view of the societal problems that citizens expect the government to address and strong views on how best to address those problems. Political scientists use the term *iron triangle* to describe long-term collaborative efforts among bureaucrats in a government agency, the members of an interest group, and the members of a legislative committee to get their mutual concerns on the agenda and then to formulate the policies they deem necessary to address those concerns. *Issue networks,* which are temporary collaborations among bureaucrats, elected officials, and the members of several interest groups, also engage in lobbying to set the agenda, as well as to influence policy formulation. Bureaucrats who want to get their concerns and proposed programs on the agenda may work to create issue networks as well as iron triangles. For more about iron triangles and issue networks, see Chapter 7.

Policy Formulation

The second stage of the policy process, policy formulation, involves defining a problem that has made it to the agenda and setting a plan of action (a policy) to address the problem. (Note, however, that not all concerns that reach an elected official's agenda—or even the agendas of numerous elected officials—go further in the policy process.) Although anyone can formulate a public policy, only elected officials can officially introduce policy proposals into the lawmaking process. Thus individuals and groups outside government, as well as bureaucrats, must identify members of Congress to introduce policy proposals for legislative action. The president can also make policy by issuing an executive order, an authority that lies outside the legislative process (see Chapter 12).

Because bureaucrats often have specialized knowledge of societal problems, elected officials rely on bureaucrats when formulating policies. House and Senate committees frequently call on bureaucrats to review and comment on bills that, if approved, they will implement and to testify in the hearings in which congressional members investigate and study problems. Thus bureaucrats regularly take part in policy formulation, whether at their own impetus or at the request of elected officials.

In recognition of bureaucrats' expertise, Congress often includes vague or ambiguous language in bills and relies on bureaucrats to fill in the program details after a bill is passed, during the policy implementation stage. Vague legislative language may also reflect the congressional sponsors' need to win majority votes in both the House and the Senate and to secure presidential approval of the policy. Fuzzy language means that if the bill becomes law, bureaucrats will need to discern what the policy is directing them to do before they can implement it.

> Kathleen Sebelius, secretary of the Department of Health and Human Services, testifies in front of the Senate Appropriations Committee on the proposed budget estimates for her department in June of 2009. As secretary of health and human services, she oversees the formulation of bills relevant to her department, including the department's budget request, and the department's implementation of policy.

Policy Approval

When Congress and the president vote to approve or reject the formulated policy, which is in the form of a proposed piece of legislation—a bill—they have reached the third stage, policy approval. Bills detailing the government's plan to address a problem are called authorization bills; when

authorization law
a law that provides the plan of action to address a given societal concern and identifies the executive branch unit that will put the plan into effect

Congress and the president, or Congress alone over a president's veto, approves such bills, the laws thus created authorize government action. **Authorization laws** not only provide the plan of action to address a given societal concern but also identify the executive branch unit that will put the plan into effect. The law may authorize an existing executive unit to carry out the policy, or it may establish a new unit to do the job. Presidential executive orders, another form of public policy, direct bureaucrats in how to implement policy. Yet bureaucracies cannot implement a public policy until they have legal authority to spend money.

Resource Allocation

In the next phase of the policy process, resource allocation, Congress and the president specify how much money each bureaucracy will be authorized to spend during the budget year. Through the budget process (see Chapter 15), Congress and the president formulate appropriation bills, which are plans for the distribution of government revenue to government entities, including bureaucracies, legislative bodies, and judicial bodies. Approved appropriation bills—**appropriation laws**—give bureaucracies the legal authority to spend money.

appropriation law
a law that gives bureaucracies and other government entities the legal authority to spend money

Bureaucrats play three key roles in the budget process. First, at the request of the president, bureaucrats develop an annual budget request for their agencies. Second, before Congress approves the appropriation bills that distribute government revenues to the agencies, it calls on bureaucrats to justify their budget requests. In turn, bureaucrats lobby members of Congress to allocate to their agencies the funds they requested. With limited money available, bureaucracies typically do not receive all the funding they request. Therefore bureaucracies compete with one another for their piece of the limited budget pie. Once Congress and the president approve the appropriation bills, bureaucrats take on their third role in the budget process; they spend money to put the public policy into action.

Policy Implementation

Bureaucrats are at the center of the second-to-last stage of the policy cycle, policy implementation. In this phase, bureaucrats must first interpret the law and then carry it out. Congress and the president delegate to bureaucrats the authority to determine the best way to implement the policy; this authority is called **administrative discretion.** Applying administrative discretion, bureaucrats make the day-to-day decisions related to executing policy programs and enforcing the necessary rules and standards. Elected officials risk the loss of control over the content of public policy when they delegate administrative discretion to bureaucrats. However, they have numerous tools to limit this risk, which we discuss later in this chapter's section on federal bureaucratic accountability.

administrative discretion
the authority delegated to bureaucrats to use their expertise and judgment when determining how to implement public policy

Bureaucrats, specifically those in independent agencies, use administrative discretion to establish programs, rules, regulations, and standards necessary for the effective and efficient implementation of policy. The process by which bureaucrats translate vague law into concrete plans of action is a quasi-legislative ("as-if legislative") process. It is "quasi-legislative" because bureaucrats in the executive branch, not legislators, make policy as they fill in the details needed to implement legislation. **Administrative rule making** is the name of this process by which upper-level bureaucrats use their administrative discretion and their expertise in the policy area to create rules, regulations, and standards that the bureaucracy will then enforce. For example, recognizing its lack of expertise in the specifics of how to prevent air and water pollution, Congress delegated to the Environmental Protection Agency (EPA) the authority to establish policy. The EPA sets specific pollution emissions standards to implement the Clean Water and Clean Air acts. Although Congress does not approve these EPA administrative standards, importantly, the standards have the force of law.

administrative rule making
the process by which an independent commission or agency fills in the details of a vague law by formulating, proposing, and approving rules, regulations, and standards that will be enforced to implement the policy

Agencies involved in administrative rule making also have a quasi-judicial ("as-if judicial") role. Through **administrative adjudication,** they determine when their rules are violated, and they impose penalties on the violators. Citizens who disagree with an agency's application of its administrative rules or those whom an agency finds guilty of violating its rules may challenge the agency's decisions through a lawsuit. Indeed, several states successfully sued the EPA in 2007 for its failure to set carbon dioxide emissions standards and

administrative adjudication
the process by which agencies resolve disputes over the implementation of their administrative rules

hence its inadequate implementation of the Clean Air Act. Claiming that the EPA was still not properly implementing the law, Massachusetts attorney general Martha Coakley, along with the attorneys general of seventeen other states, as well as two cities and eleven environmental interest groups, successfully sued the EPA in April 2008.[12]

Policy Evaluation

The last stage of the policy process is policy evaluation—the assessment of the intended and unintended effects of policy implementation. People do not assess government success by the number of laws passed or by the promises made in the language of the laws. Rather, the effectiveness and the efficiency of public service delivery are what matter to the public. The implementation of policy by bureaucrats is thus the key to citizens' satisfaction with government—and the key to government success.

Since the 1970s, U.S. taxpayers have called for increased transparency in government, including evaluations of public policy implementation to determine how effectively government is using their tax dollars. The corruption of the administration of President Richard Nixon—which featured Nixon's misuse of the Internal Revenue Service to collect information on opponents, as well as the infamous White House cover-up of the break-in at the Democratic Party headquarters in the Watergate Building—partially explains the call for greater transparency in government. The publication in 1973 of political scientists Jeffrey L. Pressman and Aaron B. Wildavsky's study of a federally funded economic development program also fueled outcries for increased transparency and evaluations.[13] Their landmark research concluded that it is "amazing that federal programs work at all" given the hurdles that policy implementers encounter.

As a result, policy evaluation has become a larger component of the workload of legislators and bureaucrats in recent decades than it ever was before. Because elected officials and citizens want proof of the efficiency and the effectiveness of implemented policies, agencies must document what they do and its impact. Because citizens do not elect bureaucrats, they do not have the opportunity to fire civil servants whose performance is unsatisfactory. Therefore citizens defer the responsibility for bureaucratic accountability to members of Congress, the president, and the judges who preside over the courts because these elected and appointed government officials have legal means to monitor bureaucrats' work and to hold them accountable.

Federal Bureaucratic Accountability

When it comes to public service, everyone is watching. The courts, through the mechanism of lawsuits, review the actions of the executive and legislative branches to ensure that they are constitutional and legal. Congress and the president, as the creators and funders of bureaucracies, can threaten to revamp or eliminate any bureaucracy, or to decrease its funding, if its performance falls short of expectations. Congress and the president not only structure bureaucracies to foster efficient, effective, and accountable public service but also pass laws to increase self-policing by bureaucrats.

People outside government, including many ordinary citizens, also keep a close eye on bureaucracies. National **sunshine laws** open up government functions and documents to the public, ensuring transparency and the public's right to know about government business and decision making. But these laws are effective only if citizens know about them and take advantage of them.

sunshine laws
legislation that opens up government functions and documents to the public

Accountability to the People

One of the first national sunshine laws for the enhancement of bureaucratic accountability to the people was the Administrative Procedure Act (APA) of 1946. The APA responded to citizens' and interest groups' concerns about the fast growth in the number of agencies involved in administrative rule making and about the lack of transparency and accountability of the bureaucratic rule makers. The APA, which applies to all federal agencies except those specifically excluded by legislation, standardized rule-making procedures and requires bureaucracies to publicize their proposed rules in the *Federal Register,* a daily national government publication. They also must publish an invitation for people to offer comments on the agency's proposals.

Once the agency collects and reviews the people's comments, it must publish its approved rules in the *Federal Register.* To facilitate this open process, the national government Web site www.regulations.gov posts proposed administrative rules and accepts electronically submitted comments on the rules. In this way, people can have a voice in administrative rule making. Such citizen input is essential to democracy, because bureaucrats propose and approve more administrative rules each year than the pieces of legislation proposed and approved by Congress and the president.

The Freedom of Information Act (FOIA) is a 1966 amendment to the APA. The FOIA requires national agencies to give citizens access to government documents upon request and at a reasonable cost. After the terrorist attacks on September 11, 2001, however, the national government denied an increasing percentage of such requests in the name of national security. The decreased access to government documents has heightened tensions between people advocating government confidentiality on the one hand, and individuals cherishing democratic openness and those dedicated to holding the national bureaucracy accountable on the other hand. The American Society of Newspaper Editors was so concerned about the diminished access that it established Sunshine Week (first held March 13–20, 2005) to educate citizens about their right to know and to request information about what the bureaucracy is doing.

Another law that aims to make the federal bureaucracy open and responsive to the people is the Government in the Sunshine Act of 1976. This act of Congress requires all multiheaded national agencies, except those in the Executive Office of the President (EOP), to conduct open, public meetings where citizens can testify and present their concerns about these agencies' actions (past, current, and potential) and the procedures by which they make decisions.

National agencies are now also using the Internet to make government more transparent. In September 2000, the General Services Administration (GSA) of the national government launched its FirstGov Web site, the national government's one-stop portal to national, state, local, and tribal government agency Web sites. This portal puts government information and services at your fingertips. In 2007, the GSA renamed the Web site USA.gov (www .usa.gov) in response to feedback from users who wanted a name that was easier to remember.

Strongly supporting the use of the Internet as a means to enhance citizen access to government information and services, Congress approved and President George W. Bush signed into law the E-Government Act of 2002. This law established a Federal Chief Information Officer within the Office of Management and Budget. Moreover, it requires national agencies to use Internet-based information technology. President Barack Obama promised that under his administration the federal government will provide Americans with an "unprecedented level of openness, collaboration, and efficiency and effectiveness through the use of information technology."[14]

Private organizations that monitor and evaluate the activities of bureaucrats have certainly taken advantage of sunshine laws and e-government. For example, in 2007, Congress passed legislation to establish an independent, bipartisan commission to investigate U.S. wartime contracting in Iraq and Afghanistan. Senator Claire McCaskill (D-Missouri), the bill's cosponsor, praised "POGO's [the Project on Government Oversight] work in supporting these provisions, along with the support of other watchdog groups including Taxpayers for Common Sense, the Government Accountability Project, OMBWatch, Common Cause, U.S. PIRG and Iraq and Afghanistan Veterans of America."[15] In addition to taking advantage of their right to government documents under the FOIA, watchdog groups are more likely than the average citizen to use government Web sites to track bureaucratic activities.

In a democracy, bureaucrats, like elected officials, operate in a fishbowl. Working face to face, or computer screen to computer screen, with the people whom they serve, they are in full view of anyone interested in monitoring them. Sunshine laws and e-government provide citizens with the means to find out what is going on in the bureaucracy. When citizens or watchdog groups identify a problem with bureaucratic operations, they frequently turn to the media to bring public attention to the issue, because the media are always ready to report on bureaucratic inefficiency and impropriety. A more expensive option for citizen and interest group action against bureaucratic waste and misconduct is the filing of a lawsuit.

Accountability to the Courts

As bureaucratic agencies implement policy, they must comply with constitutional guarantees of due process and equal protection of laws. A citizen believing that bureaucrats have violated those rights can challenge bureaucratic actions through the agency's quasi-judicial processes, discussed earlier. If the citizen is not satisfied with the result of this quasi-judicial recourse, he or she can sue the agency through the courts.

Through the litigation process, the U.S. judicial system seeks to ensure that administrative agencies conduct their quasi-legislative and quasi-judicial functions in compliance with the constitutional guarantees of due process (in the Fifth and Fourteenth amendments) as well as the Administrative Procedure Act of 1946. In 2006, for example, federal district judge Richard Leon ruled that the Federal Emergency Management Agency (FEMA) procedures and notices to Hurricane Katrina victims were so difficult to understand that evacuees were deprived of due process because they were unable to determine what the process was. According to ACORN, a housing advocacy group that brought the lawsuit, as many as 11,000 families may have been wrongfully denied long-term housing assistance by the lack of due process in FEMA procedures.[16]

Accountability to Congress

Bureaucrats must always keep in mind the preferences and the agenda of Congress if they want to survive, for Congress approves the legislation that creates, regulates, and funds bureaucracies. The Senate has an additional mechanism for promoting bureaucratic accountability, in that more than one-quarter of the president's appointees are subject to Senate confirmation. The confirmation process for top bureaucrats gives senators a degree of influence over the leadership and direction of executive departments and agencies.

Another means by which Congress encourages bureaucratic accountability is the monitoring of bureaucracies' policy implementation, a form of legislative oversight. When the media, citizens, or interest groups bring concerns

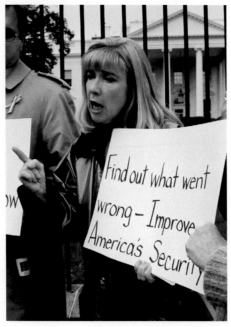

> Individual citizens and interest groups frequently pressure the government to investigate scandals and disasters to find out what went wrong and what the government can do to prevent future misbehavior and disasters. Sally Regenhard, founder of the Skyscraper Safety Campaign, participates in a vigil in front of the White House urging the formation of an independent commission to investigate the terrorist attacks of September 11, 2001. Ms. Regenhard's son, a probationary New York City firefighter, perished in the World Trade Center collapse.

about a bureaucracy's policy implementation to the attention of legislators, Congress might launch an investigation. If, consequently, Congress and the president are dissatisfied with that bureaucracy's performance or behavior, they can cut its budget, modify its legal authority, or even eliminate the agency.

In most cases, oversight does not occur unless citizens, interest groups, and the media push for congressional action, as occurred in the aftermath of September 11, 2001, when public pressure forced Congress to create the 9/11 Commission to investigate the terrorist attacks on the World Trade Center in New York City and on the Pentagon in Arlington, Virginia. An evaluation of bureaucratic performance can also be required in the authorization legislation by a **sunset clause,** which forces the expiration of the program or policy after a specified number of years unless Congress reauthorizes it through new legislation.

sunset clause
a clause in legislation that sets an expiration date for the authorized program/policy unless Congress re-authorizes it

Accountability to the President

The president also has several tools for holding bureaucracies accountable. Like Congress, the president can use the authorization and appropriation processes to ensure accountability. In addition, because most top political appointees serve at the president's pleasure, they are responsive to the president's policy preferences—and in this way, they and their agencies are accountable to the president.

Today, the Office of Management and Budget, an EOP agency, is the key lever in the president's efforts to hold the bureaucracy accountable. The OMB evaluates bureaucratic performance for the president. On the basis of OMB performance assessments, the president proposes budget increases or decreases, agency growth or elimination, or even a reorganization of the executive branch in which agencies are consolidated.

In addition to overseeing performance evaluations of bureaucratic agencies, the OMB spearheads the development of the president's budget, controls the implementation of appropriation laws, and regulates administrative rule making. Through its Office of Information and Regulatory Affairs (OIRA), the OMB ensures that regulations created by executive branch agencies are not "unnecessarily costly"[17] and support the president's policy preferences.

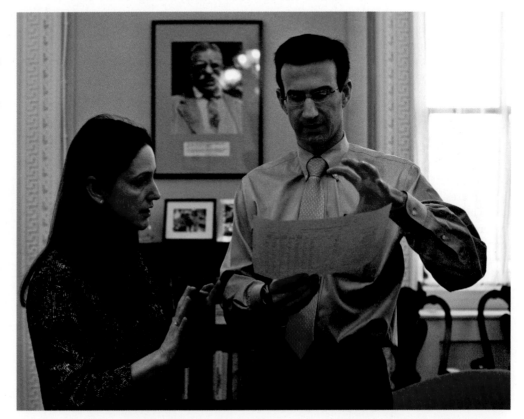

> Peter Orszag, President Obama's first Office of Management and Budget director, reviews documents in his office in February 2009. Upon his announced resignation from the OMB in June 2010, President Obama credited Orszag with helping to identify more than one hundred programs for elimination because they had outlived their purpose.

Internal Accountability

The president, Congress, the courts, and ordinary citizens have multiple means by which to hold bureaucrats accountable. But bureaucrats, who themselves are taxpayers, also worry about inefficiency and waste in public service. Legislated codes of behavior and whistle-blower protections help to foster accountability from within bureaucracies.

CODES OF BEHAVIOR AND THE ETHICS IN GOVERNMENT ACT To ensure the best public service, bureaucracies have codes of behavior. These codes specify guidelines for ethical, efficient, and effective behavior on the part of bureaucrats. Each government agency has its own such code. In addition, in 1992, the Office of Government Ethics published a comprehensive set of ethical standards for national bureaucrats. Moreover, many of the professions in which bureaucrats are members (lawyers, doctors, nurses, accountants, engineers, and so on) also have established codes of behavior. Importantly, however, codes of behavior are just guidelines. They do not stipulate what a bureaucrat should do in a given situation. Thus bureaucrats must use discretion when applying such codes to their daily work of providing public service.

The Ethics in Government Act of 1978 established the United States Office of Government Ethics (OGE), which is charged with preventing conflicts of interest by bureaucrats (political appointees, SES bureaucrats, and civil servants). A **conflict of interest** arises when a public servant is in a position to make a decision or take an action from which he or she can personally benefit. In such a situation, the public servant's private interest is in conflict with his or her responsibility to serve the public interest. A key to the prevention of conflicts of interest is the requirement that top government officials must disclose their finances.

conflict of interest
in the case of public servants, the situation in which they can personally benefit from a decision they make or an action they take in the process of doing their jobs

WHISTLE-BLOWER PROTECTIONS AND INSPECTORS GENERAL Whistle-blower laws offer an additional means of internal accountability in the national bureaucracy. The 1978 Civil Service Reform Act provided some protections to civil servant **whistle-blowers**—employees who disclose government misconduct, waste, mismanagement, abuse of authority, or a threat to public health or safety. The CSRA established the Office of Special Counsel to protect whistle-blowers' job security. Then in 1986, thanks to the lobbying efforts of many groups, including the Project on Government Oversight, Congress approved the False Claims Act. This law allows for a monetary reward for government whistle-blowers who expose fraud that harms the U.S. government.

whistle-blower
a civil servant who discloses mismanagement, fraud, waste, corruption, and/or threats to public health and safety to the government

In another attempt to improve internal accountability, Congress approved the Inspector General Act in 1978. This law aims to ensure the integrity of public service by creating government watchdogs, called **inspectors general,** appointed by the president and embedded in government agencies to monitor policy implementation and investigate alleged misconduct. The law requires the appointment of the inspectors general without regard to their political affiliation and strictly on the basis of their abilities in accounting, auditing, or investigation. "We're supposed to check our politics at the door and call things as we see them. If we uncover things that reflect badly on the government, we're legally and morally obliged to report it. We're obliged to do that for the good of the country." So explained Clark Ervin, who held the position of inspector general at the State and Homeland Security departments.[18]

inspectors general
political appointees who work within a government agency to ensure the integrity of public service by investigating allegations of misconduct by bureaucrats

In summary, whistle-blower protection laws and inspectors general enhance the ability of the bureaucrats themselves to police the agencies in which they work, and sunshine laws give government outsiders various instruments for monitoring the bureaucracy. But many citizens and government officials believe that more needs to be done to improve bureaucrats' record of performance.

Can Bureaucratic Performance Be Improved?

In the United States, bureaucrats perform every job imaginable. They generally do their job so well that we rarely think about how their work positively affects us around the clock. We and our elected officials are nevertheless quick to bash the bureaucracy at the slightest hint of inefficiency. Similarly, the media seize upon any opportunity to report on problems with bureaucrats and bureaucracies. Our public discourse infrequently covers bureaucrats' *good* performance. When was the last time you heard a news report or were a party to a friendly conversation that praised a public servant?

Yet the U.S. Postal Service delivers hundreds of millions of pieces of mail six days a week, and rarely is a letter or a package lost. Thousands of planes safely take off from and land at U.S. airports every hour, guided by federal bureaucrats in the person of air traffic controllers. Millions of senior citizens receive a monthly Social Security check on time every month. Even more people travel the interstate highway systems without incident each day.

Public administration and policy scholar Charles Goodsell has found that two-thirds to three-fourths of Americans report their encounters with government bureaucrats and bureaucracy as "satisfactory."[19] However, research consistently shows that some national agencies perform better than do others.

The Best-Performing Bureaucracies

Political scientists William T. Gormley and Steven Balla reviewed national performance data and summarized the characteristics of national agencies that perform well.[20] They found that numerous factors correlate with better-performing bureaucracies—factors that individual bureaucrats have little control over. They include legislative language that clearly states the goal of the legislation and provides high levels of administrative discretion, allowing bureaucrats to determine the best way to achieve the goal. Better-performing bureaucracies tend to be those with easily measured goals, especially goals that include providing resources to citizens (such as Social Security checks) as opposed to taking resources (tax collection). Another factor correlated with good performance is high levels of support from elected officials, the media, and diverse groups of citizens for the legislated goal and the implementing agency. High levels of support typically result in an agency receiving ample resources. Effective leaders who develop and maintain high levels of support from government officials and interested parties outside government are also important to well-performing bureaucracies.

Does Contracting-Out Improve Performance?

In addition to analyzing citizen satisfaction with public bureaucracies, Charles Goodsell has analyzed the body of research that assesses the efficiency of public policy implementation by government bureaucrats compared with the efficiency of private organizations. He has found that "the assumption that business always does better than government is not upheld."[21] In fact, Goodsell reports that "despite antigovernment rhetoric to the contrary, the federal government achieves essentially the same degree of satisfaction for its services as corporate America does for its products."[22] Nevertheless, many commentators and elected officials argue that private businesses are more efficient than are governments and therefore that more public service should be outsourced to private businesses.

Contracting-out to private businesses certainly decreases the number of bureaucrats on the national payroll. But does outsourcing foster more efficient and effective public service? Does it save taxpayer dollars? The evidence strongly suggests otherwise.

Outsourcing government work can lead to waste, fraud, overpricing, and corruption. In its evaluation of contract waste and fraud in Hurricane Katrina relief, the House of Representatives Government Reform Committee reported that "the main problems were no-bid contracts, layers of subcontracting that inflated costs, and a lack of oversight on the completion of work."[23] What causes these inefficiencies?

First, for-profit organizations must make a profit to survive. As contract law experts note, for many private government contractors, overestimating the costs of the work and then reaping illegally high profits are a common reality. Second, holding bureaucrats accountable for their performance is not easy in general, and determining whom to hold accountable for delays, cost overruns, and quality issues is complicated when policy implementation occurs through the shadow bureaucracy.[24] Unlike government bodies, private businesses can legally function behind closed doors—unless and until concerned citizens,

> In August 2007, the I-135W bridge in Minneapolis collapsed, killing thirteen people. Barely one year after the collapse, the new replacement bridge opened to traffic. The private construction firm contracted by the state of Minnesota to design and build the new bridge completed the job three months earlier than the state's deadline and less than 2 percent over budget—unusual for a project of this magnitude. The success of this $234 million contract can be attributed to cooperation among local, state, and federal bureaucracies, all moving with record speed, as well as an innovative arrangement with the private contractor.

watchdog groups, the media, and government officials force the doors open through congressional investigations or lawsuits.

Citizens' Role in Bureaucratic Performance

Citizens turn to the government to provide services and solve problems. As we have discussed, the government's success in serving the people well depends on many factors. Ultimately, even if all other factors correlated with a well-performing bureaucracy are in place, the bureaucracy will fail without the participation and compliance of the people it serves. The effectiveness of public policies depends on people's knowledge of and compliance with the law. It depends on their applying for the government programs for which they qualify and their conformity to the rules, regulations, standards, and directions of bureaucrats. This symbiotic relationship is essential to the success of government.

CONCLUSION

THINKING CRITICALLY ABOUT WHAT'S NEXT IN THE BUREAUCRACY

Candidates, elected officials, and the media perpetually criticize government bureaucrats and bureaucracies. At the same time, they do not typically bring attention to or compliment bureaucrats for work satisfactorily or well done. In reality, citizens take for granted the overwhelming majority of public services because they are provided day-in and day-out without problem. And although citizens typically use the terms *bureaucrat* and *bureaucracy* to insult public servants and government agencies, 61 percent of respondents to a summer 2009 Gallup poll indicated they were satisfied with their most recent interaction with a federal government agency.[25]

Numerous groups, including the Partnership for Public Service, are working to improve the image of public service and to inspire quality college graduates to work as public servants. Will such efforts succeed, or will the bureaucracy remain a target of criticism from citizens, candidates, and elected officials? Will the best and the brightest respond to the call to serve as a large proportion of federal employees retire in the next decade?

Many critics of the bureaucracy argue that private-sector for-profit and nonprofit organizations can provide better-quality public services for less money. However, studies done to support that theory have produced mixed findings. Moreover, several private organizations with government contracts have been involved in scandals regarding their provision of services and materials to victims of natural disasters and man-made disasters both on U.S. soil and abroad. Given these realities, will the volume of public service outsourced to private organizations continue to increase?

Summary

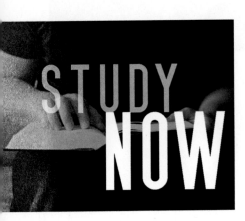

1. Bureaucrats and Bureaucracy
Traditionally, bureaucrats are defined as employees in the executive branch of government who are hired to deliver public services. Today, however, many private-sector employees—the so-called shadow bureaucrats—also implement public policy. Although most people think of government agencies when they hear the word *bureaucracy,* a bureaucracy is any large, hierarchical organization featuring a division of labor, specialization of tasks, standard operating procedures, and a chain of command.

2. Federal Bureaucrats
The national government hires almost 3 million civilians into the executive branch to administer public policies. The president appoints a small percentage of these bureaucrats. The government hires the overwhelming majority of national bureaucrats on the basis of merit, using a hiring process that includes open competition and equal opportunity. As a result, the national bureaucracy features a more diverse representation of the people than do the elective institutions of the federal government.

3. State, Local, and Shadow Bureaucrats
The overall number of national bureaucrats has been stable over the past few decades. However, the number of state, local, and shadow bureaucrats has grown significantly because of the proliferation of grants-in-aid and the practice of contracting-out more and more public service.

4. The Evolution and Organization of the Federal Bureaucracy
The federal bureaucracy has grown tremendously in size, scope, and complexity since 1789. Political scientists typically put government agencies in one of five categories—departments, independent administrative agencies, independent regulatory commissions, government corporations, and Executive Office of the President agencies. But this categorization oversimplifies the diversity of structure, size, and function of the thousands of national bureaucracies.

5. Federal Bureaucrats' Roles in Public Policy
Federal bureaucrats do much more than implement policy. Bureaucrats lobby elected officials in all stages of the policy cycle to get their concerns, and the concerns of the citizens who are their clients, addressed. Elected officials frequently defer to the expertise of bureaucrats when it comes to determining the detailed programs, rules, and standards that are needed to serve the people. Citizen satisfaction with government is deeply dependent on the efficient and effective work of bureaucrats.

6. Federal Bureaucratic Accountability
Elected officials delegate administrative discretion to bureaucrats. Interested parties inside and outside government closely scrutinize bureaucrats' use of this discretion. Taxpayers, clients, the media, and interest groups, as well as the president, Congress, and the courts, hold bureaucrats accountable. In addition to sunshine laws and ethics codes, the structure of national bureaucracies lends itself to accountability.

7. Can Bureaucratic Performance Be Improved?

All those who scrutinize bureaucracies are quick to find fault and slow to offer praise. Certainly, not every agency is evaluated as performing well, but for the most part, citizens report that their interactions with government bureaucrats are at least satisfactory.

Key Terms

administrative
adjudication 418

administrative discretion 418

administrative rule
making 418

appropriation law 418

authorization law 418

bureaucracy 405

bureaucrats 403

civil servants 407

conflict of interest 423

contracting-out (privatizing,
outsourcing) 403

department 413

government corporation 415

independent administrative
agency 414

independent regulatory
commission 415

inspectors general 423

merit-based civil service 407

plum book 405

politics-administration
dichotomy 416

senior executive service
(SES) 409

shadow bureaucrats 403

sunset clause 422

sunshine laws 419

whistle-blower 423

For Review

1. List and describe the structural characteristics of bureaucratic organizations.

2. Compare and contrast the following categories of bureaucrats: political appointees, civil servants, senior executive service bureaucrats, and shadow bureaucrats.

3. What accounts for the fact that the national budget and the scope of its responsibilities have continued to grow in recent decades, yet the number of its civilian employees has remained stable?

4. Differentiate the five categories of national bureaucracies by discussing differences in their structures and the type of services they provide.

5. Describe the role that bureaucrats play at each stage of the policy process.

6. Distinguish between internal and external means of bureaucratic accountability and give some examples of each.

7. According to Gormley and Balla, what are three or four characteristics of bureaucracies that perform well?

For Critical Thinking and Discussion

1. Do citizens expect too much from government and hence from bureaucrats and bureaucracies? Explain your answer.

2. Does the profit motive of private businesses threaten the efficient use of taxpayer money when public services are contracted-out? Why or why not?

3. Identify at least one public service that you believe the national government should not contract-out to private-sector organizations, and defend your choice(s).

4. How often do you interact with national bureaucrats? What about state bureaucrats? Local bureaucrats? Give some recent examples of each interaction. Can you identify some shadow bureaucrats that have provided you with public services?

5. Compose a list of public services provided to you since you woke up this morning. Were you satisfied with the services? Which of those services do people generally take for granted?

MULTIPLE CHOICE: Choose the lettered item that answers the question correctly.

1. The number of federal civilian bureaucrats is
   a. almost 3 million.
   b. almost 5 million.
   c. almost 13 million.
   d. almost 20 million.

2. The youngest department in the national bureaucracy is the department of
   a. energy.
   b. homeland security.
   c. state.
   d. veterans affairs.

3. The demographics of what category of federal employee are most comparable to those of the population as a whole?
   a. elected officials
   b. civil servants
   c. political appointees
   d. senior executive service employees

4. The legislation that created the federal merit-based civil service system was the
   a. Civil Rights Act (1964).
   b. Civil Service Reform Act (1978).
   c. Pendleton Act (1883).
   d. Title IX (1972).

5. The independent administrative agency that is the central personnel office for the federal bureaucracy today is the
   a. EOP.   c. MSPB.
   b. FLRA.   d. OPM.

6. In what category of federal bureaucracies are secretaries the top appointed officials?
   a. department
   b. independent administrative agency
   c. independent regulatory commission
   d. government corporation

7. Bureaucracies in which category are expected to make enough money to cover their costs?
   a. department
   b. independent administrative agency
   c. independent regulatory commission
   d. government corporation

8. Bureaucrats make policy, using the administrative discretion that Congress delegates to them, at the stage of the policy process that is called
   a. policy formulation.
   b. policy approval.
   c. policy implementation.
   d. policy evaluation.

9. All of the following are merit principles except
   a. competence.   c. political neutrality.
   b. open competition.   d. Senate confirmation.

10. Political appointees who work within a government agency to ensure the integrity of public service by investigating allegations of misconduct by bureaucrats are
    a. inspectors general.
    b. shadow bureaucrats.
    c. watchdogs.
    d. whistle-blowers.

FILL IN THE BLANKS.

11. A _____ is an organization with the following characteristics: a division of labor; workers hired based on competence to do a specialized task; standard operating procedures; and a vertical chain of command.

12. The hiring system initially used by the federal government, which allowed the president to hire anyone he wanted based on whatever qualifications he decided on, is the _____ system.

13. People hired and paid by private for-profit and nonprofit organizations that implement public policy through a government contract are _____ .

14. _____ is the authority delegated to bureaucrats to use their expertise and judgment when determining how to implement public policy.

15. Laws that force the government to be transparent by holding open meetings and providing citizens with requested information at a reasonable cost are collectively known as _____ .

Answers: 1. a; **2.** b; **3.** b; **4.** c; **5.** d; **6.** a; **7.** d; **8.** c; **9.** d; **10.** a; **11.** bureaucracy; **12.** patronage; **13.** shadow bureaucrats; **14.** Administrative discretion; **15.** sunshine laws.

RESOURCES FOR RESEARCH AND ACTION

Internet Resources

Office of Management and Budget
www.whitehouse.gov.omb This Web site provides access to the current and previous federal budget documents and historical budget tables.

Regulations.gov
www.regulations.gov You can review proposed and approved rules, regulations, and standards of federal executive agencies and submit your comments about them.

U.S. Government Printing Office
www.gpoaccess.gov/gmanual/browse This Web site allows you to view the most current U.S. Government Manual as well as several older editions of the manual.

USA.gov
www.usa.gov Use this site as a one-stop portal to national, state, and local government officials, agencies, and documents.

Internet Activism

Like the U.S. population as a whole, the bureaucracy is "graying." More than 40 percent of the national workforce is now eligible for retirement. That means growth in job opportunities, especially for college graduates looking for secure jobs with good compensation (pay and benefits). To find out more about government job opportunities as well as apprenticeships, fellowships, and internships, visit the Web site of the Office of Personnel Management (OPM):
www.usajobs.gov

YouTube
www.youtube.com/RecoveryBoard Recovery Board Chairman Earl Devaney explains how citizens can use the recovery.gov Web site to hold the federal government accountable for its spending by becoming a "citizen inspector general."

Blog
http://blog.usa.gov/roller/govgab Federal bureaucrats from the Office of Citizen Services and Communications at the U.S. General Service Administration encounter on a daily basis a staggering amount of information about the government and its services. Go to the blog to learn about services from which you can benefit.

Facebook
www.facebook.com/partnershipforpublicservice The Partnership for Public Service's mission is to revitalize the federal government by inspiring a new generation to serve and by transforming the way government works.

Recommended Readings

Goodsell, Charles T. *The Case for Bureaucracy: A Public Administration Polemic,* 4th ed. Washington, DC: CQ Press, 2004. A review of the common myths and criticisms of bureaucracy, with evidence to show that they are indeed unsupported.

Gormley, William T., Jr. and Steven J. Balla. *Bureaucracy and Democracy: Accountability and Performance.* Washington, DC: CQ Press, 2004. Uses case studies and examples to illustrate what the national bureaucracy does and why it is important, and draws on social science theories to describe how bureaucracy works and the complex and conflicting demands put on it.

Kettl, Donald F. *System Under Stress: Homeland Security and American Politics.* Washington, DC: CQ Press, 2004. Analysis of the environmental factors that led to the creation of the newest cabinet-level department, the Department of Homeland Security, with an examination of the intergovernmental nature of the endeavor to protect homeland security.

Stillman, Richard. *The American Bureaucracy: The Core of Modern Government.* Chicago: Nelson-Hall Publishers, 1996. A comprehensive introductory textbook in public administration, with excellent description and analysis of bureaucracies (national, state, and local) in the United States.

Wilson, James Q. 1989. *Bureaucracy: What Government Agencies Do and Why They Do It.* New York: Basic Books, 1989. A classic treatise on what government agencies do and why they function as they do, with analysis on how they might become more responsible and efficient.

Movies of Interest

Pentagon Papers (2003)
In this made-for-TV movie, a Department of Defense bureaucrat, Daniel Ellsberg, has access to classified documents that he decides should be brought to the public's attention. The documents detail the secret history of U.S. involvement in Vietnam, which includes bureaucrats misinforming decision makers and the public. Ellsberg risks his career and his freedom to try to get the truth to the public. Based on a true story.

Mississippi Burning (1989)
Two committed FBI agents, with very different personal styles, investigate the disappearance of three civil rights workers during the 1960s. Based on a true story.

Serpico (1973)
The story of a New York City police officer who is living his dream of being a cop. His dream job turns life threatening when he blows the whistle on corruption in the police force, the existence of which shows that not all of Serpico's coworkers are as committed to public service as he is. Based on a true story.

The
Judiciary

THEN

A common-law tradition imported from England dominated in the U.S. legal system.

NOW

Through code law and further interpretation of common law, the courts respond to unprecedented developments, from a torrent of technology to a continuing terrorist threat.

NEXt

Will new laws successfully address the complexities of issues including technological advances and the terrorist menace?

Will shifting Supreme Court ideology influence government actions in response to the ever-present threat of terrorism?

Will courts with specific policy expertise supplant legislatures' policy making in areas such as technology?

In this chapter, we survey the foundations, structure, and workings of the contemporary U.S. judiciary. We examine how the courts are responding to the ongoing, and sometimes unprecedented, changes occurring in contemporary society. We conclude by looking at how individuals, as well as the other branches of the government and the courts themselves, check judicial power.

FIRST, we examine *the origins of the U.S. judiciary.*

SECOND, we consider *the basis of U.S. law,* including common law and code law.

THIRD, we focus on the *sources of U.S. law,* including constitutions, statutes, judicial decisions, executive orders, and administrative law.

FOURTH, we examine *the structure of the federal court system.*

FIFTH, we look at the criteria used in *selecting judges for the federal bench.*

SIXTH, we survey *the U.S. Supreme Court today,* including its jurisdiction and the procedures by which the Court chooses, considers, and decides a case.

SEVENTH, we examine *judges as policy makers.*

EIGHTH, we probe the various *checks on U.S. courts.* These checks come from the executive and legislative branches of the government, police and other law enforcement agents, interest groups, the courts themselves, and the ordinary citizens who most directly experience the impact of a court decision.

judiciary
the branch of government comprising the courts and the judges who preside over them

We think of the courts primarily

as places where citizens turn when they have a dispute that they need to resolve. We venture into a courtroom when we encounter some difficult legal issue with either the government or a private individual or group. The resolution of disputes is indeed the primary function of the courts in the United States. But courts and judges are concerned with other, more significant and far-reaching endeavors. In this chapter, we consider how the judiciary, consisting of the federal and state court systems, provides one of the most important defenses that citizens have against abuses of power by the executive and legislative branches. In recognition of the judiciary's role as protector of civil liberties and civil rights, the American people typically award courts higher approval ratings than the other institutions of government.[1]

In *Federalist* No. 78, Alexander Hamilton explains that the Constitution intentionally structures the judiciary to be the weakest branch of government. But the judiciary has evolved significantly, to the point that it shares an equal role with the other two branches. Today, the courts play a central role in ensuring that power remains in balance among the three branches of government on the federal level, as well as between the federal government and the states.

Judges have powers that go well beyond the immediate case they are considering. This authority allows them to make law for future generations. In fact, on both the national and the state level, lawmaking is a shared enterprise among the three branches—legislative, executive, and judicial. Although the Constitution created a government characterized by a separation of powers, lawmaking is far less compartmentalized.[2] It is simplistic to think that legislatures make law, executives enforce it, and courts interpret it; rather, lawmaking is a part of what all three branches are empowered to do.

The Origins of the U.S. Judiciary

The foundations of the U.S. **judiciary**—the branch of government comprising courts and the judges who preside over them—reach back to American colonial history and the early years of the republic that took shape after the colonies broke with England. The U.S. Constitution created the framework for the judiciary. The structure and the authority of the federal judiciary have evolved further, and continuously, through compromises forged over the last 200-plus years.

The Constitution and the Judiciary Act of 1789: Establishing the Supreme Court and the Federal District Courts

During the debates over the ratification of the Constitution, the Anti-Federalists and the Federalists had sparred over what the powers of the national judiciary should be. The Anti-Federalists had warned that a too powerful national judiciary would erode states' rights. For their part, the Federalists had contended that a strong national court would be necessary to moderate conflicts between the states. Ultimately, the Constitution named the **U.S. Supreme Court** as the high court of the land, but the framers intentionally did not make the Court's powers specific. Only by saying little about the specific powers of the Supreme Court were they able to reach agreement on the judiciary.

One of the most important of the framers' compromises was to establish only one national court, the Supreme Court, and to empower Congress to create all lower national courts. Congress accordingly set up these inferior courts in the earliest days of its first session, when it passed the Judiciary Act of 1789, creating the federal district courts.[3] The federal district courts' geographic jurisdictions matched state boundaries, with at least one federal court in every state. Congress intended that these courts would have strong ties to the states in which they were located and expected that in many cases federal judges would apply state, not federal, law. These federal district courts drew strength from their ties to the states, but the federal judiciary was quite weak, with little authority.

Marbury v. Madison and the Principle of Judicial Review

Shortly after his election in 1800, President Thomas Jefferson barred the Supreme Court from meeting in the 1801–1802 term. Jefferson was concerned about the out-of-power Federalists' potential use of the federal judiciary to maintain control in the national government. Jefferson was perhaps right to worry, because in the following term, in the landmark case **Marbury v. Madison** (1803), the Federalist-led Supreme Court grabbed for itself the power of judicial review.[4] **Judicial review** is the Court's authority to review and to strike down laws passed by the other branches of the national government (see Chapter 2).

In the *Marbury* case, the Court argued something that it had never argued before: that it had the power not only to review acts of Congress and the president but also to decide whether those laws were consistent with the Constitution, and to strike down those laws that conflicted with constitutional principles. Legal scholar Joel B. Grossman observes that in *Marbury*, "[John] Marshall made it abundantly clear that the meaning of the Constitution was rarely self-contained and obvious and that those who interpreted it—a role he staked out for the federal courts but one that did not reach its full flowering until the mid-twentieth century—made a difference."[5] Judicial review is the most significant power the Supreme Court exercises. Over time, the Court has extended this power to apply not only to acts of Congress and the chief executive but also to laws passed by state legislatures and executives, as well as to state court rulings.[6]

The Judiciary Act of 1891: Expanding the Federal Courts

The middle level in the federal court structure, the courts of appeals, also known as **circuit courts** of appeals, were created some one hundred years after the *Marbury* decision, through the Judiciary Act of 1891. This law sought to relieve the heavy caseload that the U.S. Supreme Court faced after Congress had gradually expanded the jurisdiction of the federal courts to include criminal cases during the nineteenth century.

Until the advent of separate circuit courts of appeals, federal district court judges and even Supreme Court justices had needed to ride by horseback around the circuits to hear intermediate-level appeals cases. They sometimes traveled thousands of miles in a year in the practice, which became known as **circuit riding.** Over time, they began to bitterly bemoan the hardships they faced in serving the geographically expanding country and the increasing case docket. But it took a long time for the states and their representatives in Congress to become convinced of the necessity of **courts of appeals**—courts that review previous decisions made by courts in the federal or state judicial

U.S. Supreme Court
high court with a limited original jurisdiction whose decisions may not be appealed; it serves as the court of last resort in the U.S. judiciary

Marbury v. Madison
the 1803 Supreme Court case that established the power of judicial review

judicial review
court authority to determine that an action taken by any government official or governing body violates the Constitution

circuit courts
also known as *courts of appeals;* the middle level in the federal court structure, the courts of appeals

circuit riding
the practice of traveling around the circuits by early Supreme Court justices and district court judges to hear appeals cases

courts of appeals
intermediate appellate courts in the federal system that review the application of law in previous decisions made by courts in the federal or state judicial system

> Historically, federal district court judges and even Supreme Court justices rode by horseback around their geographic circuit to hear cases. The harsh demands placed on judges by circuit riding spurred the creation of federal courts of appeals that would review the application of the law in previously-decided cases.

system. These courts were charged exclusively with reviewing the application of law in previous court decisions rather than reviewing evidence or facts of the cases.

The Judiciary Act of 1891 divided the courts of appeals into nine geographic units, with each unit number corresponding to a circuit. The assumption in carving out these units was that each state should be grouped with states likely to have similar political cultures. Today, there are twelve courts of appeals covering designated regions, and the thirteenth hears specific kinds of cases, among them cases involving international trade, governmental contracts, and patents. By creating these separate courts of appeals, Congress significantly reduced the Supreme Court's workload: in 1890, 623 cases were filed with the Court, but just two years later, after passage of the Judiciary Act, that number fell by more than half, to 275. The act also eliminated the requirement of circuit riding, thus easing the burden on Supreme Court justices. Significantly, in using statutes rooted in the common-law tradition, the Congress itself was creating a relatively new form of law: code law.

The Basis of U.S. Law

U.S. law combines two kinds of law: *common law*, which is made principally by judges reaching decisions in cases, and *code law*, enacted primarily by legislators (and often referred to as *statutory law*) and by chief executives.[7] Although the U.S. legal system has roots in a common-law system, most legal disputes today center on disagreements involving the interpretation of code law.

Civil law is the body of law dealing with the rights of private citizens. In civil law cases, there is a conflict between private individuals in which one party alleges that some action or inaction by the other party, the defendant, has caused harm to him or her. **Criminal law** is the body of law dealing with conduct considered so harmful to society as a whole that it is prohibited by statute, and is prosecuted and punished by the government. Criminal law cases are always filed by the government against the defendant.

Because criminal cases are concerned with the breach of an obligation owed by the individual to the larger society, criminal cases always involve either a state government or the national government (though sometimes civil cases can involve a government entity). For example, when the baseball legend and home run–record breaker Barry Bonds was indicted for allegedly having lied to federal authorities investigating the sale of steroids, the criminal case was filed as *The United States of America v. Barry Lamar Bonds*. In contrast, civil cases typically pit individual against individual, as in *Dawn Simorangkir* (also known as the "Boudoir Queen") *v. Courtney Love*, a case in which Simorangkir alleged that celebrity Love used Twitter and other online platforms to publish "delusional accusations and lies" and "threats of harm" concerning the fashion designer.[8] Civil cases typically center on the breach of some obligation owed by one individual to another. The most common civil cases are concerned with the family, a contractual matter, or a negligent injury to a person or property (known as a **tort**).

Common Law

Law created by courts through the cases they decide is called **common law,** and it binds all courts considering similar cases in the future. To understand how common law functions in the American legal system, consider the 2005 case of Terri Schiavo, the woman at the center of a very controversial debate about an individual's right to die. When Schiavo became ill and collapsed in 1990, her brain lost oxygen and she lapsed into what doctors call a persistent vegetative state, or PVS. A person in a PVS can breathe on his or her own but has very limited brain activity and requires artificial food and hydration. Terri remained in this terrible state for years. Then in 1998, Terri's husband, Michael Schiavo, asked a Florida state court to issue an order that would allow the discontinuance of artificial food and hydration. When the state court issued the order, Terri's family filed a motion to block the removal of the feeding tube. Over the next seven years, the disputing parties battled out the case of Terri Schiavo in the state and federal courts. The courts had to determine whether Terri would have wanted to terminate life support. That determination must have been difficult for the judges, who had to puzzle out Terri's intent by listening to her loved ones'

civil law
the body of law dealing with the rights of private citizens

criminal law
the body of law dealing with conduct so harmful to society as a whole that it is prohibited by statute, and is prosecuted and punished by the government

tort
a wrongful act involving a personal injury or harm to one's property or reputation

common law
law made by judges who decide cases and articulate legal principles in their opinions; based on the British system

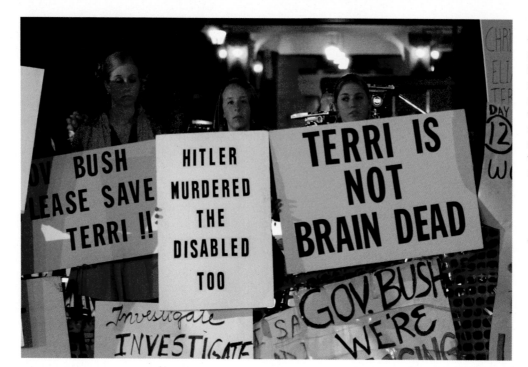

> Law created by courts through the cases they decide is called common law. In the 2005 case of Terri Schiavo, the courts created common law concerning an individual's right to die, focusing specifically on what Schiavo would have chosen if she had been competent. The court decision that established the right to discontinue food and hydration is now part of U.S. common law.

testimony on Terri's comments, before her accident, about how she would have wanted to live if she were ever in such a state.

Competent individuals have a right to discontinue food and hydration without government interference. The Supreme Court recognized this right in the case *Cruzan v. Missouri Department of Health* (1990). The *Cruzan* case concerned Nancy Cruzan, who also was in a persistent vegetative state and for whom the family sought to discontinue food and hydration. The state of Missouri had intervened, arguing that the family had not provided sufficient evidence that Ms. Cruzan would have wanted this termination. Ultimately, however, the family prevailed.

The *Cruzan* case is important because it created new law. The Supreme Court's decision in this case established that the Constitution's due process clause, which states, "No state shall make or enforce any law which shall abridge the privileges or immunities of citizens of the United States; nor shall any state deprive any person of life, liberty, or property, without due process of law," protected the right to discontinue food and hydration. This right was assumed in the *Schiavo* case. The courts were not trying to puzzle out whether Terri Schiavo had the right to discontinue food and hydration, since *Cruzan* had already established this right. Instead, the judicial deliberations focused solely on whether this was a choice that Terri herself would have made if she had been competent.[9] The court decision that established the right to discontinue food and hydration is now part of U.S. common law.

HISTORICAL BASIS OF COMMON LAW   England began using the common law as a means of unifying the country in the 1100s, when local courts began to write down this national, or "common," law to make it easy to use. Nobles soon realized that the law might be applied to limiting the power of the king and could protect them against unfair and arbitrary actions by the monarchy. Most significant in the creation of common law was the Magna Carta ("Great Charter") of 1215, the first document to list the rights and protections granted to individuals in England. The Magna Carta is one of the core documents in the evolution of constitutional law.

In the common-law system, the jury provides a key check on the powers of the government. The English colonists of North America and later the framers of the Constitution embraced the right to a jury trial. This right rests on the belief that a jury of one's peers is best able to place itself in the shoes of the accused and to make a determination about whether a wrong has been committed. Serving on a jury, like voting in an election or volunteering for an interest group, is an important form of citizen engagement.

THE PRINCIPLE OF *STARE DECISIS* In the evolution of the American judicial system, the colonists relied on the principle of *stare decisis,* a Latin phrase that means "let the decision stand." ***Stare decisis*** means that in deciding cases, judges must abide by the legal **precedent,** that is, the legal authority that earlier cases established, even in the instance of laws handed down hundreds of years before and in a society that was far different. The principle of *stare decisis* ensures that common law is not very quick to change. *Stare decisis* also ensures a consistency of legal expectations for individuals and the legal community. Common law was the predominant form of law in the United States in the nineteenth century.

stare decisis
from the Latin "let the decision stand," the principle that binds judges to rely upon the holdings of past judges in deciding cases

precedent
legal authority established by earlier cases

Code Law

By the early twentieth century, rapid changes in society and the economy demanded much faster responses in the law than what common law could provide. Legislators in Congress and the states responded to those changes by creating laws to regulate the behavior of individuals and organizations and to deal with a vast array of new issues. The kind of law they developed is known as **code law.** Code law differs from common law in that it traditionally is formulated by legislators through statutes, whereas common law is created through judicial decisions.

code law
laws created by legislators to regulate the behavior of individuals and organizations

A similar, continuously changing social environment prevails today. Because of the steady flow of change and the fast pace of contemporary life, particularly due to nonstop technological advances, the prior body of law has become inadequate to deal with unprecedented developments in commerce, communication, and even crime. In creating code law responsive to these new realities, legislators have had to become more knowledgeable and specialized about the topics of the laws they write. They have had to rely heavily on experts—police attempting to enforce laws; business and industry leaders; other specialists—to help shape how laws are written. Code law functions very differently from common law. When legislatures or executives make law, they can move quickly in response to some pressing crisis or problem. They can decide to change course and even take a totally unprecedented approach to a situation.

Sources of U.S. Law

We have seen that code law and common law coexist in the United States and that judges, legislators, and presidents all contribute to lawmaking. What's more, these officials often cooperate in the lawmaking enterprise, interacting to clarify ambiguous provisions in the code law or to apply the common law to more specific situations. These lawmakers collectively create law that is distinct, but they do so in different ways, as we consider in this discussion.

In this section, we examine the five sources of laws in the United States:

- the U.S. and state constitutions
- statutes
- judicial decisions
- executive orders
- administrative and regulatory law

These sources differ not only in who makes the law but also in their place in the hierarchy of the U.S. legal system. Moreover, lawmakers create law not only at the national level but in all fifty state governments as well.

The Federal and State Constitutions

Atop the hierarchy of the sources of U.S. law are constitutions—the U.S. Constitution and the constitutions of the fifty states. Constitutions are the highest form of law, taking precedence over all other laws, and they are the primary organizational blueprint for the federal and state governments. Constitutions delineate the powers of the government and the limitations on those powers. They also establish the structure and the function of each of the branches—executive, legislative, and judicial—and define the relationship between the federal and state governments and between the government and the individual.

The body of law that comes out of the courts in cases involving constitutional interpretation is known as **constitutional law.** In cases concerning a provision of the federal Constitution, the high court is the U.S. Supreme Court, and its decisions bind all Americans, including Congress and the president.

If the president or the members of Congress do not like the outcome of a particular case, they may test the Supreme Court's ruling by passing a law challenging the decision. (In the instance of state high court cases, a governor or the state legislature can take a similar action.) Legislatures and executives also may try to circumvent a Court decision by changing the law through a constitutional amendment. For example, since 1963, some members of Congress have sought to blunt the impact of a series of Supreme Court decisions establishing that prayer in public schools violates the Constitution's separation of church and state. These legislators have introduced into the House and the Senate various constitutional amendments that would allow vocal prayer or mandate a "moment of silence" in public schools. None of these proposed amendments has garnered the two-thirds supermajority vote in Congress necessary to move the amendment to the next stage in the ratification process. Yet some representatives in Congress continue to seek to negate the Court's decision by amending the Constitution.

Statutes

Laws written by legislatures are called **statutes.** Statutory lawmaking is the hallmark of any code-law system. In such a system, legislative law reflects the core principles of the government system. For example, the **U.S. Code** is a compilation of all the laws ever passed by the U.S. Congress, and it reflects that body's priorities and concerns. The U.S. Code has fifty sections spanning a range of issues including agriculture, bankruptcy, highways, the postal service, and war and defense.

Judicial Decisions

When a judge or a panel of judges decides a case, they sometimes write an opinion that justifies their decision and explains how they have applied principles of *stare decisis.* These judicial opinions then become part of the common law.

Under what circumstances do judges write an opinion? To answer that question, we must consider the resources for appealing cases on the federal and state levels. The federal court system comprises two levels of appeals, or appellate, court: the circuit courts of appeals, previously described, and the U.S. Supreme Court, which has the final say in cases. The state systems generally feature two appeals levels, and the final appellate court is the court of last resort, performing much the same function as the U.S. Supreme Court.[10] Judges serving in *courts of last resort*—that is, the U.S. Supreme Court and the state high courts—almost always write opinions in cases, and those opinions have the force of law. The Supreme Court's decisions govern all similar cases heard in all the federal courts and become the law of the land; a state high court's decisions become law in that state.

Executive Orders

Article II, Section 1, of the U.S. Constitution states that "the executive power shall be vested in [the] president of the United States." This power has been interpreted to allow the president to issue orders that create and guide the bureaucracy in implementing policy. Because executive orders have the force and effect of law, they represent a crucial tool in the president's lawmaking toolbox. Historically, presidents have sometimes used executive orders to create policy that may not have garnered sufficient legislative support. For example, Chapter 12 describes President Harry Truman's use of executive orders to desegregate the military in 1948.

constitutional law
the body of law that comes out of the courts in cases involving the interpretation of the Constitution

statute
a law enacted by Congress or by state legislatures to deal with particular issues or problems, sometimes more detailed and comprehensive than the common law

U.S. Code
a compilation of all the laws passed by the U.S. Congress

Glossary terms

dual court system
a two-part judicial system such as that of the United States, which has both federal and state courts

trial court
the court in which a case is first heard and which determines the facts of a case

jurisdiction
the power of a court to hear a case and to resolve it, given to a court by either a constitution or a statute

federal question
a question of law based on interpretation of the U.S. Constitution, federal laws, or treaties

diversity of citizenship
the circumstance in which the parties in a legal case are from different states or the case involves a U.S. citizen and a foreign government

A president or a governor can enact an executive order without input from the other branches of government, though executive orders are subject to judicial review and depend on Congress for funding. As described in Chapter 12, President Bush used executive orders extensively to address a wide range of issues. These included prohibiting new investment in Burma to punish that nation's repressive regime and improving the coordination and effectiveness of bureaucracies administering youth programs in the United States.[11]

Administrative Law

In addition to the executive order, presidents and governors have another source of lawmaking power: they head a vast bureaucracy of agencies that have their own lawmaking authority. As we saw in Chapter 13, bureaucrats get their power directly from the Congress or the state legislatures. By delegating significant power to bureaucratic administrators with expertise in specific policy areas, Congress and the state legislatures help to ensure the effective implementation of the laws they pass.

Why, specifically, must legislators delegate such power? The reason is that lawmakers typically write vague or ambiguous bills. They do so to increase the chances that representatives and senators with differing ideologies will find a given bill acceptable for passage into law. But the result of vague or ambiguous wording might be that the law, once passed, is difficult to implement. Thus legislators must turn to bureaucrats with expertise and specialized knowledge to help them to administer the law.

This delegation of authority gives administrators substantial power. It allows them to act as quasi- ("as if") legislators in creating administrative rules, implementing them, and interpreting those rules as well. Administrative rule making fleshes out the broad principles in the statutory law, much of which is interpreted by the federal courts.

The Federal Court System

Article III of the Constitution created only one court—the Supreme Court—and left it to Congress to create any additional federal courts that the country might need. As we saw earlier in this chapter, Congress responded with a series of laws that created inferior (or lower) courts in the form of federal district courts and federal appellate courts (or courts of appeals).

In addition to these constitutionally and legislatively created courts, each state has its own independent state court system structured by state constitutions. Because the U.S. judicial system has both federal and state courts, it is said to be a **dual court system.** Figure 14.1 shows that nearly every case, whether tried in a federal or a state court, originates in a **trial court**—the court in which a case is first heard and which determines the facts of a case.[12]

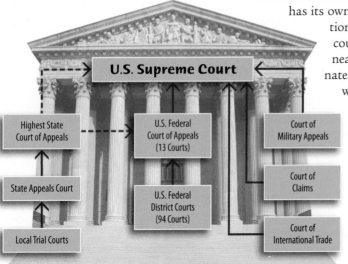

FIGURE 14.1

The U.S. Court System

U.S. Supreme Court

Highest State Court of Appeals

State Appeals Court

Local Trial Courts

U.S. Federal Court of Appeals (13 Courts)

U.S. Federal District Courts (94 Courts)

Court of Military Appeals

Court of Claims

Court of International Trade

Jurisdiction of Federal Courts

The ability of a court to hear a case depends on whether that court has **jurisdiction**—the authority of a court to hear and decide a case. Federal jurisdiction is strictly defined by Article III, Section 2, of the Constitution. In this passage, federal courts are empowered to hear only cases involving a federal question or a diversity of citizenship. A **federal question** is a question of law based on interpretation of the U.S. Constitution, federal laws, or treaties. **Diversity of citizenship** means that the parties in the case are individuals from different states or that the case involves a U.S. citizen and a foreign government. It may also mean that the suit centers on the complaint of one or more states against another state or states.

When a court has **original jurisdiction** over a case, that court is the first court to hear the case—no other court has yet considered the legal issues in this case. In instances of original jurisdiction, the court must decide what happened in the case and must apply the existing law to resolve the dispute. In contrast, **appellate jurisdiction** empowers a court to review the decision of the court that has already heard a case. Usually, the appellate court is called upon to decide not what happened but, rather, whether the first court correctly applied or interpreted the law.

In the federal courts, the federal district courts have original jurisdiction in most cases. The U.S. courts of appeals handle first-level appeals of decisions made in those federal district courts. Most cases that reach the Supreme Court come to it under its appellate jurisdiction.

The Structure of the Federal Courts

The U.S. court system is a dual system in two ways. First, as noted above, parallel federal and state court systems operate largely independently of each other and make law in specific areas. Second, each of these systems has both trial courts and appellate courts. In the brief discussions that follow, we consider the different kinds of courts in the federal system.

FEDERAL DISTRICT COURTS The federal judiciary is structured hierarchically, similar to a pyramid. There are ninety-four federal district courts at the bottom of this pyramid. These are the trial courts in this system, and they do much of the work of the federal judiciary. The function of trial courts is straightforward: judges or juries decide what happened in a case and then apply the law. For example, in a terrorism case, the judge or the jury assesses whether the defendant is guilty of committing acts of terror as defined by federal law. If the defendant is found guilty, the court then looks to the law to impose a penalty. Federal district courts operate throughout the United States; every state must have at least one.

U.S. COURTS OF APPEALS At the middle level of the federal judicial pyramid are thirteen courts of appeals. As Figure 14.2 on page 440 shows, twelve of these courts cover specific regions (circuits) plus the Federal Circuit located in the District of Columbia. The thirteenth court of appeals covers specific kinds of cases, involving such matters as international trade, government contracts, and patents. Congress has authorized 179 judgeships for these courts of appeals, though typically there are vacancies.

The size of each circuit varies depending on the size of the court's constituency and its caseload. Today, the smallest circuit is the First Circuit, which consists of six judgeships; the largest, the Ninth, has twenty-eight.[13] Each circuit court of appeals is supervised by a chief judge. The chief judge is the individual on the bench who has the most seniority but is under age 65. The judges who hear a case typically include a three-judge panel made up of the courts of appeals judges. They are sometimes joined by visiting judges (usually from the corresponding federal district of the court of appeals) and retired judges. In deciding cases, the judges read briefs submitted by lawyers, which argue their clients' case, and then may hear oral arguments. During this process, no new facts are admitted into evidence; instead, the court of appeals focuses on questions of procedure or the application of law that occurred in a decision of the lower court.

The Judiciary Act of 1891 carved out only nine geographic units for the courts of appeals. The increased number of circuit courts to the thirteen of the present day (see Figure 14.2) occurred through a process by which Congress split up existing circuits. Each new division has typically reflected Congress's desire to keep together states with similar legal and political cultures.

Courts of appeals have no original jurisdiction—that is, these courts do not decide the facts of a case. Rather, as appellate courts, they review the legal procedures of a preceding case and decide whether the law was applied appropriately given the facts already admitted into evidence. Courts of appeals are the courts of last resort for most federal cases,

original jurisdiction
the power of a court to hear a case first, before other courts have decided it

appellate jurisdiction
the authority of a court to review the the application or interpretation of the law in previous decisions reached by another court in a case

The Federal Circuit Courts of Appeals

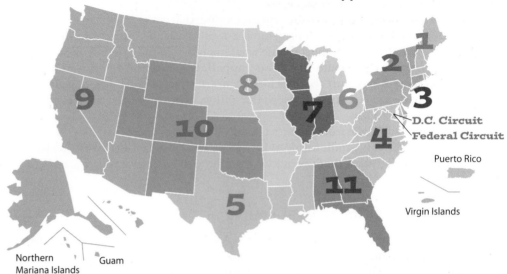

FIGURE 14.2 ▇ How many U.S. circuit courts of appeals are there today? What are the circuits (regions) they cover, and what determines the size of each circuit? What kinds of cases does an additional, special court of appeals (not shown in the map) cover?

because after a case has been decided by the appellate court, there is no automatic right to an appeal. Although some cases may be appealed to the U.S. Supreme Court, the Court ultimately chooses to hear only a small fraction of those.

SPECIAL COURTS In addition to the federal district courts and the courts of appeals, Congress, acting under Article I of the Constitution, created several specialized courts. These include the Court of International Trade, the U.S. Court of Military Appeals, the U.S. Tax Court, and the U.S. Court of Veterans' Appeals.

In recent years, media coverage has highlighted the activities of another kind of specialized court, the Foreign Intelligence Surveillance Act (FISA) court. It was established by Congress in a 1978 act that spells out the procedures for the collection of human and electronic intelligence.[14] During the George W. Bush administration, FISA courts were charged with determining whether an individual could be subject to warrantless surveillance of his or her communications (see Chapter 4).

FISA courts are evidence of a notable trend in how the judicial branch is coping with the growing complexity of the types of cases that come before the courts. This trend involves increasing specialization, both by law, as in the creation of special courts such as FISA courts, and by practice, as when judges develop an "informal" expertise in a policy area—say, DNA testing or software patent law. Legal scholar Lawrence Baum assesses this trend as an effort by the courts to gain and apply the kind of expertise characteristic of the administrative agencies of the government:

> Whether judicial specialization is established by law or develops in practice, it reflects an effort to gain the perceived strengths of administrative agencies while retaining the form and name of the courts. The efficiency and expertise that are ascribed to specialization can help courts keep up with their caseloads and perhaps improve the quality of decision-making.[15]

Although this specialization may occur in both state and federal courts, it is not possible for the highest court in the land, the U.S. Supreme Court, to limit its expertise.

THE U.S. SUPREME COURT WITHIN THE FEDERAL SYSTEM At the top of the federal judicial pyramid sits the U.S. Supreme Court. Although this court has a very limited original jurisdiction (which we examine later in this chapter), it hears appeals from both the federal and the state courts when cases decided there concern a federal constitutional question or when federal law is involved.

Nine judges, called **justices,** sit on the Supreme Court. One of these justices has been specially selected by the president to serve as the **chief justice,** the judge who provides both organizational and intellectual leadership on the Court. The chief justice has the same voting power as the other justices, called the associate justices. But he or she has an important, distinctive role in the decision-making process. When the chief justice agrees with the majority, he or she chooses whether to write the majority opinion or assign it to another justice. The current chief justice is John Roberts, whom President George W. Bush appointed in 2005.

Selecting Judges for the Federal Bench

In both 2009 and 2010, President Barack Obama faced one of the most important decisions of his presidency, a decision that would have implications for policy decades after his presidency had ended. In May 2009, Obama announced Sonia Sotomayor as his nominee for the seat that had been occcupied by Supreme Court Justice David Souter, who had retired at the end of the Court's 2008–2009 term. The following year, he selected Elena Kagan as his nominee to replace retiring Associate Justice John Paul Stevens. Obama's selections of Sotomayor and Kagan illustrate the differing characteristics presidents might emphasize when selecting judges for the federal bench.

In selecting Sonia Sotomayor, who had sat on the second circuit of the U.S. Court of Appeals since 1998, Obama sought a competent individual who would win Senate confirmation. Obama also wanted to make his mark on a Supreme Court whose ideology has been greatly shaped by the appointments of his predecessor, President George W. Bush, who had appointed two conservatives—Chief Justice John Roberts and Associate Justice Samuel Alito—to the Court. Finally, following his election, President Obama had been pressured by both Latino constituents and interest groups to appoint the Court's first Latino member.

Obama's selection of Kagan was perhaps more surprising. Kagan, who served as the Dean of the Harvard Law School, had never served as a judge. Though there was precedent for nonjudges being appointed to the Court, that career path was not the usual one. But in Kagan, many analysts believe that Obama saw traits that far outweighed her lack of experience on the bench. Throughout her career, Kagan had gained a reputation as a conciliator—a peacemaker who could bring divergent ideological sides together, a characteristic that could prove important given the often divided nature of the Court. In addition to her impeccable

Changing Caseloads: Fraud on the Internet

	THEN (2001)*	NOW (2009)**
Number of complaints processed by the federal government's Internet Fraud Complaint Center and referred to law enforcement agencies	16,775	275,284
Cumulative losses by victims of cybercrimes whose cases were processed by the federal government's Internet Fraud Complaint Center	$17.8 million	$265 million
Top three reported offenses	Internet auction fraud (43%) Nondelivery of merchandise and payment (20%) Nigerian letter fraud (10%)	Nondelivery of merchandise and/or payment (33%) Internet auction fraud (25%) Credit/debit card fraud (9%)

WHAT'S NEXT?

> Have you been, or do you know anyone who has been, a victim of Internet fraud?

> Will cyberfraud continue to grow, in keeping with the present trend? What will be the impact of any growth on the court system?

> What new forms might Internet crime take in the future?

* www.ic3.gov/media/annualreport/2001_IFCCReport.pdf.
** www.ic3.gov/media/2009/090331.aspx.

justice
any of the nine judges who sit on the Supreme Court

chief justice
the leading justice on the Supreme Court, who provides both organizational and intellectual leadership

> With her mother holding the Bible and her brother looking on, Sonia Sotomayor is sworn in by Chief Justice John Roberts. President Obama's 2009 appointee to the Supreme Court was the Court's first Latino member.

academic credentials, because she had not served as a judge, Kagan was not saddled with an enormous record of judicial opinions that could have been used against her during the confirmation process. Kagan is the fourth woman to serve on the Court (three women sit today, and Associate Justice Sandra Day O'Connor retired from the bench in 2006), the first member in forty years appointed without a judicial background (the last being the late Chief Justice William Rehnquist). Kagan is the eighth Jewish person to serve on the Court, which currently has three Jewish members. The criteria important for Obama's selections are typical for presidents faced with the nomination of a member of the U.S. Supreme Court.

Once Supreme Court and other federal court judges are confirmed by the Senate, they serve for life, as long as they do not commit any impeachable offense. While lifetime tenure is controversial (see "Thinking Critically About Democracy"), it also means that such appointees often are the longest-lasting legacies of the presidents who appoint them. Chief Justice John Roberts, who was appointed to the Court at age 50, and Associate Justices Sonia Sotomayor and Elena Kagan, who were 55 and 50, respectively, when appointed, will each likely serve on the Court for about thirty years.

The Senate's Role in Appointment and Confirmation

The president and the Senate share power in the selection of federal court judges and Supreme Court justices. In this way, the nomination and confirmation process serves as a check on the respective powers of the presidency and the Senate.

senatorial courtesy

A custom that allows senators from the president's political party to veto the president's choice of federal district court judge in the senator's state

In the case of the federal district court judges, a custom known as **senatorial courtesy** gives senators—though only those who are of the same political party as the president—a powerful voice in choosing the district court judges who will serve in their state. Under this tradition, a senator from the same political party as the president can block the president's choice of a federal district court judge in the senator's state.

Because circuit courts of appeals judges and Supreme Court justices serve more than one state, the individual senators from any one state play a far less powerful role in the appointment of these judges than they do in the selection of district court judges. Rather, in the selection procedure for circuit court judges and U.S. Supreme Court justices, the Senate Judiciary Committee, composed of eighteen senators, takes the lead. Committee members are charged with gathering information about each nominee and providing it to the full Senate. The Senate Judiciary Committee also typically votes on the nominee, and the full Senate uses this vote to signal whether the nominee is acceptable. Sometimes the judiciary committee does not make a recommendation about a candidate, as when members split their vote 7–7 on the nomination of Clarence Thomas to be a U.S. Supreme Court justice in 1991.

Judicial Competence

Competence is of central concern for nominees to the circuit courts of appeals and the Supreme Court. Appeals court judges and Supreme Court justices first and foremost must be qualified, and some nominees in recent decades have been rejected because of senatorial doubts about their qualifications. The Senate rejected two nominees of President Richard Nixon because of such concerns. And when President George W. Bush nominated his White House counsel Harriet Miers as an associate Supreme Court justice in 2005, he was forced to withdraw his nomination because of concerns about Miers's lack of qualifications. Those objections strongly indicated that Miers would face a steep uphill climb in achieving

SHOULD THERE BE A CONSTITUTIONAL AMENDMENT MANDATING A RETIREMENT AGE FOR SUPREME COURT JUSTICES?

The Issue: Some states require top judges to retire at age 70 or 75, but a Supreme Court justice has a lifetime tenure. Thus a Supreme Court justice can potentially serve well beyond the age at which most people retire from their professional lives. In 2006, Justice Sandra Day O'Connor stepped down from the Court at age 76. But O'Connor was an exception. Justice John Paul Stevens sat on the bench until 2010, when, at age 90, he retired. Chief Justice William Rehnquist presided until his death at age 80 in 2005. Such precedents—given the cognitive and physical problems generally associated with old age—have given rise to questions about the wisdom of allowing justices to serve on the Supreme Court for life. Some Americans believe that the country needs a constitutional amendment to mandate a specific retirement age for the justices. Others disagree, although some of these naysayers propose alternative means of ensuring judicial competence.

Should there be a constitutional amendment mandating a retirement age for Supreme Court justices? Here is what the various camps have to say.

Yes: The country needs a constitutional amendment that modifies the framers' specification of a life term for Supreme Court justices. Relevant is the work of legal scholar David J. Garrow. His research on Supreme Court justices' "mental decrepitude" has emphasized that many former Supreme Court justices themselves, including Earl Warren and Potter Stewart, did not oppose a constitutional amendment limiting tenure to age 75—*if* such an age limit were imposed on members of Congress and the president as well. Moreover, in *Gregory v. Ashcroft* (1991), which addressed the constitutionality of a mandatory retirement age of 70 for state court judges, Justice Sandra Day O'Connor opined that a mandatory retirement age of 70 could be in the public interest.*

No: A constitutional amendment requiring a mandatory retirement age for Supreme Court justices constitutes age discrimination. Such an amendment violates the framers' intentions, because the Constitution explicitly states that justices may serve for life. Through such an amendment, the United States would lose the expertise, wisdom, and perspective of older jurists. Thus the Constitution should not be amended to set a specific age for retirement from the Court.

Other approaches: A constitutional amendment that would apply across the board to all Supreme Court justices, regardless of their health status, denies citizens the invaluable experience of some older justices whose health may not be in decline. Society can address the challenge of ensuring competence on the Court by other means. For example, the ever-watchful media could publicize the behaviors of justices whose health seems to be impeding their ability to perform their duties. In addition, or alternatively, Congress could aggressively monitor the mental and physical health of Supreme Court justices by requiring the justices to provide health information to a special congressional monitoring committee.

What do you think?

① Do the potential advantages of preventing an elderly, mentally diminished Supreme Court justice from serving outweigh the benefits (wisdom, experience, and so on) that might come from the continued service of this jurist or other aging justices? Explain.

② Should the country pass a constitutional amendment setting a mandatory retirement age for Supreme Court justices? Why or why not?

③ What alternative solutions beyond those proposed here might address the problem of ensuring competence on the Court?

* *Gregory v. Ashcroft*, 501 U.S. 452 (1991).

> Born in 1920, Associate Justice John Paul Stevens retired from the U.S. Supreme Court in 2010, at age 90.

Senate confirmation. (Some in the media argued, however, that the questions about Miers's competence were in part a political smoke screen—a ploy by certain conservative Republican senators who would be voting on her nomination to reject the Republican nominee because her ideological outlook may not have been conservative enough for them.)[16]

Ideology and Selection to the Bench

Once the Senate establishes the competence of a circuit court or Supreme Court candidate, attention shifts to the nominee's ideology—his or her worldview. Mindful that federal judges typically serve far beyond their own tenure, presidents often regard these nominations as a way of cementing their own legacies. They give the nod to judges, and more significantly, to Supreme Court justices, with whom they are ideologically compatible. When President Barack Obama chose Sonia Sotomayor to serve on the Court, he chose a person who held liberal views consistent with his own. In Elena Kagan, he found a nominee who, though holding liberal views, could build bridges with the conservative members of the Court. At the same time, it appeared that Kagan was on the record as someone who "supported assertions of executive power."[17] When George W. Bush nominated John Roberts, he chose an individual who shared the president's own policy views, particularly with regard to issues such as abortion, church and state relations, and criminal due process protections.

A Supreme Court justice's (and a circuit court judge's) ideology can shift over time, however. President Richard Nixon selected Justice Harry Blackmun to serve on the Supreme Court because of Blackmun's conservative record in deciding cases involving civil rights and civil liberties. But Blackmun, who wrote the Court's opinion in *Roe v. Wade*—the decision guaranteeing a woman's right to abortion—and who was a vocal critic of capital punishment once seated on the Court, was a serious disappointment to Nixon. Still, in most instances, a justice's worldview remains fairly constant. Justices' ideologies are reinforced by the presence of stable ideological blocs on the Supreme Court, which may bolster long-held beliefs and discourage the rethinking of issues from a completely new perspective. This reality underscores why the nomination and confirmation process is so important: the president and the Senate are banking on their assumption that the nominee's demonstrated ideology or perspective will color how he or she sees issues and cases that come before the Court in the future.[18]

Representation of Demographic Groups

Faced with the prospect of appointing a successor to replace the retiring Associate Justice David Souter, President Barack Obama encountered significant pressure from constituents and from interest groups (which created expectation in the media) to appoint the first Hispanic justice to the Court. (See "Analyzing the Sources.") Obama obliged, selecting Sonia Sotomayor, who sat on the second circuit of the U.S. Court of Appeals and is of Puerto Rican descent. In selecting Sotomayor, Obama named the first Hispanic and third woman to the Court. Other presidents have faced similar expectations: when Thurgood Marshall, the Supreme Court's first African American jurist retired in 1991, political analysts and the media expected President George H. W. Bush to appoint another African American to the seat. Bush obliged and appointed Clarence Thomas to the Court. Even though the federal courts effectively underrepresent the population at large, because judges are overwhelmingly male, white, Protestant, and upper middle class, the current Supreme Court has a relatively diverse composition. In recent decades, an informal demographic composition of the Court has evolved with an African American seat (currently occupied by Associate Justice Clarence Thomas), a Jewish seat (now there are three Jewish associate justices: Stephen Breyer, Ruth Bader Ginsburg, and Elena Kagan), a Roman Catholic seat (now actually several such seats, with Chief Justice John Roberts and Associate Justices Anthony Kennedy, Antonin Scalia, Clarence Thomas, and Samuel Alito all being Catholic), a woman's seat (held exclusively for over a decade by Sandra Day O'Connor, who served on the Court from 1981 to 2006; she was joined on the Court by Ruth Bader Ginsburg in 1993; Ginsburg was joined by Sotomayor in 2009 and Kagan in 2010), and now a Hispanic seat (occupied by Sotomayor).

ANALYZING THE SOURCES

THE DEMOGRAPHIC BALANCE ON THE SUPREME COURT

> In this cartoon by Ed Fischer, a Republican senator considers the nomination of U.S. Supreme Court Justice Sonia Sotomayor while voters, representing 40 million Hispanic voters, look on.

Evaluating the Evidence

① Why would the cartoon specify that Republican legislators might be cautious in considering Hispanic voters when considering the Sotomayor nomination?

② What does the size of the Hispanic man and woman indicate about the strength of the Hispanic vote in shaping the outcome of some elections?

③ As it turned out, only 9 Republican U.S. Senators voted for Sotomayor's confirmation. Republican senators from both Texas and Arizona (where Hispanics constitute a sizeable proportion of the electorate) voted against her nomination. Among those voting for Sotomayor was Senator Mel Martinez of Florida. Do you think Hispanic voters will consider their senators' position on the Sotomayor nomination in future Senate elections? Why or why not?

The impulse to recognize specific seats that reflect major groups in the population serves the goal of **symbolic representation,** which is the representation on the Court of the country's leading demographic groups. There is an implicit assumption that a justice occupying one of these seats will best serve the concerns of the racial, ethnic, gender, or other group to which he or she belongs. That is, the Latino justice will take the perspective of Latinos, the female justice will consider the policy preferences of women, and so on. In fact, however, the representation may be more symbolic than real because the issues of importance to Latinos, women, or any other group are hardly monolithic. These issues are so multidimensional that no one person could speak for all the members' concerns. Nevertheless, many public figures and citizens say that the Court should mirror as closely as possible the main contours of the national demographic profile.

Clearly, the nomination and confirmation of federal judges does not take place in a vacuum. Beyond presidents' and senators' concerns about judicial qualifications, ideology, and demographic representation, these players are acutely aware of what their constituencies will think of any nominee and of what might happen at the confirmation hearings. For that reason, they continuously gauge public opinion throughout the nomination and confirmation process. In addition to being mindful of the voters, the president and the senators calculate how interest groups, particularly those that helped to put them in office, will view the nominee. In nominating John Roberts, George W. Bush sought to ensure that his nominee would be acceptable to one of his core constituencies, conservative voters.

symbolic representation
the attempt to ensure that the Supreme Court includes representatives of major demographic groups, such as women, African Americans, Jews, and Catholics

Interest groups often have a significant voice in the confirmation hearings. Some groups almost always participate in the hearings, among them the American Bar Association, labor and civil rights organizations, law enforcement groups, and business interests. These groups do not hesitate to let the members of the Senate Judiciary Committee know clearly whether they support or oppose a given candidate.

The U.S. Supreme Court Today

The decisions of the U.S. Supreme Court's nine justices are binding on all other courts in the country, and no other court may overturn them. Decision making on the Court is a multistep process that provides many opportunities for conflict and compromise. As a **collegial court,** which means it is made up of a panel of justices, Supreme Court justices must work closely together as they navigate the process. The need for compromise on the Court is especially intense because of the sheer number of cases it hears and the fact that its decisions are final.

collegial court
a court made up of a group of judges who must evaluate a case together and decide on the outcome; significant compromise and negotiation take place as members try to build a majority coalition

The Supreme Court's Jurisdiction

In the vast majority of cases, the Supreme Court is reviewing a decision made by a lower court rather than exercising original jurisdiction. The framers limited the Supreme Court's original jurisdiction to only those cases that concern ambassadors, public ministers, and consuls, and those involving two or more states. But over time, Congress, in cooperation with the Court, has decided that the Court should retain original jurisdiction only in cases involving suits between two or more states.

Choosing Cases for Review

Approximately 7,000 petitions are filed with the Court each year, each asking for the review of a case already decided. Each case is one that a party or parties are appealing from

> The current U.S. Supreme Court. Front from left are Associate Justices Clarence Thomas and Antonin Scalia, Chief Justice John Roberts, and Associate Justices Anthony Kennedy and Ruth Bader Ginsburg. Top from left are Associate Justices Sonia Sotomayor, Stephen Breyer, Samuel Alito, and Elena Kagan.

some other court because one or both sides dispute the decision in the case. Ultimately, the justices write decisions in only eighty to ninety cases, however. How do they decide which cases to hear? Like the other stages of the decision-making process, "deciding to decide," as Supreme Court scholar H. W. Perry puts it, is a joint activity.[19]

The decision to place a case on the Supreme Court's agenda is a collaborative one. Important in this process is the role of Supreme Court clerks. These young lawyers, who are recommended for the positions by certain "feeder professors" at selective law schools, are charged with drafting a **pool memo,** a description of the facts of the case, the pertinent legal arguments, and a recommendation as to whether the case should be taken.

The chief justice distributes a list of selected cases, the **discuss list,** to the other justices before a regularly scheduled conference. A chief justice's decision as to whether to include a given case on the discuss list is based primarily on review of the Supreme Court clerks' pool memos. On Fridays throughout the Court's term, which lasts from October to June, the justices meet in conference to discuss the cases on the list.[20] At this point, they vote on whether to issue a writ of *certiorari*—a Latin term roughly translated as "a request to make certain"—for specific cases. The **writ of *certiorari*** is a higher court's order to a lower court to make available the records of a past case so that the higher court can determine whether mistakes were made during the lower-court trial that would justify a review of the case.[21] The writ of *certiorari* falls within the Court's discretionary jurisdiction, meaning that the Court can choose whether to hear such cases (unlike those cases that have a mandatory appeal to the U.S. Supreme Court).

Cases on the U.S. Supreme Court's docket

Original jurisdiction

Applications for review by appeal or writ of *certiorari* from federal and state courts (justices use Rule of Four to determine docket)

1 Briefs submitted by both sides; amicus curiae briefs filed by interested parties

2 Oral arguments presented by attorneys for each side

3 Justices' conference: cases discussed; nonbinding votes taken; opinion writing assigned

4 Justices' opinions drafted and circulated for comment

5 Court's final decision announced

FIGURE 14.3

Decision Making on the Supreme Court

The justices determine whether they will consider a case according to a practice known as the **Rule of Four,** under which the justices will hear a case if four or more of nine justices decide they want to hear it. They do not need to give reasons for wanting or not wanting to hear a case—they simply must vote. The vast majority of the cases the Court hears reach the justices through a writ of *certiorari*, reflecting its role as primarily an appellate court.

On the Docket: Considering the Case

When a case makes its way onto the Court docket, the parties in the litigation shift into high gear (see Figure 14.3). The petitioner (the party that sought the Court's review in the first place) usually has forty-five days to file a written **brief**—a document detailing the legal argument for the desired outcome—with the Court. After the filing of this brief, the opposing party (the respondent) has thirty days to file its own brief with the Court.

Today, *amicus curiae* briefs are a common part of Supreme Court litigation. Filed within a specified time period by a person or group that is not party to the lawsuit, an ***amicus curiae* brief,** or **"friend of the court" brief,** is a document that aims to influence the Court's decision. Some cases trigger the filing of many *amicus* briefs; the largest number of such briefs (ninety) ever filed in a Supreme Court case came in two cases involving affirmative action at the University of Michigan.[22]

Amicus curiae briefs seek to provide information that jurists need to resolve cases and can be very influential. In the University of Michigan cases, a wide variety of interested parties, ranging from the MTV network to the Law School Admissions Council, filed

pool memo
description written by Court clerks of the facts of a case filed with the Court, the pertinent legal arguments, and a recommendation as to whether the case should be taken

discuss list
compiled by the chief justice, the list of cases on review that he thinks may be appropriate for the Court to hear

writ of *certiorari*
Latin for "a request to make certain"; this is an order to a lower court to produce a certified record of a case so that the appellate court can determine whether any errors occurred during trial that warrant review of the case

Rule of Four
practice by which the Supreme Court justices determine if they will hear a case if four or more justices want to hear it

brief
a document detailing the legal argument for the desired outcome in a court case

***amicus curiae* brief ("friend of the court" brief)**
document submitted by parties interested in a certain case or issue in an attempt to provide the Court with information that may be used to decide the case

briefs describing their views on how racial equality has been and can be achieved in various settings. Judges often use the information or the legal arguments contained in *amicus curiae* briefs to decide cases.[23] The use of these briefs democratizes the judicial system by opening it up to lobbying that is similar to lobbying in the other branches of government. And the participation of interest groups and other organized interests in the judicial decision-making process provides an avenue for citizen engagement and civic discourse.[24] But the playing field for these groups is not level: like lobbyists in the other branches of government, some groups are more influential than others. Elite interest groups, benefiting from members' influence and richer resources, are likelier to have their views heard in a court case than groups with less privileged members.[25]

oral arguments
the stage when appeals court judges or Supreme Court justices meet with the petitioner and the respondent to ask questions about the legal interpretations or information contained in their briefs

In docketing a case, the clerk of the court selects a date for **oral arguments**—attorneys' formal spoken arguments that lay out why the Court should rule in their client's favor. Heard in the Supreme Court's public gallery, oral arguments give the justices the opportunity to ask the parties and their lawyers specific questions about the arguments in their briefs. In typical cases, each side's lawyers have thirty minutes to make a statement to the Court and to answer the justices' questions. Although the public gallery is very grand, and the mood is often somber and formal, the justices can sometimes be less than polite toward one another and the lawyers during the oral arguments. The justices frequently interrupt the attorneys during their opening statements and responses to questions and sometimes seem to ignore the lawyers entirely, instead talking with one another. This discourse takes place entirely within public view, and transcripts (and sometimes even tapes) are readily available to the public.

Meeting in Conference: The Deliberative Stage

After the justices have listened to the oral arguments in the case, they meet in conference to deliberate. At this point, each justice will signal his or her likely vote on the case and discuss the legal issues in play. We have few clues as to how the justices interact in conference, because those proceedings are entirely closed to the public. The late chief justice William Rehnquist once described conferences in which the most junior associate justice was seated closest to the door and was charged with answering any knocks on the door that might come about during deliberation.[26] But other than the anecdotal descriptions we have from justices, once a case enters this phase, it is in a kind of black box. We can only guess about how the justices deliberate and make their decisions, because there is no public record of the proceedings.

We do know that the justices must work together at the deliberation stage if they hope to reach a decision that a majority of them will sign. Because cases are decided by majority rule, there is a strong incentive to cooperate. The chief justice plays a vital role in this process. After the likely votes of the other justices are tallied in the conference, the chief justice decides whether he is with the majority. If he is, he chooses whether he wants to write the majority opinion. If he declines, he can assign the task to one of the other justices in the likely majority. If the chief justice is not with the majority, the senior member of this majority decides whether to write the opinion or assign the opinion to another justice. By the time the justices have finished with the conference, they will have already read the briefs in the case, heard the oral arguments, and listened to one another's views. In assigning the majority opinion, the senior member is effectively giving a stamp of approval to the view of the case that either he or she or some other member of the Court has articulated.

The assignment of the opinion is a crucial stage. The justice who writes the opinion must consider the positions of the other justices, especially those who are likely to vote with him or her in the majority. No justice who is assigned with writing the majority opinion can afford to ignore the policy views of the other justices. At the opinion-writing stage, the justices must cooperate and try to hammer out a decision that at least five of them will agree to. Their discussion about the case often centers on the legal arguments that the parties have advanced or on the underlying factual issues.

Deciding How to Vote: Voting Blocs on the Court

How does each justice decide how to vote in a particular case? Frequently, the justices vote in blocs—those with similar views tend to vote together, especially in similar cases. By the late 1990s and early 2000s, Supreme Court watchers could predict with a great deal of certainty how specific justices would line up to vote in cases involving abortion restrictions, for example.

These voting blocs work as a kind of shorthand for the justices, who often look to other, like-minded justices to decide how they should vote in certain cases.[27] In cases involving broad areas of the law, such as civil rights and civil liberties, and in cases concerned with the separation of powers, the justices are remarkably predictable.[28] Their decision making follows patterns, with many justices voting together term after term. For example, in case after case brought before the Rehnquist Court (from 1986 to 2005, when William Rehnquist was chief justice), four of the nine justices lined up on each side and Justice Sandra Day O'Connor cast the swing vote that determined the outcome in those closely divided cases.[29]

In terms of political stance, we tend to talk about the justices as either conservative or liberal, with conservative justices tending to favor the state and state interests in cases involving civil liberties or civil rights, and liberal justices tending to favor the individual in these cases. The justices are arrayed in groups on a kind of spectrum, and Justice O'Connor occupied the central position for many years. Because the Court was so closely divided, she exercised significant power in the decision-making process.

Writing the Opinion

At the opinion-writing stage, give-and-take comes into play among the justices, especially if the case is particularly close so that the justice writing the majority opinion must lock in all the available votes. This is an important consideration because at this point the justices are still free to change their minds about how they will vote or whose opinion they will join.[30] Although there are no records of the justices' deliberations, it is likely that the first draft of most majority opinions is modified to reflect the desires of at least some of the justices who agree to sign it.

There are significant incentives for the author of the draft opinion to take into account the perspectives not only of the justices who agree with his or her conclusions but also of those who disagree. The reason is that the majority draft may not be the only draft circulating among the justices. When the justices disagree about a decision, it is likely that other drafts also circulate. Some of these drafts may become concurring opinions; others may become dissenting opinions. **Concurring opinions** agree with how the majority opinion decides the case but disagree with at least some of the legal arguments or conclusions reached in this majority opinion. **Dissenting opinions** not only disagree with these arguments and conclusions but also reject the underlying decision in the case.[31]

As drafts of the majority, concurring, and dissenting opinions circulate, the justices continue to gauge the level of support for each. It does not appear to be unusual for majority opinions to become concurring opinions and vice versa. Again, the ability of the justices to persuade their colleagues on the Court is the primary indicator of which opinion will prevail as the majority decision.

After the opinions are written and signed off on, the Court announces the decision by publishing it. On rare occasions, the justices read their majority opinions, and sometimes their concurring and dissenting opinions, from the bench.

The Supreme Court Today: The Roberts Court

Many legal scholars say the Roberts Court, particularly in the absence of the strong moderate voice of Sandra Day O'Connor and with the addition of the conservative Alito, has been tilting more conservatively than the Rehnquist Court, in which O'Connor played the pivotal balancing role.[32] But President Obama's 2009 appointment of Sonia Sotomayor, considered more liberal than the justices appointed by President George W. Bush, seems to have altered public opinion concerning the Supreme Court's ideology. Figure 14.4 (on page 450) shows the shifts in public opinion that have accompanied these changes in the composition of the court.

Today, half of all Americans consider the ideology of the Court "about right," while an increasing number (from 21 to 28 percent between 2008 and 2009) believe the Court is too

concurring opinion
judicial opinion agreeing with how the majority decides the case but disagreeing with at least some of the legal interpretations or conclusions reached by the majority

dissenting opinion
judicial opinion disagreeing both with the majority's disposition of a case and with their legal interpretations and conclusions

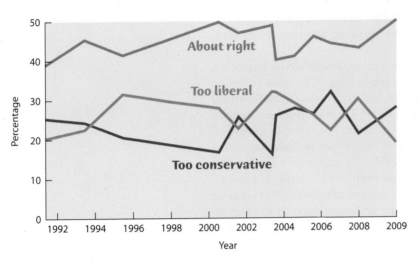

FIGURE 14.4

Citizens' Views on Supreme Court Ideology

SOURCE: Gallup News Service, www.gallup.com/poll/4732/Supreme-Court.aspx.

conservative. Paralleling this trend is a decreasing percentage (30 to 19 percent) who believe the Court is too liberal.[33] Despite the evidence that increasing numbers of Americans believe the Court is too liberal, the short track record established by the Roberts Court thus far indicates that the outcome of many cases undertaken by the Court have had a decidedly conservative flavor; for example, the 2007 decision regarding affirmative action in which the Court ruled that judicial decisions concerning the use of racial criteria in higher education do not apply to public high school admission policies.[34] This decision illuminates a distinct trend of the Court today: the justices' willingness to limit the authority of the states and the other branches of government. In another example, the Roberts Court weakened a key provision of a landmark campaign finance law, the Bipartisan Campaign Finance Reform Act of 2002, by loosening restrictions on campaign television ads. The Court's recent conservatism is also evident in a case in which the justices upheld a federal ban on partial birth abortion, a procedure in which labor is induced and suction is used to remove a fetus.[35]

Many other important cases that the Roberts Court has chosen to hear deal with the balance of power between individuals and government, often reaching a conservative decision by a slim (5–4) margin. Though not divisive, one important case involved a 13-year-old suing her school district after being strip-searched when school officials suspected that she had provided over-the-counter ibuprofen to a classmate. In an 8–1 decision, the court ruled that although it was reasonable to search a student's backpack and outer garments, a strip search violated the student's right to privacy and was unreasonable.[36] Another more closely divided case dealt with when federal courts may act to enforce federal mandates on states. By a 5–4 decision, the Court made it easier for state schools to shed federal supervision of their English-language education program, a decision that will affect other state institutions, including prisons.[37] In another 5–4 decision, the Court dealt a blow to the criminal justice system in forty states by requiring that crime lab analysts testify in criminal proceedings, instead of allowing reports written by the analysts to substitute as evidence.[38] At the time of the ruling, laws in only ten states complied with the ruling.

Figure 14.5 shows the ideological distribution of the Supreme Court today and highlights its slight tilt toward the conservative side, with Justices Clarence Thomas, Antonin Scalia, and Samuel Alito, and Chief Justice Roberts, reflecting a conservative viewpoint and Justices Sonia Sotomayor and Ruth Bader Ginsburg taking a more liberal stance on many issues. In the center are Justice Anthony Kennedy, a moderate conservative, and Justices Stephen Breyer and Elena Kagan, moderate liberals.

Judges as Policy Makers

Courts make law—common law—by deciding cases and establishing legal principles that bind future litigants and judges. The lawmaking function of courts ensures that judges have a powerful role as public policy makers.[39] This is particularly true of judges who serve in appellate courts such as the state supreme courts, the federal circuit courts of appeals, and the U.S. Supreme Court.

Because of their policy-making role, judges participate in a larger political discourse that goes far beyond the concerns of individual litigants. As we consider in this section, judges are not free to act completely independently of the other branches of the government, but they *are* able to weigh in on some of the country's most important issues. Supreme Court Justice Antonin Scalia has colorfully described the crucial role that judges play in using the law to create policy. As Scalia sees it, the ideal judge is "one who has the intelligence to

Sotomayor   Ginsburg   Kagan   Breyer   Kennedy   Roberts   Alito   Scalia   Thomas

FIGURE 14.5 ■ **THE IDEOLOGICAL DISTRIBUTION OF THE SUPREME COURT TODAY** In what direction does today's supreme court tilt with respect to ideology? How could that slant change? Given the current presidential administration, what is the likelihood that it will?

discern the best rule of law for the case at hand and then the skill to perform the broken-field running through earlier cases that leaves him free to impose that rule: distinguishing one prior case on the left, straight-arming another on the right, high-stepping away from another precedent about to tackle him from the rear, until (bravo!) he reaches the goal—good law."[40] Most recently, the courts have been called upon to resolve issues related to the war on terror, the death penalty (see "Global Context"), the powers of the chief executive, freedom of speech, abortion, euthanasia, and affirmative action.

judicial activism
an approach to judicial decision making whereby judges apply their authority to bring about specific social goals

What does it mean to be a policy maker? Recall from Chapter 13 that policy makers are individuals who have authority to influence, or to determine, solutions—public policies—that address the issues and problems a society faces. After choosing a policy, the policy maker must stand ready to adapt it to changed situations or new challenges.

Activism Versus Restraint

When considering the courts' role as policy makers, legal analysts often categorize judges and justices as exercising either judicial activism or judicial restraint. **Judicial activism** refers to the courts' practice of applying their authority to bring about particular social goals. It reflects the notion that the role of the courts is to check the power of the federal and state executive and legislative branches when those governmental entities exceed their authority.

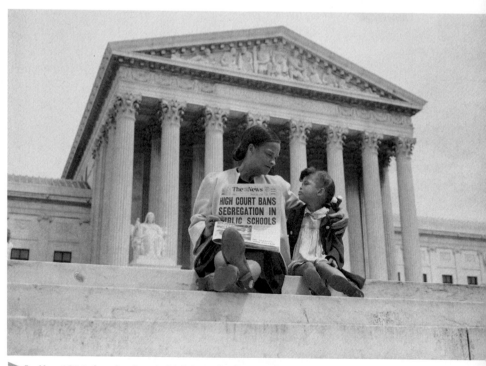

> In May 1954, in a landmark decision, the U.S. Supreme Court ruled unconstitutional segregation in American public schools.

GLOBAL CONTEXT

JUDGES AS POLICY MAKERS: THE DEATH PENALTY WORLDWIDE

The United States is the only industrialized Western democracy that executes its citizens as punishment for crimes committed. In nations where the death penalty is legal, an argument often heard in favor of the death penalty is that it deters crime. But surveys undertaken by the United Nations indicate that "it is not prudent to accept the hypothesis that capital punishment deters murder to a marginally greater extent than does the threat and application of the supposedly lesser punishment of life imprisonment."

In 2008, the executions performed in China, Iran, Saudi Arabia, the United States, Pakistan, and Iraq accounted for more than 95 percent of executions worldwide. According to Amnesty International, in 2008, nearly 2,400 people were executed in 25 countries around the world and 8,864 people were sentenced to death in 52 countries. Amnesty International reports that in 2008, executions almost doubled from 1,252 in 2007 to 2,390. As shown in the accompanying table, the United States ranks fourth, behind only China, Iran, and Saudi Arabia in the number of executions it carried out.

While several international human rights treaties—including the International Covenant on Civil and Political Rights, the American Convention on Human Rights, and the Convention on the Rights of the Child—prohibit death sentences for minors (under 18 years of age) who commit crimes, seven countries—China, the Democratic Republic of Congo, Iran, Nigeria, Pakistan, Saudi Arabia, and Yemen—execute individuals who were minors when they committed the crime for which they were sentenced to death. The U.S. Supreme Court ruled that the execution of juveniles was unconstitutional in 2005, but between 1990 and the Court's ruling, the United States executed 19 people for crimes they committed as juveniles, some of whom were still juveniles when executed.

Opponents of the death penalty mainly cite humanitarian reasons, but concerns also have emerged about the execution of innocents. Since 1973, states have released more than 107 prisoners from death row after evidence of their innocence was presented to the courts. The problem of the potential execution of innocent convicts became so acute that Illinois Governor George Ryan declared a moratorium on the implementation of the death penalty after 13 death row inmates were exonerated in that state. Currently, more than 3,300 prisoners sit on death row in the United States.

COUNTRIES WITH THE MOST CONFIRMED EXECUTIONS IN 2008

1. China (1,718)
2. Iran (346)
3. Saudi Arabia (102)
4. United States (37)
5. Pakistan (36)
6. Iraq (34)

COUNTRIES WITH A DEATH PENALTY FOR ORDINARY CRIMES

Afghanistan	Guinea	Qatar
Antigua and Barbuda	Guyana	Saint Christopher & Nevis
Bahamas	India	Saint Lucia
Bahrain	Indonesia	Saint Vincent & Grenadines
Bangladesh	Iran	Saudi Arabia
Barbados	Iraq	Sierra Leone
Belarus	Jamaica	Singapore
Belize	Japan	Somalia
Botswana	Jordan	Sudan
Burundi	Kazakstan	Syria
Cameroon	Korea (North)	Taiwan
Chad	Kuwait	Tajikistan
China	Lebanon	Thailand
Comoros	Lesotho	Trinidad and Tobago
Congo (Democratic Republic)	Libya	Uganda
Cuba	Malaysia	United Arab Emirates
Dominica	Mongolia	United States of America
Egypt	Nigeria	Viet Nam
Equatorial Guinea	Oman	Yemen
Ethiopia	Pakistan	Zimbabwe
Guatemala	Palestinian Authority	

SOURCE: Death Penalty Information Center, http://www.deathpenaltyinfo.org/death-penalty-international-perspective.

During the Warren Court (the tenure of Chief Justice Earl Warren, from 1953 to 1969), the Supreme Court took an activist stance, most notably in rejecting the constitutionality of racial segregation. By barring southern states from segregation in a variety of contexts—including schools and other public facilities—the activist Warren Court powerfully bolstered the efforts of civil rights activists. The activism of the Warren Court was also instrumental in shaping the modern rights of the accused. During Warren's tenure, the Supreme Court established *Miranda* rights for individuals accused of a crime[41] and mandated that states provide counsel to such defendants when they cannot afford an attorney.[42] The Warren Court's activism also shaped modern definitions of the privacy rights of individuals,[43] which would later form the framework for the Court's thinking about abortion rights. (See Chapter 4 for further discussion of those cases.) Supported by presidents who enforced its rulings, the Warren Court took on a leadership role in changing the nature of U.S. society.

Some judges reject the idea that the courts' role is to actively check legislative and executive authority. Noting that officials in those branches are elected to carry out the people's will, these judges observe **judicial restraint**—the limiting of their own power as judges. Practitioners of judicial restraint believe that the judiciary, as the least democratic branch of government, should not check the power of the democratically elected executive and legislative branches unless their actions clearly violate the Constitution.[44]

By tradition, judicial activism and judicial restraint are linked, respectively, with the liberal and conservative ideologies. That neat categorization, however, breaks down when one tries to apply it to recent courts. The Rehnquist Court (1986–2005) was both conservative and activist.[45] That Court chose to hear a case, *Planned Parenthood of Southeastern Pennsylvania v. Casey* (1992), that checked the authority of the state of Pennsylvania to implement a state law that limits access to abortion. In its decision, the Court laid the framework for the tightening of abortion laws in many states by clarifying what measures the states could take in restricting abortions.

judicial restraint
an approach to judicial decision making whereby judges defer to the democratically elected legislative and executive branches of government

Competing Legal Interpretations

When judges and lawyers consider a case, the common-law tradition—specifically, the principle of *stare decisis*—means that they must consider past cases with similar facts and legal questions. They must be guided by how courts in those cases have interpreted the underlying legal issues. As we have seen, the legal principles that come out of those cases constitute case law.

But even though *stare decisis* binds jurists and attorneys to prior case law, this does not mean that judges, in ruling on new cases, simply apply previous decisions to new circumstances. Rather, in interpreting the legal precedent, they typically choose among several cases related to the legal issues at stake, and their choice often determines the outcome of the present case. For that reason, law school students become skilled at identifying the line of cases that might help them to succeed in making a particular argument. They must assume, however, that the lawyer on the other side of the courtroom will also select cases that best support that attorney's chances for success.

Checks on the Courts

The U.S. judiciary is a powerful institution. It operates as the equal of the legislative and executive branches of government yet is insulated from the influence of those other institutions. Nonetheless, judges and justices face checks and constraints that limit how they decide cases, make law, and act as policy makers. Among the most important checks on the judiciary's power are the other branches of government. But the law enforcement community, lawyers, interest groups, and individual citizens also check the courts and constrain their activism, as we next consider.

The Inner Ring: Legislatures and Chief Executives

Formidable checks on the judiciary come from what some analysts call the *inner ring*—the other core institutions of the government, namely, the legislative and executive branches.

> Congress and the president can check the courts' power of judicial review by enacting new laws. In 1976, Congress passed the Pregnancy Discrimination Act, which amended Title VII of the 1964 Civil Rights Act to state explicitly that sex discrimination encompassed pregnancy discrimination, after the Supreme Court had narrowly interpreted Title VII's bans on sex discrimination.

Article II of the Constitution explicitly gives the legislative and executive branches crucial checks on the structure of the courts. It grants Congress the power to create all federal courts other than the Supreme Court and gives both the president and the federal legislature important powers in determining who sits on all federal courts. Indeed, the procedures for choosing the judges who will serve on the federal bench afford both of these branches significant control over the judiciary. Executives check the judiciary through their appointment authority, and the legislature does so through the confirmation process.

Beyond giving the president a check on the judiciary by specifying the executive's power to appoint judges, the Constitution also empowers the chief executive to grant pardons to individuals for violations of the law. A further check on judges results from the courts' reliance on the executive branch for the enforcement of their decisions. Specifically, if presidents fail to direct the bureaucracy to carry out judicial decisions, those decisions carry little weight. Frequently, it is executive implementation that gives teeth to the judiciary's decisions.

The Constitution also creates a legislative check on the judiciary because the framers established only the Supreme Court and left it up to Congress to create the lower federal courts. In addition, Article I allows Congress to control the Supreme Court's appellate docket and even to remove whole categories of cases from the Court's consideration. Congress also can control the number of judges or justices who serve in the federal judiciary and can increase this number to get a majority of judges or justices to choose a preferred policy outcome. The two houses of Congress moreover have a central role in deciding whether to impeach federal judges. The House issues the articles of impeachment, and the Senate conducts the impeachment trial. Finally, Congress initiates the process of constitutional amendment. In fact, in several cases Congress has embarked on such amendment procedures in direct response to a Court decision with which members of Congress or their constituencies have disagreed. For example, the Twenty-Sixth Amendment, which standardized the voting age to 18 years of age, came about after the Supreme Court ruled that states could set their own age limits for state elections.[46]

Additional constitutional checks also limit the power of the judges. So although the courts can check the lawmaking power of the legislative and executive branches by exercising judicial review (which, to recap, is the courts' power to decide whether the laws passed by the other branches are constitutional), the legislature and the executive can check the courts' power of judicial review through the creation of new laws. For example, Title VII of the 1964 Civil Rights Act bars sex discrimination in employment. In decisions reached in 1974 and 1976, the Supreme Court interpreted this prohibition narrowly, concluding that Congress did not mean to bar discrimination on the basis of pregnancy when it passed Title VII. Many legislators were angered by those decisions. Consequently, in 1976, Congress passed the Pregnancy Discrimination Act, which amended Title VII to state explicitly that sex discrimination encompassed pregnancy discrimination. The Court could do nothing to respond to this new law because Congress used the law specifically to clarify the Civil Rights Act. Only if the new act had been in conflict with the Constitution could the Court have taken action.

The Gatekeepers: Participants in the Judicial Process

Participants in the judicial process—especially law enforcement officers and interest groups concerned with issues of law—also provide checks on how judges and justices decide cases, make law, and act as policy makers.

LAW ENFORCERS' CHECKS ON THE JUDICIARY   One way in which law enforcement officials check the judiciary is through the exercise of *discretion*. Every day, police officers face situations in which they must decide whether to investigate wrongdoing and whether to arrest suspects engaged in illegal acts. The use of discretion by the police and others who are in the front line of law enforcement means these citizens are effectively deciding how and whether to enforce the laws made by courts, legislatures, and chief executives.

For many years, local law enforcement agents closed their eyes to spousal abuse, for example. If they investigated domestic violence, they often treated the perpetrator much more leniently than they would have if the person had not been married to the victim. That decision to be less aggressive in enforcing the law against assault and battery in such cases made some sense, because police knew that entering a home where spousal abuse was occurring was dangerous and that the victim would be unlikely to cooperate in prosecuting his or her attacker. Police often acted on their own, disregarding what the lawmaking institutions, including the courts, required them to do. Only when victims or their families successfully sued police departments for their failure to act did agencies throughout the country begin to treat spousal abuse cases more seriously.

INTEREST GROUPS' CHECKS ON THE JUDICIARY Legal scholar Andrew Jay Koshner argues that interest groups have transformed how the judiciary operates.[47] Often, lawyers and law firms assist interest groups in bringing their concerns to the judiciary. For example, when lawyers for the National Association for the Advancement of Colored People (NAACP) hit a roadblock in their attempts to persuade state legislatures to eliminate segregation in public schools, they pressed civil rights advocacy groups to go to court. The result was the landmark Supreme Court ruling in *Brown v. Board of Education* (1954), which established that segregation in public schools violated the equal protection guarantees in the Fourteenth Amendment.[48]

Experienced and trusted interest groups also constrain the courts by providing them with essential information. Courts need such information, especially in highly complex or technical cases involving issues far outside judges' expertise. Depending on what information and arguments they provide, these groups can constrain the courts' options in a case. When a court decides, for example, to rely on information detailed in the brief of the American College of Obstetrics and Gynecology, a mainstream physicians' group, and virtually to ignore information provided by the pro-life group Physicians for Life, the court is legitimizing one group over the other and giving special access to the preferred group. This favored group's lawyers can provide information that helps them to advance their legal argument and that, in so doing, can limit the court's options and effectively constrain the judges in their decision making.

Intra-Court Constraints

Confirmed judges and justices also face powerful internal constraints on their judicial actions. For lower-court judges, the higher courts, or those courts' decisions in previous cases, impose limitations. Federal district court and appeals court judges, for example, do not diverge far from Supreme Court precedent because if they did so, they would risk having their decisions overturned.

Even the Supreme Court faces substantial constraints, some of which arise from dynamics inside the Court itself. The relationships and interactions among the justices seem to place serious restrictions on their decisions. We have seen, for example, that compromise and negotiation are a central part of the Court's decision making, particularly at the opinion-writing stage. Justices who can persuade others to sign their opinions exercise significant power. This power takes a different form than it does in the other branches. Whereas in the executive and legislative branches the players exercise the power of the purse and engage in overt forms of vote trading, in the judiciary this power is based on legal reasoning and persuasion.

The Outer Ring: The Users

In addition to these various other influences on the courts, an "outer ring" of *users*—the people whom a law directly affects—can considerably constrain the actions of judges. In the many cases where these users are the general public, the courts must consider how this public will receive their decisions and interpretations.

Indeed, public opinion seems to have a distinct impact on what the courts do, especially appellate courts such as the U.S. Supreme Court. The Court rarely issues a decision that is completely out of step with the thinking of the majority of the population. This trend is confirmed by the comparatively high levels of approval of the Court among Americans, illustrated in Figure 14.6 on page 456. In fact, most cases seem to follow public opinion. When

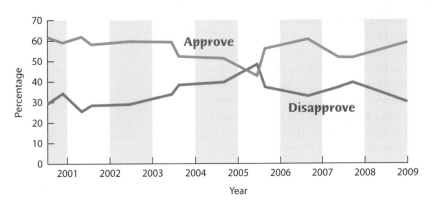

FIGURE 14.6

The Supreme Court's high approval ratings indicate that while the Constitution may be the foremost determinant of Court decisions, often these decisions reflect public opinion.

SOURCE: Gallup News Service, June 19, 2009.

> In the many capital punishment cases decided since *Gregg v. Georgia* (1976), the justices have upheld capital punishment in general but have barred states from imposing it on juveniles and people with mental disabilities, using public opinion polls to justify their rulings. The lethal injection death chamber in the prison in Huntsville, Texas, shown here, is one of the most active in the nation.

the Court does break with public opinion, as it has in prohibiting prayer in the public schools, it opens itself up to harsh criticism by the president, Congress, interest groups, and the general public.

But sometimes in the case of a landmark decision that is out of touch with public sentiment, the Court's ruling and people's opinions align over time. This shift can occur either because later courts adjust the original, controversial decision or, less commonly, because the Supreme Court's decision changes public opinion. One example of the interplay between public opinion and judicial decisions can be seen in Court rulings concerning the death penalty. In the case of *Furman v. Georgia* (1972), the Supreme Court prohibited capital punishment as it was practiced at the time, finding that it violated the Eighth Amendment prohibition against cruel and unusual punishment. The *Furman* decision evoked a public outcry that led many state legislatures to modify their laws governing capital punishment. In 1976, the Court upheld this new generation of laws in *Gregg v. Georgia,* and public opinion has continued to be central to how the Court handles cases involving capital punishment. In the many cases brought to trial since *Gregg,* the justices have used the public opinion polls to justify the Court's decision to uphold capital punishment in general but to bar states from imposing it on juveniles and people with mental disabilities.

Users can also constrain the courts by threatening to ignore their rulings. When members of the public disagree with judicial decisions, or with any law for that matter, they can engage in civil disobedience. In acts of civil disobedience, individuals or groups flout the law to make a larger point about its underlying unfairness. Keep in mind that the courts have little ability to enforce their decisions, and if people refuse to recognize those decisions and the other branches of the government fail to enforce them, the courts risk losing their authority and power. Fear of losing authority may partly explain why judicial decisions rarely fall out of step with the larger public stance on an issue. Like the inner ring and the gatekeepers, the outer ring imposes significant constraints on courts and probably limits how judges handle cases and interpret laws. These constraints may not be written into the U.S. Constitution as the checks are, but they are nonetheless very powerful and probably have a significant impact on how judges decide cases.

CONCLUSION

THINKING CRITICALLY ABOUT WHAT'S NEXT FOR THE JUDICIARY

Rooted in a common-law tradition and framed by the Constitution, the American judiciary in its early form strongly reflected its English heritage, with its emphasis on law made by judges. Over the past two-plus centuries, the judiciary has evolved powerfully to accommodate a broad spectrum of societal changes in a continuously growing country.

The judiciary has proved remarkably responsive to the sweeping societal changes that have occurred since those early beginnings. Specifically, the judicial branch has expanded to reflect both the rising population and citizens' increased use of courts to settle disputed matters. At the same time, the body of law that the courts interpret and apply has developed well beyond its common-law origins into a system based heavily on more explicit code law.

In the coming years, the judicial system will face questions that are likely to grow in number and complexity. Future courts will be challenged to interpret new laws addressing a host of thorny issues, including many currently unresolved dimensions of technology and terrorism. For example, how can the courts effectively apply laws—dealing with everything from child pornography to hate speech—given the anonymity and global reach of the Internet? How will the courts balance issues of privacy with the urgent need to provide common security? Furthermore, *entirely new* problems, arising from forces in play today and to come in the future, will require the wisdom of the best and brightest judges. Deciding cases centered on these currently unknown issues also will vitally involve the input of experts and well-informed citizens. These issues may include, for example, new legal questions emerging as a result of the tide of new immigrants, related demographic shifts, and the country's mounting energy problems.

We can anticipate how the judicial branch will meet these and other new demands by examining the strategies the courts have brought to bear in the past. We can see that the judiciary has responded to societal changes in incremental ways, through both revisions in code law and increased judicial specialization. Today, special FISA courts are determining whether the domestic wiretapping of personal communications is warranted. Perhaps it will come to pass that activist courts with expertise in the technology of terrorism will play a more central role in policy making. A key question is, will the incremental change in judicial specialization that has thus far characterized the courts be sufficient in a world that is rushing forward at so high a rate of speed? And another important question is, how will shifting Supreme Court ideology figure into the mix?

Despite the uncertainties, the courts will remain a bastion in defense of individual liberties and rights. And public opinion of the judiciary will likely continue to run high, particularly when this institution is compared with the other branches of the government.

Summary

1. The Origins of the U.S. Judiciary
The Constitution and the Judiciary Act of 1789 created a weak judiciary. The Constitution specified only the Supreme Court and left it to Congress to establish lower courts. In the landmark case *Marbury v. Madison* (1803), the Court asserted the principle of *judicial review*, which empowered the courts to check the democratically elected branches of government. The Judiciary Act of 1891 expanded the federal court system by creating federal appellate courts.

2. The Basis of U.S. Law
The American legal system has its basis in both common law and code law. Common law is created when judges reach decisions and write opinions in cases. Code law is made by the legislative and executive branches when they pass statutes or create regulations. There are advantages and disadvantages to both common law and code law. Common law has the advantage of stability over time, but it is also slow to change when social, political, or economic conditions shift. Code law has the advantage of being quickly amendable to meet the needs of a rapidly changing society, but the resulting instability can undercut well-established principles.

3. Sources of U.S. Law
There are five sources of law in the American system: the federal and state constitutions, statutes, judicial decisions, executive orders, and administrative law. Constitutions take precedence over all other laws, in that when a conflict arises between a constitutional provision and some other law, the constitutional provision prevails and the other law is struck down. Both the federal government and the fifty state governments take part in the

lawmaking enterprise. There are also fifty-one legal systems in operation: the federal court system and the systems in place in the fifty states.

4. The Federal Court System

The Constitution expressly established only the Supreme Court, and Congress created the appeals and district courts in a series of laws, beginning in 1789. The Supreme Court has almost total control over the cases it will hear, and compromise and negotiation mark deliberations among the justices. This Court is the United States' highest court, and its decisions are binding on both the lower federal courts and all the state courts.

5. Selecting Judges for the Federal Bench

Federal judges and justices are nominated by the president and confirmed by the Senate. In evaluating nominees, senators examine the nominee's competence and ideology and consider how the nominee's demographic characteristics might represent the population at large.

6. The U.S. Supreme Court Today

Although the Supreme Court has limited original jurisdiction, it is the highest court in the land. The justices choose to hear only a fraction of cases that come before them. The cases they select tend to have broad repercussions in their application. To date, the current Supreme Court, headed by Chief Justice John Roberts, has been conservative in its ideology and activist in its willingness to check the states and other branches of government.

7. Judges as Policy Makers

Judges are influential actors in the policy-making enterprise. They choose among several policy options in deciding cases. Although U.S. legal culture encourages the view that there is only one way for a case to be decided, the reality is that judges often draw from multiple legal interpretations in deciding cases and weigh these options in determining which best promotes the goal or social good that they think should receive priority.

8. Checks on the Courts

Powerful constraints limit what judges and justices in the U.S. legal system may do. The influences that can constrain policy making come from both outside and inside the judiciary. Outside influences include an inner ring consisting of legislatures and executives, a ring of gatekeepers comprising law enforcers and interest groups, and an outer ring of users, the people whom the laws directly affect. Within the judicial system, on the Supreme Court itself, legal precedent and the need to build coalitions restrict the justices' actions. Even in light of these various constraints, however, U.S. courts and judges play a crucial role in lawmaking and policy making.

Key Terms

amicus curiae brief ("friend of the court" brief) 447
appellate jurisdiction 439
brief 447
chief justice 441
circuit courts 433
circuit riding 433
civil law 434
code law 436
collegial court 446
common law 434
concurring opinion 449
constitutional law 437
courts of appeals 433

criminal law 434
discuss list 447
dissenting opinion 449
diversity of citizenship 438
dual court system 438
federal question 438
judicial activism 451
judicial restraint 453
judicial review 433*
judiciary 432
jurisdiction 438
justice 441
Marbury v. Madison 433*
oral arguments 448

original jurisdiction 439
pool memo 447
precedent 436
Rule of Four 447
senatorial courtesy 442
stare decisis 436
statute 437
symbolic representation 445
tort 434
trial court 438
U.S. Code 437
U.S. Supreme Court 433
writ of *certiorari* 447

*Judicial review and *Marbury v. Madison* were introduced in Chapter 2.

For Review

1. What is the basis of the American legal system? Why is it unusual for a nation-state to blend the two traditions that are the core of this system? What are the advantages and disadvantages of these two traditions?

2. What are the five sources of law in the U.S. legal system? What is the relationship among these five sources?

3. What is the structure of the federal court system? Does this system have more or less power than the state court system? Explain.

4. How are federal judges chosen? Who tends to be chosen? How does the selection process differ for federal district court judges, circuit court judges, and Supreme Court justices? In what ways do conflict and compromise characterize the selection process for all these judges?

5. Outline the stages by which the Supreme Court decides cases. Why do we say that negotiation and compromise are a part of every one of these stages?

6. In what ways do federal judges participate in civic discourse as policy makers? Outline the ways in which this participation is either checked by the Constitution or constrained by internal and external actors.

For Critical Thinking and Discussion

1. How did the American legal system come to be a blend of the common law and code law traditions? Which tradition better suits today's political, social, and economic realities? Why?

2. What is your view on the shared lawmaking by the three branches of American government? Are you satisfied that this shared system benefits the country? Can you think of some negatives to the U.S. system?

3. The Supreme Court has the power of judicial review, that is, the power to strike down federal and state laws that it views as in conflict with the U.S. Constitution. Can you think of any reasons why it would not be a good thing to allow the Court to overturn laws passed by the democratically elected branches?

4. When a president nominates a prospective federal judge, a number of factors are at play, and the nominee's qualifications are only one of these. What are these other factors? Should they be in play? Why or why not? In what ways do these factors reinforce or undermine democratic principles?

5. Which do you think impose greater limitations on policy making by federal courts: constitutional checks or intra-court and external constraints? Why?

MULTIPLE CHOICE: Choose the lettered item that answers the question correctly.

1. The notion that it is the role of the Court to check the power of the federal and state executive and legislative branches when those governmental entities exceed their authority is called
   a. judicial review.
   b. judicial constraint.
   c. judicial restraint.
   d. writ of *certiorari*.

2. The high court with a limited original jurisdiction whose decision may not be appealed is called:
   a. the U.S. Court of Appeals.
   b. the U.S. Supreme Court.
   c. federal District Court.
   d. the U.S. Superior Court.

3. The middle level of the federal court structure is
   a. circuit courts.
   b. courts of appeals.
   c. the U.S. Supreme Court.
   d. (a) and (b).

4. *Stare decisis* means
   a. "I have decided."
   b. "The king has decided."
   c. "Decided by God."
   d. "Let the decision stand."

5. Law created by legislators to regulate the behavior of individuals and organizations is called
   a. common law.
   b. code law.
   c. constitutional law.
   d. judicial law.

6. Federal courts are empowered to hear only cases
   a. involving a federal question.
   b. involving diversity of citizenship.
   c. involving statutory law.
   d. (a) or (b).

7. Legal authority established by earlier cases is called
   a. precedent.
   b. statutory law.
   c. tort law.
   d. oral law.

8. A wrongful act involving personal injury or harm to one's property or reputation is called
   a. administrative law.
   b. statutory law.
   c. tort law.
   d. oral law.

9. The practice by which the Supreme Court justices determine if they will hear a case is called
   a. the Rule of Two.
   b. the Rule of Four.
   c. the Rule of Six.
   d. the Rule of Eight.

10. The list of cases on review that the Chief Justice thinks may be appropriate for the Court to hear is called
    a. an *amicus curiae* brief.
    b. a pool memo.
    c. a discuss list.
    d. an opinion.

FILL IN THE BLANK.

11. The practice of traveling around the circuits by early Supreme Court justices and district court judges to hear appeals cases is called _____.

12. The description written by Court clerks of the facts of the case filed with the Court, the pertinent legal arguments, and a recommendation as to whether the case should be taken is called a _____.

13. A judicial opinion agreeing with how the majority decides the case but disagreeing with at least some of the legal interpretations or conclusions reached by the majority is called a _____.

14. A custom that allows senators from the president's political party to veto the president's choice of federal district court judge in the senator's state is called _____.

15. An approach to judicial decision making whereby judges apply their authority to bring about specific goals is called _____.

Answers: 1. a; 2. b; 3. d; 4. d; 5. b; 6. d; 7. a; 8. c; 9. b; 10. c; 11. circuit riding; 12. pool memo; 13. concurring opinion; 14. senatorial courtesy; 15. judicial activism.

RESOURCES FOR RESEARCH AND ACTION

Internet Resources

FindLaw
www.findlaw.com This Web site provides a wealth of information about lawmaking in the federal and state judiciaries, as well as ongoing cases in the news. It allows users easy access to federal and state code law, case law, and regulatory law. It also helps pre-law and law students stay connected to helpful information about legal education and practice.

Oyez
www.oyez.org/oyez/frontpage This interactive Web site allows you to access recordings of the oral arguments in a select group of cases. You can also visit the site to take a virtual tour of the Supreme Court building and to learn interesting trivia about the Court, including a list of the most active lawyers before the Court.

Legal Information Institute (LII)
http://straylight.law.cornell.edu This is a valuable resource for doing research not only on the U.S. Supreme Court but also on the other courts in the federal and state judiciaries. The site provides an excellent catalog of statutory, regulatory, and administrative laws, as well as executive orders. It also allows you to search for all sources of law in a particular area of the law, including not only federal and state court decisions but laws coming out of the other branches as well.

U.S. Supreme Court
www.supremecourtus.gov The official Web site of the U.S. Supreme Court is an excellent resource for doing research on the Court. You can access the briefs and oral argument transcripts for cases currently before the Court, as well as cases recently decided. The site also allows easy access to nearly all cases that the Court has decided, including historical decisions.

Internet Activism

Twitter
Follow **@SCOTUSOpinions** for links to the latest opinions from the U.S. Supreme Court.

Recommended Readings

Friedman, Leon. *Justices of the United States Supreme Court.* 2010. This chronological biography of Supreme Court justices examines each Supreme Court justice's education and legal background.

McGuire, Kevin T. *Understanding the Supreme Court: Cases and Controversies.* New York: McGraw-Hill, 2002. A book that uses real cases to examine the selection of justices, the Supreme Court's decision-making procedures, the influence of interest groups, and the impact of Court rulings.

Samuels, Suzanne U. *Law, Politics and Society: An Introduction to American Law.* Boston: Houghton Mifflin, 2006. A comprehensive survey of the foundations of the American legal system, lawmaking by institutions and groups, and law and public policy.

Savage, David G. *Guide to the U.S. Supreme Court.* Washington, DC: Congressional Quarterly, 2010. This volume contains a thorough description of the U.S. Supreme Court, including its origins, its functions, and its impact.

Tarr, G. Alan. *Judicial Process and Judicial Policymaking.* Belmont, CA: Thomson/Wadsworth, 2006. A broad outline of the institutions and main actors in the U.S. judicial system, explaining both judicial decision making and policy making.

van Geel, T. R. *Understanding Supreme Court Opinions.* New York: Pearson/Longman, 2005. An introduction to Supreme Court opinions and to the justices' use of different schools of legal argument and interpretation in those opinions.

Movies of Interest

The Runaway Jury (2003)
This film provides critical examination of the role of the jury in the American judicial system.

Monster's Ball (2001)
Probing the issues of capital punishment and racism in a personal way, this film explores the relationships among a white executioner, his African American prisoner, and their families.

A Civil Action (1998)
Based on a real-life story, this engrossing film takes the viewer through the pitfalls of civil litigation in a series of cases involving the pollution of a Massachusetts town's water supply by several corporations and businesses.

Gideon's Trumpet (1980)
This classic film starring Henry Fonda traces the true story of Clarence Gideon's fight to have a counsel appointed to his case at the expense of the state. *Gideon v. Wainwright* was the 1963 Supreme Court's decision that extended state-appointed attorneys to all criminal defendants.

12 Angry Men (1957)
Henry Fonda starred in and produced this classic drama depicting the acrimonious deliberations of a jury in a death penalty case.

AA-CAR

DON'T LET YOUR JOB SEARCH
BECOME A WAITING GAME

Experience the Industries highest
standard of client care. Discover a
better way to advance your career.
Don't let your job search become a
waiting game, be pro-active and
take control.

UNPARALLED RESOURCES
ALL SEGMENTS OF BUSINESS AND IND

AA-CAREERS

Associated offices in most major U.S. Ci

AA -
CAREERS

FREE

RESUME
CRITIQUE

Economic Policy

THEN

The federal government played a limited role in the economy, and there was consensus about the need for a balanced federal budget.

NOW

The federal government makes policy to achieve national economic health, and borrowing to balance the federal budget is the norm.

NEXT

Will continuing globalization impede the government's ability to maintain a healthy national economy?

Will the national government enact major tax, spending, or regulatory reforms in the wake of the Great Recession?

Will your generation and future generations achieve the American dream?

economic policy, a body of diverse policies geared toward promoting its nation's economic health. Since World War II, the United States' economic policy has made it the dominant force in the global economy. But participants in the 2008 World Economic Forum—an annual meeting of thousands of corporate chief executive officers, government officials, and intellectuals—came to some sobering conclusions. The consensus was that the United States has fallen from its pedestal as the world's economic leader because of its colossal national debt and its deep reliance on imported oil, as well as the serious problems within its financial institutions.[1]

From President George Washington's terms in office to the current administration, the involvement of the national government in the nation's economy has evolved dramatically. Today, the national government enacts a variety of laws that seek to ensure economic prosperity. These laws include tax laws, laws that regulate economic activity in the domestic and international marketplaces, laws that protect the health and safety of workers and consumers, and spending policies that encourage economic growth as well as provide for the public good. In addition, the Federal Reserve—the United States' central banking system—makes policy decisions that affect the amount of money in circulation and hence consumer prices and employment rates.

Debates about the proper role for the national government in creating and maintaining a healthy economy have been ongoing since the birth of the American republic. The economic downturn experienced by the United States beginning in 2007 intensified the tone and the volume of debates about U.S. economic policy among elected and appointed officials at the national and state levels, economists, corporate leaders, and taxpayers. As these debates raged, and the global economy faltered, the U.S. national debt continued to grow, surpassing $12.4 trillion.

Economic Health and the American Dream

The American national government seeks a healthy economy so that it can raise the revenue it needs to serve the people in compliance with the mission laid out in the Preamble to the Constitution: to establish justice, ensure domestic tranquility, provide for the common defense, promote the general welfare, and secure the blessings of liberty today and in the future. On a more personal level, many U.S. citizens desire a healthy economy so that they can achieve the **American dream**—a financially secure, happy, and healthy life, with upward social mobility, attained through an individual's hard work and persistence.

Despite its name, the American dream's promise is not limited to Americans: people around the globe widely aspire to these same ideals. Hundreds of thousands of foreigners immigrate to the United States each year—most legally, some illegally—in search of the American dream. The primary cause of immigration is poverty. Foreign peoples come to the United States to get jobs that will provide more for them and their families than the jobs that their home country can provide. U.S. immigration policy (see Chapter 16) accommodates immigration on a limited basis, imposing an annual cap on the number of immigrants allowed legal entrance and giving preference to immigrants with family members living permanently in the United States, as well as those with high-level job skills needed in select segments of the U.S. economy.

This chapter explores U.S. economic policy from its roots to the present.

FIRST, we consider *economic health and the American dream*—how economic prosperity is essential to the ability of people to be financially secure and to realize the American dream.

SECOND, we examine *the American economy* and the national government's use of policy tools to create and maintain a healthy economy.

THIRD, we focus on various *economic theories that shape economic policy*.

FOURTH, we examine the data used in *measuring economic health*, exploring both traditional and other measures of prosperity.

FIFTH, we look at *fiscal policy*—the taxing and spending decisions made by Congress and the president—*and economic health*.

SIXTH, we survey the goals of *monetary policy and the Federal Reserve System's* role in setting it.

SEVENTH, we probe government's *regulatory policy*.

EIGHTH, we look at *trade policy in the global economy*—its evolution over time and its focus today.

NINTH, we assess the *U.S. economy and the American dream today*, in the context of the *global economy*.

economic policy
a government's body of diverse policies geared toward promoting the nation's economic health

American dream
the belief that in the United States hard work and persistence will reap a financially secure, happy, and healthy life, with upward social mobility

The desire for enough money to buy not only what we require to meet our basic needs (food, shelter, and clothing) but also what many people would consider luxuries seems natural to most Americans. In developed countries such as the United States, "luxuries" typically include owning a home instead of renting, owning a car or two, dining at a nice restaurant now and then, taking vacations, and sending children to good schools. The American dream includes sustaining this middle-class lifestyle through retirement and expecting our children's lives to be even better than our own.

Clearly, it takes money to live the American dream. For some, being born into a wealthy family or just dumb luck (winning the lottery!) may provide the means to live the American dream. For most individuals, however, the ability to earn enough money to attain the American dream is the product of several factors, including their education level, their work ethic, and the availability of well-paying jobs.

Why are you attending college? Are you taking classes to develop your intellectual capacities? To better understand yourself and the world around you? To get a better-paying job so you can live the American dream? If you read your college's mission statement, you will find that your institution hopes to facilitate all those accomplishments. Probably the easiest accomplishment to measure is gaining a well-paying job, and personal income is a logical measure of a well-paying job. Table 15.1 shows that personal income is positively correlated with educational attainment; generally, the more education you acquire, the higher your personal income will be. In addition, Table 15.1 shows that race and sex—two factors that you cannot control—are also correlated with personal income. So earning a college degree is the best step you can take in your quest to live the American dream. However, for women and nonwhite men, the income benefits of a college education are muted.

Although you may be able to increase your level of education, and you have some control over your work ethic, the availability of well-paying jobs commensurate with your level of education is not within your control. The health of the national economy determines the availability of jobs and their compensation (pay and benefits). So, although achieving the American dream depends on individual attributes and opportunities to develop those attributes, the health of the national economy also plays a major role.

A healthy national economy—with low unemployment, stable prices, and high productivity—supports a nation's ability to raise sufficient revenue to serve its people. The better the economy's performance, the greater the **tax base:** the overall wealth (income and assets, such as property) of citizens and corporations that governments tax to raise revenue.

The American Economy

In the United States and other countries, national government policies influence the **economy,** a system for producing, distributing,

tax base

the overall wealth (income and assets of citizens and corporations) that the government can tax to raise revenue

economy

a system for producing, distributing, and consuming goods and services

Education, Race, Sex, and Mean Personal Income

TABLE 15.1

	High School	Associate's Degree	Bachelor's Degree	Master's Degree	Doctoral Degree
All groups	$31,286	$39,746	$57,181	$70,186	$ 95,565
Female	$24,234	$33,276	$43,127	$54,772	$ 69,251
Male	$36,839	$47,190	$70,898	$86,966	$108,941
Black	$27,179	$36,445	$46,502	$56,398	$ 96,092
Female	$24,724	$34,774	$41,560	$51,695	$*
Male	$29,640	$38,921	$53,029	$63,801	$*
Hispanic	$27,604	$35,348	$44,696	$68,040	$*
Female	$22,283	$29,884	$38,584	$54,263	$*
Male	$30,932	$42,140	$50,805	$81,069	$*
White	$32,223	$40,373	$58,652	$71,321	$ 97,254
Female	$24,276	$33,223	$42,846	$54,532	$ 69,778
Male	$38,214	$48,444	$73,477	$89,678	$110,480

* Too few earning PhDs to meet statistical standards for reliability.

SOURCE: U.S. Census Bureau, *Statistical Abstract of the United States: 2010,* 129th Ed. (Washington, DC: 2009), Table 227, www.census.gov/statab/www/.

POLITICAL INQUIRY

On average, do women or men make more money? Does this pattern hold for blacks, Hispanics, and whites? On average, people of which racial/ethnic background earn the most money? Which group earns the least? Do these patterns hold for all levels of education? What are some of the possible explanations for these patterns?

and consuming goods and services. Economic policies are those aimed at creating and/or maintaining a healthy economy. Economists view a healthy economy as one in which unemployment is low, the prices of consumer goods are relatively stable, and the productivity of individual workers, and of the economy as a whole, is increasing.

Although labeled as a capitalist economy, the U.S. economy is not an example of pure capitalism. In a **pure capitalist economy,** private individuals and companies own the modes of producing goods and services, and the government does *not* enact laws aimed at influencing the marketplace transactions that distribute those goods and services. In other words, a pure capitalist economy has a government-free marketplace. Although private ownership of the modes of production dominates the U.S. marketplace, it is not a government-free marketplace. National government policies in some cases encourage, and in other cases mandate, certain business practices that the government deems essential to sustain a healthy economy, as well as a clean environment and a safe and productive citizenry. Because of the many national policies enacted to influence the economy, the U.S. economy is an example of a **regulated capitalist economy (mixed economy),** not a pure capitalist economy.

People around the world want their governments to engage in actions that ensure a healthy economy. Yet the actions a government takes to ensure a healthy economy depend on the economic theories its lawmakers follow. In the United States, Democrats and Republicans traditionally disagree on economic policies, each justifying their policy preferences with different economic theories. Next, we survey several economic theories that have influenced U.S. national economic policy in various historical periods.

Economic Theories That Shape Economic Policy

Today's debates about the proper role of the national government in the economy are nothing new. It was the lack of an economic role for the national government and the poor health of the economy under the Articles of Confederation that sparked the call for a constitutional convention in 1787. The framers of the new system of government established by the Constitution envisioned a national government much more involved in the economy. Moreover, although citizens initially supported a very limited role for the government in the economy—a *laissez-faire* economic policy—as the national economy evolved and experienced ups and downs, citizens and corporations sought greater government involvement in the economy, and economists developed new theories about the proper role for governments in creating and maintaining a healthy economy: Keynesian economics, supply-side economics, and monetarism.

Laissez-Faire Economics: An Unrealized Policy

Until the late 1800s, a majority of the American people believed that the national government should take a relatively **laissez-faire,** or "hands-off," stance with regard to the marketplace. That is, they thought that the government should neither encourage nor discourage (through its laws) business practices that affected economic health. In his *Wealth of Nations* (1776), economist Adam Smith described the principles underlying the theory of laissez-faire. Smith's classical capitalist argument emphasized that the most effective means of supporting a strong and stable economy in the long term is to allow unregulated competition in the marketplace. According to Smith, people's pursuit of their self-interest in an unregulated marketplace would yield a healthy economy. Although it supported a hands-off approach in general, the national government became involved in economic activity as early as 1789, when Congress approved and President George Washington (1789–1797) signed the first import tariff (tax on imported goods).

As a manufacturing economy replaced the farming-dominated economy during the nineteenth century, the general laissez-faire stance of the national government disappeared. Technological advances fueled industrialization and the movement of workers from farms to manufacturing jobs in the cities. As immigrants flocked to the United States in search

---

pure capitalist economy
an economy in which private individuals and companies own the modes of producing goods and services, and the government does not enact laws aimed at influencing the marketplace transactions that distribute those goods and services

regulated capitalist economy (mixed economy)
an economy in which the government enacts policies to influence the health of the economy

laissez-faire
hands-off stance of a government in regard to the marketplace

of the American dream, the supply of cheap labor ballooned. Giant corporations formed, and individuals with money to invest accumulated great wealth. Monopolies and trusts also developed, limiting competition in a variety of industries. **Income inequality,** the gap in the proportion of national income held by the few at the top of the income ladder compared with the many on the lower rungs, grew. At the same time, the quality of life for most working-class citizens deteriorated as additional family members, including children, needed to work to pay for life's basic necessities. As fewer and fewer people achieved the American dream, even with all family members working, many Americans began to look to the federal government to improve working and living conditions.

In the late nineteenth century, the federal government began to respond to workers' demands for better wages and working conditions and to business owners' calls for uniform (national) rules and regulations for business practices to replace the existing hodgepodge of state-imposed regulations. Moreover, by the early twentieth century, the national government took steps to protect public health by passing laws regulating the

> In the late eighteenth and early nineteenth centuries, income inequality forced many American families to rely on the income brought home by their children to help pay the bills. By 1900, large numbers of children worked in mines, glass factories, textiles, agriculture, canneries, and home industries such as cigar making. Here two little girls work in a hosiery mill in 1910.

income inequality
the gap in the proportion of national income held by the richest compared to that held by the poorest

processing of foods and drugs, and the cleanliness and safety of manufacturing plants. Though not directed at the health of the economy, such regulations increased the costs of doing business, hence affecting the economy. In addition to regulating working conditions, the national government began to use the tool of immigration policy to bolster the national economy and the wages of American-born workers. For example, the Chinese Exclusion Act of 1882 disallowed immigrants from China, who were willing to work to build the railroads for lower wages than American-born workers. The contemporary public debate about the impact of immigrants on the U.S. economy—in terms of wages, working conditions, and the cost of health, education, and welfare policies—is discussed in Chapter 16.

Clearly, the national government never fully implemented laissez-faire. Moreover, as the national economy grew with industrialization, Americans accepted and even called for a mixed economy featuring regulated capitalism. Today, consensus continues on the need for some level of government involvement in the marketplace to ensure a healthy and sustainable economy, environment, and standard of living. But debate continues over how much government involvement is appropriate and what specific policies the government should enact.

Keynesian Economics

Before the Great Depression of the 1930s, government officials and economists believed that a **balanced budget,** a budget in which the government's expenditures (costs of doing business) are equal to or less than its revenues (money raised from taxes), was important for a healthy economy. Yet officials and economists recognized that during wartime the government might need to engage in **deficit spending,** spending more than is raised through taxes, to pay for the military effort.

During the Great Depression, when unemployment rates soared to 25 percent, President Franklin D. Roosevelt (1933–1945) and Congress supported deficit spending to address the severe economic depression that engulfed the nation. The Roosevelt administration implemented numerous economic regulations and a number of innovative work and public

balanced budget
a budget in which the government's expenditures are equal to or less than its revenues

deficit spending
government expenditures costing more than is raised in taxes, leading to borrowing and debt

assistance programs. Those policies drove up government spending at a time of shrinking government revenues. A key objective of the government's increased spending was to trigger economic growth by lowering unemployment rates, thereby increasing demand for goods (because more employed people means more people with money to spend), thus boosting the national economy. Deficit spending, Roosevelt said, would provide the solution to the American people's economic woes.

The new economic theory of John Maynard Keynes supported Roosevelt's unprecedented peacetime deficit spending. **Keynesian economics** recommends that during a **recession**—an economic downturn during which unemployment is high and the production of goods and services is low—the national government should increase its spending (to create jobs) and decrease taxes (so that people have more money to spend) to stimulate the economy. Based on this theory, during a **depression,** which is a long-term and severe recession, deficit spending is justified. During times of rapid economic growth—an **economic boom,** which is the opposite of a recession/depression—Keynesian theory recommends cutting government spending and possibly increasing taxes. In the long term, deficit spending during recessions and collecting a surplus when the economy is booming should lead to a balanced budget. Hence Keynesian economic theory advocates using **fiscal policy,** the combination of tax policy and spending policy, to ensure a healthy economy.

In February 2008, following the tenets of Keynesian economics, Congress and President George W. Bush (2001–2009) approved tax refunds for citizens totaling $168 billion and tax cuts for select businesses. In September 2008, Congress and the president pledged to spend $300 billion to rescue two top mortgage companies (Fannie Mae and Freddie Mac) and the American International Group (AIG), a major international insurance and financial services organization. The Bush administration continued these fiscal policies in the fall of 2008 by winning approval from Congress for $700 billion to bail out faltering Wall Street financial institutions.

President Barack Obama (2009–present) and Congress continued to use fiscal policy to stimulate the sagging economy by enacting the American Recovery and Reinvestment Act (ARRA), which authorized $787 billion in combined tax cuts and federal spending, in February 2009. The ARRA tax cuts and increased federal spending compose what the media and government officials refer to as a "stimulus package." The goals of the ARRA were to create and save jobs, jump-start the nation's economy, and build the foundation for long-

Keynesian economics
theory that recommends that during a recession the national government should increase its spending and decrease taxes, and during a boom, it should cut spending and increase taxes

recession
an economic downturn during which unemployment is high and the production of goods and services is low

depression
a long-term and severe recession

economic boom
rapid economic growth

fiscal policy
government spending and taxing and their effect on the economy

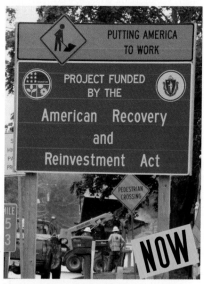

> Created in 1935 as one component of President Roosevelt's effort to end the Great Depression, the Works Projects Administration (WPA) put millions of unemployed people to work on public works projects such as highway and building construction. In his efforts to address the growing U.S. unemployment rate during the severe global recession of 2007–2009, President Obama signed into law the American Recovery and Reinvestment Act (ARRA), aimed at creating 3.5 million jobs, in February 2009. By June 2009, ARRA stimulus funds were being spent on hundreds of construction projects throughout the country.

term economic growth. Whereas Keynesian economics has shaped the economic policies of Democratic and Republican administrations from Roosevelt to Bush to Obama, President Ronald Reagan (1981–1989) implemented a different economic theory in his efforts to deal with the economic downturn that began during the late 1970s.

Supply-Side Economics

President Reagan introduced the nation to a competing economic theory, **supply-side economics,** which advocates tax cuts and a decrease in government regulation to stimulate the economy in times of recession. Supply-siders argue that the government collects so much money in income taxes from workers that they are discouraged from working more than they absolutely need to (because any extra effort will just mean they pay more in taxes). In addition, high taxes drain the economy because they diminish people's ability to save and corporations' ability to invest to increase productivity. Therefore, the theory goes, if the government cuts taxes, workers will be more productive and people will have more money to save and invest, thus stimulating economic growth. Supply-siders also argue that because government regulation increases the cost of producing goods, **deregulation**—reducing or eliminating restrictions on business—will contribute to increased production at the same cost, thus increasing the supply of goods.

Republican President George H. W. Bush (1989–1993) initially continued the supply-side economic policies of Reagan, but before the end of his presidency, Bush broke his promise not to raise taxes in an attempt to begin to address the growing **national debt**—the total amount of money owed to others due to borrowing. In addition to increasing taxes, he signed into law new regulations. Democratic President Bill Clinton (1993–2001) battled a Republican-dominated Congress for most of his presidency. Clinton's proposed spending increases were muted by Congress, and Congress pushed for tax cuts. As a result of those policies and economic growth, by the end of the 1990s, the national government was no longer engaging in deficit spending.

President George W. Bush (2001–2009), working with a Republican-dominated Congress for most of his presidency, initially pursued supply-side economics by cutting taxes and deregulating. However, as the recession that began in 2007 persisted, the Bush administration and Congress approved increased spending to prevent the collapse of numerous financial institutions.

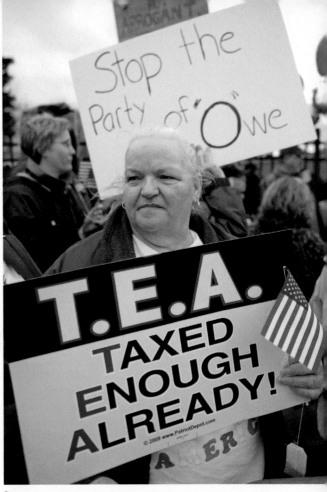

> April 15th is tax day, the day that citizens must pay their federal income taxes. Anti-tax protests are common on tax day. Critics of President Obama marked tax day 2009 with "tea party" protests across the country, including this one in Staten Island, New York. Tea Party protests are reminiscent of the 1773 Boston Tea Party revolt against British colonial taxes.

Monetarism

Economist Milton Friedman, a onetime supporter of Keynesian economics, is today best known for yet another economic theory, **monetarism,** which advocates that the government's proper role in promoting a healthy economy is the regulation of the money supply to ensure that the rate of inflation remains low. **Inflation** refers to a rising price level for consumer goods, which decreases the purchasing power of money. The Bureau of Labor Statistics provides an inflation calculator (www.bls.gov/data/inflation_calculator.htm) that allows you to determine what yesterday's dollar is worth today because of inflation. For example, according to the calculator, $1.25 in 2009 bought what $1.00 in 2000 could buy.

Monetarists believe that *too much* money in circulation leads to a high inflation rate, which slows economic growth as people spend less because of higher prices. In addition, as the rate of inflation increases, investors begin to worry about the health of the economy, and investments may decline as a result, ultimately limiting economic growth. On the flip side, the monetarists say, *too little* money in circulation means there is not enough for new investments and that consequently new jobs are not created; this situation, too, retards

supply-side economics
theory that advocates cutting taxes and deregulating business to stimulate the economy

deregulation
reduction or elimination of regulatory restrictions on firms and industries

national debt
the total amount of money the national government owes to its creditors

monetarism
theory that says the government's proper economic role is to control the rate of inflation by controlling the amount of money in circulation

inflation
the decreased value of money as evidenced by increased prices

economic growth. Today, monetarists target an inflation rate of 1–3 percent per year to ensure an adequate money supply for a healthy economy. They believe that the national government must use its monetary policy to maintain this level of inflation.

Should One Economic Theory Predominate?

Although economists, government officials, and citizens broadly agree that the government should act to ensure a healthy economy, there is perpetual debate over how involved the government should be in the economy and what specific policy actions it should take. Where people stand in this debate depends on which economic theory they advocate. Each theory supports the use of different government policies to promote a healthy economy. Before we discuss these various policies that theoretically promote economic health, we consider how governments measure economic health. Once we know what a healthy economy looks like, we can then consider the effects that various policies have on the performance of the economy.

Measuring Economic Health

Economists and government officials describe a healthy economy as one that has the following characteristics: expanding gross domestic product (GDP); increasing level of worker productivity; low unemployment rate; low inflation rate.

These traditional measures of economic health together provide a useful snapshot of how the national economy is doing. Other measures of economic health focus on the general well-being of the people by accounting for factors such as rates of poverty and literacy and the financial situation of households. These less traditional measures include the United Nations Human Development Index, real median household income, income inequality, and the poverty rate.

Traditional Measures of Economic Health

Most economists assume that growth in the gross domestic product translates into a prosperous nation with improving living standards—hence progress toward living the American dream. **Gross domestic product (GDP)** is the total market value of all goods and services produced within a country's borders. Another assumption made by most economists is that high productivity, or output per worker, also fosters improved living standards. Rising GDP and productivity are signs of an expanding economy, which means the production of more goods and services—and thus the availability of more goods and services for consumers.

Economists also expect a healthy economy to correlate with a low level of inflation. When inflation rises, consumers' purchasing power falls and they cannot buy as much this year with the same amount of money they spent last year. The government agency known as the Bureau of Labor Statistics publishes the **consumer price index (CPI)**, which measures the average change in prices over time of a "market basket" of goods and services, including food, clothing, shelter, fuel, transportation costs, and selected medical costs. The CPI is the most commonly used measure of inflation's impact on people. According to economists, when the economy is healthy, the inflation rate (measured by the change in CPI) ranges between 1 and 3 percent.

A low unemployment rate, 5 percent or less, is also characteristic of a healthy economy, according to economists. When more people are working, the financial situation of families overall should improve. In addition, in a growing economy with falling unemployment, government revenues should increase (since there is more corporate and personal income to tax), and government spending for social welfare programs should decrease (because fewer people should need public assistance). These trends create a healthier financial situation for government. (For a closer look at what the GDP and unemployment rates measure, see "Analyzing the Sources.")

gross domestic product (GDP)
the total value of all goods and services produced within a country's borders

consumer price index (CPI)
the most common measure of inflation, it gauges the average change in prices over time of a "market basket" of goods and services including food, clothing, shelter, fuels, transportation costs, and selected medical costs

GDP AND UNEMPLOYMENT RATES: WHAT DO THEY MEASURE?

Traditionally, no measure of economic health has been as widely accepted as gross domestic product (GDP), although some economists argue that a more accurate economic assessment would add a quality-of-life measure to the value of GDP. Employment status clearly correlates with a person's quality of life, but some economists and government officials have also questioned the current means by which the government measures this indicator.

The Gross Domestic Product

The U.S. Commerce Department calculates the *gross domestic product (GDP)*, which it defines as the total value of all goods and services produced within a country's borders for a specified period, usually one year. The GDP is calculated from the following formula:

$$GDP = C + G + I + NX$$

where

C is the total amount of *consumer spending* to purchase goods and services

G is the total amount of *government spending* to purchase goods and services

I is the total amount of money *businesses invest* in new capital resources (such as equipment, computers and software, automobiles, and facilities)

NX is the nation's total net exports, which is the difference between the value of all its exports and the value of all its imports

The Unemployment Rate

Every month, the Bureau of Labor Statistics of the Department of Labor reports the *unemployment rate,* which is the percent of people who are actively looking for work but who do not have jobs. To calculate the unemployment rate, each month more than 2,000 trained Census Bureau employees (the Census Bureau is within the Department of Commerce) interview people in 60,000 households that are representative of the households across the United States. Collectively these interviews are called the Current Population Survey (CPS).

The Census Bureau classifies individuals as employed if they did any work at all for pay or profit during the survey week, including part-time and temporary work. The Bureau also counts as employed people who have a job but did not work during the survey week because they were on vacation, ill, experiencing child-care problems, taking care of some other family or personal obligation, on maternity or paternity leave, involved in an industrial dispute, or prevented from working by bad weather.

The CPS classifies persons as *unemployed* if they meet the following criteria:

1. They do not have a job.

2. They have actively looked for work in the preceding four weeks.

3. They are currently available for work.

Therefore, people who do not have a job and have stopped looking for work are not counted as unemployed.

Evaluating the Evidence

① The GDP does not include the value of unpaid work done in the home, such as home-cooked meals, child care, adult care, house cleaning, and clothes cleaning. Should it include those costs? Why or why not?

② Does the fact that the "unemployment" rate does not account for people who have given up hope of finding a job and therefore have stopped looking for work call into question the rate's accuracy? Justify your answer.

③ What measure, or combination of measures, would you argue provides citizens with the most accurate picture of the health of the economy? Explain your answer.

In sum, a high or rising GDP, high or increasing rate of productivity, low inflation rate, and low unemployment rate suggest a healthy national economy. Yet as the U.S. Department of Commerce's Bureau of Economic Analysis points out, "While the GDP is used as an indicator of economic progress, it is not a measure of well-being."[2] Therefore we next describe other measures that attempt to assess the well-being of the people, which most people expect is a product of a healthy economy.

Other Measures of Economic Health

Human Development Index (HDI)
UN-created measure to determine how well a country's economy is providing for a long and healthy life, educational opportunities, and a decent standard of living

The United Nations (UN) created the **Human Development Index (HDI)** to measure the standard of living of the people of various nations. As discussed in the "Global Context" box, the HDI assesses three components of human development that people in prosperous nations should be able to enjoy: a long and healthy life, educational opportunities, and a decent standard of daily living. These measures of economic health shed light on the ability of people to earn enough to *enjoy a decent quality of life*. Thus they are probing into something quite different from the traditional measures of national economic health that we have just discussed.

With an HDI score of .956 (1.0 is the highest score possible), the United States ranked thirteenth out of 182 countries in the *Human Development Report 2010*.[3] How do we know what this rank means to American households and their ability to live the American dream? Additional measures—looking at household income, income inequality, and the level of poverty within the population—can help us answer this question.

real income
earned income adjusted for inflation

household income
total pretax earnings of all residents over the age of 15 living in a home

median household income
the middle of all household incomes—50 percent of households have incomes less than the median and 50 percent have incomes greater than the median

Real median household income is an important measure of the financial well-being of American households. **Real income** is income adjusted for inflation so that it can be compared across years. **Household income** is the total pretax earnings of all residents over the age of 15 living in a home. **Median household income** is the income level in the middle of all household incomes; 50 percent of the households have incomes less than the median and 50 percent have incomes greater than the median. An increase in real median household income should characterize a healthy, expanding economy if we assume that increases in workers' productivity will translate into increases in workers' incomes.

To determine whether people at all income levels are benefiting from a healthy economy, the government calculates changes in the percentage of the total national income possessed by households in five income groups. Specifically, the government divides U.S. households into five *quintiles*, each composed of 20 percent of the households in the nation, based on total household income. The bottom group (bottom quintile) is composed of the 20 percent of households with the lowest incomes, and the top quintile comprises the 20 percent of households with the highest incomes. The government then determines the percentage of the total national income possessed by each quintile. Changes in the percentage of the total income held by each quintile over time indicate whether income inequality is growing or shrinking. The ideal is to see a shrinking of income inequality as the national economy expands.

poverty
the condition of lacking sufficient income to purchase the necessities for an adequate living standard

poverty rate
proportion of the population living below the poverty line as established by the national government

poverty thresholds
an annually updated set of income measures (adjusted for family size) that defines who is living in poverty

The ideal healthy economy would also ensure that all workers earn enough to stay out of **poverty**—the condition of lacking sufficient income to purchase the necessities for an adequate living standard. The **poverty rate** is the percentage of the population with income below the nationally designated poverty level. The U.S. Census Bureau calculates the poverty rate by using its **poverty thresholds**—an annually updated set of income measures (adjusted for family size) that define who is living in poverty. According to the poverty thresholds for 2008, a family of four, with two children under the age of 18 years, earning less than $21,834 was living in poverty.[4] A family of the same size and makeup earning $21,835 was not living in poverty.

So we have seen that not only traditional economic measures such as GDP, productivity, inflation, and employment serve as indicators of national economic health, but also other measures shed light on the quality of life of people in the United States. With this context in mind, we next explore the way the national government uses fiscal policy to promote a healthy national economy that provides benefits to individuals and households.

GLOBAL CONTEXT

NATIONAL ECONOMIES AND HUMAN DEVELOPMENT

The United Nations Development Programme (UNDP) focuses on the question, How does the economic development of a country translate, or fail to translate, into improved well-being for its inhabitants? In an effort to understand the complex relationships between a country's economic development, its inhabitants' incomes, and their well-being, the UNDP created the Human Development Index (HDI). The HDI uses three components to assess the most fundamental aspects of people's lives. The UNDP maintains that the HDI provides a more complete picture of a country's development than do traditional measures of economic development, such as the GDP.

How will the global recession affect the pattern of improvement in HDI scores?

The first component of the HDI is a long and healthy life, as measured by life expectancy at birth. The second component is knowledge, measured by adult literacy rates and enrollment in primary, secondary, and tertiary schools. The third component is a decent standard of living, which is measured by GDP per capita (per person inhabiting the country). The closer to 1 a country's HDI score is, the better the living standard in the country. The accompanying table compares the top five and the bottom five nations, based on their HDI scores in 2009.

TOP FIVE NATIONS	BOTTOM FIVE NATIONS
1. Norway (.971)	178. Mali (.371)
2. Australia (.970)	179. Central African Republic (.369)
3. Iceland (.969)	180. Sierra Leone (.365)
4. Canada (.966)	181. Afghanistan (.352)
5. Ireland (.965)	182. Niger (.340)

Between 1990 and 2009, HDI scores in all regions of the world have increased, in part because of improvements in health and education. Progress is slower in some years and regions, however, and incomes in the poorest countries have been problematic. In addition, many countries have experienced setbacks from regional economic downturns, civil wars and other conflict-related causes, and epidemics. Indeed, inequality in the distribution of the world's income persists.

SOURCE: http://hdr.undp.org/en/.

Fiscal Policy and Economic Health

As noted earlier, fiscal policy comprises a government's spending and tax policies. The national government, through its budget process, annually approves a twelve-month plan for raising revenue and spending revenue. The twelve-month accounting period for revenue raising and spending is a **fiscal year (FY).** The national government's fiscal year runs from October 1 through September 30 of the following calendar year, and is named for the calendar year in which it ends. Therefore the federal FY 2011 began on October 1, 2010 and ends on September 30, 2011.

National government expenditures accounted for 25 percent of the GDP of the United States in 2009—unquestionably, a substantial percentage of national economic output.[5] Although government spending certainly can create jobs, its primary goal is to provide the services necessary to fulfill the Constitution's mission. The other side of the coin, tax policy, raises revenue needed by the national government to serve the people. Although the main goal of tax policy is to collect revenue, taxation also decreases the amount of money taxpayers have to spend in the marketplace and corporations have to invest. Hence, taxation may

fiscal year (FY)

the twelve-month accounting period for revenue raising and spending, which for the national government begins on October 1 and ends on September 30 of the following year

progressive tax

a tax that takes a larger percentage of the income of wealthier taxpayers and a smaller percentage of the income of lower-income taxpayers

proportional tax (flat tax)

a tax that takes the same percentage of each taxpayer's income

regressive tax

a tax that takes a greater percentage of the income of lower-income earners than of higher-income earners

tax expenditures

also called *tax breaks* or loopholes; government financial supports that allow individuals and corporations to pay reduced taxes, to encourage behaviors that foster the public good

reduce consumer demand for goods and services, with possible effects on the unemployment rate as well as company profits. It may also affect investment, which contributes to economic growth. Thus tax policy, like spending policy, powerfully affects the economy.

To understand fiscal policy, we look next at the sources of the funds the federal government uses to run the nation, as well as the spending decisions that Congress and the president must make.

Tax Policy

The Constitution delegates the power of the purse to Congress. By the authority of the Constitution, Congress formulates and approves *tax laws* to raise money along with *appropriation laws*—legislation that authorizes the spending of government money for a fiscal year. The Constitution specifies that the House must introduce revenue-raising bills before the Senate can consider them. The House Ways and Means Committee and the Senate Finance Committee are the congressional standing committees from which tax bills emerge.

Figure 15.1 presents the tax mix proposed in the FY 2011 budget. Today, the national tax on individual income is the largest revenue source for the national government. The federal individual income tax is imposed on each individual's *earned income* (salaries and wages) and *unearned income* (profits made from investments).

The second-largest revenue category, social insurance, includes taxes collected for Social Security and Medicare. Because employers deduct from workers' paychecks the amount they owe for social insurance taxes, these taxes are referred to as *payroll taxes*. The federal government's third-largest revenue source is corporate income taxes. The national government also collects *excise taxes,* which are taxes levied against a specific item such as gasoline or liquor, *estate and gift taxes,* and *customs duties* (import taxes).

Taxes levied by the federal government do not affect the income of all taxpayers in the same way. The national income tax is a **progressive tax** because it takes a larger percentage of the income of wealthier taxpayers and a smaller percentage of the income of less-well-off taxpayers. Most taxpayers view a progressive tax, theoretically based on a person's ability to pay, as fair. Some people believe that a **proportional tax (flat tax),** which takes the same percentage of each taxpayer's income, is fairer than a progressive tax. A flat tax of 10 percent would equal $3,500 for a person earning $35,000 and $13,500 for a person earning $135,000. Although these two taxpayers pay a different amount of money in taxes, the *proportion* of their income collected is the same—hence the name proportional tax. Taxes can also be regressive. A **regressive tax** takes a greater percentage of the income of lower-income earners than of higher-income earners. States' sales taxes are the prime example of a regressive tax.

Taxes may affect various taxpayers differently because the government grants **tax expenditures** (better known as *tax breaks* or *tax loopholes*). These are government financial supports to individuals and corporations to encourage behaviors that ostensibly enhance the public good. Tax breaks and loopholes allow taxpayers to pay lower taxes on their income than they would otherwise pay. For example, to encourage home ownership, the government gives tax breaks to individuals paying interest on a home mortgage. The government also offers tax breaks to businesses for job creation and worker retraining.

State and local governments, as well as nonprofit organizations that provide a public service, pay no federal taxes. Thus we say that they are exempt from federal taxes. Included in this group of tax-exempt organizations are the overwhelming majority of colleges and universities, which are public or nonprofit institutions. They are tax exempt because they provide the public good of higher education without making a profit; they must invest any surplus money back into the institution.

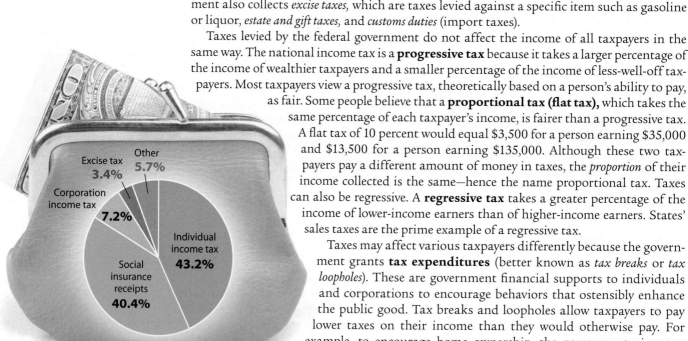

Excise tax 3.4%

Other 5.7%

Corporation income tax 7.2%

Individual income tax 43.2%

Social insurance receipts 40.4%

FY 2011 Executive Budget Revenue

POLITICAL INQUIRY

FIGURE 15.1 ▓ **What is the government's top source of revenue in the FY 2011 executive budget? Do you project that the revenue from this source will remain high in future budgets? Why or why not? What are the other two main sources that provide national revenue? How do you think they may change in future budgets?**

Tax expenditures and tax cuts would not be such a big concern if the government raised enough money to balance its budget. Unfortunately, deficit spending is the norm for the national government. How is the government spending all this money?

Spending Policy

Decisions the federal government makes about spending significantly affect both the national economy and the ability of individuals to achieve their American dream. Although setting the budget is an annual process, with Congress and the president approving a spending plan one fiscal year at a time, not all national government spending is approved annually.

For the government to spend money, Congress and the president must enact laws that establish **budget authority,** which is the legal authority for agencies to obligate government spending. Programs granted budget authority through annual appropriation acts are **discretionary spending** programs. There are two categories of discretionary spending programs: security programs and nonsecurity programs. As Figure 15.2 indicates, security spending is a bigger piece of the budget pie than is nonsecurity spending. Security program spending includes expenditures for the Department of Defense, the Department of Homeland Security, and international affairs. Nonsecurity spending covers an array of activities and programs, including the administration of justice, agriculture, education, energy, environment, health, housing, income security for the poor and disabled, and transportation.

Congress and the president deliberate each year over how much budget authority to include in annual appropriation acts for these discretionary spending programs. Typically, Democrats and Republicans differ on their priorities for discretionary spending programs. As the share of the budget spent on discretionary spending has been shrinking, because of the growing share that goes to *mandatory spending,* the partisan battles between Democrats and Republicans become even more intense.

Figure 15.2 shows that the largest share of the national budget pays for **mandatory spending,** which includes programs whose budget authority is provided in laws other than annual appropriation acts. The budget authority for mandatory spending is established in the authorization legislation that created the program, and is *open ended* because it obligates the government to pay for the program every year, whatever the cost may be, as long as the program exists. Social Security (income security for retired Americans and people with certain disabilities), Medicare (health insurance for the elderly), and Medicaid (health insurance for low-income individuals) are prime examples of mandatory spending programs. Because the government is legally obligated to pay back money it borrows, payments for the national debt also fall within the category of mandatory spending.

In the annual budget process, Congress and the president do not make annual decisions about most of the money spent by the national government because most expenditures are mandatory. Other than interest payments on the debt, mandatory spending could be controlled by Congress and the president by rewriting the legislation that established these open-ended budget obligations. Recent attempts to rewrite the legislation that created the Social Security retirement program have shown that many mandatory programs are politically difficult to change. This is partly because elected officials fear the impact such changes would have on their reelection prospects, and partly because of partisanship. Not only do Democrats and Republicans disagree on the proper reforms, but also members of both parties disagree among themselves on specific reforms. Hence mandatory spending continues to grow as a percentage of the federal budget.

Creating Fiscal Policy Through the National Budget Process

The federal government creates its programs through authorization legislation that specifies the program's goals and establishes whether its budget authority is obligated for the life of the program

budget authority

authority provided by law for agencies to spend government funds

discretionary spending

payment on programs for which Congress and the president must approve budget authority each year in appropriation legislation

mandatory spending

government spending for debt and programs whose budget authority is provided in legislation other than annual appropriation acts; this budget authority is open ended, obligating the government to pay for the program as long as it exists

Discretionary nonsecurity spending — Discretionary security spending — Mandatory spending

13.6%   23.3%   63.1%

FIGURE 15.2

Federal Expenditures by Budget Categories: FY 2011 Executive Budget

SOURCE: Table S-4 at www.whitehouse.gov/omb/budget/fy2011/assets/tables.pdf.

(mandatory spending) or must be set annually (discretionary spending). In an annual appropriation process, Congress and the president establish yearly funding for discretionary spending programs and possibly change tax policy to increase revenue raised—to pay the bills—or to cut taxes in an effort to stimulate the economy. This process begins in the executive branch.

THE PRESIDENT'S EXECUTIVE BUDGET   The budget process officially starts about a year and a half before the beginning of the fiscal year for which budget authority will be obligated. For example, work on the budget for FY 2011 began during the spring of 2009. The process begins when the Office of Management and Budget (OMB) sends the president's budget priorities (policy and financing preferences) to the executive branch agencies. Executive branch agencies use the president's guidelines to formulate their funding requests. Typically, these requests are incremental changes (small increases) to their current fiscal year's budget authority.

The budget requests work their way back up the executive branch hierarchy to the OMB. The OMB reviews the budget requests, conducts hearings in which the agencies justify their requests, and analyzes the requests in light of economic forecasts. The OMB then submits its budget recommendations to the president, who works with the OMB to create a proposed fiscal plan for the entire national government for the upcoming fiscal year. The OMB drafts a budget document and a budget message, collectively labeled the **executive budget,** which explains the president's fiscal plan. The president is required by law to submit the executive budget to Congress by the first Monday in February, eight months before the fiscal year begins.

CONGRESSIONAL ACTION   Once Congress receives the president's executive budget, the Congressional Budget Office (CBO), the legislative branch's counterpart to the OMB, swings into action. The CBO analyzes the executive budget in light of economic forecasts and predicted government revenues. The House Budget Committee and the Senate Budget Committee use the CBO's analysis, along with reports from other congressional committees, to develop the **concurrent budget resolution,** which establishes a binding expenditure ceiling (the maximum amount that can be spent) and a binding revenue floor (the minimum amount that must be raised) as well as proposed expenditure levels for major policy categories. The House and the Senate must both agree to the concurrent budget resolution. This agreement is to occur by April 15, less than six months before the fiscal year begins.

After approval of the concurrent budget resolution, the House and the Senate Appropriations Committees each draft appropriation bills to provide budget authority for discretionary programs. To comply with the concurrent budget resolution, Congress may also need to revise the legislation that authorized selected government programs. For example, the House and Senate may have to agree to change the open-ended budget authority in existing legislation to comply with the expenditure ceiling in the concurrent budget resolution. Or they may have to agree to changes in tax legislation to meet the revenue floor specified in the concurrent resolution. **Budget reconciliation** is the annual process of rewriting authorization legislation to comply with the concurrent budget resolution. The deadline for completion of the reconciliation process is June 15, less than four months before the fiscal year begins.

Congress has until the end of June to approve the twelve appropriation bills that fund the national government for the upcoming fiscal year. This timetable leaves two months for the president to approve the bills so that by October 1 the national government can begin the new fiscal year with budget authority for discretionary spending programs. If Congress and the president fail to approve one or more of the appropriation bills by October 1, Congress must approve a **continuing resolution** to authorize agencies not covered by approved appropriation laws to continue to spend money within their previous budget year's levels.

The nature of the annual budget process is such that, at any given time, some government body in the executive or legislative branch is preparing a future budget, even as the executive branch is implementing the current budget. At the same time, the Government

> Congress received President Barack Obama's 2011 executive budget on Capitol Hill on February 1, 2010. The executive branch's work on the 2011 budget began in the spring of 2009 when the OMB sent President Obama's budget priorities to the government agencies.

executive budget
the budget document and budget message that explains the president's fiscal plan

concurrent budget resolution
document approved by the House and Senate at the beginning of their budget process that establishes a binding expenditure ceiling and a binding revenue floor as well as proposed expenditure levels for major policy categories

budget reconciliation
the annual process of rewriting authorization legislation to comply with the expenditure ceiling and revenue floor of the concurrent budget resolution for the upcoming fiscal year

continuing resolution
an agreement of the House and Senate that authorizes agencies not covered by approved appropriation laws to continue to spend money within their previous budget year's levels

Accountability Office (GAO) is evaluating the implementation of the previous fiscal year's budget. Thus budgeting is a perpetual government activity, one that takes up a great deal of national officials' time.

Deficit Spending, Debt, and Economic Health

Most Americans highly value the ideal of a balanced budget, in which, as we have seen, the government spends no more than the revenues that it raises. Although the nation had a **budget surplus** (money left over when all expenses are paid) for several years at the end of the 1990s, **budget deficits** (more money spent than collected through revenues) recurred as the first decade of the twenty-first century unfolded. Indeed, deficit spending has become the norm, not the exception (see Figure 15.3). In February 2010, President Obama estimated the FY 2010 deficit would be $1.6 trillion. What impact does fiscal policy dominated by deficit spending have on the nation's economic health?

A government that engages in deficit spending borrows money and hence goes into debt. Even as politicians, some economists, and many concerned citizens call for a balanced budget—with some people even proposing a constitutional amendment mandating this objective—deficit spending continues, and so the national debt grows. The long-term impact of debt is the legal obligation to pay back not only the money initially borrowed (the *principal*) but also *interest*, an additional amount of money equal to a percentage of the amount initially borrowed. In the case of government borrowing, future generations

budget surplus
money left over after all expenses are paid

budget deficit
more money spent than collected through revenues

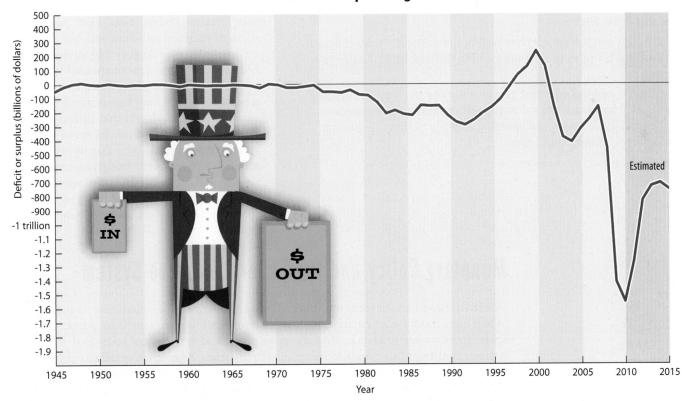

Federal Deficit Spending Since 1945

FIGURE 15.3 ▦ What do we mean by a budget deficit and a budget surplus? What trend in deficit spending does the graph indicate? In what recent years has there been a surplus rather than a deficit? What government expenditures do you think explain the rise in deficit spending since 2002?

SOURCE: Table 1.1, www.whitehouse.gov.omb/budget/Historicals.

The Federal Government's Financial Status

THEN (FY 2000)	NOW (FY 2010)
$1.7 trillion total budget outlay	$3.7 trillion total budget outlay*
$409 billion Social Security outlay	$722 billion Social Security outlay*
$236 billion surplus	$1.6 trillion deficit*
$5.6 trillion national debt	$13.8 trillion national debt*
$6 trillion legal debt ceiling	$14.3 trillion legal debt ceiling

WHAT'S NEXT?

> Will Congress and the president engage in the politically risky endeavor of cutting spending to stop the growing national debt? Explain what discretionary spending you think it is politically feasible for elected federal officials to cut.

> Will Congress and the president engage in the politically risky endeavor of increasing tax rates to stop the growing national debt? Justify your answer.

> Will Congress and the president continue to raise the legal debt ceiling (the limit on how much the national government can borrow) instead of making difficult taxing and spending changes to stop the growing national debt? Justify your answer.

* These are estimates from the FY 2011 Executive Budget.

must pay back the debt of their parents and grandparents. Today, to pay off the $12.4 trillion national debt, each citizen would have to chip in about $40,176.[6]

Public debate is ongoing about the economic impact of long-term deficit spending and the colossal national debt, which is more than three times the amount of money the national government spends in one year. Some economists argue that the more money the national government borrows, the less money businesses can borrow to invest and expand the economy. In addition, many citizens grow increasingly concerned that today's deficit spending will burden future generations with the bill for current policies. Complicating the picture, as the debt incurred from decades of deficit spending accumulates, the debt payment is becoming a larger proportion of the annual federal budget, increasing the percentage of the budget that pays for mandatory spending.

For the government to stop its deficit spending and ultimately reduce its debt, it must increase taxes, cut expenditures, or both. Elected officials do not like to reduce spending, however, because budget cuts often mean that some of their constituents will lose a service or their jobs. Nor do they like to raise taxes, because higher taxes mean that some citizens must give even more of their income to the government and thus have less to spend, invest, or save. Elected officials fear that citizens harmed by spending cuts and tax increases will not vote for them on Election Day. While elected officials struggle with budget decisions and their impact on reelection hopes, appointed officials, whom citizens cannot hold accountable through the ballot box, make monetary policy.

Monetary Policy and the Federal Reserve System

The federal government seeks to influence the value of money by controlling its availability. When more money is in circulation, it is lower in value; consequently, consumers need to spend more money to keep buying the same goods and services. Inflation is at work. The costs of running a business also increase with inflation. As a result of increased costs and decreased sales (because fewer people can maintain their level of spending), businesses may choose to lay off workers. To avert these potential problems, the Federal Reserve, the nation's central banking system, works to maximize employment, ensure stable prices (keep inflation low), and moderate long-term interest rates.

Congress and President Woodrow Wilson (1913–1921) established the Federal Reserve System (the Fed) in 1913. The Fed is composed of the Board of Governors (a government agency whose members the president nominates and the Senate must confirm), twelve Federal Reserve Banks, and the Federal Open Market Committee (FOMC). The Board of Governors, the president of the Federal Reserve Bank of New York, and the presidents of four other

Federal Reserve Banks, who serve on a rotating basis, make up the FOMC. Today, the Fed's responsibilities include (1) setting **monetary policy**—the body of government policies aimed at maintaining price stability; (2) supervising and regulating banking institutions; (3) maintaining the stability of financial markets; and (4) providing financial services to depository institutions, the national government, and foreign official institutions—central banks of other nations, and international organizations such as the International Monetary Fund.

The Fed has three primary tools for setting monetary policy. It can raise or lower the *reserve requirement*—the amount of money that financial institutions must keep out of circulation. In times of high inflation, the Fed may raise the reserve requirement to decrease the amount of money available through credit, hence decreasing the money supply. The Fed can also raise or lower the *discount rate*—the interest charged to financial institutions that borrow money from the Federal Reserve bank—and thereby make it more or less costly to borrow money. The Fed action that most influences the money supply, however, is its decision to buy or sell Treasury Securities (bills, notes, and bonds, which represent loans of money to the government to meet expenditures not covered by tax revenues). The Fed sells Treasury Securities when it wants to decrease the money supply and buys them to increase the supply.

Beyond its authority to set monetary policy, the Fed exerts supervisory and some regulatory authority over about 3,000 banks that are members of the Federal Reserve System (including all commercial banks chartered by the national government and those state-chartered banks that choose to join the Federal Reserve System), companies that control banks, and the U.S. activities of foreign banks. However, the Fed is not the only federal agency supervising and regulating the banking and financial industries. For example, the Office of the Comptroller of the Currency (OCC)—created in 1863 as a bureau within the Treasury Department—also charters, supervises, and regulates national banks. The Federal Deposit Insurance Corporation (FDIC)—an independent agency established in 1933—supervises state-chartered banks that are not members of the Federal Reserve System. Since the mid-1800s, the national government has created numerous regulatory agencies charged with ensuring the safety and soundness of the nation's banking and financial industries and systems, with the ultimate goal of promoting a healthy national economy.

Regulatory Policy

As stated by Adam Smith in 1776, in theory, the competition that characterizes a free, unregulated market serves the public good by producing the range of high-quality and affordable products and services that citizens need or demand. Free-market advocates assume that competition provides for the public good. Yet at times, the competition of a free, unregulated market may harm consumers, workers, and the environment.

Indeed, competition among private entities, each trying to make a profit, may threaten public safety and health. Consider, for example, the unsafe products, including dangerous food and drugs, that may be manufactured and sold to make a profit. Think about production and manufacturing processes that may pollute the air, water, and land, creating conditions that are injurious to public health. Competition may also lead firms to cut salaries and benefits to ensure their profits, or their very survival. Such cuts decrease workers' ability to earn wages and benefits that keep them in the middle class, or even out of poverty. Unsafe and unhealthful working conditions may be another "cost" that workers "pay" so that firms can hold down or reduce production expenses. Moreover, if marketplace competition results in a few firms driving out their competition, they then have the power to raise prices or produce goods of lower quality, harming consumers.

Recently, the United States experienced a failure in the financial market to channel funds from savers to borrowers because of risky decisions by numerous financial and banking institutions. Loans and credit lines extended to people without the means to repay the borrowed money sparked an increase in the number of people who could not pay their mortgages and therefore lost their homes. Hundreds of billions of dollars worth of mortgage-related investments went bad by the fall of 2008, and several large, prominent financial and banking companies collapsed. President Bush and Congress began discussions

monetary policy
the body of government policies, controlled by the Federal Reserve System, aimed at influencing the supply of money in the marketplace to maintain price stability

about the need for new regulations for the banking and financial industries to prevent similar market failures in the future. Congress and President Obama's administration continued those discussions, focusing on protecting consumers of the banking and financial industries. In the summer of 2010, President Obama signed legislation establishing the Bureau of Consumer Financial Protection, an independent unit within the Fed. The Bureau of Consumer Financial Protection has the authority to regulate a wide range of financial products, including mortgages and credit cards, and to collect and monitor consumer complaints about the financial and banking industries, and a responsibility to educate consumers about financial products and services.

In the U.S. economy today, the government regulates marketplace practices to protect the public. This regulation occurs in two broad categories: business regulation and social regulation. **Business regulation** includes government policies that aim to preserve competition in the marketplace. **Social regulation** refers to government policies directed at protecting workers, consumers, and the environment from the harm caused by marketplace competition. In Chapter 13, we surveyed the administrative rule-making process by which executive branch agencies establish business and social regulations. In this discussion, we trace the evolution of these two types of regulatory policy.

Business Regulation

The federal government created the first agency for the purpose of regulating business, the Interstate Commerce Commission (ICC), in 1887. The ICC initially regulated the prices of and services provided by the railroad industry to protect the livelihood of farmers who relied on the nation's rail lines to transport their goods to distant markets. Next, in 1914, the federal government established regulations to prevent large corporations from engaging in business practices that harmed marketplace competition and established the Federal Trade Commission (FTC) to oversee these regulations.[7]

In 1934, during the Great Depression, the government created the Securities and Exchange Commission (SEC) to regulate and make transparent the nation's stock markets and financial markets. Another regulation of the Depression era, the National Labor Relations Act of 1935 (commonly known as the Wagner Act), authorized the national government to

business regulation
government rules, regulations, and standards directed at protecting competition in the marketplace

social regulation
government rules and regulations aimed at protecting workers, consumers, and the environment from market failure

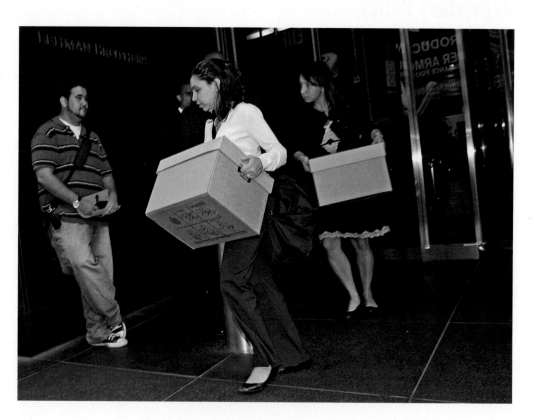

> Women carry their belongings from the headquarters of Lehman Brothers in New York in September 2008 after the 158-year-old investment bank filed for bankruptcy. Because of the credit crisis and devalued real estate market that devastated banking and financial institutions such as Lehman Brothers, the federal government proposed new regulations for these institutions.

regulate interactions between management and labor unions. The Wagner Act empowered union members by guaranteeing the right of workers to unionize and elect representatives to bargain collectively with management for improved wages and working conditions. Moreover, the Wagner Act outlawed certain management practices that Congress considered unfair to labor—and hence a potential threat to the economy. Then in 1947, Congress overrode President Harry Truman's (1945–1953) veto and passed the Labor-Management Relations Act (Taft-Hartley Act), which identified and outlawed labor practices Congress deemed unfair and restricted the right to unionize to nonsupervisory employees only.

Thus within fifty years of the creation of the first regulatory agency, the ICC, the national government had put in place a full range of business regulations. From regulating prices and standards in industries, to criminalizing business practices that restrict marketplace competition, to making stock transactions transparent, to regulating labor-management relations—today, the government regulates the marketplace in a wide variety of ways in the interest of creating and maintaining a healthy economy.

Social Regulation

The national government also uses social regulatory policy—which aims to protect the public's health and safety—to safeguard workers, consumers, and the environment from the potential harm created by the competitive quest for profits in the marketplace. Like business regulation, social regulation has an economic impact because it increases the costs of doing business.

EARLY SOCIAL REGULATION Scholars see precedents for social regulation in two 1906 laws that protected *public* health—the Pure Food and Drug Act and the Meat Inspection Act. Upton Sinclair's descriptions of the dangerous and unsanitary conditions in the Chicago meatpacking industry in his novel *The Jungle* motivated President Theodore Roosevelt (1901–1909) to sign those two laws. The Pure Food and Drug Act created the Food and Drug Administration (FDA) and charged it with testing all foods and drugs produced for human consumption. It also requires individuals to present prescriptions from licensed physicians to purchase certain drugs and mandates the use of warning labels on habit-forming drugs. The Meat Inspection Act requires government inspection of animals that are slaughtered and processed for human consumption and establishes standards of cleanliness for slaughterhouses and meat processing plants.

The federal government first addressed working conditions that jeopardized *workers'* health when it enacted the Fair Labor Standards Act (FLSA) in 1938. The FLSA established standards for a legal workweek, overtime pay for those working more than the standard workweek, minimum wages, record keeping of workers' hours, and limits on child labor. President Franklin D. Roosevelt characterized the law as the "most far-reaching, far-sighted program to the benefit of workers ever adopted."[8]

CONSUMER AND ENVIRONMENTAL PROTECTION In the 1960s, the government focused anew on growing concerns about product quality and safety. In his 1965 book *Unsafe at Any Speed,* attorney and consumer advocate Ralph Nader warned that "a great problem of contemporary life is how to control the power of economic interests which ignore the harmful effects of their applied science and technology."[9] Although Nader's book targeted the unsafe cars rolling off the assembly lines of the U.S. auto industry, his warning was equally relevant to the countless American industries that were discharging chemicals and toxins into the environment. Nader's book ignited a consumer safety movement, and a related environmental movement was born with the first Earth Day in 1970.

Lobbying by concerned citizens and interest groups led to passage of the Environmental Protection Act of 1970 and the Consumer Product Safety Act (CPSA) of 1973. These far-reaching federal laws aimed to regulate business practices that threatened consumers' health and safety as well as the environment. The federal Consumer Product Safety Commission (CPSC), created through the CPSA, is charged by law with protecting the public from unreasonable risk of injury associated with more than 15,000 consumer products,

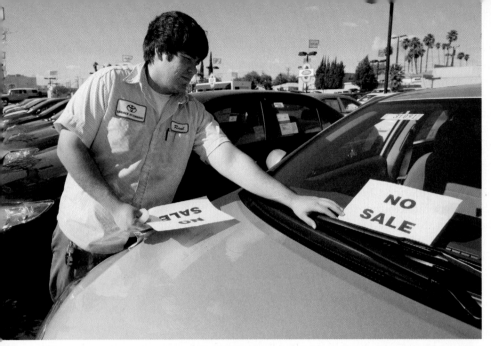

including toys, products for children, products for inside and outside the home, and products made for sports and recreation. The CPSA can recall such products if it deems them unsafe, just as the FDA can recall food and prescription medicines it judges to be unsafe. The CPSC and the FDA post recall information on their Web sites (www.cpsc.gov/; www.fda.gov/opacom/Enforce.html).

The financial and economic free fall that began in 2007 sparked a national conversation about the need for additional regulation of the financial and banking industries. In 2009, President Obama and Treasury Secretary Timothy Geithner proposed restructuring the numerous existing federal agencies that regulate the financial banking industries. In addition, they proposed the creation of a new agency to oversee financial products sold to consumers to protect consumers and the economy. In 2010, Congress and President Obama created the Bureau of Consumer Financial Protection.

THE COSTS OF REGULATION Market regulation has unquestionably lowered the risk of harm to citizens and the environment caused by marketplace competition. It also has cushioned economic downfalls. But the burden of government regulations has driven up the cost of doing business, and in the end, consumers pay for this cost. In many industries, this increased cost poses greater problems for smaller firms than for larger ones. The higher costs caused by regulation may also put U.S. industries and firms at a competitive disadvantage in the global marketplace, because many other countries do not impose regulations. Therefore the production costs of firms in other countries are often lower than those in the United States.

The lack of regulations imposed by governments in other nations is a growing concern in the United States. The FDA and the CPSC are recalling numerous products manufactured in foreign countries, and even some products manufactured in the United States that use ingredients or components from foreign sources. Because of these concerns, trade policy and the interdependence of the global economy are prominent contemporary issues.

> Employee Raul Quecada places a "No Sale" sign on a Toyota a day after Toyota Motor Corporation announced it would stop sales of some of its top-selling vehicles to fix a sticking gas pedal problem. This action followed several voluntary safety recalls Toyota announced (September 2007, October 2009, January 2010) after the number of gas pedal problems sparked media attention and concerns among the public. In February 2010, the National Traffic and Safety Administration, the regulatory agency to which automakers must report defects, initiated an investigation to determine if Toyota conducted the three recalls in a timely manner.

Trade Policy in the Global Economy

The next time you are shopping, try to purchase only American-made products. Is it possible? Stores in the United States offer products that are domestic (that is, American-made) as well as imported (made overseas by American or foreign companies). Moreover, many American-made products have imported components and ingredients. For example, U.S. International Trade Commission data show that ingredients for food products are imported from more than one hundred countries.[10] Today, marketplaces in every country offer products grown and produced in countries from throughout the world. Hence national economies are integrated and interdependent—holistically forming the **global economy.**

To navigate in this global economy, each nation has its own **trade policy**—a collection of tax laws and regulations that support the country's international commerce. In addition, international organizations whose mission is to establish trade rules for all nations to follow have created a global trade policy. The goal of trade policy, like the other economic policies we have discussed, is ostensibly to promote prosperous economies.

global economy
the worldwide economy created by the integration and interdependence of national economies

trade policy
a collection of tax laws and regulations that supports the country's international commerce

Trade Policy: Protectionist or Free Trade?

A government's trade policy takes one of two basic forms: free trade or protectionism. **Protectionist trade policy** aims at protecting domestic producers and businesses from foreign competition through tariffs and nontariff trade barriers. A **tariff** is a special tax on imported goods. **Nontariff trade barriers** include government social and business regulations as well as government **subsidies**—tax breaks or another kind of financial support that encourages behaviors the government deems beneficial to the public good. Most subsidies are given to producers or distributors of goods to promote economic growth. Proponents of national government subsidies to U.S. farmers argue that to decrease these subsidies would place the farmers at a competitive disadvantage because European farmers receive even larger subsidies from their governments. Regulations include restrictions such as limits on the number of imports allowed into the country and bans on the sale of imports that the government deems unsafe. For example, in 2007 the national government blocked imports of wheat gluten from a company in China after the FDA recalled a brand of pet food manufactured in Canada that contained this wheat gluten. The pet food caused cats and dogs throughout the United States to become ill and even to die.

From the 1790s until the 1930s, protectionism was the aim of U.S. trade policy. As the first secretary of the treasury, Alexander Hamilton argued successfully that taxes on imported goods could be set high enough to protect American-made products in the domestic marketplace. In 1930, even as the American economy was failing, Congress hiked tariffs 20 percent—so high that it set off an international tariff war. This tariff hike fueled the Great Depression, whose economic toll was global in scope.

After World War II, the United States and its international partners gradually shifted toward a **free trade policy,** which aims at lowering or eliminating tariffs and nontariff barriers to trade. Free trade policies decrease the costs of bringing products to markets throughout the world and, in this way, open markets to a greater diversity of products and brisker competition. When other nations eliminate tariffs, American companies can participate in the global marketplace at a lower cost. These opportunities encourage an increase in the supply of U.S. goods and thus lead to an expansion of the U.S. economy. By the same token, when the United States eliminates its tariffs, more foreign products make their way into the American marketplace, increasing the diversity of consumer goods and producer competition and decreasing consumer prices in the United States.

International Trade Agreements

In 1947, the United States and twenty-three other nations signed the General Agreement on Tariffs and Trade (GATT). This multilateral agreement on guidelines for conducting international trade had three basic objectives. First, the signatory countries would not discriminate against one another in trade matters. Second, the signatory countries would work toward eliminating all tariff and regulatory barriers to trade among their countries. Third, the signatory countries would consult and negotiate with one another to resolve any trade conflicts or damages caused by trading activities of another signatory country. Through multilateral negotiations, the GATT established the guidelines for international trade and resolved trade disputes from 1947 to 1995.

Then in 1995, the World Trade Organization (WTO) came into being. The WTO continues the GATT's advocacy of free trade and punishment of protectionism. Specifically, the WTO monitors adherence to international trade rules and resolves charges of rule violations raised by any of its over 130 member countries. The WTO Ministerial Conference meets every two years to discuss and deliberate on international trade rules. The meetings have become magnets for massive and sometimes violent demonstrations by protesters from around the world who believe that free trade is harming the environment, impeding human development in developing countries, and hurting the poor in all countries.

protectionist trade policy
establishment of trade barriers to protect domestic goods from foreign competition

tariff
a special tax on imported goods

nontariff trade barriers
business and social regulations as well as subsidies aimed at creating a competitive advantage in trade

subsidy
a tax break or another kind of financial support that encourages behaviors the government deems beneficial to the public good

free trade policy
elimination of tariffs and nontariff trade barriers so that international trade is expanded

Opponents of free trade argue that the deregulation of nontrade barriers has exacerbated deplorable working conditions, child labor problems, and poverty. (See "Thinking Critically About Democracy.")

In the 1990s, bipartisan support for free trade in the U.S. Congress produced regional trade agreements such as the North American Free Trade Agreement (NAFTA), which the United States, Canada, and Mexico signed in 1993. NAFTA eliminated barriers to trade and financial investments across the economies of the three nations. Yet by the beginning of the twenty-first century, congressional legislators' concerns about possible damage to living standards and the health of the global environment, which many argue are caused by free trade, were growing, as was the nation's **trade deficit** (a negative balance of trade in which imports exceed exports).

Activists throughout the world are advocating policies to limit some of the harms they ascribe to free trade. Environmental groups fight for environmental protections to be included in international trade agreements. The International Labor Organization—a United Nations agency that promotes internationally recognized human and worker rights—advocates for bans on forced labor and child labor, prohibitions against discrimination in personnel decisions and policies, and safeguards for the rights of workers to organize and bargain collectively with employers, all of which are forms of social regulation. Groups concerned about human development worry that free trade agreements ignore the economic status of small family farmers, artisans whose goods are sold in local markets, and poor people in general. In addition to these global concerns, American activists look closer to home, concerned about the impact of free trade on American living standards.

trade deficit
a negative balance of trade in which imports exceed exports

The U.S. Economy, the Global Economy, and the American Dream Today

Between 2000 and 2006, according to traditional measures of economic health—GDP, unemployment rates, and rates of inflation—the U.S. economy was expanding; however, it was the weakest economic expansion since World War II.[11] During the same period, in American households, the real median household income decreased[12] and the poverty rate crept up to 12.3 percent.[13] Moreover, income inequality grew. According to the U.S. Census Bureau, by 2007 the bottom quintile (20 percent of the population) possessed just 3.4 percent of the total national income, while the top quintile held 50.5 percent, the largest share of the national income held by the top quintile since 1967.[14] Alan Greenspan, the renowned economist who chaired the Federal Reserve from 1987 to 2005, testified to Congress's Joint Economic Committee in 2005 about this paradox of a growing economy that disproportionately benefits those at the top: "This is not the type of thing which a democratic society—a capitalist democratic society—can really accept without addressing." He even suggested that this income gap seriously threatened the stability of the U.S. economy.[15]

Indeed, in 2007 the economy began to stagnate. The Fed used monetary policy to try to stimulate the economy, cutting interest rates six times between September 2007 and March 2008. However, by February 2008, some in the media and the government were forecasting an economic downturn as consumer prices increased at the same time that economic growth (as measured by change in the GDP) was stagnating.[16] Senator Christopher Dodd (D-Connecticut), chairman of the Senate Banking Committee, stated, "The current economic situation is more than merely a 'slowdown' or a 'downturn.' It is a crisis of confidence among consumers and investors."[17] This "crisis in confidence" sparked a call for the Fed to increase its regulation of the banking and financial investment industries in spring 2008.

President George W. Bush and Congress attempted to use fiscal policy to address this economic situation. In February 2008, they approved tax rebates totaling $168 billion and tax cuts for select businesses. Then in October 2008, as we have seen, President Bush signed the $700 billion Emergency Economic Stabilization Act, allowing the federal government to buy assets from the biggest banks to shore them up and restore confidence in the financial system.

IS FREE TRADE MERELY A RACE TO THE BOTTOM?

The Issue: Since World War II, world powers—including governments and influential nongovernmental organizations (NGOs)—have worked to expand international trade. Although the founders of this globalization movement envisioned a "race to the top" with respect to living standards, today a global debate rages on the pros and cons of free trade. Supporters of free trade argue that it is the path out of poverty. Opponents insist that free trade has set off a brutal "race to the bottom" because of market failures.

Yes: Free trade sets off a race to the bottom. Free trade encourages today's corporations to move their jobs to countries where business and social regulation is weak or nonexistent. Consequently, the workers in producer nations lose jobs to lower-paid foreign workers toiling in deplorable conditions. Foreign plants, with weak or nonexistent environmental regulations to follow, also create major environmental hazards that spill across national borders.

No: Free trade spreads wealth. Free trade opens new markets for products from all countries. New markets increase demand for products, hence creating jobs in the producing countries. As consumers enjoy a greater variety of products at lower costs, the standard of living improves, especially for lower-income households. History shows that in the long term, this type of economic transition—economic development—improves the quality of life for workers as everyone benefits financially.

Other approaches: Creative capitalism can ameliorate a race to the bottom. Under creative capitalism, governments, businesses, and nonprofit organizations work together to ensure that current global economic forces benefit profit-making corporations while also addressing societal problems. For example, the (RED) Campaign is a coordinated effort in which corporations have pledged a percentage of their profits from select products to purchase medications needed to fight AIDS in Africa. Creative capitalism does not tinker with free trade, but it does encourage corporations to develop a social consciousness for which consumers reward them. The profits of free trade benefit the poor as well as the corporations.

What do you think?

① Are U.S. companies that create jobs in foreign countries interested in improving those countries' working conditions and pay and in protecting the environment? Explain.

② In the long term, what effect will a global laissez-faire policy have on the quality of life of the world's population as a whole?

③ How can the benefits of global economic development decrease income inequality?

In his FY 2010 executive budget (published in February 2009), President Barack Obama summarized the economic status of the nation and the actions his administration planned to take in response to it: "We start 2009 in the midst of a crisis unlike any we have seen in our lifetime. Our economy is in a deep recession that threatens to be deeper and longer than any since the Great Depression. . . . The time has come to usher in a new era—a new era of responsibility in which we act not only to save and create new jobs, but also to lay a new foundation of growth upon which we can renew the promise of America." Obama then highlighted the planned investments in clean energy, education, health care, and infrastructure (such as roads, bridges, schools, and broadband lines) that are part of the American Recovery and Reinvestment Act (2009). The hope was that these investments would maintain and create jobs. He also discussed the need for government to be more transparent and accountable to the people, beginning with the necessity of cutting deficit spending.

In February 2010, a year after the enactment of the ARRA, while Congress was debating the content of proposed new stimulus packages, economists, government officials, and citizens were assessing the effect of the 2009 stimulus package. Because most people worry about being employed during poor economic times, many people focused on the national unemployment rate, which was close to 10 percent. Critics of the ARRA claimed this high rate of unemployment was proof that the stimulus package did not work—it did not save or create jobs. However, others argued that without the ARRA's tax cuts and increased

TAKE YOUR CHILD TO WORK DAY 2009

UNEMPLOYMENT →

Source: Chan Lowe/South Florida Sun-Sentinel.

spending, the unemployment rate would have been even higher. In addition, by the end of 2009, even though salaries and wages on average had decreased, consumer spending was up. Corporate spending had surged by the end of 2009, as tax credits for corporate investment were expiring. Clearly, the Great Recession was not over, but there was little doubt among most economists that the U.S. economy would have declined even further without the 2009 ARRA.[18]

The recession, which began in 2007 and deepened throughout 2008 and 2009, was a global phenomenon. Rising unemployment, shrinking confidence in financial institutions, decreasing availability of credit and hence decreasing investment, and slow economic growth were economic realities in countries throughout the world. In November 2008, leaders of twenty countries met in Washington, D.C., for an emergency economic summit and agreed to work together to address the global recession. Central banks in European and Asian countries took actions to encourage investment and to shore up financial institutions. Many nations also put in place stimulus packages—taxing and spending plans—to combat the worst global economic crisis since the Great Depression.

It was during the Great Depression that historian James Truslow Adams coined the term "American dream." In his book *The Epic of America* (1931), Adams argued that what made America a unique nation was its inhabitants' "dream of a better, richer, and happier life" for all citizens based on equal "opportunity for each according to his [or her] ability or achievement."[19] For many, the American dream has come to mean owning a home, providing their children with good educational opportunities so they can advance in life, and saving for retirement. For others, it means being rich. Today, Americans tell pollsters that they are living better than their parents did. At the same time, Americans tell pollsters that today's children will *not* be able to live better than *their* parents did.[20] Indeed, *New York Times* columnist Bob Herbert summarized several studies of the millennial generation (those born between 1980 and 2000) by stating that it "is in danger of being left out of the American dream—the first American generation to do less well economically than their parents."[21] Is the American dream doing better economically than your parents? Is it being rich? Or is the American dream living in a nation that has a stable, healthy economy and an equal opportunity to achieve (measured by home ownership, high levels of education, and comfortable retirement) according to your ability and effort? If the American dream is the last, can government policies—fiscal, monetary, regulatory, and trade—ensure a healthy national economy in today's interdependent global economy? In addition, can government domestic policies—which we discuss in Chapter 16—ensure equal opportunity for citizens to achieve according to their ability and effort?

CONCLUSION

THINKING CRITICALLY ABOUT WHAT'S NEXT IN ECONOMIC POLICY

Governments throughout the world seek to maintain healthy economies using economic policy. U.S. economic policy comprises taxing and spending policies (fiscal policy), monetary policy, regulatory policy, and trade policy. Today, the economic decisions made by the president, Congress, and the Fed are influenced by the realities of the global economy. Just as the economic policy decisions made in other countries throughout the world can affect the economic health of the United States, the economic policies made by the U.S. national government can affect the economic health of nations all over the globe. What impact will continuing globalization have on the U.S. government's ability to maintain a healthy national economy?

The global recession that began in 2007 has reinvigorated long-standing debates on the proper role of government in maintaining a healthy economy. As the recession developed, the national government attempted to address its immediate effects with limited tax cuts and spending increases to shore up unemployment and health benefits, and to protect and create jobs. In addition, taxpayers became partial owners of some businesses when the government bought assets of collapsing businesses. However, many politicians, economists, and citizens argue that the nation needs major changes to current fiscal, monetary, and regulatory policies to ensure long-term economic health. People are again beginning to call for a constitutional amendment mandating a balanced budget. Will national elected and appointed officials enact major tax, spending, and regulatory reforms in the wake of the Great Recession?

The viability of the American dream depends on a healthy national economy. Even before the current recession began, income inequality was growing. The gap between those who have the largest share of the nation's wealth and everyone else has expanded in the last few decades. Will your generation and future generations be able to achieve the American dream?

Summary

1. Economic Health and the American Dream
Though work ethic and education level influence personal income, a healthy national economy is essential to the ability of people to live a financially secure, happy, and healthy life—to realize the American dream. The health of the economy influences the availability of jobs with adequate levels of compensation (salaries and benefits).

2. The Nature of the American Economy
The national government's economic policy is aimed at establishing and maintaining a healthy economy so that it can raise the money necessary to fulfill its mission of serving the people. Because the government implements many policies that encourage, and sometimes mandate, certain business practices in the interest of creating and maintaining a healthy economy, the United States has what is known as a regulated capitalist economy.

3. Economic Theories That Shape Economic Policy
The national government's efforts to achieve and maintain a healthy economy have expanded as lawmakers have embraced various economic theories, among them Keynesian economics, supply-side economics, and monetarism. The specific policies implemented by the government depend on the particular economic theories government officials adopt. In recent decades, Democrats and Republicans have followed different economic theories, with the result that taxing, spending, and regulatory policies have frequently shifted.

4. Measuring Economic Health
Traditional measures of economic health include worker productivity, GDP, rate of inflation, and rate of unemployment. Other measures include real median household income, income inequality, rate of poverty, and the Human Development Index. Together, they can be used to assess how well a prosperous national economy enables its citizens to live the American dream. Unfortunately, many times this diversity of measures yields conflicting assessments of economic health: the nation's economy may be growing at the same time that the financial status of households is stagnating or even declining.

5. Fiscal Policy and Its Impact on the Health of the Economy
Taxing and spending decisions by the president and Congress influence how much money consumers have to spend, save, and invest; how much profit firms make and how much they have to invest in expanding business; and how much the government has to spend in order

to serve the people. Deficit spending is a persistent reality of U.S. fiscal policy, creating economic problems in the long term.

6. Monetary Policy and the Federal Reserve System

The Fed, directed by a group of appointed officials, works to keep inflation and unemployment low by regulating the amount of money in circulation in the economy. Aimed at creating and maintaining price stability, monetary policy is a component of U.S. economic policy.

7. Regulatory Policy

By the late 1800s, the laissez-faire ideal concerning government regulation of marketplace competition and business practices was clearly not the reality. Today, business regulation (to ensure competition) and social regulation (to protect workers, consumers, and the environment) are pervasive components of the U.S. economy, despite ongoing calls by business, some economists, and politicians (more apt to be Republicans than Democrats) to deregulate.

8. Trade Policy in the Global Economy

Protectionist trade policy dominated the United States until after World War II. Then free trade policy became the goal of international agreements and U.S. trade policy. Today, debate continues over the domestic and global effects (positive and negative) of free trade policy in the global economy.

9. The U.S. Economy, the Global Economy, and the American Dream Today

The recent global recession, the worst since the Great Depression of the 1930s, has sparked conversations about the nature of the American dream and whether or not it is achievable in the global economy.

Key Terms

American dream 464

balanced budget 467

budget authority 475

budget deficit 477

budget reconciliation 476

budget surplus 477

business regulation 480

concurrent budget
    resolution 476

consumer price index
    (CPI) 470

continuing resolution 476

deficit spending 467

depression 468

deregulation 469

discretionary spending 475

economic boom 468

economic policy 464

economy 465

executive budget 476

fiscal policy 468

fiscal year (FY) 473

free trade policy 483

global economy 482

gross domestic product
    (GDP) 470

household income 472

Human Development Index
    (HDI) 472

income inequality 467

inflation 469

Keynesian economics 468

laissez-faire 466

mandatory spending 475

median household income 472

monetarism 469

monetary policy 479

national debt 469

nontariff trade barriers 483

poverty 472

poverty rate 472

poverty thresholds 472

progressive tax 474

proportional tax
    (flat tax) 474

protectionist trade policy 483

pure capitalist economy 466

real income 472

recession 468

regressive tax 474

regulated capitalist economy
    (mixed economy) 466

social regulation 480

subsidy 483

supply-side economics 469

tariff 483

tax base 465

tax expenditures 474

trade deficit 484

trade policy 482

For Review

1. What is the American dream? Describe one impact each of the following national policies can have on the American dream: tax policy, spending policy, business regulation, social regulation, monetary policy, trade policy.

2. What distinguishes a pure capitalist economy from a regulated capitalist economy?

3. Differentiate among Keynesian economics, supply-side economics, and monetarism.

4. Explain at least four measures of economic health.

5. What is fiscal policy and who makes it?

6. What is monetary policy and who makes it?

7. Distinguish between business regulation and social regulation. Indicate how each type of regulation affects the economy.

8. Differentiate between the goals as well as the techniques of free trade policy and protectionist trade policy.

9. What is the health of the U.S. economy as well as the American dream at the beginning of the twenty-first century?

For Critical Thinking and Discussion

1. If you were president of the United States and wanted to balance the annual budget, what programs' cost cuts do you think you could get American taxpayers to support? What tax increases or new taxes do you think you could get American taxpayers to support? Explain your choices.

2. Consider your family's financial situation. What economic policy would you propose the national government implement to improve your family's financial situation? Explain.

3. Which type of tax do you think is the most fair, progressive, proportional, or regressive? Explain your choice.

4. If the national government deregulates with regard to environmental protection, product safety, and/or working conditions, would there be negative consequences? Give some examples, or explain why there would not be any.

5. Some politicians have suggested that a flat income tax of about 17 percent could raise about the same amount of revenue for the national government as the current progressive income tax and should replace it. Politically speaking, who would support such a proposal, and who would oppose it?

PRACTICE QUIZ

MULTIPLE CHOICE: Choose the lettered item that answers the question correctly.

1. The economic theory that advocates the use of fiscal policy to create and maintain a healthy economy is called
   a. Keynesian economics.
   b. laissez-faire economics.
   c. monetarism.
   d. supply-side economics.

2. Which of the following is *not* included in the mandatory spending category of the national government?
   a. debt payments   c. Medicare
   b. education   d. Social Security

3. The officials that approve fiscal policy are
   a. Congress (on its own).
   b. Congress and the president.
   c. Congress, the president, and the Fed.
   d. the Fed (on its own).

4. The officials that approve monetary policy are
   a. Congress (on its own).
   b. Congress and the president.
   c. Congress, the president, and the Fed.
   d. the Fed (on its own).

5. The policy that decreases the costs of bringing products to markets throughout the world by lowering or eliminating tariffs and deregulating is called
   a. free trade policy.
   b. monetary policy.
   c. protectionist trade policy.
   d. regulatory policy.

6. The policy in which the national government engages to protect consumers, workers, and the environment from the harm of marketplace competition is called
   a. business regulation.
   b. deregulation.
   c. protectionist trade policy.
   d. social regulation.

7. Based on its impact on taxpayers' income, what type of tax is the state sales tax?
   a. flat   c. proportional
   b. progressive   d. regressive

8. The largest revenue source for the national government is
   a. corporate income taxes.
   b. import taxes.
   c. individual income taxes.
   d. social insurance taxes.

9. During what president's administrations did the national government first adopt Keynesian economic principles to create and maintain a healthy national economy?
   a. George Washington
   b. Franklin Delano Roosevelt
   c. Ronald Reagan
   d. George W. Bush

10. During what president's administration did the national government adopt the American Recovery and Reinvestment Act to address a great recession?
    a. Franklin Delano Roosevelt
    b. Ronald Reagan
    c. George W. Bush
    d. Barack Obama

FILL IN THE BLANKS.

11. When it spends more money than it collects in taxes, the government is engaging in _____ .

12. _____ refers to the rising prices of consumer goods, which means the value of the dollar has decreased.

13. The date on which the national 2011 fiscal year (FY 2011) began is _____ .

14. The _____ is a nongovernmental organization that advocates for free trade policy, monitors adherence to international trade rules, and resolves charges of trade rule violation raised by its member countries.

15. The collection of national tax policies and spending policies is referred to as _____ policy.

RESOURCES FOR RESEARCH AND ACTION

Internet Resources

American Enterprise Institute (AEI)
www.aei.org The AEI sponsors research on government policy and economic policy and advocates limited government involvement in the marketplace.

American Institute for Economic Research
www.aier.org This nonprofit research and educational organization provides studies and information on economic and financial issues.

Bureau of Economic Analysis (BEA)
www.bea.doc.gov The BEA, an agency in the Department of Commerce, produces and disseminates data on regional, national, and international economies.

Economic Policy Institute
http://epinet.org This nonprofit organization aims to broaden public debate on strategies to achieve a prosperous and fair economy.

Office of Management and Budget (OMB)
www.whitehouse.gov/omb The OMB's site has links to the most recent executive budget and historical budget documents.

U.S. Census Bureau
www.census.gov The Census Bureau, a bureau in the Department of Commerce, collects and disseminates data about the people and economy of the nation.

Internet Activism

Public Citizen, founded by Ralph Nader in 1971, is a national, nonprofit, public interest organization engaged in research and advocacy on a multitude of issues, including reform of the financial system, protections for consumers and workers, equitable trade, and globalization. To learn more about these economic issues and the role you can play in Public Citizen's lobbying efforts, visit **www.facebook.com/publiccitizen** or **www.citizen.org**.

Twitter
http://twitter.com/OnSafety Get notified about U.S. Consumer Product Safety Commission's safety alerts and recalls.

YouTube
www.youtube.com/watch?v=6_7jaEO3pPs The landmark National Debt Clock in New York City is running out of room as the debt expands to fourteen-digit numbers.

Facebook
www.facebook.com/taxfoundation The Tax Foundation is a nonpartisan, nonprofit research institution founded in 1937 to educate Americans about sound tax policy at all levels of government. Its economic and policy analysis is guided by the principles of neutrality, simplicity, transparency, and stability.

Recommended Readings

Derber, Charles. *People Before Profit*. New York: Picador, 2003. A disturbing analysis of globalization to date with a blueprint for a new form of globalization that will lead to a more stable and just global community.

Lieberman, Carl. *Making Economic Policy*. Englewood Cliffs, NJ: Prentice Hall, 1991. A concise yet comprehensive overview of economic policies, including spending policy, tax policy, monetary policy, economic regulation, and economic subsidies.

Schick, Allen. *The Federal Budget*. Washington, DC: Brookings Institute, 2000. A comprehensive, in-depth consideration of the national budget process.

Woodward, Bob. *Maestro: Greenspan's Fed and the American Boom*. New York: Simon & Schuster, 2000. A probing look into how the Fed operated under the leadership of Alan Greenspan from 1987 to 2000. The effect of the evolving global economy on the economic health of the United States is an intriguing part of Woodward's account.

Movies of Interest

Cinderella Man (2005)
Based on the life of prizefighter Jim Braddock, this film movingly depicts the common person's struggle to survive the Great Depression and the hopes and inspiration that one person's rise from the bottom can evoke in the population at large.

Enron: The Smartest Guys in the Room (2005)
Based on the best-selling book of the same title, this documentary spotlights the human drama of Enron's fall—the biggest corporate scandal in American history—including the company's collapse, the elimination of thousands of jobs, and the loss of $60 billion in market value and $2 billion in pension plans.

Commanding Heights: The Battle for the World Economy (2002)
This documentary exploration of the political side of today's global economy looks at the people, ideas, and events that fostered the liberalization of trade policies around the globe.

Domestic Policy

THEN

In the 1930s, radical new federal government policies created a safety net that enabled economically distressed citizens to provide for their basic needs.

NOW

The federal government faces a host of domestic policy issues, from the high cost of maintaining the safety net to environmental degradation, scarce energy supplies, homeland security threats, and calls for immigration reform.

NEXT

Will global warming and worldwide environmental degradation force U.S. policy makers to sign international treaties?

Will the perpetually increasing costs of income security programs and health care force U.S. policy makers to enact major legislative reforms?

Will demographic change owing to high immigration today bring new issues to tomorrow's domestic policy agenda?

Independence and the U.S. Constitution, American government must ensure a just and safe society in which citizens can live their lives freely, in pursuit of their happiness. Essential to the achievement of these goals are the preservation and protection of the natural environment so that future generations can enjoy a quality of life comparable to today's. And implicit in these founding documents is that government policy makers must recognize the long-term impact of their policies, as well as their lack of policies, on citizens, their communities, and the nation at large.

In our federal system, when citizens bring societal problems to the attention of government officials, the ensuing legislative and public debates typically revolve around several key questions. First, government officials must decide whether the problem is one that government should address. If the answer to that fundamental question is yes, then additional questions follow. What level of government has legal authority to address the problem? What level of government has the financial resources? What is the most cost-effective means to deal with the problem? Beyond the expected positive effects of a policy's implementation, what unexpected costs and negative consequences might occur?

Citizen Engagement and Domestic Policy

The Constitution established a government that is by and for the people. Previous chapters have explored the many ways in which individuals and groups engage with government officials and political processes to influence what government does and does not do. Yet a widespread national affliction is *NIMBY*, or "not-in-my-backyard" syndrome. People with NIMBY syndrome decline to participate in politics until a government action or inaction threatens them directly. Lobbying government officials is a common first step in citizen engagement, and it may be as basic as making a phone call, sending an e-mail, or writing a letter. Citizens may also use lawsuits to press government officials to focus on issues of concern and to address them through policy making.

Complicating the work of U.S. policy makers, the diversity of citizens' needs and expectations for government action means that almost every call for government action sparks a call for either a different action or no action. The plurality of citizens' needs, individuals' constantly changing priorities, and their range of political ideologies make for an ongoing public conversation and legislative debate over which policies warrant government spending and who will pay the taxes to cover the bills. Democrats and Republicans frequently disagree on these matters. Democrats typically are liberal in inclination and tend to support **safety nets**—programs ensuring that every citizen's basic physiological needs (food, water, shelter, health care, and a clean environment) are met. Republicans more commonly have a conservative ideology and focus more on public safety and national security issues. Ultimately, elected officials—whose career goal, after all, is to get reelected—find it much easier to add new policies and programs, and consequently to drive up government expenses, than to eliminate programs or to decrease program costs.

As we have seen in preceding chapters, the government makes policy in several ways. For one, Congress and the president set policy by approving *authorization bills,* which establish a policy and identify who will implement it, and *appropriation bills,* which authorize the spending of national revenue. Federal, state, local, and shadow bureaucrats also make policy, through both the administrative rule-making process and their daily use of admin-

---

In this chapter, we survey national domestic policies that are most directly related to the basic needs of a sustainable, safe country where citizens can live healthy lives in pursuit of their happiness.

FIRST, we review the role of *citizen engagement* in establishing *domestic policy.*

SECOND, we consider the *tools of domestic policy,* the array of public programs by which the government provides for citizens' basic needs.

THIRD, we look at *environmental policy,* the government's efforts to preserve the environment, conserve scarce resources, and control pollution.

FOURTH, we examine *energy policy,* specifically looking at the problems of rising energy consumption and Americans' reliance on nonrenewable fossil fuels.

FIFTH, we consider *income security programs*—in particular, safety-net policies for citizens in financial need.

SIXTH, we probe *health care policy,* where soaring costs are prompting ongoing research and experimentation with new models.

SEVENTH, we discuss *homeland security* policy, which is directed at preventing and responding to natural and man-made disasters.

EIGHTH, we examine legislators' efforts at reforming *immigration policy* to address citizens' concerns over the masses of unauthorized immigrants streaming into the country.

safety net
a collection of public policies ensuring that the basic physiological needs of citizens are met

istrative discretion. In addition, the presidential power of the executive order amounts to making policy, because it gives the president the authority to tell bureaucrats how to carry out a national policy. Finally, the federal judiciary, through the various cases that come before the courts, has policy-making power by virtue of its authority to declare unconstitutional the laws made by the legislative and executive branches of national, state, and local government (the authority of judicial review). The courts also resolve conflicts over the meaning and proper implementation of laws. In summary, each of the three branches of the national government has policy-making authority that it uses to fulfill the government's constitutionally established mission to serve present and future generations.

Since 1788 (when the states ratified the U.S. Constitution), the national government's scope of responsibility for addressing domestic matters has gradually expanded as citizens and groups have lobbied to press for their interests. Federal authority now covers a diverse collection of public policies. Today's national budget lists seventeen superfunctions of the federal government (see Table 16.1).[1] The numbers in the table show that most federal government functions and most government spending are directed at *domestic* policy matters: 72.5 percent for domestic policies and 21.0 percent for foreign and defense policies. The remaining percentage pays the interest on the national debt incurred by past borrowing to cover deficit spending.

Because it would be impossible for us to examine every domestic policy program, we limit our focus in this chapter to a subset of national homeland policies. Specifically, we concentrate on policies that address the most basic of human needs and are essential to sustaining life, liberty, and opportunities to pursue happiness: environmental, energy, income security, health care, and homeland security policies. We also look at the controversial policy

TABLE 16.1

National Budget Superfunctions and Expenditures:
Total Proposed National Budget Authority, 2011—$3,833,861 million ($3.8 trillion)

Defense and Foreign Policy ($803,940 million; 21.0% of budget outlays)*	National defense ($749,748 million; 19.5%)
	International affairs ($54,192 million; 1.4%)
Domestic Policy ($2,779,212 million; 72.5%)	General science, space, and technology ($31,554 million; 0.8%)
	Energy ($24,863 million; 0.6%)
	Natural resources and environment ($42,537 million; 1.1%)
	Agriculture ($25,590 million; 0.7%)
	Commerce and housing credit ($22,127 million; 0.6%)
	Transportation ($104,189 million; 2.7%)
	Community and regional development ($31,973 million; 0.8%)
	Education, training, employment, and social services ($126,399 million; 3.3%)
	Health ($400,661 million; 10.5%)
	Medicare ($497,341 million; 13.0%)
	Income security ($595,005 million; 15.5%)
	Social Security ($736,284 million; 19.2%)
	Veterans benefits and services ($124,539 million; 3.3%)
	Administration of justice ($57,280 million; 1.5%)
	General government ($27,670 million; 0.7%)
Net Interest ($250,709 million; 6.5%)	

*Numbers in parentheses represent (1) total outlay for each function and (2) percentage of total budget outlay, rounded to the nearest tenth of a percent.

SOURCE: Budget of the United States Fiscal Year 2011, Historical Tables, Table 3.1, www.whitehouse.gov/omb/budget/Historicals/.

> Jayme Bozik assists her husband, U.S. Army Sargeant Joey Bozik, with his physical therapy at Walter Reed Army Medical Center in Washington, D. C. The national government hires doctors, nurses, physical therapists, and other health professions to work in military hospitals, providing medical services to injured military personnel.

area of immigration, defined by some as a national security concern, by others as an economic issue, and by still others as a humanitarian cause reflecting the United States' roots and highest ideals.

Tools of Domestic Policy

The national government attempts to address citizens' problems and to provide benefits and services to the people by using various policy tools. Domestic policy tools include laws and regulations, direct provision of public goods, cash transfer payments, loans, loan guarantees, insurance, and contracting-out the provision of public goods to nongovernmental entities.

Laws and Regulations

At the federal, state, and local levels alike, government strives to accomplish its domestic policy goals by creating laws with which individuals and organizations must comply. These include environmental laws, national narcotics laws, and laws addressing work standards and conditions. Many laws assign administrative agencies the authority to establish the specific rules, regulations, and standards that are essential to effective implementation of the laws.

The overwhelming majority of people and organizations comply with most laws and regulations. But because some individuals and organizations fail to do so, the government must monitor compliance. For example, the government hires inspectors to monitor adherence to rules that limit industrial plants' emissions of pollutants, and hires police officers to monitor compliance with laws that prohibit narcotic drug use. The government counts on citizens, interest groups, and the media to assist in overseeing compliance—and in reporting violators.

Direct Provision of Public Goods

direct provision
the policy tool whereby the government that creates a policy hires public servants to provide the service

In addition to creating rules of behavior through law and regulations, governments provide services and benefits. Using the domestic policy tool of **direct provision,** governments hire public servants—bureaucrats who receive a government paycheck—to dispense the service. For example, veterans hospitals hire doctors, nurses, and physical therapists to administer health care to veterans; the U.S. Postal Service hires mail carriers, postal clerks, and postal processing machine operators to deliver billions of pieces of mail each week. To provide for the country's common defense, the national government employs millions of military personnel. The workers hired by the national government to provide these services directly are on the payroll of the national government.

Cash Transfers

cash transfer
the direct provision of cash (in forms including checks, debit cards, and tax breaks) to eligible individuals or to providers of goods or services to eligible individuals

in-kind assistance
a cash transfer in which the government pays cash to those who provide goods or services to eligible individuals

Another instrument of government policy is the **cash transfer**—the direct provision of cash (in various forms) to eligible individuals or to the providers of goods or services to eligible individuals. **In-kind assistance** is a form of a cash transfer in which the government pays cash to those who provide goods or services to eligible individuals. Approximately 60 percent of the money spent by the national government goes toward cash transfers to citizens. Today, the majority of U.S. citizens receive cash payments of some kind from the federal government at some time during their lives.

Examples of cash transfers include unemployment and Social Security checks, Pell grants to college students, grants-in-aid to state and local governments (see Chapter 3), and tax breaks and subsidies to individuals and corporations (see Chapter 15). Medicaid, the government program that provides health care for the poor, is an example of an in-kind assistance, cash transfer program. The Medicaid recipient receives medical care at no cost or at a reduced cost because the government pays health care providers for their services. The Supplemental Nutrition Assistance Program (SNAP), the new name for the food stamp program created in 1964, is another example of in-kind assistance. The government provides cash to the stores that accept SNAP vouchers or debit cards for food purchases.

The main cash transfer programs are of two kinds, depending upon their sources of revenue. For **noncontributory programs,** the general revenues collected by the government pay for the program. This means that a proportion of the money collected from all taxpayers funds the cash transfer. Temporary Assistance to Needy Families, the income security program for families with children who have no or very low income, is an example of a noncontributory cash-transfer program. In contrast, **contributory programs,** or **social insurance programs,** are funded by revenue collected specifically for these programs, and they benefit only those who have paid into the programs. Social insurance programs are **entitlement programs,** meaning the government guarantees the program's benefits to all who meet the eligibility criteria. Thus workers who pay the payroll tax for Social Security will receive Social Security checks when they retire.

With a **direct subsidy,** another type of cash transfer, the government provides financial support to specific persons or organizations that engage in activities that the government believes benefit the public good. Individual farmers and agricultural corporations, for example, receive money from the government to grow specified crops or to limit how much they grow. College students receiving Pell grants, which do not need to be paid back, are also recipients of direct subsidies funded through the federal government's general revenue.

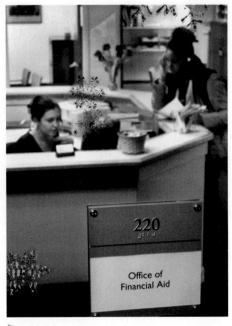

> The federal government assists college students through cash transfers such as Pell grants, student loans, and loan guarantees. College financial aid offices play a role in administering these grant and loan programs.

noncontributory program
a benefit provided to a targeted population, paid for by a proportion of the money collected from all taxpayers

contributory program (social insurance program)
a benefit provided only to those who paid the specific tax created to fund the benefit

entitlement program
a government benefit guaranteed to all who meet the eligibility requirements

direct subsidy
a cash transfer from general revenues to particular persons or private companies engaged in activities that the national government believes support the public good

Loans, Loan Guarantees, and Insurance

In addition to using tax breaks and grants to encourage behaviors that accomplish its goals, the national government lends money to individuals and organizations, and it guarantees loans made by private businesses. Some examples are government loan programs to assist individuals in purchasing homes, reflecting the widespread belief that home ownership promotes the general welfare and domestic tranquility, and Perkins loans, which pay some of the college expenses of students from very-low-income families. In addition, the government guarantees banks that it will repay the loans they provide to college students if the students cannot repay the loans themselves; these guaranteed loans are called Stafford loans. If the government did not guarantee them, it is unlikely that banks, which are profit-making organizations, would lend thousands of dollars to unemployed young people to pay for college costs.

The national government is also in the insurance business. The Federal Deposit Insurance Corporation (FDIC) is one example of a national insurance program. The FDIC insures bank deposits in member banks to encourage people to save money not only for their own sake but also for the good of the national economy.

> Depositors, fearful that the money they had deposited had been lost, besieged banks such as this one in Passaic, New Jersey, after Wall Street crashed and the Great Depression began in 1929. To protect depositors' money, in 1933 the federal government created the Federal Deposit Insurance Corporation (FDIC), which insures bank deposits. During the Great Recession that began in 2008, the federal government temporarily increased the insurance limit from $100,000 to $250,000. The limit is scheduled to revert to $100,000 on January 1, 2014.

Contracting-Out

The government also contracts with private and nonprofit organizations to produce essential resources or to deliver services historically provided by the government. One example of contracting-out, or outsourcing (see Chapter 13), is its contracts with corporations such as Lockheed Martin and Boeing to build the planes and missiles it needs to defend the country.

By means of contracting-out and the other various tools we have surveyed, the government delivers goods and services to its citizens now and in the future. In the rest of this chapter, we examine how government uses these tools to implement overall policy in several domestic policy areas, including the environment, energy, income security, health care, homeland security, and immigration.

Environmental Policy

At the most basic level, providing for the general welfare means ensuring that people have the basic necessities for sustaining life. These needs include clean and drinkable water, breathable air, and unpolluted land on which to grow food safe for consumption. No one argues against a clean environment. Yet there is no consensus on how to achieve and maintain one. In addition, appeals for environmental protection often conflict with demands for ample supplies of energy and for economic development. For example, the extraction of coal and oil from the earth, as well as the development of nuclear energy, poses immediate as well as long-term threats to the environment. They also create jobs.

Environmental protection includes conserving natural resources and limiting the pollution emitted into the air and water and onto the land. By the late 1960s and 1970s, several environmental crises had brought the harm humans had caused to the natural environment, plants, animals, and people into stark view.

Environmental Degradation

Since the 1940s, farmers have used chemicals to destroy insects, weeds, fungi, and other living organisms that harm their crops. The threats such pesticides pose to air, water, and land became the focus of public concern and political debate after the publication of Rachel Carson's eye-opening best seller *Silent Spring* in 1962. Carson's book documented how pesticides were contaminating the environment and getting into human food. The use of chemicals, she warned, threatened the existence not only of birds—whose extinction would mean a silent spring—but of humankind itself. Although the chemical industry tried to discredit Carson's findings, President John F. Kennedy (1961–1963) established a special panel to investigate them, and the panel found support for Carson's concerns.

Then, in 1969, those growing apprehensions became a spectacular reality when the heavily polluted Cuyahoga River in northeastern Ohio caught fire (again!). Around the same time, arsenic was found in the Kansas River, and millions of fish went belly-up in major waterways such as Lake Superior, killed by the chemicals and untreated waste emitted by industrial plants and local sewage systems. In response, state and local governments banned fishing in many waterways, including Lake Erie, because of their excessive pollution.

The mounting environmental crises and additional governmental studies brought amplified calls to action from both citizens'

> In April 2010, more than one billion people around the world celebrated the 40th anniversary of Earth Day by engaging in teach-ins, clean-ups, and lobbying efforts. In Washington, D. C., members of the Washington Nationals professional baseball team, including infielder Ronnie Belliard, collaborated with students from the Charles E. Smith Jewish Day School to clean up the banks of the Anacostia River, which flows along side the Nationals' baseball stadium.

groups and elected officials during the 1960s and 1970s. U.S. Senator Gaylord Nelson (D-Wisconsin) responded by founding Earth Day. He later recollected that "all across the country, evidence of environmental degradation was appearing. . . . The people were concerned, but the politicians were not. . . . Suddenly, the idea occurred to me—why not organize a huge grassroots protest over what was happening to our environment?"[2]

Nelson's vision of a day of educational rallies in Washington, D.C., became a reality on April 22, 1970, when more than 200,000 people gathered on the National Mall. Millions more congregated across the country to draw attention to environmental concerns. Earth Day 1970 was so successful at bringing attention to the environmental cause that many consider it the beginning of the environmental movement. Celebrated every year with rallies and teach-ins involving millions of people worldwide, Earth Day keeps concerns about environmental degradation on the public policy agenda.

Environmental Protection

A cascade of groundbreaking national legislation followed the first Earth Day. The Environmental Protection Act of 1970 established the Environmental Protection Agency (EPA) to oversee the implementation of laws protecting the quality of air, water, and land. The Environmental Protection Act mandates that all construction projects receiving federal funding begin with an environmental impact study analyzing the project's effects on the environment and on endangered species. The act also has a sunshine component requiring the government to invite citizens' comments on proposed projects. Under these provisions of the law, environmental interest groups frequently bring lawsuits challenging the quality and accuracy of environmental impact studies and developers' lack of compliance with the sunshine provisions. Developers and parties probing into new energy sources view such lawsuits as a waste of time and money. But in fact, this litigation, combined with the broader work of various environmental groups, has become a driving force in environmental protection today.

CLEAN AIR The landmark Clean Air Act of 1970 delegates authority to the EPA to set air quality standards while giving state governments enforcement responsibility. Today, states in turn typically delegate some of their enforcement responsibilities to local governments. If states and their local governments do not enforce compliance with the national standards, the EPA can take over.

To bolster compliance with the Clean Air Act, the law gives citizens the right to sue those who are violating the standards. Citizens also have the right to sue the EPA if it does not enforce the Clean Air Act. Citizens and environmental interest groups have availed themselves of their right to sue, pushing the government and industries to comply with the law. For example, in 2007, Massachusetts and eleven other states, three cities, and several environmental groups successfully challenged the EPA and President George W. Bush's interpretation of the law, when the U.S. Supreme Court determined that carbon dioxide is a pollutant that the EPA has the authority to regulate.[3]

CLEAN WATER The Clean Water Act is actually the 1972 Federal Water Pollution Control Act as amended over the years. This law, which has the goal of making waterways clean enough to swim in and to eat fish from, authorizes the EPA to set water quality standards and to require permits for anyone discharging contaminants into any waterway. However, the direct discharge of pollutants into waterways is not the only source of water pollution. Runoff from farms, which carries animal waste and pesticides into waterways, also contributes heavily to the problem. The Department of Agriculture joins forces with the EPA to prevent this indirect source of pollution.

Under the Clean Water Act, state and local governments must monitor water quality, issue permits to those discharging waste into waterways, and enforce the national standards. If states and localities fail to carry out these mandated responsibilities, the EPA can step in and do the job. The law also provides for federal loans to local governments, funneled through state governments, for building wastewater treatment plants.

The Safe Drinking Water Act of 1974 authorizes the EPA to establish purity standards for drinking water. Because states or localities typically operate water systems, this act effectively requires the EPA to regulate state and local governments. The act provides for national grants to state and local governments for research and for improving their water systems.

Water problems extend far beyond U.S. borders. For insight into international efforts to address water issues, see "Global Context."

CLEAN LAND The United States produces more solid waste—from household garbage to toxic by-products of manufacturing—per person than any other country. If not properly disposed of or treated, all waste has the potential to harm the environment, as well as plants, animals, and people. Some toxic by-products, such as the radioactive nuclear wastes produced in manufacturing nuclear weapons and generating nuclear power, cannot be treated or disposed of, but they dissipate over time—from one hundred years for low-level radioactive waste to hundreds of thousands of years for high-level radioactive waste.

Citizens with resources, including money and the time to organize or to join an existing organization, are able to fight the location of undesirable land uses in their communities. Lower-income communities are more likely than more affluent cities and towns to bear the burden of housing waste storage facilities. **Environmental racism** is the term used to describe the higher incidence of environmental threats and subsequent health problems in lower-income communities, which frequently are also communities dominated by people of color.[4]

The Resource Conservation and Recovery Act of 1976, administered by the EPA, regulates the disposal of solid and hazardous wastes and encourages recycling. Although this act authorized the cleanup of toxic waste sites, and the government identified thousands of such sites in the 1970s, no national funding was made available for the cleanup. Then in 1980, as Congress was debating how to address potential harm caused by toxic waste sites, an abandoned site for the storage, treatment, and disposal of hazardous waste in Elizabeth, New Jersey, exploded.[5] Shortly thereafter, Congress approved the Comprehensive Environmental Response, Compensation and Liability Act of 1980 (known as the Superfund law) to pay for cleanup of the nation's most toxic waste dumps.

Because U.S. air quality and water quality have improved tremendously since the 1970s, many citizens and government officials have shifted their attention to other societal concerns. At the same time, U.S. industries have become more resistant to legislative proposals

environmental racism
the term for the higher incidence of environmental threats and subsequent health problems in lower-income communities, which frequently are also communities dominated by people of color

GLOBAL CONTEXT

CLEAN WATER FOR A HEALTHY WORLD

Clean water is necessary for life. It is necessary for drinking, growing safe and healthy food (crops and domestic animals, including fish), preparing food, preventing illness (through personal hygiene, cleaning, washing, and waste disposal), and caring for the sick. Most people in North America and Europe take for granted their access to toilets and drinkable water, and are not aware of the spreading water crisis. But more than one out of six people in the world lack access to drinkable water. More than one in three people worldwide do not have access to toilets or latrines. As a result, diseases related to unsafe drinking water, inadequate sanitation, and poor hygiene cause more than 2 million global deaths a year, most of them children under 5 years of age.*

> **What are some of the potential barriers to providing millions more people around the globe with clean water, the essential ingredient for life?**

Currently, the water crisis is limited to certain countries and regions in the world, with the populations of Asia and Africa particularly hard-hit. Yet with the world's population poised to grow by at least 40 percent over the next fifty years, and with increased economic development and urbanization, the demand for clean water to drink and to grow healthy food has the potential to develop into a worldwide crisis.**

Recognizing as crucial the need to protect and manage water resources for a healthy world, the United Nation's General Assembly established the UN International Decade for Action on Water, 2005–2015. UN member states agreed to reduce by half the proportion of people without clean drinking water by 2015. To achieve this goal, in each year of the Decade for Action on Water, 100 million additional people (or 274,000 people each day) will need to gain access to clean, drinkable water.† With the efforts of governments, nongovernmental organizations, and activists throughout the world, the United Nations International Children's Emergency Fund (UNICEF)—an organization dedicated to the protection, survival, and development of children and mothers—predicts that this target will be met.§

> More than one out of six people in the world lack drinkable water, and so they drink water from polluted wells or wells infested with parasites, such as this one in the Ivory Coast. The lack of safe drinking water results in more than 2 million global deaths each year caused by water-related diseases.

*www.un.org/waterforlifedecade/pdf/waterforlifebklt-e.pdf.
**Ibid.
†Ibid.
§www.unicef.org/voy/explore/wes/explore_2711.html.

to stiffen environmental standards and are increasingly challenging the implementation of environmental laws. In addition, a growing private property rights movement is challenging restrictions on land use that have been put in place in the name of environmental protection. Although no one is arguing against a clean environment, tensions persist between the need for environmental protection and other policy areas. The increasing demand for cheap energy is one such area.

The environmental threats and damage created by energy production, accidents during the extraction of energy sources such as coal and oil, and energy consumption are evident worldwide. In April 2010, the United States witnessed the deaths of twenty-nine coal miners in West Virginia and eleven oil rig workers in the Gulf of Mexico. In both cases, explosions occurred as private companies extracted natural resources, killing the workers. In addition to the loss of life, the oil rig explosion created an environmental disaster whose total damage to wildlife, the livelihoods of thousands of people, and the economy of numerous communities we will not know for decades. The national government began investigating the causes of these accidents immediately, and calls for better government oversight and increased regulation of the coal mining and oil industries followed quickly.

International, national, state, and local policies are focusing on limiting the threats to the environment posed by energy production and consumption. An additional energy concern for the United States is its reliance on nonrenewable energy sources, as we next consider.

Energy Policy

Energy creation—the production of electricity and heat, as well as fuels to power automobiles, trucks, planes, trains, and other transport vehicles—is essential to the prosperity of the U.S. economy and to the American way of life. The United States uses more energy than any other country in the world, and its demand for energy continues to rise. What underlies this increasing demand? Industrial and commercial expansion, the construction of larger houses, and soaring computer use all have contributed to the ballooning demand for electricity. Robust sales of trucks for personal use, as well as of gas-guzzling sport utility vehicles (SUVs), have driven up consumers' demand for gasoline. Moreover, the transportation system in the United States relies more heavily on passenger cars than is the case in other countries, where public transportation links cities to one another and to suburbs more effectively. The ever-rising energy demands of the U.S. economy and the lifestyle of U.S. residents are problematic for several reasons, as we shall see.

Energy and Global Warming

greenhouse effect
the heating of the earth's atmosphere as a result of humans' burning of fossil fuels and the resultant buildup of carbon dioxide and other gases

global warming
rising temperature of the earth as a result of pollution that traps solar heat, keeping the air warmer than it would otherwise be

Most energy consumed in the United States is produced by burning fossil fuels—oil, coal, and natural gas. Burning fossil fuels pollutes the air. The pollution produced from burning fossil fuels is not just a national problem; it is a global problem. Mounting evidence indicates that pollution from burning fossil fuels has increased temperatures worldwide, creating a **greenhouse effect**—so-called because in a greenhouse, the walls and roof trap solar heat, keeping the temperature inside warmer than it is outside. **Global warming,** the gradual average increase in the earth's temperature, is the result of pollution that traps solar heat in the earth's atmosphere.

International fears about the potential harm of global warming led to a treaty called the Kyoto Protocol of 1997. Countries that ratify the Kyoto Protocol agree to work toward eliminating the greenhouse effect by reducing their emissions of carbon dioxide and other gases believed to cause it. Although 184 countries have ratified the treaty, the United States has not.

Even though the federal government has opted not to ratify the Kyoto Protocol, many state and local governments are collectively working to meet its provisions, with the goal of showing the national government the benefits of abiding by it. Currently, ten Northeast and mid-Atlantic states have agreed to the Regional Greenhouse Gas Initiative (RGGI). The RGGI commits those states to capping emissions from power plants and to reducing emissions by 10 percent by 2018.

President Barack Obama (2009–present) came into office with the reduction of global warming as one of his top priorities. With his support, the House of Representatives approved the American Clean Energy and Security Act in June 2009. In July 2009, the Senate Energy and Natural Resources Committee approved the Clean Energy and Leadership Act. Both the House and the Senate bills propose a change in the direction of the nation's energy policy by imposing the first-ever federal limits on carbon dioxide and other pollutants

> In response to their disappointment over the perceived weakness of the U.S. House's American Clean Energy and Security Act, environmentalists draped a banner over South Dakota's Mount Rushmore in July 2009 to urge President Obama and other world leaders meeting in Italy to develop a strong global strategy for reducing greenhouse emissions.

linked to global warming. Al Gore, who won a Nobel Peace Prize in 2007 for his work on global warming, posted a statement on his Web site declaring this bill "an essential first step towards solving the climate crisis."

National Energy Policy

Today, energy policy debates focus on the nation's reliance on *nonrenewable energy sources*—crude oil, natural gas, coal, and nuclear power—and calls to increase the use of *renewable energy sources*—solar, geothermal, wind, hydropower, and biomass. Figure 16.1 on page 504 shows the current mix of U.S. energy sources. Those who advocate the use of renewable energy cite the environmental threats that result from burning fossil fuels, the nonrenewable nature of fossil fuels as an energy source, and the nation's reliance on imported petroleum.[6]

According to the U.S. Energy Information Administration, in 2008, 93 percent of U.S. energy came from nonrenewable sources. Petroleum is the largest U.S. energy source, providing close to 40 percent of U.S. energy. In 2008, the United States imported almost 60 percent of the petroleum that it consumed.[7] This heavy reliance on foreign oil concerns citizens and government officials because of the volatile political environments in some oil-producing countries in the Middle East and South America, and because of conflicts between U.S. policies and the policies of some of those countries.

THE OPEC EMBARGO AND CARTER'S RESPONSE In 1973, for example, the Arab members of the Organization of Petroleum Exporting Countries (OPEC) implemented an embargo on oil supplies. This embargo was a reaction to U.S. support of Israel in that nation's Yom Kippur War of 1973 against Egypt and Syria over disputed lands. Outraged by what they saw as U.S. interference, OPEC member nations refused to sell oil to the United States and western European nations that supported Israel in the war. This

Energy Sources*

Renewable Energy Sources*
(7% of energy sources)

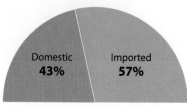

Sources of U.S. Crude Oil**

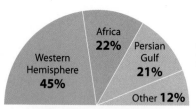

Imported Crude Oil**

POLITICAL INQUIRY

FIGURE 16.1 ■ U.S. ENERGY SOURCES
Should U.S. citizens be concerned about the proportion of energy coming from nonrenewable sources? Explain your answer. What might explain why the proportion of energy coming from renewable sources is so low? From what part of the globe does the majority of U.S. petroleum (crude oil) come?

*HTTP://TONTO.EIA.DOE.GOV/ENERGYEXPLAINED/INDEX_CFM?PAGE=ABOUT_HOME
**http://tonton.eia.doe.gov/energy_in_brief/foreign_oil_dependence.cfm.

five-month oil embargo, followed by OPEC production limits that kept oil prices high, and produced hours-long waits in gas station lines, forced the United States to set national energy policies.

In 1975, the national government established the Strategic Petroleum Reserve, a growing supply of crude oil stored away in case of a future energy emergency or an interruption in the U.S. supply of imported oil. That same year, Congress also set fuel-efficiency standards for passenger cars and light trucks, the Corporate Average Fuel Economy (CAFÉ) standards. In 2007, more than thirty-five years after establishing CAFÉ, Congress significantly increased the fuel-efficiency standards for the first time. Automobile producers must meet the new 35-miles-per-gallon standard, up from 25 miles per gallon, by the year 2020.[8] However, it was not until May 2009, during President Barack Obama's administration, that the Department of Transportation finalized the rules needed to enforce the new CAFÉ standards.

In 1976, the federal government established the Department of Energy to develop and oversee a comprehensive national energy plan. In 1977, President Jimmy Carter (1977–1981) declared an "energy crisis" and announced energy conservation measures such as the regulation of temperature settings in public buildings and tax incentives to insulate homes. In addition, government regulation of oil and natural gas prices was curtailed during Carter's presidency.[9] Although the government had historically regulated the prices of those energy resources, the expectation was that if prices rose on the basis of supply and demand, people would conserve. Carter's energy policies also included increased financial support for research and development of alternative energy sources such as solar, wind, geothermal, and renewable biomass.

With deregulation, oil prices jumped by 1980 to more than ten times their 1972 level. But by 1986, oil prices began to fall. With lower prices through the 1990s came reduced federal government support for research and development of alternative energy sources. The public, too, lost interest in energy conservation, and the demand for energy grew, as did the production of gas-guzzling automobiles.

AN ENERGY POLICY FOCUSED ON FOSSIL FUELS In 2001, Secretary of Energy Spencer Abraham sounded an alarm: "America faces a major energy-supply crisis over the next two decades. The failure to meet this challenge will threaten our nation's economic prosperity, compromise our national security, and literally alter the way we live our lives."[10] In response, President George W. Bush appointed Vice President Dick Cheney—a former oil company executive—to preside over a task force charged with formulating a new national energy policy. The result was an energy policy emphasizing the increased production of fossil fuels. This policy was in stark contrast to the conservation approach developed in the 1970s. Moreover, Bush's 2002 budget drastically cut funding for conservation initiatives and for research on alternative, renewable energy sources.

By the winter of 2005, government officials and citizens were increasingly concerned over the price and availability of oil. Hurricane Katrina had taken a toll on domestic oil production. The Iraq War and tensions with Iran jeopardized the stability of imports from the Middle East. President Hugo Chavez of Venezuela, the number 3 U.S. oil supplier, was also threatening to limit the availability of his country's oil.

In response, President Bush emphasized in his 2006 State of the Union address how essential affordable energy is to the United States' success in the world economy. He stressed that Americans' "addiction" to oil must be reduced. Bush called for a 22 percent increase in funding for research in alternative renewable energy sources such as solar and wind, as well as nuclear energy, and recommended increased use of coal. The president also called for expanded research in alternative means to power automobiles, including electricity, hydrogen, and ethanol (produced from corn, wood chips, and switchgrass).

FUTURE DIRECTIONS   In 2009, the U.S. House and Senate worked on clean energy bills. Under the proposed policies, energy companies would pay a price for the greenhouse pollution they create through the purchase of pollution allowances, or they could shift to using cleaner, renewable energy, including solar, wind, and geothermal power, or to cleaner nuclear energy. Automakers would be required to make more fuel-efficient cars. Members of Congress who supported the bills and President Obama argued that another outcome would be creation of new green jobs—such as making or installing solar panels and wind turbines, developing equipment to harness carbon emissions, and producing energy-efficient lightbulbs, washing machines, and other home appliances. President Obama called on all Americans to support clean energy legislation, which, he argued, would "open the door to a clean energy economy and a better future for America."[11]

Today, limited supplies and high costs of traditional energy sources, along with the environmental impact of the continuing use of fossil fuels, threaten the quality of life of Americans and people around the globe. Americans are looking to national and state government for public policy solutions to these energy-related and environmental concerns. In a similar way, during the 1930s, Americans had turned to the national government to address the economic downturn that was impeding millions of Americans' ability to enjoy a decent quality of life, as we next consider.

Income Security Programs

Before the Great Depression of the 1930s, Americans who could not provide for their basic needs relied on relief from family, friends, charities, and, in some cases, local or state government. During the Depression, however, the excessively weak economy left one-quarter of the U.S. labor force unemployed. Families lost jobs, savings, and homes. Charities were overwhelmed. State and local governments lacked the resources to assist the millions of people without incomes. Citizens, as well as state and local governments, looked to the federal government for assistance.

Within his first one hundred days in office, President Franklin D. Roosevelt (1933–1945) proposed a sequence of revolutionary bills to stimulate and regulate sectors of the depressed economy and to provide income to the needy. His administration's radical proposals placed the national government at the center of issues it had historically left to local and state governments. Those and the subsequent New Deal policies approved in Roosevelt's first few years in office created jobs, established a more regulated capitalist economy (see Chapter 15), and provided income security for retired citizens and a safety net for people in financial need. Many of the New Deal programs are still in place today, though in modified form.

Noncontributory safety-net programs, which are funded through general tax revenues, engender a good deal of debate. Conservatives typically oppose these programs on the grounds that hard work, not government handouts, should be the source of the income individuals need to sustain themselves. Liberals are more inclined to support noncontributory safety-net programs. They make the case that systemic factors, not individual characteristics, prevent many people from earning enough income to sustain themselves. Although you would be hard pressed to find someone who argues against contributory safety-net programs (also called *social insurance programs*), there is an ongoing debate over the best means of funding such programs and the proper level of benefits. The largest contributory income security program, in cost and people served, is the Old-Age and Survivors component of Social Security.

Social Security

The Social Security Act of 1935, a centerpiece of the New Deal, established a range of landmark income security programs. To this day, these programs provide financial assistance to the elderly, disabled, dependent, and unemployed.

OLD-AGE AND SURVIVORS INSURANCE

The Social Security Act established the Old-Age and Survivors Insurance (OASI) Program, which initially provided income to individuals or families when a worker covered by the program retired. This contributory cash transfer program is the traditional retirement insurance component of Social Security; most people are aware of it and anticipate benefiting from it in retirement. OASI is a social insurance entitlement program, funded by contributions that employees as well as employers make. Each year, the federal government establishes the amount of earnings subject to the Social Security tax, which is called the *covered income*. Employees and employers each pay 6.2 percent (for a total of 12.4 percent) of the employee's covered income for Social Security. In 2010, income up to $106,800 was subject to the tax.

A formula that accounts for how much individuals paid into Social Security over their years of employment determines the amount of each beneficiary's monthly Social Security check. The more money invested, the greater the check. Because OASI is an **indexed benefit,** the government makes regularly scheduled, automatic cost of living adjustments (COLAs), increasing the benefit based on the rate of inflation. The 1937 Federal Insurance Contribution Act (FICA) established the pay-as-you-go funding mechanism for OASI. Through FICA contributions, current workers and employers deposit money in the Social Security Trust Fund, and the government uses the money contributed today to pay today's beneficiaries. The money left over after today's payments are made is invested so that the trust fund will grow; income from investments will be combined with future FICA revenues to pay for future Social Security checks.

Because Social Security is an entitlement, and because the government cannot predict how long a Social Security recipient will live—and therefore how many checks the recipient will receive during his or her lifetime—the government cannot control or predict the annual cost of Social Security.

Most people collect more from Social Security than they pay into the fund, and the number of retirees is growing. With the increasing number of retirees and with those retirees living longer lives, the pay-as-you-go system will eventually reach the point of not covering the full costs of OASI. The surplus money in the Social Security Trust Fund is already shrinking. This situation generates intense public debate over what the national government should do to ensure that Social Security funds are available for workers who are currently contributing to the program.

The Future of Old Age and Survivors Insurance (OASI)

	THEN (1937)	NOW (2010)
Percentage of workers covered*	60%	97%
Payroll tax collected from employee to fund OASI*	1% on wages up to $3,000	6.2% on wages up to $106,800
Payroll tax collected from employer to fund OASI*	1% on wages up to $3,000	6.2% on wages up to $106,800
Number of workers paying into OASI per retiree*	16	3
Normal retirement age*	65	67 (for those born after 1959)
Total receipts**	$747 million	$695,462 million (end of 2008)
Total benefit payments**	$ 1 million	$509,337 million (end of 2008)
Assets at end of year**	$766 million	$2,202,886 million (end of 2008)

WHAT'S NEXT?

> With only three workers paying into the system for every one retiree and retirees living longer, the system is not sustainable. What can the government do to bring more money into the system to pay benefits to future retirees?

> Currently, all workers who pay into the system can apply for OASI benefits at their normal retirement age, even workers who continue to work and those earning money through investments, including millionaires and billionaires. Will government officials have the political will to cut the benefits of millionaires and billionaires to ensure security income to other beneficiaries? Explain your answer.

> The Social Security Trustees report indicates that within 30 to 75 years, the OASI trust fund will be depleted. Is there a particular Social Security reform, or combination of reforms, that you believe most U.S. citizens would support? Explain.

*www.newyorklife.com/cda/0,3254,5786,00.html.
**www.ssa.gov/OACT/STATS/table4a1.html.

indexed benefit
a government benefit with an automatic cost of living increase based on the rate of inflation

AMENDMENTS TO THE SOCIAL SECURITY ACT Congress amended the Social Security Act in 1939 to provide benefits to the dependents and surviving spouse of a deceased worker. In 1956, the act was further amended to assist workers who, because of physical or mental disabilities, had to stop working after age 50 but before the OASI-designated retirement age. The new benefit program thus created, called Social Security Disability Insurance (SSDI), provides income to those covered by the Social Security program and to their families if they meet the guidelines for disability. Similarly to OASI, SSDI is a contributory (social insurance) program.

In 1972, Congress again amended the Social Security Act by establishing the Supplemental Security Income (SSI) program, a noncontributory program. Recipients of SSI include low-income elderly people whose Social Security benefits are so low they cannot provide for themselves, individuals with disabilities, and blind people. Unlike other Social Security programs, SSI is a **means-tested benefit,** meaning that the eligibility criteria to receive the benefit include a government-specified income level, which is very low.

The Social Security Act of 1935 created other income security programs, including unemployment compensation and Aid to Dependent Children. Three years after passage of the Social Security Act, the Roosevelt administration also enacted a minimum wage, and several decades later, in 1975, Congress established an additional income security program known as the Earned Income Tax Credit. We now turn to these other income security programs.

means-tested benefit
a benefit for which eligibility is based on having an income below a specified amount, typically based on a percentage of the poverty guideline

Unemployment Compensation

Together, employees, employers, the federal government, and state governments fund the unemployment compensation program created by the Social Security Act of 1935. Through this program, employees who lose their jobs through no fault of their own can collect unemployment compensation for up to twenty-six weeks. An employee fired for cause (not doing the job, doing it poorly, or violating work rules or the law) cannot receive unemployment compensation.

During economic recessions, the national government has sometimes extended the twenty-six-week benefit period if the unemployment rate remains high for a long time. For example, in February 2009, the federal government approved a new, temporary unemployment program to provide up to twenty additional weeks of unemployment benefits to certain workers. This extension was added to a 2008 extension that provided up to thirteen additional weeks of benefits to workers in states with unemployment rates of at least 6 percent. The federal government paid for these additional thirty-three weeks of extended benefits.[12]

Minimum Wage

In addition to guaranteeing some income for workers who lose their jobs through no fault of their own, Congress in 1938 enacted the Fair Labor Standards Act, which established a minimum wage. The aim was to guarantee most employed workers a **living wage**—a wage high enough to keep them out of poverty. The federal government has amended this law several times to expand minimum wage coverage to additional job categories, yet there are still many exceptions to it. Workers not guaranteed the federal minimum wage include full-time students, youths under 20 years of age for the first ninety days of their employment, workers who earn tips, commissioned sales employees, farm laborers, and seasonal and recreational workers. (Why do you think these workers are excluded from the minimum wage?) For workers guaranteed the minimum wage, employers must pay overtime (equal to one and a half times an employee's regular hourly rate) for all hours over 40 worked during a workweek.

In 1938, the government set the federal minimum wage at twenty-five cents per hour. Unlike the Social Security retirement program, OASI, the minimum wage benefit is not indexed to other economic factors and so does not automatically receive a COLA to keep up with inflation. Congress and the president must approve new legislation if the minimum wage is to increase. (Why do you think OASI is indexed to receive automatic COLAs and the minimum wage is not?)

Proposals to raise the minimum wage are always controversial, as revealed by the intense debate that preceded legislation in May 2007 that increased the national minimum wage

living wage
a wage high enough to keep workers and their families out of poverty and to allow them to enjoy a basic living standard

from $5.15 (the wage set in 1997) to $7.25 per hour. Senate Democrats, led by the late Senator Edward Kennedy (D-Massachusetts), included the provision for the minimum wage hike in a bill to continue funding for the Iraq War. In that way, they won needed votes from those who did not support the wage increase but did support the war funding. Speaker of the House Nancy Pelosi (D-California) said of the increase, "We are raising wages for the hardest-working Americans."[13]

State and local governments can establish a minimum wage higher than the federal minimum for covered workers, and they can extend a minimum wage to workers not covered by the federal minimum wage. In 2009, thirteen states and the District of Columbia had minimum wages higher than the new national $7.25 an hour.[14] But even in instances of these more generous benefits, the harsh reality is that many minimum wage workers, as well as many people earning several dollars over the national minimum wage—whom we collectively call the working poor—are still living in poverty. Hence, today's minimum wage is not a living wage. To reduce the financial hardship of minimum and low-wage workers, the national government established the Earned Income Tax Credit program.

Earned Income Tax Credit

In addition to providing cash transfers and regulating wages, the government supports income security through programs offering tax breaks. One of these is the Earned Income Tax Credit (EITC) program, established in 1975.

Citizens with low to moderate earned income from employment or from self-employment who file an income tax return are eligible for EITC benefits. Working parents are eligible for larger tax credits than are workers without children. The amount of the tax credit decreases (eventually reaching zero) as earned income increases.

According to the Center on Budget and Policy Priorities (CBPP), a research organization concerned with the status of poor people, in 2009 the EITC kept an estimated 6.6 million people out of poverty, including 3.3 million children. The CBPP claims, "There is broad bipartisan agreement that a two-parent family with two children with a full-time, minimum-wage worker should not have to raise its children in poverty. At the minimum wage's current level, such a family can move out of poverty only if it receives the EITC as well as food stamps."[15] Yet the antipoverty program with which many Americans are most familiar began in 1935 as Aid to Dependent Children.

Temporary Assistance to Needy Families

The Social Security Act established Aid to Dependent Children (ADC), which evolved into Aid to Families with Dependent Children (AFDC) and was then replaced by Temporary Assistance to Needy Families (TANF). Initially supporting stay-at-home single widows with children, the ADC program evolved into TANF, with its emphasis on assisting needy single-parent and two-parent families with children. The focus moreover has changed from one of encouraging women to stay home with their children to one of requiring recipients to work (those in single- and dual-parent households) and requiring fathers (particularly those not living with their children) to take on greater financial responsibilities for their children.

Federal grants and state funds paid for the ADC and AFDC noncontributory cash transfer, entitlement programs, and a formula in the national law determined what percentage of each state's annual program cost the federal government would cover. The federal law also gave each state discretion to determine the level of benefits as well as the eligibility criteria for program recipients in that state. (See "Analyzing the Sources" for data on the level of state benefits.) However, as mandated by federal law, eligibility criteria for AFDC in every state included the presence of children under the age of 18 and a means test indicating no or very low family income.

Beginning in the late 1950s, the number of households headed by women with children living in poverty began to increase, a development referred to as the **feminization of poverty.** Although the overwhelming majority of AFDC beneficiaries were children, myths

feminization of poverty
the phenomenon of increasing numbers of unmarried, divorced, and separated women with children living in poverty

ANALYZING THE SOURCES

DO TANF MONTHLY BENEFITS KEEP FAMILIES OUT OF POVERTY?

Each state establishes the TANF benefit levels for its recipients. The map indicates the 2008 TANF per-month benefit levels in each state for a family of three (one adult and two children) with no income.

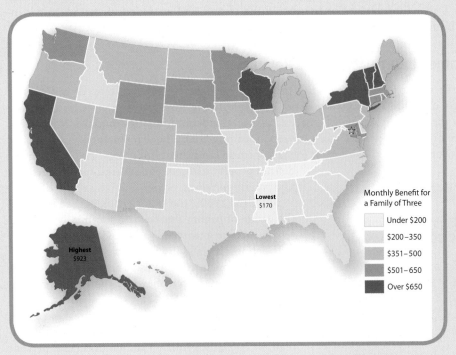

Lowest $170

Highest $923

Monthly Benefit for a Family of Three
- Under $200
- $200–350
- $351–500
- $501–650
- Over $650

SOURCE: Liz Schott and Zachary Levinson, "TANF Benefits Are Low and Have Not Kept Pace with Inflation" (Washington, DC: Center on Budget Policy and Priorities, November 24, 2008).

Evaluating the Evidence

① On the basis of the information in the map, determine the annual income provided to a family of three in your home state; in the state with the highest benefit; and in the state with the lowest benefit. How does your home state's benefit compare with the highest and lowest state benefits?

② Compare the annual incomes you identified in item 1 with the data supplied in Table 16.2 on page 510 to determine whether the family of three in these three states would be defined as living in poverty according to the Department of Health and Human Services (HHS) poverty guidelines. Report your findings.

③ Do a second comparison to see whether the families in these states would be eligible for programs available to families based on 185 percent of the income in the HHS poverty guidelines, found in Table 16.2. Report your findings.

---

about a poor work ethic and irresponsible sexual practices on the part of their typically single mothers fueled many calls for reform.

With passage of the Family Support Act (FSA) of 1988, the federal government adopted the objective of cultivating self-sufficiency in AFDC recipients. The FSA drove up the expense of the aid programs substantially, because it required states to provide job training, child care, and health benefits. In the long-term, the FSA was expected to decrease in cost as welfare recipients became self-sufficient workers. The short-term cost spike, however, led to calls for further welfare reform. In response, the federal government offered states waivers from some of the AFDC grant conditions to encourage experimentation with new forms of income security for low-income families with children.

On the national level, in 1996, President Bill Clinton (1993–2001) signed the Personal Responsibility and Work Opportunity Reconciliation Act (PRWORA), which radically changed both the nature and the provision of income security for low-income families with children. PRWORA replaced the AFDC entitlement program and several other grant assistance programs for low-income families with one grant, Temporary Assistance to Needy Families (TANF). Unlike AFDC, TANF is not an entitlement program.

Although PRWORA gives state governments a great deal of flexibility in determining TANF eligibility, benefits, and programs, it comes with several very specific regulations. For example, a family can receive benefits only for two consecutive years and a lifetime maximum of five years. Moreover, program beneficiaries must work or be enrolled in an educational or a training program that prepares them for work. In addition, female TANF recipients must identify their children's fathers so that these men can be required to provide financial support for their children. Ultimately, the success of this radical approach to welfare reform depends on the availability of jobs that pay well and offer benefits; hence its success depends on the overall health of the U.S. economy.

Congress included $5 billion in the 2009 American Recovery and Reinvestment Act (ARRA) for a temporary TANF Emergency Contingency Fund. The ARRA contained tax breaks and new spending aimed at stimulating the national economy as the Great Recession that began in 2007 continued. A state could apply for additional TANF grant money from the TANF Emergency Contingency Fund if its TANF caseload increased or if it increased the benefits provided to TANF recipients.[16]

Government Definitions of Poverty

poverty guidelines
a simplified version of the Census Bureau's poverty thresholds developed each year by the Department of Health and Human Services; used to set financial eligibility criteria for benefits

Despite the various income security programs we have considered, tens of millions of Americans, including millions who work full-time, live in *poverty*—the condition of lacking sufficient income to purchase the necessities for an adequate living standard. Millions of others are one problem away from poverty, meaning that a health emergency, significant car repair, family relations issue, or job layoff could land them in poverty. The government defines poverty using two measures: *poverty thresholds* and *poverty guidelines*.

Since the 1960s, the U.S. Census Bureau has used the gauge of *poverty thresholds*—an annually updated set of income measures (adjusted for family size) that define who is living in poverty (see Chapter 15). The government uses these thresholds to collect data on how many families and individuals are living in poverty.

Using 100 percent of the poverty threshold as the definition of poverty, according to the Census Bureau, in 2009, 39.8 million individuals (13.2 percent of the U.S. population) were living in poverty. There were 14.1 million children below the age of 18 years (19 percent) living in poverty, and almost 3.7 million people over the age of 64 (9.7 percent) in the same situation. The poverty rate among blacks was 24.7 percent; Hispanics, 23.2 percent; Asians, 11.8 percent; and non-Hispanic whites, 8.6 percent.[17]

Government agencies that offer additional safety-net programs beyond those we have considered so far do not use the Census Bureau's poverty thresholds to determine eligibility. Instead, many use the Department of Health and Human Services' (HHS) **poverty guidelines,** a version of the poverty thresholds simplified for administrative use. Table 16.2 presents the HHS Poverty Guidelines for 2009/2010.

Most (in-kind assistance) safety-net programs allow families with incomes of a certain percentage above the HHS poverty guidelines (say, 185 percent)

TABLE 16.2

Poverty Guidelines for the Forty-Eight Contiguous States and Washington, D.C., 2009/2010 ($ per year)

Persons in Household	100 Percent of Poverty	185 Percent of Poverty
1	10,830	20,036
2	14,570	26,955
3	18,310	33,874
4	22,050	40,793
5	25,790	47,712
6	29,530	54,631
7	33,370	61,550
8	37,010	68,469
For each additional person add	3,740	

SOURCE: http://liheap.ncat.org/profiles/povertytables/FY2010/popstate.htm.

POLITICAL INQUIRY

What quality of life could you, as a single person, achieve at the income of 100 percent of the poverty guideline? What quality of life could you, as a single person, achieve at the income of 185 percent of the poverty guideline?

to receive benefits. Administrators recognize that families with even those income levels experience difficulties in meeting their basic needs. Programs that use the HHS poverty guidelines as the basis for determining eligibility include the Supplemental Nutrition Assistance Program (SNAP) and the National School Lunch Program. These programs target the problem of **food insecurity,** the situation in which people have limited or uncertain ability to obtain, in socially acceptable ways, enough nutritious food to sustain a healthy and active life.

Housing insecurity—the condition in which people have limited or uncertain ability to obtain, in socially acceptable ways, housing that is affordable, safe, of decent quality, and permanent—is another problem for a growing proportion of the U.S. population. According to the Joint Center for Housing Studies at Harvard University, "The nation's housing challenges are escalating. Affordability is worsening, inadequate conditions persist, and crowding is more common."[18] The National Coalition for the Homeless estimates that more than 3 million people (1 percent of the entire U.S. population) experience homelessness in a given year.[19] About 40 percent of the homeless are children under the age of 18. Forty-nine percent are African American (compared with 11 percent of the general population). Twenty-three percent are veterans (compared with 13 percent of the general population).

Today, most federal revenue spent on housing assistance is in the form of tax breaks to homeowners, developers, and property owners who rent to low-income householders. But the programs that are most in the public eye are means-tested public housing and housing voucher (Section 8 rent subsidy) programs for which low-income households can apply. According to the Department of Housing and Urban Development (HUD), the availability of these forms of housing assistance is very limited, not close to meeting the demand.[20]

food insecurity
situation in which people have limited or uncertain ability to obtain, in socially acceptable ways, enough nutritious food to live a healthy and active life

housing insecurity
situation in which people have limited or uncertain ability to obtain, in socially acceptable ways, affordable, safe, and decent-quality permanent housing

Health Care Policy

Lack of health insurance is an additional problem for low-income households. Further, it is a growing challenge for middle-income households because the number of employers providing medical insurance for their employees (at no cost or a shared cost) has decreased in recent years as the cost of medical care has skyrocketed.

According to the U.S. Census Bureau, in 2008, 46.3 million people in the United States (15.4 percent) were without health insurance. Among those uninsured, 7.3 million (9.9 percent) were under 18 years of age. Approximately 67 percent of those with insurance had private insurance; 58.6 percent of people were covered by employer-provided insurance. Twenty-nine percent of those insured were covered by government health programs, just over 14 percent were covered by Medicaid, and another 14 percent were covered by Medicare.[21] These two programs were established in 1965 as part of President Lyndon Johnson's (1963–1969) "Great Society" plan, which included government programs to address the effects of poverty during a time of national economic prosperity. Medicare and Medicaid are part of today's safety net.

Medicaid

Title XIX, added to the Social Security Act in 1965, created Medicaid—a joint federal-state entitlement program providing health care to people meeting the means test. Because the national legislation delegates substantial discretion to state governments regarding eligibility and benefits, there are really fifty different Medicaid programs.

In this cash transfer program, state governments pay health care providers, and then the national government reimburses the states for a percentage of those bills. The national government's share of each state's cost is based on a formula that takes into account the state's wealth. The national government pays as little as 50 percent of the Medicaid bill in the fourteen wealthiest states and as much as 77 percent in the poorest state, Mississippi.[22]

Medicaid beneficiaries fit into one of five broad categories: (1) pregnant women and children under 6 with family income at or below 133 percent of the federal poverty guideline; (2) children ages 6 to 19 with a family income at or below 100 percent of the poverty guidelines; (3) low-income adults who care for children under age 18; (4) low-income adults who are blind, disabled, or living in a nursing home or a long-term care facility; (5) individuals who receive Supplemental Security Income. States have discretion to provide Medicaid to some additional groups, as defined by the national government. Many states cover children up to age 21 who are living on their own.[23]

The State Children's Health Insurance Program (SCHIP), established in 1997, covers medical costs for low-income uninsured children under the age of 19 who are not eligible for Medicaid. In this joint federal-state cash transfer program, eligibility is based on a family income that is generally less than 200 percent of the HHS poverty guideline. States participating in SCHIP can expand their current Medicaid program to cover these children, or they can create a new program that provides the standard coverage mandated by the national government.

Although most of those who benefit from Medicaid are women and children, the bulk of Medicaid spending covers the health care costs of the elderly. The largest percentage of Medicaid spending pays for nursing home and long-term care services, which Medicare does not cover.

Medicare

In 1965, President Lyndon Johnson signed legislation enacting Medicare, a program that provides health insurance to persons over age 65 and those under 65 who have been receiving SSDI for at least two years. Today, Medicare has four components.

Part A, Medicare's Hospital Insurance Program, is a social insurance program funded by a 1.45 percent tax paid by employees and employers that helps to pay for hospital stays. (This tax and the Social Security tax make up the "FICA" deduction from your paychecks.) All who pay into Medicare are eligible for Part A benefits when they reach the age of 65. Also eligible for Part A are persons under age 65 who have been receiving SSDI for at least two years.

All persons eligible for Part A and any persons over age 65, even if they are not eligible for Part A, can opt into *Part B,* Medicare's Supplemental Medical Insurance. Part B covers a percentage of physician costs and other outpatient health care expenses, such as laboratory fees and ambulance services.

In 1997, Congress established a third Medicare component, *Part C,* Medicare + Choice. This component allows Medicare beneficiaries to choose private health plans that provide them with the same coverage found in Medicare Parts A and B.

Under pressure from the American Association of Retired Persons (AARP) and other senior citizen interest groups, Congress proposed and President George W. Bush signed the Medicare Prescription Drug, Improvement, and Modernization Act in 2003. This act established Medicare *Part D,* the core of which is a prescription drug plan that took effect in 2006. A complicated program, Part D requires Medicare beneficiaries to choose a prescription drug plan provided by a private insurer if they do not already have prescription coverage through another health plan.

> On March 23, 2010, nearly a century after President Teddy Roosevelt first called for health care reform, and thirteen months after stating that "health care reform cannot wait, it must not wait, and it will not wait another year." President Barack Obama signed into law the Patient Protection and Affordable Care Act. Joining the president at the signing were Democratic congressional members and Vice President Joe Biden. Not present at the signing is even one Republican. The partisan battle over passage of this major health care reform did not end with its signing. It is ongoing as the national government attempts to implement the act.

The Patient Protection and Affordable Care Act

In February 2009, as he began his presidency, President Barack Obama staked out health care reform as one of his top priorities. Of the anticipated battle over health care reform, President Obama stated, "I suffer no illusions that this will be an easy process. It will be hard. But I also know that nearly a century after Teddy Roosevelt first called for reform, the cost of our health care has weighed down our economy and the conscience of our nation long enough. So let there be no doubt: health care reform cannot wait, it must not wait, and it will not wait another year."[24]

SHOULD ALL PEOPLE BE REQUIRED TO HAVE HEALTH INSURANCE?

The Issue: People who claim that U.S. health care is second-to-none support their claim by pointing to quick adoption of new medical technologies, patient participation in treatment decisions, prompt care, and the fact that the United States spends more per person on care than any other country. However, critics of U.S. health care point out that the United States has shorter life expectancy and higher infant mortality rates than most other wealthy industrialized countries. There is consensus that these are the two most reliable factors to compare health care systems. Critics also note that the United States is the only wealthy industrialized country in the world without some form of universal health care to ensure that everyone has access to some level of medical care. Moreover, approximately 45 million individuals in the United States do not have health insurance at some point each year. Should all people be required to have health insurance?

Yes: People without health insurance experience poorer health and die younger. The nation's economy is also harmed by reduced employment and job productivity, higher costs of public health programs, and diminished public health from lack of access to preventive care for those without insurance. Ultimately, people who pay health insurance premiums and taxpayers are burdened with paying the costs of health care for the uninsured through higher premiums and taxes, respectively. Those who can afford health care should be legally required to purchase it so as not to be a burden on the rest of us. The government should provide health insurance for those who cannot afford it.

No: First, it is unconstitutional to force individuals to purchase health insurance. The freedom to choose how they spend their money is a foundational right of American citizens. In addition, if the government has to insure all those who cannot afford insurance, we will experience further loss of personal freedom because the government will increase taxes on smoking, fast food, soda, and so on to pay for it. Moreover, uninsured Americans *do* have access to health care through nonprofits and public hospitals. Current law makes it illegal for any hospital to refuse emergency medical services because of a lack of insurance.

Other approaches: The national government requires employees and employers to pay into income security programs (Social Security and unemployment compensation). It also requires employers and employees to pay into the Medicare system (health insurance for retired citizens). Therefore, there is legal precedent for the national government to require employees and employers to pay into a health insurance system. The government could extend Medicaid coverage to nonemployed Americans who cannot afford to purchase their own health insurance.

What do you think?

① Is health care a right? Is it a privilege? Explain your answer.

② Do you think the lack of universal health insurance coverage is a large enough threat to public health that the national government should ensure that every individual has coverage? Explain your answer.

③ Is there a particular health care reform, or combination of reforms, that you believe the majority of U.S. citizens would support? Explain.

On March 23, 2010, President Barack Obama signed into law the Patient Protection and Affordable Care Act. However, the battle over health care reform did not end with the president's signing of this act. Congressional Republicans vowed to repeal the law. Attorneys general in more than a dozen states filed lawsuits against the federal government, contending that some provisions in the new law are unconstitutional. What is in this controversial, landmark legislation? The law's goal is to expand coverage to 32 million Americans who are currently uninsured through modifications to current government programs, new regulations imposed on the insurance industry and employers, and a requirement that all individuals acquire insurance. At the same time, the law attempts to contain health care costs.

The law expands Medicaid coverage to families earning 133 percent of the federal poverty level. It also requires states to expand Medicaid coverage to childless adults starting in 2014. Another means by which the law expands coverage is by making illegal (by 2014) the current insurance industry practice of denying coverage to people with preexisting conditions. In addition, insurance companies must now allow children to stay on their parents' insurance plans until age 26.

The law mandates that by 2014, everyone (with some exceptions for low-income people) must purchase health insurance, if it is not provided through their employer or a government program, or face an annual fine. The federal government will make subsidies available to individuals with income between 133 percent and 400 percent of the federal poverty level to help them purchase insurance. The law also calls for the establishment of health insurance exchanges in which uninsured and self-employed individuals will be able to purchase health insurance with federal subsidies. Moreover, employers with more than fifty employees will have to provide health insurance or pay annual fines for each of their employees who receive federal subsidies to purchase insurance.

For seniors participating in the Medicare Part D prescription program, the new law closes a gap in prescription coverage by providing rebates and discounts on brand-name drugs. To pay for the new government-provided benefits, the law imposes a new tax on indoor tanning services, on insurance companies that provide expensive, high-end insurance plans, and on investment income of higher-earning individuals and families.

After signing the Patient Protection and Affordable Care Act, President Obama said it "enshrines the core principle that everybody should have some basic security when it comes to their health care."[25] However, controversy continues over how the new law implements this core principle. (See "Thinking Critically About Democracy.")

Homeland Security

The government's responsibility does not stop with ensuring basic necessities such as a clean environment, affordable energy, a secure income, sufficient food, shelter, and health care. Federal, state, and local governments also cooperate to prevent threats to personal safety, home, and health. Such threats may come from natural disasters such as hurricanes and earthquakes or from human-made calamities such as terrorist attacks.

President George W. Bush and Congress established the Department of Homeland Security in 2002 in response to the September 11, 2001, terrorist attacks. The department's mission is to improve the coordination of efforts to prevent and respond to disasters, both human-made and natural, within U.S. borders. Homeland security is a central theme in contemporary U.S. domestic policy and an ever-present concern in Americans' daily lives.

Four Challenges for Policy Makers

Four significant challenges present themselves in homeland security policy deliberations. The first is how much intrusion into citizens' lives, in the name of prevention, is acceptable. The second challenge is the appropriate level and distribution of national grants-in-aid to state and local governments for improved communication systems and response capabilities. A third challenge has to do with the intergovernmental aspect of homeland security. The issue is, how much discretion should state and local governments have in administering the federal grants-in-aid? Although this is a common concern with respect to intergovernmental efforts for any policy area, the stakes can be very high and the finger-pointing and blaming can be especially vigorous when homeland disasters arise.

The fourth challenge for policy makers is how to ensure that national, state, and local bureaucrats, as well as other first responders, are able to coordinate their efforts to prevent and respond to homeland disasters. Communication, leadership, authority, and cooperation have all proven to be problematic during homeland disasters.

The Importance of Intergovernmental Coordination

Homeland security can succeed only as an intergovernmental effort. The prevention of attacks relies on intelligence collected by local and state law enforcement as well as federal agencies such as the Central Intelligence Agency (CIA), the National Security Agency (NSA), and the Federal Bureau of Investigation (FBI). Typically, the first responders to attacks and natural disasters are police officers, firefighters, emergency medical technicians, and other public servants hired by local governments. Federal and state agencies, when necessary, support first responders. The Department of Homeland Security agencies that back up first responders are the Federal Emergency Management Agency (FEMA), the Office of Domestic Preparedness, and the National Biological Warfare Defense Analysis Center.

Hurricane Katrina and its aftermath in September 2005 presented the first real test of the response capacity of the Department of Homeland Security. The department failed the test according to citizens living in the states damaged by the hurricane, along with local and state government officials, the media, and Bush administration investigators. According to the Bush administration's *Fact Sheet: The Federal Response to Hurricane Katrina: Lessons Learned,* the hurricane and the subsequent flooding of New Orleans "exposed significant flaws in our national preparedness for catastrophic events and our capacity to respond to them."[26] The report highlights the crucial need for the integration of homeland security plans across national, state, and local government, as well as across organizations in the private and nonprofit sector.

Clearly, intergovernmental efforts are essential if we are to have secure homes, health, and opportunities to pursue happiness within the borders of the United States—the mission of domestic policy. The efforts of individual citizens are also vital.

Another facet of the Department of Homeland Security's work is the implementation of immigration policy and border security. Continuing concerns about potential acts of terrorism on U.S. soil, as well as debates over the economic effects of the increasing number of immigrants coming to the United States, have placed immigration policy reform high on the national agenda.

Immigration Policy

The majority of immigrants to the United States are young people seeking two goals: reunification with family members residing here and work that will provide a better quality of life than they are able to achieve in their home countries. U.S. immigration policy, the collection of laws that specify which people the government will authorize to immigrate to the United States, allows approximately 1 million immigrants, in four categories, to immigrate legally each year. Figure 16.2 shows that these legal immigrants come from around the globe. In addition to the legal newcomers, about 500,000 unauthorized immigrants come into the United States annually. After the events of 9/11, citizens and their elected representatives, concerned about the impact of both authorized and unauthorized immigrants, began to analyze immigration policy anew. Debate on immigration policy reform has been ongoing ever since.

Authorized and Unauthorized Immigration

Federal immigration policy determines who may immigrate to the United States as permanent residents and as temporary visitors (such as tourists, students, and guest workers). Since the Immigration and Nationality Act of 1965, the largest category of immigrants authorized to come to the United States permanently are those seeking to reunify with family members who are either U.S. citizens or authorized permanent residents. The second-largest category comprises individuals welcomed for their employment skills; this group includes highly skilled professionals and wealthy entrepreneurs expected to invest in job creation. Persons to whom the United States offers humanitarian protection from persecution (or likely persecution) because of race, religion, nationality, membership in a particular social group, or political views compose the third-largest category of authorized immigrants. The smallest category of permanent authorized immigrants gain entry through the country-quota system, which allows up to 25,000 people per country per year (selected by lottery) to

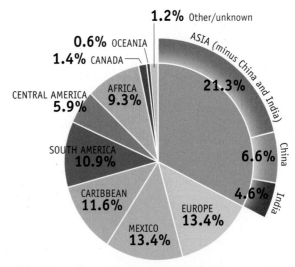

POLITICAL INQUIRY

FIGURE 16.2 ■ GLOBAL SCOPE OF U.S. IMMIGRATION What world region is the source of most U.S. immigrants today? With respect to the Americas, what country or larger geographical unit is the source of most immigrants to the United States?

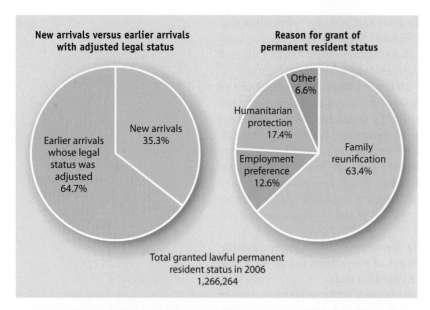

New arrivals versus earlier arrivals with adjusted legal status

- New arrivals 35.3%
- Earlier arrivals whose legal status was adjusted 64.7%

Reason for grant of permanent resident status

- Other 6.6%
- Humanitarian protection 17.4%
- Employment preference 12.6%
- Family reunification 63.4%

Total granted lawful permanent resident status in 2006
1,266,264

POLITICAL INQUIRY

FIGURE 16.3 ■ LEGAL IMMIGRATION TO THE UNITED STATES For immigrants who were granted lawful permanent residence in 2006, what percentages, respectively, were (1) new arrivals and (2) earlier arrivals whose legal status was adjusted? What factor accounted for the most grants of permanent status?

enter the United States legally.[27] Figure 16.3 presents the breakdown of authorized and unauthorized immigrants for 2006.

Who is *not* eligible for permanent authorized immigration to the United States? In addition to foreigners who do not fall within one of the categories described above, foreign nationals perceived to be anarchists or political extremists have been excluded since 1901, when a Polish anarchist assassinated President William McKinley (1897–1901). More recently, in 2002, the USA PATRIOT Act established new criteria for denying entry to the United States. Today, the national government can deny authorized immigration to foreigners who are perceived as a security or terrorist threat, have a criminal history, have previously been removed from the United States, or present a health risk.[28]

Why do half a million immigrants enter the United States without authorization each year? There are several answers to that question. One is that economic opportunities are better than those available in the home country. Yet unless an individual fits into one of the four categories for authorized immigration, he or she has no basis on which to apply for permanent, legal entry into the United States. Another reason for the large volume of unauthorized immigration is that individuals applying for immigration under the family reunification category or through their country's quota system come up against the annual U.S. quota of 25,000 per country. There is a wide gap between the number allowed under this quota and the number of applications. The result is a backlog of millions of applications that may mean up to a twenty-year wait for authorized immigration.[29] These are just some of the obstacles that explain why approximately 500,000 unauthorized immigrants enter the United States each year.

Proposed Immigration Policy Reforms

The flood of unauthorized immigrants creates financial and other stresses and strains that have prompted calls for immigration reform. Although unauthorized immigrants are not eligible for safety-net benefits such as programs for income security and food security, all children born on U.S. soil—even those born to unauthorized immigrants—are citizens and hence are eligible for these benefits. Moreover, the government guarantees a public education to all children, citizens and unauthorized immigrants alike. State and local governments cover approximately 92 percent of the cost of public education, and the national government funds the remaining 8 percent. And with respect to legal rights, the Fourteenth Amendment to the Constitution guarantees all people, not just citizens, due process before the government can infringe on their life, liberty, or pursuit of happiness, as well as equal protection of the law. Typically, the costs of these constitutional guarantees fall to state and local governments. Most unauthorized immigrants *do* pay taxes and so are contributing to government revenues collected to pay these bills. Yet their tax contributions do not cover these costs, just as the taxes collected from low-income citizens and authorized immigrants do not cover the costs of their safety-net benefits.

Given the financial burden of supporting the 10 million unauthorized immigrants residing in the United States in 2005, and in light of concerns about the ease with which terrorists (posing as well-intended immigrants) might gain entry into the country, Congress and President Bush worked intensively, yet unsuccessfully, to reform immigration policy. Without immigration reform, the federal government increased spending to install fencing along the U.S.-Mexico border and to post additional border patrol agents on the border.

Responding to the lack of national government immigration reform, numerous state and local governments began enacting their own immigration laws. According to the National Conference of State Legislatures, during 2007, state lawmakers introduced at least 1,100 immigration bills. That was double the number of state immigration bills submitted in 2006. Local governments also enacted laws pertaining to immigrants. Immigration reform was an issue in the 2008 presidential campaign as well, with Barack Obama saying he would work on it in his first year as president. However, by April 2010, the national government still had not taken up the issue of immigration reform. Then on April 23, 2010, Arizona governor Jan Brewer signed an immigration law that sparked protests and lawsuits. Civil rights organizations argued that the law would lead to racial profiling. The federal government sued Arizona claiming portions of the law were unconstitutional because they abridged the federal government's authority over immigration policy. In July 2010, a federal District Court judge blocked the implementation of several provisions of the law while allowing other provisions to go into effect. Arizona appealed this decision to the Ninth U.S. Circuit Court of Appeals, which scheduled a hearing for early November 2010. Ultimately, Arizona's immigration law forced national lawmakers to move immigration reform up on their policy agenda.

> Members of the U.S. Army install part of the fence along the border near Puerto Palomas, Mexico. The federal government is building a 745-mile fence along the U.S.-Mexico border to reduce the flow of illegal migrants into the United States.

CONCLUSION

THINKING CRITICALLY ABOUT WHAT'S NEXT IN DOMESTIC POLICY

A healthy environment is essential to human health, happiness, and survival. Reliance on nonrenewable energy sources, specifically fossil fuels, as well as the volumes of waste produced by the world's growing population, harm the global environment. Pollution and environmental degradation do not recognize the borders between countries. Emission caps in the northeastern United States do not compensate for the lack of caps elsewhere in the country, or in the world. Will worldwide environmental degradation force U.S. policy makers to sign international treaties?

Ensuring a healthy and safe society in which citizens can live their lives freely, in pursuit of their happiness, means more than protecting air, water, and land quality. During the Great Depression, the national government established income security programs to ensure at least a minimum quality of life for U.S. citizens. During the economic boom of the 1960s, the national government continued its efforts to ensure at least a minimum quality of life by creating national health care programs for the elderly, persons with disabilities, and very-low-income families. Today, the ever-increasing costs of ensuring a just and safe society in which citizens can live their lives freely, in pursuit of happiness, is forcing U.S. policy makers to take a hard look at income security and health care programs. Will the perpetually increasing costs of income security programs and health care force U.S. policy makers to enact major legislative reforms?

Each year, millions of immigrants enter the United States, some legally and others illegally, to take advantage of the quality of life in the United States. Throughout U.S. history, immigrants have been essential to the workforce and hence the economic health of the nation. High levels of immigration since the early 1990s have produced a U.S. population that is much more diverse in race, ethnicity, religion, and languages. Will demographic change owing to high immigration today bring new issues to tomorrow's domestic policy agenda?

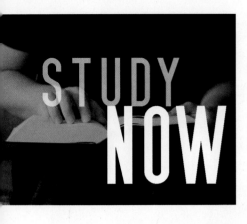

Summary

1. Citizen Engagement and Domestic Policy

U.S. domestic policy addresses internal problems that threaten the people's well-being, domestic tranquility, and civil liberties, and a decent standard of living. The exponential growth in the number and range of domestic policies since the Constitution's ratification in 1788 is the product of the responses of elected representatives to citizens' and interest groups' lobbying efforts as well as national crises.

2. Tools of Domestic Policy

The national government uses various policy tools to accomplish its domestic goals. These include laws, regulations, direct provision of public goods, cash transfers, loans, loan guarantees, insurance plans, and contracting-out.

3. Environmental Policy

Since the 1970s, the federal government has assumed the primary role in formulating environmental policy. Through its regulatory policy, supplemented with grants-in-aid and loans, the national government has devolved the implementation of environmental protection to state and local governments. The tensions between the competing goals of environmental protection, economic development, and ensuring an ample supply of affordable energy are ongoing.

4. Energy Policy

Economic development and the high standard of living that is the American way have driven up energy demand. Given U.S. reliance on imported oil, much of it from politically unstable foreign nations, the internal situation of other countries strongly affects U.S. energy supplies and hence prices. Most U.S. energy is produced by the burning of nonrenewable fossil fuels, which harms the natural environment. This damage has led to an energy policy that includes funding for research and the development of alternative, renewable energy sources for the long term and conservation efforts for the short term.

5. Income Security Programs

The idea that the government should provide a safety net for citizens in financial need took shape through key components of President Franklin D. Roosevelt's New Deal. The government expanded that safety net with President Lyndon Johnson's Great Society programs. The national government meets its responsibility to provide a safety net through income security, food security, and housing security policies.

6. Health Care Policy

Health care costs are rising steadily for all. Even with the protections of Medicare and Medicaid, and even with the recent expansion of these programs, millions of people, including many employed adults, do not have health insurance. Given the steeply rising national and state expenditures for health care, and the large percentage of citizens lacking health insurance, research into and experimentation with new health care policies is ongoing.

7. Homeland Security

The Department of Homeland Security's mission is to prevent terrorist attacks and to respond to domestic disasters (human-made and natural). To accomplish this mission, the national government uses the policy tools of direct provision and grants-in-aid, working in collaboration with state and local governments.

8. Immigration Policy

Approximately 1.5 million authorized and unauthorized immigrants come to the United States each year seeking family reunification, asylum from persecution, and a better quality of life. Concerns over taxpayer costs to provide for immigrants and over the ease with which terrorists might gain entrance into the United States have sparked new efforts for immigration policy reforms.

Key Terms

cash transfer 496

contributory program (social insurance program) 497

direct provision 496

direct subsidy 497

entitlement program 497

environmental racism 500

feminization of poverty 508

food insecurity 511

global warming 502

greenhouse effect 502

housing insecurity 511

indexed benefit 506

in-kind assistance 496

living wage 507

means-tested benefit 507

noncontributory program 497

poverty guidelines 510

safety net 494

For Review

1. Explain the NIMBY syndrome.

2. Describe four or five of the domestic policy tools used by the federal government.

3. Discuss how the federal policy tools used for environmental protection make intergovernmental relations a key component of environmental policy.

4. Explain how concerns about environmental protection, as well as the political situation in oil-producing countries, influence national energy policy.

5. Use the following terms to distinguish between OASI and TANF: contributory program, noncontributory program, means-tested program, and entitlement program.

6. Differentiate between Medicaid and Medicare in terms of who benefits from each program.

7. What is the mission of the Department of Homeland Security?

8. For what reasons do hundreds of thousands of foreigners come to the United States as unauthorized immigrants each year?

For Critical Thinking and Discussion

1. Many critics of current environmental policy argue that government regulation of pollution amounts to ineffective policy. Some claim that using cash transfer tools, including tax expenditures, grants, and direct subsidies, would be more effective. Explain how the government could use at least one of the cash transfer tools to protect the environment.

2. Which cash transfer programs (including tax expenditures) will the majority of Americans benefit from at some point in their lives? Explain.

3. Explain how at least two of the programs discussed in this chapter are important to a sustainable community.

4. What might explain why Social Security and Medicare are entitlements but TANF is not an entitlement? Keep in mind the nature of the programs (contributory or noncontributory) and the populations each program targets.

5. Frequently, a crisis or a disaster is the catalyst for revolutionary, new public policies. Discuss one or two crises or disasters that have occurred in your lifetime and that led to major changes in public policy.

MULTIPLE CHOICE: Choose the lettered item that answers the question correctly.

1. The largest national cash transfer program is
   a. SNAP.
   b. Social Security.
   c. Temporary Assistance to Needy Families (TANF).
   d. unemployment compensation.

2. The largest component (in cost and number of people served) of Social Security is
   a. COLA.   c. SSDI.
   b. OASI.   d. SSI.

3. Pell grants and financial support to farmers for growing or limiting the growth of crops are two examples of the policy tool of
   a. contributory cash transfer.
   b. direct subsidy.
   c. insurance.
   d. loan guarantee.

4. All of the following safety-net programs were created during President Franklin D. Roosevelt's administrations *except*
   a. Medicaid.
   b. the minimum wage.
   c. Social Security's Old-Age and Survivors Insurance.
   d. unemployment compensation.

5. The environmental movement began in the
   a. 1890s.   c. 1970s.
   b. 1930s.   d. 1990s.

6. What is the current national minimum wage?
   a. $5.50.
   b. $6.75.
   c. $7.25.
   d. $8.00.

7. The disaster that prompted the national government to establish the Department of Homeland Security is
   a. the Great Depression.
   b. Hurricane Katrina.
   c. Love Canal.
   d. the terrorist attacks on 9/11.

8. The largest category of immigrants to the United States consists of
   a. authorized immigrants seeking family reunification.
   b. authorized immigrants with professional skills and/or wealth.
   c. authorized immigrants seeking humanitarian protection from persecution.
   d. unauthorized immigrants.

9. The entitlement retirement income program created in 1935 is
   a. EITC.
   b. OASI.
   c. SSDI.
   d. TANF.

10. The income security program that is subject to a regular COLA is
    a. minimum wage.
    b. OASI.
    c. TANF.
    d. unemployment compensation.

FILL IN THE BLANKS.

11. _____ is the national program that provides health insurance to the elderly.

12. _____ is the national program that provides health insurance to low-income citizens.

13. A (An) _____ program guarantees a benefit to all who meet the program's eligibility criteria, regardless of the total cost to the government.

14. An indexed benefit is one that automatically increases to keep up with inflation. The increase is a COLA, which stands for _____ .

15. A (An) _____ benefit has a government-specified income level (typically based on the poverty guidelines) as one of its eligibility criteria.

Internet Resources

Center for Budget and Policy Priorities
www.cbpp.org The center focuses on the impact of public policies on low-income households. On the Web site, you will find links to numerous reports elaborating on the effects of public policies on such households.

Environmental Protection Agency
www.epa.gov/history/topics This section of the EPA's Web site provides historical overviews of toxic waste sites that the government has worked to clean up.

USA Government Information
www.usa.gov This easy-to-use first stop for government information offers links to government agencies and their programs.

Internet Activism

Is there an issue you are passionate about? Do you want the government to address it? If your answer is yes, then visit **www.freethechildren.com/youthzone/media/sevensteps**. This Web site provides a step-by-step guide to political engagement, from researching an issue, through developing the agenda for and running a meeting of peers, to creating a blueprint for social action.

Blog
www.offthechartsblog.org The Center on Budget and Policy Priorities is a nonprofit, nonpartisan policy organization working at the federal and state levels on fiscal policy and public programs that affect low- and moderate-income families and individuals.

Facebook
www.facebook.com/pages/Ecological-Footprint-Quiz-Myfoot printorg/111090025594739?ref=ts Take the Ecological Footprint quiz to determine how your lifestyle affects the environment.

Youtube
www.youtube.com/watch?v=Q3JToii4Aq4 For a quick overview of the history of immigration to the United States through 2007, the last year that the U.S. House or Senate passed an immigration bill, watch this video.

Recommended Readings

Carson, Rachel. *Silent Spring.* New York: Houghton Mifflin, 1962. Thorough and alarming description of how the pesticide DDT harmed the food chain, caused cancer and genetic damage, and threatened the world as we know it.

Ehrenreich, Barbara. *Nickel and Dimed: On (Not) Getting By in America.* New York: Henry Holt, 2001. Documentation of the author's experiences when she joined the millions of Americans working full-time, year-round, for wages higher than the minimum wage ($6 to $7 per hour) in jobs with no benefits.

Gore, Al. *Earth in the Balance: Ecology and the Human Spirit.* Boston: Houghton Mifflin, 1992. Comprehensive assessment of the major post–Cold War threat to the United States and the world: planetary destruction due to overpopulation, deforestation, soil erosion, air pollution, and water pollution. Written before his more popularly known *An Inconvenient Truth,* Gore recommends far-reaching and specific governmental and corporate actions.

Kettl, Donald. *System Under Stress: Homeland Security and American Politics,* 2nd ed. Washington, D.C.: CQ Press, 2007. Comprehensive presentation of the massive bureaucratic reorganization that created the Department of Homeland Security. The effectiveness of this reorganization is assessed in light of the disastrous governmental response to Hurricane Katrina.

Movies of Interest

An Inconvenient Truth (2006)
A rallying cry for citizens and government to address the problem of global warming, this documentary presents the science of global warming as it follows Al Gore's environmental advocacy from his college years to today.

United 93 (2006)
An account of the fate of United Flight 93—the fourth plane hijacked on September 11, 2001—this fact-based film documents the plight of the passengers (who had become aware of the other hijackings) and their struggle to prevent another catastrophe. It also reveals the national government's lack of preparedness for the emergency.

A Civil Action (1998)
This movie highlights the enormous expense (financial and emotional) of proving in a court of law that a large corporation's chemical waste pollution caused the leukemia that killed children from eight families.

The Grapes of Wrath (1940)
The winner of two Academy Awards, this movie, set during the Great Depression, tells the story of the Joad family (and their acquaintances) as they struggle to meet their basic needs, first in the Oklahoma Dust Bowl and later in California.

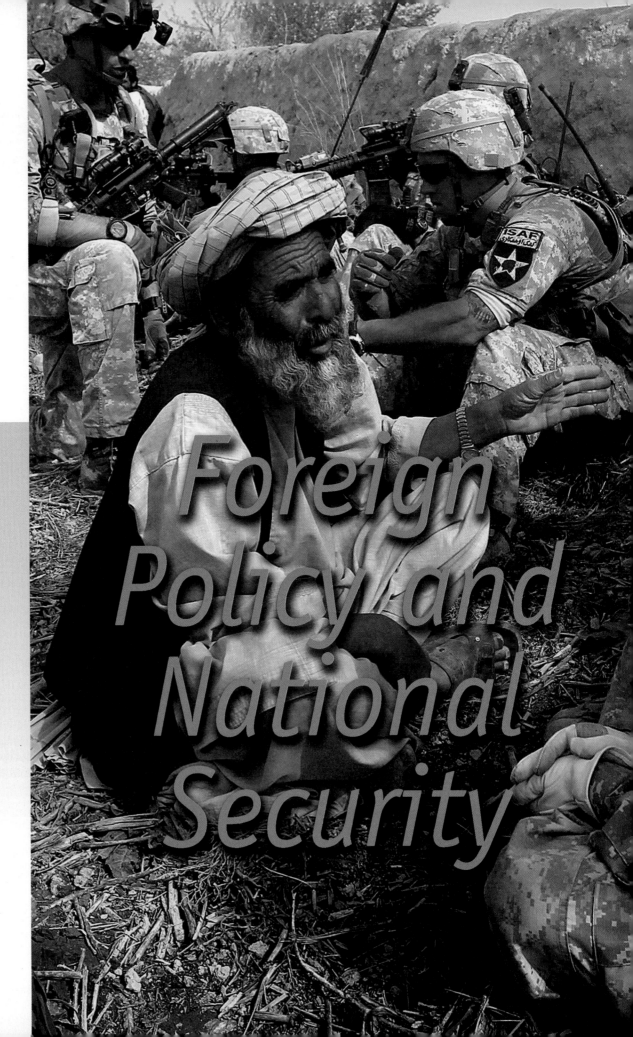

CHAPTER

17

Foreign Policy and National Security

THEN

The emergence of the United States as a superpower and the Cold War dominated U.S. foreign policy in the aftermath of World War II.

NOW

The war on terror defines U.S. foreign and national security policy.

NEXT

What long-term repercussions will the wars in Afghanistan and Iraq and ongoing tensions with Iran and North Korea have on the future of U.S. foreign policy and the United States' role as world leader?

How will the continuing threat of terrorism against the United States influence foreign and national security policy in the future?

Will U.S. foreign policy in the coming years increasingly reflect a clash of civilizations between Western democracies and fundamentalist Islamic states?

This chapter provides a framework for your study of foreign policy and national security.

FIRST, we examine *the tools of U.S. foreign policy.*

SECOND, we analyze the question of *who decides: the creators and shapers of foreign policy.*

THIRD, we look at *U.S. foreign policy in historical context,* tracing its development from the ratification of the Constitution until World War II.

FOURTH, we analyze *the postwar era* and the status of *the United States as superpower.*

FIFTH, since it has become clear that Cold War policies are no longer relevant, we consider *U.S. foreign policy after 9/11.*

SIXTH, we take a look at *future challenges in American foreign policy.*

The conventional view is that

foreign policy is all about wizened old statesmen negotiating treaties and about sophisticated ambassadors clinking wine glasses at chic cocktail parties. It is true that top government officials in Washington, D.C., formulate foreign policy—the politics and the programs by which the United States conducts its relations with other countries and furthers American interests around the globe. But the broader, everyday reality of U.S. foreign policy is that individual American citizens play an important part in shaping and implementing the programs decided upon by foreign policy makers. Citizens play their part by staying informed about policy makers' decisions on war, peace, trade issues, and policies that ensure national security in the post-9/11 world, and expressing their personal views to their representatives in government and through the ballot box.

Of all the country's policy arenas, the foreign policy arena is the most volatile. During the past sixty years, the goals of U.S. foreign policy have shifted significantly, from preventing the spread of communism in the post–World War II era, to redefining the national foreign policy agenda as the world's only superpower in the 1990s, to responding to the terrorist attacks of September 11, 2001. As the objectives and the worldviews of policy makers have changed in concert with unprecedented world developments, so too have their priorities and the instruments available to them in implementing U.S. foreign policy.

The Tools of U.S. Foreign Policy

Government officials use a variety of instruments to shape foreign policy. Among these are diplomacy, trade and economic policies, and military options.

Diplomacy

diplomacy
the conduct of international relations, particularly involving the negotiation of treaties and other agreements between nations

Covering a gamut of situations, diplomacy is often foreign policy makers' tool of choice. **Diplomacy** can be generally defined as the conduct of international relations, particularly involving the negotiation of treaties and other agreements between nations. It can include an occurrence as mundane as the communication between two embassies when a citizen of one country commits a crime in another. Or it can involve an event as significant as a major summit attended by world leaders. When diplomacy works, we typically do not hear about it.

foreign service officers
the diplomatic and consular staff at U.S. embassies abroad

Among the central figures in the diplomatic arena are **foreign service officers,** the diplomatic and consular staff at American embassies abroad. Foreign service officers, who are employees of the Department of State, conduct formal communications among nations. They are frequently responsible for negotiating many types of international agreements, including economic and trade policies.

Trade and Economic Policies

normal trade relations (NTR) status
the international trade principle holding that the least restrictive trade conditions (best tariff rates) offered to any one national trading partner will be offered to every other nation in a trading network (also known as *most favored nations*)

U.S. foreign policy makers rely on trade policies, economic aid (foreign aid), and economic penalties to compel foreign governments to conform to the United States' will. Consider the example of most favored nation status. In international trade, conferring **normal trade relations (NTR) status** means that a country grants to a particular trading partner the same, least restrictive trade conditions (that is, the lowest tariff rates) that the country offers to its other favored trading partners—its "most favored nations." U.S. foreign policy makers can bestow most favored nation status on a country to influence it to enact policies the United States prefers. Conversely, they can withhold this status to punish a nation that does not institute policies supportive of the United States' goals. For example, the United States withheld most favored nation status from Vietnam for many years, in an attempt to get the Vietnamese to account for American prisoners of war and soldiers missing in action in the Vietnam War.

Governments also use trade agreements as a tool of foreign policy. Among the most important of these agreements in the United States is the North American Free Trade Agreement (NAFTA), whose members include the United States, Mexico, and Canada. NAFTA eliminated barriers to trade and financial investments across the economies of the three nations.

Beyond trade policy, American diplomats frequently use economic enticements in the form of foreign aid to pressure other countries into enacting and enforcing policies that the United States supports. After the terrorist attacks of September 11, 2001, for example, the George W. Bush administration sought the cooperation of the Pakistani government in Operation Enduring Freedom, the U.S. military offensive in neighboring Afghanistan. The United States sought to overthrow the Islamic fundamentalist Taliban regime, which had harbored and provided training grounds for terrorists, and to capture 9/11 mastermind Osama bin Laden, who was believed to be hiding in Afghanistan. Before the 9/11 terrorist strikes on domestic U.S. targets, Pakistan had received comparatively little aid from the United States. In fact, the United States had imposed sanctions on Pakistan because of its pursuit of nuclear weapons, its history of domestic coups, and its track record of defaulting on international loans. But after 9/11 and because of Pakistan's proximity to Afghanistan (they share a 1,500-mile-long border), Pakistan became a focal point of the U.S. war on terror. To encourage (and finance) the country's cooperation, the Bush administration waived the sanctions on Pakistan.[1] Moreover, whereas Pakistan had received only about $3.4 million in aid from the United States in the year before the terrorist attacks, in 2002 the country was the beneficiary of over $1 billion in U.S. aid. Although aid levels tapered off to between $400 million and $600 million annually between 2003 and 2007, the Bush administration requested $785 million for Pakistan in 2008.[2] The Obama administration continued the policy of relying on economic enticements to compel compliance. In 2009, the administration sought and won congressional approval for a $7.5 billion aid bill, to be disbursed over five years. The bill includes prohibitions against the use of the funds for nuclear proliferation, to support terrorist groups, or to pay for attacks in neighboring countries. And it reserves the right to end aid to the Pakistanis if they fail to crack down on militants.[3] The aid has proven effective in paving the way for warmer Pakistani-U.S. relations: the United States regularly uses Pakistani air bases to launch attacks into Afghanistan, and it continues to rely on Pakistani intelligence for information about terror network activity.

American foreign policy makers also rely on economic strategies to punish countries whose policies or behavior the U.S. government disapproves of. In February 2010, President Barack Obama announced that the United States and its allies were developing a host of **sanctions**—penalties that halt economic exchanges (and that may include boycotts and a suspension of cultural exchanges)—on Iran. The Obama administration and its western European allies object to Iran's pursuit of nuclear weapons. Obama's announcement came after Iranian state media reported that the nation had begun the uranium enrichment process. Iran stated that the uranium would be used for medical research, but the administration

sanctions
penalties that halt economic relations

rejected that claim. However, as former Senator Christopher Dodd (D-Connecticut), who chaired the Banking, Housing, and Urban Affairs Committee, noted, "Economic sanctions are a critical element of U.S. policy toward Iran. But sanctions alone are not sufficient. They must be used as effective leverage, undertaken as part of a coherent, coordinated, comprehensive diplomatic and political strategy which firmly seeks to deter Iran's nuclear ambitions and other actions which pose a threat to regional stability."[4]

Almost a century ago, President Woodrow Wilson made this observation:

> A nation that is boycotted is a nation that is in sight of surrender. Apply this economic, peaceful, silent, deadly remedy and there will be no need for force. It does not cost a life outside the nation boycotted, but it brings a pressure upon the nation which, in my judgment, no modern nation could resist.[5]

globalism
the interconnectedness between nations in contemporary times

But others argue that sanctions actually may worsen conditions, particularly for the poorest people in a sanctioned nation.[6] And given the high levels of **globalism,** or interconnectedness, among the world's countries today, a nation on which boycotts or sanctions are imposed often has recourse—sometimes in the form of aid from allies—to withstand the pressure of the economic penalty.

The Military Option

Since September 11, 2001, the United States has been involved in a multifront war that prominently features military actions in Afghanistan and Iraq. The September 11 terrorist strikes and subsequent U.S. government actions demonstrate how the creators of foreign policy use the military option as an instrument of foreign policy. Hungry for an enemy after the deadly attacks on American soil, the United States targeted Afghanistan's Taliban regime. The Taliban had supported and harbored members of **al-Qaeda,** the radical international Islamic fundamentalist terror organization that took credit for the 9/11 bloodshed. Foreign intelligence had pointed to Osama bin Laden, a Saudi millionaire living in Afghanistan, as the engineer of the attacks. U.S. military action in Afghanistan continues today.

al-Qaeda
a radical international Islamic fundamentalist terror organization

But the bases of world terrorist activity today transcend national borders. The nineteen 9/11 terrorists themselves were not citizen-soldiers of any one country but, rather, nationals from Saudi Arabia, the United Arab Emirates, Egypt, and Lebanon. They had trained in various nations, including Afghanistan, and had been supported by citizens of still other countries. Thus no single, clear nation-state was the enemy. Without a concrete enemy (over which a victory could be defined and declared), the Bush administration requested, and Congress passed, a formal declaration of a "war on terror."

Then–Secretary of State Colin Powell subsequently made a case to the United Nations and to the American people alleging that U.S. intelligence indicated that the Saddam Hussein regime in Iraq was harboring **weapons of mass destruction (WMDs)**—nuclear, chemical, and biological weapons.[7] In response to what at the time appeared to be a credible threat, on March 18, 2003, American troops invaded Iraq. The military strike toppled the Hussein regime, which the United States had supported for years through foreign aid.[8] Following the invasion, weapons inspectors conducted a thorough search of suspected weapons sites, but no WMDs were ever found, leaving many critics of the Bush administration to question the administration's motives and to ask whether the intelligence community had been pressured by administration officials to find intelligence rationalizing the war in Iraq.[9] Nonetheless, the military effort continues today.

weapons of mass destruction (WMDs)
nuclear, chemical, and biological weapons

When they use the military as an instrument of foreign policy, policy makers send a strong signal. When military conflict occurs on a grand scale—for the United States, that would include today's wars in the Mideast, as well as the Gulf War (1990-1991), the Vietnam War (1965-1975), the Korean War (1950-1953), and the two world wars (1914-1918 and 1939-1945), the goal often is **regime change,** the replacement of a country's government with another government by facilitating the deposing of its leader or leading political party. That is, rather than attempting to change another nation's policies, the wars are fought to end the reign of the enemy nations' leaders. On the other hand, most military action by the United States in the past century has occurred on a smaller scale, as policy mak-

regime change
the replacement of a country's government with another government by facilitating the deposing of its leader or leading political party

ers have sought to change the policy in another country or perhaps to protect U.S. interests or allies. For example, in 1999 during the Clinton administration, the United States took military action in Kosovo in the former Yugoslavia to halt ethnic cleansing in that region. Other military actions—in Somalia (1992–1994), Bosnia (beginning in 1993), and Panama (1989)—have also been on a limited scale with specific and smaller goals than those of the major conflicts.

Who Decides? The Creators and Shapers of Foreign Policy

In the United States, the executive and legislative branches are the primary foreign policy makers, with the president and the executive branch playing the dominant role. That said, a wide variety of interests—from the media, to interest groups, to other nations, and even private individuals—provide the context of the foreign policy process and contribute to shaping the policy outcomes of that process.

The President and the Executive Branch

The president of the United States is the foremost foreign policy actor in the world. This vast power partially derives from the constitutionally prescribed duties of the president, particularly the role of commander in chief of the U.S. armed forces. But presidents' foreign policy powers also have roots in the way the institution of the presidency has evolved and continues to evolve. Other government institutions, especially the U.S. Congress, have some ability to rein in the foreign policy authority of the president. But presidential resources such as cabinet departments and the national intelligence community, as well as the executive prestige that supplements presidents' legal and administrative powers, mean that U.S. presidents in the twenty-first century are the central figures in the foreign policy arena.

THE DEPARTMENTS OF STATE AND DEFENSE In the executive branch, the departments of State and Defense take the lead in advising the president about foreign and military policy issues. Specifically, the Department of State, headed by the secretary of state, has more than 30,000 employees located both within the United States and abroad. (State Department employees work at more than three hundred U.S. consular offices around the world.) These staff members are organized according to topical specialty (trade policy, environmental policy, and so on) and geographic area specialty (the Middle East or Southeast Asia, for example). Political appointees hold many of the top ambassadorial posts. These ambassadors and the career members of the foreign service who staff each **country desk**—the official operation of the U.S. government in each country with diplomatic ties to the United States—help to shape and administer U.S. foreign policy in that country.

country desk
the official operation of the U.S. government in each country that has diplomatic ties to the United States

The Department of Defense, often referred to as the Pentagon for its five-sided headquarters, is headed by the secretary of defense. The modern Department of Defense traces its history to the end of World War II, although it is the successor of the Department of War established at the nation's founding. The Defense Department is the cabinet department that oversees all branches of the U.S. military. Thus, although the Army, Navy, Marines, Air Force, and Coast Guard operate independently, administratively they are part of the Department of Defense. The commanding officers of each branch of the military, plus a chairperson and a vice chairperson, make up the Joint Chiefs of Staff, important military advisers to the president. Increasingly, both the State and the Defense departments rely on private contractors to perform some functions typically associated with these respective departments, particularly overseas.

THE NATIONAL SECURITY COUNCIL AND THE INTELLIGENCE COMMUNITY
As discussed in Chapter 12, the National Security Council, consisting of the vice president, the secretary of state, the secretary of the treasury, the secretary of defense, and the national

> The national security advisor has traditionally competed with the secretary of state for influence over foreign policy. Here, National Security Advisor James Jones chats with Secretary of State Hillary Clinton. Competition between the two advisors often stems from the differing time frames emphasized by each agency, with the NSC focusing more on short-term crises while the State Department emphasizes a long-term strategic view of global affairs.

director of national intelligence (DNI)
the person responsible for coordinating and overseeing all the intelligence agencies within the executive branch

security adviser, advises and assists the president on national security and foreign policy.

Through the input of the National Security Council, the president's administration considers the country's top security matters. The NSC also coordinates foreign policy approaches among the various government agencies that will implement them. A recent addition to the foreign policy apparatus, the national security adviser has traditionally competed with the secretary of state for influence over foreign policy—and for influence over the president as well. The tension between the two advisers also stems from the differing approaches each agency takes in shaping foreign policy. Frequently, the State Department has a long-term view of world affairs and advocates for foreign policies in keeping with long-term goals. In contrast, the National Security Council focuses more on short-term crises and objectives. These competing viewpoints have at times sparked media wars between the leaders of these foreign policy bureaucracies. Perhaps none of these battles was more contentious than the one between President Jimmy Carter's (1977–1981) secretary of state Cyrus Vance and Zbigniew Brzezinski, his national security adviser. Brzezinski publicly attacked Vance because he disagreed with Vance's push for increased diplomacy with the Soviet Union, advocating instead a tougher, more hawkish strategy.

A key resource in presidential foreign policy making is the intelligence community. Chief among the agencies in this community is the Central Intelligence Agency (CIA). This independent agency of the federal government is responsible for collecting, analyzing, evaluating, and disseminating foreign intelligence to the president and senior national policy makers. The CIA's roots are the World War II–era Office of Special Services. Like the NSC, the modern CIA was created by the National Security Act of 1947 at the dawn of the Cold War to monitor the actions of the expansionist Soviet Union. Since that time, the CIA has expanded its mission, using agents to penetrate the governments of foreign countries, influence their politics, and foment insurrections when the president has deemed such tactics necessary to promote American interests.

The clandestine nature of the CIA's activities prompted some members of Congress to raise questions about the agency's operations abroad. In 1975, the Select Committee to Study Governmental Operations with Respect to Intelligence—called the Church Committee after its chair, Senator Frank Church (D-Idaho)—began investigations into whether the CIA and the FBI had engaged in illegal activities while gathering intelligence. Those probes led to a series of reforms aimed at increasing Congress's oversight of the CIA's activities. Primary among the reforms was creation of the Senate Select Committee on Intelligence. Today, this committee and the House Intelligence Committee are the congressional watchdogs that oversee intelligence operations. Then, in the mid-1990s, following the collapse of communism, members of Congress again challenged the CIA's mission and operations. These critics complained that the agency was behind the times in remaining focused on an enemy that no longer existed. Evidence that operatives working for foreign governments had infiltrated the CIA led to even louder congressional demands for reform of the agency's operations.

These calls for reform gained strength in the aftermath of the 9/11 attacks. Congress, the media, and the independent 9/11 Commission pointed fingers at both the domestic intelligence service—the Federal Bureau of Investigation (FBI)—and the Central Intelligence Agency for failing to anticipate and to avert the terrorist strikes. Congress scrutinized both agencies for lapses in intelligence and apprehension. Because the CIA and the FBI had been seriously understaffed in Arabic translators, neither agency had had the means to interpret intercepted messages that might have enabled them to prevent the tragedy.

Spurred by the 9/11 Commission's findings, in 2005 President Bush announced the appointment of a national intelligence czar, called the **director of national intelligence (DNI).** This individual is responsible for coordinating and overseeing all the intelligence agencies within the executive branch.

DO THE GENEVA CONVENTIONS APPLY WHEN TERRORISTS HAVE SO DRASTICALLY ALTERED THE RULES OF WAR?

The Issue: The Geneva Conventions are a set of four treaties signed in Geneva, Switzerland, in 1949, in the aftermath of World War II. The conventions established standards for the protection of humanitarian concerns under international law. They apply to injured or ill members of the armed forces, prisoners of war, and civilians. Article 13 of the Third Geneva Convention, which specifically guides the treatment of prisoners of war, states that "prisoners of war must at all times be humanely treated. Any unlawful act or omission by the Detaining Power causing death or seriously endangering the health of a prisoner of war in its custody is prohibited, and will be regarded as a serious breach of the present Convention. In particular, no prisoner of war may be subjected to physical mutilation or to medical or scientific experiments of any kind which are not justified by the medical, dental or hospital treatment of the prisoner concerned and carried out in his interest. Likewise, prisoners of war must at all times be protected, particularly against acts of violence or intimidation and against insults and public curiosity. Measures of reprisal against prisoners of war are prohibited."*

Beginning in 2002, U.S. military authorities at the United States' Guantánamo Bay Naval Base in Cuba have detained about 775 "enemy combatants." Captured primarily in Afghanistan, these individuals were transported to Guantánamo for questioning. Although authorities in the Bush and Obama administrations have released nearly two-thirds of the prisoners, over 200 remain. As designated enemy combatants, the prisoners have not enjoyed the legal rights granted to individuals charged with a crime in the United States. In effect, the detainees at Guantánamo do not have the legal rights that those charged with a crime in the United States typically enjoy—no right to a lawyer, a trial, or *habeas corpus* (which, as you may recall, is a petition that allows a prisoner to go to a court where a judge will determine whether he or she is being held illegally).

Yes: The Geneva Conventions clearly apply in this situation. As many human rights organizations, including Amnesty International, argue, the detention of prisoners at Guantánamo amounts to a violation of the Geneva Conventions. Specifically, as these critics cite, there have been emphatic allegations of torture by individuals who have been released. Furthermore, the indefinite nature of the detentions—combined with the captors' acknowledged practices of sleep deprivation and constant light exposure, plus the disrespect of the Muslim religion on the part of some—constitutes the abuse of their human rights in violation of the Geneva Conventions. The moral high ground usually occupied by the United States is at stake, and if the United States does not accord these prisoners' rights consistent with the Geneva Convention, our own soldiers will be at risk of having their rights denied when they are captured by enemy forces.

No: The Geneva Conventions do not apply when the rules of engagement of war have changed so drastically. The Bush administration convincingly argued that the Geneva Conventions apply only to "prisoners of war" (POWs) and not to "unlawful combatants." Because the nature of the war on terror and of the tactics used by terrorists is in stark contrast to accepted international conventions of war, the treatment of combatants in that war should also vary. The Supreme Court has thus far agreed with the Bush administration's assessment that holding enemy combatants is legal.**

Other approaches: The Geneva Conventions do not apply to detainees at Guantánamo because they are not conventional enemy combatants, but the detainees should be afforded their human rights. In times like these, when international terrorist organizations do not follow centuries-old rules of engagement in warfare, the United States cannot follow antiquated rules and expect to keep its citizens safe. Therefore, detention can prevent further terrorist attacks if potential terrorists are prevented from carrying them out. Nevertheless, the detainees are entitled to humane treatment and to a hearing before an impartial judge to determine if they are truly a threat.

What do you think?

① Are the prisoners held at Guantánamo different from the prisoners of war held in other wars? If so, how?

② Are the Geneva Conventions, drafted soon after the conclusion of World War II, still applicable in the post-9/11 world, in which terrorism is such an urgent problem in international affairs?

* You can read the rules and explore other topics at this International Committee of the Red Cross site: www.icrc.org/ihl.nsf/7c4d08d9b287a42141256739003e636b/6fef854a3517b75ac125641e004a9e68.
** *Hamdi v. Rumsfeld*, 542 U.S. 507 (2004).

Congress

Along with the president, Congress enjoys significant constitutional authority in foreign policy making. The constitutional provisions that outline congressional authority with respect to foreign relations include, prominently, Congress's power to declare war. In modern times, however, presidential administrations have circumvented this congressional power by using U.S. troops without a formal congressional declaration of war. Such was the case in the Vietnam War, for example.

War Powers Act
law that limits presidential use of military forces to sixty days, with an automatic extension of thirty additional days if the president requests such an extension

In response to this presidential tactic, Congress in 1973 passed the **War Powers Act.** This law limits presidential use of military forces to sixty days, with an automatic extension of thirty additional days if the president requests such an extension. But the nature of modern warfare has quickly made the War Powers Act less effective than in the days of traditional warfare, since most modern warfare (the Iraq War being an exception) is measured in weeks rather than months. Thus it has been possible for modern presidents to wage full-scale wars without congressional involvement. Because of this reality, some critics have argued that designating war powers to the president is a cowardly decision. Representative Ron Paul (R-Texas), a conservative Republican presidential candidate in 2008, observed that "Congress would rather give up its most important authorized power to the President and the [United Nations] than risk losing an election if the war goes badly."[10] Other critics contend that the war powers law itself violates the constitutional provision for the separation of powers by mitigating both the president's power as commander in chief and Congress's authority to declare war.

But Congress's ability to shape foreign policy does not rest merely with its authority to declare war. Congressional powers with respect to foreign relations also include the authority of the U.S. Senate to ratify treaties, as well as to confirm presidential appointees to ambassadorial posts and to cabinet positions (including those of the secretaries of defense and state). Furthermore, one of Congress's greatest powers is its national legislature's control of the purse strings. This control means that although the president can order troops into action, the members of Congress must authorize spending for such an operation. This tension between Congress and the president is plainly evident in the numerous congressional votes to allocate funds for the war in Iraq, particularly after the Democratic Party won control of Congress in the midterm elections of 2006. Although the Democrats in Congress would have preferred not to allocate as much money to the war effort, their hands were tied because they did not want to relinquish their obligations to the troops already deployed in Iraq, nor did they want to alienate constituents in the military or defense communities who were benefiting from the increased expenditures.

The Military-Industrial Complex

In his farewell address, President Dwight D. Eisenhower (1953–1961), Supreme Allied Commander of Europe during World War II, warned the nation of the influence of the expanding military-industrial complex. Eisenhower stressed that the American people and their representatives in government must "guard against the acquisition of unwarranted influence" and noted that "only an alert and knowledgeable citizenry can compel the proper meshing of the industrial and military machinery of defense with our peaceful methods and goals so that security and liberty may prosper together."[11]

Eisenhower was describing the mutually advantageous—and potentially corrupting—collusion among the U.S. armed forces, the defense industry, and Congress. These three entities have the potential to develop "unwarranted influence" over foreign policy in general and defense spending in particular, for several reasons. First, the goals of the military and the goals of the defense industry often intersect. Consider, for example, the military's need to supply soldiers with the appropriate equipment to fight wars. Both the military complex and the defense industry benefit from doing so: the military wants to protect its troops and help ensure their success on the battleground, and the defense industry seeks to sell such goods to the military—and reap a healthy profit.

A second reason that the military-industrial complex has the potential to be so highly influential is the close personal and professional relationships that flourish between the

> Governments attempt to shape public opinion, especially in wartime. During World War II, posters urged Americans to buy war bonds, but during the Vietnam War, journalists—especially television reporters—allowed Americans to see a harsher image of war. In an indelible 1972 image of that war, 9-year-old Kim Phuc, who had stripped off her burning clothes, flees an aerial napalm attack. Kim Phuc is now a Canadian citizen, and her spoken essay, "The Long Road to Forgiveness," was broadcast on National Public Radio in 2008.

individuals in the military and their counterparts in the defense industry. These relationships are similar to the associations that develop in the case of iron triangles (see Chapter 13). Indeed, many retired military personnel often put their military expertise to work in "retirement jobs" with defense contractors or as congressional lobbyists.

For many congressional districts throughout the United States, spending by the federal government for military bases, personnel, and defense contracts represents an important infusion of money into the local economy. When this economic influence is combined with the clout members of the military, veterans, their interest groups, and their families can wield, we can see why many members of Congress support the military-industrial complex.

The Media

Because of the pervasiveness and reach of the media, foreign policy decisions provide prime fodder for news reporting. But the media go well beyond monitoring and reporting on foreign policy; they also frequently play a role in shaping the country's foreign policy and in influencing the conduct of that policy.

Since the beginning of the twentieth century, the U.S. government has used the news media in an organized way to promote its foreign policy priorities. During World War I, newspapers ran ads calling on Americans to take all kinds of actions to help the war effort, from cleaning their plates and planting "victory gardens" (to conserve food supplies for soldiers) to buying war bonds to help finance the war. By World War II, filmmakers spurred Americans to action, from enlisting in the armed services to conserving food fats and saving scrap metal for the war effort. In those various wartime initiatives, the media worked hand in hand with the government and generally took a highly patriotic and supportive stance. By the era of the Vietnam War, however, journalists, particularly television reporters stationed among U.S. troops in the faraway Asian country, painted a grimmer, more realistic canvas, focusing on the ravages of war that most Americans had never before seen.

> The media play an important role in keeping tabs on those who carry out foreign policy on the ground. In April 2004, the news magazine program *60 Minutes II* broadcast an investigation of prisoner abuses at the Abu Ghraib prison in Baghdad, Iraq. Among the images shown was this one from late 2003 showing Pfc. Lynndie England holding a leash attached to an Iraqi detainee. England and several other soldiers serving at the prison were convicted by the Army courts-martial. England served 521 days for inflicting sexual, physical, and psychological abuse on Iraqi prisoners of war. Though the soldiers claimed they were instructed by superiors to engage in the abuse, no commanding officers were convicted.

As for the news media's influence over the conduct and substance of foreign policy, it can take a variety of forms, including the following:

- *Agenda setting and public awareness.* By focusing public attention on policy makers in a certain area of the world or on a particular aspect of foreign policy, the media have an impact on setting the policy agenda. During the current conflict in Afghanistan, for example, the news media highlight the war's casualties. Newspapers report the names and sometimes print the photographs of soldiers killed in action; TV news specials scroll the names and hometowns of fallen U.S. troops and civilians. This coverage reminds policy makers and the American public alike about the human costs of war and can have an effect on subsequent policy-making decisions.
- *Investigations.* The media play a powerful role in determining that U.S. foreign policy is being implemented in a way that the policy makers intended. The news media also help to ensure that the men and women who carry out foreign policy "in the trenches" of real life cease to commit or rectify any abuses they may be committing. Consider the media coverage surrounding U.S. soldiers' scandalous abuse of enemy prisoners at the Abu Ghraib prison in Iraq. Graphic photos published in print and online of American soldiers tormenting naked captives reached readers all over the world. These photos heightened public awareness of the culture that appeared to be prevalent at the prison and led to the court-martial of twelve soldiers.

Public Opinion

Hot-button foreign policy issues such as the abuse of prisoners and the fighting of costly wars generate high levels of media coverage. The public might voice strong opinions on these issues in the wake of the saturated media reporting. Yet when it comes to foreign policy matters, public opinion is rarely the strong force that it can be in setting the domestic policy agenda. In general, people tend to be less concerned, less informed, and less interested in foreign policy matters than in domestic issues. Thus the public at large is likely to accept the views and actions of the individuals who make their country's foreign policy.

Public opinion plays a comparatively small role in shaping foreign policy for several reasons. First, foreign policy is made incrementally, over years and decades, and keeping up with international developments in different parts of the world is not something that many individuals or even news organizations do. Often, international issues must reach crisis proportions before media coverage becomes significant and exerts an impact on public opinion.

Many Americans also feel less connected to foreign policy decisions than they do to domestic policy issues. Individuals may feel empathetic toward Chinese citizens who endure human rights violations at the hands of their government or may express sympathy toward North Korean famine victims. Yet their compassion goes only so far, because those incidents have less bearing on their own lives than, say, whether their mortgage payments will increase because of Federal Reserve policy or whether more student loans will be available to pay their tuition. Despite the disconnect between most people's everyday lives and pressing issues in foreign policy, individuals nonetheless can and do influence foreign policy decisions, as we now consider.

Private Citizens

public diplomat
an individual outside government who promotes his or her country's interests and thus helps to shape international perceptions of that nation

Individuals can have an impact on the foreign policy process. Consider the various educational exchange programs that arrange for students from one country to visit another. In effect, such visitors act as **public diplomats**—individuals who promote their country's interests by shaping the host country's perception of their homeland, not only through educational but also through business or entertainment initiatives that advance mutual understanding.

A world conflict can become an influence in American foreign policy, too, when individuals take personal causes that are related to their ethnic origins to the White House and Congress. The influence of domestic interests on foreign policy, called **intermestics,** plays a distinct part in foreign policy making.

Among the most powerful examples of intermestics is the importance of large numbers of Cuban immigrants in Florida, many of them refugees or descendants of refugees from the regime of Fidel Castro. This influential group has swayed U.S. policy toward the imposition of an embargo against the Castro government since 1962, as well as encouraged tightened travel and currency restrictions between the United States and Cuba.

> Individuals can have an impact on the foreign policy process. Here, Music Director Lorin Maazel conducts the New York Philharmonic Orchestra near a North Korean flag during a rehearsal at the East Pyongyang Grand Theater in Pyongyang, North Korea, in 2008. The Philharmonic was the first major American cultural group to visit North Korea and the largest delegation from the United States ever to visit that isolated nation.

U.S. Foreign Policy in Historical Context: Isolationism and Intervention

As those who make and shape U.S. foreign policy continue to confront the challenges of a new century, they can look back on two broad historical traditions with respect to American foreign relations: isolationism and intervention. Historically, an initial policy of **isolationism,** a foreign policy characterized by a country's unwillingness to participate in international affairs, gave way to **interventionism,** the willingness of a country to take part and intervene in international situations, including another country's affairs.

intermestics
the influence of domestic interests on foreign policy

isolationism
a foreign policy characterized by a nation's unwillingness to participate in international affairs

interventionism
a foreign policy characterized by a nation's willingness to participate and intervene in international situations, including another country's affairs

The Constitutional Framework and Early Foreign Policy Making

In drafting the Constitution, the founders sought to remove the United States from international affairs. They reasoned that it was best for the new American republic to stay out of the deadly wars that had plagued Europe for centuries and because of which many Americans had left their native lands. Because of that isolationist outlook, the founders structured the Constitution so that responsibility for conducting foreign affairs rests exclusively with the national government rather than with the states.

THE CONSTITUTION AND FOREIGN POLICY POWERS The Constitution provides for shared responsibility for foreign policy making in the national government between the executive and the legislative branches. The Constitution grants the president very specific powers. These include powers related to the role of commander in chief, to making treaties, and to appointing and receiving ambassadors. In comparison, Congress's powers in foreign policy making are broader. Moreover, the Constitution structures executive and legislative powers as complementary. Note that the Constitution provides for checks and balances: although the president is commander in chief, Congress declares war and raises and supports an army and navy. Political scientist Roger Davidson has termed the give-and-take between presidential and congressional power "an invitation to struggle," reflecting the founders' attempt to ensure that neither entity dominates the process.[12]

EARLY ISOLATIONISM In keeping with the founders' emphasis on isolationism, President George Washington's Farewell Address in 1796 warned the young government against involving the United States in entangling alliances. Washington feared that membership in such international associations would draw a war-weary people and a war-weakened nation into further conflicts. He refused to accept the advice of either his secretary of state, Thomas Jefferson, who favored an alliance with France, or his treasury secretary, Alexander Hamilton, who wanted stronger ties to Great Britain. As a general who knew firsthand about the ravages of war and who also was the first American leader to connect foreign and defense policy, Washington set the tone for the United States' role in the world for the next two hundred years.

> *Burning of the Frigate Philadelphia in the Harbor of Tripoli, February 16, 1804,* a painting by Edward Moran (1829–1901), shows the USS *Philadelphia* aflame in Tripoli Harbor during the Barbary Wars.

impressment
the forcible removal of merchant sailors from U.S. ships on the spurious grounds that the sailors were deserters from the British Navy

FOREIGN TRADE AND THE EROSION OF U.S. ISOLATIONISM During Washington's tenure as president and in successive administrations, the United States' primary activity in the international arena was trade. Rich in natural resources and blessed with an industrious labor force, the United States sought to increase its wealth by selling raw materials and supplies to all sides in the Napoleonic wars (1792-1815), the latest in the never-ending series of European conflicts. The French empire took exception to the United States' provision of supplies to its enemies, and when France captured ships that it alleged were bound for enemy ports, the United States was forced into an undeclared naval war with France in the 1790s.

Neutral international trade was a difficult feat to accomplish in the American republic's early years. American ships had to cross sea lanes where neutrality was not the governing principle; instead, pirates, warring nations, and the allies of warring nations controlled the seas, and nationality counted for little. When pirates off the Barbary Coast of Africa seized ships and their crews, which they held for ransom, the United States fought the Barbary Wars (1801-1805 and 1815) against the North African Barbary states (what are now Morocco, Algeria, Tunisia, and Libya).

Throughout the early part of the nineteenth century, the seas proved a difficult place for American sailors. During that time, the British Navy began the practice of **impressment,** or forcing merchant sailors off U.S. ships—in effect, kidnapping them—on the spurious grounds that American sailors were "deserters" from the British Navy. In protest of this policy, Congress passed the Embargo Act of 1807, which forced U.S. ships to obtain approval from the American government before departing for foreign ports. But the British continued impressments, and the Embargo Act seriously curtailed the amount of U.S. goods being exported. Overall, the Embargo Act harmed the U.S. economy, as the decline in trade spurred more economic woes.

The tensions between the United States and Great Britain escalated as the practice of impressment continued. When the United States sought to increase its territory northward into Canada (then still part of the British Empire), the United States and Great Britain fought the War of 1812 over the United States' desire to annex portions of Canada and to put a halt to the practice of impressments. The war was relatively short-lived, ending with the signing of the Treaty of Ghent in 1814, when the British decided that their military resources could be better used against France in the Napoleonic wars.

Hegemony and National Expansion: From the Monroe Doctrine to the Roosevelt Corollary

After the conclusion of the War of 1812 in 1814 and of the Napoleonic wars in 1815, peace settled over the United States and Europe. Still, some American politicians feared that European nations—especially France, Spain, and Russia—would attempt to assert or reassert their influence in the Western Hemisphere. Thus, the view arose in American foreign policy-making circles that the United States should establish hegemony over its own hemisphere. In 1823, President James Monroe declared that "the American continents by the free and independent condition which they have assumed and maintain, are henceforth not to be considered as subjects for future colonization by any European power." Known as the **Monroe Doctrine,** this declaration sounded more like bravado than policy, because the United States was still too weak militarily to chase a European power away from South America, Central America, or the Caribbean. But the United States' interest in preventing the colonization of the Americas was consistent with the interest of the British, who did not want to see European rivals dominating in the Americas. Thus Monroe's doctrine had the backing of the still-formidable British fleet.

With the Americas out of play, European countries were expanding their colonial empires in Africa and the Middle East during the first half of the nineteenth century. Meanwhile, the United States also extended its territories westward and solidified its borders. Supporters of the theory of **manifest destiny**—the idea that it was the United States' destiny to expand throughout the North American continent—used this concept to rationalize the spread of U.S. territory. As the philosophy of manifest destiny took hold on the popular imagination, the United States expanded west to the Pacific Ocean, as well as south and southwest.

During this era, too, the United States became increasingly active in profitable international trade, particularly with China and Japan. To facilitate this Pacific trade—which was a primary goal of American policy makers—the United States acquired the islands of Hawaii, Wake, and Midway and part of Samoa in the 1890s. In 1898, on the pretext of ending Spanish abuses in Cuba and instigated by a jingoistic (extremely nationalistic and aggressive) President William McKinley and press, the United States decided to fight Spain, which by then was the weakest of the colonial powers. The United States won the Spanish-American War handily, and the victory increased the country's international prestige.

Theodore Roosevelt, who later became president, achieved enormous national popularity during the Spanish-American War for his leadership of the Rough Riders, a cavalry regiment. Their charge up San Juan Hill in Cuba in 1898 was the war's bloodiest and most famous battle. As spoils, the United States obtained the Philippines, Guam, Puerto Rico, and—temporarily—Cuba from Spain. Roosevelt supported the United States' entry into the war and later, as president (1901–1909), added his own famous dictum to the Monroe Doctrine: the **Roosevelt Corollary.** He announced that to ensure stability in the region, the United States had the right to act as an "international police power" and intervene in Latin America—and indeed, the entire Western Hemisphere—if the situation in any country warranted the intervention of a "civilized society."

After Roosevelt became president, the United States intervened in Panama, where U.S.-backed revolutionaries won independence from Colombia in 1903. The United States then immediately began construction on the Panama Canal in 1904. The canal improved the flow of trade by reducing the length of time ships took to travel between the Atlantic and Pacific oceans. It also accomplished one of Roosevelt's more cherished dreams: to show off U.S. naval power. At one point, Roosevelt decided to send the navy around the world strictly for public relations reasons, as a "show of force." Congress protested the cost of this endeavor, however. To outsmart Congress, Roosevelt, who had

Monroe Doctrine
President James Monroe's 1823 declaration that the Americas should not be considered subjects for future colonization by any European power

manifest destiny
the idea that it was the United States' destiny to spread throughout the North American continent; used to rationalize the expansion of U.S. territory

Roosevelt Corollary
the idea, advanced by President Theodore Roosevelt, that the United States had the right to act as an "international police power" in the Western Hemisphere to ensure stability in the region

> The Panama Canal improved the flow of international trade by reducing the length of time ships took to travel between the Atlantic and Pacific oceans. This is an aerial view of the Gatun Locks.

enough funds in the treasury for half the trip, sent the troops as far as Tokyo Bay. To "bring the boys home," Congress had to ante up the rest of the money.

World War I and the End of U.S. Isolationism

Encouraged by its successful efforts at colonization and strong enough by this time to ignore George Washington's admonition about avoiding foreign entanglements, the nation became embroiled in two major European wars in the twentieth century: World War I and World War II. The United States' isolation from the world ended with these two wars, even though strong isolationist forces in Congress and the White House continued to play a role during the first half of the twentieth century.

World War I came about primarily because of the balance of power system that dominated the world's foreign policy decisions from the end of the Napoleonic wars in 1815 until the conclusion of World War I in 1918. The **balance of power system** was a system of international alliances that, in theory, would balance the power of one group of nations against the power of another group and thus discourage war. For nearly a century, that attempt to bring order to international relations worked, and Europe enjoyed a long period of peace. But a flaw of the balance of power system was that a relatively small skirmish could escalate into a major international incident because of agreements for **collective defense**—the idea that allied nations agree to defend one another in the face of invasion—that were inherent in the system. Such was the case in 1914 in Sarajevo when a young Bosnian Serb student assassinated Archduke Ferdinand, heir to the Austro-Hungarian throne. The assassin was a member of a group seeking Bosnia's independence from the Austro-Hungarian empire. The empire demanded that Serbia respond to the assassination, and when it determined that Serbia had not so responded, it declared war. Austria-Hungary's declaration of war led to a sweeping domino effect that had the European continent in full-scale war within weeks of that initial declaration because of those alliances and collective defense obligations between nations.

The United States entered World War I in 1917, three years after the conflict began and largely at the behest of Britain. U.S. participation led President Woodrow Wilson to formulate the first conceptual framework for world governance that had ever been articulated. The most effective way to maintain peace, Wilson believed, was through **collective security**—the idea that peace could be achieved if nations agreed to collectively oppose any nation that attacked another country. By using this approach, nations at peace could prevent war by working together to restrain the lawlessness inherent in more unstable parts of the world.

Internationalism and the League of Nations

In negotiating the end of World War I at the Paris Peace Conference, Wilson sought to organize a **League of Nations,** a representative body that would ensure the collective security of nations. Wilson was successful in convincing representatives at the Paris meetings of the need for such an organization. But he was less successful in convincing Congress of the merits of the League of Nations. In 1918, the Republican-controlled Senate—Wilson was a Democrat—refused to ratify the Treaty of Versailles, which included among the terms for ending World War I the formation of the League of Nations. Without the United States, the League died a natural death before being replaced near the end of World War II by the United Nations.

In the dawning days of World War I, the United States was still heeding George Washington's call to avoid entangling alliances. At the war's conclusion, isolationism remained a key tenet of U.S. foreign policy. In the years immediately following the war, trade reasserted itself as the key component of U.S. foreign policy. The industrial revolution was in full swing, and the United States depended upon the import of raw materials and the export of manufactured goods to grease the wheels of its prosperous economy in the 1920s. During this time, however, Europe was healing from the ravages of World War I, and growth in its manufacturing sector meant serious competition for American industry.

The U.S. economy suffered another blow in 1929 when the stock market crashed, marking the beginning of the Great Depression. To protect American industry from interna-

---

balance of power system
a system of international alliances that, in theory, would balance the power of one group of nations against the power of another group and thus discourage war

collective defense
the concept that allied nations agree to defend one another in the face of an invasion

collective security
the idea that peace could be achieved if nations agreed to collectively oppose any nation that attacked another country

League of Nations
a representative body founded in the aftermath of World War I to establish the collective security of nations

tional competition, in 1930 Congress passed the Smoot-Hawley Tariff, which imposed a significant tax on imported goods. Confronted with this measure, other nations responded in kind, placing tariffs on American goods imported into their countries. The result? International trade dropped dramatically, and the economies of various nations, burdened by lower demand for the goods they produced, faltered. Industrialists, as well as citizens who saw the economic impact of an isolated United States, began to question the isolationism that had characterized U.S. foreign policy to date—from the era of Washington to the era of Smoot-Hawley.

World War II: U.S. Foreign Policy at a Crossroads

World War I was supposed to be the "war to end all wars." In hindsight, however, many observers believed that the victors only sowed the seeds of World War II (1939–1945). By impoverishing the defeated Germany through the imposition of huge reparations (compensation paid by a defeated nation to the victors for war damages) and the loss of 13 percent of its territory, the Treaty of Versailles (1919) created the environment that gave Adolf Hitler, the fascist leader of Germany, the opportunity to succeed politically. With his aggressive foreign policy, Hitler aimed to expand the German homeland at the expense of non-Germanic populations.

Influenced by a strong isolationist group in Congress, the United States waited until two years after the official start of the war in 1939 to declare war. Following a deadly Japanese attack on the U.S. naval base at Pearl Harbor, Hawaii, in December 1941, the United States declared war first on Japan and then on the other Axis powers (Germany and Italy) after those countries declared war on the United States. Following years of fighting on multiple fronts, in August 1945 the United States dropped two atomic bombs on the Japanese cities of Hiroshima and Nagasaki. Those devastating attacks ended the war.

The question remains whether the United States would have joined the efforts of the Allies (the United States, England, France, China, and the Soviet Union) sooner had policy makers known about the **Holocaust**—the murder by Hitler and his subordinates of 6 million Jews, along with political dissidents, Catholics, homosexuals, the disabled, and gypsies. Newspapers did not report the genocide until 1943, well after the war was under way. The experience of fighting World War II and dealing with its aftermath forced U.S. policy makers to reassess the country's role in the world, as well as the policies that governed its entire approach to foreign affairs.

Holocaust
the genocide perpetrated by Adolf Hitler and the Nazis against 6 million Jews, along with political dissidents, Catholics, homosexuals, the disabled, and gypsies

The Postwar Era: The United States as Superpower

The post–World War II era saw the emergence of two of the Allied victors, the United States and the Soviet Union, as **superpowers**—leader nations with dominating influence in international affairs. The United States' role as superpower in a new international system, and the relationship between these superpowers, would shape America's foreign policy for the remainder of the twentieth century. Increasingly important in this new era was the role that **multilateral** (many-sided, or supported by numerous nations) organizations and agreements would play.

superpowers
leader nations with dominating influence in international affairs

multilateral
many-sided; having the support of numerous nations

International Agreements and Organizations

In the aftermath of World War II, the United States was intent on avoiding the mistakes of the Treaty of Versailles, which many policy makers felt had led directly to the conditions that produced the war. They proceeded to address those mistakes one by one, often forming international organizations equipped to respond to the public policy challenges confronting the postwar world.

A key component of the postwar recovery effort was the **Marshall Plan.** Named for Secretary of State George Marshall, the program provided the funds necessary for Western

Marshall Plan
the U.S. government program that provided funds necessary for Western European countries to rebuild after World War II

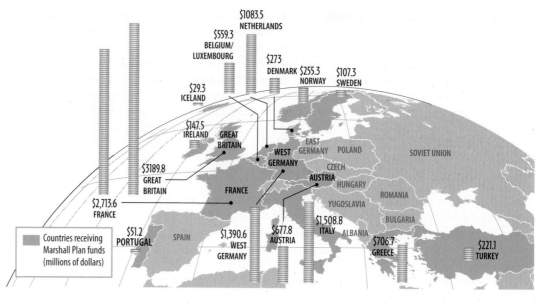

FIGURE 17.1

Recipients of Marshall Plan Aid, 1948–1951

SOURCE: www.cnn.com/SPECIALS/cold.war/episodes/03/maps.

European countries—even the United States' enemies from World War II—to rebuild. War-ravaged nations, including defeated (West) Germany, soon became economic powerhouses, thanks to initial help from the Marshall Plan. Ironically, by forcing the Germans to demilitarize as a condition of their surrender, the Allies freed Germany from spending large amounts of its own tax money on defense, thus enabling the German people to devote more of their resources to economic development. Other countries impoverished by war also benefited from the Marshall Plan (see Figure 17.1), creating new markets for U.S. products. Eastern European nations, now securely under Soviet influence, were prevented from participating. Because of the plan's success in Western Europe, the United States recognized that economic development and peace were intertwined, that economic stability was critical if future wars were to be prevented, and that an international approach was preferable to isolationism in foreign policy.

THE UNITED NATIONS The Allied victors of World War II recognized the need for a structure to ensure collective security. In that spirit, U.S. officials organized a meeting in San Francisco in 1945 with fifty U.S. allies, all of whom agreed to create the **United Nations (UN)**. Participants hoped that this international body, through collective security, would develop the capacity to prevent future wars. The charter of the United Nations created these components:

■ A Security Council with eleven members, five of which—including the United States, the Soviet Union (now Russia), China, Great Britain, and France—are permanent members with the power to veto any action taken by the council. Today, the Security Council consists of fifteen members, with the permanent members and their veto power remaining unchanged.

■ A General Assembly consisting of all the member nations, each with a single vote (in 1945, there were 51 member nations; today there are 192).

■ A Secretariat headed by a secretary-general with a staff at UN headquarters in New York. The secretary-general in 2010 is Ban Ki-moon of South Korea.

■ Several specialized organizations to handle specific public policy challenges, including the Economic and Social Council, the Trusteeship Council, and the International Court at The Hague.

The United Nations' mission includes the promotion of economic and social development. Since its founding, it has added peacekeeping to its functions and has had some lim-

United Nations (UN)

established in 1945, an international body intended to prevent future wars by achieving collective security and peace ited success in that endeavor in areas of the former Yugoslavia, the Middle East, and Africa. But in the immediate post–World War II era, the ability of the United Nations in general, and of the Security Council in particular, to provide for collective security was seriously undermined by the presence of the Soviet Union on the Security Council. Because the Soviet Union was a permanent member with veto power, any attempt by the Security Council to thwart Soviet aggression was blocked by the Soviets' veto.

NATO   It did not take long for the United States and the Western democracies to be disappointed by the inability of the United Nations to provide for collective security. The UN's failure to halt the militaristic expansion of the Soviet sphere of influence particularly troubled them. Their frustrations led the United States and its Western allies to attempt to bring order to international relations through the creation of regional security alliances. **Regional security alliances** typically involve a superpower and nations that are ideologically similar in a particular area of the world.

The first regional security alliance was the **North Atlantic Treaty Organization (NATO).** Established in 1949, NATO created a structure for regional security for its fifteen member nations through a declaration that "an armed attack against one or more NATO nations . . . shall be considered an attack against them all."[13] Through the formation of NATO, the United States made a specific commitment to defend Western Europe in the event of a Soviet attack. In response to the creation of NATO, the Soviet Union and its seven satellite states in Eastern Europe formed a similar regional security alliance, the **Warsaw Pact,** in 1955.

The success of NATO at holding Soviet expansion into Western Europe at bay motivated the creation of the **Southeast Asia Treaty Organization (SEATO),** whose goal was to prevent communist encroachment in Southeast Asia. SEATO was a decidedly weaker organization than NATO; decisions had to be reached unanimously and rarely were. For example, SEATO was unable to agree to intervene in Cambodia, Laos, or Vietnam because member nations, including France, Pakistan, and the Philippines, objected to intervention.

Both NATO and the Warsaw Pact reflected the tensions and the rivalry that existed between the United States and the Soviet Union. They also reflected the failure of the United Nations to provide for collective security, that is, the security of *all* nations. Instead, the regional security alliances more closely resembled the balance of power alliances established after the Napoleonic wars.

INTERNATIONAL FINANCIAL ORGANIZATIONS

In addition to establishing the United Nations and NATO for the purposes of conflict management and security, the United States recognized the need to relinquish a great deal of its own economic power in exchange for the economic stability that would come from international financial institutions. Doing so would benefit the global economy in general but also the U.S. economy in particular.

To that end, in 1944, an international agreement made in Bretton Woods, New Hampshire—the Bretton Woods Agreement—established the International Monetary Fund. The delegates to the meeting charged the **International Monetary Fund (IMF)** with regulating the monetary relationship among nations, including the establishment of exchange rates for major currencies around the world. To the present day, IMF member states provide the resources the IMF needs to operate through a formula by which nations pay amounts roughly proportional to the size of their economies. Based on these IMF contribution quotas, nations are allocated votes proportional to their contributions. Thus the IMF perpetuates the dominance of the high-contributing economic powerhouses. Today, the United States has nearly 20 percent of the IMF votes. The Bretton Woods agreement also established the institution that would become the **World Bank,** which initially focused on lending money to countries devastated in World War II. Today, the World Bank lends money to developing nations to help them become self-sufficient.

Still reeling from the effects of high tariffs on international trade during the Depression, the United States also encouraged an international agreement that would heal the economies of nations by lowering tariffs and promoting international trade. In 1948, twenty-three nations signed the General Agreement on Tariffs and Trade (GATT). The GATT is based on the most favored nation principle.

In 1995, the **World Trade Organization (WTO)** replaced the GATT. Whereas the GATT was a series of agreements among nations, the WTO is an actual organization that

regional security alliance
an alliance typically between a superpower and nations that are ideologically similar in a particular region

North Atlantic Treaty Organization (NATO)
an international mutual defense alliance formed in 1949 that created a structure for regional security for its fifteen member nations

Warsaw Pact
regional security structure formed in 1955 by the Soviet Union and its seven satellite states in Eastern Europe in response to the creation of NATO

Southeast Asia Treaty Organization (SEATO)
regional security agreement whose goal was to prevent communist encroachment in the countries of Southeast Asia

International Monetary Fund (IMF)
institution charged with regulating monetary relationships among nations, including establishment of exchange rates for major world currencies; established in 1944 by the Bretton Woods Agreement

World Bank
international financial institution created by the Bretton Woods Agreement of 1944 and charged with lending money to nations in need

World Trade Organization (WTO)
organization created in 1995 to negotiate, implement, and enforce international trade agreements

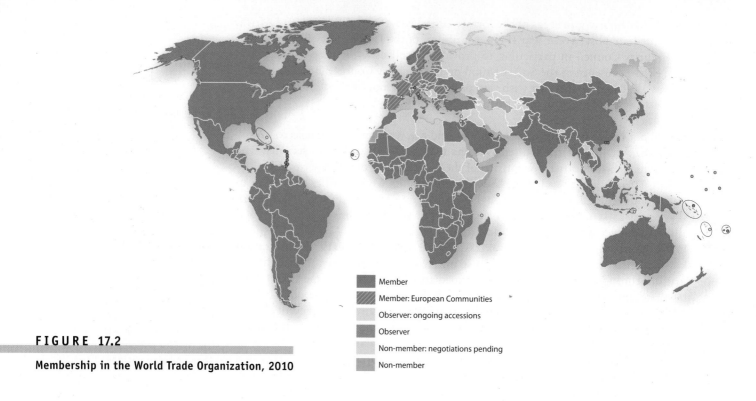

FIGURE 17.2

Membership in the World Trade Organization, 2010

Member

Member: European Communities

Observer: ongoing accessions

Observer

Non-member: negotiations pending

Non-member

negotiates, implements, and enforces international trade agreements. Today, the WTO consists of 153 member nations (see Figure 17.2). Although it has a one-nation, one-vote policy, this policy is moot because the largest economies have the greatest say. The organization's goal—to remove all types of trade barriers, including obstacles to investment—is more ambitious than that of the GATT.

The Cold War: Superpowers in Collision

During World War II, the United States, Great Britain, and the Soviet Union were allies against the Nazis. But events at the wartime Yalta Conference in 1945—the second of three wartime conferences among British, U.S., and Soviet leaders—sowed the seeds of what would become known as the Cold War. The **Cold War** refers to the political, ideological, and military conflict that lasted from 1945 until 1990 between communist nations, led by the Soviet Union, and Western democracies, led by the United States. Each leader came to the Yalta Conference with an agenda. The United States' Franklin Roosevelt needed Soviet help in battling Japan in the naval wars of the Pacific. England's Winston Churchill sought democratic elections in Eastern Europe. And Soviet Premier Joseph Stalin wanted Eastern Europe as a Soviet sphere of influence, arguing that the Soviet Union's national security depended on its hegemony in the region.

At the conference, Stalin agreed to allow free elections in the region, but he later broke that promise. In response, former British prime minister Churchill warned Americans in a 1946 speech that the Soviets were dividing Europe with an "Iron Curtain." Churchill's characterization was accurate, because Stalin's brutal dictatorship, combined with the force of the Soviet Red Army, would install a communist government in every Eastern European nation. When Stalin also refused to cooperate in the planned cooperative allied occupation of Germany, the result was the division of Germany into separate zones, one administered by the Soviet Union and the other three by the United States, Great Britain, and France. In 1948, when the Soviets backed communist guerillas who were attempting to take over Greece and Turkey, U.S. president Harry Truman (1945–1953) committed the United States to "support free people who are resisting attempted subjugation by armed minorities or by outside pressures."[14] This policy—the United States' foreign policy commitment to assist efforts to resist communism—was called the **Truman Doctrine.**

Cold War

the political, ideological, and military conflict that lasted from 1945 until 1990 between communist nations led by the Soviet Union and Western democracies led by the United States

Truman Doctrine

articulated by President Harry Truman, a foreign policy commitment by the United States to assist countries' efforts to resist communism in the Cold War era

POLITICAL INQUIRY

U.S. Efforts to Contain Communism: Korea, Cuba, and Vietnam

The Truman Doctrine reflected the ideas of George F. Kennan, the State Department's Soviet expert at the time. Specifically, Kennan advocated the principle of **containment,** the policy of preventing the spread of communism, mainly by providing military and economic aid as well as political advice to beleaguered countries that were vulnerable to communist takeover. Kennan argued, "It is clear that the main element of any United States policy toward the Soviet Union must be that of a long-term vigilant containment of Russian expansive tendencies."[15] The idea of containment would spur the United States to fight in two protracted wars, the Korean War and the Vietnam War, to contain communism.

THE KOREAN WAR, 1950–1953 The first military effort the United States engaged in to check the spread of communism occurred in 1950. In June of that year, North Korea, with the backing of Stalin and the Soviet Union, invaded South Korea in an attempt to reunify the Korean peninsula under communism. During that summer, the United States sent in forces as part of a United Nations force to help the South Koreans repel the attack. The defensive strategy quickly succeeded, but by October the United States changed military strategy. Instead of merely containing the spread of communism, the United States sought to reunify North and South Korea—and, in doing so, to depose the communists from North Korea. But as U.S. and South Korean forces edged north, they also came closer and closer to the North Korea–China border.

That October, China, wary of a potential invasion, came to the aid of fellow communists in North Korea. The two countries' combined forces repelled the United Nations forces back to the 38th parallel, the original border between North and South Korea. Over the next two years, U.S. forces (as part of the UN contingent), North and South Koreans, and Chinese soldiers would continue to do battle, with very little territory changing hands. When an armistice was reached in July 1953, the border established was the 38th parallel—exactly what it had been before the war—although a demilitarized zone (DMZ) was created. Today, U.S. and South Korean troops still patrol one side of the DMZ, while North Korean troops patrol the other.

The Korean War marked an escalation and expansion of the Cold War. Not only was the war the first occasion in which the two superpowers clashed militarily, but it also brought

containment
Cold War-era policy of preventing the spread of communism, mainly by providing military and economic aid as well as political advice to countries vulnerable to a communist takeover

limited war
a combatant country's self-imposed limitation on the tactics and strategy it uses, particularly its avoidance of the use of nuclear weapons

brinkmanship
Cold War-era practice of fooling the enemy by going to the edge (the brink), even if the party using the strategy had no intention of following through

domino theory
the principle that if one nation fell to communism, other nations in its geographic vicinity would also succumb

the Cold War outside the boundaries of Europe. Significantly, the outbreak of the Korean War also gave rise to the concept of **limited war**—a combatant country's self-imposed limitation on the tactics and strategy it uses, particularly its avoidance of the deployment of nuclear weapons. The idea of limited war would set the stage for subsequent conflicts.

THE CUBAN MISSILE CRISIS, 1962   Another tactic of U.S. foreign policy during the Cold War was brinkmanship, a term coined by John Foster Dulles, the secretary of state under President Dwight D. Eisenhower (1953–1961). In essence, **brinkmanship** meant fooling the enemy by going to the edge (the brink), even if the party employing brinkmanship had no intention of following through to its logical conclusion.

The Cuban Missile Crisis in October 1962 turned out to be a perfect example of brinkmanship, even though that was not the intention of President John F. Kennedy (1961–1963). Reacting to Soviet premier Nikita Khrushchev's decision to put ballistic missiles in Cuba, Kennedy imposed a naval blockade around that island nation and warned the Soviet Union to withdraw its missiles, or else—never specifying what he meant by "or else." Although this confrontation seemed like brinkmanship, it was no bluff; rather, it was an act of bravado that could easily have led to nuclear war. Luckily for the United States and the rest of the world, the Soviets backed down, withdrew their missiles, and entered a period of improved relations with the United States.[16]

THE VIETNAM CONFLICT, 1965–1975   The United States' involvement in the war in Vietnam was motivated in large part by policy makers' acceptance of the **domino theory,** the principle that if one nation fell to communism, other nations in its geographic vicinity would also succumb. As described by President Dwight Eisenhower, "You have broader considerations that might follow what you would call the 'falling domino' principle. You have a row of dominoes set up, you knock over the first one, and what will happen to the last one is the certainty that it will go over very quickly. So you could have a beginning of a disintegration that would have the most profound influences."[17]

And so the United States again sought to contain the spread of communism in Southeast Asia. Although Vietnam was not of particular strategic importance to the United States, it represented the second "domino" in the faraway region. U.S. involvement in Vietnam started in the late 1950s, and by 1963, the United States became enmeshed in an all-out ground, naval, and air war there. The United States supported the South Vietnamese against the North Vietnamese in the decade-long civil war that would take the lives of almost 60,000 U.S. soldiers and at least 3 million Vietnamese soldiers and civilians. On April 29, 1975, when the South Vietnamese capital, Saigon, fell to the North Vietnamese Vietcong forces, the event marked the first military failure by the United States in its efforts to contain communism.

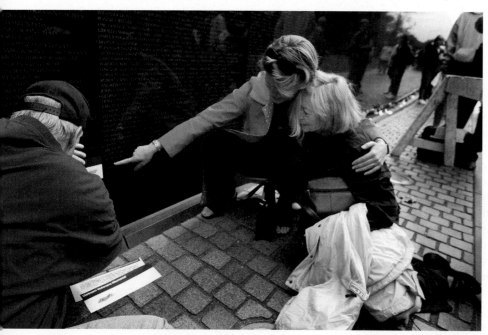

> A widow is comforted as she watches a stoneworker carve the name of her husband on the Vietnam Veterans Memorial in Washington, D.C., in 2005. Names appear on the wall according to the date the service member was killed in action.

Détente: A Thaw in the Cold War Chill

Richard M. Nixon (1969–1974) was elected to the presidency in 1968, largely on his promise to conclude the war in Vietnam. Although several years would pass before the war ended, Nixon's approach to the top foreign policy issues of the day marked a departure from that of his predecessors. Specifically, the **Nixon Doctrine** emphasized the responsibility of U.S. allies to provide for their own national defense and security and sought to improve relations with the two communist world powers, the Soviet Union and China. As early as 1970, his administration sought **détente,** or the easing of tensions between the United States and its communist rivals. In keeping with this idea, the Nixon administration normalized diplomatic relations with China and began a series of nuclear arms control talks that would occur throughout the 1970s. Critics of the Nixon Doctrine argued that President Nixon's approach to foreign policy was accommodationist—that it sought the easy solution and ignored the moral and philosophical implications of improving relations between the Western democracies and their communist rivals.

Part of the motivation for détente was the recognition that any escalation of tensions between the superpowers would increase the probability of nuclear war. Since the early 1960s, the United States and the Soviet Union had engaged in a nuclear arms race in which each country attempted to surpass the other's nuclear capability. According to the doctrine of **mutual assured destruction (MAD),** if one nation attacked another with nuclear weapons, the other would be capable of retaliating, and *would* retaliate, with such force as to assure mutual annihilation. The advent of intercontinental ballistic missiles (ICBMs) meant that both the United States and the Soviet Union were capable of sending nuclear warheads through space to targets in their rivals' homelands. The goal of the arms race (which would continue through the 1980s) was first-strike capability, meaning that each nation sought the ability to use nuclear weapons against another nation and eliminate the possibility of that nation's retaliating in a second-strike attack.

Many foreign policy makers in both the United States and the Soviet Union believed in the power of **deterrence,** the idea that nations would be less likely to engage in nuclear war if the adversaries each had first-strike capability. But Nixon and his primary foreign policy adviser, Henry Kissinger (who served first as Nixon's national security adviser and then as his secretary of state), sought negotiations with the Soviets that would dampen the arms race.

SALT I AND SALT II   In 1972, the United States and the Soviet Union concluded two and a half years of **strategic arms limitation talks (SALT talks)** that focused on cooling the superheated nuclear arms race between the two superpowers. The resulting treaty, **SALT I,** limited the two countries' antiballistic missiles (ABMs) and froze the number of offensive missiles that each nation could have at the number they already possessed, plus the number they had under construction.

The SALT II strategic arms limitation talks, begun during the Nixon administration and continuing through the Jimmy Carter presidency (1977–1981), resulted in the signing of the SALT II treaty in 1979. The **SALT II** treaty set an overall limit on all strategic nuclear launchers, including ICBMs, submarine-launched ballistic missiles (SLBMs), and cruise missiles. SALT II also limited the number of missiles that could carry multiple independently targeted reentry vehicles (MIRVs) with nuclear warheads, and limited each nation to the development of only one new type of ICBM.

Later in 1979, however, the Soviet Union invaded Afghanistan, sparking a new round of U.S.-Soviet tensions. In response, President Jimmy Carter withdrew the SALT II treaty from consideration for ratification by the Senate. Nevertheless, Carter announced (as did his successor, Ronald Reagan) that the United States would abide by all the terms of SALT II as long as the Soviet Union complied as well. During his one term in office, Carter also sought to engage the world in a campaign for human rights, while at the same time attempting to convert the vast U.S. military apparatus to peacetime functions—a policy known as **defense conversion.**

The Reagan Years and Soviet Collapse

Ronald Reagan's presidency (1981–1989) marked a pivotal time in U.S.-Soviet relations. On the one hand, the Reagan administration pushed for a *reduction* in missiles and nuclear warheads, not merely a limitation on increases. Because of this new direction, Reagan named

Nixon Doctrine
policy emphasizing the responsibility of U.S. allies to provide for their own national defense and security, aimed at improving relations with the communist nations, including the Soviet Union and China

détente
easing of tensions between the United States and its communist rivals

mutual assured destruction (MAD)
the doctrine that if one nation attacked another with nuclear weapons, the other would be capable of retaliating and would retaliate with such force as to assure mutual annihilation

deterrence
the idea that nations would be less likely to engage in nuclear war if adversaries each had first-strike capability

strategic arms limitation talks (SALT talks)
discussions between the United States and the Soviet Union in the 1970s that focused on cooling down the nuclear arms race between the two superpowers

SALT I
treaty signed in 1972 by the United States and the Soviet Union limiting the two countries' antiballistic missiles and freezing the number of offensive missiles that each nation could have at the number they already possessed, plus the number they had under construction

SALT II
treaty signed in 1979 by the United States and the Soviet Union that set an overall limit on strategic nuclear launchers, limited the number of missiles that could carry multiple independently targeted reentry vehicles (MIRVs) with nuclear warheads, and limited each nation to the development of only one new type of intercontinental ballistic missile (ICBM)

defense conversion
President Jimmy Carter's attempt to convert the nation's vast military apparatus to peacetime functions

strategic arms reduction talks (START talks)

talks between the United States and the Soviet Union in which reductions in missiles and nuclear warheads, not merely a limitation on increases, were negotiated

strategic defense initiative (SDI, or "Star Wars")

a ballistic missile defense system advocated by President Ronald Reagan

these arms reduction talks the **strategic arms reduction talks (START talks).** Despite this overture, the Reagan administration was passionate in the pursuit of a ballistic missile defense system, called the **strategic defense initiative (SDI, or "Star Wars").** In protest of the development of this system, the Soviet Union walked out of the START meeting in 1983. The two superpowers would return to the table in 1985, after Reagan won reelection with a resounding victory.

In 1987, the United States and the Soviet Union signed the Intermediate-Range Nuclear Forces Treaty (INF), the first agreement that resulted in the destruction of nuclear weapons. It eliminated an entire class of weapons—those with an intermediate range of between 300 and 3,800 miles. A pathbreaking treaty, the INF shaped future arms control talks. It provided for reductions in the number of nuclear weapons, established the principle of equality because both nations ended up with the same number of weapons (in this case, zero), and, through the establishment of on-site inspections, provided a means of verifying compliance.

In retrospect, many analysts credit the Soviet Union's eventual collapse to President Reagan. During his tenure, Reagan ratcheted up the rhetoric with his many speeches referring to the Soviet Union as "the Evil Empire." Under his administration, the U.S. defense budget also doubled, with much of the expenditure going toward the SDI. The Soviets reacted with fear and a surge in spending. These developments all came at a time when the Soviet Union was dealing with dissatisfied nationalities within its borders, as the fifteen republics that eventually would break away pressed for secession. The last straw, however, was the country's troubled economy, because to compete with the U.S. ballistic missile system, the Soviet Union had to increase its military budget to the point where its economy collapsed—and with it, the government.

Post-Soviet Times: The United States as Solo Superpower in an Era of Wars

The START talks, which had resumed in 1985, resulted in a long-awaited agreement that reduced the number of long-range strategic nuclear weapons to 3,000 for each side. In 1991, the agreement was signed by U.S. president George H. W. Bush and Soviet president Mikhail Gorbachev, whose tenure had ushered in the ideas of *glasnost* (openness) and *perestroika* (economic restructuring) in the Soviet Union. That same year, after an attempted coup failed, the Soviet Union ended and Russia had its first democratically elected president, Boris Yeltsin.

Upon Yeltsin's election, in another series of talks called START II, Yeltsin agreed to even deeper cuts in nuclear weapons. Importantly, he also assented to the eventual elimination of all land-based missiles with multiple warheads (MIRVs). The START II agreement of 1992 between the superpowers was fully implemented in 2003 and significantly decreased the likelihood of a massive nuclear attack.

The 1990s proved to be a novel time in U.S. foreign relations. For the first time in over half a century, the United States was without an enemy, and it found itself the world's lone superpower. The tumult following the collapse of communism ushered in an era of wars—many of them fueled by long-standing ethnic rivalries or disputes—and the creation of new borders and new nations. By the start of the new century, fourteen wars were going on around the globe. Some, such as the decades-long conflict in Northern Ireland, now seem to be resolved. Others seemed intractable, such as the conflict in the Middle East over the Palestinian question. Still others, such as the tribal wars in Africa, were all too often manipulated by foreign interests and by corrupt indigenous leaders who were reluctant to give up their power. And other events—such as fighting that erupted between UN and U.S. forces against Somali militia fighters loyal to warlord Mohamed Farrah Aidid in 1993; the 1998 attacks on U.S. embassies in Nairobi, Kenya, and Dar es Salaam, Tanzania; and the 2000 suicide bombing of the U.S. Navy guided missile destroyer USS *Cole* in the port of Aden, Yemen—were harbingers of clashes to come. It was as if a giant hand had lifted a rock at the end of the Cold War, freeing long-submerged problems to crawl out and presenting new challenges for U.S. foreign policy makers as the United States assumed its role as the world's leader.

U.S. Foreign Policy After 9/11

American foreign policy makers' challenges in the 1990s pale in comparison with those they have faced since the terrorist attacks of September 11, 2001. The incidents on that day have profoundly defined and determined recent American foreign policy.

The Bush Doctrine: A Clash of Civilizations

One prism for viewing the 9/11 attacks is that posited by political scientist Samuel P. Huntington. He asserts that "the clash of civilizations will be the battle lines of the future."[18] Huntington's **clash of civilizations thesis** asserts that bitter cultural conflict will continue and escalate between modern Western democracies and fundamentalist Islamic states. Huntington, whose thesis remains controversial, argues that the ideological divisions that characterized the twentieth century—the clash between communism and democratic capitalism, for example—will be replaced by an older source of conflict: cultural and religious identity. Huntington initially posited his ideas in 1993, and his theories seemed particularly relevant during the 1990s when ethnic and religious warfare broke out in Bosnia and in parts of Africa. After 9/11, Huntington's neoconservative theory appeared to have significantly shaped the foreign policy of the George W. Bush administration.

Huntington's clash of civilizations thesis provides one explanation of *why* contemporary U.S. foreign policy has focused on the areas that it has. President George W. Bush himself articulated his views on the *how* of that policy's implementation. According to the **Bush Doctrine,** unilateral action (action by the United States alone) directly targeted at enemies is both justifiable and feasible. The Bush Doctrine also asserted that the United States should use its role as the world's only remaining superpower to spread democracy and to create conditions of security that will benefit itself and its allies.

WAR IN AFGHANISTAN The United States' first response to the 9/11 attacks was based on the connection of Osama bin Laden and the al-Qaeda terror network to the masterminding and execution of those attacks. For several years before 9/11, the fundamentalist Taliban regime in Afghanistan had allowed al-Qaeda training camps to operate in that country. In retaliation for the 9/11 strikes, in late 2001 the United States, a coalition of allies, and anti-Taliban rebels from within Afghanistan attacked the training camps and the Taliban government itself. Within weeks the Taliban government fell. By toppling the Taliban as the leaders of Afghanistan, the United States fulfilled the policy goal of regime change.

The multilateral forces worked to create first an interim government in Afghanistan and then, in 2004, a democratically elected government. Nonetheless, U.S. forces and those of its allies must still deal with continued attacks from Taliban forces, and Osama bin Laden, believed to have escaped to the mountains of neighboring Pakistan, remains at large.

Defining U.S. Foreign Policy

THEN (1984)	NOW (2011)
The Cold War was the defining feature of U.S. foreign policy.	The U.S. presence in Afghanistan and Iraq is the defining feature of the nation's foreign policy.
The United States and the Soviet Union competed as the two world superpowers.	The United States is the world's only superpower.
The arms race resulted in unprecedented military spending.	A multifront war and national security needs result in unprecedented defense spending.

WHAT'S NEXT?

> What new realities will shape U.S. foreign and national defense policy?

> Will the United States continue as the world's only superpower? How will a superpower be defined in the future? Will the term refer to military or economic might or a combination of these (and/or other) factors?

> What impact will continued spending have on the U.S. and global economy?

clash of civilizations thesis
Samuel Huntington's idea that bitter cultural conflict will continue and escalate between modern Western democracies and fundamentalist Islamic states

Bush Doctrine
the argument, articulated by President George W. Bush, that unilateral action directly targeted at an enemy is both justifiable and feasible

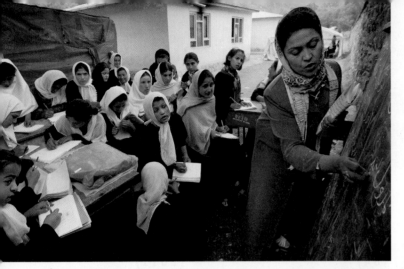

> One impact of the war in Afghanistan has been increased educational opportunities for women. Here Afghan girls listen to their teacher during language class in an open-air classroom after space ran out in their school. Shortages of supplies and overcrowded classrooms are commonplace, since the nation's girls, who had been prohibited from attending school under the Taliban regime, now may receive an education, though they are often still at great risk.

preventive war
the strategy of waging war on countries regarded as threatening in order to avoid future conflicts

Although the U.S. invasion of Afghanistan occurred largely in response to the Taliban's support of al-Qaeda, the invasion also demonstrated the potential consequences for nations that support terrorism against the United States.

WAR IN IRAQ After the Taliban's fall, President Bush set his sights on changing another regime: that of Iraq's Saddam Hussein. During the presidency of Bush's father, George H. W. Bush (1989–1993), the United States had gone to war with Iraq when that country invaded Kuwait, an ally of the United States. During the younger Bush's 2003 State of the Union address, the president claimed that Iraq possessed weapons of mass destruction (WMDs) and said that the Iraqis were attempting to purchase the components of nuclear weapons. In the ensuing weeks, the Bush administration made a case for going to war with Hussein's regime to both the UN Security Council and the American people. In doing so, Bush introduced the concept of **preventive war,** the strategy of waging war on countries regarded as threatening to the United States in order to avoid future conflicts.

The concept of preventive war represents a shift in policy from responding to attacks to anticipating attacks. The idea of preventive war is in part an outgrowth of the drastically altered nature of warfare. The biological, chemical, and nuclear weapons of today can cross borders with far deadlier efficiency than troops, ships, or aircraft. In addition, U.S. enemies no longer declare themselves as openly as they did before. The national defense policy makers who advocate preventive war thus argue that the only way to defend the country against these various new threats is to invade *before* the fact, in hopes of deterring another attack.

The invasion of Iraq in March 2003 was initially successful in toppling Saddam Hussein's regime. Despite insurgency violence that prevented peace from taking root, elections were finally held in 2004 and 2005, and power officially passed to an elected government. In the face of continued violence, the Bush administration enacted a military surge policy, resulting in the addition of more than 20,000 troops in Baghdad and Al Anbar province. Though not ending the conflict, the surge strategy was credited with quelling much of the insurgent violence in these areas.

In addition to the violence that has continued to plague Iraq, political turmoil has been characteristic of this nation. In March 2010, parliamentary elections were held—and large numbers of Iraqis defied the threat of violence and actual attacks to cast their ballots in one of the most open and competitive elections Iraq has had. The results were so close that only two seats separated the top two political parties, which then had to form a coalition with other parties to acquire the requisite number of seats to govern. Despite those challenges, the election was widely viewed as a success.

Nation building in Iraq proved troublesome—far more so than the rebuilding of Japan after World War II, for example. There, U.S. general Douglas MacArthur undertook the task of reconstructing the nation and creating a system of democratic self-governance. It took four years, but when MacArthur left for duty in Korea, Japan was as close to democracy as any Far Eastern country. Japan's feudal aristocracy was abolished, the country had a new constitution that empowered the legislature to make laws, civil liberties and collective bargaining were guaranteed, the legal equality of the sexes was established, and citizens had been given the right of *habeas corpus*. MacArthur also suspended banks that had financed the war, destroyed (at least temporarily) the giant monopolies, and refused to allow "war profiteers" to invade Japan at the expense of local businesses.

Fifty years later, as the United States sought to rebuild Iraq's war-torn infrastructure and feed its people after toppling Hussein's regime, a powerful insurgency thwarted American efforts. Unlike MacArthur, the U.S. military had allowed widespread looting in the early days of the occupation, including the looting of munitions warehouses. These munitions later helped to arm the insurgents. Also unlike MacArthur, who had some familiarity with Japanese culture, few commanders knew either the Arabic language or Iraqi culture and rituals. Even fewer knew how to stem the war profiteering of the multinational corporations that had also "invaded" the country.

The Obama Doctrine: A New Tone in U.S. Foreign Policy

With the election of President Barack Obama, it seemed that a new era in U.S. foreign policy had begun. As a candidate, Obama had called for an end to U.S. presence in Iraq and a change in the tenor of U.S. foreign policy. Of particular note was Obama's position that he would meet with Iranian leader Mahmoud Ahmadinejad to pressure the Iranian leader to give up Iran's efforts to develop a nuclear weapon. (See "Global Context.") Obama's position was controversial because Ahmadinejad has used strong rhetoric against Israel, a key ally of the United States. Throughout his tenure both as a candidate and as president, Obama has used language that would seem to reject Huntington's clash of civilizations thesis, which was instrumental in shaping Bush administration policy. For example, in what was billed as an "address to the Muslim world," given in Egypt in 2009, Obama referred to the differences between his worldview and those of his predecessors:

> Violent extremists have exploited these tensions in a small but potent minority of Muslims. The attacks of September 11th, 2001, and the continued efforts of these extremists to engage in violence against civilians has led some in my country to view Islam as inevitably hostile not only to America and Western countries, but also to human rights. This has bred more fear and mistrust.
>
> So long as our relationship is defined by our differences, we will empower those who sow hatred rather than peace, and who promote conflict rather than the cooperation that can help all of our people achieve justice and prosperity. This cycle of suspicion and discord must end.
>
> I have come here to seek a new beginning between the United States and Muslims around the world; one based upon mutual interest and mutual respect; and one based upon the truth that America and Islam are not exclusive, and need not be in competition. Instead, they overlap, and share common principles—principles of justice and progress; tolerance and the dignity of all human beings.

From his rhetoric, it appears that President Obama has rejected the idea that the United States and Islamic nations are destined to clash, instead seeking to build bridges between the United States and the Muslim nations. Nonetheless, many are surprised at how similar Obama and Bush administrations policies are, despite the change in rhetoric. For example, some analysts say that the success of President Bush's "surge strategy" in Iraq was the guiding principle behind President Obama's troop surge in Afghanistan. While ramping up the United States' involvement in Afghanistan, though, the Obama administration continues to scale back involvement in Iraq and has pledged to withdraw military forces from Iraq by 2011.

Future Challenges in American Foreign Policy

The volatility and the complexity of events in the global arena show no sign of abating. In the foreseeable future and beyond, U.S. foreign policy makers will undoubtedly continue to face a number of pressing issues. Certainly among the most urgent of these problems is the ongoing, acute threat of further terrorism directed at domestic and foreign targets. Issues such as the environment, human rights, and technology promise to remain a fixture on the U.S. foreign policy agenda in the years to come.

The Ongoing Threat of Terrorism

As the terrorist attacks of 9/11 tragically demonstrated, foreign affairs can be unpredictable. There are nonetheless some clear challenges that U.S. foreign policy makers are certain to confront in the years to come. First among these is the continued threat of terrorism. As a tactic, terrorism has proven enormously effective in accomplishing the goals of the attackers. Specifically, terrorism breeds terror—it has disrupted economies, created instability, and acted as a polarizing force.

The increasing availability of chemical and biological weapons to both nations and terror groups also promises to be a tough challenge for U.S. and other foreign policy makers. The potential, enormous damage of these weapons of mass destruction cannot be underestimated.

THE UNITED STATES AND IRAN—A COMPLEX HISTORY

We can trace today's tense and complex relations between the United States and Iran back to 1951. That year, the democratically elected prime minister of Iran, Mohammed Mossadegh, nationalized the country's oil reserves, meaning that the government took over ownership of reserves that had been held by private corporations. Mossadegh's bold stroke set off a furious reaction by then–British prime minister Winston Churchill. Churchill and President Dwight Eisenhower, who was concerned about the increasing Soviet influence in Iran, agreed to enlist the Central Intelligence Agency in orchestrating a coup to depose Mossadegh in 1953.* The coup attempt eventually succeeded, and Mohammad Reza Pahlavi, Iran's monarch (Shah), installed as prime minister Fazlollah Zahedi, the choice of Great Britain and the United States.

Are Western democracies and fundamentalist Islamic states such as Iran destined to clash?

With continued British and U.S. support, the Shah modernized Iran's infrastructure. His autocratic rule, however, opened him to criticism by Ayatollah Ruhollah Khomeini, an influential Islamic Iranian cleric. Khomeini was exiled from the country but remained a vocal critic of both the Shah and the United States, which he characterized as "the Great Satan."

In early 1978, individuals from a broad coalition of Iranians—including students, Marxists, and pro-democracy activists—took to the streets protesting the Shah's oppressive government and calling for Khomeini's return. The demonstrations evolved into what became known as the Iranian revolution and forced the Shah to flee Iran in January 1979. When a victorious Khomeini returned to Iran shortly after, many Iranians embraced the stern cleric. And although various groups had sought to depose the Shah, the Iranian people at large soon voted to make Iran an Islamic republic with Khomeini as its leader.

During the Iranian uprisings in 1979, students had seized control of the U.S. embassy in Tehran and taken its personnel as hostages. The students claimed that the diplomats were CIA agents plotting a coup against the Khomeini government, as indeed had occurred in 1953. During this time, tensions between the United States and Iran were sky-high, and fifty-two Americans were held hostage for 444 days. Khomeini supported the students' actions. Part of the American response was to freeze more than $12 billion in Iranian assets in the United States. Although the United States later returned a sizeable portion of those assets, other parts remain frozen as the United States awaits the resolution of property disputes that arose out of the revolution. To the present day, this issue is a point of sharp contention between the two countries.

Closely monitoring the bitter relations between the United States and its allies and Iran, Saddam Hussein, the president of neighboring Iraq, decided to exploit the ill will that Westerners felt for the Khomeini regime and the chaos that had accompanied the Iranian revolution. Hussein's Iraqi army invaded Iran in 1980, setting off the Iran-Iraq War. The United States backed Iraq in this six-year war, in which Hussein used chemical weapons against Iranian soldiers and civilians.

Over the next fifteen years, relations between the United States and Iran remained contentious. The United States denounced Iran's support of terrorist organizations and its pursuit of nuclear weapons. In 1995, the Clinton administration imposed economic sanctions on Iran. These sanctions were expanded with the passage of the Iran-Libya Sanctions Act of 1996, which penalized foreign corporations that invested in Iran's energy industry. This measure was a severe blow to the Iranian economy. In 1997, reformist Mohammad Khatami was elected president of Iran with a platform of strengthening democracy in Iran. Khatami made overtures to the United States, and for several years, the icy American-Iranian relations seemed to be thawing. When the terrorist attacks of September 11 occurred, young Iranians took to the streets in spontaneous demonstrations of support for the U.S. victims of the attacks.

That the good will had dissolved, however, was apparent when George W. Bush characterized Iran as part of an "axis of evil" in his 2002 State of the Union speech. Relations chilled primarily because of Iran's pursuit of nuclear weapons. Since that time, the harsh rhetoric has continued between the United States and Iran, with President Barack Obama seeking sanctions against Iran in response to its continuing pursuit of nuclear weapons.

> Iranian women light candles in Mother Square in Tehran on September 18, 2001, in memory of victims of the September 11th terrorist attacks on the United States.

* www.nytimes.com/library/world/mideast/041600iran-cia-index.html.

INTERNATIONAL APPROVAL OF U.S. LEADERSHIP

The graphs below show the percentage approving and disapproving of U.S. leadership worldwide, and in Europe, Africa, the Americas, and Asia from 2006 through 2009.

Do you approve or disapprove of the job performance of the leadership of the United States?

 % Approve   % Disapprove ● % Don't know/Refused

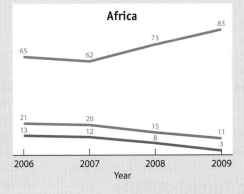

SOURCE: www.gallup.com/poll/125720/Global-Perceptions-Leadership-Improve-2009.aspx.

Evaluating the Evidence

① What is the overall trend regarding approval rating of U.S. leadership? What accounts for changes in the overall trend?

② Where specifically is U.S. leadership viewed most favorably? Least favorably?

③ Where have views of leadership changed the most? Why do you think this is the case?

FIGURE 17.3 ■ **THE NUCLEAR CLUB** What, if anything, do most or all of the countries that gave up or ended their nuclear programs have in common, either among themselves or with the countries that have nuclear capability? What do most or all of the countries that have nuclear capability—either declared or undeclared—have in common? What conclusions can you draw about these commonalities?

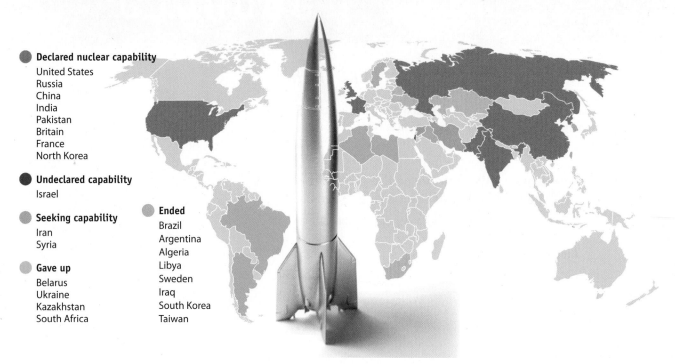

● **Declared nuclear capability**
United States
Russia
China
India
Pakistan
Britain
France
North Korea

● **Undeclared capability**
Israel

● **Seeking capability**
Iran
Syria

● **Gave up**
Belarus
Ukraine
Kazakhstan
South Africa

● **Ended**
Brazil
Argentina
Algeria
Libya
Sweden
Iraq
South Korea
Taiwan

Not all challenges to come are new, however. The continued proliferation of nuclear weapons presents a serious problem to foreign policy makers throughout the world. Figure 17.3 shows that eight nations have a declared nuclear weapons capability, including India and Pakistan; that another, Israel, has the undeclared potential; and that yet another, Iran, is seeking such potential. The fact that dangerous WMDs are in such wide distribution increases the likelihood of their use—either accidentally or intentionally.

Environmental Issues

In 2007, former vice president Al Gore won the Nobel Peace Prize for his work in raising public awareness of the critically important issue of rapid global climate change. This problem and other environmental concerns that by their very nature are worldwide challenges promise to remain on the United States' foreign policy agenda deep into the future. Specifically, the failure of the United States to ratify the Kyoto Protocol—an international agreement whose objective is to reduce global warming by lowering the amount of greenhouse gas emissions—makes it likely that the warming of Planet Earth will be a continuing and increasingly urgent focus of U.S. foreign policy makers. Other environmental concerns that are sure to have a secure place in foreign policy makers' agendas for the future include the enormous world consumption of fossil fuels, the deterioration of the oceans, worldwide deforestation, and ongoing air and water contamination.

Technology's Potential in Foreign Affairs

Although there are many uncertainties about what's next in the foreign policy arena, one certainty is that the impact of technology—as a tool in foreign policy and in citizens' efforts to influence the policies and institutions of government—will continue to increase. The impact of new technologies could be seen in 2009, when activists protesting Iranian elections initially relied on cell phones and the

Internet to spread word of demonstrations. During the protests, citizens and journalists photographed, videoed, and transmitted images of the massive demonstrations. Because such technologies enable citizens to see how governments in other countries work, a number of countries have thrown off the shackles of one-person or one-party rule. Finding Western democracy preferable to their own form of government, in 2004, 48 million voters in the Ukraine overturned dubious election results and ousted the first victor, Prime Minister Viktor Yanukovych, installing in his stead another Viktor: Viktor Yushenko. The electronic media broadcast the "orange revolution" in the Ukraine—so called for the orange flags and orange garments of the protesters—for viewers around the world to see. The increasing inability of countries, including China and North Korea, to limit access to technology and information from around the world will prove empowering to people everywhere.

CONCLUSION

THINKING CRITICALLY ABOUT WHAT'S NEXT IN FOREIGN POLICY

In retrospect, the development of the United States' foreign policy over time seems to have followed a natural progression as the nation itself grew and changed. The nation's initial isolationism, spawned by a healthy suspicion of foreign powers and their motives, gave way to international relations in the limited sphere of trade. Then, in both World War I and World War II, the importance of global alliances in helping to shape U.S. foreign policy became evident. With the end of World War II, the United States emerged as a superpower whose foreign policy came to be defined largely by its relations with its chief rival in the global arena, the Soviet Union. After the collapse of the Soviet empire in the 1990s, the foreign policy arena was murky as U.S. and world policy makers searched for a new prism through which to view the nations of the world. Could policy makers have anticipated the threat of terrorism that was to come?

On September 11, 2001, U.S. foreign policy instantly acquired a new focus. Their morning hardly going according to their daily planners, a shaken president and his aides scrambled to respond appropriately to the unforeseen and unprecedented terrorist attacks on U.S. soil. They asked the same question that the millions of Americans who watched the unbelievable events unfold on television asked: Why? Ultimately, the administration's responses to the terrorist strikes showed that significant cultural and political differences separate the United States and the other Western democracies on the one hand, and fundamentalist non-Western states that harbor terrorists on the other hand. The attacks crystallized perceptions both among U.S. policy makers and in the general public that no longer could the terrorist states be viewed simply as potential threats or as insignificant to the United States' interests. Do those perceptions remain widely held by the public and policy makers today?

Since assuming the presidency in January 2009, the Obama administration has signaled a departure from the tenor of the Bush administration. But it remains unclear whether Obama's more conciliatory approach will prove effective in building relations with Arab and Muslim nations. It also remains to be seen whether national security measures put in place by both Bush and Obama administrations will effectively deter future terror attacks on the United States.

Given the distinctive nature of those who practice terrorism—their lack of geographic boundaries and their refusal to abide by the conventional rules of war—such a conflict surely would differ starkly from the last major clash of ideologies, the Cold War. In view of the unique qualities of terrorism, it is difficult to anticipate how the continued threat of terrorist acts will shape U.S. foreign policy. The randomness of terrorism confounds policy makers and other experts and prevents them from making accurate predictions and determining adequate modes of defense. Nonetheless, given the high stakes of another potential attack, the threat of terrorism—and the imperative to prevent it—clearly will remain a defining characteristic of U.S. foreign policy in the decades to come.

STUDY NOW

Summary

1. The Tools of U.S. Foreign Policy

The government officials who formulate U.S. foreign policy rely on diplomacy, by which nations conduct political negotiations with one another and settle disagreements. They also rely on economic policy to cajole other nations into enacting policies that the United States supports, and on military force, if needed, to force other countries to align with U.S. interests.

2. Who Decides? The Creators and Shapers of Foreign Policy

Because the Constitution grants important foreign policy-making powers to the president, the president along with the executive branch is the primary foreign policy maker in the United States. Congress also plays an important role in creating foreign policy, particularly through its decision making with respect to declaring war and appropriating funds. Interest groups, the media, and private individuals also influence the foreign policy process.

3. U.S. Foreign Policy in Historical Context: Isolationism and Intervention

The conduct of foreign policy was at first influenced by a suspicion of foreign affairs. As the U.S. economy developed, government and business interests primarily concentrated on maximizing profits through international trade. In the twentieth century, the balance of power system drew the United States into global conflict in World War I. Although the United States retreated into an isolationist position during the Great Depression, an alliance with the British and Japan's attack on the U.S. naval base at Pearl Harbor, Hawaii, precipitated U.S. entry into World War II.

4. The Postwar Era: The United States as Superpower

After the Second World War, the United States and the Soviet Union emerged as competing superpowers locked in a Cold War of clashing ideologies. This rivalry defined U.S. foreign policy for half a century. During this period, international organizations charged with ensuring security and facilitating economic relations among nations were established. During the Cold War, the United States also attempted to curb the spread of communism on the Korean peninsula, in Cuba, and in Vietnam. President Richard Nixon initiated a period of détente; President Ronald Reagan outspent the Soviets and forced the collapse of the Soviet economy. The end of communism in the Soviet Union and Eastern Europe meant drastic changes in the context of international relations.

5. U.S. Foreign Policy After 9/11

With the terrorist attacks of September 11, 2001, a new era in U.S. foreign policy commenced, seeming to reflect acceptance of the theory that a clash of civilizations—warfare over cultural and religious differences—was inevitable. In espousing the tenets of the Bush Doctrine, administration officials promoted the strategy of preventive war. After 9/11, foreign policy officials also pursued a program of regime change in both Afghanistan and Iraq, while also setting their sights on the regimes in Iran and North Korea. Though striking a different rhetorical tone, the Obama administration has continued many of the Bush administration's foreign policy practices.

6. Future Challenges in American Foreign Policy

Among the greatest challenges for the United States in the foreign policy arena are the continued threat of terrorism and the accumulation of nuclear, chemical, and biological weapons. Environmental challenges and the impact of technology will also serve as focal points in the future.

Key Terms

al-Qaeda 526
balance of power system 536
brinkmanship 542
Bush Doctrine 545

clash of civilizations
thesis 545
Cold War 540
collective defense 536

collective security 536
containment 541
country desk 527
defense conversion 543

For Review

1. What are the primary tools that policy makers use in the foreign policy process?

2. Why is the president the primary foreign policy maker in the United States? What tools do presidents have to assist them in creating foreign policy? Who are the other actors in foreign policy decision making?

3. How did the United States evolve from a nation that emphasized isolationism in its early years to internationalism in the post–World War II era? What factors spurred this transformation?

4. How did the Cold War between the United States and the Soviet Union affect U.S. foreign policy? How did it influence relations between the United States and other nations?

5. September 11, 2001, led to a significant shift in how the United States viewed itself and the world. What theories best explain how the United States now sees itself in the post-9/11 global context?

6. What specific, major challenges will U.S. foreign policy makers face in the years to come?

For Critical Thinking and Discussion

1. How have the 9/11 terrorist attacks changed the structure of the foreign policy-making apparatus in the executive branch?

2. How did World War II change the way the United States was perceived by other nations around the world? How did the war alter U.S. policy makers' perceptions of what the international order should look like?

3. In retrospect, was the theory of containment an accurate description of how the United States should have attempted to stem the tide of communism during the Cold War? Why or why not?

4. Does Samuel Huntington's clash of civilizations theory accurately reflect the current state of world affairs? Explain. What present-day realities are in keeping with Huntington's theory? What other realities defy it?

5. What additional challenges, beyond those we examined in the text, are likely to face the makers of U.S. foreign policy in the next decade?

PRACTICE QUIZ

MULTIPLE CHOICE: Choose the lettered item that answers the question correctly.

1. The conduct of international relations, particularly involving the negotiation of treaties and other agreements between countries, is called
   a. brinkmanship.
   b. diplomacy.
   c. counterintelligence.
   d. intermestics.

2. _____ is a radical international Islamic fundamentalist terror organization.
   a. GATT
   b. The IRA
   c. Al-Qaeda
   d. The WTO

3. The replacement of a country's government with another government by facilitating the deposing of its leader or leading political party is called
   a. regime change.
   b. bilateralism.
   c. brinkmanship.
   d. globalism.

4. The official operation of the U.S. government in each country that has diplomatic ties to the United States is called the
   a. American seat.
   b. nation's chair.
   c. country desk.
   d. capital consul.

5. Since 2005, the person responsible for coordinating and overseeing all the intelligence agencies within the executive branch has been
   a. the Director of Homeland Security.
   b. the Director of the Federal Bureau of Investigation.
   c. the Director of the Central Intelligence Agency.
   d. the Director of National Intelligence.

6. The law that limits presidential use of military forces to sixty days, with an automatic extension of thirty additional days if the president requests such an extension, is
   a. the Gulf of Tonkin Resolution.
   b. the War Powers Act.
   c. the Defense Authorization Act.
   d. the Executive Military Control Act.

7. An individual outside government who promotes his or her country's interests and thus helps to shape international perceptions of that nation is called a
   a. professional diplomat.
   b. public diplomat.
   c. a foreign service officer.
   d. a foreign advocate.

8. The influence of domestic interests on foreign policy is called
   a. globalism.
   b. domestic influence peddling.
   c. domestic engineering.
   d. intermestics.

9. A foreign policy characterized by a nation's unwillingness to participate in international affairs is called
   a. isolationism.
   b. interventionism.
   c. bilateralism.
   d. globalism.

10. A foreign policy characterized by a nation's willingness to participate and intervene in international situations, including another country's affairs is called
    a. isolationism.
    b. interventionism.
    c. bilateralism.
    d. globalism.

FILL IN THE BLANKS.

11. _____ are the diplomatic and consular staff at U.S. embassies abroad.

12. _____ is the international trade principle holding that the least restrictive trade conditions offered to any one national trading partner will be offered to every other nation in a trading network.

13. The interconnectedness between nations in contemporary times is called _____ .

14. Nuclear, chemical, and biological weapons are known as _____ .

15. The _____ is an organization created in 1995 to negotiate, implement, and enforce international trade agreements.

Answer: 1. b; 2. c; 3. a; 4. c; 5. d; 6. b; 7. b; 8. d; 9. a; 10. b; 11. Foreign service officers; 12. Normal trade relations status; 13. globalism; 14. weapons of mass destruction, or WMDs; 15. World Trade Organization

Internet Resources

American Democracy Now Web site
www.mhhe.com/harrison2e Consult the book's Web site for study guides, interactive activities, simulations, and current hotlinks for additional information on American foreign policy.

Central Intelligence Agency
https://www.cia.gov This is the official Web site of the CIA. Its *World Factbook,* available online at this site, is an excellent resource for research on various nations. The site also hosts news and information, history, and career opportunities.

North Atlantic Treaty Organization
www.nato.int This site hosts an informative eLibrary as well as an impressive multimedia collection of documentation about NATO-related events and history.

State Department and Defense Department
www.state.gov and www.defenselink.mil These government sites offer a plethora of information from these two cabinet departments. Included are news and information, policy statements, career opportunities, virtual tours, and reports.

World Bank
www.worldbank.org This site explains the World Bank's policy priorities and offers data, research reports, and a wide variety of related international news.

Internet Activism

Visit **www.un.org/en** to learn about United Nations' priorities and activities concerning peace and security, development, human rights, humanitarian affairs, and international law, as well as the UN structure.

Twitter
senatorlugar Follow Sen. Richard Lugar, the ranking member of the Senate Foreign Relations Committee.

YouTube
www.youtube.com/watch?v=6BlqlwCKkeY Watch President Obama's watershed speech to the Muslim world in Cairo, Egypt.

Facebook
www.facebook.com/home.php#!/foreign.policy .magazine?ref=ts Like *Foreign Policy* magazine.

Recommended Readings

Allison, Graham. *Nuclear Terrorism: The Ultimate Preventable Catastrophe.* New York: Times Books, 2004, and *The Essence of Decision: Explaining the Cuban Missile Crisis,* Boston: Little Brown, 1971. This key scholar of U.S. foreign policy making uses the Cuban Missile Crisis as a model to explain foreign policy making. In his more recent work, he analyzes the foreign policy dilemma of nuclear terrorism.

Cameron, Fraser. *U.S. Foreign Policy after the Cold War.* New York: Routledge, 2002. This introduction to U.S. foreign policy looks at some aspects of U.S. foreign policy from the perspective of their domestic origins. Critical of the United States' unilateralism, Cameron also details relations between the United States and the European Union.

Huntington, Samuel P. *The Clash of Civilizations and the Remaking of World Order.* New York: Simon & Schuster, 1998. Huntington asserts that Western democracies are engaged in a clash of civilizations, particularly with Islamic societies.

Jervis, Robert. *American Foreign Policy in a New Era.* New York: Routledge, 2005. A noted foreign policy scholar explains the issues and influences on American foreign policy in today's international circumstances.

Keohane, Robert. *Neo-Realism and Its Critics,* New York: Columbia University Press, 1986. This classic work explains neorealism, a theory that emphasizes the power of state actors in international affairs.

Movies of Interest

The Hurt Locker (2008)
This 2009 Oscar-winning film follows the story of a U.S. Army Explosive Ordnance Disposal (EOD) team during the war in Iraq.

The Good Shepherd (2006)
Directed by Robert De Niro and starring Matt Damon, Alec Baldwin, and Angelina Jolie, this film traces the creation of the CIA and its evolution through the Cold War.

The Killing Fields (1984)
Based on a true story, this film tells the story of an American journalist and his Cambodian guide during the vicious genocide by Cambodia's Khmer Rouge regime during the Vietnam War.

Breaker Morant (1980)
Based on a true story, this courtroom drama tells the story of three Australian soldiers who are court-martialed for shooting prisoners during the Boer War in South Africa (1899–1902).

Dr. Strangelove or: How I Learned to Stop Worrying and Love the Bomb (1964)
This Stanley Kubrick film probes the dangers of the Cold War when an insane army general tries to start a nuclear war over the objections of political leaders and other generals.

The Mouse That Roared (1959)
This Peter Sellers comedy takes a satirical look at how the United States used foreign aid to ensure the support of allies. It features a fictional impoverished European nation that invades the United States with the goal of losing so that it can receive foreign aid.

State and Local Government

THEN

Responding to calls to give citizens a stronger voice in their government, state and local governments adopted processes that facilitate direct democracy.

NOW

Citizens are increasingly using initiatives and referenda to constrain taxing and spending by state and local governments and to bypass legislators.

NEXT

As the U.S. population becomes ever more diverse, what new services and benefits will citizens call on state and local governments to provide?

Will states continue to experiment with public policies that address nationwide problems?

Will the success of initiatives and referenda at the state and local levels lead to a movement to adopt these processes at the national level?

This chapter surveys the institutions and policies of state and local governments. We also look at the roles of state government in national politics.

FIRST, we examine citizen engagement in state and local government by way of the exercise of *direct democracy* at the state and local levels.

SECOND, we review the constitutional documents of state and local government, specifically the common principles and constructs of *state constitutions and local charters.*

THIRD, we consider the *diversity in political cultures, people, environments, and resources* that affect the processes and policy making of state and local governments.

FOURTH, we focus on *state and local government budgets* to understand what goods and services they provide to citizens and how they pay for them.

FIFTH, we look at the *responsibilities of state and local governments in national politics:* both the formal and the informal responsibilities that have developed over the years.

SIXTH, we focus on the *institutions of state government,* examining the commonalities and differences from state to state and contrasting state and federal institutions.

SEVENTH, we survey *local governments* and differentiate among general-purpose and single-purpose local governments.

open meeting laws
laws requiring legislative bodies and executive agencies of government to conduct policy-making meetings in public

The founding fathers created a

federal system of government with dual sovereignty. In 1789, one newly created national government shared sovereign power with twelve state governments. (The thirteenth state, Rhode Island, joined the union in 1790.) The Constitution of the United States distributed powers and responsibilities among those governments. The Constitution delegated enumerated and implied powers to the national government. The Tenth Amendment, ratified by the states in 1791, reserved for the states and the people all powers that the Constitution did not delegate to the national government. State governments created local governments with whom they shared their reserved powers. Over the course of U.S. history, the differentiation between enumerated, implied, and reserved powers has proven to be murky. Although dual sovereignty still exists, intergovernmental relations is pervasive as national, state, and local governments work together to provide for and protect Americans.

Today, 1 national government, 50 state governments, and 89,527 local governments serve the people living in the United States. There is great diversity among these tens of thousands of governments. There are differences in government structures and processes, revenue-raising strategies, services and benefits, and rights guaranteed to and responsibilities imposed on the citizens by the numerous governments in whose jurisdictions they live. Yet with all this diversity, there also exist many commonalities across the tens of thousands of governments.

This chapter explores similarities and differences among the national, state, and local governments in the United States. We begin with a discussion of direct democracy, a form of democracy that exists in state and local governments but not in the national government. We then review similarities and differences between the U.S. Constitution and state constitutions. Following an examination of the diversity in political cultures, people, environments, and resources that affect processes and policies of state and local governments, we survey state and local fiscal policies, responsibilities to national politics, and institutional structures.

Direct Democracy: Letting the People Decide

In the United States, governments at the national, state, and local levels are all representative democracies in which citizens elect officials to create and approve public policies for them. To verify that representative democracy functions properly, governments have enacted sunshine laws that open their processes to public view and participation. For example, national, state, and local governments all have **open meeting laws** requiring legislative bodies, as well as executive agencies, to conduct their policy-making meetings in public. Open meeting laws typically require advance public notice of the meetings of policy-making bodies in a general circulation newspaper.

Many state and local governments couple representative democracy with *direct democracy*—a system of procedures that allow citizens to vote directly to approve or reject proposed public policies or to force an elected official from office before the completion of his or her term (see Chapter 1). In contrast to states and localities, the U.S. national government does not provide for direct democracy.

Although many local governments have provided for direct democracy since their creation, South Dakota in 1898 became the first state to adopt direct democracy. Subsequently, between 1898 and 1918, twenty-four states adopted some form of direct democracy as a result of the Progressive movement, a mass movement that called for changes in state and local government processes to expand citizens' ability to have a voice in policy making and to hold their elected officials accountable. Progressives argued that these reforms would force government at all levels to be more responsive to the people and less beholden to well-funded special interest groups. The benefit, the Progressives said, would be a more democratic government. President Theodore Roosevelt (1901–1909) argued that direct democracy should be used to "correct [representative government] whenever it becomes misrepresentative."[1]

Referenda and Initiatives

Direct democracy takes various forms. Whatever the form, the final stage involves citizens' voting on a **ballot measure**—a proposed piece of legislation, a constitutional amendment, or some other policy proposal placed on the Election Day ballot for voters to approve or reject. The various forms of direct democracy differ in who formulates the proposed law and what process is required for getting it on the ballot.

The *referendum* is a ballot measure that gives citizens veto power by allowing them to vote to approve or reject legislation or a constitutional amendment that the state legislature has proposed. All fifty states allow for a **legislative referendum,** a ballot measure whereby voters approve or reject a law or an amendment *proposed* by state officials. States use the legislative referendum (among other procedures), for example, to amend their constitutions. In this process, proposed amendments to a state constitution must appear on the ballot for citizens to approve or reject (in all states except Delaware, where legislators, not citizens, approve constitutional amendments). Twenty-four states also use the **popular referendum,** a measure that allows citizens, by collecting signatures in a petition drive, to put before voters specific legislation that the legislature has *previously approved*. In effect, the popular referendum allows voters to repeal laws that their legislators already have passed.

The *initiative* is a ballot measure, formulated by an individual or a group, that allows citizens themselves to propose legislation or state constitutional amendments through petitions signed by a specified number of registered voters. By using the tool of the initiative, citizens in twenty-one states and in almost 60 percent of U.S. cities can write legislative bills and force their state or local governments to place the bills on the ballot for citizens to approve or reject on Election Day. Twenty-four states allow their citizens to use the initiative process to place proposed state constitutional amendments on the ballot. Through the initiative procedure, citizens can bypass their elected officials to create and approve laws. Figure 18.1 on page 560 identifies the states that have initiative and/or referendum processes.

Referenda and initiatives are a large (and growing) factor in state policy making, and citizens use them even more frequently in local policy making. State ballots featured about 500 initiatives in the eighty years between 1900 and 1980, or an average of about 6 per year.[2] The success of California's Proposition 13 (1978) ignited tremendous growth in ballot measures. Between 1980 and 2009, 998 initiatives were placed on ballots, or an average of 34 initiatives per year.[3] The People's Initiative to Limit Property Taxation (Proposition 13) amended California's constitution. It set a cap on local property tax increases and required a supermajority vote of state legislators to approve increases in tax rates, thus making it more difficult for lawmakers to raise revenues.

In 2009, 32 ballot measures were on ballots in seven states. Although that number was far short

ballot measure
any proposed policy that, as the result of an initiative or a referendum, wins a place on the ballot for voters to approve or reject

legislative referendum
a ballot measure whereby voters approve or reject a law or an amendment proposed by state officials

popular referendum
a measure that allows citizens, by collecting signatures in a petition drive, to put before voters specific legislation that the legislature has previously approved

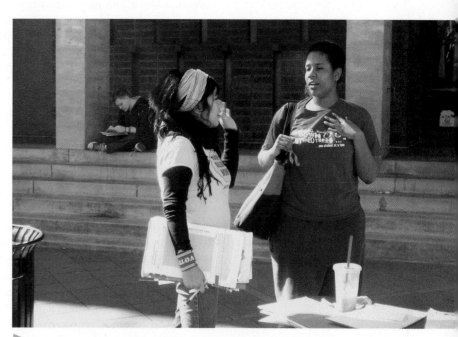

> **A student volunteer for Tuition Relief Now collects signatures on a petition to place the College Affordability Act on California's 2008 ballot.**

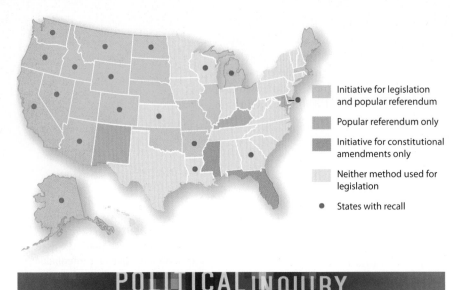

Legend:

- Initiative for legislation and popular referendum
- Popular referendum only
- Initiative for constitutional amendments only
- Neither method used for legislation
- ● States with recall

FIGURE 18.1 ■ STATES WITH INITIATIVE, REFERENDUM, AND RECALL PROCESSES In what part(s) of the country do states tend to allow their citizens the most options for participating in the political process by affecting legislation or amending their state constitutions? Where do citizens have the least ability to do so? How might the history of these areas of the country have influenced these policies?

NOTE: All states except Delaware have referenda on state constitutional amendments.

of the more than 150 ballot measures in 2008, there are always fewer measures in odd-numbered-year elections because many states do not hold elections in those years, and in states that allow initiatives, the state law typically prohibits initiatives in odd-numbered years. The headline issues among the 2009 ballot measures were same-sex marriage rights, tax limits, expenditure limits, and medical marijuana.[4]

Clearly, citizens are increasingly using initiatives and referenda as means to participate personally and to influence public policy making. Some scholars attribute the rising use of direct democracy to citizens' growing frustration with government and to their willingness to take policy matters into their own hands. Others note that an "initiative industry" has arisen, featuring professionals whom citizens and interest groups can hire to collect signatures and coordinate media campaigns in support of or opposition to initiatives. Although they come with a high price tag, such professionals make it easier for citizens to initiate ballot measures and may even encourage them to attempt to influence their state and local governments by exercising their right to direct democracy.[5]

The increased use of direct democracy is not limited to the United States. European nations also have direct democracy provisions in their laws. However, the procedures typically used in Europe differ from those used by state and local governments in the United States. (See "Global Context.")

Proponents of direct democracy applaud the growing use of these various means of increasing government responsiveness. They say that the availability of these tools fosters citizen engagement in policy making and that this trend is good for democratic government. Election Day ballot measures stimulate public conversations on public issues and mobilize voters, as indicated by higher voter turnout rates. Opponents of direct democracy note that citizens' drives to get signatures on petitions, as well as the campaigns to persuade voters to approve or reject ballot measures, are very costly, making it a tool for well-funded, well-organized special interests and wealthy individuals to influence government. Moreover, opponents argue that on Election Day, voters cannot discern from the brief statement they read on the ballot the intricacies of proposed policies, and therefore they cannot cast an educated vote. The job of elected officials is to understand complex policy issues and to make the best decisions for their constituents. If voters do not like the decisions of their elected officials, they can turn them out of office by not reelecting them and, in some states, by recalling them.

Recall of Elected Officials

Another instrument of direct democracy in the United States is *recall*—a procedure allowing citizens to remove an elected official from office before the end of the individual's term. The recall is unique to about one-third of the states and 60 percent of cities; Figure 18.1 indicates which states have recall. Recall requires a legally specified number of signatures on a petition to force a vote. The number of signatures required is typically a percentage of the number of registered voters who participated in the last election for that office; 25 percent is the most common requirement.[6]

DIRECT DEMOCRACY IN EUROPE

Direct democracy in European nations looks quite different from direct democracy in the United States. Unlike the U.S. Constitution, which does not provide for the use of either an initiative or a referendum, the constitutions of at least thirty European countries contain provisions for national direct democracy. (Some European countries, among them Switzerland, have had national direct democracy since the early 1800s.) Moreover, in the United States, state and local governments have exercised various forms of direct democracy since before ratification of the U.S. Constitution, whereas in Europe, direct democracy is relatively new among local governments. Beyond these differences, the direct democracy processes that local governments in Europe use contrast notably with those used by state and local governments in the United States.

What issue will be the next common concern addressed by local referenda in Europe and in state and local ballot measures in the United States?

In European nations, a common component of direct democracy at the local level is the requirement that local governing councils must approve any ballot measure—whether it is initiated by citizens or formulated by a legislature—before the measure can appear on the ballot. There is no citizen initiative in European nations comparable to the U.S. initiative, which allows American citizens to bypass the local or state legislature by collecting the legally required number of signatures on a petition to place a proposal on the ballot. Direct democracy in Europe more closely resembles the U.S. referendum process, in which voters approve or reject legislation or a constitutional amendment proposed or passed by the state or local legislature.

In recent years, environmental protection and conservation have become issues of common concern in U.S. state and local government ballot measures (initiatives and referenda) and local referenda in European countries. Citizens and interest groups on both continents are using direct democracy to encourage environmental protection and sustainability.

SOURCE: Michael Smith, "Is Direct Democracy Good for the Environment? A Re-examination of the Link from the Perspective of Central and Eastern Europe," presented at the When Voters Make Laws: How Direct Democracy Is Reshaping American Cities Symposium at the University of Southern California, April 7, 2007.

States vary as to how they handle the recall procedure and how they replace a recalled official. For example, in Wisconsin when citizens vote to recall an elected official, the state holds a subsequent primary election for the position and, later, a general election. In contrast, in California, on the same day that citizens cast their ballot in the recall election, they also vote to elect an official to replace the incumbent if the majority of voters approve the recall.

In 2003, more than 1.5 million Californians (well over the state-required minimum of 12 percent of the 2002 turnout, or 900,000 signatures) signed a recall petition.[7] The recall petition charged Governor Gray Davis with "gross mismanagement of California finances by overspending taxpayers' money, threatening public safety by cutting funds to local governments, failing to account for the exorbitant cost of energy, and failing in general to deal with the state's major problems until they get to crisis stage."[8] On the same day that California voters approved Davis's recall, they selected former actor Arnold Schwarzenegger of *Terminator* fame from a field of 135 candidates to replace Davis.[9]

The 2003 recall of Governor Davis was the first gubernatorial recall since North Dakotans recalled Governor Lynn J. Frazier in 1921, and only the second recall of a governor in U.S. history.[10] In September 2009, the Ingham County Election Commission approved a petition to recall Michigan Governor Jennifer Granholm. The recall effort failed to get the

> Arnold Schwarzenegger was sworn in as the governor of California in 2003, after Californians recalled Governor Gray Davis and elected Schwarzenegger from a field of 135 candidates. In 2009, the campaign to recall Michigan Governor Jennifer Granholm failed to garner the 950,000 signatures required to place the recall question on the ballot.

950,000 signatures required to place the recall question on the ballot.[11] At the local level, the volume of recalls is growing. In 2009, citizens initiated close to three hundred recall campaigns. Most local recall efforts make it to the ballot.[12]

State Constitutions and Local Charters

Recalls, referenda, and initiatives occur in state and local governments because state constitutions allow for these forms of direct democracy. Each state's constitution, and the state laws written in compliance with it, defines that state's governing processes and legal authority. This legal basis includes the state's authority to create local governments, which the U.S. Constitution does not mention at all. In this section, we first look at the basic components of state constitutions and their differences with respect to the U.S. Constitution. We then examine local **charters**—the constitutional documents approved by state governments to establish local governments.

charter
the constitution of a local government

The Elements of State Constitutions

Similarly to the U.S. Constitution, state constitutions include

- an enumeration of fundamental rights (bill of rights)
- a division of powers among three branches of government
- an impeachment process
- a constitutional amendment process

Unlike the U.S. Constitution, the majority of state constitutions also contain

- allowances for direct democracy
- provisions for the creation of local governments
- provisions for public education
- a balanced budget requirement
- guidelines for conducting elections

State law (constitutional law and statutes) frequently offers broader fundamental rights than the U.S. Constitution and national law guarantee. For example, although the U.S. Constitution does *not* guarantee a right to "clean air, pure water, and to the preservation of the natural, scenic, historic and esthetic values of the environment," the state constitution of Pennsylvania does. Twenty state constitutions provide that equal rights under the law shall not be denied because of sex, but the U.S. Constitution has no comparable equal rights amendment. According to the U.S. Supreme Court, the rights established by the U.S. Constitution are the minimum rights that governments must guarantee. Therefore state and local governments can establish additional rights.

State constitutions are generally longer than the U.S. Constitution. The reason is that the U.S. Constitution presents only broad foundational principles and procedures, whereas the state constitutions spell out not only fundamental rights but also details of policy matters—the latter, for example, in sections on educational policy and business regulation. In addition, state constitutions discuss local governments, which the U.S. Constitution does not mention at all.

Local Charters: How Much Local Discretion?

When a state government establishes a local government, the state government specifies the local government's structures, institutions, and responsibilities in a constitutional document called a charter. Traditionally, state governments wrote and approved local government charters that specified not only the structures but also the functions of local government. Following **Dillon's Rule,** a principle articulated by Iowa Supreme Court judge John Forrest Dillon in 1868 and employed in hundreds of U.S. court decisions, local governments are creatures of the state that created them, and as such, they have only the powers expressly mentioned in their state-written and approved charters and those necessarily implied by the formally expressed powers.

In recent decades, however, most states have allowed for **home rule** by giving their citizens the opportunity to write, adopt, and amend local government charters at the city and county levels. A citizens' commission typically drafts these so-called **home rule charters,** which voters then accept or reject. These charters typically give the local government greater discretion in its activities than do state-developed charters. In comparison with local governments based on Dillon's rule, localities with home rule have discretion to determine the extent of their powers and responsibilities, as long as they comply with limits imposed by their state and by the U.S. Constitution.

In 1973, Congress enacted the District of Columbia Home Rule Act. This act devolved certain congressional powers for the governance of Washington, D.C., the federal district that is the nation's capital city, to local government. The federal law includes the District Home Rule Charter, which provides for the citizens living in DC to elect a mayor and thirteen members to a city council. Under the District Home Rule Charter, Congress maintains its constitutionally granted authority over the city, with authority to veto laws enacted by the city government and over the city's budget. In 1980, DC citizens passed an initiative calling for a constitutional convention. In 1982, the citizens ratified a constitution for a new state, New Columbia. The battle over statehood for Washington, D.C., continues today and is debated in this chapter's "Thinking Critically About Democracy" feature (see page 564).

Dillon's rule
the ruling articulated by Judge John Forrest Dillon in 1872 that local governments are creatures of the state that created them, and they have only the powers expressly mentioned in the charters written and approved by the state and those necessarily implied by the formally expressed powers

home rule
the opportunity provided by state government for citizens to write, adopt, and amend local government charters at the city and county levels

home rule charter
local government constitution written and approved by citizens following state-mandated procedures, including a referendum

SHOULD WASHINGTON, D.C., BECOME THE FIFTY-FIRST STATE OF THE UNION?

The Issue: The residents of Washington, D.C.—who are a larger population than the state of Wyoming—use the rallying cry of "taxation without representation" in their movement for statehood. Washington, D.C., is a city (Washington) and a federal district (the District of Columbia). Since the national government enacted the DC Home Rule Act of 1973, DC residents elect a local government composed of a mayor and a thirteen-member city council, but Congress can veto any laws made by the local government and maintains authority over DC's budget. The residents of Washington, D.C., pay the highest federal taxes per capita, but they have no voting representatives in either the House or the Senate. Before the Twenty-Third Amendment (1961), they also had no vote in presidential elections. Should Washington, D.C., become the fifty-first state?

Yes: Statehood would give the almost 600,000 citizens living in DC the same representation in Congress that citizens elsewhere in the nation have. It would eliminate the undemocratic policy of federal taxation without representation. In addition, it would give the DC citizens a government whose constitutional responsibility and primary focus is to attend to the day-to-day matters that affect their lives, liberties, and pursuit of happiness. Citizens in all other locations in the country have a state government that can focus all its attention on state residents. Congress would be out of the business of overseeing the legislation and administration of a city—one less concern on the overflowing congressional agenda.

No: The Constitution established a federal district as the permanent location for the nation's capital. To grant Washington, D.C., statehood would violate the intent of the founding fathers. In addition, if DC became a state, Congress, whose members meet and many of whom live in DC almost year-round, would be inclined to favor New Columbia (the name proposed for DC when it gains statehood). Moreover, because the citizens of DC vote overwhelmingly Democratic, DC statehood would likely add two Democratic Senators to a very partisan and closely divided Senate.

Other approaches: Congress could redraw the city lines so that the federal district included only the National Mall (including the U.S. Capitol, the White House, and the Supreme Court building). Then the state of Maryland could reclaim the remaining city land, which it had given to the national government to establish the capital city. DC residents would become citizens of the state of Maryland, with all rights of national and state citizenship, including full representation in Congress.

What do you think?

① Should U.S. citizens living in Washington, D.C., be guaranteed the same right to elect voting members to the House of Representatives and the Senate as citizens living elsewhere throughout the nation? Justify your answer.

② Is the fact that DC residents vote overwhelmingly Democratic relevant to the debate over statehood? Explain your answer.

③ Is there another approach that would address the complaint of "taxation without representation"?

Today, fifty state governments, each with its own constitution, and tens of thousands of local governments serve the diverse expectations and day-to-day needs of more than 300 million Americans.

Diversity in Political Cultures, People, Environments, and Resources

The Constitution of the United States distributes power and responsibilities to the national and state governments. According to this constitutional distribution, the national government is responsible for defense, foreign relations, interstate and foreign commerce, and promoting the general welfare—matters that affect the nation as a whole. By comparison, states and their local governments bear responsibility for the distinct day-to-day needs and demands of the people who live within their jurisdictions. Between 1789 and the 1960s, the national government became more and more involved in day-to-day domestic matters. Since the late 1970s, the federal government has relinquished much of its involvement in domestic issues, leaving state and local governments to step into the gap. The breadth of state and local policies, along with the size of their budgets and bureaucracies, is evidence of their increasingly central role in the lives of Americans.

The particular needs and demands each state and local government must address are the product of many factors, including residents' demographics (characteristics such as age, ethnicity, religion, income level, and educational attainment), the local environment, and resources. A state's resources (natural and financial resources alike), as well as its political culture, influence its capacity and willingness to meet the needs and demands of the people dwelling within its borders. The great diversity in people, environments, resources, and political cultures both within and across states affects the structures and public policies of state and local governments.

Political Culture and Its Effect on Governing

The dominant shared views among the people of a community concerning what the appropriate purposes and roles of government are, as well as who should participate in government, make up the *political culture*. Political scientist Daniel Elazar distinguished among three types of political culture to explain state and regional differences in "political processes, institutional structures, political behavior, and policies and programs of state and local government."[13] The three political cultures Elazar identified are traditionalistic, individualistic, and moralistic.[14]

In a **traditionalistic political culture,** government's primary purpose is to preserve the status quo—to keep things as they currently are. Further, the expectation is that the participants in government should come from among society's elite, not from the population at large. States where a traditionalistic political culture dominates tend to have relatively lower voter turnout and lower levels of mass participation than other states. These states are also less likely to have provisions for direct democracy.

In an **individualistic political culture,** citizens view politics as a means by which an individual can improve his or her economic and social status. Those who participate in politics do so for their own benefit. In areas where an individualistic political culture dominates, the primary purpose of government depends on the goals of those who get involved. These states also tend not to allow for direct democracy.

Concern for the collective good of society is the impetus for government action according to the **moralistic political culture.** In states dominated by this political culture, people feel an obligation to participate in government and to ensure that government is serving those who cannot provide for themselves. Mass political participation is common in such states, as are the processes of direct democracy. Voter turnout tends to be higher in states with a moralistic political culture than in those with traditionalistic or individualistic cultures.

Political scientist Joel Lieske extended Elazar's study of political culture to local governments. He identified ten subcultures that help to explain differences in political behaviors, policy preferences, and political institutions created by local governments. Lieske argued that the following socializing agents influence the political culture of a community of people: racial and ethnic kinship ties, value systems, and lifestyles.[15] In addition to these socializing agents, the local economy, distribution of income, life cycle, and environmental constraints, which include natural resources and climate, influence political culture.[16]

A community's political culture influences its governing processes, its people's political behavior and preferences, and ultimately public policy decisions. Therefore demographic and environmental differences throughout the country yield a variety of public policies across states as well as within them.

People: Dealing with Demographics

Demographic differences from state to state and from locality to locality place varying demands on state and local governments. In Mississippi, 20 percent of the population live in poverty; in New Hampshire, about 6 percent do.[17] The greater the percentage of a state's

traditionalistic political culture
the view that the purpose of government is to maintain the status quo and that participants in government should come from society's elite

individualistic political culture
the view that the decision to take part in government is an individual choice, and those who choose to participate determine the purpose of government and personally benefit from their participation

moralistic political culture
the view that the purpose of government is to serve the public good, including providing for those who are disadvantaged, and that all citizens should participate in government

> State and local governments fund English as a Second Language (E.S.L) classes in elementary and secondary schools in localities where a large portion of the student body speak a language other than English at home. State and local governments also assist in funding E.S.L. programs for adults in community centers such as this one in Queens, New York.

population living below the poverty line, the greater the demand on state and local government budgets for safety-net provisions such as school lunch programs and subsidized housing. Similarly, the larger the proportion of children living in a state, the higher the demand for public elementary and secondary education. And the greater the proportion of a state's population that is elderly, the more extensive the need for Medicaid (the joint federal-state health insurance program for low-income citizens, which includes coverage for nursing home care).

Another demographic difference that affects governmental expenditures can be seen in California, where about 40 percent of the residents speak a language other than English at home. This places demands on state and local governments to provide English as a Second Language (ESL) programs in public schools.[18] Because of this intrastate diversity, some school districts in California must cope with as many as forty different primary languages, whereas others need to handle two or three primary languages. Moreover, California residents need multilingual police officers, hospital workers, social workers, and emergency medical workers. West Virginia, where only about 3 percent of the residents speak a language other than English at home, does not have the same need for multilingual public servants and services.[19]

Environment and Resources: Variations in Needs and Tax Capacity

Climate significantly influences the demands citizens place on state and local governments and the services governments must provide for their citizens. States vulnerable to blizzards, tornadoes, and hurricanes all face unique demands, whether these be plowing and salting roadways in a snowstorm or alerting residents to a fierce approaching windstorm. State and local governments can address these localized problems more efficiently than the national government, but when climatic emergencies spread across state borders, the national government may need to step in.

Similarly, a region's natural resources affect public policies, the types of jobs available in the economy, and a government's ability to raise revenue (tax capacity). Oil is a natural resource that positively affects the economies of Texas and Alaska by creating jobs. Because the government can tax those who extract oil from the land, oil reserves also influence the tax policies in these states. A tax on the extraction of any natural resource, from fish in streams, to lumber in forests, to oil in the land, is a *severance tax*. Texas and Alaska raise so much revenue from their oil severance taxes that they are among the seven states that do not need to impose an individual income tax on their citizens to balance their budgets.

Many other examples illustrate the influence of climate and natural resources on a state's political and economic profile. The climate and natural resources of Hawaii have made tourism a vital industry there. The midwestern Plains states (Ohio, Indiana, Illinois, Michigan, Minnesota, and Wisconsin) are called America's breadbasket owing to the agricultural enterprise and related industries (such as food processing) that dominate the economies of those states. Compared with other states, Indiana has the greatest percentage of its labor force employed in manufacturing. The state policies needed to regulate and support each type of economic activity vary considerably, depending on whether farming, tourism, or manufacturing is the dominant industry.

> Because of the great diversity across the states in climate and resources, state and local governments differ widely in the public services they provide, in the types of industries that fuel their economies, and in their ability to raise the revenue they need to serve their residents.

Climate, natural resources, and the demographic profile of residents also affect a jurisdiction's *tax base*—its wealth, in the form of personal income, property, and other assets, that the government can tax. The financial resources of a government are a product of the tax base. Given the diversity of people, climate, and natural resources, as well as the diversity of political cultures that influences decisions about taxing and spending, it is not surprising that some states and localities have more money to spend than others do, which means that taxes and public services differ from state to state.

State and Local Government Budgets

A government's budget is its central policy document. It reveals how the government is spending its financial resources and where it is getting the money to pay the bills. The constitutions of all states except Vermont require state legislators to achieve a balanced budget. How do they approach this challenge? On what do state and local governments spend their money? Where do they get the revenue to balance their budgets?

Balanced Budgets

For forty-nine states and their local governments, the balanced budget requirement means that they must balance their **operating budgets,** which include all the costs of day-to-day government operations. That is, the government must raise enough money during the budget year, without borrowing, to pay for these expenses. In the case of governments, typical examples of operating budget expenditures include salaries and benefits, utility bills, office supplies, and rent.

Although state and local governments cannot borrow money to pay for their day-to-day operations, they can borrow money (go into debt) for *capital projects*. These include expensive building projects and purchases from which citizens will benefit for many years. Because a state or local government typically cannot raise enough money through its taxes, user fees, and grants-in-aid in one year both to balance its operating budget and to build new highways, or to purchase new computer systems, states' laws allow them to borrow money to pay for these expensive projects. Such capital project expenditures and revenues are included in the **capital budget,** to which the annual balanced budget mandate does not apply.

operating budget
a budget that accounts for all the costs of day-to-day government operations and covers such items as salaries and benefits, utilities, office supplies, and rent

capital budget
a budget that accounts for the costs and revenues for expensive building and purchasing projects from which citizens will benefit for many years and for which governments can borrow money

State and Local Expenditures on Day-to-Day Domestic Matters

On what goods and services do state and local governments spend their money? Figure 18.2 shows the total expenditures of state and local governments in selected policy areas. This figure illustrates the diversity of services provided by state and local governments, most of them related to daily domestic matters, for these are the matters reserved to the states (and the local governments they create) by the Tenth Amendment of the U.S. Constitution.

State and local governments spend most of their money paying the salaries and benefits of their employees. The fifty state governments employ about 5 million people, and the 89,000-plus local governments employ more than 14 million.[20] These millions of state and local employees serve in just about every occupation imaginable, with many of them involved in providing **essential services,** the everyday work required to prevent chaos and hazardous conditions in society. As long as they receive these services, citizens seldom think about them; but if they experience an interruption in even one essential service, they become alarmed, outraged, or seriously endangered or inconvenienced. Essential service providers include elementary and secondary schoolteachers, police officers, firefighters, sanitation workers, medical care personnel, and road and bridge maintenance crews. Table 18.1 presents data on state and local government spending per capita on selected services. Let's take a close-up look at just a few of the essential services state and local workers provide: public education, public health, and public safety.

essential services
public services provided by state and local governments on a daily basis to prevent chaos and hazardous conditions in society

PUBLIC EDUCATION   State constitutions guarantee equal and effective education, and states typically create school districts (a type of local government) to provide elementary and secondary education. All states have a compulsory education law, which means that children must go to school until they achieve the age or grade level specified by their state government. The overwhelming majority of U.S. children attend public schools, with only about 10 percent in private schools and about 2 percent homeschooled.[21] In view of the fact that almost 17 percent of the U.S. population is enrolled in public elementary and secondary schools at any given time, it is no wonder that the majority of local government employees are dedicated to providing elementary and secondary education.[22]

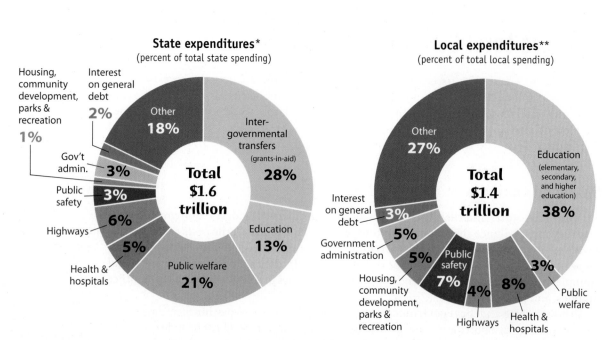

*CALCULATED from U.S. Census Bureau, *Statistical Abstract of the United States: 2010* (Washington DC: U.S. Government Printing Office, 2010), Table 442.

**CALCULATED from U.S. Census Bureau, *Statistical Abstract of the United States: 2010* (Washington DC: U.S. Government Printing Office, 2010), Table 444.

FIGURE 18.2

Expenditures of State and Local Governments

State and Local Government Spending Per Capita on Selected Services

TABLE 18.1

Service	Highest per capita state	Lowest per capita state
Fire protection	Rhode Island ($230)	Pennsylvania ($46)
Health and hospitals	Wyoming ($1,753)	North Dakota ($158)
Highways	Alaska ($1,925)	Georgia ($291)
Parks and recreation	Colorado ($221)	Maine ($51)
Police protection	Delaware ($489)	West Virginia ($131)
Welfare	New York ($2,239)	Nevada ($719)

SOURCE: *Governing State & Local Sourcebook*, http://sourcebook.governing.com/index.jsp.

According to the National Center for Public Policy and Higher Education, in 2006, state and county governments provided higher education in 1,520 public colleges and universities, educating 78 percent of enrolled undergraduates.[23] The majority of these institutions (944) were two-year colleges. California had the highest number of public colleges and universities, with 110 two-year institutions and 34 four-year institutions. Rhode Island had the fewest, with 2 four-year public institutions and 1 two-year public institution.

In a comparison of policy costs, on average, educational policy makes up the largest proportion of state and local budgets. States vary widely, though, with respect to both the amount of money and the proportion of their budgets that they spend on public education. In the 2005–2006 school year, New Jersey spent the most—$13,781 per elementary and secondary school pupil. In that same year, Utah spent the least—$5,347 per pupil. Per-pupil state support of higher education in 2006 ranged from a high of $9,733 in Hawaii to a low of $2,361 in Colorado.[24]

Since the 1970s, lawsuits challenging state elementary and secondary school financing systems have become common. State courts have ruled intrastate inequities in spending between school districts to be in violation of state constitutions. More recently, state courts are determining whether states are providing an adequate education to all children. While courts focus on the results, states may need to increase their funding in order to provide the resources needed to offer an adequate educational experience.[25]

PUBLIC HEALTH AND SAFETY   Another major responsibility of state and local governments is to ensure public health and safety, which involves a broad range of state and local government activity. Medicaid, for example, competes with education as the most expensive item in state budgets. Although rising Medicaid costs are ballooning state expenditures for public health, fewer state employees provide health services than education services.

Other public health- and safety-related protections funded at the state and local levels include the provision of safe drinking water and the proper disposal of garbage and sewage to prevent disease. State and local governments also establish building codes to ensure the safe construction of homes and other structures. They pass codes related to the use of smoke detectors, handrails on staircases, functioning fire escapes in high-rise buildings, and sanitary conditions in restaurants. They regulate personal behavior by means of criminal laws, speed limits, legal drinking ages, and laws specifying the blood alcohol content that defines "driving under the

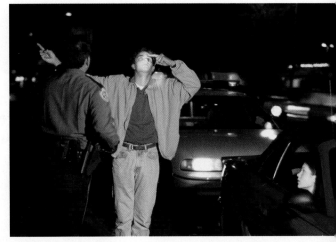

> State and local governments are responsible for essential services, including elementary and secondary education and the protection of public health and safety. One means of ensuring public safety is the regulation of individual behavior, such as the enforcement of state laws that prohibit driving under the influence of alcohol.

influence." State laws requiring the immunization of children before they are allowed to attend school also promote public health and safety.

Since the terrorist attacks of 9/11, public safety—often referred to as homeland security now—has warranted increased attention from the national government. This attention has meant both new national policies and additional federal grant moneys for state and local governments, which employ first responders. The Department of Homeland Security, established in 2003, relies on the work of state and local police, firefighters, and emergency medical technicians to ensure domestic safety and security.

State Government Revenues

How do state and local governments raise the money needed to balance their operating budgets? Figure 18.3 shows the sources of state and local government revenues.

Other than grants-in-aid from the federal government, the largest revenue source for state governments (as a group) is the sales tax, although not all states impose a sales tax. Among the forty-five states that do collect a sales tax, the tax most commonly falls on purchases of goods, not on the costs of hiring someone—such as a lawyer, an accountant, or a hairdresser—to provide a service. Yet the states that tax purchased goods do not all tax the same goods or use the same tax rate. Take groceries, for example. Mississippi has a 7 percent sales tax on all groceries purchased. Virginia's sales tax on groceries is only 2.5 percent. Pennsylvania does not collect a sales tax on unprepared food purchased, but it does impose a 6 percent sales tax on ready-to-eat store- and restaurant-prepared foods.

Today, debate continues over the collection of sales taxes on Internet and online purchases. According to federal law, states can require only companies that have a physical presence in the state to collect sales taxes. So, if the vendor from which you make an Internet purchase is located in another state, your state government cannot force the vendor to collect a sales tax on the purchase. (Did you know that you, the purchaser, are legally obligated to pay this uncollected sales tax when you file your state taxes?) As the volume of Internet purchases continues to increase, and as citizens buy relatively fewer goods in local stores, many states are losing urgently needed sales tax revenue—and thus are vigorously lobbying for changes in the federal law.

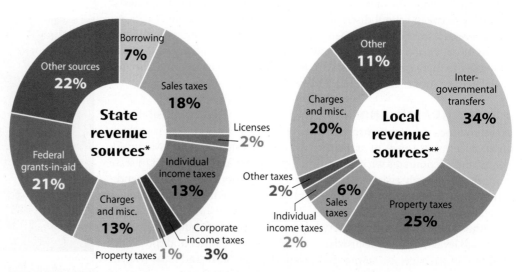

FIGURE 18.3

State and Local Revenue Sources

*CALCULATED from U.S. Census Bureau, *Statistical Abstract of the United States: 2010* (Washington, DC: U.S. Government Printing Office, 2010), Table 439.

**CALCULATED from U.S. Census Bureau, *Statistical Abstract of the United States: 2010* (Washington, DC: U.S. Government Printing Office, 2010), Table 443.

State governments also raise money through excise taxes. These taxes on the purchase of gasoline, tobacco, alcohol, and other items aim not only to raise revenue but also to reduce consumption of these products. In addition, state governments typically tax inheritances, large monetary gifts, and, as noted, the extraction of natural resources (severance taxes). Moreover, all but seven states—Alaska, Florida , Nevada, South Dakota, Texas, Washington, and Wyoming—collect personal income taxes.[26]

Beyond the variety of taxes they impose, states raise revenue by charging fees for some of the services they provide, such as higher education (through tuition at state colleges and universities) and hospital care. Some states, such as Pennsylvania and New Hampshire, even make money on the sale of liquor because they own the liquor stores in the state.

Local Government Revenues

How do local governments raise funds? A major revenue source for local governments is grants from their state government. The primary source of local government tax revenue, however, is the property tax. The property tax is imposed on the value of property a person owns (typically land and buildings, although some states also place a property tax on the value of household furnishings, clothing, and jewelry).

Unfortunately for local governments, the property tax is the most criticized tax, for several reasons. First, unlike the income tax, which (as a percentage of income) people view as based on their ability to pay, the property tax depends on the value of a person's property, which may not correlate with income and hence with that person's ability to pay. For people on a fixed income (such as Social Security), increases in property taxes mean they must pay a larger proportion of their income to hold on to their home. Further, unlike sales and income taxes, property taxes go up almost annually.

Owing to inflation, the operating costs of local governments rise every year. This increase occurs even when they are providing the same services as in the preceding year. Thus they need to raise more money each year if they are to balance their budgets. One way local governments collect more money is by increasing the property tax rate. Increases in the property tax rate take place through an annual vote (either by local government officials or by citizens in a referendum). Upon approval of the new tax rate, citizens receive a bill for their full property tax obligation and then write a check to pay the bill. This process makes the property tax a more "visible" burden to taxpayers than the sales tax, which people typically pay without much thought and do not track on an annual basis. It is also more visible than the income tax, which the government automatically deducts from individuals' paychecks, frequently without their close monitoring.

Recognizing that property taxes alone sometimes do not cover localities' full financial needs, state governments are increasingly allowing local governments to collect revenues through additional channels. Some state governments have given selected local governments the authority to collect sales taxes, and at least thirteen states allow some local governments to collect income taxes. The majority of states have authorized their local governments to collect fees for goods and services such as sewerage service and utilities.

State and local governments differ with respect to the value of their available taxable resources, as well as in their decisions about which resources to tax, and at what rate. Because the governments of the fifty states and of the tens of thousands of U.S. localities have unequal financial capacities to provide for their citizens, they sometimes compete with one another for resources. For example, state and local governments vie with one another to attract new companies because the arrival of new firms means job creation, which expands the tax base. Newly created jobs mean more people working and thus more revenue raised through income taxes—and perhaps also through sales taxes because employed people usually have more money to spend than unemployed people do. To bring in new companies, state and local governments may provide tax breaks for businesses, or they may spend money on schools, parks, and improved public safety to enhance the quality of life in their communities. State and local governments also compete for national grant money that they can put toward balancing their budgets.

The Federal Government as a Fiscal Equalizer

The federal government offers state and local governments grants-in-aid to implement national policy preferences. It also provides grants to balance the interstate (among states) and intrastate (within a state) differences in financial capacity to meet the needs of the population at large. Through grant programs, which typically distribute more money to states and localities with the greatest mismatch between their resources and their citizens' needs, the federal government acts as a fiscal equalizer. Through its grants, the national government tries to ensure that all states can adequately serve their citizens.

For example, the national government distributes Medicaid grants to the states on the basis of a formula that ensures the greatest assistance for states with the lowest per capita income. Accordingly, in 2008, the federal budget covered 76 percent of Mississippi's Medicaid cost, based on data indicating that Mississippi had the lowest per capita income and the largest percentage of people in poverty among all the states. This was the highest national cost sharing for Medicaid among all the states. Twelve states received the lowest national cost sharing—50 percent—for Medicaid: California, Colorado, Connecticut, Delaware, Illinois, Maryland, Massachusetts, Minnesota, New Hampshire, New Jersey, New York, and Virginia.[27] Table 18.2 presents data on federal grant spending.

The ability of the federal government to be a fiscal equalizer for state and local governments is limited. The great recession that began in 2007 hit state and local governments hard. Typically, job losses during a recession create revenue shortfalls for state governments that rely on sales and individual income taxes for a large proportion of their revenues, and employment is one of the last parts of the economy to bounce back. Even though the 2009 economic stimulus package (the American Recovery and Reinvestment Act)[28] provided state and local governments with $280 billion in federal grants—$48 billion of which was intended to stabilize fiscally stressed state budgets[29]—states may face budget deficits as high as $350 billion in 2010 and 2011.[30]

Even though the national economy was showing signs of growth by the end of 2009, state and local governments usually experience their worst budget years in the two years after a recession ends.[31] Therefore, state and local governments have not seen the worst of the recession. Moreover, because state constitutions require state and local governments to balance their budgets, state and local governments will have to either raise more revenue (with increases in taxes or user fees) or cut spending (which means decreases in services). As

TABLE 18.2

Federal Aid to State and Local Governments

	Highest	Lowest
Total in millions	California ($56,402)*	Delaware ($1,241)**
As percent of total revenue	Mississippi (30.7%)	Virginia (11.6%)
Per capita	Wyoming ($3,988)	Virginia ($934)

*$1,556 per capita.
**$2,120 per capita.

SOURCE: *Governing State & Local Sourcebook*, http://sourcebook.governing.com/index.jsp.

POLITICAL INQUIRY

Why does California have the highest total of federal grant dollars but a per capita amount that is more than half of Wyoming's federal aid per capita? Keeping in mind the federal government's role as a fiscal equalizer, what does the comparison of Mississippi's federal aid as a percent of total revenue with Virginia's indicate about the tax base of Mississippi compared with that of Virginia?

Vermont Governor Jim Douglas warned in February 2010, for state and local governments "the worst probably is yet to come."[32]

Responsibilities of State and Local Governments in National Politics

The U.S. Constitution describes certain state obligations to the national government, and hence these are formal responsibilities. Other state responsibilities to the federal government have developed informally over time. In this section, we explore the main formal and informal responsibilities of state and local governments to the national government.

States in National Politics: Formal Roles

The U.S. Constitution established state government authority in several areas of national import (all of which have been discussed in previous chapters):

- conducting national elections
- determining the process by which electors for the Electoral College are selected
- redrawing House districts (redistricting) after congressional reapportionment
- ratifying amendments to the U.S. Constitution

These are the formal roles of state governments in national politics. Today, most states delegate to local governments the responsibility of conducting elections, including those for national offices. In many states, there are ongoing efforts to reform the process of choosing electors for the Electoral College and redistricting.

States in National Politics: Informal Functions

In addition to those constitutionally based roles for state governments, the states, by tradition, perform various informal functions in national politics and government. Two such functions are serving as a training ground for federal government officials and acting as a laboratory for innovative and experimental public policies.

TRAINING GROUNDS FOR NATIONAL OFFICE Since 1921, the overwhelming majority of members of Congress have had prior local or state government experience, or both. Presidents also develop experience serving in state government.

Political scientists have identified three common pathways to the presidency over the course of U.S. history: the Senate, the vice presidency, and a governorship. Four of the last six presidents—Jimmy Carter, Ronald Reagan, Bill Clinton, and George W. Bush—used their position as governor as a steppingstone to the White House. President Reagan said that being governor "was the best training school for" the presidency.[33] Reagan's vice president, George H. W. Bush, successfully ran for the presidency in 1988, but before his success, no sitting vice president had been elected to the presidency since Martin Van Buren in 1836. Yet Americans widely view their vice president as in training for the presidency because the second-in-command is only "a heartbeat away" from the office. Since 1960, only two sitting U.S. senators have been elected to the presidency—John F. Kennedy and Barack Obama. Therefore, for the last four decades, governorships have served as the primary training ground for presidents.

Although career politicians typically advance from local to state to national positions, sometimes the movement occurs in the other direction—from national to state office. In 2008, ten sitting governors had previous experience serving in Congress.[34] That national officials are running for governor suggests a growing prestige for the gubernatorial office.

LABORATORIES FOR NEW PUBLIC POLICIES State and local governments are worth watching if you are looking for innovative public policies. States and localities develop creative policies to deal with domestic matters that are reserved to them by the Constitution, as well as to carry out the authority for policy making that the national government devolves to them through mandates and grants (as discussed in Chapter 3). State and local governments also set policies for domestic problems they believe the national government is not addressing appropriately. In particular, state governments are leading the way with innovative programs for environmental protection and health care.

Dissatisfied with the national government's response to various environmental concerns of national and global context and scope, state and local governments have taken matters into their own hands. Through both legislative action and citizen initiatives, states and localities, deeply concerned about the lack of national action to address global warming, have enacted laws requiring or encouraging utilities to increase their use of alternative energy, including solar and wind power.[35] The city government of Boulder, Colorado, became the first government in the United States to impose a tax on the use of electricity generated by the burning of fossil fuels. Voters in Boulder approved the tax in a 2006 ballot measure, expecting that the tax would promote conservation and consequently decrease the carbon emissions that scientists link to global warming.[36]

States have also taken the lead in health care policy making, stepping in when the national government failed to deliver. While serving as First Lady (1993–2001), Hillary Rodham Clinton worked diligently, but unsuccessfully, for a national universal health care plan. The plan was to institute publicly funded, national medical services that would cover most or all of the health care expenses of citizens who do not have their own, private health insurance. In 2006, Massachusetts and Vermont passed legislation aimed at providing health care to all their states' residents. In addition, with support from federal Medicaid funding, state governments across the country have experimented with programs that provide health insurance specifically to children.

States monitor one another's experiments closely. When policy makers in a given state see an innovative program working effectively, they often adopt it, making the necessary adjustments to meet the distinct needs of their own citizens. In turn, the national government sometimes adopts successful state programs, as in 1996 when Congress passed the Personal Responsibility and Work Opportunity Reconciliation Act, a national welfare reform bill that combined components of several experimental state welfare programs.

> Wind energy is among the world's fastest growing sources of energy. In the United States, the state of Texas is leading the way in wind energy growth. Many Texas landowners have leased their lands to wind turbine developers. In Texas, and other states where wind power development is occurring, state and local laws regulate its development. Moreover, state-government tax incentives are one of the driving forces behind the growth in wind energy.

In summary, as the national government has placed ever-greater demands on state and local governments without always providing sufficient funding to address crucial policy issues, the states have become more creative in devising appropriate public policy solutions. States are also addressing problems when concerned citizens are not satisfied with the remedies provided—or not provided—by the national government. Finally, when an innovative policy works in one state, other states, and even the national government, are often inclined to adopt it.

Having surveyed the constitutional basis of state and local governments, as well as their responsibilities to their citizens and the nation, we now examine the structures and institutions by which state and local governments exercise their authority. Because no two states and no two local governments are identical, we will focus on the most common structures and institutions.

Institutions of State Government

The state constitutions in effect at the time of the ratification of the Articles of Confederation (1781) and the U.S. Constitution (1789) had all established three branches of government with a system of checks and balances. This state government structure became the model for the national government created by the U.S. Constitution. Although the constitutions of all the states have been amended numerous times over the centuries, and many have been totally replaced several times, the basic structures of state governments have not changed. Each state government's structure is unique, but the legislative, executive, and judicial institutions of all the states share several common characteristics that we now consider.

Legislative Branch: Formulating and Approving Policy

The basic functions of state legislatures resemble those of their federal counterpart, Congress. The primary functions of state legislatures are policy formulation and policy approval. In addition, state legislatures monitor the executive branch's implementation of policy. Further, individual state legislators, like members of Congress, assist their constituents in solving problems they may be experiencing with the various levels of government.

The state legislature, typically called the General Assembly, is bicameral (two chambered) in all states except Nebraska, which has a unicameral (single chamber) legislature. A state with a bicameral legislature commonly calls the chamber that has more members the House, and the smaller chamber the Senate. Nebraskans call their unicameral legislature the Senate. The number of legislators in each state legislature varies widely. The figure in "Analyzing the Sources" on page 576 presents the number of legislators per million people, for each state. As you can see from the graphic, the number of state legislators does not correlate with the state population.

State senators usually serve a four-year term of office; state representatives, a two-year term. Fifteen states have set term limits for legislators—incumbents can run for reelection for the same position only a set number of times. Not surprisingly, citizens (not state legislators) took the lead in establishing most of these term limits, using the state's initiative processes.

There is generally more diversity of gender, ethnicity, and race among state legislators than among national legislators. In 2010, for example, 24 percent of the total number of state legislators (7,382) were women (1,799 legislators). In New Hampshire, 38 percent of the legislators were women, but in South Carolina, only 10 percent of the lawmakers were women.[37] The predominance of a moralistic political culture (see page 565) appears to correlate with higher proportions of women elected to state legislatures, as does the presence in the population of relatively high numbers of educated, professional women—women who are more likely to have a sense of political efficacy and are more willing and able to run for office.

The racial and ethnic diversity within a state's population generally correlates with the diverse composition of its state legislature. For example, in 2009 Mississippi had the highest proportion of African Americans in its state legislature (29 percent) as well as the highest

ANALYZING THE SOURCES

HOW REPRESENTATIVE IS EACH STATE'S LEGISLATURE?

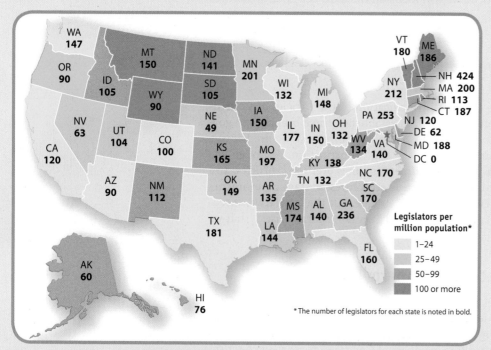

As the map shows, the state's population does not determine the number of state legislators. In the case of New Hampshire residents, 324 legislators represent every 1 million people. For Californians, only 3 legislators represent every 1 million people.

Evaluating the Evidence

① After you examine the map, review Figure 18.1. Assuming that you are interested in having your voice heard by your elected officials, which state would you rather live in? Why?

② Considering all the figures in this chapter, discuss the geographic pattern of states that provide greater levels of democracy—as in government by and for the people.

③ On the basis of the figures in this chapter, which states would you characterize as having a moralistic political culture? Explain.

---

proportion of African Americans in its state population (37 percent). Nine states—Hawaii, Idaho, Iowa, Maine, Montana, North Dakota, South Dakota, Utah, and Wyoming—had no African American state legislators. All of these states are in the bottom fifteen states when ranked by the proportion of African Americans in their population. In 2009, 9 percent of the legislators from all fifty states were African American. As for Latino state lawmakers, in 2009 New Mexico's legislature had the largest representation, with 44 percent in the legislature. New Mexico is also the state with the largest proportion of Latino residents, with 45 percent. Overall, 3 percent of state legislators were Latino.[38]

Unlike members of the U.S. House and Senate, the overwhelming majority of state legislators (85 percent) serve on a part-time basis. Most state legislatures convene annually from January to May or June. Seven state legislatures convene only every other year.

Regardless of the variations from state to state with respect to the number of legislators, their terms of office, their demographic characteristics, and whether the job is full- or part-time, all state legislatures have the same primary function: to formulate public policy. Further, they all share with their states' governors the authority to approve public policy as part of the system of checks and balances that accommodates the separation of basic governing functions. Approved state policy is put into action by employees of the executive branch.

Executive Branch: Putting Policy into Action

The executive branch of state government implements public policy. Approximately 5 million people work in the executive branches of the fifty state governments. In addition to those who directly implement policy, states have numerous appointed and elected executive branch officials who assist in formulating policy and supervising its implementation.

Unlike citizens voting in the national presidential election, who elect individuals to only two executive branch positions (the presidency and the vice presidency), citizens in almost all states have the opportunity to elect people to *several* of the state executive branch positions. **Plural executive system** refers to a government structure in which citizens elect more than two officials to the executive branch (Figure 18.4). Whereas the average number of statewide elected executive officials is seven, North Dakota elects the most (twelve). Each statewide elected executive branch official oversees a specific policy or functional area of state government, with the governor bearing responsibility for the remaining areas. The more elected statewide executive officials, the more people with whom the governor must share authority—and hence the weaker the governor.

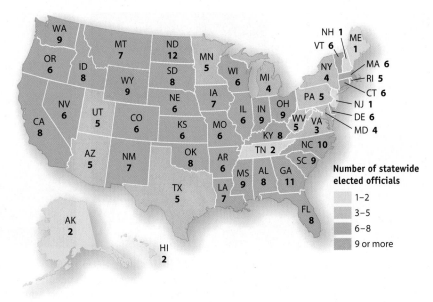

FIGURE 18.4

Total Number of Statewide Elected Officials for Each State, Executive Branch

SOURCE: State totals from Kendra A. Hovey and Harold A. Hovey, *CQ's State Fact Finder 2007* (Washington, DC: CQ Press, 2007), p. 113.

plural executive system
a state and local government structure in which the citizens elect more than two people to top positions in the executive branch of government

GOVERNOR The best-known elected official in state government is the governor. (Can you name your governor? What about your state legislators?) Unlike the majority of state legislators, the governor is a full-time official. Moreover, the governor gets more media coverage than do legislators. Thus citizens can more easily learn about and track the governor's positions and actions than they can the work of their elected state legislators. Once the majority of legislators approve a bill, the governor can sign it into law or reject it with a veto. The governor's one vote—to approve or to reject a bill—draws more media attention than does the vote of any individual legislator.

Just as the president launches the budget process by presenting Congress with a proposed budget, the majority of governors begin the state budget procedure by drafting an executive budget they put before the state legislature. Compared with Congress, state legislatures typically have more limits on their authority to modify the executive budget. On the basis of the modified executive budget, the legislature writes specific appropriation bills that allocate spending by state departments and agencies. Most governors can use a line-item veto, the authority to eliminate one or more funding lines in appropriation bills while approving the remainder of the bill. The line-item veto is a tool that governors can and do wield to balance the state budget.

Once a bill becomes law, the governor must ensure its efficient, effective, and legal implementation. To that end, governors have the authority to appoint numerous people to top positions in the executive branch. In addition, governors can reorganize the departments and agencies in the executive branch to improve their efficiency and performance in implementing the law. Governors can also mandate specific activities and procedures on the part of executive branch bureaucrats by issuing executive orders.

In another responsibility of gubernatorial office, the governor serves as commander in chief of the state's National Guard. In this capacity, the governor can call on the National Guard to respond to state emergencies and crises, including natural disasters (for example, floods, blizzards, landslides, and hurricanes), civil unrest (such as riots), and terrorist attacks (such as those on September 11, 2001).

> Although governors are commander-in-chief of their state's National Guard, the president can supersede the governors' authority over the National Guard by federalizing troops and deploying them on behalf of the federal government. In 1957, Arkansas Governor Orval Faubus called on the Arkansas National Guard to prevent nine African American students from entering Little Rock's Central High School. In response, President Eisenhower federalized the National Guard troops, ordering them to protect the civil rights of the students as they integrated Central High. Today, National Guard troops are deployed worldwide, including in Kabul, Afghanistan, as part of the war on terrorism.

Whereas the nation elected its first minority male president in 2008, and has never elected a woman to serve as president, a diversity of gender, race, and ethnicity is evident among the nation's governors. In 2010, six of the fifty governors, and nine of the forty-two lieutenant governors were women.[39] In addition, there were two African American governors, one Latino, one Asian American, and one Arab American. Because of the plural executive structure of state government, there are many more opportunities for citizens to get elected to executive positions on the state than on the national level.

OTHER STATEWIDE ELECTED EXECUTIVES States vary with respect to both how many elected executive branch officials they have and what positions those officials hold. All but seven states elect lieutenant governors, and many elect other statewide officials.

The lieutenant governor is in line to succeed the governor if the latter is unable to complete the term of office. States without the lieutenant governor position designate some other elected official to succeed a governor who cannot complete his or her term. Lieutenant governors also typically act as the president of their states' senates, presiding over Senate meetings and casting tie-breaking votes.

More than forty states have plural executive systems, which typically include the state attorney general, secretary of state, treasurer, and auditor. What are the responsibilities of these officials? The attorney general is the chief law enforcement officer in the state and represents the state in lawsuits. The secretary of state is the official record keeper. In addition to maintaining the legislative records, administrative rules, executive orders, and constitutional changes, the secretary of state keeps records of information relevant to elections, such as campaign finance reports, petitions by candidates to get on the Election Day ballot, and lists of registered voters. The state treasurer pays the state's bills, and the auditor reviews state spending to ensure that it is legal, efficient, and effective.

The statewide executive officials elected by citizens do not serve under the governor. Elected independently of the governor, they may even be members of a political party other than the governor's party. Because they serve for fixed terms (usually four years) and must satisfy the voters, not the governor, if they are to win reelection, these officials need not be loyal to the governor's priorities. The majority of state executives elected statewide, including governors, have term limits—usually a limit of two consecutive terms.

Judicial Branch: Resolving Questions of Law

In addition to electing state legislators and (on average) seven state executive branch officials, citizens in most states elect judges to serve in the state court system. Each of the fifty states has its own court system that is independent of the national judicial system. State judges must uphold both their state's constitution and the U.S. Constitution. Lawsuits that involve state and local laws are resolved in state courts. If such cases also involve questions of federal law or the U.S. Constitution, they may move into the federal court system.

State courts hear thousands more criminal and civil cases than do the national courts. In the process of resolving these cases, state judges may have to interpret the meaning of laws and previous court decisions. State judges also have the authority of judicial review; that is, they can declare acts of the state and local legislative and executive officials to be unconstitutional.

STRUCTURE OF STATE COURT SYSTEMS Although the primary responsibilities of the courts across the fifty states are the same, judicial structures and procedures differ from state to state. Here, we look briefly at certain commonalities in judicial organization and process.

State *trial courts* have *original* jurisdiction: they are responsible for determining whether the accused person is guilty or not guilty based on the evidence presented in court. All states have two levels of trial courts. The lower-level trial courts hear less serious cases than do the upper-level trial courts. In contrast to trial courts, *appellate courts* have *appellate* jurisdiction: they review the legality and fairness of trial and lower appellate court procedures and decisions in the cases brought to them through an appeal. Thus appellate courts do not determine guilt. Rather, they ensure due process through their review of judges' decisions made in lower courts—decisions on issues such as what evidence lawyers can submit for jurors to consider and what questions lawyers can ask of witnesses. The appellate judges review trial transcripts and lawyers' arguments to determine whether the judges made the correct decisions. The majority of states have two levels of appellate courts: the intermediate-level court and the court of last resort. Figure 18.5 summarizes the structure of and the selection process for the state court systems.

	Jurisdiction	Type of Trial	Judges
Court of last resort	Appellate	Bench only	Panel, most commonly elected
Intermediate appeals court	Mandatory appellate	Bench only	Panel, most commonly merit selection process
Major trial courts	Original and *de novo* from minor trial courts*	Jury or bench	One judge, most commonly elected
Minor trial courts	Original	Bench	One judge, most commonly elected

* Note: *De novo* (Latin for *anew*) because no written transcript is kept of the proceedings in minor trial courts; when there is an appeal there must be a new trial, and this is conducted in the major trial court.

POLITICAL INQUIRY

FIGURE 18.5 ■ STRUCTURE OF STATE COURT SYSTEMS How does the structure of the typical state court system differ from the structure of the federal court system? How does the selection of federal judges differ from the selection of state judges? What are the advantages and disadvantages of each type of judicial selection process?

Judges decide what laws mean and ensure due process. How are judges selected to ensure that they have the proper qualifications for this essential role in our democracy?

JUDGES Whereas the president appoints and the Senate confirms federal judges, the states use a variety of methods to select their judges. Some states use one selection process for trial judges and a different procedure for appellate judges. State judges may be (1) elected, (2) appointed, or (3) chosen through a process that combines an initial appointment with a subsequent retention election. Each state's law specifies the judicial selection procedure(s) the state will follow.

In states that grant judgeships through an electoral process, voters typically select judges through a nonpartisan election, a type of election not used at the national level of government. In a **nonpartisan election,** the candidates are not selected by a political party, and party affiliations do not appear on the ballot. In contrast, in a **partisan election,** political parties select candidates, and the ballot lists each candidate's party affiliation. State governments adopted nonpartisan judicial elections during the Progressive Era of the late 1800s and early 1900s—the same era when state governments were adopting direct democracy. Progressive reformers maintained that nonpartisan elections would encourage voters to pay greater attention to the candidates' qualifications than to their party affiliations and limit the influence of party organizations on both election outcomes and public policy.

Debates over appointing rather than electing judges, and over partisan rather than nonpartisan judicial elections, have led more and more states to adopt a **merit selection process,** which combines an initial appointment with a subsequent election. Proponents of this selection method believe that it combines the best of the electoral and appointive processes. Although merit selection procedures vary from state to state, they have some common elements. The process usually begins with the governor appointing citizens to a nonpartisan nominating committee. The nominating committee sends a list of qualified judicial candidates to the governor, who then appoints judges from the list of nominees. After a one- or two-year term, the appointed judge stands for a noncompetitive **retention election,** in which the judge runs unopposed and voters vote "yes" to keep the judge on the bench or "no" to remove the judge. Typically, a vote to retain the judge means a second term of eight or ten years. At the end of the term, the judge must again go through a retention election to remain on the bench.

The question of which government each judge actually works for can be a source of confusion for citizens. Even though voters elect trial judges to hear cases that arise in one city, borough, township, or county, the state government typically funds all the trial courts, as well as the appellate courts, in the state. Hence individuals who appear to be city or county judges are in fact judges working in the state court system at large. Local governments do not have a separate judicial branch. Some local governments do not even have distinct legislative and executive branches. Instead, one governmental body (a council, a commission, a board, or an authority) has responsibility for both the legislative and the executive functions, as we next consider.

Local Governments

Scholars categorize local governments as either *general-purpose* or *single-purpose* governments on the basis of the variety of services they dispense. Most citizens live within the borders of at least two general-purpose local governments (such as a county and a municipal government) and at least one single-purpose local government (typically a school district). In this section, we differentiate among these general-purpose and single-purpose governments.

General-Purpose Local Governments

As the term suggests, **general-purpose government** provides numerous and varied services, in multiple policy areas, to the people living within its borders. The fifty states have 39,044 such governments, yet not all states have all varieties of general-purpose govern-

---

nonpartisan election

an election in which candidates are not nominated by political parties and the ballot does not include party affiliations

partisan election

an election in which candidates are nominated by political parties and the ballot lists each candidate's political party affiliation

merit selection process

a process for selecting judges in which a nonpartisan committee nominates candidates, the governor or legislature appoints judges from among those candidates to a short term of service, and then the appointed judges face a retention election at the end of the short term

retention election

a noncompetitive election in which an incumbent judge's name is on the ballot and voters decide whether the judge should be retained

general-purpose government

a government providing services in numerous and diverse policy and functional areas to the residents living within its borders

municipal government

self-governing general-purpose government—including city, borough, and town governments—created by states to provide goods and services within a densely populated area ments.[40] Municipal, township, and county governments are three forms of general-purpose governments.

Municipal governments are self-governing political jurisdictions created by states to provide goods and services to a densely populated area within the state. Municipal governments include city, borough, and town governments. These governments provide day-to-day services and benefits to citizens. **Townships,** which also deliver day-to-day services, are units of government that serve people living outside municipalities, in rural areas where the population is more dispersed than in areas served by municipal governments.

Day-to-day services provided by municipal and township governments include public safety, zoning regulations for land use, road maintenance, parks and recreation, and libraries. The larger the population of a municipality or township, the more numerous and diverse the services its government provides. Very large cities may have their own mass transportation systems, colleges, hospitals, and jails. Townships and smaller municipalities typically do not provide such services. Instead, county governments may provide these services in the less densely populated areas in which townships and smaller municipalities are located.

Most states initially created **county governments** to assist with the implementation of state policy in geographic subdivisions of the state. Although historically county governments were not self-governing and did not make many of their own public policies, the picture is changing. Today's county governments are taking on increased responsibilities and engaging in more policy making than in years past. County governments provide a growing list of services and benefits, including law enforcement, corrections, highway maintenance, property assessment, tax collection, the recording of legal documents (from voter registration to land transactions), higher education, nursing home care, parks and recreation, and land use planning. Because a single county typically contains numerous municipalities and townships, the services rendered by each of these general-purpose local governments somewhat depend on what services the other local governments with jurisdiction over some of the same geographical area are providing.

There are three basic structures of general-purpose governments: the commission form, the council-mayor form, and the council-manager form. These forms are differentiated by the way the executive and legislative functions are distributed among elected and appointed government officials.

In the **commission** form, which is more common in county and township governments than in other general-purpose governments, voters elect a body of officials who collectively hold the legislative and executive reins of the government. In this form of general-purpose government, there is no independently elected chief executive, and so the commission oversees day-to-day government affairs.

The **council-mayor** form of municipal government is comparable to the **council-executive** form of county government, with both composed of a legislative body, elected by voters, and an independently elected chief executive. Within the council-mayor form of government, political scientists differentiate strong mayors from weak mayors. **Strong mayors** have the traditional powers delegated to elected chief executives (veto power, power to formulate the budget, and power to appoint many executive branch officials). **Weak mayors** have fewer, if any, powers traditionally delegated to elected chief executives.

The **council-manager** (also called **commission-administrator**) form of government, found in many counties and the majority of cities, features an elected body with legislative and executive powers; this council, or commission, hires a professional manager/administrator to oversee the government's daily operations. The appointed manager has no authority to vote on policy but does advise the elected council members on policy matters.

As national and state governments have devolved more responsibilities to general-purpose local governments, and as citizens' demands for services have mounted, general-purpose governments have sought to lighten their workload and decrease their spending. One approach they have used is to establish collaborative working relationships with one or more other local governments in their region. One type of collaborative relationship is a **Council of Governments (COG),** which is a regional agency composed of representatives from several local governments that are sharing resources to address one or more mutual problems. Another type of collaboration is the consolidation of services. In this case, two or more local governments provide services to their communities through one unit, such as

township
a unit of government that serves people living outside municipalities, in rural areas where the population is more dispersed than in areas served by municipal governments

county government
a general-purpose local government created by states to assist them in implementing policy in geographic subdivisions of the state

commission
a form of local government that is more common in county and township governments than in other general-purpose governments and for which voters elect a body of officials who collectively hold legislative and executive powers

council-mayor (council-executive)
a form of general-purpose local government comprising (1) a legislative body elected by voters and (2) an independently elected chief executive

strong mayor
an elected municipal government executive who holds the powers traditionally delegated to elected chief executives (veto power, power to formulate the budget, and power to appoint many executive branch officials)

weak mayor
an elected municipal government executive who holds few, if any, of the powers traditionally delegated to elected chief executives

council-manager (commission-administrator)
a form of general-purpose local government found in many counties and the majority of cities; it is composed of an elected body with legislative and executive powers whose members hire a professional manager to oversee the government's day-to-day operations

Council of Governments (COG)
a regional agency composed of representatives from several local governments who share resources to address one or more mutual problems

a joint police department. In some cases, two local governments have also been consolidated into one. However, voters in most states must approve the consolidation of existing local governments through a referendum, and in the majority of cases, voters do not approve such consolidations because they do not want to lose the local government they know. Voters also fear consolidation will mean poorer-quality services.[41]

In contrast to these collaborative approaches to lightening their burden, general-purpose governments (individually or collectively) can create a new government and delegate to it one specific responsibility, such as fire protection or the management of the sewer system. The newly created local government, with one specific responsibility—known as a single-purpose government—is an independently functioning entity.

Growth in State and Local Governments

	THEN (1957)*	NOW (2010)**
National	1	1
State	48	50
County	3,047	3,033
Municipalities and townships	34,381	36,011
School districts	50,446	13,051
Special districts	14,405	37,381

WHAT'S NEXT?

> Will the conditions that encourage general-purpose governments to create new single-purpose governments change any time in the near future?

> If the number of single-purpose governments continues to grow, what might cause citizens to become more aware of them and to pay more attention to them?

> Will cost concerns encourage citizens to support the consolidation of more local government services, and even consolidation of local governments?

> Will the movement to gain statehood for the District of Columbia win congressional approval, increasing the number of states to fifty-one?

* U.S. Census Bureau, *Statistical Abstract of the United States: 1959*, 80th ed. (Washington, DC: U.S. Government Printing Office, 1959), Table 502.

** U.S. Census Bureau, *Statistical Abstract of the United States: 2010*, 129th ed. (Washington, DC: U.S. Government Printing Office, 2010), Table 416.

Single-Purpose Local Governments

Tens of thousands of general-purpose local governments exist, but there are even more single-purpose governments, and the number keeps growing. A **single-purpose government** provides one service or function to the people living within its borders. The most visible of these governments are school districts. Political scientists usually discuss school districts separately from other single-purpose governments because there are so many of them and because state, not local, governments created them. The number of school districts varies tremendously from state to state; Texas has 1,089, and Virginia has only one. In addition to the 13,051 school district governments in the United States, there are 37,381 other single-purpose governments.[42]

Single-purpose governments typically have a structure comparable to the commission form of general-purpose government and fall into two types: districts and authorities. The most common distinction between a district and an authority is that a district can impose and collect taxes to pay for its services, but an authority cannot do so. Instead, the authority must raise money by selling or renting its services or resources. For example, a water authority sells water, a sewer authority charges for the use of sewers, and a parking authority charges for the use of its parking spaces. In addition, because authorities do not have to deal with the same personnel and financial constraints that general-purpose governments must confront, they have more flexibility in their operations.

Most people are aware of the general-purpose local governments under which they live. Few, however, know much about the single-purpose governments in their community, other than the school district. Moreover, because the NIMBY (not-in-my-backyard) syndrome is alive and well, people rarely take advantage of the open meetings conducted by government—national, state, general-purpose local government, or single-purpose local government—until or unless an action (or a proposed action) of government negatively af-

single-purpose government
a government providing one service or function for residents living within its borders

fects them. Yet democratic governments rest on the principle that government is *by* and *for* the people. For many citizens, the *by* dimension creates an obligation to participate at least reactively, if not proactively. State and local governments provide countless, rich opportunities for citizen participation.

CONCLUSION

THINKING CRITICALLY ABOUT WHAT'S NEXT IN STATE AND LOCAL GOVERNMENT

Contemporary migration of people from locality to locality and from state to state, as well as immigration of people from other countries, fuels intrastate and interstate diversity. Intrastate and interstate diversity in cultures, resources, climate, and demographics produces different political processes and a large variety of public policies as state and local governments respond to the demands of their residents. As the U.S. population becomes ever more diverse, what new services and benefits will citizens call on state and local governments to provide?

State and local governments have always served as laboratories for innovative policies to address long-existing problems as well as for creative policies to address new problems. Over the last half century, the national government has devolved to the states responsibility for many societal problems that have a nationwide affect. Moreover, during economic downturns, state and local governments become even more innovative as they must continue to serve their citizens while experiencing decreased revenues. The economic forecast for state and local governments in the near future is grim. Will states be able to continue to experiment with public policies that address nationwide problems in dire economic times?

At the state and local levels of government, citizens have been successful in reining in tax increases and spending increases through their use of initiatives and referenda. They have also used these modes of direct democracy to enact policies that their elected officials were unable or unwilling to enact. At the same time, citizen displeasure with gridlock in national policy making has been growing. Will the success of initiatives and referenda at the state and local levels lead to a movement to adopt these processes at the national level?

Summary

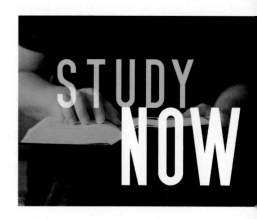

1. Direct Democracy: Letting the People Decide
State and local governments give U.S. citizens opportunities for direct democracy that are not available in the national government. All states provide for some form of referendum, and about 40 percent of the states also provide for citizen initiatives. In addition, about one-third of the states allow citizens to recall elected state officials with whom they are dissatisfied.

2. State Constitutions and Local Charters
Each state has its own constitution, which authorizes state legislators to create local governments through the process of approving local government charters. According to Dillon's rule, the responsibilities of local governments are limited to only those specified in their charters. In recent decades, state governments have expanded their use of home rule charters, approved by local voters, that provide local governments with greater discretion.

3. Diversity in Political Cultures, People, Environment, and Resources
The great diversity in the fifty states affects the demands placed on state and local governments. It also influences the political processes and the policy choices of these

governments, as well as their financial capacity. The more than 89,000 state and local governments operating in the United States can better address this diversity than could one national government.

4. State and Local Government Budgets

Although the U.S. Constitution does not require the national government to balance its budget, state constitutions do mandate balanced state and local operating budgets. The ability of state and local governments to provide the day-to-day services for which they are responsible, many of which are essential to public safety and health, depends on their tax base. Because some states and localities have smaller tax bases than do others, the federal government takes on the role of fiscal equalizer to support those with weaker financial capacities.

5. Responsibilities of State and Local Governments in National Politics

The Constitution delegates to state governments a role in national elections, in the redistricting of national House districts, and in the ratification of amendments to the U.S. Constitution. In addition, state and local governments provide future national officials with government experience, and they test innovative public policies that, if successful, other state and local governments, and even the federal government, might adopt.

6. Institutions of State Government

Although the institutions of the fifty states share certain commonalities, such as a system that balances power among three branches of government, each state government is unique. In addition, state governments differ from the national government in that most states have a plural executive system and most elect rather than appoint state judges.

7. Local Governments

One useful way to differentiate among local governments in the United States is to categorize them as either general-purpose or single-purpose governments. General-purpose governments, which include cities, counties, boroughs, and townships, dispense a variety of services to their citizens. Single-purpose governments, such as school districts that provide elementary and secondary education, deliver one specific service to their citizens.

Key Terms

ballot measure 559

capital budget 567

charter 562

commission 581

Council of Governments (COG) 581

council-manager (commission-administrator) 581

council-mayor (council-executive) 581

county government 580

Dillon's rule 563

essential services 568

general-purpose government 580

home rule 563

home rule charter 563

individualistic political culture 565

legislative referendum 559

merit selection process 580

moralistic political culture 565

municipal government 580

nonpartisan election 580

open meeting laws 558

operating budget 567

partisan election 580

plural executive system 577

popular referendum 559

retention election 580

single-purpose government 582

strong mayor 581

township 580

traditionalistic political culture 565

weak mayor 581

For Review

1. How does direct democracy differ from representative democracy?

2. Differentiate between Dillon's rule and home rule.

3. Explain how diversity in political culture, people, and resources puts different demands on state and local governments and therefore leads to different policies.

4. What essential services do state and local governments provide?

5. Describe two informal functions of the states in national politics.

6. Identify some differences between the three branches of national government and the three branches of state governments.

7. Differentiate between general-purpose governments and single-purpose governments, and give examples of each.

For Critical Thinking and Discussion

1. Which of the many governments that you have interacted with has had the biggest impact on your life to date? What government will have the greatest impact on you after you graduate from college? In your retirement years?

2. Think about the distinctions the text makes among traditionalistic, individualistic, and moralistic political cultures. What would you say is the dominant political culture on your college campus? What is it in your home community? Do you think it would be possible to change these political cultures? Explain.

3. What would be the impact on state and local governments, as well as citizens, if the national government stopped acting as a fiscal equalizer?

4. Given the growth of the international direct democracy movement, do you think Congress would approve, and the states would ratify, an amendment to the U.S. Constitution that authorizes the use of direct democracy (initiative, referendum, and recall) at the national level of government? Explain why or why not.

5. Because the U.S. Constitution establishes minimums in terms of civil rights, states can establish additional rights, such as a voting age lower than 18. Some have called for states to lower the voting age to 16 years old for school board elections. Present an argument in support of this proposal. Present an argument against this proposal.

6. Given the fiscal stress that all governments (national, state, and local) are experiencing, note one national, one state, and one local public service that you are willing to have eliminated. Discuss the negative impacts of your proposed cuts.

7. Voter participation in state and local elections is lower than in national elections. What do you think explains this phenomenon? Discuss one proposal for local government action that you think might increase voter participation in local elections.

MULTIPLE CHOICE: Choose the lettered item that answers the question correctly.

1. All of the following are direct democracy processes except
   a. electing government officials.
   b. initiative.
   c. recall.
   d. referendum.

2. The direct democracy process that includes *citizens* drafting public policy, which is then placed on the Election Day ballot, is called
   a. initiative.
   b. legislative referendum.
   c. popular referendum.
   d. recall.

3. Higher levels of voter turnout occur in states dominated by a(n)
   a. individualistic political culture.
   b. moralistic political culture.
   c. traditionalistic political culture.
   d. libertarian political culture.

4. A state's capital budget can include the costs for all the following items except
   a. bridge and highway construction.
   b. computer systems purchases.
   c. state office buildings construction.
   d. salaries and benefits.

5. The primary source of tax revenue for state governments is
   a. excise taxes.
   b. personal income taxes.
   c. property taxes.
   d. sales taxes.

6. The primary source of tax revenue for local governments is
   a. excise taxes.
   b. personal income taxes.
   c. property taxes.
   d. sales taxes.

7. On average, citizens elect people to the greatest number of positions in
   a. the national executive branch.
   b. the national legislative branch.
   c. the state executive branch.
   d. the state legislative branch.

8. All of the following are examples of general-purpose local governments except
   a. boroughs.
   b. cities.
   c. counties.
   d. school districts.

9. The fastest-growing category of government is
   a. municipal government.
   b. single-purpose government.
   c. state government.
   d. township.

10. Three branches of government are clearly identifiable in
    a. national, state, and local governments.
    b. national and state governments.
    c. state and local governments.
    d. only the national government.

FILL IN THE BLANKS.

11. The California tax-reform ballot measure known as _____ is credited with sparking an increase in citizen use of ballot measures that began in the 1980s and continues today.

12. In forty-nine states, the _____ budget, which covers the costs of day-to-day government functions, must be balanced.

13. The everyday public services provided by state and local governments that are required to prevent chaos and hazardous conditions are collectively labeled _____ services.

14. The overwhelming majority of states have a _____ system that allows voters to elect, on average, seven state executive officials.

15. In a _____ election, candidates are not selected by political parties and the Election Day ballot does not list the candidates' party affiliations.

Answers: 1. a; 2. a; 3. b; 4. d; 5. d; 6. c; 7. c; 8. d; 9. b; 10. b; 11. Proposition 13; 12. operating; 13. essential; 14. plural executive; 15. nonpartisan.

Internet Resources

Census Bureau's Quick Facts
http://quickfacts.census.gov This site is your one stop for state-by-state statistics.

Council of State Governments
www.csg.org A resource for state governments, this site offers training for state leaders and information on the best innovative approaches to the problems confronting states. This Web site also offers current news regarding government in all fifty states.

The National Council of State Legislators
www.ncsl.org This site is a resource for state governments and individuals interested in improving state government operations and understanding state issues, as well as issues of federalism and intergovernmental relations.

The National Governors Association
www.nga.org This site is a source of information on governors, collaborative lobbying efforts of governors, and the impact of national laws on state governments.

Internet Activism

Blog
To join a conversation about your state's government, review the state-by-state list of blogs at **www.stateline.org/live/resources/State_blogs.** To join a conversation about a specific state policy issue of concern to you, review the list of policy blogs at **www.stateline.org/live/resources/Issue_blogs.**

Twitter
http://twitter.com/NCSLCOMM The Communications Division of the National Council of State Legislators (NCSL), the bipartisan organization that serves legislators and staff of states, commonwealths and territories, tweets about state governing bodies, proposed and newly enacted legislation, reports and surveys.

Facebook
www.facebook.com/governing GOVERNING connects America's governors, mayors, state legislators, local council members, other senior governmental officials, and students of state and local government by providing intelligence and analysis on management, policy, and politics to help guide and inspire innovative leaders across state and local government.

YouTube
www.youtube.com/watch?v=6JI4orbn1Nk President Obama addressed the National Governors Association in February 2010 discussing his administration's cooperative work with state governments during the current economic downturn.

Recommended Readings

Beyle, Thad L. *State and Local Government: 2007–2008.* Washington, DC: CQ Press, 2007. The most recent edition of a collection of news articles on the problems and concerns that state and local governments are confronting. Each section begins with an analysis of the most important issues relevant to that section's topic. Topics include politics, media, state institutions, and local governments.

Elazar, Daniel J. *American Federalism: A View from the States,* 2nd ed. New York: Harper & Row, 1972. The seminal work on the political cultures of states.

Maddex, Robert L. *State Constitutions of the United States,* 2nd ed. Washington, DC: CQ Press, 2006. A comprehensive overview of the constitutions of all fifty states, U.S. territories, and Washington, D.C. Covers constitutional history, fundamental rights, branches of government, amendment procedures, special provisions such as direct democracy, and trends in constitutional reforms.

Van Horn, Carl. *The State of the States,* 4th ed. Washington, DC: CQ Press, 2005. A collection of readings that provide a solid overview of the important issues confronting state governments and the behavior of state governmental institutions in the 1980s and early 1990s.

Movies of Interest

The Town That Was (2007)
This film tells the story of the battle in the 1980s between the people of Centralia, Pennsylvania, and the state government over the state's decision to raze the town and relocate its 1,600 citizens. State officials argued that these drastic measures would cost less than the estimated half-billion dollars needed to extinguish the coal mine fire burning below the town since 1962. The film centers on John Lokitis, the youngest of the eleven remaining Centralia residents.

All the King's Men (2006)
Based on a novel by Robert Penn Warren, this film follows the career of Willie Stark, a southern politician running for governor, who woos the citizens of Louisiana with promises of policies to support the lower economic classes. The novel loosely re-creates aspects of the life of Louisiana governor Huey Long.

Jaws (1975)
This popular super-thriller traces the battle between the new, yet experienced, police chief and the mayor over how to handle the crisis posed by a great white shark feasting in the waters off their small island resort town as the Fourth of July approaches. The chief, hired to protect the town's people and tourists, wants to close the beach. The mayor puts tourism and the needed revenue it will bring to the town above the people's safety.

APPENDIX A

THE DECLARATION OF INDEPENDENCE

In Congress, July 4, 1776

THE UNANIMOUS DECLARATION OF THE THIRTEEN UNITED STATES OF AMERICA

When in the Course of human Events, it becomes necessary for one People to dissolve the Political Bands which have connected them with another, and to assume, among the Powers of the Earth, the separate and equal Station to which the Laws of Nature and of Nature's God entitle them, a decent Respect to the Opinions of Mankind requires that they should declare the Causes which impel them to the Separation.

We hold these Truths to be self-evident, that all Men are created equal, that they are endowed, by their Creator, with certain unalienable Rights, that among these are Life, Liberty, and the Pursuit of Happiness.—That to secure these Rights, Governments are instituted among Men, deriving their just Powers from the Consent of the Governed, that whenever any Form of Government becomes destructive of these Ends, it is the Right of the People to alter or to abolish it, and to institute new Government, laying its Foundation on such Principles, and organizing its Powers in such Form, as to them shall seem most likely to effect their Safety and Happiness. Prudence, indeed, will dictate, that Governments long established, should not be changed for light and transient Causes; and accordingly all Experience hath shewn, that Mankind are more disposed to suffer, while Evils are sufferable, than to right themselves by abolishing the Forms to which they are accustomed. But when a long Train of Abuses and Usurpations, pursuing invariably the same Object, evinces a Design to reduce them under absolute Despotism, it is their Right, it is their Duty, to throw off such Government, and to provide new Guards for their future Security. Such has been the patient Sufferance of these Colonies; and such is now the Necessity which constrains them to alter their former Systems of Government. The History of the present King of Great-Britain is a History of repeated Injuries and Usurpations, all having in direct Object the Establishment of an absolute Tyranny over these States. To prove this, let Facts be submitted to a candid World.

He has refused his Assent to Laws, the most wholesome and necessary for the public Good.

He has forbidden his Governors to pass Laws of immediate and pressing Importance, unless suspended in their Operation till his Assent should be obtained; and when so suspended, he has utterly neglected to attend to them.

He has refused to pass other Laws for the Accommodation of large Districts of People, unless those People would relinquish the Right of Representation in the Legislature, a Right inestimable to them, and formidable to Tyranny only.

He has called together Legislative Bodies at Places unusual, uncomfortable, and distant from the Depository of their public Records, for the sole Purpose of fatiguing them into Compliance with his Measures.

He has dissolved Representative Houses repeatedly, for opposing with manly Firmness his Invasions on the Rights of the People.

He has refused for a long Time, after such Dissolutions, to cause others to be elected; whereby the Legislative Powers, incapable of Annihilation, have returned to the People at large for their exercise; the State remaining, in the mean Time, exposed to all the Dangers of Invasion from without, and Convulsions within.

He has endeavoured to prevent the Population of these States; for that Purpose obstructing the Laws for Naturalization of Foreigners; refusing to pass others to encourage their Migrations hither, and raising the Conditions of new Appropriations of Lands.

He has obstructed the Administration of Justice, by refusing his Assent to Laws for establishing Judiciary Powers.

He has made Judges dependent on his Will alone, for the Tenure of their Offices, and the Amount and Payment of their Salaries.

He has erected a Multitude of new Offices, and sent hither Swarms of Officers to harrass our People, and eat out their Substance.

He has kept among us, in Times of Peace, Standing Armies, without the Consent of our Legislatures.

He has affected to render the Military independent of and superior to the Civil Power.

He has combined with others to subject us to a Jurisdiction foreign to our Constitution, and unacknowledged by our Laws; giving his Assent to their Acts of pretended Legislation:

For quartering large Bodies of Armed Troops among us:

For protecting them, by a mock Trial, from Punishment for any Murders which they should commit on the Inhabitants of these States:

For cutting off our Trade with all Parts of the World:

For imposing Taxes on us without our Consent:

For depriving us, in many Cases, of the Benefits of Trial by Jury:

For transporting us beyond Seas to be tried for pretended Offences:

For abolishing the free System of English Laws in a neighbouring Province, establishing therein an arbitrary Government, and enlarging its Boundaries, so as to render it at once an Example and fit Instrument for introducing the same absolute Rule into these Colonies:

For taking away our Charters, abolishing our most valuable Laws, and altering fundamentally the Forms of our Governments:

For suspending our own Legislatures, and declaring themselves invested with Power to legislate for us in all Cases whatsoever.

He has abdicated Government here, by declaring us out of his Protection, and waging War against us.

He has plundered our Seas, ravaged our Coasts, burnt our Towns, and destroyed the Lives of our People.

He is, at this Time, transporting large Armies of foreign Mercenaries to complete the Works of Death, Desolation, and Tyranny, already begun with Circumstances of Cruelty and Perfidy, scarcely paralleled in the most barbarous Ages, and totally unworthy the Head of a civilized Nation.

He has constrained our fellow Citizens taken Captive on the high Seas to bear Arms against their Country, to become the Executioners of their Friends and Brethren, or to fall themselves by their Hands.

He has excited domestic Insurrections amongst us, and has endeavoured to bring on the Inhabitants of our Frontiers, the merciless Indian Savages, whose known Rule of Warfare, is an undistinguished Destruction, of all Ages, Sexes and Conditions.

In every Stage of these Oppressions we have Petitioned for Redress in the most humble Terms: Our repeated Petitions have been answered only by repeated Injury. A Prince, whose Character is thus marked by every Act which may define a Tyrant, is unfit to be the Ruler of a free People.

Nor have we been wanting in Attentions to our British Brethren. We have warned them, from Time to Time of Attempts by their Legislature to extend an unwarrantable Jurisdiction over us. We have reminded them of the Circumstances of our Emigration and Settlement here. We have appealed to their native Justice and Magnanimity, and we have conjured them by the Ties of our common Kindred to disavow these Usurpations, which would inevitably interrupt our Connections and Correspondence. They too have been deaf to the Voice of Justice and of Consanguinity. We must, therefore, acquiesce in the Necessity, which denounces our Separation, and hold them, as we hold the Rest of Mankind, Enemies in War, in Peace Friends.

We, therefore, the Representatives of the UNITED STATES OF AMERICA, in General Congress Assembled, appealing to the Supreme Judge of the World for the Rectitude of our Intentions, do, in the Name, and by Authority of the good People of these Colonies, solemnly Publish and Declare, That these United Colonies are, and of Right ought to be, Free and Independent States; that they are absolved from all Allegiance to the British Crown, and that all political Connection between them and the State of Great-Britain, is and ought to be totally dissolved; and that as Free and Independent States, they have full Power to levy War, conclude Peace, contract Alliances, establish Commerce, and to do all other Acts and Things which Independent States may of Right do. And for the Support of this Declaration, with a firm Reliance on the Protection of Divine Providence, we mutually pledge to each other our Lives, our Fortunes, and our sacred Honour.

John Hancock.

NEW-HAMPSHIRE
Josiah Bartlett
William Whipple
Matthew Thornton

MASSACHUSETTS BAY
Samuel Adams
John Adams
Robert Treat Paine
Elbridge Gerry

RHODE ISLAND
Stephen Hopkins
William Ellery

CONNECTICUT
Roger Sherman
Samuel Huntington
William Williams
Oliver Wolcott

NEW YORK
William Floyd
Philip Livingston
Francis Lewis
Lewis Morris

NEW JERSEY
Richard Stockton
John Witherspoon
Francis Hopkinson
John Hart
Abraham Clark

PENNSYLVANIA
Robert Morris
Benjamin Rush
Benjamin Franklin
John Morton
George Clymer
James Smith
George Taylor
James Wilson
George Ross

DELAWARE
Caesar Rodney
George Read
Thomas McKean

MARYLAND
Samuel Chase
William Paca
Thomas Stone
Charles Carroll

VIRGINIA
George Wythe
Richard Henry Lee
Thomas Jefferson
Benjamin Harrison
Thomas Nelson, Jr.
Francis Lightfoot Lee
Carter Braxton

NORTH CAROLINA
William Hooper
Joseph Hewes
John Penn

SOUTH CAROLINA
Edward Rutledge
Thomas Heyward, Jr.
Thomas Lynch, Jr.
Arthur Middleton

GEORGIA
Button Gwinnett
Lyman Hall
George Walton

APPENDIX B

THE FEDERALIST NO. 10

November 22, 1787

JAMES MADISON

TO THE PEOPLE OF THE STATE OF NEW YORK:

Among the numerous advantages promised by a well constructed Union, none deserves to be more accurately developed than its tendency to break and control the violence of faction. The friend of popular governments never finds himself so much alarmed for their character and fate, as when he contemplates their propensity to this dangerous vice. He will not fail, therefore, to set a due value on any plan which, without violating the principles to which he is attached, provides a proper cure for it. The instability, injustice, and confusion introduced into the public councils, have, in truth, been the mortal diseases under which popular governments have everywhere perished; as they continue to be the favorite and fruitful topics from which the adversaries to liberty derive their most specious declamations. The valuable improvements made by the American constitutions on the popular models, both ancient and modern, cannot certainly be too much admired; but it would be an unwarrantable partiality, to contend that they have as effectually obviated the danger on this side, as was wished and expected. Complaints are everywhere heard from our most considerate and virtuous citizens, equally the friends of public and private faith, and of public and personal liberty, that our governments are too unstable, that the public good is disregarded in the conflicts of rival parties, and that measures are too often decided, not according to the rules of justice and the rights of the minor party, but by the superior force of an interested and overbearing majority. However anxiously we may wish that these complaints had no foundation, the evidence, of known facts will not permit us to deny that they are in some degree true. It will be found, indeed, on a candid review of our situation, that some of the distresses under which we labor have been erroneously charged on the operation of our governments; but it will be found, at the same time, that other causes will not alone account for many of our heaviest misfortunes; and, particularly, for that prevailing and increasing distrust of public engagements, and alarm for private rights, which are echoed from one end of the continent to the other. These must be chiefly, if not wholly, effects of the unsteadiness and injustice with which a factious spirit has tainted our public administrations.

By a faction, I understand a number of citizens, whether amounting to a majority or a minority of the whole, who are united and actuated by some common impulse of passion, or of interest, adversed to the rights of other citizens, or to the permanent and aggregate interests of the community.

There are two methods of curing the mischiefs of faction: the one, by removing its causes; the other, by controlling its effects.

There are again two methods of removing the causes of faction: the one, by destroying the liberty which is essential to its existence; the other, by giving to every citizen the same opinions, the same passions, and the same interests.

It could never be more truly said than of the first remedy, that it was worse than the disease. Liberty is to faction what air is to fire, an aliment without which it instantly expires. But it could not be less folly to abolish liberty, which is essential to political life, because it nourishes faction, than it would be to wish the annihilation of air, which is essential to animal life, because it imparts to fire its destructive agency.

The second expedient is as impracticable as the first would be unwise. As long as the reason of man continues fallible, and he is at liberty to exercise it, different opinions will be formed. As long as the connection subsists between his reason and his self-love, his opinions and his passions will have a reciprocal influence on each other; and the former will be objects to which the latter will attach themselves. The diversity in the faculties of men, from which the rights of property originate, is not less an insuperable obstacle to a uniformity of interests. The protection of these faculties is the first object of government. From the protection of different and unequal faculties of acquiring property, the possession of different degrees and kinds of property immediately results; and from the influence of these on the sentiments and views of the respective proprietors, ensues a division of the society into different interests and parties.

The latent causes of faction are thus sown in the nature of man; and we see them everywhere brought into different degrees of activity, according to the different circumstances of civil society. A zeal for different opinions concerning religion, concerning government, and many other points, as well of speculation as of practice; an attachment to different leaders ambitiously contending for pre-eminence and power; or to persons of other descriptions whose fortunes have been interesting to the human passions, have, in turn, divided mankind into parties, inflamed them with mutual animosity, and rendered them much more disposed to vex and oppress each other than to co-operate for their common good. So strong is this propensity of mankind to fall into mutual animosities, that where no substantial occasion presents itself, the most frivolous and fanciful distinctions have been sufficient to kindle their unfriendly passions and excite their most violent conflicts. But the most common and durable source of factions has been the various and unequal distribution of property. Those who hold and those who are without property have ever formed distinct interests in society. Those who are creditors, and those who are debtors, fall under a like discrimination. A landed interest, a manufacturing interest, a mercantile interest, a moneyed interest, with many lesser interests, grow up of necessity in civilized nations, and divide them into different classes, actuated by different sentiments and views. The regulation of these various and interfering interests forms the principal task of modern legislation, and involves the spirit of party and faction in the necessary and ordinary operations of the government.

No man is allowed to be a judge in his own cause, because his interest would certainly bias his judgment, and, not improbably, corrupt his integrity. With equal, nay with greater reason, a body of men are unfit to be both judges and parties at the same time; yet what are many of the most important acts of legislation, but so many judicial determinations, not indeed concerning the rights of single persons, but concerning the rights of large bodies of citizens? And what are the different classes of legislators but advocates and parties to the causes which they determine? Is a law proposed concerning private debts? It is a question to which the creditors are parties on one side and the debtors on the other. Justice ought to hold the balance between them. Yet the parties are, and must be, themselves the judges; and the most numerous party, or, in other words, the most powerful faction must be expected to prevail. Shall domestic manufactures be encouraged, and in what degree, by restrictions on foreign manufactures? are questions which would be differently decided by the landed and the manufacturing classes, and probably by neither with a sole regard to justice and the public good. The apportionment of taxes on the various descriptions of property is an act which seems to require the most exact impartiality; yet there is, perhaps, no legislative act in which greater opportunity and temptation are given to a predominant party to trample on the rules of justice. Every shilling with which they overburden the inferior number, is a shilling saved to their own pockets.

It is in vain to say that enlightened statesmen will be able to adjust these clashing interests, and render them all subservient to the public good. Enlightened statesmen will not always be at the helm. Nor, in many cases, can such an adjustment be made at all without taking into view indirect and remote considerations, which will rarely prevail over the immediate interest which one party may find in disregarding the rights of another or the good of the whole.

The inference to which we are brought is, that the causes of faction cannot be removed, and that relief is only to be sought in the means of controlling its *effects*.

If a faction consists of less than a majority, relief is supplied by the republican principle, which enables the majority to defeat its sinister views by regular vote. It may clog the administration, it may convulse the society; but it will be unable to execute and mask its violence under the forms of the Constitution. When a majority is included in a faction, the form of popular government, on the other hand, enables it to sacrifice to its ruling passion or interest both the public good and the rights of other citizens. To secure the public good and private rights against the danger of such a faction, and at the same time to preserve the spirit and the form of popular government, is then the great object to which our inquiries are directed. Let me add that it is the great desideratum by which this form of government can be rescued from the opprobrium under which it has so long labored, and be recommended to the esteem and adoption of mankind.

By what means is this object attainable? Evidently by one of two only. Either the existence of the same passion or interest in a majority at the same time must be prevented, or the majority, having such coexistent passion or interest, must be rendered, by their number and local situation, unable to concert and carry into effect schemes of oppression. If the impulse and the opportunity be suffered to coincide, we well know that neither moral nor religious motives can be relied on as an adequate control. They are not found to be such on the injustice and violence of individuals, and lose their efficacy in proportion to the number combined together, that is, in proportion as their efficacy becomes needful.

From this view of the subject it may be concluded that a pure democracy, by which I mean a society consisting of a small number of citizens, who assemble and administer the government in person, can admit of no cure for the mischiefs of faction. A common passion or interest will, in almost every case, be felt by a majority of the whole; a communication and concert result from the form of government itself; and there is nothing to check the inducements to sacrifice the weaker party or an obnoxious individual. Hence it is that such democracies have ever been spectacles of turbulence and contention; have ever been found incompatible with personal security or the rights of property; and have in general been as short in their lives as they have been violent in their deaths. Theoretic politicians, who have patronized this species of government, have erroneously supposed that by reducing mankind to a perfect equality in their political rights, they would, at the same time, be perfectly equalized and assimilated in their possessions, their opinions, and their passions.

A republic, by which I mean a government in which the scheme of representation takes place, opens a different prospect, and promises the cure for which we are seeking. Let us examine the points in which it varies from pure democracy, and we shall comprehend both the nature of the cure and the efficacy which it must derive from the Union.

The two great points of difference between a democracy and a republic are: first, the delegation of the government, in the latter, to a small number of citizens elected by the rest; secondly, the greater number of citizens, and greater sphere of country, over which the latter may be extended.

The effect of the first difference is, on the one hand, to refine and enlarge the public views, by passing them through the medium of a chosen body of citizens, whose wisdom may best discern the true interest of their country, and whose patriotism and love of justice will be least likely to sacrifice it to temporary or partial considerations. Under such a regulation, it may well happen that the public voice, pronounced by the representatives of the people, will be more consonant to the public good than if pronounced by the people themselves, convened for the purpose. On the other hand, the effect may be inverted. Men of factious tempers, of local prejudices, or of sinister designs, may, by intrigue, by corruption, or by other means, first obtain the suffrages, and then betray the interests, of the people. The question resulting is, whether small or extensive republics are more favorable to the election of proper guardians of the public weal; and it is clearly decided in favor of the latter by two obvious considerations:

In the first place, it is to be remarked that, however small the republic may be, the representatives must be raised to a certain number, in order to guard against the cabals of a few; and that, however large it may be, they must be limited to a certain number, in order to guard against the confusion of a multitude. Hence, the number of representatives in the two cases not being in proportion to that of the two constituents, and being proportionally greater in the small republic, it follows that, if the proportion of fit characters be not less in the large than in the small republic, the former will present a greater option, and consequently a greater probability of a fit choice.

In the next place, as each representative will be chosen by a greater number of citizens in the large than in the small republic, it will be more difficult for unworthy candidates to practice with success the vicious arts by which elections are too often carried; and the suffrages of the people being more free, will be more likely to centre in men who possess the most attractive merit and the most diffusive and established characters.

It must be confessed that in this, as in most other cases, there is a mean, on both sides of which inconveniences will be found to lie. By enlarging too much the number of electors, you render the representatives too little acquainted with all their local circumstances and lesser interests; as by reducing it too much, you render him unduly attached to these, and too little fit to comprehend and pursue great and national objects. The federal Constitution forms a happy combination in this respect; the great and aggregate interests being referred to the national, the local and particular to the State legislatures.

The other point of difference is, the greater number of citizens and extent of territory which may be brought within the compass of republican than of democratic government; and it is this circumstance principally which renders factious combinations less to be dreaded in the former than in the latter. The smaller the society, the fewer probably will be the distinct parties and interests composing it; the fewer the distinct parties and interests, the more frequently will a majority be found of the same party; and the smaller the number of individuals composing a majority, and the smaller the compass within which they are placed, the more easily will they concert and execute their plans of oppression. Extend the sphere, and you take in a greater variety of parties and interests; you make it less probable that a majority of the whole will have a common motive to invade the rights of other citizens; or if such a common motive exists, it will be more difficult for all who feel it to discover their own strength, and to act in unison with each other. Besides other impediments, it may be remarked that, where there is a consciousness of unjust or dis-

honorable purposes, communication is always checked by distrust in proportion to the number whose concurrence is necessary.

Hence, it clearly appears, that the same advantage which a republic has over a democracy, in controlling the effects of faction, is enjoyed by a large over a small republic,—is enjoyed by the Union over the States composing it. Does the advantage consist in the substitution of representatives whose enlightened views and virtuous sentiments render them superior to local prejudices and schemes of injustice? It will not be denied that the representation of the Union will be most likely to possess these requisite endowments. Does it consist in the greater security afforded by a greater variety of parties, against the event of any one party being able to outnumber and oppress the rest? In an equal degree does the increased variety of parties comprised within the Union, increase this security? Does it, in fine, consist in the greater obstacles opposed to the concert and accomplishment of the secret wishes of an unjust and interested majority? Here, again, the extent of the Union gives it the most palpable advantage.

The influence of factious leaders may kindle a flame within their particular States, but will be unable to spread a general conflagration through the other States. A religious sect may degenerate into a political faction in a part of the Confederacy; but the variety of sects dispersed over the entire face of it must secure the national councils against any danger from that source. A rage for paper money, for an abolition of debts, for an equal division of property, or for any other improper or wicked project, will be less apt to pervade the whole body of the Union than a particular member of it; in the same proportion as such a malady is more likely to taint a particular county or district, than an entire State.

In the extent and proper structure of the Union, therefore, we behold a republican remedy for the diseases most incident to republican government. And according to the degree of pleasure and pride we feel in being republicans, ought to be our zeal in cherishing the spirit and supporting the character of Federalists.

Publius

February 6, 1788

JAMES MADISON

To the People of the State of New York:

To what expedient, then, shall we finally resort, for maintaining in practice the necessary partition of power among the several departments, as laid down in the Constitution? The only answer that can be given is, that as all these exterior provisions are found to be inadequate, the defect must be supplied, by so contriving the interior structure of the government as that its several constituent parts may, by their mutual relations, be the means of keeping each other in their proper places. Without presuming to undertake a full development of this important idea, I will hazard a few general observations, which may perhaps place it in a clearer light, and enable us to form a more correct judgment of the principles and structure of the government planned by the convention.

In order to lay a due foundation for that separate and distinct exercise of the different powers of government, which to a certain extent is admitted on all hands to be essential to the preservation of liberty, it is evident that each department should have a will of its own; and consequently should be so constituted that the members of each should have as little agency as possible in the appointment of the members of the others. Were this principle rigorously adhered to, it would require that all the appointments for the supreme executive, legislative, and judiciary magistracies should be drawn from the same fountain of authority, the people, through channels having no communication whatever with one another. Perhaps such a plan of constructing the several departments would be less difficult in practice than it may in contemplation appear. Some difficulties, however, and some additional expense would attend the execution of it. Some deviations, therefore, from the principle must be admitted. In the constitution of the judiciary department in particular, it might be inexpedient to insist rigorously on the principle: first, because peculiar qualifications being essential in the members, the primary consideration ought to be to select that mode of choice which best secures these qualifications; secondly, because the permanent tenure by which the appointments are held in that department, must soon destroy all sense of dependence on the authority conferring them.

It is equally evident, that the members of each department should be as little dependent as possible on those of the others, for the emoluments annexed to their offices. Were the executive magistrate, or the judges, not independent of the legislature in this particular, their independence in every other would be merely nominal.

But the great security against a gradual concentration of the several powers in the same department, consists in giving to those who administer each department the necessary constitutional means and personal motives to resist encroachments of the others. The provision for defense must in this, as in all other cases, be made commensurate to the danger of attack. Ambition must be made to counteract ambition. The interest of the man must be connected with the constitutional rights of the place. It may be a reflection on human nature, that such devices should be necessary to control the abuses of government. But what is government itself, but the greatest of all reflections on human nature? If men were angels, no government would be necessary. If angels were to govern men, neither external nor internal controls on government would be necessary. In framing a government which is to be administered by men over men, the great difficulty lies in this: you must first enable the government to control the governed; and in the next place oblige it to control itself. A dependence on the people is, no doubt, the primary control on the government; but experience has taught mankind the necessity of auxiliary precautions.

This policy of supplying, by opposite and rival interests, the defect of better motives, might be traced through the whole system of human affairs, private as well as public. We see it particularly displayed in all the subordinate distributions of power, where the constant aim is to divide and arrange the several offices in such a manner as that each may be a check on the other—that the private interest of every individual may be a sentinel over the public rights. These inventions of prudence cannot be less requisite in the distribution of the supreme powers of the State.

But it is not possible to give to each department an equal power of self-defense. In republican government, the legislative authority necessarily predominates. The remedy for this inconveniency is to divide the legislature into different branches; and to render them, by different modes of election and different principles of action, as little connected with each other as the nature of their common functions and their common dependence on the society will admit. It may even be necessary to guard against dangerous encroachments by still further precautions. As the weight of the legislative authority requires that it should be thus divided, the weakness of the executive may require, on the other hand, that it should be fortified. An absolute negative on the legislature appears, at first view, to be the natural defense with which the executive magistrate should be armed. But perhaps it would be neither altogether safe nor alone sufficient. On ordinary occasions it might not be exerted with the requisite firmness, and on extraordinary occasions it might be perfidiously abused. May not this defect of an absolute negative be supplied by some qualified connection between this weaker department and the weaker branch of the stronger department, by which the latter may be led to support the constitutional rights of the former, without being too much detached from the rights of its own department?

If the principles on which these observations are founded be just, as I persuade myself they are, and they be applied as a criterion to the several State constitutions, and to the federal Constitution it will be found that if the latter does not perfectly correspond with them, the former are infinitely less able to bear such a test.

There are, moreover, two considerations particularly applicable to the federal system of America, which place that system in a very interesting point of view.

First. In a single republic, all the power surrendered by the people is submitted to the administration of a single government; and the usurpations are guarded against by a division of the government into distinct and separate departments. In the compound republic of America, the power surrendered by the people is first divided between two distinct governments, and then the portion allotted to each subdivided among distinct and separate departments. Hence a double security arises to the rights of the people. The different governments will control each other, at the same time that each will be controlled by itself.

Second. It is of great importance in a republic not only to guard the society against the oppression of its rulers, but to guard one part of the society against the injustice of the other part. Different interests necessarily exist in different classes of citizens. If a majority be united by a common interest, the rights of the minority will be insecure. There are but two methods of providing against this evil: the one by creating a will in the community independent of the majority—that is, of the society itself; the other, by comprehending in the society so many separate descriptions of citizens as will render an unjust combination of a majority of the whole very improbable, if not impracticable. The first method prevails in all governments possessing an hereditary or self-appointed authority. This, at best, is but a precarious security; because a power independent of the society may as well espouse the unjust views of the major, as the rightful interests of the minor party, and may possibly be turned against both parties. The second method will be exemplified in the federal republic of the United States. Whilst all authority in it will be derived from and dependent on the society, the society itself will be broken into so many parts, interests, and classes of citizens, that the rights of individuals, or of the minority, will be in little danger from interested combinations of the majority. In a free government the security for civil rights must be the same as that for religious rights. It consists in the one case in the multiplicity of interests, and

in the other in the multiplicity of sects. The degree of security in both cases will depend on the number of interests and sects; and this may be presumed to depend on the extent of country and number of people comprehended under the same government. This view of the subject must particularly recommend a proper federal system to all the sincere and considerate friends of republican government, since it shows that in exact proportion as the territory of the Union may be formed into more circumscribed Confederacies, or States oppressive combinations of a majority will be facilitated: the best security, under the republican forms, for the rights of every class of citizens, will be diminished: and consequently the stability and independence of some member of the government, the only other security, must be proportionately increased. Justice is the end of government. It is the end of civil society. It ever has been and ever will be pursued until it be obtained, or until liberty be lost in the pursuit. In a society under the forms of which the stronger faction can readily unite and oppress the weaker, anarchy may as truly be said to reign as in a state of nature, where the weaker individual is not secured against the violence of the stronger; and as, in the latter state, even the stronger individuals are prompted, by the uncertainty of their condition, to submit to a government which may protect the weak as well as themselves; so, in the former state, will the more powerful factions or parties be gradually induced, by a like motive, to wish for a government which will protect all parties, the weaker as well as the more powerful. It can be little doubted that if the State of Rhode Island was separated from the Confederacy and left to itself, the insecurity of rights under the popular form of government within such narrow limits would be displayed by such reiterated oppressions of factious majorities that some power altogether independent of the people would soon be called for by the voice of the very factions whose misrule had proved the necessity of it. In the extended republic of the United States, and among the great variety of interests, parties, and sects which it embraces, a coalition of a majority of the whole society could seldom take place on any other principles than those of justice and the general good; whilst there being thus less danger to a minor from the will of a major party, there must be less pretext, also, to provide for the security of the former, by introducing into the government a will not dependent on the latter, or, in other words, a will independent of the society itself. It is no less certain than it is important, notwithstanding the contrary opinions which have been entertained, that the larger the society, provided it lie within a practical sphere, the more duly capable it will be of self-government. And happily for the *republican cause*, the practicable sphere may be carried to a very great extent, by a judicious modification and mixture of the *federal principle*.

Publius

THE DECLARATION OF SENTIMENTS

Seneca Falls Conference, 1848

When, in the course of human events, it becomes necessary for one portion of the family of man to assume among the people of the earth a position different from that which they have hitherto occupied, but one to which the laws of nature and of nature's God entitle them, a decent respect to the opinions of mankind requires that they should declare the causes that impel them to such a course.

We hold these truths to be self-evident: that all men and women are created equal; that they are endowed by their Creator with certain inalienable rights; that among these are life, liberty, and the pursuit of happiness; that to secure these rights governments are instituted, deriving their just powers from the consent of the governed. Whenever any form of government becomes destructive of these ends, it is the right of those who suffer from it to refuse allegiance to it, and to insist upon the institution of a new government, laying its foundation on such principles, and organizing its powers in such form, as to them shall seem most likely to effect their safety and happiness. Prudence, indeed, will dictate that governments long established should not be changed for light and transient causes; and accordingly all experience hath shown that mankind are more disposed to suffer, while evils are sufferable, than to right themselves by abolishing the forms to which they are accustomed. But when a long train of abuses and usurpations, pursuing invariably the same object, evinces a design to reduce them under absolute despotism, it is their duty to throw off such government, and to provide new guards for their future security. Such has been the patient sufferance of the women under this government, and such is now the necessity which constrains them to demand the equal station to which they are entitled.

The history of mankind is a history of repeated injuries and usurpations on the part of man toward woman, having in direct object the establishment of an absolute tyranny over her. To prove this, let facts be submitted to a candid world.

He has never permitted her to exercise her inalienable right to the elective franchise.

He has compelled her to submit to laws, in the formation of which she had no voice.

He has withheld from her rights which are given to the most ignorant and degraded men—both natives and foreigners.

Having deprived her of this first right of a citizen, the elective franchise, thereby leaving her without representation in the halls of legislation, he has oppressed her on all sides.

He has made her, if married, in the eye of the law, civilly dead.

He has taken from her all right in property, even to the wages she earns.

He has made her, morally, an irresponsible being, as she can commit many crimes with impunity, provided they be done in the presence of her husband. In the covenant of marriage, she is compelled to promise obedience to her husband, he becoming, to all intents and purposes, her master—the law giving him power to deprive her of her liberty, and to administer chastisement.

He has so framed the laws of divorce, as to what shall be the proper causes, and in case of separation, to whom the guardianship of the children shall be given, as to be wholly regardless of the happiness of women—the law, in all cases, going upon a false supposition of the supremacy of man, and giving all power into his hands.

After depriving her of all rights as a married woman, if single, and the owner of property, he has taxed her to support a government which recognizes her only when her property can be made profitable to it.

He has monopolized nearly all the profitable employments, and from those she is permitted to follow, she receives but a scanty remuneration. He closes against her all the avenues to wealth and distinction which he considers most honorable to himself. As a teacher of theology, medicine, or law, she is not known.

He has denied her the facilities for obtaining a thorough education, all colleges being closed against her.

He allows her in church, as well as state, but a subordinate position, claiming apostolic authority for her exclusion from the ministry, and, with some exceptions, from any public participation in the affairs of the church.

He has created a false public sentiment by giving to the world a different code of morals for men and women, by which moral delinquencies which exclude women from society, are not only tolerated, but deemed of little account in man.

He has usurped the prerogative of Jehovah himself, claiming it as his right to assign for her a sphere of action, when that belongs to her conscience and to her God.

He has endeavored, in every way that he could, to destroy her confidence in her own powers, to lessen her self-respect, and to make her willing to lead a dependent and abject life.

Now, in view of this entire disfranchisement of one-half the people of this country, their social and religious degradation—in view of the unjust laws above mentioned, and because women do feel themselves aggrieved, oppressed, and fraudulently deprived of their most sacred rights, we insist that they have immediate admission to all the rights and privileges which belong to them as citizens of the United States.

In entering upon the great work before us, we anticipate no small amount of misconception, misrepresentation, and ridicule; but we shall use every instrumentality within our power to effect our object. We shall employ agents, circulate tracts, petition the State and national Legislatures, and endeavor to enlist the pulpit and the press in our behalf. We hope this Convention will be followed by a series of Conventions, embracing every part of the country.

Firmly relying upon the final triumph of the Right and the True, we do this day affix our signatures to this declaration.

Harriet Cady Eaton
Elizabeth M'Clintock
Mary M'Clintock
Margaret Pryor
Eunice Newton Foote
Margaret Schooley
Catherine F. Stebbins
Mary Ann Frink
Lydia Mount
Delia Matthews
Catharine C. Paine
Mary H. Hallowell
Sarah Hallowell
Catharine Shaw
Deborah Scott
Mary Gilbert
Sophrone Taylor
Cynthia Davis
Hannah Plant
Lucy Jones
Sarah Whitney
Elizabeth Conklin
Lucretia Coffin Mott
Mary Ann M'Clintock
Susan Quinn
Mary S. Mirror
Phebe King
Julia Ann Drake
Charlotte Woodard
Martha Underhill
Dorothy Matthews
Eunice Baker

Sarah R. Woods
Lydia Gild
Sarah Hoffman
Elizabeth Leslie
Martha Ridley
Rachel D. Bonnel
Betsey Tewksbury
Rhoda Palmer
Margaret Jenkins
Cynthia Fuller
Mary Martin
P. A. Culvert
Susan R. Doty
Rebecca Race
Martha Coffin Wright
Jane C. Hunt
Sarah A. Mosher
Mary E. Vail
Lucy Spaulding
Lavinia Latham
Sarah Smith
Eliza Martin
Maria E. Wilbur
Elizabeth D. Smith
Caroline Barker
Ann Porter
Experience Gibbs
Antoinette E. Segur
Hannah J. Latham
Sarah Sisson
Malvina Seymour
Phebe Mosher

Joel Bunker
Isaac Van Tassel
Thomas Dell
E. W. Capron
Stephen Shear
Henry Hatley
Amy Post
Frederick Douglass
Richard P. Hunt
Samuel D. Tillman
Justin Williams
Elisha Foote
Henry W. Seymour
David Salding
William G. Barker
Elias J. Doty
John Jones
William S. Dell
William Burroughs
Azaliah Schooley
Robert Smalldridge
Jacob Matthews
Charles L. Hoskins
Thomas M'Clintock
Saron Phillips
Jacob Chamberlain
Johnathan Metcalf
Nathan J. Milliken
S. E. Woodworth
Edward F. Underhill
George W. Pryor

GLOSSARY

A

absentee voting The casting of a ballot in advance by mail in situations where illness, travel, or other circumstances prevent voters from voting in their precinct.

administrative adjudication The process by which agencies resolve disputes over the implementation of their administrative rules.

administrative discretion The authority delegated to bureaucrats to use their expertise and judgment when determining how to implement public policy.

administrative rule making The process by which an independent commission or agency fills in the details of a vague law by formulating, proposing, and approving rules, regulations, and standards that will be enforced to implement the policy.

advice and consent The Senate's authority to approve or reject the president's top appointments.

affirmative action In the employment arena, intentional efforts to recruit, hire, train, and promote underutilized categories of workers (women and minority men); in higher education, intentional efforts to diversify the student body.

agency review Part of the committee or subcommittee process of considering a bill, wherein committee members ask executive agencies that would administer the law for written comments on the measure.

agenda setting The determination by Congress of which public issues the government should consider for legislation.

agents of socialization The individuals, organizations, and institutions that facilitate the acquisition of political views.

al-Qaeda A radical international Islamic fundamentalist terror organization.

American dream The belief that in the United States hard work and persistence will reap a financially secure, happy and healthy life, with upward social mobility.

amicus curiae brief ("friend of the court" brief) A document submitted by parties interested in a certain case or issue in an attempt to provide the Court with information that may be used to decide the case.

Anti-Federalists Individuals who opposed ratification of the Constitution because they were deeply suspicious of the powers it gave to the national government and of the impact these powers would have on states' authority and individual freedoms.

appellate jurisdiction The authority of a court to review the decision reached by another court in a case.

appropriation law A law that gives bureaucracies and other government entities the legal authority to spend money.

approval ratings The percentage of survey respondents who say that they "approve" or "strongly approve" of the way the president is doing his job.

articles of impeachment Charges against the president during an impeachment.

attentive public The segment of voters who pay careful attention to political issues.

Australian ballot A secret ballot prepared by the government, distributed to all eligible voters, and, when balloting is completed, counted by government officials in an unbiased fashion, without corruption or regard to individual preferences.

authoritarianism A system of government in which the government holds strong powers but is checked by some forces.

authorization law A law that provides the plan of action to address a given societal concern and identifies the executive branch unit that will put the plan into effect.

B

bad tendency test A standard established in the 1925 case *Gitlow v. New York,* whereby any speech that has the tendency to incite crime or disturb the public peace can be silenced.

balance of power system A system of international alliances that, in theory, would balance the power of one group of nations against the power of another group and thus discourage war.

balanced budget A budget in which the government's expenditures are equal to or less than its revenues.

balanced ticket The selection of a running mate who brings diversity of ideology, geographic region, age, gender, race, or ethnicity to the slate.

ballot measure Any proposed policy that, as the result of an initiative or a referendum, wins a place on the ballot for voters to approve or reject.

bandwidth The amount of data that can travel through a network in a given time period.

bicameral Describes a legislative body composed of two chambers.

bill A proposed piece of legislation.

bill of rights A written list of citizens' liberties within a constitution that establishes a limited government by ensuring that both the people and the government know what freedoms the government cannot violate.

Bill of Rights The first ten amendments to the Constitution, which were ratified in 1791, constituting an enumeration of the individual liberties with which the government is forbidden to interfere.

Black Codes Laws passed immediately after the Civil War by the confederate states that limited the rights of "freemen" (former slaves).

blanket primary A type of primary that allows voters to vote in either party's primary, and voters can choose to vote in *both* parties' primaries for different offices.

block grant The intergovernmental transfer of money that has fewer conditions of aid than a categorical grant and is used for broadly defined policy areas; it is distributed based on complicated formulas.

blogosphere A community, or social network, of bloggers.

brief A document detailing the legal argument for the desired outcome in a court case.

brinkmanship The Cold War–era practice of fooling the enemy by going to the edge (the brink), even if the party using the brinkmanship strategy had no intention of following it through.

Brown v. Board of Education of Topeka This 1954 Supreme Court decision ruled that segregated schools violated the equal protection clause of the Fourteenth Amendment.

budget authority The authority provided by law for agencies to obligate government spending.

budget deficit More money spent than collected through revenues.

budget reconciliation The annual process of rewriting authorization legislation to comply with the expenditure ceiling and revenue floor of the concurrent budget resolution for the upcoming fiscal year.

budget surplus Money left over after all expenses are paid.

bureaucracy Any organization with a hierarchical structure; most commonly used to designate a government agency or the collection of all national executive branch organizations.

bureaucrats People employed in a government executive branch unit to implement public policy; a public administrator; a public servant.

Bush Doctrine The argument, articulated by President George W. Bush, that unilateral action directly targeted at an enemy is both justifiable and feasible.

business regulation Government rules, regulations, and standards, directed at protecting competition in the marketplace.

C

cabinet The group of experts chosen by the president to serve as advisers on running the country.

campaign consultant A paid professional who specializes in the overall management of political campaigns or an aspect of campaigns.

campaign manager A professional whose duties comprise a variety of strategic and managerial tasks, from fund-raising to staffing a campaign.

campaign strategy The blueprint for the campaign, including a budget and fund-raising plan, an advertising strategy, a staffing plan.

candidate committees Organizations that candidates form to support their individual election.

candidate-centered campaign A campaign in which the individual seeking election, rather than an entire party slate, is the focus.

capital budget A budget that accounts for the costs and revenues for expensive building and purchasing projects from which citizens will benefit for many years and for which governments can borrow money.

capitalism An economic system in which the means of producing wealth are privately owned and operated to produce profits.

casework Personal work by a member of Congress on behalf of a constituent or group of constituents, typically aimed at getting the government to do something the constituent wants done.

cash transfer The direct provision of cash (in forms including checks, debit cards, and tax breaks) to eligible individuals or to providers of goods or services to eligible individuals.

categorical formula grant The intergovernmental transfer of money for a specified program area for which the amount of money a government is eligible to receive is based on a legislated formula.

categorical project grant The intergovernmental transfer of money for a specified program area for which recipients compete by proposing specific projects they want to implement.

caucus A meeting of all members of the political party in one chamber in which they elect leaders, approve committee assignments, and elect committee chairpersons.

centralized federalism The relationship between the national and state governments whereby the national government imposes its policy preferences on state governments.

chad A ready-made perforation on a punch card ballot.

charter The constitution of a local government.

checks and balances The mechanisms by which each branch of government can monitor and limit the functions of the other branches.

chief justice The leading justice on the Supreme Court, who provides both organizational and intellectual leadership.

chief of staff Among the most important staff members of the White House Office (WHO); serves as both an adviser to the president and the manager of the WHO.

circuit courts Also known as *courts of appeals;* the middle level in the federal court structure.

circuit riding The practice of traveling around the circuits by early Supreme Court justices and district court judges to hear appeals cases.

citizens Those members of the polity who, through birth or naturalization, enjoy the rights, privileges, and responsibilities attached to membership in a given nation.

civic engagement Individual and collective actions designed to identify and address issues of public concern.

civil disobedience Active, but nonviolent, refusal to comply with laws or governmental policies that are morally objectionable.

civil law The body of law dealing with the rights of private citizens.

civil liberties Constitutionally established guarantees that protect citizens, opinions, and property against arbitrary government interference.

civil rights The rights and privileges guaranteed to all citizens under the equal protection and due process clauses of the Fifth and Fourteenth amendments; the idea that individuals are protected from discrimination based on characteristics such as race, national origin, religion, and sex.

civil servants Bureaucrats hired through a merit-based personnel system who have job protection.

clash of civilizations thesis Samuel Huntington's idea that bitter cultural conflict will continue and escalate between modern Western democracies and fundamentalist Islamic states.

clear and present danger test A standard established in the 1919 Supreme Court case *Schenck v. U.S.* whereby the government may silence speech or expression when there is a clear and present danger that this speech will bring about some harm that the government has the power to prevent.

clear and probable danger test A standard established in the 1951 case *Dennis v. U.S.* whereby the government could suppress speech to avoid grave danger, even if the probability of the dangerous result was relatively remote; replaced by the imminent lawless action (incitement) test in 1969.

climate control The practice of using public outreach to build favorable public opinion of an organization.

closed primary A type of primary in which voting in a party's primary is limited to members of that party.

cloture A procedural move in which a supermajority of sixty senators agrees to end a filibuster.

coattail effect The phenomenon by which candidates running for a lower-level office such as city council benefit in an election from the popularity of a top-of-ticket nominee.

code law Laws created by legislators to regulate the behavior of individuals and organizations.

Cold War The political, ideological, and military conflict that lasted from 1945 until 1990 between communist nations led by the Soviet Union and Western democracies led by the United States.

collective defense The concept that allied nations agree to defend one another in the face of an invasion.

collective goods Outcomes shared by the general public; also called *public goods*.

collective security The idea that peace could be achieved if nations agreed to collectively oppose any nation that attacked another country.

collegial court A court made up of a group of judges who must evaluate a case together and decide on the outcome; significant compromise and negotiation take place as members try to build a majority coalition.

commercial speech Advertising statements that describe products.

commission A form of local government that is more common in county and township governments than in other general-purpose governments and for which voters elect a body of officials who collectively hold legislative and executive powers.

common law Law made by judges who decide cases and articulate legal principles in their opinions; based upon the British system.

concurrent budget resolution A document approved by the House and the Senate at the beginning of their budget process that establishes binding expenditure ceilings and a binding revenue floor as well as proposed expenditure levels for major policies.

concurrent powers The basic governing functions of all sovereign governments; in the United States, they are held by the national, state, and local governments and include the authority to tax, to make policy, and to implement policy, and the power of eminent domain.

concurring opinion A judicial opinion agreeing with how the majority decides the case but disagreeing with at least some of the legal interpretations or conclusions reached by the majority.

confederal system A structure of government in which several independent sovereign governments agree to cooperate on specified governmental matters while retaining sovereignty over all other governmental matters within their jurisdictions.

confederation A union of independent states in which each state retains its sovereignty, rights, and power, which is not by their agreement expressly delegated to a central governing body.

conference committee A bicameral, bipartisan committee composed of legislators whose job is to reconcile two versions of a bill.

conflict of interest In the case of public servants, the situation in which they can personally benefit from a decision they make or an action they take in the process of doing their jobs.

conflicted federalism The current status of national-state relations that involve the conflicting elements of dual, cooperative, and centralized federalisms.

Connecticut Compromise (Great Compromise) At the constitutional convention, the compromise between the Virginia Plan and the New Jersey Plan that created a bicameral legislature with one chamber's representation based on population and the other chamber having two members for each state.

consent of the governed The idea that, in a democracy, the government's power derives from the consent of the people.

conservatism An ideology that emphasizes preserving tradition and relying on community and family as mechanisms of continuity in society.

constitution The fundamental principles of a government and the basic structure and procedures by which the government operates to fulfill those principles; may be written or unwritten.

constitutional law The body of law that comes out of the courts in cases involving the interpretation of the Constitution.

constitutionalism Government that is structured by law, and in which the power of government is limited.

consumer price index (CPI) The most common measure of inflation, it measures the average change in prices over time of a "market basket" of goods and services.

containment The Cold War–era policy of preventing the spread of communism, mainly by providing military and economic aid as well as political advice to countries vulnerable to a communist takeover.

continuing resolution An agreement of the House and Senate that authorizes agencies not covered by approved appropriation laws to continue to spend money within their previous budget year's levels.

contracting-out Also called *outsourcing* or *privatizing;* a process by which the government contracts with a private for-profit or nonprofit organization to provide public services, such as disaster relief, or resources needed by the government, such as fighter planes.

contributory program (social insurance program) A benefit provided only to those who paid the specific tax created to fund the benefit.

convergence The merging of various forms of media, including newspapers, television stations, radio networks, and blogs, under one corporate roof and one set of business editorial leaders.

cooperative federalism The relationship between the national and state governments whereby the two levels of government work together to address domestic matters reserved to the states, driven by the policy priorities of the states.

Council of Governments (COG) A regional agency composed of representatives from several local governments who share resources to address one or more mutual problems.

council-manager (commission-administrator) A form of general-purpose local government found in many counties and the majority of cities; it is composed of an elected body with legislative and executive powers whose members hire a professional manager to oversee the government's day-to-day operations.

council-mayor (council-executive) A form of general-purpose local government comprising (1) a legislative body elected by voters and (2) an independently elected chief executive.

county government A general-purpose local government created by states to assist them in implementing policy in geographic subdivisions of the state.

country desk The official operation of the U.S. government in each country that has diplomatic ties to the United States.

courts of appeals The intermediate appellate courts in the federal system that review previous decisions made by courts in the federal or state judicial system.

creationism A theory of the creation of the earth and humankind that is based on a literal interpretation of the biblical story of Genesis.

criminal due process rights Safeguards for those accused of crime; these rights constrain government conduct in investigating crimes, trying cases, and punishing offenders.

criminal law The body of law dealing with conduct so harmful to society as a whole that it is prohibited by statute, and is prosecuted and punished by the government.

cross pressuring The presence of two conditions or traits that pull a voter toward different political parties.

D

de facto segregation Segregation caused by the fact that people tend to live in neighborhoods with others of their own race, religion, or ethnic group.

de jure segregation Segregation mandated by law.

dealignment The situation in which fewer voters support the two major political parties, instead identifying themselves as independent, or splitting their ticket between candidates from more than one party

defense conversion President Jimmy Carter's attempt to convert the nation's vast military apparatus to peacetime functions.

deficit spending Government expenditures costing more than is raised in taxes, leading to borrowing and debt.

democracy Government in which supreme power of governance lies in the hands of its citizens.

department One of fifteen executive branch units responsible for a broadly defined policy area and whose top administrator (secretary) is appointed by the president, is confirmed by the Senate, and serves at the discretion of the president.

depression A long-term and severe recession.

deregulation The reduction or elimination of regulatory restrictions on firms and industries.

détente The easing of tensions between the United States and its communist rivals.

deterrence The idea that nations would be less likely to engage in nuclear war if adversaries each had first-strike capability.

devolution The process whereby the national government returns policy responsibilities to state and/or local governments.

digital divide The inequality of access to computers and Internet connections.

Dillon's rule The ruling articulated by Judge John Forrest Dillon in 1872 that local governments are creatures of the state that created them, and they have only the powers expressly mentioned in the charters written and approved by the state and those necessarily implied by the formally expressed powers.

diplomacy The conduct of international relations, particularly involving the negotiation of treaties and other agreements between nations.

direct democracy A system of government that allows citizens to vote directly to approve or reject proposed public policies or to force an elected official from office before the completion of his or her term.

direct provision A policy tool whereby the government that creates a policy hires public servants to provide the service.

direct subsidy A cash transfer from general revenues to particular persons or private companies engaged in activities that the national government believes support the public good.

director of national intelligence (DNI) The person responsible for coordinating and overseeing all the intelligence agencies within the executive branch.

discharge petition A special tactic used to extract a bill from a committee to have it considered by the entire House.

discretionary spending Payment on programs for which Congress and the president must approve budget authority each year in appropriation legislation.

discuss list Compiled by the chief justice, the list of cases on review that he thinks may be appropriate for the Court to hear.

dissenting opinion A judicial opinion disagreeing both with the majority's disposition of a case and with their legal interpretations and conclusions.

diversity of citizenship The circumstance in which the parties in a legal case are from different states or the case involves a U.S. citizen and a foreign government.

divided government The situation that exists when Congress is controlled by one party and the presidency by the other.

divine right of kings The assertion that monarchies, as a manifestation of God's

will, could rule absolutely without regard to the will or well-being of their subjects.

domino theory The principle that if one nation fell to communism, other nations in its geographic vicinity also would succumb.

double jeopardy The trying of a person for the same crime that he or she has been cleared of in court; barred by the Fifth Amendment.

dual court system A two-part judicial system such as that of the United States, which has both federal and state courts.

dual federalism The relationship between the national and state governments, dominant between 1789 and 1932, whereby the two levels of government functioned independently of each other to address their distinct constitutional responsibilities.

dual sovereignty A system of government in which ultimate governing authority is divided between two levels of government, a central government and regional governments, with each level having ultimate authority over different policy matters.

due process The legal safeguards that prevent the government from arbitrarily depriving citizens of life, liberty, or property; guaranteed by the Fifth and Fourteenth amendments.

E

earmark A designation within a spending bill that provides for a specific expenditure.

e-campaigning The practice of mobilizing voters using the Internet.

economic boom Rapid economic growth.

economic incentives Motivation to join an interest group because the group works for policies that will provide members with material benefits.

economic policy A government's body of diverse policies geared toward promoting the nation's economic health.

economy A system for producing, distributing, and consuming goods and services.

efficacy Citizens' belief that they have the ability to achieve something desirable and that the government listens to people like them.

electioneering Working to influence the election of candidates who support the organization's issues.

Electoral College A group of people elected by voters in each state to elect the president and the vice president.

elite theory A theory that holds that a group of wealthy, educated individuals wields most political power.

emergency powers Broad powers exercised by the president during times of national crisis.

entitlement program A government benefit guaranteed to all who meet the eligibility requirements.

enumerated powers The powers of the national government that are listed in the Constitution.

environmental racism The term for the higher incidence of environmental threats and subsequent health problems in lower-income communities, which frequently are also communities dominated by people of color.

equal protection clause The Fourteenth Amendment clause stating that no state shall "deny to any person within its jurisdiction the equal protection of the laws."

essential services Public services provided by state and local governments on a daily basis to prevent chaos and hazardous conditions in society.

establishment clause The First Amendment clause that bars the government from passing any law "respecting an establishment of religion"; often interpreted as a separation of church and state but increasingly questioned.

exclusionary rule The criminal procedural rule stating that evidence obtained illegally cannot be used in a trial.

executive agreement An international agreement between the United States and other nations, not subject to Senate approval and only in effect during the administration of the president who negotiates the agreement.

executive budget The budget document and budget message that explains the president's fiscal plan.

Executive Office of the President (EOP) The offices, counsels, and boards that help the president to carry out his day-to-day responsibilities.

executive order The power of the president to issue orders that carry the force of law.

executive privilege The right of the chief executive and members of the administration to withhold information from Congress or the courts, or the right to refuse to appear before legislative or judicial bodies.

exit polls Polls conducted at polling places on Election Day to project the winner of an election before the polls close.

expressed powers Presidential powers enumerated in the Constitution.

extradition The return of a person accused of a crime to the state in which the crime was committed upon the request of that state's governor.

F

fairness doctrine The requirement that stations provide equal time to all parties regarding important public issues and equal access to airtime to all candidates for public office.

federal question A question of law based on interpretation of the U.S. Constitution, federal laws, or treaties.

federal system A governmental structure with two levels of government and in which each level has sovereignty over different governmental functions and policy matters.

The Federalist Papers A series of essays, written by James Madison, Alexander Hamilton, and John Jay, that argued for the ratification of the Constitution.

Federalists Individuals who supported the new Constitution as presented by the Constitutional Convention in 1787.

feminization of poverty The phenomenon of increasing numbers of unmarried, divorced, and separated women with children living in poverty.

fighting words Speech that is likely to bring about public disorder or chaos; the Supreme Court has held that this speech may be banned in public places to ensure the preservation of public order.

filibuster A procedural move by a member of the Senate to attempt to halt passage of a bill, during which the senator can speak for an unlimited time on the Senate floor.

fireside chats President Franklin Roosevelt's radio addresses to the country.

fiscal federalism The relationship between the national government and state and local governments whereby the national government provides grant money to state and local governments.

fiscal policy Government spending and taxing and their effect on the economy.

fiscal year (FY) The twelve-month accounting period for revenue raising and spending, which for the national government begins on October 1 and ends on September 30 of the following year.

527 A tax-exempt group that raises money for political activities, much like those allowed under the soft money loophole.

food insecurity The situation in which people have a limited or an uncertain ability to obtain, in socially acceptable ways, enough nutritious food to live a healthy and active life.

foreign service officers The diplomatic and consular staff at U.S. embassies abroad.

framing The process by which the media set a context that helps people understand important events and matters of shared interest.

free exercise clause The First Amendment clause prohibiting the government from enacting laws prohibiting an individual's practice of his or her religion; often in contention with the establishment clause.

free rider problem The phenomenon of someone deriving benefit from others' actions.

free trade policy The elimination of tariffs and nontariff trade barriers so that international trade is expanded.

freedom of assembly The right to form or join any type of organization, political party, or club without penalty.

full faith and credit clause The constitutional clause that requires states to comply with and uphold the public acts, records, and judicial decisions of other states.

fund-raising consultant A professional who works with candidates in identifying likely contributors to the campaign and arranging events and meetings with donors.

G

gender gap The measurable difference in the way women and men vote for candidates and in the way they view political issues.

general election An election that determines which candidates win the offices being sought.

general-purpose government A government providing services in numerous and diverse policy and functional areas to the residents living within its borders.

generational effect The impact of an important external event in shaping the views of a generation.

gerrymandering The drawing of legislative district boundaries to benefit an incumbent, a political party, or another group.

global economy The worldwide economy created by the integration and interdependence of national economies.

global warming The rising temperature of the earth as a result of pollution that traps solar heat, keeping the air warmer than it would otherwise be.

globalism The interconnectedness between nations in contemporary times.

GOTV Get out the vote.

government The institution that creates and implements policy and laws that guide the conduct of the nation and its citizens.

government corporation An executive branch unit that sells a service and is expected to be financially self-sufficient.

grandfather clause A clause exempting individuals from voting conditions such as poll taxes or literacy tests if they or their ancestor had voted before 1870, thus sparing most white voters in the South.

grant-in-aid (intergovernmental transfer) The transfer of money from one government to another government (or from a government to a nonprofit organization, a for-profit organization, or an individual) that does not need to be paid back.

grassroots organizing Tasks that involve direct contact with voters or potential voters.

greenhouse effect The heating of the earth's atmosphere as a result of humans' burning of fossil fuels and the resultant buildup of carbon dioxide and other gases.

gross domestic product (GDP) The total value of all goods and services produced by labor and properties within a country's borders.

H

habeas corpus An ancient right that protects an individual in custody from being held without the right to be heard in a court of law.

hard money Regulated campaign contributions that can specifically advocate the election of a candidate.

hate crime A crime committed against a person, property, or society, where the offender is motivated, in part or in whole, by his or her bias against the victim because of the victim's race, religion, disability, sexual orientation, or ethnicity.

hearings Sessions held by committees or subcommittees to gather information and views from experts.

heightened scrutiny test (intermediate scrutiny test) The guidelines used most frequently by the courts to determine the legality of sex-based discrimination; on the basis of this test, sex-based discrimination is legal if the government can prove that it is substantially related to the achievement of an important public interest.

Holocaust The genocide perpetrated by Adolf Hitler and the Nazis of six million Jews, along with political dissidents, Catholics, homosexuals, and gypsies.

home rule The opportunity provided by state government for citizens to write, adopt, and amend local government charters at the city and county levels.

home rule charter A local government constitution written and approved by citizens following state-mandated procedures that include a referendum.

honeymoon period A time early in a new president's administration characterized by optimistic approval by the public.

hopper A wooden box that sits on a desk at the front of the House of Representatives, into which House members place bills they want to introduce.

horizontal federalism The state-to-state relationships created by the U.S. Constitution.

House majority leader The leader of the majority party, who helps the Speaker develop and implement strategy and work with other members of the House of Representatives.

House minority leader The leader of the minority party, whose job mirrors that of the majority leader but without the power that comes from holding a majority in the House of Representatives.

household income The total pretax earnings of all residents over the age of 15 living in a home.

housing insecurity The situation in which people have limited or uncertain ability to obtain, in socially acceptable ways, affordable, safe, and decent-quality permanent housing.

Human Development Index (HDI) A UN-created measure to determine how well a country's economy is providing for a long and healthy life, educational opportunity, and a decent standard of living.

I

imminent lawless action test (incitement test) A standard established in the 1969 *Brandenburg v. Ohio* case whereby speech is restricted only if it goes beyond mere advocacy, or words, to create a high likelihood of imminent disorder or lawlessness.

impeach Formally charging a government official with not fulfilling constitutional duties or with committing a high crime or misdemeanor.

impeachment The power of the House of Representatives to formally accuse the president (and other high-ranking officials, including the vice president and federal judges) of crimes.

implied powers The powers of the national government that are not enumerated in the Constitution but that Congress claims are necessary and proper for the national government to fulfill its enumerated powers in accordance with the necessary and proper clause of the Constitution.

impressment The forcible removal of merchant sailors from U.S. ships on the spurious grounds that the sailors were deserters from the British Navy.

income inequality The gap in the proportion of national income held by the richest compared with that held by the poorest.

incorporation The process by which the Bill of Rights protections were applied to state governments.

incumbency The situation of already holding the office that is up for reelection.

independent Often used as a synonym for unaffiliated voter.

independent administrative agency An executive branch unit created by Congress and the president that is responsible for a narrowly defined function and whose governing board is intended to be protected from partisan politics.

independent expenditures Outlays by PACs and others, typically for advertising for or against a candidate, but uncoordinated with a candidate's campaign.

independent regulatory commission An executive branch unit responsible for developing standards of behavior within specific industries and businesses, monitoring compliance with these standards, and imposing sanctions on violators.

indexed benefit A government benefit with an automatic cost of living increase based on the rate of inflation.

indirect democracy Sometimes called a *representative democracy*, a system in which citizens elect representatives who decide policies on behalf of their constituents.

individualistic political culture The view that the decision to take part in government is an individual choice and those who choose to participate determine the purpose of government and personally benefit from their participation.

inflation The decreased value of money as evidenced by increased prices.

information equilibrium The dissemination of information outside traditional channels of control.

infotainment News shows that combine entertainment and news, a hybrid of the words *information* and *entertainment*.

inherent characteristics Individual attributes such as race, national origin, religion, and sex.

inherent powers Presidential powers that are implied in the Constitution.

initiative A direct democracy process in which citizens draft a desired policy and get a state-specified number of signatures on a petition in support of the proposal so that it is placed on the ballot for voters to approve or reject.

in-kind assistance A cash transfer in which the government pays cash to those who provide goods or services to eligible individuals.

inspectors general Political appointees who work within a government agency to ensure the integrity of public service by investigating allegations of misconduct by bureaucrats.

instant runoff election A special runoff election in which the computerized voting machine simulates the elimination of last-place voter-getters.

instructed delegate model A model of representation in which legislators, as representatives of their constituents, should vote in keeping with the constituents' views, even if those views contradict the legislator's personal views.

intelligent design The theory that the apparent design in the universe and in living things is the product of an intelligent cause rather than of an undirected process such as natural selection: its primary proponents believe that the designer is God and seek to redefine science to accept supernatural explanations.

interest groups Organizations that seek to achieve some of their goals by influencing government decision making.

intergovernmental lobbying Efforts by groups representing state and local governments to influence national domestic policy.

intergovernmental relations (IGR) The collaborative efforts of two or more levels of government working to serve the public.

intermestics The influence of domestic interests on foreign policy.

International Monetary Fund (IMF) The institution charged with regulating monetary relationships among nations, including establishment of exchange rates for major world currencies; established in 1944 by the Bretton Woods Agreement.

interstate compacts Agreements between states that Congress has the authority to review and reject.

interventionism A foreign policy characterized by a nation's willingness to participate and intervene in international situations, including another country's affairs.

iron triangle The interaction of mutual interests among members of Congress, executive agencies, and organized interests during policy making.

isolationism A foreign policy characterized by a nation's unwillingness to participate in international affairs.

issue network The web of connections among those concerned about a policy and those who create and administer the policy.

J

Jim Crow laws Laws requiring the strict separation of racial groups, with whites and "nonwhites" required to attend separate schools, work in different jobs, and use segregated public accommodations, such as transportation and restaurants.

joint committee A bicameral committee composed of members of both chambers of Congress.

joint referral The practice, abolished in the 104th Congress, by which a bill could be referred to two different committees for consideration.

journalism The practice of gathering and reporting events.

judicial activism An approach to judicial decision making whereby judges apply their authority to bring about specific social goals.

judicial restraint An approach to judicial decision making whereby judges defer to the democratically elected legislative and executive branches of government.

judicial review Court authority to determine that an action taken by any government official or governing body violates the Constitution.

judiciary The branch of government comprising the state and federal courts and the judges who preside over them.

jurisdiction The power of a court to hear a case and to resolve it, given to a court by either a constitution or a statute.

justice Any of the nine judges who sit on the Supreme Court.

K

Keynesian economics The theory that recommends that during a recession the national government increase its spending and decrease taxes, and during a boom, cut spending and increase taxes.

L

laissez-faire The hands-off stance of a government in regard to the marketplace.

lead committee The primary committee considering a bill.

League of Nations A representative body founded in the aftermath of World War I to establish the collective security of nations.

legislative referendum A ballot measure whereby voters approve or reject a law or an amendment proposed by state officials.

legitimacy A quality conferred on government by citizens who believe that its exercise of power is right and proper.

Lemon **test** A three-part test established by the Supreme Court in the 1971 case *Lemon v. Kurtzman* to determine whether government aid to parochial schools is constitutional; the test is also applied to other cases involving the establishment clause.

letter to the editor A letter in which a reader responds to a story in a newspaper, knowing that the letter might be published in that paper.

libel False written statements about others that harm their reputation.

liberalism An ideology that advocates change in the social, political, and economic realms to better protect the well-being of individuals and to produce equality within society.

libertarianism An ideology whose advocates believe that government should take a "hands off" approach in most matters.

liberty The most essential quality of American democracy; it is both the freedom from governmental interference in citizens' lives and the freedom to pursue happiness.

limited government Government that is restricted in what it can do so that the rights of the people are protected.

limited war A combatant country's self-imposed limitation on the tactics and strategy it uses, particularly its avoidance of the use of nuclear weapons.

line-item veto The power of the president to strike out specific line items on an appropriations bill while allowing the rest of the bill to become law; declared unconstitutional by the Supreme Court in 1997.

literacy test A test to determine eligibility to vote; designed so that few African Americans would pass.

living wage A wage high enough to keep workers and their families out of poverty and to allow them to enjoy a basic living standard.

lobby To communicate directly with policy makers on an interest group's behalf.

logrolling The practice of members of Congress agreeing to vote for a bill in exchange for their colleague's vote on another bill.

loyal opposition A role that the party out of power plays, highlighting its objections to policies and priorities of the government in power.

M

majority rule The idea that in a democracy, only policies with 50 percent plus one vote are enacted, and only candidates that win 50 percent plus one vote are elected.

majority whip A go-between with the majority leadership and party members in the House of Representatives.

majority-minority district A legislative district composed of a majority of a given minority community—say, African Americans—the intent of which is to make it likely that a member of that minority will be elected to Congress.

mandates Clauses in legislation that direct state and local governments to comply with national legislation and national standards.

mandatory spending Government spending for debt and programs whose budget authority is provided in legislation other than annual appropriation acts; this budget authority is open ended, obligating the government to pay for the program as long as it exists.

manifest destiny The idea that it was the United States' destiny to spread throughout the North American continent; used to rationalize the expansion of U.S. territory.

Marbury v. Madison The 1803 Supreme Court case that established the power of judicial review, which allows the Court to strike down laws passed by the other branches that it views to be in conflict with the Constitution.

margin of error Also called *sampling error;* a statistical calculation of the difference in results between a poll of the sample and a poll of the entire population.

marketplace of ideas A concept at the core of the freedoms of expression and press, based on the belief that true and free political discourse depends upon a free and unrestrained discussion of ideas.

markup The process by which the members of legislative committees "mark up" a bill with suggested language for changes and amendments.

Marshall Plan The U.S. government program that provided funds necessary for Western European countries to rebuild after World War II.

McCullogh v. Maryland The 1819 case that established that the necessary and proper clause justifies broad understandings of enumerated powers.

means-tested benefit A benefit for which eligibility is based on having an income below a specified amount, typically based on a percentage of the poverty guideline.

media Tools used to store and deliver information or data.

media consultant A professional who brings the campaign message to voters by creating handouts and all forms of media ads.

media segmentation The breaking down of the media according to the specific audiences they target.

median household income The middle of all household incomes—50 percent of households have incomes less than the median and 50 percent have incomes greater than the median.

merit-based civil service A personnel system in which bureaucrats are hired on the basis of the principles of competence, equal opportunity (open competition), and political neutrality; once hired, these public servants have job protection.

merit selection process A process for selecting judges in which a nonpartisan committee nominates candidates, the governor or legislature appoints judges from among those candidates to a short term of service, and then the appointed judges face a retention election at the end of the short term.

minority whip The go-between with the minority leadership, whose job mirrors that of the majority whip but without the power that comes from holding a majority in the House of Representatives.

Miranda **rights** A criminal procedural rule, established in the 1966 case *Miranda v. Arizona,* requiring police to inform criminal suspects, on their arrest, of their legal rights, such as the right to remain silent and the

right to counsel; these warnings must be read to suspects before interrogation.

monarchy A government in which a member of a royal family, usually a king or queen, has absolute authority over a territory and its government.

monetarism The theory that says the government's proper economic role is to control the rate of inflation by controlling the amount of money in circulation.

monetary policy The body of government policies, controlled by the Federal Reserve System, aimed at influencing the supply of money in the marketplace to maintain price stability.

Monroe Doctrine President James Monroe's 1823 declaration that the Americas should not be considered subjects for future colonization by any European power.

moralistic political culture The view that the purpose of government is to serve the public good, including providing for those who are disadvantaged, and that all citizens should participate in government.

muckraking Criticism and exposés of corruption in government and industry by journalists at the turn of the twentieth century.

multilateral Many-sided; having the support of numerous nations.

municipal government Self-governing general-purpose government—including city, borough, and town governments—created by states to provide goods and services within a densely populated area.

mutual assured destruction (MAD) The doctrine that if one nation attacked another with nuclear weapons, the other would be capable of retaliating and would retaliate with such force as to assure mutual annihilation.

N

narrowcasting The practice of aiming media content at specific segments of the public.

national debt The total amount of money the government owes to others due to borrowing.

National Security Council (NSC) Consisting of top foreign policy advisers and relevant cabinet officials, this is an arm of the Executive Office of the President that the president consults on matters of foreign policy and national security.

natural law The assertion that standards that govern human behavior are derived from the nature of humans themselves and can be universally applied.

natural rights (unalienable rights) The rights possessed by all humans as a gift from nature, or God, including the rights to life, liberty and the pursuit of happiness.

naturalization The process of becoming a citizen by means other than birth, as in the case of immigrants.

necessary and proper clause (elastic clause) A clause in Article I, section 8, of the Constitution that gives Congress the power to do whatever it deems necessary and constitutional to meet its enumerated obligations; the basis for the implied powers.

neoconservatism An ideology that advocates military over diplomatic solutions in foreign policy and is less concerned with restraining government activity in domestic politics than traditional conservatives.

Net neutrality The idea that Internet traffic—e-mail, Web site content, videos, and phone calls—should flow without interference or discrimination by those who own or run the Internet pipeline.

netroots The Internet-centered political efforts on behalf of candidates and causes.

New Deal Franklin Roosevelt's broad social welfare program in which the government would bear the responsibility of providing a "safety net" to protect the weakest members of society.

New Deal coalition The group composed of southern Democrats, northern city dwellers, immigrants, the poor, Catholics, labor union members, blue-collar workers, African Americans, and women that elected FDR to the presidency four times.

New Jersey Plan The proposal presented in response to the Virginia Plan by the less populous states at the Constitutional Convention, which called for a unicameral national legislature in which all states would have an equal voice (equal representation), an executive office composed of several people elected by Congress, and a Supreme Court whose members would be appointed by the executive office.

new judicial federalism The practice whereby state judges base decisions regarding civil rights and liberties on their state's constitution, rather than the U.S. Constitution, when their state's constitution guarantees more than minimum rights.

new media Cable television, the Internet, blogs, and satellite technology.

Nixon Doctrine Policy emphasizing the responsibility of U.S. allies to provide for their own national defense and security, aimed at improving relations with the communist nations, including the Soviet Union and China.

noncontributory program A benefit provided to a targeted population, paid for by a proportion of the money collected from all taxpayers.

nonpartisan election An election in which the candidates are not nominated by political parties and the ballot does not include party affiliations.

nontariff trade barriers Business and social regulations as well as subsidies aimed at creating a competitive advantage in trade.

normal trade relations (NTR) status The international trade principle holding that the least restrictive trade conditions (best tariff rates) offered to any one national trading partner will be offered to every other nation in a trading network (also known as *most favored nations*).

North Atlantic Treaty Organization (NATO) An international mutual defense alliance formed in 1949 that created a structure for regional security for its fifteen member nations.

O

obscenity Indecent or offensive speech or expression.

Office of Management and Budget (OMB) The office that creates the president's annual budget.

office-block ballot A type of ballot that arranges all the candidates for a particular office under the name of that office.

oligarchy A government in which an elite few hold power.

ombudsperson A role in which an elected or appointed leader acts as an advocate for citizens by listening to and investigating complaints against a government agency.

open meeting laws Laws requiring legislative bodies and executive agencies of government to conduct policy-making meetings in public.

open primary A type of primary in which both parties' ballots are available in the voting booth, and the voters simply select one on which to register their preferences.

operating budget A budget that accounts for all the costs of day-to-day government operations and covers such items as salaries and benefits, utilities, office supplies, and rent.

oral arguments The stage when appeals court judges or Supreme Court justices meet with the petitioner and the respondent to ask questions about the legal interpretations or information contained in their briefs.

ordinary scrutiny test The guidelines the courts used between 1873 and 1976 to determine the legality of sex-based discrimination; on the basis of this test, sex-based discrimination is legal if it is a reasonable means by which the government can achieve a legitimate public interest.

original jurisdiction The power of a court to hear a case first, before other courts have decided it.

outsourcing The situation in which the government signs contracts with private-sector employers to do work previously provided by government workers.

oversight The process by which the legislative branch "checks" the executive branch to ensure that the laws Congress has passed are being administered in keeping with legislators' intent.

P

partisan election An election in which candidates are nominated by political parties and the ballot lists each candidate's political party affiliation.

party identifiers Individuals who identify themselves as a member of one party or the other.

party in government The partisan identifications of elected leaders in local, county, state, and federal government.

party in the electorate Individuals who identify with or tend to support a party.

party organization The formal party apparatus, including committees, party leaders, conventions, and workers.

party system The categorization of the number and competitiveness of political parties in a polity.

party-column ballot A ballot that organizes the candidates by political party.

patronage The system in which a party leader rewarded political supporters with jobs or government contracts in exchange for their support of the party.

penny press Newspapers that sold for a penny in the 1830s.

platform The formal statement of a party's principles and policy objectives.

Plessy v. Ferguson 1896 Supreme Court ruling creating the separate but equal doctrine.

plum book A publication that lists the top jobs in the bureaucracy to which the president will appoint people through the patronage system.

plural executive system A state and local government structure in which the citizens elect more than two people to top positions in the executive branch of government.

pluralist theory A theory that holds that policy making is a competition among diverse interest groups that ensure the representation of individual interests.

pocket veto A special presidential veto of a bill passed at the conclusion of a legislative session, whereby the president waits ten days without signing the bill, and the bill dies.

police powers The states' reserved powers to protect the health, safety, lives, and properties of residents in a state.

political action committee (PAC) A group that raises and spends money to influence the outcome of an election.

political culture The people's collective beliefs and attitudes about government and political processes.

political engagement Citizen actions that are intended to solve public problems through political means.

political ideology An integrated system of ideas or beliefs about political values in general and the role of government in particular.

political machines Big-city organizations that exerted control over many aspects of life and lavishly rewarded supporters.

political party An organization that recruits, nominates, and elects party members to office in order to control the government.

political socialization The process by which we develop our political values and opinions.

politics The process of deciding who gets benefits in society and who is excluded from benefiting.

politics-administration dichotomy The concept that elected government officials, who are accountable to the voters, create and approve public policy, and then competent, politically neutral bureaucrats implement the public policy.

poll tax A fee for voting; levied to prevent poor African Americans in the South from voting.

pool memo Description written by Court clerks of the facts of a case filed with the Court, the pertinent legal arguments, and a recommendation as to whether the case should be taken.

popular referendum A measure that allows citizens, by collecting signatures in a petition drive, to put before voters specific legislation that the legislature has previously approved.

popular sovereignty The theory that government is created by the people and depends on the people for the authority to rule.

population In a poll, the group of people whose opinions are of interest and/or about whom information is desired.

populism A philosophy supporting the rights and empowerment of the masses as opposed to elites.

pork barrel Legislators' appropriations of funds for special projects located within their congressional districts.

poverty The condition of lacking the income sufficient to purchase the necessities for an adequate living standard.

poverty guidelines A simplified version of the poverty thresholds developed each year by the Department of Health and Human Services; used to set financial eligibility criteria for benefits.

poverty rate The proportion of the population living below the poverty line as established by the national government.

poverty thresholds A set of income measures adjusted for family size that the Census Bureau establishes each year to define poverty for data collection purposes.

precedent Legal authority established by earlier cases.

preemption The constitutionally based principle that allows a national law to supersede state or local laws.

president pro tempore Also called *president pro tem;* theoretically, the chair of the Senate in the vice president's absence; in reality, an honorary title, with the senator of the majority party having the longest record of continuous service being elected to the position.

press secretary The president's spokesperson to the media.

preventive war The strategy of waging war on countries that are regarded as threatening in order to avoid future conflicts.

primary election An election in which voters choose the party's candidates who will run in the later general election.

priming Bringing certain policies on issues to the public agenda through media coverage.

prior restraint A form of censorship by the government whereby it blocks the publication of news stories viewed as libelous or harmful.

privileges and immunities The Constitution's requirement that a state extend to other states' citizens the privileges and immunities it provides for its citizens.

progressive tax A tax that takes a larger percentage of the income of wealthier taxpayers and a smaller percentage of the income of lower-income taxpayers.

property Anything that can be owned.

proportional representation system An electoral structure in which political parties win the number of parliamentary seats equal to the percentage of the vote the party receives.

proportional (flat) tax A tax that takes the same percentage of each taxpayer's income.

proposition A proposed measure placed on the ballot in an initiative election.

prospective voting A method of evaluating candidates in which voters focus on candidates' positions on issues important to them and vote for the candidates who best represent their views.

prosumers Individuals who simultaneously consume information and news and produce information in the form of videos, blogs, and Web sites.

protectionist trade policy The establishment of trade barriers to protect domestic goods from foreign competition.

public agenda The public issues that most demand the attention of government officials.

public diplomat An individual outside government who promotes his or her country's interests and thus contributes to shaping international perceptions of the nation.

public goods Services governments provide that are available to everyone, like clean air, clean water, airport security, and highways.

public opinion The public's expressed views about an issue at a specific point in time.

public opinion poll A survey of a given population's opinion on an issue or a candidate at a particular point in time.

pure capitalist economy An economy in which private individuals and companies own the modes of producing goods and services, and the government does not enact laws aimed at influencing the marketplace transactions that distribute those goods and services.

purposive incentives Motivation to join an interest group based on the belief in the group's cause from an ideological or a moral standpoint.

push polls A special type of poll that both provides information to campaigns about candidate strengths and weaknesses and attempts to skew public opinion about a candidate.

Q

quota sample A method by which pollsters structure a sample so that it is representative of the characteristics of the target population.

R

rally 'round the flag effect The peaks in presidential approval ratings during short-term military action.

random sampling A scientific method of selection for a poll in which each member of the population has an equal chance at being included in the sample.

rational abstention thesis A theory that some individuals decide the costs of voting are not worth the effort when compared with the benefits.

rational choice theory The idea that from an economic perspective it is not rational for people to participate in collective action when they can secure the collective good without participating.

real income Earned income adjusted for inflation.

realignment A shift in party allegiances or electoral support.

reapportionment Reallocation of seats in the House of Representatives to each state based on changes in the state's population since the last census.

recall A direct democracy measure by which citizens can remove an elected official from office before the end of his or her term.

recession An economic downturn during which unemployment is high and the production of goods and services is low.

Reconstruction era The time after the Civil War between 1866 and 1877 when the institutions and infrastructure of the South were rebuilt.

redistricting The redrawing of congressional district boundaries within each state, based on the reapportionment from the census.

referendum A direct democracy measure that places public policy drafted by government officials on the ballot for voters to approve or reject.

regime change The replacement of a country's government with another government by facilitating the deposing of its leader or leading political party.

regional security alliance An alliance typically between a superpower and nations that are ideologically similar in a particular region.

regressive tax A tax that takes a greater percentage of the income of lower-income earners than of higher-income earners.

regulated capitalist economy (mixed economy) An economy in which the government enacts policies to influence the health of the economy.

regulatory law (administrative law) A law made by executive and regulatory agencies, often pursuant to a delegation of lawmaking power from Congress.

regulatory policies Policies that mandate individual and group (corporate) behaviors that foster the general welfare.

rendition The transfer of suspected terrorists to other nations for imprisonment and interrogation; this practice circumvents U.S. law, which requires due process and prohibits torture.

report A legislative committee's explanation to the full chamber of a bill and its intent.

republic A government that derives its authority from the people and in which citizens elect government officials to represent them in the processes by which laws are made; a representative democracy.

reserved powers The matters referred to in the Tenth Amendment over which states retain sovereignty.

responsible party model Political scientists' view that a function of a party is to offer a clear choice to voters by establishing priorities or policy stances different from those of rival parties.

retention election A noncompetitive election in which an incumbent judge's name is on the ballot and voters decide whether the judge should be retained.

retrospective voting A method of evaluating candidates in which voters evaluate incumbent candidates and decide whether to support them based on their past performance.

right to privacy The right of an individual to be left alone and to make decisions freely, without the interference of others.

Roosevelt Corollary The idea advanced by President Theodore Roosevelt, stating that the United States had the right to act as an "international police power" in the Western Hemisphere to ensure stability in the region.

Rule of Four The Supreme Court practice by which the Court will agree to hear a case that comes to it under its discretionary jurisdiction if four or more justices vote to hear it.

Rules Committee One of the most important committees in the House, which decides the length of debate and the scope of amendments that will be allowed on a bill.

run-off election A follow-up election that is held when no candidate receives the majority of votes cast in the original election.

S

safety net A collection of public policies ensuring that the basic physiological needs of citizens are met.

salient Having resonance, in relation to a voting issue, reflecting intense interest.

SALT I The treaty signed in 1972 by the United States and the Soviet Union limiting the two countries' antiballistic missiles and freezing the number of offensive missiles that each nation could have at the number they already possessed, plus the number they had under construction.

SALT II The treaty signed in 1979 by the United States and the Soviet Union that set an overall limit on strategic nuclear launchers, limited the number of missiles that could carry multiple independently targeted reentry vehicles (MIRVs) with nuclear warheads, and limited each nation to the development of only one new type of intercontinental ballistic missile (ICBM).

sampling error Also called *margin of error;* a statistical calculation of the difference in results between a poll of a randomly drawn sample and a poll of the entire population.

sanctions Penalties that halt economic relations.

select committee A congressional committee created to consider a specific policy issue or address a specific concern.

selective incorporation The process by which, over time, the Supreme Court applied those freedoms that served some fundamental principle of liberty or justice to the states, thus rejecting total incorporation.

Senate majority leader The most powerful position in the Senate; the majority leader manages the legislative process and schedules debate on legislation.

Senate minority leader The leader of the minority party in the Senate, who works with the majority leader in negotiating legislation.

senatorial courtesy A custom that allows senators from the president's political party to veto the president's choice of federal district court judge in the senator's state.

senior executive service (SES) A unique personnel system for top managerial, supervisory, and policy positions offering less job security but higher pay than the merit-based civil service system.

seniority system The system in which the member with the longest continuous tenure on a standing committee is given preference when the committee chooses its chair.

separate but equal doctrine Established by the Supreme Court in *Plessy v. Ferguson*, it said that separate but equal facilities for whites and nonwhites do not violate the Fourteenth Amendment's equal protection clause.

separation of powers The Constitution's delegation of authority for the primary governing functions among three branches of government so that no one group of government officials controls all the governing functions.

shadow bureaucrats People hired and paid by private for-profit and nonprofit organizations that implement public policy through a government contract.

signing statement A written message that the president issues upon signing a bill into law.

single-issue groups Groups that focus on one issue.

single-purpose government A government providing services in one policy or functional area to residents living within its borders.

slander False verbal statements about others that harm their reputation.

social capital The ways in which our lives are improved in many ways by social connections.

social contract An agreement between the people and their leaders in which the people agree to give up some liberties so that their other liberties are protected.

social contract theory The idea that individuals possess free will, and every individual is equally endowed with the God-given right of self-determination and the ability to consent to be governed.

social movement The organized action of a broad segment of society to demand and effect improvement in the treatment of a specific group.

social regulation The government rules and regulations aimed at protecting workers, consumers, and the environment from market failure.

socialism An ideology that advocates economic equality, theoretically achieved by having the government or workers own the means of production (businesses and industry).

soft money loophole The Supreme Court's interpretation of campaign finance law that enabled political parties to raise unlimited funds for party-building activities such as voter registration drives and get-out-the-vote (GOTV) efforts.

solidary incentives The motivation to join an interest group based on the companionship and the satisfaction derived from socializing with others that it offers.

Southeast Asia Treaty Organization (SEATO) A regional security agreement whose goal was to prevent communist encroachment in the countries of Southeast Asia.

sovereignty Having ultimate authority to govern, with no legal superior.

Speaker of the House The leader of the House of Representatives, chosen by the majority party.

spoils system The practice of rewarding political supporters with jobs.

standing committee A permanent committee in Congress, with a defined legislative jurisdiction.

standing to sue The ability to bring lawsuits in court.

stare decisis From the Latin "let the decision stand," the principle that binds judges to rely upon the holdings of past judges in deciding cases.

statute A law enacted by Congress or by state legislatures to deal with particular issues or problems, sometimes more detailed and comprehensive than the common law.

statutory powers Powers explicitly granted to presidents by congressional action.

steering The practice by which realtors steered African American families to certain neighborhoods and white families to others.

strategic arms limitation talks (SALT talks) Discussions between the United States and the Soviet Union in the 1970s that focused on cooling down the nuclear arms race between the two superpowers.

strategic arms reduction talks (START talks) Talks between the United States and the Soviet Union in which reductions in

missiles and nuclear warheads, not merely a limitation on increases, were negotiated.

strategic defense initiative (SDI, or "Star Wars") A ballistic missile defense system advocated by President Ronald Reagan.

stratified sampling A process of random sampling in which the national population is divided into fourths and representative counties and metropolitan statistical areas are selected as representative of the national population.

straw poll A poll conducted in an unscientific manner, used to predict election outcomes.

strict scrutiny test Guidelines the courts use to determine the legality of all but sex-based discrimination; on the basis of this test, discrimination is legal if it is a necessary means by which the government can achieve a compelling public interest.

strong mayor An elected municipal government executive who holds the powers traditionally delegated to elected chief executives (veto power, power to formulate the budget, and power to appoint many executive branch officials).

subcommittee A subordinate committee in Congress that typically handles specific areas of a standing committee's jurisdiction.

subsidy A tax break or another kind of financial support that encourages behaviors the government deems beneficial to the public good.

sunset clause A clause in legislation that sets an expiration date for the authorized program/policy unless Congress reauthorizes it.

sunshine laws Legislation that opens up government functions and documents to the public.

Super Tuesday The Tuesday in early March on which the most primary elections are held, many of them in southern states; provided the basis for Super-Duper Tuesday in 2008.

superpowers Leader nations with dominating influence in international affairs.

supply-side economics The theory that advocates cutting taxes and deregulating business to stimulate the economy.

supremacy clause The paragraph in Article VI that makes the Constitution, and the treaties and laws created in compliance with it, the supreme law of the land.

supreme law of the land The U.S. Constitution's description of its own authority, meaning that all laws made by governments within the United States must be in compliance with the Constitution.

suspect classifications Distinctions based on race, religion, national origin, and sex, which are assumed to be illegitimate.

symbolic representation The attempt to ensure that the Supreme Court is representative of major demographic groups, such as women, African Americans, Jews, and Catholics.

symbolic speech Nonverbal "speech" in the form of an action such as picketing, flag burning, or wearing an armband to signify a protest.

T

take care clause The constitutional basis for inherent powers, which states that the president "shall take Care that the Laws be faithfully executed."

talk radio A format featuring conversations and interviews about topics of interest, along with call-ins from listeners.

tariff A special tax on imported goods.

tax base The overall *wealth* (income and assets of citizens and corporations) that the government can tax to raise revenue.

tax expenditures (Also, *tax breaks* or *loopholes*), government financial supports that allow individuals and corporations to pay reduced taxes, to encourage behaviors that foster the public good.

Tea Party movement A grassroots, conservative protest movement that opposed recent government actions, including stimulus spending and health care reform.

telegenic The quality of looking good on TV.

third party A party organized in opposition or as an alternative to the existing parties in a two-party system.

Three-Fifths Compromise The negotiated agreement by the delegates to the Constitutional Convention to count each slave as three-fifths of a free man for the purpose of representation and taxes.

ticket splitting The situation in which voters vote for candidates from more than one party.

time, place, and manner restrictions Regulations regarding when, where, or how expression may occur; must be content neutral.

tort A wrongful act involving a personal injury or harm to one's property or reputation.

total incorporation The theory that the Fourteenth Amendment's due process clause requires the states to uphold all freedoms in the Bill of Rights; rejected by the Supreme Court in favor of selective incorporation.

totalitarianism A system of government in which the government essentially controls every aspect of people's lives.

township A unit of government that serves people living outside municipalities, in rural areas where the population is more dispersed than in areas served by municipal governments.

tracking polls Polls that measure changes in public opinion over the course of days, weeks, or months by repeatedly asking respondents the same questions and measuring changes in their responses.

trade deficit A negative balance of trade in which imports exceed exports.

trade policy A collection of tax laws and regulations that supports the country's international commerce.

traditionalistic political culture The view that the purpose of government is to maintain the status quo and that participants in government should come from the society's elite.

trial court The court in which a case is first heard and which determines the facts of a case.

Truman Doctrine Articulated by President Harry Truman, a foreign policy commitment by the United States to assist countries' efforts to resist communism in the Cold War era.

trustee model A model of representation in which a member of the House or the Senate follows his or her own conscience when deciding issue positions.

turnout rate The proportion of eligible voters who actually voted.

U

umbrella organizations Interest groups that represent collective groups of industries or corporations.

unanimous consent An agreement by every senator to the terms of debate on a given piece of legislation.

unicameral Describes a legislative body with a single chamber.

unitary system A governmental structure in which one central government has sovereignty, although it may create regional governments to which it delegates responsibilities.

United Nations (UN) Established in 1945, an international body whose founders hoped would develop the capacity to prevent future wars by achieving collective security and peace.

U.S. Code A compilation of all the laws passed by the U.S. Congress.

U.S. Supreme Court High court with a limited original jurisdiction whose decisions may not be appealed; it serves as the court of last resort in the U.S. judiciary.

V

vblog A video Weblog.

veto An executive power held by the president, who can reject a bill and return it to Congress with reasons for the rejection.

Virginia Plan The new governmental structure proposed by the Virginia delegation to the Constitutional Convention; it consisted of a bicameral legislature (Congress), an executive elected by the legislature, and a separate national judiciary; state representation in Congress would be proportional, based on state population; the people would elect members to the lower house, and members of the lower house would elect the members of the upper house.

voter fatigue The condition in which voters grow tired of all candidates by the time Election Day arrives, and may thus be less likely to vote.

W

War Powers Act A law that limits presidential use of military forces to sixty days, with an automatic extension of thirty additional days if the president requests such an extension.

Warsaw Pact A regional security structure formed in 1955 by the Soviet Union and its seven satellite states in Eastern Europe in response to the creation of the North Atlantic Treaty Organization (NATO).

Watergate During the Nixon administration, a scandal involving burglaries and the subsequent cover-up by high-level administration officials.

weak mayor An elected municipal government executive who holds few, if any, of the powers traditionally delegated to elected chief executives.

weapons of mass destruction (WMDs) Nuclear, chemical, and biological weapons.

whistle-blower A civil servant who discloses mismanagement, fraud, waste, corruption, and/or threats to public health and safety to the government.

White House counsel The president's lawyer.

White House Office (WHO) The office that develops policies and protects the president's legal and political interests.

white primary A primary election in which a party's nominees for general election were chosen but in which only white people were allowed to vote.

winner-take-all An electoral system in which the candidate who receives the most votes wins that office, even if that total is not a majority.

Works Progress Administration (WPA) A New Deal program that would employ 8.5 million people at a cost of more than $11 million between 1935 and 1943.

World Bank The international financial institution created by the Bretton Woods Agreement of 1944 and charged with lending money to nations in need.

World Trade Organization (WTO) The organization created in 1995 to negotiate, implement, and enforce international trade agreements.

writ of *certiorari* Latin for "a request to make certain"; this is an order to a lower court to produce a certified record of a case so that the appellate court can determine whether any errors occurred during trial that warrant review of the case.

Y

yellow journalism An irresponsible, sensationalist approach to news reporting, so named after the yellow ink used in the "Yellow Kid" cartoons in the *New York World*.

REFERENCES

CHAPTER 1

1. Rogers Smith, *Civic Ideals: Conflicting Visions of Citizenship in U.S. History* (New Haven, CT: Yale University Press, 1997).
2. Robert A. Dahl, *Who Governs? Democracy and Power in an American City* (New Haven, CT: Yale University Press, 1961).
3. E. E. Schattschneider, *The Semi-Sovereign People* (New York: Holt, Rinehart, and Winston, 1960).
4. E. J. Dionne Jr., *Why Americans Hate Politics: The Death of the Democratic Process,* 2nd ed. (New York: Touchstone, 1992).
5. Gallup Poll, "Trust in Government," www.gallup.com/poll/5392/Trust-Government.aspx.
6. Institute of Politics at Harvard University, "Attitudes Towards Politics and Public Service: A National Survey of College Undergraduates," April 11-20, 2000, www.iop.harvard.edu/pdfs/survey/2000.pdf.
7. Ibid.
8. Ibid.
9. Ibid.
10. Barbara Roswell, "From Service-Learning to Service Politics: A Conversation with Rick Battistoni," http://reflectionsjournal.org/Articles/V3.N1.Battistoni.Rick.Roswell.Barbara.pdf.
11. Michael Delli Carpini, Director Pew Charitable Trusts, www.apa.org/ed/slce/civicengagement.html.
12. S. E. Finer, *The History of Government*, 3 vols. (London: Oxford University Press, 1997).
13. Martin A. Reddish, *The Constitution as Political Structure* (London: Oxford University Press, 1995).
14. Theodore Sky, *To Provide for the General Welfare: A History of the Federal Spending Power* (Newark, DE: University of Delaware Press, 2003).
15. David Epstein, *The Political Theory of the Federalist* (Chicago: University of Chicago Press, 1984).
16. Thomas Hobbes, *Leviathan* (1651; New York: Oxford University Press, 1996), chap. 14.
17. *New York Times,* "America Enduring," September 11, 2002, http://query.nytimes.com/gst/fullpage.html?res=9A00E0DE1431F932A2575AC0A9649C8B63&scp=1&sq=america+enduring&st=nyt.
18. Oscar Handlin and Mary Handlin, *The Dimensions of Liberty* (Cambridge, MA: Harvard University Press, 1961).
19. Richard Labunski, *James Madison and the Struggle for the Bill of Rights* (London: Oxford University Press, 2006).
20. Jack N. Rakove, *Original Meanings: Politics and Ideas in the Making of the Constitution* (New York: Knopf, 1996).
21. Ira Katznelson and Martin Shefter, eds., *Shaped by War and Trade: International Influences on American Political Development* (Princeton, NJ: Princeton University Press, 2002).
22. *Wing Hing v. City of Eureka* (Calif), 1886.
23. Clyde W. Barrow, *Critical Theories of the State: Marxist, Neo-Marxist, Post-Marxist* (Madison: University of Wisconsin Press, 1993).
24. Seymour Martin Lipset and Gary Marks, *It Didn't Happen Here: Why Socialism Failed in the United States* (New York: W. W. Norton, 2001).
25. Giovanni Sartori and Peter Mair, *Parties and Party Systems: A Framework for Analysis* (Oxford, England: European Consortium for Political Research).

CHAPTER 2

1. www.u-s-history.com/pages/h1211.html.
2. www.yale.edu/lawweb/avalon/amerrev/parliament/stamp_act_1765.htm.
3. www.historyplace.com/unitedstates/revolution/rev-prel.htm.
4. J. Alan Rogers, "Colonial Opposition to the Quartering of Troops During the French and Indian War," *Military Affairs* (1970): 7.
5. www.manhattanrarebooks-history.com/declaratory_act.htm.
6. http://ahp.gatech.edu/townshend_act_1767.html.
7. Russell Bourne, *Cradle of Violence: How Boston's Waterfront Mobs Ignited the American Revolution* (Hoboken, NJ: Wiley, 2006).
8. www.u-s-history.com/pages/h675.html.
9. C. Brian Kelly, *Best Little Stories from the American Revolution* (Nashville, TN: Cumberland House, 1999).
10. www.bostonteapartyship.com/.
11. www.ushistory.org/declaration/related/intolerable.htm.
12. www.usconstitution.net/intol.html#Rights.
13. www.usconstitution.net/assocart.html.
14. For further discussion of the impact of *Common Sense* on colonial attitudes and beliefs, see Edmund S. Morgan, *The Birth of the Republic: 1763-89* (Chicago: University of Chicago Press, 1992), 71-76.
15. www.geocities.com/presfacts/8/lee.html.
16. You can find these constitutions at http://avalon.law.yale.edu/subject_menus/18th.asp.
17. Jack N. Rakove, "A Tradition Born of Strife," in *American Politics: Classic and Contemporary Readings,* 6th ed., ed. Allan J. Cigler and Burdett A. Loomis (Boston: Houghton Mifflin, 2005), 4-5.
18. www.fordham.edu/halsall/mod/iroquois.html.
19. For an excellent discussion of how the Articles benefited the states, see Keith L. Dougherty, *Collective Action Under the Articles of Confederation* (New York: Cambridge University Press, 2001), 76-82.
20. http://avalon.law.yale.edu/18th_century/annapoli.asp.
21. Charles Beard, *An Economic Interpretation of the Constitution of the United States* (New York: Macmillan, 1913).
22. www.usconstitution.net/consttop_ccon.html.
23. www.africanaonline.com/slavery_timeline.htm.
24. Alexander Hamilton, "Federalist No. 9," *The Federalist Papers* (Cutchogue, NY: Buccaneer Books, 1992), 37.
25. James Madison, "Federalist No. 51," *The Federalist Papers* (Cutchogue, NY: Buccaneer Books, 1992), 261-65.
26. James Madison, "Federalist No. 10," *The Federalist Papers* (Cutchogue, NY: Buccaneer Books, 1992), 42-49.
27. Alexander Hamilton, "Federalist No. 84," *The Federalist Papers* (Cutchogue, NY: Buccaneer Books, 1992), 436-37.
28. Thomas Jefferson, Letter to James Madison on the Bill of Rights debate, March 15, 1789. Courtesy of Eigen's Political & Historical Quotations.
29. Larry M. Lane and Judith J. Lane, "The Columbian Patriot: Mercy Otis Warren and the Constitution," in *Women, Politics, and the Constitution,* ed. Naomi B. Lunn (New York: Harrington Park Press, 1990), 17-31.

30. John P. Roche, "The Founding Fathers: A Reform Caucus in Action," *American Political Science Review,* LV (1961).

31. Alexander Hamilton, "Federalist No. 78," *The Federalist Papers* (Cutchogue, NY: Buccaneer Books, 1992), 395–96.

32. Courtesy of Eigen's Political and Historical Quotations, www.politicalquotes.org/Quotedisplay.aspx?DocID=22447.

33. *Plessy v. Ferguson,* 163 U.S. 537 (1896).

34. *Brown v. Board of Education,* 347 U.S. 483 (1954).

35. Thomas Marshall, "Representing Public Opinion: American Courts and the Appeals Process," *Politics and Policy* 31, no. 4 (December 2003): 726–39.

CHAPTER 3

1. http://edocket.access.gpo.gov/2009/pdf/E9-27427.pdf.

2. U.S. Census, "Federal Grants-in-Aid to State and Local Governments," www.census.gov/compendia/statab/tables 90s414.pdf.

3. *Marbury v. Madison,* 5 U.S. 137 (1803).

4. Joe R. Feagin and Clairece Booher Feagin, *Racial and Ethnic Relations,* 7th ed. (Upper Saddle River, NJ: Prentice Hall, 2003), 131.

5. Dennis L. Dresang and James J. Gosling, *Politics and Policy in American States and Communities,* 4th ed. (New York: Pearson Longman, 2004), 88.

6. *McCulloch v. Maryland,* 17 U.S. 316 (1819).

7. *Gibbons v. Ogden,* 22 U.S. 1 (1824).

8. *United States v. Lopez,* 514 U.S. 549 (1995).

9. www.oyez.org/cases/1990-1999/1994/1994_93_1260/.

10. *Helvering v. Davis,* 301 U.S. 619 (1937).

11. CNN, *CNN Reports: Katrina – State of Emergency* (Kansas City, KS: Andrews McMeel Publishing, 2005), 10.

12. Ibid., 11.

13. Ibid., 16.

14. Ibid., 176.

15. Ibid., 46.

16. *Pruneyard Shopping Center & Fred Sahadi v. Michael Robins et al.,* 447 U.S. 74, 100 S. Ct. 2035.

17. David B. Walker, *The Rebirth of Federalism,* 2nd ed. (New York: Chatham House, 2000).

18. *National League of Cities v. Usery,* 426 U.S. 833 (1976).

19. *Garcia v. San Antonio Transportation Authority,* 469 U.S. 528 (1985).

20. *United States v. Oakland Cannabis Buyers' Cooperative,* 532 U.S. 483 (2001).

21. www.drugpolicy.org/marijuana/medical/challenges/cases/conant/.

22. *Raich v. Gonzales,* 545 U.S. 1 (2005).

23. *Bush v. Gore,* 531 U.S. 98 (2000).

24. See, for example, David B. Walker, *The Rebirth of Federalism.*

25. Josh Goodman, "Where Have All the Dollars Gone?" *Governing* (October 2009): 45–48.

26. *Massachusetts v. Mellon,* 262 U.S. 447 (1923).

27. *South Dakota v. Dole,* 483 U.S. 208 (1987).

28. www2.potsdam.edu/hansondj/LegalDrinkingAge.html.

29. www.nih.gov/about/researchresultsforthepublic/AlcoholRelatedTrafficDeaths.pdf.

30. Goodman, "Where Have All the Dollars Gone?" 45–48.

CHAPTER 4

1. Stephen L. Carter, *The Dissent of the Governed: Law, Religion, and Loyalty* (Cambridge, MA: Harvard University Press, 1998).

2. For an accessible and lively account of the central role of liberty in the American Revolution, see Thomas Fleming, *Liberty! The American Revolution* (New York: Viking, 1997).

3. For a history of civil liberties in wartime, see Geoffrey R. Stone, *Perilous Times: Free Speech in Wartime from the Sedition Act of 1798 to the War on Terrorism* (New York: W. W. Norton, 2004).

4. *Barron v. Baltimore,* 32 U.S. 243 (1833).

5. See *Hurtado v. California,* 110 U.S. 516 (1884) and *Turning v. New Jersey,* 211 U.S. 78 (1908) for a discussion of the standard the Court uses to determine whether a particular liberty should be incorporated into the Fourteenth Amendment.

6. *Gitlow v. New York,* 268 U.S. 652 (1925).

7. *Near v. Minnesota,* 283 U.S. 697 (1931).

8. *Palko v. Connecticut,* 302 U.S. 319 (1937).

9. Presidential Proclamation of September 24, 1862, by President Abraham Lincoln, suspending the writ of habeas corpus.

10. For two detailed accounts of the acts, see John C. Miller, *Crisis in Freedom: The Alien and Sedition Acts* (Boston: Little, Brown, 1951), and James Morton Smith, *Freedom's Fetters: The Alien and Sedition Laws and American Civil Liberties* (Ithaca, NY: Cornell University Press, 1956).

11. Ron Fournier, "Bush Orders Terrorist Trials by Military Tribunals," Associated Press, November 13, 2001. Executive order available at www.whitehouse.gov/news/releases/releases/2001/11/20011113-27.html.

12. Associated Press, "Obama Administration Considering DC Trial for Guantanamo Detainee Riduan Isamuddin, aka Hambali," January 15, 2010, www.nydailynews.com/news/national/2010/01/15/2010-01-15_administration_considering_dc_for_gitmo_detainee.html.

13. Charlie Savage, "Detainees Will Still Be Held, but Not Tried, Official Says," January 22, 2010, www.nytimes.com/2010/01/22/us/22gitmo.html?hpw.

14. *Schenck v. United States,* 249 U.S. 47 (1919).

15. *Gitlow v. New York.*

16. *Dennis v. U.S.,* 341 U.S. 494 (1951).

17. *Brandenburg v. Ohio,* 395 U.S. 444 (1969).

18. *U.S. v. O'Brien,* 391 U.S. 367 (1968).

19. *Tinker et al. v. Des Moines Independent Community School District et al.,* 393 U.S. 503 (1969).

20. For a discussion of *Tinker* and similar cases, see Jamin B. Baskin, *We the Students: Supreme Court Cases for and About Students* (Washington, DC: CQ Press, 2000).

21. *Texas v. Johnson,* 491 U.S. 397 (1989).

22. *U.S. v. Eichman,* 496 U.S. 310 (1990).

23. *Citizens United v. Federal Election Commission,* 558 U.S. _____ (2010).

24. *Miller v. California,* 413 U.S. 15 (1973).

25. *Chaplinsky v. New Hampshire,* 315 U.S. 568 (1942).

26. *Reno v. ACLU,* 521 U.S. 844 (1997); *U.S. v. Playboy Entertainment Group,* 529 U.S. 803 (2000).

27. *Ashcroft v. Free Speech Coalition,* 535 U.S. 234 (2002).

28. James Risen and Eric Lightblau, "Bush Lets U.S. Spy on Callers Without Courts," *New York Times,* December 16, 2005.

29. Marc Ambinder, "Shut Up: It's Still a Secret," *The Atlantic,* April 7, 2009; www.theatlantic.com/politics/archive/2009/04/shut-up-its-still-a-secret/7304/.

30. David Kravets, "Obama Sides with Bush in Spy Case," January 22, 2009, www.wired.com/threatlivelevel/2009/01/obama-sides-wit/; Wayne Madsen, "Warrantless Electronic Surveillance Continues at Bush Levels under Obama," December 16, 2009, http://onlinejournal.com/artman/publish/article_5383.shtml.

31. *New York Times v. U.S.,* 403 U.S. 713 (1971).

32. www.gallup.com/poll/1690/Religion.aspx.

33. The phrase "wall of separation" first appeared in Thomas Jefferson's 1802 letter to the Danbury Baptist Association. This letter is available at the Library of Congress Web site: www.loc.gov/loc/lcib/9806/danpre.html.

34. For a discussion of the doctrine of accommodationism, see Kenneth D. Wald, *Religion and Politics in the United States,* 3rd ed. (Washington, DC: CQ Press, 1997). For a discussion of neutrality, see Robert Booth Fowler, Allen D. Hertzke, and Laura R. Olson, *Religion and Politics in America: Faith, Culture, & Strategic Choices,* 2nd ed. (Boulder, CO: Westview Press, 1999).

35. *Everson v. Board of Education,* 330 U.S. 1 (1947).

36. *Lemon v. Kurtzman,* 403 U.S. 602 (1971).

37. *Zelman v. Simmons-Harris,* 539 U.S. 639 (2002).

38. *Engel v. Vitale,* 370 U.S. 421 (1962).

39. See, for example, the U.S. District Court ruling in *Tammy Kitzmiller et al. v. Dover Area School District et al.,* 400 F. Supp. 2d 707 (M.D. Pa. 2005).

40. *Prince v. Massachusetts,* 321 U.S. 158 (1944).

41. *Employment Division, Department of Human Resources of the State of Oregon et al. v. Smith,* 494 U.S. 872 (1990).

42. *Griswold v. Connecticut,* 381 U.S. 479 (1965).

43. *Roberts v. U.S. Jaycees,* 468 U.S. 609 (1984).

44. *Roe v. Wade,* 410 U.S. 113 (1973).

45. *Planned Parenthood v. Casey,* 505 U.S. 833 (1992).

46. *Cruzan v. Director, Missouri Department of Health,* 497 U.S. 261 (1990).

47. Ibid.
48. *Bowers v. Hardwick,* 478 U.S. 186 (1986).
49. *Lawrence v. Texas,* 539 U.S. 558 (2003).
50. This is a point of agreement among the Court's opinion, the concurring opinion, and the dissenting opinion issued in *Lawrence v. Texas,* 539 U.S. 558 (2003).
51. *Weeks v. U.S.,* 232 U.S. 383 (1914).
52. *Mapp v. Ohio,* 367 U.S. 643 (1961).
53. See Chief Justice Warren E. Burger's dissent in *Coolidge v. New Hampshire,* 403 U.S. 443.
54. *Segura v. U.S.,* 468 U.S. 796 (1984).
55. *U.S. v. Leon,* 468 U.S. 897 (1984).
56. *California v. Greenwood,* 486 U.S. 35 (1988).
57. *Miranda v. Arizona,* 384 U.S. 436 (1966).
58. *Gideon v. Wainwright,* 312 U.S. 335 (1963).
59. *Furman v. Georgia,* 408 U.S. 238 (1972).
60. The de facto moratorium on the death penalty ended in 1976 in a series of cases starting with *Gregg v. Georgia,* 428 U.S. 153 (1976).
61. *Baze v. Rees,* 553 U.S. (2008).
62. *Wilkerson v. Utah,* 99 U.S. 130 (1878).
63. For a strong argument against gun control, see John R. Lott Jr., *More Guns, Less Crime: Understanding Crime and Gun Control Laws* (Chicago: University of Chicago Press, 1998).
64. For a detailed look at different historical interpretations of the Second Amendment, see Carl T. Bogus, ed., *The Second Amendment in Law and History: Historians and Constitutional Scholars on the Right to Bear Arms* (New York: New Press, 2000).
65. For an articulation of this argument, see Carl T. Bogus, "What Does the Second Amendment Restrict? A Collective Rights Analysis," *Constitutional Commentary* 18, no. 3 (Winter 2001): 485–516.
66. *McDonald v. City of Chicago,* 561 U.S. _____ (2010).
67. *District of Columbia v. Heller,* 554 U.S. (2008).
68. www.millionmommarch.org.
69. http://2asisters.org.
70. For a recent report, see ACLU, "History Repeated: The Dangers of Domestic Spying by Federal Law Enforcement," May 29, 2007, www.aclu.org/images/asset_upload _file893_29902.pdf.
71. Larry Siems, "Why We're Challenging the FAA," July 22, 2009, www.aclu.org/blog/ national-security/why-were-challenging -FAA.
72. ACLU, "No Real Threat: The Pentagon's Secret Database on Peaceful Protest," January 17, 2007, available at www.aclu.org/ safefree/spyfiles/27988pub20070117.html.
73. Jo Mannies, "Ashcroft Defends Bush on Spying," St. Louis *Post-Dispatch,* February 10, 2008.
74. The full title of the law (H.R. 3162) is the Uniting and Strengthening America by Providing Appropriate Tools Required to Intercept and Obstruct Terrorism (USA PATRIOT) Act of 2001.
75. Protect America Act of 2007 (Pub.L. 110-55, S. 1927) signed into law by George W. Bush on August 5, 2007.

76. Offices of Inspectors General of the Department of Defense, Department of Justice, the Central Intelligence Agency, the National Security Agency, and the Office of the Director of National Intelligence, "Unclassified Report on the President's Surveillance Progam," Report No. 2009-0013-AS, July 10, 2009.
77. For an articulation of this argument, see Charles Krauthammer, "The Truth About Torture," *The Weekly Standard,* December 5, 2005.
78. For an articulation of this viewpoint, see Andrew Sullivan, "The Abolition of Torture," *New Republic,* December 19, 2005.
79. The full text of the Detainee Treatment Act of 2005 (H.R. 2863, Title X) is available at http://thomas.loc.gov/cgi-bin/query/ R?r109:FLD001:S10909.
80. The full text of a statement delivered by Condoleezza Rice, the former U.S. secretary of state, at Andrews Air Force base in Maryland is available at www.timesonline .co.uk/tol/news/world/us_and_americas/ article745995.ece.
81. European Parliament report, January 22, 2006, "Alleged Secret Detentions and Unlawful Inter-State Transfers Involving Council of Europe Member States."
82. United States Department of Justice, "Special Task Force on Interrogations and Transfer Policies Issues Its Recommendations to the President," August 24, 2009, www.justice.gov/opa/pr/2009/August/09 -ag-835.html.
83. David A. Harris, "'Flying While Arab,' Immigration Issues, and Lessons from the Racial Profiling Controversy," testimony before the U.S. Commission on Civil Rights (October 12, 2001).
84. Eric Love, "Obama Administration Official Ignores Non-Muslim Terrorists," Alternet, June 8, 2010, http://blogs.alternet.org/ speakeasy/2010/06/08/obama -administration-only-muslims-can-be -terrorists/; Spencer Hsu, "Nawar Shora Takes Battle for Arab and Muslim Rights Inside the TSA," Washingtonpost.com, March 19, 2010, www.washingtonpost.com wp-dyn/content/article/2010/03/18/ AR2010031805190.html.

CHAPTER 5

1. Rolan J. Pennock, "Rights, Natural Rights, and Human Rights—A General View," in *Human Rights,* ed. J. R. Pennock and J. W. Chapman (New York: New York University Press, 1981).
2. *Loving v. Virginia,* 388 U.S. 1 (1967).
3. Donald E. Lively, *The Constitution and Race* (New York: Praeger, 1992).
4. John Hope Franklin, *From Slavery to Freedom,* 7th ed. (New York: McGraw-Hill, 1994).
5. *Dred Scott v. Sandford,* 60 U.S. 393 (1857).
6. *Plessy v. Ferguson,* 163 U.S. 537 (1896).

7. George T. Blakey, *Hard Times and New Deal in Kentucky, 1929–1939* (Lexington: University of Kentucky Press, 1986).
8. Richard Kluger, *Simple Justice: The History of* Brown v. Board of Education *and Black America's Struggle for Equality* (New York: Knopf, 1976).
9. Raymond Wolters, *The Burden of Brown: Thirty Years of School Desegregation* (Knoxville: University of Tennessee Press, 1984).
10. Jo Ann Robinson, *The Montgomery Bus Boycott and the Women Who Started It* (Knoxville: University of Tennessee Press, 1987).
11. Taylor Branch, *Parting the Waters: America During the King Years, 1954–1963* (New York: Simon & Schuster, 1988).
12. *Browder v. Gale,* 142 F. Supp. 707 (1956).
13. John Lewis, *Walking with the Wind: A Memoir of the Movement* (New York: Simon & Schuster, 1998).
14. David J. Garrow, *Protest at Selma: Martin Luther King, Jr., and the Voting Rights Act of 1965* (New Haven, CT: Yale University Press, 1978).
15. Taylor Branch, *Pillar of Fire: America in the King Years 1963–65* (New York: Simon & Schuster, 1998).
16. Stokely Carmichael, "What We Want," *New York Review of Books,* September 22, 1966: 5–7.
17. Stokely Carmichael and Mike Thelwell, "Toward Black Liberation," *Massachusetts Review* 7 (1966): 639–51.
18. Steven Lawson, *Black Ballots: Voting Rights in the South, 1944–1969* (New York: Columbia University Press, 1976).
19. www.census.gov/prod/2001pubs/statab/ sec08.pdf.
20. *Bradwell v. Illinois,* 83 U.S. 130 (1873).
21. *Minor v. Happersett,* 88 U.S. 162 (1875).
22. www.now.org/history/purpos66.html.
23. *Reed v. Reed,* 404 U.S. 71 (1971).
24. *Craig v. Boren,* 429 U.S. 190 (1976).
25. *U.S. v. Virginia,* 518 U.S. 515 (1996).
26. Joe R. Feagin and Clairece Booher Feagin, *Racial and Ethnic Relations* (Upper Saddle River, NJ: Prentice Hall, 2003), 135.
27. www.nigc.gov/ReadingRoom/ PressReleases/PressReleasesMain/ PR113062009/tabid/918/Default.aspx.
28. Feagin and Feagin, *Racial and Ethnic Relations,* 135.
29. www.naacpldf.org/content/pdf/austin2/ Navajo_Nation_Brief_14.pdf.
30. http://pewhispanic.org/files/factsheets/ hispanics2007/Table-3.pdf.
31. Based on author's calculations using data from the William C. Velasquez Institute, www.wcvi.org/latino_voter_research/ latino_voter_statistics.html.
32. www.lulac.org/about/history.html.
33. Ibid.
34. *Mendez v. Westminister,* 64 F. Supp. 544 (1946).
35. Feagin and Feagin, *Racial and Ethnic Relations,* 218.
36. *Corpus Christi Independent School District v. Cisneros,* 404 U.S. 1211 (1971).

37. Texas State Historical Association, "The Handbook of Texas Online," www.tshaonline.org/handbook/online/articles/CC/jrc2.html.
38. www.naleo.org/directory. html.
39. http://minorityhealth.hhs.gov/templates/content.aspx?ID=3005.
40. Feagin and Feagin, *Racial and Ethnic Relations,* 278 and 310.
41. Ibid., 315.
42. http://www.aasc.ucla.edu/archives/pa_07_08.asp.
43. www.access-board.gov/about/laws/ada-amendments.htm.
44. *Bowers v. Hardwick,* 478 U.S. 186 (1986).
45. *Lawrence v. Texas,* 539 U.S. 558 (2003).
46. Jon W. Davidson, "Celebrating Recent LGBT Legislative Advances," www.lambdalegal.org/our-work/publications/facts-backgrounds/recent-lgbt-advances.html.
47. *Romer v. Evans,* 517 U.S. 620 (1996).
48. www.lambdalegal.org/publications/articles/nationwide-status-same-sex-relationships.html#9.
49. www.adl.org/99hatecrime/state_hate_crime_laws.pdf.
50. *Regents of the University of California v. Bakke,* 438 U.S. 265 (1978).
51. Ward Connerly, "College Admissions, Let's Not Break the Law," 2007, www.acri.org/chairman.html.
52. www.acri.org/.
53. *Grutter v. Bollinger,* 539 U.S. 306 (2003).
54. *Parents Involved in Community Schools v. Seattle School District No. 1 et al.,* 551 U.S. _____ (2007) and *Meredith v. Jefferson County Board of Education,* 551 U.S. _____ (2007).

CHAPTER 6

1. Steven Pinker, *How the Mind Works* (W. W. Norton, 1997), viii.
2. Aaron Nelson, "Update: Kids Tell Adults to 'Go Vote,'" *The Brownsville Herald,* November 7, 2006.
3. V. O. Key Jr., *Public Opinion and American Democracy* (New York: Knopf, 1961), 8.
4. Mark Hugo Lopez, Peter Levine, Deborah Both, Abby Kiesa, Emily Kirby, and Karlo Marcelo, *The 2006 Civic and Political Health of the Nation: A Detailed Look at How Youth Participate in Politics and Communities* (College Park, MD: Circle: The Center for Information and Research on Civic Learning and Engagement, 2006), 4.
5. Ibid.
6. Sidney Verba, Kay Lehman Schlozman, and Henry E. Brady, *Voice and Equality: Civic Voluntarism in American Politics* (Cambridge, MA: Harvard University Press, 1995), 439.
7. David L. Leal, Matt A. Barreto, Jongho Lee, and Rodolfo O. de la Garza, "The Latino Vote in the 2004 Election," *PS: Political Science and Politics* (2005): 46.
8. Lopez et al., *The 2006 Civic and Political Health of the Nation,* 20–21.

9. Karlo Barrios Marcelo, Mark Hugo Lopez, and Emily Hoban Kirby, *Civic Engagement Among Young Men and Women* (College Park, MD: Circle: The Center for Information and Research on Civic Learning and Engagement, 2007), 12.
10. David W. Moore, "Death Penalty Gets Less Support from Britons, Canadians Than Americans," Gallup News Service, February 20, 2006.
11. Elizabeth Noelle-Neumann, *The Spiral of Silence: Public Opinion—Our Social Skin,* 2nd ed. (Chicago: University of Chicago Press, 1993).
12. Susan Herbst, *Numbered Voices: How Opinion Polling Has Shaped American Politics* (Chicago: University of Chicago Press, 1993).
13. Robert S. Erikson, Gerald C. Wright, and John P. McIver, *Statehouse Democracy: Public Opinion and Policy in the American States* (New York: Cambridge University Press, 1994).
14. Walter Lippmann, *Public Opinion* (1929; repr. London: Free Press, 1997), 114.
15. "George Gallup, 1901-1984: Founder, The Gallup Organization," http://gallup.com/content/?ci=21364.
16. Herbert Asher, *Polling and the Public: What Every Citizen Should Know* (Washington, DC: CQ Press, 2001).
17. Ibid., 2.
18. Joseph Carroll, "Many Americans Use Multiple Labels to Describe Their Ideology," December 6, 2006, www.gallup.com/poll/25771/Many-Americans-Use-Multiple-Labels-Describe-Their-Ideology.aspx.
19. Randolph Grossman and Douglas Weiland, "The Use of Telephone Directories as a Sample Frame: Patterns of Bias Revisited, *Journal of Advertising* 7 (1978): 31–36.
20. Stephen J. Blumberg and Julian V. Luke, "Coverage Bias in Traditional Telephone Surveys of Low-Income and Young Adults," *Public Opinion Quarterly* 71 (2007): 734–49.
21. Clyde Tucker, J. Michael Brick, and Brian Meekins, "Household Telephone Service and Usage Patterns in the United States in 2004: Implications for Telephone Samples," *Public Opinion Quarterly* 71 (2007): 3–22.
22. "Wireless Solution: Early Release Estimates from the National Health Interview Survey, July–December 2008," National Health Center for Health Statistics, Centers for Disease Control and Prevention, May 2009.
23. Blumberg and Luke, "Coverage Bias in Traditional Telephone Surveys of Low-Income and Young Adults," 734–49.
24. Ibid.
25. George Terhanian and John Bremer, "Confronting the Selection-Bias and Learning Effects Problems Associated with Internet Research," Harris Interactive white paper, August 16, 2000.
26. G. Terhanian, R. Smith, J. Bremer, and R. K. Thomas, "Exploiting Analytical Advances: Minimizing the Biases Associated with Internet-Based Surveys of Non-Random Samples," *ARF/ESOMAR: Worldwide Online Measurement* 248 (2001): 247–72.

27. Irving Crespi, *Pre-Election Polling: Sources of Accuracy & Error* (New York: Russell Sage Foundation, 1988).
28. Benjamin I. Page and Robert Y. Shapiro, *The Rational Public: Fifty Years of Trends in Americans' Policy Preferences* (Chicago: University of Chicago Press, 1992).
29. Frank Newport, *Polling Matters: Why Leaders Must Listen to the Wisdom of the People* (New York: Warner Books, 2004).
30. James A. Stimson, *Tides of Consent: How Public Opinion Shapes American Politics* (Cambridge: Cambridge University Press, 2004).
31. Frank Newport, "U.S. Satisfaction at 15%, Lowest Since 1992," April 14, 2008, www.gallup.com/poll/106498/US-Satisfaction-15-Lowest-Since-1992.aspx.
32. Frank Newport and Joseph Carroll, "Iraq Versus Vietnam: A Comparison of Public Opinion," August 24, 2005, www.galluppoll.com/content/default.aspx?ci=18097&pg=2.
33. Jeffrey M. Jones and Joseph Carroll, "National Satisfaction Level Dips to 25%, One of Lowest Since 1979," May 16, 2007, www.galluppoll.com/content/?ci=27601&pg=1.
34. David W. Moore, "Top Ten Gallup Presidential Approval Ratings," Gallup press release, September 24, 2001.

CHAPTER 7

1. Frank R. Baumgartner and Beth L. Leech, *Basic Interests: The Importance of Groups in Politics and in Political Science* (Princeton, NJ: Princeton University Press, 1998).
2. Peggy Daniels and Carol Schwartz, *Encyclopedia of Associations 1996* (Detroit: Gale Research, 1995).
3. Alexis De Tocqueville, *Democracy in America: The Complete and Unabridged Volumes I and II* (1835–1840; New York: Bantam, 2000), 51.
4. Everett Carll Ladd, *The Ladd Report* (New York: Free Press, 1999).
5. Publius (James Madison), *Federalist #10,* 1787, www.ourdocuments.gov/doc.php?doc=10.
6. Robert D. Putnam, *Bowling Alone: The Collapse and Revival of American Community* (New York: Touchstone, 2000).
7. Claude S. Fischer, "Bowling Alone: What's the Score?" *Social Networks* 27 (May): 155–67.
8. E. E. Schattschneider, *The Semi-Sovereign People* (New York: Holt, Rinehart, and Winston, 1960), 132.
9. Earl Latham, *The Group Basis of Politics* (Ithaca, NY: Cornell University Press, 1952).
10. David B. Truman, *The Governmental Process* (New York: Knopf, 1951).
11. Hugh Davis Graham, *The Civil Rights Era: Origins and Development of National Policy, 1960–1972* (London: Oxford University Press, 1990).
12. Sidney Verba, Kay Schlozman, and Nancy Burns, *The Private Roots of Public Action: Gender, Equality, and Political Participation*

(Cambridge, MA: Harvard University Press, 2001).

13. Quoted in Mark P. Petracca, *The Politics of Interests* (Boulder, CO: Westview, 1992), 347.

14. www.ama-assn.org/ama/pub/health-system-reform/repeal-medicare-sgr-video.shtml.

15. Julie Greene, *Pure and Simple Politics: The American Federation of Labor and Political Activism, 1881–1917* (New York: Cambridge University Press, 1998).

16. Elizabeth Sanders, *Roots of Reform: Farmers, Workers, and the American State, 1877–1917* (Chicago: University of Chicago Press, 1998).

17. Sharon E. Jarvis, Lisa Montoya, and Emily Mulvoy, "The Civic Participation of Working Youth and College Students: Working Paper 36" (Austin, TX: The Annette Strauss Institute for Civic Participation, and CIRCLE, the Center for Information and Research on Civic Learning and Engagement, 2005).

18. James Q. Wilson, *Political Organizations* (New York: Basic Books, 1973).

19. Dennis Hastert, *Speaker: Lessons from Forty Years in Coaching and Politics* (Washington, DC: Regnery Publishing, 2004), 256.

20. Jeffrey Berry, *The Interest Group Society,* 3rd ed. (New York: Longman, 1997).

21. Martin J. Smith, *Pressures, Power and Policy: Policy Networks and State Autonomy in Britain and the United States* (Pittsburgh, PA: University of Pittsburgh, 1994).

22. Herbert Alexander, *Money in Politics* (Washington, DC: Public Affairs Press, 1972).

23. Frank Sorauf, *Money in American Elections* (New York: Little, Brown, 1988).

24. Frank Sorauf, *Inside Campaign Finance: Myths and Realities* (New Haven, CT: Yale University Press, 1992).

25. Gary C. Jacobson, *Money in Congressional Elections* (New Haven, CT: Yale University Press, 1980).

26. Allan J. Cigler and Burdett A. Loomis, *Interest Group Politics* (Washington, DC: CQ Press, 1991).

27. Lucy G. Barber, *Marching on Washington: The Forging of an American Political Tradition* (Los Angeles: University of California Press, 2002).

28. www.cc.org/mission.cfm.

29. *Citizens United v. Federal Election Commission,* 558 U.S. _____ (2010).

30. American Music Conference Newsletter, "Sesame Street's Elmo Visits Congress on Behalf of Music Education," www.amc-music.com/AMCNews/newsletterSp02/elmo_dc.html.

31. Louise Overacker, *Money in Elections* (New York: Macmillan, 1932), 378.

CHAPTER 8

1. E. E. Schattschneider, *Party Government* (New York: Farrar & Rinehart, 1942), 1.

2. L. Sandy Maisel and Kara Z. Buckley, *Parties and Elections in America,* 4th ed. (Lanham, MD: Rowman & Littlefield, 2004).

3. Jo Freeman, *A Room at a Time: How Women Entered Party Politics* (New York: Rowman & Littlefield, 2000).

4. Ibid.

5. Melanie Gustafson, Kristie Miller, and Elisabeth Israels Perry, *We Have Come to Stay: American Women and Political Parties, 1880–1960* (Albuquerque: University of New Mexico Press, 1999).

6. V. O. Key, *Politics, Parties, and Pressure Groups* (New York: Thomas Y. Crowell, 1964).

7. Seymour Martin Lipset and Stein Rokkan, *Party Systems and Voter Alignments* (New York: Free Press, 1967).

8. The Pew Research Center for the People and the Press, "Beyond Red vs. Blue: Republicans Divided About Role of Government—Democrats by Social and Personal Values" (Washington, DC: The Pew Research Center for the People and the Press, 2005).

9. Geoffrey Layman, *The Great Divide: Religious and Cultural Conflict in American Party Politics* (New York: Columbia University Press, 2002).

10. Walter Dean Burnham, *Critical Elections and the Mainsprings of American Politics* (New York: W. W. Norton, 1997).

11. John Aldrich, *Why Parties? The Origin and Transformation of Party Politics in America* (Chicago: University of Chicago Press, 1995).

12. *Buckley v. Valeo,* 424 U.S. 1 (1976).

13. Regina Dougherty, "Divided Government Defines the Era," in *America at the Polls: 1996,* ed. Regina Dougherty, Everett C. Ladd, David Wilber, and Lynn Zayachkiwsky (Storrs, CT: Roper Center for Public Opinion Research, 1997).

14. Richard Hofstadter, "A Constitution Against Parties: Madisonian Pluralism and the Anti-Party Tradition," *Government and Opposition* 4, no. 3 (1969), 345–66.

15. Jefferson and Washington quoted in Richard Hofstadter, *The Idea of a Party System: The Rise of Legitimate Opposition in the United States, 1780–1840* (Berkeley: University of California Press, 1969), 2, 123.

16. Hofstadter, *The Idea of a Party System.*

17. James L. Sundquist, *Dynamics of the Party System: Alignment and Realignment of Political Parties in the United States* (Washington, DC: Brookings, 1983).

18. Everett C. Ladd, *American Political Parties* (New York: W. W. Norton, 1970).

19. David R. Mayhew, *Electoral Realignments: A Critique of an American Genre* (New Haven, CT: Yale University Press, 2002).

20. William Nisbet Chambers, *Political Parties in a New Nation: The American Experience, 1776–1809* (New York: Oxford University Press, 1963).

21. Lance Banning, *The Jeffersonian Persuasion: Evolution of a Party Ideology* (Ithaca, NY: Cornell University Press, 1978).

22. Richard L. McCormick, *The Party Period and Public Policy: American Politics from the Age of Jackson to the Progressive Era* (New York: Oxford University Press, 1986).

23. Jules Witcover, *Party of the People: A History of the Democrats* (New York: Random House, 2003).

24. Lee Benson, *The Concept of Jacksonian Democracy* (Princeton, NJ: Princeton University Press, 1961).

25. Aileen Kraditor, *The Ideas of the Woman Suffrage Movement, 1890–1920* (New York: W. W. Norton, 1981).

26. Eric Foner, *Free Soil, Free Labor, Free Men: The Ideology of the Republican Party Before the Civil War* (New York: Oxford University Press, 1995).

27. William E. Gienapp, *The Origins of the Republican Party, 1852–1856* (New York: Oxford University Press, 1987).

28. Witcover, *Party of the People.*

29. McCormick, *The Party Period and Public Policy.*

30. Joel H. Silbey, *The Partisan Imperative: The Dynamics of American Politics Before the Civil War* (New York: Oxford University Press, 1985).

31. Lewis L. Gould, *Grand Old Party: A History of the Republicans* (New York: Random House, 2003).

32. Paul Kleppner, *The Third Electoral System, 1853–1892: Parties, Voters, and Political Cultures* (Chapel Hill: University of North Carolina Press, 1979).

33. Quoted in A. James Reichley, "Party Politics in a Federal Polity," in *Challenges to Party Government,* ed. John Kenneth White and Jerome M. Mileur (Carbondale: Southern Illinois University, 1992), 48.

34. Kristi Anderson, *After Suffrage* (Chicago: University of Chicago Press, 1996), 30.

35. John Petrocik, *Party Coalitions: Realignment and the Decline of the New Deal Party System* (Chicago: University of Chicago Press, 1981).

36. David G. Lawrence, *The Collapse of the Democratic Majority: Realignment, Dealignment, and Electoral Change from Franklin Roosevelt to Bill Clinton* (New York: Westview, 1997).

37. Edward G. Carmines, John P. McIver, and James A. Stimson, "Unrealized Partisanship: A Theory of Dealignment," *Journal of Politics* 49 (1987): 376–400.

38. www.galluppoll.com/content/default.aspx?ci=24655&pg=2.

39. David Karol, Hans Noel, John Zaller, and Marty Cohen, "Polls or Pols? The Real Driving Force Behind Presidential Nominations," www.brookings.edu/articles/2003/summer_politics_cohen.aspx.

40. Arend Lijphardt, *Electoral Systems and Party Systems: A Study of Twenty-Seven Democracies, 1945–1990* (New York: Oxford University Press, 1994).

41. Lipset and Rokkan, *Party Systems and Voter Alignments.*

42. Maurice Duverger, *Political Parties* (New York: Wiley, 1951).

43. Gary Orren, "The Changing Styles of American Party Politics," in *The Future of*

American Political Parties: The Challenge of Governance, ed. Joel L. Fleishman (Englewood Cliffs, NJ: Prentice Hall, 1982), 31.

44. This basis for this argument can be found in Larry J. Sabato and Bruce Larson, *The Party's Just Begun: Shaping Political Parties for America's Future,* 2nd ed. (New York: Longman, 2001).

45. Steven J. Rosenstone, Roy L. Behr, and Edward H. Lazarus, *Third Parties in America,* 2nd ed. (Princeton, NJ: Princeton University Press, 1996).

46. Stefan Halper and Jonathon Clarke, *America Alone: The Neo-Conservatives and the Global Order* (London: Cambridge University Press, 2004).

CHAPTER 9

1. V. O. Key, *The Responsible Electorate* (Cambridge, MA: Harvard University Press, 1966).

2. Samuel C. Patterson and Gregory A. Caldeira, "Getting Out the Vote: Participation in Gubernatorial Elections," *American Political Science Review* 77 (1983): 675–89.

3. Barbara Norrander, *Super Tuesday: Regional Politics and Presidential Primaries* (Lexington: University of Kentucky Press, 1992).

4. Thomas E. Cronin, *Direct Democracy: The Politics of Initiative, Referendum, and Recall* (Cambridge, MA: Harvard University Press, 1999).

5. David Broder, *Democracy Derailed: Initiative Campaigns and the Power of Money* (New York: Harvest Books, 2001).

6. *Perry v. Schwarzenegger,* 704 F. Supp. 2d 921 (N.D. Cal. 2010).

7. John F. Bibby, *Politics, Parties, and Elections in America* (Belmont, CA: Wadsworth, 2000), 253.

8. Pat Buchanan on NBC's *Today Show,* "The American Presidency Project," November 9, 2000, www.presidency.ucsb.edu/showflorida2000.php?fileid=buchanan11-09.

9. Ibid.

10. Mark Trahant, "Vote by Mail? OK, So I Was Wrong . . . ," *Seattle Post-Intelligencer,* September 25, 2005, http://seattlepi.nwsource.com/opinion/242020_trahant25.html.

11. Pippa Norris, ed., *Politics and the Press: The News Media and Their Influences* (Boulder, CO: Lynne Rienner Publishers, 1997).

12. Ben Smith, "The Next Bob Shrum?" *Politico,* February 6, 2007, www.politico.com/news/stories/0207/2667.html.

13. See, for example, Matthew Dowd, "Campaign Organization and Strategy," in *Electing the President 2004: An Insider's View,* ed. Kathleen Hall Jamieson (Philadelphia: University of Pennsylvania Press, 2006).

14. Vivé Griffith, "The Influence of Media in Presidential Politics," Think Democracy Project, University of Texas at Austin, www.utexas.edu/features/archive/2004/election_media.html.

15. Jose Antonio Vargas, "Obama Raised Half a Billion Online," January 20, 2008, http://voices.washingtonpost.com/44/2008/11/20/obama_raised_half_a_billion_on.html.

16. www.articles.latimes.com/2007/mar/11/nation/na-actblue11

17. Gary Jacobson, *Money and Congressional Elections* (New Haven, CT: Yale University Press, 1980).

18. David Adamany, "Money, Politics and Democracy," *American Political Science Review* 71 (1977): 289–304.

19. *Buckley v. Valeo,* 424 U.S. (1976).

20. See Anthony Corrado, Thomas E. Mann, Dan Ortiz, Trevor Potter, and Frank Sorauf, *Campaign Finance Reform: A Sourcebook* (Washington, DC: Brookings Institute, 1997).

21. *Federal Election Commission v. National Conservative PAC,* 470 U.S. 480 (1985).

22. *McConnell v. Federal Election Commission,* 540 U.S. 93 (2003).

23. *Federal Election Commission v. Wisconsin Right to Life, Inc.,* 551 U.S. (2007).

24. Norman H. Nie, Sidney Verba, and John R. Petrocik, *The Changing American Voter* (Cambridge, MA: Harvard University Press, 1976).

25. Angus Campbell, Philip Converse, Warren Miller, and Donald Stokes, *The American Voter* (New York: Wiley, 1960).

26. Jan Leighley and Jonathan Nagler, "Who Votes Now? And Does It Matter?" (paper presented at the annual meeting of the Midwest Political Science Association Chicago, 2007).

27. Norman H. Nie, Jane Junn, and Kenneth Stehlik-Barry, *Education and Democratic Citizenship in America* (Chicago: University of Chicago Press, 1996).

28. Jan E. Leighley and Jonathan Nagler, "Socioeconomic Class Bias in Turnout, 1964–1988: The Voters Remain the Same," *American Political Science Review* 86 (1992): 725–36.

29. The Annenberg National Election Study (ANES), "Voter Turnout 1948–2004," www.electionstudies.org/nesguide/2ndtable/t6a_2_2.htm.

30. Kim Nguyen and James Garand, "The Effects of Income Inequality on Political Attitudes and Behavior" (paper presented at the annual meeting of the Midwest Political Science Association, Chicago, 2007).

31. Richard A. Brody, "The Puzzle of Political Participation in America," in *The New American Political System,* ed. Anthony King (Washington, DC: American Enterprise Institute for Public Policy Research, 1978), 287–324.

32. www.census.gov/Press-Release/www/releases/archives/voting/013995.html.

33. Pippa Norris, "Retrospective Voting in the 1984 Presidential Election: Peace, Prosperity, and Patriotism," *Political Studies* 35 (1987): 289–300.

34. Daniel M. Shea, *Campaign Craft: The Strategies, Tactics, and Art of Political Campaign Management* (Westport, CT: Praeger, 1996).

35. Nie, Verba, and Petrocik, *The Changing American Voter.*

36. Samuel Kernell, "Presidential Popularity and Negative Voting," *American Political Science Review* 71 (1977): 44–66.

37. Shanto Iyengar and Jennifer A. McGrady, *Media Politics: A Citizen's Guide* (New York: W. W. Norton, 2006).

38. Warren E. Miller, "Disinterest, Disaffection, and Participation," *Political Behavior* 2 (1980): 7–32.

39. E. E. Schattschneider, *The Semi-Sovereign People* (New York: Holt, Rinehart, and Winston, 1960).

40. Pew Research Center for People and the Press, "Beyond Red Versus Blue: Profiles of the Typology Groups," 2005, http://people-press.org/reports/display.php3?PageID=949.

41. Barbara Norrander and Bernard N. Grofman, "A Rational Choice Model of Citizen Participation in High and Low Commitment Electoral Activities," *Public Choice* 57 (1988): 187–92.

42. Sidney Verba and Norman H. Nie, *Participation in America: Political Democracy and Social Equality* (New York: Harper & Row, 1972).

43. Arend Lijphart, "Compulsory Voting Is the Best Way to Keep Democracy Strong," *The Chronicle of Higher Education,* October 18, 1996: B3–4.

44. Ruy A. Teixeira, "Just How Much Difference Does Turnout Really Make?" *The American Enterprise,* July/August, 1992: 52–59.

CHAPTER 10

1. www.guardian.co.uk/media/pda/2010/feb/16/george-polk-awards.

2. Pippa Norris, *Women, Media and Politics* (New York: Oxford, 1997).

3. David Weinberger, www.hillwatch.com/PPRC/Quotes/Internet_and_Politics.aspx.

4. On April 7, 2005, General Motors pulled its advertising from the *Los Angeles Times* after columnist Dan McNeil, who covers the automotive trade for the newspaper, published several columns critical of GM, including one that chastised the company for not pursuing hybrid technology but, rather, pushing gas-guzzling SUVs and another that called for the "impeachment" of two of the company's top executives.

5. New editions of all of these works are available: Tarbell (New York: Norton, 1969); Steffens (New York: Sangamore Press, 1957); and Sinclair (Cambridge, MA: B. Bentley, 1971).

6. Mark Wheeler, *Politics and the Mass Media* (Oxford: Blackwell, 1997), 228.

7. Robert Smith, "Running for Office via the Web," *NPR: Morning Edition,* January 23, 2007.

8. Howard Rheingold, "Using Participatory Media and Public Voice to Encourage Civic Engagement," in *Civic Life Online: Learning How Digital Media Can Engage Youth,* ed. Lance W. Bennett, The John D. and Catherine T. MacArthur Foundation Series on

Digital Media and Learning (Cambridge, MA: MIT Press, 2008).

9. Norman H. Nie, Irena Stepanikova, Heili Pals, Lu Zheng, and Xiaobin He, *Ten Years after the Birth of the Internet: How Do Americans Use the Internet in Their Daily Lives?* www.stanford.edu/group/siqss/research/time_study_files/ProjectReport2005.pdf.

10. See Howard Kurtz, *Spin Cycle–How the White House and the Media Manipulate the News* (New York: Simon & Schuster, 1998).

11. Christine Gibbs Springer, "Mastering Strategic Conversations," *PA Times,* September 2006.

12. Jodi Wilgoren, "Shadowed by Threats, Judge Finds New Horror," *New York Times,* March 2, 2005, 1. See also Martin and Susan J. Tolchin, *A World Ignited: How Apostles of Ethnic, Religious and Racial Hatred Torch the Globe* (Lanham, MD: Rowman & Littlefield, 2006).

13. www.internetworldstats.com/stats.htm.

14. Cass Sunstein, *Republic.Com* (Princeton, NJ: Princeton University Press, 2002).

15. Republican National Convention Speech, July 14, 1964, *Eisenhower's Post-Presidential Speeches,* www.eisenhower.archives.gov/speeches/Post-Presidential_speeches.pdf.

16. C. Richard Hofstetter, *Bias in the News: Network Television Coverage of the 1972 Election Campaign* (Columbus, OH: Ohio State University Press, 1976); Michael J. Robinson and Margaret A. Sheehan, *Over the Wire and on TV: CBS and UPI in Campaign '80* (New York: Russell Sage Foundation, 1983).

17. William P. Eveland Jr. and Dhavan V. Shah, "The Impact of Individual and Interpersonal Factors on Perceived News Media Bias," *Political Psychology* 24, no. 1 (2003): 101–17.

18. Michael Parenti, *Inventing Reality: The Politics of the Mass Media* (New York: St. Martin's Press, 1986).

19. Tim Berners-Leer, "Neutrality of the Net," http://dig.csail.mit.edu/breadcrumbs/node/132.

CHAPTER 11

1. See, for example, David E. Price, *The Congressional Experience: A View from the Hill* (Boulder, CO: Westview, 1992).

2. Richard F. Fenno Jr., *Home Style: House Members in Their Districts* (New York: Longman, 2002).

3. www.electiondataservices.com/images/File/NR_Appor08wTables.pdf.

4. *Davis v. Bandemer,* 478 U.S. 109 (1986).

5. Samuel Kernell, ed., *James Madison: The Theory and Practice of Republican Government* (Stanford, CA: Stanford University Press, 2003).

6. Richard F. Fenno Jr., *Congressional Travels* (New York: Pearson Longman, 2007).

7. Sue Thomas, *How Women Legislate* (New York: Oxford University Press, 1994).

8. Edmund Burke, *Speeches at His Arrival at Bristol,* November, 3, 1774, http://books.google.com/books?id=eNILAAAAYAAJ&pg=PA81&dq=Edmund+Burke,.+1774.+Speeches+at+His+Arrival+at+Bristol.+3+November,+3,+1774.&source=gbs_toc_r&cad=0_0.

9. Ibid.

10. Diana Evans, *Greasing the Wheels: Using Pork Barrel Projects to Build Majority Coalitions in Congress* (New York: Cambridge University Press, 2004).

11. Bret Schulte, "A Bridge (Way) Too Far," *U.S. News and World Report,* August 8, 2005, www.usnews.com/usnews/news/articles/050808/8highway.htm.

12. Citizens Against Government Waste, *2010 Congressional Pig Book Summary,* p. 63, www.cagw.org/assets/pig-book-files/2010/2010-pig-book-summary.pdf.

13. See, for example, Bruce Cain, John Ferejohn, and Morris Fiorina, *The Personal Vote: Constituency Service and Electoral Independence* (Cambridge, MA: Harvard University Press, 1987).

14. Walter F. Mondale, testimony in hearing before the Joint Committee on the Organization of Congress, July 1, 1993, www.rules.house.gov/Archives/jcoc2av.htm.

15. Walter J. Oleszek, *Congressional Procedures and the Policy Process,* 7th ed. (Washington, DC: CQ Press, 2007).

16. See Janet M. Martin, *Lessons from the Hill: The Legislative Journey of an Education Program* (New York: St. Martin's, 1994).

17. Gary Cox and Matthew D. McCubbins, *Setting the Agenda* (Cambridge: Cambridge University Press, 2004).

18. Woodrow Wilson, *Constitutional Government in the United States* (New York: Columbia University Press, 1911), 87.

19. David Butler and Bruce Cain, *Congressional Redistricting: Comparative and Theoretical Perspectives* (New York: Macmillan, 1992).

20. Christopher J. Deering and Steven S. Smith, *Committees in Congress,* 3rd ed. (Washington, DC: Congressional Quarterly, 1997).

21. Garrison Nelson, *Committees in the U.S. Congress, 1947–1992,* 2 vols. (Washington, DC: CQ Press, 1993).

22. Steven S. Smith, Jason M. Roberts, and Ryan J. VanderWielen, *The American Congress,* 5th ed. (New York: Cambridge University Press, 2007).

23. Lawrence C. Dodd and Bruce I. Oppenheimer, *Congress Reconsidered,* 8th ed. (Washington, DC: CQ Press, 2004).

24. Sarah H. Binder, *Minority Rights, Majority Rule: Partisanship and the Development of Congress* (Cambridge: Cambridge University Press, 1997).

25. David W. Brady and Mathew D. McCubbins, *Party, Process, and Political Change in Congress: New Perspectives on the History of Congress* (Stanford, CA: Stanford University Press, 2002).

26. Joseph Martin Hernon, *Profiles in Character: Hubris and Heroism in the U.S. Senate, 1789–1990* (Armonk, NY: M. E. Sharpe, 1997).

27. Gary W. Cox, *Legislative Leviathan: Party Government in the House* (Berkeley: University of California Press, 1993).

28. Ronald M. Peters Jr., *The American Speakership: The Office in Historical Perspective,* 2nd ed. (Baltimore: Johns Hopkins University Press, 1997).

29. Susan Webb Hammond, *Congressional Caucuses in National Policy Making* (Baltimore: Johns Hopkins University Press, 2001).

30. Charles Babington and Jonathan Weisman, "Reid, Pelosi Expected to Keep Tight Rein in Both Chambers," *Washington Post,* November 10, 2006: A12.

31. Barbara Sinclair, *Majority Leadership in the US House and the Transformation of the US Senate* (Baltimore: Johns Hopkins University Press, 1990).

32. Barry C. Burden, *Personal Roots of Representation* (Princeton, NJ: Princeton University Press, 2007).

33. Sean Theriault, "Party Polarization in Congress" (paper presented at the annual meeting of the American Political Science Association, Marriott Wardman Park, Omni Shoreham, Washington Hilton, Washington,DC, September 1, 2005), www.allacademic.com/meta/p40938_index.html.

34. Michael J. Malbin, *Unelected Representatives: Congressional Staff and the Future of Representative Government* (New York: Basic Books, 1980).

35. Burdett A. Loomis, *The Contemporary Congress,* 3rd ed. (Boston: Bedford/St. Martin's, 2000).

36. John R. Wright, *Interest Groups and Congress* (New York: Allyn and Bacon, 1996).

37. R. Douglas Arnold, *The Logic of Congressional Action* (New Haven, CT: Yale University Press, 1990).

38. For a discussion of the potential goals of demographic representation, see for example, David T. Canon, "Representing Racial and Ethnic Minorities," in *The Legislative Branch,* eds. Paul J. Quirk and Sarah A. Binder (New York: Oxford University Press, 2005).

CHAPTER 12

1. George C. Edwards III, John H. Kessel, and Bert A. Rockman, eds., *Researching the Presidency: Vital Questions, New Approaches* (Pittsburgh, PA: University of Pittsburgh Press, 1993).

2. Theodore J. Lowi, *The Personal President* (Ithaca, NY: Cornell University Press, 1985).

3. Jean Reith Schroedel, *Congress, the President, and Policymaking: A Historical Analysis* (Armonk, NY: M. E. Sharpe, 1994).

4. William W. Lammers, *The Presidency and Domestic Policy: Comparing Leadership Styles, FDR to Clinton* (Washington, DC: CQ Press, 2000).

5. Andrew Rudalevige, *Managing the President's Program: Presidential Leadership and*

Legislative Policy Formulation (Princeton, NJ: Princeton University Press, 2002).

6. Richard A. Watson, *Presidential Vetoes and Public Policy* (Lawrence: University of Kansas Press, 1993).

7. Robert J. Spitzer, *The Presidential Veto: Touchstone of the American Presidency* (Albany: SUNY Press, 1988).

8. Sidney M. Milkis and Mchael Nelson, *The American Presidency: Origins and Development, 1776–1998,* 4th ed. (Washington, DC: CQ Press, 2003).

9. www.abanet.org/media/releases/news072406.html.

10. http://online.wsj.com/article/SB125116264837455591.html.

11. George C. Edwards III and Steven J. Wayne, *Studying the Presidency* (Knoxville: University of Tennessee Press, 1983).

12. Louis Fisher, *Presidential War Power* (Lawrence: University of Kansas Press, 1995).

13. David S. Broder, "Obama in Command," *Washington Post,* May 21, 2009, www.washingtonpost.com/wp-dyn/content/article/2009/05/20/AR2009052003029.html.

14. Jon Meacham, "A Highly Logical Approach," *Newsweek,* May 16, 2009, www.newsweek.com/id/197891.

15. Cornell G. Hooton, *Executive Governance: Presidential Administrations and Policy Change in the Federal Bureaucracy* (Armonk, NY: M. E. Sharpe, 1997).

16. O. C. Fisher, *Cactus Jack: A Biography of John Nance Garner* (Waco, TX: Texian Press), chap. 11.

17. Bill Clinton, *My Life* (New York: Knopf, 2004), 414.

18. Stephen Skowronek, *The Politics Presidents Make: Leadership from John Adams to George Bush* (Cambridge, MA: Belknap Press, 1997).

19. MaryAnne Borrelli, *The President's Cabinet: Gender, Power, and Representation* (Boulder, CO: Lynne Rienner, 2002).

20. Joel D. Aberbach and Mark A. Peterson, eds., *The Executive Branch* (New York: Oxford University Press, 2005).

21. William E. Leuchtenburg, *In the Shadow of FDR: From Harry Truman to Ronald Reagan* (Ithaca, NY: Cornell University Press, 1989).

22. Kenneth R. Mayer, *With the Stroke of a Pen: Executive Orders and Presidential Power* (Princeton, NJ: Princeton University Press, 2002).

23. www.trumanlibrary.org/9981.htm.

24. *U.S. v. Curtiss-Wright Export Corp.,* 229 U.S. 304 (1936).

25. Mark J. Rozell, *Executive Privilege: Presidential Power, Secrecy, and Accountability,* 2nd ed. rev. (Lawrence: University of Kansas Press, 2002).

26. *U.S. v. Richard M. Nixon,* 418 U.S. 683 (1974).

27. Richard Neustadt, *The Power to Persuade* (New York: Wiley, 1960).

28. *Outlook,* February 27, 1909.

29. Richard E. Neustadt, *Presidential Power and the Modern President* (New York: The Free Press, 1990).

30. George C. Edwards III with Alec M. Gallup, *Presidential Approval: A Sourcebook* [Eisenhower to Reagan] (Baltimore: Johns Hopkins University Press, 1990).

31. Jeffrey K. Tulis, *The Rhetorical Presidency* (Princeton, NJ: Princeton University Press, 1988).

32. Harry A. Bailey Jr. and Jay M. Shafritz, *The American Presidency: Historical and Contemporary Perspectives* (Pacific Grove, CA: Brooks/Cole, 1988).

33. Marc Landy and Sidney M. Milkis, *Presidential Greatness* (Lawrence: University of Kansas Press, 2000).

34. Harold J. Laski, *The American Presidency* (New York: Harper & Row, 1940).

35. William M. Goldsmith, *The Growth of Presidential Power: A Documented History,* 3 vols. (New York: Chelsea House, 1974).

36. *New York Times Co. v. U.S.,* 403 U.S. 713 (1971).

37. Statement of Sen. Howard Baker (R-TN) during the Senate Committee investigation.

38. John Dean, the Nixon presidential transcripts, March 21, 1973.

39. http://nixon.archives.gov/find/tapes/excerpts/watergate.html.

40. David Frost, *I Gave Them a Sword* (New York: William Morrow, 1978).

41. http://blog.washingtonpost.com/the-trail/2007/08/29/a_party_in_disarray.html/.

42. Barbara Gamarekian, "Washington Talk: The Presidency; First Ladies Step Further Out of Shadows," *New York Times,* March 10, 1988, B5.

43. Barbara Bush, commencement address at Wellesley College, June 1, 1990.

44. Charles C. Thach Jr., *The Creation of the Presidency, 1775–1789: A Study in Constitutional History* (Baltimore: Johns Hopkins University Press, 1969).

CHAPTER 13

1. www.whitehouse.gov/omb/budget/Historicals.

2. For a review of the literature on public service motivation, see David J. Houston, "'Walking the Walk' of Public Service Motivation: Public Employees and Charitable Gifts of Time, Blood, and Money," *Journal of Public Administration Research and Theory* 16, no. 1 (2005): 67–86.

3. David J. Houston and Lauren K. Harding, "Trust in the Public Service: A Cross-National Examination" (presented at the 66th Annual National Conference of the Midwest Political Science Association, Chicago, April 3–6, 2008).

4. Charles T. Goodsell, *The Case for Bureaucracy: A Public Administration Polemic,* 4th ed. (Washington, DC: CQ Press, 2004): 104–106.

5. Norman J. Baldwin, "Public Versus Private Employees: Debunking Stereotypes," *Review of Public Personnel Administration* 12 (Winter 1991): 1–27.

6. Goodsell, *The Case for Bureaucracy,* 106.

7. Stuart Greenfield, "Public Sector Employment: The Current Situation" (Washington, DC: The Center for State & Local Government Excellence), www.slge.org/vertical/Sites/%7BA260E1DF-5Aee-459D-84C4-876EFE1E4032%7D/uploads/%7BB4579F88-660D-49DD-8D52-F6928BD43C46%7D.pdf.

8. John T. Woolley and Gerhard Peters, "The American Presidency Project," www.presidency.ucsb.edu/ws/?pid=30436 (Santa Barbara: University of California, hosted, Gerhard Peters, database).

9. www.bls.gov/news.release/union.

10. www.opm.gov/ses/features.asp.

11. www.usaspending.gov.

12. www.msnbc.msn.com/id/23919234.

13. Jeffrey L. Pressman and Aaron Wildavsky, *Implementation: How Great Expectations in Washington Are Dashed in Oakland: Or, Why It's Amazing That Federal Programs Work at All* (Berkeley: University of California Press, 1973).

14. Office of Management and Budget, *FY 2008 Report to Congress on Implementation of the E-Government Act of 2002,* March 1, 2009:3.

15. www.pogo.org/p/x/2007impact.html#contract.

16. Shaila Dewan, "FEMA Ordered to Restore Evacuees' Housing Aid," *New York Times,* November 30, 2006.

17. William T. Gormley Jr. and Steven J. Balla, *Bureaucracy and Democracy: Accountability and Performance* (Washington DC: CQ Press, 2004), 67.

18. Matt Kelley, "Probes at NASA Plummet Under Its Current IG," *USA Today,* January 11, 2008.

19. Charles T. Goodsell, *The Case for Bureaucracy,* 139.

20. Gormley and Balla, *Bureaucracy and Democracy,* 164–78.

21. Goodsell, The Case for Bureaucracy, 54.

22. Ibid., 30.

23. www.house.gov/etheridge/Press-FEMAcontracts.htm.

24. Richard Stillman, *The American Bureaucracy: The Core of Modern Government* (Chicago: Nelson Hall Publishers, 1996), 308.

25. http://media.washingtonpost.com/wp-serv/politics/documents/gov_experience_final_111609.pdf.

CHAPTER 14

1. "More Than Half of Americans Approve of the Job the Court Is Doing, Which Is Lower Than Approval Has Been at Some Recent Points but Still Much Higher Than Public Approval of President George W. Bush and Congress." Joseph Carroll, "1/3 of Americans Say U.S. Supreme Court Is

'Too Conservative,'" Gallup News Service, October 2, 2007.

2. Christopher N. May, *Constitutional Law—National Power and Federalism: Examples and Explanations* (New York: Aspen, 2004).

3. Morton J. Horowitz, *The Transformation of American Law, 1780–1860* (Cambridge, MA: Harvard University Press, 1977).

4. Charles D. Shipan, *Designing Judicial Review* (Ann Arbor: University of Michigan Press, 1997).

5. Joel B. Grossman, "Paths to the Bench: Selecting Supreme Court Justices in a 'Juristocratic' World," in *The Judicial Branch,* ed. Kermit L. Hall and Kevin T. McGuire (Oxford: Oxford University Press, 2005), 143.

6. Robert G. McCloskey, *The American Supreme Court,* 4th ed. (Chicago: University of Chicago Press, 2005).

7. Erwin Chemerinsky, *Constitutional Law: Principles and Policies* (New York: Aspen, 2006).

8. www.citmedialaw.org/threats/simorangkir-v-love#description.

9. Robert A. Carp, Ronald Stidham, and Kenneth L. Manning, *Judicial Process in America* (Washington, DC: CQ Press, 2007).

10. Robert A. Carp and Ronald Stidham, *The Federal Courts,* 4th ed. (Washington, DC: CQ Press, 2001).

11. www.whitehouse.gov/news/releases/2008/05/20080517-2.html.

12. The exception is those cases whose original jurisdiction is the U.S. Supreme Court, which is not typically considered a trial court.

13. www.uscourts.gov/faq.html.

14. 50 U.S.C. §§1801–1811, 1821–29, 1841–46, and 1861–62.

15. Lawrence Baum, "The Future of the Judicial Branch," in *The Judicial Branch,* ed. Kermit L. Hall and Kevin T. McGuire (Oxford: Oxford University Press, 2005), 523.

16. See, for example, Hugh Hewitt, "Why the Right Was Wrong," *New York Times,* October 28, 2005, www.nytimes.com/2005/10/28/opinion/28hewitt.html?ex=1288152000&en=53aee2bcf6872884&ei=5090&partner=rssuserland&emc=rss.

17. www.nytimes.com/interactive/2010/04/09/us/politics/20100409-stevens-candidates.html.

18. Henry J. Abraham, *Justices and Presidents: A Political History of Appointments to the Supreme Court* (New York: Oxford University Press, 1974).

19. H. W. Perry Jr., *Deciding to Decide: Agenda Setting in the United States Supreme Court* (Cambridge, MA: Harvard University Press, 1994).

20. Bob Woodward, *The Brethren: Inside the Supreme Court* (New York: Simon & Schuster, 2005).

21. Henry J. Abraham, *The Judicial Process* (New York: Oxford University Press, 1998).

22. *Gratz v. Bollinger,* 539 U.S. 244 (2003) and *Grutter v. Bollinger,* 539 U.S. 306 (2003).

23. Benjamin N. Cardozo, *The Nature of the Judicial Process* (Mineola, NY: Dover, 2005).

24. Stephen Breyer, *Active Liberty: Interpreting Our Democratic Constitution* (New York: Vintage Books, 2006).

25. Gregory A. Caldeira and John R. Wright, "*Amicus Curiae* Before the Supreme Court: Who Participates, When, and How Much? *Journal of Politics* 52 (1990): 803.

26. William H. Rehnquist, *The Supreme Court* (New York: Vintage, 2002).

27. Bernard Schwartz, *Decision: How the Supreme Court Decides Cases* (New York: Oxford University Press, 1996).

28. Jeffrey A. Segal and Harold J. Spaeth, *The Supreme Court and the Attitudinal Model* (New York: Cambridge University Press, 2003).

29. Jeffrey Toobin, *The Nine: Inside the Secret World of the Supreme Court* (New York: Doubleday, 2007).

30. Lawrence Baum, *The Supreme Court* (Washington, DC: CQ Press, 2006).

31. Paul J. Wahlbeck, James F. Spriggs II, and Forrest Maltzman, "The Politics of Dissents and Concurrences on the U.S. Supreme Court," *American Politics Quarterly* 27 (1999): 488–514.

32. *New York Times,* "The Roberts Court Returns," www.nytimes.com/2007/09/30/opinion/30sun1.html; Charles Lane, "Narrow Victories Move Court to the Right," *Washington Post,* June 29, 2007, p. A04; Linda Greenhouse, "Roberts Court Is a Conservative's Dream," *International Herald Tribune,* www.iht.com/articles/2007/07/01/news/scotus.php.

33. www.gallup.com/poll/4732/Supreme-/Court.aspx.

34. *Parents Involved in Community Schools v. Seattle School District No. 1,* 551 U.S. _____ (2007).

35. *Gonzales v. Carhart,* 550 U.S. (2007).

36. *Safford Unified School District v. Redding,* 557 U.S. _____ (2009).

37. *Horne v. Flores,* 57 U.S. _____ (2009).

38. *Melendez-Diaz v. Massachusetts,* 57 U.S. _____ (2009).

39. Lee Epstein and Jack Knight, *The Choices Justices Make* (Washington, DC: CQ Press, 1998).

40. Lee Cokorinos, *The Assault on Diversity: An Organized Challenge to Racial and Gender Justice* (Lanham, MD: Rowman & Littlefield, 2003), 9.

41. *Miranda v. Arizona,* 384 U.S. 436.

42. *Gideon v. Wainwright,* 372 U.S. 335 (1963).

43. *Griswold v. Connecticut,* 381 U.S. 479 (1965).

44. Antonin Scalia, *A Matter of Interpretation: Federal Courts and the Law* (Princeton, NJ: Princeton University Press, 1998).

45. Thomas M. Keck, *The Most Activist Supreme Court in History: The Road to Modern Judicial Conservatism* (Chicago: University of Chicago Press, 2004).

46. *Oregon v. Mitchell,* 400 U.S. 112 (1970).

47. Andrew Jay Koshner, *Solving the Puzzle of Interest Group Litigation* (Westport, CT: Greenwood, 1998).

48. John E. Nowak and Ronald D. Rotunda, *Constitutional Law (Hornbook Series)* (St. Paul, MN: West, 2004).

CHAPTER 15

1. Trudy Rubin, "Global Economy Waits for Next 'Conductor,'" *Philadelphia Inquirer,* January 27, 2008.

2. Bureau of Economic Analysis, "Measuring the Economy: A Primer on GDP and the National Income and Product Accounts," September 2007, www.bea.gov/national/pdf/nipa_primer.pdf.

3. http://hdr.undp.org/en/statistics/.

4. www.census.gov/hhes/www/poverty/data/threshld/thresh08.html.

5. www.whitehouse.gov/omb/budget/Historicals/.

6. www.brillig.com/debt_clock.

7. Sherman Antitrust Act (1890); Clayton Antitrust Act (1914).

8. www.u-s-history.com/pages/h1603.html.

9. Ralph Nader, *Unsafe at Any Speed: The Designed-in Dangers of American Automobiles* (New York: Grossman Publishing, 1965), ix.

10. Alexei Barrionuevo, "Globalization in Every Loaf," *New York Times,* June 16, 2007.

11. L. Josh Bivens and John Irons, "A Feeble Recovery: The Fundamental Economic Weaknesses of the 2001–2007 Expansion," Economic Policy Institute Briefing Paper #214, May 1, 2008, www.epi.org/publications/entry/4139.

12. Jared Bernstein, "Real Wages Decline in 2007," Economic Policy Issue Brief #240, 2008, www.epi.org/content.cfm/ib240.

13. Jared Bernstein, Elise Gould, and Lawrence Mishel; "Income Picture: Poverty, Income and Health Insurance Trends in 2006," August 28, 2007, www.epi.org/content.cfm/webfeatures_econindicators_income20070828.

14. Ibid.

15. Peter Grier, "Rich-poor gap gaining attention," *Christian Science Monitor,* June 14, 2005, viewed at www.csmonitor.com/2005/0614/p01s03-usec.htm.

16. Graham Bowley, "That 70's Look: Stagflation," *New York Times,* February 21, 2008.

17. Edmund L. Andrews, "Top Officials See Bleaker Outlook for the Economy," *New York Times,* February 15, 2008.

18. David Leonhardt, "Judging Stimulus by Job Data Reveals Success," *New York Times,* February 17, 2010.

19. Quoted in David Kamp: "Rethinking the American Dream," *Vanity Fair,* April 2009.

20. David Leonhardt, "Has the Jump in Wages Met Its End?" *New York Times,* September 12, 2007.

21. Bob Herbert, "Here Come the Millennials," *New York Times,* May 13, 2008.

CHAPTER 16

1. Visit the federal government's Web site (www.whitehouse.gov/omb/expectmore/index.html) for a more complete list of domestic programs.
2. http://earthday.wilderness.org/history/.
3. *Massachusetts v. EPA*, (2007) 549 U.S., 497.
4. David Hosansky, *The Environment: A to Z* (Washington, DC: CQ Press, 2001), 80–81.
5. Ibid., 243.
6. http://tonto.eia.doe.gov/energyexplained/index.cfm?page=about_home.
7. http://tonto.eia.doe.gov/energy_in_brief/foreign_oil_dependence.cfm.
8. Bill Vlasic, "Early Target for Fuel Economy Is Expected," *New York Times,* April 22, 2008.
9. Mary Cooper, "Energy Policy," in *Economic Issues: Selections from the CQ Researcher* (Washington, DC: CQ Press), 146–49.
10. Ibid., 139.
11. Josef Herbert, "Climate Bill May Spur Energy Revolution: President Claims Measure Will Strengthen Economy," Associated Press, June 28, 2009.
12. http://opencrs.com/document/RS22915.
13. Stephen Labaton, "Congress Passes Increase in the Minimum Wage," *New York Times,* May 25, 2007.
14. www.labotlawcenter.com/t-State-Minimum-Wage-Rates.aspx.
15. Center on Budget and Policy Priorities, "Policy Basics: The Earned Income Tax Credit," December 4, 2009, www.cbpp.org/cms/index.cfm?fa+view&id+2505#.
16. LaDonna Pavetti and Dottie Rosenbaum, "Creating a Safety Net That Works When the Economy Doesn't: The Role of the Food Stamp and TANF Programs" (Washington, DC: The Center on Budget and Policy Priorities, February 25, 2010), www.cbpp.org/cms/index.cfm?fa+view&id=3096.
17. www.census.gov/hhes/www/cpstables/032009/pov/new01_100.htm.
18. Joint Center for Housing Studies of Harvard University, *The State of the Nation's Housing 2005* (Boston: Harvard University, 2005), 24.
19. www.nationalhomeless.org/publications/facts.html.
20. www.hud.gov/offices/pih/programs/hcv/about/fact_sheet.cfm.
21. www.census.gov/hhes/www/hlthins08/hlth08asc.html.
22. Kendra Hovey and Harold A. Hovey, *CQ's State Fact Finder 2007* (Washington, DC: CQ Press, 2007), 143.
23. www.cms.hhs.gov/medicaideligibility/02?areyoueligible_asp.
24. www.whitehouse.gov/the-press-office/remarks-president-barack-obama-address-joint-session-congress.
25. Sheryl Gay Stolberg and Robert Peat, "Obama Signs Health Care Overhaul Bill, With a Flourish," www.nytimes.com/2010/03/24/health/policy/24health.html.
26. www.whitehouse.gov/news/releases/2006/02/print/20060223.html.
27. Deborah Macmillan, "Overview: Federal Immigration Policy and Proposed Reforms," www.lwv.org/AM/Template.cfm?Section=LWVUSImmigrationStudy&TEMPLATE=/CM/ContentDisplay.cfm&CONTENTID=7426.
28. Ibid.
29. Patricia Hatch, "What Motivates Immigration to America," www.lwv.org/AM/Template.cfm?Section=LWVUSImmigrationStudy&CONTENTID=8179&TEMPLATE=/CM/ContentDisplay.cfm.

CHAPTER 17

1. Congressional Research Service Report to Congress, "U.S. Foreign Aid to East and Southeast Asia: Selected Recipients," August 22, 2007, www.fas.org/sgp/crs/row/RL31362.pdf, p. 31.
2. Ibid., p. 36.
3. "About Those Billions," *Newsweek,* www.newsweek.com/id/218932.
4. "Dodd Assesses Efforts by U.S. to Increase Economic, Diplomatic, Political Pressure on Iran," March 21, 2007, http://dodd.senate.gov/index.php?q=node/3793.
5. Saul K. Padover, ed., *Wilson's Ideals* (Washington, DC: American Council on Public Affairs, 1942), 108.
6. www.unicef.org/sowc97/.
7. Secretary of State Colin L. Powell, remarks to the United Nations Security Council, February 5, 2003, www.state.gov/secretary/former/powell/remarks/2003/17300.htm.
8. www.npr.org/templates/story/story.php?storyId=4859238.
9. See, for example, James Risen, *State of War: The Secret History of the CIA and the Bush Administration* (New York: Free Press, 2006).
10. "Congress Abdicates War Powers," *The New American* (November 4, 2002): 5.
11. www.ourdocuments.gov/doc.php?flash=true&doc=90.
12. Roger H. Davidson, "Invitation to Struggle: An Overview of Legislative-Executive Relations," *Annals of the American Academy of Political and Social Science* 499 (1988): 1, 9–21.
13. Article 5 of the North Atlantic Treaty, Washington D.C., April 4, 1949, www.nato.int/docu/basictxt/treaty.htm.
14. President Harry S. Truman's address before a joint session of Congress on March 12, 1947.
15. George F. Kennan, writing under the pseudonym "X," "Sources of Soviet Conduct," *Foreign Affairs* (July 1947): 25.
16. Graham T. Allison and Philip Zelikow, *Essence of Decision: Explaining the Cuban Missile Crisis,* 2nd ed. (New York: Longman, 1999).
17. www.nps.gov/archive/eise/quotes2.htm.
18. Samuel P. Huntington, "The Clash of Civilizations?" *Foreign Affairs* 72, no. 3 (Summer 1993): 22–49.

CHAPTER 18

1. Theodore Roosevelt, "Charter of Democracy," speech to the 1912 Ohio constitutional convention.
2. www.iandrinstitute.org/IRI%20Initiative%20Use%20(2006-11).pdf.
3. www.iandrinstitute.org/IRI%20Initiative%20Use%20%281904-2008%29.pdf.
4. www.ncsl.org/default.aspx?tabid=18908; www.iandrinstitute.org/BW%202009-2%20Results%20%28v1%29.pdf.
5. M. Dane Waters, "The Initiative Industry: Its Impact on the Future of the Initiative Process," www.iandrinstitute.org/New%20IRI%20Website%20Info/I&R%20Research%20and%20History/I&R%20Studies/Waters%20-%20The%20Initiative%20Industry-Its%20Impact%20on%20the%20Future%20.pdf.
6. Alan Greenblatt, "Total Recall," in *State and Local Government 2004–2005,* ed. Thad L. Beyle (Washington, DC: CQ Press, 2004), 30.
7. http://igs.berkeley.edu/library/htRecall2003.html.
8. http://vote2003.sos.ca.gov/recall/1-1-proponents-grounds.html.
9. Thad Beyle, "The California Recall and Replacement Elections of 2003," in *State and Local Government 2004–2005* (Washington, DC: CQ Press), 34.
10. M. Dane Waters, "I Couldn't Recall," in *State and Local Government 2004–2005* (Washington, DC: CQ Press), 34.
11. www.ballotpedia.org/wiki/index.php/Jennifer_Granholm_recall,_Michigan,_2010.
12. "A Case of Faulty Recall," *Governing* (December 2009): 12.
13. Joel Lieske, "The Changing Regional Subcultures of the United States: A New Cultural Measure for Understanding Political Behavior" (paper presented at 2004 Annual Meeting of the Midwest Political Science Association, Chicago, April 15–18, 2004), p. 2.
14. Daniel Elazar, *American Federalist,* 3rd ed. (New York: Harper & Row, 1984).
15. Lieske, "The Changing Regional Subcultures of the United States, 5.
16. Ibid., 6.
17. Kendra A. Hovey and Harold A. Hovey, *CQ's State Fact Finder 2007* (Washington, DC: CQ Press, 2007), 33.
18. http://quickfacts.census.gov/qfd/states/06000.html.
19. http://quickfacts.census.gov/qfd/states/54000.html.
20. U.S. Census Burau, *Statistical Abstract of the United States: 2010* (Washington, DC: U.S. Government Printing Office, 2010), Table 449.
21. Hovey and Hovey, *CQ's State Fact Finder 2007,* 210; Kevin Smith, Alan Greenblatt, and John Buntin, *Governing States and Localities* (Washington, DC: CQ Press, 2005), 421.

22. Hovey and Hovey, *CQ's State Fact Finder 2007,* 231.

23. http://measuringup.highereducation.org/compare/state_addcomparison.cfm.

24. Hovey and Hovey, *CQ's State Fact Finder 2007,* 218, 225, 226.

25. "Financing America's Public Schools," www.nga.org/cda/files/PUBLICSCHOOLS.pdf.

26. U.S. Census Bureau, *Statistical Abstract of the United States: 2006,* 125th ed. (Washington, DC: U.S. Government Printing Office, 2005), Table 439.

27. Hovey and Hovey, *CQ's State Fact Finder 2007,* 143.

28. Josh Goodman, "Where Have all the Dollars Gone?" *Governing* (October 2009): 45–48.

29. Josh Goodman, "Uneven Stimulus," *Governing* (April 2009): 17.

30. Rob Gurwitt, "Broke and Broken," *Governing* (January 2010): 19–23.

31. Liz Sidoti, "Govs Expect Worst to Come: Joblessness, Bare budgets, to Continue," *The Scranton Sunday Times,* February 21, 2010, B3.

32. Ibid.

33. Thad Beyle, ed., *State and Local Government 2004–2005* (Washington, DC, CQ Press, 2004), 110.

34. www.nga.org/portal/site/nga/menuitem.42b929b1a5b9e4eac3363d10501010a0/?vgnextoid=d54c8aaa2ebbff00VgnVCM1000001a01010aRCRD&vgnextfmt=curgov.

35. www.afdc.energy.gov/afdc/laws/state.

36. Tom Arrandale, "A Bolder Boulder," *Governing* (February 2007): 56.

37. For more information on women in elected and appointed government positions, see the Web site of the Center for Women in Politics: www.cawp.rutgers.edu.

38. Statistics on race and ethnicity in state legislatures are available at www.ncsl.org/default.aspx?tabid=14767. Statistics on race and ethnicity in state populations are available at http://quickfacts.census.gov/qfd/index.html.

39. www.cawp.rutgers.edu/fast_facts/levels_of_office/Statewide-Current.php.

40. U.S. Census Bureau, *2007 Census of Government,* "Local Government and Public School Systems by Type and State," www.census.gov/govs/cog/GovOrgTab03ss.html.

41. Mayraj Fahim, "U.S. Voters Are Not Convinced That Big Is Better in Local Government," June 2005, www.citymayors.com/government/mergers_locgov.html.

42. U.S. Census Bureau, *2007 Census of Government,* "Local Government and Public School Systems by Type and State," www.census.gov/govs/cog/GovOrgTab03ss.html.

CREDITS

war with Iraq over Kuwait, 526, 546
Bush, George W. *See also* Afghanistan, U.S. war in;
    Iraq War; war on terror
  "axis of evil" speech of, 548
  Bush Doctrine, 545
  on carbon dioxide regulation, 500
  Christian interest group support of, 229
  on discrimination lawsuit time limits, 372
  divided government under, 252
  domestic surveillance under, 124, 138, 139, 440
  economic bailout plan of, 373
  in election of 2000 (*See* election of 2000)
  energy policy under, 504
  executive orders of, 438
  on global warming, 418–419
  Guantánamo Bay detainees of, 56*f*, 116*f*, 140,
    385–386, 529
  Homeland Security Department creation, 379,
    514
  Hurricane Katrina response by, 93–94, 94*f*, 204,
    205*f*, 424, 515
  immigration reform efforts of, 516
  on Iran, 548
  loss of popular vote by, 369
  Medicare prescription drug program of, 512,
    514
  on military tribunals, 118–119
  neoconservatives and, 26, 545
  Pakistan and, 525
  politically motivated firing of U.S. attorneys, 386
  presidential power under, 392
  public opinion on, 387–388, 388*f*
  public trust in, 205*f*, 206
  regulatory policy of, 479–480
  selling of Iraq War to the public, 546
  signing statements by, 370–371, 373
  Supreme Court justices selected by, 441, 444
  tax cuts of, 468, 469, 484
  use of inherent powers, 385
  vetoes of, 370
  voting rights extension, 161
Bush, Laura, 394
Bush Doctrine, 545
Bush v. Gore, 100, 100*f*, 280
business. *See* corporations
Business and Professional Women, 165*f*
business interest groups, 226
business regulation, 479–481, 480*f*, 482
Business Roundtable, 224, 226
butterfly ballot, 280–281
Byrd, James, Jr., 175
Byrd, Robert, 354

C

cabinet, 379, 381*t*
CAFÉ (Corporate Average Fuel Economy) standards, 504
CAIR (Council on American-Islamic Relations),
  230
California
  higher education in, 569
  on medical use of marijuana, 98–99
  multilingual population in, 566
  opposing interests in, 346, 346*f*
  Proposition 8, 278–279
  Proposition 13, 559
  recall election in, 561
California Marriage Protection Act, 278–279
Cameron, David, 375
campaign consultants, 284
campaign fund-raising. *See also* Bipartisan Campaign Finance Reform Act (2002); political
  action committees

Citizens United decision and, 123, 217, 224, 231,
  288, 291
  consultants in, 284
  527 groups, 289–290
  incumbency advantages in, 339
  independent expenditures in, 288
  interest groups and, 217, 218–219, 233–236,
    233*f*, 234*f*
  Internet and, 267, 286–287
  largest donors, 236*t*
  regulation of, 287–291, 290*t*, 291*f*
  soft money in, 249, 288–289
campaign managers, 283
campaigns. *See also* campaign fund-raising
  candidate-centered politics, 261
  candidate eligibility requirements, 283–284, 283*f*
  congressional, 100, 338–340, 338*f*, 339*f*, 340*f*
  corporations and labor unions in, 123, 217,
    224, 231, 288, 291
  costs of, 338
  decision making by voters, 296–298, 297*f*, 298*f*
  endorsements in, 233–234, 374*f*
  influences on voter choice, 297–298, 298*f*
  Internet in, 266–267, 286–287, 319
  media in, 285–286, 285*f*
  national conventions, 249, 276, 292
  negative, 297–299, 298*f*
  presidential, 292–293, 292*f*
  primaries (*See* primary elections)
  professionalization of, 284–285
  reasons for running for office, 282
  technology use in, 5, 286–287
  timeline of, 292*f*
campaign strategy, 284
candidate-centered campaigns, 261
candidate committees, 256–257
capital budgets, 567
capitalism
  "creative," 485
  definition of, 17
  laissez-faire, 466–467
  in political culture, 17
  pure *vs.* regulated, 466
Capital News Group, 323
capital projects, 567
capital punishment, 135, 136*f*, 452, 452*f*, 456, 456*f*
Capitol building, 348, 348*f*
carbon dioxide emission standards, 418–419
Carmichael, Stokely, 159
Carson, Rachel, 499
Carter, Jimmy
  in arms limitation talks, 543
  civil service reform by, 408
  on energy conservation, 504
  foreign policy advisors of, 528
  hostages held by Iran and, 548
  on interest groups, 218
  presidential power and, 392
  response to OPEC embargo, 503–504
  women's support of, 192
Carter, Stephen L., 112
casework, 339, 343–344
cash transfers, 496–497, 511
Castro, Fidel, 533
categorical formula grants, 100–101
categorical project grants, 101
caucuses
  congressional, 352
  nominating, 276
CBO (Congressional Budget Office), 476
CBPP (Center on Budget and Policy Priorities), 508
cell phones
  in the Iranian election protests, 119, 308–309,
    309*f*, 324, 550–551
  public opinion polls and, 200, 201

censorship, 124–125
census, 101, 340
Census Bureau, 471
Center on Budget and Policy Priorities (CBPP), 508
Central Intelligence Agency (CIA), 140, 514, 528
centralized federalism, 96–97
chads, 279–280, 280*f*
Chamber of Commerce, 226
Chaplinsky v. New Hampshire, 123
charters, local, 84, 562, 563–564
Chavez, Cesar, 169, 169*f*
Chavez, Hugo, 504
checks and balances, 43–44, 45*f*, 56, 453–456
chemical and biological weapons, 526, 547, 548
Cheney, Dick
  energy policy of, 504
  tie-breaking vote on spending bill, 353–354
  as vice president, 378
Chertoff, Michael, 93
Chicano Movement, 169–170, 169*f*
chief executive, president as, 377
chief justice, 441
chief of staff, 381
chief of state, president as, 377
child labor laws, 481
child pornography, 123
children
  adoptions, 171*f*, 174
  food insecurity among, 511
  health care for, 511
  homeless, 511
  political socialization of, 185, 186–188, 311,
    311*f*
  in poverty, 508–510, 509*t*
  trafficking of, 154
  of unauthorized immigrants, 516
China
  contaminated pet food from, 483
  Korean War and, 541
Chinese Americans, 18, 467
Chinese Exclusion Acts, 18, 467
Christian Coalition, 229
Christian interest groups, 229–230
Christian Right, 247
Chu, Stephen, 379
Church, Frank, 528
Church Committee, 528
Churchill, Winston, 540, 541*f*, 548
CIA (Central Intelligence Agency), 140, 514, 528
circuit courts. *See* courts of appeals
circuit riding, 433, 433*f*
citizens, 8, 153
citizenship
  of adopted children, 171*f*
  of African Americans, 152, 153
  of Asian Americans, 170, 171*f*
  of Mexican Americans, 169
  of Native Americans, 167
  of women, 163
Citizens United, 217
Citizens United v. Federal Elections Commission, 123,
  217, 224, 231, 288, 291
Citizen Tube, 320
city councils, 250–251
city government. *See* local governments
city-states, ancient Greek, 12–13
The 2006 Civic and Political Health of the Nation,
  191–192
civic engagement. *See also* political participation
  agenda setting and, 345
  definition of, 7
  domestic policy and, 286–287, 494–496
  Internet and, 266–267
  social capital and, 214, 221, 274
civic participation. *See* political participation

M

Maazel, Lorin, 533*f*
MacArthur, Douglas, 546
MAD (mutual assured destruction), 543
MADD (Mothers Against Drunk Driving), 218
Madison, James
  on the Bill of Rights, 52
  at the Constitutional Convention, 44
  The Federalist Papers, 51, 51*f,* 104, A–3 to A–5,
    A–7 to A–8
  on freedom of religion, 126
  on interest groups, 214
  popular support for, 253
  on separation between church and state, 126
  on slavery compromise, 47
Magna Carta, 435
Maine, explosion of, 313–314, 313*f*
majority-minority districts, 340
majority rule, 17
majority whip, 352–353
Malcolm X, 159
MALDEF (Mexican American Legal Defense and
  Education Fund), 170
mandates, 103–104
mandatory spending, 475
manifest destiny, 535
Mapp v. Ohio, 133
Marbury v. Madison, 48, 54, 87, 433
margin of error, 201
marijuana, medical use of, 98–99
marketplace of ideas, 118
markup, 350
marriage. *See also* families
  civil unions, 95, 131*f*
  Defense of Marriage Act, 95, 131, 131*f*
  interracial, 149, 154
  same-sex, 95, 131, 131*f,* 173, 278–279
Marshall, George, 537–538
Marshall, Justice John, 433
Marshall, Justice Thurgood, 157, 444
Marshall Plan, 537–538, 538*f*
Maryland, national bank dispute in, 92
Massachusetts
  health care in, 574
  Shays's Rebellion in, 42
  in the War for Independence, 38
Massachusetts Committee of Correspondence, 38
Massachusetts v. Mellon, 102
matching funds requirement, 101
Matthew Shepard and James Byrd Jr. Hate Crimes
  Prevention Act (2009), 175
May, Catherine, 165*f*
Mayfield, Max, 93
Mayflower Compact, 13
McCain, John
  ADA and ACU ratings of, 234
  campaign finance reform by, 289
  vice presidential choice of, 379
McCain-Feingold Act. *See* Bipartisan Campaign
  Finance Reform Act
McCardell, John, Jr., 103
McCarthy, Carolyn, 282
McCarthy, Eugene, 276
McCaskill, Claire, 421
McClure's Magazine, 314
McConnell, Mitch, 289, 341*f*
McConnell v. the Federal Election Committee, 289
McCord, James W., Jr., 391
McCormick, Richard P., 253
McCubbins, Matthew D., 345
McCulloch v. Maryland, 92, 93, 96
McGovern-Fraser Commission, 276
McGrady, Jennifer A., 298
McGuinness, Martin, 258

McKinley, William, 254, 516, 535
Mead, Margaret, 4
means-tested benefits, 507
Meat Inspection Act (1906), 481
media, 308–329. *See also* Internet; newspapers;
  radio; television
  agenda setting by, 309–310
  bias in, 325–326, 326*f*
  campaign advertising, 217, 219, 288
  campaign consultants on, 284–285
  campaign transformation by, 317–319, 318*f*
  competitive elections and, 296
  convergence in, 314, 323
  declining newspaper readership, 314, 314*f*
  definition of, 308
  foreign policy role of, 531–532, 531*f*
  as forum for political conversations, 311
  framing by, 309–310
  incumbency advantages with, 339
  as information providers, 309
  new media, 314–315
  penny papers, 313
  personality *vs.* policy in, 285–286, 285*f*
  political party decline from role of, 260–261
  political socialization by, 187, 311, 311*f*
  presidential use of, 316, 316*f*
  press in history, 313–314, 313*f*
  public confidence in, 310*f*
  regulation of, 326–327
  segmented, 318
  yellow journalism, 313–314, 313*f*
media consultants, 284–285
median household income, 472
media segmentation, 318
Medicaid
  beneficiaries of, 511–512
  as cash transfer, 497
  expansion of, 513
  federal grants to states for, 572, 572*t*
  formation of, 511
  as mandatory spending, 475
  state funding for, 569
medical treatment, right to terminate, 130–131
Medicare
  as mandatory spending, 475
  prescription drug plan, 512, 514
  provisions of, 512
  taxes collected for, 474, 474*f*
Medicare Prescription Drug, Improvement, and
  Modernization Act (2003), 512, 514
men, mean personal income of, 465, 465*t. See also*
  gender differences
Menendez, Robert, 266
merit-based civil service, 406
merit selection process, of judges, 580
Merit System Protection Board (MSPB), 409
Mexican American Legal Defense and Education
  Fund (MALDEF), 170
Mexican Americans. *See also* Latinos/Latinas
  Chicano Movement, 169–170, 169*f*
  population of, 19
Mexico-U.S. border fence, 516–517, 517*f*
Miers, Harriet, 386, 442, 444
military
  budget for, 9
  commander in chief, 376–377, 377*f,* 533, 577
  Defense Department and, 527
  desegregation of, 385, 437
  Don't Ask, Don't Tell policy, 345
  in foreign policy, 526–527
  Geneva Conventions and, 529
  Guantánamo Bay detainees (*See* Guantánamo
    Bay detainees)
  impressment by British, 534
  Joint Chiefs of Staff, 527

military courts, 118–119
  Quartering Act (1765), 37, 38
  rendition, 140
  torture of detainees by, 139–140, 529, 532, 532*f*
military-industrial complex, 530–531
military tribunals, 118–119
militias, 137
Millennial Generation, 5–6, 8, 192*f,* 486. *See also*
  young people
Miller, Ola Babcock, 196, 198
Miller v. California, 123
Million Moms, 137, 137*f*
minimum legal drinking age, 102–103
minimum wage laws
  conflicted federalism and, 98
  current wage in, 507–508
  Fair Labor Standards Act creation of, 481, 507
  interest groups and, 225, 226
  as living wage, 507–508
Minneapolis I-135W bridge, 425*f*
Minor, Virginia, 163
minorities. *See also* demographics; race and ethnicity; *specific minority groups*
  in cabinet positions, 379, 381*t*
  in Congress, 358–360, 358*t,* 359*f,* 360*f*
  in federal bureaucracy, 408*f*
  Latinos as, 170
  majority-minority districts, 340
  mean personal income of, 465, 465*t*
  newsroom employment of, 315, 315*t*
  in the population, 19, 20*f,* 21*f,* 22, 22*f*
  poverty rates among, 510
  in presidential cabinets, 379
minority whip, 353
Minor v. Happersett, 163
Miranda rights, 134, 453
Miranda v. Arizona, 134
MIRVs (multiple independently targeted reentry
  vehicles), 543, 544
miscegenation laws, 154
Mississippi, African American state legislators in,
  575–576
Missouri Compromise, 151, 152
Mitchell, George, 258
Mitchell Principles, 258
mixed economy, 466, 467
monarchies, 12, 13, 14
Mondale, Walter F., 344
monetarism, 469–470
monetary policy, 478–479, 484
Monroe, James, 253, 535
Monroe Doctrine, 535
Montesquieu, Baron de, 43–44
Montgomery bus boycott, 157, 158, 158*f*
moralistic political culture, 565, 575
Moral Majority, 229
Moran, Edward, 534*f*
Moran v. Burbine, 134*t*
mortgage crisis. *See* Great Recession
Mossadegh, Mohammed, 548
most favored nation status, 525, 539
Mothers Against Drunk Driving (MADD), 218
Motion Picture Association of America (MPAA),
  226
"Motor Voter" Act, 299
Mott, Lucretia, 162
Mousavi, Mir-Hossein, 119, 324
MoveOn.org, 286, 290
MPAA (Motion Picture Association of America),
  226
MSPB (Merit System Protection Board), 409
Mubasher FM, 312, 312*f*
muckraking, 314
multilateral agreements, 537
multilingual services, 566